40 YEARS OF NME CHARTS

NEW MUSICAL EXPRESS

Dafydd Rees, Barry Lazell & Roger Osborne

BOXTREE

ACKNOWLEDGEMENTS

There are a lot of people without whom this book would not have been possible.
Special thanks must go to Andy McDuff, Alan Lewis, Fiona Foulgar, Cate Jago,
Danny Kelly and all at the New Musical Express. Also to Dick Whincup, Peter
Lassey and Phil Midgley at the Department of Computing, Scarborough Technical
College; for their enthusiasm and expert advice. To Fred Dellar, Pete Compton and
Barry Davies; to Charles 'Dr Rock' White; to Michael Randolfi for his day at the
museum; to Jo Pratt at EMI; to John Easby and Bryan Hodgson at Adverset for the
new edition; thanks also go to Jake Lingwood, and Andrew Hurman for his help
with the chart research. Photo pages by Janis Bright.

This edition published 1995 by
BOXTREE LIMITED

First published in the UK 1992 by
BOXTREE LIMITED, Broadwall House,
21 Broadwall, London SE1 9PL.

10 9 8 7 6 5 4 3 2 1

ISBN: 0 7522 0829 2

Music Charts 1952 to May 1988, © IPC Magazines Ltd.
Music Charts June 1988 to May 1994 © MRIB Ltd.

Packaged by Osborne Randolfi Books,
79 High Street, Snainton, North Yorkshire YO13 9AJ.

Linotron output by Adverset, Scarborough.

Front cover design by Design 23.

Printed and bound in Great Britain by Cox & Wyman Ltd., Reading, Berkshire.

A catalogue record for this book is available from the British Library.

The Beginning

When the *New Musical Express* published Britain's first 'Hit Parade' on November 14, 1952 Winston Churchill was Prime Minister, food rationing was still in force and Elvis was a high-school student. Every one of the hundreds of charts and listings published during the subsequent forty-three years either appeared in direct competition to the NME's pioneering effort or developed directly from it. Not many forty-somethings can claim to have revolutionized an entire industry. That, however, has been the achievement of the singles chart. It is impossible to conceive of the modern music industry without the singles charts and the LP charts that were born from them. For record companies and artists success is dictated by the charts, and trends in music are measured by reference to the charts. The theme tunes of our times are all there in the Top Ten or Twenty or Thirty.

Until that landmark date in November 1952 songs were rated only by sheet music sales. The NME chart began as a Top 12, by record sales. With the advent of rock 'n' roll the record industry exploded and carried on expanding through the next four decades. Single sales grew inexorably and a larger survey was needed. Within two years the NME chart was expanded to a Top 20, and in April 1956 it became a Top 30. In April 1983, the chart was expanded to a Top 50 as it is today.

The forty-three year history of the NME singles chart mirrors the whole lifetime of popular music culture in the second half of the twentieth century; every style, every star, every trend and every folly, be they far-reaching and influential or ephemeral and soon forgotten, is nailed down to its precise chronological context. Cultural history of the utmost importance or, if you like, an endless ramble in glorious nostalgia.

The New Musical Express Singles Charts

The charts that follow differ in some important respects from those printed weekly in the NME. The date at the head of each chart in this book is the Saturday at the end of the week in which the chart was published. In the NME this date varies from Tuesday to Thursday to Saturday as the date of compilation of the chart and publication of the paper changed.

In order to fit the space available the NME sometimes abbreviates titles of records, names of artists or names of labels. We have restored the full names wherever possible. You will notice that the same song is often recorded under slightly different titles by different artists. This is particularly true in the 1950s, when numerous cover versions would often chart simultaneously.

Under intense pressure of producing the best music weekly in Britain, mistakes were sometimes made in compiling the chart. Again these have been corrected wherever possible. In very rare cases (three only, we think) a record was missed out of a chart. In these instances we have guessed the likely position and inserted it as an extra.

Along with most other papers and magazines the NME usually misses one or two issues over the Christmas and New Year period. We have not duplicated the previous week's chart for these missing weeks, but have gone on to the next published chart.

This updated edition covers the NME singles charts from their beginning in November 1952 to the end of 1994, and has a Title Index and Artist Index at the end of the book.

3

November – December 1952

15 November 1952

1	1 HERE IN MY HEART	Al Martino (Capitol)
2	2 YOU BELONG TO ME	Jo Stafford (Columbia)
3	3 SOMEWHERE ALONG THE WAY	
		Nat King Cole (Capitol)
4	4 ISLE OF INNISFREE	Bing Crosby (Bruswick)
5	5 FEET UP	Guy Mitchell (Columbia)
6	6 HALF AS MUCH	
		Rosemary Clooney (Columbia)
7	7 HIGH NOON	Frankie Laine (Columbia)
7	7 FORGET ME NOT	Vera Lynn (Decca)
8	8 SUGARBUSH	Doris Day
		& Frankie Laine (Columbia)
8	8 BLUE TANGO	Ray Martin (Capitol)
9	9 HOMING WALTZ	Vera Lynn (Decca)
10	10 AUF WIEDERSEHEN (SWEETHEART)	
		Vera Lynn (Decca)
11	BECAUSE YOU'RE MINE	Mario Lanza (HMV)
11	COWPUNCHER'S CANTATA	
		Max Bygraves (HMV)
12	WALKING MY BABY BACK HOME	
		Johnnie Ray (Columbia)

22 November 1952

1	1 HERE IN MY HEART	Al Martino (Capitol)
5	2 FEET UP	Guy Mitchell (Columbia)
6	3 HALF AS MUCH	
		Rosemary Clooney (Columbia)
4	4 ISLE OF INNISFREE	Bing Crosby (Bruswick)
2	5 YOU BELONG TO ME	Jo Stafford (Columbia)
3	6 SOMEWHERE ALONG THE WAY	
		Nat King Cole (Capitol)
7	7 HIGH NOON	Frankie Laine (Columbia)
11	8 BECAUSE YOU'RE MINE	Mario Lanza (HMV)
-	9 TAKE MY HEART	Al Martino (Capitol)
-	10 MY LOVE AND DEVOTION	
		Doris Day (Columbia)
9	11 HOMING WALTZ	Vera Lynn (Decca)
8	12 SUGARBUSH	Doris Day & Frankie Laine
		(Columbia)

29 November 1952

1	1 HERE IN MY HEART	Al Martino (Capitol)
5	2 YOU BELONG TO ME	Jo Stafford (Columbia)
3	3 HALF AS MUCH	
		Rosemary Clooney (Columbia)
8	4 BECAUSE YOU'RE MINE	Mario Lanza (HMV)
2	5 FEET UP	Guy Mitchell (Columbia)
4	6 ISLE OF INNISFREE	Bing Crosby (Bruswick)
-	7 FORGET ME NOT	Vera Lynn (Decca)
6	8 SOMEWHERE ALONG THE WAY	
		Nat King Cole (Capitol)
11	9 HOMING WALTZ	Vera Lynn (Decca)
10	10 MY LOVE AND DEVOTION	
		Doris Day (Columbia)
7	11 HIGH NOON	Frankie Laine (Columbia)
-	12 BLUE TANGO	Ray Martin (Capitol)

6 December 1952

1	1 HERE IN MY HEART	Al Martino (Capitol)
2	2 YOU BELONG TO ME	Jo Stafford (Columbia)
4	3 BECAUSE YOU'RE MINE	Mario Lanza (HMV)
6	4 ISLE OF INNISFREE	Bing Crosby (Bruswick)
5	5 FEET UP	Guy Mitchell (Columbia)
7	6 FORGET ME NOT	Vera Lynn (Decca)
3	7 HALF AS MUCH	
		Rosemary Clooney (Columbia)
-	8 SUGARBUSH	Doris Day & Frankie Laine
		(Columbia)
-	9 COMES A-LONG A-LOVE	Kay Starr (Capitol)
-	10 ZING A LITTLE ZONG	
		Bing Crosby & Jane Wyman (Brunswick)
11	11 HIGH NOON	Frankie Laine (Columbia)
8	12 SOMEWHERE ALONG THE WAY	
		Nat King Cole (Capitol)
12	12 BLUE TANGO	Ray Martin (Capitol)

13 December 1952

1	1 HERE IN MY HEART	Al Martino (Capitol)
2	2 YOU BELONG TO ME	Jo Stafford (Columbia)
4	3 ISLE OF INNISFREE	Bing Crosby (Bruswick)
7	3 HALF AS MUCH	
		Rosemary Clooney (Columbia)
5	4 FEET UP	Guy Mitchell (Columbia)
6	5 FORGET ME NOT	Vera Lynn (Decca)
3	5 BECAUSE YOU'RE MINE	Mario Lanza (HMV)
9	6 COMES A-LONG A-LOVE	Kay Starr (Capitol)
12	7 SOMEWHERE ALONG THE WAY	
		Nat King Cole (Capitol)
8	8 SUGARBUSH	Doris Day &
		Frankie Laine (Columbia)
11	9 HIGH NOON	Frankie Laine (Columbia)
12	10 BLUE TANGO	Ray Martin (Capitol)
-	11 BRITANNIA RAG	Winnifred Atwell (Decca)
10	12 ZING A LITTLE ZONG	
		Bing Crosby & Jane Wyman (Brunswick)

20 December 1952

1	1 HERE IN MY HEART	Al Martino (Capitol)
2	2 YOU BELONG TO ME	Jo Stafford (Columbia)
3	3 ISLE OF INNISFREE	Bing Crosby (Bruswick)
4	4 FEET UP	Guy Mitchell (Columbia)
3	5 HALF AS MUCH	
		Rosemary Clooney (Columbia)
7	6 SOMEWHERE ALONG THE WAY	
		Nat King Cole (Capitol)
-	6 BECAUSE YOU'RE MINE	
		Nat King Cole (Capitol)
-	6 WHITE CHRISTMAS	Mantovani (Decca)
-	7 FAITH CAN MOVE MOUNTAINS	
		Johnnie Ray (Columbia)
-	8 TAKES TWO TO TANGO	
		Louis Armstrong (Brunswick)
-	8 SILENT NIGHT	Bing Crosby (Brunswick)
-	9 WALKIN' TO MISSOURI	Tony Brent (Columbia)
8	10 SUGARBUSH	Doris Day &
		Frankie Laine (Columbia)
5	10 BECAUSE YOU'RE MINE	Mario Lanza (HMV)
5	10 FORGET ME NOT	Vera Lynn (Decca)
-	11 JAMBALAYA	Jo Stafford (Columbia)
9	12 HIGH NOON	Frankie Laine (Columbia)

The first-ever British singles chart, ostensibly a Top 12, actually had 15 entries in it, due to the original compilers' eccentric attitude towards tied positions. This ensured that no number between 1 and 12 was omitted, regardless of whether there were duplicate entries in the position above. This was a phenomenon which would haunt the chart throughout its first year or so of existence, stretching some Top 12's almost to Top 20 length. 1952's final chart, with 17 entries, is a case in point. Musically, balladeer Al Martino was the first ruler of the roost with his debut single, and ballads and novelties were the order of the day - a close reflection of what could be heard on the radio in Britain during the post-war austerity years. Music for a teenage audience was still some years off; in fact, in 1952, the word 'teenager' was not yet in common use.

January – February 1953

3 January 1953

Last	This	Title	Artist
1	1	HERE IN MY HEART	Al Martino (Capitol)
2	2	YOU BELONG TO ME	Jo Stafford (Columbia)
-	3	COMES A-LONG A-LOVE	Kay Starr (Capitol)
4	4	FEET UP	Guy Mitchell (Columbia)
3	5	ISLE OF INNISFREE	Bing Crosby (Brunswick)
5	6	HALF AS MUCH	Rosemary Clooney (Columbia)
10	7	BECAUSE YOU'RE MINE	Mario Lanza (HMV)
8	8	TAKES TWO TO TANGO	Louis Armstrong (Brunswick)
-	8	COWPUNCHER'S CANTATA	Max Bygraves (HMV)
6	9	WHITE CHRISTMAS	Mantovani (Decca)
10	10	SUGARBUSH	Doris Day & Frankie Laine (Columbia)
-	11	FAITH CAN MOVE MOUNTAINS	Nat King Cole (Capitol)
-	12	MAKE IT SOON	Tony Brent (Columbia)
-	12	OUTSIDE OF HEAVEN	Eddie Fisher (HMV)

10 January 1953

Last	This	Title	Artist
1	1	HERE IN MY HEART	Al Martino (Capitol)
2	2	YOU BELONG TO ME	Jo Stafford (Columbia)
3	3	COMES A-LONG A-LOVE	Kay Starr (Capitol)
5	4	ISLE OF INNISFREE	
4	5	FEET UP Guy Mitchell (Columbia)	
12	6	OUTSIDE OF HEAVEN	
-	7	WALKIN' TO MISSOURI	Tony Brent (Columbia)
6	7	HALF AS MUCH	Rosemary Clooney (Columbia)
7	8	BECAUSE YOU'RE MINE	Mario Lanza (HMV)
8	9	TAKES TWO TO TANGO	Louis Armstrong (Brunswick)
-	9	FAITH CAN MOVE MOUNTAINS	Johnnie Ray (Columbia)
10	10	SUGARBUSH	Doris Day & Frankie Laine (Columbia)
-	10	THE GLOW WORM	Mills Brothers (Brunswick)
12	11	MAKE IT SOON	Tony Brent (Columbia)
11	11	FAITH CAN MOVE MOUNTAINS	Jimmy Young (Decca)
-	12	BRITANNIA RAG	Winifred Atwell (Decca)

17 January 1953

Last	This	Title	Artist
2	1	YOU BELONG TO ME	Jo Stafford (Columbia)
3	2	COMES A-LONG A-LOVE	Kay Starr (Capitol)
8	3	BECAUSE YOU'RE MINE	Mario Lanza (HMV)
6	4	OUTSIDE OF HEAVEN	Eddie Fisher (HMV)
4	5	ISLE OF INNISFREE	Bing Crosby (Brunswick)
1	6	HERE IN MY HEART	Al Martino (Capitol)
9	7	TAKES TWO TO TANGO	Louis Armstrong (Brunswick)
5	7	FEET UP	Guy Mitchell (Columbia)
12	8	BRITANNIA RAG	Winifred Atwell (Decca)
11	9	MAKE IT SOON	Tony Brent (Columbia)
7	10	WALKIN' TO MISSOURI	Tony Brent (Columbia)
-	10	DON'T LET THE STARS GET IN YOUR EYES	Perry Como (HMV)
-	11	VANESSA	Ted Heath (Decca)
-	12	FAITH CAN MOVE MOUNTAINS	Nat King Cole (Capitol)

24 January 1953

Last	This	Title	Artist
2	1	COMES A-LONG A-LOVE	Kay Starr (Capitol)
4	2	OUTSIDE OF HEAVEN	Eddie Fisher (HMV)
1	2	YOU BELONG TO ME	Jo Stafford (Columbia)
6	3	HERE IN MY HEART	Al Martino (Capitol)
3	4	BECAUSE YOU'RE MINE	Mario Lanza (HMV)
8	5	BRITANNIA RAG	Winifred Atwell (Decca)
7	6	TAKES TWO TO TANGO	Louis Armstrong (Brunswick)
-	6	COWPUNCHER'S CANTATA	Max Bygraves (HMV)
5	7	ISLE OF INNISFREE	Bing Crosby (Brunswick)
10	8	DON'T LET THE STARS GET IN YOUR EYES	Perry Como (HMV)
9	9	MAKE IT SOON	Tony Brent (Columbia)
10	11	WALKIN' TO MISSOURI	Tony Brent (Columbia)
12	12	FAITH CAN MOVE MOUNTAINS	Nat King Cole (Capitol)
-	12	EVERYTHING I HAVE IS YOURS	Eddie Fisher (HMV)

31 January 1953

Last	This	Title	Artist
2	1	OUTSIDE OF HEAVEN	Eddie Fisher (HMV)
1	2	COMES A-LONG A-LOVE	Kay Starr (Capitol)
8	3	DON'T LET THE STARS GET IN YOUR EYES	Perry Como (HMV)
4	4	BECAUSE YOU'RE MINE	Mario Lanza (HMV)
2	5	YOU BELONG TO ME	Jo Stafford (Columbia)
3	6	HERE IN MY HEART	Al Martino (Capitol)
6	7	TAKES TWO TO TANGO	Louis Armstrong (Brunswick)
5	8	BRITANNIA RAG	Winifred Atwell (Decca)
6	9	COWPUNCHER'S CANTATA	Max Bygraves (HMV)
-	10	NOW	Al Martino (Capitol)
7	11	ISLE OF INNISFREE	Bing Crosby (Brunswick)
11	12	WALKIN' TO MISSOURI	Tony Brent (Columbia)

7 February 1953

Last	This	Title	Artist
3	1	DON'T LET THE STARS GET IN YOUR EYES	Perry Como (HMV)
2	2	COMES A-LONG A-LOVE	Kay Starr (Capitol)
1	3	OUTSIDE OF HEAVEN	Eddie Fisher (HMV)
4	4	BECAUSE YOU'RE MINE	Mario Lanza (HMV)
5	5	YOU BELONG TO ME	Jo Stafford (Columbia)
6	6	HERE IN MY HEART	Al Martino (Capitol)
9	7	COWPUNCHER'S CANTATA	Max Bygraves (HMV)
-	8	EVERYTHING I HAVE IS YOURS	Eddie Fisher (HMV)
10	9	NOW	Al Martino (Capitol)
7	10	TAKES TWO TO TANGO	Louis Armstrong (Brunswick)
12	11	WALKIN' TO MISSOURI	Tony Brent (Columbia)
8	12	BRITANNIA RAG	Winifred Atwell (Decca)

14 February 1953

Last	This	Title	Artist
1	1	DON'T LET THE STARS GET IN YOUR EYES	Perry Como (HMV)
3	2	OUTSIDE OF HEAVEN	Eddie Fisher (HMV)
2	3	COMES A-LONG A-LOVE	Kay Starr (Capitol)
4	4	BECAUSE YOU'RE MINE	Mario Lanza (HMV)
6	5	HERE IN MY HEART	Al Martino (Capitol)
5	6	YOU BELONG TO ME	Jo Stafford (Columbia)
10	7	TAKES TWO TO TANGO	Louis Armstrong (Brunswick)
9	7	NOW	Al Martino (Capitol)
7	8	COWPUNCHER'S CANTATA	Max Bygraves (HMV)
8	9	EVERYTHING I HAVE IS YOURS	Eddie Fisher (HMV)
-	10	SHE WEARS RED FEATHERS	Guy Mitchell (Columbia)
-	11	BECAUSE YOU'RE MINE	Nat King Cole (Capitol)
-	11	BROKEN WINGS	Stargazers (Decca)
-	12	BROKEN WINGS	

21 February 1953

Last	This	Title	Artist
			Art & Dotty Todd (HMV)
1	1	DON'T LET THE STARS GET IN YOUR EYES	Perry Como (HMV)
2	2	OUTSIDE OF HEAVEN	Eddie Fisher (HMV)
4	3	BECAUSE YOU'RE MINE	Mario Lanza (HMV)
3	4	COMES A-LONG A-LOVE	Kay Starr (Capitol)
10	5	SHE WEARS RED FEATHERS	Guy Mitchell (Columbia)
7	6	NOW	Al Martino (Capitol)
12	7	BROKEN WINGS	Art & Dotty Todd (HMV)
5	8	HERE IN MY HEART	Al Martino (Capitol)
6	9	YOU BELONG TO ME	Jo Stafford (Columbia)
7	10	TAKES TWO TO TANGO	Louis Armstrong (Brunswick)
9	11	EVERYTHING I HAVE IS YOURS	Eddie Fisher (HMV)
8	12	COWPUNCHER'S CANTATA	Max Bygraves (HMV)
-	12	BROKEN WINGS	Dickie Valentine (Decca)

After having spent most of the weeks since the chart's inception as the Number Two bridesmaid, Jo Stafford finally became – briefly – Britain's second chart-topper in mid-January, before surrendering the top slot to fellow US female vocalist Kay Starr. British challengers to the chart-dominant Americans were still few and far between, with pianist Winifred Atwell and vocalists Max Bygraves and Tony Brent (scoring with two singles simultaneously) as the main Top 10 contenders.

28 February 1953

last week	this week	Title / Artist
1	1	DON'T LET THE STARS GET IN YOUR EYES — Perry Como (HMV)
2	2	OUTSIDE OF HEAVEN — Eddie Fisher (HMV)
5	3	SHE WEARS RED FEATHERS — Guy Mitchell (Columbia)
6	4	NOW — Al Martino (Capitol)
3	5	BECAUSE YOU'RE MINE — Mario Lanza (HMV)
7	6	BROKEN WINGS — Art & Dotty Todd (HMV)
-	7	WONDERFUL COPENHAGEN — Danny Kaye (Brunswick)
4	8	COMES A-LONG A-LOVE — Kay Starr (Capitol)
8	9	HERE IN MY HEART — Al Martino (Capitol)
11	10	EVERYTHING I HAVE IS YOURS — Eddie Fisher (HMV)
9	11	YOU BELONG TO ME — Jo Stafford (Columbia)
-	12	BROKEN WINGS — Stargazers (Decca)

7 March 1953

last week	this week	Title / Artist
1	1	DON'T LET THE STARS GET IN YOUR EYES — Perry Como (HMV)
3	2	SHE WEARS RED FEATHERS — Guy Mitchell (Columbia)
2	3	OUTSIDE OF HEAVEN — Eddie Fisher (HMV)
5	4	BECAUSE YOU'RE MINE — Mario Lanza (HMV)
4	5	NOW — Al Martino (Capitol)
6	6	BROKEN WINGS — Art & Dotty Todd (HMV)
12	7	BROKEN WINGS — Stargazers (Decca)
11	8	YOU BELONG TO ME — Jo Stafford (Columbia)
7	9	WONDERFUL COPENHAGEN — Danny Kaye (Brunswick)
-	10	COWPUNCHER'S CANTATA — Max Bygraves (HMV)
-	11	WHY DON'T YOU BELIEVE ME — Joni James (MGM)
8	11	COMES A-LONG A-LOVE — Kay Starr (Capitol)
9	12	HERE IN MY HEART — Al Martino (Capitol)

14 March 1953

last week	this week	Title / Artist
2	1	SHE WEARS RED FEATHERS — Guy Mitchell (Columbia)
1	2	DON'T LET THE STARS GET IN YOUR EYES — Perry Como (HMV)
3	3	OUTSIDE OF HEAVEN — Eddie Fisher (HMV)
5	4	NOW — Al Martino (Capitol)
4	5	BECAUSE YOU'RE MINE — Mario Lanza (HMV)
7	6	BROKEN WINGS — Stargazers (Decca)
6	7	BROKEN WINGS — Art & Dotty Todd (HMV)
9	8	WONDERFUL COPENHAGEN — Danny Kaye (Brunswick)
-	9	(HOW MUCH IS) THAT DOGGIE IN THE WINDOW — Lita Roza (Decca)
-	10	MAKE IT SOON — Tony Brent (Columbia)
12	11	HERE IN MY HEART — Al Martino (Capitol)
8	11	YOU BELONG TO ME — Jo Stafford (Columbia)
11	12	COMES A-LONG A-LOVE — Kay Starr (Capitol)
-	12	ALL THE TIME AND EVERYWHERE — Dickie Valentine (Decca)

21 March 1953

last week	this week	Title / Artist
1	1	SHE WEARS RED FEATHERS — Guy Mitchell (Columbia)
-	2	DON'T LET THE STARS GET IN YOUR EYES — Perry Como (HMV)
4	3	NOW — Al Martino (Capitol)
9	3	(HOW MUCH IS) THAT DOGGIE IN THE WINDOW — Lita Roza (Decca)
3	4	OUTSIDE OF HEAVEN — Eddie Fisher (HMV)
5	5	BECAUSE YOU'RE MINE — Mario Lanza (HMV)
8	6	WONDERFUL COPENHAGEN — Danny Kaye (Brunswick)
6	7	BROKEN WINGS — Stargazers (Decca)
12	8	COMES A-LONG A-LOVE — Kay Starr (Capitol)
10	9	MAKE IT SOON — Tony Brent (Columbia)
12	9	ALL THE TIME AND EVERYWHERE — Dickie Valentine (Decca)
7	10	BROKEN WINGS — Art & Dotty Todd (HMV)
-	11	GIRL IN THE WOOD — Frankie Laine (Columbia)
-	12	NIGHT TRAIN — Buddy Morrow (HMV)
11	12	YOU BELONG TO ME — Jo Stafford (Columbia)

28 March 1953

last week	this week	Title / Artist
1	1	SHE WEARS RED FEATHERS — Guy Mitchell (Columbia)
4	2	OUTSIDE OF HEAVEN — Eddie Fisher (HMV)
3	3	(HOW MUCH IS) THAT DOGGIE IN THE WINDOW — Lita Roza (Decca)
2	4	DON'T LET THE STARS GET IN YOUR EYES — Perry Como (HMV)
3	5	NOW — Al Martino (Capitol)
6	6	WONDERFUL COPENHAGEN — Danny Kaye (Brunswick)
5	7	BECAUSE YOU'RE MINE — Mario Lanza (HMV)
7	8	BROKEN WINGS — Stargazers (Decca)
-	9	(HOW MUCH IS) THAT DOGGIE IN THE WINDOW — Patti Page (Oriole)
9	10	ALL THE TIME AND EVERYWHERE — Dickie Valentine (Decca)
10	11	BROKEN WINGS — Art & Dotty Todd (HMV)
9	12	MAKE IT SOON — Tony Brent (Columbia)

4 April 1953

last week	this week	Title / Artist
1	1	SHE WEARS RED FEATHERS — Guy Mitchell (Columbia)
8	2	BROKEN WINGS — Stargazers (Decca)
5	3	NOW — Al Martino (Capitol)
3	4	(HOW MUCH IS) THAT DOGGIE IN THE WINDOW — Lita Roza (Decca)
4	5	DON'T LET THE STARS GET IN YOUR EYES — Perry Como (HMV)
6	6	WONDERFUL COPENHAGEN — Danny Kaye (Brunswick)
-	7	OH HAPPY DAY — Johnston Brothers (Decca)
7	8	BECAUSE YOU'RE MINE — Mario Lanza (HMV)
2	9	OUTSIDE OF HEAVEN — Eddie Fisher (HMV)
-	10	LITTLE RED MONKEY — Frank Chacksfield (Parlophone)
-	11	I BELIEVE — Frankie Laine (Philips)
-	12	MA SAYS PA SAYS — Doris Day & Johnnie Ray (Columbia)
9	12	(HOW MUCH IS) THAT DOGGIE IN THE WINDOW — Patti Page (Oriole)

11 April 1953

last week	this week	Title / Artist
2	1	BROKEN WINGS — Stargazers (Decca)
1	2	SHE WEARS RED FEATHERS — Guy Mitchell (Columbia)
4	2	(HOW MUCH IS) THAT DOGGIE IN THE WINDOW — Lita Roza (Decca)
5	3	DON'T LET THE STARS GET IN YOUR EYES — Perry Como (HMV)
3	4	NOW — Al Martino (Capitol)
6	5	WONDERFUL COPENHAGEN — Danny Kaye (Brunswick)
-	6	SOMEBODY STOLE MY GAL — Johnnie Ray (Philips)
9	7	OUTSIDE OF HEAVEN — Eddie Fisher (HMV)
11	8	I BELIEVE — Frankie Laine (Philips)
7	9	OH HAPPY DAY — Johnston Brothers (Decca)
8	10	BECAUSE YOU'RE MINE — Mario Lanza (HMV)
10	11	LITTLE RED MONKEY — Frank Chacksfield (Parlophone)
12	12	(HOW MUCH IS) THAT DOGGIE IN THE WINDOW — Patti Page (Oriole)

18 April 1953

last week	this week	Title / Artist
2	1	(HOW MUCH IS) THAT DOGGIE IN THE WINDOW — Lita Roza (Decca)
2	2	SHE WEARS RED FEATHERS — Guy Mitchell (Columbia)
1	3	BROKEN WINGS — Stargazers (Decca)
8	4	I BELIEVE — Frankie Laine (Philips)
3	5	DON'T LET THE STARS GET IN YOUR EYES — Perry Como (HMV)
9	6	OH HAPPY DAY — Johnston Brothers (Decca)
5	6	WONDERFUL COPENHAGEN — Danny Kaye (Brunswick)
7	7	OUTSIDE OF HEAVEN — Eddie Fisher (HMV)
4	8	NOW — Al Martino (Capitol)
12	9	(HOW MUCH IS) THAT DOGGIE IN THE WINDOW — Patti Page (Oriole)
10	10	BECAUSE YOU'RE MINE — Mario Lanza (HMV)
-	11	FULL TIME JOB — Doris Day & Johnnie Ray (Columbia)
11	12	LITTLE RED MONKEY — Frank Chacksfield (Parlophone)

Winning a battle against US originator Patti Page with *(How Much Is) That Doggie In The Window*, the Ted Heath band's girl vocalist Lita Roza (whose version of the song eschewed the US hit's trademark harmony self-duetting) became the first British act to reach the UK Top Three. She also went on to a week at Number One, though (by just seven days) she was beaten there by the Stargazers' version of *Broken Wings*, which thus became the first British single to top the UK chart.

April – June 1953

25 April 1953

last week	this week	Title	Artist (Label)
4	1	I BELIEVE	Frankie Laine (Philips)
2	2	SHE WEARS RED FEATHERS	Guy Mitchell (Columbia)
1	3	(HOW MUCH IS) THAT DOGGIE IN THE WINDOW	Lita Roza (Decca)
-	4	PRETTY LITTLE BLACK EYED SUSIE	Guy Mitchell (Columbia)
6	5	OH HAPPY DAY	Johnston Brothers (Decca)
3	6	BROKEN WINGS	Stargazers (Decca)
-	7	SOMEBODY STOLE MY GAL	Johnnie Ray (Philips)
6	8	WONDERFUL COPENHAGEN	Danny Kaye (Brunswick)
5	9	DON'T LET THE STARS GET IN YOUR EYES	Perry Como (HMV)
-	9	SIDE BY SIDE	Kay Starr (Capitol)
-	10	PRETEND	Nat King Cole (Capitol)
10	11	BECAUSE YOU'RE MINE	Mario Lanza (HMV)
9	12	(HOW MUCH IS) THAT DOGGIE IN THE WINDOW	Patti Page (Oriole)

2 May 1953

last week	this week	Title	Artist (Label)
1	1	I BELIEVE	Frankie Laine (Philips)
4	2	PRETTY LITTLE BLACK EYED SUSIE	Guy Mitchell (Columbia)
2	3	SHE WEARS RED FEATHERS	Guy Mitchell (Columbia)
5	4	OH HAPPY DAY	Johnston Brothers (Decca)
3	4	(HOW MUCH IS) THAT DOGGIE IN THE WINDOW	Lita Roza (Decca)
10	5	PRETEND	Nat King Cole (Capitol)
7	6	SOMEBODY STOLE MY GAL	Johnnie Ray (Philips)
9	7	SIDE BY SIDE	Kay Starr (Capitol)
6	8	BROKEN WINGS	Stargazers (Decca)
-	9	DOWNHEARTED	Eddie Fisher (HMV)
8	10	WONDERFUL COPENHAGEN	Danny Kaye (Brunswick)
-	11	IN A GOLDEN COACH	Billy Cotton & His Band, vocals by Doreen Stephens (Decca)
-	12	OUTSIDE OF HEAVEN	Eddie Fisher (HMV)

9 May 1953

last week	this week	Title	Artist (Label)
1	1	I BELIEVE	Frankie Laine (Philips)
5	2	PRETEND	Nat King Cole (Capitol)
2	3	PRETTY LITTLE BLACK EYED SUSIE	Guy Mitchell (Columbia)
4	4	OH HAPPY DAY	Johnston Brothers (Decca)
4	5	(HOW MUCH IS) THAT DOGGIE IN THE WINDOW	Lita Roza (Decca)
3	6	SHE WEARS RED FEATHERS	Guy Mitchell (Columbia)
9	7	DOWNHEARTED	Eddie Fisher (HMV)
6	8	SOMEBODY STOLE MY GAL	Johnnie Ray (Philips)
-	9	TELL ME A STORY	Frankie Laine & Jimmy Boyd (Philips)
11	10	IN A GOLDEN COACH	Billy Cotton & His Band, vocals by Doreen Stephens (Decca)
7	11	SIDE BY SIDE	Kay Starr (Capitol)
8	12	BROKEN WINGS	Stargazers (Decca)

16 May 1953

last week	this week	Title	Artist (Label)
1	1	I BELIEVE	Frankie Laine (Philips)
2	2	PRETEND	Nat King Cole (Capitol)
3	3	PRETTY LITTLE BLACK EYED SUSIE	Guy Mitchell (Columbia)
7	4	DOWNHEARTED	Eddie Fisher (HMV)
9	5	TELL ME A STORY	Frankie Laine & Jimmy Boyd (Philips)
4	6	OH HAPPY DAY	Johnston Brothers (Decca)
6	7	SHE WEARS RED FEATHERS	Guy Mitchell (Columbia)
5	7	(HOW MUCH IS) THAT DOGGIE IN THE WINDOW	Lita Roza (Decca)
11	8	SIDE BY SIDE	Kay Starr (Capitol)
10	9	IN A GOLDEN COACH	Billy Cotton & His Band, vocals by Doreen Stephens (Decca)
8	10	SOMEBODY STOLE MY GAL	Johnnie Ray (Philips)
-	11	HOLD ME THRILL ME KISS ME	Muriel Smith (Philips)
-	12	CORONATION RAG	Winifred Atwell (Decca)
-	12	LIMELIGHT	Ron Goodwin (Parlophone)

23 May 1953

last week	this week	Title	Artist (Label)
1	1	I BELIEVE	Frankie Laine (Philips)
2	2	PRETEND	Nat King Cole (Capitol)
4	3	DOWNHEARTED	Eddie Fisher (HMV)
3	4	PRETTY LITTLE BLACK EYED SUSIE	Guy Mitchell (Columbia)
5	5	TELL ME A STORY	Frankie Laine & Jimmy Boyd (Philips)
-	6	I'M WALKING BEHIND YOU	Eddie Fisher (HMV)
9	7	IN A GOLDEN COACH	Billy Cotton & His Band, vocals by Doreen Stephens (Decca)
11	8	HOLD ME THRILL ME KISS ME	Muriel Smith (Philips)
6	8	OH HAPPY DAY	Johnston Brothers (Decca)
7	9	(HOW MUCH IS) THAT DOGGIE IN THE WINDOW	Lita Roza (Decca)
-	10	LIMELIGHT	Frank Chacksfield (Decca)
12	11	LIMELIGHT	Ron Goodwin (Parlophone)
7	12	SHE WEARS RED FEATHERS	Guy Mitchell (Columbia)

30 May 1953

last week	this week	Title	Artist (Label)
1	1	I BELIEVE	Frankie Laine (Philips)
2	2	PRETEND	Nat King Cole (Capitol)
10	3	LIMELIGHT	Frank Chacksfield (Decca)
3	4	DOWNHEARTED	Eddie Fisher (HMV)
4	5	PRETTY LITTLE BLACK EYED SUSIE	Guy Mitchell (Columbia)
7	6	HOLD ME THRILL ME KISS ME	Muriel Smith (Philips)
6	7	I'M WALKING BEHIND YOU	Eddie Fisher (HMV)
7	8	IN A GOLDEN COACH	Billy Cotton & His Band, vocals by Doreen Stephens (Decca)
5	9	TELL ME A STORY	Frankie Laine & Jimmy Boyd (Philips)
-	10	MOULIN ROUGE	Mantovani (Decca)
11	11	LIMELIGHT	Ron Goodwin (Parlophone)
-	12	CORONATION RAG	Winifred Atwell (Decca)
-	12	SOMEBODY STOLE MY GAL	Johnnie Ray (Philips)

6 June 1953

last week	this week	Title	Artist (Label)
1	1	I BELIEVE	Frankie Laine (Philips)
3	2	LIMELIGHT	Frank Chacksfield (Decca)
8	3	IN A GOLDEN COACH	Billy Cotton & His Band, vocals by Doreen Stephens (Decca)
4	4	DOWNHEARTED	Eddie Fisher (HMV)
2	4	PRETEND	Nat King Cole (Capitol)
6	4	HOLD ME THRILL ME KISS ME	Muriel Smith (Philips)
12	5	CORONATION RAG	Winifred Atwell (Decca)
7	6	I'M WALKING BEHIND YOU	Eddie Fisher (HMV)
-	7	IN A GOLDEN COACH	Dickie Valentine (Decca)
10	8	MOULIN ROUGE	Mantovani (Decca)
5	9	PRETTY LITTLE BLACK EYED SUSIE	Guy Mitchell (Columbia)
11	10	LIMELIGHT	Ron Goodwin (Parlophone)
9	11	TELL ME A STORY	Frankie Laine & Jimmy Boyd (Philips)
-	11	WINDSOR WALTZ	Vera Lynn (Decca)
-	12	I'M WALKING BEHIND YOU	Dorothy Squires (Polygon)

13 June 1953

last week	this week	Title	Artist (Label)
1	1	I BELIEVE	Frankie Laine (Philips)
2	2	LIMELIGHT	Frank Chacksfield (Decca)
4	3	PRETEND	Nat King Cole (Capitol)
8	4	MOULIN ROUGE	Mantovani (Decca)
6	5	I'M WALKING BEHIND YOU	Eddie Fisher (HMV)
4	6	HOLD ME THRILL ME KISS ME	Muriel Smith (Philips)
3	7	IN A GOLDEN COACH	Billy Cotton & His Band, vocals by Doreen Stephens (Decca)
8	8	DOWNHEARTED	Eddie Fisher (HMV)
5	9	CORONATION RAG	Winifred Atwell (Decca)
10	10	TELL ME A STORY	Frankie Laine & Jimmy Boyd (Philips)
11	11	LIMELIGHT	Ron Goodwin (Parlophone)
9	12	PRETTY LITTLE BLACK EYED SUSIE	Guy Mitchell (Columbia)
-	12	SHE WEARS RED FEATHERS	Guy Mitchell (Columbia)

Frankie Laine's biggest-ever success in Britain came with the inspirational *I Believe,* which, once it hit Number One, looked like staying there for ever. In the event, it would manage a total of 18 weeks at the top, the first nine of them consecutively, thus equalling the nine-week tenure of Al Martino's *Here In My Heart. I Believe*'s full Number One stay would never be matched by another record, though the consecutive run would be beaten by David Whitfield's 10-week champion *Cara Mia* a year later.

last week	this week	20 June 1953
1	1	I BELIEVE — Frankie Laine (Philips)
3	2	PRETEND — Nat King Cole (Capitol)
6	3	HOLD ME THRILL ME KISS ME — Muriel Smith (Philips)
5	4	I'M WALKING BEHIND YOU — Eddie Fisher (HMV)
2	5	LIMELIGHT — Frank Chacksfield (Decca)
8	6	DOWNHEARTED — Eddie Fisher (HMV)
4	7	MOULIN ROUGE — Mantovani (Decca)
11	8	IN A GOLDEN COACH — Ron Goodwin (Parlophone)
7	9	IN A GOLDEN COACH — Billy Cotton & His Band, vocals by Doreen Stephens (Decca)
10	10	TELL ME A STORY — Frankie Laine & Jimmy Boyd (Philips)
12	11	PRETTY LITTLE BLACK EYED SUSIE — Guy Mitchell (Columbia)
9	12	CORONATION RAG — Winifred Atwell (Decca)

27 June 1953

last	this	
4	1	I'M WALKING BEHIND YOU — Eddie Fisher (HMV)
1	2	I BELIEVE — Frankie Laine (Philips)
3	3	HOLD ME THRILL ME KISS ME — Muriel Smith (Philips)
5	4	LIMELIGHT — Frank Chacksfield (Decca)
2	5	PRETEND — Nat King Cole (Capitol)
7	6	MOULIN ROUGE — Mantovani (Decca)
8	7	LIMELIGHT — Ron Goodwin (Parlophone)
10	8	TELL ME A STORY — Frankie Laine & Jimmy Boyd (Philips)
6	9	DOWNHEARTED — Eddie Fisher (HMV)
11	10	PRETTY LITTLE BLACK EYED SUSIE — Guy Mitchell (Columbia)
12	11	CORONATION RAG — Winifred Atwell (Decca)
9	12	IN A GOLDEN COACH — Billy Cotton & His Band, vocals by Doreen Stephens (Decca)

4 July 1953

last	this	
2	1	I BELIEVE — Frankie Laine (Philips)
4	2	LIMELIGHT — Frank Chacksfield (Decca)
1	3	I'M WALKING BEHIND YOU — Eddie Fisher (HMV)
3	4	HOLD ME THRILL ME KISS ME — Muriel Smith (Philips)
6	5	MOULIN ROUGE — Mantovani (Decca)
5	6	PRETEND — Nat King Cole (Capitol)
8	7	TELL ME A STORY — Frankie Laine & Jimmy Boyd (Philips)
9	8	DOWNHEARTED — Eddie Fisher (HMV)
7	9	LIMELIGHT — Ron Goodwin (Parlophone)
10	10	PRETTY LITTLE BLACK EYED SUSIE — Guy Mitchell (Columbia)
-	11	HOT TODDY — Ted Heath (Decca)
12	12	IN A GOLDEN COACH — Billy Cotton & His Band, vocals by Doreen Stephens (Decca)

11 July 1953

last	this	
1	1	I BELIEVE — Frankie Laine (Philips)
2	2	LIMELIGHT — Frank Chacksfield (Decca)
4	3	HOLD ME THRILL ME KISS ME — Muriel Smith (Philips)
5	4	MOULIN ROUGE — Mantovani (Decca)
3	5	I'M WALKING BEHIND YOU — Eddie Fisher (HMV)
6	6	PRETEND — Nat King Cole (Capitol)
9	7	LIMELIGHT — Ron Goodwin (Parlophone)
7	8	TELL ME A STORY — Frankie Laine & Jimmy Bo (Philips)
8	9	DOWNHEARTED — Eddie Fisher (HMV)
-	10	RACHEL — Al Martino (Capitol)
11	11	HOT TODDY — Ted Heath (Decca)
-	12	BUSHEL AND A PECK — Vivian Blaine (Brunswick)

18 July 1953

last	this	
1	1	I BELIEVE — Frankie Laine (Philips)
2	2	LIMELIGHT — Frank Chacksfield (Decca)
3	3	HOLD ME THRILL ME KISS ME — Muriel Smith (Philips)
5	4	I'M WALKING BEHIND YOU — Eddie Fisher (HMV)
4	5	MOULIN ROUGE — Mantovani (Decca)
7	6	LIMELIGHT — Ron Goodwin (Parlophone)
9	7	DOWNHEARTED — Eddie Fisher (HMV)
8	8	TELL ME A STORY — Frankie Laine & Jimmy Boyd (Philips)
6	9	PRETEND — Nat King Cole (Capitol)
10	10	RACHEL — Al Martino (Capitol)
11	11	HOT TODDY — Ted Heath (Decca)
-	12	SEVEN LONELY DAYS — Gisele McKenzie (Capitol)

25 July 1953

last	this	
1	1	I BELIEVE — Frankie Laine (Philips)
5	2	MOULIN ROUGE — Mantovani (Decca)
2	3	LIMELIGHT — Frank Chacksfield (Decca)
4	4	I'M WALKING BEHIND YOU — Eddie Fisher (HMV)
6	5	LIMELIGHT — Ron Goodwin (Parlophone)
3	6	HOLD ME THRILL ME KISS ME — Muriel Smith (Philips)
8	7	TELL ME A STORY — Frankie Laine & Jimmy Boyd (Philips)
9	8	PRETEND — Nat King Cole (Capitol)
7	9	DOWNHEARTED — Eddie Fisher (HMV)
11	10	HOT TODDY — Ted Heath (Decca)
-	11	LET'S WALK THATA-WAY — Doris Day & Johnnie Ray (Philips)
10	12	RACHEL — Al Martino (Capitol)

1 August 1953

last	this	
1	1	I BELIEVE — Frankie Laine (Philips)
3	2	LIMELIGHT — Frank Chacksfield (Decca)
4	3	I'M WALKING BEHIND YOU — Eddie Fisher (HMV)
6	4	HOLD ME THRILL ME KISS ME — Muriel Smith (Philips)
2	5	MOULIN ROUGE — Mantovani (Decca)
5	6	LIMELIGHT — Ron Goodwin (Parlophone)
8	7	PRETEND — Nat King Cole (Capitol)
11	8	LET'S WALK THATA-WAY — Doris Day & Johnnie Ray (Philips)
10	8	HOT TODDY — Ted Heath (Decca)
9	9	DOWNHEARTED — Eddie Fisher (HMV)
7	10	TELL ME A STORY — Frankie Laine & Jimmy Boyd (Philips)
-	11	SEVEN LONELY DAYS — Gisele McKenzie (Capitol)
12	12	RACHEL — Al Martino (Capitol)

8 August 1953

last	this	
1	1	I BELIEVE — Frankie Laine (Philips)
2	2	LIMELIGHT — Frank Chacksfield (Decca)
6	3	LIMELIGHT — Ron Goodwin (Parlophone)
5	4	MOULIN ROUGE — Mantovani (Decca)
3	5	I'M WALKING BEHIND YOU — Eddie Fisher (HMV)
4	6	HOLD ME THRILL ME KISS ME — Muriel Smith (Philips)
7	7	PRETEND — Nat King Cole (Capitol)
8	8	HOT TODDY — Ted Heath (Decca)
8	9	LET'S WALK THATA-WAY — Doris Day & Johnnie Ray (Philips)
-	10	SAY YOU'RE MINE AGAIN — June Hutton (Capitol)
-	11	SOMEBODY STOLE MY GAL — Johnnie Ray (Philips)
9	12	DOWNHEARTED — Eddie Fisher (HMV)
10	12	TELL ME A STORY — Frankie Laine & Jimmy Boyd (Philips)

Titles like *Coronation Rag* and *In A Golden Coach* left no doubt about the biggest event of mid-1953. The Coronation had little more effect on the chart, however (it boosted TV set sales hugely, but isn't known to have performed similarly for record players), and the chief competition to *I Believe* throughout this period (not counting the single week that Eddie Fisher sneaked at the top) came from Charlie Chaplin's lush *Limelight* movie theme, as played by Frank Chacksfield's Orchestra.

9

August – October 1953

Frank Chacksfield might have reached Number One had it not been for Ron Goodwin's similar version of *Limelight* creaming off a large proportion of sales as it, too, rode the Top 10 for several weeks. In the end, the next record to tumble *I Believe* (again, for just one week) was another orchestral film theme: Mantovani's *Moulin Rouge*. Meanwhile, UK singer Jimmy Young (the same J.Y. who has been a Radio 2 presenter for the last 25 years) had his first of several top tenners with *Eternally*.

10 October 1953 (last week / this week)

1. 1 LOOK AT THAT GIRL — Guy Mitchell (Philips)
3. 2 I BELIEVE — Frankie Laine (Philips)
2. 3 WHERE THE WIND BLOWS — Frankie Laine (Philips)
4. 4 LET'S WALK THATA-WAY — Doris Day & Johnnie Ray (Philips)
5. 5 LIMELIGHT — Frank Chacksfield (Decca)
10. 6 CAN'T I? — Nat King Cole (Capitol)
6. 7 MOULIN ROUGE — Mantovani (Decca)
7. 8 KISS — Dean Martin (Capitol)
12. 9 MOTHER NATURE AND FATHER TIME — Nat King Cole (Capitol)
-. 10 FLIRTATION WALTZ — Winifred Atwell (Decca)
8. 11 LIMELIGHT — Ron Goodwin (Parlophone)
11. 12 ETERNALLY — Jimmy Young (Decca)

17 October 1953

1. 1 LOOK AT THAT GIRL — Guy Mitchell (Philips)
2. 2 I BELIEVE — Frankie Laine (Philips)
-. 3 HEY JOE — Frankie Laine (Philips)
3. 4 WHERE THE WIND BLOWS — Frankie Laine (Philips)
5. 5 LIMELIGHT — Frank Chacksfield (Decca)
7. 6 MOULIN ROUGE — Mantovani (Decca)
9. 7 MOTHER NATURE AND FATHER TIME — Nat King Cole (Capitol)
4. 8 LET'S WALK THATA-WAY — Doris Day & Johnnie Ray (Philips)
11. 9 LIMELIGHT — Ron Goodwin (Parlophone)
8. 10 KISS — Dean Martin (Capitol)
12. 11 ETERNALLY — Jimmy Young (Decca)
-. 12 ANSWER ME — David Whitfield (Decca)

24 October 1953

3. 1 HEY JOE — Frankie Laine (Philips)
1. 2 LOOK AT THAT GIRL — Guy Mitchell (Philips)
4. 3 WHERE THE WIND BLOWS — Frankie Laine (Philips)
2. 4 I BELIEVE — Frankie Laine (Philips)
10. 5 KISS — Dean Martin (Capitol)
5. 6 LIMELIGHT — Frank Chacksfield (Decca)
-. 6 SWEDISH RHAPSODY — Mantovani (Decca)
12. 8 ANSWER ME — David Whitfield (Decca)
8. 9 LET'S WALK THATA-WAY — Doris Day & Johnnie Ray (Philips)
7. 10 MOTHER NATURE AND FATHER TIME — Nat King Cole (Capitol)
-. 11 POPPA PICCOLINO — Diana Decker (Columbia)
-. 12 DRAGNET — Ted Heath (Decca)

31 October 1953

1. 1 HEY JOE — Frankie Laine (Philips)
2. 2 LOOK AT THAT GIRL — Guy Mitchell (Philips)
-. 3 ANSWER ME — Frankie Laine (Philips)
8. 4 ANSWER ME — David Whitfield (Decca)
3. 5 WHERE THE WIND BLOWS — Frankie Laine (Philips)
4. 6 I BELIEVE — Frankie Laine (Philips)
5. 7 KISS — Dean Martin (Capitol)
11. 8 POPPA PICCOLINO — Diana Decker (Columbia)
6. 9 SWEDISH RHAPSODY — Mantovani (Decca)
-. 10 CAN'T I? — Nat King Cole (Capitol)
10. 11 MOTHER NATURE AND FATHER TIME — Nat King Cole (Capitol)
6. 12 LIMELIGHT — Frank Chacksfield (Decca)

7 November 1953

4. 1 ANSWER ME — David Whitfield (Decca)
3. 2 ANSWER ME — Frankie Laine (Philips)
1. 3 HEY JOE — Frankie Laine (Philips)
2. 4 LOOK AT THAT GIRL — Guy Mitchell (Philips)
6. 5 I BELIEVE — Frankie Laine (Philips)
-. 6 CHICKA BOOM — Guy Mitchell (Philips)
5. 7 WHERE THE WIND BLOWS — Frankie Laine (Philips)
8. 8 POPPA PICCOLINO — Diana Decker (Columbia)
9. 9 SWEDISH RHAPSODY — Mantovani (Decca)
7. 10 KISS — Dean Martin (Capitol)
-. 11 WISH YOU WERE HERE — Eddie Fisher (HMV)
-. 12 FLIRTATION WALTZ — Winifred Atwell (Decca)

14 November 1953

2. 1 ANSWER ME — Frankie Laine (Philips)
1. 2 ANSWER ME — David Whitfield (Decca)
4. 3 LOOK AT THAT GIRL — Guy Mitchell (Philips)
3. 4 HEY JOE — Frankie Laine (Philips)
9. 5 SWEDISH RHAPSODY — Mantovani (Decca)
8. 6 POPPA PICCOLINO — Diana Decker (Columbia)
5. 7 I BELIEVE — Frankie Laine (Philips)
6. 8 CHICKA BOOM — Guy Mitchell (Philips)
7. 9 WHERE THE WIND BLOWS — Frankie Laine (Philips)
-. 10 MOULIN ROUGE — Mantovani (Decca)
11. 11 WISH YOU WERE HERE — Eddie Fisher (HMV)
10. 12 KISS — Dean Martin (Capitol)

21 November 1953

1. 1 ANSWER ME — Frankie Laine (Philips)
2. 2 ANSWER ME — David Whitfield (Decca)
5. 3 SWEDISH RHAPSODY — Mantovani (Decca)
7. 4 I BELIEVE — Frankie Laine (Philips)
6. 5 POPPA PICCOLINO — Diana Decker (Columbia)
4. 6 HEY JOE — Frankie Laine (Philips)
-. 7 VAYA CON DIOS — Les Paul & Mary Ford (Capitol)
11. 8 WISH YOU WERE HERE — Eddie Fisher (HMV)
8. 9 CHICKA BOOM — Guy Mitchell (Philips)
3. 10 LOOK AT THAT GIRL — Guy Mitchell (Philips)
-. 11 CRYING IN THE CHAPEL — Lee Lawrence (Decca)
9. 12 WHERE THE WIND BLOWS — Frankie Laine (Philips)

28 November 1953

1. 1 ANSWER ME — Frankie Laine (Philips)
2. 2 ANSWER ME — David Whitfield (Decca)
3. 3 SWEDISH RHAPSODY — Mantovani (Decca)
5. 4 POPPA PICCOLINO — Diana Decker (Columbia)
6. 5 HEY JOE — Frankie Laine (Philips)
4. 6 I BELIEVE — Frankie Laine (Philips)
9. 7 CHICKA BOOM — Guy Mitchell (Philips)
-. 8 I SAW MOMMA KISSING SANTA CLAUS — Jimmy Boyd (Columbia)
-. 9 DRAGNET — Ted Heath (Decca)
10. 10 LOOK AT THAT GIRL — Guy Mitchell (Philips)
-. 11 I SAW MOMMY KISSING SANTA CLAUS — Beverley Sisters (Philips)
7. 11 VAYA CON DIOS — Les Paul & Mary Ford (Capitol)
8. 12 WISH YOU WERE HERE — Eddie Fisher (HMV)

In the week ending October 24, Frankie Laine held three of the top four slots on the chart, including the Number One position. No act since has ever equalled or surpassed such Top Four domination – but Laine didn't stop there. A week later his *Answer Me*, flying neck-and-neck with David Whitfield's cover, crashed in at Three, giving Laine *four* placings in the Top Six, again including Number One. The irony was that Whitfield's *Answer Me* then beat Frankie's version to Number One, albeit only by a week.

December 1953

5 December 1953	12 December 1953	19 December 1953
1 1 ANSWER ME Frankie Laine (Philips)	1 1 ANSWER ME Frankie Laine (Philips)	1 1 ANSWER ME Frankie Laine (Philips)
3 2 SWEDISH RHAPSODY Mantovani (Decca)	5 1 ANSWER ME David Whitfield (Decca)	1 2 ANSWER ME David Whitfield (Decca)
8 3 I SAW MOMMA KISSING SANTA CLAUS Jimmy Boyd (Columbia)	4 2 POPPA PICCOLINO Diana Decker (Columbia)	3 3 LET'S HAVE A PARTY Winifred Atwell (Philips)
4 4 POPPA PICCOLINO Diana Decker (Columbia)	7 3 LET'S HAVE A PARTY Winifred Atwell (Philips)	- 4 SWEDISH RHAPSODY Ray Martin (Columbia)
2 5 ANSWER ME David Whitfield (Decca)	2 4 SWEDISH RHAPSODY Mantovani (Decca)	4 5 SWEDISH RHAPSODY Mantovani (Decca)
7 6 CHICKA BOOM Guy Mitchell (Philips)	6 5 CHICKA BOOM Guy Mitchell (Philips)	- 6 OH MEIN PAPA Eddie Calvert (Columbia)
- 7 DRAGNET Ray Anthony & His Orches (Capitol)	- 6 I SAW MOMMY KISSING SANTA CLAUS Beverley Sisters (Philips)	6 7 I SAW MOMMY KISSING SANTA CLAUS Beverley Sisters (Philips)
- 7 LET'S HAVE A PARTY Winifred Atwell (Philips)	- 7 CRYING IN THE CHAPEL Lee Lawrence (Decca)	8 8 I SAW MOMMA KISSING SANTA CLAUS Jimmy Boyd (Columbia)
5 8 HEY JOE Frankie Laine (Philips)	3 8 I SAW MOMMA KISSING SANTA CLAUS Jimmy Boyd (Columbia)	5 9 CHICKA BOOM Guy Mitchell (Philips)
11 9 VAYA CON DIOS Les Paul & Mary Ford (Capitol)	- 8 RICOCHET Joan Regan (Decca)	7 10 CRYING IN THE CHAPEL Lee Lawrence (Decca)
6 10 I BELIEVE Frankie Laine (Philips)	11 9 WISH YOU WERE HERE Eddie Fisher (HMV)	- 11 I SAW MOMMY KISSING SANTA CLAUS Billy Cotton & His Band, vocal by the Mill Girls & the Bandits (Decca)
- 10 SWEDISH RHAPSODY Ray Martin (Columbia)	9 10 VAYA CON DIOS Les Paul & Mary Ford (Capitol)	9 12 WISH YOU WERE HERE Eddie Fisher (HMV)
12 11 WISH YOU WERE HERE Eddie Fisher (HMV)	- 11 DRAGNET Ted Heath (Decca)	- 12 CLOUD LUCKY SEVEN Guy Mitchell (Philips)
- 12 MOULIN ROUGE Mantovani (Decca)	- 12 RAGS TO RICHES David Whitfield (Decca)	

Jimmy Boyd's *I Saw Mommy Kissing Santa Claus* had been a US Top 10 hit the previous Christmas, when the boy singer had been 12 years old. Its belated UK success was shared with the Beverley Sisters' cover. The song was by British writer Tommie Connor, who also wrote the English lyrics to *Lili Marlene*! December 12's Number One was unique: there would be later examples of records tying at the top, but never again two versions of the same song.

Frankie Laine dominated the chart in 1953, spending a record 18 weeks at Number One with I Believe

January – February 1954

9 January 1954

last week	this week	Title	Artist (Label)
6	1	OH MEIN PAPA	Eddie Calvert (Columbia)
5	2	SWEDISH RHAPSODY	Mantovani (Decca)
-	3	RAGS TO RICHES	David Whitfield (Decca)
1	4	ANSWER ME	Frankie Laine (Philips)
-	5	POPPA PICCOLINO	Diana Decker (Columbia)
2	6	ANSWER ME	David Whitfield (Decca)
-	7	BLOWING WILD	Frankie Laine (Philips)
-	8	CLOUD LUCKY SEVEN	Guy Mitchell (Philips)
3	9	LET'S HAVE A PARTY	Winifred Atwell (Philips)
10	10	CRYING IN THE CHAPEL	Lee Lawrence (Decca)
-	11	DRAGNET	Ray Anthony & His Orchestra (Capitol)
-	12	RICOCHET	Joan Regan (Decca)

16 January 1954

last week	this week	Title	Artist (Label)
1	1	OH MEIN PAPA	Eddie Calvert (Columbia)
9	2	LET'S HAVE A PARTY	Winifred Atwell (Philips)
7	2	BLOWING WILD	Frankie Laine (Philips)
2	4	SWEDISH RHAPSODY	Mantovani (Decca)
8	5	CLOUD LUCKY SEVEN	Guy Mitchell (Philips)
4	6	ANSWER ME	Frankie Laine (Philips)
3	7	RAGS TO RICHES	David Whitfield (Decca)
-	8	CHICKA BOOM	Guy Mitchell (Philips)
5	9	POPPA PICCOLINO	Diana Decker (Columbia)
12	10	RICOCHET	Joan Regan (Decca)
-	11	DRAGNET	Ted Heath (Decca)
-	12	THE CREEP	Ken Mackintosh (HMV)

23 January 1954

last week	this week	Title	Artist (Label)
1	1	OH MEIN PAPA	Eddie Calvert (Columbia)
2	2	BLOWING WILD	Frankie Laine (Philips)
5	3	CLOUD LUCKY SEVEN	Guy Mitchell (Philips)
2	4	LET'S HAVE A PARTY	Winifred Atwell (Philips)
6	5	ANSWER ME	Frankie Laine (Philips)
7	6	RAGS TO RICHES	David Whitfield (Decca)
4	7	SWEDISH RHAPSODY	Mantovani (Decca)
8	8	CHICKA BOOM	Guy Mitchell (Philips)
-	9	OH MEIN PAPA	Eddie Fisher (HMV)
-	10	THE HAPPY WANDERER	Obernkirchen Children's Choir (Parlophone)
11	11	THAT'S AMORE	Dean Martin (Capitol)
10	12	RICOCHET	Joan Regan (Decca)

30 January 1954

last week	this week	Title	Artist (Label)
1	1	OH MEIN PAPA	Eddie Calvert (Columbia)
2	2	BLOWING WILD	Frankie Laine (Philips)
3	3	CLOUD LUCKY SEVEN	Guy Mitchell (Philips)
8	4	CHICKA BOOM	Guy Mitchell (Philips)
6	4	RAGS TO RICHES	David Whitfield (Decca)
4	5	LET'S HAVE A PARTY	Winifred Atwell (Philips)
5	6	ANSWER ME	Frankie Laine (Philips)
11	7	THAT'S AMORE	Dean Martin (Capitol)
10	7	THE HAPPY WANDERER	Obernkirchen Children's Choir (Parlophone)
7	8	SWEDISH RHAPSODY	Mantovani (Decca)
12	9	RICOCHET	Joan Regan (Decca)
-	10	THE CREEP	Ken Mackintosh (HMV)
-	11	ISTANBUL	Frankie Vaughan (HMV)
-	12	ANSWER ME	David Whitfield (Decca)

6 February 1954

last week	this week	Title	Artist (Label)
1	1	OH MEIN PAPA	Eddie Calvert (Columbia)
2	2	BLOWING WILD	Frankie Laine (Philips)
3	3	CLOUD LUCKY SEVEN	Guy Mitchell (Philips)
7	4	THAT'S AMORE	Dean Martin (Capitol)
4	5	RAGS TO RICHES	David Whitfield (Decca)
7	6	THE HAPPY WANDERER	Obernkirchen Children's Choir (Parlophone)
-	7	TENNESSEE WIG WALK	Bonnie Lou (Parlophone)
6	8	ANSWER ME	Frankie Laine (Philips)
8	9	SWEDISH RHAPSODY	Mantovani (Decca)
4	10	CHICKA BOOM	Guy Mitchell (Philips)
-	11	WOMAN/MAN	Jose Ferrer/Rosemary Clooney (Philips)
-	11	OH MEIN PAPA	Eddie Fisher (HMV)
-	12	DRAGNET	Ted Heath (Decca)

13 February 1954

last week	this week	Title	Artist (Label)
1	1	OH MEIN PAPA	Eddie Calvert (Columbia)
2	2	BLOWING WILD	Frankie Laine (Philips)
3	2	CLOUD LUCKY SEVEN	Guy Mitchell (Philips)
5	3	RAGS TO RICHES	David Whitfield (Decca)
7	4	TENNESSEE WIG WALK	David Whitfield (Decca)
4	5	THAT'S AMORE	Dean Martin (Capitol)
9	6	SWEDISH RHAPSODY	Mantovani (Decca)
6	7	THE HAPPY WANDERER	Obernkirchen Children's Choir (Parlophone)
8	8	ANSWER ME	Frankie Laine (Philips)
-	9	EBB TIDE	Frank Chacksfield (Decca)
11	10	WOMAN/MAN	Jose Ferrer/Rosemary Clooney (Philips)
10	11	CHICKA BOOM	Guy Mitchell (Philips)
-	12	SKIN DEEP	Ted Heath (Decca)

20 February 1954

last week	this week	Title	Artist (Label)
1	1	OH MEIN PAPA	Eddie Calvert (Columbia)
5	2	THAT'S AMORE	Dean Martin (Capitol)
3	3	RAGS TO RICHES	David Whitfield (Decca)
2	4	BLOWING WILD	Frankie Laine (Philips)
2	4	CLOUD LUCKY SEVEN	Guy Mitchell (Philips)
4	5	TENNESSEE WIG WALK	Bonnie Lou (Parlophone)
7	6	THE HAPPY WANDERER	Obernkirchen Children's Choir (Parlophone)
10	7	WOMAN/MAN	Jose Ferrer/Rosemary Clooney (Philips)
-	8	DON'T LAUGH AT ME	Norman Wisdom (Columbia)
12	9	SKIN DEEP	Ted Heath (Decca)
-	9	CUFF OF MY SHIRT	Guy Mitchell (Philips)
8	10	ANSWER ME	Frankie Laine (Philips)
-	10	THE BOOK	David Whitfield (Decca)
9	11	EBB TIDE	Frank Chacksfield (Decca)
11	11	CHICKA BOOM	Guy Mitchell (Philips)
-	12	I SEE THE MOON	Stargazers (Decca)

27 February 1954

last week	this week	Title	Artist (Label)
1	1	OH MEIN PAPA	Eddie Calvert (Columbia)
4	2	BLOWING WILD	Frankie Laine (Philips)
2	3	THAT'S AMORE	Dean Martin (Capitol)
4	4	CLOUD LUCKY SEVEN	Guy Mitchell (Philips)
5	5	TENNESSEE WIG WALK	Bonnie Lou (Parlophone)
8	6	DON'T LAUGH AT ME	Norman Wisdom (Columbia)
7	7	WOMAN/MAN	Jose Ferrer/Rosemary Clooney (Philips)
6	7	THE HAPPY WANDERER	Obernkirchen Children's Choir (Parlophone)
12	8	I SEE THE MOON	Stargazers (Decca)
3	8	RAGS TO RICHES	David Whitfield (Decca)
10	9	THE BOOK	David Whitfield (Decca)
-	10	OH MEIN PAPA	Eddie Fisher (HMV)
9	11	SKIN DEEP	Ted Heath (Decca)
-	11	SIPPIN' SODA	Guy Mitchell (Philips)
-	12	SWEDISH RHAPSODY	Mantovani (Decca)

Trumpeter king Eddie Calvert became the fifth British artist to top the UK chart, but the first to do so for more than one week, as the Stargazers, Lita Roza, Mantovani and David Whitfield had all managed in 1953. In fact, Calvert's nine-week tenure at the top with *Oh Mein Papa* (which originally came from a German-language Swiss musical titled *Schwarze Hecht*), equalled the two longest consecutive runs so far achieved by Americans, despite strong competition from Eddie Fisher's US vocal version.

March – April 1954

6 March 1954

last week	this week	Title	Artist (Label)
1	1	OH MEIN PAPA	Eddie Calvert (Columbia)
8	2	I SEE THE MOON	Stargazers (Decca)
3	3	THAT'S AMORE	Dean Martin (Capitol)
5	4	TENNESSEE WIG WALK	Bonnie Lou (Parlophone)
7	5	THE HAPPY WANDERER	Obernkirchen Children's Choir (Parlophone)
6	6	DON'T LAUGH AT ME	Norman Wisdom (Columbia)
2	7	BLOWING WILD	Frankie Laine (Philips)
4	8	CLOUD LUCKY SEVEN	Guy Mitchell (Philips)
-	9	SKIN DEEP	Duke Ellington (Philips)
9	10	THE BOOK	David Whitfield (Decca)
8	11	RAGS TO RICHES	David Whitfield (Decca)
7	12	WOMAN/MAN	Jose Ferrer/Rosemary Clooney (Philips)

13 March 1954

last week	this week	Title	Artist (Label)
2	1	I SEE THE MOON	Stargazers (Decca)
1	2	OH MEIN PAPA	Eddie Calvert (Columbia)
5	3	THE HAPPY WANDERER	Obernkirchen Children's Choir (Parlophone)
4	4	TENNESSEE WIG WALK	Bonnie Lou (Parlophone)
6	4	DON'T LAUGH AT ME	Norman Wisdom (Columbia)
7	5	BLOWING WILD	Frankie Laine (Philips)
3	6	THAT'S AMORE	Dean Martin (Capitol)
9	7	SKIN DEEP	Duke Ellington (Philips)
6	8	CLOUD LUCKY SEVEN	Guy Mitchell (Philips)
10	9	THE BOOK	David Whitfield (Decca)
11	10	RAGS TO RICHES	David Whitfield (Decca)
-	11	OH MEIN PAPA	Eddie Fisher (HMV)
-	12	MOONLIGHT SERENADE	Glenn Miller (HMV)

20 March 1954

last week	this week	Title	Artist (Label)
1	1	I SEE THE MOON	Stargazers (Decca)
3	2	THE HAPPY WANDERER	Obernkirchen Children's Choir (Parlophone)
2	3	OH MEIN PAPA	Eddie Calvert (Columbia)
4	4	TENNESSEE WIG WALK	Bonnie Lou (Parlophone)
6	5	THAT'S AMORE	Dean Martin (Capitol)
-	6	CHANGING PARTNERS	Kay Starr (Capitol)
9	6	THE BOOK	David Whitfield (Decca)
4	7	DON'T LAUGH AT ME	Norman Wisdom (Columbia)
5	8	BLOWING WILD	Frankie Laine (Philips)
8	9	CLOUD LUCKY SEVEN	Guy Mitchell (Philips)
-	10	BELL BOTTOM BLUES	Alma Cogan (HMV)
-	10	CHANGING PARTNERS	Bing Crosby (Brunswick)
7	11	SKIN DEEP	Duke Ellington (Philips)
-	12	CUFF OF MY SHIRT	Guy Mitchell (Philips)

27 March 1954

last week	this week	Title	Artist (Label)
1	1	I SEE THE MOON	Stargazers (Decca)
2	2	THE HAPPY WANDERER	Obernkirchen Children's Choir (Parlophone)
3	3	OH MEIN PAPA	Eddie Calvert (Columbia)
7	4	DON'T LAUGH AT ME	Norman Wisdom (Columbia)
6	5	THE BOOK	David Whitfield (Decca)
10	6	BELL BOTTOM BLUES	Alma Cogan (HMV)
4	7	TENNESSEE WIG WALK	Bonnie Lou (Parlophone)
6	8	CHANGING PARTNERS	Kay Starr (Capitol)
9	9	CLOUD LUCKY SEVEN	Guy Mitchell (Philips)
11	10	SKIN DEEP	Duke Ellington (Philips)
-	10	GRANADA	Frankie Laine (Philips)
5	11	THAT'S AMORE	Dean Martin (Capitol)
8	12	BLOWING WILD	Frankie Laine (Philips)

3 April 1954

last week	this week	Title	Artist (Label)
1	1	I SEE THE MOON	Stargazers (Decca)
2	2	THE HAPPY WANDERER	Obernkirchen Children's Choir (Parlophone)
3	3	OH MEIN PAPA	Eddie Calvert (Columbia)
6	4	BELL BOTTOM BLUES	Alma Cogan (HMV)
5	5	THE BOOK	David Whitfield (Decca)
4	6	DON'T LAUGH AT ME	Norman Wisdom (Columbia)
7	7	TENNESSEE WIG WALK	Bonnie Lou (Parlophone)
11	8	THAT'S AMORE	Dean Martin (Capitol)
-	9	CHANGING PARTNERS	Bing Crosby (Brunswick)
-	10	SECRET LOVE	Doris Day (Philips)
8	10	CHANGING PARTNERS	Kay Starr (Capitol)
-	11	CUFF OF MY SHIRT	Guy Mitchell (Philips)
9	12	CLOUD LUCKY SEVEN	Guy Mitchell (Philips)

10 April 1954

last week	this week	Title	Artist (Label)
1	1	I SEE THE MOON	Stargazers (Decca)
2	2	THE HAPPY WANDERER	Obernkirchen Children's Choir (Parlophone)
6	3	DON'T LAUGH AT ME	Norman Wisdom (Columbia)
10	4	CHANGING PARTNERS	Kay Starr (Capitol)
10	5	SECRET LOVE	Doris Day (Philips)
4	6	BELL BOTTOM BLUES	Alma Cogan (HMV)
5	7	THE BOOK	David Whitfield (Decca)
3	8	OH MEIN PAPA	Eddie Calvert (Columbia)
-	9	GRANADA	Frankie Laine (Philips)
-	10	SUCH A NIGHT	Johnnie Ray (Philips)
7	11	TENNESSEE WIG WALK	Bonnie Lou (Parlophone)
-	12	THE HAPPY WANDERER	Stargazers (Decca)

17 April 1954

last week	this week	Title	Artist (Label)
5	1	SECRET LOVE	Doris Day (Philips)
2	2	THE HAPPY WANDERER	Obernkirchen Children's Choir (Parlophone)
1	3	I SEE THE MOON	Stargazers (Decca)
10	4	SUCH A NIGHT	Johnnie Ray (Philips)
3	5	DON'T LAUGH AT ME	Norman Wisdom (Columbia)
4	6	CHANGING PARTNERS	Kay Starr (Capitol)
8	7	OH MEIN PAPA	Eddie Calvert (Columbia)
6	8	BELL BOTTOM BLUES	Alma Cogan (HMV)
9	9	THE KID'S LAST FIGHT	Frankie Laine (Philips)
-	10	TENDERLY	Nat King Cole (Capitol)
7	11	THE BOOK	David Whitfield (Decca)
-	12	BIMBO	Ruby Wright (Parlophone)

24 April 1954

last week	this week	Title	Artist (Label)
3	1	I SEE THE MOON	Stargazers (Decca)
1	2	SECRET LOVE	Doris Day (Philips)
4	3	SUCH A NIGHT	Johnnie Ray (Philips)
2	4	THE HAPPY WANDERER	Obernkirchen Children's Choir (Parlophone)
6	5	CHANGING PARTNERS	Kay Starr (Capitol)
8	6	BELL BOTTOM BLUES	Alma Cogan (HMV)
7	7	OH MEIN PAPA	Eddie Calvert (Columbia)
9	8	THE KID'S LAST FIGHT	Frankie Laine (Philips)
12	9	BIMBO	Ruby Wright (Parlophone)
5	10	DON'T LAUGH AT ME	Norman Wisdom (Columbia)
-	11	CHANGING PARTNERS	Bing Crosby (Brunswick)
11	12	THE BOOK	David Whitfield (Decca)

Another film song joined the fray as Doris Day's *Secret Love*, from her movie *Calamity Jane*, became the biggest hit of the late spring of 1955. It played tag at Number One with the Stargazers' tongue-in-cheek *I See The Moon* and Johnnie Ray's *Such A Night* (which had some problems with BBC airplay), before settling down to a two-month top slot tenure. The Stargazers, incidentally, after being the first UK act to have a Number One, now also became the first to secure a second (and their last).

1 May 1954

last week	this week		
3	1	SUCH A NIGHT	Johnnie Ray (Philips)
2	2	SECRET LOVE	Doris Day (Philips)
8	3	THE KID'S LAST FIGHT	Frankie Laine (Philips)
1	4	I SEE THE MOON	Stargazers (Decca)
5	5	CHANGING PARTNERS	Kay Starr (Capitol)
4	6	THE HAPPY WANDERER	Obernkirchen Children's Choir (Parlophone)
10	7	DON'T LAUGH AT ME	Norman Wisdom (Columbia)
-	8	DIME AND A DOLLAR	Guy Mitchell (Philips)
6	9	BELL BOTTOM BLUES	Alma Cogan (HMV)
7	10	OH MEIN PAPA	Eddie Calvert (Columbia)
9	11	BIMBO	Ruby Wright (Parlophone)
-	12	FRIENDS AND NEIGHBOURS	Billy Cotton & His Band, vocals by The Bandits (Decca)
12	12	THE BOOK	David Whitfield (Decca)

8 May 1954

2	1	SECRET LOVE	Doris Day (Philips)
1	2	SUCH A NIGHT	Johnnie Ray (Philips)
6	3	THE HAPPY WANDERER	Obernkirchen Children's Choir (Parlophone)
5	4	CHANGING PARTNERS	Kay Starr (Capitol)
4	5	I SEE THE MOON	Stargazers (Decca)
3	6	THE KID'S LAST FIGHT	Frankie Laine (Philips)
11	7	BIMBO	Ruby Wright (Parlophone)
-	8	MAKE LOVE TO ME	Jo Stafford (Philips)
7	9	DON'T LAUGH AT ME	Norman Wisdom (Columbia)
9	10	BELL BOTTOM BLUES	Alma Cogan (HMV)
12	11	THE BOOK	David Whitfield (Decca)
10	12	OH MEIN PAPA	Eddie Calvert (Columbia)

15 May 1954

1	1	SECRET LOVE	Doris Day (Philips)
2	2	SUCH A NIGHT	Johnnie Ray (Philips)
6	3	THE KID'S LAST FIGHT	Frankie Laine (Philips)
3	4	THE HAPPY WANDERER	Obernkirchen Children's Choir (Parlophone)
5	5	I SEE THE MOON	Stargazers (Decca)
-	6	FRIENDS AND NEIGHBOURS	Billy Cotton & His Band, vocals by The Bandits (Decca)
4	6	CHANGING PARTNERS	Kay Starr (Capitol)
9	8	DON'T LAUGH AT ME	Norman Wisdom (Columbia)
-	9	DIME AND A DOLLAR	Guy Mitchell (Philips)
-	10	SOMEONE ELSE'S ROSES	Joan Regan (Decca)
-	11	HEART OF MY HEART	Max Bygraves (HMV)
10	11	BELL BOTTOM BLUES	Alma Cogan (HMV)

22 May 1954

1	1	SECRET LOVE	Doris Day (Philips)
2	2	SUCH A NIGHT	Johnnie Ray (Philips)
6	3	FRIENDS AND NEIGHBOURS	Billy Cotton & His Band, vocals by The Bandits (Decca)
6	4	CHANGING PARTNERS	Kay Starr (Capitol)
4	5	THE HAPPY WANDERER	Obernkirchen Children's Choir (Parlophone)
3	6	THE KID'S LAST FIGHT	Frankie Laine (Philips)
10	7	SOMEONE ELSE'S ROSES	Joan Regan (Decca)
5	8	I SEE THE MOON	Stargazers (Decca)
11	9	HEART OF MY HEART	Max Bygraves (HMV)
8	10	DON'T LAUGH AT ME	Norman Wisdom (Columbia)
9	11	DIME AND A DOLLAR	Guy Mitchell (Philips)
-	12	BIMBO	Ruby Wright (Parlophone)

29 May 1954

1	1	SECRET LOVE	Doris Day (Philips)
2	2	SUCH A NIGHT	Johnnie Ray (Philips)
3	3	FRIENDS AND NEIGHBOURS	Billy Cotton & His Band, vocals by The Bandits (Decca)
5	4	THE HAPPY WANDERER	Obernkirchen Children's Choir (Parlophone)
6	5	THE KID'S LAST FIGHT	Frankie Laine (Philips)
7	6	SOMEONE ELSE'S ROSES	Joan Regan (Decca)
9	7	HEART OF MY HEART	Max Bygraves (HMV)
11	8	DIME AND A DOLLAR	Guy Mitchell (Philips)
4	9	CHANGING PARTNERS	Kay Starr (Capitol)
10	10	DON'T LAUGH AT ME	Norman Wisdom (Columbia)
8	11	I SEE THE MOON	Stargazers (Decca)
-	12	THE BOOK	David Whitfield (Decca)

5 June 1954

1	1	SECRET LOVE	Doris Day (Philips)
2	2	SUCH A NIGHT	Johnnie Ray (Philips)
3	3	FRIENDS AND NEIGHBOURS	Billy Cotton & His Band, vocals by The Bandits (Decca)
4	4	THE HAPPY WANDERER	Obernkirchen Children's Choir (Parlophone)
6	5	SOMEONE ELSE'S ROSES	Joan Regan (Decca)
5	6	THE KID'S LAST FIGHT	Frankie Laine (Philips)
7	7	HEART OF MY HEART	Max Bygraves (HMV)
9	8	CHANGING PARTNERS	Kay Starr (Capitol)
-	9	OH BABY MINE, I GET SO LONELY	Four Knights (Capitol)
8	9	DIME AND A DOLLAR	Guy Mitchell (Philips)
12	10	THE BOOK	David Whitfield (Decca)
-	11	WANTED	Perry Como (HMV)
-	12	WANTED	Al Martino (Capitol)

12 June 1954

1	1	SECRET LOVE	Doris Day (Philips)
2	2	SUCH A NIGHT	Johnnie Ray (Philips)
3	3	FRIENDS AND NEIGHBOURS	Billy Cotton & His Band, vocals by The Bandits (Decca)
4	4	THE HAPPY WANDERER	Obernkirchen Children's Choir (Parlophone)
5	5	SOMEONE ELSE'S ROSES	Joan Regan (Decca)
9	6	OH BABY MINE, I GET SO LONELY	Four Knights (Capitol)
6	7	THE KID'S LAST FIGHT	Frankie Laine (Philips)
7	8	HEART OF MY HEART	Max Bygraves (HMV)
8	9	CHANGING PARTNERS	Kay Starr (Capitol)
11	10	WANTED	Perry Como (HMV)
10	11	THE BOOK	David Whitfield (Decca)
-	12	THE LITTLE SHOEMAKER	Petula Clark (Polygon)

19 June 1954

1	1	SECRET LOVE	Doris Day (Philips)
2	2	SUCH A NIGHT	Johnnie Ray (Philips)
3	3	FRIENDS AND NEIGHBOURS	Billy Cotton & His Band, vocals by The Bandits (Decca)
10	4	WANTED	Perry Como (HMV)
4	5	THE HAPPY WANDERER	Obernkirchen Children's Choir (Parlophone)
6	6	OH BABY MINE, I GET SO LONELY	Four Knights (Capitol)
5	7	SOMEONE ELSE'S ROSES	Joan Regan (Decca)
8	8	HEART OF MY HEART	Max Bygraves (HMV)
-	9	CARA MIA	David Whitfield (Decca)
9	10	CHANGING PARTNERS	Kay Starr (Capitol)
7	11	THE KID'S LAST FIGHT	Frankie Laine (Philips)
-	12	WANTED	Al Martino (Capitol)

Petula Clark, who would become a chart regular during the later 1950s and then throughout the '60s, made her debut with *The Little Shoemaker*, a novelty not untypical of her early material, but far removed from her later commercial style(s). Ruby Wright's *Bimbo* was in a similar bag: adult novelty records with appeal to children. Everybody seemed to miss the point during this era that no material was being directly aimed at the most impressionable and potentially lucrative record buyers of all - teenagers.

June – August 1954

26 June 1954

last	this		
1	1	SECRET LOVE	Doris Day (Philips)
2	2	SUCH A NIGHT	Johnnie Ray (Philips)
9	2	CARA MIA	David Whitfield (Decca)
4	4	WANTED	Perry Como (HMV)
6	5	OH BABY MINE, I GET SO LONELY	Four Knights (Capitol)
-	6	IDLE GOSSIP	Perry Como (HMV)
3	7	FRIENDS AND NEIGHBOURS	Billy Cotton & His Band, vocals by The Bandits (Decca)
7	8	SOMEONE ELSE'S ROSES	Joan Regan (Decca)
8	9	HEART OF MY HEART	Max Bygraves (HMV)
12	10	WANTED	Al Martino (Capitol)
-	11	THE LITTLE SHOEMAKER	Petula Clark (Polygon)
5	12	THE HAPPY WANDERER	Obernkirchen Children's Choir (Parlophone)

3 July 1954

2	1	CARA MIA	David Whitfield (Decca)
1	2	SECRET LOVE	Doris Day (Philips)
2	3	SUCH A NIGHT	Johnnie Ray (Philips)
6	4	IDLE GOSSIP	Perry Como (HMV)
-	5	LITTLE THINGS MEAN A LOT	Kitty Kallen (Brunswick)
7	6	FRIENDS AND NEIGHBOURS	Billy Cotton & His Band, vocals by The Bandits (Decca)
4	7	WANTED	Perry Como (HMV)
10	8	WANTED	Al Martino (Capitol)
5	9	OH BABY MINE, I GET SO LONELY	Four Knights (Capitol)
11	10	THE LITTLE SHOEMAKER	Petula Clark (Polygon)
8	11	SOMEONE ELSE'S ROSES	Joan Regan (Decca)
9	12	HEART OF MY HEART	Max Bygraves (HMV)

10 July 1954

1	1	CARA MIA	David Whitfield (Decca)
2	2	SECRET LOVE	Doris Day (Philips)
5	3	LITTLE THINGS MEAN A LOT	Kitty Kallen (Brunswick)
4	4	IDLE GOSSIP	Perry Como (HMV)
7	5	WANTED	Perry Como (HMV)
9	6	OH BABY MINE, I GET SO LONELY	Four Knights (Capitol)
3	7	SUCH A NIGHT	Johnnie Ray (Philips)
8	8	WANTED	Al Martino (Capitol)
6	9	FRIENDS AND NEIGHBOURS	Billy Cotton & His Band, vocals by The Bandits (Decca)
10	10	THE LITTLE SHOEMAKER	Petula Clark (Polygon)
-	11	THE HAPPY WANDERER	Obernkirchen Children's Choir (Parlophone)
-	12	YOUNG AT HEART	Frank Sinatra (Capitol)

17 July 1954

1	1	CARA MIA	David Whitfield (Decca)
3	2	LITTLE THINGS MEAN A LOT	Kitty Kallen (Brunswick)
2	3	SECRET LOVE	Doris Day (Philips)
4	4	IDLE GOSSIP	Perry Como (HMV)
8	5	WANTED	Al Martino (Capitol)
5	6	WANTED	Perry Como (HMV)
7	7	SUCH A NIGHT	Johnnie Ray (Philips)
11	8	THE HAPPY WANDERER	Obernkirchen Children's Cho (Parlophone)
10	9	THE LITTLE SHOEMAKER	Petula Clark (Polygon)
6	10	OH BABY MINE, I GET SO LONELY	Four Knights (Capitol)
-	11	THREE COINS IN THE FOUNTAIN	Frank Sinatra (Capitol)
9	12	FRIENDS AND NEIGHBOURS	Billy Cotton & His Band, vocals by The Bandits (Decca)

24 July 1954

1	1	CARA MIA	David Whitfield (Decca)
2	2	LITTLE THINGS MEAN A LOT	Kitty Kallen (Brunswick)
3	3	SECRET LOVE	Doris Day (Philips)
5	4	WANTED	Al Martino (Capitol)
4	5	IDLE GOSSIP	Perry Como (HMV)
11	6	THREE COINS IN THE FOUNTAIN	Frank Sinatra (Capitol)
9	7	THE LITTLE SHOEMAKER	Petula Clark (Polygon)
6	8	WANTED	Perry Como (HMV)
7	9	SUCH A NIGHT	Johnnie Ray (Philips)
8	10	THE HAPPY WANDERER	Obernkirchen Children's Choir (Parlophone)
-	11	THE STORY OF THREE LOVES (RACHMANINOFF'S 18TH VARIATION)	Winifred Atwell (Philips)
12	12	FRIENDS AND NEIGHBOURS	Billy Cotton & His Band, vocals by The Bandits (Decca)

31 July 1954

1	1	CARA MIA	David Whitfield (Decca)
2	2	LITTLE THINGS MEAN A LOT	Kitty Kallen (Brunswick)
3	3	SECRET LOVE	Doris Day (Philips)
4	4	WANTED	Al Martino (Capitol)
6	5	THREE COINS IN THE FOUNTAIN	Frank Sinatra (Capitol)
5	6	IDLE GOSSIP	Perry Como (HMV)
8	7	WANTED	Perry Como (HMV)
7	8	THE LITTLE SHOEMAKER	Petula Clark (Polygon)
-	9	THREE COINS IN THE FOUNTAIN	Four Aces (Brunswick)
9	10	SUCH A NIGHT	Johnnie Ray (Philips)
11	11	THE STORY OF THREE LOVES (RACHMANINOFF'S 18TH VARIATION)	Winifred Atwell (Philips)
-	12	OH BABY MINE, I GET SO LONELY	Four Knights (Capitol)

7 August 1954

1	1	CARA MIA	David Whitfield (Decca)
5	2	THREE COINS IN THE FOUNTAIN	Frank Sinatra (Capitol)
2	3	LITTLE THINGS MEAN A LOT	Kitty Kallen (Brunswick)
4	4	WANTED	Al Martino (Capitol)
6	5	IDLE GOSSIP	Perry Como (HMV)
3	6	SECRET LOVE	Doris Day (Philips)
8	7	THE LITTLE SHOEMAKER	Petula Clark (Polygon)
7	8	WANTED	Perry Como (HMV)
9	9	THREE COINS IN THE FOUNTAIN	Four Aces (Brunswick)
11	10	THE STORY OF THREE LOVES (RACHMANINOFF'S 18TH VARIATION)	Winifred Atwell (Philips)
12	11	OH BABY MINE, I GET SO LONELY	Four Knights (Capitol)
10	12	SUCH A NIGHT	Johnnie Ray (Philips)

14 August 1954

1	1	CARA MIA	David Whitfield (Decca)
3	2	LITTLE THINGS MEAN A LOT	Kitty Kallen (Brunswick)
2	3	THREE COINS IN THE FOUNTAIN	Frank Sinatra (Capitol)
5	4	IDLE GOSSIP	Perry Como (HMV)
9	5	THREE COINS IN THE FOUNTAIN	Four Aces (Brunswick)
4	6	WANTED	Al Martino (Capitol)
6	7	SECRET LOVE	Doris Day (Philips)
-	8	MY FRIEND	Frankie Laine (Philips)
8	9	WANTED	Perry Como (HMV)
11	10	OH BABY MINE, I GET SO LONELY	Four Knights (Capitol)
10	11	THE STORY OF THREE LOVES (RACHMANINOFF'S 18TH VARIATION)	Winifred Atwell (Philips)
7	12	THE LITTLE SHOEMAKER	Petula Clark (Polygon)

David Whitfield's *Cara Mia*, on which he was accompanied by Mantovani & His Orchestra (a hitmaking act in their own right), was the hit which broke the existing record for consecutive weeks at Number One, staying astride the chart for 10 weeks in succession. Co-written (under a pseudonym) by Mantovani, *Cara Mia* was former Hughie Green protege Whitfield's biggest success, also reaching the US Top 10 and making him the first British male vocalist to have a million-seller in America.

last this week

21 August 1954

last	this		
1	1	CARA MIA	David Whitfield (Decca)
2	2	LITTLE THINGS MEAN A LOT	Kitty Kallen (Brunswick)
4	3	IDLE GOSSIP	Perry Como (HMV)
7	4	SECRET LOVE	Doris Day (Philips)
3	5	THREE COINS IN THE FOUNTAIN	Frank Sinatra (Capitol)
8	6	MY FRIEND	Frankie Laine (Philips)
6	7	WANTED	Al Martino (Capitol)
5	8	THREE COINS IN THE FOUNTAIN	Four Aces (Brunswick)
9	9	WANTED	Perry Como (HMV)
11	10	THE STORY OF THREE LOVES (RACHMANINOFF'S 18TH VARIATION)	Winifred Atwell (Philips)
10	11	OH BABY MINE, I GET SO LONELY	Four Knights (Capitol)
12	12	THE LITTLE SHOEMAKER	Petula Clark (Polygon)

28 August 1954

last	this		
1	1	CARA MIA	David Whitfield (Decca)
2	2	LITTLE THINGS MEAN A LOT	Kitty Kallen (Brunswick)
5	3	THREE COINS IN THE FOUNTAIN	Frank Sinatra (Capitol)
6	4	MY FRIEND	Frankie Laine (Philips)
3	5	IDLE GOSSIP	Perry Como (HMV)
4	6	SECRET LOVE	Doris Day (Philips)
-	7	BLACK HILLS OF DAKOTA	Doris Day (Philips)
7	8	WANTED	Al Martino (Capitol)
10	9	THE STORY OF THREE LOVES (RACHMANINOFF'S 18TH VARIATION)	Winifred Atwell (Philips)
8	10	THREE COINS IN THE FOUNTAIN	Four Aces (Brunswick)
-	11	LITTLE THINGS MEAN A LOT	Alma Cogan (HMV)
9	12	WANTED	Perry Como (HMV)

4 September 1954

last	this		
1	1	CARA MIA	David Whitfield (Decca)
2	2	LITTLE THINGS MEAN A LOT	Kitty Kallen (Brunswick)
3	3	THREE COINS IN THE FOUNTAIN	Frank Sinatra (Capitol)
4	4	MY FRIEND	Frankie Laine (Philips)
6	5	SECRET LOVE	Doris Day (Philips)
8	6	WANTED	Al Martino (Capitol)
5	7	IDLE GOSSIP	Perry Como (HMV)
7	8	BLACK HILLS OF DAKOTA	Doris Day (Philips)
9	9	THE STORY OF THREE LOVES (RACHMANINOFF'S 18TH VARIATION)	Winifred Atwell (Philips)
-	10	HOLD MY HAND	Don Cornell (Vogue)
11	11	LITTLE THINGS MEAN A LOT	Alma Cogan (HMV)
12	12	WANTED	Perry Como (HMV)

2 October 1954

last	this		
1	1	THREE COINS IN THE FOUNTAIN	Frank Sinatra (Capitol)
6	2	SMILE	Nat King Cole (Capitol)
2	3	CARA MIA	David Whitfield (Decca)
3	4	MY FRIEND	Frankie Laine (Philips)
4	5	HOLD MY HAND	Don Cornell (Vogue)
5	6	LITTLE THINGS MEAN A LOT	Kitty Kallen (Brunswick)
7	7	GILLY GILLY OSSENFEFFER KATZENELLEN BOGEN BY THE SEA	Max Bygraves (HMV)
10	8	SECRET LOVE	Doris Day (Philips)
9	9	BLACK HILLS OF DAKOTA	Doris Day (Philips)
-	10	SWAY	Dean Martin (Capitol)
-	10	THE STORY OF TINA	Al Martino (Capitol)
12	12	THE STORY OF TINA	Ronnie Harris (Columbia)
11	13	WEST OF ZANZIBAR	Anthony Steel & the Radio Revellers (Polygon)
8	14	IDLE GOSSIP	Perry Como (HMV)
-	15	IF I GIVE MY HEART TO YOU	Doris Day (Philips)
	16	SH-BOOM	Crew Cuts (Mercury)
	17	WANTED	Al Martino (Capitol)
	18	WANTED	Perry Como (HMV)
	19	THE STORY OF THREE LOVES (RACHMANINOFF'S 18TH VARIATION ON A THEME BY PAGANINI)	Winifred Atwell (Philips)
	20	IF I GIVE MY HEART TO YOU	Joan Regan (Decca)

11 September 1954

last	this		
2	1	LITTLE THINGS MEAN A LOT	Kitty Kallen (Brunswick)
3	2	THREE COINS IN THE FOUNTAIN	Frank Sinatra (Capitol)
1	3	CARA MIA	David Whitfield (Decca)
4	4	MY FRIEND	Frankie Laine (Philips)
10	5	HOLD MY HAND	Don Cornell (Vogue)
-	6	SMILE	Nat King Cole (Capitol)
8	7	BLACK HILLS OF DAKOTA	Doris Day (Philips)
6	7	WANTED	Al Martino (Capitol)
7	9	IDLE GOSSIP	Perry Como (HMV)
5	10	SECRET LOVE	Doris Day (Philips)
-	11	GILLY GILLY OSSENFEFFER KATZENELLEN BOGEN BY THE SEA	Max Bygraves (HMV)
-	12	WEST OF ZANZIBAR	Anthony Steel & the Radio Revellers (Polygon)

18 September 1954

last	this		
2	1	THREE COINS IN THE FOUNTAIN	Frank Sinatra (Capitol)
3	2	CARA MIA	David Whitfield (Decca)
1	3	LITTLE THINGS MEAN A LOT	Kitty Kallen (Brunswick)
5	4	HOLD MY HAND	Don Cornell (Vogue)
6	5	SMILE	Nat King Cole (Capitol)
4	6	MY FRIEND	Frankie Laine (Philips)
9	7	IDLE GOSSIP	Perry Como (HMV)
10	8	SECRET LOVE	Doris Day (Philips)
7	9	BLACK HILLS OF DAKOTA	Doris Day (Philips)
-	10	WANTED	Al Martino (Capitol)
11	11	GILLY GILLY OSSENFEFFER KATZENELLEN BOGEN BY THE SEA	Max Bygraves (HMV)
12	12	WEST OF ZANZIBAR	Anthony Steel & the Radio Revellers (Polygon)

25 September 1954

last	this		
1	1	THREE COINS IN THE FOUNTAIN	Frank Sinatra (Capitol)
2	2	CARA MIA	David Whitfield (Decca)
6	3	MY FRIEND	Frankie Laine (Philips)
4	4	HOLD MY HAND	Don Cornell (Vogue)
3	5	LITTLE THINGS MEAN A LOT	Kitty Kallen (Brunswick)
5	6	SMILE	Nat King Cole (Capitol)
11	7	GILLY GILLY OSSENFEFFER KATZENELLEN BOGEN BY THE SEA	Max Bygraves (HMV)
7	8	IDLE GOSSIP	Perry Como (HMV)
9	9	BLACK HILLS OF DAKOTA	Doris Day (Philips)
8	10	SECRET LOVE	Doris Day (Philips)
12	11	WEST OF ZANZIBAR	Anthony Steel & the Radio Revellers (Polygon)
-	12	THE STORY OF TINA	Ronnie Harris (Columbia)

Kitty Kallen was one of the first major one-hit wonders in the UK charts - Number One with *Little Things Mean A Lot*, then never heard of again. In the US, where this was 1954's biggest single, with two months at the top, she also managed a Top 10 follow-up with *In The Chapel In The Moonlight*. Winifred Atwell's *The Story Of Three Loves* was her version of that film's theme tune; the actual piece of music was *Rachmaninoff's 18th Variation On A Theme By Paganini*.

October – November 1954

last this
week

9 October 1954

last	this		
5	1	HOLD MY HAND	Don Cornell (Vogue)
6	2	LITTLE THINGS MEAN A LOT	
			Kitty Kallen (Brunswick)
2	3	SMILE	Nat King Cole (Capitol)
1	4	THREE COINS IN THE FOUNTAIN	
			Frank Sinatra (Capitol)
4	5	MY FRIEND	Frankie Laine (Philips)
3	6	CARA MIA	David Whitfield (Decca)
10	7	SWAY	Dean Martin (Capitol)
15	8	IF I GIVE MY HEART TO YOU	Doris Day (Philips)
9	9	BLACK HILLS OF DAKOTA	Doris Day (Philips)
10	10	THE STORY OF TINA	Al Martino (Capitol)
-	11	MAKE HER MINE	Nat King Cole (Capitol)
16	12	SH-BOOM	Crew Cuts (Mercury)
-	13	THERE MUST BE A REASON	
			Frankie Laine (Philips)
8	14	SECRET LOVE	Doris Day (Philips)
7	15	GILLY GILLY OSSENFEFFER KATZENELLEN	
		BOGEN BY THE SEA	Max Bygraves (HMV)
-	16	THIS OLE HOUSE	Rosemary Clooney (Philips)
12	17	THE STORY OF TINA	Ronnie Harris (Columbia)
13	18	WEST OF ZANZIBAR	Anthony Steel
			& the Radio Revellers (Polygon)
-	19	LITTLE THINGS MEAN A LOT	Alma Cogan (HMV)
19	20	THE STORY OF THREE LOVES	
		(RACHMANINOFF'S 18TH VARIATION)	
			Winifred Atwell (Philips)

16 October 1954

1	1	HOLD MY HAND	Don Cornell (Vogue)
3	2	SMILE	Nat King Cole (Capitol)
4	3	THREE COINS IN THE FOUNTAIN	
			Frank Sinatra (Capitol)
2	4	LITTLE THINGS MEAN A LOT	
			Kitty Kallen (Brunswick)
5	5	MY FRIEND	Frankie Laine (Philips)
7	6	SWAY	Dean Martin (Capitol)
6	7	CARA MIA	David Whitfield (Decca)
8	8	IF I GIVE MY HEART TO YOU	
			Doris Day (Philips)
-	9	MY SON MY SON	Vera Lynn (Decca)
16	10	THIS OLE HOUSE	Rosemary Clooney (Philips)
10	10	THE STORY OF TINA	Al Martino (Capitol)
-	12	THIS OLE HOUSE	Billie Anthony (Columbia)
12	13	SH-BOOM	Crew Cuts (Mercury)
13	14	THERE MUST BE A REASON	
			Frankie Laine (Philips)
15	15	GILLY GILLY OSSENFEFFER KATZENELLEN	
		BOGEN BY THE SEA	Max Bygraves (HMV)
9	16	BLACK HILLS OF DAKOTA	Doris Day (Philips)
-	17	AM I A TOY OR A TREASURE	Kay Starr (Capitol)
14	18	SECRET LOVE	Doris Day (Philips)
11	19	MAKE HER MINE	Nat King Cole (Capitol)
18	20	WEST OF ZANZIBAR	Anthony Steel
			& the Radio Revellers (Polygon)

23 October 1954

1	1	HOLD MY HAND	Don Cornell (Vogue)
2	2	SMILE	Nat King Cole (Capitol)
5	3	MY FRIEND	Frankie Laine (Philips)
3	4	THREE COINS IN THE FOUNTAIN	
			Frank Sinatra (Capitol)
4	5	LITTLE THINGS MEAN A LOT	
			Kitty Kallen (Brunswick)
9	6	MY SON MY SON	Vera Lynn (Decca)
7	7	CARA MIA	David Whitfield (Decca)
12	8	THIS OLE HOUSE	Billie Anthony (Columbia)
14	9	THERE MUST BE A REASON	
			Frankie Laine (Philips)
8	10	IF I GIVE MY HEART TO YOU	Doris Day (Philips)
6	11	SWAY	Dean Martin (Capitol)
13	12	SH-BOOM	Crew Cuts (Mercury)
10	13	THIS OLE HOUSE	Rosemary Clooney (Philips)
10	14	THE STORY OF TINA	Al Martino (Capitol)
-	15	HOW DO YOU SPEAK TO AN ANGEL	
			Dean Martin (Capitol)
-	16	RAIN RAIN RAIN	Frankie Laine (Philips)
-	17	THREE COINS IN THE FOUNTAIN	
			Four Aces (Brunswick)
15	18	GILLY GILLY OSSENFEFFER KATZENELLEN	
		BOGEN BY THE SEA	Max Bygraves (HMV)
-	18	LITTLE THINGS MEAN A LOT	Alma Cogan (HMV)
17	20	AM I A TOY OR A TREASURE	Kay Starr (Capitol)

30 October 1954

1	1	HOLD MY HAND	Don Cornell (Vogue)
6	2	MY SON MY SON	Vera Lynn (Decca)
2	3	SMILE	Nat King Cole (Capitol)
8	4	THIS OLE HOUSE	Billie Anthony (Columbia)
13	5	THIS OLE HOUSE	Rosemary Clooney (Philips)
10	6	IF I GIVE MY HEART TO YOU	Doris Day (Philips)
3	7	MY FRIEND	Frankie Laine (Philips)
16	8	RAIN RAIN RAIN	Frankie Laine (Philips)
5	9	LITTLE THINGS MEAN A LOT	
			Kitty Kallen (Brunswick)
-	10	IF I GIVE MY HEART TO YOU	
			Joan Regan (Decca)
9	11	THERE MUST BE A REASON	
			Frankie Laine (Philips)
4	12	THREE COINS IN THE FOUNTAIN	
			Frank Sinatra (Capitol)
7	13	CARA MIA	David Whitfield (Decca)
11	14	SWAY	Dean Martin (Capitol)
14	15	THE STORY OF TINA	Al Martino (Capitol)
12	16	SH-BOOM	Crew Cuts (Mercury)
-	17	I NEED YOU NOW	Eddie Fisher (HMV)
20	18	AM I A TOY OR A TREASURE	Kay Starr (Capitol)
15	19	HOW DO YOU SPEAK TO AN ANGEL	
			Dean Martin (Capitol)
18	20	LITTLE THINGS MEAN A LOT	Alma Cogan (HMV)

6 November 1954

2	1	MY SON MY SON	Vera Lynn (Decca)
5	2	THIS OLE HOUSE	Rosemary Clooney (Philips)
1	3	HOLD MY HAND	Don Cornell (Vogue)
3	4	SMILE	Nat King Cole (Capitol)
6	5	IF I GIVE MY HEART TO YOU	Doris Day (Philips)
4	6	THIS OLE HOUSE	Billie Anthony (Columbia)
7	7	MY FRIEND	Frankie Laine (Philips)
8	8	RAIN RAIN RAIN	Frankie Laine (Philips)
10	8	IF I GIVE MY HEART TO YOU	
			Joan Regan (Decca)
9	10	LITTLE THINGS MEAN A LOT	
			Kitty Kallen (Brunswick)
12	10	THREE COINS IN THE FOUNTAIN	
			Frank Sinatra (Capitol)
11	12	THERE MUST BE A REASON	
			Frankie Laine (Philips)
13	13	CARA MIA	David Whitfield (Decca)
16	14	SH-BOOM	Crew Cuts (Mercury)
14	15	SWAY	Dean Martin (Capitol)
17	16	I NEED YOU NOW	Eddie Fisher (HMV)
15	17	THE STORY OF TINA	Al Martino (Capitol)
-	18	WAIT FOR ME, DARLING	
			Joan Regan & the Johnston Brothers (Decca)
-	19	ENDLESS	Dickie Valentine (Decca)
-	20	GILLY GILLY OSSENFEFFER KATZENELLEN	
		BOGEN BY THE SEA	Max Bygraves (HMV)

13 November 1954

1	1	MY SON MY SON	Vera Lynn (Decca)
3	2	HOLD MY HAND	Don Cornell (Vogue)
2	3	THIS OLE HOUSE	Rosemary Clooney (Philips)
5	4	IF I GIVE MY HEART TO YOU	Doris Day (Philips)
6	5	THIS OLE HOUSE	Billie Anthony (Columbia)
8	6	IF I GIVE MY HEART TO YOU	
			Joan Regan (Decca)
4	7	SMILE	Nat King Cole (Capitol)
7	8	MY FRIEND	Frankie Laine (Philips)
10	9	LITTLE THINGS MEAN A LOT	
			Kitty Kallen (Brunswick)
8	9	RAIN RAIN RAIN	Frankie Laine (Philips)
10	11	THREE COINS IN THE FOUNTAIN	
			Frank Sinatra (Capitol)
13	12	CARA MIA	David Whitfield (Decca)
-	13	SANTO NATALE	David Whitfield (Decca)
14	14	SH-BOOM	Crew Cuts (Mercury)
15	15	SWAY	Dean Martin (Capitol)
-	16	NO ONE BUT YOU	Billy Eckstine (MGM)
-	17	A SKY BLUE SHIRT AND A RAINBOW TIE	
			Norman Brooks (London)
12	17	THERE MUST BE A REASON	
			Frankie Laine (Philips)
17	19	THE STORY OF TINA	Al Martino (Capitol)
-	20	AM I A TOY OR A TREASURE	Kay Starr (Capitol)

My Son, My Son provided Vera Lynn's only chart-topping hit (though she almost certainly would have had many more, had the chart existed prior to 1952). The song was part-written by Eddie Calvert, who had been at Number One himself earlier in the year. *This Ole House*, the song penned by Stuart Hamblen about his finding a dead man in a derelict shack, was arguably the hottest song of late 1954, with Rosemary Clooney's version hitting the top, and Billie Anthony's UK cover closely chasing it.

November – December 1954

20 November 1954

2	1	HOLD MY HAND	Don Cornell (Vogue)
3	2	THIS OLE HOUSE	Rosemary Clooney (Philips)
1	2	MY SON MY SON	Vera Lynn (Decca)
6	4	IF I GIVE MY HEART TO YOU	Joan Regan (Decca)
4	5	IF I GIVE MY HEART TO YOU	Doris Day (Philips)
5	6	THIS OLE HOUSE	Billie Anthony (Columbia)
7	7	SMILE	Nat King Cole (Capitol)
12	8	CARA MIA	David Whitfield (Decca)
16	9	NO ONE BUT YOU	Billy Eckstine (MGM)
9	10	RAIN RAIN RAIN	Frankie Laine (Philips)
13	11	SANTO NATALE	David Whitfield (Decca)
9	12	LITTLE THINGS MEAN A LOT	Kitty Kallen (Brunswick)
8	13	MY FRIEND	Frankie Laine (Philips)
17	13	THERE MUST BE A REASON	Frankie Laine (Philips)
-	15	SH-BOOM	Stan Freberg (Capitol)
-	16	I NEED YOU NOW	Eddie Fisher (HMV)
14	17	SH-BOOM	Crew Cuts (Mercury)
11	18	THREE COINS IN THE FOUNTAIN	Frank Sinatra (Capitol)
-	19	HOW DO YOU SPEAK TO AN ANGEL	Dean Martin (Capitol)
19	20	THE STORY OF TINA	Al Martino (Capitol)

27 November 1954

2	1	THIS OLE HOUSE	Rosemary Clooney (Philips)
2	2	MY SON MY SON	Vera Lynn (Decca)
4	3	IF I GIVE MY HEART TO YOU	Joan Regan (Decca)
1	4	HOLD MY HAND	Don Cornell (Vogue)
7	5	SMILE	Nat King Cole (Capitol)
11	6	SANTO NATALE	David Whitfield (Decca)
9	7	NO ONE BUT YOU	Billy Eckstine (MGM)
6	8	THIS OLE HOUSE	Billie Anthony (Columbia)
-	9	LET'S HAVE ANOTHER PARTY	Winifred Atwell (Philips)
10	10	RAIN RAIN RAIN	Frankie Laine (Philips)
5	11	IF I GIVE MY HEART TO YOU	Doris Day (Philips)
8	12	CARA MIA	David Whitfield (Decca)
13	13	THERE MUST BE A REASON	Frankie Laine (Philips)
-	14	LET'S HAVE A PARTY	Winifred Atwell (Philips)
16	14	I NEED YOU NOW	Eddie Fisher (HMV)
12	14	LITTLE THINGS MEAN A LOT	Kitty Kallen (Brunswick)
-	17	I STILL BELIEVE	Ronnie Hilton (HMV)
17	18	SH-BOOM	Crew Cuts (Mercury)
15	19	SH-BOOM	Stan Freberg (Capitol)
19	20	HOW DO YOU SPEAK TO AN ANGEL	Dean Martin (Capitol)

4 December 1954

9	1	LET'S HAVE ANOTHER PARTY	Winifred Atwell (Philips)
6	2	SANTO NATALE	David Whitfield (Decca)
1	3	THIS OLE HOUSE	Rosemary Clooney (Philips)
4	4	HOLD MY HAND	Don Cornell (Vogue)
8	5	THIS OLE HOUSE	Billie Anthony (Columbia)
3	6	IF I GIVE MY HEART TO YOU	Joan Regan (Decca)
2	7	MY SON MY SON	Vera Lynn (Decca)
7	8	NO ONE BUT YOU	Billy Eckstine (MGM)
17	9	I STILL BELIEVE	Ronnie Hilton (HMV)
11	10	IF I GIVE MY HEART TO YOU	Doris Day (Philips)
5	11	SMILE	Nat King Cole (Capitol)
10	12	RAIN RAIN RAIN	Frankie Laine (Philips)
14	13	I NEED YOU NOW	Eddie Fisher (HMV)
13	14	THERE MUST BE A REASON	Frankie Laine (Philips)
-	15	HEARTBEAT	Ruby Murray (Columbia)
14	16	LET'S HAVE A PARTY	Winifred Atwell (Philips)
-	17	I CAN'T TELL A WALTZ FROM A TANGO	Alma Cogan (HMV)
12	18	CARA MIA	David Whitfield (Decca)
20	19	HOW DO YOU SPEAK TO AN ANGEL	Dean Martin (Capitol)
14	20	LITTLE THINGS MEAN A LOT	Kitty Kallen (Brunswick)

11 December 1954

1	1	LET'S HAVE ANOTHER PARTY	Winifred Atwell (Philips)
2	2	SANTO NATALE	David Whitfield (Decca)
3	3	THIS OLE HOUSE	Rosemary Clooney (Philips)
8	4	NO ONE BUT YOU	Billy Eckstine (MGM)
7	4	MY SON MY SON	Vera Lynn (Decca)
5	6	THIS OLE HOUSE	Billie Anthony (Columbia)
4	7	HOLD MY HAND	Don Cornell (Vogue)
6	8	IF I GIVE MY HEART TO YOU	Joan Regan (Decca)
12	9	RAIN RAIN RAIN	Frankie Laine (Philips)
9	10	I STILL BELIEVE	Ronnie Hilton (HMV)
15	11	HEARTBEAT	Ruby Murray (Columbia)
10	12	IF I GIVE MY HEART TO YOU	Doris Day (Philips)
11	13	SMILE	Nat King Cole (Capitol)
13	14	I NEED YOU NOW	Eddie Fisher (HMV)
-	15	LET'S GET TOGETHER NO.1	Big Ben Banjo Band (Columbia)
-	16	PAPA LOVES MAMBO	Perry Como (HMV)
19	17	HOW DO YOU SPEAK TO AN ANGEL	Dean Martin (Capitol)
16	18	LET'S HAVE A PARTY	Winifred Atwell (Philips)
17	19	I CAN'T TELL A WALTZ FROM A TANGO	Alma Cogan (HMV)
-	20	VENI VIDI VICI	Ronnie Hilton (HMV)

18 December 1954

1	1	LET'S HAVE ANOTHER PARTY	Winifred Atwell (Philips)
2	2	SANTO NATALE	David Whitfield (Decca)
10	3	I STILL BELIEVE	Ronnie Hilton (HMV)
3	4	THIS OLE HOUSE	Rosemary Clooney (Philips)
4	5	NO ONE BUT YOU	Billy Eckstine (MGM)
15	6	LET'S GET TOGETHER NO.1	Big Ben Banjo Band (Columbia)
-	7	FINGER OF SUSPICION	Dickie Valentine (Decca)
4	8	MY SON MY SON	Vera Lynn (Decca)
9	9	RAIN RAIN RAIN	Frankie Laine (Philips)
11	10	HEARTBEAT	Ruby Murray (Columbia)
7	11	HOLD MY HAND	Don Cornell (Vogue)
6	12	THIS OLE HOUSE	Billie Anthony (Columbia)
-	13	SHAKE RATTLE AND ROLL	Bill Haley & the Comets (Brunswick)
19	14	I CAN'T TELL A WALTZ FROM A TANGO	Alma Cogan (HMV)
8	14	IF I GIVE MY HEART TO YOU	Joan Regan (Decca)
20	16	VENI VIDI VICI	Ronnie Hilton (HMV)
-	17	MR. SANDMAN	Chordettes (Columbia)
14	18	I NEED YOU NOW	Eddie Fisher (HMV)
-	19	MR. SANDMAN	Dickie Valentine (Decca)
18	20	LET'S HAVE A PARTY	Winifred Atwell (Philips)
-	20	MAMBO ITALIANO	Rosemary Clooney (Philips)
-	20	PIANO MEDLEY NO.114	Charlie Kunz (Decca)

Two records specifically released for Christmas - Winifred Atwell's singalong piano medley *Let's Have Another Party* and David Whitfield's *Santo Natale* (which means something festive in Italian) - ruled the year's final charts. More historically significant was the debut of Bill Haley on December 18 with *Shake, Rattle And Roll*, the first rock disc to make the UK chart. America's Christmas Number One was the Chordettes' *Mr Sandman*, which also made a year-end debut here alongside Dickie Valentine's cover.

Rock 'n' Roll Arrives

The unlikely figure of Bill Haley led the way when Shake, Rattle And Roll charted in Britain in December 1954. Like many other early rock 'n' roll hits the song was an R&B number widely played by black bands, including a seminal version by Big Joe Turner. Then came the film Blackboard Jungle, with Rock Around The Clock as its theme tune, and the face of popular music changed forever. With hindsight it seems extraordinary that many people thought that rock 'n' roll would be a temporary fad. Bill Haley's popularity declined but he was replaced by a flood of new singers and bands from across the Atlantic – rock 'n' roll was here to stay.
Clockwise from top left: Eddie Cochran; Bill Haley; Little Richard; The Everlys; Fats Domino

January – February 1955

8 January 1955

last	this		
7	1	FINGER OF SUSPICION	
			Dickie Valentine (Decca)
1	2	LET'S HAVE ANOTHER PARTY	
			Winifred Atwell (Philips)
20	3	MAMBO ITALIANO	Rosemary Clooney (Philips)
5	4	NO ONE BUT YOU	Billy Eckstine (MGM)
2	5	SANTA NATALE	David Whitfield (Decca)
3	6	I STILL BELIEVE	Ronnie Hilton (HMV)
11	7	HOLD MY HAND	Don Cornell (Vogue)
10	7	HEARTBEAT	Ruby Murray (Columbia)
19	9	MR. SANDMAN	Dickie Valentine (Decca)
13	10	SHAKE RATTLE AND ROLL	
			Bill Haley & His Comets (Brunswick)
17	11	MR. SANDMAN	Chordettes (Columbia)
12	12	THIS OLE HOUSE	Billie Anthony (Columbia)
14	13	I CAN'T WALTZ FROM A TANGO	
			Alma Cogan (HMV)
-	14	MR. SANDMAN	Four Aces (Brunswick)
8	14	MY SON, MY SON	
			Vera Lynn & Frank Weir & His Saxophone
			(Decca)
4	16	THIS OLE HOUSE	Rosemary Clooney (Philips)
-	17	ROCK AROUND THE CLOCK	
			Bill Haley & His Comets (Brunswick)
-	18	COUNT YOUR BLESSINGS	
			Bing Crosby (Brunswick)
9	19	RAIN RAIN RAIN	Frankie Laine (Philips)
16	20	VENI-VIDI-VICI	Ronnie Hilton (HMV)

15 January 1955

last	this		
3	1	MAMBO ITALIANO	Rosemary Clooney (Philips)
1	2	FINGER OF SUSPICION	
			Dickie Valentine (Decca)
4	3	NO ONE BUT YOU	Billy Eckstine (MGM)
6	4	I STILL BELIEVE	Ronnie Hilton (HMV)
7	5	HEARTBEAT	Ruby Murray (Columbia)
10	6	SHAKE RATTLE AND ROLL	
			Bill Haley & His Comets (Brunswick)
9	7	MR. SANDMAN	Dickie Valentine (Decca)
13	8	I CAN'T WALTZ FROM A TANGO	
			Alma Cogan (HMV)
14	9	MR. SANDMAN	Four Aces (Brunswick)
16	10	THIS OLE HOUSE	Rosemary Clooney (Philips)
19	11	RAIN RAIN RAIN	Frankie Laine (Philips)
2	12	LET'S HAVE ANOTHER PARTY	
			Winifred Atwell (Philips)
5	13	SANTA NATALE	David Whitfield (Decca)
11	14	MR. SANDMAN	Chordettes (Columbia)
7	15	HOLD MY HAND	Don Cornell (Vogue)
-	16	CHARLIE KUNZ PIANO MEDLEY NO. 114	
			Charlie Kunz (Decca)
20	17	VENI-VIDI-VICI	Ronnie Hilton (HMV)
17	18	ROCK AROUND THE CLOCK	
			Bill Haley & His Comets (Brunswick)
12	19	THIS OLE HOUSE	Billie Anthony (Columbia)
14	20	MY SON, MY SON	
			Vera Lynn & Frank Weir & His Saxophone
			(Decca)

22 January 1955

last	this		
2	1	FINGER OF SUSPICION	
			Dickie Valentine (Decca)
1	2	MAMBO ITALIANO	Rosemary Clooney (Philips)
3	3	NO ONE BUT YOU	Billy Eckstine (MGM)
6	4	SHAKE RATTLE AND ROLL	
			Bill Haley & His Comets (Brunswick)
4	5	I STILL BELIEVE	Ronnie Hilton (HMV)
8	6	I CAN'T WALTZ FROM A TANGO	
			Alma Cogan (HMV)
5	7	HEARTBEAT	Ruby Murray (Columbia)
11	8	RAIN RAIN RAIN	Frankie Laine (Philips)
7	9	MR. SANDMAN	Dickie Valentine (Decca)
10	10	THIS OLE HOUSE	Rosemary Clooney (Philips)
9	11	MR. SANDMAN	Four Aces (Brunswick)
14	12	MR. SANDMAN	Chordettes (Columbia)
19	13	THIS OLE HOUSE	Billie Anthony (Columbia)
-	14	HAPPY DAYS AND LONELY NIGHTS	
			Suzi Miller (Decca)
-	15	GIVE ME YOUR WORD	
			Tennessee Ernie Ford (Capitol)
-	16	MR. SANDMAN	Max Bygraves (HMV)
-	17	COUNT YOUR BLESSINGS	
			Bing Crosby (Brunswick)
17	18	VENI-VIDI-VICI	Ronnie Hilton (HMV)
-	19	I NEED YOU NOW	Eddie Fisher (HMV)
15	20	HOLD MY HAND	Don Cornell (Vogue)

29 January 1955

last	this		
1	1	FINGER OF SUSPICION	
			Dickie Valentine (Decca)
2	2	MAMBO ITALIANO	Rosemary Clooney (Philips)
7	3	HEARTBEAT	Ruby Murray (Columbia)
5	4	I STILL BELIEVE	Ronnie Hilton (HMV)
3	5	NO ONE BUT YOU	Billy Eckstine (MGM)
9	6	MR. SANDMAN	Dickie Valentine (Decca)
4	7	SHAKE RATTLE AND ROLL	
			Bill Haley & His Comets (Brunswick)
6	8	I CAN'T WALTZ FROM A TANGO	
			Alma Cogan (HMV)
-	9	SOFTLY, SOFTLY	Ruby Murray (Columbia)
15	10	GIVE ME YOUR WORD	
			Tennessee Ernie Ford (Capitol)
17	11	COUNT YOUR BLESSINGS	
			Bing Crosby (Brunswick)
18	12	VENI-VIDI-VICI	Ronnie Hilton (HMV)
8	13	RAIN RAIN RAIN	Frankie Laine (Philips)
-	14	HAPPY DAYS AND LONELY NIGHTS	
			Frankie Vaughan (HMV)
10	15	THIS OLE HOUSE	Rosemary Clooney (Philips)
12	16	MR. SANDMAN	Chordettes (Columbia)
11	17	MR. SANDMAN	Four Aces (Brunswick)
14	18	HAPPY DAYS AND LONELY NIGHTS	
			Suzi Miller (Decca)
13	19	THIS OLE HOUSE	Billie Anthony (Columbia)
-	20	THE NAUGHTY LADY OF SHADY LANE	
			Dean Martin (Capitol)

5 February 1955

last	this		
2	1	MAMBO ITALIANO	Rosemary Clooney (Philips)
1	2	FINGER OF SUSPICION	Dickie Valentine (Decca)
9	3	SOFTLY, SOFTLY	Ruby Murray (Columbia)
7	4	SHAKE RATTLE AND ROLL	
			Bill Haley & His Comets (Brunswick)
6	5	MR. SANDMAN	Dickie Valentine (Decca)
10	6	GIVE ME YOUR WORD	
			Tennessee Ernie Ford (Capitol)
3	7	HEARTBEAT	Ruby Murray (Columbia)
5	8	NO ONE BUT YOU	Billy Eckstine (MGM)
-	9	THE NAUGHTY LADY OF SHADY LANE	
			Ames Brothers (HMV)
20	10	THE NAUGHTY LADY OF SHADY LANE	
			Dean Martin (Capitol)
4	11	I STILL BELIEVE	Ronnie Hilton (HMV)
14	12	HAPPY DAYS AND LONELY NIGHTS	
			Frankie Vaughan (HMV)
-	13	DRINK, DRINK, DRINK (THE DRINKING SONG)	
			Mario Lanza (HMV)
-	14	MAMBO ITALIANO	Dean Martin (Capitol)
8	15	I CAN'T WALTZ FROM A TANGO	
			Alma Cogan (HMV)
-	16	HAPPY DAYS AND LONELY NIGHTS	
			Ruby Murray (Columbia)
13	17	RAIN RAIN RAIN	Frankie Laine (Philips)
15	18	THIS OLE HOUSE	Rosemary Clooney (Philips)
16	19	MR. SANDMAN	Chordettes (Columbia)
17	20	MR. SANDMAN	Four Aces (Brunswick)

12 February 1955

last	this		
1	1	MAMBO ITALIANO	Rosemary Clooney (Philips)
3	2	SOFTLY, SOFTLY	Ruby Murray (Columbia)
2	3	FINGER OF SUSPICION	
			Dickie Valentine (Decca)
6	4	GIVE ME YOUR WORD	
			Tennessee Ernie Ford (Capitol)
7	5	HEARTBEAT	Ruby Murray (Columbia)
9	6	THE NAUGHTY LADY OF SHADY LANE	
			Ames Brothers (HMV)
10	7	THE NAUGHTY LADY OF SHADY LANE	
			Dean Martin (Capitol)
8	8	NO ONE BUT YOU	Billy Eckstine (MGM)
5	9	MR. SANDMAN	Dickie Valentine (Decca)
4	10	SHAKE RATTLE AND ROLL	
			Bill Haley & His Comets (Brunswick)
-	11	LET ME GO LOVER	
			Teresa Brewer (Vogue/Coral)
11	12	I STILL BELIEVE	Ronnie Hilton (HMV)
-	13	BEYOND THE STARS	David Whitfield (Decca)
16	14	HAPPY DAYS AND LONELY NIGHTS	
			Ruby Murray (Columbia)
-	15	MOBILE	Ray Burns (Columbia)
-	16	LONELY BALLERINA	Mantovani (Decca)
12	17	HAPPY DAYS AND LONELY NIGHTS	
			Frankie Vaughan (HMV)
14	18	MAMBO ITALIANO	Dean Martin (Capitol)
15	19	I CAN'T WALTZ FROM A TANGO	
			Alma Cogan (HMV)
-	20	TEACH ME TONIGHT	
			De Castro Sisters (London)

While Dickie Valentine and Rosemary Clooney swapped back and forth at the top, Valentine also scored best in the now three-way battle (the Four Aces' version had` also charted) over *Mr Sandman* by reaching the Top Five. Bill Haley's *Rock Around The Clock* made a fairly inauspicious initial showing, but his *Shake, Rattle And Roll* became the first genuine rock'n'roll Top Five hit. The popular *Naughty Lady Of Shady Lane* turned out, innocuously, to be a small child, so BBC airplay on this title was not an issue!

February – March 1955

19 February 1955

last	this	title	artist
2	1	SOFTLY, SOFTLY	Ruby Murray (Columbia)
1	2	MAMBO ITALIANO	Rosemary Clooney (Philips)
4	3	GIVE ME YOUR WORD	Tennessee Ernie Ford (Capitol)
3	4	FINGER OF SUSPICION	Dickie Valentine (Decca)
5	5	HEARTBEAT	Ruby Murray (Columbia)
7	6	THE NAUGHTY LADY OF SHADY LANE	Dean Martin (Capitol)
10	7	SHAKE RATTLE AND ROLL	Bill Haley & His Comets (Brunswick)
6	8	THE NAUGHTY LADY OF SHADY LANE	Ames Brothers (HMV)
11	9	LET ME GO LOVER	Teresa Brewer (Vogue/Coral)
8	10	NO ONE BUT YOU	Billy Eckstine (MGM)
14	11	HAPPY DAYS AND LONELY NIGHTS	Ruby Murray (Columbia)
13	12	BEYOND THE STARS	David Whitfield (Decca)
9	13	MR. SANDMAN	Dickie Valentine (Decca)
15	14	MOBILE	Ray Burns (Columbia)
-	15	A BLOSSOM FELL	Dickie Valentine (Decca)
16	16	LET ME GO LOVER	Joan Weber (Philips)
-	17	MAJORCA	Petula Clark (Polygon)
-	18	I'LL WALK WITH GOD	Mario Lanza (HMV)
12	19	I STILL BELIEVE	Ronnie Hilton (HMV)
16	20	LONELY BALLERINA	Mantovani (Decca)

26 February 1955

last	this	title	artist
1	1	SOFTLY, SOFTLY	Ruby Murray (Columbia)
3	2	GIVE ME YOUR WORD	Tennessee Ernie Ford (Capitol)
2	3	MAMBO ITALIANO	Rosemary Clooney (Philips)
5	4	HEARTBEAT	Ruby Murray (Columbia)
4	5	FINGER OF SUSPICION	Dickie Valentine (Decca)
11	6	HAPPY DAYS AND LONELY NIGHTS	Ruby Murray (Columbia)
6	7	THE NAUGHTY LADY OF SHADY LANE	Dean Martin (Capitol)
8	8	THE NAUGHTY LADY OF SHADY LANE	Ames Brothers (HMV)
7	9	SHAKE RATTLE AND ROLL	Bill Haley & His Comets (Brunswick)
9	10	LET ME GO LOVER	Teresa Brewer (Vogue/Coral)
10	11	NO ONE BUT YOU	Billy Eckstine (MGM)
12	12	BEYOND THE STARS	David Whitfield (Decca)
-	13	A BLOSSOM FELL	Nat King Cole (Capitol)
17	14	MAJORCA	Petula Clark (Polygon)
13	15	MR. SANDMAN	Dickie Valentine (Decca)
14	16	MOBILE	Ray Burns (Columbia)
16	16	LET ME GO LOVER	Dean Martin (Capitol)
18	18	A BLOSSOM FELL	Dickie Valentine (Decca)
20	19	LONELY BALLERINA	Mantovani (Decca)
19	20	I STILL BELIEVE	Ronnie Hilton (HMV)

5 March 1955

last	this	title	artist
1	1	SOFTLY, SOFTLY	Ruby Murray (Columbia)
2	2	GIVE ME YOUR WORD	Tennessee Ernie Ford (Capitol)
3	3	MAMBO ITALIANO	Rosemary Clooney (Philips)
4	4	HEARTBEAT	Ruby Murray (Columbia)
7	5	THE NAUGHTY LADY OF SHADY LANE	Dean Martin (Capitol)
5	5	FINGER OF SUSPICION	Dickie Valentine (Decca)
6	7	HAPPY DAYS AND LONELY NIGHTS	Ruby Murray (Columbia)
12	8	BEYOND THE STARS	David Whitfield (Decca)
10	9	LET ME GO LOVER	Teresa Brewer (Vogue/Coral)
16	10	LET ME GO LOVER	Dean Martin (Capitol)
8	11	THE NAUGHTY LADY OF SHADY LANE	Ames Brothers (HMV)
16	12	MOBILE	Ray Burns (Columbia)
-	14	MAJORCA	Petula Clark (Polygon)
-	14	LET ME GO LOVER	Ruby Murray (Columbia)
9	16	SHAKE RATTLE AND ROLL	Bill Haley & His Comets (Brunswick)
18	17	A BLOSSOM FELL	Dickie Valentine (Decca)
11	18	NO ONE BUT YOU	Billy Eckstine (MGM)
15	19	MR. SANDMAN	Dickie Valentine (Decca)
-	20	SOMEBODY	Stargazers (Decca)

12 March 1955

last	this	title	artist
2	1	GIVE ME YOUR WORD	Tennessee Ernie Ford (Capitol)
1	2	SOFTLY, SOFTLY	Ruby Murray (Columbia)
3	3	MAMBO ITALIANO	Rosemary Clooney (Philips)
5	4	FINGER OF SUSPICION	Dickie Valentine (Decca)
10	5	LET ME GO LOVER	Dean Martin (Capitol)
4	6	HEARTBEAT	Ruby Murray (Columbia)
15	7	A BLOSSOM FELL	Nat King Cole (Capitol)
6	8	HAPPY DAYS AND LONELY NIGHTS	Ruby Murray (Columbia)
12	9	MOBILE	Ray Burns (Columbia)
8	9	BEYOND THE STARS	David Whitfield (Decca)
5	11	THE NAUGHTY LADY OF SHADY LANE	Dean Martin (Capitol)
14	12	LET ME GO LOVER	Ruby Murray (Columbia)
9	13	LET ME GO LOVER	Teresa Brewer (Vogue/Coral)
12	14	MAJORCA	Petula Clark (Polygon)
16	15	SHAKE RATTLE AND ROLL	Bill Haley & His Comets (Brunswick)
-	16	A BLOSSOM FELL	Ronnie Hilton (HMV)
11	17	THE NAUGHTY LADY OF SHADY LANE	Ames Brothers (HMV)
17	17	A BLOSSOM FELL	Dickie Valentine (Decca)
-	19	TOMORROW	Johnny Brandon (Polygon)
-	20	IN THE BEGINNING	Frankie Laine (Philips)

19 March 1955

last	this	title	artist
1	1	GIVE ME YOUR WORD	Tennessee Ernie Ford (Capitol)
2	2	SOFTLY, SOFTLY	Ruby Murray (Columbia)
7	3	A BLOSSOM FELL	Nat King Cole (Capitol)
9	4	MOBILE	Ray Burns (Columbia)
12	5	LET ME GO LOVER	Ruby Murray (Columbia)
3	6	MAMBO ITALIANO	Rosemary Clooney (Philips)
11	7	THE NAUGHTY LADY OF SHADY LANE	Dean Martin (Capitol)
5	8	LET ME GO LOVER	Dean Martin (Capitol)
4	9	FINGER OF SUSPICION	Dickie Valentine (Decca)
13	10	LET ME GO LOVER	Teresa Brewer (Vogue/Coral)
17	11	A BLOSSOM FELL	Dickie Valentine (Decca)
19	12	TOMORROW	Johnny Brandon (Polygon)
9	13	BEYOND THE STARS	David Whitfield (Decca)
8	14	HAPPY DAYS AND LONELY NIGHTS	Ruby Murray (Columbia)
6	15	HEARTBEAT	Ruby Murray (Columbia)
-	16	WEDDING BELLS	Eddie Fisher (HMV)
-	17	IF ANYONE FINDS THIS, I LOVE YOU	Ruby Murray & Anne Warren (Columbia)
-	18	LONELY BALLERINA	Mantovani (Decca)
15	19	SHAKE RATTLE AND ROLL	Bill Haley & His Comets (Brunswick)
16	20	A BLOSSOM FELL	Ronnie Hilton (HMV)

26 March 1955

last	this	title	artist
1	1	GIVE ME YOUR WORD	Tennessee Ernie Ford (Capitol)
2	2	SOFTLY, SOFTLY	Ruby Murray (Columbia)
8	3	LET ME GO LOVER	Dean Martin (Capitol)
3	4	A BLOSSOM FELL	Nat King Cole (Capitol)
4	5	MOBILE	Ray Burns (Columbia)
6	6	LET ME GO LOVER	Ruby Murray (Columbia)
16	7	WEDDING BELLS	Eddie Fisher (HMV)
12	8	TOMORROW	Johnny Brandon (Polygon)
11	9	A BLOSSOM FELL	Dickie Valentine (Decca)
17	10	IF ANYONE FINDS THIS, I LOVE YOU	Ruby Murray & Anne Warren (Columbia)
7	11	THE NAUGHTY LADY OF SHADY LANE	Dean Martin (Capitol)
-	12	CHERRY PINK AND APPLE BLOSSOM WHITE	Perez 'Prez' Prado & His Orchestra (HMV)
13	13	BEYOND THE STARS	David Whitfield (Decca)
10	14	LET ME GO LOVER	Teresa Brewer (Vogue/Coral)
20	15	A BLOSSOM FELL	Ronnie Hilton (HMV)
9	16	MAMBO ITALIANO	Rosemary Clooney (Philips)
9	17	FINGER OF SUSPICION	Dickie Valentine (Decca)
-	18	MAJORCA	Petula Clark (Polygon)
14	19	HAPPY DAYS AND LONELY NIGHTS	Ruby Murray (Columbia)
-	20	PRIZE OF GOLD	Joan Regan (Decca)

As Ruby Murray moved to the chart top with *Softly, Softly* she began to pile up additional entries in its wake, until on March 19 she had five songs in the Top 20 – a feat rarely matched in subsequent years, and certainly not by a female singer. On two of her hits, Ruby had competition from two other artists, and in fact, this was one of the busiest times ever for multiple hit versions of the most popular songs. Tennessee Ernie Ford was very much an exception in having the field to himself on *Give Me Your Word*.

2 April 1955

last week	this week	title	artist
1	1	GIVE ME YOUR WORD	Tennessee Ernie Ford (Capitol)
2	2	SOFTLY, SOFTLY	Ruby Murray (Columbia)
12	3	CHERRY PINK AND APPLE BLOSSOM WHITE	Perez 'Prez' Prado & His Orchestra (HMV)
4	4	A BLOSSOM FELL	Nat King Cole (Capitol)
7	5	WEDDING BELLS	Eddie Fisher (HMV)
10	6	IF ANYONE FINDS THIS, I LOVE YOU	Ruby Murray & Anne Warren (Columbia)
5	7	MOBILE	Ray Burns (Columbia)
3	8	LET ME GO LOVER	Dean Martin (Capitol)
20	9	PRIZE OF GOLD	Joan Regan (Decca)
8	10	TOMORROW	Johnny Brandon (Polygon)
-	11	UNDER THE BRIDGES OF PARIS	Eartha Kitt (HMV)
6	12	LET ME GO LOVER	Ruby Murray (Columbia)
-	13	UNDER THE BRIDGES OF PARIS	Dean Martin (Capitol)
11	14	THE NAUGHTY LADY OF SHADY LANE	Dean Martin (Capitol)
14	15	LET ME GO LOVER	Teresa Brewer (Vogue/Coral)
16	15	MAMBO ITALIANO	Rosemary Clooney (Philips)
13	15	BEYOND THE STARS	David Whitfield (Decca)
9	18	A BLOSSOM FELL	Dickie Valentine (Decca)
15	19	A BLOSSOM FELL	Ronnie Hilton (HMV)
-	20	NO MORE	McGuire Sisters (Vogue Coral)

9 April 1955

last week	this week	title	artist
1	1	GIVE ME YOUR WORD	Tennessee Ernie Ford (Capitol)
2	2	SOFTLY, SOFTLY	Ruby Murray (Columbia)
3	3	CHERRY PINK AND APPLE BLOSSOM WHITE	Perez 'Prez' Prado & His Orchestra (HMV)
6	4	IF ANYONE FINDS THIS, I LOVE YOU	Ruby Murray & Anne Warren (Columbia)
5	5	MOBILE	Ray Burns (Columbia)
9	6	PRIZE OF GOLD	Joan Regan (Decca)
4	7	A BLOSSOM FELL	Nat King Cole (Capitol)
13	8	UNDER THE BRIDGES OF PARIS	Dean Martin (Capitol)
5	9	WEDDING BELLS	Eddie Fisher (HMV)
19	10	A BLOSSOM FELL	Ronnie Hilton (HMV)
-	11	CHERRY PINK AND APPLE BLOSSOM WHITE	Eddie Calvert (Columbia)
8	12	LET ME GO LOVER	Dean Martin (Capitol)
-	13	READY, WILLING AND ABLE	Doris Day (Philips)
11	14	UNDER THE BRIDGES OF PARIS	Eartha Kitt (HMV)
-	15	IF YOU BELIEVE	Johnnie Ray (Philips)
16	16	A BLOSSOM FELL	Dickie Valentine (Decca)
10	17	TOMORROW	Johnny Brandon (Polygon)
18	18	BEYOND THE STARS	David Whitfield (Decca)
12	19	LET ME GO LOVER	Ruby Murray (Columbia)
15	20	LET ME GO LOVER	Teresa Brewer (Vogue/Coral)

16 April 1955

last week	this week	title	artist
1	1	GIVE ME YOUR WORD	Tennessee Ernie Ford (Capitol)
2	2	SOFTLY, SOFTLY	Ruby Murray (Columbia)
3	3	CHERRY PINK AND APPLE BLOSSOM WHITE	Perez 'Prez' Prado & His Orchestra (HMV)
4	4	IF ANYONE FINDS THIS, I LOVE YOU	Ruby Murray & Anne Warren (Columbia)
11	5	CHERRY PINK AND APPLE BLOSSOM WHITE	Eddie Calvert (Columbia)
8	6	UNDER THE BRIDGES OF PARIS	Dean Martin (Capitol)
13	7	READY, WILLING AND ABLE	Doris Day (Philips)
9	8	WEDDING BELLS	Eddie Fisher (HMV)
6	9	PRIZE OF GOLD	Joan Regan (Decca)
-	10	STRANGER IN PARADISE	Tony Bennett (Philips)
7	11	A BLOSSOM FELL	Nat King Cole (Capitol)
5	12	MOBILE	Ray Burns (Columbia)
13	13	LET ME GO LOVER	Dean Martin (Capitol)
-	14	MAMBO ROCK	Bill Haley & His Comets (Brunswick)
14	15	UNDER THE BRIDGES OF PARIS	Eartha Kitt (HMV)
16	16	A BLOSSOM FELL	Dickie Valentine (Decca)
17	17	TOMORROW	Johnny Brandon (Polygon)
-	18	EARTH ANGEL	Crew-Cuts (Mercury)
19	19	LET ME GO LOVER	Ruby Murray (Columbia)
20	20	LET ME GO LOVER	Teresa Brewer (Vogue/Coral)

23 April 1955

last week	this week	title	artist
1	1	GIVE ME YOUR WORD	Tennessee Ernie Ford (Capitol)
3	2	CHERRY PINK AND APPLE BLOSSOM WHITE	Perez 'Prez' Prado & His Orchestra (HMV)
10	3	STRANGER IN PARADISE	Tony Bennett (Philips)
2	4	SOFTLY, SOFTLY	Ruby Murray (Columbia)
5	5	CHERRY PINK AND APPLE BLOSSOM WHITE	Eddie Calvert (Columbia)
6	6	UNDER THE BRIDGES OF PARIS	Dean Martin (Capitol)
15	7	UNDER THE BRIDGES OF PARIS	Eartha Kitt (HMV)
4	8	IF ANYONE FINDS THIS, I LOVE YOU	Ruby Murray & Anne Warren (Columbia)
8	9	WEDDING BELLS	Eddie Fisher (HMV)
18	10	EARTH ANGEL	Crew-Cuts (Mercury)
-	11	STRANGER IN PARADISE	Tony Martin (HMV)
7	12	READY, WILLING AND ABLE	Doris Day (Philips)
12	13	MOBILE	Ray Burns (Columbia)
11	14	A BLOSSOM FELL	Nat King Cole (Capitol)
9	15	PRIZE OF GOLD	Joan Regan (Decca)
14	16	MAMBO ROCK	Bill Haley & His Comets (Brunswick)
-	17	TWEEDLE DEE	Frankie Vaughan (Philips)
13	18	LET ME GO LOVER	Dean Martin (Capitol)
-	19	SERENADE	Mario Lanza (HMV)
-	20	STRANGER IN PARADISE	Don Cornell (Vogue)
-	20	TWEEDLE DEE	Georgia Gibbs (Mercury)

30 April 1955

last week	this week	title	artist
2	1	CHERRY PINK AND APPLE BLOSSOM WHITE	Perez 'Prez' Prado & His Orchestra (HMV)
1	2	GIVE ME YOUR WORD	Tennessee Ernie Ford (Capitol)
3	3	STRANGER IN PARADISE	Tony Bennett (Philips)
5	4	CHERRY PINK AND APPLE BLOSSOM WHITE	Eddie Calvert (Columbia)
4	5	SOFTLY, SOFTLY	Ruby Murray (Columbia)
11	6	STRANGER IN PARADISE	Tony Martin (HMV)
10	7	EARTH ANGEL	Crew-Cuts (Mercury)
7	8	UNDER THE BRIDGES OF PARIS	Eartha Kitt (HMV)
12	9	READY, WILLING AND ABLE	Doris Day (Philips)
9	9	WEDDING BELLS	Eddie Fisher (HMV)
6	11	UNDER THE BRIDGES OF PARIS	Dean Martin (Capitol)
8	12	IF ANYONE FINDS THIS, I LOVE YOU	Ruby Murray & Anne Warren (Columbia)
15	13	PRIZE OF GOLD	Joan Regan (Decca)
-	14	MELODY OF LOVE	Ink Spots (Parlophone)
13	15	MOBILE	Ray Burns (Columbia)
-	16	A BLOSSOM FELL	Ronnie Hilton (HMV)
14	17	A BLOSSOM FELL	Nat King Cole (Capitol)
18	18	A BLOSSOM FELL	Dickie Valentine (Decca)
20	19	STRANGER IN PARADISE	Don Cornell (Vogue)
-	20	STRANGER IN PARADISE	Bing Crosby (Brunswick)

7 May 1955

last week	this week	title	artist
1	1	CHERRY PINK AND APPLE BLOSSOM WHITE	Perez 'Prez' Prado & His Orchestra (HMV)
3	2	STRANGER IN PARADISE	Tony Bennett (Philips)
2	3	GIVE ME YOUR WORD	Tennessee Ernie Ford (Capitol)
4	4	CHERRY PINK AND APPLE BLOSSOM WHITE	Eddie Calvert (Columbia)
5	5	EARTH ANGEL	Crew-Cuts (Mercury)
5	6	SOFTLY, SOFTLY	Ruby Murray (Columbia)
6	7	STRANGER IN PARADISE	Tony Martin (HMV)
9	8	WEDDING BELLS	Eddie Fisher (HMV)
9	9	READY, WILLING AND ABLE	Doris Day (Philips)
14	10	MELODY OF LOVE	Ink Spots (Parlophone)
8	11	UNDER THE BRIDGES OF PARIS	Eartha Kitt (HMV)
12	12	IF ANYONE FINDS THIS, I LOVE YOU	Ruby Murray & Anne Warren (Columbia)
11	13	UNDER THE BRIDGES OF PARIS	Dean Martin (Capitol)
-	14	UNCHAINED MELODY	Jimmy Young (Decca)
-	15	SERENADE	Mario Lanza (HMV)
16	16	PRIZE OF GOLD	Joan Regan (Decca)
20	17	STRANGER IN PARADISE	Bing Crosby (Brunswick)
16	18	A BLOSSOM FELL	Ronnie Hilton (HMV)
15	19	MOBILE	Ray Burns (Columbia)
-	20	I'LL WALK WITH GOD	Mario Lanza (HMV)

Multiple version mania was the hallmark of April 1955, as yet more songs were pounced upon by all and sundry. The April 30 chart contained two versions of *Cherry Pink*, two of *Under The Bridges Of Paris*, three of *A Blossom Fell* (all in adjacent positions!), and no less than four of *Stranger In Paradise* - and the multi-covered *Unchained Melody* was still to come. Untroubled by their original US R&B versions, however, were *Earth Angel* (originally by the Penguins) and *Tweedle Dee* (LaVern Baker).

May – June 1955

14 May 1955

last week	this week	title	artist
2	1	STRANGER IN PARADISE	Tony Bennett (Philips)
1	2	CHERRY PINK AND APPLE BLOSSOM WHITE	Perez 'Prez' Prado & His Orchestra (HMV)
4	3	CHERRY PINK AND APPLE BLOSSOM WHITE	Eddie Calvert (Columbia)
5	4	EARTH ANGEL	Crew-Cuts (Mercury)
3	5	GIVE ME YOUR WORD	Tennessee Ernie Ford (Capitol)
6	6	SOFTLY, SOFTLY	Ruby Murray (Columbia)
7	7	STRANGER IN PARADISE	Tony Martin (HMV)
-	8	IF YOU BELIEVE	Johnnie Ray (Philips)
8	9	WEDDING BELLS	Eddie Fisher (HMV)
12	10	IF ANYONE FINDS THIS, I LOVE YOU	Ruby Murray & Anne Warren (Columbia)
-	11	UNCHAINED MELODY	Al Hibbler (Brunswick)
11	12	UNDER THE BRIDGES OF PARIS	Eartha Kitt (HMV)
14	13	UNCHAINED MELODY	Jimmy Young (Decca)
9	14	READY, WILLING AND ABLE	Doris Day (Philips)
10	15	MELODY OF LOVE	Ink Spots (Parlophone)
16	16	PRIZE OF GOLD	Joan Regan (Decca)
-	17	UNCHAINED MELODY	Les Baxter (Capitol)
13	18	UNDER THE BRIDGES OF PARIS	Dean Martin (Capitol)
-	19	STRANGER IN PARADISE	Eddie Calvert (Columbia)
15	20	SERENADE	Mario Lanza (HMV)

21 May 1955

last week	this week	title	artist
1	1	STRANGER IN PARADISE	Tony Bennett (Philips)
3	2	CHERRY PINK AND APPLE BLOSSOM WHITE	Eddie Calvert (Columbia)
2	3	CHERRY PINK AND APPLE BLOSSOM WHITE	Perez 'Prez' Prado & His Orchestra (HMV)
5	4	GIVE ME YOUR WORD	Tennessee Ernie Ford (Capitol)
11	5	UNCHAINED MELODY	Al Hibbler (Brunswick)
4	6	EARTH ANGEL	Crew-Cuts (Mercury)
8	7	IF YOU BELIEVE	Johnnie Ray (Philips)
7	8	STRANGER IN PARADISE	Tony Martin (HMV)
6	9	SOFTLY, SOFTLY	Ruby Murray (Columbia)
10	10	IF ANYONE FINDS THIS, I LOVE YOU	Ruby Murray & Anne Warren (Columbia)
17	11	UNCHAINED MELODY	Les Baxter (Capitol)
14	12	READY, WILLING AND ABLE	Doris Day (Philips)
13	13	UNCHAINED MELODY	Jimmy Young (Decca)
9	14	WEDDING BELLS	Eddie Fisher (HMV)
12	15	UNDER THE BRIDGES OF PARIS	Eartha Kitt (HMV)
-	16	STRANGER IN PARADISE	Four Aces (Brunswick)
19	17	STRANGER IN PARADISE	Eddie Calvert (Columbia)
18	18	UNDER THE BRIDGES OF PARIS	Dean Martin (Capitol)
-	19	WHERE WILL THE DIMPLE BE?	Rosemary Clooney (Philips)
15	20	MELODY OF LOVE	Ink Spots (Parlophone)
-	20	PATHS OF PARADISE	Johnnie Ray (Philips)

28 May 1955

last week	this week	title	artist
2	1	CHERRY PINK AND APPLE BLOSSOM WHITE	Eddie Calvert (Columbia)
1	2	STRANGER IN PARADISE	Tony Bennett (Philips)
3	3	CHERRY PINK AND APPLE BLOSSOM WHITE	Perez 'Prez' Prado & His Orchestra (HMV)
5	4	UNCHAINED MELODY	Al Hibbler (Brunswick)
6	5	EARTH ANGEL	Crew-Cuts (Mercury)
4	6	GIVE ME YOUR WORD	Tennessee Ernie Ford (Capitol)
13	7	UNCHAINED MELODY	Jimmy Young (Decca)
8	8	STRANGER IN PARADISE	Tony Martin (HMV)
16	9	STRANGER IN PARADISE	Four Aces (Brunswick)
11	10	UNCHAINED MELODY	Les Baxter (Capitol)
7	11	IF YOU BELIEVE	Johnnie Ray (Philips)
9	12	SOFTLY, SOFTLY	Ruby Murray (Columbia)
19	13	WHERE WILL THE DIMPLE BE?	Rosemary Clooney (Philips)
17	14	STRANGER IN PARADISE	Eddie Calvert (Columbia)
14	15	WEDDING BELLS	Eddie Fisher (HMV)
12	16	READY, WILLING AND ABLE	Doris Day (Philips)
-	17	DREAMBOAT	Alma Cogan (HMV)
10	18	IF ANYONE FINDS THIS, I LOVE YOU	Ruby Murray & Anne Warren (Columbia)
-	19	PRIZE OF GOLD	Joan Regan (Decca)
-	20	ELEPHANT TANGO	Cyril Stapleton (Decca)
-	20	MAMA	David Whitfield (Decca)

4 June 1955

last week	this week	title	artist
1	1	CHERRY PINK AND APPLE BLOSSOM WHITE	Eddie Calvert (Columbia)
3	2	CHERRY PINK AND APPLE BLOSSOM WHITE	Perez 'Prez' Prado & His Orchestra (HMV)
2	3	STRANGER IN PARADISE	Tony Bennett (Philips)
5	4	EARTH ANGEL	Crew-Cuts (Mercury)
4	5	UNCHAINED MELODY	Al Hibbler (Brunswick)
9	6	STRANGER IN PARADISE	Four Aces (Brunswick)
7	7	UNCHAINED MELODY	Jimmy Young (Decca)
11	8	IF YOU BELIEVE	Johnnie Ray (Philips)
8	9	STRANGER IN PARADISE	Tony Martin (HMV)
17	10	DREAMBOAT	Alma Cogan (HMV)
6	11	GIVE ME YOUR WORD	Tennessee Ernie Ford (Capitol)
13	12	WHERE WILL THE DIMPLE BE?	Rosemary Clooney (Philips)
10	13	UNCHAINED MELODY	Les Baxter (Capitol)
12	14	SOFTLY, SOFTLY	Ruby Murray (Columbia)
-	15	SING IT WITH JOE	Joe 'Mr Piano' Henderson (Polygon)
-	16	I WONDER	Dickie Valentine (Decca)
14	17	STRANGER IN PARADISE	Eddie Calvert (Columbia)
16	18	READY, WILLING AND ABLE	Doris Day (Philips)
-	19	CRAZY OTTO RAG	Stargazers (Decca)
20	20	ELEPHANT TANGO	Cyril Stapleton (Decca)

11 June 1955

last week	this week	title	artist
1	1	CHERRY PINK AND APPLE BLOSSOM WHITE	Eddie Calvert (Columbia)
5	2	UNCHAINED MELODY	Al Hibbler (Brunswick)
7	3	UNCHAINED MELODY	Jimmy Young (Decca)
3	4	STRANGER IN PARADISE	Tony Bennett (Philips)
4	5	EARTH ANGEL	Crew-Cuts (Mercury)
2	6	CHERRY PINK AND APPLE BLOSSOM WHITE	Perez 'Prez' Prado & His Orchestra (HMV)
8	7	IF YOU BELIEVE	Johnnie Ray (Philips)
10	8	DREAMBOAT	Alma Cogan (HMV)
6	9	STRANGER IN PARADISE	Four Aces (Brunswick)
9	10	STRANGER IN PARADISE	Tony Martin (HMV)
12	11	WHERE WILL THE DIMPLE BE?	Rosemary Clooney (Philips)
13	12	UNCHAINED MELODY	Les Baxter (Capitol)
-	13	YOU, MY LOVE	Frank Sinatra (Capitol)
15	14	SING IT WITH JOE	Joe 'Mr Piano' Henderson (Polygon)
11	15	GIVE ME YOUR WORD	Tennessee Ernie Ford (Capitol)
16	16	I WONDER	Dickie Valentine (Decca)
14	17	SOFTLY, SOFTLY	Ruby Murray (Columbia)
19	18	CRAZY OTTO RAG	Stargazers (Decca)
-	19	THE MAN THAT GOT AWAY	Judy Garland (Philips)
-	20	UNDER THE BRIDGES OF PARIS	Eartha Kitt (HMV)

18 June 1955

last week	this week	title	artist
1	1	CHERRY PINK AND APPLE BLOSSOM WHITE	Eddie Calvert (Columbia)
2	2	UNCHAINED MELODY	Al Hibbler (Brunswick)
3	3	UNCHAINED MELODY	Jimmy Young (Decca)
4	4	STRANGER IN PARADISE	Tony Bennett (Philips)
6	5	CHERRY PINK AND APPLE BLOSSOM WHITE	Perez 'Prez' Prado & His Orchestra (HMV)
8	6	DREAMBOAT	Alma Cogan (HMV)
4	7	EARTH ANGEL	Crew-Cuts (Mercury)
11	8	WHERE WILL THE DIMPLE BE?	Rosemary Clooney (Philips)
7	9	IF YOU BELIEVE	Johnnie Ray (Philips)
10	10	STRANGER IN PARADISE	Tony Martin (HMV)
15	11	GIVE ME YOUR WORD	Tennessee Ernie Ford (Capitol)
9	12	STRANGER IN PARADISE	Four Aces (Brunswick)
16	13	I WONDER	Dickie Valentine (Decca)
14	14	SING IT WITH JOE	Joe 'Mr Piano' Henderson (Polygon)
13	15	YOU, MY LOVE	Frank Sinatra (Capitol)
17	16	SOFTLY, SOFTLY	Ruby Murray (Columbia)
12	17	UNCHAINED MELODY	Les Baxter (Capitol)
19	18	THE MAN THAT GOT AWAY	Judy Garland (Philips)
-	19	I WONDER	Jane Froman (Capitol)
-	20	UNCHAINED MELODY	Liberace (Philips)
18	20	CRAZY OTTO RAG	Stargazers (Decca)

Tony Bennett topped the chart with his *Stranger In Paradise* (a song from the stage show *Kismet*, using a melody from Borodin) despite the fierce competition. More surprisingly still, Eddie Calvert took his version of *Cherry Pink And Apple Blossom White* to Number One for a month, just a fortnight after the Perez Prado original had vacated the top slot. Meanwhile, four variations of *Unchained Melody* (theme from the film *Unchained*, hence a title which has nothing to do with its lyric) joined in the multiple versions jamboree.

25 June 1955

last week	this week	title	artist
3	1	UNCHAINED MELODY	Jimmy Young (Decca)
1	2	CHERRY PINK AND APPLE BLOSSOM WHITE	Eddie Calvert (Columbia)
2	3	UNCHAINED MELODY	Al Hibbler (Brunswick)
6	4	DREAMBOAT	Alma Cogan (HMV)
7	5	EARTH ANGEL	Crew-Cuts (Mercury)
8	6	WHERE WILL THE DIMPLE BE?	Rosemary Clooney (Philips)
10	7	STRANGER IN PARADISE	Tony Martin (HMV)
4	8	STRANGER IN PARADISE	Tony Bennett (Philips)
5	9	CHERRY PINK AND APPLE BLOSSOM WHITE	Perez 'Prez' Prado & His Orchestra (HMV)
17	10	UNCHAINED MELODY	Les Baxter (Capitol)
13	11	I WONDER	Dickie Valentine (Decca)
11	12	GIVE ME YOUR WORD	Tennessee Ernie Ford (Capitol)
9	13	IF YOU BELIEVE	Johnnie Ray (Philips)
-	14	COOL WATER	Frankie Laine (Philips)
12	15	STRANGER IN PARADISE	Four Aces (Brunswick)
-	16	STOWAWAY	Barbara Lyon (Columbia)
15	17	YOU, MY LOVE	Frank Sinatra (Capitol)
19	18	I WONDER	Jane Froman (Capitol)
14	18	SING IT WITH JOE	Joe 'Mr Piano' Henderson (Polygon)
16	20	SOFTLY, SOFTLY	Ruby Murray (Columbia)
-	20	MAMA	David Whitfield (Decca)

2 July 1955

last week	this week	title	artist
1	1	UNCHAINED MELODY	Jimmy Young (Decca)
3	2	UNCHAINED MELODY	Al Hibbler (Brunswick)
4	3	DREAMBOAT	Alma Cogan (HMV)
2	4	CHERRY PINK AND APPLE BLOSSOM WHITE	Eddie Calvert (Columbia)
5	5	EARTH ANGEL	Crew-Cuts (Mercury)
11	6	I WONDER	Dickie Valentine (Decca)
6	7	WHERE WILL THE DIMPLE BE?	Rosemary Clooney (Philips)
8	8	STRANGER IN PARADISE	Tony Bennett (Philips)
9	9	CHERRY PINK AND APPLE BLOSSOM WHITE	Perez 'Prez' Prado & His Orchestra (HMV)
7	10	STRANGER IN PARADISE	Tony Martin (HMV)
14	11	COOL WATER	Frankie Laine (Philips)
10	12	UNCHAINED MELODY	Les Baxter (Capitol)
13	13	IF YOU BELIEVE	Johnnie Ray (Philips)
14	14	I WONDER	Jane Froman (Capitol)
12	15	GIVE ME YOUR WORD	Tennessee Ernie Ford (Capitol)
-	16	EVERMORE	Ruby Murray (Columbia)
-	17	EVERY DAY OF MY LIFE	Malcolm Vaughan (HMV)
18	18	STOWAWAY	Barbara Lyon (Columbia)
20	19	MAMA	David Whitfield (Decca)
-	20	DON'T WORRY	Johnny Brandon (Polygon)
-	20	ELEPHANT TANGO	Cyril Stapleton (Decca)

9 July 1955

last week	this week	title	artist
1	1	UNCHAINED MELODY	Jimmy Young (Decca)
2	2	UNCHAINED MELODY	Al Hibbler (Brunswick)
3	3	DREAMBOAT	Alma Cogan (HMV)
4	4	CHERRY PINK AND APPLE BLOSSOM WHITE	Eddie Calvert (Columbia)
5	5	EARTH ANGEL	Crew-Cuts (Mercury)
6	6	I WONDER	Dickie Valentine (Decca)
7	7	WHERE WILL THE DIMPLE BE?	Rosemary Clooney (Philips)
16	8	EVERMORE	Ruby Murray (Columbia)
8	9	STRANGER IN PARADISE	Tony Bennett (Philips)
11	10	COOL WATER	Frankie Laine (Philips)
9	11	CHERRY PINK AND APPLE BLOSSOM WHITE	Perez 'Prez' Prado & His Orchestra (HMV)
10	12	STRANGER IN PARADISE	Tony Martin (HMV)
17	13	EVERY DAY OF MY LIFE	Malcolm Vaughan (HMV)
18	14	STOWAWAY	Barbara Lyon (Columbia)
13	14	IF YOU BELIEVE	Johnnie Ray (Philips)
12	16	UNCHAINED MELODY	Les Baxter (Capitol)
14	17	I WONDER	Jane Froman (Capitol)
-	18	EVE'RYWHERE	David Whitfield (Decca)
20	19	DON'T WORRY	Johnny Brandon (Polygon)
-	20	SOFTLY, SOFTLY	Ruby Murray (Columbia)

16 July 1955

last week	this week	title	artist
3	1	DREAMBOAT	Alma Cogan (HMV)
1	2	UNCHAINED MELODY	Jimmy Young (Decca)
2	3	UNCHAINED MELODY	Al Hibbler (Brunswick)
6	4	I WONDER	Dickie Valentine (Decca)
4	5	CHERRY PINK AND APPLE BLOSSOM WHITE	Eddie Calvert (Columbia)
8	6	EVERMORE	Ruby Murray (Columbia)
10	7	COOL WATER	Frankie Laine (Philips)
5	8	EARTH ANGEL	Crew-Cuts (Mercury)
7	9	WHERE WILL THE DIMPLE BE?	Rosemary Clooney (Philips)
-	10	ROSE MARIE	Slim Whitman (London)
13	11	EVERY DAY OF MY LIFE	Malcolm Vaughan (HMV)
9	12	STRANGER IN PARADISE	Tony Bennett (Philips)
18	13	EVE'RYWHERE	David Whitfield (Decca)
-	14	SINCERELY	McGuire Sisters (Vogue Coral)
-	15	STRANGE LADY IN TOWN	Frankie Laine (Philips)
11	16	CHERRY PINK AND APPLE BLOSSOM WHITE	Perez 'Prez' Prado & His Orchestra (HMV)
12	17	STRANGER IN PARADISE	Tony Martin (HMV)
14	18	STOWAWAY	Barbara Lyon (Columbia)
14	19	IF YOU BELIEVE	Johnnie Ray (Philips)
-	19	ELEPHANT TANGO	Cyril Stapleton (Decca)
19	20	DON'T WORRY	Johnny Brandon (Polygon)

23 July 1955

last week	this week	title	artist
1	1	DREAMBOAT	Alma Cogan (HMV)
2	2	UNCHAINED MELODY	Jimmy Young (Decca)
6	3	EVERMORE	Ruby Murray (Columbia)
10	4	ROSE MARIE	Slim Whitman (London)
4	5	I WONDER	Dickie Valentine (Decca)
5	6	CHERRY PINK AND APPLE BLOSSOM WHITE	Eddie Calvert (Columbia)
3	7	UNCHAINED MELODY	Al Hibbler (Brunswick)
8	8	COOL WATER	Frankie Laine (Philips)
8	9	EARTH ANGEL	Crew-Cuts (Mercury)
9	10	WHERE WILL THE DIMPLE BE?	Rosemary Clooney (Philips)
13	11	EVE'RYWHERE	David Whitfield (Decca)
18	12	STOWAWAY	Barbara Lyon (Columbia)
11	13	EVERY DAY OF MY LIFE	Malcolm Vaughan (HMV)
12	14	STRANGER IN PARADISE	Tony Bennett (Philips)
14	15	SINCERELY	McGuire Sisters (Vogue Coral)
15	16	STRANGE LADY IN TOWN	Frankie Laine (Philips)
-	17	YOU, MY LOVE	Frank Sinatra (Capitol)
20	18	DON'T WORRY	Johnny Brandon (Polygon)
19	19	ELEPHANT TANGO	Cyril Stapleton (Decca)
-	20	I'M IN FAVOUR OF FRIENDSHIP	Five Smith Brothers (Decca)

30 July 1955

last week	this week	title	artist
4	1	ROSE MARIE	Slim Whitman (London)
1	2	DREAMBOAT	Alma Cogan (HMV)
3	3	EVERMORE	Ruby Murray (Columbia)
8	4	COOL WATER	Frankie Laine (Philips)
2	5	UNCHAINED MELODY	Jimmy Young (Decca)
5	6	I WONDER	Dickie Valentine (Decca)
6	7	CHERRY PINK AND APPLE BLOSSOM WHITE	Eddie Calvert (Columbia)
13	8	EVERY DAY OF MY LIFE	Malcolm Vaughan (HMV)
7	9	UNCHAINED MELODY	Al Hibbler (Brunswick)
11	10	EV'RYWHERE	David Whitfield (Decca)
16	11	STRANGE LADY IN TOWN	Frankie Laine (Philips)
12	12	STOWAWAY	Barbara Lyon (Columbia)
9	13	EARTH ANGEL	Crew-Cuts (Mercury)
10	14	WHERE WILL THE DIMPLE BE?	Rosemary Clooney (Philips)
-	15	MAMA	David Whitfield (Decca)
15	16	SINCERELY	McGuire Sisters (Vogue Coral)
14	17	STRANGER IN PARADISE	Tony Bennett (Philips)
-	18	JOHN AND JULIE	Eddie Calvert (Columbia)
17	19	YOU, MY LOVE	Frank Sinatra (Capitol)
-	20	SOMETHING'S GOTTA GIVE	Sammy Davis Jr. (Brunswick)
-	20	INDIAN LOVE CALL	Slim Whitman (London)

The British version of *Unchained Melody* by Jimmy Young emerged as the chart-topper, though only by a whisker from Al Hibbler. In the US, Hibbler had similarly been beaten by a small margin, in that case by Les Baxter's orchestral version, which was the third-rated in the UK. Barbara Lyon, who charted with Stowaway, was a familiar TV personality as the daughter in *Life With The Lyons*, a sitcom based around an American family in London, and starring Ben Lyon, his wife, son and daughter as themselves.

August – September 1955

6 August 1955

last week	this		
1	1	ROSE MARIE	Slim Whitman (London)
4	2	COOL WATER	Frankie Laine (Philips)
2	3	DREAMBOAT	Alma Cogan (HMV)
3	4	EVERMORE	Ruby Murray (Columbia)
5	5	UNCHAINED MELODY	Jimmy Young (Decca)
8	6	EVERY DAY OF MY LIFE	Malcolm Vaughan (HMV)
11	7	STRANGE LADY IN TOWN	Frankie Laine (Philips)
6	8	I WONDER	Dickie Valentine (Decca)
7	9	CHERRY PINK AND APPLE BLOSSOM WHITE	Eddie Calvert (Columbia)
10	10	EVE'RYWHERE	David Whitfield (Decca)
9	11	UNCHAINED MELODY	Al Hibbler (Brunswick)
-	12	LEARNIN' THE BLUES	Frank Sinatra (Capitol)
15	13	MAMA	David Whitfield (Decca)
14	14	WHERE WILL THE DIMPLE BE?	Rosemary Clooney (Philips)
13	15	EARTH ANGEL	Crew-Cuts (Mercury)
12	16	STOWAWAY	Barbara Lyon (Columbia)
20	17	INDIAN LOVE CALL	Slim Whitman (London)
18	18	JOHN AND JULIE	Eddie Calvert (Columbia)
20	19	SOMETHING'S GOTTA GIVE	Sammy Davis Jr. (Brunswick)
16	20	SINCERELY	McGuire Sisters (Vogue Coral)

13 August 1955

last week	this		
1	1	ROSE MARIE	Slim Whitman (London)
2	2	COOL WATER	Frankie Laine (Philips)
3	3	DREAMBOAT	Alma Cogan (HMV)
4	4	EVERMORE	Ruby Murray (Columbia)
10	5	EVE'RYWHERE	David Whitfield (Decca)
7	6	STRANGE LADY IN TOWN	Frankie Laine (Philips)
6	7	EVERY DAY OF MY LIFE	Malcolm Vaughan (HMV)
7	8	I WONDER	Dickie Valentine (Decca)
5	9	UNCHAINED MELODY	Jimmy Young (Decca)
12	10	LEARNIN' THE BLUES	Frank Sinatra (Capitol)
9	11	CHERRY PINK AND APPLE BLOSSOM WHITE	Eddie Calvert (Columbia)
11	12	UNCHAINED MELODY	Al Hibbler (Brunswick)
13	13	MAMA	David Whitfield (Decca)
15	14	EARTH ANGEL	Crew-Cuts (Mercury)
18	15	JOHN AND JULIE	Eddie Calvert (Columbia)
14	16	WHERE WILL THE DIMPLE BE?	Rosemary Clooney (Philips)
-	17	YOU, MY LOVE	Frank Sinatra (Capitol)
16	18	STOWAWAY	Barbara Lyon (Columbia)
17	19	INDIAN LOVE CALL	Slim Whitman (London)
-	20	ALABAMA JUBILEE	Ferko String Band (London)

20 August 1955

last week	this		
1	1	ROSE MARIE	Slim Whitman (London)
2	2	COOL WATER	Frankie Laine (Philips)
4	3	EVERMORE	Ruby Murray (Columbia)
5	4	EVE'RYWHERE	David Whitfield (Decca)
3	5	DREAMBOAT	Alma Cogan (HMV)
10	6	LEARNIN' THE BLUES	Frank Sinatra (Capitol)
6	7	STRANGE LADY IN TOWN	Frankie Laine (Philips)
7	8	EVERY DAY OF MY LIFE	Malcolm Vaughan (HMV)
9	9	UNCHAINED MELODY	Jimmy Young (Decca)
8	10	I WONDER	Dickie Valentine (Decca)
11	11	CHERRY PINK AND APPLE BLOSSOM WHITE	Eddie Calvert (Columbia)
13	12	MAMA	David Whitfield (Decca)
12	13	UNCHAINED MELODY	Al Hibbler (Brunswick)
14	14	JOHN AND JULIE	Eddie Calvert (Columbia)
15	15	INDIAN LOVE CALL	Slim Whitman (London)
-	16	THE BREEZE AND I	Caterina Valente (Polydor)
17	17	YOU, MY LOVE	Frank Sinatra (Capitol)
14	18	EARTH ANGEL	Crew-Cuts (Mercury)
-	19	SOMETHING'S GOTTA GIVE	Sammy Davis Jr. (Brunswick)
20	20	ALABAMA JUBILEE	Ferko String Band (London)

27 August 1955

last week	this		
1	1	ROSE MARIE	Slim Whitman (London)
6	2	LEARNIN' THE BLUES	Frank Sinatra (Capitol)
2	3	COOL WATER	Frankie Laine (Philips)
4	4	EVE'RYWHERE	David Whitfield (Decca)
3	5	EVERMORE	Ruby Murray (Columbia)
8	6	EVERY DAY OF MY LIFE	Malcolm Vaughan (HMV)
15	7	INDIAN LOVE CALL	Slim Whitman (London)
16	8	THE BREEZE AND I	Caterina Valente (Polydor)
5	9	DREAMBOAT	Alma Cogan (HMV)
7	10	STRANGE LADY IN TOWN	Frankie Laine (Philips)
14	11	JOHN AND JULIE	Eddie Calvert (Columbia)
9	12	UNCHAINED MELODY	Jimmy Young (Decca)
10	13	I WONDER	Dickie Valentine (Decca)
13	14	UNCHAINED MELODY	Al Hibbler (Brunswick)
19	15	SOMETHING'S GOTTA GIVE	Sammy Davis Jr. (Brunswick)
12	16	MAMA	David Whitfield (Decca)
11	17	CHERRY PINK AND APPLE BLOSSOM WHITE	Eddie Calvert (Columbia)
-	18	MY ONE SIN	Nat King Cole (Capitol)
18	18	STARS SHINE IN YOUR EYES	Ronnie Hilton (HMV)
-	20	THAT'S HOW A LOVE SONG WAS BORN	Ray Burns (Columbia)
18	20	EARTH ANGEL	Crew-Cuts (Mercury)

3 September 1955

last week	this		
1	1	ROSE MARIE	Slim Whitman (London)
2	2	LEARNIN' THE BLUES	Frank Sinatra (Capitol)
3	3	COOL WATER	Frankie Laine (Philips)
4	4	EVE'RYWHERE	David Whitfield (Decca)
6	5	EVERY DAY OF MY LIFE	Malcolm Vaughan (HMV)
11	6	JOHN AND JULIE	Eddie Calvert (Columbia)
8	7	THE BREEZE AND I	Caterina Valente (Polydor)
7	8	INDIAN LOVE CALL	Slim Whitman (London)
5	9	EVERMORE	Ruby Murray (Columbia)
10	10	STRANGE LADY IN TOWN	Frankie Laine (Philips)
15	11	SOMETHING'S GOTTA GIVE	Sammy Davis Jr. (Brunswick)
9	12	DREAMBOAT	Alma Cogan (HMV)
13	13	MAMA	David Whitfield (Decca)
12	14	UNCHAINED MELODY	Jimmy Young (Decca)
13	15	I WONDER	Dickie Valentine (Decca)
18	16	STARS SHINE IN YOUR EYES	Ronnie Hilton (HMV)
20	17	THAT'S HOW A LOVE SONG WAS BORN	Ray Burns (Columbia)
-	18	NOT AS A STRANGER	Frank Sinatra (Capitol)
-	19	SING IT AGAIN WITH JOE	Joe 'Mr Piano' Henderson (Polygon)
14	20	UNCHAINED MELODY	Al Hibbler (Brunswick)

10 September 1955

last week	this		
1	1	ROSE MARIE	Slim Whitman (London)
2	2	LEARNIN' THE BLUES	Frank Sinatra (Capitol)
3	3	COOL WATER	Frankie Laine (Philips)
4	4	EVE'RYWHERE	David Whitfield (Decca)
7	5	THE BREEZE AND I	Caterina Valente (Polydor)
6	6	JOHN AND JULIE	Eddie Calvert (Columbia)
10	7	STRANGE LADY IN TOWN	Frankie Laine (Philips)
5	8	EVERY DAY OF MY LIFE	Malcolm Vaughan (HMV)
8	9	INDIAN LOVE CALL	Slim Whitman (London)
9	10	EVERMORE	Ruby Murray (Columbia)
11	11	SOMETHING'S GOTTA GIVE	Sammy Davis Jr. (Brunswick)
-	12	CLOSE THE DOOR	Stargazers (Decca)
16	13	STARS SHINE IN YOUR EYES	Ronnie Hilton (HMV)
-	14	LOVE ME OR LEAVE ME	Sammy Davis Jr. (Brunswick)
17	15	THAT'S HOW A LOVE SONG WAS BORN	Ray Burns (Columbia)
13	16	MAMA	David Whitfield (Decca)
12	17	DREAMBOAT	Alma Cogan (HMV)
19	18	SING IT AGAIN WITH JOE	Joe 'Mr Piano' Henderson (Polygon)
15	19	I WONDER	Dickie Valentine (Decca)
-	20	LOVE ME OR LEAVE ME	Doris Day (Philips)

Slim Whitman's *Rose Marie*, 1955's biggest-selling single, set a record at the chart-top which would remain unbroken for 36 years, when it went a week better than David Whitfield's *Cara Mia* in 1954, and stayed at Number One for an unbroken run of 11 weeks. In doing so, it held off a consistent challenge from Frankie Laine's *Cool Water* (punctuated by a similar one from Frank Sinatra with *Learnin' The Blues*) throughout most of that period. Whitman's earlier *Indian Love Call* also revived itself in support.

17 September 1955

Last week	This week	Title	Artist (Label)
1	1	ROSE MARIE	Slim Whitman (London)
2	2	LEARNIN' THE BLUES	Frank Sinatra (Capitol)
3	3	COOL WATER	Frankie Laine (Philips)
4	4	EVE'RYWHERE	David Whitfield (Decca)
5	5	THE BREEZE AND I	Caterina Valente (Polydor)
7	6	STRANGE LADY IN TOWN	Frankie Laine (Philips)
6	7	JOHN AND JULIE	Eddie Calvert (Columbia)
10	8	EVERMORE	Ruby Murray (Columbia)
8	9	EVERY DAY OF MY LIFE	Malcolm Vaughan (HMV)
12	10	CLOSE THE DOOR	Stargazers (Decca)
14	11	LOVE ME OR LEAVE ME	Sammy Davis Jr. (Brunswick)
9	12	INDIAN LOVE CALL	Slim Whitman (London)
13	13	STARS SHINE IN YOUR EYES	Ronnie Hilton (HMV)
15	14	THAT'S HOW A LOVE SONG WAS BORN	Ray Burns (Columbia)
-	15	THE MAN FROM LARAMIE	Jimmy Young (Decca)
11	16	SOMETHING'S GOTTA GIVE	Sammy Davis Jr. (Brunswick)
-	17	MY ONE SIN	Nat King Cole (Capitol)
-	18	CLOSE YOUR EYES	Tony Bennett (Philips)
16	19	MAMA	David Whitfield (Decca)
18	20	SING IT AGAIN WITH JOE	Joe 'Mr Piano' Henderson (Polygon)

24 September 1955

Last week	This week	Title	Artist (Label)
1	1	ROSE MARIE	Slim Whitman (London)
2	2	LEARNIN' THE BLUES	Frank Sinatra (Capitol)
4	3	EV'RYWHERE	David Whitfield (Decca)
3	4	COOL WATER	Frankie Laine (Philips)
8	5	EVERMORE	Ruby Murray (Columbia)
15	6	THE MAN FROM LARAMIE	Jimmy Young (Decca)
5	7	THE BREEZE AND I	Caterina Valente (Polydor)
11	8	LOVE ME OR LEAVE ME	Sammy Davis Jr. (Brunswick)
6	9	STRANGE LADY IN TOWN	Frankie Laine (Philips)
10	10	CLOSE THE DOOR	Stargazers (Decca)
7	11	JOHN AND JULIE	Eddie Calvert (Columbia)
12	12	INDIAN LOVE CALL	Slim Whitman (London)
9	13	EVERY DAY OF MY LIFE	Malcolm Vaughan (HMV)
13	14	STARS SHINE IN YOUR EYES	Ronnie Hilton (HMV)
-	15	CHINA DOLL	Slim Whitman (London)
-	16	BLUE STAR (THE 'MEDIC' THEME)	Cyril Stapleton (Decca)
-	17	BANJO'S BACK IN TOWN	Alma Cogan (HMV)
14	18	THAT'S HOW A LOVE SONG WAS BORN	Ray Burns (Columbia)
-	19	THE MAN FROM LARAMIE	Al Martino (Capitol)
-	20	BLUE STAR (THE 'MEDIC' THEME)	Charlie Applewhite (Brunswick)

1 October 1955

Last week	This week	Title	Artist (Label)
1	1	ROSE MARIE	Slim Whitman (London)
4	2	COOL WATER	Frankie Laine (Philips)
2	3	LEARNIN' THE BLUES	Frank Sinatra (Capitol)
3	4	EV'RYWHERE	David Whitfield (Decca)
6	5	THE MAN FROM LARAMIE	Jimmy Young (Decca)
10	6	CLOSE THE DOOR	Stargazers (Decca)
7	7	THE BREEZE AND I	Caterina Valente (Polydor)
5	8	EVERMORE	Ruby Murray (Columbia)
16	9	BLUE STAR (THE 'MEDIC' THEME)	Cyril Stapleton (Decca)
9	10	STRANGE LADY IN TOWN	Frankie Laine (Philips)
12	11	INDIAN LOVE CALL	Slim Whitman (London)
11	12	JOHN AND JULIE	Eddie Calvert (Columbia)
13	13	EVERY DAY OF MY LIFE	Malcolm Vaughan (HMV)
8	14	LOVE ME OR LEAVE ME	Sammy Davis Jr. (Brunswick)
14	15	STARS SHINE IN YOUR EYES	Ronnie Hilton (HMV)
-	16	THAT OLD BLACK MAGIC	Sammy Davis Jr. (Brunswick)
-	17	HEY THERE	Rosemary Clooney (Philips)
15	18	CHINA DOLL	Slim Whitman (London)
18	19	THAT'S HOW A LOVE SONG WAS BORN	Ray Burns (Columbia)
19	20	THE MAN FROM LARAMIE	Al Martino (Capitol)

8 October 1955

Last week	This week	Title	Artist (Label)
1	1	ROSE MARIE	Slim Whitman (London)
5	2	THE MAN FROM LARAMIE	Jimmy Young (Decca)
2	3	COOL WATER	Frankie Laine (Philips)
3	4	LEARNIN' THE BLUES	Frank Sinatra (Capitol)
4	5	EV'RYWHERE	David Whitfield (Decca)
9	6	BLUE STAR (THE 'MEDIC' THEME)	Cyril Stapleton (Decca)
7	7	THE BREEZE AND I	Caterina Valente (Polydor)
6	8	CLOSE THE DOOR	Stargazers (Decca)
-	9	YELLOW ROSE OF TEXAS	Mitch Miller (Philips)
10	10	INDIAN LOVE CALL	Slim Whitman (London)
-	11	HERNANDO'S HIDEAWAY	Johnston Brothers (Decca)
13	12	EVERY DAY OF MY LIFE	Malcolm Vaughan (HMV)
14	13	LOVE ME OR LEAVE ME	Sammy Davis Jr. (Brunswick)
8	14	EVERMORE	Ruby Murray (Columbia)
10	15	STRANGE LADY IN TOWN	Frankie Laine (Philips)
12	16	JOHN AND JULIE	Eddie Calvert (Columbia)
-	17	HEY THERE	Lita Roza (Decca)
17	18	HEY THERE	Rosemary Clooney (Philips)
19	19	HEY THERE	Sammy Davis Jr. (Brunswick)
15	20	STARS SHINE IN YOUR EYES	Ronnie Hilton (HMV)
-	20	HERNANDO'S HIDEAWAY	Johnnie Ray (Philips)

15 October 1955

Last week	This week	Title	Artist (Label)
2	1	THE MAN FROM LARAMIE	Jimmy Young (Decca)
3	2	COOL WATER	Frankie Laine (Philips)
6	3	BLUE STAR (THE 'MEDIC' THEME)	Cyril Stapleton (Decca)
1	4	ROSE MARIE	Slim Whitman (London)
9	5	YELLOW ROSE OF TEXAS	Mitch Miller (Philips)
5	6	EV'RYWHERE	David Whitfield (Decca)
4	7	LEARNIN' THE BLUES	Frank Sinatra (Capitol)
8	8	THE BREEZE AND I	Caterina Valente (Polydor)
8	9	CLOSE THE DOOR	Stargazers (Decca)
18	10	HEY THERE	Rosemary Clooney (Philips)
11	11	HERNANDO'S HIDEAWAY	Johnston Brothers (Decca)
20	11	HERNANDO'S HIDEAWAY	Johnnie Ray (Philips)
-	13	ROCK AROUND THE CLOCK	Bill Haley & His Comets (Brunswick)
10	14	INDIAN LOVE CALL	Slim Whitman (London)
12	15	EVERY DAY OF MY LIFE	Malcolm Vaughan (HMV)
-	16	HEY THERE	Johnnie Ray (Philips)
13	17	LOVE ME OR LEAVE ME	Sammy Davis Jr. (Brunswick)
14	18	EVERMORE	Ruby Murray (Columbia)
-	19	I'LL COME WHEN YOU CALL	Ruby Murray (Columbia)
-	20	GO ON BY	Alma Cogan (HMV)
17	20	HEY THERE	Lita Roza (Decca)

22 October 1955

Last week	This week	Title	Artist (Label)
1	1	THE MAN FROM LARAMIE	Jimmy Young (Decca)
3	2	BLUE STAR (THE 'MEDIC' THEME)	Cyril Stapleton (Decca)
5	3	YELLOW ROSE OF TEXAS	Mitch Miller (Philips)
6	4	EV'RYWHERE	David Whitfield (Decca)
4	5	ROSE MARIE	Slim Whitman (London)
2	6	COOL WATER	Frankie Laine (Philips)
8	7	THE BREEZE AND I	Caterina Valente (Polydor)
13	8	ROCK AROUND THE CLOCK	Bill Haley & His Comets (Brunswick)
16	9	HEY THERE	Johnnie Ray (Philips)
10	10	HEY THERE	Rosemary Clooney (Philips)
11	11	HERNANDO'S HIDEAWAY	Johnston Brothers (Decca)
11	12	HERNANDO'S HIDEAWAY	Johnnie Ray (Philips)
7	13	LEARNIN' THE BLUES	Frank Sinatra (Capitol)
9	14	CLOSE THE DOOR	Stargazers (Decca)
19	15	I'LL COME WHEN YOU CALL	Ruby Murray (Columbia)
16	16	HEY THERE	Ruby Murray (Columbia)
-	17	I'LL NEVER STOP LOVING YOU	Doris Day (Philips)
-	18	THE DAM BUSTERS MARCH	Central Band Of The Royal Air Force (HMV)
-	19	YELLOW ROSE OF TEXAS	Gary Miller (Nixa)
20	20	GO ON BY	Alma Cogan (HMV)

Jimmy Young scored his second consecutive Number One with *The Man From Laramie*, easily shaking off the challenge from former chart-topper Al Martino's version. Four versions of *Hey There*, the hit song from the new musical *The Pyjama Game*, vied for honours, while new rhythms in the chart included the old-time march of *Yellow Rose Of Texas* and the tango style of *Hernando's Hideaway*, both with more than one version sharing the honours. Slim Whitman now had three simultaneous Top 20 hits.

October – December 1955

29 October 1955

last	this	title	artist (label)
1	1	THE MAN FROM LARAMIE	Jimmy Young (Decca)
3	2	YELLOW ROSE OF TEXAS	Mitch Miller (Philips)
2	2	BLUE STAR (THE 'MEDIC' THEME)	Cyril Stapleton (Decca)
10	4	HERNANDO'S HIDEAWAY	Johnston Brothers (Decca)
5	5	ROSE MARIE	Slim Whitman (London)
6	6	COOL WATER	Frankie Laine (Philips)
8	7	ROCK AROUND THE CLOCK	Bill Haley & His Comets (Brunswick)
10	8	HEY THERE	Rosemary Clooney (Philips)
9	9	EV'RYWHERE	David Whitfield (Decca)
4	10	HEY THERE	Johnnie Ray (Philips)
12	11	HERNANDO'S HIDEAWAY	Johnnie Ray (Philips)
7	12	THE BREEZE AND I	Caterina Valente (Polydor)
15	13	I'LL COME WHEN YOU CALL	Ruby Murray (Columbia)
14	14	CLOSE THE DOOR	Stargazers (Decca)
15	15	LEARNIN' THE BLUES	Frank Sinatra (Capitol)
20	16	GO ON BY	Alma Cogan (HMV)
9	17	YELLOW ROSE OF TEXAS	Gary Miller (Nixa)
-	18	SONG OF THE DREAMER	Johnnie Ray (Philips)
17	19	I'LL NEVER STOP LOVING YOU	Doris Day (Philips)
-	20	BLUE STAR (THE 'MEDIC' THEME)	Ron Goodwin & His Orchestra (Parlophone)
-	20	THE MAN FROM LARAMIE	Al Martino (Capitol)

5 November 1955

last	this	title	artist (label)
1	1	THE MAN FROM LARAMIE	Jimmy Young (Decca)
4	2	HERNANDO'S HIDEAWAY	Johnston Brothers (Decca)
2	3	BLUE STAR (THE 'MEDIC' THEME)	Cyril Stapleton (Decca)
7	4	ROCK AROUND THE CLOCK	Bill Haley & His Comets (Brunswick)
2	5	YELLOW ROSE OF TEXAS	Mitch Miller (Philips)
10	6	HEY THERE	Johnnie Ray (Philips)
9	7	EV'RYWHERE	David Whitfield (Decca)
8	8	HEY THERE	Rosemary Clooney (Philips)
5	9	ROSE MARIE	Slim Whitman (London)
13	10	I'LL COME WHEN YOU CALL	Ruby Murray (Columbia)
6	11	COOL WATER	Frankie Laine (Philips)
18	12	SONG OF THE DREAMER	Johnnie Ray (Philips)
12	13	THE BREEZE AND I	Caterina Valente (Polydor)
11	14	HERNANDO'S HIDEAWAY	Johnnie Ray (Philips)
15	15	YELLOW ROSE OF TEXAS	Gary Miller (Nixa)
-	16	CLOUDBURST	Don Lang (HMV)
14	17	CLOSE THE DOOR	Stargazers (Decca)
-	18	LET'S HAVE A DING DONG	Winifred Atwell (Decca)
-	19	LOVE ME OR LEAVE ME	Sammy Davis Jr. (Brunswick)
16	20	GO ON BY	Alma Cogan (HMV)

12 November 1955

last	this	title	artist (label)
2	1	HERNANDO'S HIDEAWAY	Johnston Brothers (Decca)
4	2	ROCK AROUND THE CLOCK	Bill Haley & His Comets (Brunswick)
1	3	THE MAN FROM LARAMIE	Jimmy Young (Decca)
3	4	BLUE STAR (THE 'MEDIC' THEME)	Cyril Stapleton (Decca)
6	5	HEY THERE	Johnnie Ray (Philips)
10	6	I'LL COME WHEN YOU CALL	Ruby Murray (Columbia)
8	7	HEY THERE	Rosemary Clooney (Philips)
7	8	EV'RYWHERE	David Whitfield (Decca)
5	9	YELLOW ROSE OF TEXAS	Mitch Miller (Philips)
18	10	LET'S HAVE A DING DONG	Winifred Atwell (Decca)
12	11	SONG OF THE DREAMER	Johnnie Ray (Philips)
11	12	COOL WATER	Frankie Laine (Philips)
13	13	YELLOW ROSE OF TEXAS	Gary Miller (Nixa)
9	14	ROSE MARIE	Slim Whitman (London)
15	15	YELLOW ROSE OF TEXAS	Ronnie Hilton (HMV)
-	16	HUMMINGBIRD	Frankie Laine (Philips)
-	17	TWENTY TINY FINGERS	Stargazers (Decca)
19	18	LOVE ME OR LEAVE ME	Sammy Davis Jr. (Brunswick)
16	18	CLOUDBURST	Don Lang (HMV)
13	20	THE BREEZE AND I	Caterina Valente (Polydor)

19 November 1955

last	this	title	artist (label)
1	1	HERNANDO'S HIDEAWAY	Johnston Brothers (Decca)
3	2	THE MAN FROM LARAMIE	Jimmy Young (Decca)
2	3	ROCK AROUND THE CLOCK	Bill Haley & His Comets (Brunswick)
7	4	HEY THERE	Rosemary Clooney (Philips)
5	5	HEY THERE	Johnnie Ray (Philips)
9	6	YELLOW ROSE OF TEXAS	Mitch Miller (Philips)
4	7	BLUE STAR (THE 'MEDIC' THEME)	Cyril Stapleton (Decca)
10	8	LET'S HAVE A DING DONG	Winifred Atwell (Decca)
6	9	I'LL COME WHEN YOU CALL	Ruby Murray (Columbia)
11	10	SONG OF THE DREAMER	Johnnie Ray (Philips)
-	11	LOVE IS A MANY SPLENDORED THING	Four Aces (Brunswick)
8	12	EV'RYWHERE	David Whitfield (Decca)
17	13	TWENTY TINY FINGERS	Stargazers (Decca)
20	14	THE BREEZE AND I	Caterina Valente (Polydor)
15	15	YELLOW ROSE OF TEXAS	Ronnie Hilton (HMV)
12	16	COOL WATER	Frankie Laine (Philips)
13	17	YELLOW ROSE OF TEXAS	Gary Miller (Nixa)
14	18	ROSE MARIE	Slim Whitman (London)
-	19	MEET ME ON THE CORNER	Max Bygraves (HMV)
-	20	AIN'T THAT A SHAME	Pat Boone (London)

26 November 1955

last	this	title	artist (label)
3	1	ROCK AROUND THE CLOCK	Bill Haley & His Comets (Brunswick)
11	2	LOVE IS A MANY SPLENDORED THING	Four Aces (Brunswick)
1	3	HERNANDO'S HIDEAWAY	Johnston Brothers (Decca)
8	4	LET'S HAVE A DING DONG	Winifred Atwell (Decca)
2	5	THE MAN FROM LARAMIE	Jimmy Young (Decca)
4	6	HEY THERE	Rosemary Clooney (Philips)
6	7	YELLOW ROSE OF TEXAS	Mitch Miller (Philips)
5	8	HEY THERE	Johnnie Ray (Philips)
20	9	AIN'T THAT A SHAME	Pat Boone (London)
13	10	TWENTY TINY FINGERS	Stargazers (Decca)
19	11	MEET ME ON THE CORNER	Max Bygraves (HMV)
-	12	CHRISTMAS ALPHABET	Dickie Valentine (Decca)
7	13	BLUE STAR (THE 'MEDIC' THEME)	Cyril Stapleton (Decca)
9	14	I'LL COME WHEN YOU CALL	Ruby Murray (Columbia)
10	15	SONG OF THE DREAMER	Johnnie Ray (Philips)
-	16	OH! SUZANNAH/MEDLEY: PAT-A-CAKE/THREE BLIND MICE/JINGLE BELLS	Singing Dogs (Nixa)
17	17	WHEN YOU LOSE THE ONE YOU LOVE	David Whitfield (Decca)
18	18	SUDDENLY THERE'S A VALLEY	Petula Clark (Pye Nixa)
-	19	I'LL NEVER STOP LOVING YOU	Doris Day (Philips)
-	20	TWENTY TINY FINGERS	Coronets (Columbia)
-	20	HAWK-EYE	Frankie Laine (Philips)

3 December 1955

last	this	title	artist (label)
1	1	ROCK AROUND THE CLOCK	Bill Haley & His Comets (Brunswick)
2	2	LOVE IS A MANY SPLENDORED THING	Four Aces (Brunswick)
4	3	LET'S HAVE A DING DONG	Winifred Atwell (Decca)
12	4	CHRISTMAS ALPHABET	Dickie Valentine (Decca)
3	5	HERNANDO'S HIDEAWAY	Johnston Brothers (Decca)
7	6	YELLOW ROSE OF TEXAS	Mitch Miller (Philips)
10	7	TWENTY TINY FINGERS	Stargazers (Decca)
9	8	AIN'T THAT A SHAME	Pat Boone (London)
11	9	MEET ME ON THE CORNER	Max Bygraves (HMV)
5	10	THE MAN FROM LARAMIE	Jimmy Young (Decca)
6	11	HEY THERE	Rosemary Clooney (Philips)
8	12	HEY THERE	Johnnie Ray (Philips)
13	13	BLUE STAR (THE 'MEDIC' THEME)	Cyril Stapleton (Decca)
18	14	SUDDENLY THERE'S A VALLEY	Petula Clark (Pye Nixa)
17	15	WHEN YOU LOSE THE ONE YOU LOVE	David Whitfield (Decca)
16	16	OH! SUZANNAH/MEDLEY: PAT-A-CAKE/THREE BLIND MICE/JINGLE BELLS	Singing Dogs (Nixa)
20	17	HAWK-EYE	Frankie Laine (Philips)
-	18	CLOUDBURST	Don Lang (HMV)
-	19	SUDDENLY THERE'S A VALLEY	Lee Lawrence (Columbia)
-	20	SEVENTEEN	Frankie Vaughan (Philips)

Rock Around The Clock, the Bill Haley single which had briefly grazed the chart in January but failed to match the initial impact of Haley's *Shake, Rattle And Roll*, swept back in far more imposing style after being heard in the film *The Blackboard Jungle*, which focused on deliquency in an American school. Some of the teddy boy audience who flocked to watch the movie unfortunately opted to take up the delinquency as well as the rock'n'roll rhythm, but if cinema seats suffered, Haley's single's sales certainly did not.

10 December 1955

last week / this week

last	this		
1	1	ROCK AROUND THE CLOCK	
			Bill Haley & His Comets (Brunswick)
4	2	CHRISTMAS ALPHABET	Dickie Valentine (Decca)
2	3	LOVE IS A MANY SPLENDORED THING	
			Four Aces (Brunswick)
3	4	LET'S HAVE A DING DONG	
			Winifred Atwell (Decca)
7	5	TWENTY TINY FINGERS	Stargazers (Decca)
9	6	MEET ME ON THE CORNER	Max Bygraves (HMV)
8	7	AIN'T THAT A SHAME	Pat Boone (London)
6	8	YELLOW ROSE OF TEXAS	Mitch Miller (Philips)
14	9	SUDDENLY THERE'S A VALLEY	
			Petula Clark (Pye Nixa)
5	10	HERNANDO'S HIDEAWAY	
			Johnston Brothers (Decca)
15	11	WHEN YOU LOSE THE ONE YOU LOVE	
			David Whitfield (Decca)
17	12	HAWK-EYE	Frankie Laine (Philips)
16	13	OH! SUZANNAH/MEDLEY: PAT-A-CAKE/THREE	
		BLIND MICE/JINGLE BELLS Singing Dogs (Nixa)	
11	14	HEY THERE	Johnnie Ray (Philips)
13	15	BLUE STAR (THE 'MEDIC' THEME)	
			Cyril Stapleton (Decca)
16	16	HEY THERE	Rosemary Clooney (Philips)
-	17	ON WITH THE MOTLEY	Harry Secombe (Philips)
20	18	SEVENTEEN	Frankie Vaughan (Philips)
-	19	LET'S GET TOGETHER AGAIN	
			Big Ben Banjo Band (Columbia)
-	20	SUDDENLY THERE'S A VALLEY	
			Jo Stafford (Philips)

17 December 1955

last	this		
2	1	CHRISTMAS ALPHABET	Dickie Valentine (Decca)
1	2	ROCK AROUND THE CLOCK	
			Bill Haley & His Comets (Brunswick)
3	3	LOVE IS A MANY SPLENDORED THING	
			Four Aces (Brunswick)
4	4	LET'S HAVE A DING DONG	
			Winifred Atwell (Decca)
6	5	MEET ME ON THE CORNER	Max Bygraves (HMV)
5	5	TWENTY TINY FINGERS	Stargazers (Decca)
11	7	WHEN YOU LOSE THE ONE YOU LOVE	
			David Whitfield (Decca)
10	8	HERNANDO'S HIDEAWAY	
			Johnston Brothers (Decca)
8	9	YELLOW ROSE OF TEXAS	Mitch Miller (Philips)
7	10	AIN'T THAT A SHAME	Pat Boone (London)
12	11	HAWK-EYE	Frankie Laine (Philips)
9	12	SUDDENLY THERE'S A VALLEY	
			Petula Clark (Pye Nixa)
13	13	OH! SUZANNAH/MEDLEY: PAT-A-CAKE/THREE	
		BLIND MICE/JINGLE BELLS Singing Dogs (Nixa)	
-	14	SUDDENLY THERE'S A VALLEY	
			Lee Lawrence (Columbia)
20	15	SUDDENLY THERE'S A VALLEY	
			Jo Stafford (Philips)
17	16	ON WITH THE MOTLEY	Harry Secombe (Philips)
-	17	TWENTY TINY FINGERS	Alma Cogan (HMV)
18	18	SEVENTEEN	Frankie Vaughan (Philips)
-	19	ARRIVEDERCI DARLING (GOODBYE TO ROME)	
			Anne Shelton (HMV)
-	20	OLD PIANNA RAG	Dickie Valentine (Decca)

24 December 1955

last	this		
1	1	CHRISTMAS ALPHABET	Dickie Valentine (Decca)
2	2	ROCK AROUND THE CLOCK	
			Bill Haley & His Comets (Brunswick)
3	3	LOVE IS A MANY SPLENDORED THING	
			Four Aces (Brunswick)
5	4	MEET ME ON THE CORNER	Max Bygraves (HMV)
4	5	LET'S HAVE A DING DONG Winifred Atwell (Decca)	
5	6	TWENTY TINY FINGERS	Stargazers (Decca)
11	7	HAWK-EYE	Frankie Laine (Philips)
9	8	YELLOW ROSE OF TEXAS	Mitch Miller (Philips)
12	9	SUDDENLY THERE'S A VALLEY	
			Petula Clark (Pye Nixa)
7	10	WHEN YOU LOSE THE ONE YOU LOVE	
			David Whitfield (Decca)
8	11	HERNANDO'S HIDEAWAY	
			Johnston Brothers (Decca)
15	12	SUDDENLY THERE'S A VALLEY	
			Jo Stafford (Philips)
-	13	NEVER DO A TANGO WITH AN ESKIMO	
			Alma Cogan (HMV)
10	14	AIN'T THAT A SHAME	Pat Boone (London)
14	15	SUDDENLY THERE'S A VALLEY	
			Lee Lawrence (Columbia)
-	16	SEVENTEEN	Boyd Bennett (Parlophone)
16	17	ON WITH THE MOTLEY	Harry Secombe (Philips)
19	18	ARRIVEDERCI DARLING (GOODBYE TO ROME)	
			Anne Shelton (HMV)
-	19	SOMEONE ON YOUR MIND	Jimmy Young (Decca)
-	20	BLUEBELL POLKA Jimmy Shand (Parlophone)	
20	20	OLD PIANNA RAG	Dickie Valentine (Decca)

31 December 1955

last	this		
1	1	CHRISTMAS ALPHABET	Dickie Valentine (Decca)
2	2	ROCK AROUND THE CLOCK	
			Bill Haley & His Comets (Brunswick)
4	3	MEET ME ON THE CORNER	
			Max Bygraves (HMV)
5	4	LET'S HAVE A DING DONG	
			Winifred Atwell (Decca)
3	5	LOVE IS A MANY SPLENDORED THING	
			Four Aces (Brunswick)
6	6	TWENTY TINY FINGERS	Stargazers (Decca)
7	7	HAWK-EYE	Frankie Laine (Philips)
9	8	SUDDENLY THERE'S A VALLEY	
			Petula Clark (Pye Nixa)
	9	'JOIN IN AND SING AGAIN' MEDLEY	
			Johnston Brothers (Decca)
13	10	NEVER DO A TANGO WITH AN ESKIMO	
			Alma Cogan (HMV)
8	11	YELLOW ROSE OF TEXAS	Mitch Miller (Philips)
10	12	WHEN YOU LOSE THE ONE YOU LOVE	
			David Whitfield (Decca)
12	13	SUDDENLY THERE'S A VALLEY	
			Jo Stafford (Philips)
14	14	AIN'T THAT A SHAME	Pat Boone (London)
11	15	HERNANDO'S HIDEAWAY	
			Johnston Brothers (Decca)
19	16	SOMEONE ON YOUR MIND	Jimmy Young (Decca)
18	17	ARRIVEDERCI DARLING (GOODBYE TO ROME)	
			Anne Shelton (HMV)
-	18	LET'S GET TOGETHER AGAIN	
			Big Ben Banjo Band (Columbia)
20	18	OLD PIANNA RAG	Dickie Valentine (Decca)
20	20	BLUEBELL POLKA	Jimmy Shand (Parlophone)
-	21	ROCK A BEATIN' BOOGIE	
			Bill Haley & His Comets (Brunswick)
15	22	SUDDENLY THERE'S A VALLEY	
			Lee Lawrence (Columbia)
16	23	SEVENTEEN	Boyd Bennett (Parlophone)
-	24	TINA MARIE	Perry Como (HMV)
-	25	PICKIN' A CHICKEN	Eve Boswell (Parlophone)

With Christmas record sales booming, the NME decided, for a single week at the end of the year, to extend the chart by five places to reflect this. Pat Boone was the first of the new-breed rock singers to chart in Haley's wake, but otherwise it was a yuletide of novelties (*Christmas Alphabet*), singalongs (count them), and most bizarrely, Jimmy Shand!

Slim Whitman had the biggest-selling single of 1955 with Rose Marie.

29

January – February 1956

7 January 1956

last	this		
2	1	ROCK AROUND THE CLOCK	Bill Haley & His Comets (Brunswick)
3	2	MEET ME ON THE CORNER	Max Bygraves (HMV)
5	3	LOVE IS A MANY SPLENDORED THING	Four Aces (Brunswick)
6	4	TWENTY TINY FINGERS	Stargazers (Decca)
-	5	ROCK 'N' BEATIN' BOOGIE	Bill Haley & His Comets (Brunswick)
10	6	NEVER DO A TANGO WITH AN ESKIMO	Alma Cogan (HMV)
8	7	SUDDENLY THERE'S A VALLEY	Petula Clark (Pye Nixa)
7	8	HAWK EYE	Frankie Laine (Philips)
1	9	CHRISTMAS ALPHABET	Dickie Valentine (Decca)
4	10	LET'S HAVE A DING DONG	Winifred Atwell (Decca)
12	11	WHEN YOU LOSE THE ONE YOU LOVE	David Whitfield (Decca)
14	12	AIN'T THAT A SHAME	Pat Boone (London)
-	13	BALLAD OF DAVY CROCKETT	Bill Hayes (London)
16	14	SOMEONE ON YOUR MIND	Jimmy Young (Decca)
18	15	OLD PI-ANNA RAG	Dickie Valentine (Decca)
13	16	SUDDENLY THERE'S A VALLEY	Jo Stafford (Philips)
-	17	ROCK ISLAND LINE	Lonnie Donegan (Decca)
-	18	SIXTEEN TONS	Tennessee Ernie Ford (Capitol)
17	19	ARRIVEDERCI DARLING	Anne Shelton (HMV)
-	20	PICKIN' A CHICKEN	Eve Boswell (Parlophone)

14 January 1956

last	this		
1	1	ROCK AROUND THE CLOCK	Bill Haley & His Comets (Brunswick)
18	2	SIXTEEN TONS	Tennessee Ernie Ford (Capitol)
3	3	LOVE IS A MANY SPLENDORED THING	Four Aces (Brunswick)
5	4	ROCK A BEATIN' BOOGIE	Bill Haley & His Comets (Brunswick)
2	5	MEET ME ON THE CORNER	Max Bygraves (HMV)
6	6	NEVER DO A TANGO WITH AN ESKIMO	Alma Cogan (HMV)
13	7	BALLAD OF DAVY CROCKETT	Bill Hayes (London)
4	8	TWENTY TINY FINGERS	Stargazers (Decca)
-	9	LOVE AND MARRIAGE	Frank Sinatra (Capitol)
7	10	SUDDENLY THERE'S A VALLEY	Petula Clark (Pye Nixa)
-	11	THE BALLAD OF DAVY CROCKETT	Tennessee Ernie Ford (Capitol)
11	12	WHEN YOU LOSE THE ONE YOU LOVE	David Whitfield (Decca)
14	13	SOMEONE ON YOUR MIND	Jimmy Young (Decca)
8	14	HAWK EYE	Frankie Laine (Philips)
20	15	PICKIN' A CHICKEN	Eve Boswell (Parlophone)
17	16	ROCK ISLAND LINE	Lonnie Donegan (Decca)
12	17	AIN'T THAT A SHAME	Pat Boone (London)
15	18	OLD PI-ANNA RAG	Dickie Valentine (Decca)
-	19	ARRIVEDERCI DARLING	Edna Savage (Parlophone)
-	20	CLOUDBURST	Don Lang (HMV)
-	20	ROBIN HOOD	Gary Miller (Nixa)

21 January 1956

last	this		
2	1	SIXTEEN TONS	Tennessee Ernie Ford (Capitol)
7	2	BALLAD OF DAVY CROCKETT	Bill Hayes (London)
9	3	LOVE AND MARRIAGE	Frank Sinatra (Capitol)
4	4	ROCK A BEATIN' BOOGIE	Bill Haley & His Comets (Brunswick)
3	5	LOVE IS A MANY SPLENDORED THING	Four Aces (Brunswick)
1	6	ROCK AROUND THE CLOCK	Bill Haley & His Comets (Brunswick)
11	7	THE BALLAD OF DAVY CROCKETT	Tennessee Ernie Ford (Capitol)
5	8	MEET ME ON THE CORNER	Max Bygraves (HMV)
-	9	(LOVE IS) THE TENDER TRAP	Frank Sinatra (Capitol)
16	10	ROCK ISLAND LINE	Lonnie Donegan (Decca)
-	11	SIXTEEN TONS	Frankie Laine (Philips)
6	12	NEVER DO A TANGO WITH AN ESKIMO	Alma Cogan (HMV)
15	13	PICKIN' A CHICKEN	Eve Boswell (Parlophone)
12	14	WHEN YOU LOSE THE ONE YOU LOVE	David Whitfield (Decca)
10	15	SUDDENLY THERE'S A VALLEY	Petula Clark (Pye Nixa)
8	16	TWENTY TINY FINGERS	Stargazers (Decca)
-	17	ROBIN HOOD	Dick James (Parlophone)
13	18	SOMEONE ON YOUR MIND	Jimmy Young (Decca)
20	19	ROBIN HOOD	Gary Miller (Nixa)
-	20	THE SHIFTING, WHISPERING SANDS	Eamonn Andrews (Parlophone)

28 January 1956

last	this		
1	1	SIXTEEN TONS	Tennessee Ernie Ford (Capitol)
2	2	BALLAD OF DAVY CROCKETT	Bill Hayes (London)
7	3	THE BALLAD OF DAVY CROCKETT	Tennessee Ernie Ford (Capitol)
3	4	LOVE AND MARRIAGE	Frank Sinatra (Capitol)
5	5	LOVE IS A MANY SPLENDORED THING	Four Aces (Brunswick)
9	6	(LOVE IS) THE TENDER TRAP	Frank Sinatra (Capitol)
4	7	ROCK A BEATIN' BOOGIE	Bill Haley & His Comets (Brunswick)
6	8	ROCK AROUND THE CLOCK	Bill Haley & His Comets (Brunswick)
10	9	ROCK ISLAND LINE	Lonnie Donegan (Decca)
11	10	SIXTEEN TONS	Frankie Laine (Philips)
14	11	WHEN YOU LOSE THE ONE YOU LOVE	David Whitfield (Decca)
13	12	PICKIN' A CHICKEN	Eve Boswell (Parlophone)
19	13	ROBIN HOOD	Gary Miller (Nixa)
-	14	ONLY YOU	Hilltoppers (London)
8	15	MEET ME ON THE CORNER	Max Bygraves (HMV)
17	16	ROBIN HOOD	Dick James (Parlophone)
15	17	SUDDENLY THERE'S A VALLEY	Petula Clark (Pye Nixa)
-	18	ZAMBESI	Lou Busch (Capitol)
-	18	DREAMS CAN TELL A LIE	Nat King Cole (Capitol)
20	20	THE SHIFTING, WHISPERING SANDS	Eamon Andrews (Parlophone)
-	20	WITH YOUR LOVE	Malcolm Vaughan (HMV)
-	20	THE SHIFTING, WHISPERING SANDS, PART I	Billy Vaughn & His Orchestra (London)

4 February 1956

last	this		
1	1	SIXTEEN TONS	Tennessee Ernie Ford (Capitol)
2	2	BALLAD OF DAVY CROCKETT	Bill Hayes (London)
6	3	(LOVE IS) THE TENDER TRAP	Frank Sinatra (Capitol)
4	4	LOVE AND MARRIAGE	Frank Sinatra (Capitol)
3	5	THE BALLAD OF DAVY CROCKETT	Tennessee Ernie Ford (Capitol)
7	6	ROCK A BEATIN' BOOGIE	Bill Haley & His Comets (Brunswick)
5	7	LOVE IS A MANY SPLENDORED THING	Four Aces (Brunswick)
9	8	ROCK ISLAND LINE	Lonnie Donegan (Decca)
12	9	PICKIN' A CHICKEN	Eve Boswell (Parlophone)
13	10	ROBIN HOOD	Gary Miller (Nixa)
18	11	DREAMS CAN TELL A LIE	Nat King Cole (Capitol)
11	12	WHEN YOU LOSE THE ONE YOU LOVE	David Whitfield (Decca)
10	13	SIXTEEN TONS	Frankie Laine (Philips)
8	14	ROCK AROUND THE CLOCK	Bill Haley & His Comets (Brunswick)
14	15	ONLY YOU	Hilltoppers (London)
16	16	ROBIN HOOD	Dick James (Parlophone)
18	17	ZAMBESI	Lou Busch (Capitol)
20	18	THE SHIFTING, WHISPERING SANDS	Eamonn Andrews (Parlophone)
-	19	SUDDENLY THERE'S A VALLEY	Jo Stafford (Philips)
-	20	MY BOY FLAT TOP	Frankie Vaughan (Philips)

11 February 1956

last	this		
1	1	SIXTEEN TONS	Tennessee Ernie Ford (Capitol)
3	2	(LOVE IS) THE TENDER TRAP	Frank Sinatra (Capitol)
2	3	BALLAD OF DAVY CROCKETT	Bill Hayes (London)
-	4	MEMORIES ARE MADE OF THIS	Dean Martin (Capitol)
4	5	LOVE AND MARRIAGE	Frank Sinatra (Capitol)
6	6	ROCK A BEATIN' BOOGIE	Bill Haley & His Comets (Brunswick)
17	7	ZAMBESI	Lou Busch (Capitol)
15	8	ONLY YOU	Hilltoppers (London)
9	9	ROCK ISLAND LINE	Lonnie Donegan (Decca)
5	10	THE BALLAD OF DAVY CROCKETT	Tennessee Ernie Ford (Capitol)
10	11	ROBIN HOOD	Gary Miller (Nixa)
11	12	DREAMS CAN TELL A LIE	Nat King Cole (Capitol)
7	13	LOVE IS A MANY SPLENDORED THING	Four Aces (Brunswick)
16	14	ROBIN HOOD	Dick James (Parlophone)
9	15	PICKIN' A CHICKEN	Eve Boswell (Parlophone)
-	16	IT'S ALMOST TOMORROW	Dream Weavers (Brunswick)
-	17	YOUNG AND FOOLISH	Ronnie Hilton (HMV)
-	18	WITH YOUR LOVE	Malcolm Vaughan (HMV)
-	19	BAND OF GOLD	Don Cherry (Philips)
20	20	MY BOY FLAT TOP	Frankie Vaughan (Philips)

The biggest-selling act of the early weeks of 1956 was Tennessee Ernie Ford, who, having taken almost a year to follow up his *Give Me Your Word* chart-topper, now scored two simultaneous Top Three hits. His *Sixteen Tons* had been 's Capitol's fastest seller to date in the US, and rocketed similarly to Number One in Britain. Meanwhile, the release of Walt Disney's *Davy Crockett* TV film to the cinema here fuelled both Ford's and Bill Hayes' versions of the theme almost to the chart top in tight competition.

last week / this week

18 February 1956

4 1 MEMORIES ARE MADE OF THIS — Dean Martin (Capitol)
1 2 SIXTEEN TONS Tennessee Ernie Ford (Capitol)
7 3 ZAMBESI Lou Busch (Capitol)
2 4 (LOVE IS) THE TENDER TRAP — Frank Sinatra (Capitol)
3 5 BALLAD OF DAVY CROCKETT — Bill Hayes (London)
16 6 IT'S ALMOST TOMORROW — Dream Weavers (Brunswick)
5 7 LOVE AND MARRIAGE Frank Sinatra (Capitol)
8 8 ONLY YOU Hilltoppers (London)
- 9 ROCK AND ROLL WALTZ Kay Starr (HMV)
19 10 BAND OF GOLD Don Cherry (Philips)
12 11 DREAMS CAN TELL A LIE — Nat King Cole (Capitol)
9 12 ROCK ISLAND LINE Lonnie Donegan (Decca)
- 13 MEMORIES ARE MADE OF THIS — Dave King (Decca)
10 14 THE BALLAD OF DAVY CROCKETT — Tennessee Ernie Ford (Capitol)
6 15 ROCK A BEATIN' BOOGIE — Bill Haley & His Comets (Brunswick)
14 16 ROBIN HOOD Dick James (Parlophone)
- 17 YOUNG AND FOOLISH — Edmund Hockridge (Nixa)
11 17 ROBIN HOOD Gary Miller (Nixa)
- 19 WHO'S SORRY NOW Johnnie Ray (Philips)
- 20 THE BALLAD OF DAVY CROCKETT — Max Bygraves (HMV)

25 February 1956

1 1 MEMORIES ARE MADE OF THIS — Dean Martin (Capitol)
2 2 ZAMBESI Lou Busch (Capitol)
6 3 IT'S ALMOST TOMORROW — Dream Weavers (Brunswick)
4 4 (LOVE IS) THE TENDER TRAP — Frank Sinatra (Capitol)
2 5 SIXTEEN TONS Tennessee Ernie Ford (Capitol)
8 6 ONLY YOU Hilltoppers (London)
9 7 ROCK AND ROLL WALTZ Kay Starr (HMV)
10 8 BAND OF GOLD Don Cherry (Philips)
5 9 BALLAD OF DAVY CROCKETT — Bill Hayes (London)
11 10 DREAMS CAN TELL A LIE — Nat King Cole (Capitol)
12 11 ROCK ISLAND LINE Lonnie Donegan (Decca)
17 12 YOUNG AND FOOLISH — Edmund Hockridge (Nixa)
7 13 LOVE AND MARRIAGE Frank Sinatra (Capitol)
14 14 THE BALLAD OF DAVY CROCKETT — Tennessee Ernie Ford (Capitol)
13 15 MEMORIES ARE MADE OF THIS — Dave King (Decca)
16 16 ROBIN HOOD Dick James (Parlophone)
19 17 WHO'S SORRY NOW Johnnie Ray (Philips)
- 18 IN OLD LISBON Frank Chacksfield (Decca)
15 19 ROCK A BEATIN' BOOGIE — Bill Haley & His Comets (Brunswick)
- 20 YOUNG AND FOOLISH Ronnie Hilton (HMV)

3 March 1956

1 1 MEMORIES ARE MADE OF THIS — Dean Martin (Capitol)
2 2 ZAMBESI Lou Busch (Capitol)
3 3 IT'S ALMOST TOMORROW — Dream Weavers (Brunswick)
7 4 ROCK AND ROLL WALTZ Kay Starr (HMV)
5 5 ONLY YOU Hilltoppers (London)
8 6 BAND OF GOLD Don Cherry (Philips)
4 7 (LOVE IS) THE TENDER TRAP — Frank Sinatra (Capitol)
8 8 SIXTEEN TONS Tennessee Ernie Ford (Capitol)
11 9 ROCK ISLAND LINE Lonnie Donegan (Decca)
12 10 YOUNG AND FOOLISH — Edmund Hockridge (Nixa)
15 11 MEMORIES ARE MADE OF THIS — Dave King (Decca)
9 12 BALLAD OF DAVY CROCKETT — Bill Hayes (London)
10 13 DREAMS CAN TELL A LIE — Nat King Cole (Capitol)
16 14 ROBIN HOOD Dick James (Parlophone)
18 15 IN OLD LISBON Frank Chacksfield (Decca)
13 16 LOVE AND MARRIAGE Frank Sinatra (Capitol)
- 17 THE GREAT PRETENDER — Jimmy Parkinson (Columbia)
- 18 PICKIN' A CHICKEN Eve Boswell (Parlophone)
- 19 MY SEPTEMBER LOVE David Whitfield (Decca)
- 20 YOUNG AND FOOLISH Dean Martin (Capitol)
- 20 WITH YOUR LOVE Malcolm Vaughan (HMV)

10 March 1956

1 1 MEMORIES ARE MADE OF THIS — Dean Martin (Capitol)
2 2 ZAMBESI Lou Busch (Capitol)
3 3 IT'S ALMOST TOMORROW — Dream Weavers (Brunswick)
4 4 ROCK AND ROLL WALTZ Kay Starr (HMV)
11 5 MEMORIES ARE MADE OF THIS — Dave King (Decca)
5 6 ONLY YOU Hilltoppers (London)
6 7 BAND OF GOLD Don Cherry (Philips)
7 8 (LOVE IS) THE TENDER TRAP — Frank Sinatra (Capitol)
- 9 SEE YOU LATER, ALLIGATOR — Bill Haley & His Comets (Brunswick)
10 10 YOUNG AND FOOLISH — Edmund Hockridge (Nixa)
9 11 ROCK ISLAND LINE Lonnie Donegan (Decca)
17 12 THE GREAT PRETENDER — Jimmy Parkinson (Columbia)
13 13 DREAMS CAN TELL A LIE — Nat King Cole (Capitol)
8 14 SIXTEEN TONS Tennessee Ernie Ford (Capitol)
15 15 IN OLD LISBON Frank Chacksfield (Decca)
18 16 PICKIN' A CHICKEN Eve Boswell (Parlophone)
14 17 ROBIN HOOD Dick James (Parlophone)
- 18 ZAMBESI Eddie Calvert (Columbia)
- 19 YOUNG AND FOOLISH Ronnie Hilton (HMV)
19 20 MY SEPTEMBER LOVE David Whitfield (Decca)
- 20 TUMBLING TUMBLEWEEDS — Slim Whitman (London)

17 March 1956

3 1 IT'S ALMOST TOMORROW — Dream Weavers (Brunswick)
2 2 ZAMBESI Lou Busch (Capitol)
1 3 MEMORIES ARE MADE OF THIS — Dean Martin (Capitol)
4 4 ROCK AND ROLL WALTZ Kay Starr (HMV)
5 5 MEMORIES ARE MADE OF THIS — Dave King (Decca)
6 6 ONLY YOU Hilltoppers (London)
9 7 SEE YOU LATER, ALLIGATOR — Bill Haley & His Comets (Brunswick)
7 8 BAND OF GOLD Don Cherry (Philips)
11 9 ROCK ISLAND LINE Lonnie Donegan (Decca)
12 10 THE GREAT PRETENDER — Jimmy Parkinson (Columbia)
10 11 YOUNG AND FOOLISH — Edmund Hockridge (Nixa)
- 12 POOR PEOPLE OF PARIS — Winifred Atwell (Decca)
14 13 SIXTEEN TONS Tennessee Ernie Ford (Capitol)
8 14 (LOVE IS) THE TENDER TRAP — Frank Sinatra (Capitol)
- 15 'THE THREEPENNY OPERA' THEME — Dick Hyman Trio (MGM)
13 16 DREAMS CAN TELL A LIE — Nat King Cole (Capitol)
16 17 PICKIN' A CHICKEN Eve Boswell (Parlophone)
- 18 CHAIN GANG Jimmy Young (Decca)
20 19 TUMBLING TUMBLEWEEDS — Slim Whitman (London)
15 20 IN OLD LISBON Frank Chacksfield (Decca)

24 March 1956

1 1 IT'S ALMOST TOMORROW — Dream Weavers (Brunswick)
4 2 ROCK AND ROLL WALTZ Kay Starr (HMV)
3 3 MEMORIES ARE MADE OF THIS — Dean Martin (Capitol)
6 4 ONLY YOU Hilltoppers (London)
12 5 POOR PEOPLE OF PARIS — Winifred Atwell (Decca)
2 6 ZAMBESI Lou Busch (Capitol)
7 7 SEE YOU LATER, ALLIGATOR — Bill Haley & His Comets (Brunswick)
5 8 MEMORIES ARE MADE OF THIS — Dave King (Decca)
18 9 CHAIN GANG Jimmy Young (Decca)
8 10 BAND OF GOLD Don Cherry (Philips)
10 11 THE GREAT PRETENDER — Jimmy Parkinson (Columbia)
15 12 'THE THREEPENNY OPERA' THEME — Dick Hyman Trio (MGM)
9 13 ROCK ISLAND LINE Lonnie Donegan (Decca)
11 14 YOUNG AND FOOLISH — Edmund Hockridge (Nixa)
- 15 THE TROUBLE WITH HARRY — Alfi & Harry (London)
- 16 ZAMBESI Eddie Calvert (Columbia)
- 17 A THEME FROM "THE THREEPENNY OPERA" (MACK THE KNIFE) Billy Vaughn (Columbia)
18 18 MY SEPTEMBER LOVE David Whitfield (Decca)
- 19 JIMMY UNKNOWN Lita Roza (Decca)
16 20 DREAMS CAN TELL A LIE — Nat King Cole (Capitol)

Dean Martin's *Memories Are Made Of This* sold even faster for Capitol than *Sixteen tons,* but Dean Martin did find stiff competition from Dave King's UK cover version, which set a record of its own by being recorded on a Friday, pressed over the weekend, and in the shops by Monday. Lonnie Donegan made the Top 10 with his first release, and the lack of a UK outlet for the Platters' US hits *Only You* and *The Great Pretender* left the field to Hilltoppers and Jimmy Parkinson covers.

March – April 1956

last week	this week	**31 March 1956**
2	1	ROCK AND ROLL WALTZ Kay Starr (HMV)
1	2	IT'S ALMOST TOMORROW Dream Weavers (Brunswick)
5	3	POOR PEOPLE OF PARIS Winifred Atwell (Decca)
6	4	ZAMBESI Lou Busch (Capitol)
4	5	ONLY YOU Hilltoppers (London)
8	6	MEMORIES ARE MADE OF THIS Dave King (Decca)
3	7	MEMORIES ARE MADE OF THIS Dean Martin (Capitol)
7	8	SEE YOU LATER, ALLIGATOR Bill Haley & His Comets (Brunswick)
9	9	CHAIN GANG Jimmy Young (Decca)
12	10	'THE THREEPENNY OPERA' THEME Dick Hyman Trio (MGM)
11	11	THE GREAT PRETENDER Jimmy Parkinson (Columbia)
10	12	BAND OF GOLD Don Cherry (Philips)
16	13	ZAMBESI Eddie Calvert (Columbia)
14	14	YOUNG AND FOOLISH Edmund Hockridge (Nixa)
17	15	A THEME FROM "THE THREEPENNY OPERA" (MACK THE KNIFE) Billy Vaughn (London)
15	16	THE TROUBLE WITH HARRY Alfi & Harry (London)
19	17	JIMMY UNKNOWN Lita Roza (Decca)
-	18	WILLIE CAN Alma Cogan (HMV)
13	19	ROCK ISLAND LINE Lonnie Donegan (Decca)
-	20	NOTHIN' TO DO Michael Holliday (Columbia)

		7 April 1956
2	1	IT'S ALMOST TOMORROW Dream Weavers (Brunswick)
3	2	POOR PEOPLE OF PARIS Winifred Atwell (Decca)
1	3	ROCK AND ROLL WALTZ Kay Starr (HMV)
5	4	ONLY YOU Hilltoppers (London)
6	5	MEMORIES ARE MADE OF THIS
4	6	ZAMBESI Lou Busch (Capitol)
8	7	SEE YOU LATER, ALLIGATOR Bill Haley & His Comets
7	8	MEMORIES ARE MADE OF THIS Dean Martin (Capitol)
11	9	THE GREAT PRETENDER Jimmy Parkinson (Columbia)
9	10	CHAIN GANG Jimmy Young (Decca)
10	11	'THE THREEPENNY OPERA' THEME Dick Hyman Trio (MGM)
15	12	A THEME FROM "THE THREEPENNY OPERA" (MACK THE KNIFE) Billy Vaughn (London)
13	13	ZAMBESI Eddie Calvert (Columbia)
12	13	BAND OF GOLD Don Cherry (Philips)
17	15	JIMMY UNKNOWN
-	16	MY SEPTEMBER LOVE David Whitfield (Decca)
18	17	WILLIE CAN Alma Cogan (HMV)
-	18	THE ITALIAN THEME Cyril Stapleton (Decca)
16	19	THE TROUBLE WITH HARRY Alfi & Harry (London)
-	20	PICKIN' A CHICKEN Eve Boswell (Parlophone)

Lonnie Donegan on the Rock Island Line

		14 April 1956
2	1	POOR PEOPLE OF PARIS Winifred Atwell (Decca)
1	2	IT'S ALMOST TOMORROW Dream Weavers (Brunswick)
3	3	ROCK AND ROLL WALTZ Kay Starr (HMV)
4	4	ONLY YOU Hilltoppers (London)
6	5	ZAMBESI Lou Busch (Capitol)
5	6	MEMORIES ARE MADE OF THIS Dave King (Decca)
8	7	MEMORIES ARE MADE OF THIS Dean Martin (Capitol)
7	8	SEE YOU LATER, ALLIGATOR Bill Haley & His Comets (Brunswick)
11	9	'THE THREEPENNY OPERA' THEME Dick Hyman Trio (MGM)
9	10	THE GREAT PRETENDER Jimmy Parkinson (Columbia)
16	11	MY SEPTEMBER LOVE David Whitfield (Decca)
12	12	A THEME FROM "THE THREEPENNY OPERA" (MACK THE KNIFE) Billy Vaughn (London)
17	13	WILLIE CAN Alma Cogan (HMV)
13	14	ZAMBESI Eddie Calvert (Columbia)
10	15	CHAIN GANG Jimmy Young (Decca)
-	16	ROCK ISLAND LINE Lonnie Donegan (Decca)
13	17	BAND OF GOLD Don Cherry (Philips)
-	18	A TEAR FELL Teresa Brewer (Vogue-Coral)
-	19	I'M A FOOL Slim Whitman (London)
15	20	JIMMY UNKNOWN Lita Roza (Decca)
19	21	THE TROUBLE WITH HARRY Alfi & Harry (London)
-	22	NO OTHER LOVE Johnston Brothers (Decca)
18	23	THE ITALIAN THEME Cyril Stapleton (Decca)
-	24	SEVEN DAYS Anne Shelton (HMV)
-	25	YOU CAN'T BE TRUE TO TWO Dave King (Decca)
20	26	PICKIN' A CHICKEN Eve Boswell (Parlophone)
-	27	A THEME FROM "THE THREEPENNY OPERA" (MACK THE KNIFE) Louis Armstrong & His All Stars (Philips)
-	28	YOUNG AND FOOLISH Edmund Hockridge (Nixa)
-	29	COME NEXT SPRING Tony Bennett (Philips)
-	30	WILLIE CAN Beverley Sisters (Decca)

		21 April 1956
1	1	POOR PEOPLE OF PARIS Winifred Atwell (Decca)
3	2	ROCK AND ROLL WALTZ Kay Starr (HMV)
2	3	IT'S ALMOST TOMORROW Dream Weavers (Brunswick)
4	4	ONLY YOU Hilltoppers (London)
7	5	MEMORIES ARE MADE OF THIS Dean Martin (Capitol)
6	6	MEMORIES ARE MADE OF THIS Dave King (Decca)
5	7	ZAMBESI Lou Busch (Capitol)
8	8	SEE YOU LATER, ALLIGATOR Bill Haley & His Comets (Brunswick)
11	8	MY SEPTEMBER LOVE David Whitfield (Decca)
9	10	'THE THREEPENNY OPERA' THEME Dick Hyman Trio (MGM)
18	11	A TEAR FELL Teresa Brewer (Vogue-Coral)
10	12	THE GREAT PRETENDER Jimmy Parkinson (Columbia)
13	13	WILLIE CAN Alma Cogan (HMV)
27	14	A THEME FROM "THE THREEPENNY OPERA" (MACK THE KNIFE) Louis Armstrong & His All Stars (Philips)
-	15	NO OTHER LOVE Ronnie Hilton (HMV)
19	16	I'M A FOOL Slim Whitman (London)
12	17	À THEME FROM "THE THREEPENNY OPERA" (MACK THE KNIFE) Billy Vaughn (London)
25	18	YOU CAN'T BE TRUE TO TWO Dave King (Decca)
-	19	AIN'T MISBEHAVIN' Johnnie Ray (Philips)
17	20	BAND OF GOLD Don Cherry (Philips)
24	20	SEVEN DAYS Anne Shelton (HMV)
15	22	CHAIN GANG Jimmy Young (Decca)
26	23	PICKIN' A CHICKEN Eve Boswell (Parlophone)
30	24	WILLIE CAN Beverley Sisters (Decca)
14	25	ZAMBESI Eddie Calvert (Columbia)
20	26	JIMMY UNKNOWN Lita Roza (Decca)
-	27	STEWBALL Lonnie Donegan (Pye Nixa)
-	28	IN A PERSIAN MARKET Sammy Davis Jr. (Brunswick)
21	29	THE TROUBLE WITH HARRY Alfi & Harry (London)
16	30	ROCK ISLAND LINE Lonnie Donegan (Decca)

Following the one-week experiment with a longer chart the previous Christmas, the NME announced on the chart page of the April 14 issue: "In response to repeated requests from readers and the trade, we are increasing our list of Best-Selling records from 20 to 30, as of this week". So, the NME Top 30, the format into which the paper's singles chart settled for over a quarter of a century, was instituted, with pianist Winifred Atwell giving it a non-vocal launch at Number One.

last week	this week	28 April 1956
1	1	POOR PEOPLE OF PARIS — Winifred Atwell (Decca)
3	2	IT'S ALMOST TOMORROW — Dream Weavers (Brunswick)
2	3	ROCK AND ROLL WALTZ — Kay Starr (HMV)
15	4	NO OTHER LOVE — Ronnie Hilton (HMV)
4	5	ONLY YOU — Hilltoppers (London)
6	6	MEMORIES ARE MADE OF THIS — Dave King (Decca)
7	7	ZAMBESI — Lou Busch (Capitol)
11	8	A TEAR FELL — Teresa Brewer (Vogue-Coral)
8	9	MY SEPTEMBER LOVE — David Whitfield (Decca)
5	10	MEMORIES ARE MADE OF THIS — Dean Martin (Capitol)
8	11	SEE YOU LATER, ALLIGATOR — Bill Haley & His Comets (Brunswick)
10	12	'THE THREEPENNY' THEME — Dick Hyman Trio (MGM)
18	13	YOU CAN'T BE TRUE TO TWO — Dave King (Decca)
14	14	A THEME FROM "THE THREEPENNY OPERA" (MACK THE KNIFE) — Louis Armstrong & His All Stars (Philips)
13	15	WILLIE CAN — Alma Cogan (HMV)
-	16	LOST JOHN/STEWBALL — Lonnie Donegan (Pye Nixa)
19	17	AIN'T MISBEHAVIN' — Johnnie Ray (Philips)
12	18	THE GREAT PRETENDER — Jimmy Parkinson (Columbia)
-	19	I'LL BE HOME — Pat Boone (London)
20	20	SEVEN DAYS — Anne Shelton (HMV)
16	20	I'M A FOOL — Slim Whitman (London)
-	22	IN A LITTLE SPANISH TOWN — Bing Crosby (Brunswick)
24	23	WILLIE CAN — Beverley Sisters (Decca)
-	24	MAIN TITLE (FROM 'MAN WITH THE GOLDEN ARM') — Billy May & His Orchestra (Capitol)
30	25	ROCK ISLAND LINE — Lonnie Donegan (Decca)
25	26	ZAMBESI — Eddie Calvert (Columbia)
-	27	INNAMORATA — Dean Martin (Capitol)
17	28	A THEME FROM "THE THREEPENNY OPERA" (MACK THE KNIFE) — Billy Vaughn (London)
-	29	MOUNTAIN GREENERY — Mel Torme (Vogue-Coral)
-	30	JUKE BOX BABY — Perry Como (Capitol)
-	30	NOTHIN' TO DO — Michael Holliday (Columbia)

		5 May 1956
4	1	NO OTHER LOVE — Ronnie Hilton (HMV)
1	2	POOR PEOPLE OF PARIS — Winifred Atwell (Decca)
2	3	IT'S ALMOST TOMORROW — Dream Weavers (Brunswick)
3	4	ROCK AND ROLL WALTZ — Kay Starr (HMV)
5	5	ONLY YOU — Hilltoppers (London)
8	6	A TEAR FELL — Teresa Brewer (Vogue-Coral)
9	7	MY SEPTEMBER LOVE — David Whitfield (Decca)
14	8	A THEME FROM "THE THREEPENNY OPERA" (MACK THE KNIFE) — Louis Armstrong & His All Stars (Philips)
24	9	MAIN TITLE (FROM 'MAN WITH THE GOLDEN ARM') — Billy May & His Orchestra (Capitol)
11	10	SEE YOU LATER, ALLIGATOR — Bill Haley & His Comets (Brunswick)
13	11	YOU CAN'T BE TRUE TO TWO — Dave King (Decca)
16	12	LOST JOHN/STEWBALL — Lonnie Donegan (Pye Nixa)
10	13	MEMORIES ARE MADE OF THIS — Dean Martin (Capitol)
19	14	I'LL BE HOME — Pat Boone (London)
6	15	MEMORIES ARE MADE OF THIS — Dave King (Decca)
7	16	ZAMBESI — Lou Busch (Capitol)
15	17	WILLIE CAN — Alma Cogan (HMV)
17	18	AIN'T MISBEHAVIN' — Johnnie Ray (Philips)
12	19	'THE THREEPENNY' THEME — Dick Hyman Trio (MGM)
18	20	THE GREAT PRETENDER — Jimmy Parkinson (Columbia)
27	21	INNAMORATA — Dean Martin (Capitol)
30	22	JUKE BOX BABY — Perry Como (Capitol)
30	23	NOTHIN' TO DO — Michael Holliday (Columbia)
29	24	MOUNTAIN GREENERY — Mel Torme (Vogue-Coral)
28	25	A THEME FROM "THE THREEPENNY OPERA" (MACK THE KNIFE) — Billy Vaughn (London)
-	26	YOUNG AND FOOLISH — Edmund Hockridge (Nixa)
23	27	WILLIE CAN — Beverley Sisters (Decca)
-	28	HELL HATH NO FURY — Frankie Laine (Philips)
22	29	IN A LITTLE SPANISH TOWN — Bing Crosby (Brunswick)
20	30	SEVEN DAYS — Anne Shelton (HMV)

		12 May 1956
1	1	NO OTHER LOVE — Ronnie Hilton (HMV)
2	2	POOR PEOPLE OF PARIS — Winifred Atwell (Decca)
3	3	IT'S ALMOST TOMORROW — Dream Weavers (Brunswick)
5	3	ONLY YOU — Hilltoppers (London)
6	5	A TEAR FELL — Teresa Brewer (Vogue-Coral)
4	6	ROCK AND ROLL WALTZ — Kay Starr (HMV)
7	7	MY SEPTEMBER LOVE — David Whitfield (Decca)
12	8	LOST JOHN/STEWBALL — Lonnie Donegan (Pye Nixa)
14	9	I'LL BE HOME — Pat Boone (London)
9	10	MAIN TITLE (FROM 'MAN WITH THE GOLDEN ARM') — Billy May & His Orchestra (Capitol)
8	11	A THEME FROM "THE THREEPENNY OPERA" (MACK THE KNIFE) — Louis Armstrong & His All Stars (Philips)
11	12	YOU CAN'T BE TRUE TO TWO — Dave King (Decca)
10	13	SEE YOU LATER, ALLIGATOR — Bill Haley & His Comets (Brunswick)
15	14	MEMORIES ARE MADE OF THIS — Dave King (Decca)
-	15	HEARTBREAK HOTEL — Elvis Presley (HMV)
19	16	'THE THREEPENNY' THEME — Dick Hyman Trio (MGM)
13	17	MEMORIES ARE MADE OF THIS — Dean Martin (Capitol)
17	18	WILLIE CAN — Alma Cogan (HMV)
18	19	AIN'T MISBEHAVIN' — Johnnie Ray (Philips)
-	20	ROCK ISLAND LINE — Lonnie Donegan (Decca)
16	21	ZAMBESI — Lou Busch (Capitol)
24	22	MOUNTAIN GREENERY — Mel Torme (Vogue-Coral)
-	23	THE HAPPY WHISTLER — Don Robertson (Capitol)
20	24	THE GREAT PRETENDER — Jimmy Parkinson (Columbia)
22	25	JUKE BOX BABY — Perry Como (Capitol)
29	26	IN A LITTLE SPANISH TOWN — Bing Crosby (Brunswick)
-	27	NO OTHER LOVE — Edmund Hockridge (Nixa)
-	28	TOO YOUNG TO GO STEADY — Nat King Cole (Capitol)
-	29	I'M A FOOL — Slim Whitman (London)
21	30	INNAMORATA — Dean Martin (Capitol)

		19 May 1956
1	1	NO OTHER LOVE — Ronnie Hilton (HMV)
2	2	POOR PEOPLE OF PARIS — Winifred Atwell (Decca)
7	3	MY SEPTEMBER LOVE — David Whitfield (Decca)
5	4	A TEAR FELL — Teresa Brewer (Vogue-Coral)
6	5	ROCK AND ROLL WALTZ — Kay Starr (HMV)
3	6	IT'S ALMOST TOMORROW — Dream Weavers (Brunswick)
9	7	I'LL BE HOME — Pat Boone (London)
23	8	THE HAPPY WHISTLER — Don Robertson (Capitol)
10	9	MAIN TITLE (FROM 'MAN WITH THE GOLDEN ARM') — Billy May & His Orchestra (Capitol)
8	10	LOST JOHN/STEWBALL — Lonnie Donegan (Pye Nixa)
11	11	A THEME FROM "THE THREEPENNY OPERA" (MACK THE KNIFE) — Louis Armstrong & His All Stars (Philips)
3	12	ONLY YOU — Hilltoppers (London)
12	13	YOU CAN'T BE TRUE TO TWO — Dave King (Decca)
15	14	HEARTBREAK HOTEL — Elvis Presley (HMV)
22	15	MOUNTAIN GREENERY — Mel Torme (Vogue-Coral)
13	16	SEE YOU LATER, ALLIGATOR — Bill Haley & His Comets (Brunswick)
28	17	TOO YOUNG TO GO STEADY — Nat King Cole (Capitol)
-	18	BLUE SUEDE SHOES — Carl Perkins (London)
-	19	PORT-AU-PRINCE — Winifred Atwell & Frank Chacksfield (Decca)
20	20	ROCK ISLAND LINE — Lonnie Donegan (Decca)
24	21	THE GREAT PRETENDER — Jimmy Parkinson (Columbia)
18	22	WILLIE CAN — Alma Cogan (HMV)
14	22	MEMORIES ARE MADE OF THIS — Dave King (Decca)
27	24	NO OTHER LOVE — Edmund Hockridge (Nixa)
16	25	'THE THREEPENNY' THEME — Dick Hyman Trio (MGM)
19	26	AIN'T MISBEHAVIN' — Johnnie Ray (Philips)
17	27	MEMORIES ARE MADE OF THIS — Dean Martin (Capitol)
21	28	ZAMBESI — Lou Busch (Capitol)
-	29	ROBIN HOOD/DAVY CROCKETT — Dick James (Parlophone)
25	30	JUKE BOX BABY — Perry Como (Capitol)

British vocalist Ronnie Hilton, a prolific coverer of most of the major ballad hits of the 1950s, had his biggest success when *No Other Love*, a comparatively obscure Rodgers & Hammerstein song, gave him his only chart-topper. A more significant event in the long term, however, was the chart debut of Elvis Presley on May 12 with *Heartbreak Hotel*, which had recently hit Number One in the US. A week later, Presley's Memphis compatriot Carl Perkins joined him with US million-seller, *Blue Suede Shoes*.

May – June 1956

26 May 1956

last	this	title	artist
1	1	NO OTHER LOVE	Ronnie Hilton (HMV)
4	2	A TEAR FELL	Teresa Brewer (Vogue-Coral)
2	3	POOR PEOPLE OF PARIS	Winifred Atwell (Decca)
7	4	I'LL BE HOME	Pat Boone (London)
3	5	MY SEPTEMBER LOVE	David Whitfield (Decca)
5	6	ROCK AND ROLL WALTZ	Kay Starr (HMV)
10	7	LOST JOHN/STEWBALL	Lonnie Donegan (Pye Nixa)
14	8	HEARTBREAK HOTEL	Elvis Presley (HMV)
8	9	THE HAPPY WHISTLER	Don Robertson (Capitol)
9	10	MAIN TITLE (FROM 'MAN WITH THE GOLDEN ARM')	Billy May & His Orchestra (Capitol)
12	11	ONLY YOU	Hilltoppers (London)
11	12	A THEME FROM "THE THREEPENNY OPERA" (MACK THE KNIFE)	Louis Armstrong & His All Stars (Philips)
6	13	IT'S ALMOST TOMORROW	Dream Weavers (Brunswick)
18	14	BLUE SUEDE SHOES	Carl Perkins (London)
-	15	HOT DIGGITY (DOG ZIGGITY BOOM)	Perry Como (HMV)
-	16	BLUE SUEDE SHOES	Elvis Presley (HMV)
13	17	YOU CAN'T BE TRUE TO TWO	Dave King (Decca)
15	17	MOUNTAIN GREENERY	Mel Torme (Vogue-Coral)
17	19	TOO YOUNG TO GO STEADY	Nat King Cole (Capitol)
19	20	PORT-AU-PRINCE	Winifred Atwell & Frank Chacksfield (Decca)
20	21	ROCK ISLAND LINE	Lonnie Donegan (Decca)
16	22	SEE YOU LATER, ALLIGATOR	Bill Haley & His Comets (Brunswick)
-	23	THE SAINTS ROCK 'N' ROLL	Johnnie Ray (Philips)
26	24	AIN'T MISBEHAVIN'	Dean Martin (Capitol)
27	25	MEMORIES ARE MADE OF THIS	Jimmy Parkinson (Columbia)
21	26	THE GREAT PRETENDER	Max Bygraves (HMV)
-	27	OUT OF TOWN	Three Kayes (HMV)
-	28	IVORY TOWER	Perry Como (Capitol)
30	29	JUKE BOX BABY	Dave King (Decca)
22	30	MEMORIES ARE MADE OF THIS	

2 June 1956

last	this	title	artist
1	1	NO OTHER LOVE	Ronnie Hilton (HMV)
7	2	LOST JOHN	Lonnie Donegan (Pye Nixa)
4	3	I'LL BE HOME	Pat Boone (London)
2	4	A TEAR FELL	Teresa Brewer (Vogue-Coral)
8	5	HEARTBREAK HOTEL	Elvis Presley (HMV)
3	6	POOR PEOPLE OF PARIS	Winifred Atwell (Decca)
5	7	MY SEPTEMBER LOVE	David Whitfield (Decca)
6	8	ROCK AND ROLL WALTZ	Kay Starr (HMV)
9	9	THE HAPPY WHISTLER	Don Robertson (Capitol)
23	10	THE SAINTS ROCK 'N' ROLL	Bill Haley & His Comets (Brunswick)
11	11	ONLY YOU	Hilltoppers (London)
10	12	MAIN TITLE (FROM 'MAN WITH THE GOLDEN ARM')	Billy May & His Orchestra (Capitol)
15	13	HOT DIGGITY (DOG ZIGGITY BOOM)	Perry Como (HMV)
19	14	TOO YOUNG TO GO STEADY	Nat King Cole (Capitol)
12	15	A THEME FROM "THE THREEPENNY OPERA" (MACK THE KNIFE)	Louis Armstrong & His All Stars (Philips)
14	16	BLUE SUEDE SHOES	Carl Perkins (London)
17	17	YOU CAN'T BE TRUE TO TWO	Dave King (Decca)
17	18	MOUNTAIN GREENERY	Mel Torme (Vogue-Coral)
16	19	BLUE SUEDE SHOES	Elvis Presley (HMV)
20	20	PORT-AU-PRINCE	Winifred Atwell & Frank Chacksfield (Decca)
13	21	IT'S ALMOST TOMORROW	D:eam Weavers (Brunswick)
21	22	ROCK ISLAND LINE	Lonnie Donegan (Decca)
22	23	SEE YOU LATER, ALLIGATOR	Bill Haley & His Comets (Brunswick)
-	24	DELILAH JONES	McGuire Sisters (Vogue-Coral)
29	25	JUKE BOX BABY	Perry Como (Capitol)
-	26	MOONGLOW AND THEME FROM 'PICNIC'	Morris Stoloff (Brunswick)
27	27	OUT OF TOWN	Max Bygraves (HMV)
-	28	THE HAPPY WHISTLER	Cyril Stapleton (Decca)
-	29	NO OTHER LOVE	Edmund Hockridge (Nixa)
28	30	IVORY TOWER	Three Kayes (HMV)

9 June 1956

last	this	title	artist
1	1	NO OTHER LOVE	Ronnie Hilton (HMV)
3	2	I'LL BE HOME	Pat Boone (London)
2	3	LOST JOHN	Lonnie Donegan (Pye Nixa)
5	4	HEARTBREAK HOTEL	Elvis Presley (HMV)
4	5	A TEAR FELL	Teresa Brewer (Vogue-Coral)
13	6	HOT DIGGITY (DOG ZIGGITY BOOM)	Perry Como (HMV)
10	7	THE SAINTS ROCK 'N' ROLL	Bill Haley & His Comets (Brunswick)
7	8	MY SEPTEMBER LOVE	David Whitfield (Decca)
8	9	ROCK AND ROLL WALTZ	Kay Starr (HMV)
19	10	BLUE SUEDE SHOES	Elvis Presley (HMV)
6	11	POOR PEOPLE OF PARIS	Winifred Atwell (Decca)
14	12	TOO YOUNG TO GO STEADY	Nat King Cole (Capitol)
9	12	THE HAPPY WHISTLER	Don Robertson (Capitol)
11	14	ONLY YOU	Hilltoppers (London)
26	14	MOONGLOW AND THEME FROM 'PICNIC'	Morris Stoloff (Brunswick)
16	16	BLUE SUEDE SHOES	Carl Perkins (London)
12	17	MAIN TITLE (FROM 'MAN WITH THE GOLDEN ARM')	Billy May & His Orchestra (Capitol)
20	18	PORT-AU-PRINCE	Winifred Atwell & Frank Chacksfield (Decca)
22	19	ROCK ISLAND LINE	Lonnie Donegan (Decca)
30	20	IVORY TOWER	Three Kayes (HMV)
15	21	A THEME FROM "THE THREEPENNY OPERA" (MACK THE KNIFE)	Louis Armstrong & His All Stars (Philips)
18	22	MOUNTAIN GREENERY	Mel Torme (Vogue-Coral)
21	23	IT'S ALMOST TOMORROW	Dream Weavers (Brunswick)
-	24	AIN'T MISBEHAVIN'	Johnnie Ray (Philips)
17	25	YOU CAN'T BE TRUE TO TWO	Dave King (Decca)
28	26	THE HAPPY WHISTLER	Cyril Stapleton (Decca)
-	27	THE WAYWARD WIND	Jimmy Young (Decca)
27	28	OUT OF TOWN	Max Bygraves (HMV)
24	29	DELILAH JONES	McGuire Sisters (Vogue-Coral)
-	30	WHO ARE WE	Vera Lynn (Decca)

16 June 1956

last	this	title	artist
2	1	I'LL BE HOME	Pat Boone (London)
3	2	LOST JOHN	Lonnie Donegan (Pye Nixa)
4	3	HEARTBREAK HOTEL	Elvis Presley (HMV)
1	4	NO OTHER LOVE	Ronnie Hilton (HMV)
6	5	HOT DIGGITY (DOG ZIGGITY BOOM)	Perry Como (HMV)
7	6	THE SAINTS ROCK 'N' ROLL	Bill Haley & His Comets (Brunswick)
5	7	A TEAR FELL	Teresa Brewer (Vogue-Coral)
8	8	MY SEPTEMBER LOVE	David Whitfield (Decca)
10	9	BLUE SUEDE SHOES	Elvis Presley (HMV)
16	10	BLUE SUEDE SHOES	Carl Perkins (London)
12	11	THE HAPPY WHISTLER	Don Robertson (Capitol)
9	12	ROCK AND ROLL WALTZ	Kay Starr (HMV)
14	13	MOONGLOW AND THEME FROM 'PICNIC'	Morris Stoloff (Brunswick)
12	14	TOO YOUNG TO GO STEADY	Nat King Cole (Capitol)
11	15	POOR PEOPLE OF PARIS	Winifred Atwell (Decca)
14	16	ONLY YOU	Hilltoppers (London)
22	17	MOUNTAIN GREENERY	Mel Torme (Vogue-Coral)
28	18	OUT OF TOWN	Max Bygraves (HMV)
-	19	GAL WITH THE YALLER SHOES	Michael Holliday (Columbia)
18	20	PORT-AU-PRINCE	Winifred Atwell & Frank Chacksfield (Decca)
17	21	MAIN TITLE (FROM 'MAN WITH THE GOLDEN ARM')	Billy May & His Orchestra (Capitol)
26	22	THE HAPPY WHISTLER	Cyril Stapleton (Decca)
21	23	A THEME FROM "THE THREEPENNY OPERA" (MACK THE KNIFE)	Louis Armstrong & His All Stars (Philips)
20	24	IVORY TOWER	Three Kayes (HMV)
19	25	ROCK ISLAND LINE	Lonnie Donegan (Decca)
-	26	SONGS FOR SWINGIN' LOVERS (LP)	Frank Sinatra (Capitol)
-	27	CAROUSEL	Soundtrack (Capitol)
-	28	CAROUSEL WALTZ	Ray Martin (Columbia)
-	29	TAKE IT SATCH (EP)	Louis Armstrong (Philips)
-	30	NO OTHER LOVE	Edmund Hockridge (Nixa)

HMV rushed Elvis' cover version of *Blue Suede Shoes* on to the UK market as soon as *Heartbreak Hotel* made the chart. One of the highlights of his US TV appearances (not seen here), the song was marketed on an EP there. But in the UK, the usurping of an original with a stronger cover version was still the major (in some cases, the only) ploy in the A&R man's book - even when, as here, both versions were American. Both, in the event, made the Top 10 for Presley and Carl Perkins.

23 June 1956

last week	this week	Title — Artist (Label)
1	1	I'LL BE HOME — Pat Boone (London)
3	2	HEARTBREAK HOTEL — Elvis Presley (HMV)
2	3	LOST JOHN — Lonnie Donegan (Pye Nixa)
5	4	HOT DIGGITY (DOG ZIGGITY BOOM) — Perry Como (HMV)
4	5	NO OTHER LOVE — Ronnie Hilton (HMV)
6	6	THE SAINTS ROCK 'N' ROLL — Bill Haley & His Comets (Brunswick)
13	7	MOONGLOW AND THEME FROM 'PICNIC' — Morris Stoloff (Brunswick)
7	8	A TEAR FELL — Teresa Brewer (Vogue-Coral)
8	8	MY SEPTEMBER LOVE — David Whitfield (Decca)
9	10	BLUE SUEDE SHOES — Elvis Presley (HMV)
14	11	TOO YOUNG TO GO STEADY — Nat King Cole (Capitol)
10	12	BLUE SUEDE SHOES — Carl Perkins (London)
19	13	GAL WITH THE YALLER SHOES — Michael Holliday (Columbia)
11	14	THE HAPPY WHISTLER — Don Robertson (Capitol)
-	15	HOT DIGGITY (DOG ZIGGITY BOOM) — Michael Holliday (Columbia)
26	16	SONGS FOR SWINGIN' LOVERS (LP) — Frank Sinatra (Capitol)
17	17	MOUNTAIN GREENERY — Mel Torme (Vogue-Coral)
15	18	POOR PEOPLE OF PARIS — Winifred Atwell (Decca)
18	18	OUT OF TOWN — Max Bygraves (HMV)
20	20	PORT-AU-PRINCE — Winifred Atwell & Frank Chacksfield (Decca)
23	21	A THEME FROM "THE THREEPENNY OPERA" (MACK THE KNIFE) — Louis Armstrong & His All Stars (Philips)
12	22	ROCK AND ROLL WALTZ — Kay Starr (HMV)
22	23	THE HAPPY WHISTLER — Cyril Stapleton (Decca)
-	24	SERENADE — Slim Whitman (London)
-	25	RICH MAN, POOR MAN — Jimmy Young (Decca)
16	26	ONLY YOU — Hilltoppers (London)
21	27	MAIN TITLE (FROM 'MAN WITH THE GOLDEN ARM') — Billy May & His Orchestra (Capitol)
-	28	HOT DIGGITY (DOG ZIGGITY BOOM) — Stargazers (Decca)
-	29	EXPERIMENTS WITH MICE — Johnny Dankworth (Parlophone)
-	30	THE WAYWARD WIND — Tex Ritter (Capitol)
24	30	IVORY TOWER — Three Kayes (HMV)

30 June 1956

last week	this week	Title — Artist (Label)
1	1	I'LL BE HOME — Pat Boone (London)
2	2	HEARTBREAK HOTEL — Elvis Presley (HMV)
3	3	LOST JOHN — Lonnie Donegan (Pye Nixa)
5	4	NO OTHER LOVE — Ronnie Hilton (HMV)
4	5	HOT DIGGITY (DOG ZIGGITY BOOM) — Perry Como (HMV)
6	6	THE SAINTS ROCK 'N' ROLL — Bill Haley & His Comets (Brunswick)
8	7	MY SEPTEMBER LOVE — David Whitfield (Decca)
11	8	TOO YOUNG TO GO STEADY — Nat King Cole (Capitol)
8	9	A TEAR FELL — Teresa Brewer (Vogue-Coral)
29	10	EXPERIMENTS WITH MICE — Johnny Dankworth (Parlophone)
10	10	BLUE SUEDE SHOES — Elvis Presley (HMV)
7	12	MOONGLOW AND THEME FROM 'PICNIC' — Morris Stoloff (Brunswick)
16	13	SONGS FOR SWINGIN' LOVERS (LP) — Frank Sinatra (Capitol)
15	14	HOT DIGGITY (DOG ZIGGITY BOOM) — Michael Holliday (Columbia)
14	15	THE HAPPY WHISTLER — Don Robertson (Capitol)
-	16	ALL-STAR HIT PARADE — Various Artists (Decca)
12	17	BLUE SUEDE SHOES — Carl Perkins (London)
30	18	THE WAYWARD WIND — Tex Ritter (Capitol)
13	19	GAL WITH THE YALLER SHOES — Michael Holliday (Columbia)
-	20	WHATEVER WILL BE WILL BE — Doris Day (Philips)
-	20	THE WAYWARD WIND — Gogi Grant (London)
-	22	WHY DO FOOLS FALL IN LOVE — Teenagers featuring Frankie Lymon (Columbia)
17	23	MOUNTAIN GREENERY — Mel Torme (Vogue-Coral)
22	24	ROCK AND ROLL WALTZ — Kay Starr (HMV)
-	25	PORTUGUESE WASHERWOMAN — Joe "Fingers" Carr (Capitol)
24	25	SERENADE — Slim Whitman (London)
18	27	POOR PEOPLE OF PARIS — Winifred Atwell (Decca)
27	28	MAIN TITLE (FROM 'MAN WITH THE GOLDEN ARM') — Billy May & His Orchestra (Capitol)
-	29	WHO ARE WE — Ronnie Hilton (HMV)
18	30	OUT OF TOWN — Max Bygraves (HMV)
-	30	I'M WALKING BACKWARDS FOR CHRISTMAS/BLUEBOTTLE BLUES — Goons (Decca)

7 July 1956

last week	this week	Title — Artist (Label)
1	1	I'LL BE HOME — Pat Boone (London)
2	2	LOST JOHN — Lonnie Donegan (Pye Nixa)
3	3	HEARTBREAK HOTEL — Elvis Presley (HMV)
16	4	ALL-STAR HIT PARADE — Various Artists (Decca)
6	5	THE SAINTS ROCK 'N' ROLL — Bill Haley & His Comets (Brunswick)
30	6	I'M WALKING BACKWARDS FOR CHRISTMAS/BLUEBOTTLE BLUES — Goons (Decca)
5	7	HOT DIGGITY (DOG ZIGGITY BOOM) — Perry Como (HMV)
4	8	NO OTHER LOVE — Ronnie Hilton (HMV)
7	9	MY SEPTEMBER LOVE — David Whitfield (Decca)
10	10	EXPERIMENTS WITH MICE — Johnny Dankworth (Parlophone)
12	11	MOONGLOW AND THEME FROM 'PICNIC' — Morris Stoloff (Brunswick)
13	12	SONGS FOR SWINGIN' LOVERS (LP) — Frank Sinatra (Capitol)
22	13	WHY DO FOOLS FALL IN LOVE — Teenagers featuring Frankie Lymon (Columbia)
8	14	TOO YOUNG TO GO STEADY — Nat King Cole (Capitol)
18	15	THE WAYWARD WIND — Tex Ritter (Capitol)
20	16	THE WAYWARD WIND — Gogi Grant (London)
9	17	A TEAR FELL — Teresa Brewer (Vogue-Coral)
10	17	BLUE SUEDE SHOES — Elvis Presley (HMV)
14	19	HOT DIGGITY (DOG ZIGGITY BOOM) — Michael Holliday (Columbia)
25	20	PORTUGUESE WASHERWOMAN — Joe "Fingers" Carr (Capitol)
-	20	SKIFFLE SESSION (EP) — Lonnie Donegan (Pye Nixa)
15	22	THE HAPPY WHISTLER — Don Robertson (Capitol)
20	23	WHATEVER WILL BE WILL BE — Doris Day (Philips)
17	24	BLUE SUEDE SHOES — Carl Perkins (London)
23	25	MOUNTAIN GREENERY — Mel Torme (Vogue-Coral)
-	26	CAROUSEL — Soundtrack (Capitol)
25	27	SERENADE — Slim Whitman (London)
-	28	THE FAITHFUL HUSSAR — Ted Heath & His Music (Decca)
30	29	OUT OF TOWN — Max Bygraves (HMV)
29	30	WHO ARE WE — Ronnie Hilton (HMV)

14 July 1956

last week	this week	Title — Artist (Label)
1	1	I'LL BE HOME — Pat Boone (London)
4	2	ALL-STAR HIT PARADE — Various Artists (Decca)
3	3	HEARTBREAK HOTEL — Elvis Presley (HMV)
6	4	I'M WALKING BACKWARDS FOR CHRISTMAS/BLUEBOTTLE BLUES — Goons (Decca)
13	5	WHY DO FOOLS FALL IN LOVE — Teenagers featuring Frankie Lymon (Columbia)
7	6	HOT DIGGITY (DOG ZIGGITY BOOM) — Perry Como (HMV)
10	7	EXPERIMENTS WITH MICE — Johnny Dankworth (Parlophone)
2	7	LOST JOHN — Lonnie Donegan (Pye Nixa)
16	9	THE WAYWARD WIND — Gogi Grant (London)
9	10	MY SEPTEMBER LOVE — David Whitfield (Decca)
15	11	THE WAYWARD WIND — Tex Ritter (Capitol)
30	12	WHO ARE WE — Ronnie Hilton (HMV)
5	13	THE SAINTS ROCK 'N' ROLL — Bill Haley & His Comets (Brunswick)
8	14	NO OTHER LOVE — Ronnie Hilton (HMV)
17	15	A TEAR FELL — Teresa Brewer (Vogue-Coral)
12	16	SONGS FOR SWINGIN' LOVERS (LP) — Frank Sinatra (Capitol)
14	17	TOO YOUNG TO GO STEADY — Nat King Cole (Capitol)
11	18	MOONGLOW AND THEME FROM 'PICNIC' — Morris Stoloff (Brunswick)
17	19	BLUE SUEDE SHOES — Elvis Presley (HMV)
-	20	SWEET-OLD FASHIONED GIRL — Teresa Brewer (Vogue-Coral)
-	21	BAD PENNY BLUES — Humphrey Lyttelton & His Ban (Parlophone)
-	21	WALK HAND IN HAND — Tony Martin (HMV)
28	23	THE FAITHFUL HUSSAR — Ted Heath & His Music (Decca)
19	24	HOT DIGGITY (DOG ZIGGITY BOOM) — Michael Holliday (Columbia)
-	25	KISS ME ANOTHER — Georgia Gibbs (Mercury)
20	26	PORTUGUESE WASHERWOMAN — Joe "Fingers" Carr (Capitol)
20	27	SKIFFLE SESSION (EP) — Lonnie Donegan (Pye Nixa)
23	28	WHATEVER WILL BE WILL BE — Doris Day (Philips)
29	29	THE FAITHFUL HUSSAR — Louis Armstrong & His All Stars (Philips)
-	30	THE BIRDS AND THE BEES — Alma Cogan (HMV)

Pat Boone's *I'll Be Home*, a cover of a Flamingos R&B hit (though nobody here knew that) was his biggest UK seller and only British chart-topper. The song would continue to be popular throughout the 1950s and '60s, because its lyric made it a natural for BBC Radio's *Two-Way Family Favourites*. Frank Sinatra's LP *Songs For Swingin' Lovers*, sold like a single at a time when album sales were comparatively insignificant. Its Number 12 peak would only eventually be beaten by the Beatles' second album.

July – August 1956

21 July 1956

last week / this week

5	1	WHY DO FOOLS FALL IN LOVE — Teenagers featuring Frankie Lymon (Columbia)
1	2	I'LL BE HOME — Pat Boone (London)
2	3	ALL-STAR HIT PARADE — Various Artists (Decca)
3	4	HEARTBREAK HOTEL — Elvis Presley (HMV)
4	5	I'M WALKING BACKWARDS FOR CHRISTMAS/BLUEBOTTLE BLUES — Goons (Decca)
6	6	HOT DIGGITY (DOG ZIGGITY BOOM) — Perry Como (HMV)
7	7	EXPERIMENTS WITH MICE — Johnny Dankworth (Parlophone)
21	7	WALK HAND IN HAND — Tony Martin (HMV)
9	9	THE WAYWARD WIND — Gogi Grant (London)
7	10	LOST JOHN — Lonnie Donegan (Pye Nixa)
12	10	WHO ARE WE — Ronnie Hilton (HMV)
28	12	WHATEVER WILL BE WILL BE — Doris Day (Philips)
11	12	THE WAYWARD WIND — Tex Ritter (HMV)
18	14	MOONGLOW AND THEME FROM 'PICNIC' — Morris Stoloff (Brunswick)
16	15	SONGS FOR SWINGIN' LOVERS (LP) — Frank Sinatra (Capitol)
10	16	MY SEPTEMBER LOVE — David Whitfield (Decca)
13	17	THE SAINTS ROCK 'N' ROLL — Bill Haley & His Comets (Brunswick)
15	18	A TEAR FELL — Teresa Brewer (Vogue-Coral)
21	19	BAD PENNY BLUES — Humphrey Lyttelton & His Band (Parlophone)
-	20	LEFT BANK — Winifred Atwell (Decca)
20	21	SWEET-OLD FASHIONED GIRL — Teresa Brewer (Vogue-Coral)
17	21	TOO YOUNG TO GO STEADY — Nat King Cole (Capitol)
14	23	NO OTHER LOVE — Ronnie Hilton (HMV)
26	24	PORTUGUESE WASHERWOMAN — Joe "Fingers" Carr (Capitol)
-	25	I WANT YOU, I NEED YOU, I LOVE YOU — Elvis Presley (HMV)
23	26	THE FAITHFUL HUSSAR — Ted Heath & His Music (Decca)
29	27	THE FAITHFUL HUSSAR — Louis Armstrong & His All Stars (Philips)
30	28	THE BIRDS AND THE BEES — Alma Cogan (HMV)
24	29	HOT DIGGITY (DOG ZIGGITY BOOM) — Michael Holliday (Columbia)
-	30	BE-BOP-A-LULA — Gene Vincent (Capitol)

28 July 1956

1	1	WHY DO FOOLS FALL IN LOVE — Teenagers featuring Frankie Lymon (Columbia)
2	2	I'LL BE HOME — Pat Boone (London)
12	3	WHATEVER WILL BE WILL BE — Doris Day (Philips)
4	4	HEARTBREAK HOTEL — Elvis Presley (HMV)
7	5	WALK HAND IN HAND — Tony Martin (HMV)
3	6	ALL-STAR HIT PARADE — Various Artists (Decca)
6	7	HOT DIGGITY (DOG ZIGGITY BOOM) — Perry Como (HMV)
5	8	I'M WALKING BACKWARDS FOR CHRISTMAS/BLUEBOTTLE BLUES — Goons (Decca)
10	9	WHO ARE WE — Ronnie Hilton (HMV)
12	10	THE WAYWARD WIND — Tex Ritter (Capitol)
7	11	EXPERIMENTS WITH MICE — Johnny Dankworth (Parlophone)
9	12	THE WAYWARD WIND — Gogi Grant (London)
17	13	THE SAINTS ROCK 'N' ROLL — Bill Haley & His Comets (Brunswick)
10	14	LOST JOHN — Lonnie Donegan (Pye Nixa)
21	15	SWEET-OLD FASHIONED GIRL — Teresa Brewer (Vogue-Coral)
14	16	MOONGLOW AND THEME FROM 'PICNIC' — Morris Stoloff (Brunswick)
16	17	MY SEPTEMBER LOVE — David Whitfield (Decca)
20	18	LEFT BANK — Winifred Atwell (Decca)
-	19	WALK HAND IN HAND — Ronnie Carroll (Philips)
19	20	BAD PENNY BLUES — Humphrey Lyttelton & His Band (Parlophone)
-	20	MOUNTAIN GREENERY — Mel Torme (Vogue-Coral)
15	22	SONGS FOR SWINGIN' LOVERS (LP) — Frank Sinatra (Capitol)
21	23	TOO YOUNG TO GO STEADY — Nat King Cole (Capitol)
-	24	ROCK ISLAND LINE/HEARTBREAK HOTEL — Stan Freberg (Capitol)
28	25	THE BIRDS AND THE BEES — Alma Cogan (HMV)
26	26	THE FAITHFUL HUSSAR — Ted Heath & His Music (Decca)
-	27	LONG TALL SALLY — Pat Boone (London)
-	28	I'M IN LOVE AGAIN — Fats Domino (London)
-	29	SERENADE — Slim Whitman (London)
24	30	PORTUGUESE WASHERWOMAN — Joe "Fingers" Carr (Capitol)

4 August 1956

1	1	WHY DO FOOLS FALL IN LOVE — Teenagers featuring Frankie Lymon (Columbia)
3	2	WHATEVER WILL BE WILL BE — Doris Day (Philips)
5	3	WALK HAND IN HAND — Tony Martin (HMV)
2	4	I'LL BE HOME — Pat Boone (London)
15	5	SWEET-OLD FASHIONED GIRL — Teresa Brewer (Vogue-Coral)
9	6	WHO ARE WE — Ronnie Hilton (HMV)
4	6	HEARTBREAK HOTEL — Elvis Presley (HMV)
10	8	THE WAYWARD WIND — Tex Ritter (Capitol)
20	9	MOUNTAIN GREENERY — Mel Torme (Vogue-Coral)
7	10	HOT DIGGITY (DOG ZIGGITY BOOM) — Perry Como (Capitol)
8	10	I'M WALKING BACKWARDS FOR CHRISTMAS/BLUEBOTTLE BLUES — Goons (Decca)
13	12	THE SAINTS ROCK 'N' ROLL — Bill Haley & His Comets (Brunswick)
6	13	ALL-STAR HIT PARADE — Various Artists (Decca)
12	14	THE WAYWARD WIND — Gogi Grant (London)
11	15	EXPERIMENTS WITH MICE — Johnny Dankworth (Parlophone)
23	16	TOO YOUNG TO GO STEADY — Nat King Cole (Capitol)
18	17	LEFT BANK — Winifred Atwell (Decca)
29	18	SERENADE — Slim Whitman (London)
19	19	WALK HAND IN HAND — Ronnie Carroll (Philips)
26	20	THE FAITHFUL HUSSAR — Ted Heath & His Music (Decca)
14	21	LOST JOHN — Lonnie Donegan (Pye Nixa)
16	22	MOONGLOW AND THEME FROM 'PICNIC' — Morris Stoloff (Brunswick)
-	23	I WANT YOU, I NEED YOU, I LOVE YOU — Elvis Presley (HMV)
-	24	CAROUSEL WALTZ — Ray Martin (Columbia)
-	25	HOT DIGGITY (DOG ZIGGITY BOOM) — Michael Holliday (Columbia)
22	26	SONGS FOR SWINGIN' LOVERS (LP) — Frank Sinatra (Capitol)
17	27	MY SEPTEMBER LOVE — David Whitfield (Decca)
20	28	BAD PENNY BLUES — Humphrey Lyttelton & His Band (Parlophone)
25	29	THE BIRDS AND THE BEES — Alma Cogan (HMV)
27	30	LONG TALL SALLY — Pat Boone (London)

11 August 1956

2	1	WHATEVER WILL BE WILL BE — Doris Day (Philips)
3	2	WALK HAND IN HAND — Tony Martin (HMV)
1	3	WHY DO FOOLS FALL IN LOVE — Teenagers featuring Frankie Lymon (Columbia)
9	4	MOUNTAIN GREENERY — Mel Torme (Vogue-Coral)
5	5	SWEET-OLD FASHIONED GIRL — Teresa Brewer (Vogue-Coral)
6	6	HEARTBREAK HOTEL — Elvis Presley (HMV)
4	7	I'LL BE HOME — Pat Boone (London)
13	8	ALL-STAR HIT PARADE — Various Artists (Decca)
6	9	WHO ARE WE — Ronnie Hilton (HMV)
8	10	THE WAYWARD WIND — Tex Ritter (Capitol)
12	11	THE SAINTS ROCK 'N' ROLL — Bill Haley & His Comets (Brunswick)
15	12	EXPERIMENTS WITH MICE — Johnny Dankworth (Parlophone)
10	13	I'M WALKING BACKWARDS FOR CHRISTMAS/BLUEBOTTLE BLUES — Goons (Decca)
17	14	LEFT BANK — Winifred Atwell (Decca)
10	15	HOT DIGGITY (DOG ZIGGITY BOOM) — Perry Como (HMV)
19	16	WALK HAND IN HAND — Ronnie Carroll (Philips)
25	17	HOT DIGGITY (DOG ZIGGITY BOOM) — Michael Holliday (Columbia)
20	18	THE FAITHFUL HUSSAR — Ted Heath & His Music (Decca)
14	19	THE WAYWARD WIND — Gogi Grant (London)
27	20	MY SEPTEMBER LOVE — David Whitfield (Decca)
22	21	MOONGLOW AND THEME FROM 'PICNIC' — Morris Stoloff (Brunswick)
-	22	WHY DO FOOLS FALL IN LOVE — Alma Cogan (HMV)
23	23	I WANT YOU, I NEED YOU, I LOVE YOU — Elvis Presley (HMV)
-	24	ONLY YOU — Hilltoppers (London)
21	25	LOST JOHN — Lonnie Donegan (Pye Nixa)
16	26	TOO YOUNG TO GO STEADY — Nat King Cole (Capitol)
28	27	BAD PENNY BLUES — Humphrey Lyttelton & His Band (Parlophone)
24	28	CAROUSEL WALTZ — Ray Martin (Columbia)
-	29	ROCK ISLAND LINE/HEARTBREAK HOTEL — Stan Freberg (Capitol)
30	30	LONG TALL SALLY — Pat Boone (London)
18	30	SERENADE — Slim Whitman (London)

The Teenagers, featuring the 13-year-old Frankie Lymon on lead vocal, were the prototype for every successful young black group to chart in their wake. After Presley (who now had his third hit in two months), they brought the first real breath of teenage fresh air into a chart still basically dominated by adult music. Gene Vincent and Fats Domino also made their UK debuts. Stan Freberg parodied the more eccentric aspects of rock'n'roll; Johnny Dankworth's hit was a jazz variation on *Three Blind Mice*!

August – September 1956

18 August 1956

last week	this week	title / artist
1	1	WHATEVER WILL BE WILL BE — Doris Day (Philips)
3	2	WHY DO FOOLS FALL IN LOVE — Teenagers featuring Frankie Lymon (Columbia)
5	3	SWEET-OLD FASHIONED GIRL — Teresa Brewer (Vogue-Coral)
2	4	WALK HAND IN HAND — Tony Martin (HMV)
4	5	MOUNTAIN GREENERY — Mel Torme (Vogue-Coral)
7	6	I'LL BE HOME — Pat Boone (London)
6	7	HEARTBREAK HOTEL — Elvis Presley (HMV)
10	8	THE WAYWARD WIND — Tex Ritter (Capitol)
-	9	ROCKIN' THROUGH THE RYE — Bill Haley & His Comets (Brunswick)
11	10	THE SAINTS ROCK 'N' ROLL — Bill Haley & His Comets (Brunswick)
8	11	ALL-STAR HIT PARADE — Various Artists (Decca)
13	12	I'M WALKING BACKWARDS FOR CHRISTMAS/BLUEBOTTLE BLUES — Goons (Decca)
19	13	THE WAYWARD WIND — Gogi Grant (London)
9	14	WHO ARE WE — Ronnie Hilton (HMV)
16	15	WALK HAND IN HAND — Ronnie Carroll (Philips)
12	16	EXPERIMENTS WITH MICE — Johnny Dankworth (Parlophone)
-	17	I ALMOST LOST MY MIND — Pat Boone (London)
18	18	THE FAITHFUL HUSSAR — Ted Heath & His Music (Decca)
30	19	SERENADE — Slim Whitman (London)
14	20	LEFT BANK — Winifred Atwell (Decca)
23	21	I WANT YOU, I NEED YOU, I LOVE YOU — Elvis Presley (HMV)
15	22	HOT DIGGITY (DOG ZIGGITY BOOM) — Perry Como (HMV)
22	23	WHY DO FOOLS FALL IN LOVE — Alma Cogan (HMV)
-	24	I'M IN LOVE AGAIN — Fats Domino (London)
-	25	HOT DIGGITY/GAL WITH THE YALLER SHOES — Michael Holliday (Columbia)
20	26	MY SEPTEMBER LOVE — David Whitfield (Decca)
-	27	BLUE SUEDE SHOES — Elvis Presley (HMV)
27	28	BAD PENNY BLUES — Humphrey Lyttelton & His Band (Parlophone)
25	29	LOST JOHN — Lonnie Donegan (Pye Nixa)
-	30	WALK HAND IN HAND — Jimmy Parkinson (Columbia)

25 August 1956

last week	this week	title / artist
1	1	WHATEVER WILL BE WILL BE — Doris Day (Philips)
2	2	WHY DO FOOLS FALL IN LOVE — Teenagers featuring Frankie Lymon (Columbia)
3	3	SWEET-OLD FASHIONED GIRL — Teresa Brewer (Vogue-Coral)
4	4	WALK HAND IN HAND — Tony Martin (HMV)
5	5	MOUNTAIN GREENERY — Mel Torme (Vogue-Coral)
9	6	ROCKIN' THROUGH THE RYE — Bill Haley & His Comets (Brunswick)
7	7	HEARTBREAK HOTEL — Elvis Presley (HMV)
6	8	I'LL BE HOME — Pat Boone (London)
8	9	THE WAYWARD WIND — Tex Ritter (Capitol)
18	10	SERENADE — Slim Whitman (London)
14	11	WHO ARE WE — Ronnie Hilton (HMV)
10	12	THE SAINTS ROCK 'N' ROLL — Bill Haley & His Comets (Brunswick)
15	13	WALK HAND IN HAND — Ronnie Carroll (Philips)
17	14	I ALMOST LOST MY MIND — Pat Boone (London)
13	15	THE WAYWARD WIND — Gogi Grant (London)
-	16	BE-BOP-A-LULA — Gene Vincent (Capitol)
20	17	I WANT YOU, I NEED YOU, I LOVE YOU — Elvis Presley (HMV)
-	18	LONG TALL SALLY — Pat Boone (London)
24	19	I'M IN LOVE AGAIN — Fats Domino (London)
12	20	I'M WALKING BACKWARDS FOR CHRISTMAS/BLUEBOTTLE BLUES — Goons (Decca)
11	21	ALL-STAR HIT PARADE — Various Artists (Decca)
18	22	THE FAITHFUL HUSSAR — Ted Heath & His Music (Decca)
20	23	LEFT BANK — Winifred Atwell (Decca)
23	24	WHY DO FOOLS FALL IN LOVE — Alma Cogan (HMV)
16	25	EXPERIMENTS WITH MICE — Johnny Dankworth (Parlophone)
27	26	BLUE SUEDE SHOES — Elvis Presley (HMV)
-	27	TREASURE OF LOVE — Clyde McPhatter (London)
-	28	LAY DOWN YOUR ARMS — Anne Shelton (Philips)
-	29	SADIE'S SHAWL — Frank Cordell (HMV)
-	30	MY SON JOHN — David Whitfield (Decca)

1 September 1956

last week	this week	title / artist
1	1	WHATEVER WILL BE WILL BE — Doris Day (Philips)
2	2	WHY DO FOOLS FALL IN LOVE — Teenagers featuring Frankie Lymon (Columbia)
4	3	WALK HAND IN HAND — Tony Martin (HMV)
3	4	SWEET-OLD FASHIONED GIRL — Teresa Brewer (Vogue-Coral)
6	5	ROCKIN' THROUGH THE RYE — Bill Haley & His Comets (Brunswick)
5	5	MOUNTAIN GREENERY — Mel Torme (Vogue-Coral)
7	7	HEARTBREAK HOTEL — Elvis Presley (HMV)
10	8	SERENADE — Slim Whitman (London)
8	9	I'LL BE HOME — Pat Boone (London)
12	10	THE SAINTS ROCK 'N' ROLL — Bill Haley & His Comets (Brunswick)
9	11	THE WAYWARD WIND — Tex Ritter (Capitol)
19	12	I'M IN LOVE AGAIN — Fats Domino (London)
-	13	BORN TO BE WITH YOU — Chordettes (London)
28	14	LAY DOWN YOUR ARMS — Anne Shelton (Philips)
14	15	I ALMOST LOST MY MIND — Pat Boone (London)
11	16	WHO ARE WE — Ronnie Hilton (HMV)
13	17	WALK HAND IN HAND — Ronnie Carroll (Philips)
17	18	I WANT YOU, I NEED YOU, I LOVE YOU — Elvis Presley (HMV)
-	19	YOU ARE MY FIRST LOVE — Ruby Murray (Columbia)
16	20	BE-BOP-A-LULA — Gene Vincent (Capitol)
18	21	LONG TALL SALLY — Pat Boone (London)
30	22	MY SON JOHN — David Whitfield (Decca)
15	23	THE WAYWARD WIND — Gogi Grant (London)
-	24	BY THE FOUNTAINS OF ROME — Edmund Hockridge (Pye Nixa)
20	25	I'M WALKING BACKWARDS FOR CHRISTMAS/BLUEBOTTLE BLUES — Goons (Decca)
-	26	DONKEY CART — Frank Chacksfield (Decca)
23	27	LEFT BANK — Winifred Atwell (Decca)
22	28	THE FAITHFUL HUSSAR — Ted Heath & His Music (Decca)
-	29	MY UNFINISHED SYMPHONY — David Whitfield (Decca)
29	30	SADIE'S SHAWL — Frank Cordell (HMV)
25	30	EXPERIMENTS WITH MICE — Johnny Dankworth (Parlophone)

8 September 1956

last week	this week	title / artist
1	1	WHATEVER WILL BE WILL BE — Doris Day (Philips)
2	2	WHY DO FOOLS FALL IN LOVE — Teenagers (Columbia)
4	3	SWEET-OLD FASHIONED GIRL — Teresa Brewer (Vogue/Coral)
5	4	ROCKING THROUGH THE RYE — Bill Haley & the Comets (Brunswick)
14	5	LAY DOWN YOUR ARMS — Anne Shelton (Philips)
3	6	WALK HAND IN HAND — Tony Martin (HMV)
5	7	MOUNTAIN GREENERY — Mel Torme (Vogue/Coral)
13	8	BORN TO BE WITH YOU — Chordettes (London)
7	9	HEARTBREAK HOTEL — Elvis Presley (HMV)
10	10	SAINTS ROCK AND ROLL — Bill Haley & His Comets (Brunswick)
8	11	SERENADE — Slim Whitman (London)
12	12	I'M IN LOVE AGAIN — Fats Domino (London)
-	13	GREAT PRETENDER/ONLY YOU — Platters (Mercury)
18	14	I WANT YOU, I NEED YOU, I LOVE YOU — Elvis Presley (HMV)
15	15	I ALMOST LOST MY MIND — Pat Boone (London)
19	16	YOU ARE MY FIRST LOVE — Ruby Murray (Columbia)
9	17	I'LL BE HOME — Pat Boone (London)
21	18	LONG TALL SALLY — Pat Boone (London)
11	19	WAYWARD WIND — Tex Ritter (Capitol)
17	20	WALK HAND IN HAND — Ronnie Carroll (Philips)
24	21	FOUNTAINS OF ROME — Edmund Hockridge (Pye Nixa)
16	22	WHO ARE WE? — Ronnie Hilton (HMV)
19	23	BE BOP A LULA — Gene Vincent (Capitol)
22	24	MY SON JOHN — David Whitfield (Decca)
-	25	MY SEPTEMBER LOVE — David Whitfield (Decca)
26	26	DONKEY CART — Frank Chacksfield (Decca)
-	27	WOMAN IN LOVE — Frankie Laine (Philips)
-	28	BRING A LITTLE WATER SYLVIE /DEAD OR ALIVE — Lonnie Donegan (Pye Nixa)
30	29	EXPERIMENTS WITH MICE — John Dankworth (Parlophone)
23	30	WAYWARD WIND — Gogi Grant (London)

Doris Day's Number One hit (also known as *Que Sera Sera*) was from her movie (with James Stewart) *The Man Who Knew Too Much*, and in fact won an Oscar as the year's best song from a film. Meanwhile, the newer rock-orientated acts were finding their successes multiplying - both Pat Boone and Elvis had three simultaneous hits for several weeks, and Bill Haley had two together in the Top 10, including *Rocking Through The Rye* - the first rock number based on a traditional Scottish tune!

15 September 1956

last week	this week	Title / Artist
1	1	WHATEVER WILL BE WILL BE — Doris Day (Philips)
5	2	LAY DOWN YOUR ARMS — Anne Shelton (Philips)
6	3	WALK HAND IN HAND — Tony Martin (HMV)
3	4	SWEET-OLD FASHIONED GIRL — Teresa Brewer (Vogue-Coral)
4	5	ROCKIN' THROUGH THE RYE — Bill Haley & His Comets (Brunswick)
2	6	WHY DO FOOLS FALL IN LOVE — Teenagers featuring Frankie Lymon (Columbia)
13	7	THE GREAT PRETENDER/ONLY YOU — Platters (Mercury)
7	8	MOUNTAIN GREENERY — Mel Torme (Vogue-Coral)
-	9	THE YING TONG SONG/ BLOODNOK'S ROCK 'N' ROLL CALL — Goons (Decca)
28	10	BRING A LITTLE WATER SYLVIE /DEAD OR ALIVE — Lonnie Donegan (Pye Nixa)
27	11	A WOMAN IN LOVE — Frankie Laine (Philips)
11	12	SERENADE — Slim Whitman (London)
10	13	THE SAINTS ROCK 'N' ROLL — Bill Haley & His Comets (Brunswick)
14	14	I WANT YOU, I NEED YOU, I LOVE YOU — Elvis Presley (HMV)
8	15	BORN TO BE WITH YOU — Chordettes (London)
15	16	I ALMOST LOST MY MIND — Pat Boone (London)
17	17	I'LL BE HOME — Pat Boone (London)
20	17	BY THE FOUNTAINS OF ROME — Edmund Hockridge (Pye Nixa)
12	19	I'M IN LOVE AGAIN — Fats Domino (London)
9	20	HEARTBREAK HOTEL — Elvis Presley (HMV)
16	21	YOU ARE MY FIRST LOVE — Ruby Murray (Columbia)
20	22	WALK HAND IN HAND — Ronnie Carroll (Philips)
18	23	LONG TALL SALLY — Pat Boone (London)
-	24	LOVE ME AS THOUGH THERE WERE NO TOMORROW — Nat King Cole (Capitol)
-	25	SERENADE — Mario Lanza (HMV)
22	26	WHO ARE WE — Ronnie Hilton (HMV)
19	26	THE WAYWARD WIND — Tex Ritter (Capitol)
24	28	MY SON JOHN — David Whitfield (Decca)
-	29	RAZZLE DAZZLE — Bill Haley & His Comets (Brunswick)
-	30	TRYIN' — Hilltoppers (London)

22 September 1956

last week	this week	Title / Artist
2	1	LAY DOWN YOUR ARMS — Anne Shelton (Philips)
1	2	WHATEVER WILL BE WILL BE — Doris Day (Philips)
5	3	ROCKIN' THROUGH THE RYE — Bill Haley & His Comets (Brunswick)
9	4	THE YING TONG SONG / BLOODNOK'S ROCK 'N' ROLL CALL — Goons (Decca)
7	5	THE GREAT PRETENDER/ONLY YOU — Platters (Mercury)
4	6	SWEET-OLD FASHIONED GIRL — Teresa Brewer (Vogue-Coral)
3	6	WALK HAND IN HAND — Tony Martin (HMV)
6	6	WHY DO FOOLS FALL IN LOVE — Teenagers featuring Frankie Lymon (Columbia)
10	9	BRING A LITTLE WATER SYLVIE /DEAD OR ALIVE — Lonnie Donegan (Pye Nixa)
8	10	MOUNTAIN GREENERY — Mel Torme (Vogue-Coral)
13	11	THE SAINTS ROCK 'N' ROLL — Bill Haley & His Comets (Brunswick)
11	12	A WOMAN IN LOVE — Frankie Laine (Philips)
-	13	HOUND DOG — Elvis Presley (HMV)
12	14	SERENADE — Slim Whitman (London)
15	15	BORN TO BE WITH YOU — Chordettes (London)
14	16	I WANT YOU, I NEED YOU, I LOVE YOU — Elvis Presley (HMV)
-	17	ROCK AROUND THE CLOCK — Bill Haley & His Comets (Brunswick)
17	17	BY THE FOUNTAINS OF ROME — Edmund Hockridge (Pye Nixa)
16	19	I ALMOST LOST MY MIND — Pat Boone (London)
17	20	I'LL BE HOME — Pat Boone (London)
-	21	SEE YOU LATER, ALLIGATOR — Bill Haley & His Comets (Brunswick)
19	22	I'M IN LOVE AGAIN — Fats Domino (London)
26	23	THE WAYWARD WIND — Tex Ritter (Capitol)
20	24	HEARTBREAK HOTEL — Elvis Presley (HMV)
21	25	YOU ARE MY FIRST LOVE — Ruby Murray (Columbia)
24	26	LOVE ME AS THOUGH THERE WERE NO TOMORROW — Nat King Cole (Capitol)
-	27	BY THE FOUNTAINS OF ROME — David Hughes (Philips)
29	28	RAZZLE DAZZLE — Bill Haley & His Comets (Brunswick)
-	29	MORE — Perry Como (Capitol)
-	30	WOMAN IN LOVE — Ronnie Hilton (HMV)

29 September 1956

last week	this week	Title / Artist
1	1	LAY DOWN YOUR ARMS — Anne Shelton (Philips)
2	2	WHATEVER WILL BE WILL BE — Doris Day (Philips)
4	3	THE YING TONG SONG/ BLOODNOK'S ROCK 'N' ROLL CALL — Goons (Decca)
3	4	ROCKIN' THROUGH THE RYE — Bill Haley & His Comets (Brunswick)
13	5	HOUND DOG — Elvis Presley (HMV)
5	6	THE GREAT PRETENDER/ONLY YOU — Platters (Mercury)
9	7	BRING A LITTLE WATER SYLVIE/DEAD OR ALIVE — Lonnie Donegan (Pye Nixa)
12	8	A WOMAN IN LOVE — Frankie Laine (Philips)
6	9	WALK HAND IN HAND — Tony Martin (HMV)
6	10	SWEET-OLD FASHIONED GIRL — Teresa Brewer (Vogue-Coral)
11	11	THE SAINTS ROCK 'N' ROLL — Bill Haley & His Comets (Brunswick)
10	12	MOUNTAIN GREENERY — Mel Torme (Vogue-Coral)
17	13	ROCK AROUND THE CLOCK — Bill Haley & His Comets (Brunswick)
6	14	WHY DO FOOLS FALL IN LOVE — Teenagers featuring Frankie Lymon (Columbia)
15	15	BORN TO BE WITH YOU — Chordettes (London)
-	16	GIDDY-UP-A-DING-DONG — Freddie Bell & the Bellboys (Mercury)
28	17	RAZZLE DAZZLE — Bill Haley & His Comets (Brunswick)
14	18	SERENADE — Slim Whitman (London)
21	19	SEE YOU LATER, ALLIGATOR — Bill Haley & His Comets (Brunswick)
17	19	BY THE FOUNTAINS OF ROME — Edmund Hockridge (Pye Nixa)
16	21	I WANT YOU, I NEED YOU, I LOVE YOU — Elvis Presley (HMV)
24	22	HEARTBREAK HOTEL — Elvis Presley (HMV)
-	23	WHEN MEXICO GAVE UP THE RUMBA — Mitchell Torok (Brunswick)
-	24	BE-BOP-A-LULA — Gene Vincent (Capitol)
-	25	GLENDORA — Perry Como (HMV)
29	26	MORE — Perry Como (HMV)
-	26	MORE — Jimmy Young (Decca)
-	28	GLENDORA — Glen Mason (Parlophone)
22	29	I'M IN LOVE AGAIN — Fats Domino (London)
19	30	I ALMOST LOST MY MIND — Pat Boone (London)

6 October 1956

last week	this week	Title / Artist
1	1	LAY DOWN YOUR ARMS — Anne Shelton (Philips)
2	2	WHATEVER WILL BE WILL BE — Doris Day (Philips)
8	3	A WOMAN IN LOVE — Frankie Laine (Philips)
5	4	HOUND DOG — Elvis Presley (HMV)
4	5	ROCKIN' THROUGH THE RYE — Bill Haley & His Comets (Brunswick)
16	6	GIDDY-UP-A-DING-DONG — Freddie Bell & the Bellboys (Mercury)
3	7	THE YING TONG SONG / BLOODNOK'S ROCK 'N' ROLL CALL — Goons (Decca)
6	8	THE GREAT PRETENDER/ONLY YOU — Platters (Mercury)
7	9	BRING A LITTLE WATER SYLVIE/DEAD OR ALIVE — Lonnie Donegan (Pye Nixa)
9	10	WALK HAND IN HAND — Tony Martin (HMV)
15	11	BORN TO BE WITH YOU — Chordettes (London)
13	12	ROCK AROUND THE CLOCK — Bill Haley & His Comets (Brunswick)
17	13	RAZZLE DAZZLE — Bill Haley & His Comets (Brunswick)
12	13	MOUNTAIN GREENERY — Mel Torme (Vogue-Coral)
10	15	SWEET-OLD FASHIONED GIRL — Teresa Brewer (Vogue-Coral)
11	16	THE SAINTS ROCK 'N' ROLL — Bill Haley & His Comets (Brunswick)
14	17	WHY DO FOOLS FALL IN LOVE — Teenagers featuring Frankie Lymon (Columbia)
26	18	MORE — Perry Como (Capitol)
23	19	WHEN MEXICO GAVE UP THE RUMBA — Mitchell Torok (Brunswick)
19	20	SEE YOU LATER, ALLIGATOR — Bill Haley & His Comets (Brunswick)
-	21	YOU ARE MY FIRST LOVE — Ruby Murray (Columbia)
26	22	MORE — Jimmy Young (Decca)
24	23	BE-BOP-A-LULA — Gene Vincent (Capitol)
29	24	I'M IN LOVE AGAIN — Fats Domino (London)
-	25	LOVE ME AS THOUGH THERE WERE NO TOMORROW — Nat King Cole (Capitol)
-	26	WALK HAND IN HAND — Jimmy Parkinson (Columbia)
18	27	SERENADE — Slim Whitman (London)
-	28	TEN THOUSAND MILES — Michael Holliday (Columbia)
25	29	GLENDORA — Perry Como (HMV)
28	30	GLENDORA — Glen Mason (Parlophone)

Anne Shelton became just the third UK Artist this year to top the chart with her military-style march *Lay Down Your Arms* - a decidedly old-guard sound. Meanwhile, the releasé of the film *Rock Around The Clock* brought two former Bill Haley hits back to life, and on Sept 29 he had five simultaneous entries in the Top 20, equalling Ruby Murray's 1955 record. Elvis Presley's *Hound Dog* was his fastest-selling UK single yet, and even the Goons, in their second double-sided smash, dabbled in rock'n'roll.

13 October 1956

last week	this week	Title
1	1	LAY DOWN YOUR ARMS — Anne Shelton (Philips)
3	2	A WOMAN IN LOVE — Frankie Laine (Philips)
4	3	HOUND DOG — Elvis Presley (HMV)
2	4	WHATEVER WILL BE WILL BE — Doris Day (Philips)
8	5	THE GREAT PRETENDER/ONLY YOU — Platters (Mercury)
7	6	THE YING TONG SONG/BLOODNOK'S ROCK 'N' ROLL CALL — Goons (Decca)
6	7	GIDDY-UP-A-DING-DONG — Freddie Bell & the Bellboys (Mercury)
12	8	ROCK AROUND THE CLOCK — Bill Haley & His Comets (Brunswick)
5	9	ROCKIN' THROUGH THE RYE — Bill Haley & His Comets (Brunswick)
9	10	BRING A LITTLE WATER SYLVIE /DEAD OR ALIVE — Lonnie Donegan (Pye Nixa)
16	11	THE SAINTS ROCK 'N' ROLL — Bill Haley & His Comets (Brunswick)
11	12	BORN TO BE WITH YOU — Chordettes (London)
15	13	SWEET-OLD FASHIONED GIRL — Teresa Brewer (Vogue-Coral)
19	14	WHEN MEXICO GAVE UP THE RUMBA — Mitchell Torok (Brunswick)
18	15	MORE — Perry Como (Capitol)
10	16	WALK HAND IN HAND — Tony Martin (HMV)
13	17	RAZZLE DAZZLE — Bill Haley & His Comets (Brunswick)
13	18	MOUNTAIN GREENERY — Mel Torme (Vogue-Coral)
-	19	JUST WALKING IN THE RAIN — Johnnie Ray (Philips)
20	20	SEE YOU LATER, ALLIGATOR — Bill Haley & His Comets (Brunswick)
22	20	MORE — Jimmy Young (Decca)
24	22	I'M IN LOVE AGAIN — Fats Domino (London)
17	23	WHY DO FOOLS FALL IN LOVE — Teenagers featuring Frankie Lymon (Columbia)
28	24	TEN THOUSAND MILES — Michael Holliday (Columbia)
27	25	SERENADE — Slim Whitman (London)
25	26	LOVE ME AS THOUGH THERE WERE NO TOMORROW — Nat King Cole (Capitol)
29	27	GLENDORA — Perry Como (HMV)
-	28	RACE WITH THE DEVIL — Gene Vincent (Capitol)
-	29	SERENADE — Mario Lanza (HMV)
-	30	AUTUMN CONCERTO — Melachrino Orchestra (HMV)

20 October 1956

last week	this week	Title
2	1	A WOMAN IN LOVE — Frankie Laine (Philips)
1	2	LAY DOWN YOUR ARMS — Anne Shelton (Philips)
3	3	HOUND DOG — Elvis Presley (HMV)
7	4	GIDDY-UP-A-DING-DONG — Freddie Bell & the Bellboys (Mercury)
4	5	WHATEVER WILL BE WILL BE — Doris Day (Philips)
9	6	ROCKIN' THROUGH THE RYE — Bill Haley & His Comets (Brunswick)
10	7	BRING A LITTLE WATER SYLVIE /DEAD OR ALIVE — Lonnie Donegan (Pye Nixa)
5	8	THE GREAT PRETENDER/ONLY YOU — Platters (Mercury)
8	9	ROCK AROUND THE CLOCK — Bill Haley & His Comets (Brunswick)
6	10	THE YING TONG SONG/BLOODNOK'S ROCK 'N' ROLL CALL — Goons (Decca)
14	11	WHEN MEXICO GAVE UP THE RUMBA — Mitchell Torok (Brunswick)
20	12	SEE YOU LATER, ALLIGATOR — Bill Haley & His Comets (Brunswick)
19	13	JUST WALKING IN THE RAIN — Johnnie Ray (Philips)
15	14	MORE — Perry Como (Capitol)
17	15	RAZZLE DAZZLE — Bill Haley & His Comets (Brunswick)
20	16	MORE — Jimmy Young (Decca)
11	17	THE SAINTS ROCK 'N' ROLL — Bill Haley & His Comets (Brunswick)
12	18	BORN TO BE WITH YOU — Chordettes (London)
30	19	AUTUMN CONCERTO — Melachrino Orchestra (HMV)
27	20	GLENDORA — Perry Como (HMV)
-	21	WOMAN IN LOVE — Four Aces (Brunswick)
13	22	SWEET-OLD FASHIONED GIRL — Teresa Brewer (Vogue-Coral)
16	23	WALK HAND IN HAND — Tony Martin (HMV)
18	24	MOUNTAIN GREENERY — Mel Torme (Vogue-Coral)
-	25	TEACH YOU TO ROCK/SHORT'NIN' BREAD ROCK — Tony Crombie & His Rockets (Columbia)
26	26	LOVE ME AS THOUGH THERE WERE NO TOMORROW — Nat King Cole (Capitol)
-	27	BLUE JEAN BOP — Gene Vincent (Capitol)
-	28	I DON'T CARE — Liberace (Columbia)
24	29	TEN THOUSAND MILES — Michael Holliday (Columbia)
22	30	I'M IN LOVE AGAIN — Fats Domino (London)

27 October 1956

last week	this week	Title
1	1	A WOMAN IN LOVE — Frankie Laine (Philips)
3	2	HOUND DOG — Elvis Presley (HMV)
2	3	LAY DOWN YOUR ARMS — Anne Shelton (Philips)
4	4	GIDDY-UP-A-DING-DONG — Freddie Bell & the Bellboys (Mercury)
13	5	JUST WALKING IN THE RAIN — Johnnie Ray (Philips)
5	6	WHATEVER WILL BE WILL BE — Doris Day (Philips)
6	7	ROCKIN' THROUGH THE RYE — Bill Haley & His Comets (Brunswick)
9	8	ROCK AROUND THE CLOCK — Bill Haley & His Comets (Brunswick)
7	9	BRING A LITTLE WATER SYLVIE /DEAD OR ALIVE — Lonnie Donegan (Pye Nixa)
8	10	THE GREAT PRETENDER/ONLY YOU — Platters (Mercury)
16	11	MORE — Jimmy Young (Decca)
10	12	THE YING TONG SONG/BLOODNOK'S ROCK 'N' ROLL CALL — Goons (Decca)
14	13	MORE — Perry Como (Capitol)
11	14	WHEN MEXICO GAVE UP THE RUMBA — Mitchell Torok (Brunswick)
12	15	SEE YOU LATER, ALLIGATOR — Bill Haley & His Comets (Brunswick)
26	16	LOVE ME AS THOUGH THERE WERE NO TOMORROW — Nat King Cole (Capitol)
17	17	THE SAINTS ROCK 'N' ROLL — Bill Haley & His Comets (Brunswick)
20	18	GLENDORA — Perry Como (HMV)
21	19	WOMAN IN LOVE — Four Aces (Brunswick)
30	20	I'M IN LOVE AGAIN — Fats Domino (London)
19	21	AUTUMN CONCERTO — Melachrino Orchestra (HMV)
-	22	MAKE IT A PARTY — Winifred Atwell (Decca)
-	23	HEARTBREAK HOTEL — Elvis Presley (HMV)
15	24	RAZZLE DAZZLE — Bill Haley & His Comets (Brunswick)
-	25	A HOUSE WITH LOVE IN IT — Vera Lynn (Decca)
-	26	ROCK WITH THE CAVEMAN — Tommy Steele (Decca)
-	27	ST. THERESE OF THE ROSES — Malcolm Vaughan (HMV)
28	28	BLUE JEAN BOP — Gene Vincent (Capitol)
18	29	BORN TO BE WITH YOU — Chordettes (London)
25	30	TEACH YOU TO ROCK/SHORT'NIN' BREAD ROCK — Tony Crombie & His Rockets (Columbia)
-	30	THE GREEN DOOR — Jim Lowe (London)

3 November 1956

last week	this week	Title
1	1	A WOMAN IN LOVE — Frankie Laine (Philips)
2	2	HOUND DOG — Elvis Presley (HMV)
5	3	JUST WALKING IN THE RAIN — Johnnie Ray (Philips)
3	4	LAY DOWN YOUR ARMS — Anne Shelton (Philips)
8	5	ROCK AROUND THE CLOCK — Bill Haley & His Comets (Brunswick)
4	6	GIDDY-UP-A-DING-DONG — Freddie Bell & the Bellboys (Mercury)
7	6	ROCKIN' THROUGH THE RYE — Bill Haley & His Comets (Brunswick)
-	8	MY PRAYER — Platters (Mercury)
6	9	WHATEVER WILL BE WILL BE — Doris Day (Philips)
11	10	MORE — Jimmy Young (Decca)
13	11	MORE — Perry Como (Capitol)
14	11	WHEN MEXICO GAVE UP THE RUMBA — Mitchell Torok (Brunswick)
26	13	ROCK WITH THE CAVEMAN — Tommy Steele (Decca)
12	14	THE YING TONG SONG/BLOODNOK'S ROCK 'N' ROLL CALL — Goons (Decca)
16	15	LOVE ME AS THOUGH THERE WERE NO TOMORROW — Nat King Cole (Capitol)
9	15	BRING A LITTLE WATER SYLVIE /DEAD OR ALIVE — Lonnie Donegan (Pye Nixa)
10	17	THE GREAT PRETENDER/ONLY YOU — Platters (Mercury)
15	18	SEE YOU LATER, ALLIGATOR — Bill Haley & His Comets (Brunswick)
21	19	AUTUMN CONCERTO — Melachrino Orchestra (HMV)
22	20	MAKE IT A PARTY — Winifred Atwell (Decca)
30	21	THE GREEN DOOR — Jim Lowe (London)
28	21	BLUE JEAN BOP — Gene Vincent (Capitol)
20	23	I'M IN LOVE AGAIN — Fats Domino (London)
24	24	RAZZLE DAZZLE — Bill Haley & His Comets (Brunswick)
16	24	THE SAINTS ROCK 'N' ROLL — Bill Haley & His Comets (Brunswick)
-	26	IN THE MIDDLE OF THE HOUSE — Alma Cogan (HMV)
19	27	WOMAN IN LOVE — Four Aces (Brunswick)
25	28	A HOUSE WITH LOVE IN IT — Vera Lynn (Decca)
18	29	GLENDORA — Perry Como (HMV)
-	30	TONIGHT YOU BELONG TO ME — Patience & Prudence (London)

The Bill Haley-styled Freddie Bell & The Bellboys were lucky enough to have their *Giddy-Up-A-Ding-Dong* featured in the *Rock Around The Clock* film, as were the Platters, who sang both their first two US million sellers *Only You* and *The Great Pretender* (now finally issued as a British two-sider) in the exploitive cinema epic. Closer to home, Lonnie Donegan's skiffle style was proving a sensation in live performance, and *Bring A Little Water, Sylvie/Dead Or Alive* was his third straight top-tenner.

November – December 1956

10 November 1956

last	this	title / artist
1	1	A WOMAN IN LOVE — Frankie Laine (Philips)
2	2	HOUND DOG — Elvis Presley (HMV)
3	3	JUST WALKING IN THE RAIN — Johnnie Ray (Philips)
8	4	MY PRAYER — Platters (Mercury)
6	5	ROCKIN' THROUGH THE RYE — Bill Haley & His Comets (Brunswick)
4	6	LAY DOWN YOUR ARMS — Anne Shelton (Philips)
10	6	MORE — Jimmy Young (Decca)
8	8	GIDDY-UP-A-DING-DONG — Freddie Bell & the Bellboys (Mercury)
5	8	ROCK AROUND THE CLOCK — Bill Haley & His Comets (Brunswick)
11	10	MORE — Perry Como (Capitol)
20	11	MAKE IT A PARTY — Winifred Atwell (Decca)
15	12	LOVE ME AS THOUGH THERE WERE NO TOMORROW — Nat King Cole (Capitol)
11	13	WHEN MEXICO GAVE UP THE RUMBA — Mitchell Torok (Brunswick)
21	14	THE GREEN DOOR — Jim Lowe (London)
9	15	WHATEVER WILL BE WILL BE — Doris Day (Philips)
21	16	BLUE JEAN BOP — Gene Vincent (Capitol)
13	17	ROCK WITH THE CAVEMAN — Tommy Steele (Decca)
19	18	AUTUMN CONCERTO — Melachrino Orchestra (HMV)
17	18	THE GREAT PRETENDER/ONLY YOU — Platters (Mercury)
-	20	GREEN DOOR — Frankie Vaughan (Philips)
-	21	RIP IT UP — Bill Haley & His Comets (Brunswick)
14	22	THE YING TONG SONG/ BLOODNOK'S ROCK 'N' ROLL CALL — Goons (Decca)
15	23	BRING A LITTLE WATER SYLVIE/DEAD OR ALIVE — Lonnie Donegan (Pye Nixa)
23	24	I'M IN LOVE AGAIN — Fats Domino (London)
18	25	SEE YOU LATER, ALLIGATOR — Bill Haley & His Comets (Brunswick)
-	26	IN THE MIDDLE OF THE HOUSE — Jimmy Parkinson (Columbia)
28	27	A HOUSE WITH LOVE IN IT — Vera Lynn (Decca)
30	28	TONIGHT YOU BELONG TO ME — Patience & Prudence (London)
-	29	TWO DIFFERENT WORLDS — Ronnie Hilton (HMV)
-	30	ROCK 'N' ROLL STAGE SHOW (LP) — Bill Haley & His Comets (Brunswick)

17 November 1956

last	this	title / artist
2	1	JUST WALKING IN THE RAIN — Johnnie Ray (Philips)
1	2	A WOMAN IN LOVE — Frankie Laine (Philips)
2	3	HOUND DOG — Elvis Presley (HMV)
4	4	MY PRAYER — Platters (Mercury)
6	4	MORE — Jimmy Young (Decca)
21	6	RIP IT UP — Bill Haley & His Comets (Brunswick)
5	7	ROCKIN' THROUGH THE RYE — Bill Haley & His Comets (Brunswick)
14	8	THE GREEN DOOR — Jim Lowe (London)
20	9	GREEN DOOR — Frankie Vaughan (Philips)
6	10	LAY DOWN YOUR ARMS — Anne Shelton (Philips)
12	11	LOVE ME AS THOUGH THERE WERE NO TOMORROW — Nat King Cole (Capitol)
-	12	ST. THERESE OF THE ROSES — Malcolm Vaughan (HMV)
11	13	MAKE IT A PARTY — Winifred Atwell (Decca)
8	14	ROCK AROUND THE CLOCK — Bill Haley & His Comets (Brunswick)
8	15	GIDDY-UP-A-DING-DONG — Freddie Bell & the Bellboys (Mercury)
-	15	BLUE MOON — Elvis Presley (HMV)
13	15	WHEN MEXICO GAVE UP THE RUMBA — Mitchell Torok (Brunswick)
10	18	MORE — Perry Como (Capitol)
17	18	ROCK WITH THE CAVEMAN — Tommy Steele (Decca)
15	20	WHATEVER WILL BE WILL BE — Doris Day (Philips)
16	21	BLUE JEAN BOP — Gene Vincent (Capitol)
18	22	AUTUMN CONCERTO — Melachrino Orchestra (HMV)
18	23	THE GREAT PRETENDER/ONLY YOU — Platters (Mercury)
29	24	TWO DIFFERENT WORLDS — Ronnie Hilton (HMV)
27	25	A HOUSE WITH LOVE IN IT — Vera Lynn (Decca)
-	26	GREEN DOOR — Glen Mason (Parlophone)
23	27	BRING A LITTLE WATER SYLVIE/DEAD OR ALIVE — Lonnie Donegan (Pye Nixa)
26	27	IN THE MIDDLE OF THE HOUSE — Jimmy Parkinson (Columbia)
28	29	TONIGHT YOU BELONG TO ME — Patience & Prudence (London)
22	30	THE YING TONG SONG/ BLOODNOK'S ROCK 'N' ROLL CALL — Goons (Decca)

24 November 1956

last	this	title / artist
1	1	JUST WALKING IN THE RAIN — Johnnie Ray (Philips)
2	2	A WOMAN IN LOVE — Frankie Laine (Philips)
3	3	HOUND DOG — Elvis Presley (HMV)
9	4	GREEN DOOR — Frankie Vaughan (Philips)
4	4	MORE — Jimmy Young (Decca)
4	6	MY PRAYER — Platters (Mercury)
15	6	WHEN MEXICO GAVE UP THE RUMBA — Mitchell Torok (Brunswick)
6	8	RIP IT UP — Bill Haley & His Comets (Brunswick)
15	9	BLUE MOON — Elvis Presley (HMV)
12	10	ST. THERESE OF THE ROSES — Malcolm Vaughan (HMV)
13	11	MAKE IT A PARTY — Winifred Atwell (Decca)
7	11	ROCKIN' THROUGH THE RYE — Bill Haley & His Comets (Brunswick)
14	13	ROCK AROUND THE CLOCK — Bill Haley & His Comets (Brunswick)
8	14	THE GREEN DOOR — Jim Lowe (London)
-	15	CINDY, OH CINDY — Eddie Fisher (HMV)
18	16	MORE — Perry Como (Capitol)
11	17	LOVE ME AS THOUGH THERE WERE NO TOMORROW — Nat King Cole (Capitol)
24	18	TWO DIFFERENT WORLDS — Ronnie Hilton (HMV)
10	19	LAY DOWN YOUR ARMS — Anne Shelton (Philips)
-	20	IN THE MIDDLE OF THE HOUSE — Alma Cogan (HMV)
23	21	THE GREAT PRETENDER/ONLY YOU — Platters (Mercury)
20	22	WHATEVER WIL BE WILL BE — Doris Day (Philips)
22	22	AUTUMN CONCERTO — Melachrino Orchestra (HMV)
-	24	TRUE LOVE — Bing Crosby & Grace Kelly (Capitol)
27	25	BRING A LITTLE WATER SYLVIE/DEAD OR ALIVE — Lonnie Donegan (Pye Nixa)
25	26	A HOUSE WITH LOVE IN IT — Vera Lynn (Decca)
26	27	GREEN DOOR — Glen Mason (Parlophone)
15	28	GIDDY-UP-A-DING-DONG — Freddie Bell & the Bellboys (Mercury)
-	29	I DON'T CARE IF THE SUN DON'T SHINE — Elvis Presley (HMV)
-	30	RUDY'S ROCK — Bill Haley & His Comets (Brunswick)

1 December 1956

last	this	title / artist
1	1	JUST WALKING IN THE RAIN — Johnnie Ray (Philips)
2	2	A WOMAN IN LOVE — Frankie Laine (Philips)
4	3	GREEN DOOR — Frankie Vaughan (Philips)
6	4	MY PRAYER — Platters (Mercury)
8	5	RIP IT UP — Bill Haley & His Comets (Brunswick)
3	6	HOUND DOG — Elvis Presley (HMV)
4	7	MORE — Jimmy Young (Decca)
10	8	ST. THERESE OF THE ROSES — Malcolm Vaughan (HMV)
9	9	BLUE MOON — Elvis Presley (HMV)
6	10	WHEN MEXICO GAVE UP THE RUMBA — Mitchell Torok (Brunswick)
24	11	TRUE LOVE — Bing Crosby & Grace Kelly (Capitol)
15	12	CINDY, OH CINDY — Eddie Fisher (HMV)
11	13	MAKE IT A PARTY — Winifred Atwell (Decca)
18	13	TWO DIFFERENT WORLDS — Ronnie Hilton (HMV)
13	15	ROCK AROUND THE CLOCK — Bill Haley & His Comets (Brunswick)
14	16	THE GREEN DOOR — Jim Lowe (London)
11	17	ROCKIN' THROUGH THE RYE — Bill Haley & His Comets (Brunswick)
22	18	AUTUMN CONCERTO — Melachrino Orchestra (HMV)
17	19	LOVE ME AS THOUGH THERE WERE NO TOMORROW — Nat King Cole (Capitol)
20	20	IN THE MIDDLE OF THE HOUSE — Alma Cogan (HMV)
26	20	A HOUSE WITH LOVE IN IT — Vera Lynn (Decca)
-	22	IN THE MIDDLE OF THE HOUSE — Jimmy Parkinson (Columbia)
-	23	ROCK WITH THE CAVEMAN — Tommy Steele (Decca)
27	24	GREEN DOOR — Glen Mason (Parlophone)
16	25	MORE — Perry Como (Capitol)
-	26	BLUEBERRY HILL — Fats Domino (London)
-	27	IN THE MIDDLE OF THE HOUSE — Johnston Brothers (Decca)
-	28	CINDY, OH CINDY — Tony Brent (Columbia)
28	29	GIDDY-UP-A-DING-DONG — Freddie Bell & the Bellboys (Mercury)
-	30	THE CAT CAME BACK — Sonny James (Capitol)

Johnnie Ray's *Just Walking In The Rain* had an unusual pedigree, having been originally recorded (for Sam Phillips' Sun Records) by the Prisonaires, all inmates at the Tennessee State Penitentiary. Britain's first rock star Tommy Steele charted with his debut single, Bill Haley got an LP into the chart, and the public had three hit versions of the offbeat *Green Door* to choose from. And in case you were wondering, when Mexico gave up the Rumba, according to Torok, it was to do the rock'n'roll.

8 December 1956

last week	this week	
1	1	JUST WALKING IN THE RAIN — Johnnie Ray (Philips)
3	2	GREEN DOOR — Frankie Vaughan (Philips)
2	3	A WOMAN IN LOVE — Frankie Laine (Philips)
5	4	RIP IT UP — Bill Haley & His Comets (Brunswick)
6	5	HOUND DOG — Elvis Presley (HMV)
8	6	ST. THERESE OF THE ROSES — Malcolm Vaughan (HMV)
4	7	MY PRAYER — Platters (Mercury)
7	8	MORE — Jimmy Young (Decca)
9	9	BLUE MOON — Elvis Presley (HMV)
11	10	TRUE LOVE — Bing Crosby & Grace Kelly (Capitol)
12	11	CINDY, OH CINDY — Eddie Fisher (HMV)
10	12	WHEN MEXICO GAVE UP THE RUMBA — Mitchell Torok (Brunswick)
13	13	MAKE IT A PARTY — Winifred Atwell (Decca)
13	14	TWO DIFFERENT WORLDS — Ronnie Hilton (HMV)
-	14	SINGING THE BLUES — Guy Mitchell (Philips)
19	16	LOVE ME AS THOUGH THERE WERE NO TOMORROW — Nat King Cole (Capitol)
17	17	ROCKIN' THROUGH THE RYE — Bill Haley & His Comets (Brunswick)
20	17	A HOUSE WITH LOVE IN IT — Vera Lynn (Decca)
-	19	LOVE ME TENDER — Elvis Presley (HMV)
22	20	IN THE MIDDLE OF THE HOUSE — Jimmy Parkinson (Columbia)
-	21	THE GREAT PRETENDER/ONLY YOU — Platters (Mercury)
20	22	IN THE MIDDLE OF THE HOUSE — Alma Cogan (HMV)
-	22	CHRISTMAS ISLAND — Dickie Valentine (Decca)
-	24	FRIENDLY PERSUASION — Pat Boone (London)
18	25	AUTUMN CONCERTO — Melachrino Orchestra (HMV)
24	26	GREEN DOOR — Glen Mason (Parlophone)
16	27	THE GREEN DOOR — Jim Lowe (London)
28	28	CINDY, OH CINDY — Tony Brent (Columbia)
-	29	THAT'S RIGHT — Deep River Boys (HMV)
-	30	'JOIN IN AND SING, NO. 3' MEDLEY — Johnston Brothers (Decca)

15 December 1956

last week	this week	
1	1	JUST WALKING IN THE RAIN — Johnnie Ray (Philips)
2	2	GREEN DOOR — Frankie Vaughan (Philips)
6	3	ST. THERESE OF THE ROSES — Malcolm Vaughan (HMV)
4	4	RIP IT UP — Bill Haley & His Comets (Brunswick)
14	5	SINGING THE BLUES — Guy Mitchell (Philips)
7	6	MY PRAYER — Platters (Mercury)
11	7	CINDY, OH CINDY — Eddie Fisher (HMV)
3	8	A WOMAN IN LOVE — Frankie Laine (Philips)
5	9	HOUND DOG — Elvis Presley (HMV)
10	10	TRUE LOVE — Bing Crosby & Grace Kelly (Capitol)
13	11	MAKE IT A PARTY — Winifred Atwell (Decca)
9	11	BLUE MOON — Elvis Presley (HMV)
14	13	TWO DIFFERENT WORLDS — Ronnie Hilton (HMV)
12	14	WHEN MEXICO GAVE UP THE RUMBA — Mitchell Torok (Brunswick)
22	15	CHRISTMAS ISLAND — Dickie Valentine (Decca)
8	15	MORE — Jimmy Young (Decca)
19	17	LOVE ME TENDER — Elvis Presley (HMV)
28	18	CINDY, OH CINDY — Tony Brent (Columbia)
17	19	A HOUSE WITH LOVE IN IT — Vera Lynn (Decca)
27	20	THE GREEN DOOR — Jim Lowe (London)
17	21	ROCKIN' THROUGH THE RYE — Bill Haley & His Comets (Brunswick)
16	22	LOVE ME AS THOUGH THERE WERE NO TOMORROW — Nat King Cole (Capitol)
-	23	SINGING THE BLUES — Tommy Steele (Decca)
-	24	ROCK AROUND THE CLOCK — Bill Haley & His Comets (Brunswick)
24	25	FRIENDLY PERSUASION — Pat Boone (London)
-	26	CINDY, OH CINDY — Vince Martin (London)
26	27	GREEN DOOR — Glen Mason (Parlophone)
-	28	RUDY'S ROCK — Bill Haley & His Comets (Brunswick)
-	29	MORE — Perry Como (Capitol)
-	30	RIP IT UP — Little Richard (London)

22 December 1956

last week	this week	
1	1	JUST WALKING IN THE RAIN — Johnnie Ray (Philips)
2	2	GREEN DOOR — Frankie Vaughan (Philips)
3	3	ST. THERESE OF THE ROSES — Malcolm Vaughan (HMV)
5	4	SINGING THE BLUES — Guy Mitchell (Philips)
7	5	CINDY, OH CINDY — Eddie Fisher (HMV)
4	6	RIP IT UP — Bill Haley & His Comets (Brunswick)
10	7	TRUE LOVE — Bing Crosby & Grace Kelly (Capitol)
6	8	MY PRAYER — Platters (Mercury)
11	9	MAKE IT A PARTY — Winifred Atwell (Decca)
8	10	A WOMAN IN LOVE — Frankie Laine (Philips)
9	11	HOUND DOG — Elvis Presley (HMV)
15	12	CHRISTMAS ISLAND — Dickie Valentine (Decca)
14	13	WHEN MEXICO GAVE UP THE RUMBA — Mitchell Torok (Brunswick)
17	14	LOVE ME TENDER — Elvis Presley (HMV)
15	14	MORE — Jimmy Young (Decca)
16	16	CINDY, OH CINDY — Tony Brent (Columbia)
11	17	BLUE MOON — Elvis Presley (HMV)
18	18	TWO DIFFERENT WORLDS — Ronnie Hilton (HMV)
23	19	SINGING THE BLUES — Tommy Steele (Decca)
25	20	FRIENDLY PERSUASION — Pat Boone (London)
19	20	A HOUSE WITH LOVE IN IT — Vera Lynn (Decca)
22	22	LOVE ME AS THOUGH THERE WERE NO TOMORROW — Nat King Cole (Capitol)
-	23	I DON'T CARE IF THE SUN DON'T SHINE — Elvis Presley (HMV)
-	24	CHRISTMAS AND YOU — Dave King (Decca)
24	25	ROCK AROUND THE CLOCK — Bill Haley & His Comets (Brunswick)
28	26	RUDY'S ROCK — Bill Haley & His Comets (Brunswick)
-	27	LETTER TO A SOLDIER — Barbara Lyon (Columbia)
-	28	LONNIE DONEGAN SHOWCASE (LP) — Lonnie Donegan (Pye Nixa)
20	29	THE GREEN DOOR — Jim Lowe (London)
-	30	BLUEBERRY HILL — Fats Domino (London)

29 December 1956

last week	this week	
1	1	JUST WALKING IN THE RAIN — Johnnie Ray (Philips)
4	2	SINGING THE BLUES — Guy Mitchell (Philips)
2	3	GREEN DOOR — Frankie Vaughan (Philips)
3	3	ST. THERESE OF THE ROSES — Malcolm Vaughan (HMV)
7	5	TRUE LOVE — Bing Crosby & Grace Kelly (Capitol)
5	6	CINDY, OH CINDY — Eddie Fisher (HMV)
9	7	MAKE IT A PARTY — Winifred Atwell (Decca)
12	8	CHRISTMAS ISLAND — Dickie Valentine (Decca)
6	9	RIP IT UP — Bill Haley & His Comets (Brunswick)
8	10	MY PRAYER — Platters (Mercury)
14	11	LOVE ME TENDER — Elvis Presley (HMV)
10	12	A WOMAN IN LOVE — Frankie Laine (Philips)
14	13	MORE — Jimmy Young (Decca)
-	14	MOONLIGHT GAMBLER — Frankie Laine (Philips)
13	15	WHEN MEXICO GAVE UP THE RUMBA — Mitchell Torok (Brunswick)
11	16	HOUND DOG — Elvis Presley (HMV)
19	17	SINGING THE BLUES — Tommy Steele (Decca)
20	18	A HOUSE WITH LOVE IN IT — Vera Lynn (Decca)
20	19	FRIENDLY PERSUASION — Pat Boone (London)
16	20	CINDY, OH CINDY — Tony Brent (Columbia)
18	21	TWO DIFFERENT WORLDS — Ronnie Hilton (HMV)
17	22	BLUE MOON — Elvis Presley (HMV)
24	23	CHRISTMAS AND YOU — Dave King (Decca)
-	24	'JOIN IN AND SING, NO. 3' MEDLEY — Johnston Brothers (Decca)
30	25	BLUEBERRY HILL — Fats Domino (London)
23	26	I DON'T CARE IF THE SUN DON'T SHINE — Elvis Presley (HMV)
27	27	LETTER TO A SOLDIER — Barbara Lyon (Columbia)
-	28	ALL OF YOU — Sammy Davis Jr. (Brunswick)
28	29	LONNIE DONEGAN SHOWCASE (LP) — Lonnie Donegan (Pye Nixa)
22	30	LOVE ME AS THOUGH THERE WERE NO TOMORROW — Nat King Cole (Capitol)
26	30	RUDY'S ROCK — Bill Haley & His Comets (Brunswick)

Musically there was little bluesy about Guy Mitchell's *Singing The Blues*, but its breezy commerciality also lent itself ideally to Tommy Steele's voice, sidetracking him from rock'n'roll when he'd hardly got started in it. Elvis' first movie *Love Me Tender* opened in the UK on December 13, and the title song immediately charted to keep *Hound Dog* and both sides of *Blue Moon/I Don't Care If The Sun Don't Shine* company. Another LP made the 30 over Christmas – a 10" release by Lonnie Donegan.

Elvis Is King

Elvis hit comfortable mid-fifties America like a whirlwind. He was in Sam Phillips' words "a white boy playing black music". And that wasn't all. His stage act was outrageously sexually charged and he looked dangerous. On his early TV appearances he seemed to come from another planet from the other bland acts. After recording some classic tracks for the Sun label in Memphis he signed to RCA for the then astronomical sum of $35,000 in late 1955. He released Heartbreak Hotel and the world capitulated. His extraordinary life has been documented ad nauseam, but the charts in this book show the hold he had over the record-buyers of a whole generation.

5 January 1957

last week	this		
2	1	SINGING THE BLUES	Guy Mitchell (Philips)
1	2	JUST WALKING IN THE RAIN	Johnnie Ray (Philips)
3	3	GREEN DOOR	Frankie Vaughan (Philips)
3	4	ST. THERESE OF THE ROSES	Malcolm Vaughan (HMV)
6	5	CINDY, OH, CINDY	Eddie Fisher (HMV)
17	6	SINGING THE BLUES	Tommy Steele (Decca)
5	7	TRUE LOVE	Bing Crosby & Grace Kelly (Capitol)
16	8	HOUND DOG	Elvis Presley (HMV)
9	9	RIP IT UP	Bill Haley & His Comets (Brunswick)
12	10	A WOMAN IN LOVE	Frankie Laine (Philips)
11	11	LOVE ME TENDER	Elvis Presley (HMV)
15	12	WHEN MEXICO GAVE UP THE RUMBA	Mitchell Torok (Brunswick)
14	13	MOONLIGHT GAMBLER	Frankie Laine (Philips)
7	14	MAKE IT A PARTY	Winifred Atwell (Decca)
13	15	MORE	Jimmy Young (Decca)
19	16	FRIENDLY PERSUASION	Pat Boone (London)
10	16	MY PRAYER	Platters (Mercury)
21	18	TWO DIFFERENT WORLDS	Ronnie Hilton (HMV)
-	19	ROCKIN' THROUGH THE RYE	Bill Haley & His Comets (Brunswick)
18	19	HOUSE WITH LOVE IN IT	Vera Lynn (Decca)
25	21	BLUEBERRY HILL	Fats Domino (London)
22	22	BLUE MOON	Elvis Presley (HMV)
20	23	CINDY, OH, CINDY	Tony Brent (Columbia)
8	23	CHRISTMAS ISLAND	Dickie Valentine (Decca)
-	25	ROCK AROUND THE CLOCK	Bill Haley & His Comets (Brunswick)
29	26	LONNIE DONEGAN SHOWCASE (LP)	Lonnie Donegan (Pye Nixa)
30	27	RUDY'S ROCK	Bill Haley & His Comets (Brunswick)
27	28	LETTER TO A SOLDIER	Barbara Lyon (Columbia)
-	29	FRIENDLY PERSUASION	Four Aces (Brunswick)
26	30	I DON'T CARE IF THE SUN DON'T SHINE	Elvis Presley (HMV)

12 January 1957

6	1	SINGING THE BLUES	Tommy Steele (Decca)
1	2	SINGING THE BLUES	Guy Mitchell (Philips)
4	3	ST. THERESE OF THE ROSES	Malcolm Vaughan (HMV)
3	4	GREEN DOOR	Frankie Vaughan (Philips)
2	5	JUST WALKING IN THE RAIN	Johnnie Ray (Philips)
7	6	TRUE LOVE	Bing Crosby & Grace Kelly (Capitol)
5	7	CINDY, OH, CINDY	Eddie Fisher (HMV)
8	8	HOUND DOG	Elvis Presley (HMV)
16	9	FRIENDLY PERSUASION	Pat Boone (London)
9	10	RIP IT UP	Bill Haley & His Comets (Brunswick)
-	11	THE GARDEN OF EDEN	Frankie Vaughan (Philips)
21	12	BLUEBERRY HILL	Fats Domino (London)
11	13	LOVE ME TENDER	Elvis Presley (HMV)
10	14	A WOMAN IN LOVE	Frankie Laine (Philips)
13	15	MOONLIGHT GAMBLER	Frankie Laine (Philips)
-	15	GARDEN OF EDEN	Gary Miller (Pye Nixa)
22	17	BLUE MOON	Elvis Presley (HMV)
15	18	MORE	Jimmy Young (Decca)
-	19	I'LL BE HOME	Pat Boone (London)
12	20	WHEN MEXICO GAVE UP THE RUMBA	Mitchell Torok (Brunswick)
18	21	TWO DIFFERENT WORLDS	Ronnie Hilton (HMV)
19	22	HOUSE WITH LOVE IN IT	Vera Lynn (Decca)
-	23	GARDEN OF EDEN	Dick James (Parlophone)
19	24	ROCKIN' THROUGH THE RYE	Bill Haley & His (Brunswick)
-	25	AIN'T THAT A SHAME	Pat Boone (London)
25	26	ROCK AROUND THE CLOCK	Bill Haley & His (Brunswick)
28	27	LETTER TO A SOLDIER	Barbara Lyon (Columbia)
14	28	MAKE IT A PARTY	Winifred Atwell (Decca)
-	29	RED LIGHT, GREEN LIGHT	Mitchell Torok (Brunswick)
-	30	BRING A LITTLE WATER, SYLVIE/DEAD OR ALIVE	Lonnie Donegan (Pye Nixa)

19 January 1957

2	1	SINGING THE BLUES	Guy Mitchell (Philips)
1	2	SINGING THE BLUES	Tommy Steele (Decca)
11	3	THE GARDEN OF EDEN	Frankie Vaughan (Philips)
9	4	FRIENDLY PERSUASION	Pat Boone (London)
6	5	TRUE LOVE	Grace Kelly (Capitol)
4	6	GREEN DOOR	Frankie Vaughan (Philips)
5	7	JUST WALKING IN THE RAIN	Johnnie Ray (Philips)
3	8	ST. THERESE OF THE ROSES	Malcolm Vaughan (HMV)
7	9	CINDY, OH, CINDY	Eddie Fisher (HMV)
8	10	HOUND DOG	Elvis Presley (HMV)
10	11	RIP IT UP	Bill Haley & His Comets (Brunswick)
12	12	BLUEBERRY HILL	Fats Domino (London)
-	13	DON'T YOU ROCK ME DADDY-O	Lonnie Donegan (Pye Nixa)
15	14	GARDEN OF EDEN	Gary Miller (Pye Nixa)
13	15	LOVE ME TENDER	Elvis Presley (HMV)
15	16	MOONLIGHT GAMBLER	Frankie Laine (Philips)
17	17	BLUE MOON	Elvis Presley (HMV)
-	18	YOU, ME AND US	Alma Cogan (HMV)
21	19	TWO DIFFERENT WORLDS	Ronnie Hilton (HMV)
14	20	A WOMAN IN LOVE	Frankie Laine (Philips)
-	21	YOU DON'T OWE ME A THING/LOOK HOMEWARD ANGEL	Johnnie Ray (Philips)
25	22	AIN'T THAT A SHAME	Pat Boone (London)
23	23	GARDEN OF EDEN	Dick James (Parlophone)
-	23	THE GARDEN OF EDEN	Joe Valino (HMV)
19	25	I'LL BE HOME	Pat Boone (London)
22	26	HOUSE WITH LOVE IN IT	Vera Lynn (Decca)
20	27	WHEN MEXICO GAVE UP THE RUMBA	Mitchell Torok (Brunswick)
18	28	MORE	Jimmy Young (Decca)
24	29	ROCKIN' THROUGH THE RYE	Bill Haley & His Comets (Brunswick)
-	30	MY PRAYER	Platters (Mercury)

26 January 1957

3	1	THE GARDEN OF EDEN	Frankie Vaughan (Philips)
1	2	SINGING THE BLUES	Guy Mitchell (Philips)
4	3	FRIENDLY PERSUASION	Pat Boone (London)
2	4	SINGING THE BLUES	Tommy Steele (Decca)
5	5	TRUE LOVE	Grace Kelly (Capitol)
8	6	ST. THERESE OF THE ROSES	Malcolm Vaughan (HMV)
9	7	CINDY, OH, CINDY	Eddie Fisher (HMV)
7	8	JUST WALKING IN THE RAIN	Johnnie Ray (Philips)
6	9	GREEN DOOR	Frankie Vaughan (Philips)
12	10	BLUEBERRY HILL	Fats Domino (London)
10	10	HOUND DOG	Elvis Presley (HMV)
13	12	DON'T YOU ROCK ME DADDY-O	Lonnie Donegan (Pye Nixa)
16	13	MOONLIGHT GAMBLER	Frankie Laine (Philips)
15	13	LOVE ME TENDER	Elvis Presley (HMV)
11	15	RIP IT UP	Bill Haley & His Comets (Brunswick)
-	16	THE ADORATION WALTZ	David Whitfield (Decca)
21	17	YOU DON'T OWE ME A THING/LOOK HOMEWARD ANGEL	Johnnie Ray (Philips)
23	18	GARDEN OF EDEN	Dick James (Parlophone)
18	19	YOU, ME AND US	Alma Cogan (HMV)
29	20	ROCKIN' THROUGH THE RYE	Bill Haley & His Comets (Brunswick)
19	21	TWO DIFFERENT WORLDS	Ronnie Hilton (HMV)
14	21	GARDEN OF EDEN	Gary Miller (Pye Nixa)
-	23	YOU'LL NEVER, NEVER KNOW/IT ISN'T RIGHT	Platters (Mercury)
-	24	DON'T YOU ROCK ME DADDY-O	Vipers Skiffle Group (Parlophone)
20	25	A WOMAN IN LOVE	Frankie Laine (Philips)
17	26	BLUE MOON	Elvis Presley (HMV)
-	27	ROCK AROUND THE CLOCK	Bill Haley & His (Brunswick)
30	28	MY PRAYER	Platters (Mercury)
23	29	THE GARDEN OF EDEN	Joe Valino (HMV)
-	30	AIN'T THAT A SHAME	Fats Domino (London)

Singing The Blues provided a unique case of one version of a song replacing another at Number One - and then losing out again to the first version! There was a reassertion of ballads in the Top Ten – *Cindy, Oh Cindy*, the near-operatic *St Therese Of The Roses*, and two film songs, the *Friendly Persuasion* title song, and *True Love*, from the musical *High Society*. And Bill Haley's *Rock Around The Clock* became, in late January, the first single to sell over a million in Britain.

February 1957

2 February 1957

last	this		
2	1	SINGING THE BLUES	Guy Mitchell (Philips)
1	1	THE GARDEN OF EDEN	Frankie Vaughan (Philips)
3	3	FRIENDLY PERSUASION	Pat Boone (London)
6	4	ST. THERESE OF THE ROSES	Malcolm Vaughan (HMV)
5	5	TRUE LOVE	Bing Crosby & Grace Kelly (Capitol)
4	6	SINGING THE BLUES	Tommy Steele (Decca)
9	7	GREEN DOOR	Frankie Vaughan (Philips)
7	8	CINDY, OH, CINDY	Eddie Fisher (HMV)
12	9	DON'T YOU ROCK ME DADDY-O	Lonnie Donegan (Pye Nixa)
10	10	BLUEBERRY HILL	Fats Domino (London)
10	11	HOUND DOG	Elvis Presley (HMV)
8	12	JUST WALKING IN THE RAIN	Johnnie Ray (Philips)
13	13	MOONLIGHT GAMBLER	Frankie Laine (Philips)
24	14	DON'T YOU ROCK ME DADDY-O	Vipers Skiffle Group (Parlophone)
16	15	THE ADORATION WALTZ	David Whitfield (Decca)
17	16	YOU DON'T OWE ME A THING /LOOK HOMEWARD ANGEL	Johnnie Ray (Philips)
13	17	LOVE ME TENDER	Elvis Presley (HMV)
19	18	YOU, ME AND US	Alma Cogan (HMV)
15	18	RIP IT UP	Bill Haley & His Comets (London)
-	20	ROCK THE JOINT	Bill Haley & His Comets (London)
18	20	GARDEN OF EDEN	Dick James (Parlophone)
27	22	ROCK AROUND THE CLOCK	Bill Haley & His Comets (Brunswick)
30	23	AIN'T THAT A SHAME	Fats Domino (London)
21	24	GARDEN OF EDEN	Gary Miller (Pye Nixa)
21	25	TWO DIFFERENT WORLDS	Ronnie Hilton (HMV)
-	26	I DREAMED	Beverley Sisters (Decca)
-	27	DON'T FORBID ME	Pat Boone (London)
20	28	ROCKIN' THROUGH THE RYE	Bill Haley & His Comets (Brunswick)
-	29	HONEY CHILE	Fats Domino (London)
-	30	WHEN MEXICO GAVE UP THE RUMBA	Mitchell Torok (Brunswick)

9 February 1957

1	1	THE GARDEN OF EDEN	Frankie Vaughan (Philips)
1	2	SINGING THE BLUES	Guy Mitchell (Philips)
3	3	FRIENDLY PERSUASION	Pat Boone (London)
5	4	TRUE LOVE	Bing Crosby & Grace Kelly (Capitol)
9	5	DON'T YOU ROCK ME DADDY-O	Lonnie Donegan (Pye Nixa)
10	6	BLUEBERRY HILL	Fats Domino (London)
4	7	ST. THERESE OF THE ROSES	Malcolm Vaughan (HMV)
6	8	SINGING THE BLUES	Tommy Steele (Decca)
8	9	CINDY, OH, CINDY	Eddie Fisher (HMV)
11	10	HOUND DOG	Elvis Presley (HMV)
14	10	DON'T YOU ROCK ME DADDY-O	Vipers Skiffle Group (Parlophone)
-	12	YOUNG LOVE	Tab Hunter (London)
7	13	GREEN DOOR	Frankie Vaughan (Philips)
18	14	RIP IT UP	Bill Haley & His Comets (Brunswick)
27	15	DON'T FORBID ME	Pat Boone (London)
-	15	DON'T KNOCK ME A THING	Bill Haley & His Comets (Brunswick)
12	17	JUST WALKING IN THE RAIN	Johnnie Ray (Philips)
13	18	MOONLIGHT GAMBLER	Frankie Laine (Philips)
-	19	ROCK-A-BYE YOUR BABY WITH A DIXIE MELODY	Jerry Lewis (Brunswick)
-	20	YOUNG LOVE	Sonny James (Capitol)
20	21	ROCK THE JOINT	Bill Haley & His Comets (London)
16	21	YOU DON'T OWE ME A THING /LOOK HOMEWARD ANGEL	Johnnie Ray (Philips)
15	21	THE ADORATION WALTZ	David Whitfield (Decca)
26	24	I DREAMED	Beverley Sisters (Decca)
24	24	GARDEN OF EDEN	Gary Miller (Pye Nixa)
18	26	YOU, ME AND US	Alma Cogan (HMV)
-	27	GIVE HER MY LOVE	Johnston Brothers (Decca)
-	28	LONG TALL SALLY	Little Richard (London)
-	29	YOU'LL NEVER, NEVER KNOW /IT ISN'T RIGHT	Platters (Mercury)
-	30	CINDY, OH, CINDY	Tony Brent (Columbia)

16 February 1957

1	1	THE GARDEN OF EDEN	Frankie Vaughan (Philips)
12	2	YOUNG LOVE	Tab Hunter (London)
2	3	SINGING THE BLUES	Guy Mitchell (Philips)
15	4	DON'T FORBID ME	Pat Boone (London)
5	4	DON'T YOU ROCK ME DADDY-O	Lonnie Donegan (Pye Nixa)
3	6	FRIENDLY PERSUASION	Pat Boone (London)
15	7	DON'T KNOCK THE ROCK	Bill Haley & His Comets (Brunswick)
4	8	TRUE LOVE	Bing Crosby & Grace Kelly (Capitol)
6	9	BLUEBERRY HILL	Fats Domino (London)
7	10	ST. THERESE OF THE ROSES	Malcolm Vaughan (HMV)
9	11	CINDY, OH, CINDY	Eddie Fisher (HMV)
19	12	ROCK-A-BYE YOUR BABY WITH A DIXIE MELODY	Jerry Lewis (Brunswick)
10	13	DON'T YOU ROCK ME DADDY-O	Vipers Skiffle Group (Parlophone)
8	14	SINGING THE BLUES	Tommy Steele (Decca)
21	15	YOU DON'T OWE ME A THING /LOOK HOMEWARD ANGEL	Johnnie Ray (Philips)
10	16	HOUND DOG	Elvis Presley (HMV)
28	17	LONG TALL SALLY	Little Richard (London)
14	18	RIP IT UP	Bill Haley & His Comets (Brunswick)
20	19	YOUNG LOVE	Sonny James (Capitol)
13	20	GREEN DOOR	Frankie Vaughan (Philips)
-	21	KNEE DEEP IN THE BLUES	Guy Mitchell (Philips)
21	22	ROCK THE JOINT	Bill Haley & His Comets (London)
17	23	JUST WALKING IN THE RAIN	Johnnie Ray (Philips)
21	24	THE ADORATION WALTZ	David Whitfield (Decca)
24	25	GARDEN OF EDEN	Gary Miller (Pye Nixa)
-	26	KNEE DEEP IN THE BLUES	Tommy Steele (Decca)
-	27	THE BANANA BOAT SONG	Shirley Bassey (Philips)
18	28	MOONLIGHT GAMBLER	Frankie Laine (Philips)
-	29	MYSTERY TRAIN	Elvis Presley (HMV)
26	30	YOU, ME AND US	Alma Cogan (HMV)

23 February 1957

2	1	YOUNG LOVE	Tab Hunter (London)
1	2	THE GARDEN OF EDEN	Frankie Vaughan (Philips)
3	3	SINGING THE BLUES	Guy Mitchell (Philips)
4	4	DON'T FORBID ME	Pat Boone (London)
4	5	DON'T YOU ROCK ME DADDY-O	Lonnie Donegan (Pye Nixa)
8	6	TRUE LOVE	Bing Crosby & Grace Kelly (Capitol)
6	7	FRIENDLY PERSUASION	Pat Boone (London)
7	8	DON'T KNOCK THE ROCK	Bill Haley & His Comets (Brunswick)
9	9	BLUEBERRY HILL	Fats Domino (London)
21	10	KNEE DEEP IN THE BLUES	Guy Mitchell (Philips)
10	11	ST. THERESE OF THE ROSES	Malcolm Vaughan (HMV)
19	12	YOUNG LOVE	Sonny James (Capitol)
14	13	SINGING THE BLUES	Tommy Steele (Decca)
24	14	THE ADORATION WALTZ	David Whitfield (Decca)
26	15	KNEE DEEP IN THE BLUES	Tommy Steele (Decca)
12	16	ROCK-A-BYE YOUR BABY WITH A DIXIE MELODY	Jerry Lewis (Brunswick)
17	17	LONG TALL SALLY	Little Richard (London)
13	18	DON'T YOU ROCK ME DADDY-O	Vipers Skiffle Group (Parlophone)
-	19	YOU DON'T OWE ME A THING	Johnnie Ray (Philips)
28	20	MOONLIGHT GAMBLER	Frankie Laine (Philips)
11	21	CINDY, OH, CINDY	Eddie Fisher (HMV)
16	22	HOUND DOG	Elvis Presley (HMV)
30	23	YOU, ME AND US	Alma Cogan (HMV)
27	24	THE BANANA BOAT SONG	Shirley Bassey (Philips)
22	25	ROCK THE JOINT	Bill Haley & His Comets (London)
29	26	MYSTERY TRAIN	Elvis Presley (HMV)
-	27	LOOK HOMEWARD, ANGEL	Johnnie Ray (Philips)
-	28	LET'S ROCK 'N' ROLL	Winifred Atwell (Decca)
-	29	TUTTI FRUTTI	Little Richard (London)
18	30	RIP IT UP	Bill Haley & His Comets (Brunswick)

Fats Domino scored his first major UK success with *Blueberry Hill*, as did Little Richard with *Long Tall Sally*, a cover hit by Pat Boone some months earlier. Boone himself put two ballads in the Top Ten simultaneously, while Bill Haley's UK tour brought in another flurry (the last) of his records. Meanwhile, after five weeks of charting Johnnie Ray's *You Don't Owe Me A Thing/Look Homeward Angel* jointly, the NME was logging sufficient individual sales on each side to separate them on February 23

2 March 1957

last week	this week	entry
1	1	YOUNG LOVE — Tab Hunter (London)
2	2	THE GARDEN OF EDEN — Frankie Vaughan (Philips)
4	3	DON'T FORBID ME — Pat Boone (London)
3	4	SINGING THE BLUES — Guy Mitchell (Philips)
10	5	KNEE DEEP IN THE BLUES — Guy Mitchell (Philips)
5	6	DON'T YOU ROCK ME DADDY-O — Lonnie Donegan (Pye Nixa)
6	7	TRUE LOVE — Bing Crosby & Grace Kelly (Capitol)
7	8	FRIENDLY PERSUASION — Pat Boone (London)
14	9	THE ADORATION WALTZ — David Whitfield (Decca)
9	10	BLUEBERRY HILL — Fats Domino (London)
12	11	YOUNG LOVE — Sonny James (Capitol)
8	12	DON'T KNOCK THE ROCK — Bill Haley & His Comets (Brunswick)
17	13	LONG TALL SALLY — Little Richard (London)
16	14	ROCK-A-BYE YOUR BABY WITH A DIXIE MELODY — Jerry Lewis (Brunswick)
11	15	ST. THERESE OF THE ROSES — Malcolm Vaughan (HMV)
-	16	BANANA BOAT SONG (DAY-O) — Harry Belafonte (HMV)
20	17	MOONLIGHT GAMBLER — Frankie Laine (Philips)
15	18	KNEE DEEP IN THE BLUES — Tommy Steele (Decca)
18	19	DON'T YOU ROCK ME DADDY-O — Vipers Skiffle Group (Parlophone)
-	20	BANANA BOAT SONG — Tarriers (Columbia)
13	21	SINGING THE BLUES — Tommy Steele (Decca)
19	22	YOU DON'T OWE ME A THING — Johnnie Ray (Philips)
24	23	THE BANANA BOAT SONG — Shirley Bassey (Philips)
30	24	RIP IT UP — Bill Haley & His Comets (Brunswick)
27	25	LOOK HOMEWARD, ANGEL — Johnnie Ray (Philips)
21	26	CINDY, OH, CINDY — Eddie Fisher (HMV)
-	27	GARDEN OF EDEN — Gary Miller (Pye Nixa)
28	28	LET'S ROCK 'N' ROLL — Winifred Atwell (Decca)
26	29	MYSTERY TRAIN — Elvis Presley (HMV)
-	30	GONNA GET ALONG WITHOUT YA NOW — Patience & Prudence (London)

9 March 1957

this	entry
1	YOUNG LOVE — Tab Hunter (London)
2	DON'T FORBID ME — Pat Boone (London)
3	KNEE DEEP IN THE BLUES — Guy Mitchell (Philips)
4	SINGING THE BLUES — Guy Mitchell (Philips)
5	THE GARDEN OF EDEN — Frankie Vaughan (Philips)
6	TRUE LOVE — Bing Crosby & Grace Kelly (Capitol)
7	DON'T YOU ROCK ME DADDY-O — Lonnie Donegan (Pye Nixa)
8	FRIENDLY PERSUASION — Pat Boone (London)
9	LONG TALL SALLY — Little Richard (London)
10	BANANA BOAT SONG (DAY-O) — Harry Belafonte (HMV)
11	YOUNG LOVE — Sonny James (Capitol)
12	THE BANANA BOAT SONG — Shirley Bassey (Philips)
13	THE ADORATION WALTZ — David Whitfield (Decca)
14	BLUEBERRY HILL — Fats Domino (London)
15	DON'T KNOCK THE ROCK — Bill Haley & His Comets (Brunswick)
16	DON'T YOU ROCK ME DADDY-O — Vipers Skiffle Group (Parlophone)
17	ST. THERESE OF THE ROSES — Malcolm Vaughan (HMV)
18	KNEE DEEP IN THE BLUES — Tommy Steele (Decca)
19	BANANA BOAT SONG — Tarriers (Columbia)
20	YOU DON'T OWE ME A THING — Johnnie Ray (Philips)
21	SINGING THE BLUES — Tommy Steele (Decca)
22	ROCK-A-BYE YOUR BABY WITH A DIXIE MELODY — Jerry Lewis (Brunswick)
23	CINDY, OH, CINDY — Eddie Fisher (HMV)
24	LOOK HOMEWARD, ANGEL — Johnnie Ray (Philips)
25	MYSTERY TRAIN — Elvis Presley (HMV)
26	SHE'S GOT IT — Little Richard (London)
27	RIP IT UP — Elvis Presley (HMV)
28	MOONLIGHT GAMBLER — Frankie Laine (Philips)
29	GONNA GET ALONG WITHOUT YA NOW — Patience & Prudence (London)
30	RIP IT UP — Bill Haley & His Comets (Brunswick)

16 March 1957

this	entry
1	YOUNG LOVE — Tab Hunter (London)
2	DON'T FORBID ME — Pat Boone (London)
3	KNEE DEEP IN THE BLUES — Guy Mitchell (Philips)
4	LONG TALL SALLY — Little Richard (London)
5	DON'T YOU ROCK ME DADDY-O — Lonnie Donegan (Pye Nixa)
6	SINGING THE BLUES — Guy Mitchell (Philips)
7	BANANA BOAT SONG (DAY-O) — Harry Belafonte (HMV)
8	THE GARDEN OF EDEN — Frankie Vaughan (Philips)
9	THE BANANA BOAT SONG — Shirley Bassey (Philips)
10	TRUE LOVE — Bing Crosby & Grace Kelly (Capitol)
11	FRIENDLY PERSUASION — Pat Boone (London)
12	DON'T KNOCK THE ROCK — Bill Haley & His Comets (Brunswick)
13	THE ADORATION WALTZ — David Whitfield (Decca)
14	YOUNG LOVE — Sonny James (Capitol)
15	BANANA BOAT SONG — Tarriers (Columbia)
16	ROCK-A-BYE YOUR BABY WITH A DIXIE MELODY — Jerry Lewis (Brunswick)
17	BLUEBERRY HILL — Fats Domino (London)
18	ST. THERESE OF THE ROSES — Malcolm Vaughan (HMV)
19	THE GIRL CAN'T HELP IT — Little Richard (London)
20	THE WISDOM OF A FOOL — Norman Wisdom (Columbia)
21	YOU DON'T OWE ME A THING — Johnnie Ray (Philips)
22	GONNA GET ALONG WITHOUT YA NOW — Patience & Prudence (London)
23	KNEE DEEP IN THE BLUES — Tommy Steele (Decca)
24	LET'S ROCK 'N' ROLL — Winifred Atwell (Decca)
25	MYSTERY TRAIN — Elvis Presley (HMV)
26	DON'T YOU ROCK ME DADDY-O — Vipers Skiffle Group (Parlophone)
27	LOOK HOMEWARD, ANGEL — Johnnie Ray (Philips)
28	MOONLIGHT GAMBLER — Frankie Laine (Philips)
29	THE FAITHFUL HUSSAR (DON'T CRY MY LOVE) — Vera Lynn (Decca)
30	SHE'S GOT IT — Little Richard (London)

23 March 1957

this	entry
1	YOUNG LOVE — Tab Hunter (London)
2	DON'T FORBID ME — Pat Boone (London)
3	KNEE DEEP IN THE BLUES — Guy Mitchell (Philips)
4	LONG TALL SALLY — Little Richard (London)
5	DON'T YOU ROCK ME DADDY-O — Lonnie Donegan (Pye Nixa)
6	BANANA BOAT SONG (DAY-O) — Harry Belafonte (HMV)
7	TRUE LOVE — Bing Crosby & Grace Kelly (Capitol)
8	SINGING THE BLUES — Guy Mitchell (Philips)
9	THE BANANA BOAT SONG — Shirley Bassey (Philips)
10	FRIENDLY PERSUASION — Pat Boone (London)
11	THE GARDEN OF EDEN — Frankie Vaughan (Philips)
12	THE GIRL CAN'T HELP IT — Little Richard (London)
13	THE WISDOM OF A FOOL — Norman Wisdom (Columbia)
14	THE ADORATION WALTZ — David Whitfield (Decca)
15	YOU DON'T OWE ME A THING — Johnnie Ray (Philips)
16	DON'T KNOCK THE ROCK — Bill Haley & His Comets (Brunswick)
17	YOUNG LOVE — Sonny James (Capitol)
18	LOOK HOMEWARD, ANGEL — Johnnie Ray (Philips)
19	BANANA BOAT SONG — Tarriers (Columbia)
20	SHE'S GOT IT — Little Richard (London)
21	THE MAN WHO PLAYS THE MANDOLINO — Dean Martin (Capitol)
22	ROCK-A-BYE YOUR BABY WITH A DIXIE MELODY — Jerry Lewis (Brunswick)
23	BLUEBERRY HILL — Fats Domino (London)
24	GONNA GET ALONG WITHOUT YA NOW — Patience & Prudence (London)
25	CUMBERLAND GAP — Vipers Skiffle Group (Parlophone)
26	ST. THERESE OF THE ROSES — Malcolm Vaughan (HMV)
27	KNEE DEEP IN THE BLUES — Tommy Steele (Decca)
28	LET'S ROCK 'N' ROLL — Winifred Atwell (Decca)
29	DON'T YOU ROCK ME DADDY-O — Vipers Skiffle Group (Parlophone)
30	THE FAITHFUL HUSSAR (DON'T CRY MY LOVE) — Vera Lynn (Decca)

Bizarrely, both Guy Mitchell and Tommy Steele elected to follow their *Singing The Blues* hits with the same song, *Knee Deep In The Blues* (moreover, both were covers of Marty Robbins' follow-up to *HIS Singing The Blues*, which had been the original US version!) This time around, Mitchell was the clear winner in chart terms. Meanwhile, Little Richard reinforced his hit status with both sides of his *She's Got It/The Girl Can't Help It* single, each of which was featured in the movie of the latter title.

March – April 1957

30 March 1957

Last	This	Title	Artist (Label)
1	1	YOUNG LOVE	Tab Hunter (London)
2	2	DON'T FORBID ME	Pat Boone (London)
4	3	LONG TALL SALLY	Little Richard (London)
3	3	KNEE DEEP IN THE BLUES	Guy Mitchell (Philips)
6	5	BANANA BOAT SONG (DAY-O)	Harry Belafonte (HMV)
5	6	DON'T YOU ROCK ME DADDY-O	Lonnie Donegan (Pye Nixa)
7	7	TRUE LOVE	Bing Crosby & Grace Kelly (Capitol)
9	8	THE BANANA BOAT SONG	Shirley Bassey (Philips)
8	9	SINGING THE BLUES	Guy Mitchell (Philips)
11	10	THE GARDEN OF EDEN	Frankie Vaughan (Philips)
12	11	THE GIRL CAN'T HELP IT	Little Richard (London)
10	12	FRIENDLY PERSUASION	Pat Boone (London)
25	13	CUMBERLAND GAP	Vipers Skiffle Group (Parlophone)
13	13	THE WISDOM OF A FOOL	Norman Wisdom (Columbia)
15	15	YOU DON'T OWE ME A THING	Johnnie Ray (Philips)
14	16	THE ADORATION WALTZ	David Whitfield (Decca)
18	17	LOOK HOMEWARD, ANGEL	Johnnie Ray (Philips)
-	18	ONLY YOU	Platters (Mercury)
20	19	SHE'S GOT IT	Little Richard (London)
-	20	THE WISDOM OF A FOOL	Ronnie Carroll (Philips)
16	21	DON'T KNOCK THE ROCK	Bill Haley & His Comets (Brunswick)
-	22	MY PRAYER	Platters (Mercury)
-	23	BLUE MONDAY	Fats Domino (London)
27	23	KNEE DEEP IN THE BLUES	Tommy Steele (Decca)
-	25	MANGOS	Rosemary Clooney (Philips)
-	26	WHATEVER LOLA WANTS	Alma Cogan (HMV)
-	27	I'M NOT A JUVENILE DELINQUENT	Teenagers featuring Frankie Lymon (Columbia)
-	28	MOONLIGHT GAMBLER	Frankie Laine (Philips)
21	29	THE MAN WHO PLAYS THE MANDOLINO	Dean Martin (Capitol)
18	30	BANANA BOAT SONG	Tarriers (Columbia)

6 April 1957

Last	This	Title	Artist (Label)
1	1	YOUNG LOVE	Tab Hunter (London)
2	2	DON'T FORBID ME	Pat Boone (London)
5	3	BANANA BOAT SONG (DAY-O)	Harry Belafonte (HMV)
3	4	LONG TALL SALLY	Little Richard (London)
3	5	KNEE DEEP IN THE BLUES	Guy Mitchell (Philips)
-	6	CUMBERLAND GAP	Lonnie Donegan (Pye Nixa)
6	7	DON'T YOU ROCK ME DADDY-O	Lonnie Donegan (Pye Nixa)
7	8	TRUE LOVE	Bing Crosby & Grace Kelly (Capitol)
9	9	SINGING THE BLUES	Guy Mitchell (Philips)
11	10	THE GIRL CAN'T HELP IT	Little Richard (London)
17	11	LOOK HOMEWARD, ANGEL	Johnnie Ray (Philips)
8	12	THE BANANA BOAT SONG	Shirley Bassey (Philips)
12	13	FRIENDLY PERSUASION	Pat Boone (London)
15	14	YOU DON'T OWE ME A THING	Johnnie Ray (Philips)
19	15	SHE'S GOT IT	Little Richard (London)
13	15	CUMBERLAND GAP	Vipers Skiffle Group (Parlophone)
13	17	THE WISDOM OF A FOOL	Norman Wisdom (Columbia)
-	18	HEART	Max Bygraves (Decca)
23	19	KNEE DEEP IN THE BLUES	Tommy Steele (Decca)
-	20	MARIANNE	Hilltoppers (London)
10	21	THE GARDEN OF EDEN	Frankie Vaughan (Philips)
-	22	ROCK-A-BYE YOUR BABY WITH A DIXIE MELODY	Jerry Lewis (Brunswick)
20	23	THE WISDOM OF A FOOL	Ronnie Carroll (Philips)
27	23	I'M NOT A JUVENILE DELINQUENT	Teenagers featuring Frankie Lymon (Columbia)
16	25	THE ADORATION WALTZ	David Whitfield (Decca)
26	26	WHATEVER LOLA WANTS	Alma Cogan (HMV)
18	26	ONLY YOU	Platters (Mercury)
-	28	I'LL FIND YOU	David Whitfield (Decca)
25	29	MANGOS	Rosemary Clooney (Philips)
-	30	CRY ME A RIVER	Julie London (London)

13 April 1957

Last	This	Title	Artist (Label)
6	1	CUMBERLAND GAP	Lonnie Donegan (Pye Nixa)
3	2	BANANA BOAT SONG (DAY-O)	Harry Belafonte (HMV)
1	2	YOUNG LOVE	Tab Hunter (London)
4	4	LONG TALL SALLY	Little Richard (London)
2	5	DON'T FORBID ME	Pat Boone (London)
5	6	KNEE DEEP IN THE BLUES	Guy Mitchell (Philips)
7	7	DON'T YOU ROCK ME DADDY-O	Lonnie Donegan (Pye Nixa)
11	8	LOOK HOMEWARD, ANGEL	Johnnie Ray (Philips)
10	9	THE GIRL CAN'T HELP IT	Little Richard (London)
15	10	CUMBERLAND GAP	Vipers Skiffle Group (Parlophone)
14	12	YOU DON'T OWE ME A THING	Johnnie Ray (Philips)
9	13	SINGING THE BLUES	Guy Mitchell (Philips)
18	14	HEART	Max Bygraves (Decca)
15	15	SHE'S GOT IT	Little Richard (London)
23	16	I'M NOT A JUVENILE DELINQUENT	Teenagers featuring Frankie Lymon (Columbia)
-	17	NINETY-NINE WAYS	Tab Hunter (London)
-	18	BABY, BABY	Teenagers featuring Frankie Lymon (Columbia)
12	19	THE BANANA BOAT SONG	Shirley Bassey (Philips)
13	20	FRIENDLY PERSUASION	Pat Boone (London)
-	21	FREIGHT TRAIN	Chas McDevitt Skiffle Group & Nancy Whiskey (Oriole)
30	22	CRY ME A RIVER	Julie London (London)
17	23	THE WISDOM OF A FOOL	Norman Wisdom (Columbia)
-	24	GONNA GET ALONG WITHOUT YA NOW	Patience & Prudence (London)
-	25	I'LL TAKE YOU HOME AGAIN KATHLEEN	Slim Whitman (London)
19	26	KNEE DEEP IN THE BLUES	Tommy Steele (Decca)
20	27	MARIANNE	Hilltoppers (London)
28	28	I'LL FIND YOU	David Whitfield (Decca)
-	29	YOU'LL NEVER, NEVER KNOW /IT ISN'T RIGHT	Platters (Mercury)
26	30	ONLY YOU	Platters (Mercury)
-	30	THE WORLD IS MINE	Malcolm Vaughan (HMV)

20 April 1957

Last	This	Title	Artist (Label)
1	1	CUMBERLAND GAP	Lonnie Donegan (Pye Nixa)
2	2	YOUNG LOVE	Tab Hunter (London)
3	3	BANANA BOAT SONG (DAY-O)	Harry Belafonte (HMV)
5	4	DON'T FORBID ME	Pat Boone (London)
4	5	LONG TALL SALLY	Little Richard (London)
6	6	KNEE DEEP IN THE BLUES	Guy Mitchell (Philips)
8	7	LOOK HOMEWARD, ANGEL	Johnnie Ray (Philips)
18	8	BABY, BABY	Teenagers featuring Frankie Lymon (Columbia)
17	9	NINETY-NINE WAYS	
7	10	DON'T YOU ROCK ME DADDY-O	Lonnie Donegan (Pye Nixa)
10	11	TRUE LOVE	Bing Crosby & Grace Kelly (Capitol)
9	12	THE GIRL CAN'T HELP IT	Little Richard (London)
16	12	I'M NOT A JUVENILE DELINQUENT	Teenagers featuring Frankie Lymon (Columbia)
14	14	HEART	Max Bygraves (Decca)
25	15	I'LL TAKE YOU HOME AGAIN KATHLEEN	Slim Whitman (London)
10	16	CUMBERLAND GAP	Vipers Skiffle Group (Parlophone)
12	17	YOU DON'T OWE ME A THING	Johnnie Ray (Philips)
21	18	FREIGHT TRAIN	Chas McDevitt Skiffle Group & Nancy Whiskey (Oriole)
-	19	I'M WALKIN'	Fats Domino (London)
-	20	WHEN I FALL IN LOVE	Nat King Cole (Capitol)
13	20	SINGING THE BLUES	Guy Mitchell (Philips)
15	22	SHE'S GOT IT	Little Richard (London)
-	23	BUTTERFLY	Charlie Gracie (Parlophone)
-	24	SINGING THE BLUES	Tommy Steele (Decca)
19	25	THE BANANA BOAT SONG	Shirley Bassey (Philips)
-	26	HEART	Johnston Brothers (Decca)
22	27	CRY ME A RIVER	Julie London (London)
20	28	FRIENDLY PERSUASION	Pat Boone (London)
-	29	BUTTERFLY	Andy Williams (London)
-	30	BLUE MONDAY	Fats Domino (London)

More songs from the hit film *The Girl Can't Help It* – Fats Domino's *Blue Monday*, the Platters' *You'll Never, Never Know* and Julie London's two-year-old *Cry Me A River* – made the Top 30. Following a lull since their Number One hit, the Teenagers returned strongly with both sides of *Baby, Baby/I'm Not A Juvenile Delinquent*. Fighting off competition from the Vipers Skiffle Group, Lonnie not only scored two Top 10 hits simultaneously, but also achieved his first chart-topper with the skiffle-rocker *Cumberland Gap*.

April – May 1957

last week	this week	27 April 1957
1	1	CUMBERLAND GAP — Lonnie Donegan (Pye Nixa)
3	2	BANANA BOAT SONG (DAY-O) — Harry Belafonte (HMV)
2	3	YOUNG LOVE — Tab Hunter (London)
4	4	DON'T FORBID ME — Pat Boone (London)
5	5	LONG TALL SALLY — Little Richard (London)
8	6	BABY, BABY — Teenagers featuring Frankie Lymon (Columbia)
7	7	LOOK HOMEWARD, ANGEL — Johnnie Ray (Philips)
9	8	NINETY-NINE WAYS — Tab Hunter (London)
20	9	WHEN I FALL IN LOVE — Nat King Cole (Capitol)
10	10	DON'T YOU ROCK ME DADDY-O — Lonnie Donegan (Pye Nixa)
15	11	I'LL TAKE YOU HOME AGAIN KATHLEEN — Slim Whitman (London)
18	12	FREIGHT TRAIN — Chas McDevitt Skiffle Group & Nancy Whiskey (Oriole)
6	12	KNEE DEEP IN THE BLUES — Guy Mitchell (Philips)
14	14	HEART — Max Bygraves (Decca)
12	15	I'M NOT A JUVENILE DELINQUENT — Teenagers featuring Frankie Lymon (Columbia)
29	16	BUTTERFLY — Andy Williams (London)
11	17	TRUE LOVE — Bing Crosby & Grace Kelly (Capitol)
12	17	THE GIRL CAN'T HELP IT — Little Richard (London)
-	19	ROCK-A-BILLY — Guy Mitchell (Philips)
20	20	SINGING THE BLUES — Guy Mitchell (Philips)
23	21	BUTTERFLY — Charlie Gracie (Parlophone)
-	22	LOVE IS A GOLDEN RING — Frankie Laine (Philips)
26	23	HEART — Johnston Brothers (Decca)
17	24	YOU DON'T OWE ME A THING — Johnnie Ray (Philips)
19	25	I'M WALKIN' — Fats Domino (London)
16	25	CUMBERLAND GAP — Vipers Skiffle Group (Parlophone)
-	27	MANGOS — Rosemary Clooney (Philips)
-	28	WHY BABY WHY — Pat Boone (London)
28	29	FRIENDLY PERSUASION — Pat Boone (London)
-	30	MARIANNE — Hilltoppers (London)

last	this	4 May 1957
1	1	CUMBERLAND GAP — Lonnie Donegan (Pye Nixa)
2	2	BANANA BOAT SONG (DAY-O) — Harry Belafonte (HMV)
3	3	YOUNG LOVE — Tab Hunter (London)
6	4	BABY, BABY — Teenagers featuring Frankie Lymon (Columbia)
8	5	NINETY-NINE WAYS — Tab Hunter (London)
19	6	ROCK-A-BILLY — Guy Mitchell (Philips)
7	7	LOOK HOMEWARD, ANGEL — Johnnie Ray (Philips)
5	8	LONG TALL SALLY — Little Richard (London)
4	9	DON'T FORBID ME — Pat Boone (London)
16	10	BUTTERFLY — Andy Williams (London)
9	11	WHEN I FALL IN LOVE — Nat King Cole (Capitol)
17	12	THE GIRL CAN'T HELP IT — Little Richard (London)
12	13	FREIGHT TRAIN — Chas McDevitt Skiffle Group & Nancy Whiskey (Oriole)
11	13	I'LL TAKE YOU HOME AGAIN KATHLEEN — Slim Whitman (London)
17	15	TRUE LOVE — Bing Crosby & Grace Kelly (Capitol)
15	16	I'M NOT A JUVENILE DELINQUENT — Teenagers featuring Frankie Lymon (Columbia)
14	17	HEART — Max Bygraves (Decca)
10	17	DON'T YOU ROCK ME DADDY-O — Lonnie Donegan (Pye Nixa)
12	19	KNEE DEEP IN THE BLUES — Guy Mitchell (Philips)
20	20	SINGING THE BLUES — Guy Mitchell (Philips)
27	21	MANGOS — Rosemary Clooney (Philips)
22	22	LOVE IS A GOLDEN RING — Frankie Laine (Philips)
28	23	WHY BABY WHY — Pat Boone (London)
30	24	MARIANNE — Hilltoppers (London)
-	25	BUTTERFINGERS — Tommy Steele (Decca)
25	26	I'M WALKIN' — Fats Domino (London)
21	27	BUTTERFLY — Charlie Gracie (Parlophone)
23	28	HEART — Johnston Brothers (Decca)
-	29	THE WORLD IS MINE — Malcolm Vaughan (HMV)
-	30	ROUND AND ROUND — Jimmy Young (Decca)

last	this	11 May 1957
1	1	CUMBERLAND GAP — Lonnie Donegan (Pye Nixa)
10	2	BUTTERFLY — Andy Williams (London)
6	3	ROCK-A-BILLY — Guy Mitchell (Philips)
2	3	BANANA BOAT SONG (DAY-O) — Harry Belafonte (HMV)
4	5	BABY, BABY — Teenagers featuring Frankie Lymon (Columbia)
5	6	NINETY-NINE WAYS — Tab Hunter (London)
13	7	FREIGHT TRAIN — Chas McDevitt Skiffle Group & Nancy Whiskey (Oriole)
-	8	YES, TONIGHT, JOSEPHINE — Johnnie Ray (Philips)
11	9	WHEN I FALL IN LOVE — Nat King Cole (Capitol)
3	10	YOUNG LOVE — Tab Hunter (London)
13	11	I'LL TAKE YOU HOME AGAIN KATHLEEN — Slim Whitman (London)
7	12	LOOK HOMEWARD, ANGEL — Johnnie Ray (Philips)
-	13	TOO MUCH — Elvis Presley (HMV)
8	14	LONG TALL SALLY — Little Richard (London)
12	15	THE GIRL CAN'T HELP IT — Little Richard (London)
17	16	HEART — Max Bygraves (Decca)
23	17	WHY BABY WHY — Pat Boone (London)
-	18	CHAPEL OF THE ROSES — Malcolm Vaughan (HMV)
9	19	DON'T FORBID ME — Pat Boone (London)
22	20	LOVE IS A GOLDEN RING — Frankie Laine (Philips)
15	21	TRUE LOVE — Bing Crosby & Grace Kelly (Capitol)
26	22	I'M WALKIN' — Fats Domino (London)
16	23	I'M NOT A JUVENILE DELINQUENT — Teenagers featuring Frankie Lymon (Columbia)
27	24	BUTTERFLY — Charlie Gracie (Parlophone)
17	25	DON'T YOU ROCK ME DADDY-O — Lonnie Donegan (Pye Nixa)
21	26	MANGOS — Rosemary Clooney (Philips)
24	27	MARIANNE — Hilltoppers (London)
-	28	NORAH MALONE — Teresa Brewer (Vogue/Coral)
-	29	PARTY DOLL — Buddy Knox (Columbia)
29	30	THE WORLD IS MINE — Malcolm Vaughan (HMV)

last	this	18 May 1957
3	1	ROCK-A-BILLY — Guy Mitchell (Philips)
2	2	BUTTERFLY — Andy Williams (London)
9	3	WHEN I FALL IN LOVE — Nat King Cole (Capitol)
1	4	CUMBERLAND GAP — Lonnie Donegan (Pye Nixa)
5	5	BABY, BABY — Teenagers featuring Frankie Lymon (Columbia)
8	6	YES, TONIGHT, JOSEPHINE — Johnnie Ray (Philips)
6	7	NINETY-NINE WAYS — Tab Hunter (London)
3	8	BANANA BOAT SONG (DAY-O) — Harry Belafonte (HMV)
7	9	FREIGHT TRAIN — Chas McDevitt Skiffle Group & Nancy Whiskey (Oriole)
13	10	TOO MUCH — Elvis Presley (HMV)
11	11	I'LL TAKE YOU HOME AGAIN KATHLEEN — Slim Whitman (London)
10	12	YOUNG LOVE — Tab Hunter (London)
12	13	LOOK HOMEWARD, ANGEL — Johnnie Ray (Philips)
14	14	LONG TALL SALLY — Little Richard (London)
15	15	THE GIRL CAN'T HELP IT — Little Richard (London)
18	16	CHAPEL OF THE ROSES — Malcolm Vaughan (HMV)
24	17	BUTTERFLY — Charlie Gracie (Parlophone)
16	18	HEART — Max Bygraves (Decca)
-	19	BUTTERFINGERS — Tommy Steele (Decca)
20	19	LOVE IS A GOLDEN RING — Frankie Laine (Philips)
17	21	WHY BABY WHY — Pat Boone (London)
19	22	DON'T FORBID ME — Pat Boone (London)
27	23	MARIANNE — Hilltoppers (London)
21	24	TRUE LOVE — Bing Crosby & Grace Kelly (Capitol)
22	25	I'M WALKIN' — Fats Domino (London)
28	26	NORAH MALONE — Teresa Brewer (Vogue/Coral)
26	27	MANGOS — Rosemary Clooney (Philips)
-	28	I'M SORRY — Platters (Mercury)
-	29	SINGING THE BLUES — Tommy Steele (Decca)
29	30	PARTY DOLL — Buddy Knox (Columbia)

Guy Mitchell's (briefly) chart-topping *Rock-A-Billy* was, perversely, an energetic uptempo number which nonetheless had nothing at all to do with rockabilly - not as far as later years would understand the term, anyway. Buddy Knox's *Party Doll* (a million seller in the US) and Charlie Gracie's *Butterfly* had greater rockabilly essence, though Andy Williams's cover of the latter smoothed the edges. Williams apparently didn't think much of this track; he later purchased his early catalogue in order to keep it off the market.

May – June 1957

25 May 1957

last	this	Title / Artist
2	1	BUTTERFLY — Andy Williams (London)
1	2	ROCK-A-BILLY — Guy Mitchell (Philips)
6	3	YES, TONIGHT, JOSEPHINE — Johnnie Ray (Philips)
3	4	WHEN I FALL IN LOVE — Nat King Cole (Capitol)
4	5	CUMBERLAND GAP — Lonnie Donegan (Pye Nixa)
7	6	NINETY-NINE WAYS — Tab Hunter (London)
11	7	I'LL TAKE YOU HOME AGAIN KATHLEEN — Slim Whitman (London)
5	8	BABY, BABY — Teenagers featuring Frankie Lymon (Columbia)
10	9	TOO MUCH — Elvis Presley (HMV)
9	10	FREIGHT TRAIN — Chas McDevitt Skiffle Group & Nancy Whiskey (Oriole)
8	11	BANANA BOAT SONG (DAY-O) — Harry Belafonte (HMV)
17	12	BUTTERFLY — Charlie Gracie (Parlophone)
19	13	BUTTERFINGERS — Tommy Steele (Decca)
16	14	CHAPEL OF THE ROSES — Malcolm Vaughan (HMV)
-	15	MR WONDERFUL — Peggy Lee (Brunswick)
-	16	AROUND THE WORLD — Ronnie Hilton (HMV)
27	17	MANGOS — Rosemary Clooney (Philips)
13	18	LOOK HOMEWARD, ANGEL — Johnnie Ray (Philips)
12	19	YOUNG LOVE — Tab Hunter (London)
-	20	AROUND THE WORLD — Bing Crosby (Brunswick)
21	21	WHY BABY WHY — Pat Boone (London)
18	22	HEART — Max Bygraves (Decca)
19	23	LOVE IS A GOLDEN RING — Frankie Laine (Philips)
25	24	I'M WALKIN' — Fats Domino (London)
14	24	LONG TALL SALLY — Little Richard (London)
28	26	I'M SORRY — Platters (Mercury)
15	27	THE GIRL CAN'T HELP IT — Little Richard (London)
-	28	SHE'S GOT IT — Little Richard (London)
-	29	WE WILL MAKE LOVE — Russ Hamilton (Oriole)
24	30	TRUE LOVE — Bing Crosby & Grace Kelly (Capitol)
30	30	PARTY DOLL — Buddy Knox (Columbia)

1 June 1957

last	this	Title / Artist
1	1	BUTTERFLY — Andy Williams (London)
2	2	ROCK-A-BILLY — Guy Mitchell (Philips)
3	3	YES, TONIGHT, JOSEPHINE — Johnnie Ray (Philips)
4	4	WHEN I FALL IN LOVE — Nat King Cole (Capitol)
10	5	FREIGHT TRAIN — Chas McDevitt Skiffle Group & Nancy Whiskey (Oriole)
9	6	TOO MUCH Elvis Presley (HMV)
7	7	I'LL TAKE YOU HOME AGAIN KATHLEEN — Slim Whitman (London)
5	8	CUMBERLAND GAP — Lonnie Donegan (Pye Nixa)
6	9	NINETY-NINE WAYS — Tab Hunter (London)
15	10	MR WONDERFUL — Peggy Lee (Brunswick)
-	11	AROUND THE WORLD — Gracie Fields (Columbia)
8	12	BABY, BABY — Teenagers featuring Frankie Lymon (Columbia)
14	13	CHAPEL OF THE ROSES — Malcolm Vaughan (HMV)
16	14	AROUND THE WORLD — Ronnie Hilton (HMV)
20	14	AROUND THE WORLD — Bing Crosby (Brunswick)
13	16	BUTTERFINGERS — Tommy Steele (Decca)
12	17	BUTTERFLY — Charlie Gracie (Parlophone)
26	18	I'M SORRY — Platters (Mercury)
19	19	YOUNG LOVE — Tab Hunter (London)
11	20	BANANA BOAT SONG (DAY-O) — Harry Belafonte (HMV)
29	21	WE WILL MAKE LOVE — Russ Hamilton (Oriole)
-	22	LITTLE DARLIN' — Diamonds (Mercury)
24	22	I'M WALKIN' — Fats Domino (London)
17	24	MANGOS — Rosemary Clooney (Philips)
21	25	WHY BABY WHY — Pat Boone (London)
-	26	THE WORLD IS MINE — Malcolm Vaughan (HMV)
-	27	A WHITE SPORT COAT (AND A PINK CARNATION) — King Brothers (Parlophone)
-	27	AROUND THE WORLD — Mantovani (Decca)
28	29	SHE'S GOT IT — Little Richard (London)
-	30	STREAMLINE TRAIN — Vipers Skiffle Group (Parlophone)

8 June 1957

last	this	Title / Artist
3	1	YES, TONIGHT, JOSEPHINE — Johnnie Ray (Philips)
1	2	BUTTERFLY — Andy Williams (London)
4	3	WHEN I FALL IN LOVE — Nat King Cole (Capitol)
2	3	ROCK-A-BILLY — Guy Mitchell (Philips)
10	5	MR WONDERFUL — Peggy Lee (Brunswick)
5	6	FREIGHT TRAIN — Chas McDevitt Skiffle Group & Nancy Whiskey (Oriole)
14	7	AROUND THE WORLD — Ronnie Hilton (HMV)
11	8	AROUND THE WORLD — Gracie Fields (Columbia)
14	9	AROUND THE WORLD — Bing Crosby (Brunswick)
7	10	I'LL TAKE YOU HOME AGAIN KATHLEEN — Slim Whitman (London)
-	11	PUTTIN' ON THE STYLE /GAMBLIN' MAN — Lonnie Donegan (Pye Nixa)
6	12	TOO MUCH Elvis Presley (HMV)
8	13	CUMBERLAND GAP — Lonnie Donegan (Pye Nixa)
22	14	LITTLE DARLIN' — Diamonds (Mercury)
13	15	CHAPEL OF THE ROSES — Malcolm Vaughan (HMV)
9	16	NINETY-NINE WAYS — Tab Hunter (London)
27	17	A WHITE SPORT COAT (AND A PINK CARNATION) — King Brothers (Parlophone)
16	18	BUTTERFINGERS — Tommy Steele (Decca)
21	19	WE WILL MAKE LOVE — Russ Hamilton (Oriole)
27	20	AROUND THE WORLD — Mantovani (Decca)
18	21	I'M SORRY — Platters (Mercury)
12	22	BABY, BABY — Teenagers featuring Frankie Lymon (Columbia)
30	23	STREAMLINE TRAIN — Vipers Skiffle Group (Parlophone)
19	24	YOUNG LOVE — Tab Hunter (London)
-	25	A WHITE SPORT COAT (AND A PINK CARNATION) — Terry Dene (Decca)
17	26	BUTTERFLY — Charlie Gracie (Parlophone)
24	27	MANGOS — Rosemary Clooney (Philips)
20	28	BANANA BOAT SONG (DAY-O) — Harry Belafonte (HMV)
25	29	WHY BABY WHY — Pat Boone (London)
-	30	I'LL FIND YOU — David Whitfield (Decca)

15 June 1957

last	this	Title / Artist
1	1	YES, TONIGHT, JOSEPHINE — Johnnie Ray (Philips)
3	2	WHEN I FALL IN LOVE — Nat King Cole (Capitol)
2	3	BUTTERFLY — Andy Williams (London)
4	4	ROCK-A-BILLY — Guy Mitchell (Philips)
7	5	AROUND THE WORLD — Ronnie Hilton (HMV)
9	6	AROUND THE WORLD — Bing Crosby (Brunswick)
11	7	PUTTIN' ON THE STYLE/GAMBLIN' MAN — Lonnie Donegan (Pye Nixa)
14	8	LITTLE DARLIN' — Diamonds (Mercury)
6	9	FREIGHT TRAIN — Chas McDevitt Skiffle Group & Nancy Whiskey (Oriole)
8	10	AROUND THE WORLD — Gracie Fields (Columbia)
5	10	MR WONDERFUL — Peggy Lee (Brunswick)
12	12	TOO MUCH Elvis Presley (HMV)
15	13	CHAPEL OF THE ROSES — Malcolm Vaughan (HMV)
10	14	I'LL TAKE YOU HOME AGAIN KATHLEEN — Slim Whitman (London)
19	15	WE WILL MAKE LOVE — Russ Hamilton (Oriole)
17	16	A WHITE SPORT COAT (AND A PINK CARNATION) — King Brothers (Parlophone)
22	17	BABY, BABY — Teenagers featuring Frankie Lymon (Columbia)
21	18	I'M SORRY — Platters (Mercury)
13	19	CUMBERLAND GAP — Lonnie Donegan (Pye Nixa)
16	20	NINETY-NINE WAYS — Tab Hunter (London)
18	21	BUTTERFINGERS — Tommy Steele (Decca)
25	22	A WHITE SPORT COAT (AND A PINK CARNATION) — Terry Dene (Decca)
20	23	AROUND THE WORLD — Mantovani (Decca)
-	24	ALL SHOOK UP — Elvis Presley (HMV)
28	25	BANANA BOAT SONG (DAY-O) — Harry Belafonte (HMV)
-	26	FABULOUS — Charlie Gracie (Parlophone)
30	27	I'LL FIND YOU — David Whitfield (Decca)
-	28	GREENBACK DOLLAR — Chas McDevitt Group (Oriole)
-	29	ISLAND IN THE SUN — Harry Belafonte (RCA)
23	29	STREAMLINE TRAIN — Vipers Skiffle Group (Parlophone)

Nat King Cole's *When I Fall In Love* was not conceived as a single, and not released as one in the US. Capitol UK noted its potential and lifted it from Cole's album *Love Is The Thing*, whereupon it became his all-time biggest British hit. *Around The World In 80 Days* was packing the cinemas, and its theme song *Around The World* attracted multiple covers. Uniquely, on June 8, the Ronnie Hilton, Gracie Fields and Bing Crosby versions not only stood in the Top 10, but in adjacent slots.

22 June 1957

last week	this week	Entry
1	1	YES, TONIGHT, JOSEPHINE — Johnnie Ray (Philips)
7	2	PUTTIN' ON THE STYLE /GAMBLIN' MAN — Lonnie Donegan (Pye Nixa)
2	3	WHEN I FALL IN LOVE — Nat King Cole (Capitol)
3	4	BUTTERFLY — Andy Williams (London)
6	5	AROUND THE WORLD — Bing Crosby (Brunswick)
8	6	LITTLE DARLIN' — Diamonds (Mercury)
5	7	AROUND THE WORLD — Ronnie Hilton (HMV)
9	8	FREIGHT TRAIN — Chas McDevitt Skiffle Group & Nancy Whiskey (Oriole)
10	9	AROUND THE WORLD — Gracie Fields (Columbia)
10	10	MR WONDERFUL — Peggy Lee (Brunswick)
4	11	ROCK-A-BILLY — Guy Mitchell (Philips)
16	12	A WHITE SPORT COAT (AND A PINK CARNATION) — King Brothers (Parlophone)
15	13	WE WILL MAKE LOVE — Russ Hamilton (Oriole)
12	14	TOO MUCH — Elvis Presley (HMV)
29	15	ISLAND IN THE SUN — Harry Belafonte (RCA)
26	16	FABULOUS — Charlie Gracie (Parlophone)
14	17	I'LL TAKE YOU HOME AGAIN KATHLEEN — Slim Whitman (London)
21	18	BUTTERFINGERS — Tommy Steele (Decca)
22	18	A WHITE SPORT COAT (AND A PINK CARNATION) — Terry Dene (Decca)
13	20	CHAPEL OF THE ROSES — Malcolm Vaughan (HMV)
18	21	I'M SORRY — Platters (Mercury)
-	22	FIRE DOWN BELOW — Jeri Southern (Brunswick)
17	23	BABY, BABY — Teenagers featuring Frankie Lymon (Columbia)
-	24	SCHOOL DAY (RING! RING! GOES THE BELL) — Chuck Berry (Columbia)
-	24	I LIKE YOUR KIND OF LOVE — Andy Williams (London)
-	26	TRAVELLIN' HOME — Vera Lynn (Decca)
23	27	AROUND THE WORLD — Mantovani (Decca)
25	28	BANANA BOAT SONG (DAY-O) — Harry Belafonte (HMV)
19	29	CUMBERLAND GAP — Lonnie Donegan (Pye Nixa)
20	30	NINETY-NINE WAYS — Tab Hunter (London)

29 June 1957

last week	this week	Entry
2	1	PUTTIN' ON THE STYLE/GAMBLIN' MAN — Lonnie Donegan (Pye Nixa)
1	2	YES, TONIGHT, JOSEPHINE — Johnnie Ray (Philips)
3	3	WHEN I FALL IN LOVE — Nat King Cole (Capitol)
6	4	LITTLE DARLIN' — Diamonds (Mercury)
7	5	AROUND THE WORLD — Ronnie Hilton (HMV)
12	6	A WHITE SPORT COAT (AND A PINK CARNATION) — King Brothers (Parlophone)
7	7	ALL SHOOK UP — Elvis Presley (HMV)
5	8	AROUND THE WORLD — Bing Crosby (Brunswick)
13	9	WE WILL MAKE LOVE — Russ Hamilton (Oriole)
4	10	BUTTERFLY — Andy Williams (London)
11	11	ROCK-A-BILLY — Guy Mitchell (Philips)
10	12	MR WONDERFUL — Peggy Lee (Brunswick)
8	13	FREIGHT TRAIN — Chas McDevitt Skiffle Group & Nancy Whiskey (Oriole)
16	14	FABULOUS — Charlie Gracie (Parlophone)
9	15	AROUND THE WORLD — Gracie Fields (Columbia)
15	16	ISLAND IN THE SUN — Harry Belafonte (RCA)
18	17	BUTTERFINGERS — Tommy Steele (Decca)
14	18	TOO MUCH — Elvis Presley (HMV)
17	19	I'LL TAKE YOU HOME AGAIN KATHLEEN — Slim Whitman (London)
18	20	A WHITE SPORT COAT (AND A PINK CARNATION) — Terry Dene (Decca)
23	21	BABY, BABY — Teenagers featuring Frankie Lymon (Columbia)
20	22	CHAPEL OF THE ROSES — Malcolm Vaughan (HMV)
22	22	FIRE DOWN BELOW — Jeri Southern (Brunswick)
24	24	SCHOOL DAY (RING! RING! GOES THE BELL) — Chuck Berry (Columbia)
26	25	TRAVELLIN' HOME — Vera Lynn (Decca)
28	26	BANANA BOAT SONG (DAY-O) — Harry Belafonte (HMV)
24	27	I LIKE YOUR KIND OF LOVE — Andy Williams (London)
-	28	FORGOTTEN DREAMS — Leroy Anderson (Brunswick)
-	29	DARK MOON — Tony Brent (Columbia)
29	29	LUCILLE — Little Richard (London)

6 July 1957

last week	this week	Entry
1	1	PUTTIN' ON THE STYL /GAMBLIN' MAN — Lonnie Donegan (Pye Nixa)
7	2	ALL SHOOK UP — Elvis Presley (HMV)
2	3	YES, TONIGHT, JOSEPHINE — Johnnie Ray (Philips)
5	4	AROUND THE WORLD — Ronnie Hilton (HMV)
4	5	LITTLE DARLIN' — Diamonds (Mercury)
3	6	WHEN I FALL IN LOVE — Nat King Cole (Capitol)
12	7	MR WONDERFUL — Peggy Lee (Brunswick)
8	8	WE WILL MAKE LOVE — Russ Hamilton (Oriole)
6	9	A WHITE SPORT COAT (AND A PINK CARNATION) — King Brothers (Parlophone)
8	10	AROUND THE WORLD — Bing Crosby (Brunswick)
13	11	FREIGHT TRAIN — Chas McDevitt Skiffle Group & Nancy Whiskey (Oriole)
17	12	BUTTERFINGERS — Tommy Steele (Decca)
14	13	FABULOUS — Charlie Gracie (Parlophone)
11	14	ROCK-A-BILLY — Guy Mitchell (Philips)
10	15	BUTTERFLY — Andy Williams (London)
16	16	ISLAND IN THE SUN — Harry Belafonte (RCA)
15	17	AROUND THE WORLD — Gracie Fields (Columbia)
-	18	LOVE LETTERS IN THE SAND — Pat Boone (London)
29	18	LUCILLE — Little Richard (London)
25	20	TRAVELLIN' HOME — Vera Lynn (Decca)
19	21	I'LL TAKE YOU HOME AGAIN KATHLEEN — Slim Whitman (London)
20	22	A WHITE SPORT COAT (AND A PINK CARNATION) — Terry Dene (Decca)
23	23	I'M SORRY — Platters (Mercury)
27	24	I LIKE YOUR KIND OF LOVE — Andy Williams (London)
22	25	FIRE DOWN BELOW — Jeri Southern (Brunswick)
-	26	SCHOOL DAY — Don Lang (HMV)
29	27	DARK MOON — Tony Brent (Columbia)
-	28	WHEN ROCK AND ROLL CAME TO TRINIDAD — Nat King Cole (Capitol)
-	29	NINETY-NINE WAYS — Tab Hunter (London)
-	30	GREENBACK DOLLAR — Chas McDevitt Group (Oriole)

13 July 1957

last week	this week	Entry
2	1	ALL SHOOK UP — Elvis Presley (HMV)
1	2	PUTTIN' ON THE STYLE /GAMBLIN' MAN — Lonnie Donegan (Pye Nixa)
5	3	LITTLE DARLIN' — Diamonds (Mercury)
4	4	AROUND THE WORLD — Ronnie Hilton (HMV)
8	5	WE WILL MAKE LOVE — Russ Hamilton (Oriole)
3	6	YES, TONIGHT, JOSEPHINE — Johnnie Ray (Philips)
6	7	WHEN I FALL IN LOVE — Nat King Cole (Capitol)
9	8	A WHITE SPORT COAT (AND A PINK CARNATION) — King Brothers (Parlophone)
10	9	AROUND THE WORLD — Bing Crosby (Brunswick)
12	10	BUTTERFINGERS — Tommy Steele (Decca)
7	11	MR WONDERFUL — Peggy Lee (Brunswick)
18	12	LOVE LETTERS IN THE SAND — Pat Boone (London)
-	13	TEDDY BEAR — Elvis Presley (RCA)
13	14	FABULOUS — Charlie Gracie (Parlophone)
11	15	FREIGHT TRAIN — Chas McDevitt Skiffle Group & Nancy Whiskey (Oriole)
24	16	I LIKE YOUR KIND OF LOVE — Andy Williams (London)
15	17	BUTTERFLY — Andy Williams (London)
18	18	LUCILLE — Little Richard (London)
-	19	BYE BYE LOVE — Everly Brothers (London)
15	20	ISLAND IN THE SUN — Harry Belafonte (RCA)
22	21	A WHITE SPORT COAT (AND A PINK CARNATION) — Terry Dene (Decca)
20	22	TRAVELLIN' HOME — Vera Lynn (Decca)
23	23	ROCK-A-BILLY — Guy Mitchell (Philips)
17	24	AROUND THE WORLD — Gracie Fields (Columbia)
-	25	SCHOOL DAY (RING! RING! GOES THE BELL) — Chuck Berry (Columbia)
-	26	TOO MUCH — Elvis Presley (HMV)
27	27	DARK MOON — Tony Brent (Columbia)
-	28	START MOVIN' (IN MY DIRECTION) — Sal Mineo (Philips)
26	29	SCHOOL DAY — Don Lang (HMV)
-	30	FORGOTTEN DREAMS — Leroy Anderson (Brunswick)

With the double A-side *Puttin' On The Style/Gamblin' Man*, Lonnie Donegan scored his second chart-topper in two releases - the first British artist to do so. Elvis Presley's rush-releasd *All Shook Up* then became his first British Number One, with HMV's haste possibly influenced by the fact that its license to release new American RCA product was about to terminate - RCA's own UK label debuted in the first week of July, and Elvis' next single *Teddy Bear* marked its chart debut just a week later.

July – August 1957

In a decade totally dominated by labels marketed through the big three record companies EMI, Decca and Philips, with Pye Nixa providing most new blood, the summer of 1957 was also notable for the succes of the tiny independent Oriole label, as it scored simultaneous Top 20 entries with Chas McDevitt's skiffle-y *Freight Train* and ex-Butlin Redcoat Russ Hamilton's self-penned ballad *We Will Make Love*. Amazingly, both acts also charted in the US, though the US opted for Hamilton's UK B-side, *Rainbow*.

last week	this week	17 August 1957
1	1	ALL SHOOK UP — Elvis Presley (HMV)
5	2	LOVE LETTERS IN THE SAND — Pat Boone (London)
6	3	TEDDY BEAR — Elvis Presley (RCA)
2	4	PUTTIN' ON THE STYLE/GAMBLIN' MAN — Lonnie Donegan (Pye Nixa)
7	5	ISLAND IN THE SUN — Harry Belafonte (RCA)
3	6	LITTLE DARLIN' — Diamonds (Mercury)
4	7	WE WILL MAKE LOVE — Russ Hamilton (Oriole)
12	8	LAST TRAIN TO SAN FERNANDO — Johnny Duncan & the Blue Grass Boys (Columbia)
8	8	BYE BYE LOVE — Everly Brothers (London)
16	10	AROUND THE WORLD — Bing Crosby (Brunswick)
15	11	WITH ALL MY HEART — Petula Clark (Pye Nixa)
12	12	BUTTERFINGERS — Tommy Steele (Decca)
26	13	DIANA — Paul Anka (Columbia)
9	14	AROUND THE WORLD — Ronnie Hilton (HMV)
23	15	START MOVIN' (IN MY DIRECTION) — Terry Dene (Decca)
17	16	WHEN I FALL IN LOVE — Nat King Cole (Capitol)
14	17	A WHITE SPORT COAT (AND A PINK CARNATION) — King Brothers (Parlophone)
10	18	LUCILLE — Little Richard (London)
18	19	MR WONDERFUL — Peggy Lee (Brunswick)
11	20	YES, TONIGHT, JOSEPHINE — Johnnie Ray (Philips)
21	20	FABULOUS — Charlie Gracie (Parlophone)
19	22	START MOVIN' (IN MY DIRECTION) — Sal Mineo (Philips)
20	23	ALL STAR HIT PARADE NO.2 — Various Artists (Decca)
21	24	ANY OLD IRON — Peter Sellers (Parlophone)
29	24	I'M GONNA SIT RIGHT DOWN AND WRITE MYSELF A LETTER — Billy Williams (Vogue-Coral)
30	26	IN THE MIDDLE OF AN ISLAND — King Brothers (Parlophone)
25	26	I LIKE YOUR KIND OF LOVE — Andy Williams (London)
24	28	DARK MOON — Tony Brent (Columbia)
27	29	FORGOTTEN DREAMS — Cyril Stapleton (Decca)
-	30	WATER, WATER/A HANDFUL OF SONGS — Tommy Steele (Decca)

		24 August 1957
1	1	ALL SHOOK UP — Elvis Presley (HMV)
2	2	LOVE LETTERS IN THE SAND — Pat Boone (London)
5	3	ISLAND IN THE SUN — Harry Belafonte (RCA)
13	4	DIANA — Paul Anka (Columbia)
3	5	TEDDY BEAR — Elvis Presley (RCA)
8	6	LAST TRAIN TO SAN FERNANDO — Johnny Duncan & the Blue Grass Boys (Columbia)
7	7	BYE BYE LOVE — Everly Brothers (London)
4	8	PUTTIN' ON THE STYLE/GAMBLIN' MAN — Lonnie Donegan (Pye Nixa)
11	9	WITH ALL MY HEART — Petula Clark (Pye Nixa)
7	10	WE WILL MAKE LOVE — Russ Hamilton (Oriole)
6	11	LITTLE DARLIN' — Diamonds (Mercury)
20	12	FABULOUS — Charlie Gracie (Parlophone)
14	13	AROUND THE WORLD — Ronnie Hilton (HMV)
12	14	BUTTERFINGERS — Tommy Steele (Decca)
23	15	ALL STAR HIT PARADE NO.2 — Various Artists (Decca)
22	16	START MOVIN' (IN MY DIRECTION) — Sal Mineo (Philips)
10	17	AROUND THE WORLD — Bing Crosby (Brunswick)
28	18	DARK MOON — Tony Brent (Columbia)
16	19	WHEN I FALL IN LOVE — Nat King Cole (Capitol)
15	20	START MOVIN' (IN MY DIRECTION) — Terry Dene (Decca)
30	21	WATER, WATER/A HANDFUL OF SONGS — Tommy Steele (Decca)
17	22	A WHITE SPORT COAT (AND A PINK CARNATION) — King Brothers (Parlophone)
18	23	LUCILLE — Little Richard (London)
-	24	WANDERING EYES/I LOVE YOU SO MUCH IT HURTS — Charlie Gracie (London)
24	24	I'M GONNA SIT RIGHT DOWN AND WRITE MYSELF A LETTER — Billy Williams (Vogue-Coral)
26	26	IN THE MIDDLE OF AN ISLAND — King Brothers (Parlophone)
20	27	YES, TONIGHT, JOSEPHINE — Johnnie Ray (Philips)
-	28	IN THE MIDDLE OF A DARK, DARK NIGHT/SWEET STUFF — Guy Mitchell (Philips)
26	29	I LIKE YOUR KIND OF LOVE — Andy Williams (London)
-	30	FIRE DOWN BELOW — Shirley Bassey (Philips)

		31 August 1957
4	1	DIANA — Paul Anka (Columbia)
2	2	LOVE LETTERS IN THE SAND — Pat Boone (London)
1	3	ALL SHOOK UP — Elvis Presley (HMV)
3	4	ISLAND IN THE SUN — Harry Belafonte (RCA)
6	5	LAST TRAIN TO SAN FERNANDO — Johnny Duncan & the Blue Grass Boys (Columbia)
7	6	BYE BYE LOVE — Everly Brothers (London)
5	7	TEDDY BEAR — Elvis Presley (RCA)
12	8	FABULOUS — Charlie Gracie (Parlophone)
9	9	WITH ALL MY HEART — Petula Clark (Pye Nixa)
10	10	WE WILL MAKE LOVE — Russ Hamilton (Oriole)
8	11	PUTTIN' ON THE STYLE/GAMBLIN' MAN — Lonnie Donegan (Pye Nixa)
-	12	SHIRALEE — Tommy Steele (Decca)
21	13	WATER, WATER/A HANDFUL OF SONGS — Tommy Steele (Decca)
24	14	WANDERING EYES/I LOVE YOU SO MUCH IT HURTS — Charlie Gracie (London)
11	15	LITTLE DARLIN' — Diamonds (Mercury)
-	16	PARALYSED — Elvis Presley (HMV)
18	17	DARK MOON — Tony Brent (Columbia)
16	18	START MOVIN' (IN MY DIRECTION) — Sal Mineo (Philips)
13	19	AROUND THE WORLD — Ronnie Hilton (HMV)
14	20	BUTTERFINGERS — Tommy Steele (Decca)
15	21	ALL STAR HIT PARADE NO.2 — Various Artists (Decca)
24	22	I'M GONNA SIT RIGHT DOWN AND WRITE MYSELF A LETTER — Billy Williams (Vogue-Coral)
-	23	TAMMY — Debbie Reynolds (Vogue-Coral)
26	23	IN THE MIDDLE OF AN ISLAND — King Brothers (Parlophone)
28	25	IN THE MIDDLE OF A DARK, DARK NIGHT/SWEET STUFF — Guy Mitchell (Philips)
20	26	START MOVIN' (IN MY DIRECTION) — Terry Dene (Decca)
22	27	A WHITE SPORT COAT (AND A PINK CARNATION) — King Brothers (Parlophone)
17	28	AROUND THE WORLD — Bing Crosby (Brunswick)
-	29	BUTTERFLY — Andy Williams (London)
19	30	WHEN I FALL IN LOVE — Nat King Cole (Capitol)

		7 September 1957
1	1	DIANA — Paul Anka (Columbia)
2	2	LOVE LETTERS IN THE SAND — Pat Boone (London)
5	3	LAST TRAIN TO SAN FERNANDO — Johnny Duncan & the Blue Grass Boys (Columbia)
4	4	ISLAND IN THE SUN — Harry Belafonte (RCA)
3	5	ALL SHOOK UP — Elvis Presley (HMV)
9	6	WITH ALL MY HEART — Petula Clark (Pye Nixa)
13	7	WATER, WATER/A HANDFUL OF SONGS — Tommy Steele (Decca)
6	8	BYE BYE LOVE — Everly Brothers (London)
14	9	WANDERING EYES — Charlie Gracie (London)
7	10	TEDDY BEAR — Elvis Presley (RCA)
12	11	SHIRALEE — Tommy Steele (Decca)
15	12	LITTLE DARLIN' — Diamonds (Mercury)
10	12	WE WILL MAKE LOVE — Russ Hamilton (Oriole)
8	14	FABULOUS — Charlie Gracie (Parlophone)
16	14	PARALYSED — Elvis Presley (HMV)
11	16	PUTTIN' ON THE STYLE/GAMBLIN' MAN — Lonnie Donegan (Pye Nixa)
23	17	TAMMY — Debbie Reynolds (Vogue-Coral)
18	18	START MOVIN' (IN MY DIRECTION) — Sal Mineo (Philips)
17	19	DARK MOON — Tony Brent (Columbia)
-	20	I LOVE YOU SO MUCH IT HURTS — Charlie Gracie (Parlophone)
19	21	AROUND THE WORLD — Ronnie Hilton (HMV)
23	22	IN THE MIDDLE OF AN ISLAND — King Brothers (Parlophone)
-	23	SCARLET RIBBONS — Harry Belafonte (HMV)
-	24	ANY OLD IRON — Peter Sellers (Parlophone)
21	25	ALL STAR HIT PARADE NO.2 — Various Artists (Decca)
20	26	BUTTERFINGERS — Tommy Steele (Decca)
-	27	BUILD YOUR LOVE — Johnnie Ray (Philips)
22	27	I'M GONNA SIT RIGHT DOWN AND WRITE MYSELF A LETTER — Billy Williams (Vogue-Coral)
-	29	YOU, YOU ROMEO — Shirley Bassey (Philips)
-	30	FORGOTTEN DREAMS — Leroy Anderson (Brunswick)
26	30	START MOVIN' (IN MY DIRECTION) — Terry Dene (Decca)

America's biggest-selling single of 1957, Pat Boone's *Love Letters In The Sand*, reached its UK peak of Number Two in mid-August, unable (like Elvis' own *Teddy Bear*) to shift *All Shook Up*. The song which did end Presley's run at the top was 15-year-old Canadian Paul Anka's self-penned *Diana* - a song about Anka's crush on his family's babysitter. The Everly Brothers began their illustrious hit career with *Bye Bye Love*, and Tommy Steele had three simultaneous Top 20 entries on August 31.

51

September – October 1957

14 September 1957

last	this		
1	1	DIANA	Paul Anka (Columbia)
3	2	LAST TRAIN TO SAN FERNANDO	Johnny Duncan & the Blue Grass Boys (Columbia)
2	3	LOVE LETTERS IN THE SAND	Pat Boone (London)
4	4	ISLAND IN THE SUN	Harry Belafonte (RCA)
7	5	WATER, WATER/A HANDFUL OF SONGS	Tommy Steele (Decca)
5	6	ALL SHOOK UP	Elvis Presley (HMV)
6	7	WITH ALL MY HEART	Petula Clark (Pye Nixa)
14	8	PARALYSED	Elvis Presley (HMV)
9	9	WANDERING EYES	Charlie Gracie (London)
8	10	BYE BYE LOVE	Everly Brothers (London)
17	11	TAMMY	Debbie Reynolds (Vogue-Coral)
10	12	TEDDY BEAR	Elvis Presley (RCA)
16	13	PUTTIN' ON THE STYLE/GAMBLIN' MAN	Lonnie Donegan (Pye Nixa)
14	14	FABULOUS	Charlie Gracie (Parlophone)
12	15	LITTLE DARLIN'	Diamonds (Mercury)
11	16	SHIRALEE	Tommy Steele (Decca)
-	17	JENNY JENNY	Little Richard (London)
27	18	BUILD YOUR LOVE	Johnnie Ray (Philips)
12	19	WE WILL MAKE LOVE	Russ Hamilton (Oriole)
-	19	STARDUST	Billy Ward & the Dominoes (London)
24	21	ANY OLD IRON	Peter Sellers (Parlophone)
22	22	IN THE MIDDLE OF AN ISLAND	King Brothers (Parlophone)
23	22	SCARLET RIBBONS	Harry Belafonte (HMV)
30	24	FORGOTTEN DREAMS	Leroy Anderson (Brunswick)
27	25	I'M GONNA SIT RIGHT DOWN AND WRITE MYSELF A LETTER	Billy Williams (Vogue-Coral)
21	26	AROUND THE WORLD	Ronnie Hilton (HMV)
18	27	START MOVIN' (IN MY DIRECTION)	Sal Mineo (Philips)
19	28	DARK MOON	Tony Brent (Columbia)
20	28	I LOVE YOU SO MUCH IT HURTS	Charlie Gracie (Parlophone)
29	30	YOU, YOU ROMEO	Shirley Bassey (Philips)

21 September 1957

1	1	DIANA	Paul Anka (Columbia)
3	2	LOVE LETTERS IN THE SAND	Pat Boone (London)
2	3	LAST TRAIN TO SAN FERNANDO	Johnny Duncan & the Blue Grass Boys (Columbia)
4	4	ISLAND IN THE SUN	Harry Belafonte (RCA)
7	5	WITH ALL MY HEART	Petula Clark (Pye Nixa)
5	6	WATER, WATER/A HANDFUL OF SONGS	Tommy Steele (Decca)
6	7	ALL SHOOK UP	Elvis Presley (HMV)
9	8	WANDERING EYES	Charlie Gracie (London)
8	9	PARALYSED	Elvis Presley (HMV)
11	10	TAMMY	Debbie Reynolds (Vogue-Coral)
13	11	PUTTIN' ON THE STYLE/GAMBLIN' MAN	Lonnie Donegan (Pye Nixa)
10	12	BYE BYE LOVE	Everly Brothers (London)
12	13	TEDDY BEAR	Elvis Presley (RCA)
14	14	FABULOUS	Charlie Gracie (Parlophone)
19	15	STARDUST	Billy Ward & the Dominoes (London)
16	16	WE WILL MAKE LOVE	Russ Hamilton (Oriole)
17	16	JENNY JENNY	Little Richard (London)
18	18	BUILD YOUR LOVE	Johnnie Ray (Philips)
22	19	IN THE MIDDLE OF AN ISLAND	King Brothers (Parlophone)
22	20	SCARLET RIBBONS	Harry Belafonte (HMV)
15	21	LITTLE DARLIN'	Diamonds (Mercury)
16	22	SHIRALEE	Tommy Steele (Decca)
21	23	ANY OLD IRON	Peter Sellers (Parlophone)
-	24	GOODY GOODY	Frankie Lymon & the Teenagers (Columbia)
-	25	SHORT FAT FANNIE	Larry Williams (London)
17	26	START MOVIN' (IN MY DIRECTION)	Sal Mineo (Philips)
-	27	FREIGHT TRAIN	Chas McDevitt Skiffle Group & Nancy Whiskey (Oriole)
28	28	DARK MOON	Tony Brent (Columbia)
26	29	AROUND THE WORLD	Ronnie Hilton (HMV)
25	30	I'M GONNA SIT RIGHT DOWN AND WRITE MYSELF A LETTER	Billy Williams (Vogue-Coral)

28 September 1957

1	1	DIANA	Paul Anka (Columbia)
2	2	LOVE LETTERS IN THE SAND	Pat Boone (London)
3	3	LAST TRAIN TO SAN FERNANDO	Johnny Duncan & the Blue Grass Boys (Columbia)
5	4	WITH ALL MY HEART	Petula Clark (Pye Nixa)
4	5	ISLAND IN THE SUN	Harry Belafonte (RCA)
6	6	WATER, WATER/A HANDFUL OF SONGS	Tommy Steele (Decca)
8	7	WANDERING EYES	Charlie Gracie (London)
7	8	ALL SHOOK UP	Elvis Presley (HMV)
9	9	PARALYSED	Elvis Presley (HMV)
10	10	TAMMY	Debbie Reynolds (Vogue-Coral)
16	11	JENNY JENNY	Little Richard (London)
-	12	THAT'LL BE THE DAY	Crickets (Vogue Coral)
15	13	STARDUST	Billy Ward & the Dominoes (London)
11	14	PUTTIN' ON THE STYLE/GAMBLIN' MAN	Lonnie Donegan (Pye Nixa)
12	15	BYE BYE LOVE	Everly Brothers (London)
13	16	TEDDY BEAR	Elvis Presley (RCA)
18	17	BUILD YOUR LOVE	Johnnie Ray (Philips)
20	18	SCARLET RIBBONS	Harry Belafonte (HMV)
23	19	ANY OLD IRON	Peter Sellers (Parlophone)
19	20	IN THE MIDDLE OF AN ISLAND	King Brothers (Parlophone)
25	21	SHORT FAT FANNIE	Larry Williams (London)
-	22	PASSING STRANGERS	Billy Eckstine & Sarah Vaughan (Mercury)
-	23	REMEMBER YOU'RE MINE/GOLD MINE IN THE SKY	Pat Boone (London)
16	24	WE WILL MAKE LOVE	Russ Hamilton (Oriole)
14	25	FABULOUS	Charlie Gracie (Parlophone)
24	26	GOODY GOODY	Frankie Lymon & the Teenagers (Columbia)
-	27	WEDDING RING	Russ Hamilton (Oriole)
28	28	DARK MOON	Tony Brent (Columbia)
-	29	WHOLE LOTTA SHAKIN' GOIN' ON	Jerry Lee Lewis (London)
-	30	SEARCHIN'	Coasters (London)

5 October 1957

1	1	DIANA	Paul Anka (Columbia)
3	2	LAST TRAIN TO SAN FERNANDO	Johnny Duncan & the Blue Grass Boys (Columbia)
2	3	LOVE LETTERS IN THE SAND	Pat Boone (London)
5	4	ISLAND IN THE SUN	Harry Belafonte (RCA)
6	5	WATER, WATER/A HANDFUL OF SONGS	Tommy Steele (Decca)
4	6	WITH ALL MY HEART	Petula Clark (Pye Nixa)
10	7	TAMMY	Debbie Reynolds (Vogue-Coral)
8	8	ALL SHOOK UP	Elvis Presley (HMV)
7	9	WANDERING EYES	Charlie Gracie (London)
12	10	THAT'LL BE THE DAY	Crickets (Vogue Coral)
9	11	PARALYSED	Elvis Presley (HMV)
16	12	TEDDY BEAR	Elvis Presley (RCA)
11	13	JENNY JENNY	Little Richard (London)
13	14	STARDUST	Billy Ward & the Dominoes (London)
-	15	PARTY	Elvis Presley (RCA)
14	16	PUTTIN' ON THE STYLE/GAMBLIN' MAN	Lonnie Donegan (Pye Nixa)
23	17	REMEMBER YOU'RE MINE/GOLD MINE IN THE SKY	Pat Boone (London)
-	18	MAN ON FIRE/WANDERING EYES	Frankie Vaughan (Philips)
29	18	WHOLE LOTTA SHAKIN' GOIN' ON	Jerry Lee Lewis (London)
20	20	IN THE MIDDLE OF AN ISLAND	King Brothers (Parlophone)
19	21	ANY OLD IRON	Peter Sellers (Parlophone)
21	21	SHORT FAT FANNIE	Larry Williams (London)
17	23	BUILD YOUR LOVE	Johnnie Ray (Philips)
18	24	SCARLET RIBBONS	Harry Belafonte (HMV)
15	25	BYE BYE LOVE	Everly Brothers (London)
24	26	WE WILL MAKE LOVE	Russ Hamilton (Oriole)
22	26	PASSING STRANGERS	Billy Eckstine & Sarah Vaughan (Mercury)
27	28	WEDDING RING	Russ Hamilton (Oriole)
-	28	UP ABOVE MY HEAD/GOOD EVENING FRIENDS	Frankie Laine & Johnnie Ray (Philips)
26	30	GOODY GOODY	Frankie Lymon & the Teenagers (Columbia)

Diana quickly developed into 1957's biggest hit so far, with its nine-week Number One run the longest since Slim Whitman's 11 weeks on top in 1955. By the time its sales finally died away during 1958, *Diana* would have sold 1,180,000 copies in Britain, the third single in UK chart history to reach seven figures (the second was still awaiting release at this time). Significant chart debuts, meanwhile, came from the Crickets (led by Buddy Holly), the Coasters and 'Killer' Jerry Lee Lewis.

October – November 1957

12 October 1957

last	this	title	artist (label)
1	1	DIANA	Paul Anka (Columbia)
3	2	LOVE LETTERS IN THE SAND	Pat Boone (London)
7	3	TAMMY	Debbie Reynolds (Vogue-Coral)
2	4	LAST TRAIN TO SAN FERNANDO	Johnny Duncan & the Blue Grass Boys (Columbia)
4	5	ISLAND IN THE SUN	Harry Belafonte (RCA)
5	6	WATER, WATER/A HANDFUL OF SONGS	Tommy Steele (Decca)
6	7	WITH ALL MY HEART	Petula Clark (Pye Nixa)
9	7	WANDERING EYES	Charlie Gracie (London)
10	9	THAT'LL BE THE DAY	Crickets (Vogue Coral)
8	10	ALL SHOOK UP	Elvis Presley (HMV)
15	11	PARTY	Elvis Presley (RCA)
11	12	PARALYSED	Elvis Presley (HMV)
12	12	TEDDY BEAR	Elvis Presley (RCA)
18	14	MAN ON FIRE/WANDERING EYES	Frankie Vaughan (Philips)
17	15	REMEMBER YOU'RE MINE/GOLD MINE IN THE SKY	Pat Boone (London)
18	16	WHOLE LOTTA SHAKIN' GOIN' ON	Jerry Lee Lewis (London)
21	17	ANY OLD IRON	Peter Sellers (Parlophone)
25	18	BYE BYE LOVE	Everly Brothers (London)
-	19	MY DIXIE DARLING	Lonnie Donegan (Pye Nixa)
13	20	JENNY JENNY	Little Richard (London)
14	21	STARDUST	Billy Ward & the Dominoes (London)
21	22	SHORT FAT FANNIE	Larry Williams (London)
-	23	BE MY GIRL	Jim Dale (Parlophone)
20	24	IN THE MIDDLE OF AN ISLAND	King Brothers (Parlophone)
28	25	WEDDING RING	Russ Hamilton (Oriole)
-	26	CALL ROSIE ON THE PHONE	Guy Mitchell (Philips)
16	27	PUTTIN' ON THE STYLE/GAMBLIN' MAN	Lonnie Donegan (Pye Nixa)
23	27	BUILD YOUR LOVE	Johnnie Ray (Philips)
29	29	UP ABOVE MY HEAD/GOOD EVENING FRIENDS	Frankie Laine & Johnnie Ray (Philips)
24	30	SCARLET RIBBONS	Harry Belafonte (HMV)

19 October 1957

last	this	title	artist (label)
1	1	DIANA	Paul Anka (Columbia)
9	2	THAT'LL BE THE DAY	Crickets (Vogue Coral)
3	3	TAMMY	Debbie Reynolds (Vogue-Coral)
2	4	LOVE LETTERS IN THE SAND	Pat Boone (London)
11	5	PARTY	Elvis Presley (RCA)
5	6	ISLAND IN THE SUN	Harry Belafonte (RCA)
4	7	LAST TRAIN TO SAN FERNANDO	Johnny Duncan & the Blue Grass Boys (Columbia)
7	8	WITH ALL MY HEART	Petula Clark (Pye Nixa)
7	9	WANDERING EYES	Charlie Gracie (London)
15	10	REMEMBER YOU'RE MINE/GOLD MINE IN THE SKY	Pat Boone (London)
6	11	WATER, WATER/A HANDFUL OF SONGS	Tommy Steele (Decca)
14	12	MAN ON FIRE/WANDERING EYES	Frankie Vaughan (Philips)
12	13	TEDDY BEAR	Elvis Presley (RCA)
19	14	MY DIXIE DARLING	Lonnie Donegan (Pye Nixa)
10	15	ALL SHOOK UP	Elvis Presley (HMV)
16	16	WHOLE LOTTA SHAKIN' GOIN' ON	Jerry Lee Lewis (London)
12	17	PARALYSED	Elvis Presley (HMV)
26	17	CALL ROSIE ON THE PHONE	Guy Mitchell (Philips)
-	19	GOT A LOT O' LIVIN' TO DO	Elvis Presley (RCA)
25	20	WEDDING RING	Russ Hamilton (Oriole)
-	21	MY PERSONAL POSSESSION	Nat King Cole (Capitol)
18	22	BYE BYE LOVE	Everly Brothers (London)
21	23	STARDUST	Billy Ward & the Dominoes (London)
23	23	BE MY GIRL	Jim Dale (Parlophone)
17	25	ANY OLD IRON	Peter Sellers (Parlophone)
22	25	SHORT FAT FANNIE	Larry Williams (London)
29	27	UP ABOVE MY HEAD/GOOD EVENING FRIENDS	Frankie Laine & Johnnie Ray (Philips)
-	28	I'M GONNA SIT RIGHT DOWN AND WRITE MYSELF A LETTER	Billy Williams (Vogue-Coral)
24	29	IN THE MIDDLE OF AN ISLAND	King Brothers (Parlophone)
27	30	BUILD YOUR LOVE	Johnnie Ray (Philips)

26 October 1957

last	this	title	artist (label)
1	1	DIANA	Paul Anka (Columbia)
5	2	PARTY	Elvis Presley (RCA)
2	3	THAT'LL BE THE DAY	Crickets (Vogue Coral)
4	4	TAMMY	Debbie Reynolds (Vogue-Coral)
4	5	LOVE LETTERS IN THE SAND	Pat Boone (London)
9	6	WANDERING EYES	Charlie Gracie (London)
6	7	ISLAND IN THE SUN	Harry Belafonte (RCA)
10	8	REMEMBER YOU'RE MINE/GOLD MINE IN THE SKY	Pat Boone (London)
13	9	TEDDY BEAR	Elvis Presley (RCA)
16	10	WHOLE LOTTA SHAKIN' GOIN' ON	Jerry Lee Lewis (London)
8	11	WITH ALL MY HEART	Petula Clark (Pye Nixa)
11	12	WATER, WATER/A HANDFUL OF SONGS	Tommy Steele (Decca)
12	13	MAN ON FIRE/WANDERING EYES	Frankie Vaughan (Philips)
14	14	MY DIXIE DARLING	Lonnie Donegan (Pye Nixa)
7	15	LAST TRAIN TO SAN FERNANDO	Johnny Duncan & the Blue Grass Boys (Columbia)
15	16	ALL SHOOK UP	Elvis Presley (HMV)
17	17	CALL ROSIE ON THE PHONE	Guy Mitchell (Philips)
23	18	STARDUST	Billy Ward & the Dominoes (London)
23	19	BE MY GIRL	Jim Dale (Parlophone)
17	20	PARALYSED	Elvis Presley (HMV)
19	20	GOT A LOT O' LIVIN' TO DO	Elvis Presley (RCA)
25	22	SHORT FAT FANNIE	Larry Williams (London)
20	23	WEDDING RING	Russ Hamilton (Oriole)
-	24	STARDUST	Nat King Cole (Capitol)
25	25	UP ABOVE MY HEAD/GOOD EVENING FRIENDS	Frankie Laine & Johnnie Ray (Philips)
25	26	ANY OLD IRON	Peter Sellers (Parlophone)
-	27	BLUE, BLUE HEARTACHES	Johnny Duncan & the B Grass Boys (Columbia)
21	28	MY PERSONAL POSSESSION	Nat King Cole (Capitol)
22	29	BYE BYE LOVE	Everly Brothers (London)
29	30	IN THE MIDDLE OF AN ISLAND	King Brothers (Parlophone)

2 November 1957

last	this	title	artist (label)
3	1	THAT'LL BE THE DAY	Crickets (Vogue Coral)
4	2	TAMMY	Debbie Reynolds (Vogue-Coral)
1	3	DIANA	Paul Anka (Columbia)
2	4	PARTY	Elvis Presley (RCA)
8	5	REMEMBER YOU'RE MINE/GOLD MINE IN THE SKY	Pat Boone (London)
13	6	MAN ON FIRE/WANDERING EYES	Frankie Vaughan (Philips)
19	7	BE MY GIRL	Jim Dale (Parlophone)
10	8	WHOLE LOTTA SHAKIN' GOIN' ON	Jerry Lee Lewis (London)
12	9	WATER, WATER/A HANDFUL OF SONGS	Tommy Steele (Decca)
7	10	ISLAND IN THE SUN	Harry Belafonte (RCA)
6	11	WANDERING EYES	Charlie Gracie (London)
9	12	TEDDY BEAR	Elvis Presley (RCA)
5	13	LOVE LETTERS IN THE SAND	Pat Boone (London)
11	14	WITH ALL MY HEART	Petula Clark (Pye Nixa)
14	15	MY DIXIE DARLING	Lonnie Donegan (Pye Nixa)
16	16	ALL SHOOK UP	Elvis Presley (HMV)
15	16	LAST TRAIN TO SAN FERNANDO	Johnny Duncan & the Blue Grass Boys (Columbia)
17	18	CALL ROSIE ON THE PHONE	Guy Mitchell (Philips)
18	19	STARDUST	Billy Ward & the Dominoes (London)
-	20	TRYING TO GET TO YOU	Elvis Presley (HMV)
20	21	GOT A LOT O' LIVIN' TO DO	Elvis Presley (RCA)
-	22	GOTTA HAVE SOMETHING IN THE BANK, FRANK	Frankie Vaughan & the Kaye Sisters (Philips)
22	23	SHORT FAT FANNIE	Larry Williams (London)
-	24	LOVING YOU	Elvis Presley (RCA)
23	25	WEDDING RING	Russ Hamilton (Oriole)
20	26	PARALYSED	Elvis Presley (HMV)
24	27	STARDUST	Nat King Cole (Capitol)
30	28	IN THE MIDDLE OF AN ISLAND	King Brothers (Parlophone)
-	29	MARY'S BOY CHILD	Harry Belafonte (RCA)
-	30	HONEYCOMB	Jimmie Rodgers (Columbia)

Partly thanks to his being on two labels (HMV retained rights to issue earlier RCA material until mid-1958), and to buyers requesting the B-sides of *Teddy Bear* (Loving You) and *Party* (Got A Lot O' Livin' To Do), the chart was beginning to fill up with Elvis Presley singles. By November 2 he had seven simultaneously in the Top 30, with an additional title - *Lawdy Miss Clawdy* - waiting in the wings to enter the following week. This is a Top 30 record which has never been broken.

November 1957

9 November 1957

1 1 THAT'LL BE THE DAY Crickets (Vogue Coral)
4 2 PARTY Elvis Presley (RCA)
2 3 TAMMY Debbie Reynolds (Vogue-Coral)
3 4 DIANA Paul Anka (Columbia)
5 5 REMEMBER YOU'RE MINE/GOLD MINE IN THE SKY Pat Boone (London)
6 6 MAN ON FIRE/WANDERING EYES Frankie Vaughan (Philips)
7 7 BE MY GIRL Jim Dale (Parlophone)
22 8 GOTTA HAVE SOMETHING IN THE BANK, FRANK Frankie Vaughan & the Kaye Sisters (Philips)
8 9 WHOLE LOTTA SHAKIN' GOIN' ON Jerry Lee Lewis (London)
15 10 MY DIXIE DARLING Lonnie Donegan (Pye Nixa)
11 11 WANDERING EYES Charlie Gracie (London)
13 12 LOVE LETTERS IN THE SAND Pat Boone (London)
9 13 WATER, WATER/A HANDFUL OF SONGS Tommy Steele (Decca)
14 14 WITH ALL MY HEART Petula Clark (Pye Nixa)
12 15 TEDDY BEAR Elvis Presley (RCA)
- 16 I LOVE YOU, BABY Paul Anka (Columbia)
21 17 GOT A LOT O' LIVIN' TO DO Elvis Presley (RCA)
16 18 LAST TRAIN TO SAN FERNANDO Johnny Duncan & the Blue Grass Boys (Columbia)
10 19 ISLAND IN THE SUN Harry Belafonte (RCA)
- 20 LAWDY MISS CLAWDY Elvis Presley (HMV)
29 21 MARY'S BOY CHILD Harry Belafonte (RCA)
- 21 WAKE UP LITTLE SUSIE Everly Brothers (London)
20 23 TRYING TO GET TO YOU Elvis Presley (HMV)
18 24 CALL ROSIE ON THE PHONE Guy Mitchell (Philips)
16 25 ALL SHOOK UP Elvis Presley (HMV)
19 26 STARDUST Billy Ward & the Dominoes (London)
23 27 SHORT FAT FANNIE Larry Williams (London)
- 28 TELL ME THAT YOU LOVE ME Paul Anka (Columbia)
- 29 HE'S GOT THE WHOLE WORLD IN HIS HANDS Laurie London (Parlophone)
24 30 LOVING YOU Elvis Presley (RCA)

16 November 1957

1 1 THAT'LL BE THE DAY Crickets (Vogue Coral)
2 2 PARTY Elvis Presley (RCA)
21 3 MARY'S BOY CHILD Harry Belafonte (RCA)
3 4 TAMMY Debbie Reynolds (Vogue-Coral)
5 5 REMEMBER YOU'RE MINE/GOLD MINE IN THE SKY Pat Boone (London)
4 6 DIANA Paul Anka (Columbia)
7 7 BE MY GIRL Jim Dale (Parlophone)
8 8 GOTTA HAVE SOMETHING IN THE BANK, FRANK Frankie Vaughan & the Kaye Sisters (Philips)
16 9 I LOVE YOU, BABY Paul Anka (Columbia)
6 10 MAN ON FIRE/WANDERING EYES Frankie Vaughan (Philips)
21 11 WAKE UP LITTLE SUSIE Everly Brothers (London)
10 12 MY DIXIE DARLING Lonnie Donegan (Pye Nixa)
12 13 LOVE LETTERS IN THE SAND Pat Boone (London)
13 14 WATER, WATER/A HANDFUL OF SONGS Tommy Steele (Decca)
9 15 WHOLE LOTTA SHAKIN' GOIN' ON Jerry Lee Lewis (London)
14 16 WITH ALL MY HEART Petula Clark (Pye Nixa)
23 16 TRYING TO GET TO YOU Elvis Presley (HMV)
20 18 LAWDY MISS CLAWDY Elvis Presley (HMV)
- 19 SANTA BRING MY BABY BACK TO ME Elvis Presley (RCA)
19 20 ISLAND IN THE SUN Harry Belafonte (RCA)
11 20 WANDERING EYES Charlie Gracie (London)
15 22 TEDDY BEAR Elvis Presley (RCA)
- 23 ALONE Petula Clark (Pye Nixa)
- 24 REET PETITE Jackie Wilson (Coral)
24 25 CALL ROSIE ON THE PHONE Guy Mitchell (Philips)
28 25 TELL ME THAT YOU LOVE ME Paul Anka (Columbia)
29 27 HE'S GOT THE WHOLE WORLD IN HIS HANDS Laurie London (Parlophone)
- 27 ALONE Shepherd Sisters (HMV)
18 29 LAST TRAIN TO SAN FERNANDO Johnny Duncan & the Blue Grass Boys (Columbia)
26 30 STARDUST Billy Ward & the Dominoes (London)

23 November 1957

3 1 MARY'S BOY CHILD Harry Belafonte (RCA)
2 2 PARTY Elvis Presley (RCA)
1 3 THAT'LL BE THE DAY Crickets (Vogue Coral)
9 4 I LOVE YOU, BABY Paul Anka (Columbia)
5 5 REMEMBER YOU'RE MINE/GOLD MINE IN THE SKY Pat Boone (London)
7 6 BE MY GIRL Jim Dale (Parlophone)
4 7 TAMMY Debbie Reynolds (Vogue-Coral)
8 8 GOTTA HAVE SOMETHING IN THE BANK, FRANK Frankie Vaughan & the Kaye Sisters (Philips)
11 9 WAKE UP LITTLE SUSIE Everly Brothers (London)
6 10 DIANA Paul Anka (Columbia)
19 11 SANTA BRING MY BABY BACK TO ME Elvis Presley (RCA)
10 12 MAN ON FIRE/WANDERING EYES Frankie Vaughan (Philips)
23 13 ALONE Petula Clark (Pye Nixa)
12 14 MY DIXIE DARLING Lonnie Donegan (Pye Nixa)
18 15 LAWDY MISS CLAWDY Elvis Presley (HMV)
- 16 MA, HE'S MAKING EYES AT ME Johnny Otis Show with Marie Adams (Capitol)
16 17 TRYING TO GET TO YOU Elvis Presley (HMV)
14 18 WATER, WATER/A HANDFUL OF SONGS Tommy Steele (Decca)
27 19 ALONE Shepherd Sisters (HMV)
13 20 LOVE LETTERS IN THE SAND Pat Boone (London)
15 21 WHOLE LOTTA SHAKIN' GOIN' ON Jerry Lee Lewis (London)
- 22 ALONE Southlanders (Decca)
27 23 HE'S GOT THE WHOLE WORLD IN HIS HANDS Laurie London (Parlophone)
20 24 ISLAND IN THE SUN Harry Belafonte (RCA)
30 25 STARDUST Billy Ward & the Dominoes (London)
24 26 REET PETITE Jackie Wilson (Coral)
16 27 WITH ALL MY HEART Petula Clark (Pye Nixa)
- 28 HEY YOU! Tommy Steele (Decca)
- 29 CHICAGO/ALL THE WAY Frank Sinatra (Capitol)
20 30 WANDERING EYES Charlie Gracie (London)

30 November 1957

1 1 MARY'S BOY CHILD Harry Belafonte (RCA)
6 2 BE MY GIRL Jim Dale (Parlophone)
2 3 PARTY Elvis Presley (RCA)
4 4 I LOVE YOU, BABY Paul Anka (Columbia)
3 5 THAT'LL BE THE DAY Crickets (Vogue Coral)
9 5 WAKE UP LITTLE SUSIE Everly Brothers (London)
5 7 REMEMBER YOU'RE MINE/GOLD MINE IN THE SKY Pat Boone (London)
7 8 TAMMY Debbie Reynolds (Vogue-Coral)
8 9 GOTTA HAVE SOMETHING IN THE BANK, FRANK Frankie Vaughan & the Kaye Sisters (Philips)
16 10 MA, HE'S MAKING EYES AT ME Johnny Otis Show with Marie Adams (Capitol)
13 11 ALONE Petula Clark (Pye Nixa)
12 12 MAN ON FIRE/WANDERING EYES Frankie Vaughan (Philips)
11 13 SANTA BRING MY BABY BACK TO ME Elvis Presley (RCA)
19 14 ALONE Shepherd Sisters (HMV)
10 15 DIANA Paul Anka (Columbia)
23 16 HE'S GOT THE WHOLE WORLD IN HIS HANDS Laurie London (Parlophone)
14 17 MY DIXIE DARLING Lonnie Donegan (Pye Nixa)
26 18 REET PETITE Jackie Wilson (Coral)
22 19 ALONE Southlanders (Decca)
- 20 MY SPECIAL ANGEL Malcolm Vaughan (HMV)
18 21 WATER, WATER/A HANDFUL OF SONGS Tommy Steele (Decca)
- 22 MY SPECIAL ANGEL Bobby Helms (Brunswick)
- 23 KEEP A KNOCKIN' Little Richard (London)
24 24 ISLAND IN THE SUN Harry Belafonte (RCA)
29 25 CHICAGO/ALL THE WAY Frank Sinatra (Capitol)
- 26 PARTY POPS Russ Conway (Columbia)
- 27 FOOTPRINTS IN THE SNOW Johnny Duncan & the B Grass Boys (Columbia)
15 28 LAWDY MISS CLAWDY Elvis Presley (HMV)
21 29 WHOLE LOTTA SHAKIN' GOIN' ON Jerry Lee Lewis (London)
- 30 DEEP PURPLE Billy Ward & the Dominoes (London)

After his major successes *Banana Boat Song* and *Island In The Sun*, Harry Belafonte's *Mary's Boy Child* (a US hit over Christmas 1956) was a natural for the seasonal market. Nobody was prepared, however, for the magnitude of its success - it became the year's fastest seller, hitting Number One a full month before Christmas and staying at the top into 1958. Eight weeks after release, it passed the million mark in Britain, beating Paul Anka's *Diana* to become only the second single ever to do so.

7 December 1957

last week	this week	
1	1	MARY'S BOY CHILD — Harry Belafonte (RCA)
2	2	BE MY GIRL — Jim Dale (Parlophone)
5	3	WAKE UP LITTLE SUSIE — Everly Brothers (London)
4	4	I LOVE YOU, BABY — Paul Anka (Columbia)
10	5	MA, HE'S MAKING EYES AT ME — Johnny Otis Show with Marie Adams (Capitol)
3	6	PARTY — Elvis Presley (RCA)
20	7	MY SPECIAL ANGEL — Malcolm Vaughan (HMV)
13	8	SANTA BRING MY BABY BACK TO ME — Elvis Presley (RCA)
5	9	THAT'LL BE THE DAY — Crickets (Vogue Coral)
7	10	REMEMBER YOU'RE MINE/GOLD MINE IN THE SKY — Pat Boone (London)
11	11	ALONE — Petula Clark (Pye Nixa)
16	12	HE'S GOT THE WHOLE WORLD IN HIS HANDS — Laurie London (Parlophone)
12	13	MAN ON FIRE/WANDERING EYES — Frankie Vaughan (Philips)
9	13	GOTTA HAVE SOMETHING IN THE BANK, FRANK — Frankie Vaughan & the Kaye Sisters (Philips)
-	15	LET'S HAVE A BALL — Winifred Atwell (Decca)
8	16	TAMMY — Debbie Reynolds (Vogue-Coral)
18	17	REET PETITE — Jackie Wilson (Coral)
19	18	ALONE — Southlanders (Decca)
15	19	DIANA — Paul Anka (Columbia)
14	20	ALONE — Shepherd Sisters (HMV)
25	21	CHICAGO/ALL THE WAY — Frank Sinatra (Capitol)
23	22	KEEP A KNOCKIN' — Little Richard (London)
22	23	MY SPECIAL ANGEL — Bobby Helms (Brunswick)
17	24	MY DIXIE DARLING — Lonnie Donegan (Pye Nixa)
28	25	LAWDY MISS CLAWDY — Elvis Presley (HMV)
-	26	APRIL LOVE — Pat Boone (London)
-	26	WAKE UP LITTLE SUSIE — King Brothers (Parlophone)
26	28	PARTY POPS — Russ Conway (Columbia)
-	29	AN AFFAIR TO REMEMBER — Vic Damone (Philips)
-	30	PEGGY SUE — Buddy Holly (Coral)

14 December 1957

1	1	MARY'S BOY CHILD — Harry Belafonte (RCA)
3	2	WAKE UP LITTLE SUSIE — Everly Brothers (London)
4	3	I LOVE YOU, BABY — Paul Anka (Columbia)
5	4	MA, HE'S MAKING EYES AT ME — Johnny Otis Show with Marie Adams (Capitol)
7	5	MY SPECIAL ANGEL — Malcolm Vaughan (HMV)
2	6	BE MY GIRL — Jim Dale (Parlophone)
8	7	SANTA BRING MY BABY BACK TO ME — Elvis Presley (RCA)
11	8	ALONE — Petula Clark (Pye Nixa)
17	9	REET PETITE — Jackie Wilson (Coral)
6	10	PARTY — Elvis Presley (RCA)
15	11	LET'S HAVE A BALL — Winifred Atwell (Decca)
10	12	REMEMBER YOU'RE MINE/GOLD MINE IN THE SKY — Pat Boone (London)
19	13	DIANA — Paul Anka (Columbia)
9	14	THAT'LL BE THE DAY — Crickets (Vogue Coral)
13	15	GOTTA HAVE SOMETHING IN THE BANK, FRANK — Frankie Vaughan & the Kaye Sisters (Philips)
12	16	HE'S GOT THE WHOLE WORLD IN HIS HANDS — Laurie London (Parlophone)
21	17	CHICAGO/ALL THE WAY — Frank Sinatra (Capitol)
16	18	TAMMY — Debbie Reynolds (Vogue-Coral)
13	19	MAN ON FIRE/WANDERING EYES — Frankie Vaughan (Philips)
20	20	ALONE — Southlanders (Decca)
22	21	KEEP A KNOCKIN' — Little Richard (London)
24	22	MY DIXIE DARLING — Lonnie Donegan (Pye Nixa)
30	22	PEGGY SUE — Buddy Holly (Coral)
26	22	WAKE UP LITTLE SUSIE — King Brothers (Parlophone)
25	25	APRIL LOVE — Pat Boone (London)
26	26	PARTY POPS — Russ Conway (Columbia)
23	27	MY SPECIAL ANGEL — Bobby Helms (Brunswick)
-	28	WATER, WATER/A HANDFUL OF SONGS — Tommy Steele (Decca)
-	29	WHITE CHRISTMAS — Pat Boone (London)
20	30	ALONE — Shepherd Sisters (HMV)

21 December 1957

1	1	MARY'S BOY CHILD — Harry Belafonte (RCA)
4	2	MA, HE'S MAKING EYES AT ME — Johnny Otis Show with Marie Adams (Capitol)
2	3	WAKE UP LITTLE SUSIE — Everly Brothers (London)
3	4	I LOVE YOU, BABY — Paul Anka (Columbia)
5	5	MY SPECIAL ANGEL — Malcolm Vaughan (HMV)
6	6	BE MY GIRL — Jim Dale (Parlophone)
17	7	CHICAGO/ALL THE WAY — Frank Sinatra (Capitol)
11	8	LET'S HAVE A BALL — Winifred Atwell (Decca)
9	9	REET PETITE — Jackie Wilson (Coral)
8	10	ALONE — Petula Clark (Pye Nixa)
12	11	REMEMBER YOU'RE MINE/GOLD MINE IN THE SKY — Pat Boone (London)
-	12	GREAT BALLS OF FIRE — Jerry Lee Lewis (London)
13	13	DIANA — Paul Anka (Columbia)
10	14	PARTY — Elvis Presley (RCA)
16	14	HE'S GOT THE WHOLE WORLD IN HIS HANDS — Laurie London (Parlophone)
25	16	APRIL LOVE — Pat Boone (London)
7	17	SANTA BRING MY BABY BACK TO ME — Elvis Presley (RCA)
15	18	GOTTA HAVE SOMETHING IN THE BANK, FRANK — Frankie Vaughan & the Kaye Sisters (Philips)
-	19	JACK O' DIAMONDS — Lonnie Donegan (Pye Nixa)
-	20	KISSES SWEETER THAN WINE — Jimmie Rodgers (Columbia)
21	21	KEEP A KNOCKIN' — Little Richard (London)
14	22	THAT'LL BE THE DAY — Crickets (Vogue Coral)
22	23	PEGGY SUE — Buddy Holly (Coral)
26	24	PARTY POPS — Russ Conway (Columbia)
-	24	KISSES SWEETER THAN WINE — Frankie Vaughan (Philips)
22	26	WAKE UP LITTLE SUSIE — King Brothers (Parlophone)
27	27	MAN ON FIRE/WANDERING EYES — Frankie Vaughan (Philips)
20	27	ALONE — Southlanders (Decca)
22	29	MY DIXIE DARLING — Lonnie Donegan (Pye Nixa)
18	30	TAMMY — Debbie Reynolds (Vogue-Coral)

28 December 1957

1	1	MARY'S BOY CHILD — Harry Belafonte (RCA)
2	2	MA, HE'S MAKING EYES AT ME — Johnny Otis Show with Marie Adams (Capitol)
5	3	MY SPECIAL ANGEL — Malcolm Vaughan (HMV)
8	4	LET'S HAVE A BALL — Winifred Atwell (Decca)
7	5	CHICAGO/ALL THE WAY — Frank Sinatra (Capitol)
12	6	GREAT BALLS OF FIRE — Jerry Lee Lewis (London)
3	7	WAKE UP LITTLE SUSIE — Everly Brothers (London)
4	8	I LOVE YOU, BABY — Paul Anka (Columbia)
10	9	ALONE — Petula Clark (Pye Nixa)
8	10	REET PETITE — Jackie Wilson (Coral)
6	11	BE MY GIRL — Jim Dale (Parlophone)
13	12	DIANA — Paul Anka (Columbia)
16	13	APRIL LOVE — Pat Boone (London)
19	14	JACK O' DIAMONDS — Lonnie Donegan (Pye Nixa)
24	15	KISSES SWEETER THAN WINE — Frankie Vaughan (Philips)
14	16	PARTY — Elvis Presley (RCA)
20	17	KISSES SWEETER THAN WINE — Jimmie Rodgers (Columbia)
11	18	REMEMBER YOU'RE MINE/GOLD MINE IN THE SKY — Pat Boone (London)
14	19	HE'S GOT THE WHOLE WORLD IN HIS HANDS — Laurie London (Parlophone)
17	20	SANTA BRING MY BABY BACK TO ME — Elvis Presley (RCA)
23	21	PEGGY SUE — Buddy Holly (Coral)
22	22	THAT'LL BE THE DAY — Crickets (Vogue Coral)
-	23	OH BOY! — Crickets (Coral)
24	24	PARTY POPS — Russ Conway (Columbia)
29	25	MY DIXIE DARLING — Lonnie Donegan (Pye Nixa)
-	26	WHOLE LOTTA SHAKIN' GOIN' ON — Jerry Lee Lewis (London)
18	27	GOTTA HAVE SOMETHING IN THE BANK, FRANK — Frankie Vaughan & the Kay Sisters (Philips)
-	28	SNOWBOUND FOR CHRISTMAS — Dickie Valentine (Decca)
21	29	KEEP A KNOCKIN' — Little Richard (London)
27	30	ALONE — Southlanders (Decca)

As the Crickets' *That'll Be The Day* left the Top 10, Buddy Holly made an equally significant chart debut as a solo artist with *Peggy Sue*, just three weeks ahead of the group's own smash follow-up *Oh Boy!* The Everly Brothers' *Wake Up Little Susie* and Jerry Lee Lewis' *Great Balls Of Fire* both outpaced their first hits, while former Dominoes lead singer Jackie Wilson made the Top 10 with his first solo offering *Reet Petite* - a song which would sit atop the chart 29 Christmases later.

January 1958

4 January 1958

last	this		
1	1	MARY'S BOY CHILD	Harry Belafonte (RCA)
7	2	WAKE UP LITTLE SUSIE	Everly Brothers (London)
3	3	MY SPECIAL ANGEL	Malcolm Vaughan (HMV)
2	4	MA, HE'S MAKING EYES AT ME	Johnny Otis Show with Marie Adams (Capitol)
6	5	GREAT BALLS OF FIRE	Jerry Lee Lewis (London)
10	6	REET PETITE	Jackie Wilson (Coral)
8	7	I LOVE YOU BABY	Paul Anka (Columbia)
5	8	ALL THE WAY	Frank Sinatra (Capitol)
9	9	ALONE	Petula Clark (Pye Nixa)
12	10	DIANA	Paul Anka (Columbia)
15	11	KISSES SWEETER THAN WINE	Frankie Vaughan (Philips)
21	12	PEGGY SUE	Buddy Holly (Coral)
16	12	PARTY	Elvis Presley (RCA)
14	14	JACK O' DIAMONDS	Lonnie Donegan (Pye Nixa)
13	15	APRIL LOVE	Pat Boone (London)
17	16	KISSES SWEETER THAN WINE	Jimmie Rodgers (Columbia)
4	17	LET'S HAVE A BALL	Winifred Atwell (Decca)
30	17	ALONE	Southlanders (Decca)
19	19	HE'S GOT THE WHOLE WORLD IN HIS HANDS	Laurie London (Parlophone)
11	20	BE MY GIRL	Jim Dale (Parlophone)
27	21	GOTTA HAVE SOMETHING IN THE BANK, FRANK	Frankie Vaughan & the Kaye Sisters (Philips)
-	22	ALONE	Shepherd Sisters (HMV)
18	23	REMEMBER YOU'RE MINE	Pat Boone (London)
23	24	OH BOY!	Crickets (Coral)
20	25	SANTA BRING MY BABY BACK TO ME	Elvis Presley (RCA)
-	26	STARDUST	Billy Ward & the Dominoes (London)
-	27	SHAKE ME I RATTLE/ALONE	Kaye Sisters (Philips)
-	28	FOOTPRINTS IN THE SNOW	Johnny Duncan & the Blue Grass Boys (Columbia)
25	29	MY DIXIE DARLING	Lonnie Donegan (Pye Nixa)
29	30	KEEP A KNOCKIN'	Little Richard (London)

11 January 1958

last	this		
5	1	GREAT BALLS OF FIRE	Jerry Lee Lewis (London)
4	2	MA, HE'S MAKING EYES AT ME	Johnny Otis Show with Marie Adams (Capitol)
2	3	WAKE UP LITTLE SUSIE	Everly Brothers (London)
3	4	MY SPECIAL ANGEL	Malcolm Vaughan (HMV)
8	5	ALL THE WAY	Frank Sinatra (Capitol)
7	6	I LOVE YOU BABY	Paul Anka (Columbia)
6	7	REET PETITE	Jackie Wilson (Coral)
16	8	KISSES SWEETER THAN WINE	Jimmie Rodgers (Columbia)
12	9	PEGGY SUE	Buddy Holly (Coral)
11	10	KISSES SWEETER THAN WINE	Frankie Vaughan (Philips)
24	11	OH BOY!	Crickets (Coral)
1	12	MARY'S BOY CHILD	Harry Belafonte (RCA)
9	13	ALONE	Petula Clark (Pye Nixa)
10	14	DIANA	Paul Anka (Columbia)
15	15	APRIL LOVE	Pat Boone (London)
14	16	JACK O' DIAMONDS	Lonnie Donegan (Pye Nixa)
20	17	BE MY GIRL	Jim Dale (Parlophone)
19	17	HE'S GOT THE WHOLE WORLD IN HIS HANDS	Laurie London (Parlophone)
17	19	ALONE	Southlanders (Decca)
21	20	GOTTA HAVE SOMETHING IN THE BANK, FRANK	Frankie Vaughan & the Kaye Sisters (Philips)
17	21	LET'S HAVE A BALL	Winifred Atwell (Decca)
23	22	REMEMBER YOU'RE MINE	Pat Boone (London)
30	23	KEEP A KNOCKIN'	Little Richard (London)
12	24	PARTY	Elvis Presley (RCA)
-	25	RAUNCHY	Bill Justis (London)
-	26	COOL BABY	Charlie Gracie (London)
-	27	JUST BORN (TO BE YOUR BABY)	Jim Dale (Parlophone)
29	28	MY DIXIE DARLING	Lonnie Donegan (Pye Nixa)
-	29	THAT'LL BE THE DAY	Crickets (Vogue Coral)
-	30	BYE BYE BABY	Johnny Otis Show (Capitol)

18 January 1958

last	this		
1	1	GREAT BALLS OF FIRE	Jerry Lee Lewis (London)
2	2	MA, HE'S MAKING EYES AT ME	Johnny Otis Show with Marie Adams (Capitol)
5	3	ALL THE WAY	Frank Sinatra (Capitol)
11	4	OH BOY!	Crickets (Coral)
4	5	MY SPECIAL ANGEL	Malcolm Vaughan (HMV)
9	6	PEGGY SUE	Buddy Holly (Coral)
8	7	KISSES SWEETER THAN WINE	Jimmie Rodgers (Columbia)
10	8	KISSES SWEETER THAN WINE	Frankie Vaughan (Philips)
7	9	REET PETITE	Jackie Wilson (Coral)
6	10	I LOVE YOU BABY	Paul Anka (Columbia)
3	11	WAKE UP LITTLE SUSIE	Everly Brothers (London)
15	12	APRIL LOVE	Pat Boone (London)
13	13	ALONE	Petula Clark (Pye Nixa)
16	14	JACK O' DIAMONDS	Lonnie Donegan (Pye Nixa)
-	15	THE STORY OF MY LIFE	Michael Holliday (Columbia)
-	16	AT THE HOP	Danny & the Juniors (HMV)
17	17	HE'S GOT THE WHOLE WORLD IN HIS HANDS	Laurie London (Parlophone)
-	18	THE STORY OF MY LIFE	Gary Miller (Pye Nixa)
14	19	DIANA	Paul Anka (Columbia)
19	20	ALONE	Southlanders (Decca)
-	21	I'M LEFT, YOU'RE RIGHT, SHE'S GONE	Elvis Presley (HMV)
30	22	BYE BYE BABY	Johnny Otis Show (Capitol)
-	23	BONY MORONIE	Larry Williams (London)
12	24	MARY'S BOY CHILD	Harry Belafonte (RCA)
25	24	RAUNCHY	Bill Justis (London)
17	26	BE MY GIRL	Jim Dale (Parlophone)
22	27	REMEMBER YOU'RE MINE	Pat Boone (London)
28	28	MY DIXIE DARLING	Lonnie Donegan (Pye Nixa)
-	29	YOU SEND ME	Sam Cooke (London)
-	30	CRAZY DREAM	Jim Dale (Parlophone)

25 January 1958

last	this		
-	1	JAILHOUSE ROCK	Elvis Presley (RCA)
2	2	MA, HE'S MAKING EYES AT ME	Johnny Otis Show with Marie Adams (Capitol)
3	3	ALL THE WAY	Frank Sinatra (Capitol)
4	4	OH BOY!	Crickets (Coral)
1	5	GREAT BALLS OF FIRE	Jerry Lee Lewis (London)
6	6	PEGGY SUE	Buddy Holly (Coral)
5	6	MY SPECIAL ANGEL	Malcolm Vaughan (HMV)
15	8	THE STORY OF MY LIFE	Michael Holliday (Columbia)
9	8	REET PETITE	Jackie Wilson (Coral)
7	10	KISSES SWEETER THAN WINE	Jimmie Rodgers (Columbia)
8	11	KISSES SWEETER THAN WINE	Frankie Vaughan (Philips)
12	12	APRIL LOVE	Pat Boone (London)
10	13	I LOVE YOU BABY	Paul Anka (Columbia)
11	14	WAKE UP LITTLE SUSIE	Everly Brothers (London)
23	15	BONY MORONIE	Larry Williams (London)
16	16	AT THE HOP	Danny & the Juniors (HMV)
18	16	THE STORY OF MY LIFE	Gary Miller (Pye Nixa)
-	18	LOVE ME FOREVER	Marion Ryan (Pye Nixa)
14	19	JACK O' DIAMONDS	Lonnie Donegan (Pye Nixa)
-	20	THE STORY OF MY LIFE	Dave King (Decca)
13	21	ALONE	Petula Clark (Pye Nixa)
22	21	BYE BYE BABY	Johnny Otis Show (Capitol)
26	23	BE MY GIRL	Jim Dale (Parlophone)
30	24	CRAZY DREAM	Jim Dale (Parlophone)
21	25	I'M LEFT, YOU'RE RIGHT, SHE'S GONE	Elvis Presley (HMV)
-	26	LOVE ME FOREVER	Eydie Gorme (HMV)
27	27	REMEMBER YOU'RE MINE	Pat Boone (London)
20	28	ALONE	Southlanders (Decca)
17	29	HE'S GOT THE WHOLE WORLD IN HIS HANDS	Laurie London (Parlophone)
19	30	DIANA	Paul Anka (Columbia)

Jerry Lee Lewis scored his only chart-topper on either side of the Atlantic with *Great Balls Of Fire*, which over 30 years' later would also be the title of his biopic. The January 10 release date for Elvis Presley's *Jailhouse Rock* had to be delayed a week because the factory presses could not meet the unprecedented demand of 250,000 advance orders. On release, the single sold almost half a million in its first week, and duly entered the January 25 chart at Number One, the first time this feat had been achieved.

1 February 1958

last week	this week	title
1	1	JAILHOUSE ROCK — Elvis Presley (RCA)
8	2	THE STORY OF MY LIFE — Michael Holliday (Columbia)
4	3	OH BOY! — Crickets (Coral)
3	4	ALL THE WAY — Frank Sinatra (Capitol)
2	5	MA, HE'S MAKING EYES AT ME — Johnny Otis Show with Marie Adams (Capitol)
5	6	GREAT BALLS OF FIRE — Jerry Lee Lewis (London)
7	7	MY SPECIAL ANGEL — Malcolm Vaughan (HMV)
12	8	APRIL LOVE — Pat Boone (London)
6	9	PEGGY SUE — Buddy Holly (Coral)
10	10	KISSES SWEETER THAN WINE — Jimmie Rodgers (Columbia)
16	11	AT THE HOP — Danny & the Juniors (HMV)
8	11	REET PETITE — Jackie Wilson (Coral)
11	13	KISSES SWEETER THAN WINE — Frankie Vaughan (Philips)
16	14	THE STORY OF MY LIFE — Gary Miller (Pye Nixa)
13	15	I LOVE YOU BABY — Paul Anka (Columbia)
18	16	LOVE ME FOREVER — Marion Ryan (Pye Nixa)
15	17	BONY MORONIE — Larry Williams (London)
14	18	WAKE UP LITTLE SUSIE — Everly Brothers (London)
-	19	YOU ARE MY DESTINY — Paul Anka (Columbia)
-	20	JAILHOUSE ROCK (EP) — Elvis Presley (RCA)
21	21	BYE BYE BABY — Johnny Otis Show (Capitol)
20	22	THE STORY OF MY LIFE — Dave King (Decca)
-	23	RAUNCHY — Bill Justis (London)
26	24	LOVE ME FOREVER — Eydie Gorme (HMV)
-	25	THE STORY OF MY LIFE — Alma Cogan (HMV)
19	26	JACK O' DIAMONDS — Lonnie Donegan (Pye Nixa)
21	27	ALONE — Petula Clark (Pye Nixa)
-	28	LOVE ME FOREVER — Four Esquires (London)
-	29	PUT A LIGHT IN THE WINDOW — King Brothers (Parlophone)
-	30	AN AFFAIR TO REMEMBER — Vic Damone (Philips)

8 February 1958

last week	this week	title
1	1	JAILHOUSE ROCK — Elvis Presley (RCA)
2	2	THE STORY OF MY LIFE — Michael Holliday (Columbia)
3	3	OH BOY! — Crickets (Coral)
4	4	ALL THE WAY — Frank Sinatra (Capitol)
11	5	AT THE HOP — Danny & the Juniors (HMV)
6	6	GREAT BALLS OF FIRE — Jerry Lee Lewis (London)
16	7	LOVE ME FOREVER — Marion Ryan (Pye Nixa)
9	8	PEGGY SUE — Buddy Holly (Coral)
8	9	APRIL LOVE — Pat Boone (London)
5	10	MA, HE'S MAKING EYES AT ME — Johnny Otis Show with Marie Adams (Capitol)
7	11	MY SPECIAL ANGEL — Malcolm Vaughan (HMV)
10	12	KISSES SWEETER THAN WINE — Jimmie Rodgers (Columbia)
13	13	KISSES SWEETER THAN WINE — Frankie Vaughan (Philips)
17	14	BONY MORONIE — Larry Williams (London)
19	15	YOU ARE MY DESTINY — Paul Anka (Columbia)
-	16	MAGIC MOMENTS — Perry Como (RCA)
14	17	THE STORY OF MY LIFE — Gary Miller (Pye Nixa)
11	18	REET PETITE — Jackie Wilson (Coral)
20	19	JAILHOUSE ROCK (EP) — Elvis Presley (RCA)
21	20	BYE BYE BABY — Johnny Otis Show (Capitol)
24	21	LOVE ME FOREVER — Eydie Gorme (HMV)
23	21	RAUNCHY — Bill Justis (London)
28	23	LOVE ME FOREVER — Four Esquires (London)
15	24	I LOVE YOU BABY — Paul Anka (Columbia)
22	25	THE STORY OF MY LIFE — Dave King (Decca)
25	26	THE STORY OF MY LIFE — Alma Cogan (HMV)
-	26	RAUNCHY — Ken Mackintosh (HMV)
-	26	WITCHCRAFT — Frank Sinatra (Capitol)
-	29	I'M LEFT, YOU'RE RIGHT, SHE'S GONE — Elvis Presley (HMV)
-	30	MANDY — Eddie Calvert (Columbia)

15 February 1958

last week	this week	title
2	1	THE STORY OF MY LIFE — Michael Holliday (Columbia)
1	2	JAILHOUSE ROCK — Elvis Presley (RCA)
16	3	MAGIC MOMENTS — Perry Como (RCA)
5	4	AT THE HOP — Danny & the Juniors (HMV)
3	5	OH BOY! — Crickets (Coral)
4	6	ALL THE WAY — Frank Sinatra (Capitol)
9	7	APRIL LOVE — Pat Boone (London)
8	7	PEGGY SUE — Buddy Holly (Coral)
7	7	LOVE ME FOREVER — Marion Ryan (Pye Nixa)
15	10	YOU ARE MY DESTINY — Paul Anka (Columbia)
6	11	GREAT BALLS OF FIRE — Jerry Lee Lewis (London)
14	12	BONY MORONIE — Larry Williams (London)
10	13	MA, HE'S MAKING EYES AT ME — Johnny Otis Show with Marie Adams (Capitol)
11	14	MY SPECIAL ANGEL — Malcolm Vaughan (HMV)
21	15	RAUNCHY — Bill Justis (London)
12	16	KISSES SWEETER THAN WINE — Jimmie Rodgers (Columbia)
17	17	THE STORY OF MY LIFE — Gary Miller (Pye Nixa)
19	18	JAILHOUSE ROCK (EP) — Elvis Presley (RCA)
13	19	KISSES SWEETER THAN WINE — Frankie Vaughan (Philips)
26	20	RAUNCHY — Ken Mackintosh (HMV)
26	20	WITCHCRAFT — Frank Sinatra (Capitol)
20	22	BYE BYE BABY — Johnny Otis Show (Capitol)
-	23	CRY MY HEART — David Whitfield/Mantovani (Decca)
-	24	SUGARTIME — McGuire Sisters (Coral)
18	25	REET PETITE — Jackie Wilson (Coral)
30	26	MANDY — Eddie Calvert (Columbia)
21	26	LOVE ME FOREVER — Eydie Gorme (HMV)
-	28	PUT A LIGHT IN THE WINDOW — King Brothers (Parlophone)
-	29	SUGARTIME — Alma Cogan (HMV)
24	30	I LOVE YOU BABY — Paul Anka (Columbia)

22 February 1958

last week	this week	title
1	1	THE STORY OF MY LIFE — Michael Holliday (Columbia)
3	2	MAGIC MOMENTS — Perry Como (RCA)
2	3	JAILHOUSE ROCK — Elvis Presley (RCA)
4	4	AT THE HOP — Danny & the Juniors (HMV)
5	5	OH BOY! — Crickets (Coral)
6	6	ALL THE WAY — Frank Sinatra (Capitol)
7	7	LOVE ME FOREVER — Marion Ryan (Pye Nixa)
10	8	YOU ARE MY DESTINY — Paul Anka (Columbia)
7	9	APRIL LOVE — Pat Boone (London)
7	10	PEGGY SUE — Buddy Holly (Coral)
15	11	RAUNCHY — Bill Justis (London)
11	12	GREAT BALLS OF FIRE — Jerry Lee Lewis (London)
12	13	BONY MORONIE — Larry Williams (London)
24	14	SUGARTIME — McGuire Sisters (Coral)
20	15	WITCHCRAFT — Frank Sinatra (Capitol)
16	16	KISSES SWEETER THAN WINE — Jimmie Rodgers (Columbia)
13	17	MA, HE'S MAKING EYES AT ME — Johnny Otis Show with Marie Adams (Capitol)
14	18	MY SPECIAL ANGEL — Malcolm Vaughan (HMV)
20	19	RAUNCHY — Ken Mackintosh (HMV)
26	20	MANDY — Eddie Calvert (Columbia)
18	21	JAILHOUSE ROCK (EP) — Elvis Presley (RCA)
-	22	MAGIC MOMENTS — Ronnie Hilton (HMV)
23	22	CRY MY HEART — David Whitfield/Mantovani (Decca)
17	24	THE STORY OF MY LIFE — Gary Miller (Pye Nixa)
-	25	BUONA SERA — Louis Prima (Capitol)
19	25	KISSES SWEETER THAN WINE — Frankie Vaughan (Philips)
-	27	STOOD UP — Ricky Nelson (London)
22	28	BYE BYE BABY — Johnny Otis Show (Capitol)
26	29	LOVE ME FOREVER — Eydie Gorme (HMV)
29	30	SUGARTIME — Alma Cogan (HMV)
-	30	NO OTHER BABY — Bobby Helms (Brunswick)

Michael Holliday triumphed in a four-way battle on *The Story Of My Life* with Gary Miller, Dave King and Alma Cogan, to take the top slot from Elvis. Both this (a US hit for Marty Robbins) and the song which replaced it at the top, Perry Como's *Magic Moments*, were written by Burt Bachrach and Hal David - the first major hits for this duo, later to find consistent chart paydirt in the 1960s. Presley, meanwhile, consolidated his *Jailhouse Rock* success, with the film's soundtrack EP joining the single in the Top 20.

March 1958

1 March 1958

last	this		
2	1	MAGIC MOMENTS	Perry Como (RCA)
1	2	THE STORY OF MY LIFE	Michael Holliday (Columbia)
3	3	JAILHOUSE ROCK	Elvis Presley (RCA)
4	4	AT THE HOP	Danny & the Juniors (HMV)
7	5	LOVE ME FOREVER	Marion Ryan (Pye Nixa)
6	6	ALL THE WAY	Frank Sinatra (Capitol)
8	7	YOU ARE MY DESTINY	Paul Anka (Columbia)
5	7	OH BOY!	Crickets (Coral)
9	9	APRIL LOVE	Pat Boone (London)
10	10	PEGGY SUE	Buddy Holly (Coral)
13	11	BONY MORONIE	Larry Williams (London)
15	12	WITCHCRAFT	Frank Sinatra (Capitol)
20	13	MANDY	Eddie Calvert (Columbia)
-	13	DON'T	Elvis Presley (RCA)
12	15	GREAT BALLS OF FIRE	Jerry Lee Lewis (London)
11	16	RAUNCHY	Bill Justis (London)
18	17	MY SPECIAL ANGEL	Malcolm Vaughan (HMV)
14	18	SUGARTIME	McGuire Sisters (Coral)
17	19	MA, HE'S MAKING EYES AT ME	Johnny Otis Show with Marie Adams (Capitol)
30	20	SUGARTIME	Alma Cogan (HMV)
19	21	RAUNCHY	Ken Mackintosh (HMV)
25	22	KISSES SWEETER THAN WINE	Frankie Vaughan (Philips)
-	23	GOOD GOLLY MISS MOLLY	Little Richard (London)
16	24	KISSES SWEETER THAN WINE	Jimmie Rodgers (Columbia)
-	25	PUT A LIGHT IN THE WINDOW	King Brothers (Parlophone)
21	27	BABY LOVER	Petula Clark (Pye Nixa)
21	27	JAILHOUSE ROCK (EP)	Elvis Presley (RCA)
22	28	MAGIC MOMENTS	Ronnie Hilton (HMV)
22	29	CRY MY HEART	David Whitfield/Mantovani (Decca)
-	30	THE CLOUDS WILL SOON ROLL BY	Tony Brent (Columbia)

8 March 1958

last	this		
1	1	MAGIC MOMENTS	Perry Como (RCA)
2	2	THE STORY OF MY LIFE	Michael Holliday (Columbia)
3	3	JAILHOUSE ROCK	Elvis Presley (RCA)
4	4	AT THE HOP	Danny & the Juniors (HMV)
13	5	DON'T	Elvis Presley (RCA)
7	6	YOU ARE MY DESTINY	Paul Anka (Columbia)
5	7	LOVE ME FOREVER	Marion Ryan (Pye Nixa)
7	8	OH BOY!	Crickets (Coral)
9	9	APRIL LOVE	Pat Boone (London)
6	10	ALL THE WAY	Frank Sinatra (Capitol)
-	11	CAN'T GET ALONG WITHOUT YOU/WE ARE NOT ALONE	Frankie Vaughan (Philips)
11	12	BONY MORONIE	Larry Williams (London)
23	13	GOOD GOLLY MISS MOLLY	Little Richard (London)
13	14	MANDY	Eddie Calvert (Columbia)
-	15	NAIROBI	Tommy Steele (Decca)
10	16	PEGGY SUE	Buddy Holly (Coral)
12	17	WITCHCRAFT	Frank Sinatra (Capitol)
16	18	RAUNCHY	Bill Justis (London)
18	19	SUGARTIME	McGuire Sisters (Coral)
20	20	SUGARTIME	Alma Cogan (HMV)
-	21	CATCH A FALLING STAR	Perry Como (RCA)
15	21	GREAT BALLS OF FIRE	Jerry Lee Lewis (London)
26	23	BABY LOVER	Petula Clark (Pye Nixa)
30	24	THE CLOUDS WILL SOON ROLL BY	Tony Brent (Columbia)
-	25	SUGARTIME	Jim Dale (Parlophone)
25	26	PUT A LIGHT IN THE WINDOW	King Brothers (Parlophone)
21	27	RAUNCHY	Ken Mackintosh (HMV)
-	28	WHY DON'T THEY UNDERSTAND	George Hamilton IV (HMV)
-	29	STOOD UP	Ricky Nelson (London)
-	29	WHOLE LOTTA WOMAN	Marvin Rainwater (MGM)

15 March 1958

last	this		
1	1	MAGIC MOMENTS	Perry Como (RCA)
2	2	THE STORY OF MY LIFE	Michael Holliday (Columbia)
3	3	JAILHOUSE ROCK	Elvis Presley (RCA)
4	4	AT THE HOP	Danny & the Juniors (HMV)
5	5	DON'T	Elvis Presley (RCA)
7	6	LOVE ME FOREVER	Marion Ryan (Pye Nixa)
6	7	YOU ARE MY DESTINY	Paul Anka (Columbia)
9	8	APRIL LOVE	Pat Boone (London)
8	9	OH BOY!	Crickets (Coral)
15	10	NAIROBI	Tommy Steele (Decca)
13	11	GOOD GOLLY MISS MOLLY	Little Richard (London)
23	12	BABY LOVER	Petula Clark (Pye Nixa)
11	13	CAN'T GET ALONG WITHOUT YOU/WE ARE NOT ALONE	Frankie Vaughan (Philips)
10	14	ALL THE WAY	Frank Sinatra (Capitol)
14	15	MANDY	Eddie Calvert (Columbia)
-	16	LISTEN TO ME	Buddy Holly (Coral)
21	17	CATCH A FALLING STAR	Perry Como (RCA)
29	18	WHOLE LOTTA WOMAN	Marvin Rainwater (MGM)
16	19	PEGGY SUE	Buddy Holly (Coral)
17	20	WITCHCRAFT	Frank Sinatra (Capitol)
19	21	SUGARTIME	McGuire Sisters (Coral)
20	22	SUGARTIME	Alma Cogan (HMV)
12	23	BONY MORONIE	Larry Williams (London)
24	24	THE CLOUDS WILL SOON ROLL BY	Tony Brent (Columbia)
28	24	WHY DON'T THEY UNDERSTAND	George Hamilton IV (HMV)
-	26	IN LOVE	Michael Holliday (Columbia)
-	27	TO BE LOVED	Jackie Wilson (Coral)
-	28	MAYBE BABY	Crickets (Coral)
25	29	SUGARTIME	Jim Dale (Parlophone)
-	30	LA DEE DAH	Jackie Dennis (Decca)
-	30	SWINGIN' SHEPHERD BLUES	Ted Heath & His Music (Decca)
27	30	RAUNCHY	Ken Mackintosh (HMV)

22 March 1958

last	this		
1	1	MAGIC MOMENTS	Perry Como (RCA)
2	2	THE STORY OF MY LIFE	Michael Holliday (Columbia)
4	3	AT THE HOP	Danny & the Juniors (HMV)
3	4	JAILHOUSE ROCK	Elvis Presley (RCA)
5	5	DON'T	Elvis Presley (RCA)
10	6	NAIROBI	Tommy Steele (Decca)
7	7	YOU ARE MY DESTINY	Paul Anka (Columbia)
11	8	GOOD GOLLY MISS MOLLY	Little Richard (London)
17	9	CATCH A FALLING STAR	Perry Como (RCA)
9	10	OH BOY!	Crickets (Coral)
18	11	WHOLE LOTTA WOMAN	Marvin Rainwater (MGM)
6	12	LOVE ME FOREVER	Marion Ryan (Pye Nixa)
14	13	ALL THE WAY	Frank Sinatra (Capitol)
8	14	APRIL LOVE	Pat Boone (London)
28	15	MAYBE BABY	Crickets (Coral)
19	16	PEGGY SUE	Buddy Holly (Coral)
15	17	MANDY	Eddie Calvert (Columbia)
12	18	BABY LOVER	Petula Clark (Pye Nixa)
13	19	CAN'T GET ALONG WITHOUT YOU/WE ARE NOT ALONE	Frankie Vaughan (Philips)
20	20	WITCHCRAFT	Frank Sinatra (Capitol)
30	21	LA DEE DAH	Jackie Dennis (Decca)
30	21	SWINGIN' SHEPHERD BLUES	Ted Heath & His Music (Decca)
24	23	WHY DON'T THEY UNDERSTAND	George Hamilton IV (HMV)
-	24	TO BE LOVED	Malcolm Vaughan (HMV)
23	25	BONY MORONIE	Larry Williams (London)
22	26	SUGARTIME	Alma Cogan (HMV)
21	26	SUGARTIME	McGuire Sisters (Coral)
29	28	SUGARTIME	Jim Dale (Parlophone)
26	29	IN LOVE	Michael Holliday (Columbia)
16	30	LISTEN TO ME	Buddy Holly (Coral)

Perry Como's *Magic Moments* was already established at Number One when the other side of the single, *Catch A Falling Star* (the bigger success of the two in the US), began to attract sales attention in its own right, eventually also making the Top 10. Buddy Holly and the Crickets' 25-date British tour in March, a resounding success, gave a renewed boost to their record sales: for two weeks, two singles by Holly and two by the whole group all rode the Top 30 together, though *Listen To Me*'s run was surprisingly brief.

29 March 1958

last week	this week	Title
1	1	MAGIC MOMENTS — Perry Como (RCA)
5	2	DON'T — Elvis Presley (RCA)
2	3	THE STORY OF MY LIFE — Michael Holliday (Columbia)
6	4	NAIROBI — Tommy Steele (Decca)
11	5	WHOLE LOTTA WOMAN — Marvin Rainwater (MGM)
4	6	JAILHOUSE ROCK — Elvis Presley (RCA)
3	7	AT THE HOP — Danny & the Juniors (HMV)
21	8	LA DEE DAH — Jackie Dennis (Decca)
15	9	MAYBE BABY — Crickets (Coral)
7	10	YOU ARE MY DESTINY — Paul Anka (Columbia)
8	11	GOOD GOLLY MISS MOLLY — Little Richard (London)
9	12	CATCH A FALLING STAR — Perry Como (RCA)
18	13	BABY LOVER — Petula Clark (Pye Nixa)
14	14	APRIL LOVE — Pat Boone (London)
13	15	ALL THE WAY — Frank Sinatra (Capitol)
26	16	SUGARTIME — Alma Cogan (HMV)
12	16	LOVE ME FOREVER — Marion Ryan (Pye Nixa)
17	18	MANDY — Eddie Calvert (Columbia)
21	18	SWINGIN' SHEPHERD BLUES — Ted Heath & His Music (Decca)
10	20	OH BOY! — Crickets (Coral)
-	21	OH-OH, I'M FALLING IN LOVE AGAIN — Jimmie Rodgers (Columbia)
19	22	CAN'T GET ALONG WITHOUT YOU/WE ARE NOT ALONE — Frankie Vaughan (Philips)
-	23	SWINGIN' SHEPHERD BLUES — Moe Koffman Quartet (London)
20	24	WITCHCRAFT — Frank Sinatra (Capitol)
16	25	PEGGY SUE — Buddy Holly (Coral)
24	25	TO BE LOVED — Malcolm Vaughan (HMV)
23	27	WHY DON'T THEY UNDERSTAND — George Hamilton IV (HMV)
-	28	THE BIG BEAT — Fats Domino (London)
-	29	TO BE LOVED — Jackie Wilson (Coral)
29	30	IN LOVE — Michael Holliday (Columbia)

5 April 1958

last week	this week	Title
1	1	MAGIC MOMENTS — Perry Como (RCA)
5	2	WHOLE LOTTA WOMAN — Marvin Rainwater (MGM)
4	3	NAIROBI — Tommy Steele (Decca)
2	4	DON'T — Elvis Presley (RCA)
9	5	MAYBE BABY — Crickets (Coral)
3	6	THE STORY OF MY LIFE — Michael Holliday (Columbia)
8	7	LA DEE DAH — Jackie Dennis (Decca)
7	8	AT THE HOP — Danny & the Juniors (HMV)
18	9	MANDY — Eddie Calvert (Columbia)
-	10	TEQUILA — Champs (London)
18	10	SWINGIN' SHEPHERD BLUES — Ted Heath & His Music (Decca)
12	12	CATCH A FALLING STAR — Perry Como (RCA)
6	13	JAILHOUSE ROCK — Elvis Presley (RCA)
11	14	GOOD GOLLY MISS MOLLY — Little Richard (London)
13	15	BABY LOVER — Petula Clark (Pye Nixa)
-	16	A WONDERFUL TIME UP THERE — Pat Boone (London)
25	17	TO BE LOVED — Malcolm Vaughan (HMV)
10	18	YOU ARE MY DESTINY — Paul Anka (Columbia)
14	19	APRIL LOVE — Pat Boone (London)
21	20	OH-OH, I'M FALLING IN LOVE AGAIN — Jimmie Rodgers (Columbia)
16	21	SUGARTIME — Alma Cogan (HMV)
-	22	WHO'S SORRY NOW — Connie Francis (MGM)
22	23	CAN'T GET ALONG WITHOUT YOU/WE ARE NOT ALONE — Frankie Vaughan (Philips)
29	24	TO BE LOVED — Jackie Wilson (Coral)
28	25	THE BIG BEAT — Fats Domino (London)
15	26	ALL THE WAY — Frank Sinatra (Capitol)
16	27	LOVE ME FOREVER — Marion Ryan (Pye Nixa)
27	28	WHY DON'T THEY UNDERSTAND — George Hamilton IV (HMV)
23	29	SWINGIN' SHEPHERD BLUES — Moe Koffman Quartet (London)
20	30	OH BOY! — Crickets (Coral)

12 Apri 1958

last week	this week	Title
1	1	MAGIC MOMENTS — Perry Como (RCA)
2	2	WHOLE LOTTA WOMAN — Marvin Rainwater (MGM)
3	3	NAIROBI — Tommy Steele (Decca)
7	4	LA DEE DAH — Jackie Dennis (Decca)
5	5	MAYBE BABY — Crickets (Coral)
10	6	SWINGIN' SHEPHERD BLUES — Ted Heath & His Music (Decca)
4	7	DON'T — Elvis Presley (RCA)
6	8	THE STORY OF MY LIFE — Michael Holliday (Columbia)
10	9	TEQUILA — Champs (London)
22	10	WHO'S SORRY NOW — Connie Francis (MGM)
14	11	GOOD GOLLY MISS MOLLY — Little Richard (London)
12	12	CATCH A FALLING STAR — Perry Como (RCA)
-	13	IT'S TOO SOON TO KNOW — Pat Boone (London)
13	14	JAILHOUSE ROCK — Elvis Presley (RCA)
9	15	MANDY — Eddie Calvert (Columbia)
16	16	A WONDERFUL TIME UP THERE — Pat Boone (London)
17	17	TO BE LOVED — Malcolm Vaughan (HMV)
8	18	AT THE HOP — Danny & the Juniors (HMV)
20	19	OH-OH, I'M FALLING IN LOVE AGAIN — Jimmie Rodgers (Columbia)
25	20	THE BIG BEAT — Fats Domino (London)
19	21	APRIL LOVE — Pat Boone (London)
-	22	BREATHLESS — Jerry Lee Lewis (London)
15	23	BABY LOVER — Petula Clark (Pye Nixa)
24	24	WHY DON'T THEY UNDERSTAND — George Hamilton IV (HMV)
18	25	YOU ARE MY DESTINY — Paul Anka (Columbia)
23	26	CAN'T GET ALONG WITHOUT YOU/WE ARE NOT ALONE — Frankie Vaughan (Philips)
24	27	TO BE LOVED — Jackie Wilson (Coral)
21	28	SUGARTIME — Alma Cogan (HMV)
-	29	TEQUILA — Ted Heath & His Music (Decca)
-	30	GRAND COOLIE DAM — Lonnie Donegan (Pye Nixa)

19 April 1958

last week	this week	Title
1	1	MAGIC MOMENTS — Perry Como (RCA)
2	2	WHOLE LOTTA WOMAN — Marvin Rainwater (MGM)
6	3	SWINGIN' SHEPHERD BLUES — Ted Heath & His Music (Decca)
5	4	MAYBE BABY — Crickets (Coral)
3	5	NAIROBI — Tommy Steele (Decca)
9	6	TEQUILA — Champs (London)
16	7	A WONDERFUL TIME UP THERE — Pat Boone (London)
4	8	LA DEE DAH — Jackie Dennis (Decca)
10	9	WHO'S SORRY NOW — Connie Francis (MGM)
13	10	IT'S TOO SOON TO KNOW — Pat Boone (London)
7	11	DON'T — Elvis Presley (RCA)
22	12	BREATHLESS — Jerry Lee Lewis (London)
15	13	MANDY — Eddie Calvert (Columbia)
12	14	CATCH A FALLING STAR — Perry Como (RCA)
8	15	THE STORY OF MY LIFE — Michael Holliday (Columbia)
21	16	APRIL LOVE — Pat Boone (London)
17	17	TO BE LOVED — Malcolm Vaughan (HMV)
19	18	OH-OH, I'M FALLING IN LOVE AGAIN — Jimmie Rodgers (Columbia)
11	19	GOOD GOLLY MISS MOLLY — Little Richard (London)
14	20	JAILHOUSE ROCK — Elvis Presley (RCA)
18	21	AT THE HOP — Danny & the Juniors (HMV)
30	22	GRAND COOLIE DAM — Lonnie Donegan (Pye Nixa)
-	23	LOLLIPOP — Chordettes (London)
20	24	THE BIG BEAT — Fats Domino (London)
24	25	WHY DON'T THEY UNDERSTAND — George Hamilton IV (HMV)
25	26	YOU ARE MY DESTINY — Paul Anka (Columbia)
28	27	SUGARTIME — Alma Cogan (HMV)
29	28	TEQUILA — Ted Heath & His Music (Decca)
27	29	TO BE LOVED — Jackie Wilson (Coral)
-	30	I MAY NEVER PASS THIS WAY AGAIN — Ronnie Hilton (HMV)

The Champs' Latin-tinged *Tequila*, a US Number One hit, became the second major instrumental rock'n'roll success in the UK following *Raunchy* in February. Even so, it was outsold in the non-vocal stakes by *Swingin' Shepherd Blues*, a big band belter with just a hint of rock backbeat, and a gift for Britain's Ted Heath, whose cover saw off Moe Koffman's US original. Interestingly, Heath simultaneously issued a version of *Tequila* (which made the lower end of the chart) and he covered *Raunchy* on *Shepherd*'s B-side.

April – May 1958

26 April 1958

last week	this week	title	artist
2	1	WHOLE LOTTA WOMAN	Marvin Rainwater (MGM)
1	2	MAGIC MOMENTS	Perry Como (RCA)
3	3	SWINGIN' SHEPHERD BLUES	Ted Heath & His Music (Decca)
7	4	A WONDERFUL TIME UP THERE	Pat Boone (London)
6	5	TEQUILA	Champs (London)
9	6	WHO'S SORRY NOW	Connie Francis (MGM)
10	7	IT'S TOO SOON TO KNOW	Pat Boone (London)
5	8	NAIROBI	Tommy Steele (Decca)
12	9	BREATHLESS	Jerry Lee Lewis (London)
4	10	MAYBE BABY	Crickets (Coral)
8	11	LA DEE DAH	Jackie Dennis (Decca)
23	12	LOLLIPOP	Chordettes (London)
11	13	DON'T	Elvis Presley (RCA)
17	14	TO BE LOVED	Malcolm Vaughan (HMV)
13	15	MANDY	Eddie Calvert (Columbia)
16	16	APRIL LOVE	Pat Boone (London)
14	17	CATCH A FALLING STAR	Perry Como (RCA)
22	18	GRAND COOLIE DAM	Lonnie Donegan (Pye Nixa)
18	19	OH-OH, I'M FALLING IN LOVE AGAIN	Jimmie Rodgers (Columbia)
-	20	HAPPY GUITAR	Tommy Steele (Decca)
28	21	TEQUILA	Ted Heath & His Music (Decca)
25	22	WHY DON'T THEY UNDERSTAND	George Hamilton IV (HMV)
-	23	I MAY NEVER PASS THIS WAY AGAIN	Robert Earl (Philips)
15	24	THE STORY OF MY LIFE	Michael Holliday (Columbia)
19	25	GOOD GOLLY MISS MOLLY	Little Richard (London)
29	26	TO BE LOVED	Jackie Wilson (Coral)
26	27	YOU ARE MY DESTINY	Paul Anka (Columbia)
-	28	SWEET LITTLE SIXTEEN	Chuck Berry (London)
20	29	JAILHOUSE ROCK	Elvis Presley (RCA)
-	30	TOM HARK	Elias & His Zig Zag Jive Flutes (Columbia)

3 April 1958

last week	this week	title	artist
1	1	WHOLE LOTTA WOMAN	Marvin Rainwater (MGM)
6	2	WHO'S SORRY NOW	Connie Francis (MGM)
3	3	SWINGIN' SHEPHERD BLUES	Ted Heath & His Music (Decca)
2	4	MAGIC MOMENTS	Perry Como (RCA)
4	5	A WONDERFUL TIME UP THERE	Pat Boone (London)
5	6	TEQUILA	Champs (London)
12	7	LOLLIPOP	Chordettes (London)
9	8	BREATHLESS	Jerry Lee Lewis (London)
13	9	DON'T	Elvis Presley (RCA)
10	10	MAYBE BABY	Crickets (Coral)
-	11	LOLLIPOP	Mudlarks (Columbia)
30	12	TOM HARK	Elias & His Zig Zag Jive Flutes (Columbia)
7	13	IT'S TOO SOON TO KNOW	Pat Boone (London)
-	13	WEAR MY RING AROUND YOUR NECK	Elvis Presley (RCA)
14	15	TO BE LOVED	Malcolm Vaughan (HMV)
18	16	GRAND COOLIE DAM	Lonnie Donegan (Pye Nixa)
23	17	I MAY NEVER PASS THIS WAY AGAIN	Robert Earl (Philips)
8	18	NAIROBI	Tommy Steele (Decca)
11	19	LA DEE DAH	Jackie Dennis (Decca)
15	20	MANDY	Eddie Calvert (Columbia)
19	20	OH-OH, I'M FALLING IN LOVE AGAIN	Jimmie Rodgers (Columbia)
21	21	TEQUILA	Ted Heath & His Music (Decca)
26	23	TO BE LOVED	Jackie Wilson (Coral)
16	24	APRIL LOVE	Pat Boone (London)
20	25	HAPPY GUITAR	Tommy Steele (Decca)
28	26	SWEET LITTLE SIXTEEN	Chuck Berry (London)
17	27	CATCH A FALLING STAR	Perry Como (RCA)
-	28	TULIPS FROM AMSTERDAM /YOU NEED HANDS	Max Bygraves (Decca)
22	29	WHY DON'T THEY UNDERSTAND	George Hamilton IV (HMV)
-	30	SUGARTIME	Alma Cogan (HMV)
-	30	I MAY NEVER PASS THIS WAY AGAIN	Ronnie Hilton (HMV)

10 May 1958

last week	this week	title	artist
1	1	WHOLE LOTTA WOMAN	Marvin Rainwater (MGM)
2	2	WHO'S SORRY NOW	Connie Francis (MGM)
5	3	A WONDERFUL TIME UP THERE	Pat Boone (London)
13	4	WEAR MY RING AROUND YOUR NECK	Elvis Presley (RCA)
3	5	SWINGIN' SHEPHERD BLUES	Ted Heath & His Music (Decca)
7	6	LOLLIPOP	Chordettes (London)
12	7	TOM HARK	Elias & His Zig Zag Jive Flutes (Columbia)
16	8	GRAND COOLIE DAM	Lonnie Donegan (Pye Nixa)
6	9	TEQUILA	Champs (London)
11	10	LOLLIPOP	Mudlarks (Columbia)
8	11	BREATHLESS	Jerry Lee Lewis (London)
4	12	MAGIC MOMENTS	Perry Como (RCA)
13	13	IT'S TOO SOON TO KNOW	Pat Boone (London)
15	14	TO BE LOVED	Malcolm Vaughan (HMV)
10	15	MAYBE BABY	Crickets (Coral)
26	16	SWEET LITTLE SIXTEEN	Chuck Berry (London)
17	17	I MAY NEVER PASS THIS WAY AGAIN	Robert Earl (Philips)
19	18	LA DEE DAH	Jackie Dennis (Decca)
18	19	NAIROBI	Tommy Steele (Decca)
-	20	THE CLOUDS WILL SOON ROLL BY	Tony Brent (Columbia)
9	21	DON'T	Elvis Presley (RCA)
25	22	HAPPY GUITAR	Tommy Steele (Decca)
24	23	APRIL LOVE	Pat Boone (London)
20	24	MANDY	Eddie Calvert (Columbia)
-	25	KEWPIE DOLL	Perry Como (RCA)
27	26	CATCH A FALLING STAR	Perry Como (RCA)
-	26	KEWPIE DOLL	Frankie Vaughan (Philips)
22	28	TEQUILA	Ted Heath & His Music (Decca)
28	29	TULIPS FROM AMSTERDAM /YOU NEED HANDS	Max Bygraves (Decca)
-	30	ON THE STREET WHERE YOU LIVE	Vic Damone (Philips)

17 May 1958

last week	this week	title	artist
2	1	WHO'S SORRY NOW	Connie Francis (MGM)
3	2	A WONDERFUL TIME UP THERE	Pat Boone (London)
1	3	WHOLE LOTTA WOMAN	Marvin Rainwater (MGM)
10	4	LOLLIPOP	Mudlarks (Columbia)
4	5	WEAR MY RING AROUND YOUR NECK	Elvis Presley (RCA)
7	6	TOM HARK	Elias & His Zig Zag Jive Flutes (Columbia)
8	7	GRAND COOLIE DAM	Lonnie Donegan (Pye Nixa)
5	8	SWINGIN' SHEPHERD BLUES	Ted Heath & His Music (Decca)
6	9	LOLLIPOP	Chordettes (London)
13	10	IT'S TOO SOON TO KNOW	Pat Boone (London)
9	11	TEQUILA	Champs (London)
12	12	MAGIC MOMENTS	Perry Como (RCA)
29	13	TULIPS FROM AMSTERDAM /YOU NEED HANDS	Max Bygraves (Decca)
14	14	TO BE LOVED	Malcolm Vaughan (HMV)
17	15	I MAY NEVER PASS THIS WAY AGAIN	Robert Earl (Philips)
25	16	KEWPIE DOLL	Perry Como (RCA)
11	17	BREATHLESS	Jerry Lee Lewis (London)
16	18	SWEET LITTLE SIXTEEN	Chuck Berry (London)
30	19	ON THE STREET WHERE YOU LIVE	Vic Damone (Philips)
26	19	KEWPIE DOLL	Frankie Vaughan (Philips)
28	21	TEQUILA	Ted Heath & His Music (Decca)
22	22	HAPPY GUITAR	Tommy Steele (Decca)
-	23	TO BE LOVED	Jackie Wilson (Coral)
19	24	NAIROBI	Tommy Steele (Decca)
-	25	ON THE STREET WHERE YOU LIVE	David Whitfield (Decca)
15	26	MAYBE BABY	Crickets (Coral)
-	27	STAIRWAY OF LOVE	Michael Holliday (Columbia)
-	28	TWILIGHT TIME	Platters (Mercury)
-	29	STAIRWAY OF LOVE	Terry Dene (Decca)
20	30	THE CLOUDS WILL SOON ROLL BY	Tony Brent (Columbia)

The MGM label had its first two British Number One hit singles in immediate succession. Rocker Marvin Rainwater proved to be just a one-and-a-bit hitmaker (though his full-blooded Cherokee Indian origins guaranteed him plenty of coverage while *Whole Lotta Woman* was popular), but Connie Francis' *Who's Sorry Now* - recorded as a final fling in a session due to be her last before the label dropped her for lack of success - marked the beginning of one of the all-time most successful chart careers by any female singer.

24 May 1958

last week	this week	Title / Artist (Label)
1	1	WHO'S SORRY NOW — Connie Francis (MGM)
6	2	TOM HARK — Elias & His Zig Zag Jive Flutes (Columbia)
5	3	WEAR MY RING AROUND YOUR NECK — Elvis Presley (RCA)
2	4	A WONDERFUL TIME UP THERE — Pat Boone (London)
4	5	LOLLIPOP — Mudlarks (Columbia)
3	6	WHOLE LOTTA WOMAN — Marvin Rainwater (MGM)
7	7	GRAND COOLIE DAM — Lonnie Donegan (Pye Nixa)
8	8	LOLLIPOP — Chordettes (London)
19	9	ON THE STREET WHERE YOU LIVE — Vic Damone (Philips)
16	10	KEWPIE DOLL — Perry Como (RCA)
11	11	TULIPS FROM AMSTERDAM /YOU NEED HANDS — Max Bygraves (Decca)
19	12	KEWPIE DOLL — Frankie Vaughan (Philips)
8	13	SWINGIN' SHEPHERD BLUES — Ted Heath & His Music (Decca)
15	14	I MAY NEVER PASS THIS WAY AGAIN — Robert Earl (Philips)
-	15	SWINGIN' SHEPHERD BLUES — Ella Fitzgerald (HMV)
-	16	WITCH DOCTOR — David Seville (London)
27	17	STAIRWAY OF LOVE — Michael Holliday (Columbia)
29	18	STAIRWAY OF LOVE — Terry Dene (Decca)
-	19	WITCH DOCTOR — Don Lang (HMV)
18	20	SWEET LITTLE SIXTEEN — Chuck Berry (London)
14	21	TO BE LOVED — Malcolm Vaughan (HMV)
12	22	MAGIC MOMENTS — Perry Como (RCA)
10	23	IT'S TOO SOON TO KNOW — Pat Boone (London)
-	24	ALL I HAVE TO DO IS DREAM /CLAUDETTE — Everly Brothers (London)
11	25	TEQUILA — Champs (London)
22	26	HAPPY GUITAR — Tommy Steele (Decca)
25	26	ON THE STREET WHERE YOU LIVE — David Whitfield (Decca)
-	28	TEACHER, TEACHER — Johnny Mathis (Fontana)
28	29	TWILIGHT TIME — Platters (Mercury)
17	30	BREATHLESS — Jerry Lee Lewis (London)

31 May 1958

last week	this week	Title / Artist (Label)
1	1	WHO'S SORRY NOW — Connie Francis (MGM)
2	2	TOM HARK — Elias & His Zig Zag Jive Flutes (Columbia)
4	2	LOLLIPOP — Mudlarks (Columbia)
3	4	WEAR MY RING AROUND YOUR NECK — Elvis Presley (RCA)
4	5	A WONDERFUL TIME UP THERE — Pat Boone (London)
7	6	GRAND COOLIE DAM — Lonnie Donegan (Pye Nixa)
6	7	WHOLE LOTTA WOMAN — Marvin Rainwater (MGM)
9	8	ON THE STREET WHERE YOU LIVE — Vic Damone (Philips)
10	9	KEWPIE DOLL — Perry Como (RCA)
11	10	TULIPS FROM AMSTERDAM /YOU NEED HANDS — Max Bygraves (Decca)
16	11	WITCH DOCTOR — David Seville (London)
17	12	STAIRWAY OF LOVE — Michael Holliday (Columbia)
12	13	KEWPIE DOLL — Frankie Vaughan (Philips)
19	14	WITCH DOCTOR — Don Lang (HMV)
14	15	I MAY NEVER PASS THIS WAY AGAIN — Robert Earl (Philips)
18	16	STAIRWAY OF LOVE — Terry Dene (Decca)
15	16	SWINGIN' SHEPHERD BLUES — Ella Fitzgerald (HMV)
24	18	ALL I HAVE TO DO IS DREAM /CLAUDETTE — Everly Brothers (London)
13	19	SWINGIN' SHEPHERD BLUES — Ted Heath & His Music (Decca)
23	20	IT'S TOO SOON TO KNOW — Pat Boone (London)
8	21	LOLLIPOP — Chordettes (London)
29	22	TWILIGHT TIME — Platters (Mercury)
22	23	MAGIC MOMENTS — Perry Como (RCA)
20	24	TO BE LOVED — Malcolm Vaughan (HMV)
-	25	I MAY NEVER PASS THIS WAY AGAIN — Perry Como (RCA)
-	26	CRAZY LOVE — Paul Anka (Columbia)
-	27	THE SIGNATURE TUNE OF THE ARMY GAME — Michael Medwin, Alfie Bass, Bernard Bresslaw, Leslie Fyson (HMV)
26	28	ON THE STREET WHERE YOU LIVE — David Whitfield (Decca)
28	29	TEACHER, TEACHER — Johnny Mathis (Fontana)
25	30	TEQUILA — Champs (London)

7 June 1958

last week	this week	Title / Artist (Label)
1	1	WHO'S SORRY NOW — Connie Francis (MGM)
2	2	TOM HARK — Elias & His Zig Zag Jive Flutes (Columbia)
8	3	ON THE STREET WHERE YOU LIVE — Vic Damone (Philips)
5	4	A WONDERFUL TIME UP THERE — Pat Boone (London)
2	5	LOLLIPOP — Mudlarks (Columbia)
6	6	GRAND COOLIE DAM — Lonnie Donegan (Pye Nixa)
10	7	TULIPS FROM AMSTERDAM /YOU NEED HANDS — Max Bygraves (Decca)
12	8	STAIRWAY OF LOVE — Michael Holliday (Columbia)
14	9	WITCH DOCTOR — Don Lang (HMV)
13	10	KEWPIE DOLL — Frankie Vaughan (Philips)
4	11	WEAR MY RING AROUND YOUR NECK — Elvis Presley (RCA)
18	12	ALL I HAVE TO DO IS DREAM /CLAUDETTE — Everly Brothers (London)
9	13	KEWPIE DOLL — Perry Como (RCA)
11	14	WITCH DOCTOR — David Seville (London)
7	15	WHOLE LOTTA WOMAN — Marvin Rainwater (MGM)
16	16	TWILIGHT TIME — Platters (Mercury)
17	17	THE SIGNATURE TUNE OF THE ARMY GAME — Michael Medwin, Alfie Bass, Bernard Bresslaw, Leslie Fyson (HMV)
16	18	SWINGIN' SHEPHERD BLUES — Ella Fitzgerald (HMV)
25	19	I MAY NEVER PASS THIS WAY AGAIN — Perry Como (RCA)
20	20	IT'S TOO SOON TO KNOW — Pat Boone (London)
21	21	LOLLIPOP — Chordettes (London)
16	22	STAIRWAY OF LOVE — Terry Dene (Decca)
-	23	I DIG YOU, BABY — Marvin Rainwater (MGM)
15	24	I MAY NEVER PASS THIS WAY AGAIN — Robert Earl (Philips)
24	25	TO BE LOVED — Malcolm Vaughan (HMV)
-	26	BOOK OF LOVE — Mudlarks (Columbia)
-	27	I MAY NEVER PASS THIS WAY AGAIN — Ronnie Hilton (HMV)
19	28	SWINGIN' SHEPHERD BLUES — Ted Heath & His Music (Decca)
28	29	ON THE STREET WHERE YOU LIVE — David Whitfield (Decca)
29	30	TEACHER, TEACHER — Johnny Mathis (Fontana)

14 June 1958

last week	this week	Title / Artist (Label)
1	1	WHO'S SORRY NOW — Connie Francis (MGM)
2	2	TOM HARK — Elias & His Zig Zag Jive Flute (Columbia)
8	3	STAIRWAY OF LOVE — Michael Holliday (Columbia)
3	4	ON THE STREET WHERE YOU LIVE — Vic Damone (Philips)
9	5	WITCH DOCTOR — Don Lang (HMV)
7	6	TULIPS FROM AMSTERDAM /YOU NEED HANDS — Max Bygraves (Decca)
4	7	A WONDERFUL TIME UP THERE — Pat Boone (London)
5	8	LOLLIPOP — Mudlarks (Columbia)
12	9	ALL I HAVE TO DO IS DREAM /CLAUDETTE — Everly Brothers (London)
6	10	GRAND COOLIE DAM — Lonnie Donegan (Pye Nixa)
10	10	KEWPIE DOLL — Frankie Vaughan (Philips)
17	12	THE SIGNATURE TUNE OF THE ARMY GAME — Michael Medwin, Alfie Bass, Bernard Bresslaw, Leslie Fyson (HMV)
11	13	WEAR MY RING AROUND YOUR NECK — Elvis Presley (RCA)
13	14	KEWPIE DOLL — Perry Como (RCA)
19	15	I MAY NEVER PASS THIS WAY AGAIN — Perry Como (RCA)
16	16	TWILIGHT TIME — Platters (Mercury)
24	17	I MAY NEVER PASS THIS WAY AGAIN — Robert Earl (Philips)
14	18	WITCH DOCTOR — David Seville (London)
26	19	BOOK OF LOVE — Mudlarks (Columbia)
15	20	WHOLE LOTTA WOMAN — Marvin Rainwater (MGM)
-	21	BIG MAN — Four Preps (Capitol)
23	22	I DIG YOU, BABY — Marvin Rainwater (MGM)
18	23	SWINGIN' SHEPHERD BLUES — Ella Fitzgerald (HMV)
-	24	RETURN TO ME — Dean Martin (Capitol)
29	25	ON THE STREET WHERE YOU LIVE — David Whitfield (Decca)
20	26	IT'S TOO SOON TO KNOW — Pat Boone (London)
-	27	A VERY PRECIOUS LOVE — Doris Day (Philips)
30	28	TEACHER, TEACHER — Johnny Mathis (Fontana)
28	29	SWINGIN' SHEPHERD BLUES — Ted Heath & His Music (Decca)
22	30	STAIRWAY OF LOVE — Terry Dene (Decca)

Hit singles came no more ethnic than *Tom Hark*, an hypnotically catchy piece of kwela music from South Africa, instrumental apart from an introduction which sounded like a dice game being played. It made the outrageous rock novelty *Witch Doctor*, on which 6.5 *Special* regular Don Lang's cover sneaked the honours from its US creator David Seville (later aka the Chipmunks), sound positively pedestrian, the latter's high-pitched chorus of *"ooh-ee, ooh-ah-ah, ting-tang, wallah-wallah bing-bang"* notwithstanding.

June – July 1958

21 June 1958

last	this	
1	1	WHO'S SORRY NOW Connie Francis (MGM)
4	2	ON THE STREET WHERE YOU LIVE Vic Damone (Philips)
2	3	TOM HARK Elias & His Zig Zag Jive Flutes (Columbia)
9	4	ALL I HAVE TO DO IS DREAM /CLAUDETTE Everly Brothers (London)
6	5	TULIPS FROM AMSTERDAM /YOU NEED HANDS Max Bygraves (Decca)
3	5	STAIRWAY OF LOVE Michael Holliday (Columbia)
5	7	WITCH DOCTOR Don Lang (HMV)
12	8	THE SIGNATURE TUNE OF THE ARMY GAME Michael Medwin, Alfie Bass, Bernard Bresslaw, Leslie Fyson (HMV)
7	9	A WONDERFUL TIME UP THERE Pat Boone (London)
8	10	LOLLIPOP Mudlarks (Columbia)
10	11	KEWPIE DOLL Frankie Vaughan (Philips)
16	12	TWILIGHT TIME Platters (Mercury)
19	13	BOOK OF LOVE Mudlarks (Columbia)
10	14	GRAND COOLIE DAM Lonnie Donegan (Pye Nixa)
15	15	I MAY NEVER PASS THIS WAY AGAIN Perry Como (RCA)
21	16	BIG MAN Four Preps (Capitol)
25	17	ON THE STREET WHERE YOU LIVE David Whitfield (Decca)
18	18	WITCH DOCTOR David Seville (London)
22	19	I DIG YOU, BABY Marvin Rainwater (MGM)
17	20	I MAY NEVER PASS THIS WAY AGAIN Robert Earl (Philips)
13	21	WEAR MY RING AROUND YOUR NECK Elvis Presley (RCA)
-	22	THE PURPLE PEOPLE EATER Sheb Wooley (MGM)
14	23	KEWPIE DOLL Perry Como (RCA)
24	24	RETURN TO ME Dean Martin (Capitol)
27	25	A VERY PRECIOUS LOVE Doris Day (Philips)
26	26	IT'S TOO SOON TO KNOW Pat Boone (London)
23	27	SWINGIN' SHEPHERD BLUES Ella Fitzgerald (HMV)
28	27	TEACHER, TEACHER Johnny Mathis (Fontana)
-	29	LITTLE SERENADE Eddie Calvert (Columbia)
-	29	RAVE ON Buddy Holly (Coral)

28 June 1958

2	1	ON THE STREET WHERE YOU LIVE Vic Damone (Philips)
4	2	ALL I HAVE TO DO IS DREAM /CLAUDETTE Everly Brothers (London)
1	3	WHO'S SORRY NOW Connie Francis (MGM)
5	4	STAIRWAY OF LOVE Michael Holliday (Columbia)
8	5	THE SIGNATURE TUNE OF THE ARMY GAME Michael Medwin, Alfie Bass, Bernard Bresslaw, Leslie Fyson (HMV)
3	6	TOM HARK Elias & His Zig Zag Jive Flutes (Columbia)
7	6	WITCH DOCTOR Don Lang (HMV)
5	8	TULIPS FROM AMSTERDAM /YOU NEED HANDS Max Bygraves (Decca)
13	9	BOOK OF LOVE Mudlarks (Columbia)
16	10	BIG MAN Four Preps (Capitol)
9	11	A WONDERFUL TIME UP THERE Pat Boone (London)
12	12	TWILIGHT TIME Platters (Mercury)
11	13	KEWPIE DOLL Frankie Vaughan (Philips)
22	14	THE PURPLE PEOPLE EATER Sheb Wooley (MGM)
29	15	RAVE ON Buddy Holly (Coral)
20	16	I MAY NEVER PASS THIS WAY AGAIN Robert Earl (Philips)
24	17	RETURN TO ME Dean Martin (Capitol)
17	18	ON THE STREET WHERE YOU LIVE David Whitfield (Decca)
-	19	SUGAR MOON Pat Boone (London)
10	20	LOLLIPOP Mudlarks (Columbia)
19	21	I DIG YOU, BABY Marvin Rainwater (MGM)
14	22	GRAND COOLIE DAM Lonnie Donegan (Pye Nixa)
21	23	WEAR MY RING AROUND YOUR NECK Elvis Presley (RCA)
15	24	I MAY NEVER PASS THIS WAY AGAIN Perry Como (RCA)
18	25	WITCH DOCTOR David Seville (London)
26	26	IT'S TOO SOON TO KNOW Pat Boone (London)
25	27	A VERY PRECIOUS LOVE Doris Day (Philips)
29	28	LITTLE SERENADE Eddie Calvert (Columbia)
-	29	THE PURPLE PEOPLE EATER Jackie Dennis (Decca)
-	29	I'M SORRY I MADE YOU CRY Connie Francis (MGM)

5 July 1958

1	1	ON THE STREET WHERE YOU LIVE Vic Damone (Philips)
2	2	ALL I HAVE TO DO IS DREAM /CLAUDETTE Everly Brothers (London)
8	3	TULIPS FROM AMSTERDAM /YOU NEED HANDS Max Bygraves (Decca)
3	4	WHO'S SORRY NOW Connie Francis (MGM)
10	5	BIG MAN Four Preps (Capitol)
12	6	TWILIGHT TIME Platters (Mercury)
7	7	WITCH DOCTOR Don Lang (HMV)
9	8	BOOK OF LOVE Mudlarks (Columbia)
6	9	TOM HARK Elias & His Zig Zag Jive Flutes (Columbia)
5	10	THE SIGNATURE TUNE OF THE ARMY GAME Michael Medwin, Alfie Bass, Bernard Bresslaw, Leslie Fyson (HMV)
4	11	STAIRWAY OF LOVE Michael Holliday (Columbia)
19	12	SUGAR MOON Pat Boone (London)
14	13	THE PURPLE PEOPLE EATER Sheb Wooley (MGM)
13	14	KEWPIE DOLL Frankie Vaughan (Philips)
11	15	A WONDERFUL TIME UP THERE Pat Boone (London)
15	15	RAVE ON Buddy Holly (Coral)
24	17	I MAY NEVER PASS THIS WAY AGAIN Perry Como (RCA)
18	18	ON THE STREET WHERE YOU LIVE David Whitfield (Decca)
29	19	I'M SORRY I MADE YOU CRY Connie Francis (MGM)
27	20	A VERY PRECIOUS LOVE Doris Day (Philips)
16	20	I MAY NEVER PASS THIS WAY AGAIN Robert Earl (Philips)
22	22	GRAND COOLIE DAM Lonnie Donegan (Pye Nixa)
17	23	RETURN TO ME Dean Martin (Capitol)
21	24	I DIG YOU, BABY Marvin Rainwater (MGM)
-	25	TORERO - CHA CHA CHA Renato Carosone & His Sextet (Parlophone)
-	26	SICK AND TIRED Fats Domino (London)
-	27	TOM HARK Ted Heath & His Music (Decca)
23	28	WEAR MY RING AROUND YOUR NECK Elvis Presley (RCA)
-	29	WHEN THE BOYS TALK ABOUT THE GIRLS Valerie Carr (Columbia)
-	30	TORERO Julius LaRosa (RCA)

12 July 1958

1	1	ALL I HAVE TO DO IS DREAM /CLAUDETTE Everly Brothers (London)
1	2	ON THE STREET WHERE YOU LIVE Vic Damone (Philips)
6	3	TWILIGHT TIME Platters (Mercury)
3	4	TULIPS FROM AMSTERDAM /YOU NEED HANDS Max Bygraves (Decca)
5	5	BIG MAN Four Preps (Capitol)
4	6	WHO'S SORRY NOW Connie Francis (MGM)
12	7	SUGAR MOON Pat Boone (London)
8	8	BOOK OF LOVE Mudlarks (Columbia)
11	9	STAIRWAY OF LOVE Michael Holliday (Columbia)
15	10	RAVE ON Buddy Holly (Coral)
9	11	TOM HARK Elias & His Zig Zag Jive Flutes (Columbia)
7	12	WITCH DOCTOR Don Lang (HMV)
13	12	THE PURPLE PEOPLE EATER Sheb Wooley (MGM)
-	14	SALLY DON'T YOU GRIEVE/BETTY, BETTY, BETTY Lonnie Donegan (Pye Nixa)
10	15	THE SIGNATURE TUNE OF THE ARMY GAME Michael Medwin, Alfie Bass, Bernard Bresslaw, Leslie Fyson (HMV)
14	16	KEWPIE DOLL Frankie Vaughan (Philips)
19	17	I'M SORRY I MADE YOU CRY Connie Francis (MGM)
18	17	ON THE STREET WHERE YOU LIVE David Whitfield (Decca)
20	19	A VERY PRECIOUS LOVE Doris Day (Philips)
23	20	RETURN TO ME Dean Martin (Capitol)
15	21	A WONDERFUL TIME UP THERE Pat Boone (London)
22	22	GRAND COOLIE DAM Lonnie Donegan (Pye Nixa)
-	23	ENDLESS SLEEP Marty Wilde (Philips)
20	24	I MAY NEVER PASS THIS WAY AGAIN Robert Earl (Philips)
27	24	TOM HARK Ted Heath & His Music (Decca)
24	26	I DIG YOU, BABY Marvin Rainwater (MGM)
-	27	I'LL ALWAYS BE IN LOVE WITH YOU Michael Holliday (Columbia)
17	28	I MAY NEVER PASS THIS WAY AGAIN Perry Como (RCA)
30	29	TORERO Julius LaRosa (RCA)
-	30	OOH! MY SOUL Little Richard (London)

ITV's sitcom *The Army Game* was one of 1958's highest-rated TV programmes, so it was little surprise that a novelty vocal adaptation of the show's theme tune, featuring some of the stars in character, should become a Top 10 hit single. It and *Witch Doctor* were joined in the novelty stakes by America's fastest-selling hit of the summer, *The Purple People Eater*. It was sung by *Rawhide* actor Sheb Wooley, who was to continue his "musical" career in the 60s under the pseudonym Ben Colder, as a parodist of country hits.

last this week

19 July 1958

last	this		
1	1	ALL I HAVE TO DO IS DREAM /CLAUDETTE	Everly Brothers (London)
5	2	BIG MAN	Four Preps (Capitol)
4	3	TULIPS FROM AMSTERDAM /YOU NEED HANDS	Max Bygraves (Decca)
2	4	ON THE STREET WHERE YOU LIVE	Vic Damone (Philips)
3	5	TWILIGHT TIME	Platters (Mercury)
7	6	SUGAR MOON	Pat Boone (London)
6	7	WHO'S SORRY NOW	Connie Francis (MGM)
10	8	RAVE ON	Buddy Holly (Coral)
8	9	BOOK OF LOVE	Mudlarks (Columbia)
12	10	WITCH DOCTOR	Don Lang (HMV)
14	11	SALLY DON'T YOU GRIEVE/BETTY, BETTY, BETTY	Lonnie Donegan (Pye Nixa)
23	12	ENDLESS SLEEP	Marty Wilde (Philips)
13	13	THE PURPLE PEOPLE EATER	Sheb Wooley (MGM)
9	14	STAIRWAY OF LOVE	Michael Holliday (Columbia)
17	15	I'M SORRY I MADE YOU CRY	Connie Francis (MGM)
-	16	THE ONLY MAN ON THE ISLAND	Tommy Steele (Decca)
16	17	ON THE STREET WHERE YOU LIVE	David Whitfield (Decca)
19	18	A VERY PRECIOUS LOVE	Doris Day (Philips)
20	19	RETURN TO ME	Dean Martin (Capitol)
11	20	TOM HARK	Elias & His Zig Zag Jive Flutes (Columbia)
22	21	GRAND COOLIE DAM	Lonnie Donegan (Pye Nixa)
16	22	KEWPIE DOLL	Frankie Vaughan (Philips)
15	23	THE SIGNATURE TUNE OF THE ARMY GAME	Michael Medwin, Alfie Bass, Bernard Bresslaw, Leslie Fyson (HMV)
-	24	WHEN	Kalin Twins (Brunswick)
25	25	I MAY NEVER PASS THIS WAY AGAIN	Perry Como (RCA)
29	25	TORERO	Julius LaRosa (RCA)
24	27	I MAY NEVER PASS THIS WAY AGAIN	Robert Earl (Philips)
21	28	A WONDERFUL TIME UP THERE	Pat Boone (London)
-	29	I KNOW WHERE I'M GOING	George Hamilton IV (HMV)
-	30	WHEN THE BOYS TALK ABOUT THE GIRLS	Valerie Carr (Columbia)
26	30	I DIG YOU, BABY	Marvin Rainwater (MGM)

26 July 1958

last	this		
1	1	ALL I HAVE TO DO IS DREAM /CLAUDETTE	Everly Brothers (London)
2	2	BIG MAN	Four Preps (Capitol)
3	3	TULIPS FROM AMSTERDAM /YOU NEED HANDS	Max Bygraves (Decca)
4	4	ON THE STREET WHERE YOU LIVE	Vic Damone (Philips)
5	5	TWILIGHT TIME	Platters (Mercury)
-	6	HARD HEADED WOMAN	Elvis Presley (RCA)
8	7	RAVE ON	Buddy Holly (Coral)
6	8	SUGAR MOON	Pat Boone (London)
12	9	ENDLESS SLEEP	Marty Wilde (Philips)
7	10	WHO'S SORRY NOW	Connie Francis (MGM)
11	11	SALLY DON'T YOU GRIEVE/BETTY, BETTY, BETTY	Lonnie Donegan (Pye Nixa)
15	12	I'M SORRY I MADE YOU CRY	Connie Francis (MGM)
19	13	RETURN TO ME	Dean Martin (Capitol)
9	14	BOOK OF LOVE	Mudlarks (Columbia)
24	15	WHEN	Kalin Twins (Brunswick)
16	16	ON THE STREET WHERE YOU LIVE	David Whitfield (Decca)
18	17	A VERY PRECIOUS LOVE	Doris Day (Philips)
10	18	WITCH DOCTOR	Don Lang (HMV)
14	19	STAIRWAY OF LOVE	Michael Holliday (Columbia)
13	20	THE PURPLE PEOPLE EATER	Sheb Wooley (MGM)
16	21	THE ONLY MAN ON THE ISLAND	Tommy Steele (Decca)
23	22	THE SIGNATURE TUNE OF THE ARMY GAME	Michael Medwin, Alfie Bass, Bernard Bresslaw, Leslie Fyson (HMV)
-	23	OOH! MY SOUL	Little Richard (London)
28	24	A WONDERFUL TIME UP THERE	Pat Boone (London)
-	25	TRUDIE	Joe 'Mr Piano' Henderson (Pye Nixa)
-	26	PATRICIA	Perez Prado (RCA)
22	26	KEWPIE DOLL	Frankie Vaughan (Philips)
-	28	THINK IT OVER	Crickets (Coral)
25	28	TORERO	Julius LaRosa (RCA)
20	30	TOM HARK	Elias & His Zig Zag Jive Flutes (Columbia)

2 August 1958

last	this		
1	1	ALL I HAVE TO DO IS DREAM /CLAUDETTE	Everly Brothers (London)
6	2	HARD HEADED WOMAN	Elvis Presley (RCA)
2	3	BIG MAN	Four Preps (Capitol)
3	4	TULIPS FROM AMSTERDAM /YOU NEED HANDS	Max Bygraves (Decca)
7	5	RAVE ON	Buddy Holly (Coral)
15	6	WHEN	Kalin Twins (Brunswick)
5	7	TWILIGHT TIME	Platters (Mercury)
9	8	ENDLESS SLEEP	Marty Wilde (Philips)
13	9	RETURN TO ME	Dean Martin (Capitol)
10	10	WHO'S SORRY NOW	Connie Francis (MGM)
4	11	ON THE STREET WHERE YOU LIVE	Vic Damone (Philips)
12	12	I'M SORRY I MADE YOU CRY	Connie Francis (MGM)
8	13	SUGAR MOON	Pat Boone (London)
11	14	SALLY DON'T YOU GRIEVE/BETTY, BETTY, BETTY	Lonnie Donegan (Pye Nixa)
28	15	TORERO	Julius LaRosa (RCA)
17	16	A VERY PRECIOUS LOVE	Doris Day (Philips)
20	16	THE PURPLE PEOPLE EATER	Sheb Wooley (MGM)
16	18	ON THE STREET WHERE YOU LIVE	David Whitfield (Decca)
19	19	STAIRWAY OF LOVE	Michael Holliday (Columbia)
28	20	THINK IT OVER	Crickets (Coral)
26	21	PATRICIA	Perez Prado (RCA)
23	22	OOH! MY SOUL	Little Richard (London)
25	23	TRUDIE	Joe 'Mr Piano' Henderson (Pye Nixa)
14	23	BOOK OF LOVE	Mudlarks (Columbia)
18	25	WITCH DOCTOR	Don Lang (HMV)
-	26	THE ONLY MAN ON THE ISLAND	Vic Damone (Philips)
21	26	THE ONLY MAN ON THE ISLAND	Tommy Steele (Decca)
-	28	SPLISH SPLASH	Bobby Darin (London)
-	29	JACQUELINE	Bobby Helms (Brunswick)
-	30	WONDERFUL THINGS	Frankie Vaughan (Philips)

9 August 1958

last	this		
1	1	ALL I HAVE TO DO IS DREAM /CLAUDETTE	Everly Brothers (London)
2	2	HARD HEADED WOMAN	Elvis Presley (RCA)
6	3	WHEN	Kalin Twins (Brunswick)
3	4	BIG MAN	Four Preps (Capitol)
9	5	RETURN TO ME	Dean Martin (Capitol)
4	6	TULIPS FROM AMSTERDAM/YOU NEED HANDS	Max Bygraves (Decca)
8	7	ENDLESS SLEEP	Marty Wilde (Philips)
5	8	RAVE ON	Buddy Holly (Coral)
7	9	TWILIGHT TIME	Platters (Mercury)
13	10	SUGAR MOON	Pat Boone (London)
12	11	I'M SORRY I MADE YOU CRY	Connie Francis (MGM)
14	12	SALLY DON'T YOU GRIEVE/BETTY, BETTY, BETTY	Lonnie Donegan (Pye Nixa)
21	13	PATRICIA	Perez Prado (RCA)
11	14	ON THE STREET WHERE YOU LIVE	Vic Damone (Philips)
10	15	WHO'S SORRY NOW	Connie Francis (MGM)
20	16	THINK IT OVER	Crickets (Coral)
15	17	TORERO	Julius LaRosa (RCA)
26	18	THE ONLY MAN ON THE ISLAND	Tommy Steele (Decca)
18	19	ON THE STREET WHERE YOU LIVE	David Whitfield (Decca)
29	19	JACQUELINE	Bobby Helms (Brunswick)
23	20	TRUDIE	Joe 'Mr Piano' Henderson (Pye Nixa)
16	21	A VERY PRECIOUS LOVE	Doris Day (Philips)
30	22	WONDERFUL THINGS	Frankie Vaughan (Philips)
26	24	THE ONLY MAN ON THE ISLAND	Vic Damone (Philips)
-	25	I KNOW WHERE I'M GOING	George Hamilton IV (HMV)
16	26	THE PURPLE PEOPLE EATER	Sheb Wooley (MGM)
22	27	OOH! MY SOUL	Little Richard (London)
-	28	SPLISH SPLASH	Charlie Drake (Parlophone)
19	29	STAIRWAY OF LOVE	Michael Holliday (Columbia)
-	30	THE RIGHT TO LOVE	David Whitfield (Decca)

After two smashes, the Everly Brothers' third single *This Little Girl Of Mine* had failed in the UK, but the coupling of the ballad *All I Have To Do Is Dream* with the Roy Orbison-penned rocker *Claudette* finally established the duo once and for all, with the year's second-longest (after *Magic Moments*) Number One run. Marty Wilde, the first major British rock idol to emerge since Tommy Steele, made his chart debut with *Endless Sleep*, and Bobby Darin also scored for the first time with the novelty rocker *Splish Splash*.

August – September 1958

last week	this week	16 August 1958
1	1	ALL I HAVE TO DO IS DREAM /CLAUDETTE Everly Brothers (London)
3	2	WHEN Kalin Twins (Brunswick)
5	3	RETURN TO ME Dean Martin (Capitol)
2	4	HARD HEADED WOMAN Elvis Presley (RCA)
6	5	TULIPS FROM AMSTERDAM /YOU NEED HANDS Max Bygraves (Decca)
7	6	ENDLESS SLEEP Marty Wilde (Philips)
4	7	BIG MAN Four Preps (Capitol)
8	8	RAVE ON Buddy Holly (Coral)
9	9	TWILIGHT TIME Platters (Mercury)
13	10	PATRICIA Perez Prado (RCA)
10	11	SUGAR MOON Pat Boone (London)
15	12	WHO'S SORRY NOW Connie Francis (MGM)
16	13	THINK IT OVER Crickets (Coral)
14	14	ON THE STREET WHERE YOU LIVE Vic Damone (Philips)
20	14	TRUDIE Joe 'Mr Piano' Henderson (Pye Nixa)
12	16	SALLY DON'T YOU GRIEVE/BETTY, BETTY, BETTY Lonnie Donegan (Pye Nixa)
11	17	I'M SORRY I MADE YOU CRY Connie Francis (MGM)
17	17	TORERO Julius LaRosa (RCA)
-	19	YAKETY YAK Coasters (London)
28	20	SPLISH SPLASH Charlie Drake (Parlophone)
18	20	THE ONLY MAN ON THE ISLAND Tommy Steele (Decca)
22	22	A VERY PRECIOUS LOVE Doris Day (Philips)
25	23	I KNOW WHERE I'M GOING George Hamilton IV (HMV)
19	24	ON THE STREET WHERE YOU LIVE David Whitfield (Decca)
24	25	THE ONLY MAN ON THE ISLAND Vic Damone (Philips)
22	26	WONDERFUL THINGS Frankie Vaughan (Philips)
20	27	JACQUELINE Bobby Helms (Brunswick)
-	28	SPLISH SPLASH Bobby Darin (London)
-	29	FEVER Peggy Lee (Capitol)
-	30	EVERYBODY LOVES A LOVER Doris Day (Philips)

		23 August 1958
2	1	WHEN Kalin Twins (Brunswick)
1	2	ALL I HAVE TO DO IS DREAM /CLAUDETTE Everly Brothers (London)
3	3	RETURN TO ME Dean Martin (Capitol)
4	4	HARD HEADED WOMAN Elvis Presley (RCA)
6	5	ENDLESS SLEEP Marty Wilde (Philips)
5	6	TULIPS FROM AMSTERDAM /YOU NEED HANDS Max Bygraves (Decca)
7	7	BIG MAN Four Preps (Capitol)
8	7	RAVE ON Buddy Holly (Coral)
10	9	PATRICIA Perez Prado (RCA)
20	10	SPLISH SPLASH Charlie Drake (Parlophone)
13	11	THINK IT OVER Crickets (Coral)
-	12	POOR LITTLE FOOL Ricky Nelson (London)
11	13	SUGAR MOON Pat Boone (London)
9	14	TWILIGHT TIME Platters (Mercury)
29	15	FEVER Peggy Lee (Capitol)
19	16	YAKETY YAK Coasters (London)
12	17	WHO'S SORRY NOW Connie Francis (MGM)
14	18	ON THE STREET WHERE YOU LIVE Vic Damone (Philips)
-	19	STUPID CUPID/CAROLINA MOON Connie Francis (MGM)
-	20	LITTLE BERNADETTE Harry Belafonte (RCA)
14	21	TRUDIE Joe 'Mr Piano' Henderson (Pye Nixa)
20	22	THE ONLY MAN ON THE ISLAND Tommy Steele (Decca)
28	23	SPLISH SPLASH Bobby Darin (London)
16	24	SALLY DON'T YOU GRIEVE/BETTY, BETTY, BETTY Lonnie Donegan (Pye Nixa)
30	25	EVERYBODY LOVES A LOVER Doris Day (Philips)
17	26	I'M SORRY I MADE YOU CRY Connie Francis (MGM)
17	26	TORERO Julius LaRosa (RCA)
-	28	LITTLE TRAIN/GOTTA HAVE RAIN Max Bygraves (Decca)
22	28	A VERY PRECIOUS LOVE Doris Day (Philips)
23	30	I KNOW WHERE I'M GOING George Hamilton IV (HMV)

		30 August 1958
1	1	WHEN Kalin Twins (Brunswick)
2	2	ALL I HAVE TO DO IS DREAM/CLAUDETTE Everly Brothers (London)
3	3	RETURN TO ME Dean Martin (Capitol)
5	4	ENDLESS SLEEP Marty Wilde (Philips)
6	5	TULIPS FROM AMSTERDAM /YOU NEED HANDS Max Bygraves (Decca)
19	6	STUPID CUPID/CAROLINA MOON Connie Francis (MGM)
4	7	HARD HEADED WOMAN Elvis Presley (RCA)
15	8	FEVER Peggy Lee (Capitol)
9	9	PATRICIA Perez Prado (RCA)
7	10	RAVE ON Buddy Holly (Coral)
10	11	SPLISH SPLASH Charlie Drake (Parlophone)
12	12	BIG MAN Four Preps (Capitol)
12	13	POOR LITTLE FOOL Ricky Nelson (London)
-	14	VOLARE (NEL BLU DIPINTO DI BLU) Dean Martin (Capitol)
11	15	THINK IT OVER Crickets (Coral)
20	16	LITTLE BERNADETTE Harry Belafonte (RCA)
16	17	YAKETY YAK Coasters (London)
13	18	SUGAR MOON Pat Boone (London)
23	19	SPLISH SPLASH Bobby Darin (London)
-	20	EARLY IN THE MORNING Buddy Holly (Coral)
26	21	I'M SORRY I MADE YOU CRY Connie Francis (MGM)
17	22	WHO'S SORRY NOW Connie Francis (MGM)
18	23	ON THE STREET WHERE YOU LIVE Vic Damone (Philips)
22	23	THE ONLY MAN ON THE ISLAND Tommy Steele (Decca)
26	25	TORERO Julius LaRosa (RCA)
21	26	TRUDIE Joe 'Mr Piano' Henderson (Pye Nixa)
25	27	EVERYBODY LOVES A LOVER Doris Day (Philips)
14	27	TWILIGHT TIME Platters (Mercury)
28	29	LITTLE TRAIN/GOTTA HAVE RAIN Max Bygraves (Decca)
-	30	IF DREAMS CAME TRUE Pat Boone (London)

		6 September 1958
1	1	WHEN Kalin Twins (Brunswick)
3	2	RETURN TO ME Dean Martin (Capitol)
2	3	ALL I HAVE TO DO IS DREAM/CLAUDETTE Everly Brothers (London)
6	4	STUPID CUPID/CAROLINA MOON Connie Francis (MGM)
14	5	VOLARE (NEL BLU DIPINTO DI BLU) Dean Martin (Capitol)
4	6	ENDLESS SLEEP Marty Wilde (Philips)
8	7	FEVER Peggy Lee (Capitol)
9	8	PATRICIA Perez Prado (RCA)
13	9	POOR LITTLE FOOL Ricky Nelson (London)
11	10	SPLISH SPLASH Charlie Drake (Parlophone)
7	11	HARD HEADED WOMAN Elvis Presley (RCA)
17	12	YAKETY YAK Coasters (London)
10	13	RAVE ON Buddy Holly (Coral)
5	14	TULIPS FROM AMSTERDAM /YOU NEED HANDS Max Bygraves (Decca)
-	15	VOLARE (NEL BLU DIPINTO DI BLU) Domenico Modugno (Oriole)
16	16	LITTLE BERNADETTE Harry Belafonte (RCA)
20	17	EARLY IN THE MORNING Buddy Holly (Coral)
12	18	BIG MAN Four Preps (Capitol)
26	19	TRUDIE Joe 'Mr Piano' Henderson (Pye Nixa)
-	20	GIRL OF MY DREAMS Tony Brent (Columbia)
22	21	WHO'S SORRY NOW Connie Francis (MGM)
18	22	SUGAR MOON Pat Boone (London)
15	23	THINK IT OVER Crickets (Coral)
-	24	MOON TALK Perry Como (RCA)
-	25	MAD PASSIONATE LOVE Bernard Bresslaw (HMV)
30	26	IF DREAMS CAME TRUE Pat Boone (London)
-	26	REBEL ROUSER Duane Eddy (London)
19	28	SPLISH SPLASH Bobby Darin (London)
23	29	THE ONLY MAN ON THE ISLAND Tommy Steele (Decca)
27	30	TWILIGHT TIME Platters (Mercury)

The chart saw its second bout this year of multiple Buddy Holly activity, as *Rave On* and the Crickets' *Think It Over* were joined in the Top 20 by Holly's cover of Bobby Darin's *Early In The Morning*. The latter's *Splish Splash*, meanwhile, had lost out to the unlikely UK cover version by miniscule comedian Charlie Drake, who adapted the rocker to his familiar TV persona, and snatched the Top 10 honours. Ricky Nelson had his first major UK hit with his fifth US million-seller, and guitar man Duane Eddy debuted.

September – October 1958

13 September 1958

last week	this week	title / artist
1	1	WHEN — Kalin Twins (Brunswick)
4	2	STUPID CUPID/CAROLINA MOON — Connie Francis (MGM)
2	3	RETURN TO ME — Dean Martin (Capitol)
5	4	VOLARE (NEL BLU DIPINTO DI BLU) — Dean Martin (Capitol)
3	5	ALL I HAVE TO DO IS DREAM /CLAUDETTE — Everly Brothers (London)
6	6	ENDLESS SLEEP — Marty Wilde (Philips)
10	7	SPLISH SPLASH — Charlie Drake (Parlophone)
9	8	POOR LITTLE FOOL — Ricky Nelson (London)
7	9	FEVER — Peggy Lee (Capitol)
15	10	VOLARE (NEL BLU DIPINTO DI BLU) — Domenico Modugno (Oriole)
8	11	PATRICIA — Perez Prado (RCA)
25	12	MAD PASSIONATE LOVE — Bernard Bresslaw (HMV)
14	13	TULIPS FROM AMSTERDAM /YOU NEED HANDS — Max Bygraves (Decca)
12	14	YAKETY YAK — Coasters (London)
11	14	HARD HEADED WOMAN — Elvis Presley (RCA)
-	16	BIRD DOG — Everly Brothers (London)
13	17	RAVE ON — Buddy Holly (Coral)
20	18	GIRL OF MY DREAMS — Tony Brent (Columbia)
26	19	REBEL ROUSER — Duane Eddy (London)
16	20	LITTLE BERNADETTE — Harry Belafonte (RCA)
28	21	SPLISH SPLASH — Bobby Darin (London)
21	21	WHO'S SORRY NOW — Connie Francis (MGM)
19	23	TRUDIE — Joe 'Mr Piano' Henderson (Pye Nixa)
17	24	EARLY IN THE MORNING — Buddy Holly (Coral)
26	25	IF DREAMS CAME TRUE — Pat Boone (London)
24	25	MOON TALK — Perry Como (RCA)
22	27	SUGAR MOON — Pat Boone (London)
-	27	WONDERFUL THINGS — Frankie Vaughan (Philips)
-	29	MOVE IT — Cliff Richard (Columbia)
30	30	TWILIGHT TIME — Platters (Mercury)

20 September 1958

last week	this week	title / artist
1	1	WHEN — Kalin Twins (Brunswick)
2	2	STUPID CUPID/CAROLINA MOON — Connie Francis (MGM)
4	3	VOLARE (NEL BLU DIPINTO DI BLU) — Dean Martin (Capitol)
3	4	RETURN TO ME — Dean Martin (Capitol)
5	5	ALL I HAVE TO DO IS DREAM /CLAUDETTE — Everly Brothers (London)
8	6	POOR LITTLE FOOL — Ricky Nelson (London)
9	7	FEVER — Peggy Lee (Capitol)
7	8	SPLISH SPLASH — Charlie Drake (Parlophone)
11	9	PATRICIA — Perez Prado (RCA)
6	10	ENDLESS SLEEP — Marty Wilde (Philips)
12	11	MAD PASSIONATE LOVE — Bernard Bresslaw (HMV)
10	11	VOLARE (NEL BLU DIPINTO DI BLU) — Domenico Modugno (Oriole)
13	13	TULIPS FROM AMSTERDAM /YOU NEED HANDS — Max Bygraves (Decca)
23	14	TRUDIE — Joe 'Mr Piano' Henderson (Pye Nixa)
14	15	YAKETY YAK — Coasters (London)
18	16	GIRL OF MY DREAMS — Tony Brent (Columbia)
16	16	BIRD DOG — Everly Brothers (London)
25	18	IF DREAMS CAME TRUE — Pat Boone (London)
-	19	BORN TOO LATE — Poni-Tails (HMV)
19	20	REBEL ROUSER — Duane Eddy (London)
14	21	HARD HEADED WOMAN — Elvis Presley (RCA)
-	22	BIG MAN — Four Preps (Capitol)
17	23	RAVE ON — Buddy Holly (Coral)
20	24	LITTLE BERNADETTE — Harry Belafonte (RCA)
25	25	MOON TALK — Perry Como (RCA)
24	26	EARLY IN THE MORNING — Buddy Holly (Coral)
29	27	MOVE IT — Cliff Richard (Columbia)
27	28	WONDERFUL THINGS — Frankie Vaughan (Philips)
21	29	WHO'S SORRY NOW — Connie Francis (MGM)
21	30	SPLISH SPLASH — Bobby Darin (London)

27 September 1958

last week	this week	title / artist
2	1	STUPID CUPID/CAROLINA MOON — Connie Francis (MGM)
3	2	VOLARE (NEL BLU DIPINTO DI BLU) — Dean Martin (Capitol)
1	3	WHEN — Kalin Twins (Brunswick)
4	4	RETURN TO ME — Dean Martin (Capitol)
7	5	FEVER — Peggy Lee (Capitol)
6	6	POOR LITTLE FOOL — Ricky Nelson (London)
11	7	MAD PASSIONATE LOVE — Bernard Bresslaw (HMV)
16	8	BIRD DOG — Everly Brothers (London)
8	9	SPLISH SPLASH — Charlie Drake (Parlophone)
10	10	ENDLESS SLEEP — Marty Wilde (Philips)
9	11	PATRICIA — Perez Prado (RCA)
5	12	ALL I HAVE TO DO IS DREAM /CLAUDETTE — Everly Brothers (London)
19	13	BORN TOO LATE — Poni-Tails (HMV)
11	14	VOLARE (NEL BLU DIPINTO DI BLU) — Domenico Modugno (Oriole)
15	15	YAKETY YAK — Coasters (London)
13	16	TULIPS FROM AMSTERDAM /YOU NEED HANDS — Max Bygraves (Decca)
14	17	TRUDIE — Joe 'Mr Piano' Henderson (Pye Nixa)
18	18	IF DREAMS CAME TRUE — Pat Boone (London)
16	18	GIRL OF MY DREAMS — Tony Brent (Columbia)
27	20	MOVE IT — Cliff Richard (Columbia)
20	21	REBEL ROUSER — Duane Eddy (London)
-	22	A CERTAIN SMILE — Johnny Mathis (Fontana)
21	23	HARD HEADED WOMAN — Elvis Presley (RCA)
25	24	MOON TALK — Perry Como (RCA)
-	25	LITTLE STAR — Elegants (HMV)
-	26	MIDNIGHT — Paul Anka (Columbia)
-	27	EVERYBODY LOVES A LOVER — Doris Day (Philips)
24	28	LITTLE BERNADETTE — Harry Belafonte (RCA)
-	28	LONESOME TRAVELLER — Lonnie Donegan (Pye Nixa)
28	30	WONDERFUL THINGS — Frankie Vaughan (Philips)

4 October 1958

last week	this week	title / artist
1	1	STUPID CUPID/CAROLINA MOON — Connie Francis (MGM)
2	2	VOLARE (NEL BLU DIPINTO DI BLU) — Dean Martin (Capitol)
3	3	WHEN — Kalin Twins (Brunswick)
6	4	POOR LITTLE FOOL — Ricky Nelson (London)
8	5	BIRD DOG — Everly Brothers (London)
7	6	MAD PASSIONATE LOVE — Bernard Bresslaw (HMV)
4	7	RETURN TO ME — Dean Martin (Capitol)
9	8	SPLISH SPLASH — Charlie Drake (Parlophone)
-	9	KING CREOLE — Elvis Presley (RCA)
5	10	FEVER — Peggy Lee (Capitol)
13	11	BORN TOO LATE — Poni-Tails (HMV)
20	12	MOVE IT — Cliff Richard (Columbia)
11	13	PATRICIA — Perez Prado (RCA)
22	14	A CERTAIN SMILE — Johnny Mathis (Fontana)
12	15	ALL I HAVE TO DO IS DREAM /CLAUDETTE — Everly Brothers (London)
18	16	IF DREAMS CAME TRUE — Pat Boone (London)
10	16	ENDLESS SLEEP — Marty Wilde (Philips)
18	18	GIRL OF MY DREAMS — Tony Brent (Columbia)
16	19	TULIPS FROM AMSTERDAM /YOU NEED HANDS — Max Bygraves (Decca)
24	20	MOON TALK — Perry Como (RCA)
17	20	TRUDIE — Joe 'Mr Piano' Henderson (Pye Nixa)
14	22	VOLARE (NEL BLU DIPINTO DI BLU) — Domenico Modugno (Oriole)
15	23	YAKETY YAK — Coasters (London)
21	24	REBEL ROUSER — Duane Eddy (London)
-	25	IT'S ALL IN THE GAME — Tommy Edwards (MGM)
26	26	VOLARE (NEL BLU DIPINTO DI BLU) — Marino Marini Quartet (Durium)
-	27	WESTERN MOVIES — Olympics (HMV)
28	28	LITTLE BERNADETTE — Harry Belafonte (RCA)
25	29	LITTLE STAR — Elegants (HMV)
23	30	HARD HEADED WOMAN — Elvis Presley (RCA)

One of the most significant chart debuts of the whole year looked fairly inconsequential during its first couple of weeks, as Cliff Richard's *Move It* came slowly into the bottom reaches. However, when Cliff was signed by producer Jack Good to appear on ITV's *Oh Boy!* show, and immediately made a huge impact on the teenage TV audience, *Move It* - initially marketed by EMI as the B-side to the limp *Schoolboy Crush* (which Good despised and *Oh Boy!* ignored) - accelerated up the chart in ever-increasing bounds.

October – November 1958

11 October 1958

last	this	
1	1	STUPID CUPID/CAROLINA MOON Connie Francis (MGM)
2	2	VOLARE (NEL BLU DIPINTO DI BLU) Dean Martin (Capitol)
3	3	WHEN Kalin Twins (Brunswick)
9	4	KING CREOLE Elvis Presley (RCA)
12	5	MOVE IT Cliff Richard (Columbia)
5	6	BIRD DOG Everly Brothers (London)
11	7	BORN TOO LATE Poni-Tails (HMV)
6	8	MAD PASSIONATE LOVE Bernard Bresslaw (HMV)
4	9	POOR LITTLE FOOL Ricky Nelson (London)
7	10	RETURN TO ME Dean Martin (Capitol)
14	10	A CERTAIN SMILE Johnny Mathis (Fontana)
22	12	VOLARE (NEL BLU DIPINTO DI BLU) Domenico Modugno (Oriole)
25	13	IT'S ALL IN THE GAME Tommy Edwards (MGM)
26	13	VOLARE (NEL BLU DIPINTO DI BLU) Marino Marini Quartet (Durium)
-	15	COME PRIMA Marino Marini Quartet(Durium)
10	16	FEVER Peggy Lee (Capitol)
27	17	WESTERN MOVIES Olympics (HMV)
8	18	SPLISH SPLASH Charlie Drake (Parlophone)
20	19	MOON TALK Perry Como (RCA)
16	20	IF DREAMS CAME TRUE Pat Boone (London)
13	20	PATRICIA Perez Prado (RCA)
24	22	REBEL ROUSER Duane Eddy (London)
16	23	ENDLESS SLEEP Marty Wilde (Philips)
20	24	TRUDIE Joe 'Mr Piano' Henderson (Pye Nixa)
18	25	GIRL OF MY DREAMS Tony Brent (Columbia)
19	26	TULIPS FROM AMSTERDAM /YOU NEED HANDS Max Bygraves (Decca)
-	27	AM I WASTING MY TIME Frankie Vaughan (Philips)
-	28	MY TRUE LOVE Jack Scott (London)
15	29	ALL I HAVE TO DO IS DREAM/CLAUDETTE Everly Brothers (London)
-	30	GINGER BREAD Frankie Avalon (HMV)

18 October 1958

last	this	
1	1	STUPID CUPID/CAROLINA MOON Connie Francis (MGM)
4	2	KING CREOLE Elvis Presley (RCA)
2	3	VOLARE (NEL BLU DIPINTO DI BLU) Dean Martin (Capitol)
5	4	MOVE IT Cliff Richard (Columbia)
7	5	BORN TOO LATE Poni-Tails (HMV)
6	6	BIRD DOG Everly Brothers (London)
10	7	A CERTAIN SMILE Johnny Mathis (Fontana)
3	8	WHEN Kalin Twins (Brunswick)
8	9	MAD PASSIONATE LOVE Bernard Bresslaw (HMV)
15	10	COME PRIMA Marino Marini Quartet (Durium)
9	11	POOR LITTLE FOOL Ricky Nelson (London)
13	12	IT'S ALL IN THE GAME Tommy Edwards (MGM)
12	13	VOLARE (NEL BLU DIPINTO DI BLU) Domenico Modugno (Oriole)
-	14	SOMEDAY (YOU'LL WANT ME TO WANT YOU) Jodie Sands (HMV)
-	15	MORE THAN EVER (COME PRIMA) Malcolm Vaughan (HMV)
10	16	RETURN TO ME Dean Martin (Capitol)
13	17	VOLARE (NEL BLU DIPINTO DI BLU) Marino Marini (Durium)
17	18	WESTERN MOVIES Olympics (HMV)
22	19	REBEL ROUSER Duane Eddy (London)
20	20	IF DREAMS CAME TRUE Pat Boone (London)
28	20	MY TRUE LOVE Jack Scott (London)
20	22	PATRICIA Perez Prado (RCA)
19	23	MOON TALK Perry Como (RCA)
-	24	SUSIE DARLIN' Robin Luke (London)
27	25	AM I WASTING MY TIME Frankie Vaughan (Philips)
-	26	TEA FOR TWO CHA-CHA Tommy Dorsey Orchestra starring Warren Covington (Brunswick)
26	27	TULIPS FROM AMSTERDAM /YOU NEED HANDS Max Bygraves (Decca)
16	28	FEVER Peggy Lee (Capitol)
18	29	SPLISH SPLASH Charlie Drake (Parlophone)
25	30	GIRL OF MY DREAMS Tony Brent (Columbia)

25 October 1958

last	this	
1	1	STUPID CUPID/CAROLINA MOON Connie Francis (MGM)
10	2	COME PRIMA Marino Marini Quartet (Durium)
4	2	MOVE IT Cliff Richard (Columbia)
2	4	KING CREOLE Elvis Presley (RCA)
6	5	BIRD DOG Everly Brothers (London)
12	6	IT'S ALL IN THE GAME Tommy Edwards (MGM)
7	7	A CERTAIN SMILE Johnny Mathis (Fontana)
5	8	BORN TOO LATE Poni-Tails (HMV)
3	9	VOLARE (NEL BLU DIPINTO DI BLU) Dean Martin (Capitol)
15	10	MORE THAN EVER (COME PRIMA) Malcolm Vaughan (HMV)
9	11	MAD PASSIONATE LOVE Bernard Bresslaw (HMV)
11	12	POOR LITTLE FOOL Ricky Nelson (London)
-	13	HOOTS MON Lord Rockingham's XI (Decca)
18	14	WESTERN MOVIES Olympics (HMV)
17	16	VOLARE (NEL BLU DIPINTO DI BLU) Marino MariniQuartet (Durium)
13	17	VOLARE (NEL BLU DIPINTO DI BLU) Domenico Modugno (Oriole)
14	18	SOMEDAY (YOU'LL WANT ME TO WANT YOU) Jodie Sands (HMV)
22	19	PATRICIA Perez Prado (RCA)
19	20	REBEL ROUSER Duane Eddy (London)
20	21	IF DREAMS CAME TRUE Pat Boone (London)
23	22	MOON TALK Perry Como (RCA)
-	23	TRUDIE Joe 'Mr Piano' Henderson (Pye Nixa)
16	24	RETURN TO ME Dean Martin (Capitol)
24	25	SUSIE DARLIN' Robin Luke (London)
20	25	MY TRUE LOVE Jack Scott (London)
26	27	TEA FOR TWO CHA-CHA Tommy Dorsey Orchestra starring Warren Covington (Brunswick)
-	28	VOLARE Charlie Drake (Parlophone)
28	29	FEVER Peggy Lee (Capitol)
-	30	MORE THAN EVER Robert Earl (Philips)

1 November 1958

last	this	
1	1	STUPID CUPID/CAROLINA MOON Connie Francis (MGM)
2	2	COME PRIMA Marino Marini Quartet (Durium)
5	3	BIRD DOG Everly Brothers (London)
2	4	MOVE IT Cliff Richard (Columbia)
7	5	A CERTAIN SMILE Johnny Mathis (Fontana)
6	6	IT'S ALL IN THE GAME Tommy Edwards (MGM)
4	7	KING CREOLE Elvis Presley (RCA)
8	7	BORN TOO LATE Poni-Tails (HMV)
13	9	HOOTS MON Lord Rockingham's XI (Decca)
9	10	VOLARE (NEL BLU DIPINTO DI BLU) Dean Martin (Capitol)
12	11	POOR LITTLE FOOL Ricky Nelson (London)
14	12	WESTERN MOVIES Olympics (HMV)
10	13	MORE THAN EVER (COME PRIMA) Malcolm Vaughan (HMV)
16	14	VOLARE (NEL BLU DIPINTO DI BLU) Marino Marini Quartet (Durium)
11	15	MAD PASSIONATE LOVE Bernard Bresslaw (HMV)
15	16	WHEN Kalin Twins (Brunswick)
17	17	VOLARE (NEL BLU DIPINTO DI BLU) Domenico Modugno (Oriole)
25	18	MY TRUE LOVE Jack Scott (London)
18	19	SOMEDAY (YOU'LL WANT ME TO WANT YOU) Jodie Sands (HMV)
20	20	REBEL ROUSER Duane Eddy (London)
27	21	TEA FOR TWO CHA-CHA Tommy Dorsey Orchestra starring Warren Covington (Brunswick)
22	22	MOON TALK Perry Como (RCA)
19	23	PATRICIA Perez Prado (RCA)
-	24	I'LL GET BY Connie Francis (MGM)
21	25	IF DREAMS CAME TRUE Pat Boone (London)
30	26	MORE THAN EVER Robert Earl (Philips)
23	27	TRUDIE Joe 'Mr Piano' Henderson (Pye Nixa)
24	28	RETURN TO ME Dean Martin (Capitol)
25	29	SUSIE DARLIN' Robin Luke (London)
28	30	VOLARE Charlie Drake (Parlophone)

The Italian song *Volare (Nel Blu Dipinto Di Blu)*, the winner of the 1958 San Remo Song Festival, was easily the most-covered number of the Autumn. After Dean Martin swept to Number Two with an English-langauge version of it in quick succession to his *Return To Me*, the original Italian version by its composer Domenico Modugno (the bigger seller in the US) also hit the Top 20, neck-and-neck with a second Italian rendition by Marino Marini's Quartet, and comic Charlie Drake again did a novelty cover.

November 1958

last week	this week	8 November 1958
6	1	IT'S ALL IN THE GAME Tommy Edwards (MGM)
2	2	COME PRIMA Marino Marini Quartet (Durium)
3	3	BIRD DOG Everly Brothers (London)
1	4	STUPID CUPID/CAROLINA MOON Connie Francis (MGM)
9	5	HOOTS MON Lord Rockingham's XI (Decca)
5	6	A CERTAIN SMILE Johnny Mathis (Fontana)
4	7	MOVE IT Cliff Richard (Columbia)
13	8	MORE THAN EVER (COME PRIMA) Malcolm Vaughan (HMV)
7	9	KING CREOLE Elvis Presley (RCA)
8	10	BORN TOO LATE Poni-Tails (HMV)
18	11	MY TRUE LOVE Jack Scott (London)
21	12	TEA FOR TWO CHA-CHA Tommy Dorsey Orchestra starring Warren Covington (Brunswick)
12	13	WESTERN MOVIES Olympics (HMV)
10	14	VOLARE (NEL BLU DIPINTO DI BLU) Dean Martin (Capitol)
15	15	MAD PASSIONATE LOVE Bernard Bresslaw (HMV)
11	16	POOR LITTLE FOOL Ricky Nelson (London)
22	17	MOON TALK Perry Como (RCA)
19	17	SOMEDAY (YOU'LL WANT ME TO WANT YOU) Jodie Sands (HMV)
-	19	LOVE MAKES THE WORLD GO 'ROUND Perry Como (RCA)
16	20	WHEN Kalin Twins (Brunswick)
17	21	VOLARE (NEL BLU DIPINTO DI BLU) Domenico Modugno (Oriole)
24	22	I'LL GET BY Connie Francis (MGM)
14	23	VOLARE (NEL BLU DIPINTO DI BLU) Marino Marini Quartet (Durium)
-	24	SUMMERTIME BLUES Eddie Cochran (London)
28	25	RETURN TO ME Dean Martin (Capitol)
23	26	PATRICIA Perez Prado (RCA)
25	27	IF DREAMS CAME TRUE Pat Boone (London)
-	28	SOMEDAY (YOU'LL WANT ME TO WANT YOU) Ricky Nelson (London)
-	29	ROCKIN' ROBIN Bobby Day (London)
20	30	REBEL ROUSER Duane Eddy (London)

last week	this week	15 November 1958
1	1	IT'S ALL IN THE GAME Tommy Edwards (MGM)
3	2	BIRD DOG Everly Brothers (London)
5	3	HOOTS MON Lord Rockingham's XI (Decca)
2	4	COME PRIMA Marino Marini Quartet (Durium)
6	5	A CERTAIN SMILE Johnny Mathis (Fontana)
4	6	STUPID CUPID/CAROLINA MOON Connie Francis (MGM)
7	7	MOVE IT Cliff Richard (Columbia)
8	8	MORE THAN EVER (COME PRIMA) Malcolm Vaughan (HMV)
11	9	MY TRUE LOVE Jack Scott (London)
9	10	KING CREOLE Elvis Presley (RCA)
12	11	TEA FOR TWO CHA-CHA Tommy Dorsey Orchestra starring Warren Covington (Brunswick)
10	12	BORN TOO LATE Poni-Tails (HMV)
19	13	LOVE MAKES THE WORLD GO 'ROUND Perry Como (RCA)
17	14	SOMEDAY (YOU'LL WANT ME TO WANT YOU) Jodie Sands (HMV)
14	15	VOLARE (NEL BLU DIPINTO DI BLU) Dean Martin (Capitol)
23	16	VOLARE (NEL BLU DIPINTO DI BLU) Marino Marini Quartet (Durium)
16	17	POOR LITTLE FOOL Ricky Nelson (London)
17	17	MOON TALK Perry Como (RCA)
13	18	WESTERN MOVIES Olympics (HMV)
-	20	IT'S ONLY MAKE BELIEVE Conway Twitty (MGM)
-	21	COME ON LET'S GO Tommy Steele (Decca)
21	22	VOLARE (NEL BLU DIPINTO DI BLU) Domenico Modugno (Oriole)
24	23	SUMMERTIME BLUES Eddie Cochran (London)
28	24	SOMEDAY (YOU'LL WANT ME TO WANT YOU) Ricky Nelson (London)
22	25	I'LL GET BY Connie Francis (MGM)
15	26	MAD PASSIONATE LOVE Bernard Bresslaw (HMV)
20	27	WHEN Kalin Twins (Brunswick)
-	28	LONNIE'S SKIFFLE PARTY Lonnie Donegan (Pye Nixa)
-	29	MR. SUCCESS Frank Sinatra (Capitol)
29	30	ROCKIN' ROBIN Bobby Day (London)

last week	this week	22 November 1958
1	1	IT'S ALL IN THE GAME Tommy Edwards (MGM)
3	2	HOOTS MON Lord Rockingham's XI (Decca)
2	3	BIRD DOG Everly Brothers (London)
5	4	A CERTAIN SMILE Johnny Mathis (Fontana)
8	5	MORE THAN EVER (COME PRIMA) Malcolm Vaughan (HMV)
20	6	IT'S ONLY MAKE BELIEVE Conway Twitty (MGM)
4	7	COME PRIMA Marino Marini Quartet (Durium)
7	8	MOVE IT Cliff Richard (Columbia)
6	9	STUPID CUPID/CAROLINA MOON Connie Francis (MGM)
11	10	TEA FOR TWO CHA-CHA Tommy Dorsey Orchestra starring Warren Covington (Brunswick)
13	11	LOVE MAKES THE WORLD GO 'ROUND Perry Como (RCA)
10	12	KING CREOLE Elvis Presley (RCA)
-	13	TOM DOOLEY Lonnie Donegan (Pye Nixa)
24	14	SOMEDAY (YOU'LL WANT ME TO WANT YOU) Ricky Nelson (London)
9	15	MY TRUE LOVE Jack Scott (London)
14	16	SOMEDAY (YOU'LL WANT ME TO WANT YOU) Jodie Sands (HMV)
21	16	COME ON LET'S GO Tommy Steele (Decca)
12	18	BORN TOO LATE Poni-Tails (HMV)
25	19	I'LL GET BY Connie Francis (MGM)
-	20	TOM DOOLEY Kingston Trio (Capitol)
18	20	WESTERN MOVIES Olympics (HMV)
-	22	FALLIN' Connie Francis (MGM)
-	23	SUSIE DARLIN' Robin Luke (London)
-	23	HIGH CLASS BABY Cliff Richard (Columbia)
23	25	SUMMERTIME BLUES Eddie Cochran (London)
28	26	LONNIE'S SKIFFLE PARTY Lonnie Donegan (Pye Nixa)
-	27	I GOT A FEELING Ricky Nelson (London)
-	28	MORE THAN EVER Robert Earl (Philips)
-	29	MANDOLINS IN THE MOONLIGHT Perry Como (RCA)
15	30	VOLARE (NEL BLU DIPINTO DI BLU) Dean Martin (Capitol)
22	30	VOLARE (NEL BLU DIPINTO DI BLU) Domenico Modugno (Oriole)

last week	this week	29 November 1958
2	1	HOOTS MON Lord Rockingham's XI (Decca)
1	2	IT'S ALL IN THE GAME Tommy Edwards (MGM)
6	3	IT'S ONLY MAKE BELIEVE Conway Twitty (MGM)
4	4	A CERTAIN SMILE Johnny Mathis (Fontana)
7	5	COME PRIMA Marino Marini Quartet (Durium)
13	6	TOM DOOLEY Lonnie Donegan (Pye Nixa)
3	7	BIRD DOG Everly Brothers (London)
5	8	MORE THAN EVER (COME PRIMA) Malcolm Vaughan (HMV)
11	9	LOVE MAKES THE WORLD GO 'ROUND Perry Como (RCA)
8	10	MOVE IT Cliff Richard (Columbia)
10	11	TEA FOR TWO CHA-CHA Tommy Dorsey Orchestra starring Warren Covington (Brunswick)
14	12	SOMEDAY (YOU'LL WANT ME TO WANT YOU) Ricky Nelson (London)
9	13	STUPID CUPID/CAROLINA MOON Connie Francis (MGM)
23	14	HIGH CLASS BABY Cliff Richard (Columbia)
16	15	COME ON LET'S GO Tommy Steele (Decca)
15	16	MY TRUE LOVE Jack Scott (London)
20	17	TOM DOOLEY Kingston Trio (Capitol)
25	18	SUMMERTIME BLUES Eddie Cochran (London)
29	19	MANDOLINS IN THE MOONLIGHT Perry Como (RCA)
22	20	FALLIN' Connie Francis (MGM)
12	20	KING CREOLE Elvis Presley (RCA)
16	22	SOMEDAY (YOU'LL WANT ME TO WANT YOU) Jodie Sands (HMV)
26	23	LONNIE'S SKIFFLE PARTY Lonnie Donegan (Pye Nixa)
19	24	I'LL GET BY Connie Francis (MGM)
-	25	MARY'S BOY CHILD Harry Belafonte (RCA)
18	26	BORN TOO LATE Poni-Tails (HMV)
30	27	VOLARE (NEL BLU DIPINTO DI BLU) Dean Martin (Capitol)
28	28	MORE THAN EVER Robert Earl (Philips)
-	28	POOR LITTLE FOOL Ricky Nelson (London)
-	30	MORE PARTY POPS Russ Conway (Columbia)

Marino Marini's *Volare*, a big seller in its own right, was only the simultaneously-charting B-side to his own Italian hit song *Come Prima*, which soared much higher to rest at Number Two. Translated into English as *More Than Ever*, the song also gave Top Five honours to Malcolm Vaughan. Tommy Edwards' chart-topping *It's All In The Game* was actually his second recording of the song (written by former US Vice-President Charles Dawes in 1912); he had first cut it, without any notable success, back in 1951.

6 December 1958

last week	this week	Title / Artist (Label)
1	1	HOOTS MON — Lord Rockingham's XI (Decca)
3	2	IT'S ONLY MAKE BELIEVE — Conway Twitty (MGM)
6	3	TOM DOOLEY — Lonnie Donegan (Pye Nixa)
2	3	IT'S ALL IN THE GAME — Tommy Edwards (MGM)
4	5	A CERTAIN SMILE — Johnny Mathis (Fontana)
11	6	TEA FOR TWO CHA-CHA — Tommy Dorsey Orchestra starring Warren Covington (Brunswick)
8	7	MORE THAN EVER (COME PRIMA) — Malcolm Vaughan (HMV)
17	8	TOM DOOLEY — Kingston Trio (Capitol)
14	9	HIGH CLASS BABY — Cliff Richard (Columbia)
9	10	LOVE MAKES THE WORLD GO 'ROUND — Perry Como (RCA)
12	10	SOMEDAY (YOU'LL WANT ME TO WANT YOU) — Ricky Nelson (London)
5	12	COME PRIMA — Marino Marini Quartet (Durium)
7	13	BIRD DOG — Everly Brothers (London)
15	14	COME ON LET'S GO — Tommy Steele (Decca)
10	15	MOVE IT — Cliff Richard (Columbia)
13	16	STUPID CUPID/CAROLINA MOON — Connie Francis (MGM)
22	17	SOMEDAY (YOU'LL WANT ME TO WANT YOU) — Jodie Sands (HMV)
16	18	MY TRUE LOVE — Jack Scott (London)
18	19	SUMMERTIME BLUES — Eddie Cochran (London)
25	20	MARY'S BOY CHILD — Harry Belafonte (RCA)
19	21	MANDOLINS IN THE MOONLIGHT — Perry Como (RCA)
24	22	I'LL GET BY — Connie Francis (MGM)
-	23	SUSIE DARLIN' — Robin Luke (London)
-	24	THE DAY THE RAINS CAME — Jane Morgan (London)
30	25	MORE PARTY POPS — Russ Conway (Columbia)
26	26	FALLIN' — Connie Francis (MGM)
20	27	KING CREOLE — Elvis Presley (RCA)
23	28	LONNIE'S SKIFFLE PARTY — Lonnie Donegan (Pye Nixa)
-	29	TOPSY (PART 1 AND 2) — Cozy Cole (London)
-	30	GEE BUT IT'S LONELY — Pat Boone (London)

13 December 1958

last week	this week	Title / Artist (Label)
1	1	HOOTS MON — Lord Rockingham's XI (Decca)
2	2	IT'S ONLY MAKE BELIEVE — Conway Twitty (MGM)
3	3	TOM DOOLEY — Lonnie Donegan (Pye Nixa)
3	4	IT'S ALL IN THE GAME — Tommy Edwards (MGM)
6	5	TEA FOR TWO CHA-CHA — Tommy Dorsey Orchestra starring Warren Covington (Brunswick)
8	6	TOM DOOLEY — Kingston Trio (Capitol)
9	7	HIGH CLASS BABY — Cliff Richard (Columbia)
10	8	LOVE MAKES THE WORLD GO 'ROUND — Perry Como (RCA)
10	9	SOMEDAY (YOU'LL WANT ME TO WANT YOU) — Ricky Nelson (London)
7	10	MORE THAN EVER (COME PRIMA) — Malcolm Vaughan (HMV)
12	11	COME PRIMA — Marino Marini Quartet (Durium)
5	11	A CERTAIN SMILE — Johnny Mathis (Fontana)
14	13	COME ON LET'S GO — Tommy Steele (Decca)
24	14	THE DAY THE RAINS CAME — Jane Morgan (London)
13	15	BIRD DOG — Everly Brothers (London)
21	16	MANDOLINS IN THE MOONLIGHT — Perry Como (RCA)
20	17	MARY'S BOY CHILD — Harry Belafonte (RCA)
-	18	REAL LOVE — Ruby Murray (Columbia)
17	19	SOMEDAY (YOU'LL WANT ME TO WANT YOU) — Jodie Sands (HMV)
16	20	STUPID CUPID/CAROLINA MOON — Connie Francis (MGM)
25	21	MORE PARTY POPS — Russ Conway (Columbia)
19	22	SUMMERTIME BLUES — Eddie Cochran (London)
28	23	LONNIE'S SKIFFLE PARTY — Lonnie Donegan (Pye Nixa)
23	24	SUSIE DARLIN' — Robin Luke (London)
15	25	MOVE IT — Cliff Richard (Columbia)
26	26	FALLIN' — Connie Francis (MGM)
-	27	THE SON OF MARY — Harry Belafonte (RCA)
27	27	KING CREOLE — Elvis Presley (RCA)
-	29	MR. SUCCESS — Frank Sinatra (Capitol)
18	30	MY TRUE LOVE — Jack Scott (London)

20 December 1958

last week	this week	Title / Artist (Label)
2	1	IT'S ONLY MAKE BELIEVE — Conway Twitty (MGM)
1	2	HOOTS MON — Lord Rockingham's XI (Decca)
3	3	TOM DOOLEY — Lonnie Donegan (Pye Nixa)
5	4	TEA FOR TWO CHA-CHA — Tommy Dorsey Orchestra starring Warren Covington (Brunswick)
4	5	IT'S ALL IN THE GAME — Tommy Edwards (MGM)
6	6	TOM DOOLEY — Kingston Trio (Capitol)
8	7	LOVE MAKES THE WORLD GO 'ROUND — Perry Como (RCA)
7	8	HIGH CLASS BABY — Cliff Richard (Columbia)
10	9	MORE THAN EVER (COME PRIMA) — Malcolm Vaughan (HMV)
17	10	MARY'S BOY CHILD — Harry Belafonte (RCA)
14	11	THE DAY THE RAINS CAME — Jane Morgan (London)
13	12	COME ON LET'S GO — Tommy Steele (Decca)
11	13	A CERTAIN SMILE — Johnny Mathis (Fontana)
11	14	COME PRIMA — Marino Marini Quartet (Durium)
9	15	SOMEDAY (YOU'LL WANT ME TO WANT YOU) — Ricky Nelson (London)
21	16	MORE PARTY POPS — Russ Conway (Columbia)
16	17	MANDOLINS IN THE MOONLIGHT — Perry Como (RCA)
27	18	THE SON OF MARY — Harry Belafonte (RCA)
18	18	REAL LOVE — Ruby Murray (Columbia)
15	20	BIRD DOG — Everly Brothers (London)
19	21	SOMEDAY (YOU'LL WANT ME TO WANT YOU) — Jodie Sands (HMV)
27	22	KING CREOLE — Elvis Presley (RCA)
26	23	FALLIN' — Connie Francis (MGM)
24	24	MOVE IT — Cliff Richard (Columbia)
20	25	STUPID CUPID/CAROLINA MOON — Connie Francis (MGM)
-	25	WINTER WONDERLAND — Johnny Mathis (Fontana)
29	25	MR. SUCCESS — Frank Sinatra (Capitol)
-	28	AS I LOVE YOU — Shirley Bassey (Philips)
-	28	WOMAN FROM LIBERIA — Jimmie Rodgers (Columbia)
-	30	TO KNOW HIM IS TO LOVE HIM — Teddy Bears (London)

27 December 1958

last week	this week	Title / Artist (Label)
1	1	IT'S ONLY MAKE BELIEVE — Conway Twitty (MGM)
2	2	HOOTS MON — Lord Rockingham's XI (Decca)
3	3	TOM DOOLEY — Lonnie Donegan (Pye Nixa)
4	4	TEA FOR TWO CHA-CHA — Tommy Dorsey Orchestra starring Warren Covington (Brunswick)
5	4	IT'S ALL IN THE GAME — Tommy Edwards (MGM)
6	6	TOM DOOLEY — Kingston Trio (Capitol)
7	7	LOVE MAKES THE WORLD GO 'ROUND — Perry Como (RCA)
11	8	THE DAY THE RAINS CAME — Jane Morgan (London)
8	9	HIGH CLASS BABY — Cliff Richard (Columbia)
12	10	COME ON LET'S GO — Tommy Steele (Decca)
9	11	MORE THAN EVER (COME PRIMA) — Malcolm Vaughan (HMV)
10	12	MARY'S BOY CHILD — Harry Belafonte (RCA)
15	13	SOMEDAY (YOU'LL WANT ME TO WANT YOU) — Ricky Nelson (London)
17	14	A CERTAIN SMILE — Johnny Mathis (Fontana)
14	15	MANDOLINS IN THE MOONLIGHT — Perry Como (RCA)
15	15	COME PRIMA — Marino Marini Quartet (Durium)
25	17	WINTER WONDERLAND — Johnny Mathis (Fontana)
16	18	MORE PARTY POPS — Russ Conway (Columbia)
20	19	BIRD DOG — Everly Brothers (London)
18	20	REAL LOVE — Ruby Murray (Columbia)
24	21	MOVE IT — Cliff Richard (Columbia)
-	22	KISS ME, HONEY HONEY, KISS ME — Shirley Bassey (Philips)
-	23	YOU ALWAYS HURT THE ONE YOU LOVE — Connie Francis (MGM)
18	24	THE SON OF MARY — Harry Belafonte (RCA)
30	25	TO KNOW HIM IS TO LOVE HIM — Teddy Bears (London)
28	26	WOMAN FROM LIBERIA — Jimmie Rodgers (Columbia)
28	27	AS I LOVE YOU — Shirley Bassey (Philips)
25	28	STUPID CUPID/CAROLINA MOON — Connie Francis (MGM)
22	29	KING CREOLE — Elvis Presley (RCA)
-	30	CHANTILLY LACE — Big Bopper (Mercury)

Hoots Mon, the first rock instrumental to top the UK chart (and the only one with Scottish-accented vocal interjections!) gave record success to the session band which was the backbone of the *Oh Boy!* TV show. "Lord Rockingham", inasmuch as he existed at all, was band leader Harry Robinson. Harry Belafonte followed his huge Yule success of the previous year with a new Christmas ballad, *The Son Of Mary* (to the melody of *Greensleeves*), but, perversely, *Mary's Boy Child* was a much bigger chart hit all over again.

last week	this week	3 January 1959
1	1	IT'S ONLY MAKE BELIEVE Conway Twitty (MGM)
2	2	HOOTS MON Lord Rockingham's XI (Decca)
4	3	TEA FOR TWO CHA-CHA Tommy Dorsey (Brunswick)
3	4	TOM DOOLEY Lonnie Donegan (Pye Nixa)
6	5	TOM DOOLEY Kingston Trio (Capitol)
8	6	THE DAY THE RAINS CAME Jane Morgan (London)
7	7	LOVE MAKES THE WORLD GO ROUND Perry Como (RCA)
4	8	IT'S ALL IN THE GAME Tommy Edwards (MGM)
9	9	HIGH CLASS BABY Cliff Richard (Columbia)
18	10	MORE PARTY POPS Russ Conway (Columbia)
10	11	COME ON LET'S GO Tommy Steele (Decca)
13	12	SOMEDAY Ricky Nelson (London)
11	13	MORE THAN EVER (COME PRIMA) Malcolm Vaughan (HMV)
15	14	MANDOLINS IN THE MOONLIGHT Perry Como (RCA)
12	15	MARY'S BOY CHILD Harry Belafonte (RCA)
-	16	BABY FACE Little Richard (London)
22	17	KISS ME, HONEY HONEY, KISS ME Shirley Bassey (Philips)
23	17	YOU ALWAYS HURT THE ONE YOU LOVE Connie Francis (MGM)
15	19	COME PRIMA Marino Marini Quartet (Durium)
25	20	TO KNOW HIM IS TO LOVE HIM Teddy Bears (London)
24	21	THE SON OF MARY Harry Belafonte (RCA)
29	22	KING CREOLE Elvis Presley (RCA)
-	23	MY UKELELE Max Bygraves (Decca)
14	24	A CERTAIN SMILE Johnny Mathis (Fontana)
-	25	CANNONBALL Duane Eddy (London)
-	26	MR. SUCCESS Frank Sinatra (Capitol)
26	27	WOMAN FROM LIBERIA Jimmie Rodgers (Columbia)
21	27	MOVE IT Cliff Richard (Columbia)
17	29	WINTER WONDERLAND Johnny Mathis (Fontana)
20	30	REAL LOVE Ruby Murray (Columbia)

10 January 1959
1 1 IT'S ONLY MAKE BELIEVE Conway Twitty (MGM)
2 2 HOOTS MON Lord Rockingham's XI (Decca)
4 3 TOM DOOLEY Lonnie Donegan (Pye Nixa)
3 4 TEA FOR TWO CHA-CHA Tommy Dorsey (Brunswick)
6 5 THE DAY THE RAINS CAME Jane Morgan (London)
7 6 LOVE MAKES THE WORLD GO ROUND Perry Como (RCA)
5 7 TOM DOOLEY Kingston Trio (Capitol)
9 8 HIGH CLASS BABY Cliff Richard (Columbia)
16 9 BABY FACE Little Richard (London)
20 10 TO KNOW HIM IS TO LOVE HIM Teddy Bears (London)
8 11 IT'S ALL IN THE GAME Tommy Edwards (MGM)
11 12 COME ON LET'S GO Tommy Steele (Decca)
14 13 MANDOLINS IN THE MOONLIGHT Perry Como (RCA)
17 14 KISS ME, HONEY HONEY, KISS ME Shirley Bassey (Philips)
17 14 YOU ALWAYS HURT THE ONE YOU LOVE Connie Francis (MGM)
12 14 SOMEDAY Ricky Nelson (London)
13 17 MORE THAN EVER (COME PRIMA) Malcolm Vaughan (HMV)
27 18 WOMAN FROM LIBERIA Jimmie Rodgers (Columbia)
23 19 MY UKELELE Max Bygraves (Decca)
24 20 A CERTAIN SMILE Johnny Mathis (Fontana)
10 21 MORE PARTY POPS Russ Conway (Columbia)
30 22 REAL LOVE Ruby Murray (Columbia)
- 23 CHANTILLY LACE Big Bopper (Mercury)
25 23 CANNONBALL Duane Eddy (London)
- 25 AS I LOVE YOU Shirley Bassey (Philips)
22 26 KING CREOLE Elvis Presley (RCA)
19 27 COME PRIMA Marino Marini Quartet (Durium)
- 28 AM I WASTING MY TIME Frankie Vaughan (Philips)
- 29 QUEEN OF THE HOP Bobby Darin (London)
- 30 THE WORLD OUTSIDE Ronnie Hilton (HMV)

17 January 1959
1 1 IT'S ONLY MAKE BELIEVE Conway Twitty (MGM)
5 2 THE DAY THE RAINS CAME Jane Morgan (London)
2 3 HOOTS MON Lord Rockingham's XI (Decca)
3 4 TOM DOOLEY Lonnie Donegan (Pye Nixa)
10 5 TO KNOW HIM IS TO LOVE HIM Teddy Bears (London)
4 6 TEA FOR TWO CHA-CHA Tommy Dorsey (Brunswick)
9 7 BABY FACE Little Richard (London)
6 8 LOVE MAKES THE WORLD GO ROUND Perry Como (RCA)
14 9 KISS ME, HONEY HONEY, KISS ME Shirley Bassey (Philips)
8 10 HIGH CLASS BABY Cliff Richard (Columbia)
12 10 COME ON LET'S GO Tommy Steele (Decca)
7 12 TOM DOOLEY Kingston Trio (Capitol)
13 13 MANDOLINS IN THE MOONLIGHT Perry Como (RCA)
14 13 YOU ALWAYS HURT THE ONE YOU LOVE Connie Francis (MGM)
11 15 IT'S ALL IN THE GAME Tommy Edwards (MGM)
25 16 AS I LOVE YOU Shirley Bassey (Philips)
- 17 SMOKE GETS IN YOUR EYES Platters (Mercury)
23 18 CHANTILLY LACE Big Bopper (Mercury)
18 18 WOMAN FROM LIBERIA Jimmie Rodgers (Columbia)
19 20 MY UKELELE Max Bygraves (Decca)
14 21 SOMEDAY Ricky Nelson (London)
23 22 CANNONBALL Duane Eddy (London)
17 23 MORE THAN EVER (COME PRIMA) Malcolm Vaughan (HMV)
29 24 QUEEN OF THE HOP Bobby Darin (London)
- 24 YOU'RE THE TOP CHA Al Saxon (Fontana)
22 26 REAL LOVE Ruby Murray (Columbia)
28 27 AM I WASTING MY TIME Frankie Vaughan (Philips)
- 28 I'LL REMEMBER TONIGHT Pat Boone (London)
30 29 THE WORLD OUTSIDE Ronnie Hilton (HMV)
- 30 HEARTBEAT Buddy Holly (Coral)

24 January 1959
2 1 THE DAY THE RAINS CAME Jane Morgan (London)
7 2 BABY FACE Little Richard (London)
- 3 I GOT STUNG/ONE NIGHT Elvis Presley (RCA)
5 4 TO KNOW HIM IS TO LOVE HIM Teddy Bears (London)
1 5 IT'S ONLY MAKE BELIEVE Conway Twitty (MGM)
9 6 KISS ME, HONEY HONEY, KISS ME Shirley Bassey (Philips)
6 7 TEA FOR TWO CHA-CHA Tommy Dorsey (Brunswick)
3 8 HOOTS MON Lord Rockingham's XI (Decca)
16 9 AS I LOVE YOU Shirley Bassey (Philips)
12 10 TOM DOOLEY Kingston Trio (Capitol)
4 11 TOM DOOLEY Lonnie Donegan (Pye Nixa)
8 12 LOVE MAKES THE WORLD GO ROUND Perry Como (RCA)
10 13 COME ON LET'S GO Tommy Steele (Decca)
17 14 SMOKE GETS IN YOUR EYES Platters (Mercury)
13 15 YOU ALWAYS HURT THE ONE YOU LOVE Connie Francis (MGM)
18 16 CHANTILLY LACE Big Bopper (Mercury)
24 17 YOU'RE THE TOP CHA Al Saxon (Fontana)
13 18 MANDOLINS IN THE MOONLIGHT Perry Como (RCA)
- 18 PROBLEMS Everly Brothers (London)
10 18 HIGH CLASS BABY Cliff Richard (Columbia)
29 21 THE WORLD OUTSIDE Ronnie Hilton (HMV)
22 22 CANNONBALL Duane Eddy (London)
- 22 HIGH SCHOOL CONFIDENTIAL Jerry Lee Lewis (London)
- 24 THE WORLD OUTSIDE Russ Conway (Columbia)
20 25 MY UKELELE Max Bygraves (Decca)
21 26 SOMEDAY Ricky Nelson (London)
15 27 IT'S ALL IN THE GAME Tommy Edwards (MGM)
- 28 I'LL BE WITH YOU IN APPLE BLOSSOM TIME Rosemary June (Pye International)
- 29 THE WORLD OUTSIDE Four Aces (Brunswick)
- 30 LAST NIGHT ON THE BACK PORCH Alma Cogan (HMV)
18 30 WOMAN FROM LIBERIA Jimmie Rodgers (Columbia)

The Teddy Bears' *To Know Him Is To Love Him* was the world's introduction to erratic music genius Phil Spector. As well as being a member of the teenage high school trio which sang the hit, Spector produced the single and also wrote the song, supposedly inspired by the inscription on his father's tombstone. Little Richard, who had publicly retired from rock'n'roll late in 1957 to become an evangelist, was still scoring with old tracks held by his label for later release: *Baby Face* was his biggest-ever UK hit.

January – February 1959

31 January 1959

3 1 I GOT STUNG/ONE NIGHT Elvis Presley (RCA)
4 2 TO KNOW HIM IS TO LOVE HIM Teddy Bears (London)
2 3 BABY FACE Little Richard (London)
6 4 KISS ME, HONEY HONEY, KISS ME Shirley Bassey (Philips)
1 4 THE DAY THE RAINS CAME Jane Morgan (London)
9 6 AS I LOVE YOU Shirley Bassey (Philips)
5 7 IT'S ONLY MAKE BELIEVE Conway Twitty (MGM)
18 8 PROBLEMS Everly Brothers (London)
14 9 SMOKE GETS IN YOUR EYES Platters (Mercury)
11 10 TOM DOOLEY Lonnie Donegan (Pye Nixa)
7 11 TEA FOR TWO CHA-CHA Tommy Dorsey (Brunswick)
16 12 CHANTILLY LACE Big Bopper (Mercury)
10 13 TOM DOOLEY Kingston Trio (Capitol)
8 14 HOOTS MON Lord Rockingham's XI (Decca)
18 15 MANDOLINS IN THE MOONLIGHT Perry Como (RCA)
13 16 COME ON LET'S GO Tommy Steele (Decca)
15 17 YOU ALWAYS HURT THE ONE YOU LOVE Connie Francis (MGM)
22 18 HIGH SCHOOL CONFIDENTIAL Jerry Lee Lewis (London)
12 19 LOVE MAKES THE WORLD GO ROUND Perry Como (RCA)
- 20 (ALL OF A SUDDEN) MY HEART SINGS Paul Anka (Columbia)
21 20 THE WORLD OUTSIDE Ronnie Hilton (HMV)
17 22 YOU'RE THE TOP CHA Al Saxon (Fontana)
26 23 SOMEDAY Ricky Nelson (London)
- 24 THERE MUST BE A WAY Joni James (MGM)
- 25 LIVIN' LOVIN' DOLL Cliff Richard (Columbia)
28 26 I'LL BE WITH YOU IN APPLE BLOSSOM TIME Rosemary June (Pye International)
30 27 LAST NIGHT ON THE BACK PORCH Alma Cogan (HMV)
29 27 THE WORLD OUTSIDE Four Aces (Brunswick)
- 29 A PUB WITH NO BEER Slim Dusty (Columbia)
- 30 THAT'S MY DOLL Frankie Vaughan (Philips)

7 February 1959

1 1 I GOT STUNG/ONE NIGHT Elvis Presley (RCA)
2 2 TO KNOW HIM IS TO LOVE HIM Teddy Bears (London)
6 3 AS I LOVE YOU Shirley Bassey (Philips)
4 4 KISS ME, HONEY HONEY, KISS ME Shirley Bassey (Philips)
3 5 BABY FACE Little Richard (London)
8 6 PROBLEMS Everly Brothers (London)
4 7 THE DAY THE RAINS CAME Jane Morgan (London)
9 7 SMOKE GETS IN YOUR EYES Platters (Mercury)
- 9 DOES YOUR CHEWING GUM LOSE ITS FLAVOUR Lonnie Donegan (Pye Nixa)
7 10 IT'S ONLY MAKE BELIEVE Conway Twitty (MGM)
11 11 TEA FOR TWO CHA-CHA Tommy Dorsey (Brunswick)
20 12 (ALL OF A SUDDEN) MY HEART SINGS Paul Anka (Columbia)
10 13 TOM DOOLEY Lonnie Donegan (Pye Nixa)
18 14 HIGH SCHOOL CONFIDENTIAL Jerry Lee Lewis (London)
14 15 HOOTS MON Lord Rockingham's XI (Decca)
26 16 I'LL BE WITH YOU IN APPLE BLOSSOM TIME Rosemary June (Pye International)
12 17 CHANTILLY LACE Big Bopper (Mercury)
20 18 THE WORLD OUTSIDE Ronnie Hilton (HMV)
13 18 TOM DOOLEY Kingston Trio (Capitol)
29 20 A PUB WITH NO BEER Slim Dusty (Columbia)
- 21 I'LL REMEMBER TONIGHT Pat Boone (London)
- 21 WEE TOM Lord Rockingham's XI (Decca)
27 23 THE WORLD OUTSIDE Four Aces (Brunswick)
19 24 LOVE MAKES THE WORLD GO ROUND Perry Como (RCA)
25 25 LIVIN' LOVIN' DOLL Cliff Richard (Columbia)
17 26 YOU ALWAYS HURT THE ONE YOU LOVE Connie Francis (MGM)
15 27 MANDOLINS IN THE MOONLIGHT Perry Como (RCA)
16 28 COME ON LET'S GO Tommy Steele (Decca)
30 28 THAT'S MY DOLL Frankie Vaughan (Philips)
22 30 YOU'RE THE TOP CHA Al Saxon (Fontana)

14 February 1959

1 1 I GOT STUNG/ONE NIGHT Elvis Presley (RCA)
3 2 AS I LOVE YOU Shirley Bassey (Philips)
3 3 KISS ME, HONEY HONEY, KISS ME Shirley Bassey (Philips)
2 4 TO KNOW HIM IS TO LOVE HIM Teddy Bears (London)
5 5 BABY FACE Little Richard (London)
9 6 DOES YOUR CHEWING GUM LOSE ITS FLAVOUR Lonnie Donegan (Pye Nixa)
7 7 SMOKE GETS IN YOUR EYES Platters (Mercury)
6 8 PROBLEMS Everly Brothers (London)
7 9 THE DAY THE RAINS CAME Jane Morgan (London)
12 10 (ALL OF A SUDDEN) MY HEART SINGS Paul Anka (Columbia)
20 11 A PUB WITH NO BEER Slim Dusty (Columbia)
14 12 HIGH SCHOOL CONFIDENTIAL Jerry Lee Lewis (London)
10 13 IT'S ONLY MAKE BELIEVE Conway Twitty (MGM)
16 14 I'LL BE WITH YOU IN APPLE BLOSSOM TIME Rosemary June (Pye International)
11 15 TEA FOR TWO CHA-CHA Tommy Dorsey (Brunswick)
- 16 THE LITTLE DRUMMER BOY Beverley Sisters (Decca)
21 16 WEE TOM Lord Rockingham's XI (Decca)
23 18 THE WORLD OUTSIDE Four Aces (Brunswick)
- 19 MY HAPPINESS Connie Francis (MGM)
- 20 GIGI Billy Eckstine (Mercury)
25 20 LIVIN' LOVIN' DOLL Cliff Richard (Columbia)
13 22 TOM DOOLEY Lonnie Donegan (Pye Nixa)
18 22 THE WORLD OUTSIDE Ronnie Hilton (HMV)
- 22 THE LITTLE DRUMMER BOY The Harry Simeone Chorale (Top Rank)
15 25 HOOTS MON Lord Rockingham's XI (Decca)
17 26 CHANTILLY LACE Big Bopper (Mercury)
- 27 PETITE FLEUR Chris Barber (Pye-Nixa)
18 28 TOM DOOLEY Kingston Trio (Capitol)
- 29 THE WONDERFUL SECRET OF LOVE Robert Earl (Philips)
- 29 STAGGER LEE Lloyd Price (HMV)

21 February 1959

2 1 AS I LOVE YOU Shirley Bassey (Philips)
1 2 I GOT STUNG/ONE NIGHT Elvis Presley (RCA)
7 3 SMOKE GETS IN YOUR EYES Platters (Mercury)
6 4 DOES YOUR CHEWING GUM LOSE ITS FLAVOUR Lonnie Donegan (Pye Nixa)
3 5 KISS ME, HONEY HONEY, KISS ME Shirley Bassey (Philips)
4 6 TO KNOW HIM IS TO LOVE HIM Teddy Bears (London)
8 7 PROBLEMS Everly Brothers (London)
5 7 BABY FACE Little Richard (London)
11 9 A PUB WITH NO BEER Slim Dusty (Columbia)
9 10 THE DAY THE RAINS CAME Jane Morgan (London)
27 11 PETITE FLEUR Chris Barber (Pye-Nixa)
10 12 (ALL OF A SUDDEN) MY HEART SINGS Paul Anka (Columbia)
22 13 THE LITTLE DRUMMER BOY The Harry Simeone Chorale (Top Rank)
12 14 HIGH SCHOOL CONFIDENTIAL Jerry Lee Lewis (London)
16 15 THE LITTLE DRUMMER BOY Beverley Sisters (Decca)
19 16 MY HAPPINESS Connie Francis (MGM)
14 17 I'LL BE WITH YOU IN APPLE BLOSSOM TIME Rosemary June (Pye International)
20 18 GIGI Billy Eckstine (Mercury)
16 19 WEE TOM Lord Rockingham's XI (Decca)
15 20 TEA FOR TWO CHA-CHA Tommy Dorsey (Brunswick)
13 21 IT'S ONLY MAKE BELIEVE Conway Twitty (MGM)
- 22 I'LL REMEMBER TONIGHT Pat Boone (London)
26 23 CHANTILLY LACE Big Bopper (Mercury)
- 23 SIDE SADDLE Russ Conway (Columbia)
20 23 LIVIN' LOVIN' DOLL Cliff Richard (Columbia)
22 26 TOM DOOLEY Lonnie Donegan (Pye Nixa)
28 27 TOM DOOLEY Kingston Trio (Capitol)
29 28 THE WONDERFUL SECRET OF LOVE Robert Earl (Philips)
18 29 THE WORLD OUTSIDE Four Aces (Brunswick)
29 29 STAGGER LEE Lloyd Price (HMV)

Elvis Presley had been US Army private 53310761 for the best part of a year when the double A-side *I Got Stung/One Night* gave him his third chart-topping single; the former title had been cut in a session held during Army leave in 1958. Shirley Bassey achieved the amazing distinction of simultaneously holding both positions two and three behind Elvis on February 14, with the contrasting ballad *As I Love You* and zestful *Kiss Me, Honey Honey, Kiss Me*. The following week, the former title was Number One.

February – March 1959

28 February 1959

last week	this week	Title	Artist
1	1	AS I LOVE YOU	Shirley Bassey (Philips)
3	2	SMOKE GETS IN YOUR EYES	Platters (Mercury)
4	3	DOES YOUR CHEWING GUM LOSE ITS FLAVOUR	Lonnie Donegan (Pye Nixa)
2	4	I GOT STUNG/ONE NIGHT	Elvis Presley (RCA)
5	5	KISS ME, HONEY HONEY, KISS ME	Shirley Bassey (Philips)
9	6	A PUB WITH NO BEER	Slim Dusty (Columbia)
6	7	TO KNOW HIM IS TO LOVE HIM	Teddy Bears (London)
11	8	PETITE FLEUR	Chris Barber (Pye-Nixa)
15	9	THE LITTLE DRUMMER BOY	Beverley Sisters (Decca)
7	9	PROBLEMS	Everly Brothers (London)
12	11	(ALL OF A SUDDEN) MY HEART SINGS	Paul Anka (Columbia)
16	12	MY HAPPINESS	Connie Francis (MGM)
13	13	THE LITTLE DRUMMER BOY	The Harry Simeone Chorale (Top Rank)
7	14	BABY FACE	Little Richard (London)
29	15	STAGGER LEE	Lloyd Price (HMV)
18	16	GIGI	Billy Eckstine (Mercury)
10	16	THE DAY THE RAINS CAME	Jane Morgan (London)
28	18	THE WONDERFUL SECRET OF LOVE	Robert Earl (Philips)
-	19	TOMBOY	Perry Como (RCA)
-	20	THE LITTLE DRUMMER BOY	Michael Flanders (Parlophone)
-	20	IT DOESN'T MATTER ANYMORE	Buddy Holly (Coral)
23	22	SIDE SADDLE	Russ Conway (Columbia)
17	23	I'LL BE WITH YOU IN APPLE BLOSSOM TIME	Rosemary June (Pye International)
29	24	THE WORLD OUTSIDE	Four Aces (Brunswick)
14	25	HIGH SCHOOL CONFIDENTIAL	Jerry Lee Lewis (London)
-	26	MAYBE TOMORROW	Billy Fury (Decca)
22	27	I'LL REMEMBER TONIGHT	Pat Boone (London)
-	28	WAIT FOR ME/WILLINGLY	Malcolm Vaughan (HMV)
-	29	MANHATTAN SPIRITUAL	Reg Owen (Pye International)
-	30	THE LOVE GAME	Mudlarks (Columbia)
23	30	LIVIN' LOVIN' DOLL	Cliff Richard (Columbia)

7 March 1959

last week	this week	Title	Artist
1	1	AS I LOVE YOU	Shirley Bassey (Philips)
2	2	SMOKE GETS IN YOUR EYES	Platters (Mercury)
6	3	A PUB WITH NO BEER	Slim Dusty (Columbia)
3	4	DOES YOUR CHEWING GUM LOSE ITS FLAVOUR	Lonnie Donegan (Pye Nixa)
5	5	KISS ME, HONEY HONEY, KISS ME	Shirley Bassey (Philips)
8	6	PETITE FLEUR	Chris Barber (Pye-Nixa)
4	7	I GOT STUNG/ONE NIGHT	Elvis Presley (RCA)
22	8	SIDE SADDLE	Russ Conway (Columbia)
9	9	THE LITTLE DRUMMER BOY	Beverley Sisters (Decca)
12	10	MY HAPPINESS	Connie Francis (MGM)
11	11	(ALL OF A SUDDEN) MY HEART SINGS	Paul Anka (Columbia)
9	12	PROBLEMS	Everly Brothers (London)
7	12	TO KNOW HIM IS TO LOVE HIM	Teddy Bears (London)
14	14	BABY FACE	Little Richard (London)
15	15	STAGGER LEE	Lloyd Price (HMV)
13	16	THE LITTLE DRUMMER BOY	The Harry Simeone Chorale (Top Rank)
20	16	IT DOESN'T MATTER ANYMORE	Buddy Holly (Coral)
16	18	THE DAY THE RAINS CAME	Jane Morgan (London)
16	19	GIGI	Billy Eckstine (Mercury)
19	20	TOMBOY	Perry Como (RCA)
18	21	THE WONDERFUL SECRET OF LOVE	Robert Earl (Philips)
26	22	MAYBE TOMORROW	Billy Fury (Decca)
29	23	MANHATTAN SPIRITUAL	Reg Owen (Pye International)
-	24	THE WORLD OUTSIDE	Russ Conway (Columbia)
23	25	I'LL BE WITH YOU IN APPLE BLOSSOM TIME	Rosemary June (Pye International)
27	26	I'LL REMEMBER TONIGHT	Pat Boone (London)
20	27	THE LITTLE DRUMMER BOY	Michael Flanders (Parlophone)
30	28	LIVIN' LOVIN' DOLL	Cliff Richard (Columbia)
-	29	DONNA	Ritchie Valens (London)
-	30	DONNA	Marty Wilde (Philips)

14 March 1959

last week	this week	Title	Artist
1	1	AS I LOVE YOU	Shirley Bassey (Philips)
2	2	SMOKE GETS IN YOUR EYES	Platters (Mercury)
3	3	A PUB WITH NO BEER	Slim Dusty (Columbia)
8	4	SIDE SADDLE	Russ Conway (Columbia)
6	5	PETITE FLEUR	Chris Barber (Pye-Nixa)
5	6	KISS ME, HONEY HONEY, KISS ME	Shirley Bassey (Philips)
9	6	THE LITTLE DRUMMER BOY	Beverley Sisters (Decca)
4	8	DOES YOUR CHEWING GUM LOSE ITS FLAVOUR	Lonnie Donegan (Pye Nixa)
10	9	MY HAPPINESS	Connie Francis (MGM)
11	10	(ALL OF A SUDDEN) MY HEART SINGS	Paul Anka (Columbia)
7	11	I GOT STUNG/ONE NIGHT	Elvis Presley (RCA)
15	12	STAGGER LEE	Lloyd Price (HMV)
16	13	IT DOESN'T MATTER ANYMORE	Buddy Holly (Coral)
19	14	GIGI	Billy Eckstine (Mercury)
12	15	PROBLEMS	Everly Brothers (London)
12	16	TO KNOW HIM IS TO LOVE HIM	Teddy Bears (London)
21	17	THE WONDERFUL SECRET OF LOVE	Robert Earl (Philips)
20	18	TOMBOY	Perry Como (RCA)
16	18	THE LITTLE DRUMMER BOY	The Harry Simeone Chorale (Top Rank)
-	20	C'MON EVERYBODY	Eddie Cochran (London)
14	21	BABY FACE	Little Richard (London)
26	22	I'LL REMEMBER TONIGHT	Pat Boone (London)
23	23	MANHATTAN SPIRITUAL	Reg Owen (Pye International)
18	24	THE DAY THE RAINS CAME	Jane Morgan (London)
24	25	THE WORLD OUTSIDE	Russ Conway (Columbia)
22	26	MAYBE TOMORROW	Billy Fury (Decca)
-	27	WAIT FOR ME	Malcolm Vaughan (HMV)
-	28	VENUS	Dickie Valentine (Pye Nixa)
30	29	DONNA	Marty Wilde (Philips)
25	30	I'LL BE WITH YOU IN APPLE BLOSSOM TIME	Rosemary June (Pye International)

21 March 1959

last week	this week	Title	Artist
2	1	SMOKE GETS IN YOUR EYES	Platters (Mercury)
1	2	AS I LOVE YOU	Shirley Bassey (Philips)
4	3	SIDE SADDLE	Russ Conway (Columbia)
3	4	A PUB WITH NO BEER	Slim Dusty (Columbia)
9	5	MY HAPPINESS	Connie Francis (MGM)
5	6	PETITE FLEUR	Chris Barber (Pye-Nixa)
12	7	STAGGER LEE	Lloyd Price (HMV)
6	8	THE LITTLE DRUMMER BOY	Beverley Sisters (Decca)
14	8	GIGI	Billy Eckstine (Mercury)
13	10	IT DOESN'T MATTER ANYMORE	Buddy Holly (Coral)
8	11	DOES YOUR CHEWING GUM LOSE ITS FLAVOUR	Lonnie Donegan (Pye Nixa)
6	12	KISS ME, HONEY HONEY, KISS ME	Shirley Bassey (Philips)
10	13	(ALL OF A SUDDEN) MY HEART SINGS	Paul Anka (Columbia)
18	14	TOMBOY	Perry Como (RCA)
20	15	C'MON EVERYBODY	Eddie Cochran (London)
11	16	I GOT STUNG/ONE NIGHT	Elvis Presley (RCA)
17	17	THE WONDERFUL SECRET OF LOVE	Robert Earl (Philips)
22	18	I'LL REMEMBER TONIGHT	Pat Boone (London)
15	19	PROBLEMS	Everly Brothers (London)
23	20	MANHATTAN SPIRITUAL	Reg Owen (Pye International)
18	21	THE LITTLE DRUMMER BOY	The Harry Simeone Chorale (Top Rank)
-	22	SING LITTLE BIRDIE	Pearl Carr & Teddy Johnson (Columbia)
16	23	TO KNOW HIM IS TO LOVE HIM	Teddy Bears (London)
21	24	BABY FACE	Little Richard (London)
-	25	CIAO CIAO BAMBINA	Marino Marini (Durium)
24	25	THE DAY THE RAINS CAME	Jane Morgan (London)
27	27	WAIT FOR ME	Malcolm Vaughan (HMV)
30	28	I'LL BE WITH YOU IN APPLE BLOSSOM TIME	Rosemary June (Pye International)
29	29	DONNA	Marty Wilde (Philips)
25	30	THE WORLD OUTSIDE	Russ Conway (Columbia)

Shirley Bassey was the first and only female singer ever to dislodge Elvis Presley from the top of the UK singles chart. Slim Dusty offered a rare example of an early Australian record hitting big in Britain (the dry pub of the song was located in the outback), while Christmas apparently came late for buyers of The *Little Drummer Boy* - the Beverley Sisters' version of this Nativity song reached the Top 10 two full months after Christmas Day, and the Michael Flanders and Harry Simeone versions were selling almost as well.

March – April 1959

28 March 1959

Last	This	Title / Artist
3	1	SIDE SADDLE — Russ Conway (Columbia)
1	2	SMOKE GETS IN YOUR EYES — Platters (Mercury)
2	3	AS I LOVE YOU — Shirley Bassey (Philips)
5	4	MY HAPPINESS — Connie Francis (MGM)
6	5	PETITE FLEUR — Chris Barber (Pye-Nixa)
4	6	A PUB WITH NO BEER — Slim Dusty (Columbia)
7	7	STAGGER LEE — Lloyd Price (HMV)
8	8	GIGI — Billy Eckstine (Mercury)
10	9	IT DOESN'T MATTER ANYMORE — Buddy Holly (Coral)
8	10	THE LITTLE DRUMMER BOY — Beverley Sisters (Decca)
11	11	DOES YOUR CHEWING GUM LOSE ITS FLAVOUR — Lonnie Donegan (Pye Nixa)
15	12	C'MON EVERYBODY — Eddie Cochran (London)
13	13	(ALL OF A SUDDEN) MY HEART SINGS — Paul Anka (Columbia)
14	14	TOMBOY — Perry Como (RCA)
16	15	I GOT STUNG/ONE NIGHT — Elvis Presley (RCA)
12	16	KISS ME, HONEY HONEY, KISS ME — Shirley Bassey (Philips)
17	17	THE WONDERFUL SECRET OF LOVE — Robert Earl (Philips)
27	18	WAIT FOR ME — Malcolm Vaughan (HMV)
-	19	MAYBE TOMORROW — Billy Fury (Decca)
22	20	SING LITTLE BIRDIE — Pearl Carr & Teddy Johnson (Columbia)
29	21	DONNA — Marty Wilde (Philips)
-	22	CHARLIE BROWN — Coasters (London)
18	23	I'LL REMEMBER TONIGHT — Pat Boone (London)
20	24	MANHATTAN SPIRITUAL — Reg Owen (Pye International)
21	24	THE LITTLE DRUMMER BOY — The Harry Simeone Chorale (Top Rank)
19	26	PROBLEMS — Everly Brothers (London)
23	27	TO KNOW HIM IS TO LOVE HIM — Teddy Bears (London)
24	28	BABY FACE — Little Richard (London)
-	29	CIAO CIAO BAMBINA — Domenico Modugno (Oriole)
-	30	THE STORY OF MY LOVE — Conway Twitty (MGM)

4 April 1959

Last	This	Title / Artist
1	1	SIDE SADDLE — Russ Conway (Columbia)
2	2	SMOKE GETS IN YOUR EYES — Platters (Mercury)
9	3	IT DOESN'T MATTER ANYMORE — Buddy Holly (Coral)
3	4	AS I LOVE YOU — Shirley Bassey (Philips)
4	5	MY HAPPINESS — Connie Francis (MGM)
5	6	PETITE FLEUR — Chris Barber (Pye-Nixa)
7	7	STAGGER LEE — Lloyd Price (HMV)
6	8	A PUB WITH NO BEER — Slim Dusty (Columbia)
8	9	GIGI — Billy Eckstine (Mercury)
10	10	TOMBOY — Perry Como (RCA)
10	11	THE LITTLE DRUMMER BOY — Beverley Sisters (Decca)
20	12	SING LITTLE BIRDIE — Pearl Carr & Teddy Johnson (Columbia)
18	13	WAIT FOR ME — Malcolm Vaughan (HMV)
11	14	DOES YOUR CHEWING GUM LOSE ITS FLAVOUR — Lonnie Donegan (Pye Nixa)
21	15	DONNA — Marty Wilde (Philips)
22	16	CHARLIE BROWN — Coasters (London)
12	17	C'MON EVERYBODY — Eddie Cochran (London)
13	18	(ALL OF A SUDDEN) MY HEART SINGS — Paul Anka (Columbia)
16	19	KISS ME, HONEY HONEY, KISS ME — Shirley Bassey (Philips)
-	20	BY THE LIGHT OF THE SILVERY MOON — Little Richard (London)
15	21	I GOT STUNG/ONE NIGHT — Elvis Presley (RCA)
19	22	MAYBE TOMORROW — Billy Fury (Decca)
17	23	THE WONDERFUL SECRET OF LOVE — Robert Earl (Philips)
-	24	CIAO CIAO BAMBINA — Marino Marini (Durium)
-	25	VENUS — Dickie Valentine (Pye Nixa)
27	26	TO KNOW HIM IS TO LOVE HIM — Teddy Bears (London)
26	27	PROBLEMS — Everly Brothers (London)
23	28	I'LL REMEMBER TONIGHT — Pat Boone (London)
24	29	MANHATTAN SPIRITUAL — Reg Owen (Pye International)
28	30	BABY FACE — Little Richard (London)

11 April 1959

Last	This	Title / Artist
1	1	SIDE SADDLE — Russ Conway (Columbia)
2	2	SMOKE GETS IN YOUR EYES — Platters (Mercury)
3	3	IT DOESN'T MATTER ANYMORE — Buddy Holly (Coral)
5	4	MY HAPPINESS — Connie Francis (MGM)
6	5	PETITE FLEUR — Chris Barber (Pye-Nixa)
4	6	AS I LOVE YOU — Shirley Bassey (Philips)
7	7	STAGGER LEE — Lloyd Price (HMV)
9	8	GIGI — Billy Eckstine (Mercury)
8	9	A PUB WITH NO BEER — Slim Dusty (Columbia)
15	10	DONNA — Marty Wilde (Philips)
11	11	THE LITTLE DRUMMER BOY — Beverley Sisters (Decca)
10	12	TOMBOY — Perry Como (RCA)
16	13	CHARLIE BROWN — Coasters (London)
17	14	C'MON EVERYBODY — Eddie Cochran (London)
12	15	SING LITTLE BIRDIE — Pearl Carr & Teddy Johnson (Columbia)
13	16	WAIT FOR ME — Malcolm Vaughan (HMV)
20	17	BY THE LIGHT OF THE SILVERY MOON — Little Richard (London)
22	18	MAYBE TOMORROW — Billy Fury (Decca)
14	19	DOES YOUR CHEWING GUM LOSE ITS FLAVOUR — Lonnie Donegan (Pye Nixa)
18	20	(ALL OF A SUDDEN) MY HEART SINGS — Paul Anka (Columbia)
-	21	WITH THE WIND AND THE RAIN IN YOUR HAIR — Pat Boone (London)
-	22	ALL-AMERICAN BOY — Bill Parsons (London)
19	23	KISS ME, HONEY HONEY, KISS ME — Shirley Bassey (Philips)
	24	I GOT STUNG/ONE NIGHT — Elvis Presley (RCA)
-	25	FRENCH FOREIGN LEGION — Frank Sinatra (Capitol)
-	26	EARLY TO BED — Poni-Tails (HMV)
27	27	PROBLEMS — Everly Brothers (London)
29	28	MANHATTAN SPIRITUAL — Reg Owen (Pye International)
30	29	BABY FACE — Little Richard (London)
23	30	THE WONDERFUL SECRET OF LOVE — Robert Earl (Philips)

18 April 1959

Last	This	Title / Artist
1	1	SIDE SADDLE — Russ Conway (Columbia)
3	2	IT DOESN'T MATTER ANYMORE — Buddy Holly (Coral)
5	3	PETITE FLEUR — Chris Barber (Pye-Nixa)
2	4	SMOKE GETS IN YOUR EYES — Platters (Mercury)
10	5	DONNA — Marty Wilde (Philips)
14	6	C'MON EVERYBODY — Eddie Cochran (London)
7	7	STAGGER LEE — Lloyd Price (HMV)
13	8	CHARLIE BROWN — Coasters (London)
8	9	GIGI — Billy Eckstine (Mercury)
4	10	MY HAPPINESS — Connie Francis (MGM)
11	11	THE LITTLE DRUMMER BOY — Beverley Sisters (Decca)
6	12	AS I LOVE YOU — Shirley Bassey (Philips)
12	13	TOMBOY — Perry Como (RCA)
9	14	A PUB WITH NO BEER — Slim Dusty (Columbia)
16	15	WAIT FOR ME — Malcolm Vaughan (HMV)
15	16	SING LITTLE BIRDIE — Pearl Carr & Teddy Johnson (Columbia)
17	17	BY THE LIGHT OF THE SILVERY MOON — Little Richard (London)
18	18	MAYBE TOMORROW — Billy Fury (Decca)
20	19	(ALL OF A SUDDEN) MY HEART SINGS — Paul Anka (Columbia)
19	20	DOES YOUR CHEWING GUM LOSE ITS FLAVOUR — Lonnie Donegan (Pye Nixa)
25	21	FRENCH FOREIGN LEGION — Frank Sinatra (Capitol)
-	22	IT'S LATE — Ricky Nelson (London)
23	23	KISS ME, HONEY HONEY, KISS ME — Shirley Bassey (Philips)
-	24	THE LITTLE DRUMMER BOY — Michael Flanders (Parlophone)
21	25	WITH THE WIND AND THE RAIN IN YOUR HAIR — Pat Boone (London)
-	26	VENUS — Dickie Valentine (Pye Nixa)
26	27	EARLY TO BED — Poni-Tails (HMV)
22	28	ALL-AMERICAN BOY — Bill Parsons (London)
30	29	THE WONDERFUL SECRET OF LOVE — Robert Earl (Philips)
28	30	MANHATTAN SPIRITUAL — Reg Owen (Pye International)

Russ Conway's *Side Saddle*, the longest-resident chart record of 1959 (30 weeks in the Top 30) catapulted him to fame as Britain's leading instrumental hitmaker since Winifred Atwell. The Chris Barber Band's *Petite Fleur*, meanwhile, featuring Monty Sunshine on lead clarinett, was the precursor of the commercial flurry of trad jazz which was to come two years later. Barber, oddly, would not share in the 1961 chart successes, but *Petite Fleur* outsold most of the later competition, and was also a hit in America.

April – May 1959

25 April 1959

last week	this week	title	artist
2	1	IT DOESN'T MATTER ANYMORE	Buddy Holly (Coral)
1	2	SIDE SADDLE	Russ Conway (Columbia)
3	3	PETITE FLEUR	Chris Barber (Pye-Nixa)
-	4	A FOOL SUCH AS I/I NEED YOUR LOVE TONIGHT	Elvis Presley (RCA)
5	5	DONNA	Marty Wilde (Philips)
8	6	CHARLIE BROWN	Coasters (London)
4	7	SMOKE GETS IN YOUR EYES	Platters (Mercury)
6	8	C'MON EVERYBODY	Eddie Cochran (London)
10	9	MY HAPPINESS	Connie Francis (MGM)
7	10	STAGGER LEE	Lloyd Price (HMV)
13	11	TOMBOY	Perry Como (RCA)
9	12	GIGI	Billy Eckstine (Mercury)
14	13	A PUB WITH NO BEER	Slim Dusty (Columbia)
12	14	AS I LOVE YOU	Shirley Bassey (Philips)
11	15	THE LITTLE DRUMMER BOY	Beverley Sisters (Decca)
22	16	IT'S LATE	Ricky Nelson (London)
15	17	WAIT FOR ME	Malcolm Vaughan (HMV)
21	18	FRENCH FOREIGN LEGION	Frank Sinatra (Capitol)
16	19	SING LITTLE BIRDIE	Pearl Carr & Teddy Johnson (Columbia)
-	20	COME SOFTLY TO ME	Fleetwoods (London)
18	21	MAYBE TOMORROW	Billy Fury (Decca)
26	22	VENUS	Dickie Valentine (Pye Nixa)
17	23	BY THE LIGHT OF THE SILVERY MOON	Little Richard (London)
-	24	I GO APE	Neil Sedaka (RCA)
19	25	(ALL OF A SUDDEN) MY HEART SINGS	Paul Anka (Columbia)
-	26	LOVE'S MADE A FOOL OF YOU	Crickets (Coral)
-	27	VENUS	Frankie Avalon (HMV)
20	28	DOES YOUR CHEWING GUM LOSE ITS FLAVOUR	Lonnie Donegan (Pye Nixa)
27	29	EARLY TO BED	Poni-Tails (HMV)
25	30	WITH THE WIND AND THE RAIN IN YOUR HAIR	Pat Boone (London)

2 May 1959

last week	this week	title	artist
1	1	IT DOESN'T MATTER ANYMORE	Buddy Holly (Coral)
4	2	A FOOL SUCH AS I/I NEED YOUR LOVE TONIGHT	Elvis Presley (RCA)
3	3	PETITE FLEUR	Chris Barber (Pye-Nixa)
2	4	SIDE SADDLE	Russ Conway (Columbia)
5	5	DONNA	Marty Wilde (Philips)
6	6	CHARLIE BROWN	Coasters (London)
7	7	SMOKE GETS IN YOUR EYES	Platters (Mercury)
8	8	C'MON EVERYBODY	Eddie Cochran (London)
16	9	IT'S LATE	Ricky Nelson (London)
20	10	COME SOFTLY TO ME	Fleetwoods (London)
-	11	COME SOFTLY TO ME	Frankie Vaughan & the Kaye Sisters (Philips)
-	12	I'VE WAITED SO LONG	Anthony Newley (Decca)
24	13	I GO APE	Neil Sedaka (RCA)
10	14	STAGGER LEE	Lloyd Price (HMV)
9	15	MY HAPPINESS	Connie Francis (MGM)
13	16	A PUB WITH NO BEER	Slim Dusty (Columbia)
11	17	TOMBOY	Perry Como (RCA)
12	18	GIGI	Billy Eckstine (Mercury)
14	19	AS I LOVE YOU	Shirley Bassey (Philips)
22	20	VENUS	Dickie Valentine (Pye Nixa)
27	21	VENUS	Frankie Avalon (HMV)
18	22	FRENCH FOREIGN LEGION	Frank Sinatra (Capitol)
15	23	THE LITTLE DRUMMER BOY	Beverley Sisters (Decca)
17	24	WAIT FOR ME	Malcolm Vaughan (HMV)
-	25	MAY YOU ALWAYS	Joan Regan (HMV)
19	26	SING LITTLE BIRDIE	Pearl Carr & Teddy Johnson (Columbia)
-	27	MAY YOU ALWAYS	McGuire Sisters (Coral)
-	28	LOVIN' UP A STORM	Jerry Lee Lewis (London)
21	29	MAYBE TOMORROW	Billy Fury (Decca)
23	30	BY THE LIGHT OF THE SILVERY MOON	Little Richard (London)

9 May 1959

last week	this week	title	artist
1	1	IT DOESN'T MATTER ANYMORE	Buddy Holly (Coral)
2	2	A FOOL SUCH AS I/I NEED YOUR LOVE TONIGHT	Elvis Presley (RCA)
4	3	SIDE SADDLE	Russ Conway (Columbia)
5	4	DONNA	Marty Wilde (Philips)
9	5	IT'S LATE	Ricky Nelson (London)
3	6	PETITE FLEUR	Chris Barber (Pye-Nixa)
10	7	COME SOFTLY TO ME	Fleetwoods (London)
6	8	CHARLIE BROWN	Coasters (London)
12	9	I'VE WAITED SO LONG	Anthony Newley (Decca)
11	10	COME SOFTLY TO ME	Frankie Vaughan & the K Sisters (Philips)
8	11	C'MON EVERYBODY	Eddie Cochran (London)
13	12	I GO APE	Neil Sedaka (RCA)
7	13	SMOKE GETS IN YOUR EYES	Platters (Mercury)
-	14	MEAN STREAK	Cliff Richard (Columbia)
-	15	FORT WORTH JAIL	Lonnie Donegan (Pye Nixa)
14	16	STAGGER LEE	Lloyd Price (HMV)
-	17	IDLE ON PARADE (EP)	Anthony Newley (Decca)
24	18	WAIT FOR ME	Malcolm Vaughan (HMV)
15	19	MY HAPPINESS	Connie Francis (MGM)
21	20	VENUS	Frankie Avalon (HMV)
18	21	GIGI	Billy Eckstine (Mercury)
16	22	A PUB WITH NO BEER	Slim Dusty (Columbia)
26	23	SING LITTLE BIRDIE	Pearl Carr & Teddy Johnson (Columbia)
27	24	MAY YOU ALWAYS	McGuire Sisters (Coral)
25	25	MAY YOU ALWAYS	Joan Regan (HMV)
20	26	VENUS	Dickie Valentine (Pye Nixa)
17	27	TOMBOY	Perry Como (RCA)
22	28	FRENCH FOREIGN LEGION	Frank Sinatra (Capitol)
23	29	THE LITTLE DRUMMER BOY	Beverley Sisters (Decca)
-	30	LOVE'S MADE A FOOL OF YOU	Crickets (Coral)

16 May 1959

last week	this week	title	artist
2	1	A FOOL SUCH AS I/I NEED YOUR LOVE TONIGHT	Elvis Presley (RCA)
1	2	IT DOESN'T MATTER ANYMORE	Buddy Holly (Coral)
3	3	SIDE SADDLE	Russ Conway (Columbia)
4	4	DONNA	Marty Wilde (Philips)
6	5	PETITE FLEUR	Chris Barber (Pye-Nixa)
7	6	COME SOFTLY TO ME	Fleetwoods (London)
9	7	I'VE WAITED SO LONG	Anthony Newley (Decca)
5	8	IT'S LATE	Ricky Nelson (London)
8	9	CHARLIE BROWN	Coasters (London)
10	10	COME SOFTLY TO ME	Frankie Vaughan & the Kaye Sisters (Philips)
12	11	I GO APE	Neil Sedaka (RCA)
14	12	MEAN STREAK	Cliff Richard (Columbia)
17	13	IDLE ON PARADE (EP)	Anthony Newley (Decca)
15	14	FORT WORTH JAIL	Lonnie Donegan (Pye Nixa)
11	15	C'MON EVERYBODY	Eddie Cochran (London)
20	16	VENUS	Frankie Avalon (HMV)
13	17	SMOKE GETS IN YOUR EYES	Platters (Mercury)
24	18	MAY YOU ALWAYS	McGuire Sisters (Coral)
-	19	NEVER BE ANYONE ELSE BUT YOU	Ricky Nelson (London)
-	19	GUITAR BOOGIE SHUFFLE	Bert Weedon (Top Rank)
-	21	NEVER MIND	Cliff Richard (Columbia)
-	22	WHERE WERE YOU (ON OUR WEDDING DAY)	Lloyd Price (HMV)
-	23	ROULETTE	Russ Conway (Columbia)
25	24	MAY YOU ALWAYS	Joan Regan (HMV)
16	25	STAGGER LEE	Lloyd Price (HMV)
21	26	GIGI	Billy Eckstine (Mercury)
18	27	WAIT FOR ME	Malcolm Vaughan (HMV)
27	28	TOMBOY	Perry Como (RCA)
19	29	MY HAPPINESS	Connie Francis (MGM)
-	30	COME DANCE WITH ME (LP)	Frank Sinatra (Capitol)

Buddy Holly hit Number One, almost three months after his death, for the first time since the Crickets' debut *That'll Be The Day* in 1957, and the first time at all as a solo artist. In fact, the Crickets were not on *It Doesn't Matter Anymore* (a song donated to Holly by its writer Paul Anka), since singer and group had parted in Autumn 1958, and Holly had made his last recordings in New York with the Dick Jacobs Orchestra. The Crickets, in turn, quickly scored in Holly-less form with *Love's Made A Fool Of You*.

May – June 1959

23 May 1959

last	this	title
1	1	A FOOL SUCH AS I/I NEED YOUR LOVE TONIGHT — Elvis Presley (RCA)
2	2	IT DOESN'T MATTER ANYMORE — Buddy Holly (Coral)
8	3	IT'S LATE — Ricky Nelson (London)
3	4	SIDE SADDLE — Russ Conway (Columbia)
3	5	DONNA — Marty Wilde (Philips)
7	6	I'VE WAITED SO LONG — Anthony Newley (Decca)
6	7	COME SOFTLY TO ME — Fleetwoods (London)
5	8	PETITE FLEUR — Chris Barber (Pye-Nixa)
10	9	COME SOFTLY TO ME — Frankie Vaughan & the Kaye Sisters (Philips)
12	10	MEAN STREAK — Cliff Richard (Columbia)
11	11	I GO APE — Neil Sedaka (RCA)
9	12	CHARLIE BROWN — Coasters (London)
23	13	ROULETTE — Russ Conway (Columbia)
14	14	FORT WORTH JAIL — Lonnie Donegan (Pye Nixa)
22	15	WHERE WERE YOU (ON OUR WEDDING DAY) — Lloyd Price (HMV)
19	15	GUITAR BOOGIE SHUFFLE — Bert Weedon (Top Rank)
18	17	MAY YOU ALWAYS — McGuire Sisters (Coral)
17	18	SMOKE GETS IN YOUR EYES — Platters (Mercury)
16	19	VENUS — Frankie Avalon (HMV)
27	20	WAIT FOR ME — Malcolm Vaughan (HMV)
15	21	C'MON EVERYBODY — Eddie Cochran (London)
13	22	IDLE ON PARADE (EP) — Anthony Newley (Decca)
24	23	MAY YOU ALWAYS — Joan Regan (HMV)
-	24	MARGIE — Fats Domino (London)
-	25	VENUS — Dickie Valentine (Pye Nixa)
21	26	NEVER MIND — Cliff Richard (Columbia)
-	27	IF ONLY I COULD LIVE MY LIFE AGAIN — Jane Morgan (London)
-	28	THREE STARS — Ruby Wright (Parlophone)
-	29	TAKE A MESSAGE TO MARY — Everly Brothers (London)
-	30	FOR A PENNY — Pat Boone (London)

30 May 1959

last	this	title
1	1	A FOOL SUCH AS I/I NEED YOUR LOVE TONIGHT — Elvis Presley (RCA)
2	2	IT DOESN'T MATTER ANYMORE — Buddy Holly (Coral)
3	3	IT'S LATE — Ricky Nelson (London)
6	4	I'VE WAITED SO LONG — Anthony Newley (Decca)
4	5	SIDE SADDLE — Russ Conway (Columbia)
13	6	ROULETTE — Russ Conway (Columbia)
5	7	DONNA — Marty Wilde (Philips)
8	8	PETITE FLEUR
9	9	COME SOFTLY TO ME — Frankie Vaughan & the Kaye Sisters (Philips)
7	10	COME SOFTLY TO ME — Fleetwoods (London)
11	10	I GO APE — Neil Sedaka (RCA)
10	12	MEAN STREAK — Cliff Richard (Columbia)
15	13	GUITAR BOOGIE SHUFFLE — Bert Weedon (Top Rank)
12	14	CHARLIE BROWN — Coasters (London)
17	15	MAY YOU ALWAYS — McGuire Sisters (Coral)
14	16	FORT WORTH JAIL — Lonnie Donegan (Pye Nixa)
15	17	WHERE WERE YOU (ON OUR WEDDING DAY) — Lloyd Price (HMV)
24	18	MARGIE — Fats Domino (London)
20	19	WAIT FOR ME — Malcolm Vaughan (HMV)
23	20	MAY YOU ALWAYS — Joan Regan (HMV)
19	21	VENUS — Frankie Avalon (HMV)
28	21	THREE STARS — Ruby Wright (Parlophone)
22	23	IDLE ON PARADE (EP) — Anthony Newley (Decca)
18	24	SMOKE GETS IN YOUR EYES — Platters (Mercury)
-	25	YOU MADE ME LOVE YOU — Nat King Cole (Capitol)
21	26	C'MON EVERYBODY — Eddie Cochran (London)
-	27	DREAM LOVER — Bobby Darin (London)
30	28	FOR A PENNY — Pat Boone (London)
-	29	POOR JENNY — Everly Brothers (London)
-	30	MY HAPPINESS — Connie Francis (MGM)

6 June 1959

last	this	title
1	1	A FOOL SUCH AS I/I NEED YOUR LOVE TONIGHT — Elvis Presley (RCA)
2	2	IT DOESN'T MATTER ANYMORE — Buddy Holly (Coral)
4	3	I'VE WAITED SO LONG — Anthony Newley (Decca)
3	4	IT'S LATE — Ricky Nelson (London)
6	5	ROULETTE — Russ Conway (Columbia)
5	6	SIDE SADDLE — Russ Conway (Columbia)
10	7	COME SOFTLY TO ME — Fleetwoods (London)
8	8	PETITE FLEUR — Chris Barber (Pye-Nixa)
9	9	DONNA — Marty Wilde (Philips)
13	10	GUITAR BOOGIE SHUFFLE — Bert Weedon (Top Rank)
11	11	MEAN STREAK — Cliff Richard (Columbia)
12	12	I GO APE — Neil Sedaka (RCA)
9	13	COME SOFTLY TO ME — Frankie Vaughan & the Kaye Sisters (Philips)
14	14	CHARLIE BROWN — Coasters (London)
17	15	WHERE WERE YOU (ON OUR WEDDING DAY) — Lloyd Price (HMV)
27	16	DREAM LOVER — Bobby Darin (London)
29	17	POOR JENNY — Everly Brothers (London)
15	18	MAY YOU ALWAYS — McGuire Sisters (Coral)
18	19	MARGIE — Fats Domino (London)
-	20	NEVER BE ANYONE ELSE BUT YOU — Ricky Nelson (London)
20	21	MAY YOU ALWAYS — Joan Regan (HMV)
25	22	YOU MADE ME LOVE YOU — Nat King Cole (Capitol)
16	23	FORT WORTH JAIL — Lonnie Donegan (Pye Nixa)
19	24	WAIT FOR ME — Malcolm Vaughan (HMV)
21	24	THREE STARS — Ruby Wright (Parlophone)
-	26	KANSAS CITY — Little Richard (London)
26	26	A TEENAGER IN LOVE — Marty Wilde (Philips)
-	28	GOODBYE, JIMMY GOODBYE — Ruby Murray (Columbia)
28	28	FOR A PENNY — Pat Boone (London)
26	30	C'MON EVERYBODY — Eddie Cochran (London)

13 June 1959

last	this	title
1	1	A FOOL SUCH AS I/I NEED YOUR LOVE TONIGHT — Elvis Presley (RCA)
5	2	ROULETTE — Russ Conway (Columbia)
2	3	IT DOESN'T MATTER ANYMORE — Buddy Holly (Coral)
4	4	IT'S LATE — Ricky Nelson (London)
16	5	DREAM LOVER — Bobby Darin (London)
3	6	I'VE WAITED SO LONG — Anthony Newley (Decca)
6	7	SIDE SADDLE — Russ Conway (Columbia)
26	8	A TEENAGER IN LOVE — Marty Wilde (Philips)
12	9	I GO APE — Neil Sedaka (RCA)
13	10	COME SOFTLY TO ME — Frankie Vaughan & the Kaye Sisters (Philips)
11	11	MEAN STREAK — Cliff Richard (Columbia)
10	12	GUITAR BOOGIE SHUFFLE — Bert Weedon (Top Rank)
9	13	DONNA — Marty Wilde (Philips)
8	14	PETITE FLEUR — Chris Barber (Pye-Nixa)
18	15	MAY YOU ALWAYS — McGuire Sisters (Coral)
15	16	WHERE WERE YOU (ON OUR WEDDING DAY) — Lloyd Price (HMV)
21	17	MAY YOU ALWAYS — Joan Regan (HMV)
7	18	COME SOFTLY TO ME — Fleetwoods (London)
24	19	THREE STARS — Ruby Wright (Parlophone)
17	20	POOR JENNY — Everly Brothers (London)
20	21	NEVER BE ANYONE ELSE BUT YOU — Ricky Nelson (London)
-	22	PERSONALITY — Anthony Newley (Decca)
28	23	GOODBYE, JIMMY GOODBYE — Ruby Murray (Columbia)
-	24	A TEENAGER IN LOVE — Craig Douglas (Top Rank)
24	25	WAIT FOR ME — Malcolm Vaughan (HMV)
-	26	PERSONALITY — Lloyd Price (HMV)
14	27	CHARLIE BROWN — Coasters (London)
19	28	MARGIE — Fats Domino (London)
26	28	KANSAS CITY — Little Richard (London)
22	30	YOU MADE ME LOVE YOU — Nat King Cole (Capitol)
-	30	PLEASE DON'T TOUCH — Johnny Kidd (HMV)

Elvis' *A Fool Such As I* and *I Need Your Love Tonight* were, like *I Got Stung*, tracks recorded in 1958 during leave from the Army. Russ Conway's *Roulette* gave him two simultaneous Top 10 entries, and both Ricky Nelson and the Everly Brothers charted both sides of a single independently for the first time, in both cases with contrasting rocker and ballad couplings. Ruby Wright's *Three Stars* was a tribute to Buddy Holly, Ritchie Valens and the Big Bopper, the trio who had died together earlier in the year.

20 June 1959

last week	this week	Title	Artist
2	1	ROULETTE	Russ Conway (Columbia)
1	2	A FOOL SUCH AS I/I NEED YOUR LOVE TONIGHT	Elvis Presley (RCA)
5	3	DREAM LOVER	Bobby Darin (London)
8	4	A TEENAGER IN LOVE	Marty Wilde (Philips)
6	5	I'VE WAITED SO LONG	Anthony Newley (Decca)
3	6	IT DOESN'T MATTER ANYMORE	Buddy Holly (Coral)
4	7	IT'S LATE	Ricky Nelson (London)
7	8	SIDE SADDLE	Russ Conway (Columbia)
17	9	MAY YOU ALWAYS	Joan Regan (HMV)
12	10	GUITAR BOOGIE SHUFFLE	Bert Weedon (Top Rank)
-	11	PETER GUNN	Duane Eddy (London)
9	12	I GO APE	Neil Sedaka (RCA)
11	13	MEAN STREAK	Cliff Richard (Columbia)
24	14	A TEENAGER IN LOVE	Craig Douglas (Top Rank)
21	14	NEVER BE ANYONE ELSE BUT YOU	Ricky Nelson (London)
23	16	GOODBYE, JIMMY GOODBYE	Ruby Murray (Columbia)
14	17	PETITE FLEUR	Chris Barber (Pye-Nixa)
26	18	PERSONALITY	Lloyd Price (HMV)
10	19	COME SOFTLY TO ME	Frankie Vaughan & the Kaye Sisters (Philips)
20	20	POOR JENNY	Everly Brothers (London)
22	21	PERSONALITY	Anthony Newley (Decca)
19	22	THREE STARS	Ruby Wright (Parlophone)
12	23	DONNA	Marty Wilde (Philips)
15	24	MAY YOU ALWAYS	McGuire Sisters (Coral)
16	24	WHERE WERE YOU (ON OUR WEDDING DAY)	Lloyd Price (HMV)
30	26	PLEASE DON'T TOUCH	Johnny Kidd & the Pirates (HMV)
-	27	TAKE A MESSAGE TO MARY	Everly Brothers (London)
-	28	VENUS	Dickie Valentine (Pye Nixa)
28	29	KANSAS CITY	Little Richard (London)
28	30	MARGIE	Fats Domino (London)

27 June 1959

last	this	Title	Artist
1	1	ROULETTE	Russ Conway (Columbia)
3	2	DREAM LOVER	Bobby Darin (London)
4	3	A TEENAGER IN LOVE	Marty Wilde (Philips)
2	4	A FOOL SUCH AS I/I NEED YOUR LOVE TONIGHT	Elvis Presley (RCA)
5	5	I'VE WAITED SO LONG	Anthony Newley (Decca)
8	6	SIDE SADDLE	Russ Conway (Columbia)
-	7	THE BATTLE OF NEW ORLEANS	Lonnie Donegan (Pye)
6	8	IT DOESN'T MATTER ANYMORE	Buddy Holly (Coral)
7	9	IT'S LATE	Ricky Nelson (London)
11	10	PETER GUNN	Duane Eddy (London)
21	11	PERSONALITY	Anthony Newley (Decca)
18	12	PERSONALITY	Lloyd Price (HMV)
9	12	MAY YOU ALWAYS	Joan Regan (HMV)
16	14	GOODBYE, JIMMY GOODBYE	Ruby Murray (Columbia)
14	15	A TEENAGER IN LOVE	Craig Douglas (Top Rank)
10	16	GUITAR BOOGIE SHUFFLE	Bert Weedon (Top Rank)
13	17	MEAN STREAK	Cliff Richard (Columbia)
14	18	NEVER BE ANYONE ELSE BUT YOU	Ricky Nelson (London)
22	19	THREE STARS	Ruby Wright (Parlophone)
12	20	I GO APE	Neil Sedaka (RCA)
20	21	POOR JENNY	Everly Brothers (London)
-	21	THE BATTLE OF NEW ORLEANS	Johnny Horton (Philips)
17	23	PETITE FLEUR	Chris Barber (Pye-Nixa)
24	24	MAY YOU ALWAYS	McGuire Sisters (Coral)
19	25	COME SOFTLY TO ME	Frankie Vaughan & the Kaye Sisters (Philips)
26	26	PLEASE DON'T TOUCH	Johnny Kidd & the Pirates (HMV)
29	27	KANSAS CITY	Little Richard (London)
-	28	FOR A PENNY	Pat Boone (London)
-	28	A TEENAGER IN LOVE	Dion & the Belmonts (London)
-	28	MARGO, DON'T GO	Billy Fury (Decca)

4 July 1959

last	this	Title	Artist
2	1	DREAM LOVER	Bobby Darin (London)
1	2	ROULETTE	Russ Conway (Columbia)
3	3	A TEENAGER IN LOVE	Marty Wilde (Philips)
7	4	THE BATTLE OF NEW ORLEANS	Lonnie Donegan (Pye)
4	5	A FOOL SUCH AS I/I NEED YOUR LOVE TONIGHT	Elvis Presley (RCA)
11	6	PERSONALITY	Anthony Newley (Decca)
5	7	I'VE WAITED SO LONG	Anthony Newley (Decca)
10	8	PETER GUNN	Duane Eddy (London)
6	9	SIDE SADDLE	Russ Conway (Columbia)
12	10	PERSONALITY	Lloyd Price (HMV)
9	11	IT'S LATE	Ricky Nelson (London)
12	12	MAY YOU ALWAYS	Joan Regan (HMV)
8	13	IT DOESN'T MATTER ANYMORE	Buddy Holly (Coral)
14	14	GOODBYE, JIMMY GOODBYE	Ruby Murray (Columbia)
21	15	POOR JENNY	Everly Brothers (London)
16	16	THE BATTLE OF NEW ORLEANS	Johnny Horton (Philips)
20	17	I GO APE	Neil Sedaka (RCA)
16	18	GUITAR BOOGIE SHUFFLE	Bert Weedon (Top Rank)
28	19	FOR A PENNY	Pat Boone (London)
15	20	A TEENAGER IN LOVE	Craig Douglas (Top Rank)
19	21	THREE STARS	Ruby Wright (Parlophone)
18	22	NEVER BE ANYONE ELSE BUT YOU	Ricky Nelson (London)
23	23	PETITE FLEUR	Chris Barber (Pye-Nixa)
-	24	TAKE A MESSAGE TO MARY	Everly Brothers (London)
-	25	DONNA	Marty Wilde (Philips)
24	26	MAY YOU ALWAYS	McGuire Sisters (Coral)
17	27	MEAN STREAK	Cliff Richard (Columbia)
28	28	A TEENAGER IN LOVE	Dion & the Belmonts (London)
-	28	LIPSTICK ON YOUR COLLAR	Connie Francis (MGM)
27	30	KANSAS CITY	Little Richard (London)

11 July 1959

last	this	Title	Artist
1	1	DREAM LOVER	Bobby Darin (London)
3	2	A TEENAGER IN LOVE	Marty Wilde (Philips)
4	3	THE BATTLE OF NEW ORLEANS	Lonnie Donegan (Pye)
2	4	ROULETTE	Russ Conway (Columbia)
5	5	A FOOL SUCH AS I/I NEED YOUR LOVE TONIGHT	Elvis Presley (RCA)
8	6	PETER GUNN	Duane Eddy (London)
6	7	PERSONALITY	Anthony Newley (Decca)
7	8	I'VE WAITED SO LONG	Anthony Newley (Decca)
10	9	PERSONALITY	Lloyd Price (HMV)
14	10	GOODBYE, JIMMY GOODBYE	Ruby Murray (Columbia)
11	11	IT'S LATE	Ricky Nelson (London)
9	12	SIDE SADDLE	Russ Conway (Columbia)
12	12	MAY YOU ALWAYS	Joan Regan (HMV)
15	14	POOR JENNY	Everly Brothers (London)
-	15	LIVING DOLL	Cliff Richard (Columbia)
20	16	A TEENAGER IN LOVE	Craig Douglas (Top Rank)
28	17	LIPSTICK ON YOUR COLLAR	Connie Francis (MGM)
13	18	IT DOESN'T MATTER ANYMORE	Buddy Holly (Coral)
22	19	NEVER BE ANYONE ELSE BUT YOU	Ricky Nelson (London)
24	20	TAKE A MESSAGE TO MARY	Everly Brothers (London)
17	21	I GO APE	Neil Sedaka (RCA)
20	22	THREE STARS	Ruby Wright (Parlophone)
16	23	THE BATTLE OF NEW ORLEANS	Johnny Horton (Philips)
-	24	I KNOW	Perry Como (RCA)
23	25	PETITE FLEUR	Chris Barber (Pye-Nixa)
-	26	LONELY BOY	Paul Anka (Columbia)
25	27	DONNA	Marty Wilde (Philips)
-	28	ENDLESSLY	Brook Benton (Mercury)
18	29	GUITAR BOOGIE SHUFFLE	Bert Weedon (Top Rank)
19	30	FOR A PENNY	Pat Boone (London)

Duane Eddy's *Peter Gunn*, his version of the theme to a TV series which was not even being shown in the UK, was ostensibly the B-side of his new single *Yep!* However, BBC-TV's *Juke Box Jury* opted to play *Peter Gunn*, the show's panel voted it a hit, and the interest created kick-started the track into the chart to become Eddy's biggest UK hit to date. Three versions of *A Teenager In Love*, meanwhile, vied for sales - one of the two UK covers, by Marty Wilde, actually won the race quite easily, reaching Number Two.

July – August 1959

18 July 1959

last	this	
1	1	DREAM LOVER / Bobby Darin (London)
2	2	A TEENAGER IN LOVE / Marty Wilde (Philips)
3	3	THE BATTLE OF NEW ORLEANS / Lonnie Donegan (Pye)
4	4	ROULETTE / Russ Conway (Columbia)
15	5	LIVING DOLL / Cliff Richard (Columbia)
6	6	PETER GUNN / Duane Eddy (London)
7	7	PERSONALITY / Anthony Newley (Decca)
17	8	LIPSTICK ON YOUR COLLAR / Connie Francis (MGM)
5	9	A FOOL SUCH AS I/I NEED YOUR LOVE TONIGHT / Elvis Presley (RCA)
8	10	I'VE WAITED SO LONG / Anthony Newley (Decca)
10	11	GOODBYE, JIMMY GOODBYE / Ruby Murray (Columbia)
9	12	PERSONALITY / Lloyd Price (HMV)
12	13	SIDE SADDLE / Russ Conway (Columbia)
11	14	IT'S LATE / Ricky Nelson (London)
12	15	MAY YOU ALWAYS / Joan Regan (HMV)
16	16	A TEENAGER IN LOVE / Craig Douglas (Top Rank)
19	17	NEVER BE ANYONE ELSE BUT YOU / Ricky Nelson (London)
14	18	POOR JENNY / Everly Brothers (London)
24	19	I KNOW / Perry Como (RCA)
22	20	THREE STARS / Ruby Wright (Parlophone)
18	21	IT DOESN'T MATTER ANYMORE / Buddy Holly (Coral)
20	22	TAKE A MESSAGE TO MARY / Everly Brothers (London)
21	23	I GO APE / Neil Sedaka (RCA)
-	24	WATERLOO / Stonewall Jackson (Philips)
-	25	PLEASE DON'T TOUCH / Johnny Kidd (HMV)
26	26	LONELY BOY / Paul Anka (Columbia)
23	27	THE BATTLE OF NEW ORLEANS / Johnny Horton (Philips)
28	28	ENDLESSLY / Brook Benton (Mercury)
30	29	FOR A PENNY / Pat Boone (London)
-	28	MAY YOU ALWAYS / McGuire Sisters (Coral)

25 July 1959

last	this	
1	1	DREAM LOVER / Bobby Darin (London)
3	2	THE BATTLE OF NEW ORLEANS / Lonnie Donegan (Pye)
5	3	LIVING DOLL / Cliff Richard (Columbia)
2	4	A TEENAGER IN LOVE / Marty Wilde (Philips)
-	5	A BIG HUNK O' LOVE / Elvis Presley (RCA)
4	6	ROULETTE / Russ Conway (Columbia)
8	7	LIPSTICK ON YOUR COLLAR / Connie Francis (MGM)
6	8	PETER GUNN / Duane Eddy (London)
7	9	PERSONALITY / Anthony Newley (Decca)
12	10	PERSONALITY / Lloyd Price (HMV)
11	11	GOODBYE, JIMMY GOODBYE / Ruby Murray (Columbia)
14	12	IT'S LATE / Ricky Nelson (London)
9	13	A FOOL SUCH AS I/I NEED YOUR LOVE TONIGHT / Elvis Presley (RCA)
10	14	I'VE WAITED SO LONG / Anthony Newley (Decca)
13	15	SIDE SADDLE / Russ Conway (Columbia)
19	16	I KNOW / Perry Como (RCA)
16	16	A TEENAGER IN LOVE / Craig Douglas (Top Rank)
15	18	MAY YOU ALWAYS / Joan Regan (HMV)
18	19	POOR JENNY / Everly Brothers (London)
-	20	YEP! / Duane Eddy (London)
-	20	THE HEART OF A MAN / Frankie Vaughan (Philips)
20	22	THREE STARS / Ruby Wright (Parlophone)
17	23	NEVER BE ANYONE ELSE BUT YOU / Ricky Nelson (London)
-	24	WHY SHOULD I BE LONELY? / Tony Brent (Columbia)
24	25	WATERLOO / Stonewall Jackson (Philips)
22	26	TAKE A MESSAGE TO MARY / Everly Brothers (London)
26	27	LONELY BOY / Paul Anka (Columbia)
25	27	PLEASE DON'T TOUCH / Johnny Kidd (HMV)
-	29	LA PLUME DE MA TANTE / Hugo & Luigi (RCA)
28	30	FOR A PENNY / Pat Boone (London)
-	30	RAGTIME COWBOY JOE / Chipmunks (London)

1 August 1959

last	this	
3	1	LIVING DOLL / Cliff Richard (Columbia)
1	2	DREAM LOVER / Bobby Darin (London)
2	3	THE BATTLE OF NEW ORLEANS / Lonnie Donegan (Pye)
4	4	A TEENAGER IN LOVE / Marty Wilde (Philips)
5	5	A BIG HUNK O' LOVE / Elvis Presley (RCA)
7	6	LIPSTICK ON YOUR COLLAR / Connie Francis (MGM)
6	7	ROULETTE / Russ Conway (Columbia)
9	8	PERSONALITY / Anthony Newley (Decca)
8	9	PETER GUNN / Duane Eddy (London)
12	10	IT'S LATE / Ricky Nelson (London)
11	11	GOODBYE, JIMMY GOODBYE / Ruby Murray (Columbia)
15	12	SIDE SADDLE / Russ Conway (Columbia)
16	13	A TEENAGER IN LOVE / Craig Douglas (Top Rank)
30	14	RAGTIME COWBOY JOE / Chipmunks (London)
18	15	MAY YOU ALWAYS / Joan Regan (HMV)
27	16	LONELY BOY / Paul Anka (Columbia)
20	17	YEP! / Duane Eddy (London)
20	18	THE HEART OF A MAN / Frankie Vaughan (Philips)
16	19	I KNOW / Perry Como (RCA)
10	20	PERSONALITY / Lloyd Price (HMV)
26	21	TAKE A MESSAGE TO MARY / Everly Brothers (London)
19	22	POOR JENNY / Everly Brothers (London)
13	23	A FOOL SUCH AS I/I NEED YOUR LOVE TONIGHT / Elvis Presley (RCA)
30	24	FOR A PENNY / Pat Boone (London)
14	25	I'VE WAITED SO LONG / Anthony Newley (Decca)
24	26	WHY SHOULD I BE LONELY? / Tony Brent (Columbia)
-	26	MIDNIGHT SHIFT / Buddy Holly (Brunswick)
-	28	PETITE FLEUR / Chris Barber (Pye-Nixa)
-	29	TWIXT TWELVE AND TWENTY / Pat Boone (London)
29	30	LA PLUME DE MA TANTE / Hugo & Luigi (RCA)
23	30	NEVER BE ANYONE ELSE BUT YOU / Ricky Nelson (London)

8 August 1959

last	this	
1	1	LIVING DOLL / Cliff Richard (Columbia)
2	2	DREAM LOVER / Bobby Darin (London)
3	3	THE BATTLE OF NEW ORLEANS / Lonnie Donegan (Pye)
5	4	A BIG HUNK O' LOVE / Elvis Presley (RCA)
6	5	LIPSTICK ON YOUR COLLAR / Connie Francis (MGM)
4	5	A TEENAGER IN LOVE / Marty Wilde (Philips)
7	7	ROULETTE / Russ Conway (Columbia)
8	8	PERSONALITY / Anthony Newley (Decca)
16	9	LONELY BOY / Paul Anka (Columbia)
10	10	IT'S LATE / Ricky Nelson (London)
9	11	PETER GUNN / Duane Eddy (London)
-	12	SOMEONE / Johnny Mathis (Fontana)
14	12	RAGTIME COWBOY JOE / Chipmunks (London)
11	14	GOODBYE, JIMMY GOODBYE / Ruby Murray (Columbia)
19	15	I KNOW / Perry Como (RCA)
13	15	A TEENAGER IN LOVE / Craig Douglas (Top Rank)
18	15	THE HEART OF A MAN / Frankie Vaughan (Philips)
17	18	YEP! / Duane Eddy (London)
12	19	SIDE SADDLE / Russ Conway (Columbia)
15	20	MAY YOU ALWAYS / Joan Regan (HMV)
22	21	POOR JENNY / Everly Brothers (London)
28	22	PETITE FLEUR / Chris Barber (Pye-Nixa)
29	23	TWIXT TWELVE AND TWENTY / Pat Boone (London)
-	24	SUMMER OF THE 17TH DOLL / Winifred Atwell (Decca)
21	25	TAKE A MESSAGE TO MARY / Everly Brothers (London)
-	26	ONLY SIXTEEN / Craig Douglas (Top Rank)
26	27	MIDNIGHT SHIFT / Buddy Holly (Brunswick)
26	28	WHY SHOULD I BE LONELY? / Tony Brent (Columbia)
-	29	MY MELANCHOLY BABY / Tommy Edwards (MGM)
25	29	I'VE WAITED SO LONG / Anthony Newley (Decca)

Songwriter Lionel Bart had been quite annoyed when, earlier in the year, Cliff Richard had released a single titled *Livin' Lovin' Doll*, since he figured it could be easily confused with *Living Doll*, the song he had written for Cliff's movie debut in *Serious Charge*. In the event, the earlier single, though a Top 20 hit, was quickly forgotten, while *Living Doll*, with its artfully simple strummed arrangement, transcended its movie origins to become Cliff's first Number One, first million seller, and even his first US Top 30 entry.

August – September 1959

15 August 1959

last week	this week	
1	1	LIVING DOLL — Cliff Richard (Columbia)
3	2	THE BATTLE OF NEW ORLEANS — Lonnie Donegan (Pye)
2	3	DREAM LOVER — Bobby Darin (London)
5	4	LIPSTICK ON YOUR COLLAR — Connie Francis (MGM)
4	5	A BIG HUNK O' LOVE — Elvis Presley (RCA)
5	6	A TEENAGER IN LOVE — Marty Wilde (Philips)
9	7	LONELY BOY — Paul Anka (Columbia)
7	8	ROULETTE — Russ Conway (Columbia)
15	9	THE HEART OF A MAN — Frankie Vaughan (Philips)
8	10	PERSONALITY — Anthony Newley (Decca)
12	11	RAGTIME COWBOY JOE — Chipmunks (London)
11	12	PETER GUNN — Duane Eddy (London)
12	13	SOMEONE — Johnny Mathis (Fontana)
26	14	ONLY SIXTEEN — Craig Douglas (Top Rank)
15	15	I KNOW — Perry Como (RCA)
10	16	IT'S LATE — Ricky Nelson (London)
14	17	GOODBYE, JIMMY GOODBYE — Ruby Murray (Columbia)
23	18	TWIXT TWELVE AND TWENTY — Pat Boone (London)
-	19	TALLAHASSEE LASSIE — Freddy Cannon (Top Rank)
-	20	TALLAHASSEE LASSIE — Tommy Steele (Decca)
18	21	YEP! — Duane Eddy (London)
19	22	SIDE SADDLE — Russ Conway (Columbia)
-	23	ONLY SIXTEEN — Sam Cooke (HMV)
25	24	TAKE A MESSAGE TO MARY — Everly Brothers (London)
20	25	MAY YOU ALWAYS — Joan Regan (HMV)
-	26	PERSONALITY — Lloyd Price (HMV)
27	27	MIDNIGHT SHIFT — Buddy Holly (Brunswick)
15	28	A TEENAGER IN LOVE — Craig Douglas (Top Rank)
24	29	SUMMER OF THE 17TH DOLL — Winifred Atwell (Decca)
28	29	WHY SHOULD I BE LONELY? — Tony Brent (Columbia)

22 August 1959

last week	this week	
1	1	LIVING DOLL — Cliff Richard (Columbia)
3	2	DREAM LOVER — Bobby Darin (London)
4	3	LIPSTICK ON YOUR COLLAR — Connie Francis (MGM)
2	4	THE BATTLE OF NEW ORLEANS — Lonnie Donegan (Pye)
7	5	LONELY BOY — Paul Anka (Columbia)
14	6	ONLY SIXTEEN — Craig Douglas (Top Rank)
5	7	A BIG HUNK O' LOVE — Elvis Presley (RCA)
9	8	THE HEART OF A MAN — Frankie Vaughan (Philips)
8	9	ROULETTE — Russ Conway (Columbia)
6	10	A TEENAGER IN LOVE — Marty Wilde (Philips)
10	11	PERSONALITY — Anthony Newley (Decca)
13	12	SOMEONE — Johnny Mathis (Fontana)
15	13	I KNOW — Perry Como (RCA)
11	14	RAGTIME COWBOY JOE — Chipmunks (London)
17	15	GOODBYE, JIMMY GOODBYE — Ruby Murray (Columbia)
16	16	IT'S LATE — Ricky Nelson (London)
12	17	PETER GUNN — Duane Eddy (London)
20	18	TALLAHASSEE LASSIE — Tommy Steele (Decca)
19	19	TALLAHASSEE LASSIE — Freddy Cannon (Top Rank)
18	20	TWIXT TWELVE AND TWENTY — Pat Boone (London)
22	21	SIDE SADDLE — Russ Conway (Columbia)
-	22	MONA LISA — Conway Twitty (MGM)
-	23	CHINA TEA — Russ Conway (Columbia)
-	24	THE WONDER OF YOU — Ronnie Hilton (HMV)
26	25	PERSONALITY — Lloyd Price (HMV)
21	26	YEP! — Duane Eddy (London)
28	27	A TEENAGER IN LOVE — Craig Douglas (Top Rank)
-	28	SORRY (I RAN ALL THE WAY HOME) — Impalas (MGM)
24	29	TAKE A MESSAGE TO MARY — Everly Brothers (London)
23	30	ONLY SIXTEEN — Sam Cooke (HMV)

29 August 1959

last week	this week	
1	1	LIVING DOLL — Cliff Richard (Columbia)
6	2	ONLY SIXTEEN — Craig Douglas (Top Rank)
5	3	LONELY BOY — Paul Anka (Columbia)
4	4	THE BATTLE OF NEW ORLEANS — Lonnie Donegan (Pye)
2	5	DREAM LOVER — Bobby Darin (London)
3	6	LIPSTICK ON YOUR COLLAR — Connie Francis (MGM)
8	7	THE HEART OF A MAN — Frankie Vaughan (Philips)
23	8	CHINA TEA — Russ Conway (Columbia)
9	9	ROULETTE — Russ Conway (Columbia)
12	10	SOMEONE — Johnny Mathis (Fontana)
7	10	A BIG HUNK O' LOVE — Elvis Presley (RCA)
10	12	A TEENAGER IN LOVE — Marty Wilde (Philips)
22	13	MONA LISA — Conway Twitty (MGM)
13	14	I KNOW — Perry Como (RCA)
14	15	RAGTIME COWBOY JOE — Chipmunks (London)
18	16	TALLAHASSEE LASSIE — Tommy Steele (Decca)
19	17	TALLAHASSEE LASSIE — Freddy Cannon (Top Rank)
21	18	SIDE SADDLE — Russ Conway (Columbia)
-	19	HERE COMES SUMMER — Jerry Keller (London)
15	20	GOODBYE, JIMMY GOODBYE — Ruby Murray (Columbia)
11	21	PERSONALITY — Anthony Newley (Decca)
24	22	THE WONDER OF YOU — Ronnie Hilton (HMV)
16	22	IT'S LATE — Ricky Nelson (London)
-	24	ONLY SIXTEEN — Al Saxon (Fontana)
-	25	REMEMBER WHEN — Platters (Mercury)
20	26	TWIXT TWELVE AND TWENTY — Pat Boone (London)
30	27	ONLY SIXTEEN — Sam Cooke (HMV)
-	28	HIGH HOPES — Frank Sinatra (Capitol)
-	28	GIVE! GIVE! GIVE! — Tommy Steele (Decca)
-	30	HONEYMOON SONG — Manuel & The Music Of The Mountains (Columbia)

5 September 1959

last week	this week	
1	1	LIVING DOLL — Cliff Richard (Columbia)
2	2	ONLY SIXTEEN — Craig Douglas (Top Rank)
3	3	LONELY BOY — Paul Anka (Columbia)
5	4	LIPSTICK ON YOUR COLLAR — Connie Francis (MGM)
4	5	THE BATTLE OF NEW ORLEANS — Lonnie Donegan (Pye)
7	5	THE HEART OF A MAN — Frankie Vaughan (Philips)
10	7	SOMEONE — Johnny Mathis (Fontana)
5	8	DREAM LOVER — Bobby Darin (London)
8	9	CHINA TEA — Russ Conway (Columbia)
19	10	HERE COMES SUMMER — Jerry Keller (London)
13	11	MONA LISA — Conway Twitty (MGM)
10	12	A BIG HUNK O' LOVE — Elvis Presley (RCA)
12	13	A TEENAGER IN LOVE — Marty Wilde (Philips)
9	14	ROULETTE — Russ Conway (Columbia)
15	15	RAGTIME COWBOY JOE — Chipmunks (London)
-	16	FORTY MILES OF BAD ROAD — Duane Eddy (London)
16	17	TALLAHASSEE LASSIE — Tommy Steele (Decca)
14	18	I KNOW — Perry Como (RCA)
17	19	TALLAHASSEE LASSIE — Freddy Cannon (Top Rank)
18	19	SIDE SADDLE — Russ Conway (Columbia)
-	19	SWEETER THAN YOU — Ricky Nelson (London)
22	22	THE WONDER OF YOU — Ronnie Hilton (HMV)
-	23	THE WONDER OF YOU — Ray Petersen (RCA)
27	24	ONLY SIXTEEN — Sam Cooke (HMV)
26	25	TWIXT TWELVE AND TWENTY — Pat Boone (London)
24	25	ONLY SIXTEEN — Al Saxon (Fontana)
-	27	MIDNIGHT FLYER — Nat King Cole (Capitol)
25	27	REMEMBER WHEN — Platters (Mercury)
30	29	HONEYMOON SONG — Manuel & The Music Of The Mountains (Columbia)
28	30	GIVE! GIVE! GIVE! — Tommy Steele (Decca)

More chart cover version battles raged over *Only Sixteen* (three versions, with Craig Douglas the runaway winner), *Tallahassie Lassie* (pretty much a draw between Tommy Steele and newcomer Freddy Cannon's US original, though Steele's B-side also charted), and *The Wonder Of You* (Ronnie Hilton just having the edge over America's Ray Peterson). Once again, a new Russ Conway single, *China Tea*, made the Top 10 while his previous hit was still resident there - and while *Side Saddle* was still in the Top 20.

September – October 1959

12 September 1959

last week	this week	Title / Artist
2	1	ONLY SIXTEEN — Craig Douglas (Top Rank)
1	2	LIVING DOLL — Cliff Richard (Columbia)
3	3	LONELY BOY — Paul Anka (Columbia)
10	4	HERE COMES SUMMER — Jerry Keller (London)
9	5	CHINA TEA — Russ Conway (Columbia)
4	6	LIPSTICK ON YOUR COLLAR — Connie Francis (MGM)
7	6	SOMEONE — Johnny Mathis (Fontana)
5	8	THE BATTLE OF NEW ORLEANS — Lonnie Donegan (Pye)
11	9	MONA LISA — Conway Twitty (MGM)
5	10	THE HEART OF A MAN — Frankie Vaughan (Philips)
8	11	DREAM LOVER — Bobby Darin (London)
16	12	FORTY MILES OF BAD ROAD — Duane Eddy (London)
-	13	SAL'S GOT A SUGAR LIP — Lonnie Donegan (Pye)
-	14	JUST A LITTLE TOO MUCH — Ricky Nelson (London)
-	15	('TIL) I KISSED YOU — Everly Brothers (London)
12	16	A BIG HUNK O' LOVE — Elvis Presley (RCA)
18	17	I KNOW — Perry Como (RCA)
14	18	ROULETTE — Russ Conway (Columbia)
-	19	HIGH HOPES — Frank Sinatra (Capitol)
-	20	PLENTY GOOD LOVIN' — Connie Francis (MGM)
-	21	PEGGY SUE GOT MARRIED — Buddy Holly (Coral)
19	22	SWEETER THAN YOU — Ricky Nelson (London)
19	23	SIDE SADDLE — Russ Conway (Columbia)
13	24	A TEENAGER IN LOVE — Marty Wilde (Philips)
19	25	TALLAHASSEE LASSIE — Freddy Cannon (Top Rank)
15	26	RAGTIME COWBOY JOE — Chipmunks (London)
-	27	PETER GUNN — Duane Eddy (London)
25	27	ONLY SIXTEEN — Al Saxon (Fontana)
-	29	BROKEN-HEARTED MELODY — Sarah Vaughan (Mercury)
-	30	I'M GONNA GET MARRIED — Lloyd Price (HMV)

19 September 1959

this week	Title / Artist
1	ONLY SIXTEEN — Craig Douglas (Top Rank)
2	LIVING DOLL — Cliff Richard (Columbia)
3	HERE COMES SUMMER — Jerry Keller (London)
4	LONELY BOY — Paul Anka (Columbia)
5	CHINA TEA — Russ Conway (Columbia)
6	LIPSTICK ON YOUR COLLAR — Connie Francis (MGM)
6	MONA LISA — Conway Twitty (MGM)
8	SOMEONE — Johnny Mathis (Fontana)
9	THE HEART OF A MAN — Frankie Vaughan (Philips)
10	THE BATTLE OF NEW ORLEANS — Lonnie Donegan (Pye)
11	FORTY MILES OF BAD ROAD — Duane Eddy (London)
12	DREAM LOVER — Bobby Darin (London)
13	('TIL) I KISSED YOU — Everly Brothers (London)
14	SAL'S GOT A SUGAR LIP — Lonnie Donegan (Pye)
15	I KNOW — Perry Como (RCA)
15	JUST A LITTLE TOO MUCH — Ricky Nelson (London)
17	HIGH HOPES — Frank Sinatra (Capitol)
18	BROKEN-HEARTED MELODY — Sarah Vaughan (Mercury)
19	THE THREE BELLS — Browns (RCA)
20	ROULETTE — Russ Conway (Columbia)
20	PLENTY GOOD LOVIN' — Connie Francis (MGM)
22	PEGGY SUE GOT MARRIED — Buddy Holly (Coral)
23	MIDNIGHT FLYER — Nat King Cole (Capitol)
24	SWEETER THAN YOU — Ricky Nelson (London)
25	I'M GONNA GET MARRIED — Lloyd Price (HMV)
26	TWIXT TWELVE AND TWENTY — Pat Boone (London)
27	A BIG HUNK O' LOVE — Elvis Presley (RCA)
28	TALLAHASSEE LASSIE — Freddy Cannon (Top Rank)
28	WALKIN' TALL — Frankie Vaughan (Philips)
28	A TEENAGER IN LOVE — Marty Wilde (Philips)

26 September 1959

this week	Title / Artist
1	ONLY SIXTEEN — Craig Douglas (Top Rank)
2	LIVING DOLL — Cliff Richard (Columbia)
3	HERE COMES SUMMER — Jerry Keller (London)
4	LONELY BOY — Paul Anka (Columbia)
5	MONA LISA — Conway Twitty (MGM)
6	CHINA TEA — Russ Conway (Columbia)
7	('TIL) I KISSED YOU — Everly Brothers (London)
8	THE HEART OF A MAN — Frankie Vaughan (Philips)
9	SOMEONE — Johnny Mathis (Fontana)
10	LIPSTICK ON YOUR COLLAR — Connie Francis (MGM)
11	THE THREE BELLS — Browns (RCA)
11	FORTY MILES OF BAD ROAD — Duane Eddy (London)
13	JUST A LITTLE TOO MUCH — Ricky Nelson (London)
14	THE BATTLE OF NEW ORLEANS — Lonnie Donegan (Pye)
15	HIGH HOPES — Frank Sinatra (Capitol)
15	BROKEN-HEARTED MELODY — Sarah Vaughan (Mercury)
17	SAL'S GOT A SUGAR LIP — Lonnie Donegan (Pye)
18	I KNOW — Perry Como (RCA)
18	DREAM LOVER — Bobby Darin (London)
18	PLENTY GOOD LOVIN' — Connie Francis (MGM)
21	SEA OF LOVE — Marty Wilde (Philips)
22	PEGGY SUE GOT MARRIED — Buddy Holly (Coral)
23	I'M GONNA GET MARRIED — Lloyd Price (HMV)
24	MACK THE KNIFE — Bobby Darin (London)
25	TALLAHASSEE LASSIE — Tommy Steele (Decca)
26	MIDNIGHT FLYER — Nat King Cole (Capitol)
27	HONEYMOON SONG — Manuel & The Music Of The Mountains (Columbia)
28	A TEENAGER IN LOVE — Marty Wilde (Philips)
29	TALLAHASSEE LASSIE — Freddy Cannon (Top Rank)
30	THE WAY I WALK — Jack Scott (London)

3 October 1959

this week	Title / Artist
1	ONLY SIXTEEN — Craig Douglas (Top Rank)
2	HERE COMES SUMMER — Jerry Keller (London)
3	LIVING DOLL — Cliff Richard (Columbia)
4	('TIL) I KISSED YOU — Everly Brothers (London)
5	MACK THE KNIFE — Bobby Darin (London)
6	SOMEONE — Johnny Mathis (Fontana)
7	LONELY BOY — Paul Anka (Columbia)
8	CHINA TEA — Russ Conway (Columbia)
9	MONA LISA — Conway Twitty (MGM)
10	THE THREE BELLS — Browns (RCA)
11	JUST A LITTLE TOO MUCH — Ricky Nelson (London)
12	HIGH HOPES — Frank Sinatra (Capitol)
13	PEGGY SUE GOT MARRIED — Buddy Holly (Coral)
14	THE HEART OF A MAN — Frankie Vaughan (Philips)
15	BROKEN-HEARTED MELODY — Sarah Vaughan (Mercury)
16	LIPSTICK ON YOUR COLLAR — Connie Francis (MGM)
16	SEA OF LOVE — Marty Wilde (Philips)
18	FORTY MILES OF BAD ROAD — Duane Eddy (London)
19	I KNOW — Perry Como (RCA)
20	PLENTY GOOD LOVIN' — Connie Francis (MGM)
21	THE BATTLE OF NEW ORLEANS — Lonnie Donegan (Pye)
22	SAL'S GOT A SUGAR LIP — Lonnie Donegan (Pye)
23	HONEYMOON SONG — Manuel & The Music Of The Mountains (Columbia)
24	I'M GONNA GET MARRIED — Lloyd Price (HMV)
25	DREAM LOVER — Bobby Darin (London)
26	JUST KEEP IT UP — Dee Clark (London)
26	HOLD BACK TOMORROW — Miki & Griff (Pye)
28	MIDNIGHT FLYER — Nat King Cole (Capitol)
29	TALLAHASSEE LASSIE — Freddy Cannon (Top Rank)
29	WALKIN' TALL — Frankie Vaughan (Philips)

The Everly Brothers' *(Til) I Kissed You* was recorded with the Crickets (uncredited) as the duo's session back-up band, while original Crickets leader Buddy Holly had a second posthumous hit with a song which was lyrically a sequel to his first solo success. Bobby Darin's *Mack The Knife* was America's biggest hit single of 1959, topping the chart for more than two months. In total contrast to the pop-rock of *Dream Lover*, and displaying Darin's Sinatra-like jazzy, finger-snapping side, it found him an adult audience.

10 October 1959

last week	this week	Title / Artist
2	1	HERE COMES SUMMER — Jerry Keller (London)
1	2	ONLY SIXTEEN — Craig Douglas (Top Rank)
5	3	MACK THE KNIFE — Bobby Darin (London)
3	4	LIVING DOLL — Cliff Richard (Columbia)
4	5	('TIL) I KISSED YOU — Everly Brothers (London)
6	6	SOMEONE — Johnny Mathis (Fontana)
7	7	LONELY BOY — Paul Anka (Columbia)
10	8	THE THREE BELLS — Browns (RCA)
8	9	CHINA TEA — Russ Conway (Columbia)
12	10	HIGH HOPES — Frank Sinatra (Capitol)
9	11	MONA LISA — Conway Twitty (MGM)
11	12	JUST A LITTLE TOO MUCH — Ricky Nelson (London)
16	13	SEA OF LOVE — Marty Wilde (Philips)
-	14	TRAVELLIN' LIGHT — Cliff Richard (Columbia)
18	15	FORTY MILES OF BAD ROAD — Duane Eddy (London)
15	16	BROKEN-HEARTED MELODY — Sarah Vaughan (Mercury)
14	17	THE HEART OF A MAN — Frankie Vaughan (Philips)
-	18	DYNAMITE — Cliff Richard (Columbia)
16	19	LIPSTICK ON YOUR COLLAR — Connie Francis (MGM)
13	20	PEGGY SUE GOT MARRIED — Buddy Holly (Coral)
19	21	I KNOW — Perry Como (RCA)
21	22	THE BATTLE OF NEW ORLEANS — Lonnie Donegan (Pye)
20	23	PLENTY GOOD LOVIN' — Connie Francis (MGM)
24	24	I'M GONNA GET MARRIED — Lloyd Price (HMV)
23	25	HONEYMOON SONG — Manuel & The Music Of The Mountains (Columbia)
-	26	GOODBYE, JIMMY GOODBYE — Ruby Murray (Columbia)
-	27	LONESOME — Chris Barber (Columbia)
-	27	THE THREE BELLS — Compagnons de la Chanson (Columbia)
-	29	RED RIVER ROCK — Johnny & the Hurricanes (London)
26	30	HOLD BACK TOMORROW — Miki & Griff (Pye)

17 October 1959

last week	this week	Title / Artist
3	1	MACK THE KNIFE — Bobby Darin (London)
1	2	HERE COMES SUMMER — Jerry Keller (London)
5	3	('TIL) I KISSED YOU — Everly Brothers (London)
2	4	ONLY SIXTEEN — Craig Douglas (Top Rank)
13	5	SEA OF LOVE — Marty Wilde (Philips)
8	6	THE THREE BELLS — Browns (RCA)
4	7	LIVING DOLL — Cliff Richard (Columbia)
14	8	TRAVELLIN' LIGHT — Cliff Richard (Columbia)
16	9	BROKEN-HEARTED MELODY — Sarah Vaughan (Mercury)
10	10	HIGH HOPES — Frank Sinatra (Capitol)
12	11	JUST A LITTLE TOO MUCH — Ricky Nelson (London)
11	12	MONA LISA — Conway Twitty (MGM)
6	13	SOMEONE — Johnny Mathis (Fontana)
9	14	CHINA TEA — Russ Conway (Columbia)
15	15	FORTY MILES OF BAD ROAD — Duane Eddy (London)
18	16	DYNAMITE — Cliff Richard (Columbia)
7	17	LONELY BOY — Paul Anka (Columbia)
20	18	PEGGY SUE GOT MARRIED — Buddy Holly (Coral)
-	19	MAKIN' LOVE — Floyd Robinson (RCA)
19	20	LIPSTICK ON YOUR COLLAR — Connie Francis (MGM)
17	21	THE HEART OF A MAN — Frankie Vaughan (Philips)
25	22	HONEYMOON SONG — Manuel & The Music Of The Mountains (Columbia)
-	23	SOMETHIN' ELSE — Eddie Cochran (London)
-	23	I WANT TO WALK YOU HOME — Fats Domino (London)
29	25	RED RIVER ROCK — Johnny & the Hurricanes (London)
-	26	SLEEP WALK — Santo & Johnny (Pye International)
21	27	I KNOW — Perry Como (RCA)
27	28	LONESOME — Chris Barber (Columbia)
-	28	BUT NOT FOR ME — Ella Fitzgerald (HMV)
23	28	PLENTY GOOD LOVIN' — Connie Francis (MGM)

24 October 1959

last week	this week	Title / Artist
1	1	MACK THE KNIFE — Bobby Darin (London)
3	2	('TIL) I KISSED YOU — Everly Brothers (London)
8	2	TRAVELLIN' LIGHT — Cliff Richard (Columbia)
5	4	SEA OF LOVE — Marty Wilde (Philips)
2	5	HERE COMES SUMMER — Jerry Keller (London)
6	6	THE THREE BELLS — Browns (RCA)
4	7	ONLY SIXTEEN — Craig Douglas (Top Rank)
7	8	LIVING DOLL — Cliff Richard (Columbia)
9	9	BROKEN-HEARTED MELODY — Sarah Vaughan (Mercury)
10	10	HIGH HOPES — Frank Sinatra (Capitol)
12	10	MONA LISA — Conway Twitty (MGM)
25	12	RED RIVER ROCK — Johnny & the Hurricanes (London)
19	13	MAKIN' LOVE — Floyd Robinson (RCA)
13	14	SOMEONE — Johnny Mathis (Fontana)
17	15	LONELY BOY — Paul Anka (Columbia)
15	16	FORTY MILES OF BAD ROAD — Duane Eddy (London)
11	17	JUST A LITTLE TOO MUCH — Ricky Nelson (London)
14	18	CHINA TEA — Russ Conway (Columbia)
18	19	PEGGY SUE GOT MARRIED — Buddy Holly (Coral)
-	20	ONE MORE SUNRISE (MORGEN) — Dickie Valentine (Pye)
-	21	THE THREE BELLS — Compagnons de la Chanson (Columbia)
23	22	SOMETHIN' ELSE — Eddie Cochran (London)
22	23	HONEYMOON SONG — Manuel & The Music O Mountains (Columbia)
27	24	I KNOW — Perry Como (RCA)
28	25	BUT NOT FOR ME — Ella Fitzgerald (HMV)
26	25	SLEEP WALK — Santo & Johnny (Pye International)
-	27	OLD SHEP — Clinton Ford (Oriole)
-	28	TREBLE CHANCE — Joe 'Mr Piano' Henderson (Pye)
23	29	I WANT TO WALK YOU HOME — Fats Domino (London)
21	30	THE HEART OF A MAN — Frankie Vaughan (Philips)

31 October 1959

last week	this week	Title / Artist
2	1	TRAVELLIN' LIGHT — Cliff Richard (Columbia)
1	2	MACK THE KNIFE — Bobby Darin (London)
4	3	SEA OF LOVE — Marty Wilde (Philips)
2	4	('TIL) I KISSED YOU — Everly Brothers (London)
12	5	RED RIVER ROCK — Johnny & the Hurricanes (London)
5	6	HERE COMES SUMMER — Jerry Keller (London)
9	7	BROKEN-HEARTED MELODY — Sarah Vaughan (Mercury)
7	8	ONLY SIXTEEN — Craig Douglas (Top Rank)
10	9	HIGH HOPES — Frank Sinatra (Capitol)
6	10	THE THREE BELLS — Browns (RCA)
-	11	PUT YOUR HEAD ON MY SHOULDER — Paul Anka (Columbia)
-	12	WHAT DO YOU WANT TO MAKE THOSE EYES AT ME FOR — Emile Ford (Pye)
13	13	MAKIN' LOVE — Floyd Robinson (RCA)
10	14	MONA LISA — Conway Twitty (MGM)
8	15	LIVING DOLL — Cliff Richard (Columbia)
16	16	FORTY MILES OF BAD ROAD — Duane Eddy (London)
19	17	PEGGY SUE GOT MARRIED — Buddy Holly (Coral)
20	17	ONE MORE SUNRISE (MORGEN) — Dickie Valentine (Pye)
29	19	I WANT TO WALK YOU HOME — Fats Domino (London)
17	20	JUST A LITTLE TOO MUCH — Ricky Nelson (London)
-	21	DYNAMITE — Cliff Richard (Columbia)
14	22	SOMEONE — Johnny Mathis (Fontana)
25	23	SLEEP WALK — Santo & Johnny (Pye International)
-	24	POISON IVY — Coasters (London)
22	25	SOMETHIN' ELSE — Eddie Cochran (London)
21	25	THE THREE BELLS — Compagnons de la Chanson (Columbia)
15	27	LONELY BOY — Paul Anka (Columbia)
-	28	PRIMROSE LANE — Dickie Pride (Columbia)
-	29	MR. BLUE — Mike Preston (Decca)
18	30	CHINA TEA — Russ Conway (Columbia)
-	30	MR. BLUE — David Macbeth (Pye)

Jerry Keller's *Here Comes Summer* curiously peaked in Britain just when summer was well and truly gone for another year. Cliff Richard's *Travellin' Light* stuck to the strummed teenbeat style which had been so effective on *Living Doll*, and virtually emulated the previous single's chart success, giving Cliff another month at Number One. Nevertheless, for some *Move It*-vintage fans the frantic B-side rocker *Dynamite* was preferable, and this duly made the Top 20 in its own right, while *Living Doll* also continued to sell.

November 1959

last week	this week	7 November 1959
1	1	TRAVELLIN' LIGHT — Cliff Richard (Columbia)
2	2	MACK THE KNIFE — Bobby Darin (London)
3	3	SEA OF LOVE — Marty Wilde (Philips)
5	4	RED RIVER ROCK — Johnny & the Hurricanes (London)
4	5	('TIL) I KISSED YOU — Everly Brothers (London)
9	6	HIGH HOPES — Frank Sinatra (Capitol)
12	7	WHAT DO YOU WANT TO MAKE THOSE EYES AT ME FOR — Emile Ford (Pye)
10	8	THE THREE BELLS — Browns (RCA)
11	9	PUT YOUR HEAD ON MY SHOULDER — Paul Anka (Columbia)
7	10	BROKEN-HEARTED MELODY — Sarah Vaughan (Mercury)
13	11	MAKIN' LOVE — Floyd Robinson (RCA)
6	12	HERE COMES SUMMER — Jerry Keller (London)
8	13	ONLY SIXTEEN — Craig Douglas (Top Rank)
19	14	I WANT TO WALK YOU HOME — Fats Domino (London)
14	14	MONA LISA — Conway Twitty (MGM)
17	16	ONE MORE SUNRISE (MORGEN) — Dickie Valentine (Pye)
15	17	LIVING DOLL — Cliff Richard (Columbia)
30	18	MR. BLUE David Macbeth (Pye)
22	19	SOMEONE — Johnny Mathis (Fontana)
30	20	CHINA TEA — Russ Conway (Columbia)
29	20	MR. BLUE — Mike Preston (Decca)
23	22	SLEEP WALK Santo & Johnny (Pye International)
-	23	MORGEN Ivo Robic (Polydor)
-	24	MACK THE KNIFE — Louis Armstrong (Philips)
17	25	PEGGY SUE GOT MARRIED — Buddy Holly (Coral)
21	26	DYNAMITE — Cliff Richard (Columbia)
-	27	HONEYMOON SONG — Manuel & The Music Of The Mountains (Columbia)
-	28	TEEN BEAT — Sandy Nelson (Top Rank)
24	29	POISON IVY — Coasters (London)
-	30	LITTLE DONKEY — Gracie Fields (Columbia)

this week	14 November 1959
1	TRAVELLIN' LIGHT — Cliff Richard (Columbia)
2	MACK THE KNIFE — Bobby Darin (London)
4	3 RED RIVER ROCK — Johnny & the Hurricanes (London)
7	4 WHAT DO YOU WANT TO MAKE THOSE EYES AT ME FOR — Emile Ford (Pye)
3	5 SEA OF LOVE — Marty Wilde (Philips)
5	6 ('TIL) I KISSED YOU — Everly Brothers (London)
10	7 BROKEN-HEARTED MELODY — Sarah Vaughan (Mercury)
9	8 PUT YOUR HEAD ON MY SHOULDER — Paul Anka (Columbia)
11	9 MAKIN' LOVE — Floyd Robinson (RCA)
6	10 HIGH HOPES — Frank Sinatra (Capitol)
8	11 THE THREE BELLS — Browns (RCA)
20	12 MR. BLUE Mike Preston (Decca)
-	13 OH! CAROL Neil Sedaka (RCA)
12	14 HERE COMES SUMMER — Jerry Keller (London)
17	15 LIVING DOLL — Cliff Richard (Columbia)
16	16 ONE MORE SUNRISE (MORGEN) — Dickie Valentine (Pye)
14	17 MONA LISA — Conway Twitty (MGM)
28	18 TEEN BEAT — Sandy Nelson (Top Rank)
13	19 ONLY SIXTEEN — Craig Douglas (Top Rank)
29	20 POISON IVY — Coasters (London)
20	21 CHINA TEA — Russ Conway (Columbia)
14	22 I WANT TO WALK YOU HOME — Fats Domino (London)
18	23 MR. BLUE David Macbeth (Pye)
-	24 SNOW COACH — Russ Conway (Columbia)
-	25 RAWHIDE — Frankie Laine (Philips)
-	26 SEVEN LITTLE GIRLS SITTING IN THE BACK SEAT — Avons (Columbia)
27	27 HONEYMOON SONG — Manuel & The Music Of The Mountains (Columbia)
19	28 SOMEONE — Johnny Mathis (Fontana)
25	29 PEGGY SUE GOT MARRIED — Buddy Holly (Coral)
-	30 ALWAYS — Sammy Turner (London)

this week	21 November 1959
1	1 TRAVELLIN' LIGHT — Cliff Richard (Columbia)
2	2 MACK THE KNIFE — Bobby Darin (London)
4	3 WHAT DO YOU WANT TO MAKE THOSE EYES AT ME FOR — Emile Ford (Pye)
3	4 RED RIVER ROCK — Johnny & the Hurricanes (London)
6	5 ('TIL) I KISSED YOU — Everly Brothers (London)
5	6 SEA OF LOVE — Marty Wilde (Philips)
8	7 PUT YOUR HEAD ON MY SHOULDER — Paul Anka (Columbia)
10	8 HIGH HOPES — Frank Sinatra (Capitol)
11	9 THE THREE BELLS — Browns (RCA)
13	10 OH! CAROL Neil Sedaka (RCA)
9	11 MAKIN' LOVE — Floyd Robinson (RCA)
7	11 BROKEN-HEARTED MELODY — Sarah Vaughan (Mercury)
15	13 LIVING DOLL — Cliff Richard (Columbia)
16	14 ONE MORE SUNRISE (MORGEN) — Dickie Valentine (Pye)
24	15 SNOW COACH — Russ Conway (Columbia)
18	16 TEEN BEAT — Sandy Nelson (Top Rank)
12	17 MR. BLUE — Mike Preston (Decca)
20	18 POISON IVY — Coasters (London)
-	18 WHAT DO YOU WANT? — Adam Faith (Parlophone)
-	20 LITTLE DONKEY — Beverley Sisters (Decca)
14	21 HERE COMES SUMMER — Jerry Keller (London)
25	21 RAWHIDE — Frankie Laine (Philips)
26	23 SEVEN LITTLE GIRLS SITTING IN THE BACK SEAT — Avons (Columbia)
23	23 MR. BLUE David Macbeth (Pye)
-	25 MORE AND MORE PARTY POPS — Russ Conway (Columbia)
30	26 ALWAYS — Sammy Turner (London)
-	27 VILLAGE OF ST. BERNADETTE — Anne Shelton (Philips)
-	28 LITTLE DONKEY — Gracie Fields (Columbia)
-	29 NASHVILLE BOOGIE — Bert Weedon (Top Rank)
17	30 MONA LISA — Conway Twitty (MGM)

this week	28 November 1959
1	1 TRAVELLIN' LIGHT — Cliff Richard (Columbia)
3	2 WHAT DO YOU WANT TO MAKE THOSE EYES AT ME FOR — Emile Ford (Pye)
2	3 MACK THE KNIFE — Bobby Darin (London)
4	4 RED RIVER ROCK — Johnny & the Hurricanes (London)
5	5 ('TIL) I KISSED YOU — Everly Brothers (London)
10	5 OH! CAROL Neil Sedaka (RCA)
7	7 PUT YOUR HEAD ON MY SHOULDER — Paul Anka (Columbia)
18	8 WHAT DO YOU WANT? — Adam Faith (Parlophone)
6	9 SEA OF LOVE — Marty Wilde (Philips)
11	10 BROKEN-HEARTED MELODY — Sarah Vaughan (Mercury)
16	11 TEEN BEAT — Sandy Nelson (Top Rank)
11	12 MAKIN' LOVE — Floyd Robinson (RCA)
23	13 SEVEN LITTLE GIRLS SITTING IN THE BACK SEAT — Avons (Columbia)
15	14 SNOW COACH — Russ Conway (Columbia)
9	15 THE THREE BELLS — Browns (RCA)
8	16 HIGH HOPES — Frank Sinatra (Capitol)
18	17 POISON IVY — Coasters (London)
14	17 ONE MORE SUNRISE (MORGEN) — Dickie Valentine (Pye)
21	19 RAWHIDE Frankie Laine (Philips)
17	20 MR. BLUE Mike Preston (Decca)
28	21 LITTLE DONKEY — Gracie Fields (Columbia)
-	22 PIANO PARTY — Winifred Atwell (Decca)
20	23 LITTLE DONKEY — Beverley Sisters (Decca)
13	24 LIVING DOLL — Cliff Richard (Columbia)
-	25 SEVEN LITTLE GIRLS SITTING IN THE BACK SEAT — Paul Evans & the Curls (London)
-	26 HEARTACHES BY THE NUMBER — Guy Mitchell (Philips)
25	27 MORE AND MORE PARTY POPS — Russ Conway (Columbia)
21	28 HERE COMES SUMMER — Jerry Keller (London)
29	29 NASHVILLE BOOGIE — Bert Weedon (Top Rank)
-	30 THE BEST OF EVERYTHING — Johnny Mathis (Fontana)

As Johnny & the Hurricanes' *Red River Rock* went into the Top Three, further classic rock instrumentals were charting in the shape of Santo & Johnny's *Sleep Walk* (the main inspiration for Fleetwood Mac's later *Albatross*), and drummer Sandy Nelson's *Teen Beat*.

Two versions of the extremely twee *Little Donkey* vied for early Christmas sales during November, but the major hit version of this song would actually come one Christmas later from Nina & Frederick. Frankie Laine's *Rawhide* was the TV series theme.

5 December 1959

last week	this week	
8	1	WHAT DO YOU WANT? Adam Faith (Parlophone)
2	2	WHAT DO YOU WANT TO MAKE THOSE EYES AT ME FOR Emile Ford (Pye)
1	3	TRAVELLIN' LIGHT Cliff Richard (Columbia)
5	4	OH! CAROL Neil Sedaka (RCA)
4	5	RED RIVER ROCK Johnny & the Hurricanes (London)
3	6	MACK THE KNIFE Bobby Darin (London)
7	7	PUT YOUR HEAD ON MY SHOULDER Paul Anka (Columbia)
13	8	SEVEN LITTLE GIRLS SITTING IN THE BACK SEAT Avons (Columbia)
5	9	('TIL) I KISSED YOU Everly Brothers (London)
11	10	TEEN BEAT Sandy Nelson (Top Rank)
9	11	SEA OF LOVE Marty Wilde (Philips)
14	12	SNOW COACH Russ Conway (Columbia)
19	13	RAWHIDE Frankie Laine (Philips)
22	14	PIANO PARTY Winifred Atwell (Decca)
17	15	POISON IVY Coasters (London)
17	16	ONE MORE SUNRISE (MORGEN) Dickie Valentine (Pye)
10	17	BROKEN-HEARTED MELODY Sarah Vaughan (Mercury)
-	18	LITTLE WHITE BULL Tommy Steele (Decca)
-	19	SAN MIGUEL Lonnie Donegan (Pye)
-	20	AMONG MY SOUVENIRS Connie Francis (MGM)
12	21	MAKIN' LOVE Floyd Robinson (RCA)
-	22	DECK OF CARDS Wink Martindale (London)
21	23	LITTLE DONKEY Gracie Fields (Columbia)
23	24	LITTLE DONKEY Beverley Sisters (Decca)
20	25	MR. BLUE Mike Preston (Decca)
-	26	I'LL NEVER FALL IN LOVE AGAIN Johnnie Ray (Philips)
16	26	HIGH HOPES Frank Sinatra (Capitol)
27	28	MORE AND MORE PARTY POPS Russ Conway (Columbia)
-	29	SAN MIGUEL Kingston Trio (Capitol)
15	30	THE THREE BELLS Browns (RCA)
-	30	IF YOU WERE THE ONLY BOY IN THE WORLD Stevie Marsh (Decca)
26	30	HEARTACHES BY THE NUMBER Guy Mitchell (Philips)

12 December 1959

this week	
1	WHAT DO YOU WANT? Adam Faith (Parlophone)
2	WHAT DO YOU WANT TO MAKE THOSE EYES AT ME FOR Emile Ford (Pye)
3	TRAVELLIN' LIGHT Cliff Richard (Columbia)
4	OH! CAROL Neil Sedaka (RCA)
5	SEVEN LITTLE GIRLS SITTING IN THE BACK SEAT Avons (Columbia)
6	RED RIVER ROCK Johnny & the Hurricanes (London)
7	PUT YOUR HEAD ON MY SHOULDER Paul Anka (Columbia)
7	MACK THE KNIFE Bobby Darin (London)
9	SNOW COACH Russ Conway (Columbia)
9	TEEN BEAT Sandy Nelson (Top Rank)
11	LITTLE WHITE BULL Tommy Steele (Decca)
12	AMONG MY SOUVENIRS Connie Francis (MGM)
13	RAWHIDE Frankie Laine (Philips)
14	LITTLE DONKEY Beverley Sisters (London)
15	MORE AND MORE PARTY POPS Russ Conway (Columbia)
16	PIANO PARTY Winifred Atwell (Decca)
17	MR. BLUE Mike Preston (Decca)
18	BAD BOY Marty Wilde (Philips)
19	('TIL) I KISSED YOU Everly Brothers (London)
20	SEA OF LOVE Marty Wilde (Philips)
21	ONE MORE SUNRISE (MORGEN) Dickie Valentine (Pye)
22	THE THREE BELLS Browns (RCA)
23	POISON IVY Coasters (London)
24	DECK OF CARDS Wink Martindale (London)
25	SAN MIGUEL Lonnie Donegan (Pye)
26	LIVING DOLL Cliff Richard (Columbia)
26	MAKIN' LOVE Floyd Robinson (RCA)
28	I'LL NEVER FALL IN LOVE AGAIN Johnnie Ray (Philips)
29	IF YOU WERE THE ONLY BOY IN THE WORLD Stevie Marsh (Decca)
30	MARY'S BOY CHILD Harry Belafonte (RCA)
30	LITTLE DONKEY Gracie Fields (Columbia)

19 December 1959

this week	
1	WHAT DO YOU WANT? Adam Faith (Parlophone)
1	WHAT DO YOU WANT TO MAKE THOSE EYES AT ME FOR Emile Ford (Pye)
3	OH! CAROL Neil Sedaka (RCA)
4	SEVEN LITTLE GIRLS SITTING IN THE BACK SEAT Avons (Columbia)
5	TRAVELLIN' LIGHT Cliff Richard (Columbia)
6	RED RIVER ROCK Johnny & the Hurricanes (London)
7	PUT YOUR HEAD ON MY SHOULDER Paul Anka (Columbia)
8	MORE AND MORE PARTY POPS Russ Conway (Columbia)
8	RAWHIDE Frankie Laine (Philips)
10	PIANO PARTY Winifred Atwell (Decca)
10	SNOW COACH Russ Conway (Columbia)
12	LITTLE WHITE BULL Tommy Steele (Decca)
13	AMONG MY SOUVENIRS Connie Francis (MGM)
14	JINGLE BELL ROCK Max Bygraves (Decca)
15	LITTLE DONKEY Beverley Sisters (Decca)
16	MACK THE KNIFE Bobby Darin (London)
17	SOME KIND-A EARTHQUAKE Duane Eddy (London)
18	DECK OF CARDS Wink Martindale (London)
19	STACCATO'S THEME Elmer Bernstein (Capitol)
20	BAD BOY Marty Wilde (Philips)
21	TEEN BEAT Sandy Nelson (Top Rank)
22	BE MY GUEST Fats Domino (London)
23	SAN MIGUEL Lonnie Donegan (Pye)
24	LITTLE DONKEY Gracie Fields (Columbia)
25	MR. BLUE Mike Preston (Decca)
26	MARY'S BOY CHILD Nina & Frederick (Columbia)
27	HEARTACHES BY THE NUMBER Guy Mitchell (Philips)
28	('TIL) I KISSED YOU Everly Brothers (London)
29	WE GOT LOVE Alma Cogan (HMV)
29	I'LL NEVER FALL IN LOVE AGAIN Johnnie Ray (Philips)

26 December 1959

this week	
1	WHAT DO YOU WANT TO MAKE THOSE EYES AT ME FOR Emile Ford (Pye)
2	WHAT DO YOU WANT? Adam Faith (Parlophone)
3	OH! CAROL Neil Sedaka (RCA)
4	SEVEN LITTLE GIRLS SITTING IN THE BACK SEAT Avons (Columbia)
5	MORE AND MORE PARTY POPS Russ Conway (Columbia)
6	STACCATO'S THEME Elmer Bernstein (Capitol)
7	SNOW COACH Russ Conway (Columbia)
8	TRAVELLIN' LIGHT Cliff Richard (Columbia)
9	RED RIVER ROCK Johnny & the Hurricanes (London)
10	LITTLE WHITE BULL Tommy Steele (Decca)
11	JINGLE BELL ROCK Max Bygraves (Decca)
12	AMONG MY SOUVENIRS Connie Francis (MGM)
13	PIANO PARTY Winifred Atwell (Decca)
13	RAWHIDE Frankie Laine (Philips)
15	PUT YOUR HEAD ON MY SHOULDER Paul Anka (Columbia)
15	SOME KIND-A EARTHQUAKE Duane Eddy (London)
17	BE MY GUEST Fats Domino (London)
18	BAD BOY Marty Wilde (Philips)
19	TEEN BEAT Sandy Nelson (Top Rank)
20	MACK THE KNIFE Bobby Darin (London)
21	LITTLE DONKEY Beverley Sisters (Decca)
22	HEARTACHES BY THE NUMBER Guy Mitchell (Philips)
23	REVEILLE ROCK Johnny & the Hurricanes (London)
24	IF YOU WERE THE ONLY BOY IN THE WORLD Stevie Marsh (Decca)
25	DECK OF CARDS Wink Martindale (London)
26	SAN MIGUEL Lonnie Donegan (Pye)
27	WE GOT LOVE Alma Cogan (HMV)
27	I'LL NEVER FALL IN LOVE AGAIN Johnnie Ray (Philips)
29	BUT NOT FOR ME Ella Fitzgerald (HMV)
30	IN THE MOOD Ernie Fields (London)

Adam Faith's *What Do You Want*, after a breakneck chart climb, pipped Emile Ford's debut to Number One, only to share the top slot with Ford two weeks later and surrender it the week after that. For a Number One record title to incorporate the whole title of its chart-topping predecessor into itself is an unlikely eventuality, but *What Do You Want To Make Those Eyes At Me For* did just that! Both these singles sold phenomenally, each moving in the region of 750,000 copies in the UK alone by early 1960.

January 1960

2 January 1960

last	this	Title / Artist (Label)
1	1	WHAT DO YOU WANT TO MAKE THOSE EYES AT ME FOR — Emile Ford (Pye)
2	2	WHAT DO YOU WANT? — Adam Faith (Parlophone)
4	3	SEVEN LITTLE GIRLS SITTING IN THE BACK SEAT — Avons (Columbia)
3	4	OH CAROL — Neil Sedaka (RCA)
8	5	TRAVELLIN' LIGHT — Cliff Richard (Columbia)
13	6	RAWHIDE — Frankie Laine (Philips)
11	7	JINGLE BELL ROCK — Max Bygraves (Decca)
6	8	STACCATO'S THEME — Elmer Bernstein (Capitol)
7	8	SNOW COACH — Russ Conway (Columbia)
10	10	LITTLE WHITE BULL — Tommy Steele (Decca)
5	11	MORE AND MORE PARTY POPS — Russ Conway (Columbia)
12	12	AMONG MY SOUVENIRS — Connie Francis (MGM)
13	13	SOME KIND-A EARTHQUAKE — Duane Eddy (London)
18	14	BAD BOY — Marty Wilde (Philips)
13	15	PIANO PARTY — Winifred Atwell (Decca)
21	16	LITTLE DONKEY — Beverley Sisters (Decca)
15	17	PUT YOUR HEAD ON MY SHOULDER — Paul Anka (Columbia)
22	17	HEARTACHES BY THE NUMBER — Guy Mitchell (Philips)
20	19	MACK THE KNIFE — Bobby Darin (London)
9	19	RED RIVER ROCK — Johnny & the Hurricanes (London)
23	19	REVEILLE ROCK — Johnny & the Hurricanes (London)
19	22	TEEN BEAT — Sandy Nelson (Top Rank)
25	23	DECK OF CARDS — Wink Martindale (London)
-	24	WAY DOWN YONDER IN NEW ORLEANS — Freddy Cannon (Top Rank)
17	25	BE MY GUEST — Fats Domino (London)
27	26	WE GOT LOVE — Alma Cogan (HMV)
24	27	IF YOU WERE THE ONLY BOY IN THE WORLD — Stevie Marsh (Decca)
30	28	IN THE MOOD — Ernie Fields (London)
-	28	STARRY EYED — Michael Holliday (Columbia)
-	28	LIVING DOLL — Cliff Richard (Columbia)

9 January 1960

last	this	Title / Artist (Label)
1	1	WHAT DO YOU WANT TO MAKE THOSE EYES AT ME FOR — Emile Ford (Pye)
2	2	WHAT DO YOU WANT? — Adam Faith (Parlophone)
4	3	OH CAROL — Neil Sedaka (RCA)
3	4	SEVEN LITTLE GIRLS SITTING IN THE BACK SEAT — Avons (Columbia)
8	5	STACCATO'S THEME — Elmer Bernstein (Capitol)
10	6	LITTLE WHITE BULL — Tommy Steele (Decca)
14	7	BAD BOY — Marty Wilde (Philips)
6	8	RAWHIDE — Frankie Laine (Philips)
5	9	TRAVELLIN' LIGHT — Cliff Richard (Columbia)
19	10	RED RIVER ROCK — Johnny & the Hurricanes (London)
12	11	AMONG MY SOUVENIRS — Connie Francis (MGM)
13	12	SOME KIND-A EARTHQUAKE — Duane Eddy (London)
25	13	BE MY GUEST — Fats Domino (London)
28	14	STARRY EYED — Michael Holliday (Columbia)
11	15	MORE AND MORE PARTY POPS — Russ Conway (Columbia)
17	16	HEARTACHES BY THE NUMBER — Guy Mitchell (Philips)
19	17	REVEILLE ROCK — Johnny & the Hurricanes (London)
28	18	IN THE MOOD — Ernie Fields (London)
22	18	TEEN BEAT — Sandy Nelson (Top Rank)
24	20	WAY DOWN YONDER IN NEW ORLEANS — Freddy Cannon (Top Rank)
8	20	SNOW COACH — Russ Conway (Columbia)
17	22	PUT YOUR HEAD ON MY SHOULDER — Paul Anka (Columbia)
19	23	MACK THE KNIFE — Bobby Darin (London)
-	24	DANCE WITH ME — Drifters (London)
7	25	JINGLE BELL ROCK — Max Bygraves (Decca)
-	26	I'LL STAY SINGLE — Jerry Lordan (Parlophone)
-	26	I'LL NEVER FALL IN LOVE AGAIN — Johnnie Ray (Philips)
-	28	WILD CAT — Gene Vincent (Capitol)
15	29	PIANO PARTY — Winifred Atwell (Decca)
26	29	WE GOT LOVE — Alma Cogan (HMV)

16 January 1960

last	this	Title / Artist (Label)
1	1	WHAT DO YOU WANT TO MAKE THOSE EYES AT ME FOR — Emile Ford (Pye)
2	2	WHAT DO YOU WANT? — Adam Faith (Parlophone)
3	3	OH CAROL — Neil Sedaka (RCA)
5	4	STACCATO'S THEME — Elmer Bernstein (Capitol)
14	5	STARRY EYED — Michael Holliday (Columbia)
4	6	SEVEN LITTLE GIRLS SITTING IN THE BACK SEAT — Avons (Columbia)
6	7	LITTLE WHITE BULL — Tommy Steele (Decca)
8	8	RAWHIDE — Frankie Laine (Philips)
7	9	BAD BOY — Marty Wilde (Philips)
20	10	WAY DOWN YONDER IN NEW ORLEANS — Freddy Cannon (Top Rank)
13	11	BE MY GUEST — Fats Domino (London)
12	12	WHY — Anthony Newley (Decca)
9	12	TRAVELLIN' LIGHT — Cliff Richard (Columbia)
17	14	REVEILLE ROCK — Johnny & the Hurricanes (London)
18	15	IN THE MOOD — Ernie Fields (London)
16	15	HEARTACHES BY THE NUMBER — Guy Mitchell (Philips)
12	17	SOME KIND-A EARTHQUAKE — Duane Eddy (London)
18	18	TEEN BEAT — Sandy Nelson (Top Rank)
-	19	TOO GOOD — Little Tony (Decca)
10	20	RED RIVER ROCK — Johnny & the Hurricanes (London)
28	21	WILD CAT — Gene Vincent (Capitol)
22	22	PUT YOUR HEAD ON MY SHOULDER — Paul Anka (Columbia)
24	23	DANCE WITH ME — Drifters (London)
11	24	AMONG MY SOUVENIRS — Connie Francis (MGM)
-	25	EXPRESSO BONGO (EP) — Cliff Richard (Columbia)
26	26	I'LL STAY SINGLE — Jerry Lordan (Parlophone)
-	27	WHEN YOU ASK ABOUT LOVE — Crickets (Coral)
-	28	DECK OF CARDS — Wink Martindale (London)
-	29	TOO YOUNG — Bill Forbes (Columbia)
-	30	I WANNA BE LOVED — Ricky Nelson (London)

23 January 1960

last	this	Title / Artist (Label)
1	1	WHAT DO YOU WANT TO MAKE THOSE EYES AT ME FOR — Emile Ford (Pye)
12	2	WHY — Anthony Newley (Decca)
5	3	STARRY EYED — Michael Holliday (Columbia)
2	4	WHAT DO YOU WANT? — Adam Faith (Parlophone)
10	5	WAY DOWN YONDER IN NEW ORLEANS — Freddy Cannon (Top Rank)
3	6	OH CAROL — Neil Sedaka (RCA)
4	7	STACCATO'S THEME — Elmer Bernstein (Capitol)
7	8	LITTLE WHITE BULL — Tommy Steele (Decca)
15	9	HEARTACHES BY THE NUMBER — Guy Mitchell (Philips)
-	10	A VOICE IN THE WILDERNESS — Cliff Richard (Columbia)
8	11	RAWHIDE — Frankie Laine (Philips)
6	12	SEVEN LITTLE GIRLS SITTING IN THE BACK SEAT — Avons (Columbia)
9	13	BAD BOY — Marty Wilde (Philips)
11	14	BE MY GUEST — Fats Domino (London)
14	15	REVEILLE ROCK — Johnny & the Hurricanes (London)
15	16	IN THE MOOD — Ernie Fields (London)
23	17	DANCE WITH ME — Drifters (London)
25	18	EXPRESSO BONGO (EP) — Cliff Richard (Columbia)
12	19	TRAVELLIN' LIGHT — Cliff Richard (Columbia)
-	20	WHY — Frankie Avalon (HMV)
24	21	AMONG MY SOUVENIRS — Connie Francis (MGM)
19	21	TOO GOOD — Little Tony (Decca)
-	23	SUMMER SET — Mr Acker Bilk (Columbia)
21	24	WILD CAT — Gene Vincent (Capitol)
20	25	RED RIVER ROCK — Johnny & the Hurricanes (London)
-	26	THE BIG HURT — Maureen Evans (Oriole)
-	27	POOR ME — Adam Faith (Parlophone)
-	28	HALLELUJAH, I LOVE HER SO — Eddie Cochran (London)
-	28	PRETTY BLUE EYES — Craig Douglas (Top Rank)
-	30	MACK THE KNIFE — Bobby Darin (London)
28	30	DECK OF CARDS — Wink Martindale (London)

Tommy Steele's *Little White Bull* came from his unlikely movie *Tommy The Toreador*, a mixture of schmaltz and bullfighting. Rather more impressive was Cliff Richard's role as a malleable young rock singer in *Expresso Bongo* with Lawrence Harvey. The EP of the film's songs immediately sold like a single, while *A Voice In The Wilderness* was extracted from it. Both made the Top 20. The Drifters made their UK chart debut, as did Jerry Lordan, who would write *Apache* for The Shadows.

30 January 1960

last week	this week		
3	1	STARRY EYED	Michael Holliday (Columbia)
2	2	WHY	Anthony Newley (Decca)
1	3	WHAT DO YOU WANT TO MAKE THOSE EYES AT ME FOR	Emile Ford (Pye)
10	4	A VOICE IN THE WILDERNESS	Cliff Richard (Columbia)
5	5	WAY DOWN YONDER IN NEW ORLEANS	Freddy Cannon (Top Rank)
9	6	HEARTACHES BY THE NUMBER	Guy Mitchell (Philips)
4	7	WHAT DO YOU WANT?	Adam Faith (Parlophone)
6	7	OH CAROL	Neil Sedaka (RCA)
7	9	STACCATO'S THEME	Elmer Bernstein (Capitol)
12	10	SEVEN LITTLE GIRLS SITTING IN THE BACK SEAT	Avons (Columbia)
8	11	LITTLE WHITE BULL	Tommy Steele (Decca)
11	12	RAWHIDE	Frankie Laine (Philips)
16	13	IN THE MOOD	Ernie Fields (London)
14	14	BE MY GUEST	Fats Domino (London)
23	15	SUMMER SET	Mr Acker Bilk (Columbia)
18	15	EXPRESSO BONGO (EP)	Cliff Richard (Columbia)
-	17	HARBOUR LIGHTS	Platters (Mercury)
27	18	POOR ME	Adam Faith (Parlophone)
-	19	MISTY	Johnny Mathis (Fontana)
20	20	WHY	Frankie Avalon (HMV)
19	21	TRAVELLIN' LIGHT	Cliff Richard (Columbia)
17	22	DANCE WITH ME	Drifters (London)
21	23	TOO GOOD	Little Tony (Decca)
-	24	LA MER (BEYOND THE SEA)	Bobby Darin (London)
28	25	PRETTY BLUE EYES	Craig Douglas (Top Rank)
-	25	WHAT MORE DO YOU WANT	Frankie Vaughan (Philips)
26	27	THE BIG HURT	Maureen Evans (Oriole)
-	28	EL PASO	Marty Robbins (Fontana)
21	29	AMONG MY SOUVENIRS	Connie Francis (MGM)
13	29	BAD BOY	Marty Wilde (Philips)

6 February 1960

2	1	WHY	Anthony Newley (Decca)
4	2	A VOICE IN THE WILDERNESS	Cliff Richard (Columbia)
1	3	STARRY EYED	Michael Holliday (Columbia)
5	4	WAY DOWN YONDER IN NEW ORLEANS	Freddy Cannon (Top Rank)
6	5	HEARTACHES BY THE NUMBER	Guy Mitchell (Philips)
3	6	WHAT DO YOU WANT TO MAKE THOSE EYES AT ME FOR	Emile Ford (Pye)
18	7	POOR ME	Adam Faith (Parlophone)
7	8	WHAT DO YOU WANT?	Adam Faith (Parlophone)
7	9	OH CAROL	Neil Sedaka (RCA)
9	10	STACCATO'S THEME	Elmer Bernstein (Capitol)
11	10	LITTLE WHITE BULL	Tommy Steele (Decca)
25	12	PRETTY BLUE EYES	Craig Douglas (Top Rank)
12	13	RAWHIDE	Frankie Laine (Philips)
15	14	EXPRESSO BONGO (EP)	Cliff Richard (Columbia)
24	15	LA MER (BEYOND THE SEA)	Bobby Darin (London)
19	15	MISTY	Johnny Mathis (Fontana)
15	17	SUMMER SET	Mr Acker Bilk (Columbia)
14	17	BE MY GUEST	Fats Domino (London)
17	17	HARBOUR LIGHTS	Platters (Mercury)
13	20	IN THE MOOD	Ernie Fields (London)
-	21	ON A SLOW BOAT TO CHINA	Emile Ford (Pye)
-	22	HALLELUJAH, I LOVE HER SO	Eddie Cochran (London)
10	23	SEVEN LITTLE GIRLS SITTING IN THE BACK SEAT	Avons (Columbia)
28	24	EL PASO	Marty Robbins (Fontana)
-	25	TEEN BEAT	Sandy Nelson (Top Rank)
25	26	WHAT MORE DO YOU WANT	Frankie Vaughan (Philips)
20	27	WHY	Frankie Avalon (HMV)
-	28	I'LL NEVER FALL IN LOVE AGAIN	Johnnie Ray (Philips)
-	29	HAPPY ANNIVERSARY	Joan Regan (Pye)
29	30	AMONG MY SOUVENIRS	Connie Francis (MGM)

13 February 1960

1	1	WHY	Anthony Newley (Decca)
2	2	A VOICE IN THE WILDERNESS	Cliff Richard (Columbia)
4	3	WAY DOWN YONDER IN NEW ORLEANS	Freddy Cannon (Top Rank)
7	4	POOR ME	Adam Faith (Parlophone)
3	5	STARRY EYED	Michael Holliday (Columbia)
12	6	PRETTY BLUE EYES	Craig Douglas (Top Rank)
21	6	ON A SLOW BOAT TO CHINA	Emile Ford (Pye)
15	8	LA MER (BEYOND THE SEA)	Bobby Darin (London)
6	9	WHAT DO YOU WANT TO MAKE THOSE EYES AT ME FOR	Emile Ford (Pye)
5	10	HEARTACHES BY THE NUMBER	Guy Mitchell (Philips)
17	11	SUMMER SET	Mr Acker Bilk (Columbia)
15	12	MISTY	Johnny Mathis (Fontana)
-	13	RUNNING BEAR	Johnny Preston (Mercury)
10	14	STACCATO'S THEME	Elmer Bernstein (Capitol)
8	14	WHAT DO YOU WANT?	Adam Faith (Parlophone)
17	16	HARBOUR LIGHTS	Platters (Mercury)
10	17	LITTLE WHITE BULL	Tommy Steele (Decca)
13	18	RAWHIDE	Frankie Laine (Philips)
24	19	EL PASO	Marty Robbins (Fontana)
9	20	OH CAROL	Neil Sedaka (RCA)
-	21	YOU GOT WHAT IT TAKES	Marv Johnson (London)
-	22	LET IT BE ME	Everly Brothers (London)
14	23	EXPRESSO BONGO (EP)	Cliff Richard (Columbia)
22	24	HALLELUJAH, I LOVE HER SO	Eddie Cochran (London)
-	25	YOU GOT WHAT IT TAKES	Johnny Kidd & the Pirates (HMV)
-	26	STRICTLY ELVIS (EP)	Elvis Presley (RCA)
27	27	WHY	Frankie Avalon (HMV)
20	27	IN THE MOOD	Ernie Fields (London)
-	29	TIME AND THE RIVER	Nat King Cole (Capitol)
-	30	THE BIG HURT	Toni Fisher (Top Rank)

20 February 1960

1	1	WHY	Anthony Newley (Decca)
2	2	A VOICE IN THE WILDERNESS	Cliff Richard (Columbia)
4	3	POOR ME	Adam Faith (Parlophone)
3	4	WAY DOWN YONDER IN NEW ORLEANS	Freddy Cannon (Top Rank)
6	5	ON A SLOW BOAT TO CHINA	Emile Ford (Pye)
6	6	PRETTY BLUE EYES	Craig Douglas (Top Rank)
5	7	STARRY EYED	Michael Holliday (Columbia)
13	8	RUNNING BEAR	Johnny Preston (Mercury)
8	9	LA MER (BEYOND THE SEA)	Bobby Darin (London)
10	10	HEARTACHES BY THE NUMBER	Guy Mitchell (Philips)
9	11	WHAT DO YOU WANT TO MAKE THOSE EYES AT ME FOR	Emile Ford (Pye)
11	12	SUMMER SET	Mr Acker Bilk (Columbia)
12	13	MISTY	Johnny Mathis (Fontana)
14	14	WHAT DO YOU WANT?	Adam Faith (Parlophone)
21	15	YOU GOT WHAT IT TAKES	Marv Johnson (London)
16	16	HARBOUR LIGHTS	Platters (Mercury)
14	17	STACCATO'S THEME	Elmer Bernstein (Capitol)
18	18	RAWHIDE	Frankie Laine (Philips)
17	19	LITTLE WHITE BULL	Tommy Steele (Decca)
-	20	BONNIE CAME BACK	Duane Eddy (London)
22	20	LET IT BE ME	Everly Brothers (London)
-	22	BE MINE	Lance Fortune (Pye)
19	22	EL PASO	Marty Robbins (Fontana)
20	24	OH CAROL	Neil Sedaka (RCA)
-	25	BE MY GUEST	Fats Domino (London)
-	26	LUCKY DEVIL	Frank Ifield (Columbia)
24	27	HALLELUJAH, I LOVE HER SO	Eddie Cochran (London)
25	28	YOU GOT WHAT IT TAKES	Johnny Kidd & the Pirates (HMV)
-	29	HAPPY ANNIVERSARY	Joan Regan (Pye)
23	30	EXPRESSO BONGO (EP)	Cliff Richard (Columbia)

Anthony Newley's *Why* was one of a rare breed of British cover versions, which in terms of quality and performance, far outshone their US models – though enough people did prefer Frankie Avalon's original to give it a Top 20 place. Marty Robbin's western story song *El Paso* had been a US chart-topper, and at almost five minutes, was by far the longest hit single of the era. Eddie Cochran, on a UK tour with Gene Vincent, scored with Ray Charles' *Hallelujah, I Love Her So*.

February – March 1960

27 February 1960

last	this		
1	1	WHY	Anthony Newley (Decca)
3	2	POOR ME	Adam Faith (Parlophone)
4	3	WAY DOWN YONDER IN NEW ORLEANS	Freddy Cannon (Top Rank)
6	4	PRETTY BLUE EYES	Craig Douglas (Top Rank)
2	4	A VOICE IN THE WILDERNESS	Cliff Richard (Columbia)
5	6	ON A SLOW BOAT TO CHINA	Emile Ford (Pye)
8	7	RUNNING BEAR	Johnny Preston (Mercury)
9	8	LA MER (BEYOND THE SEA)	Bobby Darin (London)
7	9	STARRY EYED	Michael Holliday (Columbia)
12	10	SUMMER SET	Mr Acker Bilk (Columbia)
16	11	HARBOUR LIGHTS	Platters (Mercury)
15	12	YOU GOT WHAT IT TAKES	Marv Johnson (London)
22	13	BE MINE	Lance Fortune (Pye)
11	14	WHAT DO YOU WANT TO MAKE THOSE EYES AT ME FOR	Emile Ford (Pye)
13	15	MISTY	Johnny Mathis (Fontana)
10	16	HEARTACHES BY THE NUMBER	Guy Mitchell (Philips)
20	17	BONNIE CAME BACK	Duane Eddy (London)
20	18	LET IT BE ME	Everly Brothers (London)
25	19	BE MY GUEST	Fats Domino (London)
14	20	WHAT DO YOU WANT?	Adam Faith (Parlophone)
18	21	RAWHIDE	Frankie Laine (Philips)
26	22	LUCKY DEVIL	Frank Ifield (Columbia)
-	23	TIME AND THE RIVER	Nat King Cole (Capitol)
-	24	DELAWARE	Perry Como (RCA)
24	24	WHO COULD BE BLUER?	Jerry Lordan (Parlophone)
22	26	EL PASO	Marty Robbins (Fontana)
24	27	OH CAROL	Neil Sedaka (RCA)
-	28	IT'S TIME TO CRY	Paul Anka (Columbia)
30	29	EXPRESSO BONGO (EP)	Cliff Richard (Columbia)
28	30	YOU GOT WHAT IT TAKES	Johnny Kidd & the Pirates (HMV)

5 March 1960

last	this		
2	1	POOR ME	Adam Faith (Parlophone)
1	2	WHY	Anthony Newley (Decca)
7	3	RUNNING BEAR	Johnny Preston (Mercury)
6	4	ON A SLOW BOAT TO CHINA	Emile Ford (Pye)
4	5	A VOICE IN THE WILDERNESS	Cliff Richard (Columbia)
3	6	WAY DOWN YONDER IN NEW ORLEANS	Freddy Cannon (Top Rank)
4	7	PRETTY BLUE EYES	Craig Douglas (Top Rank)
24	8	DELAWARE	Perry Como (RCA)
10	9	SUMMER SET	Mr Acker Bilk (Columbia)
8	10	LA MER (BEYOND THE SEA)	Bobby Darin (London)
13	11	BE MINE	Lance Fortune (Pye)
17	12	BONNIE CAME BACK	Duane Eddy (London)
12	12	YOU GOT WHAT IT TAKES	Marv Johnson (London)
9	14	STARRY EYED	Michael Holliday (Columbia)
11	14	HARBOUR LIGHTS	Platters (Mercury)
24	16	WHO COULD BE BLUER?	Jerry Lordan (Parlophone)
-	17	ROYAL EVENT	Russ Conway (Columbia)
-	18	THEME FROM 'A SUMMER PLACE'	Percy Faith (Philips)
18	19	LET IT BE ME	Everly Brothers (London)
15	20	MISTY	Johnny Mathis (Fontana)
14	21	WHAT DO YOU WANT TO MAKE THOSE EYES AT ME FOR	Emile Ford (Pye)
19	22	BE MY GUEST	Fats Domino (London)
22	23	LUCKY DEVIL	Frank Ifield (Columbia)
-	24	HIT AND MISS	John Barry Seven (Columbia)
-	25	CALIFORNIA HERE I COME	Freddy Cannon (Top Rank)
21	26	RAWHIDE	Frankie Laine (Philips)
16	27	HEARTACHES BY THE NUMBER	Guy Mitchell (Philips)
26	28	EL PASO	Marty Robbins (Fontana)
23	29	TIME AND THE RIVER	Nat King Cole (Capitol)
27	29	OH CAROL	Neil Sedaka (RCA)

12 March 1960

last	this		
1	1	POOR ME	Adam Faith (Parlophone)
3	2	RUNNING BEAR	Johnny Preston (Mercury)
8	3	DELAWARE	Perry Como (RCA)
4	4	ON A SLOW BOAT TO CHINA	Emile Ford (Pye)
2	5	WHY	Anthony Newley (Decca)
6	6	WAY DOWN YONDER IN NEW ORLEANS	Freddy Cannon (Top Rank)
18	7	THEME FROM 'A SUMMER PLACE'	Percy Faith (Philips)
5	8	A VOICE IN THE WILDERNESS	Cliff Richard (Columbia)
12	9	YOU GOT WHAT IT TAKES	Marv Johnson (London)
9	10	SUMMER SET	Mr Acker Bilk (Columbia)
7	11	PRETTY BLUE EYES	Craig Douglas (Top Rank)
11	12	BE MINE	Lance Fortune (Pye)
-	13	WHAT IN THE WORLD'S COME OVER YOU?	Jack Scott (Top Rank)
10	14	LA MER (BEYOND THE SEA)	Bobby Darin (London)
15	15	WHO COULD BE BLUER?	Jerry Lordan (Parlophone)
17	16	ROYAL EVENT	Russ Conway (Columbia)
-	16	LOOKING HIGH, HIGH, HIGH	Bryan Johnson (Decca)
12	18	BONNIE CAME BACK	Duane Eddy (London)
14	19	HARBOUR LIGHTS	Platters (Mercury)
25	20	CALIFORNIA HERE I COME	Freddy Cannon (Top Rank)
19	21	LET IT BE ME	Everly Brothers (London)
24	22	HIT AND MISS	John Barry Seven (Columbia)
-	23	FINGS AIN'T WOT THEY USED TO BE	Max Bygraves (Decca)
-	23	WILD ONE	Bobby Rydell (Columbia)
14	25	STARRY EYED	Michael Holliday (Columbia)
-	26	COLETTE	Billy Fury (Decca)
20	27	MISTY	Johnny Mathis (Fontana)
-	28	TEEN ANGEL	Mark Dinning (MGM)
-	29	DARKTOWN STRUTTERS' BALL	Joe Brown (Decca)
22	30	BE MY GUEST	Fats Domino (London)

19 March 1960

last	this		
2	1	RUNNING BEAR	Johnny Preston (Mercury)
1	2	POOR ME	Adam Faith (Parlophone)
3	3	DELAWARE	Perry Como (RCA)
7	4	THEME FROM 'A SUMMER PLACE'	Percy Faith (Philips)
9	5	YOU GOT WHAT IT TAKES	Marv Johnson (London)
13	6	WHAT IN THE WORLD'S COME OVER YOU?	Jack Scott (Top Rank)
5	7	WHY	Anthony Newley (Decca)
4	8	ON A SLOW BOAT TO CHINA	Emile Ford (Pye)
12	9	BE MINE	Lance Fortune (Pye)
10	10	SUMMER SET	Mr Acker Bilk (Columbia)
23	11	FINGS AIN'T WOT THEY USED TO BE	Max Bygraves (Decca)
11	12	PRETTY BLUE EYES	Craig Douglas (Top Rank)
8	13	A VOICE IN THE WILDERNESS	Cliff Richard (Columbia)
15	14	WHO COULD BE BLUER?	Jerry Lordan (Parlophone)
6	15	WAY DOWN YONDER IN NEW ORLEANS	Freddy Cannon (Top Rank)
-	16	HANDY MAN	Jimmy Jones (MGM)
23	17	WILD ONE	Bobby Rydell (Columbia)
16	18	ROYAL EVENT	Russ Conway (Columbia)
26	19	COLETTE	Billy Fury (Decca)
16	20	LOOKING HIGH, HIGH, HIGH	Bryan Johnson (Decca)
22	21	HIT AND MISS	John Barry Seven (Columbia)
-	22	BEATNIK FLY	Johnny & the Hurricanes (London)
14	23	LA MER (BEYOND THE SEA)	Bobby Darin (London)
29	24	DARKTOWN STRUTTERS' BALL	Joe Brown (Decca)
-	25	COUNTRY BOY	Fats Domino (London)
20	26	CALIFORNIA HERE I COME	Freddy Cannon (Top Rank)
19	27	HARBOUR LIGHTS	Platters (Mercury)
18	28	BONNIE CAME BACK	Duane Eddy (London)
28	29	TEEN ANGEL	Mark Dinning (MGM)
21	30	LET IT BE ME	Everly Brothers (London)

Poor Me had taken considerably longer to climb the chart than *What Do You Want*, but nevertheless secured Adam Faith two Number Ones with his first two hits. Russ Conway's *Royal Event* was in celebration of the birth of Prince Andrew, while the John Barry Seven's *Hit And Miss* was the theme to BBC TV's top-rating *Juke Box Jury* show. Perry Como's *Delaware* was notable for name-checking US states in appalling puns ('Why did Cali phone ya', 'Where has Orry gone', etc.).

March – April 1960

26 March 1960

last week	this week	title	artist (label)
-	1	MY OLD MAN'S A DUSTMAN	Lonnie Donegan (Pye)
1	2	RUNNING BEAR	Johnny Preston (Mercury)
3	3	DELAWARE	Perry Como (RCA)
2	4	POOR ME	Adam Faith (Parlophone)
4	5	THEME FROM 'A SUMMER PLACE'	Percy Faith (Philips)
5	6	YOU GOT WHAT IT TAKES	Marv Johnson (London)
6	7	WHAT IN THE WORLD'S COME OVER YOU?	Jack Scott (Top Rank)
11	8	FINGS AIN'T WOT THEY USED TO BE	Max Bygraves (Decca)
22	9	BEATNIK FLY	Johnny & the Hurricanes (London)
8	10	ON A SLOW BOAT TO CHINA	Emile Ford (Pye)
7	11	WHY	Anthony Newley (Decca)
-	12	FALL IN LOVE WITH YOU	Cliff Richard (Columbia)
10	13	SUMMER SET	Mr Acker Bilk (Columbia)
-	14	DO YOU MIND?	Anthony Newley (Decca)
16	15	HANDY MAN	Jimmy Jones (MGM)
17	16	WILD ONE	Bobby Rydell (Columbia)
9	17	BE MINE	Lance Fortune (Pye)
12	18	PRETTY BLUE EYES	Craig Douglas (Top Rank)
13	19	A VOICE IN THE WILDERNESS	Cliff Richard (Columbia)
14	20	WHO COULD BE BLUER?	Jerry Lordan (Parlophone)
-	21	WILLIE AND THE HAND JIVE	Cliff Richard (Columbia)
19	22	COLETTE	Billy Fury (Decca)
21	23	HIT AND MISS	John Barry Seven (Columbia)
15	24	WAY DOWN YONDER IN NEW ORLEANS	Freddy Cannon (Top Rank)
25	25	COUNTRY BOY	Fats Domino (London)
18	26	ROYAL EVENT	Russ Conway (Columbia)
23	27	LA MER (BEYOND THE SEA)	Bobby Darin (London)
20	28	LOOKING HIGH, HIGH, HIGH	Bryan Johnson (Decca)
-	29	MY HEART	Gene Vincent (Capitol)
27	30	HARBOUR LIGHTS	Platters (Mercury)

2 April 1960

last week	this week	title	artist (label)
1	1	MY OLD MAN'S A DUSTMAN	Lonnie Donegan (Pye)
8	2	FINGS AIN'T WOT THEY USED TO BE	Max Bygraves (Decca)
2	3	RUNNING BEAR	Johnny Preston (Mercury)
12	4	FALL IN LOVE WITH YOU	Cliff Richard (Columbia)
5	5	THEME FROM 'A SUMMER PLACE'	Percy Faith (Philips)
3	6	DELAWARE	Perry Como (RCA)
7	7	WHAT IN THE WORLD'S COME OVER YOU?	Jack Scott (Top Rank)
6	8	YOU GOT WHAT IT TAKES	Marv Johnson (London)
15	9	HANDY MAN	Jimmy Jones (MGM)
4	10	POOR ME	Adam Faith (Parlophone)
14	11	DO YOU MIND?	Anthony Newley (Decca)
9	12	BEATNIK FLY	Johnny & the Hurricanes (London)
16	13	WILD ONE	Bobby Rydell (Columbia)
13	14	SUMMER SET	Mr Acker Bilk (Columbia)
11	15	WHY	Anthony Newley (Decca)
10	16	ON A SLOW BOAT TO CHINA	Emile Ford (Pye)
17	17	BE MINE	Lance Fortune (Pye)
23	18	HIT AND MISS	John Barry Seven (Columbia)
20	19	WHO COULD BE BLUER?	Jerry Lordan (Parlophone)
-	20	CLEMENTINE	Bobby Darin (London)
-	21	HE'LL HAVE TO GO	Jim Reeves (RCA)
22	22	WILLIE AND THE HAND JIVE	Cliff Richard (Columbia)
25	23	COUNTRY BOY	Fats Domino (London)
18	24	PRETTY BLUE EYES	Craig Douglas (Top Rank)
22	25	COLETTE	Billy Fury (Decca)
28	26	LOOKING HIGH, HIGH, HIGH	Bryan Johnson (Decca)
-	27	STAIRWAY TO HEAVEN	Neil Sedaka (RCA)
-	28	FOOTSTEPS	
19	29	A VOICE IN THE WILDERNESS	Cliff Richard (Columbia)
29	30	MY HEART	Gene Vincent (Capitol)

9 April 1960

last week	this week	title	artist (label)
1	1	MY OLD MAN'S A DUSTMAN	Lonnie Donegan (Pye)
4	2	FALL IN LOVE WITH YOU	Cliff Richard (Columbia)
-	3	STUCK ON YOU	Elvis Presley (RCA)
9	4	HANDY MAN	Jimmy Jones (MGM)
2	5	FINGS AIN'T WOT THEY USED TO BE	Max Bygraves (Decca)
3	6	RUNNING BEAR	Johnny Preston (Mercury)
5	7	THEME FROM 'A SUMMER PLACE'	Percy Faith (Philips)
11	8	DO YOU MIND?	Anthony Newley (Decca)
12	9	BEATNIK FLY	Johnny & the Hurricanes (London)
8	10	YOU GOT WHAT IT TAKES	Marv Johnson (London)
7	11	WHAT IN THE WORLD'S COME OVER YOU?	Jack Scott (Top Rank)
13	12	WILD ONE	Bobby Rydell (Columbia)
6	13	DELAWARE	Perry Como (RCA)
20	14	CLEMENTINE	Bobby Darin (London)
10	15	POOR ME	Adam Faith (Parlophone)
23	16	COUNTRY BOY	Fats Domino (London)
21	17	HE'LL HAVE TO GO	Jim Reeves (RCA)
22	18	WILLIE AND THE HAND JIVE	Cliff Richard (Columbia)
17	19	BE MINE	Lance Fortune (Pye)
16	20	ON A SLOW BOAT TO CHINA	Emile Ford (Pye)
27	21	STAIRWAY TO HEAVEN	Neil Sedaka (RCA)
14	22	SUMMER SET	Mr Acker Bilk (Columbia)
28	23	FOOTSTEPS	Steve Lawrence (HMV)
-	24	SWEET NOTHIN'S	Brenda Lee (Brunswick)
15	25	WHY	Anthony Newley (Decca)
26	26	LOOKING HIGH, HIGH, HIGH	Bryan Johnson (Decca)
18	27	HIT AND MISS	John Barry Seven (Columbia)
25	28	COLETTE	Billy Fury (Decca)
19	29	WHO COULD BE BLUER?	Jerry Lordan (Parlophone)
30	30	MY HEART	Gene Vincent (Capitol)

16 April 1960

last week	this week	title	artist (label)
1	1	MY OLD MAN'S A DUSTMAN	Lonnie Donegan (Pye)
3	2	STUCK ON YOU	Elvis Presley (RCA)
2	3	FALL IN LOVE WITH YOU	Cliff Richard (Columbia)
4	4	HANDY MAN	Jimmy Jones (MGM)
8	5	DO YOU MIND?	Anthony Newley (Decca)
5	6	FINGS AIN'T WOT THEY USED TO BE	Max Bygraves (Decca)
7	7	THEME FROM 'A SUMMER PLACE'	Percy Faith (Philips)
9	8	BEATNIK FLY	Johnny & the Hurricanes (London)
6	9	RUNNING BEAR	Johnny Preston (Mercury)
14	10	CLEMENTINE	Bobby Darin (London)
-	11	SOMEONE ELSE'S BABY	Adam Faith (Parlophone)
12	12	WILD ONE	Bobby Rydell (Columbia)
13	13	DELAWARE	Perry Como (RCA)
10	14	YOU GOT WHAT IT TAKES	Marv Johnson (London)
24	15	SWEET NOTHIN'S	Brenda Lee (Brunswick)
-	16	CATHY'S CLOWN	Everly Brothers (Warner Bros)
11	17	WHAT IN THE WORLD'S COME OVER YOU?	Jack Scott (Top Rank)
26	18	LOOKING HIGH, HIGH, HIGH	Bryan Johnson (Decca)
16	19	COUNTRY BOY	Fats Domino (London)
17	20	HE'LL HAVE TO GO	Jim Reeves (RCA)
15	21	POOR ME	Adam Faith (Parlophone)
27	22	HIT AND MISS	John Barry Seven (Columbia)
23	23	FOOTSTEPS	Steve Lawrence (HMV)
21	24	STAIRWAY TO HEAVEN	Neil Sedaka (RCA)
19	25	BE MINE	Lance Fortune (Pye)
29	26	WHO COULD BE BLUER?	Jerry Lordan (Parlophone)
22	27	SUMMER SET	Mr Acker Bilk (Columbia)
18	28	WILLIE AND THE HAND JIVE	Cliff Richard (Columbia)
20	29	ON A SLOW BOAT TO CHINA	Emile Ford (Pye)
25	30	WHY	Anthony Newley (Decca)

Lonnie Donegan's *My Old Man's A Dustman,* an archetypal music-hall comedy song, boosted by a London Palladium show TV play as the song was released, caught the popular imagination like nothing he had cut previously. Slamming its way instantly to Number One with over a quarter of a million sales in its first week, it made Donegan the first British act to have a pole position entry, and only the second artist in history, after Elvis in 1958, to achieve this. *Dustman* eventually sold over a million.

April – May 1960

23 April 1960

last week	this week		
5	1	DO YOU MIND?	Anthony Newley (Decca)
2	2	STUCK ON YOU	Elvis Presley (RCA)
1	3	MY OLD MAN'S A DUSTMAN	Lonnie Donegan (Pye)
3	4	FALL IN LOVE WITH YOU	Cliff Richard (Columbia)
4	5	HANDY MAN	Jimmy Jones (MGM)
16	6	CATHY'S CLOWN	Everly Brothers (Warner Bros)
11	7	SOMEONE ELSE'S BABY	Adam Faith (Parlophone)
15	8	SWEET NOTHIN'S	Brenda Lee (Brunswick)
6	9	FINGS AIN'T WOT THEY USED TO BE	Max Bygraves (Decca)
7	10	THEME FROM 'A SUMMER PLACE'	Percy Faith (Philips)
-	11	STANDING ON THE CORNER	King Brothers (Parlophone)
8	12	BEATNIK FLY	Johnny & the Hurricanes (London)
10	13	CLEMENTINE	Bobby Darin (London)
22	14	FOOTSTEPS	Steve Lawrence (HMV)
9	15	RUNNING BEAR	Johnny Preston (Mercury)
12	16	WILD ONE	Bobby Rydell (Columbia)
13	17	DELAWARE	Perry Como (RCA)
20	17	HE'LL HAVE TO GO	Jim Reeves (RCA)
17	19	WHAT IN THE WORLD'S COME OVER YOU?	Jack Scott (Top Rank)
14	20	YOU GOT WHAT IT TAKES	Marv Johnson (London)
21	21	POOR ME	Adam Faith (Parlophone)
19	22	COUNTRY BOY	Fats Domino (London)
-	23	MACK THE KNIFE	Ella Fitzgerald (HMV)
-	23	CRADLE OF LOVE	Johnny Preston (Mercury)
-	25	TEASE ME	Keith Kelly (Parlophone)
18	26	LOOKING HIGH, HIGH, HIGH	Bryan Johnson (Decca)
22	27	HIT AND MISS	John Barry Seven (Columbia)
24	28	STAIRWAY TO HEAVEN	Neil Sedaka (RCA)
-	29	STANDING ON THE CORNER	Four Lads (Philips)
30	30	WHY	Anthony Newley (Decca)

30 April 1960

last week	this week		
6	1	CATHY'S CLOWN	Everly Brothers (Warner Bros)
1	2	DO YOU MIND?	Anthony Newley (Decca)
7	3	SOMEONE ELSE'S BABY	Adam Faith (Parlophone)
5	4	HANDY MAN	Jimmy Jones (MGM)
4	5	FALL IN LOVE WITH YOU	Cliff Richard (Columbia)
3	6	MY OLD MAN'S A DUSTMAN	Lonnie Donegan (Pye)
11	7	STANDING ON THE CORNER	King Brothers (Parlophone)
2	8	STUCK ON YOU	Elvis Presley (RCA)
8	9	SWEET NOTHIN'S	Brenda Lee (Brunswick)
9	10	FINGS AIN'T WOT THEY USED TO BE	Max Bygraves (Decca)
10	11	THEME FROM 'A SUMMER PLACE'	Percy Faith (Philips)
-	12	SHAZAM	Duane Eddy (London)
14	13	FOOTSTEPS	Steve Lawrence (HMV)
23	14	CRADLE OF LOVE	Johnny Preston (Mercury)
15	15	RUNNING BEAR	Johnny Preston (Mercury)
12	16	BEATNIK FLY	Johnny & the Hurricanes (London)
16	17	WILD ONE	Bobby Rydell (Columbia)
13	18	CLEMENTINE	Bobby Darin (London)
23	19	MACK THE KNIFE	Ella Fitzgerald (HMV)
17	20	HE'LL HAVE TO GO	Jim Reeves (RCA)
19	21	WHAT IN THE WORLD'S COME OVER YOU?	Jack Scott (Top Rank)
27	22	HIT AND MISS	John Barry Seven (Columbia)
28	23	STAIRWAY TO HEAVEN	Neil Sedaka (RCA)
20	24	YOU GOT WHAT IT TAKES	Marv Johnson (London)
17	25	DELAWARE	Perry Como (RCA)
25	25	TEASE ME	Keith Kelly (Parlophone)
29	27	STANDING ON THE CORNER	Four Lads (Philips)
21	28	POOR ME	Adam Faith (Parlophone)
26	29	LOOKING HIGH, HIGH, HIGH	Bryan Johnson (Decca)
-	30	CHATTANOOGA CHOO CHOO	Ernie Fields (London)

7 May 1960

last week	this week		
1	1	CATHY'S CLOWN	Everly Brothers (Warner Bros)
3	2	SOMEONE ELSE'S BABY	Adam Faith (Parlophone)
2	3	DO YOU MIND?	Anthony Newley (Decca)
5	4	FALL IN LOVE WITH YOU	Cliff Richard (Columbia)
4	5	HANDY MAN	Jimmy Jones (MGM)
7	6	STANDING ON THE CORNER	King Brothers (Parlophone)
8	7	STUCK ON YOU	Elvis Presley (RCA)
9	8	SWEET NOTHIN'S	Brenda Lee (Brunswick)
12	9	SHAZAM	Duane Eddy (London)
6	10	MY OLD MAN'S A DUSTMAN	Lonnie Donegan (Pye)
13	11	FOOTSTEPS	Steve Lawrence (HMV)
14	12	CRADLE OF LOVE	Johnny Preston (Mercury)
11	13	THEME FROM 'A SUMMER PLACE'	Percy Faith (Philips)
-	14	THE HEART OF A TEENAGE GIRL	Craig Douglas (Top Rank)
10	15	FINGS AIN'T WOT THEY USED TO BE	Max Bygraves (Decca)
16	16	BEATNIK FLY	Johnny & the Hurricanes (London)
19	17	MACK THE KNIFE	Ella Fitzgerald (HMV)
18	18	CLEMENTINE	Bobby Darin (London)
17	19	WILD ONE	Bobby Rydell (Columbia)
20	20	HE'LL HAVE TO GO	Jim Reeves (RCA)
23	21	STAIRWAY TO HEAVEN	Neil Sedaka (RCA)
25	22	TEASE ME	Keith Kelly (Parlophone)
15	23	RUNNING BEAR	Johnny Preston (Mercury)
21	24	WHAT IN THE WORLD'S COME OVER YOU?	Jack Scott (Top Rank)
28	25	POOR ME	Adam Faith (Parlophone)
27	26	STANDING ON THE CORNER	Four Lads (Philips)
22	27	HIT AND MISS	John Barry Seven (Columbia)
29	28	LOOKING HIGH, HIGH, HIGH	Bryan Johnson (Decca)
25	29	DELAWARE	Perry Como (RCA)
30	30	CHATTANOOGA CHOO CHOO	Ernie Fields (London)

14 May 1960

last week	this week		
1	1	CATHY'S CLOWN	Everly Brothers (Warner Bros)
2	2	SOMEONE ELSE'S BABY	Adam Faith (Parlophone)
3	3	DO YOU MIND?	Anthony Newley (Decca)
4	4	HANDY MAN	Jimmy Jones (MGM)
9	5	SHAZAM	Duane Eddy (London)
8	6	SWEET NOTHIN'S	Brenda Lee (Brunswick)
6	7	STANDING ON THE CORNER	King Brothers (Parlophone)
4	8	FALL IN LOVE WITH YOU	Cliff Richard (Columbia)
12	9	CRADLE OF LOVE	Johnny Preston (Mercury)
11	10	FOOTSTEPS	Steve Lawrence (HMV)
7	11	STUCK ON YOU	Elvis Presley (RCA)
13	12	THEME FROM 'A SUMMER PLACE'	Percy Faith (Philips)
-	13	THREE STEPS TO HEAVEN	Eddie Cochran (London)
14	14	THE HEART OF A TEENAGE GIRL	Craig Douglas (Top Rank)
15	15	FINGS AIN'T WOT THEY USED TO BE	Max Bygraves (Decca)
10	16	MY OLD MAN'S A DUSTMAN	Lonnie Donegan (Pye)
16	16	BEATNIK FLY	Johnny & the Hurricanes (London)
22	18	TEASE ME	Keith Kelly (Parlophone)
21	19	STAIRWAY TO HEAVEN	Neil Sedaka (RCA)
-	20	SIXTEEN REASONS	Connie Stevens (Warner Bros)
-	21	OOH-LA-LA	Keith Kelly (Parlophone)
-	22	KOOKIE KOOKIE	Edd Byrnes & Connie Stevens (Warner Bros)
19	23	WILD ONE	Bobby Rydell (Columbia)
17	24	MACK THE KNIFE	Ella Fitzgerald (HMV)
24	25	WHAT IN THE WORLD'S COME OVER YOU?	Jack Scott (Top Rank)
18	26	CLEMENTINE	Bobby Darin (London)
26	27	STANDING ON THE CORNER	Four Lads (Philips)
-	28	I LOVE THE WAY YOU LOVE	Marv Johnson (London)
20	29	HE'LL HAVE TO GO	Jim Reeves (RCA)
-	30	LET THE LITTLE GIRL DANCE	Billy Bland (London)

Though it made Number One with ease in the US, Elvis Presley's first post-Army recording *Stuck On You* was surprisingly held from the top here, first by Lonnie Donegan, then by Anthony Newley's second consecutive chart-topper *Do You Mind*. The biggest record this spring was, however, the Everly Brothers' *Cathy's Clown*, thier first recording for their new label Warner Bros, and also Warner first release in the UK. Its nine week Number One run was the longest since Paul Anka's *Diana* in 1957.

21 May 1960

last week	this week	Title / Artist (Label)
1	1	CATHY'S CLOWN — Everly Brothers (Warner Bros)
2	2	SOMEONE ELSE'S BABY — Adam Faith (Parlophone)
9	3	CRADLE OF LOVE — Johnny Preston (Mercury)
4	4	HANDY MAN — Jimmy Jones (MGM)
3	5	DO YOU MIND? — Anthony Newley (Decca)
5	6	SHAZAM — Duane Eddy (London)
6	6	SWEET NOTHIN'S — Brenda Lee (Brunswick)
8	8	FALL IN LOVE WITH YOU — Cliff Richard (Columbia)
10	9	FOOTSTEPS — Steve Lawrence (HMV)
13	10	THREE STEPS TO HEAVEN — Eddie Cochran (London)
7	11	STANDING ON THE CORNER — King Brothers (Parlophone)
11	12	STUCK ON YOU — Elvis Presley (RCA)
14	13	THE HEART OF A TEENAGE GIRL — Craig Douglas (Top Rank)
19	14	STAIRWAY TO HEAVEN — Neil Sedaka (RCA)
30	15	LET THE LITTLE GIRL DANCE — Billy Bland (London)
15	15	FINGS AIN'T WOT THEY USED TO BE — Max Bygraves (Decca)
12	17	THEME FROM 'A SUMMER PLACE' — Percy Faith (Philips)
18	18	TEASE ME — Keith Kelly (Parlophone)
16	19	MY OLD MAN'S A DUSTMAN — Lonnie Donegan (Pye)
16	20	BEATNIK FLY — Johnny & the Hurricanes (London)
26	21	CLEMENTINE — Bobby Darin (London)
29	22	HE'LL HAVE TO GO — Jim Reeves (RCA)
-	23	ROBOT MAN — Connie Francis (MGM)
20	23	SIXTEEN REASONS — Connie Stevens (Warner Bros)
-	25	THAT'S YOU — Nat King Cole (Capitol)
-	26	MAMA — Connie Francis (MGM)
-	27	BIG TIME — Adam Faith (Parlophone)
-	27	MILORD — Edith Piaf (Columbia)
22	29	KOOKIE KOOKIE — Edd Byrnes & Connie Stevens (Warner Bros)
24	30	MACK THE KNIFE — Ella Fitzgerald (HMV)

28 May 1960

last week	this week	Title / Artist (Label)
1	1	CATHY'S CLOWN — Everly Brothers (Warner Bros)
3	2	CRADLE OF LOVE — Johnny Preston (Mercury)
2	3	SOMEONE ELSE'S BABY — Adam Faith (Parlophone)
4	3	HANDY MAN — Jimmy Jones (MGM)
6	5	SWEET NOTHIN'S — Brenda Lee (Brunswick)
6	6	SHAZAM — Duane Eddy (London)
10	7	THREE STEPS TO HEAVEN — Eddie Cochran (London)
5	8	DO YOU MIND? — Anthony Newley (Decca)
26	9	MAMA — Connie Francis (MGM)
9	10	FOOTSTEPS — Steve Lawrence (HMV)
8	11	FALL IN LOVE WITH YOU — Cliff Richard (Columbia)
14	12	STAIRWAY TO HEAVEN — Neil Sedaka (RCA)
11	13	STANDING ON THE CORNER — King Brothers (Parlophone)
13	14	THE HEART OF A TEENAGE GIRL — Craig Douglas (Top Rank)
12	15	STUCK ON YOU — Elvis Presley (RCA)
22	16	HE'LL HAVE TO GO — Jim Reeves (RCA)
-	17	I WANNA GO HOME — Lonnie Donegan (Pye)
-	18	LUCKY FIVE — Russ Conway (Columbia)
-	19	THE URGE — Freddy Cannon (Top Rank)
25	19	THAT'S YOU — Nat King Cole (Capitol)
15	21	LET THE LITTLE GIRL DANCE — Billy Bland (London)
27	22	MILORD — Edith Piaf (Columbia)
23	23	ROBOT MAN — Connie Francis (MGM)
20	24	BEATNIK FLY — Johnny & the Hurricanes (London)
-	25	TRUE LOVE WAYS — Buddy Holly (Coral)
17	26	THEME FROM 'A SUMMER PLACE' — Percy Faith (Philips)
23	26	SIXTEEN REASONS — Connie Stevens (Warner Bros)
-	28	THAT'S LOVE — Billy Fury (Decca)
-	29	YOU'LL NEVER KNOW WHAT YOU'RE MISSIN' — Emile Ford (Pye)
-	30	GOT A GIRL — Four Preps (Capitol)
-	30	SWEET DREAMS — Dave Sampson (Columbia)

4 June 1960

last week	this week	Title / Artist (Label)
1	1	CATHY'S CLOWN — Everly Brothers (Warner Bros)
2	2	CRADLE OF LOVE — Johnny Preston (Mercury)
3	3	HANDY MAN — Jimmy Jones (MGM)
5	4	SWEET NOTHIN'S — Brenda Lee (Brunswick)
3	5	SOMEONE ELSE'S BABY — Adam Faith (Parlophone)
6	6	SHAZAM — Duane Eddy (London)
10	7	FOOTSTEPS — Steve Lawrence (HMV)
7	8	THREE STEPS TO HEAVEN — Eddie Cochran (London)
9	9	MAMA — Connie Francis (MGM)
8	10	DO YOU MIND? — Anthony Newley (Decca)
17	11	I WANNA GO HOME — Lonnie Donegan (Pye)
23	11	ROBOT MAN — Connie Francis (MGM)
18	13	LUCKY FIVE — Russ Conway (Columbia)
16	14	HE'LL HAVE TO GO — Jim Reeves (RCA)
11	15	FALL IN LOVE WITH YOU — Cliff Richard (Columbia)
21	16	LET THE LITTLE GIRL DANCE — Billy Bland (London)
12	17	STAIRWAY TO HEAVEN — Neil Sedaka (RCA)
26	18	SIXTEEN REASONS — Connie Stevens (Warner Bros)
19	19	THAT'S YOU — Nat King Cole (Capitol)
19	20	THE URGE — Freddy Cannon (Top Rank)
14	20	THE HEART OF A TEENAGE GIRL — Craig Douglas (Top Rank)
30	22	GOT A GIRL — Four Preps (Capitol)
13	23	STANDING ON THE CORNER — King Brothers (Parlophone)
28	24	THAT'S LOVE — Billy Fury (Decca)
29	25	YOU'LL NEVER KNOW WHAT YOU'RE MISSIN' — Emile Ford (Pye)
15	26	STUCK ON YOU — Elvis Presley (RCA)
-	27	AIN'T MISBEHAVIN' — Tommy Bruce (Columbia)
30	27	SWEET DREAMS — Dave Sampson (Columbia)
26	29	THEME FROM 'A SUMMER PLACE' — Percy Faith (Philips)
22	30	MILORD — Edith Piaf (Columbia)

11 June 1960

last week	this week	Title / Artist (Label)
1	1	CATHY'S CLOWN — Everly Brothers (Warner Bros)
2	2	CRADLE OF LOVE — Johnny Preston (Mercury)
3	3	HANDY MAN — Jimmy Jones (MGM)
4	4	SWEET NOTHIN'S — Brenda Lee (Brunswick)
8	5	THREE STEPS TO HEAVEN — Eddie Cochran (London)
6	6	SHAZAM — Duane Eddy (London)
11	7	I WANNA GO HOME — Lonnie Donegan (Pye)
9	8	MAMA — Connie Francis (MGM)
11	9	ROBOT MAN — Connie Francis (MGM)
5	10	SOMEONE ELSE'S BABY — Adam Faith (Parlophone)
14	11	HE'LL HAVE TO GO — Jim Reeves (RCA)
18	12	SIXTEEN REASONS — Connie Stevens (Warner Bros)
19	13	THAT'S YOU — Nat King Cole (Capitol)
17	14	STAIRWAY TO HEAVEN — Neil Sedaka (RCA)
16	15	LET THE LITTLE GIRL DANCE — Billy Bland (London)
13	16	LUCKY FIVE — Russ Conway (Columbia)
7	17	FOOTSTEPS — Steve Lawrence (HMV)
27	18	AIN'T MISBEHAVIN' — Tommy Bruce (Columbia)
10	19	DO YOU MIND? — Anthony Newley (Decca)
-	20	RIVER, STAY 'WAY FROM MY DOOR — Frank Sinatra (Capitol)
15	21	FALL IN LOVE WITH YOU — Cliff Richard (Columbia)
24	22	THAT'S LOVE — Billy Fury (Decca)
-	23	DOWN YONDER — Johnny & the Hurricanes (London)
20	24	THE URGE — Freddy Cannon (Top Rank)
20	25	THE HEART OF A TEENAGE GIRL — Craig Douglas (Top Rank)
-	26	MUSTAPHA — Bob Azzam (Decca)
30	27	MILORD — Edith Piaf (Columbia)
23	28	STANDING ON THE CORNER — King Brothers (Parlophone)
27	28	SWEET DREAMS — Dave Sampson (Columbia)
25	30	YOU'LL NEVER KNOW WHAT YOU'RE MISSIN' — Emile Ford (Pye)

Cathy's Clown prevented both Adam Faith from making history by achieving Number Ones with his first three hits, and also Johnny Preston from scoring two in a row with *Running Bear* and *Cradle Of Love*. Connie Francis achieved the amazing feat of putting both contrasting sides of *Mama/Robot Man* in the Top Ten independently. The latter rock number, cut specifically for the UK, was a late substitute after the original B-side, Paul Anka's song *Teddy* was withdrawn. *Robot Man* was never released in the US.

June – July 1960

	18 June 1960
1 1	CATHY'S CLOWN Everly Brothers (Warner Bros)
2 2	CRADLE OF LOVE Johnny Preston (Mercury)
5 3	THREE STEPS TO HEAVEN Eddie Cochran (London)
3 4	HANDY MAN Jimmy Jones (MGM)
7 5	I WANNA GO HOME Lonnie Donegan (Pye)
6 6	SHAZAM Duane Eddy (London)
9 7	ROBOT MAN Connie Francis (MGM)
18 8	AIN'T MISBEHAVIN' Tommy Bruce (Columbia)
4 9	SWEET NOTHIN'S Brenda Lee (Brunswick)
8 10	MAMA Connie Francis (MGM)
12 11	SIXTEEN REASONS Connie Stevens (Warner Bros)
14 12	STAIRWAY TO HEAVEN Neil Sedaka (RCA)
23 13	DOWN YONDER Johnny & the Hurricanes (London)
- 14	GOOD TIMIN' Jimmy Jones (MGM)
17 15	FOOTSTEPS Steve Lawrence (HMV)
10 16	SOMEONE ELSE'S BABY Adam Faith (Parlophone)
20 17	RIVER, STAY 'WAY FROM YOUR DOOR Frank Sinatra (Capitol)
26 18	MUSTAPHA Bob Azzam (Decca)
11 19	HE'LL HAVE TO GO Jim Reeves (RCA)
16 20	LUCKY FIVE Russ Conway (Columbia)
- 20	ANGELA JONES Michael Cox (Triumph)
15 22	LET THE LITTLE GIRL DANCE Billy Bland (London)
13 22	THAT'S YOU Nat King Cole (Capitol)
30 24	YOU'LL NEVER KNOW WHAT YOU'RE MISSIN' Emile Ford (Pye)
19 25	DO YOU MIND? Anthony Newley (Decca)
21 26	FALL IN LOVE WITH YOU Cliff Richard (Columbia)
22 27	THAT'S LOVE Billy Fury (Decca)
- 28	ROMANTICA Jane Morgan (London)
28 28	SWEET DREAMS Dave Sampson (Columbia)
- 28	PISTOL PACKIN' MAMA Gene Vincent (Capitol)

	25 June 1960
1 1	CATHY'S CLOWN Everly Brothers (Warner Bros)
3 2	THREE STEPS TO HEAVEN Eddie Cochran (London)
7 3	ROBOT MAN Connie Francis (MGM)
14 4	GOOD TIMIN' Jimmy Jones (MGM)
4 4	HANDY MAN Jimmy Jones (MGM)
8 6	AIN'T MISBEHAVIN' Tommy Bruce (Columbia)
2 6	CRADLE OF LOVE Johnny Preston (Mercury)
5 8	I WANNA GO HOME Lonnie Donegan (Pye)
9 9	SWEET NOTHIN'S Brenda Lee (Brunswick)
13 10	DOWN YONDER Johnny & the Hurricanes (London)
10 11	MAMA Connie Francis (MGM)
11 12	SIXTEEN REASONS Connie Stevens (Warner Bros)
19 13	HE'LL HAVE TO GO Jim Reeves (RCA)
12 14	STAIRWAY TO HEAVEN Neil Sedaka (RCA)
6 15	SHAZAM Duane Eddy (London)
17 16	RIVER, STAY 'WAY FROM MY DOOR Frank Sinatra (Capitol)
20 17	ANGELA JONES Michael Cox (Triumph)
- 18	MADE YOU Adam Faith (Parlophone)
28 19	PISTOL PACKIN' MAMA Gene Vincent (Capitol)
15 20	FOOTSTEPS Steve Lawrence (HMV)
18 21	MUSTAPHA Bob Azzam (Decca)
22 22	THAT'S YOU Nat King Cole (Capitol)
20 23	LUCKY FIVE Russ Conway (Columbia)
- 24	WHAT A MOUTH Tommy Steele (Decca)
28 25	ROMANTICA Jane Morgan (London)
22 26	LET THE LITTLE GIRL DANCE Billy Bland (London)
- 27	THE URGE Freddy Cannon (Top Rank)
- 28	SHAKIN' ALL OVER Johnny Kidd & the Pirates (HMV)
- 29	BILL BAILEY, WON'T YOU PLEASE COME HOME Bobby Darin (London)
- 30	WHY DIDN'T YOU TELL ME Marke Anthony (Decca)
24 30	YOU'LL NEVER KNOW WHAT YOU'RE MISSIN' Emile Ford (Pye)

	2 July 1960
4 1	GOOD TIMIN' Jimmy Jones (MGM)
6 2	AIN'T MISBEHAVIN' Tommy Bruce (Columbia)
2 3	THREE STEPS TO HEAVEN Eddie Cochran (London)
1 4	CATHY'S CLOWN Everly Brothers (Warner Bros)
3 5	ROBOT MAN Connie Francis (MGM)
24 6	WHAT A MOUTH Tommy Steele (Decca)
- 7	PLEASE DON'T TEASE Cliff Richard (Columbia)
6 8	CRADLE OF LOVE Johnny Preston (Mercury)
18 9	MADE YOU Adam Faith (Parlophone)
10 10	DOWN YONDER Johnny & the Hurricanes (London)
11 11	MAMA Connie Francis (MGM)
8 12	I WANNA GO HOME Lonnie Donegan (Pye)
4 12	HANDY MAN Jimmy Jones (MGM)
17 14	ANGELA JONES Michael Cox (Triumph)
12 15	SIXTEEN REASONS Connie Stevens (Warner Bros)
28 16	SHAKIN' ALL OVER Johnny Kidd & the Pirates (HMV)
13 17	HE'LL HAVE TO GO Jim Reeves (RCA)
16 18	RIVER, STAY 'WAY FROM MY DOOR Frank Sinatra (Capitol)
19 19	PISTOL PACKIN' MAMA Gene Vincent (Capitol)
- 20	WHEN JOHNNY COMES MARCHING HOME Adam Faith (Parlophone)
9 20	SWEET NOTHIN'S Brenda Lee (Brunswick)
15 22	SHAZAM Duane Eddy (London)
14 23	STAIRWAY TO HEAVEN Neil Sedaka (RCA)
21 24	MUSTAPHA Bob Azzam (Decca)
- 25	PAPER ROSES Anita Bryant (London)
- 26	GREEN FIELDS Brothers Four (Philips)
- 26	LOVE IS LIKE A VIOLIN Ken Dodd (Decca)
- 28	I'M SORRY Brenda Lee (Brunswick)
25 28	ROMANTICA Jane Morgan (London)
- 30	GREEN FIELDS Beverley Sisters (Columbia)

	9 July 1960
1 1	GOOD TIMIN' Jimmy Jones (MGM)
2 2	AIN'T MISBEHAVIN' Tommy Bruce (Columbia)
7 3	PLEASE DON'T TEASE Cliff Richard (Columbia)
4 4	WHAT A MOUTH Tommy Steele (Decca)
5 5	ROBOT MAN Connie Francis (MGM)
9 6	MADE YOU Adam Faith (Parlophone)
3 7	THREE STEPS TO HEAVEN Eddie Cochran (London)
4 7	CATHY'S CLOWN Everly Brothers (Warner Bros)
16 9	SHAKIN' ALL OVER Johnny Kidd & the Pirates (HMV)
11 10	MAMA Connie Francis (MGM)
14 11	ANGELA JONES Michael Cox (Triumph)
10 12	DOWN YONDER Johnny & the Hurricanes (London)
12 13	HANDY MAN Jimmy Jones (MGM)
12 14	I WANNA GO HOME Lonnie Donegan (Pye)
20 15	WHEN JOHNNY COMES MARCHING HOME Adam Faith (Parlophone)
20 16	SWEET NOTHIN'S Brenda Lee (Brunswick)
8 17	CRADLE OF LOVE Johnny Preston (Mercury)
18 18	RIVER, STAY 'WAY FROM MY DOOR Frank Sinatra (Capitol)
19 19	PISTOL PACKIN' MAMA Gene Vincent (Capitol)
15 20	SIXTEEN REASONS Connie Stevens (Warner Bros)
28 21	I'M SORRY Brenda Lee (Brunswick)
17 22	HE'LL HAVE TO GO Jim Reeves (RCA)
- 23	LOOK FOR A STAR Garry Mills (Top Rank)
- 24	BILL BAILEY Bobby Darin (London)
- 24	ANGELA JONES Johnny Ferguson (MGM)
26 26	GREEN FIELDS Brothers Four (Philips)
- 27	WALKING THE FLOOR OVER YOU Pat Boone (London)
27 27	PAPER ROSES Kaye Sisters (Philips)
- 29	ITSY BITSY TEENY WEENY YELLOW POLKA DOT BIKINI Brian Hyland (London)
30 30	GREEN FIELDS Beverley Sisters (Columbia)

Lonnie Donegan's *I Wanna Go Home* was based on the traditional song *The Wreck Of the John B*, as was the Beach Boys' *Sloop John B* six years later. Eddie Cochran's ironically-titled *Three Steps To Heaven* gave him his biggest-ever UK success, just two months after his tragic death. Michael Cox's *Angela Jones* brought quick succes to independent Triumph Records run by producer Joe Meek, while Adam Faith joined the elite who had placed both sides of a single in the Top Twenty simultaneously.

July – August 1960

16 July 1960

last week	this week	Title — Artist
1	1	GOOD TIMIN' — Jimmy Jones (MGM)
3	2	PLEASE DON'T TEASE — Cliff Richard (Columbia)
2	3	AIN'T MISBEHAVIN' — Tommy Bruce (Columbia)
9	4	SHAKIN' ALL OVER — Johnny Kidd & the Pirates (HMV)
6	5	MADE YOU — Adam Faith (Parlophone)
5	6	ROBOT MAN — Connie Francis (MGM)
4	7	WHAT A MOUTH — Tommy Steele (Decca)
23	8	LOOK FOR A STAR — Garry Mills (Top Rank)
11	9	ANGELA JONES — Michael Cox (Triumph)
7	10	THREE STEPS TO HEAVEN — Eddie Cochran (London)
15	11	WHEN JOHNNY COMES MARCHING HOME — Adam Faith (Parlophone)
12	12	MAMA — Connie Francis (MGM)
7	13	CATHY'S CLOWN — Everly Brothers (Warner Bros)
21	14	I'M SORRY — Brenda Lee (Brunswick)
14	15	I WANNA GO HOME — Lonnie Donegan (Pye)
-	16	WHEN WILL I BE LOVED — Everly Brothers (London)
29	17	ITSY BITSY TEENY WEENY YELLOW POLKA DOT BIKINI — Brian Hyland (London)
12	17	DOWN YONDER — Johnny & the Hurricanes (London)
27	19	PAPER ROSES — Kaye Sisters (Philips)
-	20	ELVIS IS BACK (LP) — Elvis Presley (RCA)
19	21	PISTOL PACKIN' MAMA — Gene Vincent (Capitol)
-	22	THE LADY IS A TRAMP — Buddy Greco (Fontana)
13	23	HANDY MAN — Jimmy Jones (MGM)
24	24	ANGELA JONES — Johnny Ferguson (MGM)
-	25	IF SHE SHOULD COME TO YOU — Anthony Newley (Decca)
18	26	RIVER, STAY 'WAY FROM MY DOOR — Frank Sinatra (Capitol)
-	27	ANGRY — Marty Wilde (Philips)
16	28	SWEET NOTHIN'S — Brenda Lee (Brunswick)
27	29	WALKING THE FLOOR OVER YOU — Pat Boone (London)
-	29	LOVE IS LIKE A VIOLIN — Ken Dodd (Decca)
-	29	COME BACK AGAIN — Anne Shelton (Philips)

23 July 1960

last week	this week	Title — Artist
2	1	PLEASE DON'T TEASE — Cliff Richard (Columbia)
1	2	GOOD TIMIN' — Jimmy Jones (MGM)
4	3	SHAKIN' ALL OVER — Johnny Kidd & the Pirates (HMV)
3	4	AIN'T MISBEHAVIN' — Tommy Bruce (Columbia)
8	5	LOOK FOR A STAR — Garry Mills (Top Rank)
16	6	WHEN WILL I BE LOVED — Everly Brothers (London)
7	7	WHAT A MOUTH — Tommy Steele (Decca)
9	8	ANGELA JONES — Michael Cox (Triumph)
6	9	ROBOT MAN — Connie Francis (MGM)
25	10	IF SHE SHOULD COME TO YOU — Anthony Newley (Decca)
5	11	MADE YOU — Adam Faith (Parlophone)
11	12	WHEN JOHNNY COMES MARCHING HOME — Adam Faith (Parlophone)
10	13	THREE STEPS TO HEAVEN — Eddie Cochran (London)
15	14	I WANNA GO HOME — Lonnie Donegan (Pye)
-	15	BECAUSE THEY'RE YOUNG — Duane Eddy (London)
17	15	ITSY BITSY TEENY WEENY YELLOW POLKA DOT BIKINI — Brian Hyland (London)
20	17	ELVIS IS BACK (LP) — Elvis Presley (RCA)
29	18	LOVE IS LIKE A VIOLIN — Ken Dodd (Decca)
12	19	MAMA — Connie Francis (MGM)
-	19	APACHE — Shadows (Columbia)
14	21	I'M SORRY — Brenda Lee (Brunswick)
19	22	PAPER ROSES — Kaye Sisters (Philips)
-	23	MAIS OUI — King Brothers (Parlophone)
13	24	CATHY'S CLOWN — Everly Brothers (Warner Bros)
27	25	ANGRY — Marty Wilde (Philips)
17	26	DOWN YONDER — Johnny & the Hurricanes (London)
-	27	BANJO BOY — Valerie Masters (Fontana)
29	27	COME BACK AGAIN — Anne Shelton (Philips)
21	27	PISTOL PACKIN' MAMA — Gene Vincent (Capitol)
22	30	THE LADY IS A TRAMP — Buddy Greco (Fontana)
23	30	HANDY MAN — Jimmy Jones (MGM)

30 July 1960

last week	this week	Title — Artist
1	1	PLEASE DON'T TEASE — Cliff Richard (Columbia)
2	2	GOOD TIMIN' — Jimmy Jones (MGM)
3	3	SHAKIN' ALL OVER — Johnny Kidd & the Pirates (HMV)
4	4	AIN'T MISBEHAVIN' — Tommy Bruce (Columbia)
5	5	LOOK FOR A STAR — Garry Mills (Top Rank)
6	6	WHEN WILL I BE LOVED — Everly Brothers (London)
19	7	APACHE — Shadows (Columbia)
-	8	A MESS OF BLUES — Elvis Presley (RCA)
10	9	IF SHE SHOULD COME TO YOU — Anthony Newley (Decca)
11	10	MADE YOU — Adam Faith (Parlophone)
15	11	BECAUSE THEY'RE YOUNG — Duane Eddy (London)
15	11	ITSY BITSY TEENY WEENY YELLOW POLKA DOT BIKINI — Brian Hyland (London)
9	13	ROBOT MAN — Connie Francis (MGM)
7	14	WHAT A MOUTH — Tommy Steele (Decca)
-	15	TIE ME KANGAROO DOWN SPORT — Rolf Harris (Columbia)
12	16	WHEN JOHNNY COMES MARCHING HOME — Adam Faith (Parlophone)
8	17	ANGELA JONES — Michael Cox (Triumph)
19	18	MAMA — Connie Francis (MGM)
18	19	LOVE IS LIKE A VIOLIN — Ken Dodd (Decca)
13	20	THREE STEPS TO HEAVEN — Eddie Cochran (London)
-	21	THE GIRL OF MY BEST FRIEND — Elvis Presley (RCA)
14	22	I WANNA GO HOME — Lonnie Donegan (Pye)
22	23	PAPER ROSES — Kaye Sisters (Philips)
-	24	TRAIN OF LOVE — Alma Cogan (HMV)
17	24	ELVIS IS BACK (LP) — Elvis Presley (RCA)
23	26	MAIS OUI — King Brothers (Parlophone)
21	27	I'M SORRY — Brenda Lee (Brunswick)
30	28	HANDY MAN — Jimmy Jones (MGM)
-	28	PAPA LOVES MAMA — Donald Peers (Columbia)
27	30	BANJO BOY — Valerie Masters (Fontana)

6 August 1960

last week	this week	Title — Artist
1	1	PLEASE DON'T TEASE — Cliff Richard (Columbia)
2	2	GOOD TIMIN' — Jimmy Jones (MGM)
3	3	SHAKIN' ALL OVER — Johnny Kidd & the Pirates (HMV)
8	4	A MESS OF BLUES — Elvis Presley (RCA)
7	5	APACHE — Shadows (Columbia)
5	6	LOOK FOR A STAR — Garry Mills (Top Rank)
11	7	BECAUSE THEY'RE YOUNG — Duane Eddy (London)
6	8	WHEN WILL I BE LOVED — Everly Brothers (London)
9	9	IF SHE SHOULD COME TO YOU — Anthony Newley (Decca)
11	10	ITSY BITSY TEENY WEENY YELLOW POLKA DOT BIKINI — Brian Hyland (London)
4	11	AIN'T MISBEHAVIN' — Tommy Bruce (Columbia)
13	12	ROBOT MAN — Connie Francis (MGM)
16	13	WHEN JOHNNY COMES MARCHING HOME — Adam Faith (Parlophone)
15	14	TIE ME KANGAROO DOWN SPORT — Rolf Harris (Columbia)
10	15	MADE YOU — Adam Faith (Parlophone)
18	16	MAMA — Connie Francis (MGM)
23	17	PAPER ROSES — Kaye Sisters (Philips)
14	18	WHAT A MOUTH — Tommy Steele (Decca)
19	19	LOVE IS LIKE A VIOLIN — Ken Dodd (Decca)
27	20	I'M SORRY — Brenda Lee (Brunswick)
26	21	MAIS OUI — King Brothers (Parlophone)
22	22	I WANNA GO HOME — Lonnie Donegan (Pye)
-	23	AS LONG AS HE NEEDS ME — Shirley Bassey (Columbia)
20	24	THREE STEPS TO HEAVEN — Eddie Cochran (London)
21	25	THE GIRL OF MY BEST FRIEND — Elvis Presley (RCA)
24	26	TRAIN OF LOVE — Alma Cogan (HMV)
17	26	ANGELA JONES — Michael Cox (Triumph)
-	28	ANGELA JONES — Johnny Ferguson (MGM)
24	29	ELVIS IS BACK (LP) — Elvis Presley (RCA)
28	30	HANDY MAN — Jimmy Jones (MGM)

Elvis Is Back, the singers first album to be recorded since he emerged from the US Army, sold massively by 1960 album standards, oudoing all but 19 of the country's best-selling singles during its week of release, and doing even better the following week.

The Shadows, who had recorded several singles with minimal succes up to this time, suddenly hit a magical instrumental formula with *Apache,* written by Jerry Lordan, who had had two hits as a vocalist earlier in the year.

August – September 1960

last week	this week	13 August 1960
1	1	PLEASE DON'T TEASE — Cliff Richard (Columbia)
5	2	APACHE — Shadows (Columbia)
4	3	A MESS OF BLUES — Elvis Presley (RCA)
2	4	GOOD TIMIN' — Jimmy Jones (MGM)
3	5	SHAKIN' ALL OVER — Johnny Kidd & the Pirates (HMV)
8	6	WHEN WILL I BE LOVED — Everly Brothers (London)
7	7	BECAUSE THEY'RE YOUNG — Duane Eddy (London)
6	8	LOOK FOR A STAR — Garry Mills (Top Rank)
9	8	IF SHE SHOULD COME TO YOU — Anthony Newley (Decca)
10	10	ITSY BITSY TEENY WEENY YELLOW POLKA DOT BIKINI — Brian Hyland (London)
14	11	TIE ME KANGAROO DOWN SPORT — Rolf Harris (Columbia)
11	12	AIN'T MISBEHAVIN' — Tommy Bruce (Columbia)
20	13	I'M SORRY — Brenda Lee (Brunswick)
17	14	PAPER ROSES — Kaye Sisters (Philips)
25	14	THE GIRL OF MY BEST FRIEND — Elvis Presley (RCA)
21	16	MAIS OUI — King Brothers (Parlophone)
23	17	AS LONG AS HE NEEDS ME — Shirley Bassey (Columbia)
12	18	ROBOT MAN — Connie Francis (MGM)
13	19	WHEN JOHNNY COMES MARCHING HOME — Adam Faith (Parlophone)
18	20	WHAT A MOUTH — Tommy Steele (Decca)
15	21	MADE YOU — Adam Faith (Parlophone)
-	22	WALKING TO NEW ORLEANS — Fats Domino (London)
19	23	LOVE IS LIKE A VIOLIN — Ken Dodd (Decca)
22	23	I WANNA GO HOME — Lonnie Donegan (Pye)
16	25	MAMA — Connie Francis (MGM)
26	26	TRAIN OF LOVE — Alma Cogan (HMV)
26	27	ANGELA JONES — Michael Cox (Triumph)
-	27	FEEL SO FINE — Johnny Preston (Mercury)
30	29	HANDY MAN — Jimmy Jones (MGM)
29	30	ELVIS IS BACK (LP) — Elvis Presley (RCA)

last week	this week	20 August 1960
2	1	APACHE — Shadows (Columbia)
1	2	PLEASE DON'T TEASE — Cliff Richard (Columbia)
3	3	A MESS OF BLUES — Elvis Presley (RCA)
7	4	BECAUSE THEY'RE YOUNG — Duane Eddy (London)
5	5	SHAKIN' ALL OVER — Johnny Kidd & the Pirates (HMV)
6	6	WHEN WILL I BE LOVED — Everly Brothers (London)
11	7	TIE ME KANGAROO DOWN SPORT — Rolf Harris (Columbia)
8	7	IF SHE SHOULD COME TO YOU — Anthony Newley (Decca)
4	9	GOOD TIMIN' — Jimmy Jones (MGM)
13	10	I'M SORRY — Brenda Lee (Brunswick)
10	11	ITSY BITSY TEENY WEENY YELLOW POLKA DOT BIKINI — Brian Hyland (London)
8	12	LOOK FOR A STAR — Garry Mills (Top Rank)
14	13	PAPER ROSES — Kaye Sisters (Philips)
17	14	AS LONG AS HE NEEDS ME — Shirley Bassey (Columbia)
14	15	THE GIRL OF MY BEST FRIEND — Elvis Presley (RCA)
16	16	MAIS OUI — King Brothers (Parlophone)
-	17	EVERYBODY'S SOMEBODY'S FOOL — Connie Francis (MGM)
27	18	FEEL SO FINE — Johnny Preston (Mercury)
-	19	TELL LAURA I LOVE HER — Ricky Valance (Columbia)
12	20	AIN'T MISBEHAVIN' — Tommy Bruce (Columbia)
23	21	LOVE IS LIKE A VIOLIN — Ken Dodd (Decca)
22	22	WALKING TO NEW ORLEANS — Fats Domino (London)
19	23	WHEN JOHNNY COMES MARCHING HOME — Adam Faith (Parlophone)
23	24	I WANNA GO HOME — Lonnie Donegan (Pye)
25	25	MAMA — Connie Francis (MGM)
26	26	TRAIN OF LOVE — Alma Cogan (HMV)
-	27	MULE SKINNER BLUES — Fendermen (Top Rank)
28	28	ONLY THE LONELY — Roy Orbison (London)
29	29	HANDY MAN — Jimmy Jones (MGM)
20	30	WHAT A MOUTH — Tommy Steele (Decca)

last week	this week	27 August 1960
1	1	APACHE — Shadows (Columbia)
2	2	PLEASE DON'T TEASE — Cliff Richard (Columbia)
4	3	BECAUSE THEY'RE YOUNG — Duane Eddy (London)
3	4	A MESS OF BLUES — Elvis Presley (RCA)
6	5	WHEN WILL I BE LOVED — Everly Brothers (London)
5	6	SHAKIN' ALL OVER — Johnny Kidd & the Pirates (HMV)
7	7	IF SHE SHOULD COME TO YOU — Anthony Newley (Decca)
7	8	TIE ME KANGAROO DOWN SPORT — Rolf Harris (Columbia)
17	9	EVERYBODY'S SOMEBODY'S FOOL — Connie Francis (MGM)
10	10	I'M SORRY — Brenda Lee (Brunswick)
9	11	GOOD TIMIN' — Jimmy Jones (MGM)
15	12	THE GIRL OF MY BEST FRIEND — Elvis Presley (RCA)
-	13	LORELEI — Lonnie Donegan (Pye)
14	14	AS LONG AS HE NEEDS ME — Shirley Bassey (Columbia)
11	14	ITSY BITSY TEENY WEENY YELLOW POLKA DOT BIKINI — Brian Hyland (London)
13	16	PAPER ROSES — Kaye Sisters (Philips)
19	17	TELL LAURA I LOVE HER — Ricky Valance (Columbia)
21	18	LOVE IS LIKE A VIOLIN — Ken Dodd (Decca)
28	19	ONLY THE LONELY — Roy Orbison (London)
16	20	MAIS OUI — King Brothers (Parlophone)
12	20	LOOK FOR A STAR — Garry Mills (Top Rank)
-	22	IMAGE OF A GIRL — Mark Wynter (Decca)
18	23	FEEL SO FINE — Johnny Preston (Mercury)
20	24	AIN'T MISBEHAVIN' — Tommy Bruce (Columbia)
25	25	MAMA — Connie Francis (MGM)
-	26	MADE YOU — Adam Faith (Parlophone)
22	27	WALKING TO NEW ORLEANS — Fats Domino (London)
27	27	MULE SKINNER BLUES — Fendermen (Top Rank)
-	29	IMAGE OF A GIRL — Nelson Keene (HMV)
30	29	WHAT A MOUTH — Tommy Steele (Decca)

last week	this week	3 September 1960
1	1	APACHE — Shadows (Columbia)
3	2	BECAUSE THEY'RE YOUNG — Duane Eddy (London)
2	3	PLEASE DON'T TEASE — Cliff Richard (Columbia)
4	4	A MESS OF BLUES — Elvis Presley (RCA)
5	5	WHEN WILL I BE LOVED — Everly Brothers (London)
7	6	IF SHE SHOULD COME TO YOU — Anthony Newley (Decca)
9	7	EVERYBODY'S SOMEBODY'S FOOL — Connie Francis (MGM)
12	8	THE GIRL OF MY BEST FRIEND — Elvis Presley (RCA)
18	9	LOVE IS LIKE A VIOLIN — Ken Dodd (Decca)
14	10	AS LONG AS HE NEEDS ME — Shirley Bassey (Columbia)
6	11	SHAKIN' ALL OVER — Johnny Kidd & the Pirates (HMV)
17	12	TELL LAURA I LOVE HER — Ricky Valance (Columbia)
13	13	LORELEI — Lonnie Donegan (Pye)
8	14	TIE ME KANGAROO DOWN SPORT — Rolf Harris (Columbia)
10	15	I'M SORRY — Brenda Lee (Brunswick)
19	16	ONLY THE LONELY — Roy Orbison (London)
11	17	GOOD TIMIN' — Jimmy Jones (MGM)
16	17	PAPER ROSES — Kaye Sisters (Philips)
14	19	ITSY BITSY TEENY WEENY YELLOW POLKA DOT BIKINI — Brian Hyland (London)
23	20	FEEL SO FINE — Johnny Preston (Mercury)
20	21	LOOK FOR A STAR — Garry Mills (Top Rank)
22	22	IMAGE OF A GIRL — Mark Wynter (Decca)
20	23	MAIS OUI — King Brothers (Parlophone)
-	24	I JUST GO FOR YOU — Jimmy Jones (MGM)
29	24	IMAGE OF A GIRL — Nelson Keene (HMV)
-	26	VOLARE — Bobby Rydell (Columbia)
-	27	BROKEN DOLL — Tommy Bruce (Columbia)
-	28	CARIBBEAN HONEYMOON — Frank Weir (Oriole)
27	29	WALKING TO NEW ORLEANS — Fats Domino (London)
-	29	PLEASE HELP ME I'M FALLING — Hank Locklin (RCA)
-	29	LET'S THINK ABOUT LIVING — Bob Luman (Warner Bros)

Elvis's US follow-up single to *Stuck On You, It's Now Or Never*, ran into copyright problems in the UK – a result of being based on the 1901 Italian composition *O Sole Mio* (a tune used much later in a series of adverts for a particular ice-cream). With speculation that it might take seven years to clear release rights, RCA issued the B-side *A Mess Of Blues* and coupled it with *The Girl Of My Best Friend*, a track from the *Elvis Is Back* LP. When both sides reached the Top Ten this decision was clearly justified.

10 September 1960

last week	this week	Title	Artist
1	1	APACHE	Shadows (Columbia)
2	2	BECAUSE THEY'RE YOUNG	Duane Eddy (London)
3	3	PLEASE DON'T TEASE	Cliff Richard (Columbia)
4	4	A MESS OF BLUES	Elvis Presley (RCA)
5	5	WHEN WILL I BE LOVED	Everly Brothers (London)
8	6	THE GIRL OF MY BEST FRIEND	Elvis Presley (RCA)
10	7	AS LONG AS HE NEEDS ME	Shirley Bassey (Columbia)
7	8	EVERYBODY'S SOMEBODY'S FOOL	Connie Francis (MGM)
12	9	TELL LAURA I LOVE HER	Ricky Valance (Columbia)
17	10	PAPER ROSES	Kaye Sisters (Philips)
9	11	LOVE IS LIKE A VIOLIN	Ken Dodd (Decca)
16	12	ONLY THE LONELY	Roy Orbison (London)
15	13	I'M SORRY	Brenda Lee (Brunswick)
6	14	IF SHE SHOULD COME TO YOU	Anthony Newley (Decca)
11	15	SHAKIN' ALL OVER	Johnny Kidd & the Pirates (HMV)
14	16	TIE ME KANGAROO DOWN SPORT	Rolf Harris (Columbia)
13	17	LORELEI	Lonnie Donegan (Pye)
19	18	ITSY BITSY TEENY WEENY YELLOW POLKA DOT BIKINI	Brian Hyland (London)
26	19	VOLARE	Bobby Rydell (Columbia)
17	20	GOOD TIMIN'	Jimmy Jones (MGM)
29	21	PLEASE HELP ME I'M FALLING	Hank Locklin (RCA)
20	22	FEEL SO FINE	Johnny Preston (Mercury)
21	23	LOOK FOR A STAR	Garry Mills (Top Rank)
21	24	IMAGE OF A GIRL	Mark Wynter (Decca)
-	25	WALK DON'T RUN	Ventures (Top Rank)
24	26	IMAGE OF A GIRL	Nelson Keene (HMV)
28	27	CARIBBEAN HONEYMOON	Frank Weir (Oriole)
-	28	WHITE CLIFFS OF DOVER	Mr Acker Bilk (Columbia)
23	29	MAIS OUI	King Brothers (Parlophone)
27	30	BROKEN DOLL	Tommy Bruce (Columbia)

17 September 1960

last week	this week	Title	Artist
1	1	APACHE	Shadows (Columbia)
2	2	BECAUSE THEY'RE YOUNG	Duane Eddy (London)
4	3	A MESS OF BLUES	Elvis Presley (RCA)
9	4	TELL LAURA I LOVE HER	Ricky Valance (Columbia)
12	5	ONLY THE LONELY	Roy Orbison (London)
6	6	THE GIRL OF MY BEST FRIEND	Elvis Presley (RCA)
3	7	PLEASE DON'T TEASE	Cliff Richard (Columbia)
7	8	AS LONG AS HE NEEDS ME	Shirley Bassey (Columbia)
8	9	EVERYBODY'S SOMEBODY'S FOOL	Connie Francis (MGM)
10	10	PAPER ROSES	Kaye Sisters (Philips)
5	11	WHEN WILL I BE LOVED	Everly Brothers (London)
-	12	HOW ABOUT THAT!	Adam Faith (Parlophone)
11	13	LOVE IS LIKE A VIOLIN	Ken Dodd (Decca)
14	14	IF SHE SHOULD COME TO YOU	Anthony Newley (Decca)
15	15	SHAKIN' ALL OVER	Johnny Kidd & the Pirates (HMV)
16	16	TIE ME KANGAROO DOWN SPORT	Rolf Harris (Columbia)
17	17	LORELEI	Lonnie Donegan (Pye)
13	18	I'M SORRY	Brenda Lee (Brunswick)
25	19	WALK DON'T RUN	Ventures (Top Rank)
-	20	WALK DON'T RUN	John Barry Seven (Columbia)
19	21	VOLARE	Bobby Rydell (Columbia)
21	22	PLEASE HELP ME I'M FALLING	Hank Locklin (RCA)
24	23	IMAGE OF A GIRL	Mark Wynter (Decca)
18	24	ITSY BITSY TEENY WEENY YELLOW POLKA DOT BIKINI	Brian Hyland (London)
-	25	NICE 'N' EASY	Frank Sinatra (Capitol)
27	26	CARIBBEAN HONEYMOON	Frank Weir (Oriole)
22	27	FEEL SO FINE	Johnny Preston (Mercury)
20	28	GOOD TIMIN'	Jimmy Jones (MGM)
28	29	WHITE CLIFFS OF DOVER	Mr Acker Bilk (Columbia)
-	30	I JUST GO FOR YOU	Jimmy Jones (MGM)

24 September 1960

last week	this week	Title	Artist
1	1	APACHE	Shadows (Columbia)
5	2	ONLY THE LONELY	Roy Orbison (London)
4	3	TELL LAURA I LOVE HER	Ricky Valance (Columbia)
2	4	BECAUSE THEY'RE YOUNG	Duane Eddy (London)
12	5	HOW ABOUT THAT!	Adam Faith (Parlophone)
3	6	A MESS OF BLUES	Elvis Presley (RCA)
-	7	NINE TIMES OUT OF TEN	Cliff Richard (Columbia)
8	8	AS LONG AS HE NEEDS ME	Shirley Bassey (Columbia)
6	9	THE GIRL OF MY BEST FRIEND	Elvis Presley (RCA)
9	10	EVERYBODY'S SOMEBODY'S FOOL	Connie Francis (MGM)
7	11	PLEASE DON'T TEASE	Cliff Richard (Columbia)
19	12	WALK DON'T RUN	Ventures (Top Rank)
10	13	PAPER ROSES	Kaye Sisters (Philips)
11	14	WHEN WILL I BE LOVED	Everly Brothers (London)
-	15	SO SAD	Everly Brothers (Warner Bros)
20	16	WALK DON'T RUN	John Barry Seven (Columbia)
22	17	PLEASE HELP ME I'M FALLING	Hank Locklin (RCA)
21	18	VOLARE	Bobby Rydell (Columbia)
-	19	LUCILLE	Everly Brothers (Warner Bros)
26	20	CARIBBEAN HONEYMOON	Frank Weir (Oriole)
15	21	SHAKIN' ALL OVER	Johnny Kidd & the Pirates (HMV)
13	22	LOVE IS LIKE A VIOLIN	Ken Dodd (Decca)
23	23	IMAGE OF A GIRL	Mark Wynter (Decca)
14	24	IF SHE SHOULD COME TO YOU	Anthony Newley (Decca)
18	25	I'M SORRY	Brenda Lee (Brunswick)
-	26	PASSING BREEZE	Russ Conway (Columbia)
-	26	LET'S THINK ABOUT LIVING	Bob Luman (Warner Bros)
-	28	CHAIN GANG	Sam Cooke (RCA)
17	29	LORELEI	Lonnie Donegan (Pye)
-	30	LET'S HAVE A PARTY	Wanda Jackson (Capitol)

1 October 1960

last week	this week	Title	Artist
3	1	TELL LAURA I LOVE HER	Ricky Valance (Columbia)
7	2	NINE TIMES OUT OF TEN	Cliff Richard (Columbia)
2	3	ONLY THE LONELY	Roy Orbison (London)
5	4	HOW ABOUT THAT!	Adam Faith (Parlophone)
1	5	APACHE	Shadows (Columbia)
4	6	BECAUSE THEY'RE YOUNG	Duane Eddy (London)
8	7	THE GIRL OF MY BEST FRIEND	Elvis Presley (RCA)
8	8	AS LONG AS HE NEEDS ME	Shirley Bassey (Columbia)
12	9	WALK DON'T RUN	Ventures (Top Rank)
16	10	WALK DON'T RUN	John Barry Seven (Columbia)
15	11	SO SAD	Everly Brothers (Warner Bros)
6	12	A MESS OF BLUES	Elvis Presley (RCA)
10	13	EVERYBODY'S SOMEBODY'S FOOL	Connie Francis (MGM)
19	14	LUCILLE	Everly Brothers (Warner Bros)
17	15	PLEASE HELP ME I'M FALLING	Hank Locklin (RCA)
13	16	PAPER ROSES	Kaye Sisters (Philips)
14	17	WHEN WILL I BE LOVED	Everly Brothers (London)
28	18	CHAIN GANG	Sam Cooke (RCA)
26	19	PASSING BREEZE	Russ Conway (Columbia)
26	20	LET'S THINK ABOUT LIVING	Bob Luman (Warner Bros)
22	21	LOVE IS LIKE A VIOLIN	Ken Dodd (Decca)
-	22	ROCKING GOOSE	Johnny & the Hurricanes (London)
11	23	PLEASE DON'T TEASE	Cliff Richard (Columbia)
20	24	CARIBBEAN HONEYMOON	Frank Weir (Oriole)
-	25	IMAGE OF A GIRL	Nelson Keene (HMV)
18	26	VOLARE	Bobby Rydell (Columbia)
-	26	NICE 'N' EASY	Frank Sinatra (Capitol)
-	28	MACDONALD'S CAVE	Piltdown Men (Capitol)
-	29	EE-O-ELEVEN	Sammy Davis Jr. (Brunswick)
-	29	WHAT A MOUTH	Tommy Steele (Decca)

Both Cliff Richard's *Please Don't Tease* and its follow-up *Nine Times Out Of Ten.* were selected as hit material by a panel of fans, who were played a number of newly-recorded tracks at Abbey Road studios. Cliff may well have hoped to replace the Shadows at Number One with *Nine Times* (since *Apache* had dethroned *Tease*), but in the event it was label-mate Ricky Valance who went to the top with *Tell Laura I Love Her*, controversial because of its boy-dies-for-girl lyric.

October 1960

last week / this week

8 October 1960

last	this	
1	1	TELL LAURA I LOVE HER — Ricky Valance (Columbia)
3	2	ONLY THE LONELY — Roy Orbison (London)
4	3	HOW ABOUT THAT! — Adam Faith (Parlophone)
2	4	NINE TIMES OUT OF TEN — Cliff Richard (Columbia)
11	5	SO SAD — Everly Brothers (Warner Bros)
5	6	APACHE — Shadows (Columbia)
8	7	AS LONG AS HE NEEDS ME — Shirley Bassey (Columbia)
10	8	WALK DON'T RUN — John Barry Seven (Columbia)
9	9	WALK DON'T RUN — Ventures (Top Rank)
7	10	THE GIRL OF MY BEST FRIEND — Elvis Presley (RCA)
6	11	BECAUSE THEY'RE YOUNG — Duane Eddy (London)
12	12	A MESS OF BLUES — Elvis Presley (RCA)
13	13	EVERYBODY'S SOMEBODY'S FOOL — Connie Francis (MGM)
15	14	PLEASE HELP ME I'M FALLING — Hank Locklin (RCA)
14	15	LUCILLE — Everly Brothers (Warner Bros)
20	16	LET'S THINK ABOUT LIVING — Bob Luman (Warner Bros)
18	17	CHAIN GANG — Sam Cooke (RCA)
26	18	NICE 'N' EASY — Frank Sinatra (Capitol)
22	19	ROCKING GOOSE — Johnny & the Hurricanes (London)
-	20	DREAMIN' — Johnny Burnette (London)
19	20	PASSING BREEZE — Russ Conway (Columbia)
-	22	THEM THERE EYES — Emile Ford (Pye)
16	23	PAPER ROSES — Kaye Sisters (Philips)
28	24	MACDONALD'S CAVE — Piltdown Men (Capitol)
-	25	RESTLESS — Johnny Kidd & the Pirates (HMV)
25	26	IMAGE OF A GIRL — Nelson Keene (HMV)
-	27	HAPPY-GO-LUCKY BLUES — Tommy Steele (Decca)
24	27	CARIBBEAN HONEYMOON — Frank Weir (Oriole)
-	28	KIDDIO — Brook Benton (Mercury)
-	29	ALONG CAME CAROLINE — Michael Cox (HMV)
21	29	LOVE IS LIKE A VIOLIN — Ken Dodd (Decca)

15 October 1960

last	this	
2	1	ONLY THE LONELY — Roy Orbison (London)
1	2	TELL LAURA I LOVE HER — Ricky Valance (Columbia)
7	3	AS LONG AS HE NEEDS ME — Shirley Bassey (Columbia)
3	3	HOW ABOUT THAT! — Adam Faith (Parlophone)
5	5	SO SAD — Everly Brothers (Warner Bros)
4	6	NINE TIMES OUT OF TEN — Cliff Richard (Columbia)
6	7	APACHE — Shadows (Columbia)
17	8	CHAIN GANG — Sam Cooke (RCA)
10	9	THE GIRL OF MY BEST FRIEND — Elvis Presley (RCA)
9	10	WALK DON'T RUN — Ventures (Top Rank)
8	11	WALK DON'T RUN — John Barry Seven (Columbia)
16	12	LET'S THINK ABOUT LIVING — Bob Luman (Warner Bros)
14	13	PLEASE HELP ME I'M FALLING — Hank Locklin (RCA)
20	14	DREAMIN' — Johnny Burnette (London)
12	15	A MESS OF BLUES — Elvis Presley (RCA)
19	16	ROCKING GOOSE — Johnny & the Hurricanes (London)
11	17	BECAUSE THEY'RE YOUNG — Duane Eddy (London)
13	18	EVERYBODY'S SOMEBODY'S FOOL — Connie Francis (MGM)
18	19	NICE 'N' EASY — Frank Sinatra (Capitol)
20	20	PASSING BREEZE — Russ Conway (Columbia)
25	21	RESTLESS — Johnny Kidd & the Pirates (HMV)
15	22	LUCILLE — Everly Brothers (Warner Bros)
22	22	THEM THERE EYES — Emile Ford (Pye)
24	22	MACDONALD'S CAVE — Piltdown Men (Capitol)
-	25	MY LOVE FOR YOU — Johnny Mathis (Fontana)
-	26	NEVER ON SUNDAY — Don Costa (London)
-	27	SHORT'NIN' BREAD — Viscounts (Pye)
-	28	SUNDAY DATE — Flee-Rekkers (Pye)
-	29	WONDROUS PLACE — Billy Fury (Decca)
-	30	NEVER ON SUNDAY — Manuel & His Music Of The Mountains (Columbia)

22 October 1960

last	this	
1	1	ONLY THE LONELY — Roy Orbison (London)
3	2	AS LONG AS HE NEEDS ME — Shirley Bassey (Columbia)
2	3	TELL LAURA I LOVE HER — Ricky Valance (Columbia)
4	4	HOW ABOUT THAT! — Adam Faith (Parlophone)
6	5	NINE TIMES OUT OF TEN — Cliff Richard (Columbia)
11	6	WALK DON'T RUN — John Barry Seven (Columbia)
5	7	SO SAD — Everly Brothers (Warner Bros)
8	8	CHAIN GANG — Sam Cooke (RCA)
12	9	LET'S THINK ABOUT LIVING — Bob Luman (Warner Bros)
7	10	APACHE — Shadows (Columbia)
10	11	WALK DON'T RUN — Ventures (Top Rank)
14	12	DREAMIN' — Johnny Burnette (London)
9	13	THE GIRL OF MY BEST FRIEND — Elvis Presley (RCA)
13	14	PLEASE HELP ME I'M FALLING — Hank Locklin (RCA)
22	15	MACDONALD'S CAVE — Piltdown Men (Capitol)
16	16	ROCKING GOOSE — Johnny & the Hurricanes (London)
15	17	A MESS OF BLUES — Elvis Presley (RCA)
25	18	MY LOVE FOR YOU — Johnny Mathis (Fontana)
20	19	PASSING BREEZE — Russ Conway (Columbia)
18	20	EVERYBODY'S SOMEBODY'S FOOL — Connie Francis (MGM)
22	21	THEM THERE EYES — Emile Ford (Pye)
17	22	BECAUSE THEY'RE YOUNG — Duane Eddy (London)
26	23	NEVER ON SUNDAY — Don Costa (London)
-	24	TOP TEEN BABY — Garry Mills (Top Rank)
21	25	RESTLESS — Johnny Kidd & the Pirates (HMV)
30	25	NEVER ON SUNDAY — Manuel & His Music Of The Mountains (Columbia)
27	25	SHORT'NIN' BREAD — Viscounts (Pye)
-	28	LEARNING THE GAME — Buddy Holly (Coral)
-	29	LONELY — Eddie Cochran (London)
19	30	NICE 'N' EASY — Frank Sinatra (Capitol)

29 October 1960

last	this	
1	1	ONLY THE LONELY — Roy Orbison (London)
2	2	AS LONG AS HE NEEDS ME — Shirley Bassey (Columbia)
3	3	TELL LAURA I LOVE HER — Ricky Valance (Columbia)
4	4	HOW ABOUT THAT! — Adam Faith (Parlophone)
12	5	DREAMIN' — Johnny Burnette (London)
9	6	LET'S THINK ABOUT LIVING — Bob Luman (Warner Bros)
6	7	WALK DON'T RUN — John Barry Seven (Columbia)
8	8	CHAIN GANG — Sam Cooke (RCA)
5	9	NINE TIMES OUT OF TEN — Cliff Richard (Columbia)
16	10	ROCKING GOOSE — Johnny & the Hurricanes (London)
7	11	SO SAD — Everly Brothers (Warner Bros)
10	12	APACHE — Shadows (Columbia)
14	13	PLEASE HELP ME I'M FALLING — Hank Locklin (RCA)
15	14	MACDONALD'S CAVE — Piltdown Men (Capitol)
18	15	MY LOVE FOR YOU — Johnny Mathis (Fontana)
13	16	THE GIRL OF MY BEST FRIEND — Elvis Presley (RCA)
11	16	WALK DON'T RUN — Ventures (Top Rank)
22	18	BECAUSE THEY'RE YOUNG — Duane Eddy (London)
23	19	NEVER ON SUNDAY — Don Costa (London)
17	20	A MESS OF BLUES — Elvis Presley (RCA)
30	21	NICE 'N' EASY — Frank Sinatra (Capitol)
-	22	LUCILLE — Everly Brothers (Warner Bros)
21	23	THEM THERE EYES — Emile Ford (Pye)
19	24	PASSING BREEZE — Russ Conway (Columbia)
25	25	NEVER ON SUNDAY — Manuel & His Music Of The Mountains (Columbia)
24	25	TOP TEEN BABY — Garry Mills (Top Rank)
25	27	SHORT'NIN' BREAD — Viscounts (Pye)
-	28	WONDROUS PLACE — Billy Fury (Decca)
28	28	LEARNING THE GAME — Buddy Holly (Coral)
29	30	LONELY — Eddie Cochran (London)
-	30	MR. CUSTER — Charlie Drake (Parlophone)

Roy Orbison made the top with what was his first UK release, but only after four years on three labels in the US with a string of unsuccessful releases. Shirley Bassey's single which Orbison kept from Number One was the major song from Lionel Bart's new stage musical *Oliver*. Johnny Burnette, like Orbison, had been recording since the mid-fifties with little succes, notably as the leader of the Rock 'n' Roll Trio, whose rockabilly recordings were later regarded as classics. He died in 1964.

November 1960

5 November 1960

last week	this week	
-	1	IT'S NOW OR NEVER — Elvis Presley (RCA)
1	2	ONLY THE LONELY — Roy Orbison (London)
2	3	AS LONG AS HE NEEDS ME — Shirley Bassey (Columbia)
5	4	DREAMIN' — Johnny Burnette (London)
10	5	ROCKING GOOSE — Johnny & the Hurricanes (London)
6	6	LET'S THINK ABOUT LIVING — Bob Luman (Warner Bros)
8	7	CHAIN GANG — Sam Cooke (RCA)
11	8	SO SAD — Everly Brothers (Warner Bros)
4	9	HOW ABOUT THAT! — Adam Faith (Parlophone)
9	10	NINE TIMES OUT OF TEN — Cliff Richard (Columbia)
7	11	WALK DON'T RUN — John Barry Seven (Columbia)
14	12	MACDONALD'S CAVE — Piltdown Men (Capitol)
3	13	TELL LAURA I LOVE HER — Ricky Valance (Columbia)
15	14	MY LOVE FOR YOU — Johnny Mathis (Fontana)
-	15	MY HEART HAS A MIND OF ITS OWN — Connie Francis (MGM)
13	16	PLEASE HELP ME I'M FALLING — Hank Locklin (RCA)
-	17	MILORD — Edith Piaf (Columbia)
16	18	WALK DON'T RUN — Ventures (Top Rank)
-	19	SAVE THE LAST DANCE FOR ME — Drifters (London)
30	20	MR. CUSTER — Charlie Drake (Parlophone)
12	21	APACHE — Shadows (Columbia)
25	22	NEVER ON SUNDAY — Manuel & His Music Of The Mountains (Columbia)
19	23	NEVER ON SUNDAY — Don Costa (London)
-	24	BLUE ANGEL — Roy Orbison (London)
23	25	THEM THERE EYES — Emile Ford (Pye)
25	25	TOP TEEN BABY — Garry Mills (Top Rank)
16	27	THE GIRL OF MY BEST FRIEND — Elvis Presley (RCA)
18	28	BECAUSE THEY'RE YOUNG — Duane Eddy (London)
-	29	SORRY ROBBIE — Bert Weedon (Top Rank)
-	30	MILORD — Frankie Vaughan (Philips)

12 November 1960

last week	this week	
1	1	IT'S NOW OR NEVER — Elvis Presley (RCA)
3	2	AS LONG AS HE NEEDS ME — Shirley Bassey (Columbia)
2	3	ONLY THE LONELY — Roy Orbison (London)
4	4	DREAMIN' — Johnny Burnette (London)
5	5	ROCKING GOOSE — Johnny & the Hurricanes (London)
15	6	MY HEART HAS A MIND OF ITS OWN — Connie Francis (MGM)
6	7	LET'S THINK ABOUT LIVING — Bob Luman (Warner Bros)
12	8	MACDONALD'S CAVE — Piltdown Men (Capitol)
19	9	SAVE THE LAST DANCE FOR ME — Drifters (London)
20	10	MR. CUSTER — Charlie Drake (Parlophone)
-	11	GOODNESS GRACIOUS ME — Peter Sellers & Sophia Loren (Parlophone)
11	12	WALK DON'T RUN — John Barry Seven (Columbia)
14	13	MY LOVE FOR YOU — Johnny Mathis (Fontana)
7	14	CHAIN GANG — Sam Cooke (RCA)
9	15	HOW ABOUT THAT! — Adam Faith (Parlophone)
-	16	MAN OF MYSTERY — Shadows (Columbia)
10	17	NINE TIMES OUT OF TEN — Cliff Richard (Columbia)
-	18	KOMMOTION — Duane Eddy (London)
8	19	SO SAD — Everly Brothers (Warner Bros)
17	20	MILORD — Edith Piaf (Columbia)
24	21	BLUE ANGEL — Roy Orbison (London)
13	22	TELL LAURA I LOVE HER — Ricky Valance (Columbia)
-	23	SHORT'NIN' BREAD — Viscounts (Pye)
16	24	PLEASE HELP ME I'M FALLING — Hank Locklin (RCA)
25	25	THEM THERE EYES — Emile Ford (Pye)
29	25	SORRY ROBBIE — Bert Weedon (Top Rank)
-	27	JUST AS MUCH AS EVER — Nat King Cole (Capitol)
-	28	TODAY'S TEARDROPS — Roy Orbison (London)
25	29	TOP TEEN BABY — Garry Mills (Top Rank)
18	30	WALK DON'T RUN — Ventures (Top Rank)

19 November 1960

last week	this week	
1	1	IT'S NOW OR NEVER — Elvis Presley (RCA)
2	2	AS LONG AS HE NEEDS ME — Shirley Bassey (Columbia)
4	3	DREAMIN' — Johnny Burnette (London)
3	4	ONLY THE LONELY — Roy Orbison (London)
6	5	MY HEART HAS A MIND OF ITS OWN — Connie Francis (MGM)
5	6	ROCKING GOOSE — Johnny & the Hurricanes (London)
9	7	SAVE THE LAST DANCE FOR ME — Drifters (London)
11	8	GOODNESS GRACIOUS ME — Peter Sellers & Sophia Loren (Parlophone)
16	9	MAN OF MYSTERY — Shadows (Columbia)
13	10	MY LOVE FOR YOU — Johnny Mathis (Fontana)
-	11	THE STRANGER — Shadows (Columbia)
7	12	LET'S THINK ABOUT LIVING — Bob Luman (Warner Bros)
18	13	KOMMOTION — Duane Eddy (London)
8	14	MACDONALD'S CAVE — Piltdown Men (Capitol)
10	15	MR. CUSTER — Charlie Drake (Parlophone)
20	16	MILORD — Edith Piaf (Columbia)
-	17	LITTLE DONKEY — Nina & Frederick (Columbia)
15	18	HOW ABOUT THAT! — Adam Faith (Parlophone)
14	19	CHAIN GANG — Sam Cooke (RCA)
27	20	JUST AS MUCH AS EVER — Nat King Cole (Capitol)
17	21	NINE TIMES OUT OF TEN — Cliff Richard (Columbia)
19	22	SO SAD — Everly Brothers (Warner Bros)
21	22	BLUE ANGEL — Roy Orbison (London)
25	24	SORRY ROBBIE — Bert Weedon (Top Rank)
25	25	THEM THERE EYES — Emile Ford (Pye)
12	26	WALK DON'T RUN — John Barry Seven (Columbia)
-	26	MILORD — Frankie Vaughan (Philips)
-	28	ROCKIN' ALONE — Miki & Griff (Pye)
-	29	NEVER ON SUNDAY — Manuel & His Music Of The Mountains (Columbia)
-	30	DON'T BE CRUEL — Bill Black's Combo (London)

26 November 1960

last week	this week	
1	1	IT'S NOW OR NEVER — Elvis Presley (RCA)
7	2	SAVE THE LAST DANCE FOR ME — Drifters (London)
8	3	GOODNESS GRACIOUS ME — Peter Sellers & Sophia Loren (Parlophone)
2	4	AS LONG AS HE NEEDS ME — Shirley Bassey (Columbia)
6	4	ROCKING GOOSE — Johnny & the Hurricanes (London)
5	6	MY HEART HAS A MIND OF ITS OWN — Connie Francis (MGM)
3	7	DREAMIN' — Johnny Burnette (London)
9	8	MAN OF MYSTERY — Shadows (Columbia)
-	9	OL' MACDONALD — Frank Sinatra (Capitol)
17	10	LITTLE DONKEY — Nina & Frederick (Columbia)
4	11	ONLY THE LONELY — Roy Orbison (London)
11	12	THE STRANGER — Shadows (Columbia)
-	13	STRAWBERRY FAIR — Anthony Newley (Decca)
14	14	LIVELY — Lonnie Donegan (Pye)
13	15	KOMMOTION — Duane Eddy (London)
10	16	MY LOVE FOR YOU — Johnny Mathis (Fontana)
12	17	LET'S THINK ABOUT LIVING — Bob Luman (Warner Bros)
15	18	MILORD — Edith Piaf (Columbia)
15	19	MR. CUSTER — Charlie Drake (Parlophone)
14	20	MACDONALD'S CAVE — Piltdown Men (Capitol)
20	21	JUST AS MUCH AS EVER — Nat King Cole (Capitol)
-	22	EVEN MORE PARTY POPS — Russ Conway (Columbia)
22	23	BLUE ANGEL — Roy Orbison (London)
-	24	POETRY IN MOTION — Johnny Tillotson (London)
-	25	LONELY PUP — Adam Faith (Parlophone)
-	26	PERFIDIA — Ventures (London)
22	27	SO SAD — Everly Brothers (Warner Bros)
26	28	MILORD — Frankie Vaughan (Philips)
24	28	SORRY ROBBIE — Bert Weedon (Top Rank)
30	30	DON'T BE CRUEL — Bill Black's Combo (London)
29	30	NEVER ON SUNDAY — Manuel & His Music Of The Mountains (Columbia)

Its copyright problems solved relatively quickly, *It's Now Or Never* was cleared for UK release and ammassed a staggering advance order from dealers of almost half a million – the largest ever known at this time. Its immediate Number One entry was the only the third in chart history, and Presley's second after *Jailhouse Rock*. Such was the customer demand that first weekend that at least one London record shop closed for normal business and concentrated simply on selling huge stocks of *It's Now Or Never*.

December 1960

It's Now Or Never held Number One for nine weeks, equalling the run of *Cathy's Clown* earlier in the year. On December 13 it passed the million sales mark in Britain, having achieved this total in a new record time of six and a half weeks. Frank Sinatra and instrumental group the Piltdown Men had – on the same label – vastly different interpretations of the same traditional song. Ray Charles made his UK chart debut and both Cliff Richard and the Shadows had both sides of their singles in the charts.

1   1   IT'S NOW OR NEVER
           Elvis Presley (RCA)
2   2   SAVE THE LAST DANCE FOR ME
           Drifters (London)
4   3   POETRY IN MOTION
           Johnny Tillotson (London)
3   4   I LOVE YOU
           Cliff Richard (Columbia)
5   5   LONELY PUP
           Adam Faith (Parlophone)
7   6   LITTLE DONKEY
           Nina & Frederick (Columbia)
6   7   STRAWBERRY FAIR
           Anthony Newley (Decca)
8   8   GOODNESS GRACIOUS ME
           Peter Sellers & Sophia Loren
           (Parlophone)
11   9   MAN OF MYSTERY
           Shadows (Columbia)
9   10   ROCKING GOOSE
           Johnny & the Hurricanes
           (London)
12   11   GURNEY SLADE
           Max Harris (Fontana)
10   12   PERFIDIA
           Ventures (London)
14   13   AS LONG AS HE NEEDS ME
           Shirley Bassey (Columbia)
17   14   COUNTING TEARDROPS
           Emile Ford (Pye)
-   15   STRAWBERRY BLONDE
           Frank D'Rone (Mercury)
25   16   PORTRAIT OF MY LOVE
           Matt Monro (Parlophone)
30   17   SWAY
           Bobby Rydell (Columbia)
20   18   LIVELY
           Lonnie Donegan (Pye)
15   19   MY LOVE FOR YOU
           Johnny Mathis (Fontana)
20   19   BLUE ANGEL
           Roy Orbison (London)
13   21   MY HEART HAS A MIND OF ITS
           OWN
           Connie Francis (MGM)
27   22   BUONA SERA
           Mr Acker Bilk (Columbia)
16   23   EVEN MORE PARTY POPS
           Russ Conway (Columbia)
19   24   LITTLE GIRL
           Marty Wilde (Philips)
24   25   LIKE STRANGERS
           Everly Brothers (London)
27   26   MILORD
           Edith Piaf (Columbia)
29   27   G.I. BLUES (LP)
           Elvis Presley (RCA)
30   28   TILL   Tony Bennett (Philips)
-   28   IT'S YOU THAT I LOVE
           Marion Ryan (Pye Nixa)
18   30   DREAMIN'
           Johnny Burnette (London)

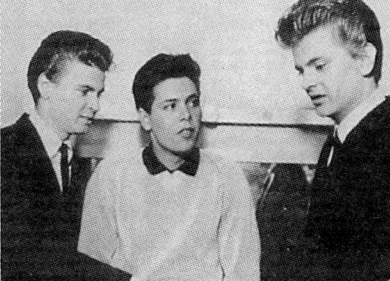

Charting in 1960 – the Everly Brothers (seen here with Cliff who was also making hits), Ray Charles and Nat 'King' Cole. To come in 1961, Helen Shapiro.

January 1961

7 January 1961

last week	this week	title / artist
3	1	POETRY IN MOTION — Johnny Tillotson (London)
2	2	SAVE THE LAST DANCE FOR ME — Drifters (London)
4	3	I LOVE YOU — Cliff Richard (Columbia)
1	4	IT'S NOW OR NEVER — Elvis Presley (RCA)
4	5	LONELY PUP — Adam Faith (Parlophone)
10	6	ROCKING GOOSE — Johnny & the Hurricanes (London)
8	7	GOODNESS GRACIOUS ME — Peter Sellers & Sophia Loren (Parlophone)
12	8	PERFIDIA — Ventures (London)
7	9	STRAWBERRY FAIR — Anthony Newley (Decca)
9	10	MAN OF MYSTERY — Shadows (Columbia)
19	11	BLUE ANGEL — Roy Orbison (London)
14	12	COUNTING TEARDROPS — Emile Ford (Pye)
16	13	PORTRAIT OF MY LOVE — Matt Monro (Parlophone)
15	14	STRAWBERRY BLONDE — Frank D'Rone (Mercury)
24	14	LITTLE GIRL — Marty Wilde (Philips)
22	16	BUONA SERA — Mr Acker Bilk (Columbia)
17	16	SWAY — Bobby Rydell (Columbia)
11	18	GURNEY SLADE — Max Harris (Fontana)
-	19	STAY — Maurice Williams & the Zodiac (Top Rank)
13	20	AS LONG AS HE NEEDS ME — Shirley Bassey (Columbia)
6	21	LITTLE DONKEY — Nina & Frederick (Columbia)
28	22	TILL — Tony Bennett (Philips)
25	23	LIKE STRANGERS — Everly Brothers (London)
21	24	MY HEART HAS A MIND OF ITS OWN — Connie Francis (MGM)
18	25	LIVELY — Lonnie Donegan (Pye)
-	26	CHARIOT — Rhet Stoller (Decca)
30	27	DREAMIN' — Johnny Burnette (London)
27	28	G.I. BLUES (LP) — Elvis Presley (RCA)
28	28	IT'S YOU THAT I LOVE — Marion Ryan (Columbia)
-	30	BLACK STOCKINGS — John Barry Seven (Columbia)
19	30	MY LOVE FOR YOU — Johnny Mathis (Fontana)

14 January 1961

last week	this week	title / artist
1	1	POETRY IN MOTION — Johnny Tillotson (London)
3	2	I LOVE YOU — Cliff Richard (Columbia)
2	3	SAVE THE LAST DANCE FOR ME — Drifters (London)
4	4	IT'S NOW OR NEVER — Elvis Presley (RCA)
8	5	PERFIDIA — Ventures (London)
13	6	PORTRAIT OF MY LOVE — Matt Monro (Parlophone)
12	7	COUNTING TEARDROPS — Emile Ford (Pye)
5	8	LONELY PUP — Adam Faith (Parlophone)
7	9	GOODNESS GRACIOUS ME — Peter Sellers & Sophia Loren (Parlophone)
11	10	BLUE ANGEL — Roy Orbison (London)
6	11	ROCKING GOOSE — Johnny & the Hurricanes (London)
16	12	BUONA SERA — Mr Acker Bilk (Columbia)
16	13	SWAY — Bobby Rydell (Columbia)
10	14	MAN OF MYSTERY — Shadows (Columbia)
9	15	STRAWBERRY FAIR — Anthony Newley (Decca)
14	16	LITTLE GIRL — Marty Wilde (Philips)
19	16	STAY — Maurice Williams & the Zodiacs (Top Rank)
-	18	PEPE — Duane Eddy (London)
23	18	LIKE STRANGERS — Everly Brothers (London)
14	20	STRAWBERRY BLONDE — Frank D'Rone (Mercury)
-	21	NORTH TO ALASKA — Johnny Horton (Philips)
18	22	GURNEY SLADE — Max Harris (Fontana)
30	23	BLACK STOCKINGS — John Barry Seven (Columbia)
21	23	LITTLE DONKEY — Nina & Frederick (Columbia)
-	25	MANY TEARS AGO — Connie Francis (MGM)
-	26	YOU'RE SIXTEEN — Johnny Burnette (London)
26	26	CHARIOT — Rhet Stoller (Decca)
-	28	DOLL HOUSE — King Brothers (Parlophone)
-	29	BANGERS AND MASH — Peter Sellers & Sophia Loren (Parlophone)
-	30	PEPE — Russ Conway (Columbia)

21 January 1961

last week	this week	title / artist
1	1	POETRY IN MOTION — Johnny Tillotson (London)
-	2	ARE YOU LONESOME TONIGHT? — Elvis Presley (RCA)
2	3	I LOVE YOU — Cliff Richard (Columbia)
3	4	SAVE THE LAST DANCE FOR ME — Drifters (London)
6	5	PORTRAIT OF MY LOVE — Matt Monro (Parlophone)
18	6	PEPE — Duane Eddy (London)
4	7	IT'S NOW OR NEVER — Elvis Presley (RCA)
5	8	PERFIDIA — Ventures (London)
7	9	COUNTING TEARDROPS — Emile Ford (Pye)
12	10	BUONA SERA — Mr Acker Bilk (Columbia)
9	11	GOODNESS GRACIOUS ME — Peter Sellers & Sophia Loren (Parlophone)
13	12	SWAY — Bobby Rydell (Columbia)
26	13	YOU'RE SIXTEEN — Johnny Burnette (London)
16	13	STAY — Maurice Williams & the Zodiacs (Top Rank)
28	15	DOLL HOUSE — King Brothers (Parlophone)
18	16	LIKE STRANGERS — Everly Brothers (London)
25	17	MANY TEARS AGO — Connie Francis (MGM)
8	18	LONELY PUP — Adam Faith (Parlophone)
10	19	BLUE ANGEL — Roy Orbison (London)
16	20	LITTLE GIRL — Marty Wilde (Philips)
15	21	STRAWBERRY FAIR — Anthony Newley (Decca)
29	21	BANGERS AND MASH — Peter Sellers & Sophia Loren (Parlophone)
14	21	MAN OF MYSTERY — Shadows (Columbia)
30	24	PEPE — Russ Conway (Columbia)
-	24	PILTDOWN RIDES AGAIN — Piltdown Men (Capitol)
-	26	RUBBER BALL — Marty Wilde (Philips)
21	27	NORTH TO ALASKA — Johnny Horton (Philips)
11	27	ROCKING GOOSE — Johnny & the Hurricanes (London)
26	29	CHARIOT — Rhet Stoller (Decca)
-	30	A THOUSAND STARS — Billy Fury (Decca)

28 January 1961

last week	this week	title / artist
2	1	ARE YOU LONESOME TONIGHT? — Elvis Presley (RCA)
1	2	POETRY IN MOTION — Johnny Tillotson (London)
5	3	PORTRAIT OF MY LOVE — Matt Monro (Parlophone)
6	4	PEPE — Duane Eddy (London)
3	5	I LOVE YOU — Cliff Richard (Columbia)
-	6	SAILOR — Petula Clark (Pye)
9	7	COUNTING TEARDROPS — Emile Ford (Pye)
10	8	BUONA SERA — Mr Acker Bilk (Columbia)
4	9	SAVE THE LAST DANCE FOR ME — Drifters (London)
13	10	STAY — Maurice Williams & the Zodiacs (Top Rank)
13	11	YOU'RE SIXTEEN — Johnny Burnette (London)
8	11	PERFIDIA — Ventures (London)
-	13	RUBBER BALL — Bobby Vee (London)
17	14	MANY TEARS AGO — Connie Francis (MGM)
7	15	IT'S NOW OR NEVER — Elvis Presley (RCA)
26	16	RUBBER BALL — Marty Wilde (Philips)
-	17	SAILOR — Anne Shelton (Philips)
16	18	LIKE STRANGERS — Everly Brothers (London)
15	19	DOLL HOUSE — King Brothers (Parlophone)
11	19	GOODNESS GRACIOUS ME — Peter Sellers & Sophia Loren (Parlophone)
12	21	SWAY — Bobby Rydell (Columbia)
27	22	NORTH TO ALASKA — Johnny Horton (Philips)
24	23	PILTDOWN RIDES AGAIN — Piltdown Men (Capitol)
20	23	LITTLE GIRL — Marty Wilde (Philips)
21	25	MAN OF MYSTERY — Shadows (Columbia)
24	26	PEPE — Russ Conway (Columbia)
-	27	NEW ORLEANS — U.S. Bonds (Top Rank)
-	28	SERENATA — Sarah Vaughan (Columbia)
29	29	CHARIOT — Rhet Stoller (Decca)
21	30	BANGERS AND MASH — Peter Sellers & Sophia Loren (Parlophone)

Elvis Presley's *Are You Lonesome Tonight* just failed to emulate *It's Now Or Never*'s entry at Number One, debuting at Two behind a very strongly selling Johnny Tillotson. It still proved to be one of Presley's biggest-ever UK sellers, with sales of over 800,000 by the end of its chart run. Peter Sellers and Sophia Loren teamed up again for *Bangers And Mash*, originally intended as the B-side of *Goodness Gracious Me*, but thought strong enough to sell on its own. It did, but only fleetingly.

last week	this week	4 February 1961
1	1	ARE YOU LONESOME TONIGHT? Elvis Presley (RCA)
6	2	SAILOR Petula Clark (Pye)
2	3	POETRY IN MOTION Johnny Tillotson (London)
4	4	PEPE Duane Eddy (London)
3	5	PORTRAIT OF MY LOVE Matt Monro (Parlophone)
11	6	YOU'RE SIXTEEN Johnny Burnette (London)
5	7	I LOVE YOU Cliff Richard (Columbia)
13	8	RUBBER BALL Bobby Vee (London)
16	9	RUBBER BALL Marty Wilde (Philips)
7	10	COUNTING TEADROPS Emile Ford (Pye)
17	10	SAILOR Anne Shelton (Philips)
8	12	BUONA SERA Mr Acker Bilk (Columbia)
15	13	IT'S NOW OR NEVER Elvis Presley (RCA)
14	14	MANY TEARS AGO Connie Francis (MGM)
10	15	STAY Maurice Williams & the Zodiacs (Top Rank)
23	16	PILTDOWN RIDES AGAIN Piltdown Men (Capitol)
11	17	PERFIDIA Ventures (London)
21	18	SWAY Bobby Rydell (Columbia)
9	19	SAVE THE LAST DANCE FOR ME Drifters (London)
26	20	PEPE Russ Conway (Columbia)
18	21	LIKE STRANGERS Everly Brothers (London)
19	22	DOLL HOUSE King Brothers (Parlophone)
-	23	A THOUSAND STARS Billy Fury (Decca)
23	24	LITTLE GIRL Marty Wilde (Philips)
-	25	A SCOTTISH SOLDIER Andy Stewart (Top Rank)
27	26	NEW ORLEANS U.S. Bonds (Top Rank)
29	27	CHARIOT Rhet Stoller (Decca)
-	28	C'EST SI BON Conway Twitty (MGM)
-	29	WHAT TO DO Buddy Holly (Coral)
-	30	FIRST TASTE OF LOVE Ben E. King (London)

		11 February 1961
1	1	ARE YOU LONESOME TONIGHT? Elvis Presley (RCA)
2	2	SAILOR Petula Clark (Pye)
8	3	RUBBER BALL Bobby Vee (London)
6	4	YOU'RE SIXTEEN Johnny Burnette (London)
4	5	PEPE Duane Eddy (London)
3	6	POETRY IN MOTION Johnny Tillotson (London)
9	7	RUBBER BALL Marty Wilde (Philips)
10	8	SAILOR Anne Shelton (Philips)
5	9	PORTRAIT OF MY LOVE Matt Monro (Parlophone)
-	10	F.B.I. Shadows (Columbia)
12	11	BUONA SERA Mr Acker Bilk (Columbia)
-	12	WALK RIGHT BACK Everly Brothers (Warner Bros)
14	13	MANY TEARS AGO Connie Francis (MGM)
-	14	WHO AM I? Adam Faith (Parlophone)
7	15	I LOVE YOU Cliff Richard (Columbia)
-	16	CALENDAR GIRL Neil Sedaka (RCA)
15	17	STAY Maurice Williams & the Zodiacs (Top Rank)
20	18	PEPE Russ Conway (Columbia)
10	18	COUNTING TEADROPS Emile Ford (Pye)
26	20	NEW ORLEANS U.S. Bonds (Top Rank)
18	21	SWAY Bobby Rydell (Columbia)
-	22	WILL YOU LOVE ME TOMORROW? Shirelles (Top Rank)
16	23	PILTDOWN RIDES AGAIN Piltdown Men (Capitol)
13	24	IT'S NOW OR NEVER Elvis Presley (RCA)
25	24	A SCOTTISH SOLDIER Andy Stewart (Top Rank)
-	26	LET'S JUMP THE BROOMSTICK Brenda Lee (Brunswick)
28	27	C'EST SI BON Conway Twitty (MGM)
23	28	A THOUSAND STARS Billy Fury (Decca)
-	29	EBONY EYES Everly Brothers (Warner Bros)
17	29	PERFIDIA Ventures (London)
-	29	GINCHY Bert Weedon (Top Rank)

		18 February 1961
1	1	ARE YOU LONESOME TONIGHT? Elvis Presley (RCA)
2	2	SAILOR Petula Clark (Pye)
3	3	RUBBER BALL Bobby Vee (London)
4	4	YOU'RE SIXTEEN Johnny Burnette (London)
10	4	F.B.I. Shadows (Columbia)
12	6	WALK RIGHT BACK Everly Brothers (Warner Bros)
5	7	PEPE Duane Eddy (London)
14	8	WHO AM I? Adam Faith (Parlophone)
9	9	PORTRAIT OF MY LOVE Matt Monro (Parlophone)
22	10	WILL YOU LOVE ME TOMORROW? Shirelles (Top Rank)
8	11	SAILOR Anne Shelton (Philips)
7	12	RUBBER BALL Marty Wilde (Philips)
16	13	CALENDAR GIRL Neil Sedaka (RCA)
6	13	POETRY IN MOTION Johnny Tillotson (London)
11	15	BUONA SERA Mr Acker Bilk (Columbia)
12	16	MANY TEARS AGO Connie Francis (MGM)
15	17	I LOVE YOU Cliff Richard (Columbia)
18	18	COUNTING TEADROPS Emile Ford (Pye)
29	19	EBONY EYES Everly Brothers (Warner Bros)
20	20	NEW ORLEANS U.S. Bonds (Top Rank)
24	21	A SCOTTISH SOLDIER Andy Stewart (Top Rank)
26	22	LET'S JUMP THE BROOMSTICK Brenda Lee (Brunswick)
-	23	THIS IS IT Adam Faith (Parlophone)
18	24	PEPE Russ Conway (Columbia)
23	25	PILTDOWN RIDES AGAIN Piltdown Men (Capitol)
28	26	A THOUSAND STARS Billy Fury (Decca)
-	27	MYSTERY GIRL Jess Conrad (Decca)
21	27	SWAY Bobby Rydell (Columbia)
17	29	STAY Maurice Williams & the Zodiacs (Top Rank)
27	30	C'EST SI BON Conway Twitty (MGM)

		25 February 1961
1	1	ARE YOU LONESOME TONIGHT? Elvis Presley (RCA)
2	2	SAILOR Petula Clark (Pye)
6	3	WALK RIGHT BACK Everly Brothers (Warner Bros)
4	4	F.B.I. Shadows (Columbia)
3	5	RUBBER BALL Bobby Vee (London)
10	6	WILL YOU LOVE ME TOMORROW? Shirelles (Top Rank)
8	7	WHO AM I? Adam Faith (Parlophone)
4	8	YOU'RE SIXTEEN Johnny Burnette (London)
13	9	CALENDAR GIRL Neil Sedaka (RCA)
7	10	PEPE Duane Eddy (London)
9	11	PORTRAIT OF MY LOVE Matt Monro (Parlophone)
-	12	RIDERS IN THE SKY Ramrods (London)
15	13	BUONA SERA Mr Acker Bilk (Columbia)
-	14	ARE YOU SURE Allisons (Fontana)
22	15	LET'S JUMP THE BROOMSTICK Brenda Lee (Brunswick)
11	15	SAILOR Anne Shelton (Philips)
19	17	EBONY EYES Everly Brothers (Warner Bros)
-	18	GATHER IN THE MUSHROOMS Benny Hill (Pye)
13	19	POETRY IN MOTION Johnny Tillotson (London)
27	20	MYSTERY GIRL Jess Conrad (Decca)
20	20	NEW ORLEANS U.S. Bonds (Top Rank)
12	21	RUBBER BALL Marty Wilde (Philips)
25	23	PILTDOWN RIDES AGAIN Piltdown Men (Capitol)
-	24	WHEELS String-A-Longs (London)
24	25	PEPE Russ Conway (Columbia)
-	26	JA-DA Johnny & the Hurricanes (London)
18	27	COUNTING TEADROPS Emile Ford (Pye)
21	28	A SCOTTISH SOLDIER Andy Stewart (Top Rank)
16	29	MANY TEARS AGO Connie Francis (MGM)
17	30	I LOVE YOU Cliff Richard (Columbia)

After being absent from the chart for almost thre years, Petula Clarke made a spectacular comeback with *Sailor*, a cover of the German-language hit *Seeman* by Lolita (who also had the US hit version in an English translation). Only the huge sales of Elvis' single prevented Pet from having a lengthy Number One run, and she clung doggedly to Number Two for five weeks. Even so, there were still enough buyers left over for Anne Shelton's version of the song, which climbed to Number Eight.

March 1961

4 March 1961

last week	this week		
3	1	WALK RIGHT BACK	Everly Brothers (Warner Bros)
2	2	SAILOR	Petula Clark (Pye)
6	3	WILL YOU LOVE ME TOMORROW?	Shirelles (Top Rank)
14	4	ARE YOU SURE	Allisons (Fontana)
1	5	ARE YOU LONESOME TONIGHT?	Elvis Presley (RCA)
4	6	F.B.I.	Shadows (Columbia)
7	7	WHO AM I?	Adam Faith (Parlophone)
9	8	CALENDAR GIRL	Neil Sedaka (RCA)
12	9	RIDERS IN THE SKY	Ramrods (London)
5	10	RUBBER BALL	Bobby Vee (London)
-	11	THEME FOR A DREAM	Cliff Richard (Columbia)
8	12	YOU'RE SIXTEEN	Johnny Burnette (London)
26	13	JA-DA	Johnny & the Hurricanes (London)
15	14	LET'S JUMP THE BROOMSTICK	Brenda Lee (Brunswick)
24	14	WHEELS	String-A-Longs (London)
10	16	PEPE	Duane Eddy (London)
21	17	NEW ORLEANS	U.S. Bonds (Top Rank)
-	18	SAMANTHA	Kenny Ball & His Jazzmen (Pye Jazz)
20	18	MYSTERY GIRL	Jess Conrad (Decca)
11	20	PORTRAIT OF MY LOVE	Matt Monro (Parlophone)
13	21	BUONA SERA	Mr Acker Bilk (Columbia)
15	22	SAILOR	Anne Shelton (Philips)
18	23	GATHER IN THE MUSHROOMS	Benny Hill (Pye)
17	24	EBONY EYES	Everly Brothers (Warner Bros)
-	25	BABY SITTIN' BOOGIE	Buzz Clifford (Fontana)
-	26	AFRICAN WALTZ	Johnny Dankworth (Columbia)
21	27	RUBBER BALL	Marty Wilde (Philips)
25	28	PEPE	Russ Conway (Columbia)
-	29	DREAM GIRL	Mark Wynter (Decca)
28	30	A SCOTTISH SOLDIER	Andy Stewart (Top Rank)

11 March 1961

1	1	WALK RIGHT BACK	Everly Brothers (Warner Bros)
4	2	ARE YOU SURE	Allisons (Fontana)
11	3	THEME FOR A DREAM	Cliff Richard (Columbia)
3	4	WILL YOU LOVE ME TOMORROW?	Shirelles (Top Rank)
-	5	WOODEN HEART	Elvis Presley (RCA)
2	6	SAILOR	Petula Clark (Pye)
9	7	RIDERS IN THE SKY	Ramrods (London)
5	8	ARE YOU LONESOME TONIGHT?	Elvis Presley (RCA)
6	9	F.B.I.	Shadows (Columbia)
7	10	WHO AM I?	Adam Faith (Parlophone)
8	10	CALENDAR GIRL	Neil Sedaka (RCA)
18	12	SAMANTHA	Kenny Ball & His Jazzmen (Pye Jazz)
14	13	WHEELS	String-A-Longs (London)
-	14	MY KIND OF GIRL	Matt Monro (Parlophone)
14	15	LET'S JUMP THE BROOMSTICK	Brenda Lee (Brunswick)
13	16	JA-DA	Johnny & the Hurricanes (London)
10	17	RUBBER BALL	Bobby Vee (London)
23	18	GATHER IN THE MUSHROOMS	Benny Hill (Pye)
18	19	MYSTERY GIRL	Jess Conrad (Decca)
12	20	YOU'RE SIXTEEN	Johnny Burnette (London)
-	21	EXODUS	Ferrante & Teicher (London)
16	22	PEPE	Duane Eddy (London)
29	23	DREAM GIRL	Mark Wynter (Decca)
-	24	MARRY ME	Mike Preston (Decca)
25	25	BABY SITTIN' BOOGIE	Buzz Clifford (Fontana)
21	26	BUONA SERA	Mr Acker Bilk (Columbia)
17	27	NEW ORLEANS	U.S. Bonds (Top Rank)
26	27	AFRICAN WALTZ	Johnny Dankworth (Columbia)
-	29	WHAT AM I GONNA DO	Emile Ford (Pye)
-	29	EMOTIONS	Brenda Lee (Brunswick)
-	29	GOODNIGHT, MRS. FLINTSTONE	Piltdown Men (Capitol)

18 March 1961

1	1	WALK RIGHT BACK	Everly Brothers (Warner Bros)
3	2	THEME FOR A DREAM	Cliff Richard (Columbia)
5	3	WOODEN HEART	Elvis Presley (RCA)
2	4	ARE YOU SURE	Allisons (Fontana)
4	5	WILL YOU LOVE ME TOMORROW?	Shirelles (Top Rank)
14	6	MY KIND OF GIRL	Matt Monro (Parlophone)
21	7	EXODUS	Ferrante & Teicher (London)
9	8	F.B.I.	Shadows (Columbia)
6	9	SAILOR	Petula Clark (Pye)
7	10	RIDERS IN THE SKY	Ramrods (London)
10	11	WHO AM I?	Adam Faith (Parlophone)
8	12	ARE YOU LONESOME TONIGHT?	Elvis Presley (RCA)
10	13	CALENDAR GIRL	Neil Sedaka (RCA)
12	14	SAMANTHA	Kenny Ball & His Jazzmen (Pye Jazz)
-	15	AND THE HEAVENS CRIED	Anthony Newley (Decca)
13	16	WHEELS	String-A-Longs (London)
15	17	LET'S JUMP THE BROOMSTICK	Brenda Lee (Brunswick)
16	18	JA-DA	Johnny & the Hurricanes (London)
-	19	EXODUS	Semprini (HMV)
29	20	GOODNIGHT, MRS. FLINTSTONE	Piltdown Men (Capitol)
25	21	BABY SITTIN' BOOGIE	Buzz Clifford (Fontana)
-	22	LAZY RIVER	Bobby Darin (London)
23	23	DREAM GIRL	Mark Wynter (Decca)
18	24	GATHER IN THE MUSHROOMS	Benny Hill (Pye)
24	25	MARRY ME	Mike Preston (Decca)
27	26	AFRICAN WALTZ	Johnny Dankworth (Columbia)
20	27	YOU'RE SIXTEEN	Johnny Burnette (London)
19	28	MYSTERY GIRL	Jess Conrad (Decca)
17	29	RUBBER BALL	Bobby Vee (London)
22	30	PEPE	Duane Eddy (London)

25 March 1961

3	1	WOODEN HEART	Elvis Presley (RCA)
4	2	ARE YOU SURE	Allisons (Fontana)
1	3	WALK RIGHT BACK	Everly Brothers (Warner Bros)
2	4	THEME FOR A DREAM	Cliff Richard (Columbia)
6	5	MY KIND OF GIRL	Matt Monro (Parlophone)
5	6	WILL YOU LOVE ME TOMORROW?	Shirelles (Top Rank)
7	7	EXODUS	Ferrante & Teicher (London)
22	8	LAZY RIVER	Bobby Darin (London)
15	9	AND THE HEAVENS CRIED	Anthony Newley (Decca)
10	10	RIDERS IN THE SKY	Ramrods (London)
16	11	WHEELS	String-A-Longs (London)
8	12	F.B.I.	Shadows (Columbia)
13	13	CALENDAR GIRL	Neil Sedaka (RCA)
14	14	SAMANTHA	Kenny Ball & His Jazzmen (Pye Jazz)
20	15	GOODNIGHT, MRS. FLINTSTONE	Piltdown Men (Capitol)
11	16	WHO AM I?	Adam Faith (Parlophone)
9	17	SAILOR	Petula Clark (Pye)
25	18	MARRY ME	Mike Preston (Decca)
19	19	EXODUS	Semprini (HMV)
12	20	ARE YOU LONESOME TONIGHT?	Elvis Presley (RCA)
17	21	LET'S JUMP THE BROOMSTICK	Brenda Lee (Brunswick)
-	22	SEVENTY-SIX TROMBONES	King Brothers (Parlophone)
18	23	JA-DA	Johnny & the Hurricanes (London)
21	24	BABY SITTIN' BOOGIE	Buzz Clifford (Fontana)
-	24	WHERE THE BOYS ARE	Connie Francis (MGM)
23	26	DREAM GIRL	Mark Wynter (Decca)
26	27	AFRICAN WALTZ	Johnny Dankworth (Columbia)
24	28	GATHER IN THE MUSHROOMS	Benny Hill (Pye)
-	29	'TIL THERE WAS YOU	Peggy Lee (Capitol)
-	30	WARPAINT	Brook Brothers (Pye)

As the Everly Brothers hit the top with *Walk Right Back* (the B-side *Ebony Eyes* also getting enough sales to make the Top 20), they faced an immediate challenge from a similar UK duo. The Bob and John Allison's *Are You Sure* was the winner of the 1961 Song For Europe competition, and eventually became runner-up in the Eurovision Song Contest itself. However, it was Elvis, whom the Everlys had dethroned from Number One, who actually replaced them, with the *G.I. Blues* song *Wooden Heart*.

last week	this week	1 April 1961
1	1	WOODEN HEART — Elvis Presley (RCA)
2	2	ARE YOU SURE — Allisons (Fontana)
4	3	THEME FOR A DREAM — Cliff Richard (Columbia)
3	4	WALK RIGHT BACK — Everly Brothers (Warner Bros)
5	5	MY KIND OF GIRL — Matt Monro (Parlophone)
7	6	EXODUS — Ferrante & Teicher (London)
8	7	LAZY RIVER — Bobby Darin (London)
6	8	WILL YOU LOVE ME TOMORROW? — Shirelles (Top Rank)
9	9	AND THE HEAVENS CRIED — Anthony Newley (Decca)
12	10	F.B.I. — Shadows (Columbia)
14	11	SAMANTHA — Kenny Ball & His Jazzmen (Pye Jazz)
24	12	WHERE THE BOYS ARE — Connie Francis (MGM)
10	13	RIDERS IN THE SKY — Ramrods (London)
11	14	WHEELS — String-A-Longs (London)
13	15	CALENDAR GIRL — Neil Sedaka (RCA)
24	16	BABY SITTIN' BOOGIE — Buzz Clifford (Fontana)
16	17	MARRY ME — Mike Preston (Decca)
-	18	YOU'RE DRIVING ME CRAZY — Temperance Seven (Parlophone)
19	19	WHO AM I? — Adam Faith (Parlophone)
27	20	AFRICAN WALTZ — Johnny Dankworth (Columbia)
30	21	WARPAINT — Brook Brothers (Pye)
-	21	DON'T TREAT ME LIKE A CHILD — Helen Shapiro (Columbia)
15	23	GOODNIGHT, MRS. FLINTSTONE — Piltdown Men (Capitol)
23	24	JA-DA — Johnny & the Hurricanes (London)
18	25	EXODUS — Semprini (HMV)
22	26	SEVENTY-SIX TROMBONES — King Brothers (Parlophone)
20	26	ARE YOU LONESOME TONIGHT? — Elvis Presley (RCA)
17	28	SAILOR — Petula Clark (Pye)
21	29	LET'S JUMP THE BROOMSTICK — Brenda Lee (Brunswick)
29	30	'TIL THERE WAS YOU — Peggy Lee (Capitol)

last	this	8 April 1961
2	1	ARE YOU SURE — Allisons (Fontana)
1	2	WOODEN HEART — Elvis Presley (RCA)
3	3	THEME FOR A DREAM — Cliff Richard (Columbia)
4	4	WALK RIGHT BACK — Everly Brothers (Warner Bros)
7	5	LAZY RIVER — Bobby Darin (London)
5	6	MY KIND OF GIRL — Matt Monro (Parlophone)
6	7	EXODUS — Ferrante & Teicher (London)
9	8	AND THE HEAVENS CRIED — Anthony Newley (Decca)
8	9	WILL YOU LOVE ME TOMORROW? — Shirelles (Top Rank)
12	10	WHERE THE BOYS ARE — Connie Francis (MGM)
11	11	F.B.I. — Shadows (Columbia)
11	12	SAMANTHA — Kenny Ball & His Jazzmen (Pye Jazz)
18	13	YOU'RE DRIVING ME CRAZY — Temperance Seven (Parlophone)
16	14	BABY SITTIN' BOOGIE — Buzz Clifford (Fontana)
13	15	RIDERS IN THE SKY — Ramrods (London)
14	16	WHEELS — String-A-Longs (London)
19	17	WHO AM I? — Adam Faith (Parlophone)
20	18	AFRICAN WALTZ — Johnny Dankworth (Columbia)
-	19	GEE WHIZ IT'S YOU — Cliff Richard (Columbia)
21	20	WARPAINT — Brook Brothers (Pye)
26	21	SEVENTY-SIX TROMBONES — King Brothers (Parlophone)
16	22	MARRY ME — Mike Preston (Decca)
21	23	DON'T TREAT ME LIKE A CHILD — Helen Shapiro (Columbia)
15	24	CALENDAR GIRL — Neil Sedaka (RCA)
23	25	GOODNIGHT, MRS. FLINTSTONE — Piltdown Men (Capitol)
-	26	BLUE MOON — Marcels (Pye International)
26	27	ARE YOU LONESOME TONIGHT? — Elvis Presley (RCA)
-	28	GOOD TIME BABY — Bobby Rydell (Columbia)
24	29	JA-DA — Johnny & the Hurricanes (London)
28	30	SAILOR — Petula Clark (Pye)

last	this	15 April 1961
2	1	WOODEN HEART — Elvis Presley (RCA)
1	2	ARE YOU SURE — Allisons (Fontana)
4	3	WALK RIGHT BACK — Everly Brothers (Warner Bros)
5	4	LAZY RIVER — Bobby Darin (London)
3	5	THEME FOR A DREAM — Cliff Richard (Columbia)
13	6	YOU'RE DRIVING ME CRAZY — Temperance Seven (Parlophone)
7	7	EXODUS — Ferrante & Teicher (London)
8	8	AND THE HEAVENS CRIED — Anthony Newley (Decca)
10	9	WHERE THE BOYS ARE — Connie Francis (MGM)
11	10	F.B.I. — Shadows (Columbia)
6	11	MY KIND OF GIRL — Matt Monro (Parlophone)
9	12	WILL YOU LOVE ME TOMORROW? — Shirelles (Top Rank)
12	13	SAMANTHA — Kenny Ball & His Jazzmen (Pye Jazz)
26	14	BLUE MOON — Marcels (Pye International)
14	15	BABY SITTIN' BOOGIE — Buzz Clifford (Fontana)
20	16	WARPAINT — Brook Brothers (Pye)
17	17	WHO AM I? — Adam Faith (Parlophone)
18	18	AFRICAN WALTZ — Johnny Dankworth (Columbia)
19	19	GEE WHIZ IT'S YOU — Cliff Richard (Columbia)
23	19	DON'T TREAT ME LIKE A CHILD — Helen Shapiro (Columbia)
16	21	WHEELS — String-A-Longs (London)
-	22	THE MUSKRAT RUMBLE — Freddy Cannon (Top Rank)
-	23	(I WANNA) LOVE MY LIFE AWAY — Gene Pitney (London)
15	24	RIDERS IN THE SKY — Ramrods (London)
25	25	SEVENTY-SIX TROMBONES — King Brothers (Parlophone)
22	25	MARRY ME — Mike Preston (Decca)
28	27	GOOD TIME BABY — Bobby Rydell (Columbia)
29	28	JA-DA — Johnny & the Hurricanes (London)
-	29	LITTLE BOY SAD — Johnny Burnette (London)
-	30	A HUNDRED POUNDS OF CLAY — Craig Douglas (Top Rank)

last	this	22 April 1961
2	1	ARE YOU SURE — Allisons (Fontana)
1	2	WOODEN HEART — Elvis Presley (RCA)
4	3	LAZY RIVER — Bobby Darin (London)
6	4	YOU'RE DRIVING ME CRAZY — Temperance Seven (Parlophone)
14	5	BLUE MOON — Marcels (Pye International)
7	6	EXODUS — Ferrante & Teicher (London)
3	7	WALK RIGHT BACK — Everly Brothers (Warner Bros)
9	8	WHERE THE BOYS ARE — Connie Francis (MGM)
5	9	THEME FOR A DREAM — Cliff Richard (Columbia)
19	10	GEE WHIZ IT'S YOU — Cliff Richard (Columbia)
16	11	WARPAINT — Brook Brothers (Pye)
10	12	F.B.I. — Shadows (Columbia)
8	13	AND THE HEAVENS CRIED — Anthony Newley (Decca)
13	14	SAMANTHA — Kenny Ball & His Jazzmen (Pye Jazz)
12	15	WILL YOU LOVE ME TOMORROW? — Shirelles (Top Rank)
11	16	MY KIND OF GIRL — Matt Monro (Parlophone)
18	17	AFRICAN WALTZ — Johnny Dankworth (Columbia)
30	18	A HUNDRED POUNDS OF CLAY — Craig Douglas (Top Rank)
19	18	DON'T TREAT ME LIKE A CHILD — Helen Shapiro (Columbia)
29	20	LITTLE BOY SAD — Johnny Burnette (London)
22	21	THE MUSKRAT RUMBLE — Freddy Cannon (Top Rank)
15	22	BABY SITTIN' BOOGIE — Buzz Clifford (Fontana)
-	23	THEME FROM DIXIE — Duane Eddy (London)
-	24	HOW WONDERFUL TO KNOW — Pearl Carr & Teddy Johnson (Columbia)
23	25	(I WANNA) LOVE MY LIFE AWAY — Gene Pitney (London)
17	26	WHO AM I? — Adam Faith (Parlophone)
21	27	WHEELS — String-A-Longs (London)
25	28	SEVENTY-SIX TROMBONES — King Brothers (Parlophone)
27	29	GOOD TIME BABY — Bobby Rydell (Columbia)
24	30	RIDERS IN THE SKY — Ramrods (London)

In a game of nip-and-tuck, the Allisons and Elvis Presley shared the top slot through April. Interestingly, the Presley song had not been a single in the US, but it was a Number One hit all over Europe, with British sales reaching three quarters of a million. Notable chart debuts included Gene Pitney and 14-year-old Helen Shapiro, while Craig Douglas' *A Hundred Pounds Of Clay* had to be re-recorded to be sure of airplay, after the BBC had objected to religious references in the original lyric.

April – May 1961

29 April 1961

last week	this week	Title	Artist (Label)
4	1	YOU'RE DRIVING ME CRAZY	Temperance Seven (Parlophone)
2	2	WOODEN HEART	Elvis Presley (RCA)
5	3	BLUE MOON	Marcels (Pye International)
3	4	LAZY RIVER	Bobby Darin (London)
1	5	ARE YOU SURE	Allisons (Fontana)
10	6	GEE WHIZ IT'S YOU	Cliff Richard (Columbia)
6	7	EXODUS	Ferrante & Teicher (London)
18	8	A HUNDRED POUNDS OF CLAY	Craig Douglas (Top Rank)
23	9	THEME FROM DIXIE	Duane Eddy (London)
18	10	DON'T TREAT ME LIKE A CHILD	Helen Shapiro (Columbia)
8	11	WHERE THE BOYS ARE	Connie Francis (MGM)
17	12	AFRICAN WALTZ	Johnny Dankworth (Columbia)
9	13	THEME FOR A DREAM	Cliff Richard (Columbia)
11	14	WARPAINT	Brook Brothers (Pye)
7	15	WALK RIGHT BACK	Everly Brothers (Warner Bros)
-	16	ON THE REBOUND	Floyd Cramer (RCA)
20	17	LITTLE BOY SAD	Johnny Burnette (London)
24	18	HOW WONDERFUL TO KNOW	Pearl Carr & Teddy Johnson (Columbia)
14	19	SAMANTHA	Kenny Ball & His Jazzmen (Pye Jazz)
13	20	AND THE HEAVENS CRIED	Anthony Newley (Decca)
12	21	F.B.I.	Shadows (Columbia)
-	22	EASY GOING ME	Adam Faith (Parlophone)
22	23	BABY SITTIN' BOOGIE	Buzz Clifford (Fontana)
15	24	WILL YOU LOVE ME TOMORROW?	Shirelles (Top Rank)
16	25	MY KIND OF GIRL	Matt Monro (Parlophone)
-	25	RUNAWAY	Del Shannon (London)
28	27	SEVENTY-SIX TROMBONES	King Brothers (Parlophone)
-	27	CORONATION STREET	Geoff Love (Columbia)
21	29	THE MUSKRAT RUMBLE	Freddy Cannon (Top Rank)
-	30	MORE THAN I CAN SAY	Bobby Vee (London)

6 May 1961

last week	this week	Title	Artist (Label)
3	1	BLUE MOON	Marcels (Pye International)
1	2	YOU'RE DRIVING ME CRAZY	Temperance Seven (Parlophone)
2	3	WOODEN HEART	Elvis Presley (RCA)
4	4	LAZY RIVER	Bobby Darin (London)
9	5	THEME FROM DIXIE	Duane Eddy (London)
16	6	ON THE REBOUND	Floyd Cramer (RCA)
8	7	A HUNDRED POUNDS OF CLAY	Craig Douglas (Top Rank)
10	8	DON'T TREAT ME LIKE A CHILD	Helen Shapiro (Columbia)
7	9	EXODUS	Ferrante & Teicher (London)
6	9	GEE WHIZ IT'S YOU	Cliff Richard (Columbia)
12	11	AFRICAN WALTZ	Johnny Dankworth (Columbia)
5	12	ARE YOU SURE	Allisons (Fontana)
14	13	WARPAINT	Brook Brothers (Pye)
30	13	MORE THAN I CAN SAY	Bobby Vee (London)
17	15	LITTLE BOY SAD	Johnny Burnette (London)
22	16	EASY GOING ME	Adam Faith (Parlophone)
11	17	WHERE THE BOYS ARE	Connie Francis (MGM)
25	18	RUNAWAY	Del Shannon (London)
18	19	HOW WONDERFUL TO KNOW	Pearl Carr & Teddy Johnson (Columbia)
19	20	SAMANTHA	Kenny Ball & His Jazzmen (Pye Jazz)
-	21	WHAT'D I SAY	Jerry Lee Lewis (London)
-	22	MOTHER-IN-LAW	Ernie K-Doe (London)
-	23	BUT I DO	Clarence 'Frogman' Henry (Pye International)
21	24	F.B.I.	Shadows (Columbia)
13	25	THEME FOR A DREAM	Cliff Richard (Columbia)
15	26	WALK RIGHT BACK	Everly Brothers (Warner Bros)
23	27	BABY SITTIN' BOOGIE	Buzz Clifford (Fontana)
-	28	MY BLUE HEAVEN	Frank Sinatra (Capitol)
-	29	THE MAGNIFICENT SEVEN	Al Caiola (HMV)
27	29	CORONATION STREET	Geoff Love (Columbia)

13 May 1961

last week	this week	Title	Artist (Label)
1	1	BLUE MOON	Marcels (Pye International)
2	2	YOU'RE DRIVING ME CRAZY	Temperance Seven (Parlophone)
6	3	ON THE REBOUND	Floyd Cramer (RCA)
18	4	RUNAWAY	Del Shannon (London)
8	5	DON'T TREAT ME LIKE A CHILD	Helen Shapiro (Columbia)
13	6	MORE THAN I CAN SAY	Bobby Vee (London)
5	7	THEME FROM DIXIE	Duane Eddy (London)
3	8	WOODEN HEART	Elvis Presley (RCA)
-	9	THE FRIGHTENED CITY	Shadows (Columbia)
11	10	AFRICAN WALTZ	Johnny Dankworth (Columbia)
16	11	EASY GOING ME	Adam Faith (Parlophone)
21	12	WHAT'D I SAY	Jerry Lee Lewis (London)
9	12	GEE WHIZ IT'S YOU	Cliff Richard (Columbia)
7	14	A HUNDRED POUNDS OF CLAY	Craig Douglas (Top Rank)
13	15	WARPAINT	Brook Brothers (Pye)
9	15	EXODUS	Ferrante & Teicher (London)
4	17	LAZY RIVER	Bobby Darin (London)
-	18	I STILL LOVE YOU ALL	Kenny Ball & His Jazzmen (Pye Jazz)
15	19	LITTLE BOY SAD	Johnny Burnette (London)
12	20	ARE YOU SURE	Allisons (Fontana)
23	21	BUT I DO	Clarence 'Frogman' Henry (Pye International)
19	22	HOW WONDERFUL TO KNOW	Pearl Carr & Teddy Johnson (Columbia)
-	23	HAVE A DRINK ON ME	Lonnie Donegan (Pye)
22	24	MOTHER-IN-LAW	Ernie K-Doe (London)
20	25	SAMANTHA	Kenny Ball & His Jazzmen (Pye Jazz)
17	26	WHERE THE BOYS ARE	Connie Francis (MGM)
-	27	YOU'LL NEVER KNOW	Shirley Bassey (Columbia)
-	28	WORDS	Allisons (Fontana)
-	29	THE MAGNIFICENT SEVEN	John Barry Seven (Columbia)
24	29	F.B.I.	Shadows (Columbia)
28	29	MY BLUE HEAVEN	Frank Sinatra (Capitol)

20 May 1961

last week	this week	Title	Artist (Label)
4	1	RUNAWAY	Del Shannon (London)
1	2	BLUE MOON	Marcels (Pye International)
2	3	YOU'RE DRIVING ME CRAZY	Temperance Seven (Parlophone)
6	4	MORE THAN I CAN SAY	Bobby Vee (London)
3	5	ON THE REBOUND	Floyd Cramer (RCA)
9	6	THE FRIGHTENED CITY	Shadows (Columbia)
5	7	DON'T TREAT ME LIKE A CHILD	Helen Shapiro (Columbia)
8	8	WOODEN HEART	Elvis Presley (RCA)
27	9	YOU'LL NEVER KNOW	Shirley Bassey (Columbia)
12	10	WHAT'D I SAY	Jerry Lee Lewis (London)
7	11	THEME FROM DIXIE	Duane Eddy (London)
11	12	EASY GOING ME	Adam Faith (Parlophone)
21	13	BUT I DO	Clarence 'Frogman' Henry (Pye International)
10	14	AFRICAN WALTZ	Johnny Dankworth (Columbia)
15	15	WARPAINT	Brook Brothers (Pye)
19	16	LITTLE BOY SAD	Johnny Burnette (London)
23	16	HAVE A DRINK ON ME	Lonnie Donegan (Pye)
14	16	A HUNDRED POUNDS OF CLAY	Craig Douglas (Top Rank)
12	19	GEE WHIZ IT'S YOU	Cliff Richard (Columbia)
18	20	I STILL LOVE YOU ALL	Kenny Ball & His Jazzmen (Pye Jazz)
15	20	EXODUS	Ferrante & Teicher (London)
22	22	HOW WONDERFUL TO KNOW	Pearl Carr & Teddy Johnson (Columbia)
-	22	LITTLE DEVIL	Neil Sedaka (RCA)
17	24	LAZY RIVER	Bobby Darin (London)
28	25	WORDS	Allisons (Fontana)
29	26	MY BLUE HEAVEN	Frank Sinatra (Capitol)
-	27	HALFWAY TO PARADISE	Billy Fury (Decca)
-	28	SPURS SONG	Totnamites (Oriole)
20	29	ARE YOU SURE	Allisons (Fontana)
-	30	I'VE TOLD EVERY LITTLE STAR	Linda Scott (Columbia)

The Marcels' crazed doo-wop reading of *Blue Moon*, dominated by *"bom-ba-ba-bom"*'s from the group's bass singer, found no favour at all with the song's composer Richard Rodgers, who heavily denounced what he saw as an insulting treatment. This did not stop the single from topping both the US and British charts. Whether Rodgers refused to accept the royalties is not on record! Most significant chart debut this month came from Del Shannon, whose self-penned *Runaway* was 1961's top seller.

27 May 1961

last week	this week	Title — Artist (Label)
–	1	SURRENDER — Elvis Presley (RCA)
1	2	RUNAWAY — Del Shannon (London)
5	3	ON THE REBOUND — Floyd Cramer (RCA)
6	4	THE FRIGHTENED CITY — Shadows (Columbia)
4	5	MORE THAN I CAN SAY — Bobby Vee (London)
9	6	YOU'LL NEVER KNOW — Shirley Bassey (Columbia)
2	7	BLUE MOON — Marcels (Pye International)
3	8	YOU'RE DRIVING ME CRAZY — Temperance Seven (Parlophone)
13	9	BUT I DO — Clarence 'Frogman' Henry (Pye International)
7	10	DON'T TREAT ME LIKE A CHILD — Helen Shapiro (Columbia)
10	11	WHAT'D I SAY — Jerry Lee Lewis (London)
12	12	EASY GOING ME — Adam Faith (Parlophone)
16	13	HAVE A DRINK ON ME — Lonnie Donegan (Pye)
22	14	LITTLE DEVIL — Neil Sedaka (RCA)
11	15	THEME FROM DIXIE — Duane Eddy (London)
16	16	A HUNDRED POUNDS OF CLAY — Craig Douglas (Top Rank)
8	17	WOODEN HEART — Elvis Presley (RCA)
27	18	HALFWAY TO PARADISE — Billy Fury (Decca)
15	19	WARPAINT — Brook Brothers (Pye)
19	20	GEE WHIZ IT'S YOU — Cliff Richard (Columbia)
14	21	AFRICAN WALTZ — Johnny Dankworth (Columbia)
20	22	EXODUS — Ferrante & Teicher (London)
20	23	I STILL LOVE YOU ALL — Kenny Ball & His Jazzmen (Pye Jazz)
16	24	LITTLE BOY SAD — Johnny Burnette (London)
26	25	MY BLUE HEAVEN — Frank Sinatra (Capitol)
30	26	I'VE TOLD EVERY LITTLE STAR — Linda Scott (Columbia)
–	27	HELLO MARY LOU — Ricky Nelson (London)
–	28	WHY NOT NOW — Matt Monro (Parlophone)
28	29	SPURS SONG — Totnamites (Oriole)
22	30	HOW WONDERFUL TO KNOW — Pearl Carr & Teddy Johnson (Columbia)

3 June 1961

last week	this week	Title — Artist (Label)
1	1	SURRENDER — Elvis Presley (RCA)
2	2	RUNAWAY — Del Shannon (London)
4	3	THE FRIGHTENED CITY — Shadows (Columbia)
5	4	MORE THAN I CAN SAY — Bobby Vee (London)
3	5	ON THE REBOUND — Floyd Cramer (RCA)
6	6	YOU'LL NEVER KNOW — Shirley Bassey (Columbia)
9	7	BUT I DO — Clarence 'Frogman' Henry (Pye International)
7	8	BLUE MOON — Marcels (Pye International)
11	9	WHAT'D I SAY — Jerry Lee Lewis (London)
8	10	YOU'RE DRIVING ME CRAZY — Temperance Seven (Parlophone)
13	11	HAVE A DRINK ON ME — Lonnie Donegan (Pye)
14	12	LITTLE DEVIL — Neil Sedaka (RCA)
10	13	DON'T TREAT ME LIKE A CHILD — Helen Shapiro (Columbia)
12	14	EASY GOING ME — Adam Faith (Parlophone)
18	15	HALFWAY TO PARADISE — Billy Fury (Decca)
27	16	HELLO MARY LOU — Ricky Nelson (London)
23	17	I STILL LOVE YOU ALL — Kenny Ball & His Jazzmen (Pye Jazz)
17	18	WOODEN HEART — Elvis Presley (RCA)
26	19	I'VE TOLD EVERY LITTLE STAR — Linda Scott (Columbia)
15	20	THEME FROM DIXIE — Duane Eddy (London)
–	21	RUNNING SCARED — Roy Orbison (London)
19	22	WARPAINT — Brook Brothers (Pye)
22	23	EXODUS — Ferrante & Teicher (London)
21	24	AFRICAN WALTZ — Johnny Dankworth (Columbia)
24	25	LITTLE BOY SAD — Johnny Burnette (London)
28	26	WHY NOT NOW — Matt Monro (Parlophone)
–	27	WELL I ASK YOU — Eden Kane (Decca)
–	28	SHE SHE LITTLE SHEILA — Gene Vincent (Capitol)
16	29	A HUNDRED POUNDS OF CLAY — Craig Douglas (Top Rank)
20	30	GEE WHIZ IT'S YOU — Cliff Richard (Columbia)

10 June 1961

last week	this week	Title — Artist (Label)
1	1	SURRENDER — Elvis Presley (RCA)
2	2	RUNAWAY — Del Shannon (London)
3	3	THE FRIGHTENED CITY — Shadows (Columbia)
6	4	YOU'LL NEVER KNOW — Shirley Bassey (Columbia)
7	5	BUT I DO — Clarence 'Frogman' Henry (Pye International)
4	6	MORE THAN I CAN SAY — Bobby Vee (London)
5	7	ON THE REBOUND — Floyd Cramer (RCA)
11	8	HAVE A DRINK ON ME — Lonnie Donegan (Pye)
12	9	LITTLE DEVIL — Neil Sedaka (RCA)
9	10	WHAT'D I SAY — Jerry Lee Lewis (London)
16	11	HELLO MARY LOU — Ricky Nelson (London)
15	12	HALFWAY TO PARADISE — Billy Fury (Decca)
8	13	BLUE MOON — Marcels (Pye International)
10	14	YOU'RE DRIVING ME CRAZY — Temperance Seven (Parlophone)
13	15	DON'T TREAT ME LIKE A CHILD — Helen Shapiro (Columbia)
21	16	RUNNING SCARED — Roy Orbison (London)
19	17	I'VE TOLD EVERY LITTLE STAR — Linda Scott (Columbia)
27	18	WELL I ASK YOU — Eden Kane (Decca)
18	19	WOODEN HEART — Elvis Presley (RCA)
22	20	WARPAINT — Brook Brothers (Pye)
20	21	THEME FROM DIXIE — Duane Eddy (London)
17	22	I STILL LOVE YOU ALL — Kenny Ball & His Jazzmen (Pye Jazz)
–	23	TRAVELLIN' MAN — Ricky Nelson (London)
14	24	EASY GOING ME — Adam Faith (Parlophone)
23	25	EXODUS — Ferrante & Teicher (London)
24	26	AFRICAN WALTZ — Johnny Dankworth (Columbia)
–	27	HALF OF MY HEART — Emile Ford (Piccadilly)
28	28	SHE SHE LITTLE SHEILA — Gene Vincent (Capitol)
–	29	TRANSISTOR RADIO — Benny Hill (Pye)
–	30	CLIMB EV'RY MOUNTAIN — Tony Bennett (Philips)
26	30	WHY NOT NOW — Matt Monro (Parlophone)

17 June 1961

last week	this week	Title — Artist (Label)
1	1	SURRENDER — Elvis Presley (RCA)
2	2	RUNAWAY — Del Shannon (London)
5	3	BUT I DO — Clarence 'Frogman' Henry (Pye International)
3	4	THE FRIGHTENED CITY — Shadows (Columbia)
4	5	YOU'LL NEVER KNOW — Shirley Bassey (Columbia)
–	6	PASADENA — Temperance Seven (Parlophone)
8	7	HAVE A DRINK ON ME — Lonnie Donegan (Pye)
12	8	HALFWAY TO PARADISE — Billy Fury (Decca)
17	8	I'VE TOLD EVERY LITTLE STAR — Linda Scott (Columbia)
11	10	HELLO MARY LOU — Ricky Nelson (London)
–	11	TEMPTATION — Everly Brothers (Warner Bros)
9	12	LITTLE DEVIL — Neil Sedaka (RCA)
6	13	MORE THAN I CAN SAY — Bobby Vee (London)
–	14	POP GOES THE WEASEL — Anthony Newley (Decca)
10	15	WHAT'D I SAY — Jerry Lee Lewis (London)
16	16	RUNNING SCARED — Roy Orbison (London)
18	17	WELL I ASK YOU — Eden Kane (Decca)
15	18	DON'T TREAT ME LIKE A CHILD — Helen Shapiro (Columbia)
14	19	YOU'RE DRIVING ME CRAZY — Temperance Seven (Parlophone)
7	20	ON THE REBOUND — Floyd Cramer (RCA)
13	21	BLUE MOON — Marcels (Pye International)
23	22	TRAVELLIN' MAN — Ricky Nelson (London)
19	23	WOODEN HEART — Elvis Presley (RCA)
30	24	WHY NOT NOW — Matt Monro (Parlophone)
–	25	BREAKIN' IN A BRAND NEW BROKEN HEART — Connie Francis (MGM)
29	25	TRANSISTOR RADIO — Benny Hill (Pye)
–	27	MARCHETA — Karl Denver (Decca)
27	28	HALF OF MY HEART — Emile Ford (Piccadilly)
28	29	SHE SHE LITTLE SHEILA — Gene Vincent (Capitol)
–	30	BELLS OF AVIGNON — Max Bygraves (Decca)

Surrender, advance oders for which exceeded 400,000, was Elvis' second instant chart-topper in four releases. Like *It's Now Or Never*, the song was an adaptation with new lyrics of an Italian ballad, in this case, *Turna A Sorrento*. The Shadows' *The Frightened City* was their adaptation of the theme from a British gangster movie of the same title, while the Totnamites' *Spurs Song* (forerunner of all dreadful football hits) was a tribute to Tottenham Hotspur securing the 1961 League and Cup double.

June – July 1961

24 June 1961

2 1 RUNAWAY
Del Shannon (London)
1 2 SURRENDER
Elvis Presley (RCA)
11 3 TEMPTATION
Everly Brothers (Warner Bros)
3 4 BUT I DO
Clarence 'Frogman' Henry
(Pye International)
6 4 PASADENA
Temperance Seven (Parlophone)
10 6 HELLO MARY LOU
Ricky Nelson (London)
8 7 HALFWAY TO PARADISE
Billy Fury (Decca)
5 8 YOU'LL NEVER KNOW
Shirley Bassey (Columbia)
4 9 THE FRIGHTENED CITY
Shadows (Columbia)
- 10 A GIRL LIKE YOU
Cliff Richard (Columbia)
7 11 HAVE A DRINK ON ME
Lonnie Donegan (Pye)
14 12 POP GOES THE WEASEL
Anthony Newley (Decca)
16 12 RUNNING SCARED
Roy Orbison (London)
13 14 MORE THAN I CAN SAY
Bobby Vee (London)
8 15 I'VE TOLD EVERY LITTLE STAR
Linda Scott (Columbia)
17 16 WELL I ASK YOU
Eden Kane (Decca)
12 17 LITTLE DEVIL Neil Sedaka (RCA)
20 18 ON THE REBOUND
Floyd Cramer (RCA)
18 19 DON'T TREAT ME LIKE A CHILD
Helen Shapiro (Columbia)
22 20 TRAVELLIN' MAN
Ricky Nelson (London)
21 21 BLUE MOON
Marcels (Pye International)
25 22 BREAKIN' IN A BRAND NEW
BROKEN HEART
Connie Francis (MGM)
29 23 SHE SHE LITTLE SHEILA
Gene Vincent (Capitol)
28 24 HALF OF MY HEART
Emile Ford (Piccadilly)
15 25 WHAT'D I SAY
Jerry Lee Lewis (London)
- 26 WEEKEND
Eddie Cochran (London)
27 27 MARCHETA Karl Denver (Decca)
- 28 ONCE IN EVERY LIFETIME
Ken Dodd (Decca)
19 28 YOU'RE DRIVING ME CRAZY
Temperance Seven (Parlophone)
- 30 RING OF FIRE
Duane Eddy (London)
25 30 TRANSISTOR RADIO
Benny Hill (Pye)

1 July 1961

1 1 RUNAWAY
Del Shannon (London)
3 2 TEMPTATION
Everly Brothers (Warner Bros)
4 3 PASADENA
Temperance Seven (Parlophone)
10 4 A GIRL LIKE YOU
Cliff Richard (Columbia)
2 5 SURRENDER
Elvis Presley (RCA)
6 6 HELLO MARY LOU
Ricky Nelson (London)
4 7 BUT I DO
Clarence 'Frogman' Henry
(Pye International)
7 8 HALFWAY TO PARADISE
Billy Fury (Decca)
9 9 THE FRIGHTENED CITY
Shadows (Columbia)
12 10 RUNNING SCARED
Roy Orbison (London)
16 11 WELL I ASK YOU
Eden Kane (Decca)
8 12 YOU'LL NEVER KNOW
Shirley Bassey (Columbia)
12 13 POP GOES THE WEASEL
Anthony Newley (Decca)
11 14 HAVE A DRINK ON ME
Lonnie Donegan (Pye)
15 15 I'VE TOLD EVERY LITTLE STAR
Linda Scott (Columbia)
17 16 LITTLE DEVIL Neil Sedaka (RCA)
30 17 RING OF FIRE
Duane Eddy (London)
27 18 MARCHETA
Karl Denver (Decca)
14 19 MORE THAN I CAN SAY
Bobby Vee (London)
- 20 MOODY RIVER
Pat Boone (London)
21 TIME Craig Douglas (Top Rank)
25 22 WHAT'D I SAY
Jerry Lee Lewis (London)
- 23 EXCLUSIVELY YOURS
Mark Wynter (Decca)
22 24 BREAKIN' IN A BRAND NEW
BROKEN HEART
Connie Francis (MGM)
20 24 TRAVELLIN' MAN
Ricky Nelson (London)
24 26 HALF OF MY HEART
Emile Ford (Piccadilly)
23 27 SHE SHE LITTLE SHEILA
Gene Vincent (Capitol)
26 28 WEEKEND
Eddie Cochran (London)
- 28 BABY I DON'T CARE
Buddy Holly (Coral)
- 28 STAND BY ME
Ben E. King (London)
19 28 DON'T TREAT ME LIKE A CHILD
Helen Shapiro (Columbia)

8 July 1961

1 1 RUNAWAY
Del Shannon (London)
2 2 TEMPTATION
Everly Brothers (Warner Bros)
6 3 HELLO MARY LOU
Ricky Nelson (London)
4 4 A GIRL LIKE YOU
Cliff Richard (Columbia)
3 4 PASADENA
Temperance Seven (Parlophone)
8 6 HALFWAY TO PARADISE
Billy Fury (Decca)
5 7 SURRENDER
Elvis Presley (RCA)
7 8 BUT I DO
Clarence 'Frogman' Henry
(Pye International)
11 9 WELL I ASK YOU
Eden Kane (Decca)
10 10 RUNNING SCARED
Roy Orbison (London)
13 11 POP GOES THE WEASEL
Anthony Newley (Decca)
9 12 THE FRIGHTENED CITY
Shadows (Columbia)
12 13 YOU'LL NEVER KNOW
Shirley Bassey (Columbia)
21 14 TIME Craig Douglas (Top Rank)
15 15 I'VE TOLD EVERY LITTLE STAR
Linda Scott (Columbia)
24 16 BREAKIN' IN A BRAND NEW
BROKEN HEART
Connie Francis (MGM)
18 17 MARCHETA
Karl Denver (Decca)
14 18 HAVE A DRINK ON ME
Lonnie Donegan (Pye)
17 19 RING OF FIRE
Duane Eddy (London)
- 20 NATURE BOY
Bobby Darin (London)
28 21 WEEKEND
Eddie Cochran (London)
- 22 YOU DON'T KNOW
Helen Shapiro (Columbia)
16 23 LITTLE DEVIL
Neil Sedaka (RCA)
20 24 MOODY RIVER
Pat Boone (London)
19 24 MORE THAN I CAN SAY
Bobby Vee (London)
23 26 EXCLUSIVELY YOURS
Mark Wynter (Decca)
28 27 STAND BY ME
Ben E. King (London)
28 28 BABY I DON'T CARE
Buddy Holly (Coral)
- 29 THE BOLL WEEVIL SONG
Brook Benton (Mercury)
- 30 HIGH VOLTAGE
Johnny & the Hurricanes
(London)

15 July 1961

2 1 TEMPTATION
Everly Brothers (Warner Bros)
1 2 RUNAWAY
Del Shannon (London)
3 3 HELLO MARY LOU
Ricky Nelson (London)
9 4 WELL I ASK YOU
Eden Kane (Decca)
6 5 HALFWAY TO PARADISE
Billy Fury (Decca)
4 6 A GIRL LIKE YOU
Cliff Richard (Columbia)
4 7 PASADENA
Temperance Seven (Parlophone)
8 8 BUT I DO
Clarence 'Frogman' Henry
(Pye International)
10 9 RUNNING SCARED
Roy Orbison (London)
7 10 SURRENDER
Elvis Presley (RCA)
- 11 YOU ALWAYS HURT THE ONE
YOU LOVE
Clarence 'Frogman' Henry
(Pye International)
22 11 YOU DON'T KNOW
Helen Shapiro (Columbia)
11 13 POP GOES THE WEASEL
Anthony Newley (Decca)
14 14 TIME Craig Douglas (Top Rank)
24 15 MOODY RIVER
Pat Boone (London)
16 16 BREAKIN' IN A BRAND NEW
BROKEN HEART
Connie Francis (MGM)
12 17 THE FRIGHTENED CITY
Shadows (Columbia)
21 18 WEEKEND
Eddie Cochran (London)
- 19 ROMEO Petula Clark (Pye)
28 19 BABY I DON'T CARE
Buddy Holly (Coral)
19 21 RING OF FIRE
Duane Eddy (London)
13 22 YOU'LL NEVER KNOW
Shirley Bassey (Columbia)
20 23 NATURE BOY
Bobby Darin (London)
17 23 MARCHETA Karl Denver (Decca)
- 25 THAT'S MY HOME
Mr Acker Bilk (Columbia)
18 26 HAVE A DRINK ON ME
Lonnie Donegan (Pye)
27 27 STAND BY ME
Ben E. King (London)
29 28 THE BOLL WEEVIL SONG
Brook Benton (Mercury)
30 28 HIGH VOLTAGE
Johnny & the Hurricanes
(London)
15 30 I'VE TOLD EVERY LITTLE STAR
Linda Scott (Columbia)

Having been shouldered back to second place by *Surrender* for a month, Del Shannon proved the remarkable resilience of *Runaway* by re-securing the Number One slot for three more weeks once the Presley hit paused for breath. Ricky Nelson's *Hello Mary Lou*, his first UK top tenner for over two years, was written by Gene Pitney, who with only one minor hit of his own so far, was piling up the songwriting royalties, having also (under a pseudonym) penned the Bobby Vee/Marty Wilde smash *Rubber Ball*.

22 July 1961

last week	this week	Title / Artist (Label)
4	1	WELL I ASK YOU / Eden Kane (Decca)
1	2	TEMPTATION / Everly Brothers (Warner Bros)
2	3	RUNAWAY Del Shannon (London)
3	4	HELLO MARY LOU / Ricky Nelson (London)
6	5	A GIRL LIKE YOU / Cliff Richard (Columbia)
7	6	PASADENA / Temperance Seven (Parlophone)
5	7	HALFWAY TO PARADISE / Billy Fury (Decca)
11	8	YOU DON'T KNOW / Helen Shapiro (Columbia)
9	9	YOU ALWAYS HURT THE ONE YOU LOVE / Clarence 'Frogman' Henry (Pye International)
8	10	BUT I DO / Clarence 'Frogman' Henry (Pye International)
9	11	RUNNING SCARED / Roy Orbison (London)
19	12	ROMEO Petula Clark (Pye)
10	13	SURRENDER / Elvis Presley (RCA)
13	14	POP GOES THE WEASEL / Anthony Newley (Decca)
14	15	TIME Craig Douglas (Top Rank)
15	16	MOODY RIVER / Pat Boone (London)
18	16	WEEKEND / Eddie Cochran (London)
17	18	THE FRIGHTENED CITY / Shadows (Columbia)
21	19	RING OF FIRE / Duane Eddy (London)
-	20	QUARTER TO THREE / U.S. Bonds (Top Rank)
-	20	DUM DUM Brenda Lee (Brunswick)
19	22	BABY I DON'T CARE / Buddy Holly (Coral)
25	23	THAT'S MY HOME / Mr Acker Bilk (Columbia)
-	24	QUITE A PARTY / Fireballs (Pye International)
-	25	OLD SMOKIE Johnny & the Hurricanes (London)
16	26	BREAKIN' IN A BRAND NEW BROKEN HEART / Connie Francis (MGM)
22	27	YOU'LL NEVER KNOW / Shirley Bassey (Columbia)
30	28	I'VE TOLD EVERY LITTLE STAR / Linda Scott (Columbia)
-	29	DON'T YOU KNOW IT / Adam Faith (Parlophone)
28	30	THE BOLL WEEVIL SONG / Brook Benton (Mercury)
23	30	NATURE BOY / Bobby Darin (London)

29 July 1961

	Title / Artist (Label)
1	WELL I ASK YOU / Eden Kane (Decca)
2	TEMPTATION / Everly Brothers (Warner Bros)
8	YOU DON'T KNOW / Helen Shapiro (Columbia)
3	RUNAWAY / Del Shannon (London)
5	A GIRL LIKE YOU / Cliff Richard (Columbia)
9	YOU ALWAYS HURT THE ONE YOU LOVE / Clarence 'Frogman' Henry (Pye International)
4	HELLO MARY LOU / Ricky Nelson (London)
7	HALFWAY TO PARADISE / Billy Fury (Decca)
6	PASADENA / Temperance Seven (Parlophone)
12	ROMEO Petula Clark (Pye)
29	DON'T YOU KNOW IT / Adam Faith (Parlophone)
11	RUNNING SCARED / Roy Orbison (London)
10	BUT I DO / Clarence 'Frogman' Henry (Pye International)
16	MOODY RIVER / Pat Boone (London)
14	TIME Craig Douglas (Top Rank)
-	MARCHETA Karl Denver (Decca)
16	WEEKEND / Eddie Cochran (London)
22	BABY I DON'T CARE / Buddy Holly (Coral)
13	SURRENDER / Elvis Presley (RCA)
20	QUARTER TO THREE / U.S. Bonds (Top Rank)
-	CLIMB EV'RY MOUNTAIN / Shirley Bassey (Columbia)
26	BREAKIN' IN A BRAND NEW BROKEN HEART / Connie Francis (MGM)
23	THAT'S MY HOME / Mr Acker Bilk (Columbia)
24	QUITE A PARTY / Fireballs (Pye International)
20	DUM DUM / Brenda Lee (Brunswick)
18	THE FRIGHTENED CITY / Shadows (Columbia)
25	OLD SMOKIE / Johnny & the Hurricanes (London)
14	POP GOES THE WEASEL / Anthony Newley (Decca)
30	NATURE BOY / Bobby Darin (London)
30	THE BOLL WEEVIL SONG / Brook Benton (Mercury)

5 August 1961

	Title / Artist (Label)
3	YOU DON'T KNOW / Helen Shapiro (Columbia)
1	WELL I ASK YOU / Eden Kane (Decca)
2	TEMPTATION / Everly Brothers (Warner Bros)
9	PASADENA / Temperance Seven (Parlophone)
8	HALFWAY TO PARADISE / Billy Fury (Decca)
6	YOU ALWAYS HURT THE ONE YOU LOVE / Clarence 'Frogman' Henry (Pye International)
4	RUNAWAY / Del Shannon (London)
10	ROMEO Petula Clark (Pye)
11	DON'T YOU KNOW IT / Adam Faith (Parlophone)
5	A GIRL LIKE YOU / Cliff Richard (Columbia)
7	HELLO MARY LOU / Ricky Nelson (London)
-	JOHNNY REMEMBER ME / John Leyton (Top Rank)
14	TIME Craig Douglas (Top Rank)
20	QUARTER TO THREE / U.S. Bonds (Top Rank)
16	MARCHETA / Karl Denver (Decca)
13	BUT I DO / Clarence 'Frogman' Henry (Pye International)
18	BABY I DON'T CARE / Buddy Holly (Coral)
21	CLIMB EV'RY MOUNTAIN / Shirley Bassey (Columbia)
12	RUNNING SCARED / Roy Orbison (London)
-	REACH FOR THE STARS / Shirley Bassey (Columbia)
14	MOODY RIVER / Pat Boone (London)
23	THAT'S MY HOME / Mr Acker Bilk (Columbia)
18	SURRENDER / Elvis Presley (RCA)
17	WEEKEND / Eddie Cochran (London)
24	QUITE A PARTY / Fireballs (Pye International)
27	POP GOES THE WEASEL / Anthony Newley (Decca)
27	OLD SMOKIE / Johnny & the Hurricanes (London)
29	NATURE BOY / Bobby Darin (London)
25	DUM DUM / Brenda Lee (Brunswick)
26	THE FRIGHTENED CITY / Shadows (Columbia)

12 August 1961

	Title / Artist (Label)
1	YOU DON'T KNOW / Helen Shapiro (Columbia)
2	WELL I ASK YOU / Eden Kane (Decca)
12	JOHNNY REMEMBER ME / John Leyton (Top Rank)
3	TEMPTATION / Everly Brothers (Warner Bros)
8	ROMEO Petula Clark (Pye)
5	HALFWAY TO PARADISE / Billy Fury (Decca)
4	PASADENA / Temperance Seven (Parlophone)
6	YOU ALWAYS HURT THE ONE YOU LOVE / Clarence 'Frogman' Henry (Pye International)
9	DON'T YOU KNOW IT / Adam Faith (Parlophone)
7	RUNAWAY / Del Shannon (London)
11	HELLO MARY LOU / Ricky Nelson (London)
10	A GIRL LIKE YOU / Cliff Richard (Columbia)
13	TIME Craig Douglas (Top Rank)
14	QUARTER TO THREE / U.S. Bonds (Top Rank)
18	CLIMB EV'RY MOUNTAIN / Shirley Bassey (Columbia)
20	REACH FOR THE STARS / Shirley Bassey (Columbia)
15	MARCHETA / Karl Denver (Decca)
22	THAT'S MY HOME / Mr Acker Bilk (Columbia)
16	BUT I DO / Clarence 'Frogman' Henry (Pye International)
20	MOODY RIVER / Pat Boone (London)
-	CUPID Sam Cooke (RCA)
17	BABY I DON'T CARE / Buddy Holly (Coral)
24	WEEKEND / Eddie Cochran (London)
-	HOW MANY TEARS / Bobby Vee (London)
23	SURRENDER / Elvis Presley (RCA)
28	DUM DUM / Brenda Lee (Brunswick)
25	QUITE A PARTY / Fireballs (Pye International)
19	RUNNING SCARED / Roy Orbison (London)
30	THE FRIGHTENED CITY / Shadows (Columbia)
-	A SCOTTISH SOLDIER / Andy Stewart (Top Rank)

The growling, impassioned style of Eden Kane on *Well I Ask You* (his first single had been the rather less promising *Hot Chocolate Crazy!*) was quite a contrast to the light teenbeat voices which were prevalent in the chart in mid-1961 - as indeed were the rich boyish tones of Helen Shapiro, who skipped easily to Number One with her second single, and the high vocal gymnastics of Glaswegian Karl Denver, making his debut with *Marcheta*, and due to be a chart regular for the next three years.

August – September 1961

19 August 1961

last	this		
1	1	YOU DON'T KNOW	Helen Shapiro (Columbia)
3	2	JOHNNY REMEMBER ME	John Leyton (Top Rank)
2	3	WELL I ASK YOU	Eden Kane (Decca)
5	4	ROMEO	Petula Clark (Pye)
6	5	HALFWAY TO PARADISE	Billy Fury (Decca)
7	6	PASADENA	Temperance Seven (Parlophone)
8	7	YOU ALWAYS HURT THE ONE YOU LOVE	Clarence 'Frogman' Henry (Pye International)
13	8	TIME Craig Douglas (Top Rank)	
16	9	REACH FOR THE STARS	Shirley Bassey (Columbia)
9	10	DON'T YOU KNOW IT	Adam Faith (Parlophone)
15	11	CLIMB EV'RY MOUNTAIN	Shirley Bassey (Columbia)
4	12	TEMPTATION	Everly Brothers (Warner Bros)
14	13	QUARTER TO THREE	U.S. Bonds (Top Rank)
11	13	HELLO MARY LOU	Ricky Nelson (London)
12	15	A GIRL LIKE YOU	Cliff Richard (Columbia)
10	16	RUNAWAY	Del Shannon (London)
18	17	THAT'S MY HOME	Mr Acker Bilk (Columbia)
22	18	BABY I DON'T CARE	Buddy Holly (Coral)
21	19	CUPID Sam Cooke (RCA)	
17	20	MARCHETA	Karl Denver (Decca)
19	21	BUT I DO	Clarence 'Frogman' Henry (Pye International)
23	22	WEEKEND	Eddie Cochran (London)
24	23	HOW MANY TEARS	Bobby Vee (London)
27	24	QUITE A PARTY	Fireballs (Pye International)
29	25	THE FRIGHTENED CITY	Shadows (Columbia)
25	26	SURRENDER	Elvis Presley (RCA)
28	27	RUNNING SCARED	Roy Orbison (London)
20	28	MOODY RIVER	Pat Boone (London)
-	29	NATURE BOY	Bobby Darin (London)
-	30	WRITING ON THE WALL	Tommy Steele (Decca)

26 August 1961

2	1	JOHNNY REMEMBER ME	John Leyton (Top Rank)
1	2	YOU DON'T KNOW	Helen Shapiro (Columbia)
3	3	WELL I ASK YOU	Eden Kane (Decca)
5	4	HALFWAY TO PARADISE	Billy Fury (Decca)
4	5	ROMEO Petula Clark (Pye)	
9	6	REACH FOR THE STARS	Shirley Bassey (Columbia)
13	7	QUARTER TO THREE	U.S. Bonds (Top Rank)
15	8	A GIRL LIKE YOU	Cliff Richard (Columbia)
7	9	YOU ALWAYS HURT THE ONE YOU LOVE	Clarence 'Frogman' Henry (Pye International)
8	10	TIME Craig Douglas (Top Rank)	
13	11	HELLO MARY LOU	Ricky Nelson (London)
10	12	DON'T YOU KNOW IT	Adam Faith (Parlophone)
11	13	CLIMB EV'RY MOUNTAIN	Shirley Bassey (Columbia)
18	14	BABY I DON'T CARE	Buddy Holly (Coral)
19	15	CUPID Sam Cooke (RCA)	
6	16	PASADENA	Temperance Seven (Parlophone)
17	17	THAT'S MY HOME	Mr Acker Bilk (Columbia)
20	18	MARCHETA	Karl Denver (Decca)
12	19	TEMPTATION	Everly Brothers (Warner Bros)
23	19	HOW MANY TEARS	Bobby Vee (London)
16	21	RUNAWAY	Del Shannon (London)
-	22	AIN'T GONNA WASH FOR A WEEK	Brook Brothers (Pye)
22	23	WEEKEND	Eddie Cochran (London)
30	24	WRITING ON THE WALL	Tommy Steele (Decca)
29	25	NATURE BOY	Bobby Darin (London)
-	26	WHAT KIND OF FOOL AM I	Anthony Newley (Decca)
28	27	MOODY RIVER	Pat Boone (London)
-	28	TOO MANY BEAUTIFUL GIRLS	Clinton Ford (Oriole)
24	29	QUITE A PARTY	Fireballs (Pye International)
25	30	THE FRIGHTENED CITY	Shadows (Columbia)

2 September 1961

1	1	JOHNNY REMEMBER ME	John Leyton (Top Rank)
2	1	YOU DON'T KNOW	Helen Shapiro (Columbia)
6	3	REACH FOR THE STARS	Shirley Bassey (Columbia)
5	4	ROMEO Petula Clark (Pye)	
3	5	WELL I ASK YOU	Eden Kane (Decca)
4	6	HALFWAY TO PARADISE	Billy Fury (Decca)
8	7	A GIRL LIKE YOU	Cliff Richard (Columbia)
17	8	THAT'S MY HOME	Mr Acker Bilk (Columbia)
7	9	QUARTER TO THREE	U.S. Bonds (Top Rank)
9	10	YOU ALWAYS HURT THE ONE YOU LOVE	Clarence 'Frogman' Henry (Pye International)
13	11	CLIMB EV'RY MOUNTAIN	Shirley Bassey (Columbia)
15	12	CUPID Sam Cooke (RCA)	
10	13	TIME Craig Douglas (Top Rank)	
11	14	HELLO MARY LOU	Ricky Nelson (London)
16	15	PASADENA	Temperance Seven (Parlophone)
12	16	DON'T YOU KNOW IT	Adam Faith (Parlophone)
19	16	HOW MANY TEARS	Bobby Vee (London)
19	18	TEMPTATION	Everly Brothers (Warner Bros)
14	19	BABY I DON'T CARE	Buddy Holly (Coral)
-	20	SOMEDAY (YOU'LL BE SORRY)	Kenny Ball & His Jazzmen (Pye Jazz)
22	20	AIN'T GONNA WASH FOR A WEEK B:ook Brothers (Pye)	
-	20	MICHAEL ROW THE BOAT	Lonnie Donegan (Pye)
-	23	GIRLS	Johnny Burnette (London)
18	24	MARCHETA Karl Denver (Decca)	
26	25	WHAT KIND OF FOOL AM I	Anthony Newley (Decca)
-	26	SAY IT WITH FLOWERS	Dorothy Squires & Russ Conway (Columbia)
24	27	WRITING ON THE WALL	Tommy Steele (Decca)
-	28	WHEELS CHA CHA	Joe Loss (HMV)
-	29	TRUE LOVE Terry Lightfoot & His Jazzmen (Columbia)	
-	30	THERE I'VE SAID IT AGAIN	Al Saxon (Piccadilly)
21	30	RUNAWAY	Del Shannon (London)

9 September 1961

1	1	JOHNNY REMEMBER ME	John Leyton (Top Rank)
1	2	YOU DON'T KNOW	Helen Shapiro (Columbia)
-	3	WILD IN THE COUNTRY	Elvis Presley (RCA)
3	4	REACH FOR THE STARS	Shirley Bassey (Columbia)
5	5	WELL I ASK YOU	Eden Kane (Decca)
-	6	KON-TIKI Shadows (Columbia)	
4	7	ROMEO	Petula Clark (Pye)
6	8	HALFWAY TO PARADISE	Billy Fury (Decca)
8	9	THAT'S MY HOME	Mr Acker Bilk (Columbia)
16	10	HOW MANY TEARS	Bobby Vee (London)
12	11	CUPID Sam Cooke (RCA)	
9	12	QUARTER TO THREE	U.S. Bonds (Top Rank)
13	13	TIME Craig Douglas (Top Rank)	
14	13	HELLO MARY LOU	Ricky Nelson (London)
20	15	MICHAEL ROW THE BOAT	Lonnie Donegan (Pye)
7	16	A GIRL LIKE YOU	Cliff Richard (Columbia)
-	17	MICHAEL Highwaymen (HMV)	
10	18	YOU ALWAYS HURT THE ONE YOU LOVE	Clarence 'Frogman' Henry (Pye International)
11	19	CLIMB EV'RY MOUNTAIN	Shirley Bassey (Columbia)
-	20	GET LOST	Eden Kane (Decca)
-	21	TOGETHER	Connie Francis (MGM)
22	22	AIN'T GONNA WASH FOR A WEEK Brook Brothers (Pye)	
24	23	MARCHETA	Karl Denver (Decca)
20	24	SOMEDAY (YOU'LL BE SORRY)	Kenny Ball & His Jazzmen (Pye Jazz)
-	25	JEALOUSY	Billy Fury (Decca)
18	26	TEMPTATION	Everly Brothers (Warner Bros)
25	27	WHAT KIND OF FOOL AM I	Anthony Newley (Decca)
15	27	PASADENA	Temperance Seven (Parlophone)
16	29	DON'T YOU KNOW IT	Adam Faith (Parlophone)
-	29	YOU'LL ANSWER TO ME	Cleo Laine (Fontana)
29	29	TRUE LOVE	Terry Lightfoot & His Jazzmen (Columbia)

Actor/singer John Leyton, who had recorded earlier for independent producer Joe Meek without success, gave both Meek and himself their first Number One success with *Johnny Remember Me*. Leyton had featured the song in an episode of the TV drama series *Harper's West One*, in which he guested as ficticious rock star Johnny St Cyr ("sincere"– geddit?), and this kick-started the record. Writer Geoff Goddard had toned down the overt death references in the song's lyric, to ensure BBC airplay.

September – October 1961

16 September 1961

last week	this week		
1	1	JOHNNY REMEMBER ME	John Leyton (Top Rank)
2	2	YOU DON'T KNOW	Helen Shapiro (Columbia)
6	3	KON-TIKI	Shadows (Columbia)
3	4	WILD IN THE COUNTRY	Elvis Presley (RCA)
4	5	REACH FOR THE STARS	Shirley Bassey (Columbia)
15	6	MICHAEL ROW THE BOAT	Lonnie Donegan (Pye)
5	7	WELL I ASK YOU	Eden Kane (Decca)
11	8	CUPID	Sam Cooke (RCA)
17	9	MICHAEL	Highwaymen (HMV)
7	10	ROMEO	Petula Clark (Pye)
9	11	THAT'S MY HOME	Mr Acker Bilk (Columbia)
21	12	TOGETHER	Connie Francis (MGM)
12	13	QUARTER TO THREE	U.S. Bonds (Top Rank)
8	14	HALFWAY TO PARADISE	Billy Fury (Decca)
25	15	JEALOUSY	Billy Fury (Decca)
10	16	HOW MANY TEARS	Bobby Vee (London)
20	17	GET LOST	Eden Kane (Decca)
22	18	AIN'T GONNA WASH FOR A WEEK	Brook Brothers (Pye)
-	19	HATS OFF TO LARRY	Del Shannon (London)
24	20	SOMEDAY (YOU'LL BE SORRY)	Kenny Ball & His Jazzmen (Pye Jazz)
-	20	I FEEL SO BAD	Elvis Presley (RCA)
-	22	SEA OF HEARTBREAK	Don Gibson (RCA)
13	23	HELLO MARY LOU	Ricky Nelson (London)
-	24	DRIVIN' HOME	Duane Eddy (London)
29	25	YOU'LL ANSWER TO ME	Cleo Laine (Fontana)
19	26	CLIMB EV'RY MOUNTAIN	Shirley Bassey (Columbia)
13	26	TIME Craig Douglas (Top Rank)	
16	28	A GIRL LIKE YOU	Cliff Richard (Columbia)
-	29	BREAKAWAY	Springfields (Philips)
23	30	MARCHETA	Karl Denver (Decca)

23 September 1961

last week	this week		
4	1	WILD IN THE COUNTRY	Elvis Presley (RCA)
1	2	JOHNNY REMEMBER ME	John Leyton (Top Rank)
2	3	YOU DON'T KNOW	Helen Shapiro (Columbia)
3	4	KON-TIKI	Shadows (Columbia)
5	5	REACH FOR THE STARS	Shirley Bassey (Columbia)
9	6	MICHAEL	Highwaymen (HMV)
15	7	JEALOUSY	Billy Fury (Decca)
8	8	CUPID	Sam Cooke (RCA)
19	9	HATS OFF TO LARRY	Del Shannon (London)
17	10	GET LOST	Eden Kane (Decca)
6	11	MICHAEL ROW THE BOAT	Lonnie Donegan (Pye)
11	12	THAT'S MY HOME	Mr Acker Bilk (Columbia)
12	13	TOGETHER	Connie Francis (MGM)
18	14	AIN'T GONNA WASH FOR A WEEK	Brook Brothers (Pye)
16	15	HOW MANY TEARS	Bobby Vee (London)
25	16	YOU'LL ANSWER TO ME	Cleo Laine (Fontana)
10	17	ROMEO	Petula Clark (Pye)
7	18	WELL I ASK YOU	Eden Kane (Decca)
22	19	SEA OF HEARTBREAK	Don Gibson (RCA)
14	20	HALFWAY TO PARADISE	Billy Fury (Decca)
20	21	I FEEL SO BAD	Elvis Presley (RCA)
13	22	QUARTER TO THREE	U.S. Bonds (Top Rank)
29	23	BREAKAWAY	Springfields (Philips)
26	24	CLIMB EV'RY MOUNTAIN	Shirley Bassey (Columbia)
-	25	SAY IT WITH FLOWERS	Dorothy Squires & Russ Conway (Columbia)
30	26	MARCHETA	Karl Denver (Decca)
-	27	FRANKIE AND JOHNNY	Brook Benton (Mercury)
-	27	I'M GONNA KNOCK ON YOUR DOOR	Eddie Hodges (London)
24	29	DRIVIN' HOME	Duane Eddy (London)
20	30	SOMEDAY (YOU'LL BE SORRY)	Kenny Ball & His Jazzmen (Pye Jazz)
-	30	LUMBERED	Lonnie Donegan (Pye)

30 September 1961

last week	this week		
2	1	JOHNNY REMEMBER ME	John Leyton (Top Rank)
1	2	WILD IN THE COUNTRY	Elvis Presley (RCA)
4	3	KON-TIKI	Shadows (Columbia)
6	4	MICHAEL	Highwaymen (HMV)
7	5	JEALOUSY	Billy Fury (Decca)
3	6	YOU DON'T KNOW	Helen Shapiro (Columbia)
5	7	REACH FOR THE STARS	Shirley Bassey (Columbia)
10	8	GET LOST	Eden Kane (Decca)
16	9	YOU'LL ANSWER TO ME	Cleo Laine (Fontana)
9	9	HATS OFF TO LARRY	Del Shannon (London)
13	11	TOGETHER	Connie Francis (MGM)
11	12	MICHAEL ROW THE BOAT	Lonnie Donegan (Pye)
-	13	WALKIN' BACK TO HAPPINESS	Helen Shapiro (Columbia)
8	14	CUPID	Sam Cooke (RCA)
-	15	GRANADA	Frank Sinatra (Reprise)
19	16	SEA OF HEARTBREAK	Don Gibson (RCA)
-	17	SUCU SUCU	Laurie Johnson (Pye)
12	18	THAT'S MY HOME	Mr Acker Bilk (Columbia)
14	19	AIN'T GONNA WASH FOR A WEEK	Brook Brothers (Pye)
-	20	MUSKRAT	Everly Brothers (Warner Bros)
15	21	HOW MANY TEARS	Bobby Vee (London)
21	22	I FEEL SO BAD	Elvis Presley (RCA)
22	23	QUARTER TO THREE	U.S. Bonds (Top Rank)
20	24	HALFWAY TO PARADISE	Billy Fury (Decca)
23	24	BREAKAWAY	Springfields (Philips)
-	26	WHEELS CHA CHA	Joe Loss (HMV)
-	27	AMOR	Ben E. King (London)
25	28	SAY IT WITH FLOWERS	Dorothy Squires & Russ Conway (Columbia)
18	29	WELL I ASK YOU	Eden Kane (Decca)
27	30	I'M GONNA KNOCK ON YOUR DOOR	Eddie Hodges (London)

7 October 1961

last week	this week		
4	1	MICHAEL Highwaymen (HMV)	
2	2	WILD IN THE COUNTRY	Elvis Presley (RCA)
13	2	WALKIN' BACK TO HAPPINESS	Helen Shapiro (Columbia)
5	4	JEALOUSY Billy Fury (Decca)	
1	5	JOHNNY REMEMBER ME	John Leyton (Top Rank)
3	6	KON-TIKI	Shadows (Columbia)
9	7	YOU'LL ANSWER TO ME	Cleo Laine (Fontana)
8	8	GET LOST	Eden Kane (Decca)
9	9	HATS OFF TO LARRY	Del Shannon (London)
17	10	SUCU SUCU	Laurie Johnson (Pye)
6	11	YOU DON'T KNOW	Helen Shapiro (Columbia)
15	11	GRANADA	Frank Sinatra (Reprise)
-	13	WILD WIND	John Leyton (Top Rank)
7	14	REACH FOR THE STARS	Shirley Bassey (Columbia)
11	15	TOGETHER	Connie Francis (MGM)
12	16	MICHAEL ROW THE BOAT	Lonnie Donegan (Pye)
-	17	BLESS YOU	Tony Orlando (Fontana)
20	18	MUSKRAT	Everly Brothers (Warner Bros)
-	19	HARD HEARTED HANNAH	Temperance Seven (Parlophone)
18	20	THAT'S MY HOME	Mr Acker Bilk (Columbia)
14	21	CUPID	Sam Cooke (RCA)
16	22	SEA OF HEARTBREAK	Don Gibson (RCA)
29	23	WELL I ASK YOU	Eden Kane (Decca)
19	24	AIN'T GONNA WASH FOR A WEEK	Brook Brothers (Pye)
27	25	AMOR	Ben E. King (London)
26	26	WHEELS CHA CHA	Joe Loss (HMV)
30	27	I'M GONNA KNOCK ON YOUR DOOR	Eddie Hodges (London)
24	28	BREAKAWAY	Springfields (Philips)
-	29	TRIBUTE TO BUDDY HOLLY	Mike Berry (HMV)
28	30	SAY IT WITH FLOWERS	Dorothy Squires & Russ Conway (Columbia)

A battle royal developed around the simple folk-style ditty *Michael*, as the US hit version by the Highwaymen (a polite, harmony reading) battled with the robust cover by Britain's Lonnie Donegan, who also extended the song's title. They were so different that some people probably bought both. In the event the Highwaymen repeated their transatlantic Number One success - though Lonnie also got his B-side to number 30. The Springfields (featuring Dusty) made their chart debut with the equally folky *Breakaway*.

October – November 1961

14 October 1961

last	this	
2	1	WALKIN' BACK TO HAPPINESS — Helen Shapiro (Columbia)
13	2	WILD WIND — John Leyton (Top Rank)
7	3	YOU'LL ANSWER TO ME — Cleo Laine (Fontana)
1	4	MICHAEL — Highwaymen (HMV)
4	5	JEALOUSY — Billy Fury (Decca)
6	6	KON-TIKI — Shadows (Columbia)
10	7	SUCU SUCU — Laurie Johnson (Pye)
9	8	HATS OFF TO LARRY — Del Shannon (London)
2	9	WILD IN THE COUNTRY — Elvis Presley (RCA)
15	10	TOGETHER — Connie Francis (MGM)
8	10	GET LOST — Eden Kane (Decca)
11	12	GRANADA — Frank Sinatra (Reprise)
5	13	JOHNNY REMEMBER ME — John Leyton (Top Rank)
17	14	BLESS YOU — Tony Orlando (Fontana)
-	15	YOU MUST HAVE BEEN A BEAUTIFUL BABY — Bobby Darin (London)
-	16	MY BOOMERANG WON'T COME BACK — Charlie Drake (Parlophone)
-	17	MEXICALI ROSE — Karl Denver (Decca)
11	18	YOU DON'T KNOW — Helen Shapiro (Columbia)
-	18	WHO BUT THE BOMP — Viscounts (Pye)
14	20	REACH FOR THE STARS — Shirley Bassey (Columbia)
18	21	MUSKRAT — Everly Brothers (Warner Bros)
-	22	SUCU SUCU — Nina & Frederick (Columbia)
16	23	MICHAEL ROW THE BOAT — Lonnie Donegan (Pye)
22	24	SEA OF HEARTBREAK — Don Gibson (RCA)
-	25	CHILI BOM BOM — Temperance Seven (Parlophone)
-	26	CRYING — Roy Orbison (London)
21	27	CUPID — Sam Cooke (RCA)
25	28	AMOR — Ben E. King (London)
28	29	BREAKAWAY — Springfields (Philips)
24	30	AIN'T GONNA WASH FOR A WEEK — Brook Brothers (Pye)

21 October 1961

last	this	
1	1	WALKIN' BACK TO HAPPINESS — Helen Shapiro (Columbia)
2	2	WILD WIND — John Leyton (Top Rank)
4	3	MICHAEL — Highwaymen (HMV)
-	4	WHEN THE GIRL IN YOUR ARMS IS THE GIRL IN YOUR HEART — Cliff Richard (Columbia)
3	5	YOU'LL ANSWER TO ME — Cleo Laine (Fontana)
5	6	JEALOUSY — Billy Fury (Decca)
7	6	SUCU SUCU — Laurie Johnson (Pye)
6	8	KON-TIKI — Shadows (Columbia)
9	9	HATS OFF TO LARRY — Del Shannon (London)
14	10	BLESS YOU — Tony Orlando (Fontana)
17	11	MEXICALI ROSE — Karl Denver (Decca)
9	12	WILD IN THE COUNTRY — Elvis Presley (RCA)
10	13	GET LOST — Eden Kane (Decca)
15	14	YOU MUST HAVE BEEN A BEAUTIFUL BABY — Bobby Darin (London)
-	15	HIT THE ROAD JACK — Ray Charles (HMV)
16	16	MY BOOMERANG WON'T COME BACK — Charlie Drake (Parlophone)
10	17	TOGETHER — Connie Francis (MGM)
12	17	GRANADA — Frank Sinatra (Reprise)
18	19	WHO BUT THE BOMP — Viscounts (Pye)
22	20	SUCU SUCU — Nina & Frederick (Columbia)
21	21	MUSKRAT — Everly Brothers (Warner Bros)
-	22	LET'S GET TOGETHER — Hayley Mills (Decca)
-	23	GOT A FUNNY FEELING — Cliff Richard (Columbia)
13	24	JOHNNY REMEMBER ME — John Leyton (Top Rank)
18	25	YOU DON'T KNOW — Helen Shapiro (Columbia)
-	26	TRIBUTE TO BUDDY HOLLY — Mike Berry (HMV)
-	27	THE MOUNTAIN'S HIGH — Dick & Deedee (London)
20	28	REACH FOR THE STARS — Shirley Bassey (Columbia)
24	28	SEA OF HEARTBREAK — Don Gibson (RCA)
-	30	COME SEPTEMBER — Bobby Darin & His Orchestra (London)

28 October 1961

last	this	
1	1	WALKIN' BACK TO HAPPINESS — Helen Shapiro (Columbia)
4	2	WHEN THE GIRL IN YOUR ARMS IS THE GIRL IN YOUR HEART — Cliff Richard (Columbia)
2	3	WILD WIND — John Leyton (Top Rank)
6	4	SUCU SUCU — Laurie Johnson (Pye)
15	5	HIT THE ROAD JACK — Ray Charles (HMV)
5	6	YOU'LL ANSWER TO ME — Cleo Laine (Fontana)
3	7	MICHAEL — Highwaymen (HMV)
10	8	BLESS YOU — Tony Orlando (Fontana)
11	9	MEXICALI ROSE — Karl Denver (Decca)
14	10	YOU MUST HAVE BEEN A BEAUTIFUL BABY — Bobby Darin (London)
-	11	TAKE FIVE — Dave Brubeck Quartet (Fontana)
6	12	JEALOUSY — Billy Fury (Decca)
9	13	HATS OFF TO LARRY — Del Shannon (London)
-	14	BIG BAD JOHN — Jimmy Dean (Philips)
8	15	KON-TIKI — Shadows (Columbia)
16	16	MY BOOMERANG WON'T COME BACK — Charlie Drake (Parlophone)
22	17	LET'S GET TOGETHER — Hayley Mills (Decca)
12	18	WILD IN THE COUNTRY — Elvis Presley (RCA)
13	19	GET LOST — Eden Kane (Decca)
-	20	THE TIME HAS COME — Adam Faith (Parlophone)
17	21	TOGETHER — Connie Francis (MGM)
-	22	YOU DON'T KNOW WHAT YOU'VE GOT — Ral Donner (Parlophone)
-	22	TAKE GOOD CARE OF MY BABY — Bobby Vee (London)
17	24	GRANADA — Frank Sinatra (Reprise)
27	25	THE MOUNTAIN'S HIGH — Dick & Deedee (London)
19	25	WHO BUT THE BOMP — Viscounts (Pye)
25	27	YOU DON'T KNOW — Helen Shapiro (Columbia)
20	28	SUCU SUCU — Nina & Frederick (Columbia)
26	29	TRIBUTE TO BUDDY HOLLY — Mike Berry (HMV)
21	30	MUSKRAT — Everly Brothers (Warner Bros)

4 November 1961

last	this	
1	1	WALKIN' BACK TO HAPPINESS — Helen Shapiro (Columbia)
-	2	HIS LATEST FLAME — Elvis Presley (RCA)
2	3	WHEN THE GIRL IN YOUR ARMS IS THE GIRL IN YOUR HEART — Cliff Richard (Columbia)
5	4	HIT THE ROAD JACK — Ray Charles (HMV)
3	5	WILD WIND — John Leyton (Top Rank)
11	6	TAKE FIVE — Dave Brubeck Quartet (Fontana)
14	7	BIG BAD JOHN — Jimmy Dean (Philips)
22	8	TAKE GOOD CARE OF MY BABY — Bobby Vee (London)
4	9	SUCU SUCU — Laurie Johnson (Pye)
9	10	MEXICALI ROSE — Karl Denver (Decca)
20	11	THE TIME HAS COME — Adam Faith (Parlophone)
8	12	BLESS YOU — Tony Orlando (Fontana)
6	13	YOU'LL ANSWER TO ME — Cleo Laine (Fontana)
10	14	YOU MUST HAVE BEEN A BEAUTIFUL BABY — Bobby Darin (London)
7	15	MICHAEL — Highwaymen (HMV)
17	16	LET'S GET TOGETHER — Hayley Mills (Decca)
16	17	MY BOOMERANG WON'T COME BACK — Charlie Drake (Parlophone)
-	18	LITTLE SISTER — Elvis Presley (RCA)
12	19	JEALOUSY — Billy Fury (Decca)
13	20	HATS OFF TO LARRY — Del Shannon (London)
22	21	YOU DON'T KNOW WHAT YOU'VE GOT — Ral Donner (Parlophone)
15	22	KON-TIKI — Shadows (Columbia)
-	23	MOON RIVER — Danny Williams (HMV)
19	24	GET LOST — Eden Kane (Decca)
-	25	RUNAROUND SUE — Dion (Top Rank)
-	25	I'M A MOODY GUY — Shane Fenton & the Fentones (Parlophone)
25	27	THE MOUNTAIN'S HIGH — Dick & Deedee (London)
18	28	WILD IN THE COUNTRY — Elvis Presley (RCA)
28	29	SUCU SUCU — Nina & Frederick (Columbia)
24	30	GRANADA — Frank Sinatra (Reprise)

Helen Shapiro cemented her success with a second consecutive Number One in *Walkin' Back To Happiness*. Writers John Schroeder and Mike Hawker had been given a weekend to come up with Helen's third hit, as Rank's *Look At Life* series wanted to film her in the studio cutting it. After two fruitless days, they finally got the inspiration for *Walkin'* while out dejectedly buying their breakfast on Monday morning. It became her biggest seller, and even grazed the US chart, no mean feat in 1961.

November – December 1961

last this week

11 November 1961

LW	TW	Title / Artist
2	1	HIS LATEST FLAME — Elvis Presley (RCA)
1	2	WALKIN' BACK TO HAPPINESS — Helen Shapiro (Columbia)
8	3	TAKE GOOD CARE OF MY BABY — Bobby Vee (London)
7	4	BIG BAD JOHN — Jimmy Dean (Philips)
3	5	WHEN THE GIRL IN YOUR ARMS IS THE GIRL IN YOUR HEART — Cliff Richard (Columbia)
4	6	HIT THE ROAD JACK — Ray Charles (HMV)
6	7	TAKE FIVE — Dave Brubeck Quartet (Fontana)
11	8	THE TIME HAS COME — Adam Faith (Parlophone)
10	9	MEXICALI ROSE — Karl Denver (Decca)
9	10	SUCU SUCU — Laurie Johnson (Pye)
12	11	BLESS YOU — Tony Orlando (Fontana)
14	12	YOU MUST HAVE BEEN A BEAUTIFUL BABY — Bobby Darin (London)
23	13	MOON RIVER — Danny Williams (HMV)
5	14	WILD WIND — John Leyton (Top Rank)
16	15	LET'S GET TOGETHER — Hayley Mills (Decca)
17	16	MY BOOMERANG WON'T COME BACK — Charlie Drake (Parlophone)
-	17	TOWER OF STRENGTH — Frankie Vaughan (Philips)
13	18	YOU'LL ANSWER TO ME — Cleo Laine (Fontana)
25	19	RUNAROUND SUE — Dion (Top Rank)
15	20	MICHAEL — Highwaymen (HMV)
18	21	LITTLE SISTER — Elvis Presley (RCA)
29	22	SUCU SUCU — Nina & Frederick (Columbia)
25	23	I'M A MOODY GUY — Shane Fenton & the Fentones (Parlophone)
19	24	JEALOUSY — Billy Fury (Decca)
21	25	YOU DON'T KNOW WHAT YOU'VE GOT — Ral Donner (Parlophone)
22	26	KON-TIKI — Shadows (Columbia)
-	27	THIS TIME — Troy Shondell (London)
-	28	TOMORROW'S CLOWN — Marty Wilde (Philips)
29	29	HEY LOOK ME OVER — Ronnie Hilton (HMV)
-	30	MIDNIGHT IN MOSCOW — Kenny Ball & His Jazzmen (Pye Jazz)

18 November 1961

LW	TW	Title / Artist
1	1	HIS LATEST FLAME — Elvis Presley (RCA)
3	2	TAKE GOOD CARE OF MY BABY — Bobby Vee (London)
4	3	BIG BAD JOHN — Jimmy Dean (Philips)
2	4	WALKIN' BACK TO HAPPINESS — Helen Shapiro (Columbia)
8	5	THE TIME HAS COME — Adam Faith (Parlophone)
5	6	WHEN THE GIRL IN YOUR ARMS IS THE GIRL IN YOUR HEART — Cliff Richard (Columbia)
6	7	HIT THE ROAD JACK — Ray Charles (HMV)
7	8	TAKE FIVE — Dave Brubeck Quartet (Fontana)
17	9	TOWER OF STRENGTH — Frankie Vaughan (Philips)
19	10	RUNAROUND SUE — Dion (Top Rank)
13	10	MOON RIVER — Danny Williams (HMV)
10	12	SUCU SUCU — Laurie Johnson (Pye)
11	13	BLESS YOU — Tony Orlando (Fontana)
9	14	MEXICALI ROSE — Karl Denver (Decca)
-	14	THE SAVAGE — Shadows (Columbia)
12	16	YOU MUST HAVE BEEN A BEAUTIFUL BABY — Bobby Darin (London)
30	17	MIDNIGHT IN MOSCOW — Kenny Ball & His Jazzmen (Pye Jazz)
15	18	LET'S GET TOGETHER — Hayley Mills (Decca)
18	19	YOU'LL ANSWER TO ME — Cleo Laine (Fontana)
-	19	RUNAROUND — Doug Sheldon (Decca)
14	21	WILD WIND — John Leyton (Top Rank)
22	22	THIS TIME — Troy Shondell (London)
16	23	MY BOOMERANG WON'T COME BACK — Charlie Drake (Parlophone)
23	24	I'M A MOODY GUY — Shane Fenton & the Fentones (Parlophone)
-	25	LET TRUE LOVE BEGIN — Nat King Cole (Capitol)
-	26	HATS OFF TO LARRY — Del Shannon (London)
21	27	LITTLE SISTER — Elvis Presley (RCA)
-	28	EVERLOVIN' — Ricky Nelson (London)
28	28	TOMORROW'S CLOWN — Marty Wilde (Philips)
26	30	KON-TIKI — Shadows (Columbia)

25 November 1961

LW	TW	Title / Artist
1	1	HIS LATEST FLAME — Elvis Presley (RCA)
2	2	TAKE GOOD CARE OF MY BABY — Bobby Vee (London)
9	3	TOWER OF STRENGTH — Frankie Vaughan (Philips)
3	4	BIG BAD JOHN — Jimmy Dean (Philips)
4	5	WALKIN' BACK TO HAPPINESS — Helen Shapiro (Columbia)
10	6	MOON RIVER — Danny Williams (HMV)
5	7	THE TIME HAS COME — Adam Faith (Parlophone)
8	8	TAKE FIVE — Dave Brubeck Quartet (Fontana)
14	9	THE SAVAGE — Shadows (Columbia)
6	10	WHEN THE GIRL IN YOUR ARMS IS THE GIRL IN YOUR HEART — Cliff Richard (Columbia)
17	11	MIDNIGHT IN MOSCOW — Kenny Ball & His Jazzmen (Pye Jazz)
10	11	RUNAROUND SUE — Dion (Top Rank)
7	13	HIT THE ROAD JACK — Ray Charles (HMV)
12	14	SUCU SUCU — Laurie Johnson (Pye)
14	15	MEXICALI ROSE — Karl Denver (Decca)
-	16	I'LL GET BY — Shirley Bassey (Columbia)
17	17	MOON RIVER — Henry Mancini (RCA)
16	18	YOU MUST HAVE BEEN A BEAUTIFUL BABY — Bobby Darin (London)
24	19	I'M A MOODY GUY — Shane Fenton & the Fentones (Parlophone)
23	20	MY BOOMERANG WON'T COME BACK — Charlie Drake (Parlophone)
13	21	BLESS YOU — Tony Orlando (Fontana)
18	22	LET'S GET TOGETHER — Hayley Mills (Decca)
21	23	WILD WIND — John Leyton (Top Rank)
22	24	THIS TIME — Troy Shondell (London)
-	25	CREOLE JAZZ — Mr Acker Bilk (Columbia)
25	25	LET TRUE LOVE BEGIN — Nat King Cole (Capitol)
19	27	RUNAROUND SUE — Doug Sheldon (Decca)
19	28	YOU'LL ANSWER TO ME — Cleo Laine (Fontana)
28	29	EVERLOVIN' — Ricky Nelson (London)
-	30	SUCU SUCU — Nina & Frederick (Columbia)
-	30	SEPTEMBER IN THE RAIN — Dinah Washington (Mercury)

2 December 1961

LW	TW	Title / Artist
3	1	TOWER OF STRENGTH — Frankie Vaughan (Philips)
2	1	TAKE GOOD CARE OF MY BABY — Bobby Vee (London)
6	3	MOON RIVER — Danny Williams (HMV)
1	4	HIS LATEST FLAME — Elvis Presley (RCA)
4	5	BIG BAD JOHN — Jimmy Dean (Philips)
7	6	THE TIME HAS COME — Adam Faith (Parlophone)
5	7	WALKIN' BACK TO HAPPINESS — Helen Shapiro (Columbia)
8	8	TAKE FIVE — Dave Brubeck Quartet (Fontana)
11	9	MIDNIGHT IN MOSCOW — Kenny Ball & His Jazzmen (Py Jazz)
16	10	I'LL GET BY — Shirley Bassey (Columbia)
11	11	RUNAROUND SUE — Dion (Top Rank)
9	12	THE SAVAGE — Shadows (Columbia)
10	13	WHEN THE GIRL IN YOUR ARMS IS THE GIRL IN YOUR HEART — Cliff Richard (Columbia)
13	14	HIT THE ROAD JACK — Ray Charles (HMV)
15	15	MEXICALI ROSE — Karl Denver (Decca)
16	16	YOU MUST HAVE BEEN A BEAUTIFUL BABY — Bobby Darin (London)
24	17	THIS TIME — Troy Shondell (London)
14	18	SUCU SUCU — Laurie Johnson (Pye)
22	19	LET'S GET TOGETHER — Hayley Mills (Decca)
17	20	MOON RIVER — Henry Mancini (RCA)
-	20	DON'T BRING LULU — Dorothy Provine (Warner Bros)
-	22	STRANGER ON THE SHORE — Mr Acker Bilk (Columbia)
19	23	I'M A MOODY GUY — Shane Fenton & the Fentones (Parlophone)
-	24	YOU'RE THE ONLY GOOD THING (THAT'S HAPPENED TO ME) — Jim Reeves (RCA)
-	25	MY FRIEND THE SEA — Petula Clark (Pye)
25	25	I CRIED FOR YOU — Ricky Stevens (Columbia)
-	27	HELEN (EP) — Helen Shapiro (Columbia)
21	28	BLESS YOU — Tony Orlando (Fontana)
-	29	CHARLESTON — Temperance Seven (Parlophone)
-	30	JEANNIE JEANNIE JEANNIE — Eddie Cochran (London)

After disapointing sales on Wild In The Country, Elvis marched back to form with *His Latest Flame*, the B-side *Little Sister* also picking up chartworthy sales. He was dethroned by not one record but two, as Frankie Vaughan's *Tower Of Strength* and Bobby Vee's *Take Good Care Of My Baby* shared Number One on December 2. The Vaughan disc was a new arrangement of an American hit by Gene McDaniels, whose earlier *A Hundred Pounds Of Clay* had also been successfuly covered here by Craig Douglas.

December 1961

9 December 1961

LW	TW	Title / Artist (Label)
1	1	TOWER OF STRENGTH — Frankie Vaughan (Philips)
3	2	MOON RIVER — Danny Williams (HMV)
1	3	TAKE GOOD CARE OF MY BABY — Bobby Vee (London)
4	4	HIS LATEST FLAME — Elvis Presley (RCA)
8	5	TAKE FIVE — Dave Brubeck Quartet (Fontana)
5	6	BIG BAD JOHN — Jimmy Dean (Philips)
10	7	I'LL GET BY — Shirley Bassey (Columbia)
9	8	MIDNIGHT IN MOSCOW — Kenny Ball & His Jazzmen (Pye Jazz)
7	9	WALKIN' BACK TO HAPPINESS — Helen Shapiro (Columbia)
6	10	THE TIME HAS COME — Adam Faith (Parlophone)
22	11	STRANGER ON THE SHORE — Mr Acker Bilk (Columbia)
12	12	THE SAVAGE — Shadows (Columbia)
11	13	RUNAROUND SUE — Dion (Top Rank)
25	14	I CRIED FOR YOU — Ricky Stevens (Columbia)
24	15	YOU'RE THE ONLY GOOD THING (THAT'S HAPPENED TO ME) — Jim Reeves (RCA)
29	16	CHARLESTON — Temperance Seven (Parlophone)
-	17	JOHNNY WILL — Pat Boone (London)
14	18	HIT THE ROAD JACK — Ray Charles (HMV)
20	18	DON'T BRING LULU — Dorothy Provine (Warner Bros)
15	20	MEXICALI ROSE — Karl Denver (Decca)
-	21	SO LONG BABY — Del Shannon (London)
16	22	YOU MUST HAVE BEEN A BEAUTIFUL BABY — Bobby Darin (London)
-	23	TOY BALLOONS — Russ Conway (Columbia)
13	24	WHEN THE GIRL IN YOUR ARMS IS THE GIRL IN YOUR HEART — Cliff Richard (Columbia)
25	25	MY FRIEND THE SEA — Petula Clark (Pye)
20	25	MOON RIVER — Henry Mancini (RCA)
-	27	BAMBINO — Springfields (Philips)
-	27	TALL DARK STRANGER — Rose Brennan (Philips)
-	28	LET TRUE LOVE BEGIN — Nat King Cole (Capitol)
-	28	I LOVE HOW YOU LOVE ME — Jimmy Crawford (Columbia)

16 December 1961

LW	TW	Title / Artist (Label)
1	1	TOWER OF STRENGTH — Frankie Vaughan (Philips)
2	2	MOON RIVER — Danny Williams (HMV)
3	3	TAKE GOOD CARE OF MY BABY — Bobby Vee (London)
11	4	STRANGER ON THE SHORE — Mr Acker Bilk (Columbia)
8	5	MIDNIGHT IN MOSCOW — Kenny Ball & His Jazzmen (Pye Jazz)
7	6	I'LL GET BY — Shirley Bassey (Columbia)
17	7	JOHNNY WILL — Pat Boone (London)
-	8	LET THERE BE DRUMS — Sandy Nelson (London)
4	8	HIS LATEST FLAME — Elvis Presley (RCA)
5	10	TAKE FIVE — Dave Brubeck Quartet (Fontana)
9	11	WALKIN' BACK TO HAPPINESS — Helen Shapiro (Columbia)
12	12	MY FRIEND THE SEA — Petula Clark (Pye)
10	13	THE TIME HAS COME — Adam Faith (Parlophone)
21	14	SO LONG BABY — Del Shannon (London)
14	15	I CRIED FOR YOU — Ricky Stevens (Columbia)
6	16	BIG BAD JOHN — Jimmy Dean (Philips)
18	17	DON'T BRING LULU — Dorothy Provine (Warner Bros)
12	18	THE SAVAGE — Shadows (Columbia)
-	19	I'D NEVER FIND ANOTHER YOU — Billy Fury (Decca)
23	20	TOY BALLOONS — Russ Conway (Columbia)
-	21	MRS. MILLS MEDLEY — Mrs. Mills (Parlophone)
-	22	HAPPY BIRTHDAY SWEET SIXTEEN — Neil Sedaka (RCA)
16	22	CHARLESTON — Temperance Seven (Parlophone)
24	24	YOU'RE THE ONLY GOOD THING (THAT'S HAPPENED TO ME) — Jim Reeves (RCA)
13	25	RUNAROUND SUE — Dion (Top Rank)
27	25	BAMBINO — Springfields (Philips)
28	27	I LOVE HOW YOU LOVE ME — Jimmy Crawford (Columbia)
-	27	BABY'S FIRST CHRISTMAS — Connie Francis (MGM)
24	29	WHEN THE GIRL IN YOUR ARMS IS THE GIRL IN YOUR HEART — Cliff Richard (Columbia)
-	30	I UNDERSTAND — G-Clefs (London)
-	30	SEPTEMBER IN THE RAIN — Dinah Washington (Mercury)

23 December 1961

LW	TW	Title / Artist (Label)
1	1	TOWER OF STRENGTH — Frankie Vaughan (Philips)
2	2	MOON RIVER — Danny Williams (HMV)
4	3	STRANGER ON THE SHORE — Mr Acker Bilk (Columbia)
8	4	LET THERE BE DRUMS — Sandy Nelson (London)
5	5	MIDNIGHT IN MOSCOW — Kenny Ball & His Jazzmen (Pye Jazz)
7	6	JOHNNY WILL — Pat Boone (London)
3	6	TAKE GOOD CARE OF MY BABY — Bobby Vee (London)
6	8	I'LL GET BY — Shirley Bassey (Columbia)
11	9	WALKIN' BACK TO HAPPINESS — Helen Shapiro (Columbia)
22	10	HAPPY BIRTHDAY SWEET SIXTEEN — Neil Sedaka (RCA)
12	11	MY FRIEND THE SEA — Petula Clark (Pye)
10	12	TAKE FIVE — Dave Brubeck Quartet (Fontana)
17	13	DON'T BRING LULU — Dorothy Provine (Warner Bros)
14	13	SO LONG BABY — Del Shannon (London)
16	15	BIG BAD JOHN — Jimmy Dean (Philips)
19	16	I'D NEVER FIND ANOTHER YOU — Billy Fury (Decca)
8	16	HIS LATEST FLAME — Elvis Presley (RCA)
15	16	I CRIED FOR YOU — Ricky Stevens (Columbia)
20	19	TOY BALLOONS — Russ Conway (Columbia)
21	20	MRS. MILLS MEDLEY — Mrs. Mills (Parlophone)
24	21	YOU'RE THE ONLY GOOD THING (THAT'S HAPPENED TO ME) — Jim Reeves (RCA)
13	22	THE TIME HAS COME — Adam Faith (Parlophone)
29	23	WHEN THE GIRL IN YOUR ARMS IS THE GIRL IN YOUR HEART — Cliff Richard (Columbia)
-	24	MULTIPLICATION — Bobby Darin (London)
25	25	BAMBINO — Springfields (Philips)
22	26	CHARLESTON — Temperance Seven (Parlophone)
-	27	GIVE US A KISS FOR CHRISTMAS — Lionel Bart (Decca)
18	28	THE SAVAGE — Shadows (Columbia)
27	29	BABY'S FIRST CHRISTMAS — Connie Francis (MGM)
-	30	GOODBYE CRUEL WORLD — James Darren (Pye International)
-	30	KING KONG — Terry Lightfoot & His Jazzmen (Columbia)

30 December 1961

LW	TW	Title / Artist (Label)
2	1	MOON RIVER — Danny Williams (HMV)
3	2	STRANGER ON THE SHORE — Mr Acker Bilk (Columbia)
1	2	TOWER OF STRENGTH — Frankie Vaughan (Philips)
6	4	JOHNNY WILL — Pat Boone (London)
5	5	MIDNIGHT IN MOSCOW — Kenny Ball & His Jazzmen (Pye Jazz)
4	6	LET THERE BE DRUMS — Sandy Nelson (London)
6	7	TAKE GOOD CARE OF MY BABY — Bobby Vee (London)
10	8	HAPPY BIRTHDAY SWEET SIXTEEN — Neil Sedaka (RCA)
16	9	I'D NEVER FIND ANOTHER YOU — Billy Fury (Decca)
24	10	MULTIPLICATION — Bobby Darin (London)
13	11	SO LONG BABY — Del Shannon (London)
13	12	DON'T BRING LULU — Dorothy Provine (Warner Bros)
11	13	MY FRIEND THE SEA — Petula Clark (Pye)
19	14	TOY BALLOONS — Russ Conway (Columbia)
21	15	YOU'RE THE ONLY GOOD THING (THAT'S HAPPENED TO ME) — Jim Reeves (RCA)
9	16	WALKIN' BACK TO HAPPINESS — Helen Shapiro (Columbia)
16	17	I CRIED FOR YOU — Ricky Stevens (Columbia)
8	18	I'LL GET BY — Shirley Bassey (Columbia)
15	19	BIG BAD JOHN — Jimmy Dean (Philips)
12	20	TAKE FIVE — Dave Brubeck Quartet (Fontana)
-	21	I UNDERSTAND — G-Clefs (London)
-	22	RUN TO HIM — Bobby Vee (London)
16	23	HIS LATEST FLAME — Elvis Presley (RCA)
26	24	CHARLESTON — Temperance Seven (Parlophone)
30	25	GOODBYE CRUEL WORLD — James Darren (Pye International)
20	26	MRS. MILLS MEDLEY — Mrs. Mills (Parlophone)
30	27	KING KONG — Terry Lightfoot & His Jazzmen (Columbia)
23	28	WHEN THE GIRL IN YOUR ARMS IS THE GIRL IN YOUR HEART — Cliff Richard (Columbia)
-	29	SEPTEMBER IN THE RAIN — Dinah Washington (Mercury)
-	30	COME ALONG PLEASE — Bob Wallis (Pye Jazz)

The end of 1961 had a somewhat instrumental look about the upper chart reaches, as Kenny Ball had his biggest hit yet with his trad arrangement of a Russian tune as *Midnight In Moscow*. Sandy Nelson belatedly followed *Teen Beat* with another rock drum showcase on *Let There Be Drums*, and Acker Bilk eschewed his jazz style completely for the clarinet-and-strings piece *Stranger On The Shore*, the theme to a children's TV series. Both Bilk's and Ball's discs would become US million-sellers during 1962.

January 1962

6 January 1962

last week	this	Title / Artist (Label)
2	1	STRANGER ON THE SHORE — Mr Acker Bilk (Columbia)
1	2	MOON RIVER — Danny Williams (HMV)
2	3	TOWER OF STRENGTH — Frankie Vaughan (Philips)
6	4	LET THERE BE DRUMS — Sandy Nelson (London)
4	5	JOHNNY WILL — Pat Boone (London)
5	6	MIDNIGHT IN MOSCOW — Kenny Ball & His Jazzmen (Pye Jazz)
8	7	HAPPY BIRTHDAY SWEET SIXTEEN — Neil Sedaka (RCA)
9	8	I'D NEVER FIND ANOTHER YOU — Billy Fury (Decca)
10	9	MULTIPLICATION — Bobby Darin (London)
11	10	SO LONG BABY — Del Shannon (London)
14	11	TOY BALLOONS — Russ Conway (Columbia)
7	12	TAKE GOOD CARE OF MY BABY — Bobby Vee (London)
12	13	DON'T BRING LULU — Dorothy Provine (Warner Bros)
15	14	YOU'RE THE ONLY GOOD THING (THAT'S HAPPENED TO ME) — Jim Reeves (RCA)
-	15	LET'S TWIST AGAIN — Chubby Checker (Columbia)
21	16	I UNDERSTAND — G-Clefs (London)
22	17	RUN TO HIM — Bobby Vee (London)
13	18	MY FRIEND THE SEA — Petula Clark (Pye)
16	19	WALKIN' BACK TO HAPPINESS — Helen Shapiro (Columbia)
19	20	BIG BAD JOHN — Jimmy Dean (Philips)
20	21	TAKE FIVE — Dave Brubeck Quartet (Fontana)
-	22	THE TWIST — Chubby Checker (Columbia)
17	23	I CRIED FOR YOU — Ricky Stevens (Columbia)
18	24	I'LL GET BY — Shirley Bassey (Columbia)
-	25	SON THIS IS SHE — John Leyton (HMV)
25	26	GOODBYE CRUEL WORLD — James Darren (Pye International)
-	27	THE LANGUAGE OF LOVE — John D. Loudermilk (RCA)
23	28	HIS LATEST FLAME — Elvis Presley (RCA)
24	29	CHARLESTON — Temperance Seven (Parlophone)
30	30	COME ALONG PLEASE — Bob Wallis (Pye Jazz)

13 January 1962

last week	this	Title / Artist (Label)
-	1	THE YOUNG ONES — Cliff Richard (Columbia)
1	2	STRANGER ON THE SHORE — Mr Acker Bilk (Columbia)
4	3	LET THERE BE DRUMS — Sandy Nelson (London)
8	4	I'D NEVER FIND ANOTHER YOU — Billy Fury (Decca)
9	5	MULTIPLICATION — Bobby Darin (London)
2	6	MOON RIVER — Danny Williams (HMV)
15	7	LET'S TWIST AGAIN — Chubby Checker (Columbia)
7	8	HAPPY BIRTHDAY SWEET SIXTEEN — Neil Sedaka (RCA)
6	9	MIDNIGHT IN MOSCOW — Kenny Ball & His Jazzmen (Pye Jazz)
5	10	JOHNNY WILL — Pat Boone (London)
22	11	THE TWIST — Chubby Checker (Columbia)
17	12	RUN TO HIM — Bobby Vee (London)
27	13	THE LANGUAGE OF LOVE — John D. Loudermilk (RCA)
3	14	TOWER OF STRENGTH — Frankie Vaughan (Philips)
10	15	SO LONG BABY — Del Shannon (London)
-	16	THE LION SLEEPS TONIGHT — Tokens (RCA)
11	17	TOY BALLOONS — Russ Conway (Columbia)
25	18	SON THIS IS SHE — John Leyton (HMV)
12	19	TAKE GOOD CARE OF MY BABY — Bobby Vee (London)
14	20	YOU'RE THE ONLY GOOD THING (THAT'S HAPPENED TO ME) — Jim Reeves (RCA)
13	21	DON'T BRING LULU — Dorothy Provine (Warner Bros)
16	22	I UNDERSTAND — G-Clefs (London)
21	23	TAKE FIVE — Dave Brubeck Quartet (Fontana)
18	24	MY FRIEND THE SEA — Petula Clark (Pye)
19	25	WALKIN' BACK TO HAPPINESS — Helen Shapiro (Columbia)
26	26	GOODBYE CRUEL WORLD — James Darren (Pye International)
23	27	I CRIED FOR YOU — Ricky Stevens (Columbia)
-	28	PEPPERMINT TWIST — Danny Peppermint & the Jumping Jacks (London)
-	29	WALK ON BY — Leroy Van Dyke (Mercury)
-	30	SEPTEMBER IN THE RAIN — Dinah Washington (Mercury)

20 January 1962

last week	this	Title / Artist (Label)
1	1	THE YOUNG ONES — Cliff Richard (Columbia)
2	2	STRANGER ON THE SHORE — Mr Acker Bilk (Columbia)
4	3	I'D NEVER FIND ANOTHER YOU — Billy Fury (Decca)
7	4	LET'S TWIST AGAIN — Chubby Checker (Columbia)
5	5	MULTIPLICATION — Bobby Darin (London)
3	6	LET THERE BE DRUMS — Sandy Nelson (London)
8	7	HAPPY BIRTHDAY SWEET SIXTEEN — Neil Sedaka (RCA)
12	8	RUN TO HIM — Bobby Vee (London)
11	9	THE TWIST — Chubby Checker (Columbia)
9	10	JOHNNY WILL — Pat Boone (London)
9	11	MIDNIGHT IN MOSCOW — Kenny Ball & His Jazzmen (Pye Jazz)
6	12	MOON RIVER — Danny Williams (HMV)
16	13	THE LION SLEEPS TONIGHT — Tokens (RCA)
29	14	WALK ON BY — Leroy Van Dyke (Mercury)
13	15	THE LANGUAGE OF LOVE — John D. Loudermilk (RCA)
-	16	CRYING IN THE RAIN — Everly Brothers (Warner Bros)
18	17	SON THIS IS SHE — John Leyton (HMV)
-	18	FORGET ME NOT — Eden Kane (Decca)
15	19	SO LONG BABY — Del Shannon (London)
22	20	I UNDERSTAND — G-Clefs (London)
18	21	TAKE GOOD CARE OF MY BABY — Bobby Vee (London)
26	22	GOODBYE CRUEL WORLD — James Darren (Pye International)
14	23	TOWER OF STRENGTH — Frankie Vaughan (Philips)
17	24	TOY BALLOONS — Russ Conway (Columbia)
20	25	YOU'RE THE ONLY GOOD THING (THAT'S HAPPENED TO ME) — Jim Reeves (RCA)
24	26	MY FRIEND THE SEA — Petula Clark (Pye)
21	27	DON'T BRING LULU — Dorothy Provine (Warner Bros)
30	28	SEPTEMBER IN THE RAIN — Dinah Washington (Mercury)
23	29	TAKE FIVE — Dave Brubeck Quartet (Fontana)
25	30	WALKIN' BACK TO HAPPINESS — Helen Shapiro (Columbia)

27 January 1962

last week	this	Title / Artist (Label)
1	1	THE YOUNG ONES — Cliff Richard (Columbia)
4	2	LET'S TWIST AGAIN — Chubby Checker (Columbia)
3	3	I'D NEVER FIND ANOTHER YOU — Billy Fury (Decca)
7	4	HAPPY BIRTHDAY SWEET SIXTEEN — Neil Sedaka (RCA)
2	5	STRANGER ON THE SHORE — Mr Acker Bilk (Columbia)
5	6	MULTIPLICATION — Bobby Darin (London)
18	7	FORGET ME NOT — Eden Kane (Decca)
8	8	RUN TO HIM — Bobby Vee (London)
14	9	WALK ON BY — Leroy Van Dyke (Mercury)
6	10	LET THERE BE DRUMS — Sandy Nelson (London)
9	11	THE TWIST — Chubby Checker (Columbia)
16	12	CRYING IN THE RAIN — Everly Brothers (Warner Bros)
11	13	MIDNIGHT IN MOSCOW — Kenny Ball & His Jazzmen (Pye Jazz)
13	14	THE LION SLEEPS TONIGHT — Tokens (RCA)
12	15	MOON RIVER — Danny Williams (HMV)
-	16	LONESOME — Adam Faith (Parlophone)
10	17	JOHNNY WILL — Pat Boone (London)
15	18	THE LANGUAGE OF LOVE — John D. Loudermilk (RCA)
17	19	SON THIS IS SHE — John Leyton (HMV)
-	20	THE COMANCHEROS — Lonnie Donegan (Pye)
-	21	JEANNIE — Danny Williams (HMV)
-	22	D-DARLING — Anthony Newley (Decca)
22	23	GOODBYE CRUEL WORLD — James Darren (Pye International)
25	24	YOU'RE THE ONLY GOOD THING (THAT'S HAPPENED TO ME) — Jim Reeves (RCA)
19	25	SO LONG BABY — Del Shannon (London)
26	26	DON'T BRING LULU — Dorothy Provine (Warner Bros)
-	27	PEPPERMINT TWIST — Joey Dee & the Starliters (Columbia)
28	28	SEPTEMBER IN THE RAIN — Dinah Washington (Mercury)
20	29	I UNDERSTAND — G-Clefs (London)
24	30	TOY BALLOONS — Russ Conway (Columbia)

With *The Young Ones* - a song in which he initially had so little faith that he wanted it released as the B-side of the single - Cliff Richard joined Elvis and Lonnie Donegan in the ultra-select club of straight-in-at-Number-One hitmakers. Boosted by (and, in turn, boosting) Cliff and the Shadow's film musical of the same title, which was a huge box office hit in the UK, this would become his all-time most successful single domestically, with British sales alone topping a million.

February 1962

last/this week — 3 February 1962

Last	This	Title / Artist
1	1	THE YOUNG ONES — Cliff Richard (Columbia)
2	2	LET'S TWIST AGAIN — Chubby Checker (Columbia)
7	3	FORGET ME NOT — Eden Kane (Decca)
-	4	ROCK-A-HULA BABY — Elvis Presley (RCA)
6	5	MULTIPLICATION — Bobby Darin (London)
3	6	HAPPY BIRTHDAY SWEET SIXTEEN — Neil Sedaka (RCA)
3	7	I'D NEVER FIND ANOTHER YOU — Billy Fury (Decca)
5	8	STRANGER ON THE SHORE — Mr Acker Bilk (Columbia)
9	9	WALK ON BY — Leroy Van Dyke (Mercury)
10	10	LET THERE BE DRUMS — Sandy Nelson (London)
11	11	THE TWIST — Chubby Checker (Columbia)
8	12	RUN TO HIM — Bobby Vee (London)
12	13	CRYING IN THE RAIN — Everly Brothers (Warner Bros)
16	13	LONESOME — Adam Faith (Parlophone)
27	15	PEPPERMINT TWIST — Joey Dee & the Starliters (Columbia)
20	16	THE COMANCHEROS — Lonnie Donegan (Pye)
14	17	THE LION SLEEPS TONIGHT — Tokens (RCA)
18	18	THE LANGUAGE OF LOVE — John D. Loudermilk (RCA)
21	19	JEANNIE — Danny Williams (HMV)
22	20	D-DARLING — Anthony Newley (Decca)
19	21	SON THIS IS SHE — John Leyton (HMV)
17	22	JOHNNY WILL — Pat Boone (London)
23	23	YOU'RE THE ONLY GOOD THING (THAT'S HAPPENED TO ME) — Jim Reeves (RCA)
13	24	MIDNIGHT IN MOSCOW — Kenny Ball & His Jazzmen (Pye Jazz)
15	24	MOON RIVER — Danny Williams (HMV)
-	26	DON'T STOP TWIST — Frankie Vaughan (Philips)
-	27	A LITTLE BITTY TEAR — Miki & Griff (Pye)
-	28	WIMOWEH — Karl Denver (Decca)
-	29	HE'S OLD ENOUGH TO KNOW BETTER — Brook Brothers (Pye)
-	30	CAN'T HELP FALLING IN LOVE — Elvis Presley (RCA)

10 February 1962

Last	This	Title / Artist
1	1	THE YOUNG ONES — Cliff Richard (Columbia)
4	2	ROCK-A-HULA BABY — Elvis Presley (RCA)
3	3	LET'S TWIST AGAIN — Chubby Checker (Columbia)
	4	FORGET ME NOT — Eden Kane (Decca)
9	5	WALK ON BY — Leroy Van Dyke (Mercury)
6	6	HAPPY BIRTHDAY SWEET SIXTEEN — Neil Sedaka (RCA)
	7	MULTIPLICATION — Bobby Darin (London)
7	8	I'D NEVER FIND ANOTHER YOU — Billy Fury (Decca)
8	9	STRANGER ON THE SHORE — Mr Acker Bilk (Columbia)
13	10	CRYING IN THE RAIN — Everly Brothers (Warner Bros)
15	11	PEPPERMINT TWIST — Joey Dee & the Starliters (Columbia)
-	11	A LITTLE BITTY TEAR — Burl Ives (Brunswick)
12	11	RUN TO HIM — Bobby Vee (London)
13	14	LONESOME — Adam Faith (Parlophone)
16	15	THE COMANCHEROS — Lonnie Donegan (Pye)
19	16	JEANNIE — Danny Williams (HMV)
11	17	THE TWIST — Chubby Checker (Columbia)
10	18	LET THERE BE DRUMS — Sandy Nelson (London)
30	19	CAN'T HELP FALLING IN LOVE — Elvis Presley (RCA)
26	20	DON'T STOP TWIST — Frankie Vaughan (Philips)
17	21	THE LION SLEEPS TONIGHT — Tokens (RCA)
24	22	MIDNIGHT IN MOSCOW — Kenny Ball & His Jazzmen (Pye Jazz)
28	23	WIMOWEH — Karl Denver (Decca)
20	24	D-DARLING — Anthony Newley (Decca)
27	25	A LITTLE BITTY TEAR — Miki & Griff (Pye)
-	26	IT'S A RAGGY WALTZ — Dave Brubeck Quartet (Fontana)
18	27	THE LANGUAGE OF LOVE — John D. Loudermilk (RCA)
-	28	LESSONS IN LOVE — Allisons (Fontana)
-	28	SOFTLY AS I LEAVE YOU — Matt Monro (Parlophone)
24	28	MOON RIVER — Danny Williams (HMV)

17 February 1962

Last	This	Title / Artist
1	1	THE YOUNG ONES — Cliff Richard (Columbia)
3	2	LET'S TWIST AGAIN — Chubby Checker (Columbia)
2	3	ROCK-A-HULA BABY — Elvis Presley (RCA)
4	4	FORGET ME NOT — Eden Kane (Decca)
5	5	WALK ON BY — Leroy Van Dyke (Mercury)
10	6	CRYING IN THE RAIN — Everly Brothers (Warner Bros)
11	7	A LITTLE BITTY TEAR — Burl Ives (Brunswick)
6	8	HAPPY BIRTHDAY SWEET SIXTEEN — Neil Sedaka (RCA)
8	9	I'D NEVER FIND ANOTHER YOU — Billy Fury (Decca)
11	10	RUN TO HIM — Bobby Vee (London)
9	11	STRANGER ON THE SHORE — Mr Acker Bilk (Columbia)
11	12	PEPPERMINT TWIST — Joey Dee & the Starliters (Columbia)
7	13	MULTIPLICATION — Bobby Darin (London)
23	14	WIMOWEH — Karl Denver (Decca)
14	15	LONESOME — Adam Faith (Parlophone)
15	16	THE COMANCHEROS — Lonnie Donegan (Pye)
16	17	JEANNIE — Danny Williams (HMV)
19	18	CAN'T HELP FALLING IN LOVE — Elvis Presley (RCA)
20	19	DON'T STOP TWIST — Frankie Vaughan (Philips)
28	20	SOFTLY AS I LEAVE YOU — Matt Monro (Parlophone)
17	21	THE TWIST — Chubby Checker (Columbia)
18	22	LET THERE BE DRUMS — Sandy Nelson (London)
-	23	MARCH OF THE SIAMESE CHILDREN — Kenny Ball & His Jazzmen (Pye Jazz)
-	24	TELL ME WHAT HE SAID — Helen Shapiro (Columbia)
26	25	IT'S A RAGGY WALTZ — Dave Brubeck Quartet (Fontana)
-	26	I'LL SEE YOU IN MY DREAMS — Pat Boone (London)
22	27	MIDNIGHT IN MOSCOW — Kenny Ball & His Jazzmen (Pye Jazz)
-	28	TONIGHT — Shirley Bassey (Columbia)
-	29	THE WANDERER — Dion (HMV)
28	30	MOON RIVER — Danny Williams (HMV)

24 February 1962

Last	This	Title / Artist
2	1	LET'S TWIST AGAIN — Chubby Checker (Columbia)
1	2	THE YOUNG ONES — Cliff Richard (Columbia)
3	3	ROCK-A-HULA BABY — Elvis Presley (RCA)
4	4	FORGET ME NOT — Eden Kane (Decca)
14	5	WIMOWEH — Karl Denver (Decca)
5	6	WALK ON BY — Leroy Van Dyke (Mercury)
23	7	MARCH OF THE SIAMESE CHILDREN — Kenny Ball & His Jazzmen (Pye Jazz)
6	8	CRYING IN THE RAIN — Everly Brothers (Warner Bros)
18	9	CAN'T HELP FALLING IN LOVE — Elvis Presley (RCA)
7	10	A LITTLE BITTY TEAR — Burl Ives (Brunswick)
10	11	RUN TO HIM — Bobby Vee (London)
11	12	STRANGER ON THE SHORE — Mr Acker Bilk (Columbia)
8	13	HAPPY BIRTHDAY SWEET SIXTEEN — Neil Sedaka (RCA)
9	14	I'D NEVER FIND ANOTHER YOU — Billy Fury (Decca)
13	15	MULTIPLICATION — Bobby Darin (London)
24	16	TELL ME WHAT HE SAID — Helen Shapiro (Columbia)
29	17	THE WANDERER — Dion (HMV)
20	18	SOFTLY AS I LEAVE YOU — Matt Monro (Parlophone)
26	19	I'LL SEE YOU IN MY DREAMS — Pat Boone (London)
12	20	PEPPERMINT TWIST — Joey Dee & the Starliters (Columbia)
17	21	JEANNIE — Danny Williams (HMV)
15	22	LONESOME — Adam Faith (Parlophone)
16	23	THE COMANCHEROS — Lonnie Donegan (Pye)
19	24	DON'T STOP TWIST — Frankie Vaughan (Philips)
-	25	RING-A-DING GIRL — Ronnie Carroll (Philips)
-	26	A HOLE IN THE GROUND — Bernard Cribbins (Parlophone)
22	27	LET THERE BE DRUMS — Sandy Nelson (London)
-	28	TWISTIN THE NIGHT AWAY — Sam Cooke (RCA)
28	29	TONIGHT — Shirley Bassey (Columbia)
-	30	LESSON ONE — Russ Conway (Columbia)

Twist fever hit the UK early in 1962, shortly after the two-year-old dance craze's huge resurrection in the US. The charts started to fill with twist records as artists jumped on the bandwagon. But undisputed king of the genre was Chubby Checker, whose *The Twist* (from 1960) and *Let's Twist Again* (from '61) led the way. While the former song was a second-time-around Number One in America, the latter was (and has remained) the more popular here, eventually toppling *The Young Ones* from the chart top.

3 March 1962

last	this	Entry
1	1	LET'S TWIST AGAIN — Chubby Checker (Columbia)
2	2	THE YOUNG ONES — Cliff Richard (Columbia)
7	3	MARCH OF THE SIAMESE CHILDREN — Kenny Ball & His Jazzmen (Pye Jazz)
5	4	WIMOWEH — Karl Denver (Decca)
9	5	CAN'T HELP FALLING IN LOVE — Elvis Presley (RCA)
16	6	TELL ME WHAT HE SAID — Helen Shapiro (Columbia)
3	7	ROCK-A-HULA BABY — Elvis Presley (RCA)
4	8	FORGET ME NOT — Eden Kane (Decca)
10	9	A LITTLE BITTY TEAR — Burl Ives (Brunswick)
8	10	CRYING IN THE RAIN — Everly Brothers (Warner Bros)
6	11	WALK ON BY — Leroy Van Dyke (Mercury)
-	12	WONDERFUL LAND — Shadows (Columbia)
12	13	STRANGER ON THE SHORE — Mr Acker Bilk (Columbia)
18	13	SOFTLY AS I LEAVE YOU — Matt Monro (Parlophone)
13	15	HAPPY BIRTHDAY SWEET SIXTEEN — Neil Sedaka (RCA)
20	16	PEPPERMINT TWIST — Joey Dee & the Starliters (Columbia)
26	17	A HOLE IN THE GROUND — Bernard Cribbins (Parlophone)
19	18	I'LL SEE YOU IN MY DREAMS — Pat Boone (London)
17	18	THE WANDERER — Dion (HMV)
11	18	RUN TO HIM — Bobby Vee (London)
14	21	I'D NEVER FIND ANOTHER YOU — Billy Fury (Decca)
21	22	JEANNIE — Danny Williams (HMV)
-	23	LESSONS IN LOVE — Allisons (Fontana)
25	24	RING-A-DING GIRL — Ronnie Carroll (Philips)
30	25	LESSON ONE — Russ Conway (Columbia)
29	26	TONIGHT — Shirley Bassey (Columbia)
-	27	PIANISSIMO — Ken Dodd (Decca)
23	28	THE COMANCHEROS — Lonnie Donegan (Pye)
-	29	IT'S A RAGGY WALTZ — Dave Brubeck Quartet (Fontana)
28	29	TWISTIN' THE NIGHT AWAY — Sam Cooke (RCA)
24	29	DON'T STOP TWIST — Frankie Vaughan (Philips)

10 March 1962

last	this	Entry
3	1	MARCH OF THE SIAMESE CHILDREN — Kenny Ball & His Jazzmen (Pye Jazz)
1	2	LET'S TWIST AGAIN — Chubby Checker (Columbia)
4	3	WIMOWEH — Karl Denver (Decca)
2	4	THE YOUNG ONES — Cliff Richard (Columbia)
6	4	TELL ME WHAT HE SAID — Helen Shapiro (Columbia)
12	6	WONDERFUL LAND — Shadows (Columbia)
5	7	CAN'T HELP FALLING IN LOVE — Elvis Presley (RCA)
7	8	ROCK-A-HULA BABY — Elvis Presley (RCA)
13	9	STRANGER ON THE SHORE — Mr Acker Bilk (Columbia)
10	10	CRYING IN THE RAIN — Everly Brothers (Warner Bros)
8	11	FORGET ME NOT — Eden Kane (Decca)
13	12	SOFTLY AS I LEAVE YOU — Matt Monro (Parlophone)
9	13	A LITTLE BITTY TEAR — Burl Ives (Brunswick)
17	14	A HOLE IN THE GROUND — Bernard Cribbins (Parlophone)
11	14	WALK ON BY — Leroy Van Dyke (Mercury)
18	16	THE WANDERER — Dion (HMV)
29	17	TWISTIN' THE NIGHT AWAY — Sam Cooke (RCA)
-	18	DREAM BABY — Roy Orbison (London)
18	19	I'LL SEE YOU IN MY DREAMS — Pat Boone (London)
-	20	LETTER FULL OF TEARS — Billy Fury (Decca)
21	21	NEVER GOODBYE — Karl Denver (Decca)
-	22	THEME FROM Z CARS (JOHNNY TODD) — Johnny Keating (Piccadilly)
22	23	JEANNIE — Danny Williams (HMV)
25	24	LESSON ONE — Russ Conway (Columbia)
15	24	HAPPY BIRTHDAY SWEET SIXTEEN — Neil Sedaka (RCA)
-	26	I AIN'T GOT NOBODY — Buddy Greco (Fontana)
23	27	LESSONS IN LOVE — Allisons (Fontana)
-	28	BRAZILIAN LOVE SONG — Nat King Cole (Capitol)
16	28	PEPPERMINT TWIST — Joey Dee & the Starliters (Columbia)
27	30	PIANISSIMO — Ken Dodd (Decca)
-	30	LISTEN TO ME — Buddy Holly (Coral)

17 March 1962

last	this	Entry
6	1	WONDERFUL LAND — Shadows (Columbia)
1	2	MARCH OF THE SIAMESE CHILDREN — Kenny Ball & His Jazzmen (Pye Jazz)
4	3	TELL ME WHAT HE SAID — Helen Shapiro (Columbia)
2	4	LET'S TWIST AGAIN — Chubby Checker (Columbia)
7	5	CAN'T HELP FALLING IN LOVE — Elvis Presley (RCA)
3	6	WIMOWEH — Karl Denver (Decca)
4	7	THE YOUNG ONES — Cliff Richard (Columbia)
8	8	ROCK-A-HULA BABY — Elvis Presley (RCA)
14	9	A HOLE IN THE GROUND — Bernard Cribbins (Parlophone)
17	10	TWISTIN' THE NIGHT AWAY — Sam Cooke (RCA)
9	11	STRANGER ON THE SHORE — Mr Acker Bilk (Columbia)
18	12	DREAM BABY — Roy Orbison (London)
16	13	THE WANDERER — Dion (HMV)
12	14	SOFTLY AS I LEAVE YOU — Matt Monro (Parlophone)
10	15	CRYING IN THE RAIN — Everly Brothers (Warner Bros)
14	16	WALK ON BY — Leroy Van Dyke (Mercury)
20	17	LETTER FULL OF TEARS — Billy Fury (Decca)
13	18	A LITTLE BITTY TEAR — Burl Ives (Brunswick)
11	19	FORGET ME NOT — Eden Kane (Decca)
26	20	I AIN'T GOT NOBODY — Buddy Greco (Fontana)
-	21	HEY! BABY — Bruce Channel (Mercury)
-	22	FANLIGHT FANNY — Clinton Ford (Oriole)
19	23	I'LL SEE YOU IN MY DREAMS — Pat Boone (London)
22	24	THEME FROM Z CARS (JOHNNY TODD) — Johnny Keating (Piccadilly)
21	25	NEVER GOODBYE — Karl Denver (Decca)
23	26	JEANNIE — Danny Williams (HMV)
28	27	BRAZILIAN LOVE SONG — Nat King Cole (Capitol)
30	28	LISTEN TO ME — Buddy Holly (Coral)
-	29	DUKE OF EARL — Gene Chandler (Columbia)
24	29	LESSON ONE — Russ Conway (Columbia)
-	29	DR. KILDARE THEME (THREE STARS WILL SHINE TONIGHT) — Johnnie Spence (Parlophone)

24 March 1962

last	this	Entry
1	1	WONDERFUL LAND — Shadows (Columbia)
3	2	TELL ME WHAT HE SAID — Helen Shapiro (Columbia)
5	3	CAN'T HELP FALLING IN LOVE — Elvis Presley (RCA)
2	4	MARCH OF THE SIAMESE CHILDREN — Kenny Ball & His Jazzmen (Pye Jazz)
4	5	LET'S TWIST AGAIN — Chubby Checker (Columbia)
6	6	WIMOWEH — Karl Denver (Decca)
9	7	A HOLE IN THE GROUND — Bernard Cribbins (Parlophone)
10	8	TWISTIN' THE NIGHT AWAY — Sam Cooke (RCA)
21	9	HEY! BABY — Bruce Channel (Mercury)
12	10	DREAM BABY — Roy Orbison (London)
11	11	STRANGER ON THE SHORE — Mr Acker Bilk (Columbia)
7	12	THE YOUNG ONES — Cliff Richard (Columbia)
8	13	ROCK-A-HULA BABY — Elvis Presley (RCA)
13	14	THE WANDERER — Dion (HMV)
14	15	SOFTLY AS I LEAVE YOU — Matt Monro (Parlophone)
24	16	THEME FROM Z CARS (JOHNNY TODD) — Johnny Keating (Piccadilly)
17	17	LETTER FULL OF TEARS — Billy Fury (Decca)
-	17	HEY LITTLE GIRL — Del Shannon (London)
29	19	DR. KILDARE THEME (THREE STARS WILL SHINE TONIGHT) — Johnnie Spence (Parlophone)
-	20	WHEN MY LITTLE GIRL IS SMILING — Drifters (London)
18	21	A LITTLE BITTY TEAR — Burl Ives (Brunswick)
16	22	WALK ON BY — Leroy Van Dyke (Mercury)
23	23	I'LL SEE YOU IN MY DREAMS — Pat Boone (London)
20	23	I AIN'T GOT NOBODY — Buddy Greco (Fontana)
19	25	FORGET ME NOT — Eden Kane (Decca)
25	26	NEVER GOODBYE — Karl Denver (Decca)
22	27	FANLIGHT FANNY — Clinton Ford (Oriole)
-	28	HEAVEN'S PLAN — Mark Wynter (Decca)
27	29	BRAZILIAN LOVE SONG — Nat King Cole (Capitol)
-	30	THEME FROM Z CARS (JOHNNY TODD) — Norrie Paramor (Columbia)

Strong individual sales on both sides of Elvis Presley's *Rock-A-Hula Baby/Can't Help Falling in Love* ironically prevented the single from topping the chart, though since the sides reached Numbers Two and Three respectively, there was hardly a problem. It was instead the Shadows who swept all before them; *Wonderful Land* was written by Jerry Lordan, who had given the group *Apache*, and was their first instrumental to be augmented by strings. Top in its third week, it remained there for two months.

March – April 1962

last / this week

31 March 1962	7 April 1962	14 April 1962	21 April 1962

31 March 1962

1 1 WONDERFUL LAND Shadows (Columbia)
2 2 TELL ME WHAT HE SAID Helen Shapiro (Columbia)
3 3 CAN'T HELP FALLING IN LOVE Elvis Presley (RCA)
4 4 MARCH OF THE SIAMESE CHILDREN Kenny Ball & His Jazzmen (Pye Jazz)
9 5 HEY! BABY Bruce Channel (Mercury)
10 6 DREAM BABY Roy Orbison (London)
5 7 LET'S TWIST AGAIN Chubby Checker (Columbia)
8 7 TWISTIN' THE NIGHT AWAY Sam Cooke (RCA)
6 9 WIMOWEH Karl Denver (Decca)
7 10 A HOLE IN THE GROUND Bernard Cribbins (Parlophone)
11 11 STRANGER ON THE SHORE Mr Acker Bilk (Columbia)
12 12 THE YOUNG ONES Cliff Richard (Columbia)
15 13 SOFTLY AS I LEAVE YOU Del Monro (Parlophone)
17 14 HEY LITTLE GIRL Del Shannon (London)
26 15 NEVER GOODBYE Karl Denver (Decca)
14 16 THE WANDERER Dion (HMV)
20 17 WHEN MY LITTLE GIRL IS SMILING Drifters (London)
13 18 ROCK-A-HULA BABY Elvis Presley (RCA)
16 19 THEME FROM Z CARS (JOHNNY TODD) Johnny Keating (Piccadilly)
- 20 SLOW TWISTN' Chubby Checker (Columbia)
- 21 LOVE ME WARM AND TENDER Paul Anka (RCA)
17 21 LETTER FULL OF TEARS Billy Fury (Decca)
- 23 WHEN MY LITTLE GIRL IS SMILING Jimmy Justice (Pye)
19 23 DR. KILDARE THEME (THREE STARS WILL SHINE TONIGHT) Johnnie Spence (Parlophone)
28 25 HEAVEN'S PLAN Mark Wynter (Decca)
- 26 TEACH ME TO TWIST Chubby Checker & Bobby Rydell (Columbia)
21 27 A LITTLE BITTY TEAR Burl Ives (Brunswick)
- 28 WHEN MY LITTLE GIRL IS SMILING Craig Douglas (Top Rank)
23 29 I AIN'T GOT NOBODY Buddy Greco (Fontana)
27 30 FANLIGHT FANNY Clinton Ford (Oriole)
- 30 SPEAK TO ME PRETTY Brenda Lee (Brunswick)

7 April 1962

1 1 WONDERFUL LAND Shadows (Columbia)
5 2 HEY! BABY Bruce Channel (Mercury)
2 3 TELL ME WHAT HE SAID Helen Shapiro (Columbia)
6 4 DREAM BABY Roy Orbison (London)
7 5 TWISTIN' THE NIGHT AWAY Sam Cooke (RCA)
3 6 CAN'T HELP FALLING IN LOVE Elvis Presley (RCA)
9 7 WIMOWEH Karl Denver (Decca)
7 8 LET'S TWIST AGAIN Chubby Checker (Columbia)
23 9 WHEN MY LITTLE GIRL IS SMILING Jimmy Justice (Pye)
4 10 MARCH OF THE SIAMESE CHILDREN Kenny Ball & His Jazzmen (Pye Jazz)
11 11 STRANGER ON THE SHORE Mr Acker Bilk (Columbia)
15 12 NEVER GOODBYE Karl Denver (Decca)
13 13 SOFTLY AS I LEAVE YOU Matt Monro (Parlophone)
14 14 HEY LITTLE GIRL Del Shannon (London)
10 15 A HOLE IN THE GROUND Bernard Cribbins (Parlophone)
23 16 DR. KILDARE THEME (THREE STARS WILL SHINE TONIGHT) Johnnie Spence (Parlophone)
28 17 WHEN MY LITTLE GIRL IS SMILING Craig Douglas (Top Rank)
21 18 LOVE ME WARM AND TENDER Paul Anka (RCA)
12 18 THE YOUNG ONES Cliff Richard (Columbia)
19 20 THEME FROM Z CARS (JOHNNY TODD) Johnny Keating (Piccadilly)
- 21 THEME FROM Z CARS (JOHNNY TODD) Norrie Paramor (Columbia)
17 22 WHEN MY LITTLE GIRL IS SMILING Drifters (London)
20 23 SLOW TWISTN' Chubby Checker (Columbia)
16 24 THE WANDERER Dion (HMV)
- 24 THE MAIGRET THEME Joe Loss (HMV)
18 26 ROCK-A-HULA BABY Elvis Presley (RCA)
21 27 LETTER FULL OF TEARS Billy Fury (Decca)
- 28 WHAT KIND OF FOOL AM I Sammy Davis Jr. (Reprise)
25 28 HEAVEN'S PLAN Mark Wynter (Decca)
30 30 SPEAK TO ME PRETTY Brenda Lee (Brunswick)

14 April 1962

1 1 WONDERFUL LAND Shadows (Columbia)
2 2 HEY! BABY Bruce Channel (Mercury)
4 3 DREAM BABY Roy Orbison (London)
5 4 TWISTIN' THE NIGHT AWAY Sam Cooke (RCA)
9 4 WHEN MY LITTLE GIRL IS SMILING Jimmy Justice (Pye)
3 6 TELL ME WHAT HE SAID Helen Shapiro (Columbia)
14 7 HEY LITTLE GIRL Del Shannon (London)
6 8 CAN'T HELP FALLING IN LOVE Elvis Presley (RCA)
12 9 NEVER GOODBYE Karl Denver (Decca)
8 10 LET'S TWIST AGAIN Chubby Checker (Columbia)
10 11 MARCH OF THE SIAMESE CHILDREN Kenny Ball & His Jazzmen (Pye Jazz)
7 12 WIMOWEH Karl Denver (Decca)
16 13 DR. KILDARE THEME (THREE STARS WILL SHINE TONIGHT) Johnnie Spence (Parlophone)
18 14 LOVE ME WARM AND TENDER Paul Anka (RCA)
17 14 WHEN MY LITTLE GIRL IS SMILING Craig Douglas (Top Rank)
30 14 SPEAK TO ME PRETTY Brenda Lee (Brunswick)
20 17 THEME FROM Z CARS (JOHNNY TODD) Johnny Keating (Piccadilly)
11 18 STRANGER ON THE SHORE Mr Acker Bilk (Columbia)
15 19 A HOLE IN THE GROUND Bernard Cribbins (Parlophone)
24 20 THE MAIGRET THEME Joe Loss (HMV)
- 21 THE PARTY'S OVER Lonnie Donegan (Pye)
23 22 SLOW TWISTN' Chubby Checker (Columbia)
13 22 SOFTLY AS I LEAVE YOU Matt Monro (Parlophone)
26 24 ROCK-A-HULA BABY Elvis Presley (RCA)
22 25 WHEN MY LITTLE GIRL IS SMILING Drifters (London)
21 26 THEME FROM Z CARS (JOHNNY TODD) Norrie Paramor (Columbia)
- 27 LOVE LETTERS Ketty Lester (London)
- 27 YOUNG WORLD Rick Nelson (London)
- 29 NUT ROCKER B. Bumble & the Stingers (Top Rank)
18 29 THE YOUNG ONES Cliff Richard (Columbia)
- 29 EV'RYBODY'S TWISTIN' Frank Sinatra (Reprise)

21 April 1962

1 1 WONDERFUL LAND Shadows (Columbia)
2 2 HEY! BABY Bruce Channel (Mercury)
4 3 WHEN MY LITTLE GIRL IS SMILING Jimmy Justice (Pye)
3 4 DREAM BABY Roy Orbison (London)
4 5 TWISTIN' THE NIGHT AWAY Sam Cooke (RCA)
14 6 SPEAK TO ME PRETTY Brenda Lee (Brunswick)
7 7 HEY LITTLE GIRL Del Shannon (London)
6 8 TELL ME WHAT HE SAID Helen Shapiro (Columbia)
8 9 CAN'T HELP FALLING IN LOVE Elvis Presley (RCA)
9 10 NEVER GOODBYE Karl Denver (Decca)
27 11 LOVE LETTERS Ketty Lester (London)
13 12 DR. KILDARE THEME (THREE STARS WILL SHINE TONIGHT) Johnnie Spence (Parlophone)
14 13 WHEN MY LITTLE GIRL IS SMILING Craig Douglas (Top Rank)
10 14 LET'S TWIST AGAIN Chubby Checker (Columbia)
29 15 NUT ROCKER B. Bumble & the Stingers (Top Rank)
21 16 THE PARTY'S OVER Lonnie Donegan (Pye)
29 17 EV'RYBODY'S TWISTIN' Frank Sinatra (Reprise)
17 18 THEME FROM Z CARS (JOHNNY TODD) Johnny Keating (Piccadilly)
22 19 SLOW TWISTN' Chubby Checker (Columbia)
12 19 WIMOWEH Karl D nver (Decca)
20 19 THE MAIGRET THEME Joe Loss (HMV)
11 22 MARCH OF THE SIAMESE CHILDREN Kenny Ball & His Jazzmen (Pye Jazz)
22 23 SOFTLY AS I LEAVE YOU Matt Monro (Parlophone)
19 24 A HOLE IN THE GROUND Bernard Cribbins (Parlophone)
18 25 STRANGER ON THE SHORE Mr Acker Bilk (Columbia)
14 26 LOVE ME WARM AND TENDER Paul Anka (RCA)
- 26 THE WONDERFUL WORLD OF THE YOUNG Danny Williams (HMV)
27 28 YOUNG WORLD Rick Nelson (London)
24 28 ROCK-A-HULA BABY Elvis Presley (RCA)
29 30 THE YOUNG ONES Cliff Richard (Columbia)

The twist continued to be flavour of the day, as not only Sam Cooke but also the unlikely Frank Sinatra got in on the act with twist-style hits. Meanwhile, there were several close battles being fought in the chart, as two *"Baby"*s battled for the Number Two slot (Bruce Channel's *Hey!* just pipping Roy Orbison's *Dream*), two versions of TV's *Z Cars* theme paced each other, and a three-way race on *When My Little Girl Is Smiling* was won by the rank outsider, newcomer Jimmy Justice.

28 April 1962

last week	this week	Title / Artist (Label)
1	1	WONDERFUL LAND — Shadows (Columbia)
2	2	HEY! BABY — Bruce Channel (Mercury)
3	3	WHEN MY LITTLE GIRL IS SMILING — Jimmy Justice (Pye)
4	4	DREAM BABY — Roy Orbison (London)
7	5	HEY LITTLE GIRL — Del Shannon (London)
5	6	TWISTIN' THE NIGHT AWAY — Sam Cooke (RCA)
6	6	SPEAK TO ME PRETTY — Brenda Lee (Brunswick)
15	8	NUT ROCKER — B. Bumble & the Stingers (Top Rank)
26	9	THE WONDERFUL WORLD OF THE YOUNG — Danny Williams (HMV)
11	10	LOVE LETTERS — Ketty Lester (London)
10	11	NEVER GOODBYE — Karl Denver (Decca)
25	12	STRANGER ON THE SHORE — Mr Acker Bilk (Columbia)
8	13	TELL ME WHAT HE SAID — Helen Shapiro (Columbia)
17	13	EV'RYBODY'S TWISTIN' — Frank Sinatra (Reprise)
13	15	WHEN MY LITTLE GIRL IS SMILING — Craig Douglas (Top Rank)
9	16	CAN'T HELP FALLING IN LOVE — Elvis Presley (RCA)
16	17	THE PARTY'S OVER — Lonnie Donegan (Pye)
14	18	LET'S TWIST AGAIN — Chubby Checker (Columbia)
12	19	DR. KILDARE THEME (THREE STARS WILL SHINE TONIGHT) — Johnnie Spence (Parlophone)
18	20	THEME FROM Z CARS (JOHNNY TODD) — Johnny Keating (Piccadilly)
19	21	THE MAIGRET THEME — Joe Loss (HMV)
26	22	LOVE ME WARM AND TENDER — Paul Anka (RCA)
19	23	SLOW TWISTN' — Chubby Checker (Columbia)
19	24	WIMOWEH — Karl Denver (Decca)
28	25	ROCK-A-HULA BABY — Elvis Presley (RCA)
23	26	SOFTLY AS I LEAVE YOU — Matt Monro (Parlophone)
28	27	YOUNG WORLD — Rick Nelson (London)
-	28	I'M GONNA CLIP YOUR WINGS — Frankie Vaughan (Philips)
22	29	MARCH OF THE SIAMESE CHILDREN — Kenny Ball & His Jazzmen (Pye Jazz)
24	30	A HOLE IN THE GROUND — Bernard Cribbins (Parlophone)

5 May 1962

last week	this week	Title / Artist (Label)
1	1	WONDERFUL LAND — Shadows (Columbia)
8	2	NUT ROCKER — B. Bumble & the Stingers (Top Rank)
2	3	HEY! BABY — Bruce Channel (Mercury)
4	4	SPEAK TO ME PRETTY — Brenda Lee (Brunswick)
3	5	WHEN MY LITTLE GIRL IS SMILING — Jimmy Justice (Pye)
5	6	HEY LITTLE GIRL — Del Shannon (London)
4	7	DREAM BABY — Roy Orbison (London)
10	8	LOVE LETTERS — Ketty Lester (London)
6	9	TWISTIN' THE NIGHT AWAY — Sam Cooke (RCA)
9	10	THE WONDERFUL WORLD OF THE YOUNG — Danny Williams (HMV)
17	11	THE PARTY'S OVER — Lonnie Donegan (Pye)
12	12	STRANGER ON THE SHORE — Mr Acker Bilk (Columbia)
15	13	WHEN MY LITTLE GIRL IS SMILING — Craig Douglas (Top Rank)
13	14	EV'RYBODY'S TWISTIN' — Frank Sinatra (Reprise)
11	15	NEVER GOODBYE — Karl Denver (Decca)
16	16	CAN'T HELP FALLING IN LOVE — Elvis Presley (RCA)
-	17	AS YOU LIKE IT — Adam Faith (Parlophone)
18	18	LET'S TWIST AGAIN — Chubby Checker (Columbia)
20	19	THEME FROM Z CARS (JOHNNY TODD) — Johnny Keating (Piccadilly)
21	20	THE MAIGRET THEME — Joe Loss (HMV)
27	21	YOUNG WORLD — Rick Nelson (London)
13	22	TELL ME WHAT HE SAID — Helen Shapiro (Columbia)
-	23	LET'S TALK ABOUT LOVE — Helen Shapiro (Columbia)
19	24	DR. KILDARE THEME (THREE STARS WILL SHINE TONIGHT) — Johnnie Spence (Parlophone)
23	25	SLOW TWISTN' — Chubby Checker (Columbia)
-	25	KING OF CLOWNS — Neil Sedaka (RCA)
22	27	LOVE ME WARM AND TENDER — Paul Anka (RCA)
-	28	JOHNNY ANGEL — Shelley Fabares (Pye International)
-	28	DON'T BREAK THE HEART THAT LOVES YOU — Connie Francis (MGM)
-	28	LOVER PLEASE — Maureen & the Vernon Girls (Decca)

12 May 1962

last week	this week	Title / Artist (Label)
2	1	NUT ROCKER — B. Bumble & the Stingers (Top Rank)
1	2	WONDERFUL LAND — Shadows (Columbia)
-	3	GOOD LUCK CHARM — Elvis Presley (RCA)
6	4	HEY LITTLE GIRL — Del Shannon (London)
4	5	SPEAK TO ME PRETTY — Brenda Lee (Brunswick)
5	5	WHEN MY LITTLE GIRL IS SMILING — Jimmy Justice (Pye)
-	6	I'M LOOKING OUT THE WINDOW — Cliff Richard (Columbia)
8	8	LOVE LETTERS — Ketty Lester (London)
3	9	HEY! BABY — Bruce Channel (Mercury)
7	10	DREAM BABY — Roy Orbison (London)
17	11	AS YOU LIKE IT — Adam Faith (Parlophone)
10	12	THE WONDERFUL WORLD OF THE YOUNG — Danny Williams (HMV)
11	13	THE PARTY'S OVER — Lonnie Donegan (Pye)
9	14	TWISTIN' THE NIGHT AWAY — Sam Cooke (RCA)
12	15	STRANGER ON THE SHORE — Mr Acker Bilk (Columbia)
15	16	NEVER GOODBYE — Karl Denver (Decca)
23	17	LET'S TALK ABOUT LOVE — Helen Shapiro (Columbia)
14	17	EV'RYBODY'S TWISTIN' — Frank Sinatra (Reprise)
-	19	LAST NIGHT WAS MADE FOR LOVE — Billy Fury (Decca)
13	20	WHEN MY LITTLE GIRL IS SMILING — Craig Douglas (Top Rank)
16	20	CAN'T HELP FALLING IN LOVE — Elvis Presley (RCA)
-	22	COME OUTSIDE — Mike Sarne (Parlophone)
21	23	YOUNG WORLD — Rick Nelson (London)
-	24	LONELY CITY — John Leyton (HMV)
28	25	LOVER PLEASE — Maureen & the Vernon Girls (Decca)
18	26	LET'S TWIST AGAIN — Chubby Checker (Columbia)
28	27	JOHNNY ANGEL — Shelley Fabares (Pye International)
25	27	KING OF CLOWNS — Neil Sedaka (RCA)
27	29	LOVE ME WARM AND TENDER — Paul Anka (RCA)
28	29	DON'T BREAK THE HEART THAT LOVES YOU — Connie Francis (MGM)

19 May 1962

last week	this week	Title / Artist (Label)
3	1	GOOD LUCK CHARM — Elvis Presley (RCA)
6	2	I'M LOOKING OUT THE WINDOW — Cliff Richard (Columbia)
1	3	NUT ROCKER — B. Bumble & the Stingers (Top Rank)
8	4	LOVE LETTERS — Ketty Lester (London)
2	5	WONDERFUL LAND — Shadows (Columbia)
5	6	SPEAK TO ME PRETTY — Brenda Lee (Brunswick)
11	7	AS YOU LIKE IT — Adam Faith (Parlophone)
4	8	HEY LITTLE GIRL — Del Shannon (London)
6	9	WHEN MY LITTLE GIRL IS SMILING — Jimmy Justice (Pye)
9	10	HEY! BABY — Bruce Channel (Mercury)
22	11	COME OUTSIDE — Mike Sarne (Parlophone)
19	12	LAST NIGHT WAS MADE FOR LOVE — Billy Fury (Decca)
12	13	THE WONDERFUL WORLD OF THE YOUNG — Danny Williams (HMV)
10	14	DREAM BABY — Roy Orbison (London)
14	15	TWISTIN' THE NIGHT AWAY — Sam Cooke (RCA)
17	16	LET'S TALK ABOUT LOVE — Helen Shapiro (Columbia)
24	17	LONELY CITY — John Leyton (HMV)
15	18	STRANGER ON THE SHORE — Mr Acker Bilk (Columbia)
17	19	EV'RYBODY'S TWISTIN' — Frank Sinatra (Reprise)
13	20	THE PARTY'S OVER — Lonnie Donegan (Pye)
27	21	KING OF CLOWNS — Neil Sedaka (RCA)
-	22	THE GREEN LEAVES OF SUMMER — Kenny Ball & His Jazzmen (Pye Jazz)
16	22	NEVER GOODBYE — Karl Denver (Decca)
25	22	LOVER PLEASE — Maureen & the Vernon Girls (Decca)
-	25	I DON'T KNOW WHY — Eden Kane (Decca)
-	26	GINNY COME LATELY — Brian Hyland (HMV)
23	27	YOUNG WORLD — Rick Nelson (London)
-	28	A PICTURE OF YOU — Joe Brown (Piccadilly)
-	29	HOW CAN I MEET HER — Everly Brothers (Warner Bros)
-	30	JOHNNY ANGEL — Patti Lynn (Fontana)
-	30	JEZEBEL — Marty Wilde (Philips)

The BBC might have been expected to ban B. Bumble & The Stingers' *Nut Rocker*, which gave a manic piano workout to the recognisable melody of Tchaikovsky's *Nutcracker March*, but surprisingly it got airtime and soared all the way to the top. Significantly the "group" (maverick entrepreneur Kim Fowley with some session men) never had another hit until *Nut Rocker* itself re-charted in 1972. *Stranger On The Shore* went back up the chart when Acker Bilk appeared on TV's *This Is Your Life*.

May – June 1962

26 May 1962

LW	TW	Title	Artist (Label)
1	1	GOOD LUCK CHARM	Elvis Presley (RCA)
2	2	I'M LOOKING OUT THE WINDOW	Cliff Richard (Columbia)
3	3	NUT ROCKER	B. Bumble & the Stingers (Top Rank)
4	4	LOVE LETTERS	Ketty Lester (London)
7	5	AS YOU LIKE IT	Adam Faith (Parlophone)
11	6	COME OUTSIDE	Mike Sarne (Parlophone)
5	6	WONDERFUL LAND	Shadows (Columbia)
12	8	LAST NIGHT WAS MADE FOR LOVE	Billy Fury (Decca)
25	9	I DON'T KNOW WHY	Eden Kane (Decca)
26	10	GINNY COME LATELY	Brian Hyland (HMV)
6	11	SPEAK TO ME PRETTY	Brenda Lee (Brunswick)
22	12	THE GREEN LEAVES OF SUMMER	Kenny Ball & His Jazzmen (Pye Jazz)
18	13	STRANGER ON THE SHORE	Mr Acker Bilk (Columbia)
8	14	HEY LITTLE GIRL	Del Shannon (London)
13	15	THE WONDERFUL WORLD OF THE YOUNG	Danny Williams (HMV)
9	16	WHEN MY LITTLE GIRL IS SMILING	Jimmy Justice (Pye)
28	17	A PICTURE OF YOU	Joe Brown (Piccadilly)
16	17	LET'S TALK ABOUT LOVE	Helen Shapiro (Columbia)
-	19	DO YOU WANT TO DANCE	Cliff Richard (Columbia)
15	20	TWISTIN' THE NIGHT AWAY	Sam Cooke (RCA)
19	21	EV'RYBODY'S TWISTIN'	Frank Sinatra (Reprise)
20	22	THE PARTY'S OVER	Lonnie Donegan (Pye)
10	23	HEY! BABY	Bruce Channel (Mercury)
22	23	LOVER PLEASE	Maureen & the Vernon Girls (Decca)
17	25	LONELY CITY	John Leyton (HMV)
14	26	DREAM BABY	Roy Orbison (London)
29	27	HOW CAN I MEET HER	Everly Brothers (Warner Bros)
-	28	DEEP IN THE HEART OF TEXAS	Duane Eddy (RCA)
-	28	BESAME MUCHO	Jet Harris (Decca)
-	28	SWINGING IN THE RAIN	Norman Vaughan (Pye)
30	28	JEZEBEL	Marty Wilde (Philips)

2 June 1962

LW	TW	Title	Artist (Label)
1	1	GOOD LUCK CHARM	Elvis Presley (RCA)
6	2	COME OUTSIDE	Mike Sarne (Parlophone)
2	3	I'M LOOKING OUT THE WINDOW	Cliff Richard (Columbia)
3	4	NUT ROCKER	B. Bumble & the Stingers (Top Rank)
5	5	AS YOU LIKE IT	Adam Faith (Parlophone)
8	6	LAST NIGHT WAS MADE FOR LOVE	Billy Fury (Decca)
9	7	I DON'T KNOW WHY	Eden Kane (Decca)
10	8	GINNY COME LATELY	Brian Hyland (HMV)
4	9	LOVE LETTERS	Ketty Lester (London)
17	10	A PICTURE OF YOU	Joe Brown (Piccadilly)
12	11	THE GREEN LEAVES OF SUMMER	Kenny Ball & His Jazzmen (Pye Jazz)
6	12	WONDERFUL LAND	Shadows (Columbia)
19	13	DO YOU WANT TO DANCE	Cliff Richard (Columbia)
13	14	STRANGER ON THE SHORE	Mr Acker Bilk (Columbia)
15	15	THE WONDERFUL WORLD OF THE YOUNG	Danny Williams (HMV)
16	16	WHEN MY LITTLE GIRL IS SMILING	Jimmy Justice (Pye)
11	17	SPEAK TO ME PRETTY	Brenda Lee (Brunswick)
25	18	LONELY CITY	John Leyton (HMV)
-	19	UNSQUARE DANCE	Dave Brubeck Quartet (CBS)
14	20	HEY LITTLE GIRL	Del Shannon (London)
23	20	LOVER PLEASE	Maureen & the Vernon Girls (Decca)
28	22	DEEP IN THE HEART OF TEXAS	Duane Eddy (RCA)
17	23	LET'S TALK ABOUT LOVE	Helen Shapiro (Columbia)
21	24	EV'RYBODY'S TWISTIN'	Frank Sinatra (Reprise)
-	25	THE RIVER'S RUN DRY	Vince Hill (Piccadilly)
22	26	THE PARTY'S OVER	Lonnie Donegan (Pye)
28	27	JEZEBEL	Marty Wilde (Philips)
-	28	GINNY COME LATELY	Steve Perry (Decca)
-	29	A LITTLE LOVE, A LITTLE KISS	Karl Denver (Decca)
27	30	HOW CAN I MEET HER	Everly Brothers (Warner Bros)
28	30	SWINGING IN THE RAIN	Norman Vaughan (Pye)

9 June 1962

LW	TW	Title	Artist (Label)
1	1	GOOD LUCK CHARM	Elvis Presley (RCA)
2	2	COME OUTSIDE	Mike Sarne (Parlophone)
3	3	I'M LOOKING OUT THE WINDOW	Cliff Richard (Columbia)
4	4	NUT ROCKER	B. Bumble & the Stingers (Top Rank)
10	5	A PICTURE OF YOU	Joe Brown (Piccadilly)
8	5	GINNY COME LATELY	Brian Hyland (HMV)
5	7	AS YOU LIKE IT	Adam Faith (Parlophone)
6	8	LAST NIGHT WAS MADE FOR LOVE	Billy Fury (Decca)
7	9	I DON'T KNOW WHY	Eden Kane (Decca)
13	10	DO YOU WANT TO DANCE	Cliff Richard (Columbia)
9	11	LOVE LETTERS	Ketty Lester (London)
11	12	THE GREEN LEAVES OF SUMMER	Kenny Ball & His Jazzmen (Pye Jazz)
14	13	STRANGER ON THE SHORE	Mr Acker Bilk (Columbia)
12	14	WONDERFUL LAND	Shadows (Columbia)
18	15	LONELY CITY	John Leyton (HMV)
29	16	A LITTLE LOVE, A LITTLE KISS	Karl Denver (Decca)
17	17	SPEAK TO ME PRETTY	Brenda Lee (Brunswick)
20	18	HEY LITTLE GIRL	Del Shannon (London)
19	19	UNSQUARE DANCE	Dave Brubeck Quartet (CBS)
22	19	DEEP IN THE HEART OF TEXAS	Duane Eddy (RCA)
15	21	THE WONDERFUL WORLD OF THE YOUNG	Danny Williams (HMV)
16	22	WHEN MY LITTLE GIRL IS SMILING	Jimmy Justice (Pye)
-	23	AIN'T THAT FUNNY	Jimmy Justice (Pye)
-	24	DR. KILDARE THEME (THREE STARS WILL SHINE TONIGHT)	Richard Chamberlain (MGM)
20	24	LOVER PLEASE	Maureen & the Vernon Girls (Decca)
26	26	GINNY COME LATELY	Steve Perry (Decca)
-	27	SHARING YOU	Bobby Vee (Liberty)
30	28	HOW CAN I MEET HER	Everly Brothers (Warner Bros)
25	29	THE RIVER'S RUN DRY	Vince Hill (Piccadilly)
27	29	JEZEBEL	Marty Wilde (Philips)

16 June 1962

LW	TW	Title	Artist (Label)
1	1	GOOD LUCK CHARM	Elvis Presley (RCA)
2	2	COME OUTSIDE	Mike Sarne (Parlophone)
3	3	I'M LOOKING OUT THE WINDOW	Cliff Richard (Columbia)
5	4	A PICTURE OF YOU	Joe Brown (Piccadilly)
5	5	GINNY COME LATELY	Brian Hyland (HMV)
8	6	LAST NIGHT WAS MADE FOR LOVE	Billy Fury (Decca)
7	7	AS YOU LIKE IT	Adam Faith (Parlophone)
4	8	NUT ROCKER	B. Bumble & the Stingers (Top Rank)
9	9	I DON'T KNOW WHY	Eden Kane (Decca)
12	10	THE GREEN LEAVES OF SUMMER	Kenny Ball & His Jazzmen (Pye Jazz)
16	11	A LITTLE LOVE, A LITTLE KISS	Karl Denver (Decca)
10	12	DO YOU WANT TO DANCE	Cliff Richard (Columbia)
13	13	STRANGER ON THE SHORE	Mr Acker Bilk (Columbia)
24	14	DR. KILDARE THEME (THREE STARS WILL SHINE TONIGHT)	Richard Chamberlain (MGM)
19	15	UNSQUARE DANCE	Dave Brubeck Quartet (CBS)
11	16	LOVE LETTERS	Ketty Lester (London)
23	17	AIN'T THAT FUNNY	Jimmy Justice (Pye)
21	18	THE WONDERFUL WORLD OF THE YOUNG	Danny Williams (HMV)
-	19	FOLLOW THAT DREAM (EP)	Elvis Presley (RCA)
14	19	WONDERFUL LAND	Shadows (Columbia)
15	21	LONELY CITY	John Leyton (HMV)
27	22	SHARING YOU	Bobby Vee (Liberty)
28	23	HOW CAN I MEET HER	Everly Brothers (Warner Bros)
-	24	I CAN'T STOP LOVING YOU	Ray Charles (HMV)
29	25	JEZEBEL	Marty Wilde (Philips)
22	26	WHEN MY LITTLE GIRL IS SMILING	Jimmy Justice (Pye)
17	27	SPEAK TO ME PRETTY	Brenda Lee (Brunswick)
18	28	HEY LITTLE GIRL	Del Shannon (London)
19	29	DEEP IN THE HEART OF TEXAS	Duane Eddy (RCA)
-	30	ENGLISH COUNTRY GARDEN	Jimmie Rodgers (Columbia)
-	30	SOLDIER BOY	Shirelles (HMV)

Two weeks after Cliff Richard's *I'm Looking Out The Window* charted, its contrasting B-side, a rocking revival of Bobby Freeman's 1958 US hit *Do You Want To Dance*, made an appearance in its own right, eventually joining the A-side in the Top 10. Dave Brubeck had his third hit single in a row, quite a feat for an experimental modern jazzman. His *Unsquare Dance* proved the acid test for amateur hand-clappers, however - in 7/4 time, it was well-nigh impossible to clap to correctly in rhythm.

23 June 1962

last week	this week	
2	1	COME OUTSIDE — Mike Sarne (Parlophone)
1	2	GOOD LUCK CHARM — Elvis Presley (RCA)
4	3	A PICTURE OF YOU — Joe Brown (Piccadilly)
3	4	I'M LOOKING OUT THE WINDOW — Cliff Richard (Columbia)
5	5	GINNY COME LATELY — Brian Hyland (HMV)
6	6	LAST NIGHT WAS MADE FOR LOVE — Billy Fury (Decca)
9	7	I DON'T KNOW WHY — Eden Kane (Decca)
24	8	I CAN'T STOP LOVING YOU — Ray Charles (HMV)
7	9	AS YOU LIKE IT — Adam Faith (Parlophone)
8	10	NUT ROCKER — B. Bumble & the Stingers (Top Rank)
14	11	DR. KILDARE THEME (THREE STARS WILL SHINE TONIGHT) — Richard Chamberlain (MGM)
12	12	DO YOU WANT TO DANCE — Cliff Richard (Columbia)
17	13	AIN'T THAT FUNNY — Jimmy Justice (Pye)
10	14	THE GREEN LEAVES OF SUMMER — Kenny Ball & His Jazzmen (Pye Jazz)
13	15	STRANGER ON THE SHORE — Mr Acker Bilk (Columbia)
19	16	FOLLOW THAT DREAM (EP) — Elvis Presley (RCA)
11	17	A LITTLE LOVE, A LITTLE KISS — Karl Denver (Decca)
22	18	SHARING YOU — Bobby Vee (Liberty)
30	19	ENGLISH COUNTRY GARDEN — Jimmie Rodgers (Columbia)
15	20	UNSQUARE DANCE — Dave Brubeck Quartet (CBS)
18	21	THE WONDERFUL WORLD OF THE YOUNG — Danny Williams (HMV)
23	22	HOW CAN I MEET HER — Everly Brothers (Warner Bros)
-	23	YES, MY DARLING DAUGHTER — Eydie Gorme (CBS)
25	23	JEZEBEL — Marty Wilde (Philips)
21	25	LONELY CITY — John Leyton (HMV)
-	26	HERE COMES THAT FEELING — Brenda Lee (Brunswick)
30	27	SOLDIER BOY — Shirelles (HMV)
-	28	FAR AWAY — Shirley Bassey (Columbia)
-	28	CONSCIENCE — James Darren (Pye International)
-	28	THE RIVER'S RUN DRY — Vince Hill (Piccadilly)

30 June 1962

1	1	COME OUTSIDE — Mike Sarne (Parlophone)
3	2	A PICTURE OF YOU — Joe Brown (Piccadilly)
2	3	GOOD LUCK CHARM — Elvis Presley (RCA)
8	4	I CAN'T STOP LOVING YOU — Ray Charles (HMV)
5	5	GINNY COME LATELY — Brian Hyland (HMV)
4	6	I'M LOOKING OUT THE WINDOW — Cliff Richard (Columbia)
6	7	LAST NIGHT WAS MADE FOR LOVE — Billy Fury (Decca)
7	8	I DON'T KNOW WHY — Eden Kane (Decca)
26	9	HERE COMES THAT FEELING — Brenda Lee (Brunswick)
14	10	THE GREEN LEAVES OF SUMMER — Kenny Ball & His Jazzmen (Pye Jazz)
12	11	DO YOU WANT TO DANCE — Cliff Richard (Columbia)
13	12	AIN'T THAT FUNNY — Jimmy Justice (Pye)
15	13	STRANGER ON THE SHORE — Mr Acker Bilk (Columbia)
9	14	AS YOU LIKE IT — Adam Faith (Parlophone)
11	15	DR. KILDARE THEME (THREE STARS WILL SHINE TONIGHT) — Richard Chamberlain (MGM)
16	16	FOLLOW THAT DREAM (EP) — Elvis Presley (RCA)
19	16	ENGLISH COUNTRY GARDEN — Jimmie Rodgers (Columbia)
23	18	YES, MY DARLING DAUGHTER — Eydie Gorme (CBS)
10	19	NUT ROCKER — B. Bumble & the Stingers (Top Rank)
18	20	SHARING YOU — Bobby Vee (Liberty)
17	21	A LITTLE LOVE, A LITTLE KISS — Karl Denver (Decca)
20	22	UNSQUARE DANCE — Dave Brubeck Quartet (CBS)
-	23	OUR FAVOURITE MELODIES — Craig Douglas (Columbia)
-	24	YA YA TWIST — Petula Clark (Pye)
22	25	HOW CAN I MEET HER — Everly Brothers (Warner Bros)
-	26	PALISADES PARK — Freddy Cannon (Stateside)
28	27	CONSCIENCE — James Darren (Pye International)
-	28	DON'T EVER CHANGE — Crickets (Liberty)
27	28	SOLDIER BOY — Shirelles (HMV)
28	30	FAR AWAY — Shirley Bassey (Columbia)
-	30	STEEL MEN — Rog Whittaker (Fontana)

7 July 1962

2	1	A PICTURE OF YOU — Joe Brown (Piccadilly)
4	2	I CAN'T STOP LOVING YOU — Ray Charles (HMV)
1	3	COME OUTSIDE — Mike Sarne (Parlophone)
3	4	GOOD LUCK CHARM — Elvis Presley (RCA)
5	5	GINNY COME LATELY — Brian Hyland (HMV)
6	6	I'M LOOKING OUT THE WINDOW — Cliff Richard (Columbia)
9	7	HERE COMES THAT FEELING — Brenda Lee (Brunswick)
10	8	THE GREEN LEAVES OF SUMMER — Kenny Ball & His Jazzmen (Pye Jazz)
7	9	LAST NIGHT WAS MADE FOR LOVE — Billy Fury (Decca)
16	10	ENGLISH COUNTRY GARDEN — Jimmie Rodgers (Columbia)
16	11	FOLLOW THAT DREAM (EP) — Elvis Presley (RCA)
13	12	STRANGER ON THE SHORE — Mr Acker Bilk (Columbia)
12	13	AIN'T THAT FUNNY — Jimmy Justice (Pye)
8	14	I DON'T KNOW WHY — Eden Kane (Decca)
14	15	AS YOU LIKE IT — Adam Faith (Parlophone)
18	16	YES, MY DARLING DAUGHTER — Eydie Gorme (CBS)
20	17	SHARING YOU — Bobby Vee (Liberty)
23	18	OUR FAVOURITE MELODIES — Craig Douglas (Columbia)
-	18	I REMEMBER YOU — Frank Ifield (Columbia)
15	20	DR. KILDARE THEME (THREE STARS WILL SHINE TONIGHT) — Richard Chamberlain (MGM)
28	20	DON'T EVER CHANGE — Crickets (Liberty)
21	22	A LITTLE LOVE, A LITTLE KISS — Karl Denver (Decca)
24	24	YA YA TWIST — Petula Clark (Pye)
-	23	TEARS — Danny Williams (HMV)
11	25	DO YOU WANT TO DANCE — Cliff Richard (Columbia)
22	26	UNSQUARE DANCE — Dave Brubeck Quartet (CBS)
-	27	RIGHT SAID FRED — Bernard Cribbins (Parlophone)
-	28	JOHNNY GET ANGRY — Joanie Sommers (Warner Bros)
26	29	PALISADES PARK — Freddy Cannon (Stateside)
-	29	ORANGE BLOSSOM SPECIAL — Spotnicks (Oriole)
30	29	STEEL MEN — Rog Whittaker (Fontana)

14 July 1962

2	1	I CAN'T STOP LOVING YOU — Ray Charles (HMV)
1	2	A PICTURE OF YOU — Joe Brown (Piccadilly)
3	3	COME OUTSIDE — Mike Sarne (Parlophone)
18	4	I REMEMBER YOU — Frank Ifield (Columbia)
4	5	GOOD LUCK CHARM — Elvis Presley (RCA)
5	6	GINNY COME LATELY — Brian Hyland (HMV)
7	7	HERE COMES THAT FEELING — Brenda Lee (Brunswick)
10	8	ENGLISH COUNTRY GARDEN — Jimmie Rodgers (Columbia)
6	9	I'M LOOKING OUT THE WINDOW — Cliff Richard (Columbia)
8	10	THE GREEN LEAVES OF SUMMER — Kenny Ball & His Jazzmen (Pye Jazz)
9	11	LAST NIGHT WAS MADE FOR LOVE — Billy Fury (Decca)
20	12	DON'T EVER CHANGE — Crickets (Liberty)
18	13	OUR FAVOURITE MELODIES — Craig Douglas (Columbia)
12	14	STRANGER ON THE SHORE — Mr Acker Bilk (Columbia)
16	15	YES, MY DARLING DAUGHTER — Eydie Gorme (CBS)
11	15	FOLLOW THAT DREAM (EP) — Elvis Presley (RCA)
27	17	RIGHT SAID FRED — Bernard Cribbins (Parlophone)
13	18	AIN'T THAT FUNNY — Jimmy Justice (Pye)
17	19	SHARING YOU — Bobby Vee (Liberty)
23	20	YA YA TWIST — Petula Clark (Pye)
-	21	SPEEDY GONZALES — Pat Boone (London)
22	22	A LITTLE LOVE, A LITTLE KISS — Karl Denver (Decca)
14	23	I DON'T KNOW WHY — Eden Kane (Decca)
23	23	TEARS — Danny Williams (HMV)
29	25	PALISADES PARK — Freddy Cannon (Stateside)
15	26	AS YOU LIKE IT — Adam Faith (Parlophone)
20	27	DR. KILDARE THEME (THREE STARS WILL SHINE TONIGHT) — Richard Chamberlain (MGM)
25	28	DO YOU WANT TO DANCE — Cliff Richard (Columbia)
-	29	AL DI LA — Emilio Pericoli (Warner Bros)
-	30	LITTLE MISS LONELY — Helen Shapiro (Columbia)

Mike Sarne's novelty chart-topper *Come Outside* was a duet, the uncredited "bird" being Wendy Richard, much later of *Are You Being Served?* and *East Enders* fame. Ray Charles' *I Can't Stop Loving You* was America's fastest-selling Number One hit this summer, and moved almost as quickly to the top in the UK. Elvis' *Follow That Dream* EP, containing four songs from his latest film, became the highest chart-placed EP yet when it reached 11. Roger Whittaker started his chart career as plain 'Rog'.

July – August 1962

last this
week

		21 July 1962
4	1	I REMEMBER YOU / Frank Ifield (Columbia)
1	2	I CAN'T STOP LOVING YOU / Ray Charles (HMV)
2	3	A PICTURE OF YOU / Joe Brown (Piccadilly)
3	4	COME OUTSIDE / Mike Sarne (Parlophone)
21	5	SPEEDY GONZALES / Pat Boone (London)
5	6	GOOD LUCK CHARM / Elvis Presley (RCA)
7	7	HERE COMES THAT FEELING / Brenda Lee (Brunswick)
12	8	DON'T EVER CHANGE / Crickets (Liberty)
8	9	ENGLISH COUNTRY GARDEN / Jimmie Rodgers (Columbia)
13	10	OUR FAVOURITE MELODIES / Craig Douglas (Columbia)
18	11	AIN'T THAT FUNNY / Jimmy Justice (Pye)
15	12	YES, MY DARLING DAUGHTER / Eydie Gorme (CBS)
6	13	GINNY COME LATELY / Brian Hyland (HMV)
20	14	YA YA TWIST / Petula Clark (Pye)
17	15	RIGHT SAID FRED / Bernard Cribbins (Parlophone)
10	16	THE GREEN LEAVES OF SUMMER / Kenny Ball & His Jazzmen (Pye Jazz)
19	16	SHARING YOU / Bobby Vee (Liberty)
30	18	LITTLE MISS LONELY / Helen Shapiro (Columbia)
11	19	LAST NIGHT WAS MADE FOR LOVE / Billy Fury (Decca)
9	20	I'M LOOKING OUT THE WINDOW / Cliff Richard (Columbia)
14	21	STRANGER ON THE SHORE / Mr Acker Bilk (Columbia)
25	22	PALISADES PARK / Freddy Cannon (Stateside)
-	23	LET THERE BE LOVE / Nat King Cole/George Shearing (Capitol)
15	24	FOLLOW THAT DREAM (EP) / Elvis Presley (RCA)
22	25	A LITTLE LOVE, A LITTLE KISS / Karl Denver (Decca)
26	26	I'M JUST A BABY / Louise Cordet (Decca)
-	27	CINDY'S BIRTHDAY / Shane Fenton (Parlophone)
-	28	FAR AWAY / Shirley Bassey (Columbia)
-	29	BREAKING UP IS HARD TO DO / Neil Sedaka (RCA)
23	30	I DON'T KNOW WHY / Eden Kane (Decca)
29	30	AL DI LA / Emilio Pericoli (Warner Bros)
-	30	ADIOS AMIGO / Jim Reeves (RCA)

		28 July 1962
1	1	I REMEMBER YOU / Frank Ifield (Columbia)
2	2	I CAN'T STOP LOVING YOU / Ray Charles (HMV)
5	3	SPEEDY GONZALES / Pat Boone (London)
3	4	A PICTURE OF YOU / Joe Brown (Piccadilly)
4	5	COME OUTSIDE / Mike Sarne (Parlophone)
8	6	DON'T EVER CHANGE / Crickets (Liberty)
7	7	HERE COMES THAT FEELING / Brenda Lee (Brunswick)
9	8	ENGLISH COUNTRY GARDEN / Jimmie Rodgers (Columbia)
10	9	OUR FAVOURITE MELODIES / Craig Douglas (Columbia)
6	10	GOOD LUCK CHARM / Elvis Presley (RCA)
15	11	RIGHT SAID FRED / Bernard Cribbins (Parlophone)
18	12	LITTLE MISS LONELY / Helen Shapiro (Columbia)
23	13	LET THERE BE LOVE / Nat King Cole/George Shearing (Capitol)
11	14	AIN'T THAT FUNNY / Jimmy Justice (Pye)
14	15	YA YA TWIST / Petula Clark (Pye)
21	16	STRANGER ON THE SHORE / Mr Acker Bilk (Columbia)
-	17	THINGS / Bobby Darin (London)
12	18	YES, MY DARLING DAUGHTER / Eydie Gorme (CBS)
13	18	GINNY COME LATELY / Brian Hyland (HMV)
16	20	THE GREEN LEAVES OF SUMMER / Kenny Ball & His Jazzmen (Pye Jazz)
26	21	I'M JUST A BABY / Louise Cordet (Decca)
20	22	I'M LOOKING OUT THE WINDOW / Cliff Richard (Columbia)
27	23	CINDY'S BIRTHDAY / Shane Fenton (Parlophone)
30	23	AL DI LA / Emilio Pericoli (Warner Bros)
16	23	SHARING YOU / Bobby Vee (Liberty)
22	26	PALISADES PARK / Freddy Cannon (Stateside)
-	26	ONCE UPON A DREAM / Billy Fury (Decca)
24	28	FOLLOW THAT DREAM (EP) / Elvis Presley (RCA)
30	29	ADIOS AMIGO / Jim Reeves (RCA)
29	29	BREAKING UP IS HARD TO DO / Neil Sedaka (RCA)

		4 August 1962
1	1	I REMEMBER YOU / Frank Ifield (Columbia)
3	2	SPEEDY GONZALES / Pat Boone (London)
2	3	I CAN'T STOP LOVING YOU / Ray Charles (HMV)
4	4	A PICTURE OF YOU / Joe Brown (Piccadilly)
6	5	DON'T EVER CHANGE / Crickets (Liberty)
5	6	COME OUTSIDE / Mike Sarne (Parlophone)
7	7	HERE COMES THAT FEELING / Brenda Lee (Brunswick)
-	8	GUITAR TANGO / Shadows (Columbia)
12	9	LITTLE MISS LONELY / Helen Shapiro (Columbia)
8	10	ENGLISH COUNTRY GARDEN / Jimmie Rodgers (Columbia)
17	11	THINGS / Bobby Darin (London)
11	12	RIGHT SAID FRED / Bernard Cribbins (Parlophone)
15	13	YA YA TWIST / Petula Clark (Pye)
13	14	LET THERE BE LOVE / Nat King Cole/George Shearing (Capitol)
9	15	OUR FAVOURITE MELODIES / Craig Douglas (Columbia)
10	16	GOOD LUCK CHARM / Elvis Presley (RCA)
26	17	ONCE UPON A DREAM / Billy Fury (Decca)
29	18	BREAKING UP IS HARD TO DO / Neil Sedaka (RCA)
16	19	STRANGER ON THE SHORE / Mr Acker Bilk (Columbia)
14	20	AIN'T THAT FUNNY / Jimmy Justice (Pye)
21	21	I'M JUST A BABY / Louise Cordet (Decca)
23	22	SHARING YOU / Bobby Vee (Liberty)
29	23	ADIOS AMIGO / Jim Reeves (RCA)
18	24	YES, MY DARLING DAUGHTER / Eydie Gorme (CBS)
18	25	GINNY COME LATELY / Brian Hyland (HMV)
28	25	FOLLOW THAT DREAM (EP) / Elvis Presley (RCA)
23	27	CINDY'S BIRTHDAY / Shane Fenton (Parlophone)
23	28	AL DI LA / Emilio Pericoli (Warner Bros)
-	29	GOTTA SEE BABY TONIGHT / Mr Acker Bilk (Columbia)
-	30	VACATION / Connie Francis (MGM)
-	30	ROSES ARE RED / Bobby Vinton (Columbia)

		11 August 1962
1	1	I REMEMBER YOU / Frank Ifield (Columbia)
2	2	SPEEDY GONZALES / Pat Boone (London)
3	3	I CAN'T STOP LOVING YOU / Ray Charles (HMV)
8	4	GUITAR TANGO / Shadows (Columbia)
4	5	A PICTURE OF YOU / Joe Brown (Piccadilly)
5	6	DON'T EVER CHANGE / Crickets (Liberty)
11	7	THINGS / Bobby Darin (London)
9	8	LITTLE MISS LONELY / Helen Shapiro (Columbia)
-	9	ROSES ARE RED / Ronnie Carroll (Philips)
14	10	LET THERE BE LOVE / Nat King Cole/George Shearing (Capitol)
12	11	RIGHT SAID FRED / Bernard Cribbins (Parlophone)
17	12	ONCE UPON A DREAM / Billy Fury (Decca)
7	13	HERE COMES THAT FEELING / Brenda Lee (Brunswick)
6	14	COME OUTSIDE / Mike Sarne (Parlophone)
10	15	ENGLISH COUNTRY GARDEN / Jimmie Rodgers (Columbia)
13	16	YA YA TWIST / Petula Clark (Pye)
18	17	BREAKING UP IS HARD TO DO / Neil Sedaka (RCA)
30	18	ROSES ARE RED / Bobby Vinton (Columbia)
16	19	GOOD LUCK CHARM / Elvis Presley (RCA)
15	20	OUR FAVOURITE MELODIES / Craig Douglas (Columbia)
30	21	VACATION / Connie Francis (MGM)
21	22	I'M JUST A BABY / Louise Cordet (Decca)
19	23	STRANGER ON THE SHORE / Mr Acker Bilk (Columbia)
22	24	SHARING YOU / Bobby Vee (Liberty)
20	25	AIN'T THAT FUNNY / Jimmy Justice (Pye)
23	26	ADIOS AMIGO / Jim Reeves (RCA)
-	27	SEALED WITH A KISS / Brian Hyland (HMV)
29	28	GOTTA SEE BABY TONIGHT / Mr Acker Bilk (Columbia)
25	29	FOLLOW THAT DREAM (EP) / Elvis Presley (RCA)
-	30	DANCIN' PARTY / Chubby Checker (Columbia)

Frank Ifield had been recording for a couple of years (with just one minor hit in *Lucky Devil*), when suddenly a revival of the 1942 song *I Remember You* (from the film *The Fleet's In*) changed his world. In the normally "soft" summer sales period, it sold 102,000 copies in one day during the week it hit Number One. By the end of the year - by which time it had also made the US Top Five - its domestic sales were 6000 over the one million mark. It spent eight weeks at the top.

18 August 1962

last week	this week	
1	1	I REMEMBER YOU — Frank Ifield (Columbia)
2	2	SPEEDY GONZALES — Pat Boone (London)
7	3	THINGS — Bobby Darin (London)
3	4	I CAN'T STOP LOVING YOU — Ray Charles (HMV)
4	4	GUITAR TANGO — Shadows (Columbia)
9	6	ROSES ARE RED — Ronnie Carroll (Philips)
6	7	DON'T EVER CHANGE — Crickets (Liberty)
8	8	LITTLE MISS LONELY — Helen Shapiro (Columbia)
5	9	A PICTURE OF YOU — Joe Brown (Piccadilly)
12	9	ONCE UPON A DREAM — Billy Fury (Decca)
10	11	LET THERE BE LOVE — Nat King Cole/George Shearing (Capitol)
17	12	BREAKING UP IS HARD TO DO — Neil Sedaka (RCA)
18	13	ROSES ARE RED — Bobby Vinton (Columbia)
27	14	SEALED WITH A KISS — Brian Hyland (HMV)
21	15	VACATION — Connie Francis (MGM)
13	16	HERE COMES THAT FEELING — Brenda Lee (Brunswick)
11	17	RIGHT SAID FRED — Bernard Cribbins (Parlophone)
14	18	COME OUTSIDE — Mike Sarne (Parlophone)
29	19	FOLLOW THAT DREAM (EP) — Elvis Presley (RCA)
15	20	ENGLISH COUNTRY GARDEN — Jimmie Rodgers (Columbia)
16	21	YA YA TWIST — Petula Clark (Pye)
23	22	STRANGER ON THE SHORE — Mr Acker Bilk (Columbia)
-	23	MAIN TITLE THEME (FROM THE MAN WITH THE GOLDEN ARM) — Jet Harris (Decca)
-	24	BALLAD OF PALADIN — Duane Eddy (RCA)
26	24	ADIOS AMIGO — Jim Reeves (RCA)
28	26	GOTTA SEE BABY TONIGHT — Mr Acker Bilk (Columbia)
30	27	DANCIN' PARTY — Chubby Checker (Columbia)
22	27	I'M JUST A BABY — Louise Cordet (Decca)
19	27	GOOD LUCK CHARM — Elvis Presley (RCA)
-	30	PICK A BALE OF COTTON — Lonnie Donegan (Pye)
-	30	ROSES ARE RED — David Macbeth

25 August 1962

last week	this week	
1	1	I REMEMBER YOU — Frank Ifield (Columbia)
2	2	SPEEDY GONZALES — Pat Boone (London)
3	3	THINGS — Bobby Darin (London)
6	4	ROSES ARE RED — Ronnie Carroll (Philips)
4	4	GUITAR TANGO — Shadows (Columbia)
4	6	I CAN'T STOP LOVING YOU — Ray Charles (HMV)
9	7	ONCE UPON A DREAM — Billy Fury (Decca)
14	8	SEALED WITH A KISS — Brian Hyland (HMV)
12	9	BREAKING UP IS HARD TO DO — Neil Sedaka (RCA)
11	10	LET THERE BE LOVE — Nat King Cole/George Shearing (Capitol)
8	11	LITTLE MISS LONELY — Helen Shapiro (Columbia)
9	12	A PICTURE OF YOU — Joe Brown (Piccadilly)
15	13	VACATION — Connie Francis (MGM)
7	14	DON'T EVER CHANGE — Crickets (Liberty)
-	15	SO DO I — Kenny Ball & His Jazzmen (Pye Jazz)
13	15	ROSES ARE RED — Bobby Vinton (Columbia)
27	17	DANCIN' PARTY — Chubby Checker (Columbia)
23	18	MAIN TITLE THEME (FROM THE MAN WITH THE GOLDEN ARM) — Jet Harris (Decca)
24	19	BALLAD OF PALADIN — Duane Eddy (RCA)
27	20	I'M JUST A BABY — Louise Cordet (Decca)
30	20	PICK A BALE OF COTTON — Lonnie Donegan (Pye)
18	22	COME OUTSIDE — Mike Sarne (Parlophone)
16	23	HERE COMES THAT FEELING — Brenda Lee (Brunswick)
17	24	RIGHT SAID FRED — Bernard Cribbins (Parlophone)
20	25	ENGLISH COUNTRY GARDEN — Jimmie Rodgers (Columbia)
19	26	FOLLOW THAT DREAM (EP) — Elvis Presley (RCA)
-	27	SPANISH HARLEM — Jimmy Justice (Pye)
22	28	STRANGER ON THE SHORE — Mr Acker Bilk (Columbia)
-	29	YOU KNOW WHAT I MEAN — Vernons Girls (Decca)
26	30	GOTTA SEE BABY TONIGHT — Mr Acker Bilk (Columbia)

1 September 1962

last week	this week	
1	1	I REMEMBER YOU — Frank Ifield (Columbia)
4	2	ROSES ARE RED — Ronnie Carroll (Philips)
2	3	SPEEDY GONZALES — Pat Boone (London)
3	4	THINGS — Bobby Darin (London)
5	5	GUITAR TANGO — Shadows (Columbia)
8	6	SEALED WITH A KISS — Brian Hyland (HMV)
9	7	BREAKING UP IS HARD TO DO — Neil Sedaka (RCA)
7	8	ONCE UPON A DREAM — Billy Fury (Decca)
6	9	I CAN'T STOP LOVING YOU — Ray Charles (HMV)
19	10	BALLAD OF PALADIN — Duane Eddy (RCA)
15	11	SO DO I — Kenny Ball & His Jazzmen (Pye Jazz)
10	12	LET THERE BE LOVE — Nat King Cole/George Shearing (Capitol)
13	13	VACATION — Connie Francis (MGM)
-	13	SHE'S NOT YOU — Elvis Presley (RCA)
15	15	ROSES ARE RED — Bobby Vinton (Columbia)
20	16	PICK A BALE OF COTTON — Lonnie Donegan (Pye)
18	16	MAIN TITLE THEME (FROM THE MAN WITH THE GOLDEN ARM) — Jet Harris (Decca)
-	18	WILL I WHAT — Mike Sarne (Parlophone)
11	19	LITTLE MISS LONELY — Helen Shapiro (Columbia)
17	20	DANCIN' PARTY — Chubby Checker (Columbia)
14	20	DON'T EVER CHANGE — Crickets (Liberty)
-	22	DON'T THAT BEAT ALL — Adam Faith (Parlophone)
12	23	A PICTURE OF YOU — Joe Brown (Piccadilly)
20	24	I'M JUST A BABY — Louise Cordet (Decca)
27	24	SPANISH HARLEM — Jimmy Justice (Pye)
-	26	SOME PEOPLE (EP) — Valerie Mountain & the Eagles (Pye)
-	27	PETER AND THE WOLF — Clyde Valley Stompers (Parlophone)
-	27	ADIOS AMIGO — Jim Reeves (RCA)
30	29	GOTTA SEE BABY TONIGHT — Mr Acker Bilk (Columbia)
24	30	RIGHT SAID FRED — Bernard Cribbins (Parlophone)

8 September 1962

last week	this week	
1	1	I REMEMBER YOU — Frank Ifield (Columbia)
2	2	ROSES ARE RED — Ronnie Carroll (Philips)
4	3	THINGS — Bobby Darin (London)
3	4	SPEEDY GONZALES — Pat Boone (London)
6	5	SEALED WITH A KISS — Brian Hyland (HMV)
13	6	SHE'S NOT YOU — Elvis Presley (RCA)
7	7	BREAKING UP IS HARD TO DO — Neil Sedaka (RCA)
5	8	GUITAR TANGO — Shadows (Columbia)
-	9	IT'LL BE ME — Cliff Richard (Columbia)
8	10	ONCE UPON A DREAM — Billy Fury (Decca)
10	11	BALLAD OF PALADIN — Duane Eddy (RCA)
9	12	I CAN'T STOP LOVING YOU — Ray Charles (HMV)
16	13	PICK A BALE OF COTTON — Lonnie Donegan (Pye)
22	14	DON'T THAT BEAT ALL — Adam Faith (Parlophone)
18	15	WILL I WHAT — Mike Sarne (Parlophone)
11	16	SO DO I — Kenny Ball & His Jazzmen (Pye Jazz)
16	17	MAIN TITLE THEME (FROM THE MAN WITH THE GOLDEN ARM) — Jet Harris (Decca)
12	18	LET THERE BE LOVE — Nat King Cole/George Shearing (Capitol)
-	19	SOME PEOPLE — Carol Deene (HMV)
13	20	VACATION — Connie Francis (MGM)
-	21	SOME PEOPLE — Jet Harris (Decca)
-	22	THE LOCO-MOTION — Little Eva (London)
26	22	SOME PEOPLE (EP) — Valerie Mountain & the Eagles
24	24	SPANISH HARLEM — Jimmy Justice (Pye)
27	24	ADIOS AMIGO — Jim Reeves (RCA)
15	26	ROSES ARE RED — Bobby Vinton (Columbia)
-	27	WHAT NOW MY LOVE — Shirley Bassey (Columbia)
20	27	DON'T EVER CHANGE — Crickets (Liberty)
19	29	LITTLE MISS LONELY — Helen Shapiro (Columbia)
20	30	DANCIN' PARTY — Chubby Checker (Columbia)

As the summer of 1962 drew to a close, there was no sign that a savage revolution was soon to sweep through popular music. It would have seemed most unlikely during August that Pat Boone, enjoying one of his biggest sellers with *Speedy Gonzales*, was having his penultimate hit, or that *Pick A Bale Of Cotton* would be Lonnie Donegan's last. Helen Shapiro never made the Top 20 again after *Little Miss Lonely*, or Connie Francis after *Vacation*. Up in Liverpool, Ringo had just joined the Beatles.

September – October 1962

Telstar, the instrumental hit that writer/producer Joe Meek was inspired to pen after being impressed by the achievements of the telecommunications satellite of the same name (which relayed the first transatlantic TV pictures), wasted no time in becoming the hottest record of Autumn '62. It would eventually top the US chart too, giving the Tornados the accolade of being the first British group to achieve this feat. Meanwhile, Buddy Holly scored posthumously with the never-before-heard *Reminiscing*.

October – November 1962

13 October 1962

last week	this week	Title	Artist (Label)
1	1	TELSTAR	Tornados (Decca)
4	2	SHEILA	Tommy Roe (HMV)
4	3	IT MIGHT AS WELL RAIN UNTIL SEPTEMBER	Carole King (London)
6	4	THE LOCO-MOTION	Little Eva (London)
2	5	SHE'S NOT YOU	Elvis Presley (RCA)
3	6	IT'LL BE ME	Cliff Richard (Columbia)
8	7	YOU DON'T KNOW ME	Ray Charles (HMV)
13	8	RAMBLIN' ROSE	Nat King Cole (Capitol)
12	9	WHAT NOW MY LOVE	Shirley Bassey (Columbia)
7	10	I REMEMBER YOU	Frank Ifield (Columbia)
21	11	VENUS IN BLUE JEANS	Mark Wynter (Pye)
10	12	DON'T THAT BEAT ALL	Adam Faith (Parlophone)
9	13	SEALED WITH A KISS	Brian Hyland (HMV)
14	14	ROSES ARE RED	Ronnie Carroll (Philips)
16	15	LONELY	Mr Acker Bilk (Columbia)
17	16	IT STARTED ALL OVER AGAIN	Brenda Lee (Brunswick)
15	17	BREAKING UP IS HARD TO DO	Neil Sedaka (RCA)
11	18	THINGS	Bobby Darin (London)
-	19	SHERRY	Four Seasons (Stateside)
23	20	GUITAR TANGO	Shadows (Columbia)
19	21	BALLAD OF PALADIN	Duane Eddy (RCA)
18	22	REMINISCING	Buddy Holly (Coral)
-	23	LET'S DANCE	Chris Montez (London)
27	24	SPANISH HARLEM	Jimmy Justice (Pye)
30	25	BLUE WEEKEND	Karl Denver (Decca)
20	26	SPEEDY GONZALES	Pat Boone (London)
-	27	DEVIL WOMAN	Marty Robbins (CBS)
-	28	IF A MAN ANSWERS	Bobby Darin (Capitol)
22	29	MAIN TITLE THEME (FROM THE MAN WITH THE GOLDEN ARM)	Jet Harris (Decca)
-	30	THE SWISS MAID	Del Shannon (London)

20 October 1962

last week	this week	Title	Artist (Label)
1	1	TELSTAR	Tornados (Decca)
4	2	THE LOCO-MOTION	Little Eva (London)
3	3	IT MIGHT AS WELL RAIN UNTIL SEPTEMBER	Carole King (London)
2	4	SHEILA	Tommy Roe (HMV)
8	5	RAMBLIN' ROSE	Nat King Cole (Capitol)
7	6	YOU DON'T KNOW ME	Ray Charles (HMV)
5	7	SHE'S NOT YOU	Elvis Presley (RCA)
11	8	VENUS IN BLUE JEANS	Mark Wynter (Pye)
6	9	IT'LL BE ME	Cliff Richard (Columbia)
9	10	WHAT NOW MY LOVE	Shirley Bassey (Columbia)
23	11	LET'S DANCE	Chris Montez (London)
19	12	SHERRY	Four Seasons (Stateside)
10	13	I REMEMBER YOU	Frank Ifield (Columbia)
12	14	DON'T THAT BEAT ALL	Adam Faith (Parlophone)
15	15	LONELY	Mr Acker Bilk (Columbia)
30	16	THE SWISS MAID	Del Shannon (London)
16	17	IT STARTED ALL OVER AGAIN	Brenda Lee (Brunswick)
14	18	ROSES ARE RED	Ronnie Carroll (Philips)
27	19	DEVIL WOMAN	Marty Robbins (CBS)
13	20	SEALED WITH A KISS	Brian Hyland (HMV)
28	21	IF A MAN ANSWERS	Bobby Darin (Capitol)
18	22	THINGS	Bobby Darin (London)
-	23	SEND ME THE PILLOW YOU DREAM ON	Johnny Tillotson (London)
20	24	GUITAR TANGO	Shadows (Columbia)
-	25	THE PAY-OFF	Kenny Ball & His Jazzmen (Pye Jazz)
22	26	REMINISCING	Buddy Holly (Coral)
17	27	BREAKING UP IS HARD TO DO	Neil Sedaka (RCA)
-	28	BOBBY'S GIRL	Susan Maughan (Philips)
25	29	BLUE WEEKEND	Karl Denver (Decca)
21	30	BALLAD OF PALADIN	Duane Eddy (RCA)

27 October 1962

last week	this week	Title	Artist (Label)
1	1	TELSTAR	Tornados (Decca)
2	2	THE LOCO-MOTION	Little Eva (London)
4	3	SHEILA	Tommy Roe (HMV)
5	4	RAMBLIN' ROSE	Nat King Cole (Capitol)
3	5	IT MIGHT AS WELL RAIN UNTIL SEPTEMBER	Carole King (London)
8	6	VENUS IN BLUE JEANS	Mark Wynter (Pye)
11	7	LET'S DANCE	Chris Montez (London)
-	8	LOVESICK BLUES	Frank Ifield (Columbia)
6	9	YOU DON'T KNOW ME	Ray Charles (HMV)
10	10	WHAT NOW MY LOVE	Shirley Bassey (Columbia)
16	11	THE SWISS MAID	Del Shannon (London)
12	12	SHERRY	Four Seasons (Stateside)
7	13	SHE'S NOT YOU	Elvis Presley (RCA)
19	14	DEVIL WOMAN	Marty Robbins (CBS)
9	15	IT'LL BE ME	Cliff Richard (Columbia)
-	16	SHE TAUGHT ME HOW TO YODEL	Frank Ifield (Columbia)
13	17	I REMEMBER YOU	Frank Ifield (Columbia)
15	18	LONELY	Mr Acker Bilk (Columbia)
-	19	NO ONE CAN MAKE MY SUNSHINE SMILE	Everly Brothers (Warner Bros)
14	20	DON'T THAT BEAT ALL	Adam Faith (Parlophone)
17	21	IT STARTED ALL OVER AGAIN	Brenda Lee (Brunswick)
23	22	SEND ME THE PILLOW YOU DREAM ON	Johnny Tillotson (London)
25	23	THE PAY-OFF	Kenny Ball & His Jazzmen (Pye Jazz)
21	24	IF A MAN ANSWERS	Bobby Darin (Capitol)
28	25	BOBBY'S GIRL	Susan Maughan (Philips)
-	26	BECAUSE OF LOVE	Billy Fury (Decca)
-	27	LOVE ME DO	Beatles (Parlophone)
26	28	REMINISCING	Buddy Holly (Coral)
18	29	ROSES ARE RED	Ronnie Carroll (Philips)
-	30	THE JAMES BOND THEME	John Barry (Columbia)

3 November 1962

last week	this week	Title	Artist (Label)
1	1	TELSTAR	Tornados (Decca)
8	2	LOVESICK BLUES	Frank Ifield (Columbia)
7	2	LET'S DANCE	Chris Montez (London)
2	4	THE LOCO-MOTION	Little Eva (London)
6	5	VENUS IN BLUE JEANS	Mark Wynter (Pye)
5	6	IT MIGHT AS WELL RAIN UNTIL SEPTEMBER	Carole King (London)
11	7	THE SWISS MAID	Del Shannon (London)
3	8	SHEILA	Tommy Roe (HMV)
4	9	RAMBLIN' ROSE	Nat King Cole (Capitol)
12	10	SHERRY	Four Seasons (Stateside)
10	11	WHAT NOW MY LOVE	Shirley Bassey (Columbia)
14	12	DEVIL WOMAN	Marty Robbins (CBS)
9	13	YOU DON'T KNOW ME	Ray Charles (HMV)
13	14	SHE'S NOT YOU	Elvis Presley (RCA)
19	15	NO ONE CAN MAKE MY SUNSHINE SMILE	Everly Brothers (Warner Bros)
25	15	BOBBY'S GIRL	Susan Maughan (Philips)
16	17	SHE TAUGHT ME HOW TO YODEL	Frank Ifield (Columbia)
-	18	KID GALAHAD (EP)	Elvis Presley (RCA)
17	19	I REMEMBER YOU	Frank Ifield (Columbia)
18	20	LONELY	Mr Acker Bilk (Columbia)
-	21	SUN ARISE	Rolf Harris (Columbia)
22	22	SEND ME THE PILLOW YOU DREAM ON	Johnny Tillotson (London)
30	23	THE JAMES BOND THEME	John Barry (Columbia)
26	23	BECAUSE OF LOVE	Billy Fury (Decca)
-	25	OH LONESOME ME	Craig Douglas (Decca)
15	25	IT'LL BE ME	Cliff Richard (Columbia)
-	27	KEEP AWAY FROM OTHER GIRLS	Helen Shapiro (Columbia)
23	28	THE PAY-OFF	Kenny Ball & His Jazzmen (Pye Jazz)
-	29	IF ONLY TOMORROW	Ronnie Carroll (Philips)
-	29	WARMED OVER KISSES	Brian Hyland (HMV)

Carole King, veteran of many hits as a writer, made her first (and only, until the 1970s) chart appearance as a performer, while her babysitter Little Eva cleaned up with Goffin & King's *The Loco-Motion*, one of the all-time classic dance discs (still in London's catalogue and selling 15 years later.) Frank Ifield followed his million seller with a two-sided hit, the Yodel number getting a boost from a London Palladium TV plug the weekend after release. The Beatles made their (minor) chart debut on October 27.

November – December 1962

10 November 1962

last week	this week	Title / Artist (label)
2	1	LOVESICK BLUES — Frank Ifield (Columbia)
2	2	LET'S DANCE — Chris Montez (London)
1	2	TELSTAR — Tornados (Decca)
7	4	THE SWISS MAID — Del Shannon (London)
4	5	THE LOCO-MOTION — Little Eva (London)
5	6	VENUS IN BLUE JEANS — Mark Wynter (Pye)
10	7	SHERRY — Four Seasons (Stateside)
6	8	IT MIGHT AS WELL RAIN UNTIL SEPTEMBER — Carole King (London)
9	9	RAMBLIN' ROSE — Nat King Cole (Capitol)
8	10	SHEILA — Tommy Roe (HMV)
12	11	DEVIL WOMAN — Marty Robbins (CBS)
15	12	BOBBY'S GIRL — Susan Maughan (Philips)
15	13	NO ONE CAN MAKE MY SUNSHINE SMILE — Everly Brothers (Warner Bros)
11	14	WHAT NOW MY LOVE — Shirley Bassey (Columbia)
18	15	KID GALAHAD (EP) — Elvis Presley (RCA)
14	16	SHE'S NOT YOU — Frank Ifield (Columbia)
17	17	SHE TAUGHT ME HOW TO YODEL — Frank Ifield (Columbia)
19	18	I REMEMBER YOU — Frank Ifield (Columbia)
13	19	YOU DON'T KNOW ME — Ray Charles (HMV)
25	19	OH LONESOME ME — Craig Douglas (Decca)
23	21	THE JAMES BOND THEME — John Barry (Columbia)
-	22	(DANCE WITH THE) GUITAR MAN — Duane Eddy (RCA)
20	23	LONELY — Mr Acker Bilk (Columbia)
23	24	BECAUSE OF LOVE — Billy Fury (Decca)
-	25	IT ONLY TOOK A MINUTE — Joe Brown (Piccadilly)
21	26	SUN ARISE — Rolf Harris (Columbia)
29	27	IF ONLY TOMORROW — Ronnie Carroll (Philips)
29	28	WARMED OVER KISSES — Brian Hyland (HMV)
22	28	SEND ME THE PILLOW YOU DREAM ON — Johnny Tillotson (London)
-	30	LOVE ME TENDER — Richard Chamberlain (MGM)
-	30	MUST BE MADISON — Joe Loss (HMV)

17 November 1962

last week	this week	Title / Artist (label)
1	1	LOVESICK BLUES — Frank Ifield (Columbia)
2	2	LET'S DANCE — Chris Montez (London)
4	3	THE SWISS MAID — Del Shannon (London)
2	3	TELSTAR — Tornados (Decca)
6	5	VENUS IN BLUE JEANS — Mark Wynter (Pye)
12	6	BOBBY'S GIRL — Susan Maughan (Philips)
7	7	SHERRY — Four Seasons (Stateside)
5	8	THE LOCO-MOTION — Little Eva (London)
11	9	DEVIL WOMAN — Marty Robbins (CBS)
9	10	RAMBLIN' ROSE — Nat King Cole (Capitol)
13	11	NO ONE CAN MAKE MY SUNSHINE SMILE — Everly Brothers (Warner Bros)
8	12	IT MIGHT AS WELL RAIN UNTIL SEPTEMBER — Carole King (London)
10	13	SHEILA — Tommy Roe (HMV)
22	14	(DANCE WITH THE) GUITAR MAN — Duane Eddy (RCA)
19	15	OH LONESOME ME — Craig Douglas (Decca)
30	16	LOVE ME TENDER — Richard Chamberlain (MGM)
15	17	KID GALAHAD (EP) — Elvis Presley (RCA)
30	18	MUST BE MADISON — Joe Loss (HMV)
26	19	SUN ARISE — Rolf Harris (Columbia)
21	20	THE JAMES BOND THEME — John Barry (Columbia)
-	21	MAIN ATTRACTION — Pat Boone (London)
17	22	SHE TAUGHT ME HOW TO YODEL — Frank Ifield (Columbia)
19	23	YOU DON'T KNOW ME — Ray Charles (HMV)
24	23	BECAUSE OF LOVE — Billy Fury (Decca)
14	25	WHAT NOW MY LOVE — Shirley Bassey (Columbia)
18	26	I REMEMBER YOU — Frank Ifield (Columbia)
-	27	DESFINADO — Stan Getz & Charlie Byrd (HMV)
16	28	SHE'S NOT YOU — Elvis Presley (RCA)
25	29	IT ONLY TOOK A MINUTE — Joe Brown (Piccadilly)
-	29	LIMBO ROCK — Chubby Checker (Cameo-Parkway)
-	29	CAN CAN '62 — Peter Jay & the Jaywalkers (Decca)

24 November 1962

last week	this week	Title / Artist (label)
1	1	LOVESICK BLUES — Frank Ifield (Columbia)
2	2	LET'S DANCE — Chris Montez (London)
3	3	THE SWISS MAID — Del Shannon (London)
6	4	BOBBY'S GIRL — Susan Maughan (Philips)
3	5	TELSTAR — Tornados (Decca)
9	6	DEVIL WOMAN — Marty Robbins (CBS)
5	7	VENUS IN BLUE JEANS — Mark Wynter (Pye)
7	8	SHERRY — Four Seasons (Stateside)
11	9	NO ONE CAN MAKE MY SUNSHINE SMILE — Everly Brothers (Warner Bros)
8	10	THE LOCO-MOTION — Little Eva (London)
14	11	(DANCE WITH THE) GUITAR MAN — Duane Eddy (RCA)
10	12	RAMBLIN' ROSE — Nat King Cole (Capitol)
19	13	SUN ARISE — Rolf Harris (Columbia)
15	14	OH LONESOME ME — Craig Douglas (Decca)
16	15	LOVE ME TENDER — Richard Chamberlain (MGM)
-	16	A FOREVER KIND OF LOVE — Bobby Vee (Liberty)
13	17	SHEILA — Tommy Roe (HMV)
12	18	IT MIGHT AS WELL RAIN UNTIL SEPTEMBER — Carole King (London)
23	19	BECAUSE OF LOVE — Billy Fury (Decca)
18	20	MUST BE MADISON — Joe Loss (HMV)
22	21	SHE TAUGHT ME HOW TO YODEL — Frank Ifield (Columbia)
27	22	DESFINADO — Stan Getz & Charlie Byrd (HMV)
20	23	THE JAMES BOND THEME — John Barry (Columbia)
-	24	NEXT DOOR TO AN ANGEL — Neil Sedaka (RCA)
29	25	IT ONLY TOOK A MINUTE — Joe Brown (Piccadilly)
17	26	KID GALAHAD (EP) — Elvis Presley (RCA)
21	27	MAIN ATTRACTION — Pat Boone (London)
29	28	CAN CAN '62 — Peter Jay & the Jaywalkers (Decca)
-	29	SUSIE DARLIN' — Tommy Roe (HMV)
-	30	JAMES (HOLD THE LADDER STEADY) — Carol Deene (HMV)

1 December 1962

last week	this week	Title / Artist (label)
1	1	LOVESICK BLUES — Frank Ifield (Columbia)
2	2	LET'S DANCE — Chris Montez (London)
3	3	THE SWISS MAID — Del Shannon (London)
4	4	BOBBY'S GIRL — Susan Maughan (Philips)
-	5	RETURN TO SENDER — Elvis Presley (RCA)
6	6	DEVIL WOMAN — Marty Robbins (CBS)
7	7	TELSTAR — Tornados (Decca)
11	8	(DANCE WITH THE) GUITAR MAN — Duane Eddy (RCA)
13	8	SUN ARISE — Rolf Harris (Columbia)
9	10	NO ONE CAN MAKE MY SUNSHINE SMILE — Everly Brothers (Warner Bros)
8	11	SHERRY — Four Seasons (Stateside)
16	12	A FOREVER KIND OF LOVE — Bobby Vee (Liberty)
7	12	VENUS IN BLUE JEANS — Mark Wynter (Pye)
10	14	THE LOCO-MOTION — Little Eva (London)
23	15	THE JAMES BOND THEME — John Barry (Columbia)
12	16	RAMBLIN' ROSE — Nat King Cole (Capitol)
27	17	MAIN ATTRACTION — Pat Boone (London)
14	17	OH LONESOME ME — Craig Douglas (Decca)
25	19	IT ONLY TOOK A MINUTE — Joe Brown (Piccadilly)
20	20	MUST BE MADISON — Joe Loss (HMV)
19	21	BECAUSE OF LOVE — Billy Fury (Decca)
15	22	LOVE ME TENDER — Richard Chamberlain (MGM)
-	23	ROCKIN' AROUND THE CHRISTMAS TREE — Brenda Lee (Brunswick)
22	24	DESFINADO — Stan Getz & Charlie Byrd (HMV)
18	25	IT MIGHT AS WELL RAIN UNTIL SEPTEMBER — Carole King (London)
29	26	SUSIE DARLIN' — Tommy Roe (HMV)
-	27	HEARTACHES — Patsy Cline (Brunswick)
17	28	SHEILA — Tommy Roe (HMV)
30	29	JAMES (HOLD THE LADDER STEADY) — Carol Deene (HMV)
-	30	I REMEMBER YOU — Frank Ifield (Columbia)
24	30	NEXT DOOR TO AN ANGEL — Neil Sedaka (RCA)

Late 1962 introduced at least three new "sounds": the unique falsetto vocal blend of Frankie Valli and the Four Seasons on *Sherry*, the jazzy rhythm of Bossa Nova as heard on Stan Getz & Charlie Byrd's *Desafinado*, and the unmistakeable twang of the James Bond theme, as introduced in *Dr No*, and reprised in every Bond film through the subsequent 30 years. Though John Barry scored many of those later movies, he did not actually write the Theme (Monty Norman did), but he recorded the original hit.

8 December 1962

last week	this week	title / artist
1	1	LOVESICK BLUES — Frank Ifield (Columbia)
5	2	RETURN TO SENDER — Elvis Presley (RCA)
2	3	LET'S DANCE — Chris Montez (London)
8	4	(DANCE WITH THE) GUITAR MAN — Duane Eddy (RCA)
8	5	SUN ARISE — Rolf Harris (Columbia)
3	5	THE SWISS MAID — Del Shannon (London)
4	7	BOBBY'S GIRL — Susan Maughan (Philips)
6	8	DEVIL WOMAN — Marty Robbins (CBS)
7	9	TELSTAR — Tornados (Decca)
-	10	THE NEXT TIME — Cliff Richard (Columbia)
12	11	VENUS IN BLUE JEANS — Mark Wynter (Pye)
11	12	SHERRY — Four Seasons (Stateside)
17	13	MAIN ATTRACTION — Pat Boone (London)
-	13	BACHELOR BOY — Cliff Richard (Columbia)
12	15	A FOREVER KIND OF LOVE — Bobby Vee (Liberty)
19	16	IT ONLY TOOK A MINUTE — Joe Brown (Piccadilly)
10	17	NO ONE CAN MAKE MY SUNSHINE SMILE — Everly Brothers (Warner Bros)
23	18	ROCKIN' AROUND THE CHRISTMAS TREE — Brenda Lee (Brunswick)
15	19	THE JAMES BOND THEME — John Barry (Columbia)
20	19	MUST BE MADISON — Joe Loss (HMV)
24	21	DESFINADO — Stan Getz & Charlie Byrd (HMV)
22	22	LOVE ME TENDER — Richard Chamberlain (MGM)
21	23	BECAUSE OF LOVE — Billy Fury (Decca)
16	24	RAMBLIN' ROSE — Nat King Cole (Capitol)
17	24	OH LONESOME ME — Craig Douglas (Decca)
27	26	HEARTACHES — Patsy Cline (Brunswick)
14	27	THE LOCO-MOTION — Little Eva (London)
-	28	ALWAYS YOU AND ME — Russ Conway (Columbia)
-	28	BABY TAKE A BOW — Adam Faith (Parlophone)
-	30	LIKE I DO — Maureen Evans (Oriole)

15 December 1962

last week	this week	title / artist
2	1	RETURN TO SENDER — Elvis Presley (RCA)
1	2	LOVESICK BLUES — Frank Ifield (Columbia)
5	3	SUN ARISE — Rolf Harris (Columbia)
10	4	THE NEXT TIME — Cliff Richard (Columbia)
7	5	BOBBY'S GIRL — Susan Maughan (Philips)
4	6	(DANCE WITH THE) GUITAR MAN — Duane Eddy (RCA)
3	7	LET'S DANCE — Chris Montez (London)
5	8	THE SWISS MAID — Del Shannon (London)
18	9	ROCKIN' AROUND THE CHRISTMAS TREE — Brenda Lee (Brunswick)
9	10	TELSTAR — Tornados (Decca)
8	11	DEVIL WOMAN — Marty Robbins (CBS)
-	12	DANCE ON — Shadows (Columbia)
13	13	BACHELOR BOY — Cliff Richard (Columbia)
16	14	IT ONLY TOOK A MINUTE — Joe Brown (Piccadilly)
13	15	MAIN ATTRACTION — Pat Boone (London)
21	16	DESFINADO — Stan Getz & Charlie Byrd (HMV)
12	17	SHERRY — Four Seasons (Stateside)
15	18	A FOREVER KIND OF LOVE — Bobby Vee (Liberty)
19	19	MUST BE MADISON — Joe Loss (HMV)
28	20	BABY TAKE A BOW — Adam Faith (Parlophone)
11	21	VENUS IN BLUE JEANS — Mark Wynter (Pye)
30	22	LIKE I DO — Maureen Evans (Oriole)
-	23	YOUR CHEATING HEART — Ray Charles (HMV)
17	24	NO ONE CAN MAKE MY SUNSHINE SMILE — Everly Brothers (Warner Bros)
19	25	THE JAMES BOND THEME — John Barry (Columbia)
-	26	GOSSIP CALYPSO — Bernard Cribbins (Parlophone)
27	27	THE LOCO-MOTION — Little Eva (London)
22	28	LOVE ME TENDER — Richard Chamberlain (MGM)
-	29	UP ON THE ROOF — Kenny Lynch (HMV)
-	30	ME AND MY SHADOW — Frank Sinatra & Sammy Davis Jr. (Reprise)

22 December 1962

last week	this week	title / artist
1	1	RETURN TO SENDER — Elvis Presley (RCA)
3	2	SUN ARISE — Rolf Harris (Columbia)
2	3	LOVESICK BLUES — Frank Ifield (Columbia)
4	3	THE NEXT TIME — Cliff Richard (Columbia)
6	5	(DANCE WITH THE) GUITAR MAN — Duane Eddy (RCA)
12	6	DANCE ON — Shadows (Columbia)
5	7	BOBBY'S GIRL — Susan Maughan (Philips)
9	8	ROCKIN' AROUND THE CHRISTMAS TREE — Brenda Lee (Brunswick)
7	9	LET'S DANCE — Chris Montez (London)
10	10	TELSTAR — Tornados (Decca)
8	11	THE SWISS MAID — Del Shannon (London)
14	12	IT ONLY TOOK A MINUTE — Joe Brown (Piccadilly)
13	13	BACHELOR BOY — Cliff Richard (Columbia)
11	14	DEVIL WOMAN — Marty Robbins (CBS)
15	15	MAIN ATTRACTION — Pat Boone (London)
23	15	YOUR CHEATING HEART — Ray Charles (HMV)
20	17	BABY TAKE A BOW — Adam Faith (Parlophone)
29	18	UP ON THE ROOF — Kenny Lynch (HMV)
-	19	GO AWAY LITTLE GIRL — Mark Wynter (Pye)
22	20	LIKE I DO — Maureen Evans (Oriole)
16	20	DESFINADO — Stan Getz & Charlie Byrd (HMV)
19	22	MUST BE MADISON — Joe Loss (HMV)
18	23	A FOREVER KIND OF LOVE — Bobby Vee (Liberty)
30	24	ME AND MY SHADOW — Frank Sinatra & Sammy Davis Jr. (Reprise)
17	25	SHERRY — Four Seasons (Stateside)
24	26	NO ONE CAN MAKE MY SUNSHINE SMILE — Everly Brothers (Warner Bros)
-	27	UP ON THE ROOF — Julie Grant (Pye)
26	28	GOSSIP CALYPSO — Bernard Cribbins (Parlophone)
-	29	HE'S A REBEL — Crystals (London)
-	30	ISLAND OF DREAMS — Springfields (Philips)

29 December 1962

last week	this week	title / artist
3	1	THE NEXT TIME — Cliff Richard (Columbia)
1	2	RETURN TO SENDER — Elvis Presley (RCA)
6	3	DANCE ON — Shadows (Columbia)
2	4	SUN ARISE — Rolf Harris (Columbia)
3	5	LOVESICK BLUES — Frank Ifield (Columbia)
5	6	(DANCE WITH THE) GUITAR MAN — Duane Eddy (RCA)
8	6	ROCKIN' AROUND THE CHRISTMAS TREE — Brenda Lee (Brunswick)
9	8	LET'S DANCE — Chris Montez (London)
13	9	BACHELOR BOY — Cliff Richard (Columbia)
7	10	BOBBY'S GIRL — Susan Maughan (Philips)
12	11	IT ONLY TOOK A MINUTE — Joe Brown (Piccadilly)
10	12	TELSTAR — Tornados (Decca)
18	13	UP ON THE ROOF — Kenny Lynch (HMV)
15	14	MAIN ATTRACTION — Pat Boone (London)
15	14	YOUR CHEATING HEART — Ray Charles (HMV)
11	16	THE SWISS MAID — Del Shannon (London)
19	17	GO AWAY LITTLE GIRL — Mark Wynter (Pye)
22	18	MUST BE MADISON — Joe Loss (HMV)
24	19	ME AND MY SHADOW — Frank Sinatra & Sammy Davis Jr. (Reprise)
20	20	LIKE I DO — Maureen Evans (Oriole)
20	20	DESFINADO — Stan Getz & Charlie Byrd (HMV)
14	22	DEVIL WOMAN — Marty Robbins (CBS)
23	23	A FOREVER KIND OF LOVE — Bobby Vee (Liberty)
28	24	GOSSIP CALYPSO — Bernard Cribbins (Parlophone)
30	25	ISLAND OF DREAMS — Springfields (Philips)
17	26	BABY TAKE A BOW — Adam Faith (Parlophone)
-	27	DON'T YOU THINK IT'S TIME — Mike Berry & the Outlaws (HMV)
-	28	MERRY CHRISTMAS YOU SUCKERS — Paddy Roberts
-	29	UP ON THE ROOF — Drifters (London)
27	29	UP ON THE ROOF — Julie Grant (Pye)

The first taste of *Summer Holiday*, Cliff Richard's movie follow-up to *The Young Ones*, was the release of the single *The Next Time/Bachelor Boy*. Both sides were plugged by Cliff and the Shadows on TV's Palladium show the weekend before release, and both immediately sold like crazy, the ballad *The Next Time* taking the initial advantage and dethroning Elvis' film song (from *Girls! Girls! Girls!*) *Return To Sender* as the year closed. Note that three different versions of *Up On The Roof* charted in successive weeks.

January 1963

5 January 1963

3 1 DANCE ON / Shadows (Columbia)
2 2 RETURN TO SENDER / Elvis Presley (RCA)
1 3 THE NEXT TIME / Cliff Richard (Columbia)
4 4 SUN ARISE / Rolf Harris (Columbia)
6 5 DANCE WITH THE GUITAR MAN / Duane Eddy (RCA)
9 5 BACHELOR BOY / Cliff Richard (Columbia)
5 7 LOVESICK BLUES / Frank Ifield (Columbia)
7 8 BOBBY'S GIRL / Susan Maughan (Philips)
11 9 IT ONLY TOOK A MINUTE / Joe Brown (Piccadilly)
12 9 TELSTAR Tornados (Decca)
8 11 LET'S DANCE / Chris Montez (London)
20 12 DESAFINADO / Stan Getz & Charlie Byrd (HMV)
17 13 GO AWAY LITTLE GIRL / Mark Wynter (Pye)
14 14 YOUR CHEATING HEART / Ray Charles (HMV)
20 14 LIKE I DO / Maureen Evans (Oriole)
13 16 UP ON THE ROOF / Kenny Lynch (HMV)
16 17 THE SWISS MAID / Del Shannon (London)
23 18 A FOREVER KIND OF LOVE / Bobby Vee (Liberty)
19 19 ME AND MY SHADOW / Frank Sinatra & Sammy Davis Jr. (Reprise)
29 20 UP ON THE ROOF / Julie Grant (Pye)
26 21 BABY TAKE A BOW / Adam Faith (Parlophone)
6 22 ROCKIN' AROUND THE CHRISTMAS TREE / Brenda Lee (Brunswick)
14 23 THE MAIN ATTRACTION / Pat Boone (London)
27 24 DON'T YOU THINK IT'S TIME / Mike Berry & the Outlaws (HMV)
18 25 MUST BE MADISON / Joe Loss (HMV)
- 26 COMIN' HOME BABY / Mel Torme (London)
- 27 JUST FOR KICKS / Mike Sarne (Parlophone)
22 28 DEVIL WOMAN / Marty Robbins (CBS)
- 29 HE'S A REBEL / Crystals (London)
- 30 GONNA GO FISHIN' / Hank Locklin (RCA)

12 January 1963

1 1 DANCE ON / Shadows (Columbia)
2 2 RETURN TO SENDER / Elvis Presley (RCA)
3 3 THE NEXT TIME / Cliff Richard (Columbia)
5 4 BACHELOR BOY / Cliff Richard (Columbia)
5 5 DANCE WITH THE GUITAR MAN / Duane Eddy (RCA)
7 6 LOVESICK BLUES / Frank Ifield (Columbia)
4 7 SUN ARISE / Rolf Harris (Columbia)
9 8 TELSTAR Tornados (Decca)
9 9 IT ONLY TOOK A MINUTE / Joe Brown (Piccadilly)
13 10 GO AWAY LITTLE GIRL / Mark Wynter (Pye)
14 11 LIKE I DO / Maureen Evans (Oriole)
16 12 UP ON THE ROOF / Kenny Lynch (HMV)
8 12 BOBBY'S GIRL / Susan Maughan (Philips)
11 14 LET'S DANCE / Chris Montez (London)
- 15 GLOBETROTTER / Tornados (Decca)
26 16 COMIN' HOME BABY / Mel Torme (London)
12 17 DESAFINADO / Stan Getz & Charlie Byrd (HMV)
24 18 DON'T YOU THINK IT'S TIME / Mike Berry & the Outlaws (HMV)
14 19 YOUR CHEATING HEART / Ray Charles (HMV)
- 20 DIAMONDS / Jet Harris & Tony Meehan (Decca)
17 21 THE SWISS MAID / Del Shannon (London)
19 22 ME AND MY SHADOW / Frank Sinatra & Sammy Davis Jr. (Reprise)
18 23 A FOREVER KIND OF LOVE / Bobby Vee (Liberty)
23 24 THE MAIN ATTRACTION / Pat Boone (London)
29 25 HE'S A REBEL / Crystals (London)
20 25 UP ON THE ROOF / Julie Grant (Pye)
- 27 RUBY ANN / Marty Robbins (CBS)
- 28 CHARMAINE Bachelors (Decca)
25 29 MUST BE MADISON / Joe Loss (HMV)
30 30 GONNA GO FISHIN' / Hank Locklin (RCA)
27 30 JUST FOR KICKS / Mike Sarne (Parlophone)

19 January 1963

1 1 DANCE ON / Shadows (Columbia)
2 2 RETURN TO SENDER / Elvis Presley (RCA)
3 3 THE NEXT TIME / Cliff Richard (Columbia)
4 4 BACHELOR BOY / Cliff Richard (Columbia)
20 5 DIAMONDS / Jet Harris & Tony Meehan (Decca)
15 6 GLOBETROTTER / Tornados (Decca)
11 7 LIKE I DO / Maureen Evans (Oriole)
16 8 COMIN' HOME BABY / Mel Torme (London)
6 9 LOVESICK BLUES / Frank Ifield (Columbia)
5 10 DANCE WITH THE GUITAR MAN / Duane Eddy (RCA)
12 11 UP ON THE ROOF / Kenny Lynch (HMV)
10 12 GO AWAY LITTLE GIRL / Mark Wynter (Pye)
18 13 DON'T YOU THINK IT'S TIME / Mike Berry & the Outlaws (HMV)
7 13 SUN ARISE / Rolf Harris (Columbia)
8 15 TELSTAR Tornados (Decca)
9 16 IT ONLY TOOK A MINUTE / Joe Brown (Piccadilly)
- 17 LITTLE TOWN FLIRT / Del Shannon (London)
12 18 BOBBY'S GIRL / Susan Maughan (Philips)
25 19 HE'S A REBEL / Crystals (London)
- 20 BIG GIRLS DON'T CRY / Four Seasons (Stateside)
14 21 LET'S DANCE / Chris Montez (London)
17 22 DESAFINADO / Stan Getz & Charlie Byrd (HMV)
23 23 A FOREVER KIND OF LOVE / Bobby Vee (Liberty)
19 24 YOUR CHEATING HEART / Ray Charles (HMV)
25 24 UP ON THE ROOF / Julie Grant (Pye)
- 26 ALL ALONE AM I / Brenda Lee (Brunswick)
28 27 CHARMAINE / Bachelors (Decca)
27 28 RUBY ANN / Marty Robbins (CBS)
22 29 ME AND MY SHADOW / Frank Sinatra & Sammy Davis Jr. (Reprise)
- 29 LOOP-DE-LOOP / Frankie Vaughan (Philips)

26 January 1963

5 1 DIAMONDS / Jet Harris & Tony Meehan (Decca)
1 2 DANCE ON / Shadows (Columbia)
4 3 BACHELOR BOY / Cliff Richard (Columbia)
6 4 GLOBETROTTER / Tornados (Decca)
2 5 RETURN TO SENDER / Elvis Presley (RCA)
7 6 LIKE I DO / Maureen Evans (Oriole)
3 7 THE NEXT TIME / Cliff Richard (Columbia)
13 8 DON'T YOU THINK IT'S TIME / Mike Berry & the Outlaws (HMV)
8 9 COMIN' HOME BABY / Mel Torme (London)
17 10 LITTLE TOWN FLIRT / Del Shannon (London)
11 11 UP ON THE ROOF / Kenny Lynch (HMV)
12 12 GO AWAY LITTLE GIRL / Mark Wynter (Pye)
10 13 DANCE WITH THE GUITAR MAN / Duane Eddy (RCA)
20 14 BIG GIRLS DON'T CRY / Four Seasons (Stateside)
26 15 ALL ALONE AM I / Brenda Lee (Brunswick)
13 16 SUN ARISE / Rolf Harris (Columbia)
- 17 THE WAYWARD WIND / Frank Ifield (Columbia)
- 17 ISLAND OF DREAMS / Springfields (Philips)
9 19 LOVESICK BLUES / Frank Ifield (Columbia)
- 20 SOME KINDA FUN / Chris Montez (London)
- 21 LOO-BE-LOO Chucks (Decca)
15 22 TELSTAR Tornados (Decca)
- 23 A TASTE OF HONEY / Mr Acker Bilk (Columbia)
18 24 BOBBY'S GIRL / Susan Maughan (Philips)
16 25 IT ONLY TOOK A MINUTE / Joe Brown (Piccadilly)
19 26 HE'S A REBEL / Crystals (London)
27 27 CHARMAINE / Bachelors (Decca)
29 28 LOOP-DE-LOOP / Frankie Vaughan (Philips)
- 29 SUKIYAKI / Kenny Ball & His Jazzmen (Pye Jazz)
22 30 DESAFINADO / Stan Getz & Charlie Byrd (HMV)

A month dominated by intrumentals, as the Shadows clung to the top slot for three weeks, to be replaced by the first single from ex-members Harris & Meehan (written by Jerry Lordan, writer of the Shads' previous two chart-toppers, *Apache* and *Wonderful Land*). The other notable achievement was Cliff Richard's double-sided success. *Bachelor Boy* peaked at Number Three only four weeks after *The Next Time* had made the top - the most successful independent placings by two sides of a single in UK chart history.

February 1963

2 February 1963

LW	TW	Title	Artist (Label)
1	1	DIAMONDS	Jet Harris & Tony Meehan (Decca)
4	2	GLOBETROTTER	Tornados (Decca)
2	3	DANCE ON	Shadows (Columbia)
3	4	BACHELOR BOY	Cliff Richard (Columbia)
6	5	LIKE I DO	Maureen Evans (Oriole)
8	6	DON'T YOU THINK IT'S TIME	Mike Berry & the Outlaws (HMV)
10	7	LITTLE TOWN FLIRT	Del Shannon (London)
17	8	THE WAYWARD WIND	Frank Ifield (Columbia)
5	9	RETURN TO SENDER	Elvis Presley (RCA)
7	10	THE NEXT TIME	Cliff Richard (Columbia)
9	11	COMIN' HOME BABY	Mel Torme (London)
11	12	UP ON THE ROOF	Kenny Lynch (HMV)
12	13	GO AWAY LITTLE GIRL	Mark Wynter (Pye)
14	14	BIG GIRLS DON'T CRY	Four Seasons (Stateside)
15	15	ALL ALONE AM I	Brenda Lee (Brunswick)
20	16	SOME KINDA FUN	Chris Montez (London)
-	17	PLEASE PLEASE ME	Beatles (Parlophone)
23	18	A TASTE OF HONEY	Mr Acker Bilk (Columbia)
28	19	LOOP-DE-LOOP	Frankie Vaughan (Philips)
21	20	LOO-BE-LOO	Chucks (Decca)
17	20	ISLAND OF DREAMS	Springfields (Philips)
-	22	MY LITTLE GIRL	Crickets (Liberty)
13	23	DANCE WITH THE GUITAR MAN	Duane Eddy (RCA)
29	24	SUKIYAKI	Kenny Ball & His Jazzmen (Pye Jazz)
27	25	CHARMAINE	Bachelors (Decca)
-	26	WALK RIGHT IN	Rooftop Singers (Fontana)
19	27	LOVESICK BLUES	Frank Ifield (Columbia)
16	28	SUN ARISE	Rolf Harris (Columbia)
-	29	HAVA NAGILA	Spotnicks (Oriole)
25	30	IT ONLY TOOK A MINUTE	Joe Brown (Piccadilly)

9 February 1963

LW	TW	Title	Artist (Label)
1	1	DIAMONDS	Jet Harris & Tony Meehan (Decca)
8	2	THE WAYWARD WIND	Frank Ifield (Columbia)
2	3	GLOBETROTTER	Tornados (Decca)
7	4	LITTLE TOWN FLIRT	Del Shannon (London)
17	5	PLEASE PLEASE ME	Beatles (Parlophone)
4	6	BACHELOR BOY	Cliff Richard (Columbia)
19	7	LOOP-DE-LOOP	Frankie Vaughan (Philips)
6	8	DON'T YOU THINK IT'S TIME	Mike Berry & the Outlaws (HMV)
3	9	DANCE ON	Shadows (Columbia)
5	10	LIKE I DO	Maureen Evans (Oriole)
14	11	ALL ALONE AM I	Brenda Lee (Brunswick)
10	12	THE NEXT TIME	Cliff Richard (Columbia)
26	13	WALK RIGHT IN	Rooftop Singers (Fontana)
20	14	ISLAND OF DREAMS	Springfields (Philips)
24	15	SUKIYAKI	Kenny Ball & His Jazzmen (Pye Jazz)
14	15	BIG GIRLS DON'T CRY	Four Seasons (Stateside)
-	17	THE NIGHT HAS A THOUSAND EYES	Bobby Vee (Liberty)
9	18	RETURN TO SENDER	Elvis Presley (RCA)
18	19	A TASTE OF HONEY	Mr Acker Bilk (Columbia)
16	20	SOME KINDA FUN	Chris Montez (London)
20	21	LOO-BE-LOO	Chucks (Decca)
12	22	UP ON THE ROOF	Kenny Lynch (HMV)
11	23	COMIN' HOME BABY	Mel Torme (London)
13	24	GO AWAY LITTLE GIRL	Mark Wynter (Pye)
22	25	MY LITTLE GIRL	Crickets (Liberty)
29	26	HAVA NAGILA	Spotnicks (Oriole)
-	27	TELL HIM	Billie Davis (Decca)
25	28	CHARMAINE	Bachelors (Decca)
-	29	WHAT NOW	Adam Faith (Parlophone)
30	30	IT'S UP TO YOU	Rick Nelson (London)

16 February 1963

LW	TW	Title	Artist (Label)
1	1	DIAMONDS	Jet Harris & Tony Meehan (Decca)
2	2	THE WAYWARD WIND	Frank Ifield (Columbia)
5	3	PLEASE PLEASE ME	Beatles (Parlophone)
4	4	LITTLE TOWN FLIRT	Del Shannon (London)
7	5	LOOP-DE-LOOP	Frankie Vaughan (Philips)
17	6	THE NIGHT HAS A THOUSAND EYES	Bobby Vee (Liberty)
14	7	ISLAND OF DREAMS	Springfields (Philips)
3	8	GLOBETROTTER	Tornados (Decca)
6	9	BACHELOR BOY	Cliff Richard (Columbia)
10	10	LIKE I DO	Maureen Evans (Oriole)
11	11	ALL ALONE AM I	Brenda Lee (Brunswick)
8	12	DON'T YOU THINK IT'S TIME	Mike Berry & the Outlaws (HMV)
15	13	SUKIYAKI	Kenny Ball & His Jazzmen (Pye Jazz)
13	14	WALK RIGHT IN	Rooftop Singers (Fontana)
12	15	THE NEXT TIME	Cliff Richard (Columbia)
15	16	BIG GIRLS DON'T CRY	Four Seasons (Stateside)
-	17	THAT'S WHAT LOVE WILL DO	Joe Brown (Piccadilly)
9	18	DANCE ON	Shadows (Columbia)
19	19	A TASTE OF HONEY	Mr Acker Bilk (Columbia)
20	20	SOME KINDA FUN	Chris Montez (London)
27	21	TELL HIM	Billie Davis (Decca)
26	22	HAVA NAGILA	Spotnicks (Oriole)
21	23	LOO-BE-LOO	Chucks (Decca)
28	24	CHARMAINE	Bachelors (Decca)
30	25	IT'S UP TO YOU	Rick Nelson (London)
-	26	HEY PAULA	Paul & Paula (Philips)
18	27	RETURN TO SENDER	Elvis Presley (RCA)
-	28	LIKE I'VE NEVER BEEN GONE	Billy Fury (Decca)
25	29	MY LITTLE GIRL	Crickets (Liberty)
29	30	WHAT NOW	Adam Faith (Parlophone)

23 February 1963

LW	TW	Title	Artist (Label)
3	1	PLEASE PLEASE ME	Beatles (Parlophone)
2	1	THE WAYWARD WIND	Frank Ifield (Columbia)
1	3	DIAMONDS	Jet Harris & Tony Meehan (Decca)
6	4	THE NIGHT HAS A THOUSAND EYES	Bobby Vee (Liberty)
5	5	LOOP-DE-LOOP	Frankie Vaughan (Philips)
4	6	LITTLE TOWN FLIRT	Del Shannon (London)
17	7	THAT'S WHAT LOVE WILL DO	Joe Brown (Piccadilly)
7	8	ISLAND OF DREAMS	Springfields (Philips)
-	9	SUMMER HOLIDAY	Cliff Richard (Columbia)
13	10	SUKIYAKI	Kenny Ball & His Jazzmen (Pye Jazz)
14	11	WALK RIGHT IN	Rooftop Singers (Fontana)
11	12	ALL ALONE AM I	Brenda Lee (Brunswick)
28	13	LIKE I'VE NEVER BEEN GONE	Billy Fury (Decca)
10	14	LIKE I DO	Maureen Evans (Oriole)
8	15	GLOBETROTTER	Tornados (Decca)
9	16	BACHELOR BOY	Cliff Richard (Columbia)
12	17	DON'T YOU THINK IT'S TIME	Mike Berry & the Outlaws (HMV)
15	18	THE NEXT TIME	Cliff Richard (Columbia)
26	19	HEY PAULA	Paul & Paula (Philips)
22	20	HAVA NAGILA	Spotnicks (Oriole)
21	21	TELL HIM	Billie Davis (Decca)
19	22	A TASTE OF HONEY	Mr Acker Bilk (Columbia)
24	23	CHARMAINE	Bachelors (Decca)
-	24	HI-LILI HI-LO	Richard Chamberlain (MGM)
-	25	DANCING SHOES	Cliff Richard (Columbia)
16	26	BIG GIRLS DON'T CRY	Four Seasons (Stateside)
20	27	SOME KINDA FUN	Chris Montez (London)
18	28	DANCE ON	Shadows (Columbia)
23	29	LOO-BE-LOO	Chucks (Decca)
-	30	BOSS GUITAR	Duane Eddy (RCA)

Here was the first hint that the Beatles were really a force to be reckoned with. Having just missed the Top 30 in its first week on sale, *Please Please Me* then took just four weeks from its debut at 17 to the top. Its equally-shared peak stance with *The Wayward Wind* at the month-end didn't detract from Frank Ifield's own achievement - he became the first UK artist to send three consecutive singles to Number One. Note also three rock instrumentals in the top three slots on February 2 - a unique occurrence.

March 1963

	2 March 1963		9 March 1963		16 March 1963		23 March 1963
1	1 PLEASE PLEASE ME Beatles (Parlophone)	4	1 SUMMER HOLIDAY Cliff Richard (Columbia)	1	1 SUMMER HOLIDAY Cliff Richard (Columbia)	1	1 SUMMER HOLIDAY Cliff Richard (Columbia)
1	2 THE WAYWARD WIND Frank Ifield (Columbia)	1	2 PLEASE PLEASE ME Beatles (Parlophone)	2	2 PLEASE PLEASE ME Beatles (Parlophone)	4	2 FOOT TAPPER Shadows (Columbia)
4	3 THE NIGHT HAS A THOUSAND EYES Bobby Vee (Liberty)	6	3 THAT'S WHAT LOVE WILL DO Joe Brown (Piccadilly)	5	3 LIKE I'VE NEVER BEEN GONE Billy Fury (Decca)	3	3 LIKE I'VE NEVER BEEN GONE Billy Fury (Decca)
9	4 SUMMER HOLIDAY Cliff Richard (Columbia)	3	4 THE NIGHT HAS A THOUSAND EYES Bobby Vee (Liberty)	11	4 FOOT TAPPER Shadows (Columbia)	2	4 PLEASE PLEASE ME Beatles (Parlophone)
5	5 LOOP-DE-LOOP Frankie Vaughan (Philips)	9	5 LIKE I'VE NEVER BEEN GONE Billy Fury (Decca)	3	5 THAT'S WHAT LOVE WILL DO Joe Brown (Piccadilly)	5	5 THAT'S WHAT LOVE WILL DO Joe Brown (Piccadilly)
7	6 THAT'S WHAT LOVE WILL DO Joe Brown (Piccadilly)	2	6 THE WAYWARD WIND Frank Ifield (Columbia)	4	6 THE NIGHT HAS A THOUSAND EYES Bobby Vee (Liberty)	10	6 CHARMAINE Bachelors (Decca)
3	7 DIAMONDS Jet Harris & Tony Meehan (Decca)	5	7 LOOP-DE-LOOP Frankie Vaughan (Philips)	6	7 THE WAYWARD WIND Frank Ifield (Columbia)	17	7 FROM A JACK TO A KING Ned Miller (London)
8	8 ISLAND OF DREAMS Springfields (Philips)	19	8 ONE BROKEN HEART FOR SALE Elvis Presley (RCA)	8	8 ONE BROKEN HEART FOR SALE Elvis Presley (RCA)	9	8 ISLAND OF DREAMS Springfields (Philips)
13	9 LIKE I'VE NEVER BEEN GONE Billy Fury (Decca)	8	9 ISLAND OF DREAMS Springfields (Philips)	9	9 ISLAND OF DREAMS Springfields (Philips)	6	9 THE NIGHT HAS A THOUSAND EYES Bobby Vee (Liberty)
6	10 LITTLE TOWN FLIRT Del Shannon (London)	7	10 DIAMONDS Jet Harris & Tony Meehan (Decca)	13	10 CHARMAINE Bachelors (Decca)	8	10 ONE BROKEN HEART FOR SALE Elvis Presley (RCA)
11	11 WALK RIGHT IN Rooftop Singers (Fontana)	-	11 FOOT TAPPER Shadows (Columbia)	14	11 HEY PAULA Paul & Paula (Philips)	15	11 RHYTHM OF THE RAIN Cascades (Warner Bros)
10	12 SUKIYAKI Kenny Ball & His Jazzmen (Pye Jazz)	17	12 TELL HIM Billie Davis (Decca)	7	12 LOOP-DE-LOOP Frankie Vaughan (Philips)	19	12 BROWN-EYED HANDSOME MAN Buddy Holly (Coral)
23	13 CHARMAINE Bachelors (Decca)	13	13 CHARMAINE Bachelors (Decca)	12	13 TELL HIM Billie Davis (Decca)	7	13 THE WAYWARD WIND Frank Ifield (Columbia)
12	14 ALL ALONE AM I Brenda Lee (Brunswick)	15	14 HEY PAULA Paul & Paula (Philips)	25	14 SAY WONDERFUL THINGS Ronnie Carroll (Philips)	14	14 SAY WONDERFUL THINGS Ronnie Carroll (Philips)
19	15 HEY PAULA Paul & Paula (Philips)	11	15 WALK RIGHT IN Rooftop Singers (Fontana)	22	15 RHYTHM OF THE RAIN Cascades (Warner Bros)	11	14 HEY PAULA Paul & Paula (Philips)
20	16 HAVA NAGILA Spotnicks (Oriole)	16	16 HAVA NAGILA Spotnicks (Oriole)	10	16 DIAMONDS Jet Harris & Tony Meehan (Decca)	13	16 TELL HIM Billie Davis (Decca)
21	17 TELL HIM Billie Davis (Decca)	14	17 ALL ALONE AM I Brenda Lee (Brunswick)	21	17 FROM A JACK TO A KING Ned Miller (London)	-	17 HOW DO YOU DO IT? Gerry & the Pacemakers (Columbia)
15	18 GLOBETROTTER Tornados (Decca)	25	18 CUPBOARD LOVE John Leyton (HMV)	16	18 HAVA NAGILA Spotnicks (Oriole)	-	18 ROBOT Tornados (Decca)
-	19 ONE BROKEN HEART FOR SALE Elvis Presley (RCA)	10	19 LITTLE TOWN FLIRT Del Shannon (London)	-	19 BROWN-EYED HANDSOME MAN Buddy Holly (Coral)	12	19 LOOP-DE-LOOP Frankie Vaughan (Philips)
24	20 HI-LILI HI-LO Richard Chamberlain (MGM)	12	20 SUKIYAKI Kenny Ball & His Jazzmen (Pye Jazz)	18	20 CUPBOARD LOVE John Leyton (HMV)	-	20 LET'S TURKEY TROT Little Eva (London)
14	21 LIKE I DO Maureen Evans (Oriole)	29	21 FROM A JACK TO A KING Ned Miller (London)	15	21 WALK RIGHT IN Rooftop Singers (Fontana)	20	21 CUPBOARD LOVE John Leyton (HMV)
16	22 BACHELOR BOY Cliff Richard (Columbia)	27	22 RHYTHM OF THE RAIN Cascades (Warner Bros)	20	22 SUKIYAKI Kenny Ball & His Jazzmen (Pye Jazz)	-	22 THE FOLK SINGER Tommy Roe (HMV)
17	23 DON'T YOU THINK IT'S TIME Mike Berry & the Outlaws (HMV)	22	23 BACHELOR BOY Cliff Richard (Columbia)	19	23 LITTLE TOWN FLIRT Del Shannon (London)	16	23 DIAMONDS Jet Harris & Tony Meehan (Decca)
22	24 A TASTE OF HONEY Mr Acker Bilk (Columbia)	20	24 HI-LILI HI-LO Richard Chamberlain (MGM)	24	24 HI-LILI HI-LO Richard Chamberlain (MGM)	27	23 IN DREAMS Roy Orbison (London)
-	25 CUPBOARD LOVE John Leyton (HMV)	-	25 SAY WONDERFUL THINGS Ronnie Carroll (Philips)	17	25 ALL ALONE AM I Brenda Lee (Brunswick)	24	25 HI-LILI HI-LO Richard Chamberlain (MGM)
25	26 DANCING SHOES Cliff Richard (Columbia)	27	26 THE NEXT TIME Cliff Richard (Columbia)	23	26 BACHELOR BOY Cliff Richard (Columbia)	-	26 SO IT WILL ALWAYS BE Everly Brothers (Warner Bros)
-	27 RHYTHM OF THE RAIN Cascades (Warner Bros)	-	27 BOSS GUITAR Duane Eddy (RCA)	-	27 IN DREAMS Roy Orbison (London)	21	26 WALK RIGHT IN Rooftop Singers (Fontana)
18	27 THE NEXT TIME Cliff Richard (Columbia)	21	27 LIKE I DO Maureen Evans (Oriole)	30	28 OLD SMOKEY LOCOMOTION Little Eva (London)	-	28 GOOD GOLLY MISS MOLLY Jerry Lee Lewis (London)
-	29 FROM A JACK TO A KING Ned Miller (London)	18	29 GLOBETROTTER Tornados (Decca)	-	29 MY KIND OF GIRL Frank Sinatra (Reprise)	28	29 OLD SMOKEY LOCOMOTION Little Eva (London)
29	30 LOO-BE-LOO Chucks (Decca)	-	30 OLD SMOKEY LOCOMOTION Little Eva (London)	29	30 GLOBETROTTER Tornados (Decca)	-	30 COUNT ON ME Julie Grant (Pye)

Cliff's *Summer Holiday* couldn't equal the sales of *The Young Ones* a year earlier, but was comfortably the month's biggest single (with its B-side also making a small showing). A more significant event was the stalling of Elvis Presley's *One Broken Heart* For Sale at only No.8, after a string of Presley chart-toppers. The single was slated for its pitiful length (1 min 34 secs), but the winds of musical change were also stirring. Meanwhile, Little Eva joined the elite few to chart both sides of a single simultaneously.

March – April 1963

last week / this week

30 March 1963

last	this	title / artist (label)
2	1	FOOT TAPPER — Shadows (Columbia)
1	2	SUMMER HOLIDAY — Cliff Richard (Columbia)
17	3	HOW DO YOU DO IT? — Gerry & the Pacemakers (Columbia)
7	4	FROM A JACK TO A KING — Ned Miller (London)
3	5	LIKE I'VE NEVER BEEN GONE — Billy Fury (Decca)
6	6	CHARMAINE — Bachelors (Decca)
14	7	SAY WONDERFUL THINGS — Ronnie Carroll (Philips)
5	8	THAT'S WHAT LOVE WILL DO — Joe Brown (Piccadilly)
4	9	PLEASE PLEASE ME — Beatles (Parlophone)
8	10	ISLAND OF DREAMS — Springfields (Philips)
11	11	RHYTHM OF THE RAIN — Cascades (Warner Bros)
12	12	BROWN-EYED HANDSOME MAN — Buddy Holly (Coral)
9	13	THE NIGHT HAS A THOUSAND EYES — Bobby Vee (Liberty)
16	14	TELL HIM — Billie Davis (Decca)
14	15	HEY PAULA — Paul & Paula (Philips)
10	16	ONE BROKEN HEART FOR SALE — Elvis Presley (RCA)
13	17	THE WAYWARD WIND — Frank Ifield (Columbia)
20	18	LET'S TURKEY TROT — Little Eva (London)
22	19	THE FOLK SINGER — Tommy Roe (HMV)
18	19	ROBOT — Tornados (Decca)
-	21	SAY I WON'T BE THERE — Springfields (Philips)
23	22	IN DREAMS — Roy Orbison (London)
-	23	MR. BASS MAN — Johnny Cymbal (London)
26	23	SO IT WILL ALWAYS BE — Everly Brothers (Warner Bros)
-	25	THE END OF THE WORLD — Skeeter Davis (RCA)
-	26	WALK LIKE A MAN — Four Seasons (Stateside)
-	27	ALL ALONE AM I — Brenda Lee (Brunswick)
21	28	CUPBOARD LOVE — John Leyton (HMV)
-	29	CAN YOU FORGIVE ME — Karl Denver (Decca)
19	30	LOOP-DE-LOOP — Frankie Vaughan (Philips)

6 April 1963

last	this	title / artist (label)
3	1	HOW DO YOU DO IT? — Gerry & the Pacemakers (Columbia)
1	2	FOOT TAPPER — Shadows (Columbia)
4	3	FROM A JACK TO A KING — Ned Miller (London)
2	4	SUMMER HOLIDAY — Cliff Richard (Columbia)
7	5	SAY WONDERFUL THINGS — Ronnie Carroll (Philips)
5	6	LIKE I'VE NEVER BEEN GONE — Billy Fury (Decca)
11	7	RHYTHM OF THE RAIN — Cascades (Warner Bros)
6	8	CHARMAINE — Bachelors (Decca)
12	9	BROWN-EYED HANDSOME MAN — Buddy Holly (Coral)
8	10	THAT'S WHAT LOVE WILL DO — Joe Brown (Piccadilly)
19	11	THE FOLK SINGER — Tommy Roe (HMV)
10	12	ISLAND OF DREAMS — Springfields (Philips)
9	13	PLEASE PLEASE ME — Beatles (Parlophone)
21	14	SAY I WON'T BE THERE — Springfields (Philips)
19	14	ROBOT — Tornados (Decca)
26	16	WALK LIKE A MAN — Four Seasons (Stateside)
15	17	HEY PAULA — Paul & Paula (Philips)
22	18	IN DREAMS — Roy Orbison (London)
18	19	LET'S TURKEY TROT — Little Eva (London)
25	20	THE END OF THE WORLD — Skeeter Davis (RCA)
14	21	TELL HIM — Billie Davis (Decca)
23	22	MR. BASS MAN — Johnny Cymbal (London)
23	23	SO IT WILL ALWAYS BE — Everly Brothers (Warner Bros)
16	24	ONE BROKEN HEART FOR SALE — Elvis Presley (RCA)
13	25	THE NIGHT HAS A THOUSAND EYES — Bobby Vee (Liberty)
28	26	CUPBOARD LOVE — John Leyton (HMV)
-	26	CAN'T GET USED TO LOSING YOU — Andy Williams (CBS)
-	28	LOSING YOU — Brenda Lee (Brunswick)
-	29	CODE OF LOVE — Mike Sarne (Parlophone)
-	30	I WANNA BE AROUND — Tony Bennett (CBS)
-	30	MY LITTLE BABY — Mike Berry (HMV)

13 April 1963

last	this	title / artist (label)
1	1	HOW DO YOU DO IT? — Gerry & the Pacemakers (Columbia)
3	2	FROM A JACK TO A KING — Ned Miller (London)
2	3	FOOT TAPPER — Shadows (Columbia)
7	4	RHYTHM OF THE RAIN — Cascades (Warner Bros)
5	5	SAY WONDERFUL THINGS — Ronnie Carroll (Philips)
4	5	SUMMER HOLIDAY — Cliff Richard (Columbia)
9	7	BROWN-EYED HANDSOME MAN — Buddy Holly (Coral)
14	8	SAY I WON'T BE THERE — Springfields (Philips)
6	9	LIKE I'VE NEVER BEEN GONE — Billy Fury (Decca)
11	10	THE FOLK SINGER — Tommy Roe (HMV)
8	11	CHARMAINE — Bachelors (Decca)
-	12	NOBODY'S DARLIN' BUT MINE — Frank Ifield (Columbia)
16	13	WALK LIKE A MAN — Four Seasons (Stateside)
19	14	LET'S TURKEY TROT — Little Eva (London)
18	15	IN DREAMS — Roy Orbison (London)
12	16	ISLAND OF DREAMS — Springfields (Philips)
14	16	ROBOT — Tornados (Decca)
26	18	CAN'T GET USED TO LOSING YOU — Andy Williams (CBS)
10	19	THAT'S WHAT LOVE WILL DO — Joe Brown (Piccadilly)
28	20	LOSING YOU — Brenda Lee (Brunswick)
20	21	THE END OF THE WORLD — Skeeter Davis (RCA)
13	22	PLEASE PLEASE ME — Beatles (Parlophone)
22	22	MR. BASS MAN — Johnny Cymbal (London)
23	24	SO IT WILL ALWAYS BE — Everly Brothers (Warner Bros)
17	25	HEY PAULA — Paul & Paula (Philips)
-	26	OUR DAY WILL COME — Ruby & the Romantics (London)
24	27	ONE BROKEN HEART FOR SALE — Elvis Presley (RCA)
29	28	CODE OF LOVE — Mike Sarne (Parlophone)
26	29	CUPBOARD LOVE — John Leyton (HMV)
-	30	COUNT ON ME — Julie Grant (Pye)

20 April 1963

last	this	title / artist (label)
1	1	HOW DO YOU DO IT? — Gerry & the Pacemakers (Columbia)
2	2	FROM A JACK TO A KING — Ned Miller (London)
7	3	BROWN-EYED HANDSOME MAN — Buddy Holly (Coral)
3	4	FOOT TAPPER — Shadows (Columbia)
8	5	SAY I WON'T BE THERE — Springfields (Philips)
-	6	FROM ME TO YOU — Beatles (Parlophone)
4	7	RHYTHM OF THE RAIN — Cascades (Warner Bros)
10	8	THE FOLK SINGER — Tommy Roe (HMV)
5	9	SAY WONDERFUL THINGS — Ronnie Carroll (Philips)
12	10	NOBODY'S DARLIN' BUT MINE — Frank Ifield (Columbia)
15	11	IN DREAMS — Roy Orbison (London)
5	12	SUMMER HOLIDAY — Cliff Richard (Columbia)
18	13	CAN'T GET USED TO LOSING YOU — Andy Williams (CBS)
13	14	WALK LIKE A MAN — Four Seasons (Stateside)
11	15	CHARMAINE — Bachelors (Decca)
9	16	LIKE I'VE NEVER BEEN GONE — Billy Fury (Decca)
20	17	LOSING YOU — Brenda Lee (Brunswick)
14	18	LET'S TURKEY TROT — Little Eva (London)
16	19	ROBOT — Tornados (Decca)
22	20	MR. BASS MAN — Johnny Cymbal (London)
16	21	ISLAND OF DREAMS — Springfields (Philips)
21	22	THE END OF THE WORLD — Skeeter Davis (RCA)
19	23	THAT'S WHAT LOVE WILL DO — Joe Brown (Piccadilly)
24	24	SO IT WILL ALWAYS BE — Everly Brothers (Warner Bros)
-	25	CASABLANCA — Kenny Ball & His Jazzmen (Pye Jazz)
26	26	CAN YOU FORGIVE ME — Karl Denver (Decca)
27	27	HE'S SO FINE — Chiffons (Stateside)
30	28	COUNT ON ME — Julie Grant (Pye)
25	29	HEY PAULA — Paul & Paula (Philips)
26	30	OUR DAY WILL COME — Ruby & the Romantics (London)

Foot Tapper gave the Shadows three chart-toppers out of four singles, but it was to be their final No.1. More significant was the instant success of EMI's second Liverpool group Gerry & the Pacemakers, whose Beatle-rejected *How Do You Do It?* outsold *Please Please Me*. Such was the ever-growing excitement around the Beatles, though, that *From Me To You* built big advance orders, and slammed into the chart at No.6 in its first week of release. The Springfields were at the peak of their chart career.

April – May 1963

last week / this week

27 April 1963

last	this		
6	1	FROM ME TO YOU	Beatles (Parlophone)
1	2	HOW DO YOU DO IT?	Gerry & the Pacemakers (Columbia)
2	3	FROM A JACK TO A KING	Ned Miller (London)
10	4	NOBODY'S DARLIN' BUT MINE	Frank Ifield (Columbia)
5	5	SAY I WON'T BE THERE	Springfields (Philips)
3	6	BROWN-EYED HANDSOME MAN	Buddy Holly (Coral)
11	7	IN DREAMS	Roy Orbison (London)
8	7	THE FOLK SINGER	Tommy Roe (HMV)
13	7	CAN'T GET USED TO LOSING YOU	Andy Williams (CBS)
4	10	FOOT TAPPER	Shadows (Columbia)
7	11	RHYTHM OF THE RAIN	Cascades (Warner Bros)
14	12	WALK LIKE A MAN	Four Seasons (Stateside)
12	13	SUMMER HOLIDAY	Cliff Richard (Columbia)
9	14	SAY WONDERFUL THINGS	Ronnie Carroll (Philips)
17	15	LOSING YOU	Brenda Lee (Brunswick)
-	16	SCARLETT O'HARA	Jet Harris & Tony Meehan (Decca)
27	17	HE'S SO FINE	Chiffons (Stateside)
16	18	LIKE I'VE NEVER BEEN GONE	Billy Fury (Decca)
15	19	CHARMAINE	Bachelors (Decca)
18	20	LET'S TURKEY TROT	Little Eva (London)
22	21	THE END OF THE WORLD	Skeeter Davis (RCA)
-	22	TWO KINDS OF TEARDROPS	Del Shannon (London)
19	23	ROBOT	Tornados (Decca)
25	24	CASABLANCA	Kenny Ball & His Jazzmen (Pye Jazz)
28	24	COUNT ON ME	Julie Grant (Pye)
20	26	MR. BASS MAN	Johnny Cymbal (London)
24	27	SO IT WILL ALWAYS BE	Everly Brothers (Warner Bros)
26	28	CAN YOU FORGIVE ME	Karl Denver (Decca)
-	29	DECK OF CARDS	Wink Martindale (London)
-	30	IT'S MY WAY OF LOVING YOU	Miki & Griff (Pye)

4 May 1963

last	this		
1	1	FROM ME TO YOU	Beatles (Parlophone)
2	2	HOW DO YOU DO IT?	Gerry & the Pacemakers (Columbia)
3	3	FROM A JACK TO A KING	Ned Miller (London)
4	4	NOBODY'S DARLIN' BUT MINE	Frank Ifield (Columbia)
7	5	CAN'T GET USED TO LOSING YOU	Andy Williams (CBS)
7	6	IN DREAMS	Roy Orbison (London)
5	7	SAY I WON'T BE THERE	Springfields (Philips)
16	8	SCARLETT O'HARA	Jet Harris & Tony Meehan (Decca)
11	9	RHYTHM OF THE RAIN	Cascades (Warner Bros)
6	10	BROWN-EYED HANDSOME MAN	Buddy Holly (Coral)
22	11	TWO KINDS OF TEARDROPS	Del Shannon (London)
7	12	THE FOLK SINGER	Tommy Roe (HMV)
15	13	LOSING YOU	Brenda Lee (Brunswick)
17	14	HE'S SO FINE	Chiffons (Stateside)
10	15	FOOT TAPPER	Shadows (Columbia)
12	16	WALK LIKE A MAN	Four Seasons (Stateside)
14	17	SAY WONDERFUL THINGS	Ronnie Carroll (Philips)
24	18	CASABLANCA	Kenny Ball & His Jazzmen (Pye Jazz)
13	19	SUMMER HOLIDAY	Cliff Richard (Columbia)
29	20	DECK OF CARDS	Wink Martindale (London)
20	21	LET'S TURKEY TROT	Little Eva (London)
-	22	DO YOU WANT TO KNOW A SECRET?	Billy J. Kramer & the Dakotas (Parlophone)
24	23	COUNT ON ME	Julie Grant (Pye)
18	24	LIKE I'VE NEVER BEEN GONE	Billy Fury (Decca)
21	25	THE END OF THE WORLD	Skeeter Davis (RCA)
-	26	ISLAND OF DREAMS	Springfields (Philips)
-	27	PIPELINE	Chantays (London)
-	28	MY WAY	Eddie Cochran (Liberty)
30	29	IT'S MY WAY OF LOVING YOU	Miki & Griff (Pye)
27	30	SO IT WILL ALWAYS BE	Everly Brothers (Warner Bros)
-	30	YOUNG LOVERS	Paul & Paula (Philips)

11 May 1963

last	this		
1	1	FROM ME TO YOU	Beatles (Parlophone)
2	2	HOW DO YOU DO IT?	Gerry & the Pacemakers (Columbia)
8	3	SCARLETT O'HARA	Jet Harris & Tony Meehan (Decca)
4	4	NOBODY'S DARLIN' BUT MINE	Frank Ifield (Columbia)
5	5	CAN'T GET USED TO LOSING YOU	Andy Williams (CBS)
3	6	FROM A JACK TO A KING	Ned Miller (London)
6	7	IN DREAMS	Roy Orbison (London)
11	8	TWO KINDS OF TEARDROPS	Del Shannon (London)
7	9	SAY I WON'T BE THERE	Springfields (Philips)
-	10	LUCKY LIPS	Cliff Richard (Columbia)
22	11	DO YOU WANT TO KNOW A SECRET?	Billy J. Kramer & the Dakotas (Parlophone)
13	12	LOSING YOU	Brenda Lee (Brunswick)
9	13	RHYTHM OF THE RAIN	Cascades (Warner Bros)
14	14	HE'S SO FINE	Chiffons (Stateside)
10	15	BROWN-EYED HANDSOME MAN	Buddy Holly (Coral)
12	16	THE FOLK SINGER	Tommy Roe (HMV)
16	17	WALK LIKE A MAN	Four Seasons (Stateside)
18	18	CASABLANCA	Kenny Ball & His Jazzmen (Pye Jazz)
27	19	PIPELINE	Chantays (London)
20	20	DECK OF CARDS	Wink Martindale (London)
15	21	FOOT TAPPER	Shadows (Columbia)
17	22	SAY WONDERFUL THINGS	Ronnie Carroll (Philips)
19	23	SUMMER HOLIDAY	Cliff Richard (Columbia)
28	24	MY WAY	Eddie Cochran (Liberty)
30	24	YOUNG LOVERS	Paul & Paula (Philips)
23	26	COUNT ON ME	Julie Grant (Pye)
-	27	LITTLE BAND OF GOLD	James Gilreath (Pye International)
24	28	LIKE I'VE NEVER BEEN GONE	Billy Fury (Decca)
30	29	SO IT WILL ALWAYS BE	Everly Brothers (Warner Bros)
29	29	IT'S MY WAY OF LOVING YOU	Miki & Griff (Pye)

18 May 1963

last	this		
1	1	FROM ME TO YOU	Beatles (Parlophone)
3	2	SCARLETT O'HARA	Jet Harris & Tony Meehan (Decca)
5	3	CAN'T GET USED TO LOSING YOU	Andy Williams (CBS)
10	4	LUCKY LIPS	Cliff Richard (Columbia)
2	5	HOW DO YOU DO IT?	Gerry & the Pacemakers (Columbia)
11	5	DO YOU WANT TO KNOW A SECRET?	Billy J. Kramer & the Dakotas (Parlophone)
7	7	IN DREAMS	Roy Orbison (London)
8	8	TWO KINDS OF TEARDROPS	Del Shannon (London)
4	9	NOBODY'S DARLIN' BUT MINE	Frank Ifield (Columbia)
6	10	FROM A JACK TO A KING	Ned Miller (London)
14	11	HE'S SO FINE	Chiffons (Stateside)
12	12	LOSING YOU	Brenda Lee (Brunswick)
24	13	YOUNG LOVERS	Paul & Paula (Philips)
9	14	SAY I WON'T BE THERE	Springfields (Philips)
20	15	DECK OF CARDS	Wink Martindale (London)
19	16	PIPELINE	Chantays (London)
18	17	CASABLANCA	Kenny Ball & His Jazzmen (Pye Jazz)
13	18	RHYTHM OF THE RAIN	Cascades (Warner Bros)
15	18	BROWN-EYED HANDSOME MAN	Buddy Holly (Coral)
27	20	LITTLE BAND OF GOLD	James Gilreath (Pye International)
-	21	WHEN WILL YOU SAY I LOVE YOU	Billy Fury (Decca)
16	22	THE FOLK SINGER	Tommy Roe (HMV)
22	23	SAY WONDERFUL THINGS	Ronnie Carroll (Philips)
17	24	WALK LIKE A MAN	Four Seasons (Stateside)
24	25	MY WAY	Eddie Cochran (Liberty)
-	26	TAKE THESE CHAINS FROM MY HEART	Ray Charles (HMV)
-	27	IF YOU GOTTA MAKE A FOOL OF SOMEBODY	Freddie & the Dreamers (Columbia)
-	28	FORGET HIM	Bobby Rydell (Cameo Parkway)
-	29	JUST LISTEN TO MY HEART	Spotnicks (Oriole)
23	30	SUMMER HOLIDAY	Cliff Richard (Columbia)

This time, the Beatles reached the chart top in only their second week, and while Liverpool dominated at both Numbers One and Two for most of this month, the city's (and manager Brian Epstein's) third big-breaking group, Billy J Kramer & the Dakotas, made an immediate mark with their cover of a track from the Beatles' debut album. The oddest Top 30 entry was *Deck Of Cards*, back after more than three years, and outselling its initial release, after a chance play on BBC Radio's *Two-Way Family Favourites*.

last week / this week

25 May 1963

Last	This	Title — Artist (Label)
1	1	FROM ME TO YOU — Beatles (Parlophone)
2	2	SCARLETT O'HARA — Jet Harris & Tony Meehan (Decca)
5	3	DO YOU WANT TO KNOW A SECRET? — Billy J. Kramer & the Dakotas (Parlophone)
4	4	LUCKY LIPS — Cliff Richard (Columbia)
3	5	CAN'T GET USED TO LOSING YOU — Andy Williams (CBS)
8	6	TWO KINDS OF TEARDROPS — Del Shannon (London)
7	7	IN DREAMS — Roy Orbison (London)
5	8	HOW DO YOU DO IT? — Gerry & the Pacemakers (Columbia)
9	9	NOBODY'S DARLIN' BUT MINE — Frank Ifield (Columbia)
26	10	TAKE THESE CHAINS FROM MY HEART — Ray Charles (HMV)
21	11	WHEN WILL YOU SAY I LOVE YOU — Billy Fury (Decca)
10	12	FROM A JACK TO A KING — Ned Miller (London)
13	13	DECK OF CARDS — Wink Martindale (London)
13	14	YOUNG LOVERS — Paul & Paula (Philips)
12	15	LOSING YOU — Brenda Lee (Brunswick)
11	16	HE'S SO FINE — Chiffons (Stateside)
16	17	PIPELINE — Chantays (London)
27	18	IF YOU GOTTA MAKE A FOOL OF SOMEBODY — Freddie & the Dreamers (Columbia)
28	19	FORGET HIM — Bobby Rydell (Cameo Parkway)
14	20	SAY I WON'T BE THERE — Springfields (Philips)
18	21	BROWN-EYED HANDSOME MAN — Buddy Holly (Coral)
20	22	LITTLE BAND OF GOLD — James Gilreath (Pye International)
17	23	CASABLANCA — Kenny Ball & His Jazzmen (Pye Jazz)
–	24	SHY GIRL — Mark Wynter (Pye)
22	25	THE FOLK SINGER — Tommy Roe (HMV)
25	26	MY WAY — Eddie Cochran (Liberty)
–	27	LET'S GO STEADY AGAIN — Neil Sedaka (RCA)
–	28	SHY GIRL — Cascades (Warner Bros)
–	29	FIREBALL — Don Spencer (HMV)
–	30	HARVEST OF LOVE — Benny Hill (Pye)

1 June 1963

Last	This	Title — Artist (Label)
3	1	DO YOU WANT TO KNOW A SECRET? — Billy J. Kramer & the Dakotas (Parlophone)
1	1	FROM ME TO YOU — Beatles (Parlophone)
2	3	SCARLETT O'HARA — Jet Harris & Tony Meehan (Decca)
4	4	LUCKY LIPS — Cliff Richard (Columbia)
7	5	IN DREAMS — Roy Orbison (London)
11	6	WHEN WILL YOU SAY I LOVE YOU — Billy Fury (Decca)
5	7	CAN'T GET USED TO LOSING YOU — Andy Williams (CBS)
6	8	TWO KINDS OF TEARDROPS — Del Shannon (London)
10	9	TAKE THESE CHAINS FROM MY HEART — Ray Charles (HMV)
–	9	I LIKE IT — Gerry & the Pacemakers (Columbia)
13	11	DECK OF CARDS — Wink Martindale (London)
14	12	YOUNG LOVERS — Paul & Paula (Philips)
8	13	HOW DO YOU DO IT? — Gerry & the Pacemakers (Columbia)
9	14	NOBODY'S DARLIN' BUT MINE — Frank Ifield (Columbia)
18	15	IF YOU GOTTA MAKE A FOOL OF SOMEBODY — Freddie & the Dreamers (Columbia)
–	16	FALLING — Roy Orbison (London)
12	17	FROM A JACK TO A KING — Ned Miller (London)
15	18	LOSING YOU — Brenda Lee (Brunswick)
19	19	FORGET HIM — Bobby Rydell (Cameo Parkway)
24	20	SHY GIRL — Mark Wynter (Pye)
17	21	PIPELINE — Chantays (London)
16	22	HE'S SO FINE — Chiffons (Stateside)
30	23	HARVEST OF LOVE — Benny Hill (Pye)
–	24	OUT OF MY MIND — Johnny Tillotson (London)
28	25	SHY GIRL — Cascades (Warner Bros)
–	25	ANOTHER SATURDAY NIGHT — Sam Cooke (RCA)
27	27	LET'S GO STEADY AGAIN — Neil Sedaka (RCA)
20	28	SAY I WON'T BE THERE — Springfields (Philips)
21	29	BROWN-EYED HANDSOME MAN — Buddy Holly (Coral)
22	30	LITTLE BAND OF GOLD — James Gilreath (Pye International)

8 June 1963

Last	This	Title — Artist (Label)
1	1	DO YOU WANT TO KNOW A SECRET? — Billy J. Kramer & the Dakotas (Parlophone)
2	2	FROM ME TO YOU — Beatles (Parlophone)
3	3	SCARLETT O'HARA — Jet Harris & Tony Meehan (Decca)
9	4	I LIKE IT — Gerry & the Pacemakers (Columbia)
6	5	WHEN WILL YOU SAY I LOVE YOU — Billy Fury (Decca)
9	6	TAKE THESE CHAINS FROM MY HEART — Ray Charles (HMV)
4	7	LUCKY LIPS — Cliff Richard (Columbia)
5	8	IN DREAMS — Roy Orbison (London)
8	9	TWO KINDS OF TEARDROPS — Del Shannon (London)
15	10	IF YOU GOTTA MAKE A FOOL OF SOMEBODY — Freddie & the Dreamers (Columbia)
11	11	DECK OF CARDS — Wink Martindale (London)
–	12	ATLANTIS — Shadows (Columbia)
7	13	CAN'T GET USED TO LOSING YOU — Andy Williams (CBS)
16	14	FALLING — Roy Orbison (London)
12	15	YOUNG LOVERS — Paul & Paula (Philips)
–	16	THE ICE CREAM MAN — Tornados (Decca)
18	17	LOSING YOU — Brenda Lee (Brunswick)
23	18	HARVEST OF LOVE — Benny Hill (Pye)
19	19	FORGET HIM — Bobby Rydell (Cameo Parkway)
20	20	SHY GIRL — Mark Wynter (Pye)
21	21	PIPELINE — Chantays (London)
14	22	NOBODY'S DARLIN' BUT MINE — Frank Ifield (Columbia)
13	23	HOW DO YOU DO IT? — Gerry & the Pacemakers (Columbia)
27	24	LET'S GO STEADY AGAIN — Neil Sedaka (RCA)
–	25	BO DIDDLEY — Buddy Holly (Coral)
25	26	ANOTHER SATURDAY NIGHT — Sam Cooke (RCA)
22	27	HE'S SO FINE — Chiffons (Stateside)
17	28	FROM A JACK TO A KING — Ned Miller (London)
24	29	OUT OF MY MIND — Johnny Tillotson (London)
30	30	LITTLE BAND OF GOLD — James Gilreath (Pye International)

15 June 1963

Last	This	Title — Artist (Label)
4	1	I LIKE IT — Gerry & the Pacemakers (Columbia)
1	2	DO YOU WANT TO KNOW A SECRET? — Billy J. Kramer & the Dakotas (Parlophone)
2	3	FROM ME TO YOU — Beatles (Parlophone)
6	4	TAKE THESE CHAINS FROM MY HEART — Ray Charles (HMV)
10	4	IF YOU GOTTA MAKE A FOOL OF SOMEBODY — Freddie & the Dreamers (Columbia)
5		WHEN WILL YOU SAY I LOVE YOU — Billy Fury (Decca)
12	6	ATLANTIS — Shadows (Columbia)
3	8	SCARLETT O'HARA — Jet Harris & Tony Meehan (Decca)
11	9	DECK OF CARDS — Wink Martindale (London)
7	10	LUCKY LIPS — Cliff Richard (Columbia)
25	11	BO DIDDLEY — Buddy Holly (Coral)
8	12	IN DREAMS — Roy Orbison (London)
14	13	FALLING — Roy Orbison (London)
9	14	TWO KINDS OF TEARDROPS — Del Shannon (London)
15	15	YOUNG LOVERS — Paul & Paula (Philips)
16	16	THE ICE CREAM MAN — Tornados (Decca)
18	17	HARVEST OF LOVE — Benny Hill (Pye)
13	18	CAN'T GET USED TO LOSING YOU — Andy Williams (CBS)
19	19	FORGET HIM — Bobby Rydell (Cameo Parkway)
21	20	PIPELINE — Chantays (London)
22	21	NOBODY'S DARLIN' BUT MINE — Frank Ifield (Columbia)
–	22	IT'S MY PARTY — Lesley Gore (Mercury)
–	23	IT'S BEEN NICE — Everly Brothers (Warner Bros)
–	24	INDIAN LOVE CALL — Karl Denver (Decca)
26	25	ANOTHER SATURDAY NIGHT — Sam Cooke (RCA)
–	26	AIN'T THAT A SHAME — Four Seasons (Stateside)
20	26	SHY GIRL — Mark Wynter (Pye)
–	28	DA DOO RON RON — Crystals (London)
23	29	HOW DO YOU DO IT? — Gerry & the Pacemakers (Columbia)
–	30	SHE'S NEW TO YOU — Susan Maughan (Philips)

Assorted Liverpudlians played hand-me-on at No.1, while Jet Harris & Tony Meehan followed a chart-toppping instrumental with a similar No. 2. Over four years after his death, Buddy Holly too was confounding trends, quickly following his fourth-best-selling solo single, *Brown-Eyed Handsome Man*, with *Bo Diddley*. Both songs were from his 1963 LP *Reminiscing*, and featured accompaniment by the Fireballs. Don Spencer's hit of that title was from Gerry Anderson's TV show *Fireball XL5*.

June – July 1963

last this
week

22 June 1963

1 1 I LIKE IT — Gerry & the Pacemakers (Columbia)
4 2 IF YOU GOTTA MAKE A FOOL OF SOMEBODY — Freddie & the Dreamers (Columbia)
6 3 ATLANTIS Shadows (Columbia)
4 4 TAKE THESE CHAINS FROM MY HEART Ray Charles (HMV)
3 5 FROM ME TO YOU Beatles (Parlophone)
2 6 DO YOU WANT TO KNOW A SECRET? Billy J. Kramer & the Dakotas (Parlophone)
6 7 WHEN WILL YOU SAY I LOVE YOU Billy Fury (Decca)
9 8 DECK OF CARDS Wink Martindale (London)
13 9 FALLING Roy Orbison (London)
11 10 BO DIDDLEY Buddy Holly (Coral)
8 11 SCARLETT O'HARA Jet Harris & Tony Meehan (Decca)
12 12 IN DREAMS Roy Orbison (London)
10 13 LUCKY LIPS Cliff Richard (Columbia)
28 14 DA DOO RON RON Crystals (London)
15 15 YOUNG LOVERS Paul & Paula (Philips)
22 16 IT'S MY PARTY Lesley Gore (Mercury)
14 17 TWO KINDS OF TEARDROPS Del Shannon (London)
19 18 FORGET HIM Bobby Rydell (Cameo Parkway)
- 19 WELCOME TO MY WORLD Jim Reeves (RCA)
16 19 THE ICE CREAM MAN Tornados (Decca)
18 21 CAN'T GET USED TO LOSING YOU Andy Williams (CBS)
- 22 HEY MAMA Frankie Vaughan (Philips)
20 23 PIPELINE Chantays (London)
26 24 SHY GIRL Mark Wynter (Pye)
- 25 RONDO Kenny Ball & His Jazzmen (Pye Jazz)
25 26 ANOTHER SATURDAY NIGHT Sam Cooke (RCA)
24 26 INDIAN LOVE CALL Karl Denver (Decca)
23 28 IT'S BEEN NICE Everly Brothers (Warner Bros)
26 28 AIN'T THAT A SHAME Four Seasons (Stateside)
17 28 HARVEST OF LOVE Benny Hill (Pye)
21 28 NOBODY'S DARLIN' BUT MINE Frank Ifield (Columbia)

29 June 1963

1 1 I LIKE IT — Gerry & the Pacemakers (Columbia)
3 2 ATLANTIS Shadows (Columbia)
2 3 IF YOU GOTTA MAKE A FOOL OF SOMEBODY — Freddie & the Dreamers (Columbia)
4 4 TAKE THESE CHAINS FROM MY HEART Ray Charles (HMV)
8 5 DECK OF CARDS Wink Martindale (London)
5 6 FROM ME TO YOU Beatles (Parlophone)
6 7 DO YOU WANT TO KNOW A SECRET? Billy J. Kramer & the Dakotas (Parlophone)
7 8 WHEN WILL YOU SAY I LOVE YOU Billy Fury (Decca)
9 9 FALLING Roy Orbison (London)
- 10 CONFESSIN' (THAT I LOVE YOU) Frank Ifield (Columbia)
10 11 BO DIDDLEY Buddy Holly (Coral)
14 12 DA DOO RON RON Crystals (London)
16 13 IT'S MY PARTY Lesley Gore (Mercury)
13 14 LUCKY LIPS Cliff Richard (Columbia)
11 15 SCARLETT O'HARA Jet Harris & Tony Meehan (Decca)
18 15 FORGET HIM Bobby Rydell (Cameo Parkway)
19 17 WELCOME TO MY WORLD Jim Reeves (RCA)
12 18 IN DREAMS Roy Orbison (London)
19 19 THE ICE CREAM MAN Tornados (Decca)
- 20 BOBBY TOMORROW Bobby Vee (Liberty)
21 21 CAN'T GET USED TO LOSING YOU Andy Williams (CBS)
17 22 TWO KINDS OF TEARDROPS Del Shannon (London)
15 23 YOUNG LOVERS Paul & Paula (Philips)
22 23 HEY MAMA Frankie Vaughan (Philips)
25 25 RONDO Kenny Ball & His Jazzmen (Pye Jazz)
- 26 SWING THAT HAMMER Mike Cotton's Jazzmen (Columbia)
- 27 TWIST AND SHOUT Isley Brothers (Stateside)
- 28 SUKIYAKI Kyu Sakamoto (HMV)
23 29 PIPELINE Chantays (London)
28 30 NOBODY'S DARLIN' BUT MINE Frank Ifield (Columbia)

6 July 1963

1 1 I LIKE IT — Gerry & the Pacemakers (Columbia)
2 2 ATLANTIS Shadows (Columbia)
10 3 CONFESSIN' (THAT I LOVE YOU) Frank Ifield (Columbia)
3 4 IF YOU GOTTA MAKE A FOOL OF SOMEBODY — Freddie & the Dreamers (Columbia)
4 5 TAKE THESE CHAINS FROM MY HEART Ray Charles (HMV)
5 6 DECK OF CARDS Wink Martindale (London)
6 7 FROM ME TO YOU Beatles (Parlophone)
11 8 BO DIDDLEY Buddy Holly (Coral)
9 9 FALLING Roy Orbison (London)
12 10 DA DOO RON RON Crystals (London)
13 11 IT'S MY PARTY Lesley Gore (Mercury)
7 12 DO YOU WANT TO KNOW A SECRET? Billy J. Kramer & the Dakotas (Parlophone)
- 13 DEVIL IN DISGUISE Elvis Presley (RCA)
8 14 WHEN WILL YOU SAY I LOVE YOU Billy Fury (Decca)
17 15 WELCOME TO MY WORLD Jim Reeves (RCA)
15 16 FORGET HIM Bobby Rydell (Cameo Parkway)
14 17 LUCKY LIPS Cliff Richard (Columbia)
15 18 SCARLETT O'HARA Jet Harris & Tony Meehan (Decca)
- 19 TWIST AND SHOUT Brian Poole & the Tremeloes (Decca)
28 20 SUKIYAKI Kyu Sakamoto (HMV)
20 21 BOBBY TOMORROW Bobby Vee (Liberty)
27 22 TWIST AND SHOUT Isley Brothers (Stateside)
18 23 IN DREAMS Roy Orbison (London)
- 24 SWEETS FOR MY SWEET Searchers (Pye)
23 24 HEY MAMA Frankie Vaughan (Philips)
- 26 NATURE'S TIME FOR LOVE Joe Brown (Piccadilly)
19 27 THE ICE CREAM MAN Tornados (Decca)
25 28 RONDO Kenny Ball & His Jazzmen (Pye Jazz)
- 29 WALKIN' TALL Adam Faith (Parlophone)
- 30 YOU CAN NEVER STOP ME LOVING YOU Kenny Lynch (HMV)
- 30 IT'S TOO LATE NOW Swinging Blue Jeans (HMV)

13 July 1963

3 1 CONFESSIN' (THAT I LOVE YOU) Frank Ifield (Columbia)
1 2 I LIKE IT — Gerry & the Pacemakers (Columbia)
13 3 DEVIL IN DISGUISE Elvis Presley (RCA)
2 4 ATLANTIS Shadows (Columbia)
24 5 SWEETS FOR MY SWEET Searchers (Pye)
5 6 TAKE THESE CHAINS FROM MY HEART Ray Charles (HMV)
15 7 WELCOME TO MY WORLD Jim Reeves (RCA)
4 8 IF YOU GOTTA MAKE A FOOL OF SOMEBODY — Freddie & the Dreamers (Columbia)
6 8 DECK OF CARDS Wink Martindale (London)
10 10 DA DOO RON RON Crystals (London)
11 11 IT'S MY PARTY Lesley Gore (Mercury)
8 12 BO DIDDLEY Buddy Holly (Coral)
19 13 TWIST AND SHOUT Brian Poole & the Tremeloes (Decca)
9 14 FALLING Roy Orbison (London)
7 15 FROM ME TO YOU Beatles (Parlophone)
16 16 FORGET HIM Bobby Rydell (Cameo Parkway)
12 17 DO YOU WANT TO KNOW A SECRET? Billy J. Kramer & the Dakotas (Parlophone)
20 18 SUKIYAKI Kyu Sakamoto (HMV)
30 19 YOU CAN NEVER STOP ME LOVING YOU Kenny Lynch (HMV)
24 20 HEY MAMA Frankie Vaughan (Philips)
14 21 WHEN WILL YOU SAY I LOVE YOU Billy Fury (Decca)
22 21 TWIST AND SHOUT Isley Brothers (Stateside)
17 23 LUCKY LIPS Cliff Richard (Columbia)
21 24 BOBBY TOMORROW Bobby Vee (Liberty)
27 25 THE ICE CREAM MAN Tornados (Decca)
18 26 SCARLETT O'HARA Jet Harris & Tony Meehan (Decca)
23 27 IN DREAMS Roy Orbison (London)
29 28 WALKIN' TALL Adam Faith (Parlophone)
26 29 NATURE'S TIME FOR LOVE Joe Brown (Piccadilly)
- 30 THE GOOD LIFE Tony Bennett (CBS)

By the end of June, EMI's Columbia and Parlophone labels had held the Number One slot for 20 weeks - and the streak carried on into July as *Confessin'* gave Frank Ifield his fourth chart-topper from five singles. Elvis returned in stronger form with the recently-recorded *(You're The) Devil In Disguise*, Brian Poole & the Tremeloes jumped on the fact that *Twist And Shout* was the most popular dancehall track on the Beatles' LP, and enough were buying the year-old Isley Brothers original to chart that too.

last week	this week	20 July 1963
1	1	CONFESSIN' (THAT I LOVE YOU) Frank Ifield (Columbia)
3	2	DEVIL IN DISGUISE Elvis Presley (RCA)
2	3	I LIKE IT Gerry & the Pacemakers (Columbia)
5	4	SWEETS FOR MY SWEET Searchers (Pye)
4	5	ATLANTIS Shadows (Columbia)
10	6	DA DOO RON RON Crystals (London)
13	7	TWIST AND SHOUT Brian Poole & the Tremeloes (Decca)
8	8	DECK OF CARDS Wink Martindale (London)
6	9	TAKE THESE CHAINS FROM MY HEART Ray Charles (HMV)
7	10	WELCOME TO MY WORLD Jim Reeves (RCA)
12	11	BO DIDDLEY Buddy Holly (Coral)
11	12	IT'S MY PARTY Lesley Gore (Mercury)
-	13	TWIST AND SHOUT (EP) Beatles (Parlophone)
8	14	IF YOU GOTTA MAKE A FOOL OF SOMEBODY Freddie & the Dreamers (Columbia)
15	15	FROM ME TO YOU Beatles (Parlophone)
18	16	SUKIYAKI Kyu Sakamoto (HMV)
14	17	FALLING Roy Orbison (London)
19	18	YOU CAN NEVER STOP ME LOVING YOU Kenny Lynch (HMV)
16	19	FORGET HIM Bobby Rydell (Cameo Parkway)
-	19	THEME FROM 'THE LEGION'S LAST PATROL' Ken Thorne (HMV)
17	21	DO YOU WANT TO KNOW A SECRET? Billy J. Kramer & the Dakotas (Parlophone)
21	22	TWIST AND SHOUT Isley Brothers (Stateside)
28	23	WALKIN' TALL Adam Faith (Parlophone)
-	23	I WONDER Brenda Lee (Brunswick)
20	25	HEY MAMA Frankie Vaughan (Philips)
24	26	BOBBY TOMORROW Bobby Vee (Liberty)
30	27	THE GOOD LIFE Tony Bennett (CBS)
-	28	MISTER PORTER Mickie Most (Decca)
-	29	I'LL NEVER GET OVER YOU Johnny Kidd & the Pirates (HMV)
23	30	LUCKY LIPS Cliff Richard (Columbia)

last	this	27 July 1963
1	1	CONFESSIN' (THAT I LOVE YOU) Frank Ifield (Columbia)
2	2	DEVIL IN DISGUISE Elvis Presley (RCA)
4	3	SWEETS FOR MY SWEET Searchers (Pye)
6	4	DA DOO RON RON Crystals (London)
7	5	TWIST AND SHOUT Brian Poole & the Tremeloes (Decca)
3	6	I LIKE IT Gerry & the Pacemakers (Columbia)
5	7	ATLANTIS Shadows (Columbia)
13	8	TWIST AND SHOUT (EP) Beatles (Parlophone)
12	9	IT'S MY PARTY Lesley Gore (Mercury)
9	10	TAKE THESE CHAINS FROM MY HEART Ray Charles (HMV)
10	11	WELCOME TO MY WORLD Jim Reeves (RCA)
8	12	DECK OF CARDS Wink Martindale (London)
16	13	SUKIYAKI Kyu Sakamoto (HMV)
11	14	BO DIDDLEY Buddy Holly (Coral)
18	15	YOU CAN NEVER STOP ME LOVING YOU Kenny Lynch (HMV)
19	16	THEME FROM 'THE LEGION'S LAST PATROL' Ken Thorne (HMV)
-	17	SO MUCH IN LOVE Tymes (Cameo Parkway)
15	18	FROM ME TO YOU Beatles (Parlophone)
23	19	I WONDER Brenda Lee (Brunswick)
20	20	IN SUMMER Billy Fury (Decca)
14	21	IF YOU GOTTA MAKE A FOOL OF SOMEBODY Freddie & the Dreamers (Columbia)
17	22	FALLING Roy Orbison (London)
-	22	WIPE OUT Surfaris (London)
19	24	FORGET HIM Bobby Rydell (Cameo Parkway)
25	24	HEY MAMA Frankie Vaughan (Philips)
23	26	WALKIN' TALL Adam Faith (Parlophone)
21	27	DO YOU WANT TO KNOW A SECRET? Billy J. Kramer & the Dakotas (Parlophone)
-	28	BY THE WAY Big Three (Decca)
29	28	I'LL NEVER GET OVER YOU Johnny Kidd & the Pirates (HMV)
-	30	COME ON HOME Springfields (Philips)

last	this	3 August 1963
3	1	SWEETS FOR MY SWEET Searchers (Pye)
1	2	CONFESSIN' (THAT I LOVE YOU) Frank Ifield (Columbia)
2	3	DEVIL IN DISGUISE Elvis Presley (RCA)
5	4	TWIST AND SHOUT Brian Poole & the Tremeloes (Decca)
4	5	DA DOO RON RON Crystals (London)
8	6	TWIST AND SHOUT (EP) Beatles (Parlophone)
7	7	ATLANTIS Shadows (Columbia)
13	8	SUKIYAKI Kyu Sakamoto (HMV)
6	9	I LIKE IT Gerry & the Pacemakers (Columbia)
10	10	TAKE THESE CHAINS FROM MY HEART Ray Charles (HMV)
9	10	IT'S MY PARTY Lesley Gore (Mercury)
20	12	IN SUMMER Billy Fury (Decca)
11	13	WELCOME TO MY WORLD Jim Reeves (RCA)
12	14	DECK OF CARDS Wink Martindale (London)
15	15	YOU CAN NEVER STOP ME LOVING YOU Kenny Lynch (HMV)
16	16	THEME FROM 'THE LEGION'S LAST PATROL' Ken Thorne (HMV)
19	17	I WONDER Brenda Lee (Brunswick)
22	18	WIPE OUT Surfaris (London)
-	19	BAD TO ME Billy J. Kramer & the Dakotas (Parlophone)
14	20	BO DIDDLEY Buddy Holly (Coral)
28	20	I'LL NEVER GET OVER YOU Johnny Kidd & the Pirates (HMV)
28	22	BY THE WAY Big Three (Decca)
17	22	SO MUCH IN LOVE Tymes (Cameo Parkway)
24	24	HEY MAMA Frankie Vaughan (Philips)
21	25	IF YOU GOTTA MAKE A FOOL OF SOMEBODY Freddie & the Dreamers (Columbia)
-	26	COME ON Rolling Stones (Decca)
18	27	FROM ME TO YOU Beatles (Parlophone)
-	28	THE CRUEL SEA Dakotas (Parlophone)
-	29	JUST LIKE EDDIE Heinz (Decca)
30	30	WIPE OUT Saints (Pye)

last	this	10 August 1963
1	1	SWEETS FOR MY SWEET Searchers (Pye)
2	2	CONFESSIN' (THAT I LOVE YOU) Frank Ifield (Columbia)
3	3	DEVIL IN DISGUISE Elvis Presley (RCA)
6	4	TWIST AND SHOUT (EP) Beatles (Parlophone)
4	5	TWIST AND SHOUT Brian Poole & the Tremeloes (Decca)
5	6	DA DOO RON RON Crystals (London)
19	7	BAD TO ME Billy J. Kramer & the Dakotas (Parlophone)
12	8	IN SUMMER Billy Fury (Decca)
8	9	SUKIYAKI Kyu Sakamoto (HMV)
18	10	WIPE OUT Surfaris (London)
7	11	ATLANTIS Shadows (Columbia)
16	12	THEME FROM 'THE LEGION'S LAST PATROL' Ken Thorne (HMV)
9	13	I LIKE IT Gerry & the Pacemakers (Columbia)
15	14	YOU CAN NEVER STOP ME LOVING YOU Kenny Lynch (HMV)
10	15	TAKE THESE CHAINS FROM MY HEART Ray Charles (HMV)
10	16	IT'S MY PARTY Lesley Gore (Mercury)
20	17	I'LL NEVER GET OVER YOU Johnny Kidd & the Pirates (HMV)
13	18	WELCOME TO MY WORLD Jim Reeves (RCA)
14	19	DECK OF CARDS Wink Martindale (London)
17	20	I WONDER Brenda Lee (Brunswick)
22	21	SO MUCH IN LOVE Tymes (Cameo Parkway)
-	22	YOU DON'T HAVE TO BE A BABY TO CRY Caravelles (Decca)
29	23	JUST LIKE EDDIE Heinz (Decca)
28	24	THE CRUEL SEA Dakotas (Parlophone)
-	25	THE GOOD LIFE Tony Bennett (CBS)
-	26	I'M TELLING YOU NOW Freddie & the Dreamers (Columbia)
26	27	COME ON Rolling Stones (Decca)
22	28	BY THE WAY Big Three (Decca)
20	29	BO DIDDLEY Buddy Holly (Coral)
-	30	AFTER YOU'VE GONE Alice Babs (Fontana)
-	30	ONLY THE HEARTACHES Houston Wells (Parlophone)

First Ifield, and then Pye's first Liverpool signing the Searchers, just kept Presley from re-establishing his chart-topping credentials. The Beatles stepped in and overrode the *Twist And Shout* chart debate between Brian Poole and the Isleys by releasing their own version on a 4-track EP from their album. This debuted only two places below the previous highest slot reached by an EP (Elvis' *Follow That Dream* in 1962), and broke that record the following week, before equalling the No. 4 peak of the Poole single.

August – September 1963

last week	this week	17 August 1963
1	1	SWEETS FOR MY SWEET Searchers (Pye)
7	2	BAD TO ME Billy J. Kramer & the Dakotas (Parlophone)
2	3	CONFESSIN' (THAT I LOVE YOU) Beatles (Parlophone)
4	4	TWIST AND SHOUT (EP) Frank Ifield (Columbia)
8	5	IN SUMMER Billy Fury (Decca)
5	6	TWIST AND SHOUT Brian Poole & the Tremeloes (Decca)
26	7	I'M TELLING YOU NOW Freddie & the Dreamers (Columbia)
3	8	DEVIL IN DISGUISE Elvis Presley (RCA)
12	9	THEME FROM 'THE LEGION'S LAST PATROL' Ken Thorne (HMV)
10	10	WIPE OUT Surfaris (London)
6	11	DA DOO RON RON Crystals (London)
9	12	SUKIYAKI Kyu Sakamoto (HMV)
17	13	I'LL NEVER GET OVER YOU Johnny Kidd & the Pirates (HMV)
22	14	YOU DON'T HAVE TO BE A BABY TO CRY Caravelles (Decca)
14	15	YOU CAN NEVER STOP ME LOVING YOU Kenny Lynch (HMV)
11	15	ATLANTIS Shadows (Columbia)
18	17	WELCOME TO MY WORLD Jim Reeves (RCA)
23	18	JUST LIKE EDDIE Heinz (Decca)
15	19	TAKE THESE CHAINS FROM MY HEART Ray Charles (HMV)
13	20	I LIKE IT Gerry & the Pacemakers (Columbia)
21	21	SO MUCH IN LOVE Tymes (Cameo Parkway)
16	22	IT'S MY PARTY Lesley Gore (Mercury)
24	23	THE CRUEL SEA Dakotas (Parlophone)
20	24	I WONDER Brenda Lee (Brunswick)
27	25	COME ON Rolling Stones (Decca)
19	26	DECK OF CARDS Wink Martindale (London)
-	27	ACAPULCO 1922 Kenny Ball & His Jazzmen (Pye Jazz)
-	28	DANCE ON Kathy Kirby (Decca)
28	29	BY THE WAY Big Three (Decca)
30	29	ONLY THE HEARTACHES Houston Wells (Parlophone)

		24 August 1963
2	1	BAD TO ME Billy J. Kramer & the Dakotas (Parlophone)
1	2	SWEETS FOR MY SWEET Searchers (Pye)
7	3	I'M TELLING YOU NOW Freddie & the Dreamers (Columbia)
5	4	IN SUMMER Billy Fury (Decca)
4	5	TWIST AND SHOUT (EP) Beatles (Parlophone)
-	6	IT'S ALL IN THE GAME Cliff Richard (Columbia)
3	7	CONFESSIN' (THAT I LOVE YOU) Frank Ifield (Columbia)
10	8	WIPE OUT Surfaris (London)
9	9	THEME FROM 'THE LEGION'S LAST PATROL' Ken Thorne (HMV)
6	10	TWIST AND SHOUT Brian Poole & the Tremeloes (Decca)
13	11	I'LL NEVER GET OVER YOU Johnny Kidd & the Pirates (HMV)
8	12	DEVIL IN DISGUISE Elvis Presley (RCA)
14	13	YOU DON'T HAVE TO BE A BABY TO CRY Caravelles (Decca)
11	14	DA DOO RON RON Crystals (London)
28	15	DANCE ON Kathy Kirby (Decca)
16	16	JUST LIKE EDDIE Heinz (Decca)
12	16	SUKIYAKI Kyu Sakamoto (HMV)
-	18	I WANT TO STAY HERE Steve & Eydie (CBS)
23	19	THE CRUEL SEA Dakotas (Parlophone)
25	20	COME ON Rolling Stones (Decca)
15	21	YOU CAN NEVER STOP ME LOVING YOU Kenny Lynch (HMV)
-	22	STILL Karl Denver (Decca)
15	23	ATLANTIS Shadows (Columbia)
27	24	ACAPULCO 1922 Kenny Ball & His Jazzmen (Pye Jazz)
24	24	I WONDER Brenda Lee (Brunswick)
17	26	WELCOME TO MY WORLD Jim Reeves (RCA)
29	27	BY THE WAY Big Three (Decca)
-	28	SURFIN' USA Beach Boys (Capitol)
-	29	SURF CITY Jan & Dean (Liberty)
-	30	WHISPERING Bachelors (Decca)

		31 August 1963
1	1	BAD TO ME Billy J. Kramer & the Dakotas (Parlophone)
-	2	SHE LOVES YOU Beatles (Parlophone)
3	3	I'M TELLING YOU NOW Freddie & the Dreamers (Columbia)
6	4	IT'S ALL IN THE GAME Cliff Richard (Columbia)
2	5	SWEETS FOR MY SWEET Searchers (Pye)
11	6	I'LL NEVER GET OVER YOU Johnny Kidd & the Pirates (HMV)
13	7	YOU DON'T HAVE TO BE A BABY TO CRY Caravelles (Decca)
8	8	WIPE OUT Surfaris (London)
9	9	THEME FROM 'THE LEGION'S LAST PATROL' Ken Thorne (HMV)
5	10	TWIST AND SHOUT (EP) Beatles (Parlophone)
18	10	I WANT TO STAY HERE Steve & Eydie (CBS)
4	12	IN SUMMER Billy Fury (Decca)
16	13	JUST LIKE EDDIE Heinz (Decca)
7	14	CONFESSIN' (THAT I LOVE YOU) Frank Ifield (Columbia)
10	15	TWIST AND SHOUT Brian Poole & the Tremeloes (Decca)
15	16	DANCE ON Kathy Kirby (Decca)
22	17	STILL Karl Denver (Decca)
16	18	SUKIYAKI Kyu Sakamoto (HMV)
19	19	THE CRUEL SEA Dakotas (Parlophone)
-	20	TWO SILHOUETTES Del Shannon (London)
12	21	DEVIL IN DISGUISE Elvis Presley (RCA)
26	21	WELCOME TO MY WORLD Jim Reeves (RCA)
14	23	DA DOO RON RON Crystals (London)
-	24	I WANNA STAY HERE Miki & Griff (Pye)
20	25	COME ON Rolling Stones (Decca)
21	26	YOU CAN NEVER STOP ME LOVING YOU Kenny Lynch (HMV)
30	27	WHISPERING Bachelors (Decca)
28	28	SURFIN' USA Beach Boys (Capitol)
24	29	ACAPULCO 1922 Kenny Ball & His Jazzmen (Pye Jazz)
29	30	SURF CITY Jan & Dean (Liberty)

		7 September 1963
2	1	SHE LOVES YOU Beatles (Parlophone)
1	2	BAD TO ME Billy J. Kramer & the Dakotas (Parlophone)
3	3	I'M TELLING YOU NOW Freddie & the Dreamers (Columbia)
4	4	IT'S ALL IN THE GAME Cliff Richard (Columbia)
6	5	I'LL NEVER GET OVER YOU Johnny Kidd & the Pirates (HMV)
7	6	YOU DON'T HAVE TO BE A BABY TO CRY Caravelles (Decca)
10	7	I WANT TO STAY HERE Steve & Eydie (CBS)
13	8	JUST LIKE EDDIE Heinz (Decca)
5	8	SWEETS FOR MY SWEET Searchers (Pye)
9	10	THEME FROM 'THE LEGION'S LAST PATROL' Ken Thorne (HMV)
8	11	WIPE OUT Surfaris (London)
12	12	IN SUMMER Billy Fury (Decca)
10	13	TWIST AND SHOUT (EP) Beatles (Parlophone)
16	14	DANCE ON Kathy Kirby (Decca)
14	15	CONFESSIN' (THAT I LOVE YOU) Frank Ifield (Columbia)
24	16	I WANNA STAY HERE Miki & Griff (Pye)
17	17	STILL Karl Denver (Decca)
27	18	WHISPERING Bachelors (Decca)
-	19	APPLEJACK Jet Harris & Tony Meehan (Decca)
20	20	STILL Ken Dodd (Columbia)
15	21	TWIST AND SHOUT Brian Poole & the Tremeloes (Decca)
25	22	COME ON Rolling Stones (Decca)
20	22	TWO SILHOUETTES Del Shannon (London)
-	24	FRANKIE AND JOHNNY Sam Cooke (RCA)
30	25	SURF CITY Jan & Dean (Liberty)
-	26	WISHING Buddy Holly (Coral)
19	27	THE CRUEL SEA Dakotas (Parlophone)
21	28	DEVIL IN DISGUISE Elvis Presley (RCA)
29	29	ACAPULCO 1922 Kenny Ball & His Jazzmen (Pye Jazz)
18	30	SUKIYAKI Kyu Sakamoto (HMV)

Billy J Kramer had a second chart-topper, this time with a Lennon/McCartney song unrecorded by the Beatles. They didn't need it, as *She Loves You* proved by debuting spectacularly at Number Two: this record would ignite full-blown Beatlemania and become Britain's all-time biggest-selling single until the late 1970s. America's surf music boom was finding some success here, via the Surfaris' instrumental *Wipe Out*, and debuts by the Beach Boys and Jan & Dean. The Rolling Stones' first single *Come On* peaked at 20.

14 September 1963

last week	this week	Entry
1	1	SHE LOVES YOU Beatles (Parlophone)
2	2	BAD TO ME Billy J. Kramer & the Dakotas (Parlophone)
4	3	IT'S ALL IN THE GAME Cliff Richard (Columbia)
3	4	I'M TELLING YOU NOW Freddie & the Dreamers (Columbia)
7	5	I WANT TO STAY HERE Steve & Eydie (CBS)
5	6	I'LL NEVER GET OVER YOU Johnny Kidd & the Pirates (HMV)
6	7	YOU DON'T HAVE TO BE A BABY TO CRY Caravelles (Decca)
8	8	JUST LIKE EDDIE Heinz (Decca)
19	9	APPLEJACK Jet Harris & Tony Meehan (Decca)
11	10	WIPE OUT Surfaris (London)
10	11	THEME FROM 'THE LEGION'S LAST PATROL' Ken Thorne (HMV)
8	12	SWEETS FOR MY SWEET Searchers (Pye)
14	13	DANCE ON Kathy Kirby (Decca)
17	14	STILL Karl Denver (Decca)
15	15	TWIST AND SHOUT (EP) Beatles (Parlophone)
16	16	WHISPERING Bachelors (Decca)
26	17	WISHING Buddy Holly (Coral)
16	17	I WANNA STAY HERE Miki & Griff (Pye)
-	19	DO YOU LOVE ME Brian Poole & the Tremeloes (Decca)
12	20	IN SUMMER Billy Fury (Decca)
15	21	CONFESSIN' (THAT I LOVE YOU) Frank Ifield (Columbia)
20	22	STILL Ken Dodd (Columbia)
-	23	IF I HAD A HAMMER Trini Lopez (Reprise)
25	24	SURF CITY Jan & Dean (Liberty)
22	25	TWO SILHOUETTES Del Shannon (London)
21	26	TWIST AND SHOUT Brian Poole & the Tremeloes (Decca)
22	27	COME ON Rolling Stones (Decca)
27	28	THE CRUEL SEA Dakotas (Parlophone)
24	29	FRANKIE AND JOHNNY Sam Cooke (RCA)
-	29	THE GOOD LIFE Tony Bennett (CBS)
-	29	NO ONE Ray Charles (HMV)

21 September 1963

last week	this week	Entry
1	1	SHE LOVES YOU Beatles (Parlophone)
3	2	IT'S ALL IN THE GAME Cliff Richard (Columbia)
5	3	I WANT TO STAY HERE Steve & Eydie (CBS)
2	4	BAD TO ME Billy J. Kramer & the Dakotas (Parlophone)
6	5	I'LL NEVER GET OVER YOU Johnny Kidd & the Pirates (HMV)
4	6	I'M TELLING YOU NOW Freddie & the Dreamers (Columbia)
19	7	DO YOU LOVE ME Brian Poole & the Tremeloes (Decca)
7	8	YOU DON'T HAVE TO BE A BABY TO CRY Caravelles (Decca)
9	9	APPLEJACK Jet Harris & Tony Meehan (Decca)
8	9	JUST LIKE EDDIE Heinz (Decca)
-	11	THEN HE KISSED ME Crystals (London)
14	12	STILL Karl Denver (Decca)
23	13	IF I HAD A HAMMER Trini Lopez (Reprise)
10	14	WIPE OUT Surfaris (London)
11	14	THEME FROM 'THE LEGION'S LAST PATROL' Ken Thorne (HMV)
-	16	SHINDIG Shadows (Columbia)
13	17	DANCE ON Kathy Kirby (Decca)
17	18	WISHING Buddy Holly (Coral)
15	19	TWIST AND SHOUT (EP) Beatles (Parlophone)
17	20	I WANNA STAY HERE Miki & Griff (Pye)
22	21	STILL Ken Dodd (Columbia)
16	22	WHISPERING Bachelors (Decca)
12	23	SWEETS FOR MY SWEET Searchers (Pye)
20	24	IN SUMMER Billy Fury (Decca)
21	25	CONFESSIN' (THAT I LOVE YOU) Frank Ifield (Columbia)
-	25	HELLO MUDDAH HELLO FADDAH Allan Sherman (Warner Bros)
-	27	SEARCHIN' Hollies (Parlophone)
29	28	FRANKIE AND JOHNNY Sam Cooke (RCA)
-	29	MEAN WOMAN BLUES Roy Orbison (London)
-	30	HELLO LITTLE GIRL Fourmost (Parlophone)
-	30	ONLY THE HEARTACHES Houston Wells (Parlophone)

28 September 1963

last week	this week	Entry
1	1	SHE LOVES YOU Beatles (Parlophone)
7	2	DO YOU LOVE ME Brian Poole & the Tremeloes (Decca)
2	3	IT'S ALL IN THE GAME Cliff Richard (Columbia)
11	4	THEN HE KISSED ME Crystals (London)
3	5	I WANT TO STAY HERE Steve & Eydie (CBS)
9	6	APPLEJACK Jet Harris & Tony Meehan (Decca)
13	7	IF I HAD A HAMMER Trini Lopez (Reprise)
4	8	BAD TO ME Billy J. Kramer & the Dakotas (Parlophone)
9	9	JUST LIKE EDDIE Heinz (Decca)
16	10	SHINDIG Shadows (Columbia)
5	11	I'LL NEVER GET OVER YOU Johnny Kidd & the Pirates (HMV)
18	12	WISHING Buddy Holly (Coral)
-	13	BLUE BAYOU Roy Orbison (London)
8	14	YOU DON'T HAVE TO BE A BABY TO CRY Caravelles (Decca)
6	15	I'M TELLING YOU NOW Freddie & the Dreamers (Columbia)
-	16	AIN'T GONNA KISS YA (EP) Searchers (Pye)
29	17	MEAN WOMAN BLUES Roy Orbison (London)
-	18	THE FIRST TIME Adam Faith (Parlophone)
12	19	STILL Karl Denver (Decca)
22	20	WHISPERING Bachelors (Decca)
25	21	HELLO MUDDAH HELLO FADDAH Allan Sherman (Warner Bros)
30	22	HELLO LITTLE GIRL Fourmost (Parlophone)
14	22	THEME FROM 'THE LEGION'S LAST PATROL' Ken Thorne (HMV)
21	24	STILL Ken Dodd (Columbia)
17	25	DANCE ON Kathy Kirby (Decca)
27	26	SEARCHIN' Hollies (Parlophone)
-	27	EVERYBODY Tommy Roe (HMV)
14	28	WIPE OUT Surfaris (London)
25	29	CONFESSIN' (THAT I LOVE YOU) Frank Ifield (Columbia)
-	30	DO YOU LOVE ME Dave Clark Five (Columbia)

5 October 1963

last week	this week	Entry
2	1	DO YOU LOVE ME Brian Poole & the Tremeloes (Decca)
1	2	SHE LOVES YOU Beatles (Parlophone)
4	3	THEN HE KISSED ME Crystals (London)
7	4	IF I HAD A HAMMER Trini Lopez (Reprise)
5	5	I WANT TO STAY HERE Steve & Eydie (CBS)
10	6	SHINDIG Shadows (Columbia)
13	7	BLUE BAYOU Roy Orbison (London)
6	8	APPLEJACK Jet Harris & Tony Meehan (Decca)
9	9	JUST LIKE EDDIE Heinz (Decca)
3	10	IT'S ALL IN THE GAME Cliff Richard (Columbia)
18	11	THE FIRST TIME Adam Faith (Parlophone)
16	12	AIN'T GONNA KISS YA (EP) Searchers (Pye)
8	13	BAD TO ME Billy J. Kramer & the Dakotas (Parlophone)
17	14	MEAN WOMAN BLUES Roy Orbison (London)
12	15	WISHING Buddy Holly (Coral)
11	15	I'LL NEVER GET OVER YOU Johnny Kidd & the Pirates (HMV)
-	17	I (WHO HAVE NOTHING) Shirley Bassey (Columbia)
21	18	HELLO MUDDAH HELLO FADDAH Allan Sherman (Warner Bros)
26	19	SEARCHIN' Hollies (Parlophone)
22	20	HELLO LITTLE GIRL Fourmost (Parlophone)
14	21	YOU DON'T HAVE TO BE A BABY TO CRY Caravelles (Decca)
20	22	WHISPERING Bachelors (Decca)
27	22	EVERYBODY Tommy Roe (HMV)
24	24	STILL Ken Dodd (Columbia)
30	25	DO YOU LOVE ME Dave Clark Five (Columbia)
-	26	SOMEBODY ELSE'S GIRL Billy Fury (Decca)
19	27	STILL Karl Denver (Decca)
-	28	MY BOYFRIEND'S BACK Angels (Mercury)
25	28	DANCE ON Kathy Kirby (Decca)
-	30	MEMPHIS TENNESSEE Dave Berry (Decca)

Brian Poole took some revenge for *Twist And Shout* by toppling the Beatles with *Do You Love Me*, far outselling the competing version by the Dave Clark Five in the process. The Phil Spector girl group hits were finding their UK peak by now, as the Crystals' *Then He Kissed Me* proved a spectacular follow-up to *Da Doo Ron Ron*. The Searchers emulated the Beatles with a Top 20 EP, and Roy Orbison charted both sides of his single after choosing to promote *Mean Woman Blues* first on TV's *Ready Steady Go!*

October – November 1963

12 October 1963

last	this	
1	1	DO YOU LOVE ME — Brian Poole & the Tremeloes (Decca)
3	2	THEN HE KISSED ME — Crystals (London)
2	3	SHE LOVES YOU — Beatles (Parlophone)
4	4	IF I HAD A HAMMER — Trini Lopez (Reprise)
11	5	THE FIRST TIME — Adam Faith (Parlophone)
7	6	BLUE BAYOU — Roy Orbison (London)
-	7	YOU'LL NEVER WALK ALONE — Gerry & the Pacemakers (Columbia)
6	7	SHINDIG Shadows (Columbia)
17	9	I (WHO HAVE NOTHING) — Shirley Bassey (Columbia)
8	10	APPLEJACK — Jet Harris & Tony Meehan (Decca)
10	11	IT'S ALL IN THE GAME — Cliff Richard (Columbia)
9	12	JUST LIKE EDDIE Heinz (Decca)
5	13	I WANT TO STAY HERE — Steve & Eydie (CBS)
12	14	AIN'T GONNA KISS YA (EP) — Searchers (Pye)
22	15	EVERYBODY Tommy Roe (HMV)
15	16	WISHING Buddy Holly (Coral)
20	17	HELLO LITTLE GIRL — Fourmost (Parlophone)
18	17	HELLO MUDDAH HELLO FADDAH — Allan Sherman (Warner Bros)
19	19	SEARCHIN' — Hollies (Parlophone)
26	20	SOMEBODY ELSE'S GIRL — Billy Fury (Decca)
-	21	MEMPHIS TENNESSEE — Chuck Berry (Pye International)
15	22	I'LL NEVER GET OVER YOU — Johnny Kidd & the Pirates (HMV)
27	23	STILL Karl Denver (Decca)
14	23	MEAN WOMAN BLUES — Roy Orbison (London)
25	25	DO YOU LOVE ME — Dave Clark Five (Columbia)
13	26	BAD TO ME — Billy J. Kramer & the Dakotas (Parlophone)
22	27	WHISPERING — Bachelors (Decca)
30	28	MEMPHIS TENNESSEE — Dave Berry (Decca)
21	29	YOU DON'T HAVE TO BE A BABY TO CRY — Caravelles (Decca)
24	30	STILL Ken Dodd (Columbia)
-	30	MISS YOU — Jimmy Young (Columbia)

19 October 1963

last	this	
1	1	DO YOU LOVE ME — Brian Poole & the Tremeloes (Decca)
2	2	THEN HE KISSED ME — Crystals (London)
7	3	YOU'LL NEVER WALK ALONE — Gerry & the Pacemakers (Columbia)
3	4	SHE LOVES YOU — Beatles (Parlophone)
5	5	THE FIRST TIME — Adam Faith (Parlophone)
6	6	BLUE BAYOU — Roy Orbison (London)
4	7	IF I HAD A HAMMER — Trini Lopez (Reprise)
9	8	I (WHO HAVE NOTHING) — Shirley Bassey (Columbia)
7	9	SHINDIG Shadows (Columbia)
17	10	HELLO LITTLE GIRL — Fourmost (Parlophone)
19	10	SEARCHIN' — Hollies (Parlophone)
10	12	APPLEJACK Jet Harris & Tony Meehan (Decca)
15	13	EVERYBODY Tommy Roe (HMV)
11	14	IT'S ALL IN THE GAME — Cliff Richard (Columbia)
14	15	AIN'T GONNA KISS YA (EP) — Searchers (Pye)
12	16	JUST LIKE EDDIE Heinz (Decca)
21	17	MEMPHIS TENNESSEE — Chuck Berry (Pye International)
18	17	HELLO MUDDAH HELLO FADDAH — Allan Sherman (Warner Bros)
23	19	MEAN WOMAN BLUES — Roy Orbison (London)
23	20	STILL Karl Denver (Decca)
13	21	I WANT TO STAY HERE — Steve & Eydie (CBS)
16	22	WISHING Buddy Holly (Coral)
20	23	SOMEBODY ELSE'S GIRL — Billy Fury (Decca)
25	24	DO YOU LOVE ME — Dave Clark Five (Columbia)
-	25	BE MY BABY — Ronettes (London)
30	25	MISS YOU — Jimmy Young (Columbia)
28	27	MEMPHIS TENNESSEE — Dave Berry (Decca)
27	28	WHISPERING Bachelors (Decca)
-	28	MULE TRAIN — Frank Ifield (Columbia)
-	30	LOVE OF THE LOVED — Cilla Black (Parlophone)
30	30	FOOLS RUSH IN — Rick Nelson (Brunswick)
-	30	DRAGONFLY — Tornados (Decca)

26 October 1963

last	this	
3	1	YOU'LL NEVER WALK ALONE — Gerry & the Pacemakers (Columbia)
1	2	DO YOU LOVE ME — Brian Poole & the Tremeloes (Decca)
4	3	SHE LOVES YOU — Beatles (Parlophone)
2	4	THEN HE KISSED ME — Crystals (London)
8	5	I (WHO HAVE NOTHING) — Shirley Bassey (Columbia)
6	6	BLUE BAYOU — Roy Orbison (London)
7	7	IF I HAD A HAMMER — Trini Lopez (Reprise)
5	8	THE FIRST TIME — Adam Faith (Parlophone)
25	9	BE MY BABY — Ronettes (London)
17	10	MEMPHIS TENNESSEE — Chuck Berry (Pye International)
-	11	BOSSA NOVA BABY — Elvis Presley (RCA)
10	12	HELLO LITTLE GIRL — Fourmost (Parlophone)
-	13	SUGAR AND SPICE — Searchers (Pye)
14	14	SHINDIG Shadows (Columbia)
13	15	EVERYBODY Tommy Roe (HMV)
10	16	SEARCHIN' — Hollies (Parlophone)
27	17	MEMPHIS TENNESSEE — Dave Berry (Decca)
30	18	FOOLS RUSH IN — Rick Nelson (Brunswick)
25	19	MISS YOU — Jimmy Young (Columbia)
12	20	APPLEJACK — Jet Harris & Tony Meehan (Decca)
15	21	AIN'T GONNA KISS YA (EP) — Searchers (Pye)
19	22	MEAN WOMAN BLUES — Roy Orbison (London)
23	23	SOMEBODY ELSE'S GIRL — Billy Fury (Decca)
14	24	IT'S ALL IN THE GAME — Cliff Richard (Columbia)
18	24	HELLO MUDDAH HELLO FADDAH — Allan Sherman (Warner Bros)
20	26	STILL Karl Denver (Decca)
16	27	JUST LIKE EDDIE Heinz (Decca)
24	28	DO YOU LOVE ME — Dave Clark Five (Columbia)
28	29	MULE TRAIN Frank Ifield (Columbia)
22	30	WISHING Buddy Holly (Coral)
21	30	I WANT TO STAY HERE — Steve & Eydie (CBS)

2 November 1963

last	this	
1	1	YOU'LL NEVER WALK ALONE — Gerry & the Pacemakers (Columbia)
3	2	SHE LOVES YOU — Beatles (Parlophone)
2	3	DO YOU LOVE ME — Brian Poole & the Tremeloes (Decca)
5	4	I (WHO HAVE NOTHING) — Shirley Bassey (Columbia)
6	5	BLUE BAYOU — Roy Orbison (London)
13	6	SUGAR AND SPICE — Searchers (Pye)
4	7	THEN HE KISSED ME — Crystals (London)
9	8	BE MY BABY — Ronettes (London)
10	9	MEMPHIS TENNESSEE — Chuck Berry (Pye International)
8	10	THE FIRST TIME — Adam Faith (Parlophone)
7	11	IF I HAD A HAMMER — Trini Lopez (Reprise)
12	12	HELLO LITTLE GIRL — Fourmost (Parlophone)
11	13	BOSSA NOVA BABY — Elvis Presley (RCA)
18	14	FOOLS RUSH IN — Rick Nelson (Brunswick)
19	15	MISS YOU — Jimmy Young (Columbia)
17	16	MEMPHIS TENNESSEE — Dave Berry (Decca)
15	17	EVERYBODY — Tommy Roe (HMV)
-	18	BLOWIN' IN THE WIND — Peter Paul & Mary (Warner Bros)
-	19	SUE'S GOTTA BE MINE — Del Shannon (London)
14	20	SHINDIG Shadows (Columbia)
22	21	MEAN WOMAN BLUES — Roy Orbison (London)
-	22	YOUR MOMMA'S OUT OF TOWN — Carter-Lewis (Oriole)
23	23	SOMEBODY ELSE'S GIRL — Billy Fury (Decca)
16	23	SEARCHIN' — Hollies (Parlophone)
29	25	MULE TRAIN — Frank Ifield (Columbia)
26	26	STILL — Karl Denver (Decca)
-	27	RED SAILS IN THE SUNSET — Fats Domino (HMV)
20	28	APPLEJACK — Jet Harris & Tony Meehan (Decca)
-	28	GUILTY — Jim Reeves (RCA)
27	30	JUST LIKE EDDIE — Heinz (Decca)

As *You'll Never Walk Alone* soared to Number One, Gerry & the Pacemakers became not only the third UK act within a year to have three consecutive chart-topping singles, but also the first act ever to achive the feat with their first three releases - a record they would hold until fellow Liverpudlians Frankie Goes To Hollywood matched it in 1984. Dave Berry's UK cover of *Memphis Tennessee* prompted the reissue of the Chuck Berry original, enhancing his godfather role to the emerging UK R&B group boom.

last week	this week	9 November 1963
1	1	YOU'LL NEVER WALK ALONE Gerry & the Pacemakers (Columbia)
2	2	SHE LOVES YOU Beatles (Parlophone)
8	3	BE MY BABY Ronettes (London)
6	4	SUGAR AND SPICE Searchers (Pye)
5	5	BLUE BAYOU Roy Orbison (London)
3	6	DO YOU LOVE ME Brian Poole & the Tremeloes (Decca)
4	7	I (WHO HAVE NOTHING) Shirley Bassey (Columbia)
9	8	MEMPHIS TENNESSEE Chuck Berry (Pye International)
7	9	THEN HE KISSED ME Crystals (London)
10	10	THE FIRST TIME Adam Faith (Parlophone)
11	11	IF I HAD A HAMMER Trini Lopez (Reprise)
14	12	FOOLS RUSH IN Rick Nelson (Brunswick)
-	13	SECRET LOVE Kathy Kirby (Decca)
13	14	BOSSA NOVA BABY Elvis Presley (RCA)
-	15	DON'T TALK TO HIM Cliff Richard (Columbia)
12	16	HELLO LITTLE GIRL Fourmost (Parlophone)
-	17	MARIA ELENA Los Indios Tabajaras (RCA)
18	18	BLOWIN' IN THE WIND Peter Paul & Mary (Warner Bros)
15	19	MISS YOU Jimmy Young (Columbia)
16	20	MEMPHIS TENNESSEE Dave Berry (Decca)
19	21	SUE'S GOTTA BE MINE Del Shannon (London)
-	22	I'LL KEEP YOU SATISFIED Billy J. Kramer & the Dakotas (Parlophone)
-	23	YOU WERE MADE FOR ME Freddie & the Dreamers (Columbia)
21	24	MEAN WOMAN BLUES Roy Orbison (London)
22	25	YOUR MOMMA'S OUT OF TOWN Carter-Lewis (Oriole)
17	26	EVERYBODY Tommy Roe (HMV)
-	27	BUSTED Ray Charles (HMV)
-	28	FROM RUSSIA WITH LOVE Matt Monro (Parlophone)
27	29	RED SAILS IN THE SUNSET Fats Domino (HMV)
-	30	THE BEATLES' HITS (EP) Beatles (Parlophone)
-	30	I WANNA BE YOUR MAN Rolling Stones (Decca)

		16 November 1963
1	1	YOU'LL NEVER WALK ALONE Gerry & the Pacemakers (Columbia)
2	2	SHE LOVES YOU Beatles (Parlophone)
4	3	SUGAR AND SPICE Searchers (Pye)
3	4	BE MY BABY Ronettes (London)
15	5	DON'T TALK TO HIM Cliff Richard (Columbia)
13	6	SECRET LOVE Kathy Kirby (Decca)
7	7	I (WHO HAVE NOTHING) Shirley Bassey (Columbia)
22	8	I'LL KEEP YOU SATISFIED Billy J. Kramer & the Dakotas (Parlophone)
5	9	BLUE BAYOU Roy Orbison (London)
8	10	MEMPHIS TENNESSEE Chuck Berry (Pye International)
6	11	DO YOU LOVE ME Brian Poole & the Tremeloes (Decca)
17	12	MARIA ELENA Los Indios Tabajaras (RCA)
23	13	YOU WERE MADE FOR ME Freddie & the Dreamers (Columbia)
12	14	FOOLS RUSH IN Rick Nelson (Brunswick)
9	15	THEN HE KISSED ME Crystals (London)
18	16	BLOWIN' IN THE WIND Peter Paul & Mary (Warner Bros)
10	17	THE FIRST TIME Adam Faith (Parlophone)
11	17	IF I HAD A HAMMER Trini Lopez (Reprise)
-	19	IT'S ALMOST TOMORROW Mark Wynter (Pye)
27	20	BUSTED Ray Charles (HMV)
30	21	I WANNA BE YOUR MAN Rolling Stones (Decca)
16	22	HELLO LITTLE GIRL Fourmost (Parlophone)
28	23	FROM RUSSIA WITH LOVE Matt Monro (Parlophone)
25	24	YOUR MOMMA'S OUT OF TOWN Carter-Lewis (Oriole)
14	25	BOSSA NOVA BABY Elvis Presley (RCA)
20	26	MEMPHIS TENNESSEE Dave Berry (Decca)
-	27	BEATLES No.1 (EP) Beatles (Parlophone)
26	28	EVERYBODY Tommy Roe (HMV)
19	28	MISS YOU Jimmy Young (Columbia)
21	30	SUE'S GOTTA BE MINE Del Shannon (London)

		23 November 1963
2	1	SHE LOVES YOU Beatles (Parlophone)
1	2	YOU'LL NEVER WALK ALONE Gerry & the Pacemakers (Columbia)
5	3	DON'T TALK TO HIM Cliff Richard (Columbia)
8	4	I'LL KEEP YOU SATISFIED Billy J. Kramer & the Dakotas (Parlophone)
3	5	SUGAR AND SPICE Searchers (Pye)
6	6	SECRET LOVE Kathy Kirby (Decca)
13	7	YOU WERE MADE FOR ME Freddie & the Dreamers (Columbia)
4	8	BE MY BABY Ronettes (London)
12	9	MARIA ELENA Los Indios Tabajaras (RCA)
7	10	I (WHO HAVE NOTHING) Shirley Bassey (Columbia)
9	11	BLUE BAYOU Roy Orbison (London)
10	12	MEMPHIS TENNESSEE Chuck Berry (Pye International)
19	13	IT'S ALMOST TOMORROW Mark Wynter (Pye)
16	14	BLOWIN' IN THE WIND Peter Paul & Mary (Warner Bros)
14	15	FOOLS RUSH IN Rick Nelson (Brunswick)
15	16	THEN HE KISSED ME Crystals (London)
11	17	DO YOU LOVE ME Brian Poole & the Tremeloes (Decca)
-	17	I ONLY WANT TO BE WITH YOU Dusty Springfield (Philips)
17	19	IF I HAD A HAMMER Trini Lopez (Reprise)
24	20	YOUR MOMMA'S OUT OF TOWN Carter-Lewis (Oriole)
-	20	MONEY Bern Elliott & the Fenmen (Decca)
-	20	DEEP PURPLE Nino Tempo & April Stevens (London)
21	23	I WANNA BE YOUR MAN Rolling Stones (Decca)
27	24	BEATLES No.1 (EP) Beatles (Parlophone)
28	25	MISS YOU Jimmy Young (Columbia)
20	26	BUSTED Ray Charles (HMV)
-	27	GLAD ALL OVER Dave Clark Five (Columbia)
17	27	THE FIRST TIME Adam Faith (Parlophone)
-	29	TWIST AND SHOUT (EP) Beatles (Parlophone)
-	30	THE BEATLES' HITS (EP) Beatles (Parlophone)

		30 November 1963
1	1	SHE LOVES YOU Beatles (Parlophone)
3	2	DON'T TALK TO HIM Cliff Richard (Columbia)
7	3	YOU WERE MADE FOR ME Freddie & the Dreamers (Columbia)
2	4	YOU'LL NEVER WALK ALONE Gerry & the Pacemakers (Columbia)
6	5	SECRET LOVE Kathy Kirby (Decca)
4	6	I'LL KEEP YOU SATISFIED Billy J. Kramer & the Dakotas (Parlophone)
8	7	BE MY BABY Ronettes (London)
5	7	SUGAR AND SPICE Searchers (Pye)
9	9	MARIA ELENA Los Indios Tabajaras (RCA)
17	10	I ONLY WANT TO BE WITH YOU Dusty Springfield (Philips)
27	11	GLAD ALL OVER Dave Clark Five (Columbia)
10	12	I (WHO HAVE NOTHING) Shirley Bassey (Columbia)
11	13	BLUE BAYOU Roy Orbison (London)
13	14	IT'S ALMOST TOMORROW Mark Wynter (Pye)
-	15	WITH THE BEATLES (LP) Beatles (Parlophone)
29	16	TWIST AND SHOUT (EP) Beatles (Parlophone)
20	17	MONEY Bern Elliott & the Fenmen (Decca)
12	18	MEMPHIS TENNESSEE Chuck Berry (Pye International)
14	19	BLOWIN' IN THE WIND Peter Paul & Mary (Warner Bros)
-	20	COUNTRY BOY Heinz (Decca)
-	21	I CAN DANCE Brian Poole & the Tremeloes (Decca)
17	22	DO YOU LOVE ME Brian Poole & the Tremeloes (Decca)
-	23	HUNGRY FOR LOVE Johnny Kidd & the Pirates (HMV)
-	23	DOMINIQUE Singing Nun (Philips)
16	25	THEN HE KISSED ME Crystals (London)
24	26	BEATLES No.1 (EP) Beatles (Parlophone)
-	27	FROM RUSSIA WITH LOVE Matt Monro (Parlophone)
20	27	DEEP PURPLE Nino Tempo & April Stevens (London)
20	29	YOUR MOMMA'S OUT OF TOWN Carter-Lewis (Oriole)
26	30	BUSTED Ray Charles (HMV)
15	30	FOOLS RUSH IN Rick Nelson (Brunswick)

She Loves You passed the UK million sales mark, confounding the usual chart rules by returning to Number One for a second run. The Beatles were beginning to occupy the chart wholesale, however, as the *Twist And Shout* EP also resurged, and their other two EPs, *The Beatles' Hits* (i.e. the three previous singles) and *The Beatles' No.1* (selling on *I Saw Her Standing There*) joined it. Dusty Springfield made an impact with her first solo release, and the Ronettes leapfrogged the Crystals' success with *Be My Baby*.

December 1963

7 December 1963

last week	this	
-	1	I WANT TO HOLD YOUR HAND Beatles (Parlophone)
1	2	SHE LOVES YOU Beatles (Parlophone)
2	3	DON'T TALK TO HIM Cliff Richard (Columbia)
3	4	YOU WERE MADE FOR ME Freddie & the Dreamers (Columbia)
5	4	SECRET LOVE Kathy Kirby (Decca)
4	6	YOU'LL NEVER WALK ALONE Gerry & the Pacemakers (Columbia)
6	7	I'LL KEEP YOU SATISFIED Billy J. Kramer & the Dakotas (Parlophone)
9	7	MARIA ELENA Los Indios Tabajaras (RCA)
11	9	GLAD ALL OVER Dave Clark Five (Columbia)
10	10	I ONLY WANT TO BE WITH YOU Dusty Springfield (Philips)
15	11	WITH THE BEATLES (LP) Beatles (Parlophone)
7	12	BE MY BABY Ronettes (London)
23	13	DOMINIQUE Singing Nun (Philips)
14	14	IT'S ALMOST TOMORROW Mark Wynter (Pye)
16	15	TWIST AND SHOUT (EP) Beatles (Parlophone)
17	16	MONEY Bern Elliott & the Fenmen (Decca)
7	16	SUGAR AND SPICE Searchers (Pye)
-	18	TWENTY FOUR HOURS FROM TULSA Gene Pitney (United Artists)
-	19	BEATLES HITS (EP) Beatles (Parlophone)
-	20	GERONIMO Shadows (Columbia)
12	21	I (WHO HAVE NOTHING) Shirley Bassey (Columbia)
-	21	STAY Hollies (Parlophone)
27	23	DEEP PURPLE Nino Tempo & April Stevens (London)
23	24	HUNGRY FOR LOVE Johnny Kidd & the Pirates (HMV)
20	25	COUNTRY BOY Heinz (Decca)
-	25	I WANNA BE YOUR MAN Rolling Stones (Decca)
13	27	BLUE BAYOU Roy Orbison (London)
-	28	ALL I WANT FOR CHRISTMAS IS A BEATLE Dora Bryan (Fontana)
21	29	I CAN DANCE Brian Poole & the Tremeloes (Decca)
-	30	NOT TOO LITTLE NOT TOO MUCH Chris Sandford (Decca)

14 December 1963

last	this	
1	1	I WANT TO HOLD YOUR HAND Beatles (Parlophone)
2	2	SHE LOVES YOU Beatles (Parlophone)
4	3	SECRET LOVE Kathy Kirby (Decca)
4	4	YOU WERE MADE FOR ME Freddie & the Dreamers (Columbia)
9	5	GLAD ALL OVER Dave Clark Five (Columbia)
3	6	DON'T TALK TO HIM Cliff Richard (Columbia)
10	7	I ONLY WANT TO BE WITH YOU Dusty Springfield (Philips)
8	8	MARIA ELENA Los Indios Tabajaras (RCA)
13	9	DOMINIQUE Singing Nun (Philips)
18	10	TWENTY FOUR HOURS FROM TULSA Gene Pitney (United Artists)
7	11	I'LL KEEP YOU SATISFIED Billy J. Kramer & the Dakotas (Parlophone)
15	12	TWIST AND SHOUT (EP) Beatles (Parlophone)
20	12	GERONIMO Shadows (Columbia)
11	14	WITH THE BEATLES (LP) Beatles (Parlophone)
6	15	YOU'LL NEVER WALK ALONE Gerry & the Pacemakers (Columbia)
-	16	SWINGING ON A STAR Big Dee Irwin (Colpix)
19	17	BEATLES HITS (EP) Beatles (Parlophone)
14	17	IT'S ALMOST TOMORROW Mark Wynter (Pye)
28	19	ALL I WANT FOR CHRISTMAS IS A BEATLE Dora Bryan (Fontana)
20	20	I WANNA BE YOUR MAN Rolling Stones (Decca)
21	21	COUNTRY BOY Heinz (Decca)
16	22	MONEY Bern Elliott & the Fenmen (Decca)
23	23	DEEP PURPLE Nino Tempo & April Stevens (London)
24	24	HUNGRY FOR LOVE Johnny Kidd & the Pirates (HMV)
21	25	STAY Hollies (Parlophone)
12	26	BE MY BABY Ronettes (London)
30	27	NOT TOO LITTLE NOT TOO MUCH Chris Sandford (Decca)
26	28	WE ARE IN LOVE Adam Faith (Parlophone)
-	29	THE BEATLES NO.1 (EP) Beatles (Parlophone)
-	30	FROM RUSSIA WITH LOVE Matt Monro (Parlophone)

21 December 1963

last	this	
1	1	I WANT TO HOLD YOUR HAND Beatles (Parlophone)
2	2	SHE LOVES YOU Beatles (Parlophone)
5	2	GLAD ALL OVER Dave Clark Five (Columbia)
4	4	YOU WERE MADE FOR ME Freddie & the Dreamers (Columbia)
3	4	SECRET LOVE Kathy Kirby (Decca)
7	6	I ONLY WANT TO BE WITH YOU Dusty Springfield (Philips)
9	7	DOMINIQUE Singing Nun (Philips)
10	8	TWENTY FOUR HOURS FROM TULSA Gene Pitney (United Artists)
6	9	DON'T TALK TO HIM Cliff Richard (Columbia)
8	10	MARIA ELENA Los Indios Tabajaras (RCA)
12	11	GERONIMO Shadows (Columbia)
11	12	I'LL KEEP YOU SATISFIED Billy J. Kramer & the Dakotas (Parlophone)
16	13	SWINGING ON A STAR Big Dee Irwin (Colpix)
12	14	TWIST AND SHOUT (EP) Beatles (Parlophone)
20	15	I WANNA BE YOUR MAN Rolling Stones (Decca)
15	16	YOU'LL NEVER WALK ALONE Gerry & the Pacemakers (Columbia)
14	17	WITH THE BEATLES (LP) Beatles (Parlophone)
19	18	ALL I WANT FOR CHRISTMAS IS A BEATLE Dora Bryan (Fontana)
17	19	IT'S ALMOST TOMORROW Mark Wynter (Pye)
17	20	BEATLES HITS (EP) Beatles (Parlophone)
22	21	MONEY Bern Elliott & the Fenmen (Decca)
25	22	STAY Hollies (Parlophone)
27	23	NOT TOO LITTLE NOT TOO MUCH Chris Sandford (Decca)
28	24	WE ARE IN LOVE Adam Faith (Parlophone)
-	25	KISS ME QUICK Elvis Presley (RCA)
-	26	I CAN DANCE Brian Poole & the Tremeloes (Decca)
23	27	DEEP PURPLE Nino Tempo & April Stevens (London)
-	28	STEPTOE AND SON AT THE PALACE Harry H. Corbett (Pye)
-	29	I (WHO HAVE NOTHING) Shirley Bassey (Columbia)
21	30	COUNTRY BOY Heinz (Decca)

28 December 1963

last	this	
1	1	I WANT TO HOLD YOUR HAND Beatles (Parlophone)
2	2	GLAD ALL OVER Dave Clark Five (Columbia)
7	3	DOMINIQUE Singing Nun (Philips)
2	4	SHE LOVES YOU Beatles (Parlophone)
4	5	SECRET LOVE Kathy Kirby (Decca)
6	6	I ONLY WANT TO BE WITH YOU Dusty Springfield (Philips)
8	7	TWENTY FOUR HOURS FROM TULSA Gene Pitney (United Artists)
4	8	YOU WERE MADE FOR ME Freddie & the Dreamers (Columbia)
13	9	SWINGING ON A STAR Big Dee Irwin (Colpix)
10	10	MARIA ELENA Los Indios Tabajaras (RCA)
9	11	DON'T TALK TO HIM Cliff Richard (Columbia)
15	12	I WANNA BE YOUR MAN Rolling Stones (Decca)
14	13	TWIST AND SHOUT (EP) Beatles (Parlophone)
11	14	GERONIMO Shadows (Columbia)
17	15	WITH THE BEATLES (LP) Beatles (Parlophone)
18	16	ALL I WANT FOR CHRISTMAS IS A BEATLE Dora Bryan (Fontana)
25	17	KISS ME QUICK Elvis Presley (RCA)
-	18	HIPPY HIPPY SHAKE Swinging Blue Jeans (HMV)
16	19	YOU'LL NEVER WALK ALONE Gerry & the Pacemakers (Columbia)
20	20	BEATLES HITS (EP) Beatles (Parlophone)
23	21	NOT TOO LITTLE NOT TOO MUCH Chris Sandford (Decca)
12	22	I'LL KEEP YOU SATISFIED Billy J. Kramer & the Dakotas (Parlophone)
24	23	WE ARE IN LOVE Adam Faith (Parlophone)
19	24	IT'S ALMOST TOMORROW Mark Wynter (Pye)
22	25	STAY Hollies (Parlophone)
-	26	DO YOU REALLY LOVE ME TOO (FOOL'S ERRAND) Billy Fury (Decca)
-	27	IF I RULED THE WORLD Harry Secombe (Philips)
28	28	STEPTOE AND SON AT THE PALACE Wilfrid Brambell & Harry H. Corbett (Pye)
29	29	I (WHO HAVE NOTHING) Shirley Bassey (Columbia)
30	30	COUNTRY BOY Heinz (Decca)

This was the Beatlemania Christmas, when the group sold almost as many records as the rest of the market combined. *I Want To Hold Your Hand* debuted at Number One, deposing *She Loves You*, and sold a million during its first week on the market, having accrued 950,000 advance orders. Meanwhile, the *With The Beatles* album sold like a single (normal LP sales then were a fraction of today's), so was placed in the Top 30, where, at No.11, it reached the highest singles chart placing ever for an album.

Beatlemania

Top: still from Help!; (centre) working with producer George Martin in 1963; (bottom) a bizarre publicity pic from 1966.

At the height of their success the Fab Four were selling almost as many records in Britain as the whole of the rest of the music industry put together. Their impact in America was, if anything even greater than in Britain, because of their strangeness. Most American teenagers had hardly heard an English accent, never mind a Scouse one. A wave of Beatles singles were released simultaneously in the US leading to the famous Billboard chart of 28 March 1964 when they occupied the top five places. The end of the Beatles more or less coincided with the end of the sixties – a decade that will always be associated with them and their music. After all, as has often been said, the Beatles wrote the theme music to those years.

January 1964

4 January 1964

1	1	I WANT TO HOLD YOUR HAND Beatles (Parlophone)
2	2	GLAD ALL OVER Dave Clark Five (Columbia)
4	3	SHE LOVES YOU Beatles (Parlophone)
6	4	I ONLY WANT TO BE WITH YOU Dusty Springfield (Philips)
3	5	DOMINIQUE Singing Nun (Philips)
7	6	TWENTY-FOUR HOURS FROM TULSA Gene Pitney (United Artists)
5	7	SECRET LOVE Kathy Kirby (Decca)
8	8	YOU WERE MADE FOR ME Freddie & the Dreamers (Columbia)
9	9	SWINGING ON A STAR Big Dee Irwin (Colpix)
18	9	HIPPY HIPPY SHAKE Swinging Blue Jeans (HMV)
10	11	MARIA ELENA Los Indios Tabajaras (RCA)
11	12	DON'T TALK TO HIM Cliff Richard (Columbia)
12	12	I WANNA BE YOUR MAN Rolling Stones (Decca)
14	14	GERONIMO Shadows (Columbia)
17	15	KISS ME QUICK Elvis Presley (RCA)
19	16	YOU'LL NEVER WALK ALONE Gerry & the Pacemakers (Columbia)
13	17	TWIST AND SHOUT (EP) Beatles (Parlophone)
25	18	STAY Hollies (Parlophone)
20	19	BEATLES HITS (EP) Beatles (Parlophone)
15	20	WITH THE BEATLES (LP) Beatles (Parlophone)
23	21	WE ARE IN LOVE Adam Faith (Parlophone)
21	22	NOT TOO LITTLE NOT TOO MUCH Chris Sandford (Decca)
22	23	I'LL KEEP YOU SATISFIED Billy J. Kramer & the Dakotas (Parlophone)
24	24	IT'S ALMOST TOMORROW Mark Wynter (Pye)
26	25	DO YOU REALLY LOVE ME TOO (FOOL'S ERRAND) Billy Fury (Decca)
-	26	MONEY Bern Elliott & the Fenmen (Decca)
16	27	ALL I WANT FOR CHRISTMAS IS A BEATLE Dora Bryan (Fontana)
28	28	STEPTOE AND SON AT THE PALACE Wilfrid Brambell & Harry H. Corbett (Pye)
-	29	BEATLES NO. 1 (EP) Beatles (Parlophone)
-	30	HUNGRY FOR LOVE Johnny Kidd (HMV)

11 January 1964

1	1	I WANT TO HOLD YOUR HAND Beatles (Parlophone)
2	2	GLAD ALL OVER Dave Clark Five (Columbia)
9	3	HIPPY HIPPY SHAKE Swinging Blue Jeans (HMV)
6	4	TWENTY-FOUR HOURS FROM TULSA Gene Pitney (United Artists)
4	5	I ONLY WANT TO BE WITH YOU Dusty Springfield (Philips)
3	6	SHE LOVES YOU Beatles (Parlophone)
9	7	SWINGING ON A STAR Big Dee Irwin (Colpix)
8	8	YOU WERE MADE FOR ME Freddie & the Dreamers (Columbia)
5	9	DOMINIQUE Singing Nun (Philips)
7	10	SECRET LOVE Kathy Kirby (Decca)
18	11	STAY Hollies (Parlophone)
12	11	I WANNA BE YOUR MAN Rolling Stones (Decca)
15	13	KISS ME QUICK Elvis Presley (RCA)
12	14	DON'T TALK TO HIM Cliff Richard (Columbia)
11	15	MARIA ELENA Los Indios Tabajaras (RCA)
17	16	TWIST AND SHOUT (EP) Beatles (Parlophone)
25	17	DO YOU REALLY LOVE ME TOO (FOOL'S ERRAND) Billy Fury (Decca)
16	18	YOU'LL NEVER WALK ALONE Gerry & the Pacemakers (Columbia)
14	19	GERONIMO Shadows (Columbia)
20	20	WITH THE BEATLES (LP) Beatles (Parlophone)
21	20	WE ARE IN LOVE Adam Faith (Parlophone)
19	22	BEATLES HITS (EP) Beatles (Parlophone)
22	23	NOT TOO LITTLE NOT TOO MUCH Chris Sandford (Decca)
26	24	MONEY Bern Elliott & the Fenmen (Decca)
-	25	I'M IN LOVE Fourmost (Parlophone)
26	26	BABY I LOVE YOU Ronettes (London)
-	26	IF I RULED THE WORLD Harry Secombe (Philips)
23	28	I'LL KEEP YOU SATISFIED Billy J. Kramer & the Dakotas (Parlophone)
30	29	HUNGRY FOR LOVE Johnny Kidd (HMV)
29	30	BEATLES NO. 1 (EP) Beatles (Parlophone)

18 January 1964

2	1	GLAD ALL OVER Dave Clark Five (Columbia)
3	2	HIPPY HIPPY SHAKE Swinging Blue Jeans (HMV)
1	3	I WANT TO HOLD YOUR HAND Beatles (Parlophone)
4	4	TWENTY-FOUR HOURS FROM TULSA Gene Pitney (United Artists)
5	5	I ONLY WANT TO BE WITH YOU Dusty Springfield (Philips)
7	6	SWINGING ON A STAR Big Dee Irwin (Colpix)
6	7	SHE LOVES YOU Beatles (Parlophone)
11	8	STAY Hollies (Parlophone)
11	9	I WANNA BE YOUR MAN Rolling Stones (Decca)
8	10	YOU WERE MADE FOR ME Freddie & the Dreamers (Columbia)
13	11	KISS ME QUICK Elvis Presley (RCA)
9	12	DOMINIQUE Singing Nun (Philips)
20	13	WE ARE IN LOVE Adam Faith (Parlophone)
-	13	I'M THE ONE Gerry & the Pacemakers (Columbia)
10	15	SECRET LOVE Kathy Kirby (Decca)
17	16	DO YOU REALLY LOVE ME TOO (FOOL'S ERRAND) Billy Fury (Decca)
-	17	AS USUAL Brenda Lee (Brunswick)
-	18	DON'T BLAME ME Frank Ifield (Columbia)
-	18	NEEDLES AND PINS Searchers (Pye)
14	20	DON'T TALK TO HIM Cliff Richard (Columbia)
25	21	I'M IN LOVE Fourmost (Parlophone)
18	22	YOU'LL NEVER WALK ALONE Gerry & the Pacemakers (Columbia)
26	22	BABY I LOVE YOU Ronettes (London)
16	24	TWIST AND SHOUT (EP) Beatles (Parlophone)
-	25	WHISPERING Nino Tempo & April Stevens (London)
-	26	SAY IT ISN'T SO Frank Ifield (Columbia)
15	27	MARIA ELENA Los Indios Tabajaras (RCA)
-	28	ROLLING STONES (EP) Rolling Stones (Decca)
29	29	5-4-3-2-1 Manfred Mann (HMV)
-	30	LOUIE LOUIE Kingsmen (Pye International)
-	30	I THINK OF YOU Merseybeats (Fontana)
19	30	GERONIMO Shadows (Columbia)

25 January 1964

1	1	GLAD ALL OVER Dave Clark Five (Columbia)
2	2	HIPPY HIPPY SHAKE Swinging Blue Jeans (HMV)
3	3	I WANT TO HOLD YOUR HAND Beatles (Parlophone)
18	4	NEEDLES AND PINS Searchers (Pye)
13	5	I'M THE ONE Gerry & the Pacemakers (Columbia)
5	6	I ONLY WANT TO BE WITH YOU Dusty Springfield (Philips)
4	7	TWENTY-FOUR HOURS FROM TULSA Gene Pitney (United Artists)
8	8	STAY Hollies (Parlophone)
6	9	SWINGING ON A STAR Big Dee Irwin (Colpix)
17	10	AS USUAL Brenda Lee (Brunswick)
18	11	DON'T BLAME ME Frank Ifield (Columbia)
21	12	I'M IN LOVE Fourmost (Parlophone)
29	12	5-4-3-2-1 Manfred Mann (HMV)
7	14	SHE LOVES YOU Beatles (Parlophone)
16	15	DO YOU REALLY LOVE ME TOO (FOOL'S ERRAND) Billy Fury (Decca)
13	16	WE ARE IN LOVE Adam Faith (Parlophone)
9	17	I WANNA BE YOUR MAN Rolling Stones (Decca)
11	18	KISS ME QUICK Elvis Presley (RCA)
28	19	ROLLING STONES (EP) Rolling Stones (Decca)
10	20	YOU WERE MADE FOR ME Freddie & the Dreamers (Columbia)
12	21	DOMINIQUE Singing Nun (Philips)
30	22	LOUIE LOUIE Kingsmen (Pye International)
20	23	DON'T TALK TO HIM Cliff Richard (Columbia)
15	24	SECRET LOVE Kathy Kirby (Decca)
22	24	BABY I LOVE YOU Ronettes (London)
25	26	WHISPERING Nino Tempo & April Stevens (London)
26	27	SAY IT ISN'T SO Frank Ifield (Columbia)
-	28	THE DAVE CLARK FIVE (EP) Dave Clark Five (Columbia)
27	28	MARIA ELENA Los Indios Tabajaras (RCA)
24	30	TWIST AND SHOUT (EP) Beatles (Parlophone)

Tabloid newspapers trumpeted "London replaces Liverpool" as the Dave Clark Five took over at Number One from the Beatles, apparently oblivious to the fact that *I Want To Hold Your Hand* had to move down at some point, and absolutely anything could have been next in line. Manfred Mann's debut chartmaker *5-4-3-2-1* was the new theme for ITV's *Ready Steady Go!*, and the Rolling Stones and the Dave Clark Five joined the Beatles in the big-selling EP stakes, both with eponymous first EP releases.

February 1964

last / this week

1 February 1964

last	this	
4	1	NEEDLES AND PINS — Searchers (Pye)
2	2	HIPPY HIPPY SHAKE — Swinging Blue Jeans (HMV)
1	3	GLAD ALL OVER — Dave Clark Five (Columbia)
5	4	I'M THE ONE — Gerry & the Pacemakers (Columbia)
7	5	TWENTY-FOUR HOURS FROM TULSA — Gene Pitney (United Artists)
3	6	I WANT TO HOLD YOUR HAND — Beatles (Parlophone)
6	7	I ONLY WANT TO BE WITH YOU — Dusty Springfield (Philips)
8	8	STAY — Hollies (Parlophone)
11	9	DON'T BLAME ME — Frank Ifield (Columbia)
10	10	AS USUAL — Brenda Lee (Brunswick)
12	10	5-4-3-2-1 — Manfred Mann (HMV)
9	12	SWINGING ON A STAR — Big Dee Irwin (Colpix)
16	13	WE ARE IN LOVE — Adam Faith (Parlophone)
-	14	DIANE — Bachelors (Decca)
12	15	I'M IN LOVE — Fourmost (Parlophone)
15	16	DO YOU REALLY LOVE ME TOO (FOOL'S ERRAND) — Billy Fury (Decca)
22	17	LOUIE LOUIE — Kingsmen (Pye International)
14	18	SHE LOVES YOU — Beatles (Parlophone)
19	19	ROLLING STONES (EP) — Rolling Stones (Decca)
-	20	I THINK OF YOU — Merseybeats (Fontana)
-	20	FOR YOU — Rick Nelson (Brunswick)
18	22	KISS ME QUICK — Elvis Presley (RCA)
17	22	I WANNA BE YOUR MAN — Rolling Stones (Decca)
-	24	CANDY MAN — Brian Poole & the Tremeloes (Decca)
24	25	BABY I LOVE YOU — Ronettes (London)
26	26	WHISPERING — Nino Tempo & April Stevens (London)
-	27	SONG OF MEXICO — Tony Meehan (Decca)
28	28	THE DAVE CLARK FIVE (EP) — Dave Clark Five (Columbia)
-	29	MY BABY LEFT ME — Dave Berry (Decca)
23	30	DON'T TALK TO HIM — Cliff Richard (Columbia)

8 February 1964

last	this	
1	1	NEEDLES AND PINS — Searchers (Pye)
2	2	I'M THE ONE — Gerry & the Pacemakers (Columbia)
2	3	HIPPY HIPPY SHAKE — Swinging Blue Jeans (HMV)
14	4	DIANE — Bachelors (Decca)
3	5	GLAD ALL OVER — Dave Clark Five (Columbia)
10	6	5-4-3-2-1 — Manfred Mann (HMV)
10	7	AS USUAL — Brenda Lee (Brunswick)
5	8	TWENTY-FOUR HOURS FROM TULSA — Gene Pitney (United Artists)
9	9	DON'T BLAME ME — Frank Ifield (Columbia)
6	10	I WANT TO HOLD YOUR HAND — Beatles (Parlophone)
11	11	STAY — Hollies (Parlophone)
20	12	I THINK OF YOU — Merseybeats (Fontana)
7	13	I ONLY WANT TO BE WITH YOU — Dusty Springfield (Philips)
-	14	I'M THE LONELY ONE — Cliff Richard (Columbia)
15	15	I'M IN LOVE — Fourmost (Parlophone)
25	16	BABY I LOVE YOU — Ronettes (London)
24	17	CANDY MAN — Brian Poole & the Tremeloes (Decca)
-	18	ALL MY LOVING (EP) — Beatles (Parlophone)
-	18	ANYONE WHO HAD A HEART — Cilla Black (Parlophone)
17	18	LOUIE LOUIE — Kingsmen (Pye International)
13	21	WE ARE IN LOVE — Adam Faith (Parlophone)
16	22	DO YOU REALLY LOVE ME TOO (FOOL'S ERRAND) — Billy Fury (Decca)
12	23	SWINGING ON A STAR — Big Dee Irwin (Colpix)
19	24	ROLLING STONES (EP) — Rolling Stones (Decca)
20	25	FOR YOU — Rick Nelson (Brunswick)
29	26	MY BABY LEFT ME — Dave Berry (Decca)
22	27	I WANNA BE YOUR MAN — Rolling Stones (Decca)
22	28	KISS ME QUICK — Elvis Presley (RCA)
18	29	SHE LOVES YOU — Beatles (Parlophone)
-	30	EIGHT BY TEN — Ken Dodd (Columbia)

15 February 1964

last	this	
1	1	NEEDLES AND PINS — Searchers (Pye)
2	2	I'M THE ONE — Gerry & the Pacemakers (Columbia)
4	3	DIANE — Bachelors (Decca)
6	4	5-4-3-2-1 — Manfred Mann (HMV)
18	5	ANYONE WHO HAD A HEART — Cilla Black (Parlophone)
3	5	HIPPY HIPPY SHAKE — Swinging Blue Jeans (HMV)
5	7	GLAD ALL OVER — Dave Clark Five (Columbia)
7	8	AS USUAL — Brenda Lee (Brunswick)
12	9	I THINK OF YOU — Merseybeats (Fontana)
14	10	I'M THE LONELY ONE — Cliff Richard (Columbia)
17	11	CANDY MAN — Brian Poole & the Tremeloes (Decca)
8	12	TWENTY-FOUR HOURS FROM TULSA — Gene Pitney (United Artists)
16	13	BABY I LOVE YOU — Ronettes (London)
9	14	DON'T BLAME ME — Frank Ifield (Columbia)
18	15	ALL MY LOVING (EP) — Beatles (Parlophone)
10	16	I WANT TO HOLD YOUR HAND — Beatles (Parlophone)
18	16	LOUIE LOUIE — Kingsmen (Pye International)
11	18	STAY — Hollies (Parlophone)
15	19	I'M IN LOVE — Fourmost (Parlophone)
24	20	ROLLING STONES (EP) — Rolling Stones (Decca)
23	21	SWINGING ON A STAR — Big Dee Irwin (Colpix)
25	22	FOR YOU — Rick Nelson (Brunswick)
13	23	I ONLY WANT TO BE WITH YOU — Dusty Springfield (Philips)
30	24	EIGHT BY TEN — Ken Dodd (Columbia)
21	25	WE ARE IN LOVE — Adam Faith (Parlophone)
26	26	BOYS CRY — Eden Kane (Fontana)
26	27	MY BABY LEFT ME — Dave Berry (Decca)
22	28	DO YOU REALLY LOVE ME TOO — Billy Fury (Decca)
-	29	TOP SIX NO.1 (EP) — Various (Top Six)
-	30	NADINE (IS IT YOU?) — Chuck Berry (Pye International)
30	30	UM, UM, UM, UM, UM, UM — Major Lance (Columbia)

22 February 1964

last	this	
5	1	ANYONE WHO HAD A HEART — Cilla Black (Parlophone)
1	2	NEEDLES AND PINS — Searchers (Pye)
3	3	DIANE — Bachelors (Decca)
2	4	I'M THE ONE — Gerry & the Pacemakers (Columbia)
4	5	5-4-3-2-1 — Manfred Mann (HMV)
9	6	I THINK OF YOU — Merseybeats (Fontana)
	7	BITS AND PIECES — Dave Clark Five (Columbia)
11	8	CANDY MAN — Brian Poole & the Tremeloes (Decca)
8	9	AS USUAL — Brenda Lee (Brunswick)
5	10	HIPPY HIPPY SHAKE — Swinging Blue Jeans (HMV)
10	11	I'M THE LONELY ONE — Cliff Richard (Columbia)
7	12	GLAD ALL OVER — Dave Clark Five (Columbia)
15	13	ALL MY LOVING (EP) — Beatles (Parlophone)
13	14	BABY I LOVE YOU — Ronettes (London)
20	15	ROLLING STONES (EP) — Rolling Stones (Decca)
14	16	DON'T BLAME ME — Frank Ifield (Columbia)
22	17	FOR YOU — Rick Nelson (Brunswick)
12	17	TWENTY-FOUR HOURS FROM TULSA — Gene Pitney (United Artists)
16	19	LOUIE LOUIE — Kingsmen (Pye International)
16	20	I WANT TO HOLD YOUR HAND — Beatles (Parlophone)
-	21	STAY AWHILE — Dusty Springfield (Philips)
26	22	BOYS CRY — Eden Kane (Fontana)
-	23	OVER YOU — Freddie & the Dreamers (Columbia)
29	24	TOP SIX NO.1 (EP) — Various (Top Six)
18	25	STAY — Hollies (Parlophone)
-	26	LET ME GO, LOVER — Kathy Kirby (Decca)
19	27	I'M IN LOVE — Fourmost (Parlophone)
-	28	BORNE ON THE WIND — Roy Orbison (London)
-	29	YOU WERE THERE — Heinz (Decca)
21	30	SWINGING ON A STAR — Big Dee Irwin (Colpix)

Needles And Pins, the Searchers' cover of a minor US hit by Jackie De Shannon (written by Sonny Bono, later half of Sonny & Cher) gave them two Number Ones from three singles, while also preventing Gerry & the Pacemakers from achieving a record four chart-toppers from their first four singles. Cilla Black's *Anyone Who had A Heart* was an opportunist cover of Dionne Warwick's latest US hit, but it became the best-selling single in Britain by a female singer to date, with sales of over 850,000.

February – March 1964

29 February 1964

last week	this week	
1	1	ANYONE WHO HAD A HEART — Cilla Black (Parlophone)
3	2	DIANE — Bachelors (Decca)
7	3	BITS AND PIECES — Dave Clark Five (Columbia)
2	4	NEEDLES AND PINS — Searchers (Pye)
6	5	I THINK OF YOU — Merseybeats (Fontana)
4	6	I'M THE ONE — Gerry & the Pacemakers (Columbia)
5	7	5-4-3-2-1 — Manfred Mann (HMV)
8	8	CANDY MAN — Brian Poole & the Tremeloes (Decca)
9	9	AS USUAL — Brenda Lee (Brunswick)
11	10	I'M THE LONELY ONE — Cliff Richard (Columbia)
	10	NOT FADE AWAY — Rolling Stones (Decca)
10	12	HIPPY HIPPY SHAKE — Swinging Blue Jeans (HMV)
23	13	OVER YOU — Freddie & the Dreamers (Columbia)
21	14	STAY AWHILE — Dusty Springfield (Philips)
17	15	FOR YOU — Rick Nelson (Brunswick)
22	16	BOYS CRY — Eden Kane (Fontana)
14	17	BABY I LOVE YOU — Ronettes (London)
26	18	LET ME GO, LOVER — Kathy Kirby (Decca)
15	18	ROLLING STONES (EP) — Rolling Stones (Decca)
-	20	I LOVE YOU BECAUSE — Jim Reeves (RCA)
13	21	ALL MY LOVING (EP) — Beatles (Parlophone)
12	22	GLAD ALL OVER — Dave Clark Five (Columbia)
28	23	BORNE ON THE WIND — Roy Orbison (London)
20	24	I WANT TO HOLD YOUR HAND — Beatles (Parlophone)
29	25	YOU WERE THERE — Heinz (Decca)
17	26	TWENTY-FOUR HOURS FROM TULSA — Gene Pitney (United Artists)
-	27	LITTLE CHILDREN — Billy J. Kramer & the Dakotas (Parlophone)
-	28	THAT BELONGS TO YESTERDAY — Gene Pitney (United Artists)
-	29	NADINE (IS IT YOU?) — Chuck Berry (Pye International)
16	29	DON'T BLAME ME — Frank Ifield (Columbia)
19	29	LOUIE LOUIE — Kingsmen (Pye International)

7 March 1964

last week	this week	
1	1	ANYONE WHO HAD A HEART — Cilla Black (Parlophone)
3	2	BITS AND PIECES — Dave Clark Five (Columbia)
2	3	DIANE — Bachelors (Decca)
5	4	I THINK OF YOU — Merseybeats (Fontana)
10	5	NOT FADE AWAY — Rolling Stones (Decca)
4	5	NEEDLES AND PINS — Searchers (Pye)
27	7	LITTLE CHILDREN — Billy J. Kramer & the Dakotas (Parlophone)
6	8	I'M THE ONE — Gerry & the Pacemakers (Columbia)
8	9	CANDY MAN — Brian Poole & the Tremeloes (Decca)
16	10	BOYS CRY — Eden Kane (Fontana)
7	11	5-4-3-2-1 — Manfred Mann (HMV)
13	12	OVER YOU — Freddie & the Dreamers (Columbia)
14	13	STAY AWHILE — Dusty Springfield (Philips)
10	14	I'M THE LONELY ONE — Cliff Richard (Columbia)
9	15	AS USUAL — Brenda Lee (Brunswick)
-	16	JUST ONE LOOK — Hollies (Parlophone)
28	17	THAT BELONGS TO YESTERDAY — Gene Pitney (United Artists)
20	18	I LOVE YOU BECAUSE — Jim Reeves (RCA)
18	19	LET ME GO, LOVER — Kathy Kirby (Decca)
18	20	ROLLING STONES (EP) — Rolling Stones (Decca)
23	21	BORNE ON THE WIND — Roy Orbison (London)
21	22	ALL MY LOVING (EP) — Beatles (Parlophone)
-	23	THEME FOR YOUNG LOVERS — Shadows (Columbia)
15	24	FOR YOU — Rick Nelson (Brunswick)
17	25	BABY I LOVE YOU — Ronettes (London)
25	26	YOU WERE THERE — Heinz (Decca)
12	27	HIPPY HIPPY SHAKE — Swinging Blue Jeans (HMV)
24	28	I WANT TO HOLD YOUR HAND — Beatles (Parlophone)
-	29	KING OF KINGS — Ezz Reco & the Launchers (Columbia)
29	30	DON'T BLAME ME — Frank Ifield (Columbia)

14 March 1964

last week	this week	
1	1	ANYONE WHO HAD A HEART — Cilla Black (Parlophone)
2	2	BITS AND PIECES — Dave Clark Five (Columbia)
7	3	LITTLE CHILDREN — Billy J. Kramer & the Dakotas (Parlophone)
3	4	DIANE — Bachelors (Decca)
5	5	NOT FADE AWAY — Rolling Stones (Decca)
4	6	I THINK OF YOU — Merseybeats (Fontana)
16	7	JUST ONE LOOK — Hollies (Parlophone)
10	8	BOYS CRY — Eden Kane (Fontana)
5	9	NEEDLES AND PINS — Searchers (Pye)
12	10	OVER YOU — Freddie & the Dreamers (Columbia)
8	11	I'M THE ONE — Gerry & the Pacemakers (Columbia)
9	12	CANDY MAN — Brian Poole & the Tremeloes (Decca)
17	13	THAT BELONGS TO YESTERDAY — Gene Pitney (United Artists)
18	14	I LOVE YOU BECAUSE — Jim Reeves (RCA)
13	15	STAY AWHILE — Dusty Springfield (Philips)
19	16	LET ME GO, LOVER — Kathy Kirby (Decca)
-	17	TELL ME WHEN — Applejacks (Decca)
23	18	THEME FOR YOUNG LOVERS — Shadows (Columbia)
21	19	BORNE ON THE WIND — Roy Orbison (London)
14	20	I'M THE LONELY ONE — Cliff Richard (Columbia)
15	21	AS USUAL — Brenda Lee (Brunswick)
11	22	5-4-3-2-1 — Manfred Mann (HMV)
26	23	YOU WERE THERE — Heinz (Decca)
22	24	ALL MY LOVING (EP) — Beatles (Parlophone)
25	25	BABY I LOVE YOU — Ronettes (London)
20	26	ROLLING STONES (EP) — Rolling Stones (Decca)
29	27	KING OF KINGS — Ezz Reco & the Launchers (Columbia)
-	28	EIGHT BY TEN — Ken Dodd (Columbia)
-	29	IT'S AN OPEN SECRET — Joy Strings (Regal Zonophone)
-	30	IF HE TELLS YOU — Adam Faith (Parlophone)

21 March 1964

last week	this week	
3	.1	LITTLE CHILDREN — Billy J. Kramer & the Dakotas (Parlophone)
1	2	ANYONE WHO HAD A HEART — Cilla Black (Parlophone)
5	3	NOT FADE AWAY — Rolling Stones (Decca)
2	4	BITS AND PIECES — Dave Clark Five (Columbia)
7	5	JUST ONE LOOK — Hollies (Parlophone)
4	6	DIANE — Bachelors (Decca)
14	7	I LOVE YOU BECAUSE — Jim Reeves (RCA)
6	8	I THINK OF YOU — Merseybeats (Fontana)
8	9	BOYS CRY — Eden Kane (Fontana)
13	10	THAT BELONGS TO YESTERDAY — Gene Pitney (United Artists)
11	11	I BELIEVE — Bachelors (Decca)
10	12	OVER YOU — Freddie & the Dreamers (Columbia)
17	13	TELL ME WHEN — Applejacks (Decca)
18	14	THEME FOR YOUNG LOVERS — Shadows (Columbia)
12	15	CANDY MAN — Brian Poole & the Tremeloes (Decca)
16	16	LET ME GO, LOVER — Kathy Kirby (Decca)
15	17	STAY AWHILE — Dusty Springfield (Philips)
9	18	NEEDLES AND PINS — Searchers (Pye)
19	19	BORNE ON THE WIND — Roy Orbison (London)
-	20	GOOD GOLLY MISS MOLLY — Swinging Blue Jeans (HMV)
-	21	A WORLD WITHOUT LOVE — Peter & Gordon (Columbia)
-	22	MY BOY LOLLIPOP — Millie (Fontana)
11	23	I'M THE ONE — Gerry & the Pacemakers (Columbia)
-	24	VIVA LAS VEGAS — Elvis Presley (RCA)
27	25	KING OF KINGS — Ezz Reco & the Launchers (Columbia)
29	26	IT'S AN OPEN SECRET — Joy Strings (Regal Zonophone)
26	27	ROLLING STONES (EP) — Rolling Stones (Decca)
30	28	IF HE TELLS YOU — Adam Faith (Parlophone)
24	29	ALL MY LOVING (EP) — Beatles (Parlophone)
28	30	EIGHT BY TEN — Ken Dodd (Columbia)

Little Children, Billy J Kramer & the Dakotas' first non-Beatle-penned single (it was an American composition by Mort Shuman and John McFarland) proved to be their biggest seller, while Gene Pitney's *That Girl Belongs To Yesterday* came not from his most prevalent writing sources (himself or Bacharach & David), but from Rolling Stones Mick Jagger and Keith Richard, whom Pitney met in London during the recording sessions for their first album. The Joy Strings were a Salvation Army vocal group!

March – April 1964

28 March 1964

Last	This	Title
-	1	CAN'T BUY ME LOVE — Beatles (Parlophone)
1	2	LITTLE CHILDREN — Billy J. Kramer & the Dakotas (Parlophone)
5	3	JUST ONE LOOK — Hollies (Parlophone)
3	4	NOT FADE AWAY — Rolling Stones (Decca)
11	5	I BELIEVE — Bachelors (Decca)
4	6	BITS AND PIECES — Dave Clark Five (Columbia)
7	7	I LOVE YOU BECAUSE — Jim Reeves (RCA)
2	8	ANYONE WHO HAD A HEART — Cilla Black (Parlophone)
10	8	THAT BELONGS TO YESTERDAY — Gene Pitney (United Artists)
13	10	TELL ME WHEN — Applejacks (Decca)
6	11	DIANE — Bachelors (Decca)
9	12	BOYS CRY — Eden Kane (Fontana)
21	13	A WORLD WITHOUT LOVE — Peter & Gordon (Columbia)
14	14	THEME FOR YOUNG LOVERS — Shadows (Columbia)
8	15	I THINK OF YOU — Merseybeats (Fontana)
20	16	GOOD GOLLY MISS MOLLY — Swinging Blue Jeans (HMV)
24	17	VIVA LAS VEGAS — Elvis Presley (RCA)
12	18	OVER YOU — Freddie & the Dreamers (Columbia)
15	19	CANDY MAN — Brian Poole and the Tremeloes (Decca)
16	20	LET ME GO, LOVER — Kathy Kirby (Decca)
22	21	MY BOY LOLLIPOP — Millie (Fontana)
19	21	BORNE ON THE WIND — Roy Orbison (London)
17	23	STAY AWHILE — Dusty Springfield (Philips)
28	24	IF HE TELLS YOU — Adam Faith (Parlophone)
-	25	MOVE OVER DARLING — Doris Day (CBS)
25	26	KING OF KINGS — Ezz Reco & the Launchers (Columbia)
26	27	IT'S AN OPEN SECRET — Joy Strings (Regal Zonophone)
23	28	I'M THE ONE — Gerry & the Pacemakers (Columbia)
-	29	MOCKING BIRD HILL — Migil Five (Pye)
27	30	ROLLING STONES (EP) — Rolling Stones (Decca)

4 April 1964

Last	This	Title
1	1	CAN'T BUY ME LOVE — Beatles (Parlophone)
5	2	I BELIEVE — Bachelors (Decca)
2	3	LITTLE CHILDREN — Billy J. Kramer & the Dakotas (Parlophone)
3	4	JUST ONE LOOK — Hollies (Parlophone)
13	5	A WORLD WITHOUT LOVE — Peter & Gordon (Columbia)
4	5	NOT FADE AWAY — Rolling Stones (Decca)
7	7	I LOVE YOU BECAUSE — Jim Reeves (RCA)
8	8	THAT BELONGS TO YESTERDAY — Gene Pitney (United Artists)
10	9	TELL ME WHEN — Applejacks (Decca)
6	10	BITS AND PIECES — Dave Clark Five (Columbia)
8	11	ANYONE WHO HAD A HEART — Cilla Black (Parlophone)
11	12	DIANE — Bachelors (Decca)
16	13	GOOD GOLLY MISS MOLLY — Swinging Blue Jeans (HMV)
14	14	THEME FOR YOUNG LOVERS — Shadows (Columbia)
21	15	MY BOY LOLLIPOP — Millie (Fontana)
17	16	VIVA LAS VEGAS — Elvis Presley (RCA)
29	17	MOCKING BIRD HILL — Migil Five (Pye)
15	18	I THINK OF YOU — Merseybeats (Fontana)
12	19	BOYS CRY — Eden Kane (Fontana)
19	20	CANDY MAN — Brian Poole and the Tremeloes (Decca)
25	21	MOVE OVER DARLING — Doris Day (CBS)
18	22	OVER YOU — Freddie & the Dreamers (Columbia)
23	23	STAY AWHILE — Dusty Springfield (Philips)
-	24	JULIET — Four Pennies (Philips)
20	25	LET ME GO, LOVER — Kathy Kirby (Decca)
21	26	BORNE ON THE WIND — Roy Orbison (London)
24	27	IF HE TELLS YOU — Adam Faith (Parlophone)
26	28	KING OF KINGS — Ezz Reco & the Launchers (Columbia)
-	29	ONLY YOU — Mark Wynter (Pye)
-	30	NEEDLES AND PINS — Searchers (Pye)

11 April 1964

Last	This	Title
1	1	CAN'T BUY ME LOVE — Beatles (Parlophone)
2	2	I BELIEVE — Bachelors (Decca)
5	2	A WORLD WITHOUT LOVE — Peter & Gordon (Columbia)
4	4	LITTLE CHILDREN — Billy J. Kramer & the Dakotas (Parlophone)
4	5	JUST ONE LOOK — Hollies (Parlophone)
7	6	I LOVE YOU BECAUSE — Jim Reeves (RCA)
5	7	NOT FADE AWAY — Rolling Stones (Decca)
9	8	TELL ME WHEN — Applejacks (Decca)
8	9	THAT BELONGS TO YESTERDAY — Gene Pitney (United Artists)
15	10	MY BOY LOLLIPOP — Millie (Fontana)
13	11	GOOD GOLLY MISS MOLLY — Swinging Blue Jeans (HMV)
10	12	BITS AND PIECES — Dave Clark Five (Columbia)
17	13	MOCKING BIRD HILL — Migil Five (Pye)
11	14	ANYONE WHO HAD A HEART — Cilla Black (Parlophone)
14	15	THEME FOR YOUNG LOVERS — Shadows (Columbia)
21	16	MOVE OVER DARLING — Doris Day (CBS)
16	17	VIVA LAS VEGAS — Elvis Presley (RCA)
-	18	EVERYTHING'S ALRIGHT — Mojos (Decca)
12	19	DIANE — Bachelors (Decca)
19	20	BOYS CRY — Eden Kane (Fontana)
24	21	JULIET — Four Pennies (Philips)
18	22	I THINK OF YOU — Merseybeats (Fontana)
-	23	HI-HEEL SNEAKERS — Tommy Tucker (Pye Int.)
-	24	THINK — Brenda Lee (Brunswick)
20	25	CANDY MAN — Brian Poole and the Tremeloes (Decca)
-	26	TOP SIX NO.3 — Various (Top Six)
-	27	IT'S SO NICE — Gamblers (Decca)
25	28	LET ME GO, LOVER — Kathy Kirby (Decca)
28	29	KING OF KINGS — Ezz Reco & the Launchers (Columbia)
22	30	OVER YOU — Freddie & the Dreamers (Columbia)

18 April 1964

Last	This	Title
1	1	CAN'T BUY ME LOVE — Beatles (Parlophone)
2	2	A WORLD WITHOUT LOVE — Peter & Gordon (Columbia)
2	3	I BELIEVE — Bachelors (Decca)
4	4	LITTLE CHILDREN — Billy J. Kramer & the Dakotas (Parlophone)
8	5	TELL ME WHEN — Applejacks (Decca)
10	6	MY BOY LOLLIPOP — Millie (Fontana)
6	7	I LOVE YOU BECAUSE — Jim Reeves (RCA)
-	8	DON'T THROW YOUR LOVE AWAY — Searchers (Pye)
7	9	NOT FADE AWAY — Rolling Stones (Decca)
5	10	JUST ONE LOOK — Hollies (Parlophone)
16	11	MOVE OVER DARLING — Doris Day (CBS)
9	12	THAT BELONGS TO YESTERDAY — Gene Pitney (United Artists)
11	13	GOOD GOLLY MISS MOLLY — Swinging Blue Jeans (HMV)
13	14	MOCKING BIRD HILL — Migil Five (Pye)
18	15	EVERYTHING'S ALRIGHT — Mojos (Decca)
12	16	BITS AND PIECES — Dave Clark Five (Columbia)
15	17	THEME FOR YOUNG LOVERS — Shadows (Columbia)
-	18	WALK ON BY — Dionne Warwick (Pye International)
21	19	JULIET — Four Pennies (Philips)
-	20	DON'T LET THE SUN CATCH YOU CRYING — Gerry & the Pacemakers (Columbia)
-	21	HUBBLE BUBBLE TOIL AND TROUBLE — Manfred Mann (HMV)
-	22	DON'T TURN AROUND — Merseybeats (Fontana)
17	23	VIVA LAS VEGAS — Elvis Presley (RCA)
23	24	HI-HEEL SNEAKERS — Tommy Tucker (Pye)
24	25	THINK — Brenda Lee (Brunswick)
14	26	ANYONE WHO HAD A HEART — Cilla Black (Parlophone)
20	26	BOYS CRY — Eden Kane (Fontana)
-	28	BABY LET ME TAKE YOU HOME — Animals (Columbia)
-	29	ANGRY AT THE BIG OAK TREE — Frank Ifield (Columbia)
19	30	DIANE — Bachelors (Decca)

Can't Buy Me Love amassed the biggest advance order for a single ever known in Britain: over a million. By the end of its first week on the market, it had sold 1,226,000 copies, and was obviously an instant Number One - first-week entries at the top would be the norm for Beatles singles over the next couple of years. It also prevented the Bachelors from emulating Frankie Laine's 1953 chart-topping achievement with their revival of *I Believe*. Doris Day returned to the chart after a six-year absence.

April – May 1964

25 April 1964

last	this		
2	1	A WORLD WITHOUT LOVE	Peter & Gordon (Columbia)
3	2	I BELIEVE	Bachelors (Decca)
1	3	CAN'T BUY ME LOVE	Beatles (Parlophone)
8	3	DON'T THROW YOUR LOVE AWAY	Searchers (Pye)
6	5	MY BOY LOLLIPOP	Millie (Fontana)
7	6	I LOVE YOU BECAUSE	Jim Reeves (RCA)
5	7	TELL ME WHEN	Applejacks (Decca)
11	8	MOVE OVER DARLING	Doris Day (CBS)
4	9	LITTLE CHILDREN	Billy J. Kramer & the Dakotas (Parlophone)
14	10	MOCKING BIRD HILL	Migil Five (Pye)
20	11	DON'T LET THE SUN CATCH YOU CRYING	Gerry & the Pacemakers (Columbia)
9	11	NOT FADE AWAY	Rolling Stones (Decca)
15	13	EVERYTHING'S ALRIGHT	Mojos (Decca)
18	14	WALK ON BY	Dionne Warwick (Pye International)
21	15	HUBBLE BUBBLE TOIL AND TROUBLE	Manfred Mann (HMV)
10	16	JUST ONE LOOK	Hollies (Parlophone)
13	17	GOOD GOLLY MISS MOLLY	Swinging Blue Jeans (HMV)
22	18	DON'T TURN AROUND	Merseybeats (Fontana)
28	19	BABY LET ME TAKE YOU HOME	Animals (Columbia)
19	19	JULIET	Four Pennies (Philips)
12	21	THAT BELONGS TO YESTERDAY	Gene Pitney (United Artists)
17	22	THEME FOR YOUNG LOVERS	Shadows (Columbia)
-	23	THE ROLLING STONES (LP)	Rolling Stones (Decca)
23	24	VIVA LAS VEGAS	Elvis Presley (RCA)
24	25	HI-HEEL SNEAKERS	Tommy Tucker (Pye)
25	26	THINK	Brenda Lee (Brunswick)
16	27	BITS AND PIECES	Dave Clark Five (Columbia)
-	28	A LITTLE LOVING	Fourmost (Parlophone)
30	29	DIANE	Bachelors (Decca)
29	29	ANGRY AT THE BIG OAK TREE	Frank Ifield (Columbia)

2 May 1964

last	this		
1	1	A WORLD WITHOUT LOVE	Peter & Gordon (Columbia)
3	2	DON'T THROW YOUR LOVE AWAY	Searchers (Pye)
2	3	I BELIEVE	Bachelors (Decca)
5	4	MY BOY LOLLIPOP	Millie (Fontana)
3	5	CAN'T BUY ME LOVE	Beatles (Parlophone)
6	6	I LOVE YOU BECAUSE	Jim Reeves (RCA)
11	7	DON'T LET THE SUN CATCH YOU CRYING	Gerry & the Pacemakers (Columbia)
8	8	MOVE OVER DARLING	Doris Day (CBS)
19	9	JULIET	Four Pennies (Philips)
14	10	WALK ON BY	Dionne Warwick (Pye International)
15	11	HUBBLE BUBBLE TOIL AND TROUBLE	Manfred Mann (HMV)
10	12	MOCKING BIRD HILL	Migil Five (Pye)
13	13	EVERYTHING'S ALRIGHT	Mojos (Decca)
18	14	DON'T TURN AROUND	Merseybeats (Fontana)
19	15	BABY LET ME TAKE YOU HOME	Animals (Columbia)
-	15	IT'S OVER	Roy Orbison (London)
28	17	A LITTLE LOVING	Fourmost (Parlophone)
7	18	TELL ME WHEN	Applejacks (Decca)
11	19	NOT FADE AWAY	Rolling Stones (Decca)
9	20	LITTLE CHILDREN	Billy J. Kramer & the Dakotas (Parlophone)
-	21	NON HO L'ETA PER AMARTI	Gigliola Cinquetti (Decca)
-	22	CONSTANTLY	Cliff Richard (Columbia)
23	23	THE ROLLING STONES (LP)	Rolling Stones (Decca)
16	24	JUST ONE LOOK	Hollies (Parlophone)
17	25	GOOD GOLLY MISS MOLLY	Swinging Blue Jeans (HMV)
-	26	IF I LOVED YOU	Richard Anthony (Columbia)
29	27	ANGRY AT THE BIG OAK TREE	Frank Ifield (Columbia)
25	27	HI-HEEL SNEAKERS	Tommy Tucker (Pye)
29	29	DIANE	Bachelors (Decca)
-	30	BABY IT'S YOU	Dave Berry (Decca)
-	30	I WILL	Billy Fury (Decca)

9 May 1964

last	this		
2	1	DON'T THROW YOUR LOVE AWAY	Searchers (Pye)
4	2	MY BOY LOLLIPOP	Millie (Fontana)
3	3	I BELIEVE	Bachelors (Decca)
1	4	A WORLD WITHOUT LOVE	Peter & Gordon (Columbia)
9	5	JULIET	Four Pennies (Philips)
7	6	DON'T LET THE SUN CATCH YOU CRYING	Gerry & the Pacemakers (Columbia)
5	7	CAN'T BUY ME LOVE	Beatles (Parlophone)
6	8	I LOVE YOU BECAUSE	Jim Reeves (RCA)
10	9	WALK ON BY	Dionne Warwick (Pye International)
8	10	MOVE OVER DARLING	Doris Day (CBS)
15	11	IT'S OVER	Roy Orbison (London)
17	12	A LITTLE LOVING	Fourmost (Parlophone)
12	13	MOCKING BIRD HILL	Migil Five (Pye)
11	14	HUBBLE BUBBLE TOIL AND TROUBLE	Manfred Mann (HMV)
22	15	CONSTANTLY	Cliff Richard (Columbia)
14	16	DON'T TURN AROUND	Merseybeats (Fontana)
13	17	EVERYTHING'S ALRIGHT	Mojos (Decca)
15	18	BABY LET ME TAKE YOU HOME	Animals (Columbia)
-	18	YOU'RE MY WORLD	Cilla Black (Parlophone)
-	20	THE RISE AND FALL OF FLINGEL BUNT	Shadows (Columbia)
19	21	NOT FADE AWAY	Rolling Stones (Decca)
30	22	I WILL	Billy Fury (Decca)
21	23	NON HO L'ETA PER AMARTI	Gigliola Cinquetti (Decca)
18	24	TELL ME WHEN	Applejacks (Decca)
26	25	IF I LOVED YOU	Richard Anthony (Columbia)
20	26	LITTLE CHILDREN	Billy J. Kramer & the Dakotas (Parlophone)
23	27	THE ROLLING STONES (LP)	Rolling Stones (Decca)
-	28	YOU'RE THE ONE	Kathy Kirby (Decca)
27	29	ANGRY AT THE BIG OAK TREE	Frank Ifield (Columbia)
-	30	CAN'T BUY ME LOVE	Ella Fitzgerald (Verve)

16 May 1964

last	this		
5	1	JULIET	Four Pennies (Philips)
2	2	MY BOY LOLLIPOP	Millie (Fontana)
1	3	DON'T THROW YOUR LOVE AWAY	Searchers (Pye)
3	4	I BELIEVE	Bachelors (Decca)
18	5	YOU'RE MY WORLD	Cilla Black (Parlophone)
11	6	IT'S OVER	Roy Orbison (London)
12	7	A LITTLE LOVING	Fourmost (Parlophone)
6	8	DON'T LET THE SUN CATCH YOU CRYING	Gerry & the Pacemakers (Columbia)
15	9	CONSTANTLY	Cliff Richard (Columbia)
9	9	WALK ON BY	Dionne Warwick (Pye International)
4	11	A WORLD WITHOUT LOVE	Peter & Gordon (Columbia)
8	12	I LOVE YOU BECAUSE	Jim Reeves (RCA)
7	13	CAN'T BUY ME LOVE	Beatles (Parlophone)
20	14	THE RISE AND FALL OF FLINGEL BUNT	Shadows (Columbia)
16	15	DON'T TURN AROUND	Merseybeats (Fontana)
13	16	MOCKING BIRD HILL	Migil Five (Pye)
10	17	MOVE OVER DARLING	Doris Day (CBS)
23	18	NON HO L'ETA PER AMARTI	Gigliola Cinquetti (Decca)
-	19	NO PARTICULAR PLACE TO GO	Chuck Berry (Pye International)
22	19	I WILL	Billy Fury (Decca)
14	21	HUBBLE BUBBLE TOIL AND TROUBLE	Manfred Mann (HMV)
17	22	EVERYTHING'S ALRIGHT	Mojos (Decca)
18	23	BABY LET ME TAKE YOU HOME	Animals (Columbia)
28	24	YOU'RE THE ONE	Kathy Kirby (Decca)
-	25	SOMEONE, SOMEONE	Brian Poole & the Tremeloes (Decca)
29	26	ANGRY AT THE BIG OAK TREE	Frank Ifield (Columbia)
24	27	TELL ME WHEN	Applejacks (Decca)
21	28	NOT FADE AWAY	Rolling Stones (Decca)
-	29	SUSPICION	Terry Stafford (London)
-	30	SHOUT	Lulu & the Luvvers (Decca)

Peter & Gordon wrested Number One from the Beatles with a Lennon/McCartney composition (the duo's Peter Asher was the brother of Paul McCartney's then-girlfriend, actress Jane Asher). The Rolling Stones' debut album sold in hit single-like quantities, Ella Fitzgerald covered *Can't Buy Me Love* in a swinging jazz style, and both Cliff Richard and Cilla Black charted with English translations of Italian ballads. Italy, meanwhile, won the Eurovision Song Contest with *Non Ho L'Eta Per Amarti*.

last week	this	**23 May 1964**
1	1	JULIET Four Pennies (Philips)
5	2	YOU'RE MY WORLD Cilla Black (Parlophone)
6	3	IT'S OVER Roy Orbison (London)
2	4	MY BOY LOLLIPOP Millie (Fontana)
9	5	CONSTANTLY Cliff Richard (Columbia)
7	6	A LITTLE LOVING Fourmost (Parlophone)
3	7	DON'T THROW YOUR LOVE AWAY Searchers (Pye)
4	8	I BELIEVE Bachelors (Decca)
19	9	NO PARTICULAR PLACE TO GO Chuck Berry (Pye International)
9	10	WALK ON BY Dionne Warwick (Pye International)
14	11	THE RISE AND FALL OF FLINGEL BUNT Shadows (Columbia)
8	12	DON'T LET THE SUN CATCH YOU CRYING Gerry & the Pacemakers (Columbia)
12	13	I LOVE YOU BECAUSE Jim Reeves (RCA)
18	14	NON HO L'ETA PER AMARTI Gigliola Cinquetti (Decca)
-	15	MY GUY Mary Wells (Stateside)
19	16	I WILL Billy Fury (Decca)
-	17	I LOVE YOU BABY Freddie & the Dreamers (Columbia)
16	18	MOCKING BIRD HILL Migil Five (Pye)
15	19	DON'T TURN AROUND Merseybeats (Fontana)
17	20	MOVE OVER DARLING Doris Day (CBS)
11	21	A WORLD WITHOUT LOVE Peter & Gordon (Columbia)
13	22	CAN'T BUY ME LOVE Beatles (Parlophone)
25	23	SOMEONE, SOMEONE Brian Poole & the Tremeloes (Decca)
-	24	HERE I GO AGAIN Hollies (Parlophone)
24	25	YOU'RE THE ONE Kathy Kirby (Decca)
26	26	ANGRY AT THE BIG OAK TREE Frank Ifield (Columbia)
22	27	EVERYTHING'S ALRIGHT Mojos (Decca)
-	28	IF I LOVED YOU Richard Anthony (Columbia)
30	29	SHOUT Lulu & the Luvvers (Decca)
29	30	SUSPICION Terry Stafford (London)

		30 May 1964
2	1	YOU'RE MY WORLD Cilla Black (Parlophone)
1	2	JULIET Four Pennies (Philips)
3	3	IT'S OVER Roy Orbison (London)
4	4	MY BOY LOLLIPOP Millie (Fontana)
5	5	CONSTANTLY Cliff Richard (Columbia)
6	6	A LITTLE LOVING Fourmost (Parlophone)
9	7	NO PARTICULAR PLACE TO GO Chuck Berry (Pye International)
11	8	THE RISE AND FALL OF FLINGEL BUNT Shadows (Columbia)
15	9	MY GUY Mary Wells (Stateside)
7	10	DON'T THROW YOUR LOVE AWAY Searchers (Pye)
10	11	WALK ON BY Dionne Warwick (Pye International)
24	12	HERE I GO AGAIN Hollies (Parlophone)
8	13	I BELIEVE Bachelors (Decca)
23	14	SOMEONE, SOMEONE Brian Poole & the Tremeloes (Decca)
12	15	DON'T LET THE SUN CATCH YOU CRYING Gerry & the Pacemakers (Columbia)
14	16	NON HO L'ETA PER AMARTI Gigliola Cinquetti (Decca)
17	17	I LOVE YOU BABY Freddie & the Dreamers (Columbia)
29	18	SHOUT Lulu & the Luvvers (Decca)
25	19	YOU'RE THE ONE Kathy Kirby (Decca)
13	20	I LOVE YOU BECAUSE Jim Reeves (RCA)
16	21	I WILL Billy Fury (Decca)
-	22	CAN'T YOU SEE THAT SHE'S MINE Dave Clark Five (Columbia)
18	23	MOCKING BIRD HILL Migil Five (Pye)
22	24	CAN'T BUY ME LOVE Beatles (Parlophone)
21	25	A WORLD WITHOUT LOVE Peter & Gordon (Columbia)
-	26	I WISH YOU WOULD Yardbirds (Columbia)
-	27	DON'T LET THE RAIN COME DOWN (CROOKED LITTLE MAN) Ronnie Hilton (HMV)
19	28	DON'T TURN AROUND Merseybeats (Fontana)
30	29	SUSPICION Terry Stafford (London)
28	30	IF I LOVED YOU Richard Anthony (Columbia)

		6 June 1964
1	1	YOU'RE MY WORLD Cilla Black (Parlophone)
3	2	IT'S OVER Roy Orbison (London)
2	3	JULIET Four Pennies (Philips)
7	4	NO PARTICULAR PLACE TO GO Chuck Berry (Pye International)
5	5	CONSTANTLY Cliff Richard (Columbia)
8	6	THE RISE AND FALL OF FLINGEL BUNT Shadows (Columbia)
9	6	MY GUY Mary Wells (Stateside)
12	8	HERE I GO AGAIN Hollies (Parlophone)
4	9	MY BOY LOLLIPOP Millie (Fontana)
14	10	SOMEONE, SOMEONE Brian Poole & the Tremeloes (Decca)
6	11	A LITTLE LOVING Fourmost (Parlophone)
18	12	SHOUT Lulu & the Luvvers (Decca)
11	13	WALK ON BY Dionne Warwick (Pye International)
22	14	CAN'T YOU SEE THAT SHE'S MINE Dave Clark Five (Columbia)
16	15	NON HO L'ETA PER AMARTI Gigliola Cinquetti (Decca)
-	16	HELLO DOLLY Louis Armstrong (London)
13	17	I BELIEVE Bachelors (Decca)
20	18	I LOVE YOU BECAUSE Jim Reeves (RCA)
19	19	RAMONA Bachelors (Decca)
21	20	I WILL Billy Fury (Decca)
10	21	DON'T THROW YOUR LOVE AWAY Searchers (Pye)
17	22	I LOVE YOU BABY Freddie & the Dreamers (Columbia)
19	23	YOU'RE THE ONE Kathy Kirby (Decca)
27	24	DON'T LET THE RAIN COME DOWN (CROOKED LITTLE MAN) Ronnie Hilton (HMV)
-	25	NOBODY I KNOW Peter & Gordon (Columbia)
-	26	HELLO DOLLY Frankie Vaughan (Philips)
-	27	AIN'T SHE SWEET Beatles (Polydor)
-	27	NEAR YOU Migil Five (Pye)
15	29	DON'T LET THE SUN CATCH YOU CRYING Gerry & the Pacemakers (Columbia)
-	29	YOU'RE NO GOOD Swinging Blue Jeans (HMV)

		13 June 1964
1	1	YOU'RE MY WORLD Cilla Black (Parlophone)
2	2	IT'S OVER Roy Orbison (London)
6	3	MY GUY Mary Wells (Stateside)
4	4	NO PARTICULAR PLACE TO GO Chuck Berry (Pye International)
8	5	HERE I GO AGAIN Hollies (Parlophone)
10	6	SOMEONE, SOMEONE Brian Poole & the Tremeloes (Decca)
3	7	JULIET Four Pennies (Philips)
5	8	CONSTANTLY Cliff Richard (Columbia)
16	9	HELLO DOLLY Louis Armstrong (London)
6	10	THE RISE AND FALL OF FLINGEL BUNT Shadows (Columbia)
19	11	RAMONA Bachelors (Decca)
12	12	SHOUT Lulu & the Luvvers (Decca)
9	13	MY BOY LOLLIPOP Millie (Fontana)
11	14	A LITTLE LOVING Fourmost (Parlophone)
15	15	NON HO L'ETA PER AMARTI Gigliola Cinquetti (Decca)
13	16	WALK ON BY Dionne Warwick (Pye International)
29	17	YOU'RE NO GOOD Swinging Blue Jeans (HMV)
14	18	CAN'T YOU SEE THAT SHE'S MINE Dave Clark Five (Columbia)
18	19	I LOVE YOU BECAUSE Jim Reeves (RCA)
20	20	I WILL Billy Fury (Decca)
25	20	NOBODY I KNOW Peter & Gordon (Columbia)
26	20	HELLO DOLLY Frankie Vaughan (Philips)
24	23	DON'T LET THE RAIN COME DOWN (CROOKED LITTLE MAN) Ronnie Hilton (HMV)
27	24	AIN'T SHE SWEET Beatles (Polydor)
22	25	I LOVE YOU BABY Freddie & the Dreamers (Columbia)
23	26	YOU'RE THE ONE Kathy Kirby (Decca)
27	27	NEAR YOU Migil Five (Pye)
-	28	I LOVE BEING IN LOVE WITH YOU Adam Faith (Parlophone)
17	29	I BELIEVE Bachelors (Decca)
-	30	HELLO DOLLY Kenny Ball (Pye)

Mary Wells' *My Guy*, a chart-topper in the US, was the first UK hit from the Tamla Motown stable - though ironically it was Mary's last recording for the label, as she was in the process of leaving for a new deal with 20th Century Fox records, which would prove to be a major career error. Chuck Berry made the Top 10 with a song which used the same melody as his 1957 hit *School Day*, while *Hello Dolly*, the hit song from the new Broadway musical of the same name, had three instant competing Top 30 versions.

June – July 1964

20 June 1964

last	this	
2	1	IT'S OVER Roy Orbison (London)
1	2	YOU'RE MY WORLD Cilla Black (Parlophone)
6	3	SOMEONE, SOMEONE Brian Poole & the Tremeloes (Decca)
5	4	HERE I GO AGAIN Hollies (Parlophone)
9	5	HELLO DOLLY Louis Armstrong (London)
3	5	MY GUY Mary Wells (Stateside)
4	7	NO PARTICULAR PLACE TO GO Chuck Berry (Pye International)
11	8	RAMONA Bachelors (Decca)
12	9	SHOUT Lulu & the Luvvers (Decca)
10	10	THE RISE AND FALL OF FLINGEL BUNT Shadows (Columbia)
8	11	CONSTANTLY Cliff Richard (Columbia)
18	12	CAN'T YOU SEE THAT SHE'S MINE Dave Clark Five (Columbia)
7	13	JULIET Four Pennies (Philips)
20	14	NOBODY I KNOW Peter & Gordon (Columbia)
15	15	HOLD ME P.J. Proby (Decca)
17	16	YOU'RE NO GOOD Swinging Blue Jeans (HMV)
19	17	I LOVE YOU BECAUSE Jim Reeves (RCA)
13	18	MY BOY LOLLIPOP Millie (Fontana)
15	19	NON HO L'ETA PER AMARTI Gigliola Cinquetti (Decca)
20	20	HELLO DOLLY Frankie Vaughan (Philips)
14	21	A LITTLE LOVING Fourmost (Parlophone)
16	22	WALK ON BY Dionne Warwick (Pye International)
25	23	I LOVE YOU BABY Freddie & the Dreamers (Columbia)
-	24	DIMPLES John Lee Hooker (Stateside)
-	24	BAMALAMA BAMALOO Little Richard (London)
30	26	HELLO DOLLY Kenny Ball (Pye)
20	27	I WILL Billy Fury (Decca)
-	28	I WON'T FORGET YOU Jim Reeves (RCA)
-	29	BABY WHAT'S WRONG Downliners Sect (Columbia)
-	30	I WISH YOU WOULD Yardbirds (Columbia)

27 June 1964

last	this	
1	1	IT'S OVER Roy Orbison (London)
3	2	SOMEONE, SOMEONE Brian Poole & the Tremeloes (Decca)
5	3	HELLO DOLLY Louis Armstrong (London)
2	4	YOU'RE MY WORLD Cilla Black (Parlophone)
8	5	RAMONA Bachelors (Decca)
6	6	MY GUY Mary Wells (Stateside)
4	7	HERE I GO AGAIN Hollies (Parlophone)
16	8	YOU'RE NO GOOD Swinging Blue Jeans (HMV)
14	9	NOBODY I KNOW Peter & Gordon (Columbia)
-	10	HOUSE OF THE RISING SUN Animals (Columbia)
12	11	CAN'T YOU SEE THAT SHE'S MINE Dave Clark Five (Columbia)
9	11	SHOUT Lulu & the Luvvers (Decca)
10	13	THE RISE AND FALL OF FLINGEL BUNT Shadows (Columbia)
15	14	HOLD ME P.J. Proby (Decca)
28	15	I WON'T FORGET YOU Jim Reeves (RCA)
7	16	NO PARTICULAR PLACE TO GO Chuck Berry (Pye International)
20	17	HELLO DOLLY Frankie Vaughan (Philips)
11	18	CONSTANTLY Cliff Richard (Columbia)
-	19	KISSIN' COUSINS Elvis Presley (RCA)
17	20	I LOVE YOU BECAUSE Jim Reeves (RCA)
24	21	DIMPLES John Lee Hooker (Stateside)
13	22	JULIET Four Pennies (Philips)
19	23	NON HO L'ETA PER AMARTI Gigliola Cinquetti (Decca)
26	24	HELLO DOLLY Kenny Ball (Pye)
24	24	BAMALAMA BAMALOO Little Richard (London)
-	26	CHAPEL OF LOVE Dixie Cups (Pye International)
-	27	NEAR YOU Migil Five (Pye)
21	28	A LITTLE LOVING Fourmost (Parlophone)
-	29	AIN'T SHE SWEET Beatles (Polydor)
27	30	I WILL Billy Fury (Decca)

4 July 1964

last	this	
10	1	HOUSE OF THE RISING SUN Animals (Columbia)
1	2	IT'S OVER Roy Orbison (London)
2	3	SOMEONE, SOMEONE Brian Poole & the Tremeloes (Decca)
3	4	HELLO DOLLY Louis Armstrong (London)
14	5	HOLD ME P.J. Proby (Decca)
8	6	YOU'RE NO GOOD Swinging Blue Jeans (HMV)
-	7	IT'S ALL OVER NOW Rolling Stones (Decca)
5	8	RAMONA Bachelors (Decca)
9	9	NOBODY I KNOW Peter & Gordon (Columbia)
15	10	I WON'T FORGET YOU Jim Reeves (RCA)
6	11	MY GUY Mary Wells (Stateside)
4	12	YOU'RE MY WORLD Cilla Black (Parlophone)
-	13	LONG TALL SALLY (EP) Beatles (Parlophone)
19	14	KISSIN' COUSINS Elvis Presley (RCA)
7	15	HERE I GO AGAIN Hollies (Parlophone)
11	16	CAN'T YOU SEE THAT SHE'S MINE Dave Clark Five (Columbia)
11	17	SHOUT Lulu & the Luvvers (Decca)
-	18	ON THE BEACH Cliff Richard (Columbia)
17	18	HELLO DOLLY Frankie Vaughan (Philips)
13	20	THE RISE AND FALL OF FLINGEL BUNT Shadows (Columbia)
20	21	I LOVE YOU BECAUSE Jim Reeves (RCA)
16	22	NO PARTICULAR PLACE TO GO Chuck Berry (Pye International)
26	23	CHAPEL OF LOVE Dixie Cups (Pye International)
21	24	DIMPLES John Lee Hooker (Stateside)
24	25	BAMALAMA BAMALOO Little Richard (London)
-	26	SWEET WILLIAM Millie (Fontana)
24	27	HELLO DOLLY Kenny Ball (Pye)
18	28	CONSTANTLY Cliff Richard (Columbia)
-	29	I JUST DON'T KNOW WHAT TO DO WITH MYSELF Dusty Springfield (Philips)
-	30	LIKE DREAMERS DO Applejacks (Decca)
-	30	WHY NOT TONIGHT Mojos (Decca)

11 July 1964

last	this	
1	1	HOUSE OF THE RISING SUN Animals (Columbia)
7	2	IT'S ALL OVER NOW Rolling Stones (Decca)
5	3	HOLD ME P.J. Proby (Decca)
2	4	IT'S OVER Roy Orbison (London)
6	5	YOU'RE NO GOOD Swinging Blue Jeans (HMV)
3	6	SOMEONE, SOMEONE Brian Poole & the Tremeloes (Decca)
10	7	I WON'T FORGET YOU Jim Reeves (RCA)
4	8	HELLO DOLLY Louis Armstrong (London)
14	9	KISSIN' COUSINS Elvis Presley (RCA)
8	10	RAMONA Bachelors (Decca)
13	11	LONG TALL SALLY (EP) Beatles (Parlophone)
9	12	NOBODY I KNOW Peter & Gordon (Columbia)
18	13	ON THE BEACH Cliff Richard (Columbia)
29	14	I JUST DON'T KNOW WHAT TO DO WITH MYSELF Dusty Springfield (Philips)
26	15	SWEET WILLIAM Millie (Fontana)
11	16	MY GUY Mary Wells (Stateside)
16	17	CAN'T YOU SEE THAT SHE'S MINE Dave Clark Five (Columbia)
17	18	HELLO DOLLY Frankie Vaughan (Philips)
17	19	SHOUT Lulu & the Luvvers (Decca)
23	20	CHAPEL OF LOVE Dixie Cups (Pye International)
-	21	TOBACCO ROAD Nashville Teens (Decca)
-	22	WISHIN' AND HOPIN' Merseybeats (Fontana)
30	23	LIKE DREAMERS DO Applejacks (Decca)
15	24	HERE I GO AGAIN Hollies (Parlophone)
-	25	NEAR YOU Migil Five (Pye)
12	26	YOU'RE MY WORLD Cilla Black (Parlophone)
24	27	DIMPLES John Lee Hooker (Stateside)
-	28	CALL UP THE GROUPS Barron Knights (Columbia)
21	28	I LOVE YOU BECAUSE Jim Reeves (RCA)
30	30	WHY NOT TONIGHT Mojos (Decca)

The Animals' four-minute-plus arrangement of the traditional blues number, plugged on *Ready Steady Go!* on the day of release, was an instant sensation, its Number One success repeated around the world (though the group's US label was afraid its length would make radio shy away, and so shortened the American single considerably). The Beatles' *Long Tall Sally* EP was their first to contain songs not previously issued on singles or albums, while *Ain't She Sweet* was a relic of their 1961 Hamburg days.

18 July 1964

last week / this week

-	1	A HARD DAY'S NIGHT Beatles (Parlophone)
2	2	IT'S ALL OVER NOW Rolling Stones (Decca)
1	3	HOUSE OF THE RISING SUN Animals (Columbia)
3	4	HOLD ME P.J. Proby (Decca)
7	5	I WON'T FORGET YOU Jim Reeves (RCA)
14	5	I JUST DON'T KNOW WHAT TO DO WITH MYSELF Dusty Springfield (Philips)
13	7	ON THE BEACH Cliff Richard (Columbia)
5	8	YOU'RE NO GOOD Swinging Blue Jeans (HMV)
6	9	SOMEONE, SOMEONE Brian Poole & the Tremeloes (Decca)
28	10	CALL UP THE GROUPS Barron Knights (Columbia)
9	10	KISSIN' COUSINS Elvis Presley (RCA)
4	12	IT'S OVER Roy Orbison (London)
8	13	HELLO DOLLY Louis Armstrong (London)
11	14	LONG TALL SALLY (EP) Beatles (Parlophone)
21	15	TOBACCO ROAD Nashville Teens (Decca)
-	15	SOMEDAY WE'RE GONNA LOVE AGAIN Searchers (Pye)
10	17	RAMONA Bachelors (Decca)
15	18	SWEET WILLIAM Millie (Fontana)
22	19	WISHIN' AND HOPIN' Merseybeats (Fontana)
18	20	HELLO DOLLY Frankie Vaughan (Philips)
12	21	NOBODY I KNOW Peter & Gordon (Columbia)
16	22	MY GUY Mary Wells (Stateside)
25	23	NEAR YOU Migil Five (Pye)
23	24	LIKE DREAMERS DO Applejacks (Decca)
-	25	DO WAH DIDDY DIDDY Manfred Mann (HMV)
17	26	CAN'T YOU SEE THAT SHE'S MINE Dave Clark Five (Columbia)
-	27	HELLO DOLLY Kenny Ball (Pye Jazz)
-	28	I GET AROUND Beach Boys (Capitol)
-	29	A HARD DAY'S NIGHT (LP) Beatles (Parlophone)
26	30	YOU'RE MY WORLD Cilla Black (Parlophone)

25 July 1964

1	1	A HARD DAY'S NIGHT Beatles (Parlophone)
2	2	IT'S ALL OVER NOW Rolling Stones (Decca)
5	3	I JUST DON'T KNOW WHAT TO DO WITH MYSELF Dusty Springfield (Philips)
3	4	HOUSE OF THE RISING SUN Animals (Columbia)
10	5	CALL UP THE GROUPS Barron Knights (Columbia)
4	6	HOLD ME P.J. Proby (Decca)
25	7	DO WAH DIDDY DIDDY Manfred Mann (HMV)
5	8	I WON'T FORGET YOU Jim Reeves (RCA)
15	9	TOBACCO ROAD Nashville Teens (Decca)
7	9	ON THE BEACH Cliff Richard (Columbia)
15	11	SOMEDAY WE'RE GONNA LOVE AGAIN Searchers (Pye)
8	12	YOU'RE NO GOOD Swinging Blue Jeans (HMV)
10	13	KISSIN' COUSINS Elvis Presley (RCA)
9	14	SOMEONE, SOMEONE Brian Poole & the Tremeloes (Decca)
19	15	WISHIN' AND HOPIN' Merseybeats (Fontana)
13	16	HELLO DOLLY Louis Armstrong (London)
12	17	IT'S OVER Roy Orbison (London)
14	18	LONG TALL SALLY (EP) Beatles (Parlophone)
28	19	I GET AROUND Beach Boys (Capitol)
-	20	IT'S ONLY MAKE BELIEVE Billy Fury (Decca)
17	21	RAMONA Bachelors (Decca)
18	22	SWEET WILLIAM Millie (Fontana)
29	23	A HARD DAY'S NIGHT (LP) Beatles (Parlophone)
22	24	MY GUY Mary Wells (Stateside)
-	25	(THEY CALL HER) LA BAMBA Crickets (Liberty)
20	26	HELLO DOLLY Frankie Vaughan (Philips)
-	27	CHAPEL OF LOVE Dixie Cups (Pye International)
24	28	LIKE DREAMERS DO Applejacks (Decca)
30	29	YOU'RE MY WORLD Cilla Black (Parlophone)
21	30	NOBODY I KNOW Peter & Gordon (Columbia)

1 August 1964

1	1	A HARD DAY'S NIGHT Beatles (Parlophone)
2	2	IT'S ALL OVER NOW Rolling Stones (Decca)
7	3	DO WAH DIDDY DIDDY Manfred Mann (HMV)
3	4	I JUST DON'T KNOW WHAT TO DO WITH MYSELF Dusty Springfield (Philips)
5	5	CALL UP THE GROUPS Barron Knights (Columbia)
9	6	ON THE BEACH Cliff Richard (Columbia)
4	7	HOUSE OF THE RISING SUN Animals (Columbia)
8	8	TOBACCO ROAD Nashville Teens (Decca)
6	9	HOLD ME P.J. Proby (Decca)
8	10	I WON'T FORGET YOU Jim Reeves (RCA)
11	11	SOMEDAY WE'RE GONNA LOVE AGAIN Searchers (Pye)
15	12	WISHIN' AND HOPIN' Merseybeats (Fontana)
20	13	IT'S ONLY MAKE BELIEVE Billy Fury (Decca)
19	14	I GET AROUND Beach Boys (Capitol)
12	14	YOU'RE NO GOOD Swinging Blue Jeans (HMV)
13	16	KISSIN' COUSINS Elvis Presley (RCA)
-	17	FROM A WINDOW Billy J. Kramer & the Dakotas (Parlophone)
14	18	SOMEONE, SOMEONE Brian Poole & the Tremeloes (Decca)
17	19	IT'S OVER Roy Orbison (London)
18	20	LONG TALL SALLY (EP) Beatles (Parlophone)
-	20	FERRIS WHEEL Everly Brothers (Warner Bros)
23	22	A HARD DAY'S NIGHT (LP) Beatles (Parlophone)
16	23	HELLO DOLLY Louis Armstrong (London)
21	23	RAMONA Bachelors (Decca)
-	23	I FOUND OUT THE HARD WAY Four Pennies (Philips)
-	26	YOU'LL NEVER GET TO HEAVEN Dionne Warwick (Pye International)
25	27	(THEY CALL HER) LA BAMBA Crickets (Liberty)
26	28	HELLO DOLLY Frankie Vaughan (Philips)
30	29	NOBODY I KNOW Peter & Gordon (Columbia)
24	30	MY GUY Mary Wells (Stateside)

8 August 1964

1	1	A HARD DAY'S NIGHT Beatles (Parlophone)
3	2	DO WAH DIDDY DIDDY Manfred Mann (HMV)
2	3	IT'S ALL OVER NOW Rolling Stones (Decca)
4	4	I JUST DON'T KNOW WHAT TO DO WITH MYSELF Dusty Springfield (Philips)
5	5	CALL UP THE GROUPS Barron Knights (Columbia)
8	6	TOBACCO ROAD Nashville Teens (Decca)
6	7	ON THE BEACH Cliff Richard (Columbia)
10	8	I WON'T FORGET YOU Jim Reeves (RCA)
14	9	I GET AROUND Beach Boys (Capitol)
7	10	HOUSE OF THE RISING SUN Animals (Columbia)
11	11	SOMEDAY WE'RE GONNA LOVE AGAIN Searchers (Pye)
9	12	HOLD ME P.J. Proby (Decca)
13	13	IT'S ONLY MAKE BELIEVE Billy Fury (Decca)
26	14	YOU'LL NEVER GET TO HEAVEN Dionne Warwick (Pye International)
-	15	IT'S FOR YOU Cilla Black (Parlophone)
12	15	WISHIN' AND HOPIN' Merseybeats (Fontana)
-	17	HAVE I THE RIGHT Honeycombs (Pye)
17	17	FROM A WINDOW Billy J. Kramer & the Dakotas (Parlophone)
20	19	FERRIS WHEEL Everly Brothers (Warner Bros)
23	20	I FOUND OUT THE HARD WAY Four Pennies (Philips)
14	21	YOU'RE NO GOOD Swinging Blue Jeans (HMV)
22	22	A HARD DAY'S NIGHT (LP) Beatles (Parlophone)
16	23	KISSIN' COUSINS Elvis Presley (RCA)
18	24	SOMEONE, SOMEONE Brian Poole & the Tremeloes (Decca)
19	25	IT'S OVER Roy Orbison (London)
-	26	THINKING OF YOU BABY Dave Clark Five (Columbia)
20	27	LONG TALL SALLY (EP) Beatles (Parlophone)
23	28	HELLO DOLLY Louis Armstrong (London)
-	29	THE GIRL FROM IPANEMA Stan Getz/Joao Gilberto (Verve)
27	30	(THEY CALL HER) LA BAMBA Crickets (Liberty)

As their first film opened (with 170 prints doing heavy box office around the country) the Beatles set another record by charting both the title single and the soundtrack album (which contained both sides of said single, and had 250,000 advance orders in its own right) simultaneously. Both Billy J Kramer and Cilla Black returned to Lennon/McCartney compositions for their latest hits, while Manfred Mann's *Do Wah Diddy Diddy* was a revival of a little-known US recording by R&B group the Exciters.

August – September 1964

last week	this week	15 August 1964
2	1	DO WAH DIDDY DIDDY Manfred Mann (HMV)
1	2	A HARD DAY'S NIGHT Beatles (Parlophone)
3	3	IT'S ALL OVER NOW Rolling Stones (Decca)
5	4	CALL UP THE GROUPS Barron Knights (Columbia)
4	5	I JUST DON'T KNOW WHAT TO DO WITH MYSELF Dusty Springfield (Philips)
6	6	TOBACCO ROAD Nashville Teens (Decca)
17	7	HAVE I THE RIGHT Honeycombs (Pye)
7	8	ON THE BEACH Cliff Richard (Columbia)
8	9	I WON'T FORGET YOU Jim Reeves (RCA)
9	10	I GET AROUND Beach Boys (Capitol)
13	11	IT'S ONLY MAKE BELIEVE Billy Fury (Decca)
15	12	IT'S FOR YOU Cilla Black (Parlophone)
17	13	FROM A WINDOW Billy J. Kramer & the Dakotas (Parlophone)
20	14	I FOUND OUT THE HARD WAY Four Pennies (Philips)
11	15	SOMEDAY WE'RE GONNA LOVE AGAIN Searchers (Pye)
15	16	WISHIN' AND HOPIN' Merseybeats (Fontana)
14	17	YOU'LL NEVER GET TO HEAVEN Dionne Warwick (Pye International)
10	18	HOUSE OF THE RISING SUN Animals (Columbia)
-	19	YOU REALLY GOT ME Kinks (Pye)
19	20	FERRIS WHEEL Everly Brothers (Warner Bros)
12	21	HOLD ME P.J. Proby (Decca)
29	22	THE GIRL FROM IPANEMA Stan Getz/Joao Gilberto (Verve)
26	23	THINKING OF YOU BABY Dave Clark Five (Columbia)
-	24	I WOULDN'T TRADE YOU FOR THE WORLD Bachelors (Decca)
-	25	THE WEDDING Julie Rogers (Mercury)
23	26	KISSIN' COUSINS Elvis Presley (RCA)
-	27	HAPPINESS Ken Dodd (Columbia)
21	28	YOU'RE NO GOOD Swinging Blue Jeans (HMV)
28	29	HELLO DOLLY Louis Armstrong (London)
-	30	HOW CAN I TELL HER Fourmost (Parlophone)

last week	this week	22 August 1964
1	1	DO WAH DIDDY DIDDY Manfred Mann (HMV)
7	2	HAVE I THE RIGHT Honeycombs (Pye)
2	3	A HARD DAY'S NIGHT Beatles (Parlophone)
4	4	CALL UP THE GROUPS Barron Knights (Columbia)
6	5	TOBACCO ROAD Nashville Teens (Decca)
9	6	I WON'T FORGET YOU Jim Reeves (RCA)
3	7	IT'S ALL OVER NOW Rolling Stones (Decca)
19	8	YOU REALLY GOT ME Kinks (Pye)
12	9	IT'S FOR YOU Cilla Black (Parlophone)
10	10	I GET AROUND Beach Boys (Capitol)
5	11	I JUST DON'T KNOW WHAT TO DO WITH MYSELF Dusty Springfield (Philips)
8	12	ON THE BEACH Cliff Richard (Columbia)
11	13	IT'S ONLY MAKE BELIEVE Billy Fury (Decca)
-	13	FIVE BY FIVE (EP) Rolling Stones (Decca)
24	15	I WOULDN'T TRADE YOU FOR THE WORLD Bachelors (Decca)
14	16	I FOUND OUT THE HARD WAY Four Pennies (Philips)
13	17	FROM A WINDOW Billy J. Kramer & the Dakotas (Parlophone)
15	18	SOMEDAY WE'RE GONNA LOVE AGAIN Searchers (Pye)
-	19	SUCH A NIGHT Elvis Presley (RCA)
-	20	SHE'S NOT THERE Zombies (Decca)
-	21	THE CRYING GAME Dave Berry (Decca)
-	22	I LOVE YOU BECAUSE Jim Reeves (RCA)
17	23	YOU'LL NEVER GET TO HEAVEN Dionne Warwick (Pye International)
18	24	HOUSE OF THE RISING SUN Animals (Columbia)
23	25	THINKING OF YOU BABY Dave Clark Five (Columbia)
16	26	WISHIN' AND HOPIN' Merseybeats (Fontana)
20	27	FERRIS WHEEL Everly Brothers (Warner Bros)
-	28	AS TEARS GO BY Marianne Faithfull (Decca)
30	29	HOW CAN I TELL HER Fourmost (Parlophone)
-	30	TWELVE STEPS TO LOVE Brian Poole & the Tremeloes (Decca)

last week	this week	29 August 1964
2	1	HAVE I THE RIGHT Honeycombs (Pye)
1	2	DO WAH DIDDY DIDDY Manfred Mann (HMV)
8	3	YOU REALLY GOT ME Kinks (Pye)
6	4	I WON'T FORGET YOU Jim Reeves (RCA)
3	5	A HARD DAY'S NIGHT Beatles (Parlophone)
5	6	TOBACCO ROAD Nashville Teens (Decca)
4	7	CALL UP THE GROUPS Barron Knights (Columbia)
9	8	IT'S FOR YOU Cilla Black (Parlophone)
13	9	FIVE BY FIVE (EP) Rolling Stones (Decca)
7	10	IT'S ALL OVER NOW Rolling Stones (Decca)
10	11	I GET AROUND Beach Boys (Capitol)
21	12	THE CRYING GAME Dave Berry (Decca)
15	13	I WOULDN'T TRADE YOU FOR THE WORLD Bachelors (Decca)
19	13	SUCH A NIGHT Elvis Presley (RCA)
12	15	ON THE BEACH Cliff Richard (Columbia)
13	16	IT'S ONLY MAKE BELIEVE Billy Fury (Decca)
20	17	SHE'S NOT THERE Zombies (Decca)
16	18	I FOUND OUT THE HARD WAY Four Pennies (Philips)
17	19	FROM A WINDOW Billy J. Kramer & the Dakotas (Parlophone)
22	19	I LOVE YOU BECAUSE Jim Reeves (RCA)
21	21	RAG DOLL Four Seasons (Philips)
11	22	I JUST DON'T KNOW WHAT TO DO WITH MYSELF Dusty Springfield (Philips)
28	23	AS TEARS GO BY Marianne Faithfull (Decca)
23	24	YOU'LL NEVER GET TO HEAVEN Dionne Warwick (Pye International)
-	25	I'M INTO SOMETHING GOOD Herman's Hermits (Columbia)
-	26	THE WEDDING Julie Rogers (Mercury)
27	27	EVERYBODY LOVES SOMEBODY Dean Martin (Reprise)
28	28	YOU NEVER CAN TELL Chuck Berry (Pye International)
18	29	SOMEDAY WE'RE GONNA LOVE AGAIN Searchers (Pye)
30	30	TWELVE STEPS TO LOVE Brian Poole & the Tremeloes (Decca)
-	30	A HARD DAY'S NIGHT (LP) Beatles (Parlophone)

last week	this week	5 September 1964
1	1	HAVE I THE RIGHT Honeycombs (Pye)
3	2	YOU REALLY GOT ME Kinks (Pye)
2	3	DO WAH DIDDY DIDDY Manfred Mann (HMV)
4	4	I WON'T FORGET YOU Jim Reeves (RCA)
13	5	I WOULDN'T TRADE YOU FOR THE WORLD Bachelors (Decca)
11	6	THE CRYING GAME Dave Berry (Decca)
9	7	FIVE BY FIVE (EP) Rolling Stones (Decca)
5	8	A HARD DAY'S NIGHT Beatles (Parlophone)
25	9	I'M INTO SOMETHING GOOD Herman's Hermits (Columbia)
21	10	RAG DOLL Four Seasons (Philips)
6	11	TOBACCO ROAD Nashville Teens (Decca)
8	12	IT'S FOR YOU Cilla Black (Parlophone)
23	13	AS TEARS GO BY Rolling Stones (Decca)
13	14	SUCH A NIGHT Elvis Presley (RCA)
	15	WHERE DID OUR LOVE GO Supremes (Stateside)
11	16	I GET AROUND Beach Boys (Capitol)
10	17	IT'S ALL OVER NOW Rolling Stones (Decca)
7	18	CALL UP THE GROUPS Barron Knights (Columbia)
17	19	SHE'S NOT THERE Zombies (Decca)
27	20	EVERYBODY LOVES SOMEBODY Dean Martin (Reprise)
19	21	I LOVE YOU BECAUSE Jim Reeves (RCA)
30	22	A HARD DAY'S NIGHT (LP) Beatles (Parlophone)
23	23	YOU NEVER CAN TELL Chuck Berry (Pye International)
15	24	ON THE BEACH Cliff Richard (Columbia)
19	25	FROM A WINDOW Billy J. Kramer & the Dakotas (Parlophone)
16	26	IT'S ONLY MAKE BELIEVE Billy Fury (Decca)
-	27	I SHOULD HAVE KNOWN BETTER Naturals (Parlophone)
18	28	I FOUND OUT THE HARD WAY Four Pennies (Philips)
-	29	TOGETHER P.J. Proby (Decca)
-	30	IT'S GONNA BE ALRIGHT Gerry & the Pacemakers (Columbia)
26	30	THE WEDDING Julie Rogers (Mercury)

The Honeycombs' *Have I The Right* gave their producer Joe Meek what would be his last Number One success. The Rolling Stones' *Five By Five* EP contained previously-unheard material recorded in Chicago during their first US tour. Jim Reeves' sales suddenly took an upturn following his death in a plane crash: *I Won't Forget You* went back into the Top Five, and *I Love You Because* made a strong re-entry. Notable chart debutantes were the Supremes, Zombies, Marianne Faithfull and Herman's Hermits.

12 September 1964

last week	this	Title / Artist
2	1	YOU REALLY GOT ME — Kinks (Pye)
1	2	HAVE I THE RIGHT — Honeycombs (Pye)
9	3	I'M INTO SOMETHING GOOD — Herman's Hermits (Columbia)
5	4	I WOULDN'T TRADE YOU FOR THE WORLD — Bachelors (Decca)
4	5	I WON'T FORGET YOU — Jim Reeves (RCA)
6	6	THE CRYING GAME — Dave Berry (Decca)
15	7	WHERE DID OUR LOVE GO — Supremes (Stateside)
3	8	DO WAH DIDDY DIDDY — Manfred Mann (HMV)
10	9	RAG DOLL — Four Seasons (Philips)
7	10	FIVE BY FIVE (EP) — Rolling Stones (Decca)
13	11	AS TEARS GO BY — Marianne Faithfull (Decca)
8	12	A HARD DAY'S NIGHT — Beatles (Parlophone)
19	13	SHE'S NOT THERE — Zombies (Decca)
12	14	IT'S FOR YOU — Cilla Black (Parlophone)
20	15	EVERYBODY LOVES SOMEBODY — Dean Martin (Reprise)
14	16	SUCH A NIGHT — Elvis Presley (RCA)
-	17	IS IT TRUE — Brenda Lee (Brunswick)
-	18	RHYTHM AND GREENS — Shadows (Columbia)
30	19	THE WEDDING — Julie Rogers (Mercury)
16	20	I GET AROUND — Beach Boys (Capitol)
21	21	I LOVE YOU BECAUSE — Jim Reeves (RCA)
11	22	TOBACCO ROAD — Nashville Teens (Decca)
29	23	TOGETHER — P.J. Proby (Decca)
17	23	IT'S ALL OVER NOW — Rolling Stones (Decca)
30	25	IT'S GONNA BE ALRIGHT — Gerry & the Pacemakers (Columbia)
18	26	CALL UP THE GROUPS — Barron Knights (Columbia)
-	27	BREAD AND BUTTER — Newbeats (Hickory)
-	28	OH, PRETTY WOMAN — Roy Orbison (London)
27	29	I SHOULD HAVE KNOWN BETTER — Naturals (Parlophone)
26	30	IT'S ONLY MAKE BELIEVE — Billy Fury (Decca)

19 September 1964

	Title / Artist
3 1	I'M INTO SOMETHING GOOD — Herman's Hermits (Columbia)
1 2	YOU REALLY GOT ME — Kinks (Pye)
9 3	RAG DOLL — Four Seasons (Philips)
2 4	HAVE I THE RIGHT — Honeycombs (Pye)
4 5	I WOULDN'T TRADE YOU FOR THE WORLD — Bachelors (Decca)
7 6	WHERE DID OUR LOVE GO — Supremes (Stateside)
5 7	I WON'T FORGET YOU — Jim Reeves (RCA)
6 8	THE CRYING GAME — Dave Berry (Decca)
11 9	AS TEARS GO BY — Marianne Faithfull (Decca)
28 10	OH, PRETTY WOMAN — Roy Orbison (London)
19 11	THE WEDDING — Julie Rogers (Mercury)
8 12	DO WAH DIDDY DIDDY — Manfred Mann (HMV)
13 13	SHE'S NOT THERE — Zombies (Decca)
10 14	FIVE BY FIVE (EP) — Rolling Stones (Decca)
23 15	TOGETHER — P.J. Proby (Decca)
15 16	EVERYBODY LOVES SOMEBODY — Dean Martin (Reprise)
17 17	IS IT TRUE — Brenda Lee (Brunswick)
12 18	A HARD DAY'S NIGHT — Beatles (Parlophone)
16 19	SUCH A NIGHT — Elvis Presley (RCA)
21 20	I LOVE YOU BECAUSE — Jim Reeves (RCA)
18 21	RHYTHM AND GREENS — Shadows (Columbia)
27 22	BREAD AND BUTTER — Newbeats (Hickory)
14 23	IT'S FOR YOU — Cilla Black (Parlophone)
25 24	IT'S GONNA BE ALRIGHT — Gerry & the Pacemakers (Columbia)
- 25	I'M CRYING — Animals (Columbia)
26 26	I SHOULD HAVE KNOWN BETTER — Naturals (Parlophone)
- 27	HOW SOON — Henry Mancini (RCA)
23 28	IT'S ALL OVER NOW — Rolling Stones (Decca)
- 29	WHEN YOU WALK IN THE ROOM — Searchers (Pye)
30 30	COME TO ME — Julie Grant (Pye)
- 30	WE'RE THROUGH — Hollies (Parlophone)

26 September 1964

	Title / Artist
1 1	I'M INTO SOMETHING GOOD — Herman's Hermits (Columbia)
6 2	WHERE DID OUR LOVE GO — Supremes (Stateside)
3 3	RAG DOLL — Four Seasons (Philips)
5 4	I WOULDN'T TRADE YOU FOR THE WORLD — Bachelors (Decca)
10 5	OH, PRETTY WOMAN — Roy Orbison (London)
2 6	YOU REALLY GOT ME — Kinks (Pye)
7 7	I WON'T FORGET YOU — Jim Reeves (RCA)
4 8	HAVE I THE RIGHT — Honeycombs (Pye)
9 9	AS TEARS GO BY — Marianne Faithfull (Decca)
11 10	THE WEDDING — Julie Rogers (Mercury)
8 11	THE CRYING GAME — Dave Berry (Decca)
15 12	TOGETHER — P.J. Proby (Decca)
16 13	EVERYBODY LOVES SOMEBODY — Dean Martin (Reprise)
13 14	SHE'S NOT THERE — Zombies (Decca)
25 15	I'M CRYING — Animals (Columbia)
22 16	BREAD AND BUTTER — Newbeats (Hickory)
12 17	DO WAH DIDDY DIDDY — Manfred Mann (HMV)
20 18	I LOVE YOU BECAUSE — Jim Reeves (RCA)
14 19	FIVE BY FIVE (EP) — Rolling Stones (Decca)
17 20	IS IT TRUE — Brenda Lee (Brunswick)
30 21	WE'RE THROUGH — Hollies (Parlophone)
29 22	WHEN YOU WALK IN THE ROOM — Searchers (Pye)
27 23	HOW SOON — Henry Mancini (RCA)
- 24	WALK AWAY — Matt Monro (Parlophone)
19 25	SUCH A NIGHT — Elvis Presley (RCA)
- 26	HAPPINESS — Ken Dodd (Columbia)
18 27	A HARD DAY'S NIGHT — Beatles (Parlophone)
21 28	RHYTHM AND GREENS — Shadows (Columbia)
30 29	COME TO ME — Julie Grant (Pye)
28 30	IT'S ALL OVER NOW — Rolling Stones (Decca)

3 October 1964

	Title / Artist
1 1	I'M INTO SOMETHING GOOD — Herman's Hermits (Columbia)
5 2	OH, PRETTY WOMAN — Roy Orbison (London)
2 3	WHERE DID OUR LOVE GO — Supremes (Stateside)
3 4	RAG DOLL — Four Seasons (Philips)
4 5	I WOULDN'T TRADE YOU FOR THE WORLD — Bachelors (Decca)
10 6	THE WEDDING — Julie Rogers (Mercury)
7 7	I WON'T FORGET YOU — Jim Reeves (RCA)
6 8	YOU REALLY GOT ME — Kinks (Pye)
12 8	TOGETHER — P.J. Proby (Decca)
15 10	I'M CRYING — Animals (Columbia)
13 11	EVERYBODY LOVES SOMEBODY — Dean Martin (Reprise)
9 12	AS TEARS GO BY — Marianne Faithfull (Decca)
8 13	HAVE I THE RIGHT — Honeycombs (Pye)
22 14	WHEN YOU WALK IN THE ROOM — Searchers (Pye)
21 15	WE'RE THROUGH — Hollies (Parlophone)
11 16	THE CRYING GAME — Dave Berry (Decca)
16 17	BREAD AND BUTTER — Newbeats (Hickory)
20 18	IS IT TRUE — Brenda Lee (Brunswick)
23 19	HOW SOON — Henry Mancini (RCA)
24 20	WALK AWAY — Matt Monro (Parlophone)
14 20	SHE'S NOT THERE — Zombies (Decca)
19 22	FIVE BY FIVE (EP) — Rolling Stones (Decca)
18 23	I LOVE YOU BECAUSE — Jim Reeves (RCA)
- 24	MAYBE I KNOW — Lesley Gore (Mercury)
17 25	DO WAH DIDDY DIDDY — Manfred Mann (HMV)
- 26	IT'S GONNA BE ALRIGHT — Gerry & the Pacemakers (Columbia)
25 27	SUCH A NIGHT — Elvis Presley (RCA)
- 28	SEVEN DAFFODILS — Cherokees (Columbia)
- 29	ONE WAY LOVE — Cliff Bennett & the Rebel Rousers (Parlophone)
- 30	BYE BYE BABY — Tony Jackson (Pye)

Rag Doll, a US chart-topper, brought the Four Seasons back into UK contention after an absence of more than a year, while Lesley Gore's *Maybe I Know* was also her first British hit since her initial success with *It's My Party*. Brenda Lee came to Britain to record *Is It True* with producer Mickie Most (responsible for the Animals' and Herman's Hermits' chart-toppers). The Shadows' *Rhythm And Greens* was the title theme from a half-hour comedy film made by the group, which went on cinema B-release.

October 1964

146

10 October 1964

last week	this week	
2	1	OH, PRETTY WOMAN Roy Orbison (London)
1	2	I'M INTO SOMETHING GOOD Herman's Hermits (Columbia)
3	3	WHERE DID OUR LOVE GO Supremes (Stateside)
6	4	THE WEDDING Julie Rogers (Mercury)
4	5	RAG DOLL Four Seasons (Philips)
10	6	I'M CRYING Animals (Columbia)
5	7	I WOULDN'T TRADE YOU FOR THE WORLD Bachelors (Decca)
8	8	TOGETHER P.J. Proby (Decca)
14	9	WHEN YOU WALK IN THE ROOM Searchers (Pye)
15	10	WE'RE THROUGH Hollies (Parlophone)
11	11	EVERYBODY LOVES SOMEBODY Dean Martin (Reprise)
-	12	(THERE'S) ALWAYS SOMETHING THERE TO REMIND ME Sandie Shaw (Pye)
-	13	TWELFTH OF NEVER Cliff Richard (Columbia)
20	14	WALK AWAY Matt Monro (Parlophone)
7	15	I WON'T FORGET YOU Jim Reeves (RCA)
19	16	HOW SOON Henry Mancini (RCA)
12	17	AS TEARS GO BY Marianne Faithfull (Decca)
8	18	YOU REALLY GOT ME Kinks (Pye)
18	19	IS IT TRUE Brenda Lee (Brunswick)
29	20	ONE WAY LOVE Cliff Bennett and the Rebel Rousers (Parlophone)
17	20	BREAD AND BUTTER Newbeats (Hickory)
13	22	HAVE I THE RIGHT Honeycombs (Pye)
24	23	MAYBE I KNOW Lesley Gore (Mercury)
16	24	THE CRYING GAME Dave Berry (Decca)
30	25	BYE BYE BABY Tony Jackson (Pye)
-	26	REACH OUT FOR ME Dionne Warwick (Pye Int.)
-	27	SUMMER IS OVER Frank Ifield (Columbia)
-	28	UM, UM, UM, UM, UM, UM Wayne Fontana & the Mindbenders (Fontana)
-	29	QUESTIONS I CAN'T ANSWER Heinz (Columbia)
-	30	THREE LITTLE WORDS Applejacks (Decca)
20	30	SHE'S NOT THERE Zombies (Decca)

17 October 1964

last week	this week	
1	1	OH, PRETTY WOMAN Roy Orbison (London)
12	2	(THERE'S) ALWAYS SOMETHING THERE TO REMIND ME Sandie Shaw (Pye)
3	3	WHERE DID OUR LOVE GO Supremes (Stateside)
2	4	I'M INTO SOMETHING GOOD Herman's Hermits (Columbia)
4	5	THE WEDDING Julie Rogers (Mercury)
9	6	WHEN YOU WALK IN THE ROOM Searchers (Pye)
10	7	WE'RE THROUGH Hollies (Parlophone)
6	8	I'M CRYING Animals (Columbia)
13	8	TWELFTH OF NEVER Cliff Richard (Columbia)
14	10	WALK AWAY Matt Monro (Parlophone)
5	11	RAG DOLL Four Seasons (Philips)
16	12	HOW SOON Henry Mancini (RCA)
7	13	I WOULDN'T TRADE YOU FOR THE WORLD Bachelors (Decca)
8	14	TOGETHER P.J. Proby (Decca)
11	15	EVERYBODY LOVES SOMEBODY Dean Martin (Reprise)
15	16	I WON'T FORGET YOU Jim Reeves (RCA)
20	17	ONE WAY LOVE Cliff Bennett & the Rebel Rousers (Parlophone)
23	18	MAYBE I KNOW Lesley Gore (Mercury)
28	19	UM, UM, UM, UM, UM, UM Wayne Fontana & the Mindbenders (Fontana)
-	20	SHA LA LA Manfred Mann (HMV)
20	21	BREAD AND BUTTER Newbeats (Hickory)
26	22	REACH OUT FOR ME Dionne Warwick (Pye Int.)
19	23	IS IT TRUE Brenda Lee (Brunswick)
27	24	SUMMER IS OVER Frank Ifield (Columbia)
-	25	GOLDFINGER Shirley Bassey (Columbia)
17	26	AS TEARS GO BY Marianne Faithfull (Decca)
-	27	REMEMBER (WALKIN' IN THE SAND) Shangri-Las (Red Bird)
30	28	THREE LITTLE WORDS Applejacks (Decca)
18	29	YOU REALLY GOT ME Kinks (Pye)
-	30	DANCING IN THE STREET Martha & the Vandellas (Stateside)

24 October 1964

last week	this week	
1	1	OH, PRETTY WOMAN Roy Orbison (London)
2	2	(THERE'S) ALWAYS SOMETHING THERE TO REMIND ME Sandie Shaw (Pye)
8	3	TWELFTH OF NEVER Cliff Richard (Columbia)
5	4	THE WEDDING Julie Rogers (Mercury)
10	5	WALK AWAY Matt Monro (Parlophone)
3	6	WHERE DID OUR LOVE GO Supremes (Stateside)
7	7	WHEN YOU WALK IN THE ROOM Searchers (Pye)
7	8	WE'RE THROUGH Hollies (Parlophone)
4	9	I'M INTO SOMETHING GOOD Herman's Hermits (Columbia)
12	10	HOW SOON Henry Mancini (RCA)
8	11	I'M CRYING Animals (Columbia)
17	12	ONE WAY LOVE Cliff Bennett & the Rebel Rousers (Parlophone)
20	13	SHA LA LA Manfred Mann (HMV)
11	14	RAG DOLL Four Seasons (Philips)
13	15	I WOULDN'T TRADE YOU FOR THE WORLD Bachelors (Decca)
16	16	I WON'T FORGET YOU Jim Reeves (RCA)
-	17	BABY LOVE Supremes (Stateside)
14	18	TOGETHER P.J. Proby (Decca)
-	19	HE'S IN TOWN Rockin' Berries (Piccadilly)
19	20	UM, UM, UM, UM, UM, UM Wayne Fontana & the Mindbenders (Fontana)
15	21	EVERYBODY LOVES SOMEBODY Dean Martin (Reprise)
25	22	GOLDFINGER Shirley Bassey (Columbia)
18	23	MAYBE I KNOW Lesley Gore (Mercury)
28	24	THREE LITTLE WORDS Applejacks (Decca)
22	25	REACH OUT FOR ME Dionne Warwick (Pye Int.)
-	26	ANY WAY YOU WANT IT Dave Clark Five (Columbia)
27	27	REMEMBER (WALKIN' IN THE SAND) Shangri-Las (Red Bird)
24	28	SUMMER IS OVER Frank Ifield (Columbia)
-	29	WALK TALL Val Doonican (Decca)
-	30	IS IT BECAUSE Honeycombs (Pye)

31 October 1964

last week	this week	
2	1	(THERE'S) ALWAYS SOMETHING THERE TO REMIND ME Sandie Shaw (Pye)
1	2	OH, PRETTY WOMAN Roy Orbison (London)
17	3	BABY LOVE Supremes (Stateside)
4	4	THE WEDDING Julie Rogers (Mercury)
5	5	WALK AWAY Matt Monro (Parlophone)
13	6	SHA LA LA Manfred Mann (HMV)
3	7	TWELFTH OF NEVER Cliff Richard (Columbia)
7	8	WHEN YOU WALK IN THE ROOM Searchers (Pye)
10	9	HOW SOON Henry Mancini (RCA)
8	10	WE'RE THROUGH Hollies (Parlophone)
6	11	WHERE DID OUR LOVE GO Supremes (Stateside)
12	12	ONE WAY LOVE Cliff Bennett & the Rebel Rousers (Parlophone)
-	13	TOKYO MELODY Helmut Zacharias (Polydor)
9	14	I'M INTO SOMETHING GOOD Herman's Hermits (Columbia)
11	15	I'M CRYING Animals (Columbia)
19	16	HE'S IN TOWN Rockin' Berries (Piccadilly)
-	17	DON'T BRING ME DOWN Pretty Things (Fontana)
20	18	UM, UM, UM, UM, UM, UM Wayne Fontana & the Mindbenders (Fontana)
-	18	AIN'T THAT LOVING YOU BABY Elvis Presley (RCA)
-	20	GOOGLE EYE Nashville Teens (Decca)
22	21	GOLDFINGER Shirley Bassey (Columbia)
27	22	REMEMBER (WALKIN' IN THE SAND) Shangri-Las (Red Bird)
16	23	I WON'T FORGET YOU Jim Reeves (RCA)
15	24	I WOULDN'T TRADE YOU FOR THE WORLD Bachelors (Decca)
24	25	THREE LITTLE WORDS Applejacks (Decca)
26	26	ANY WAY YOU WANT IT Dave Clark Five (Columbia)
21	27	EVERYBODY LOVES SOMEBODY Dean Martin (Reprise)
14	28	RAG DOLL Four Seasons (Philips)
-	29	ALL DAY AND ALL OF THE NIGHT Kinks (Pye)
25	30	REACH OUT FOR ME Dionne Warwick (Pye Int.)
-	30	NOW WE'RE THRU' Poets (Decca)

Roy Orbison's *Oh, Pretty Woman* was his all-time biggest seller both in Britain and the US, and came at a time when Orbison was the only solo American male artist to still be scoring consistent major UK hits in the face of the almost total dominance of domestic rock music here. His *It's Over*, earlier in the year, had been the first US single to top the British chart for 18 months (since the end of 1962), and *Oh, Pretty Woman* was the second. Sandie Shaw, who was next to Number One, was a protegee of Adam Faith.

7 November 1964

last week	this week		
1	1	(THERE'S) ALWAYS SOMETHING THERE TO REMIND ME	Sandie Shaw (Pye)
2	2	OH, PRETTY WOMAN	Roy Orbison (London)
3	3	BABY LOVE	Supremes (Stateside)
6	4	SHA LA LA Manfred Mann (HMV)	
5	5	WALK AWAY	Matt Monro (Parlophone)
4	6	THE WEDDING	Julie Rogers (Mercury)
18	7	UM, UM, UM, UM, UM, UM	Wayne Fontana & the Mindbenders (Fontana)
16	8	HE'S IN TOWN	Rockin' Berries (Piccadilly)
13	9	TOKYO MELODY	Helmut Zacharias (Polydor)
8	10	WHEN YOU WALK IN THE ROOM	Searchers (Pye)
17	11	DON'T BRING ME DOWN	Pretty Things (Fontana)
29	12	ALL DAY AND ALL OF THE NIGHT	Kinks (Pye)
7	13	TWELFTH OF NEVER	Cliff Richard (Columbia)
20	14	GOOGLE EYE	Nashville Teens (Decca)
22	15	REMEMBER (WALKIN' IN THE SAND)	Shangri-Las (Red Bird)
9	16	HOW SOON Henry Mancini (RCA)	
18	17	AIN'T THAT LOVING YOU BABY	Elvis Presley (RCA)
12	18	ONE WAY LOVE	Cliff Bennett & the Rebel Rousers (Parlophone)
10	19	WE'RE THROUGH	Hollies (Parlophone)
11	20	WHERE DID OUR LOVE GO	Supremes (Stateside)
-	21	LOSING YOU	Dusty Springfield (Philips)
30	22	NOW WE'RE THRU'	Poets (Decca)
15	23	I'M CRYING Animals (Columbia)	
26	24	ANY WAY YOU WANT IT	Dave Clark Five (Columbia)
14	24	I'M INTO SOMETHING GOOD	Herman's Hermits (Columbia)
-	26	THERE'S A HEARTACHE FOLLOWING ME	Jim Reeves (RCA)
-	27	THE WILD SIDE OF LIFE	Tommy Quickly (Pye)
-	28	BLACK GIRL	Four Pennies (Philips)
24	29	I WOULDN'T TRADE YOU FOR THE WORLD	Bachelors (Decca)
-	30	WHEN I GROW UP (TO BE A MAN)	Beach Boys (Capitol)
-	30	WALK TALL Val Doonican (Decca)	

14 November 1964

last week	this week		
3	1	BABY LOVE	Supremes (Stateside)
7	2	UM, UM, UM, UM, UM, UM	Wayne Fontana & the Mindbenders (Fontana)
12	3	ALL DAY AND ALL OF THE NIGHT	Kinks (Pye)
2	4	OH, PRETTY WOMAN	Roy Orbison (London)
8	5	HE'S IN TOWN	Rockin' Berries (Piccadilly)
1	6	(THERE'S) ALWAYS SOMETHING THERE TO REMIND ME	Sandie Shaw (Pye)
4	7	SHA LA LA Manfred Mann (HMV)	
9	8	TOKYO MELODY	Helmut Zacharias (Polydor)
11	9	DON'T BRING ME DOWN	Pretty Things (Fontana)
5	10	WALK AWAY	Matt Monro (Parlophone)
15	11	REMEMBER (WALKIN' IN THE SAND)	Shangri-Las (Red Bird)
6	12	THE WEDDING	Julie Rogers (Mercury)
14	13	GOOGLE EYE	Nashville Teens (Decca)
26	14	THERE'S A HEARTACHE FOLLOWING ME	Jim Reeves (RCA)
10	15	WHEN YOU WALK IN THE ROOM	Searchers (Pye)
13	16	TWELFTH OF NEVER	Cliff Richard (Columbia)
17	17	AIN'T THAT LOVING YOU BABY	Elvis Presley (RCA)
21	18	LOSING YOU	Dusty Springfield (Philips)
16	19	HOW SOON	Henry Mancini (RCA)
-	19	I'M GONNA BE STRONG	Gene Pitney (Stateside)
-	21	DOWNTOWN Petula Clark (Pye)	
18	22	ONE WAY LOVE	Cliff Bennett & the Rebel Rousers (Parlophone)
-	22	I UNDERSTAND	Freddie & the Dreamers (Columbia)
30	24	WALK TALL	Val Doonican (Decca)
28	25	BLACK GIRL	Four Pennies (Philips)
-	26	GOLDFINGER	Shirley Bassey (Columbia)
22	27	NOW WE'RE THRU'	Poets (Decca)
19	28	WE'RE THROUGH	Hollies (Parlophone)
30	29	WHEN I GROW UP (TO BE A MAN)	Beach Boys (Capitol)
27	30	THE WILD SIDE OF LIFE	Tommy Quickly (Pye)

21 November 1964

last week	this week		
-	1	LITTLE RED ROOSTER	Rolling Stones (Decca)
1	2	BABY LOVE	Supremes (Stateside)
3	3	ALL DAY AND ALL OF THE NIGHT	Kinks (Pye)
2	4	UM, UM, UM, UM, UM, UM	Wayne Fontana & the Mindbenders (Fontana)
5	5	HE'S IN TOWN	Rockin' Berries (Piccadilly)
19	6	I'M GONNA BE STRONG	Gene Pitney (Stateside)
7	7	SHA LA LA Manfred Mann (HMV)	
4	8	OH, PRETTY WOMAN	Roy Orbison (London)
9	9	DON'T BRING ME DOWN	Pretty Things (Fontana)
11	10	REMEMBER (WALKIN' IN THE SAND)	Shangri-Las (Red Bird)
18	11	LOSING YOU	Dusty Springfield (Philips)
8	12	TOKYO MELODY	Helmut Zacharias (Polydor)
21	13	DOWNTOWN Petula Clark (Pye)	
14	13	THERE'S A HEARTACHE FOLLOWING ME	Jim Reeves (RCA)
6	15	(THERE'S) ALWAYS SOMETHING THERE TO REMIND ME	Sandie Shaw (Pye)
10	16	WALK AWAY	Matt Monro (Parlophone)
13	17	GOOGLE EYE	Nashville Teens (Decca)
-	18	PRETTY PAPER	Roy Orbison (London)
12	19	THE WEDDING	Julie Rogers (Mercury)
25	20	BLACK GIRL	Four Pennies (Philips)
16	21	TWELFTH OF NEVER	Cliff Richard (Columbia)
24	22	WALK TALL	Val Doonican (Decca)
22	23	I UNDERSTAND	Freddie & the Dreamers (Columbia)
15	24	WHEN YOU WALK IN THE ROOM	Searchers (Pye)
19	25	HOW SOON	Henry Mancini (RCA)
17	26	AIN'T THAT LOVING YOU BABY	Elvis Presley (RCA)
26	27	GOLDFINGER	Shirley Bassey (Columbia)
30	28	THE WILD SIDE OF LIFE	Tommy Quickly (Pye)
29	29	WHEN I GROW UP (TO BE A MAN)	Beach Boys (Capitol)
-	30	SHOW ME GIRL	Herman's Hermits (Columbia)

28 November 1964

last week	this week		
1	1	LITTLE RED ROOSTER	Rolling Stones (Decca)
2	2	BABY LOVE	Supremes (Stateside)
3	3	ALL DAY AND ALL OF THE NIGHT	Kinks (Pye)
6	4	I'M GONNA BE STRONG	Gene Pitney (Stateside)
5	5	HE'S IN TOWN	Rockin' Berries (Piccadilly)
4	6	UM, UM, UM, UM, UM, UM	Wayne Fontana & the Mindbenders (Fontana)
13	7	DOWNTOWN Petula Clark (Pye)	
9	8	DON'T BRING ME DOWN	Pretty Things (Fontana)
13	9	THERE'S A HEARTACHE FOLLOWING ME	Jim Reeves (RCA)
11	10	LOSING YOU	Dusty Springfield (Philips)
7	11	SHA LA LA Manfred Mann (HMV)	
8	12	OH, PRETTY WOMAN	Roy Orbison (London)
12	13	TOKYO MELODY	Helmut Zacharias (Polydor)
10	14	REMEMBER (WALKIN' IN THE SAND)	Shangri-Las (Red Bird)
18	15	PRETTY PAPER	Roy Orbison (London)
22	16	WALK TALL	Val Doonican (Decca)
16	17	WALK AWAY	Matt Monro (Parlophone)
15	18	(THERE'S) ALWAYS SOMETHING THERE TO REMIND ME	Sandie Shaw (Pye)
20	19	BLACK GIRL	Four Pennies (Philips)
19	20	THE WEDDING	Julie Rogers (Mercury)
30	21	SHOW ME GIRL	Herman's Hermits (Columbia)
17	22	GOOGLE EYE	Nashville Teens (Decca)
23	23	I UNDERSTAND	Freddie & the Dreamers (Columbia)
26	24	AIN'T THAT LOVING YOU BABY	Elvis Presley (RCA)
-	25	A MESSAGE TO MARTHA (KENTUCKY BLUEBIRD)	Adam Faith (Parlophone)
-	26	MARCH OF THE MODS	Joe Loss (HMV)
-	27	DANCING IN THE STREET	Martha & the Vandellas (Stateside)
29	28	WHEN I GROW UP (TO BE A MAN)	Beach Boys (Capitol)
-	29	TERRY	Twinkle (Decca)
28	30	THE WILD SIDE OF LIFE	Tommy Quickly (Pye)

With *Baby Love* coming quickly on the heels of their Number Two hit *Where Did Our Love Go*, the Supremes became the first Tamla Motown act to score a Number One in Britain. In the US they would do even better - both these two singles and the next three would take them to the chart-top. Here, *Baby Love*'s brief tenure was terminated by the Rolling Stones, whose most traditional blues recording yet, *Little Red Rooster*, made them the fifth act in chart history to have a single debut at Number One.

December 1964

5 December 1964

last	this	
-	1	I FEEL FINE Beatles (Parlophone)
1	2	LITTLE RED ROOSTER Rolling Stones (Decca)
4	3	I'M GONNA BE STRONG Gene Pitney (Stateside)
7	4	DOWNTOWN Petula Clark (Pye)
3	5	ALL DAY AND ALL OF THE NIGHT Kinks (Pye)
2	6	BABY LOVE Supremes (Stateside)
5	7	HE'S IN TOWN Rockin' Berries (Piccadilly)
6	8	UM, UM, UM, UM, UM, UM Wayne Fontana & the Mindbenders (Fontana)
16	9	WALK TALL Val Doonican (Decca)
15	10	PRETTY PAPER Roy Orbison (London)
8	11	DON'T BRING ME DOWN Pretty Things (Fontana)
9	12	THERE'S A HEARTACHE FOLLOWING ME Jim Reeves (RCA)
10	13	LOSING YOU Dusty Springfield (Philips)
25	14	A MESSAGE TO MARTHA (KENTUCKY BLUEBIRD) Adam Faith (Parlophone)
23	15	I UNDERSTAND Freddie & the Dreamers (Columbia)
11	16	SHA LA LA Manfred Mann (HMV)
13	17	TOKYO MELODY Helmut Zacharias (Polydor)
19	18	BLACK GIRL Four Pennies (Philips)
14	18	REMEMBER (WALKIN' IN THE SAND) Shangri-Las (Red Bird)
12	20	OH, PRETTY WOMAN Roy Orbison (London)
-	21	I COULD EASILY FALL (IN LOVE WITH YOU) Cliff Richard (Columbia)
17	22	WALK AWAY Matt Monro (Parlophone)
-	23	NO ARMS CAN EVER HOLD YOU Bachelors (Decca)
21	24	SHOW ME GIRL Herman's Hermits (Columbia)
29	25	TERRY Twinkle (Decca)
-	26	GENIE WITH THE LIGHT BROWN LAMP Shadows (Columbia)
20	27	THE WEDDING Julie Rogers (Mercury)
27	28	DANCING IN THE STREET Martha & the Vandellas (Stateside)
22	29	GOOGLE EYE Nashville Teens (Decca)
-	30	GONE, GONE, GONE Everly Brothers (Warner Bros)
-	30	BLUE CHRISTMAS Elvis Presley (RCA)

12 December 1964

last	this	
1	1	I FEEL FINE Beatles (Parlophone)
3	2	I'M GONNA BE STRONG Gene Pitney (Stateside)
2	2	LITTLE RED ROOSTER Rolling Stones (Decca)
4	4	DOWNTOWN Petula Clark (Pye)
10	6	PRETTY PAPER
5	7	ALL DAY AND ALL OF THE NIGHT Kinks (Pye)
6	8	BABY LOVE Supremes (Stateside)
15	9	I UNDERSTAND Freddie & the Dreamers (Columbia)
21	10	I COULD EASILY FALL (IN LOVE WITH YOU) Cliff Richard (Columbia)
14	11	A MESSAGE TO MARTHA (KENTUCKY BLUEBIRD) Adam Faith (Parlophone)
8	12	UM, UM, UM, UM, UM, UM Wayne Fontana & the Mindbenders (Fontana)
-	13	SOMEWHERE P.J. Proby (Liberty)
23	14	NO ARMS CAN EVER HOLD YOU Bachelors (Decca)
12	14	THERE'S A HEARTACHE FOLLOWING ME Jim Reeves (RCA)
30	16	BLUE CHRISTMAS Elvis Presley (RCA)
13	17	LOSING YOU Dusty Springfield (Philips)
11	18	DON'T BRING ME DOWN Pretty Things (Fontana)
26	19	GENIE WITH THE LIGHT BROWN LAMP Shadows (Columbia)
25	20	TERRY Twinkle (Decca)
21	21	WHAT HAVE THEY DONE TO THE RAIN Searchers (Pye)
7	22	HE'S IN TOWN Rockin' Berries (Piccadilly)
24	23	SHOW ME GIRL Herman's Hermits (Columbia)
22	24	WALK AWAY Matt Monro (Parlophone)
-	24	GIRL DON'T COME Sandie Shaw (Pye)
18	26	BLACK GIRL Four Pennies (Philips)
17	27	TOKYO MELODY Helmut Zacharias (Polydor)
-	28	BEATLES FOR SALE (LP) Beatles (Parlophone)
-	29	YEH YEH Georgie Fame & the Blue Flames (Columbia)
-	30	BABY I NEED YOUR LOVING Fourmost (Parlophone)
-	30	CAST YOUR FATE TO THE WIND Sounds Orchestral (Piccadilly)

19 December 1964

last	this	
1	1	I FEEL FINE Beatles (Parlophone)
2	2	I'M GONNA BE STRONG Gene Pitney (Stateside)
4	3	DOWNTOWN Petula Clark (Pye)
2	4	LITTLE RED ROOSTER Rolling Stones (Decca)
5	5	WALK TALL Val Doonican (Decca)
9	6	I UNDERSTAND & the Dreamers (Columbia)
13	7	SOMEWHERE P.J. Proby (Liberty)
14	8	NO ARMS CAN EVER HOLD YOU Bachelors (Decca)
6	9	PRETTY PAPER Roy Orbison (London)
10	10	I COULD EASILY FALL (IN LOVE WITH YOU) Cliff Richard (Columbia)
16	11	BLUE CHRISTMAS Elvis Presley (RCA)
11	12	A MESSAGE TO MARTHA (KENTUCKY BLUEBIRD) Adam Faith (Parlophone)
8	13	BABY LOVE Supremes (Stateside)
29	14	YEH YEH Georgie Fame & the Blue Flames (Columbia)
20	15	TERRY Twinkle (Decca)
14	16	THERE'S A HEARTACHE FOLLOWING ME Jim Reeves (RCA)
24	17	GIRL DON'T COME Sandie Shaw (Pye)
7	18	ALL DAY AND ALL OF THE NIGHT Kinks (Pye)
21	19	WHAT HAVE THEY DONE TO THE RAIN Searchers (Pye)
19	19	GENIE WITH THE LIGHT BROWN LAMP Shadows (Columbia)
12	21	UM, UM, UM, UM, UM, UM Wayne Fontana & the Mindbenders (Fontana)
17	22	LOSING YOU Dusty Springfield (Philips)
-	23	GO NOW Moody Blues (Decca)
28	24	BEATLES FOR SALE (LP) Beatles (Parlophone)
22	25	HE'S IN TOWN Rockin' Berries (Piccadilly)
24	26	WALK AWAY Matt Monro (Parlophone)
-	27	LIKE A CHILD Julie Rogers (Mercury)
30	28	CAST YOUR FATE TO THE WIND Sounds Orchestral (Piccadilly)
-	29	CHRISTMAS WILL BE JUST ANOTHER LONELY DAY Brenda Lee (Brunswick)
-	30	FERRY CROSS THE MERSEY Gerry & the Pacemakers (Columbia)

26 December 1964

last	this	
1	1	I FEEL FINE Beatles (Parlophone)
3	2	DOWNTOWN Petula Clark (Pye)
2	3	I'M GONNA BE STRONG Gene Pitney (Stateside)
5	4	WALK TALL Val Doonican (Decca)
7	5	SOMEWHERE P.J. Proby (Liberty)
14	6	YEH YEH Georgie Fame & the Blue Flames (Columbia)
8	7	NO ARMS CAN EVER HOLD YOU Bachelors (Decca)
6	8	I UNDERSTAND Freddie & the Dreamers (Columbia)
4	9	LITTLE RED ROOSTER Rolling Stones (Decca)
10	10	I COULD EASILY FALL (IN LOVE WITH YOU) Cliff Richard (Columbia)
15	11	TERRY Twinkle (Decca)
17	12	GIRL DON'T COME Sandie Shaw (Pye)
9	13	PRETTY PAPER Roy Orbison (London)
11	14	BLUE CHRISTMAS Elvis Presley (RCA)
12	15	A MESSAGE TO MARTHA (KENTUCKY BLUEBIRD) Adam Faith (Parlophone)
23	16	GO NOW Moody Blues (Decca)
16	17	THERE'S A HEARTACHE FOLLOWING ME Jim Reeves (RCA)
19	18	WHAT HAVE THEY DONE TO THE RAIN Searchers (Pye)
13	18	BABY LOVE Supremes (Stateside)
19	19	GENIE WITH THE LIGHT BROWN LAMP Shadows (Columbia)
30	21	FERRY CROSS THE MERSEY Gerry & the Pacemakers (Columbia)
24	22	BEATLES FOR SALE (LP) Beatles (Parlophone)
18	23	ALL DAY AND ALL OF THE NIGHT Kinks (Pye)
26	24	WALK AWAY Matt Monro (Parlophone)
28	25	CAST YOUR FATE TO THE WIND Sounds Orchestral (Piccadilly)
29	26	CHRISTMAS WILL BE JUST ANOTHER LONELY DAY Brenda Lee (Brunswick)
21	27	UM, UM, UM, UM, UM, UM Wayne Fontana & the Mindbenders (Fontana)
27	28	LIKE A CHILD Julie Rogers (Mercury)
-	29	MRS. MILLS' PARTY MEDLEY Mrs. Mills (HMV)
22	30	LOSING YOU Dusty Springfield (Philips)

With a 750,000 advance order, the Beatles' *I Feel Fine* was inevitably an instant Number One, and was the first time that two successive chart-toppers had each debuted in that position. Also unsurprising was the group's fourth album, *Beatles For Sale*, reaching the singles chart as its two predecessors had done. Petula Clark made a chart return after 18 months in the wilderness with *Downtown*, a Tony Hatch song which heralded a more aggressive commercial style for her. It would go on to top the US chart in 1965.

last week	this week	2 January 1965
1	1	I FEEL FINE / Beatles (Parlophone)
2	2	DOWNTOWN Petula Clark (Pye)
4	3	WALK TALL / Val Doonican (Decca)
5	4	SOMEWHERE / P.J. Proby (Liberty)
6	5	YEH YEH / Georgie Fame & the Blue Flames (Columbia)
3	6	I'M GONNA BE STRONG / Gene Pitney (Stateside)
10	7	I COULD EASILY FALL (IN LOVE WITH YOU) / Cliff Richard (Columbia)
7	8	NO ARMS CAN EVER HOLD YOU / Bachelors (Decca)
11	9	TERRY Twinkle (Decca)
8	10	I UNDERSTAND Freddie & the Dreamers (Columbia)
12	11	GIRL DON'T COME / Sandie Shaw (Pye)
9	12	LITTLE RED ROOSTER / Rolling Stones (Decca)
14	13	BLUE CHRISTMAS / Elvis Presley (RCA)
18	14	WHAT HAVE THEY DONE TO THE RAIN / Searchers (Pye)
13	15	PRETTY PAPER / Roy Orbison (London)
20	16	GENIE WITH THE LIGHT BROWN LAMP Shadows (Columbia)
15	17	A MESSAGE TO MARTHA (KENTUCKY BLUEBIRD) / Adam Faith (Parlophone)
17	18	THERE'S A HEARTACHE FOLLOWING ME / Jim Reeves (RCA)
16	19	GO NOW Moody Blues (Decca)
21	20	FERRY CROSS THE MERSEY / Gerry & the Pacemakers (Columbia)
26	21	CHRISTMAS WILL BE JUST ANOTHER LONELY DAY / Brenda Lee (Brunswick)
28	22	LIKE A CHILD / Julie Rogers (Mercury)
24	23	WALK AWAY / Matt Monro (Parlophone)
22	24	BEATLES FOR SALE (LP) / Beatles (Parlophone)
25	24	CAST YOUR FATE TO THE WIND / Sounds Orchestral (Piccadilly)
23	26	ALL DAY AND ALL OF THE NIGHT / Kinks (Pye)
18	27	BABY LOVE / Supremes (Stateside)
30	28	LOSING YOU / Dusty Springfield (Philips)
29	29	MRS. MILLS PARTY MEDLEY / Mrs. Mills (HMV)
-	30	ET MEME Francoise Hardy (Pye)

		9 January 1965
1	1	I FEEL FINE / Beatles (Parlophone)
5	2	YEH YEH / Georgie Fame & the Blue Flames (Columbia)
2	3	DOWNTOWN Petula Clark (Pye)
4	4	SOMEWHERE / P.J. Proby (Liberty)
3	5	WALK TALL / Val Doonican (Decca)
11	6	GIRL DON'T COME / Sandie Shaw (Pye)
7	7	I COULD EASILY FALL (IN LOVE WITH YOU) / Cliff Richard (Columbia)
9	8	TERRY Twinkle (Decca)
19	9	GO NOW Moody Blues (Decca)
8	10	NO ARMS CAN EVER HOLD YOU / Bachelors (Decca)
6	11	I'M GONNA BE STRONG / Gene Pitney (Stateside)
10	12	I UNDERSTAND Freddie & the Dreamers (Columbia)
20	13	FERRY CROSS THE MERSEY / Gerry & the Pacemakers (Columbia)
14	14	WHAT HAVE THEY DONE TO THE RAIN / Searchers (Pye)
12	15	LITTLE RED ROOSTER / Rolling Stones (Decca)
24	16	CAST YOUR FATE TO THE WIND / Sounds Orchestral (Piccadilly)
16	17	GENIE WITH THE LIGHT BROWN LAMP Shadows (Columbia)
17	18	A MESSAGE TO MARTHA (KENTUCKY BLUEBIRD) / Adam Faith (Parlophone)
15	19	PRETTY PAPER / Roy Orbison (London)
-	20	I'M LOST WITHOUT YOU / Billy Fury (Decca)
22	21	LIKE A CHILD / Julie Rogers (Mercury)
18	22	THERE'S A HEARTACHE FOLLOWING ME / Jim Reeves (RCA)
-	23	BABY PLEASE DON'T GO / Them (Decca)
24	24	BEATLES FOR SALE (LP) / Beatles (Parlophone)
13	25	BLUE CHRISTMAS / Elvis Presley (RCA)
26	26	ALL DAY AND ALL OF THE NIGHT / Kinks (Pye)
27	27	BABY LOVE / Supremes (Stateside)
30	28	ET MEME Francoise Hardy (Pye)
-	29	GOIN' OUT OF MY HEAD / Dodie West (Decca)
-	30	GOIN' OUT OF MY HEAD / Little Anthony and the Imperials (United Artists)

		16 January 1965
2	1	YEH YEH / Georgie Fame & the Blue Flames (Columbia)
1	2	I FEEL FINE Beatles (Parlophone)
9	3	GO NOW Moody Blues (Decca)
6	4	GIRL DON'T COME / Sandie Shaw (Pye)
8	5	TERRY Twinkle (Decca)
4	6	SOMEWHERE / P.J. Proby (Liberty)
3	7	DOWNTOWN Petula Clark (Pye)
13	8	FERRY CROSS THE MERSEY / Gerry & the Pacemakers (Columbia)
5	9	WALK TALL Val Doonican (Decca)
7	10	I COULD EASILY FALL (IN LOVE WITH YOU) / Cliff Richard (Columbia)
16	11	CAST YOUR FATE TO THE WIND / Sounds Orchestral (Piccadilly)
10	12	NO ARMS CAN EVER HOLD YOU / Bachelors (Decca)
20	13	I'M LOST WITHOUT YOU / Billy Fury (Decca)
-	14	COME TOMORROW / Manfred Mann (HMV)
23	14	BABY PLEASE DON'T GO / Them (Decca)
14	16	WHAT HAVE THEY DONE TO THE RAIN / Searchers (Pye)
-	17	YOU'VE LOST THAT LOVIN' FEELIN' Cilla Black (Parlophone)
11	18	I'M GONNA BE STRONG / Gene Pitney (Stateside)
12	19	I UNDERSTAND Freddie & the Dreamers (Columbia)
15	20	LITTLE RED ROOSTER / Rolling Stones (Decca)
-	21	THE THREE BELLS Brian Poole & the Tremeloes (Decca)
17	22	GENIE WITH THE LIGHT BROWN LAMP Shadows (Columbia)
-	23	LEADER OF THE PACK / Shangri-Las (Red Bird)
-	24	YOU'VE LOST THAT LOVIN' FEELIN' / Righteous Brothers (London)
-	25	DANCE, DANCE, DANCE / Beach Boys (Capitol)
-	26	GETTING MIGHTY CROWDED / Betty Everett (Fontana)
18	27	A MESSAGE TO MARTHA (KENTUCKY BLUEBIRD) / Adam Faith (Parlophone)
21	28	LIKE A CHILD / Julie Rogers (Mercury)
-	29	PROMISED LAND / Chuck Berry (Pye International)
22	30	THERE'S A HEARTACHE FOLLOWING ME Jim Reeves (RCA)

		23 January 1965
3	1	GO NOW Moody Blues (Decca)
1	2	YEH YEH / Georgie Fame & the Blue Flames (Columbia)
5	3	TERRY Twinkle (Decca)
4	4	GIRL DON'T COME / Sandie Shaw (Pye)
17	5	YOU'VE LOST THAT LOVIN' FEELIN' Cilla Black (Parlophone)
11	5	CAST YOUR FATE TO THE WIND / Sounds Orchestral (Piccadilly)
2	7	I FEEL FINE / Beatles (Parlophone)
14	8	COME TOMORROW / Manfred Mann (HMV)
8	9	FERRY CROSS THE MERSEY / Gerry & the Pacemakers (Columbia)
24	10	YOU'VE LOST THAT LOVIN' FEELIN' / Righteous Brothers (London)
14	11	BABY PLEASE DON'T GO / Them (Decca)
6	12	SOMEWHERE P.J. Proby (Liberty)
-	13	TIRED OF WAITING FOR YOU / Kinks (Pye)
7	14	DOWNTOWN Petula Clark (Pye)
9	15	WALK TALL Val Doonican (Decca)
30	16	KEEP SEARCHIN' (WE'LL FOLLOW THE SUN) Del Shannon (Stateside)
13	17	I'M LOST WITHOUT YOU / Billy Fury (Decca)
10	18	I COULD EASILY FALL (IN LOVE WITH YOU) / Cliff Richard (Columbia)
23	19	LEADER OF THE PACK / Shangri-Las (Red Bird)
21	20	THE THREE BELLS Brian Poole & the Tremeloes (Decca)
-	21	THE ROLLING STONES NO.2 (LP) / Rolling Stones (Decca)
-	22	THE SPECIAL YEARS / Val Doonican (Decca)
26	23	GETTING MIGHTY CROWDED / Betty Everett (Fontana)
-	24	I'LL NEVER FIND ANOTHER YOU / Seekers (Columbia)
25	25	DANCE, DANCE, DANCE / Beach Boys (Capitol)
16	25	WHAT HAVE THEY DONE TO THE RAIN / Searchers (Pye)
29	27	PROMISED LAND / Chuck Berry (Pye International)
12	28	NO ARMS CAN EVER HOLD YOU / Bachelors (Decca)
-	29	BABY I NEED YOUR LOVING / Fourmost (Parlophone)
18	29	I'M GONNA BE STRONG / Gene Pitney (Stateside)
-	29	WHAT IN THE WORLD'S COME OVER YOU / Rockin' Berries (Piccadilly)

Apart from the Beatles, Gerry and the Pacemakers were the only British Beat Boom group to be given their own starring feature film. *Ferry Across The Mersey* turned out to be a fairly minor cinema work, but its title song did return the group to the Top Ten – though for the last time. Two songs about deaths on motorbikes – *Terry* and *Leader Of The Pack* were in the charts simultaneously, while the Moody Blues reached the top with their chart debut – a cover version of a small US hit by Bessie Banks.

January – February 1965

30 January 1965

last week	this week	Entry
1	1	GO NOW Moody Blues (Decca)
10	2	YOU'VE LOST THAT LOVIN' FEELIN' Righteous Brothers (London)
13	3	TIRED OF WAITING FOR YOU Kinks (Pye)
8	4	COME TOMORROW Manfred Mann (HMV)
5	5	YOU'VE LOST THAT LOVIN' FEELIN' Cilla Black (Parlophone)
5	6	CAST YOUR FATE TO THE WIND Sounds Orchestral (Piccadilly)
2	7	YEH YEH Georgie Fame & the Blue Flames (Columbia)
3	8	TERRY Twinkle (Decca)
16	9	KEEP SEARCHIN' (WE'LL FOLLOW THE SUN) Del Shannon (Stateside)
11	10	BABY PLEASE DON'T GO Them (Decca)
4	11	GIRL DON'T COME Sandie Shaw (Pye)
9	12	FERRY CROSS THE MERSEY Gerry & the Pacemakers (Columbia)
7	13	I FEEL FINE Beatles (Parlophone)
22	14	THE SPECIAL YEARS Val Doonican (Decca)
12	15	SOMEWHERE P.J. Proby (Liberty)
20	16	THE THREE BELLS Brian Poole & the Tremeloes (Decca)
19	17	LEADER OF THE PACK Shangri-Las (Red Bird)
24	18	I'LL NEVER FIND ANOTHER YOU Seekers (Columbia)
14	19	DOWNTOWN Petula Clark (Pye)
23	20	GETTING MIGHTY CROWDED Betty Everett (Fontana)
17	21	I'M LOST WITHOUT YOU Billy Fury (Decca)
21	22	THE ROLLING STONES NO.2 (LP) Rolling Stones (Decca)
25	23	DANCE, DANCE, DANCE Beach Boys (Capitol)
29	24	WHAT IN THE WORLD'S COME OVER YOU Rockin' Berries (Piccadilly)
15	25	WALK TALL Val Doonican (Decca)
27	26	PROMISED LAND Chuck Berry (Pye International)
18	27	I COULD EASILY FALL (IN LOVE WITH YOU) Cliff Richard (Columbia)
-	28	COME SEE ABOUT ME Supremes (Stateside)
-	29	WHATCHA GONNA DO ABOUT IT Doris Troy (Atlantic)
-	30	YES I WILL Hollies (Parlophone)

6 February 1965

last week	this week	Entry
2	1	YOU'VE LOST THAT LOVIN' FEELIN' Righteous Brothers (London)
3	2	TIRED OF WAITING FOR YOU Kinks (Pye)
1	3	GO NOW Moody Blues (Decca)
9	4	KEEP SEARCHIN' (WE'LL FOLLOW THE SUN) Del Shannon (Stateside)
4	5	COME TOMORROW Manfred Mann (HMV)
6	6	CAST YOUR FATE TO THE WIND Sounds Orchestral (Piccadilly)
5	7	YOU'VE LOST THAT LOVIN' FEELIN' Cilla Black (Parlophone)
14	8	THE SPECIAL YEARS Val Doonican (Decca)
18	9	I'LL NEVER FIND ANOTHER YOU Seekers (Columbia)
10	10	BABY PLEASE DON'T GO Them (Decca)
8	11	TERRY Twinkle (Decca)
7	12	YEH YEH Georgie Fame & the Blue Flames (Columbia)
12	13	FERRY CROSS THE MERSEY Gerry & the Pacemakers (Columbia)
-	14	DON'T LET ME BE MISUNDERSTOOD Animals (Columbia)
17	15	LEADER OF THE PACK Shangri-Las (Red Bird)
11	16	GIRL DON'T COME Sandie Shaw (Pye)
16	17	THE THREE BELLS Brian Poole & the Tremeloes (Decca)
-	18	THE GAME OF LOVE Wayne Fontana & the Mindbenders (Fontana)
-	19	FUNNY HOW LOVE CAN BE Ivy League (Piccadilly)
21	20	I'M LOST WITHOUT YOU Billy Fury (Decca)
24	21	WHAT IN THE WORLD'S COME OVER YOU Rockin' Berries (Piccadilly)
30	22	YES I WILL Hollies (Parlophone)
13	23	I FEEL FINE Beatles (Parlophone)
-	24	IT HURTS SO MUCH (TO SEE YOU GO) Jim Reeves (RCA)
20	25	GETTING MIGHTY CROWDED Betty Everett (Fontana)
19	26	DOWNTOWN Petula Clark (Pye)
15	27	SOMEWHERE P.J. Proby (Liberty)
28	28	COME SEE ABOUT ME Supremes (Stateside)
23	29	DANCE, DANCE, DANCE Beach Boys (Capitol)
-	30	TELL HER NO Zombies (Decca)

13 February 1965

last week	this week	Entry
2	1	TIRED OF WAITING FOR YOU Kinks (Pye)
1	2	YOU'VE LOST THAT LOVIN' FEELIN' Righteous Brothers (London)
9	3	I'LL NEVER FIND ANOTHER YOU Seekers (Columbia)
4	4	KEEP SEARCHIN' (WE'LL FOLLOW THE SUN) Del Shannon (Stateside)
3	5	GO NOW Moody Blues (Decca)
18	6	THE GAME OF LOVE Wayne Fontana & the Mindbenders (Fontana)
8	7	THE SPECIAL YEARS Val Doonican (Decca)
14	8	DON'T LET ME BE MISUNDERSTOOD Animals (Columbia)
5	9	COME TOMORROW Manfred Mann (HMV)
6	10	CAST YOUR FATE TO THE WIND Sounds Orchestral (Piccadilly)
19	11	FUNNY HOW LOVE CAN BE Ivy League (Piccadilly)
24	12	IT HURTS SO MUCH (TO SEE YOU GO) Jim Reeves (RCA)
7	13	YOU'VE LOST THAT LOVIN' FEELIN' Cilla Black (Parlophone)
10	14	BABY PLEASE DON'T GO Them (Decca)
15	15	LEADER OF THE PACK Shangri-Las (Red Bird)
22	16	YES I WILL Hollies (Parlophone)
11	17	TERRY Twinkle (Decca)
17	18	THE THREE BELLS Brian Poole & the Tremeloes (Decca)
13	19	FERRY CROSS THE MERSEY Gerry & the Pacemakers (Columbia)
12	20	YEH YEH Georgie Fame & the Blue Flames (Columbia)
-	21	IT'S NOT UNUSUAL Tom Jones (Decca)
20	22	I'M LOST WITHOUT YOU Billy Fury (Decca)
21	23	WHAT IN THE WORLD'S COME OVER YOU Rockin' Berries (Piccadilly)
16	23	GIRL DON'T COME Sandie Shaw (Pye)
-	25	MARY ANNE Shadows (Columbia)
25	26	GETTING MIGHTY CROWDED Betty Everett (Fontana)
-	27	GOODNIGHT Roy Orbison (London)
29	28	DANCE, DANCE, DANCE Beach Boys (Capitol)
-	29	I MUST BE SEEING THINGS Gene Pitney (Stateside)
28	30	COME SEE ABOUT ME Supremes (Stateside)

20 February 1965

last week	this week	Entry
3	1	I'LL NEVER FIND ANOTHER YOU Seekers (Columbia)
1	2	TIRED OF WAITING FOR YOU Kinks (Pye)
2	3	YOU'VE LOST THAT LOVIN' FEELIN' Righteous Brothers (London)
6	4	THE GAME OF LOVE Wayne Fontana & the Mindbenders (Fontana)
4	5	KEEP SEARCHIN' (WE'LL FOLLOW THE SUN) Del Shannon (Stateside)
8	6	DON'T LET ME BE MISUNDERSTOOD Animals (Columbia)
7	7	THE SPECIAL YEARS Val Doonican (Decca)
11	8	FUNNY HOW LOVE CAN BE Ivy League (Piccadilly)
12	9	IT HURTS SO MUCH (TO SEE YOU GO) Jim Reeves (RCA)
21	10	IT'S NOT UNUSUAL Tom Jones (Decca)
9	11	COME TOMORROW Manfred Mann (HMV)
5	12	GO NOW Moody Blues (Decca)
27	13	GOODNIGHT Roy Orbison (London)
10	14	CAST YOUR FATE TO THE WIND Sounds Orchestral (Piccadilly)
29	15	I MUST BE SEEING THINGS Gene Pitney (Stateside)
16	16	YES I WILL Hollies (Parlophone)
25	17	MARY ANNE Shadows (Columbia)
15	18	LEADER OF THE PACK Shangri-Las (Red Bird)
14	19	BABY PLEASE DON'T GO Them (Decca)
13	20	YOU'VE LOST THAT LOVIN' FEELIN' Cilla Black (Parlophone)
-	21	COME AND STAY WITH ME Marianne Faithfull (Decca)
-	22	SILHOUETTES Herman's Hermits (Columbia)
-	23	I'LL STOP AT NOTHING Sandie Shaw (Pye)
22	24	I'M LOST WITHOUT YOU Billy Fury (Decca)
-	25	HONEY I NEED Pretty Things (Fontana)
17	26	TERRY Twinkle (Decca)
19	27	FERRY CROSS THE MERSEY Gerry & the Pacemakers (Columbia)
20	28	YEH YEH Georgie Fame & the Blue Flames (Columbia)
18	29	THE THREE BELLS Brian Poole & the Tremeloes (Decca)
23	30	WHAT IN THE WORLD'S COME OVER YOU Rockin' Berries (Piccadilly)
-	30	GOLDEN LIGHTS Twinkle (Decca)

Cilla Black's cover of *You've Lost That Lovin' Feelin'* looked inevitably like being the major UK hit version, based on her huge success profile against the totally unknown status of America's Righteous Brothers. However Rolling Stones manager Andrew Oldham took an unsolicited music press ad extolling the virtues of the original and the duo were brought over for a promotional visit, including Ready Steady Go! The outcome was a Number One for the Righteous Brothers and one of pop's classic songs.

27 February 1965

last week	this week		
1	1	I'LL NEVER FIND ANOTHER YOU	Seekers (Columbia)
10	2	IT'S NOT UNUSUAL	Tom Jones (Decca)
4	3	THE GAME OF LOVE	Wayne Fontana & the Mindbenders (Fontana)
6	4	DON'T LET ME BE MISUNDERSTOOD	Animals (Columbia)
2	5	TIRED OF WAITING FOR YOU	Kinks (Pye)
8	6	FUNNY HOW LOVE CAN BE	Ivy League (Piccadilly)
7	7	THE SPECIAL YEARS	Val Doonican (Decca)
15	8	I MUST BE SEEING THINGS	Gene Pitney (Stateside)
3	9	YOU'VE LOST THAT LOVIN' FEELIN'	Righteous Brothers (London)
22	10	SILHOUETTES	Herman's Hermits (Columbia)
5	11	KEEP SEARCHIN' (WE'LL FOLLOW THE SUN)	Del Shannon (Stateside)
21	12	COME AND STAY WITH ME	Marianne Faithfull (Decca)
9	13	IT HURTS SO MUCH (TO SEE YOU GO)	Jim Reeves (RCA)
23	14	I'LL STOP AT NOTHING	Sandie Shaw (Pye)
13	15	GOODNIGHT	Roy Orbison (London)
16	16	YES I WILL	Hollies (Parlophone)
11	17	COME TOMORROW	Manfred Mann (HMV)
25	18	HONEY I NEED	Pretty Things (Fontana)
19	19	MARY ANNE	Shadows (Columbia)
12	20	GO NOW	Moody Blues (Decca)
14	21	CAST YOUR FATE TO THE WIND	Sounds Orchestral (Piccadilly)
-	22	I APOLOGISE	P.J. Proby (Liberty)
18	22	LEADER OF THE PACK	Shangri-Las (Red Bird)
-	24	STOP FEELING SORRY FOR YOURSELF	Adam Faith (Parlophone)
30	24	GOLDEN LIGHTS	Twinkle (Decca)
-	26	YOUR HURTIN' KINDA LOVE	Dusty Springfield (Philips)
27	27	THE 'IN' CROWD	Dobie Gray (London)
28	28	I CAN'T EXPLAIN	Who (Brunswick)
29	29	CAN'T YOU HEAR MY HEARTBEAT	Goldie & the Gingerbreads (Decca)
-	30	PAPER TIGER	Sue Thompson (Hickory)

6 March 1965

2	1	IT'S NOT UNUSUAL	Tom Jones (Decca)
1	2	I'LL NEVER FIND ANOTHER YOU	Seekers (Columbia)
10	3	SILHOUETTES	Herman's Hermits (Columbia)
3	4	THE GAME OF LOVE	Wayne Fontana & the Mindbenders (Fontana)
14	5	I'LL STOP AT NOTHING	Sandie Shaw (Pye)
4	6	DON'T LET ME BE MISUNDERSTOOD	Animals (Columbia)
8	7	I MUST BE SEEING THINGS	Gene Pitney (Stateside)
-	8	THE LAST TIME	Rolling Stones (Decca)
12	9	COME AND STAY WITH ME	Marianne Faithfull (Decca)
6	10	FUNNY HOW LOVE CAN BE	Ivy League (Piccadilly)
16	11	YES I WILL	Hollies (Parlophone)
7	12	THE SPECIAL YEARS	Val Doonican (Decca)
22	13	I APOLOGISE	P.J. Proby (Liberty)
5	14	TIRED OF WAITING FOR YOU	Kinks (Pye)
13	15	IT HURTS SO MUCH (TO SEE YOU GO)	Jim Reeves (RCA)
15	16	GOODNIGHT	Roy Orbison (London)
19	17	MARY ANNE	Shadows (Columbia)
18	18	HONEY I NEED	Pretty Things (Fontana)
-	19	IN THE MEANTIME	Georgie Fame & the Blue Flames (Columbia)
9	20	YOU'VE LOST THAT LOVIN' FEELIN'	Righteous Brothers (London)
24	21	GOLDEN LIGHTS	Twinkle (Decca)
11	22	KEEP SEARCHIN' (WE'LL FOLLOW THE SUN)	Del Shannon (Stateside)
-	23	CONCRETE AND CLAY	Unit 4 + 2 (Decca)
-	24	GOODBYE MY LOVE	Searchers (Pye)
-	25	WINDMILL IN OLD AMSTERDAM	Ronnie Hilton (HMV)
27	26	THE 'IN' CROWD	Dobie Gray (London)
28	26	I CAN'T EXPLAIN	Who (Brunswick)
29	28	CAN'T YOU HEAR MY HEARTBEAT	Goldie & the Gingerbreads (Decca)
-	29	DIGGING MY POTATOES	Heinz (Columbia)
24	30	STOP FEELING SORRY FOR YOURSELF	Adam Faith (Parlophone)
-	30	SOMEONE MUST HAVE HURT YOU A LOT	Frankie Vaughan (Philips)

13 March 1965

8	1	THE LAST TIME	Rolling Stones (Decca)
1	2	IT'S NOT UNUSUAL	Tom Jones (Decca)
2	3	I'LL NEVER FIND ANOTHER YOU	Seekers (Columbia)
3	4	SILHOUETTES	Herman's Hermits (Columbia)
5	5	I'LL STOP AT NOTHING	Sandie Shaw (Pye)
4	6	THE GAME OF LOVE	Wayne Fontana & the Mindbenders (Fontana)
9	7	COME AND STAY WITH ME	Marianne Faithfull (Decca)
6	8	DON'T LET ME BE MISUNDERSTOOD	Animals (Columbia)
7	9	I MUST BE SEEING THINGS	Gene Pitney (Stateside)
24	10	GOODBYE MY LOVE	Searchers (Pye)
11	11	YES I WILL	Hollies (Parlophone)
10	12	FUNNY HOW LOVE CAN BE	Ivy League (Piccadilly)
13	13	I APOLOGISE	P.J. Proby (Liberty)
18	14	HONEY I NEED	Pretty Things (Fontana)
12	15	THE SPECIAL YEARS	Val Doonican (Decca)
19	16	IN THE MEANTIME	Georgie Fame & the Blue Flames (Columbia)
16	17	GOODNIGHT	Roy Orbison (London)
15	18	IT HURTS SO MUCH (TO SEE YOU GO)	Jim Reeves (RCA)
-	19	YOU'RE MY BREAKING MY HEART	Keely Smith (Reprise)
14	20	TIRED OF WAITING FOR YOU	Kinks (Pye)
17	20	MARY ANNE	Shadows (Columbia)
23	22	CONCRETE AND CLAY	Unit 4 + 2 (Decca)
-	23	SHE'S LOST YOU	Zephyrs (Columbia)
-	24	I KNOW A PLACE	Petula Clark (Pye)
-	25	THE MINUTE YOU'RE GONE	Cliff Richard (Columbia)
21	26	GOLDEN LIGHTS	Twinkle (Decca)
26	27	THE 'IN' CROWD	Dobie Gray (London)
-	28	DO THE CLAM	Elvis Presley (RCA)
-	29	I DON'T WANT TO GO ON WITHOUT YOU	Moody Blues (Decca)
-	30	FOR YOUR LOVE	Yardbirds (Columbia)

20 March 1965

1	1	THE LAST TIME	Rolling Stones (Decca)
2	2	IT'S NOT UNUSUAL	Tom Jones (Decca)
4	3	SILHOUETTES	Herman's Hermits (Columbia)
3	4	I'LL NEVER FIND ANOTHER YOU	Seekers (Columbia)
7	5	COME AND STAY WITH ME	Marianne Faithfull (Decca)
5	6	I'LL STOP AT NOTHING	Sandie Shaw (Pye)
10	7	GOODBYE MY LOVE	Searchers (Pye)
6	8	THE GAME OF LOVE	Wayne Fontana & the Mindbenders (Fontana)
9	9	I MUST BE SEEING THINGS	Gene Pitney (Stateside)
11	10	YES I WILL	Hollies (Parlophone)
14	11	HONEY I NEED	Pretty Things (Fontana)
13	12	I APOLOGISE	P.J. Proby (Liberty)
8	13	DON'T LET ME BE MISUNDERSTOOD	Animals (Columbia)
22	14	CONCRETE AND CLAY	Unit 4 + 2 (Decca)
25	15	THE MINUTE YOU'RE GONE	Cliff Richard (Columbia)
24	16	I KNOW A PLACE	Petula Clark (Pye)
16	17	IN THE MEANTIME	Georgie Fame & the Blue Flames (Columbia)
19	17	YOU'RE MY BREAKING MY HEART	Keely Smith (Reprise)
28	19	DO THE CLAM	Elvis Presley (RCA)
17	20	GOODNIGHT	Roy Orbison (London)
15	21	THE SPECIAL YEARS	Val Doonican (Decca)
12	22	FUNNY HOW LOVE CAN BE	Ivy League (Piccadilly)
-	23	I CAN'T EXPLAIN	Who (Brunswick)
23	24	SHE'S LOST YOU	Zephyrs (Columbia)
20	25	MARY ANNE	Shadows (Columbia)
30	26	FOR YOUR LOVE	Yardbirds (Columbia)
-	27	A WINDMILL IN OLD AMSTERDAM	Ronnie Hilton (HMV)
29	28	I DON'T WANT TO GO ON WITHOUT YOU	Moody Blues (Decca)
-	29	CATCH THE WIND	Donovan (Pye)
-	30	REELIN' AND ROCKIN'	Dave Clark Five (Columbia)

P J Proby's *I Apologise* seemed an appropriate title at the time, following several trouser-splitting incidents on stage which had resulted in Proby facing bans from theatre circuits and TV shows. The Rolling Stones' *The Last Time*, ostensibly a Jagger/Richard composition, but in fact closely based on the Staple Singers' gospel number *This May Be The Last Time*, gave the group not only their second Number One, but their biggest selling UK single. The Who and Donovan made their chart debuts.

March – April 1965

27 March 1965

last	this	Title / Artist
1	1	THE LAST TIME — Rolling Stones (Decca)
3	2	SILHOUETTES — Herman's Hermits (Columbia)
2	3	IT'S NOT UNUSUAL — Tom Jones (Decca)
5	4	COME AND STAY WITH ME — Marianne Faithfull (Decca)
7	5	GOODBYE MY LOVE — Searchers (Pye)
4	6	I'LL NEVER FIND ANOTHER YOU — Seekers (Columbia)
14	7	CONCRETE AND CLAY — Unit 4 + 2 (Decca)
6	8	I'LL STOP AT NOTHING — Sandie Shaw (Pye)
15	9	THE MINUTE YOU'RE GONE — Cliff Richard (Columbia)
11	10	HONEY I NEED — Pretty Things (Fontana)
29	11	CATCH THE WIND — Donovan (Pye)
26	12	FOR YOUR LOVE — Yardbirds (Columbia)
10	13	YES I WILL — Hollies (Parlophone)
9	14	I MUST BE SEEING THINGS — Gene Pitney (Stateside)
8	15	THE GAME OF LOVE — Wayne Fontana & the Mindbenders (Fontana)
17	16	YOU'RE MY BREAKING MY HEART — Keely Smith (Reprise)
12	17	I APOLOGISE — P.J. Proby (Liberty)
23	18	I CAN'T EXPLAIN — Who (Brunswick)
16	19	I KNOW A PLACE — Petula Clark (Pye)
17	20	IN THE MEANTIME — Georgie Fame & the Blue Flames (Columbia)
-	21	THE TIMES THEY ARE A-CHANGIN' — Bob Dylan (CBS)
19	22	DO THE CLAM — Elvis Presley (RCA)
13	23	DON'T LET ME BE MISUNDERSTOOD — Animals (Columbia)
24	23	SHE'S LOST YOU — Zephyrs (Columbia)
-	25	STOP! IN THE NAME OF LOVE — Supremes (Tamla Motown)
-	25	HERE COMES THE NIGHT — Them (Decca)
-	27	FIND MY WAY BACK HOME — Nashville Teens (Decca)
-	28	LITTLE THINGS — Dave Berry (Decca)
-	29	I'LL BE THERE — Gerry & the Pacemakers (Columbia)
30	30	REELIN' AND ROCKIN' — Dave Clark Five (Columbia)

3 April 1965

last	this	Title / Artist
1	1	THE LAST TIME — Rolling Stones (Decca)
7	2	CONCRETE AND CLAY — Unit 4 + 2 (Decca)
9	3	THE MINUTE YOU'RE GONE — Cliff Richard (Columbia)
12	4	FOR YOUR LOVE — Yardbirds (Columbia)
3	5	IT'S NOT UNUSUAL — Tom Jones (Decca)
2	6	SILHOUETTES — Herman's Hermits (Columbia)
4	7	COME AND STAY WITH ME — Marianne Faithfull (Decca)
5	8	GOODBYE MY LOVE — Searchers (Pye)
11	9	CATCH THE WIND — Donovan (Pye)
21	10	THE TIMES THEY ARE A-CHANGIN' — Bob Dylan (CBS)
6	11	I'LL NEVER FIND ANOTHER YOU — Seekers (Columbia)
25	12	HERE COMES THE NIGHT — Them (Decca)
8	13	I'LL STOP AT NOTHING — Sandie Shaw (Pye)
18	14	I CAN'T EXPLAIN — Who (Brunswick)
16	15	YOU'RE MY BREAKING MY HEART — Keely Smith (Reprise)
25	16	STOP! IN THE NAME OF LOVE — Supremes (Tamla Motown)
29	17	I'LL BE THERE — Gerry & the Pacemakers (Columbia)
10	18	HONEY I NEED — Pretty Things (Fontana)
28	19	LITTLE THINGS — Dave Berry (Decca)
-	20	I DON'T WANT TO GO ON WITHOUT YOU — Moody Blues (Decca)
-	21	EVERYBODY'S GONNA BE HAPPY — Kinks (Pye)
30	22	REELIN' AND ROCKIN' — Dave Clark Five (Columbia)
14	23	I MUST BE SEEING THINGS — Gene Pitney (Stateside)
13	24	YES I WILL — Hollies (Parlophone)
19	25	I KNOW A PLACE — Petula Clark (Pye)
-	26	POP GO THE WORKERS — Barron Knights (Columbia)
-	27	NOWHERE TO RUN — Martha & the Vandellas (Tamla Motown)
20	28	IN THE MEANTIME — Georgie Fame & the Blue Flames (Columbia)
22	29	DO THE CLAM — Elvis Presley (RCA)
-	30	KING OF THE ROAD — Roger Miller (Philips)
-	30	HAWAIIAN WEDDING SONG — Julie Rogers (Mercury)

10 April 1965

last	this	Title / Artist
4	1	FOR YOUR LOVE — Yardbirds (Columbia)
3	1	THE MINUTE YOU'RE GONE — Cliff Richard (Columbia)
2	3	CONCRETE AND CLAY — Unit 4 + 2 (Decca)
1	4	THE LAST TIME — Rolling Stones (Decca)
12	5	HERE COMES THE NIGHT — Them (Decca)
9	6	CATCH THE WIND — Donovan (Pye)
16	7	STOP! IN THE NAME OF LOVE — Supremes (Tamla Motown)
5	8	IT'S NOT UNUSUAL — Tom Jones (Decca)
10	9	THE TIMES THEY ARE A-CHANGIN' — Bob Dylan (CBS)
14	10	I CAN'T EXPLAIN — Who (Brunswick)
8	11	GOODBYE MY LOVE — Searchers (Pye)
6	12	SILHOUETTES — Herman's Hermits (Columbia)
15	12	YOU'RE MY BREAKING MY HEART — Keely Smith (Reprise)
7	14	COME AND STAY WITH ME — Marianne Faithfull (Decca)
19	15	LITTLE THINGS — Dave Berry (Decca)
17	16	I'LL BE THERE — Gerry & the Pacemakers (Columbia)
20	17	I DON'T WANT TO GO ON WITHOUT YOU — Moody Blues (Decca)
26	18	POP GO THE WORKERS — Barron Knights (Columbia)
21	19	EVERYBODY'S GONNA BE HAPPY — Kinks (Pye)
11	19	I'LL NEVER FIND ANOTHER YOU — Seekers (Columbia)
-	21	BRING IT ON HOME TO ME — Animals (Columbia)
30	22	KING OF THE ROAD — Roger Miller (Philips)
13	23	I'LL STOP AT NOTHING — Sandie Shaw (Pye)
27	24	NOWHERE TO RUN — Martha & the Vandellas (Tamla Motown)
30	25	HAWAIIAN WEDDING SONG — Julie Rogers (Mercury)
22	26	REELIN' AND ROCKIN' — Dave Clark Five (Columbia)
-	27	ALL OVER THE WORLD — Francoise Hardy (Pye)
23	28	I MUST BE SEEING THINGS — Gene Pitney (Stateside)
-	29	TRUE LOVE FOR EVERMORE — Bachelors (Decca)
29	30	DO THE CLAM — Elvis Presley (RCA)

17 April 1965

last	this	Title / Artist
-	1	TICKET TO RIDE — Beatles (Parlophone)
1	2	THE MINUTE YOU'RE GONE — Cliff Richard (Columbia)
5	3	HERE COMES THE NIGHT — Them (Decca)
1	4	FOR YOUR LOVE — Yardbirds (Columbia)
3	5	CONCRETE AND CLAY — Unit 4 + 2 (Decca)
6	6	CATCH THE WIND — Donovan (Pye)
4	7	THE LAST TIME — Rolling Stones (Decca)
7	8	STOP! IN THE NAME OF LOVE — Supremes (Tamla Motown)
21	9	BRING IT ON HOME TO ME — Animals (Columbia)
9	10	THE TIMES THEY ARE A-CHANGIN' — Bob Dylan (CBS)
15	11	LITTLE THINGS — Dave Berry (Decca)
18	12	POP GO THE WORKERS — Barron Knights (Columbia)
10	13	I CAN'T EXPLAIN — Who (Brunswick)
22	14	KING OF THE ROAD — Roger Miller (Philips)
12	15	YOU'RE MY BREAKING MY HEART — Keely Smith (Reprise)
8	16	IT'S NOT UNUSUAL — Tom Jones (Decca)
16	17	I'LL BE THERE — Gerry & the Pacemakers (Columbia)
12	18	SILHOUETTES — Herman's Hermits (Columbia)
17	19	I DON'T WANT TO GO ON WITHOUT YOU — Moody Blues (Decca)
19	20	I'LL NEVER FIND ANOTHER YOU — Seekers (Columbia)
-	21	TRUE LOVE WAYS — Peter & Gordon (Columbia)
14	22	COME AND STAY WITH ME — Marianne Faithfull (Decca)
11	23	GOODBYE MY LOVE — Searchers (Pye)
-	24	A WORLD OF OUR OWN — Seekers (Columbia)
19	25	EVERYBODY'S GONNA BE HAPPY — Kinks (Pye)
27	26	ALL OVER THE WORLD — Francoise Hardy (Pye)
29	27	TRUE LOVE FOR EVERMORE — Bachelors (Decca)
26	28	REELIN' AND ROCKIN' — Dave Clark Five (Columbia)
-	29	OH NO, NOT MY BABY — Manfred Mann (HMV)
-	30	I'M GONNA GET THERE SOMEHOW — Val Doonican (Decca)

Of the two singles sharing the April 10 Number One slot, Cliff Richard's *The Minute You're Gone* was one of several tracks he had cut in Nashville the previous year with US producer Billy Sherrill. The Yardbird's *For Your Love* was their last single to feature guitarist Eric Clapton, who reportedly quit the group in disgust over its commercial trappings. Bob Dylan's first UK single was the title track of an album already riding the LP charts, while the Supremes' *Stop!* was the first single on Motown's own UK label.

24 April 1965

last week	this week	title / artist
1	1	TICKET TO RIDE — Beatles (Parlophone)
2	2	THE MINUTE YOU'RE GONE — Cliff Richard (Columbia)
3	3	HERE COMES THE NIGHT — Them (Decca)
5	4	CONCRETE AND CLAY — Unit 4 + 2 (Decca)
4	5	FOR YOUR LOVE — Yardbirds (Columbia)
14	6	KING OF THE ROAD — Roger Miller (Philips)
9	7	BRING IT ON HOME TO ME — Animals (Columbia)
8	8	STOP! IN THE NAME OF LOVE — Supremes (Tamla Motown)
12	9	POP GO THE WORKERS — Barron Knights (Columbia)
11	10	LITTLE THINGS — Dave Berry (Decca)
7	11	THE LAST TIME — Rolling Stones (Decca)
6	12	CATCH THE WIND — Donovan (Pye)
15	13	YOU'RE MY BREAKING MY HEART — Keely Smith (Reprise)
10	14	THE TIMES THEY ARE A-CHANGIN' — Bob Dylan (CBS)
13	15	I CAN'T EXPLAIN — Who (Brunswick)
24	16	A WORLD OF OUR OWN — Seekers (Columbia)
21	17	TRUE LOVE WAYS — Peter & Gordon (Columbia)
-	18	WONDERFUL WORLD — Herman's Hermits (Columbia)
-	19	A LITTLE YOU — Freddie & the Dreamers (Columbia)
17	20	I'LL BE THERE — Gerry & the Pacemakers (Columbia)
20	20	I'LL NEVER FIND ANOTHER YOU — Seekers (Columbia)
29	22	OH NO, NOT MY BABY — Manfred Mann (HMV)
25	23	EVERYBODY'S GONNA BE HAPPY — Kinks (Pye)
26	24	ALL OVER THE WORLD — Francoise Hardy (Pye)
-	25	SOMETHING BETTER BEGINNING — Honeycombs (Pye)
-	26	NOWHERE TO RUN — Martha & the Vandellas (Tamla Motown)
16	26	IT'S NOT UNUSUAL — Tom Jones (Decca)
-	28	AT THE CLUB — Drifters (Atlantic)
23	29	GOODBYE MY LOVE — Searchers (Pye)
-	30	WHERE ARE YOU NOW — Jackie Trent (Pye)

1 May 1965

this week	title / artist
1	TICKET TO RIDE — Beatles (Parlophone)
2	KING OF THE ROAD — Roger Miller (Philips)
3	HERE COMES THE NIGHT — Them (Decca)
4	THE MINUTE YOU'RE GONE — Cliff Richard (Columbia)
5	BRING IT ON HOME TO ME — Animals (Columbia)
6	A WORLD OF OUR OWN — Seekers (Columbia)
7	POP GO THE WORKERS — Barron Knights (Columbia)
8	LITTLE THINGS — Dave Berry (Decca)
9	TRUE LOVE WAYS — Peter & Gordon (Columbia)
10	CATCH THE WIND — Donovan (Pye)
11	CONCRETE AND CLAY — Unit 4 + 2 (Decca)
12	STOP! IN THE NAME OF LOVE — Supremes (Tamla Motown)
13	OH NO, NOT MY BABY — Manfred Mann (HMV)
14	YOU'RE MY BREAKING MY HEART — Keely Smith (Reprise)
15	FOR YOUR LOVE — Yardbirds (Columbia)
16	WONDERFUL WORLD — Herman's Hermits (Columbia)
17	WHERE ARE YOU NOW — Jackie Trent (Pye)
18	THE LAST TIME — Rolling Stones (Decca)
19	THE TIMES THEY ARE A-CHANGIN' — Bob Dylan (CBS)
20	SUBTERRANEAN HOMESICK BLUES — Bob Dylan (CBS)
21	ONCE UPON A TIME — Tom Jones (Decca)
22	A LITTLE YOU — Freddie & the Dreamers (Columbia)
23	I'VE BEEN WRONG BEFORE — Cilla Black (Parlophone)
23	NOT UNTIL THE NEXT TIME — Jim Reeves (RCA)
25	I CAN'T EXPLAIN — Who (Brunswick)
26	I'LL NEVER FIND ANOTHER YOU — Seekers (Columbia)
27	ALL OVER THE WORLD — Francoise Hardy (Pye)
28	I'LL BE THERE — Gerry & the Pacemakers (Columbia)
29	SOMETHING BETTER BEGINNING — Honeycombs (Pye)
30	THAT'S WHY I'M CRYING — Ivy League (Piccadilly)
30	NOWHERE TO RUN — Martha & the Vandellas (Tamla Motown)

8 May 1965

this week	title / artist
1	TICKET TO RIDE — Beatles (Parlophone)
2	KING OF THE ROAD — Roger Miller (Philips)
3	A WORLD OF OUR OWN — Seekers (Columbia)
4	BRING IT ON HOME TO ME — Animals (Columbia)
5	HERE COMES THE NIGHT — Them (Decca)
6	SUBTERRANEAN HOMESICK BLUES — Bob Dylan (CBS)
7	POP GO THE WORKERS — Barron Knights (Columbia)
8	TRUE LOVE WAYS — Peter & Gordon (Columbia)
8	WHERE ARE YOU NOW — Jackie Trent (Pye)
10	THE MINUTE YOU'RE GONE — Cliff Richard (Columbia)
11	OH NO, NOT MY BABY — Manfred Mann (HMV)
12	LITTLE THINGS — Dave Berry (Decca)
13	WONDERFUL WORLD — Herman's Hermits (Columbia)
14	CATCH THE WIND — Donovan (Pye)
15	STOP! IN THE NAME OF LOVE — Supremes (Tamla Motown)
16	NOT UNTIL THE NEXT TIME — Jim Reeves (RCA)
17	CONCRETE AND CLAY — Unit 4 + 2 (Decca)
18	YOU'RE MY BREAKING MY HEART — Keely Smith (Reprise)
19	ALL OVER THE WORLD — Francoise Hardy (Pye)
20	THIS LITTLE BIRD — Marianne Faithfull (Decca)
21	FOR YOUR LOVE — Yardbirds (Columbia)
22	THE TIMES THEY ARE A-CHANGIN' — Bob Dylan (CBS)
22	THE LAST TIME — Rolling Stones (Decca)
24	I'VE BEEN WRONG BEFORE — Cilla Black (Parlophone)
25	SOMETHING BETTER BEGINNING — Honeycombs (Pye)
26	THAT'S WHY I'M CRYING — Ivy League (Piccadilly)
27	ONCE UPON A TIME — Tom Jones (Decca)
28	I'LL NEVER FIND ANOTHER YOU — Seekers (Columbia)
29	A LITTLE YOU — Freddie & the Dreamers (Columbia)
30	POOR MAN'S SON — Rockin' Berries (Piccadilly)

15 May 1965

this week	title / artist
1	TICKET TO RIDE — Beatles (Parlophone)
2	A WORLD OF OUR OWN — Seekers (Columbia)
3	KING OF THE ROAD — Roger Miller (Philips)
4	WHERE ARE YOU NOW — Jackie Trent (Pye)
5	TRUE LOVE WAYS — Peter & Gordon (Columbia)
6	SUBTERRANEAN HOMESICK BLUES — Bob Dylan (CBS)
7	WONDERFUL WORLD — Herman's Hermits (Columbia)
8	BRING IT ON HOME TO ME — Animals (Columbia)
9	OH NO, NOT MY BABY — Manfred Mann (HMV)
10	THIS LITTLE BIRD — Marianne Faithfull (Decca)
11	HERE COMES THE NIGHT — Them (Decca)
12	LONG LIVE LOVE — Sandie Shaw (Pye)
13	POP GO THE WORKERS — Barron Knights (Columbia)
14	THE MINUTE YOU'RE GONE — Cliff Richard (Columbia)
15	THE CLAPPING SONG — Shirley Ellis (London)
15	NOT UNTIL THE NEXT TIME — Jim Reeves (RCA)
17	LITTLE THINGS — Dave Berry (Decca)
18	POOR MAN'S SON — Rockin' Berries (Piccadilly)
19	CATCH THE WIND — Donovan (Pye)
20	ALL OVER THE WORLD — Francoise Hardy (Pye)
21	STOP! IN THE NAME OF LOVE — Supremes (Tamla Motown)
22	I'VE BEEN WRONG BEFORE — Cilla Black (Parlophone)
23	THAT'S WHY I'M CRYING — Ivy League (Piccadilly)
24	WE SHALL OVERCOME — Joan Baez (Fontana)
25	SOMETHING BETTER BEGINNING — Honeycombs (Pye)
26	ONCE UPON A TIME — Tom Jones (Decca)
27	YOU'RE MY BREAKING MY HEART — Keely Smith (Reprise)
28	THAT'S HOW STRONG MY LOVE IS — In Crowd (Parlophone)
29	CONCRETE AND CLAY — Unit 4 + 2 (Decca)
30	THE TIMES THEY ARE A-CHANGIN' — Bob Dylan (CBS)

Bob Dylan scored two Top Ten hits in rapid succession following the rush-release of his newly-recorded *Subterranean Homesick Blues*, a precursor of the new rock-oriented material which would take him to a commercial peak and provoke cries of 'Judas!' from purist folk followers. By contrast Tom Jones' follow up to his chart-topping *It's Not Unusual*, th undistinguished *Once Upon A Time*, barely did the business at all, leaving Jones looking like a one-hit wonder at this stage, though his live act was booming.

May – June 1965

22 May 1965

last	this		
4	1	WHERE ARE YOU NOW	Jackie Trent (Pye)
2	2	A WORLD OF OUR OWN	Seekers (Columbia)
12	3	LONG LIVE LOVE	Sandie Shaw (Pye)
1	4	TICKET TO RIDE	Beatles (Parlophone)
5	5	TRUE LOVE WAYS	Peter & Gordon (Columbia)
3	6	KING OF THE ROAD	Roger Miller (Philips)
10	7	THIS LITTLE BIRD	Marianne Faithfull (Decca)
6	8	SUBTERRANEAN HOMESICK BLUES	Bob Dylan (CBS)
15	9	THE CLAPPING SONG	Shirley Ellis (London)
7	10	WONDERFUL WORLD	Herman's Hermits (Columbia)
18	11	POOR MAN'S SON	Rockin' Berries (Piccadilly)
8	12	BRING IT ON HOME TO ME	Animals (Columbia)
9	13	OH NO, NOT MY BABY	Manfred Mann (HMV)
15	14	NOT UNTIL THE NEXT TIME	Jim Reeves (RCA)
13	15	POP GO THE WORKERS	Barron Knights (Columbia)
11	16	HERE COMES THE NIGHT	Them (Decca)
-	17	TRAINS AND BOATS AND PLANES	Burt Bacharach (London)
20	18	ALL OVER THE WORLD	Francoise Hardy (Pye)
23	19	THAT'S WHY I'M CRYING	Ivy League (Piccadilly)
-	20	IKO IKO	Dixie Cups (Red Bird)
-	21	MARIE	Bachelors (Decca)
14	22	THE MINUTE YOU'RE GONE	Cliff Richard (Columbia)
-	23	THE PRICE OF LOVE	Everly Brothers (Warner Bros)
-	24	TRAINS AND BOATS AND PLANES	Billy J. Kramer & the Dakotas (Parlophone)
-	24	NEVER BEEN IN LOVE LIKE THIS BEFORE	Unit 4 + 2 (Decca)
-	26	HOW LONG HAS IT BEEN	Jim Reeves (RCA)
24	27	WE SHALL OVERCOME	Joan Baez (Fontana)
22	27	I'VE BEEN WRONG BEFORE	Cilla Black (Parlophone)
17	29	LITTLE THINGS	Dave Berry (Decca)
-	30	LOVE HER	Walker Brothers (Philips)

29 May 1965

last	this		
3	1	LONG LIVE LOVE	Sandie Shaw (Pye)
1	2	WHERE ARE YOU NOW	Jackie Trent (Pye)
2	3	A WORLD OF OUR OWN	Seekers (Columbia)
5	4	TRUE LOVE WAYS	Peter & Gordon (Columbia)
7	5	THIS LITTLE BIRD	Marianne Faithfull (Decca)
11	6	POOR MAN'S SON	Rockin' Berries (Piccadilly)
9	7	THE CLAPPING SONG	Shirley Ellis (London)
6	8	KING OF THE ROAD	Roger Miller (Philips)
17	9	TRAINS AND BOATS AND PLANES	Burt Bacharach (London)
4	10	TICKET TO RIDE	Beatles (Parlophone)
8	11	SUBTERRANEAN HOMESICK BLUES	Bob Dylan (CBS)
21	12	MARIE	Bachelors (Decca)
14	13	NOT UNTIL THE NEXT TIME	Jim Reeves (RCA)
-	14	CRYING IN THE CHAPEL	Elvis Presley (RCA)
23	15	THE PRICE OF LOVE	Everly Brothers (Warner Bros)
18	16	ALL OVER THE WORLD	Francoise Hardy (Pye)
10	17	WONDERFUL WORLD	Herman's Hermits (Columbia)
12	18	BRING IT ON HOME TO ME	Animals (Columbia)
24	19	TRAINS AND BOATS AND PLANES	Billy J. Kramer & the Dakotas (Parlophone)
20	20	IKO IKO	Dixie Cups (Red Bird)
15	21	POP GO THE WORKERS	Barron Knights (Columbia)
-	22	SET ME FREE	Kinks (Pye)
24	23	NEVER BEEN IN LOVE LIKE THIS BEFORE	Unit 4 + 2 (Decca)
27	24	WE SHALL OVERCOME	Joan Baez (Fontana)
13	25	OH NO, NOT MY BABY	Manfred Mann (HMV)
-	26	COME HOME	Dave Clark Five (Columbia)
19	26	THAT'S WHY I'M CRYING	Ivy League (Piccadilly)
30	28	LOVE HER	Walker Brothers (Philips)
26	29	HOW LONG HAS IT BEEN	Jim Reeves (RCA)
-	30	I'M ALIVE	Hollies (Parlophone)
-	30	ANYWAY ANYHOW ANYWHERE	Who (Brunswick)

5 June 1965

last	this		
1	1	LONG LIVE LOVE	Sandie Shaw (Pye)
3	2	A WORLD OF OUR OWN	Seekers (Columbia)
15	3	THE PRICE OF LOVE	Everly Brothers (Warner Bros)
7	4	THE CLAPPING SONG	Shirley Ellis (London)
9	5	TRAINS AND BOAT AND PLANES	Burt Bacharach (London)
14	6	CRYING IN THE CHAPEL	Elvis Presley (RCA)
6	7	POOR MAN'S SON	Rockin' Berries (Piccadilly)
4	8	TRUE LOVE WAYS	Peter & Gordon (Columbia)
2	9	WHERE ARE YOU NOW	Jackie Trent (Pye)
5	10	THIS LITTLE BIRD	Marianne Faithfull (Decca)
12	11	MARIE	Bachelors (Decca)
19	12	TRAINS AND BOATS AND PLANES	Billy J. Kramer & the Dakotas (Parlophone)
30	13	I'M ALIVE	Hollies (Parlophone)
8	14	KING OF THE ROAD	Roger Miller (Philips)
26	15	COME HOME	Dave Clark Five (Columbia)
22	16	SET ME FREE	Kinks (Pye)
11	17	SUBTERRANEAN HOMESICK BLUES	Bob Dylan (CBS)
10	18	TICKET TO RIDE	Beatles (Parlophone)
13	19	NOT UNTIL THE NEXT TIME	Jim Reeves (RCA)
16	20	ALL OVER THE WORLD	Francoise Hardy (Pye)
30	21	ANYWAY ANYHOW ANYWHERE	Who (Brunswick)
-	22	COLOURS	Donovan (Pye)
23	23	STINGRAY	Shadows (Columbia)
23	24	NEVER BEEN IN LOVE LIKE THIS BEFORE	Unit 4 + 2 (Decca)
28	24	LOVE HER	Walker Brothers (Philips)
17	26	WONDERFUL WORLD	Herman's Hermits (Columbia)
20	27	IKO IKO	Dixie Cups (Red Bird)
-	28	ENGINE, ENGINE NO.9	Roger Miller (Philips)
-	29	FROM THE BOTTOM OF MY HEART	Moody Blues (Decca)
-	30	MY CHILD	Connie Francis (MGM)

12 June 1965

last	this		
3	1	THE PRICE OF LOVE	Everly Brothers (Warner Bros)
1	2	LONG LIVE LOVE	Sandie Shaw (Pye)
6	3	CRYING IN THE CHAPEL	Elvis Presley (RCA)
4	4	THE CLAPPING SONG	Shirley Ellis (London)
5	5	TRAINS AND BOATS AND PLANES	Burt Bacharach (London)
7	6	POOR MAN'S SON	Rockin' Berries (Piccadilly)
2	7	A WORLD OF OUR OWN	Seekers (Columbia)
13	8	I'M ALIVE	Hollies (Parlophone)
11	9	MARIE	Bachelors (Decca)
12	10	TRAINS AND BOATS AND PLANES	Billy J. Kramer & the Dakotas (Parlophone)
8	11	TRUE LOVE WAYS	Peter & Gordon (Columbia)
10	12	THIS LITTLE BIRD	Marianne Faithfull (Decca)
9	13	WHERE ARE YOU NOW	Jackie Trent (Pye)
16	14	SET ME FREE	Kinks (Pye)
22	15	COLOURS	Donovan (Pye)
15	16	COME HOME	Dave Clark Five (Columbia)
21	17	ANYWAY ANYHOW ANYWHERE	Who (Brunswick)
24	18	LOVE HER	Walker Brothers (Philips)
23	19	STINGRAY	Shadows (Columbia)
14	20	KING OF THE ROAD	Roger Miller (Philips)
24	21	NEVER BEEN IN LOVE LIKE THIS BEFORE	Unit 4 + 2 (Decca)
30	22	MY CHILD	Connie Francis (MGM)
-	23	ON MY WORD	Cliff Richard (Columbia)
29	24	FROM THE BOTTOM OF MY HEART	Moody Blues (Decca)
-	25	IT AIN'T ME BABE	Johnny Cash (CBS)
-	26	LOOKING THRU THE EYES OF LOVE	Gene Pitney (Stateside)
-	27	HEART FULL OF SOUL	Yardbirds (Columbia)
18	28	TICKET TO RIDE	Beatles (Parlophone)
19	29	NOT UNTIL THE NEXT TIME	Jim Reeves (RCA)
-	30	HELP ME RHONDA	Beach Boys (Capitol)
-	30	I'LL STAY BY YOU	Kenny Lynch (HMV)

Jackie Trent's *Where Are You Now* was the featured song in a TV drama serial titled *It's Dark Outside*, and the TV exposure (even though Jackie herself wasn't featured) undoubtedly helped boost it to the chart top. The Walker Brothers made their debut with *Love Her*, a song originally recorded by the Everly Brothers, while the Everlys themselves came back with renewed vigour and a more R&B-based style on *The Price Of Love* which gave them their first hit since *Temptation* four years earlier.

June – July 1965

19 June 1965

last week	this week	title	artist
3	1	CRYING IN THE CHAPEL	Elvis Presley (RCA)
1	2	THE PRICE OF LOVE	Everly Brothers (Warner Bros)
8	3	I'M ALIVE	Hollies (Parlophone)
2	4	LONG LIVE LOVE	Sandie Shaw (Pye)
5	5	TRAINS AND BOATS AND PLANES	Burt Bacharach (London)
4	6	THE CLAPPING SONG	Shirley Ellis (London)
15	7	COLOURS	Donovan (Pye)
6	8	POOR MAN'S SON	Rockin' Berries (Piccadilly)
14	9	SET ME FREE	Kinks (Pye)
7	10	A WORLD OF OUR OWN	Seekers (Columbia)
26	11	LOOKING THRU THE EYES OF LOVE	Gene Pitney (Stateside)
9	12	MARIE	Bachelors (Decca)
-	13	GOT LIVE IF YOU WANT IT (EP)	Rolling Stones (Decca)
17	14	ANYWAY ANYHOW ANYWHERE	Who (Brunswick)
24	15	FROM THE BOTTOM OF MY HEART	Moody Blues (Decca)
23	16	ON MY WORD	Cliff Richard (Columbia)
21	17	NEVER BEEN IN LOVE LIKE THIS BEFORE	Unit 4 + 2 (Decca)
10	18	TRAINS AND BOATS AND PLANES	Billy J. Kramer & the Dakotas (Parlophone)
-	18	THE ONE IN THE MIDDLE (EP)	Manfred Mann (HMV)
16	20	COME HOME	Dave Clark Five (Columbia)
12	21	THIS LITTLE BIRD	Marianne Faithfull (Decca)
19	21	STINGRAY	Shadows (Columbia)
27	23	HEART FULL OF SOUL	Yardbirds (Columbia)
11	24	TRUE LOVE WAYS	Peter & Gordon (Columbia)
25	25	IT AIN'T ME BABE	Johnny Cash (CBS)
22	26	MY CHILD	Connie Francis (MGM)
30	27	I'LL STAY BY YOU	Kenny Lynch (HMV)
-	28	LEAVE A LITTLE LOVE	Lulu (Decca)
18	29	LOVE HER	Walker Brothers (Philips)
30	30	HELP ME RHONDA	Beach Boys (Capitol)
-	30	MAGGIE'S FARM	Bob Dylan (CBS)
-	30	SHE'S ABOUT A MOVER	Sir Douglas Quintet (London)

26 June 1965

this week	title	artist
1	CRYING IN THE CHAPEL	Elvis Presley (RCA)
2	I'M ALIVE	Hollies (Parlophone)
3	THE PRICE OF LOVE	Everly Brothers (Warner Bros)
4	LOOKING THRU THE EYES OF LOVE	Gene Pitney (Stateside)
5	COLOURS	Donovan (Pye)
6	LONG LIVE LOVE	Sandie Shaw (Pye)
7	TRAINS AND BOATS AND PLANES	Burt Bacharach (London)
8	GOT LIVE IF YOU WANT IT (EP)	Rolling Stones (Decca)
9	THE CLAPPING SONG	Shirley Ellis (London)
10	THE ONE IN THE MIDDLE (EP)	Manfred Mann (HMV)
11	SET ME FREE	Kinks (Pye)
12	POOR MAN'S SON	Rockin' Berries (Piccadilly)
13	ANYWAY ANYHOW ANYWHERE	Who (Brunswick)
14	LEAVE A LITTLE LOVE	Lulu (Decca)
15	ON MY WORD	Cliff Richard (Columbia)
15	A WORLD OF OUR OWN	Seekers (Columbia)
17	MARIE	Bachelors (Decca)
18	HEART FULL OF SOUL	Yardbirds (Columbia)
19	IN THE MIDDLE OF NOWHERE	Dusty Springfield (Philips)
20	TO KNOW YOU IS TO LOVE YOU	Peter & Gordon (Columbia)
20	NEVER BEEN IN LOVE LIKE THIS BEFORE	Unit 4 + 2 (Decca)
22	FROM THE BOTTOM OF MY HEART	Moody Blues (Decca)
22	WOOLY BULLY	Sam the Sham & the Pharaohs (MGM)
24	MR. TAMBOURINE MAN	Byrds (CBS)
25	COME HOME	Dave Clark Five (Columbia)
26	MAGGIE'S FARM	Bob Dylan (CBS)
27	SHE'S ABOUT A MOVER	Sir Douglas Quintet (London)
28	TRAINS AND BOATS AND PLANES	Billy J. Kramer & the Dakotas (Parlophone)
29	I'LL STAY BY YOU	Kenny Lynch (HMV)
29	IT'S JUST A LITTLE BIT TOO LATE	Wayne Fontana (Fontana)
29	TOSSING AND TURNING	Ivy League (Piccadilly)

3 July 1965

this week	title	artist
1	I'M ALIVE	Hollies (Parlophone)
2	CRYING IN THE CHAPEL	Elvis Presley (RCA)
3	LOOKING THRU THE EYES OF LOVE	Gene Pitney (Stateside)
4	THE PRICE OF LOVE	Everly Brothers (Warner Bros)
5	COLOURS	Donovan (Pye)
6	THE ONE IN THE MIDDLE (EP)	Manfred Mann (HMV)
7	GOT LIVE IF YOU WANT IT (EP)	Rolling Stones (Decca)
8	MR. TAMBOURINE MAN	Byrds (CBS)
9	HEART FULL OF SOUL	Yardbirds (Columbia)
10	TO KNOW YOU IS TO LOVE YOU	Peter & Gordon (Columbia)
11	LEAVE A LITTLE LOVE	Lulu (Decca)
12	THE CLAPPING SONG	Shirley Ellis (London)
13	ANYWAY ANYHOW ANYWHERE	Who (Brunswick)
14	LONG LIVE LOVE	Sandie Shaw (Pye)
15	TRAINS AND BOATS AND PLANES	Burt Bacharach (London)
16	IN THE MIDDLE OF NOWHERE	Dusty Springfield (Philips)
17	ON MY WORD	Cliff Richard (Columbia)
18	TOSSING AND TURNING	Ivy League (Piccadilly)
19	WOOLY BULLY	Sam the Sham & the Pharaohs (MGM)
20	SET ME FREE	Kinks (Pye)
21	FROM THE BOTTOM OF MY HEART	Moody Blues (Decca)
22	POOR MAN'S SON	Rockin' Berries (Piccadilly)
23	SHE'S ABOUT A MOVER	Sir Douglas Quintet (London)
24	A WORLD OF OUR OWN	Seekers (Columbia)
25	NEVER BEEN IN LOVE LIKE THIS BEFORE	Unit 4 + 2 (Decca)
26	HELP ME RHONDA	Beach Boys (Capitol)
27	MARIE	Bachelors (Decca)
28	COME HOME	Dave Clark Five (Columbia)
29	IT AIN'T ME BABE	Johnny Cash (CBS)
30	MAGGIE'S FARM	Bob Dylan (CBS)

10 July 1965

this week	title	artist
1	I'M ALIVE	Hollies (Parlophone)
2	CRYING IN THE CHAPEL	Elvis Presley (RCA)
3	MR. TAMBOURINE MAN	Byrds (CBS)
4	HEART FULL OF SOUL	Yardbirds (Columbia)
5	LOOKING THRU THE EYES OF LOVE	Gene Pitney (Stateside)
6	TO KNOW YOU IS TO LOVE YOU	Peter & Gordon (Columbia)
7	IN THE MIDDLE OF NOWHERE	Dusty Springfield (Philips)
8	COLOURS	Donovan (Pye)
9	THE ONE IN THE MIDDLE (EP)	Manfred Mann (HMV)
10	TOSSING AND TURNING	Ivy League (Piccadilly)
10	LEAVE A LITTLE LOVE	Lulu (Decca)
12	THE PRICE OF LOVE	Everly Brothers (Warner Bros)
12	GOT LIVE IF YOU WANT IT (EP)	Rolling Stones (Decca)
14	WOOLY BULLY	Sam the Sham & the Pharaohs (MGM)
15	ON MY WORD	Cliff Richard (Columbia)
16	THERE BUT FOR FORTUNE	Joan Baez (Fontana)
17	ANYWAY ANYHOW ANYWHERE	Who (Brunswick)
18	LONG LIVE LOVE	Sandie Shaw (Pye)
19	FROM THE BOTTOM OF MY HEART	Moody Blues (Decca)
20	GOODBYEEE	Peter Cook & Dudley Moore (Decca)
21	SHE'S ABOUT A MOVER	Sir Douglas Quintet (London)
22	I CAN'T HELP MYSELF (SUGAR PIE, HONEY BUNCH)	Four Tops (Tamla Motown)
23	YOU'VE GOT YOUR TROUBLES	Fortunes (Decca)
24	THE CLAPPING SONG	Shirley Ellis (London)
25	CRY TO ME	Pretty Things (Fontana)
26	HELP ME RHONDA	Beach Boys (Capitol)
27	LET THE WATER RUN DOWN	P.J. Proby (Liberty)
28	HE'S GOT NO LOVE	Searchers (Pye)
29	THE BALLAD OF SPOTTY MULDOON	Peter Cook (Decca)
30	SET ME FREE	Kinks (Pye)

Crying In The Chapel had originally been recorded by Elvis in 1960 as part of the sessions for his gospel album *His Hand In Mine*. RCA held the track back at the time as having possible commercial potential away from the LP. Eventually issued as a 1965 Easter special single in the US, it proved the original decision correct by making the Top Three in the US, as well as Number One here. This would be Elvis Presley's last UK chart-topper until *In The Ghetto* in July 1969.

July – August 1965

17 July 1965

last	this	title
3	1	MR. TAMBOURINE MAN — Byrds (CBS)
4	2	HEART FULL OF SOUL — Yardbirds (Columbia)
1	3	I'M ALIVE — Hollies (Parlophone)
10	4	TOSSING AND TURNING — Ivy League (Piccadilly)
2	5	CRYING IN THE CHAPEL — Elvis Presley (RCA)
6	6	TO KNOW YOU IS TO LOVE YOU — Peter & Gordon (Columbia)
7	7	IN THE MIDDLE OF NOWHERE — Dusty Springfield (Philips)
5	8	LOOKING THRU THE EYES OF LOVE — Gene Pitney (Stateside)
10	9	LEAVE A LITTLE LOVE — Lulu (Decca)
9	10	THE ONE IN THE MIDDLE (EP) — Manfred Mann (HMV)
14	11	WOOLY BULLY — Sam the Sham & the Pharaohs (MGM)
16	12	THERE BUT FOR FORTUNE — Joan Baez (Fontana)
8	13	COLOURS — Donovan (Pye)
12	14	GOT LIVE IF YOU WANT IT (EP) — Rolling Stones (Decca)
12	15	THE PRICE OF LOVE — Everly Brothers (Warner Bros)
23	16	YOU'VE GOT YOUR TROUBLES — Fortunes (Decca)
17	17	ANYWAY ANYHOW ANYWHERE — Who (Brunswick)
20	18	GOODBYEEE — Peter Cook & Dudley Moore (Decca)
28	19	HE'S GOT NO LOVE — Searchers (Pye)
25	20	CRY TO ME — Pretty Things (Fontana)
-	21	WITH THESE HANDS — Tom Jones (Decca)
15	22	ON MY WORD — Cliff Richard (Columbia)
22	23	I CAN'T HELP MYSELF (SUGAR PIE, HONEY BUNCH) — Four Tops (Tamla Motown)
19	24	FROM THE BOTTOM OF MY HEART — Moody Blues (Decca)
27	25	LET THE WATER RUN DOWN — P.J. Proby (Liberty)
21	26	SHE'S ABOUT A MOVER — Sir Douglas Quintet (London)
-	27	WE GOTTA GET OUT OF THIS PLACE — Animals (Columbia)
26	28	HELP ME RHONDA — Beach Boys (Capitol)
29	29	THE BALLAD OF SPOTTY MULDOON — Peter Cook (Decca)
-	30	CATCH US IF YOU CAN — Dave Clark Five (Columbia)

24 July 1965

last	this	title
1	1	MR. TAMBOURINE MAN — Byrds (CBS)
2	2	HEART FULL OF SOUL — Yardbirds (Columbia)
4	3	TOSSING AND TURNING — Ivy League (Piccadilly)
16	4	YOU'VE GOT YOUR TROUBLES — Fortunes (Decca)
7	5	IN THE MIDDLE OF NOWHERE — Dusty Springfield (Philips)
3	6	I'M ALIVE — Hollies (Parlophone)
27	7	WE GOTTA GET OUT OF THIS PLACE — Animals (Columbia)
12	8	THERE BUT FOR FORTUNE — Joan Baez (Fontana)
5	9	CRYING IN THE CHAPEL — Elvis Presley (RCA)
6	10	TO KNOW YOU IS TO LOVE YOU — Peter & Gordon (Columbia)
8	11	LOOKING THRU THE EYES OF LOVE — Gene Pitney (Stateside)
11	12	WOOLY BULLY — Sam the Sham & the Pharaohs (MGM)
19	13	HE'S GOT NO LOVE — Searchers (Pye)
10	14	THE ONE IN THE MIDDLE (EP) — Manfred Mann (HMV)
9	15	LEAVE A LITTLE LOVE — Lulu (Decca)
30	16	CATCH US IF YOU CAN — Dave Clark Five (Columbia)
21	17	WITH THESE HANDS — Tom Jones (Decca)
25	18	LET THE WATER RUN DOWN — P.J. Proby (Liberty)
18	19	GOODBYEEE — Peter Cook & Dudley Moore (Decca)
20	20	CRY TO ME — Pretty Things (Fontana)
-	21	SAY YOU'RE MY GIRL — Roy Orbison (London)
14	22	GOT LIVE IF YOU WANT IT (EP) — Rolling Stones (Decca)
-	23	TOO MANY RIVERS — Brenda Lee (Brunswick)
-	24	IN THOUGHTS OF YOU — Billy Fury (Decca)
23	25	I CAN'T HELP MYSELF — Four Tops (Tamla Motown)
-	26	A WALK IN THE BLACK FOREST — Horst Jankowski (Mercury)
-	27	THIS WORLD IS NOT MY HOME — Jim Reeves (RCA)
26	28	SHE'S ABOUT A MOVER — Sir Douglas Quintet (London)
22	29	ON MY WORD — Cliff Richard (Columbia)
-	30	I WANT CANDY — Brian Poole & the Tremeloes (Decca)

31 July 1965

last	this	title
-	1	HELP! — Beatles (Parlophone)
1	2	MR. TAMBOURINE MAN — Byrds (CBS)
4	3	YOU'VE GOT YOUR TROUBLES — Fortunes (Decca)
7	4	WE GOTTA GET OUT OF THIS PLACE — Animals (Columbia)
3	5	TOSSING AND TURNING — Ivy League (Piccadilly)
2	6	HEART FULL OF SOUL — Yardbirds (Columbia)
8	7	THERE BUT FOR FORTUNE — Joan Baez (Fontana)
5	8	IN THE MIDDLE OF NOWHERE — Dusty Springfield (Philips)
16	9	CATCH US IF YOU CAN — Dave Clark Five (Columbia)
13	10	HE'S GOT NO LOVE — Searchers (Pye)
12	11	WOOLY BULLY — Sam the Sham & the Pharaohs (MGM)
6	12	I'M ALIVE — Hollies (Parlophone)
9	13	CRYING IN THE CHAPEL — Elvis Presley (RCA)
17	14	WITH THESE HANDS — Tom Jones (Decca)
10	15	TO KNOW YOU IS TO LOVE YOU — Peter & Gordon (Columbia)
24	16	IN THOUGHTS OF YOU — Billy Fury (Decca)
14	17	THE ONE IN THE MIDDLE (EP) — Manfred Mann (HMV)
11	18	LOOKING THRU THE EYES OF LOVE — Gene Pitney (Stateside)
-	19	EVERYONE'S GONE TO THE MOON — Jonathan King (Decca)
26	20	A WALK IN THE BLACK FOREST — Horst Jankowski (Mercury)
23	21	TOO MANY RIVERS — Brenda Lee (Brunswick)
15	22	LEAVE A LITTLE LOVE — Lulu (Decca)
21	23	SAY YOU'RE MY GIRL — Roy Orbison (London)
-	24	SUMMER NIGHTS — Marianne Faithfull (Decca)
26	25	THIS WORLD IS NOT MY HOME — Jim Reeves (RCA)
20	26	CRY TO ME — Pretty Things (Fontana)
19	27	GOODBYEEE — Peter Cook & Dudley Moore (Decca)
18	28	LET THE WATER RUN DOWN — P.J. Proby (Liberty)
-	29	ZORBA'S DANCE — Marcello Minerbi (Durium)
-	30	LIKE WE USED TO BE — Georgie Fame & the Blue Flames (Columbia)

7 August 1965

last	this	title
1	1	HELP! — Beatles (Parlophone)
3	2	YOU'VE GOT YOUR TROUBLES — Fortunes (Decca)
4	3	WE GOTTA GET OUT OF THIS PLACE — Animals (Columbia)
2	4	MR. TAMBOURINE MAN — Byrds (CBS)
9	5	CATCH US IF YOU CAN — Dave Clark Five (Columbia)
5	6	TOSSING AND TURNING — Ivy League (Piccadilly)
7	7	THERE BUT FOR FORTUNE — Joan Baez (Fontana)
6	8	HEART FULL OF SOUL — Yardbirds (Columbia)
19	9	EVERYONE'S GONE TO THE MOON — Jonathan King (Decca)
8	10	IN THE MIDDLE OF NOWHERE — Dusty Springfield (Philips)
14	11	WITH THESE HANDS — Tom Jones (Decca)
10	12	HE'S GOT NO LOVE — Searchers (Pye)
11	13	WOOLY BULLY — Sam the Sham & the Pharaohs (MGM)
16	14	IN THOUGHTS OF YOU — Billy Fury (Decca)
29	15	ZORBA'S DANCE — Marcello Minerbi (Durium)
20	16	A WALK IN THE BLACK FOREST — Horst Jankowski (Mercury)
24	17	SUMMER NIGHTS — Marianne Faithfull (Decca)
21	18	TOO MANY RIVERS — Brenda Lee (Brunswick)
12	19	I'M ALIVE — Hollies (Parlophone)
25	20	THIS WORLD IS NOT MY HOME — Jim Reeves (RCA)
13	21	CRYING IN THE CHAPEL — Elvis Presley (RCA)
23	22	SAY YOU'RE MY GIRL — Roy Orbison (London)
15	23	TO KNOW YOU IS TO LOVE YOU — Peter & Gordon (Columbia)
-	24	UNCHAINED MELODY — Righteous Brothers (London)
17	25	THE ONE IN THE MIDDLE (EP) — Manfred Mann (HMV)
-	26	DON'T MAKE MY BABY BLUE — Shadows (Columbia)
26	27	CRY TO ME — Pretty Things (Fontana)
28	28	LET THE WATER RUN DOWN — P.J. Proby (Liberty)
18	29	LOOKING THRU THE EYES OF LOVE — Gene Pitney (Stateside)
30	30	LIKE WE USED TO BE — Georgie Fame & the Blue Flames (Columbia)

A British equivalent of the San Remo Song Festival was held in Brighton in 1965, intended as the first of an annual series, but destined to be a one-off. Several of the artists and songs in the televised event found chart success, like Kenny Lynch's *I'll Stand By You* (first in the contest), Lulu's *Leave A Little Love* (second), the Ivy League's *Tossing And Turning*, and Manfred Mann's *The One In The Middle*, which was the title of the group's EP (though the Dylan song *With God On Our Side* was the main selling point).

August – September 1965

14 August 1965

1	1	HELP! Beatles (Parlophone)
2	2	YOU'VE GOT YOUR TROUBLES Fortunes (Decca)
3	3	WE GOTTA GET OUT OF THIS PLACE Animals (Columbia)
5	4	CATCH US IF YOU CAN Dave Clark Five (Columbia)
9	5	EVERYONE'S GONE TO THE MOON Jonathan King (Decca)
4	6	MR. TAMBOURINE MAN Byrds (CBS)
7	7	THERE BUT FOR FORTUNE Joan Baez (Fontana)
6	8	TOSSING AND TURNING Ivy League (Piccadilly)
14	9	IN THOUGHTS OF YOU Billy Fury (Decca)
11	10	WITH THESE HANDS Tom Jones (Decca)
15	11	ZORBA'S DANCE Marcello Minerbi (Durium)
17	12	SUMMER NIGHTS Marianne Faithfull (Decca)
16	13	A WALK IN THE BLACK FOREST Horst Jankowski (Mercury)
13	14	WOOLY BULLY Sam the Sham & the Pharaohs (MGM)
12	15	HE'S GOT NO LOVE Searchers (Pye)
8	16	HEART FULL OF SOUL Yardbirds (Columbia)
-	17	I GOT YOU BABE Sonny & Cher (Atlantic)
-	18	SEE MY FRIEND Kinks (Pye)
-	19	ALL I REALLY WANT TO DO Byrds (CBS)
18	19	TOO MANY RIVERS Brenda Lee (Brunswick)
10	21	IN THE MIDDLE OF NOWHERE Dusty Springfield (Philips)
20	22	THIS WORLD IS NOT MY HOME Jim Reeves (RCA)
26	22	DON'T MAKE MY BABY BLUE Shadows (Columbia)
30	24	LIKE WE USED TO BE Georgie Fame & the Blue Flames (Columbia)
24	25	UNCHAINED MELODY Righteous Brothers (London)
-	26	HELP! (LP) Beatles (Parlophone)
22	27	SAY YOU'RE MY GIRL Roy Orbison (London)
19	28	I'M ALIVE Hollies (Parlophone)
21	29	CRYING IN THE CHAPEL Elvis Presley (RCA)
-	30	WHAT'S NEW PUSSYCAT? Tom Jones (Decca)

21 August 1965

1	1	HELP! Beatles (Parlophone)
17	2	I GOT YOU BABE Sonny & Cher (Atlantic)
5	3	EVERYONE'S GONE TO THE MOON Jonathan King (Decca)
2	4	YOU'VE GOT YOUR TROUBLES Fortunes (Decca)
3	5	WE GOTTA GET OUT OF THIS PLACE Animals (Columbia)
4	6	CATCH US IF YOU CAN Dave Clark Five (Columbia)
11	7	ZORBA'S DANCE Marcello Minerbi (Durium)
13	8	A WALK IN THE BLACK FOREST Horst Jankowski (Mercury)
19	9	ALL I REALLY WANT TO DO Byrds (CBS)
9	10	IN THOUGHTS OF YOU Billy Fury (Decca)
6	11	MR. TAMBOURINE MAN Byrds (CBS)
12	12	SUMMER NIGHTS Marianne Faithfull (Decca)
7	13	THERE BUT FOR FORTUNE Joan Baez (Fontana)
8	14	TOSSING AND TURNING Ivy League (Piccadilly)
25	15	SEE MY FRIEND Kinks (Pye)
22	17	DON'T MAKE MY BABY BLUE Shadows (Columbia)
30	18	WHAT'S NEW PUSSYCAT? Tom Jones (Decca)
10	19	WITH THESE HANDS Tom Jones (Decca)
19	20	TOO MANY RIVERS Brenda Lee (Brunswick)
-	21	THAT'S THE WAY Honeycombs (Pye)
24	22	LIKE WE USED TO BE Georgie Fame & the Blue Flames (Columbia)
14	23	WOOLY BULLY Sam the Sham & the Pharaohs (MGM)
26	24	HELP! (LP) Beatles (Parlophone)
-	25	MAKE IT EASY ON YOURSELF Walker Brothers (Philips)
-	26	ALL I REALLY WANT TO DO Cher (Liberty)
-	27	THE TIME IN BETWEEN Cliff Richard (Columbia)
15	28	HE'S GOT NO LOVE Searchers (Pye)
27	29	SAY YOU'RE MY GIRL Roy Orbison (London)
-	30	DO YOU LOVE THAT GIRL? Johnny Carr & the Cadillacs (Fontana)

28 August 1965

2	1	I GOT YOU BABE Sonny & Cher (Atlantic)
1	2	HELP! Beatles (Parlophone)
-	3	(I CAN'T GET NO) SATISFACTION Rolling Stones (Decca)
9	4	ALL I REALLY WANT TO DO Byrds (CBS)
8	5	A WALK IN THE BLACK FOREST Horst Jankowski (Mercury)
7	6	ZORBA'S DANCE Marcello Minerbi (Durium)
	7	LIKE A ROLLING STONE Bob Dylan (CBS)
3	8	EVERYONE'S GONE TO THE MOON Jonathan King (Decca)
5	9	WE GOTTA GET OUT OF THIS PLACE Animals (Columbia)
4	10	YOU'VE GOT YOUR TROUBLES Fortunes (Decca)
26	11	ALL I REALLY WANT TO DO Cher (Liberty)
6	12	CATCH US IF YOU CAN Dave Clark Five (Columbia)
18	13	WHAT'S NEW PUSSYCAT? Tom Jones (Decca)
25	14	MAKE IT EASY ON YOURSELF Walker Brothers (Philips)
17	15	DON'T MAKE MY BABY BLUE Shadows (Columbia)
15	16	UNCHAINED MELODY Righteous Brothers (London)
10	17	IN THOUGHTS OF YOU Billy Fury (Decca)
15	18	SEE MY FRIEND Kinks (Pye)
12	19	SUMMER NIGHTS Marianne Faithfull (Decca)
27	20	THE TIME IN BETWEEN Cliff Richard (Columbia)
-	21	LAUGH AT ME Sonny (Atlantic)
20	22	TOO MANY RIVERS Brenda Lee (Brunswick)
24	23	HELP! (LP) Beatles (Parlophone)
21	23	THAT'S THE WAY Honeycombs (Pye)
11	25	MR. TAMBOURINE MAN Byrds (CBS)
13	26	THERE BUT FOR FORTUNE Joan Baez (Fontana)
-	27	UNIVERSAL SOLDIER (EP) Donovan (Pye)
14	28	TOSSING AND TURNING Ivy League (Piccadilly)
-	29	JUST A LITTLE BIT BETTER Herman's Hermits (Columbia)
19	30	WITH THESE HANDS Tom Jones (Decca)
-	30	HANG ON SLOOPY McCoys (Immediate)

4 September 1965

3	1	(I CAN'T GET NO) SATISFACTION Rolling Stones (Decca)
1	2	I GOT YOU BABE Sonny & Cher (Atlantic)
2	3	HELP! Beatles (Parlophone)
5	4	A WALK IN THE BLACK FOREST Horst Jankowski (Mercury)
14	4	MAKE IT EASY ON YOURSELF Walker Brothers (Philips)
6	6	ZORBA'S DANCE Marcello Minerbi (Durium)
7	7	LIKE A ROLLING STONE Bob Dylan (CBS)
4	8	ALL I REALLY WANT TO DO Byrds (CBS)
11	9	ALL I REALLY WANT TO DO Cher (Liberty)
13	10	WHAT'S NEW PUSSYCAT? Tom Jones (Decca)
8	11	EVERYONE'S GONE TO THE MOON Jonathan King (Decca)
9	12	WE GOTTA GET OUT OF THIS PLACE Animals (Columbia)
21	13	LAUGH AT ME Sonny (Atlantic)
16	14	UNCHAINED MELODY Righteous Brothers (London)
23	15	THAT'S THE WAY Honeycombs (Pye)
-	16	LOOK THROUGH ANY WINDOW Hollies (Parlophone)
17	17	IN THOUGHTS OF YOU Billy Fury (Decca)
12	18	CATCH US IF YOU CAN Dave Clark Five (Columbia)
18	19	SEE MY FRIEND Kinks (Pye)
20	20	THE TIME IN BETWEEN Cliff Richard (Columbia)
19	21	SUMMER NIGHTS Marianne Faithfull (Decca)
15	22	DON'T MAKE MY BABY BLUE Shadows (Columbia)
10	23	YOU'VE GOT YOUR TROUBLES Fortunes (Decca)
-	24	TEARS Ken Dodd (Columbia)
27	25	UNIVERSAL SOLDIER (EP) Donovan (Pye)
23	26	HELP! (LP) Beatles (Parlophone)
-	27	WHATCHA GONNA DO ABOUT IT Small Faces (Decca)
30	28	HANG ON SLOOPY McCoys (Immediate)
-	28	IL SILENZIO Nini Rosso (Durium)
29	30	JUST A LITTLE BIT BETTER Herman's Hermits (Columbia)

As with *A Hard Day's Night* a year before, the Beatles' soundtrack album from their second film *Help!* made the singles chart along with its title track single. Sonny & Cher, who made a well-timed and highly visible UK promotional visit, reaped the benefits as *I Got You Babe* emulated its US Number One success, and solo singles by each half of the duo followed it into the chart in successive weeks. The Righteous Brothers' *Unchained Melody* was to find its real chart glory twenty-five years later!

September – October 1965

11 September 1965

last	this		
1	1	(I CAN'T GET NO) SATISFACTION	Rolling Stones (Decca)
2	2	I GOT YOU BABE	Sonny & Cher (Atlantic)
7	3	LIKE A ROLLING STONE	Bob Dylan (CBS)
4	4	MAKE IT EASY ON YOURSELF	Walker Brothers (Philips)
3	5	HELP!	Beatles (Parlophone)
4	6	A WALK IN THE BLACK FOREST	Horst Jankowski (Mercury)
6	7	ZORBA'S DANCE	Marcello Minerbi (Durium)
9	8	ALL I REALLY WANT TO DO	Cher (Liberty)
16	9	LOOK THROUGH ANY WINDOW	Hollies (Parlophone)
24	10	TEARS	Ken Dodd (Columbia)
13	11	LAUGH AT ME	Sonny (Atlantic)
10	12	WHAT'S NEW PUSSYCAT?	Tom Jones (Decca)
8	13	ALL I REALLY WANT TO DO	Byrds (CBS)
14	14	UNCHAINED MELODY	Righteous Brothers (London)
25	15	UNIVERSAL SOLDIER (EP)	Donovan (Pye)
15	16	THAT'S THE WAY	Honeycombs (Pye)
11	17	EVERYONE'S GONE TO THE MOON	Jonathan King (Decca)
28	18	IL SILENZIO	Nini Rosso (Durium)
28	19	HANG ON SLOOPY	McCoys (Immediate)
20	20	THE TIME IN BETWEEN	Cliff Richard (Columbia)
30	21	JUST A LITTLE BIT BETTER	Herman's Hermits (Columbia)
27	21	WHATCHA GONNA DO ABOUT IT	Small Faces (Decca)
12	23	WE GOTTA GET OUT OF THIS PLACE	Animals (Columbia)
-	24	EVE OF DESTRUCTION	Barry McGuire (RCA)
-	25	IT'S ALL OVER NOW BABY BLUE	Joan Baez (Fontana)
-	26	PARADISE	Frank Ifield (Columbia)
-	26	BABY DON'T GO	Sonny & Cher (Reprise)
-	28	YOU'RE MY GIRL	Rockin' Berries (Piccadilly)
22	29	DON'T MAKE MY BABY BLUE	Shadows (Columbia)
-	30	HARK	Unit 4 + 2 (Decca)

18 September 1965

1	1	(I CAN'T GET NO) SATISFACTION	Rolling Stones (Decca)
2	2	I GOT YOU BABE	Sonny & Cher (Atlantic)
4	3	MAKE IT EASY ON YOURSELF	Walker Brothers (Philips)
3	4	LIKE A ROLLING STONE	Bob Dylan (CBS)
10	5	TEARS Ken Dodd (Columbia)
9	6	LOOK THROUGH ANY WINDOW	Hollies (Parlophone)
6	7	A WALK IN THE BLACK FOREST	Horst Jankowski (Mercury)
5	8	HELP! Beatles (Parlophone)
7	9	ZORBA'S DANCE	Marcello Minerbi (Durium)
11	10	LAUGH AT ME	Sonny (Atlantic)
8	11	ALL I REALLY WANT TO DO	Cher (Liberty)
15	12	UNIVERSAL SOLDIER (EP)	Donovan (Pye)
16	13	THAT'S THE WAY	Honeycombs (Pye)
24	13	EVE OF DESTRUCTION	Barry McGuire (RCA)
12	15	WHAT'S NEW PUSSYCAT?	Tom Jones (Decca)
13	16	ALL I REALLY WANT TO DO	Byrds (CBS)
18	17	IL SILENZIO	Nini Rosso (Durium)
14	18	UNCHAINED MELODY	Righteous Brothers (London)
19	19	HANG ON SLOOPY	McCoys (Immediate)
21	20	JUST A LITTLE BIT BETTER	Herman's Hermits (Columbia)
-	21	IF YOU GOTTA GO, GO NOW	Manfred Mann (HMV)
21	21	WHATCHA GONNA DO ABOUT IT	Small Faces (Decca)
26	21	BABY DON'T GO	Sonny & Cher (Reprise)
-	24	ALMOST THERE	Andy Williams (CBS)
26	25	PARADISE	Frank Ifield (Columbia)
-	26	TRY TO UNDERSTAND	Lulu (Decca)
25	27	IT'S ALL OVER NOW BABY BLUE	Joan Baez (Fontana)
17	28	EVERYONE'S GONE TO THE MOON	Jonathan King (Decca)
-	29	RUN TO MY LOVIN' ARMS	Billy Fury (Decca)
-	30	IT'S THE SAME OLD SONG	Four Tops (Tamla Motown)

25 September 1965

5	1	TEARS Ken Dodd (Columbia)
1	2	(I CAN'T GET NO) SATISFACTION	Rolling Stones (Decca)
3	3	MAKE IT EASY ON YOURSELF	Walker Brothers (Philips)
6	4	LOOK THROUGH ANY WINDOW	Hollies (Parlophone)
2	5	I GOT YOU BABE	Sonny & Cher (Atlantic)
4	6	LIKE A ROLLING STONE	Bob Dylan (CBS)
21	7	IF YOU GOTTA GO, GO NOW	Manfred Mann (HMV)
13	7	EVE OF DESTRUCTION	Barry McGuire (RCA)
7	9	A WALK IN THE BLACK FOREST	Horst Jankowski (Mercury)
17	10	IL SILENZIO	Nini Rosso (Durium)
9	11	ZORBA'S DANCE	Marcello Minerbi (Durium)
10	12	LAUGH AT ME	Sonny (Atlantic)
20	13	JUST A LITTLE BIT BETTER	Herman's Hermits (Columbia)
13	14	THAT'S THE WAY	Honeycombs (Pye)
12	15	UNIVERSAL SOLDIER (EP)	Donovan (Pye)
19	15	HANG ON SLOOPY	McCoys (Immediate)
24	17	ALMOST THERE	Andy Williams (CBS)
8	18	HELP! Beatles (Parlophone)
11	19	ALL I REALLY WANT TO DO	Cher (Liberty)
20	20	WHATCHA GONNA DO ABOUT IT	Small Faces (Decca)
21	21	BABY DON'T GO	Sonny & Cher (Reprise)
27	22	IT'S ALL OVER NOW BABY BLUE	Joan Baez (Fontana)
29	23	RUN TO MY LOVIN' ARMS	Billy Fury (Decca)
-	24	SOME OF YOUR LOVIN'	Dusty Springfield (Philips)
18	25	UNCHAINED MELODY	Righteous Brothers (London)
-	26	PAPA'S GOT A BRAND NEW BAG	James Brown (London)
15	27	WHAT'S NEW PUSSYCAT?	Tom Jones (Decca)
-	28	IN THE MIDNIGHT HOUR	Wilson Pickett (Atlantic)
16	29	ALL I REALLY WANT TO DO	Byrds (CBS)
-	30	MESSAGE UNDERSTOOD	Sandie Shaw (Pye)
-	30	TAKE A HEART	Sorrows (Piccadilly)

2 October 1965

1	1	TEARS Ken Dodd (Columbia)
3	2	MAKE IT EASY ON YOURSELF	Walker Brothers (Philips)
7	3	IF YOU GOTTA GO, GO NOW	Manfred Mann (HMV)
4	4	LOOK THROUGH ANY WINDOW	Hollies (Parlophone)
2	5	(I CAN'T GET NO) SATISFACTION	Rolling Stones (Decca)
7	6	EVE OF DESTRUCTION	Barry McGuire (RCA)
15	7	HANG ON SLOOPY	McCoys (Immediate)
17	8	ALMOST THERE	Andy Williams (CBS)
10	9	IL SILENZIO	Nini Rosso (Durium)
13	10	JUST A LITTLE BIT BETTER	Herman's Hermits (Columbia)
5	11	I GOT YOU BABE	Sonny & Cher (Atlantic)
6	12	LIKE A ROLLING STONE	Bob Dylan (CBS)
21	13	BABY DON'T GO	Sonny & Cher (Reprise)
9	14	A WALK IN THE BLACK FOREST	Horst Jankowski (Mercury)
14	15	THAT'S THE WAY	Honeycombs (Pye)
20	16	WHATCHA GONNA DO ABOUT IT	Small Faces (Decca)
30	17	MESSAGE UNDERSTOOD	Sandie Shaw (Pye)
15	18	UNIVERSAL SOLDIER (EP)	Donovan (Pye)
11	19	ZORBA'S DANCE	Marcello Minerbi (Durium)
12	20	LAUGH AT ME Sonny (Atlantic)
28	21	IN THE MIDNIGHT HOUR	Wilson Pickett (Atlantic)
18	22	HELP! Beatles (Parlophone)
24	23	SOME OF YOUR LOVIN'	Dusty Springfield (Philips)
23	24	RUN TO MY LOVIN' ARMS	Billy Fury (Decca)
-	25	SHE NEEDS LOVE	Wayne Fontana & the Mindbenders (Fontana)
26	26	PAPA'S GOT A BRAND NEW BAG	James Brown (London)
-	27	THAT MEANS A LOT	P.J. Proby (Liberty)
22	28	IT'S ALL OVER NOW BABY BLUE	Joan Baez (Fontana)
-	29	IT'S GOOD NEWS WEEK	Hedgehoppers Anonymous (Decca)
-	29	YOU'VE GOT TO HIDE YOUR LOVE AWAY	Silkie (Fontana)
30	29	TAKE A HEART	Sorrows (Piccadilly)

The Rolling Stones' (I Can't Get No) Satisfaction was a latecomer to the UK chart having been a US Number One some months earlier. Its release here had been delayed to allow the Got Live If You Want It EP to fulfill the sales potential it showed by reaching the Top Ten. The best-selling EP currently was Donovan's Universal Soldier, a quartet of anti-war songs highlighted by the Buffy Saint-Marie penned title track. Protest from a marginally different angle was aired in Barry McGuire's Eve Of Destruction.

9 October 1965

last week	this week	
1	1	TEARS Ken Dodd (Columbia)
3	2	IF YOU GOTTA GO, GO NOW Manfred Mann (HMV)
8	3	ALMOST THERE Andy Williams (CBS)
2	4	MAKE IT EASY ON YOURSELF Walker Brothers (Philips)
6	5	EVE OF DESTRUCTION Barry McGuire (RCA)
7	6	HANG ON SLOOPY McCoys (Immediate)
4	7	LOOK THROUGH ANY WINDOW Hollies (Parlophone)
5	8	(I CAN'T GET NO) SATISFACTION Rolling Stones (Decca)
9	9	MESSAGE UNDERSTOOD Sandie Shaw (Pye)
10	10	IL SILENZIO Nini Rosso (Durium)
13	11	BABY DON'T GO Sonny & Cher (Reprise)
12	12	LIKE A ROLLING STONE Bob Dylan (CBS)
11	13	I GOT YOU BABE Sonny & Cher (Atlantic)
14	14	A WALK IN THE BLACK FOREST Horst Jankowski (Mercury)
23	15	SOME OF YOUR LOVIN' Dusty Springfield (Philips)
21	16	IN THE MIDNIGHT HOUR Wilson Pickett (Atlantic)
29	17	IT'S GOOD NEWS WEEK Hedgehoppers Anonymous (Decca)
16	18	WHATCHA GONNA DO ABOUT IT Small Faces (Decca)
10	19	JUST A LITTLE BIT BETTER Herman's Hermits (Columbia)
15	20	THAT'S THE WAY Honeycombs (Pye)
19	21	ZORBA'S DANCE Marcello Minerbi (Durium)
26	22	PAPA'S GOT A BRAND NEW BAG James Brown (London)
24	23	RUN TO MY LOVIN' ARMS Billy Fury (Decca)
-	24	EVIL HEARTED YOU Yardbirds (Columbia)
29	25	TAKE A HEART Sorrows (Piccadilly)
-	26	YESTERDAY MAN Chris Andrews (Decca)
-	27	DO YOU BELIEVE IN MAGIC Pack (Columbia)
-	28	CALIFORNIA GIRLS Beach Boys (Capitol)
27	29	THAT MEANS A LOT P.J. Proby (Liberty)
25	30	SHE NEEDS LOVE Wayne Fontana & the Mindbenders (Fontana)
-	30	I LOVE YOU, YES I DO Merseybeats (Fontana)

16 October 1965

last week	this week	
1	1	TEARS Ken Dodd (Columbia)
3	2	ALMOST THERE Andy Williams (CBS)
2	3	IF YOU GOTTA GO, GO NOW Manfred Mann (HMV)
6	4	HANG ON SLOOPY McCoys (Immediate)
5	5	EVE OF DESTRUCTION Barry McGuire (RCA)
9	6	MESSAGE UNDERSTOOD Sandie Shaw (Pye)
7	7	MAKE IT EASY ON YOURSELF Walker Brothers (Philips)
7	8	LOOK THROUGH ANY WINDOW Hollies (Parlophone)
17	9	IT'S GOOD NEWS WEEK Hedgehoppers Anonymous (Decca)
24	10	EVIL HEARTED YOU Yardbirds (Columbia)
15	11	SOME OF YOUR LOVIN' Dusty Springfield (Philips)
10	12	IL SILENZIO Nini Rosso (Durium)
8	13	(I CAN'T GET NO) SATISFACTION Rolling Stones (Decca)
11	14	BABY DON'T GO Sonny & Cher (Atlantic)
18	15	WHATCHA GONNA DO ABOUT IT Small Faces (Decca)
26	16	YESTERDAY MAN Chris Andrews (Decca)
16	17	IN THE MIDNIGHT HOUR Wilson Pickett (Atlantic)
-	18	HERE IT COMES AGAIN Fortunes (Decca)
14	19	A WALK IN THE BLACK FOREST Horst Jankowski (Mercury)
-	20	STILL I'M SAD Yardbirds (Columbia)
13	21	I GOT YOU BABE Sonny & Cher (Atlantic)
22	22	PAPA'S GOT A BRAND NEW BAG James Brown (London)
12	23	LIKE A ROLLING STONE Bob Dylan (CBS)
20	24	THAT'S THE WAY Honeycombs (Pye)
29	24	THAT MEANS A LOT P.J. Proby (Liberty)
30	26	I LOVE YOU, YES I DO Merseybeats (Fontana)
21	27	ZORBA'S DANCE Marcello Minerbi (Durium)
25	28	TAKE A HEART Sorrows (Piccadilly)
-	29	YESTERDAY Matt Monro (Parlophone)
-	30	HOME OF THE BRAVE Jody Miller (Capitol)

23 October 1965

last week	this week	
1	1	TEARS Ken Dodd (Columbia)
2	2	ALMOST THERE Andy Williams (CBS)
3	3	IF YOU GOTTA GO, GO NOW Manfred Mann (HMV)
5	4	EVE OF DESTRUCTION Barry McGuire (RCA)
4	5	HANG ON SLOOPY McCoys (Immediate)
16	6	YESTERDAY MAN Chris Andrews (Decca)
9	7	IT'S GOOD NEWS WEEK Hedgehoppers Anonymous (Decca)
6	8	MESSAGE UNDERSTOOD Sandie Shaw (Pye)
18	9	HERE IT COMES AGAIN Fortunes (Decca)
10	10	EVIL HEARTED YOU Yardbirds (Columbia)
29	11	YESTERDAY Matt Monro (Parlophone)
11	12	SOME OF YOUR LOVIN' Dusty Springfield (Philips)
20	13	STILL I'M SAD Yardbirds (Columbia)
17	14	IN THE MIDNIGHT HOUR Wilson Pickett (Atlantic)
7	15	MAKE IT EASY ON YOURSELF Walker Brothers (Philips)
15	16	WHATCHA GONNA DO ABOUT IT Small Faces (Decca)
8	17	LOOK THROUGH ANY WINDOW Hollies (Parlophone)
12	18	IL SILENZIO Nini Rosso (Durium)
14	19	BABY DON'T GO Sonny & Cher (Reprise)
13	20	(I CAN'T GET NO) SATISFACTION Rolling Stones (Decca)
22	21	PAPA'S GOT A BRAND NEW BAG James Brown (London)
-	22	LOVE IS STRANGE Everly Brothers (Warner Bros)
19	23	A WALK IN THE BLACK FOREST Horst Jankowski (Mercury)
-	24	UNTIL IT'S TIME FOR YOU TO GO Four Pennies (Philips)
-	25	BUT YOU'RE MINE Sonny & Cher (Atlantic)
23	26	LIKE A ROLLING STONE Bob Dylan (CBS)
26	26	I LOVE YOU, YES I DO Merseybeats (Fontana)
-	28	I KNOW HOW IT FEELS TO BE LOVED Nashville Teens (Decca)
24	29	THAT MEANS A LOT P.J. Proby (Liberty)
27	30	ZORBA'S DANCE Marcello Minerbi (Durium)
28	30	TAKE A HEART Sorrows (Piccadilly)

30 October 1965

last week	this week	
1	1	TEARS Ken Dodd (Columbia)
6	2	YESTERDAY MAN Chris Andrews (Decca)
-	3	GET OFF OF MY CLOUD Rolling Stones (Decca)
7	4	IT'S GOOD NEWS WEEK Hedgehoppers Anonymous (Decca)
2	5	ALMOST THERE Andy Williams (CBS)
11	6	YESTERDAY Matt Monro (Parlophone)
9	7	HERE IT COMES AGAIN Fortunes (Decca)
4	8	EVE OF DESTRUCTION Barry McGuire (RCA)
3	9	IF YOU GOTTA GO, GO NOW Manfred Mann (HMV)
5	9	HANG ON SLOOPY McCoys (Immediate)
10	11	EVIL HEARTED YOU Yardbirds (Columbia)
13	12	STILL I'M SAD Yardbirds (Columbia)
12	13	SOME OF YOUR LOVIN' Dusty Springfield (Philips)
-	14	IT'S MY LIFE Animals (Columbia)
8	14	MESSAGE UNDERSTOOD Sandie Shaw (Pye)
22	16	LOVE IS STRANGE Everly Brothers (Warner Bros)
14	17	IN THE MIDNIGHT HOUR Wilson Pickett (Atlantic)
-	18	POSITIVELY 4TH STREET Bob Dylan (CBS)
25	19	BUT YOU'RE MINE Sonny & Cher (Atlantic)
16	20	WHATCHA GONNA DO ABOUT IT Small Faces (Decca)
24	21	UNTIL IT'S TIME FOR YOU TO GO Four Pennies (Philips)
28	22	I KNOW HOW IT FEELS TO BE LOVED Nashville Teens (Decca)
-	23	THE CARNIVAL IS OVER Seekers (Columbia)
18	24	IL SILENZIO Nini Rosso (Durium)
19	25	BABY DON'T GO Sonny & Cher (Reprise)
-	26	1-2-3 Len Barry (Brunswick)
-	27	SOMETHING Georgie Fame & the Blue Flames (Columbia)
-	27	BABY I'M YOURS Peter & Gordon (Columbia)
15	27	MAKE IT EASY ON YOURSELF Walker Brothers (Philips)
26	30	I LOVE YOU, YES I DO Merseybeats (Fontana)

Though Ken Dodd had interspersed his comedy career with occasional hit records since 1961, none caused a stir until *Tears*. A singalong with enormous silent majority appeal, it stayed at Number One for six weeks and became the year's biggest hit with sales of over one and a half million. Another balladeer Matt Monro took advantage of the Beatles' decision not to release *Yesterday* from their *Help!* LP as a UK single, and scored a Top Ten hit with it. The Beatles' version topped the US chart.

November 1965

6 November 1965

last	this	Entry
3	1	GET OFF OF MY CLOUD — Rolling Stones (Decca)
2	2	YESTERDAY MAN — Chris Andrews (Decca)
1	3	TEARS — Ken Dodd (Columbia)
7	4	HERE IT COMES AGAIN — Fortunes (Decca)
4	5	IT'S GOOD NEWS WEEK — Hedgehoppers Anonymous (Decca)
6	6	YESTERDAY — Matt Monro (Parlophone)
14	7	IT'S MY LIFE — Animals (Columbia)
5	8	ALMOST THERE — Andy Williams (CBS)
12	9	STILL I'M SAD — Yardbirds (Columbia)
11	10	EVIL HEARTED YOU — Yardbirds (Columbia)
23	11	THE CARNIVAL IS OVER — Seekers (Columbia)
8	12	EVE OF DESTRUCTION — Barry McGuire (RCA)
18	13	POSITIVELY 4TH STREET — Bob Dylan (CBS)
16	14	LOVE IS STRANGE — Everly Brothers (Warner Bros)
26	15	1-2-3 — Len Barry (Brunswick)
-	16	MY GENERATION — Who (Brunswick)
-	17	A LOVER'S CONCERTO — Toys (Stateside)
9	18	HANG ON SLOOPY — McCoys (Immediate)
13	19	SOME OF YOUR LOVIN' — Dusty Springfield (Philips)
9	20	IF YOU GOTTA GO, GO NOW — Manfred Mann (HMV)
27	21	BABY I'M YOURS — Peter & Gordon (Columbia)
21	22	UNTIL IT'S TIME FOR YOU TO GO — Four Pennies (Philips)
19	23	BUT YOU'RE MINE — Sonny & Cher (Atlantic)
14	24	MESSAGE UNDERSTOOD — Sandie Shaw (Pye)
-	25	WIND ME UP (LET ME GO) — Cliff Richard (Columbia)
27	26	SOMETHING — Georgie Fame & the Blue Flames (Columbia)
17	27	IN THE MIDNIGHT HOUR — Wilson Pickett (Atlantic)
22	28	IN THE CHAPEL IN THE MOONLIGHT — Bachelors (Decca)
22	28	I KNOW HOW IT FEELS TO BE LOVED — Nashville Teens (Decca)
-	30	TURQUOISE — Donovan (Pye)
-	30	TREAT HER RIGHT — Roy Head (Vocalion)

13 November 1965

last	this	Entry
1	1	GET OFF OF MY CLOUD — Rolling Stones (Decca)
2	2	YESTERDAY MAN — Chris Andrews (Decca)
16	3	MY GENERATION — Who (Brunswick)
15	4	1-2-3 — Len Barry (Brunswick)
7	5	IT'S MY LIFE — Animals (Columbia)
4	6	HERE IT COMES AGAIN — Fortunes (Decca)
11	7	THE CARNIVAL IS OVER — Seekers (Columbia)
3	8	TEARS — Ken Dodd (Columbia)
6	9	YESTERDAY — Matt Monro (Parlophone)
5	10	IT'S GOOD NEWS WEEK — Hedgehoppers Anonymous (Decca)
17	11	A LOVER'S CONCERTO — Toys (Stateside)
9	12	STILL I'M SAD — Yardbirds (Columbia)
8	13	ALMOST THERE — Andy Williams (CBS)
10	14	EVIL HEARTED YOU — Yardbirds (Columbia)
13	15	POSITIVELY 4TH STREET — Bob Dylan (CBS)
14	16	LOVE IS STRANGE — Everly Brothers (Warner Bros)
25	17	WIND ME UP (LET ME GO) — Cliff Richard (Columbia)
-	18	TELL ME WHY — Elvis Presley (RCA)
-	19	IS IT REALLY OVER — Jim Reeves (RCA)
-	20	PRINCESS IN RAGS — Gene Pitney (Stateside)
28	21	IN THE CHAPEL IN THE MOONLIGHT — Bachelors (Decca)
-	22	I'M GONNA TAKE YOU THERE — Dave Berry (Decca)
12	23	EVE OF DESTRUCTION — Barry McGuire (RCA)
-	24	OUR LOVE IS SLIPPING AWAY — Ivy League (Piccadilly)
30	25	TREAT HER RIGHT — Roy Head (Vocalion)
20	26	IF YOU GOTTA GO, GO NOW — Manfred Mann (HMV)
-	27	DON'T BRING ME YOUR HEARTACHES — Paul & Barry Ryan (Decca)
-	28	CRAWLING BACK — Roy Orbison (London)
-	29	WHO WHO HURT — Beryl Marsden (Columbia)
26	30	SOMETHING — Georgie Fame & the Blue Flames (Columbia)
21	30	BABY I'M YOURS — Peter & Gordon (Columbia)

20 November 1965

last	this	Entry
1	1	GET OFF OF MY CLOUD — Rolling Stones (Decca)
4	2	1-2-3 — Len Barry (Brunswick)
7	3	THE CARNIVAL IS OVER — Seekers (Columbia)
3	4	MY GENERATION — Who (Brunswick)
2	5	YESTERDAY MAN — Chris Andrews (Decca)
5	6	IT'S MY LIFE — Animals (Columbia)
6	7	HERE IT COMES AGAIN — Fortunes (Decca)
8	8	TEARS — Ken Dodd (Columbia)
11	9	A LOVER'S CONCERTO — Toys (Stateside)
9	10	YESTERDAY — Matt Monro (Parlophone)
17	11	WIND ME UP (LET ME GO) — Cliff Richard (Columbia)
15	12	POSITIVELY 4TH STREET — Bob Dylan (CBS)
12	13	STILL I'M SAD — Yardbirds (Columbia)
18	14	TELL ME WHY — Elvis Presley (RCA)
20	15	PRINCESS IN RAGS — Gene Pitney (Stateside)
14	16	EVIL HEARTED YOU — Yardbirds (Columbia)
10	17	IT'S GOOD NEWS WEEK — Hedgehoppers Anonymous (Decca)
13	18	ALMOST THERE — Andy Williams (CBS)
16	19	LOVE IS STRANGE — Everly Brothers (Warner Bros)
19	20	IS IT REALLY OVER — Jim Reeves (RCA)
27	21	DON'T BRING ME YOUR HEARTACHES — Paul & Barry Ryan (Decca)
-	22	YOU'RE THE ONE — Petula Clark (Pye)
-	22	THE RIVER — Ken Dodd (Columbia)
24	24	OUR LOVE IS SLIPPING AWAY — Ivy League (Piccadilly)
-	25	LET'S HANG ON — Four Seasons (Philips)
21	26	IN THE CHAPEL IN THE MOONLIGHT — Bachelors (Decca)
28	27	CRAWLING BACK — Roy Orbison (London)
22	28	I'M GONNA TAKE YOU THERE — Dave Berry (Decca)
30	29	BABY I'M YOURS — Peter & Gordon (Columbia)
29	30	WHO YOU GONNA HURT — Beryl Marsden (Columbia)

27 November 1965

last	this	Entry
2	1	1-2-3 — Len Barry (Brunswick)
3	2	THE CARNIVAL IS OVER — Seekers (Columbia)
4	3	MY GENERATION — Who (Brunswick)
1	4	GET OFF OF MY CLOUD — Rolling Stones (Decca)
5	5	YESTERDAY MAN — Chris Andrews (Decca)
8	6	TEARS — Ken Dodd (Columbia)
9	7	A LOVER'S CONCERTO — Toys (Stateside)
11	8	WIND ME UP (LET ME GO) — Cliff Richard (Columbia)
6	9	IT'S MY LIFE — Animals (Columbia)
15	10	PRINCESS IN RAGS — Gene Pitney (Stateside)
7	11	HERE IT COMES AGAIN — Fortunes (Decca)
12	12	POSITIVELY 4TH STREET — Bob Dylan (CBS)
10	13	YESTERDAY — Matt Monro (Parlophone)
22	14	THE RIVER — Ken Dodd (Columbia)
-	15	MARIA — P.J. Proby (Liberty)
25	16	LET'S HANG ON — Four Seasons (Philips)
14	17	TELL ME WHY — Elvis Presley (RCA)
21	18	DON'T BRING ME YOUR HEARTACHES — Paul & Barry Ryan (Decca)
13	19	STILL I'M SAD — Yardbirds (Columbia)
18	20	ALMOST THERE — Andy Williams (CBS)
16	21	EVIL HEARTED YOU — Yardbirds (Columbia)
-	22	HOW CAN YOU TELL — Sandie Shaw (Pye)
-	23	RESCUE ME — Fontella Bass (Chess)
22	24	YOU'RE THE ONE — Petula Clark (Pye)
24	25	OUR LOVE IS SLIPPING AWAY — Ivy League (Piccadilly)
20	26	IS IT REALLY OVER — Jim Reeves (RCA)
17	27	IT'S GOOD NEWS WEEK — Hedgehoppers Anonymous (Decca)
-	28	TO WHOM IT CONCERNS — Chris Andrews (Decca)
-	28	UNTIL IT'S TIME FOR YOU TO GO — Four Pennies (Philips)
-	30	I LEFT MY HEART IN SAN FRANCISCO — Tony Bennett (CBS)

Get Off My Cloud gave the Stones a quartet of consecutive Number One singles, the only other group to have achieved this being the Beatles. The Yardbirds joined the exclusive coterie of acts to have placed both sides of a single independently in the Top Ten at the Top Ten, as *Still I'm Sad* and *Evil Hearted You* peaked together on November 6. Elvis Presley's *Tell Me Why* was a previous unreleased 1957 recording, while Tony Bennett's *I Left My Heart In San Francisco* had originally been released in 1962.

December 1965

last week	this week	4 December 1965	
2	1	THE CARNIVAL IS OVER	Seekers (Columbia)
1	2	1-2-3	Len Barry (Brunswick)
3	3	MY GENERATION	Who (Brunswick)
6	4	TEARS	Ken Dodd (Columbia)
8	4	WIND ME UP (LET ME GO)	Cliff Richard (Columbia)
7	6	A LOVER'S CONCERTO	Toys (Stateside)
14	7	THE RIVER	Ken Dodd (Columbia)
4	8	GET OFF OF MY CLOUD	Rolling Stones (Decca)
5	9	YESTERDAY MAN	Chris Andrews (Decca)
15	10	MARIA	P.J. Proby (Liberty)
10	11	PRINCESS IN RAGS	Gene Pitney (Stateside)
12	12	POSITIVELY 4TH STREET	Bob Dylan (CBS)
16	13	LET'S HANG ON	Four Seasons (Philips)
18	14	DON'T BRING ME YOUR HEARTACHES	Paul & Barry Ryan (Decca)
9	15	IT'S MY LIFE	Animals (Columbia)
23	16	RESCUE ME	Fontella Bass (Chess)
28	17	TO WHOM IT CONCERNS	Chris Andrews (Decca)
13	18	YESTERDAY	Matt Monro (Parlophone)
26	19	IS IT REALLY OVER	Jim Reeves (RCA)
22	20	HOW CAN YOU TELL	Sandie Shaw (Pye)
11	21	HERE IT COMES AGAIN	Fortunes (Decca)
17	22	TELL ME WHY	Elvis Presley (RCA)
24	23	YOU'RE THE ONE	Petula Clark (Pye)
-	23	MY SHIP IS COMING IN	Walker Brothers (Philips)
-	25	THE WAR LORD	Shadows (Columbia)
30	26	I LEFT MY HEART IN SAN FRANCISCO	Tony Bennett (CBS)
-	26	CRAWLING BACK	Roy Orbison (London)
-	28	TURN! TURN! TURN!	Byrds (CBS)
-	29	STANDING IN THE RUINS	Keely Smith (Reprise)
28	30	UNTIL IT'S TIME FOR YOU TO GO	Four Pennies (Philips)
-	30	DOWN CAME THE RAIN	Mister Murray (Fontana)

last week	this week	11 December 1965	
-	1	DAY TRIPPER/WE CAN WORK IT OUT	Beatles (Parlophone)
1	2	THE CARNIVAL IS OVER	Seekers (Columbia)
2	3	1-2-3	Len Barry (Brunswick)
4	4	WIND ME UP (LET ME GO)	Cliff Richard (Columbia)
3	5	MY GENERATION	Who (Brunswick)
7	6	THE RIVER	Ken Dodd (Columbia)
6	7	A LOVER'S CONCERTO	Toys (Stateside)
4	8	TEARS	Ken Dodd (Columbia)
10	9	MARIA	P.J. Proby (Liberty)
11	10	PRINCESS IN RAGS	Gene Pitney (Stateside)
16	11	RESCUE ME	Fontella Bass (Chess)
13	12	LET'S HANG ON	Four Seasons (Philips)
9	13	YESTERDAY MAN	Chris Andrews (Decca)
17	14	TO WHOM IT CONCERNS	Chris Andrews (Decca)
12	15	POSITIVELY 4TH STREET	Bob Dylan (CBS)
8	15	GET OFF OF MY CLOUD	Rolling Stones (Decca)
23	17	MY SHIP IS COMING IN	Walker Brothers (Philips)
19	18	IS IT REALLY OVER	Jim Reeves (RCA)
14	19	DON'T BRING ME YOUR HEARTACHES	Paul & Barry Ryan (Decca)
-	20	KEEP ON RUNNING	Spencer Davis Group (Fontana)
15	21	IT'S MY LIFE	Animals (Columbia)
20	22	HOW CAN YOU TELL	Sandie Shaw (Pye)
-	23	I LEFT MY HEART IN SAN FRANCISCO	Tony Bennett (CBS)
18	24	YESTERDAY	Matt Monro (Parlophone)
-	25	YOU MAKE IT MOVE	Dave Dee, Dozy, Beaky, Mick & Tich (Fontana)
-	26	TILL THE END OF THE DAY	Kinks (Pye)
21	27	HERE IT COMES AGAIN	Fortunes (Decca)
22	27	TELL ME WHY	Elvis Presley (RCA)
-	29	MY GIRL	Otis Redding (Atlantic)
25	30	THE WAR LORD	Shadows (Columbia)

last week	this week	18 December 1965	
1	1	DAY TRIPPER/WE CAN WORK IT OUT	Beatles (Parlophone)
2	2	THE CARNIVAL IS OVER	Seekers (Columbia)
6	3	THE RIVER	Ken Dodd (Columbia)
3	4	1-2-3	Len Barry (Brunswick)
5	5	MY GENERATION	Who (Brunswick)
4	6	WIND ME UP (LET ME GO)	Cliff Richard (Columbia)
11	7	RESCUE ME	Fontella Bass (Chess)
8	8	TEARS	Ken Dodd (Columbia)
7	9	A LOVER'S CONCERTO	Toys (Stateside)
9	10	MARIA	P.J. Proby (Liberty)
12	11	LET'S HANG ON	Four Seasons (Philips)
14	12	TO WHOM IT CONCERNS	Chris Andrews (Decca)
17	13	MY SHIP IS COMING IN	Walker Brothers (Philips)
10	14	PRINCESS IN RAGS	Gene Pitney (Stateside)
20	15	KEEP ON RUNNING	Spencer Davis Group (Fontana)
15	16	GET OFF OF MY CLOUD	Rolling Stones (Decca)
15	17	POSITIVELY 4TH STREET	Bob Dylan (CBS)
18	18	IS IT REALLY OVER	Jim Reeves (RCA)
26	19	TILL THE END OF THE DAY	Kinks (Pye)
30	20	THE WAR LORD	Shadows (Columbia)
29	21	MY GIRL	Otis Redding (Atlantic)
27	22	TELL ME WHY	Elvis Presley (RCA)
25	23	YOU MAKE IT MOVE	Dave Dee, Dozy, Beaky, Mick & Tich (Fontana)
-	24	A MUST TO AVOID	Herman's Hermits (Columbia)
-	25	YOU'VE GOT TO BE CRUEL TO BE KIND	Unit 4 + 2 (Decca)
-	26	FAREWELL ANGELINA	Joan Baez (Fontana)
-	27	MERRY GENTLE POPS	Barron Knights (Columbia)
-	28	IF I NEEDED SOMEONE	Hollies (Parlophone)
-	29	THE VERY THOUGHT OF YOU	Tony Bennett (CBS)
-	30	IT WAS EASIER TO HURT HER	Wayne Fontana (Fontana)
-	30	TAKE ME FOR WHAT I'M WORTH	Searchers (Pye)

last week	this week	25 December 1965	
1	1	DAY TRIPPER/WE CAN WORK IT OUT	Beatles (Parlophone)
2	2	THE CARNIVAL IS OVER	Seekers (Columbia)
3	3	THE RIVER	Ken Dodd (Columbia)
6	4	WIND ME UP (LET ME GO)	Cliff Richard (Columbia)
4	5	1-2-3	Len Barry (Brunswick)
8	6	TEARS	Ken Dodd (Columbia)
15	7	KEEP ON RUNNING	Spencer Davis Group (Fontana)
13	7	MY SHIP IS COMING IN	Walker Brothers (Philips)
10	9	MARIA	P.J. Proby (Liberty)
7	10	RESCUE ME	Fontella Bass (Chess)
9	11	A LOVER'S CONCERTO	Toys (Stateside)
5	12	MY GENERATION	Who (Brunswick)
12	13	TO WHOM IT CONCERNS	Chris Andrews (Decca)
11	14	LET'S HANG ON	Four Seasons (Philips)
27	15	MERRY GENTLE POPS	Barron Knights (Columbia)
20	16	THE WAR LORD	Shadows (Columbia)
21	17	MY GIRL	Otis Redding (Atlantic)
14	18	PRINCESS IN RAGS	Gene Pitney (Stateside)
17	19	POSITIVELY 4TH STREET	Bob Dylan (CBS)
-	20	A HARD DAY'S NIGHT	Peter Sellers (Parlophone)
19	21	TILL THE END OF THE DAY	Kinks (Pye)
24	22	A MUST TO AVOID	Herman's Hermits (Columbia)
25	23	YOU'VE GOT TO BE CRUEL TO BE KIND	Unit 4 + 2 (Decca)
23	24	YOU MAKE IT MOVE	Dave Dee, Dozy, Beaky, Mick & Tich (Fontana)
22	25	TELL ME WHY	Elvis Presley (RCA)
-	26	SPANISH FLEA	Herb Alpert & the Tijuana Brass (Pye International)
-	27	I LEFT MY HEART IN SAN FRANCISCO	Tony Bennett (CBS)
-	28	THE WATER IS OVER MY HEAD	Rockin' Berries (Piccadilly)
26	29	FAREWELL ANGELINA	Joan Baez (Fontana)
16	30	GET OFF OF MY CLOUD	Rolling Stones (Decca)

For the first time the Beatles had a single with two nominated A-sides. The NME found it impossible from th outset to judge the comparative popularity of *Day Tripper* and *We Can Work It Out* (buyers were simply asking for 'the new Beatles single') so they were confined to one joint chart entry. The coupling sold over one million in the UK by early 1966, as did the New Seekers' *The Carnival Is Over*. Meanwhile Peter Sellers (as Richard III) personalised *A Hard Day's Night*.

The British Boom

The Beatles started what became an explosion of British groups in the early and mid-sixties. Beat groups doing other people's songs were followed by a generation of hugely talented songwriters who formed the nucleus of groups that were to take the world by storm.
The Rolling Stones opened up an audience for black R&B music made into classic pop. Bands like the Animals reaped the rewards, and the Who proudly dubbed their music 'Maximum R&B'. But these bands and others like the Kinks and the Small Faces brought a peculiarly English flavour to their music, which subsequently went down a storm in America.

Clockwise from top left: the Hollies; the Rolling Stones; the Who's Pete Townshend; Herman's Hermits

162

1 January 1966

Last	This	Title
1	1	DAY TRIPPER/WE CAN WORK IT OUT Beatles (Parlophone)
3	2	THE RIVER Ken Dodd (Columbia)
2	3	THE CARNIVAL IS OVER Seekers (Columbia)
7	4	KEEP ON RUNNING Spencer Davis Group (Fontana)
6	5	TEARS Ken Dodd (Columbia)
4	6	WIND ME UP (LET ME GO) Cliff Richard (Columbia)
10	7	RESCUE ME Fontella Bass (Chess)
8	8	MY SHIP IS COMING IN Walker Brothers (Philips)
9	9	1-2-3 Len Barry (Brunswick)
15	10	MERRY GENTLE POPS Barron Knights (Columbia)
14	11	LET'S HANG ON Four Seasons (Philips)
9	12	MARIA P.J. Proby (Liberty)
12	13	MY GENERATION Who (Brunswick)
13	14	TO WHOM IT CONCERNS Chris Andrews (Decca)
20	15	A HARD DAY'S NIGHT Peter Sellers (Parlophone)
21	16	TILL THE END OF THE DAY Kinks (Pye)
11	17	A LOVER'S CONCERTO Toys (Stateside)
22	18	A MUST TO AVOID Herman's Hermits (Columbia)
24	19	YOU MAKE IT MOVE Dave Dee, Dozy, Beaky, Mick & Tich (Fontana)
26	20	SPANISH FLEA Herb Alpert & the Tijuana Brass (Pye International)
17	21	MY GIRL Otis Redding (Atlantic)
27	22	I LEFT MY HEART IN SAN FRANCISCO Tony Bennett (CBS)
28	23	WATER IS OVER MY HEAD Rockin' Berries (Piccadilly)
-	24	YESTERDAY MAN Chris Andrews (Decca)
16	25	THE WAR LORD Shadows (Columbia)
-	26	IS IT REALLY OVER Jim Reeves (RCA)
23	27	YOU'VE GOT TO BE CRUEL TO BE KIND Unit 4 + 2 (Decca)
18	28	PRINCESS IN RAGS Gene Pitney (Stateside)
-	29	ENGLAND SWINGS Roger Miller (Philips)
-	30	THE VERY THOUGHT OF YOU Tony Bennett (CBS)

8 January 1966

Last	This	Title
1	1	DAY TRIPPER/WE CAN WORK IT OUT Beatles (Parlophone)
4	2	KEEP ON RUNNING Spencer Davis Group (Fontana)
2	3	THE RIVER Ken Dodd (Columbia)
3	4	THE CARNIVAL IS OVER Seekers (Columbia)
8	5	MY SHIP IS COMING IN Walker Brothers (Philips)
5	6	TEARS Ken Dodd (Columbia)
7	7	RESCUE ME Fontella Bass (Chess)
11	8	LET'S HANG ON Four Seasons (Philips)
6	9	WIND ME UP (LET ME GO) Cliff Richard (Columbia)
16	10	TILL THE END OF THE DAY Kinks (Pye)
10	11	MERRY GENTLE POPS Barron Knights (Columbia)
9	12	1-2-3 Len Barry (Brunswick)
13	13	MY GENERATION Who (Brunswick)
14	14	TO WHOM IT CONCERNS Chris Andrews (Decca)
15	15	A HARD DAY'S NIGHT Peter Sellers (Parlophone)
18	16	A MUST TO AVOID Herman's Hermits (Columbia)
12	17	MARIA P.J. Proby (Liberty)
20	18	SPANISH FLEA Herb Alpert & the Tijuana Brass (Pye International)
22	19	I LEFT MY HEART IN SAN FRANCISCO Tony Bennett (CBS)
-	20	BYE BYE BLUES Bert Kaempfert (Polydor)
29	21	ENGLAND SWINGS Roger Miller (Philips)
21	22	MY GIRL Otis Redding (Atlantic)
17	23	A LOVER'S CONCERTO Toys (Stateside)
-	24	IF I NEEDED SOMEONE Hollies (Parlophone)
19	25	YOU MAKE IT MOVE Dave Dee, Dozy, Beaky, Mick & Tich (Fontana)
30	26	THE VERY THOUGHT OF YOU Tony Bennett (CBS)
-	27	MIDNIGHT TO SIX MAN Pretty Things (Fontana)
-	28	HELLO, DOLLY! Bachelors (Decca)
28	29	PRINCESS IN RAGS Gene Pitney (Stateside)
24	30	YESTERDAY MAN Chris Andrews (Decca)

15 January 1966

Last	This	Title
2	1	KEEP ON RUNNING Spencer Davis Group (Fontana)
1	2	DAY TRIPPER/WE CAN WORK IT OUT Beatles (Parlophone)
3	3	THE RIVER Ken Dodd (Columbia)
5	4	MY SHIP IS COMING IN Walker Brothers (Philips)
4	5	THE CARNIVAL IS OVER Seekers (Columbia)
8	6	LET'S HANG ON Four Seasons (Philips)
18	7	SPANISH FLEA Herb Alpert & the Tijuana Brass (Pye International)
10	8	TILL THE END OF THE DAY Kinks (Pye)
16	9	A MUST TO AVOID Herman's Hermits (Columbia)
7	10	RESCUE ME Fontella Bass (Chess)
6	11	TEARS Ken Dodd (Columbia)
11	12	MERRY GENTLE POPS Barron Knights (Columbia)
9	13	WIND ME UP (LET ME GO) Cliff Richard (Columbia)
14	14	MY GIRL Otis Redding (Atlantic)
-	15	MICHELLE Overlanders (Pye)
15	16	A HARD DAY'S NIGHT Peter Sellers (Parlophone)
14	17	TO WHOM IT CONCERNS Chris Andrews (Decca)
12	18	1-2-3 Len Barry (Brunswick)
25	19	YOU MAKE IT MOVE Dave Dee, Dozy, Beaky, Mick & Tich (Fontana)
21	20	ENGLAND SWINGS Roger Miller (Philips)
-	21	YOU WERE ON MY MIND Crispian St. Peters (Decca)
13	22	MY GENERATION Who (Brunswick)
-	23	TAKE ME FOR WHAT I'M WORTH Searchers (Pye)
20	24	BYE BYE BLUES Bert Kaempfert (Polydor)
-	25	LIKE A BABY Len Barry (Brunswick)
-	26	MIRROR, MIRROR Pinkerton's Assorted Colours (Decca)
27	27	MIDNIGHT TO SIX MAN Pretty Things (Fontana)
24	28	IF I NEEDED SOMEONE Hollies (Parlophone)
-	29	SECOND HAND ROSE Barbra Streisand (CBS)
-	30	TAKE ME TO YOUR HEART AGAIN Vince Hill (Columbia)

22 January 1966

Last	This	Title
1	1	KEEP ON RUNNING Spencer Davis Group (Fontana)
2	2	DAY TRIPPER/WE CAN WORK IT OUT Beatles (Parlophone)
7	3	SPANISH FLEA Herb Alpert & the Tijuana Brass (Pye International)
15	4	MICHELLE Overlanders (Pye)
6	5	LET'S HANG ON Four Seasons (Philips)
4	6	MY SHIP IS COMING IN Walker Brothers (Philips)
9	7	A MUST TO AVOID Herman's Hermits (Columbia)
5	8	THE CARNIVAL IS OVER Seekers (Columbia)
3	9	THE RIVER Ken Dodd (Columbia)
8	10	TILL THE END OF THE DAY Kinks (Pye)
14	11	MY GIRL Otis Redding (Atlantic)
13	12	WIND ME UP (LET ME GO) Cliff Richard (Columbia)
10	13	RESCUE ME Fontella Bass (Chess)
-	14	LOVE'S JUST A BROKEN HEART Cilla Black (Parlophone)
-	15	MICHELLE David & Jonathan (Columbia)
11	16	TEARS Ken Dodd (Columbia)
25	17	LIKE A BABY Len Barry (Brunswick)
20	18	ENGLAND SWINGS Roger Miller (Philips)
23	19	TAKE ME FOR WHAT I'M WORTH Searchers (Pye)
21	20	YOU WERE ON MY MIND Crispian St. Peters (Decca)
29	21	SECOND HAND ROSE Barbra Streisand (CBS)
12	22	MERRY GENTLE POPS Barron Knights (Columbia)
18	23	1-2-3 Len Barry (Brunswick)
-	24	A GROOVY KIND OF LOVE Mindbenders (Fontana)
16	25	A HARD DAY'S NIGHT Peter Sellers (Parlophone)
26	26	MIRROR, MIRROR Pinkerton's Assorted Colours (Decca)
30	27	TAKE ME TO YOUR HEART AGAIN Vince Hill (Columbia)
17	28	TO WHOM IT CONCERNS Chris Andrews (Decca)
-	29	THE VERY THOUGHT OF YOU Tony Bennett (CBS)
19	30	YOU MAKE IT MOVE Dave Dee, Dozy, Beaky, Mick & Tich (Fontana)

The Spencer Davis Group, with the teenager Steve Winwood on lead vocals, began their big year in the strongest possible way by deposing the Beatles at the chart top. Bert Kaempfert, the German musician and producer, had been the first man to record the Beatles when they backed Tony Sheridan in Hamburg in 1961. He scored an instrumental hit with his orchestra with *Bye Bye Blues*. Herman's Hermits' *A Must To Avoid* was famed for its badly articulated chorus – the song was generally known as 'Muscular Boy'!

January – February 1966

Michelle was the most popular track on the Beatles' *Rubber Soul* album, and the obvious target of single cover versions. Former folk-style group the Overlanders got in first and had the Number One. David & Jonathan (otherwise songwriters Roger Cook and Roger Greenaway who had penned *You've Got Your Troubles* for the Fortunes) also made the Top Ten (and had the US Top 20 hit). Nancy Sinatra, daughter of Frank, had an international chart-topper with *These Boots Are Made For Walkin'*.

February – March 1966

26 February 1966

last week	this week	
1	1	19TH NERVOUS BREAKDOWN Rolling Stones (Decca)
2	2	THESE BOOTS ARE MADE FOR WALKIN' Nancy Sinatra (Reprise)
4	3	A GROOVY KIND OF LOVE Mindbenders (Fontana)
5	4	MY LOVE Petula Clark (Pye)
3	5	YOU WERE ON MY MIND Crispian St. Peters (Decca)
11	6	INSIDE LOOKING OUT Animals (Decca)
12	6	SHA-LA-LA-LA-LEE Small Faces (Decca)
15	8	BARBARA ANN Beach Boys (Capitol)
6	9	LOVE'S JUST A BROKEN HEART Cilla Black (Parlophone)
9	10	SPANISH FLEA Herb Alpert and the Tijuana Brass (Pye International)
27	11	BACKSTAGE Gene Pitney (Stateside)
8	12	MIRROR, MIRROR Pinkerton's Assorted Colours (Decca)
13	13	UPTIGHT (EVERYTHING'S ALRIGHT) Stevie Wonder (Tamla Motown)
10	14	TOMORROW Sandie Shaw (Pye)
7	15	MICHELLE Overlanders (Pye)
16	16	GIRL Truth (Pye)
-	17	LIGHTNIN' STRIKES Lou Christie (MGM)
24	18	MAKE THE WORLD GO AWAY Eddy Arnold (RCA)
17	19	LITTLE BY LITTLE Dusty Springfield (Philips)
24	20	THIS GOLDEN RING Fortunes (Decca)
14	20	SECOND HAND ROSE Barbra Streisand (CBS)
23	22	GET OUT OF MY LIFE WOMAN Lee Dorsey (Stateside)
21	22	YOU'VE COME BACK P.J. Proby (Liberty)
29	24	JENNY TAKE A RIDE Mitch Ryder and the Detroit Wheels (Stateside)
-	25	BLUE RIVER Elvis Presley (RCA)
-	26	WHAT NOW MY LOVE Sonny & Cher (Atlantic)
-	27	YOU DON'T LOVE ME Gary Walker (CBS)
-	28	I GOT YOU (I FEEL GOOD) James Brown (Pye International)
-	29	I CAN'T LET GO Hollies (Parlophone)
-	30	634-5789 Wilson Pickett (Atlantic)

5 March 1966

1	1	19TH NERVOUS BREAKDOWN Rolling Stones (Decca)
2	2	THESE BOOTS ARE MADE FOR WALKIN' Nancy Sinatra (Reprise)
3	3	A GROOVY KIND OF LOVE Mindbenders (Fontana)
6	4	SHA-LA-LA-LA-LEE Small Faces (Decca)
8	5	BARBARA ANN Beach Boys (Capitol)
4	6	MY LOVE Petula Clark (Pye)
6	7	INSIDE LOOKING OUT Animals (Decca)
11	8	BACKSTAGE Gene Pitney (Stateside)
17	9	LIGHTNIN' STRIKES Lou Christie (MGM)
29	10	I CAN'T LET GO Hollies (Parlophone)
18	11	MAKE THE WORLD GO AWAY Eddy Arnold (RCA)
5	12	YOU WERE ON MY MIND Crispian St. Peters (Decca)
10	13	SPANISH FLEA Herb Alpert and the Tijuana Brass (Pye International)
26	14	WHAT NOW MY LOVE Sonny & Cher (Atlantic)
20	15	THIS GOLDEN RING Fortunes (Decca)
-	16	THE SUN AIN'T GONNA SHINE ANYMORE Walker Brothers (Philips)
12	17	MIRROR, MIRROR Pinkerton's Assorted Colours (Decca)
13	18	UPTIGHT (EVERYTHING'S ALRIGHT) Stevie Wonder (Tamla Motown)
14	19	TOMORROW Sandie Shaw (Pye)
-	19	SHAPES OF THINGS Yardbirds (Columbia)
9	21	LOVE'S JUST A BROKEN HEART Cilla Black (Parlophone)
25	22	BLUE RIVER Elvis Presley (RCA)
24	22	JENNY TAKE A RIDE Mitch Ryder and the Detroit Wheels (Stateside)
16	24	GIRL Truth (Pye)
-	25	DEDICATED FOLLOWER OF FASHION Kinks (Pye)
19	25	LITTLE BY LITTLE Dusty Springfield (Philips)
22	27	GET OUT OF MY LIFE WOMAN Lee Dorsey (Stateside)
15	28	MICHELLE Overlanders (Pye)
27	29	YOU DON'T LOVE ME Gary Walker (CBS)
28	30	I GOT YOU (I FEEL GOOD) James Brown (Pye International)
-	30	BABY NEVER SAY GOODBYE Unit 4 + 2 (Decca)

12 March 1966

10	1	I CAN'T LET GO Hollies (Parlophone)
4	2	SHA-LA-LA-LA-LEE Small Faces (Decca)
3	3	A GROOVY KIND OF LOVE Mindbenders (Fontana)
5	4	BARBARA ANN Beach Boys (Capitol)
16	5	THE SUN AIN'T GONNA SHINE ANYMORE Walker Brothers (Philips)
8	6	BACKSTAGE Gene Pitney (Stateside)
2	7	THESE BOOTS ARE MADE FOR WALKIN' Nancy Sinatra (Reprise)
1	8	19TH NERVOUS BREAKDOWN Rolling Stones (Decca)
11	9	MAKE THE WORLD GO AWAY Eddy Arnold (RCA)
6	10	MY LOVE Petula Clark (Pye)
19	11	SHAPES OF THINGS Yardbirds (Columbia)
9	12	LIGHTNIN' STRIKES Lou Christie (MGM)
7	13	INSIDE LOOKING OUT Animals (Decca)
25	14	DEDICATED FOLLOWER OF FASHION Kinks (Pye)
12	15	YOU WERE ON MY MIND Crispian St. Peters (Decca)
13	16	SPANISH FLEA Herb Alpert and the Tijuana Brass (Pye International)
15	17	THIS GOLDEN RING Fortunes (Decca)
14	17	WHAT NOW MY LOVE Sonny & Cher (Atlantic)
22	19	BLUE RIVER Elvis Presley (RCA)
-	19	SUBSTITUTE Who (Reaction)
18	21	UPTIGHT (EVERYTHING'S ALRIGHT) Stevie Wonder (Tamla Motown)
-	22	HOLD TIGHT Dave Dee, Dozy, Beaky, Mick & Tich (Fontana)
17	23	MIRROR, MIRROR Pinkerton's Assorted Colours (Decca)
19	24	TOMORROW Sandie Shaw (Pye)
29	25	YOU DON'T LOVE ME Gary Walker (CBS)
30	26	I GOT YOU (I FEEL GOOD) James Brown (Pye International)
22	27	JENNY TAKE A RIDE Mitch Ryder and the Detroit Wheels (Stateside)
30	28	BABY NEVER SAY GOODBYE Unit 4 + 2 (Decca)
25	29	LITTLE BY LITTLE Dusty Springfield (Philips)
21	30	LOVE'S JUST A BROKEN HEART Cilla Black (Parlophone)

19 March 1966

5	1	THE SUN AIN'T GONNA SHINE ANYMORE Walker Brothers (Philips)
1	1	I CAN'T LET GO Hollies (Parlophone)
2	3	SHA-LA-LA-LA-LEE Small Faces (Decca)
4	4	BARBARA ANN Beach Boys (Capitol)
11	5	SHAPES OF THINGS Yardbirds (Columbia)
9	6	MAKE THE WORLD GO AWAY Eddy Arnold (RCA)
6	7	BACKSTAGE Gene Pitney (Stateside)
3	8	A GROOVY KIND OF LOVE Mindbenders (Fontana)
7	9	THESE BOOTS ARE MADE FOR WALKIN' Nancy Sinatra (Reprise)
14	10	DEDICATED FOLLOWER OF FASHION Kinks (Pye)
12	11	LIGHTNIN' STRIKES Lou Christie (MGM)
10	12	MY LOVE Petula Clark (Pye)
8	13	19TH NERVOUS BREAKDOWN Rolling Stones (Decca)
-	14	ELUSIVE BUTTERFLY Bob Lind (Fontana)
19	15	SUBSTITUTE Who (Reaction)
13	16	INSIDE LOOKING OUT Animals (Decca)
16	17	SPANISH FLEA Herb Alpert and the Tijuana Brass (Pye International)
26	18	I GOT YOU James Brown (Pye International)
-	19	ELUSIVE BUTTERFLY Val Doonican (Decca)
17	20	WHAT NOW MY LOVE Sonny & Cher (Atlantic)
19	21	BLUE RIVER Elvis Presley (RCA)
22	22	HOLD TIGHT Dave Dee, Dozy, Beaky, Mick & Tich (Fontana)
-	23	WOMAN Peter & Gordon (Columbia)
15	24	YOU WERE ON MY MIND Crispian St. Peters (Decca)
-	25	MAY EACH DAY Andy Williams (CBS)
17	26	THIS GOLDEN RING Fortunes (Decca)
-	27	LOVE ME WITH ALL OF YOUR HEART Bachelors (Decca)
-	28	THE SOUND OF SILENCE Bachelors (Decca)
25	29	YOU DON'T LOVE ME Gary Walker (CBS)
-	30	I MET A GIRL Shadows (Columbia)

The Beach Boys had their biggest UK success yet with *Barbara Ann* which was originally a throwaway track on a fairly disposable album, *Beach Boys Party*. An impromptu but infectious live workout of an old US doo-wop hit by the Regents, it featured Dean Torrance (of Jan & Dean) handling the lead vocal line. 1966 would be the Beach Boys' most successful year ever in the UK singles chart. The Walker Brothers had a second Number One with a revival of Frankie Valli's first (unsuccessful) solo single.

March – April 1966

last week	this week	26 March 1966
1	1	THE SUN AIN'T GONNA SHINE ANYMORE — Walker Brothers (Philips)
1	2	I CAN'T LET GO — Hollies (Parlophone)
6	3	MAKE THE WORLD GO AWAY — Eddy Arnold (RCA)
5	4	SHAPES OF THINGS — Yardbirds (Columbia)
4	5	BARBARA ANN — Beach Boys (Capitol)
10	6	DEDICATED FOLLOWER OF FASHION — Kinks (Pye)
14	7	ELUSIVE BUTTERFLY — Bob Lind (Fontana)
3	7	SHA-LA-LA-LEE — Small Faces (Decca)
7	9	BACKSTAGE — Gene Pitney (Stateside)
9	10	THESE BOOTS ARE MADE FOR WALKIN' — Nancy Sinatra (Reprise)
11	11	LIGHTNIN' STRIKES — Lou Christie (MGM)
19	12	ELUSIVE BUTTERFLY — Val Doonican (Decca)
8	13	A GROOVY KIND OF LOVE — Mindbenders (Fontana)
20	14	WHAT NOW MY LOVE — Sonny & Cher (Atlantic)
-	15	SOMEBODY HELP ME — Spencer Davis Group (Fontana)
28	16	THE SOUND OF SILENCE — Bachelors (Decca)
22	17	HOLD TIGHT — Dave Dee, Dozy, Beaky, Mick & Tich (Fontana)
15	17	SUBSTITUTE — Who (Reaction)
12	19	MY LOVE — Petula Clark (Pye)
-	20	BLUE TURNS TO GREY — Cliff Richard (Columbia)
27	21	LOVE ME WITH ALL OF YOUR HEART — Bachelors (Decca)
23	22	WOMAN — Peter & Gordon (Columbia)
13	23	19TH NERVOUS BREAKDOWN — Rolling Stones (Decca)
16	24	INSIDE LOOKING OUT — Animals (Decca)
17	25	SPANISH FLEA — Herb Alpert & the Tijuana Brass (Pye International)
18	25	I GOT YOU — James Brown (Pye International)
25	27	MAY EACH DAY — Andy Williams (CBS)
21	28	BLUE RIVER — Elvis Presley (RCA)
-	29	HEARTACHES — Vince Hill (Columbia)
30	30	I MET A GIRL — Shadows (Columbia)

		2 April 1966
1	1	THE SUN AIN'T GONNA SHINE ANYMORE — Walker Brothers (Philips)
2	2	I CAN'T LET GO — Hollies (Parlophone)
7	3	ELUSIVE BUTTERFLY — Bob Lind (Fontana)
3	4	MAKE THE WORLD GO AWAY — Eddy Arnold (RCA)
4	5	SHAPES OF THINGS — Yardbirds (Columbia)
6	6	DEDICATED FOLLOWER OF FASHION — Kinks (Pye)
15	7	SOMEBODY HELP ME — Spencer Davis Group (Fontana)
12	8	ELUSIVE BUTTERFLY — Val Doonican (Decca)
16	9	THE SOUND OF SILENCE — Bachelors (Decca)
5	10	BARBARA ANN — Beach Boys (Capitol)
17	11	HOLD TIGHT — Dave Dee, Dozy, Beaky, Mick & Tich (Fontana)
17	12	SUBSTITUTE — Who (Reaction)
7	13	SHA-LA-LA-LEE — Small Faces (Decca)
14	14	WHAT NOW MY LOVE — Sonny & Cher (Atlantic)
9	15	BACKSTAGE — Gene Pitney (Stateside)
10	16	THESE BOOTS ARE MADE FOR WALKIN' — Nancy Sinatra (Reprise)
-	17	BANG BANG (MY BABY SHOT ME DOWN) — Cher (Liberty)
11	18	LIGHTNIN' STRIKES — Lou Christie (MGM)
20	19	BLUE TURNS TO GREY — Cliff Richard (Columbia)
-	20	I PUT A SPELL ON YOU — Alan Price Set (Decca)
-	21	ALFIE — Cilla Black (Parlophone)
13	22	A GROOVY KIND OF LOVE — Mindbenders (Fontana)
-	23	YOU WON'T BE LEAVING — Herman's Hermits (Columbia)
-	24	SOME DAY ONE DAY — Seekers (Columbia)
25	25	YOU DON'T HAVE TO SAY YOU LOVE ME — Dusty Springfield (Philips)
19	26	MY LOVE — Petula Clark (Pye)
21	27	LOVE ME WITH ALL OF YOUR HEART — Bachelors (Decca)
-	28	SUPER GIRL — Graham Bonney (Columbia)
25	29	SPANISH FLEA — Herb Alpert & the Tijuana Brass (Pye International)
-	29	THAT'S NICE — Neil Christian (Strike)
-	29	THE BALLAD OF THE GREEN BERETS — Staff Sgt Barry Sadler (RCA)

		9 April 1966
1	1	THE SUN AIN'T GONNA SHINE ANYMORE — Walker Brothers (Philips)
7	2	SOMEBODY HELP ME — Spencer Davis Group (Fontana)
3	3	ELUSIVE BUTTERFLY — Bob Lind (Fontana)
6	4	DEDICATED FOLLOWER OF FASHION — Kinks (Pye)
11	5	HOLD TIGHT — Dave Dee, Dozy, Beaky, Mick & Tich (Fontana)
8	6	ELUSIVE BUTTERFLY — Val Doonican (Decca)
9	7	THE SOUND OF SILENCE — Bachelors (Decca)
2	8	I CAN'T LET GO — Hollies (Parlophone)
12	9	SUBSTITUTE — Who (Reaction)
5	10	SHAPES OF THINGS — Yardbirds (Columbia)
25	11	YOU DON'T HAVE TO SAY YOU LOVE ME — Dusty Springfield (Philips)
4	12	MAKE THE WORLD GO AWAY — Eddy Arnold (RCA)
17	13	BANG BANG (MY BABY SHOT ME DOWN) — Cher (Liberty)
21	14	ALFIE — Cilla Black (Parlophone)
20	15	I PUT A SPELL ON YOU — Alan Price Set (Decca)
10	16	BARBARA ANN — Beach Boys (Capitol)
14	17	WHAT NOW MY LOVE — Sonny & Cher (Atlantic)
19	18	BLUE TURNS TO GREY — Cliff Richard (Columbia)
-	19	THE PIED PIPER — Crispian St. Peters (Decca)
23	20	YOU WON'T BE LEAVING — Herman's Hermits (Columbia)
13	21	SHA-LA-LA-LEE — Small Faces (Decca)
16	22	THESE BOOTS ARE MADE FOR WALKIN' — Nancy Sinatra (Reprise)
15	23	BACKSTAGE — Gene Pitney (Stateside)
24	24	SOME DAY ONE DAY — Seekers (Columbia)
29	25	THAT'S NICE — Neil Christian (Strike)
18	25	LIGHTNIN' STRIKES — Lou Christie (MGM)
28	27	SUPER GIRL — Graham Bonney (Columbia)
-	28	DAYDREAM — Lovin' Spoonful (Pye International)
-	29	HOMEWARD BOUND — Simon & Garfunkel (CBS)
-	30	TWINKLE TOES — Roy Orbison (London)

		16 April 1966
2	1	SOMEBODY HELP ME — Spencer Davis Group (Fontana)
1	2	THE SUN AIN'T GONNA SHINE ANYMORE — Walker Brothers (Philips)
5	3	HOLD TIGHT — Dave Dee, Dozy, Beaky, Mick & Tich (Fontana)
11	4	YOU DON'T HAVE TO SAY YOU LOVE ME — Dusty Springfield (Philips)
7	5	THE SOUND OF SILENCE — Bachelors (Decca)
6	6	ELUSIVE BUTTERFLY — Val Doonican (Decca)
14	7	ALFIE — Cilla Black (Parlophone)
9	8	SUBSTITUTE — Who (Reaction)
13	9	BANG BANG (MY BABY SHOT ME DOWN) — Cher (Liberty)
3	10	ELUSIVE BUTTERFLY — Bob Lind (Fontana)
4	11	DEDICATED FOLLOWER OF FASHION — Kinks (Pye)
12	12	MAKE THE WORLD GO AWAY — Eddy Arnold (RCA)
15	13	I PUT A SPELL ON YOU — Alan Price Set (Decca)
19	14	THE PIED PIPER — Crispian St. Peters (Decca)
8	15	I CAN'T LET GO — Hollies (Parlophone)
10	16	SHAPES OF THINGS — Yardbirds (Columbia)
28	17	DAYDREAM — Lovin' Spoonful (Pye International)
24	18	SOME DAY ONE DAY — Seekers (Columbia)
18	19	BLUE TURNS TO GREY — Cliff Richard (Columbia)
29	20	HOMEWARD BOUND — Simon & Garfunkel (CBS)
16	21	BARBARA ANN — Beach Boys (Capitol)
25	22	THAT'S NICE — Neil Christian (Strike)
30	23	TWINKLE TOES — Roy Orbison (London)
-	24	BALLAD OF THE GREEN BERETS — Staff Sgt Barry Sadler (RCA)
17	24	WHAT NOW MY LOVE — Sonny & Cher (Atlantic)
27	26	SUPER GIRL — Graham Bonney (Columbia)
-	27	WALKIN' MY CAT NAMED DOG — Norma Tanega (Stateside)
21	28	SHA-LA-LA-LEE — Small Faces (Decca)
20	29	YOU WON'T BE LEAVING — Herman's Hermits (Columbia)
22	30	THESE BOOTS ARE MADE FOR WALKIN' — Nancy Sinatra (Reprise)

Two versions of the folky *Elusive Butterfly*, by its writer Bob Lind and Val Doonican, shared Top Ten honours. The Bachelors' version of *Sound Of Silence* succeeded where Simon & Garfunkel's US chart-topper had failed in Britain (and the Irish trio's B-side also made the 30). The Seekers entered with a song co-written by Paul Simon with their own Bruce Woodley, and Simon & Garfunkel themselves made chart amends with *Homeward Bound*, a song which Paul Simon penned while on tour in Britain.

23 April 1966

last week	this week	title
4	1	YOU DON'T HAVE TO SAY YOU LOVE ME — Dusty Springfield (Philips)
1	2	SOMEBODY HELP ME — Spencer Davis Group (Fontana)
3	3	HOLD TIGHT — Dave Dee, Dozy, Beaky, Mick & Tich (Fontana)
5	4	THE SOUND OF SILENCE — Bachelors (Decca)
9	5	BANG BANG (MY BABY SHOT ME DOWN) — Cher (Liberty)
2	6	THE SUN AIN'T GONNA SHINE ANYMORE — Walker Brothers (Philips)
8	7	SUBSTITUTE — Who (Reaction)
7	8	ALFIE — Cilla Black (Parlophone)
14	9	THE PIED PIPER — Crispian St. Peters (Decca)
17	10	DAYDREAM — Lovin' Spoonful (Pye International)
6	11	ELUSIVE BUTTERFLY — Val Doonican (Decca)
13	12	I PUT A SPELL ON YOU — Alan Price Set (Decca)
10	13	ELUSIVE BUTTERFLY — Bob Lind (Fontana)
11	14	DEDICATED FOLLOWER OF FASHION — Kinks (Pye)
20	15	HOMEWARD BOUND — Simon & Garfunkel (CBS)
18	16	SOME DAY ONE DAY — Seekers (Columbia)
12	17	MAKE THE WORLD GO AWAY — Eddy Arnold (RCA)
-	18	PRETTY FLAMINGO — Manfred Mann (HMV)
-	19	SLOOP JOHN B — Beach Boys (Capitol)
19	20	BLUE TURNS TO GREY — Cliff Richard (Columbia)
-	21	FRANKIE AND JOHNNY — Elvis Presley (RCA)
22	22	THAT'S NICE — Neil Christian (Strike)
29	23	YOU WON'T BE LEAVING — Herman's Hermits (Columbia)
-	24	SOMETHING ON MY MIND — Chris Andrews (Decca)
-	25	SHOTGUN WEDDING — Roy C (Island)
24	25	BALLAD OF THE GREEN BERETS — Staff Sgt Barry Sadler (RCA)
-	27	HIGHWAY CODE — Master Singers (Parlophone)
26	28	SUPER GIRL — Graham Bonney (Columbia)
16	29	SHAPES OF THINGS — Yardbirds (Columbia)
-	30	SOUL AND INSPIRATION — Righteous Brothers (Verve)
27	30	WALKIN' MY CAT NAMED DOG — Norma Tanega (Stateside)

30 April 1966

last week	this week	title
1	1	YOU DON'T HAVE TO SAY YOU LOVE ME — Dusty Springfield (Philips)
5	2	BANG BANG (MY BABY SHOT ME DOWN) — Cher (Liberty)
18	3	PRETTY FLAMINGO — Manfred Mann (HMV)
10	4	DAYDREAM — Lovin' Spoonful (Pye International)
3	5	HOLD TIGHT — Dave Dee, Dozy, Beaky, Mick & Tich (Fontana)
9	6	THE PIED PIPER — Crispian St. Peters (Decca)
2	7	SOMEBODY HELP ME — Spencer Davis Group (Fontana)
4	8	THE SOUND OF SILENCE — Bachelors (Decca)
8	9	ALFIE — Cilla Black (Parlophone)
7	10	SUBSTITUTE — Who (Reaction)
19	11	SLOOP JOHN B — Beach Boys (Capitol)
12	12	I PUT A SPELL ON YOU — Alan Price Set (Decca)
6	13	THE SUN AIN'T GONNA SHINE ANYMORE — Walker Brothers (Philips)
15	14	HOMEWARD BOUND — Simon & Garfunkel (CBS)
11	15	ELUSIVE BUTTERFLY — Val Doonican (Decca)
16	16	SOME DAY ONE DAY — Seekers (Columbia)
25	17	SHOTGUN WEDDING — Roy C (Island)
13	18	ELUSIVE BUTTERFLY — Bob Lind (Fontana)
14	19	DEDICATED FOLLOWER OF FASHION — Kinks (Pye)
21	20	FRANKIE AND JOHNNY — Elvis Presley (RCA)
30	20	SOUL AND INSPIRATION — Righteous Brothers (Verve)
27	22	HIGHWAY CODE — Master Singers (Parlophone)
17	23	MAKE THE WORLD GO AWAY — Eddy Arnold (RCA)
30	24	WALKIN' MY CAT NAMED DOG — Norma Tanega (Stateside)
22	25	THAT'S NICE — Neil Christian (Strike)
25	26	BALLAD OF THE GREEN BERETS — Staff Sgt Barry Sadler (RCA)
20	27	BLUE TURNS TO GREY — Cliff Richard (Columbia)
-	28	HOW DOES THAT GRAB YOU DARLIN' — Nancy Sinatra (Reprise)
-	29	TAKE IT OR LEAVE IT — Searchers (Pye)
-	30	A HARD DAY'S NIGHT — Ramsey Lewis Trio (Chess)
-	30	WALKIN' MY CAT NAMED DOG — Barry McGuire (RCA)

7 May 1966

last week	this week	title
3	1	PRETTY FLAMINGO — Manfred Mann (HMV)
1	2	YOU DON'T HAVE TO SAY YOU LOVE ME — Dusty Springfield (Philips)
4	3	DAYDREAM — Lovin' Spoonful (Pye International)
2	4	BANG BANG (MY BABY SHOT ME DOWN) — Cher (Liberty)
11	5	SLOOP JOHN B — Beach Boys (Capitol)
6	6	THE PIED PIPER — Crispian St. Peters (Decca)
5	7	HOLD TIGHT — Dave Dee, Dozy, Beaky, Mick & Tich (Fontana)
8	8	THE SOUND OF SILENCE — Bachelors (Decca)
9	9	ALFIE — Cilla Black (Parlophone)
7	10	SOMEBODY HELP ME — Spencer Davis Group (Fontana)
14	11	HOMEWARD BOUND — Simon & Garfunkel (CBS)
17	12	SHOTGUN WEDDING — Roy C (Island)
10	13	SUBSTITUTE — Who (Reaction)
16	14	SOME DAY ONE DAY — Seekers (Columbia)
12	15	I PUT A SPELL ON YOU — Alan Price Set (Decca)
15	16	ELUSIVE BUTTERFLY — Val Doonican (Decca)
20	17	SOUL AND INSPIRATION — Righteous Brothers (Verve)
23	18	MAKE THE WORLD GO AWAY — Eddy Arnold (RCA)
24	19	WALKIN' MY CAT NAMED DOG — Norma Tanega (Stateside)
28	20	HOW DOES THAT GRAB YOU DARLIN' — Nancy Sinatra (Reprise)
-	21	SORROW — Merseys (Fontana)
13	22	THE SUN AIN'T GONNA SHINE ANYMORE — Walker Brothers (Philips)
25	23	THAT'S NICE — Neil Christian (Strike)
-	24	COME ON HOME — Wayne Fontana (Fontana)
29	25	TAKE IT OR LEAVE IT — Searchers (Pye)
22	26	HIGHWAY CODE — Master Singers (Parlophone)
27	27	WILD THING — Troggs (Fontana)
-	28	SOMETHING ON MY MIND — Chris Andrews (Decca)
20	29	FRANKIE AND JOHNNY — Elvis Presley (RCA)
26	30	THE BALLAD OF THE GREEN BERETS — Staff Sgt Barry Sadler (RCA)

14 May 1966

last week	this week	title
1	1	PRETTY FLAMINGO — Manfred Mann (HMV)
3	2	DAYDREAM — Lovin' Spoonful (Pye International)
5	3	SLOOP JOHN B — Beach Boys (Capitol)
2	4	YOU DON'T HAVE TO SAY YOU LOVE ME — Dusty Springfield (Philips)
6	5	THE PIED PIPER — Crispian St. Peters (Decca)
4	6	BANG BANG (MY BABY SHOT ME DOWN) — Cher (Liberty)
12	7	SHOTGUN WEDDING — Roy C (Island)
7	8	HOLD TIGHT — Dave Dee, Dozy, Beaky, Mick & Tich (Fontana)
9	9	ALFIE — Cilla Black (Parlophone)
8	10	THE SOUND OF SILENCE — Bachelors (Decca)
11	11	HOMEWARD BOUND — Simon & Garfunkel (CBS)
27	12	WILD THING — Troggs (Fontana)
21	13	SORROW — Merseys (Fontana)
10	14	SOMEBODY HELP ME — Spencer Davis Group (Fontana)
17	15	SOUL AND INSPIRATION — Righteous Brothers (Verve)
14	16	SOME DAY ONE DAY — Seekers (Columbia)
-	16	HEY GIRL — Small Faces (Decca)
15	18	I PUT A SPELL ON YOU — Alan Price Set (Decca)
16	19	ELUSIVE BUTTERFLY — Val Doonican (Decca)
-	20	RAINY DAY WOMEN NOS. 12 & 35 — Bob Dylan (CBS)
13	21	SUBSTITUTE — Who (Reaction)
20	22	HOW DOES THAT GRAB YOU DARLIN' — Nancy Sinatra (Reprise)
19	23	WALKIN' MY CAT NAMED DOG — Norma Tanega (Stateside)
23	24	THAT'S NICE — Neil Christian (Strike)
24	25	COME ON HOME — Wayne Fontana (Fontana)
29	26	FRANKIE AND JOHNNY — Elvis Presley (RCA)
-	27	PROMISES — Ken Dodd (Columbia)
26	27	HIGHWAY CODE — Master Singers (Parlophone)
-	29	CALIFORNIA DREAMIN' — Mamas & Papas (RCA)
30	30	ONCE — Geneveve (CBS)
-	30	STRANGERS IN THE NIGHT — Frank Sinatra (Reprise)

Dusty Springfield finally had a Number One after several years of solo hits, while Manfred Mann topped the chart again for the first time since *Doo Wah Diddy Diddy*. Barry Sadler's *Green Berets* was a right-wing exhortation of America's fighting forces, and struck a major patriotic note in the US where it reportedly sold five million copies. UK reaction was more muted, with the Master Singers' acapella harmony rendition of excerpts from the *Highway Code* actually selling rather better.

May – June 1966

21 May 1966

last week	this week	
1	1	PRETTY FLAMINGO — Manfred Mann (HMV)
3	2	SLOOP JOHN B — Beach Boys (Capitol)
12	3	WILD THING — Troggs (Fontana)
2	4	DAYDREAM — Lovin' Spoonful (Pye International)
-	5	PAINT IT BLACK — Rolling Stones (Decca)
7	6	SHOTGUN WEDDING — Roy C (Island)
30	7	STRANGERS IN THE NIGHT — Frank Sinatra (Reprise)
4	8	YOU DON'T HAVE TO SAY YOU LOVE ME — Dusty Springfield (Philips)
13	9	SORROW — Merseys (Fontana)
20	10	RAINY DAY WOMEN NOS. 12 & 35 — Bob Dylan (CBS)
5	11	THE PIED PIPER — Crispian St. Peters (Decca)
-	12	MONDAY MONDAY — Mamas & Papas (RCA)
16	13	HEY GIRL — Small Faces (Decca)
6	14	BANG BANG (MY BABY SHOT ME DOWN) — Cher (Liberty)
27	15	PROMISES — Ken Dodd (Columbia)
8	16	HOLD TIGHT — Dave Dee, Dozy, Beaky, Mick & Tich (Fontana)
-	17	WHEN A MAN LOVES A WOMAN — Percy Sledge (Atlantic)
9	18	ALFIE — Cilla Black (Parlophone)
11	19	HOMEWARD BOUND — Simon & Garfunkel (CBS)
15	20	SOUL AND INSPIRATION — Righteous Brothers (Verve)
10	21	THE SOUND OF SILENCE — Bachelors (Decca)
25	22	COME ON HOME — Wayne Fontana (Fontana)
22	23	HOW DOES THAT GRAB YOU DARLIN' — Nancy Sinatra (Reprise)
30	24	ONCE — Geneveve (CBS)
29	25	CALIFORNIA DREAMIN' — Mamas & Papas (RCA)
18	26	I PUT A SPELL ON YOU — Alan Price Set (Decca)
-	27	I LOVE HER — Paul & Barry Ryan (Decca)
14	28	SOMEBODY HELP ME — Spencer Davis Group (Fontana)
19	29	ELUSIVE BUTTERFLY — Val Doonican (Decca)
-	29	CAN'T LIVE WITHOUT YOU — Mindbenders (Fontana)
16	29	SOME DAY ONE DAY — Seekers (Columbia)

28 May 1966

last week	this week	
5	1	PAINT IT BLACK — Rolling Stones (Decca)
3	2	WILD THING — Troggs (Fontana)
7	3	STRANGERS IN THE NIGHT — Frank Sinatra (Reprise)
1	4	PRETTY FLAMINGO — Manfred Mann (HMV)
2	5	SLOOP JOHN B — Beach Boys (Capitol)
9	6	SORROW — Merseys (Fontana)
12	7	MONDAY MONDAY — Mamas & Papas (RCA)
6	8	SHOTGUN WEDDING — Roy C (Island)
10	9	RAINY DAY WOMEN NOS. 12 & 35 — Bob Dylan (CBS)
4	10	DAYDREAM — Lovin' Spoonful (Pye International)
15	11	PROMISES — Ken Dodd (Columbia)
13	12	HEY GIRL — Small Faces (Decca)
17	13	WHEN A MAN LOVES A WOMAN — Percy Sledge (Atlantic)
8	14	YOU DON'T HAVE TO SAY YOU LOVE ME — Dusty Springfield (Philips)
11	15	THE PIED PIPER — Crispian St. Peters (Decca)
14	16	BANG BANG (MY BABY SHOT ME DOWN) — Cher (Liberty)
22	17	COME ON HOME — Wayne Fontana (Fontana)
-	18	NOTHING COMES EASY — Sandie Shaw (Pye)
27	19	I LOVE HER — Paul & Barry Ryan (Decca)
19	20	HOMEWARD BOUND — Simon & Garfunkel (CBS)
18	21	ALFIE — Cilla Black (Parlophone)
29	22	CAN'T LIVE WITHOUT YOU — Mindbenders (Fontana)
16	23	HOLD TIGHT — Dave Dee, Dozy, Beaky, Mick & Tich (Fontana)
25	24	CALIFORNIA DREAMIN' — Mamas & Papas (RCA)
23	25	HOW DOES THAT GRAB YOU DARLIN' — Nancy Sinatra (Reprise)
24	26	ONCE — Geneveve (CBS)
21	27	THE SOUND OF SILENCE — Bachelors (Decca)
20	28	SOUL AND INSPIRATION — Righteous Brothers (Verve)
-	29	THAT'S NICE — Neil Christian (Strike)
-	30	HIGHWAY CODE — Master Singers (Parlophone)

4 June 1966

last week	this week	
3	1	STRANGERS IN THE NIGHT — Frank Sinatra (Reprise)
1	2	PAINT IT BLACK — Rolling Stones (Decca)
2	3	WILD THING — Troggs (Fontana)
7	4	MONDAY MONDAY — Mamas & Papas (RCA)
6	5	SORROW — Merseys (Fontana)
4	6	PRETTY FLAMINGO — Manfred Mann (HMV)
5	7	SLOOP JOHN B — Beach Boys (Capitol)
13	8	WHEN A MAN LOVES A WOMAN — Percy Sledge (Atlantic)
11	9	PROMISES — Ken Dodd (Columbia)
8	10	SHOTGUN WEDDING — Roy C (Island)
9	11	RAINY DAY WOMEN NOS. 12 & 35 — Bob Dylan (CBS)
12	12	HEY GIRL — Small Faces (Decca)
10	13	DAYDREAM — Lovin' Spoonful (Pye International)
17	14	COME ON HOME — Wayne Fontana (Fontana)
18	15	NOTHING COMES EASY — Sandie Shaw (Pye)
15	16	THE PIED PIPER — Crispian St. Peters (Decca)
-	17	DON'T BRING ME DOWN — Animals (Decca)
19	18	I LOVE HER — Paul & Barry Ryan (Decca)
14	19	YOU DON'T HAVE TO SAY YOU LOVE ME — Dusty Springfield (Philips)
16	20	BANG BANG (MY BABY SHOT ME DOWN) — Cher (Liberty)
	21	NOT RESPONSIBLE — Tom Jones (Decca)
22	22	CAN'T LIVE WITHOUT YOU — Mindbenders (Fontana)
23	23	HOLD TIGHT — Dave Dee, Dozy, Beaky, Mick & Tich (Fontana)
-	23	STOP HER ON SIGHT — Edwin Starr (Polydor)
20	25	HOMEWARD BOUND — Simon & Garfunkel (CBS)
21	26	ALFIE — Cilla Black (Parlophone)
24	27	CALIFORNIA DREAMIN' — Mamas & Papas (RCA)
-	28	EIGHT MILES HIGH — Byrds (CBS)
28	29	SOUL AND INSPIRATION — Righteous Brothers (Verve)
-	30	TWINKIE LEE — Gary Walker (CBS)
-	30	OVER UNDER SIDEWAYS DOWN — Yardbirds (Columbia)

11 June 1966

last week	this week	
1	1	STRANGERS IN THE NIGHT — Frank Sinatra (Reprise)
2	2	PAINT IT BLACK — Rolling Stones (Decca)
4	3	MONDAY MONDAY — Mamas & Papas (RCA)
3	4	WILD THING — Troggs (Fontana)
5	5	SORROW — Merseys (Fontana)
8	6	WHEN A MAN LOVES A WOMAN — Percy Sledge (Atlantic)
9	7	PROMISES — Ken Dodd (Columbia)
17	8	DON'T BRING ME DOWN — Animals (Decca)
7	9	SLOOP JOHN B — Beach Boys (Capitol)
11	10	RAINY DAY WOMEN NOS. 12 & 35 — Bob Dylan (CBS)
6	11	PRETTY FLAMINGO — Manfred Mann (HMV)
10	12	SHOTGUN WEDDING — Roy C (Island)
12	13	HEY GIRL — Small Faces (Decca)
-	14	DON'T ANSWER ME — Cilla Black (Parlophone)
30	15	OVER UNDER SIDEWAYS DOWN — Yardbirds (Columbia)
15	16	NOTHING COMES EASY — Sandie Shaw (Pye)
14	17	COME ON HOME — Wayne Fontana (Fontana)
-	18	RIVER DEEP - MOUNTAIN HIGH — Ike & Tina Turner (London)
-	19	NOBODY NEEDS YOUR LOVE — Gene Pitney (Stateside)
19	20	YOU DON'T HAVE TO SAY YOU LOVE ME — Dusty Springfield (Philips)
21	21	NOT RESPONSIBLE — Tom Jones (Decca)
-	22	SUNNY AFTERNOON — Kinks (Pye)
23	23	STOP HER ON SIGHT — Edwin Starr (Polydor)
13	24	DAYDREAM — Lovin' Spoonful (Pye International)
18	25	I LOVE HER — Paul & Barry Ryan (Decca)
16	26	THE PIED PIPER — Crispian St. Peters (Decca)
30	27	TWINKIE LEE — Gary Walker (CBS)
-	28	SWEET TALKIN' GUY — Chiffons (Stateside)
-	29	OPUS 17 (DON'T YOU WORRY 'BOUT ME) — Four Seasons (Philips)
22	30	CAN'T LIVE WITHOUT YOU — Mindbenders (Fontana)

With daughter Nancy turning out the hits, it seemed appropriate that Frank Sinatra should return to the singles chart. *Strangers In The Night* was the theme to the film *A Man Could Get Killed*, composed by Bert Kaempfert who was having a good year in the charts. The tune's publisher had noted the hit potential of the originally instrumental theme, and commissioned lyrics from Eddie Snyder and Charles Singleton specifically with Sinatra in mind. It was his first UK chart-topper since 1954.

last week	this week	18 June 1966		25 June 1966		2 July 1966		9 July 1966

18 June 1966

last	this		
1	1	STRANGERS IN THE NIGHT	Frank Sinatra (Reprise)
-	2	PAPERBACK WRITER	Beatles (Parlophone)
3	3	MONDAY MONDAY	Mamas & Papas (RCA)
2	4	PAINT IT BLACK	Rolling Stones (Decca)
5	5	SORROW	Merseys (Fontana)
8	6	DON'T BRING ME DOWN	Animals (Decca)
6	7	WHEN A MAN LOVES A WOMAN	Percy Sledge (Atlantic)
4	8	WILD THING	Troggs (Fontana)
14	9	DON'T ANSWER ME	Cilla Black (Parlophone)
22	10	SUNNY AFTERNOON	Kinks (Pye)
7	11	PROMISES	Ken Dodd (Columbia)
18	12	RIVER DEEP - MOUNTAIN HIGH	Ike & Tina Turner (London)
9	13	SLOOP JOHN B	Beach Boys (Capitol)
15	14	OVER UNDER SIDEWAYS DOWN	Yardbirds (Columbia)
19	15	NOBODY NEEDS YOUR LOVE	Gene Pitney (Stateside)
10	16	RAINY DAY WOMEN NOS. 12 & 35	Bob Dylan (CBS)
16	17	NOTHING COMES EASY	Sandie Shaw (Pye)
13	17	HEY GIRL	Small Faces (Decca)
12	19	SHOTGUN WEDDING	Roy C (Island)
11	20	PRETTY FLAMINGO	Manfred Mann (HMV)
17	21	COME ON HOME	Wayne Fontana (Fontana)
-	22	HIDEAWAY	Dave Dee, Dozy, Beaky, Mick & Tich (Fontana)
21	23	NOT RESPONSIBLE	Tom Jones (Decca)
23	24	STOP HER ON SIGHT	Edwin Starr (Polydor)
29	25	OPUS 17 (DON'T YOU WORRY 'BOUT ME)	Four Seasons (Philips)
-	26	IT'S A MAN'S MAN'S MAN'S WORLD	James Brown (Pye International)
28	27	SWEET TALKIN' GUY	Chiffons (Stateside)
27	28	TWINKIE LEE	Gary Walker (CBS)
-	29	LANA	Roy Orbison (London)
-	30	LADY JANE	David Garrick (Piccadilly)

25 June 1966

2	1	PAPERBACK WRITER	Beatles (Parlophone)
1	2	STRANGERS IN THE NIGHT	Frank Sinatra (Reprise)
3	3	MONDAY MONDAY	Mamas & Papas (RCA)
10	4	SUNNY AFTERNOON	Kinks (Pye)
9	5	DON'T ANSWER ME	Cilla Black (Parlophone)
12	6	RIVER DEEP - MOUNTAIN HIGH	Ike & Tina Turner (London)
15	7	NOBODY NEEDS YOUR LOVE	Gene Pitney (Stateside)
7	8	WHEN A MAN LOVES A WOMAN	Percy Sledge (Atlantic)
11	9	PROMISES	Ken Dodd (Columbia)
5	10	SORROW	Merseys (Fontana)
4	11	PAINT IT BLACK	Rolling Stones (Decca)
6	12	DON'T BRING ME DOWN	Animals (Decca)
14	13	OVER UNDER SIDEWAYS DOWN	Yardbirds (Columbia)
22	14	HIDEAWAY	Dave Dee, Dozy, Beaky, Mick & Tich (Fontana)
8	15	WILD THING	Troggs (Fontana)
13	16	SLOOP JOHN B	Beach Boys (Capitol)
26	17	IT'S A MAN'S MAN'S MAN'S WORLD	James Brown (Pye International)
-	18	GET AWAY	Georgie Fame & the Blue Flames (Columbia)
-	19	BUS STOP	Hollies (Parlophone)
29	20	LANA	Roy Orbison (London)
25	21	OPUS 17 (DON'T YOU WORRY 'BOUT ME)	Four Seasons (Philips)
17	22	NOTHING COMES EASY	Sandie Shaw (Pye)
-	23	I NEED YOU (EP)	Walker Brothers (Philips)
30	24	LADY JANE	David Garrick (Piccadilly)
23	25	NOT RESPONSIBLE	Tom Jones (Decca)
-	26	I AM A ROCK	Simon & Garfunkel (CBS)
21	27	COME ON HOME	Wayne Fontana (Fontana)
19	28	SHOTGUN WEDDING	Roy C (Island)
20	29	PRETTY FLAMINGO	Manfred Mann (HMV)
-	30	SITTIN' ON A FENCE	Twice As Much (Immediate)

2 July 1966

1	1	PAPERBACK WRITER	Beatles (Parlophone)
2	2	STRANGERS IN THE NIGHT	Frank Sinatra (Reprise)
4	3	SUNNY AFTERNOON	Kinks (Pye)
7	4	NOBODY NEEDS YOUR LOVE	Gene Pitney (Stateside)
6	5	RIVER DEEP - MOUNTAIN HIGH	Ike & Tina Turner (London)
19	6	BUS STOP	Hollies (Parlophone)
5	7	DON'T ANSWER ME	Cilla Black (Parlophone)
8	8	WHEN A MAN LOVES A WOMAN	Percy Sledge (Atlantic)
18	9	GET AWAY	Georgie Fame & the Blue Flames (Columbia)
3	10	MONDAY MONDAY	Mamas & Papas (RCA)
14	11	HIDEAWAY	Dave Dee, Dozy, Beaky, Mick & Tich (Fontana)
9	12	PROMISES	Ken Dodd (Columbia)
13	13	OVER UNDER SIDEWAYS DOWN	Yardbirds (Columbia)
12	14	DON'T BRING ME DOWN	Animals (Decca)
10	15	SORROW	Merseys (Fontana)
20	16	LANA	Roy Orbison (London)
17	17	IT'S A MAN'S MAN'S MAN'S WORLD	James Brown (Pye International)
11	18	PAINT IT BLACK	Rolling Stones (Decca)
-	19	I COULDN'T LIVE WITHOUT YOUR LOVE	Petula Clark (Pye)
16	20	SLOOP JOHN B	Beach Boys (Capitol)
21	21	OPUS 17 (DON'T YOU WORRY 'BOUT ME)	Four Seasons (Philips)
23	22	I NEED YOU (EP)	Walker Brothers (Philips)
-	23	OUT OF TIME	Chris Farlowe (Immediate)
15	24	WILD THING	Troggs (Fontana)
-	25	THIS DOOR SWINGS BOTH WAYS	Herman's Hermits (Columbia)
26	26	I AM A ROCK	Simon & Garfunkel (CBS)
27	27	BLACK IS BLACK	Los Bravos (Decca)
-	28	THE MORE I SEE YOU	Chris Montez (Pye International)
-	29	MAMA	Dave Berry (Decca)
28	30	SHOTGUN WEDDING	Roy C (Island)

9 July 1966

3	1	SUNNY AFTERNOON	Kinks (Pye)
4	2	NOBODY NEEDS YOUR LOVE	Gene Pitney (Stateside)
6	3	BUS STOP	Hollies (Parlophone)
1	4	PAPERBACK WRITER	Beatles (Parlophone)
5	5	RIVER DEEP - MOUNTAIN HIGH	Ike & Tina Turner (London)
2	6	STRANGERS IN THE NIGHT	Frank Sinatra (Reprise)
9	7	GET AWAY	Georgie Fame & the Blue Flames (Columbia)
11	8	HIDEAWAY	Dave Dee, Dozy, Beaky, Mick & Tich (Fontana)
19	9	I COULDN'T LIVE WITHOUT YOUR LOVE	Petula Clark (Pye)
8	10	WHEN A MAN LOVES A WOMAN	Percy Sledge (Atlantic)
7	11	DON'T ANSWER ME	Cilla Black (Parlophone)
10	12	MONDAY MONDAY	Mamas & Papas (RCA)
23	13	OUT OF TIME	Chris Farlowe (Immediate)
16	14	LANA	Roy Orbison (London)
28	15	THE MORE I SEE YOU	Chris Montez (Pye International)
13	16	OVER UNDER SIDEWAYS DOWN	Yardbirds (Columbia)
27	17	BLACK IS BLACK	Los Bravos (Decca)
17	18	IT'S A MAN'S MAN'S MAN'S WORLD	James Brown (Pye International)
-	19	GOIN' BACK	Dusty Springfield (Philips)
12	20	PROMISES	Ken Dodd (Columbia)
25	21	THIS DOOR SWINGS BOTH WAYS	Herman's Hermits (Columbia)
-	22	LOVE LETTERS	Elvis Presley (RCA)
14	23	DON'T BRING ME DOWN	Animals (Decca)
26	24	I AM A ROCK	Simon & Garfunkel (CBS)
15	25	SORROW	Merseys (Fontana)
22	26	I NEED YOU (EP)	Walker Brothers (Philips)
-	27	SITTIN' ON A FENCE	Twice As Much (Immediate)
21	28	OPUS 17 (DON'T YOU WORRY 'BOUT ME)	Four Seasons (Philips)
20	29	SLOOP JOHN B	Beach Boys (Capitol)
29	29	MAMA	Dave Berry (Decca)

The strength of Sinatra's chart-topper prevented the Beatles from scoring their customary first-week Number One entry with *Paperback Writer*. Ike & Tina Turner made the Top Five with *River Deep – Mountain High*, a disc which had scored only minimally in the US and caused the producer Phil Spector – who saw it as a magnum opus – to virtually close down his Philles record label and temporarily retire. Chis Montez returned after being absent since *Some Kinda Fun* in 1963.

July – August 1966

16 July 1966

last week	this week	Title	Artist
1	1	SUNNY AFTERNOON	Kinks (Pye)
2	2	NOBODY NEEDS YOUR LOVE	Gene Pitney (Stateside)
7	3	GET AWAY	Georgie Fame & the Blue Flames (Columbia)
5	4	RIVER DEEP - MOUNTAIN HIGH	Ike & Tina Turner (London)
3	5	BUS STOP	Hollies (Parlophone)
13	6	OUT OF TIME	Chris Farlowe (Immediate)
9	7	I COULDN'T LIVE WITHOUT YOUR LOVE	Petula Clark (Pye)
6	8	STRANGERS IN THE NIGHT	Frank Sinatra (Reprise)
4	9	PAPERBACK WRITER	Beatles (Parlophone)
17	10	BLACK IS BLACK	Los Bravos (Decca)
8	11	HIDEAWAY	Dave Dee, Dozy, Beaky, Mick & Tich (Fontana)
22	12	LOVE LETTERS	Elvis Presley (RCA)
15	13	THE MORE I SEE YOU	Chris Montez (Pye International)
19	14	GOIN' BACK	Dusty Springfield (Philips)
10	15	WHEN A MAN LOVES A WOMAN	Percy Sledge (Atlantic)
11	16	DON'T ANSWER ME	Cilla Black (Parlophone)
14	17	LANA	Roy Orbison (London)
12	18	MONDAY MONDAY	Mamas & Papas (RCA)
--	19	WITH A GIRL LIKE YOU	Troggs (Fontana)
18	20	IT'S A MAN'S MAN'S MAN'S WORLD	James Brown (Pye International)
--	21	(BABY) YOU DON'T HAVE TO TELL ME	Walker Brothers (Philips)
29	22	MAMA	Dave Berry (Decca)
27	23	SITTIN' ON A FENCE	Twice As Much (Immediate)
20	24	PROMISES	Ken Dodd (Columbia)
21	25	THIS DOOR SWINGS BOTH WAYS	Herman's Hermits (Columbia)
29	26	SLOOP JOHN B	Beach Boys (Capitol)
24	26	I AM A ROCK	Simon & Garfunkel (CBS)
-	28	A PLACE IN THE SUN	Shadows (Columbia)
-	29	CAN I TRUST YOU	Bachelors (Decca)
26	30	I NEED YOU (EP)	Walker Brothers (Philips)

23 July 1966

last week	this week	Title	Artist
6	1	OUT OF TIME	Chris Farlowe (Immediate)
1	2	SUNNY AFTERNOON	Kinks (Pye)
3	3	GET AWAY	Georgie Fame & the Blue Flames (Columbia)
10	4	BLACK IS BLACK	Los Bravos (Decca)
4	5	RIVER DEEP - MOUNTAIN HIGH	Ike & Tina Turner (London)
2	6	NOBODY NEEDS YOUR LOVE	Gene Pitney (Stateside)
7	7	I COULDN'T LIVE WITHOUT YOUR LOVE	Petula Clark (Pye)
19	8	WITH A GIRL LIKE YOU	Troggs (Fontana)
13	9	THE MORE I SEE YOU	Chris Montez (Pye International)
5	10	BUS STOP	Hollies (Parlophone)
12	11	LOVE LETTERS	Elvis Presley (RCA)
14	12	GOIN' BACK	Dusty Springfield (Philips)
8	13	STRANGERS IN THE NIGHT	Frank Sinatra (Reprise)
21	14	(BABY) YOU DON'T HAVE TO TELL ME	Walker Brothers (Philips)
11	15	HIDEAWAY	Dave Dee, Dozy, Beaky, Mick & Tich (Fontana)
9	16	PAPERBACK WRITER	Beatles (Parlophone)
22	17	MAMA	Dave Berry (Decca)
17	18	LANA	Roy Orbison (London)
-	19	SUMMER IN THE CITY	Lovin' Spoonful (Kama Sutra)
16	20	DON'T ANSWER ME	Cilla Black (Parlophone)
-	21	VISIONS	Cliff Richard (Columbia)
15	22	WHEN A MAN LOVES A WOMAN	Percy Sledge (Atlantic)
23	23	SITTIN' ON A FENCE	Twice As Much (Immediate)
26	24	I AM A ROCK	Simon & Garfunkel (CBS)
28	25	A PLACE IN THE SUN	Shadows (Columbia)
-	26	HI-LILI, HI-LO	Alan Price Set (Decca)
25	27	THIS DOOR SWINGS BOTH WAYS	Herman's Hermits (Columbia)
20	28	IT'S A MAN'S MAN'S MAN'S WORLD	James Brown (Pye International)
18	29	MONDAY MONDAY	Mamas & Papas (RCA)
24	30	PROMISES	Ken Dodd (Columbia)
-	30	OOPS	Neil Christian (Strike)

30 July 1966

last week	this week	Title	Artist
1	1	OUT OF TIME	Chris Farlowe (Immediate)
8	2	WITH A GIRL LIKE YOU	Troggs (Fontana)
4	3	BLACK IS BLACK	Los Bravos (Decca)
3	4	GET AWAY	Georgie Fame & the Blue Flames (Columbia)
9	5	THE MORE I SEE YOU	Chris Montez (Pye International)
2	6	SUNNY AFTERNOON	Kinks (Pye)
7	7	I COULDN'T LIVE WITHOUT YOUR LOVE	Petula Clark (Pye)
11	8	LOVE LETTERS	Elvis Presley (RCA)
6	9	NOBODY NEEDS YOUR LOVE	Gene Pitney (Stateside)
5	10	RIVER DEEP - MOUNTAIN HIGH	Ike & Tina Turner (London)
12	11	GOIN' BACK	Dusty Springfield (Philips)
10	12	BUS STOP	Hollies (Parlophone)
17	13	MAMA	Dave Berry (Decca)
14	14	(BABY) YOU DON'T HAVE TO TELL ME	Walker Brothers (Philips)
19	15	SUMMER IN THE CITY	Lovin' Spoonful (Kama Sutra)
13	16	STRANGERS IN THE NIGHT	Frank Sinatra (Reprise)
21	17	VISIONS	Cliff Richard (Columbia)
26	18	HI-LILI, HI-LO	Alan Price Set (Decca)
-	19	GOD ONLY KNOWS	Beach Boys (Capitol)
15	20	HIDEAWAY	Dave Dee, Dozy, Beaky, Mick & Tich (Fontana)
-	21	I WANT YOU	Bob Dylan (CBS)
-	22	I LOVE HOW YOU LOVE ME	Paul & Barry Ryan (Decca)
16	23	PAPERBACK WRITER	Beatles (Parlophone)
18	23	LANA	Roy Orbison (London)
-	25	CAN I TRUST YOU	Bachelors (Decca)
-	26	LOVERS OF THE WORLD UNITE	David & Jonathan (Columbia)
22	27	WHEN A MAN LOVES A WOMAN	Percy Sledge (Atlantic)
30	28	PROMISES	Ken Dodd (Columbia)
27	29	THIS DOOR SWINGS BOTH WAYS	Herman's Hermits (Columbia)
28	30	IT'S A MAN'S MAN'S MAN'S WORLD	James Brown (Pye International)

6 August 1966

last week	this week	Title	Artist
2	1	WITH A GIRL LIKE YOU	Troggs (Fontana)
1	2	OUT OF TIME	Chris Farlowe (Immediate)
3	3	BLACK IS BLACK	Los Bravos (Decca)
5	4	THE MORE I SEE YOU	Chris Montez (Pye International)
8	5	LOVE LETTERS	Elvis Presley (RCA)
4	6	GET AWAY	Georgie Fame & the Blue Flames (Columbia)
13	7	MAMA	Dave Berry (Decca)
7	8	I COULDN'T LIVE WITHOUT YOUR LOVE	Petula Clark (Pye)
6	9	SUNNY AFTERNOON	Kinks (Pye)
15	10	SUMMER IN THE CITY	Lovin' Spoonful (Kama Sutra)
9	10	NOBODY NEEDS YOUR LOVE	Gene Pitney (Stateside)
11	12	GOIN' BACK	Dusty Springfield (Philips)
19	13	GOD ONLY KNOWS	Beach Boys (Capitol)
17	14	VISIONS	Cliff Richard (Columbia)
10	15	RIVER DEEP - MOUNTAIN HIGH	Ike & Tina Turner (London)
18	16	HI-LILI, HI-LO	Alan Price Set (Decca)
14	17	(BABY) YOU DON'T HAVE TO TELL ME	Walker Brothers (Philips)
16	18	STRANGERS IN THE NIGHT	Frank Sinatra (Reprise)
12	19	BUS STOP	Hollies (Parlophone)
-	20	I SAW HER AGAIN	Mamas & Papas (RCA)
22	21	I LOVE HOW YOU LOVE ME	Paul & Barry Ryan (Decca)
-	22	LOVING YOU IS SWEETER THAN EVER	Four Tops (Tamla Motown)
21	23	I WANT YOU	Bob Dylan (CBS)
26	24	LOVERS OF THE WORLD UNITE	David & Jonathan (Columbia)
-	25	AIN'T TOO PROUD TO BEG	Temptations (Tamla Motown)
-	26	MORE THAN LOVE	Ken Dodd (Columbia)
-	26	WARM AND TENDER LOVE	Percy Sledge (Atlantic)
23	28	PAPERBACK WRITER	Beatles (Parlophone)
28	29	PROMISES	Ken Dodd (Columbia)
-	29	GIVE ME YOUR WORD	Billy Fury (Decca)

The Walker Brothers' *(Baby) You Don't Have To Tell Me* briefly gave the trio two simultaneous hits, while their EP *I Need You* continued to sell. But the single proved not to have the strength to be a good follow-up to *Sun Ain't Gonna Shine*. On the other hand the Troggs' *Wild Thing* follow-up, *With A Girl Like You*, went one better than its predecessor and made Number One – at precisely the same time that *Wild Thing* topped the US chart. Percy Sledge was to come back into the chart with the same song 25 years later.

August – September 1966

13 August 1966

last week	this week	
1	1	WITH A GIRL LIKE YOU Troggs (Fontana)
-	2	YELLOW SUBMARINE/ELEANOR RIGBY Beatles (Parlophone)
3	3	BLACK IS BLACK Los Bravos (Decca)
4	4	THE MORE I SEE YOU Chris Montez (Pye International)
7	5	MAMA Dave Berry (Decca)
2	6	OUT OF TIME Chris Farlowe (Immediate)
13	7	GOD ONLY KNOWS Beach Boys (Capitol)
5	8	LOVE LETTERS Elvis Presley (RCA)
10	9	SUMMER IN THE CITY Lovin' Spoonful (Kama Sutra)
14	10	VISIONS Cliff Richard (Columbia)
8	11	I COULDN'T LIVE WITHOUT YOUR LOVE Petula Clark (Pye)
16	12	HI-LILI, HI-LO Alan Price Set (CBS)
12	13	GOIN' BACK Dusty Springfield (Philips)
6	14	GET AWAY Georgie Fame & the Blue Flames (Columbia)
9	15	SUNNY AFTERNOON Kinks (Pye)
20	16	I SAW HER AGAIN Mamas & Papas (RCA)
-	17	THEY'RE COMING TO TAKE ME AWAY, HA-HAAA! Napoleon XIV (Warner Brothers)
23	18	I WANT YOU Bob Dylan (CBS)
24	19	LOVERS OF THE WORLD UNITE David & Jonathan (Columbia)
18	20	STRANGERS IN THE NIGHT Frank Sinatra (Reprise)
10	21	NOBODY NEEDS YOUR LOVE Gene Pitney (Stateside)
26	22	MORE THAN LOVE Ken Dodd (Columbia)
21	23	I LOVE HOW YOU LOVE ME Paul & Barry Ryan (Decca)
15	24	RIVER DEEP - MOUNTAIN HIGH Ike & Tina Turner (London)
-	25	REVOLVER (LP) Beatles (Parlophone)
17	26	(BABY) YOU DON'T HAVE TO TELL ME Walker Brothers (Philips)
22	27	LOVING YOU IS SWEETER THAN EVER Four Tops (Tamla Motown)
25	28	AIN'T TOO PROUD TO BEG Temptations (Tamla Motown)
19	29	BUS STOP Hollies (Parlophone)
-	30	JUST LIKE A WOMAN Manfred Mann (HMV)

20 August 1966

last week	this week	
2	1	YELLOW SUBMARINE/ELEANOR RIGBY Beatles (Parlophone)
1	2	WITH A GIRL LIKE YOU Troggs (Fontana)
7	3	GOD ONLY KNOWS Beach Boys (Capitol)
5	4	MAMA Dave Berry (Decca)
3	5	BLACK IS BLACK Los Bravos (Decca)
4	6	THE MORE I SEE YOU Chris Montez (Pye International)
9	7	SUMMER IN THE CITY Lovin' Spoonful (Kama Sutra)
17	8	THEY'RE COMING TO TAKE ME AWAY, HA-HAAA! Napoleon XIV (Warner Brothers)
6	9	OUT OF TIME Chris Farlowe (Immediate)
10	10	VISIONS Cliff Richard (Columbia)
12	11	HI-LILI, HI-LO Alan Price Set (Decca)
19	12	LOVERS OF THE WORLD UNITE David & Jonathan (Columbia)
8	13	LOVE LETTERS Elvis Presley (RCA)
16	14	I SAW HER AGAIN Mamas & Papas (RCA)
-	15	ALL OR NOTHING Small Faces (Decca)
22	16	MORE THAN LOVE Ken Dodd (Columbia)
18	17	I WANT YOU Bob Dylan (CBS)
25	18	REVOLVER (LP) Beatles (Parlophone)
13	19	GOIN' BACK Dusty Springfield (Philips)
11	20	I COULDN'T LIVE WITHOUT YOUR LOVE Petula Clark (Pye)
-	21	TOO SOON TO KNOW Roy Orbison (London)
30	22	JUST LIKE A WOMAN Manfred Mann (HMV)
28	23	AIN'T TOO PROUD TO BEG Temptations (Tamla Motown)
27	24	LOVING YOU IS SWEETER THAN EVER Four Tops (Tamla Motown)
15	25	SUNNY AFTERNOON Kinks (Pye)
14	26	GET AWAY Georgie Fame & the Blue Flames (Columbia)
23	27	I LOVE HOW YOU LOVE ME Paul & Barry Ryan (Decca)
20	28	STRANGERS IN THE NIGHT Frank Sinatra (Reprise)
-	29	BAREFOOTIN' Robert Parker (Island)
-	30	GOT TO GET YOU INTO MY LIFE Cliff Bennett & the Rebel Rousers (Parlophone)

27 August 1966

last week	this week	
1	1	YELLOW SUBMARINE/ELEANOR RIGBY Beatles (Parlophone)
3	2	GOD ONLY KNOWS Beach Boys (Capitol)
2	3	WITH A GIRL LIKE YOU Troggs (Fontana)
8	4	THEY'RE COMING TO TAKE ME AWAY, HA-HAAA! Napoleon XIV (Warner Brothers)
4	5	MAMA Dave Berry (Decca)
15	6	ALL OR NOTHING Small Faces (Decca)
10	7	VISIONS Cliff Richard (Columbia)
5	8	BLACK IS BLACK Los Bravos (Decca)
7	9	SUMMER IN THE CITY Lovin' Spoonful (Kama Sutra)
11	10	HI-LILI, HI-LO Alan Price Set (Decca)
6	11	THE MORE I SEE YOU Chris Montez (Pye International)
12	12	LOVERS OF THE WORLD UNITE David & Jonathan (Columbia)
21	13	TOO SOON TO KNOW Roy Orbison (London)
14	14	I SAW HER AGAIN Mamas & Papas (RCA)
16	15	MORE THAN LOVE Ken Dodd (Columbia)
9	16	OUT OF TIME Chris Farlowe (Immediate)
22	17	JUST LIKE A WOMAN Manfred Mann (HMV)
30	18	GOT TO GET YOU INTO MY LIFE Cliff Bennett & the Rebel Rousers (Parlophone)
18	19	REVOLVER (LP) Beatles (Parlophone)
-	20	DISTANT DRUMS Jim Reeves (RCA)
17	21	I WANT YOU Bob Dylan (CBS)
13	22	LOVE LETTERS Elvis Presley (RCA)
24	23	LOVING YOU IS SWEETER THAN EVER Four Tops (Tamla Motown)
-	24	WORKING IN THE COAL MINE Lee Dorsey (Stateside)
23	25	AIN'T TOO PROUD TO BEG Temptations (Tamla Motown)
-	26	HOW SWEET IT IS (TO BE LOVED BY YOU) Jr. Walker & the All Stars (Tamla Motown)
29	27	BAREFOOTIN' Robert Parker (Island)
28	28	STRANGERS IN THE NIGHT Frank Sinatra (Reprise)
-	29	BLOWIN' IN THE WIND Stevie Wonder (Tamla Motown)
20	30	I COULDN'T LIVE WITHOUT YOUR LOVE Petula Clark (Pye)

3 September 1966

last week	this week	
1	1	YELLOW SUBMARINE/ELEANOR RIGBY Beatles (Parlophone)
2	2	GOD ONLY KNOWS Beach Boys (Capitol)
6	3	ALL OR NOTHING Small Faces (Decca)
4	4	THEY'RE COMING TO TAKE ME AWAY, HA-HAAA! Napoleon XIV (Warner Brothers)
3	5	WITH A GIRL LIKE YOU Troggs (Fontana)
5	6	MAMA Dave Berry (Decca)
13	7	TOO SOON TO KNOW Roy Orbison (London)
7	8	VISIONS Cliff Richard (Columbia)
12	9	LOVERS OF THE WORLD UNITE David & Jonathan (Columbia)
10	10	HI-LILI, HI-LO Alan Price Set (Decca)
20	11	DISTANT DRUMS Jim Reeves (RCA)
8	12	BLACK IS BLACK Los Bravos (Decca)
9	13	SUMMER IN THE CITY Lovin' Spoonful (Kama Sutra)
17	14	JUST LIKE A WOMAN Manfred Mann (HMV)
14	15	I SAW HER AGAIN Mamas & Papas (RCA)
11	16	THE MORE I SEE YOU Chris Montez (Pye International)
18	17	GOT TO GET YOU INTO MY LIFE Cliff Bennett & the Rebel Rousers (Parlophone)
15	18	MORE THAN LOVE Ken Dodd (Columbia)
24	19	WORKING IN THE COAL MINE Lee Dorsey (Stateside)
19	20	REVOLVER (LP) Beatles (Parlophone)
26	21	HOW SWEET IT IS (TO BE LOVED BY YOU) Jr. Walker & the All Stars (Tamla Motown)
16	22	OUT OF TIME Chris Farlowe (Immediate)
25	23	AIN'T TOO PROUD TO BEG Temptations (Tamla Motown)
-	24	WHEN I COME HOME Spencer Davis Group (Fontana)
21	25	I WANT YOU Bob Dylan (CBS)
23	26	LOVING YOU IS SWEETER THAN EVER Four Tops (Tamla Motown)
27	27	BAREFOOTIN' Robert Parker (Island)
30	28	I COULDN'T LIVE WITHOUT YOUR LOVE Petula Clark (Pye)
-	29	GIVE ME YOUR WORD Billy Fury (Decca)
-	30	GOODBYE BLUEBIRD Wayne Fontana (Fontana)

It was unusual for the Beatles to extract two songs from an album for immediate single release, but *Yellow Submarine/Eleanor Rigby* took little away from *Revolver* sales (it had advance orders of 300,000, and again made the singles chart). *Yellow Submarine* was the group's only single to feature Ringo on lead vocals, while *Eleanor Rigby* was essentially a Paul McCartney solo with string accompaniment. Napoleon XIV was actually a recording engineer named Jerry Samuels.

September – October 1966

10 September 1966

last week	this week	
1	1	YELLOW SUBMARINE/ELEANOR RIGBY Beatles (Parlophone)
3	2	ALL OR NOTHING Small Faces (Decca)
2	3	GOD ONLY KNOWS Beach Boys (Capitol)
11	4	DISTANT DRUMS Jim Reeves (RCA)
7	5	TOO SOON TO KNOW Roy Orbison (London)
4	6	THEY'RE COMING TO TAKE ME AWAY, HA-HAAA! Napoleon XIV (Warner Brothers)
9	7	LOVERS OF THE WORLD UNITE David & Jonathan (Columbia)
6	8	MAMA Dave Berry (Decca)
5	9	WITH A GIRL LIKE YOU Troggs (Fontana)
17	10	GOT TO GET YOU INTO MY LIFE Cliff Bennett & the Rebel Rousers (Parlophone)
8	11	VISIONS Cliff Richard (Columbia)
19	12	WORKING IN THE COAL MINE Lee Dorsey (Stateside)
-	13	I'M A BOY Who (Reaction)
14	14	JUST LIKE A WOMAN Manfred Mann (HMV)
15	15	I SAW HER AGAIN Mamas & Papas (RCA)
18	16	MORE THAN LOVE Ken Dodd (Columbia)
10	17	HI-LILI, HI-LO Alan Price Set (Decca)
-	18	LITTLE MAN Sonny & Cher (Atlantic)
-	19	YOU CAN'T HURRY LOVE Supremes (Tamla Motown)
21	20	HOW SWEET IT IS (TO BE LOVED BY YOU) Jr. Walker & the All Stars (Tamla Motown)
12	21	BLACK IS BLACK Los Bravos (Decca)
13	22	SUMMER IN THE CITY Lovin' Spoonful (Kama Sutra)
16	23	THE MORE I SEE YOU Chris Montez (Pye International)
-	24	ASHES TO ASHES Mindbenders (Fontana)
24	25	WHEN I COME HOME Spencer Davis Group (Fontana)
-	26	LAND OF 1,000 DANCES Wilson Pickett (Atlantic)
-	27	I CAN'T TURN YOU LOOSE Otis Redding (Atlantic)
-	28	BIG TIME OPERATOR Zoot Money (Columbia)
23	29	AIN'T TOO PROUD TO BEG Temptations (Tamla Motown)
-	30	WINCHESTER CATHEDRAL New Vaudeville Band (Fontana)

17 September 1966

2	1	ALL OR NOTHING Small Faces (Decca)
1	2	YELLOW SUBMARINE/ELEANOR RIGBY Beatles (Parlophone)
4	3	DISTANT DRUMS Jim Reeves (RCA)
5	4	TOO SOON TO KNOW Roy Orbison (London)
3	5	GOD ONLY KNOWS Beach Boys (Capitol)
7	6	LOVERS OF THE WORLD UNITE David & Jonathan (Columbia)
12	7	WORKING IN THE COAL MINE Lee Dorsey (Stateside)
10	8	GOT TO GET YOU INTO MY LIFE Cliff Bennett & the Rebel Rousers (Parlophone)
18	9	I'M A BOY Who (Reaction)
13	10	LITTLE MAN Sonny & Cher (Atlantic)
19	11	YOU CAN'T HURRY LOVE Supremes (Tamla Motown)
6	12	THEY'RE COMING TO TAKE ME AWAY, HA-HAAA! Napoleon XIV (Warner Brothers)
14	13	JUST LIKE A WOMAN Manfred Mann (HMV)
8	14	MAMA Dave Berry (Decca)
-	15	SUNNY Bobby Hebb (Philips)
10	16	VISIONS Cliff Richard (Columbia)
16	17	MORE THAN LOVE Ken Dodd (Columbia)
15	18	I SAW HER AGAIN Mamas & Papas (RCA)
9	19	WITH A GIRL LIKE YOU Troggs (Fontana)
-	20	WALK WITH ME Seekers (Columbia)
24	21	ASHES TO ASHES Mindbenders (Fontana)
26	22	LAND OF 1,000 DANCES Wilson Pickett (Atlantic)
30	23	WINCHESTER CATHEDRAL New Vaudeville Band (Fontana)
25	24	WHEN I COME HOME Spencer Davis Group (Fontana)
20	25	HOW SWEET IT IS (TO BE LOVED BY YOU) Jr. Walker & the All Stars (Tamla Motown)
17	26	HI-LILI, HI-LO Alan Price Set (Decca)
22	27	SUMMER IN THE CITY Lovin' Spoonful (Kama Sutra)
-	28	I DON'T CARE Los Bravos (Decca)
27	29	I CAN'T TURN YOU LOOSE Otis Redding (Atlantic)
28	30	BIG TIME OPERATOR Zoot Money (Columbia)

24 September 1966

3	1	DISTANT DRUMS Jim Reeves (RCA)
1	2	ALL OR NOTHING Small Faces (Decca)
4	3	TOO SOON TO KNOW Roy Orbison (London)
9	4	I'M A BOY Who (Reaction)
11	5	YOU CAN'T HURRY LOVE Supremes (Tamla Motown)
10	6	LITTLE MAN Sonny & Cher (Atlantic)
2	7	YELLOW SUBMARINE/ELEANOR RIGBY Beatles (Parlophone)
7	8	WORKING IN THE COAL MINE Lee Dorsey (Stateside)
8	9	GOT TO GET YOU INTO MY LIFE Cliff Bennett & the Rebel Rousers (Parlophone)
5	10	GOD ONLY KNOWS Beach Boys (Capitol)
-	11	BEND IT Dave Dee, Dozy, Beaky, Mick & Tich (Fontana)
6	12	LOVERS OF THE WORLD UNITE David & Jonathan (Columbia)
15	13	SUNNY Bobby Hebb (Philips)
24	14	WHEN I COME HOME Spencer Davis Group (Fontana)
-	15	ALL I SEE IS YOU Dusty Springfield (Philips)
21	16	ASHES TO ASHES Mindbenders (Fontana)
23	17	WINCHESTER CATHEDRAL New Vaudeville Band (Fontana)
20	18	WALK WITH ME Seekers (Columbia)
13	19	JUST LIKE A WOMAN Manfred Mann (HMV)
14	20	MAMA Dave Berry (Decca)
29	21	I CAN'T TURN YOU LOOSE Otis Redding (Atlantic)
-	22	GUANTANAMERA Sandpipers (Pye International)
-	23	ANOTHER TEAR FALLS Walker Brothers (Philips)
12	24	THEY'RE COMING TO TAKE ME AWAY, HA-HAAA! Napoleon XIV (Warner Brothers)
22	25	LAND OF 1,000 DANCES Wilson Pickett (Atlantic)
28	26	I DON'T CARE Los Bravos (Decca)
17	27	MORE THAN LOVE Ken Dodd (Columbia)
25	28	HOW SWEET IT IS (TO BE LOVED BY YOU) Jr. Walker & the All Stars (Tamla Motown)
-	29	SUNNY Georgie Fame (Columbia)
18	30	I SAW HER AGAIN Mamas & Papas (RCA)

1 October 1966

1	1	DISTANT DRUMS Jim Reeves (RCA)
4	2	I'M A BOY Who (Reaction)
5	3	YOU CAN'T HURRY LOVE Supremes (Tamla Motown)
6	4	LITTLE MAN Sonny & Cher (Atlantic)
11	5	BEND IT Dave Dee, Dozy, Beaky, Mick & Tich (Fontana)
3	6	TOO SOON TO KNOW Roy Orbison (London)
2	7	ALL OR NOTHING Small Faces (Decca)
15	8	ALL I SEE IS YOU Dusty Springfield (Philips)
17	9	WINCHESTER CATHEDRAL New Vaudeville Band (Fontana)
-	10	HAVE YOU SEEN YOUR MOTHER BABY, STANDING IN THE SHADOWS Rolling Stones (Decca)
13	11	SUNNY Bobby Hebb (Philips)
18	12	WALK WITH ME Seekers (Columbia)
7	13	YELLOW SUBMARINE/ELEANOR RIGBY Beatles (Parlophone)
8	14	WORKING IN THE COAL MINE Lee Dorsey (Stateside)
9	15	GOT TO GET YOU INTO MY LIFE Cliff Bennett & the Rebel Rousers (Parlophone)
14	16	WHEN I COME HOME Spencer Davis Group (Fontana)
22	17	GUANTANAMERA Sandpipers (Pye International)
23	18	ANOTHER TEAR FALLS Walker Brothers (Philips)
10	19	GOD ONLY KNOWS Beach Boys (Capitol)
29	20	SUNNY Georgie Fame (Columbia)
26	21	I DON'T CARE Los Bravos (Decca)
16	22	ASHES TO ASHES Mindbenders (Fontana)
12	23	LOVERS OF THE WORLD UNITE David & Jonathan (Columbia)
-	23	LADY GODIVA Peter & Gordon (Columbia)
20	25	MAMA Dave Berry (Decca)
25	26	LAND OF 1,000 DANCES Wilson Pickett (Atlantic)
-	27	IN THE ARMS OF LOVE Andy Williams (CBS)
27	28	MORE THAN LOVE Ken Dodd (Columbia)
-	28	DEAR MRS. APPLEBEE David Garrick (Piccadilly)
21	30	I CAN'T TURN YOU LOOSE Otis Redding (Atlantic)

Jim Reeves' *Distant Drums* (a song recorded by Roy Orbison on the B-side of his 1963 hit Falling) gave the singer his biggest UK hit more than two years after his death. Orbison himself came under fire from some directions over *Too Soon To Know*, which was taken to be about the recent tragic death of his wife Claudette, though the singer denied a specific connection. On a more frivolous note, Dave Dee & co's *Bend It* caused some shocked reaction, but was actually about a dance.

172

8 October 1966

last week	this week		
1	1	DISTANT DRUMS	Jim Reeves (RCA)
2	2	I'M A BOY	Who (Reaction)
5	3	BEND IT	Dave Dee, Dozy, Beaky, Mick & Tich (Fontana)
3	4	YOU CAN'T HURRY LOVE	Supremes (Tamla Motown)
9	5	WINCHESTER CATHEDRAL	New Vaudeville Band (Fontana)
4	6	LITTLE MAN	Sonny & Cher (Atlantic)
10	7	HAVE YOU SEEN YOUR MOTHER BABY, STANDING IN THE SHADOWS	Rolling Stones (Decca)
6	8	TOO SOON TO KNOW	Roy Orbison (London)
8	9	ALL I SEE IS YOU	Dusty Springfield (Philips)
12	10	WALK WITH ME	Seekers (Columbia)
11	11	SUNNY	Bobby Hebb (Philips)
17	12	GUANTANAMERA	Sandpipers (Pye International)
18	13	ANOTHER TEAR FALLS	Walker Brothers (Philips)
20	14	SUNNY	Georgie Fame (Columbia)
7	15	ALL OR NOTHING	Small Faces (Decca)
-	16	I CAN'T CONTROL MYSELF	Troggs (Page One)
21	17	I DON'T CARE	Los Bravos (Decca)
23	18	LADY GODIVA	Peter & Gordon (Columbia)
13	19	YELLOW SUBMARINE/ELEANOR RIGBY	Beatles (Parlophone)
-	20	I'VE GOT YOU UNDER MY SKIN	Four Seasons (Philips)
16	21	WHEN I COME HOME	Spencer Davis Group (Fontana)
23	22	LOVERS OF THE WORLD UNITE	David & Jonathan (Columbia)
-	22	BORN A WOMAN	Sandy Posey (MGM)
14	24	WORKING IN THE COAL MINE	Lee Dorsey (Stateside)
15	25	GOT TO GET YOU INTO MY LIFE	Cliff Bennett & the Rebel Rousers (Parlophone)
30	26	I CAN'T TURN YOU LOOSE	Otis Redding (Atlantic)
-	27	SUNNY	Cher (Liberty)
-	28	SOMEWHERE MY LOVE	Mike Sammes Singers (HMV)
28	29	DEAR MRS. APPLEBEE	David Garrick (Piccadilly)
-	30	SUMMER WIND	Frank Sinatra (Reprise)

15 October 1966

1	1	DISTANT DRUMS	Jim Reeves (RCA)
3	2	BEND IT	Dave Dee, Dozy, Beaky, Mick & Tich (Fontana)
2	3	I'M A BOY	Who (Reaction)
5	4	WINCHESTER CATHEDRAL	New Vaudeville Band (Fontana)
7	5	HAVE YOU SEEN YOUR MOTHER BABY, STANDING IN THE SHADOWS	Rolling Stones (Decca)
16	6	I CAN'T CONTROL MYSELF	Troggs (Page One)
4	7	YOU CAN'T HURRY LOVE	Supremes (Tamla Motown)
12	8	GUANTANAMERA	Sandpipers (Pye International)
6	9	LITTLE MAN	Sonny & Cher (Atlantic)
-	10	REACH OUT I'LL BE THERE	Four Tops (Tamla Motown)
9	10	ALL I SEE IS YOU	Dusty Springfield (Philips)
14	12	SUNNY	Georgie Fame (Columbia)
8	13	TOO SOON TO KNOW	Roy Orbison (London)
10	14	WALK WITH ME	Seekers (Columbia)
11	15	SUNNY	Bobby Hebb (Philips)
-	16	STOP STOP STOP	Hollies (Parlophone)
13	17	ANOTHER TEAR FALLS	Walker Brothers (Philips)
17	18	I DON'T CARE	Los Bravos (Decca)
20	19	I'VE GOT YOU UNDER MY SKIN	Four Seasons (Philips)
18	20	LADY GODIVA	Peter & Gordon (Columbia)
-	21	NO MILK TODAY	Herman's Hermits (Columbia)
-	22	HIGH TIME	Paul Jones (HMV)
28	23	SOMEWHERE MY LOVE	Mike Sammes Singers (HMV)
-	24	TIME DRAGS BY	Cliff Richard (Columbia)
-	25	ALL THAT I AM	Elvis Presley (RCA)
22	26	BORN A WOMAN	Sandy Posey (MGM)
19	27	YELLOW SUBMARINE/ELEANOR RIGBY	Beatles (Parlophone)
29	28	DEAR MRS. APPLEBEE	David Garrick (Piccadilly)
-	29	BEAUTY IS ONLY SKIN DEEP	Temptations (Tamla Motown)
-	30	IF I WERE A CARPENTER	Bobby Darin (Atlantic)

22 October 1966

1	1	DISTANT DRUMS	Jim Reeves (RCA)
10	2	REACH OUT I'LL BE THERE	Four Tops (Tamla Motown)
6	3	I CAN'T CONTROL MYSELF	Troggs (Page One)
4	4	WINCHESTER CATHEDRAL	New Vaudeville Band (Fontana)
2	5	BEND IT	Dave Dee, Dozy, Beaky, Mick & Tich (Fontana)
5	6	HAVE YOU SEEN YOUR MOTHER BABY, STANDING IN THE SHADOWS	Rolling Stones (Decca)
8	7	GUANTANAMERA	Sandpipers (Pye International)
3	8	I'M A BOY	Who (Reaction)
16	9	STOP STOP STOP	Hollies (Parlophone)
7	10	YOU CAN'T HURRY LOVE	Supremes (Tamla Motown)
10	11	ALL I SEE IS YOU	Dusty Springfield (Philips)
9	12	LITTLE MAN	Sonny & Cher (Atlantic)
12	13	SUNNY	Georgie Fame (Columbia)
21	14	NO MILK TODAY	Herman's Hermits (Columbia)
13	15	TOO SOON TO KNOW	Roy Orbison (London)
24	16	TIME DRAGS BY	Cliff Richard (Columbia)
19	17	I'VE GOT YOU UNDER MY SKIN	Four Seasons (Philips)
17	18	ANOTHER TEAR FALLS	Walker Brothers (Philips)
14	19	WALK WITH ME	Seekers (Columbia)
20	20	LADY GODIVA	Peter & Gordon (Columbia)
22	21	HIGH TIME	Paul Jones (HMV)
18	22	I DON'T CARE	Los Bravos (Decca)
25	23	ALL THAT I AM	Elvis Presley (RCA)
30	24	IF I WERE A CARPENTER	Bobby Darin (Atlantic)
-	25	A FOOL AM I	Cilla Black (Parlophone)
29	26	BEAUTY IS ONLY SKIN DEEP	Temptations (Tamla Motown)
26	27	BORN A WOMAN	Sandy Posey (MGM)
-	28	I LOVE MY DOG	Cat Stevens (Deram)
15	29	SUNNY	Bobby Hebb (Philips)
28	30	DEAR MRS. APPLEBEE	David Garrick (Piccadilly)

29 October 1966

2	1	REACH OUT I'LL BE THERE	Four Tops (Tamla Motown)
1	2	DISTANT DRUMS	Jim Reeves (RCA)
3	3	I CAN'T CONTROL MYSELF	Troggs (Page One)
9	4	STOP STOP STOP	Hollies (Parlophone)
4	5	WINCHESTER CATHEDRAL	New Vaudeville Band (Fontana)
7	6	GUANTANAMERA	Sandpipers (Pye International)
5	7	BEND IT	Dave Dee, Dozy, Beaky, Mick & Tich (Fontana)
6	8	HAVE YOU SEEN YOUR MOTHER BABY, STANDING IN THE SHADOWS	Rolling Stones (Decca)
16	9	TIME DRAGS BY	Cliff Richard (Columbia)
14	10	NO MILK TODAY	Herman's Hermits (Columbia)
8	11	I'M A BOY	Who (Reaction)
17	12	I'VE GOT YOU UNDER MY SKIN	Four Seasons (Philips)
10	13	YOU CAN'T HURRY LOVE	Supremes (Tamla Motown)
11	14	ALL I SEE IS YOU	Dusty Springfield (Philips)
21	15	HIGH TIME	Paul Jones (HMV)
25	16	A FOOL AM I	Cilla Black (Parlophone)
24	17	IF I WERE A CARPENTER	Bobby Darin (Atlantic)
15	18	TOO SOON TO KNOW	Roy Orbison (London)
19	19	WALK WITH ME	Seekers (Columbia)
26	20	BEAUTY IS ONLY SKIN DEEP	Temptations (Tamla Motown)
-	21	SEMI-DETACHED SUBURBAN MR. JAMES	Manfred Mann (HMV)
13	22	SUNNY	Georgie Fame (Columbia)
23	23	ALL THAT I AM	Elvis Presley (RCA)
27	24	BORN A WOMAN	Sandy Posey (MGM)
20	25	LADY GODIVA	Peter & Gordon (Columbia)
12	25	LITTLE MAN	Sonny & Cher (Atlantic)
-	27	WRAPPING PAPER	Cream (Reaction)
22	28	I DON'T CARE	Los Bravos (Decca)
28	29	I LOVE MY DOG	Cat Stevens (Deram)
-	30	HELP ME GIRL	Eric Burdon & the Animals (Decca)
-	30	A LOVE LIKE YOURS	Ike & Tina Turner (London)

With the Who's *I'm A Boy* being concerned with enforced sexual confusion in childhood and Dave Dee's *Bend It* being refused US airplay (they recorded a reworded version for US release), it seemed to the moralists that the apocalypse had arrived when the Troggs came up with *I Can't Control Myself* – which was promptly banned in Australia. In Britain it made *Top Of The Pops* without divine retribution falling. Then came the Stones' *Have You Seen Your Mother Baby...*

November 1966

last week	this week	5 November 1966
1	1	REACH OUT I'LL BE THERE Four Tops (Tamla Motown)
4	2	STOP STOP STOP Hollies (Parlophone)
3	3	I CAN'T CONTROL MYSELF Troggs (Page One)
2	4	DISTANT DRUMS Jim Reeves (RCA)
5	5	WINCHESTER CATHEDRAL New Vaudeville Band (Fontana)
-	6	GOOD VIBRATIONS Beach Boys (Capitol)
21	7	SEMI-DETACHED SUBURBAN MR. JAMES Manfred Mann (HMV)
15	8	HIGH TIME Paul Jones (HMV)
10	9	NO MILK TODAY Herman's Hermits (Columbia)
6	9	GUANTANAMERA Sandpipers (Pye International)
9	11	TIME DRAGS BY Cliff Richard (Columbia)
7	12	BEND IT Dave Dee, Dozy, Beaky, Mick & Tich (Fontana)
16	13	A FOOL AM I Cilla Black (Parlophone)
17	14	IF I WERE A CARPENTER Bobby Darin (Atlantic)
-	14	GIMME SOME LOVING Spencer Davis Group (Fontana)
12	16	I'VE GOT YOU UNDER MY SKIN Four Seasons (Philips)
11	17	I'M A BOY Who (Reaction)
14	18	ALL I SEE IS YOU Dusty Springfield (Philips)
8	19	HAVE YOU SEEN YOUR MOTHER BABY, STANDING IN THE SHADOWS Rolling Stones (Decca)
13	20	YOU CAN'T HURRY LOVE Supremes (Tamla Motown)
25	21	LADY GODIVA Peter & Gordon (Columbia)
-	22	PAINTER MAN Creation (Planet)
20	23	BEAUTY IS ONLY SKIN DEEP Temptations (Tamla Motown)
30	24	A LOVE LIKE YOURS Ike & Tina Turner (London)
27	25	WRAPPING PAPER Cream (Reaction)
-	25	HOLY COW Lee Dorsey (Stateside)
30	27	HELP ME GIRL Eric Burdon & the Animals (Decca)
23	28	ALL THAT I AM Elvis Presley (RCA)
18	29	TOO SOON TO KNOW Roy Orbison (London)
-	30	WHAT WOULD I BE Val Doonican (Decca)
29	30	I LOVE MY DOG Cat Stevens (Deram)

last week	this week	12 November 1966
1	1	REACH OUT I'LL BE THERE Four Tops (Tamla Motown)
6	2	GOOD VIBRATIONS Beach Boys (Capitol)
7	3	SEMI-DETACHED SUBURBAN MR. JAMES Manfred Mann (HMV)
14	4	GIMME SOME LOVING Spencer Davis Group (Fontana)
2	4	STOP STOP STOP Hollies (Parlophone)
8	6	HIGH TIME Paul Jones (HMV)
4	7	DISTANT DRUMS Jim Reeves (RCA)
3	8	I CAN'T CONTROL MYSELF Troggs (Page One)
5	9	WINCHESTER CATHEDRAL New Vaudeville Band (Fontana)
9	10	NO MILK TODAY Herman's Hermits (Columbia)
13	11	A FOOL AM I Cilla Black (Parlophone)
14	12	IF I WERE A CARPENTER Bobby Darin (Atlantic)
11	13	TIME DRAGS BY Cliff Richard (Columbia)
-	14	GUANTANAMERA Sandpipers (Pye International)
25	15	HOLY COW Lee Dorsey (Stateside)
12	16	BEND IT Dave Dee, Dozy, Beaky, Mick & Tich (Fontana)
30	17	WHAT WOULD I BE Val Doonican (Decca)
24	18	A LOVE LIKE YOURS Ike & Tina Turner (London)
27	19	HELP ME GIRL Eric Burdon & the Animals (Decca)
-	20	GREEN GREEN GRASS OF HOME Tom Jones (Decca)
16	21	I'VE GOT YOU UNDER MY SKIN Four Seasons (Philips)
28	22	ALL THAT I AM Elvis Presley (RCA)
-	23	SOMEWHERE MY LOVE Mike Sammes Singers (HMV)
-	24	RIDE ON BABY Chris Farlowe (Immediate)
23	25	BEAUTY IS ONLY SKIN DEEP Temptations (Tamla Motown)
18	26	ALL I SEE IS YOU Dusty Springfield (Philips)
22	27	PAINTER MAN Creation (Planet)
-	28	JUST ONE SMILE Gene Pitney (Stateside)
17	29	I'M A BOY Who (Reaction)
29	30	TOO SOON TO KNOW Roy Orbison (London)

last week	this week	19 November 1966
2	1	GOOD VIBRATIONS Beach Boys (Capitol)
4	2	GIMME SOME LOVING Spencer Davis Group (Fontana)
3	3	SEMI-DETACHED SUBURBAN MR. JAMES Manfred Mann (HMV)
1	4	REACH OUT I'LL BE THERE Four Tops (Tamla Motown)
5	5	STOP STOP STOP Hollies (Parlophone)
6	6	HIGH TIME Paul Jones (HMV)
20	7	GREEN GREEN GRASS OF HOME Tom Jones (Decca)
7	8	DISTANT DRUMS Jim Reeves (RCA)
17	9	WHAT WOULD I BE Val Doonican (Decca)
15	10	HOLY COW Lee Dorsey (Stateside)
8	11	I CAN'T CONTROL MYSELF Troggs (Page One)
11	12	A FOOL AM I Cilla Black (Parlophone)
12	13	IF I WERE A CARPENTER Bobby Darin (Atlantic)
9	14	WINCHESTER CATHEDRAL New Vaudeville Band (Fontana)
10	15	NO MILK TODAY Herman's Hermits (Columbia)
13	16	TIME DRAGS BY Cliff Richard (Columbia)
28	17	JUST ONE SMILE Gene Pitney (Stateside)
14	18	GUANTANAMERA Sandpipers (Pye International)
19	19	HELP ME GIRL Eric Burdon & the Animals (Decca)
-	20	MY MIND'S EYE Small Faces (Decca)
18	21	A LOVE LIKE YOURS Ike & Tina Turner (London)
-	22	WHAT BECOMES OF THE BROKENHEARTED Jimmy Ruffin (Tamla Motown)
25	23	BEAUTY IS ONLY SKIN DEEP Temptations (Tamla Motown)
-	24	WHITE CLIFFS OF DOVER Righteous Brothers (London)
24	25	RIDE ON BABY Chris Farlowe (Immediate)
22	26	ALL THAT I AM Elvis Presley (RCA)
21	27	I'VE GOT YOU UNDER MY SKIN Four Seasons (Philips)
23	28	SOMEWHERE MY LOVE Mike Sammes Singers (HMV)
-	29	FRIDAY ON MY MIND Easybeats (United Artists)
30	30	FA FA FA FA FA FA FA (SAD SONG) Otis Redding (Atlantic)
-	30	READY STEADY WHO (EP) Who (Reaction)

last week	this week	26 November 1966
1	1	GOOD VIBRATIONS Beach Boys (Capitol)
7	2	GREEN GREEN GRASS OF HOME Tom Jones (Decca)
2	3	GIMME SOME LOVING Spencer Davis Group (Fontana)
3	4	SEMI-DETACHED SUBURBAN MR. JAMES Manfred Mann (HMV)
4	5	REACH OUT I'LL BE THERE Four Tops (Tamla Motown)
9	6	WHAT WOULD I BE Val Doonican (Decca)
10	7	HOLY COW Lee Dorsey (Stateside)
6	8	HIGH TIME Paul Jones (HMV)
20	9	MY MIND'S EYE Small Faces (Decca)
5	10	STOP STOP STOP Hollies (Parlophone)
8	11	DISTANT DRUMS Jim Reeves (RCA)
17	12	JUST ONE SMILE Gene Pitney (Stateside)
13	13	IF I WERE A CARPENTER Bobby Darin (Atlantic)
22	14	WHAT BECOMES OF THE BROKENHEARTED Jimmy Ruffin (Tamla Motown)
12	15	A FOOL AM I Cilla Black (Parlophone)
11	16	I CAN'T CONTROL MYSELF Troggs (Page One)
29	17	FRIDAY ON MY MIND Easybeats (United Artists)
18	18	GUANTANAMERA Sandpipers (Pye International)
14	19	WINCHESTER CATHEDRAL New Vaudeville Band (Fontana)
20	20	A LOVE LIKE YOURS Ike & Tina Turner (London)
19	21	HELP ME GIRL Eric Burdon & the Animals (Decca)
15	22	NO MILK TODAY Herman's Hermits (Columbia)
28	23	SOMEWHERE MY LOVE Mike Sammes Singers (HMV)
16	24	TIME DRAGS BY Cliff Richard (Columbia)
-	25	MORNINGTOWN RIDE Seekers (Columbia)
-	26	DEAD END STREET Kinks (Pye)
24	26	WHITE CLIFFS OF DOVER Righteous Brothers (London)
27	28	I'VE GOT YOU UNDER MY SKIN Four Seasons (Philips)
-	29	IT'S LOVE Ken Dodd (Columbia)
30	30	FA FA FA FA FA FA FA (SAD SONG) Otis Redding (Atlantic)

The Beach Boys, or at least writer/producer Brian Wilson, had spent upwards of nine months piecing together the musical collage that was *Good Vibrations*. Such long-term devotion was justified on release, with unique critical acclaim for the single (and the related album *Pet Sounds*) and commercial success to match – it topped both US and UK charts. A measure of Wilson's achievement is that it is still regarded as the peak of the Beach Boys' achievement over twenty-five years later.

3 December 1966

last week	this week	Title / Artist (Label)
2	1	GREEN GREEN GRASS OF HOME — Tom Jones (Decca)
1	2	GOOD VIBRATIONS — Beach Boys (Capitol)
3	3	GIMME SOME LOVING — Spencer Davis Group (Fontana)
6	4	WHAT WOULD I BE — Val Doonican (Decca)
4	5	SEMI-DETACHED SUBURBAN MR. JAMES — Manfred Mann (HMV)
9	6	MY MIND'S EYE — Small Faces (Decca)
7	7	HOLY COW — Lee Dorsey (Stateside)
12	8	JUST ONE SMILE — Gene Pitney (Stateside)
5	9	REACH OUT I'LL BE THERE — Four Tops (Tamla Motown)
14	10	WHAT BECOMES OF THE BROKENHEARTED — Jimmy Ruffin (Tamla Motown)
25	11	MORNINGTOWN RIDE — Seekers (Columbia)
8	12	HIGH TIME — Paul Jones (HMV)
11	13	DISTANT DRUMS — Jim Reeves (RCA)
26	14	DEAD END STREET — Kinks (Pye)
17	15	FRIDAY ON MY MIND — Easybeats (United Artists)
-	16	YOU KEEP ME HANGIN' ON — Supremes (Tamla Motown)
10	17	STOP STOP STOP — Hollies (Parlophone)
13	18	IF I WERE A CARPENTER — Bobby Darin (Atlantic)
20	19	A LOVE LIKE YOURS — Ike & Tina Turner (London)
16	20	I CAN'T CONTROL MYSELF — Troggs (Page One)
21	21	HELP ME GIRL — Eric Burdon & the Animals (Decca)
15	22	A FOOL AM I — Cilla Black (Parlophone)
22	23	NO MILK TODAY — Herman's Hermits (Columbia)
30	24	FA FA FA FA FA FA (SAD SONG) — Otis Redding (Atlantic)
-	25	THERE WON'T BE MANY COMING HOME — Roy Orbison (London)
18	26	GUANTANAMERA — Sandpipers (Pye International)
19	27	WINCHESTER CATHEDRAL — New Vaudeville Band (Fontana)
-	28	THINK SOMETIMES ABOUT ME — Sandie Shaw (Pye)
26	29	WHITE CLIFFS OF DOVER — Righteous Brothers (London)
-	30	UNDER NEW MANAGEMENT — Barron Knights (Columbia)

10 December 1966

last	this	Title / Artist (Label)
1	1	GREEN GREEN GRASS OF HOME — Tom Jones (Decca)
4	2	WHAT WOULD I BE — Val Doonican (Decca)
2	3	GOOD VIBRATIONS — Beach Boys (Capitol)
6	4	MY MIND'S EYE — Small Faces (Decca)
11	5	MORNINGTOWN RIDE — Seekers (Columbia)
3	6	GIMME SOME LOVING — Spencer Davis Group (Fontana)
8	7	JUST ONE SMILE — Gene Pitney (Stateside)
14	8	DEAD END STREET — Kinks (Pye)
10	9	WHAT BECOMES OF THE BROKENHEARTED — Jimmy Ruffin (Tamla Motown)
15	10	FRIDAY ON MY MIND — Easybeats (United Artists)
7	11	HOLY COW — Lee Dorsey (Stateside)
5	12	SEMI-DETACHED SUBURBAN MR. JAMES — Manfred Mann (HMV)
16	13	YOU KEEP ME HANGIN' ON — Supremes (Tamla Motown)
9	14	REACH OUT I'LL BE THERE — Four Tops (Tamla Motown)
13	15	DISTANT DRUMS — Jim Reeves (RCA)
25	16	THERE WON'T BE MANY COMING HOME — Roy Orbison (London)
-	17	SUNSHINE SUPERMAN — Donovan (Pye)
-	18	WALK WITH FAITH IN YOUR HEART — Bachelors (Decca)
12	19	HIGH TIME — Paul Jones (HMV)
20	20	IF EVERY DAY WAS LIKE CHRISTMAS — Elvis Presley (RCA)
24	21	FA FA FA FA FA FA (SAD SONG) — Otis Redding (Atlantic)
-	22	SAVE ME — Dave Dee, Dozy, Beaky, Mick & Tich (Fontana)
-	23	I'M READY FOR LOVE — Martha & the Vandellas (Tamla Motown)
19	24	A LOVE LIKE YOURS — Ike & Tina Turner (London)
28	25	THINK SOMETIMES ABOUT ME — Sandie Shaw (Pye)
17	26	STOP STOP STOP — Hollies (Parlophone)
29	27	WHITE CLIFFS OF DOVER — Righteous Brothers (London)
18	28	IF I WERE A CARPENTER — Bobby Darin (Atlantic)
-	29	IT'S LOVE — Ken Dodd (Columbia)
-	30	EAST WEST — Herman's Hermits (Columbia)

17 December 1966

last	this	Title / Artist (Label)
1	1	GREEN GREEN GRASS OF HOME — Tom Jones (Decca)
2	2	WHAT WOULD I BE — Val Doonican (Decca)
5	3	MORNINGTOWN RIDE — Seekers (Columbia)
3	4	GOOD VIBRATIONS — Beach Boys (Capitol)
4	5	MY MIND'S EYE — Small Faces (Decca)
9	6	WHAT BECOMES OF THE BROKENHEARTED — Jimmy Ruffin (Tamla Motown)
17	7	SUNSHINE SUPERMAN — Donovan (Pye)
12	7	YOU KEEP ME HANGIN' ON — Supremes (Tamla Motown)
6	9	GIMME SOME LOVING — Spencer Davis Group (Fontana)
8	10	DEAD END STREET — Kinks (Pye)
10	11	FRIDAY ON MY MIND — Easybeats (United Artists)
7	12	JUST ONE SMILE — Gene Pitney (Stateside)
20	13	IF EVERY DAY WAS LIKE CHRISTMAS — Elvis Presley (RCA)
22	14	SAVE ME — Dave Dee, Dozy, Beaky, Mick & Tich (Fontana)
12	15	SEMI-DETACHED SUBURBAN MR. JAMES — Manfred Mann (HMV)
11	16	HOLY COW — Lee Dorsey (Stateside)
15	17	DISTANT DRUMS — Jim Reeves (RCA)
18	18	WALK WITH FAITH IN YOUR HEART — Bachelors (Decca)
-	19	UNDER NEW MANAGEMENT — Barron Knights (Columbia)
-	20	IN THE COUNTRY — Cliff Richard (Columbia)
-	21	CALL HER YOUR SWEETHEART — Frank Ifield (Columbia)
16	22	THERE WON'T BE MANY COMING HOME — Roy Orbison (London)
19	23	HIGH TIME — Paul Jones (HMV)
14	24	REACH OUT I'LL BE THERE — Four Tops (Tamla Motown)
25	25	HAPPY JACK — Who (Reaction)
21	26	FA FA FA FA FA FA (SAD SONG) — Otis Redding (Atlantic)
-	27	ANY WAY THAT YOU WANT ME — Troggs (Page One)
-	28	PAMELA PAMELA — Wayne Fontana (Fontana)
25	29	THINK SOMETIMES ABOUT ME — Sandie Shaw (Pye)
-	30	DEADLIER THAN THE MALE — Walker Brothers (Philips)

24 December 1966

last	this	Title / Artist (Label)
1	1	GREEN GREEN GRASS OF HOME — Tom Jones (Decca)
3	2	MORNINGTOWN RIDE — Seekers (Columbia)
2	3	WHAT WOULD I BE — Val Doonican (Decca)
7	4	SUNSHINE SUPERMAN — Donovan (Pye)
5	5	MY MIND'S EYE — Small Faces (Decca)
6	6	WHAT BECOMES OF THE BROKENHEARTED — Jimmy Ruffin (Tamla Motown)
7	7	YOU KEEP ME HANGIN' ON — Supremes (Tamla Motown)
10	8	DEAD END STREET — Kinks (Pye)
11	9	FRIDAY ON MY MIND — Easybeats (United Artists)
14	10	SAVE ME — Dave Dee, Dozy, Beaky, Mick & Tich (Fontana)
13	11	IF EVERY DAY WAS LIKE CHRISTMAS — Elvis Presley (RCA)
4	12	GOOD VIBRATIONS — Beach Boys (Capitol)
25	13	HAPPY JACK — Who (Reaction)
20	14	IN THE COUNTRY — Cliff Richard (Columbia)
9	15	GIMME SOME LOVING — Spencer Davis Group (Fontana)
12	16	JUST ONE SMILE — Gene Pitney (Stateside)
18	17	WALK WITH FAITH IN YOUR HEART — Bachelors (Decca)
27	18	ANY WAY THAT YOU WANT ME — Troggs (Page One)
19	19	UNDER NEW MANAGEMENT — Barron Knights (Columbia)
17	20	DISTANT DRUMS — Jim Reeves (RCA)
16	21	HOLY COW — Lee Dorsey (Stateside)
15	22	SEMI-DETACHED SUBURBAN MR. JAMES — Manfred Mann (HMV)
22	23	THERE WON'T BE MANY COMING HOME — Roy Orbison (London)
21	24	CALL HER YOUR SWEETHEART — Frank Ifield (Columbia)
28	25	PAMELA PAMELA — Wayne Fontana (Fontana)
24	26	REACH OUT I'LL BE THERE — Four Tops (Tamla Motown)
23	27	HIGH TIME — Paul Jones (HMV)
-	28	HEART — Rita Pavone (RCA)
26	29	FA FA FA FA FA FA (SAD SONG) — Otis Redding (Atlantic)
30	30	DEADLIER THAN THE MALE — Walker Brothers (Philips)

Tom Jones had been slighty in the chart doldrums when he decided to record a song interpreted by Jerry Lee Lewis on the latter's *Country Songs For City Folks* album. Jones' recording of *Green Green Grass Of Home* brought him his all-time most successful single, selling over a million in the UK and emerging as the year's biggest hit. At this time he was being wooed by Motown records in the States and was tempted by the chance of recording in Detroit, but his Decca contract was firm until 1970.

December 1966

1	1	GREEN GREEN GRASS OF HOME Tom Jones (Decca)
2	2	MORNINGTOWN RIDE Seekers (Columbia)
3	3	WHAT WOULD I BE Val Doonican (Decca)
4	4	SUNSHINE SUPERMAN Donovan (Pye)
7	5	YOU KEEP ME HANGIN' ON Supremes (Tamla Motown)
6	6	WHAT BECOMES OF THE BROKENHEARTED Jimmy Ruffin (Tamla Motown)
10	7	SAVE ME Dave Dee, Dozy, Beaky, Mick & Tich (Fontana)
8	8	DEAD END STREET Kinks (Pye)
13	9	HAPPY JACK Who (Reaction)
5	10	MY MIND'S EYE Small Faces (Decca)
11	11	IF EVERY DAY WAS LIKE CHRISTMAS Elvis Presley (RCA)
9	12	FRIDAY ON MY MIND Easybeats (United Artists)
14	12	IN THE COUNTRY Cliff Richard (Columbia)
17	14	ANY WAY THAT YOU WANT ME Troggs (Page One)
12	15	GOOD VIBRATIONS Beach Boys (Capitol)
19	16	UNDER NEW MANAGEMENT Barron Knights (Columbia)
15	17	GIMME SOME LOVING Spencer Davis Group (Fontana)
17	18	WALK WITH FAITH IN YOUR HEART Bachelors (Decca)
16	19	JUST ONE SMILE Gene Pitney (Stateside)
20	20	DISTANT DRUMS Jim Reeves (RCA)
25	21	PAMELA PAMELA Wayne Fontana (Fontana)
21	22	HOLY COW Lee Dorsey (Stateside)
22	23	SEMI-DETACHED SUBURBAN MR. JAMES Manfred Mann (HMV)
24	24	CALL HER YOUR SWEETHEART Frank Ifield (Columbia)
23	25	THERE WON'T BE MANY COMING HOME Roy Orbison (London)
27	26	HIGH TIME Paul Jones (HMV)
-	27	(I KNOW) I'M LOSING YOU Temptations (Tamla Motown)
26	28	REACH OUT I'LL BE THERE Four Tops (Tamla Motown)
-	29	SITTING IN THE PARK Georgie Fame (Columbia)
30	30	DEADLIER THAN THE MALE Walker Brothers (Philips)

In another good year for British acts Welsh beefcake Tom Jones (seen here later in his career) ended on top. The Small Faces were at Number Ten.

last week	this week	7 January 1967		14 January 1967		21 January 1967		28 January 1967

7 January 1967

last	this	
1	1	GREEN GREEN GRASS OF HOME Tom Jones (Decca)
2	2	MORNINGTOWN RIDE Seekers (Columbia)
7	3	SAVE ME Dave Dee, Dozy, Beaky, Mick & Tich (Fontana)
4	4	SUNSHINE SUPERMAN Donovan (Pye)
3	5	WHAT WOULD I BE Val Doonican (Decca)
9	6	HAPPY JACK Who (Reaction)
14	7	ANY WAY THAT YOU WANT ME Troggs (Page One)
8	8	DEAD END STREET Kinks (Pye)
12	9	IN THE COUNTRY Cliff Richard (Columbia)
5	10	YOU KEEP ME HANGIN' ON Supremes (Tamla Motown)
6	11	WHAT BECOMES OF THE BROKENHEARTED Jimmy Ruffin (Tamla Motown)
10	12	MY MIND'S EYE Small Faces (Decca)
12	13	FRIDAY ON MY MIND Easybeats (United Artists)
16	14	UNDER NEW MANAGEMENT Barron Knights (Columbia)
15	15	GOOD VIBRATIONS Beach Boys (Capitol)
29	16	SITTING IN THE PARK Georgie Fame (Columbia)
21	17	PAMELA PAMELA Wayne Fontana (Fontana)
18	18	WALK WITH FAITH IN YOUR HEART Bachelors (Decca)
20	19	DISTANT DRUMS Jim Reeves (RCA)
24	20	CALL HER YOUR SWEETHEART Frank Ifield (Columbia)
17	21	GIMME SOME LOVING Spencer Davis Group (Fontana)
11	22	IF EVERY DAY WAS LIKE CHRISTMAS Elvis Presley (RCA)
27	23	(I KNOW) I'M LOSING YOU Temptations (Tamla Motown)
-	24	I FEEL FREE Cream (Reaction)
25	25	THERE WON'T BE MANY COMING HOME Roy Orbison (London)
30	25	DEADLIER THAN THE MALE Walker Brothers (Philips)
-	27	NIGHT OF FEAR Move (Deram)
19	28	JUST ONE SMILE Gene Pitney (Stateside)
-	29	I'M A BELIEVER Monkees (RCA)
28	30	REACH OUT I'LL BE THERE Four Tops (Tamla Motown)

14 January 1967

last	this	
1	1	GREEN GREEN GRASS OF HOME Tom Jones (Decca)
29	2	I'M A BELIEVER Monkees (RCA)
2	3	MORNINGTOWN RIDE Seekers (Columbia)
6	4	HAPPY JACK Who (Reaction)
4	5	SUNSHINE SUPERMAN Donovan (Pye)
3	6	SAVE ME Dave Dee, Dozy, Beaky, Mick & Tich (Fontana)
7	7	ANY WAY THAT YOU WANT ME Troggs (Page One)
9	8	IN THE COUNTRY Cliff Richard (Columbia)
5	9	WHAT WOULD I BE Val Doonican (Decca)
10	10	YOU KEEP ME HANGIN' ON Supremes (Tamla Motown)
8	11	DEAD END STREET Kinks (Pye)
-	12	STANDING IN THE SHADOWS OF LOVE Four Tops (Tamla Motown)
16	13	SITTING IN THE PARK Georgie Fame (Columbia)
27	14	NIGHT OF FEAR Move (Deram)
-	15	MATTHEW AND SON Cat Stevens (Deram)
17	16	PAMELA PAMELA Wayne Fontana (Fontana)
13	17	FRIDAY ON MY MIND Easybeats (United Artists)
24	18	I FEEL FREE Cream (Reaction)
11	19	WHAT BECOMES OF THE BROKENHEARTED Jimmy Ruffin (Tamla Motown)
23	20	(I KNOW) I'M LOSING YOU Temptations (Tamla Motown)
12	21	MY MIND'S EYE Small Faces (Decca)
-	22	MUSTANG SALLY Wilson Pickett (Atlantic)
15	23	GOOD VIBRATIONS Beach Boys (Capitol)
-	24	HEY JOE Jimi Hendrix Experience (Polydor)
14	25	UNDER NEW MANAGEMENT Barron Knights (Columbia)
20	26	CALL HER YOUR SWEETHEART Frank Ifield (Columbia)
18	27	WALK WITH FAITH IN YOUR HEART Bachelors (Decca)
25	28	THERE WON'T BE MANY COMING HOME Roy Orbison (London)
-	29	SINGLE GIRL Sandy Posey (MGM)
-	30	NASHVILLE CATS Lovin' Spoonful (Kama Sutra)
-	30	SUGAR TOWN Nancy Sinatra (Reprise)

21 January 1967

last	this	
2	1	I'M A BELIEVER Monkees (RCA)
1	2	GREEN GREEN GRASS OF HOME Tom Jones (Decca)
4	3	HAPPY JACK Who (Reaction)
3	4	MORNINGTOWN RIDE Seekers (Columbia)
12	5	STANDING IN THE SHADOWS OF LOVE Four Tops (Tamla Motown)
7	6	ANY WAY THAT YOU WANT ME Troggs (Page One)
15	7	MATTHEW AND SON Cat Stevens (Deram)
14	8	NIGHT OF FEAR Move (Deram)
6	9	SAVE ME Dave Dee, Dozy, Beaky, Mick & Tich (Fontana)
5	10	SUNSHINE SUPERMAN Donovan (Pye)
24	11	HEY JOE Jimi Hendrix Experience (Polydor)
8	12	IN THE COUNTRY Cliff Richard (Columbia)
13	13	SITTING IN THE PARK Georgie Fame (Columbia)
18	14	I FEEL FREE Cream (Reaction)
16	15	PAMELA PAMELA Wayne Fontana (Fontana)
9	16	WHAT WOULD I BE Val Doonican (Decca)
-	17	LET'S SPEND THE NIGHT TOGETHER Rolling Stones (Decca)
11	18	DEAD END STREET Kinks (Pye)
10	19	YOU KEEP ME HANGIN' ON Supremes (Tamla Motown)
-	20	I'VE BEEN A BAD BAD BOY Paul Jones (HMV)
29	21	SINGLE GIRL Sandy Posey (MGM)
30	22	SUGAR TOWN Nancy Sinatra (Reprise)
20	23	(I KNOW) I'M LOSING YOU Temptations (Tamla Motown)
26	24	CALL HER YOUR SWEETHEART Frank Ifield (Columbia)
17	25	FRIDAY ON MY MIND Easybeats (United Artists)
30	26	NASHVILLE CATS Lovin' Spoonful (Kama Sutra)
23	27	GOOD VIBRATIONS Beach Boys (Capitol)
19	28	WHAT BECOMES OF THE BROKENHEARTED Jimmy Ruffin (Tamla Motown)
-	29	RUBY TUESDAY Rolling Stones (Decca)
-	30	HEART Rita Pavone (RCA)

28 January 1967

last	this	
1	1	I'M A BELIEVER Monkees (RCA)
7	2	MATTHEW AND SON Cat Stevens (Deram)
2	3	GREEN GREEN GRASS OF HOME Tom Jones (Decca)
8	4	NIGHT OF FEAR Move (Deram)
17	5	LET'S SPEND THE NIGHT TOGETHER Rolling Stones (Decca)
5	6	STANDING IN THE SHADOWS OF LOVE Four Tops (Tamla Motown)
3	7	HAPPY JACK Who (Reaction)
11	8	HEY JOE Jimi Hendrix Experience (Polydor)
20	9	I'VE BEEN A BAD BAD BOY Paul Jones (HMV)
4	10	MORNINGTOWN RIDE Seekers (Columbia)
14	11	I FEEL FREE Cream (Reaction)
13	12	SITTING IN THE PARK Georgie Fame (Columbia)
12	13	IN THE COUNTRY Cliff Richard (Columbia)
6	14	ANY WAY THAT YOU WANT ME Troggs (Page One)
15	15	PAMELA PAMELA Wayne Fontana (Fontana)
10	16	SUNSHINE SUPERMAN Donovan (Pye)
-	17	LET ME CRY ON YOUR SHOULDER Ken Dodd (Columbia)
9	18	SAVE ME Dave Dee, Dozy, Beaky, Mick & Tich (Fontana)
21	19	SINGLE GIRL Sandy Posey (MGM)
29	20	RUBY TUESDAY Rolling Stones (Decca)
22	21	SUGAR TOWN Nancy Sinatra (Reprise)
-	22	I'M A MAN Spencer Davis Group (Fontana)
16	22	WHAT WOULD I BE Val Doonican (Decca)
-	24	SNOOPY VS. THE RED BARON Royal Guardsmen (Stateside)
19	25	YOU KEEP ME HANGIN' ON Supremes (Tamla Motown)
24	26	CALL HER YOUR SWEETHEART Frank Ifield (Columbia)
-	27	YOU ONLY YOU Rita Pavone (RCA)
23	28	(I KNOW) I'M LOSING YOU Temptations (Tamla Motown)
-	29	IT TAKES TWO Marvin Gaye & Kim Weston (Tamla Motown)
-	30	TELL IT TO THE RAIN Four Seasons (Philips)
-	30	98.6 Keith (Mercury)

Jimi Hendrix, who had arrived in Britain only late in 1966 at the urging of Chas Chandler, the former Animals bassist who became his producer and co-manager, scored instantly with his first UK recording *Hey Joe*. Even bigger, though, was the arrival of the Monkees, whose TV series, already huge in the US, began on British screens on January 7. Immediately after the first show, *I'm A Believer* leapt from 29 to Number Two in one bound, prior to a month at Number One and 750,000 UK sales inside 10 weeks.

February 1967

last week	this week	4 February 1967
1	1	I'M A BELIEVER — Monkees (RCA)
2	2	MATTHEW AND SON — Cat Stevens (Deram)
4	3	NIGHT OF FEAR — Move (Deram)
5	4	LET'S SPEND THE NIGHT TOGETHER — Rolling Stones (Decca)
9	5	I'VE BEEN A BAD BAD BOY — Paul Jones (HMV)
3	6	GREEN GREEN GRASS OF HOME — Tom Jones (Decca)
6	7	STANDING IN THE SHADOWS OF LOVE — Four Tops (Tamla Motown)
8	8	HEY JOE — Jimi Hendrix Experience (Polydor)
7	9	HAPPY JACK — Who (Reaction)
22	10	I'M A MAN — Spencer Davis Group (Fontana)
12	11	SITTING IN THE PARK — Georgie Fame (Columbia)
11	12	I FEEL FREE — Cream (Reaction)
15	12	PAMELA PAMELA — Wayne Fontana (Fontana)
10	14	MORNINGTOWN RIDE — Seekers (Columbia)
17	15	LET ME CRY ON YOUR SHOULDER — Ken Dodd (Columbia)
-	15	RELEASE ME — Engelbert Humperdinck (Decca)
-	17	HERE COMES MY BABY — Tremeloes (CBS)
21	18	SUGAR TOWN — Nancy Sinatra (Reprise)
24	19	SNOOPY VS. THE RED BARON — Royal Guardsmen (Stateside)
20	20	RUBY TUESDAY — Rolling Stones (Decca)
27	21	YOU ONLY YOU — Rita Pavone (RCA)
29	22	IT TAKES TWO — Marvin Gaye & Kim Weston (Tamla Motown)
-	23	PEEK-A-BOO — New Vaudeville Band (Fontana)
13	24	IN THE COUNTRY — Cliff Richard (Columbia)
19	25	SINGLE GIRL — Sandy Posey (MGM)
-	26	LAST TRAIN TO CLARKSVILLE — Monkees (RCA)
-	26	I WON'T COME IN WHILE HE'S THERE — Jim Reeves (RCA)
30	28	98.6 — Keith (Mercury)
14	29	ANY WAY THAT YOU WANT ME — Troggs (Page One)
16	30	SUNSHINE SUPERMAN — Donovan (Pye)

		11 February 1967
1	1	I'M A BELIEVER — Monkees (RCA)
4	2	LET'S SPEND THE NIGHT TOGETHER — Rolling Stones (Decca)
-	3	THIS IS MY SONG — Petula Clark (Pye)
2	4	MATTHEW AND SON — Cat Stevens (Deram)
5	5	I'VE BEEN A BAD BAD BOY — Paul Jones (HMV)
3	6	NIGHT OF FEAR — Move (Deram)
8	7	HEY JOE — Jimi Hendrix Experience (Polydor)
6	8	GREEN GREEN GRASS OF HOME — Tom Jones (Decca)
15	9	RELEASE ME — Engelbert Humperdinck (Decca)
10	10	I'M A MAN — Spencer Davis Group (Fontana)
15	11	LET ME CRY ON YOUR SHOULDER — Ken Dodd (Columbia)
18	12	SUGAR TOWN — Nancy Sinatra (Reprise)
26	13	I WON'T COME IN WHILE HE'S THERE — Jim Reeves (RCA)
17	14	HERE COMES MY BABY — Tremeloes (CBS)
7	15	STANDING IN THE SHADOWS OF LOVE — Four Tops (Tamla Motown)
22	16	IT TAKES TWO — Marvin Gaye & Kim Weston (Tamla Motown)
23	17	PEEK-A-BOO — New Vaudeville Band (Fontana)
19	18	SNOOPY VS. THE RED BARON — Royal Guardsmen (Stateside)
12	19	I FEEL FREE — Cream (Reaction)
12	20	PAMELA PAMELA — Wayne Fontana (Fontana)
-	21	MELLOW YELLOW — Donovan (Pye)
14	22	MORNINGTOWN RIDE — Seekers (Columbia)
9	23	HAPPY JACK — Who (Reaction)
25	24	SINGLE GIRL — Sandy Posey (MGM)
11	25	SITTING IN THE PARK — Georgie Fame (Columbia)
20	26	RUBY TUESDAY — Rolling Stones (Decca)
26	27	LAST TRAIN TO CLARKSVILLE — Monkees (RCA)
21	28	YOU ONLY YOU — Rita Pavone (RCA)
24	29	IN THE COUNTRY — Cliff Richard (Columbia)
-	30	EDELWEISS — Vince Hill (Columbia)

		18 February 1967
3	1	THIS IS MY SONG — Petula Clark (Pye)
9	2	RELEASE ME — Engelbert Humperdinck (Decca)
1	3	I'M A BELIEVER — Monkees (RCA)
2	4	LET'S SPEND THE NIGHT TOGETHER — Rolling Stones (Decca)
4	5	MATTHEW AND SON — Cat Stevens (Deram)
5	6	I'VE BEEN A BAD BAD BOY — Paul Jones (HMV)
14	7	HERE COMES MY BABY — Tremeloes (CBS)
8	8	SNOOPY VS. THE RED BARON — Royal Guardsmen (Stateside)
6	9	NIGHT OF FEAR — Move (Deram)
12	10	SUGAR TOWN — Nancy Sinatra (Reprise)
10	11	I'M A MAN — Spencer Davis Group (Fontana)
13	12	I WON'T COME IN WHILE HE'S THERE — Jim Reeves (RCA)
17	13	PEEK-A-BOO — New Vaudeville Band (Fontana)
21	14	MELLOW YELLOW — Donovan (Pye)
11	15	LET ME CRY ON YOUR SHOULDER — Ken Dodd (Columbia)
16	16	IT TAKES TWO — Marvin Gaye & Kim Weston (Tamla Motown)
7	16	HEY JOE — Jimi Hendrix Experience (Polydor)
8	18	GREEN GREEN GRASS OF HOME — Tom Jones (Decca)
30	19	EDELWEISS — Vince Hill (Columbia)
-	20	INDESCRIBABLY BLUE — Elvis Presley (RCA)
-	21	STAY WITH ME BABY — Walker Brothers (Philips)
26	22	RUBY TUESDAY — Rolling Stones (Decca)
-	23	GIVE IT TO ME — Troggs (Page One)
-	24	ON A CAROUSEL — Hollies (Parlophone)
24	25	SINGLE GIRL — Sandy Posey (MGM)
15	26	STANDING IN THE SHADOWS OF LOVE — Four Tops (Tamla Motown)
27	27	LAST TRAIN TO CLARKSVILLE — Monkees (RCA)
-	28	I'VE PASSED THIS WAY BEFORE — Jimmy Ruffin (Tamla Motown)
-	29	THERE'S A KIND OF HUSH (ALL OVER THE WORLD) — Herman's Hermits (Columbia)
-	30	DETROIT CITY — Tom Jones (Decca)
-	30	MICHAEL (THE LOVER) — Geno Washington (Piccadilly)

		25 February 1967
1	1	THIS IS MY SONG — Petula Clark (Pye)
2	2	RELEASE ME — Engelbert Humperdinck (Decca)
-	3	PENNY LANE/STRAWBERRY FIELDS FOREVER — Beatles (Parlophone)
3	4	I'M A BELIEVER — Monkees (RCA)
7	5	HERE COMES MY BABY — Tremeloes (CBS)
8	6	SNOOPY VS. THE RED BARON — Royal Guardsmen (Stateside)
4	7	LET'S SPEND THE NIGHT TOGETHER — Rolling Stones (Decca)
13	8	PEEK-A-BOO — New Vaudeville Band (Fontana)
14	9	MELLOW YELLOW — Donovan (Pye)
24	10	ON A CAROUSEL — Hollies (Parlophone)
12	11	I WON'T COME IN WHILE HE'S THERE — Jim Reeves (RCA)
6	12	I'VE BEEN A BAD BAD BOY — Paul Jones (HMV)
19	13	EDELWEISS — Vince Hill (Columbia)
5	14	MATTHEW AND SON — Cat Stevens (Deram)
10	15	SUGAR TOWN — Nancy Sinatra (Reprise)
16	16	IT TAKES TWO — Marvin Gaye & Kim Weston (Tamla Motown)
11	17	I'M A MAN — Spencer Davis Group (Fontana)
30	18	DETROIT CITY — Tom Jones (Decca)
29	19	THERE'S A KIND OF HUSH (ALL OVER THE WORLD) — Herman's Hermits (Columbia)
9	20	NIGHT OF FEAR — Move (Deram)
15	21	LET ME CRY ON YOUR SHOULDER — Ken Dodd (Columbia)
25	22	SINGLE GIRL — Sandy Posey (MGM)
16	23	HEY JOE — Jimi Hendrix Experience (Polydor)
23	24	GIVE IT TO ME — Troggs (Page One)
18	25	GREEN GREEN GRASS OF HOME — Tom Jones (Decca)
27	26	LAST TRAIN TO CLARKSVILLE — Monkees (RCA)
-	27	GEORGY GIRL — Seekers (Columbia)
20	28	INDESCRIBABLY BLUE — Elvis Presley (RCA)
22	29	RUBY TUESDAY — Rolling Stones (Decca)
-	30	RUN TO THE DOOR — Clinton Ford (Piccadilly)
28	30	I'VE PASSED THIS WAY BEFORE — Jimmy Ruffin (Tamla Motown)

This Is My Song was written by the then 77-year-old Charlie Chaplin, for the Sophia Loren/Marlon Brando film *A Countess From Hong Kong*, and was recorded first by Petula Clark in French and German before she (not initially overly impressed by the song) cut an English version. In the event, it provided her first UK Number One hit; she had previously topped the US chart with *Downtown* and *My Love*. Meanwhile, the Monkees' earlier single, *Last Train To Clarksville*, reawoke to join *I'm A Believer* in the Top 30.

4 March 1967

last week	this week	Title	Artist (Label)
2	1	RELEASE ME	Engelbert Humperdinck (Decca)
1	2	THIS IS MY SONG	Petula Clark (Pye)
3	3	PENNY LANE/STRAWBERRY FIELDS FOREVER	Beatles (Parlophone)
5	4	HERE COMES MY BABY	Tremeloes (CBS)
13	5	EDELWEISS	Vince Hill (Columbia)
10	6	ON A CAROUSEL	Hollies (Parlophone)
4	7	I'M A BELIEVER	Monkees (RCA)
6	8	SNOOPY VS. THE RED BARON	Royal Guardsmen (Stateside)
9	9	MELLOW YELLOW	Donovan (Pye)
8	10	PEEK-A-BOO	New Vaudeville Band (Fontana)
18	11	DETROIT CITY	Tom Jones (Decca)
19	12	THERE'S A KIND OF HUSH (ALL OVER THE WORLD)	Herman's Hermits (Columbia)
7	13	LET'S SPEND THE NIGHT TOGETHER	Rolling Stones (Decca)
11	14	I WON'T COME IN WHILE HE'S HERE	Jim Reeves (RCA)
27	15	GEORGY GIRL	Seekers (Columbia)
24	16	GIVE IT TO ME	Troggs (Page One)
16	17	IT TAKES TWO	Marvin Gaye & Kim Weston (Tamla Motown)
14	18	MATTHEW AND SON	Cat Stevens (Deram)
21	19	LET ME CRY ON YOUR SHOULDER	Ken Dodd (Columbia)
15	20	SUGAR TOWN	Nancy Sinatra (Reprise)
12	21	I'VE BEEN A BAD BAD BOY	Paul Jones (HMV)
-	22	I'LL TRY ANYTHING	Dusty Springfield (Philips)
23	23	I'M A MAN	Spencer Davis Group (Fontana)
22	24	SINGLE GIRL	Sandy Posey (MGM)
25	25	GREEN GREEN GRASS OF HOME	Tom Jones (Decca)
30	26	I'VE PASSED THIS WAY BEFORE	Jimmy Ruffin (Tamla Motown)
-	27	LOVE IS HERE AND NOW YOU'RE GONE	Supremes (Tamla Motown)
-	28	THEN YOU CALL TELL ME GOODBYE	Casinos (President)
-	28	STAY WITH ME BABY	Walker Brothers (Philips)
-	30	THIS IS MY SONG	Harry Secombe (Philips)

11 March 1967

last week	this week	Title	Artist (Label)
1	1	RELEASE ME	Engelbert Humperdinck (Decca)
3	2	PENNY LANE/STRAWBERRY FIELDS FOREVER	Beatles (Parlophone)
2	3	THIS IS MY SONG	Petula Clark (Pye)
4	4	HERE COMES MY BABY	Tremeloes (CBS)
5	5	EDELWEISS	Vince Hill (Columbia)
6	6	ON A CAROUSEL	Hollies (Parlophone)
11	7	DETROIT CITY	Tom Jones (Decca)
8	8	SNOOPY VS. THE RED BARON	Royal Guardsmen (Stateside)
12	9	THERE'S A KIND OF HUSH (ALL OVER THE WORLD)	Herman's Hermits (Columbia)
15	10	GEORGY GIRL	Seekers (Columbia)
7	11	I'M A BELIEVER	Monkees (RCA)
9	12	MELLOW YELLOW	Donovan (Pye)
10	13	PEEK-A-BOO	New Vaudeville Band (Fontana)
30	14	THIS IS MY SONG	Harry Secombe (Philips)
16	15	GIVE IT TO ME	Troggs (Page One)
14	16	I WON'T COME IN WHILE HE'S HERE	Jim Reeves (RCA)
17	17	IT TAKES TWO	Marvin Gaye & Kim Weston (Tamla Motown)
-	18	MEMORIES ARE MADE OF THIS	Val Doonican (Decca)
13	19	LET'S SPEND THE NIGHT TOGETHER	Rolling Stones (Decca)
22	20	I'LL TRY ANYTHING	Dusty Springfield (Philips)
-	21	I CAN'T MAKE IT	Small Faces (Decca)
-	22	SIMON SMITH AND HIS AMAZING DANCING BEAR	Alan Price Set (Decca)
23	23	SINGLE GIRL	Sandy Posey (MGM)
27	24	LOVE IS HERE AND NOW YOU'RE GONE	Supremes (Tamla Motown)
25	25	I'VE PASSED THIS WAY BEFORE	Jimmy Ruffin (Tamla Motown)
-	26	RUN TO THE DOOR	Clinton Ford (Piccadilly)
20	27	SUGAR TOWN	Nancy Sinatra (Reprise)
19	28	LET ME CRY ON YOUR SHOULDER	Ken Dodd (Columbia)
28	29	STAY WITH ME BABY	Walker Brothers (Philips)
-	30	I WAS KAISER BILL'S BATMAN	Whistling Jack Smith (Deram)

18 March 1967

last week	this week	Title	Artist (Label)
1	1	RELEASE ME	Engelbert Humperdinck (Decca)
2	2	PENNY LANE/STRAWBERRY FIELDS FOREVER	Beatles (Parlophone)
3	3	THIS IS MY SONG	Petula Clark (Pye)
5	4	EDELWEISS	Vince Hill (Columbia)
6	5	ON A CAROUSEL	Hollies (Parlophone)
9	6	THERE'S A KIND OF HUSH (ALL OVER THE WORLD)	Herman's Hermits (Columbia)
4	7	HERE COMES MY BABY	Tremeloes (CBS)
10	8	GEORGY GIRL	Seekers (Columbia)
14	9	THIS IS MY SONG	Harry Secombe (Philips)
7	10	DETROIT CITY	Tom Jones (Decca)
8	11	SNOOPY VS. THE RED BARON	Royal Guardsmen (Stateside)
18	12	MEMORIES ARE MADE OF THIS	Val Doonican (Decca)
13	13	PEEK-A-BOO	New Vaudeville Band (Fontana)
11	14	I'M A BELIEVER	Monkees (RCA)
22	14	SIMON SMITH AND HIS AMAZING DANCING BEAR	Alan Price Set (Decca)
30	16	I WAS KAISER BILL'S BATMAN	Whistling Jack Smith (Deram)
20	17	I'LL TRY ANYTHING	Dusty Springfield (Philips)
15	18	GIVE IT TO ME	Troggs (Page One)
12	19	MELLOW YELLOW	Donovan (Pye)
16	20	I WON'T COME IN WHILE HE'S HERE	Jim Reeves (RCA)
24	21	LOVE IS HERE AND NOW YOU'RE GONE	Supremes (Tamla Motown)
-	22	PUPPET ON A STRING	Sandie Shaw (Pye)
23	23	IT TAKES TWO	Marvin Gaye & Kim Weston (Tamla Motown)
-	24	TOUCH ME, TOUCH ME	Dave Dee, Dozy, Beaky, Mick & Tich (Fontana)
-	25	THEN YOU CALL TELL ME GOODBYE	Casinos (President)
-	26	JUST WHAT YOU WANT	John's Children (Columbia)
26	27	RUN TO THE DOOR	Clinton Ford (Piccadilly)
-	28	AL CAPONE	Prince Buster (Blue Beat)
21	29	I CAN'T MAKE IT	Small Faces (Decca)
25	30	I'VE PASSED THIS WAY BEFORE	Jimmy Ruffin (Tamla Motown)

25 March 1967

last week	this week	Title	Artist (Label)
1	1	RELEASE ME	Engelbert Humperdinck (Decca)
4	2	EDELWEISS	Vince Hill (Columbia)
3	3	THIS IS MY SONG	Petula Clark (Pye)
9	4	THIS IS MY SONG	Harry Secombe (Philips)
2	5	PENNY LANE/STRAWBERRY FIELDS FOREVER	Beatles (Parlophone)
5	6	ON A CAROUSEL	Hollies (Parlophone)
14	7	SIMON SMITH AND HIS AMAZING DANCING BEAR	Alan Price Set (Decca)
8	8	GEORGY GIRL	Seekers (Columbia)
6	9	THERE'S A KIND OF HUSH (ALL OVER THE WORLD)	Herman's Hermits (Columbia)
16	10	I WAS KAISER BILL'S BATMAN	Whistling Jack Smith (Deram)
22	11	PUPPET ON A STRING	Sandie Shaw (Pye)
10	12	DETROIT CITY	Tom Jones (Decca)
-	13	SOMETHIN' STUPID	Frank & Nancy Sinatra (Reprise)
11	14	SNOOPY VS. THE RED BARON	Royal Guardsmen (Stateside)
7	15	HERE COMES MY BABY	Tremeloes (CBS)
18	16	GIVE IT TO ME	Troggs (Page One)
12	17	MEMORIES ARE MADE OF THIS	Val Doonican (Decca)
17	18	I'LL TRY ANYTHING	Dusty Springfield (Philips)
13	19	PEEK-A-BOO	New Vaudeville Band (Fontana)
-	20	IT'S ALL OVER	Cliff Richard (Columbia)
29	21	I CAN'T MAKE IT	Small Faces (Decca)
14	22	I'M A BELIEVER	Monkees (RCA)
21	22	LOVE IS HERE AND NOW YOU'RE GONE	Supremes (Tamla Motown)
24	24	TOUCH ME, TOUCH ME	Dave Dee, Dozy, Beaky, Mick & Tich (Fontana)
28	25	AL CAPONE	Prince Buster (Blue Beat)
-	26	KNOCK ON WOOD	Eddie Floyd (Atlantic)
19	27	MELLOW YELLOW	Donovan (Pye)
23	28	IT TAKES TWO	Marvin Gaye & Kim Weston (Tamla Motown)
25	29	THEN YOU CALL TELL ME GOODBYE	Casinos (President)
-	30	GONNA GET ALONG WITHOUT YOU	Trini Lopez (Reprise)

Engelbert Humperdinck, formerly a no-hit singer named Gerry Dorsey, was the biggest-selling singles act in Britain during 1967, thanks to striking a significant public chord with some strong MOR ballads and an appeal more romantic than his raunchier management stable-mate Tom Jones. *Release Me*, a country song of some years' vintage acieved the notable feat of holding the Beatles at Number Two with one of their most highly-regarded singles, *Penny Lane/Strawberry Fields Forever*.

April 1967

1 April 1967

last	this	
1	1	RELEASE ME — Engelbert Humperdinck (Decca)
4	2	THIS IS MY SONG — Harry Secombe (Philips)
11	3	PUPPET ON A STRING — Sandie Shaw (Pye)
2	4	EDELWEISS Vince Hill (Columbia)
10	5	I WAS KAISER BILL'S BATMAN — Whistling Jack Smith (Deram)
7	6	SIMON SMITH AND HIS AMAZING DANCING BEAR — Alan Price Set (Decca)
13	7	SOMETHIN' STUPID — Frank & Nancy Sinatra (Reprise)
3	8	THIS IS MY SONG — Petula Clark (Pye)
8	9	GEORGY GIRL Seekers (Columbia)
5	10	PENNY LANE/STRAWBERRY FIELDS FOREVER — Beatles (Parlophone)
6	11	ON A CAROUSEL — Hollies (Parlophone)
17	12	MEMORIES ARE MADE OF THIS — Val Doonican (Decca)
9	13	THERE'S A KIND OF HUSH (ALL OVER THE WORLD) — Herman's Hermits (Columbia)
20	14	IT'S ALL OVER — Cliff Richard (Columbia)
12	15	DETROIT CITY Tom Jones (Decca)
16	16	GIVE IT TO ME Troggs (Page One)
25	17	AL CAPONE — Prince Buster (Blue Beat)
22	17	I'M A BELIEVER Monkees (RCA)
18	19	I'LL TRY ANYTHING — Dusty Springfield (Philips)
-	20	BECAUSE I LOVE YOU — Georgie Fame (CBS)
14	21	SNOOPY VS. THE RED BARON — Royal Guardsmen (Stateside)
22	21	LOVE IS HERE AND NOW YOU'RE GONE — Supremes (Tamla Motown)
26	23	KNOCK ON WOOD — Eddie Floyd (Atlantic)
24	24	TOUCH ME, TOUCH ME — Dave Dee, Dozy, Beaky, Mick & Tich (Fontana)
-	25	PURPLE HAZE — Jimi Hendrix Experience (Track)
-	26	ARNOLD LAYNE — Pink Floyd (Columbia)
-	27	BERNADETTE — Four Tops (Tamla Motown)
15	28	HERE COMES MY BABY — Tremeloes (CBS)
-	29	HA! HA! SAID THE CLOWN — Manfred Mann (Fontana)
21	30	I CAN'T MAKE IT — Small Faces (Decca)
-	30	HAPPY TOGETHER — Turtles (London)

8 April 1967

1	1	RELEASE ME — Engelbert Humperdinck (Decca)
2	2	THIS IS MY SONG — Harry Secombe (Philips)
7	3	SOMETHIN' STUPID — Frank & Nancy Sinatra (Reprise)
3	4	PUPPET ON A STRING — Sandie Shaw (Pye)
6	5	SIMON SMITH AND HIS AMAZING DANCING BEAR — Alan Price Set (Decca)
4	6	EDELWEISS Vince Hill (Columbia)
5	7	I WAS KAISER BILL'S BATMAN — Whistling Jack Smith (Deram)
-	8	A LITTLE BIT ME, A LITTLE BIT YOU Monkees (RCA)
14	8	IT'S ALL OVER — Cliff Richard (Columbia)
8	10	THIS IS MY SONG — Petula Clark (Pye)
29	11	HA! HA! SAID THE CLOWN — Manfred Mann (Fontana)
10	12	PENNY LANE/STRAWBERRY FIELDS FOREVER — Beatles (Parlophone)
9	13	GEORGY GIRL — Seekers (Columbia)
12	14	MEMORIES ARE MADE OF THIS — Val Doonican (Decca)
13	15	THERE'S A KIND OF HUSH (ALL OVER THE WORLD) — Herman's Hermits (Columbia)
27	16	BERNADETTE — Four Tops (Tamla Motown)
11	17	ON A CAROUSEL — Hollies (Parlophone)
24	18	TOUCH ME, TOUCH ME — Dave Dee, Dozy, Beaky, Mick & Tich (Fontana)
20	19	BECAUSE I LOVE YOU — Georgie Fame (CBS)
17	20	I'M A BELIEVER Monkees (RCA)
15	21	DETROIT CITY — Tom Jones (Decca)
30	22	HAPPY TOGETHER — Turtles (London)
25	23	PURPLE HAZE — Jimi Hendrix Experience (Track)
17	24	AL CAPONE — Prince Buster (Blue Beat)
-	25	SEVEN DRUNKEN NIGHTS — Dubliners (Major Minor)
23	26	KNOCK ON WOOD — Eddie Floyd (Atlantic)
21	27	LOVE IS HERE AND NOW YOU'RE GONE — Supremes (Tamla Motown)
16	28	GIVE IT TO ME Troggs (Page One)
19	29	I'LL TRY ANYTHING — Dusty Springfield (Philips)
-	30	YOU'VE GOT WHAT IT TAKES — Dave Clark Five (Columbia)

15 April 1967

3	1	SOMETHIN' STUPID — Frank & Nancy Sinatra (Reprise)
4	2	PUPPET ON A STRING — Sandie Shaw (Pye)
1	3	RELEASE ME — Engelbert Humperdinck (Decca)
8	4	A LITTLE BIT ME, A LITTLE BIT YOU Monkees (RCA)
2	5	THIS IS MY SONG — Harry Secombe (Philips)
11	6	HA! HA! SAID THE CLOWN — Manfred Mann (Fontana)
5	7	SIMON SMITH AND HIS AMAZING DANCING BEAR — Alan Price Set (Decca)
8	8	IT'S ALL OVER — Cliff Richard (Columbia)
7	9	I WAS KAISER BILL'S BATMAN — Whistling Jack Smith (Deram)
6	10	EDELWEISS Vince Hill (Columbia)
23	11	PURPLE HAZE — Jimi Hendrix Experience (Track)
16	12	BERNADETTE — Four Tops (Tamla Motown)
-	13	I'M GONNA GET ME A GUN — Cat Stevens (Deram)
10	14	THIS IS MY SONG — Petula Clark (Pye)
13	15	GEORGY GIRL Seekers (Columbia)
12	16	PENNY LANE/STRAWBERRY FIELDS FOREVER — Beatles (Parlophone)
19	17	BECAUSE I LOVE YOU — Georgie Fame (CBS)
25	18	SEVEN DRUNKEN NIGHTS — Dubliners (Major Minor)
22	19	HAPPY TOGETHER — Turtles (London)
18	20	TOUCH ME, TOUCH ME — Dave Dee, Dozy, Beaky, Mick & Tich (Fontana)
14	21	MEMORIES ARE MADE OF THIS — Val Doonican (Decca)
-	22	DEDICATED TO THE ONE I LOVE — Mamas & Papas (RCA)
-	23	I CAN HEAR THE GRASS GROW — Move (Deram)
26	24	KNOCK ON WOOD — Eddie Floyd (Atlantic)
-	24	ARNOLD LAYNE — Pink Floyd (Columbia)
-	26	HI HO SILVER LINING — Jeff Beck (Columbia)
24	27	AL CAPONE — Prince Buster (Blue Beat)
30	28	YOU'VE GOT WHAT IT TAKES — Dave Clark Five (Columbia)
-	29	JIMMY MACK — Martha & the Vandellas (Tamla Motown)
15	30	THERE'S A KIND OF HUSH (ALL OVER THE WORLD) — Herman's Hermits (Columbia)

22 April 1967

2	1	PUPPET ON A STRING — Sandie Shaw (Pye)
1	2	SOMETHIN' STUPID — Frank & Nancy Sinatra (Reprise)
4	3	A LITTLE BIT ME, A LITTLE BIT YOU Monkees (RCA)
6	4	HA! HA! SAID THE CLOWN — Manfred Mann (Fontana)
3	5	RELEASE ME — Engelbert Humperdinck (Decca)
5	6	THIS IS MY SONG — Harry Secombe (Philips)
11	7	PURPLE HAZE — Jimi Hendrix Experience (Track)
12	8	BERNADETTE — Four Tops (Tamla Motown)
8	9	IT'S ALL OVER — Cliff Richard (Columbia)
7	10	SIMON SMITH AND HIS AMAZING DANCING BEAR — Alan Price Set (Decca)
13	11	I'M GONNA GET ME A GUN — Cat Stevens (Deram)
9	12	I WAS KAISER BILL'S BATMAN — Whistling Jack Smith (Deram)
18	13	SEVEN DRUNKEN NIGHTS — Dubliners (Major Minor)
17	14	BECAUSE I LOVE YOU — Georgie Fame (CBS)
23	15	I CAN HEAR THE GRASS GROW — Move (Deram)
10	16	EDELWEISS Vince Hill (Columbia)
19	17	HAPPY TOGETHER — Turtles (London)
22	18	DEDICATED TO THE ONE I LOVE — Mamas & Papas (RCA)
-	19	FUNNY FAMILIAR FORGOTTEN FEELINGS Tom Jones (Decca)
29	20	JIMMY MACK — Martha & the Vandellas (Tamla Motown)
15	21	GEORGY GIRL Seekers (Columbia)
-	22	THE BOAT THAT I ROW — Lulu (Columbia)
27	23	AL CAPONE — Prince Buster (Blue Beat)
26	24	HI HO SILVER LINING — Jeff Beck (Columbia)
24	24	KNOCK ON WOOD — Eddie Floyd (Atlantic)
16	26	PENNY LANE/STRAWBERRY FIELDS FOREVER — Beatles (Parlophone)
21	26	MEMORIES ARE MADE OF THIS — Val Doonican (Decca)
20	28	TOUCH ME, TOUCH ME — Dave Dee, Dozy, Beaky, Mick & Tich (Fontana)
14	29	THIS IS MY SONG — Petula Clark (Pye)
-	30	MAROC 7 Shadows (Columbia)

The spring of 1967 was a high point for romantic ballads and MOR songs, in the wake of *This Is My Song* and *Release Me*. Harry Secombe's version of the former, in a very different arrangement from Pet Clark's, almost emulated her success with weeks, while Vince Hill hit Number Two with the *Sound Of Music* song *Edelweiss*, Cliff covered the Everly Brothers' wistful *It's All Over*, and Frank & Nancy Sinatra cut a cosy duet on the easy-going *Somethin' Stupid*, topping the chart on both sides of the Atlantic.

April – May 1967

29 April 1967

last week	this week		
1	1	PUPPET ON A STRING	Sandie Shaw (Pye)
2	2	SOMETHIN' STUPID	Frank & Nancy Sinatra (Reprise)
3	3	A LITTLE BIT ME, A LITTLE BIT YOU	Monkees (RCA)
4	4	HA! HA! SAID THE CLOWN	Manfred Mann (Fontana)
7	5	PURPLE HAZE	Jimi Hendrix Experience (Track)
5	6	RELEASE ME	Engelbert Humperdinck (Decca)
8	7	BERNADETTE	Four Tops (Tamla Motown)
11	8	I'M GONNA GET ME A GUN	Cat Stevens (Deram)
13	9	SEVEN DRUNKEN NIGHTS	Dubliners (Major Minor)
18	10	DEDICATED TO THE ONE I LOVE	Mamas & Papas (RCA)
15	11	I CAN HEAR THE GRASS GROW	Move (Deram)
6	12	THIS IS MY SONG	Harry Secombe (Philips)
19	13	FUNNY FAMILIAR FORGOTTEN FEELINGS	Tom Jones (Decca)
17	14	HAPPY TOGETHER	Turtles (London)
22	15	THE BOAT THAT I ROW	Lulu (Columbia)
9	16	IT'S ALL OVER	Cliff Richard (Columbia)
12	17	I WAS KAISER BILL'S BATMAN	Whistling Jack Smith (Deram)
10	18	SIMON SMITH AND HIS AMAZING DANCING BEAR	Alan Price Set (Decca)
14	19	BECAUSE I LOVE YOU	Georgie Fame (CBS)
-	19	PICTURES OF LILY	Who (Track)
24	21	KNOCK ON WOOD	Eddie Floyd (Atlantic)
20	22	JIMMY MACK	Martha & the Vandellas (Tamla Motown)
24	23	HI HO SILVER LINING	Jeff Beck (Columbia)
-	24	SILENCE IS GOLDEN	Tremeloes (CBS)
30	25	MAROC 7	Shadows (Columbia)
-	26	SWEET SOUL MUSIC	Arthur Conley (Atlantic)
-	27	GONNA GIVE HER ALL THE LOVE I'VE GOT	Jimmy Ruffin (Tamla Motown)
23	28	AL CAPONE	Prince Buster (Blue Beat)
16	29	EDELWEISS	Vince Hill (Columbia)
21	30	GEORGY GIRL	Seekers (Columbia)

6 May 1967

1	1	PUPPET ON A STRING	Sandie Shaw (Pye)
2	2	SOMETHIN' STUPID	Frank & Nancy Sinatra (Reprise)
3	3	A LITTLE BIT ME, A LITTLE BIT YOU	Monkees (RCA)
10	4	DEDICATED TO THE ONE I LOVE	Mamas & Papas (RCA)
5	5	PURPLE HAZE	Jimi Hendrix Experience (Track)
4	6	HA! HA! SAID THE CLOWN	Manfred Mann (Fontana)
11	7	I CAN HEAR THE GRASS GROW	Move (Deram)
13	8	FUNNY FAMILIAR FORGOTTEN FEELINGS	Tom Jones (Decca)
9	9	SEVEN DRUNKEN NIGHTS	Dubliners (Major Minor)
15	10	THE BOAT THAT I ROW	Lulu (Columbia)
8	11	I'M GONNA GET ME A GUN	Cat Stevens (Deram)
19	12	PICTURES OF LILY	Who (Track)
24	13	SILENCE IS GOLDEN	Tremeloes (CBS)
6	14	RELEASE ME	Engelbert Humperdinck (Decca)
7	15	BERNADETTE	Four Tops (Tamla Motown)
14	16	HAPPY TOGETHER	Turtles (London)
23	17	HI HO SILVER LINING	Jeff Beck (Columbia)
16	18	IT'S ALL OVER	Cliff Richard (Columbia)
12	19	THIS IS MY SONG	Harry Secombe (Philips)
26	20	SWEET SOUL MUSIC	Arthur Conley (Atlantic)
17	21	I WAS KAISER BILL'S BATMAN	Whistling Jack Smith (Deram)
27	22	GONNA GIVE HER ALL THE LOVE I'VE GOT	Jimmy Ruffin (Tamla Motown)
21	23	KNOCK ON WOOD	Eddie Floyd (Atlantic)
22	24	JIMMY MACK	Martha & the Vandellas (Tamla Motown)
25	25	MAROC 7	Shadows (Columbia)
-	26	NEW YORK MINING DISASTER 1941	Bee Gees (Polydor)
-	27	BIRDS AND BEES	Warm Sounds (Deram)
-	28	GET ME TO THE WORLD ON TIME	Electric Prunes (Reprise)
19	29	BECAUSE I LOVE YOU	Georgie Fame (CBS)
18	30	SIMON SMITH AND HIS AMAZING DANCING BEAR	Alan Price Set (Decca)

13 May 1967

1	1	PUPPET ON A STRING	Sandie Shaw (Pye)
4	2	DEDICATED TO THE ONE I LOVE	Mamas & Papas (RCA)
2	3	SOMETHIN' STUPID	Frank & Nancy Sinatra (Reprise)
13	4	SILENCE IS GOLDEN	Tremeloes (CBS)
5	5	PURPLE HAZE	Jimi Hendrix Experience (Track)
10	6	THE BOAT THAT I ROW	Lulu (Columbia)
12	7	PICTURES OF LILY	Who (Track)
7	8	I CAN HEAR THE GRASS GROW	Move (Deram)
3	9	A LITTLE BIT ME, A LITTLE BIT YOU	Monkees (RCA)
8	10	FUNNY FAMILIAR FORGOTTEN FEELINGS	Tom Jones (Decca)
9	11	SEVEN DRUNKEN NIGHTS	Dubliners (Major Minor)
6	12	HA! HA! SAID THE CLOWN	Manfred Mann (Fontana)
11	13	I'M GONNA GET ME A GUN	Cat Stevens (Deram)
16	14	HAPPY TOGETHER	Turtles (London)
14	15	RELEASE ME	Engelbert Humperdinck (Decca)
15	16	BERNADETTE	Four Tops (Tamla Motown)
-	17	WATERLOO SUNSET	Kinks (Pye)
17	18	HI HO SILVER LINING	Jeff Beck (Columbia)
20	19	SWEET SOUL MUSIC	Arthur Conley (Atlantic)
-	20	THEN I KISSED HER	Beach Boys (Capitol)
26	21	NEW YORK MINING DISASTER 1941	Bee Gees (Polydor)
-	22	THE FIRST CUT IS THE DEEPEST	P.P. Arnold (Immediate)
18	23	IT'S ALL OVER	Cliff Richard (Columbia)
-	24	THE WIND CRIES MARY	Jimi Hendrix Experience (Track)
27	25	BIRDS AND BEES	Warm Sounds (Deram)
-	26	FINCHLEY CENTRAL	New Vaudeville Band (Fontana)
-	27	CASINO ROYALE	Herb Alpert & the Tijuana Brass (A&M)
25	28	MAROC 7	Shadows (Columbia)
23	29	KNOCK ON WOOD	Eddie Floyd (Atlantic)
-	30	IF I WERE A RICH MAN	Topol (CBS)

20 May 1967

4	1	SILENCE IS GOLDEN	Tremeloes (CBS)
2	2	DEDICATED TO THE ONE I LOVE	Mamas & Papas (RCA)
1	3	PUPPET ON A STRING	Sandie Shaw (Pye)
7	4	PICTURES OF LILY	Who (Track)
3	5	SOMETHIN' STUPID	Frank & Nancy Sinatra (Reprise)
6	6	THE BOAT THAT I ROW	Lulu (Columbia)
17	7	WATERLOO SUNSET	Kinks (Pye)
11	8	SEVEN DRUNKEN NIGHTS	Dubliners (Major Minor)
10	9	FUNNY FAMILIAR FORGOTTEN FEELINGS	Tom Jones (Decca)
5	10	PURPLE HAZE	Jimi Hendrix Experience (Track)
9	11	A LITTLE BIT ME, A LITTLE BIT YOU	Monkees (RCA)
20	12	THEN I KISSED HER	Beach Boys (Capitol)
24	13	THE WIND CRIES MARY	Jimi Hendrix Experience (Track)
8	14	I CAN HEAR THE GRASS GROW	Move (Deram)
19	15	SWEET SOUL MUSIC	Arthur Conley (Atlantic)
21	16	NEW YORK MINING DISASTER 1941	Bee Gees (Polydor)
12	17	HA! HA! SAID THE CLOWN	Manfred Mann (Fontana)
18	18	HI HO SILVER LINING	Jeff Beck (Columbia)
14	19	HAPPY TOGETHER	Turtles (London)
15	20	RELEASE ME	Engelbert Humperdinck (Decca)
26	21	FINCHLEY CENTRAL	New Vaudeville Band (Fontana)
-	22	THE HAPPENING	Supremes (Tamla Motown)
27	23	CASINO ROYALE	Herb Alpert & the Tijuana Brass (A&M)
22	24	THE FIRST CUT IS THE DEEPEST	P.P. Arnold (Immediate)
13	25	I'M GONNA GET ME A GUN	Cat Stevens (Deram)
25	26	BIRDS AND BEES	Warm Sounds (Deram)
29	27	IF I WERE A RICH MAN	Topol (CBS)
-	28	MUSIC TO WATCH GIRLS BY	Andy Williams (CBS)
-	29	ROSES OF PICARDY	Vince Hill (Columbia)
28	30	MAROC 7	Shadows (Columbia)

Neil Diamond, still some years from UK chart success as a performer, was becoming a very successful songwriter. Having penned the Monkees' *I'm A Believer*, he was also responsible for the group's follow-up, *A Little Bit Me, A Little Bit You*, and for Lulu's *The Boat That I Row*. Meanwhile, Jimi Hendrix (who guested on Lulu's UK TV show, and toured in the US with the Monkees, though is not known to have worked with Neil Diamond!) had two simultanous, and contrasting, Top 20 entries.

May – June 1967

27 May 1967

last week	this week	Title / Artist
1	1	SILENCE IS GOLDEN — Tremeloes (CBS)
7	2	WATERLOO SUNSET — Kinks (Pye)
2	3	DEDICATED TO THE ONE I LOVE — Mamas & Papas (RCA)
4	4	PICTURES OF LILY — Who (Track)
3	5	PUPPET ON A STRING — Sandie Shaw (Pye)
12	6	THEN I KISSED HER — Beach Boys (Capitol)
13	7	THE WIND CRIES MARY — Jimi Hendrix Experience (Track)
6	8	THE BOAT THAT I ROW — Lulu (Columbia)
8	9	SEVEN DRUNKEN NIGHTS — Dubliners (Major Minor)
5	10	SOMETHIN' STUPID — Frank & Nancy Sinatra (Reprise)
-	11	A WHITER SHADE OF PALE — Procol Harum (Deram)
9	12	FUNNY FAMILIAR FORGOTTEN FEELINGS — Tom Jones (Decca)
15	13	SWEET SOUL MUSIC — Arthur Conley (Atlantic)
22	14	THE HAPPENING — Supremes (Tamla Motown)
16	15	NEW YORK MINING DISASTER 1941 — Bee Gees (Polydor)
-	16	THERE GOES MY EVERYTHING — Engelbert Humperdinck (Decca)
11	17	A LITTLE BIT ME, A LITTLE BIT YOU — Monkees (RCA)
10	18	PURPLE HAZE — Jimi Hendrix Experience (Track)
18	19	HI HO SILVER LINING — Jeff Beck (Columbia)
21	20	FINCHLEY CENTRAL — New Vaudeville Band (Fontana)
14	21	I CAN HEAR THE GRASS GROW — Move (Deram)
23	22	CASINO ROYALE — Herb Alpert & the Tijuana Brass (A&M)
29	23	ROSES OF PICARDY — Vince Hill (Columbia)
24	24	THE FIRST CUT IS THE DEEPEST — P.P. Arnold (Immediate)
-	25	WALKING IN THE RAIN — Walker Brothers (Philips)
28	25	MUSIC TO WATCH GIRLS BY — Andy Williams (CBS)
27	27	IF I WERE A RICH MAN — Topol (CBS)
-	28	I GOT RHYTHM — Happenings (Stateside)
26	29	BIRDS AND BEES — Warm Sounds (Deram)
-	29	GROOVIN' — Young Rascals (Atlantic)

3 June 1967

this week	Title / Artist
1	SILENCE IS GOLDEN — Tremeloes (CBS)
2	WATERLOO SUNSET — Kinks (Pye)
3	A WHITER SHADE OF PALE — Procol Harum (Deram)
4	DEDICATED TO THE ONE I LOVE — Mamas & Papas (RCA)
5	THEN I KISSED HER — Beach Boys (Capitol)
6	THERE GOES MY EVERYTHING — Engelbert Humperdinck (Decca)
7	THE HAPPENING — Supremes (Tamla Motown)
8	THE WIND CRIES MARY — Jimi Hendrix Experience (Track)
9	PICTURES OF LILY — Who (Track)
10	PUPPET ON A STRING — Sandie Shaw (Pye)
11	SEVEN DRUNKEN NIGHTS — Dubliners (Major Minor)
12	SWEET SOUL MUSIC — Arthur Conley (Atlantic)
13	THE BOAT THAT I ROW — Lulu (Columbia)
14	FUNNY FAMILIAR FORGOTTEN FEELINGS — Tom Jones (Decca)
15	SOMETHIN' STUPID — Frank & Nancy Sinatra (Reprise)
16	FINCHLEY CENTRAL — New Vaudeville Band (Fontana)
17	NEW YORK MINING DISASTER 1941 — Bee Gees (Polydor)
18	THE FIRST CUT IS THE DEEPEST — P.P. Arnold (Immediate)
19	ROSES OF PICARDY — Vince Hill (Columbia)
20	GROOVIN' — Young Rascals (Atlantic)
21	CASINO ROYALE — Herb Alpert & the Tijuana Brass (A&M)
22	IF I WERE A RICH MAN — Topol (CBS)
23	WALKING IN THE RAIN — Walker Brothers (Philips)
24	NIGHT OF THE LONG GRASS — Troggs (Page One)
25	DON'T SLEEP IN THE SUBWAY — Petula Clark (Pye)
26	SGT. PEPPER'S LONELY HEARTS CLUB BAND (LP) — Beatles (Parlophone)
26	GIVE ME TIME — Dusty Springfield (Philips)
28	I GOT RHYTHM — Happenings (Stateside)
29	A LITTLE BIT ME, A LITTLE BIT YOU — Monkees (RCA)
30	I CAN HEAR THE GRASS GROW — Move (Deram)

10 June 1967

last week	this week	Title / Artist
3	1	A WHITER SHADE OF PALE — Procol Harum (Deram)
1	2	SILENCE IS GOLDEN — Tremeloes (CBS)
6	3	THERE GOES MY EVERYTHING — Engelbert Humperdinck (Decca)
2	4	WATERLOO SUNSET — Kinks (Pye)
4	5	DEDICATED TO THE ONE I LOVE — Mamas & Papas (RCA)
5	6	THEN I KISSED HER — Beach Boys (Capitol)
7	7	THE HAPPENING — Supremes (Tamla Motown)
8	8	THE WIND CRIES MARY — Jimi Hendrix Experience (Track)
12	9	SWEET SOUL MUSIC — Arthur Conley (Atlantic)
16	10	FINCHLEY CENTRAL — New Vaudeville Band (Fontana)
9	10	PICTURES OF LILY — Who (Track)
10	12	PUPPET ON A STRING — Sandie Shaw (Pye)
-	13	CARRIE ANNE — Hollies (Parlophone)
11	14	SEVEN DRUNKEN NIGHTS — Dubliners (Major Minor)
-	15	OKAY! — Dave Dee, Dozy, Beaky, Mick & Tich (Fontana)
20	15	GROOVIN' — Young Rascals (Atlantic)
26	17	GIVE ME TIME — Dusty Springfield (Philips)
19	18	ROSES OF PICARDY — Vince Hill (Columbia)
-	19	PAPER SUN — Traffic (Island)
25	20	DON'T SLEEP IN THE SUBWAY — Petula Clark (Pye)
26	21	SGT. PEPPER'S LONELY HEARTS CLUB BAND (LP) — Beatles (Parlophone)
18	22	THE FIRST CUT IS THE DEEPEST — P.P. Arnold (Immediate)
15	23	SOMETHIN' STUPID — Frank & Nancy Sinatra (Reprise)
14	24	FUNNY FAMILIAR FORGOTTEN FEELINGS — Tom Jones (Decca)
22	24	IF I WERE A RICH MAN — Topol (CBS)
13	26	THE BOAT THAT I ROW — Lulu (Columbia)
21	27	CASINO ROYALE — Herb Alpert & the Tijuana Brass (A&M)
24	28	NIGHT OF THE LONG GRASS — Troggs (Page One)
23	29	WALKING IN THE RAIN — Walker Brothers (Philips)
17	30	NEW YORK MINING DISASTER 1941 — Bee Gees (Polydor)

17 June 1967

last week	this week	Title / Artist
1	1	A WHITER SHADE OF PALE — Procol Harum (Deram)
3	2	THERE GOES MY EVERYTHING — Engelbert Humperdinck (Decca)
2	3	SILENCE IS GOLDEN — Tremeloes (CBS)
4	4	WATERLOO SUNSET — Kinks (Pye)
7	5	THE HAPPENING — Supremes (Tamla Motown)
13	6	CARRIE ANNE — Hollies (Parlophone)
5	7	DEDICATED TO THE ONE I LOVE — Mamas & Papas (RCA)
6	8	THEN I KISSED HER — Beach Boys (Capitol)
15	9	OKAY! — Dave Dee, Dozy, Beaky, Mick & Tich (Fontana)
9	10	SWEET SOUL MUSIC — Arthur Conley (Atlantic)
10	11	FINCHLEY CENTRAL — New Vaudeville Band (Fontana)
15	12	GROOVIN' — Young Rascals (Atlantic)
8	13	THE WIND CRIES MARY — Jimi Hendrix Experience (Track)
19	14	PAPER SUN — Traffic (Island)
20	15	DON'T SLEEP IN THE SUBWAY — Petula Clark (Pye)
18	16	ROSES OF PICARDY — Vince Hill (Columbia)
12	17	PUPPET ON A STRING — Sandie Shaw (Pye)
22	18	THE FIRST CUT IS THE DEEPEST — P.P. Arnold (Immediate)
-	19	HERE COMES THE NICE — Small Faces (Immediate)
24	20	IF I WERE A RICH MAN — Topol (CBS)
28	21	NIGHT OF THE LONG GRASS — Troggs (Page One)
10	21	PICTURES OF LILY — Who (Track)
-	23	WHAT GOOD AM I — Cilla Black (Parlophone)
-	23	I'LL COME RUNNING — Cliff Richard (Columbia)
-	25	SEVEN ROOMS OF GLOOM — Four Tops (Tamla Motown)
17	26	GIVE ME TIME — Dusty Springfield (Philips)
21	27	SGT. PEPPER'S LONELY HEARTS CLUB BAND (LP) — Beatles (Parlophone)
14	28	SEVEN DRUNKEN NIGHTS — Dubliners (Major Minor)
-	29	STRANGE BREW — Cream (Reaction)
-	30	RESPECT — Aretha Franklin (Atlantic)

The Tremeloes went to the Four Seasons back-catalogue, and specifically to the B-side of *Rag Doll*, for *Silence Is Golden*. Meanwhile, newcomers Procol Harum went to J.S. Bach, and very specifically his *Suite No.3 in D Major (Air On The G String)*, for the musical framework of *A Whiter Shade Of Pale*, a lyrically surrealistic, languid song which caught the whole mood of 1967's emerging "Summer of Love", and along with the Beatles' *Sgt. Pepper* album - which charted a week later - still stands as an icon of the era.

24 June 1967

last / this week

1 1 A WHITER SHADE OF PALE — Procol Harum (Deram)
2 2 THERE GOES MY EVERYTHING — Engelbert Humperdinck (Decca)
6 3 CARRIE ANNE — Hollies (Parlophone)
3 4 SILENCE IS GOLDEN — Tremeloes (CBS)
4 5 WATERLOO SUNSET — Kinks (Pye)
9 6 OKAY! — Dave Dee, Dozy, Beaky, Mick & Tich (Fontana)
5 7 THE HAPPENING — Supremes (Tamla Motown)
14 8 PAPER SUN — Traffic (Island)
10 9 SWEET SOUL MUSIC — Arthur Conley (Atlantic)
12 10 GROOVIN' — Young Rascals (Atlantic)
8 11 THEN I KISSED HER — Beach Boys (Capitol)
19 12 HERE COMES THE NICE — Small Faces (Immediate)
7 13 DEDICATED TO THE ONE I LOVE — Mamas & Papas (RCA)
11 14 FINCHLEY CENTRAL — New Vaudeville Band (Fontana)
- 15 SHE'D RATHER BE WITH ME — Turtles (London)
15 16 DON'T SLEEP IN THE SUBWAY — Petula Clark (Pye)
20 17 IF I WERE A RICH MAN — Topol (CBS)
23 18 WHAT GOOD AM I — Cilla Black (Parlophone)
23 19 I'LL COME RUNNING — Cliff Richard (Columbia)
29 20 STRANGE BREW — Cream (Reaction)
- 21 ALTERNATE TITLE — Monkees (RCA)
16 22 ROSES OF PICARDY — Vince Hill (Columbia)
25 23 SEVEN ROOMS OF GLOOM — Four Tops (Tamla Motown)
21 24 NIGHT OF THE LONG GRASS — Troggs (Page One)
30 25 RESPECT — Aretha Franklin (Atlantic)
- 26 IT MUST BE HIM — Vikki Carr (Liberty)
18 27 THE FIRST CUT IS THE DEEPEST — P.P. Arnold (Immediate)
17 27 PUPPET ON A STRING — Sandie Shaw (Pye)
13 29 THE WIND CRIES MARY — Jimi Hendrix Experience (Track)
27 30 SGT. PEPPER'S LONELY HEARTS CLUB BAND (LP) — Beatles (Parlophone)

1 July 1967

1 1 A WHITER SHADE OF PALE — Procol Harum (Deram)
2 2 THERE GOES MY EVERYTHING — Engelbert Humperdinck (Decca)
3 3 CARRIE ANNE — Hollies (Parlophone)
8 4 PAPER SUN — Traffic (Island)
6 5 OKAY! — Dave Dee, Dozy, Beaky, Mick & Tich (Fontana)
21 6 ALTERNATE TITLE — Monkees (RCA)
15 7 SHE'D RATHER BE WITH ME — Turtles (London)
10 8 GROOVIN' — Young Rascals (Atlantic)
4 9 SILENCE IS GOLDEN — Tremeloes (CBS)
12 10 HERE COMES THE NICE — Small Faces (Immediate)
7 11 THE HAPPENING — Supremes (Tamla Motown)
5 12 WATERLOO SUNSET — Kinks (Pye)
9 13 SWEET SOUL MUSIC — Arthur Conley (Atlantic)
16 14 DON'T SLEEP IN THE SUBWAY — Petula Clark (Pye)
20 15 STRANGE BREW — Cream (Reaction)
17 16 IF I WERE A RICH MAN — Topol (CBS)
26 17 IT MUST BE HIM — Vikki Carr (Liberty)
23 18 SEVEN ROOMS OF GLOOM — Four Tops (Tamla Motown)
11 19 THEN I KISSED HER — Beach Boys (Capitol)
25 20 RESPECT — Aretha Franklin (Atlantic)
18 21 WHAT GOOD AM I — Cilla Black (Parlophone)
13 22 DEDICATED TO THE ONE I LOVE — Mamas & Papas (RCA)
14 23 FINCHLEY CENTRAL — New Vaudeville Band (Fontana)
24 24 NIGHT OF THE LONG GRASS — Troggs (Page One)
22 25 ROSES OF PICARDY — Vince Hill (Columbia)
19 26 I'LL COME RUNNING — Cliff Richard (Columbia)
- 27 SEE EMILY PLAY — Pink Floyd (Columbia)
29 28 THE WIND CRIES MARY — Jimi Hendrix Experience (Track)
27 29 PUPPET ON A STRING — Sandie Shaw (Pye)
30 30 SGT. PEPPER'S LONELY HEARTS CLUB BAND (LP) — Beatles (Parlophone)

8 July 1967

1 1 A WHITER SHADE OF PALE — Procol Harum (Deram)
2 2 THERE GOES MY EVERYTHING — Engelbert Humperdinck (Decca)
6 3 ALTERNATE TITLE — Monkees (RCA)
7 4 SHE'D RATHER BE WITH ME — Turtles (London)
3 5 CARRIE ANNE — Hollies (Parlophone)
4 6 PAPER SUN — Traffic (Island)
5 7 OKAY! — Dave Dee, Dozy, Beaky, Mick & Tich (Fontana)
8 8 GROOVIN' — Young Rascals (Atlantic)
17 9 IT MUST BE HIM — Vikki Carr (Liberty)
10 10 HERE COMES THE NICE — Small Faces (Immediate)
14 11 DON'T SLEEP IN THE SUBWAY — Petula Clark (Pye)
15 12 STRANGE BREW — Cream (Reaction)
18 13 SEVEN ROOMS OF GLOOM — Four Tops (Tamla Motown)
16 14 IF I WERE A RICH MAN — Topol (CBS)
9 15 SILENCE IS GOLDEN — Tremeloes (CBS)
20 16 RESPECT — Aretha Franklin (Atlantic)
11 17 THE HAPPENING — Supremes (Tamla Motown)
27 18 SEE EMILY PLAY — Pink Floyd (Columbia)
13 19 SWEET SOUL MUSIC — Arthur Conley (Atlantic)
12 20 WATERLOO SUNSET — Kinks (Pye)
21 21 WHAT GOOD AM I — Cilla Black (Parlophone)
23 22 FINCHLEY CENTRAL — New Vaudeville Band (Fontana)
25 23 ROSES OF PICARDY — Vince Hill (Columbia)
19 24 THEN I KISSED HER — Beach Boys (Capitol)
26 25 I'LL COME RUNNING — Cliff Richard (Columbia)
- 26 CLAIRE — Paul & Barry Ryan (Decca)
- 27 LET'S PRETEND — Lulu (Columbia)
- 28 ANNABELLA — John Walker (Philips)
22 29 DEDICATED TO THE ONE I LOVE — Mamas & Papas (RCA)
- 30 TAKE ME IN YOUR ARMS AND LOVE ME — Gladys Knight & the Pips (Tamla Motown)

15 July 1967

- 1 ALL YOU NEED IS LOVE — Beatles (Parlophone)
3 2 ALTERNATE TITLE — Monkees (RCA)
1 3 A WHITER SHADE OF PALE — Procol Harum (Deram)
4 4 SHE'D RATHER BE WITH ME — Turtles (London)
2 5 THERE GOES MY EVERYTHING — Engelbert Humperdinck (Decca)
9 6 IT MUST BE HIM — Vikki Carr (Liberty)
5 7 CARRIE ANNE — Hollies (Parlophone)
6 8 PAPER SUN — Traffic (Island)
8 9 GROOVIN' — Young Rascals (Atlantic)
18 10 SEE EMILY PLAY — Pink Floyd (Columbia)
10 11 HERE COMES THE NICE — Small Faces (Immediate)
13 12 SEVEN ROOMS OF GLOOM — Four Tops (Tamla Motown)
7 13 OKAY! — Dave Dee, Dozy, Beaky, Mick & Tich (Fontana)
12 14 STRANGE BREW — Cream (Reaction)
16 15 RESPECT — Aretha Franklin (Atlantic)
11 16 DON'T SLEEP IN THE SUBWAY — Petula Clark (Pye)
14 17 IF I WERE A RICH MAN — Topol (CBS)
- 18 SAN FRANCISCO (BE SURE TO WEAR SOME FLOWERS IN YOUR HAIR) — Scott McKenzie (CBS)
30 19 TAKE ME IN YOUR ARMS AND LOVE ME — Gladys Knight & the Pips (Tamla Motown)
17 20 THE HAPPENING — Supremes (Tamla Motown)
- 21 I WAS MADE TO LOVE HER — Stevie Wonder (Tamla Motown)
19 22 SWEET SOUL MUSIC — Arthur Conley (Atlantic)
26 23 CLAIRE — Paul & Barry Ryan (Decca)
- 24 SHAKE — Otis Redding (Stax)
28 25 ANNABELLA — John Walker (Philips)
- 26 UP AND AWAY — Johnny Mann Singers (Liberty)
15 27 SILENCE IS GOLDEN — Tremeloes (CBS)
- 28 JUST LOVING YOU — Anita Harris (CBS)
- 29 WHEN YOU'RE YOUNG AND IN LOVE — Marvelettes (Tamla Motown)
27 30 LET'S PRETEND — Lulu (Columbia)

A Whiter Shade Of Pale, which seemed to transcend a lot of pop-snobbery boundaries, sold over 800,000 copies, enough to prevent Engelbert Humperdinck from having his second Number One with *There Goes My Everything*, even though that, too, sold more than 750,000. Traffic, the group formed by Steve Winwood following his departure from the Spencer Davis Group, quickly scored with *Paper Sun*, while the Monkees' *Alternate Title* was, literally, a UK-only alternative to the original title: *Randy Scouse Git*.

July – August 1967

last week / this week

22 July 1967

last	this	
1	1	ALL YOU NEED IS LOVE — Beatles (Parlophone)
2	2	ALTERNATE TITLE — Monkees (RCA)
6	3	IT MUST BE HIM — Vikki Carr (Liberty)
4	4	SHE'D RATHER BE WITH ME — Turtles (London)
3	5	A WHITER SHADE OF PALE — Procol Harum (Deram)
5	6	THERE GOES MY EVERYTHING — Engelbert Humperdinck (Decca)
18	7	SAN FRANCISCO (BE SURE TO WEAR SOME FLOWERS IN YOUR HAIR) — Scott McKenzie (CBS)
10	8	SEE EMILY PLAY — Pink Floyd (Columbia)
7	9	CARRIE ANNE — Hollies (Parlophone)
15	10	RESPECT — Aretha Franklin (Atlantic)
9	11	GROOVIN' — Young Rascals (Atlantic)
11	12	HERE COMES THE NICE — Small Faces (Immediate)
8	13	PAPER SUN — Traffic (Island)
12	14	SEVEN ROOMS OF GLOOM — Four Tops (Tamla Motown)
21	15	I WAS MADE TO LOVE HER — Stevie Wonder (Tamla Motown)
14	16	STRANGE BREW — Cream (Reaction)
19	17	TAKE ME IN YOUR ARMS AND LOVE ME — Gladys Knight & the Pips (Tamla Motown)
30	18	LET'S PRETEND — Lulu (Columbia)
-	19	TRAMP — Otis Redding & Carla Thomas (Stax)
26	20	UP UP AND AWAY — Johnny Mann Singers (Liberty)
28	21	JUST LOVING YOU — Anita Harris (CBS)
-	21	YOU ONLY LIVE TWICE — Nancy Sinatra (Reprise)
17	23	IF I WERE A RICH MAN — Topol (CBS)
22	24	SWEET SOUL MUSIC — Arthur Conley (Atlantic)
-	25	TONIGHT IN TOKYO — Sandie Shaw (Pye)
13	26	OKAY! — Dave Dee, Dozy, Beaky, Mick & Tich (Fontana)
16	27	DON'T SLEEP IN THE SUBWAY — Petula Clark (Pye)
-	28	DEATH OF A CLOWN — Dave Davies (Pye)
-	29	TRYING TO FORGET — Jim Reeves (RCA)
25	30	ANNABELLA — John Walker (Philips)

29 July 1967

1	ALL YOU NEED IS LOVE — Beatles (Parlophone)
7	2 SAN FRANCISCO (BE SURE TO WEAR SOME FLOWERS IN YOUR HAIR) — Scott McKenzie (CBS)
3	3 IT MUST BE HIM — Vikki Carr (Liberty)
2	4 ALTERNATE TITLE — Monkees (RCA)
4	5 SHE'D RATHER BE WITH ME — Turtles (London)
5	6 A WHITER SHADE OF PALE — Procol Harum (Deram)
6	7 THERE GOES MY EVERYTHING — Engelbert Humperdinck (Decca)
8	8 SEE EMILY PLAY — Pink Floyd (Columbia)
20	9 UP UP AND AWAY — Johnny Mann Singers (Liberty)
28	10 DEATH OF A CLOWN — Dave Davies (Pye)
15	11 I WAS MADE TO LOVE HER — Stevie Wonder (Tamla Motown)
18	12 LET'S PRETEND — Lulu (Columbia)
10	13 RESPECT — Aretha Franklin (Atlantic)
-	14 I'LL NEVER FALL IN LOVE AGAIN — Tom Jones (Decca)
21	15 JUST LOVING YOU — Anita Harris (CBS)
19	16 TRAMP — Otis Redding & Carla Thomas (Stax)
11	17 GROOVIN' — Young Rascals (Atlantic)
21	18 YOU ONLY LIVE TWICE — Nancy Sinatra (Reprise)
17	19 TAKE ME IN YOUR ARMS AND LOVE ME — Gladys Knight & the Pips (Tamla Motown)
23	20 IF I WERE A RICH MAN — Topol (CBS)
9	21 CARRIE ANNE — Hollies (Parlophone)
14	22 SEVEN ROOMS OF GLOOM — Four Tops (Tamla Motown)
30	23 ANNABELLA — John Walker (Philips)
-	24 007 (SHANTY TOWN) — Desmond Dekker (Pyramid)
13	25 PAPER SUN — Traffic (Island)
-	26 MARTA — Bachelors (Decca)
12	27 HERE COMES THE NICE — Small Faces (Immediate)
29	28 TRYING TO FORGET — Jim Reeves (RCA)
-	29 WITH A LITTLE HELP FROM MY FRIENDS — Young Idea (Columbia)
-	30 WHEN YOU'RE YOUNG AND IN LOVE — Marvelettes (Tamla Motown)

5 August 1967

1	ALL YOU NEED IS LOVE — Beatles (Parlophone)
2	2 SAN FRANCISCO (BE SURE TO WEAR SOME FLOWERS IN YOUR HAIR) — Scott McKenzie (CBS)
3	3 IT MUST BE HIM — Vikki Carr (Liberty)
10	4 DEATH OF A CLOWN — Dave Davies (Pye)
14	4 I'LL NEVER FALL IN LOVE AGAIN — Tom Jones (Decca)
4	6 ALTERNATE TITLE — Monkees (RCA)
5	7 SHE'D RATHER BE WITH ME — Turtles (London)
9	8 UP UP AND AWAY — Johnny Mann Singers (Liberty)
8	9 SEE EMILY PLAY — Pink Floyd (Columbia)
11	10 I WAS MADE TO LOVE HER — Stevie Wonder (Tamla Motown)
7	11 THERE GOES MY EVERYTHING — Engelbert Humperdinck (Decca)
12	12 LET'S PRETEND — Lulu (Columbia)
15	13 JUST LOVING YOU — Anita Harris (CBS)
6	14 A WHITER SHADE OF PALE — Procol Harum (Deram)
18	15 YOU ONLY LIVE TWICE — Nancy Sinatra (Reprise)
13	16 RESPECT — Aretha Franklin (Atlantic)
16	17 TRAMP — Otis Redding & Carla Thomas (Stax)
24	18 007 (SHANTY TOWN) — Desmond Dekker (Pyramid)
19	19 TAKE ME IN YOUR ARMS AND LOVE ME — Gladys Knight & the Pips (Tamla Motown)
-	20 CREEQUE ALLEY — Mamas & Papas (RCA)
21	21 CARRIE ANNE — Hollies (Parlophone)
-	22 JACKSON — Nancy Sinatra & Lee Hazlewood (Reprise)
-	23 EVEN THE BAD TIMES ARE GOOD — Tremeloes (CBS)
17	23 GROOVIN' — Young Rascals (Atlantic)
-	25 GIN HOUSE — Amen Corner (Deram)
22	26 SEVEN ROOMS OF GLOOM — Four Tops (Tamla Motown)
28	27 TRYING TO FORGET — Jim Reeves (RCA)
23	27 ANNABELLA — John Walker (Philips)
26	29 MARTA — Bachelors (Decca)
-	29 TONIGHT IN TOKYO — Sandie Shaw (Pye)

12 August 1967

2	1 SAN FRANCISCO (BE SURE TO WEAR SOME FLOWERS IN YOUR HAIR) — Scott McKenzie (CBS)
1	2 ALL YOU NEED IS LOVE — Beatles (Parlophone)
4	3 I'LL NEVER FALL IN LOVE AGAIN — Tom Jones (Decca)
4	4 DEATH OF A CLOWN — Dave Davies (Pye)
10	5 I WAS MADE TO LOVE HER — Stevie Wonder (Tamla Motown)
8	6 UP UP AND AWAY — Johnny Mann Singers (Liberty)
3	7 IT MUST BE HIM — Vikki Carr (Liberty)
13	8 JUST LOVING YOU — Anita Harris (CBS)
7	9 SHE'D RATHER BE WITH ME — Turtles (London)
6	10 ALTERNATE TITLE — Monkees (RCA)
9	11 SEE EMILY PLAY — Pink Floyd (Columbia)
11	12 THERE GOES MY EVERYTHING — Engelbert Humperdinck (Decca)
20	13 CREEQUE ALLEY — Mamas & Papas (RCA)
12	14 LET'S PRETEND — Lulu (Columbia)
18	15 007 (SHANTY TOWN) — Desmond Dekker (Pyramid)
15	16 YOU ONLY LIVE TWICE — Nancy Sinatra (Reprise)
14	17 A WHITER SHADE OF PALE — Procol Harum (Deram)
17	18 TRAMP — Otis Redding & Carla Thomas (Stax)
23	19 EVEN THE BAD TIMES ARE GOOD — Tremeloes (CBS)
-	20 THE HOUSE THAT JACK BUILT — Alan Price Set (Decca)
25	21 GIN HOUSE — Amen Corner (Deram)
19	22 TAKE ME IN YOUR ARMS AND LOVE ME — Gladys Knight & the Pips (Tamla Motown)
29	23 MARTA — Bachelors (Decca)
27	24 TRYING TO FORGET — Jim Reeves (RCA)
22	25 JACKSON — Nancy Sinatra & Lee Hazlewood (Reprise)
16	26 RESPECT — Aretha Franklin (Atlantic)
-	27 A BAD NIGHT — Cat Stevens (Deram)
-	28 TIME SELLER — Spencer Davis Group (Fontana)
26	29 SEVEN ROOMS OF GLOOM — Four Tops (Tamla Motown)
21	30 CARRIE ANNE — Hollies (Parlophone)

The Beatles premiered *All You Need Is Love* via a guest-laden live-in-the-studio performance for the first globally-linked TV show, *Our World* - probably the most widely-seen promotional shot of all time. Certainly the single, bearing what was essentially the slogan of summer '67, restored the group's chart fortunes which had lapsed slightly with *Penny Lane/Strawberry Fields*. Elsewhere, Nancy Sinatra had a successful James Bond movie theme, and reggae newcomer Desmond Dekker also evoked 007.

last week	this week	19 August 1967
1	1	SAN FRANCISCO (BE SURE TO WEAR SOME FLOWERS IN YOUR HAIR) Scott McKenzie (CBS)
3	2	I'LL NEVER FALL IN LOVE AGAIN Tom Jones (Decca)
2	3	ALL YOU NEED IS LOVE Beatles (Parlophone)
4	4	DEATH OF A CLOWN Dave Davies (Pye)
6	5	UP UP AND AWAY Johnny Mann Singers (Liberty)
5	6	I WAS MADE TO LOVE HER Stevie Wonder (Tamla Motown)
8	7	JUST LOVING YOU Anita Harris (CBS)
7	8	IT MUST BE HIM Vikki Carr (Liberty)
19	9	EVEN THE BAD TIMES ARE GOOD Tremeloes (CBS)
9	10	SHE'D RATHER BE WITH ME Turtles (London)
20	11	THE HOUSE THAT JACK BUILT Alan Price Set (Decca)
13	12	CREEQUE ALLEY Mamas & Papas (RCA)
12	13	THERE GOES MY EVERYTHING Engelbert Humperdinck (Decca)
21	14	GIN HOUSE Amen Corner (Deram)
10	15	ALTERNATE TITLE Monkees (RCA)
15	16	007 (SHANTY TOWN) Desmond Dekker (Pyramid)
18	17	TRAMP Otis Redding & Carla Thomas (Stax)
11	18	SEE EMILY PLAY Pink Floyd (Columbia)
16	19	YOU ONLY LIVE TWICE Nancy Sinatra (Reprise)
-	20	ITCHYCOO PARK Small Faces (Decca)
27	21	A BAD NIGHT Cat Stevens (Deram)
-	22	PLEASANT VALLEY SUNDAY Monkees (RCA)
-	23	YOU KEEP ME HANGIN' ON Vanilla Fudge (Atlantic)
14	24	LET'S PRETEND Lulu (Columbia)
-	25	EXCERPT FROM A TEENAGE OPERA Keith West (Parlophone)
24	26	TRYING TO FORGET Jim Reeves (RCA)
-	27	THE DAY I MET MARIE Cliff Richard (Columbia)
28	28	TIME SELLER Spencer Davis Group (Fontana)
25	29	JACKSON Nancy Sinatra & Lee Hazlewood (Reprise)
17	30	A WHITER SHADE OF PALE Procol Harum (Deram)

last week	this week	26 August 1967
1	1	SAN FRANCISCO (BE SURE TO WEAR SOME FLOWERS IN YOUR HAIR) Scott McKenzie (CBS)
2	2	I'LL NEVER FALL IN LOVE AGAIN Tom Jones (Decca)
6	3	I WAS MADE TO LOVE HER Stevie Wonder (Tamla Motown)
11	4	THE HOUSE THAT JACK BUILT Alan Price Set (Decca)
9	5	EVEN THE BAD TIMES ARE GOOD Tremeloes (CBS)
3	6	ALL YOU NEED IS LOVE Beatles (Parlophone)
4	7	DEATH OF A CLOWN Dave Davies (Pye)
7	8	JUST LOVING YOU Anita Harris (CBS)
5	9	UP UP AND AWAY Johnny Mann Singers (Liberty)
8	10	IT MUST BE HIM Vikki Carr (Liberty)
22	11	PLEASANT VALLEY SUNDAY Monkees (RCA)
12	12	CREEQUE ALLEY Mamas & Papas (RCA)
-	13	WE LOVE YOU Rolling Stones (Decca)
-	14	THE LAST WALTZ Engelbert Humperdinck (Decca)
20	15	ITCHYCOO PARK Small Faces (Decca)
-	16	HEROES AND VILLAINS Beach Boys (Capitol)
14	17	GIN HOUSE Amen Corner (Deram)
25	18	EXCERPT FROM A TEENAGE OPERA Keith West (Parlophone)
17	19	TRAMP Otis Redding & Carla Thomas (Stax)
10	20	SHE'D RATHER BE WITH ME Turtles (London)
27	21	THE DAY I MET MARIE Cliff Richard (Columbia)
19	22	YOU ONLY LIVE TWICE Nancy Sinatra (Reprise)
23	23	YOU KEEP ME HANGIN' ON Vanilla Fudge (Atlantic)
13	24	THERE GOES MY EVERYTHING Engelbert Humperdinck (Decca)
16	25	007 (SHANTY TOWN) Desmond Dekker (Pyramid)
18	26	SEE EMILY PLAY Pink Floyd (Columbia)
29	27	JACKSON Nancy Sinatra & Lee Hazlewood (Reprise)
-	28	THERE MUST BE A WAY Frankie Vaughan (Columbia)
-	29	THE BURNING OF THE MIDNIGHT LAMP Jimi Hendrix Experience (Track)
15	30	ALTERNATE TITLE Monkees (RCA)

last week	this week	2 September 1967
1	1	SAN FRANCISCO (BE SURE TO WEAR SOME FLOWERS IN YOUR HAIR) Scott McKenzie (CBS)
2	2	I'LL NEVER FALL IN LOVE AGAIN Tom Jones (Decca)
14	3	THE LAST WALTZ Engelbert Humperdinck (Decca)
4	4	THE HOUSE THAT JACK BUILT Alan Price Set (Decca)
5	5	EVEN THE BAD TIMES ARE GOOD Tremeloes (CBS)
3	6	I WAS MADE TO LOVE HER Stevie Wonder (Tamla Motown)
13	7	WE LOVE YOU Rolling Stones (Decca)
8	8	JUST LOVING YOU Anita Harris (CBS)
6	9	ALL YOU NEED IS LOVE Beatles (Parlophone)
11	10	PLEASANT VALLEY SUNDAY Monkees (RCA)
16	11	HEROES AND VILLAINS Beach Boys (Capitol)
12	12	ITCHYCOO PARK Small Faces (Decca)
18	13	EXCERPT FROM A TEENAGE OPERA Keith West (Parlophone)
7	14	DEATH OF A CLOWN Dave Davies (Pye)
9	15	UP UP AND AWAY Johnny Mann Singers (Liberty)
10	16	IT MUST BE HIM Vikki Carr (Liberty)
12	17	CREEQUE ALLEY Mamas & Papas (RCA)
29	18	THE BURNING OF THE MIDNIGHT LAMP Jimi Hendrix Experience (Track)
17	19	GIN HOUSE Amen Corner (Deram)
23	20	YOU KEEP ME HANGIN' ON Vanilla Fudge (Atlantic)
-	21	LET'S GO TO SAN FRANCISCO Flowerpot Men (Deram)
21	21	THE DAY I MET MARIE Cliff Richard (Columbia)
21	23	YOU ONLY LIVE TWICE Nancy Sinatra (Reprise)
25	24	007 (SHANTY TOWN) Desmond Dekker (Pyramid)
28	25	THERE MUST BE A WAY Frankie Vaughan (Columbia)
20	26	SHE'D RATHER BE WITH ME Turtles (London)
-	27	HOLE IN MY SHOE Traffic (Island)
24	28	THERE GOES MY EVERYTHING Engelbert Humperdinck (Decca)
19	29	TRAMP Otis Redding & Carla Thomas (Stax)
-	30	A BAD NIGHT Cat Stevens (Deram)

last week	this week	9 September 1967
3	1	THE LAST WALTZ Engelbert Humperdinck (Decca)
1	2	SAN FRANCISCO (BE SURE TO WEAR SOME FLOWERS IN YOUR HAIR) Scott McKenzie (CBS)
2	3	I'LL NEVER FALL IN LOVE AGAIN Tom Jones (Decca)
7	4	WE LOVE YOU Rolling Stones (Decca)
13	5	EXCERPT FROM A TEENAGE OPERA Keith West (Parlophone)
5	6	EVEN THE BAD TIMES ARE GOOD Tremeloes (CBS)
4	7	THE HOUSE THAT JACK BUILT Alan Price Set (Decca)
6	8	I WAS MADE TO LOVE HER Stevie Wonder (Tamla Motown)
8	9	JUST LOVING YOU Anita Harris (CBS)
11	10	HEROES AND VILLAINS Beach Boys (Capitol)
10	11	PLEASANT VALLEY SUNDAY Monkees (RCA)
12	12	ITCHYCOO PARK Small Faces (Decca)
9	13	ALL YOU NEED IS LOVE Beatles (Parlophone)
21	14	LET'S GO TO SAN FRANCISCO Flowerpot Men (Deram)
18	15	THE BURNING OF THE MIDNIGHT LAMP Jimi Hendrix Experience (Track)
20	16	YOU KEEP ME HANGIN' ON Vanilla Fudge (Atlantic)
-	17	REFLECTIONS Diana Ross & the Supremes (Tamla Motown)
27	17	HOLE IN MY SHOE Traffic (Island)
25	19	THERE MUST BE A WAY Frankie Vaughan (Columbia)
15	20	UP UP AND AWAY Johnny Mann Singers (Liberty)
21	21	THE DAY I MET MARIE Cliff Richard (Columbia)
17	22	CREEQUE ALLEY Mamas & Papas (RCA)
16	23	IT MUST BE HIM Vikki Carr (Liberty)
19	24	GIN HOUSE Amen Corner (Deram)
14	25	DEATH OF A CLOWN Dave Davies (Pye)
30	26	A BAD NIGHT Cat Stevens (Deram)
28	27	THERE GOES MY EVERYTHING Engelbert Humperdinck (Decca)
29	28	TRAMP Otis Redding & Carla Thomas (Stax)
23	29	YOU ONLY LIVE TWICE Nancy Sinatra (Reprise)
-	30	BLACK VELVET BAND Dubliners (Major Minor)

It seemed fitting that *All You Need Is Love* should surrender Number One to Scott McKenzie's hymn to the joys of love-filled San Francisco. The song was written by John Phillips of the Mamas & Papas, whose autobiographical *Creeque Alley* was also riding high. The "Flowerpot Men", composed of elite UK session singers, cleverly capitalised on all this with the absurdly commercial *Let's Go To San Francisco*, while Keith West's hit was actually an excerpt from nothing, except West's imagination.

September – October 1967

16 September 1967

last week	this week	
1	1	THE LAST WALTZ Engelbert Humperdinck (Decca)
3	2	I'LL NEVER FALL IN LOVE AGAIN Tom Jones (Decca)
5	3	EXCERPT FROM A TEENAGE OPERA Keith West (Parlophone)
2	4	SAN FRANCISCO (BE SURE TO WEAR SOME FLOWERS IN YOUR HAIR) Scott McKenzie (CBS)
12	5	ITCHYCOO PARK Small Faces (Decca)
6	6	EVEN THE BAD TIMES ARE GOOD Tremeloes (CBS)
4	7	WE LOVE YOU Rolling Stones (Decca)
14	8	LET'S GO TO SAN FRANCISCO Flowerpot Men (Deram)
17	9	REFLECTIONS Diana Ross & the Supremes (Tamla Motown)
9	10	JUST LOVING YOU Anita Harris (CBS)
7	11	THE HOUSE THAT JACK BUILT Alan Price Set (Decca)
8	12	I WAS MADE TO LOVE HER Stevie Wonder (Tamla Motown)
10	13	HEROES AND VILLAINS Beach Boys (Capitol)
21	14	THE DAY I MET MARIE Cliff Richard (Columbia)
15	15	THE BURNING OF THE MIDNIGHT LAMP Jimi Hendrix Experience (Track)
11	16	PLEASANT VALLEY SUNDAY Monkees (RCA)
19	17	THERE MUST BE A WAY Frankie Vaughan (Columbia)
-	18	FLOWERS IN THE RAIN Move (Regal Zonophone)
17	19	HOLE IN MY SHOE Traffic (Island)
13	20	ALL YOU NEED IS LOVE Beatles (Parlophone)
30	21	BLACK VELVET BAND Dubliners (Major Minor)
16	22	YOU KEEP ME HANGIN' ON Vanilla Fudge (Atlantic)
22	23	CREEQUE ALLEY Mamas & Papas (RCA)
-	24	GOOD TIMES Eric Burdon & the Animals (MGM)
24	25	GIN HOUSE Amen Corner (Deram)
-	26	YOU'RE MY EVERYTHING Temptations (Tamla Motown)
25	27	DEATH OF A CLOWN Dave Davies (Pye)
-	28	MASSACHUSETTS Bee Gees (Polydor)
20	28	UP UP AND AWAY Johnny Mann Singers (Liberty)
29	30	YOU ONLY LIVE TWICE Nancy Sinatra (Reprise)

23 September 1967

last week	this week	
1	1	THE LAST WALTZ Engelbert Humperdinck (Decca)
3	2	EXCERPT FROM A TEENAGE OPERA Keith West (Parlophone)
5	3	ITCHYCOO PARK Small Faces (Decca)
2	4	I'LL NEVER FALL IN LOVE AGAIN Tom Jones (Decca)
8	5	LET'S GO TO SAN FRANCISCO Flowerpot Men (Deram)
9	6	REFLECTIONS Diana Ross & the Supremes (Tamla Motown)
4	7	SAN FRANCISCO (BE SURE TO WEAR SOME FLOWERS IN YOUR HAIR) Scott McKenzie (CBS)
18	8	FLOWERS IN THE RAIN Move (Regal Zonophone)
6	9	EVEN THE BAD TIMES ARE GOOD Tremeloes (CBS)
10	10	JUST LOVING YOU Anita Harris (CBS)
19	11	HOLE IN MY SHOE Traffic (Island)
14	12	THE DAY I MET MARIE Cliff Richard (Columbia)
7	13	WE LOVE YOU Rolling Stones (Decca)
17	14	THERE MUST BE A WAY Frankie Vaughan (Columbia)
13	15	HEROES AND VILLAINS Beach Boys (Capitol)
12	16	I WAS MADE TO LOVE HER Stevie Wonder (Tamla Motown)
15	17	THE BURNING OF THE MIDNIGHT LAMP Jimi Hendrix Experience (Track)
11	18	THE HOUSE THAT JACK BUILT Alan Price Set (Decca)
28	19	MASSACHUSETTS Bee Gees (Polydor)
21	20	BLACK VELVET BAND Dubliners (Major Minor)
24	21	GOOD TIMES Eric Burdon & the Animals (MGM)
-	22	THE LETTER Box Tops (Stateside)
16	23	PLEASANT VALLEY SUNDAY Monkees (RCA)
22	24	YOU KEEP ME HANGIN' ON Vanilla Fudge (Atlantic)
-	25	FIVE LITTLE FINGERS Frankie McBride (Emerald)
-	26	ODE TO BILLIE JOE Bobbie Gentry (Capitol)
-	27	THERE GOES MY EVERYTHING Engelbert Humperdinck (Decca)
-	28	THE WORLD WE KNEW Frank Sinatra (Reprise)
28	29	UP UP AND AWAY Johnny Mann Singers (Liberty)
26	30	YOU'RE MY EVERYTHING Temptations (Tamla Motown)

30 September 1967

last week	this week	
1	1	THE LAST WALTZ Engelbert Humperdinck (Decca)
2	2	EXCERPT FROM A TEENAGE OPERA Keith West (Parlophone)
8	3	FLOWERS IN THE RAIN Move (Regal Zonophone)
6	4	REFLECTIONS Diana Ross & the Supremes (Tamla Motown)
11	5	HOLE IN MY SHOE Traffic (Island)
3	6	ITCHYCOO PARK Small Faces (Decca)
5	7	LET'S GO TO SAN FRANCISCO Flowerpot Men (Deram)
4	8	I'LL NEVER FALL IN LOVE AGAIN Tom Jones (Decca)
14	9	THERE MUST BE A WAY Frankie Vaughan (Columbia)
7	10	SAN FRANCISCO (BE SURE TO WEAR SOME FLOWERS IN YOUR HAIR) Scott McKenzie (CBS)
12	11	THE DAY I MET MARIE Cliff Richard (Columbia)
22	12	THE LETTER Box Tops (Stateside)
19	13	MASSACHUSETTS Bee Gees (Polydor)
10	14	JUST LOVING YOU Anita Harris (CBS)
9	15	EVEN THE BAD TIMES ARE GOOD Tremeloes (CBS)
20	16	BLACK VELVET BAND Dubliners (Major Minor)
-	17	WHEN WILL THE GOOD APPLES FALL Seekers (Columbia)
13	18	WE LOVE YOU Rolling Stones (Decca)
26	19	ODE TO BILLIE JOE Bobbie Gentry (Capitol)
25	20	FIVE LITTLE FINGERS Frankie McBride (Emerald)
21	21	GOOD TIMES Eric Burdon & the Animals (MGM)
15	22	HEROES AND VILLAINS Beach Boys (Capitol)
-	23	FROM THE UNDERWORLD Herd (Fontana)
16	24	I WAS MADE TO LOVE HER Stevie Wonder (Tamla Motown)
17	25	THE BURNING OF THE MIDNIGHT LAMP Jimi Hendrix Experience (Track)
-	26	THE LETTER Mindbenders (Fontana)
27	27	THERE GOES MY EVERYTHING Engelbert Humperdinck (Decca)
24	28	YOU KEEP ME HANGIN' ON Vanilla Fudge (Atlantic)
-	29	KING MIDAS IN REVERSE Hollies (Parlophone)
-	30	TRY MY WORLD Georgie Fame (CBS)

7 October 1967

last week	this week	
1	1	THE LAST WALTZ Engelbert Humperdinck (Decca)
5	2	HOLE IN MY SHOE Traffic (Island)
3	3	FLOWERS IN THE RAIN Move (Regal Zonophone)
4	4	REFLECTIONS Diana Ross & the Supremes (Tamla Motown)
13	5	MASSACHUSETTS Bee Gees (Polydor)
2	6	EXCERPT FROM A TEENAGE OPERA Keith West (Parlophone)
9	7	THERE MUST BE A WAY Frankie Vaughan (Columbia)
6	8	ITCHYCOO PARK Small Faces (Decca)
7	9	LET'S GO TO SAN FRANCISCO Flowerpot Men (Deram)
12	10	THE LETTER Box Tops (Stateside)
11	11	THE DAY I MET MARIE Cliff Richard (Columbia)
8	12	I'LL NEVER FALL IN LOVE AGAIN Tom Jones (Decca)
16	13	BLACK VELVET BAND Dubliners (Major Minor)
19	14	ODE TO BILLIE JOE Bobbie Gentry (Capitol)
10	15	SAN FRANCISCO (BE SURE TO WEAR SOME FLOWERS IN YOUR HAIR) Scott McKenzie (CBS)
17	16	WHEN WILL THE GOOD APPLES FALL Seekers (Columbia)
14	17	JUST LOVING YOU Anita Harris (CBS)
23	18	FROM THE UNDERWORLD Herd (Fontana)
-	18	HOMBURG Procol Harum (Regal Zonophone)
20	20	FIVE LITTLE FINGERS Frankie McBride (Emerald)
29	21	KING MIDAS IN REVERSE Hollies (Parlophone)
-	22	YOU'RE MY EVERYTHING Temptations (Tamla Motown)
21	23	GOOD TIMES Eric Burdon & the Animals (MGM)
-	24	LOVE LETTERS IN THE SAND Vince Hill (Columbia)
-	25	BABY NOW THAT I'VE FOUND YOU Foundations (Pye)
-	26	YOU'VE NOT CHANGED Sandie Shaw (Pye)
22	27	HEROES AND VILLAINS Beach Boys (Capitol)
25	28	THE BURNING OF THE MIDNIGHT LAMP Jimi Hendrix Experience (Track)
30	29	TRY MY WORLD Georgie Fame (CBS)
26	29	THE LETTER Mindbenders (Fontana)
15	29	EVEN THE BAD TIMES ARE GOOD Tremeloes (CBS)

The Last Waltz, almost pointedly the antithesis of all that the progessive end of the pop spectrum was about this year, became Engelbert's second UK million-seller, topping seven figures inside two months. The Move's *Flowers In The Rain* ws the first single to be played on Radio 1, while Traffic's *Hole In My Shoe* (many years later a source of inspiration for a hippy Young One named neil) showcased the group's most mercurial member, Dave Mason. The Herd's *From The Underworld* took its inspiration from Orpheus In!

last week	this week	14 October 1967
1	1	THE LAST WALTZ — Engelbert Humperdinck (Decca)
5	2	MASSACHUSETTS — Bee Gees (Polydor)
2	3	HOLE IN MY SHOE — Traffic (Island)
3	4	FLOWERS IN THE RAIN — Move (Regal Zonophone)
4	5	REFLECTIONS — Diana Ross & the Supremes (Tamla Motown)
7	6	THERE MUST BE A WAY — Frankie Vaughan (Columbia)
10	7	THE LETTER — Box Tops (Stateside)
6	8	EXCERPT FROM A TEENAGE OPERA — Keith West (Parlophone)
8	9	ITCHYCOO PARK — Small Faces (Decca)
18	10	FROM THE UNDERWORLD — Herd (Fontana)
18	11	HOMBURG — Procol Harum (Regal Zonophone)
16	12	WHEN WILL THE GOOD APPLES FALL — Seekers (Columbia)
13	13	BLACK VELVET BAND — Dubliners (Major Minor)
9	14	LET'S GO TO SAN FRANCISCO — Flowerpot Men (Deram)
11	15	THE DAY I MET MARIE — Cliff Richard (Columbia)
14	16	ODE TO BILLIE JOE — Bobbie Gentry (Capitol)
12	17	I'LL NEVER FALL IN LOVE AGAIN — Tom Jones (Decca)
21	18	KING MIDAS IN REVERSE — Hollies (Parlophone)
-	19	PLAYGROUND — Anita Harris (CBS)
25	20	BABY NOW THAT I'VE FOUND YOU — Foundations (Pye)
26	21	YOU'VE NOT CHANGED — Sandie Shaw (Pye)
24	22	LOVE LETTERS IN THE SAND — Vince Hill (Columbia)
-	23	ZABADAK! — Dave Dee, Dozy, Beaky, Mick & Tich (Fontana)
17	23	JUST LOVING YOU — Anita Harris (CBS)
22	25	YOU'RE MY EVERYTHING — Temptations (Tamla Motown)
15	26	SAN FRANCISCO (BE SURE TO WEAR SOME FLOWERS IN YOUR HAIR) — Scott McKenzie (CBS)
20	27	FIVE LITTLE FINGERS — Frankie McBride (Emerald)
23	28	GOOD TIMES — Eric Burdon & the Animals (MGM)
-	29	YOU KEEP RUNNING AWAY — Four Tops (Tamla Motown)
29	30	EVEN THE BAD TIMES ARE GOOD — Tremeloes (CBS)

last	this	21 October 1967
2	1	MASSACHUSETTS — Bee Gees (Polydor)
1	2	THE LAST WALTZ — Engelbert Humperdinck (Decca)
3	3	HOLE IN MY SHOE — Traffic (Island)
4	4	FLOWERS IN THE RAIN — Move (Regal Zonophone)
6	5	THERE MUST BE A WAY — Frankie Vaughan (Columbia)
7	6	THE LETTER — Box Tops (Stateside)
11	7	HOMBURG — Procol Harum (Regal Zonophone)
5	8	REFLECTIONS — Diana Ross & the Supremes (Tamla Motown)
10	9	FROM THE UNDERWORLD — Herd (Fontana)
20	10	BABY NOW THAT I'VE FOUND YOU — Foundations (Pye)
8	11	EXCERPT FROM A TEENAGE OPERA — Keith West (Parlophone)
23	12	ZABADAK! — Dave Dee, Dozy, Beaky, Mick & Tich (Fontana)
12	13	WHEN WILL THE GOOD APPLES FALL — Seekers (Columbia)
16	14	ODE TO BILLIE JOE — Bobbie Gentry (Capitol)
13	15	BLACK VELVET BAND — Dubliners (Major Minor)
9	16	ITCHYCOO PARK — Small Faces (Decca)
15	17	THE DAY I MET MARIE — Cliff Richard (Columbia)
18	18	KING MIDAS IN REVERSE — Hollies (Parlophone)
14	19	LET'S GO TO SAN FRANCISCO — Flowerpot Men (Deram)
29	20	YOU KEEP RUNNING AWAY — Four Tops (Tamla Motown)
-	21	AUTUMN ALMANAC — Kinks (Pye)
19	22	PLAYGROUND — Anita Harris (CBS)
23	23	JUST LOVING YOU — Anita Harris (CBS)
25	24	YOU'RE MY EVERYTHING — Temptations (Tamla Motown)
17	25	I'LL NEVER FALL IN LOVE AGAIN — Tom Jones (Decca)
-	26	BIG SPENDER — Shirley Bassey (United Artists)
21	27	YOU'VE NOT CHANGED — Sandie Shaw (Pye)
27	28	FIVE LITTLE FINGERS — Frankie McBride (Emerald)
-	29	I CAN SEE FOR MILES — Who (Track)
-	30	LOVE IS ALL AROUND — Troggs (Page One)

last	this	28 October 1967
1	1	MASSACHUSETTS — Bee Gees (Polydor)
2	2	THE LAST WALTZ — Engelbert Humperdinck (Decca)
3	3	HOLE IN MY SHOE — Traffic (Island)
10	4	BABY NOW THAT I'VE FOUND YOU — Foundations (Pye)
7	5	HOMBURG — Procol Harum (Regal Zonophone)
5	6	THERE MUST BE A WAY — Frankie Vaughan (Columbia)
12	7	ZABADAK! — Dave Dee, Dozy, Beaky, Mick & Tich (Fontana)
6	8	THE LETTER — Box Tops (Stateside)
4	9	FLOWERS IN THE RAIN — Move (Regal Zonophone)
9	10	FROM THE UNDERWORLD — Herd (Fontana)
8	11	REFLECTIONS — Diana Ross & the Supremes (Tamla Motown)
13	12	WHEN WILL THE GOOD APPLES FALL — Seekers (Columbia)
14	13	ODE TO BILLIE JOE — Bobbie Gentry (Capitol)
30	14	LOVE IS ALL AROUND — Troggs (Page One)
11	14	EXCERPT FROM A TEENAGE OPERA — Keith West (Parlophone)
29	16	I CAN SEE FOR MILES — Who (Track)
21	17	AUTUMN ALMANAC — Kinks (Pye)
15	18	BLACK VELVET BAND — Dubliners (Major Minor)
-	19	THERE IS A MOUNTAIN — Donovan (Pye)
-	20	SAN FRANCISCAN NIGHTS — Eric Burdon & the Animals (MGM)
18	20	KING MIDAS IN REVERSE — Hollies (Parlophone)
27	22	YOU'VE NOT CHANGED — Sandie Shaw (Pye)
20	23	YOU KEEP RUNNING AWAY — Four Tops (Tamla Motown)
23	24	JUST LOVING YOU — Anita Harris (CBS)
17	25	THE DAY I MET MARIE — Cliff Richard (Columbia)
-	26	IF THE WHOLE WORLD STOPPED LOVIN' — Val Doonican (Pye)
-	27	I'M WONDERING — Stevie Wonder (Tamla Motown)
24	28	YOU'RE MY EVERYTHING — Temptations (Tamla Motown)
16	29	ITCHYCOO PARK — Small Faces (Decca)
26	30	BIG SPENDER — Shirley Bassey (United Artists)

last	this	4 November 1967
1	1	MASSACHUSETTS — Bee Gees (Polydor)
4	2	BABY NOW THAT I'VE FOUND YOU — Foundations (Pye)
7	3	ZABADAK! — Dave Dee, Dozy, Beaky, Mick & Tich (Fontana)
2	4	THE LAST WALTZ — Engelbert Humperdinck (Decca)
3	5	HOLE IN MY SHOE — Traffic (Island)
6	6	THERE MUST BE A WAY — Frankie Vaughan (Columbia)
5	7	HOMBURG — Procol Harum (Regal Zonophone)
10	8	FROM THE UNDERWORLD — Herd (Fontana)
8	9	THE LETTER — Box Tops (Stateside)
17	10	AUTUMN ALMANAC — Kinks (Pye)
9	11	FLOWERS IN THE RAIN — Move (Regal Zonophone)
14	12	LOVE IS ALL AROUND — Troggs (Page One)
11	13	REFLECTIONS — Diana Ross & the Supremes (Tamla Motown)
19	14	THERE IS A MOUNTAIN — Donovan (Pye)
20	15	SAN FRANCISCAN NIGHTS — Eric Burdon & the Animals (MGM)
13	16	ODE TO BILLIE JOE — Bobbie Gentry (Capitol)
12	17	WHEN WILL THE GOOD APPLES FALL — Seekers (Columbia)
22	18	YOU'VE NOT CHANGED — Sandie Shaw (Pye)
16	19	I CAN SEE FOR MILES — Who (Track)
24	20	JUST LOVING YOU — Anita Harris (CBS)
26	21	IF THE WHOLE WORLD STOPPED LOVIN' — Val Doonican (Pye)
23	22	YOU KEEP RUNNING AWAY — Four Tops (Tamla Motown)
28	23	YOU'RE MY EVERYTHING — Temptations (Tamla Motown)
30	24	BIG SPENDER — Shirley Bassey (United Artists)
18	25	BLACK VELVET BAND — Dubliners (Major Minor)
27	25	I'M WONDERING — Stevie Wonder (Tamla Motown)
14	27	EXCERPT FROM A TEENAGE OPERA — Keith West (Parlophone)
20	28	KING MIDAS IN REVERSE — Hollies (Parlophone)
29	29	ITCHYCOO PARK — Small Faces (Decca)
25	30	THE DAY I MET MARIE — Cliff Richard (Columbia)

The balladeers continued to flourish, as Vince Hill revived Pat Boone's *Love Letters In The Sand*, and Frankie Vaughan and Shirley Bassey both returned to the Top 30 after absences measured in years. Meanwhile, the Hollies stalled at the lower end of the 20 with the – by their commercial standards – very experimental *King Midas In Reverse*. The public's inability to cope this shift in the group's direction particularly upset Graham Nash, whose project *King Midas* mainly was, and spurred his decision to leave.

November – December 1967

11 November 1967

last week	this week	title	artist
2	1	BABY NOW THAT I'VE FOUND YOU	Foundations (Pye)
1	2	MASSACHUSETTS	Bee Gees (Polydor)
3	3	ZABADAK!	Dave Dee, Dozy, Beaky, Mick & Tich (Fontana)
4	4	THE LAST WALTZ	Engelbert Humperdinck (Decca)
10	5	AUTUMN ALMANAC	Kinks (Pye)
12	6	LOVE IS ALL AROUND	Troggs (Page One)
6	7	THERE MUST BE A WAY	Frankie Vaughan (Columbia)
8	8	FROM THE UNDERWORLD	Herd (Fontana)
14	9	THERE IS A MOUNTAIN	Donovan (Pye)
5	10	HOLE IN MY SHOE	Traffic (Island)
15	11	SAN FRANCISCAN NIGHTS	Eric Burdon & the Animals (MGM)
7	12	HOMBURG	Procol Harum (Regal Zonophone)
19	13	I CAN SEE FOR MILES	Who (Track)
18	14	YOU'VE NOT CHANGED	Sandie Shaw (Pye)
-	15	LET THE HEARTACHES BEGIN	Long John Baldry (Pye)
11	16	FLOWERS IN THE RAIN	Move (Regal Zonophone)
9	17	THE LETTER	Box Tops (Stateside)
21	18	IF THE WHOLE WORLD STOPPED LOVIN'	Val Doonican (Pye)
-	19	EVERYBODY KNOWS	Dave Clark Five (Columbia)
-	20	CARELESS HANDS	Des O'Connor (Columbia)
17	21	WHEN WILL THE GOOD APPLES FALL	Seekers (Columbia)
20	22	JUST LOVING YOU	Anita Harris (CBS)
13	23	REFLECTIONS	Diana Ross & the Supremes (Tamla Motown)
16	24	ODE TO BILLIE JOE	Bobbie Gentry (Capitol)
25	25	I'M WONDERING	Stevie Wonder (Tamla Motown)
-	26	I FEEL LOVE COMING ON	Felice Taylor (President)
24	27	BIG SPENDER	Shirley Bassey (United Artists)
25	28	BLACK VELVET BAND	Dubliners (Major Minor)
22	29	YOU KEEP RUNNING AWAY	Four Tops (Tamla Motown)
23	30	YOU'RE MY EVERYTHING	Temptations (Tamla Motown)

18 November 1967

last week	this week	title	artist
1	1	BABY NOW THAT I'VE FOUND YOU	Foundations (Pye)
3	2	ZABADAK!	Dave Dee, Dozy, Beaky, Mick & Tich (Fontana)
2	3	MASSACHUSETTS	Bee Gees (Polydor)
4	4	THE LAST WALTZ	Engelbert Humperdinck (Decca)
6	4	LOVE IS ALL AROUND	Troggs (Page One)
5	6	AUTUMN ALMANAC	Kinks (Pye)
15	7	LET THE HEARTACHES BEGIN	Long John Baldry (Pye)
9	8	THERE IS A MOUNTAIN	Donovan (Pye)
7	9	THERE MUST BE A WAY	Frankie Vaughan (Columbia)
19	10	EVERYBODY KNOWS	Dave Clark Five (Columbia)
18	11	IF THE WHOLE WORLD STOPPED LOVIN'	Val Doonican (Pye)
11	12	SAN FRANCISCAN NIGHTS	Eric Burdon & the Animals (MGM)
13	13	I CAN SEE FOR MILES	Who (Track)
8	14	FROM THE UNDERWORLD	Herd (Fontana)
12	15	HOMBURG	Procol Harum (Regal Zonophone)
10	16	HOLE IN MY SHOE	Traffic (Island)
20	17	CARELESS HANDS	Des O'Connor (Columbia)
14	18	YOU'VE NOT CHANGED	Sandie Shaw (Pye)
-	19	ALL MY LOVE	Cliff Richard (Columbia)
-	20	SO TIRED	Frankie Vaughan (Columbia)
26	21	I FEEL LOVE COMING ON	Felice Taylor (President)
25	22	I'M WONDERING	Stevie Wonder (Tamla Motown)
16	23	FLOWERS IN THE RAIN	Move (Regal Zonophone)
27	24	BIG SPENDER	Shirley Bassey (United Artists)
21	25	WHEN WILL THE GOOD APPLES FALL	Seekers (Columbia)
17	26	THE LETTER	Box Tops (Stateside)
22	27	JUST LOVING YOU	Anita Harris (CBS)
29	28	YOU KEEP RUNNING AWAY	Four Tops (Tamla Motown)
-	29	SOMETHING'S GOTTEN HOLD OF MY HEART	Gene Pitney (Stateside)
-	29	BE MINE	Tremeloes (CBS)

25 November 1967

last week	this week	title	artist
1	1	BABY NOW THAT I'VE FOUND YOU	Foundations (Pye)
7	2	LET THE HEARTACHES BEGIN	Long John Baldry (Pye)
10	3	EVERYBODY KNOWS	Dave Clark Five (Columbia)
2	4	ZABADAK!	Dave Dee, Dozy, Beaky, Mick & Tich (Fontana)
4	4	LOVE IS ALL AROUND	Troggs (Page One)
4	6	THE LAST WALTZ	Engelbert Humperdinck (Decca)
3	7	MASSACHUSETTS	Bee Gees (Polydor)
6	8	AUTUMN ALMANAC	Kinks (Pye)
8	9	THERE IS A MOUNTAIN	Donovan (Pye)
11	10	IF THE WHOLE WORLD STOPPED LOVIN'	Val Doonican (Pye)
9	11	THERE MUST BE A WAY	Frankie Vaughan (Columbia)
17	12	CARELESS HANDS	Des O'Connor (Columbia)
19	13	ALL MY LOVE	Cliff Richard (Columbia)
12	14	SAN FRANCISCAN NIGHTS	Eric Burdon & the Animals (MGM)
13	15	I CAN SEE FOR MILES	Who (Track)
29	16	SOMETHING'S GOTTEN HOLD OF MY HEART	Gene Pitney (Stateside)
21	17	I FEEL LOVE COMING ON	Felice Taylor (President)
20	18	SO TIRED	Frankie Vaughan (Columbia)
-	19	WORLD	Bee Gees (Polydor)
-	19	I'M COMING HOME	Tom Jones (Decca)
14	21	FROM THE UNDERWORLD	Herd (Fontana)
18	22	YOU'VE NOT CHANGED	Sandie Shaw (Pye)
-	23	DAYDREAM BELIEVER	Monkees (RCA)
15	24	HOMBURG	Procol Harum (Regal Zonophone)
27	25	JUST LOVING YOU	Anita Harris (CBS)
16	26	HOLE IN MY SHOE	Traffic (Island)
24	27	BIG SPENDER	Shirley Bassey (United Artists)
22	28	I'M WONDERING	Stevie Wonder (Tamla Motown)
25	29	WHEN WILL THE GOOD APPLES FALL	Seekers (Columbia)
-	30	WILD HONEY	Beach Boys (Capitol)

2 December 1967

last week	this week	title	artist
2	1	LET THE HEARTACHES BEGIN	Long John Baldry (Pye)
3	2	EVERYBODY KNOWS	Dave Clark Five (Columbia)
-	3	HELLO GOODBYE	Beatles (Parlophone)
1	4	BABY NOW THAT I'VE FOUND YOU	Foundations (Pye)
4	5	LOVE IS ALL AROUND	Troggs (Page One)
10	6	IF THE WHOLE WORLD STOPPED LOVIN'	Val Doonican (Pye)
6	7	THE LAST WALTZ	Engelbert Humperdinck (Decca)
16	8	SOMETHING'S GOTTEN HOLD OF MY HEART	Gene Pitney (Stateside)
13	9	ALL MY LOVE	Cliff Richard (Columbia)
4	10	ZABADAK!	Dave Dee, Dozy, Beaky, Mick & Tich (Fontana)
12	11	CARELESS HANDS	Des O'Connor (Columbia)
19	12	I'M COMING HOME	Tom Jones (Decca)
9	13	THERE IS A MOUNTAIN	Donovan (Pye)
19	14	WORLD	Bee Gees (Polydor)
7	15	MASSACHUSETTS	Bee Gees (Polydor)
8	16	AUTUMN ALMANAC	Kinks (Pye)
17	17	I FEEL LOVE COMING ON	Felice Taylor (President)
23	18	DAYDREAM BELIEVER	Monkees (RCA)
11	19	THERE MUST BE A WAY	Frankie Vaughan (Columbia)
15	20	I CAN SEE FOR MILES	Who (Track)
18	21	SO TIRED	Frankie Vaughan (Columbia)
-	22	HERE WE GO ROUND THE MULBERRY BUSH	Traffic (Island)
14	23	SAN FRANCISCAN NIGHTS	Eric Burdon & the Animals (MGM)
-	24	KITES	Simon Dupree & the Big Sound (Parlophone)
-	25	IN AND OUT OF LOVE	Diana Ross & the Supremes (Tamla Motown)
27	26	BIG SPENDER	Shirley Bassey (United Artists)
-	27	THANK U VERY MUCH	Scaffold (Parlophone)
-	28	SAM	Keith West (Parlophone)
-	29	SOUL MAN	Sam & Dave (Stax)
-	30	I HEARD A HEART BREAK LAST NIGHT	Jim Reeves (RCA)

The Dave Clark Five's *Everybody Knows*, their first Top 10 hit for two-and-a-half years, was potentially a mite confusing to later chroniclers of the group's work, since it was the second single of that title the group had recorded - the first having been their early 1965 follow-up to *Any Way You Want It*, which did not reach the Top 30. The two songs were completely different and were written by different people, but the potential for mixing them up (by DJs, album compilers, etc) still exists, except among afficionados.

9 December 1967

last week	this week	Title
3	1	HELLO GOODBYE — Beatles (Parlophone)
1	2	LET THE HEARTACHES BEGIN — Long John Baldry (Pye)
2	3	EVERYBODY KNOWS — Dave Clark Five (Columbia)
8	4	SOMETHING'S GOTTEN HOLD OF MY HEART — Gene Pitney (Stateside)
6	5	IF THE WHOLE WORLD STOPPED LOVIN' — Val Doonican (Pye)
11	6	CARELESS HANDS — Des O'Connor (Columbia)
12	7	I'M COMING HOME — Tom Jones (Decca)
9	8	ALL MY LOVE — Cliff Richard (Columbia)
7	9	THE LAST WALTZ — Engelbert Humperdinck (Decca)
14	10	WORLD — Bee Gees (Polydor)
5	11	LOVE IS ALL AROUND — Troggs (Page One)
4	12	BABY NOW THAT I'VE FOUND YOU — Foundations (Pye)
18	13	DAYDREAM BELIEVER — Monkees (RCA)
17	14	I FEEL LOVE COMING ON — Felice Taylor (President)
22	15	HERE WE GO ROUND THE MULBERRY BUSH — Traffic (Island)
10	16	ZABADAK! — Dave Dee, Beaky, Mick & Tich (Fontana)
27	17	THANK U VERY MUCH — Scaffold (Parlophone)
13	18	THERE IS A MOUNTAIN — Donovan (Pye)
24	19	KITES — Simon Dupree & the Big Sound (Parlophone)
19	20	THERE MUST BE A WAY — Frankie Vaughan (Columbia)
25	21	IN AND OUT OF LOVE — Diana Ross & the Supremes (Tamla Motown)
21	22	SO TIRED — Frankie Vaughan (Columbia)
16	23	AUTUMN ALMANAC — Kinks (Pye)
26	24	BIG SPENDER — Shirley Bassey (United Artists)
20	25	I CAN SEE FOR MILES — Who (Track)
15	26	MASSACHUSETTS — Bee Gees (Polydor)
-	27	TIN SOLDIER — Small Faces (Decca)
-	28	JACKIE — Scott Walker (Philips)
-	29	WILD HONEY — Beach Boys (Capitol)
23	30	SAN FRANCISCAN NIGHTS — Eric Burdon & the Animals (MGM)

16 December 1967

last week	this week	Title
1	1	HELLO GOODBYE — Beatles (Parlophone)
2	2	LET THE HEARTACHES BEGIN — Long John Baldry (Pye)
4	3	SOMETHING'S GOTTEN HOLD OF MY HEART — Gene Pitney (Stateside)
3	4	EVERYBODY KNOWS — Dave Clark Five (Columbia)
5	5	IF THE WHOLE WORLD STOPPED LOVIN' — Val Doonican (Pye)
6	6	CARELESS HANDS — Des O'Connor (Columbia)
7	7	I'M COMING HOME — Tom Jones (Decca)
10	8	WORLD — Bee Gees (Polydor)
8	9	ALL MY LOVE — Cliff Richard (Columbia)
-	10	MAGICAL MYSTERY TOUR (EP) — Beatles (Parlophone)
13	11	DAYDREAM BELIEVER — Monkees (RCA)
17	12	THANK U VERY MUCH — Scaffold (Parlophone)
9	13	THE LAST WALTZ — Engelbert Humperdinck (Decca)
15	14	HERE WE GO ROUND THE MULBERRY BUSH — Traffic (Island)
19	15	KITES — Simon Dupree & the Big Sound (Parlophone)
11	16	LOVE IS ALL AROUND — Troggs (Page One)
12	17	BABY NOW THAT I'VE FOUND YOU — Foundations (Pye)
21	18	IN AND OUT OF LOVE — Diana Ross & the Supremes (Tamla Motown)
14	19	I FEEL LOVE COMING ON — Felice Taylor (President)
-	20	WALK AWAY RENEE — Four Tops (Tamla Motown)
16	21	ZABADAK! — Dave Dee, Dozy, Beaky, Mick & Tich (Fontana)
20	22	THERE MUST BE A WAY — Frankie Vaughan (Columbia)
26	23	TIN SOLDIER — Small Faces (Decca)
-	24	SUSANNAH'S STILL ALIVE — Dave Davies (Pye)
28	25	JACKIE — Scott Walker (Philips)
-	26	THE BALLAD OF BONNIE AND CLYDE — Georgie Fame (CBS)
18	27	THERE IS A MOUNTAIN — Donovan (Pye)
22	28	SO TIRED — Frankie Vaughan (Columbia)
24	29	BIG SPENDER — Shirley Bassey (United Artists)
23	30	AUTUMN ALMANAC — Kinks (Pye)

23 December 1967

last week	this week	Title
1	1	HELLO GOODBYE — Beatles (Parlophone)
5	2	IF THE WHOLE WORLD STOPPED LOVIN' — Val Doonican (Pye)
2	3	LET THE HEARTACHES BEGIN — Long John Baldry (Pye)
3	4	SOMETHING'S GOTTEN HOLD OF MY HEART — Gene Pitney (Stateside)
7	5	I'M COMING HOME — Tom Jones (Decca)
6	6	CARELESS HANDS — Des O'Connor (Columbia)
4	7	EVERYBODY KNOWS — Dave Clark Five (Columbia)
10	8	MAGICAL MYSTERY TOUR (EP) — Beatles (Parlophone)
8	9	WORLD — Bee Gees (Polydor)
12	10	THANK U VERY MUCH — Scaffold (Parlophone)
15	11	KITES — Simon Dupree & the Big Sound (Parlophone)
9	12	ALL MY LOVE — Cliff Richard (Columbia)
11	13	DAYDREAM BELIEVER — Monkees (RCA)
20	14	WALK AWAY RENEE — Four Tops (Tamla Motown)
18	15	IN AND OUT OF LOVE — Diana Ross & the Supremes (Tamla Motown)
14	16	HERE WE GO ROUND THE MULBERRY BUSH — Traffic (Island)
13	17	THE LAST WALTZ — Engelbert Humperdinck (Decca)
26	18	THE BALLAD OF BONNIE AND CLYDE — Georgie Fame (CBS)
24	19	JACKIE — Scott Walker (Philips)
16	20	LOVE IS ALL AROUND — Troggs (Page One)
17	21	BABY NOW THAT I'VE FOUND YOU — Foundations (Pye)
23	22	TIN SOLDIER — Small Faces (Decca)
19	23	I FEEL LOVE COMING ON — Felice Taylor (President)
21	24	ZABADAK! — Dave Dee, Dozy, Beaky, Mick & Tich (Fontana)
22	25	THERE MUST BE A WAY — Frankie Vaughan (Columbia)
24	26	SUSANNAH'S STILL ALIVE — Dave Davies (Pye)
29	27	BIG SPENDER — Shirley Bassey (United Artists)
-	28	THE OTHER MAN'S GRASS (IS ALWAYS GREENER) — Petula Clark (Pye)
27	29	THERE IS A MOUNTAIN — Donovan (Pye)
30	30	AUTUMN ALMANAC — Kinks (Pye)

30 December 1967

last week	this week	Title
1	1	HELLO GOODBYE — Beatles (Parlophone)
8	2	MAGICAL MYSTERY TOUR (EP) — Beatles (Parlophone)
2	3	IF THE WHOLE WORLD STOPPED LOVIN' — Val Doonican (Pye)
5	4	I'M COMING HOME — Tom Jones (Decca)
6	5	CARELESS HANDS — Des O'Connor (Columbia)
14	6	WALK AWAY RENEE — Four Tops (Tamla Motown)
13	7	DAYDREAM BELIEVER — Monkees (RCA)
10	8	THANK U VERY MUCH — Scaffold (Parlophone)
4	9	SOMETHING'S GOTTEN HOLD OF MY HEART — Gene Pitney (Stateside)
18	10	THE BALLAD OF BONNIE AND CLYDE — Georgie Fame (CBS)
9	11	WORLD — Bee Gees (Polydor)
3	12	LET THE HEARTACHES BEGIN — Long John Baldry (Pye)
11	13	KITES — Simon Dupree & the Big Sound (Parlophone)
7	14	EVERYBODY KNOWS — Dave Clark Five (Columbia)
15	15	IN AND OUT OF LOVE — Diana Ross & the Supremes (Tamla Motown)
16	16	HERE WE GO ROUND THE MULBERRY BUSH — Traffic (Island)
17	17	THE LAST WALTZ — Engelbert Humperdinck (Decca)
19	18	JACKIE — Scott Walker (Philips)
12	19	ALL MY LOVE — Cliff Richard (Columbia)
22	20	TIN SOLDIER — Small Faces (Decca)
20	21	LOVE IS ALL AROUND — Troggs (Page One)
28	22	THE OTHER MAN'S GRASS — Petula Clark (Pye)
26	23	SUSANNAH'S STILL ALIVE — Dave Davies (Pye)
25	24	THERE MUST BE A WAY — Frankie Vaughan (Columbia)
23	25	I FEEL LOVE COMING ON — Felice Taylor (President)
27	26	BIG SPENDER — Shirley Bassey (United Artists)
21	27	BABY NOW THAT I'VE FOUND YOU — Foundations (Pye)
24	28	ZABADAK! — Dave Dee, Dozy, Beaky, Mick & Tich (Fontana)
29	29	THERE IS A MOUNTAIN — Donovan (Pye)
30	30	AUTUMN ALMANAC — Kinks (Pye)

Hello Goodbye took until its second week to hit Number One, but it still dominated the Christmas sales just as Beatles singles in 1963, 1964 and 1965 had done. Its main challenge came from the group's *Magical Mystery Tour* soundtrack, which, though an LP in the US, was a six-track double-EP package in the UK. Priced at twice the cost of a normal single, it still outsold almost everything in sight (going in lots of Christmas stockings), and in making Number 2, was the highest-placed EP ever at this time.

January 1968

6 January 1968

last week	this week	Title	Artist (Label)
1	1	HELLO GOODBYE	Beatles (Parlophone)
2	2	MAGICAL MYSTERY TOUR (EP)	Beatles (Parlophone)
3	3	IF THE WHOLE WORLD STOPPED LOVIN'	Val Doonican (Pye)
4	4	I'M COMING HOME	Tom Jones (Decca)
7	5	DAYDREAM BELIEVER	Monkees (RCA)
6	6	WALK AWAY RENEE	Four Tops (Tamla Motown)
8	7	THANK U VERY MUCH	Scaffold (Parlophone)
9	8	SOMETHING'S GOTTEN HOLD OF MY HEART	Gene Pitney (Stateside)
11	9	WORLD	Bee Gees (Polydor)
5	10	CARELESS HANDS	Des O'Connor (Columbia)
13	11	KITES	Simon Dupree & the Big Sound (Parlophone)
10	12	THE BALLAD OF BONNIE AND CLYDE	Georgie Fame (CBS)
16	13	HERE WE GO ROUND THE MULBERRY BUSH	Traffic (Island)
12	14	LET THE HEARTACHES BEGIN	Long John Baldry (Pye)
19	15	ALL MY LOVE	Cliff Richard (Columbia)
14	16	EVERYBODY KNOWS	Dave Clark Five (Columbia)
15	17	IN AND OUT OF LOVE	Diana Ross & the Supremes (Tamla Motown)
22	18	THE OTHER'S MAN GRASS	Petula Clark (Pye)
17	19	THE LAST WALTZ	Engelbert Humperdinck (Decca)
23	20	SUSANNAH'S STILL ALIVE	Dave Davies (Pye)
18	21	JACKIE	Scott Walker (Philips)
20	22	TIN SOLDIER	Small Faces (Immediate)
21	23	LOVE IS ALL AROUND	Troggs (Page One)
24	24	THERE MUST BE A WAY	Frankie Vaughan (Columbia)
25	25	I FEEL LOVE COMING ON	Felice Taylor (President)
27	26	BABY NOW THAT I'VE FOUND YOU	Foundations (Pye)
26	27	BIG SPENDER	Shirley Bassey (United Artists)
28	28	ZABADAK!	Dave Dee, Dozy, Beaky, Mick & Tich (Fontana)
29	29	THERE IS A MOUNTAIN	Donovan (Pye)
-	30	CHAIN OF FOOLS	Aretha Franklin (Atlantic)

13 January 1968

		Title	Artist (Label)
1	1	HELLO GOODBYE	Beatles (Parlophone)
5	2	DAYDREAM BELIEVER	Monkees (RCA)
6	3	WALK AWAY RENEE	Four Tops (Tamla Motown)
2	4	MAGICAL MYSTERY TOUR (EP)	Beatles (Parlophone)
12	5	THE BALLAD OF BONNIE AND CLYDE	Georgie Fame (CBS)
4	6	I'M COMING HOME	Tom Jones (Decca)
7	7	THANK U VERY MUCH	Scaffold (Parlophone)
9	8	WORLD	Bee Gees (Polydor)
11	9	KITES	Simon Dupree & the Big Sound (Parlophone)
3	10	IF THE WHOLE WORLD STOPPED LOVIN'	Val Doonican (Pye)
8	11	SOMETHING'S GOTTEN HOLD OF MY HEART	Gene Pitney (Stateside)
10	12	CARELESS HANDS	Des O'Connor (Columbia)
13	13	HERE WE GO ROUND THE MULBERRY BUSH	Traffic (Island)
17	14	IN AND OUT OF LOVE	Diana Ross & the Supremes (Tamla Motown)
15	15	ALL MY LOVE	Cliff Richard (Columbia)
22	15	TIN SOLDIER	Small Faces (Immediate)
-	16	AM I THAT EASY TO FORGET	Engelbert Humperdinck (Decca)
18	17	THE OTHER'S MAN GRASS	Petula Clark (Pye)
14	18	LET THE HEARTACHES BEGIN	Long John Baldry (Pye)
-	20	EVERLASTING LOVE	Love Affair (CBS)
-	21	PARADISE LOST	Herd (Fontana)
20	22	SUSANNAH'S STILL ALIVE	Dave Davies (Pye)
-	22	JUDY IN DISGUISE (WITH GLASSES)	John Fred & His Playboy Band (Pye Int)
-	24	EVERYTHING I AM	Plastic Penny (Page One)
-	25	GIMME LITTLE SIGN	Brenton Wood (Liberty)
19	26	THE LAST WALTZ	Engelbert Humperdinck (Decca)
16	27	EVERYBODY KNOWS	Dave Clark Five (Columbia)
21	27	JACKIE	Scott Walker (Philips)
30	29	CHAIN OF FOOLS	Aretha Franklin (Atlantic)
23	30	LOVE IS ALL AROUND	Troggs (Page One)

20 January 1968

		Title	Artist (Label)
5	1	THE BALLAD OF BONNIE AND CLYDE	Georgie Fame (CBS)
3	2	WALK AWAY RENEE	Four Tops (Tamla Motown)
2	3	DAYDREAM BELIEVER	Monkees (RCA)
1	4	HELLO GOODBYE	Beatles (Parlophone)
20	5	EVERLASTING LOVE	Love Affair (CBS)
4	6	MAGICAL MYSTERY TOUR (EP)	Beatles (Parlophone)
16	7	AM I THAT EASY TO FORGET	Engelbert Humperdinck (Decca)
6	8	I'M COMING HOME	Tom Jones (Decca)
8	9	WORLD	Bee Gees (Polydor)
7	10	THANK U VERY MUCH	Scaffold (Parlophone)
9	11	KITES	Simon Dupree & the Big Sound (Parlophone)
15	12	TIN SOLDIER	Small Faces (Immediate)
22	13	JUDY IN DISGUISE (WITH GLASSES)	John Fred & His Playboy Band (Pye Int)
10	14	IF THE WHOLE WORLD STOPPED LOVIN'	Val Doonican (Pye)
24	15	EVERYTHING I AM	Plastic Penny (Page One)
21	16	PARADISE LOST	Herd (Fontana)
11	17	SOMETHING'S GOTTEN HOLD OF MY HEART	Gene Pitney (Stateside)
13	18	HERE WE GO ROUND THE MULBERRY BUSH	Traffic (Island)
14	19	IN AND OUT OF LOVE	Diana Ross & the Supremes (Tamla Motown)
12	20	CARELESS HANDS	Des O'Connor (Columbia)
-	21	DARLIN'	Beach Boys (Capitol)
25	22	GIMME LITTLE SIGN	Brenton Wood (Liberty)
18	23	LET THE HEARTACHES BEGIN	Long John Baldry (Pye)
17	24	THE OTHER'S MAN GRASS	Petula Clark (Pye)
-	25	NIGHTS IN WHITE SATIN	Moody Blues (Deram)
-	26	SHE WEARS MY RING	Solomon King (Columbia)
-	27	THE MIGHTY QUINN	Manfred Mann (Fontana)
-	28	SUDDENLY YOU LOVE ME	Tremeloes (CBS)
19	29	ALL MY LOVE	Cliff Richard (Columbia)
-	30	MR. SECOND CLASS	Spencer Davis (United Artists)

27 January 1968

		Title	Artist (Label)
5	1	EVERLASTING LOVE	Love Affair (CBS)
1	2	THE BALLAD OF BONNIE AND CLYDE	Georgie Fame (CBS)
7	3	AM I THAT EASY TO FORGET	Engelbert Humperdinck (Decca)
3	4	DAYDREAM BELIEVER	Monkees (RCA)
2	5	WALK AWAY RENEE	Four Tops (Tamla Motown)
13	6	JUDY IN DISGUISE (WITH GLASSES)	Playboy Band (Pye Int)
4	7	HELLO GOODBYE	Beatles (Parlophone)
6	8	MAGICAL MYSTERY TOUR (EP)	Beatles (Parlophone)
15	9	EVERYTHING I AM	Plastic Penny (Page One)
12	10	TIN SOLDIER	Small Faces (Immediate)
27	11	THE MIGHTY QUINN	Manfred Mann (Fontana)
8	12	I'M COMING HOME	Tom Jones (Decca)
26	13	SHE WEARS MY RING	Solomon King (Columbia)
-	14	I CAN TAKE OR LEAVE YOUR LOVING	Herman's Hermits (Columbia)
14	15	SUDDENLY YOU LOVE ME	Tremeloes (CBS)
9	16	WORLD	Bee Gees (Polydor)
-	17	BEND ME, SHAPE ME	Amen Corner (Deram)
10	17	THANK U VERY MUCH	Scaffold (Parlophone)
16	19	PARADISE LOST	Herd (Fontana)
22	20	GIMME LITTLE SIGN	Brenton Wood (Liberty)
14	21	IF THE WHOLE WORLD STOPPED LOVIN'	Val Doonican (Pye)
21	22	DARLIN'	Beach Boys (Capitol)
11	23	KITES	Simon Dupree & the Big Sound (Parlophone)
25	24	NIGHTS IN WHITE SATIN	Moody Blues (Deram)
19	25	IN AND OUT OF LOVE	Diana Ross & the Supremes (Tamla Motown)
18	26	HERE WE GO ROUND THE MULBERRY BUSH	Traffic (Island)
17	27	SOMETHING'S GOTTEN HOLD OF MY HEART	Gene Pitney (Stateside)
24	28	THE OTHER'S MAN GRASS	Petula Clark (Pye)
-	29	ANNIVERSARY WALTZ	Anita Harris (CBS)
-	30	THE BEST PART OF BREAKING UP	Symbols (President)

Georgie Fame's *The Ballad Of Bonnie And Clyde* had nothing to do with the *Bonnie And Clyde* movie except shared inspiration, though the film's popularity probably helped the record to sell. Its staccato gunfire conclusion was created by studio overdubbing of a gunshot special effect record. Love Affair's *Everlasting Love* caused a minor furore when it was revealed that singer Steve Ellis was the only member of the group who actually appeared on the record – not in fact an unusual state of affairs in the sixties.

3 February 1968

last week	this week	
1	1	EVERLASTING LOVE Love Affair (CBS)
3	2	AM I THAT EASY TO FORGET Engelbert Humperdinck (Decca)
6	3	JUDY IN DISGUISE (WITH GLASSES) John Fred & His Playboy Band (Pye Int)
2	4	THE BALLAD OF BONNIE AND CLYDE Georgie Fame (CBS)
11	5	THE MIGHTY QUINN Manfred Mann (Fontana)
13	6	SHE WEARS MY RING Solomon King (Columbia)
17	7	BEND ME, SHAPE ME Amen Corner (Deram)
14	8	SUDDENLY YOU LOVE ME Tremeloes (CBS)
9	9	EVERYTHING I AM Plastic Penny (Page One)
4	10	DAYDREAM BELIEVER Monkees (RCA)
5	11	WALK AWAY RENEE Four Tops (Tamla Motown)
10	12	TIN SOLDIER Small Faces (Immediate)
14	13	I CAN TAKE OR LEAVE YOUR LOVING Herman's Hermits (Columbia)
20	14	GIMME LITTLE SIGN Brenton Wood (Liberty)
8	15	MAGICAL MYSTERY TOUR (EP) Beatles (Parlophone)
7	16	HELLO GOODBYE Beatles (Parlophone)
22	17	DARLIN' Beach Boys (Capitol)
12	18	I'M COMING HOME Tom Jones (Decca)
19	19	PARADISE LOST Herd (Fontana)
29	20	ANNIVERSARY WALTZ Anita Harris (CBS)
-	21	BACK ON MY FEET AGAIN Foundations (Pye)
-	22	DON'T STOP THE CARNIVAL Alan Price Set (Decca)
-	23	PICTURES OF MATCHSTICK MEN Status Quo (Pye)
16	24	WORLD Bee Gees (Polydor)
-	25	WORDS Bee Gees (Polydor)
24	26	NIGHTS IN WHITE SATIN Moody Blues (Deram)
30	27	THE BEST PART OF BREAKING UP Symbols (President)
-	28	BEND ME, SHAPE ME American Breed (Stateside)
21	29	IF THE WHOLE WORLD STOPPED LOVIN' Val Doonican (Pye)
23	30	KITES Simon Dupree & the Big Sound (Parlophone)
-	30	HONEY CHILE Martha & the Vandellas (Tamla Motown)

10 February 1968

last week	this week	
1	1	EVERLASTING LOVE Love Affair (CBS)
2	2	AM I THAT EASY TO FORGET Engelbert Humperdinck (Decca)
5	3	THE MIGHTY QUINN Manfred Mann (Fontana)
6	4	SHE WEARS MY RING Solomon King (Columbia)
7	5	BEND ME, SHAPE ME Amen Corner (Deram)
3	6	JUDY IN DISGUISE (WITH GLASSES) John Fred & His Playboy Band (Pye Int)
8	7	SUDDENLY YOU LOVE ME Tremeloes (CBS)
13	8	I CAN TAKE OR LEAVE YOUR LOVING Herman's Hermits (Columbia)
14	9	GIMME LITTLE SIGN Brenton Wood (Liberty)
4	10	THE BALLAD OF BONNIE AND CLYDE Georgie Fame (CBS)
9	11	EVERYTHING I AM Plastic Penny (Page One)
17	12	DARLIN' Beach Boys (Capitol)
12	13	TIN SOLDIER Small Faces (Immediate)
10	14	DAYDREAM BELIEVER Monkees (RCA)
11	15	WALK AWAY RENEE Four Tops (Tamla Motown)
25	16	WORDS Bee Gees (Polydor)
23	17	PICTURES OF MATCHSTICK MEN Status Quo (Pye)
21	18	BACK ON MY FEET AGAIN Foundations (Pye)
20	19	ANNIVERSARY WALTZ Anita Harris (CBS)
-	20	FIRE BRIGADE Move (Regal Zonophone)
18	21	I'M COMING HOME Tom Jones (Decca)
22	22	DON'T STOP THE CARNIVAL Alan Price Set (Decca)
15	23	MAGICAL MYSTERY TOUR (EP) Beatles (Parlophone)
28	24	BEND ME, SHAPE ME American Breed (Stateside)
26	25	NIGHTS IN WHITE SATIN Moody Blues (Deram)
-	26	SO MUCH LOVE Tony Blackburn (MGM)
19	27	PARADISE LOST Herd (Fontana)
27	27	THE BEST PART OF BREAKING UP Symbols (President)
-	29	TODAY Sandie Shaw (Pye)
-	30	DEAR DELILAH Grapefruit (RCA)

17 February 1968

last week	this week	
3	1	THE MIGHTY QUINN Manfred Mann (Fontana)
1	2	EVERLASTING LOVE Love Affair (CBS)
5	3	BEND ME, SHAPE ME Amen Corner (Deram)
4	4	SHE WEARS MY RING Solomon King (Columbia)
2	5	AM I THAT EASY TO FORGET Engelbert Humperdinck (Decca)
7	6	SUDDENLY YOU LOVE ME Tremeloes (CBS)
6	7	JUDY IN DISGUISE (WITH GLASSES) John Fred & His Playboy Band (Pye Int)
9	8	GIMME LITTLE SIGN Brenton Wood (Liberty)
8	9	I CAN TAKE OR LEAVE YOUR LOVING Herman's Hermits (Columbia)
17	10	PICTURES OF MATCHSTICK MEN Status Quo (Pye)
20	11	FIRE BRIGADE Move (Regal Zonophone)
16	13	WORDS Bee Gees (Polydor)
-	14	CINDERELLA ROCKEFELLA Esther & Abi Ofarim (Philips)
10	15	THE BALLAD OF BONNIE AND CLYDE Georgie Fame (CBS)
22	16	DON'T STOP THE CARNIVAL Alan Price Set (Decca)
11	17	EVERYTHING I AM Plastic Penny (Page One)
18	18	BACK ON MY FEET AGAIN Foundations (Pye)
19	19	ANNIVERSARY WALTZ Anita Harris (CBS)
14	19	DAYDREAM BELIEVER Monkees (RCA)
13	21	TIN SOLDIER Small Faces (Immediate)
-	22	ROSIE Don Partridge (Columbia)
29	23	TODAY Sandie Shaw (Pye)
-	24	GREEN TAMBOURINE Lemon Pipers (Pye International)
24	25	BEND ME, SHAPE ME American Breed (Stateside)
-	26	WHAT A WONDERFUL WORLD Louis Armstrong (HMV)
21	26	I'M COMING HOME Tom Jones (Decca)
26	28	SO MUCH LOVE Tony Blackburn (MGM)
-	29	THE LEGEND OF XANADU Dave Dee, Dozy, Beaky, Mick & Tich (Fontana)
30	29	DEAR DELILAH Grapefruit (RCA)

24 February 1968

last week	this week	
1	1	THE MIGHTY QUINN Manfred Mann (Fontana)
14	2	CINDERELLA ROCKEFELLA Esther & Abi Ofarim (Philips)
4	3	SHE WEARS MY RING Solomon King (Columbia)
3	4	BEND ME, SHAPE ME Amen Corner (Deram)
2	5	EVERLASTING LOVE Love Affair (CBS)
6	6	SUDDENLY YOU LOVE ME Tremeloes (CBS)
10	7	PICTURES OF MATCHSTICK MEN Status Quo (Pye)
5	8	AM I THAT EASY TO FORGET Engelbert Humperdinck (Decca)
11	9	FIRE BRIGADE Move (Regal Zonophone)
8	10	GIMME LITTLE SIGN Brenton Wood (Liberty)
7	11	JUDY IN DISGUISE (WITH GLASSES) John Fred & His Playboy Band (Pye Int)
29	12	THE LEGEND OF XANADU Dave Dee, Dozy, Beaky, Mick & Tich (Fontana)
13	13	DARLIN' Beach Boys (Capitol)
13	14	WORDS Bee Gees (Polydor)
9	15	I CAN TAKE OR LEAVE YOUR LOVING Herman's Hermits (Columbia)
16	15	DON'T STOP THE CARNIVAL Alan Price Set (Decca)
22	17	ROSIE Don Partridge (Columbia)
18	18	BACK ON MY FEET AGAIN Foundations (Pye)
19	19	ANNIVERSARY WALTZ Anita Harris (CBS)
24	20	GREEN TAMBOURINE Lemon Pipers (Pye International)
23	21	TODAY Sandie Shaw (Pye)
-	22	JENNIFER JUNIPER Donovan (Pye)
-	23	(SITTIN' ON) THE DOCK OF THE BAY Otis Redding (Stax)
17	24	EVERYTHING I AM Plastic Penny (Page One)
26	25	WHAT A WONDERFUL WORLD Louis Armstrong (HMV)
19	26	DAYDREAM BELIEVER Monkees (RCA)
-	26	NIGHTS IN WHITE SATIN Moody Blues (Deram)
28	28	SO MUCH LOVE Tony Blackburn (MGM)
-	29	GUITAR MAN Elvis Presley (RCA)
15	30	THE BALLAD OF BONNIE AND CLYDE Georgie Fame (CBS)

John Fred's *Judy In Disguise (With Glasses)* was widely held to be a pun on the Beatles' *Lucy In The Sky With Diamonds*, though the two tracks are so different that any supposed link has to be a joke. No joke, perhaps surprisingly, was Radio One DJ Tony Blackburn's chart outing with *So Much Love* – this was a serious and moderately tuneful cover of a Ben E King song. Status Quo, with colourful outfits and a self-consciously 'progressive' song, made their chart debut.

March 1968

last this week

2 March 1968

2	1	CINDERELLA ROCKEFELLA — Esther & Abi Ofarim (Philips)
1	2	THE MIGHTY QUINN — Manfred Mann (Fontana)
12	3	THE LEGEND OF XANADU — Dave Dee, Dozy, Beaky, Mick & Tich (Fontana)
3	4	SHE WEARS MY RING — Solomon King (Columbia)
9	5	FIRE BRIGADE — Move (Regal Zonophone)
7	6	PICTURES OF MATCHSTICK MEN — Status Quo (Pye)
4	7	BEND ME, SHAPE ME — Amen Corner (Deram)
5	8	EVERLASTING LOVE — Love Affair (CBS)
6	9	SUDDENLY YOU LOVE ME — Tremeloes (CBS)
17	10	ROSIE — Don Partridge (Columbia)
13	11	DARLIN' — Beach Boys (Capitol)
10	12	GIMME LITTLE SIGN — Brenton Wood (Liberty)
22	13	JENNIFER JUNIPER — Donovan (Pye)
8	14	AM I THAT EASY TO FORGET — Engelbert Humperdinck (Decca)
20	15	GREEN TAMBOURINE — Lemon Pipers (Pye International)
14	16	WORDS — Bee Gees (Polydor)
11	17	JUDY IN DISGUISE (WITH GLASSES) — John Fred & His Playboy Band (Pye Int)
18	18	BACK ON MY FEET AGAIN — Foundations (Pye)
15	19	DON'T STOP THE CARNIVAL — Alan Price Set (Decca)
19	20	ANNIVERSARY WALTZ — Anita Harris (CBS)
-	21	DELILAH — Tom Jones (Decca)
15	22	I CAN TAKE OR LEAVE YOUR LOVING — Herman's Hermits (Columbia)
23	23	(SITTIN' ON) THE DOCK OF THE BAY — Otis Redding (Stax)
-	24	ME, THE PEACEFUL HEART — Lulu (Columbia)
29	25	GUITAR MAN — Elvis Presley (RCA)
-	26	LOVE IS BLUE — Paul Mauriat & His Orchestra (Philips)
25	27	WHAT A WONDERFUL WORLD — Louis Armstrong (HMV)
-	28	NEVERTHELESS — Frankie Vaughan (Columbia)
-	29	LOVE IS BLUE — Jeff Beck (Columbia)
-	30	LITTLE GIRL — Troggs (Page One)
-	30	VALLEY OF THE DOLLS — Dionne Warwick (Pye International)

9 March 1968

1	1	CINDERELLA ROCKEFELLA — Esther & Abi Ofarim (Philips)
3	2	THE LEGEND OF XANADU — Dave Dee, Dozy, Beaky, Mick & Tich (Fontana)
5	3	FIRE BRIGADE — Move (Regal Zonophone)
2	4	THE MIGHTY QUINN — Manfred Mann (Fontana)
10	5	ROSIE — Don Partridge (Columbia)
4	6	SHE WEARS MY RING — Solomon King (Columbia)
13	7	JENNIFER JUNIPER — Donovan (Pye)
6	8	PICTURES OF MATCHSTICK MEN — Status Quo (Pye)
15	9	GREEN TAMBOURINE — Lemon Pipers (Pye International)
21	10	DELILAH — Tom Jones (Decca)
7	11	BEND ME, SHAPE ME — Amen Corner (Deram)
11	12	DARLIN'
24	13	ME, THE PEACEFUL HEART — Lulu (Columbia)
16	14	WORDS — Bee Gees (Polydor)
23	15	(SITTIN' ON) THE DOCK OF THE BAY — Otis Redding (Stax)
9	16	SUDDENLY YOU LOVE ME — Tremeloes (CBS)
12	17	GIMME LITTLE SIGN — Brenton Wood (Liberty)
8	18	EVERLASTING LOVE — Love Affair (CBS)
18	19	BACK ON MY FEET AGAIN — Foundations (Pye)
14	20	AM I THAT EASY TO FORGET — Engelbert Humperdinck (Decca)
25	21	GUITAR MAN — Elvis Presley (RCA)
20	22	ANNIVERSARY WALTZ — Anita Harris (CBS)
26	23	LOVE IS BLUE — Paul Mauriat & His Orchestra (Philips)
27	24	WHAT A WONDERFUL WORLD — Louis Armstrong (HMV)
19	25	DON'T STOP THE CARNIVAL — Alan Price Set (Decca)
30	26	LITTLE GIRL — Troggs (Page One)
29	27	LOVE IS BLUE — Jeff Beck (Columbia)
-	28	NO FACE, NO NAME, NO NUMBER — Traffic (Island)
-	29	DEAR DELILAH — Grapefruit (RCA)
17	30	JUDY IN DISGUISE (WITH GLASSES) — John Fred & His Playboy Band (Pye Int)

16 March 1968

1	1	CINDERELLA ROCKEFELLA — Esther & Abi Ofarim (Philips)
2	2	THE LEGEND OF XANADU — Dave Dee, Dozy, Beaky, Mick & Tich (Fontana)
5	3	ROSIE — Don Partridge (Columbia)
10	4	DELILAH — Tom Jones (Decca)
3	5	FIRE BRIGADE — Move (Regal Zonophone)
7	6	JENNIFER JUNIPER — Donovan (Pye)
15	7	(SITTIN' ON) THE DOCK OF THE BAY — Otis Redding (Stax)
4	8	THE MIGHTY QUINN — Manfred Mann (Fontana)
6	9	SHE WEARS MY RING — Solomon King (Columbia)
9	10	GREEN TAMBOURINE — Lemon Pipers (Pye International)
13	11	ME, THE PEACEFUL HEART — Lulu (Columbia)
12	12	DARLIN' — Beach Boys (Capitol)
8	13	PICTURES OF MATCHSTICK MEN — Status Quo (Pye)
11	14	BEND ME, SHAPE ME — Amen Corner (Deram)
14	15	WORDS — Bee Gees (Polydor)
24	16	WHAT A WONDERFUL WORLD — Louis Armstrong (HMV)
23	17	LOVE IS BLUE — Paul Mauriat & His Orchestra (Philips)
21	18	GUITAR MAN — Elvis Presley (RCA)
20	19	AM I THAT EASY TO FORGET — Engelbert Humperdinck (Decca)
-	20	IF I WERE A CARPENTER — Four Tops (Tamla Motown)
17	21	GIMME LITTLE SIGN — Brenton Wood (Liberty)
16	22	SUDDENLY YOU LOVE ME — Tremeloes (CBS)
-	23	STEP INSIDE LOVE — Cilla Black (Parlophone)
19	24	BACK ON MY FEET AGAIN — Foundations (Pye)
-	25	NEVERTHELESS — Frankie Vaughan (Columbia)
18	26	EVERLASTING LOVE — Love Affair (CBS)
29	27	DEAR DELILAH — Grapefruit (RCA)
30	28	JUDY IN DISGUISE (WITH GLASSES) — John Fred & His Playboy Band (Pye International)
22	29	ANNIVERSARY WALTZ — Anita Harris (CBS)
28	30	NO FACE, NO NAME, NO NUMBER — Traffic (Island)

23 March 1968

1	1	CINDERELLA ROCKEFELLA — Esther & Abi Ofarim (Philips)
2	2	THE LEGEND OF XANADU — Dave Dee, Dozy, Beaky, Mick & Tich (Fontana)
4	3	DELILAH — Tom Jones (Decca)
3	4	ROSIE — Don Partridge (Columbia)
7	5	(SITTIN' ON) THE DOCK OF THE BAY — Otis Redding (Stax)
-	6	LADY MADONNA — Beatles (Parlophone)
6	7	JENNIFER JUNIPER — Donovan (Pye)
5	8	FIRE BRIGADE — Move (Regal Zonophone)
11	9	ME, THE PEACEFUL HEART — Lulu (Columbia)
10	10	GREEN TAMBOURINE — Lemon Pipers (Pye International)
16	11	WHAT A WONDERFUL WORLD — Louis Armstrong (HMV)
9	12	SHE WEARS MY RING — Solomon King (Columbia)
12	13	DARLIN' — Beach Boys (Capitol)
20	14	IF I WERE A CARPENTER — Four Tops (Tamla Motown)
-	15	CONGRATULATIONS — Cliff Richard (Columbia)
23	16	STEP INSIDE LOVE — Cilla Black (Parlophone)
8	17	THE MIGHTY QUINN — Manfred Mann (Fontana)
17	18	LOVE IS BLUE — Paul Mauriat & His Orchestra (Philips)
18	19	GUITAR MAN — Elvis Presley (RCA)
15	20	WORDS — Bee Gees (Polydor)
13	21	PICTURES OF MATCHSTICK MEN — Status Quo (Pye)
14	22	BEND ME, SHAPE ME — Amen Corner (Deram)
27	23	DEAR DELILAH — Grapefruit (RCA)
19	24	AM I THAT EASY TO FORGET — Engelbert Humperdinck (Decca)
25	25	NEVERTHELESS — Frankie Vaughan (Columbia)
26	26	THEME FROM VALLEY OF THE DOLLS — Dionne Warwick (Pye Int)
21	27	GIMME LITTLE SIGN — Brenton Wood (Liberty)
22	28	SUDDENLY YOU LOVE ME — Tremeloes (CBS)
24	29	BACK ON MY FEET AGAIN — Foundations (Pye)
-	30	SIMON SAYS — 1910 Fruitgum Company (Pye International)

Israeli husband-and-wife team Esther & Abi (actually Abraham) Ofarim had the surprise hit of the spring with their honky-tonk flavoured novelty *Cinderella Rockefella*. Hated by rock fans with a rare passion it was probably less overly pretentious than Dave Dee's melodramatic epic (with Dee cracking a bullwhip with relish on *Top Of The Pops*) which the Ofarims kept at Number Two. By a strange coincidence Tom Jones' *Delilah* and Grapefruit's *Dear Delilah* – unconnected songs – charted just a week apart.

30 March 1968

last week	this week	Title / Artist
6	1	LADY MADONNA — Beatles (Parlophone)
3	2	DELILAH — Tom Jones (Decca)
1	3	CINDERELLA ROCKEFELLA — Esther & Abi Ofarim (Philips)
5	4	(SITTIN' ON) THE DOCK OF THE BAY — Otis Redding (Stax)
2	5	THE LEGEND OF XANADU — Dave Dee, Dozy, Beaky, Mick & Tich (Fontana)
11	6	WHAT A WONDERFUL WORLD — Louis Armstrong (HMV)
15	7	CONGRATULATIONS — Cliff Richard (Columbia)
4	8	ROSIE — Don Partridge (Columbia)
7	9	JENNIFER JUNIPER — Donovan (Pye)
9	10	ME, THE PEACEFUL HEART — Lulu (Columbia)
16	11	STEP INSIDE LOVE — Cilla Black (Parlophone)
14	12	IF I WERE A CARPENTER — Four Tops (Tamla Motown)
8	13	FIRE BRIGADE — Move (Regal Zonophone)
12	14	SHE WEARS MY RING — Solomon King (Columbia)
18	15	LOVE IS BLUE — Paul Mauriat & His Orchestra (Philips)
10	16	GREEN TAMBOURINE — Lemon Pipers (Pye International)
-	17	IF I ONLY HAD TIME — John Rowles (MCA)
13	18	DARLIN' — Beach Boys (Capitol)
19	19	GUITAR MAN — Elvis Presley (RCA)
-	20	VALLERI — Monkees (RCA)
-	21	CAN'T TAKE MY EYES OFF YOU — Andy Williams (CBS)
-	22	AIN'T NOTHIN' BUT A HOUSEPARTY — Showstoppers (Beacon)
30	23	SIMON SAYS — 1910 Fruitgum Company (Pye International)
-	24	CAPTAIN OF YOUR SHIP — Reparata & the Delrons (Bell)
24	25	AM I THAT EASY TO FORGET — Engelbert Humperdinck (Decca)
17	26	THE MIGHTY QUINN — Manfred Mann (Fontana)
26	27	THEME FROM VALLEY OF THE DOLLS — Dionne Warwick (Pye Int)
22	28	BEND ME, SHAPE ME — Amen Corner (Deram)
23	29	DEAR DELILAH — Grapefruit (RCA)
20	30	WORDS — Bee Gees (Polydor)

6 April 1968

last week	this week	Title / Artist
1	1	LADY MADONNA — Beatles (Parlophone)
2	2	DELILAH — Tom Jones (Decca)
6	3	WHAT A WONDERFUL WORLD — Louis Armstrong (HMV)
7	4	CONGRATULATIONS — Cliff Richard (Columbia)
4	5	(SITTIN' ON) THE DOCK OF THE BAY — Otis Redding (Stax)
3	6	CINDERELLA ROCKEFELLA — Esther & Abi Ofarim (Philips)
11	7	STEP INSIDE LOVE — Cilla Black (Parlophone)
5	8	THE LEGEND OF XANADU — Dave Dee, Dozy, Beaky, Mick & Tich (Fontana)
12	9	IF I WERE A CARPENTER — Four Tops (Tamla Motown)
17	10	IF I ONLY HAD TIME — John Rowles (MCA)
8	11	ROSIE — Don Partridge (Columbia)
10	12	ME, THE PEACEFUL HEART — Lulu (Columbia)
15	13	LOVE IS BLUE — Paul Mauriat & His Orchestra (Philips)
9	14	JENNIFER JUNIPER — Donovan (Pye)
20	15	VALLERI — Monkees (RCA)
22	16	AIN'T NOTHIN' BUT A HOUSEPARTY — Showstoppers (Beacon)
21	17	CAN'T TAKE MY EYES OFF YOU — Andy Williams (CBS)
23	18	SIMON SAYS — 1910 Fruitgum Company (Pye International)
13	19	FIRE BRIGADE — Move (Regal Zonophone)
14	20	SHE WEARS MY RING — Solomon King (Columbia)
23	21	CAPTAIN OF YOUR SHIP — Reparata & the Delrons (Bell)
-	22	JENNIFER ECCLES — Hollies (Parlophone)
18	23	DARLIN' — Beach Boys (Capitol)
-	24	SOMETHING HERE IN MY HEART — Paper Dolls (Pye)
-	25	SOMEWHERE IN THE COUNTRY — Gene Pitney (Stateside)
-	26	I CAN'T LET MAGGIE GO — Honeybus (Deram)
-	27	LITTLE GREEN APPLES — Roger Miller (Mercury)
16	28	GREEN TAMBOURINE — Lemon Pipers (Pye International)
-	29	CRY LIKE A BABY — Box Tops (Bell)
19	30	GUITAR MAN — Elvis Presley (RCA)

13 April 1968

last week	this week	Title / Artist
4	1	CONGRATULATIONS — Cliff Richard (Columbia)
3	2	WHAT A WONDERFUL WORLD — Louis Armstrong (HMV)
2	3	DELILAH — Tom Jones (Decca)
1	4	LADY MADONNA — Beatles (Parlophone)
5	5	(SITTIN' ON) THE DOCK OF THE BAY — Otis Redding (Stax)
10	6	IF I ONLY HAD TIME — John Rowles (MCA)
7	7	STEP INSIDE LOVE — Cilla Black (Parlophone)
18	8	SIMON SAYS — 1910 Fruitgum Company (Pye International)
9	9	IF I WERE A CARPENTER — Four Tops (Tamla Motown)
6	10	CINDERELLA ROCKEFELLA — Esther & Abi Ofarim (Philips)
16	11	AIN'T NOTHIN' BUT A HOUSEPARTY — Showstoppers (Beacon)
17	12	CAN'T TAKE MY EYES OFF YOU — Andy Williams (CBS)
22	13	JENNIFER ECCLES — Hollies (Parlophone)
15	14	VALLERI — Monkees (RCA)
8	15	THE LEGEND OF XANADU — Dave Dee, Dozy, Beaky, Mick & Tich (Fontana)
13	16	LOVE IS BLUE — Paul Mauriat & His Orchestra (Philips)
24	17	SOMETHING HERE IN MY HEART — Paper Dolls (Pye)
21	18	CAPTAIN OF YOUR SHIP — Reparata & the Delrons (Bell)
11	19	ROSIE — Don Partridge (Columbia)
26	20	I CAN'T LET MAGGIE GO — Honeybus (Deram)
29	21	CRY LIKE A BABY — Box Tops (Bell)
14	22	JENNIFER JUNIPER — Donovan (Pye)
23	23	ME, THE PEACEFUL HEART — Lulu (Columbia)
25	24	SOMEWHERE IN THE COUNTRY — Gene Pitney (Stateside)
-	25	FOREVER CAME TODAY — Diana Ross & the Supremes (Tamla Motown)
-	26	I DON'T WANT OUR LOVING TO DIE — Herd (Fontana)
20	27	SHE WEARS MY RING — Solomon King (Columbia)
-	28	RAINBOW VALLEY — Love Affair (CBS)
-	29	LAZY SUNDAY — Small Faces (Immediate)
-	30	ROCK AROUND THE CLOCK — Bill Haley & the Comets (MCA)

20 April 1968

last week	this week	Title / Artist
2	1	WHAT A WONDERFUL WORLD — Louis Armstrong (HMV)
1	2	CONGRATULATIONS — Cliff Richard (Columbia)
6	3	IF I ONLY HAD TIME — John Rowles (MCA)
3	4	DELILAH — Tom Jones (Decca)
8	5	SIMON SAYS — 1910 Fruitgum Company (Pye International)
4	6	LADY MADONNA — Beatles (Parlophone)
13	7	JENNIFER ECCLES — Hollies (Parlophone)
12	8	CAN'T TAKE MY EYES OFF YOU — Andy Williams (CBS)
5	9	(SITTIN' ON) THE DOCK OF THE BAY — Otis Redding (Stax)
7	10	STEP INSIDE LOVE — Cilla Black (Parlophone)
11	11	AIN'T NOTHIN' BUT A HOUSEPARTY — Showstoppers (Beacon)
9	12	IF I WERE A CARPENTER — Four Tops (Tamla Motown)
14	13	VALLERI — Monkees (RCA)
17	14	SOMETHING HERE IN MY HEART — Paper Dolls (Pye)
18	15	CAPTAIN OF YOUR SHIP — Reparata & the Delrons (Bell)
20	16	I CAN'T LET MAGGIE GO — Honeybus (Deram)
29	17	LAZY SUNDAY — Small Faces (Immediate)
10	18	CINDERELLA ROCKEFELLA — Esther & Abi Ofarim (Philips)
19	19	CRY LIKE A BABY — Box Tops (Bell)
24	20	SOMEWHERE IN THE COUNTRY — Gene Pitney (Stateside)
16	21	LOVE IS BLUE — Paul Mauriat & His Orchestra (Philips)
26	22	I DON'T WANT OUR LOVING TO DIE — Herd (Fontana)
15	23	THE LEGEND OF XANADU — Dave Dee, Dozy, Beaky, Mick & Tich (Fontana)
-	24	WHITE HORSES — Jacky (Philips)
-	25	HELLO, HOW ARE YOU — Easybeats (United Artists)
19	26	ROSIE — Don Partridge (Columbia)
25	27	FOREVER CAME TODAY — Diana Ross & the Supremes (Tamla Motown)
-	28	PRETTY BROWN EYES — Jim Reeves (RCA)
30	29	ROCK AROUND THE CLOCK — Bill Haley & the Comets (MCA)
-	30	JUMBO — Bee Gees (Polydor)
-	30	LITTLE GREEN APPLES — Roger Miller (Mercury)

Lady Madonna was conceived by Paul McCartney as a tribute to the style of Fats Domino – and was paid the ultimate compliment when, a few months later, Fats decided it suited him too and covered it. Cliff Richard, to many people's surprise, appeared on Cilla Black's TV show singing 1968's six UK Songs For Europe. *Congratulations* proved the winner, was promptly issued as Cliff's next single and gave him his first Number One for three years. At the Eurovision Song Contest it came second.

April – May 1968

27 April 1968

last	this	
1	1	WHAT A WONDERFUL WORLD Louis Armstrong (HMV)
2	2	CONGRATULATIONS Cliff Richard (Columbia)
5	3	SIMON SAYS 1910 Fruitgum Company (Pye International)
3	4	IF I ONLY HAD TIME John Rowles (MCA)
7	5	JENNIFER ECCLES Hollies (Parlophone)
8	6	CAN'T TAKE MY EYES OFF YOU Andy Williams (CBS)
4	7	DELILAH Tom Jones (Decca)
17	8	LAZY SUNDAY Small Faces (Immediate)
11	9	AIN'T NOTHIN' BUT A HOUSEPARTY Showstoppers (Beacon)
14	10	SOMETHING HERE IN MY HEART Paper Dolls (Pye)
16	11	I CAN'T LET MAGGIE GO Honeybus (Deram)
6	12	LADY MADONNA Beatles (Parlophone)
9	13	(SITTIN' ON) THE DOCK OF THE BAY Otis Redding (Stax)
15	14	CAPTAIN OF YOUR SHIP Reparata & the Delrons (Bell)
19	15	CRY LIKE A BABY Box Tops (Bell)
13	16	VALLERI Monkees (RCA)
10	17	STEP INSIDE LOVE Cilla Black (Parlophone)
22	18	I DON'T WANT OUR LOVING TO DIE Herd (Fontana)
-	19	A MAN WITHOUT LOVE Engelbert Humperdinck (Decca)
20	20	SOMEWHERE IN THE COUNTRY Gene Pitney (Stateside)
30	21	LITTLE GREEN APPLES Roger Miller (Mercury)
24	22	WHITE HORSES Jacky (Philips)
12	23	IF I WERE A CARPENTER Four Tops (Tamla Motown)
18	24	CINDERELLA ROCKEFELLA Esther & Abi Ofarim (Philips)
-	25	HONEY Bobby Goldsboro (United Artists)
27	26	FOREVER CAME TODAY Diana Ross & the Supremes (Tamla Motown)
21	27	LOVE IS BLUE Paul Mauriat & His Orchestra (Philips)
25	28	HELLO, HOW ARE YOU Easybeats (United Artists)
26	29	ROSIE Don Partridge (Columbia)
-	30	PEGGY SUE Buddy Holly (MCA)

4 May 1968

1	1	WHAT A WONDERFUL WORLD Louis Armstrong (HMV)
3	2	SIMON SAYS 1910 Fruitgum Company (Pye International)
8	3	LAZY SUNDAY Small Faces (Immediate)
4	4	IF I ONLY HAD TIME John Rowles (MCA)
2	5	CONGRATULATIONS Cliff Richard (Columbia)
6	6	CAN'T TAKE MY EYES OFF YOU Andy Williams (CBS)
19	7	A MAN WITHOUT LOVE Engelbert Humperdinck (Decca)
5	8	JENNIFER ECCLES Hollies (Parlophone)
9	9	AIN'T NOTHIN' BUT A HOUSEPARTY Showstoppers (Beacon)
10	10	SOMETHING HERE IN MY HEART Paper Dolls (Pye)
18	11	I DON'T WANT OUR LOVING TO DIE Herd (Fontana)
7	12	DELILAH Tom Jones (Decca)
11	13	I CAN'T LET MAGGIE GO Honeybus (Deram)
15	14	CRY LIKE A BABY Box Tops (Bell)
22	15	WHITE HORSES Jacky (Philips)
25	16	HONEY Bobby Goldsboro (United Artists)
-	17	YOUNG GIRL Union Gap (CBS)
14	18	CAPTAIN OF YOUR SHIP Reparata & the Delrons (Bell)
20	19	SOMEWHERE IN THE COUNTRY Gene Pitney (Stateside)
28	20	HELLO, HOW ARE YOU Easybeats (United Artists)
21	21	LITTLE GREEN APPLES Roger Miller (Mercury)
16	22	VALLERI Monkees (RCA)
12	23	LADY MADONNA Beatles (Parlophone)
13	24	(SITTIN' ON) THE DOCK OF THE BAY Otis Redding (Stax)
26	25	FOREVER CAME TODAY Diana Ross & the Supremes (Tamla Motown)
17	26	STEP INSIDE LOVE Cilla Black (Parlophone)
-	27	RAINBOW VALLEY Love Affair (CBS)
23	28	IF I WERE A CARPENTER Four Tops (Tamla Motown)
-	29	JOANNA Scott Walker (Philips)
-	30	SLEEPY JOE Herman's Hermits (Columbia)

11 May 1968

1	1	WHAT A WONDERFUL WORLD Louis Armstrong (HMV)
2	2	SIMON SAYS 1910 Fruitgum Company (Pye International)
3	3	LAZY SUNDAY Small Faces (Immediate)
7	4	A MAN WITHOUT LOVE Engelbert Humperdinck (Decca)
17	5	YOUNG GIRL Union Gap (CBS)
16	6	HONEY Bobby Goldsboro (United Artists)
4	7	IF I ONLY HAD TIME John Rowles (MCA)
11	8	I DON'T WANT OUR LOVING TO DIE Herd (Fontana)
6	9	CAN'T TAKE MY EYES OFF YOU Andy Williams (CBS)
5	10	CONGRATULATIONS Cliff Richard (Columbia)
15	11	WHITE HORSES Jacky (Philips)
9	12	AIN'T NOTHIN' BUT A HOUSEPARTY Showstoppers (Beacon)
8	13	JENNIFER ECCLES Hollies (Parlophone)
13	14	I CAN'T LET MAGGIE GO Honeybus (Deram)
10	15	SOMETHING HERE IN MY HEART Paper Dolls (Pye)
14	16	CRY LIKE A BABY Box Tops (Bell)
12	17	DELILAH Tom Jones (Decca)
27	18	RAINBOW VALLEY Love Affair (CBS)
19	19	SOMEWHERE IN THE COUNTRY Gene Pitney (Stateside)
29	20	JOANNA Scott Walker (Philips)
20	21	HELLO, HOW ARE YOU Easybeats (United Artists)
-	22	HELULE, HELULE Tremeloes (CBS)
30	23	SLEEPY JOE Herman's Hermits (Columbia)
-	24	DO YOU KNOW THE WAY TO SAN JOSE Dionne Warwick (Pye International)
-	25	THIS WHEEL'S ON FIRE Julie Driscoll & the Brian Auger Trinity (Marmalade)
21	26	LITTLE GREEN APPLES Roger Miller (Mercury)
25	27	FOREVER CAME TODAY Diana Ross & the Supremes (Tamla Motown)
-	28	WONDERBOY Kinks (Pye)
-	29	WHEN WE WERE YOUNG Solomon King (Columbia)
-	30	ROCK AROUND THE CLOCK Bill Haley & the Comets (MCA)

18 May 1968

5	1	YOUNG GIRL Union Gap (CBS)
1	2	WHAT A WONDERFUL WORLD Louis Armstrong (HMV)
6	3	HONEY Bobby Goldsboro (United Artists)
4	4	A MAN WITHOUT LOVE Engelbert Humperdinck (Decca)
3	5	LAZY SUNDAY Small Faces (Immediate)
2	6	SIMON SAYS 1910 Fruitgum Company (Pye International)
8	7	I DON'T WANT OUR LOVING TO DIE Herd (Fontana)
9	8	CAN'T TAKE MY EYES OFF YOU Andy Williams (CBS)
7	9	IF I ONLY HAD TIME John Rowles (MCA)
11	10	WHITE HORSES Jacky (Philips)
18	11	RAINBOW VALLEY Love Affair (CBS)
20	12	JOANNA Scott Walker (Philips)
23	13	SLEEPY JOE Herman's Hermits (Columbia)
10	14	CONGRATULATIONS Cliff Richard (Columbia)
22	15	HELULE, HELULE Tremeloes (CBS)
12	16	AIN'T NOTHIN' BUT A HOUSEPARTY Showstoppers (Beacon)
13	17	JENNIFER ECCLES Hollies (Parlophone)
16	18	CRY LIKE A BABY Box Tops (Bell)
14	19	I CAN'T LET MAGGIE GO Honeybus (Deram)
25	20	THIS WHEEL'S ON FIRE Julie Driscoll & the Brian Auger Trinity (Marmalade)
15	21	SOMETHING HERE IN MY HEART Paper Dolls (Pye)
21	22	HELLO, HOW ARE YOU Easybeats (United Artists)
17	23	DELILAH Tom Jones (Decca)
19	24	SOMEWHERE IN THE COUNTRY Gene Pitney (Stateside)
26	25	LITTLE GREEN APPLES Roger Miller (Mercury)
29	26	WHEN WE WERE YOUNG Solomon King (Columbia)
-	27	U.S. MALE Elvis Presley (RCA)
30	28	ROCK AROUND THE CLOCK Bill Haley & the Comets (MCA)
24	29	DO YOU KNOW THE WAY TO SAN JOSE Dionne Warwick (Pye International)
-	30	SURPRISE SURPRISE Troggs (Page One)

If Esther & Abi Ofarim were a surprise to many at Number One, the appearance of 67 year-old Louis Armstrong in pole position with a non-jazz, non-trumpet vocal ballad was an almighty shock. Once again the silent majority of non-typical record buyers triumphed over the taste-makers and trend-followers. More was on the way in the form of Bobby Goldsboro's *Honey* – a tear-jerking emotional tale of three-tissue proportions, already ensconced at Number One in the States.

May – June 1968

195

25 May 1968

last week	this week	Title	Artist (Label)
1	1	YOUNG GIRL	Union Gap (CBS)
3	2	HONEY	Bobby Goldsboro (United Artists)
4	3	A MAN WITHOUT LOVE	Engelbert Humperdinck (Decca)
2	4	WHAT A WONDERFUL WORLD	Louis Armstrong (HMV)
7	5	I DON'T WANT OUR LOVING TO DIE	Herd (Fontana)
5	6	LAZY SUNDAY	Small Faces (Immediate)
12	7	JOANNA	Scott Walker (Philips)
11	8	RAINBOW VALLEY	Love Affair (CBS)
6	9	SIMON SAYS	1910 Fruitgum Company (Pye International)
10	10	WHITE HORSES	Jacky (Philips)
13	11	SLEEPY JOE	Herman's Hermits (Columbia)
15	12	HELULE, HELULE	Tremeloes (CBS)
8	13	CAN'T TAKE MY EYES OFF YOU	Andy Williams (CBS)
9	14	IF I ONLY HAD TIME	John Rowles (MCA)
20	15	THIS WHEEL'S ON FIRE	Julie Driscoll & the Brian Auger Trinity (Marmalade)
29	16	DO YOU KNOW THE WAY TO SAN JOSE	Dionne Warwick (Pye International)
27	17	U.S. MALE	Elvis Presley (RCA)
14	18	CONGRATULATIONS	Cliff Richard (Columbia)
16	19	AIN'T NOTHIN' BUT A HOUSEPARTY	Showstoppers (Beacon)
18	20	CRY LIKE A BABY	Box Tops (Bell)
22	21	HELLO, HOW ARE YOU	Easybeats (United Artists)
23	22	DELILAH	Tom Jones (Decca)
26	22	WHEN WE WERE YOUNG	Solomon King (Columbia)
21	24	SOMETHING HERE IN MY HEART	Paper Dolls (Pye)
17	25	JENNIFER ECCLES	Hollies (Parlophone)
-	26	ANY OLD TIME YOU'RE LONELY AND SAD	Foundations (Pye)
-	26	I PRETEND	Des O'Connor (Columbia)
24	26	SOMEWHERE IN THE COUNTRY	Gene Pitney (Stateside)
19	29	I CAN'T LET MAGGIE GO	Honeybus (Deram)
-	30	BABY COME BACK	Equals (President)

1 June 1968

last week	this week	Title	Artist (Label)
1	1	YOUNG GIRL	Union Gap (CBS)
2	2	HONEY	Bobby Goldsboro (United Artists)
3	3	A MAN WITHOUT LOVE	Engelbert Humperdinck (Decca)
5	4	I DON'T WANT OUR LOVING TO DIE	Herd (Fontana)
4	5	WHAT A WONDERFUL WORLD	Louis Armstrong (HMV)
8	6	RAINBOW VALLEY	Love Affair (CBS)
7	7	JOANNA	Scott Walker (Philips)
6	8	LAZY SUNDAY	Small Faces (Immediate)
9	9	SIMON SAYS	1910 Fruitgum Company (Pye International)
12	10	HELULE, HELULE	Tremeloes (CBS)
15	11	THIS WHEEL'S ON FIRE	Julie Driscoll & the Brian Auger Trinity (Marmalade)
-	12	JUMPIN' JACK FLASH	Rolling Stones (Decca)
10	13	WHITE HORSES	Jacky (Philips)
11	14	SLEEPY JOE	Herman's Hermits (Columbia)
16	15	DO YOU KNOW THE WAY TO SAN JOSE	Dionne Warwick (Pye International)
13	16	CAN'T TAKE MY EYES OFF YOU	Andy Williams (CBS)
17	17	U.S. MALE	Elvis Presley (RCA)
14	18	IF I ONLY HAD TIME	John Rowles (MCA)
26	19	I PRETEND	Des O'Connor (Columbia)
-	20	BLUE EYES	Don Partridge (Columbia)
19	21	AIN'T NOTHIN' BUT A HOUSEPARTY	Showstoppers (Beacon)
-	22	TIME FOR LIVIN'	Association (Warner Bros)
30	23	BABY COME BACK	Equals (President)
-	24	HURDY GURDY MAN	Donovan (Pye)
-	25	ANYONE FOR TENNIS	Cream (Polydor)
22	26	WHEN WE WERE YOUNG	Solomon King (Columbia)
20	27	CRY LIKE A BABY	Box Tops (Bell)
-	27	LOVIN' THINGS	Marmalade (CBS)
22	29	DELILAH	Tom Jones (Decca)
-	30	THINK	Aretha Franklin (Atlantic)

8 June 1968

last week	this week	Title	Artist (Label)
1	1	YOUNG GIRL	Union Gap (CBS)
2	2	HONEY	Bobby Goldsboro (United Artists)
3	3	A MAN WITHOUT LOVE	Engelbert Humperdinck (Decca)
12	4	JUMPIN' JACK FLASH	Rolling Stones (Decca)
4	5	I DON'T WANT OUR LOVING TO DIE	Herd (Fontana)
7	6	JOANNA	Scott Walker (Philips)
6	7	RAINBOW VALLEY	Love Affair (CBS)
11	8	THIS WHEEL'S ON FIRE	Julie Driscoll & the Brian Auger Trinity (Marmalade)
15	9	DO YOU KNOW THE WAY TO SAN JOSE	Dionne Warwick (Pye International)
5	10	WHAT A WONDERFUL WORLD	Louis Armstrong (HMV)
10	11	HELULE, HELULE	Tremeloes (CBS)
8	12	LAZY SUNDAY	Small Faces (Immediate)
20	13	BLUE EYES	Don Partridge (Columbia)
9	14	SIMON SAYS	1910 Fruitgum Company (Pye International)
24	15	HURDY GURDY MAN	Donovan (Pye)
14	16	SLEEPY JOE	Herman's Hermits (Columbia)
17	17	U.S. MALE	Elvis Presley (RCA)
19	18	I PRETEND	Des O'Connor (Columbia)
27	19	LOVIN' THINGS	Marmalade (CBS)
23	20	BABY COME BACK	Equals (President)
13	21	WHITE HORSES	Jacky (Philips)
16	22	CAN'T TAKE MY EYES OFF YOU	Andy Williams (CBS)
22	23	TIME FOR LIVIN'	Association (Warner Bros)
26	24	WHEN WE WERE YOUNG	Solomon King (Columbia)
25	25	ANYONE FOR TENNIS	Cream (Polydor)
18	26	IF I ONLY HAD TIME	John Rowles (MCA)
-	26	SON OF HICKORY HOLLER'S TRAMP	O.C. Smith (CBS)
30	28	THINK	Aretha Franklin (Atlantic)
-	29	HAPPY SONG	Otis Redding (Stax)
29	30	DELILAH	Tom Jones (Decca)

15 June 1968

last week	this week	Title	Artist (Label)
1	1	YOUNG GIRL	Union Gap (CBS)
4	2	JUMPIN' JACK FLASH	Rolling Stones (Decca)
2	3	HONEY	Bobby Goldsboro (United Artists)
3	4	A MAN WITHOUT LOVE	Engelbert Humperdinck (Decca)
8	5	THIS WHEEL'S ON FIRE	Julie Driscoll & the Brian Auger Trinity (Marmalade)
13	6	BLUE EYES	Don Partridge (Columbia)
15	7	HURDY GURDY MAN	Donovan (Pye)
9	8	DO YOU KNOW THE WAY TO SAN JOSE	Dionne Warwick (Pye International)
7	9	RAINBOW VALLEY	Love Affair (CBS)
5	10	I DON'T WANT OUR LOVING TO DIE	Herd (Fontana)
6	11	JOANNA	Scott Walker (Philips)
20	12	BABY COME BACK	Equals (President)
18	13	I PRETEND	Des O'Connor (Columbia)
11	14	HELULE, HELULE	Tremeloes (CBS)
10	15	WHAT A WONDERFUL WORLD	Louis Armstrong (HMV)
19	16	LOVIN' THINGS	Marmalade (CBS)
14	17	SIMON SAYS	1910 Fruitgum Company (Pye International)
16	18	SLEEPY JOE	Herman's Hermits (Columbia)
12	19	LAZY SUNDAY	Small Faces (Immediate)
26	20	SON OF HICKORY HOLLER'S TRAMP	O.C. Smith (CBS)
23	21	TIME FOR LIVIN'	Association (Warner Bros)
21	22	WHITE HORSES	Jacky (Philips)
17	23	U.S. MALE	Elvis Presley (RCA)
-	24	BOY	Lulu (Columbia)
25	25	ANYONE FOR TENNIS	Cream (Polydor)
22	26	CAN'T TAKE MY EYES OFF YOU	Andy Williams (CBS)
-	27	NOW	Val Doonican (Pye)
29	28	HAPPY SONG	Otis Redding (Stax)
-	29	MY NAME IS JACK	Manfred Mann (Fontana)
28	30	THINK	Aretha Franklin (Atlantic)

The Union Gap were led by vocalist Gary Puckett who failed to get an individual credit on the chart-topping *Young Girl* (or its US Top Ten predecessor *Woman, Woman* which had not charted in Britain), but would be duly identified on the follow-up *Lady Willpower*. Cream's almost whimsical hit *Anyone For Tennis*, an out-take from the group's *Wheels Of Fire* album session, was strangely used in the US as the theme to a biker movie entitled *The Strange Seven*. The Stones returned to form with *Jumpin' Jack Flash*.

last week	this week	22 June 1968	
2	1	JUMPIN' JACK FLASH	Rolling Stones (Decca)
1	2	YOUNG GIRL	Union Gap (CBS)
7	3	HURDY GURDY MAN	Donovan (Pye)
6	4	BLUE EYES	Don Partridge (Columbia)
3	5	HONEY	Bobby Goldsboro (United Artists)
12	6	BABY COME BACK	Equals (President)
5	7	THIS WHEEL'S ON FIRE	Julie Driscoll & the Brian Auger Trinity (Marmalade)
13	8	I PRETEND	Des O'Connor (Columbia)
8	9	DO YOU KNOW THE WAY TO SAN JOSE	Dionne Warwick (Pye International)
4	10	A MAN WITHOUT LOVE	Engelbert Humperdinck (Decca)
20	11	SON OF HICKORY HOLLER'S TRAMP	O.C. Smith (CBS)
16	12	LOVIN' THINGS	Marmalade (CBS)
9	13	RAINBOW VALLEY	Love Affair (CBS)
10	14	I DON'T WANT OUR LOVING TO DIE	Herd (Fontana)
11	15	JOANNA	Scott Walker (Philips)
29	16	MY NAME IS JACK	Manfred Mann (Fontana)
24	17	BOY	Lulu (Columbia)
15	18	WHAT A WONDERFUL WORLD	Louis Armstrong (HMV)
14	19	HELULE, HELULE	Tremeloes (CBS)
17	20	SIMON SAYS	1910 Fruitgum Company (Pye International)
-	21	YESTERDAY HAS GONE	Cupid's Inspiration (Nems)
21	22	TIME FOR LIVIN'	Association (Warner Bros)
-	23	HUSH ... NOT A WORD TO MARY	John Rowles (MCA)
18	24	SLEEPY JOE	Herman's Hermits (Columbia)
22	25	WHITE HORSES	Jacky (Philips)
-	25	YUMMY YUMMY YUMMY	Ohio Express (Pye International)
-	27	TRIBUTE TO A KING	William Bell (Stax)
-	28	ONE MORE DANCE	Esther & Abi Ofarim (Philips)
19	29	LAZY SUNDAY	Small Faces (Immediate)
-	30	QUANDO M'INNAMORO (A MAN WITHOUT LOVE)	Sandpipers (A&M)

last week	this week	29 June 1968	
1	1	JUMPIN' JACK FLASH	Rolling Stones (Decca)
6	2	BABY COME BACK	Equals (President)
3	3	HURDY GURDY MAN	Donovan (Pye)
4	4	BLUE EYES	Don Partridge (Columbia)
2	5	YOUNG GIRL	Union Gap (CBS)
8	6	I PRETEND	Des O'Connor (Columbia)
7	7	THIS WHEEL'S ON FIRE	Julie Driscoll & the Brian Auger Trinity (Marmalade)
11	8	SON OF HICKORY HOLLER'S TRAMP	O.C. Smith (CBS)
12	9	LOVIN' THINGS	Marmalade (CBS)
5	10	HONEY	Bobby Goldsboro (United Artists)
16	11	MY NAME IS JACK	Manfred Mann (Fontana)
9	12	DO YOU KNOW THE WAY TO SAN JOSE	Dionne Warwick (Pye International)
21	13	YESTERDAY HAS GONE	Cupid's Inspiration (Nems)
10	14	A MAN WITHOUT LOVE	Engelbert Humperdinck (Decca)
17	15	BOY	Lulu (Columbia)
23	15	HUSH ... NOT A WORD TO MARY	John Rowles (MCA)
25	17	YUMMY YUMMY YUMMY	Ohio Express (Pye International)
13	18	RAINBOW VALLEY	Love Affair (CBS)
28	19	ONE MORE DANCE	Esther & Abi Ofarim (Philips)
-	20	D.W. WASHBURN	Monkees (RCA)
14	21	I DON'T WANT OUR LOVING TO DIE	Herd (Fontana)
15	21	JOANNA	Scott Walker (Philips)
-	23	MONY MONY	Tommy James & the Shondells (Major Minor)
18	24	WHAT A WONDERFUL WORLD	Louis Armstrong (HMV)
-	25	MACARTHUR PARK	Richard Harris (RCA)
22	26	TIME FOR LIVIN'	Association (Warner Bros)
-	27	WHERE WILL YOU BE	Sue Nicholls (Pye)
-	28	DOGS	Who (Track)
-	29	THINK	Aretha Franklin (Atlantic)
25	30	WHITE HORSES	Jacky (Philips)

last week	this week	6 July 1968	
2	1	BABY COME BACK	Equals (President)
1	2	JUMPIN' JACK FLASH	Rolling Stones (Decca)
8	3	SON OF HICKORY HOLLER'S TRAMP	O.C. Smith (CBS)
4	4	BLUE EYES	Don Partridge (Columbia)
6	5	I PRETEND	Des O'Connor (Columbia)
3	6	HURDY GURDY MAN	Donovan (Pye)
5	7	YOUNG GIRL	Union Gap (CBS)
11	8	MY NAME IS JACK	Manfred Mann (Fontana)
9	9	LOVIN' THINGS	Marmalade (CBS)
13	10	YESTERDAY HAS GONE	Cupid's Inspiration (Nems)
17	11	YUMMY YUMMY YUMMY	Ohio Express (Pye International)
7	12	THIS WHEEL'S ON FIRE	Julie Driscoll & the Brian Auger Trinity (Marmalade)
10	13	HONEY	Bobby Goldsboro (United Artists)
15	14	HUSH ... NOT A WORD TO MARY	John Rowles (MCA)
23	15	MONY MONY	Tommy James & the Shondells (Major Minor)
12	16	DO YOU KNOW THE WAY TO SAN JOSE	Dionne Warwick (Pye International)
19	17	ONE MORE DANCE	Esther & Abi Ofarim (Philips)
25	18	MACARTHUR PARK	Richard Harris (RCA)
15	19	BOY	Lulu (Columbia)
20	20	D.W. WASHBURN	Monkees (RCA)
14	21	A MAN WITHOUT LOVE	Engelbert Humperdinck (Decca)
-	22	I'LL LOVE YOU FOREVER TODAY	Cliff Richard (Columbia)
24	23	WHAT A WONDERFUL WORLD	Louis Armstrong (HMV)
27	24	WHERE WILL YOU BE	Sue Nicholls (Pye)
-	24	I CLOSE MY EYES AND COUNT TO TEN	Dusty Springfield (Philips)
26	26	FIRE	Arthur Brown (Track)
18	27	RAINBOW VALLEY	Love Affair (CBS)
-	28	GOTTA SEE JANE	R. Dean Taylor (Tamla Motown)
-	29	AMERICA	Nice (Immediate)
-	30	U.S. MALE	Elvis Presley (RCA)

last week	this week	13 July 1968	
1	1	BABY COME BACK	Equals (President)
3	2	SON OF HICKORY HOLLER'S TRAMP	O.C. Smith (CBS)
5	3	I PRETEND	Des O'Connor (Columbia)
2	4	JUMPIN' JACK FLASH	Rolling Stones (Decca)
10	5	YESTERDAY HAS GONE	Cupid's Inspiration (Nems)
11	6	YUMMY YUMMY YUMMY	Ohio Express (Pye International)
6	7	HURDY GURDY MAN	Donovan (Pye)
9	8	LOVIN' THINGS	Marmalade (CBS)
4	9	BLUE EYES	Don Partridge (Columbia)
8	10	MY NAME IS JACK	Manfred Mann (Fontana)
15	11	MONY MONY	Tommy James & the Shondells (Major Minor)
18	12	MACARTHUR PARK	Richard Harris (RCA)
14	13	HUSH ... NOT A WORD TO MARY	John Rowles (MCA)
7	14	YOUNG GIRL	Union Gap (CBS)
17	15	ONE MORE DANCE	Esther & Abi Ofarim (Philips)
26	16	FIRE	Arthur Brown (Track)
24	17	I CLOSE MY EYES AND COUNT TO TEN	Dusty Springfield (Philips)
-	18	THIS GUY'S IN LOVE WITH YOU	Herb Alpert (A&M)
24	19	WHERE WILL YOU BE	Sue Nicholls (Pye)
20	20	D.W. WASHBURN	Monkees (RCA)
16	21	DO YOU KNOW THE WAY TO SAN JOSE	Dionne Warwick (Pye International)
28	22	GOTTA SEE JANE	R. Dean Taylor (Tamla Motown)
12	23	THIS WHEEL'S ON FIRE	Julie Driscoll & the Brian Auger Trinity (Marmalade)
-	24	IF YOU DON'T WANT MY LOVE	Robert John (CBS)
-	25	LAST NIGHT IN SOHO	Dave Dee, Dozy, Beaky, Mick & Tich (Fontana)
13	26	HONEY	Bobby Goldsboro (United Artists)
-	27	MRS. ROBINSON	Simon & Garfunkel (CBS)
22	28	I'LL LOVE YOU FOREVER TODAY	Cliff Richard (Columbia)
-	29	HELP YOURSELF	Tom Jones (Decca)
-	29	SOME THINGS YOU NEVER GET USED TO	Diana Ross & the Supremes (Tamla Motown)

Some odd records were finding chart success. Manfred Mann's *My Name Is Jack* was a John Simon song about an inmate of a home for the mentally disturbed, Esther and Abi Ofarim's *One More Dance* was even more camp than *Cinderella Rockefella*, and seemed to be a satire on European aristocratic mores. The Who's *Dogs*, seemingly released as a joke, concerned itself with greyhound racing. O C Smith's *Hickory Holler* was, in contrast, merely the tale of a man whose mother was the town whore.

July – August 1968

20 July 1968

1 1 BABY COME BACK Equals (President)
2 2 SON OF HICKORY HOLLER'S TRAMP O.C. Smith (CBS)
3 3 I PRETEND Des O'Connor (Columbia)
5 4 YESTERDAY HAS GONE Cupid's Inspiration (Nems)
11 5 MONY MONY Tommy James & the Shondells (Major Minor)
6 6 YUMMY YUMMY YUMMY Ohio Express (Pye International)
12 7 MACARTHUR PARK Richard Harris (RCA)
10 8 MY NAME IS JACK Manfred Mann (Fontana)
16 9 FIRE Arthur Brown (Track)
8 10 LOVIN' THINGS Marmalade (CBS)
4 11 JUMPIN' JACK FLASH Rolling Stones (Decca)
7 12 HURDY GURDY MAN Donovan (Pye)
18 13 THIS GUY'S IN LOVE WITH YOU Herb Alpert (A&M)
17 14 I CLOSE MY EYES AND COUNT TO TEN Dusty Springfield (Philips)
9 15 BLUE EYES Don Partridge (Columbia)
27 16 MRS. ROBINSON Simon & Garfunkel (CBS)
13 17 HUSH ... NOT A WORD TO MARY John Rowles (MCA)
14 18 YOUNG GIRL Union Gap (CBS)
19 19 WHERE WILL YOU BE Sue Nicholls (Pye)
15 20 ONE MORE DANCE Esther & Abi Ofarim (Philips)
25 21 LAST NIGHT IN SOHO Dave Dee, Dozy, Beaky, Mick & Tich (Fontana)
29 22 HELP YOURSELF Tom Jones (Decca)
22 22 GOTTA SEE JANE R. Dean Taylor (Tamla Motown)
20 24 D.W. WASHBURN Monkees (RCA)
- 25 DAYS Kinks (Pye)
- 26 KEEP ON Bruce Channel (Bell)
- 27 THE UNIVERSAL Small Faces (Immediate)
29 28 SOME THINGS YOU NEVER GET USED TO Diana Ross & the Supremes (Tamla Motown)
- 29 AMERICA Nice (Immediate)
- 30 YOUR TIME HASN'T COME YET BABY Elvis Presley (RCA)

27 July 1968

5 1 MONY MONY Tommy James & the Shondells (Major Minor)
1 2 BABY COME BACK Equals (President)
3 3 I PRETEND Des O'Connor (Columbia)
2 4 SON OF HICKORY HOLLER'S TRAMP O.C. Smith (CBS)
9 5 FIRE Arthur Brown (Track)
7 6 MACARTHUR PARK Richard Harris (RCA)
6 6 YUMMY YUMMY YUMMY Ohio Express (Pye International)
4 8 YESTERDAY HAS GONE Cupid's Inspiration (Nems)
13 9 THIS GUY'S IN LOVE WITH YOU Herb Alpert (A&M)
16 10 MRS. ROBINSON Simon & Garfunkel (CBS)
22 11 HELP YOURSELF Tom Jones (Decca)
14 12 I CLOSE MY EYES AND COUNT TO TEN Dusty Springfield (Philips)
8 13 MY NAME IS JACK Manfred Mann (Fontana)
21 14 LAST NIGHT IN SOHO Dave Dee, Dozy, Beaky, Mick & Tich (Fontana)
17 15 HUSH ... NOT A WORD TO MARY John Rowles (MCA)
11 16 JUMPIN' JACK FLASH Rolling Stones (Decca)
19 17 WHERE WILL YOU BE Sue Nicholls (Pye)
10 18 LOVIN' THINGS Marmalade (CBS)
- 19 DANCE TO THE MUSIC Sly & the Family Stone (Direction)
20 20 ONE MORE DANCE Esther & Abi Ofarim (Philips)
- 21 SUNSHINE GIRL Herman's Hermits (Columbia)
25 22 DAYS Kinks (Pye)
27 23 THE UNIVERSAL Small Faces (Immediate)
26 24 KEEP ON Bruce Channel (Bell)
15 25 BLUE EYES Don Partridge (Columbia)
12 26 HURDY GURDY MAN Donovan (Pye)
22 26 GOTTA SEE JANE R. Dean Taylor (Tamla Motown)
- 28 HERE COMES THE JUDGE Pigmeat Markham (Chess)
28 29 SOME THINGS YOU NEVER GET USED TO Diana Ross & the Supremes (Tamla Motown)
18 30 YOUNG GIRL Union Gap (CBS)

3 August 1968

1 1 MONY MONY Tommy James & the Shondells (Major Minor)
5 2 FIRE Arthur Brown (Track)
3 3 I PRETEND Des O'Connor (Columbia)
10 4 MRS. ROBINSON Simon & Garfunkel (CBS)
9 5 THIS GUY'S IN LOVE WITH YOU Herb Alpert (A&M)
2 6 BABY COME BACK Equals (President)
6 7 MACARTHUR PARK Richard Harris (RCA)
11 8 HELP YOURSELF Tom Jones (Decca)
12 9 I CLOSE MY EYES AND COUNT TO TEN Dusty Springfield (Philips)
6 10 YUMMY YUMMY YUMMY Ohio Express (Pye International)
4 11 SON OF HICKORY HOLLER'S TRAMP O.C. Smith (CBS)
14 12 LAST NIGHT IN SOHO Dave Dee, Dozy, Beaky, Mick & Tich (Fontana)
8 13 YESTERDAY HAS GONE Cupid's Inspiration (Nems)
21 14 SUNSHINE GIRL Herman's Hermits (Columbia)
19 15 DANCE TO THE MUSIC Sly & the Family Stone (Direction)
23 16 THE UNIVERSAL Small Faces (Immediate)
22 17 DAYS Kinks (Pye)
17 18 WHERE WILL YOU BE Sue Nicholls (Pye)
24 19 KEEP ON Bruce Channel (Bell)
13 19 MY NAME IS JACK Manfred Mann (Fontana)
- 21 DO IT AGAIN Beach Boys (Capitol)
28 22 HERE COMES THE JUDGE Pigmeat Markham (Chess)
15 23 HUSH ... NOT A WORD TO MARY John Rowles (MCA)
20 24 ONE MORE DANCE Esther & Abi Ofarim (Philips)
26 25 GOTTA SEE JANE R. Dean Taylor (Tamla Motown)
- 26 AMERICA Nice (Immediate)
18 27 LOVIN' THINGS Marmalade (CBS)
25 28 BLUE EYES Don Partridge (Columbia)
16 29 JUMPIN' JACK FLASH Rolling Stones (Decca)
- 30 LOVE GROWS Gene Pitney (Stateside)

10 August 1968

1 1 MONY MONY Tommy James & the Shondells (Major Minor)
2 2 FIRE Arthur Brown (Track)
3 3 I PRETEND Des O'Connor (Columbia)
8 4 HELP YOURSELF Tom Jones (Decca)
4 5 MRS. ROBINSON Simon & Garfunkel (CBS)
9 6 I CLOSE MY EYES AND COUNT TO TEN Dusty Springfield (Philips)
5 7 THIS GUY'S IN LOVE WITH YOU Herb Alpert (A&M)
12 8 LAST NIGHT IN SOHO Dave Dee, Dozy, Beaky, Mick & Tich (Fontana)
7 9 MACARTHUR PARK Richard Harris (RCA)
14 10 SUNSHINE GIRL Herman's Hermits (Columbia)
15 11 DANCE TO THE MUSIC Sly & the Family Stone (Direction)
6 12 BABY COME BACK Equals (President)
10 13 YUMMY YUMMY YUMMY Ohio Express (Pye International)
17 14 DAYS Kinks (Pye)
11 15 SON OF HICKORY HOLLER'S TRAMP O.C. Smith (CBS)
19 16 KEEP ON Bruce Channel (Bell)
21 17 DO IT AGAIN Beach Boys (Capitol)
16 18 THE UNIVERSAL Small Faces (Immediate)
13 19 YESTERDAY HAS GONE Cupid's Inspiration (Nems)
18 20 WHERE WILL YOU BE Sue Nicholls (Pye)
- 21 I'VE GOTTA GET A MESSAGE TO YOU Bee Gees (Polydor)
- 22 HIGH IN THE SKY Amen Corner (Deram)
22 23 HERE COMES THE JUDGE Pigmeat Markham (Chess)
- 24 HARD TO HANDLE Otis Redding (Atlantic)
19 25 MY NAME IS JACK Manfred Mann (Fontana)
23 26 HUSH ... NOT A WORD TO MARY John Rowles (MCA)
- 27 YOUR TIME HASN'T COME YET BABY Elvis Presley (RCA)
26 28 AMERICA Nice (Immediate)
- 29 HERE COMES THE JUDGE Shorty Long (Tamla Motown)
25 30 GOTTA SEE JANE R. Dean Taylor (Tamla Motown)

Tommy James' stomping *Mony Mony*, the summer of '68's foremost dance disc, acquired its unusual title when James, in the process of writing the track and looking for a suitable hook, glanced out of the windowand saw the Mutual Of New York insurance building spelling out the initials M.O.N.Y. in the darkness. Inspiration flashed and a hit was born. Presumably if Tommy had looked out of a different window the song might have become *Wimpy Wimpy* or *Honda Honda*.

August – September 1968

17 August 1968

last week	this week	
1	1	MONY MONY — Tommy James & the Shondells (Major Minor)
4	2	HELP YOURSELF — Tom Jones (Decca)
2	3	FIRE — Arthur Brown (Track)
7	4	THIS GUY'S IN LOVE WITH YOU — Herb Alpert (A&M)
3	5	I PRETEND — Des O'Connor (Columbia)
6	6	I CLOSE MY EYES AND COUNT TO TEN — Dusty Springfield (Philips)
10	7	SUNSHINE GIRL — Herman's Hermits (Columbia)
5	8	MRS. ROBINSON — Simon & Garfunkel (CBS)
8	9	LAST NIGHT IN SOHO — Dave Dee, Dozy, Beaky, Mick & Tich (Fontana)
11	10	DANCE TO THE MUSIC — Sly & the Family Stone (Direction)
16	11	KEEP ON — Bruce Channel (Bell)
17	12	DO IT AGAIN — Beach Boys (Capitol)
22	13	HIGH IN THE SKY — Amen Corner (Deram)
21	14	I'VE GOTTA GET A MESSAGE TO YOU — Bee Gees (Polydor)
14	14	DAYS — Kinks (Pye)
-	16	I SAY A LITTLE PRAYER — Aretha Franklin (Atlantic)
9	17	MACARTHUR PARK — Richard Harris (RCA)
12	18	BABY COME BACK — Equals (President)
13	19	YUMMY YUMMY YUMMY — Ohio Express (Pye International)
18	20	THE UNIVERSAL — Small Faces (Immediate)
15	21	SON OF HICKORY HOLLER'S TRAMP — O.C. Smith (CBS)
23	22	HERE COMES THE JUDGE — Pigmeat Markham (Chess)
20	23	WHERE WILL YOU BE — Sue Nicholls (Pye)
-	24	ON THE ROAD AGAIN — Canned Heat (Liberty)
24	25	HARD TO HANDLE — Otis Redding (Atlantic)
-	26	LAUREL AND HARDY — Equals (President)
-	27	DREAM A LITTLE DREAM OF ME — Anita Harris (CBS)
-	28	LADY WILLPOWER — Gary Puckett and the Union Gap (CBS)
30	29	GOTTA SEE JANE — R. Dean Taylor (Tamla Motown)
-	30	ONE MORE DANCE — Esther & Abi Ofarim (Philips)

24 August 1968

last week	this week	
2	1	HELP YOURSELF — Tom Jones (Decca)
1	2	MONY MONY — Tommy James & the Shondells (Major Minor)
3	3	FIRE — Arthur Brown (Track)
4	4	THIS GUY'S IN LOVE WITH YOU — Herb Alpert (A&M)
14	5	I'VE GOTTA GET A MESSAGE TO YOU — Bee Gees (Polydor)
12	6	DO IT AGAIN — Beach Boys (Capitol)
7	7	SUNSHINE GIRL — Herman's Hermits (Columbia)
6	8	I CLOSE MY EYES AND COUNT TO TEN — Dusty Springfield (Philips)
5	9	I PRETEND — Des O'Connor (Columbia)
10	10	DANCE TO THE MUSIC — Sly & the Family Stone (Direction)
8	11	MRS. ROBINSON — Simon & Garfunkel (CBS)
13	12	HIGH IN THE SKY — Amen Corner (Deram)
16	13	I SAY A LITTLE PRAYER — Aretha Franklin (Atlantic)
11	14	KEEP ON — Bruce Channel (Bell)
9	15	LAST NIGHT IN SOHO — Dave Dee, Dozy, Beaky, Mick & Tich (Fontana)
14	16	DAYS — Kinks (Pye)
24	17	ON THE ROAD AGAIN — Canned Heat (Liberty)
-	18	HOLD ME TIGHT — Johnny Nash (Regal Zonophone)
20	19	THE UNIVERSAL — Small Faces (Immediate)
17	20	MACARTHUR PARK — Richard Harris (RCA)
27	21	DREAM A LITTLE DREAM OF ME — Anita Harris (CBS)
22	22	SON OF HICKORY HOLLER'S TRAMP — O.C. Smith (CBS)
25	23	HARD TO HANDLE — Otis Redding (Atlantic)
-	24	YOUR TIME HASN'T COME YET BABY — Elvis Presley (RCA)
-	25	DREAM A LITTLE DREAM OF ME — Mama Cass (RCA)
28	26	LADY WILLPOWER — Gary Puckett and the Union Gap (CBS)
19	27	YUMMY YUMMY YUMMY — Ohio Express (Pye International)
22	28	HERE COMES THE JUDGE — Pigmeat Markham (Chess)
-	29	WE CAN HELP YOU — Alan Bown (Music Factory)
-	30	C'MON MARIANNE — Grapefruit (RCA)

31 August 1968

last week	this week	
1	1	HELP YOURSELF — Tom Jones (Decca)
5	2	I'VE GOTTA GET A MESSAGE TO YOU — Bee Gees (Polydor)
4	3	THIS GUY'S IN LOVE WITH YOU — Herb Alpert (A&M)
6	4	DO IT AGAIN — Beach Boys (Capitol)
2	5	MONY MONY — Tommy James & the Shondells (Major Minor)
13	6	I SAY A LITTLE PRAYER — Aretha Franklin (Atlantic)
3	7	FIRE — Arthur Brown (Track)
12	8	HIGH IN THE SKY — Amen Corner (Deram)
7	9	SUNSHINE GIRL — Herman's Hermits (Columbia)
10	10	DANCE TO THE MUSIC — Sly & the Family Stone (Direction)
18	11	HOLD ME TIGHT — Johnny Nash (Regal Zonophone)
8	12	I CLOSE MY EYES AND COUNT TO TEN — Dusty Springfield (Philips)
17	13	ON THE ROAD AGAIN — Canned Heat (Liberty)
9	14	I PRETEND — Des O'Connor (Columbia)
14	15	KEEP ON — Bruce Channel (Bell)
11	16	MRS. ROBINSON — Simon & Garfunkel (CBS)
16	17	DAYS — Kinks (Pye)
25	18	DREAM A LITTLE DREAM OF ME — Mama Cass (RCA)
24	19	YOUR TIME HASN'T COME YET BABY — Elvis Presley (RCA)
-	20	JESAMINE — Casuals (Decca)
21	21	DREAM A LITTLE DREAM OF ME — Anita Harris (CBS)
15	22	LAST NIGHT IN SOHO — Dave Dee, Dozy, Beaky, Mick & Tich (Fontana)
23	23	HARD TO HANDLE — Otis Redding (Atlantic)
26	24	LADY WILLPOWER — Gary Puckett and the Union Gap (CBS)
-	25	ELEANOR RIGBY — Ray Charles (Stateside)
29	26	WE CAN HELP YOU — Alan Bown (Music Factory)
-	27	VOICES IN THE SKY — Moody Blues (Deram)
22	28	SON OF HICKORY HOLLER'S TRAMP — O.C. Smith (CBS)
19	29	THE UNIVERSAL — Small Faces (Immediate)
-	30	LAUREL AND HARDY — Equals (President)

7 September 1968

last week	this week	
2	1	I'VE GOTTA GET A MESSAGE TO YOU — Bee Gees (Polydor)
4	2	DO IT AGAIN — Beach Boys (Capitol)
-	3	HEY JUDE — Beatles (Parlophone)
3	4	THIS GUY'S IN LOVE WITH YOU — Herb Alpert (A&M)
6	5	I SAY A LITTLE PRAYER — Aretha Franklin (Atlantic)
1	6	HELP YOURSELF — Tom Jones (Decca)
8	7	HIGH IN THE SKY — Amen Corner (Deram)
11	8	HOLD ME TIGHT — Johnny Nash (Regal Zonophone)
5	9	MONY MONY — Tommy James & the Shondells (Major Minor)
13	10	ON THE ROAD AGAIN — Canned Heat (Liberty)
9	11	SUNSHINE GIRL — Herman's Hermits (Columbia)
7	12	FIRE — Arthur Brown (Track)
10	12	DANCE TO THE MUSIC — Sly & the Family Stone (Direction)
18	14	DREAM A LITTLE DREAM OF ME — Mama Cass (RCA)
14	15	I PRETEND — Des O'Connor (Columbia)
15	16	KEEP ON — Bruce Channel (Bell)
24	17	LADY WILLPOWER — Gary Puckett and the Union Gap (CBS)
-	18	THOSE WERE THE DAYS — Mary Hopkin (Apple)
12	19	I CLOSE MY EYES AND COUNT TO TEN — Dusty Springfield (Philips)
20	20	JESAMINE — Casuals (Decca)
17	21	DAYS — Kinks (Pye)
23	22	HARD TO HANDLE — Otis Redding (Atlantic)
-	23	LITTLE ARROWS — Leapy Lee (MCA)
27	24	VOICES IN THE SKY — Moody Blues (Deram)
21	25	DREAM A LITTLE DREAM OF ME — Anita Harris (CBS)
19	26	YOUR TIME HASN'T COME YET BABY — Elvis Presley (RCA)
-	27	ICE IN THE SUN — Status Quo (Pye)
25	28	ELEANOR RIGBY — Ray Charles (Stateside)
30	29	LAUREL AND HARDY — Equals (President)
16	30	MRS. ROBINSON — Simon & Garfunkel (CBS)

It may have seemed slightly ironic that Herb Alpert should score his biggest British chart success with a number which featured his voice rather than either his trumpet or his Tijuana Brass. In fact Alpert had been a vocalist before forming his instrumental ensemble or founding A&M records. Aretha Franklin succeeded where Dionne Warwick had failed in the UK with *I Say A Little Prayer*, and Grapefruit also squeezed into the Top 30 where the Four Seasons had earlier failed with *C'mon Marianne*.

September – October 1968

14 September 1968

3 1 HEY JUDE — Beatles (Parlophone)
1 2 I'VE GOTTA GET A MESSAGE TO YOU — Bee Gees (Polydor)
2 3 DO IT AGAIN — Beach Boys (Capitol)
5 4 I SAY A LITTLE PRAYER — Aretha Franklin (Atlantic)
8 5 HOLD ME TIGHT — Johnny Nash (Regal Zonophone)
18 6 THOSE WERE THE DAYS — Mary Hopkin (Apple)
7 7 HIGH IN THE SKY — Amen Corner (Deram)
4 8 THIS GUY'S IN LOVE WITH YOU — Herb Alpert (A&M)
10 9 ON THE ROAD AGAIN — Canned Heat (Liberty)
6 10 HELP YOURSELF — Tom Jones (Decca)
14 11 DREAM A LITTLE DREAM OF ME — Mama Cass (RCA)
20 12 JESAMINE — Casuals (Decca)
17 13 LADY WILLPOWER — Gary Puckett & the Union Gap (CBS)
11 14 SUNSHINE GIRL — Herman's Hermits (Columbia)
9 15 MONY MONY — Tommy James & the Shondells (Major Minor)
23 16 LITTLE ARROWS — Leapy Lee (MCA)
12 17 DANCE TO THE MUSIC — Sly & the Family Stone (Direction)
22 18 HARD TO HANDLE — Otis Redding (Atlantic)
12 19 FIRE — Arthur Brown (Track)
16 20 KEEP ON — Bruce Channel (Bell)
27 21 ICE IN THE SUN — Status Quo (Pye)
15 22 I PRETEND — Des O'Connor (Columbia)
25 23 DREAM A LITTLE DREAM OF ME — Anita Harris (CBS)
19 24 I CLOSE MY EYES AND COUNT TO TEN — Dusty Springfield (Philips)
- 25 AMERICA — Nice (Immediate)
- 26 CLASSICAL GAS Mason Williams (Warner Bros)
24 27 VOICES IN THE SKY — Moody Blues (Deram)
- 28 NEED YOUR LOVE SO BAD — Fleetwood Mac (Blue Horizon)
29 29 I LIVE FOR THE SUN — Vanity Fare (Page One)
- 30 HELLO I LOVE YOU — Doors (Elektra)
- 30 C'MON MARIANNE — Grapefruit (RCA)

21 September 1968

1 1 HEY JUDE — Beatles (Parlophone)
6 2 THOSE WERE THE DAYS — Mary Hopkin (Apple)
2 3 I'VE GOTTA GET A MESSAGE TO YOU — Bee Gees (Polydor)
3 4 DO IT AGAIN — Beach Boys (Capitol)
4 5 I SAY A LITTLE PRAYER — Aretha Franklin (Atlantic)
5 6 HOLD ME TIGHT — Johnny Nash (Regal Zonophone)
12 7 JESAMINE — Casuals (Decca)
7 8 HIGH IN THE SKY — Amen Corner (Deram)
8 9 THIS GUY'S IN LOVE WITH YOU — Herb Alpert (A&M)
9 10 ON THE ROAD AGAIN — Canned Heat (Liberty)
10 11 HELP YOURSELF — Tom Jones (Decca)
13 12 LADY WILLPOWER — Gary Puckett & the Union Gap (CBS)
16 13 LITTLE ARROWS — Leapy Lee (MCA)
11 13 DREAM A LITTLE DREAM OF ME — Mama Cass (RCA)
21 15 ICE IN THE SUN — Status Quo (Pye)
18 16 HARD TO HANDLE — Otis Redding (Atlantic)
26 17 CLASSICAL GAS — Mason Williams (Warner Bros)
14 18 SUNSHINE GIRL — Herman's Hermits (Columbia)
22 19 I PRETEND — Des O'Connor (Columbia)
29 20 I LIVE FOR THE SUN — Vanity Fare (Page One)
17 21 DANCE TO THE MUSIC — Sly & the Family Stone (Direction)
- 22 A DAY WITHOUT LOVE — Love Affair (CBS)
23 23 VOICES IN THE SKY — Moody Blues (Deram)
25 24 AMERICA — Nice (Immediate)
30 25 HELLO I LOVE YOU — Doors (Elektra)
- 26 THE WEIGHT — Band (Capitol)
- 27 LES BICYCLETTES DE BELSIZE — Engelbert Humperdinck (Decca)
20 28 KEEP ON — Bruce Channel (Bell)
- 29 YESTERDAY'S DREAMS — Four Tops (Tamla Motown)
30 30 C'MON MARIANNE — Grapefruit (RCA)

28 September 1968

1 1 HEY JUDE — Beatles (Parlophone)
2 2 THOSE WERE THE DAYS — Mary Hopkin (Apple)
7 3 JESAMINE — Casuals (Decca)
3 4 I'VE GOTTA GET A MESSAGE TO YOU — Bee Gees (Polydor)
6 5 HOLD ME TIGHT — Johnny Nash (Regal Zonophone)
5 6 I SAY A LITTLE PRAYER — Aretha Franklin (Atlantic)
4 7 DO IT AGAIN — Beach Boys (Capitol)
13 8 LITTLE ARROWS — Leapy Lee (MCA)
12 9 LADY WILLPOWER — Gary Puckett & the Union Gap (CBS)
10 10 ON THE ROAD AGAIN — Canned Heat (Liberty)
8 11 HIGH IN THE SKY — Amen Corner (Deram)
9 12 THIS GUY'S IN LOVE WITH YOU — Herb Alpert (A&M)
13 13 DREAM A LITTLE DREAM OF ME — Mama Cass (RCA)
15 14 ICE IN THE SUN — Status Quo (Pye)
17 15 CLASSICAL GAS Mason Williams (Warner Bros)
11 16 HELP YOURSELF — Tom Jones (Decca)
27 17 LES BICYCLETTES DE BELSIZE — Engelbert Humperdinck (Decca)
16 18 HARD TO HANDLE — Otis Redding (Atlantic)
25 19 HELLO I LOVE YOU — Doors (Elektra)
22 20 A DAY WITHOUT LOVE — Love Affair (CBS)
- 21 THE RED BALLOON — Dave Clark Five (Columbia)
20 22 I LIVE FOR THE SUN — Vanity Fare (Page One)
19 23 I PRETEND — Des O'Connor (Columbia)
- 24 MY LITTLE LADY — Tremeloes (CBS)
26 25 THE WEIGHT — Band (Capitol)
- 26 THE GOOD, THE BAD AND THE UGLY — Leroy Holmes (United Artists)
- 27 THE WRECK OF THE ANTOINETTE — Dave Dee, Dozy, Beaky, Mick & Tich (Fontana)
24 28 AMERICA — Nice (Immediate)
- 29 LIGHT MY FIRE — Jose Feliciano (RCA)
29 29 YESTERDAY'S DREAMS — Four Tops (Tamla Motown)
23 29 VOICES IN THE SKY — Moody Blues (Deram)

5 October 1968

2 1 THOSE WERE THE DAYS — Mary Hopkin (Apple)
1 2 HEY JUDE — Beatles (Parlophone)
3 3 JESAMINE — Casuals (Decca)
8 4 LITTLE ARROWS — Leapy Lee (MCA)
5 5 HOLD ME TIGHT — Johnny Nash (Regal Zonophone)
4 6 I'VE GOTTA GET A MESSAGE TO YOU — Bee Gees (Polydor)
9 7 LADY WILLPOWER — Gary Puckett & the Union Gap (CBS)
6 8 I SAY A LITTLE PRAYER — Aretha Franklin (Atlantic)
7 9 DO IT AGAIN — Beach Boys (Capitol)
15 10 CLASSICAL GAS — Mason Williams (Warner Bros)
17 11 LES BICYCLETTES DE BELSIZE — Engelbert Humperdinck (Decca)
10 12 ON THE ROAD AGAIN — Canned Heat (Liberty)
11 13 HIGH IN THE SKY — Amen Corner (Deram)
21 14 THE RED BALLOON — Dave Clark Five (Columbia)
20 15 A DAY WITHOUT LOVE — Love Affair (CBS)
14 16 ICE IN THE SUN — Status Quo (Pye)
13 17 DREAM A LITTLE DREAM OF ME — Mama Cass (RCA)
24 18 MY LITTLE LADY — Tremeloes (CBS)
19 19 HELLO I LOVE YOU — Doors (Elektra)
18 20 HARD TO HANDLE — Otis Redding (Atlantic)
22 21 I LIVE FOR THE SUN — Vanity Fare (Page One)
16 22 HELP YOURSELF — Tom Jones (Decca)
- 23 THE GOOD, THE BAD AND THE UGLY — Hugo Montenegro (RCA)
29 24 YESTERDAY'S DREAMS — Four Tops (Tamla Motown)
12 25 THIS GUY'S IN LOVE WITH YOU — Herb Alpert (A&M)
29 26 LIGHT MY FIRE — Jose Feliciano (RCA)
- 27 LISTEN TO ME — Hollies (Parlophone)
28 28 AMERICA — Nice (Immediate)
- 29 MARIANNE — Cliff Richard (Columbia)
25 30 THE WEIGHT — Band (Capitol)
27 30 THE WRECK OF THE ANTOINETTE — Dave Dee, Dozy, Beaky, Mick & Tich (Fontana)

September 1968 saw the Beatles launch their Apple label. Although the group themselves were still contracted to Parlophone, their subsequent singles would appear on the Apple imprint with Parlophone catalogue numbers. Hey Jude was the first release to adopt this procedure. The first single by an Apple artist proper was Mary Hopkins' *Those Were The Days*, which fittingly took over the top slot from *Hey Jude*. Mary Hopkins had been an *Opportunity Knocks* winner on TV.

October – November 1968

12 October 1968

last week	this week	
1	1	THOSE WERE THE DAYS — Mary Hopkin (Apple)
3	2	JESAMINE — Casuals (Decca)
2	3	HEY JUDE — Beatles (Parlophone)
4	4	LITTLE ARROWS — Leapy Lee (MCA)
5	5	HOLD ME TIGHT — Johnny Nash (Regal Zonophone)
7	6	LADY WILLPOWER — Gary Puckett & the Union Gap (CBS)
14	7	THE RED BALLOON — Dave Clark Five (Columbia)
6	8	I'VE GOTTA GET A MESSAGE TO YOU — Bee Gees (Polydor)
18	9	MY LITTLE LADY — Tremeloes (CBS)
11	10	LES BICYCLETTES DE BELSIZE — Engelbert Humperdinck (Decca)
8	11	I SAY A LITTLE PRAYER — Aretha Franklin (Atlantic)
10	12	CLASSICAL GAS — Mason Williams (Warner Bros)
15	13	A DAY WITHOUT LOVE — Love Affair (CBS)
16	14	ICE IN THE SUN — Status Quo (Pye)
9	15	DO IT AGAIN — Beach Boys (Capitol)
13	16	HIGH IN THE SKY — Amen Corner (Deram)
19	17	HELLO I LOVE YOU — Doors (Elektra)
23	18	THE GOOD, THE BAD AND THE UGLY — Hugo Montenegro (RCA)
26	19	LIGHT MY FIRE — Jose Feliciano (RCA)
27	20	LISTEN TO ME — Hollies (Parlophone)
20	21	I LIVE FOR THE SUN — Vanity Fare (Page One)
17	22	DREAM A LITTLE DREAM OF ME — Mama Cass (RCA)
12	23	ON THE ROAD AGAIN — Canned Heat (Liberty)
30	24	THE WRECK OF THE ANTOINETTE — Dave Dee, Dozy, Beaky, Mick & Tich (Fontana)
-	25	ONLY ONE WOMAN — Marbles (Polydor)
29	26	MARIANNE — Cliff Richard (Columbia)
20	27	HARD TO HANDLE — Otis Redding (Atlantic)
22	28	HELP YOURSELF — Tom Jones (Decca)
30	29	THE WEIGHT — Band (Capitol)
-	29	WITH A LITTLE HELP FROM MY FRIENDS — Joe Cocker (Regal Zonophone)

19 October 1968

last week	this week	
1	1	THOSE WERE THE DAYS — Mary Hopkin (Apple)
4	2	LITTLE ARROWS — Leapy Lee (MCA)
2	3	JESAMINE — Casuals (Decca)
3	4	HEY JUDE — Beatles (Parlophone)
9	5	MY LITTLE LADY — Tremeloes (CBS)
7	6	THE RED BALLOON — Dave Clark Five (Columbia)
6	7	LADY WILLPOWER — Gary Puckett & the Union Gap (CBS)
10	8	LES BICYCLETTES DE BELSIZE — Engelbert Humperdinck (Decca)
13	9	A DAY WITHOUT LOVE — Love Affair (CBS)
20	10	LISTEN TO ME — Hollies (Parlophone)
18	11	THE GOOD, THE BAD AND THE UGLY — Hugo Montenegro (RCA)
12	12	CLASSICAL GAS — Mason Williams (Warner Bros)
29	13	WITH A LITTLE HELP FROM MY FRIENDS — Joe Cocker (Regal Zonophone)
5	13	HOLD ME TIGHT — Johnny Nash (Regal Zonophone)
14	15	ICE IN THE SUN — Status Quo (Pye)
25	16	ONLY ONE WOMAN — Marbles (Polydor)
19	17	LIGHT MY FIRE — Jose Feliciano (RCA)
24	18	THE WRECK OF THE ANTOINETTE — Dave Dee, Dozy, Beaky, Mick & Tich (Fontana)
8	19	I'VE GOTTA GET A MESSAGE TO YOU — Bee Gees (Polydor)
17	20	HELLO I LOVE YOU — Doors (Elektra)
11	21	I SAY A LITTLE PRAYER — Aretha Franklin (Atlantic)
15	22	DO IT AGAIN — Beach Boys (Capitol)
26	23	MARIANNE — Cliff Richard (Columbia)
29	24	THE WEIGHT — Band (Capitol)
-	25	THE GOOD, THE BAD AND THE UGLY — Leroy Holmes (United Artists)
16	26	HIGH IN THE SKY — Amen Corner (Deram)
23	27	ON THE ROAD AGAIN — Canned Heat (Liberty)
-	28	SUNSHINE OF YOUR LOVE — Cream (Polydor)
-	29	HEARTACHE — Roy Orbison (London)
-	30	YOU'RE ALL I NEED TO GET BY — Marvin Gaye & Tammi Terrell (Tamla Motown)

26 October 1968

last week	this week	
1	1	THOSE WERE THE DAYS — Mary Hopkin (Apple)
2	2	LITTLE ARROWS — Leapy Lee (MCA)
3	3	JESAMINE — Casuals (Decca)
4	4	HEY JUDE — Beatles (Parlophone)
5	5	MY LITTLE LADY — Tremeloes (CBS)
13	6	WITH A LITTLE HELP FROM MY FRIENDS — Joe Cocker (Regal Zonophone)
10	7	LISTEN TO ME — Hollies (Parlophone)
8	8	LES BICYCLETTES DE BELSIZE — Engelbert Humperdinck (Decca)
11	9	THE GOOD, THE BAD AND THE UGLY — Hugo Montenegro (RCA)
9	10	A DAY WITHOUT LOVE — Love Affair (CBS)
16	11	ONLY ONE WOMAN — Marbles (Polydor)
6	12	THE RED BALLOON — Dave Clark Five (Columbia)
7	13	LADY WILLPOWER — Gary Puckett & the Union Gap (CBS)
17	14	LIGHT MY FIRE — Jose Feliciano (RCA)
18	15	THE WRECK OF THE ANTOINETTE — Dave Dee, Dozy, Beaky, Mick & Tich (Fontana)
13	16	HOLD ME TIGHT — Johnny Nash (Regal Zonophone)
12	17	CLASSICAL GAS — Mason Williams (Warner Bros)
-	18	ALL ALONG THE WATCHTOWER — Jimi Hendrix Experience (Track)
15	18	ICE IN THE SUN — Status Quo (Pye)
-	20	THIS OLD HEART OF MINE — Isley Brothers (Tamla Motown)
-	21	ELOISE — Barry Ryan (MGM)
19	22	I'VE GOTTA GET A MESSAGE TO YOU — Bee Gees (Polydor)
21	22	I SAY A LITTLE PRAYER — Aretha Franklin (Atlantic)
23	24	MARIANNE — Cliff Richard (Columbia)
20	25	HELLO I LOVE YOU — Doors (Elektra)
28	26	SUNSHINE OF YOUR LOVE — Cream (Polydor)
-	26	MAGIC BUS — Who (Track)
28	27	IF I KNEW THEN WHAT I KNOW NOW — Val Doonican (Pye)
-	29	BREAKING DOWN THE WALLS OF HEARTACHE — Bandwagon (Direction)
27	29	ON THE ROAD AGAIN — Canned Heat (Liberty)
-	29	HARPER VALLEY P.T.A. — Jeannie C. Riley (Polydor)

2 November 1968

last week	this week	
1	1	THOSE WERE THE DAYS — Mary Hopkin (Apple)
6	2	WITH A LITTLE HELP FROM MY FRIENDS — Joe Cocker (Regal Zonophone)
9	3	THE GOOD, THE BAD AND THE UGLY — Hugo Montenegro (RCA)
2	4	LITTLE ARROWS — Leapy Lee (MCA)
11	5	ONLY ONE WOMAN — Marbles (Polydor)
5	6	MY LITTLE LADY — Tremeloes (CBS)
7	7	LISTEN TO ME — Hollies (Parlophone)
3	8	JESAMINE — Casuals (Decca)
20	9	THIS OLD HEART OF MINE — Isley Brothers (Tamla Motown)
8	10	LES BICYCLETTES DE BELSIZE — Engelbert Humperdinck (Decca)
14	11	LIGHT MY FIRE — Jose Feliciano (RCA)
10	12	A DAY WITHOUT LOVE — Love Affair (CBS)
4	13	HEY JUDE — Beatles (Parlophone)
21	13	ELOISE — Barry Ryan (MGM)
18	15	ALL ALONG THE WATCHTOWER — Jimi Hendrix Experience (Track)
12	16	THE RED BALLOON — Dave Clark Five (Columbia)
15	17	THE WRECK OF THE ANTOINETTE — Dave Dee, Dozy, Beaky, Mick & Tich (Fontana)
29	18	BREAKING DOWN THE WALLS OF HEARTACHE — Bandwagon (Direction)
13	19	LADY WILLPOWER — Gary Puckett and the Union Gap (CBS)
-	20	MEXICO — Long John Baldry (Pye)
-	21	YOU'RE ALL I NEED TO GET BY — Marvin Gaye & Tammi Terrell (Tamla Motown)
26	22	MAGIC BUS — Who (Track)
-	23	AIN'T GOT NO - I GOT LIFE — Nina Simone (RCA)
28	24	IF I KNEW THEN WHAT I KNOW NOW — Val Doonican (Pye)
-	24	ELENORE — Turtles (London)
-	26	IT'S IN HIS KISS — Betty Everett (President)
-	27	MAY I HAVE THE NEXT DREAM WITH YOU — Malcolm Roberts (Major Minor)
-	28	RUDI'S IN LOVE — Locomotive (Parlophone)
26	29	SUNSHINE OF YOUR LOVE — Cream (Polydor)
-	30	SUNSHINE COTTAGE — Herd (Fontana)

Imaginative cover versions were making their chart presence felt. Jose Feliciano's slowed-down acoustic version of *Light My Fire* was a world apart from the Doors original, while Joe Cocker's interpretation of Lennon/McCartney's *With A Little Help from My Friends* turned a bouncy Ringo showcase into an impassioned soul ballad, to great effect (and Number One sales). Jimi Hendrix took Dylan's stark original of *All Along The Watchtower* and virtually invented heavy metal with his version of it.

November 1968

9 November 1968

last week	this week	
2	1	WITH A LITTLE HELP FROM MY FRIENDS Joe Cocker (Regal Zonophone)
3	2	THE GOOD, THE BAD AND THE UGLY Hugo Montenegro (RCA)
1	3	THOSE WERE THE DAYS Mary Hopkin (Apple)
9	4	THIS OLD HEART OF MINE Isley Brothers (Tamla Motown)
5	5	ONLY ONE WOMAN Marbles (Polydor)
13	6	ELOISE Barry Ryan (MGM)
11	7	LIGHT MY FIRE Jose Feliciano (RCA)
4	8	LITTLE ARROWS Leapy Lee (MCA)
7	9	LISTEN TO ME Hollies (Parlophone)
6	10	MY LITTLE LADY Tremeloes (CBS)
8	11	JESAMINE Casuals (Decca)
15	12	ALL ALONG THE WATCHTOWER Jimi Hendrix Experience (Track)
18	13	BREAKING DOWN THE WALLS OF HEARTACHE Bandwagon (Direction)
20	14	MEXICO Long John Baldry (Pye)
13	15	HEY JUDE Beatles (Parlophone)
10	16	LES BICYCLETTES DE BELSIZE Engelbert Humperdinck (Decca)
12	17	A DAY WITHOUT LOVE Love Affair (CBS)
17	18	THE WRECK OF THE ANTOINETTE Dave Dee, Dozy, Beaky, Mick & Tich (Fontana)
24	19	ELENORE Turtles (London)
27	20	MAY I HAVE THE NEXT DREAM WITH YOU Malcolm Roberts (Major Minor)
21	21	YOU'RE ALL I NEED TO GET BY Marvin Gaye & Tammi Terrell (Tamla Motown)
16	22	THE RED BALLOON Dave Clark Five (Columbia)
-	23	HARPER VALLEY P.T.A. Jeannie C. Riley (Polydor)
23	24	AIN'T GOT NO - I GOT LIFE Nina Simone (RCA)
22	25	MAGIC BUS Who (Track)
28	26	RUDI'S IN LOVE Locomotive (Parlophone)
24	27	IF I KNEW THEN WHAT I KNOW NOW Val Doonican (Pye)
19	28	LADY WILLPOWER Gary Puckett & the Union Gap (CBS)
-	29	WAIT FOR ME MARY-ANNE Marmalade (CBS)
-	30	HELLO I LOVE YOU Doors (Elektra)

16 November 1968

last week	this week	
2	1	THE GOOD, THE BAD AND THE UGLY Hugo Montenegro (RCA)
6	2	ELOISE Barry Ryan (MGM)
1	3	WITH A LITTLE HELP FROM MY FRIENDS Joe Cocker (Regal Zonophone)
4	4	THIS OLD HEART OF MINE Isley Brothers (Tamla Motown)
3	5	THOSE WERE THE DAYS Mary Hopkin (Apple)
5	6	ONLY ONE WOMAN Marbles (Polydor)
7	7	LIGHT MY FIRE Jose Feliciano (RCA)
13	8	BREAKING DOWN THE WALLS OF HEARTACHE Bandwagon (Direction)
12	9	ALL ALONG THE WATCHTOWER Jimi Hendrix Experience (Track)
8	10	LITTLE ARROWS Leapy Lee (MCA)
14	11	MEXICO Long John Baldry (Pye)
19	12	ELENORE Turtles (London)
10	13	MY LITTLE LADY Tremeloes (CBS)
9	14	LISTEN TO ME Hollies (Parlophone)
11	15	JESAMINE Casuals (Decca)
23	16	HARPER VALLEY P.T.A. Jeannie C. Riley (Polydor)
20	17	MAY I HAVE THE NEXT DREAM WITH YOU Malcolm Roberts (Major Minor)
27	18	IF I KNEW THEN WHAT I KNOW NOW Val Doonican (Pye)
24	19	AIN'T GOT NO - I GOT LIFE Nina Simone (RCA)
16	20	LES BICYCLETTES DE BELSIZE Engelbert Humperdinck (Decca)
26	21	RUDI'S IN LOVE Locomotive (Parlophone)
22	22	YOU'RE ALL I NEED TO GET BY Marvin Gaye & Tammi Terrell (Tamla Motown)
-	23	I'M A TIGER Lulu (Columbia)
15	24	HEY JUDE Beatles (Parlophone)
25	25	MAGIC BUS Who (Track)
18	26	THE WRECK OF THE ANTOINETTE Dave Dee, Dozy, Beaky, Mick & Tich (Fontana)
-	27	LILY THE PINK Scaffold (Parlophone)
22	28	THE RED BALLOON Dave Clark Five (Columbia)
17	29	A DAY WITHOUT LOVE Love Affair (CBS)
-	30	SUNSHINE COTTAGE Herd (Fontana)

23 November 1968

last week	this week	
2	1	ELOISE Barry Ryan (MGM)
1	2	THE GOOD, THE BAD AND THE UGLY Hugo Montenegro (RCA)
4	3	THIS OLD HEART OF MINE Isley Brothers (Tamla Motown)
8	4	BREAKING DOWN THE WALLS OF HEARTACHE Bandwagon (Direction)
3	5	WITH A LITTLE HELP FROM MY FRIENDS Joe Cocker (Regal Zonophone)
9	6	ALL ALONG THE WATCHTOWER Jimi Hendrix Experience (Track)
5	7	THOSE WERE THE DAYS Mary Hopkin (Apple)
6	8	ONLY ONE WOMAN Marbles (Polydor)
12	9	ELENORE Turtles (London)
7	10	LIGHT MY FIRE Jose Feliciano (RCA)
19	11	AIN'T GOT NO - I GOT LIFE Nina Simone (RCA)
27	12	LILY THE PINK Scaffold (Parlophone)
23	13	I'M A TIGER Lulu (Columbia)
11	14	MEXICO Long John Baldry (Pye)
17	15	MAY I HAVE THE NEXT DREAM WITH YOU Malcolm Roberts (Major Minor)
18	16	IF I KNEW THEN WHAT I KNOW NOW Val Doonican (Pye)
16	17	HARPER VALLEY P.T.A. Jeannie C. Riley (Polydor)
10	18	LITTLE ARROWS Leapy Lee (MCA)
22	19	YOU'RE ALL I NEED TO GET BY Marvin Gaye & Tammi Terrell (Tamla Motown)
14	20	LISTEN TO ME Hollies (Parlophone)
13	21	MY LITTLE LADY Tremeloes (CBS)
15	22	JESAMINE Casuals (Decca)
20	23	LES BICYCLETTES DE BELSIZE Engelbert Humperdinck (Decca)
21	24	RUDI'S IN LOVE Locomotive (Parlophone)
-	25	I'M THE URBAN SPACEMAN Bonzo Dog Doo Dah Band (Liberty)
-	26	RACE WITH THE DEVIL Gun (CBS)
-	27	RAIN AND TEARS Aphrodite's Child (Mercury)
24	28	HEY JUDE Beatles (Parlophone)
-	29	I'M IN A DIFFERENT WORLD Four Tops (Tamla Motown)
26	30	THE WRECK OF THE ANTOINETTE Dave Dee, Dozy, Beaky, Mick & Tich (Fontana)

30 November 1968

last week	this week	
1	1	ELOISE Barry Ryan (MGM)
2	2	THE GOOD, THE BAD AND THE UGLY Hugo Montenegro (RCA)
3	3	THIS OLD HEART OF MINE Isley Brothers (Tamla Motown)
4	4	BREAKING DOWN THE WALLS OF HEARTACHE Bandwagon (Direction)
12	5	LILY THE PINK Scaffold (Parlophone)
11	6	AIN'T GOT NO - I GOT LIFE Nina Simone (RCA)
9	7	ELENORE Turtles (London)
6	8	ALL ALONG THE WATCHTOWER Jimi Hendrix Experience (Track)
13	9	I'M A TIGER Lulu (Columbia)
17	10	HARPER VALLEY P.T.A. Jeannie C. Riley (Polydor)
5	11	WITH A LITTLE HELP FROM MY FRIENDS Joe Cocker (Regal Zonophone)
16	12	IF I KNEW THEN WHAT I KNOW NOW Val Doonican (Pye)
15	13	MAY I HAVE THE NEXT DREAM WITH YOU Malcolm Roberts (Major Minor)
-	14	ONE TWO THREE O'LEARY Des O'Connor (Columbia)
10	15	LIGHT MY FIRE Jose Feliciano (RCA)
7	16	THOSE WERE THE DAYS Mary Hopkin (Apple)
8	17	ONLY ONE WOMAN Marbles (Polydor)
-	18	BUILD ME UP BUTTERCUP Foundations (Pye)
19	19	YOU'RE ALL I NEED TO GET BY Marvin Gaye & Tammi Terrell (Tamla Motown)
-	20	THE BEATLES (LP) Beatles (Parlophone)
18	20	LITTLE ARROWS Leapy Lee (MCA)
-	22	A MINUTE OF YOUR TIME Tom Jones (Decca)
24	23	RUDI'S IN LOVE Locomotive (Parlophone)
26	24	RACE WITH THE DEVIL Gun (CBS)
25	25	I'M THE URBAN SPACEMAN Bonzo Dog Doo Dah Band (Liberty)
-	26	QUICK JOEY SMALL Kasenetz-Katz Singing Orchestral Circus (Buddah)
-	27	DON'T FORGET TO CATCH ME Cliff Richard (Columbia)
14	28	MEXICO Long John Baldry (Pye)
-	29	PRIVATE NUMBER William Bell & Judy Clay (Stax)
-	30	LOVE CHILD Diana Ross & the Supremes (Tamla Motown)

Ennio Morricone's dramatic and inventive music for the early Clint Eastwood 'spaghetti westerns' finally translated into pop sales when Hugo Montenegro's arrangement (closely mirroring Morricone's) of *The Good, The Bad And The Ugly*, theme from the third of the 'Dollars' series, was a major hit both in the US and Britain. When he reached Number One here Montenegro was engaged in scoring the music for the Elvis Presley western *Charro*, which incorporated many elements from the Sergio Leone movies.

December 1968

7 December 1968

last week	this week	title / artist
5	1	LILY THE PINK — Scaffold (Parlophone)
2	2	THE GOOD, THE BAD AND THE UGLY — Hugo Montenegro (RCA)
1	3	ELOISE — Barry Ryan (MGM)
3	4	THIS OLD HEART OF MINE — Isley Brothers (Tamla Motown)
4	5	BREAKING DOWN THE WALLS OF HEARTACHE — Bandwagon (Direction)
6	6	AIN'T GOT NO - I GOT LIFE — Nina Simone (RCA)
14	7	ONE TWO THREE O'LEARY — Des O'Connor (Columbia)
9	8	I'M A TIGER — Lulu (Columbia)
7	9	ELENORE — Turtles (London)
18	10	BUILD ME UP BUTTERCUP — Foundations (Pye)
10	11	HARPER VALLEY P.T.A. — Jeannie C. Riley (Polydor)
13	12	MAY I HAVE THE NEXT DREAM WITH YOU — Malcolm Roberts (Major Minor)
8	13	ALL ALONG THE WATCHTOWER — Jimi Hendrix Experience (Track)
12	14	IF I KNEW THEN WHAT I KNOW NOW — Val Doonican (Pye)
22	15	A MINUTE OF YOUR TIME — Tom Jones (Decca)
24	16	RACE WITH THE DEVIL — Gun (CBS)
25	17	I'M THE URBAN SPACEMAN — Bonzo Dog Doo Dah Band (Liberty)
29	18	PRIVATE NUMBER — William Bell & Judy Clay (Stax)
16	19	THOSE WERE THE DAYS — Mary Hopkin (Apple)
11	20	WITH A LITTLE HELP FROM MY FRIENDS — Joe Cocker (Regal Zonophone)
30	21	LOVE CHILD — Diana Ross & the Supremes (Tamla Motown)
-	22	SABRE DANCE — Love Sculpture (Parlophone)
17	23	ONLY ONE WOMAN — Marbles (Polydor)
20	24	THE BEATLES (LP) — Beatles (Parlophone)
26	25	QUICK JOEY SMALL — Kasenetz-Katz Singing Orchestral Circus (Buddah)
-	26	ATLANTIS — Donovan (Pye)
19	26	YOU'RE ALL I NEED TO GET BY — Marvin Gaye & Tammi Terrell (Tamla Motown)
15	28	LIGHT MY FIRE — Jose Feliciano (RCA)
-	29	I'M IN A DIFFERENT WORLD — Four Tops (Tamla Motown)
-	30	LES BICYCLETTES DE BELSIZE — Engelbert Humperdinck (Decca)

14 December 1968

last week	this week	title / artist
1	1	LILY THE PINK — Scaffold (Parlophone)
2	2	THE GOOD, THE BAD AND THE UGLY — Hugo Montenegro (RCA)
7	3	ONE TWO THREE O'LEARY — Des O'Connor (Columbia)
10	4	BUILD ME UP BUTTERCUP — Foundations (Pye)
6	5	AIN'T GOT NO - I GOT LIFE — Nina Simone (RCA)
5	6	BREAKING DOWN THE WALLS OF HEARTACHE — Bandwagon (Direction)
8	7	I'M A TIGER — Lulu (Columbia)
4	8	THIS OLD HEART OF MINE — Isley Brothers (Tamla Motown)
12	9	MAY I HAVE THE NEXT DREAM WITH YOU — Malcolm Roberts (Major Minor)
3	10	ELOISE — Barry Ryan (MGM)
17	11	I'M THE URBAN SPACEMAN — Bonzo Dog Doo Dah Band (Liberty)
9	12	ELENORE — Turtles (London)
22	13	SABRE DANCE — Love Sculpture (Parlophone)
15	14	A MINUTE OF YOUR TIME — Tom Jones (Decca)
16	15	RACE WITH THE DEVIL — Gun (CBS)
11	16	HARPER VALLEY P.T.A. — Jeannie C. Riley (Polydor)
18	17	PRIVATE NUMBER — William Bell & Judy Clay (Stax)
21	18	LOVE CHILD — Diana Ross & the Supremes (Tamla Motown)
14	19	IF I KNEW THEN WHAT I KNOW NOW — Val Doonican (Pye)
13	20	ALL ALONG THE WATCHTOWER — Jimi Hendrix Experience (Track)
-	21	SON OF A PREACHER MAN — Dusty Springfield (Philips)
-	22	OB-LA-DI, OB-LA-DA — Marmalade (CBS)
25	23	QUICK JOEY SMALL — Kasenetz-Katz Singing Orchestral Circus (Buddah)
26	24	ATLANTIS — Donovan (Pye)
30	25	LES BICYCLETTES DE BELSIZE — Engelbert Humperdinck (Decca)
19	26	THOSE WERE THE DAYS — Mary Hopkin (Apple)
-	27	DON'T FORGET TO CATCH ME — Cliff Richard (Columbia)
-	28	ALBATROSS — Fleetwood Mac (Blue Horizon)
24	29	THE BEATLES (LP) — Beatles (Parlophone)
-	30	LITTLE ARROWS — Leapy Lee (MCA)

21 December 1968

last week	this week	title / artist
1	1	LILY THE PINK — Scaffold (Parlophone)
3	2	ONE TWO THREE O'LEARY — Des O'Connor (Columbia)
4	3	BUILD ME UP BUTTERCUP — Foundations (Pye)
5	4	AIN'T GOT NO - I GOT LIFE — Nina Simone (RCA)
2	5	THE GOOD, THE BAD AND THE UGLY — Hugo Montenegro (RCA)
11	6	I'M THE URBAN SPACEMAN — Bonzo Dog Doo Dah Band (Liberty)
9	7	MAY I HAVE THE NEXT DREAM WITH YOU — Malcolm Roberts (Major Minor)
13	8	SABRE DANCE — Love Sculpture (Parlophone)
7	9	I'M A TIGER — Lulu (Columbia)
6	10	BREAKING DOWN THE WALLS OF HEARTACHE — Bandwagon (Direction)
15	11	RACE WITH THE DEVIL — Gun (CBS)
14	12	A MINUTE OF YOUR TIME — Tom Jones (Decca)
22	13	OB-LA-DI, OB-LA-DA — Marmalade (CBS)
10	14	ELOISE — Barry Ryan (MGM)
28	15	ALBATROSS — Fleetwood Mac (Blue Horizon)
8	16	THIS OLD HEART OF MINE — Isley Brothers (Tamla Motown)
16	17	HARPER VALLEY P.T.A. — Jeannie C. Riley (Polydor)
17	18	PRIVATE NUMBER — William Bell & Judy Clay (Stax)
18	19	LOVE CHILD — Diana Ross & the Supremes (Tamla Motown)
21	20	SON OF A PREACHER MAN — Dusty Springfield (Philips)
12	21	ELENORE — Turtles (London)
19	22	IF I KNEW THEN WHAT I KNOW NOW — Val Doonican (Pye)
23	23	QUICK JOEY SMALL — Kasenetz-Katz Singing Orchestral Circus (Buddah)
-	24	STOP HER ON SIGHT — Edwin Starr (Polydor)
-	25	I SHALL BE RELEASED — Tremeloes (CBS)
-	26	OB-LA-DI, OB-LA-DA — Bedrocks (Columbia)
26	27	THOSE WERE THE DAYS — Mary Hopkin (Apple)
27	28	DON'T FORGET TO CATCH ME — Cliff Richard (Columbia)
24	29	ATLANTIS — Donovan (Pye)
-	30	TOY — Casuals (Decca)
-	30	SOMETHING'S HAPPENING — Herman's Hermits (Columbia)

28 December 1968

last week	this week	title / artist
1	1	LILY THE PINK — Scaffold (Parlophone)
2	2	ONE TWO THREE O'LEARY — Des O'Connor (Columbia)
3	3	BUILD ME UP BUTTERCUP — Foundations (Pye)
4	4	AIN'T GOT NO - I GOT LIFE — Nina Simone (RCA)
6	5	I'M THE URBAN SPACEMAN — Bonzo Dog Doo Dah Band (Liberty)
8	6	SABRE DANCE — Love Sculpture (Parlophone)
5	7	THE GOOD, THE BAD AND THE UGLY — Hugo Montenegro (RCA)
13	8	OB-LA-DI, OB-LA-DA — Marmalade (CBS)
7	9	MAY I HAVE THE NEXT DREAM WITH YOU — Malcolm Roberts (Major Minor)
10	10	RACE WITH THE DEVIL — Gun (CBS)
9	11	I'M A TIGER — Lulu (Columbia)
15	12	ALBATROSS — Fleetwood Mac (Blue Horizon)
12	13	A MINUTE OF YOUR TIME — Tom Jones (Decca)
18	14	PRIVATE NUMBER — William Bell & Judy Clay (Stax)
10	15	BREAKING DOWN THE WALLS OF HEARTACHE — Bandwagon (Direction)
19	16	LOVE CHILD — Diana Ross & the Supremes (Tamla Motown)
26	17	OB-LA-DI, OB-LA-DA — Bedrocks (Columbia)
20	18	SON OF A PREACHER MAN — Dusty Springfield (Philips)
14	19	ELOISE — Barry Ryan (MGM)
17	20	HARPER VALLEY P.T.A. — Jeannie C. Riley (Polydor)
16	21	THIS OLD HEART OF MINE — Isley Brothers (Tamla Motown)
25	22	I SHALL BE RELEASED — Tremeloes (CBS)
24	23	STOP HER ON SIGHT — Edwin Starr (Polydor)
30	24	SOMETHING'S HAPPENING — Herman's Hermits (Columbia)
23	25	QUICK JOEY SMALL — Kasenetz-Katz Singing Orchestral Circus (Buddah)
22	26	IF I KNEW THEN WHAT I KNOW NOW — Val Doonican (Pye).
21	27	ELENORE — Turtles (London)
27	28	THOSE WERE THE DAYS — Mary Hopkin (Apple)
29	29	ATLANTIS — Donovan (Pye)
28	30	DON'T FORGET TO CATCH ME — Cliff Richard (Columbia)

On the face of it a psychiatrist might have had a field day analysing artists who could fill a chart with record titles like *Lily The Pink, One Two Three O'Leary, Ob-La-Di, Ob-La-Da* or *I'm TheUrban Spaceman*, let alone a song about Atlantis or a girl who thought she was a tiger. He might have found it interesting to analyse the motives of the record-buying public that put the Scaffold hit at Number One, or Des O'Connor just below. But it was after all the silly Christmas season.

Sweet Soul Music

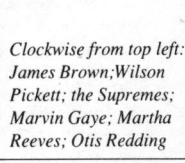

In the early sixties a new kind of black music began to emerge in America. An amalgam of gospel, R&B, southern swing and a touch of jazz, it became known as soul. In its commercial form as seen in Britain it was initially almost entirely nurtured by two extraordinary record companies, each with their own distinctive sound. Atlantic produced the gutsy and raw sound of Otis Redding, Wilson Pickett and Aretha Franklin, while Tamla Motown gave us the smooth, seductive and hypnotically danceable songs of the Supremes, the Four Tops, Smokey Robinson, Martha Reeves, Marvin Gaye, Stevie Wonder and a host of others. And of course there was James Brown – comparatively commercially unsuccessful but hugely influential. Black music was a comparative rarity in the British charts before soul came along. By the late sixties it was the principal competition to British home-grown music.

Clockwise from top left: James Brown;Wilson Pickett; the Supremes; Marvin Gaye; Martha Reeves; Otis Redding

January 1969

Rock intrumentals had been out of chart favour for some years by 1969, but suddenly there were two in the Top 10. Love Sculpture, led by guitarist Dave Edmunds (later to score as a soloist) had what was almost a straight version of Khachaturian's *Sabre Dance* in terms of tempo and melody - except that it was taken as a blistering guitar solo. Fleetwood Mac's *Albatross* reflected guitarist Peter Green's fascination with earlier rock instrumental forms, and was clearly influenced by Santo & Johnny's *Sleep Walk*.

1 February 1969

last week	this week	
1	1	ALBATROSS — Fleetwood Mac (Blue Horizon)
2	2	OB-LA-DI, OB-LA-DA — Marmalade (CBS)
3	3	FOR ONCE IN MY LIFE — Stevie Wonder (Tamla Motown)
8	4	BLACKBERRY WAY — Move (Regal Zonophone)
4	5	SOMETHING'S HAPPENING — Herman's Hermits (Columbia)
7	6	PRIVATE NUMBER — William Bell & Judy Clay (Stax)
9	7	FOX ON THE RUN — Manfred Mann (Fontana)
12	8	YOU GOT SOUL — Johnny Nash (Major Minor)
6	9	LILY THE PINK — Scaffold (Parlophone)
5	10	BUILD ME UP BUTTERCUP — Foundations (Pye)
14	11	STOP HER ON SIGHT — Edwin Starr (Tamla Motown)
20	12	DANCING IN THE STREET — Martha & the Vandellas (Tamla Motown)
28	13	TO LOVE SOMEBODY — Nina Simone (RCA)
10	14	SABRE DANCE — Love Sculpture (Parlophone)
19	15	I GUESS I'LL ALWAYS LOVE YOU — Isley Brothers (Tamla Motown)
21	16	PLEASE DON'T GO — Donald Peers (Columbia)
16	17	LOVE CHILD — Diana Ross & the Supremes (Tamla Motown)
11	18	I'M THE URBAN SPACEMAN — Bonzo Dog Doo-Dah Band (Liberty)
-	19	PEOPLE — Tymes (Direction)
-	20	(IF PARADISE WAS) HALF AS NICE — Amen Corner (Immediate)
25	21	QUICK JOEY SMALL — Kasenetz-Katz Singing Orchestral Circus (Buddah)
30	22	I'LL PICK A ROSE FOR MY ROSE — Marv Johnson (Tamla Motown)
13	23	SON OF A PREACHER MAN — Dusty Springfield (Philips)
-	24	I'M GONNA MAKE YOU LOVE ME — Diana Ross & the Supremes & the Temptations (Tamla Motown)
15	25	AIN'T GOT NO - I GOT LIFE — Nina Simone (RCA)
26	26	LOVE STORY — Jethro Tull (Island)
17	27	A MINUTE OF YOUR TIME — Tom Jones (Decca)
27	28	GOING UP THE COUNTRY — Canned Heat (Liberty)
-	29	SOUL SISTER, BROWN SUGAR — Sam & Dave (Atlantic)
17	30	OB-LA-DI, OB-LA-DA — Bedrocks (Columbia)

8 February 1969

last week	this week	
1	1	ALBATROSS — Fleetwood Mac (Blue Horizon)
4	2	BLACKBERRY WAY — Move (Regal Zonophone)
3	3	FOR ONCE IN MY LIFE — Stevie Wonder (Tamla Motown)
2	4	OB-LA-DI, OB-LA-DA — Marmalade (CBS)
7	5	FOX ON THE RUN — Manfred Mann (Fontana)
5	6	SOMETHING'S HAPPENING — Herman's Hermits (Columbia)
8	7	YOU GOT SOUL — Johnny Nash (Major Minor)
6	8	PRIVATE NUMBER — William Bell & Judy Clay (Stax)
12	9	DANCING IN THE STREET — Martha & the Vandellas (Tamla Motown)
13	10	TO LOVE SOMEBODY — Nina Simone (RCA)
20	11	(IF PARADISE WAS) HALF AS NICE — Amen Corner (Immediate)
16	12	PLEASE DON'T GO — Donald Peers (Columbia)
24	13	I'M GONNA MAKE YOU LOVE ME — Diana Ross & the Supremes & the Temptations (Tamla Motown)
11	14	STOP HER ON SIGHT — Edwin Starr (Tamla Motown)
9	15	LILY THE PINK — Scaffold (Parlophone)
15	16	I GUESS I'LL ALWAYS LOVE YOU — Isley Brothers (Tamla Motown)
10	17	BUILD ME UP BUTTERCUP — Foundations (Pye)
22	18	I'LL PICK A ROSE FOR MY ROSE — Marv Johnson (Tamla Motown)
19	19	PEOPLE — Tymes (Direction)
-	20	WHERE DO YOU GO TO MY LOVELY — Peter Sarstedt (United Artists)
21	21	QUICK JOEY SMALL — Kasenetz-Katz Singing Orchestral Circus (Buddah)
26	22	LOVE STORY — Jethro Tull (Island)
-	23	MOVE IN A LITTLE CLOSER — Harmony Grass (RCA)
-	23	THE WAY IT USED TO BE — Engelbert Humperdinck (Decca)
17	25	LOVE CHILD — Diana Ross & the Supremes (Tamla Motown)
-	26	MRS. ROBINSON (EP) — Simon & Garfunkel (CBS)
14	27	SABRE DANCE — Love Sculpture (Parlophone)
-	28	HEY JUDE — Wilson Pickett (Atlantic)
29	29	SOUL SISTER, BROWN SUGAR — Sam & Dave (Atlantic)
-	30	WICHITA LINEMAN — Glen Campbell (Ember)

15 February 1969

last week	this week	
2	1	BLACKBERRY WAY — Move (Regal Zonophone)
1	2	ALBATROSS — Fleetwood Mac (Blue Horizon)
3	3	FOR ONCE IN MY LIFE — Stevie Wonder (Tamla Motown)
11	4	(IF PARADISE WAS) HALF AS NICE — Amen Corner (Immediate)
7	5	YOU GOT SOUL — Johnny Nash (Major Minor)
13	6	I'M GONNA MAKE YOU LOVE ME — Diana Ross & the Supremes & the Temptations (Tamla Motown)
9	7	DANCING IN THE STREET — Martha & the Vandellas (Tamla Motown)
10	8	TO LOVE SOMEBODY — Nina Simone (RCA)
20	9	WHERE DO YOU GO TO MY LOVELY — Peter Sarstedt (United Artists)
12	10	PLEASE DON'T GO — Donald Peers (Columbia)
4	11	OB-LA-DI, OB-LA-DA — Marmalade (CBS)
5	12	FOX ON THE RUN — Manfred Mann (Fontana)
16	13	I GUESS I'LL ALWAYS LOVE YOU — Isley Brothers (Tamla Motown)
18	14	I'LL PICK A ROSE FOR MY ROSE — Marv Johnson (Tamla Motown)
6	15	SOMETHING'S HAPPENING — Herman's Hermits (Columbia)
19	16	PEOPLE — Tymes (Direction)
8	17	PRIVATE NUMBER — William Bell & Judy Clay (Stax)
23	18	THE WAY IT USED TO BE — Engelbert Humperdinck (Decca)
29	19	SOUL SISTER, BROWN SUGAR — Sam & Dave (Atlantic)
30	20	WICHITA LINEMAN — Glen Campbell (Ember)
26	20	MRS. ROBINSON — Simon & Garfunkel (CBS)
23	22	MOVE IN A LITTLE CLOSER — Harmony Grass (RCA)
-	23	YOU AIN'T LIVIN' TILL YOU'RE LOVIN' — Marvin Gaye & Tammi Terrell (Tamla Motown)
-	24	GOING UP THE COUNTRY — Canned Heat (Liberty)
14	25	STOP HER ON SIGHT — Edwin Starr (Tamla Motown)
26	26	LOVE STORY — Jethro Tull (Island)
-	27	SHE'S NOT THERE — Neil MacArthur (Deram)
27	28	HEY JUDE — Wilson Pickett (Atlantic)
-	28	MONSIEUR DUPONT — Sandie Shaw (Pye)
25	30	LOVE CHILD — Diana Ross & the Supremes (Tamla Motown)

22 February 1969

last week	this week	
4	1	(IF PARADISE WAS) HALF AS NICE — Amen Corner (Immediate)
9	2	WHERE DO YOU GO TO MY LOVELY — Peter Sarstedt (United Artists)
1	3	BLACKBERRY WAY — Move (Regal Zonophone)
6	4	I'M GONNA MAKE YOU LOVE ME — Diana Ross & the Supremes & the Temptations (Tamla Motown)
2	5	ALBATROSS — Fleetwood Mac (Blue Horizon)
7	5	DANCING IN THE STREET — Martha & the Vandellas (Tamla Motown)
5	7	YOU GOT SOUL — Johnny Nash (Major Minor)
3	8	FOR ONCE IN MY LIFE — Stevie Wonder (Tamla Motown)
10	9	PLEASE DON'T GO — Donald Peers (Columbia)
8	10	TO LOVE SOMEBODY — Nina Simone (RCA)
18	11	THE WAY IT USED TO BE — Engelbert Humperdinck (Decca)
14	12	I'LL PICK A ROSE FOR MY ROSE — Marv Johnson (Tamla Motown)
13	13	I GUESS I'LL ALWAYS LOVE YOU — Isley Brothers (Tamla Motown)
11	14	OB-LA-DI, OB-LA-DA — Marmalade (CBS)
16	15	PEOPLE — Tymes (Direction)
20	16	WICHITA LINEMAN — Glen Campbell (Ember)
12	17	FOX ON THE RUN — Manfred Mann (Fontana)
19	18	SOUL SISTER, BROWN SUGAR — Sam & Dave (Atlantic)
-	19	MRS. ROBINSON — Simon & Garfunkel (CBS)
17	20	PRIVATE NUMBER — William Bell & Judy Clay (Stax)
15	21	SOMETHING'S HAPPENING — Herman's Hermits (Columbia)
23	22	YOU AIN'T LIVIN' TILL YOU'RE LOVIN' — Marvin Gaye & Tammi Terrell (Tamla Motown)
-	23	SURROUND YOURSELF WITH SORROW — Cilla Black (Parlophone)
28	24	HEY JUDE — Wilson Pickett (Atlantic)
-	24	YOU'VE LOST THAT LOVIN' FEELIN' — Righteous Brothers (London)
22	26	MOVE IN A LITTLE CLOSER — Harmony Grass (RCA)
-	27	I HEARD IT THROUGH THE GRAPEVINE — Marvin Gaye (Tamla Motown)
28	27	MONSIEUR DUPONT — Sandie Shaw (Pye)
24	29	GOING UP THE COUNTRY — Canned Heat (Liberty)
-	30	WHITE ROOM — Cream (Polydor)
25	30	STOP HER ON SIGHT — Edwin Starr (Tamla Motown)

Motown music saw one of its most successful chart phases early in 1969, thanks to both a strong flow of current product, and a policy of re-promoting old releases thought not to have maximised their potential first time around. In the latter category, Martha & the Vandellas' *Dancing In The Street*, a minor hit when released in 1964, was now in the Top 10, while the Isley Brothers' *I Guess I'll Always Love You* was a revived oldie which had not originally sold at all. An average 25% of February's hits were Motown singles.

March 1969

1 March 1969

last week	this week	
2	1	WHERE DO YOU GO TO MY LOVELY Peter Sarstedt (United Artists)
1	2	(IF PARADISE WAS) HALF AS NICE Amen Corner (Immediate)
4	3	I'M GONNA MAKE YOU LOVE ME Diana Ross & the Supremes & the Temptations (Tamla Motown)
5	4	DANCING IN THE STREET Martha & the Vandellas (Tamla Motown)
3	5	BLACKBERRY WAY Move (Regal Zonophone)
9	6	PLEASE DON'T GO Donald Peers (Columbia)
5	7	ALBATROSS Fleetwood Mac (Blue Horizon)
11	8	THE WAY IT USED TO BE Engelbert Humperdinck (Decca)
7	9	YOU GOT SOUL Johnny Nash (Major Minor)
16	10	WICHITA LINEMAN Glen Campbell (Ember)
12	11	I'LL PICK A ROSE FOR MY ROSE Marv Johnson (Tamla Motown)
8	12	FOR ONCE IN MY LIFE Stevie Wonder (Tamla Motown)
18	13	SOUL SISTER, BROWN SUGAR Sam & Dave (Atlantic)
13	14	I GUESS I'LL ALWAYS LOVE YOU Isley Brothers (Tamla Motown)
10	15	TO LOVE SOMEBODY Nina Simone (RCA)
23	16	SURROUND YOURSELF WITH SORROW Cilla Black (Parlophone)
15	17	PEOPLE Tymes (Direction)
27	18	I HEARD IT THROUGH THE GRAPEVINE Marvin Gaye (Tamla Motown)
27	19	MONSIEUR DUPONT Sandie Shaw (Pye)
-	20	FIRST OF MAY Bee Gees (Polydor)
19	21	MRS. ROBINSON (EP) Simon & Garfunkel (CBS)
-	22	GENTLE ON MY MIND Dean Martin (Reprise)
14	23	OB-LA-DI, OB-LA-DA Marmalade (CBS)
24	24	YOU'VE LOST THAT LOVIN' FEELIN' Righteous Brothers (London)
17	25	FOX ON THE RUN Manfred Mann (Fontana)
22	26	YOU AIN'T LIVIN' TILL YOU'RE LOVIN' Marvin Gaye & Tammi Terrell (Tamla Motown)
29	27	GOING UP THE COUNTRY Canned Heat (Liberty)
-	28	IF I CAN DREAM Elvis Presley (RCA)
30	29	WHITE ROOM Cream (Polydor)
24	30	HEY JUDE Wilson Pickett (Atlantic)

8 March 1969

last week	this week	
1	1	WHERE DO YOU GO TO MY LOVELY Peter Sarstedt (United Artists)
2	2	(IF PARADISE WAS) HALF AS NICE Amen Corner (Immediate)
3	3	I'M GONNA MAKE YOU LOVE ME Diana Ross & the Supremes & the Temptations (Tamla Motown)
8	4	THE WAY IT USED TO BE Engelbert Humperdinck (Decca)
16	5	SURROUND YOURSELF WITH SORROW Cilla Black (Parlophone)
6	6	PLEASE DON'T GO Donald Peers (Columbia)
10	7	WICHITA LINEMAN Glen Campbell (Ember)
4	8	DANCING IN THE STREET Martha & the Vandellas (Tamla Motown)
18	9	I HEARD IT THROUGH THE GRAPEVINE Marvin Gaye (Tamla Motown)
11	10	I'LL PICK A ROSE FOR MY ROSE Marv Johnson (Tamla Motown)
22	11	GENTLE ON MY MIND Dean Martin (Reprise)
5	12	BLACKBERRY WAY Move (Regal Zonophone)
19	13	MONSIEUR DUPONT Sandie Shaw (Pye)
13	14	SOUL SISTER, BROWN SUGAR Sam & Dave (Atlantic)
24	15	YOU'VE LOST THAT LOVIN' FEELIN' Righteous Brothers (London)
7	16	ALBATROSS Fleetwood Mac (Blue Horizon)
9	17	YOU GOT SOUL Johnny Nash (Major Minor)
20	18	FIRST OF MAY Bee Gees (Polydor)
28	19	IF I CAN DREAM Elvis Presley (RCA)
-	20	GOOD TIMES (BETTER TIMES) Cliff Richard (Columbia)
14	21	I GUESS I'LL ALWAYS LOVE YOU Isley Brothers (Tamla Motown)
-	22	I SPY (FOR THE FBI) Jamo Thomas (Polydor)
12	23	FOR ONCE IN MY LIFE Stevie Wonder (Tamla Motown)
15	24	TO LOVE SOMEBODY Nina Simone (RCA)
-	25	SORRY SUZANNE Hollies (Parlophone)
-	26	WINDMILLS OF YOUR MIND Noel Harrison (Reprise)
-	27	I CAN HEAR MUSIC Beach Boys (Capitol)
16	28	PEOPLE Tymes (Direction)
23	29	OB-LA-DI, OB-LA-DA Marmalade (CBS)
-	30	MOCKINGBIRD Inez & Charlie Foxx (United Artists)

15 March 1969

last week	this week	
1	1	WHERE DO YOU GO TO MY LOVELY Peter Sarstedt (United Artists)
5	2	SURROUND YOURSELF WITH SORROW Cilla Black (Parlophone)
9	3	I HEARD IT THROUGH THE GRAPEVINE Marvin Gaye (Tamla Motown)
2	4	(IF PARADISE WAS) HALF AS NICE Amen Corner (Immediate)
3	5	I'M GONNA MAKE YOU LOVE ME Diana Ross & the Supremes & the Temptations (Tamla Motown)
7	6	WICHITA LINEMAN Glen Campbell (Ember)
11	7	GENTLE ON MY MIND Dean Martin (Reprise)
4	8	THE WAY IT USED TO BE Engelbert Humperdinck (Decca)
13	9	MONSIEUR DUPONT Sandie Shaw (Pye)
6	10	PLEASE DON'T GO Donald Peers (Columbia)
15	11	YOU'VE LOST THAT LOVIN' FEELIN' Righteous Brothers (London)
18	12	FIRST OF MAY Bee Gees (Polydor)
9	13	I'LL PICK A ROSE FOR MY ROSE Marv Johnson (Tamla Motown)
20	14	GOOD TIMES (BETTER TIMES) Cliff Richard (Columbia)
19	15	IF I CAN DREAM Elvis Presley (RCA)
8	16	DANCING IN THE STREET Martha & the Vandellas (Tamla Motown)
25	17	SORRY SUZANNE Hollies (Parlophone)
14	18	SOUL SISTER, BROWN SUGAR Sam & Dave (Atlantic)
-	19	GAMES PEOPLE PLAY Joe South (Capitol)
26	20	WINDMILLS OF YOUR MIND Noel Harrison (Reprise)
27	21	I CAN HEAR MUSIC Beach Boys (Capitol)
12	22	BLACKBERRY WAY Move (Regal Zonophone)
-	23	GET READY Temptations (Tamla Motown)
-	24	ONE ROAD Love Affair (CBS)
29	25	MOCKINGBIRD Inez & Charlie Foxx (United Artists)
-	26	BOOM-BANG-A-BANG Lulu (Columbia)
-	27	ALL THE LOVE IN THE WORLD Consortium (Pye)
22	28	I SPY (FOR THE FBI) Jamo Thomas (Polydor)
28	29	PEOPLE Tymes (Direction)
-	30	THE BAD BAD OLD DAYS Foundations (Pye)

22 March 1969

last week	this week	
1	1	WHERE DO YOU GO TO MY LOVELY Peter Sarstedt (United Artists)
3	2	I HEARD IT THROUGH THE GRAPEVINE Marvin Gaye (Tamla Motown)
2	3	SURROUND YOURSELF WITH SORROW Cilla Black (Parlophone)
8	4	THE WAY IT USED TO BE Engelbert Humperdinck (Decca)
6	5	WICHITA LINEMAN Glen Campbell (Ember)
7	6	GENTLE ON MY MIND Dean Martin (Reprise)
9	7	MONSIEUR DUPONT Sandie Shaw (Pye)
12	8	FIRST OF MAY Bee Gees (Polydor)
5	9	I'M GONNA MAKE YOU LOVE ME Diana Ross & the Supremes & the Temptations (Tamla Motown)
4	10	(IF PARADISE WAS) HALF AS NICE Amen Corner (Immediate)
17	11	SORRY SUZANNE Hollies (Parlophone)
11	12	YOU'VE LOST THAT LOVIN' FEELIN' Righteous Brothers (London)
10	13	PLEASE DON'T GO Donald Peers (Columbia)
15	14	IF I CAN DREAM Elvis Presley (RCA)
14	15	GOOD TIMES (BETTER TIMES) Cliff Richard (Columbia)
13	16	I'LL PICK A ROSE FOR MY ROSE Marv Johnson (Tamla Motown)
20	17	WINDMILLS OF YOUR MIND Noel Harrison (Reprise)
30	18	THE BAD BAD OLD DAYS Foundations (Pye)
17	19	SOUL SISTER, BROWN SUGAR Sam & Dave (Atlantic)
25	20	BOOM-BANG-A-BANG Lulu (Columbia)
19	21	GAMES PEOPLE PLAY Joe South (Capitol)
21	22	I CAN HEAR MUSIC Beach Boys (Capitol)
24	23	ONE ROAD Love Affair (CBS)
22	24	GET READY Temptations (Tamla Motown)
16	25	DANCING IN THE STREET Martha & the Vandellas (Tamla Motown)
-	26	PINBALL WIZARD Who (Track)
-	27	IT'S TOO LATE Long John Baldry (Pye)
-	28	DON JUAN Dave Dee, Dozy, Beaky, Mick & Tich (Fontana)
27	29	ALL THE LOVE IN THE WORLD Consortium (Pye)
-	30	PASSING STRANGERS Billy Eckstine & Sarah Vaughsn (Mercury)

Peter Sarstedt, newly topping the chart, was the younger brother of Richard Sarstedt - otherwise known as Eden Kane - who had beaten his sibling to the top by the best part of eight years by hitting number one in 1961 with *Well I Ask You*. Elsewhere, Donald Peers and Dean Martin were the latest balladeers to return from chart obscurity with Top 10 hits; Martin's *Gentle On My Mind* had been a US hit for Glen Campbell, now finally scoring too in Britain with his Jim Webb-penned *Wichita Lineman*.

March – April 1969

29 March 1969

last week	this week		
2	1	I HEARD IT THROUGH THE GRAPEVINE	Marvin Gaye (Tamla Motown)
1	2	WHERE DO YOU GO TO MY LOVELY	Peter Sarstedt (United Artists)
6	3	GENTLE ON MY MIND	Dean Martin (Reprise)
3	4	SURROUND YOURSELF WITH SORROW	Cilla Black (Parlophone)
4	5	THE WAY IT USED TO BE	Engelbert Humperdinck (Decca)
10	6	SORRY SUZANNE	Hollies (Parlophone)
8	7	FIRST OF MAY	Bee Gees (Polydor)
5	8	WICHITA LINEMAN	Glen Campbell (Ember)
7	9	MONSIEUR DUPONT	Sandie Shaw (Pye)
20	10	GAMES PEOPLE PLAY	Joe South (Capitol)
12	11	YOU'VE LOST THAT LOVIN' FEELIN'	Righteous Brothers (London)
18	12	THE BAD BAD OLD DAYS	Foundations (Pye)
14	13	IF I CAN DREAM	Elvis Presley (RCA)
24	14	GET READY	Temptations (Tamla Motown)
15	15	GOOD TIMES (BETTER TIMES)	Cliff Richard (Columbia)
13	16	PLEASE DON'T GO	Donald Peers (Columbia)
20	17	BOOM-BANG-A-BANG	Lulu (Columbia)
23	18	ONE ROAD	Love Affair (CBS)
17	19	WINDMILLS OF YOUR MIND	Noel Harrison (Reprise)
22	20	I CAN HEAR MUSIC	Beach Boys (Capitol)
9	21	I'M GONNA MAKE YOU LOVE ME	Diana Ross & the Supremes the Temptations (Tamla Motown)
-	22	THE ISRAELITES	Desmond Dekker & the Aces (Pyramid)
-	23	MARIA ELENA	Gene Pitney (Stateside)
10	24	(IF PARADISE WAS) HALF AS NICE	Amen Corner (Immediate)
30	25	PASSING STRANGERS	Billy Eckstein & Sarah Vaughan (Mercury)
-	26	HARLEM SHUFFLE	Bob & Earl (Island)
28	27	DON JUAN	Dave Dee, Dozy, Beaky, Mick & Tich (Fontana)
16	28	I'LL PICK A ROSE FOR MY ROSE	Marv Johnson (Tamla Motown)
-	29	I SPY	Jamo Thomas (Polydor)
-	30	I DON'T KNOW WHY	Stevie Wonder (Tamla Motown)

5 April 1969

1	I HEARD IT THROUGH THE GRAPEVINE	Marvin Gaye (Tamla Motown)
2	GENTLE ON MY MIND	Dean Martin (Reprise)
3	SORRY SUZANNE	Hollies (Parlophone)
4	THE BAD BAD OLD DAYS	Foundations (Pye)
5	SURROUND YOURSELF WITH SORROW	Cilla Black (Parlophone)
5	WHERE DO YOU GO TO MY LOVELY	Peter Sarstedt (United Artists)
7	GAMES PEOPLE PLAY	Joe South (Capitol)
8	BOOM-BANG-A-BANG	Lulu (Columbia)
9	FIRST OF MAY	Bee Gees (Polydor)
10	GET READY	Temptations (Tamla Motown)
11	MONSIEUR DUPONT	Sandie Shaw (Pye)
12	THE WAY IT USED TO BE	Engelbert Humperdinck (Decca)
13	WICHITA LINEMAN	Glen Campbell (Ember)
14	THE ISRAELITES	Desmond Dekker & the Aces (Pyramid)
15	I CAN HEAR MUSIC	Beach Boys (Capitol)
16	PLEASE DON'T GO	Donald Peers (Columbia)
17	GOOD TIMES (BETTER TIMES)	Cliff Richard (Columbia)
18	YOU'VE LOST THAT LOVIN' FEELIN'	Righteous Brothers (London)
19	IF I CAN DREAM	Elvis Presley (RCA)
20	WINDMILLS OF YOUR MIND	Noel Harrison (Reprise)
21	ONE ROAD	Love Affair (CBS)
22	PINBALL WIZARD	Who (Track)
23	HELLO WORLD	Tremeloes (CBS)
24	HARLEM SHUFFLE	Bob & Earl (Island)
25	I DON'T KNOW WHY	Stevie Wonder (Tamla Motown)
26	GOODBYE	Mary Hopkin (Apple)
27	SANCTUS (FROM MISSA LUBA)	Les Troubadours Du Roi Badouin (Philips)
28	PASSING STRANGERS	Billy Eckstein & Sarah Vaughan (Mercury)
29	CUPID	Johnny Nash (Major Minor)
30	DON JUAN	Dave Dee, Dozy, Beaky, Mick & Tich (Fontana)

12 April 1969

1	I HEARD IT THROUGH THE GRAPEVINE	Marvin Gaye (Tamla Motown)
2	GENTLE ON MY MIND	Dean Martin (Reprise)
3	BOOM-BANG-A-BANG	Lulu (Columbia)
4	SORRY SUZANNE	Hollies (Parlophone)
5	THE BAD BAD OLD DAYS	Foundations (Pye)
6	THE ISRAELITES	Desmond Dekker & the Aces (Pyramid)
7	GAMES PEOPLE PLAY	Joe South (Capitol)
8	MONSIEUR DUPONT	Sandie Shaw (Pye)
9	FIRST OF MAY	Bee Gees (Polydor)
10	WINDMILLS OF YOUR MIND	Noel Harrison (Reprise)
11	GET READY	Temptations (Tamla Motown)
12	GOOD TIMES (BETTER TIMES)	Cliff Richard (Columbia)
13	WHERE DO YOU GO TO MY LOVELY	Peter Sarstedt (United Artists)
14	I CAN HEAR MUSIC	Beach Boys (Capitol)
15	SURROUND YOURSELF WITH SORROW	Cilla Black (Parlophone)
16	PINBALL WIZARD	Who (Track)
17	GOODBYE	Mary Hopkin (Apple)
18	HARLEM SHUFFLE	Bob & Earl (Island)
19	PASSING STRANGERS	Billy Eckstein & Sarah Vaughan (Mercury)
20	IF I CAN DREAM	Elvis Presley (RCA)
21	THE WAY IT USED TO BE	Engelbert Humperdinck (Decca)
22	HELLO WORLD	Tremeloes (CBS)
23	I DON'T KNOW WHY	Stevie Wonder (Tamla Motown)
24	WICHITA LINEMAN	Glen Campbell (Ember)
25	YOU'VE LOST THAT LOVIN' FEELIN'	Righteous Brothers (London)
26	CUPID	Johnny Nash (Major Minor)
27	(I'M A) ROAD RUNNER	Jr. Walker & the All Stars (Tamla Motown)
28	ONE ROAD	Love Affair (CBS)
29	DON JUAN	Dave Dee, Dozy, Beaky, Mick & Tich (Fontana)
30	CROSSTOWN TRAFFIC	Jimi Hendrix (Track)

19 April 1969

1	THE ISRAELITES	Desmond Dekker & the Aces (Pyramid)
2	I HEARD IT THROUGH THE GRAPEVINE	Marvin Gaye (Tamla Motown)
3	GENTLE ON MY MIND	Dean Martin (Reprise)
4	BOOM-BANG-A-BANG	Lulu (Columbia)
5	THE BAD BAD OLD DAYS	Foundations (Pye)
6	SORRY SUZANNE	Hollies (Parlophone)
7	GOODBYE	Mary Hopkin (Apple)
8	GAMES PEOPLE PLAY	Joe South (Capitol)
9	WINDMILLS OF YOUR MIND	Noel Harrison (Reprise)
10	PINBALL WIZARD	Who (Track)
11	I CAN HEAR MUSIC	Beach Boys (Capitol)
12	GET READY	Temptations (Tamla Motown)
13	GOOD TIMES (BETTER TIMES)	Cliff Richard (Columbia)
14	MONSIEUR DUPONT	Sandie Shaw (Pye)
15	HARLEM SHUFFLE	Bob & Earl (Island)
16	WHERE DO YOU GO TO MY LOVELY	Peter Sarstedt (United Artists)
17	FIRST OF MAY	Bee Gees (Polydor)
18	CUPID	Johnny Nash (Major Minor)
19	I DON'T KNOW WHY	Stevie Wonder (Tamla Motown)
20	SURROUND YOURSELF WITH SORROW	Cilla Black (Parlophone)
21	PASSING STRANGERS	Billy Eckstein & Sarah Vaughan (Mercury)
22	IF I CAN DREAM	Elvis Presley (RCA)
23	COME BACK AND SHAKE ME	Clodagh Rodgers (RCA)
24	THE WAY IT USED TO BE	Engelbert Humperdinck (Decca)
25	HELLO WORLD	Tremeloes (CBS)
26	(I'M A) ROAD RUNNER	Jr. Walker & the All Stars (Tamla Motown)
27	MY WAY	Frank Sinatra (Reprise)
28	DICK-A-DUM-DUM (KING'S ROAD)	Des O'Connor (Columbia)
29	MICHAEL AND THE SLIPPER TREE	Equals (President)

As Marvin Gaye hit the chart-top with *I Heard It Through The Grapevine*, his all-time biggest UK success, the sound of Motown past also continued to echo down the Top 30: the Temptations' *Get Ready* and Jr. Walker's *(I'm A) Road Runner*, both from the mid-1960s, found reissue paydirt. The fad for reviving old soul singles was also widening, however, with Bob & Earl's *Harlem Shuffle* and Jamo Thomas' *I Spy (For The FBI)* finally getting some of the glory too after several years as afficionados' favourites.

207

April – May 1969

26 April 1969

last / this week

last	this		
1	1	THE ISRAELITES	Desmond Dekker & the Aces (Pyramid)
7	2	GOODBYE Mary Hopkin (Apple)	
-	3	GET BACK	Beatles (Apple)
2	4	I HEARD IT THROUGH THE GRAPEVINE	Marvin Gaye (Tamla Motown)
3	5	GENTLE ON MY MIND	Dean Martin (Reprise)
10	6	PINBALL WIZARD	Who (Track)
4	7	BOOM-BANG-A-BANG	Lulu (Columbia)
5	8	THE BAD BAD OLD DAYS	Foundations (Pye)
18	9	CUPID	Johnny Nash (Major Minor)
23	10	COME BACK AND SHAKE ME	Clodagh Rodgers (RCA)
15	11	HARLEM SHUFFLE	Bob & Earl (Island)
9	12	WINDMILLS OF YOUR MIND	Noel Harrison (Reprise)
11	13	I CAN HEAR MUSIC	Beach Boys (Capitol)
6	14	SORRY SUZANNE	Hollies (Parlophone)
8	15	GAMES PEOPLE PLAY	Joe South (Capitol)
27	16	MY WAY	Frank Sinatra (Reprise)
19	17	I DON'T KNOW WHY	Stevie Wonder (Tamla Motown)
12	18	GET READY	Temptations (Tamla Motown)
26	19	(I'M A) ROAD RUNNER	Jr. Walker & the All Stars (Tamla Motown)
13	20	GOOD TIMES (BETTER TIMES)	Cliff Richard (Columbia)
-	21	MAN OF THE WORLD	Fleetwood Mac (Immediate)
14	22	MONSIEUR DUPONT	Sandie Shaw (President)
29	23	MICHAEL AND THE SLIPPER TREE	Equals (President)
25	24	HELLO WORLD	Tremeloes (CBS)
21	25	PASSING STRANGERS	Sarah Vaughan & Billy Eckstine (Mercury)
20	26	SURROUND YOURSELF WITH SORROW	Cilla Black (Parlophone)
16	27	WHERE DO YOU GO TO MY LOVELY	Peter Sarstedt (United Artists)
-	28	PLASTIC MAN	Kinks (Pye)
17	29	FIRST OF MAY	Bee Gees (Polydor)
22	30	IF I CAN DREAM	Elvis Presley (RCA)
-	30	BADGE	Cream (Polydor)

3 May 1969

3	1	GET BACK	Beatles (Apple)
2	2	GOODBYE	Mary Hopkin (Apple)
1	3	THE ISRAELITES	Desmond Dekker & the Aces (Pyramid)
6	4	PINBALL WIZARD	Who (Track)
10	5	COME BACK AND SHAKE ME	Clodagh Rodgers (RCA)
9	6	CUPID	Johnny Nash (Major Minor)
5	7	GENTLE ON MY MIND	Dean Martin (Reprise)
11	8	HARLEM SHUFFLE	Bob & Earl (Island)
4	9	I HEARD IT THROUGH THE GRAPEVINE	Marvin Gaye (Tamla Motown)
19	10	(I'M A) ROAD RUNNER	Jr. Walker & the All Stars (Tamla Motown)
12	11	WINDMILLS OF YOUR MIND	Noel Harrison (Reprise)
16	12	MY WAY	Frank Sinatra (Reprise)
7	13	BOOM-BANG-A-BANG	Lulu (Columbia)
17	14	I DON'T KNOW WHY	Stevie Wonder (Tamla Motown)
8	15	THE BAD BAD OLD DAYS	Foundations (Pye)
21	16	MAN OF THE WORLD	Fleetwood Mac (Immediate)
-	17	MY SENTIMENTAL FRIEND	Herman's Hermits (Columbia)
13	18	I CAN HEAR MUSIC	Beach Boys (Capitol)
14	19	SORRY SUZANNE	Hollies (Parlophone)
15	20	GAMES PEOPLE PLAY	Joe South (Capitol)
30	21	BADGE	Cream (Polydor)
-	22	BEHIND A PAINTED SMILE	Isley Brothers (Tamla Motown)
25	23	PASSING STRANGERS	Sarah Vaughan & Billy Eckstine (Mercury)
23	24	MICHAEL AND THE SLIPPER TREE	Equals (President)
18	25	GET READY	Temptations (Tamla Motown)
-	26	DIZZY	Tommy Roe (Stateside)
-	27	COLOUR OF MY LOVE	Jefferson (Pye)
24	28	HELLO WORLD	Tremeloes (CBS)
28	29	PLASTIC MAN	Kinks (Pye)
-	30	I'M LIVING IN SHAME	Diana Ross & the Supremes (Tamla Motown)

10 May 1969

1	1	GET BACK	Beatles (Apple)
2	2	GOODBYE Mary Hopkin (Apple)	
5	3	COME BACK AND SHAKE ME	Clodagh Rodgers (RCA)
3	4	THE ISRAELITES	Desmond Dekker & the Aces (Pyramid)
4	5	PINBALL WIZARD	Who (Track)
6	6	CUPID	Johnny Nash (Major Minor)
8	7	HARLEM SHUFFLE	Bob & Earl (Island)
12	8	MY WAY	Frank Sinatra (Reprise)
17	9	MY SENTIMENTAL FRIEND	Herman's Hermits (Columbia)
10	10	(I'M A) ROAD RUNNER	Jr. Walker & the All Stars (Tamla Motown)
7	11	GENTLE ON MY MIND	Dean Martin (Reprise)
16	12	MAN OF THE WORLD	Fleetwood Mac (Immediate)
11	13	WINDMILLS OF YOUR MIND	Noel Harrison (Reprise)
22	14	BEHIND A PAINTED SMILE	Isley Brothers (Tamla Motown)
-	15	THE BOXER	Simon & Garfunkel (CBS)
14	16	I DON'T KNOW WHY	Stevie Wonder (Tamla Motown)
9	17	I HEARD IT THROUGH THE GRAPEVINE	Marvin Gaye (Tamla Motown)
13	18	BOOM-BANG-A-BANG	Lulu (Columbia)
15	19	THE BAD BAD OLD DAYS	Foundations (Pye)
26	20	DIZZY	Tommy Roe (Stateside)
27	21	COLOUR OF MY LOVE	Jefferson (Pye)
23	22	PASSING STRANGERS	Sarah Vaughan & Billy Eckstine (Mercury)
30	23	I'M LIVING IN SHAME	Diana Ross & the Supremes (Tamla Motown)
21	24	BADGE	Cream (Polydor)
-	25	AQUARIUS/LET THE SUN SHINE IN (MEDLEY) Fifth Dimension (Liberty)	
-	25	RAGAMUFFIN MAN	Manfred Mann (Fontana)
18	27	SORRY SUZANNE	Hollies (Parlophone)
-	28	YOU'VE MADE ME SO VERY HAPPY	Blood Sweat & Tears (CBS)
18	29	I CAN HEAR MUSIC	Beach Boys (Capitol)
-	30	GALVESTON	Glen Campbell (Ember)

17 May 1969

1	1	GET BACK	Beatles (Apple)
3	2	COME BACK AND SHAKE ME	Clodagh Rodgers (RCA)
2	3	GOODBYE Mary Hopkin (Apple)	
9	4	MY SENTIMENTAL FRIEND	Herman's Hermits (Columbia)
5	5	PINBALL WIZARD	Who (Track)
12	6	MAN OF THE WORLD	Fleetwood Mac (Immediate)
14	6	BEHIND A PAINTED SMILE	Isley Brothers (Tamla Motown)
8	6	MY WAY	Frank Sinatra (Reprise)
4	9	THE ISRAELITES	Desmond Dekker & the Aces (Pyramid)
15	10	THE BOXER	Simon & Garfunkel (CBS)
6	11	CUPID	Johnny Nash (Major Minor)
10	12	(I'M A) ROAD RUNNER	Jr. Walker & the All Stars (Tamla Motown)
7	13	HARLEM SHUFFLE	Bob & Earl (Island)
20	14	DIZZY	Tommy Roe (Stateside)
11	15	GENTLE ON MY MIND	Dean Martin (Reprise)
25	16	RAGAMUFFIN MAN	Manfred Mann (Fontana)
23	17	I'M LIVING IN SHAME	Diana Ross & the Supremes (Tamla Motown)
13	18	WINDMILLS OF YOUR MIND	Noel Harrison (Reprise)
24	19	BADGE	Cream (Polydor)
16	20	I DON'T KNOW WHY	Stevie Wonder (Tamla Motown)
21	21	COLOUR OF MY LOVE	Jefferson (Pye)
30	22	GALVESTON	Glen Campbell (Ember)
25	23	AQUARIUS/LET THE SUN SHINE IN (MEDLEY) Fifth Dimension (Liberty)	
-	24	LOVE ME TONIGHT	Tom Jones (Decca)
-	24	TRACKS OF MY TEARS	Smokey Robinson & the Miracles (Tamla Motown)
22	26	PASSING STRANGERS	Sarah Vaughan & Billy Eckstine (Mercury)
28	27	YOU'VE MADE ME SO VERY HAPPY	Blood Sweat & Tears (CBS)
-	28	TIME IS TIGHT	Booker T. & the MG's (Stax)
-	29	BLUER THAN BLUE	Rolf Harris (Columbia)
-	30	I THREW IT ALL AWAY	Bob Dylan (CBS)
-	30	THINK IT ALL OVER	Sandie Shaw (Pye)

Desmond Dekker's *The Israelites* was reggae's first crossover Number One hit, would one day be the source of a successful Vitalite spread TV ad jingle, and also - odd though it seemed at the time - had a great influence, later admitted, on Paul Simon, who was to investigate reggae rhythms aplenty a couple of years later when he began to work solo. An even more esoteric sound was the drum chant of *Sanctus*, a single whose release and success were entirely due to it being heavily featured in the controversial film *If*.

May – June 1969

24 May 1969

last week	this week		
1	1	GET BACK	Beatles (Apple)
6	2	MAN OF THE WORLD	Fleetwood Mac (Immediate)
4	3	MY SENTIMENTAL FRIEND	Herman's Hermits (Columbia)
6	4	BEHIND A PAINTED SMILE	Isley Brothers (Tamla Motown)
6	5	MY WAY	Frank Sinatra (Reprise)
14	6	DIZZY	Tommy Roe (Stateside)
2	7	COME BACK AND SHAKE ME	Clodagh Rodgers (RCA)
3	8	GOODBYE	Mary Hopkin (Apple)
10	9	THE BOXER	Simon & Garfunkel (CBS)
5	10	PINBALL WIZARD	Who (Track)
12	11	(I'M A) ROAD RUNNER	Jr. Walker & the All Stars (Tamla Motown)
24	12	LOVE ME TONIGHT	Tom Jones (Decca)
16	13	RAGAMUFFIN MAN	Manfred Mann (Fontana)
9	14	THE ISRAELITES	Desmond Dekker & the Aces (Pyramid)
13	15	HARLEM SHUFFLE	Bob & Earl (Island)
11	16	CUPID	Johnny Nash (Major Minor)
17	17	I'M LIVING IN SHAME	Diana Ross & the Supremes (Tamla Motown)
22	18	GALVESTON	Glen Campbell (Ember)
24	19	TRACKS OF MY TEARS	Smokey Robinson & the Miracles (Tamla Motown)
15	20	GENTLE ON MY MIND	Dean Martin (Reprise)
23	21	AQUARIUS/LET THE SUN SHINE IN (MEDLEY)	Fifth Dimension (Liberty)
19	22	BADGE	Cream (Polydor)
28	23	TIME IS TIGHT	Booker T. & the MG's (Stax)
-	24	SNAKE IN THE GRASS	Dave Dee, Dozy, Beaky, Mick & Tich (Fontana)
30	25	I THREW IT ALL AWAY	Bob Dylan (CBS)
-	26	DICK-A-DUM-DUM (KING'S ROAD)	Des O'Connor (Columbia)
21	27	COLOUR OF MY LOVE	Jefferson (Pye)
26	28	PASSING STRANGERS	Sarah Vaughan & Billy Eckstine (Mercury)
-	29	(YOUR LOVE KEEPS LIFTING ME) HIGHER AND HIGHER	Jackie Wilson (MCA)
20	30	I DON'T KNOW WHY	Stevie Wonder (Tamla Motown)
-	30	I'D RATHER GO BLIND	Chicken Shack (Blue Horizon)

31 May 1969

last week	this week		
1	1	GET BACK	Beatles (Apple)
6	2	DIZZY	Tommy Roe (Stateside)
2	3	MAN OF THE WORLD	Fleetwood Mac (Immediate)
3	4	MY SENTIMENTAL FRIEND	Herman's Hermits (Columbia)
5	5	MY WAY	Frank Sinatra (Reprise)
4	6	BEHIND A PAINTED SMILE	Isley Brothers (Tamla Motown)
9	7	THE BOXER	Simon & Garfunkel (CBS)
13	8	RAGAMUFFIN MAN	Manfred Mann (Fontana)
12	9	LOVE ME TONIGHT	Tom Jones (Decca)
7	10	COME BACK AND SHAKE ME	Clodagh Rodgers (RCA)
18	11	GALVESTON	Glen Campbell (Ember)
8	12	GOODBYE	Mary Hopkin (Apple)
11	13	(I'M A) ROAD RUNNER	Jr. Walker & the All Stars (Tamla Motown)
21	14	AQUARIUS/LET THE SUN SHINE IN (MEDLEY)	Fifth Dimension (Liberty)
10	15	PINBALL WIZARD	Who (Track)
23	16	TIME IS TIGHT	Booker T. & the MG's (Stax)
19	17	TRACKS OF MY TEARS	Smokey Robinson & the Miracles (Tamla Motown)
17	18	I'M LIVING IN SHAME	Diana Ross & the Supremes (Tamla Motown)
22	19	BADGE	Cream (Polydor)
-	20	OH HAPPY DAY	Edwin Hawkins Singers (Buddah)
15	21	HARLEM SHUFFLE	Bob & Earl (Island)
30	22	I'D RATHER GO BLIND	Chicken Shack (Blue Horizon)
25	23	I THREW IT ALL AWAY	Bob Dylan (CBS)
26	24	DICK-A-DUM-DUM (KING'S ROAD)	Des O'Connor (Columbia)
24	25	SNAKE IN THE GRASS	Dave Dee, Dozy, Beaky, Mick & Tich (Fontana)
14	25	THE ISRAELITES	Desmond Dekker & the Aces (Pyramid)
27	27	(YOUR LOVE KEEPS LIFTING ME) HIGHER AND HIGHER	Jackie Wilson (MCA)
16	28	CUPID	Johnny Nash (Major Minor)
20	29	GENTLE ON MY MIND	Dean Martin (Reprise)
-	30	GIMME GIMME GOOD LOVIN'	Crazy Elephant (Major Minor)
-	30	LIVING IN THE PAST	Jethro Tull (Island)

7 June 1969

last week	this week		
2	1	DIZZY	Tommy Roe (Stateside)
1	2	GET BACK	Beatles (Apple)
3	3	MAN OF THE WORLD	Fleetwood Mac (Immediate)
5	4	MY WAY	Frank Sinatra (Reprise)
4	5	MY SENTIMENTAL FRIEND	Herman's Hermits (Columbia)
7	6	THE BOXER	Simon & Garfunkel (CBS)
20	7	OH HAPPY DAY	Edwin Hawkins Singers (Buddah)
8	7	RAGAMUFFIN MAN	Manfred Mann (Fontana)
16	9	TIME IS TIGHT	Booker T. & the MG's (Stax)
9	9	LOVE ME TONIGHT	Tom Jones (Decca)
-	11	THE BALLAD OF JOHN AND YOKO	Beatles (Apple)
6	11	BEHIND A PAINTED SMILE	Isley Brothers (Tamla Motown)
14	13	AQUARIUS/LET THE SUN SHINE IN (MEDLEY)	Fifth Dimension (Liberty)
27	14	(YOUR LOVE KEEPS LIFTING ME) HIGHER AND HIGHER	Jackie Wilson (MCA)
11	15	GALVESTON	Glen Campbell (Ember)
10	16	COME BACK AND SHAKE ME	Clodagh Rodgers (RCA)
17	17	TRACKS OF MY TEARS	Smokey Robinson & the Miracles (Tamla Motown)
24	18	DICK-A-DUM-DUM (KING'S ROAD)	Des O'Connor (Columbia)
13	19	(I'M A) ROAD RUNNER	Jr. Walker & the All Stars (Tamla Motown)
12	20	GOODBYE	Mary Hopkin (Apple)
18	21	I'M LIVIN' IN SHAME	Diana Ross & the Supremes (Tamla Motown)
21	22	I'D RATHER GO BLIND	Chicken Shack (Blue Horizon)
30	23	GIMME GIMME GOOD LOVIN'	Crazy Elephant (Major Minor)
-	24	PROUD MARY	Creedence Clearwater Revival (Liberty)
21	25	I THREW IT ALL AWAY	Bob Dylan (CBS)
19	26	BADGE	Cream (Polydor)
30	26	LIVING IN THE PAST	Jethro Tull (Island)
-	28	BIG SHIP	Cliff Richard (Columbia)
15	29	PINBALL WIZARD	Who (Track)
25	30	SNAKE IN THE GRASS	Dave Dee, Dozy, Beaky, Mick & Tich (Fontana)

14 June 1969

last week	this week		
1	1	DIZZY	Tommy Roe (Stateside)
11	2	THE BALLAD OF JOHN AND YOKO	Beatles (Apple)
7	3	OH HAPPY DAY	Edwin Hawkins Singers (Buddah)
2	4	GET BACK	Beatles (Apple)
3	5	MAN OF THE WORLD	Fleetwood Mac (Immediate)
4	6	MY WAY	Frank Sinatra (Reprise)
9	7	TIME IS TIGHT	Booker T. & the MG's (Stax)
6	8	THE BOXER	Simon & Garfunkel (CBS)
7	9	RAGAMUFFIN MAN	Manfred Mann (Fontana)
14	10	(YOUR LOVE KEEPS LIFTING ME) HIGHER AND HIGHER	Jackie Wilson (MCA)
9	11	LOVE ME TONIGHT	Tom Jones (Decca)
5	12	MY SENTIMENTAL FRIEND	Herman's Hermits (Columbia)
11	13	BEHIND A PAINTED SMILE	Isley Brothers (Tamla Motown)
17	14	TRACKS OF MY TEARS	Smokey Robinson & the Miracles (Tamla Motown)
13	15	AQUARIUS/LET THE SUN SHINE IN (MEDLEY)	Fifth Dimension (Liberty)
15	16	GALVESTON	Glen Campbell (Ember)
22	17	I'D RATHER GO BLIND	Chicken Shack (Blue Horizon)
18	18	DICK-A-DUM-DUM (KING'S ROAD)	Des O'Connor (Columbia)
23	19	GIMME GIMME GOOD LOVIN'	Crazy Elephant (Major Minor)
26	20	LIVING IN THE PAST	Jethro Tull (Island)
28	21	BIG SHIP	Cliff Richard (Columbia)
24	22	PROUD MARY	Creedence Clearwater Revival (Liberty)
25	23	I THREW IT ALL AWAY	Bob Dylan (CBS)
20	24	GOODBYE	Mary Hopkin (Apple)
16	25	COME BACK AND SHAKE ME	Clodagh Rodgers (RCA)
-	26	FROZEN ORANGE JUICE	Peter Sarstedt (United Artists)
-	27	HAPPY HEART	Andy Williams (CBS)
-	28	TOMORROW TOMORROW	Bee Gees (Polydor)
-	29	A WAY OF LIFE	Family Dogg (Bell)
-	30	WHAT IS A MAN	Four Tops (Tamla Motown)

Get Back was the first Beatles single to credit an additional player (Billy Preston), and also the first to be chased so rapidly by its follow-up: it was still in its last of five weeks at Number One when *The Ballad Of John And Yoko* was released, and Tommy Roe had only two weeks' grace with *Dizzy*, before *John And Yoko*, in turn, made Number One. Written by John Lennon as a celebration of his recent marriage, it was recorded in an off-duty session involving only himself and Paul McCartney, the latter also playing drums.

June – July 1969

21 June 1969

last	this	
2	1	THE BALLAD OF JOHN AND YOKO Beatles (Apple)
3	2	OH HAPPY DAY Edwin Hawkins Singers (Buddah)
1	3	DIZZY Tommy Roe (Stateside)
7	4	TIME IS TIGHT Booker T. & the MG's (Stax)
10	5	(YOUR LOVE KEEPS LIFTING ME) HIGHER AND HIGHER Jackie Wilson (MCA)
4	6	GET BACK Beatles (Apple)
6	7	MY WAY Frank Sinatra (Reprise)
5	8	MAN OF THE WORLD Fleetwood Mac (Immediate)
8	9	THE BOXER Simon & Garfunkel (CBS)
20	10	LIVING IN THE PAST Jethro Tull (Island)
14	11	TRACKS OF MY TEARS Smokey Robinson & the Miracles (Tamla Motown)
19	12	GIMME GIMME GOOD LOVIN' Crazy Elephant (Major Minor)
11	13	LOVE ME TONIGHT Tom Jones (Decca)
21	14	BIG SHIP Cliff Richard (Columbia)
22	15	PROUD MARY Creedence Clearwater Revival (Liberty)
9	16	RAGAMUFFIN MAN Manfred Mann (Fontana)
-	17	IN THE GHETTO Elvis Presley (RCA)
17	18	I'D RATHER GO BLIND Chicken Shack (Blue Horizon)
26	19	FROZEN ORANGE JUICE Peter Sarstedt (United Artists)
18	20	DICK-A-DUM-DUM (KING'S ROAD) Des O'Connor (Columbia)
-	21	BREAK AWAY Beach Boys (Capitol)
16	22	GALVESTON Glen Campbell (Ember)
12	23	MY SENTIMENTAL FRIEND Herman's Hermits (Columbia)
13	24	BEHIND A PAINTED SMILE Isley Brothers (Tamla Motown)
28	25	TOMORROW TOMORROW Bee Gees (Polydor)
-	26	WET DREAM Max Romeo (Unity)
-	27	SOMETHING IN THE AIR Thunderclap Newman (Track)
-	28	LIGHTS OF CINCINNATI Scott Walker (Philips)
29	29	A WAY OF LIFE Family Dogg (Bell)
30	30	WHAT IS A MAN Four Tops (Tamla Motown)

28 June 1969

last	this	
1	1	THE BALLAD OF JOHN AND YOKO Beatles (Apple)
2	2	OH HAPPY DAY Edwin Hawkins Singers (Buddah)
10	3	LIVING IN THE PAST Jethro Tull (Island)
4	4	TIME IS TIGHT Booker T. & the MG's (Stax)
17	5	IN THE GHETTO Elvis Presley (RCA)
3	6	DIZZY Tommy Roe (Stateside)
27	7	SOMETHING IN THE AIR Thunderclap Newman (Track)
14	8	BIG SHIP Cliff Richard (Columbia)
5	9	(YOUR LOVE KEEPS LIFTING ME) HIGHER AND HIGHER Jackie Wilson (MCA)
6	10	GET BACK Beatles (Apple)
18	11	I'D RATHER GO BLIND Chicken Shack (Blue Horizon)
11	12	TRACKS OF MY TEARS Smokey Robinson & the Miracles (Tamla Motown)
7	13	MY WAY Frank Sinatra (Reprise)
15	14	PROUD MARY Creedence Clearwater Revival (Liberty)
29	14	A WAY OF LIFE Family Dogg (Bell)
21	16	BREAK AWAY Beach Boys (Capitol)
8	17	MAN OF THE WORLD Fleetwood Mac (Immediate)
9	18	THE BOXER Simon & Garfunkel (CBS)
19	19	FROZEN ORANGE JUICE Peter Sarstedt (United Artists)
12	20	GIMME GIMME GOOD LOVIN' Crazy Elephant (Major Minor)
28	21	LIGHTS OF CINCINNATI Scott Walker (Philips)
13	22	LOVE ME TONIGHT Tom Jones (Decca)
26	23	WET DREAM Max Romeo (Unity)
-	24	BABY MAKE IT SOON Marmalade (CBS)
22	25	GALVESTON Glen Campbell (Ember)
20	26	DICK-A-DUM-DUM (KING'S ROAD) Des O'Connor (Columbia)
-	27	HELLO SUSIE Amen Corner (Immediate)
25	28	TOMORROW TOMORROW Bee Gees (Polydor)
16	29	RAGAMUFFIN MAN Manfred Mann (Fontana)
-	30	WITHOUT HER Herb Alpert (A&M)

5 July 1969

last	this	
7	1	SOMETHING IN THE AIR Thunderclap Newman (Track)
5	2	IN THE GHETTO Elvis Presley (RCA)
1	3	THE BALLAD OF JOHN AND YOKO Beatles (Apple)
3	4	LIVING IN THE PAST Jethro Tull (Island)
2	5	OH HAPPY DAY Edwin Hawkins Singers (Buddah)
4	6	TIME IS TIGHT Booker T. & the MG's (Stax)
14	7	A WAY OF LIFE Family Dogg (Bell)
14	8	PROUD MARY Creedence Clearwater Revival (Liberty)
16	9	BREAK AWAY Beach Boys (Capitol)
6	10	DIZZY Tommy Roe (Stateside)
19	11	FROZEN ORANGE JUICE Peter Sarstedt (United Artists)
8	12	BIG SHIP Cliff Richard (Columbia)
9	13	(YOUR LOVE KEEPS LIFTING ME) HIGHER AND HIGHER Jackie Wilson (MCA)
11	14	I'D RATHER GO BLIND Chicken Shack (Blue Horizon)
27	15	HELLO SUSIE Amen Corner (Immediate)
12	16	TRACKS OF MY TEARS Smokey Robinson & the Miracles (Tamla Motown)
21	16	LIGHTS OF CINCINNATI Scott Walker (Philips)
20	18	GIMME GIMME GOOD LOVIN' Crazy Elephant (Major Minor)
-	19	WHAT IS A MAN Four Tops (Tamla Motown)
24	20	BABY MAKE IT SOON Marmalade (CBS)
10	21	GET BACK Beatles (Apple)
23	22	WET DREAM Max Romeo (Unity)
13	23	MY WAY Frank Sinatra (Reprise)
-	24	IT MEK Desmond Dekker (Pyramid)
-	25	HAPPY HEART Andy Williams (CBS)
17	26	MAN OF THE WORLD Fleetwood Mac (Immediate)
-	27	IT'S YOUR THING Isley Brothers (Major Minor)
-	28	MAKE ME AN ISLAND Joe Dolan (Pye)
22	28	LOVE ME TONIGHT Tom Jones (Decca)
30	30	WITHOUT HER Herb Alpert (A&M)

12 July 1969

last	this	
1	1	SOMETHING IN THE AIR Thunderclap Newman (Track)
2	2	IN THE GHETTO Elvis Presley (RCA)
7	3	A WAY OF LIFE Family Dogg (Bell)
4	4	LIVING IN THE PAST Jethro Tull (Island)
3	5	THE BALLAD OF JOHN AND YOKO Beatles (Apple)
15	6	HELLO SUSIE Amen Corner (Immediate)
9	6	BREAK AWAY Beach Boys (Capitol)
6	8	TIME IS TIGHT Booker T. & the MG's (Stax)
5	9	OH HAPPY DAY Edwin Hawkins Singers (Buddah)
8	10	PROUD MARY Creedence Clearwater Revival (Liberty)
11	11	FROZEN ORANGE JUICE Peter Sarstedt (United Artists)
16	12	LIGHTS OF CINCINNATI Scott Walker (Philips)
18	13	GIMME GIMME GOOD LOVIN' Crazy Elephant (Major Minor)
10	14	DIZZY Tommy Roe (Stateside)
-	15	HONKY TONK WOMEN Rolling Stones (Decca)
12	16	BIG SHIP Cliff Richard (Columbia)
20	17	BABY MAKE IT SOON Marmalade (CBS)
24	18	IT MEK Desmond Dekker (Pyramid)
-	19	THAT'S THE WAY GOD PLANNED IT Billy Preston (Apple)
14	20	I'D RATHER GO BLIND Chicken Shack (Blue Horizon)
13	21	(YOUR LOVE KEEPS LIFTING ME) HIGHER AND HIGHER Jackie Wilson (MCA)
19	22	WHAT IS A MAN Four Tops (Tamla Motown)
-	22	GIVE PEACE A CHANCE Plastic Ono Band (Apple)
16	24	TRACKS OF MY TEARS Smokey Robinson & the Miracles (Tamla Motown)
27	25	IT'S YOUR THING Isley Brothers (Major Minor)
28	26	MAKE ME AN ISLAND Joe Dolan (Pye)
22	27	WET DREAM Max Romeo (Unity)
23	27	MY WAY Frank Sinatra (Reprise)
-	29	WHEN TWO WORLDS COLLIDE Jim Reeves (RCA)
-	30	CONVERSATIONS Cilla Black (Parlophone)
-	30	SAVED BY THE BELL Robin Gibb (Polydor)

Thunderclap Newman, protegees of the Who's Pete Townshend, were an offbeat ensemble who included a teenage bass player and a mature, bearded ex-policeman pianist (Andy Newman, after whom the group was named). *Something In The Air*, like *A Whiter Shade Of Pale* two years before, somehow encapsulated the mood of its particular summer. Max Romeo's *Wet Dream* was a reggae opus of overt teenage lust (although he, very unconvincingly, denied it). Radio 1 refused even to name the record.

19 July 1969

last week	this week	Title / Artist (Label)
2	1	IN THE GHETTO — Elvis Presley (RCA)
1	2	SOMETHING IN THE AIR — Thunderclap Newman (Track)
15	3	HONKY TONK WOMEN — Rolling Stones (Decca)
6	4	HELLO SUSIE — Amen Corner (Immediate)
3	5	A WAY OF LIFE — Family Dogg (Bell)
6	6	BREAK AWAY — Beach Boys (Capitol)
22	7	GIVE PEACE A CHANCE — Plastic Ono Band (Apple)
5	8	THE BALLAD OF JOHN AND YOKO — Beatles (Apple)
19	9	THAT'S THE WAY GOD PLANNED IT — Billy Preston (Apple)
10	10	PROUD MARY — Creedence Clearwater Revival (Liberty)
4	11	LIVING IN THE PAST — Jethro Tull (Island)
18	12	IT MEK — Desmond Dekker (Pyramid)
17	13	BABY MAKE IT SOON — Marmalade (CBS)
8	14	TIME IS TIGHT — Booker T. & the MG's (Stax)
11	15	FROZEN ORANGE JUICE — Peter Sarstedt (United Artists)
13	16	GIMME GIMME GOOD LOVIN' — Crazy Elephant (Major Minor)
9	17	OH HAPPY DAY — Edwin Hawkins Singers (Buddah)
12	18	LIGHTS OF CINCINNATI — Scott Walker (Philips)
30	19	SAVED BY THE BELL — Robin Gibb (Polydor)
22	20	WHAT IS A MAN — Four Tops (Tamla Motown)
27	21	WET DREAM — Max Romeo (Unity)
14	22	DIZZY — Tommy Roe (Stateside)
16	23	BIG SHIP — Cliff Richard (Columbia)
30	24	CONVERSATIONS — Cilla Black (Parlophone)
25	25	IT'S YOUR THING — Isley Brothers (Major Minor)
-	26	GOODNIGHT MIDNIGHT — Clodagh Rodgers (RCA)
26	27	MAKE ME AN ISLAND — Joe Dolan (Pye)
29	28	WHEN TWO WORLDS COLLIDE — Jim Reeves (RCA)
-	29	BARABAJAGAL (LOVE IS HOT) — Donovan & the Jeff Beck Group (Pye)
-	30	MY CHERIE AMOUR — Stevie Wonder (Tamla Motown)

26 July 1969

last week	this week	Title / Artist (Label)
3	1	HONKY TONK WOMEN — Rolling Stones (Decca)
1	2	IN THE GHETTO — Elvis Presley (RCA)
7	3	GIVE PEACE A CHANCE — Plastic Ono Band (Apple)
2	4	SOMETHING IN THE AIR — Thunderclap Newman (Track)
4	5	HELLO SUSIE — Amen Corner (Immediate)
9	6	THAT'S THE WAY GOD PLANNED IT — Billy Preston (Apple)
19	7	SAVED BY THE BELL — Robin Gibb (Polydor)
5	8	A WAY OF LIFE — Family Dogg (Bell)
12	9	IT MEK — Desmond Dekker (Pyramid)
13	10	BABY MAKE IT SOON — Marmalade (CBS)
6	11	BREAK AWAY — Beach Boys (Capitol)
10	12	PROUD MARY — Creedence Clearwater Revival (Liberty)
8	13	THE BALLAD OF JOHN AND YOKO — Beatles (Apple)
18	14	LIGHTS OF CINCINNATI — Scott Walker (Philips)
11	15	LIVING IN THE PAST — Jethro Tull (Island)
26	16	GOODNIGHT MIDNIGHT — Clodagh Rodgers (RCA)
16	17	GIMME GIMME GOOD LOVIN' — Crazy Elephant (Major Minor)
14	18	TIME IS TIGHT — Booker T. & the MG's (Stax)
27	18	MAKE ME AN ISLAND — Joe Dolan (Pye)
24	20	CONVERSATIONS — Cilla Black (Parlophone)
15	21	FROZEN ORANGE JUICE — Peter Sarstedt (United Artists)
30	22	MY CHERIE AMOUR — Stevie Wonder (Tamla Motown)
28	23	WHEN TWO WORLDS COLLIDE — Jim Reeves (RCA)
21	24	WET DREAM — Max Romeo (Unity)
-	25	I CAN SING A RAINBOW/LOVE IS BLUE — Dells (Chess)
17	26	OH HAPPY DAY — Edwin Hawkins Singers (Buddah)
29	27	BARABAJAGAL (LOVE IS HOT) — Donovan & the Jeff Beck Group (Pye)
20	28	WHAT IS A MAN — Four Tops (Tamla Motown)
25	29	IT'S YOUR THING — Isley Brothers (Major Minor)
-	30	BRINGING ON BACK THE GOOD TIMES — Love Affair (CBS)

2 August 1969

last week	this week	Title / Artist (Label)
1	1	HONKY TONK WOMEN — Rolling Stones (Decca)
3	2	GIVE PEACE A CHANCE — Plastic Ono Band (Apple)
2	3	IN THE GHETTO — Elvis Presley (RCA)
7	4	SAVED BY THE BELL — Robin Gibb (Polydor)
4	5	SOMETHING IN THE AIR — Thunderclap Newman (Track)
16	6	GOODNIGHT MIDNIGHT — Clodagh Rodgers (RCA)
5	7	HELLO SUSIE — Amen Corner (Immediate)
6	8	THAT'S THE WAY GOD PLANNED IT — Billy Preston (Apple)
10	9	BABY MAKE IT SOON — Marmalade (CBS)
9	10	IT MEK — Desmond Dekker (Pyramid)
18	11	MAKE ME AN ISLAND — Joe Dolan (Pye)
8	12	A WAY OF LIFE — Family Dogg (Bell)
11	13	BREAK AWAY — Beach Boys (Capitol)
22	14	MY CHERIE AMOUR — Stevie Wonder (Tamla Motown)
20	15	CONVERSATIONS — Cilla Black (Parlophone)
13	16	THE BALLAD OF JOHN AND YOKO — Beatles (Apple)
12	17	PROUD MARY — Creedence Clearwater Revival (Liberty)
27	18	BARABAJAGAL (LOVE IS HOT) — Donovan & the Jeff Beck Group (Pye)
25	19	I CAN SING A RAINBOW/LOVE IS BLUE — Dells (Chess)
30	20	BRINGING ON BACK THE GOOD TIMES — Love Affair (CBS)
17	21	GIMME GIMME GOOD LOVIN' — Crazy Elephant (Major Minor)
24	22	WET DREAM — Max Romeo (Unity)
18	23	TIME IS TIGHT — Booker T. & the MG's (Stax)
-	24	EARLY IN THE MORNING — Vanity Fare (Page One)
14	25	LIGHTS OF CINCINNATI — Scott Walker (Philips)
-	26	TOO BUSY THINKING ABOUT MY BABY — Marvin Gaye (Tamla Motown)
23	27	WHEN TWO WORLDS COLLIDE — Jim Reeves (RCA)
15	28	LIVING IN THE PAST — Jethro Tull (Island)
-	29	PEACEFUL — Georgie Fame (CBS)
-	30	CURLY — Move (Regal Zonophone)

9 August 1969

last week	this week	Title / Artist (Label)
1	1	HONKY TONK WOMEN — Rolling Stones (Decca)
4	2	SAVED BY THE BELL — Robin Gibb (Polydor)
2	3	GIVE PEACE A CHANCE — Plastic Ono Band (Apple)
3	4	IN THE GHETTO — Elvis Presley (RCA)
6	5	GOODNIGHT MIDNIGHT — Clodagh Rodgers (RCA)
11	6	MAKE ME AN ISLAND — Joe Dolan (Pye)
14	7	MY CHERIE AMOUR — Stevie Wonder (Tamla Motown)
10	8	IT MEK — Desmond Dekker (Pyramid)
8	9	THAT'S THE WAY GOD PLANNED IT — Billy Preston (Apple)
9	10	BABY MAKE IT SOON — Marmalade (CBS)
5	11	SOMETHING IN THE AIR — Thunderclap Newman (Track)
15	12	CONVERSATIONS — Cilla Black (Parlophone)
7	13	HELLO SUSIE — Amen Corner (Immediate)
18	14	BARABAJAGAL (LOVE IS HOT) — Donovan & the Jeff Beck Group (Pye)
19	15	I CAN SING A RAINBOW/LOVE IS BLUE — Dells (Chess)
24	16	EARLY IN THE MORNING — Vanity Fare (Page One)
20	17	BRINGING ON BACK THE GOOD TIMES — Love Affair (CBS)
12	18	A WAY OF LIFE — Family Dogg (Bell)
22	19	WET DREAM — Max Romeo (Unity)
26	20	TOO BUSY THINKING ABOUT MY BABY — Marvin Gaye (Tamla Motown)
27	21	WHEN TWO WORLDS COLLIDE — Jim Reeves (RCA)
29	22	PEACEFUL — Georgie Fame (CBS)
13	23	BREAK AWAY — Beach Boys (Capitol)
30	24	CURLY — Move (Regal Zonophone)
16	25	THE BALLAD OF JOHN AND YOKO — Beatles (Apple)
-	26	HEATHER HONEY — Tommy Roe (Stateside)
-	27	IN THE YEAR 2525 — Zager & Evans (RCA)
-	28	VIVA BOBBY JOE — Equals (President)
-	29	I'M A BETTER MAN — Engelbert Humperdinck (Decca)
-	30	THUS SPAKE ZARATHUSTRA — Philharmonia Orchestra (Columbia)

Elvis scored his first chart-topper for four years with *In The Ghetto*, a strong social conscience song taken from his critically-rated *From Elvis In Memphis* album, cut in his home town earlier in the year. John Lennon's first Plastic Ono Band opus was recorded in virtually open session in a Toronto hotel room, while Stevie Wonder's *My Cherie Amour* was notable in being the B-side of his previous chart entry *I Don't Know Why*, now re-promoted in its own right following wide airplay in the US.

August – September 1969

Possibly the oddest Number One lyric ever was Zager & Evans' *In The Year 2525*, a millenia-spanning yarn predicting mankind's future until such time as the Almighty decided enough was enough. Like most unconventional records, this one was almost equally adored and loathed. The French language made its chart presence felt on Fairport convention's single, which was a Gallic translation of Dylan's *If You Gotta Go, Go Now*, and on the extremely sensuous *Je T'Aime*, by real-life lovers Birkin and Gainsbourg.

September – October 1969

13 September 1969

last week	this week	
1	1	IN THE YEAR 2525 Zager & Evans (RCA)
8	2	BAD MOON RISING Creedence Clearwater Revival (Liberty)
6	3	DON'T FORGET TO REMEMBER Bee Gees (Polydor)
3	4	TOO BUSY THINKING ABOUT MY BABY Marvin Gaye (Tamla Motown)
12	5	JE T'AIME Jane Birkin & Serge Gainsbourg (Fontana)
7	6	VIVA BOBBY JOE Equals (President)
5	7	MY CHERIE AMOUR Stevie Wonder (Tamla Motown)
10	8	NATURAL BORN BUGIE Humble Pie (Immediate)
3	9	HONKY TONK WOMEN Rolling Stones (Decca)
2	10	SAVED BY THE BELL Robin Gibb (Polydor)
14	11	GOOD MORNING STARSHINE Oliver (CBS)
11	12	EARLY IN THE MORNING Vanity Fare (Page One)
9	13	MAKE ME AN ISLAND Joe Dolan (Pye)
13	14	CURLY Move (Regal Zonophone)
24	15	I'LL NEVER FALL IN LOVE AGAIN Bobbie Gentry (Capitol)
15	16	BRINGING ON BACK THE GOOD TIMES Love Affair (CBS)
20	17	CLOUD NINE Temptations (Tamla Motown)
17	18	WET DREAM Max Romeo (Unity)
26	19	CLEAN UP YOUR OWN BACKYARD Elvis Presley (RCA)
-	20	BIRTH Peddlers (CBS)
18	21	SI TU DOIS PARTIR Fairport Convention (Island)
16	22	CONVERSATIONS Cilla Black (Parlophone)
25	23	I'M A BETTER MAN Engelbert Humperdinck (Decca)
29	24	PUT YOURSELF IN MY PLACE Isley Brothers (Tamla Motown)
-	25	TEARS IN THE WIND Chicken Shack (Blue Horizon)
27	26	MARRAKESH EXPRESS Crosby Stills & Nash (Atlantic)
30	27	IT'S GETTING BETTER Mama Cass (Stateside)
19	28	GIVE PEACE A CHANCE Plastic Ono Band (Apple)
27	29	SOUL CLAP '69 Booker T. & the MG's (Stax)
-	30	THROW DOWN A LINE Cliff Richard & Hank Marvin (Columbia)

20 September 1969

last week	this week	
2	1	BAD MOON RISING Creedence Clearwater Revival (Liberty)
3	2	DON'T FORGET TO REMEMBER Bee Gees (Polydor)
1	3	IN THE YEAR 2525 Zager & Evans (RCA)
5	4	JE T'AIME Jane Birkin & Serge Gainsbourg (Fontana)
8	5	NATURAL BORN BUGIE Humble Pie (Immediate)
4	6	TOO BUSY THINKING ABOUT MY BABY Marvin Gaye (Tamla Motown)
6	7	VIVA BOBBY JOE Equals (President)
7	8	MY CHERIE AMOUR Stevie Wonder (Tamla Motown)
11	9	GOOD MORNING STARSHINE Oliver (CBS)
15	10	I'LL NEVER FALL IN LOVE AGAIN Bobbie Gentry (Capitol)
9	11	HONKY TONK WOMEN Rolling Stones (Decca)
10	12	SAVED BY THE BELL Robin Gibb (Polydor)
17	13	CLOUD NINE Temptations (Tamla Motown)
14	14	CURLY Move (Regal Zonophone)
26	15	MARRAKESH EXPRESS Crosby Stills & Nash (Atlantic)
13	16	MAKE ME AN ISLAND Joe Dolan (Pye)
30	17	THROW DOWN A LINE Cliff Richard & Hank Marvin (Columbia)
20	18	BIRTH Peddlers (CBS)
24	19	PUT YOURSELF IN MY PLACE Isley Brothers (Tamla Motown)
27	19	IT'S GETTING BETTER Mama Cass (Stateside)
23	21	I'M A BETTER MAN Engelbert Humperdinck (Decca)
19	22	CLEAN UP YOUR OWN BACKYARD Elvis Presley (RCA)
12	23	EARLY IN THE MORNING Vanity Fare (Page One)
-	24	LAY LADY LAY Bob Dylan (CBS)
18	25	WET DREAM Max Romeo (Unity)
-	26	I'M GONNA MAKE YOU MINE Lou Christie (Buddah)
-	27	A BOY NAMED SUE Johnny Cash (CBS)
-	28	HARE KRISHNA MANTRA Radha Krishna Temple (Apple)
-	29	25 MILES Edwin Starr (Tamla Motown)
-	30	SOUL DEEP Box Tops (Bell)

27 September 1969

last week	this week	
1	1	BAD MOON RISING Creedence Clearwater Revival (Liberty)
4	2	JE T'AIME Jane Birkin & Serge Gainsbourg (Fontana/Major Minor)
2	3	DON'T FORGET TO REMEMBER Bee Gees (Polydor)
10	4	I'LL NEVER FALL IN LOVE AGAIN Bobbie Gentry (Capitol)
5	5	NATURAL BORN BUGIE Humble Pie (Immediate)
3	6	IN THE YEAR 2525 Zager & Evans (RCA)
6	7	TOO BUSY THINKING ABOUT MY BABY Marvin Gaye (Tamla Motown)
9	8	GOOD MORNING STARSHINE Oliver (CBS)
7	9	VIVA BOBBY JOE Equals (President)
27	10	A BOY NAMED SUE Johnny Cash (CBS)
17	11	THROW DOWN A LINE Cliff Richard & Hank Marvin (Columbia)
28	12	HARE KRISHNA MANTRA Radha Krishna Temple (Apple)
8	13	MY CHERIE AMOUR Stevie Wonder (Tamla Motown)
19	14	IT'S GETTING BETTER Mama Cass (Stateside)
11	15	HONKY TONK WOMEN Rolling Stones (Decca)
19	16	PUT YOURSELF IN MY PLACE Isley Brothers (Tamla Motown)
18	17	BIRTH Peddlers (CBS)
12	18	SAVED BY THE BELL Robin Gibb (Polydor)
16	19	MAKE ME AN ISLAND Joe Dolan (Pye)
13	19	CLOUD NINE Temptations (Tamla Motown)
26	21	I'M GONNA MAKE YOU MINE Lou Christie (Buddah)
15	22	MARRAKESH EXPRESS Crosby Stills & Nash (Atlantic)
30	23	SOUL DEEP Box Tops (Bell)
25	24	WET DREAM Max Romeo (Unity)
24	25	LAY LADY LAY Bob Dylan (CBS)
-	26	LOVE AT FIRST SIGHT Sounds Nice (Parlophone)
-	27	I SECOND THAT EMOTION Diana Ross & the Supremes the Temptations (Tamla Motown)
22	28	CLEAN UP YOUR OWN BACKYARD Elvis Presley (RCA)
23	29	EARLY IN THE MORNING Vanity Fare (Page One)
14	30	CURLY Move (Regal Zonophone)

4 October 1969

last week	this week	
1	1	BAD MOON RISING Creedence Clearwater Revival (Liberty)
2	2	JE T'AIME Jane Birkin & Serge Gainsbourg (Fontana/Major Minor)
4	3	I'LL NEVER FALL IN LOVE AGAIN Bobbie Gentry (Capitol)
3	4	DON'T FORGET TO REMEMBER Bee Gees (Polydor)
10	5	A BOY NAMED SUE Johnny Cash (CBS)
7	6	TOO BUSY THINKING ABOUT MY BABY Marvin Gaye (Tamla Motown)
11	7	THROW DOWN A LINE Cliff Richard & Hank Marvin (Columbia)
8	8	GOOD MORNING STARSHINE Oliver (CBS)
5	9	NATURAL BORN BUGIE Humble Pie (Immediate)
6	10	IN THE YEAR 2525 Zager & Evans (RCA)
14	11	IT'S GETTING BETTER Mama Cass (Stateside)
25	12	LAY LADY LAY Bob Dylan (CBS)
9	13	VIVA BOBBY JOE Equals (President)
16	14	PUT YOURSELF IN MY PLACE Isley Brothers (Tamla Motown)
12	15	HARE KRISHNA MANTRA Radha Krishna Temple (Apple)
20	16	CLOUD NINE Temptations (Tamla Motown)
21	17	I'M GONNA MAKE YOU MINE Lou Christie (Buddah)
27	17	I SECOND THAT EMOTION Diana Ross & the Supremes the Temptations (Tamla Motown)
-	19	NOBODY'S CHILD Karen Young (Major Minor)
23	20	SOUL DEEP Box Tops (Bell)
13	21	MY CHERIE AMOUR Stevie Wonder (Tamla Motown)
22	22	MARRAKESH EXPRESS Crosby Stills & Nash (Atlantic)
17	23	BIRTH Peddlers (CBS)
18	24	SAVED BY THE BELL Robin Gibb (Polydor)
-	25	DO WHAT YOU GOTTA DO Four Tops (Tamla Motown)
15	26	HONKY TONK WOMEN Rolling Stones (Decca)
-	27	SPACE ODDITY David Bowie (Philips)
28	28	CLEAN UP YOUR OWN BACKYARD Elvis Presley (RCA)
24	29	WET DREAM Max Romeo (Unity)
26	30	LOVE AT FIRST SIGHT Sounds Nice (Parlophone)
-	30	AM I THE SAME GIRL Dusty Springfield (Philips)

When the BBC refused to play *Je T'Aime*, the Fontana label, which had released the single, got cold feet and decided to withdraw it. At this, the opportunistic independent Major Minor acquired the rights and simultaneously reissued it, thus not stalling the record's chart progress at all - in fact, for a week or so, most dealers had stocks of both releases on their shelves. Bob Dylan's *Lay Lady Lay*, meanwhile was written to order for (but eventually turned down by) the hit film *Midnight Cowboy*.

October – November 1969

11 October 1969
(last week / this week / title)

3 1 I'LL NEVER FALL IN LOVE AGAIN Bobbie Gentry (Capitol)
1 2 BAD MOON RISING Creedence Clearwater Revival (Liberty)
2 3 JE T'AIME Jane Birkin & Serge Gainsbourg (Fontana/Major Minor)
5 4 A BOY NAMED SUE Johnny Cash (CBS)
12 5 LAY LADY LAY Bob Dylan (CBS)
4 6 DON'T FORGET TO REMEMBER Bee Gees (Polydor)
7 7 THROW DOWN A LINE Cliff Richard & Hank Marvin (Columbia)
8 8 GOOD MORNING STARSHINE Mama Cass (Stateside)
11 9 IT'S GETTING BETTER
19 10 NOBODY'S CHILD Karen Young (Major Minor)
17 11 I'M GONNA MAKE YOU MINE Lou Christie (Buddah)
15 11 HARE KRISHNA MANTRA Radha Krishna Temple (Apple)
6 13 TOO BUSY THINKING ABOUT MY BABY Marvin Gaye (Tamla Motown)
10 14 IN THE YEAR 2525 Zager & Evans (RCA)
14 15 PUT YOURSELF IN MY PLACE Isley Brothers (Tamla Motown)
9 16 NATURAL BORN BUGIE Humble Pie (Immediate)
17 17 I SECOND THAT EMOTION Diana Ross & the Supremes the Temptations (Tamla Motown)
27 18 SPACE ODDITY David Bowie (Philips)
30 19 LOVE AT FIRST SIGHT Sounds Nice (Parlophone)
25 20 DO WHAT YOU GOTTA DO Four Tops (Tamla Motown)
- 20 HE AIN'T HEAVY - HE'S MY BROTHER Hollies (Parlophone)
- 22 OH WELL Fleetwood Mac (Reprise)
13 23 VIVA BOBBY JOE Equals (President)
16 24 CLOUD NINE Temptations (Tamla Motown)
30 25 AM I THE SAME GIRL Dusty Springfield (Philips)
20 26 SOUL DEEP Box Tops (Bell)
23 26 BIRTH Peddlers (CBS)
- 28 SUGAR SUGAR Archies (RCA)
- 29 EVERYBODY'S TALKIN' Nilsson (RCA)
24 30 SAVED BY THE BELL Robin Gibb (Polydor)

18 October 1969

1 1 I'LL NEVER FALL IN LOVE AGAIN Bobbie Gentry (Capitol)
3 2 JE T'AIME Jane Birkin & Serge Gainsbourg (Fontana/Major Minor)
4 3 A BOY NAMED SUE Johnny Cash (CBS)
5 4 LAY LADY LAY Bob Dylan (CBS)
2 5 BAD MOON RISING Creedence Clearwater Revival (Liberty)
11 6 I'M GONNA MAKE YOU MINE Lou Christie (Buddah)
20 7 HE AIN'T HEAVY - HE'S MY BROTHER Hollies (Parlophone)
10 8 NOBODY'S CHILD Karen Young (Major Minor)
18 9 SPACE ODDITY David Bowie (Philips)
7 10 THROW DOWN A LINE Cliff Richard & Hank Marvin (Columbia)
9 11 IT'S GETTING BETTER Mama Cass (Stateside)
22 12 OH WELL Fleetwood Mac (Reprise)
8 13 GOOD MORNING STARSHINE Oliver (CBS)
28 14 SUGAR SUGAR Archies (RCA)
6 15 DON'T FORGET TO REMEMBER Bee Gees (Polydor)
11 16 HARE KRISHNA MANTRA Radha Krishna Temple (Apple)
17 17 DO WHAT YOU GOTTA DO Four Tops (Tamla Motown)
15 18 PUT YOURSELF IN MY PLACE Isley Brothers (Tamla Motown)
29 19 EVERYBODY'S TALKIN' Nilsson (RCA)
19 20 LOVE AT FIRST SIGHT Sounds Nice (Parlophone)
17 21 I SECOND THAT EMOTION Diana Ross & the Supremes the Temptations (Tamla Motown)
13 22 TOO BUSY THINKING ABOUT MY BABY Marvin Gaye (Tamla Motown)
- 23 LOVE'S BEEN GOOD TO ME Frank Sinatra (Reprise)
14 24 IN THE YEAR 2525 Zager & Evans (RCA)
16 25 NATURAL BORN BUGIE Humble Pie (Immediate)
24 26 CLOUD NINE Temptations (Tamla Motown)
- 27 GOLDEN SLUMBERS/CARRY THAT WEIGHT White Trash (Apple)
- 28 THE HUNT Barry Ryan (Polydor)
25 29 AM I THE SAME GIRL Dusty Springfield (Philips)
- 30 PENNY ARCADE Roy Orbison (London)

25 October 1969

1 1 I'LL NEVER FALL IN LOVE AGAIN Bobbie Gentry (Capitol)
6 2 I'M GONNA MAKE YOU MINE Lou Christie (Buddah)
7 3 HE AIN'T HEAVY - HE'S MY BROTHER Hollies (Parlophone)
14 4 SUGAR SUGAR Archies (RCA)
2 5 JE T'AIME Jane Birkin & Serge Gainsbourg (Major Minor)
3 6 A BOY NAMED SUE Johnny Cash (CBS)
9 7 SPACE ODDITY David Bowie (Philips)
4 8 LAY LADY LAY Bob Dylan (CBS)
12 9 OH WELL Fleetwood Mac (Reprise)
8 10 NOBODY'S CHILD Karen Young (Major Minor)
5 11 BAD MOON RISING Creedence Clearwater Revival (Liberty)
11 12 IT'S GETTING BETTER Mama Cass (Stateside)
13 13 GOOD MORNING STARSHINE Oliver (CBS)
17 14 DO WHAT YOU GOTTA DO Four Tops (Tamla Motown)
- 15 RETURN OF DJANGO Upsetters (Upsetter)
20 16 LOVE AT FIRST SIGHT Sounds Nice (Parlophone)
23 17 LOVE'S BEEN GOOD TO ME Frank Sinatra (Reprise)
10 18 THROW DOWN A LINE Cliff Richard & Hank Marvin (Columbia)
19 19 EVERYBODY'S TALKIN' Nilsson (RCA)
15 20 DON'T FORGET TO REMEMBER Bee Gees (Polydor)
16 21 HARE KRISHNA MANTRA Radha Krishna Temple (Apple)
- 22 AND THE SUN WILL SHINE Jose Feliciano (RCA)
- 23 DELTA LADY Joe Cocker (Regal Zonophone)
18 24 PUT YOURSELF IN MY PLACE Isley Brothers (Tamla Motown)
21 25 I SECOND THAT EMOTION Diana Ross & the Supremes the Temptations (Tamla Motown)
22 26 TOO BUSY THINKING ABOUT MY BABY Marvin Gaye (Tamla Motown)
27 27 WHAT DOES IT TAKE Jr. Walker & the All Stars (Tamla Motown)
30 28 PENNY ARCADE Roy Orbison (London)
28 29 THE HUNT Barry Ryan (Polydor)
- 30 SOUL DEEP Box Tops (Bell)
27 30 GOLDEN SLUMBERS/CARRY THAT WEIGHT White Trash (Apple)

1 November 1969

4 1 SUGAR SUGAR Archies (RCA)
3 2 HE AIN'T HEAVY - HE'S MY BROTHER Hollies (Parlophone)
2 3 I'M GONNA MAKE YOU MINE Lou Christie (Buddah)
1 4 I'LL NEVER FALL IN LOVE AGAIN Bobbie Gentry (Capitol)
9 5 OH WELL Fleetwood Mac (Reprise)
7 6 SPACE ODDITY David Bowie (Philips)
5 7 JE T'AIME Jane Birkin & Serge Gainsbourg (Major Minor)
10 8 NOBODY'S CHILD Karen Young (Major Minor)
6 9 A BOY NAMED SUE Johnny Cash (CBS)
17 10 LOVE'S BEEN GOOD TO ME Frank Sinatra (Reprise)
14 11 DO WHAT YOU GOTTA DO Four Tops (Tamla Motown)
15 12 RETURN OF DJANGO Upsetters (Upsetter)
8 13 LAY LADY LAY Bob Dylan (CBS)
23 14 DELTA LADY Joe Cocker (Regal Zonophone)
11 15 BAD MOON RISING Creedence Clearwater Revival (Liberty)
12 16 IT'S GETTING BETTER Mama Cass (Stateside)
19 17 EVERYBODY'S TALKIN' Nilsson (RCA)
27 18 WHAT DOES IT TAKE Jr. Walker & the All Stars (Tamla Motown)
13 19 GOOD MORNING STARSHINE Oliver (CBS)
- 20 WONDERFUL WORLD, BEAUTIFUL PEOPLE Jimmy Cliff (Trojan)
16 21 LOVE AT FIRST SIGHT Sounds Nice (Parlophone)
20 22 DON'T FORGET TO REMEMBER Bee Gees (Polydor)
- 23 THE LIQUIDATOR Harry J. All Stars (Trojan)
- 24 LONG SHOT KICK THE BUCKET Pioneers (Trojan)
22 25 AND THE SUN WILL SHINE Jose Feliciano (RCA)
18 26 THROW DOWN A LINE Cliff Richard & Hank Marvin (Columbia)
- 27 SWEET DREAM Jethro Tull (Chrysalis)
24 28 PUT YOURSELF IN MY PLACE Isley Brothers (Tamla Motown)
28 28 PENNY ARCADE Roy Orbison (London)
- 30 GIN GAN GOOLIE Scaffold (Parlophone)

Bobbie Gentry's *I'll Never Fall In Love Again* was a Bacharach/David song from their musical *Promises, Promises*, and not the same song as Tom Jones' identically-titled Number Two hit of two years previously (which was written by Lonnie Donegan) - although, coincidentally, Jones was having a belated US top-tenner with his record at this very time, while Gentry's single was not a hit in her homeland. Oh - and neither of these songs was the same as Johnnie Ray's late 1959 hit *I'll Never Fall In Love Again*!

214

8 November 1969

last week	this week	
1	1	SUGAR SUGAR Archies (RCA)
5	2	OH WELL Fleetwood Mac (Reprise)
2	3	HE AIN'T HEAVY - HE'S MY BROTHER Hollies (Parlophone)
3	4	I'M GONNA MAKE YOU MINE Lou Christie (Buddah)
12	5	RETURN OF DJANGO Upsetters (Upsetter)
6	6	SPACE ODDITY David Bowie (Philips)
4	7	I'LL NEVER FALL IN LOVE AGAIN Bobbie Gentry (Capitol)
14	8	DELTA LADY Joe Cocker (Regal Zonophone)
8	9	NOBODY'S CHILD Karen Young (Major Minor)
9	10	A BOY NAMED SUE Johnny Cash (CBS)
7	11	JE T'AIME Jane Birkin & Serge Gainsbourg (Major Minor)
11	12	DO WHAT YOU GOTTA DO Four Tops (Tamla Motown)
10	13	LOVE'S BEEN GOOD TO ME Frank Sinatra (Reprise)
13	14	LAY LADY LAY Bob Dylan (CBS)
20	15	WONDERFUL WORLD, BEAUTIFUL PEOPLE Jimmy Cliff (Trojan)
18	16	WHAT DOES IT TAKE Jr. Walker & the All Stars (Tamla Motown)
-	17	SOMETHING/COME TOGETHER Beatles (Apple)
-	18	(CALL ME) NUMBER ONE Tremeloes (CBS)
17	19	EVERYBODY'S TALKIN' Nilsson (RCA)
16	20	IT'S GETTING BETTER Mama Cass (Stateside)
27	21	SWEET DREAM Jethro Tull (Chrysalis)
15	22	BAD MOON RISING Creedence Clearwater Revival (Liberty)
-	23	COLD TURKEY Plastic Ono Band (Apple)
23	24	THE LIQUIDATOR Harry J. All Stars (Trojan)
24	25	LONG SHOT KICK THE BUCKET Pioneers (Trojan)
19	26	GOOD MORNING STARSHINE Oliver (CBS)
-	27	TERESA Joe Dolan (Pye)
21	28	LOVE AT FIRST SIGHT Sounds Nice (Parlophone)
25	29	AND THE SUN WILL SHINE Jose Feliciano (RCA)
-	30	I MISS YOU BABY Marvin Johnson (Tamla Motown)
-		RUBY DON'T TAKE YOUR LOVE TO TOWN Kenny Rogers & the First Edition (Reprise)

15 November 1969

last week	this week	
2	1	OH WELL Fleetwood Mac (Reprise)
1	2	SUGAR SUGAR Archies (RCA)
3	3	HE AIN'T HEAVY - HE'S MY BROTHER Hollies (Parlophone)
5	4	RETURN OF DJANGO Upsetters (Upsetter)
4	5	I'M GONNA MAKE YOU MINE Lou Christie (Buddah)
18	6	(CALL ME) NUMBER ONE Tremeloes (CBS)
8	7	DELTA LADY Joe Cocker (Regal Zonophone)
15	8	WONDERFUL WORLD, BEAUTIFUL PEOPLE Jimmy Cliff (Trojan)
13	9	LOVE'S BEEN GOOD TO ME Frank Sinatra (Reprise)
17	10	SOMETHING/COME TOGETHER Beatles (Apple)
9	11	NOBODY'S CHILD Karen Young (Major Minor)
6	12	SPACE ODDITY David Bowie (Philips)
21	13	SWEET DREAM Jethro Tull (Chrysalis)
16	14	WHAT DOES IT TAKE Jr. Walker & the All Stars (Tamla Motown)
10	15	A BOY NAMED SUE Johnny Cash (CBS)
23	16	COLD TURKEY Plastic Ono Band (Apple)
7	17	I'LL NEVER FALL IN LOVE AGAIN Bobbie Gentry (Capitol)
12	18	DO WHAT YOU GOTTA DO Four Tops (Tamla Motown)
27	19	TERESA Joe Dolan (Pye)
30	20	RUBY DON'T TAKE YOUR LOVE TO TOWN Kenny Rogers & the First Edition (Reprise)
11	21	JE T'AIME Jane Birkin & Serge Gainsbourg (Major Minor)
25	22	LONG SHOT KICK THE BUCKET Pioneers (Trojan)
19	23	EVERYBODY'S TALKIN' Nilsson (RCA)
30	24	I MISS YOU BABY Marvin Johnson (Tamla Motown)
24	25	THE LIQUIDATOR Harry J. All Stars (Trojan)
-	26	GREEN RIVER Creedence Clearwater Revival (Liberty)
14	27	LAY LADY LAY Bob Dylan (CBS)
29	28	AND THE SUN WILL SHINE Jose Feliciano (RCA)
-	28	BILJO Clodagh Rodgers (RCA)
-	30	YESTER-ME, YESTER-YOU, YESTERDAY Stevie Wonder (Tamla Motown)

22 November 1969

last week	this week	
2	1	SUGAR SUGAR Archies (RCA)
1	2	OH WELL Fleetwood Mac (Reprise)
6	3	(CALL ME) NUMBER ONE Tremeloes (CBS)
4	4	RETURN OF DJANGO Upsetters (Upsetter)
10	5	SOMETHING/COME TOGETHER Beatles (Apple)
8	6	WONDERFUL WORLD, BEAUTIFUL PEOPLE Jimmy Cliff (Trojan)
3	7	HE AIN'T HEAVY - HE'S MY BROTHER Hollies (Parlophone)
13	8	SWEET DREAM Jethro Tull (Chrysalis)
14	9	WHAT DOES IT TAKE Jr. Walker & the All Stars (Tamla Motown)
9	10	LOVE'S BEEN GOOD TO ME Frank Sinatra (Reprise)
20	11	RUBY DON'T TAKE YOUR LOVE TO TOWN Kenny Rogers & the First Edition (Reprise)
7	12	DELTA LADY Joe Cocker (Regal Zonophone)
16	13	COLD TURKEY Plastic Ono Band (Apple)
30	14	YESTER-ME, YESTER-YOU, YESTERDAY Stevie Wonder (Tamla Motown)
11	15	NOBODY'S CHILD Karen Young (Major Minor)
5	16	I'M GONNA MAKE YOU MINE Lou Christie (Buddah)
25	17	THE LIQUIDATOR Harry J. All Stars (Trojan)
28	18	BILJO Clodagh Rodgers (RCA)
19	19	TERESA Joe Dolan (Pye)
22	20	LONG SHOT KICK THE BUCKET Pioneers (Trojan)
12	21	SPACE ODDITY David Bowie (Philips)
26	22	GREEN RIVER Creedence Clearwater Revival (Liberty)
18	23	DO WHAT YOU GOTTA DO Four Tops (Tamla Motown)
24	24	I MISS YOU BABY Marvin Johnson (Tamla Motown)
-	25	WINTER WORLD OF LOVE Engelbert Humperdinck (Decca)
-	26	THE ONION SONG Marvin Gaye & Tammi Terrell (Tamla Motown)
-	27	MELTING POT Blue Mink (Philips)
-	28	PROUD MARY Checkmates Ltd. (A&M)
15	29	A BOY NAMED SUE Johnny Cash (CBS)
-	30	NO MULES FOOL Family (Reprise)

29 November 1969

last week	this week	
1	1	SUGAR SUGAR Archies (RCA)
3	2	(CALL ME) NUMBER ONE Tremeloes (CBS)
2	3	OH WELL Fleetwood Mac (Reprise)
14	4	YESTER-ME, YESTER-YOU, YESTERDAY Stevie Wonder (Tamla Motown)
5	5	SOMETHING/COME TOGETHER Beatles (Apple)
4	6	RETURN OF DJANGO Upsetters (Upsetter)
6	7	WONDERFUL WORLD, BEAUTIFUL PEOPLE Jimmy Cliff (Trojan)
11	8	RUBY DON'T TAKE YOUR LOVE TO TOWN Kenny Rogers & the First Edition (Reprise)
8	9	SWEET DREAM Jethro Tull (Chrysalis)
9	10	WHAT DOES IT TAKE Jr. Walker & the All Stars (Tamla Motown)
10	11	LOVE'S BEEN GOOD TO ME Frank Sinatra (Reprise)
25	12	WINTER WORLD OF LOVE Engelbert Humperdinck (Decca)
7	13	HE AIN'T HEAVY - HE'S MY BROTHER Hollies (Parlophone)
27	14	MELTING POT Blue Mink (Philips)
17	15	THE LIQUIDATOR Harry J. All Stars (Trojan)
18	16	BILJO Clodagh Rodgers (RCA)
13	17	COLD TURKEY Plastic Ono Band (Apple)
12	18	DELTA LADY Joe Cocker (Regal Zonophone)
22	19	GREEN RIVER Creedence Clearwater Revival (Liberty)
15	20	NOBODY'S CHILD Karen Young (Major Minor)
19	21	TERESA Joe Dolan (Pye)
26	22	THE ONION SONG Marvin Gaye & Tammi Terrell (Tamla Motown)
-	23	TWO LITTLE BOYS Rolf Harris (Columbia)
16	24	I'M GONNA MAKE YOU MINE Lou Christie (Buddah)
20	25	LONG SHOT KICK THE BUCKET Pioneers (Trojan)
24	26	I MISS YOU BABY Marvin Johnson (Tamla Motown)
-	27	LEAVIN' (DURHAM TOWN) Roger Whittaker (Columbia)
-	28	SUSPICIOUS MINDS Elvis Presley (RCA)
29	29	LOVE IS ALL Malcolm Roberts (Major Minor)
30	30	LONELINESS Des O'Connor (Columbia)

The Archies were that rare breed of Number One hitmaker - the group that doesn't exist. A musical spin-off from the Archie comic book in the States, developed by Don Kirshner, the man who had originally been behind the Monkees, they had a run of hits in the US, though *Sugar Sugar* was the one big international success - it sold not far short of a million copies in the UK alone. The group heard on the record were all experienced sessioneers, the lead voice on *Sugar Sugar* belonging to Ron Dante.

December 1969

6 December 1969

last week	this week		
4	1	YESTER-ME, YESTER-YOU, YESTERDAY	Stevie Wonder (Tamla Motown)
1	2	SUGAR SUGAR	Archies (RCA)
8	3	RUBY DON'T TAKE YOUR LOVE TO TOWN	Kenny Rogers & the First Edition (Reprise)
2	4	(CALL ME) NUMBER ONE	Tremeloes (CBS)
5	5	SOMETHING/COME TOGETHER	Beatles (Apple)
14	6	MELTING POT	Blue Mink (Philips)
3	7	OH WELL	Fleetwood Mac (Reprise)
23	8	TWO LITTLE BOYS	Rolf Harris (Columbia)
9	9	SWEET DREAM	Jethro Tull (Chrysalis)
12	10	WINTER WORLD OF LOVE	Engelbert Humperdinck (Decca)
7	11	WONDERFUL WORLD, BEAUTIFUL PEOPLE	Jimmy Cliff (Trojan)
28	12	SUSPICIOUS MINDS	Elvis Presley (RCA)
6	13	RETURN OF DJANGO	Upsetters (Upsetter)
15	14	THE LIQUIDATOR	Harry J. All Stars (Trojan)
10	15	WHAT DOES IT TAKE	Jr. Walker & the All Stars (Tamla Motown)
18	16	GREEN RIVER	Creedence Clearwater Revival (Liberty)
11	17	LOVE'S BEEN GOOD TO ME	Frank Sinatra (Reprise)
22	18	THE ONION SONG	Marvin Gaye & Tammi Terrell (Tamla Motown)
16	19	BILJO	Clodagh Rodgers (RCA)
17	20	COLD TURKEY	Plastic Ono Band (Apple)
-	21	WITHOUT LOVE	Tom Jones (Decca)
27	22	LEAVIN' (DURHAM TOWN)	Roger Whittaker (Columbia)
13	23	HE AIN'T HEAVY - HE'S MY BROTHER	Hollies (Parlophone)
29	23	LOVE IS ALL	Malcolm Roberts (Major Minor)
21	25	TERESA	Joe Dolan (Pye)
20	25	NOBODY'S CHILD	Karen Young (Major Minor)
-	27	PROUD MARY	Checkmates Ltd. (A&M)
-	28	TRACY	Cuff Links (MCA)
30	29	LONELINESS	Des O'Connor (Columbia)
26	30	I MISS YOU BABY	Marv Johnson (Tamla Motown)

13 December 1969

last week	this week		
3	1	RUBY DON'T TAKE YOUR LOVE TO TOWN	Kenny Rogers & the First Edition (Reprise)
1	2	YESTER-ME, YESTER-YOU, YESTERDAY	Stevie Wonder (Tamla Motown)
2	3	SUGAR SUGAR	Archies (RCA)
8	4	TWO LITTLE BOYS	Rolf Harris (Columbia)
6	5	MELTING POT	Blue Mink (Philips)
4	6	(CALL ME) NUMBER ONE	Tremeloes (CBS)
12	7	SUSPICIOUS MINDS	Elvis Presley (RCA)
10	8	WINTER WORLD OF LOVE	Engelbert Humperdinck (Decca)
5	9	SOMETHING/COME TOGETHER	Beatles (Apple)
18	10	THE ONION SONG	Marvin Gaye & Tammi Terrell (Tamla Motown)
9	11	SWEET DREAM	Jethro Tull (Chrysalis)
14	12	THE LIQUIDATOR	Harry J. All Stars (Trojan)
7	13	OH WELL	Fleetwood Mac (Reprise)
22	14	LEAVIN' (DURHAM TOWN)	Roger Whittaker (Columbia)
11	15	WONDERFUL WORLD, BEAUTIFUL PEOPLE	Jimmy Cliff (Trojan)
28	16	TRACY	Cuff Links (MCA)
23	16	LOVE IS ALL	Malcolm Roberts (Major Minor)
-	18	ALL I HAVE TO DO IS DREAM	Bobbie Gentry & Glen Campbell (Capitol)
13	19	RETURN OF DJANGO	Upsetters (Upsetter)
16	20	GREEN RIVER	Creedence Clearwater Revival (Liberty)
21	21	WITHOUT LOVE	Tom Jones (Decca)
17	22	LOVE'S BEEN GOOD TO ME	Frank Sinatra (Reprise)
15	23	WHAT DOES IT TAKE	Jr. Walker & the All Stars (Tamla Motown)
-	24	THE HIGHWAY SONG	Nancy Sinatra (Reprise)
19	25	BILJO	Clodagh Rodgers (RCA)
29	26	LONELINESS	Des O'Connor (Columbia)
-	27	GOOD OLD ROCK'N'ROLL	Dave Clark Five (Columbia)
20	28	COLD TURKEY	Plastic Ono Band (Apple)
27	29	PROUD MARY	Checkmates Ltd. (A&M)
-	30	WITH THE EYES OF A CHILD	Cliff Richard (Columbia)

20 December 1969

last week	this week		
4	1	TWO LITTLE BOYS	Rolf Harris (Columbia)
1	2	RUBY DON'T TAKE YOUR LOVE TO TOWN	Kenny Rogers & the First Edition (Reprise)
2	3	YESTER-ME, YESTER-YOU, YESTERDAY	Stevie Wonder (Tamla Motown)
3	4	SUGAR SUGAR	Archies (RCA)
5	5	MELTING POT	Blue Mink (Philips)
7	6	SUSPICIOUS MINDS	Elvis Presley (RCA)
8	7	WINTER WORLD OF LOVE	Engelbert Humperdinck (Decca)
10	8	THE ONION SONG	Marvin Gaye & Tammi Terrell (Tamla Motown)
18	9	ALL I HAVE TO DO IS DREAM	Bobbie Gentry & Glen Campbell (Capitol)
6	10	(CALL ME) NUMBER ONE	Tremeloes (CBS)
16	11	LOVE IS ALL	Malcolm Roberts (Major Minor)
16	12	TRACY	Cuff Links (MCA)
21	13	WITHOUT LOVE	Tom Jones (Decca)
9	14	SOMETHING/COME TOGETHER	Beatles (Apple)
20	15	GREEN RIVER	Creedence Clearwater Revival (Liberty)
14	16	LEAVIN' (DURHAM TOWN)	Roger Whittaker (Columbia)
15	17	WONDERFUL WORLD, BEAUTIFUL PEOPLE	Jimmy Cliff (Trojan)
11	18	SWEET DREAM	Jethro Tull (Chrysalis)
27	19	GOOD OLD ROCK'N'ROLL	Dave Clark Five (Columbia)
24	20	THE HIGHWAY SONG	Nancy Sinatra (Reprise)
26	21	LONELINESS	Des O'Connor (Columbia)
13	22	OH WELL	Fleetwood Mac (Reprise)
12	23	THE LIQUIDATOR	Harry J. All Stars (Trojan)
-	24	NOBODY'S CHILD	Karen Young (Major Minor)
19	25	RETURN OF DJANGO	Upsetters (Upsetter)
23	26	WHAT DOES IT TAKE	Jr. Walker & the All Stars (Tamla Motown)
30	27	WITH THE EYES OF A CHILD	Cliff Richard (Columbia)
22	28	LOVE'S BEEN GOOD TO ME	Frank Sinatra (Reprise)
25	29	BILJO	Clodagh Rodgers (RCA)
-	30	SOMEDAY WE'LL BE TOGETHER	Diana Ross & the Supremes (Tamla Motown)

27 December 1969

last week	this week		
1	1	TWO LITTLE BOYS	Rolf Harris (Columbia)
2	2	RUBY DON'T TAKE YOUR LOVE TO TOWN	Kenny Rogers & the First Edition (Reprise)
5	3	MELTING POT	Blue Mink (Philips)
4	4	SUGAR SUGAR	Archies (RCA)
3	5	YESTER-ME, YESTER-YOU, YESTERDAY	Stevie Wonder (Tamla Motown)
6	6	SUSPICIOUS MINDS	Elvis Presley (RCA)
9	7	ALL I HAVE TO DO IS DREAM	Bobbie Gentry & Glen Campbell (Capitol)
7	8	WINTER WORLD OF LOVE	Engelbert Humperdinck (Decca)
12	9	TRACY	Cuff Links (MCA)
8	10	THE ONION SONG	Marvin Gaye & Tammi Terrell (Tamla Motown)
13	10	WITHOUT LOVE	Tom Jones (Decca)
10	12	(CALL ME) NUMBER ONE	Tremeloes (CBS)
11	13	LOVE IS ALL	Malcolm Roberts (Major Minor)
16	14	LEAVIN' (DURHAM TOWN)	Roger Whittaker (Columbia)
21	15	LONELINESS	Des O'Connor (Columbia)
19	16	GOOD OLD ROCK'N'ROLL	Dave Clark Five (Columbia)
15	16	GREEN RIVER	Creedence Clearwater Revival (Liberty)
27	18	WITH THE EYES OF A CHILD	Cliff Richard (Columbia)
17	19	WONDERFUL WORLD, BEAUTIFUL PEOPLE	Jimmy Cliff (Trojan)
20	20	THE HIGHWAY SONG	Nancy Sinatra (Reprise)
14	21	SOMETHING/COME TOGETHER	Beatles (Apple)
23	22	THE LIQUIDATOR	Harry J. All Stars (Trojan)
25	23	RETURN OF DJANGO	Upsetters (Upsetter)
24	24	NOBODY'S CHILD	Karen Young (Major Minor)
30	25	SOMEDAY WE'LL BE TOGETHER	Diana Ross & the Supremes (Tamla Motown)
18	26	SWEET DREAM	Jethro Tull (Chrysalis)
-	27	BUT YOU LOVE ME DADDY	Jim Reeves (RCA)
-	28	COMIN' HOME	Delaney & Bonnie (Atlantic)
-	29	IF I THOUGHT YOU'D EVER CHANGE YOUR MIND	Cilla Black (Parlophone)
-	30	SEVENTH SON	Georgie Fame (CBS)

Blue Mink's *Melting Pot*, a cheerful exhortation to racial harmony, was a product of another grouping of the elite of Britain's session scene, its lead vocalists being Madelaine Bell and songwriter Roger Cook (also formerly half of David & Jonathan). *Melting Pot* looked like being the Christmas Number One early in December, but was pipped by the inevitable year-end novelty in the form of Rolf Harris' *Two Little Boys*, a revival of a song from the early part of the century dealing with loyalty in the face of death. Heavy stuff .

3 January 1970

last week	this week	
1	1	TWO LITTLE BOYS — Rolf Harris (Columbia)
2	2	RUBY DON'T TAKE YOUR LOVE TO TOWN — Kenny Rogers & the First Edition (Reprise)
3	3	MELTING POT — Blue Mink (Philips)
4	4	SUGAR SUGAR — Archies (RCA)
5	5	YESTER-ME, YESTER-YOU, YESTERDAY — Stevie Wonder (Tamla Motown)
6	6	SUSPICIOUS MINDS — Elvis Presley (RCA)
7	7	ALL I HAVE TO DO IS DREAM — Bobbie Gentry & Glen Campbell (Capitol)
8	8	WINTER WORLD OF LOVE — Engelbert Humperdinck (Decca)
9	9	TRACY — Cuff Links (MCA)
10	9	WITHOUT LOVE — Tom Jones (Decca)
10	11	THE ONION SONG — Marvin Gaye & Tammi Terrell (Tamla Motown)
16	12	GOOD OLD ROCK'N'ROLL — Dave Clark Five (Columbia)
12	13	(CALL ME) NUMBER ONE — Tremeloes (CBS)
13	14	LOVE IS ALL — Malcolm Roberts (Major Minor)
14	15	LEAVIN' (DURHAM TOWN) — Roger Whittaker (Columbia)
22	16	THE LIQUIDATOR — Harry J. All Stars (Trojan)
16	17	GREEN RIVER — Creedence Clearwater Revival (Liberty)
15	18	LONELINESS — Des O'Connor (Columbia)
18	19	WITH THE EYES OF A CHILD — Cliff Richard (Columbia)
21	20	SOMETHING/COME TOGETHER — Beatles (Apple)
20	21	THE HIGHWAY SONG — Nancy Sinatra (Reprise)
25	22	SOMEDAY WE'LL BE TOGETHER AGAIN — Diana Ross & the Supremes (Tamla Motown)
27	23	BUT YOU LOVE ME DADDY — Jim Reeves (RCA)
19	24	WONDERFUL WORLD, BEAUTIFUL PEOPLE — Jimmy Cliff (Trojan)
28	25	COMIN' HOME — Delaney & Bonnie (Atlantic)
26	26	SWEET DREAM — Jethro Tull (Chrysalis)
-	27	LOVE'S BEEN GOOD TO ME — Frank Sinatra (Reprise)
-	28	REFLECTIONS OF MY LIFE — Marmalade (Decca)
24	29	NOBODY'S CHILD — Karen Young (Major Minor)
29	30	IF I THOUGHT YOU'D EVER CHANGE YOUR MIND — Cilla Black (Parlophone)

10 January 1970

last week	this week	
1	1	TWO LITTLE BOYS — Rolf Harris (Columbia)
2	2	RUBY DON'T TAKE YOUR LOVE TO TOWN — Kenny Rogers & the First Edition (Reprise)
3	3	MELTING POT — Blue Mink (Philips)
7	4	ALL I HAVE TO DO IS DREAM — Bobbie Gentry & Glen Campbell (Capitol)
4	5	SUGAR SUGAR — Archies (RCA)
6	6	SUSPICIOUS MINDS — Elvis Presley (RCA)
9	7	TRACY — Cuff Links (MCA)
5	8	YESTER-ME, YESTER-YOU, YESTERDAY — Stevie Wonder (Tamla Motown)
12	9	GOOD OLD ROCK'N'ROLL — Dave Clark Five (Columbia)
9	10	WITHOUT LOVE — Tom Jones (Decca)
8	11	WINTER WORLD OF LOVE — Engelbert Humperdinck (Decca)
11	12	THE ONION SONG — Marvin Gaye & Tammi Terrell (Tamla Motown)
13	13	(CALL ME) NUMBER ONE — Tremeloes (CBS)
16	14	THE LIQUIDATOR — Harry J. All Stars (Trojan)
17	15	GREEN RIVER — Creedence Clearwater Revival (Liberty)
15	16	LEAVIN' (DURHAM TOWN) — Roger Whittaker (Columbia)
28	17	REFLECTIONS OF MY LIFE — Marmalade (Decca)
18	18	LONELINESS — Des O'Connor (Columbia)
19	19	WITH THE EYES OF A CHILD — Cliff Richard (Columbia)
22	20	SOMEDAY WE'LL BE TOGETHER AGAIN — Diana Ross & the Supremes (Tamla Motown)
14	21	LOVE IS ALL — Malcolm Roberts (Major Minor)
21	22	THE HIGHWAY SONG — Nancy Sinatra (Reprise)
24	23	WONDERFUL WORLD, BEAUTIFUL PEOPLE — Jimmy Cliff (Trojan)
23	24	BUT YOU LOVE ME DADDY — Jim Reeves (RCA)
30	25	IF I THOUGHT YOU'D EVER CHANGE YOUR MIND — Cilla Black (Parlophone)
25	26	COMIN' HOME — Delaney & Bonnie (Atlantic)
20	27	SOMETHING/COME TOGETHER — Beatles (Apple)
26	28	SWEET DREAM — Jethro Tull (Chrysalis)
29	29	NOBODY'S CHILD — Karen Young (Major Minor)
27	30	LOVE'S BEEN GOOD TO ME — Frank Sinatra (Reprise)

17 January 1970

last week	this week	
1	1	TWO LITTLE BOYS — Rolf Harris (Columbia)
7	2	TRACY — Cuff Links (MCA)
3	3	MELTING POT — Blue Mink (Philips)
4	4	ALL I HAVE TO DO IS DREAM — Bobbie Gentry & Glen Campbell (Capitol)
2	5	RUBY DON'T TAKE YOUR LOVE TO TOWN — Kenny Rogers & the First Edition (Reprise)
6	6	SUSPICIOUS MINDS — Elvis Presley (RCA)
5	7	SUGAR SUGAR — Archies (RCA)
9	8	GOOD OLD ROCK'N'ROLL — Dave Clark Five (Columbia)
17	9	REFLECTIONS OF MY LIFE — Marmalade (Decca)
8	10	YESTER-ME, YESTER-YOU, YESTERDAY — Stevie Wonder (Tamla Motown)
10	11	WITHOUT LOVE — Tom Jones (Decca)
14	12	THE LIQUIDATOR — Harry J. All Stars (Trojan)
11	13	WINTER WORLD OF LOVE — Engelbert Humperdinck (Decca)
12	14	THE ONION SONG — Marvin Gaye & Tammi Terrell (Tamla Motown)
16	15	LEAVIN' (DURHAM TOWN) — Roger Whittaker (Columbia)
18	16	SOMEDAY WE'LL BE TOGETHER AGAIN — Diana Ross & the Supremes (Tamla Motown)
-	17	COME AND GET IT — Badfinger (Apple)
-	18	FRIENDS — Arrival (Decca)
15	19	GREEN RIVER — Creedence Clearwater Revival (Liberty)
18	20	LONELINESS — Des O'Connor (Columbia)
25	21	IF I THOUGHT YOU'D EVER CHANGE YOUR MIND — Cilla Black (Parlophone)
24	22	BUT YOU LOVE ME DADDY — Jim Reeves (RCA)
13	23	(CALL ME) NUMBER ONE — Tremeloes (CBS)
-	24	SHE SOLD ME MAGIC — Lou Christie (Buddah)
26	25	COMIN' HOME — Delaney & Bonnie (Atlantic)
-	26	LET IT ALL HANG OUT — Jonathan King (Decca)
22	27	THE HIGHWAY SONG — Nancy Sinatra (Reprise)
18	28	WITH THE EYES OF A CHILD — Cliff Richard (Columbia)
-	29	SEVENTH SON — Georgie Fame (CBS)
-	30	VICTORIA — Kinks (Pye)

24 January 1970

last week	this week	
1	1	TWO LITTLE BOYS — Rolf Harris (Columbia)
2	2	TRACY — Cuff Links (MCA)
4	3	ALL I HAVE TO DO IS DREAM — Bobbie Gentry & Glen Campbell (Capitol)
6	4	SUSPICIOUS MINDS — Elvis Presley (RCA)
9	5	REFLECTIONS OF MY LIFE — Marmalade (Decca)
5	6	RUBY DON'T TAKE YOUR LOVE TO TOWN — Kenny Rogers & the First Edition (Reprise)
17	7	COME AND GET IT — Badfinger (Apple)
3	8	MELTING POT — Blue Mink (Philips)
8	9	GOOD OLD ROCK'N'ROLL — Dave Clark Five (Columbia)
18	10	FRIENDS — Arrival (Decca)
7	11	SUGAR SUGAR — Archies (RCA)
16	12	SOMEDAY WE'LL BE TOGETHER AGAIN — Diana Ross & the Supremes (Tamla Motown)
11	13	WITHOUT LOVE — Tom Jones (Decca)
15	14	LEAVIN' (DURHAM TOWN) — Roger Whittaker (Columbia)
-	15	LOVE GROWS — Edison Lighthouse (Bell)
12	16	THE LIQUIDATOR — Harry J. All Stars (Trojan)
10	17	YESTER-ME, YESTER-YOU, YESTERDAY — Stevie Wonder (Tamla Motown)
25	18	COMIN' HOME — Delaney & Bonnie (Atlantic)
-	19	WEDDING BELL BLUES — Fifth Dimension (Liberty)
22	20	BUT YOU LOVE ME DADDY — Jim Reeves (RCA)
13	21	WINTER WORLD OF LOVE — Engelbert Humperdinck (Decca)
-	22	I'M A MAN — Chicago (CBS)
-	22	I CAN'T GET NEXT TO YOU — Temptations (Tamla Motown)
-	24	LEAVING ON A JET PLANE — Peter, Paul & Mary (Warner Bros)
19	25	GREEN RIVER — Creedence Clearwater Revival (Liberty)
24	26	SHE SOLD ME MAGIC — Lou Christie (Buddah)
14	26	THE ONION SONG — Marvin Gaye & Tammi Terrell (Tamla Motown)
26	28	LET IT ALL HANG OUT — Jonathan King (Decca)
-	29	HITCHIN' A RIDE — Vanity Fare (Page One)
-	30	BOTH SIDES NOW — Judy Collins (Elektra)

Tracy hitmakers the Cuff Links were, like the Archies, a shadowy studio aggregation with no public face. The similarity didn't end there – lead singer on the Cuff Links records was also the versatile Ron Dante. *Someday We'll Be Together* was Diana Ross's last single with the Supremes, and pre-announced as such – to some the title seemed to be hedging her bets with regard to her solo career. Badfinger's *Come And Get It* was from the film *The Magic Christian*, starring Peter Sellers and Ringo Starr.

January – February 1970

31 January 1970

last	this	
5	1	REFLECTIONS OF MY LIFE Marmalade (Decca)
1	2	TWO LITTLE BOYS Rolf Harris (Columbia)
15	3	LOVE GROWS Edison Lighthouse (Bell)
7	4	COME AND GET IT Badfinger (Apple)
10	5	FRIENDS Arrival (Decca)
3	6	ALL I HAVE TO DO IS DREAM Bobbie Gentry & Glen Campbell (Capitol)
2	7	TRACY Cuff Links (MCA)
6	8	RUBY DON'T TAKE YOUR LOVE TO TOWN Kenny Rogers & the First Edition (Reprise)
4	9	SUSPICIOUS MINDS Elvis Presley (RCA)
12	10	SOMEDAY WE'LL BE TOGETHER AGAIN Diana Ross & the Supremes (Tamla Motown)
24	11	LEAVING ON A JET PLANE Peter, Paul & Mary (Warner Bros)
9	12	GOOD OLD ROCK'N'ROLL Dave Clark Five (Columbia)
22	13	I'M A MAN Chicago (CBS)
8	14	MELTING POT Blue Mink (Philips)
11	15	SUGAR SUGAR Archies (RCA)
-	16	THE WITCH'S PROMISE/TEACHER Jethro Tull (Chrysalis)
22	17	I CAN'T GET NEXT TO YOU Temptations (Tamla Motown)
16	18	THE LIQUIDATOR Harry J. All Stars (Trojan)
18	19	COMIN' HOME Delaney & Bonnie (Atlantic)
29	20	HITCHIN' A RIDE Vanity Fare (Page One)
19	21	WEDDING BELL BLUES Fifth Dimension (Liberty)
13	22	WITHOUT LOVE Tom Jones (Decca)
20	23	BUT YOU LOVE ME DADDY Jonathan King (Decca)
28	24	LET IT ALL HANG OUT Jonathan King (Decca)
14	24	LEAVIN' (DURHAM TOWN) Roger Whittaker (Columbia)
-	26	LET'S WORK TOGETHER Canned Heat (Liberty)
-	26	VENUS Shocking Blue (Penny Farthing)
30	28	BOTH SIDES NOW Judy Collins (Elektra)
17	29	YESTER-ME, YESTER-YOU, YESTERDAY Stevie Wonder (Tamla Motown)
26	30	SHE SOLD ME MAGIC Lou Christie (Buddah)

7 February 1970

3	1	LOVE GROWS Edison Lighthouse (Bell)
1	2	REFLECTIONS OF MY LIFE Marmalade (Decca)
4	3	COME AND GET IT Badfinger (Apple)
2	4	TWO LITTLE BOYS Rolf Harris (Columbia)
5	5	FRIENDS Arrival (Decca)
11	6	LEAVING ON A JET PLANE Peter, Paul & Mary (Warner Bros)
16	7	THE WITCH'S PROMISE/TEACHER Jethro Tull (Chrysalis)
13	8	I'M A MAN Chicago (CBS)
8	9	RUBY DON'T TAKE YOUR LOVE TO TOWN Kenny Rogers & the First Edition (Reprise)
6	10	ALL I HAVE TO DO IS DREAM Bobbie Gentry & Glen Campbell (Capitol)
7	11	TRACY Cuff Links (MCA)
10	12	SOMEDAY WE'LL BE TOGETHER AGAIN Diana Ross & the Supremes (Tamla Motown)
17	13	I CAN'T GET NEXT TO YOU Temptations (Tamla Motown)
9	14	SUSPICIOUS MINDS Elvis Presley (RCA)
-	15	TEMMA HARBOUR Mary Hopkin (Apple)
26	16	LET'S WORK TOGETHER Canned Heat (Liberty)
12	17	GOOD OLD ROCK'N'ROLL Dave Clark Five (Columbia)
28	18	BOTH SIDES NOW Judy Collins (Elektra)
26	19	VENUS Shocking Blue (Penny Farthing)
20	20	HITCHIN' A RIDE Vanity Fare (Page One)
21	21	WEDDING BELL BLUES Fifth Dimension (Liberty)
-	22	I WANT YOU BACK Jackson Five (Tamla Motown)
15	23	SUGAR SUGAR Archies (RCA)
14	24	MELTING POT Blue Mink (Philips)
24	25	LET IT ALL HANG OUT Jonathan King (Decca)
-	26	JUST A LITTLE MISUNDERSTANDING Contours (Tamla Motown)
22	27	WITHOUT LOVE Tom Jones (Decca)
24	28	LEAVIN' (DURHAM TOWN) Roger Whittaker (Columbia)
-	29	GIRLIE Peddlers (CBS)
23	29	BUT YOU LOVE ME DADDY Jim Reeves (RCA)

14 February 1970

1	1	LOVE GROWS Edison Lighthouse (Bell)
6	2	LEAVING ON A JET PLANE Peter, Paul & Mary (Warner Bros)
7	3	THE WITCH'S PROMISE/ TEACHER Jethro Tull (Chrysalis)
3	4	COME AND GET IT Badfinger (Apple)
2	5	REFLECTIONS OF MY LIFE Marmalade (Decca)
15	6	TEMMA HARBOUR Mary Hopkin (Apple)
4	7	TWO LITTLE BOYS Rolf Harris (Columbia)
8	8	I'M A MAN Chicago (CBS)
5	9	FRIENDS Arrival (Decca)
16	10	LET'S WORK TOGETHER Canned Heat (Liberty)
13	11	I CAN'T GET NEXT TO YOU Temptations (Tamla Motown)
19	12	VENUS Shocking Blue (Penny Farthing)
9	13	RUBY DON'T TAKE YOUR LOVE TO TOWN Kenny Rogers & the First Edition (Reprise)
22	14	I WANT YOU BACK Jackson Five (Tamla Motown)
10	15	ALL I HAVE TO DO IS DREAM Bobbie Gentry & Glen Campbell (Capitol)
20	16	HITCHIN' A RIDE Vanity Fare (Page One)
12	17	SOMEDAY WE'LL BE TOGETHER AGAIN Diana Ross & the Supremes (Tamla Motown)
18	18	BOTH SIDES NOW Judy Collins (Elektra)
11	18	TRACY Cuff Links (MCA)
-	20	WAND'RIN STAR Lee Marvin (Paramount)
14	21	SUSPICIOUS MINDS Elvis Presley (RCA)
-	22	MY BABY LOVES LOVIN' White Plains (Deram)
21	23	WEDDING BELL BLUES Fifth Dimension (Liberty)
26	24	JUST A LITTLE MISUNDERSTANDING Contours (Tamla Motown)
-	25	ELIZABETHAN REGGAE Boris Gardner (Duke)
-	26	YEARS MAY COME, YEARS MAY GO Herman's Hermits (Columbia)
17	27	GOOD OLD ROCK'N'ROLL Dave Clark Five (Columbia)
-	28	NA NA HEY HEY KISS HIM GOODBYE Steam (Fontana)
-	29	UNITED WE STAND Brotherhood of Man (Deram)
25	30	LET IT ALL HANG OUT Jonathan King (Decca)

21 February 1970

1	1	LOVE GROWS Edison Lighthouse (Bell)
10	2	LET'S WORK TOGETHER Canned Heat (Liberty)
2	3	LEAVING ON A JET PLANE Peter, Paul & Mary (Warner Bros)
14	4	I WANT YOU BACK Jackson Five (Tamla Motown)
6	5	TEMMA HARBOUR Mary Hopkin (Apple)
3	6	THE WITCH'S PROMISE/ TEACHER Jethro Tull (Chrysalis)
12	7	VENUS Shocking Blue (Penny Farthing)
20	8	WAND'RIN STAR Lee Marvin (Paramount)
4	9	COME AND GET IT Badfinger (Apple)
7	10	TWO LITTLE BOYS Rolf Harris (Columbia)
8	11	I'M A MAN Chicago (CBS)
22	11	MY BABY LOVES LOVIN' White Plains (Deram)
5	13	REFLECTIONS OF MY LIFE Marmalade (Decca)
11	14	I CAN'T GET NEXT TO YOU Temptations (Tamla Motown)
29	15	UNITED WE STAND Brotherhood of Man (Deram)
26	16	YEARS MAY COME, YEARS MAY GO Herman's Hermits (Columbia)
-	17	INSTANT KARMA John Ono Lennon/Plastic Ono Band (Apple)
16	18	HITCHIN' A RIDE Vanity Fare (Page One)
18	19	BOTH SIDES NOW Judy Collins (Elektra)
9	20	FRIENDS Arrival (Decca)
23	21	WEDDING BELL BLUES Fifth Dimension (Liberty)
13	21	RUBY DON'T TAKE YOUR LOVE TO TOWN Kenny Rogers & the First Edition (Reprise)
24	23	JUST A LITTLE MISUNDERSTANDING Contours (Tamla Motown)
15	24	ALL I HAVE TO DO IS DREAM Bobbie Gentry & Glen Campbell (Capitol)
28	25	NA NA HEY HEY KISS HIM GOODBYE Steam (Fontana)
17	26	SOMEDAY WE'LL BE TOGETHER AGAIN Diana Ross & the Supremes (Tamla Motown)
-	27	DOWN ON THE CORNER Creedence Clearwater Revival (Liberty)
25	28	ELIZABETHAN REGGAE Boris Gardner (Duke)
21	29	SUSPICIOUS MINDS Elvis Presley (RCA)
-	30	RAINDROPS KEEP FALLING ON MY HEAD Sacha Distel (Warner Bros)

The lead singer on Edison Lighthouse's *Love Grows* was not a member of the group, but top session singer Tony Burrows. So in demand were Burrows services at the time that he found himself appearing simultaneously on two other hit singles – Brotherhood Of Man's *United We Stand* and White Plains' *My Baby Loves Lovin'*. On one edition of *Top Of The Pops* he was required to appear three times in rapid succession, desperately trying to look sufficiently different in each incarnation.

February – March 1970

28 February 1970

last week	this week	
4	1	I WANT YOU BACK — Jackson Five (Tamla Motown)
8	2	WAND'RIN STAR — Lee Marvin (Paramount)
1	3	LOVE GROWS — Edison Lighthouse (Bell)
2	4	LET'S WORK TOGETHER — Canned Heat (Liberty)
17	5	INSTANT KARMA — John Ono Lennon/Plastic Ono Band (Apple)
3	6	LEAVING ON A JET PLANE — Peter, Paul & Mary (Warner Bros)
5	7	TEMMA HARBOUR — Mary Hopkin (Apple)
11	8	MY BABY LOVES LOVIN' — White Plains (Deram)
7	9	VENUS — Shocking Blue (Penny Farthing)
15	10	UNITED WE STAND — Brotherhood of Man (Deram)
6	11	THE WITCH'S PROMISE/TEACHER — Jethro Tull (Chrysalis)
16	12	YEARS MAY COME, YEARS MAY GO — Herman's Hermits (Columbia)
10	13	TWO LITTLE BOYS — Rolf Harris (Columbia)
9	14	COME AND GET IT — Badfinger (Apple)
11	15	I'M A MAN — Chicago (CBS)
19	16	BOTH SIDES NOW — Judy Collins (Elektra)
28	17	ELIZABETHAN REGGAE — Boris Gardner (Duke)
18	18	HITCHIN' A RIDE — Vanity Fare (Page One)
25	19	NA NA HEY HEY KISS HIM GOODBYE — Steam (Fontana)
30	20	RAINDROPS KEEP FALLING ON MY HEAD — Sacha Distel (Warner Bros)
14	21	I CAN'T GET NEXT TO YOU — Temptations (Tamla Motown)
13	22	REFLECTIONS OF MY LIFE — Marmalade (Decca)
-	23	DON'T CRY DADDY — Elvis Presley (RCA)
-	23	BRIDGE OVER TROUBLED WATER — Simon & Garfunkel (CBS)
21	25	WEDDING BELL BLUES — Fifth Dimension (Liberty)
27	26	DOWN ON THE CORNER — Creedence Clearwater Revival (Liberty)
21	27	RUBY DON'T TAKE YOUR LOVE TO TOWN — Kenny Rogers & the First Edition (Reprise)
23	28	JUST A LITTLE MISUNDERSTANDING — Contours (Tamla Motown)
26	29	SOMEDAY WE'LL BE TOGETHER AGAIN — Diana Ross & the Supremes (Tamla Motown)
-	30	SOMETHING'S BURNING — Kenny Rogers & the First Edition (Reprise)

7 March 1970

last week	this week	
2	1	WAND'RIN STAR — Lee Marvin (Paramount)
1	2	I WANT YOU BACK — Jackson Five (Tamla Motown)
4	3	LET'S WORK TOGETHER — Canned Heat (Liberty)
3	4	LOVE GROWS — Edison Lighthouse (Bell)
5	5	INSTANT KARMA — John Ono Lennon/Plastic Ono Band (Apple)
10	6	UNITED WE STAND — Brotherhood of Man (Deram)
6	7	LEAVING ON A JET PLANE — Peter, Paul & Mary (Warner Bros)
8	8	MY BABY LOVES LOVIN' — White Plains (Deram)
7	9	TEMMA HARBOUR — Mary Hopkin (Apple)
9	10	VENUS — Shocking Blue (Penny Farthing)
23	11	BRIDGE OVER TROUBLED WATER — Simon & Garfunkel (CBS)
12	12	YEARS MAY COME, YEARS MAY GO — Herman's Hermits (Columbia)
20	13	RAINDROPS KEEP FALLING ON MY HEAD — Sacha Distel (Warner Bros)
19	14	NA NA HEY HEY KISS HIM GOODBYE — Steam (Fontana)
16	15	BOTH SIDES NOW — Judy Collins (Elektra)
11	16	THE WITCH'S PROMISE/TEACHER — Jethro Tull (Chrysalis)
17	17	ELIZABETHAN REGGAE — Boris Gardner (Duke)
-	18	THAT SAME OLD FEELING — Pickettywitch (Pye)
23	18	DON'T CRY DADDY — Elvis Presley (RCA)
13	20	TWO LITTLE BOYS — Rolf Harris (Columbia)
14	21	COME AND GET IT — Badfinger (Apple)
30	22	SOMETHING'S BURNING — Kenny Rogers & the First Edition (Reprise)
15	23	I'M A MAN — Chicago (CBS)
-	24	FAREWELL IS A LONELY SOUND — Jimmy Ruffin (Tamla Motown)
28	25	JUST A LITTLE MISUNDERSTANDING — Contours (Tamla Motown)
21	26	I CAN'T GET NEXT TO YOU — Temptations (Tamla Motown)
26	27	DOWN ON THE CORNER — Creedence Clearwater Revival (Liberty)
-	28	SYMPATHY — Rare Bird (Charisma)
-	29	YOU'RE SUCH A GOOD LOOKINGWOMAN — Joe Dolan (Pye)
22	30	REFLECTIONS OF MY LIFE — Marmalade (Decca)

14 March 1970

last week	this week	
1	1	WAND'RIN STAR — Lee Marvin (Paramount)
2	2	I WANT YOU BACK — Jackson Five (Tamla Motown)
11	3	BRIDGE OVER TROUBLED WATER — Simon & Garfunkel (CBS)
3	4	LET'S WORK TOGETHER — Canned Heat (Liberty)
5	5	INSTANT KARMA — John Ono Lennon/Plastic Ono Band (Apple)
12	6	YEARS MAY COME, YEARS MAY GO — Herman's Hermits (Columbia)
4	7	LOVE GROWS — Edison Lighthouse (Bell)
6	8	UNITED WE STAND — Brotherhood of Man (Deram)
-	9	LET IT BE — Beatles (Apple)
8	9	MY BABY LOVES LOVIN' — White Plains (Deram)
14	11	NA NA HEY HEY KISS HIM GOODBYE — Steam (Fontana)
7	12	LEAVING ON A JET PLANE — Peter, Paul & Mary (Warner Bros)
13	13	RAINDROPS KEEP FALLING ON MY HEAD — Sacha Distel (Warner Bros)
18	14	DON'T CRY DADDY — Elvis Presley (RCA)
18	15	THAT SAME OLD FEELING — Pickettywitch (Pye)
9	16	TEMMA HARBOUR — Mary Hopkin (Apple)
10	17	VENUS — Shocking Blue (Penny Farthing)
22	18	SOMETHING'S BURNING — Kenny Rogers & the First Edition (Reprise)
17	19	ELIZABETHAN REGGAE — Boris Gardner (Duke)
15	20	BOTH SIDES NOW — Judy Collins (Elektra)
-	21	EVERYBODY GET TOGETHER — Dave Clark Five (Columbia)
-	22	YOUNG GIFTED AND BLACK — Bob & Marcia (Harry J)
-	22	CAN'T HELP FALLIN' IN LOVE — Andy Williams (CBS)
29	24	YOU'RE SUCH A GOOD LOOKINGWOMAN — Joe Dolan (Pye)
-	25	NOBODY'S FOOL — Jim Reeves (RCA)
27	26	DOWN ON THE CORNER — Creedence Clearwater Revival (Liberty)
28	27	SYMPATHY — Rare Bird (Charisma)
24	27	FAREWELL IS A LONELY SOUND — Jimmy Ruffin (Tamla Motown)
16	29	THE WITCH'S PROMISE/TEACHER — Jethro Tull (Chrysalis)
-	29	JOY OF LIVING — Cliff Richard & Hank Marvin (Columbia)

21 March 1970

last week	this week	
1	1	WAND'RIN STAR — Lee Marvin (Paramount)
3	2	BRIDGE OVER TROUBLED WATER — Simon & Garfunkel (CBS)
9	3	LET IT BE — Beatles (Apple)
2	4	I WANT YOU BACK — Jackson Five (Tamla Motown)
15	5	THAT SAME OLD FEELING — Pickettywitch (Pye)
4	6	LET'S WORK TOGETHER — Canned Heat (Liberty)
11	7	NA NA HEY HEY KISS HIM GOODBYE — Steam (Fontana)
5	8	INSTANT KARMA — John Ono Lennon/Plastic Ono Band (Apple)
14	9	DON'T CRY DADDY — Elvis Presley (RCA)
22	9	CAN'T HELP FALLIN' IN LOVE — Andy Williams (CBS)
6	11	YEARS MAY COME, YEARS MAY GO — Herman's Hermits (Columbia)
13	12	RAINDROPS KEEP FALLING ON MY HEAD — Sacha Distel (Warner Bros)
18	13	SOMETHING'S BURNING — Kenny Rogers & the First Edition (Reprise)
22	14	YOUNG GIFTED AND BLACK — Bob & Marcia (Harry J)
8	15	UNITED WE STAND — Brotherhood of Man (Deram)
7	16	LOVE GROWS — Edison Lighthouse (Bell)
9	17	MY BABY LOVES LOVIN' — White Plains (Deram)
12	18	LEAVING ON A JET PLANE — Peter, Paul & Mary (Warner Bros)
21	19	EVERYBODY GET TOGETHER — Dave Clark Five (Columbia)
24	20	YOU'RE SUCH A GOOD LOOKINGWOMAN — Joe Dolan (Pye)
27	21	FAREWELL IS A LONELY SOUND — Jimmy Ruffin (Tamla Motown)
19	22	ELIZABETHAN REGGAE — Boris Gardner (Duke)
17	23	VENUS — Shocking Blue (Penny Farthing)
27	24	SYMPATHY — Rare Bird (Charisma)
29	24	JOY OF LIVING — Cliff Richard & Hank Marvin (Columbia)
16	26	TEMMA HARBOUR — Mary Hopkin (Apple)
25	27	NOBODY'S FOOL — Jim Reeves (RCA)
-	28	I CAN'T HELP MYSELF (SUGAR PIE, HONEY BUNCH) — Four Tops (Tamla Motown)
-	29	I'LL GO ON HOPING — Des O'Connor (Columbia)
-	30	WHY MUST WE FALL IN LOVE — Diana Ross & the Supremes & the Temptations (Tamla Motown)

A most unexpected success was Lee Marvin's *Wand'rin Star*, taken from the soundtrack of the film *Paint Your Wagon*, in which he co-starred with Clint Eastwood (who warbled *I Talk To The Trees* on the B-side of this single). It would be an understatement to suggest Marvin could not sing – one review of *Wand'rin Star* compared his voice unfavourably to a Moog synthesiser – but the sheer outrageousness of the performance seemed to work to the song's advantage. He never attempted a follow-up though.

March – April 1970

28 March 1970

last wk	this wk	Title / Artist
2	1	BRIDGE OVER TROUBLED WATER Simon & Garfunkel (CBS)
1	2	WAND'RIN STAR Lee Marvin (Paramount)
3	3	LET IT BE Beatles (Apple)
9	4	CAN'T HELP FALLING IN LOVE Andy Williams (CBS)
5	5	THAT SAME OLD FEELING Pickettywitch (Pye)
14	6	YOUNG GIFTED AND BLACK Bob & Marcia (Harry J)
9	7	DON'T CRY DADDY Elvis Presley (RCA)
7	8	NA NA HEY HEY KISS HIM GOODBYE Steam (Fontana)
4	9	I WANT YOU BACK Jackson Five (Tamla Motown)
13	10	SOMETHING'S BURNING Kenny Rogers & the First Edition (Reprise)
11	11	YEARS MAY COME, YEARS MAY GO Herman's Hermits (Columbia)
6	12	LET'S WORK TOGETHER Canned Heat (Liberty)
19	13	EVERYBODY GET TOGETHER Dave Clark Five (Columbia)
-	14	KNOCK KNOCK WHO'S THERE Mary Hopkin (Apple)
8	15	INSTANT KARMA John Ono Lennon/Plastic Ono Band (Apple)
12	16	RAINDROPS KEEP FALLING ON MY HEAD Sacha Distel (Warner Bros)
21	17	FAREWELL IS A LONELY SOUND Jimmy Ruffin (Tamla Motown)
15	18	UNITED WE STAND Brotherhood of Man (Deram)
20	19	YOU'RE SUCH A GOOD LOOKINGWOMAN Joe Dolan (Pye)
28	20	I CAN'T HELP MYSELF (SUGAR PIE, HONEY BUNCH) Four Tops (Tamla Motown)
16	21	LOVE GROWS Edison Lighthouse (Bell)
30	22	WHY MUST WE FALL IN LOVE Diana Ross & the Supremes & the Temptations (Tamla Motown)
17	23	MY BABY LOVES LOVIN' White Plains (Deram)
22	24	ELIZABETHAN REGGAE Boris Gardner (Duke)
24	25	SYMPATHY Rare Bird (Charisma)
27	26	NOBODY'S FOOL Jim Reeves (RCA)
-	27	WHO DO YOU LOVE Juicy Lucy (Vertigo)
-	28	GOOD MORNING FREEDOM Blue Mink (Philips)
-	29	SPIRIT IN THE SKY Norman Greenbaum (Reprise)
24	30	JOY OF LIVING Cliff Richard & Hank Marvin (Columbia)

4 April 1970

last wk	this wk	Title / Artist
1	1	BRIDGE OVER TROUBLED WATER Simon & Garfunkel (CBS)
4	2	CAN'T HELP FALLING IN LOVE Andy Williams (CBS)
14	3	KNOCK KNOCK WHO'S THERE Mary Hopkin (Apple)
2	4	WAND'RIN STAR Lee Marvin (Paramount)
5	5	THAT SAME OLD FEELING Pickettywitch (Pye)
6	6	YOUNG GIFTED AND BLACK Bob & Marcia (Harry J)
3	7	LET IT BE Beatles (Apple)
8	8	NA NA HEY HEY KISS HIM GOODBYE Steam (Fontana)
7	9	DON'T CRY DADDY Elvis Presley (RCA)
10	10	SOMETHING'S BURNING Kenny Rogers & the First Edition (Reprise)
13	11	EVERYBODY GET TOGETHER Dave Clark Five (Columbia)
9	12	I WANT YOU BACK Jackson Five (Tamla Motown)
17	13	FAREWELL IS A LONELY SOUND Jimmy Ruffin (Tamla Motown)
29	14	SPIRIT IN THE SKY Norman Greenbaum (Reprise)
19	15	YOU'RE SUCH A GOOD LOOKINGWOMAN Joe Dolan (Pye)
20	16	I CAN'T HELP MYSELF (SUGAR PIE, HONEY BUNCH) Four Tops (Tamla Motown)
11	17	YEARS MAY COME, YEARS MAY GO Herman's Hermits (Columbia)
-	18	ALL KINDS OF EVERYTHING Dana (Rex)
27	19	WHO DO YOU LOVE Juicy Lucy (Vertigo)
12	20	LET'S WORK TOGETHER Canned Heat (Liberty)
-	21	GIMME DAT DING Pipkins (Columbia)
15	22	INSTANT KARMA John Ono Lennon/Plastic Ono Band (Apple)
26	23	NOBODY'S FOOL Jim Reeves (RCA)
28	24	GOOD MORNING FREEDOM Blue Mink (Philips)
18	25	UNITED WE STAND Brotherhood of Man (Deram)
22	26	WHY MUST WE FALL IN LOVE Diana Ross & the Supremes & the Temptations (Tamla Motown)
-	27	WHEN JULIE COMES AROUND Cuff Links (MCA)
-	28	TRAVELLIN' BAND Creedence Clearwater Revival (Liberty)
-	29	NEVER HAD A DREAM COME TRUE Stevie Wonder (Tamla Motown)
-	30	I'LL GO ON HOPING Des O'Connor (Columbia)

11 April 1970

last wk	this wk	Title / Artist
1	1	BRIDGE OVER TROUBLED WATER Simon & Garfunkel (CBS)
2	2	CAN'T HELP FALLING IN LOVE Andy Williams (CBS)
3	3	KNOCK KNOCK WHO'S THERE Mary Hopkin (Apple)
6	4	YOUNG GIFTED AND BLACK Bob & Marcia (Harry J)
18	5	ALL KINDS OF EVERYTHING Dana (Rex)
14	6	SPIRIT IN THE SKY Norman Greenbaum (Reprise)
4	7	WAND'RIN STAR Lee Marvin (Paramount)
10	8	SOMETHING'S BURNING Kenny Rogers & the First Edition (Reprise)
5	9	THAT SAME OLD FEELING Pickettywitch (Pye)
7	10	LET IT BE Beatles (Apple)
16	11	I CAN'T HELP MYSELF (SUGAR PIE, HONEY BUNCH) Four Tops (Tamla Motown)
13	12	FAREWELL IS A LONELY SOUND Jimmy Ruffin (Tamla Motown)
21	13	GIMME DAT DING Pipkins (Columbia)
8	14	NA NA HEY HEY KISS HIM GOODBYE Steam (Fontana)
15	15	YOU'RE SUCH A GOOD LOOKINGWOMAN Joe Dolan (Pye)
9	16	DON'T CRY DADDY Elvis Presley (RCA)
11	17	EVERYBODY GET TOGETHER Dave Clark Five (Columbia)
19	18	WHO DO YOU LOVE Juicy Lucy (Vertigo)
12	19	I WANT YOU BACK Jackson Five (Tamla Motown)
29	20	NEVER HAD A DREAM COME TRUE Stevie Wonder (Tamla Motown)
28	21	TRAVELLIN' BAND Creedence Clearwater Revival (Liberty)
24	22	GOOD MORNING FREEDOM Blue Mink (Philips)
27	23	WHEN JULIE COMES AROUND Cuff Links (MCA)
17	24	YEARS MAY COME, YEARS MAY GO Herman's Hermits (Columbia)
30	25	I'LL GO ON HOPING Des O'Connor (Columbia)
-	26	THE SEEKER Who (Track)
-	27	RAG MAMA RAG Band (Capitol)
-	28	HOUSE OF THE RISING SUN Frijid Pink (Deram)
-	29	JOY OF LIVING Cliff Richard & Hank Marvin (Columbia)
23	30	NOBODY'S FOOL Jim Reeves (RCA)

18 April 1970

last wk	this wk	Title / Artist
1	1	BRIDGE OVER TROUBLED WATER Simon & Garfunkel (CBS)
5	2	ALL KINDS OF EVERYTHING Dana (Rex)
6	3	SPIRIT IN THE SKY Norman Greenbaum (Reprise)
2	4	CAN'T HELP FALLING IN LOVE Andy Williams (CBS)
3	5	KNOCK KNOCK WHO'S THERE Mary Hopkin (Apple)
4	6	YOUNG GIFTED AND BLACK Bob & Marcia (Harry J)
13	7	GIMME DAT DING Pipkins (Columbia)
8	8	SOMETHING'S BURNING Kenny Rogers & the First Edition (Reprise)
9	9	THAT SAME OLD FEELING Pickettywitch (Pye)
7	10	WAND'RIN STAR Lee Marvin (Paramount)
11	11	I CAN'T HELP MYSELF (SUGAR PIE, HONEY BUNCH) Four Tops (Tamla Motown)
12	12	FAREWELL IS A LONELY SOUND Jimmy Ruffin (Tamla Motown)
10	13	LET IT BE Beatles (Apple)
22	14	WHEN JULIE COMES AROUND Cuff Links (MCA)
18	15	WHO DO YOU LOVE Juicy Lucy (Vertigo)
22	16	GOOD MORNING FREEDOM Blue Mink (Philips)
15	17	YOU'RE SUCH A GOOD LOOKINGWOMAN Joe Dolan (Pye)
20	18	NEVER HAD A DREAM COME TRUE Stevie Wonder (Tamla Motown)
21	19	TRAVELLIN' BAND Creedence Clearwater Revival (Liberty)
16	20	DON'T CRY DADDY Elvis Presley (RCA)
14	21	NA NA HEY HEY KISS HIM GOODBYE Steam (Fontana)
17	22	EVERYBODY GET TOGETHER Dave Clark Five (Columbia)
-	23	DO THE FUNKY CHICKEN Rufus Thomas (Stax)
28	24	HOUSE OF THE RISING SUN Frijid Pink (Deram)
-	25	GOVINDA Radha Krishna Temple (Apple)
-	26	DAUGHTER OF DARKNESS Tom Jones (Decca)
26	27	THE SEEKER Who (Track)
-	28	WHY MUST WE FALL IN LOVE Diana Ross & the Supremes & the Temptations (Tamla Motown)
19	29	I WANT YOU BACK Jackson Five (Tamla Motown)
25	30	I'LL GO ON HOPING Des O'Connor (Columbia)

Paul Simon admitted that he originally wrote *Bridge Over Troubled Water* with Aretha Franklin in mind – and indeed Aretha eventually recorded and had a hit with the song. In 1970 though it was Simon & Garfunkel's own version, along with its parent album of the same title which had the critics raving and the public buying in droves. On a more mundane note, May Hopkin's *Knock Knock Who's There* was the year's UK Eurovision entry. Almost inevitably it came second – one position better than in the chart.

25 April 1970

last week	this week	
3	1	SPIRIT IN THE SKY Norman Greenbaum (Reprise)
2	2	ALL KINDS OF EVERYTHING Dana (Rex)
1	3	BRIDGE OVER TROUBLED WATER Simon & Garfunkel (CBS)
4	4	CAN'T HELP FALLING IN LOVE Andy Williams (CBS)
7	5	GIMME DAT DING Pipkins (Columbia)
5	6	KNOCK KNOCK WHO'S THERE Mary Hopkin (Apple)
6	7	YOUNG GIFTED AND BLACK Bob & Marcia (Harry J)
18	8	NEVER HAD A DREAM COME TRUE Stevie Wonder (Tamla Motown)
12	9	FAREWELL IS A LONELY SOUND Jimmy Ruffin (Tamla Motown)
14	10	WHEN JULIE COMES AROUND Cuff Links (MCA)
11	11	I CAN'T HELP MYSELF (SUGAR PIE, HONEY BUNCH) Four Tops (Tamla Motown)
19	12	TRAVELLIN' BAND Creedence Clearwater Revival (Liberty)
16	13	GOOD MORNING FREEDOM Blue Mink (Philips)
10	14	WAND'RIN STAR Lee Marvin (Paramount)
9	15	THAT SAME OLD FEELING Pickettywitch (Pye)
8	16	SOMETHING'S BURNING Kenny Rogers & the First Edition (Reprise)
15	17	WHO DO YOU LOVE Juicy Lucy (Vertigo)
24	18	HOUSE OF THE RISING SUN Frijid Pink (Deram)
23	19	DO THE FUNKY CHICKEN Rufus Thomas (Stax)
-	20	BACK HOME England World Cup Squad (Pye)
27	21	THE SEEKER Who (Track)
17	23	YOU'RE SUCH A GOOD LOOKINGWOMAN Joe Dolan (Pye)
26	24	DAUGHTER OF DARKNESS Tom Jones (Decca)
-	25	I'VE GOT YOU ON MY MIND White Plains (Deram)
13	26	LET IT BE Beatles (Apple)
-	27	I DON'T BELIEVE IN IF ANY MORE Roger Whittaker (Columbia)
20	28	DON'T CRY DADDY Elvis Presley (RCA)
-	29	BRONTOSAURUS Move (Regal Zonophone)
25	30	GOVINDA Radha Krishna Temple (Apple)

2 May 1970

1	1	SPIRIT IN THE SKY Norman Greenbaum (Reprise)
2	2	ALL KINDS OF EVERYTHING Dana (Rex)
3	3	BRIDGE OVER TROUBLED WATER Simon & Garfunkel (CBS)
5	4	GIMME DAT DING Pipkins (Columbia)
8	5	NEVER HAD A DREAM COME TRUE Stevie Wonder (Tamla Motown)
4	6	CAN'T HELP FALLING IN LOVE Andy Williams (CBS)
21	7	BACK HOME England World Cup Squad (Pye)
12	8	TRAVELLIN' BAND Creedence Clearwater Revival (Liberty)
6	9	KNOCK KNOCK WHO'S THERE Mary Hopkin (Apple)
7	10	YOUNG GIFTED AND BLACK Bob & Marcia (Harry J)
9	11	FAREWELL IS A LONELY SOUND Jimmy Ruffin (Tamla Motown)
13	12	GOOD MORNING FREEDOM Blue Mink (Philips)
10	13	WHEN JULIE COMES AROUND Cuff Links (MCA)
14	14	HOUSE OF THE RISING SUN Frijid Pink (Deram)
20	15	RAG MAMA RAG Band (Capitol)
24	16	DAUGHTER OF DARKNESS Tom Jones (Decca)
11	17	I CAN'T HELP MYSELF (SUGAR PIE, HONEY BUNCH) Four Tops (Tamla Motown)
17	18	WHO DO YOU LOVE Juicy Lucy (Vertigo)
-	19	I CAN'T TELL THE BOTTOM FROM THE TOP Hollies (Parlophone)
19	20	DO THE FUNKY CHICKEN Rufus Thomas (Stax)
25	20	I'VE GOT YOU ON MY MIND White Plains (Deram)
14	22	WAND'RIN STAR Lee Marvin (Paramount)
16	23	SOMETHING'S BURNING Kenny Rogers & the First Edition (Reprise)
21	24	THE SEEKER Who (Track)
29	25	BRONTOSAURUS Move (Regal Zonophone)
27	26	I DON'T BELIEVE IN IF ANY MORE Roger Whittaker (Columbia)
15	27	THAT SAME OLD FEELING Pickettywitch (Pye)
-	28	EL CONDOR PASA Julie Felix (RAK)
-	29	DO YOU LOVE ME Deep Feeling (Page One)
30	30	GOVINDA Radha Krishna Temple (Apple)

9 May 1970

7	1	BACK HOME England World Cup Squad (Pye)
1	2	SPIRIT IN THE SKY Norman Greenbaum (Reprise)
3	3	ALL KINDS OF EVERYTHING Dana (Rex)
8	4	TRAVELLIN' BAND Creedence Clearwater Revival (Liberty)
5	5	NEVER HAD A DREAM COME TRUE Stevie Wonder (Tamla Motown)
6	6	CAN'T HELP FALLING IN LOVE Andy Williams (CBS)
11	7	FAREWELL IS A LONELY SOUND Jimmy Ruffin (Tamla Motown)
4	8	GIMME DAT DING Pipkins (Columbia)
14	9	HOUSE OF THE RISING SUN Frijid Pink (Deram)
3	10	BRIDGE OVER TROUBLED WATER Simon & Garfunkel (CBS)
13	11	WHEN JULIE COMES AROUND Cuff Links (MCA)
19	12	I CAN'T TELL THE BOTTOM FROM THE TOP Hollies (Parlophone)
12	13	GOOD MORNING FREEDOM Blue Mink (Philips)
16	14	DAUGHTER OF DARKNESS Tom Jones (Decca)
15	15	RAG MAMA RAG Band (Capitol)
20	16	DO THE FUNKY CHICKEN Rufus Thomas (Stax)
10	17	YOUNG GIFTED AND BLACK Bob & Marcia (Harry J)
9	18	KNOCK KNOCK WHO'S THERE Mary Hopkin (Apple)
23	19	THE SEEKER Who (Track)
-	20	QUESTION Moody Blues (Threshold)
-	21	YELLOW RIVER Christie (CBS)
26	22	I DON'T BELIEVE IN IF ANY MORE Roger Whittaker (Columbia)
17	23	I CAN'T HELP MYSELF (SUGAR PIE, HONEY BUNCH) Four Tops (Tamla Motown)
25	23	BRONTOSAURUS Move (Regal Zonophone)
18	25	WHO DO YOU LOVE Juicy Lucy (Vertigo)
28	26	EL CONDOR PASA Julie Felix (RAK)
20	27	I'VE GOT YOU ON MY MIND White Plains (Deram)
-	28	UP THE LADDER TO THE ROOF Supremes (Tamla Motown)
-	29	HONEY COME BACK Glen Campbell (Capitol)
-	30	ABRAHAM MARTIN AND JOHN Marvin Gaye (Tamla Motown)

16 May 1970

1	1	BACK HOME England World Cup Squad (Pye)
2	2	SPIRIT IN THE SKY Norman Greenbaum (Reprise)
9	3	HOUSE OF THE RISING SUN Frijid Pink (Deram)
14	4	DAUGHTER OF DARKNESS Tom Jones (Decca)
3	5	ALL KINDS OF EVERYTHING Dana (Rex)
4	6	TRAVELLIN' BAND Creedence Clearwater Revival (Liberty)
12	7	I CAN'T TELL THE BOTTOM FROM THE TOP Hollies (Parlophone)
5	8	NEVER HAD A DREAM COME TRUE Stevie Wonder (Tamla Motown)
10	9	BRIDGE OVER TROUBLED WATER Simon & Garfunkel (CBS)
20	10	QUESTION Moody Blues (Threshold)
6	11	CAN'T HELP FALLING IN LOVE Andy Williams (CBS)
21	12	YELLOW RIVER Christie (CBS)
11	13	WHEN JULIE COMES AROUND Cuff Links (MCA)
23	14	BRONTOSAURUS Move (Regal Zonophone)
8	15	GIMME DAT DING Pipkins (Columbia)
22	16	I DON'T BELIEVE IN IF ANY MORE Roger Whittaker (Columbia)
16	17	DO THE FUNKY CHICKEN Rufus Thomas (Stax)
7	18	FAREWELL IS A LONELY SOUND Jimmy Ruffin (Tamla Motown)
13	19	GOOD MORNING FREEDOM Blue Mink (Philips)
19	20	THE SEEKER Who (Track)
15	21	RAG MAMA RAG Band (Capitol)
29	22	HONEY COME BACK Glen Campbell (Capitol)
17	23	YOUNG GIFTED AND BLACK Bob & Marcia (Harry J)
-	23	ABC Jackson Five (Tamla Motown)
26	25	EL CONDOR PASA Julie Felix (RAK)
27	26	I'VE GOT YOU ON MY MIND White Plains (Deram)
18	27	KNOCK KNOCK WHO'S THERE Mary Hopkin (Apple)
-	28	GROOVIN' WITH MR. BLOE Mr. Bloe (DJM)
28	28	UP THE LADDER TO THE ROOF Supremes (Tamla Motown)
-	30	KENTUCKY RAIN Elvis Presley (RCA)
-	30	EVERYTHING IS BEAUTIFUL Ray Stevens (CBS)

Norman Greenbaum, formerly the leading light of the household-name group Dr West's Medicine Show & Jug Band (their best known record was *The Eggplant That Ate Chicago*), topped the chart with *Spirit In The Sky*. Its catchy riff was borrowed from Canned Heat's *On The Road Again* and it got a lot of promotional help from the new pirate radio station Radio Northsea, which plugged the record to death. US group Frigid Pink revived *House Of The Rising Sun* as a heavy metal guitar workout.

May – June 1970

23 May 1970

LW	TW	Entry
1	1	BACK HOME — England World Cup Squad (Pye)
10	2	QUESTION — Moody Blues (Threshold)
2	3	SPIRIT IN THE SKY — Norman Greenbaum (Reprise)
12	4	YELLOW RIVER Christie (CBS)
3	5	HOUSE OF THE RISING SUN — Frijid Pink (Deram)
14	6	BRONTOSAURUS — Move (Regal Zonophone)
7	7	I CAN'T TELL THE BOTTOM FROM THE TOP Hollies (Parlophone)
4	8	DAUGHTER OF DARKNESS — Tom Jones (Decca)
6	9	TRAVELLIN' BAND — Creedence Clearwater Revival (Liberty)
5	10	ALL KINDS OF EVERYTHING — Dana (Rex)
16	11	I DON'T BELIEVE IN IF ANY MORE — Roger Whittaker (Columbia)
22	12	HONEY COME BACK — Glen Campbell (Capitol)
8	13	NEVER HAD A DREAM COME TRUE — Stevie Wonder (Tamla Motown)
23	14	ABC — Jackson Five (Tamla Motown)
17	14	DO THE FUNKY CHICKEN — Rufus Thomas (Stax)
11	16	CAN'T HELP FALLIN' IN LOVE — Andy Williams (CBS)
20	17	THE SEEKER Who (Track)
9	18	BRIDGE OVER TROUBLED WATER — Simon & Garfunkel (CBS)
13	19	WHEN JULIE COMES AROUND — Cuff Links (MCA)
30	20	EVERYTHING IS BEAUTIFUL — Ray Stevens (CBS)
21	21	RAG MAMA RAG — Band (Capitol)
28	22	GROOVIN' WITH MR. BLOE — Mr. Bloe (DJM)
18	23	FAREWELL IS A LONELY SOUND — Jimmy Ruffin (Tamla Motown)
28	24	UP THE LADDER TO THE ROOF — Supremes (Tamla Motown)
-	25	ABRAHAM MARTIN AND JOHN — Marvin Gaye (Tamla Motown)
15	26	GIMME DAT DING — Pipkins (Columbia)
25	27	EL CONDOR PASA — Julie Felix (RAK)
26	28	I'VE GOT YOU ON MY MIND — White Plains (Deram)
30	29	KENTUCKY RAIN — Elvis Presley (RCA)
-	30	DON'T YOU KNOW — Butterscotch (RCA)

30 May 1970

LW	TW	Entry
2	1	QUESTION — Moody Blues (Threshold)
4	2	YELLOW RIVER Christie (CBS)
1	3	BACK HOME — England World Cup Squad (Pye)
3	4	SPIRIT IN THE SKY — Norman Greenbaum (Reprise)
5	5	HOUSE OF THE RISING SUN — Frijid Pink (Deram)
6	6	BRONTOSAURUS — Move (Regal Zonophone)
8	7	DAUGHTER OF DARKNESS — Tom Jones (Decca)
12	8	HONEY COME BACK — Glen Campbell (Capitol)
7	9	I CAN'T TELL THE BOTTOM FROM THE TOP Hollies (Parlophone)
11	10	I DON'T BELIEVE IN IF ANY MORE — Roger Whittaker (Columbia)
14	11	DO THE FUNKY CHICKEN — Rufus Thomas (Stax)
22	12	GROOVIN' WITH MR. BLOE — Mr. Bloe (DJM)
9	13	TRAVELLIN' BAND — Creedence Clearwater Revival (Liberty)
14	14	ABC — Jackson Five (Tamla Motown)
20	14	EVERYTHING IS BEAUTIFUL — Ray Stevens (CBS)
24	16	UP THE LADDER TO THE ROOF — Supremes (Tamla Motown)
30	17	DON'T YOU KNOW — Butterscotch (RCA)
18	18	THE SEEKER Who (Track)
10	19	ALL KINDS OF EVERYTHING — Dana (Rex)
27	20	EL CONDOR PASA — Julie Felix (RAK)
16	21	CAN'T HELP FALLIN' IN LOVE — Andy Williams (CBS)
18	22	BRIDGE OVER TROUBLED WATER — Simon & Garfunkel (CBS)
13	23	NEVER HAD A DREAM COME TRUE — Stevie Wonder (Tamla Motown)
25	24	ABRAHAM MARTIN AND JOHN — Marvin Gaye (Tamla Motown)
26	25	I'VE GOT YOU ON MY MIND — White Plains (Deram)
21	26	RAG MAMA RAG — Band (Capitol)
29	27	KENTUCKY RAIN — Elvis Presley (RCA)
-	28	COTTONFIELDS — Beach Boys (Capitol)
-	29	THE GREEN MANALISHI — Fleetwood Mac (Reprise)
-	29	BET YER LIFE I DO — Herman's Hermits (RAK)

6 June 1970

LW	TW	Entry
2	1	YELLOW RIVER Christie (CBS)
1	2	QUESTION — Moody Blues (Threshold)
3	3	BACK HOME — England World Cup Squad (Pye)
8	4	HONEY COME BACK — Glen Campbell (Capitol)
12	5	GROOVIN' WITH MR. BLOE — Mr. Bloe (DJM)
16	6	UP THE LADDER TO THE ROOF — Supremes (Tamla Motown)
10	7	I DON'T BELIEVE IN IF ANY MORE — Roger Whittaker (Columbia)
14	8	ABC — Jackson Five (Tamla Motown)
14	9	EVERYTHING IS BEAUTIFUL — Ray Stevens (CBS)
6	10	BRONTOSAURUS — Move (Regal Zonophone)
28	11	COTTONFIELDS — Beach Boys (Capitol)
4	12	SPIRIT IN THE SKY — Norman Greenbaum (Reprise)
5	13	HOUSE OF THE RISING SUN — Frijid Pink (Deram)
7	14	DAUGHTER OF DARKNESS — Tom Jones (Decca)
-	15	IN THE SUMMERTIME — Mungo Jerry (Dawn)
29	16	THE GREEN MANALISHI — Fleetwood Mac (Reprise)
24	17	ABRAHAM MARTIN AND JOHN — Marvin Gaye (Tamla Motown)
17	18	DON'T YOU KNOW — Butterscotch (RCA)
9	19	I CAN'T TELL THE BOTTOM FROM THE TOP Hollies (Parlophone)
11	20	DO THE FUNKY CHICKEN — Rufus Thomas (Stax)
25	21	I'VE GOT YOU ON MY MIND — White Plains (Deram)
-	22	IT'S ALL IN THE GAME — Four Tops (Tamla Motown)
27	22	KENTUCKY RAIN — Elvis Presley (RCA)
-	24	SALLY — Gerry Monroe (Chapter One)
20	25	EL CONDOR PASA — Julie Felix (RAK)
13	26	TRAVELLIN' BAND Creedence Clearwater Revival (Liberty)
29	27	BET YER LIFE I DO — Herman's Hermits (RAK)
-	28	AMERICAN WOMAN — Guess Who (RCA)
-	29	GOODBYE SAM, HELLO SAMANTHA — Cliff Richard (Columbia)
-	30	TAKE TO THE MOUNTAINS — Richard Barnes (Philips)
-	30	DOWN THE DUSTPIPE — Status Quo (Pye)

13 June 1970

LW	TW	Entry
15	1	IN THE SUMMERTIME — Mungo Jerry (Dawn)
1	2	YELLOW RIVER Christie (CBS)
2	3	QUESTION — Moody Blues (Threshold)
5	4	GROOVIN' WITH MR. BLOE — Mr. Bloe (DJM)
4	5	HONEY COME BACK — Glen Campbell (Capitol)
3	6	BACK HOME — England World Cup Squad (Pye)
9	7	EVERYTHING IS BEAUTIFUL — Ray Stevens (CBS)
6	8	UP THE LADDER TO THE ROOF — Supremes (Tamla Motown)
8	9	ABC — Jackson Five (Tamla Motown)
11	10	COTTONFIELDS — Beach Boys (Capitol)
17	11	ABRAHAM MARTIN AND JOHN — Marvin Gaye (Tamla Motown)
7	12	I DON'T BELIEVE IN IF ANY MORE — Roger Whittaker (Columbia)
16	13	THE GREEN MANALISHI — Fleetwood Mac (Reprise)
24	13	SALLY — Gerry Monroe (Chapter One)
12	15	SPIRIT IN THE SKY — Norman Greenbaum (Reprise)
22	16	IT'S ALL IN THE GAME — Four Tops (Tamla Motown)
14	17	DAUGHTER OF DARKNESS — Tom Jones (Decca)
-	18	ALL RIGHT NOW — Free (Island)
18	19	DON'T YOU KNOW — Butterscotch (RCA)
27	20	BET YER LIFE I DO — Herman's Hermits (RAK)
29	21	GOODBYE SAM, HELLO SAMANTHA — Cliff Richard (Columbia)
30	22	DOWN THE DUSTPIPE — Status Quo (Pye)
28	23	AMERICAN WOMAN — Guess Who (RCA)
22	24	KENTUCKY RAIN — Elvis Presley (RCA)
-	25	WHAT IS TRUTH — Johnny Cash (CBS)
13	26	HOUSE OF THE RISING SUN — Frijid Pink (Deram)
10	26	BRONTOSAURUS — Move (Regal Zonophone)
20	28	DO THE FUNKY CHICKEN — Rufus Thomas (Stax)
-	29	I WILL SURVIVE — Arrival (Decca)
-	30	GROUPIE GIRL — Tony Joe White (Monument)

England's 1970 World Cup Squad fared better with their 'musical' venture *Back Home* (and there was a football-shaped sleeve to boot) than they eventually did in the defence of their 1966 world title. *Up The Ladder To The Roof* introduced the Supremes with new lead singer Jean Terrell (sister of boxer Ernie), while Marvin Gaye's version of *Abraham, Martin & John*, taken off one of his albums specifically for the UK market, succeeded here where Dion's original US million-seller had failed in 1968.

20 June 1970

last week	this week	Title / Artist
1	1	IN THE SUMMERTIME — Mungo Jerry (Dawn)
2	2	YELLOW RIVER — Christie (CBS)
4	3	GROOVIN' WITH MR. BLOE — Mr. Bloe (DJM)
5	4	HONEY COME BACK — Glen Campbell (Capitol)
10	5	COTTONFIELDS — Beach Boys (Capitol)
6	6	BACK HOME — England World Cup Squad (Pye)
11	7	ABRAHAM MARTIN AND JOHN — Marvin Gaye (Tamla Motown)
8	8	UP THE LADDER TO THE ROOF — Supremes (Tamla Motown)
13	9	SALLY — Gerry Monroe (Chapter One)
7	10	QUESTION — Moody Blues (Threshold)
7	11	EVERYTHING IS BEAUTIFUL — Ray Stevens (CBS)
13	12	THE GREEN MANALISHI — Fleetwood Mac (Reprise)
16	13	IT'S ALL IN THE GAME — Four Tops (Tamla Motown)
9	14	ABC — Jackson Five (Tamla Motown)
18	15	ALL RIGHT NOW — Free (Island)
21	16	GOODBYE SAM, HELLO SAMANTHA — Cliff Richard (Columbia)
12	16	I DON'T BELIEVE IN IF ANY MORE — Roger Whittaker (Columbia)
22	18	DOWN THE DUSTPIPE — Status Quo (Pye)
29	19	I WILL SURVIVE — Arrival (Decca)
20	19	BET YER LIFE I DO — Herman's Hermits (RAK)
15	21	SPIRIT IN THE SKY — Norman Greenbaum (Reprise)
24	22	KENTUCKY RAIN — Elvis Presley (RCA)
-	23	LOVE OF THE COMMON PEOPLE — Nicky Thomas (Trojan)
19	24	DON'T YOU KNOW — Butterscotch (RCA)
23	25	AMERICAN WOMAN — Guess Who (RCA)
25	26	WHAT IS TRUTH — Johnny Cash (CBS)
17	26	DAUGHTER OF DARKNESS — Tom Jones (Decca)
-	28	PSYCHEDELIC SHACK — Temptations (Tamla Motown)
30	29	GROUPIE GIRL — Tony Joe White (Monument)
-	30	UP AROUND THE BEND — Creedence Clearwater Revival (Liberty)

27 June 1970

last week	this week	Title / Artist
1	1	IN THE SUMMERTIME — Mungo Jerry (Dawn)
3	2	GROOVIN' WITH MR. BLOE — Mr. Bloe (DJM)
5	3	COTTONFIELDS — Beach Boys (Capitol)
4	4	HONEY COME BACK — Glen Campbell (Capitol)
9	4	SALLY — Gerry Monroe (Chapter One)
15	6	ALL RIGHT NOW — Free (Island)
16	7	GOODBYE SAM, HELLO SAMANTHA — Cliff Richard (Columbia)
	8	ABRAHAM MARTIN AND JOHN — Marvin Gaye (Tamla Motown)
2	9	YELLOW RIVER — Christie (CBS)
12	10	THE GREEN MANALISHI — Fleetwood Mac (Reprise)
8	11	UP THE LADDER TO THE ROOF — Supremes (Tamla Motown)
11	12	EVERYTHING IS BEAUTIFUL — Ray Stevens (CBS)
13	13	IT'S ALL IN THE GAME — Four Tops (Tamla Motown)
10	14	QUESTION — Moody Blues (Threshold)
19	15	I WILL SURVIVE — Arrival (Decca)
14	16	ABC — Jackson Five (Tamla Motown)
6	17	BACK HOME — England World Cup Squad (Pye)
18	18	DOWN THE DUSTPIPE — Status Quo (Pye)
23	19	LOVE OF THE COMMON PEOPLE — Nicky Thomas (Trojan)
30	20	UP AROUND THE BEND — Creedence Clearwater Revival (Liberty)
26	21	WHAT IS TRUTH — Johnny Cash (CBS)
22	22	KENTUCKY RAIN — Elvis Presley (RCA)
16	23	I DON'T BELIEVE IN IF ANY MORE — Roger Whittaker (Columbia)
28	24	PSYCHEDELIC SHACK — Temptations (Tamla Motown)
19	25	BET YER LIFE I DO — Herman's Hermits (RAK)
-	26	SOMETHING — Shirley Bassey (United Artists)
25	27	AMERICAN WOMAN — Guess Who (RCA)
29	28	GROUPIE GIRL — Tony Joe White (Monument)
24	29	DON'T YOU KNOW — Butterscotch (RCA)
21	29	SPIRIT IN THE SKY — Norman Greenbaum (Reprise)

4 July 1970

last week	this week	Title / Artist
1	1	IN THE SUMMERTIME — Mungo Jerry (Dawn)
6	2	ALL RIGHT NOW — Free (Island)
2	3	GROOVIN' WITH MR. BLOE — Mr. Bloe (DJM)
3	4	COTTONFIELDS — Beach Boys (Capitol)
4	5	SALLY — Gerry Monroe (Chapter One)
7	6	GOODBYE SAM, HELLO SAMANTHA — Cliff Richard (Columbia)
13	7	IT'S ALL IN THE GAME — Four Tops (Tamla Motown)
20	8	UP AROUND THE BEND — Creedence Clearwater Revival (Liberty)
9	9	YELLOW RIVER — Christie (CBS)
4	10	HONEY COME BACK — Glen Campbell (Capitol)
10	11	THE GREEN MANALISHI — Fleetwood Mac (Reprise)
8	12	ABRAHAM MARTIN AND JOHN — Marvin Gaye (Tamla Motown)
11	13	UP THE LADDER TO THE ROOF — Supremes (Tamla Motown)
15	14	I WILL SURVIVE — Arrival (Decca)
12	15	EVERYTHING IS BEAUTIFUL — Ray Stevens (CBS)
18	16	DOWN THE DUSTPIPE — Status Quo (Pye)
19	17	LOVE OF THE COMMON PEOPLE — Nicky Thomas (Trojan)
26	18	SOMETHING — Shirley Bassey (United Artists)
28	19	GROUPIE GIRL — Tony Joe White (Monument)
27	20	AMERICAN WOMAN — Guess Who (RCA)
14	21	QUESTION — Moody Blues (Threshold)
-	22	LOLA — Kinks (Pye)
22	23	KENTUCKY RAIN — Elvis Presley (RCA)
17	24	BACK HOME — England World Cup Squad (Pye)
-	24	VEHICLE — Ides of March (Warner Bros)
23	26	I DON'T BELIEVE IN IF ANY MORE — Roger Whittaker (Columbia)
16	27	ABC — Jackson Five (Tamla Motown)
21	28	WHAT IS TRUTH — Johnny Cash (CBS)
-	29	BIG YELLOW TAXI — Joni Mitchell (Reprise)
-	30	REACH OUT AND TOUCH — Diana Ross (Tamla Motown)
30	30	SIGNED, SEALED, DELIVERED, I'M YOURS — Stevie Wonder (Tamla Motown)

11 July 1970

last week	this week	Title / Artist
2	1	ALL RIGHT NOW — Free (Island)
1	2	IN THE SUMMERTIME — Mungo Jerry (Dawn)
3	3	GROOVIN' WITH MR. BLOE — Mr. Bloe (DJM)
5	4	SALLY — Gerry Monroe (Chapter One)
6	5	GOODBYE SAM, HELLO SAMANTHA — Cliff Richard (Columbia)
4	6	COTTONFIELDS — Beach Boys (Capitol)
8	7	UP AROUND THE BEND — Creedence Clearwater Revival (Liberty)
7	7	IT'S ALL IN THE GAME — Four Tops (Tamla Motown)
16	9	DOWN THE DUSTPIPE — Status Quo (Pye)
18	10	SOMETHING — Shirley Bassey (United Artists)
10	11	HONEY COME BACK — Glen Campbell (Capitol)
11	12	THE GREEN MANALISHI — Fleetwood Mac (Reprise)
9	13	YELLOW RIVER — Christie (CBS)
17	14	LOVE OF THE COMMON PEOPLE — Nicky Thomas (Trojan)
22	15	LOLA — Kinks (Pye)
12	16	ABRAHAM MARTIN AND JOHN — Marvin Gaye (Tamla Motown)
14	17	I WILL SURVIVE — Arrival (Decca)
15	18	EVERYTHING IS BEAUTIFUL — Ray Stevens (CBS)
19	19	GROUPIE GIRL — Tony Joe White (Monument)
13	20	UP THE LADDER TO THE ROOF — Supremes (Tamla Motown)
20	21	AMERICAN WOMAN — Guess Who (RCA)
-	22	LADY D'ARBANVILLE — Cat Stevens (Island)
-	23	THE WONDER OF YOU — Elvis Presley (RCA)
-	24	NEANDERTHAL MAN — Hotlegs (Fontana)
24	25	VEHICLE — Ides of March (Warner Bros)
-	26	BET YER LIFE I DO — Herman's Hermits (RAK)
30	26	SIGNED, SEALED, DELIVERED, I'M YOURS — Stevie Wonder (Tamla Motown)
24	28	BACK HOME — England World Cup Squad (Pye)
-	29	LOVE LIKE A MAN — Ten Years After (Deram)
21	30	QUESTION — Moody Blues (Threshold)

Mungo Jerry's lucky break was, as complete unknowns, upstaging the likes of the Grateful Dead at the quaintly named Hollywood festival (it was held in the depths of rural England) and having the attendant music press raving over their performance. The rollicking *In The Summertime*, released on the crest of this publicity wave, was then an almost instant Number One. In later years its exhortation to *'have a drink have a drive'* and *'do a ton and twenty-five'* would probably have been condemned.

July – August 1970

last this week

18 July 1970

last	this	
1	1	ALL RIGHT NOW — Free (Island)
2	2	IN THE SUMMERTIME — Mungo Jerry (Dawn)
7	3	IT'S ALL IN THE GAME — Four Tops (Tamla Motown)
7	4	UP AROUND THE BEND — Creedence Clearwater Revival (Liberty)
15	5	LOLA — Kinks (Pye)
3	6	GROOVIN' WITH MR. BLOE — Mr. Bloe (DJM)
10	7	SOMETHING — Shirley Bassey (United Artists)
14	8	LOVE OF THE COMMON PEOPLE — Nicky Thomas (Trojan)
5	9	GOODBYE SAM, HELLO SAMANTHA — Cliff Richard (Columbia)
4	10	SALLY — Gerry Monroe (Chapter One)
6	11	COTTONFIELDS — Beach Boys (Capitol)
9	12	DOWN THE DUSTPIPE — Status Quo (Pye)
22	13	LADY D'ARBANVILLE — Cat Stevens (Island)
12	14	THE GREEN MANALISHI MAN — Fleetwood Mac (Reprise)
11	15	HONEY COME BACK — Glen Campbell (Capitol)
23	16	THE WONDER OF YOU — Elvis Presley (RCA)
16	17	ABRAHAM MARTIN AND JOHN — Marvin Gaye (Tamla Motown)
13	18	YELLOW RIVER — Christie (CBS)
-	19	I'LL SAY FOREVER MY LOVE — Jimmy Ruffin (Tamla Motown)
24	20	NEANDERTHAL MAN — Hotlegs (Fontana)
17	21	I WILL SURVIVE — Arrival (Decca)
29	22	LOVE LIKE A MAN — Ten Years After (Deram)
26	23	SIGNED, SEALED, DELIVERED, I'M YOURS — Stevie Wonder (Tamla Motown)
19	24	GROUPIE GIRL — Tony Joe White (Monument)
18	25	EVERYTHING IS BEAUTIFUL — Ray Stevens (CBS)
-	26	SAD OLD KINDA MOVIE — Pickettywitch (Pye)
20	27	UP THE LADDER TO THE ROOF — Supremes (Tamla Motown)
-	28	BIG YELLOW TAXI — Joni Mitchell (Reprise)
21	29	AMERICAN WOMAN — Guess Who (RCA)
25	30	VEHICLE — Ides of March (Warner Bros)

25 July 1970

last	this	
1	1	ALL RIGHT NOW — Free (Island)
2	2	IN THE SUMMERTIME — Mungo Jerry (Dawn)
3	3	IT'S ALL IN THE GAME — Four Tops (Tamla Motown)
5	4	LOLA — Kinks (Pye)
4	5	UP AROUND THE BEND — Creedence Clearwater Revival (Liberty)
7	6	SOMETHING — Shirley Bassey (United Artists)
16	7	THE WONDER OF YOU — Elvis Presley (RCA)
13	8	LADY D'ARBANVILLE — Cat Stevens (Island)
8	9	LOVE OF THE COMMON PEOPLE — Nicky Thomas (Trojan)
9	10	GOODBYE SAM, HELLO SAMANTHA — Cliff Richard (Columbia)
6	11	GROOVIN' WITH MR. BLOE — Mr. Bloe (DJM)
10	12	SALLY — Gerry Monroe (Chapter One)
11	13	COTTONFIELDS — Beach Boys (Capitol)
19	14	I'LL SAY FOREVER MY LOVE — Jimmy Ruffin (Tamla Motown)
20	15	NEANDERTHAL MAN — Hotlegs (Fontana)
26	16	SAD OLD KINDA MOVIE — Pickettywitch (Pye)
12	17	DOWN THE DUSTPIPE — Status Quo (Pye)
22	18	LOVE LIKE A MAN — Ten Years After (Deram)
15	19	HONEY COME BACK — Glen Campbell (Capitol)
14	20	THE GREEN MANALISHI MAN — Fleetwood Mac (Reprise)
23	21	SIGNED, SEALED, DELIVERED, I'M YOURS — Stevie Wonder (Tamla Motown)
-	22	A SONG OF JOY — Miguel Rios (A&M)
28	23	BIG YELLOW TAXI — Joni Mitchell (Reprise)
18	24	YELLOW RIVER — Christie (CBS)
-	25	NATURAL SINNER — Fair Weather (RCA)
25	26	EVERYTHING IS BEAUTIFUL — Ray Stevens (CBS)
24	27	GROUPIE GIRL — Tony Joe White (Monument)
-	28	WHERE ARE YOU GOING TO MY LOVE? — Brotherhood of Man (Deram)
-	29	REACH OUT AND TOUCH — Diana Ross (Tamla Motown)
-	30	RAINBOW — Marmalade (Decca)

1 August 1970

last	this	
4	1	LOLA — Kinks (Pye)
1	2	ALL RIGHT NOW — Free (Island)
7	3	THE WONDER OF YOU — Elvis Presley (RCA)
2	4	IN THE SUMMERTIME — Mungo Jerry (Dawn)
6	5	SOMETHING — Shirley Bassey (United Artists)
3	6	IT'S ALL IN THE GAME — Four Tops (Tamla Motown)
15	6	NEANDERTHAL MAN — Hotlegs (Fontana)
5	8	UP AROUND THE BEND — Creedence Clearwater Revival (Liberty)
8	9	LADY D'ARBANVILLE — Cat Stevens (Island)
9	10	LOVE OF THE COMMON PEOPLE — Nicky Thomas (Trojan)
14	11	I'LL SAY FOREVER MY LOVE — Jimmy Ruffin (Tamla Motown)
18	12	LOVE LIKE A MAN — Ten Years After (Deram)
13	13	COTTONFIELDS — Beach Boys (Capitol)
10	14	GOODBYE SAM, HELLO SAMANTHA — Cliff Richard (Columbia)
16	15	SAD OLD KINDA MOVIE — Pickettywitch (Pye)
11	16	GROOVIN' WITH MR. BLOE — Mr. Bloe (DJM)
23	17	BIG YELLOW TAXI — Joni Mitchell (Reprise)
12	18	SALLY — Gerry Monroe (Chapter One)
21	19	SIGNED, SEALED, DELIVERED, I'M YOURS — Stevie Wonder (Tamla Motown)
22	20	A SONG OF JOY — Miguel Rios (A&M)
17	21	DOWN THE DUSTPIPE — Status Quo (Pye)
30	22	RAINBOW — Marmalade (Decca)
19	23	HONEY COME BACK — Glen Campbell (Capitol)
20	24	THE GREEN MANALISHI MAN — Fleetwood Mac (Reprise)
25	25	NATURAL SINNER — Fair Weather (RCA)
24	26	YELLOW RIVER — Christie (CBS)
28	27	WHERE ARE YOU GOING TO MY LOVE? — Brotherhood of Man (Deram)
-	28	SWEET INSPIRATION — Johnny Johnson & the Bandwagon (Bell)
27	29	GROUPIE GIRL — Tony Joe White (Monument)
-	30	25 OR 6 TO 4 — Chicago (CBS)
-	30	THE LETTER — Joe Cocker (Regal Zonophone)

8 August 1970

last	this	
3	1	THE WONDER OF YOU — Elvis Presley (RCA)
1	2	LOLA — Kinks (Pye)
2	3	ALL RIGHT NOW — Free (Island)
6	4	NEANDERTHAL MAN — Hotlegs (Fontana)
5	5	SOMETHING — Shirley Bassey (United Artists)
4	6	IN THE SUMMERTIME — Mungo Jerry (Dawn)
11	7	I'LL SAY FOREVER MY LOVE — Jimmy Ruffin (Tamla Motown)
6	8	IT'S ALL IN THE GAME — Four Tops (Tamla Motown)
9	9	LADY D'ARBANVILLE — Cat Stevens (Island)
12	10	LOVE LIKE A MAN — Ten Years After (Deram)
8	11	UP AROUND THE BEND — Creedence Clearwater Revival (Liberty)
22	12	RAINBOW — Marmalade (Decca)
10	13	LOVE OF THE COMMON PEOPLE — Nicky Thomas (Trojan)
17	14	BIG YELLOW TAXI — Joni Mitchell (Reprise)
19	15	SIGNED, SEALED, DELIVERED, I'M YOURS — Stevie Wonder (Tamla Motown)
15	16	SAD OLD KINDA MOVIE — Pickettywitch (Pye)
13	17	COTTONFIELDS — Beach Boys (Capitol)
20	18	A SONG OF JOY — Miguel Rios (A&M)
25	19	NATURAL SINNER — Fair Weather (RCA)
14	20	GOODBYE SAM, HELLO SAMANTHA — Cliff Richard (Columbia)
27	21	WHERE ARE YOU GOING TO MY LOVE? — Brotherhood of Man (Deram)
-	22	THE LOVE YOU SAVE — Jackson Five (Tamla Motown)
18	23	SALLY — Gerry Monroe (Chapter One)
16	24	GROOVIN' WITH MR. BLOE — Mr. Bloe (DJM)
-	25	TEARS OF A CLOWN — Smokey Robinson & the Miracles (Tamla Motown)
30	26	25 OR 6 TO 4 — Chicago (CBS)
28	27	SWEET INSPIRATION — Johnny Johnson & the Bandwagon (Bell)
26	28	YELLOW RIVER — Christie (CBS)
23	29	HONEY COME BACK — Glen Campbell (Capitol)
21	30	DOWN THE DUSTPIPE — Status Quo (Pye)

Lola very nearly caused BBC airplay problems for the Kinks, since its mention of Coca-Cola transgressed the 'no tradenames' rule. With this in mind Ray Davies interrupted a US visit to fly back to London and re-edit a version for the Beeb which inserted the more general *'cherry'* in place of *'Coca'*, and thus passed muster. Normal copies in the shops remained as before, and nobody, except presumably the BBC's advertising-alert squad, was really aware of the problem or the change.

August – September 1970

15 August 1970

LW	TW	Title / Artist (Label)
1	1	THE WONDER OF YOU — Elvis Presley (RCA)
4	2	NEANDERTHAL MAN — Hotlegs (Fontana)
2	3	LOLA — Kinks (Pye)
5	4	SOMETHING — Shirley Bassey (United Artists)
3	5	LADY D'ARBANVILLE — Cat Stevens (Island)
6	6	ALL RIGHT NOW — Free (Island)
10	7	LOVE LIKE A MAN — Ten Years After (Deram)
7	8	I'LL SAY FOREVER MY LOVE — Jimmy Ruffin (Tamla Motown)
12	9	RAINBOW — Marmalade (Decca)
15	10	SIGNED, SEALED, DELIVERED, I'M YOURS — Stevie Wonder (Tamla Motown)
8	11	IT'S ALL IN THE GAME — Four Tops (Tamla Motown)
6	12	IN THE SUMMERTIME — Mungo Jerry (Dawn)
25	13	TEARS OF A CLOWN — Smokey Robinson & the Miracles (Tamla Motown)
19	14	NATURAL SINNER — Fair Weather (RCA)
14	15	BIG YELLOW TAXI — Joni Mitchell (Reprise)
22	16	THE LOVE YOU SAVE — Jackson Five (Tamla Motown)
11	17	UP AROUND THE BEND — Creedence Clearwater Revival (Liberty)
18	18	A SONG OF JOY — Miguel Rios (A&M)
13	19	LOVE OF THE COMMON PEOPLE — Nicky Thomas (Trojan)
26	20	25 OR 6 TO 4 — Chicago (CBS)
16	21	SAD OLD KINDA MOVIE — Pickettywitch (Pye)
27	22	SWEET INSPIRATION — Johnny Johnson & the Bandwagon (Bell)
17	23	COTTONFIELDS — Beach Boys (Capitol)
-	24	IT'S SO EASY — Andy Williams (CBS)
20	25	GOODBYE SAM, HELLO SAMANTHA — Cliff Richard (Columbia)
21	26	WHERE ARE YOU GOING TO MY LOVE? — Brotherhood of Man (Deram)
23	27	GROOVIN' WITH MR. BLOE — Mr. Bloe (DJM)
-	28	MR. PRESIDENT — Dozy, Beaky, Mick & Tich (Fontana)
-	29	MAKE IT WITH YOU — Bread (Elektra)
-	30	WILD WORLD — Jimmy Cliff (Island)

22 August 1970

LW	TW	Title / Artist (Label)
1	1	THE WONDER OF YOU — Elvis Presley (RCA)
2	2	NEANDERTHAL MAN — Hotlegs (Fontana)
3	3	LOLA — Kinks (Pye)
4	4	SOMETHING — Shirley Bassey (United Artists)
13	5	TEARS OF A CLOWN — Smokey Robinson & the Miracles (Tamla Motown)
9	6	RAINBOW — Marmalade (Decca)
14	7	NATURAL SINNER — Fair Weather (RCA)
6	8	ALL RIGHT NOW — Free (Island)
7	9	LOVE LIKE A MAN — Ten Years After (Deram)
20	10	25 OR 6 TO 4 — Chicago (CBS)
16	11	THE LOVE YOU SAVE — Jackson Five (Tamla Motown)
8	12	I'LL SAY FOREVER MY LOVE — Jimmy Ruffin (Tamla Motown)
10	13	SIGNED, SEALED, DELIVERED, I'M YOURS — Stevie Wonder (Tamla Motown)
5	14	LADY D'ARBANVILLE — Cat Stevens (Island)
15	15	BIG YELLOW TAXI — Joni Mitchell (Reprise)
12	16	IN THE SUMMERTIME — Mungo Jerry (Dawn)
-	17	MAMA TOLD ME NOT TO COME — Three Dog Night (Stateside)
22	18	SWEET INSPIRATION — Johnny Johnson & the Bandwagon (Bell)
17	19	A SONG OF JOY — Miguel Rios (A&M)
11	20	IT'S ALL IN THE GAME — Four Tops (Tamla Motown)
17	21	UP AROUND THE BEND — Creedence Clearwater Revival (Liberty)
30	22	WILD WORLD — Jimmy Cliff (Island)
-	23	I (WHO HAVE NOTHING) — Tom Jones (Decca)
24	24	IT'S SO EASY — Andy Williams (CBS)
29	25	MAKE IT WITH YOU — Bread (Elektra)
19	26	LOVE OF THE COMMON PEOPLE — Nicky Thomas (Trojan)
21	27	SAD OLD KINDA MOVIE — Pickettywitch (Pye)
23	28	COTTONFIELDS — Beach Boys (Capitol)
-	29	GIVE ME JUST A LITTLE MORE TIME — Chairmen of the Board (Invictus)
-	30	LOVE IS LIFE — Hot Chocolate (RAK)

29 August 1970

LW	TW	Title / Artist (Label)
5	1	TEARS OF A CLOWN — Smokey Robinson & the Miracles (Tamla Motown)
1	2	THE WONDER OF YOU — Elvis Presley (RCA)
2	3	NEANDERTHAL MAN — Hotlegs (Fontana)
6	4	RAINBOW — Marmalade (Decca)
4	5	SOMETHING — Shirley Bassey (United Artists)
3	6	LOLA — Kinks (Pye)
7	7	NATURAL SINNER — Fair Weather (RCA)
17	8	MAMA TOLD ME NOT TO COME — Three Dog Night (Stateside)
10	9	25 OR 6 TO 4 — Chicago (CBS)
11	10	THE LOVE YOU SAVE — Jackson Five (Tamla Motown)
18	11	SWEET INSPIRATION — Johnny Johnson & the Bandwagon (Bell)
15	12	BIG YELLOW TAXI — Joni Mitchell (Reprise)
9	13	LOVE LIKE A MAN — Ten Years After (Deram)
22	14	WILD WORLD — Jimmy Cliff (Island)
30	15	LOVE IS LIFE — Hot Chocolate (RAK)
12	15	I'LL SAY FOREVER MY LOVE — Jimmy Ruffin (Tamla Motown)
29	17	GIVE ME JUST A LITTLE MORE TIME — Chairmen of the Board (Invictus)
16	18	IN THE SUMMERTIME — Mungo Jerry (Dawn)
25	19	MAKE IT WITH YOU — Bread (Elektra)
23	20	I (WHO HAVE NOTHING) — Tom Jones (Decca)
13	21	SIGNED, SEALED, DELIVERED, I'M YOURS — Stevie Wonder (Tamla Motown)
8	22	ALL RIGHT NOW — Free (Island)
24	23	IT'S SO EASY — Andy Williams (CBS)
14	24	LADY D'ARBANVILLE — Cat Stevens (Island)
19	25	A SONG OF JOY — Miguel Rios (A&M)
20	26	IT'S ALL IN THE GAME — Four Tops (Tamla Motown)
26	27	LOVE OF THE COMMON PEOPLE — Nicky Thomas (Trojan)
28	28	COTTONFIELDS — Beach Boys (Capitol)
-	29	BLACK NIGHT — Deep Purple (Harvest)
27	30	SAD OLD KINDA MOVIE — Pickettywitch (Pye)

5 September 1970

LW	TW	Title / Artist (Label)
1	1	TEARS OF A CLOWN — Smokey Robinson & the Miracles (Tamla Motown)
2	2	THE WONDER OF YOU — Elvis Presley (RCA)
8	3	MAMA TOLD ME NOT TO COME — Three Dog Night (Stateside)
17	4	GIVE ME JUST A LITTLE MORE TIME — Chairmen of the Board (Invictus)
4	5	RAINBOW — Marmalade (Decca)
3	6	NEANDERTHAL MAN — Hotlegs (Fontana)
9	7	25 OR 6 TO 4 — Chicago (CBS)
15	8	LOVE IS LIFE — Hot Chocolate (RAK)
19	9	MAKE IT WITH YOU — Bread (Elektra)
7	10	NATURAL SINNER — Fair Weather (RCA)
14	11	WILD WORLD — Jimmy Cliff (Island)
11	12	SWEET INSPIRATION — Johnny Johnson & the Bandwagon (Bell)
5	13	SOMETHING — Shirley Bassey (United Artists)
10	14	THE LOVE YOU SAVE — Jackson Five (Tamla Motown)
6	15	LOLA — Kinks (Pye)
13	16	LOVE LIKE A MAN — Ten Years After (Deram)
-	17	YOU CAN GET IT IF YOU REALLY WANT — Desmond Dekker (Trojan)
23	18	IT'S SO EASY — Andy Williams (CBS)
20	19	I (WHO HAVE NOTHING) — Tom Jones (Decca)
-	20	DON'T PLAY THAT SONG — Aretha Franklin (Atlantic)
12	21	BIG YELLOW TAXI — Joni Mitchell (Reprise)
15	22	I'LL SAY FOREVER MY LOVE — Jimmy Ruffin (Tamla Motown)
18	23	IN THE SUMMERTIME — Mungo Jerry (Dawn)
-	24	WHICH WAY YOU GOIN' BILLY — Poppy Family (Decca)
-	25	MONTEGO BAY — Bobby Bloom (Polydor)
22	26	ALL RIGHT NOW — Free (Island)
-	27	LONG AS I CAN SEE THE LIGHT — Creedence Clearwater Revival (Liberty)
21	28	SIGNED, SEALED, DELIVERED, I'M YOURS — Stevie Wonder (Tamla Motown)
24	29	LADY D'ARBANVILLE — Cat Stevens (Island)
-	30	JIMMY MACK — Martha & the Vandellas (Tamla Motown)

The 1950s oldie *The Wonder Of You* was released in a version recorded live by Elvis in Las Vegas, and was to be his last chart-topper in his lifetime. Smokey Robinson & the Miracles' *Tears Of A Clown*, which took over at Number One, was an LP track spotted as a likely single winner by Motown's UK division. Only after it topped the UK chart did the parent company in America decided to release it as a single. It then proceeded to make it to the top of the chart in the States too.

September – October 1970

12 September 1970

last	this	
1	1	TEARS OF A CLOWN — Smokey Robinson & the Miracles (Tamla Motown)
2	2	THE WONDER OF YOU — Elvis Presley (RCA)
3	3	MAMA TOLD ME NOT TO COME — Three Dog Night (Stateside)
4	4	GIVE ME JUST A LITTLE MORE TIME — Chairmen of the Board (Invictus)
9	5	MAKE IT WITH YOU — Bread (Elektra)
5	6	RAINBOW — Marmalade (Decca)
8	7	LOVE IS LIFE — Hot Chocolate (RAK)
7	8	25 OR 6 TO 4 — Chicago (CBS)
-	9	BAND OF GOLD — Freda Payne (Invictus)
11	10	WILD WORLD — Jimmy Cliff (Island)
11	11	SWEET INSPIRATION — Johnny Johnson & the Bandwagon (Bell)
6	12	NEANDERTHAL MAN — Hotlegs (Fontana)
13	13	SOMETHING — Shirley Bassey (United Artists)
17	14	YOU CAN GET IT IF YOU REALLY WANT — Desmond Dekker (Trojan)
10	15	NATURAL SINNER — Fair Weather (RCA)
18	16	IT'S SO EASY — Andy Williams (CBS)
25	17	MONTEGO BAY — Bobby Bloom (Polydor)
24	18	WHICH WAY YOU GOIN' BILLY — Poppy Family (Decca)
19	19	I (WHO HAVE NOTHING) — Tom Jones (Decca)
20	20	DON'T PLAY THAT SONG — Aretha Franklin (Atlantic)
15	21	LOLA — Kinks (Pye)
30	22	JIMMY MACK — Martha & the Vandellas (Tamla Motown)
14	23	THE LOVE YOU SAVE — Jackson Five (Tamla Motown)
-	24	STRANGE BAND/THE WEAVER'S ANSWER — Family (Reprise)
16	25	LOVE LIKE A MAN — Ten Years After (Deram)
27	26	LONG AS I CAN SEE THE LIGHT — Creedence Clearwater Revival (Liberty)
-	27	I AIN'T GOT TIME ANY MORE — Cliff Richard (Columbia)
-	28	AIN'T NO MOUNTAIN HIGH ENOUGH — Diana Ross (Tamla Motown)
21	29	BIG YELLOW TAXI — Joni Mitchell (Reprise)
22	30	I'LL SAY FOREVER MY LOVE — Jimmy Ruffin (Tamla Motown)

19 September 1970

last	this	
1	1	TEARS OF A CLOWN — Smokey Robinson & the Miracles (Tamla Motown)
4	2	GIVE ME JUST A LITTLE MORE TIME — Chairmen of the Board (Invictus)
3	3	MAMA TOLD ME NOT TO COME — Three Dog Night (Stateside)
9	4	BAND OF GOLD — Freda Payne (Invictus)
2	5	THE WONDER OF YOU — Elvis Presley (RCA)
5	6	MAKE IT WITH YOU — Bread (Elektra)
10	7	WILD WORLD — Jimmy Cliff (Island)
7	8	LOVE IS LIFE — Hot Chocolate (RAK)
18	9	WHICH WAY YOU GOIN' BILLY — Poppy Family (Decca)
17	10	MONTEGO BAY — Bobby Bloom (Polydor)
14	11	YOU CAN GET IT IF YOU REALLY WANT — Desmond Dekker (Trojan)
8	12	25 OR 6 TO 4 — Chicago (CBS)
6	13	RAINBOW — Marmalade (Decca)
11	14	SWEET INSPIRATION — Johnny Johnson & the Bandwagon (Bell)
15	15	IT'S SO EASY — Andy Williams (CBS)
20	16	DON'T PLAY THAT SONG — Aretha Franklin (Atlantic)
22	17	JIMMY MACK — Martha & the Vandellas (Tamla Motown)
28	18	AIN'T NO MOUNTAIN HIGH ENOUGH — Diana Ross (Tamla Motown)
24	19	STRANGE BAND/THE WEAVER'S ANSWER — Family (Reprise)
19	20	I (WHO HAVE NOTHING) — Tom Jones (Decca)
12	21	NEANDERTHAL MAN — Hotlegs (Fontana)
13	22	SOMETHING — Shirley Bassey (United Artists)
26	23	LONG AS I CAN SEE THE LIGHT — Creedence Clearwater Revival (Liberty)
15	24	NATURAL SINNER — Fair Weather (RCA)
-	25	(THEY LONG TO BE) CLOSE TO YOU — Carpenters (A&M)
27	26	I AIN'T GOT TIME ANY MORE — Cliff Richard (Columbia)
-	27	SWEETHEART — Engelbert Humperdinck (Decca)
25	28	LOVE LIKE A MAN — Ten Years After (Deram)
21	29	LOLA — Kinks (Pye)
-	30	BLACK NIGHT — Deep Purple (Harvest)

26 September 1970

last	this	
4	1	BAND OF GOLD — Freda Payne (Invictus)
2	2	GIVE ME JUST A LITTLE MORE TIME — Chairmen of the Board (Invictus)
1	3	TEARS OF A CLOWN — Smokey Robinson & the Miracles (Tamla Motown)
11	4	YOU CAN GET IT IF YOU REALLY WANT — Desmond Dekker (Trojan)
3	5	MAMA TOLD ME NOT TO COME — Three Dog Night (Stateside)
10	6	MONTEGO BAY — Bobby Bloom (Polydor)
6	7	MAKE IT WITH YOU — Bread (Elektra)
8	8	LOVE IS LIFE — Hot Chocolate (RAK)
7	9	WILD WORLD — Jimmy Cliff (Island)
9	10	WHICH WAY YOU GOIN' BILLY — Poppy Family (Decca)
5	11	THE WONDER OF YOU — Elvis Presley (RCA)
16	12	DON'T PLAY THAT SONG — Aretha Franklin (Atlantic)
18	13	AIN'T NO MOUNTAIN HIGH ENOUGH — Diana Ross (Tamla Motown)
19	14	STRANGE BAND/THE WEAVER'S ANSWER — Family (Reprise)
30	15	BLACK NIGHT — Deep Purple (Harvest)
17	16	JIMMY MACK — Martha & the Vandellas (Tamla Motown)
25	17	(THEY LONG TO BE) CLOSE TO YOU — Carpenters (A&M)
15	18	IT'S SO EASY — Andy Williams (CBS)
12	19	25 OR 6 TO 4 — Chicago (CBS)
14	20	SWEET INSPIRATION — Johnny Johnson & the Bandwagon (Bell)
22	21	SOMETHING — Shirley Bassey (United Artists)
-	22	ME AND MY LIFE — Tremeloes (CBS)
-	23	BLACK PEARL — Horace Faith (Trojan)
23	24	LONG AS I CAN SEE THE LIGHT — Creedence Clearwater Revival (Liberty)
13	25	RAINBOW — Marmalade (Decca)
-	26	PARANOID — Black Sabbath (Vertigo)
20	27	I (WHO HAVE NOTHING) — Tom Jones (Decca)
27	28	SWEETHEART — Engelbert Humperdinck (Decca)
-	29	BALL OF CONFUSION — Temptations (Tamla Motown)
-	30	STILL WATER (LOVE) — Four Tops (Tamla Motown)

3 October 1970

last	this	
1	1	BAND OF GOLD — Freda Payne (Invictus)
4	2	YOU CAN GET IT IF YOU REALLY WANT — Desmond Dekker (Trojan)
6	3	MONTEGO BAY — Bobby Bloom (Polydor)
2	4	GIVE ME JUST A LITTLE MORE TIME — Chairmen of the Board (Invictus)
3	5	TEARS OF A CLOWN — Smokey Robinson & the Miracles (Tamla Motown)
15	6	BLACK NIGHT — Deep Purple (Harvest)
10	7	WHICH WAY YOU GOIN' BILLY — Poppy Family (Decca)
17	8	(THEY LONG TO BE) CLOSE TO YOU — Carpenters (A&M)
13	9	AIN'T NO MOUNTAIN HIGH ENOUGH — Diana Ross (Tamla Motown)
8	10	LOVE IS LIFE — Hot Chocolate (RAK)
7	11	MAKE IT WITH YOU — Bread (Elektra)
12	12	DON'T PLAY THAT SONG — Aretha Franklin (Atlantic)
9	13	WILD WORLD — Jimmy Cliff (Island)
5	14	MAMA TOLD ME NOT TO COME — Three Dog Night (Stateside)
11	15	THE WONDER OF YOU — Elvis Presley (RCA)
14	16	STRANGE BAND/THE WEAVER'S ANSWER — Family (Reprise)
26	17	PARANOID — Black Sabbath (Vertigo)
22	18	ME AND MY LIFE — Tremeloes (CBS)
16	19	JIMMY MACK — Martha & the Vandellas (Tamla Motown)
18	20	IT'S SO EASY — Andy Williams (CBS)
24	21	AS LONG AS I CAN SEE THE LIGHT — Creedence Clearwater Revival (Liberty)
19	22	25 OR 6 TO 4 — Chicago (CBS)
23	23	BLACK PEARL — Horace Faith (Trojan)
-	24	OUR WORLD — Blue Mink (Philips)
29	25	BALL OF CONFUSION — Temptations (Tamla Motown)
21	26	SOMETHING — Shirley Bassey (United Artists)
28	27	SWEETHEART — Engelbert Humperdinck (Decca)
30	28	STILL WATER — Four Tops (Tamla Motown)
-	29	WOODSTOCK — Matthews Southern Comfort (Uni)
-	30	I AIN'T GOT TIME ANY MORE — Cliff Richard (Columbia)

Motown's erstwhile top songwriting trio, Lamont Dozier and brothers Brian and Eddie Holland, departed the fold at the end of the sixties in search of greater creative control. This they gained via their own independent Invicta label. This got off to a notable start in the UK with its first two releases; on September 20 Freda Payne's *Band Of Gold* was topping the chart (it had taken only three weeks to get there) while the Chairmen Of The Board's *Give Me Just A Little More Time* stood at Number 10.

10 October 1970

Last	This	Title	Artist
1	1	BAND OF GOLD	Freda Payne (Invictus)
6	2	BLACK NIGHT	Deep Purple (Harvest)
2	3	YOU CAN GET IT IF YOU REALLY WANT	Desmond Dekker (Trojan)
3	4	MONTEGO BAY	Bobby Bloom (Polydor)
7	5	WHICH WAY YOU GOIN' BILLY	Poppy Family (Decca)
17	6	PARANOID	Black Sabbath (Vertigo)
8	7	(THEY LONG TO BE) CLOSE TO YOU	Carpenters (A&M)
9	8	AIN'T NO MOUNTAIN HIGH ENOUGH	Diana Ross (Tamla Motown)
4	9	GIVE ME JUST A LITTLE MORE TIME	Chairmen of the Board (Invictus)
18	10	ME AND MY LIFE	Tremeloes (CBS)
5	11	TEARS OF A CLOWN	Smokey Robinson & the Miracles (Tamla Motown)
16	12	STRANGE BAND/THE WEAVER'S ANSWER	Family (Reprise)
10	13	LOVE IS LIFE	Hot Chocolate (RAK)
12	14	DON'T PLAY THAT SONG	Aretha Franklin (Atlantic)
22	15	BLACK PEARL	Horace Faith (Trojan)
15	16	THE WONDER OF YOU	Elvis Presley (RCA)
11	17	MAKE IT WITH YOU	Bread (Elektra)
-	18	GASOLINE ALLEY BRED	Hollies (Parlophone)
25	18	BALL OF CONFUSION	Temptations (Tamla Motown)
28	20	STILL WATER	Four Tops (Tamla Motown)
14	21	MAMA TOLD ME NOT TO COME	Three Dog Night (Stateside)
24	22	OUR WORLD	Blue Mink (Philips)
21	23	AS LONG AS I CAN SEE THE LIGHT	Creedence Clearwater Revival (Liberty)
13	24	WILD WORLD	Jimmy Cliff (Island)
-	25	PATCHES	Clarence Carter (Atlantic)
19	26	JIMMY MACK	Martha & the Vandellas (Tamla Motown)
29	27	WOODSTOCK	Matthews Southern Comfort (Uni)
20	28	IT'S SO EASY	Andy Williams (CBS)
22	29	25 OR 6 TO 4	Chicago (CBS)
-	30	GET UP I FEEL LIKE BEING A SEX MACHINE	James Brown (Polydor)

17 October 1970

Last	This	Title	Artist
1	1	BAND OF GOLD	Freda Payne (Invictus)
2	2	BLACK NIGHT	Deep Purple (Harvest)
3	3	YOU CAN GET IT IF YOU REALLY WANT	Desmond Dekker (Trojan)
6	4	PARANOID	Black Sabbath (Vertigo)
7	5	(THEY LONG TO BE) CLOSE TO YOU	Carpenters (A&M)
8	6	AIN'T NO MOUNTAIN HIGH ENOUGH	Diana Ross (Tamla Motown)
4	7	MONTEGO BAY	Bobby Bloom (Polydor)
10	8	ME AND MY LIFE	Tremeloes (CBS)
20	9	STILL WATER	Four Tops (Tamla Motown)
15	10	BLACK PEARL	Horace Faith (Trojan)
18	11	BALL OF CONFUSION	Temptations (Tamla Motown)
5	12	WHICH WAY YOU GOIN' BILLY	Poppy Family (Decca)
25	13	PATCHES	Clarence Carter (Atlantic)
18	13	GASOLINE ALLEY BRED	Hollies (Parlophone)
27	15	WOODSTOCK	Matthews Southern Comfort (Uni)
9	16	GIVE ME JUST A LITTLE MORE TIME	Chairmen of the Board (Invictus)
14	17	DON'T PLAY THAT SONG	Aretha Franklin (Atlantic)
12	18	STRANGE BAND/THE WEAVER'S ANSWER	Family (Reprise)
16	19	THE WONDER OF YOU	Elvis Presley (RCA)
11	20	TEARS OF A CLOWN	Smokey Robinson & the Miracles (Tamla Motown)
-	21	RUBY TUESDAY	Melanie (Buddah)
30	22	GET UP I FEEL LIKE BEING A SEX MACHINE	James Brown (Polydor)
22	23	OUR WORLD	Blue Mink (Philips)
17	24	MAKE IT WITH YOU	Bread (Elektra)
23	25	AS LONG AS I CAN SEE THE LIGHT	Creedence Clearwater Revival (Liberty)
26	26	JIMMY MACK	Martha & the Vandellas (Tamla Motown)
-	27	WAR	Edwin Starr (Tamla Motown)
13	28	LOVE IS LIFE	Hot Chocolate (RAK)
28	29	IT'S SO EASY	Andy Williams (CBS)
-	30	EVERYTHING A MAN COULD EVER NEED	Glen Campbell (Capitol)
-	30	THE TIPS OF MY FINGERS	Des O'Connor (Columbia)

24 October 1970

Last	This	Title	Artist
1	1	BAND OF GOLD	Freda Payne (Invictus)
2	2	BLACK NIGHT	Deep Purple (Harvest)
5	3	(THEY LONG TO BE) CLOSE TO YOU	Carpenters (A&M)
15	4	WOODSTOCK	Matthews Southern Comfort (Uni)
13	5	PATCHES	Clarence Carter (Atlantic)
8	6	ME AND MY LIFE	Tremeloes (CBS)
4	7	PARANOID	Black Sabbath (Vertigo)
6	8	AIN'T NO MOUNTAIN HIGH ENOUGH	Diana Ross (Tamla Motown)
7	9	MONTEGO BAY	Bobby Bloom (Polydor)
3	10	YOU CAN GET IT IF YOU REALLY WANT	Desmond Dekker (Trojan)
11	11	BALL OF CONFUSION	Temptations (Tamla Motown)
10	12	BLACK PEARL	Horace Faith (Trojan)
9	13	STILL WATER (LOVE)	Four Tops (Tamla Motown)
21	14	RUBY TUESDAY	Melanie (Buddah)
12	15	WHICH WAY YOU GOIN' BILLY	Poppy Family (Decca)
13	16	GASOLINE ALLEY BRED	Hollies (Parlophone)
30	17	TIPS OF MY FINGERS	Des O'Connor (Columbia)
18	18	STRANGE BAND/THE WEAVER'S ANSWER	Family (Reprise)
16	19	GIVE ME JUST A LITTLE MORE TIME	Chairmen of the Board (Invictus)
22	20	GET UP I FEEL LIKE BEING A SEX MACHINE	James Brown (Polydor)
27	20	WAR	Edwin Starr (Tamla Motown)
17	22	DON'T PLAY THAT SONG	Aretha Franklin (Atlantic)
-	22	NEW WORLD IN THE MORNING	Roger Whittaker (Columbia)
23	24	OUR WORLD	Blue Mink (Philips)
-	25	THE WITCH	Rattles (Decca)
-	26	IT'S WONDERFUL TO BE LOVED	Jimmy Ruffin (Tamla Motown)
20	27	TEARS OF A CLOWN	Smokey Robinson & the Miracles (Tamla Motown)
-	28	INDIAN RESERVATION	Don Fardon (Young Blood)
19	29	THE WONDER OF YOU	Elvis Presley (RCA)
-	29	PRETTY WOMAN	Juicy Lucy (Vertigo)

31 October 1970

Last	This	Title	Artist
2	1	BLACK NIGHT	Deep Purple (Harvest)
5	2	PATCHES	Clarence Carter (Atlantic)
4	3	WOODSTOCK	Matthews Southern Comfort (Uni)
1	4	BAND OF GOLD	Freda Payne (Invictus)
5	5	ME AND MY LIFE	Tremeloes (CBS)
7	6	PARANOID	Black Sabbath (Vertigo)
3	7	(THEY LONG TO BE) CLOSE TO YOU	Carpenters (A&M)
11	8	BALL OF CONFUSION	Temptations (Tamla Motown)
14	9	RUBY TUESDAY	Melanie (Buddah)
8	10	AIN'T NO MOUNTAIN HIGH ENOUGH	Diana Ross (Tamla Motown)
13	11	STILL WATER (LOVE)	Four Tops (Tamla Motown)
20	12	WAR	Edwin Starr (Tamla Motown)
10	13	YOU CAN GET IT IF YOU REALLY WANT	Desmond Dekker (Trojan)
16	14	GASOLINE ALLEY BRED	Hollies (Parlophone)
9	15	MONTEGO BAY	Bobby Bloom (Polydor)
12	16	BLACK PEARL	Horace Faith (Trojan)
17	17	TIPS OF MY FINGERS	Des O'Connor (Columbia)
25	18	THE WITCH	Rattles (Decca)
26	18	IT'S WONDERFUL TO BE LOVED	Jimmy Ruffin (Tamla Motown)
15	20	WHICH WAY YOU GOIN' BILLY	Poppy Family (Decca)
28	21	INDIAN RESERVATION	Don Fardon (Young Blood)
22	22	NEW WORLD IN THE MORNING	Roger Whittaker (Columbia)
24	23	OUR WORLD	Blue Mink (Philips)
20	24	GET UP I FEEL LIKE BEING A SEX MACHINE	James Brown (Polydor)
-	25	SAN BERNARDINO	Christie (CBS)
-	26	JULIE DO YA LOVE ME	White Plains (Deram)
18	27	STRANGE BAND/THE WEAVER'S ANSWER	Family (Reprise)
-	28	HEAVEN IS HERE	Julie Felix (RAK)
29	28	THE WONDER OF YOU	Elvis Presley (RCA)
-	30	THINK ABOUT YOUR CHILDREN	Mary Hopkin (Apple)
-	30	MY WAY	Frank Sinatra (Reprise)

Deep Purple became the first of the newer breed of heavy rock bands (many of whom – Led Zeppelin being the prime example – refused to issue singles) to top the chart with *Black Night*. Compatriots Black Sabbath, who at this time were fronted by wildlife-loving Ozzy Osbourne, marched close behind with *Paranoid*. In contrast Melanie made the Top 10 with a personalization of the Rolling Stones' *Ruby Tuesday*, and Horace Faith had an early reggae hit with *Black Pearl*.

November 1970

7 November 1970

last	this	Title	Artist
3	1	WOODSTOCK	Matthews Southern Comfort (Uni)
2	2	PATCHES	Clarence Carterr (Atlantic)
5	3	ME AND MY LIFE	Tremeloes (CBS)
4	4	BAND OF GOLD	Freda Payne (Invictus)
1	5	BLACK NIGHT	Deep Purple (Harvest)
12	6	WAR	Edwin Starr (Tamla Motown)
8	7	BALL OF CONFUSION	Temptations (Tamla Motown)
9	8	RUBY TUESDAY	Melanie (Buddah)
11	9	STILL WATER (LOVE)	Four Tops (Tamla Motown)
6	10	PARANOID	Black Sabbath (Vertigo)
18	11	THE WITCH	Rattles (Decca)
7	12	(THEY LONG TO BE) CLOSE TO YOU	Carpenters (A&M)
10	12	AIN'T NO MOUNTAIN HIGH ENOUGH	Diana Ross (Tamla Motown)
21	14	INDIAN RESERVATION	Don Fardon (Young Blood)
18	15	IT'S WONDERFUL TO BE LOVED	Jimmy Ruffin (Tamla Motown)
15	16	MONTEGO BAY	Bobby Bloom (Polydor)
13	17	YOU CAN GET IT IF YOU REALLY WANT IT	Desmond Dekker (Trojan)
14	18	GASOLINE ALLEY BRED	Hollies (Parlophone)
17	19	TIPS OF MY FINGERS	Des O'Connor (Columbia)
22	20	NEW WORLD IN THE MORNING	Roger Whittaker (Columbia)
25	21	SAN BERNARDINO	Christie (CBS)
26	22	JULIE DO YA LOVE ME	White Plains (Deram)
16	23	BLACK PEARL	Horace Faith (Trojan)
28	24	HEAVEN IS HERE	Julie Felix (RAK)
-	25	VOODOO CHILE	Jimi Hendrix (Track)
20	26	WHICH WAY 'OU GOIN' BILLY	Poppy Family (Decca)
24	27	GET I FEEL LIKE BEING A SEX MACHINE	James Brown (Polydor)
-	28	SNOWBIRD	Anne Murray (Capitol)
30	29	THINK ABOUT YOUR CHILDREN	Mary Hopkin (Apple)
-	30	WHOLE LOTTA LOVE	C.C.S. (RAK)

14 November 1970

last	this	Title	Artist
1	1	WOODSTOCK	Matthews Southern Comfort (Uni)
2	2	PATCHES	Clarence Carterr (Atlantic)
6	3	WAR	Edwin Starr (Tamla Motown)
5	4	BLACK NIGHT	Deep Purple (Harvest)
3	5	ME AND MY LIFE	Tremeloes (CBS)
11	6	THE WITCH	Rattles (Decca)
14	7	INDIAN RESERVATION	Don Fardon (Young Blood)
8	8	RUBY TUESDAY	Melanie (Buddah)
7	8	BALL OF CONFUSION	Temptations (Tamla Motown)
25	10	VOODOO CHILE	Jimi Hendrix (Track)
9	11	STILL WATER (LOVE)	Four Tops (Tamla Motown)
4	12	BAND OF GOLD	Freda Payne (Invictus)
10	13	PARANOID	Black Sabbath (Vertigo)
15	14	IT'S WONDERFUL TO BE LOVED	Jimmy Ruffin (Tamla Motown)
22	15	JULIE DO YA LOVE ME	White Plains (Deram)
12	16	(THEY LONG TO BE) CLOSE TO YOU	Carpenters (A&M)
21	17	SAN BERNARDINO	Christie (CBS)
19	18	TIPS OF MY FINGERS	Des O'Connor (Columbia)
12	19	AIN'T NO MOUNTAIN HIGH ENOUGH	Diana Ross (Tamla Motown)
20	20	NEW WORLD IN THE MORNING	Roger Whittaker (Columbia)
24	21	HEAVEN IS HERE	Julie Felix (RAK)
30	22	WHOLE LOTTA LOVE	C.C.S. (RAK)
-	23	CRACKLIN' ROSIE	Neil Diamond (Uni)
29	24	THINK ABOUT YOUR CHILDREN	Mary Hopkin (Apple)
18	25	GASOLINE ALLEY BRED	Hollies (Parlophone)
16	26	MONTEGO BAY	Bobby Bloom (Polydor)
-	27	MORE GOOD OLD ROCK'N'ROLL	Bobby Bloom (Polydor)
17	27	YOU CAN GET IT IF YOU REALLY WANT IT	Desmond Dekker (Trojan)
-	29	RIDE A WHITE SWAN	T. Rex (Fly)
-	30	YOU'VE GOT ME DANGLING ON A STRING	Chairmen of the Board (Invictus)

21 November 1970

last	this	Title	Artist
1	1	WOODSTOCK	Matthews Southern Comfort (Uni)
3	2	WAR	Edwin Starr (Tamla Motown)
7	3	INDIAN RESERVATION	Don Fardon (Young Blood)
2	4	PATCHES	Clarence Carterr (Atlantic)
10	5	VOODOO CHILE	Jimi Hendrix (Track)
17	6	SAN BERNARDINO	Christie (CBS)
6	7	THE WITCH	Rattles (Decca)
8	8	RUBY TUESDAY	Melanie (Buddah)
5	9	ME AND MY LIFE	Tremeloes (CBS)
15	10	JULIE DO YA LOVE ME	White Plains (Deram)
14	11	IT'S WONDERFUL TO BE LOVED	Jimmy Ruffin (Tamla Motown)
23	12	CRACKLIN' ROSIE	Neil Diamond (Uni)
22	13	WHOLE LOTTA LOVE	C.C.S. (RAK)
4	14	BLACK NIGHT	Deep Purple (Harvest)
8	15	BALL OF CONFUSION	Temptations (Tamla Motown)
-	16	I HEAR YOU KNOCKING	Dave Edmunds (MAM)
13	17	PARANOID	Black Sabbath (Vertigo)
11	18	STILL WATER (LOVE)	Four Tops (Tamla Motown)
-	19	I'VE LOST YOU	Elvis Presley (RCA)
12	20	BAND OF GOLD	Freda Payne (Invictus)
24	21	THINK ABOUT YOUR CHILDREN	Mary Hopkin (Apple)
29	22	RIDE A WHITE SWAN	T. Rex (Fly)
20	23	NEW WORLD IN THE MORNING	Roger Whittaker (Columbia)
30	24	YOU'VE GOT ME DANGLING ON A STRING	Chairmen of the Board (Invictus)
18	25	TIPS OF MY FINGERS	Des O'Connor (Columbia)
16	26	(THEY LONG TO BE) CLOSE TO YOU	Carpenters (A&M)
-	27	I'LL BE THERE	Jackson Five (Tamla Motown)
21	28	HEAVEN IS HERE	Julie Felix (RAK)
19	29	AIN'T NO MOUNTAIN HIGH ENOUGH	Diana Ross (Tamla Motown)
27	30	MORE GOOD OLD ROCK'N'ROLL	Dave Clark Five (Columbia)

28 November 1970

last	this	Title	Artist
5	1	VOODOO CHILE	Jimi Hendrix (Track)
3	2	INDIAN RESERVATION	Don Fardon (Young Blood)
16	3	I HEAR YOU KNOCKING	Dave Edmunds (MAM)
1	4	WOODSTOCK	Matthews Southern Comfort (Uni)
12	5	CRACKLIN' ROSIE	Neil Diamond (Uni)
2	6	WAR	Edwin Starr (Tamla Motown)
6	7	SAN BERNARDINO	Christie (CBS)
11	8	IT'S WONDERFUL TO BE LOVED	Jimmy Ruffin (Tamla Motown)
10	9	JULIE DO YA LOVE ME	White Plains (Deram)
22	10	RIDE A WHITE SWAN	T. Rex (Fly)
4	11	PATCHES	Clarence Carter (Atlantic)
7	12	THE WITCH	Rattles (Decca)
19	13	I'VE LOST YOU	Elvis Presley (RCA)
8	14	RUBY TUESDAY	Melanie (Buddah)
24	15	YOU'VE GOT ME DANGLING ON A STRING	Chairmen of the Board (Invictus)
13	16	WHOLE LOTTA LOVE	C.C.S. (RAK)
-	17	IT'S ONLY MAKE BELIEVE	Glen Campbell (Capitol)
9	18	ME AND MY LIFE	Tremeloes (CBS)
-	19	WHEN I'M DEAD AND GONE	McGuinness Flint (Capitol)
15	20	BALL OF CONFUSION	Temptations (Tamla Motown)
27	21	I'LL BE THERE	Jackson Five (Tamla Motown)
20	22	BAND OF GOLD	Freda Payne (Invictus)
21	23	THINK ABOUT YOUR CHILDREN	Mary Hopkin (Apple)
14	24	BLACK NIGHT	Deep Purple (Harvest)
23	25	NEW WORLD IN THE MORNING	Roger Whittaker (Columbia)
-	26	HOME LOVIN' MAN	Andy Williams (CBS)
-	27	IN MY CHAIR	Status Quo (Pye)
-	28	MY PRAYER	Gerry Monroe (Chapter One)
-	29	IT'S A SHAME	Motown Spinners (Tamla Motown)
18	30	STILL WATER (LOVE)	Four Tops (Tamla Motown)

Matthew's Southern Comfort's version of Joni Mitchell's *Woodstock*, a smooth countrified rendition with a pedal-steel break, was markedly different from both the writer's original and Crosby, Stills Nash & Young's chunky rock version from earlier in the year. Nevertheless it became the biggest-selling cover of the song both in the UK and the US. Revivals of the song tended to be based on Ian Matthew's successful interpretation. Neil Diamond finally made his chart debut and the newly abridged T. Rex also arrived.

5 December 1970

last week	this week		
3	1	I HEAR YOU KNOCKING	Dave Edmunds (MAM)
1	2	VOODOO CHILE	Jimi Hendrix (Track)
5	3	CRACKLIN' ROSIE	Neil Diamond (Uni)
2	4	INDIAN RESERVATION	Don Fardon (Young Blood)
10	4	RIDE A WHITE SWAN	T. Rex (Fly)
13	6	I'VE LOST YOU	Elvis Presley (RCA)
26	7	HOME LOVING MAN	Andy Williams (CBS)
6	8	WAR	Edwin Starr (Tamla Motown)
19	9	WHEN I'M DEAD AND GONE	McGuinness Flint (Capitol)
17	10	IT'S ONLY MAKE BELIEVE	Glen Campbell (Capitol)
9	11	JULIE DO YA LOVE ME	White Plains (Deram)
7	12	SAN BERNARDINO	Christie (CBS)
8	13	IT'S WONDERFUL TO BE LOVED	Jimmy Ruffin (Tamla Motown)
15	14	YOU'VE GOT ME DANGLING ON A STRING	Chairmen of the Board (Invictus)
4	15	WOODSTOCK	Matthews Southern Comfort (Uni)
21	16	I'LL BE THERE	Jackson Five (Tamla Motown)
16	17	WHOLE LOTTA LOVE	C.C.S. (RAK)
11	18	PATCHES	Clarence Carter (Atlantic)
28	19	MY PRAYER	Gerry Monroe (Chapter One)
27	20	IN MY CHAIR	Status Quo (Pye)
12	21	THE WITCH	Rattles (Decca)
29	22	IT'S A SHAME	Motown Spinners (Tamla Motown)
23	23	THINK ABOUT YOUR CHILDREN	Mary Hopkin (Apple)
25	24	NEW WORLD IN THE MORNING	Roger Whittaker (Columbia)
14	25	RUBY TUESDAY	Melanie (Buddah)
-	26	NOTHING RHYMED	Gilbert O'Sullivan (MAM)
-	27	MY WAY	Frank Sinatra (Reprise)
17	28	ME AND MY LIFE	Tremeloes (CBS)
22	29	BAND OF GOLD	Freda Payne (Invictus)
-	30	LADY BARBARA	Peter Noone & Herman's Hermits (RAK)

12 December 1970

1	I HEAR YOU KNOCKING	Dave Edmunds (MAM)
3	2 CRACKLIN' ROSIE	Neil Diamond (Uni)
9	3 WHEN I'M DEAD AND GONE	McGuinness Flint (Capitol)
4	4 RIDE A WHITE SWAN	T. Rex (Fly)
4	5 INDIAN RESERVATION	Don Fardon (Young Blood)
2	6 VOODOO CHILE	Jimi Hendrix (Track)
14	7 YOU'VE GOT ME DANGLING ON A STRING	Chairmen of the Board (Invictus)
7	8 HOME LOVING MAN	Andy Williams (CBS)
19	9 MY PRAYER	Gerry Monroe (Chapter One)
10	10 IT'S ONLY MAKE BELIEVE	Glen Campbell (Capitol)
16	11 I'LL BE THERE	Jackson Five (Tamla Motown)
6	12 I'VE LOST YOU	Elvis Presley (RCA)
26	13 NOTHING RHYMED	Gilbert O'Sullivan (MAM)
11	14 JULIE DO YA LOVE ME	White Plains (Deram)
13	15 IT'S WONDERFUL TO BE LOVED	Jimmy Ruffin (Tamla Motown)
12	16 SAN BERNARDINO	Christie (CBS)
15	17 WOODSTOCK	Matthews Southern Comfort (Uni)
-	18 (BLAME IT ON THE) PONY EXPRESS	Johnny Johnson & the Bandwagon (Bell)
8	19 WAR	Edwin Starr (Tamla Motown)
22	20 IT'S A SHAME	Motown Spinners (Tamla Motown)
17	21 WHOLE LOTTA LOVE	C.C.S. (RAK)
27	22 MY WAY	Frank Sinatra (Reprise)
20	23 IN MY CHAIR	Status Quo (Pye)
-	24 GRANDAD	Clive Dunn (Columbia)
30	24 LADY BARBARA	Peter Noone & Herman's Hermits (RAK)
24	26 NEW WORLD IN THE MORNING	Roger Whittaker (Columbia)
18	27 PATCHES	Clarence Carter (Atlantic)
25	27 RUBY TUESDAY	Melanie (Buddah)
-	29 THE TIPS OF MY FINGERS	Des O'Connor (Columbia)
-	30 APEMAN	Kinks (Pye)

19 December 1970

1	I HEAR YOU KNOCKING	Dave Edmunds (MAM)
3	2 WHEN I'M DEAD AND GONE	McGuinness Flint (Capitol)
2	3 CRACKLIN' ROSIE	Neil Diamond (Uni)
8	4 HOME LOVING MAN	Andy Williams (CBS)
10	5 IT'S ONLY MAKE BELIEVE	Glen Campbell (Capitol)
4	6 RIDE A WHITE SWAN	T. Rex (Fly)
13	7 NOTHING RHYMED	Gilbert O'Sullivan (MAM)
7	8 YOU'VE GOT ME DANGLING ON A STRING	Chairmen of the Board (Invictus)
24	9 GRANDAD	Clive Dunn (Columbia)
9	10 MY PRAYER	Gerry Monroe (Chapter One)
11	11 I'LL BE THERE	Jackson Five (Tamla Motown)
6	12 VOODOO CHILE	Jimi Hendrix (Track)
5	13 INDIAN RESERVATION	Don Fardon (Young Blood)
12	14 I'VE LOST YOU	Elvis Presley (RCA)
18	15 (BLAME IT ON THE) PONY EXPRESS	Johnny Johnson & the Bandwagon (Bell)
24	16 LADY BARBARA	Peter Noone & Herman's Hermits (RAK)
14	17 JULIE DO YA LOVE ME	White Plains (Deram)
22	18 MY WAY	Frank Sinatra (Reprise)
21	19 WHOLE LOTTA LOVE	C.C.S. (RAK)
19	20 WAR	Edwin Starr (Tamla Motown)
20	21 IT'S A SHAME	Motown Spinners (Tamla Motown)
30	22 APEMAN	Kinks (Pye)
16	23 SAN BERNARDINO	Christie (CBS)
17	24 WOODSTOCK	Matthews Southern Comfort (Uni)
23	25 IN MY CHAIR	Status Quo (Pye)
-	26 DEEPER AND DEEPER	Freda Payne (Invictus)
-	27 BROKEN HEARTED	Ken Dodd (Columbia)
29	27 THE TIPS OF MY FINGERS	Des O'Connor (Columbia)
-	29 YOU'RE READY NOW	Frankie Valli (Philips)
15	30 IT'S WONDERFUL TO BE LOVED	Jimmy Ruffin (Tamla Motown)

26 December 1970

2	1 WHEN I'M DEAD AND GONE	McGuinness Flint (Capitol)
1	2 I HEAR YOU KNOCKING	Dave Edmunds (MAM)
8	3 GRANDAD Clive Dunn (Columbia)	
5	4 IT'S ONLY MAKE BELIEVE	Glen Campbell (Capitol)
3	5 CRACKLIN' ROSIE	Neil Diamond (Uni)
4	6 HOME LOVING MAN	Andy Williams (CBS)
6	7 RIDE A WHITE SWAN T. Rex (Fly)	
7	8 NOTHING RHYMED	Gilbert O'Sullivan (MAM)
9	9 I'LL BE THERE	Jackson Five (Tamla Motown)
8	10 YOU'VE GOT ME DANGLING ON A STRING	Chairmen of the Board (Invictus)
10	11 MY PRAYER	Gerry Monroe (Chapter One)
15	12 (BLAME IT ON THE) PONY EXPRESS Johnny Johnson & the	Bandwagon (Bell)
13	13 INDIAN RESERVATION	Don Fardon (Young Blood)
12	14 VOODOO CHILE	Jimi Hendrix (Track)
16	15 LADY BARBARA	Peter Noone & Herman's Hermits (RAK)
14	16 I'VE LOST YOU	Elvis Presley (RCA)
18	17 MY WAY Frank Sinatra (Reprise)	
21	18 IT'S A SHAME	Motown Spinners (Tamla Motown)
17	19 JULIE DO YA LOVE ME	White Plains (Deram)
22	20 APEMAN Kinks (Pye)	
27	21 BROKEN HEARTED	Ken Dodd (Columbia)
19	22 WHOLE LOTTA LOVE	C.C.S. (RAK)
23	23 SAN BERNARDINO Christie (CBS)	
-	24 AMAZING GRACE	Judy Collins (Elektra)
24	25 WOODSTOCK	Matthews Southern Comfort (Uni)
-	25 SNOWBIRD	Anne Murray (Capitol)
20	27 WAR	Edwin Starr (Tamla Motown)
30	28 IT'S WONDERFUL TO BE LOVED	Jimmy Ruffin (Tamla Motown)
-	29 NEW WORLD IN THE MORNING	Roger Whittaker (Columbia)
-	30 LONELY DAYS	Bee Gees (Polydor)
-	30 BLACK SKIN BLUE EYED BOYS	Equals (President)

I Hear You Knocking was originally a US R&B hit for Smiley Lewis in the early fifties and further popularised by his New Orleans compatriot Fats Domino later in that decade. Dave Edmunds' revival bowed to the fifties idiom and added a Creedence Clearwater Revival-style rhythm, guaranteeing Edmunds the Christmas season's most stompable party record. Gilbert O'Sullivan debuted with *Nothing Rhymed* – his wacky PR image tending to obscure the strength of his songwriting.

January 1971

last week	this week	2 January 1971

2 January 1971

3	1	GRANDAD — Clive Dunn (Columbia)
1	2	WHEN I'M DEAD AND GONE — McGuinness Flint (Capitol)
2	3	I HEAR YOU KNOCKING — Dave Edmunds (MAM)
5	4	CRACKLIN' ROSIE — Neil Diamond (Uni)
4	5	IT'S ONLY MAKE BELIEVE — Glen Campbell (Capitol)
7	6	RIDE A WHITE SWAN — T. Rex (Fly)
6	7	HOME LOVIN' MAN — Andy Williams (CBS)
8	8	NOTHING RHYMED — Gilbert O'Sullivan (MAM)
9	9	I'LL BE THERE — Jackson Five (Tamla Motown)
12	10	(BLAME IT ON THE) PONY EXPRESS — Johnny Johnson & the Bandwagon (Bell)
11	11	MY PRAYER — Gerry Monroe (Chapter One)
10	12	YOU'VE GOT ME DANGLING ON A STRING — Chairmen Of The Board (Invictus)
15	13	LADY BARBARA — Peter Noone & Herman's Hermits (RAK)
13	14	INDIAN RESERVATION — Don Fardon (Young Blood)
21	15	BROKEN HEARTED — Ken Dodd (Columbia)
17	16	MY WAY — Frank Sinatra (Reprise)
18	17	IT'S A SHAME — Motown Spinners (Tamla Motown)
16	18	I'VE LOST YOU — Elvis Presley (RCA)
14	19	VOODOO CHILE — Jimi Hendrix (Track)
20	20	APEMAN — Kinks (Pye)
19	21	JULIE DO YA LOVE ME — White Plains (Deram)
-	22	YOU DON'T HAVE TO SAY YOU LOVE ME — Elvis Presley (RCA)
24	23	AMAZING GRACE — Judy Collins (Elektra)
30	24	BLACK SKIN BLUE EYED BOYS — Equals (President)
-	25	YOU'RE READY NOW — Frankie Valli (Philips)
22	26	WHOLE LOTTA LOVE — C.C.S. (RAK)
25	27	SNOWBIRD — Anne Murray (Capitol)
-	28	MY WAY — Dorothy Squires (President)
29	29	NEW WORLD IN THE MORNING — Roger Whittaker (Columbia)
28	30	IT'S WONDERFUL TO BE LOVED — Jimmy Ruffin (Tamla Motown)

9 January 1971

1	1	GRANDAD — Clive Dunn (Columbia)
2	2	WHEN I'M DEAD AND GONE — McGuinness Flint (Capitol)
6	3	RIDE A WHITE SWAN — T. Rex (Fly)
3	4	I HEAR YOU KNOCKING — Dave Edmunds (MAM)
4	5	CRACKLIN' ROSIE — Neil Diamond (Uni)
5	6	IT'S ONLY MAKE BELIEVE — Glen Campbell (Capitol)
8	7	NOTHING RHYMED — Gilbert O'Sullivan (MAM)
7	8	HOME LOVIN' MAN — Andy Williams (CBS)
9	9	I'LL BE THERE — Jackson Five (Tamla Motown)
10	10	(BLAME IT ON THE) PONY EXPRESS — Johnny Johnson & the Bandwagon (Bell)
12	11	YOU'VE GOT ME DANGLING ON A STRING — Chairmen Of The Board (Invictus)
11	12	MY PRAYER — Gerry Monroe (Chapter One)
13	13	LADY BARBARA — Peter Noone & Herman's Hermits (RAK)
17	14	IT'S A SHAME — Motown Spinners (Tamla Motown)
25	15	YOU'RE READY NOW — Frankie Valli (Philips)
24	16	BLACK SKIN BLUE EYED BOYS — Equals (President)
16	17	MY WAY — Frank Sinatra (Reprise)
20	18	APEMAN — Kinks (Pye)
19	19	VOODOO CHILE — Jimi Hendrix (Track)
21	20	JULIE DO YA LOVE ME — White Plains (Deram)
23	21	AMAZING GRACE — Judy Collins (Elektra)
22	22	YOU DON'T HAVE TO SAY YOU LOVE ME — Elvis Presley (RCA)
14	23	INDIAN RESERVATION — Don Fardon (Young Blood)
15	24	BROKEN HEARTED — Ken Dodd (Columbia)
18	25	I'VE LOST YOU — Elvis Presley (RCA)
30	26	IT'S WONDERFUL TO BE LOVED BY YOU — Jimmy Ruffin (Tamla Motown)
27	27	SNOWBIRD — Anne Murray (Capitol)
26	28	WHOLE LOTTA LOVE — C.C.S. (RAK)
-	29	LONELY DAYS — Bee Gees (Polydor)
28	30	MY WAY — Dorothy Squires (President)

16 January 1971

1	1	GRANDAD — Clive Dunn (Columbia)
2	2	WHEN I'M DEAD AND GONE — McGuinness Flint (Capitol)
3	3	RIDE A WHITE SWAN — T. Rex (Fly)
4	4	I HEAR YOU KNOCKING — Dave Edmunds (MAM)
9	5	I'LL BE THERE — Jackson Five (Tamla Motown)
6	6	IT'S ONLY MAKE BELIEVE — Glen Campbell (Capitol)
5	7	CRACKLIN' ROSIE — Neil Diamond (Uni)
7	8	NOTHING RHYMED — Gilbert O'Sullivan (MAM)
10	9	(BLAME IT ON THE) PONY EXPRESS — Johnny Johnson & the Bandwagon (Bell)
8	10	HOME LOVIN' MAN — Andy Williams (CBS)
18	11	APEMAN — Kinks (Pye)
16	12	BLACK SKIN BLUE EYED BOYS — Equals (President)
15	13	YOU'RE READY NOW — Frankie Valli (Philips)
21	14	AMAZING GRACE — Judy Collins (Elektra)
22	15	YOU DON'T HAVE TO SAY YOU LOVE ME — Elvis Presley (RCA)
11	16	YOU'VE GOT ME DANGLING ON A STRING — Chairmen Of The Board (Invictus)
13	17	LADY BARBARA — Peter Noone & Herman's Hermits (RAK)
14	18	IT'S A SHAME — Motown Spinners (Tamla Motown)
12	19	MY PRAYER — Gerry Monroe (Chapter One)
24	20	BROKEN HEARTED — Ken Dodd (Columbia)
17	21	MY WAY — Frank Sinatra (Reprise)
-	22	THE PUSHBIKE SONG — Mixtures (Polydor)
23	23	INDIAN RESERVATION — Don Fardon (Young Blood)
27	24	SNOWBIRD — Anne Murray (Capitol)
-	25	STONED LOVE — Supremes (Tamla Motown)
29	26	LONELY DAYS — Bee Gees (Polydor)
-	27	LAS VEGAS — Tony Christie (MCA)
-	28	RUPERT — Jackie Lee (Pye)
-	29	WE'VE ONLY JUST BEGUN — Carpenters (A&M)
-	30	SHE'S A LADY — Tom Jones (Decca)

23 January 1971

1	1	GRANDAD — Clive Dunn (Columbia)
3	2	RIDE A WHITE SWAN — T. Rex (Fly)
2	3	WHEN I'M DEAD AND GONE — McGuinness Flint (Capitol)
5	4	I'LL BE THERE — Jackson Five (Tamla Motown)
9	5	(BLAME IT ON THE) PONY EXPRESS — Johnny Johnson & the Bandwagon (Bell)
11	5	APEMAN — Kinks (Pye)
4	7	I HEAR YOU KNOCKING — Dave Edmunds (MAM)
6	8	IT'S ONLY MAKE BELIEVE — Glen Campbell (Capitol)
12	9	BLACK SKIN BLUE EYED BOYS — Equals (President)
15	10	YOU DON'T HAVE TO SAY YOU LOVE ME — Elvis Presley (RCA)
14	11	AMAZING GRACE — Judy Collins (Elektra)
13	12	YOU'RE READY NOW — Frankie Valli (Philips)
7	13	CRACKLIN' ROSIE — Neil Diamond (Uni)
-	14	MY SWEET LORD — George Harrison (Apple)
10	15	HOME LOVIN' MAN — Andy Williams (CBS)
22	16	THE PUSHBIKE SONG — Mixtures (Polydor)
8	17	NOTHING RHYMED — Gilbert O'Sullivan (MAM)
25	18	STONED LOVE — Supremes (Tamla Motown)
16	19	YOU'VE GOT ME DANGLING ON A STRING — Chairmen Of The Board (Invictus)
-	20	CANDIDA — Dawn (Bell)
16	21	LADY BARBARA — Peter Noone & Herman's Hermits (RAK)
30	22	SHE'S A LADY — Tom Jones (Decca)
28	22	RUPERT — Jackie Lee (Pye)
-	24	NO MATTER WHAT — Badfinger (Apple)
21	24	MY WAY — Frank Sinatra (Reprise)
-	26	SUNNY HONEY GIRL — Cliff Richard (Columbia)
29	27	WE'VE ONLY JUST BEGUN — Carpenters (A&M)
20	28	BROKEN HEARTED — Ken Dodd (Columbia)
26	29	LONELY DAYS — Bee Gees (Polydor)
-	30	MAN FROM NAZARETH — John Paul Joans (RAK)
-	30	YOUR SONG — Elton John (DJM)

In the US the Jackson 5's *I'll Be There* was their fourth straight chart-topper from their first four Motown singles, and the biggest seller of the four. This was also the first single to demonstrate Michael Jackson's ballad singing style. The song oddly wasn't covered by any other artist until Mariah Carey finally revived it in 1992, just as this book was going to press. Frankie Valli's first UK solo hit was a re-issued 1966 oldie which had found favour with club dancers in this country.

30 January 1971

last week	this week	title	artist
14	1	MY SWEET LORD	George Harrison (Apple)
1	2	GRANDAD	Clive Dunn (Columbia)
2	3	RIDE A WHITE SWAN	T. Rex (Fly)
16	4	THE PUSHBIKE SONG	Mixtures (Polydor)
5	5	APEMAN	Kinks (Pye)
4	6	I'LL BE THERE	Jackson Five (Tamla Motown)
11	7	AMAZING GRACE	Judy Collins (Elektra)
3	8	WHEN I'M DEAD AND GONE	McGuinness Flint (Capitol)
7	9	I HEAR YOU KNOCKING	Dave Edmunds (MAM)
9	10	BLACK SKIN BLUE EYED BOYS	Equals (President)
18	11	STONED LOVE	Supremes (Tamla Motown)
10	12	YOU DON'T HAVE TO SAY YOU LOVE ME	Elvis Presley (RCA)
5	13	(BLAME IT ON THE) PONY EXPRESS	Johnny Johnson & the Bandwagon (Bell)
8	14	IT'S ONLY MAKE BELIEVE	Glen Campbell (Capitol)
24	15	NO MATTER WHAT	Badfinger (Apple)
20	16	CANDIDA	Dawn (Bell)
12	17	YOU'RE READY NOW	Frankie Valli (Philips)
22	18	SHE'S A LADY	Tom Jones (Decca)
-	19	RESURRECTION SHUFFLE	Ashton Gardner & Dyke (Capitol)
15	20	HOME LOVIN' MAN	Andy Williams (CBS)
13	21	CRACKLIN' ROSIE	Neil Diamond (Uni)
30	22	YOUR SONG	Elton John (DJM)
17	23	NOTHING RHYMED	Gilbert O'Sullivan (MAM)
-	24	IT'S THE SAME OLD SONG	Weathermen (B&C)
24	25	MY WAY	Frank Sinatra (Reprise)
30	26	MAN FROM NAZARETH	John Paul Joans (RAK)
-	27	LAS VEGAS	Tony Christie (MCA)
26	28	SUNNY HONEY GIRL	Cliff Richard (Columbia)
22	29	RUPERT	Jackie Lee (Pye)
-	30	HEAVY MAKES YOU HAPPY	Bobby Bloom (Polydor)

6 February 1971

last week	this week	title	artist
1	1	MY SWEET LORD	George Harrison (Apple)
4	2	THE PUSHBIKE SONG	Mixtures (Polydor)
2	3	GRANDAD	Clive Dunn (Columbia)
7	4	AMAZING GRACE	Judy Collins (Elektra)
5	5	APEMAN	Kinks (Pye)
3	6	RIDE A WHITE SWAN	T. Rex (Fly)
6	7	I'LL BE THERE	Jackson Five (Tamla Motown)
11	8	STONED LOVE	Supremes (Tamla Motown)
15	9	NO MATTER WHAT	Badfinger (Apple)
19	10	RESURRECTION SHUFFLE	Ashton Gardner & Dyke (Capitol)
10	11	BLACK SKIN BLUE EYED BOYS	Equals (President)
12	12	YOU DON'T HAVE TO SAY YOU LOVE ME	Elvis Presley (RCA)
16	13	CANDIDA	Dawn (Bell)
21	14	YOUR SONG	Elton John (DJM)
17	15	YOU'RE READY NOW	Frankie Valli (Philips)
8	16	WHEN I'M DEAD AND GONE	McGuinness Flint (Capitol)
18	17	SHE'S A LADY	Tom Jones (Decca)
9	18	I HEAR YOU KNOCKING	Dave Edmunds (MAM)
14	19	IT'S ONLY MAKE BELIEVE	Glen Campbell (Capitol)
21	20	CRACKLIN' ROSIE	Neil Diamond (Uni)
13	21	(BLAME IT ON THE) PONY EXPRESS	Johnny Johnson & the Bandwagon (Bell)
24	22	IT'S THE SAME OLD SONG	Weathermen (B&C)
27	23	LAS VEGAS	Tony Christie (MCA)
28	24	SUNNY HONEY GIRL	Cliff Richard (Columbia)
26	25	MAN FROM NAZARETH	John Paul Joans (RAK)
20	26	HOME LOVIN' MAN	Andy Williams (CBS)
-	27	I'M THE ONE YOU NEED	Smokey Robinson & the Miracles (Tamla Motown)
29	28	RUPERT	Jackie Lee (Pye)
25	29	MY WAY	Frank Sinatra (Reprise)
-	30	IT'S IMPOSSIBLE	Perry Como (RCA)

13 February 1971

last week	this week	title	artist
1	1	MY SWEET LORD	George Harrison (Apple)
2	2	THE PUSHBIKE SONG	Mixtures (Polydor)
7	3	STONED LOVE	Supremes (Tamla Motown)
10	4	RESURRECTION SHUFFLE	Ashton Gardner & Dyke (Capitol)
4	5	AMAZING GRACE	Judy Collins (Elektra)
13	6	CANDIDA	Dawn (Bell)
9	7	NO MATTER WHAT	Badfinger (Apple)
14	8	YOUR SONG	Elton John (DJM)
5	9	APEMAN	Kinks (Pye)
3	10	GRANDAD	Clive Dunn (Columbia)
6	11	RIDE A WHITE SWAN	T. Rex (Fly)
17	12	SHE'S A LADY	Tom Jones (Decca)
7	13	I'LL BE THERE	Jackson Five (Tamla Motown)
15	14	YOU'RE READY NOW	Frankie Valli (Philips)
12	15	YOU DON'T HAVE TO SAY YOU LOVE ME	Elvis Presley (RCA)
11	16	BLACK SKIN BLUE EYED BOYS	Equals (President)
22	17	IT'S THE SAME OLD SONG	Weathermen (B&C)
23	18	LAS VEGAS	Tony Christie (MCA)
16	19	WHEN I'M DEAD AND GONE	McGuinness Flint (Capitol)
24	20	SUNNY HONEY GIRL	Cliff Richard (Columbia)
30	21	IT'S IMPOSSIBLE	Perry Como (RCA)
28	22	RUPERT	Jackie Lee (Pye)
20	23	CRACKLIN' ROSIE	Neil Diamond (Uni)
27	24	I'M THE ONE YOU NEED	Smokey Robinson & the Miracles (Tamla Motown)
-	25	FORGET ME NOT	Martha Reeves & the Vandellas (Tamla Motown)
21	26	(BLAME IT ON THE) PONY EXPRESS	Johnny Johnson & the Bandwagon (Bell)
-	27	SONG OF MY LIFE	Petula Clark (Pye)
-	28	IT'S UP TO YOU	Edison Lighthouse (Bell)
-	29	EVERYTHING'S TUESDAY	Chairmen Of The Board (Invictus)
19	30	IT'S ONLY MAKE BELIEVE	Glen Campbell (Capitol)
-	30	I THINK I LOVE YOU	Partridge Family (Bell)

20 February 1971

last week	this week	title	artist
1	1	MY SWEET LORD	George Harrison (Apple)
2	2	THE PUSHBIKE SONG	Mixtures (Polydor)
3	3	STONED LOVE	Supremes (Tamla Motown)
4	4	RESURRECTION SHUFFLE	Ashton Gardner & Dyke (Capitol)
5	5	AMAZING GRACE	Judy Collins (Elektra)
8	6	YOUR SONG	Elton John (DJM)
7	7	NO MATTER WHAT	Badfinger (Apple)
6	8	CANDIDA	Dawn (Bell)
21	9	IT'S IMPOSSIBLE	Perry Como (RCA)
9	10	APEMAN	Kinks (Pye)
10	11	GRANDAD	Clive Dunn (Columbia)
12	12	SHE'S A LADY	Tom Jones (Decca)
11	13	RIDE A WHITE SWAN	T. Rex (Fly)
17	14	IT'S THE SAME OLD SONG	Weathermen (B&C)
13	15	I'LL BE THERE	Jackson Five (Tamla Motown)
14	16	YOU'RE READY NOW	Frankie Valli (Philips)
25	17	FORGET ME NOT	Martha Reeves & the Vandellas (Tamla Motown)
15	18	YOU DON'T HAVE TO SAY YOU LOVE ME	Elvis Presley (RCA)
16	19	BLACK SKIN BLUE EYED BOYS	Equals (President)
24	20	I'M THE ONE YOU NEED	Smokey Robinson & the Miracles (Tamla Motown)
18	21	LAS VEGAS	Tony Christie (MCA)
23	22	CRACKLIN' ROSIE	Neil Diamond (Uni)
26	23	(BLAME IT ON THE) PONY EXPRESS	Johnny Johnson & the Bandwagon (Bell)
20	24	SUNNY HONEY GIRL	Cliff Richard (Columbia)
21	25	RUPERT	Jackie Lee (Pye)
30	26	I THINK I LOVE YOU	Partridge Family (Bell)
-	27	SWEET CAROLINE	Neil Diamond (Uni)
-	28	BABY JUMP	Mungo Jerry (Dawn)
-	29	STONEY END	Barbra Streisand (CBS)
-	30	WHO PUT THE LIGHTS OUT	Dana (Rex)

George Harrison's *My Sweet Lord*, taken from his ambitious triple solo album *All Things Must Pass*, was one of the most successful singles by an ex-Beatle, selling almost 800,000 copies in the UK. This was beaten only by former Fabs singles *Mull Of Kintyre* and *Imagine*. The success was eventually blighted however when Harrison lost a legal suit declaring that he had 'unconsciously plagiarised' the song's melody from the Chiffon's 1963 hit *He's So Fine*, and thus lost his royalties from it.

February – March 1971

last week / this week

27 February 1971

last	this		
1	1	MY SWEET LORD	George Harrison (Apple)
4	2	RESURRECTION SHUFFLE	Ashton Gardner & Dyke (Capitol)
2	3	THE PUSHBIKE SONG	Mixtures (Polydor)
3	4	STONED LOVE	Supremes (Tamla Motown)
5	5	AMAZING GRACE	Judy Collins (Elektra)
9	5	IT'S IMPOSSIBLE	Perry Como (RCA)
6	7	YOUR SONG	Elton John (DJM)
7	8	NO MATTER WHAT	Badfinger (Apple)
8	9	CANDIDA	Dawn (Bell)
28	10	BABY JUMP	Mungo Jerry (Dawn)
20	11	I'M THE ONE YOU NEED	Smokey Robinson & the Miracles (Tamla Motown)
17	12	FORGET ME NOT	Martha Reeves & the Vandellas (Tamla Motown)
10	13	APEMAN	Kinks (Pye)
11	14	GRANDAD	Clive Dunn (Columbia)
14	14	IT'S THE SAME OLD SONG	Weathermen (B&C)
12	16	SHE'S A LADY	Tom Jones (Decca)
27	17	SWEET CAROLINE	Neil Diamond (Uni)
23	18	SUNNY HONEY GIRL	Cliff Richard (Columbia)
25	19	RUPERT	Jackie Lee (Pye)
-	20	EVERYTHING'S TUESDAY	Chairmen Of The Board (Invictus)
13	21	RIDE A WHITE SWAN	T. Rex (Fly)
-	22	ROSE GARDEN	Lynn Anderson (CBS)
30	23	WHO PUT THE LIGHTS OUT	Dana (Rex)
-	24	CHESTNUT MARE	Byrds (CBS)
18	25	YOU DON'T HAVE TO SAY YOU LOVE ME	Elvis Presley (RCA)
16	26	YOU'RE READY NOW	Frankie Valli (Philips)
-	27	TOMORROW NIGHT	Atomic Rooster (B&C)
-	28	ROSE GARDEN	New World (RAK)
26	29	I THINK I LOVE YOU	Partridge Family (Bell)
-	30	I WILL DRINK THE WINE	Frank Sinatra (Reprise)

6 March 1971

last	this		
1	1	MY SWEET LORD	George Harrison (Apple)
5	2	IT'S IMPOSSIBLE	Perry Como (RCA)
3	3	THE PUSHBIKE SONG	Mixtures (Polydor)
2	4	RESURRECTION SHUFFLE	Ashton Gardner & Dyke (Capitol)
10	5	BABY JUMP	Mungo Jerry (Dawn)
5	6	AMAZING GRACE	Judy Collins (Elektra)
4	7	STONED LOVE	Supremes (Tamla Motown)
-	8	ANOTHER DAY	Paul McCartney (Apple)
22	9	ROSE GARDEN	Lynn Anderson (CBS)
17	10	SWEET CAROLINE	Neil Diamond (Uni)
7	10	YOUR SONG	Elton John (DJM)
9	12	CANDIDA	Dawn (Bell)
8	13	NO MATTER WHAT	Badfinger (Apple)
12	14	FORGET ME NOT	Martha Reeves & the Vandellas (Tamla Motown)
11	15	I'M THE ONE YOU NEED	Smokey Robinson & the Miracles (Tamla Motown)
27	16	TOMORROW NIGHT	Atomic Rooster (B&C)
29	17	I THINK I LOVE YOU	Partridge Family (Bell)
20	18	EVERYTHING'S TUESDAY	Chairmen Of The Board (Invictus)
24	19	CHESTNUT MARE	Byrds (CBS)
19	20	RUPERT	Jackie Lee (Pye)
28	21	ROSE GARDEN	New World (RAK)
23	22	WHO PUT THE LIGHTS OUT	Dana (Rex)
14	23	IT'S THE SAME OLD SONG	Weathermen (B&C)
24	24	GRANDAD	Clive Dunn (Columbia)
-	24	HOT LOVE	T. Rex (Fly)
16	26	SHE'S A LADY	Tom Jones (Decca)
18	27	SUNNY HONEY GIRL	Cliff Richard (Columbia)
13	28	APEMAN	Kinks (Pye)
21	29	RIDE A WHITE SWAN	T. Rex (Fly)
30	30	I WILL DRINK THE WINE	Frank Sinatra (Reprise)

13 March 1971

last	this		
5	1	BABY JUMP	Mungo Jerry (Dawn)
8	2	ANOTHER DAY	Paul McCartney (Apple)
1	3	MY SWEET LORD	George Harrison (Apple)
2	4	IT'S IMPOSSIBLE	Perry Como (RCA)
3	5	THE PUSHBIKE SONG	Mixtures (Polydor)
10	6	SWEET CAROLINE	Neil Diamond (Uni)
9	7	ROSE GARDEN	Lynn Anderson (CBS)
4	8	RESURRECTION SHUFFLE	Ashton Gardner & Dyke (Capitol)
7	9	STONED LOVE	Supremes (Tamla Motown)
24	10	HOT LOVE	T. Rex (Fly)
6	11	AMAZING GRACE	Judy Collins (Elektra)
16	12	TOMORROW NIGHT	Atomic Rooster (B&C)
10	13	YOUR SONG	Elton John (DJM)
14	14	FORGET ME NOT	Martha Reeves & the Vandellas (Tamla Motown)
19	15	CHESTNUT MARE	Byrds (CBS)
18	16	EVERYTHING'S TUESDAY	Chairmen Of The Board (Invictus)
15	17	I'M THE ONE YOU NEED	Smokey Robinson & the Miracles (Tamla Motown)
22	18	WHO PUT THE LIGHTS OUT	Dana (Rex)
30	19	I WILL DRINK THE WINE	Frank Sinatra (Reprise)
13	20	NO MATTER WHAT	Badfinger (Apple)
17	21	I THINK I LOVE YOU	Partridge Family (Bell)
12	22	CANDIDA	Dawn (Bell)
21	23	ROSE GARDEN	New World (RAK)
-	24	BRIDGET THE MIDGET	Ray Stevens (CBS)
23	25	IT'S THE SAME OLD SONG	Weathermen (B&C)
-	26	STRANGE KIND OF WOMAN	Deep Purple (Harvest)
-	27	LOVE THE ONE YOU'RE WITH	Stephen Stills (Atlantic)
28	28	APEMAN	Kinks (Pye)
-	29	STONEY END	Barbra Streisand (CBS)
20	30	RUPERT	Jackie Lee (Pye)

20 March 1971

last	this		
2	1	ANOTHER DAY	Paul McCartney (Apple)
1	2	BABY JUMP	Mungo Jerry (Dawn)
7	3	ROSE GARDEN	Lynn Anderson (CBS)
10	4	HOT LOVE	T. Rex (Fly)
3	5	MY SWEET LORD	George Harrison (Apple)
4	6	IT'S IMPOSSIBLE	Perry Como (RCA)
5	7	THE PUSHBIKE SONG	Mixtures (Polydor)
6	8	SWEET CAROLINE	Neil Diamond (Uni)
12	9	TOMORROW NIGHT	Atomic Rooster (B&C)
11	10	AMAZING GRACE	Judy Collins (Elektra)
16	11	EVERYTHING'S TUESDAY	Chairmen Of The Board (Invictus)
18	12	WHO PUT THE LIGHTS OUT	Dana (Rex)
9	13	STONED LOVE	Supremes (Tamla Motown)
14	14	FORGET ME NOT	Martha Reeves & the Vandellas (Tamla Motown)
8	15	RESURRECTION SHUFFLE	Ashton Gardner & Dyke (Capitol)
26	16	STRANGE KIND OF WOMAN	Deep Purple (Harvest)
19	17	I WILL DRINK THE WINE	Frank Sinatra (Reprise)
15	18	CHESTNUT MARE	Byrds (CBS)
23	19	ROSE GARDEN	New World (RAK)
-	20	POWER TO THE PEOPLE	John Lennon/Plastic Ono Band (Apple)
-	21	JACK IN THE BOX	Clodagh Rodgers (RCA)
22	22	I'M THE ONE YOU NEED	Smokey Robinson & the Miracles (Tamla Motown)
24	23	BRIDGET THE MIDGET	Ray Stevens (CBS)
13	24	YOUR SONG	Elton John (DJM)
21	25	I THINK I LOVE YOU	Partridge Family (Bell)
-	26	IF NOT FOR YOU	Olivia Newton-John (Pye International)
20	27	NO MATTER WHAT	Badfinger (Apple)
22	28	CANDIDA	Dawn (Bell)
-	29	THERE GOES MY EVERYTHING	Elvis Presley (RCA)
-	30	THEME FROM LOVE STORY	Andy Williams (CBS)

Baby Jump gave Mungo Jerry two consecutive chart-topping singles, while with *Another Day* Paul McCartney became the second ex-Beatle to have a UK Number One. Perry Como returned to the Top Three for the first time since 1960 with *It's Impossible* and his contemporary Frank Sinatra continued his renewed chart streak with *I Will Drink The Wine*. America's TV show stars the Partridge Family began to emulate their US success (two million-selling singles already) with *I Think I Love You*.

27 March 1971

last week	this week	Title	Artist (Label)
4	1	HOT LOVE	T. Rex (Fly)
1	2	ANOTHER DAY	Paul McCartney (Apple)
3	3	ROSE GARDEN	Lynn Anderson (CBS)
2	4	BABY JUMP	Mungo Jerry (Dawn)
6	5	IT'S IMPOSSIBLE	Perry Como (RCA)
16	6	STRANGE KIND OF WOMAN	Deep Purple (Harvest)
5	7	MY SWEET LORD	George Harrison (Apple)
23	8	BRIDGET THE MIDGET	Ray Stevens (CBS)
8	9	SWEET CAROLINE	Neil Diamond (Uni)
9	10	TOMORROW NIGHT	Atomic Rooster (B&C)
20	10	POWER TO THE PEOPLE	John Lennon/Plastic Ono Band (Apple)
21	12	JACK IN THE BOX	Clodagh Rodgers (RCA)
7	13	THE PUSHBIKE SONG	Mixtures (Polydor)
10	14	AMAZING GRACE	Judy Collins (Elektra)
26	15	IF NOT FOR YOU	Olivia Newton-John (Pye International)
11	16	EVERYTHING'S TUESDAY	Chairmen Of The Board (Invictus)
17	17	I WILL DRINK THE WINE	Frank Sinatra (Reprise)
29	18	THERE GOES MY EVERYTHING	Elvis Presley (RCA)
12	19	WHO PUT THE LIGHTS OUT	Dana (Rex)
30	20	THEME FROM LOVE STORY	Andy Williams (CBS)
-	21	WALKIN'	C.C.S. (RAK)
19	22	ROSE GARDEN	New World (RAK)
15	23	RESURRECTION SHUFFLE	Ashton Gardner & Dyke (Capitol)
-	24	YOU COULD'VE BEEN A LADY	Hot Chocolate (RAK)
13	25	STONED LOVE	Supremes (Tamla Motown)
14	26	FORGET ME NOT	Martha Reeves & the Vandellas (Tamla Motown)
24	27	YOUR SONG	Elton John (DJM)
18	28	CHESTNUT MARE	Byrds (CBS)
-	29	FUNNY FUNNY	Sweet (RCA)
-	30	LOVE THE ONE YOU'RE WITH	Stephen Stills (Atlantic)

3 April 1971

last week	this week	Title	Artist (Label)
1	1	HOT LOVE	T. Rex (Fly)
3	2	ROSE GARDEN	Lynn Anderson (CBS)
2	3	ANOTHER DAY	Paul McCartney (Apple)
8	4	BRIDGET THE MIDGET	Ray Stevens (CBS)
4	5	BABY JUMP	Mungo Jerry (Dawn)
12	6	JACK IN THE BOX	Clodagh Rodgers (RCA)
10	7	POWER TO THE PEOPLE	John Lennon/Plastic Ono Band (Apple)
20	8	THEME FROM LOVE STORY	Andy Williams (CBS)
9	9	SWEET CAROLINE	Neil Diamond (Uni)
6	10	STRANGE KIND OF WOMAN	Deep Purple (Harvest)
5	11	IT'S IMPOSSIBLE	Perry Como (RCA)
17	12	I WILL DRINK THE WINE	Frank Sinatra (Reprise)
7	13	MY SWEET LORD	George Harrison (Apple)
21	14	WALKIN'	C.C.S. (RAK)
15	15	IF NOT FOR YOU	Olivia Newton-John (Pye International)
18	16	THERE GOES MY EVERYTHING	Elvis Presley (RCA)
10	17	TOMORROW NIGHT	Atomic Rooster (B&C)
14	18	AMAZING GRACE	Judy Collins (Elektra)
13	19	THE PUSHBIKE SONG	Mixtures (Polydor)
16	20	EVERYTHING'S TUESDAY	Chairmen Of The Board (Invictus)
22	21	ROSE GARDEN	New World (RAK)
19	22	WHO PUT THE LIGHTS OUT	Dana (Rex)
29	23	FUNNY FUNNY	Sweet (RCA)
-	24	LET'S SAY GOODBYE TOMORROW	Jimmy Ruffin (Tamla Motown)
28	25	CHESTNUT MARE	Byrds (CBS)
24	25	YOU COULD'VE BEEN A LADY	Hot Chocolate (RAK)
-	27	REMEMBER ME	Diana Ross (Tamla Motown)
23	28	RESURRECTION SHUFFLE	Ashton Gardner & Dyke (Capitol)
25	29	MY WAY	Frank Sinatra (Reprise)
-	30	DOUBLE BARREL	Dave & Ansell Collins (Technique)

10 April 1971

last week	this week	Title	Artist (Label)
1	1	HOT LOVE	T. Rex (Fly)
4	2	BRIDGET THE MIDGET	Ray Stevens (CBS)
2	3	ROSE GARDEN	Lynn Anderson (CBS)
3	4	ANOTHER DAY	Paul McCartney (Apple)
6	5	JACK IN THE BOX	Clodagh Rodgers (RCA)
7	6	POWER TO THE PEOPLE	John Lennon/Plastic Ono Band (Apple)
8	7	THEME FROM LOVE STORY	Andy Williams (CBS)
15	8	IF NOT FOR YOU	Olivia Newton-John (Pye International)
16	9	THERE GOES MY EVERYTHING	Elvis Presley (RCA)
5	10	BABY JUMP	Mungo Jerry (Dawn)
11	11	IT'S IMPOSSIBLE	Perry Como (RCA)
14	12	WALKIN'	C.C.S. (RAK)
12	13	I WILL DRINK THE WINE	Frank Sinatra (Reprise)
10	14	STRANGE KIND OF WOMAN	Deep Purple (Harvest)
27	15	REMEMBER ME	Diana Ross (Tamla Motown)
30	16	DOUBLE BARREL	Dave & Ansell Collins (Technique)
18	17	AMAZING GRACE	Judy Collins (Elektra)
13	18	MY SWEET LORD	George Harrison (Apple)
23	18	FUNNY FUNNY	Sweet (RCA)
9	20	SWEET CAROLINE	Neil Diamond (Uni)
-	21	MOZART 40TH SYMPHONY	Waldo de los Rios (A&M)
17	22	TOMORROW NIGHT	Atomic Rooster (B&C)
-	23	SOMETHING OLD SOMETHING NEW	Fantastics (Bell)
19	24	THE PUSHBIKE SONG	Mixtures (Polydor)
25	25	CHESTNUT MARE	Byrds (CBS)
26	26	YOU COULD'VE BEEN A LADY	Hot Chocolate (RAK)
24	27	LET'S SAY GOODBYE TOMORROW	Jimmy Ruffin (Tamla Motown)
21	28	ROSE GARDEN	New World (RAK)
-	29	MAMA'S PEARL	Jackson Five (Tamla Motown)
22	30	WHO PUT THE LIGHTS OUT	Dana (Rex)

17 April 1971

last week	this week	Title	Artist (Label)
1	1	HOT LOVE	T. Rex (Fly)
2	2	BRIDGET THE MIDGET	Ray Stevens (CBS)
7	3	THEME FROM LOVE STORY	Andy Williams (CBS)
3	4	ROSE GARDEN	Lynn Anderson (CBS)
5	5	JACK IN THE BOX	Clodagh Rodgers (RCA)
8	6	IF NOT FOR YOU	Olivia Newton-John (Pye International)
12	7	WALKIN'	C.C.S. (RAK)
9	8	THERE GOES MY EVERYTHING	Elvis Presley (RCA)
15	9	REMEMBER ME	Diana Ross (Tamla Motown)
4	10	ANOTHER DAY	Paul McCartney (Apple)
16	11	DOUBLE BARREL	Dave & Ansell Collins (Technique)
21	12	MOZART 40TH SYMPHONY	Waldo de los Rios (A&M)
11	13	IT'S IMPOSSIBLE	Perry Como (RCA)
6	14	POWER TO THE PEOPLE	John Lennon/Plastic Ono Band (Apple)
10	15	BABY JUMP	Mungo Jerry (Dawn)
18	16	FUNNY FUNNY	Sweet (RCA)
23	17	SOMETHING OLD SOMETHING NEW	Fantastics (Bell)
14	18	STRANGE KIND OF WOMAN	Deep Purple (Harvest)
13	19	I WILL DRINK THE WINE	Frank Sinatra (Reprise)
-	20	KNOCK THREE TIMES	Dawn (Bell)
17	21	AMAZING GRACE	Judy Collins (Elektra)
29	22	MAMA'S PEARL	Jackson Five (Tamla Motown)
26	23	YOU COULD'VE BEEN A LADY	Hot Chocolate (RAK)
-	24	SILVERY RAIN	Cliff Richard (Columbia)
18	25	MY SWEET LORD	George Harrison (Apple)
-	26	MOZART 40	Sovereign Collection (Capitol)
20	27	SWEET CAROLINE	Neil Diamond (Uni)
22	28	TOMORRCW NIGHT	Atomic Rooster (B&C)
27	29	LET'S SAY GOODBYE TOMORROW	Jimmy Ruffin (Tamla Motown)
-	30	DREAM BABY	Glen Campbell (Capitol)

Hot Love confirmed the arrival of former hippy songwriter/poet Marc Bolan (who, to all intents and purposes, was T. Rex) as a commercial mainstream rocker. He had a sly gift for straightforward Chuck Berry-style riffs with an off-beat lyric and a newly-acquired pop vocal delivery. He was aided in the vocal department by Howard Kaylan and Mark Volman, former vocalists with the Turtles, who sang back-up on several early 1970s hits before relaunching themselves as Flo & Eddie.

April – May 1971

last week	this week	24 April 1971	
1	1	HOT LOVE	T. Rex (Fly)
2	2	BRIDGET THE MIDGET	Ray Stevens (CBS)
11	3	DOUBLE BARREL	Dave & Ansell Collins (Technique)
3	4	THEME FROM LOVE STORY	Andy Williams (CBS)
4	5	ROSE GARDEN	Lynn Anderson (CBS)
7	6	WALKIN'	C.C.S. (RAK)
12	7	MOZART 40TH SYMPHONY	Waldo de los Rios (A&M)
6	7	IF NOT FOR YOU	Olivia Newton-John (Pye International)
5	9	JACK IN THE BOX	Clodagh Rodgers (RCA)
9	10	REMEMBER ME	Diana Ross (Tamla Motown)
20	11	KNOCK THREE TIMES	Dawn (Bell)
-	12	IT DON'T COME EASY	Ringo Starr (Apple)
17	13	SOMETHING OLD SOMETHING NEW	Fantastics (Bell)
8	14	THERE GOES MY EVERYTHING	Elvis Presley (RCA)
14	15	POWER TO THE PEOPLE	John Lennon/Plastic Ono Band (Apple)
10	16	ANOTHER DAY	Paul McCartney (Apple)
-	17	ROSETTA	Georgie Fame & Alan Price (CBS)
-	18	BROWN SUGAR	Rolling Stones (Rolling Stones)
16	18	FUNNY FUNNY	Sweet (RCA)
15	20	BABY JUMP	Mungo Jerry (Dawn)
13	21	IT'S IMPOSSIBLE	Perry Como (RCA)
22	22	MAMA'S PEARL	Jackson Five (Tamla Motown)
-	23	MY LITTLE ONE	Marmalade (Decca)
18	24	STRANGE KIND OF WOMAN	Deep Purple (Harvest)
24	25	SILVERY RAIN	Cliff Richard (Columbia)
19	26	I WILL DRINK THE WINE	Frank Sinatra (Reprise)
23	27	YOU COULD'VE BEEN A LADY	Hot Chocolate (RAK)
26	27	MOZART 40	Sovereign Collection (Capitol)
-	29	JUST SEVEN NUMBERS	Four Tops (Tamla Motown)
21	30	AMAZING GRACE	Judy Collins (Elektra)

last week	this week	1 May 1971	
3	1	DOUBLE BARREL	Dave & Ansell Collins (Technique)
7	2	MOZART 40TH SYMPHONY	Waldo de los Rios (A&M)
1	3	HOT LOVE	T. Rex (Fly)
11	4	KNOCK THREE TIMES	Dawn (Bell)
4	5	THEME FROM LOVE STORY	Andy Williams (CBS)
10	6	REMEMBER ME	Diana Ross (Tamla Motown)
17	7	ROSETTA	Georgie Fame & Alan Price (CBS)
18	8	BROWN SUGAR	Rolling Stones (Rolling Stones)
12	8	IT DON'T COME EASY	Ringo Starr (Apple)
2	10	BRIDGET THE MIDGET	Ray Stevens (CBS)
13	11	SOMETHING OLD SOMETHING NEW	Fantastics (Bell)
6	12	WALKIN'	C.C.S. (RAK)
5	13	ROSE GARDEN	Lynn Anderson (CBS)
7	14	IF NOT FOR YOU	Olivia Newton-John (Pye International)
18	15	FUNNY FUNNY	Sweet (RCA)
9	16	JACK IN THE BOX	Clodagh Rodgers (RCA)
14	17	THERE GOES MY EVERYTHING	Elvis Presley (RCA)
22	18	MAMA'S PEARL	Jackson Five (Tamla Motown)
-	19	JIG-A-JIG	East of Eden (Deram)
-	20	DIDN'T I (BLOW YOUR MIND THIS TIME)	Delfonics (Bell)
23	21	MY LITTLE ONE	Marmalade (Decca)
16	22	ANOTHER DAY	Paul McCartney (Apple)
15	23	POWER TO THE PEOPLE	John Lennon/Plastic Ono Band (Apple)
-	24	INDIANA WANTS ME	R. Dean Taylor (Tamla Motown)
25	25	SILVERY RAIN	Cliff Richard (Columbia)
24	26	STRANGE KIND OF WOMAN	Deep Purple (Harvest)
-	26	SUGAR SUGAR	Sakkarin (RCA)
-	28	UN BANC, UN ARBRE, UNE RUE	Severine (Philips)
20	29	BABY JUMP	Mungo Jerry (Dawn)
30	30	AMAZING GRACE	Judy Collins (Elektra)

last week	this week	8 May 1971	
1	1	DOUBLE BARREL	Dave & Ansell Collins (Technique)
4	2	KNOCK THREE TIMES	Dawn (Bell)
8	3	BROWN SUGAR	Rolling Stones (Rolling Stones)
3	4	HOT LOVE	T. Rex (Fly)
8	5	IT DON'T COME EASY	Ringo Starr (Apple)
2	6	MOZART 40TH SYMPHONY	Waldo de los Rios (A&M)
6	7	REMEMBER ME	Diana Ross (Tamla Motown)
5	8	THEME FROM LOVE STORY	Andy Williams (CBS)
7	9	ROSETTA	Georgie Fame & Alan Price (CBS)
10	10	BRIDGET THE MIDGET	Ray Stevens (CBS)
12	11	WALKIN'	C.C.S. (RAK)
24	12	INDIANA WANTS ME	R. Dean Taylor (Tamla Motown)
11	13	SOMETHING OLD SOMETHING NEW	Fantastics (Bell)
20	14	DIDN'T I (BLOW YOUR MIND THIS TIME)	Delfonics (Bell)
14	15	IF NOT FOR YOU	Olivia Newton-John (Pye International)
19	16	JIG-A-JIG	East of Eden (Deram)
18	17	MAMA'S PEARL	Jackson Five (Tamla Motown)
17	18	THERE GOES MY EVERYTHING	Elvis Presley (RCA)
13	19	ROSE GARDEN	Lynn Anderson (CBS)
15	20	FUNNY FUNNY	Sweet (RCA)
28	21	UN BANC, UN ARBRE, UNE RUE	Severine (Philips)
-	22	HEAVEN MUST HAVE SENT YOU	Elgins (Tamla Motown)
21	23	MY LITTLE ONE	Marmalade (Decca)
-	24	IT'S A SIN TO TELL A LIE	Gerry Monroe (Chapter One)
-	25	MALT AND BARLEY BLUES	McGuinness Flint (Capitol)
-	26	I THINK OF YOU	Perry Como (RCA)
26	27	SUGAR SUGAR	Sakkarin (RCA)
-	28	I AM, I SAID	Neil Diamond (Uni)
26	29	STRANGE KIND OF WOMAN	Deep Purple (Harvest)
22	30	ANOTHER DAY	Paul McCartney (Apple)

last week	this week	15 May 1971	
3	1	BROWN SUGAR	Rolling Stones (Rolling Stones)
2	2	KNOCK THREE TIMES	Dawn (Bell)
1	3	DOUBLE BARREL	Dave & Ansell Collins (Technique)
6	4	MOZART 40TH SYMPHONY	Waldo de los Rios (A&M)
5	5	IT DON'T COME EASY	Ringo Starr (Apple)
7	6	REMEMBER ME	Diana Ross (Tamla Motown)
8	7	THEME FROM LOVE STORY	Andy Williams (CBS)
16	8	JIG-A-JIG	East of Eden (Deram)
12	9	INDIANA WANTS ME	R. Dean Taylor (Tamla Motown)
4	10	HOT LOVE	T. Rex (Fly)
25	11	MALT AND BARLEY BLUES	McGuinness Flint (Capitol)
13	12	SOMETHING OLD SOMETHING NEW	Fantastics (Bell)
10	13	BRIDGET THE MIDGET	Ray Stevens (CBS)
27	14	SUGAR SUGAR	Sakkarin (RCA)
14	15	DIDN'T I (BLOW YOUR MIND THIS TIME)	Delfonics (Bell)
11	16	WALKIN'	C.C.S. (RAK)
-	17	MY BROTHER JAKE	Free (Island)
17	18	MAMA'S PEARL	Jackson Five (Tamla Motown)
9	19	ROSETTA	Georgie Fame & Alan Price (CBS)
15	20	IF NOT FOR YOU	Olivia Newton-John (Pye International)
19	21	ROSE GARDEN	Lynn Anderson (CBS)
22	22	HEAVEN MUST HAVE SENT YOU	Elgins (Tamla Motown)
24	23	IT'S A SIN TO TELL A LIE	Gerry Monroe (Chapter One)
28	24	I AM, I SAID	Neil Diamond (Uni)
-	25	GOOD OLD ARSENAL	Arsenal F.C. (Pye)
21	26	UN BANC, UN ARBRE, UNE RUE	Severine (Philips)
18	27	THERE GOES MY EVERYTHING	Elvis Presley (RCA)
23	28	MY LITTLE ONE	Marmalade (Decca)
-	29	WE CAN WORK IT OUT	Stevie Wonder (Tamla Motown)
-	30	JUST SEVEN NUMBERS	Four Tops (Tamla Motown)

Brown Sugar marked the severing of the Rolling Stones' former recording deal with Decca (a generally acrimonious partnership in the latter years) and the establishment of their own label. In the UK (though hardly anywhere else in the world) the single had an additional bonus track on the B-side – a straightforward cover of Chuck Berry's *Let It Rock*. This track has never been made available in any other form – apparently the performance was so impromptu that no proper master tape exists.

234

May – June 1971

22 May 1971

last week	this week	
2	1	KNOCK THREE TIMES — Dawn (Bell)
1	2	BROWN SUGAR — Rolling Stones (Rolling Stones)
9	3	INDIANA WANTS ME — R. Dean Taylor (Tamla Motown)
3	4	DOUBLE BARREL — Dave & Ansell Collins (Technique)
4	5	MOZART 40TH SYMPHONY — Waldo de los Rios (A&M)
8	6	JIG-A-JIG — East of Eden (Deram)
5	7	IT DON'T COME EASY — Ringo Starr (Apple)
6	8	REMEMBER ME — Diana Ross (Tamla Motown)
11	9	MALT AND BARLEY BLUES — McGuinness Flint (Capitol)
17	10	MY BROTHER JAKE — Free (Island)
26	11	UN BANC, UN ARBRE, UNE RUE — Severine (Philips)
14	12	SUGAR SUGAR — Sakkarin (RCA)
22	13	HEAVEN MUST HAVE SENT YOU — Elgins (Tamla Motown)
7	14	THEME FROM LOVE STORY — Andy Williams (CBS)
15	15	DIDN'T I (BLOW YOUR MIND THIS TIME) — Delfonics (Bell)
25	16	GOOD OLD ARSENAL — Arsenal F.C. (Pye)
24	17	I AM, I SAID — Neil Diamond (Uni)
10	17	HOT LOVE — T. Rex (Fly)
19	19	ROSETTA — Georgie Fame & Alan Price (CBS)
12	20	SOMETHING OLD SOMETHING NEW — Fantastics (Bell)
23	21	IT'S A SIN TO TELL A LIE — Gerry Monroe (Chapter One)
29	22	WE CAN WORK IT OUT — Stevie Wonder (Tamla Motown)
-	23	RAGS TO RICHES — Elvis Presley (RCA)
-	24	JUST MY IMAGINATION — Temptations (Tamla Motown)
16	25	WALKIN' — C.C.S. (RAK)
28	25	MY LITTLE ONE — Marmalade (Decca)
13	27	BRIDGET THE MIDGET — Ray Stevens (CBS)
-	28	FUNNY FUNNY — Sweet (RCA)
-	29	MR. TAMBOURINE MAN — Johnny Johnson & the Bandwagon (Bell)
27	30	THERE GOES MY EVERYTHING — Elvis Presley (RCA)

29 May 1971

last week	this week	
1	1	KNOCK THREE TIMES — Dawn (Bell)
3	2	INDIANA WANTS ME — R. Dean Taylor (Tamla Motown)
2	3	BROWN SUGAR — Rolling Stones (Rolling Stones)
9	4	MALT AND BARLEY BLUES — McGuinness Flint (Capitol)
6	5	JIG-A-JIG — East of Eden (Deram)
5	6	MOZART 40TH SYMPHONY — Waldo de los Rios (A&M)
7	7	IT DON'T COME EASY — Ringo Starr (Apple)
10	8	MY BROTHER JAKE — Free (Island)
9	9	I AM, I SAID — Neil Diamond (Uni)
13	10	HEAVEN MUST HAVE SENT YOU — Elgins (Tamla Motown)
4	11	DOUBLE BARREL — Dave & Ansell Collins (Technique)
8	12	REMEMBER ME — Diana Ross (Tamla Motown)
11	13	UN BANC, UN ARBRE, UNE RUE — Severine (Philips)
12	14	SUGAR SUGAR — Sakkarin (RCA)
23	15	RAGS TO RICHES — Elvis Presley (RCA)
21	16	IT'S A SIN TO TELL A LIE — Gerry Monroe (Chapter One)
-	17	I DID WHAT I DID FOR MARIA — Tony Christie (MCA)
15	18	DIDN'T I (BLOW YOUR MIND THIS TIME) — Delfonics (Bell)
16	19	GOOD OLD ARSENAL — Arsenal F.C. (Pye)
24	20	JUST MY IMAGINATION — Temptations (Tamla Motown)
14	21	THEME FROM LOVE STORY — Andy Williams (CBS)
-	22	I THINK OF YOU — Perry Como (RCA)
-	23	RAIN — Bruce Ruffin (Trojan)
-	24	OH YOU PRETTY THING — Peter Noone (RAK)
-	25	PAY TO THE PIPER — Chairmen Of The Board (Invictus)
22	26	WE CAN WORK IT OUT — Stevie Wonder (Tamla Motown)
27	27	HOT LOVE — T. Rex (Fly)
20	28	SOMETHING OLD SOMETHING NEW — Fantastics (Bell)
25	29	MY LITTLE ONE — Marmalade (Decca)
-	30	HEY WILLY — Hollies (Parlophone)
29	30	MR. TAMBOURINE MAN — Johnny Johnson & the Bandwagon (Bell)

5 June 1971

last week	this week	
1	1	KNOCK THREE TIMES — Dawn (Bell)
3	2	BROWN SUGAR — Rolling Stones (Rolling Stones)
5	3	JIG-A-JIG — East of Eden (Deram)
4	4	MALT AND BARLEY BLUES — McGuinness Flint (Capitol)
8	5	MY BROTHER JAKE — Free (Island)
2	6	INDIANA WANTS ME — R. Dean Taylor (Tamla Motown)
9	7	I AM, I SAID — Neil Diamond (Uni)
10	8	HEAVEN MUST HAVE SENT YOU — Elgins (Tamla Motown)
17	9	I DID WHAT I DID FOR MARIA — Tony Christie (MCA)
7	10	IT DON'T COME EASY — Ringo Starr (Apple)
13	11	UN BANC, UN ARBRE, UNE RUE — Severine (Philips)
15	12	RAGS TO RICHES — Elvis Presley (RCA)
6	13	MOZART 40TH SYMPHONY — Waldo de los Rios (A&M)
11	14	DOUBLE BARREL — Dave & Ansell Collins (Technique)
12	15	REMEMBER ME — Diana Ross (Tamla Motown)
-	16	BANNER MAN — Blue Mink (Regal Zonophone)
14	17	SUGAR SUGAR — Sakkarin (RCA)
20	18	JUST MY IMAGINATION — Temptations (Tamla Motown)
-	19	I'M GONNA RUN AWAY FROM YOU — Tami Lynn (Mojo)
22	20	I THINK OF YOU — Perry Como (RCA)
24	21	OH YOU PRETTY THING — Peter Noone (RAK)
16	22	IT'S A SIN TO TELL A LIE — Gerry Monroe (Chapter One)
-	23	LADY ROSE — Mungo Jerry (Dawn)
23	23	RAIN — Bruce Ruffin (Trojan)
30	25	HEY WILLY — Hollies (Parlophone)
-	26	HE'S GONNA STEP ON YOU AGAIN — John Kongos (Fly)
26	27	WE CAN WORK IT OUT — Stevie Wonder (Tamla Motown)
18	28	DIDN'T I (BLOW YOUR MIND THIS TIME) — Delfonics (Bell)
21	28	THEME FROM LOVE STORY — Andy Williams (CBS)
19	30	GOOD OLD ARSENAL — Arsenal F.C. (Pye)

12 June 1971

last week	this week	
5	1	MY BROTHER JAKE — Free (Island)
1	2	KNOCK THREE TIMES — Dawn (Bell)
9	3	I DID WHAT I DID FOR MARIA — Tony Christie (MCA)
7	4	I AM, I SAID — Neil Diamond (Uni)
6	5	INDIANA WANTS ME — R. Dean Taylor (Tamla Motown)
4	6	MALT AND BARLEY BLUES — McGuinness Flint (Capitol)
8	7	HEAVEN MUST HAVE SENT YOU — Elgins (Tamla Motown)
2	8	BROWN SUGAR — Rolling Stones (Rolling Stones)
19	9	I'M GONNA RUN AWAY FROM YOU — Tami Lynn (Mojo)
23	10	LADY ROSE — Mungo Jerry (Dawn)
16	11	BANNER MAN — Blue Mink (Regal Zonophone)
12	12	RAGS TO RICHES — Elvis Presley (RCA)
3	13	JIG-A-JIG — East of Eden (Deram)
21	14	OH YOU PRETTY THING — Peter Noone (RAK)
-	15	CHIRPY CHIRPY CHEEP CHEEP — Middle of the Road (RCA)
20	16	I THINK OF YOU — Perry Como (RCA)
26	17	HE'S GONNA STEP ON YOU AGAIN — John Kongos (Fly)
25	18	HEY WILLY — Hollies (Parlophone)
11	19	UN BANC, UN ARBRE, UNE RUE — Severine (Philips)
13	20	MOZART 40TH SYMPHONY — Waldo de los Rios (A&M)
10	21	IT DON'T COME EASY — Ringo Starr (Apple)
18	22	JUST MY IMAGINATION — Temptations (Tamla Motown)
23	23	RAIN — Bruce Ruffin (Trojan)
-	24	LAZYBONES — Jonathan King (Decca)
15	25	REMEMBER ME — Diana Ross (Tamla Motown)
14	26	DOUBLE BARREL — Dave & Ansell Collins (Technique)
-	27	I DON'T BLAME YOU AT ALL — Smokey Robinson & the Miracles (Tamla Motown)
22	28	IT'S A SIN TO TELL A LIE — Gerry Monroe (Chapter One)
17	29	SUGAR SUGAR — Sakkarin (RCA)
28	30	DIDN'T I (BLOW YOUR MIND THIS TIME) — Delfonics (Bell)

Dawn's *Knock Three Times* was a deliberate (and commercially successful) attempt to recreate the sound and feel of the mid-sixties songs by the Drifters. The group began an anonymous studio aggregation (with a stable-mate female group named Dusk, who had a small US hit with *Angel Baby*), but although he was not initially given an individual credit on the records, the lead singer was soon revealed to be Tony Orlando, former 1961 hitmaker with Bless You, and now a top sessioneer.

235

June – July 1971

Scottish group Middle Of The Road (whose repertoire matched their name exactly) had become major stars in Italy before the success of the mindless but ultra-commercial *Chirpy Chirpy Cheep Cheep* brought them back to the UK, where they managed three Top 10 hits in a row. Among other first-time chartmakers, John Kongos hailed from South Africa, Hurricane Smith was former Beatles and Pink Floyd engineer Norman Smith, and Medicine Head were the sole commercial success from John Peel's Dandelion label.

July – August 1971

last week	this week	17 July 1971
1	1	CHIRPY CHIRPY CHEEP CHEEP Middle of the Road (RCA)
2	2	CO-CO Sweet (RCA)
3	3	DON'T LET IT DIE Hurricane Smith (Columbia)
11	4	BLACK AND WHITE Greyhound (Trojan)
4	5	BANNER MAN Blue Mink (Regal Zonophone)
5	6	HE'S GONNA STEP ON YOU AGAIN John Kongos (Fly)
13	7	ME AND YOU AND A DOG NAMED BOO Lobo (Philips)
8	8	JUST MY IMAGINATION Temptations (Tamla Motown)
25	9	GET IT ON T. Rex (Fly)
7	10	I'M GONNA RUN AWAY FROM YOU Tami Lynn (Mojo)
12	11	PIED PIPER Bob & Marcia (Trojan)
18	12	TOM TOM TURNAROUND New World (RAK)
16	13	RIVER DEEP, MOUNTAIN HIGH Supremes & Four Tops (Tamla Motown)
10	14	I DID WHAT I DID FOR MARIA Tony Christie (MCA)
14	15	WHEN YOU ARE A KING White Plains (Deram)
6	16	LADY ROSE Mungo Jerry (Dawn)
17	17	MONKEY SPANNER Dave & Ansell Collins (Technique)
9	18	I DON'T BLAME YOU AT ALL Smokey Robinson & the Miracles (Tamla Motown)
22	19	LA-LA MEANS I LOVE YOU Delfonics (Bell)
19	20	PICTURES IN THE SKY Medicine Head (Dandelion)
15	21	KNOCK THREE TIMES Dawn (Bell)
24	22	TONIGHT Move (Harvest)
27	23	STREET FIGHTING MAN Rolling Stones (Decca)
23	24	LEAP UP AND DOWN (AND WAVE YOUR KNICKERS IN THE AIR) St. Cecilia (Polydor)
26	25	IF YOU COULD READ MY MIND Gordon Lightfoot (Reprise)
-	26	GIRLS ARE OUT TO GET YOU Fascinations (Mojo)
29	27	GET DOWN AND GET WITH IT Slade (Polydor)
-	28	THE DEVIL'S ANSWER Atomic Rooster (B&C)
-	29	WON'T GET FOOLED AGAIN Who (Track)
20	30	I AM, I SAID Neil Diamond (Uni)
-	30	WATCHING THE RIVER FLOW Bob Dylan (CBS)

		24 July 1971
1	1	CHIRPY CHIRPY CHEEP CHEEP Middle of the Road (RCA)
9	2	GET IT ON T. Rex (Fly)
2	3	CO-CO Sweet (RCA)
7	4	ME AND YOU AND A DOG NAMED BOO Lobo (Philips)
4	5	BLACK AND WHITE Greyhound (Trojan)
3	6	DON'T LET IT DIE Hurricane Smith (Columbia)
17	7	MONKEY SPANNER Dave & Ansell Collins (Technique)
12	8	TOM TOM TURNAROUND New World (RAK)
5	9	BANNER MAN Blue Mink (Regal Zonophone)
8	10	JUST MY IMAGINATION Temptations (Tamla Motown)
6	11	HE'S GONNA STEP ON YOU AGAIN John Kongos (Fly)
13	12	RIVER DEEP, MOUNTAIN HIGH Supremes & Four Tops (Tamla Motown)
15	13	WHEN YOU ARE A KING White Plains (Deram)
22	14	TONIGHT Move (Harvest)
19	15	LA-LA MEANS I LOVE YOU Delfonics (Bell)
10	16	I'M GONNA RUN AWAY FROM YOU Tami Lynn (Mojo)
11	17	PIED PIPER Bob & Marcia (Trojan)
24	18	LEAP UP AND DOWN (AND WAVE YOUR KNICKERS IN THE AIR) St. Cecilia (Polydor)
23	19	STREET FIGHTING MAN Rolling Stones (Decca)
18	20	I DON'T BLAME YOU AT ALL Smokey Robinson & the Miracles (Tamla Motown)
-	21	NEVER ENDING SONG OF LOVE New Seekers (Philips)
28	22	THE DEVIL'S ANSWER Atomic Rooster (B&C)
29	23	WON'T GET FOOLED AGAIN Who (Track)
20	24	PICTURES IN THE SKY Medicine Head (Dandelion)
16	25	LADY ROSE Mungo Jerry (Dawn)
-	26	HELLO BUDDY Tremeloes (CBS)
27	27	GET DOWN AND GET WITH IT Slade (Polydor)
14	28	I DID WHAT I DID FOR MARIA Tony Christie (MCA)
-	29	NEVER CAN SAY GOODBYE Jackson Five (Tamla Motown)
25	30	IF YOU COULD READ MY MIND Gordon Lightfoot (Reprise)

		31 July 1971
2	1	GET IT ON T. Rex (Fly)
1	2	CHIRPY CHIRPY CHEEP CHEEP Middle of the Road (RCA)
3	3	CO-CO Sweet (RCA)
5	4	BLACK AND WHITE Greyhound (Trojan)
4	5	ME AND YOU AND A DOG NAMED BOO Lobo (Philips)
8	6	TOM TOM TURNAROUND New World (RAK)
7	7	MONKEY SPANNER Dave & Ansell Collins (Technique)
21	8	NEVER ENDING SONG OF LOVE New Seekers (Philips)
6	9	DON'T LET IT DIE Hurricane Smith (Columbia)
10	10	JUST MY IMAGINATION Temptations (Tamla Motown)
14	11	TONIGHT Move (Harvest)
12	12	RIVER DEEP, MOUNTAIN HIGH Supremes & Four Tops (Tamla Motown)
22	13	THE DEVIL'S ANSWER Atomic Rooster (B&C)
17	14	PIED PIPER Bob & Marcia (Trojan)
23	15	WON'T GET FOOLED AGAIN Who (Track)
9	16	BANNER MAN Blue Mink (Regal Zonophone)
19	17	STREET FIGHTING MAN Rolling Stones (Decca)
-	18	I'M STILL WAITING Diana Ross (Tamla Motown)
18	19	LEAP UP AND DOWN (AND WAVE YOUR KNICKERS IN THE AIR) St. Cecilia (Polydor)
-	20	IN MY OWN TIME Family (Reprise)
27	20	GET DOWN AND GET WITH IT Slade (Polydor)
15	22	LA-LA MEANS I LOVE YOU Delfonics (Bell)
16	23	I'M GONNA RUN AWAY FROM YOU Tami Lynn (Mojo)
12	24	WHEN YOU ARE A KING White Plains (Deram)
20	25	I DON'T BLAME YOU AT ALL Smokey Robinson & the Miracles (Tamla Motown)
11	26	HE'S GONNA STEP ON YOU AGAIN John Kongos (Fly)
-	27	HEARTBREAK HOTEL/HOUND DOG/DON'T BE CRUEL Elvis Presley (RCA)
-	28	WE WILL Gilbert O'Sullivan (MAM)
-	29	WATCHING THE RIVER FLOW Bob Dylan (CBS)
26	30	HELLO BUDDY Tremeloes (CBS)

		7 August 1971
1	1	GET IT ON T. Rex (Fly)
8	2	NEVER ENDING SONG OF LOVE New Seekers (Philips)
2	3	CHIRPY CHIRPY CHEEP CHEEP Middle of the Road (RCA)
18	4	I'M STILL WAITING Diana Ross (Tamla Motown)
13	5	THE DEVIL'S ANSWER Atomic Rooster (B&C)
5	7	ME AND YOU AND A DOG NAMED BOO Lobo (Philips)
6	8	TOM TOM TURNAROUND New World (RAK)
4	9	BLACK AND WHITE Greyhound (Trojan)
7	10	MONKEY SPANNER Dave & Ansell Collins (Technique)
20	11	IN MY OWN TIME Family (Reprise)
19	12	LEAP UP AND DOWN (AND WAVE YOUR KNICKERS IN THE AIR) St. Cecilia (Polydor)
11	13	TONIGHT Move (Harvest)
15	14	WON'T GET FOOLED AGAIN Who (Track)
9	15	DON'T LET IT DIE Hurricane Smith (Columbia)
22	16	LA-LA MEANS I LOVE YOU Delfonics (Bell)
20	16	GET DOWN AND GET WITH IT Slade (Polydor)
10	18	JUST MY IMAGINATION Temptations (Tamla Motown)
12	19	RIVER DEEP, MOUNTAIN HIGH Supremes & Four Tops (Tamla Motown)
27	20	HEARTBREAK HOTEL/HOUND DOG/DON'T BE CRUEL Elvis Presley (RCA)
29	21	WATCHING THE RIVER FLOW Bob Dylan (CBS)
17	22	STREET FIGHTING MAN Rolling Stones (Decca)
16	23	BANNER MAN Blue Mink (Regal Zonophone)
-	24	WHAT ARE YOU DOING SUNDAY Dawn (Bell)
-	25	PICTURES IN THE SKY Medicine Head (Dandelion)
-	26	SOLDIER BLUE Buffy Sainte-Marie (RCA)
-	27	NEVER CAN SAY GOODBYE Jackson Five (Tamla Motown)
23	28	I'M GONNA RUN AWAY FROM YOU Tami Lynn (Mojo)
14	29	PIED PIPER Bob & Marcia (Trojan)
26	30	HE'S GONNA STEP ON YOU AGAIN John Kongos (Fly)

Slade's *Get Down And Get With It*, a cover of a Little Richard number was the precursor to one of the most impressive hit runs of the seventies. The group had only recently ceased to be Ambrose Slade and were saddled with a spurious boots-and-braces skinhead image which they would wisely ditch in favour of a lucrative leap on the gaudy bandwagon of glam-rock. The knicker-waving St. Cecilia were of course a concoction of the fertile imagination of Jonathan King.

August – September 1971

14 August 1971

last week	this week	Title / Artist (Label)
1	1	GET IT ON — T. Rex (Fly)
2	2	NEVER ENDING SONG OF LOVE — New Seekers (Philips)
4	3	I'M STILL WAITING — Diana Ross (Tamla Motown)
6	4	THE DEVIL'S ANSWER — Atomic Rooster (B&C)
7	5	ME AND YOU AND A DOG NAMED BOO — Lobo (Philips)
3	6	CHIRPY CHIRPY CHEEP CHEEP — Middle of the Road (RCA)
11	7	IN MY OWN TIME — Family (Reprise)
8	8	TOM TOM TURNAROUND — New World (RAK)
10	9	MONKEY SPANNER — Dave & Ansell Collins (Technique)
14	10	WON'T GET FOOLED AGAIN — Who (Track)
5	11	CO-CO — Sweet (RCA)
16	12	GET DOWN AND GET WITH IT — Slade (Polydor)
13	13	TONIGHT — Move (Harvest)
16	14	LA-LA MEANS I LOVE YOU — Delfonics (Bell)
9	15	BLACK AND WHITE — Greyhound (Trojan)
12	16	LEAP UP AND DOWN (AND WAVE YOUR KNICKERS IN THE AIR) — St. Cecilia (Polydor)
20	17	HEARTBREAK HOTEL/HOUND DOG/DON'T BE CRUEL — Elvis Presley (RCA)
26	18	SOLDIER BLUE — Buffy Sainte-Marie (RCA)
18	19	JUST MY IMAGINATION — Temptations (Tamla Motown)
19	20	RIVER DEEP, MOUNTAIN HIGH — Supremes & Four Tops (Tamla Motown)
24	21	WHAT ARE YOU DOING SUNDAY — Dawn (Bell)
-	22	MOVE ON UP — Curtis Mayfield (Buddah)
21	23	WATCHING THE RIVER FLOW — Bob Dylan (CBS)
-	24	IT'S TOO LATE — Carole King (A&M)
27	25	NEVER CAN SAY GOODBYE — Jackson Five (Tamla Motown)
-	26	HEY GIRL DON'T BOTHER ME — Tams (Probe)
15	27	DON'T LET IT DIE — Hurricane Smith (Columbia)
22	28	STREET FIGHTING MAN — Rolling Stones (Decca)
-	29	WE WILL — Gilbert O'Sullivan (MAM)
25	30	PICTURES IN THE SKY — Medicine Head (Dandelion)

21 August 1971

last week	this week	Title / Artist (Label)
2	1	NEVER ENDING SONG OF LOVE — New Seekers (Philips)
1	2	GET IT ON — T. Rex (Fly)
3	3	I'M STILL WAITING — Diana Ross (Tamla Motown)
4	4	THE DEVIL'S ANSWER — Atomic Rooster (B&C)
7	5	IN MY OWN TIME — Family (Reprise)
8	6	TOM TOM TURNAROUND — New World (RAK)
21	7	WHAT ARE YOU DOING SUNDAY — Dawn (Bell)
6	8	CHIRPY CHIRPY CHEEP CHEEP — Middle of the Road (RCA)
10	9	WON'T GET FOOLED AGAIN — Who (Track)
5	10	ME AND YOU AND A DOG NAMED BOO — Lobo (Philips)
18	11	SOLDIER BLUE — Buffy Sainte-Marie (RCA)
17	12	HEARTBREAK HOTEL/HOUND DOG/DON'T BE CRUEL — Elvis Presley (RCA)
11	13	CO-CO — Sweet (RCA)
16	14	LEAP UP AND DOWN (AND WAVE YOUR KNICKERS IN THE AIR) — St. Cecilia (Polydor)
24	15	IT'S TOO LATE — Carole King (A&M)
-	16	BANGLA DESH — George Harrison (Apple)
14	17	LA-LA MEANS I LOVE YOU — Delfonics (Bell)
22	18	MOVE ON UP — Curtis Mayfield (Buddah)
9	19	MONKEY SPANNER — Dave & Ansell Collins (Technique)
12	20	GET DOWN AND GET WITH IT — Slade (Polydor)
15	21	BLACK AND WHITE — Greyhound (Trojan)
-	22	LET YOUR YEAH BE YEAH — Pioneers (Trojan)
23	23	WATCHING THE RIVER FLOW — Bob Dylan (CBS)
25	24	NEVER CAN SAY GOODBYE — Jackson Five (Tamla Motown)
-	25	NATHAN JONES — Supremes (Tamla Motown)
13	26	TONIGHT — Move (Harvest)
20	27	RIVER DEEP, MOUNTAIN HIGH — Supremes & Four Tops (Tamla Motown)
-	28	BACK STREET LUV — Curved Air (Warner Bros)
29	29	WE WILL — Gilbert O'Sullivan (MAM)
26	30	HEY GIRL DON'T BOTHER ME — Tams (Probe)

28 August 1971

last week	this week	Title / Artist (Label)
3	1	I'M STILL WAITING — Diana Ross (Tamla Motown)
1	2	NEVER ENDING SONG OF LOVE — New Seekers (Philips)
7	3	WHAT ARE YOU DOING SUNDAY — Dawn (Bell)
5	4	IN MY OWN TIME — Family (Reprise)
2	5	GET IT ON — T. Rex (Fly)
4	6	THE DEVIL'S ANSWER — Atomic Rooster (B&C)
11	7	SOLDIER BLUE — Buffy Sainte-Marie (RCA)
6	8	TOM TOM TURNAROUND — New World (RAK)
9	9	WON'T GET FOOLED AGAIN — Who (Track)
16	10	BANGLA DESH — George Harrison (Apple)
15	11	IT'S TOO LATE — Carole King (A&M)
12	12	HEARTBREAK HOTEL/HOUND DOG/DON'T BE CRUEL — Elvis Presley (RCA)
30	13	HEY GIRL DON'T BOTHER ME — Tams (Probe)
18	14	MOVE ON UP — Curtis Mayfield (Buddah)
8	15	CHIRPY CHIRPY CHEEP CHEEP — Middle of the Road (RCA)
22	16	LET YOUR YEAH BE YEAH — Pioneers (Trojan)
14	17	LEAP UP AND DOWN (AND WAVE YOUR KNICKERS IN THE AIR) — St. Cecilia (Polydor)
10	18	ME AND YOU AND A DOG NAMED BOO — Lobo (Philips)
28	19	BACK STREET LUV — Curved Air (Warner Bros)
17	20	LA-LA MEANS I LOVE YOU — Delfonics (Bell)
29	21	WE WILL — Gilbert O'Sullivan (MAM)
23	22	WATCHING THE RIVER FLOW — Bob Dylan (CBS)
20	23	GET DOWN AND GET WITH IT — Slade (Polydor)
12	24	CO-CO — Sweet (RCA)
19	25	MONKEY SPANNER — Dave & Ansell Collins (Technique)
25	26	NATHAN JONES — Supremes (Tamla Motown)
-	27	DID YOU EVER — Nancy Sinatra & Lee Hazlewood (Reprise)
-	28	AT THE TOP OF THE STAIRS — Formations (Mojo)
21	29	BLACK AND WHITE — Greyhound (Trojan)
27	30	RIVER DEEP, MOUNTAIN HIGH — Supremes & Four Tops (Tamla Motown)

4 September 1971

last week	this week	Title / Artist (Label)
1	1	I'M STILL WAITING — Diana Ross (Tamla Motown)
2	2	NEVER ENDING SONG OF LOVE — New Seekers (Philips)
3	3	WHAT ARE YOU DOING SUNDAY — Dawn (Bell)
13	4	HEY GIRL DON'T BOTHER ME — Tams (Probe)
11	5	IT'S TOO LATE — Carole King (A&M)
4	6	IN MY OWN TIME — Family (Reprise)
5	7	GET IT ON — T. Rex (Fly)
16	8	LET YOUR YEAH BE YEAH — Pioneers (Trojan)
7	9	SOLDIER BLUE — Buffy Sainte-Marie (RCA)
10	10	BANGLA DESH — George Harrison (Apple)
14	11	MOVE ON UP — Curtis Mayfield (Buddah)
6	12	THE DEVIL'S ANSWER — Atomic Rooster (B&C)
19	13	BACK STREET LUV — Curved Air (Warner Bros)
26	14	NATHAN JONES — Supremes (Tamla Motown)
27	15	DID YOU EVER — Nancy Sinatra & Lee Hazlewood (Reprise)
9	16	WON'T GET FOOLED AGAIN — Who (Track)
8	17	TOM TOM TURNAROUND — New World (RAK)
12	18	HEARTBREAK HOTEL/HOUND DOG/DON'T BE CRUEL — Elvis Presley (RCA)
21	19	WE WILL — Gilbert O'Sullivan (MAM)
17	20	LEAP UP AND DOWN (AND WAVE YOUR KNICKERS IN THE AIR) — St. Cecilia (Polydor)
23	21	GET DOWN AND GET WITH IT — Slade (Polydor)
14	22	CHIRPY CHIRPY CHEEP CHEEP — Middle of the Road (RCA)
25	23	MONKEY SPANNER — Dave & Ansell Collins (Technique)
19	24	LA-LA MEANS I LOVE YOU — Delfonics (Bell)
28	25	AT THE TOP OF THE STAIRS — Formations (Mojo)
-	26	MAGGIE MAY — Rod Stewart (Mercury)
-	27	TAP TURNS ON THE WATER — C.C.S. (RAK)
24	28	CO-CO — Sweet (RCA)
18	29	ME AND YOU AND A DOG NAMED BOO — Lobo (Philips)
-	30	CHAIRMAN OF THE BOARD — Chairmen Of The Board (Invictus)

Like Smokey Robinson & the Miracles' *Tears Of A Clown* a year earlier, Diana Ross's *I'm Still Waiting* was originally an album track. It was extracted as a single by Motown's UK wing at the urging of Radio One's *Breakfast Show* DJ Tony Blackburn, who plugged the song incessantly. He was certainly a major factor in helping it fulfill the potential he claimed for it. *It's Too Late* gave Carole King her first success as a performer since 1962's *It Might As Well Rain Until September.*

September – October 1971

11 September 1971

last week	this week	Title / Artist
1	1	I'M STILL WAITING — Diana Ross (Tamla Motown)
4	2	HEY GIRL DON'T BOTHER ME — Tams (Probe)
2	3	NEVER ENDING SONG OF LOVE — New Seekers (Philips)
3	4	WHAT ARE YOU DOING SUNDAY — Dawn (Bell)
13	5	BACK STREET LUV — Curved Air (Warner Bros)
9	6	SOLDIER BLUE — Buffy Sainte-Marie (RCA)
6	7	IN MY OWN TIME — Family (Reprise)
15	8	DID YOU EVER — Nancy Sinatra & Lee Hazlewood (Reprise)
8	9	LET YOUR YEAH BE YEAH — Pioneers (Trojan)
5	10	IT'S TOO LATE — Carole King (A&M)
14	11	NATHAN JONES — Supremes (Tamla Motown)
11	12	MOVE ON UP — Curtis Mayfield (Buddah)
10	13	BANGLA DESH — George Harrison (Apple)
26	14	MAGGIE MAY — Rod Stewart (Mercury)
-	15	I BELIEVE (IN LOVE) — Hot Chocolate (RAK)
7	16	GET IT ON — T. Rex (Fly)
12	17	THE DEVIL'S ANSWER — Atomic Rooster (B&C)
17	18	TOM TOM TURNAROUND — New World (RAK)
19	19	WE WILL — Gilbert O'Sullivan (MAM)
-	20	FOR ALL WE KNOW — Shirley Bassey (United Artists)
-	21	YOU'VE GOT A FRIEND — James Taylor (Warner Bros)
16	22	WON'T GET FOOLED AGAIN — Who (Track)
27	23	TAP TURNS ON THE WATER — C.C.S. (RAK)
17	24	HEARTBREAK HOTEL/HOUND DOG/DON'T BE CRUEL — Elvis Presley (RCA)
-	25	COUSIN NORMAN — Marmalade (Decca)
-	26	WHEN LOVE COMES ROUND AGAIN — Ken Dodd (Columbia)
25	27	AT THE TOP OF THE STAIRS — Formations (Mojo)
21	28	GET DOWN AND GET WITH IT — Slade (Polydor)
-	29	MOON SHADOW — Cat Stevens (Island)
-	30	ANOTHER TIME, ANOTHER PLACE — Engelbert Humperdinck (Decca)

18 September 1971

last week	this week	Title / Artist
2	1	HEY GIRL DON'T BOTHER ME — Tams (Probe)
1	2	I'M STILL WAITING — Diana Ross (Tamla Motown)
3	3	DID YOU EVER — Nancy Sinatra & Lee Hazlewood (Reprise)
11	4	NATHAN JONES — Supremes (Tamla Motown)
10	5	IT'S TOO LATE — Carole King (A&M)
4	6	WHAT ARE YOU DOING SUNDAY — Dawn (Bell)
5	7	BACK STREET LUV — Curved Air (Warner Bros)
3	8	NEVER ENDING SONG OF LOVE — New Seekers (Philips)
9	9	LET YOUR YEAH BE YEAH — Pioneers (Trojan)
6	10	SOLDIER BLUE — Buffy Sainte-Marie (RCA)
14	11	MAGGIE MAY — Rod Stewart (Mercury)
21	12	YOU'VE GOT A FRIEND — James Taylor (Warner Bros)
15	13	I BELIEVE (IN LOVE) — Hot Chocolate (RAK)
20	14	FOR ALL WE KNOW — Shirley Bassey (United Artists)
23	15	TAP TURNS ON THE WATER — C.C.S. (RAK)
25	16	COUSIN NORMAN — Marmalade (Decca)
17	17	IN MY OWN TIME — Family (Reprise)
-	18	TWEEDLE DEE, TWEEDLE DUM — Middle of the Road (RCA)
13	19	BANGLA DESH — George Harrison (Apple)
12	20	MOVE ON UP — Curtis Mayfield (Buddah)
19	21	WE WILL — Gilbert O'Sullivan (MAM)
16	22	GET IT ON — T. Rex (Fly)
-	23	FREEDOM COME, FREEDOM GO — Fortunes (Capitol)
18	24	TOM TOM TURNAROUND — New World (RAK)
-	25	DADDY DON'T YOU WALK SO FAST — Daniel Boone (Penny Farthing)
26	26	WHEN LOVE COMES ROUND AGAIN — Ken Dodd (Columbia)
30	27	ANOTHER TIME, ANOTHER PLACE — Engelbert Humperdinck (Decca)
-	28	CHAIRMEN OF THE BOARD — Chairmen Of The Board (Invictus)
27	29	AT THE TOP OF THE STAIRS — Formations (Mojo)
-	30	LIFE IS A LONG SONG — Jethro Tull (Chrysalis)

25 September 1971

last week	this week	Title / Artist
1	1	HEY GIRL DON'T BOTHER ME — Tams (Probe)
3	2	DID YOU EVER — Nancy Sinatra & Lee Hazlewood (Reprise)
2	3	I'M STILL WAITING — Diana Ross (Tamla Motown)
11	4	MAGGIE MAY — Rod Stewart (Mercury)
13	5	I BELIEVE (IN LOVE) — Hot Chocolate (RAK)
4	6	NATHAN JONES — Supremes (Tamla Motown)
7	7	BACK STREET LUV — Curved Air (Warner Bros)
15	8	TAP TURNS ON THE WATER — C.C.S. (RAK)
12	9	YOU'VE GOT A FRIEND — James Taylor (Warner Bros)
5	10	IT'S TOO LATE — Carole King (A&M)
14	11	FOR ALL WE KNOW — Shirley Bassey (United Artists)
18	12	TWEEDLE DEE, TWEEDLE DUM — Middle of the Road (RCA)
10	13	SOLDIER BLUE — Buffy Sainte-Marie (RCA)
16	14	COUSIN NORMAN — Marmalade (Decca)
8	15	NEVER ENDING SONG OF LOVE — New Seekers (Philips)
6	16	WHAT ARE YOU DOING SUNDAY — Dawn (Bell)
9	17	LET YOUR YEAH BE YEAH — Pioneers (Trojan)
30	18	LIFE IS A LONG SONG — Jethro Tull (Chrysalis)
25	19	DADDY DON'T YOU WALK SO FAST — Daniel Boone (Penny Farthing)
17	20	IN MY OWN TIME — Family (Reprise)
23	21	FREEDOM COME, FREEDOM GO — Fortunes (Capitol)
25	22	WHEN LOVE COMES ROUND AGAIN — Ken Dodd (Columbia)
21	23	WE WILL — Gilbert O'Sullivan (MAM)
-	24	KEEP ON DANCING — Bay City Rollers (Bell)
27	25	ANOTHER TIME, ANOTHER PLACE — Engelbert Humperdinck (Decca)
19	26	BANGLA DESH — George Harrison (Apple)
22	27	GET IT ON — T. Rex (Fly)
20	28	MOVE ON UP — Curtis Mayfield (Buddah)
-	29	YOU DON'T HAVE TO BE IN THE ARMY TO FIGHT IN THE WAR — Mungo Jerry (Dawn)
-	30	HEARTBREAK HOTEL/HOUND DOG/DON'T BE CRUEL — Elvis Presley (RCA)

2 October 1971

last week	this week	Title / Artist
4	1	MAGGIE MAY — Rod Stewart (Mercury)
1	2	HEY GIRL DON'T BOTHER ME — Tams (Probe)
2	3	DID YOU EVER — Nancy Sinatra & Lee Hazlewood (Reprise)
5	4	I BELIEVE (IN LOVE) — Hot Chocolate (RAK)
8	5	TAP TURNS ON THE WATER — C.C.S. (RAK)
12	6	TWEEDLE DEE, TWEEDLE DUM — Middle of the Road (RCA)
9	7	YOU'VE GOT A FRIEND — James Taylor (Warner Bros)
14	8	COUSIN NORMAN — Marmalade (Decca)
6	9	NATHAN JONES — Supremes (Tamla Motown)
11	10	FOR ALL WE KNOW — Shirley Bassey (United Artists)
3	11	I'M STILL WAITING — Diana Ross (Tamla Motown)
13	12	SOLDIER BLUE — Buffy Sainte-Marie (RCA)
7	13	BACK STREET LUV — Curved Air (Warner Bros)
10	14	IT'S TOO LATE — Carole King (A&M)
18	15	LIFE IS A LONG SONG — Jethro Tull (Chrysalis)
19	16	DADDY DON'T YOU WALK SO FAST — Daniel Boone (Penny Farthing)
21	17	FREEDOM COME, FREEDOM GO — Fortunes (Capitol)
15	18	NEVER ENDING SONG OF LOVE — New Seekers (Philips)
16	19	WHAT ARE YOU DOING SUNDAY — Dawn (Bell)
25	20	ANOTHER TIME, ANOTHER PLACE — Engelbert Humperdinck (Decca)
17	21	LET YOUR YEAH BE YEAH — Pioneers (Trojan)
-	22	MOON SHADOW — Cat Stevens (Island)
-	23	WITCH QUEEN OF NEW ORLEANS — Redbone (Epic)
24	24	KEEP ON DANCING — Bay City Rollers (Bell)
-	25	BUTTERFLY — Danyel Gerard (CBS)
20	26	IN MY OWN TIME — Family (Reprise)
26	27	BANGLA DESH — George Harrison (Apple)
-	28	SIMPLE GAME — Four Tops (Tamla Motown)
-	29	SUPERSTAR — Carpenters (A&M)
-	30	SULTANA — Titanic (CBS)

In the wake of several successful revivals of soul singles from the 1960s (including Tammi Lynn's *I'm Gonna Run Away From You* and the Delfonics' *Didn't I* and *La-La Means I Love You*) the Tams' *Hey Girl Don't Bother Me*, originally released without chart success in 1965, was a surprise chart-topper. Rod Stewart's *Maggie May* had begun as a B-side of his version of Tim Hardin's *Reason To Believe*, but quickly asserted itself as the stronger side, to open Stewart's solo hit career with a Number One.

October 1971

9 October 1971

last week	this week	Title / Artist (Label)
1	1	MAGGIE MAY — Rod Stewart (Mercury)
2	2	HEY GIRL DON'T BOTHER ME — Tams (Probe)
5	3	TAP TURNS ON THE WATER — C.C.S. (RAK)
6	4	TWEEDLE DEE, TWEEDLE DUM — Middle of the Road (RCA)
3	5	DID YOU EVER — Nancy Sinatra & Lee Hazlewood (Reprise)
7	6	YOU'VE GOT A FRIEND — James Taylor (Warner Bros)
10	7	FOR ALL WE KNOW — Shirley Bassey (United Artists)
8	8	COUSIN NORMAN — Marmalade (Decca)
4	9	I BELIEVE (IN LOVE) — Hot Chocolate (RAK)
15	10	LIFE IS A LONG SONG — Jethro Tull (Chrysalis)
17	11	FREEDOM COME, FREEDOM GO — Fortunes (Capitol)
9	12	NATHAN JONES — Supremes (Tamla Motown)
23	13	WITCH QUEEN OF NEW ORLEANS — Redbone (Epic)
11	14	I'M STILL WAITING — Diana Ross (Tamla Motown)
12	15	SOLDIER BLUE — Buffy Sainte-Marie (RCA)
28	16	SIMPLE GAME — Four Tops (Tamla Motown)
30	17	SULTANA — Titanic (CBS)
13	18	BACK STREET LUV — Curved Air (Warner Bros)
20	19	ANOTHER TIME, ANOTHER PLACE — Engelbert Humperdinck (Decca)
24	20	KEEP ON DANCING — Bay City Rollers (Bell)
16	21	DADDY DON'T YOU WALK SO FAST — Daniel Boone (Penny Farthing)
22	22	MOON SHADOW — Cat Stevens (Island)
14	23	IT'S TOO LATE — Carole King (A&M)
-	24	YOU DON'T HAVE TO BE IN THE ARMY TO FIGHT IN THE WAR — Mungo Jerry (Dawn)
18	25	NEVER ENDING SONG OF LOVE — New Seekers (Philips)
29	26	SUPERSTAR — Carpenters (A&M)
-	27	SPANISH HARLEM — Aretha Franklin (Atlantic)
25	28	BUTTERFLY — Danyel Gerard (CBS)
-	29	MAMMY BLUE — Los Pop-Tops (A&M)
19	30	WHAT ARE YOU DOING SUNDAY — Dawn (Bell)

16 October 1971

last week	this week	Title / Artist (Label)
1	1	MAGGIE MAY — Rod Stewart (Mercury)
2	2	HEY GIRL DON'T BOTHER ME — Tams (Probe)
4	3	TWEEDLE DEE, TWEEDLE DUM — Middle of the Road (RCA)
6	4	YOU'VE GOT A FRIEND — James Taylor (Warner Bros)
5	5	DID YOU EVER — Nancy Sinatra & Lee Hazlewood (Reprise)
3	6	TAP TURNS ON THE WATER — C.C.S. (RAK)
13	7	WITCH QUEEN OF NEW ORLEANS — Redbone (Epic)
7	8	FOR ALL WE KNOW — Shirley Bassey (United Artists)
8	9	COUSIN NORMAN — Marmalade (Decca)
11	10	FREEDOM COME, FREEDOM GO — Fortunes (Capitol)
17	11	SULTANA — Titanic (CBS)
10	12	LIFE IS A LONG SONG — Jethro Tull (Chrysalis)
16	13	SIMPLE GAME — Four Tops (Tamla Motown)
9	14	I BELIEVE (IN LOVE) — Hot Chocolate (RAK)
12	15	NATHAN JONES — Supremes (Tamla Motown)
28	16	BUTTERFLY — Danyel Gerard (CBS)
19	17	ANOTHER TIME, ANOTHER PLACE — Engelbert Humperdinck (Decca)
20	18	KEEP ON DANCING — Bay City Rollers (Bell)
24	19	YOU DON'T HAVE TO BE IN THE ARMY TO FIGHT IN THE WAR — Mungo Jerry (Dawn)
21	20	DADDY DON'T YOU WALK SO FAST — Daniel Boone (Penny Farthing)
22	21	MOON SHADOW — Cat Stevens (Island)
27	22	SPANISH HARLEM — Aretha Franklin (Atlantic)
15	23	SOLDIER BLUE — Buffy Sainte-Marie (RCA)
26	24	SUPERSTAR — Carpenters (A&M)
18	25	BACK STREET LUV — Curved Air (Warner Bros)
-	26	THE NIGHT THEY DROVE OLD DIXIE DOWN — Joan Baez (Vanguard)
29	27	MAMMY BLUE — Los Pop-Tops (A&M)
28	28	BRANDY — Scott English (Horse)
14	29	I'M STILL WAITING — Diana Ross (Tamla Motown)
-	30	TILL — Tom Jones (Decca)

23 October 1971

last week	this week	Title / Artist (Label)
1	1	MAGGIE MAY — Rod Stewart (Mercury)
7	2	WITCH QUEEN OF NEW ORLEANS — Redbone (Epic)
13	3	SIMPLE GAME — Four Tops (Tamla Motown)
4	4	YOU'VE GOT A FRIEND — James Taylor (Warner Bros)
3	5	TWEEDLE DEE, TWEEDLE DUM — Middle of the Road (RCA)
8	6	FOR ALL WE KNOW — Shirley Bassey (United Artists)
11	7	SULTANA — Titanic (CBS)
5	8	DID YOU EVER — Nancy Sinatra & Lee Hazlewood (Reprise)
10	9	FREEDOM COME, FREEDOM GO — Fortunes (Capitol)
6	10	TAP TURNS ON THE WATER — C.C.S. (RAK)
2	11	HEY GIRL DON'T BOTHER ME — Tams (Probe)
16	12	BUTTERFLY — Danyel Gerard (CBS)
9	13	COUSIN NORMAN — Marmalade (Decca)
22	14	SPANISH HARLEM — Aretha Franklin (Atlantic)
12	15	LIFE IS A LONG SONG — Jethro Tull (Chrysalis)
26	16	THE NIGHT THEY DROVE OLD DIXIE DOWN — Joan Baez (Vanguard)
18	17	KEEP ON DANCING — Bay City Rollers (Bell)
30	18	TILL — Tom Jones (Decca)
14	19	I BELIEVE (IN LOVE) — Hot Chocolate (RAK)
17	20	ANOTHER TIME, ANOTHER PLACE — Engelbert Humperdinck (Decca)
-	21	TIRED OF BEING ALONE — Al Green (London)
18	22	YOU DON'T HAVE TO BE IN THE ARMY TO FIGHT IN THE WAR — Mungo Jerry (Dawn)
24	23	SUPERSTAR — Carpenters (A&M)
15	24	NATHAN JONES — Supremes (Tamla Motown)
20	25	DADDY DON'T YOU WALK SO FAST — Daniel Boone (Penny Farthing)
21	26	MOON SHADOW — Cat Stevens (Island)
-	27	BURUNDI BLACK — Burundi Steiphenson Black (Barclay)
28	28	BRANDY — Scott English (Horse)
27	29	MAMMY BLUE — Los Pop-Tops (A&M)
23	30	SOLDIER BLUE — Buffy Sainte-Marie (RCA)

30 October 1971

last week	this week	Title / Artist (Label)
1	1	MAGGIE MAY — Rod Stewart (Mercury)
2	2	WITCH QUEEN OF NEW ORLEANS — Redbone (Epic)
3	3	SIMPLE GAME — Four Tops (Tamla Motown)
6	4	FOR ALL WE KNOW — Shirley Bassey (United Artists)
4	5	YOU'VE GOT A FRIEND — James Taylor (Warner Bros)
8	6	SULTANA — Titanic (CBS)
5	7	TWEEDLE DEE, TWEEDLE DUM — Middle of the Road (RCA)
9	8	FREEDOM COME, FREEDOM GO — Fortunes (Capitol)
16	9	THE NIGHT THEY DROVE OLD DIXIE DOWN — Joan Baez (Vanguard)
8	10	DID YOU EVER — Nancy Sinatra & Lee Hazlewood (Reprise)
14	11	SPANISH HARLEM — Aretha Franklin (Atlantic)
12	12	BUTTERFLY — Danyel Gerard (CBS)
18	13	TILL — Tom Jones (Decca)
21	14	TIRED OF BEING ALONE — Al Green (London)
10	15	TAP TURNS ON THE WATER — C.C.S. (RAK)
23	16	SUPERSTAR — Carpenters (A&M)
17	17	KEEP ON DANCING — Bay City Rollers (Bell)
11	18	HEY GIRL DON'T BOTHER ME — Tams (Probe)
20	19	ANOTHER TIME, ANOTHER PLACE — Engelbert Humperdinck (Decca)
28	20	BRANDY — Scott English (Horse)
-	21	SURRENDER — Diana Ross (Tamla Motown)
19	22	I BELIEVE (IN LOVE) — Hot Chocolate (RAK)
15	23	LIFE IS A LONG SONG — Jethro Tull (Chrysalis)
27	24	BURUNDI BLACK — Burundi Steiphenson Black (Barclay)
-	25	LOOK AROUND — Vince Hill (Columbia)
-	25	LET'S SEE ACTION — Who (Track)
22	27	YOU DON'T HAVE TO BE IN THE ARMY TO FIGHT IN THE WAR — Mungo Jerry (Dawn)
-	28	I WILL RETURN — Springwater (Polydor)
-	29	BANKS OF THE OHIO — Olivia Newton-John (Pye International)
13	30	COUSIN NORMAN — Marmalade (Decca)
-	30	CHINATOWN — Move (Harvest)

Shirley Bassey took a cover version of the Carpenters' *For All We Know* into the Top 10 as the duo themselves charted with their cover of Delaney & Bonnie's *Superstar*. The Bay City Rollers debuted with a revival of a 1960s US hit by the Gentrys. The Four Tops' *Simple Game* was a former Moody Blues B-side which the Motown group recorded in a session produced by Tony Clarke, the Moody Blues' own producer. Redbone were, unusually, a US red indian rock band led by brothers Pat and Lolly Vegas.

last week	this	6 November 1971
1	1	MAGGIE MAY Rod Stewart (Mercury)
2	2	WITCH QUEEN OF NEW ORLEANS Redbone (Epic)
14	3	TIRED OF BEING ALONE Al Green (London)
6	4	SULTANA Titanic (CBS)
3	5	SIMPLE GAME Four Tops (Tamla Motown)
9	6	THE NIGHT THEY DROVE OLD DIXIE DOWN Joan Baez (Vanguard)
13	7	TILL Tom Jones (Decca)
4	8	FOR ALL WE KNOW Shirley Bassey (United Artists)
-	9	COS I LUV YOU Slade (Polydor)
7	10	TWEEDLE DEE, TWEEDLE DUM Middle of the Road (RCA)
11	11	SPANISH HARLEM Aretha Franklin (Atlantic)
8	12	FREEDOM COME, FREEDOM GO Fortunes (Capitol)
5	13	YOU'VE GOT A FRIEND James Taylor (Warner Bros)
17	14	KEEP ON DANCING Bay City Rollers (Bell)
28	15	I WILL RETURN Springwater (Polydor)
12	16	BUTTERFLY Danyel Gerard (CBS)
20	17	BRANDY Scott English (Horse)
16	18	SUPERSTAR Carpenters (A&M)
10	19	DID YOU EVER Nancy Sinatra & Lee Hazlewood (Reprise)
29	20	BANKS OF THE OHIO Olivia Newton-John (Pye International)
25	21	LOOK AROUND Vince Hill (Columbia)
-	22	JOHNNY REGGAE Piglets (Bell)
21	23	SURRENDER Diana Ross (Tamla Motown)
25	24	LET'S SEE ACTION Who (Track)
19	25	ANOTHER TIME, ANOTHER PLACE Engelbert Humperdinck (Decca)
-	26	RUN BABY RUN Newbeats (London)
-	27	GYPSIES, TRAMPS AND THIEVES Cher (MCA)
15	28	TAP TURNS ON THE WATER C.C.S. (RAK)
30	29	CHINATOWN Move (Harvest)
24	30	BURUNDI BLACK Burundi Steiphenson Black (Barclay)

		13 November 1971
9	1	COS I LUV YOU Slade (Polydor)
2	2	WITCH QUEEN OF NEW ORLEANS Redbone (Epic)
1	3	MAGGIE MAY Rod Stewart (Mercury)
3	4	TIRED OF BEING ALONE Al Green (London)
7	5	TILL Tom Jones (Decca)
5	6	SIMPLE GAME Four Tops (Tamla Motown)
6	7	THE NIGHT THEY DROVE OLD DIXIE DOWN Joan Baez (Vanguard)
4	8	SULTANA Titanic (CBS)
22	9	JOHNNY REGGAE Piglets (Bell)
15	10	I WILL RETURN Springwater (Polydor)
20	11	BANKS OF THE OHIO Olivia Newton-John (Pye International)
17	12	BRANDY Scott English (Horse)
27	13	GYPSIES, TRAMPS AND THIEVES Cher (MCA)
21	14	LOOK AROUND Vince Hill (Columbia)
8	15	FOR ALL WE KNOW Shirley Bassey (United Artists)
14	16	KEEP ON DANCING Bay City Rollers (Bell)
23	17	SURRENDER Diana Ross (Tamla Motown)
26	18	RUN BABY RUN Newbeats (London)
10	19	TWEEDLE DEE, TWEEDLE DUM Middle of the Road (RCA)
11	20	SPANISH HARLEM Aretha Franklin (Atlantic)
12	21	FREEDOM COME, FREEDOM GO Fortunes (Capitol)
24	22	LET'S SEE ACTION Carpenters (A&M)
18	23	SUPERSTAR Carpenters (A&M)
29	24	CHINATOWN Move (Harvest)
13	25	YOU'VE GOT A FRIEND James Taylor (Warner Bros)
-	26	ERNIE (THE FASTEST MILKMAN IN THE WEST) Benny Hill (Columbia)
19	27	DID YOU EVER Nancy Sinatra & Lee Hazlewood (Reprise)
25	28	ANOTHER TIME, ANOTHER PLACE Engelbert Humperdinck (Decca)
16	29	BUTTERFLY Danyel Gerard (CBS)
-	30	PUT YOURSELF IN MY PLACE Elgins (Tamla Motown)

		20 November 1971
1	1	COS I LUV YOU Slade (Polydor)
10	2	I WILL RETURN Springwater (Polydor)
5	3	TILL Tom Jones (Decca)
9	4	JOHNNY REGGAE Piglets (Bell)
3	5	MAGGIE MAY Rod Stewart (Mercury)
4	6	TIRED OF BEING ALONE Al Green (London)
13	7	GYPSIES, TRAMPS AND THIEVES Cher (MCA)
2	8	WITCH QUEEN OF NEW ORLEANS Redbone (Epic)
11	9	BANKS OF THE OHIO Olivia Newton-John (Pye International)
7	10	THE NIGHT THEY DROVE OLD DIXIE DOWN Joan Baez (Vanguard)
6	11	SIMPLE GAME Four Tops (Tamla Motown)
8	12	SULTANA Titanic (CBS)
18	13	RUN BABY RUN Newbeats (London)
14	14	LOOK AROUND Vince Hill (Columbia)
12	15	BRANDY Scott English (Horse)
16	16	JEEPSTER T. Rex (Fly)
17	17	SURRENDER Diana Ross (Tamla Motown)
26	18	ERNIE (THE FASTEST MILKMAN IN THE WEST) Benny Hill (Columbia)
23	19	SUPERSTAR Carpenters (A&M)
15	20	FOR ALL WE KNOW Shirley Bassey (United Artists)
20	21	SPANISH HARLEM Aretha Franklin (Atlantic)
16	22	KEEP ON DANCING Bay City Rollers (Bell)
19	23	TWEEDLE DEE, TWEEDLE DUM Middle of the Road (RCA)
22	24	LET'S SEE ACTION Who (Track)
24	25	CHINATOWN Move (Harvest)
-	26	YOU'VE GOT TO HAVE LOVE IN YOUR HEART Supremes & Four Tops (Tamla Motown)
-	27	BURUNDI BLACK Burundi Steiphenson Black (Barclay)
21	28	FREEDOM COME, FREEDOM GO Fortunes (Capitol)
25	29	YOU'VE GOT A FRIEND James Taylor (Warner Bros)
29	30	BUTTERFLY Danyel Gerard (CBS)

		27 November 1971
1	1	COS I LUV YOU Slade (Polydor)
4	2	JOHNNY REGGAE Piglets (Bell)
7	3	GYPSIES, TRAMPS AND THIEVES Cher (MCA)
2	4	I WILL RETURN Springwater (Polydor)
3	5	TILL Tom Jones (Decca)
16	6	JEEPSTER T. Rex (Fly)
9	7	BANKS OF THE OHIO Olivia Newton-John (Pye International)
18	8	ERNIE (THE FASTEST MILKMAN IN THE WEST) Benny Hill (Columbia)
5	9	MAGGIE MAY Rod Stewart (Mercury)
13	10	RUN BABY RUN Newbeats (London)
6	11	TIRED OF BEING ALONE Al Green (London)
17	12	SURRENDER Diana Ross (Tamla Motown)
-	13	TOKOLOSHE MAN John Kongos (Fly)
10	14	THE NIGHT THEY DROVE OLD DIXIE DOWN Joan Baez (Vanguard)
14	15	LOOK AROUND Vince Hill (Columbia)
8	16	WITCH QUEEN OF NEW ORLEANS Redbone (Epic)
11	17	SIMPLE GAME Four Tops (Tamla Motown)
24	18	LET'S SEE ACTION Who (Track)
12	19	SULTANA Titanic (CBS)
19	20	SUPERSTAR Carpenters (A&M)
25	21	CHINATOWN Move (Harvest)
15	22	BRANDY Scott English (Horse)
-	23	SING A SONG OF FREEDOM Cliff Richard (Columbia)
20	24	FOR ALL WE KNOW Shirley Bassey (United Artists)
-	25	SOMETHING TELLS ME Cilla Black (Parlophone)
26	26	YOU'VE GOT TO HAVE LOVE IN YOUR HEART Supremes & Four Tops (Tamla Motown)
27	27	BURUNDI BLACK Burundi Steiphenson Black (Barclay)
22	28	KEEP ON DANCING Bay City Rollers (Bell)
-	29	IS THIS THE WAY TO AMARILLO Tony Christie (MCA)
21	30	SPANISH HARLEM Aretha Franklin (Atlantic)

Unusually two rock instrumentals made the Top 10 late in 1971. The Dutch group Titanic's oddly-titled *Sultana* was followed by Springwater's *I Will Return* – this group name concealing the identity of guitarist Phil Cordell. The Newbeats' *Run Baby Run* was another re-issue of a formerly unsuccessful release of 1965, while *Johnny Reggae* by the Piglets was a further spoof release from the irreverent and commercially astute Jonathan King, with actress Adrienne Posta handling the 'vocal'.

241

December 1971

last this week

4 December 1971

last	this		
8	1	ERNIE (THE FASTEST MILKMAN IN THE WEST)	Benny Hill (Columbia)
6	2	JEEPSTER	T. Rex (Fly)
1	3	COS I LUV YOU	Slade (Polydor)
3	4	GYPSIES, TRAMPS AND THIEVES	Cher (MCA)
2	5	JOHNNY REGGAE	Piglets (Bell)
7	6	BANKS OF THE OHIO	Olivia Newton-John (Pye International)
13	7	TOKOLOSHE MAN	John Kongos (Fly)
5	8	TILL	Tom Jones (Decca)
4	9	I WILL RETURN	Springwater (Polydor)
12	10	SURRENDER	Diana Ross (Tamla Motown)
10	11	RUN BABY RUN	Newbeats (London)
-	12	THEME FROM SHAFT	Isaac Hayes (Stax)
9	13	MAGGIE MAY	Rod Stewart (Mercury)
25	14	SOMETHING TELLS ME	Cilla Black (Parlophone)
11	15	TIRED OF BEING ALONE	Al Green (London)
15	16	LOOK AROUND	Vince Hill (Columbia)
18	17	LET'S SEE ACTION	Who (Track)
14	18	THE NIGHT THEY DROVE OLD DIXIE DOWN	Joan Baez (Vanguard)
23	19	SING A SONG OF FREEDOM	Cliff Richard (Columbia)
16	20	WITCH QUEEN OF NEW ORLEANS	Redbone (Epic)
17	21	SIMPLE GAME	Four Tops (Tamla Motown)
-	22	HOOKED ON A FEELING	Jonathan King (Decca)
-	23	NO MATTER HOW I TRY	Gilbert O'Sullivan (MAM)
26	24	YOU'VE GOT TO HAVE LOVE IN YOUR HEART	Supremes & Four Tops (Tamla Motown)
27	25	BURUNDI BLACK	Burundi Stephenson Black (Barclay)
22	26	BRANDY	Scott English (Horse)
21	27	CHINATOWN	Move (Harvest)
19	28	SULTANA	Titanic (CBS)
29	29	IS THIS THE WAY TO AMARILLO	Tony Christie (MCA)
24	30	FOR ALL WE KNOW	Shirley Bassey (United Artists)

11 December 1971

last	this		
1	1	ERNIE (THE FASTEST MILKMAN IN THE WEST)	Benny Hill (Columbia)
2	2	JEEPSTER	T. Rex (Fly)
7	3	TOKOLOSHE MAN	John Kongos (Fly)
4	4	GYPSIES, TRAMPS AND THIEVES	Cher (MCA)
3	5	COS I LUV YOU	Slade (Polydor)
12	6	THEME FROM SHAFT	Isaac Hayes (Stax)
5	7	JOHNNY REGGAE	Piglets (Bell)
8	8	TILL	Tom Jones (Decca)
6	9	BANKS OF THE OHIO	Olivia Newton-John (Pye International)
23	10	NO MATTER HOW I TRY	Gilbert O'Sullivan (MAM)
14	11	SOMETHING TELLS ME	Cilla Black (Parlophone)
9	12	I WILL RETURN	Springwater (Polydor)
10	13	SURRENDER	Diana Ross (Tamla Motown)
11	14	RUN BABY RUN	Newbeats (London)
19	15	SING A SONG OF FREEDOM	Cliff Richard (Columbia)
-	16	IT MUST BE LOVE	Labi Siffre (Pye International)
17	17	LET'S SEE ACTION	Who (Track)
29	18	IS THIS THE WAY TO AMARILLO	Tony Christie (MCA)
-	19	SOFTLY WHISPERING I LOVE YOU	Congregation (Columbia)
24	20	YOU'VE GOT TO HAVE LOVE IN YOUR HEART	Supremes & Four Tops (Tamla Motown)
25	21	BURUNDI BLACK	Burundi Stephenson Black (Barclay)
13	22	MAGGIE MAY	Rod Stewart (Mercury)
-	23	FIREBALL	Deep Purple (Harvest)
20	24	WITCH QUEEN OF NEW ORLEANS	Redbone (Epic)
16	25	LOOK AROUND	Vince Hill (Columbia)
30	26	FOR ALL WE KNOW	Shirley Bassey (United Artists)
22	27	HOOKED ON A FEELING	Jonathan King (Decca)
-	28	SOLEY SOLEY	Middle of the Road (RCA)
-	29	RIDERS ON THE STORM	Doors (Elektra)
26	30	BRANDY	Scott English (Horse)

18 December 1971

last	this		
1	1	ERNIE (THE FASTEST MILKMAN IN THE WEST)	Benny Hill (Columbia)
2	2	JEEPSTER	T. Rex (Fly)
3	3	TOKOLOSHE MAN	John Kongos (Fly)
6	4	THEME FROM SHAFT	Isaac Hayes (Stax)
10	5	NO MATTER HOW I TRY	Gilbert O'Sullivan (MAM)
4	6	GYPSIES, TRAMPS AND THIEVES	Cher (MCA)
5	7	COS I LUV YOU	Slade (Polydor)
11	8	SOMETHING TELLS ME	Cilla Black (Parlophone)
9	9	BANKS OF THE OHIO	Olivia Newton-John (Pye International)
19	10	SOFTLY WHISPERING I LOVE YOU	Congregation (Columbia)
16	11	IT MUST BE LOVE	Labi Siffre (Pye International)
28	12	SOLEY SOLEY	Middle of the Road (RCA)
13	13	TILL	Tom Jones (Decca)
7	14	JOHNNY REGGAE	Piglets (Bell)
14	15	RUN BABY RUN	Newbeats (London)
15	16	SING A SONG OF FREEDOM	Cliff Richard (Columbia)
18	17	IS THIS THE WAY TO AMARILLO	Tony Christie (MCA)
23	18	FIREBALL	Deep Purple (Harvest)
13	19	SURRENDER	Diana Ross (Tamla Motown)
-	20	I'D LIKE TO TEACH THE WORLD TO SING	New Seekers (Polydor)
12	21	I WILL RETURN	Springwater (Polydor)
17	22	LET'S SEE ACTION	Who (Track)
29	23	RIDERS ON THE STORM	Doors (Elektra)
21	24	BURUNDI BLACK	Burundi Stephenson Black (Barclay)
-	25	MORNING	Val Doonican (Philips)
-	26	SLEEPY SHORES	Johnny Pearson (Penny Farthing)
20	27	YOU'VE GOT TO HAVE LOVE IN YOUR HEART	Supremes & Four Tops (Tamla Motown)
-	28	I JUST CAN'T HELP BELIEVING	Elvis Presley (RCA)
26	29	FOR ALL WE KNOW	Shirley Bassey (United Artists)
-	30	ALL I EVER NEED IS YOU	Sonny & Cher (MCA)

25 December 1971

last	this		
1	1	ERNIE (THE FASTEST MILKMAN IN THE WEST)	Benny Hill (Columbia)
2	2	JEEPSTER	T. Rex (Fly)
4	3	THEME FROM SHAFT	Isaac Hayes (Stax)
10	4	SOFTLY WHISPERING I LOVE YOU	Congregation (Columbia)
8	5	SOMETHING TELLS ME	Cilla Black (Parlophone)
20	6	I'D LIKE TO TEACH THE WORLD TO SING	New Seekers (Polydor)
5	7	NO MATTER HOW I TRY	Gilbert O'Sullivan (MAM)
3	8	TOKOLOSHE MAN	John Kongos (Fly)
6	9	GYPSIES, TRAMPS AND THIEVES	Cher (MCA)
11	10	IT MUST BE LOVE	Labi Siffre (Pye International)
12	11	SOLEY SOLEY	Middle of the Road (RCA)
9	12	BANKS OF THE OHIO	Olivia Newton-John (Pye International)
7	13	COS I LUV YOU	Slade (Polydor)
26	14	SLEEPY SHORES	Johnny Pearson (Penny Farthing)
13	15	TILL	Tom Jones (Decca)
18	16	FIREBALL	Deep Purple (Harvest)
28	17	I JUST CAN'T HELP BELIEVING	Elvis Presley (RCA)
17	18	IS THIS THE WAY TO AMARILLO	Tony Christie (MCA)
24	19	MORNING	Val Doonican (Philips)
14	20	JOHNNY REGGAE	Piglets (Bell)
-	21	MOTHER OF MINE	Neil Reid (Decca)
15	22	RUN BABY RUN	Newbeats (London)
-	23	FAMILY AFFAIR	Sly & the Family Stone (Epic)
22	24	HOOKED ON A FEELING	Jonathan King (Decca)
16	25	SING A SONG OF FREEDOM	Cliff Richard (Columbia)
-	26	THE PERSUADERS	John Barry Seven (CBS)
27	27	YOU'VE GOT TO HAVE LOVE IN YOUR HEART	Supremes & Four Tops (Tamla Motown)
24	28	BURUNDI BLACK	Burundi Stephenson Black (Barclay)
-	28	KARA KARA	New World (RAK)
19	30	SURRENDER	Diana Ross (Tamla Motown)

Benny Hill's High Noon-styled saga of amorous milkman Ernie was actually based on an earlier American song – *The Ballad Of Irving* by novelty hitmaker Frank Gallup. Hill cornered the customary Christmas novelty market, and aided by an early example of the promo video, in which he and TV show sidekick Henry McGee dramatised the saga of Ernie and Two-Ton Ted from Teddington, the comedian managed to hold T. Rex's sure-fire chart-topper *Jeepster* at Number Two through December.

Glam Rock

By the early seventies pop music was rapidly becoming a house divided. There were 'progressive' bands who refused to issue singles and whose fans looked down on what they saw as the cheap, tacky world of commercial chart-oriented music. And there were those who produced slick, catchy singles aimed straight at the Top Ten. The man who went some way towards bridging this gap was David Bowie. His music was successful on singles and albums, critically acclaimed and great pop. He also brought in the era disparagingly known as Glam Rock. Partly as a reaction against the over-serious side of rock music with its heroes clad in patched and faded jeans, bands began to camp it up. T Rex and the likes of the Sweet and even Slade dressed the part. And then came Gary Glitter with his glorious parody of a pop star.

Twenty years later it took a jeans advert to remind us that beneath the sequins Marc Bolan had been producing some great music.

Top: Marc Bolan; below: a later incarnation of David Bowie; bottom right: Gary Glitter

January 1972

last week	this week	1 January 1972

1 January 1972

1 1 ERNIE (THE FASTEST MILKMAN IN THE WEST)   Benny Hill (Columbia)
5 2 SOMETHING TELLS ME   Cilla Black (Parlophone)
6 3 I'D LIKE TO TEACH THE WORLD TO SING   New Seekers (Polydor)
2 4 JEEPSTER   T. Rex (Fly)
7 5 NO MATTER HOW I TRY   Gilbert O'Sullivan (MAM)
4 6 SOFTLY WHISPERING I LOVE YOU   Congregation (Columbia)
3 7 THEME FROM SHAFT   Isaac Hayes (Stax)
8 8 TOKOLOSHE MAN   John Kongos (Fly)
11 9 SOLEY SOLEY   Middle of the Road (RCA)
9 10 GYPSIES, TRAMPS & THIEVES   Cher (MCA)
10 11 IT MUST BE LOVE   Labi Siffre (Pye)
17 12 I JUST CAN'T HELP BELIEVING   Elvis Presley (RCA)
14 13 SLEEPY SHORES   Johnny Pearson (Penny Farthing)
15 13 TILL   Tom Jones (Decca)
12 15 BANKS OF THE OHIO   Olivia Newton-John (Pye)
21 16 MOTHER OF MINE   Neil Reid (Decca)
18 17 IS THIS THE WAY TO AMARILLO   Tony Christie (MCA)
19 18 MORNING   Val Doonican (Philips)
13 19 COS I LUV YOU   Slade (Polydor)
16 20 FIREBALL   Deep Purple (Harvest)
28 21 KARA KARA   New World (Rak)
25 22 SING A SONG OF FREEDOM   Cliff Richard (Columbia)
24 23 HOOKED ON A FEELING   Jonathan King (Decca)
28 24 BURUNDI BLACK   Burundi Stephenson Black (Barclay)
22 25 RUN BABY RUN   Newbeats (London)
- 26 BRAND NEW KEY   Melanie (Buddah)
20 27 JOHNNY REGGAE   Piglets (Bell)
27 28 YOU'VE GOT TO HAVE LOVE IN YOUR HEART   Supremes & Four Tops (Tamla Motown)
26 29 THE PERSUADERS   John Barry Orchestra (CBS)
- 30 FOR ALL WE KNOW   Shirley Bassey (United Artists)

8 January 1972

3 1 I'D LIKE TO TEACH THE WORLD TO SING   New Seekers (Polydor)
1 2 ERNIE (THE FASTEST MILKMAN IN THE WEST)   Benny Hill (Columbia)
7 3 THEME FROM SHAFT   Isaac Hayes (Stax)
2 4 SOMETHING TELLS ME   Cilla Black (Parlophone)
5 5 NO MATTER HOW I TRY   Gilbert O'Sullivan (MAM)
4 6 JEEPSTER   T. Rex (Fly)
6 6 SOFTLY WHISPERING I LOVE YOU   Congregation (Columbia)
9 8 SOLEY SOLEY   Middle of the Road (RCA)
13 9 SLEEPY SHORES   Johnny Pearson (Penny Farthing)
8 10 TOKOLOSHE MAN   John Kongos (Fly)
11 11 IT MUST BE LOVE   Labi Siffre (Pye)
12 12 I JUST CAN'T HELP BELIEVING   Elvis Presley (RCA)
16 13 MOTHER OF MINE   Neil Reid (Decca)
10 14 GYPSIES, TRAMPS & THIEVES   Cher (MCA)
15 15 BANKS OF THE OHIO   Olivia Newton-John (Pye)
18 16 MORNING   Val Doonican (Philips)
19 17 COS I LUV YOU   Slade (Polydor)
- 18 FAMILY AFFAIR   Sly & The Family Stone (Epic)
20 19 FIREBALL   Deep Purple (Harvest)
17 20 IS THIS THE WAY TO AMARILLO   Tony Christie (MCA)
- 21 A HORSE WITH NO NAME   America (Warner Bros)
26 22 BRAND NEW KEY   Melanie (Buddah)
29 23 THE PERSUADERS   John Barry Orchestra (CBS)
- 24 THEME FROM THE ONEDIN LINE   Vienna Philharmonic Orchestra (Decca)
13 25 TILL   Tom Jones (Decca)
- 26 MORNING HAS BROKEN   Cat Stevens (Island)
- 27 STAY WITH ME   Faces (Warner Bros)
21 28 KARA KARA   New World (Rak)
23 29 HOOKED ON A FEELING   Jonathan King (Decca)
22 30 SING A SONG OF FREEDOM   Cliff Richard (Columbia)

15 January 1972

1 1 I'D LIKE TO TEACH THE WORLD TO SING   New Seekers (Polydor)
8 2 SOLEY SOLEY   Middle of the Road (RCA)
3 3 THEME FROM SHAFT   Isaac Hayes (Stax)
9 4 SLEEPY SHORES   Johnny Pearson (Penny Farthing)
4 5 SOMETHING TELLS ME   Cilla Black (Parlophone)
12 6 I JUST CAN'T HELP BELIEVING   Elvis Presley (RCA)
6 7 SOFTLY WHISPERING I LOVE YOU   Congregation (Columbia)
2 8 ERNIE (THE FASTEST MILKMAN IN THE WEST)   Benny Hill (Columbia)
5 9 NO MATTER HOW I TRY   Gilbert O'Sullivan (MAM)
6 10 JEEPSTER   T. Rex (Fly)
13 11 MOTHER OF MINE   Neil Reid (Decca)
21 12 A HORSE WITH NO NAME   America (Warner Bros)
11 13 IT MUST BE LOVE   Labi Siffre (Pye)
22 14 BRAND NEW KEY   Melanie (Buddah)
16 15 MORNING   Val Doonican (Philips)
26 15 MORNING HAS BROKEN   Cat Stevens (Island)
27 17 STAY WITH ME   Faces (Warner Bros)
10 18 TOKOLOSHE MAN   John Kongos (Fly)
18 19 FAMILY AFFAIR   Sly & The Family Stone (Epic)
28 20 KARA KARA   New World (Rak)
14 21 GYPSIES, TRAMPS & THIEVES   Cher (MCA)
19 22 FIREBALL   Deep Purple (Harvest)
23 23 THE PERSUADERS   John Barry Orchestra (CBS)
- 24 WHERE DID OUR LOVE GO   Donnie Elbert (London)
24 25 THEME FROM THE ONEDIN LINE   Vienna Philharmonic Orchestra (Decca)
- 26 MOON RIVER   Greyhound (Trojan)
15 27 BANKS OF THE OHIO   Olivia Newton-John (Pye)
20 28 IS THIS THE WAY TO AMARILLO   Tony Christie (MCA)
29 29 HOOKED ON A FEELING   Jonathan King (Decca)
30 30 SING A SONG OF FREEDOM   Cliff Richard (Columbia)
- 30 LET'S STAY TOGETHER   Al Green (London)

22 January 1972

1 1 I'D LIKE TO TEACH THE WORLD TO SING   New Seekers (Polydor)
12 2 A HORSE WITH NO NAME   America (Warner Bros)
14 3 BRAND NEW KEY   Melanie (Buddah)
11 4 MOTHER OF MINE   Neil Reid (Decca)
2 5 SOLEY SOLEY   Middle of the Road (RCA)
7 6 SOFTLY WHISPERING I LOVE YOU   Congregation (Columbia)
6 7 I JUST CAN'T HELP BELIEVING   Elvis Presley (RCA)
4 8 SLEEPY SHORES   Johnny Pearson (Penny Farthing)
17 9 STAY WITH ME   Faces (Warner Bros)
15 10 MORNING HAS BROKEN   Cat Stevens (Island)
8 11 ERNIE (THE FASTEST MILKMAN IN THE WEST)   Benny Hill (Columbia)
9 12 NO MATTER HOW I TRY   Gilbert O'Sullivan (MAM)
3 13 THEME FROM SHAFT   Isaac Hayes (Stax)
10 14 JEEPSTER   T. Rex (Fly)
24 14 WHERE DID OUR LOVE GO   Donnie Elbert (London)
5 16 SOMETHING TELLS ME   Cilla Black (Parlophone)
19 17 FAMILY AFFAIR   Sly & The Family Stone (Epic)
13 18 IT MUST BE LOVE   Labi Siffre (Pye)
23 19 THE PERSUADERS   John Barry Orchestra (CBS)
30 20 LET'S STAY TOGETHER   Al Green (London)
25 21 THEME FROM THE ONEDIN LINE   Vienna Philharmonic Orchestra (Decca)
15 22 MORNING   Val Doonican (Philips)
26 23 MOON RIVER   Greyhound (Trojan)
20 24 KARA KARA   New World (Rak)
- 25 HAVE YOU SEEN HER   Chi-Lites (MCA)
- 26 IF YOU REALLY LOVE ME   Stevie Wonder (Tamla Motown)
- 27 CAN'T LET YOU GO   Barry Ryan (Polydor)
- 28 AMERICAN PIE   Don McLean (United Artists)
22 29 FIREBALL   Deep Purple (Harvest)
21 30 GYPSIES, TRAMPS & THIEVES   Cher (MCA)

Adapted from Coca-Cola's most famous TV advert, the New Seekers' *I'd Like To Teach The World To Sing* was to be the biggest seller of the first half of 1972. TV also had a hand in the success of Cilla Black's hit, which she used as her weekly show theme, Neil Reid's *Mother Of Mine* (a TV talent show 'found' him), Johnny Pearson's *Sleepy Shores* (theme from the series *Owen MD*), John Barry's *The Persuaders* (the Roger Moore/Tony Curtis series), and the classically-originated *Onedin Line* theme.

January – February 1972

last	this	29 January 1972		5 February 1972		12 February 1972		19 February 1972
1	1	I'D LIKE TO TEACH THE WORLD TO SING New Seekers (Polydor)	3 1	A HORSE WITH NO NAME America (Warner Bros)	2 1	TELEGRAM SAM T. Rex (T. Rex)	2 1	SON OF MY FATHER Chicory Tip (CBS)
4	2	MOTHER OF MINE Neil Reid (Decca)	12 2	TELEGRAM SAM T. Rex (T. Rex)	12 2	SON OF MY FATHER Chicory Tip (CBS)	1 2	TELEGRAM SAM T. Rex (T. Rex)
2	3	A HORSE WITH NO NAME America (Warner Bros)	1 3	I'D LIKE TO TEACH THE WORLD TO SING New Seekers (Polydor)	3 3	I'D LIKE TO TEACH THE WORLD TO SING New Seekers (Polydor)	4 3	HAVE YOU SEEN HER Chi-Lites (MCA)
3	4	BRAND NEW KEY Melanie (Buddah)	2 4	MOTHER OF MINE Neil Reid (Decca)	10 4	HAVE YOU SEEN HER Chi-Lites (MCA)	6 4	MOTHER OF MINE Neil Reid (Decca)
9	5	STAY WITH ME Faces (Warner Bros)	4 5	BRAND NEW KEY Melanie (Buddah)	1 5	A HORSE WITH NO NAME America (Warner Bros)	17 5	LOOK WOT YOU DUN Slade (Polydor)
7	6	I JUST CAN'T HELP BELIEVING Elvis Presley (RCA)	5 6	STAY WITH ME Faces (Warner Bros)	4 6	MOTHER OF MINE Neil Reid (Decca)	10 6	LET'S STAY TOGETHER Al Green (London)
14	7	WHERE DID OUR LOVE GO Donnie Elbert (London)	9 7	LET'S STAY TOGETHER Al Green (London)	6 7	STAY WITH ME Faces (Warner Bros)	3 7	I'D LIKE TO TEACH THE WORLD TO SING New Seekers (Polydor)
10	8	MORNING HAS BROKEN Cat Stevens (Island)	7 8	WHERE DID OUR LOVE GO Donnie Elbert (London)	8 8	WHERE DID OUR LOVE GO Donnie Elbert (London)	11 8	AMERICAN PIE Don McLean (United Artists)
20	9	LET'S STAY TOGETHER Al Green (London)	6 9	I JUST CAN'T HELP BELIEVING Elvis Presley (RCA)	5 9	BRAND NEW KEY Melanie (Buddah)	5 9	A HORSE WITH NO NAME America (Warner Bros)
8	10	SLEEPY SHORES Johnny Pearson (Penny Farthing)	15 10	HAVE YOU SEEN HER Chi-Lites (MCA)	7 10	LET'S STAY TOGETHER Al Green (London)	16 10	STORM IN A TEACUP Fortunes (Capitol)
5	11	SOLEY SOLEY Middle of the Road (RCA)	8 11	MORNING HAS BROKEN Cat Stevens (Island)	16 11	AMERICAN PIE Don McLean (United Artists)	12 11	ALL I EVER NEED IS YOU Sonny & Cher (MCA)
-	12	TELEGRAM SAM T. Rex (T. Rex)	30 12	SON OF MY FATHER Chicory Tip (CBS)	17 12	ALL I EVER NEED IS YOU Sonny & Cher (MCA)	19 12	DAY AFTER DAY Badfinger (Apple)
6	13	SOFTLY WHISPERING I LOVE YOU Congregation (Columbia)	17 13	MOON RIVER Greyhound (Trojan)	13 13	MOON RIVER Greyhound (Trojan)	7 13	STAY WITH ME Faces (Warner Bros)
17	14	FAMILY AFFAIR Sly & The Family Stone (Epic)	14 14	FAMILY AFFAIR Sly & The Family Stone (Epic)	14 14	FAMILY AFFAIR Sly & The Family Stone (Epic)	9 14	BRAND NEW KEY Melanie (Buddah)
25	15	HAVE YOU SEEN HER Chi-Lites (MCA)	16 15	THE PERSUADERS John Barry Orchestra (CBS)	9 15	I JUST CAN'T HELP BELIEVING Elvis Presley (RCA)	8 15	WHERE DID OUR LOVE GO Donnie Elbert (London)
19	16	THE PERSUADERS John Barry Orchestra (CBS)	21 16	AMERICAN PIE Don McLean (United Artists)	23 16	STORM IN A TEACUP Fortunes (Capitol)	13 16	MOON RIVER Greyhound (Trojan)
23	17	MOON RIVER Greyhound (Trojan)	27 17	ALL I EVER NEED IS YOU Sonny & Cher (MCA)	30 17	LOOK WOT YOU DUN Slade (Polydor)	20 17	BABY I'M A WANT YOU Bread (Elektra)
12	18	NO MATTER HOW I TRY Gilbert O'Sullivan (MAM)	19 18	BABY I'M A WANT YOU Bread (Elektra)	11 18	MORNING HAS BROKEN Cat Stevens (Island)	- 18	WITHOUT YOU Nilsson (RCA)
-	19	BABY I'M A WANT YOU Bread (Elektra)	11 19	SOLEY SOLEY Middle of the Road (RCA)	25 19	DAY AFTER DAY Badfinger (Apple)	21 19	MY WORLD Bee Gees (Polydor)
13	20	THEME FROM SHAFT Isaac Hayes (Stax)	10 20	SLEEPY SHORES Johnny Pearson (Penny Farthing)	18 20	BABY I'M A WANT YOU Bread (Elektra)	18 20	MORNING HAS BROKEN Cat Stevens (Island)
28	21	AMERICAN PIE Don McLean (United Artists)	24 21	IF YOU REALLY LOVE ME Stevie Wonder (Tamla Motown)	28 21	MY WORLD Bee Gees (Polydor)	15 21	I JUST CAN'T HELP BELIEVING Elvis Presley (RCA)
11	22	ERNIE (THE FASTEST MILKMAN IN THE WEST) Benny Hill (Columbia)	13 22	SOFTLY WHISPERING I LOVE YOU Congregation (Columbia)	21 22	IF YOU REALLY LOVE ME Stevie Wonder (Tamla Motown)	- 22	GOT TO BE THERE Michael Jackson (Tamla Motown)
16	23	SOMETHING TELLS ME Cilla Black (Parlophone)	- 23	STORM IN A TEACUP Fortunes (Capitol)	15 23	THE PERSUADERS John Barry Orchestra (CBS)	14 23	FAMILY AFFAIR Sly & The Family Stone (Epic)
26	24	IF YOU REALLY LOVE ME Stevie Wonder (Tamla Motown)	18 24	NO MATTER HOW I TRY Gilbert O'Sullivan (MAM)	20 24	SLEEPY SHORES Johnny Pearson (Penny Farthing)	22 24	IF YOU REALLY LOVE ME Stevie Wonder (Tamla Motown)
22	25	MORNING Val Doonican (Philips)	- 25	DAY AFTER DAY Badfinger (Apple)	- 25	SUPERSTAR (REMEMBER HOW YOU GOT WHERE YOU ARE) Temptations (Tamla Motown)	- 25	POPPA JOE Sweet (RCA)
21	26	THEME FROM THE ONEDIN LINE Vienna Philharmonic Orchestra (Decca)	26 26	THEME FROM THE ONEDIN LINE Vienna Philharmonic Orchestra (Decca)	19 26	SOLEY SOLEY Middle of the Road (RCA)	24 26	SLEEPY SHORES Johnny Pearson (Penny Farthing)
-	27	ALL I EVER NEED IS YOU Sonny & Cher (MCA)	22 27	ERNIE (THE FASTEST MILKMAN IN THE WEST) Benny Hill (Columbia)	- 27	MORNING Val Doonican (Philips)	- 27	SAY YOU DON'T MIND Colin Blunstone (Epic)
24	28	KARA KARA New World (Rak)	- 28	MY WORLD Bee Gees (Polydor)	26 28	THEME FROM THE ONEDIN LINE Vienna Philharmonic Orchestra (Decca)	25 28	SUPERSTAR (REMEMBER HOW YOU GOT WHERE YOU ARE) Temptations (Tamla Motown)
14	29	JEEPSTER T. Rex (Fly)	28 29	KARA KARA New World (Rak)	22 29	SOFTLY WHISPERING I LOVE YOU Congregation (Columbia)	- 29	MOTHER AND CHILD REUNION Paul Simon (CBS)
-	30	SON OF MY FATHER Chicory Tip (CBS)	- 30	LOOK WOT YOU DUN Slade (Polydor)	24 30	NO MATTER HOW I TRY Gilbert O'Sullivan (MAM)	- 30	DAY BY DAY Holly Sherwood (Bell)

The chart-topping debut by acoustic trio America was to be their biggest UK success. Formed here (they were from US service familes), they returned to the US to put together a string of American hits. T. Rex's first release on their own label kept up the group's 1971 chart momentum, delivering a third Number One with *Telegram Sam*. Chicory Tip's *Son Of My Father*, a cover of a German hit by Giorgio (Moroder), was the first major UK smash to make extensive use of the synthesiser.

245

February – March 1972

26 February 1972

1	1	SON OF MY FATHER	Chicory Tip (CBS)
5	2	LOOK WOT YOU DUN	Slade (Polydor)
8	3	AMERICAN PIE	Don McLean (United Artists)
3	4	HAVE YOU SEEN HER	Chi-Lites (MCA)
2	5	TELEGRAM SAM	T. Rex (T. Rex)
18	6	WITHOUT YOU	Nilsson (RCA)
4	7	MOTHER OF MINE	Neil Reid (Decca)
10	8	STORM IN A TEACUP	Fortunes (Capitol)
6	9	LET'S STAY TOGETHER	Al Green (London)
12	10	DAY AFTER DAY	Badfinger (Apple)
22	11	GOT TO BE THERE	Michael Jackson (Tamla Motown)
11	12	ALL I EVER NEED IS YOU	Sonny & Cher (MCA)
7	13	I'D LIKE TO TEACH THE WORLD TO SING	New Seekers (Polydor)
9	14	A HORSE WITH NO NAME	America (Warner Bros)
25	15	POPPA JOE	Sweet (RCA)
29	16	MOTHER AND CHILD REUNION	Paul Simon (CBS)
27	17	SAY YOU DON'T MIND	Colin Blunstone (Epic)
19	18	MY WORLD	Bee Gees (Polydor)
14	19	BRAND NEW KEY	Melanie (Buddah)
17	20	BABY I 'M A WANT YOU	Bread (Elektra)
15	21	WHERE DID OUR LOVE GO	Donnie Elbert (London)
13	22	STAY WITH ME	Faces (Warner Bros)
30	23	DAY BY DAY	Holly Sherwood (Bell)
16	24	MOON RIVER	Greyhound (Trojan)
21	25	I JUST CAN'T HELP BELIEVING	Elvis Presley (RCA)
24	26	IF YOU REALLY LOVE ME	Stevie Wonder (Tamla Motown)
28	27	SUPERSTAR (REMEMBER HOW YOU GOT WHERE YOU ARE)	Temptations (Tamla Motown)
20	28	MORNING HAS BROKEN	Cat Stevens (Island)
26	29	SLEEPY SHORES	Johnny Pearson (Penny Farthing)
23	30	FAMILY AFFAIR	Sly & The Family Stone (Epic)

4 March 1972

3	1	AMERICAN PIE	Don McLean (United Artists)
1	2	SON OF MY FATHER	Chicory Tip (CBS)
6	3	WITHOUT YOU	Nilsson (RCA)
11	4	GOT TO BE THERE	Michael Jackson (Tamla Motown)
2	5	LOOK WOT YOU DUN	Slade (Polydor)
8	6	STORM IN A TEACUP	Fortunes (Capitol)
4	7	HAVE YOU SEEN HER	Chi-Lites (MCA)
16	8	MOTHER AND CHILD REUNION	Paul Simon (CBS)
5	9	TELEGRAM SAM	T. Rex (T. Rex)
10	10	DAY AFTER DAY	Badfinger (Apple)
7	11	MOTHER OF MINE	Neil Reid (Decca)
15	12	POPPA JOE	Sweet (RCA)
-	13	BLUE IS THE COLOUR	Chelsea F C (Penny Farthing)
12	14	ALL I EVER NEED IS YOU	Sonny & Cher (MCA)
9	15	LET'S STAY TOGETHER	Al Green (London)
17	16	SAY YOU DON'T MIND	Colin Blunstone (Epic)
-	17	I CAN'T HELP MYSELF	Donnie Elbert (Avco)
-	18	BEG, STEAL OR BORROW	New Seekers (Polydor)
13	19	I'D LIKE TO TEACH THE WORLD TO SING	New Seekers (Polydor)
18	20	MY WORLD	Bee Gees (Polydor)
-	21	GIVE IRELAND BACK TO THE IRISH	Wings (Apple)
-	22	MEET ME ON THE CORNER	Lindisfarne (Charisma)
14	23	A HORSE WITH NO NAME	America (Warner Bros)
-	24	ALONE AGAIN (NATURALLY)	Gilbert O'Sullivan (MAM)
19	25	BRAND NEW KEY	Melanie (Buddah)
24	26	MOON RIVER	Greyhound (Trojan)
-	27	FLOY JOY	Supremes (Tamla Motown)
20	28	BABY I 'M A WANT YOU	Bread (Elektra)
-	29	THE BABY	Hollies (Polydor)
23	30	DAY BY DAY	Holly Sherwood (Bell)

11 March 1972

3	1	WITHOUT YOU	Nilsson (RCA)
1	2	AMERICAN PIE	Don McLean (United Artists)
2	3	SON OF MY FATHER	Chicory Tip (CBS)
4	4	GOT TO BE THERE	Michael Jackson (Tamla Motown)
8	5	MOTHER AND CHILD REUNION	Paul Simon (CBS)
5	6	LOOK WOT YOU DUN	Slade (Polydor)
6	7	STORM IN A TEACUP	Fortunes (Capitol)
13	8	BLUE IS THE COLOUR	Chelsea F C (Penny Farthing)
18	9	BEG, STEAL OR BORROW	New Seekers (Polydor)
12	10	POPPA JOE	Sweet (RCA)
24	11	ALONE AGAIN (NATURALLY)	Gilbert O'Sullivan (MAM)
10	12	DAY AFTER DAY	Badfinger (Apple)
22	13	MEET ME ON THE CORNER	Lindisfarne (Charisma)
17	14	I CAN'T HELP MYSELF	Donnie Elbert (Avco)
16	15	SAY YOU DON'T MIND	Colin Blunstone (Epic)
7	16	HAVE YOU SEEN HER	Chi-Lites (MCA)
11	17	MOTHER OF MINE	Neil Reid (Decca)
21	18	GIVE IRELAND BACK TO THE IRISH	Wings (Apple)
9	19	TELEGRAM SAM	T. Rex (T. Rex)
20	20	MY WORLD	Bee Gees (Polydor)
27	21	FLOY JOY	Supremes (Tamla Motown)
14	22	ALL I EVER NEED IS YOU	Sonny & Cher (MCA)
29	23	THE BABY	Hollies (Polydor)
15	24	LET'S STAY TOGETHER	Al Green (London)
-	25	HOLD YOUR HEAD UP	Argent (Epic)
-	26	FLIRT	Jonathan King (Decca)
-	27	DESIDERATA	Les Crane (Warner Bros)
19	28	I'D LIKE TO TEACH THE WORLD TO SING	New Seekers (Polydor)
-	29	LOVIN' YOU AIN'T EASY	Pagliaro (Pye)
23	30	A HORSE WITH NO NAME	America (Warner Bros)

18 March 1972

1	1	WITHOUT YOU	Nilsson (RCA)
2	2	AMERICAN PIE	Don McLean (United Artists)
9	3	BEG, STEAL OR BORROW	New Seekers (Polydor)
4	4	GOT TO BE THERE	Michael Jackson (Tamla Motown)
3	5	SON OF MY FATHER	Chicory Tip (CBS)
11	6	ALONE AGAIN (NATURALLY)	Gilbert O'Sullivan (MAM)
5	7	MOTHER AND CHILD REUNION	Paul Simon (CBS)
13	8	MEET ME ON THE CORNER	Lindisfarne (Charisma)
8	9	BLUE IS THE COLOUR	Chelsea F C (Penny Farthing)
6	10	LOOK WOT YOU DUN	Slade (Polydor)
14	11	I CAN'T HELP MYSELF	Donnie Elbert (Avco)
17	12	MOTHER OF MINE	Neil Reid (Decca)
18	13	GIVE IRELAND BACK TO THE IRISH	Wings (Apple)
10	14	POPPA JOE	Sweet (RCA)
12	15	DAY AFTER DAY	Badfinger (Apple)
16	16	SAY YOU DON'T MIND	Colin Blunstone (Epic)
7	17	STORM IN A TEACUP	Fortunes (Capitol)
21	18	FLOY JOY	Supremes (Tamla Motown)
25	19	HOLD YOUR HEAD UP	Argent (Epic)
27	20	DESIDERATA	Les Crane (Warner Bros)
26	21	FLIRT	Jonathan King (Decca)
16	22	HAVE YOU SEEN HER	Chi-Lites (MCA)
23	23	THE BABY	Hollies (Polydor)
-	24	IT'S ONE OF THOSE NIGHTS (YES LOVE)	Partridge Family (Bell)
-	25	WHAT IS LIFE	Olivia Newton-John (Pye)
20	26	MY WORLD	Bee Gees (Polydor)
-	27	BROTHER	C. C. S. (Rak)
19	28	TELEGRAM SAM	T. Rex (T. Rex)
-	29	JESUS	Cliff Richard (Columbia)
28	30	I'D LIKE TO TEACH THE WORLD TO SING	New Seekers (Polydor)

Don McLean's *American Pie* was one of the most enigmatic debut hits for years: while irresistibly catchy, it was difficult to be sure just what the lyrics were all about, although various hints suggested that it was McLean's personal version of the history of rock'n'roll, with the death of Buddy Holly as a focus. The artist has always refused to divulge anything further. Paul McCartney's hit was BBC-banned for its outright political statement, and the Hollies tried out a new lead singer, Michael Rikfors, on *The Baby*.

25 March 1972

last week	this week	
1	1	WITHOUT YOU Nilsson (RCA)
3	2	BEG, STEAL OR BORROW New Seekers (Polydor)
2	3	AMERICAN PIE Don McLean (United Artists)
6	4	ALONE AGAIN (NATURALLY) Gilbert O'Sullivan (MAM)
8	5	MEET ME ON THE CORNER Lindisfarne (Charisma)
7	6	MOTHER AND CHILD REUNION Paul Simon (CBS)
4	7	GOT TO BE THERE Michael Jackson (Tamla Motown)
5	8	SON OF MY FATHER Chicory Tip (CBS)
10	9	HOLD YOUR HEAD UP Argent (Epic)
18	10	FLOY JOY Supremes (Tamla Motown)
11	11	I CAN'T HELP MYSELF Donnie Elbert (Avco)
20	12	DESIDERATA Les Crane (Warner Bros)
9	13	BLUE IS THE COLOUR Chelsea F C (Penny Farthing)
24	14	IT'S ONE OF THOSE NIGHTS (YES LOVE) Partridge Family (Bell)
12	15	MOTHER OF MINE Neil Reid (Decca)
16	16	SAY YOU DON'T MIND Colin Blunstone (Epic)
14	17	POPPA JOE Sweet (RCA)
10	18	LOOK WOT YOU DUN Slade (Polydor)
13	19	GIVE IRELAND BACK TO THE IRISH Wings (Apple)
15	20	DAY AFTER DAY Badfinger (Apple)
17	21	STORM IN A TEACUP Fortunes (Capitol)
23	22	THE BABY Hollies (Polydor)
27	23	BROTHER C. C. S. (Rak)
21	24	FLIRT Jonathan King (Decca)
28	25	JESUS Cliff Richard (Columbia)
-	26	HEART OF GOLD Neil Young (Reprise)
25	27	WHAT IS LIFE Olivia Newton-John (Pye)
-	28	SWEET TALKIN' GUY Chiffons (London)
-	29	SMOKE GETS IN YOUR EYES Blue Haze (A&M)
-	30	TOO BEAUTIFUL TO LAST Engelbert Humperdinck (Decca)

1 April 1972

1	1	WITHOUT YOU Nilsson (RCA)
2	2	BEG, STEAL OR BORROW New Seekers (Polydor)
4	3	ALONE AGAIN (NATURALLY) Gilbert O'Sullivan (MAM)
3	4	AMERICAN PIE Don McLean (United Artists)
5	5	MEET ME ON THE CORNER Lindisfarne (Charisma)
9	6	HOLD YOUR HEAD UP Argent (Epic)
6	7	MOTHER AND CHILD REUNION Paul Simon (CBS)
10	8	FLOY JOY Supremes (Tamla Motown)
12	9	DESIDERATA Les Crane (Warner Bros)
12	10	IT'S ONE OF THOSE NIGHTS (YES LOVE) Partridge Family (Bell)
7	11	GOT TO BE THERE Michael Jackson (Tamla Motown)
11	12	I CAN'T HELP MYSELF Donnie Elbert (Avco)
27	13	SWEET TALKIN' GUY Chiffons (London)
27	14	WHAT IS LIFE Olivia Newton-John (Pye)
8	15	SON OF MY FATHER Chicory Tip (CBS)
13	16	BLUE IS THE COLOUR Chelsea F C (Penny Farthing)
30	17	TOO BEAUTIFUL TO LAST Engelbert Humperdinck (Decca)
25	18	HEART OF GOLD Neil Young (Reprise)
19	19	GIVE IRELAND BACK TO THE IRISH Wings (Apple)
-	20	THE YOUNG NEW MEXICAN PUPPETEER Tom Jones (Decca)
15	21	MOTHER OF MINE Neil Reid (Decca)
-	22	CRYING, LAUGHING, LOVING, LYING Labi Siffre (Pye)
-	23	SACRAMENTO Middle Of The Road (RCA)
17	24	POPPA JOE Sweet (RCA)
-	25	UNTIL IT'S TIME FOR YOU TO GO Elvis Presley (RCA)
-	26	BACK OFF BOOGALOO Ringo Starr (Apple)
23	27	BROTHER C. C. S. (Rak)
18	28	LOOK WOT YOU DUN Slade (Polydor)
29	29	SMOKE GETS IN YOUR EYES Blue Haze (A&M)
-	30	BERNADETTE Four Tops (Tamla Motown)

8 April 1972

1	1	WITHOUT YOU Nilsson (RCA)
2	2	BEG, STEAL OR BORROW New Seekers (Polydor)
3	3	ALONE AGAIN (NATURALLY) Gilbert O'Sullivan (MAM)
6	4	HOLD YOUR HEAD UP Argent (Epic)
4	5	AMERICAN PIE Don McLean (United Artists)
5	6	MEET ME ON THE CORNER Lindisfarne (Charisma)
9	7	DESIDERATA Les Crane (Warner Bros)
8	8	FLOY JOY Supremes (Tamla Motown)
13	9	SWEET TALKIN' GUY Chiffons (London)
7	10	MOTHER AND CHILD REUNION Paul Simon (CBS)
10	11	IT'S ONE OF THOSE NIGHTS (YES LOVE) Partridge Family (Bell)
-	12	AMAZING GRACE Royal Scots Dragoon Guards, Pipes, Drums & Band (RCA)
18	13	HEART OF GOLD Neil Young (Reprise)
20	14	THE YOUNG NEW MEXICAN PUPPETEER Tom Jones (Decca)
26	15	BACK OFF BOOGALOO Ringo Starr (Apple)
14	16	WHAT IS LIFE Olivia Newton-John (Pye)
11	17	GOT TO BE THERE Michael Jackson (Tamla Motown)
12	18	I CAN'T HELP MYSELF Donnie Elbert (Avco)
17	19	TOO BEAUTIFUL TO LAST Engelbert Humperdinck (Decca)
25	20	UNTIL IT'S TIME FOR YOU TO GO Elvis Presley (RCA)
16	21	BLUE IS THE COLOUR Chelsea F C (Penny Farthing)
22	22	CRYING, LAUGHING, LOVING, LYING Labi Siffre (Pye)
23	23	SACRAMENTO Middle Of The Road (RCA)
27	24	BROTHER C. C. S. (Rak)
15	25	SON OF MY FATHER Chicory Tip (CBS)
29	26	SMOKE GETS IN YOUR EYES Blue Haze (A&M)
-	27	TURN YOUR RADIO ON Ray Stevens (CBS)
30	28	BERNADETTE Four Tops (Tamla Motown)
24	29	POPPA JOE Sweet (RCA)
19	30	GIVE IRELAND BACK TO THE IRISH Wings (Apple)

15 April 1972

1	1	WITHOUT YOU Nilsson (RCA)
12	2	AMAZING GRACE Royal Scots Dragoon Guards, Pipes, Drums & Band (RCA)
9	3	SWEET TALKIN' GUY Chiffons (London)
4	4	HOLD YOUR HEAD UP Argent (Epic)
2	5	BEG, STEAL OR BORROW New Seekers (Polydor)
3	6	ALONE AGAIN (NATURALLY) Gilbert O'Sullivan (MAM)
6	7	MEET ME ON THE CORNER Lindisfarne (Charisma)
7	8	DESIDERATA Les Crane (Warner Bros)
13	9	HEART OF GOLD Neil Young (Reprise)
15	10	BACK OFF BOOGALOO Ringo Starr (Apple)
11	11	IT'S ONE OF THOSE NIGHTS (YES LOVE) Partridge Family (Bell)
8	12	FLOY JOY Supremes (Tamla Motown)
14	13	THE YOUNG NEW MEXICAN PUPPETEER Tom Jones (Decca)
5	14	AMERICAN PIE Don McLean (United Artists)
-	15	DEBORA Tyrannosaurus Rex (Magni Fly)
16	16	WHAT IS LIFE Olivia Newton-John (Pye)
-	17	RUN RUN RUN Jo Jo Gunne (Asylum)
22	18	CRYING, LAUGHING, LOVING, LYING Labi Siffre (Pye)
10	19	MOTHER AND CHILD REUNION Paul Simon (CBS)
20	20	UNTIL IT'S TIME FOR YOU TO GO Elvis Presley (RCA)
19	21	TOO BEAUTIFUL TO LAST Engelbert Humperdinck (Decca)
24	22	BROTHER C. C. S. (Rak)
-	23	RADANCER Marmalade (Decca)
18	24	I CAN'T HELP MYSELF Donnie Elbert (Avco)
-	25	COULD IT BE FOREVER David Cassidy (Bell)
-	26	I AM WHAT I AM Greyhound (Trojan)
-	27	DOWN BY THE LAZY RIVER Osmonds (MGM)
-	28	NEVER BEFORE Deep Purple (Purple)
-	29	STIR IT UP Johnny Nash (CBS)
-	30	A THING CALLED LOVE Johnny Cash (CBS)
28	30	BERNADETTE Four Tops (Tamla Motown)

Harry Nilsson's biggest hit single was written by Pete Ham and Tom Evans of Badfinger - an ironic twist for an artist equally known as a prolific songwriter. *Without You* sold consistently well enough to keep the New Seekers from a second consecutive chart-topper, with the song which they took to second place for Britain in the Eurovision Song Contest. Gilbert O'Sullivan's *Alone Again (Naturally)* was, internationally, his biggest seller, topping the US chart for six weeks.

April – May 1972

last week	this week	22 April 1972
2	1	AMAZING GRACE — Royal Scots Dragoon Guards, Pipes, Drums & Band (RCA)
1	2	WITHOUT YOU — Nilsson (RCA)
3	3	SWEET TALKIN' GUY — Chiffons (London)
10	3	BACK OFF BOOGALOO — Ringo Starr (Apple)
4	5	HOLD YOUR HEAD UP — Argent (Epic)
15	6	DEBORA — Tyrannosaurus Rex (Magni Fly)
9	7	HEART OF GOLD — Neil Young (Reprise)
17	8	RUN RUN RUN — Jo Jo Gunne (Asylum)
13	9	THE YOUNG NEW MEXICAN PUPPETEER — Tom Jones (Decca)
5	10	BEG, STEAL OR BORROW — New Seekers (Polydor)
6	11	ALONE AGAIN (NATURALLY) — Gilbert O'Sullivan (MAM)
11	12	IT'S ONE OF THOSE NIGHTS (YES LOVE) — Partridge Family (Bell)
18	13	CRYING, LAUGHING, LOVING, LYING — Labi Siffre (Pye)
8	14	DESIDERATA — Les Crane (Warner Bros)
23	15	RADANCER — Marmalade (Decca)
-	16	COME WHAT MAY — Vicky Leandros (Philips)
7	17	MEET ME ON THE CORNER — Lindisfarne (Charisma)
16	18	WHAT IS LIFE — Olivia Newton-John (Pye)
20	19	UNTIL IT'S TIME FOR YOU TO GO — Elvis Presley (RCA)
25	19	COULD IT BE FOREVER — David Cassidy (Bell)
14	21	AMERICAN PIE — Don McLean (United Artists)
12	22	FLOY JOY — Supremes (Tamla Motown)
29	23	STIR IT UP — Johnny Nash (CBS)
30	24	A THING CALLED LOVE — Johnny Cash (CBS)
24	25	I CAN'T HELP MYSELF — Donnie Elbert (Avco)
26	26	I AM WHAT I AM — Greyhound (Trojan)
-	27	RUNNIN' AWAY — Sly & the Family Stone (Epic)
19	28	MOTHER AND CHILD REUNION — Paul Simon (CBS)
-	29	TAKE A LOOK AROUND — Temptations (Tamla Motown)
-	30	ROCKET MAN — Elton John (DJM)

last	this	29 April 1972
1	1	AMAZING GRACE — Royal Scots Dragoon Guards, Pipes, Drums & Band (RCA)
3	2	BACK OFF BOOGALOO — Ringo Starr (Apple)
2	3	WITHOUT YOU — Nilsson (RCA)
3	4	SWEET TALKIN' GUY — Chiffons (London)
8	5	RUN RUN RUN — Jo Jo Gunne (Asylum)
16	6	COME WHAT MAY — Vicky Leandros (Philips)
9	7	THE YOUNG NEW MEXICAN PUPPETEER — Tom Jones (Decca)
6	8	DEBORA — Tyrannosaurus Rex (Magnify)
7	9	HEART OF GOLD — Neil Young (Reprise)
19	10	UNTIL IT'S TIME FOR YOU TO GO — Elvis Presley (RCA)
5	11	HOLD YOUR HEAD UP — Argent (Epic)
15	12	RADANCER — Marmalade (Decca)
10	13	BEG, STEAL OR BORROW — New Seekers (Polydor)
11	14	ALONE AGAIN NATURALLY — Gilbert O'Sullivan (MAM)
23	15	STIR IT UP — Johnny Nash (CBS)
19	16	COULD IT BE FOREVER — David Cassidy (Bell)
24	17	A THING CALLED LOVE — Johnny Cash (CBS)
14	18	DESIDERATA — Les Crane (Warner Bros.)
13	19	CRYING, LAUGHING, LOVING, LYING — Labi Siffre (Pye International)
12	20	IT'S ONE OF THOSE NIGHTS (YES LOVE) — Partridge Family (Bell)
30	21	ROCKET MAN — Elton John (DJM)
18	22	WHAT IS LIFE — Olivia Newton-John (Pye International)
29	23	TAKE A LOOK AROUND — Temptations (Tamla Motown)
27	24	RUNNIN' AWAY — Sly & the Family Stone (Epic)
26	25	I AM WHAT I AM — Greyhound (Trojan)
22	26	FLOY JOY — Supremes (Tamla Motown)
17	27	MEET ME ON THE CORNER — Lindisfarne (Charisma)
-	28	A WHITER SHADE OF PALE — Procol Harum (Magnify)
-	29	SACRAMENTO — Middle Of The Road (RCA)
21	30	AMERICAN PIE — Don McLean (United Artists)

last	this	6 May 1972
1	1	AMAZING GRACE — Royal Scots Dragoon Guards, Pipes, Drums & Band (RCA)
6	2	COME WHAT MAY — Vicky Leandros (Philips)
4	3	SWEET TALKIN' GUY — Chiffons (London)
2	4	BACK OFF BOOGALOO — Ringo Starr (Apple)
5	5	RUN RUN RUN — Jo Jo Gunne (Asylum)
17	6	A THING CALLED LOVE — Johnny Cash (CBS)
8	7	DEBORA — Tyrannosaurus Rex (Magni Fly)
16	8	COULD IT BE FOREVER — David Cassidy (Bell)
8	9	WITHOUT YOU — Nilsson (RCA)
15	10	STIR IT UP — Johnny Nash (CBS)
12	11	RADANCER — Marmalade (Decca)
21	12	ROCKET MAN — Elton John (DJM)
-	13	TUMBLING DICE — Rolling Stones (Rolling Stones)
7	14	THE YOUNG NEW MEXICAN PUPPETEER — Tom Jones (Decca)
10	15	UNTIL IT'S TIME FOR YOU TO GO — Elvis Presley (RCA)
23	16	TAKE A LOOK AROUND — Temptations (Tamla Motown)
24	17	RUNNIN' AWAY — Sly & the Family Stone (Epic)
8	18	HEART OF GOLD — Neil Young (Reprise)
11	19	HOLD YOUR HEAD UP — Argent (Epic)
13	20	BEG, STEAL OR BORROW — New Seekers (Polydor)
19	21	CRYING, LAUGHING, LOVING, LYING — Labi Siffre (Pye)
-	22	OH BABE WHAT WOULD YOU SAY — Hurricane Smith (Columbia)
-	23	OPEN UP — Mungo Jerry (Dawn)
-	24	ME AND JULIO DOWN BY THE SCHOOL YARD — Paul Simon (CBS)
-	25	LITTLE PIECE OF LEATHER — Donnie Elbert (London)
18	26	DESIDERATA — Les Crane (Warner Bros)
28	27	A WHITER SHADE OF PALE — Procol Harum (Magni Fly)
-	28	AT THE CLUB/SATURDAY NIGHT AT THE MOVIES — Drifters (Atlantic)
-	29	BEAUTIFUL SUNDAY — Daniel Boone (Penny Farthing)
14	30	ALONE AGAIN (NATURALLY) — Gilbert O'Sullivan (MAM)

last	this	13 May 1972
1	1	AMAZING GRACE — Royal Scots Dragoon Guards, Pipes, Drums & Band (RCA)
2	2	COME WHAT MAY
8	3	COULD IT BE FOREVER — David Cassidy (Bell)
6	4	A THING CALLED LOVE — Johnny Cash (CBS)
13	5	TUMBLING DICE — Rolling Stones (Rolling Stones)
12	6	ROCKET MAN — Elton John (DJM)
4	7	BACK OFF BOOGALOO — Ringo Starr (Apple)
5	8	RUN RUN RUN — Jo Jo Gunne (Asylum)
11	9	RADANCER — Marmalade (Decca)
3	10	SWEET TALKIN' GUY — Chiffons (London)
16	11	TAKE A LOOK AROUND — Temptations (Tamla Motown)
10	12	STIR IT UP — Johnny Nash (CBS)
7	13	DEBORA — Tyrannosaurus Rex (Magni Fly)
-	14	METAL GURU — T. Rex (T. Rex Wax Co)
14	15	THE YOUNG NEW MEXICAN PUPPETEER — Tom Jones (Decca)
17	16	RUNNIN' AWAY — Sly & the Family Stone (Epic)
9	17	WITHOUT YOU — Nilsson (RCA)
28	18	AT THE CLUB/SATURDAY NIGHT AT THE MOVIES — Drifters (Atlantic)
22	19	OH BABE WHAT WOULD YOU SAY — Hurricane Smith (Columbia)
15	20	UNTIL IT'S TIME FOR YOU TO GO — Elvis Presley (RCA)
23	21	OPEN UP — Mungo Jerry (Dawn)
24	22	ME AND JULIO DOWN BY THE SCHOOL YARD — Paul Simon (CBS)
29	23	BEAUTIFUL SUNDAY — Daniel Boone (Penny Farthing)
-	24	WADE IN THE WATER — Ramsey Lewis (Chess)
19	25	HOLD YOUR HEAD UP — Argent (Epic)
21	26	CRYING, LAUGHING, LOVING, LYING — Labi Siffre (Pye)
25	27	LITTLE PIECE OF LEATHER — Donnie Elbert (London)
27	28	A WHITER SHADE OF PALE — Procol Harum (Magni Fly)
30	29	ALONE AGAIN (NATURALLY) — Gilbert O'Sullivan (MAM)
18	30	HEART OF GOLD — Neil Young (Reprise)

Amazing indeed was the runaway success of the Band of the Royal Scots Dragoon Guards with *Amazing Grace*, particularly after Judy Collins' long chart run with her vocal version of the same song. This would not be the last time that the uniquely emotional sound of the Scottish pipes would be (literally) instrumental in hoisting the sales of a pop record to new heights. Elsewhere, *Come What May* was the year's Eurovision winner, while Tyrannosaurus Rex' *Debora* was a reissue of their first (1968) single.

20 May 1972

last week	this week	
14	1	METAL GURU — T. Rex (T. Rex Wax Co)
6	2	ROCKET MAN Elton John (DJM)
1	3	AMAZING GRACE Royal Scots Dragoon Guards, Pipes, Drums & Band (RCA)
4	4	A THING CALLED LOVE Johnny Cash (CBS)
3	5	COULD IT BE FOREVER David Cassidy (Bell)
2	6	COME WHAT MAY Vicky Leandros (Philips)
5	7	TUMBLING DICE Rolling Stones (Rolling Stones)
9	8	RADANCER Marmalade (Decca)
19	9	OH BABE WHAT WOULD YOU SAY Hurricane Smith (Columbia)
18	10	AT THE CLUB/SATURDAY NIGHT AT THE MOVIES Drifters (Atlantic)
8	11	RUN RUN RUN Jo Jo Gunne (Asylum)
11	12	TAKE A LOOK AROUND Temptations (Tamla Motown)
12	13	STIR IT UP Johnny Nash (CBS)
7	14	BACK OFF BOOGALOO Ringo Starr (Apple)
10	15	SWEET TALKIN' GUY Chiffons (London)
16	16	RUNNIN' AWAY Sly & the Family Stone (Epic)
-	17	LADY ELEANOR Lindisfarne (Charisma)
-	18	LEEDS UNITED Leeds United F C (Chapter One)
13	19	DEBORA Tyrannosaurus Rex (Magni Fly)
28	20	A WHITER SHADE OF PALE Procol Harum (Magni Fly)
15	21	THE YOUNG NEW MEXICAN PUPPETEER Tom Jones (Decca)
21	22	OPEN UP Mungo Jerry (Dawn)
-	23	AMAZING GRACE Judy Collins (Elektra)
27	24	LITTLE PIECE OF LEATHER Donnie Elbert (London)
17	25	WITHOUT YOU Nilsson (RCA)
22	26	ME AND JULIO DOWN BY THE SCHOOL YARD Paul Simon (CBS)
-	27	VINCENT Don McLean (United Artists)
23	28	BEAUTIFUL SUNDAY Daniel Boone (Penny Farthing)
-	29	ROCKIN' ROBIN Michael Jackson (Tamla Motown)
-	30	SISTER JANE New World (RAK)

27 May 1972

last week	this week	
1	1	METAL GURU — T. Rex (T. Rex Wax Co)
5	2	COULD IT BE FOREVER David Cassidy (Bell)
2	3	ROCKET MAN Elton John (DJM)
4	4	A THING CALLED LOVE Johnny Cash (CBS)
6	5	COME WHAT MAY Vicky Leandros (Philips)
3	6	AMAZING GRACE Royal Scots Dragoon Guards, Pipes, Drums & Band (RCA)
10	7	AT THE CLUB/SATURDAY NIGHT AT THE MOVIES Drifters (Atlantic)
9	8	OH BABE WHAT WOULD YOU SAY Hurricane Smith (Columbia)
7	9	TUMBLING DICE Rolling Stones (Rolling Stones)
27	10	VINCENT Don McLean (United Artists)
17	11	LADY ELEANOR Lindisfarne (Charisma)
8	12	RADANCER Marmalade (Decca)
20	13	A WHITER SHADE OF PALE Procol Harum (Magni Fly)
11	14	RUN RUN RUN Jo Jo Gunne (Asylum)
12	15	TAKE A LOOK AROUND Temptations (Tamla Motown)
18	16	LEEDS UNITED Leeds United F C (Chapter One)
30	17	SISTER JANE New World (RAK)
15	18	SWEET TALKIN' GUY Chiffons (London)
23	19	AMAZING GRACE Judy Collins (Elektra)
26	20	ME AND JULIO DOWN BY THE SCHOOL YARD Paul Simon (CBS)
14	21	BACK OFF BOOGALOO Ringo Starr (Apple)
13	22	STIR IT UP Johnny Nash (CBS)
22	23	OPEN UP Mungo Jerry (Dawn)
16	24	RUNNIN' AWAY Sly & the Family Stone (Epic)
-	25	DOOBEDOOD'NDOOBE, DOOBEDOOD'NDOOBE Diana Ross (Tamla Motown)
-	26	CALIFORNIA MAN Move (Harvest)
-	27	ISN'T LIFE STRANGE Moody Blues (Threshold)
24	28	LITTLE PIECE OF LEATHER Donnie Elbert (London)
-	29	DON'T LET HIM TOUCH YOU Angelettes (Decca)
-	30	SONG SUNG BLUE Neil Diamond (Uni)

3 June 1972

last week	this week	
1	1	METAL GURU T. Rex (T. Rex Wax Co)
3	2	ROCKET MAN Elton John (DJM)
8	3	OH BABE WHAT WOULD YOU SAY Hurricane Smith (Columbia)
2	4	COULD IT BE FOREVER David Cassidy (Bell)
10	5	VINCENT Don McLean (United Artists)
7	6	AT THE CLUB/SATURDAY NIGHT AT THE MOVIES Drifters (Atlantic)
11	7	LADY ELEANOR Lindisfarne (Charisma)
5	8	COME WHAT MAY Vicky Leandros (Philips)
4	9	A THING CALLED LOVE Johnny Cash (CBS)
9	10	TUMBLING DICE Rolling Stones (Rolling Stones)
13	11	A WHITER SHADE OF PALE Procol Harum (Magni Fly)
26	12	CALIFORNIA MAN Move (Harvest)
6	13	AMAZING GRACE Royal Scots Dragoon Guards, Pipes, Drums & Band (RCA)
17	14	SISTER JANE New World (RAK)
16	15	LEEDS UNITED Leeds United F C (Chapter One)
27	16	ISN'T LIFE STRANGE Moody Blues (Threshold)
15	17	TAKE A LOOK AROUND Temptations (Tamla Motown)
25	18	DOOBEDOOD'NDOOBE, DOOBEDOOD'NDOOBE Diana Ross (Tamla Motown)
20	19	ME AND JULIO DOWN BY THE SCHOOL YARD Paul Simon (CBS)
23	20	OPEN UP Mungo Jerry (Dawn)
-	21	ROCKIN' ROBIN Michael Jackson (Tamla Motown)
-	22	THE FIRST TIME EVER I SAW YOUR FACE Roberta Flack (Atlantic)
12	23	RADANCER Marmalade (Decca)
-	24	JUNGLE FEVER Chakachas (Polydor)
22	25	STIR IT UP Johnny Nash (CBS)
-	26	LITTLE BIT OF LOVE Free (Island)
-	27	WHAT'S YOUR NAME Chicory Tip (CBS)
-	28	MARY HAD A LITTLE LAMB Wings (Apple)
-	29	OH GIRL Chi-Lites (MCA)
28	30	LITTLE PIECE OF LEATHER Donnie Elbert (London)

10 June 1972

last week	this week	
1	1	METAL GURU T. Rex (T. Rex Wax Co)
5	2	VINCENT Don McLean (United Artists)
2	3	ROCKET MAN Elton John (DJM)
3	4	OH BABE WHAT WOULD YOU SAY Hurricane Smith (Columbia)
6	5	AT THE CLUB/SATURDAY NIGHT AT THE MOVIES Drifters (Atlantic)
12	6	CALIFORNIA MAN Move (Harvest)
4	7	COULD IT BE FOREVER David Cassidy (Bell)
7	8	LADY ELEANOR Lindisfarne (Charisma)
14	9	SISTER JANE New World (RAK)
28	10	MARY HAD A LITTLE LAMB Wings (Apple)
16	11	ISN'T LIFE STRANGE Moody Blues (Threshold)
11	12	A WHITER SHADE OF PALE Procol Harum (Magni Fly)
8	13	COME WHAT MAY Vicky Leandros (Philips)
13	14	AMAZING GRACE Royal Scots Dragoon Guards, Pipes, Drums & Band (RCA)
20	15	ROCKIN' ROBIN Michael Jackson (Tamla Motown)
-	16	TAKE ME BAK 'OME Slade (Polydor)
18	17	DOOBEDOOD'NDOOBE, DOOBEDOOD'NDOOBE Diana Ross (Tamla Motown)
9	18	A THING CALLED LOVE Johnny Cash (CBS)
10	19	TUMBLING DICE Rolling Stones (Rolling Stones)
26	20	WHAT'S YOUR NAME Chicory Tip (CBS)
19	21	ME AND JULIO DOWN BY THE SCHOOL YARD Paul Simon (CBS)
24	22	JUNGLE FEVER Chakachas (Polydor)
-	23	I'LL TAKE YOU THERE Staple Singers (Stax)
15	24	LEEDS UNITED Leeds United F C (Chapter One)
20	25	OPEN UP Mungo Jerry (Dawn)
-	26	SONG SUNG BLUE Neil Diamond (Uni)
17	27	TAKE A LOOK AROUND Temptations (Tamla Motown)
-	28	I'VE BEEN LONELY FOR SO LONG Frederick Knight (Stax)
22	29	THE FIRST TIME EVER I SAW YOUR FACE Roberta Flack (Atlantic)
-	30	AMAZING GRACE Judy Collins (Elektra)

Marc Bolan mania had reached its peak as T.Rex' *Metal Guru* held solidly to Number One, denying the slot to Elton John and David Cassidy – the latter with his first UK solo hit outside the Partridge Family (his early US million-seller *Cherish*, inexplicably unreleased here at the time, was tucked away on the B-side.) The Drifters had their biggest success since *Save The Last Dance For Me* with the astute coupling of two former mid-1960s A-sides, while Leeds United emulated the earlier success of rivals Chelsea.

June – July 1972

17 June 1972

last	this	
2	1	VINCENT — Don McLean (United Artists)
1	2	METAL GURU — T. Rex (T. Rex Wax Co)
15	3	ROCKIN' ROBIN — Michael Jackson (Tamla Motown)
4	4	OH BABE WHAT WOULD YOU SAY — Hurricane Smith (Columbia)
5	5	AT THE CLUB/SATURDAY NIGHT AT THE MOVIES — Drifters (Atlantic)
6	6	CALIFORNIA MAN — Move (Harvest)
8	7	LADY ELEANOR — Lindisfarne (Charisma)
10	8	MARY HAD A LITTLE LAMB — Wings (Apple)
16	9	TAKE ME BAK 'OME — Slade (Polydor)
3	10	ROCKET MAN — Elton John (DJM)
9	11	SISTER JANE — New World (RAK)
7	12	COULD IT BE FOREVER — David Cassidy (Bell)
17	13	DOOBEDOOD'NDOOBE, DOOBEDOOD'NDOOBE — Diana Ross (Tamla Motown)
20	14	WHAT'S YOUR NAME — Chicory Tip (CBS)
11	15	ISN'T LIFE STRANGE — Moody Blues (Threshold)
12	16	A WHITER SHADE OF PALE — Procol Harum (Magni Fly)
26	17	SONG SUNG BLUE — Neil Diamond (Uni)
13	18	COME WHAT MAY — Vicky Leandros (Philips)
14	19	AMAZING GRACE — Royal Scots Dragoon Guards, Pipes, Drums & Band (RCA)
22	20	I'LL TAKE YOU THERE — Staple Singers (Stax)
29	21	THE FIRST TIME EVER I SAW YOUR FACE — Roberta Flack (Atlantic)
-	22	ROCK AND ROLL PARTS 1 AND 2 — Gary Glitter (Bell)
18	23	A THING CALLED LOVE — Johnny Cash (CBS)
-	24	OH GIRL — Chi-Lites (MCA)
28	25	I'VE BEEN LONELY FOR SO LONG — Frederick Knight (Stax)
24	26	LEEDS UNITED — Leeds United F C (Chapter One)
19	27	TUMBLING DICE — Rolling Stones (Rolling Stones)
-	28	SUPERSONIC ROCKET SHIP — Kinks (RCA)
-	29	LITTLE WILLY — Sweet (RCA)
-	30	LITTLE BIT OF LOVE — Free (Island)

24 June 1972

last	this	
1	1	VINCENT — Don McLean (United Artists)
9	2	TAKE ME BAK 'OME — Slade (Polydor)
3	3	ROCKIN' ROBIN — Michael Jackson (Tamla Motown)
6	4	CALIFORNIA MAN — Move (Harvest)
2	5	METAL GURU — T. Rex (T. Rex Wax Co)
8	6	MARY HAD A LITTLE LAMB — Wings (Apple)
5	7	AT THE CLUB/SATURDAY NIGHT AT THE MOVIES — Drifters (Atlantic)
4	8	OH BABE WHAT WOULD YOU SAY — Hurricane Smith (Columbia)
11	9	SISTER JANE — New World (RAK)
22	10	ROCK AND ROLL PARTS 1 AND 2 — Gary Glitter (Bell)
7	11	LADY ELEANOR — Lindisfarne (Charisma)
29	12	LITTLE WILLY — Sweet (RCA)
17	13	SONG SUNG BLUE — Neil Diamond (Uni)
10	14	ROCKET MAN — Elton John (DJM)
24	15	OH GIRL — Chi-Lites (MCA)
-	16	PUPPY LOVE — Donny Osmond (MGM)
13	17	DOOBEDOOD'NDOOBE, DOOBEDOOD'NDOOBE — Diana Ross (Tamla Motown)
30	18	LITTLE BIT OF LOVE — Free (Island)
14	19	WHAT'S YOUR NAME — Chicory Tip (CBS)
20	20	I'LL TAKE YOU THERE — Staple Singers (Stax)
21	21	THE FIRST TIME EVER I SAW YOUR FACE — Roberta Flack (Atlantic)
-	22	OOH-WAKKA-DOO-WAKKA-DAY — Gilbert O'Sullivan (MAM)
28	23	SUPERSONIC ROCKET SHIP — Kinks (RCA)
25	24	I'VE BEEN LONELY FOR SO LONG — Frederick Knight (Stax)
12	25	COULD IT BE FOREVER — David Cassidy (Bell)
-	26	NUT ROCKER — B Bumble & the Stingers (Stateside)
-	27	I CAN SEE CLEARLY NOW — Johnny Nash (CBS)
18	28	COME WHAT MAY — Vicky Leandros (Philips)
15	29	ISN'T LIFE STRANGE — Moody Blues (Threshold)
-	30	JOIN TOGETHER — Who (Track)
-	30	AN AMERICAN TRILOGY — Elvis Presley (RCA)

1 July 1972

last	this	
1	1	VINCENT — Don McLean (United Artists)
10	2	ROCK AND ROLL PARTS 1 AND 2 — Gary Glitter (Bell)
2	3	TAKE ME BAK 'OME — Slade (Polydor)
3	4	ROCKIN' ROBIN — Michael Jackson (Tamla Motown)
16	5	PUPPY LOVE — Donny Osmond (MGM)
12	6	LITTLE WILLY — Sweet (RCA)
6	7	MARY HAD A LITTLE LAMB — Wings (Apple)
4	8	CALIFORNIA MAN — Move (Harvest)
7	9	AT THE CLUB/SATURDAY NIGHT AT THE MOVIES — Drifters (Atlantic)
5	10	METAL GURU — T. Rex (T. Rex Wax Co)
22	11	OOH-WAKKA-DOO-WAKKA-DAY — Gilbert O'Sullivan (MAM)
15	12	OH GIRL — Chi-Lites (MCA)
13	13	SONG SUNG BLUE — Neil Diamond (Uni)
18	14	LITTLE BIT OF LOVE — Free (Island)
9	15	SISTER JANE — New World (RAK)
21	16	THE FIRST TIME EVER I SAW YOUR FACE — Roberta Flack (Atlantic)
8	17	OH BABE WHAT WOULD YOU SAY — Hurricane Smith (Columbia)
30	18	AN AMERICAN TRILOGY — Elvis Presley (RCA)
-	19	CIRCLES — New Seekers (Polydor)
11	20	LADY ELEANOR — Lindisfarne (Charisma)
26	21	NUT ROCKER — B Bumble & the Stingers (Stateside)
30	22	JOIN TOGETHER — Who (Track)
-	23	WALKIN' IN THE RAIN WITH THE ONE I LOVE — Love Unlimited (Uni)
23	24	SUPERSONIC ROCKET SHIP — Kinks (RCA)
24	24	I'VE BEEN LONELY FOR SO LONG — Frederick Knight (Stax)
20	26	I'LL TAKE YOU THERE — Staple Singers (Stax)
27	27	I CAN SEE CLEARLY NOW — Johnny Nash (CBS)
-	28	BETCHA BY GOLLY WOW — Stylistics (Avco)
-	29	SYLVIA'S MOTHER — Dr Hook & the Medicine Show (CBS)
17	30	DOOBEDOOD'NDOOBE, DOOBEDOOD'NDOOBE — Diana Ross (Tamla Motown)

8 July 1972

last	this	
3	1	TAKE ME BAK 'OME — Slade (Polydor)
5	2	PUPPY LOVE — Donny Osmond (MGM)
2	3	ROCK AND ROLL PARTS 1 AND 2 — Gary Glitter (Bell)
1	4	VINCENT — Don McLean (United Artists)
6	5	LITTLE WILLY — Sweet (RCA)
4	6	ROCKIN' ROBIN — Michael Jackson (Tamla Motown)
8	7	CALIFORNIA MAN — Move (Harvest)
19	8	CIRCLES — New Seekers (Polydor)
11	9	OOH-WAKKA-DOO-WAKKA-DAY — Gilbert O'Sullivan (MAM)
7	10	MARY HAD A LITTLE LAMB — Wings (Apple)
9	11	AT THE CLUB/SATURDAY NIGHT AT THE MOVIES — Drifters (Atlantic)
13	11	SONG SUNG BLUE — Neil Diamond (Uni)
18	13	AN AMERICAN TRILOGY — Elvis Presley (RCA)
14	14	LITTLE BIT OF LOVE — Free (Island)
22	15	JOIN TOGETHER — Who (Track)
15	16	THE FIRST TIME EVER I SAW YOUR FACE — Roberta Flack (Atlantic)
12	17	OH GIRL — Chi-Lites (MCA)
27	18	I CAN SEE CLEARLY NOW — Johnny Nash (CBS)
23	19	WALKIN' IN THE RAIN WITH THE ONE I LOVE — Love Unlimited (Uni)
21	20	NUT ROCKER — B Bumble & the Stingers (Stateside)
29	21	SYLVIA'S MOTHER — Dr Hook & the Medicine Show (CBS)
24	22	I'VE BEEN LONELY FOR SO LONG — Frederick Knight (Stax)
10	23	METAL GURU — T. Rex (T. Rex Wax Co)
15	24	SISTER JANE — New World (RAK)
26	25	I'LL TAKE YOU THERE — Staple Singers (Stax)
24	26	SUPERSONIC ROCKET SHIP — Kinks (RCA)
28	27	BETCHA BY GOLLY WOW — Stylistics (Avco)
17	28	OH BABE WHAT WOULD YOU SAY — Hurricane Smith (Columbia)
20	29	LADY ELEANOR — Lindisfarne (Charisma)
-	30	WORKING ON A BUILDING OF LOVE — Chairmen Of The Board (Invictus)

Don McLean's second chart-topper offered less of a mystery to its buyers, being a tribute to Vincent Van Gogh. Some of the most consistently successful acts of the 1970s made their chart debuts: Gary Glitter with *Rock And Roll Parts 1&2* (at the time of this release, the name referred to the entire band, not just the singer), the Stylistics with *Betcha By Golly Wow*, and 14-year-old Donny Osmond with *Puppy Love* - the first UK flowering of the Osmonds phenomenon which had given them several US million-sellers.

15 July 1972

last	this		
2	1	PUPPY LOVE	Donny Osmond (MGM)
3	2	ROCK AND ROLL PARTS 1 AND 2	Gary Glitter (Bell)
5	3	LITTLE WILLY	Sweet (RCA)
1	4	TAKE ME BAK 'OME	Slade (Polydor)
8	5	CIRCLES New Seekers (Polydor)	
21	6	SYLVIA'S MOTHER Dr Hook &	the Medicine Show (CBS)
4	7	VINCENT	Don McLean (United Artists)
18	8	I CAN SEE CLEARLY NOW	Johnny Nash (CBS)
9	9	OOH-WAKKA-DOO-WAKKA-DAY	Gilbert O'Sullivan (MAM)
13	10	AN AMERICAN TRILOGY	Elvis Presley (RCA)
15	11	JOIN TOGETHER	Who (Track)
19	12	WALKIN' IN THE RAIN WITH THE ONE I LOVE	Love Unlimited (Uni)
6	13	ROCKIN' ROBIN Michael Jackson (Tamla Motown)	
7	14	CALIFORNIA MAN	Move (Harvest)
20	15	NUT ROCKER B Bumble & the	Stingers (Stateside)
22	16	I'VE BEEN LONELY FOR SO LONG Frederick Knight (Stax)	
10	17	MARY HAD A LITTLE LAMB	Wings (Apple)
16	18	THE FIRST TIME EVER I SAW YOUR FACE	Roberta Flack (Atlantic)
14	19	LITTLE BIT OF LOVE Free (Island)	
11	20	SONG SUNG BLUE	Neil Diamond (Uni)
27	21	BETCHA BY GOLLY WOW	Stylistics (Avco)
17	22	OH GIRL Chi-Lites (MCA)	
-	23	BREAKING UP IS HARD TO DO	Partridge Family (Bell)
25	24	I'LL TAKE YOU THERE	Staple Singers (Stax)
11	25	AT THE CLUB/SATURDAY NIGHT AT THE MOVIES Drifters (Atlantic)	
-	26	STARMAN David Bowie (RCA)	
24	27	SISTER JANE New World (RAK)	
-	28	TRAGEDY Argent (Epic)	
26	29	SUPERSONIC ROCKET SHIP	Kinks (RCA)
-	30	MAD ABOUT YOU	Bruce Ruffin (Rhino)

22 July 1972

last	this		
1	1	PUPPY LOVE	Donny Osmond (MGM)
2	2	ROCK AND ROLL PARTS 1 AND 2	Gary Glitter (Bell)
6	3	SYLVIA'S MOTHER Dr Hook &	the Medicine Show (CBS)
8	4	I CAN SEE CLEARLY NOW	Johnny Nash (CBS)
5	5	CIRCLES New Seekers (Polydor)	
3	6	LITTLE WILLY Sweet (RCA)	
4	7	TAKE ME BAK 'OME	Slade (Polydor)
23	8	BREAKING UP IS HARD TO DO	Partridge Family (Bell)
11	9	JOIN TOGETHER	Who (Track)
12	10	WALKIN' IN THE RAIN WITH THE ONE I LOVE Love Unlimited (Uni)	
9	11	OOH-WAKKA-DOO-WAKKA-DAY	Gilbert O'Sullivan (MAM)
10	12	AN AMERICAN TRILOGY	Elvis Presley (RCA)
26	13	STARMAN David Bowie (RCA)	
7	14	VINCENT	Don McLean (United Artists)
13	15	ROCKIN' ROBIN	Michael Jackson (Tamla Motown)
-	16	SEASIDE SHUFFLE Terry Dactyl	& the Dinosaurs (UK)
15	17	NUT ROCKER B Bumble & the	Stingers (Stateside)
-	18	SILVER MACHINE	Hawkwind (United Artists)
21	19	BETCHA BY GOLLY WOW	Stylistics (Avco)
17	20	MARY HAD A LITTLE LAMB	Wings (Apple)
14	21	CALIFORNIA MAN	Move (Harvest)
18	22	THE FIRST TIME EVER I SAW YOUR FACE	Roberta Flack (Atlantic)
30	23	MAD ABOUT YOU	Bruce Ruffin (Rhino)
19	24	LITTLE BIT OF LOVE Free (Island)	
-	25	MY GUY	Mary Wells (Tamla Motown)
-	26	SCHOOL'S OUT	Alice Cooper (Warner Bros)
20	27	SONG SUNG BLUE	Neil Diamond (Uni)
16	28	I'VE BEEN LONELY FOR SO LONG Frederick Knight (Stax)	
-	29	AUTOMATICALLY SUNSHINE	Supremes (Tamla Motown)
27	30	SISTER JANE New World (RAK)	

29 July 1972

last	this		
1	1	PUPPY LOVE	Donny Osmond (MGM)
2	2	ROCK AND ROLL PARTS 1 AND 2	Gary Glitter (Bell)
3	3	SYLVIA'S MOTHER Dr Hook &	the Medicine Show (CBS)
7	4	BREAKING UP IS HARD TO DO	Partridge Family (Bell)
4	5	I CAN SEE CLEARLY NOW	Johnny Nash (CBS)
5	6	CIRCLES New Seekers (Polydor)	
16	7	SEASIDE SHUFFLE Terry Dactyl	& the Dinosaurs (UK)
26	8	SCHOOL'S OUT	Alice Cooper (Warner Bros)
9	9	JOIN TOGETHER	Who (Track)
13	10	STARMAN David Bowie (RCA)	
6	11	LITTLE WILLY	Sweet (RCA)
7	12	TAKE ME BAK 'OME	Slade (Polydor)
18	13	SILVER MACHINE	Hawkwind (United Artists)
10	14	WALKIN' IN THE RAIN WITH THE ONE I LOVE Love Unlimited (Uni)	
23	15	MAD ABOUT YOU	Bruce Ruffin (Rhino)
19	16	BETCHA BY GOLLY WOW	Stylistics (Avco)
12	17	AN AMERICAN TRILOGY	Elvis Presley (RCA)
11	18	OOH-WAKKA-DOO-WAKKA-DAY	Gilbert O'Sullivan (MAM)
29	19	AUTOMATICALLY SUNSHINE	Supremes (Tamla Motown)
-	20	POPCORN Hot Butter (Pye Int.)	
25	21	MY GUY	Mary Wells (Tamla Motown)
17	22	NUT ROCKER B Bumble & the	Stingers (Stateside)
15	23	ROCKIN' ROBIN	Michael Jackson (Tamla Motown)
22	24	THE FIRST TIME EVER I SAW YOUR FACE	Roberta Flack (Atlantic)
14	25	VINCENT	Don McLean (United Artists)
27	26	SONG SUNG BLUE	Neil Diamond (Uni)
28	27	I'VE BEEN LONELY FOR SO LONG Frederick Knight (Stax)	
21	28	CALIFORNIA MAN	Move (Harvest)
24	29	LITTLE BIT OF LOVE Free (Island)	
20	30	MARY HAD A LITTLE LAMB	Wings (Apple)

5 August 1972

last	this		
1	1	PUPPY LOVE	Donny Osmond (MGM)
8	2	SCHOOL'S OUT	Alice Cooper (Warner Bros)
7	3	SEASIDE SHUFFLE Terry Dactyl	& the Dinosaurs (UK)
3	4	SYLVIA'S MOTHER Dr Hook &	the Medicine Show (CBS)
4	5	BREAKING UP IS HARD TO DO	Partridge Family (Bell)
2	6	ROCK AND ROLL PARTS 1 AND 2	Gary Glitter (Bell)
13	7	SILVER MACHINE	Hawkwind (United Artists)
5	8	I CAN SEE CLEARLY NOW	Johnny Nash (CBS)
10	9	STARMAN David Bowie (RCA)	
6	10	CIRCLES New Seekers (Polydor)	
15	10	MAD ABOUT YOU	Bruce Ruffin (Rhino)
20	12	POPCORN Hot Butter (Pye Int.)	
19	13	AUTOMATICALLY SUNSHINE	Supremes (Tamla Motown)
9	14	JOIN TOGETHER	Who (Track)
21	15	MY GUY	Mary Wells (Tamla Motown)
16	16	BETCHA BY GOLLY WOW	Stylistics (Avco)
11	17	LITTLE WILLY	Sweet (RCA)
14	18	WALKIN' IN THE RAIN WITH THE ONE I LOVE Love Unlimited (Uni)	
12	19	TAKE ME BAK 'OME	Slade (Polydor)
18	20	OOH-WAKKA-DOO-WAKKA-DAY	Gilbert O'Sullivan (MAM)
-	21	WORKING ON A BUILDING OF LOVE Chairmen Of The Board (Invictus)	
22	22	NUT ROCKER B Bumble & the	Stingers (Stateside)
17	23	AN AMERICAN TRILOGY	Elvis Presley (RCA)
-	24	IT'S FOUR IN THE MORNING	Faron Young (Mercury)
25	25	10538 OVERTURE Electric Light	Orchestra (Harvest)
24	26	THE FIRST TIME EVER I SAW YOUR FACE	Roberta Flack (Atlantic)
26	27	SONG SUNG BLUE	Neil Diamond (Uni)
27	28	I'VE BEEN LONELY FOR SO LONG Frederick Knight (Stax)	
23	29	ROCKIN' ROBIN	Michael Jackson (Tamla Motown)
25	30	VINCENT	Don McLean (United Artists)

Puppy Love, which held off all comers for a month, set the pattern for Donny Osmond's solo singles, which were generally revivals of teenage ballads of the 1950s and '60s - this song had been a 1960 million-seller for its writer, Paul Anka. Donny's heart-throb rival David Cassidy was also following the revival route with the Partridge Family, via Neil Sedaka's *Breaking Up Is Hard To Do* which went higher than the 1962 original. The Kinks' *Supersonic Rocket Ship* would be their last hit for over a decade.

251

August – September 1972

12 August 1972

last week	this week	Entry
2	1	SCHOOL'S OUT Alice Cooper (Warner Bros)
1	2	PUPPY LOVE Donny Osmond (MGM)
3	3	SEASIDE SHUFFLE Terry Dactyl & the Dinosaurs (UK)
12	4	POPCORN Hot Butter (Pye Int.)
5	5	BREAKING UP IS HARD TO DO Partridge Family (Bell)
7	6	SILVER MACHINE Hawkwind (United Artists)
4	7	SYLVIA'S MOTHER Dr Hook & the Medicine Show (CBS)
6	8	ROCK AND ROLL PARTS 1 AND 2 Gary Glitter (Bell)
8	9	I CAN SEE CLEARLY NOW Johnny Nash (CBS)
10	10	MAD ABOUT YOU Bruce Ruffin (Rhino)
13	11	AUTOMATICALLY SUNSHINE Supremes (Tamla Motown)
15	12	MY GUY Mary Wells (Tamla Motown)
9	13	STARMAN David Bowie (RCA)
25	14	10538 OVERTURE Electric Light Orchestra (Harvest)
16	15	BETCHA BY GOLLY WOW Stylistics (Avco)
10	16	CIRCLES New Seekers (Polydor)
21	17	WORKING ON A BUILDING OF LOVE Chairmen Of The Board (Invictus)
24	18	IT'S FOUR IN THE MORNING Faron Young (Mercury)
-	19	THE LOCO-MOTION Little Eva (London)
14	20	JOIN TOGETHER Who (Track)
17	21	LITTLE WILLY Sweet (RCA)
-	22	LAYLA Derek & the Dominoes (Polydor)
18	23	WALKIN' IN THE RAIN WITH THE ONE I LOVE Love Unlimited (Uni)
-	24	WATCH ME Labi Siffre (Pye)
-	25	YOU WEAR IT WELL Rod Stewart (Mercury)
-	26	TOO BUSY THINKING ABOUT MY BABY Mardi Gras (Bell)
-	27	RUN TO ME Bee Gees (Polydor)
19	28	TAKE ME BAK 'OME Slade (Polydor)
-	29	ALL THE YOUNG DUDES Mott The Hoople (CBS)
27	30	SONG SUNG BLUE Neil Diamond (Uni)

19 August 1972

Last	This	Entry
1	1	SCHOOL'S OUT Alice Cooper (Warner Bros)
3	2	SEASIDE SHUFFLE Terry Dactyl & the Dinosaurs (UK)
4	3	POPCORN Hot Butter (Pye Int.)
6	4	SILVER MACHINE Hawkwind (United Artists)
2	5	PUPPY LOVE Donny Osmond (MGM)
5	6	BREAKING UP IS HARD TO DO Partridge Family (Bell)
7	7	SYLVIA'S MOTHER Dr Hook & the Medicine Show (CBS)
8	8	ROCK AND ROLL PARTS 1 AND 2 Gary Glitter (Bell)
14	9	10538 OVERTURE Electric Light Orchestra (Harvest)
18	10	IT'S FOUR IN THE MORNING Faron Young (Mercury)
9	11	I CAN SEE CLEARLY NOW Johnny Nash (CBS)
10	12	MAD ABOUT YOU Bruce Ruffin (Rhino)
25	13	YOU WEAR IT WELL Rod Stewart (Mercury)
29	14	ALL THE YOUNG DUDES Mott The Hoople (CBS)
19	15	THE LOCO-MOTION Little Eva (London)
22	16	LAYLA Derek & the Dominoes (Polydor)
11	17	AUTOMATICALLY SUNSHINE Supremes (Tamla Motown)
15	18	BETCHA BY GOLLY WOW Stylistics (Avco)
12	19	MY GUY Mary Wells (Tamla Motown)
27	20	RUN TO ME Bee Gees (Polydor)
13	21	STARMAN David Bowie (RCA)
16	22	CIRCLES New Seekers (Polydor)
24	23	WATCH ME Labi Siffre (Pye)
17	24	WORKING ON A BUILDING OF LOVE Chairmen Of The Board (Invictus)
-	25	LEAN ON ME Bill Withers (A&M)
-	26	CONQUISTADOR Procol Harum (Chrysalis)
26	27	TOO BUSY THINKING ABOUT MY BABY Mardi Gras (Bell)
-	28	I GET THE SWEETEST FEELING Jackie Wilson (MCA)
-	29	WHERE IS THE LOVE Roberta Flack & Donny Hathaway (Atlantic)
21	30	LITTLE WILLY Sweet (RCA)

26 August 1972

Last	This	Entry
1	1	SCHOOL'S OUT Alice Cooper (Warner Bros)
2	2	SEASIDE SHUFFLE Terry Dactyl & the Dinosaurs (UK)
13	3	YOU WEAR IT WELL Rod Stewart (Mercury)
4	4	SILVER MACHINE Hawkwind (United Artists)
3	5	POPCORN Hot Butter (Pye Int.)
5	6	PUPPY LOVE Donny Osmond (MGM)
14	7	ALL THE YOUNG DUDES Mott The Hoople (CBS)
16	8	LAYLA Derek & the Dominoes (Polydor)
6	9	BREAKING UP IS HARD TO DO Partridge Family (Bell)
9	10	10538 OVERTURE Electric Light Orchestra (Harvest)
15	11	THE LOCO-MOTION Little Eva (London)
7	12	SYLVIA'S MOTHER Dr Hook & the Medicine Show (CBS)
20	13	RUN TO ME Bee Gees (Polydor)
10	14	IT'S FOUR IN THE MORNING Faron Young (Mercury)
11	15	I CAN SEE CLEARLY NOW Johnny Nash (CBS)
12	16	MAD ABOUT YOU Bruce Ruffin (Rhino)
8	17	ROCK AND ROLL PARTS 1 AND 2 Gary Glitter (Bell)
17	18	AUTOMATICALLY SUNSHINE Supremes (Tamla Motown)
28	19	I GET THE SWEETEST FEELING Jackie Wilson (MCA)
18	20	BETCHA BY GOLLY WOW Stylistics (Avco)
22	21	CIRCLES New Seekers (Polydor)
-	22	STANDING IN THE ROAD
25	23	LEAN ON ME Bill Withers (A&M)
-	24	VIRGINIA PLAIN Roxy Music (Island)
21	25	STARMAN David Bowie (RCA)
24	26	WORKING ON A BUILDING OF LOVE Chairmen Of The Board (Invictus)
27	27	TOO BUSY THINKING ABOUT MY BABY Mardi Gras (Bell)
26	28	CONQUISTADOR Procol Harum (Chrysalis)
29	29	WHERE IS THE LOVE Roberta Flack & Donny Hathaway (Atlantic)
23	30	WATCH ME Labi Siffre (Pye)

2 September 1972

Last	This	Entry
3	1	YOU WEAR IT WELL Rod Stewart (Mercury)
1	2	SCHOOL'S OUT Alice Cooper (Warner Bros)
7	3	ALL THE YOUNG DUDES Mott The Hoople (CBS)
5	4	POPCORN Hot Butter (Pye Int.)
8	5	LAYLA Derek & the Dominoes (Polydor)
4	6	SILVER MACHINE Hawkwind (United Artists)
2	7	SEASIDE SHUFFLE Terry Dactyl & the Dinosaurs (UK)
-	8	MAMA WEER ALL CRAZEE NOW Slade (Polydor)
14	9	IT'S FOUR IN THE MORNING Faron Young (Mercury)
22	10	STANDING IN THE ROAD Blackfoot Sue (Jam)
10	11	10538 OVERTURE Electric Light Orchestra (Harvest)
13	12	RUN TO ME Bee Gees (Polydor)
9	13	BREAKING UP IS HARD TO DO Partridge Family (Bell)
-	14	SUGAR ME Lynsey De Paul (MAM)
11	15	THE LOCO-MOTION Little Eva (London)
19	16	I GET THE SWEETEST FEELING Jackie Wilson (MCA)
6	17	PUPPY LOVE Donny Osmond (MGM)
24	18	VIRGINIA PLAIN Roxy Music (Island)
14	19	I CAN SEE CLEARLY NOW Johnny Nash (CBS)
23	20	LEAN ON ME Bill Withers (A&M)
-	21	AIN'T NO SUNSHINE Michael Jackson (Tamla Motown)
27	22	TOO BUSY THINKING ABOUT MY BABY Mardi Gras (Bell)
17	23	ROCK AND ROLL PARTS 1 AND 2 Gary Glitter (Bell)
-	24	JOURNEY Duncan Browne (RAK)
29	25	WHERE IS THE LOVE Roberta Flack & Donny Hathaway (Atlantic)
28	26	CONQUISTADOR Procol Harum (Chrysalis)
16	27	MAD ABOUT YOU Bruce Ruffin (Rhino)
26	28	WORKING ON A BUILDING OF LOVE Chairmen Of The Board (Invictus)
12	29	SYLVIA'S MOTHER Dr Hook & the Medicine Show (CBS)
30	30	WATCH ME Labi Siffre (Pye)

Alice Cooper's *School's Out* raised a triumphal note around the world during the school summer holidays of 1972. Like Gary Glitter, the Alice Cooper name initially referred to the entire group, but settled on the outrageously theatrical lead singer, Vince Fournier, who has been Alice ever since. Also holiday-orientated was *Seaside Shuffle*, rescued from previous non-success by Jonathan King for his UK label. Terry Dactyl & the Dinosaurs were better known as gigging band Brett Marvin & The Thunderbolts.

9 September 1972

last week	this week		
1	1	YOU WEAR IT WELL	Rod Stewart (Mercury)
8	2	MAMA, WEER ALL CRAZEE NOW	Slade (Polydor)
10	3	STANDING IN THE ROAD	Blackfoot Sue (Jam)
3	4	ALL THE YOUNG DUDES	Mott The Hoople (CBS)
9	5	IT'S FOUR IN THE MORNING	Faron Young (Mercury)
2	6	SCHOOL'S OUT	Alice Cooper (Warner Bros.)
5	7	LAYLA	Derek & the Dominos (Polydor)
6	8	SILVER MACHINE	Hawkwind (United Artists)
14	9	SUGAR ME	Lynsey De Paul (MAM)
16	10	I GET THE SWEETEST FEELING	Jackie Wilson (MCA)
4	11	POPCORN	Hot Butter (Pye International)
15	12	THE LOCO-MOTION	Little Eva (London)
12	13	RUN TO ME	Bee Gees (Polydor)
18	14	VIRGINIA PLAIN	Roxy Music (Island)
21	15	AIN'T NO SUNSHINE	Michael Jackson (Tamla Motown)
7	16	SEASIDE SHUFFLE	Terry Dactyl & the Dinosaurs (UK)
20	17	LEAN ON ME	Bill Withers (A&M)
13	18	BREAKING UP IS HARD TO DO	Partridge Family (Bell)
11	19	10538 OVERTURE	Electric Light Orchestra (Harvest)
24	20	JOURNEY	Duncan Browne (RAK)
22	21	TOO BUSY THINKING ABOUT MY BABY	Mardi Gras (Bell)
17	22	PUPPY LOVE	Donny Osmond (MGM)
19	23	I CAN SEE CLEARLY NOW	Johnny Nash (CBS)
-	24	HONKY CAT	Elton John (DJM)
23	25	ROCK AND ROLL PART 1 AND 2	Gary Glitter (Bell)
25	26	WHERE IS THE LOVE	Roberta Flack & Donny Hathaway (Atlantic)
26	27	CONQUISTADOR	Procol Harum (Chrysalis)
-	28	COME ON OVER TO MY PLACE	Drifters (Atlantic)
27	29	MAD ABOUT YOU	Bruce Ruffin (Rhino)
28	30	WORKING ON A BUILDING OF LOVE	Chairmen Of The Board (Invictus)

16 September 1972

2	1	MAMA WEER ALL CRAZEE NOW	Slade (Polydor)
1	2	YOU WEAR IT WELL	Rod Stewart (Mercury)
3	3	STANDING IN THE ROAD	Blackfoot Sue (Jam)
9	4	SUGAR ME	Lynsey De Paul (MAM)
14	5	VIRGINIA PLAIN	Roxy Music (Island)
7	6	LAYLA	Derek & the Dominoes (Polydor)
5	7	IT'S FOUR IN THE MORNING	Faron Young (Mercury)
15	8	AIN'T NO SUNSHINE	Michael Jackson (Tamla Motown)
4	9	ALL THE YOUNG DUDES	Mott The Hoople (CBS)
10	10	I GET THE SWEETEST FEELING	Jackie Wilson (MCA)
6	11	SCHOOL'S OUT	Alice Cooper (Warner Bros)
8	12	SILVER MACHINE	Hawkwind (United Artists)
12	13	THE LOCO-MOTION	Little Eva (London)
17	14	LEAN ON ME	Bill Withers (A&M)
-	15	CHILDREN OF THE REVOLUTION	T. Rex (T. Rex)
13	16	RUN TO ME	Bee Gees (Polydor)
-	17	WALK IN THE NIGHT	Jr Walker & The All Stars (Tamla Motown)
20	18	JOURNEY	Duncan Browne (RAK)
11	19	POPCORN	Hot Butter (Pye Int.)
-	20	TOO YOUNG	Donny Osmond (MGM)
-	21	LIVING IN HARMONY	Cliff Richard (Columbia)
21	22	TOO BUSY THINKING ABOUT MY BABY	Mardi Gras (Bell)
19	23	10538 OVERTURE	Electric Light Orchestra (Harvest)
-	24	BIG SIX	Judge Dread (Big Shot)
-	25	HOW CAN I BE SURE	David Cassidy (Bell)
-	26	SUZANNE BEWARE OF THE DEVIL	Dandy Livingstone (Horse)
24	27	HONKY CAT	Elton John (DJM)
-	28	STARMAN	David Bowie (RCA)
16	29	SEASIDE SHUFFLE	Terry Dactyl & the Dinosaurs (UK)
-	30	WIG WAM BAM	Sweet (RCA)

23 September 1972

1	1	MAMA WEER ALL CRAZEE NOW	Slade (Polydor)
2	2	YOU WEAR IT WELL	Rod Stewart (Mercury)
15	3	CHILDREN OF THE REVOLUTION	T. Rex (T. Rex)
7	4	IT'S FOUR IN THE MORNING	Faron Young (Mercury)
5	5	VIRGINIA PLAIN	Roxy Music (Island)
4	6	SUGAR ME	Lynsey De Paul (MAM)
25	7	HOW CAN I BE SURE	David Cassidy (Bell)
3	8	STANDING IN THE ROAD	Blackfoot Sue (Jam)
8	9	AIN'T NO SUNSHINE	Michael Jackson (Tamla Motown)
20	10	TOO YOUNG	Donny Osmond (MGM)
21	10	LIVING IN HARMONY	Cliff Richard (Columbia)
10	12	I GET THE SWEETEST FEELING	Jackie Wilson (MCA)
9	13	ALL THE YOUNG DUDES	Mott The Hoople (CBS)
6	14	LAYLA	Derek & the Dominoes (Polydor)
-	15	COME ON OVER TO MY PLACE	Drifters (Atlantic)
14	16	LEAN ON ME	Bill Withers (A&M)
24	17	BIG SIX	Judge Dread (Big Shot)
17	19	WALK IN THE NIGHT	Jr Walker & The All Stars (Tamla Motown)
-	20	MOULDY OLD DOUGH	Lieutenant Pigeon (Decca)
12	21	SILVER MACHINE	Hawkwind (United Artists)
19	22	POPCORN	Hot Butter (Pye Int.)
-	23	WHO WAS IT	Hurricane Smith (Columbia)
13	24	THE LOCO-MOTION	Little Eva (London)
27	25	HONKY CAT	Elton John (DJM)
26	26	SUZANNE BEWARE OF THE DEVIL	Dandy Livingstone (Horse)
11	27	SCHOOL'S OUT	Alice Cooper (Warner Bros)
22	28	TOO BUSY THINKING ABOUT MY BABY	Mardi Gras (Bell)
18	29	JOURNEY	Duncan Browne (RAK)
-	30	LONG COOL WOMAN IN A BLACK DRESS	Hollies (Parlophone)

30 September 1972

3	1	CHILDREN OF THE REVOLUTION	T. Rex (T. Rex)
7	2	HOW CAN I BE SURE	David Cassidy (Bell)
1	3	MAMA WEER ALL CRAZEE NOW	Slade (Polydor)
10	4	TOO YOUNG	Donny Osmond (MGM)
20	5	MOULDY OLD DOUGH	Lieutenant Pigeon (Decca)
4	6	IT'S FOUR IN THE MORNING	Faron Young (Mercury)
2	7	YOU WEAR IT WELL	Rod Stewart (Mercury)
18	8	WIG WAM BAM	Sweet (RCA)
6	9	SUGAR ME	Lynsey De Paul (MAM)
5	10	VIRGINIA PLAIN	Roxy Music (Island)
9	11	AIN'T NO SUNSHINE	Michael Jackson (Tamla Motown)
10	12	LIVING IN HARMONY	Cliff Richard (Columbia)
15	13	COME ON OVER TO MY PLACE	Drifters (Atlantic)
26	14	SUZANNE BEWARE OF THE DEVIL	Dandy Livingstone (Horse)
17	15	BIG SIX	Judge Dread (Big Shot)
-	16	I DIDN'T KNOW I LOVED YOU (TILL I SAW YOU ROCK'N'ROLL)	Gary Glitter (Bell)
12	17	I GET THE SWEETEST FEELING	Jackie Wilson (MCA)
8	18	STANDING IN THE ROAD	Blackfoot Sue (Jam)
-	19	YOU'RE A LADY	Peter Skellern (Decca)
19	20	WALK IN THE NIGHT	Jr Walker & The All Stars (Tamla Motown)
23	21	WHO WAS IT	Hurricane Smith (Columbia)
-	22	BURNING LOVE	Elvis Presley (RCA)
-	23	JOHN, I'M ONLY DANCING	David Bowie (RCA)
14	24	LAYLA	Derek & the Dominoes (Polydor)
25	25	HONKY CAT	Elton John (DJM)
-	26	LIGHT UP THE FIRE	Parchment (Pye)
16	27	LEAN ON ME	Bill Withers (A&M)
13	28	ALL THE YOUNG DUDES	Mott The Hoople (CBS)
22	29	POPCORN	Hot Butter (Pye Int.)
-	30	MAYBE I KNOW	Seashells (CBS)

Virginia Plain proved to be a potent debut release for newcomers Roxy Music, hotly tipped by many critics as a name to watch. A second impressive Top 10 debut was *Sugar Me*, from Lynsey De Paul, who had found success a few months earlier as writer of the Fortunes' *Storm In A Teacup*. Meanwhile, as another singer/songwriter, Bill Withers, scored with *Lean On Me*, Michael Jackson hit the Top 10 with a cover of Withers' previous US million-seller *Ain't No Sunshine*, which had failed to chart in the UK.

October 1972

7 October 1972

last	this	
2	1	HOW CAN I BE SURE David Cassidy (Bell)
5	2	MOULDY OLD DOUGH Lieutenant Pigeon (Decca)
1	3	CHILDREN OF THE REVOLUTION T. Rex (T. Rex)
8	4	WIG WAM BAM Sweet (RCA)
4	5	TOO YOUNG Donny Osmond (MGM)
3	6	MAMA WEER ALL CRAZEE NOW Slade (Polydor)
19	7	YOU'RE A LADY Peter Skellern (Decca)
16	8	I DIDN'T KNOW I LOVED YOU (TILL I SAW YOU ROCK'N'ROLL) Gary Glitter (Bell)
13	9	COME ON OVER TO MY PLACE Drifters (Atlantic)
22	10	BURNING LOVE Elvis Presley (RCA)
6	11	IT'S FOUR IN THE MORNING Faron Young (Mercury)
14	12	SUZANNE BEWARE OF THE DEVIL Dandy Livingstone (Horse)
15	13	BIG SIX Judge Dread (Big Shot)
10	14	VIRGINIA PLAIN Roxy Music (Island)
12	15	LIVING IN HARMONY Cliff Richard (Columbia)
7	16	YOU WEAR IT WELL Rod Stewart (Mercury)
11	17	AIN'T NO SUNSHINE Michael Jackson (Tamla Motown)
23	18	JOHN, I'M ONLY DANCING David Bowie (RCA)
20	19	WALK IN THE NIGHT Jr Walker & The All Stars (Tamla Motown)
-	20	DONNA 10 c.c. (UK)
-	21	BACK STABBERS O'Jays (CBS)
17	22	I GET THE SWEETEST FEELING Jackie Wilson (MCA)
9	23	SUGAR ME Lynsey De Paul (MAM)
18	24	STANDING IN THE ROAD Blackfoot Sue (Jam)
-	25	IN A BROKEN DREAM Python Lee Jackson (Youngblood)
21	26	WHO WAS IT Hurricane Smith (Columbia)
-	27	THERE ARE MORE QUESTIONS THAN ANSWERS Johnny Nash (CBS)
-	28	ELECTED Alice Cooper (Warner Bros)
25	29	HONKY CAT Elton John (DJM)
29	30	POPCORN Hot Butter (Pye Int.)

14 October 1972

last	this	
2	1	MOULDY OLD DOUGH Lieutenant Pigeon (Decca)
1	2	HOW CAN I BE SURE David Cassidy (Bell)
8	3	I DIDN'T KNOW I LOVED YOU (TILL I SAW YOU ROCK'N'ROLL) Gary Glitter (Bell)
7	4	YOU'RE A LADY Peter Skellern (Decca)
4	5	WIG WAM BAM Sweet (RCA)
3	6	CHILDREN OF THE REVOLUTION T. Rex (T. Rex)
5	7	TOO YOUNG Donny Osmond (MGM)
10	8	BURNING LOVE Elvis Presley (RCA)
20	9	DONNA 10 c.c. (UK)
25	10	IN A BROKEN DREAM Python Lee Jackson (Youngblood)
12	11	SUZANNE BEWARE OF THE DEVIL Dandy Livingstone (Horse)
21	12	BACK STABBERS O'Jays (CBS)
6	13	MAMA WEER ALL CRAZEE NOW Slade (Polydor)
9	14	COME ON OVER TO MY PLACE Drifters (Atlantic)
18	15	JOHN, I'M ONLY DANCING David Bowie (RCA)
13	16	BIG SIX Judge Dread (Big Shot)
11	17	IT'S FOUR IN THE MORNING Faron Young (Mercury)
27	18	THERE ARE MORE QUESTIONS THAN ANSWERS Johnny Nash (CBS)
28	19	ELECTED Alice Cooper (Warner Bros)
15	20	LIVING IN HARMONY Cliff Richard (Columbia)
17	21	AIN'T NO SUNSHINE Michael Jackson (Tamla Motown)
-	22	GUITAR MAN Bread (Elektra)
19	23	WALKIN' IN THE RAIN WITH THE ONE I LOVE Love Unlimited (Uni)
14	24	VIRGINIA PLAIN Roxy Music (Island)
-	25	BURLESQUE Family (Reprise)
-	26	AMERICA Simon & Garfunkel (CBS)
23	27	SUGAR ME Lynsey De Paul (MAM)
-	28	ELMO JAMES Chairmen Of The Board (Invictus)
-	29	GOODBYE TO LOVE Carpenters (A&M)
16	30	YOU WEAR IT WELL Rod Stewart (Mercury)

21 October 1972

last	this	
1	1	MOULDY OLD DOUGH Lieutenant Pigeon (Decca)
3	2	I DIDN'T KNOW I LOVED YOU (TILL I SAW YOU ROCK'N'ROLL) Gary Glitter (Bell)
4	3	YOU'RE A LADY Peter Skellern (Decca)
5	4	WIG WAM BAM Sweet (RCA)
8	5	BURNING LOVE Elvis Presley (RCA)
10	6	IN A BROKEN DREAM Python Lee Jackson (Youngblood)
2	7	HOW CAN I BE SURE David Cassidy (Bell)
9	8	DONNA 10 c.c. (UK)
19	9	ELECTED Alice Cooper (Warner Bros)
7	10	TOO YOUNG Donny Osmond (MGM)
15	11	JOHN, I'M ONLY DANCING David Bowie (RCA)
6	12	CHILDREN OF THE REVOLUTION T. Rex (T. Rex)
12	13	BACK STABBERS O'Jays (CBS)
18	14	THERE ARE MORE QUESTIONS THAN ANSWERS Johnny Nash (CBS)
16	15	BIG SIX Judge Dread (Big Shot)
17	16	IT'S FOUR IN THE MORNING Faron Young (Mercury)
22	17	GUITAR MAN Bread (Elektra)
11	18	SUZANNE BEWARE OF THE DEVIL Dandy Livingstone (Horse)
29	19	GOODBYE TO LOVE Carpenters (A&M)
28	20	ELMO JAMES Chairmen Of The Board (Invictus)
14	21	COME ON OVER TO MY PLACE Drifters (Atlantic)
-	22	CLAIR Gilbert O'Sullivan (MAM)
25	23	BURLESQUE Family (Reprise)
-	24	HALLELUJAH FREEDOM Junior Campbell (Deram)
26	25	AMERICA Simon & Garfunkel (CBS)
-	26	LOOP DI LOVE Shag (UK)
24	27	VIRGINIA PLAIN Roxy Music (Island)
13	28	MAMA WEER ALL CRAZEE NOW Slade (Polydor)
23	29	WALK IN THE NIGHT Jr Walker & The All Stars (Tamla Motown)
-	30	OH CAROL Neil Sedaka (RCA)

28 October 1972

last	this	
1	1	MOULDY OLD DOUGH Lieutenant Pigeon (Decca)
8	2	DONNA 10 c.c. (UK)
6	3	IN A BROKEN DREAM Python Lee Jackson (Youngblood)
3	4	YOU'RE A LADY Peter Skellern (Decca)
9	5	ELECTED Alice Cooper (Warner Bros)
5	6	BURNING LOVE Elvis Presley (RCA)
2	7	I DIDN'T KNOW I LOVED YOU (TILL I SAW YOU ROCK'N'ROLL)
22	8	CLAIR Gilbert O'Sullivan (MAM)
4	9	WIG WAM BAM Sweet (RCA)
7	10	HOW CAN I BE SURE David Cassidy (Bell)
19	11	GOODBYE TO LOVE Carpenters (A&M)
11	12	JOHN, I'M ONLY DANCING David Bowie (RCA)
14	13	THERE ARE MORE QUESTIONS THAN ANSWERS Johnny Nash (CBS)
13	14	BACK STABBERS O'Jays (CBS)
17	15	GUITAR MAN Bread (Elektra)
20	16	ELMO JAMES Chairmen Of The Board (Invictus)
15	17	BIG SIX Judge Dread (Big Shot)
26	18	LOOP DI LOVE Shag (UK)
24	19	HALLELUJAH FREEDOM Junior Campbell (Deram)
10	20	TOO YOUNG Donny Osmond (MGM)
23	21	BURLESQUE Family (Reprise)
12	22	CHILDREN OF THE REVOLUTION T. Rex (T. Rex)
-	23	LEADER OF THE PACK Shangri-Las (Kama Sutra)
16	24	IT'S FOUR IN THE MORNING Faron Young (Mercury)
18	25	SUZANNE BEWARE OF THE DEVIL Dandy Livingstone (Horse)
25	26	AMERICA Simon & Garfunkel (CBS)
21	27	COME ON OVER TO MY PLACE Drifters (Atlantic)
30	28	OH CAROL Neil Sedaka (RCA)
27	29	VIRGINIA PLAIN Roxy Music (Island)
-	30	HERE I GO AGAIN Archie Bell & the Drells (Atlantic)

A novelty instrumental was the month's runaway best-seller. *Mouldy Old Dough*, which had 'slept' for months before charting, featured the beaming middle-aged figure of Hilda Woodward, mother of the group's full-time keyboards player Rob Woodward, well to the front on TV appearances. 10 c.c., Jonathan King protegees at this time, debuted with the 1950s pastiche *Donna*, as did Peter Skellern with the idiosyncratic *You're A Lady*, and Python Lee Jackson featured the uncredited vocals of Rod Stewart.

November 1972

4 November 1972

last week	this week	Title	Artist (Label)
1	1	MOULDY OLD DOUGH	Lieutenant Pigeon (Decca)
2	2	DONNA	10 c.c. (UK)
5	3	ELECTED	Alice Cooper (Warner Bros)
8	4	CLAIR	Gilbert O'Sullivan (MAM)
3	5	IN A BROKEN DREAM	Python Lee Jackson (Youngblood)
7	6	I DIDN'T KNOW I LOVED YOU (TILL I SAW YOU ROCK'N'ROLL)	Gary Glitter (Bell)
6	7	BURNING LOVE	Elvis Presley (RCA)
18	8	LOOP DI LOVE	Shag (UK)
15	9	GUITAR MAN	Bread (Elektra)
13	10	THERE ARE MORE QUESTIONS THAN ANSWERS	Johnny Nash (CBS)
11	11	GOODBYE TO LOVE	Carpenters (A&M)
4	12	YOU'RE A LADY	Peter Skellern (Decca)
19	13	HALLELUJAH FREEDOM	Junior Campbell (Deram)
9	14	WIG WAM BAM	Sweet (RCA)
12	15	JOHN, I'M ONLY DANCING	David Bowie (RCA)
21	16	BURLESQUE	Family (Reprise)
23	17	LEADER OF THE PACK	Shangri-Las (Kama Sutra)
16	18	ELMO JAMES	Chairmen Of The Board (Invictus)
14	19	BACK STABBERS	O'Jays (CBS)
17	20	BIG SIX	Judge Dread (Big Shot)
10	21	HOW CAN I BE SURE	David Cassidy (Bell)
26	22	AMERICA	Simon & Garfunkel (CBS)
-	23	LET'S DANCE	Chris Montez (London)
-	24	MY DING-A-LING	Chuck Berry (Chess)
-	25	NEW ORLEANS	Harley Quinne (Bell)
30	26	HERE I GO AGAIN	Archie Bell & the Drells (Atlantic)
-	27	WHY CAN'T WE BE LOVERS	Holland & Dozier (Invictus)
-	28	CROCODILE ROCK	Elton John (DJM)
28	29	OH CAROL	Neil Sedaka (RCA)
20	30	TOO YOUNG	Donny Osmond (MGM)

11 November 1972

last week	this week	Title	Artist (Label)
4	1	CLAIR	Gilbert O'Sullivan (MAM)
1	2	MOULDY OLD DOUGH	Lieutenant Pigeon (Decca)
2	3	DONNA	10 c.c. (UK)
8	4	LOOP DI LOVE	Shag (UK)
3	5	ELECTED	Alice Cooper (Warner Bros)
5	6	IN A BROKEN DREAM	Python Lee Jackson (Youngblood)
17	7	LEADER OF THE PACK	Shangri-Las (Kama Sutra)
24	8	MY DING-A-LING	Chuck Berry (Chess)
11	9	GOODBYE TO LOVE	Carpenters (A&M)
7	10	BURNING LOVE	Elvis Presley (RCA)
13	11	HALLELUJAH FREEDOM	Junior Campbell (Deram)
10	12	THERE ARE MORE QUESTIONS THAN ANSWERS	Johnny Nash (CBS)
6	13	I DIDN'T KNOW I LOVED YOU (TILL I SAW YOU ROCK'N'ROLL)	Gary Glitter (Bell)
16	14	BURLESQUE	Family (Reprise)
12	15	YOU'RE A LADY	Peter Skellern (Decca)
23	16	LET'S DANCE	Chris Montez (London)
9	17	GUITAR MAN	Bread (Elektra)
-	18	WHY	Donny Osmond (MGM)
20	19	BIG SIX	Judge Dread (Big Shot)
-	20	I'M STONE IN LOVE WITH YOU	Stylistics (Avco)
-	21	HI HO SILVER LINING	Jeff Beck (RAK)
26	22	HERE I GO AGAIN	Archie Bell & the Drells (Atlantic)
25	23	NEW ORLEANS	Harley Quinne (Bell)
28	24	CROCODILE ROCK	Elton John (DJM)
14	25	WIG WAM BAM	Sweet (RCA)
27	26	WHY CAN'T WE BE LOVERS	Holland & Dozier (Invictus)
18	27	ELMO JAMES	Chairmen Of The Board (Invictus)
-	28	CRAZY HORSES	Osmonds (MGM)
19	29	BACK STABBERS	O'Jays (CBS)
29	30	OH CAROL	Neil Sedaka (RCA)

18 November 1972

last week	this week	Title	Artist (Label)
1	1	CLAIR	Gilbert O'Sullivan (MAM)
8	2	MY DING-A-LING	Chuck Berry (Chess)
2	3	MOULDY OLD DOUGH	Lieutenant Pigeon (Decca)
7	4	LEADER OF THE PACK	Shangri-Las (Kama Sutra)
18	5	WHY	Donny Osmond (MGM)
3	6	DONNA	10 c.c. (UK)
4	7	LOOP DI LOVE	Shag (UK)
28	8	CRAZY HORSES	Osmonds (MGM)
9	9	GOODBYE TO LOVE	Carpenters (A&M)
11	10	HALLELUJAH FREEDOM	Junior Campbell (Deram)
6	11	IN A BROKEN DREAM	Python Lee Jackson (Youngblood)
5	12	ELECTED	Alice Cooper (Warner Bros)
16	13	LET'S DANCE	Chris Montez (London)
24	14	CROCODILE ROCK	Elton John (DJM)
20	15	I'M STONE IN LOVE WITH YOU	Stylistics (Avco)
22	16	HERE I GO AGAIN	Archie Bell & the Drells (Atlantic)
21	17	HI HO SILVER LINING	Jeff Beck (RAK)
12	18	THERE ARE MORE QUESTIONS THAN ANSWERS	Johnny Nash (CBS)
14	19	BURLESQUE	Family (Reprise)
-	20	LOOKIN' THROUGH THE WINDOWS	Jackson Five (Tamla Motown)
-	21	WHAT MADE MILWAUKEE FAMOUS/ANGEL	Rod Stewart (Mercury)
23	22	NEW ORLEANS	Harley Quinne (Bell)
10	23	BURNING LOVE	Elvis Presley (RCA)
30	24	OH CAROL	Neil Sedaka (RCA)
19	25	BIG SIX	Judge Dread (Big Shot)
15	26	YOU'RE A LADY	Peter Skellern (Decca)
17	27	GUITAR MAN	Bread (Elektra)
13	28	I DIDN'T KNOW I LOVED YOU (TILL I SAW YOU ROCK'N'ROLL)	Gary Glitter (Bell)
26	29	WHY CAN'T WE BE LOVERS	Holland & Dozier (Invictus)
-	30	JOHN, I'M ONLY DANCING	David Bowie (RCA)

25 November 1972

last week	this week	Title	Artist (Label)
2	1	MY DING-A-LING	Chuck Berry (Chess)
1	2	CLAIR	Gilbert O'Sullivan (MAM)
8	3	CRAZY HORSES	Osmonds (MGM)
5	4	WHY	Donny Osmond (MGM)
4	5	LEADER OF THE PACK	Shangri-Las (Kama Sutra)
14	6	CROCODILE ROCK	Elton John (DJM)
7	7	LOOP DI LOVE	Shag (UK)
15	8	I'M STONE IN LOVE WITH YOU	Stylistics (Avco)
3	9	MOULDY OLD DOUGH	Lieutenant Pigeon (Decca)
21	10	WHAT MADE MILWAUKEE FAMOUS/ANGEL	Rod Stewart (Mercury)
13	11	LET'S DANCE	Chris Montez (London)
6	12	DONNA	10 c.c. (UK)
20	13	LOOKIN' THROUGH THE WINDOWS	Jackson Five (Tamla Motown)
9	14	GOODBYE TO LOVE	Carpenters (A&M)
-	15	GUDBUY T' JANE	Slade (Polydor)
17	16	HI HO SILVER LINING	Jeff Beck (RAK)
12	17	ELECTED	Alice Cooper (Warner Bros)
16	18	HERE I GO AGAIN	Archie Bell & the Drells (Atlantic)
11	19	IN A BROKEN DREAM	Python Lee Jackson (Youngblood)
10	20	HALLELUJAH FREEDOM	Junior Campbell (Deram)
24	21	OH CAROL	Neil Sedaka (RCA)
22	22	NEW ORLEANS	Harley Quinne (Bell)
-	23	LAY DOWN	Strawbs (A&M)
19	24	BURLESQUE	Family (Reprise)
18	25	THERE ARE MORE QUESTIONS THAN ANSWERS	Johnny Nash (CBS)
27	26	GUITAR MAN	Bread (Elektra)
-	27	KEEPER OF THE CASTLE	Four Tops (Probe)
-	28	BEN	Michael Jackson (Tamla Motown)
-	29	YOU'LL ALWAYS BE A FRIEND	Hot Chocolate (RAK)
-	30	I DON'T BELIEVE IN MIRACLES	Colin Blunstone (Epic)

Chuck Berry's *My Ding-A-Ling*, his first hit for nearly eight years, topped both the British and US charts, and was his all-time biggest seller. Recorded in the UK, during a live performance at the Lanchester Arts Festival, this risque audience-participation novelty was despised by many Berry fans, and upset Mrs Mary Whitehouse, who tried (without success) to get the BBC to ban it. Chuck merely laughed all the way to the bank, and also kept *Crazy Horses*, the first UK smash by the collective Osmonds, from the chart top.

December 1972

last this
week

2 December 1972

1 1 MY DING-A-LING
Chuck Berry (Chess)
3 2 CRAZY HORSES
Osmonds (MGM)
15 3 GUDBUY T' JANE
Slade (Polydor)
4 4 WHY Donny Osmond (MGM)
2 5 CLAIR Gilbert O'Sullivan (MAM)
6 6 CROCODILE ROCK
Elton John (DJM)
10 7 WHAT MADE MILWAUKEE
FAMOUS/ANGEL
Rod Stewart (Mercury)
8 8 I'M STONE IN LOVE WITH YOU
Stylistics (Avco)
5 9 LEADER OF THE PACK
Shangri-Las (Kama Sutra)
13 10 LOOKIN' THROUGH THE
WINDOWS
Jackson Five (Tamla Motown)
11 11 LET'S DANCE
Chris Montez (London)
7 12 LOOP DI LOVE Shag (UK)
28 13 BEN Michael Jackson
(Tamla Motown)
23 14 LAY DOWN Strawbs (A&M)
9 15 MOULDY OLD DOUGH
Lieutenant Pigeon (Decca)
14 16 GOODBYE TO LOVE
Carpenters (A&M)
21 17 OH CAROL Neil Sedaka (RCA)
16 18 HI HO SILVER LINING
Jeff Beck (RAK)
- 19 ROCK ME BABY
David Cassidy (Bell)
27 20 KEEPER OF THE CASTLE
Four Tops (Probe)
18 21 HERE I GO AGAIN Archie Bell &
the Drells (Atlantic)
- 22 STAY WITH ME Blue Mink
(Regal Zonophone)
- 23 HELP ME MAKE IT THROUGH THE
NIGHT Gladys Knight &
the Pips (Tamla Motown)
12 24 DONNA 10 c.c. (UK)
29 25 YOU'LL ALWAYS BE A FRIEND
Hot Chocolate (RAK)
17 26 ELECTED
Alice Cooper (Warner Bros)
- 27 LITTLE DRUMMER BOY Royal
Scots Dragoon Guards, Pipes,
Drums & Band (RCA)
- 28 BABY DON'T GET HOOKED ON
ME Mac Davis (CBS)
- 29 BIG SIX Judge Dread (Big Shot)
30 30 I DON'T BELIEVE IN MIRACLES
Colin Blunstone (Epic)

9 December 1972

1 1 MY DING-A-LING
Chuck Berry (Chess)
3 2 GUDBUY T' JANE
Slade (Polydor)
2 3 CRAZY HORSES
Osmonds (MGM)
7 4 WHAT MADE MILWAUKEE
FAMOUS/ANGEL
Rod Stewart (Mercury)
6 5 CROCODILE ROCK
Elton John (DJM)
4 6 WHY Donny Osmond (MGM)
10 7 LOOKIN' THROUGH THE
WINDOWS
Jackson Five (Tamla Motown)
14 8 LAY DOWN Strawbs (A&M)
13 9 BEN Michael Jackson
(Tamla Motown)
8 10 I'M STONE IN LOVE WITH YOU
Stylistics (Avco)
22 11 STAY WITH ME
Faces (Warner Bros)
5 12 CLAIR Gilbert O'Sullivan (MAM)
9 13 LEADER OF THE PACK
Shangri-Las (Kama Sutra)
19 14 ROCK ME BABY
David Cassidy (Bell)
- 15 SOLID GOLD EASY ACTION
T. Rex (T. Rex)
18 16 HI HO SILVER LINING
Jeff Beck (RAK)
20 17 KEEPER OF THE CASTLE
Four Tops (Probe)
- 18 SHOTGUN WEDDING Roy C (UK)
11 19 LET'S DANCE
Chris Montez (London)
23 20 HELP ME MAKE IT THROUGH THE
NIGHT Gladys Knight &
the Pips (Tamla Motown)
- 21 LONG HAIRED LOVER FROM
LIVERPOOL
Little Jimmy Osmond (MGM)
- 22 HAPPY XMAS (WAR IS OVER)
John & Yoko/Plastic Ono Band
(Apple)
17 23 OH CAROL Neil Sedaka (RCA)
- 24 NIGHTS IN WHITE SATIN
Moody Blues (Deram)
15 25 MOULDY OLD DOUGH
Lieutenant Pigeon (Decca)
12 26 LOOP DI LOVE Shag (UK)
16 27 GOODBYE TO LOVE
Carpenters (A&M)
- 28 BALL PARK INCIDENT
Wizzard (Harvest)
- 29 BIG SEVEN Judge Dread
(Big Shot)
25 30 YOU'LL ALWAYS BE A FRIEND
Hot Chocolate (RAK)

16 December 1972

2 1 GUDBUY T' JANE
Slade (Polydor)
1 2 MY DING-A-LING
Chuck Berry (Chess)
3 3 CRAZY HORSES
Osmonds (MGM)
4 4 WHAT MADE MILWAUKEE
FAMOUS/ANGEL
Rod Stewart (Mercury)
9 5 BEN Michael Jackson
(Tamla Motown)
5 6 CROCODILE ROCK
Elton John (DJM)
15 7 SOLID GOLD EASY ACTION
T. Rex (T. Rex)
21 8 LONG HAIRED LOVER FROM
LIVERPOOL
Little Jimmy Osmond (MGM)
6 9 WHY Donny Osmond (MGM)
7 10 LOOKIN' THROUGH THE
WINDOWS
Jackson Five (Tamla Motown)
8 11 LAY DOWN Strawbs (A&M)
14 12 ROCK ME BABY
David Cassidy (Bell)
22 13 HAPPY XMAS (WAR IS OVER)
John & Yoko/Plastic Ono Band
(Apple)
18 14 SHOTGUN WEDDING Roy C (UK)
11 15 STAY WITH ME
Blue Mink (Regal Zonophone)
24 16 NIGHTS IN WHITE SATIN
Moody Blues (Deram)
20 17 HELP ME MAKE IT THROUGH THE
NIGHT Gladys Knight &
the Pips (Tamla Motown)
10 18 I'M STONE IN LOVE WITH YOU
Stylistics (Avco)
- 19 LITTLE DRUMMER BOY Royal
Scots Dragoon Guards, Pipes,
Drums & Band (RCA)
- 20 HI HI HI Wings (Parlophone)
12 21 CLAIR Gilbert O'Sullivan (MAM)
17 22 KEEPER OF THE CASTLE
Four Tops (Probe)
16 23 HI HO SILVER LINING
Jeff Beck (RAK)
29 24 BIG SEVEN
Judge Dread (Big Shot)
13 25 LEADER OF THE PACK
Shangri-Las (Kama Sutra)
- 26 THE JEAN GENIE
David Bowie (RCA)
23 27 OH CAROL Neil Sedaka (RCA)
19 28 LET'S DANCE
Chris Montez (London)
- 29 GETTING A DRAG
Lynsey De Paul (MAM)
28 30 BALL PARK INCIDENT
Wizzard (Harvest)

23 December 1972

3 1 LONG HAIRED LOVER FROM
LIVERPOOL
Little Jimmy Osmond (MGM)
1 2 GUDBUY T' JANE
Slade (Polydor)
7 3 SOLID GOLD EASY ACTION
T. Rex (T. Rex)
2 4 MY DING-A-LING
Chuck Berry (Chess)
13 5 HAPPY XMAS (WAR IS OVER)
John & Yoko/Plastic Ono Band
(Apple)
5 6 BEN Michael Jackson
(Tamla Motown)
3 7 CRAZY HORSES
Osmonds (MGM)
6 8 CROCODILE ROCK
Elton John (DJM)
14 9 SHOTGUN WEDDING Roy C (UK)
16 10 NIGHTS IN WHITE SATIN
Moody Blues (Deram)
4 11 WHAT MADE MILWAUKEE
FAMOUS/ANGEL
Rod Stewart (Mercury)
15 12 STAY WITH ME
Blue Mink (Regal Zonophone)
9 13 WHY Donny Osmond (MGM)
20 14 HI HI HI Wings (Parlophone)
24 15 BIG SEVEN
Judge Dread (Big Shot)
19 16 LITTLE DRUMMER BOY Royal
Scots Dragoon Guards, Pipes,
Drums & Band (RCA)
10 17 LOOKIN' THROUGH THE
WINDOWS
Jackson Five (Tamla Motown)
11 18 LAY DOWN Strawbs (A&M)
12 19 ROCK ME BABY
David Cassidy (Bell)
17 20 HELP ME MAKE IT THROUGH THE
NIGHT Gladys Knight &
the Pips (Tamla Motown)
26 21 THE JEAN GENIE
David Bowie (RCA)
- 22 YOU'RE SO VAIN
Carly Simon (Elektra)
23 23 HI HO SILVER LINING
Jeff Beck (RAK)
22 24 KEEPER OF THE CASTLE
Four Tops (Probe)
- 25 DESPERATE DAN
Lieutenant Pigeon (Decca)
- 26 WISHING WELL
Free (Island)
30 27 BALL PARK INCIDENT
Wizzard (Harvest)
- 28 I'M ON MY WAY TO A BETTER
PLACE Chairmen Of The Board
(Invictus)
25 29 LEADER OF THE PACK
Shangri-Las (Kama Sutra)
- 30 CAN'T KEEP IT IN
Cat Stevens (Island)

Nine-year-old youngest Osmond brother Little Jimmy's *Long-Haired Lover From Liverpool* had been a comparatively minor US hit, but was released here at precisely the right moment during the rapid acceleration of Osmond-mania among the UK's female teen masses, while also being ideal for the traditionally novelty-hungry Christmas market. It was the biggest-selling of any of the Osmonds' releases in this country, shifting 985,000 copies, and headed an Osmonds-dominated Christmas chart.

First came teeny-boppers, then even younger weeny-boppers. The objects of their adulation got younger and younger as well, until Little Jimmy Osmond swept all before him. One for the Mums and Dads maybe?

Left: David Cassidy
Below: The Osmonds – individual hit-makers were Marie (second from left) Donny (fourth from left) and of course Little Jimmy at the front.

January 1973

6 January 1973

last	this	
1	1	LONG HAIRED LOVER FROM LIVERPOOL Little Jimmy Osmond (MGM)
3	2	SOLID GOLD EASY ACTION T. Rex (T. Rex)
4	3	GUDBUY T'JANE Slade (Polydor)
2	4	HAPPY XMAS (WAR IS OVER) John & Yoko/Plastic Ono Band (Apple)
5	5	CRAZY HORSES Osmonds (MGM)
6	6	MY DING-A-LING Chuck Berry (Chess)
7	7	BEN Michael Jackson (Tamla Motown)
13	8	THE JEAN GENIE David Bowie (RCA)
8	9	SHOTGUN WEDDING Roy C (UK)
10	10	NIGHTS IN WHITE SATIN Moody Blues (Deram)
9	11	CROCODILE ROCK Elton John (DJM)
20	12	BALL PARK INCIDENT Wizzard (Harvest)
22	13	HELP ME MAKE IT THROUGH THE NIGHT Gladys Knight & the Pips (Tamla Motown)
16	14	HI HI HI Wings (Parlophone)
12	15	WHY Donny Osmond (MGM)
18	16	YOU'RE SO VAIN Carly Simon (Elektra)
14	17	WHAT MADE MILWAUKEE FAMOUS/ANGEL Rod Stewart (Mercury)
14	18	LITTLE DRUMMER BOY Royal Scots Dragoon Guards, Pipes, Drums & Band (RCA)
11	19	STAY WITH ME Blue Mink (Regal Zonophone)
23	20	BIG SEVEN Judge Dread (Big Shot)
17	21	ROCK ME BABY David Cassidy (Bell)
21	22	LAY DOWN Strawbs (A&M)
19	23	ALWAYS ON MY MIND Elvis Presley (RCA)
30	24	DESPERATE DAN Lieutenant Pigeon (Decca)
25	25	CAN'T KEEP IT IN Cat Stevens (Island)
-	26	I'M ON MY WAY TO A BETTER PLACE Chairmen Of The Board (Invictus)
30	27	IT'S GETTING A DRAG Lynsey De Paul (MAM)
-	28	SING DON'T SPEAK Blackfoot Sue (Jam)
-	29	WISHING WELL Free (Island)
24	30	LOOKIN' THROUGH THE WINDOWS Jackson Five (Tamla Motown)

13 January 1973

last	this	
1	1	LONG HAIRED LOVER FROM LIVERPOOL Little Jimmy Osmond (MGM)
8	2	THE JEAN GENIE David Bowie (RCA)
2	3	SOLID GOLD EASY ACTION T. Rex (T. Rex)
14	4	HI HI HI Wings (Parlophone)
12	5	BALL PARK INCIDENT Wizzard (Harvest)
3	6	GUDBUY T'JANE Slade (Polydor)
16	7	YOU'RE SO VAIN Carly Simon (Elektra)
9	8	SHOTGUN WEDDING Roy C (UK)
5	9	CRAZY HORSES Osmonds (MGM)
7	10	BEN Michael Jackson (Tamla Motown)
6	11	MY DING-A-LING Chuck Berry (Chess)
10	12	NIGHTS IN WHITE SATIN Moody Blues (Deram)
4	13	HAPPY XMAS (WAR IS OVER) John & Yoko/Plastic Ono Band (Apple)
20	14	BIG SEVEN Judge Dread (Big Shot)
13	15	HELP ME MAKE IT THROUGH THE NIGHT Gladys Knight & the Pips (Tamla Motown)
11	16	CROCODILE ROCK Elton John (DJM)
15	17	WHY Donny Osmond (MGM)
23	18	ALWAYS ON MY MIND Elvis Presley (RCA)
-	19	BLOCKBUSTER Sweet (RCA)
24	20	DESPERATE DAN Lieutenant Pigeon (Decca)
25	21	CAN'T KEEP IT IN Cat Stevens (Island)
29	22	WISHING WELL Free (Island)
17	23	WHAT MADE MILWAUKEE FAMOUS/ANGEL Rod Stewart (Mercury)
19	24	STAY WITH ME Blue Mink (Regal Zonophone)
-	25	RELAY Who (Track)
27	26	IT'S GETTING A DRAG Lynsey De Paul (MAM)
-	27	COME SOFTLY TO ME New Seekers (Polydor)
21	28	ROCK ME BABY David Cassidy (Bell)
28	29	SING DON'T SPEAK Blackfoot Sue (Jam)
-	30	IF YOU DON'T KNOW ME BY NOW Harold Melvin & The Blue Notes (CBS)

20 January 1973

last	this	
2	1	THE JEAN GENIE David Bowie (RCA)
1	2	LONG HAIRED LOVER FROM LIVERPOOL Little Jimmy Osmond (MGM)
4	3	HI HI HI Wings (Parlophone)
4	4	YOU'RE SO VAIN Carly Simon (Elektra)
5	5	BALL PARK INCIDENT Wizzard (Harvest)
19	6	BLOCKBUSTER Sweet (RCA)
3	7	SOLID GOLD EASY ACTION T. Rex (T. Rex)
9	8	CRAZY HORSES Osmonds (MGM)
14	9	BIG SEVEN Judge Dread (Big Shot)
6	10	GUDBUY T'JANE Slade (Polydor)
18	11	ALWAYS ON MY MIND Elvis Presley (RCA)
22	12	WISHING WELL Free (Island)
12	13	NIGHTS IN WHITE SATIN Moody Blues (Deram)
8	14	SHOTGUN WEDDING Roy C (UK)
21	15	CAN'T KEEP IT IN Cat Stevens (Island)
10	16	BEN Michael Jackson (Tamla Motown)
15	17	HELP ME MAKE IT THROUGH THE NIGHT Gladys Knight & the Pips (Tamla Motown)
11	18	MY DING-A-LING Chuck Berry (Chess)
20	19	DESPERATE DAN Lieutenant Pigeon (Decca)
-	20	PAPA WAS A ROLLING STONE Temptations (Tamla Motown)
-	21	ME AND MRS JONES Billy Paul (Epic)
16	22	CROCODILE ROCK Elton John (DJM)
-	23	PAPER PLANE Status Quo (Vertigo)
25	24	RELAY Who (Track)
17	25	WHY Donny Osmond (MGM)
30	26	IF YOU DON'T KNOW ME BY NOW Harold Melvin & The Blue Notes (CBS)
27	27	COME SOFTLY TO ME New Seekers (Polydor)
13	28	HAPPY XMAS (WAR IS OVER) John & Yoko/Plastic Ono Band (Apple)
-	29	WHISKEY IN THE JAR Thin Lizzy (Decca)
24	30	STAY WITH ME Blue Mink (Regal Zonophone)

27 January 1973

last	this	
6	1	BLOCKBUSTER Sweet (RCA)
1	2	THE JEAN GENIE David Bowie (RCA)
2	3	LONG HAIRED LOVER FROM LIVERPOOL Little Jimmy Osmond (MGM)
4	4	YOU'RE SO VAIN Carly Simon (Elektra)
3	5	HI HI HI Wings (Parlophone)
5	6	BALL PARK INCIDENT Wizzard (Harvest)
12	7	WISHING WELL Free (Island)
11	8	ALWAYS ON MY MIND Elvis Presley (RCA)
26	9	IF YOU DON'T KNOW ME BY NOW Harold Melvin & The Blue Notes (CBS)
21	10	ME AND MRS JONES Billy Paul (Epic)
20	11	PAPA WAS A ROLLING STONE Temptations (Tamla Motown)
-	12	DO YOU WANNA TOUCH ME (OH YEAH) Gary Glitter (Bell)
23	13	PAPER PLANE Status Quo (Vertigo)
15	14	CAN'T KEEP IT IN Cat Stevens (Island)
9	15	BIG SEVEN Judge Dread (Big Shot)
7	16	SOLID GOLD EASY ACTION T. Rex (T. Rex)
8	17	CRAZY HORSES Osmonds (MGM)
-	18	DANIEL Elton John (DJM)
17	19	HELP ME MAKE IT THROUGH THE NIGHT Gladys Knight & the Pips (Tamla Motown)
14	20	SHOTGUN WEDDING Roy C (UK)
19	21	DESPERATE DAN Lieutenant Pigeon (Decca)
24	22	RELAY Who (Track)
13	23	NIGHTS IN WHITE SATIN Moody Blues (Deram)
27	24	COME SOFTLY TO ME New Seekers (Polydor)
10	25	GUDBUY T'JANE Slade (Polydor)
16	26	BEN Michael Jackson (Tamla Motown)
-	27	PART OF THE UNION Strawbs (A&M)
-	28	HOCUS POCUS Focus (Polydor)
-	29	ROLL OVER BEETHOVEN Electric Light Orchestra (Harvest)
29	30	WHISKEY IN THE JAR Thin Lizzy (Decca)

Wings' *Hi Hi Hi* hit the Top Three despite getting very little airplay: Radio 1 considered the title to have drug connotations, and refused to programme it, playing instead the B-side, *C Moon* - which was never listed on the chart, suggesting that buyers weren't naming it as the title they wanted. David Bowie's first chart-topper proved short-lived, with a week at the summit. Sweet's *Blockbuster*, which replaced it, used an identical riff - whether this was apparent to RCA (which issued both singles) is not clear.

last week	this	3 February 1973
1	1	BLOCKBUSTER — Sweet (RCA)
12	2	DO YOU WANNA TOUCH ME (OH YEAH) — Gary Glitter (Bell)
4	3	YOU'RE SO VAIN — Carly Simon (Elektra)
2	4	THE JEAN GENIE — David Bowie (RCA)
3	5	LONG HAIRED LOVER FROM LIVERPOOL — Little Jimmy Osmond (MGM)
18	6	DANIEL — Elton John (DJM)
9	7	IF YOU DON'T KNOW ME BY NOW — Harold Melvin & The Blue Notes (CBS)
7	8	WISHING WELL — Free (Island)
6	9	BALL PARK INCIDENT — Wizzard (Harvest)
5	10	HI HI HI — Wings (Parlophone)
10	11	ME AND MRS JONES — Billy Paul (Epic)
27	12	PART OF THE UNION — Strawbs (A&M)
13	13	PAPER PLANE — Status Quo (Vertigo)
11	14	PAPA WAS A ROLLING STONE — Temptations (Tamla Motown)
14	15	CAN'T KEEP IT IN — Cat Stevens (Island)
15	16	BIG SEVEN — Judge Dread (Big Shot)
8	17	ALWAYS ON MY MIND — Elvis Presley (RCA)
29	18	ROLL OVER BEETHOVEN — Electric Light Orchestra (Harvest)
22	19	RELAY — Who (Track)
-	20	SYLVIA — Focus (Polydor)
19	21	HELP ME MAKE IT THROUGH THE NIGHT — Gladys Knight & the Pips (Tamla Motown)
30	22	WHISKEY IN THE JAR — Thin Lizzy (Decca)
-	23	SUPERSTITION — Stevie Wonder (Tamla Motown)
24	24	DESPERATE DAN — Lieutenant Pigeon (Decca)
17	25	CRAZY HORSES — Osmonds (MGM)
17	26	NIGHTS IN WHITE SATIN — Moody Blues (Deram)
26	27	BEN — Michael Jackson (Tamla Motown)
16	28	SOLID GOLD EASY ACTION — T. Rex (T. Rex)
-	29	BIG CITY — Dandy Livingstone (Horse)
-	30	TAKE ME GIRL, I'M READY — Jr Walker & The All Stars (Tamla Motown)

10 February 1973

1	1	BLOCKBUSTER — Sweet (RCA)
2	2	DO YOU WANNA TOUCH ME (OH YEAH) — Gary Glitter (Bell)
12	3	PART OF THE UNION — Strawbs (A&M)
6	4	DANIEL — Elton John (DJM)
3	5	YOU'RE SO VAIN — Carly Simon (Elektra)
5	6	LONG HAIRED LOVER FROM LIVERPOOL — Little Jimmy Osmond (MGM)
8	7	WISHING WELL — Free (Island)
11	8	ME AND MRS JONES — Billy Paul (Epic)
18	9	ROLL OVER BEETHOVEN — Electric Light Orchestra (Harvest)
4	10	THE JEAN GENIE — David Bowie (RCA)
13	11	PAPER PLANE — Status Quo (Vertigo)
7	12	IF YOU DON'T KNOW ME BY NOW — Harold Melvin & The Blue Notes (CBS)
20	13	SYLVIA — Focus (Polydor)
23	14	SUPERSTITION — Stevie Wonder (Tamla Motown)
9	15	BALL PARK INCIDENT — Wizzard (Harvest)
22	16	WHISKEY IN THE JAR — Thin Lizzy (Decca)
14	17	PAPA WAS A ROLLING STONE — Temptations (Tamla Motown)
10	18	HI HI HI — Wings (Parlophone)
17	19	ALWAYS ON MY MIND — Elvis Presley (RCA)
15	20	CAN'T KEEP IT IN — Cat Stevens (Island)
16	21	BIG SEVEN — Judge Dread (Big Shot)
30	22	TAKE ME GIRL, I'M READY — Jr Walker & The All Stars (Tamla Motown)
-	23	TAKE ME HOME COUNTRY ROADS — Olivia Newton-John (Pye)
21	24	HELP ME MAKE IT THROUGH THE NIGHT — Gladys Knight & the Pips (Tamla Motown)
19	25	RELAY — Who (Track)
27	26	BEN — Michael Jackson (Tamla Motown)
29	27	BIG CITY — Dandy Livingstone (Horse)
-	28	HOCUS POCUS — Focus (Polydor)
25	29	CRAZY HORSES — Osmonds (MGM)
-	30	THERE'S GONNA BE A SHOWDOWN — Archie Bell & the Drells (Atlantic)

17 February 1973

1	1	BLOCKBUSTER — Sweet (RCA)
2	2	DO YOU WANNA TOUCH ME (OH YEAH) — Gary Glitter (Bell)
3	3	PART OF THE UNION — Strawbs (A&M)
4	4	DANIEL — Elton John (DJM)
5	5	YOU'RE SO VAIN — Carly Simon (Elektra)
13	6	SYLVIA — Focus (Polydor)
9	7	ROLL OVER BEETHOVEN — Electric Light Orchestra (Harvest)
11	8	PAPER PLANE — Status Quo (Vertigo)
9	9	ME AND MRS JONES — Billy Paul (Epic)
7	10	WISHING WELL — Free (Island)
12	11	IF YOU DON'T KNOW ME BY NOW — Harold Melvin & The Blue Notes (CBS)
14	12	SUPERSTITION — Stevie Wonder (Tamla Motown)
6	13	LONG HAIRED LOVER FROM LIVERPOOL — Little Jimmy Osmond (MGM)
16	14	WHISKEY IN THE JAR — Thin Lizzy (Decca)
17	15	PAPA WAS A ROLLING STONE — Temptations (Tamla Motown)
22	16	TAKE ME GIRL, I'M READY — Jr Walker & The All Stars (Tamla Motown)
-	17	LOOKING THRU' THE EYES OF LOVE — Partridge Family (Bell)
23	18	TAKE ME HOME COUNTRY ROADS — Olivia Newton-John (Pye)
15	19	BALL PARK INCIDENT — Wizzard (Harvest)
10	20	THE JEAN GENIE — David Bowie (RCA)
21	21	BIG SEVEN — Judge Dread (Big Shot)
20	22	CAN'T KEEP IT IN — Cat Stevens (Island)
-	23	REELIN' AND ROCKIN' — Chuck Berry (Chess)
28	24	HOCUS POCUS — Focus (Polydor)
19	25	ALWAYS ON MY MIND — Elvis Presley (RCA)
18	26	HI HI HI — Wings (Parlophone)
-	27	HELLO HURRAY — Alice Cooper (Warner Bros)
-	28	BABY I LOVE YOU — Dave Edmunds (Rockfield)
24	29	HELP ME MAKE IT THROUGH THE NIGHT — Gladys Knight & the Pips (Tamla Motown)
27	30	BIG CITY — Dandy Livingstone (Horse)

24 February 1973

3	1	PART OF THE UNION — Strawbs (A&M)
1	2	BLOCKBUSTER — Sweet (RCA)
2	3	DO YOU WANNA TOUCH ME (OH YEAH) — Gary Glitter (Bell)
6	4	SYLVIA — Focus (Polydor)
4	5	DANIEL — Elton John (DJM)
7	6	ROLL OVER BEETHOVEN — Electric Light Orchestra (Harvest)
-	7	CINDY INCIDENTALLY — Faces (Warner Bros)
4	8	WHISKEY IN THE JAR — Thin Lizzy (Decca)
12	9	SUPERSTITION — Stevie Wonder (Tamla Motown)
8	10	PAPER PLANE — Status Quo (Vertigo)
5	11	YOU'RE SO VAIN — Carly Simon (Elektra)
17	12	LOOKING THRU' THE EYES OF LOVE — Partridge Family (Bell)
28	13	BABY I LOVE YOU — Dave Edmunds (Rockfield)
18	14	TAKE ME HOME COUNTRY ROADS — Olivia Newton-John (Pye)
10	15	WISHING WELL — Free (Island)
27	16	HELLO HURRAY — Alice Cooper (Warner Bros)
9	17	ME AND MRS JONES — Billy Paul (Epic)
11	18	IF YOU DON'T KNOW ME BY NOW — Harold Melvin & The Blue Notes (CBS)
24	19	HOCUS POCUS — Focus (Polydor)
13	20	LONG HAIRED LOVER FROM LIVERPOOL — Little Jimmy Osmond (MGM)
16	21	TAKE ME GIRL, I'M READY — Jr Walker & The All Stars (Tamla Motown)
23	22	REELIN' AND ROCKIN' — Chuck Berry (Chess)
15	23	PAPA WAS A ROLLING STONE — Temptations (Tamla Motown)
-	24	DOCTOR MY EYES — Jackson Five (Tamla Motown)
21	25	BIG SEVEN — Judge Dread (Big Shot)
-	26	PINBALL WIZARD/SEE ME FEEL ME — New Seekers (Polydor)
-	27	KILLING ME SOFTLY WITH HIS SONG — Roberta Flack (Atlantic)
19	28	BALL PARK INCIDENT — Wizzard (Harvest)
-	29	WHY CAN'T WE LIVE TOGETHER — Timmy Thomas (Mojo)
-	30	FEEL THE NEED IN ME — Detroit Emeralds (Janus)

Somewhat unexpectedly, the continuing success of Sweet held Gary Glitter from the chart top; unsurprisingly, Blockbuster was the group's biggest-selling single. Meanwhile, as ELO took a classically-fused revival of his *Roll Over Beethoven* into the Top 10, Chuck Berry charted another UK live recording in the form of *Reelin' And Rockin'*. This song had been the B-side of Chuck's 1958 hit *Sweet Little Sixteen*. Thin Lizzy's chart debut *Whiskey In The Jar*, had taken over two months to start selling.

March 1973

3 March 1973

last week	this week	Title / Artist
1	1	PART OF THE UNION — Strawbs (A&M)
2	2	BLOCKBUSTER — Sweet (RCA)
7	3	CINDY INCIDENTALLY — Faces (Warner Bros)
4	4	SYLVIA — Focus (Polydor)
3	5	DO YOU WANNA TOUCH ME (OH YEAH) — Gary Glitter (Bell)
8	6	WHISKEY IN THE JAR — Thin Lizzy (Decca)
13	7	BABY I LOVE YOU — Dave Edmunds (Rockfield)
9	8	SUPERSTITION — Stevie Wonder (Tamla Motown)
5	9	DANIEL — Elton John (DJM)
12	10	LOOKING THRU' THE EYES OF LOVE — Partridge Family (Bell)
6	11	ROLL OVER BEETHOVEN — Electric Light Orchestra (Harvest)
16	12	HELLO HURRAY — Alice Cooper (Warner Bros)
-	13	CUM ON FEEL THE NOIZE — Slade (Polydor)
24	14	DOCTOR MY EYES — Jackson Five (Tamla Motown)
30	15	FEEL THE NEED IN ME — Detroit Emeralds (Janus)
27	16	KILLING ME SOFTLY WITH HIS SONG — Roberta Flack (Atlantic)
14	17	TAKE ME HOME COUNTRY ROADS — Olivia Newton-John (Pye)
21	18	TAKE ME GIRL, I'M READY — Jr Walker & The All Stars (Tamla Motown)
-	19	GONNA MAKE YOU AN OFFER YOU CAN'T REFUSE — Jimmy Helms (Cube)
19	20	HOCUS POCUS — Focus (Polydor)
10	21	PAPER PLANE — Status Quo (Vertigo)
26	22	PINBALL WIZARD/SEE ME FEEL ME — New Seekers (Polydor)
11	23	YOU'RE SO VAIN — Carly Simon (Elektra)
-	24	STEP INTO A DREAM — White Plains (Deram)
29	25	WHY CAN'T WE LIVE TOGETHER — Timmy Thomas (Mojo)
20	26	LONG HAIRED LOVER FROM LIVERPOOL — Little Jimmy Osmond (MGM)
15	27	WISHING WELL — Free (Island)
25	28	BIG SEVEN — Judge Dread (Big Shot)
22	29	REELIN' AND ROCKIN' — Chuck Berry (Chess)
17	30	ME AND MRS JONES — Billy Paul (Epic)

10 March 1973

last week	this week	Title / Artist
13	1	CUM ON FEEL THE NOIZE — Slade (Polydor)
3	2	CINDY INCIDENTALLY — Faces (Warner Bros)
1	3	PART OF THE UNION — Strawbs (A&M)
15	4	FEEL THE NEED IN ME — Detroit Emeralds (Janus)
4	5	SYLVIA — Focus (Polydor)
-	6	20TH CENTURY BOY — T. Rex (T. Rex)
12	7	HELLO HURRAY — Alice Cooper (Warner Bros)
2	8	BLOCKBUSTER — Sweet (RCA)
16	9	KILLING ME SOFTLY WITH HIS SONG — Roberta Flack (Atlantic)
6	10	WHISKEY IN THE JAR — Thin Lizzy (Decca)
7	11	BABY I LOVE YOU — Dave Edmunds (Rockfield)
14	12	DOCTOR MY EYES — Jackson Five (Tamla Motown)
19	13	GONNA MAKE YOU AN OFFER YOU CAN'T REFUSE — Jimmy Helms (Cube)
10	14	LOOKING THRU' THE EYES OF LOVE — Partridge Family (Bell)
5	15	DO YOU WANNA TOUCH ME (OH YEAH) — Gary Glitter (Bell)
8	16	SUPERSTITION — Stevie Wonder (Tamla Motown)
22	17	PINBALL WIZARD/SEE ME FEEL ME — New Seekers (Polydor)
-	18	THE TWELFTH OF NEVER — Donny Osmond (MGM)
9	19	DANIEL — Elton John (DJM)
11	20	ROLL OVER BEETHOVEN — Electric Light Orchestra (Harvest)
20	21	HOCUS POCUS — Focus (Polydor)
25	22	WHY CAN'T WE LIVE TOGETHER — Timmy Thomas (Mojo)
24	23	STEP INTO A DREAM — White Plains (Deram)
17	24	TAKE ME HOME COUNTRY ROADS — Olivia Newton-John (Pye)
23	25	YOU'RE SO VAIN — Carly Simon (Elektra)
26	26	LONG HAIRED LOVER FROM LIVERPOOL — Little Jimmy Osmond (MGM)
-	27	THAT'S WHEN THE MUSIC TAKES ME — Neil Sedaka (RCA)
28	28	HEART OF STONE — Kenny (RAK)
18	29	TAKE ME GIRL, I'M READY — Jr Walker & The All Stars (Tamla Motown)
-	30	NICE ONE CYRIL — Cockerel Chorus (Youngblood)

17 March 1973

last week	this week	Title / Artist
1	1	CUM ON FEEL THE NOIZE — Slade (Polydor)
6	2	20TH CENTURY BOY — T. Rex (T. Rex)
18	3	THE TWELFTH OF NEVER — Donny Osmond (MGM)
7	4	HELLO HURRAY — Alice Cooper (Warner Bros)
4	5	FEEL THE NEED IN ME — Detroit Emeralds (Janus)
9	6	KILLING ME SOFTLY WITH HIS SONG — Roberta Flack (Atlantic)
2	7	CINDY INCIDENTALLY — Faces (Warner Bros)
13	8	GONNA MAKE YOU AN OFFER YOU CAN'T REFUSE — Jimmy Helms (Cube)
11	9	BABY I LOVE YOU — Dave Edmunds (Rockfield)
3	10	PART OF THE UNION — Strawbs (A&M)
5	11	SYLVIA — Focus (Polydor)
12	12	DOCTOR MY EYES — Jackson Five (Tamla Motown)
10	13	WHISKEY IN THE JAR — Thin Lizzy (Decca)
8	14	BLOCKBUSTER — Sweet (RCA)
17	15	PINBALL WIZARD/SEE ME FEEL ME — New Seekers (Polydor)
30	16	NICE ONE CYRIL — Cockerel Chorus (Youngblood)
14	17	LOOKING THRU' THE EYES OF LOVE — Partridge Family (Bell)
22	18	WHY CAN'T WE LIVE TOGETHER — Timmy Thomas (Mojo)
-	19	POWER TO ALL OUR FRIENDS — Cliff Richard (EMI)
27	20	THAT'S WHEN THE MUSIC TAKES ME — Neil Sedaka (RCA)
28	21	HEART OF STONE — Kenny (RAK)
-	22	NEVER NEVER NEVER — Shirley Bassey (United Artists)
15	23	DO YOU WANNA TOUCH ME (OH YEAH) — Gary Glitter (Bell)
-	24	THE LOOK OF LOVE — Gladys Knight & the Pips (Tamla Motown)
16	25	SUPERSTITION — Stevie Wonder (Tamla Motown)
-	26	GET DOWN — Gilbert O'Sullivan (MAM)
-	27	PYJAMARAMA — Roxy Music (Island)
24	28	TAKE ME HOME COUNTRY ROADS — Olivia Newton-John (Pye)
23	29	STEP INTO A DREAM — White Plains (Deram)
-	30	LOVE TRAIN — O'Jays (CBS)

24 March 1973

last week	this week	Title / Artist
1	1	CUM ON FEEL THE NOIZE — Slade (Polydor)
2	2	20TH CENTURY BOY — T. Rex (T. Rex)
3	3	THE TWELFTH OF NEVER — Donny Osmond (MGM)
5	4	FEEL THE NEED IN ME — Detroit Emeralds (Janus)
6	5	KILLING ME SOFTLY WITH HIS SONG — Roberta Flack (Atlantic)
4	6	HELLO HURRAY — Alice Cooper (Warner Bros)
8	7	GONNA MAKE YOU AN OFFER YOU CAN'T REFUSE — Jimmy Helms (Cube)
19	8	POWER TO ALL OUR FRIENDS — Cliff Richard (EMI)
7	9	CINDY INCIDENTALLY — Faces (Warner Bros)
18	10	WHY CAN'T WE LIVE TOGETHER — Timmy Thomas (Mojo)
26	11	GET DOWN — Gilbert O'Sullivan (MAM)
9	12	BABY I LOVE YOU — Dave Edmunds (Rockfield)
13	13	PINBALL WIZARD/SEE ME FEEL ME — New Seekers (Polydor)
12	14	DOCTOR MY EYES — Jackson Five (Tamla Motown)
11	15	SYLVIA — Focus (Polydor)
16	16	NICE ONE CYRIL — Cockerel Chorus (Youngblood)
21	17	HEART OF STONE — Kenny (RAK)
22	18	NEVER NEVER NEVER — Shirley Bassey (United Artists)
10	19	PART OF THE UNION — Strawbs (A&M)
29	20	LOVE TRAIN — O'Jays (CBS)
27	21	PYJAMARAMA — Roxy Music (Island)
-	22	TIE A YELLOW RIBBON ROUND THE OLE OAK TREE — Dawn (Bell)
17	23	LOOKING THRU' THE EYES OF LOVE — Partridge Family (Bell)
13	24	WHISKEY IN THE JAR — Thin Lizzy (Decca)
20	25	THAT'S WHEN THE MUSIC TAKES ME — Neil Sedaka (RCA)
24	26	THE LOOK OF LOVE — Gladys Knight & the Pips (Tamla Motown)
14	27	BLOCKBUSTER — Sweet (RCA)
-	28	I'M A CLOWN/SOME KIND OF A SUMMER — David Cassidy (Bell)
29	29	STEP INTO A DREAM — White Plains (Deram)
23	30	DO YOU WANNA TOUCH ME (OH YEAH) — Gary Glitter (Bell)

Slade got their biggest sales year underway with *Cum On Feel The Noize*, which vaulted to the top in its second week; this was to be a pattern for the group's next few singles, which were now exceeding the sales of those of T. Rex - *20th Century Boy* was held at Number Two by *Cum On*. This was also the finest UK hour for Slade's label-mates, the Dutch instrumental band Focus, who scored simultaneous Top 20 hits with *Sylvia* and their earlier *Hocus Pocus* (which featured a yodelling solo!).

31 March 1973

last week	this week	Title
3	1	THE TWELFTH OF NEVER — Donny Osmond (MGM)
1	2	CUM ON FEEL THE NOIZE — Slade (Polydor)
8	3	POWER TO ALL OUR FRIENDS — Cliff Richard (EMI)
2	4	20TH CENTURY BOY — T. Rex (T. Rex)
11	5	GET DOWN — Gilbert O'Sullivan (MAM)
4	6	FEEL THE NEED IN ME — Detroit Emeralds (Janus)
5	7	KILLING ME SOFTLY WITH HIS SONG — Roberta Flack (Atlantic)
22	8	TIE A YELLOW RIBBON ROUND THE OLE OAK TREE — Dawn (Bell)
7	9	GONNA MAKE YOU AN OFFER YOU CAN'T REFUSE — Jimmy Helms (Cube)
18	10	NEVER NEVER NEVER — Shirley Bassey (United Artists)
17	11	HEART OF STONE — Kenny (RAK)
20	12	LOVE TRAIN — O'Jays (CBS)
6	13	HELLO HURRAY — Alice Cooper (Warner Bros)
28	14	I'M A CLOWN/SOME KIND OF A SUMMER — David Cassidy (Bell)
10	15	WHY CAN'T WE LIVE TOGETHER — Timmy Thomas (Mojo)
16	16	NICE ONE CYRIL — Cockerel Chorus (Youngblood)
9	17	CINDY INCIDENTALLY — Faces (Warner Bros)
21	17	PYJAMARAMA — Roxy Music (Island)
12	19	BABY I LOVE YOU — Dave Edmunds (Rockfield)
26	20	THE LOOK OF LOVE — Gladys Knight & the Pips (Tamla Motown)
-	21	TWEEDLE DEE — Jimmy Osmond (MGM)
25	22	THAT'S WHEN THE MUSIC TAKES ME — Neil Sedaka (RCA)
12	23	PINBALL WIZARD/SEE ME FEEL ME — New Seekers (Polydor)
14	24	DOCTOR MY EYES — Jackson Five (Tamla Motown)
29	25	STEP INTO A DREAM — White Plains (Deram)
15	26	SYLVIA — Focus (Polydor)
-	27	AMANDA — Stuart Gillies (A&M)
27	28	BLOCKBUSTER — Sweet (RCA)
-	29	CALIFORNIA SAGA/CALIFORNIA — Beach Boys (Reprise)
-	30	CRAZY — Mud (RAK)

7 April 1973

last week	this week	Title
1	1	THE TWELFTH OF NEVER — Donny Osmond (MGM)
5	2	GET DOWN — Gilbert O'Sullivan (MAM)
3	3	POWER TO ALL OUR FRIENDS — Cliff Richard (EMI)
8	4	TIE A YELLOW RIBBON ROUND THE OLE OAK TREE — Dawn (Bell)
14	5	I'M A CLOWN/SOME KIND OF A SUMMER — David Cassidy (Bell)
2	6	CUM ON FEEL THE NOIZE — Slade (Polydor)
4	7	20TH CENTURY BOY — T. Rex (T. Rex)
7	8	KILLING ME SOFTLY WITH HIS SONG — Roberta Flack (Atlantic)
11	9	HEART OF STONE — Kenny (RAK)
6	10	FEEL THE NEED IN ME — Detroit Emeralds (Janus)
12	11	LOVE TRAIN — O'Jays (CBS)
10	12	NEVER NEVER NEVER — Shirley Bassey (United Artists)
15	13	WHY CAN'T WE LIVE TOGETHER — Timmy Thomas (Mojo)
17	13	PYJAMARAMA — Roxy Music (Island)
9	15	GONNA MAKE YOU AN OFFER YOU CAN'T REFUSE — Jimmy Helms (Cube)
16	16	NICE ONE CYRIL — Cockerel Chorus (Youngblood)
21	17	TWEEDLE DEE — Jimmy Osmond (MGM)
30	18	CRAZY — Mud (RAK)
13	19	HELLO HURRAY — Alice Cooper (Warner Bros)
20	20	THE LOOK OF LOVE — Gladys Knight & the Pips (Tamla Motown)
-	21	HELLO! HELLO! I'M BACK AGAIN — Gary Glitter (Bell)
-	22	ALL BECAUSE OF YOU — Geordie (EMI)
22	23	THAT'S WHEN THE MUSIC TAKES ME — Neil Sedaka (RCA)
-	24	DUELLING BANJOS — Deliverance Soundtrack /Eric Weissberg & Steve Mandel (Warner Bros)
-	25	GOD GAVE ROCK AND ROLL TO YOU — Argent (Epic)
-	26	MY LOVE — Paul McCartney & Wings (EMI)
17	27	CINDY INCIDENTALLY — Faces (Warner Bros)
-	28	BY THE DEVIL — Blue Mink (EMI)
29	29	CALIFORNIA SAGA/CALIFORNIA — Beach Boys (Reprise)
-	30	BREAK UP TO MAKE UP — Stylistics (Avco)

14 April 1973

last week	this week	Title
2	1	GET DOWN — Gilbert O'Sullivan (MAM)
4	2	TIE A YELLOW RIBBON ROUND THE OLE OAK TREE — Dawn (Bell)
5	3	I'M A CLOWN/SOME KIND OF A SUMMER — David Cassidy (Bell)
1	4	THE TWELFTH OF NEVER — Donny Osmond (MGM)
3	5	POWER TO ALL OUR FRIENDS — Cliff Richard (EMI)
17	6	TWEEDLE DEE — Jimmy Osmond (MGM)
21	7	HELLO! HELLO! I'M BACK AGAIN — Gary Glitter (Bell)
12	8	NEVER NEVER NEVER — Shirley Bassey (United Artists)
11	9	LOVE TRAIN — O'Jays (CBS)
13	10	PYJAMARAMA — Roxy Music (Island)
8	11	KILLING ME SOFTLY WITH HIS SONG — Roberta Flack (Atlantic)
9	12	HEART OF STONE — Kenny (RAK)
6	13	CUM ON FEEL THE NOIZE — Slade (Polydor)
18	14	CRAZY — Mud (RAK)
10	15	FEEL THE NEED IN ME — Detroit Emeralds (Janus)
13	16	WHY CAN'T WE LIVE TOGETHER — Timmy Thomas (Mojo)
22	17	ALL BECAUSE OF YOU — Geordie (EMI)
7	18	20TH CENTURY BOY — T. Rex (T. Rex)
-	19	DRIVE-IN SATURDAY — David Bowie (RCA)
-	20	AMANDA — Stuart Gillies (A&M)
20	21	THE LOOK OF LOVE — Gladys Knight & the Pips (Tamla Motown)
24	21	DUELLING BANJOS — Deliverance Soundtrack /Eric Weissberg & Steve Mandel (Warner Bros)
19	23	HELLO HURRAY — Alice Cooper (Warner Bros)
26	24	MY LOVE — Paul McCartney & Wings (EMI)
25	25	GOD GAVE ROCK AND ROLL TO YOU — Argent (Epic)
16	26	NICE ONE CYRIL — Cockerel Chorus (Youngblood)
28	27	BY THE DEVIL — Blue Mink (EMI)
-	28	GOOD GRIEF CHRISTINA — Chicory Tip (CBS)
23	29	THAT'S WHEN THE MUSIC TAKES ME — Neil Sedaka (RCA)
15	30	GONNA MAKE YOU AN OFFER YOU CAN'T REFUSE — Jimmy Helms (Cube)

21 April 1973

last week	this week	Title
2	1	TIE A YELLOW RIBBON ROUND THE OLE OAK TREE — Dawn (Bell)
1	2	GET DOWN — Gilbert O'Sullivan (MAM)
7	3	HELLO! HELLO! I'M BACK AGAIN — Gary Glitter (Bell)
3	4	I'M A CLOWN/SOME KIND OF A SUMMER — David Cassidy (Bell)
6	5	TWEEDLE DEE — Jimmy Osmond (MGM)
10	6	PYJAMARAMA — Roxy Music (Island)
9	7	LOVE TRAIN — O'Jays (CBS)
4	8	THE TWELFTH OF NEVER — Donny Osmond (MGM)
8	9	NEVER NEVER NEVER — Shirley Bassey (United Artists)
19	10	DRIVE-IN SATURDAY — David Bowie (RCA)
5	11	POWER TO ALL OUR FRIENDS — Cliff Richard (EMI)
17	12	ALL BECAUSE OF YOU — Geordie (EMI)
14	13	CRAZY — Mud (RAK)
24	14	MY LOVE — Paul McCartney & Wings (EMI)
12	15	HEART OF STONE — Kenny (RAK)
-	16	BROTHER LOUIE — Hot Chocolate (RAK)
20	17	AMANDA — Stuart Gillies (A&M)
16	18	WHY CAN'T WE LIVE TOGETHER — Timmy Thomas (Mojo)
11	19	KILLING ME SOFTLY WITH HIS SONG — Roberta Flack (Atlantic)
15	20	FEEL THE NEED IN ME — Detroit Emeralds (Janus)
21	21	DUELLING BANJOS — Deliverance Soundtrack /Eric Weissberg & Steve Mandel (Warner Bros)
28	22	GOOD GRIEF CHRISTINA — Chicory Tip (CBS)
25	23	GOD GAVE ROCK AND ROLL TO YOU — Argent (Epic)
-	24	BIG EIGHT — Judge Dread (Big Shot)
-	25	MEAN GIRL — Status Quo (Pye)
23	26	HELLO HURRAY — Alice Cooper (Warner Bros)
-	27	THE RIGHT THING TO DO — Carly Simon (Elektra)
-	28	HEY MAMA — Joe Brown (Ammo)
-	29	GIVING IT ALL AWAY — Roger Daltrey (Track)
13	30	CUM ON FEEL THE NOIZE — Slade (Polydor)

Cliff Richard's *Power To All Our Friends* was his second (and last) shot at representing the UK in the Eurovision Song Contest. It came third, and third was as high as it managed to chart, in contrast to the international No.1 success of *Congratulations*. Cliff was the only artist to have previously charted in the UK with the much-recorded *The Twelfth Of Never*, but Donny Osmond's new revival now eclipsed that version, while his brother Jimmy also followed up with a revived 1950s song.

April – May 1973

28 April 1973

last week	this week	Title
1	1	TIE A YELLOW RIBBON ROUND THE OLE OAK TREE — Dawn (Bell)
3	2	HELLO! HELLO! I'M BACK AGAIN — Gary Glitter (Bell)
2	3	GET DOWN — Gilbert O'Sullivan (MAM)
4	4	I'M A CLOWN/SOME KIND OF A SUMMER — David Cassidy (Bell)
10	5	DRIVE-IN SATURDAY — David Bowie (RCA)
5	6	TWEEDLE DEE — Jimmy Osmond (MGM)
6	7	PYJAMARAMA — Roxy Music (Island)
7	8	LOVE TRAIN — O'Jays (CBS)
12	9	ALL BECAUSE OF YOU — Geordie (EMI)
9	10	NEVER NEVER NEVER — Shirley Bassey (United Artists)
14	11	MY LOVE — Paul McCartney & Wings (EMI)
8	12	THE TWELFTH OF NEVER — Donny Osmond (MGM)
16	13	BROTHER LOUIE — Hot Chocolate (RAK)
17	13	AMANDA — Stuart Gillies (A&M)
11	15	POWER TO ALL OUR FRIENDS — Cliff Richard (EMI)
-	16	SEE MY BABY JIVE — Wizzard (Harvest)
13	17	CRAZY — Mud (RAK)
29	18	GIVING IT ALL AWAY — Roger Daltrey (Track)
21	19	DUELLING BANJOS — Deliverance Soundtrack /Eric Weissberg & Steve Mandel (Warner Bros)
22	20	GOOD GRIEF CHRISTINA — Chicory Tip (CBS)
24	21	BIG EIGHT — Judge Dread (Big Shot)
15	22	HEART OF STONE — Kenny (RAK)
23	23	GOD GAVE ROCK AND ROLL TO YOU — Argent (Epic)
25	24	MEAN GIRL — Status Quo (Pye)
-	25	COULD IT BE I'M FALLING IN LOVE — Detroit Spinners (Atlantic)
-	26	NO MORE MR NICE GUY — Alice Cooper (Warner Bros)
20	27	FEEL THE NEED IN ME — Detroit Emeralds (Janus)
19	28	KILLING ME SOFTLY WITH HIS SONG — Roberta Flack (Atlantic)
18	29	WHY CAN'T WE LIVE TOGETHER — Timmy Thomas (Mojo)
-	30	AND I LOVE HER SO — Perry Como (RCA)

5 May 1973

last week	this week	Title
1	1	TIE A YELLOW RIBBON ROUND THE OLE OAK TREE — Dawn (Bell)
2	2	HELLO! HELLO! I'M BACK AGAIN — Gary Glitter (Bell)
3	3	GET DOWN — Gilbert O'Sullivan (MAM)
5	4	DRIVE-IN SATURDAY — David Bowie (RCA)
4	5	I'M A CLOWN/SOME KIND OF A SUMMER — David Cassidy (Bell)
9	6	ALL BECAUSE OF YOU — Geordie (EMI)
11	7	MY LOVE — Paul McCartney & Wings (EMI)
6	8	TWEEDLE DEE — Jimmy Osmond (MGM)
13	9	BROTHER LOUIE — Hot Chocolate (RAK)
16	10	SEE MY BABY JIVE — Wizzard (Harvest)
18	11	GIVING IT ALL AWAY — Roger Daltrey (Track)
10	12	NEVER NEVER NEVER — Shirley Bassey (United Artists)
16	13	NO MORE MR NICE GUY — Alice Cooper (Warner Bros)
7	14	PYJAMARAMA — Roxy Music (Island)
12	15	THE TWELFTH OF NEVER — Donny Osmond (MGM)
8	16	LOVE TRAIN — O'Jays (CBS)
20	17	GOOD GRIEF CHRISTINA — Chicory Tip (CBS)
17	18	CRAZY — Mud (RAK)
13	19	AMANDA — Stuart Gillies (A&M)
15	20	POWER TO ALL OUR FRIENDS — Cliff Richard (EMI)
21	20	BIG EIGHT — Judge Dread (Big Shot)
23	22	GOD GAVE ROCK AND ROLL TO YOU — Argent (Epic)
19	23	DUELLING BANJOS — Deliverance Soundtrack /Eric Weissberg & Steve Mandel (Warner Bros)
25	24	COULD IT BE I'M FALLING IN LOVE — Detroit Spinners (Atlantic)
30	25	AND I LOVE HER SO — Perry Como (RCA)
-	26	WONDERFUL DREAM — Ann-Marie David (Epic)
29	27	MEAN GIRL — Status Quo (Pye)
24	28	WHY CAN'T WE LIVE TOGETHER — Timmy Thomas (Mojo)
27	29	FEEL THE NEED IN ME — Detroit Emeralds (Janus)
-	30	HELL-RAISER — Sweet (RCA)

12 May 1973

last week	this week	Title
1	1	TIE A YELLOW RIBBON ROUND THE OLE OAK TREE — Dawn (Bell)
2	2	HELLO! HELLO! I'M BACK AGAIN — Gary Glitter (Bell)
30	3	HELL-RAISER — Sweet (RCA)
10	4	SEE MY BABY JIVE — Wizzard (Harvest)
4	5	DRIVE-IN SATURDAY — David Bowie (RCA)
9	6	BROTHER LOUIE — Hot Chocolate (RAK)
11	7	GIVING IT ALL AWAY — Roger Daltrey (Track)
7	8	MY LOVE — Paul McCartney & Wings (EMI)
13	9	NO MORE MR NICE GUY — Alice Cooper (Warner Bros)
6	10	ALL BECAUSE OF YOU — Geordie (EMI)
3	11	GET DOWN — Gilbert O'Sullivan (MAM)
8	12	TWEEDLE DEE — Jimmy Osmond (MGM)
25	13	AND I LOVE HER SO — Perry Como (RCA)
5	14	I'M A CLOWN/SOME KIND OF A SUMMER — David Cassidy (Bell)
17	15	GOOD GRIEF CHRISTINA — Chicory Tip (CBS)
20	15	BIG EIGHT — Judge Dread (Big Shot)
12	17	NEVER NEVER NEVER — Shirley Bassey (United Artists)
28	18	MEAN GIRL — Status Quo (Pye)
26	19	WONDERFUL DREAM — Ann-Marie David (Epic)
18	20	CRAZY — Mud (RAK)
24	21	COULD IT BE I'M FALLING IN LOVE — Detroit Spinners (Atlantic)
14	22	PYJAMARAMA — Roxy Music (Island)
-	23	ALSO SPRACH ZARATHUSTRA (2001) — Deodato (Creed Taylor)
16	24	LOVE TRAIN — O'Jays (CBS)
19	25	AMANDA — Stuart Gillies (A&M)
-	26	ONE AND ONE IS ONE — Medicine Head (Polydor)
-	27	BROKENDOWN ANGEL — Nazareth (Mooncrest)
15	28	THE TWELFTH OF NEVER — Donny Osmond (MGM)
29	29	FEEL THE NEED IN ME — Detroit Emeralds (Janus)
22	30	GOD GAVE ROCK AND ROLL TO YOU — Argent (Epic)

19 May 1973

last week	this week	Title
1	1	TIE A YELLOW RIBBON ROUND THE OLE OAK TREE — Dawn (Bell)
3	2	HELL-RAISER — Sweet (RCA)
4	3	SEE MY BABY JIVE — Wizzard (Harvest)
2	4	HELLO! HELLO! I'M BACK AGAIN — Gary Glitter (Bell)
6	5	BROTHER LOUIE — Hot Chocolate (RAK)
7	6	GIVING IT ALL AWAY — Roger Daltrey (Track)
13	7	AND I LOVE HER SO — Perry Como (RCA)
8	8	MY LOVE — Paul McCartney & Wings (EMI)
5	9	DRIVE-IN SATURDAY — David Bowie (RCA)
9	10	NO MORE MR NICE GUY — Alice Cooper (Warner Bros)
23	11	ALSO SPRACH ZARATHUSTRA (2001) — Deodato (Creed Taylor)
26	12	ONE AND ONE IS ONE — Medicine Head (Polydor)
19	13	WONDERFUL DREAM — Ann-Marie David (Epic)
10	14	ALL BECAUSE OF YOU — Geordie (EMI)
27	15	BROKENDOWN ANGEL — Nazareth (Mooncrest)
18	16	MEAN GIRL — Status Quo (Pye)
21	17	COULD IT BE I'M FALLING IN LOVE — Detroit Spinners (Atlantic)
11	18	GET DOWN — Gilbert O'Sullivan (MAM)
15	19	BIG EIGHT — Judge Dread (Big Shot)
15	20	GOOD GRIEF CHRISTINA — Chicory Tip (CBS)
-	21	WALK ON THE WILD SIDE — Lou Reed (RCA)
12	22	TWEEDLE DEE — Jimmy Osmond (MGM)
17	23	NEVER NEVER NEVER — Shirley Bassey (United Artists)
-	24	YOU WANT IT YOU GOT IT — Detroit Emeralds (Westbound)
14	25	I'M A CLOWN/SOME KIND OF A SUMMER — David Cassidy (Bell)
20	26	CRAZY — Mud (RAK)
-	27	THE RIGHT THING TO DO — Carly Simon (Elektra)
25	28	LOVE TRAIN — O'Jays (CBS)
-	29	CAN THE CAN — Suzi Quatro (RAK)
-	30	I'VE BEEN DRINKING — Jeff Beck/Rod Stewart (RAK)

Dawn, with Tony Orlando still individually uncredited, had their all-time biggest hit in *Tie A Yellow Ribbon Round The Ole Oak Tree*, which was the year's top single internationally. In the UK, it prevented both Gary Glitter and Sweet from regaining No.1 status, and eventually sold over 960,000 copies. Meanwhile, *Giving It All Away* was Roger Daltrey's first (and biggest) solo success , and Luxembourg's Eurovision winner by Ann-Marie David replaced Cliff Richard's short-lived UK entry in the chart.

26 May 1973

last week	this week	title
3	1	SEE MY BABY JIVE — Wizzard (Harvest)
1	2	TIE A YELLOW RIBBON ROUND THE OLE OAK TREE — Dawn (Bell)
2	3	HELL-RAISER — Sweet (RCA)
7	4	AND I LOVE HER SO — Perry Como (RCA)
12	5	ONE AND ONE IS ONE — Medicine Head (Polydor)
6	6	GIVING IT ALL AWAY — Roger Daltrey (Track)
11	7	ALSO SPRACH ZARATHUSTRA (2001) — Deodato (Creed Taylor)
5	8	BROTHER LOUIE — Hot Chocolate (RAK)
15	9	BROKENDOWN ANGEL — Nazareth (Mooncrest)
4	10	HELLO! HELLO! I'M BACK AGAIN — Gary Glitter (Bell)
29	11	CAN THE CAN — Suzi Quatro (RAK)
17	12	COULD IT BE I'M FALLING IN LOVE — Detroit Spinners (Atlantic)
9	13	DRIVE-IN SATURDAY — David Bowie (RCA)
8	14	MY LOVE — Paul McCartney & Wings (EMI)
13	15	WONDERFUL DREAM — Ann-Marie David (Epic)
10	16	NO MORE MR NICE GUY — Alice Cooper (Warner Bros)
-	17	YOU ARE THE SUNSHINE OF MY LIFE — Stevie Wonder (Tamla Motown)
21	18	WALK ON THE WILD SIDE — Lou Reed (RCA)
16	19	MEAN GIRL — Status Quo (Pye)
20	20	GOOD GRIEF CHRISTINA — Chicory Tip (CBS)
24	21	YOU WANT IT YOU GOT IT — Detroit Emeralds (Westbound)
14	22	ALL BECAUSE OF YOU — Geordie (EMI)
-	23	WALKING IN THE RAIN — Partridge Family (Bell)
18	24	GET DOWN — Gilbert O'Sullivan (MAM)
30	25	I'VE BEEN DRINKING — Jeff Beck/Rod Stewart (RAK)
-	26	RUBBER BULLETS — 10 c.c. (UK)
23	27	NEVER NEVER NEVER — Shirley Bassey (United Artists)
19	28	BIG EIGHT — Judge Dread (Big Shot)
-	29	STUCK IN THE MIDDLE WITH YOU — Stealers Wheel (A&M)
-	30	HELP IT ALONG/TOMORROW RISING — Cliff Richard (EMI)

2 June 1973

1	1	SEE MY BABY JIVE — Wizzard (Harvest)
11	2	CAN THE CAN — Suzi Quatro (RAK)
5	3	ONE AND ONE IS ONE — Medicine Head (Polydor)
4	4	AND I LOVE HER SO — Perry Como (RCA)
2	5	TIE A YELLOW RIBBON ROUND THE OLE OAK TREE — Dawn (Bell)
3	6	HELL-RAISER — Sweet (RCA)
9	7	BROKENDOWN ANGEL — Nazareth (Mooncrest)
17	8	YOU ARE THE SUNSHINE OF MY LIFE — Stevie Wonder (Tamla Motown)
7	9	ALSO SPRACH ZARATHUSTRA (2001) — Deodato (Creed Taylor)
18	10	WALK ON THE WILD SIDE — Lou Reed (RCA)
12	11	COULD IT BE I'M FALLING IN LOVE — Detroit Spinners (Atlantic)
6	12	GIVING IT ALL AWAY — Roger Daltrey (Track)
10	13	HELLO! HELLO! I'M BACK AGAIN — Gary Glitter (Bell)
26	14	RUBBER BULLETS — 10 c.c. (UK)
8	15	BROTHER LOUIE — Hot Chocolate (RAK)
23	16	WALKING IN THE RAIN — Partridge Family (Bell)
21	17	YOU WANT IT YOU GOT IT — Detroit Emeralds (Westbound)
15	18	WONDERFUL DREAM — Ann-Marie David (Epic)
14	19	MY LOVE — Paul McCartney & Wings (EMI)
13	20	DRIVE-IN SATURDAY — David Bowie (RCA)
29	21	STUCK IN THE MIDDLE WITH YOU — Stealers Wheel (A&M)
19	22	MEAN GIRL — Status Quo (Pye)
21	23	ARMED AND EXTREMELY DANGEROUS — First Choice (Bell)
20	24	GOOD GRIEF CHRISTINA — Chicory Tip (CBS)
16	25	NO MORE MR NICE GUY — Alice Cooper (Warner Bros)
-	26	ALBATROSS — Fleetwood Mac (CBS)
25	27	I'VE BEEN DRINKING — Jeff Beck/Rod Stewart (RAK)
-	28	POLK SALAD ANNIE — Elvis Presley (RCA)
-	29	NEITHER ONE OF US — Gladys Knight and the Pips (Tamla Motown)
-	30	FRANKENSTEIN — Edgar Winter Group (Epic)

9 June 1973

2	1	CAN THE CAN — Suzi Quatro (RAK)
1	2	SEE MY BABY JIVE — Wizzard (Harvest)
3	3	ONE AND ONE IS ONE — Medicine Head (Polydor)
4	4	AND I LOVE HER SO — Perry Como (RCA)
8	5	YOU ARE THE SUNSHINE OF MY LIFE — Stevie Wonder (Tamla Motown)
14	6	RUBBER BULLETS — 10 c.c. (UK)
5	7	TIE A YELLOW RIBBON ROUND THE OLE OAK TREE — Dawn (Bell)
6	8	HELL-RAISER — Sweet (RCA)
7	9	BROKENDOWN ANGEL — Nazareth (Mooncrest)
10	10	WALK ON THE WILD SIDE — Lou Reed (RCA)
21	11	STUCK IN THE MIDDLE WITH YOU — Stealers Wheel (A&M)
9	12	ALSO SPRACH ZARATHUSTRA (2001) — Deodato (Creed Taylor)
26	13	ALBATROSS — Fleetwood Mac (CBS)
17	14	YOU WANT IT YOU GOT IT — Detroit Emeralds (Westbound)
11	15	COULD IT BE I'M FALLING IN LOVE — Detroit Spinners (Atlantic)
16	16	WALKING IN THE RAIN — Partridge Family (Bell)
-	17	GIVE ME LOVE (GIVE ME PEACE ON EARTH) — George Harrison (Apple)
23	18	ARMED AND EXTREMELY DANGEROUS — First Choice (Bell)
30	19	FRANKENSTEIN — Edgar Winter Group (Epic)
12	20	GIVING IT ALL AWAY — Roger Daltrey (Track)
-	21	SWEET ILLUSION — Junior Campbell (Deram)
15	22	BROTHER LOUIE — Hot Chocolate (RAK)
28	23	POLK SALAD ANNIE — Elvis Presley (RCA)
-	24	WELCOME HOME — Peters & Lee (Philips)
20	25	DRIVE-IN SATURDAY — David Bowie (RCA)
13	26	HELLO! HELLO! I'M BACK AGAIN — Gary Glitter (Bell)
18	27	WONDERFUL DREAM — Ann-Marie David (Epic)
-	28	LIVE AND LET DIE — Wings (EMI)
-	29	SNOOPY VERSUS THE RED BARON — Hot Shots (Mooncrest)
22	30	MEAN GIRL — Status Quo (Pye)

16 June 1973

1	1	CAN THE CAN — Suzi Quatro (RAK)
3	2	ONE AND ONE IS ONE — Medicine Head (Polydor)
2	3	SEE MY BABY JIVE — Wizzard (Harvest)
6	4	RUBBER BULLETS — 10 c.c. (UK)
4	5	AND I LOVE HER SO — Perry Como (RCA)
5	6	YOU ARE THE SUNSHINE OF MY LIFE — Stevie Wonder (Tamla Motown)
13	7	ALBATROSS — Fleetwood Mac (CBS)
11	8	STUCK IN THE MIDDLE WITH YOU — Stealers Wheel (A&M)
17	9	GIVE ME LOVE (GIVE ME PEACE ON EARTH) — George Harrison (Apple)
16	10	WALKING IN THE RAIN — Partridge Family (Bell)
7	11	TIE A YELLOW RIBBON ROUND THE OLE OAK TREE — Dawn (Bell)
18	12	ARMED AND EXTREMELY DANGEROUS — First Choice (Bell)
10	13	WALK ON THE WILD SIDE — Lou Reed (RCA)
21	14	SWEET ILLUSION — Junior Campbell (Deram)
-	15	THE GROOVER — T. Rex (EMI)
9	16	BROKENDOWN ANGEL — Nazareth (Mooncrest)
28	17	LIVE AND LET DIE — Wings (EMI)
8	18	HELL-RAISER — Sweet (RCA)
24	19	WELCOME HOME — Peters & Lee (Philips)
29	20	SNOOPY VERSUS THE RED BARON — Hot Shots (Mooncrest)
19	21	FRANKENSTEIN — Edgar Winter Group (Epic)
15	22	COULD IT BE I'M FALLING IN LOVE — Detroit Spinners (Atlantic)
12	23	ALSO SPRACH ZARATHUSTRA (2001) — Deodato (Creed Taylor)
-	24	I'M GONNA LOVE YOU JUST A LITTLE BIT MORE BABY — Barry White (Pye)
-	25	STANDING ON THE INSIDE — Neil Sedaka (MGM)
-	26	NEITHER ONE OF US — Gladys Knight & the Pips (Tamla Motown)
14	27	YOU WANT IT YOU GOT IT — Detroit Emeralds (Westbound)
23	28	POLK SALAD ANNIE — Elvis Presley (RCA)
-	29	BORN TO BE WITH YOU — Dave Edmunds (Rockfield)
-	30	HALLELUJAH DAY — Jackson Five (Tamla Motown)

Former John Peel protegees Medicine Head scored their biggest success in post-Peel commercial mode, but they couldn't outsell pint-sized UK-domiciled American rocker Suzi Quatro's Number One debut. Fleetwood Mac's 1969 chart-topper *Albatross* was reissued to become almost as big a success all over again, while the Jeff Beck/Rod Stewart hit was also a reissued oldie - from 1968's Jeff Beck Group days, it had originally been the B-side of the chartmaking *Love Is Blue*.

June – July 1973

23 June 1973

last	this		
1	1	CAN THE CAN	Suzi Quatro (RAK)
4	2	RUBBER BULLETS	10 c.c. (UK)
7	3	ALBATROSS	Fleetwood Mac (CBS)
2	4	ONE AND ONE IS ONE	Medicine Head (Polydor)
15	5	THE GROOVER	T. Rex (EMI)
8	6	STUCK IN THE MIDDLE WITH YOU	Stealers Wheel (A&M)
3	7	SEE MY BABY JIVE	Wizzard (Harvest)
5	8	AND I LOVE HER SO	Perry Como (RCA)
9	9	GIVE ME LOVE (GIVE ME PEACE ON EARTH)	George Harrison (Apple)
10	10	WALKING IN THE RAIN	Partridge Family (Bell)
20	11	SNOOPY VERSUS THE RED BARON	Hot Shots (Mooncrest)
6	12	YOU ARE THE SUNSHINE OF MY LIFE	Stevie Wonder (Tamla Motown)
19	13	WELCOME HOME	Peters & Lee (Philips)
17	14	LIVE AND LET DIE	Wings (EMI)
12	15	ARMED AND EXTREMELY DANGEROUS	First Choice (Bell)
11	16	TIE A YELLOW RIBBON ROUND THE OLE OAK TREE	Dawn (Bell)
14	17	SWEET ILLUSION	Junior Campbell (Deram)
13	18	WALK ON THE WILD SIDE	Lou Reed (RCA)
30	19	HALLELUJAH DAY	Jackson Five (Tamla Motown)
24	20	I'M GONNA LOVE YOU JUST A	Barry White (Pye)
21	21	FRANKENSTEIN	Edgar Winter Group (Epic)
16	22	BROKENDOWN ANGEL	Nazareth (Mooncrest)
-	23	CAN YOU DO IT	Geordie (EMI)
25	24	STANDING ON THE INSIDE	Neil Sedaka (MGM)
29	25	BORN TO BE WITH YOU	Dave Edmunds (Rockfield)
-	26	TAKE ME TO THE MARDI GRAS	Paul Simon (CBS)
27	27	YOU WANT IT YOU GOT IT	Detroit Emeralds (Westbound)
28	28	POLK SALAD ANNIE	Elvis Presley (RCA)
-	29	ROCK-A-DOODLE-DOO	Linda Lewis (Raft)
26	30	NEITHER ONE OF US	Gladys Knight & the Pips (Tamla Motown)

30 June 1973

last	this		
2	1	RUBBER BULLETS	10 c.c. (UK)
3	2	ALBATROSS	Fleetwood Mac (CBS)
5	3	THE GROOVER	T. Rex (EMI)
13	4	WELCOME HOME	Peters & Lee (Philips)
11	5	SNOOPY VERSUS THE RED BARON	Hot Shots (Mooncrest)
1	6	CAN THE CAN	Suzi Quatro (RAK)
-	7	SKWEEZE ME, PLEEZE ME	Slade (Polydor)
6	8	STUCK IN THE MIDDLE WITH YOU	Stealers Wheel (A&M)
9	9	GIVE ME LOVE (GIVE ME PEACE ON EARTH)	George Harrison (Apple)
14	10	LIVE AND LET DIE	Wings (EMI)
8	11	AND I LOVE HER SO	Perry Como (RCA)
4	12	ONE AND ONE IS ONE	Medicine Head (Polydor)
7	13	SEE MY BABY JIVE	Wizzard (Harvest)
25	14	BORN TO BE WITH YOU	Dave Edmunds (Rockfield)
10	15	WALKING IN THE RAIN	Partridge Family (Bell)
17	16	SWEET ILLUSION	Junior Campbell (Deram)
26	17	TAKE ME TO THE MARDI GRAS	Paul Simon (CBS)
-	18	LIFE ON MARS	David Bowie (RCA)
16	19	TIE A YELLOW RIBBON ROUND THE OLE OAK TREE	Dawn (Bell)
23	20	CAN YOU DO IT	Geordie (EMI)
15	21	ARMED AND EXTREMELY DANGEROUS	First Choice (Bell)
12	22	YOU ARE THE SUNSHINE OF MY LIFE	Stevie Wonder (Tamla Motown)
20	23	I'M GONNA LOVE YOU JUST A	Barry White (Pye)
29	24	ROCK-A-DOODLE-DOO	Linda Lewis (Raft)
-	25	HONALOOCHIE BOOGIE	Mott The Hoople (CBS)
19	26	HALLELUJAH DAY	Jackson Five (Tamla Motown)
24	27	STANDING ON THE INSIDE	Neil Sedaka (MGM)
21	28	FRANKENSTEIN	Edgar Winter Group (Epic)
22	29	BROKENDOWN ANGEL	Nazareth (Mooncrest)
27	30	YOU WANT IT YOU GOT IT	Detroit Emeralds (Westbound)

7 July 1973

last	this		
7	1	SKWEEZE ME, PLEEZE ME	Slade (Polydor)
4	2	WELCOME HOME	Peters & Lee (Philips)
1	3	RUBBER BULLETS	10 c.c. (UK)
2	4	ALBATROSS	Fleetwood Mac (CBS)
5	5	SNOOPY VERSUS THE RED BARON	Hot Shots (Mooncrest)
14	6	BORN TO BE WITH YOU	Dave Edmunds (Rockfield)
3	7	THE GROOVER	T. Rex (EMI)
9	8	GIVE ME LOVE (GIVE ME PEACE ON EARTH)	George Harrison (Apple)
18	9	LIFE ON MARS	David Bowie (RCA)
10	10	LIVE AND LET DIE	Wings (EMI)
17	11	TAKE ME TO THE MARDI GRAS	Paul Simon (CBS)
8	12	STUCK IN THE MIDDLE WITH YOU	Stealers Wheel (A&M)
6	13	CAN THE CAN	Suzi Quatro (RAK)
24	14	ROCK-A-DOODLE-DOO	Linda Lewis (Raft)
20	15	CAN YOU DO IT	Geordie (EMI)
11	16	AND I LOVE HER SO	Perry Como (RCA)
23	17	I'M GONNA LOVE YOU JUST A LITTLE BIT MORE BABY	Barry White (Pye)
25	18	HONALOOCHIE BOOGIE	Mott The Hoople (CBS)
26	19	HALLELUJAH DAY	Jackson Five (Tamla Motown)
16	20	SWEET ILLUSION	Junior Campbell (Deram)
12	21	ONE AND ONE IS ONE	Medicine Head (Polydor)
15	22	WALKING IN THE RAIN	Partridge Family (Bell)
-	23	STEP BY STEP	Joe Simon (Mojo)
-	24	FINDERS KEEPERS	Chairmen Of The Board (Invictus)
22	25	YOU ARE THE SUNSHINE OF MY LIFE	Stevie Wonder (Tamla Motown)
19	26	TIE A YELLOW RIBBON ROUND THE OLE OAK TREE	Dawn (Bell)
-	27	RANDY	Blue Mink (EMI)
21	28	ARMED AND EXTREMELY DANGEROUS	First Choice (Bell)
-	29	PILLOW TALK	Sylvia (London)
13	30	SEE MY BABY JIVE	Wizzard (Harvest)

14 July 1973

last	this		
1	1	SKWEEZE ME, PLEEZE ME	Slade (Polydor)
2	2	WELCOME HOME	Peters & Lee (Philips)
9	3	LIFE ON MARS	David Bowie (RCA)
3	4	RUBBER BULLETS	10 c.c. (UK)
6	5	BORN TO BE WITH YOU	Dave Edmunds (Rockfield)
4	6	ALBATROSS	Fleetwood Mac (CBS)
10	7	LIVE AND LET DIE	Wings (EMI)
11	8	TAKE ME TO THE MARDI GRAS	Paul Simon (CBS)
5	9	SNOOPY VERSUS THE RED BARON	Hot Shots (Mooncrest)
8	10	GIVE ME LOVE (GIVE ME PEACE ON EARTH)	George Harrison (Apple)
18	11	HONALOOCHIE BOOGIE	Mott The Hoople (CBS)
14	12	ROCK-A-DOODLE-DOO	Linda Lewis (Raft)
7	13	THE GROOVER	T. Rex (EMI)
23	14	STEP BY STEP	Joe Simon (Mojo)
24	15	FINDERS KEEPERS	Chairmen Of The Board (Invictus)
12	16	STUCK IN THE MIDDLE WITH YOU	Stealers Wheel (A&M)
27	17	RANDY	Blue Mink (EMI)
16	18	AND I LOVE HER SO	Perry Como (RCA)
-	19	SATURDAY NIGHT'S ALRIGHT FOR FIGHTING	Elton John (DJM)
29	20	PILLOW TALK	Sylvia (London)
26	21	TIE A YELLOW RIBBON ROUND THE OLE OAK TREE	Dawn (Bell)
-	22	ALRIGHT ALRIGHT ALRIGHT	Mungo Jerry (Dawn)
19	23	HALLELUJAH DAY	Jackson Five (Tamla Motown)
20	24	SWEET ILLUSION	Junior Campbell (Deram)
-	25	GOIN' HOME	Osmonds (MGM)
-	26	FREE ELECTRIC BAND	Albert Hammond (Mums)
17	27	I'M GONNA LOVE YOU JUST A LITTLE BIT MORE BABY	Barry White (Pye)
21	28	ONE AND ONE IS ONE	Medicine Head (Polydor)
13	29	CAN THE CAN	Suzi Quatro (RAK)
-	30	TAKE ME HOME	Junior Walker & the All Stars (Tamla Motown)

The Hot Shots' reggae styling of the former Royal Guardsmen novelty *Snoopy Versus The Red Baron*, masterminded by Jonathan King, was one of 1973's odder hit revivals. The Partridge Family and Dave Edmunds were also scoring with updates of old songs, while Mungo Jerry's hit was an Anglicization of a former French hit. Paul Simon's *Take Me To The Mardi Gras* was a substitute for his current US hit *Kodachrome* (the B-side here), due to the BBC's refusal to play a song containing a commercial name.

July – August 1973

last week	this	21 July 1973
2	1	WELCOME HOME — Peters & Lee (Philips)
1	2	SKWEEZE ME, PLEEZE ME — Slade (Polydor)
3	3	LIFE ON MARS — David Bowie (RCA)
19	4	SATURDAY NIGHT'S ALRIGHT FOR FIGHTING — Elton John (DJM)
5	5	BORN TO BE WITH YOU — Dave Edmunds (Rockfield)
22	6	ALRIGHT ALRIGHT ALRIGHT — Mungo Jerry (Dawn)
-	7	I'M THE LEADER OF THE GANG — Gary Glitter (Bell)
25	8	GOIN' HOME — Osmonds (MGM)
8	9	TAKE ME TO THE MARDI GRAS — Paul Simon (CBS)
17	10	RANDY — Blue Mink (EMI)
9	11	SNOOPY VERSUS THE RED BARON — Hot Shots (Mooncrest)
14	12	STEP BY STEP — Joe Simon (Mojo)
4	13	RUBBER BULLETS — 10 c.c. (UK)
20	14	PILLOW TALK — Sylvia (London)
6	15	ALBATROSS — Fleetwood Mac (CBS)
12	16	ROCK-A-DOODLE-DOO — Linda Lewis (Raft)
11	17	HONALOOCHIE BOOGIE — Mott The Hoople (CBS)
7	18	LIVE AND LET DIE — Wings (EMI)
15	19	FINDERS KEEPERS — Chairmen Of The Board (Invictus)
10	20	GIVE ME LOVE (GIVE ME PEACE ON EARTH) — George Harrison (Apple)
-	21	HYPNOSIS — Mud (RAK)
26	22	FREE ELECTRIC BAND — Albert Hammond (Mums)
18	23	AND I LOVE HER SO — Perry Como (RCA)
-	24	GAYE — Clifford T Ward (Charisma)
11	25	CAN YOU DO IT — Geordie (EMI)
21	26	TIE A YELLOW RIBBON ROUND THE OLE OAK TREE — Dawn (Bell)
-	27	TOUCH ME IN THE MORNING — Diana Ross (Tamla Motown)
-	28	SPANISH EYES — Al Martino (Capitol)
-	29	I SAW THE LIGHT — Todd Rundgren (Bearsville)
-	30	YESTERDAY ONCE MORE — Carpenters (A&M)

		28 July 1973
1	1	WELCOME HOME — Peters & Lee (Philips)
7	2	I'M THE LEADER OF THE GANG — Gary Glitter (Bell)
6	3	ALRIGHT ALRIGHT ALRIGHT — Mungo Jerry (Dawn)
3	4	LIFE ON MARS — David Bowie (RCA)
8	5	GOIN' HOME — Osmonds (MGM)
2	6	SKWEEZE ME, PLEEZE ME — Slade (Polydor)
4	7	SATURDAY NIGHT'S ALRIGHT FOR FIGHTING — Elton John (DJM)
24	8	GAYE — Clifford T Ward (Charisma)
10	9	RANDY — Blue Mink (EMI)
14	10	PILLOW TALK — Sylvia (London)
9	11	TAKE ME TO THE MARDI GRAS — Paul Simon (CBS)
5	12	BORN TO BE WITH YOU — Dave Edmunds (Rockfield)
12	13	STEP BY STEP — Joe Simon (Mojo)
11	14	SNOOPY VERSUS THE RED BARON — Hot Shots (Mooncrest)
30	15	YESTERDAY ONCE MORE — Carpenters (A&M)
27	16	TOUCH ME IN THE MORNING — Diana Ross (Tamla Motown)
17	17	BAD BAD BOY — Nazareth (Mooncrest)
21	18	HYPNOSIS — Mud (RAK)
22	19	FREE ELECTRIC BAND — Albert Hammond (Mums)
13	20	RUBBER BULLETS — 10 c.c. (UK)
28	21	SPANISH EYES — Al Martino (Capitol)
19	22	FINDERS KEEPERS — Chairmen Of The Board (Invictus)
26	23	TIE A YELLOW RIBBON ROUND THE OLE OAK TREE — Dawn (Bell)
15	24	ALBATROSS — Fleetwood Mac (CBS)
- 25		48 CRASH — Suzi Quatro (RAK)
18	26	LIVE AND LET DIE — Wings (EMI)
17	27	HONALOOCHIE BOOGIE — Mott The Hoople (CBS)
16	28	ROCK-A-DOODLE-DOO — Linda Lewis (Raft)
20	29	GIVE ME LOVE (GIVE ME PEACE ON EARTH) — George Harrison (Apple)
25	30	CAN YOU DO IT — Geordie (EMI)

		4 August 1973
2	1	I'M THE LEADER OF THE GANG — Gary Glitter (Bell)
3	2	ALRIGHT ALRIGHT ALRIGHT — Mungo Jerry (Dawn)
1	3	WELCOME HOME — Peters & Lee (Philips)
4	4	LIFE ON MARS — David Bowie (RCA)
5	5	GOIN' HOME — Osmonds (MGM)
7	6	SATURDAY NIGHT'S ALRIGHT FOR FIGHTING — Elton John (DJM)
15	7	YESTERDAY ONCE MORE — Carpenters (A&M)
8	8	GAYE — Clifford T Ward (Charisma)
25	9	48 CRASH — Suzi Quatro (RAK)
9	10	RANDY — Blue Mink (EMI)
6	11	SKWEEZE ME, PLEEZE ME — Slade (Polydor)
21	12	SPANISH EYES — Al Martino (Capitol)
16	13	TOUCH ME IN THE MORNING — Diana Ross (Tamla Motown)
17	14	BAD BAD BOY — Nazareth (Mooncrest)
10	15	PILLOW TALK — Sylvia (London)
12	16	BORN TO BE WITH YOU — Dave Edmunds (Rockfield)
18	17	HYPNOSIS — Mud (RAK)
11	18	TAKE ME TO THE MARDI GRAS — Paul Simon (CBS)
-	19	YING TONG SONG — Goons (Decca)
-	20	YOU CAN DO MAGIC — Limmie & the Family Cookin' (Avco)
13	21	STEP BY STEP — Joe Simon (Mojo)
14	22	SNOOPY VERSUS THE RED BARON — Hot Shots (Mooncrest)
19	23	FREE ELECTRIC BAND — Albert Hammond (Mums)
22	24	FINDERS KEEPERS — Chairmen Of The Board (Invictus)
-	25	ALL RIGHT NOW — Free (Island)
-	26	LIKE SISTER LIKE BROTHER — Drifters (Bell)
-	27	I'M DOIN' FINE NOW — New York City (RCA)
24	28	ALBATROSS — Fleetwood Mac (CBS)
20	29	RUBBER BULLETS — 10 c.c. (UK)
-	30	SUMMER (THE FIRST TIME) — Bobby Goldsboro (United Artists)

		11 August 1973
1	1	I'M THE LEADER OF THE GANG — Gary Glitter (Bell)
2	2	ALRIGHT ALRIGHT ALRIGHT — Mungo Jerry (Dawn)
3	3	WELCOME HOME — Peters & Lee (Philips)
7	4	YESTERDAY ONCE MORE — Carpenters (A&M)
9	5	48 CRASH — Suzi Quatro (RAK)
5	6	GOIN' HOME — Osmonds (MGM)
4	7	LIFE ON MARS — David Bowie (RCA)
12	8	SPANISH EYES — Al Martino (Capitol)
14	9	BAD BAD BOY — Nazareth (Mooncrest)
13	10	TOUCH ME IN THE MORNING — Diana Ross (Tamla Motown)
19	11	YING TONG SONG — Goons (Decca)
20	12	YOU CAN DO MAGIC — Limmie & the Family Cookin' (Avco)
10	13	RANDY — Blue Mink (EMI)
8	14	GAYE — Clifford T Ward (Charisma)
6	15	SATURDAY NIGHT'S ALRIGHT FOR FIGHTING — Elton John (DJM)
25	16	ALL RIGHT NOW — Free (Island)
17	17	HYPNOSIS — Mud (RAK)
23	18	FREE ELECTRIC BAND — Albert Hammond (Mums)
23	19	PILLOW TALK — Sylvia (London)
30	20	SUMMER (THE FIRST TIME) — Bobby Goldsboro (United Artists)
-	21	RISING SUN — Medicine Head (Polydor)
11	22	SKWEEZE ME, PLEEZE ME — Slade (Polydor)
26	23	LIKE SISTER LIKE BROTHER — Drifters (Bell)
27	24	I'M DOIN' FINE NOW — New York City (RCA)
-	25	SMARTY PANTS — First Choice (Bell)
-	26	DANCING ON A SATURDAY NIGHT — Barry Blue (Bell)
16	27	BORN TO BE WITH YOU — Dave Edmunds (Rockfield)
-	28	I'M FREE — Roger Daltrey with the London Symphony Orchestra (Ode)
-	29	LIVE AND LET DIE — Wings (EMI)
18	30	TAKE ME TO THE MARDI GRAS — Paul Simon (CBS)

East End pub-singing duo Peters & Lee, discovered by television, confounded all prevailing musical trends with their chart-toppinbg success, while former schoolteacher Clifford T Ward also brought a gentler touch to the Top 10 with *Gaye*. Three more reissues of oldies - Al Martino's *Spanish Eyes* (1966), the Goons' *Ying Tong Song* (1956) and Free's *All Right Now* (1970) made the Top 20. *Free Electric Band* was the sole UK success for expatriot Albert Hammond, formerly of 1969 hit group Family Dogg.

August – September 1973

last week	this week	18 August 1973
1	1	I'M THE LEADER OF THE GANG — Gary Glitter (Bell)
4	2	YESTERDAY ONCE MORE — Carpenters (A&M)
5	3	48 CRASH — Suzi Quatro (RAK)
3	4	WELCOME HOME — Peters & Lee (Philips)
2	5	ALRIGHT ALRIGHT ALRIGHT — Mungo Jerry (Dawn)
8	6	SPANISH EYES — Al Martino (Capitol)
12	7	YOU CAN DO MAGIC — Limmie & the Family Cookin' (Avco)
6	8	GOIN' HOME — Osmonds (MGM)
9	9	BAD BAD BOY — Nazareth (Mooncrest)
10	10	TOUCH ME IN THE MORNING — Diana Ross (Tamla Motown)
11	11	YING TONG SONG — Goons (Decca)
7	12	LIFE ON MARS — David Bowie (RCA)
26	13	DANCING ON A SATURDAY NIGHT — Barry Blue (Bell)
16	14	ALL RIGHT NOW — Free (Island)
28	15	I'M FREE — Roger Daltrey with the London Symphony Orchestra (Ode)
25	16	SMARTY PANTS — First Choice (Bell)
21	17	RISING SUN — Medicine Head (Polydor)
20	18	SUMMER (THE FIRST TIME) — Bobby Goldsboro (United Artists)
24	19	I'M DOIN' FINE NOW — New York City (RCA)
14	20	GAYE — Clifford T Ward (Charisma)
23	21	LIKE SISTER LIKE BROTHER — Drifters (Bell)
18	22	FREE ELECTRIC BAND — Albert Hammond (Mums)
17	23	HYPNOSIS — Mud (RAK)
13	24	RANDY — Blue Mink (EMI)
-	25	YOUNG LOVE — Donny Osmond (MGM)
-	26	SAY, HAS ANYBODY SEEN MY SWEET GYPSY ROSE — Dawn (Bell)
19	27	PILLOW TALK — Sylvia (London)
-	28	FOOL — Elvis Presley (RCA)
22	29	SKWEEZE ME, PLEEZE ME — Slade (Polydor)
15	30	SATURDAY NIGHT'S ALRIGHT FOR FIGHTING — Elton John (DJM)

last	this	25 August 1973
1	1	I'M THE LEADER OF THE GANG — Gary Glitter (Bell)
2	2	YESTERDAY ONCE MORE — Carpenters (A&M)
13	3	DANCING ON A SATURDAY NIGHT — Barry Blue (Bell)
7	4	YOU CAN DO MAGIC — Limmie & the Family Cookin' (Avco)
4	5	WELCOME HOME — Peters & Lee (Philips)
6	6	SPANISH EYES — Al Martino (Capitol)
3	7	48 CRASH — Suzi Quatro (RAK)
16	8	SMARTY PANTS — First Choice (Bell)
25	9	YOUNG LOVE — Donny Osmond (MGM)
5	10	ALRIGHT ALRIGHT ALRIGHT — Mungo Jerry (Dawn)
17	11	RISING SUN — Medicine Head (Polydor)
10	12	TOUCH ME IN THE MORNING — Diana Ross (Tamla Motown)
11	13	YING TONG SONG — Goons (Decca)
21	14	LIKE SISTER LIKE BROTHER — Drifters (Bell)
9	15	BAD BAD BOY — Nazareth (Mooncrest)
18	16	SUMMER (THE FIRST TIME) — Bobby Goldsboro (United Artists)
15	17	I'M FREE — Roger Daltrey with the London Symphony Orchestra (Ode)
14	18	ALL RIGHT NOW — Free (Island)
8	19	GOIN' HOME — Osmonds (MGM)
19	20	I'M DOIN' FINE NOW — New York City (RCA)
26	21	SAY, HAS ANYBODY SEEN MY SWEET GYPSY ROSE — Dawn (Bell)
12	22	LIFE ON MARS — David Bowie (RCA)
23	23	HYPNOSIS — Mud (RAK)
20	24	GAYE — Clifford T Ward (Charisma)
22	25	FREE ELECTRIC BAND — Albert Hammond (Mums)
24	26	RANDY — Blue Mink (EMI)
-	27	DEAR ELAINE — Roy Wood (Harvest)
-	28	ROCK ON — David Essex (CBS)
-	29	NATURAL HIGH — Bloodstone (Decca)
-	30	I'VE BEEN HURT — Guy Darrell (Santa Ponsa)

last	this	1 September 1973
9	1	YOUNG LOVE — Donny Osmond (MGM)
3	2	DANCING ON A SATURDAY NIGHT — Barry Blue (Bell)
2	3	YESTERDAY ONCE MORE — Carpenters (A&M)
8	4	SMARTY PANTS — First Choice (Bell)
1	5	I'M THE LEADER OF THE GANG — Gary Glitter (Bell)
6	6	SPANISH EYES — Al Martino (Capitol)
4	7	YOU CAN DO MAGIC — Limmie & the Family Cookin' (Avco)
14	8	LIKE SISTER LIKE BROTHER — Drifters (Bell)
11	9	RISING SUN — Medicine Head (Polydor)
5	10	WELCOME HOME — Peters & Lee (Philips)
16	11	SUMMER (THE FIRST TIME) — Bobby Goldsboro (United Artists)
7	12	48 CRASH — Suzi Quatro (RAK)
17	13	I'M FREE — Roger Daltrey with the London Symphony Orchestra (Ode)
12	14	TOUCH ME IN THE MORNING — Diana Ross (Tamla Motown)
10	15	ALRIGHT ALRIGHT ALRIGHT — Mungo Jerry (Dawn)
21	16	SAY, HAS ANYBODY SEEN MY SWEET GYPSY ROSE — Dawn (Bell)
20	17	I'M DOIN' FINE NOW — New York City (RCA)
27	18	DEAR ELAINE — Roy Wood (Harvest)
-	19	ANGEL FINGERS — Wizzard (Harvest)
13	20	YING TONG SONG — Goons (Decca)
-	21	PICK UP THE PIECES — Hudson Ford (A&M)
15	22	BAD BAD BOY — Nazareth (Mooncrest)
-	23	FOOL — Elvis Presley (RCA)
-	24	THE DEAN AND I — 10 c.c. (UK)
28	25	ROCK ON — David Essex (CBS)
22	26	LIFE ON MARS — David Bowie (RCA)
18	27	ALL RIGHT NOW — Free (Island)
-	28	ANGIE — Rolling Stones (Rolling Stones)
-	29	FOR THE GOOD TIMES — Perry Como (RCA)
19	30	GOIN' HOME — Osmonds (MGM)

last	this	8 September 1973
1	1	YOUNG LOVE — Donny Osmond (MGM)
2	2	DANCING ON A SATURDAY NIGHT — Barry Blue (Bell)
7	3	YOU CAN DO MAGIC — Limmie & the Family Cookin' (Avco)
3	4	YESTERDAY ONCE MORE — Carpenters (A&M)
8	5	LIKE SISTER LIKE BROTHER — Drifters (Bell)
19	6	ANGEL FINGERS — Wizzard (Harvest)
6	7	SPANISH EYES — Al Martino (Capitol)
4	8	SMARTY PANTS — First Choice (Bell)
21	9	PICK UP THE PIECES — Hudson Ford (A&M)
11	10	SUMMER (THE FIRST TIME) — Bobby Goldsboro (United Artists)
16	11	SAY, HAS ANYBODY SEEN MY SWEET GYPSY ROSE — Dawn (Bell)
9	12	RISING SUN — Medicine Head (Polydor)
10	13	WELCOME HOME — Peters & Lee (Philips)
25	14	ROCK ON — David Essex (CBS)
28	15	ANGIE — Rolling Stones (Rolling Stones)
13	16	I'M FREE — Roger Daltrey with the London Symphony Orchestra (Ode)
5	17	I'M THE LEADER OF THE GANG — Gary Glitter (Bell)
17	18	I'M DOIN' FINE NOW — New York City (RCA)
-	19	OH NO, NOT MY BABY — Rod Stewart (Mercury)
24	20	THE DEAN AND I — 10 c.c. (UK)
12	21	48 CRASH — Suzi Quatro (RAK)
23	22	FOOL — Elvis Presley (RCA)
18	23	DEAR ELAINE — Roy Wood (Harvest)
14	24	TOUCH ME IN THE MORNING — Diana Ross (Tamla Motown)
-	25	I'VE BEEN HURT — Guy Darrell (Santa Ponsa)
29	26	FOR THE GOOD TIMES — Perry Como (RCA)
-	27	ELECTRIC LADY — Geordie (EMI)
15	28	ALRIGHT ALRIGHT ALRIGHT — Mungo Jerry (Dawn)
27	29	ALL RIGHT NOW — Free (Island)
-	30	I THINK OF YOU — Detroit Emeralds (Westbound)

Donny Osmond became the second artist to take *Young Love* to Number One, 16 years after Tab Hunter. Donny's single far outsold *Goin' Home* by the collective Osmonds. Roy Wood scored twice in the charts, via his own *Dear Elaine* and Wizzard's second consecutive chart-topper *Angel Fingers*. David Essex, also finding cinema fame in *That'll Be The Day*, made his chart debut with *Rock On*, while Elvis Presley's *Fool* was a flip-over of his US Top 20 hit *Steamroller Blues*.

September – October 1973

15 September 1973

last week	this week	Title / Artist
6	1	ANGEL FINGERS — Wizzard (Harvest)
14	2	ROCK ON — David Essex (CBS)
2	3	YOUNG LOVE — Donny Osmond (MGM)
2	4	DANCING ON A SATURDAY NIGHT — Barry Blue (Bell)
15	5	ANGIE — Rolling Stones (Rolling Stones)
9	6	PICK UP THE PIECES — Hudson Ford (A&M)
5	7	LIKE SISTER LIKE BROTHER — Drifters (Bell)
19	8	OH NO, NOT MY BABY — Rod Stewart (Mercury)
4	9	YESTERDAY ONCE MORE — Carpenters (A&M)
7	10	SPANISH EYES — Al Martino (Capitol)
3	11	YOU CAN DO MAGIC — Limmie & the Family Cookin' (Avco)
11	12	SAY, HAS ANYBODY SEEN MY SWEET GYPSY ROSE — Dawn (Bell)
10	13	SUMMER (THE FIRST TIME) — Bobby Goldsboro (United Artists)
20	14	THE DEAN AND I — 10 c.c. (UK)
16	15	I'M FREE — Roger Daltrey with the London Symphony Orchestra (Ode)
12	16	RISING SUN — Medicine Head (Polydor)
8	17	SMARTY PANTS — First Choice (Bell)
22	18	FOOL — Elvis Presley (RCA)
13	19	WELCOME HOME — Peters & Lee (Philips)
-	20	MONSTER MASH — Bobby 'Boris' Pickett & the Crypt Kickers (London)
23	21	DEAR ELAINE — Roy Wood (Harvest)
25	22	I'VE BEEN HURT — Guy Darrell (Santa Ponsa)
-	23	ALL THE WAY FROM MEMPHIS — Mott The Hoople (CBS)
26	24	FOR THE GOOD TIMES — Perry Como (RCA)
-	25	NUTBUSH CITY LIMITS — Ike & Tina Turner (United Artists)
-	26	JOYBRINGER — Manfred Mann Earthband (Vertigo)
18	27	I'M DOIN' FINE NOW — New York City (RCA)
-	28	SKYWRITER — Jackson Five (Tamla Motown)
-	29	OOH BABY — Gilbert O'Sullivan (MAM)
-	30	CAROLINE — Status Quo (Vertigo)

22 September 1973

last week	this week	Title / Artist
2	1	ROCK ON — David Essex (CBS)
5	2	ANGIE — Rolling Stones (Rolling Stones)
1	3	ANGEL FINGERS — Wizzard (Harvest)
8	4	OH NO, NOT MY BABY — Rod Stewart (Mercury)
3	5	YOUNG LOVE — Donny Osmond (MGM)
4	6	DANCING ON A SATURDAY NIGHT — Barry Blue (Bell)
6	7	PICK UP THE PIECES — Hudson Ford (A&M)
10	8	SPANISH EYES — Al Martino (Capitol)
20	9	MONSTER MASH — Bobby 'Boris' Pickett & the Crypt Kickers (London)
7	10	LIKE SISTER LIKE BROTHER — Drifters (Bell)
14	11	THE DEAN AND I — 10 c.c. (UK)
11	12	YOU CAN DO MAGIC — Limmie & the Family Cookin' (Avco)
22	13	I'VE BEEN HURT — Guy Darrell (Santa Ponsa)
18	14	FOOL — Elvis Presley (RCA)
-	15	EYE LEVEL — Simon Park Orchestra (Columbia)
12	16	SAY, HAS ANYBODY SEEN MY SWEET GYPSY ROSE — Dawn (Bell)
25	17	NUTBUSH CITY LIMITS — Ike & Tina Turner (United Artists)
13	18	SUMMER (THE FIRST TIME) — Bobby Goldsboro (United Artists)
-	19	BALLROOM BLITZ — Sweet (RCA)
9	20	YESTERDAY ONCE MORE — Carpenters (A&M)
23	21	ALL THE WAY FROM MEMPHIS — Mott The Hoople (CBS)
29	22	OOH BABY — Gilbert O'Sullivan (MAM)
26	23	JOYBRINGER — Manfred Mann Earthband (Vertigo)
15	24	I'M FREE — Roger Daltrey with the London Symphony Orchestra (Ode)
21	25	DEAR ELAINE — Roy Wood (Harvest)
28	26	SKYWRITER — Jackson Five (Tamla Motown)
16	27	RISING SUN — Medicine Head (Polydor)
24	28	FOR THE GOOD TIMES — Perry Como (RCA)
19	29	WELCOME HOME — Peters & Lee (Philips)
30	30	CAROLINE — Status Quo (Vertigo)

29 September 1973

last week	this week	Title / Artist
19	1	BALLROOM BLITZ — Sweet (RCA)
9	2	MONSTER MASH — Bobby 'Boris' Pickett & the Crypt Kickers (London)
1	3	ROCK ON — David Essex (CBS)
3	4	ANGEL FINGERS — Wizzard (Harvest)
15	5	EYE LEVEL — Simon Park Orchestra (Columbia)
4	6	OH NO, NOT MY BABY — Rod Stewart (Mercury)
2	7	ANGIE — Rolling Stones (Rolling Stones)
21	8	ALL THE WAY FROM MEMPHIS — Mott The Hoople (CBS)
17	9	NUTBUSH CITY LIMITS — Ike & Tina Turner (United Artists)
23	10	JOYBRINGER — Manfred Mann Earthband (Vertigo)
28	11	FOR THE GOOD TIMES — Perry Como (RCA)
7	12	PICK UP THE PIECES — Hudson Ford (A&M)
5	13	YOUNG LOVE — Donny Osmond (MGM)
22	14	OOH BABY — Gilbert O'Sullivan (MAM)
11	15	THE DEAN AND I — 10 c.c. (UK)
13	16	I'VE BEEN HURT — Guy Darrell (Santa Ponsa)
-	17	LAUGHING GNOME — David Bowie (Deram)
6	18	DANCING ON A SATURDAY NIGHT — Barry Blue (Bell)
30	19	CAROLINE — Status Quo (Vertigo)
8	20	SPANISH EYES — Al Martino (Capitol)
16	21	SAY, HAS ANYBODY SEEN MY SWEET GYPSY ROSE — Dawn (Bell)
10	22	LIKE SISTER LIKE BROTHER — Drifters (Bell)
14	23	FOOL — Elvis Presley (RCA)
24	24	I'M FREE — Roger Daltrey with the London Symphony Orchestra (Ode)
18	25	SUMMER (THE FIRST TIME) — Bobby Goldsboro (United Artists)
20	26	YESTERDAY ONCE MORE — Carpenters (A&M)
-	27	LET'S GET IT ON — Marvin Gaye (Tamla Motown)
-	28	SMARTY PANTS — First Choice (Bell)
26	29	SKYWRITER — Jackson Five (Tamla Motown)
29	30	WELCOME HOME — Peters & Lee (Philips)

6 October 1973

last week	this week	Title / Artist
5	1	EYE LEVEL — Simon Park Orchestra (Columbia)
1	2	BALLROOM BLITZ — Sweet (RCA)
2	3	MONSTER MASH — Bobby 'Boris' Pickett & the Crypt Kickers (London)
9	4	NUTBUSH CITY LIMITS — Ike & Tina Turner (United Artists)
4	5	ANGEL FINGERS — Wizzard (Harvest)
10	6	JOYBRINGER — Manfred Mann Earthband (Vertigo)
3	7	ROCK ON — David Essex (CBS)
17	8	LAUGHING GNOME — David Bowie (Deram)
6	9	OH NO, NOT MY BABY — Rod Stewart (Mercury)
19	10	CAROLINE — Status Quo (Vertigo)
11	11	FOR THE GOOD TIMES — Perry Como (RCA)
7	12	ANGIE — Rolling Stones (Rolling Stones)
8	13	ALL THE WAY FROM MEMPHIS — Mott The Hoople (CBS)
16	14	I'VE BEEN HURT — Guy Darrell (Santa Ponsa)
-	15	MY FRIEND STAN — Slade (Polydor)
14	16	OOH BABY — Gilbert O'Sullivan (MAM)
20	17	SPANISH EYES — Al Martino (Capitol)
-	18	GOODBYE YELLOW BRICK ROAD — Elton John (DJM)
-	19	A HARD RAIN'S A-GONNA FALL — Bryan Ferry (Island)
29	20	SKYWRITER — Jackson Five (Tamla Motown)
15	21	THE DEAN AND I — 10 c.c. (UK)
21	22	SAY, HAS ANYBODY SEEN MY SWEET GYPSY ROSE — Dawn (Bell)
13	23	YOUNG LOVE — Donny Osmond (MGM)
12	24	PICK UP THE PIECES — Hudson Ford (A&M)
18	25	DANCING ON A SATURDAY NIGHT — Barry Blue (Bell)
-	26	GHETTO CHILD — Detroit Spinners (Atlantic)
-	27	THAT LADY — Isley Brothers (Epic)
27	28	LET'S GET IT ON — Marvin Gaye (Tamla Motown)
26	29	YESTERDAY ONCE MORE — Carpenters (A&M)
24	30	I'M FREE — Roger Daltrey with the London Symphony Orchestra (Ode)

Bobby 'Boris' Pickett's classic novelty *Monster Mash* had failed to chart in the UK when it was a US Number One in 1962, but made up for the omission 11 years later as the reissue climbed to Two. Likewise, Simon Park's *Eye Level* had not achieved Top 30 status when originally released in 1972, but this bouncy orchestral piece's exposure as the theme to the successful TV detective series *Van Der Valk* pushed it all the way to the top (and an eventual million-plus UK sale) the second time around.

October – November 1973

13 October 1973

LW	TW	Title / Artist (Label)
1	1	EYE LEVEL — Simon Park Orchestra (Columbia)
2	2	BALLROOM BLITZ — Sweet (RCA)
15	3	MY FRIEND STAN — Slade (Polydor)
3	4	MONSTER MASH — Bobby 'Boris' Pickett & the Crypt Kickers (London)
4	5	NUTBUSH CITY LIMITS — Ike & Tina Turner (United Artists)
8	6	LAUGHING GNOME — David Bowie (Deram)
11	7	FOR THE GOOD TIMES — Perry Como (RCA)
6	8	JOYBRINGER — Manfred Mann Earthband (Vertigo)
10	9	CAROLINE — Status Quo (Vertigo)
5	10	ANGEL FINGERS — Wizzard (Harvest)
18	11	GOODBYE YELLOW BRICK ROAD — Elton John (DJM)
9	12	OH NO, NOT MY BABY — Rod Stewart (Mercury)
19	13	A HARD RAIN'S A -GONNA FALL — Bryan Ferry (Island)
7	14	ROCK ON — David Essex (CBS)
16	15	OOH BABY — Gilbert O'Sullivan (MAM)
-	16	PUPPY SONG/DAY DREAMER — David Cassidy (Bell)
13	17	ALL THE WAY FROM MEMPHIS — Mott The Hoople (CBS)
12	18	ANGIE — Rolling Stones (Rolling Stones)
17	19	SPANISH EYES — Al Martino (Capitol)
26	20	GHETTO CHILD — Detroit Spinners (Atlantic)
27	21	THAT LADY — Isley Brothers (Epic)
14	22	I'VE BEEN HURT — Guy Darrell (Santa Ponsa)
-	23	DECK OF CARDS — Max Bygraves (Pye)
22	24	SAY, HAS ANYBODY SEEN MY SWEET GYPSY ROSE — Dawn (Bell)
-	25	SHOW DOWN — Electric Light Orchestra (Harvest)
-	26	KNOCKIN' ON HEAVEN'S DOOR — Bob Dylan (CBS)
20	27	SKYWRITER — Jackson Five (Tamla Motown)
25	28	DANCING ON A SATURDAY NIGHT — Barry Blue (Bell)
28	29	LET'S GET IT ON — Marvin Gaye (Tamla Motown)
-	30	HIGHER GROUND — Stevie Wonder (Tamla Motown)

20 October 1973

LW	TW	Title / Artist (Label)
1	1	EYE LEVEL — Simon Park Orchestra (Columbia)
3	2	MY FRIEND STAN — Slade (Polydor)
5	3	NUTBUSH CITY LIMITS — Ike & Tina Turner (United Artists)
6	4	LAUGHING GNOME — David Bowie (Deram)
2	5	BALLROOM BLITZ — Sweet (RCA)
9	6	CAROLINE — Status Quo (Vertigo)
16	7	PUPPY SONG/DAY DREAMER — David Cassidy (Bell)
4	8	MONSTER MASH — Bobby 'Boris' Pickett & the Crypt Kickers (London)
13	9	A HARD RAIN'S A -GONNA FALL — Bryan Ferry (Island)
11	10	GOODBYE YELLOW BRICK ROAD — Elton John (DJM)
7	11	FOR THE GOOD TIMES — Perry Como (RCA)
8	12	JOYBRINGER — Manfred Mann Earthband (Vertigo)
20	13	GHETTO CHILD — Detroit Spinners (Atlantic)
25	14	SHOW DOWN — Electric Light Orchestra (Harvest)
21	15	THAT LADY — Isley Brothers (Epic)
26	16	KNOCKIN' ON HEAVEN'S DOOR — Bob Dylan (CBS)
12	17	OH NO, NOT MY BABY — Rod Stewart (Mercury)
-	18	5.15/WATER — Who (Track)
10	19	ANGEL FINGERS — Wizzard (Harvest)
24	20	SAY, HAS ANYBODY SEEN MY SWEET GYPSY ROSE — Dawn (Bell)
-	21	SORROW — David Bowie (RCA)
18	22	ANGIE — Rolling Stones (Rolling Stones)
17	23	ALL THE WAY FROM MEMPHIS — Mott The Hoople (CBS)
19	24	SPANISH EYES — Al Martino (Capitol)
14	25	ROCK ON — David Essex (CBS)
-	26	THIS FLIGHT TONIGHT — Nazareth (Mooncrest)
-	27	LET THERE BE PEACE ON EARTH — Michael Ward (Philips)
30	28	HIGHER GROUND — Stevie Wonder (Tamla Motown)
15	29	OOH BABY — Gilbert O'Sullivan (MAM)
22	30	I'VE BEEN HURT — Guy Darrell (Santa Ponsa)

27 October 1973

LW	TW	Title / Artist (Label)
1	1	EYE LEVEL — Simon Park Orchestra (Columbia)
7	2	PUPPY SONG/DAY DREAMER — David Cassidy (Bell)
2	3	MY FRIEND STAN — Slade (Polydor)
3	4	NUTBUSH CITY LIMITS — Ike & Tina Turner (United Artists)
21	5	SORROW — David Bowie (RCA)
10	6	GOODBYE YELLOW BRICK ROAD — Elton John (DJM)
9	7	A HARD RAIN'S A -GONNA FALL — Bryan Ferry (Island)
6	8	CAROLINE — Status Quo (Vertigo)
4	9	LAUGHING GNOME — David Bowie (Deram)
8	10	MONSTER MASH — Bobby 'Boris' Pickett & the Crypt Kickers (London)
11	11	FOR THE GOOD TIMES — Perry Como (RCA)
5	12	BALLROOM BLITZ — Sweet (RCA)
14	13	SHOW DOWN — Electric Light Orchestra (Harvest)
13	14	GHETTO CHILD — Detroit Spinners (Atlantic)
16	15	KNOCKIN' ON HEAVEN'S DOOR — Bob Dylan (CBS)
15	16	THAT LADY — Isley Brothers (Epic)
18	17	5.15/WATER — Who (Track)
12	18	JOYBRINGER — Manfred Mann Earthband (Vertigo)
-	19	TOP OF THE WORLD — Carpenters (A&M)
26	20	THIS FLIGHT TONIGHT — Nazareth (Mooncrest)
-	21	DECK OF CARDS — Max Bygraves (Pye)
-	22	WON'T SOMEBODY DANCE WITH ME — Lynsey De Paul (MAM)
-	23	LET ME IN — Osmonds (MGM)
-	24	LET'S GET IT ON — Marvin Gaye (Tamla Motown)
24	25	SPANISH EYES — Al Martino (Capitol)
-	26	THE DAY THAT CURLY BILLY SHOT CRAZY SAM McGEE — Hollies (Polydor)
30	27	I'VE BEEN HURT — Guy Darrell (Santa Ponsa)
-	28	PHOTOGRAPH — Ringo Starr (Apple)
20	29	SAY, HAS ANYBODY SEEN MY SWEET GYPSY ROSE — Dawn (Bell)
22	30	ANGIE — Rolling Stones (Rolling Stones)

3 November 1973

LW	TW	Title / Artist (Label)
2	1	PUPPY SONG/DAY DREAMER — David Cassidy (Bell)
5	2	SORROW — David Bowie (RCA)
1	3	EYE LEVEL — Simon Park Orchestra (Columbia)
6	4	GOODBYE YELLOW BRICK ROAD — Elton John (DJM)
8	5	CAROLINE — Status Quo (Vertigo)
3	6	MY FRIEND STAN — Slade (Polydor)
11	7	FOR THE GOOD TIMES — Perry Como (RCA)
7	8	A HARD RAIN'S A -GONNA FALL — Bryan Ferry (Island)
9	9	LAUGHING GNOME — David Bowie (Deram)
4	10	NUTBUSH CITY LIMITS — Ike & Tina Turner (United Artists)
13	11	SHOW DOWN — Electric Light Orchestra (Harvest)
14	12	GHETTO CHILD — Detroit Spinners (Atlantic)
19	13	TOP OF THE WORLD — Carpenters (A&M)
15	14	KNOCKIN' ON HEAVEN'S DOOR — Bob Dylan (CBS)
16	15	THAT LADY — Isley Brothers (Epic)
23	16	LET ME IN — Osmonds (MGM)
21	17	DECK OF CARDS — Max Bygraves (Pye)
20	18	THIS FLIGHT TONIGHT — Nazareth (Mooncrest)
17	19	5.15/WATER — Who (Track)
10	20	MONSTER MASH — Bobby 'Boris' Pickett & the Crypt Kickers (London)
12	21	BALLROOM BLITZ — Sweet (RCA)
22	22	WON'T SOMEBODY DANCE WITH ME — Lynsey De Paul (MAM)
-	23	DYNA-MITE — Mud (RAK)
-	24	LET THERE BE PEACE ON EARTH — Michael Ward (Philips)
-	25	DAYTONA DEMON — Suzi Quatro (RAK)
26	26	THE DAY THAT CURLY BILLY SHOT CRAZY SAM McGEE — Hollies (Polydor)
-	27	DREAMBOAT — Limmie & the Family Cookin' (Avco)
18	28	JOYBRINGER — Manfred Mann Earthband (Vertigo)
25	29	SPANISH EYES — Al Martino (Capitol)
-	30	DECK OF CARDS — Wink Martindale (Dot)

Eye Level sold in sufficient numbers to prevent Slade garnering another chart-topper with *My Friend Stan*. David Bowie's *The Laughing Gnome* was another formerly unsuccesful reissue: a blatant novelty in his Anthony Newley-clone mode, its chart presence was the cause of much embarrassment and annoyance in the Bowie camp, since it was in competition with his revival of the Merseys' *Sorrow*. In the event, the latter peaked two places higher. Meanwhile, *Deck Of Cards* (see 1959/1963) was back again!

November – December 1973

10 November 1973

last	this		
1	1	PUPPY SONG/DAY DREAMER	David Cassidy (Bell)
2	2	SORROW	David Bowie (RCA)
16	3	LET ME IN	Osmonds (MGM)
3	4	EYE LEVEL	Simon Park Orchestra (Columbia)
4	5	GOODBYE YELLOW BRICK ROAD	Elton John (DJM)
5	6	CAROLINE	Status Quo (Vertigo)
13	7	TOP OF THE WORLD	Carpenters (A&M)
12	8	GHETTO CHILD	Detroit Spinners (Atlantic)
7	9	FOR THE GOOD TIMES	Perry Como (RCA)
8	10	A HARD RAIN'S A -GONNA FALL	Bryan Ferry (Island)
17	11	DECK OF CARDS	Max Bygraves (Pye)
18	12	THIS FLIGHT TONIGHT	Nazareth (Mooncrest)
14	13	KNOCKIN' ON HEAVEN'S DOOR	Bob Dylan (CBS)
11	14	SHOW DOWN	Electric Light Orchestra (Harvest)
6	15	MY FRIEND STAN	Slade (Polydor)
23	16	DYNA-MITE	Mud (RAK)
9	17	LAUGHING GNOME	David Bowie (Deram)
22	18	WON'T SOMEBODY DANCE WITH ME	Lynsey De Paul (MAM)
10	19	NUTBUSH CITY LIMITS	Ike & Tina Turner (United Artists)
-	20	PHOTOGRAPH	Ringo Starr (Apple)
19	21	5.15/WATER	Who (Track)
15	22	THAT LADY	Isley Brothers (Epic)
25	23	DAYTONA DEMON	Suzi Quatro (RAK)
-	24	DO YOU WANNA DANCE	Barry Blue (Bell)
26	25	THE DAY THAT CURLY BILLY SHOT CRAZY SAM McGEE	Hollies (Polydor)
-	26	HELEN WHEELS	Paul McCartney & Wings (Apple)
24	27	LET THERE BE PEACE ON EARTH	Michael Ward (Philips)
-	28	WHEN I FALL IN LOVE	Donny Osmond (MGM)
30	29	DECK OF CARDS	Wink Martindale (Dot)
-	30	KEEP ON TRUCKIN'	Eddie Kendricks (Tamla Motown)

17 November 1973

last	this		
3	1	LET ME IN	Osmonds (MGM)
1	2	PUPPY SONG/DAY DREAMER	David Cassidy (Bell)
2	3	SORROW	David Bowie (RCA)
7	4	TOP OF THE WORLD	Carpenters (A&M)
16	5	DYNA-MITE	Mud (RAK)
20	6	PHOTOGRAPH	Ringo Starr (Apple)
28	7	WHEN I FALL IN LOVE	Donny Osmond (MGM)
6	8	CAROLINE	Status Quo (Vertigo)
5	9	GOODBYE YELLOW BRICK ROAD	Elton John (DJM)
-	10	I LOVE YOU LOVE ME LOVE	Gary Glitter (Bell)
9	11	FOR THE GOOD TIMES	Perry Como (RCA)
4	12	EYE LEVEL	Simon Park Orchestra (Columbia)
12	13	THIS FLIGHT TONIGHT	Nazareth (Mooncrest)
8	14	GHETTO CHILD	Detroit Spinners (Atlantic)
18	15	WON'T SOMEBODY DANCE WITH ME	Lynsey De Paul (MAM)
14	16	SHOW DOWN	Electric Light Orchestra (Harvest)
24	17	DO YOU WANNA DANCE	Barry Blue (Bell)
23	18	DAYTONA DEMON	Suzi Quatro (RAK)
11	19	DECK OF CARDS	Max Bygraves (Pye)
13	20	KNOCKIN' ON HEAVEN'S DOOR	Bob Dylan (CBS)
10	21	A HARD RAIN'S A -GONNA FALL	Bryan Ferry (Island)
-	22	LAMPLIGHT	David Essex (CBS)
26	23	HELEN WHEELS	Paul McCartney & Wings (Apple)
15	24	MY FRIEND STAN	Slade (Polydor)
-	25	WHY OH WHY OH WHY	Gilbert O'Sullivan (MAM)
-	26	PAPER ROSES	Marie Osmond (MGM)
30	27	KEEP ON TRUCKIN'	Eddie Kendricks (Tamla Motown)
21	28	5.15/WATER	Who (Track)
27	29	LET THERE BE PEACE ON EARTH	Michael Ward (Philips)
29	30	DECK OF CARDS	Wink Martindale (Dot)

24 November 1973

last	this		
10	1	I LOVE YOU LOVE ME LOVE	Gary Glitter (Bell)
1	2	LET ME IN	Osmonds (MGM)
5	3	DYNA-MITE	Mud (RAK)
6	4	PHOTOGRAPH	Ringo Starr (Apple)
7	5	WHEN I FALL IN LOVE	Donny Osmond (MGM)
2	6	PUPPY SONG/DAY DREAMER	David Cassidy (Bell)
3	7	SORROW	David Bowie (RCA)
17	8	DO YOU WANNA DANCE	Barry Blue (Bell)
4	9	TOP OF THE WORLD	Carpenters (A&M)
25	10	WHY OH WHY OH WHY	Gilbert O'Sullivan (MAM)
26	11	PAPER ROSES	Marie Osmond (MGM)
13	12	THIS FLIGHT TONIGHT	Nazareth (Mooncrest)
18	13	DAYTONA DEMON	Suzi Quatro (RAK)
22	14	LAMPLIGHT	David Essex (CBS)
15	15	WON'T SOMEBODY DANCE WITH ME	Lynsey De Paul (MAM)
-	16	MY COO-CA-CHOO	Alvin Stardust (Magnet)
19	17	DECK OF CARDS	Max Bygraves (Pye)
23	18	HELEN WHEELS	Paul McCartney & Wings (Apple)
11	19	FOR THE GOOD TIMES	Perry Como (RCA)
14	20	GHETTO CHILD	Detroit Spinners (Atlantic)
9	21	GOODBYE YELLOW BRICK ROAD	Elton John (DJM)
12	22	EYE LEVEL	Simon Park Orchestra (Columbia)
8	23	CAROLINE	Status Quo (Vertigo)
-	24	STREET LIFE	Roxy Music (Island)
16	25	SHOW DOWN	Electric Light Orchestra (Harvest)
27	26	KEEP ON TRUCKIN'	Eddie Kendricks (Tamla Motown)
-	27	WILD LOVE	Mungo Jerry (Dawn)
-	28	YOU WON'T FIND ANOTHER FOOL LIKE ME	New Seekers (Polydor)
20	29	KNOCKIN' ON HEAVEN'S DOOR	Bob Dylan (CBS)
-	30	TRUCK ON (TYKE)	T. Rex (EMI)

1 December 1973

last	this		
1	1	I LOVE YOU LOVE ME LOVE	Gary Glitter (Bell)
16	2	MY COO-CA-CHOO	Alvin Stardust (Magnet)
11	3	PAPER ROSES	Marie Osmond (MGM)
2	4	LET ME IN	Osmonds (MGM)
3	5	DYNA-MITE	Mud (RAK)
4	6	PHOTOGRAPH	Ringo Starr (Apple)
5	7	WHEN I FALL IN LOVE	Donny Osmond (MGM)
10	8	WHY OH WHY OH WHY	Gilbert O'Sullivan (MAM)
8	9	DO YOU WANNA DANCE	Barry Blue (Bell)
14	10	LAMPLIGHT	David Essex (CBS)
9	11	TOP OF THE WORLD	Carpenters (A&M)
18	12	HELEN WHEELS	Paul McCartney & Wings (Apple)
28	13	YOU WON'T FIND ANOTHER FOOL LIKE ME	New Seekers (Polydor)
7	14	SORROW	David Bowie (RCA)
24	15	STREET LIFE	Roxy Music (Island)
6	16	PUPPY SONG/DAY DREAMER	David Cassidy (Bell)
13	17	DAYTONA DEMON	Suzi Quatro (RAK)
-	18	ROLL AWAY THE STONE	Mott the Hoople (CBS)
-	19	AMOUREUSE	Kiki Dee (Rocket)
12	20	THIS FLIGHT TONIGHT	Nazareth (Mooncrest)
15	21	WON'T SOMEBODY DANCE WITH ME	Lynsey De Paul (MAM)
30	22	TRUCK ON (TYKE)	T. Rex (EMI)
19	23	FOR THE GOOD TIMES	Perry Como (RCA)
26	24	KEEP ON TRUCKIN'	Eddie Kendricks (Tamla Motown)
-	25	MIND GAMES	John Lennon (Apple)
17	26	DECK OF CARDS	Max Bygraves (Pye)
-	27	LOVE ON A MOUNTAIN TOP	Robert Knight (Monument)
27	28	WILD LOVE	Mungo Jerry (Dawn)
-	29	DECK OF CARDS	Wink Martindale (Dot)
22	30	EYE LEVEL	Simon Park Orchestra (Columbia)

Another classic oldie revival by Donny Osmond, but this time the group's single (a new song) outsold his solo effort. Biggest hit of the month, however – and his all-time biggest UK hit, with sales of just over one million – was Gary Glitter's *I Love You Love Me Love*. Alvin Stardust was a name clearly chosen to emulate Glitter, but the *My Coo-Ca-Choo* hitmaker was 1961/62 chart-rider Shane Fenton in relaunched guise. Another of the Osmond clan, sister Marie, debuted with the country-styled oldie *Paper Roses*.

December 1973

Slade's *Merry Xmas Everybody* was not only to be the group's biggest seller, selling 250,000 in three days and eventually topping a million in the UK, but also a perennial, re-charting several times in later years. 1973 was the first year since 1957 that the Number One Christmas single actually had a Christmas theme. It also broke an ongoing implicit embargo on Christmas records by rock acts, as Wizzard and Elton John joined Slade, and Steeleye Span offered a traditional Christmas anthem sung in Latin!

5 January 1974

last week	this week		
5	1	YOU WON'T FIND ANOTHER FOOL LIKE ME	New Seekers (Polydor)
1	2	MERRY XMAS EVERYBODY	Slade (Polydor)
7	3	THE SHOW MUST GO ON	Leo Sayer (Chrysalis)
4	4	MY COO-CA-CHOO	Alvin Stardust (Magnet)
3	5	I LOVE YOU LOVE ME LOVE	Gary Glitter (Bell)
2	6	I WISH IT COULD BE CHRISTMAS EVERYDAY	Wizzard (Harvest)
9	7	LAMPLIGHT	David Essex (CBS)
22	8	FOREVER	Roy Wood (Harvest)
11	9	LOVE ON A MOUNTAIN TOP	Robert Knight (Monument)
6	10	PAPER ROSES	Marie Osmond (MGM)
16	11	DANCE WITH THE DEVIL	Cozy Powell (RAK)
8	12	ROLL AWAY THE STONE	Mott the Hoople (CBS)
15	13	WHY OH WHY OH WHY	Gilbert O'Sullivan (MAM)
13	14	GAUDETE	Steeleye Span (Chrysalis)
17	15	RADAR LOVE	Golden Earring (Track)
24	16	VADO VIA	Drupi (A&M)
10	17	STREET LIFE	Roxy Music (Island)
12	18	POOL HALL RICHARD/I WISH IT WOULD RAIN	Faces (Warner Bros)
18	19	STEP INTO CHRISTMAS	Elton John (DJM)
20	20	TRUCK ON (TYKE)	T. Rex (EMI)
19	21	KEEP ON TRUCKIN'	Eddie Kendricks (Tamla Motown)
21	22	WHEN I FALL IN LOVE	Donny Osmond (MGM)
14	23	AMOUREUSE	Kiki Dee (Rocket)
25	24	DO YOU WANNA DANCE	Barry Blue (Bell)
26	25	LET ME IN	Osmonds (MGM)
-	26	HELEN WHEELS	Paul McCartney & Wings (Apple)
30	27	VAYA CON DIOS	Millican & Nesbitt (Pye)
-	28	ALL OF MY LIFE	Diana Ross (Tamla Motown)
23	29	DYNA-MITE	Mud (RAK)
27	30	FOR THE GOOD TIMES	Perry Como (RCA)

12 January 1974

this week		
1	YOU WON'T FIND ANOTHER FOOL LIKE ME	New Seekers (Polydor)
2	THE SHOW MUST GO ON	Leo Sayer (Chrysalis)
3	MERRY XMAS EVERYBODY	Slade (Polydor)
4	MY COO-CA-CHOO	Alvin Stardust (Magnet)
5	DANCE WITH THE DEVIL	Cozy Powell (RAK)
6	FOREVER	Roy Wood (Harvest)
7	I LOVE YOU LOVE ME LOVE	Gary Glitter (Bell)
8	POOL HALL RICHARD/I WISH IT WOULD RAIN	Faces (Warner Bros)
9	LAMPLIGHT	David Essex (CBS)
10	I WISH IT COULD BE CHRISTMAS EVERYDAY	Wizzard (Harvest)
11	LOVE ON A MOUNTAIN TOP	Robert Knight (Monument)
12	ROLL AWAY THE STONE	Mott the Hoople (CBS)
13	STREET LIFE	Roxy Music (Island)
14	PAPER ROSES	Marie Osmond (MGM)
15	RADAR LOVE	Golden Earring (Track)
16	GAUDETE	Steeleye Span (Chrysalis)
17	WHY OH WHY OH WHY	Gilbert O'Sullivan (MAM)
18	VADO VIA	Drupi (A&M)
19	SOLITAIRE	Andy Williams (CBS)
20	TRUCK ON (TYKE)	T. Rex (EMI)
21	VAYA CON DIOS	Millican & Nesbitt (Pye)
22	WHEN I FALL IN LOVE	Donny Osmond (MGM)
23	ALL OF MY LIFE	Diana Ross (Tamla Motown)
24	KEEP ON TRUCKIN'	Eddie Kendricks (Tamla Motown)
25	FOR THE GOOD TIMES	Perry Como (RCA)
26	STEP INTO CHRISTMAS	Elton John (DJM)
27	LIVING FOR THE CITY	Stevie Wonder (Tamla Motown)
28	LET ME IN	Osmonds (MGM)
29	STAR	Stealers Wheel (A&M)
30	TOP OF THE WORLD	Carpenters (A&M)

19 January 1974

last week	this week		
2	1	THE SHOW MUST GO ON	Leo Sayer (Chrysalis)
1	2	YOU WON'T FIND ANOTHER FOOL LIKE ME	New Seekers (Polydor)
5	3	DANCE WITH THE DEVIL	Cozy Powell (RAK)
4	4	MY COO-CA-CHOO	Alvin Stardust (Magnet)
15	5	RADAR LOVE	Golden Earring (Track)
8	6	POOL HALL RICHARD/I WISH IT WOULD RAIN	Faces (Warner Bros)
11	7	LOVE ON A MOUNTAIN TOP	Robert Knight (Monument)
6	8	FOREVER	Roy Wood (Harvest)
3	9	MERRY XMAS EVERYBODY	Slade (Polydor)
-	10	TEENAGE RAMPAGE	Sweet (RCA)
9	11	LAMPLIGHT	David Essex (CBS)
-	12	TIGER FEET	Mud (RAK)
7	13	I LOVE YOU LOVE ME LOVE	Gary Glitter (Bell)
12	14	ROLL AWAY THE STONE	Mott the Hoople (CBS)
14	15	PAPER ROSES	Marie Osmond (MGM)
19	16	SOLITAIRE	Andy Williams (CBS)
13	17	STREET LIFE	Roxy Music (Island)
18	18	VADO VIA	Drupi (A&M)
10	19	I WISH IT COULD BE CHRISTMAS EVERYDAY	Wizzard (Harvest)
16	20	GAUDETE	Steeleye Span (Chrysalis)
17	21	WHY OH WHY OH WHY	Gilbert O'Sullivan (MAM)
-	22	THE LOVE I LOST	Harold Melvin & the Blue Notes (Philadelphia)
-	23	THANKS FOR SAVING MY LIFE	Billy Paul (Philadelphia Int)
27	24	LIVING FOR THE CITY	Stevie Wonder (Tamla Motown)
30	25	TOP OF THE WORLD	Carpenters (A&M)
-	26	HOW COME	Ronnie Lane (GM)
25	27	FOR THE GOOD TIMES	Perry Como (RCA)
-	28	ROCKIN' ROLL BABY	Stylistics (Avco)
22	29	WHEN I FALL IN LOVE	Donny Osmond (MGM)
20	30	TRUCK ON (TYKE)	T. Rex (EMI)

26 January 1974

last week	this week		
10	1	TEENAGE RAMPAGE	Sweet (RCA)
12	2	TIGER FEET	Mud (RAK)
2	3	YOU WON'T FIND ANOTHER FOOL LIKE ME	New Seekers (Polydor)
1	4	THE SHOW MUST GO ON	Leo Sayer (Chrysalis)
3	5	DANCE WITH THE DEVIL	Cozy Powell (RAK)
5	6	RADAR LOVE	Golden Earring (Track)
4	7	MY COO-CA-CHOO	Alvin Stardust (Magnet)
16	8	SOLITAIRE	Andy Williams (CBS)
8	9	FOREVER	Roy Wood (Harvest)
6	10	POOL HALL RICHARD/I WISH IT WOULD RAIN	Faces (Warner Bros)
7	11	LOVE ON A MOUNTAIN TOP	Robert Knight (Monument)
17	12	ALL OF MY LIFE	Diana Ross (Tamla Motown)
26	13	HOW COME	Ronnie Lane (GM)
11	14	LAMPLIGHT	David Essex (CBS)
28	15	ROCKIN' ROLL BABY	Stylistics (Avco)
15	16	PAPER ROSES	Marie Osmond (MGM)
9	17	MERRY XMAS EVERYBODY	Slade (Polydor)
13	18	I LOVE YOU LOVE ME LOVE	Gary Glitter (Bell)
-	19	TEENAGE LAMENT '74	Alice Cooper (Warner Bros)
14	20	ROLL AWAY THE STONE	Mott the Hoople (CBS)
22	21	THE LOVE I LOST	Harold Melvin & the Blue Notes (Philadelphia)
23	22	THANKS FOR SAVING MY LIFE	Billy Paul (Philadelphia Int)
18	23	VADO VIA	Drupi (A&M)
24	24	LIVING FOR THE CITY	Stevie Wonder (Tamla Motown)
17	25	STREET LIFE	Roxy Music (Island)
20	26	GAUDETE	Steeleye Span (Chrysalis)
21	27	WHY OH WHY OH WHY	Gilbert O'Sullivan (MAM)
-	28	THE MAN WHO SOLD THE WORLD	Lulu (Polydor)
27	29	FOR THE GOOD TIMES	Perry Como (RCA)
-	30	HIGHWAY OF MY LIFE	Isley Brothers (Epic)

Making his debut with a Number One hit, Adam Faith protegee Leo Sayer cut a strange figure on TV performing *The Show Must Go On*, in white-face clown make up and costume in keeping with the song's lyric. The song he replaced at the top was the New Seekers' second all-time biggest hit (after *I'd Like To Teach...*), selling over 855,000. *Radar Love* was the only major UK seller by Holland's Golden Earring, while Millican & Nesbitt, newly charted with *Vaya Con Dios*, were coal miners!

February 1974

2 February 1974

last week	this week		
2	1	TIGER FEET	Mud (RAK)
1	2	TEENAGE RAMPAGE	Sweet (RCA)
13	3	HOW COME	Ronnie Lane (GM)
5	4	DANCE WITH THE DEVIL	Cozy Powell (RAK)
8	5	SOLITAIRE	Andy Williams (CBS)
4	6	THE SHOW MUST GO ON	Leo Sayer (Chrysalis)
3	7	YOU WON'T FIND ANOTHER FOOL LIKE ME	New Seekers (Polydor)
12	8	ALL OF MY LIFE	Diana Ross (Tamla Motown)
6	9	RADAR LOVE	Golden Earring (Track)
9	10	FOREVER	Roy Wood (Harvest)
15	11	ROCKIN' ROLL BABY	Stylistics (Avco)
7	12	MY COO-CA-CHOO	Alvin Stardust (Magnet)
28	13	THE MAN WHO SOLD THE WORLD	Lulu (Polydor)
10	14	POOL HALL RICHARD/I WISH IT WOULD RAIN	Faces (Warner Bros)
11	15	LOVE ON A MOUNTAIN TOP	Robert Knight (Monument)
21	16	THE LOVE I LOST	Harold Melvin & the Blue Notes (Philadelphia)
-	17	THE WOMBLING SONG	Wombles (CBS)
19	18	TEENAGE LAMENT '74	Alice Cooper (Warner Bros)
24	19	LIVING FOR THE CITY	Stevie Wonder (Tamla Motown)
14	20	LAMPLIGHT	David Essex (CBS)
23	21	VADO VIA	Drupi (A&M)
-	22	NEVER GONNA GIVE YA UP	Barry White (Pye)
22	23	THANKS FOR SAVING MY LIFE	Billy Paul (Philadelphia)
18	24	I LOVE YOU LOVE ME LOVE	Gary Glitter (Bell)
-	25	AFTER THE GOLD RUSH	Prelude (Dawn)
16	26	PAPER ROSES	Marie Osmond (MGM)
-	27	LOVE'S THEME	Love Unlimited Orchestra (Pye)
17	28	MERRY XMAS EVERYBODY	Slade (Polydor)
29	29	FOR THE GOOD TIMES	Perry Como (RCA)
26	30	GAUDETE	Steeleye Span (Chrysalis)

9 February 1974

1	1	TIGER FEET	Mud (RAK)
2	2	TEENAGE RAMPAGE	Sweet (RCA)
5	3	SOLITAIRE	Andy Williams (CBS)
13	4	THE MAN WHO SOLD THE WORLD	Lulu (Polydor)
4	5	DANCE WITH THE DEVIL	Cozy Powell (RAK)
11	6	ROCKIN' ROLL BABY	Stylistics (Avco)
8	7	ALL OF MY LIFE	Diana Ross (Tamla Motown)
6	8	THE SHOW MUST GO ON	Leo Sayer (Chrysalis)
9	9	RADAR LOVE	Golden Earring (Track)
3	10	HOW COME	Ronnie Lane (GM)
7	11	YOU WON'T FIND ANOTHER FOOL LIKE ME	New Seekers (Polydor)
10	12	FOREVER	Roy Wood (Harvest)
-	13	DEVIL GATE DRIVE	Suzi Quatro (RAK)
15	14	LOVE ON A MOUNTAIN TOP	Robert Knight (Monument)
16	15	THE LOVE I LOST	Harold Melvin & the Blue Notes (Philadelphia)
12	16	MY COO-CA-CHOO	Alvin Stardust (Magnet)
18	17	TEENAGE LAMENT '74	Alice Cooper (Warner Bros)
19	18	LIVING FOR THE CITY	Stevie Wonder (Tamla Motown)
17	19	THE WOMBLING SONG	Wombles (CBS)
22	20	NEVER GONNA GIVE YA UP	Barry White (Pye)
27	21	LOVE'S THEME	Love Unlimited Orchestra (Pye)
14	22	POOL HALL RICHARD/I WISH IT WOULD RAIN	Faces (Warner Bros)
-	23	HIGHWAYS OF MY LIFE	Isley Brothers (Epic)
-	24	MA HE'S MAKING EYES AT ME	Lena Zavaroni (Philips)
-	25	(I CAN'T GET NO) SATISFACTION	Bubble Rock (UK)
-	26	STAR	Stealer's Wheel (A&M)
-	27	TEENAGE DREAM	Marc Bolan & T. Rex (T. Rex)
26	28	PAPER ROSES	Marie Osmond (MGM)
24	29	I LOVE YOU LOVE ME LOVE	Gary Glitter (Bell)
29	30	FOR THE GOOD TIMES	Perry Como (RCA)

16 February 1974

1	1	TIGER FEET	Mud (RAK)
13	2	DEVIL GATE DRIVE	Suzi Quatro (RAK)
2	3	TEENAGE RAMPAGE	Sweet (RCA)
4	4	THE MAN WHO SOLD THE WORLD	Lulu (Polydor)
3	5	SOLITAIRE	Andy Williams (CBS)
7	6	ALL OF MY LIFE	Diana Ross (Tamla Motown)
6	7	ROCKIN' ROLL BABY	Stylistics (Avco)
5	8	DANCE WITH THE DEVIL	Cozy Powell (RAK)
19	9	THE WOMBLING SONG	Wombles (CBS)
21	10	LOVE'S THEME	Love Unlimited Orchestra (Pye)
10	11	HOW COME	Ronnie Lane (GM)
8	12	THE SHOW MUST GO ON	Leo Sayer (Chrysalis)
27	13	TEENAGE DREAM	Marc Bolan & T. Rex (T. Rex)
18	14	LIVING FOR THE CITY	Stevie Wonder (Tamla Motown)
9	15	RADAR LOVE	Golden Earring (Track)
-	16	JEALOUS MIND	Alvin Stardust (Magnet)
11	17	YOU WON'T FIND ANOTHER FOOL LIKE ME	New Seekers (Polydor)
20	18	NEVER GONNA GIVE YA UP	Barry White (Pye)
-	19	THE AIR THAT I BREATHE	Hollies (Polydor)
17	20	TEENAGE LAMENT '74	Alice Cooper (Warner Bros)
24	21	MA HE'S MAKING EYES AT ME	Lena Zavaroni (Philips)
15	22	THE LOVE I LOST	Harold Melvin & the Blue Notes (Philadelphia)
23	23	HIGHWAYS OF MY LIFE	Isley Brothers (Epic)
12	24	FOREVER	Roy Wood (Harvest)
26	25	STAR	Stealers Wheel (A&M)
-	26	YOU'RE SIXTEEN	Ringo Starr (Apple)
-	27	AFTER THE GOLD RUSH	Prelude (Dawn)
-	28	HAPPINESS IS ME AND YOU	Gilbert O'Sullivan (MAM)
-	29	SLIP AND SLIDE	Medicine Head (Polydor)
14	30	LOVE ON A MOUNTAIN TOP	Robert Knight (Monument)

23 February 1974

2	1	DEVIL GATE DRIVE	Suzi Quatro (RAK)
1	2	TIGER FEET	Mud (RAK)
4	3	THE MAN WHO SOLD THE WORLD	Lulu (Polydor)
16	4	JEALOUS MIND	Alvin Stardust (Magnet)
9	5	THE WOMBLING SONG	Wombles (CBS)
5	6	SOLITAIRE	Andy Williams (CBS)
3	7	TEENAGE RAMPAGE	Sweet (RCA)
7	8	ROCKIN' ROLL BABY	Stylistics (Avco)
6	9	ALL OF MY LIFE	Diana Ross (Tamla Motown)
19	10	THE AIR THAT I BREATHE	Hollies (Polydor)
8	11	DANCE WITH THE DEVIL	Cozy Powell (RAK)
-	12	REBEL REBEL	David Bowie (RCA)
10	13	LOVE'S THEME	Love Unlimited Orchestra (Pye)
21	14	MA HE'S MAKING EYES AT ME	Lena Zavaroni (Philips)
13	15	TEENAGE DREAM	Marc Bolan & T. Rex (T. Rex)
18	16	NEVER GONNA GIVE YA UP	Barry White (Pye)
-	17	THE MOST BEAUTIFUL GIRL	Charlie Rich (Epic)
26	18	YOU'RE SIXTEEN	Ringo Starr (Apple)
14	19	LIVING FOR THE CITY	Stevie Wonder (Tamla Motown)
12	20	THE SHOW MUST GO ON	Leo Sayer (Chrysalis)
11	21	HOW COME	Ronnie Lane (GM)
20	22	TEENAGE LAMENT '74	Alice Cooper (Warner Bros)
29	23	SLIP AND SLIDE	Medicine Head (Polydor)
27	24	AFTER THE GOLD RUSH	Prelude (Dawn)
28	25	HAPPINESS IS ME AND YOU	Gilbert O'Sullivan (MAM)
-	26	REMEMBER (SHA-LA-LA-LA)	Bay City Rollers (Bell)
25	27	STAR	Stealers Wheel (A&M)
30	28	LOVE ON A MOUNTAIN TOP	Robert Knight (Monument)
-	29	JET	Paul McCartney & Wings (Apple)
-	30	A LITTLE LOVIN'	Neil Sedaka (Polydor)

Mud's *Tiger Feet* was the group's first Number One, proving to have more sales resilience than Sweet's *Teenage Rampage*, with which it had shared a breakneck chart ascent. Lulu had her first hit for five years: a cover of David Bowie's *The Man Who Sold The World*. Chart debutantes included 10-year-old Opportunity Knocks discovery Lena Zavaroni, Prelude (whose version of Neil Young's *After The Gold Rush* was acapella), and the Wombles, who in recording terms consisted entirely of Mike Batt.

last week	this week	2 March 1974
1	1	DEVIL GATE DRIVE Suzi Quatro (RAK)
4	2	JEALOUS MIND Alvin Stardust (Magnet)
12	3	REBEL REBEL David Bowie (RCA)
5	4	THE WOMBLING SONG Wombles (CBS)
10	5	THE AIR THAT I BREATHE Hollies (Polydor)
2	6	TIGER FEET Mud (RAK)
18	7	YOU'RE SIXTEEN Ringo Starr (Apple)
3	8	THE MAN WHO SOLD THE WORLD Lulu (Polydor)
13	9	LOVE'S THEME Love Unlimited Orchestra (Pye)
26	10	REMEMBER (SHA-LA-LA-LA) Bay City Rollers (Bell)
6	11	SOLITAIRE Andy Williams (CBS)
16	12	NEVER GONNA GIVE YA UP Barry White (Pye)
17	13	THE MOST BEAUTIFUL GIRL Charlie Rich (Epic)
14	14	MA HE'S MAKING EYES AT ME Lena Zavaroni (Philips)
9	15	ALL OF MY LIFE Diana Ross (Tamla Motown)
7	16	TEENAGE RAMPAGE Sweet (RCA)
8	17	ROCKIN' ROLL BABY Stylistics (Avco)
29	18	JET Paul McCartney & Wings (Apple)
23	19	SLIP AND SLIDE Medicine Head (Polydor)
25	20	HAPPINESS IS ME AND YOU Gilbert O'Sullivan (MAM)
15	21	TEENAGE DREAM Marc Bolan & T. Rex (T. Rex)
-	22	IT'S YOU Freddie Starr (Tiffany)
-	23	BILLY DON'T BE A HERO Paper Lace (Bus Stop)
24	24	AFTER THE GOLD RUSH Prelude (Dawn)
-	25	BURN BABY BURN Hudson Ford (A&M)
19	26	LIVING FOR THE CITY Stevie Wonder (Tamla Motown)
11	27	DANCE WITH THE DEVIL Cozy Powell (RAK)
27	28	STAR Stealers Wheel (A&M)
-	29	CANDLE IN THE WIND Elton John (DJM)
-	30	UNTIL YOU COME BACK TO ME Aretha Franklin (Atlantic)

		9 March 1974
2	1	JEALOUS MIND Alvin Stardust (Magnet)
1	2	DEVIL GATE DRIVE Suzi Quatro (RAK)
5	3	THE AIR THAT I BREATHE Hollies (Polydor)
4	4	THE WOMBLING SONG Wombles (CBS)
7	5	YOU'RE SIXTEEN Ringo Starr (Apple)
10	6	REMEMBER (SHA-LA-LA-LA) Bay City Rollers (Bell)
3	7	REBEL REBEL David Bowie (RCA)
13	8	THE MOST BEAUTIFUL GIRL Charlie Rich (Epic)
23	9	BILLY DON'T BE A HERO Paper Lace (Bus Stop)
18	10	JET Paul McCartney & Wings (Apple)
12	11	NEVER GONNA GIVE YA UP Barry White (Pye)
22	12	IT'S YOU Freddie Starr (Tiffany)
14	13	MA HE'S MAKING EYES AT ME Lena Zavaroni (Philips)
6	14	TIGER FEET Mud (RAK)
29	15	CANDLE IN THE WIND Elton John (DJM)
9	16	LOVE'S THEME Love Unlimited Orchestra (Pye)
8	17	THE MAN WHO SOLD THE WORLD Lulu (Polydor)
25	18	BURN BABY BURN Hudson Ford (A&M)
11	19	SOLITAIRE Andy Williams (CBS)
24	20	AFTER THE GOLD RUSH Prelude (Dawn)
20	21	HAPPINESS IS ME AND YOU Gilbert O'Sullivan (MAM)
15	22	ALL OF MY LIFE Diana Ross (Tamla Motown)
17	23	ROCKIN' ROLL BABY Stylistics (Avco)
19	24	SLIP AND SLIDE Medicine Head (Polydor)
16	25	TEENAGE RAMPAGE Sweet (RCA)
-	26	SCHOOL LOVE Barry Blue (Bell)
30	27	UNTIL YOU COME BACK TO ME Aretha Franklin (Atlantic)
21	28	TEENAGE DREAM Marc Bolan & T. Rex (T. Rex)
-	29	I GET A LITTLE SENTIMENTAL OVER YOU New Seekers (Polydor)
-	30	SMOKIN' IN THE BOYS ROOM Brownsville Station (Philips)

		16 March 1974
1	1	JEALOUS MIND Alvin Stardust (Magnet)
3	2	THE AIR THAT I BREATHE Hollies (Polydor)
9	3	BILLY DON'T BE A HERO Paper Lace (Bus Stop)
5	4	YOU'RE SIXTEEN Ringo Starr (Apple)
8	5	THE MOST BEAUTIFUL GIRL Charlie Rich (Epic)
2	6	DEVIL GATE DRIVE Suzi Quatro (RAK)
10	7	JET Paul McCartney & Wings (Apple)
6	8	REMEMBER (SHA-LA-LA-LA) Bay City Rollers (Bell)
4	9	THE WOMBLING SONG Wombles (CBS)
15	10	CANDLE IN THE WIND Elton John (DJM)
7	11	REBEL REBEL David Bowie (RCA)
12	12	IT'S YOU Freddie Starr (Tiffany)
29	13	I GET A LITTLE SENTIMENTAL OVER YOU New Seekers (Polydor)
18	14	BURN BABY BURN Hudson Ford (A&M)
13	15	MA HE'S MAKING EYES AT ME Lena Zavaroni (Philips)
11	16	NEVER GONNA GIVE YA UP Barry White (Pye)
26	17	SCHOOL LOVE Barry Blue (Bell)
16	18	LOVE'S THEME Love Unlimited Orchestra (Pye)
24	19	SLIP AND SLIDE Medicine Head (Polydor)
17	20	THE MAN WHO SOLD THE WORLD Lulu (Polydor)
-	21	WHO DO YOU THINK YOU ARE Candlewick Green (Decca)
-	22	EVERLASTING LOVE Robert Knight (Monument)
21	23	HAPPINESS IS ME AND YOU Gilbert O'Sullivan (MAM)
14	24	TIGER FEET Mud (RAK)
27	25	UNTIL YOU COME BACK TO ME Aretha Franklin (Atlantic)
20	26	AFTER THE GOLD RUSH Prelude (Dawn)
19	27	SOLITAIRE Andy Williams (CBS)
-	28	SEVEN SEAS OF RHYE Queen (EMI)
-	29	MA-MA-MA-BELLE Electric Light Orchestra (Warner Bros)
-	30	WHO'S IN THE STRAWBERRY PATCH WITH SALLY Dawn (Bell)

		23 March 1974
3	1	BILLY DON'T BE A HERO Paper Lace (Bus Stop)
2	2	THE AIR THAT I BREATHE Hollies (Polydor)
1	3	JEALOUS MIND Alvin Stardust (Magnet)
5	4	THE MOST BEAUTIFUL GIRL Charlie Rich (Epic)
4	5	YOU'RE SIXTEEN Ringo Starr (Apple)
7	6	JET Paul McCartney & Wings (Apple)
13	7	I GET A LITTLE SENTIMENTAL OVER YOU New Seekers (Polydor)
8	8	REMEMBER (SHA-LA-LA-LA) Bay City Rollers (Bell)
10	9	CANDLE IN THE WIND Elton John (DJM)
12	10	IT'S YOU Freddie Starr (Tiffany)
17	11	SCHOOL LOVE Barry Blue (Bell)
6	12	DEVIL GATE DRIVE Suzi Quatro (RAK)
9	13	THE WOMBLING SONG Wombles (CBS)
14	14	BURN BABY BURN Hudson Ford (A&M)
16	15	NEVER GONNA GIVE YA UP Barry White (Pye)
-	16	JAMBALAYA/MR GUDER Carpenters (A&M)
28	17	SEVEN SEAS OF RHYE Queen (EMI)
-	18	EMMA Hot Chocolate (RAK)
11	19	REBEL REBEL David Bowie (RCA)
-	20	LONG LIVE LOVE Olivia Newton-John (Pye)
-	21	SEASONS IN THE SUN Terry Jacks (Bell)
22	22	EVERLASTING LOVE Robert Knight (Monument)
21	23	WHO DO YOU THINK YOU ARE Candlewick Green (Decca)
15	24	MA HE'S MAKING EYES AT ME Lena Zavaroni (Philips)
18	25	LOVE'S THEME Love Unlimited Orchestra (Pye)
-	26	SMOKIN' IN THE BOYS ROOM Brownsville Station (Philips)
25	27	UNTIL YOU COME BACK TO ME Aretha Franklin (Atlantic)
-	28	LISTEN TO THE MUSIC Doobie Brothers (Warner Bros)
29	29	SLIP AND SLIDE Medicine Head (Polydor)
30	30	WHO'S IN THE STRAWBERRY PATCH WITH SALLY Dawn (Bell)

The Bay City Rollers, who had not scored since their debut in 1971, resurged strongly, with a more teenybop image, on *Remember (Sha-La-La-La)*; it was to begin widespread 'Rollermania' as they became the biggest teen fad since the Osmonds.

Ringo put a former Johnny Burnette hit back in the Top Five, while Paul McCartney and Elton John both returned to the Top 10, but were thought by many to have even stronger B-sides (*Let Me Roll It* and *Bennie & The Jets* respectively) on their singles.

March – April 1974

30 March 1974

last	this	title / artist (label)
1	1	BILLY DON'T BE A HERO Paper Lace (Bus Stop)
4	2	THE MOST BEAUTIFUL GIRL Charlie Rich (Epic)
2	3	THE AIR THAT I BREATHE Hollies (Polydor)
7	4	I GET A LITTLE SENTIMENTAL OVER YOU New Seekers (Polydor)
18	5	EMMA Hot Chocolate (RAK)
6	6	JET Paul McCartney & Wings (Apple)
21	7	SEASONS IN THE SUN Terry Jacks (Bell)
5	8	YOU'RE SIXTEEN Ringo Starr (Apple)
17	9	SEVEN SEAS OF RHYE Queen (EMI)
8	10	REMEMBER (SHA-LA-LA-LA) Bay City Rollers (Bell)
3	11	JEALOUS MIND Alvin Stardust (Magnet)
9	12	CANDLE IN THE WIND Elton John (DJM)
11	13	SCHOOL LOVE Barry Blue (Bell)
10	14	IT'S YOU Freddie Starr (Tiffany)
16	15	JAMBALAYA/MR GUDER Carpenters (A&M)
-	16	ANGEL FACE Glitter Band (Bell)
20	17	LONG LIVE LOVE Olivia Newton-John (Pye)
-	18	YOU ARE EVERYTHING Diana Ross & Marvin Gaye (Tamla Motown)
-	19	REMEMBER ME THIS WAY Gary Glitter (Bell)
22	20	EVERLASTING LOVE Robert Knight (Monument)
13	21	THE WOMBLING SONG Wombles (CBS)
14	22	BURN BABY BURN Hudson Ford (A&M)
19	23	REBEL REBEL David Bowie (RCA)
-	24	MA-MA-MA-BELLE Electric Light Orchestra (Warner Bros)
-	25	ROCK AROUND THE CLOCK Bill Haley & His Comets (MCA)
28	26	LISTEN TO THE MUSIC Doobie Brothers (Warner Bros)
12	27	DEVIL GATE DRIVE Suzi Quatro (RAK)
27	28	UNTIL YOU COME BACK TO ME Aretha Franklin (Atlantic)
23	29	WHO DO YOU THINK YOU ARE Candlewick Green (Decca)
15	30	NEVER GONNA GIVE YA UP Barry White (Pye)

6 April 1974

last	this	title / artist (label)
1	1	BILLY DON'T BE A HERO Paper Lace (Bus Stop)
7	2	SEASONS IN THE SUN Terry Jacks (Bell)
5	3	EMMA Hot Chocolate (RAK)
19	4	REMEMBER ME THIS WAY Gary Glitter (Bell)
2	5	THE MOST BEAUTIFUL GIRL Charlie Rich (Epic)
16	6	ANGEL FACE Glitter Band (Bell)
4	7	I GET A LITTLE SENTIMENTAL OVER YOU New Seekers (Polydor)
8	8	SEVEN SEAS OF RHYE Queen (EMI)
3	9	THE AIR THAT I BREATHE Hollies (Polydor)
15	10	JAMBALAYA/MR GUDER Carpenters (A&M)
13	11	SCHOOL LOVE Barry Blue (Bell)
8	12	YOU'RE SIXTEEN Ringo Starr (Apple)
18	13	YOU ARE EVERYTHING Diana Ross & Marvin Gaye (Tamla Motown)
6	14	JET Paul McCartney & Wings (Apple)
17	15	LONG LIVE LOVE Olivia Newton-John (Pye)
12	16	CANDLE IN THE WIND Elton John (DJM)
-	17	EVERYDAY Slade (Polydor)
14	18	IT'S YOU Freddie Starr (Tiffany)
24	19	MA-MA-MA-BELLE Electric Light Orchestra (Warner Bros)
-	20	GOLDEN AGE OF ROCK'N'ROLL Mott The Hoople (CBS)
11	21	JEALOUS MIND Alvin Stardust (Magnet)
10	22	REMEMBER (SHA-LA-LA-LA) Bay City Rollers (Bell)
20	23	EVERLASTING LOVE Robert Knight (Monument)
25	24	ROCK AROUND THE CLOCK Bill Haley & His Comets (MCA)
-	25	DOCTORS ORDERS Sunny (CBS)
21	26	THE WOMBLING SONG Wombles (CBS)
-	27	THE STING Ragtimers (Pye)
-	28	I'M GONNA KNOCK ON YOUR DOOR Jimmy Osmond (MGM)
-	29	HOMELY GIRL Chi-Lites (Brunswick)
-	30	THE WAY WE WERE Barbra Streisand (CBS)

13 April 1974

last	this	title / artist (label)
2	1	SEASONS IN THE SUN Terry Jacks (Bell)
4	2	REMEMBER ME THIS WAY Gary Glitter (Bell)
3	3	EMMA Hot Chocolate (RAK)
6	4	ANGEL FACE Glitter Band (Bell)
17	5	EVERYDAY Slade (Polydor)
1	6	BILLY DON'T BE A HERO Paper Lace (Bus Stop)
13	7	YOU ARE EVERYTHING Diana Ross & Marvin Gaye (Tamla Motown)
5	8	THE MOST BEAUTIFUL GIRL Charlie Rich (Epic)
8	9	SEVEN SEAS OF RHYE Queen (EMI)
15	10	LONG LIVE LOVE Olivia Newton-John (Pye)
25	11	DOCTORS ORDERS Sunny (CBS)
7	12	I GET A LITTLE SENTIMENTAL OVER YOU New Seekers (Polydor)
-	13	THE CAT CREPT IN Mud (RAK)
10	14	JAMBALAYA/MR GUDER Carpenters (A&M)
9	15	THE AIR THAT I BREATHE Hollies (Polydor)
20	16	GOLDEN AGE OF ROCK'N'ROLL Mott The Hoople (CBS)
11	17	SCHOOL LOVE Barry Blue (Bell)
29	18	HOMELY GIRL Chi-Lites (Brunswick)
-	19	A WALKIN' MIRACLE Limmie & the Family Cookin' (Avco)
12	20	YOU'RE SIXTEEN Ringo Starr (Apple)
19	21	MA-MA-MA-BELLE Electric Light Orchestra (Warner Bros)
28	22	I'M GONNA KNOCK ON YOUR DOOR Jimmy Osmond (MGM)
18	23	IT'S YOU Freddie Starr (Tiffany)
24	24	ROCK AROUND THE CLOCK Bill Haley & His Comets (MCA)
-	25	REMEMBER YOU'RE A WOMBLE Wombles (CBS)
14	26	JET Paul McCartney & Wings (Apple)
16	27	CANDLE IN THE WIND Elton John (DJM)
-	28	LISTEN TO THE MUSIC Doobie Brothers (Warner Bros)
23	29	EVERLASTING LOVE Robert Knight (Monument)
-	30	I KNOW WHAT I LIKE Genesis (Charisma)

20 April 1974

last	this	title / artist (label)
1	1	SEASONS IN THE SUN Terry Jacks (Bell)
4	2	ANGEL FACE Glitter Band (Bell)
5	3	EVERYDAY Slade (Polydor)
2	4	REMEMBER ME THIS WAY Gary Glitter (Bell)
13	5	THE CAT CREPT IN Mud (RAK)
7	6	YOU ARE EVERYTHING Diana Ross & Marvin Gaye (Tamla Motown)
3	7	EMMA Hot Chocolate (RAK)
6	8	BILLY DON'T BE A HERO Paper Lace (Bus Stop)
11	9	DOCTORS ORDERS Sunny (CBS)
25	10	REMEMBER YOU'RE A WOMBLE Wombles (CBS)
9	11	SEVEN SEAS OF RHYE Queen (EMI)
8	12	THE MOST BEAUTIFUL GIRL Charlie Rich (Epic)
22	13	I'M GONNA KNOCK ON YOUR DOOR Jimmy Osmond (MGM)
18	14	HOMELY GIRL Chi-Lites (Brunswick)
10	15	LONG LIVE LOVE Olivia Newton-John (Pye)
19	16	A WALKIN' MIRACLE Limmie & the Family Cookin' (Avco)
16	17	GOLDEN AGE OF ROCK'N'ROLL Mott The Hoople (CBS)
14	18	JAMBALAYA/MR GUDER Carpenters (A&M)
24	19	ROCK AROUND THE CLOCK Bill Haley & His Comets (MCA)
12	20	I GET A LITTLE SENTIMENTAL OVER YOU New Seekers (Polydor)
-	21	WATERLOO Abba (Epic)
30	22	I KNOW WHAT I LIKE Genesis (Charisma)
-	23	THE STING Ragtimers (Pye)
27	24	CANDLE IN THE WIND Elton John (DJM)
15	25	THE AIR THAT I BREATHE Hollies (Polydor)
-	26	LONG LEGGED WOMAN DRESSED IN BLACK Mungo Jerry (Dawn)
21	27	MA-MA-MA-BELLE Electric Light Orchestra (Warner Bros)
-	28	HE'S MISSTRA KNOW IT ALL Stevie Wonder (Tamla Motown)
-	29	ROCK'N'ROLL SUICIDE David Bowie (RCA)
-	30	YEAR OF DECISION Three Degrees (Philadelphia)

Paper Lace, top with their first single, were Opportunity Knocks winners and protegees of hit songwriters Mitch Murray and Peter Callander. *Billy Don't Be A Hero* was a Number One in the US for Bo Donaldson & the Heywoods. Terry Jacks, who toppled Paper Lace, was a veteran of the Canadian scene, and had previously charted in 1970 with his wife Susan, as the Poppy Family on *Which Way You Goin' Billy*. Meanwhile, Bill Haley's *Rock Around The Clock* had yet another chartmaking reissue.

April – May 1974

27 April 1974

last	this	Title	Artist (Label)
5	1	THE CAT CREPT IN	Mud (RAK)
1	2	SEASONS IN THE SUN	Terry Jacks (Bell)
10	3	REMEMBER YOU'RE A WOMBLE	Wombles (CBS)
21	4	WATERLOO	Abba (Epic)
2	5	ANGEL FACE	Glitter Band (Bell)
6	6	YOU ARE EVERYTHING	Diana Ross & Marvin Gaye (Tamla Motown)
9	7	DOCTORS ORDERS	Sunny (CBS)
3	8	EVERYDAY	Slade (Polydor)
14	9	HOMELY GIRL	Chi-Lites (Brunswick)
16	10	A WALKIN' MIRACLE	Limmie & the Family Cookin' (Avco)
7	11	EMMA	Hot Chocolate (RAK)
4	12	REMEMBER ME THIS WAY	Gary Glitter (Bell)
19	13	ROCK AROUND THE CLOCK	Bill Haley & His Comets (MCA)
15	14	I'M GONNA KNOCK ON YOUR DOOR	Jimmy Osmond (MGM)
8	15	BILLY DON'T BE A HERO	Paper Lace (Bus Stop)
11	16	SEVEN SEAS OF RHYE	Queen (EMI)
28	17	HE'S MISSTRA KNOW IT ALL	Stevie Wonder (Tamla Motown)
17	18	GOLDEN AGE OF ROCK'N'ROLL	Mott The Hoople (CBS)
22	19	I KNOW WHAT I LIKE	Genesis (Charisma)
26	20	LONG LEGGED WOMAN DRESSED IN BLACK	Mungo Jerry (Dawn)
29	21	ROCK'N'ROLL SUICIDE	David Bowie (RCA)
12	22	THE MOST BEAUTIFUL GIRL	Charlie Rich (Epic)
-	23	BEHIND CLOSED DOORS	Charlie Rich (Epic)
-	24	ROCK'N'ROLL WINTER	Wizzard (Warner Bros)
18	25	JAMBALAYA/MR GUDER	Carpenters (A&M)
30	26	YEAR OF DECISION	Three Degrees (Philadelphia)
23	27	THE STING	Ragtimers (Pye)
-	28	DON'T STAY AWAY TOO LONG	Peters & Lee (Philips)
-	29	THE ENTERTAINER	Marvin Hamlisch (MCA)
-	30	SATISFACTION GUARANTEED	Harold Melvin & the Blue Notes (Philadelphia)

4 May 1974

last	this	Title	Artist (Label)
4	1	WATERLOO	Abba (Epic)
2	2	SEASONS IN THE SUN	Terry Jacks (Bell)
1	3	THE CAT CREPT IN	Mud (RAK)
3	4	REMEMBER YOU'RE A WOMBLE	Wombles (CBS)
9	5	HOMELY GIRL	Chi-Lites (Brunswick)
7	6	DOCTORS ORDERS	Sunny (CBS)
10	7	A WALKIN' MIRACLE	Limmie & the Family Cookin' (Avco)
5	8	ANGEL FACE	Glitter Band (Bell)
6	9	YOU ARE EVERYTHING	Diana Ross & Marvin Gaye (Tamla Motown)
8	10	EVERYDAY	Slade (Polydor)
24	11	ROCK'N'ROLL WINTER	Wizzard (Warner Bros)
29	12	LONG LEGGED WOMAN DRESSED IN BLACK	Mungo Jerry (Dawn)
14	13	I'M GONNA KNOCK ON YOUR DOOR	Jimmy Osmond (MGM)
17	14	HE'S MISSTRA KNOW IT ALL	Stevie Wonder (Tamla Motown)
28	15	DON'T STAY AWAY TOO LONG	Peters & Lee (Philips)
-	16	SHANG-A-LANG	Bay City Rollers (Bell)
18	17	GOLDEN AGE OF ROCK'N'ROLL	Mott The Hoople (CBS)
19	18	I KNOW WHAT I LIKE	Genesis (Charisma)
12	19	REMEMBER ME THIS WAY	Gary Glitter (Bell)
11	20	EMMA	Hot Chocolate (RAK)
21	21	ROCK'N'ROLL SUICIDE	David Bowie (RCA)
23	22	BEHIND CLOSED DOORS	Charlie Rich (Epic)
26	23	YEAR OF DECISION	Three Degrees (Philadelphia)
13	24	ROCK AROUND THE CLOCK	Bill Haley & His Comets (MCA)
-	25	SUGAR BABY LOVE	Rubettes (Polydor)
-	26	SPIDERS AND SNAKES	Jim Stafford (MGM)
16	27	SEVEN SEAS OF RHYE	Queen (EMI)
15	28	BILLY DON'T BE A HERO	Paper Lace (Bus Stop)
-	29	THE SOUND OF PHILADELPHIA	MFSB (Philadelphia)
22	30	THE MOST BEAUTIFUL GIRL	Charlie Rich (Epic)

11 May 1974

last	this	Title	Artist (Label)
1	1	WATERLOO	Abba (Epic)
5	2	HOMELY GIRL	Chi-Lites (Brunswick)
4	3	REMEMBER YOU'RE A WOMBLE	Wombles (CBS)
16	4	SHANG-A-LANG	Bay City Rollers (Bell)
3	5	THE CAT CREPT IN	Mud (RAK)
11	6	ROCK'N'ROLL WINTER	Wizzard (Warner Bros)
7	7	A WALKIN' MIRACLE	Limmie & the Family Cookin' (Avco)
2	8	SEASONS IN THE SUN	Terry Jacks (Bell)
6	9	DOCTORS ORDERS	Sunny (CBS)
15	10	DON'T STAY AWAY TOO LONG	Peters & Lee (Philips)
25	11	SUGAR BABY LOVE	Rubettes (Polydor)
23	12	YEAR OF DECISION	Three Degrees (Philadelphia)
14	13	HE'S MISSTRA KNOW IT ALL	Stevie Wonder (Tamla Motown)
12	14	LONG LEGGED WOMAN DRESSED IN BLACK	Mungo Jerry (Dawn)
9	15	YOU ARE EVERYTHING	Diana Ross & Marvin Gaye (Tamla Motown)
8	16	ANGEL FACE	Glitter Band (Bell)
22	17	BEHIND CLOSED DOORS	Charlie Rich (Epic)
26	18	SPIDERS AND SNAKES	Jim Stafford (MGM)
-	19	RED DRESS	Alvin Stardust (Magnet)
-	20	THE NIGHT CHICAGO DIED	Paper Lace (Bus Stop)
29	21	THE SOUND OF PHILADELPHIA	MFSB (Philadelphia)
-	22	I CAN'T STOP	Osmonds (MCA)
10	23	EVERYDAY	Slade (Polydor)
13	24	I'M GONNA KNOCK ON YOUR DOOR	Jimmy Osmond (MGM)
-	25	BREAK THE RULES	Status Quo (Vertigo)
21	26	ROCK'N'ROLL SUICIDE	David Bowie (RCA)
-	27	THIS TOWN AIN'T BIG ENOUGH FOR BOTH OF US	Sparks (Island)
19	28	REMEMBER ME THIS WAY	Gary Glitter (Bell)
-	29	THE ENTERTAINER	Marvin Hamlisch (MCA)
-	30	LAST TIME I SAW HIM	Diana Ross (Tamla Motown)

18 May 1974

last	this	Title	Artist (Label)
11	1	SUGAR BABY LOVE	Rubettes (Polydor)
1	2	WATERLOO	Abba (Epic)
4	3	SHANG-A-LANG	Bay City Rollers (Bell)
10	4	DON'T STAY AWAY TOO LONG	Peters & Lee (Philips)
3	5	REMEMBER YOU'RE A WOMBLE	Wombles (CBS)
2	6	HOMELY GIRL	Chi-Lites (Brunswick)
6	7	ROCK'N'ROLL WINTER	Wizzard (Warner Bros)
19	8	RED DRESS	Alvin Stardust (Magnet)
20	9	THE NIGHT CHICAGO DIED	Paper Lace (Bus Stop)
13	10	HE'S MISSTRA KNOW IT ALL	Stevie Wonder (Tamla Motown)
18	11	SPIDERS AND SNAKES	Jim Stafford (MGM)
27	12	THIS TOWN AIN'T BIG ENOUGH FOR BOTH OF US	Sparks (Island)
7	13	A WALKIN' MIRACLE	Limmie & the Family Cookin' (Avco)
14	14	LONG LEGGED WOMAN DRESSED IN BLACK	Mungo Jerry (Dawn)
8	15	SEASONS IN THE SUN	Terry Jacks (Bell)
22	16	I CAN'T STOP	Osmonds (MCA)
25	17	BREAK THE RULES	Status Quo (Vertigo)
12	18	YEAR OF DECISION	Three Degrees (Philadelphia)
9	19	DOCTORS ORDERS	Sunny (CBS)
-	20	IF I DIDN'T CARE	David Cassidy (Bell)
5	21	THE CAT CREPT IN	Mud (RAK)
17	22	BEHIND CLOSED DOORS	Charlie Rich (Epic)
21	23	THE SOUND OF PHILADELPHIA	MFSB (Philadelphia)
15	24	YOU ARE EVERYTHING	Diana Ross & Marvin Gaye (Tamla Motown)
26	25	ROCK'N'ROLL SUICIDE	David Bowie (RCA)
-	26	THERE'S A GHOST IN MY HOUSE	R Dean Taylor (Tamla Motown)
-	27	AMERICA	David Essex (CBS)
-	28	GO	Gigliola Cinquetti (CBS)
16	29	ANGEL FACE	Glitter Band (Bell)
-	30	JUDY TEEN	Cockney Rebel (EMI)

The arrival of Abba with an instant Number One hit was the result of the Eurovision Song Contest, which the group won convincingly with *Waterloo*. They were followed at the top by the Rubettes, whose stage act was rock'n'roll, but whose *Sugar Baby Love* was a Four Seasons-type pastiche, featuring the lead falsetto of Paul Da Vinci, who left the group immediately after the recording, and failed to share in their subsequent success. The Ragtimers and Marvin Hamlisch records were the same Scott Joplin tune.

May – June 1974

25 May 1974

last	this	
1	1	SUGAR BABY LOVE — Rubettes (Polydor)
4	2	DON'T STAY AWAY TOO LONG — Peters & Lee (Philips)
2	3	WATERLOO — Abba (Epic)
3	4	SHANG-A-LANG — Bay City Rollers (Bell)
12	5	THIS TOWN AIN'T BIG ENOUGH FOR BOTH OF US — Sparks (Island)
9	6	THE NIGHT CHICAGO DIED — Paper Lace (Bus Stop)
11	7	SPIDERS AND SNAKES — Jim Stafford (MGM)
6	8	HOMELY GIRL — Chi-Lites (Brunswick)
7	9	ROCK'N'ROLL WINTER — Wizzard (Warner Bros)
5	10	REMEMBER YOU'RE A WOMBLE — Wombles (CBS)
17	11	BREAK THE RULES — Status Quo (Vertigo)
8	12	RED DRESS — Alvin Stardust (Magnet)
16	13	I CAN'T STOP — Osmonds (MCA)
10	14	HE'S MISSTRA KNOW IT ALL — Stevie Wonder (Tamla Motown)
20	15	IF I DIDN'T CARE — David Cassidy (Bell)
28	16	GO — Gigliola Cinquetti (CBS)
18	17	YEAR OF DECISION — Three Degrees (Philadelphia)
13	18	A WALKIN' MIRACLE — Limmie & The Family Cookin' (Avco)
26	19	THERE'S A GHOST IN MY HOUSE — R Dean Taylor (Tamla Motown)
22	20	BEHIND CLOSED DOORS — Charlie Rich (Epic)
23	21	THE SOUND OF PHILADELPHIA — MFSB (Philadelphia)
14	22	LONG LEGGED WOMAN DRESSED IN BLACK — Mungo Jerry (Dawn)
15	23	SEASONS IN THE SUN — Terry Jacks (Bell)
30	24	JUDY TEEN — Cockney Rebel (EMI)
24	25	YOU ARE EVERYTHING — Diana Ross & Marvin Gaye (Tamla Motown)
-	26	THE 'IN' CROWD — Bryan Ferry (Island)
-	27	I SEE A STAR — Mouth & McNeal (Decca)
21	28	THE CAT CREPT IN — Mud (RAK)
27	29	AMERICA — David Essex (CBS)
-	30	CAN'T GET ENOUGH — Bad Company (Island)

1 June 1974

last	this	
1	1	SUGAR BABY LOVE — Rubettes (Polydor)
5	2	THIS TOWN AIN'T BIG ENOUGH FOR BOTH OF US — Sparks (Island)
4	3	SHANG-A-LANG — Bay City Rollers (Bell)
6	4	THE NIGHT CHICAGO DIED — Paper Lace (Bus Stop)
2	5	DON'T STAY AWAY TOO LONG — Peters & Lee (Philips)
19	6	THERE'S A GHOST IN MY HOUSE — R Dean Taylor (Tamla Motown)
12	7	RED DRESS — Alvin Stardust (Magnet)
11	8	BREAK THE RULES — Status Quo (Vertigo)
15	9	IF I DIDN'T CARE — David Cassidy (Bell)
3	10	WATERLOO — Abba (Epic)
16	11	GO — Gigliola Cinquetti (Bell)
26	12	THE 'IN' CROWD — Bryan Ferry (Island)
7	13	SPIDERS AND SNAKES — Jim Stafford (MGM)
13	14	I CAN'T STOP — Osmonds (MCA)
-	15	HEY ROCK AND ROLL — Showaddywaddy (Bell)
27	16	I SEE A STAR — Mouth & McNeal (Decca)
10	17	REMEMBER YOU'RE A WOMBLE — Wombles (CBS)
8	18	HOMELY GIRL — Chi-Lites (Brunswick)
-	19	(YOU KEEP ME) HANGIN' ON — Cliff Richard (EMI)
9	20	ROCK'N'ROLL WINTER — Wizzard (Warner Bros)
14	21	HE'S MISSTRA KNOW IT ALL — Stevie Wonder (Tamla Motown)
24	22	JUDY TEEN — Cockney Rebel (EMI)
-	23	THE STREAK — Ray Stevens (Westbound)
-	24	JARROW SONG — Alan Price (Warner Bros)
17	25	YEAR OF DECISION — Three Degrees (Philadelphia)
-	26	I WANT TO GIVE — Perry Como (RCA Victor)
22	27	LONG LEGGED WOMAN DRESSED IN BLACK — Mungo Jerry (Dawn)
30	28	CAN'T GET ENOUGH — Bad Company (Island)
-	29	THE MAN IN BLACK — Cozy Powell (RAK)
-	30	W.O.L.D. — Harry Chapin (Elektra)

8 June 1974

last	this	
1	1	SUGAR BABY LOVE — Rubettes (Polydor)
2	2	THIS TOWN AIN'T BIG ENOUGH FOR BOTH OF US — Sparks (Island)
15	3	HEY ROCK AND ROLL — Showaddywaddy (Bell)
6	4	THERE'S A GHOST IN MY HOUSE — R Dean Taylor (Tamla Motown)
4	5	THE NIGHT CHICAGO DIED — Paper Lace (Bus Stop)
23	6	THE STREAK — Ray Stevens (Westbound)
3	7	SHANG-A-LANG — Bay City Rollers (Bell)
5	8	DON'T STAY AWAY TOO LONG — Peters & Lee (Philips)
11	9	GO — Gigliola Cinquetti (CBS)
12	10	THE 'IN' CROWD — Bryan Ferry (Island)
9	11	IF I DIDN'T CARE — David Cassidy (Bell)
16	12	I SEE A STAR — Mouth & McNeal (Decca)
22	13	JUDY TEEN — Cockney Rebel (EMI)
8	14	BREAK THE RULES — Status Quo (Vertigo)
7	15	RED DRESS — Alvin Stardust (Magnet)
24	16	JARROW SONG — Alan Price (Warner Bros)
-	17	A TOUCH TOO MUCH — Arrows (RAK)
14	18	I CAN'T STOP — Osmonds (MCA)
13	19	SPIDERS AND SNAKES — Jim Stafford (MGM)
19	20	(YOU KEEP ME) HANGIN' ON — Cliff Richard (EMI)
28	21	CAN'T GET ENOUGH — Bad Company (Island)
-	22	DON'T LET THE SUN GO DOWN ON ME — Elton John (DJM)
-	23	LIVERPOOL LOU — Scaffold (Warner)
-	24	SUMMER BREEZE — Isley Brothers (Epic)
10	25	WATERLOO — Abba (Epic)
17	26	REMEMBER YOU'RE A WOMBLE — Wombles (CBS)
29	27	THE MAN IN BLACK — Cozy Powell (RAK)
-	28	WALL STREET SHUFFLE — 10 c.c. (UK)
-	29	PERSONALITY — Lena Zavaroni (Philips)
21	30	HE'S MISSTRA KNOW IT ALL — Stevie Wonder (Tamla Motown)

15 June 1974

last	this	
6	1	THE STREAK — Ray Stevens (Westbound)
3	2	HEY ROCK AND ROLL — Showaddywaddy (Bell)
2	3	THIS TOWN AIN'T BIG ENOUGH FOR BOTH OF US — Sparks (Island)
1	4	SUGAR BABY LOVE — Rubettes (Polydor)
4	5	THERE'S A GHOST IN MY HOUSE — R Dean Taylor (Tamla Motown)
13	6	JUDY TEEN — Cockney Rebel (EMI)
10	7	THE 'IN' CROWD — Bryan Ferry (Island)
16	8	JARROW SONG — Alan Price (Warner Bros)
12	9	I SEE A STAR — Mouth & McNeal (Decca)
5	10	THE NIGHT CHICAGO DIED — Paper Lace (Bus Stop)
-	11	ALWAYS YOURS — Gary Glitter (Bell)
17	12	A TOUCH TOO MUCH — Arrows (RAK)
9	13	GO — Gigliola Cinquetti (CBS)
14	14	BREAK THE RULES — Status Quo (Vertigo)
11	15	IF I DIDN'T CARE — David Cassidy (Bell)
21	16	CAN'T GET ENOUGH — Bad Company (Island)
8	17	DON'T STAY AWAY TOO LONG — Peters & Lee (Philips)
24	18	SUMMER BREEZE — Isley Brothers (Epic)
7	19	SHANG-A-LANG — Bay City Rollers (Bell)
22	20	DON'T LET THE SUN GO DOWN ON ME — Elton John (DJM)
23	21	LIVERPOOL LOU — Scaffold (Warner Bros)
20	22	(YOU KEEP ME) HANGIN' ON — Cliff Richard (EMI)
27	23	THE MAN IN BLACK — Cozy Powell (RAK)
-	24	GUILTY — Pearls (Bell)
-	25	I'D LOVE YOU TO WANT ME — Lobo (UK)
-	26	ONE MAN BAND — Leo Sayer (Chrysalis)
-	27	OOH I DO — Lynsey de Paul (Warner Bros)
28	28	IF YOU'RE READY (COME GO WITH ME) — Staple Singers (Stax)
28	29	WALL STREET SHUFFLE — 10 c.c. (UK)
19	30	SPIDERS AND SNAKES — Jim Stafford (MGM)

Sparks, the American brothers Ron and Russell Mael, made a spectacular debut with the offbeat *This Town Ain't Big Enough For Both Of Us*, but the single which displaced the Rubettes at Number One was Ray Stevens' celebration of the popular streaking craze – his first hit since the similarly silly *Bridget The Midget* in 1971. Cliff Richard's *(You Keep Me) Hangin' On* would be his final hit for nearly two years – 1975 would be the first year in Cliff's career in which he didn't have a Top 30 success.

last week	this week	22 June 1974
1	1	THE STREAK — Ray Stevens (Westbound)
11	2	ALWAYS YOURS — Gary Glitter (Bell)
2	3	HEY ROCK AND ROLL — Showaddywaddy (Bell)
8	4	JARROW SONG — Alan Price (Warner Bros)
5	5	THERE'S A GHOST IN MY HOUSE — R Dean Taylor (Tamla Motown)
12	6	A TOUCH TOO MUCH — Arrows (RAK)
6	7	JUDY TEEN — Cockney Rebel (EMI)
3	8	THIS TOWN AIN'T BIG ENOUGH FOR BOTH OF US — Sparks (Island)
26	9	ONE MAN BAND — Leo Sayer (Chrysalis)
4	10	SUGAR BABY LOVE — Rubettes (Polydor)
21	11	LIVERPOOL LOU — Scaffold (Warner Bros)
9	12	I SEE A STAR — Mouth & McNeal (Decca)
18	13	SUMMER BREEZE — Isley Brothers (Epic)
16	14	CAN'T GET ENOUGH — Bad Company (Island)
20	15	DON'T LET THE SUN GO DOWN ON ME — Elton John (DJM)
24	16	GUILTY — Pearls (Bell)
7	17	THE 'IN' CROWD — Bryan Ferry (Island)
10	18	THE NIGHT CHICAGO DIED — Paper Lace (Bus Stop)
25	19	I'D LOVE YOU TO WANT ME — Lobo (UK)
22	20	(YOU KEEP ME) HANGIN' ON — Cliff Richard (EMI)
23	21	THE MAN IN BLACK — Cozy Powell (RAK)
13	22	GO — Gigliola Cinquetti (CBS)
-	23	SHE — Charles Aznavour (Barclay)
-	24	KISSIN' IN THE BACK ROW — Drifters (Bell)
27	25	OOH I DO — Lynsey de Paul (Warner Bros)
-	26	GOING DOWN THE ROAD — Roy Wood (Harvest)
15	27	IF I DIDN'T CARE — David Cassidy (Bell)
-	28	YOUNG GIRL — Gary Puckett and the Union Gap (CBS)
28	29	IF YOU'RE READY COME GO WITH ME — Staple Singers (Stax)
29	30	WALL STREET SHUFFLE — 10 c.c. (UK)

last week	this week	29 June 1974
2	1	ALWAYS YOURS — Gary Glitter (Bell)
1	2	THE STREAK — Ray Stevens (Westbound)
3	3	HEY ROCK AND ROLL — Showaddywaddy (Bell)
23	4	SHE — Charles Aznavour (Barclay)
4	5	JARROW SONG — Alan Price (Warner Bros)
19	6	I'D LOVE YOU TO WANT ME — Lobo (UK)
5	7	THERE'S A GHOST IN MY HOUSE — R Dean Taylor (Tamla Motown)
6	8	A TOUCH TOO MUCH — Arrows (RAK)
11	9	LIVERPOOL LOU — Scaffold (Warner Bros)
7	10	JUDY TEEN — Cockney Rebel (EMI)
9	11	ONE MAN BAND — Leo Sayer (Chrysalis)
24	12	KISSIN' IN THE BACK ROW — Drifters (Bell)
16	13	GUILTY — Pearls (Bell)
26	14	GOING DOWN THE ROAD — Roy Wood (Harvest)
8	15	THIS TOWN AIN'T BIG ENOUGH FOR BOTH OF US — Sparks (Island)
13	16	SUMMER BREEZE — Isley Brothers (Epic)
30	17	WALL STREET SHUFFLE — 10 c.c. (UK)
15	18	DON'T LET THE SUN GO DOWN ON ME — Elton John (DJM)
21	19	THE MAN IN BLACK — Cozy Powell (RAK)
20	20	OOH I DO — Lynsey de Paul (Warner Bros)
-	21	BEACH BABY — First Class (UK)
-	22	DIAMOND DOGS — David Bowie (RCA)
12	23	I SEE A STAR — Mouth & McNeal (Decca)
10	24	SUGAR BABY LOVE — Rubettes (Polydor)
14	25	CAN'T GET ENOUGH — Bad Company (Island)
17	26	THE 'IN' CROWD — Bryan Ferry (Island)
-	27	BANANA ROCK — Wombles (CBS)
-	28	FOXY FOXY — Mott the Hoople (CBS)
-	29	EASY EASY — Scotland World Cup Squad (Polydor)
28	30	YOUNG GIRL — Gary Puckett and the Union Gap (CBS)

last week	this week	6 July 1974
4	1	SHE — Charles Aznavour (Barclay)
1	2	ALWAYS YOURS — Gary Glitter (Bell)
12	3	KISSIN' IN THE BACK ROW — Drifters (Bell)
6	4	I'D LOVE YOU TO WANT ME — Lobo (UK)
11	5	ONE MAN BAND — Leo Sayer (Chrysalis)
2	6	THE STREAK — Ray Stevens (Westbound)
3	7	HEY ROCK AND ROLL — Showaddywaddy (Bell)
13	8	GUILTY — Pearls (Bell)
17	9	WALL STREET SHUFFLE — 10 c.c. (UK)
-	10	THE BANGIN' MAN — Slade (Polydor)
5	11	JARROW SONG — Alan Price (Warner Bros)
7	12	THERE'S A GHOST IN MY HOUSE — R Dean Taylor (Tamla Motown)
14	13	GOING DOWN THE ROAD — Roy Wood (Harvest)
27	14	BANANA ROCK — Wombles (CBS)
-	15	TOO BIG — Suzi Quatro (RAK)
-	16	ROCK YOUR BABY — George McCrae (Jay Boy)
30	17	YOUNG GIRL — Gary Puckett and the Union Gap (CBS)
21	18	BEACH BABY — First Class (UK)
8	19	A TOUCH TOO MUCH — Arrows (RAK)
9	20	LIVERPOOL LOU — Scaffold (Warner Bros)
10	21	JUDY TEEN — Cockney Rebel (EMI)
16	22	SUMMER BREEZE — Isley Brothers (Epic)
-	23	BAND ON THE RUN — Wings (Apple)
22	24	DIAMOND DOGS — David Bowie (RCA)
25	25	CAN'T GET ENOUGH — Bad Company (Island)
19	26	THE MAN IN BLACK — Cozy Powell (RAK)
-	27	IF YOU'RE READY (COME GO WITH ME) — Staple Singers (Stax)
28	28	IF YOU GO AWAY — Terry Jacks (Bell)
-	29	JUST DON'T WANT TO BE LONELY — Main Ingredient (RCA)
-	30	MIDNIGHT AT THE OASIS — Maria Muldaur (Reprise)

last week	this week	13 July 1974
1	1	SHE — Charles Aznavour (Barclay)
3	2	KISSIN' IN THE BACK ROW — Drifters (Bell)
10	3	THE BANGIN' MAN — Slade (Polydor)
2	4	ALWAYS YOURS — Gary Glitter (Bell)
4	5	I'D LOVE YOU TO WANT ME — Lobo (UK)
17	6	YOUNG GIRL — Gary Puckett and the Union Gap (CBS)
23	7	BAND ON THE RUN — Wings (Apple)
16	8	ROCK YOUR BABY — George McCrae (Jay Boy)
9	9	WALL STREET SHUFFLE — 10 c.c. (UK)
5	10	ONE MAN BAND — Leo Sayer (Chrysalis)
14	11	BANANA ROCK — Wombles (CBS)
7	12	HEY ROCK AND ROLL — Showaddywaddy (Bell)
8	13	GUILTY — Pearls (Bell)
18	14	BEACH BABY — First Class (UK)
6	15	THE STREAK — Ray Stevens (Westbound)
13	16	GOING DOWN THE ROAD — Roy Wood (Harvest)
19	17	A TOUCH TOO MUCH — Arrows (RAK)
15	18	TOO BIG — Suzi Quatro (RAK)
28	19	IF YOU GO AWAY — Terry Jacks (Bell)
11	20	JARROW SONG — Alan Price (Warner Bros)
29	21	JUST DON'T WANT TO BE LONELY — Main Ingredient (RCA)
20	22	LIVERPOOL LOU — Scaffold (Warner Bros)
30	23	MIDNIGHT AT THE OASIS — Maria Muldaur (Reprise)
-	24	THE SIX TEENS — Sweet (RCA)
-	25	DON'T LET THE SUN GO DOWN ON ME — Elton John (DJM)
-	26	LAUGHTER IN THE RAIN — Neil Sedaka (Polydor)
-	27	SHE'S A WINNER — Intruders (Philadelphia)
24	28	DIAMOND DOGS — David Bowie (RCA)
12	29	THERE'S A GHOST IN MY HOUSE — R Dean Taylor (Tamla Motown)
-	30	WHEN WILL I SEE YOU AGAIN — Three Degrees (Philadelphia)

She by Charles Aznavour was one of those apparently timeless ballads which happen along sometimes and confound all prevailing musical trends by outselling everything else. The French song was given English lyrics by the journalist Herbert Kretzmer, and got a massive TV boost as the theme to the *Seven Faces Of Women* series; Aznavour was never able to follow it with another hit. Meanwhile, the reissue of Gary Puckett & the Union Gap's 1968 chart-topper *Young Girl* made the Top Five for a second time.

July – August 1974

20 July 1974

last	this		
1	1	SHE	Charles Aznavour (Barclay)
2	2	KISSIN' IN THE BACK ROW	Drifters (Bell)
8	3	ROCK YOUR BABY	George McCrae (Jay Boy)
3	4	THE BANGIN' MAN	Slade (Polydor)
7	5	BAND ON THE RUN	Wings (Apple)
6	6	YOUNG GIRL	Gary Puckett and the Union Gap (CBS)
5	7	I'D LOVE YOU TO WANT ME	Lobo (UK)
9	8	WALL STREET SHUFFLE	10 c.c. (UK)
10	9	ONE MAN BAND	Leo Sayer (Chrysalis)
24	10	THE SIX TEENS	Sweet (RCA)
4	11	ALWAYS YOURS	Gary Glitter (Bell)
11	12	BANANA ROCK	Wombles (CBS)
14	13	BEACH BABY	First Class (UK)
19	14	IF YOU GO AWAY	Terry Jacks (Bell)
23	15	MIDNIGHT AT THE OASIS	Maria Muldaur (Reprise)
27	16	SHE'S A WINNER	Intruders (Philadelphia)
30	17	WHEN WILL I SEE YOU AGAIN	Three Degrees (Philadelphia)
18	18	TOO BIG	Suzi Quatro (RAK)
13	19	GUILTY	Pearls (Bell)
16	20	GOING DOWN THE ROAD	Roy Wood (Harvest)
26	21	LAUGHTER IN THE RAIN	Neil Sedaka (Polydor)
21	22	JUST DON'T WANT TO BE LONELY	Main Ingredient (RCA)
12	23	HEY ROCK AND ROLL	Showaddywaddy (Bell)
-	24	MY GIRL BILL	Jim Stafford (MGM)
-	25	LIGHT OF LOVE	T. Rex (EMI)
28	26	DIAMOND DOGS	David Bowie (RCA)
-	27	BE THANKFUL FOR WHAT YOU'VE GOT	William De Vaughan (Chelsea)
-	28	TONIGHT	Rubettes (Polydor)
-	29	ROCK THE BOAT	Hues Corporation (RCA)
15	30	THE STREAK	Ray Stevens (Westbound)

27 July 1974

last	this		
3	1	ROCK YOUR BABY	George McCrae (Jay Boy)
2	2	KISSIN' IN THE BACK ROW	Drifters (Bell)
5	3	BAND ON THE RUN	Wings (Apple)
1	4	SHE	Charles Aznavour (Barclay)
6	5	YOUNG GIRL	Gary Puckett and the Union Gap (CBS)
4	6	THE BANGIN' MAN	Slade (Polydor)
17	7	WHEN WILL I SEE YOU AGAIN	Three Degrees (Philadelphia)
8	8	I'D LOVE YOU TO WANT ME	Lobo (UK)
14	9	IF YOU GO AWAY	Terry Jacks (Bell)
12	10	BANANA ROCK	Wombles (CBS)
10	11	THE SIX TEENS	Sweet (RCA)
-	12	BORN WITH A SMILE ON MY FACE	Stephanie De Sykes/Rain (Bradley)
16	13	SHE'S A WINNER	Intruders (Philadelphia)
24	14	MY GIRL BILL	Jim Stafford (MGM)
21	15	LAUGHTER IN THE RAIN	Neil Sedaka (Polydor)
8	16	WALL STREET SHUFFLE	10 c.c. (UK)
28	17	TONIGHT	Rubettes (Polydor)
15	18	MIDNIGHT AT THE OASIS	Maria Muldaur (Reprise)
-	19	YOU MAKE ME FEEL BRAND NEW	Stylistics (Avco)
13	20	BEACH BABY	First Class (UK)
11	21	ALWAYS YOURS	Gary Glitter (Bell)
-	22	AMATEUR HOUR	Sparks (Island)
25	23	LIGHT OF LOVE	T. Rex (EMI)
29	24	ROCK THE BOAT	Hues Corporation (RCA)
22	25	JUST DON'T WANT TO BE LONELY	Main Ingredient (RCA)
9	26	ONE MAN BAND	Leo Sayer (Chrysalis)
18	27	TOO BIG	Suzi Quatro (RAK)
-	28	STOP LOOK LISTEN (TO YOUR HEART)	Diana Ross & Marvin Gaye (Tamla Motown)
-	29	I SHOT THE SHERIFF	Eric Clapton (RSO)
-	30	MIKE OLDFIELD'S SINGLE (THEME FROM TUBULAR BELLS)	Mike Oldfield (Virgin)

3 August 1974

last	this		
1	1	ROCK YOUR BABY	George McCrae (Jay Boy)
7	2	WHEN WILL I SEE YOU AGAIN	Three Degrees (Philadelphia)
4	3	SHE	Charles Aznavour (Barclay)
3	4	BAND ON THE RUN	Wings (Apple)
2	5	KISSIN' IN THE BACK ROW	Drifters (Bell)
12	6	BORN WITH A SMILE ON MY FACE	Stephanie De Sykes/Rain (Bradley)
22	7	AMATEUR HOUR	Sparks (Island)
19	8	YOU MAKE ME FEEL BRAND NEW	Stylistics (Avco)
5	9	YOUNG GIRL	Gary Puckett and the Union Gap (CBS)
17	10	TONIGHT	Rubettes (Polydor)
11	11	THE SIX TEENS	Sweet (RCA)
-	12	ROCKET	Mud (RAK)
8	13	I'D LOVE YOU TO WANT ME	Lobo (UK)
9	14	IF YOU GO AWAY	Terry Jacks (Bell)
24	15	ROCK THE BOAT	Hues Corporation (RCA)
6	16	THE BANGIN' MAN	Slade (Polydor)
13	17	SHE'S A WINNER	Intruders (Philadelphia)
15	18	LAUGHTER IN THE RAIN	Neil Sedaka (Polydor)
10	19	BANANA ROCK	Wombles (CBS)
16	20	WALL STREET SHUFFLE	10 c.c. (UK)
14	21	MY GIRL BILL	Jim Stafford (MGM)
18	22	MIDNIGHT AT THE OASIS	Maria Muldaur (Reprise)
-	23	SUMMERLOVE SENSATION	Bay City Rollers (Bell)
29	24	I SHOT THE SHERIFF	Eric Clapton (RSO)
-	25	PLEASE PLEASE ME	David Cassidy (Bell)
-	26	WHAT BECOMES OF THE BROKENHEARTED	Jimmy Ruffin (Tamla Motown)
-	27	IT'S ONLY ROCK'N'ROLL	Rolling Stones (Rolling Stones)
23	28	LIGHT OF LOVE	T. Rex (EMI)
28	29	STOP LOOK LISTEN (TO YOUR HEART)	Diana Ross & Marvin Gaye (Tamla Motown)
20	30	BEACH BABY	First Class (UK)

10 August 1974

last	this		
1	1	ROCK YOUR BABY	George McCrae (Jay Boy)
2	2	WHEN WILL I SEE YOU AGAIN	Three Degrees (Philadelphia)
4	3	BAND ON THE RUN	Wings (Apple)
8	4	YOU MAKE ME FEEL BRAND NEW	Stylistics (Avco)
7	5	AMATEUR HOUR	Sparks (Island)
23	6	SUMMERLOVE SENSATION	Bay City Rollers (Bell)
6	7	BORN WITH A SMILE ON MY FACE	Stephanie De Sykes/Rain (Bradley)
15	8	ROCK THE BOAT	Hues Corporation (RCA)
12	9	ROCKET	Mud (RAK)
3	10	SHE	Charles Aznavour (Barclay)
27	11	IT'S ONLY ROCK'N'ROLL	Rolling Stones (Rolling Stones)
5	12	KISSIN' IN THE BACK ROW	Drifters (Bell)
9	13	YOUNG GIRL	Gary Puckett and the Union Gap (CBS)
17	14	SHE'S A WINNER	Intruders (Philadelphia)
26	15	WHAT BECOMES OF THE BROKENHEARTED	Jimmy Ruffin (Tamla Motown)
10	16	TONIGHT	Rubettes (Polydor)
11	17	THE SIX TEENS	Sweet (RCA)
25	18	PLEASE PLEASE ME	David Cassidy (Bell)
14	19	IF YOU GO AWAY	Terry Jacks (Bell)
24	20	I SHOT THE SHERIFF	Eric Clapton (RSO)
-	21	JUST FOR YOU	Glitter Band (Bell)
-	22	I'M LEAVING IT ALL UP TO YOU	Donny & Marie Osmond (MGM)
-	23	HELLO SUMMERTIME	Bobby Goldsboro (United Artists)
29	24	STOP LOOK LISTEN (TO YOUR HEART)	Diana Ross & Marvin Gaye (Tamla Motown)
21	25	MY GIRL BILL	Jim Stafford (MGM)
18	26	LAUGHTER IN THE RAIN	Neil Sedaka (Polydor)
19	27	BANANA ROCK	Wombles (CBS)
-	28	HONEY HONEY	Sweet Dreams (Bradleys)
-	29	SUNDOWN	Gordon Lightfoot (Reprise)
16	30	THE BANGIN' MAN	Slade (Polydor)

The top dance record of 1974, and a precursor to the disco craze of the latter '70s, George McCrae's *Rock Your Baby* was, according to legend, an afterthought recording, cut on a spare tape reel after George's vocalist wife Gwen had missed the studio session at which *she* was to have recorded the song. The Drifters' *Kissin' In The Back Row* was the second and biggest of their run of hits for Bell, made with British producers and songwriters, which constituted a new career for the group on this side of the Atlantic.

August – September 1974

17 August 1974

last week	this week	
2	1	WHEN WILL I SEE YOU AGAIN Three Degrees (Philadelphia)
1	2	ROCK YOUR BABY George McCrae (Jay Boy)
4	3	YOU MAKE ME FEEL BRAND NEW Stylistics (Avco)
6	4	SUMMERLOVE SENSATION Bay City Rollers (Bell)
9	5	ROCKET Mud (RAK)
8	6	ROCK THE BOAT Hues Corporation (RCA)
3	7	BAND ON THE RUN Wings (Apple)
15	8	WHAT BECOMES OF THE BROKENHEARTED Jimmy Ruffin (Tamla Motown)
5	9	AMATEUR HOUR Sparks (Island)
7	10	BORN WITH A SMILE ON MY FACE Stephanie De Sykes/Rain (Bradley)
11	11	IT'S ONLY ROCK'N'ROLL Rolling Stones (Rolling Stones)
20	12	I SHOT THE SHERIFF Eric Clapton (RSO)
16	13	TONIGHT Rubettes (Polydor)
22	14	I'M LEAVING IT ALL UP TO YOU Donny & Marie Osmond (MGM)
12	15	KISSIN' IN THE BACK ROW Drifters (Bell)
21	16	JUST FOR YOU Glitter Band (Bell)
23	17	HELLO SUMMERTIME Bobby Goldsboro (United Artists)
-	18	YOUR BABY AIN'T YOUR BABY ANYMORE Paul Da Vinci (Penny Farthing)
13	19	YOUNG GIRL Gary Puckett and the Union Gap (CBS)
18	20	PLEASE PLEASE ME David Cassidy (Bell)
25	21	MY GIRL BILL Jim Stafford (MGM)
14	22	SHE'S A WINNER Intruders (Philadelphia)
10	23	SHE Charles Aznavour (Barclay)
24	24	STOP LOOK LISTEN (TO YOUR HEART) Diana Ross & Marvin Gaye (Tamla Motown)
-	25	IT'S ALL UP TO YOU Jim Capaldi (Island)
29	26	SUNDOWN Gordon Lightfoot (Reprise)
28	27	HONEY HONEY Sweet Dreams (Bradleys)
-	28	MR SOFT Cockney Rebel (EMI)
17	29	THE SIX TEENS Sweet (RCA)
-	30	Y VIVA ESPANA Sylvia (Sonet)

24 August 1974

last week	this week	
1	1	WHEN WILL I SEE YOU AGAIN Three Degrees (Philadelphia)
3	2	YOU MAKE ME FEEL BRAND NEW Stylistics (Avco)
4	3	SUMMERLOVE SENSATION Bay City Rollers (Bell)
2	4	ROCK YOUR BABY George McCrae (Jay Boy)
6	5	ROCK THE BOAT Hues Corporation (RCA)
8	6	WHAT BECOMES OF THE BROKENHEARTED Jimmy Ruffin (Tamla Motown)
12	7	I SHOT THE SHERIFF Eric Clapton (RSO)
14	8	I'M LEAVING IT ALL UP TO YOU Donny & Marie Osmond (MGM)
5	9	ROCKET Mud (RAK)
11	10	IT'S ONLY ROCK'N'ROLL Rolling Stones (Rolling Stones)
10	11	BORN WITH A SMILE ON MY FACE Stephanie De Sykes/Rain (Bradley)
17	12	HELLO SUMMERTIME Bobby Goldsboro (United Artists)
16	13	JUST FOR YOU Glitter Band (Bell)
28	14	MR SOFT Cockney Rebel (EMI)
27	15	HONEY HONEY Sweet Dreams (Bradleys)
9	16	AMATEUR HOUR Sparks (Island)
7	17	BAND ON THE RUN Wings (Apple)
13	18	TONIGHT Rubettes (Polydor)
30	19	Y VIVA ESPANA Sylvia (Sonet)
-	20	LOVE ME FOR A REASON Osmonds (MGM)
-	21	ANNIE'S SONG John Denver (RCA)
18	22	YOUR BABY AIN'T YOUR BABY ANYMORE Paul Da Vinci (Penny Farthing)
25	23	IT'S ALL UP TO YOU Jim Capaldi (Island)
-	24	ROCK 'N' ROLL LADY Showaddywaddy (Bell)
-	25	KUNG FU FIGHTING Carl Douglas (Pye)
22	26	SHE'S A WINNER Intruders (Philadelphia)
26	27	SUNDOWN Gordon Lightfoot (Reprise)
20	28	PLEASE PLEASE ME David Cassidy (Bell)
24	29	STOP LOOK LISTEN (TO YOUR HEART) Diana Ross & Marvin Gaye (Tamla Motown)
-	30	NA NA NA Cozy Powell (RAK)

31 August 1974

last week	this week	
1	1	WHEN WILL I SEE YOU AGAIN Three Degrees (Philadelphia)
8	2	I'M LEAVING IT ALL UP TO YOU Donny & Marie Osmond (MGM)
2	3	YOU MAKE ME FEEL BRAND NEW Stylistics (Avco)
20	4	LOVE ME FOR A REASON Osmonds (MGM)
6	5	WHAT BECOMES OF THE BROKENHEARTED Jimmy Ruffin (Tamla Motown)
3	6	SUMMERLOVE SENSATION Bay City Rollers (Bell)
19	7	Y VIVA ESPANA Sylvia (Sonet)
14	8	MR SOFT Cockney Rebel (EMI)
15	9	HONEY HONEY Sweet Dreams (Bradleys)
13	10	JUST FOR YOU Glitter Band (Bell)
7	11	I SHOT THE SHERIFF Eric Clapton (RSO)
4	12	ROCK YOUR BABY George McCrae (Jay Boy)
5	13	ROCK THE BOAT Hues Corporation (RCA)
9	14	ROCKET Mud (RAK)
25	15	KUNG FU FIGHTING Carl Douglas (Pye)
12	16	HELLO SUMMERTIME Bobby Goldsboro (United Artists)
21	17	ANNIE'S SONG John Denver (RCA)
30	18	NA NA NA Cozy Powell (RAK)
10	19	IT'S ONLY ROCK'N'ROLL Rolling Stones (Rolling Stones)
-	20	HANG ON IN THERE BABY Johnny Bristol (MGM)
24	21	ROCK 'N' ROLL LADY Showaddywaddy (Bell)
16	22	AMATEUR HOUR Sparks (Island)
-	23	BLACK EYED BOYS Paper Lace (Bus Stop)
-	24	ANOTHER SATURDAY NIGHT Cat Stevens (Island)
-	25	RAINBOW Peters & Lee (Philips)
11	26	BORN WITH A SMILE ON MY FACE Stephanie De Sykes/Rain (Bradley)
27	27	SUNDOWN Gordon Lightfoot (Reprise)
-	28	QUEEN OF CLUBS K C and the Sunshine Band (Jayboy)
18	29	TONIGHT Rubettes (Polydor)
-	30	CAN'T GET ENOUGH OF YOUR LOVE BABE Barry White (Pye)

7 September 1974

last week	this week	
4	1	LOVE ME FOR A REASON Osmonds (MGM)
2	2	I'M LEAVING IT ALL UP TO YOU Donny & Marie Osmond (MGM)
1	3	WHEN WILL I SEE YOU AGAIN Three Degrees (Philadelphia)
15	4	KUNG FU FIGHTING Carl Douglas (Pye)
3	5	YOU MAKE ME FEEL BRAND NEW Stylistics (Avco)
6	6	SUMMERLOVE SENSATION Bay City Rollers (Bell)
5	7	WHAT BECOMES OF THE BROKENHEARTED Jimmy Ruffin (Tamla Motown)
8	8	MR SOFT Cockney Rebel (EMI)
9	9	HONEY HONEY Sweet Dreams (Bradleys)
18	10	NA NA NA Cozy Powell (RAK)
17	11	ANNIE'S SONG John Denver (RCA)
20	12	HANG ON IN THERE BABY Johnny Bristol (MGM)
16	13	HELLO SUMMERTIME Bobby Goldsboro (United Artists)
11	14	I SHOT THE SHERIFF Eric Clapton (RSO)
28	15	QUEEN OF CLUBS K C and the Sunshine Band (Jayboy)
23	16	BLACK EYED BOYS Paper Lace (Bus Stop)
-	17	YOU YOU YOU Alvin Stardust (Magnet)
21	18	ROCK 'N' ROLL LADY Showaddywaddy (Bell)
13	19	ROCK THE BOAT Hues Corporation (RCA)
30	20	CAN'T GET ENOUGH OF YOUR LOVE BABE Barry White (Pye)
12	21	ROCK YOUR BABY George McCrae (Jay Boy)
10	22	JUST FOR YOU Glitter Band (Bell)
-	23	SMOKE GETS IN YOUR EYES Bryan Ferry (Island)
14	24	ROCKET Mud (RAK)
24	25	ANOTHER SATURDAY NIGHT Cat Stevens (Island)
-	26	ROCK ME GENTLY Andy Kim (Capitol)
19	27	IT'S ONLY ROCK'N'ROLL Rolling Stones (Rolling Stones)
25	28	RAINBOW Peters & Lee (Philips)
-	29	BABY LOVE Diana Ross & the Supremes (Tamla Motown)

When Will I See You Again was the first single from Kenny Gamble and Leon Huff's Philadelphia International music stable to top the UK chart; it was then released as a single in the US and climbed to Number Two there - though oddly it was the Three Degrees' final US hit, whilst only the second of a string of major UK successes. The girls moved to Britain where the hits were coming. Meanwhile, an Osmonds resurgence saw permutations of the family back in the top two chart slots simultaneously.

September – October 1974

14 September 1974

last	this		
1	1	LOVE ME FOR A REASON	Osmonds (MGM)
5	2	KUNG FU FIGHTING	Carl Douglas (Pye)
2	3	I'M LEAVING IT ALL UP TO YOU	Donny & Marie Osmond (MGM)
4	4	Y VIVA ESPANA Sylvia (Sonet)	
12	5	ANNIE'S SONG	John Denver (RCA)
3	6	WHEN WILL I SEE YOU AGAIN	Three Degrees (Philadelphia)
6	7	YOU MAKE ME FEEL BRAND NEW	Stylistics (Avco)
13	8	HANG ON IN THERE BABY	Johnny Bristol (MGM)
9	9	MR SOFT Cockney Rebel (EMI)	
10	10	HONEY HONEY	Sweet Dreams (Bradleys)
18	11	YOU YOU YOU	Alvin Stardust (Magnet)
16	12	QUEEN OF CLUBS	K C and the Sunshine Band (Jayboy)
11	13	NA NA NA Cozy Powell (RAK)	
8	14	WHAT BECOMES OF THE BROKENHEARTED	Jimmy Ruffin (Tamla Motown)
7	15	SUMMERLOVE SENSATION	Bay City Rollers (Bell)
14	16	HELLO SUMMERTIME	Bobby Goldsboro (United Artists)
21	17	CAN'T GET ENOUGH OF YOUR LOVE BABE Barry White (Pye)	
19	18	ROCK 'N' ROLL LADY	Showaddywaddy (Bell)
30	19	BABY LOVE	Diana Ross & The Supremes (Tamla Motown)
17	20	BLACK EYED BOYS	Paper Lace (Bus Stop)
29	21	RAINBOW	Peters & Lee (Philips)
27	22	ROCK ME GENTLY	Andy Kim (Capitol)
-	23	PINBALL	Brian Protheroe (Chrysalis)
24	24	SMOKE GETS IN YOUR EYES	Bryan Ferry (Island)
26	25	ANOTHER SATURDAY NIGHT	Cat Stevens (Island)
22	26	ROCK YOUR BABY	George McCrae (Jay Boy)
20	27	ROCK THE BOAT	Hues Corporation (RCA)
15	28	I SHOT THE SHERIFF	Eric Clapton (RSO)
23	29	JUST FOR YOU	Glitter Band (Bell)
-	30	I GOT THE MUSIC IN ME	Kiki Dee Band (Rocket)

21 September 1974

this		
2	1	KUNG FU FIGHTING	Carl Douglas (Pye)
1	2	LOVE ME FOR A REASON	Osmonds (MGM)
5	3	ANNIE'S SONG	John Denver (RCA)
4	4	Y VIVA ESPANA Sylvia (Sonet)	
3	5	I'M LEAVING IT ALL UP TO YOU	Donny & Marie Osmond (MGM)
8	6	HANG ON IN THERE BABY	Johnny Bristol (MGM)
11	7	YOU YOU YOU	Alvin Stardust (Magnet)
12	8	QUEEN OF CLUBS	K C and the Sunshine Band (Jayboy)
6	9	WHEN WILL I SEE YOU AGAIN	Three Degrees (Philadelphia)
13	10	NA NA NA Cozy Powell (RAK)	
17	11	CAN'T GET ENOUGH OF YOUR LOVE BABE Barry White (Pye)	
14	12	WHAT BECOMES OF THE BROKENHEARTED	Jimmy Ruffin (Tamla Motown)
19	13	BABY LOVE	Diana Ross & The Supremes (Tamla Motown)
10	14	HONEY HONEY	Sweet Dreams (Bradleys)
9	15	MR SOFT	Cockney Rebel (EMI)
20	16	BLACK EYED BOYS	Paper Lace (Bus Stop)
7	17	YOU MAKE ME FEEL BRAND NEW	Stylistics (Avco)
24	18	SMOKE GETS IN YOUR EYES	Bryan Ferry (Island)
16	19	HELLO SUMMERTIME	Bobby Goldsboro (United Artists)
30	20	I GOT THE MUSIC IN ME	Kiki Dee Band (Rocket)
21	21	RAINBOW	Peters & Lee (Philips)
18	22	ROCK 'N' ROLL LADY	Showaddywaddy (Bell)
-	23	LONG TALL GLASSES	Leo Sayer (Chrysalis)
25	24	ANOTHER SATURDAY NIGHT	Cat Stevens (Island)
-	25	SILLY LOVE 10 c.c. (UK)	
22	26	ROCK ME GENTLY	Andy Kim (Capitol)
23	27	PINBALL	Brian Protheroe (Chrysalis)
-	28	MACHINE GUN	Commodores (Tamla Motown)
-	29	IT'S BETTER TO HAVE	Don Covay (Mercury)
-	30	THE BITCH IS BACK	Elton John (DJM)

28 September 1974

this		
1	1	KUNG FU FIGHTING	Carl Douglas (Pye)
3	2	ANNIE'S SONG	John Denver (RCA)
6	3	HANG ON IN THERE BABY	Johnny Bristol (MGM)
7	4	YOU YOU YOU	Alvin Stardust (Magnet)
2	5	LOVE ME FOR A REASON	Osmonds (MGM)
11	6	CAN'T GET ENOUGH OF YOUR LOVE BABE Barry White (Pye)	
4	7	Y VIVA ESPANA Sylvia (Sonet)	
8	8	QUEEN OF CLUBS	K C and the Sunshine Band (Jayboy)
5	9	I'M LEAVING IT ALL UP TO YOU	Donny & Marie Osmond (MGM)
16	10	BLACK EYED BOYS	Paper Lace (Bus Stop)
13	11	BABY LOVE	Diana Ross & The Supremes (Tamla Motown)
10	12	NA NA NA Cozy Powell (RAK)	
23	13	LONG TALL GLASSES	Leo Sayer (Chrysalis)
21	14	RAINBOW Peters & Lee (Philips)	
14	15	HONEY HONEY	Sweet Dreams (Bradleys)
20	16	I GOT THE MUSIC IN ME	Kiki Dee Band (Rocket)
-	17	GEE BABY	Peter Shelley (Magnet)
30	18	THE BITCH IS BACK	Elton John (DJM)
-	19	SAD SWEET DREAMER	Sweet Sensation (Pye)
26	20	ROCK ME GENTLY	Andy Kim (Capitol)
12	21	WHAT BECOMES OF THE BROKENHEARTED	Jimmy Ruffin (Tamla Motown)
18	22	SMOKE GETS IN YOUR EYES	Bryan Ferry (Island)
27	23	PINBALL	Brian Protheroe (Chrysalis)
25	24	SILLY LOVE 10 c.c. (UK)	
9	25	WHEN WILL I SEE YOU AGAIN	Three Degrees (Philadelphia)
29	26	IT'S BETTER TO HAVE	Don Covay (Mercury)
24	27	ANOTHER SATURDAY NIGHT	Cat Stevens (Island)
19	28	HELLO SUMMERTIME	Bobby Goldsboro (United Artists)
-	29	KNOCK ON WOOD	David Bowie (RCA)
17	30	YOU MAKE ME FEEL BRAND NEW	Stylistics (Avco)
22	30	ROCK 'N' ROLL LADY	Showaddywaddy (Bell)

5 October 1974

this		
1	1	KUNG FU FIGHTING	Carl Douglas (Pye)
2	2	ANNIE'S SONG	John Denver (RCA)
3	3	HANG ON IN THERE BABY	Johnny Bristol (MGM)
13	4	LONG TALL GLASSES	Leo Sayer (Chrysalis)
6	5	CAN'T GET ENOUGH OF YOUR LOVE BABE Barry White (Pye)	
4	6	YOU YOU YOU	Alvin Stardust (Magnet)
8	7	QUEEN OF CLUBS	K C and the Sunshine Band (Jayboy)
7	8	Y VIVA ESPANA Sylvia (Sonet)	
19	9	SAD SWEET DREAMER	Sweet Sensation (Pye)
5	10	LOVE ME FOR A REASON	Osmonds (MGM)
10	11	BLACK EYED BOYS	Paper Lace (Bus Stop)
29	12	KNOCK ON WOOD	David Bowie (RCA)
11	13	BABY LOVE	Diana Ross & The Supremes (Tamla Motown)
17	14	GEE BABY	Peter Shelley (Magnet)
20	15	ROCK ME GENTLY	Andy Kim (Capitol)
12	16	NA NA NA Cozy Powell (RAK)	
9	17	I'M LEAVING IT ALL UP TO YOU	Donny & Marie Osmond (MGM)
18	18	THE BITCH IS BACK	Elton John (DJM)
23	19	PINBALL	Brian Protheroe (Chrysalis)
-	20	YOU LITTLE TRUST MAKER	Tymes (RCA)
22	21	SMOKE GETS IN YOUR EYES	Bryan Ferry (Island)
27	22	ANOTHER SATURDAY NIGHT	Cat Stevens (Island)
24	23	SILLY LOVE 10 c.c. (UK)	
16	24	I GOT THE MUSIC IN ME	Kiki Dee Band (Rocket)
-	25	I GET A KICK OUT OF YOU	Gary Shearston (Charisma)
-	26	REGGAE TUNE	Andy Fairweather-Low (A&M)
-	27	FAREWELL	Rod Stewart (Mercury)
25	28	WHEN WILL I SEE YOU AGAIN	Three Degrees (Philadelphia)
26	29	IT'S BETTER TO HAVE	Don Covay (Mercury)
-	30	LIFE IS A ROCK (BUT THE RADIO ROLLED ME)	Reunion (RCA)

Kung Fu Fighting, both written and sung by Karl Douglas, was the perhaps inevitable response to the Kung Fu martial art fad, inspired by the films of Bruce Lee and the David Carradine TV series, which found wide favour in the UK in the mid-1970s. John Denver's *Annie's Song*, which perched a place below it on the chart for some weeks, was the bespectacled minstrel's sole UK chart success, despite a run of US hits which lasted well over a decade. The song was dedicated to Denver's then wife.

October – November 1974

12 October 1974

last week	this week	Title	Artist (label)
1	1	KUNG FU FIGHTING	Carl Douglas (Pye)
2	2	ANNIE'S SONG	John Denver (RCA)
14	3	GEE BABY	Peter Shelley (Magnet)
4	4	LONG TALL GLASSES	Leo Sayer (Chrysalis)
3	5	HANG ON IN THERE BABY	Johnny Bristol (MGM)
9	6	SAD SWEET DREAMER	Sweet Sensation (Pye)
15	7	ROCK ME GENTLY	Andy Kim (Capitol)
27	8	FAREWELL	Rod Stewart (Mercury)
26	9	REGGAE TUNE	Andy Fairweather-Low (A&M)
25	10	I GET A KICK OUT OF YOU	Gary Shearston (Charisma)
6	11	YOU YOU YOU	Alvin Stardust (Magnet)
7	12	QUEEN OF CLUBS	K C and the Sunshine Band (Jayboy)
5	13	CAN'T GET ENOUGH OF YOUR LOVE BABE	Barry White (Pye)
-	14	EVERYTHING I OWN	Ken Boothe (Trojan)
18	15	THE BITCH IS BACK	Elton John (DJM)
12	16	KNOCK ON WOOD	David Bowie (RCA)
11	17	BLACK EYED BOYS	Paper Lace (Bus Stop)
8	18	Y VIVA ESPANA	Sylvia (Sonet)
-	19	I CAN'T LEAVE YOU ALONE	George McCrae (Jayboy)
-	20	(YOU'RE) HAVING MY BABY	Paul Anka (United Artists)
20	21	YOU LITTLE TRUST MAKER	Tymes (RCA)
13	22	BABY LOVE	Diana Ross & The Supremes (Tamla Motown)
19	23	PINBALL	Brian Protheroe (Chrysalis)
21	24	SMOKE GETS IN YOUR EYES	Bryan Ferry (Island)
24	25	I GOT THE MUSIC IN ME	Kiki Dee Band (Rocket)
10	26	LOVE ME FOR A REASON	Osmonds (MGM)
-	27	ALL OF ME LOVES ALL OF YOU	Bay City Rollers (Bell)
-	28	SAMBA PA TI	Santana (CBS)
-	29	MACHINE GUN	Commodores (Tamla Motown)
23	30	SILLY LOVE	10 c.c. (UK)

19 October 1974

last week	this week	Title	Artist (label)
3	1	GEE BABY	Peter Shelley (Magnet)
2	2	ANNIE'S SONG	John Denver (RCA)
6	3	SAD SWEET DREAMER	Sweet Sensation (Pye)
14	4	EVERYTHING I OWN	Ken Boothe (Trojan)
7	5	ROCK ME GENTLY	Andy Kim (Capitol)
10	6	I GET A KICK OUT OF YOU	Gary Shearston (Charisma)
9	7	REGGAE TUNE	Andy Fairweather-Low (A&M)
4	8	LONG TALL GLASSES	Leo Sayer (Chrysalis)
8	9	FAREWELL	Rod Stewart (Mercury)
1	10	KUNG FU FIGHTING	Carl Douglas (Pye)
5	11	HANG ON IN THERE BABY	Johnny Bristol (MGM)
20	12	(YOU'RE) HAVING MY BABY	Paul Anka (United Artists)
19	13	I CAN'T LEAVE YOU ALONE	George McCrae (Jayboy)
16	14	KNOCK ON WOOD	David Bowie (RCA)
13	15	CAN'T GET ENOUGH OF YOUR LOVE BABE	Barry White (Pye)
27	16	ALL OF ME LOVES ALL OF YOU	Bay City Rollers (Bell)
-	17	FAR FAR AWAY	Slade (Polydor)
28	18	SAMBA PA TI	Santana (CBS)
21	19	YOU LITTLE TRUST MAKER	Tymes (RCA)
11	20	YOU YOU YOU	Alvin Stardust (Magnet)
-	21	ALL I WANT IS YOU	Roxy Music (Island)
12	22	QUEEN OF CLUBS	K C and the Sunshine Band (Jayboy)
18	23	Y VIVA ESPANA	Sylvia (Sonet)
-	24	WHATEVER GETS YOU THRU THE NIGHT	John Lennon (Apple)
-	25	HAPPY ANNIVERSARY	Slim Whitman (United Artists)
29	26	MACHINE GUN	Commodores (Tamla Motown)
15	27	THE BITCH IS BACK	Elton John (DJM)
-	28	GONNA MAKE YOU A STAR	David Essex (CBS)
-	29	LEAVE IT	Mike McGear (Warner Bros)
-	30	I'M A BELIEVER	Robert Wyatt (Virgin)

26 October 1974

last week	this week	Title	Artist (label)
4	1	EVERYTHING I OWN	Ken Boothe (Trojan)
17	2	FAR FAR AWAY	Slade (Polydor)
3	3	SAD SWEET DREAMER	Sweet Sensation (Pye)
16	4	ALL OF ME LOVES ALL OF YOU	Bay City Rollers (Bell)
1	5	GEE BABY	Peter Shelley (Magnet)
6	6	I GET A KICK OUT OF YOU	Gary Shearston (Charisma)
9	7	FAREWELL	Rod Stewart (Mercury)
28	8	GONNA MAKE YOU A STAR	David Essex (CBS)
7	9	REGGAE TUNE	Andy Fairweather-Low (A&M)
5	10	ROCK ME GENTLY	Andy Kim (Capitol)
2	11	ANNIE'S SONG	John Denver (RCA)
13	12	I CAN'T LEAVE YOU ALONE	George McCrae (Jayboy)
21	13	ALL I WANT IS YOU	Roxy Music (Island)
12	14	(YOU'RE) HAVING MY BABY	Paul Anka (United Artists)
8	15	LONG TALL GLASSES	Leo Sayer (Chrysalis)
19	16	YOU LITTLE TRUST MAKER	Tymes (RCA)
-	17	DOWN ON THE BEACH TONIGHT	Drifters (Bell)
-	18	HEY THERE LONELY GIRL	Eddie Holman (ABC)
25	19	HAPPY ANNIVERSARY	Slim Whitman (United Artists)
-	20	NEVER TURN YOUR BACK ON MOTHER EARTH	Sparks (Island)
18	21	SAMBA PA TI	Santana (CBS)
-	22	MINUETTO ALLEGRETTO	Wombles (CBS)
10	23	KUNG FU FIGHTING	Carl Douglas (Pye)
14	24	KNOCK ON WOOD	David Bowie (RCA)
-	25	KILLER QUEEN	Queen (EMI)
-	26	I HONESTLY LOVE YOU	Olivia Newton-John (EMI)
24	27	WHATEVER GETS YOU THRU THE NIGHT	John Lennon (Apple)
-	28	DA DOO RON RON	Crystals (Warner Bros)
-	29	LET'S GET TOGETHER AGAIN	Glitter Band (Bell)
-	30	LET'S PUT IT ALL TOGETHER	Stylistics (Avco)

2 November 1974

last week	this week	Title	Artist (label)
1	1	EVERYTHING I OWN	Ken Boothe (Trojan)
2	2	FAR FAR AWAY	Slade (Polydor)
4	3	ALL OF ME LOVES ALL OF YOU	Bay City Rollers (Bell)
8	4	GONNA MAKE YOU A STAR	David Essex (CBS)
14	5	(YOU'RE) HAVING MY BABY	Paul Anka (United Artists)
25	6	KILLER QUEEN	Queen (EMI)
12	7	I CAN'T LEAVE YOU ALONE	George McCrae (Jayboy)
3	8	SAD SWEET DREAMER	Sweet Sensation (Pye)
6	9	I GET A KICK OUT OF YOU	Gary Shearston (Charisma)
7	10	FAREWELL	Rod Stewart (Mercury)
13	11	ALL I WANT IS YOU	Roxy Music (Island)
5	12	GEE BABY	Peter Shelley (Magnet)
18	13	HEY THERE LONELY GIRL	Eddie Holman (ABC)
17	14	DOWN ON THE BEACH TONIGHT	Drifters (Bell)
29	15	LET'S GET TOGETHER AGAIN	Glitter Band (Bell)
20	16	NEVER TURN YOUR BACK ON MOTHER EARTH	Sparks (Island)
19	17	HAPPY ANNIVERSARY	Slim Whitman (United Artists)
10	18	ROCK ME GENTLY	Andy Kim (Capitol)
9	19	REGGAE TUNE	Andy Fairweather-Low (A&M)
11	20	ANNIE'S SONG	John Denver (RCA)
28	21	DA DOO RON RON	Crystals (Warner Bros)
26	22	I HONESTLY LOVE YOU	Olivia Newton-John (EMI)
30	23	LET'S PUT IT ALL TOGETHER	Stylistics (Avco)
15	24	LONG TALL GLASSES	Leo Sayer (Chrysalis)
16	25	YOU LITTLE TRUST MAKER	Tymes (RCA)
-	26	ROCKING SOUL	Hues Corporation (RCA)
22	27	MINUETTO ALLEGRETTO	Wombles (CBS)
-	28	HOT SHOT	Barry Blue (Bell)
21	29	SAMBA PA TI	Santana (CBS)
-	30	CAN'T GET ENOUGH OF YOUR LOVE BABE	Barry White (Pye)

The new independent Magnet label had been riding high for nearly a year with Alvin Stardust's run of Top 10 hits, but songwriter Peter Shelley's *Gee Baby* was a surprise bonus success when it attained brief Number One status. Reggae star Ken Boothe's *Everything I Own*, which replaced it, was a cover of Bread's 1972 song. The Bread original hadn't reached the Top 30 here, but in 1987 Boy George would take the song to the top again, in an identical reworking of Ken Boothe's arrangement.

November 1974

9 November 1974

last	this		
4	1	GONNA MAKE YOU A STAR	David Essex (CBS)
1	2	EVERYTHING I OWN	Ken Boothe (Trojan)
6	3	KILLER QUEEN	Queen (EMI)
2	4	FAR FAR AWAY	Slade (Polydor)
3	5	ALL OF ME LOVES ALL OF YOU	Bay City Rollers (Bell)
13	6	HEY THERE LONELY GIRL	Eddie Holman (ABC)
14	7	DOWN ON THE BEACH TONIGHT	Drifters (Bell)
5	8	(YOU'RE) HAVING MY BABY	Paul Anka (United Artists)
7	9	I CAN'T LEAVE YOU ALONE	George McCrae (Jayboy)
15	10	LET'S GET TOGETHER AGAIN	Glitter Band (Bell)
23	11	LET'S PUT IT ALL TOGETHER	Stylistics (Avco)
16	12	NEVER TURN YOUR BACK ON MOTHER EARTH	Sparks (Island)
8	13	SAD SWEET DREAMER	Sweet Sensation (Pye)
11	14	ALL I WANT IS YOU	Roxy Music (Island)
9	15	I GET A KICK OUT OF YOU	Gary Shearston (Charisma)
21	16	DA DOO RON RON	Crystals (Warner Bros)
12	17	GEE BABY	Peter Shelley (Magnet)
-	18	YOU'RE THE FIRST, THE LAST, MY EVERYTHING	Barry White (20th Century)
-	19	PEPPER BOX	Peppers (Spark)
27	20	MINUETTO ALLEGRETTO	Wombles (CBS)
26	21	ROCK'N'SOUL	Hues Corporation (RCA)
17	22	HAPPY ANNIVERSARY	Slim Whitman (United Artists)
28	23	HOT SHOT	Barry Blue (Bell)
-	24	GET YOUR LOVE BACK	Three Degrees (Philadelphia)
10	25	FAREWELL	Rod Stewart (Mercury)
22	26	I HONESTLY LOVE YOU	Olivia Newton-John (EMI)
25	27	YOU LITTLE TRUST MAKER	Tymes (RCA)
-	28	COSTAFINE TOWN	Splinter (Dark Horse)
-	29	YOU HAVEN'T DONE NOTHIN'	Stevie Wonder (Tamla Motown)
-	30	NO HONESTLY	Lynsey De Paul (Jet)

16 November 1974

this		
1	GONNA MAKE YOU A STAR	David Essex (CBS)
2	KILLER QUEEN	Queen (EMI)
3	HEY THERE LONELY GIRL	Eddie Holman (ABC)
4	EVERYTHING I OWN	Ken Boothe (Trojan)
5	ALL OF ME LOVES ALL OF YOU	Bay City Rollers (Bell)
6	DOWN ON THE BEACH TONIGH	Drifters (Bell)
7	LET'S PUT IT ALL TOGETHER	Stylistics (Avco)
8	LET'S GET TOGETHER AGAIN	Glitter Band (Bell)
9	FAR FAR AWAY	Slade (Polydor)
10	PEPPER BOX	Peppers (Spark)
11	YOU'RE THE FIRST, THE LAST, MY EVERYTHING	Barry White (20th Century)
12	(YOU'RE) HAVING MY BABY	Paul Anka (United Artists)
13	I CAN'T LEAVE YOU ALONE	George McCrae (Jayboy)
14	NEVER TURN YOUR BACK ON MOTHER EARTH	Sparks (Island)
15	ALL I WANT IS YOU	Roxy Music (Island)
16	DA DOO RON RON	Crystals (Warner Bros)
17	NO HONESTLY	Lynsey De Paul (Jet)
18	MAGIC	Pilot (EMI)
19	HAPPY ANNIVERSRAY	Slim Whitman (United Artists)
20	COSTAFINE TOWN	Splinter (Dark Horse)
21	JUNIOR'S FARM	Paul McCartney & Wings (Apple)
22	HOT SHOT	Barry Blue (Bell)
23	THE WILD ONE	Suzi Quatro (RAK)
24	I GET A KICK OUT OF YOU	Gary Shearston (Charisma)
25	TOO GOOD TO BE FORGOTTEN	Chi-Lites (Brunswick)
26	TELL HIM	Hello (Bell)
27	MINUETTO ALLEGRETTO	Wombles (CBS)
28	HOW LONG	Ace (Anchor)
29	ROCK'N'SOUL	Hues Corporation (RCA)
30	WHERE DID ALL THE GOOD TIMES GO	Donny Osmond (MGM)

23 November 1974

this		
1	GONNA MAKE YOU A STAR	David Essex (CBS)
2	KILLER QUEEN	Queen (EMI)
3	HEY THERE LONELY GIRL	Eddie Holman (ABC)
4	YOU'RE THE FIRST, THE LAST, MY EVERYTHING	Barry White (20th Century)
5	PEPPER BOX	Peppers (Spark)
6	EVERYTHING I OWN	Ken Boothe (Trojan)
7	LET'S PUT IT ALL TOGETHER	Stylistics (Avco)
8	MAGIC	Pilot (EMI)
9	ALL OF ME LOVES ALL OF YOU	Bay City Rollers (Bell)
10	JUKE BOX JIVE	Rubettes (Polydor)
11	NO HONESTLY	Lynsey De Paul (Jet)
12	DOWN ON THE BEACH TONIGHT	Drifters (Bell)
13	DA DOO RON RON	Crystals (Warner Bros)
14	THE WILD ONE	Suzi Quatro (RAK)
15	LET'S GET TOGETHER AGAIN	Glitter Band (Bell)
16	FAR FAR AWAY	Slade (Polydor)
17	TOO GOOD TO BE FORGOTTEN	Chi-Lites (Brunswick)
18	NEVER TURN YOUR BACK ON MOTHER EARTH	Sparks (Island)
19	JUNIOR'S FARM	Paul McCartney & Wings (Apple)
20	COSTAFINE TOWN	Splinter (Dark Horse)
21	OH YES! YOU'RE BEAUTIFUL	Gary Glitter (Bell)
22	(YOU'RE) HAVING MY BABY	Paul Anka (United Artists)
23	WHERE DID ALL THE GOOD TIMES GO	Donny Osmond (MGM)
24	TELL HIM	Hello (Bell)
25	YOU AIN'T SEEN NOTHING YET	Bachman-Turner Overdrive (Mercury)
26	ALL I WANT IS YOU	Roxy Music (Island)
27	HOW LONG	Ace (Anchor)
28	MY BOY	Elvis Presley (RCA)
29	I CAN'T LEAVE YOU ALONE	George McCrae (Jayboy)
30	LUCY IN THE SKY WITH DIAMONDS	Elton John (DJM)

30 November 1974

last	this		
1	1	GONNA MAKE YOU A STAR	David Essex (CBS)
4	2	YOU'RE THE FIRST, THE LAST, MY EVERYTHING	Barry White (20th Century)
10	3	JUKE BOX JIVE	Rubettes (Polydor)
2	4	KILLER QUEEN	Queen (EMI)
21	5	OH YES! YOU'RE BEAUTIFUL	Gary Glitter (Bell)
3	6	HEY THERE LONELY GIRL	Eddie Holman (ABC)
5	7	PEPPER BOX	Peppers (Spark)
11	8	NO HONESTLY	Lynsey De Paul (Jet)
17	9	TOO GOOD TO BE FORGOTTEN	Chi-Lites (Brunswick)
25	10	YOU AIN'T SEEN NOTHING YET	Bachman-Turner Overdrive (Mercury)
8	11	MAGIC	Pilot (EMI)
24	12	TELL HIM	Hello (Bell)
7	13	LET'S PUT IT ALL TOGETHER	Stylistics (Avco)
14	14	THE WILD ONE	Suzi Quatro (RAK)
6	15	EVERYTHING I OWN	Ken Boothe (Trojan)
30	16	LUCY IN THE SKY WITH DIAMONDS	Elton John (DJM)
9	17	ALL OF ME LOVES ALL OF YOU	Bay City Rollers (Bell)
19	18	JUNIOR'S FARM	Paul McCartney & Wings (Apple)
27	19	HOW LONG	Ace (Anchor)
23	20	WHERE DID ALL THE GOOD TIMES GO	Donny Osmond (MGM)
20	21	COSTAFINE TOWN	Splinter (Dark Horse)
28	22	MY BOY	Elvis Presley (RCA)
12	23	DOWN ON THE BEACH TONIGHT	Drifters (Bell)
-	24	SHA-LA-LA	Al Green (London)
13	25	DA DOO RON RON	Crystals (Warner Bros)
15	26	LET'S GET TOGETHER AGAIN	Glitter Band (Bell)
-	27	GOODBYE NOTHING TO SAY	Javells/Nosmo King (Pye)
-	28	GET DANCING	Disco Tex & the Sex-O-Lettes (Chelsea)
-	29	UNDER MY THUMB	Wayne Gibson (Pye)
-	30	ZING WENT THE STRINGS OF MY HEART	Trammps (Buddah)

David Essex' fourth hit *Gonna Make You A Star* was his biggest success, spending a month at Number One; it had no connection with his film *Stardust*, despite the title. Essex prevented Queen taking the top slot with their second top tenner. The Crystals' 1963 hit *Da Doo Ron Ron* ratified Warner Bros' new licensing deal for the Phil Spector catalogue by becoming a Top 20 hit again, while Lynsey De Paul returned to the Top 10 for the first time since her debut, with the theme from a popular TV sitcom.

December 1974

last week	this week	7 December 1974
1	1	GONNA MAKE YOU A STAR David Essex (CBS)
2	2	YOU'RE THE FIRST, THE LAST, MY EVERYTHING Barry White (20th Century)
3	3	JUKE BOX JIVE Rubettes (Polydor)
5	4	OH YES! YOU'RE BEAUTIFUL Gary Glitter (Bell)
10	5	YOU AIN'T SEEN NOTHING YET Bachman-Turner Overdrive (Mercury)
12	6	TELL HIM Hello (Bell)
12	7	KILLER QUEEN Queen (EMI)
16	8	LUCY IN THE SKY WITH DIAMONDS Elton John (DJM)
22	9	MY BOY Elvis Presley (RCA)
7	10	PEPPER BOX Peppers (Spark)
6	11	HEY THERE LONELY GIRL Eddie Holman (ABC)
9	12	TOO GOOD TO BE FORGOTTEN Chi-Lites (Brunswick)
14	13	THE WILD ONE Suzi Quatro (RAK)
19	14	HOW LONG Ace (Anchor)
11	15	MAGIC Pilot (EMI)
18	16	JUNIOR'S FARM Paul McCartney & Wings (Apple)
8	17	NO HONESTLY Lynsey De Paul (Jet)
24	18	SHA-LA-LA Al Green (London)
-	19	LONELY THIS CHRISTMAS Mud (RAK)
-	20	TELL ME WHY Alvin Stardust (Magnet)
28	21	GET DANCING Disco Tex & the Sex-O-Lettes (Chelsea)
-	22	IRE FEELINGS (SKANGA) Rupie Edwards (Cactus)
27	23	GOODBYE NOTHING TO SAY Javells/Nosmo King (Pye)
13	24	LET'S PUT IT ALL TOGETHER Stylistics (Avco)
-	25	ONLY YOU Ringo Starr (Apple)
-	26	HEY MR CHRISTMAS Showaddywaddy (Bell)
21	27	COSTAFINE TOWN Splinter (Dark Horse)
-	28	SOUND YOUR FUNKY HORN K C & the Sunshine Band (Jayboy)
29	29	UNDER MY THUMB Wayne Gibson (Pye)
30	30	ZING WENT THE STRINGS OF MY HEART Trammps (Buddah)

last week	this week	14 December 1974
2	1	YOU'RE THE FIRST, THE LAST, MY EVERYTHING Barry White (20th Century)
5	2	YOU AIN'T SEEN NOTHING YET Bachman-Turner Overdrive (Mercury)
1	3	GONNA MAKE YOU A STAR David Essex (CBS)
3	4	JUKE BOX JIVE Rubettes (Polydor)
6	5	TELL HIM Hello (Bell)
4	6	OH YES! YOU'RE BEAUTIFUL Gary Glitter (Bell)
7	7	MY BOY Elvis Presley (RCA)
19	8	LONELY THIS CHRISTMAS Mud (RAK)
21	9	GET DANCING Disco Tex & the Sex-O-Lettes (Chelsea)
8	10	LUCY IN THE SKY WITH DIAMONDS Elton John (DJM)
22	11	IRE FEELINGS (SKANGA) Rupie Edwards (Cactus)
12	12	KILLER QUEEN Queen (EMI)
-	13	YOU CAN MAKE ME DANCE, SING OR ANYTHING Faces/Rod Stewart (Warner Bros)
14	14	HOW LONG Ace (Anchor)
15	15	MAGIC Pilot (EMI)
11	16	HEY THERE LONELY GIRL Eddie Holman (ABC)
18	17	SHA-LA-LA Al Green (London)
10	18	PEPPER BOX Peppers (Spark)
-	19	STREETS OF LONDON Ralph McTell (Reprise)
12	20	TOO GOOD TO BE FORGOTTEN Chi-Lites (Brunswick)
-	21	DOWN DOWN Status Quo (Vertigo)
29	22	UNDER MY THUMB Wayne Gibson (Pye)
26	23	HEY MR CHRISTMAS Showaddywaddy (Bell)
20	24	TELL ME WHY Alvin Stardust (Magnet)
30	25	ZING WENT THE STRINGS OF MY HEART Trammps (Buddah)
13	26	THE WILD ONE Suzi Quatro (RAK)
27	27	COSTAFINE TOWN Splinter (Dark Horse)
-	28	THE BUMP Kenny (RAK)
28	29	SOUND YOUR FUNKY HORN K C & the Sunshine Band (Jayboy)
-	30	NEVER CAN SAY GOODBYE Gloria Gaynor (MGM)

last week	this week	21 December 1974
8	1	LONELY THIS CHRISTMAS Mud (RAK)
1	2	YOU'RE THE FIRST, THE LAST, MY EVERYTHING Barry White (20th Century)
2	3	YOU AIN'T SEEN NOTHING YET Bachman-Turner Overdrive (Mercury)
6	4	OH YES! YOU'RE BEAUTIFUL Gary Glitter (Bell)
19	5	STREETS OF LONDON Ralph McTell (Reprise)
7	6	MY BOY Elvis Presley (RCA)
9	7	GET DANCING Disco Tex & the Sex-O-Lettes (Chelsea)
3	8	GONNA MAKE YOU A STAR David Essex (CBS)
10	9	LUCY IN THE SKY WITH DIAMONDS Elton John (DJM)
5	10	TELL HIM Hello (Bell)
21	11	DOWN DOWN Status Quo (Vertigo)
-	12	WOMBLING MERRY CHRISTMAS The Wombles (CBS)
4	13	JUKE BOX JIVE Rubettes (Polydor)
-	14	I CAN HELP Billy Swan (Monument)
11	15	IRE FEELINGS (SKANGA) Rupie Edwards (Cactus)
-	16	THE INBETWEENIES/FATHER CHRISTMAS DO NOT TOUCH ME Goodies (Bradley)
23	17	HEY MR CHRISTMAS Showaddywaddy (Bell)
13	18	YOU CAN MAKE ME DANCE, SING OR ANYTHING Faces/Rod Stewart (Warner Bros)
20	19	TOO GOOD TO BE FORGOTTEN Chi-Lites (Brunswick)
-	20	CHRISTMAS SONG Gilbert O'Sullivan (MAM)
22	21	UNDER MY THUMB Wayne Gibson (Pye)
15	22	MAGIC Pilot (EMI)
24	23	TELL ME WHY Alvin Stardust (Magnet)
-	24	STARDUST David Essex (CBS)
30	25	NEVER CAN SAY GOODBYE Gloria Gaynor (MGM)
28	26	THE BUMP Kenny (RAK)
-	27	JUNIOR'S FARM Paul McCartney & Wings (Apple)
17	28	SHA-LA-LA Al Green (London)
12	29	KILLER QUEEN Queen (EMI)
27	30	COSTAFINE TOWN Splinter (Dark Horse)

last week	this week	28 December 1974
1	1	LONELY THIS CHRISTMAS Mud (RAK)
5	2	STREETS OF LONDON Ralph McTell (Reprise)
12	3	WOMBLING MERRY CHRISTMAS The Wombles (CBS)
3	4	YOU AIN'T SEEN NOTHING YET Bachman-Turner Overdrive (Mercury)
2	5	YOU'RE THE FIRST, THE LAST, MY EVERYTHING Barry White (20th Century)
7	6	GET DANCING Disco Tex & the Sex-O-Lettes (Chelsea)
16	7	THE INBETWEENIES/FATHER CHRISTMAS DO NOT TOUCH ME Goodies (Bradley)
6	8	MY BOY Elvis Presley (RCA)
11	9	DOWN DOWN Status Quo (Vertigo)
14	10	I CAN HELP Billy Swan (Monument)
13	11	JUKE BOX JIVE Rubettes (Polydor)
4	12	OH YES! YOU'RE BEAUTIFUL Gary Glitter (Bell)
9	13	LUCY IN THE SKY WITH DIAMONDS Elton John (DJM)
20	14	CHRISTMAS SONG Gilbert O'Sullivan (MAM)
17	15	HEY MR CHRISTMAS Showaddywaddy (Bell)
18	16	YOU CAN MAKE ME DANCE, SING OR ANYTHING Faces/Rod Stewart (Warner Bros)
10	17	TELL HIM Hello (Bell)
25	18	NEVER CAN SAY GOODBYE Gloria Gaynor (MGM)
23	19	TELL ME WHY Alvin Stardust (Magnet)
24	20	STARDUST David Essex (CBS)
26	21	THE BUMP Kenny (RAK)
-	22	MS GRACE Tymes (RCA)
-	23	SOUND YOUR FUNKY HORN K C and the Sunshine Band (Jayboy)
15	24	IRE FEELINGS (SKANGA) Rupie Edwards (Cactus)
8	25	GONNA MAKE YOU A STAR David Essex (CBS)
-	26	ARE YOU READY TO ROCK Wizzard (Warner Bros)
21	27	UNDER MY THUMB Wayne Gibson (Pye)
-	28	HELP ME MAKE IT THROUGH THE NIGHT John Holt (Trojan)
-	29	YOU CAN HAVE IT ALL George McCrae (Jayboy)
28	30	SHA-LA-LA Al Green (London)

For the second year running the top year-end single had a Christmas theme, as Mud's Les Gray turned his fondness for Elvis into a fruity pastiche on *Lonely This Christmas*. It gave the group their biggest ever seller. Christmas records were around in profusion: the Wombles had *Wombling Merry Christmas* at Number Three, while Gilbert O'Sullivan and Showaddywaddy produced Yuletide variations on their familiar styles, and the Goodies had a half-Christmassy double A-side top tenner, risqué to boot.

January 1975

4 January 1975

last week	this week	Title / Artist
1	1	LONELY THIS CHRISTMAS — Mud (RAK)
2	2	STREETS OF LONDON — Ralph McTell (Reprise)
3	3	WOMBLING MERRY CHRISTMAS — Wombles (CBS)
4	4	YOU AIN'T SEEN NOTHING YET — Bachman-Turner Overdrive (Mercury)
11	5	JUKE BOX JIVE — Rubettes (Polydor)
6	6	GET DANCING — Disco Tex & The Sex-O-Lettes (Chelsea)
5	7	YOU'RE THE FIRST, THE LAST, MY EVERYTHING — Barry White (20th Century)
7	8	THE INBETWEENIES/FATHER CHRISTMAS DO NOT TOUCH ME — Goodies (Bradley)
9	9	DOWN DOWN — Status Quo (Vertigo)
8	10	MY BOY — Elvis Presley (RCA)
13	11	LUCY IN THE SKY WITH DIAMONDS — Elton John (DJM)
10	12	I CAN HELP — Billy Swan (Monument)
14	13	CHRISTMAS SONG — Gilbert O'Sullivan (MAM)
15	14	HEY MISTER CHRISTMAS — Showaddywaddy (Bell)
16	15	YOU CAN MAKE ME DANCE, SING OR ANYTHING — /Rod Stewart (Warner Bros)
12	16	OH YES! YOU'RE BEAUTIFUL — Gary Glitter (Bell)
18	17	NEVER CAN SAY GOODBYE — Gloria Gaynor (MGM)
21	18	THE BUMP — Kenny (RAK)
17	19	TELL HIM — Hello (Bell)
20	20	STARDUST — David Essex (CBS)
23	21	SOUND YOUR FUNKY HORN — K C & The Sunshine Band (Jayboy)
22	22	MS GRACE — Tymes (RCA)
28	23	HELP ME MAKE IT THROUGH THE NIGHT — John Holt (Trojan)
19	24	TELL ME WHY — Alvin Stardust (Magnet)
24	25	IRE FEELINGS (SKANGA) — Rupie Edwards (Cactus)
26	26	ARE YOU READY TO ROCK — Wizzard (Warner Bros)
27	27	UNDER MY THUMB — Wayne Gibson (Pye)
25	28	GONNA MAKE YOU A STAR — David Essex (CBS)
-	29	CRYING OVER YOU — Ken Boothe (Trojan)
30	30	SHA-LA-LA — Al Green (London)

11 January 1975

last week	this week	Title / Artist
2	1	STREETS OF LONDON — Ralph McTell (Reprise)
9	2	DOWN DOWN — Status Quo (Vertigo)
1	3	LONELY THIS CHRISTMAS — Mud (RAK)
5	4	JUKE BOX JIVE — Rubettes (Polydor)
10	5	MY BOY — Elvis Presley (RCA)
4	6	YOU AIN'T SEEN NOTHING YET — Bachman-Turner Overdrive (Mercury)
3	7	WOMBLING MERRY CHRISTMAS — Wombles (CBS)
8	8	THE INBETWEENIES/FATHER CHRISTMAS DO NOT TOUCH ME — Goodies (Bradley)
12	9	I CAN HELP — Billy Swan (Monument)
6	10	GET DANCING — Disco Tex & The Sex-O-Lettes (Chelsea)
7	11	YOU'RE THE FIRST, THE LAST, MY EVERYTHING — Barry White (20th Century)
17	12	NEVER CAN SAY GOODBYE — Gloria Gaynor (MGM)
15	13	YOU CAN MAKE ME DANCE, SING OR ANYTHING — Faces /Rod Stewart (Warner Bros)
18	14	THE BUMP — Kenny (RAK)
11	15	LUCY IN THE SKY WITH DIAMONDS — Elton John (DJM)
22	16	MS GRACE — Tymes (RCA)
16	17	OH YES! YOU'RE BEAUTIFUL — Gary Glitter (Bell)
20	18	STARDUST — David Essex (CBS)
23	19	HELP ME MAKE IT THROUGH THE NIGHT — John Holt (Trojan)
26	20	ARE YOU READY TO ROCK — Wizzard (Warner Bros)
19	21	TELL HIM — Hello (Bell)
14	22	HEY MISTER CHRISTMAS — Showaddywaddy (Bell)
13	23	CHRISTMAS SONG — Gilbert O'Sullivan (MAM)
21	24	SOUND YOUR FUNKY HORN — K C & The Sunshine Band (Jayboy)
29	25	CRYING OVER YOU — Ken Boothe (Trojan)
24	26	TELL ME WHY — Alvin Stardust (Magnet)
27	27	UNDER MY THUMB — Wayne Gibson (Pye)
28	28	GONNA MAKE YOU A STAR — David Essex (CBS)
-	29	MORNING SIDE OF THE MOUNTAIN — Donny & Marie Osmond (MGM)
-	30	JE T'AIME — Jane Birkin & Serge Gainsbourg (Antic)

18 January 1975

last week	this week	Title / Artist
1	1	STREETS OF LONDON — Ralph McTell (Reprise)
2	2	DOWN DOWN — Status Quo (Vertigo)
12	3	NEVER CAN SAY GOODBYE — Gloria Gaynor (MGM)
14	4	THE BUMP — Kenny (RAK)
16	5	MS GRACE — Tymes (RCA)
9	6	I CAN HELP — Billy Swan (Monument)
10	7	GET DANCING Disco Tex & The Sex-O-Lettes (Chelsea)
20	8	ARE YOU READY TO ROCK — Wizzard (Warner Bros)
4	9	JUKE BOX JIVE — Rubettes (Polydor)
18	10	STARDUST David Essex (CBS)
19	11	HELP ME MAKE IT THROUGH THE NIGHT — John Holt (Trojan)
3	12	LONELY THIS CHRISTMAS — Mud (RAK)
6	13	YOU AIN'T SEEN NOTHING YET — Bachman-Turner Overdrive (Mercury)
5	14	MY BOY — Elvis Presley (RCA)
13	15	YOU CAN MAKE ME DANCE, SING OR ANYTHING — Faces /Rod Stewart (Warner Bros)
25	16	CRYING OVER YOU — Ken Boothe (Trojan)
8	17	THE INBETWEENIES/FATHER CHRISTMAS DO NOT TOUCH ME — Goodies (Bradley)
29	18	MORNING SIDE OF THE MOUNTAIN — Donny & Marie Osmond (MGM)
7	19	WOMBLING MERRY CHRISTMAS — Wombles (CBS)
15	20	LUCY IN THE SKY WITH DIAMONDS — Elton John (DJM)
-	21	PROMISED LAND — Elvis Presley (RCA)
-	22	BOOGIE ON REGGAE WOMAN — Stevie Wonder (Tamla Motown)
27	23	UNDER MY THUMB — Wayne Gibson (Pye)
11	24	YOU'RE THE FIRST, THE LAST, MY EVERYTHING — Barry White (20th Century)
-	25	JANUARY — Pilot (EMI)
-	26	YOU CAN HAVE IT ALL — George McCrae (Jayboy)
24	27	SOUND YOUR FUNKY HORN — K C & The Sunshine Band (Jayboy)
-	28	CHERI BABE — Hot Chocolate (RAK)
-	29	ROCK AND ROLL (I GAVE YOU THE BEST YEARS OF MY LIFE) — Kevin Johnson (UK)
26	30	TELL ME WHY — Alvin Stardust (Magnet)

25 January 1975

last week	this week	Title / Artist
2	1	DOWN DOWN — Status Quo (Vertigo)
3	2	NEVER CAN SAY GOODBYE — Gloria Gaynor (MGM)
1	3	STREETS OF LONDON — Ralph McTell (Reprise)
4	4	THE BUMP — Kenny (RAK)
5	5	MS GRACE — Tymes (RCA)
6	6	I CAN HELP — Billy Swan (Monument)
8	7	ARE YOU READY TO ROCK — Wizzard (Warner Bros)
11	8	HELP ME MAKE IT THROUGH THE NIGHT — John Holt (Trojan)
10	9	STARDUST David Essex (CBS)
21	10	PROMISED LAND — Elvis Presley (RCA)
25	11	JANUARY — Pilot (EMI)
16	12	CRYING OVER YOU — Ken Boothe (Trojan)
18	13	MORNING SIDE OF THE MOUNTAIN — Donny & Marie Osmond (MGM)
7	14	GET DANCING Disco Tex & The Sex-O-Lettes (Chelsea)
22	15	BOOGIE ON REGGAE WOMAN — Stevie Wonder (Tamla Motown)
-	16	GOODBYE MY LOVE — Glitter Band (Bell)
-	17	SOMETHING FOR THE GIRL WITH EVERYTHING — Sparks (Island)
-	18	SUGAR CANDY KISSES — Mac & Katie Kissoon (Polydor)
23	19	UNDER MY THUMB — Wayne Gibson (Pye)
14	20	MY BOY — Elvis Presley (RCA)
15	21	YOU CAN MAKE ME DANCE, SING OR ANYTHING — Faces /Rod Stewart (Warner Bros)
-	22	PURELY BY COINCIDENCE — Sweet Sensation (Pye)
17	23	THE INBETWEENIES/FATHER CHRISTMAS DO NOT TOUCH ME — Goodies (Bradley)
-	24	ANGIE BABY — Helen Reddy (Capitol)
9	25	JUKE BOX JIVE — Rubettes (Polydor)
29	26	ROCK AND ROLL (I GAVE YOU THE BEST YEARS OF MY LIFE) — Kevin Johnson (UK)
26	27	YOU CAN HAVE IT ALL — George McCrae (Jayboy)
13	28	YOU AIN'T SEEN NOTHING YET — Bachman-Turner Overdrive (Mercury)
12	29	LONELY THIS CHRISTMAS — Mud (RAK)
-	30	PLEASE MR POSTMAN — Carpenters (A&M)

Probably nobody was more surprised than English folk artist Ralph McTell himself to find he was top of the pop chart with a song he (and hundreds of others) had been singing around the country's folk clubs for many years. But then this was a strange January in which the previous year's Christmas songs took weeks to fade away when they would normally have dropped straight out of the chart at New Year, and Pilot had a song named after the month which prepared to rise to its peak in February!

last week	this	1 February 1975			8 February 1975			15 February 1975			22 February 1975
5	1	MS GRACE Tymes (RCA)	2	1	JANUARY Pilot (EMI)	1	1	JANUARY Pilot (EMI)	4	1	PLEASE MR POSTMAN Carpenters (A&M)
11	2	JANUARY Pilot (EMI)	1	2	MS GRACE Tymes (RCA)	3	2	SUGAR CANDY KISSES Mac & Katie Kissoon (Polydor)	1	2	JANUARY Pilot (EMI)
2	3	NEVER CAN SAY GOODBYE Gloria Gaynor (MGM)	14	3	SUGAR CANDY KISSES Mac & Katie Kissoon (Polydor)	4	3	GOODBYE MY LOVE Glitter Band (Bell)	10	3	MAKE ME SMILE Steve Harley & Cockney Rebel (EMI)
8	4	HELP ME MAKE IT THROUGH THE NIGHT John Holt (Trojan)	10	4	GOODBYE MY LOVE Glitter Band (Bell)	13	4	PLEASE MR POSTMAN Carpenters (A&M)	2	4	SUGAR CANDY KISSES Mac & Katie Kissoon (Polydor)
4	5	THE BUMP Kenny (RAK)	5	5	THE BUMP Kenny (RAK)	9	5	NOW I'M HERE Queen (EMI)	6	5	ANGIE BABY Helen Reddy (Capitol)
1	6	DOWN DOWN Status Quo (Vertigo)	3	6	NEVER CAN SAY GOODBYE Gloria Gaynor (MGM)	12	6	ANGIE BABY Helen Reddy (Capitol)	3	6	GOODBYE MY LOVE Glitter Band (Bell)
10	7	PROMISED LAND Elvis Presley (RCA)	7	7	PROMISED LAND Elvis Presley (RCA)	15	7	BLACK SUPERMAN (MUHAMMAD ALI) Johnny Wakelin & the Kinshasa Band (Pye)	15	7	SHAME SHAME SHAME Shirley & Company (All Platinum)
13	8	MORNING SIDE OF THE MOUNTAIN Donny & Marie Osmond (MGM)	13	8	PURELY BY COINCIDENCE Sweet Sensation (Pye)	2	8	MS GRACE Tymes (RCA)	7	8	BLACK SUPERMAN (MUHAMMAD ALI) Johnny Wakelin & the Kinshasa Band (Pye)
3	9	STREETS OF LONDON Ralph McTell (Reprise)	19	9	NOW I'M HERE Queen (EMI)	8	9	PURELY BY COINCIDENCE Sweet Sensation (Pye)	29	9	THE SECRETS THAT YOU KEEP Mud (RAK)
16	10	GOODBYE MY LOVE Glitter Band (Bell)	8	10	MORNING SIDE OF THE MOUNTAIN Donny & Marie Osmond (MGM)	-	10	MAKE ME SMILE Steve Harley & Cockney Rebel (EMI)	5	10	NOW I'M HERE Queen (EMI)
7	11	ARE YOU READY TO ROCK Wizzard (Warner Bros)	4	11	HELP ME MAKE IT THROUGH THE NIGHT John Holt (Trojan)	10	11	MORNING SIDE OF THE MOUNTAIN Donny & Marie Osmond (MGM)	18	11	YOUR KISS IS SWEET Syreeta (Tamla Motown)
12	12	CRYING OVER YOU Ken Boothe (Trojan)	22	12	ANGIE BABY Helen Reddy (Capitol)	7	12	PROMISED LAND Elvis Presley (RCA)	19	12	FOOTSEE Wigan's Chosen Few (Pye)
22	13	PURELY BY COINCIDENCE Sweet Sensation (Pye)	24	13	PLEASE MR POSTMAN Carpenters (A&M)	5	13	THE BUMP Kenny (RAK)	16	13	STAR ON A TV SHOW Stylistics (Avco)
18	14	SUGAR CANDY KISSES Mac & Katie Kissoon (Polydor)	20	14	BOOGIE ON REGGAE WOMAN Stevie Wonder (Tamla Motown)	6	14	NEVER CAN SAY GOODBYE Gloria Gaynor (MGM)	8	14	MS GRACE Tymes (RCA)
9	15	STARDUST David Essex (CBS)	21	15	BLACK SUPERMAN (MUHAMMAD ALI) Johnny Wakelin & the Kinshasa Band (Pye)	-	15	SHAME SHAME SHAME Shirley & Company (All Platinum)	27	15	MY EYES ADORED YOU Frankie Valli (Private Stock)
17	16	SOMETHING FOR THE GIRL WITH EVERYTHING Sparks (Island)	6	16	DOWN DOWN Status Quo (Vertigo)	17	16	STAR ON A TV SHOW Stylistics (Avco)	21	16	GOOD LOVE CAN NEVER DIE Alvin Stardust (Magnet)
6	17	I CAN HELP Billy Swan (Monument)	18	17	STAR ON A TV SHOW Stylistics (Avco)	11	17	HELP ME MAKE IT THROUGH THE NIGHT John Holt (Trojan)	13	17	THE BUMP Kenny (RAK)
-	18	STAR ON A TV SHOW Stylistics (Avco)	16	18	SOMETHING FOR THE GIRL WITH EVERYTHING Sparks (Island)	19	18	YOUR KISS IS SWEET Syreeta (Tamla Motown)	9	18	PURELY BY COINCIDENCE Sweet Sensation (Pye)
-	19	NOW I'M HERE Queen (EMI)	-	19	YOUR KISS IS SWEET Syreeta (Tamla Motown)	20	19	FOOTSEE Wigan's Chosen Few (Pye)	11	19	MORNING SIDE OF THE MOUNTAIN Donny & Marie Osmond (MGM)
15	20	BOOGIE ON REGGAE WOMAN Stevie Wonder (Tamla Motown)	27	20	FOOTSEE Wigan's Chosen Few (Pye)	14	20	BOOGIE ON REGGAE WOMAN Stevie Wonder (Tamla Motown)	-	20	IF Telly Savalas (MCA)
-	21	BLACK SUPERMAN (MUHAMMAD ALI) Johnny Wakelin & the Kinshasa Band (Pye)	-	21	GOOD LOVE CAN NEVER DIE Alvin Stardust (Magnet)	21	21	GOOD LOVE CAN NEVER DIE Alvin Stardust (Magnet)	26	21	IT MAY BE WINTER OUTSIDE Love Unlimited (20th Century)
24	22	ANGIE BABY Helen Reddy (Capitol)	28	22	IT MAY BE WINTER OUTSIDE Love Unlimited (20th Century)	27	22	ROLL ON DOWN THE HIGHWAY Bachman-Turner Overdrive (Mercury)	12	22	PROMISED LAND Elvis Presley (RCA)
26	23	ROCK AND ROLL (I GAVE YOU THE BEST YEARS OF MY LIFE) Kevin Johnson (UK)	11	23	ARE YOU READY TO ROCK Wizzard (Warner Bros)	24	23	SHOORAH! SHOORAH! Betty Wright (RCA)	23	23	SHOORAH! SHOORAH! Betty Wright (RCA)
30	24	PLEASE MR POSTMAN Carpenters (A&M)	25	24	SHOORAH! SHOORAH! Betty Wright (RCA)	18	24	SOMETHING FOR THE GIRL WITH EVERYTHING Sparks (Island)	28	24	PLEASE TELL HIM THAT I SAID HELLO Dana (GTO)
-	25	SHOORAH! SHOORAH! Betty Wright (RCA)	9	25	STREETS OF LONDON Ralph McTell (Reprise)	29	25	I'M STONE IN LOVE WITH YOU Johnny Mathis (CBS)	22	25	ROLL ON DOWN THE HIGHWAY Bachman-Turner Overdrive (Mercury)
14	26	GET DANCING Disco Tex & The Sex-O-Lettes (Chelsea)	-	26	MY EYES ADORED YOU Frankie Valli (Private Stock)	22	26	IT MAY BE WINTER OUTSIDE Love Unlimited (20th Century)	-	26	ONLY YOU CAN Fox (GTO)
-	27	FOOTSEE Wigan's Chosen Few (Pye)	-	27	ROLL ON DOWN THE HIGHWAY Bachman-Turner Overdrive (Mercury)	26	27	MY EYES ADORED YOU Frankie Valli (Private Stock)	25	27	I'M STONE IN LOVE WITH YOU Johnny Mathis (CBS)
-	28	IT MAY BE WINTER OUTSIDE Love Unlimited (20th Century)	15	28	STARDUST David Essex (CBS)	-	28	PLEASE TELL HIM THAT I SAID HELLO Dana (GTO)	-	28	HOW DOES IT FEEL Slade (Polydor)
21	29	YOU CAN MAKE ME DANCE, SING OR ANYTHING Faces /Rod Stewart (Warner Bros)	-	29	I'M STONE IN LOVE WITH YOU Johnny Mathis (CBS)	-	29	THE SECRETS THAT YOU KEEP Mud (RAK)	-	29	DREAMER Supertramp (A&M)
19	30	UNDER MY THUMB Wayne Gibson (Pye)	17	30	I CAN HELP Billy Swan (Monument)	-	30	MY LAST NIGHT WITH YOU Arrows (RAK)	-	30	SOUTH AFRICAN MAN Hamilton Bohannon (Brunswick)

Ms. Grace finally gave Philadelphia vocal group the Tymes a UK Number One, nearly 12 years after they had topped the US chart (and made their UK Top 30 debut) with *So Much In Love*. Oddly enough, this peaked at No.91 in America! The Carpenters, while fairly consistent UK hitmakers, had also waited a long time for their chart topper with the Motown oldie *Please Mr Postman*. Long absent chart returnees were Frankie Valli after five years, and Johnny Mathis after 15, scoring with a familiar Stylistics song.

March 1975

1 March 1975

last week	this week	Title
3	1	MAKE ME SMILE Steve Harley & Cockney Rebel (EMI)
20	2	IF Telly Savalas (MCA)
1	3	PLEASE MR POSTMAN Carpenters (A&M)
9	4	THE SECRETS THAT YOU KEEP Mud (RAK)
2	5	JANUARY Pilot (EMI)
7	6	SHAME SHAME SHAME Shirley & Company (All Platinum)
15	7	MY EYES ADORED YOU Frankie Valli (Private Stock)
26	8	ONLY YOU CAN Fox (GTO)
4	9	SUGAR CANDY KISSES Mac & Katie Kissoon (Polydor)
5	10	ANGIE BABY Helen Reddy (Capitol)
12	11	FOOTSEE Wigan's Chosen Few (Pye)
11	12	YOUR KISS IS SWEET Syreeta (Tamla Motown)
16	13	GOOD LOVE CAN NEVER DIE Alvin Stardust (Magnet)
27	14	I'M STONE IN LOVE WITH YOU Johnny Mathis (CBS)
8	15	BLACK SUPERMAN (MUHAMMAD ALI) Johnny Wakelin & the Kinshasa Band (Pye)
6	16	GOODBYE MY LOVE Glitter Band (Bell)
13	17	STAR ON A TV SHOW Stylistics (Avco)
10	18	NOW I'M HERE Queen (EMI)
-	19	PICK UP THE PIECES Average White Band (Atlantic)
24	20	PLEASE TELL HIM THAT I SAID HELLO Dana (GTO)
21	21	IT MAY BE WINTER OUTSIDE Love Unlimited (20th Century)
28	22	HOW DOES IT FEEL Slade (Polydor)
30	23	SOUTH AFRICAN MAN Hamilton Bohannon (Brunswick)
29	24	DREAMER Supertramp (A&M)
-	25	MY LAST NIGHT WITH YOU Arrows (RAK)
-	26	MANDY Barry Manilow (Arista)
-	27	LOVE GAMES Drifters (Bell)
23	28	SHOORAH! SHOORAH! Betty Wright (RCA)
25	29	ROLL ON DOWN THE HIGHWAY Bachman-Turner Overdrive (Mercury)
-	30	SWEET MUSIC Showaddywaddy (Bell)

8 March 1975

		Title
2	1	IF Telly Savalas (MCA)
1	2	MAKE ME SMILE Steve Harley & Cockney Rebel (EMI)
8	3	ONLY YOU CAN Fox (GTO)
4	4	THE SECRETS THAT YOU KEEP Mud (RAK)
7	5	MY EYES ADORED YOU Frankie Valli (Private Stock)
3	6	PLEASE MR POSTMAN Carpenters (A&M)
6	7	SHAME SHAME SHAME Shirley & Company (All Platinum)
21	8	IT MAY BE WINTER OUTSIDE Love Unlimited (20th Century)
-	9	YOUNG AMERICANS David Bowie (RCA)
20	10	PLEASE TELL HIM THAT I SAID HELLO Dana (GTO)
19	11	PICK UP THE PIECES Average White Band (Atlantic)
24	12	DREAMER Supertramp (A&M)
12	13	YOUR KISS IS SWEET Syreeta (Tamla Motown)
-	14	BYE BYE BABY Bay City Rollers (Bell)
14	15	I'M STONE IN LOVE WITH YOU Johnny Mathis (CBS)
9	16	SUGAR CANDY KISSES Mac & Katie Kissoon (Polydor)
11	17	FOOTSEE Wigan's Chosen Few (Pye)
13	18	GOOD LOVE CAN NEVER DIE Alvin Stardust (Magnet)
26	19	MANDY Barry Manilow (Arista)
5	20	JANUARY Pilot (EMI)
22	21	HOW DOES IT FEEL Slade (Polydor)
23	22	SOUTH AFRICAN MAN Hamilton Bohannon (Brunswick)
-	23	NO. 9 DREAM John Lennon (Apple)
25	24	MY LAST NIGHT WITH YOU Arrows (RAK)
17	25	STAR ON A TV SHOW Stylistics (Avco)
10	26	ANGIE BABY Helen Reddy (Capitol)
-	27	I CAN DO IT Rubettes (State)
-	28	THERE'S A WHOLE LOT OF LOVING Guys & Dolls (Magnet)
30	29	SWEET MUSIC Showaddywaddy (Bell)
15	30	BLACK SUPERMAN (MUHAMMAD ALI) Johnny Wakelin & the Kinshasa Band (Pye)

15 March 1975

		Title
1	1	IF Telly Savalas (MCA)
14	2	BYE BYE BABY Bay City Rollers (Bell)
3	3	ONLY YOU CAN Fox (GTO)
4	4	THE SECRETS THAT YOU KEEP Mud (RAK)
2	5	MAKE ME SMILE Steve Harley & Cockney Rebel (EMI)
5	6	MY EYES ADORED YOU Frankie Valli (Private Stock)
11	7	PICK UP THE PIECES Average White Band (Atlantic)
7	8	SHAME SHAME SHAME Shirley & Company (All Platinum)
12	9	DREAMER Supertramp (A&M)
15	10	I'M STONE IN LOVE WITH YOU Johnny Mathis (CBS)
9	11	YOUNG AMERICANS David Bowie (RCA)
29	12	SWEET MUSIC Showaddywaddy (Bell)
6	13	PLEASE MR POSTMAN Carpenters (A&M)
28	14	THERE'S A WHOLE LOT OF LOVING Guys & Dolls (Magnet)
19	15	MANDY Barry Manilow (Arista)
10	16	PLEASE TELL HIM THAT I SAID HELLO Dana (GTO)
-	17	WHAT AM I GONNA DO WITH YOU Barry White (20th Century)
27	18	I CAN DO IT Rubettes (State)
-	19	PHILADELPHIA FREEDOM Elton John Band (DJM)
16	20	FOOTSEE Wigan's Chosen Few (Pye)
8	21	IT MAY BE WINTER OUTSIDE Love Unlimited (20th Century)
21	22	HOW DOES IT FEEL Slade (Polydor)
-	23	FANCY PANTS Kenny (RAK)
-	24	GIRLS Moments & Whatnauts (All Platinum)
18	25	GOOD LOVE CAN NEVER DIE Alvin Stardust (Magnet)
-	26	PLAY ME LIKE YOU PLAY YOUR GUITAR Duane Eddy & the Rebelettes (GTO)
-	27	REACH OUT I'LL BE THERE Gloria Gaynor (MGM)
-	28	HAVING A PARTY Osmonds (MGM)
23	29	NO. 9 DREAM John Lennon (Apple)
16	30	SUGAR CANDY KISSES Mac & Katie Kissoon (Polydor)

22 March 1975

		Title
2	1	BYE BYE BABY Bay City Rollers (Bell)
1	2	IF Telly Savalas (MCA)
3	3	ONLY YOU CAN Fox (GTO)
14	4	THERE'S A WHOLE LOT OF LOVING Guys & Dolls (Magnet)
5	5	MAKE ME SMILE Steve Harley & Cockney Rebel (EMI)
7	6	PICK UP THE PIECES Average White Band (Atlantic)
4	7	THE SECRETS THAT YOU KEEP Mud (RAK)
15	8	MANDY Barry Manilow (Arista)
17	9	WHAT AM I GONNA DO WITH YOU Barry White (20th Century)
24	10	GIRLS Moments & Whatnauts (All Platinum)
6	11	MY EYES ADORED YOU Frankie Valli (Private Stock)
10	12	I'M STONE IN LOVE WITH YOU Johnny Mathis (CBS)
18	13	I CAN DO IT Rubettes (State)
23	14	FANCY PANTS Kenny (RAK)
9	15	DREAMER Supertramp (A&M)
16	16	PLEASE TELL HIM THAT I SAID HELLO Dana (GTO)
19	17	PHILADELPHIA FREEDOM Elton John Band (DJM)
26	18	PLAY ME LIKE YOU PLAY YOUR GUITAR Duane Eddy & the Rebelettes (GTO)
12	19	SWEET MUSIC Showaddywaddy (Bell)
8	20	SHAME SHAME SHAME Shirley & Company (All Platinum)
27	21	REACH OUT I'LL BE THERE Gloria Gaynor (MGM)
11	22	YOUNG AMERICANS David Bowie (RCA)
-	23	FOX ON THE RUN Sweet (RCA)
13	24	PLEASE MR POSTMAN Carpenters (A&M)
-	25	SWING YOUR DADDY Jim Gilstrap (Chelsea)
22	26	HOW DOES IT FEEL Slade (Polydor)
-	27	THE FUNKY GIBBON/SICK MAN BLUES Goodies (Bradley)
-	28	L-O-V-E Al Green (London)
28	29	HAVING A PARTY Osmonds (MGM)
-	30	WHAT IN THE WORLD'S COME OVER YOU Tam White (RAK)

Telly Savalas, star of the hit TV cop series *Kojak*, never strayed near the charts in his native USA. Here, however, his spoken-word interpretation of David Gates' song *If* (a 1971 US Top 10 hit by Bread which had failed here) took the public's fancy in a big way.

The Bay City Rollers deposed him with their biggest UK seller *Bye Bye Baby*, another cover of an old US hit (by the Four Seasons in 1965) which had missed in the UK. Slade, meanwhile, noticeably struggled with *How Does It Feel*.

29 March 1975

last week	this week	Title / Artist
1	1	BYE BYE BABY — Bay City Rollers (Bell)
4	2	THERE'S A WHOLE LOT OF LOVING — Guys & Dolls (Magnet)
3	3	ONLY YOU CAN — Fox (GTO)
2	4	IF — Telly Savalas (MCA)
14	5	FANCY PANTS — Kenny (RAK)
9	6	WHAT AM I GONNA DO WITH YOU — Barry White (20th Century)
10	7	GIRLS — Moments & Whatnauts (All Platinum)
6	8	PICK UP THE PIECES — Average White Band (Atlantic)
18	9	PLAY ME LIKE YOU PLAY YOUR GUITAR — Duane Eddy & The Rebellettes (GTO)
13	10	I CAN DO IT — Rubettes (State)
23	11	FOX ON THE RUN — Sweet (RCA)
17	12	PHILADELPHIA FREEDOM — Elton John Band (DJM)
8	13	MANDY — Barry Manilow (Arista)
27	14	THE FUNKY GIBBON/SICK MAN BLUES — Goodies (Bradley)
21	15	REACH OUT I'LL BE THERE — Gloria Gaynor (MGM)
19	16	SWEET MUSIC — Showaddywaddy (Bell)
25	17	SWING YOUR DADDY — Jim Gilstrap (Chelsea)
22	18	YOUNG AMERICANS — David Bowie (RCA)
7	19	THE SECRETS THAT YOU KEEP — Mud (RAK)
-	20	THE UGLY DUCKLING — Mike Reid (Pye)
11	21	MY EYES ADORED YOU — Frankie Valli (Private Stock)
-	22	LET ME BE THE ONE — Shadows (EMI)
-	23	SKIING IN THE SNOW — Wigan's Ovation (Spark)
16	24	PLEASE TELL HIM THAT I SAID HELLO — Dana (GTO)
5	25	MAKE ME SMILE — Steve Harley & Cockney Rebel (EMI)
12	26	I'M STONE IN LOVE WITH YOU — Johnny Mathis (CBS)
15	27	DREAMER — Supertramp (A&M)
-	28	LADY MARMALADE — Labelle (Epic)
-	29	GOOD LOVIN' GONE BAD — Bad Company (Island)
-	30	LOVE ME, LOVE MY DOG — Peter Shelley (Magnet)

5 April 1975

last week	this week	Title / Artist
1	1	BYE BYE BABY — Bay City Rollers (Bell)
2	2	THERE'S A WHOLE LOT OF LOVING — Guys & Dolls (Magnet)
11	3	FOX ON THE RUN — Sweet (RCA)
5	4	FANCY PANTS — Kenny (RAK)
7	5	GIRLS — Moments & Whatnauts (All Platinum)
6	6	WHAT AM I GONNA DO WITH YOU — Barry White (20th Century)
10	7	I CAN DO IT — Rubettes (State)
17	8	SWING YOUR DADDY — Jim Gilstrap (Chelsea)
14	9	THE FUNKY GIBBON/SICK MAN BLUES — Goodies (Bradley)
3	10	ONLY YOU CAN — Fox (GTO)
9	11	PLAY ME LIKE YOU PLAY YOUR GUITAR — Duane Eddy & The Rebellettes (GTO)
4	12	IF — Telly Savalas (MCA)
12	13	PHILADELPHIA FREEDOM — Elton John Band (DJM)
20	14	THE UGLY DUCKLING — Mike Reid (Pye)
15	15	REACH OUT I'LL BE THERE — Gloria Gaynor (MGM)
22	16	LET ME BE THE ONE — Shadows (EMI)
30	17	LOVE ME, LOVE MY DOG — Peter Shelley (Magnet)
13	18	MANDY — Barry Manilow (Arista)
8	19	PICK UP THE PIECES — Average White Band (Atlantic)
16	20	SWEET MUSIC — Showaddywaddy (Bell)
28	21	LADY MARMALADE — Labelle (Epic)
-	22	L-O-V-E — Al Green (London)
23	23	SKIING IN THE SNOW — Wigan's Ovation (Spark)
27	24	DREAMER — Supertramp (A&M)
21	25	MY EYES ADORED YOU — Frankie Valli (Private Stock)
26	26	I'M STONE IN LOVE WITH YOU — Johnny Mathis (CBS)
-	27	SING A HAPPY SONG — George McCrae (Jayboy)
-	28	WHAT IN THE WORLD'S COME OVER YOU — Tam White (RAK)
18	29	YOUNG AMERICANS — David Bowie (RCA)
-	30	IF — Yin & Yan (EMI)

12 April 1975

last week	this week	Title / Artist
1	1	BYE BYE BABY — Bay City Rollers (Bell)
2	2	THERE'S A WHOLE LOT OF LOVING — Guys & Dolls (Magnet)
3	3	FOX ON THE RUN — Sweet (RCA)
5	4	GIRLS — Moments & Whatnauts (All Platinum)
8	5	SWING YOUR DADDY — Jim Gilstrap (Chelsea)
4	6	FANCY PANTS — Kenny (RAK)
17	7	LOVE ME, LOVE MY DOG — Peter Shelley (Magnet)
7	8	I CAN DO IT — Rubettes (State)
9	9	THE FUNKY GIBBON/SICK MAN BLUES — Goodies (Bradley)
11	10	PLAY ME LIKE YOU PLAY YOUR GUITAR — Duane Eddy & The Rebellettes (GTO)
16	11	LET ME BE THE ONE — Shadows (EMI)
14	12	THE UGLY DUCKLING — Mike Reid (Pye)
13	13	PHILADELPHIA FREEDOM — Elton John Band (DJM)
6	14	WHAT AM I GONNA DO WITH YOU — Barry White (20th Century)
15	15	REACH OUT I'LL BE THERE — Gloria Gaynor (MGM)
21	16	LADY MARMALADE — Labelle (Epic)
10	17	ONLY YOU CAN — Fox (GTO)
23	18	SKIING IN THE SNOW — Wigan's Ovation (Spark)
-	19	HONEY — Bobby Goldsboro (United Artists)
22	20	L-O-V-E — Al Green (London)
12	21	IF — Telly Savalas (MCA)
-	22	HOLD ON TO LOVE — Peter Skellern (Decca)
-	23	LIFE IS A MINESTRONE — 10 c.c. (Mercury)
29	24	YOUNG AMERICANS — David Bowie (RCA)
-	25	A LITTLE LOVE AND UNDERSTANDING — Gilbert Becaud (Decca)
19	26	PICK UP THE PIECES — Average White Band (Atlantic)
18	27	MANDY — Barry Manilow (Arista)
30	28	IF — Yin & Yan (EMI)
-	29	GET DOWN TONIGHT — K C & the Sunshine Band (Jayboy)
20	30	SWEET MUSIC — Showaddywaddy (Bell)

19 April 1975

last week	this week	Title / Artist
1	1	BYE BYE BABY — Bay City Rollers (Bell)
3	2	FOX ON THE RUN — Sweet (RCA)
7	3	LOVE ME, LOVE MY DOG — Peter Shelley (Magnet)
9	4	THE FUNKY GIBBON/SICK MAN BLUES — Goodies (Bradley)
5	5	SWING YOUR DADDY — Jim Gilstrap (Chelsea)
2	6	THERE'S A WHOLE LOT OF LOVING — Guys & Dolls (Magnet)
4	7	GIRLS — Moments & Whatnauts (All Platinum)
6	8	FANCY PANTS — Kenny (RAK)
19	9	HONEY — Bobby Goldsboro (United Artists)
12	10	THE UGLY DUCKLING — Mike Reid (Pye)
23	11	LIFE IS A MINESTRONE — 10 c.c. (Mercury)
-	12	THE TEARS I CRIED — Glitter Band (Bell)
8	13	I CAN DO IT — Rubettes (State)
10	14	PLAY ME LIKE YOU PLAY YOUR GUITAR — Duane Eddy & The Rebellettes (GTO)
16	15	LADY MARMALADE — Labelle (Epic)
25	16	A LITTLE LOVE AND UNDERSTANDING — Gilbert Becaud (Decca)
11	17	LET ME BE THE ONE — Shadows (EMI)
18	18	SKIING IN THE SNOW — Wigan's Ovation (Spark)
13	19	PHILADELPHIA FREEDOM — Elton John Band (DJM)
-	20	DING-A-DONG — Teach-in (Polydor)
22	21	HOLD ON TO LOVE — Peter Skellern (Decca)
15	22	REACH OUT I'LL BE THERE — Gloria Gaynor (MGM)
-	23	TAKE GOOD CARE OF YOURSELF — Three Degrees (Philadelphia)
28	24	IF — Yin & Yan (EMI)
20	25	L-O-V-E — Al Green (London)
-	26	LOVING YOU — Minnie Riperton (Epic)
-	27	HURT SO GOOD — Susan Cadogan (Magnet)
14	28	WHAT AM I GONNA DO WITH YOU — Barry White (20th Century)
29	29	GET DOWN TONIGHT — K C & the Sunshine Band (Jayboy)
-	30	GOOD LOVIN' GONE BAD — Bad Company (Island)

Duane Eddy was back in the Top 10 for the first time in 12 years, thanks to a tailor-made number by writer/producer Tony Macaulay which was a pastiche of 1962's *(Dance With The) Guitar Man*. Duane's old chart rivals in the instrumental stakes, the Shadows, were also back after a long absence, but in vocal mode on *Let Me Be The One*, the UK's almost successful 1975 Eurovision entry. This was soon joined by the Dutch group Teach-In's *Ding-A-Dong*, the song which beat the Shads by a solitary point.

April – May 1975

26 April 1975

last	this	Title / Artist
1	1	BYE BYE BABY Bay City Rollers (Bell)
3	2	LOVE ME, LOVE MY DOG Peter Shelley (Magnet)
2	3	FOX ON THE RUN Sweet (RCA)
5	4	SWING YOUR DADDY Jim Gilstrap (Chelsea)
9	5	HONEY Bobby Goldsboro (United Artists)
4	6	THE FUNKY GIBBON/SICK MAN BLUES Goodies (Bradley)
11	7	LIFE IS A MINESTRONE 10 c.c. (Mercury)
12	8	THE TEARS I CRIED Glitter Band (Bell)
26	9	LOVING YOU Minnie Riperton (Epic)
20	10	DING-A-DONG Teach-In (Polydor)
23	11	TAKE GOOD CARE OF YOURSELF Three Degrees (Philadelphia)
6	12	THERE'S A WHOLE LOT OF LOVING Guys & Dolls (Magnet)
10	13	THE UGLY DUCKLING Mike Reid (Pye)
7	14	GIRLS Moments & Whatnauts (All Platinum)
27	15	HURT SO GOOD Susan Cadogan (Magnet)
-	16	OH BOY Mud (RAK)
18	17	SKIING IN THE SNOW Wigan's Ovation (Spark)
16	18	FANCY PANTS Kenny (RAK)
19	19	A LITTLE LOVE AND UNDERSTANDING Gilbert Becaud (Decca)
29	20	GET DOWN TONIGHT K C & The Sunshine Band (Jayboy)
14	21	PLAY ME LIKE YOU PLAY YOUR GUITAR Duane Eddy & The Rebelettes (GTO)
13	22	I CAN DO IT Rubettes (State)
21	23	HOLD ON TO LOVE Peter Skellern (Decca)
19	24	PHILADELPHIA FREEDOM Elton John Band (DJM)
17	25	LET ME BE THE ONE Shadows (EMI)
15	26	LADY MARMALADE Labelle (Epic)
25	27	L-O-V-E Al Green (London)
-	28	(YOU DON'T KNOW) HOW GLAD I AM Kiki Dee Band (Rocket)
28	29	WHAT AM I GONNA DO WITH YOU Barry White (20th Century)
22	30	REACH OUT I'LL BE THERE Gloria Gaynor (MGM)

3 May 1975

last	this	Title / Artist
5	1	HONEY Bobby Goldsboro (United Artists)
9	2	LOVING YOU Minnie Riperton (Epic)
16	3	OH BOY Mud (RAK)
1	4	BYE BYE BABY Bay City Rollers (Bell)
2	5	LOVE ME, LOVE MY DOG Peter Shelley (Magnet)
15	6	HURT SO GOOD Susan Cadogan (Magnet)
7	7	LIFE IS A MINESTRONE 10 c.c. (Mercury)
3	8	FOX ON THE RUN Sweet (RCA)
4	9	SWING YOUR DADDY Jim Gilstrap (Chelsea)
11	10	TAKE GOOD CARE OF YOURSELF Three Degrees (Philadelphia)
19	11	A LITTLE LOVE AND UNDERSTANDING Gilbert Becaud (Decca)
8	12	THE TEARS I CRIED Glitter Band (Bell)
6	13	THE FUNKY GIBBON/SICK MAN BLUES Goodies (Bradley)
-	14	LET ME TRY AGAIN Tammy Jones (Epic)
10	15	DING-A-DONG Teach-In (Polydor)
-	16	THE NIGHT Frankie Valli & The Four Seasons (Mowest)
-	17	STAND BY YOUR MAN Tammy Wynette (Epic)
23	18	HOLD ON TO LOVE Peter Skellern (Decca)
-	19	ONLY YESTERDAY Carpenters (A&M)
20	20	GET DOWN TONIGHT K C & The Sunshine Band (Jayboy)
17	21	SKIING IN THE SNOW Wigan's Ovation (Spark)
26	22	LADY MARMALADE Labelle (Epic)
-	23	WE'LL FIND OUR DAY Stephanie De Sykes (Bradley)
13	24	THE UGLY DUCKLING Mike Reid (Pye)
-	25	LOVE LIKE YOU AND ME Gary Glitter (Bell)
-	26	SORRY DOESN'T ALWAYS MAKE IT RIGHT Diana Ross (Tamla Motown)
-	27	I WANNA DANCE WIT CHOO (DO DAT DANCE) Disco-Tex & the Sex-O-Lettes (Chelsea)
-	28	WHERE IS THE LOVE Betty Wright (RCA)
-	29	TAKE YOUR MAMMA FOR A RIDE Lulu (Chelsea)
-	30	CALL ME ROUND Pilot (EMI)

10 May 1975

last	this	Title / Artist
2	1	LOVING YOU Minnie Riperton (Epic)
3	2	OH BOY Mud (RAK)
6	3	HURT SO GOOD Susan Cadogan (Magnet)
1	4	HONEY Bobby Goldsboro (United Artists)
14	5	LET ME TRY AGAIN Tammy Jones (Epic)
7	6	LIFE IS A MINESTRONE 10 c.c. (Mercury)
17	7	STAND BY YOUR MAN Tammy Wynette (Epic)
4	8	BYE BYE BABY Bay City Rollers (Bell)
10	9	TAKE GOOD CARE OF YOURSELF Three Degrees (Philadelphia I)
11	10	A LITTLE LOVE AND UNDERSTANDING Gilbert Becaud (Decca)
25	11	LOVE LIKE YOU AND ME Gary Glitter (Bell)
16	12	THE NIGHT Frankie Valli & the Four Seasons (Mowest)
5	13	LOVE ME LOVE MY DOG Peter Shelley (Magnet)
12	14	THE TEARS I CRIED Glitter Band (Bell)
19	15	ONLY YESTERDAY Carpenters (A&M)
27	16	I WANNA DANCE WITH CHOO Disco Tex & the Sex-O-Lettes (Chelsea)
15	17	DING-A-DONG Teach In (Polydor)
8	18	FOX ON THE RUN Sweet (RCA)
23	19	WE'LL FIND OUR DAY Stephanie De Sykes (Bradley)
18	20	HOLD ON TO LOVE Peter Skellern (Decca)
9	21	SWING YOUR DADDY Jim Gilstrap (Chelsea)
30	22	CALL ME ROUND Pilot (EMI)
-	23	THE WAY WE WERE Gladys Knight & the Pips (Buddah)
29	24	TAKE YOUR MAMMA FOR A RIDE Lulu (Chelsea)
24	25	THE UGLY DUCKLING Mike Reid (Pye)
22	26	LADY MARMALADE Labelle (Epic)
21	27	SKIING IN THE SNOW Wigan's Ovation (Spark)
13	28	FNUKY GIBBON/SICK MAN BLUES Goodies (Bradley's)
-	29	ONCE BITTEN TWICE SHY Ian Hunter (CBS)
20	30	GET DOWN TONIGHT KC & the Sunshine Band (Jayboy)

17 May 1975

last	this	Title / Artist
7	1	STAND BY YOUR MAN Tammy Wynette (Epic)
2	2	OH BOY Mud (RAK)
1	3	LOVING YOU Minnie Riperton (Epic)
5	4	LET ME TRY AGAIN Tammy Jones (Epic)
3	5	HURT SO GOOD Susan Cadogan (Magnet)
4	6	HONEY Bobby Goldsboro (United Artists)
12	7	THE NIGHTS Frankie Valli & The Four Seasons (Mowest)
16	8	I WANNA DANCE WIT CHOO (DO DAT DANCE) Disco-Tex & The Sex-O-Lettes (Chelsea)
15	9	ONLY YESTERDAY Carpenters (A&M)
11	10	LOVE LIKE YOU AND ME Gary Glitter (Bell)
9	11	TAKE GOOD CARE OF YOURSELF Three Degrees (Philadelphia)
10	12	A LITTLE LOVE AND UNDERSTANDING Gilbert Becaud (Decca)
14	13	THE TEARS I CRIED Glitter Band (Bell)
23	14	THE WAY WE WERE Gladys Knight & The Pips (Buddah)
8	15	BYE BYE BABY Bay City Rollers (Bell)
-	16	DON'T DO IT BABY Mac & Katie Kissoon (State)
19	17	WE'LL FIND OUR DAY Stephanie De Sykes (Bradley)
-	18	SING BABY SING Stylistics (Avco)
-	19	AUTOBAHN Kraftwerk (Vertigo)
6	20	LIFE IS A MINESTRONE 10 c.c. (Mercury)
13	21	LOVE ME, LOVE MY DOG Peter Shelley (Magnet)
-	22	THANKS FOR THE MEMORY Slade (Polydor)
29	23	ONCE BITTEN TWICE SHY Ian Hunter (CBS)
17	24	DING-A-DONG Teach-In (Polydor)
-	25	FOR YOU I'LL DO ANYTHING Barry White (20th Century)
-	26	WHISPERING GRASS Windsor Davies & Don Estelle (EMI)
20	27	HOLD ON TO LOVE Peter Skellern (Decca)
-	28	SORRY DOESN'T ALWAYS MAKE IT RIGHT Diana Ross (Tamla Motown)
-	29	IMAGINE ME, IMAGINE YOU Fox (GTO)
-	30	SEND IN THE CLOWNS Judy Collins (Elecktra)

In an astonishing example of doing it better second time around, Bobby Goldsboro's weepie *Honey*, which had peaked at Number Two in 1968, now snatched a week at Number One. Of almost the same vintage was Tammy Wynette's *Stand By Your Man*, which had originally made the US Top 20 around Christmas 1968. The Four Seasons' *The Night* was also an oldie, from their unsuccessful early '70s period with Motown. Its current hit status spun off from huge Northern Soul dancefloor success.

24 May 1975

last week	this week	
1	1	STAND BY YOUR MAN Tammy Wynette (Epic)
4	2	LET ME TRY AGAIN Tammy Jones (Epic)
18	3	SING BABY SING Stylistics (Avco)
14	4	THE WAY WE WERE Gladys Knight & The Pips (Buddah)
3	5	LOVING YOU Minnie Riperton (Epic)
8	6	I WANNA DANCE WIT CHOO (DO DAT DANCE) Disco-Tex & The Sex-O-Lettes (Chelsea)
2	7	OH BOY Mud (RAK)
9	8	ONLY YESTERDAY Carpenters (A&M)
5	9	HURT SO GOOD Susan Cadogan (Magnet)
7	10	THE NIGHT Frankie Valli & The Four Seasons (Mowest)
26	11	WHISPERING GRASS Windsor Davies & Don Estelle (EMI)
22	12	THANKS FOR THE MEMORY Slade (Polydor)
16	13	DON'T DO IT BABY Mac & Katie Kissoon (State)
10	14	LOVE LIKE YOU AND ME Gary Glitter (Bell)
19	15	AUTOBAHN Kraftwerk (Vertigo)
30	16	SEND IN THE CLOWNS Judy Collins (Elecktra)
6	17	HONEY Bobby Goldsboro (United Artists)
11	18	TAKE GOOD CARE OF YOURSELF Three Degrees (Philadelphia)
-	19	ROLL OVER LAY DOWN Status Quo (Vertigo)
12	20	A LITTLE LOVE AND UNDERSTANDING Gilbert Becaud (Decca)
23	21	ONCE BITTEN TWICE SHY Ian Hunter (CBS)
-	22	WOMBLING WHITE TIE AND TAILS Wombles (CBS)
-	23	THREE STEPS TO HEAVEN Showaddywaddy (Bell)
29	24	IMAGINE ME, IMAGINE YOU Fox (GTO)
-	25	THE ISRAELITES Desmond Dekker (Cactus)
25	26	FOR YOU I'LL DO ANYTHING Barry White 20th Century
13	27	THE TEARS I CRIED Glitter Band (Bell)
17	28	WE'LL FIND OUR DAY Stephanie De Sykes (Bradley)
-	29	I GET THE SWEETEST FEELING Jackie Wilson (Brunswick)
-	30	STAND BY ME John Lennon (Apple)

31 May 1975

last week	this week	
1	1	STAND BY YOUR MAN Tammy Wynette (Epic)
11	2	WHISPERING GRASS Windsor Davies & Don Estelle (EMI)
4	3	THE WAY WE WERE Gladys Knight & the Pips (Buddah)
3	4	SING BABY SING Stylistics (Avco)
16	5	SEND IN THE CLOWNS Judy Collins (Elektra)
23	6	THREE STEPS TO HEAVEN Showaddywaddy (Bell)
2	7	LET ME TRY AGAIN Tammy Jones (Epic)
7	8	OH BOY Mud (RAK)
12	9	THANKS FOR THE MEMORY Slade (Polydor)
19	10	ROLL OVER LADY DOWN Status Quo (Vertigo)
15	11	AUTOBAHN Kraftwerk (Vertigo)
5	12	LOVING YOU Minnie Riperton (Epic)
13	13	DON'T DO IT BABY Mac & Katie Kissoon (State)
24	14	IMAGINE ME, IMAGINE YOU Fox (GTO)
8	15	ONLY YESTERDAY Carpenters (A&M)
9	16	HURT SO GOOD Susan Cadogan (Magnet)
21	17	ONCE BITTEN TWICE SHY Ian Hunter (CBS)
6	18	I WANNA DANCE WITH CHOO Disco Tex & the Sex-O-Lettes (Chelsea)
-	19	THE PROUD ONE Osmonds (MGM)
10	20	THE NIGHT Frankie Valli & The Four Seasons (Mowest)
26	21	FOR YOU I'LL DO ANYTHING Barry White (20th Century)
29	22	I GET THE SWEETEST FEELING Jackie Wilson (Brunswick)
14	23	LOVE LIKE YOU AND ME Gary Glitter (Bell)
-	24	DISCO QUEEN Hot Chocolate (RAK)
25	25	THE ISRAELITES Desmond Dekker (Cactus)
22	26	WOMBLING WHITE TIE AND TAILS Wombles (CBS)
27	27	THE HUSTLE Van McCoy (Avco)
-	28	SWING LOW SWEET CHARIOT Eric Clapton (RSO)
18	29	TAKE GOOD CARE OF YOURSELF Three Degrees (Philadelphia)
-	30	LISTEN TO WHAT THE MAN SAID Wings (Capitol)

7 June 1975

last week	this week	
2	1	WHISPERING GRASS Windsor Davies & Don Estelle (EMI)
1	2	STAND BY YOUR MAN Tammy Wynette (Epic)
3	3	THE WAY WE WERE Gladys Knight & The Pips (Buddah)
6	4	THREE STEPS TO HEAVEN Showaddywaddy (Bell)
4	5	SING BABY SING Stylistics (Avco)
5	6	SEND IN THE CLOWNS Judy Collins (Elecktra)
19	7	THE PROUD ONE Osmonds (MGM)
9	8	THANKS FOR THE MEMORY Slade (Polydor)
10	9	ROLL OVER LAY DOWN Status Quo (Vertigo)
11	10	AUTOBAHN Kraftwerk (Vertigo)
18	11	I WANNA DANCE WIT CHOO (DO DAT DANCE) Disco-Tex & The Sex-O-Lettes (Chelsea)
-	12	I'M NOT IN LOVE 10 c.c. (Mercury)
25	13	THE ISRAELITES Desmond Dekker (Cactus)
14	14	IMAGINE ME, IMAGINE YOU Fox (GTO)
13	15	DON'T DO IT BABY Mac & Katie Kissoon (State)
7	16	LET ME TRY AGAIN Tammy Jones (Epic)
30	17	LISTEN TO WHAT THE MAN SAID Wings (Parlophone)
17	18	ONCE BITTEN TWICE SHY Ian Hunter (CBS)
28	19	SWING LOW SWEET CHARIOT Eric Clapton (RSO)
21	20	FOR YOU I'LL DO ANYTHING Barry White 20th Century
27	21	THE HUSTLE Van McCoy (Avco)
15	22	ONLY YESTERDAY Carpenters (A&M)
24	23	DISCO QUEEN Hot Chocolate (RAK)
8	24	OH BOY Mud (RAK)
-	25	DISCO STOMP Hamilton Bohannon (Brunswick)
22	26	I GET THE SWEETEST FEELING Jackie Wilson (Brunswick)
16	27	HURT SO GOOD Susan Cadogan (Magnet)
12	28	LOVING YOU Minnie Riperton (Epic)
20	29	THE NIGHT Frankie Valli & The Four Seasons (Mowest)
-	30	SENDING OUT AN S.O.S. Retta Young (All Platinum)

14 June 1975

last week	this week	
4	1	THREE STEPS TO HEAVEN Showaddywaddy (Bell)
1	2	WHISPERING GRASS Windsor Davies & Don Estelle (EMI)
12	3	I'M NOT IN LOVE 10 c.c. (Mercury)
2	4	STAND BY YOUR MAN Tammy Wynette (Epic)
7	5	THE PROUD ONE Osmonds (MGM)
3	6	THE WAY WE WERE Gladys Knight & The Pips (Buddah)
5	7	SING BABY SING Stylistics (Avco)
6	8	SEND IN THE CLOWNS Judy Collins (Elecktra)
17	9	LISTEN TO WHAT THE MAN SAID Wings (Parlophone)
21	10	THE HUSTLE Van McCoy (Avco)
9	11	ROLL OVER LAY DOWN Status Quo (Vertigo)
10	12	AUTOBAHN Kraftwerk (Vertigo)
18	13	ONCE BITTEN TWICE SHY Ian Hunter (CBS)
14	14	IMAGINE ME, IMAGINE YOU Fox (GTO)
8	15	THANKS FOR THE MEMORY Slade (Polydor)
19	16	SWING LOW SWEET CHARIOT Eric Clapton (RSO)
-	17	OH WHAT A SHAME Roy Wood (Jet)
23	18	DISCO QUEEN Hot Chocolate (RAK)
13	19	THE ISRAELITES Desmond Dekker (Cactus)
-	20	MR RAFFLES (MAN IT WAS MEAN) Steve Harley & Cockney Rebel (EMI)
11	21	I WANNA DANCE WIT CHOO (DO DAT DANCE) Disco-Tex & The Sex-O-Lettes (Chelsea)
25	22	DISCO STOMP Hamilton Bohannon (Brunswick)
-	23	WALKING IN RHYTHM Blackbyrds (Fantasy)
-	24	BABY I LOVE YOU OK Kenny (RAK)
20	25	FOR YOU I'LL DO ANYTHING Barry White 20th Century
15	26	DON'T DO IT BABY Mac & Katie Kissoon (State)
24	27	OH BOY Mud (RAK)
16	28	LET ME TRY AGAIN Tammy Jones (Epic)
-	29	DYNAMITE Tony Camillo's Bazuka (A&M)
30	30	SENDING OUT AN S.O.S. Retta Young (All Platinum)

Whispering Grass, a success for the Ink Spots in pre-chart days, became an unlikely UK chart-topper thanks to the power of a TV show. Windsor Davies and Don Estelle both starred in the Army sitcom *It Ain't Half Hot, Mum*, and they recorded the song in their show personae, Estelle turning in a virtually straight rendition in the face of "Sgt Major" interjections from Davies. The Osmonds emulated the Rollers with a successful revival of a Four Seasons (or Frankie Valli) oldie, *The Proud One*.

June – July 1975

21 June 1975	28 June 1975	5 July 1975	12 July 1975
2 1 WHISPERING GRASS Windsor Davies & Don Estelle (EMI)	3 1 I'M NOT IN LOVE 10 c.c. (Mercury)	1 1 I'M NOT IN LOVE 10cc (Mercury)	2 1 TEARS ON MY PILLOW Johnny Nash (CBS)
1 2 THREE STEPS TO HEAVEN Showaddywaddy (Bell)	1 2 WHISPERING GRASS Windsor Davies & Don Estelle (EMI)	8 2 TEARS ON MY PILLOW Johnny Nash (CBS)	1 2 I'M NOT IN LOVE 10 c. c. (Mercury)
3 3 I'M NOT IN LOVE 10 c.c. (Mercury)	2 3 THREE STEPS TO HEAVEN Showaddywaddy (Bell)	4 3 THE HUSTLE Van McCoy (Avco)	5 3 MISTY Ray Stevens (Janus)
5 4 THE PROUD ONE Osmonds (MGM)	5 4 THE HUSTLE Van McCoy (Avco)	3 4 THREE STEPS TO HEAVEN Showaddywaddy (Bell)	3 4 THE HUSTLE Van McCoy (Avco)
10 5 THE HUSTLE Van McCoy (Avco)	4 5 THE PROUD ONE Osmonds (MGM)	12 5 MISTY Ray Stevens (Janus)	15 5 HAVE YOU SEEN HER Chi-Lites (Brunswick)
8 6 SEND IN THE CLOWNS Judy Collins (Elektra)	8 6 LISTEN TO WHAT THE MAN SAID Wings (Parlophone)	2 6 WHISPERING GRASS Windsor Davies & Don Estelle (EMI)	8 6 DISCO STOMP Hamilton Bohannon (Brunswick)
7 7 SING BABY SING Stylistics (Avco)	24 7 DOING ALL RIGHT WITH THE BOYS Gary Glitter (Bell)	11 7 MOONSHINE SALLY Mud (RAK)	9 7 DOING ALL RIGHT WITH THE BOYS Gary Glitter (Bell)
9 8 LISTEN TO WHAT THE MAN SAID Wings (Parlophone)	18 8 TEARS ON MY PILLOW Johnny Nash (CBS)	9 8 DISCO STOMP Hamilton Bohannon (Brunswick)	7 8 MOONSHINE SALLY Mud (RAK)
6 9 THE WAY WE WERE Gladys Knight & The Pips (Buddah)	13 9 DISCO STOMP Hamilton Bohannon (Brunswick)	7 9 DOING ALL RIGHT WITH THE BOYS Gary Glitter (Bell)	23 9 EIGHTEEN WITH A BULLET Pete Wingfield (Island)
4 10 STAND BY YOUR MAN Tammy Wynette (Epic)	7 10 SING BABY SING Stylistics (Avco)	6 10 LISTEN TO WHAT THE MAN SAID Wings (Capitol)	6 10 WHISPERING GRASS Windsor Davies & Don Estelle (EMI)
18 11 DISCO QUEEN Hot Chocolate (RAK)	- 11 MOONSHINE SALLY Mud (RAK)	5 11 THE PROUD ONE Osmonds (MGM)	4 11 THREE STEPS TO HEAVEN Showaddywaddy (Bell)
17 12 OH WHAT A SHAME Roy Wood (Jet)	- 12 MISTY Ray Stevens (Janus)	13 12 BABY I LOVE YOU, OK Kenny (RAK)	10 12 LISTEN TO WHAT THE MAN SAID Wings (Parlophone)
22 13 DISCO STOMP Hamilton Bohannon (Brunswick)	16 13 BABY I LOVE YOU OK Kenny (RAK)	20 13 MY WHITE BICYCLE Nazareth (Mooncrest)	12 13 BABY I LOVE YOU OK Kenny (RAK)
20 14 MR RAFFLES (MAN IT WAS MEAN) Steve Harley & Cockney Rebel (EMI)	10 14 STAND BY YOUR MAN Tammy Wynette (Epic)	18 14 MR. RAFFLES (MAN IT WAS MEAN) Steve Harley & Cockney Rebel (EMI)	16 14 I DON'T LOVE YOU BUT I THINK I LIKE YOU Gilbert O'Sullivan (MAM)
11 15 ROLL OVER LAY DOWN Status Quo (Vertigo)	9 15 THE WAY WE WERE Gladys Knight & The Pips (Buddah)	23 15 HAVE YOU SEEN HER Chi-Lites (Brunswick)	- 15 GIVE A LITTLE LOVE Bay City Rollers (Bell)
24 16 BABY I LOVE YOU OK Kenny (RAK)	11 16 DISCO QUEEN Hot Chocolate (RAK)	22 16 I DON'T LOVE YOU BUT I THINK I LIKE YOU Gilbert O'Sullivan (MAM)	27 16 BLACK PUDDING BERTHA Goodies (Bradley)
23 17 WALKING IN RHYTHM Blackbyrds (Fantasy)	12 17 OH WHAT A SHAME Roy Wood (Jet)	29 17 FOE-DEE-O-DEE Rubettes (State)	13 17 MY WHITE BICYCLE Nazareth (Mooncrest)
- 18 TEARS ON MY PILLOW Johnny Nash (CBS)	14 18 MR RAFFLES (MAN IT WAS MEAN) Steve Harley & Cockney Rebel (EMI)	17 18 OH WHAT A SHAME Roy Wood (Jet)	17 18 FOE-DEE-O-DEE Rubettes (State)
13 19 ONCE BITTEN TWICE SHY Ian Hunter (CBS)	6 19 SEND IN THE CLOWNS Judy Collins (Elecktra)	24 19 MAKE THE WORLD GO AWAY Donny & Marie Osmond (MGM)	19 19 MAKE THE WORLD GO AWAY Donnie & Marie Osmond (MGM)
12 20 AUTOBAHN Kraftwerk (Vertigo)	25 20 MY WHITE BICYCLE Nazareth (Mooncrest)	27 20 MAMA NEVER TOLD ME Sister Sledge (Atlantic)	28 20 BARBADOS Typically Tropical (Gull)
16 21 SWING LOW SWEET CHARIOT Eric Clapton (RSO)	17 21 WALKING IN RHYTHM Blackbyrds (Fantasy)	10 21 SING BABY SING Stylistics (Avco)	20 21 MAMA NEVER TOLD ME Sister Sledge (Atlantic)
25 22 FOR YOU I'LL DO ANYTHING Barry White 20th Century	- 22 I DON'T LOVE YOU BUT I THINK I LIKE YOU Gilbert O'Sullivan (MAM)	- 22 D.I.V.O.R.C.E. Tammy Wynette (Epic)	11 22 THE PROUD ONE Osmonds (MGM)
- 23 MY WHITE BICYCLE Nazareth (Mooncrest)	- 23 HAVE YOU SEEN HER Chi-Lites (Brunswick)	- 23 EIGHTEEN WITH A BULLET Pete Wingfield (Island)	- 23 SEALED WITH A KISS Brian Hyland (ABC)
- 24 DOING ALL RIGHT WITH THE BOYS Gary Glitter (Bell)	- 24 MAKE THE WORLD GO AWAY Donny & Marie Osmond (MGM)	14 24 STAND BY YOUR MAN Tammy Wynette (Epic)	- 24 D.I.V.O.R.C.E. Tammy Wynette (Epic)
- 25 TAKE ME IN YOUR ARMS Doobie Brothers (Warner Bros.)	25 25 TAKE ME IN YOUR ARMS Doobie Brothers (Warner Bros)	- 25 SOMEONE SAVED MY LIFE TONIGHT Elton John (DJM)	29 25 JIVE TALKIN' Bee Gees (RSO)
29 26 DYNAMITE Tony Camillo's Bazuka (A&M)	15 26 ROLL OVER LAY DOWN Status Quo (Vertigo)	15 26 THE WAY WE WERE Gladys Knight & The Pips (Buddah)	25 26 SOMEONE SAVED MY LIFE TONIGHT Elton John (DJM)
19 27 THE ISRAELITES Desmond Dekker (Cactus)	- 27 MAMA NEVER TOLD ME Sister Sledge (Atlantic)	- 27 BLACK PUDDING BERTHA Goodies (Bradley's)	- 27 I WRITE THE SONGS David Cassidy (RCA)
15 28 THANKS FOR THE MEMORY Slade (Polydor)	19 28 ONCE BITTEN TWICE SHY Ian Hunter (CBS)	- 28 BARBADOS Typically Tropical (Gull)	14 28 MR RAFFLES (MAN IT WAS MEAN) Steve Harley & Cockney Rebel (EMI)
14 29 IMAGINE ME, IMAGINE YOU Fox (GTO)	- 29 FOE-DEE-O-DEE Rubettes (State)	- 29 JIVE TALKIN' Bee Gees (RSO)	- 29 ROLLIN' STONE David Essex (CBS)
30 30 SENDING OUT AN S.O.S. Retta Young (All Platinum)	- 30 SWEARIN' TO GOD Frankie Valli (Private Stock)	16 30 DISCO QUEEN Hot Chocolate (Rak)	18 30 OH WHAT A SHAME Roy Wood (Jet)

10 c.c.'s *I'm Not In Love*, written by Eric Stewart, became not only their biggest hit, but also a modern-day standard, forever cropping up with the likes of A *Whiter Shade Of Pale* and Led Zeppelin's *Stairway To Heaven* in polls of all-time favourites. The rest of the chart, meanwhile, was becoming crammed with revivals of old songs (*Misty, The Proud One, Three Steps To Heaven, Make The World Go Away, My White Bicycle*) and successful re-issues (*Sealed With A Kiss, The Israelites, Have You Seen Her*).

July – August 1975

19 July 1975

last week	this week	
1	1	TEARS ON MY PILLOW Johnny Nash (CBS)
3	2	MISTY Ray Stevens (Janus)
4	3	THE HUSTLE Van McCoy (Avco)
15	4	GIVE A LITTLE LOVE Bay City Rollers (Bell)
5	5	HAVE YOU SEEN HER Chi-Lites (Brunswick)
20	6	BARBADOS Typically Tropical (Gull)
2	7	I'M NOT IN LOVE 10 c.c. (Mercury)
9	8	EIGHTEEN WITH A BULLET Pete Wingfield (Island)
6	9	DISCO STOMP Hamilton Bohannon (Brunswick)
7	10	DOING ALL RIGHT WITH THE BOYS Gary Glitter (Bell)
25	11	JIVE TALKIN' Bee Gees (RSO)
23	12	SEALED WITH A KISS Brian Hyland (ABC)
8	13	MOONSHINE SALLY Mud (RAK)
24	14	D.I.V.O.R.C.E. Tammy Wynette (Epic)
17	15	MY WHITE BICYCLE Nazareth (Mooncrest)
18	16	FOE-DEE-O-DEE Rubettes (State)
11	17	THREE STEPS TO HEAVEN Showaddywaddy (Bell)
-	18	JE T'AIME Judge Dread (Cactus)
29	19	ROLLIN' STONE David Essex (CBS)
-	20	IT'S IN HIS KISS Linda Lewis (Arista)
10	21	WHISPERING GRASS Windsor Davies & Don Estelle (EMI)
16	22	BLACK PUDDING BERTHA Goodies (Bradley)
27	23	I WRITE THE SONGS David Cassidy (RCA)
19	24	MAKE THE WORLD GO AWAY Donnie & Marie Osmond (MGM)
-	25	ACTION Sweet (RCA)
12	26	LISTEN TO WHAT THE MAN SAID Wings (Parlophone)
14	27	I DON'T LOVE YOU BUT I THINK I LIKE YOU Gilbert O'Sullivan (MAM)
26	28	SOMEONE SAVED MY LIFE TONIGHT Elton John (DJM)
21	29	MAMA NEVER TOLD ME Sister Sledge (Atlantic)
-	30	FOOT STOMPIN' MUSIC Hamilton Bohannon (Brunswick)

26 July 1975

last week	this week	
4	1	GIVE A LITTLE LOVE Bay City Rollers (Bell)
6	2	BARBADOS Typically Tropical (Gull)
1	3	TEARS ON MY PILLOW Johnny Nash (CBS)
3	4	THE HUSTLE Van McCoy (Avco)
2	5	MISTY Ray Stevens (Janus)
8	6	EIGHTEEN WITH A BULLET Pete Wingfield (Island)
5	7	HAVE YOU SEEN HER Chi-Lites (Brunswick)
11	8	JIVE TALKIN' Bee Gees (RSO)
19	9	ROLLIN' STONE David Essex (CBS)
18	10	JE T'AIME Judge Dread (Cactus)
12	11	SEALED WITH A KISS Brian Hyland (ABC)
9	12	DISCO STOMP Hamilton Bohannon (Brunswick)
20	13	IT'S IN HIS KISS Linda Lewis (Arista)
7	14	I'M NOT IN LOVE 10 c.c. (Mercury)
14	15	D.I.V.O.R.C.E. Tammy Wynette(Epic)
25	16	ACTION Sweet (RCA)
23	17	I WRITE THE SONGS David Cassidy (RCA)
22	18	BLACK PUDDING BERTHA Goodies (Bradley)
-	19	IF YOU THINK YOU KNOW HOW TO LOVE ME Smokie (RAK)
29	20	MAMA NEVER TOLD ME Sister Sledge (Atlantic)
-	21	BLANKET ON THE GROUND Billie Jo Spears (United Artists)
15	22	MY WHITE BICYCLE Nazareth (Mooncrest)
10	23	DOING ALL RIGHT WITH THE BOYS Gary Glitter (Bell)
16	24	FOE-DEE-O-DEE Rubettes (State)
25	25	NEW YORK CITY T. Rex (EMI)
13	26	MOONSHINE SALLY Mud (RAK)
-	27	7-6-5-4-3-2-1 (BLOW YOUR WHISTLE) Rimshots (All Platinum)
-	28	SHERRY Adrian Baker (Magnet)
-	29	HIGHWIRE Linda Carr & The Love Squad (Chelsea)
-	30	DOLLY MY LOVE Moments (All Platinum)

2 August 1975

last week	this week	
2	1	BARBADOS Typically Tropical (Gull)
1	2	GIVE A LITTLE LOVE Bay City Rollers (Bell)
5	3	MISTY Ray Stevens (Janus)
9	4	ROLLIN' STONE David Essex (CBS)
13	5	IT'S IN HIS KISS Linda Lewis (Arista)
4	6	THE HUSTLE Van McCoy (Avco)
3	7	TEARS ON MY PILLOW Johnny Nash (CBS)
8	8	JIVE TALKIN' Bee Gees (RSO)
11	9	SEALED WITH A KISS Brian Hyland (ABC)
6	10	EIGHTEEN WITH A BULLET Pete Wingfield (Island)
7	11	HAVE YOU SEEN HER Chi-Lites (Brunswick)
19	12	IF YOU THINK YOU KNOW HOW TO LOVE ME Smokie (RAK)
10	13	JE T'AIME Judge Dread (Cactus)
16	14	ACTION Sweet (RCA)
-	15	I CAN'T GIVE YOU ANYTHING (BUT MY LOVE) Stylistics (Avco)
-	16	DELILAH Alex Harvey Band (Vertigo)
17	17	I WRITE THE SONGS David Cassidy (RCA)
15	18	D.I.V.O.R.C.E. Tammy Wynette (Epic)
28	19	SHERRY Adrian Baker (Magnet)
21	20	BLANKET ON THE GROUND Billie Jo Spears (United Artists)
25	21	NEW YORK CITY T. Rex (EMI)
14	22	I'M NOT IN LOVE 10 c.c. (Mercury)
29	23	HIGHWIRE Linda Carr & The Love Squad (Chelsea)
27	24	7-6-5-4-3-2-1 (BLOW YOUR WHISTLE) Rimshots (All Platinum)
-	25	FOOT STOMPIN' MUSIC Hamilton Bohannon (Brunswick)
30	26	DOLLY MY LOVE Moments (All Platinum)
-	27	EL BIMBO Bimbo Jet (EMI)
12	28	DISCO STOMP Hamilton Bohannon (Brunswick)
-	29	THE LAST FAREWELL Roger Whittaker (EMI)
-	30	ONE OF THESE NIGHTS Eagles (Asylum)

9 August 1975

last week	this week	
1	1	BARBADOS Typically Tropical (Gull)
2	2	GIVE A LITTLE LOVE Bay City Rollers (Bell)
8	3	JIVE TALKIN' Bee Gees (RSO)
15	4	I CAN'T GIVE YOU ANYTHING (BUT MY LOVE) Stylistics (Avco)
12	5	IF YOU THINK YOU KNOW HOW TO LOVE ME Smokie (RAK)
9	6	SEALED WITH A KISS Brian Hyland (ABC)
5	7	IT'S IN HIS KISS Linda Lewis (Arista)
16	8	DELILAH Alex Harvey Band (Vertigo)
7	9	TEARS ON MY PILLOW Johnny Nash (CBS)
3	10	MISTY Ray Stevens (Janus)
4	11	ROLLIN' STONE David Essex (CBS)
6	12	THE HUSTLE Van McCoy (Avco)
26	13	DOLLY MY LOVE Moments (All Platinum)
23	14	HIGHWIRE Linda Carr & The Love Squad (Chelsea)
13	15	JE T'AIME Judge Dread (Cactus)
14	16	ACTION Sweet (RCA)
20	17	BLANKET ON THE GROUND Billie Jo Spears (United Artists)
19	18	SHERRY Adrian Baker (Magnet)
11	19	HAVE YOU SEEN HER Chi-Lites (Brunswick)
29	20	THE LAST FAREWELL Roger Whittaker (EMI)
17	21	I WRITE THE SONGS David Cassidy (RCA)
-	22	IT'S BEEN SO LONG George McCrae (Jayboy)
24	23	7-6-5-4-3-2-1 (BLOW YOUR WHISTLE) Rimshots (All Platinum)
21	24	NEW YORK CITY T. Rex (EMI)
-	25	ONE NIGHT Mud (RAK)
-	26	FAME David Bowie (RCA)
18	27	D.I.V.O.R.C.E. Tammy Wynette (Epic)
10	28	EIGHTEEN WITH A BULLET Pete Wingfield (Island)
-	29	LOVE ME BABY Susan Cadogan (Magnet)
-	30	ROCHDALE COWBOY Mike Harding (Rubber)

Pete Wingfield's *Eighteen With A Bullet* is one of the very few chart songs to actually deal with the subject of being on the chart. Long-time R&B fan Wingfield was in personal nirvana during the week in the US when his single actually did rest at No.18 – with a bullet, (indicating strong upward progress) – in Cash Box's R&B chart. Typically Tropical's *Barbados*, despite its Caribbean idiom, was an all-British production masterminded by recording studio engineers Jeff Calvert and Max West.

291

August – September 1975

16 August 1975

last week	this week	Title / Artist
4	1	I CAN'T GIVE YOU ANYTHING (BUT MY LOVE) Stylistics (Avco)
1	2	BARBADOS Typically Tropical (Gull)
5	3	IF YOU THINK YOU KNOW HOW TO LOVE ME Smokie (RAK)
3	4	JIVE TALKIN' Bee Gees (RSO)
2	5	GIVE A LITTLE LOVE Bay City Rollers (Bell)
8	6	DELILAH Alex Harvey Band (Vertigo)
7	7	IT'S IN HIS KISS Linda Lewis (Arista)
20	8	THE LAST FAREWELL Roger Whittaker (EMI)
22	9	IT'S BEEN SO LONG George McCrae (Jayboy)
6	10	SEALED WITH A KISS Brian Hyland (ABC)
18	11	SHERRY Adrian Baker (Magnet)
17	12	BLANKET ON THE GROUND Billie Jo Spears (United Artists)
13	13	DOLLY MY LOVE Moments (All Platinum)
21	14	I WRITE THE SONGS David Cassidy (RCA)
15	15	JE T'AIME Judge Dread (Cactus)
9	16	TEARS ON MY PILLOW Johnny Nash (CBS)
24	17	NEW YORK CITY T. Rex (EMI)
14	18	HIGHWIRE Linda Carr & The Love Squad (Chelsea)
12	19	THE HUSTLE Van McCoy (Avco)
30	20	ROCHDALE COWBOY Mike Harding (Rubber)
-	21	EL BIMBO Bimbo Jet (EMI)
11	22	ROLLIN' STONE David Essex (CBS)
-	23	GET IN THE SWING Sparks (Island)
10	24	MISTY Ray Stevens (Janus)
26	25	FAME David Bowie (RCA)
-	26	BEST THING THAT EVER HAPPENED Gladys Knight & the Pips (Buddah)
-	27	THAT'S THE WAY (I LIKE IT) K C & the Sunshine Band (Jayboy)
16	28	ACTION Sweet (RCA)
-	29	DON'T THROW IT ALL AWAY Gary Benson (State)
-	30	SUMMER OF '42 Biddu Orchestra (Epic)

23 August 1975

last	this	Title / Artist
1	1	I CAN'T GIVE YOU ANYTHING (BUT MY LOVE) Stylistics (Avco)
8	2	THE LAST FAREWELL Roger Whittaker (EMI)
2	3	BARBADOS Typically Tropical (Gull)
9	4	IT'S BEEN SO LONG George McCrae (Jayboy)
3	5	IF YOU THINK YOU KNOW HOW TO LOVE ME Smokie (RAK)
4	6	JIVE TALKIN' Bee Gees (RSO)
-	7	SAILING Rod Stewart (Warner Bros)
6	8	DELILAH Alex Harvey Band (Vertigo)
12	9	BLANKET ON THE GROUND Billie Jo Spears (United Artists)
5	10	GIVE A LITTLE LOVE Bay City Rollers (Bell)
11	11	SHERRY Adrian Baker (Magnet)
13	12	DOLLY MY LOVE Moments (All Platinum)
7	13	IT'S IN HIS KISS Linda Lewis (Arista)
10	14	SEALED WITH A KISS Brian Hyland (ABC)
27	15	THAT'S THE WAY (I LIKE IT) K C & the Sunshine Band (Jayboy)
21	16	EL BIMBO Bimbo Jet (EMI)
18	17	HIGHWIRE Linda Carr & The Love Squad (Chelsea)
26	18	BEST THING THAT EVER HAPPENED Gladys Knight & the Pips (Buddah)
30	19	SUMMER OF '42 Biddu Orchestra (Epic)
17	20	NEW YORK CITY T. Rex (EMI)
-	21	LOVE ME BABY Susan Cadogan (Magnet)
25	22	FAME David Bowie (RCA)
15	23	JE T'AIME Judge Dread (Cactus)
20	24	ROCHDALE COWBOY Mike Harding (Rubber)
-	25	SUMMERTIME CITY Mike Batt (Epic)
-	26	ONE OF THESE NIGHTS Eagles (Asylum)
-	27	LOVE WON'T LET ME WAIT Major Harris (Atlantic)
23	28	GET IN THE SWING Sparks (Island)
-	29	LOVE WILL KEEP US TOGETHER Captain & Tennille (A&M)
-	30	JULIE-ANN Kenny (RAK)

30 August 1975

last	this	Title / Artist
7	1	SAILING Rod Stewart (Warner Bros)
1	2	I CAN'T GIVE YOU ANYTHING (BUT MY LOVE) Stylistics (Avco)
2	3	THE LAST FAREWELL Roger Whittaker (EMI)
4	4	IT'S BEEN SO LONG George McCrae (Jayboy)
15	5	THAT'S THE WAY (I LIKE IT) K C & the Sunshine Band (Jayboy)
3	6	BARBADOS Typically Tropical (Gull)
9	7	BLANKET ON THE GROUND Billie Jo Spears (United Artists)
5	8	IF YOU THINK YOU KNOW HOW TO LOVE ME Smokie (RAK)
12	9	DOLLY MY LOVE Moments (All Platinum)
18	10	BEST THING THAT EVER HAPPENED Gladys Knight & the Pips (Buddah)
16	11	EL BIMBO Bimbo Jet (EMI)
19	12	SUMMER OF '42 Biddu Orchestra (Epic)
-	13	DON'T THROW IT ALL AWAY Gary Benson (State)
11	14	SHERRY Adrian Baker (Magnet)
6	15	JIVE TALKIN' Bee Gees (RSO)
10	16	SEALED WITH A KISS Brian Hyland (ABC)
22	17	FAME David Bowie (RCA)
25	18	SUMMERTIME CITY Mike Batt (Epic)
10	19	GIVE A LITTLE LOVE Bay City Rollers (Bell)
-	20	A CHILD'S PRAYER Hot Chocolate (RAK)
24	21	ROCHDALE COWBOY Mike Harding (Rubber)
-	22	LOVE IN THE SUN Glitter Band (Bell)
26	23	ONE OF THESE NIGHTS Eagles (Asylum)
8	24	DELILAH Alex Harvey Band (Vertigo)
30	25	JULIE-ANN Kenny (RAK)
13	26	IT'S IN HIS KISS Linda Lewis (Arista)
-	27	SUPER WOMBLE Wombles (CBS)
-	28	PANDORA'S BOX Procol Harum (Chrysalis)
-	29	BRAZIL Ritchie Family (Polydor)
21	30	LOVE ME BABY Susan Cadogan (Magnet)

6 September 1975

last	this	Title / Artist
1	1	SAILING Rod Stewart (Warner Bros)
2	2	I CAN'T GIVE YOU ANYTHING (BUT MY LOVE) Stylistics (Avco)
3	3	THE LAST FAREWELL Roger Whittaker (EMI)
4	4	IT'S BEEN SO LONG George McCrae (Jayboy)
5	5	THAT'S THE WAY (I LIKE IT) K C & the Sunshine Band (Jayboy)
18	6	SUMMERTIME CITY Mike Batt (Epic)
7	7	BLANKET ON THE GROUND Billie Jo Spears (United Artists)
10	8	BEST THING THAT EVER HAPPENED Gladys Knight & the Pips (Buddah)
25	9	JULIE-ANN Kenny (RAK)
11	10	EL BIMBO Bimbo Jet (EMI)
-	11	MOONLIGHTING Leo Sayer (Chrysalis)
6	12	BARBADOS Typically Tropical (Gull)
9	13	DOLLY MY LOVE Moments (All Platinum)
20	14	A CHILD'S PRAYER Hot Chocolate (RAK)
-	15	FUNKY MOPED/MAGIC ROUNDABOUT Jasper Carrott (DJM)
12	16	SUMMER OF '42 Biddu Orchestra (Epic)
8	17	IF YOU THINK YOU KNOW HOW TO LOVE ME Smokie (RAK)
13	18	DON'T THROW IT ALL AWAY Gary Benson (State)
22	19	LOVE IN THE SUN Glitter Band (Bell)
23	20	ONE OF THESE NIGHTS Eagles (Asylum)
24	21	DELILAH Alex Harvey Band (Vertigo)
17	22	FAME David Bowie (RCA)
28	23	PANDORA'S BOX Procol Harum (Chrysalis)
21	24	ROCHDALE COWBOY Mike Harding (Rubber)
-	25	MOTOR BIKING Chris Spedding (RAK)
15	26	JIVE TALKIN' Bee Gees (RSO)
14	27	SHERRY Adrian Baker (Magnet)
-	28	DO IT AGAIN Steely Dan (ABC)
29	29	FOOL Al Matthews (CBS)
-	30	HEARTBEAT Showaddywaddy (Bell)

Rod Stewart's *Sailing* was his biggest-selling single in the UK, and like 10 c.c.'s *I'm Not In Love* was the one which wouldn't go away for him, probably because of the instant nostalgia inherent in both song and production. Elsewhere on the chart, the revivals continued to pile up (*Delilah, Sherry, It's In His Kiss, Je T'Aime*), while Mike Batt managed simultaneous hits both in his Womble guise (*Super Womble*) and as himself, and musical comedians Mike Harding and Jasper Carrott debuted almost simultaneously.

September – October 1975

last week	this week	13 September 1975
1	1	SAILING — Rod Stewart (Warner Bros)
3	2	THE LAST FAREWELL — Roger Whittaker (EMI)
2	3	I CAN'T GIVE YOU ANYTHING (BUT MY LOVE) — Stylistics (Avco)
6	4	SUMMERTIME CITY — Mike Batt (Epic)
5	5	THAT'S THE WAY (I LIKE IT) — K C & the Sunshine Band (Jayboy)
11	6	MOONLIGHTING — Leo Sayer (Chrysalis)
14	7	A CHILD'S PRAYER — Hot Chocolate (RAK)
4	8	IT'S BEEN SO LONG — George McCrae (Jayboy)
7	9	BLANKET ON THE GROUND — Billie Jo Spears (United Artists)
9	10	JULIE-ANN — Kenny (RAK)
15	11	FUNKY MOPED/MAGIC ROUNDABOUT — Jasper Carrott (DJM)
8	12	BEST THING THAT EVER HAPPENED — Gladys Knight & the Pips (Buddah)
23	13	PANDORA'S BOX — Procol Harum (Chrysalis)
-	14	I'M ON FIRE — 5000 VOLTS (Philips)
30	15	HEARTBEAT — Showaddywaddy (Bell)
25	16	MOTOR BIKING — Chris Spedding (RAK)
19	17	LOVE IN THE SUN — Glitter Band (Bell)
20	18	ONE OF THESE NIGHTS — Eagles (Asylum)
10	19	EL BIMBO — Bimbo Jet (EMI)
29	20	FOOL — Al Matthews (CBS)
18	21	DON'T THROW IT ALL AWAY — Gary Benson (State)
-	22	FEEL LIKE MAKIN' LOVE — Bad Company (Island)
13	23	DOLLY MY LOVE — Moments (All Platinum)
24	24	ROCHDALE COWBOY — Mike Harding (Rubber)
16	25	SUMMER OF '42 — Biddu Orchestra (Epic)
12	26	BARBADOS — Typically Tropical (Gull)
-	27	UNA PALOMA BLANCA — George Baker (Warner Bros)
-	28	UNA PALOMA BLANCA — Jonathan King (UK)
-	29	THERE GOES MY FIRST LOVE — Drifters (Bell)
28	30	DO IT AGAIN — Steely Dan (ABC)

last week	this week	20 September 1975
1	1	SAILING — Rod Stewart (Warner Bros)
6	2	MOONLIGHTING — Leo Sayer (Chrysalis)
2	3	THE LAST FAREWELL — Roger Whittaker (EMI)
14	4	I'M ON FIRE — 5000 VOLTS (Philips)
4	5	SUMMERTIME CITY — Mike Batt (Epic)
5	6	THAT'S THE WAY (I LIKE IT) — K C & the Sunshine Band (Jayboy)
7	7	A CHILD'S PRAYER — Hot Chocolate (RAK)
15	8	HEARTBEAT — Showaddywaddy (Bell)
11	9	FUNKY MOPED/MAGIC ROUNDABOUT — Jasper Carrott (DJM)
3	10	I CAN'T GIVE YOU ANYTHING (BUT MY LOVE) — Stylistics (Avco)
10	11	JULIE-ANN — Kenny (RAK)
12	12	BEST THING THAT EVER HAPPENED — Gladys Knight & the Pips (Buddah)
20	13	FOOL — Al Matthews (CBS)
8	14	IT'S BEEN SO LONG — George McCrae (Jayboy)
13	15	PANDORA'S BOX — Procol Harum (Chrysalis)
-	16	HOLD ME CLOSE — David Essex (CBS)
28	17	UNA PALOMA BLANCA — Jonathan King (UK)
16	18	MOTOR BIKING — Chris Spedding (RAK)
29	19	THERE GOES MY FIRST LOVE — Drifters (Bell)
9	20	BLANKET ON THE GROUND — Billie Jo Spears (United Artists)
-	21	FATTIE BUM BUM — Carl Malcolm (UK)
17	22	LOVE IN THE SUN — Glitter Band (Bell)
21	23	DON'T THROW IT ALL AWAY — Gary Benson (State)
18	24	ONE OF THESE NIGHTS — Eagles (Asylum)
22	25	FEEL LIKE MAKIN' LOVE — Bad Company (Island)
-	26	I ONLY HAVE EYES FOR YOU — Art Garfunkel (CBS)
27	27	UNA PALOMA BLANCA — George Baker (Warner Bros)
-	28	SING A LITTLE SONG — Desmond Dekker (Cactus)
25	29	SUMMER OF '42 — Biddu Orchestra (Epic)
30	30	IT'S TIME FOR LOVE — Chi-Lites (Brunswick)

last week	this week	27 September 1975
2	1	MOONLIGHTING — Leo Sayer (Chrysalis)
1	2	SAILING — Rod Stewart (Warner Bros)
16	3	HOLD ME CLOSE — David Essex (CBS)
4	4	I'M ON FIRE — 5000 VOLTS (Philips)
3	5	THE LAST FAREWELL — Roger Whittaker (EMI)
9	6	FUNKY MOPED/MAGIC ROUNDABOUT — Jasper Carrott (DJM)
19	7	THERE GOES MY FIRST LOVE — Drifters (Bell)
5	8	SUMMERTIME CITY — Mike Batt (Epic)
8	9	HEARTBEAT — Showaddywaddy (Bell)
7	10	A CHILD'S PRAYER — Hot Chocolate (RAK)
17	11	UNA PALOMA BLANCA — Jonathan King (UK)
21	12	FATTIE BUM BUM — Carl Malcolm (UK)
26	13	I ONLY HAVE EYES FOR YOU — Art Garfunkel (CBS)
18	14	MOTOR BIKING — Chris Spedding (RAK)
11	15	JULIE-ANN — Kenny (RAK)
6	16	THAT'S THE WAY (I LIKE IT) — K C & the Sunshine Band (Jayboy)
15	17	PANDORA'S BOX — Procol Harum (Chrysalis)
27	18	UNA PALOMA BLANCA — George Baker (Warner Bros)
10	19	I CAN'T GIVE YOU ANYTHING (BUT MY LOVE) — Stylistics (Avco)
14	20	IT'S BEEN SO LONG — George McCrae (Jayboy)
13	21	FOOL — Al Matthews (CBS)
30	22	IT'S TIME FOR LOVE — Chi-Lites (Brunswick)
12	23	BEST THING THAT EVER HAPPENED — Gladys Knight & the Pips (Buddah)
-	24	WHO LOVES YOU — Four Seasons (Warner Bros)
20	25	BLANKET ON THE GROUND — Billie Jo Spears (United Artists)
25	26	FEEL LIKE MAKIN' LOVE — Bad Company (Island)
-	27	S.O.S. — Abba (Epic)
-	28	LIKE A BUTTERFLY — Mac & Katie Kissoon (State)
-	29	FALLIN' IN LOVE — Hamilton, Joe Frank & Reynolds (Pye)
22	30	LOVE IN THE SUN — Glitter Band (Bell)

last week	this week	4 October 1975
3	1	HOLD ME CLOSE — David Essex (CBS)
2	2	SAILING — Rod Stewart (Warner Bros)
13	3	I ONLY HAVE EYES FOR YOU — Art Garfunkel (CBS)
4	4	I'M ON FIRE — 5000 VOLTS (Philips)
1	5	MOONLIGHTING — Leo Sayer (Chrysalis)
7	6	THERE GOES MY FIRST LOVE — Drifters (Bell)
6	7	FUNKY MOPED/MAGIC ROUNDABOUT — Jasper Carrott (DJM)
9	8	HEARTBEAT — Showaddywaddy (Bell)
5	9	THE LAST FAREWELL — Roger Whittaker (EMI)
12	10	FATTIE BUM BUM — Carl Malcolm (UK)
11	11	UNA PALOMA BLANCA — Jonathan King (UK)
18	12	UNA PALOMA BLANCA — George Baker (Warner Bros)
10	13	A CHILD'S PRAYER — Hot Chocolate (RAK)
14	14	MOTOR BIKING — Chris Spedding (RAK)
28	15	LIKE A BUTTERFLY — Mac & Katie Kissoon (State)
27	16	S.O.S. — Abba (Epic)
21	17	FOOL — Al Matthews (CBS)
-	18	FEELINGS — Morris Albert (Decca)
22	19	IT'S TIME FOR LOVE — Chi-Lites (Brunswick)
26	20	FEEL LIKE MAKIN' LOVE — Bad Company (Island)
8	21	SUMMERTIME CITY — Mike Batt (Epic)
-	22	SCOTCH ON THE ROCKS — Band Of The Black Watch (Spark)
24	23	WHO LOVES YOU — Four Seasons (Warner Bros)
29	24	FALLIN' IN LOVE — Hamilton, Joe Frank & Reynolds (Pye)
-	25	NO WOMAN NO CRY — Bob Marley & the Wailers (Island)
16	26	THAT'S THE WAY (I LIKE IT) — K C & the Sunshine Band (Jayboy)
17	27	PANDORA'S BOX — Procol Harum (Chrysalis)
15	28	JULIE-ANN — Kenny (RAK)
-	29	SING A LITTLE SONG — Desmond Dekker (Cactus)
-	30	CHICK-A-BOOM — 53rd & 3rd (UK)

The norm during the '50s, and common in the '60s, simultaneously charting different versions of the same song were rare by the mid-1970s, since by now artists generally tended to leave each other's material alone. In a notable exception to this rule, both the European hit version of *Una Paloma Blanca* by Dutchman George Baker, and Jonathan King's UK cover, found their way into the Top 10. Al Matthews, charting with *Fool*, would later play one of the first characters to die in the Sci-Fi movie *Alien!*

October – November 1975

Art Garfunkel took his time (five years) finding British solo success after the Simon & Garfunkel split. His solo career was extemely erratic, yet had a certain odd symmetry about it - only two of his first 12 solo singles charted, but both were Number One hits (the second being *Bright Eyes* in 1979). *I Only Have Eyes For You* took its sound, styling and arrangement lock, stock and doo-wop from the 1959 US hit version by black vocal group the Flamingos, a fact obviously lost on most of its buyers.

November 1975

8 November 1975

last week	this week	Title / Artist
2	1	SPACE ODDITY — David Bowie (RCA)
1	2	I ONLY HAVE EYES FOR YOU — Art Garfunkel (CBS)
9	3	LOVE IS THE DRUG — Roxy Music (Island)
8	4	WHAT A DIFFERENCE A DAY MAKES — Esther Phillips (Kudu)
3	5	FEELINGS — Morris Albert (Decca)
11	6	RHINESTONE COWBOY — Glen Campbell (Capitol)
16	7	BLUE GUITAR — Justin Hayward & John Lodge (Threshold)
6	8	S.O.S. — Abba (Epic)
4	9	THERE GOES MY FIRST LOVE — Drifters (Bell)
25	10	D.I.V.O.R.C.E. — Billy Connolly (Polydor)
7	11	DON'T PLAY YOUR ROCK AND ROLL TO ME — Smokie (RAK)
15	12	ISLAND GIRL — Elton John (DJM)
12	13	HOLD BACK THE NIGHT — Trammps (Buddah)
5	14	HOLD ME CLOSE — David Essex (CBS)
17	15	HIGHFLY — John Miles (Decca)
23	16	I AIN'T LYIN' — George McCrae (Jayboy)
-	17	LOVE HURTS — Jim Capaldi (Island)
10	18	IT'S TIME FOR LOVE — Chi-Lites (Brunswick)
26	19	NEW YORK GROOVE — Hello (Bell)
13	20	WHO LOVES YOU — Four Seasons (Warner Bros)
14	21	SCOTCH ON THE ROCKS — Band Of The Black Watch (Spark)
20	22	RIDE A WILD HORSE — Dee Clark (Chelsea)
-	23	IMAGINE — John Lennon (Apple)
-	24	LYIN' EYES — Eagles (Asylum)
19	25	L-L-LUCY — Mud (RAK)
27	26	DARLIN' — David Cassidy (RCA)
-	27	RIGHT BACK WHERE WE STARTED FROM — Maxine Nightingale (United Artists)
24	28	FUNKY MOPED/MAGIC ROUNDABOUT — Jasper Carrott (DJM)
-	29	ROCK ON BROTHER — Chequers (Creole)
-	30	YOU SEXY THING — Hot Chocolate (RAK)

15 November 1975

this week	Title / Artist
1	SPACE ODDITY — David Bowie (RCA)
2	LOVE IS THE DRUG — Roxy Music (Island)
3	RHINESTONE COWBOY — Glen Campbell (Capitol)
4	D.I.V.O.R.C.E. — Billy Connolly (Polydor)
5	HOLD BACK THE NIGHT — Trammps (Buddah)
6	LOVE HURTS — Jim Capaldi (Island)
7	BLUE GUITAR — Justin Hayward & John Lodge (Threshold)
8	WHAT A DIFFERENCE A DAY MAKES — Esther Phillips (Kudu)
9	I ONLY HAVE EYES FOR YOU — Art Garfunkel (CBS)
10	NEW YORK GROOVE — Hello (Bell)
11	IMAGINE — John Lennon (Apple)
12	FEELINGS — Morris Albert (Decca)
13	S.O.S. — Abba (Epic)
14	I AIN'T LYIN' — George McCrae (Jayboy)
15	RIDE A WILD HORSE — Dee Clark (Chelsea)
16	HIGHFLY — John Miles (Decca)
17	SKY HIGH — Jigsaw (Splash)
18	YOU SEXY THING — Hot Chocolate (RAK)
19	ISLAND GIRL — Elton John (DJM)
20	DON'T PLAY YOUR ROCK AND ROLL TO ME — Smokie (RAK)
21	LYIN' EYES — Eagles (Asylum)
22	THERE GOES MY FIRST LOVE — Drifters (Bell)
23	RIGHT BACK WHERE WE STARTED FROM — Maxine Nightingale (United Artists)
24	SCOTCH ON THE ROCKS — Band Of The Black Watch (Spark)
25	BOHEMIAN RHAPSODY — Queen (EMI)
26	HOLD ME CLOSE — David Essex (CBS)
27	SUPERSHIP — George Benson (CTI)
28	WHO LOVES YOU — Four Seasons (Warner Bros)
29	THIS OLD HEART OF MINE — Rod Stewart (Riva)
30	L-L-LUCY — Mud (RAK)

22 November 1975

this week	Title / Artist
1	D.I.V.O.R.C.E. — Billy Connolly (Polydor)
2	SPACE ODDITY — David Bowie (RCA)
3	LOVE HURTS — Jim Capaldi (Island)
4	LOVE IS THE DRUG — Roxy Music (Island)
5	IMAGINE — John Lennon (Apple)
6	YOU SEXY THING — Hot Chocolate (RAK)
7	RHINESTONE COWBOY — Glen Campbell (Capitol)
8	BLUE GUITAR — Justin Hayward & John Lodge (Threshold)
9	HOLD BACK THE NIGHT — Trammps (Buddah)
10	NEW YORK GROOVE — Hello (Bell)
11	SKY HIGH — Jigsaw (Splash)
12	BOHEMIAN RHAPSODY — Queen (EMI)
13	RIGHT BACK WHERE WE STARTED FROM — Maxine Nightingale (United Artists)
14	THIS OLD HEART OF MINE — Rod Stewart (Riva)
15	I AIN'T LYIN' — George McCrae (Jayboy)
16	LYIN' EYES — Eagles (Asylum)
17	WHAT A DIFFERENCE A DAY MAKES — Esther Phillips (Kudu)
18	WHY DID YOU DO IT — Stretch (Anchor)
19	MONEY HONEY — Bay City Rollers (Bell)
20	ALL AROUND MY HAT — Steeleye Span (Chrysalis)
21	DARLIN' — David Cassidy (RCA)
22	RIDE A WILD HORSE — Dee Clark (Chelsea)
23	I ONLY HAVE EYES FOR YOU — Art Garfunkel (CBS)
24	HIGHFLY — John Miles (Decca)
25	FEELINGS — Morris Albert (Decca)
26	S.O.S. — Abba (Epic)
27	ISLAND GIRL — Elton John (DJM)
28	FLY ROBIN FLY — Silver Convention (Magnet)
29	ROCKY — Austin Roberts (Private Stock)
30	IN FOR A PENNY — Slade (Polydor)

29 November 1975

this week	Title / Artist
1	YOU SEXY THING — Hot Chocolate (RAK)
2	BOHEMIAN RHAPSODY — Queen (EMI)
3	D.I.V.O.R.C.E. — Billy Connolly (Polydor)
4	LOVE HURTS — Jim Capaldi (Island)
5	THIS OLD HEART OF MINE — Rod Stewart (Riva)
6	SPACE ODDITY — David Bowie (RCA)
7	MONEY HONEY — Bay City Rollers (Bell)
8	IMAGINE — John Lennon (Apple)
9	SKY HIGH — Jigsaw (Splash)
10	LOVE IS THE DRUG — Roxy Music (Island)
11	ALL AROUND MY HAT — Steeleye Span (Chrysalis)
12	RIGHT BACK WHERE WE STARTED FROM — Maxine Nightingale (United Artists)
13	RHINESTONE COWBOY — Glen Campbell (Capitol)
14	NEW YORK GROOVE — Hello (Bell)
15	BLUE GUITAR — Justin Hayward & John Lodge (Threshold)
16	IN FOR A PENNY — Slade (Polydor)
17	LYIN' EYES — Eagles (Asylum)
18	WHY DID YOU DO IT — Stretch (Anchor)
19	DARLIN' — David Cassidy (RCA)
20	NA NA IS THE SADDEST WORD — Stylistics (Avco)
21	HOLD BACK THE NIGHT — Trammps (Buddah)
22	ROCKY — Austin Roberts (Private Stock)
23	THE TRAIL OF THE LONESOME PINE — Laurel & Hardy (United Artists)
24	FLY ROBIN FLY — Silver Convention (Magnet)
25	I AIN'T LYIN' — George McCrae (Jayboy)
26	LITTLE DARLIN' — Rubettes (State)
27	HAPPY TO BE ON AN ISLAND IN THE SUN — Demis Roussos (Philips)
28	PART TIME LOVE — Gladys Knight & The Pips (Buddah)
29	HEAVENLY — Showaddywaddy (Bell)
30	HOLY ROLLER — Nazareth (Mountain)

John Lennon's *Imagine* had been issued as a US single at the same time as the album of the same title in 1971, selling a million. It's unclear why it was unreleased then in the UK, and why its time was suddenly deemed to have come late in 1975 (it would return again, hitting Number One, in the wake of Lennon's death.) Meanwhile, David Bowie might have expected a chart-topper (as in the US) with *Fame*, but ironically he got one with a maxi-single re-issue of 1969's *Space Oddity* instead.

December 1975

6 December 1975

last	this	title / artist
2	1	BOHEMIAN RHAPSODY — Queen (EMI)
1	2	YOU SEXY THING — Hot Chocolate (RAK)
7	3	MONEY HONEY — Bay City Rollers (Bell)
4	4	LOVE HURTS — Jim Capaldi (Island)
3	5	D.I.V.O.R.C.E. — Billy Connolly (Polydor)
11	6	ALL AROUND MY HAT — Steeleye Span (Chrysalis)
20	7	NA NA IS THE SADDEST WORD — Stylistics (Avco)
5	8	THIS OLD HEART OF MINE — Rod Stewart (Riva)
8	9	IMAGINE — John Lennon (Apple)
23	10	THE TRAIL OF THE LONESOME PINE — Laurel & Hardy (United Artists)
9	11	SKY HIGH — Jigsaw (Splash)
12	12	RIGHT BACK WHERE WE STARTED FROM — Maxine Nightingale (United Artists)
-	13	SHOW ME YOU'RE A WOMAN — Mud (Private Stock)
16	14	IN FOR A PENNY — Slade (Polydor)
18	15	WHY DID YOU DO IT — Stretch (Anchor)
-	16	LET'S TWIST AGAIN — John Asher (Creole)
17	17	LYIN' EYES — Eagles (Asylum)
6	18	SPACE ODDITY — David Bowie (RCA)
19	19	DARLIN' — David Cassidy (RCA)
27	20	HAPPY TO BE ON AN ISLAND IN THE SUN — Demis Roussos (Philips)
10	21	LOVE IS THE DRUG — Roxy Music (Island)
14	22	NEW YORK GROOVE — Hello (Bell)
-	23	GOLDEN YEARS — David Bowie (RCA)
13	24	RHINESTONE COWBOY — Glen Campbell (Capitol)
-	25	LET'S TWIST AGAIN/THE TWIST — Chubby Checker (London)
22	26	ROCKY — Austin Roberts (Private Stock)
-	27	CAN I TAKE YOU HOME LITTLE GIRL — Drifters (Bell)
-	28	ART FOR ART'S SAKE — 10 c.c. (Mercury)
15	29	BLUE GUITAR — Justin Hayward & John Lodge (Threshold)
15	30	FLY ROBIN FLY — Silver Convention (Magnet)

13 December 1975

last	this	title / artist
1	1	BOHEMIAN RHAPSODY — Queen (EMI)
10	2	THE TRAIL OF THE LONESOME PINE — Laurel & Hardy (United Artists)
2	3	YOU SEXY THING — Hot Chocolate (RAK)
3	4	MONEY HONEY — Bay City Rollers (Bell)
8	5	THIS OLD HEART OF MINE — Rod Stewart (Riva)
6	6	ALL AROUND MY HAT — Steeleye Span (Chrysalis)
7	7	NA NA IS THE SADDEST WORD — Stylistics (Avco)
25	8	LET'S TWIST AGAIN/THE TWIST — Chubby Checker (London)
13	9	SHOW ME YOU'RE A WOMAN — Mud (Private Stock)
14	10	IN FOR A PENNY — Slade (Polydor)
4	11	LOVE HURTS — Jim Capaldi (Island)
20	12	HAPPY TO BE ON AN ISLAND IN THE SUN — Demis Roussos (Philips)
5	13	D.I.V.O.R.C.E. — Tammy Wynette (Epic)
11	14	SKY HIGH — Jigsaw (Splash)
23	15	GOLDEN YEARS — David Bowie (RCA)
9	16	IMAGINE — John Lennon (Apple)
-	17	RENTA SANTA — Chris Hill (Philips)
27	18	CAN I TAKE YOU HOME LITTLE GIRL — Drifters (Bell)
-	19	I BELIEVE IN FATHER CHRISTMAS — Greg Lake (Manticore)
15	20	WHY DID YOU DO IT — Stretch (Anchor)
28	21	ART FOR ART'S SAKE — 10 c.c. (Mercury)
-	22	FIRST IMPRESSIONS — Impressions (Curtom)
-	23	WIDE EYED AND LEGLESS — Andy Fairweather Low (A&M)
12	24	RIGHT BACK WHERE WE STARTED FROM — Maxine Nightingale (United Artists)
-	25	IF I COULD — David Essex (CBS)
17	26	LYIN' EYES — Eagles (Asylum)
16	27	LET'S TWIST AGAIN — John Asher (Creole)
-	28	GREEN GREEN GRASS OF HOME — Elvis Presley (RCA)
30	29	FLY ROBIN FLY — Silver Convention (Magnet)
19	30	DARLIN' — David Cassidy (RCA)

20 December 1975

last	this	title / artist
1	1	BOHEMIAN RHAPSODY — Queen (EMI)
2	2	THE TRAIL OF THE LONESOME PINE — Laurel & Hardy (United Artists)
3	3	YOU SEXY THING — Hot Chocolate (RAK)
8	4	LET'S TWIST AGAIN/THE TWIST — Chubby Checker (London)
7	5	NA NA IS THE SADDEST WORD — Stylistics (Avco)
19	6	I BELIEVE IN FATHER CHRISTMAS — Greg Lake (Manticore)
4	7	MONEY HONEY — Bay City Rollers (Bell)
9	8	SHOW ME YOU'RE A WOMAN — Mud (Private Stock)
5	9	THIS OLD HEART OF MINE — Rod Stewart (Riva)
6	10	ALL AROUND MY HAT — Steeleye Span (Chrysalis)
12	11	HAPPY TO BE ON AN ISLAND IN THE SUN — Demis Roussos (Philips)
15	12	GOLDEN YEARS — David Bowie (RCA)
17	13	RENTA SANTA — Chris Hill (Philips)
-	14	IT'S GONNA BE A COLD COLD CHRISTMAS — Dana (GTO)
21	15	ART FOR ART'S SAKE — 10 c.c. (Mercury)
16	16	IMAGINE — John Lennon (Apple)
23	17	WIDE EYED AND LEGLESS — Andy Fairweather Low (A&M)
18	18	CAN I TAKE YOU HOME LITTLE GIRL — Drifters (Bell)
14	19	SKY HIGH — Jigsaw (Splash)
11	20	LOVE HURTS — Jim Capaldi (Island)
25	21	IF I COULD — David Essex (CBS)
10	22	IN FOR A PENNY — Slade (Polydor)
-	23	GLASS OF CHAMPAGNE — Sailor (Epic)
28	24	GREEN GREEN GRASS OF HOME — Elvis Presley (RCA)
22	25	FIRST IMPRESSIONS — Impressions (Curtom)
20	26	WHY DID YOU DO IT — Stretch (Anchor)
-	27	MAMMA MIA — Abba (Epic)
-	28	(THINK OF ME) WHEREVER YOU ARE — Ken Dodd (EMI)
-	29	DO THE BUS STOP — Fatback Band (Polydor)
-	30	MAKE A DAFT NOISE FOR CHRISTMAS — Goodies (Bradley)

27 December 1975

last	this	title / artist
1	1	BOHEMIAN RHAPSODY — Queen (EMI)
6	2	I BELIEVE IN FATHER CHRISTMAS — Greg Lake (Manticore)
2	3	THE TRAIL OF THE LONESOME PINE — Laurel & Hardy (United Artists)
4	4	LET'S TWIST AGAIN/THE TWIST — Chubby Checker (London)
11	5	HAPPY TO BE ON AN ISLAND IN THE SUN — Demis Roussos (Philips)
14	6	IT'S GONNA BE A COLD COLD CHRISTMAS — Dana (GTO)
3	7	YOU SEXY THING — Hot Chocolate (RAK)
5	8	NA NA IS THE SADDEST WORD — Stylistics (Avco)
12	9	GOLDEN YEARS — David Bowie (RCA)
8	10	SHOW ME YOU'RE A WOMAN — Mud (Private Stock)
13	11	RENTA SANTA — Chris Hill (Philips)
10	12	ALL AROUND MY HAT — Steeleye Span (Chrysalis)
17	13	WIDE EYED AND LEGLESS — Andy Fairweather Low (A&M)
7	14	MONEY HONEY — Bay City Rollers (Bell)
23	15	GLASS OF CHAMPAGNE — Sailor (Epic)
15	16	ART FOR ART'S SAKE — 10 c.c. (Mercury)
18	17	CAN I TAKE YOU HOME LITTLE GIRL — Drifters (Bell)
9	18	THIS OLD HEART OF MINE — Rod Stewart (Riva)
25	19	FIRST IMPRESSIONS — Impressions (Curtom)
21	20	IF I COULD — David Essex (CBS)
30	21	MAKE A DAFT NOISE FOR CHRISTMAS — Goodies (Bradley)
28	22	(THINK OF ME) WHEREVER YOU ARE — Ken Dodd (EMI)
-	23	ITCHYCOO PARK — Small Faces (Immediate)
-	24	CHRISTMAS IN DREAMLAND/COME OUTSIDE — Judge Dread (Cactus)
27	25	MAMMA MIA — Abba (Epic)
19	26	SKY HIGH — Jigsaw (Splash)
29	27	DO THE BUS STOP — Fatback Band (Polydor)
22	28	IN FOR A PENNY — Slade (Polydor)
24	29	GREEN GREEN GRASS OF HOME — Elvis Presley (RCA)
-	30	KING OF THE COPS — Bill Howard (Penny Farthing)

1975's biggest seller was Queen's *Bohemian Rhapsody*, its two month Number One stint placing it among the elite of long-stay chart-toppers. UK sales approximated 1,190,000 – a total doubled 16 years later when the tragic death of Freddie Mercury helped propel the single to a further Number One run. Its success was due not only to the single's distinctive sound and length (almost six minutes), but also to the ground-breaking video made to promote it. The age of the music video was launched here.

January 1976

3 January 1976

LW	TW	Title / Artist
1	1	BOHEMIAN RHAPSODY — Queen (EMI)
2	2	I BELIEVE IN FATHER CHRISTMAS — Greg Lake (Manticore)
6	3	IT'S GONNA BE A COLD COLD CHRISTMAS — Dana (GTO)
3	4	THE TRAIL OF THE LONESOME PINE — Laurel & Hardy (United Artists)
4	5	LET'S TWIST AGAIN/THE TWIST — Chubby Checker (London)
5	6	HAPPY TO BE ON AN ISLAND IN THE SUN — Demis Roussos (Philips)
8	7	NA NA IS THE SADDEST WORD — Stylistics (Avco)
7	8	YOU SEXY THING — Hot Chocolate (RAK)
13	9	WIDE EYED AND LEGLESS — Andy Fairweather Low (A&M)
9	10	GOLDEN YEARS — David Bowie (RCA)
15	11	GLASS OF CHAMPAGNE — Sailor (Epic)
16	12	ART FOR ART'S SAKE — 10 c.c. (Mercury)
17	13	CAN I TAKE YOU HOME LITTLE GIRL — Drifters (Bell)
10	14	SHOW ME YOU'RE A WOMAN — Mud (RAK)
11	15	RENTA SANTA — Chris Hill (Philips)
20	16	IF I COULD — David Essex (CBS)
12	17	ALL AROUND MY HAT — Steeleye Span (Chrysalis)
-	18	IN DULCE JUBILO/HORSEBACK — Mike Oldfield (Virgin)
25	19	MAMMA MIA — Abba (Epic)
23	20	ITCHYCOO PARK — Small Faces (Immediate)
21	21	MAKE A DAFT NOISE FOR CHRISTMAS — Goodies (Bradley)
14	22	MONEY HONEY — Bay City Rollers (Bell)
24	23	CHRISTMAS IN DREADLAND/COME OUTSIDE — Judge Dread (Cactus)
27	24	DO THE BUS STOP — Fatback Band (Polydor)
19	25	FIRST IMPRESSIONS — Impressions (Curtom)
22	26	(THINK OF ME) WHEREVER YOU ARE — Ken Dodd (EMI)
18	27	THIS OLD HEART OF MINE — Rod Stewart (Riva)
30	28	KING OF THE COPS — Bill Howard (Penny Farthing)
-	29	BOTH ENDS BURNING — Roxy Music (Island)
-	30	LET'S WOMBLE TO THE PARTY TONIGHT — Wombles (CBS)

10 January 1976

LW	TW	Title / Artist
1	1	BOHEMIAN RHAPSODY — Queen (EMI)
5	2	LET'S TWIST AGAIN/THE TWIST — Chubby Checker (London)
4	3	THE TRAIL OF THE LONESOME PINE — Laurel & Hardy (United Artists)
11	4	GLASS OF CHAMPAGNE — Sailor (Epic)
2	5	I BELIEVE IN FATHER CHRISTMAS — Greg Lake (Manticore)
6	6	HAPPY TO BE ON AN ISLAND IN THE SUN — Demis Roussos (Philips)
12	7	ART FOR ART'S SAKE — 10 c.c. (Mercury)
9	8	WIDE EYED AND LEGLESS — Andy Fairweather Low (A&M)
3	9	IT'S GONNA BE A COLD COLD CHRISTMAS — Dana (GTO)
10	10	GOLDEN YEARS — David Bowie (RCA)
7	11	NA NA IS THE SADDEST WORD — Stylistics (Avco)
8	12	YOU SEXY THING — Hot Chocolate (RAK)
13	13	CAN I TAKE YOU HOME LITTLE GIRL — Drifters (Bell)
14	14	SHOW ME YOU'RE A WOMAN — Mud (RAK)
16	15	IF I COULD — David Essex (CBS)
18	16	IN DULCE JUBILO/HORSEBACK — Mike Oldfield (Virgin)
19	17	MAMMA MIA — Abba (Epic)
20	18	ITCHYCOO PARK — Small Faces (Immediate)
15	19	RENTA SANTA — Chris Hill (Philips)
28	20	KING OF THE COPS — Bill Howard (Penny Farthing)
21	21	FIRST IMPRESSIONS — Impressions (Curtom)
24	22	DO THE BUS STOP — Fatback Band (Polydor)
29	23	BOTH ENDS BURNING — Roxy Music (Island)
22	24	MONEY HONEY — Bay City Rollers (Bell)
-	25	MIDNIGHT RIDER — Paul Davidson (Tropical)
-	26	LET THE MUSIC PLAY — Barry White (20th Century)
-	27	ALL AROUND MY HAT — Steeleye Span (Chrysalis)
-	28	(THINK OF ME) WHEREVER YOU ARE — Ken Dodd (EMI)
-	29	CHRISTMAS IN DREADLAND — Judge Dread (Cactus)
-	30	I BELIEVE I'M GONNA LOVE YOU — Frank Sinatra (Reprise)

17 January 1976

LW	TW	Title / Artist
1	1	BOHEMIAN RHAPSODY — Queen (EMI)
4	2	GLASS OF CHAMPAGNE — Sailor (Epic)
2	3	LET'S TWIST AGAIN — John Asher (Creole)
8	4	WIDE EYED AND LEGLESS — Andy Fairweather Low (A&M)
17	5	MAMMA MIA — Abba (Epic)
7	6	ART FOR ART'S SAKE — 10 c.c. (Mercury)
3	7	THE TRAIL OF THE LONESOME PINE — Laurel & Hardy (United Artists)
10	8	GOLDEN YEARS — David Bowie (RCA)
20	9	KING OF THE COPS — Bill Howard (Penny Farthing)
13	10	CAN I TAKE YOU HOME LITTLE GIRL — Drifters (Bell)
6	11	HAPPY TO BE ON AN ISLAND IN THE SUN — Demis Roussos (Philips)
18	12	ITCHYCOO PARK — Small Faces (Immediate)
16	13	IN DULCE JUBILO/ON HORSEBACK — Mike Oldfield (Virgin)
5	14	I BELIEVE IN FATHER CHRISTMAS — Greg Lake (Manticore)
12	15	YOU SEXY THING — Hot Chocolate (RAK)
15	16	IF I COULD — David Essex (CBS)
26	17	LET THE MUSIC PLAY — Barry White (20th Century)
21	18	FIRST IMPRESSIONS — Impressions (Curtom)
11	19	NA NA IS THE SADDEST WORD — Stylistics (Avco)
22	20	DO THE BUS STOP — Fatback Band (Polydor)
9	21	IT'S GONNA BE A COLD COLD CHRISTMAS — Dana (GTO)
_	22	LOVE MACHINE — Miracles (Tamla Motown)
25	23	MIDNIGHT RIDER — Paul Davidson (Tropical)
24	24	WE DO IT — R & J Stone (RCA)
23	25	BOTH ENDS BURNING — Roxy Music (Island)
24	26	MONEY HONEY — Bay City Rollers (Bell)
14	27	SHOW ME YOU'RE A WOMAN — Mud (RAK)
_	28	50 WAYS TO LEAVE YOUR LOVER — Paul Simon (CBS)
_	29	EVIL WOMAN — Electric Light Orchestra (EMI)
_	30	MILKY WAY — Sheer Elegance (Pye)

24 January 1976

LW	TW	Title / Artist
2	1	GLASS OF CHAMPAGNE — Sailor (Epic)
5	2	MAMMA MIA — Abba (Epic)
1	3	BOHEMIAN RHAPSODY — Queen (EMI)
13	4	IN DULCE JUBILO/ON HORSEBACK — Mike Oldfield (Virgin)
9	5	KING OF THE COPS — Bill Howard (Penny Farthing)
6	6	ART FOR ART'S SAKE — 10 c.c. (Mercury)
22	7	LOVE MACHINE — Miracles (Tamla Motown)
4	8	WIDE EYED AND LEGLESS — Andy Fairweather Low (A&M)
24	9	WE DO IT — R & J Stone (RCA)
12	10	ITCHYCOO PARK — Small Faces (Immediate)
3	11	LET'S TWIST AGAIN/THE TWIST — Chubby Checker (London)
17	12	LET THE MUSIC PLAY — Barry White (20th Century)
29	13	EVIL WOMAN — Electric Light Orchestra (EMI)
8	14	GOLDEN YEARS — David Bowie (RCA)
-	15	FOREVER AND EVER — Slik (Bell)
11	16	HAPPY TO BE ON AN ISLAND IN THE SUN — Demis Roussos (Philips)
-	17	LOVE TO LOVE YOU BABY — Donna Summer (GTO)
23	18	MIDNIGHT RIDER — Paul Davidson (Tropical)
20	19	DO THE BUS STOP — Fatback Band (Polydor)
-	20	NO REGRETS — Walker Brothers (GTO)
-	21	ANSWER ME — Barbara Dickson (RSO)
30	22	MILKY WAY — Sheer Elegance (Pye)
7	23	THE TRAIL OF THE LONESOME PINE — Laurel & Hardy (United Artists)
25	24	BOTH ENDS BURNING — Roxy Music (Island)
16	25	IF I COULD — David Essex (CBS)
10	26	CAN I TAKE YOU HOME LITTLE GIRL — Drifters (Bell)
-	27	SUNSHINE DAY — Osibisa (Bronze)
28	28	50 WAYS TO LEAVE YOUR LOVER — Paul Simon (CBS)
-	29	WALK AWAY FROM LOVE — David Ruffin (Tamla Motown)
-	30	DEEP PURPLE — Donny & Marie Osmond (MGM)

The Miracles' *Love Machine* was their first UK hit since the group's split some years earlier from erstwhile lead singer Smokey Robinson. Unfortunately for them, it was also the last – although the song itself entered the classic soul/dance repertoire, and was later covererd by Wham! among others. Mike Oldfield's hit was an odd example of a Christmas tune – *In Dulce Jubilo* – turning into a hit after the New Year. This had only happened once before, with *Little Drummer Boy* in 1959.

297

January – February 1976

31 January 1976

last week	this week	title	artist
2	1	MAMMA MIA	Abba (Epic)
1	2	GLASS OF CHAMPAGNE	Sailor (Epic)
3	3	BOHEMIAN RHAPSODY	Queen (EMI)
7	4	LOVE MACHINE	Miracles (Tamla Motown)
9	5	WE DO IT	R & J Stone (RCA)
4	6	IN DULCE JUBILO/ON HORSEBACK	Mike Oldfield (Virgin)
5	7	KING OF THE COPS	Bill Howard (Penny Farthing)
15	8	FOREVER AND EVER	Slik (Bell)
17	9	LOVE TO LOVE YOU BABY	Donna Summer (GTO)
12	10	LET THE MUSIC PLAY	Barry White (20th Century)
18	11	MIDNIGHT RIDER	Paul Davidson (Tropical)
10	12	ITCHYCOO PARK	Small Faces (Immediate)
13	13	EVIL WOMAN	Electric Light Orchestra (EMI)
6	14	ART FOR ART'S SAKE	10 c.c. (Mercury)
21	15	ANSWER ME	Barbara Dickson (RSO)
8	16	WIDE EYED AND LEGLESS	Andy Fairweather Low (A&M)
27	17	SUNSHINE DAY	Osibisa (Bronze)
19	18	DO THE BUS STOP	Fatback Band (Polydor)
29	19	WALK AWAY FROM LOVE	David Ruffin (Tamla Motown)
28	20	50 WAYS TO LEAVE YOUR LOVER	Paul Simon (CBS)
26	21	CAN I TAKE YOU HOME LITTLE GIRL	Drifters (Bell)
-	22	LOW RIDER	War (Island)
22	23	MILKYWAY	Sheer Elegance (Pye)
11	24	LET'S TWIST AGAIN/THE TWIST	Chubby Checker (London)
24	25	BOTH ENDS BURNING	Roxy Music (Island)
-	26	BABY FACE	Wing & A Prayer Fife & Drum Corps (Atlantic)
30	27	DEEP PURPLE	Donny & Marie Osmond (MGM)
20	28	NO REGRETS	Walker Brothers (GTO)
-	29	MOONLIGHT SERENADE/LITTLE BROWN JUG/IN THE MOOD	Glenn Miller (RCA)
-	30	SQUEEZE BOX	Who (Polydor)

7 February 1976

last week	this week	title	artist
1	1	MAMMA MIA	Abba (Epic)
8	2	FOREVER AND EVER	Slik (Bell)
4	3	LOVE MACHINE	Miracles (Tamla Motown)
9	4	LOVE TO LOVE YOU BABY	Donna Summer (GTO)
5	5	WE DO IT	R & J Stone (RCA)
2	6	GLASS OF CHAMPAGNE	Sailor (Epic)
3	7	BOHEMIAN RHAPSODY	Queen (EMI)
6	8	IN DULCE JUBILO/ON HORSEBACK	Mike Oldfield (Virgin)
7	9	KING OF THE COPS	Bill Howard (Penny Farthing)
13	10	EVIL WOMAN	Electric Light Orchestra (EMI)
15	11	ANSWER ME	Barbara Dickson (RSO)
19	12	WALK AWAY FROM LOVE	David Ruffin (Tamla Motown)
11	13	MIDNIGHT RIDER	Paul Davidson (Tropical)
-	14	DECEMBER '63 (OH WHAT A NIGHT)	Four Seasons (Warner Bros)
17	15	SUNSHINE DAY	Osibisa (Bronze)
29	16	MOONLIGHT SERENADE/LITTLE BROWN JUG/IN THE MOOD	Glenn Miller (RCA)
12	17	ITCHYCOO PARK	Small Faces (Immediate)
10	18	LET THE MUSIC PLAY	Barry White (20th Century)
22	19	LOW RIDER	War (Island)
28	20	NO REGRETS	Walker Brothers (GTO)
14	21	ART FOR ART'S SAKE	10 c.c. (Mercury)
26	22	BABY FACE	Wing & A Prayer Fife & Drum Corps (Atlantic)
20	23	50 WAYS TO LEAVE YOUR LOVER	Paul Simon (CBS)
30	24	SQUEEZE BOX	Who (Polydor)
16	25	WIDE EYED AND LEGLESS	Andy Fairweather Low (A&M)
23	26	MILKYWAY	Sheer Elegance (Pye)
27	27	DEEP PURPLE	Donny & Marie Osmond (MGM)
-	28	RODRIGO'S GUITAR CONCERTO DE ARANJUEZ	Manuel & the Music Of The Mountains (EMI)
-	29	IT SHOULD HAVE BEEN ME	Yvonne Fair (Tamla Motown)
-	30	HONEY I	George McCrae (Jayboy)

14 February 1976

last week	this week	title	artist
2	1	FOREVER AND EVER	Slik (Bell)
1	2	MAMMA MIA	Abba (Epic)
14	3	DECEMBER '63 (OH WHAT A NIGHT)	Four Seasons (Warner Bros)
4	4	LOVE TO LOVE YOU BABY	Donna Summer (GTO)
5	5	WE DO IT	R & J Stone (RCA)
3	6	LOVE MACHINE	Miracles (Tamla Motown)
20	7	NO REGRETS	Walker Brothers (GTO)
16	8	MOONLIGHT SERENADE/LITTLE BROWN JUG/IN THE MOOD	Glenn Miller (RCA)
10	9	EVIL WOMAN	Electric Light Orchestra (EMI)
6	10	GLASS OF CHAMPAGNE	Sailor (Epic)
28	11	RODRIGO'S GUITAR CONCERTO DE ARANJUEZ	Manuel & the Music Of The Mountains (EMI)
7	12	BOHEMIAN RHAPSODY	Queen (EMI)
12	13	WALK AWAY FROM LOVE	David Ruffin (Tamla Motown)
9	14	KING OF THE COPS	Bill Howard (Penny Farthing)
8	15	IN DULCE JUBILO/ON HORSEBACK	Mike Oldfield (Virgin)
11	16	ANSWER ME	Barbara Dickson (RSO)
13	17	MIDNIGHT RIDER	Paul Davidson (Tropical)
18	18	LOW RIDER	War (Island)
24	19	SQUEEZE BOX	Who (Polydor)
17	20	ITCHYCOO PARK	Small Faces (Immediate)
29	21	IT SHOULD HAVE BEEN ME	Yvonne Fair (Tamla Motown)
27	22	DEEP PURPLE	Donny & Marie Osmond (MGM)
-	23	SOMETHING'S BEEN MAKING ME BLUE	Smokie (RAK)
-	24	I LOVE TO LOVE	Tina Charles (CBS)
18	25	LET THE MUSIC PLAY	Barry White (20th Century)
22	26	BABY FACE	Wing & A Prayer Fife & Drum Corps (Atlantic)
15	27	SUNSHINE DAY	Osibisa (Bronze)
-	28	THE WAY I WANT TO TOUCH YOU	Captain & Tennille (A&M)
26	29	MILKYWAY	Sheer Elegance (Pye)
23	30	50 WAYS TO LEAVE YOUR LOVER	Paul Simon (CBS)

21 February 1976

last week	this week	title	artist
3	1	DECEMBER '63 (OH WHAT A NIGHT)	Four Seasons (Warner Bros)
1	2	FOREVER AND EVER	Slik (Bell)
2	3	MAMMA MIA	Abba (Epic)
11	4	RODRIGO'S GUITAR CONCERTO DE ARANJUEZ	Manuel & the Music Of The Mountains (EMI)
6	5	LOVE MACHINE	Miracles (Tamla Motown)
4	6	LOVE TO LOVE YOU BABY	Donna Summer (GTO)
5	7	WE DO IT	R & J Stone (RCA)
24	8	I LOVE TO LOVE	Tina Charles (CBS)
7	9	NO REGRETS	Walker Brothers (GTO)
19	10	SQUEEZE BOX	Who (Polydor)
13	11	WALK AWAY FROM LOVE	David Ruffin (Tamla Motown)
17	12	LOW RIDER	War (Island)
-	13	CONVOY	C W McCall (MGM)
21	14	IT SHOULD HAVE BEEN ME	Yvonne Fair (Tamla Motown)
16	15	ANSWER ME	Barbara Dickson (RSO)
8	16	MOONLIGHT SERENADE/LITTLE BROWN JUG/IN THE MOOD	Glenn Miller (RCA)
-	17	DAT	Pluto Shervington (Opal)
26	18	BABY FACE	Wing & A Prayer Fife & Drum Corps (Atlantic)
9	19	EVIL WOMAN	Electric Light Orchestra (EMI)
-	20	LET'S CALL IT QUITS	Slade (Polydor)
-	21	RAIN	Status Quo (Vertigo)
23	22	SOMETHING'S BEEN MAKING ME BLUE	Smokie (RAK)
17	23	MIDNIGHT RIDER	Paul Davidson (Tropical)
27	24	SUNSHINE DAY	Osibisa (Bronze)
20	25	ITCHYCOO PARK	Small Faces (Immediate)
-	26	TUXEDO JUNCTION	Manhattan Transfer (Atlantic)
12	27	BOHEMIAN RHAPSODY	Queen (EMI)
14	28	KING OF THE COPS	Bill Howard (Penny Farthing)
-	29	I LOVE MUSIC	O'Jays (Philadelphia Int.)
-	30	FUNKY WEEKEND	Stylistics (Avco)

As Abba's *Mamma Mia* reached the top, it began a period of extraordinary success for the Swedish quartet during which only one of a run of seven consecutive singles would fail to make Number One. Lead singer of Slik, whose sole major hit was the chart-topping *Forever And Ever*, was Midge Ure, later to find more lasting fame with Ultravox, and then as a soloist and co-writer of *Do They Know It's Christmas*. David Ruffin, former Temptations lead singer, had his only UK solo hit.

28 February 1976

last week	this week	
1	1	DECEMBER '63 (OH WHAT A NIGHT) Four Seasons (Warner Bros)
4	2	RODRIGO'S GUITAR CONCERTO DE ARANJUEZ Manuel & the Music Of The Mountains (EMI)
8	3	I LOVE TO LOVE Tina Charles (CBS)
2	4	FOREVER AND EVER Slik (Bell)
13	5	CONVOY C W McCall (MGM)
3	6	MAMMA MIA Abba (Epic)
5	7	LOVE MACHINE Miracles (Tamla Motown)
9	8	NO REGRETS Walker Brothers (GTO)
6	9	LOVE TO LOVE YOU BABY Donna Summer (GTO)
14	10	IT SHOULD HAVE BEEN ME Yvonne Fair (Tamla Motown)
10	11	SQUEEZE BOX Who (Polydor)
21	12	RAIN Status Quo (Vertigo)
17	13	DAT Pluto Shervington (Opal)
7	14	WE DO IT R & J Stone (RCA)
16	15	MOONLIGHT SERENADE/LITTLE BROWN JUG/IN THE MOOD Glenn Miller (RCA)
12	16	LOW RIDER War (Island)
30	17	FUNKY WEEKEND Stylistics (Avco)
11	18	WALK AWAY FROM LOVE David Ruffin (Tamla Motown)
20	19	LET'S CALL IT QUITS Slade (Polydor)
15	20	ANSWER ME Barbara Dickson (RSO)
26	21	TUXEDO JUNCTION Manhattan Transfer (Atlantic)
29	22	I LOVE MUSIC O'Jays (Philadelphia Int.)
22	23	SOMETHING'S BEEN MAKING ME BLUE Smokie (RAK)
27	24	BOHEMIAN RHAPSODY Queen (EMI)
19	25	EVIL WOMAN Electric Light Orchestra (EMI)
-	26	MISS YOU NIGHTS Cliff Richard (EMI)
-	27	LOVE REALLY HURTS WITHOUT YOU Billy Ocean (GTO)
25	28	ITCHYCOO PARK Small Faces (Immediate)
28	29	KING OF THE COPS Bill Howard (Penny Farthing)
-	30	IN DULCE JUBILO/ON HORSEBACK Mike Oldfield (Virgin)

6 March 1976

3	1	I LOVE TO LOVE Tina Charles (CBS)
1	2	DECEMBER '63 (OH WHAT A NIGHT) Four Seasons (Warner Bros)
5	3	CONVOY C W McCall (MGM)
2	4	RODRIGO'S GUITAR CONCERTO DE ARANJUEZ Manuel & the Music Of The Mountains (EMI)
10	5	IT SHOULD HAVE BEEN ME Yvonne Fair (Tamla Motown)
12	6	RAIN Status Quo (Vertigo)
4	7	FOREVER AND EVER Slik (Bell)
11	8	SQUEEZE BOX Who (Polydor)
13	9	DAT Pluto Shervington (Opal)
17	10	FUNKY WEEKEND Stylistics (Avco)
19	11	LET'S CALL IT QUITS Slade (Polydor)
8	12	NO REGRETS Walker Brothers (GTO)
23	13	SOMETHING'S BEEN MAKING ME BLUE Smokie (RAK)
27	14	LOVE REALLY HURTS WITHOUT YOU Billy Ocean (GTO)
9	15	LOVE TO LOVE YOU BABY Donna Summer (GTO)
7	16	LOVE MACHINE Miracles (Tamla Motown)
6	17	MAMMA MIA Abba (Epic)
15	18	MOONLIGHT SERENADE/LITTLE BROWN JUG/IN THE MOOD Glenn Miller (RCA)
-	19	(DO THE) SPANISH HUSTLE Fatback Band (Polydor)
-	20	PEOPLE LIKE YOU, PEOPLE LIKE ME Glitter Band (Bell)
26	21	MISS YOU NIGHTS Cliff Richard (EMI)
16	22	LOW RIDER War (Island)
22	23	I LOVE MUSIC O'Jays (Philadelphia Int.)
14	24	WE DO IT R & J Stone (RCA)
-	25	YOU DON'T HAVE TO SAY YOU LOVE ME Guys'n' Dolls (Magnet)
21	26	TUXEDO JUNCTION Manhattan Transfer (Atlantic)
-	27	I WANNA STAY WITH YOU Gallagher & Lyle (A&M)
18	28	WALK AWAY FROM LOVE David Ruffin (Tamla Motown)
-	29	WEAK SPOT Evelyn Thomas (20th Century)
-	30	YOUR MAGIC PUT A SPELL ON ME L J Johnson (Philips)

13 March 1976

1	1	I LOVE TO LOVE Tina Charles (CBS)
3	2	CONVOY C.W. McCall (MGM)
2	3	DECEMBER, 1963 (OH, WHAT A NIGHT) Four Seasons (Warner Bros)
14	4	LOVE REALLY HURTS WITHOUT YOU Billy Ocean (GTO)
4	5	RODRIGO'S GUITAR CONCERTO DE ARANJUEZ Manuel & the Music Of The Mountains (EMI)
5	6	IT SHOULD HAVE BEEN ME Yvonne Fair (Tamla Motown)
6	7	RAIN Status Quo (Vertigo)
9	8	DAT Pluto Shervington (Opal)
10	9	FUNKY WEEKEND Stylistics (Avco)
25	10	YOU DON'T HAVE TO SAY YOU LOVE ME Guys 'n' Dolls (Magnet)
8	11	SQUEEZE BOX Who (Polydor)
20	12	PEOPLE LIKE YOU, PEOPLE LIKE ME Glitter Band (Bell)
23	13	I LOVE MUSIC O'Jays (Philadelphia Int)
19	14	(DO THE) SPANISH HUSTLE Fatback Band (Polydor)
21	15	MISS YOU NIGHTS Cliff Richard (EMI)
11	16	LET'S CALL IT QUITS Slade (Polydor)
7	17	FOREVER AND EVER Slik (Bell)
13	18	SOMETHING'S BEEN MAKING ME BLUE Smokie (RAK)
-	19	FALLING APART AT THE SEAMS Marmalade (Target)
-	20	LET'S DO THE LATIN HUSTLE M & O Band (Creole)
-	21	SAVE YOUR KISSES FOR ME Brotherhood Of Man (Pye)
12	22	NO REGRETS Walker Brothers (GTO)
-	23	LET'S DO THE LATIN HUSTLE Eddie Drennon & B.B.S. Unlimited (Pye)
15	24	LOVE TO LOVE YOU BABY Donna Summer (GTO)
-	25	YOU SEE THE TROUBLE WITH ME Barry White (20th Century)
-	26	CONCRETE AND CLAY Randy Edelman (20th Century)
-	27	WAKE UP EVERYBODY Harold Melvin & the Blue Notes (Philadelphia Intl)
16	28	LOVE MACHINE Miracles (Tamla Motown)
29	29	MAMMA MIA Abba (Epic)
18	30	MOONLIGHT SERENADE/LITTLE BROWN JUG/IN THE MOOD Glenn Miller (RCA)

20 March 1976

1	1	I LOVE TO LOVE Tina Charles (CBS)
4	2	LOVE REALLY HURTS WITHOUT YOU Billy Ocean (GTO)
2	3	CONVOY C W McCall (MGM)
21	4	SAVE YOUR KISSES FOR ME Brotherhood Of Man (Pye)
12	5	PEOPLE LIKE YOU, PEOPLE LIKE ME Glitter Band (Bell)
3	6	DECEMBER '63 (OH WHAT A NIGHT) Four Seasons (Warner Bros)
-	7	I WANNA STAY WITH YOU Gallagher & Lyle (A&M)
7	8	RAIN Status Quo (Vertigo)
6	9	IT SHOULD HAVE BEEN ME Yvonne Fair (Tamla Motown)
14	10	(DO THE) SPANISH HUSTLE Fatback Band (Polydor)
25	11	YOU SEE THE TROUBLE WITH ME Barry White (20th Century)
10	12	YOU DON'T HAVE TO SAY YOU LOVE ME Guys & Dolls (Magnet)
5	13	RODRIGO'S GUITAR CONCERTO DE ARANJUEZ Manuel & the Music Of The Mountains (EMI)
19	14	FALLING APART AT THE SEAMS Marmalade (Target)
9	15	FUNKY WEEKEND Stylistics (Avco)
15	16	MISS YOU NIGHTS Cliff Richard (EMI)
23	17	LET'S DO THE LATIN HUSTLE Eddie Drennan & BBS Unlimited (Pye)
26	18	CONCRETE AND CLAY Randy Edelman (20th Century)
11	19	SQUEEZE BOX Who (Polydor)
13	20	I LOVE MUSIC O'Jays (Philadelphia Int.)
-	21	YESTERDAY Beatles (Apple)
20	22	LET'S DO THE LATIN HUSTLE M & O Band (Creole)
27	23	WAKE UP EVERYBODY Harold Melvin & the Blue Notes (Philadelpia)
-	24	TAKE IT TO THE LIMIT Eagles (Asylum)
8	25	DAT Pluto Shervington (Opal)
18	26	SOMETHING'S MAKING ME BLUE Smokie (RAK)
-	27	SHIPS IN THE NIGHT Be-Bop Deluxe (Harvest)
-	28	HERE THERE AND EVERYWHERE Emmylou Harris (Reprise)
-	29	HEY MR MUSIC MAN Peters & Lee (Philips)
-	30	CITY LIGHTS David Essex (CBS)

The Four Seasons' *December '63* built upon the success of its predecessor *Who Loves You*, to give the group not only their biggest world-wide seller, but also their first UK chart-topper. The single was the first on which Frankie Valli took a vocal back seat, for once, to one of the newer Seasons, Gerry Polci. It was produced and co-written by Bob Gaudio, one of the original members of the group. C.W. McCall's *Convoy* was a celebration of the US truck-driving CB fraternity.

March – April 1976

27 March 1976

LW	TW	Title	Artist
4	1	SAVE YOUR KISSES FOR ME	Brotherhood Of Man (Pye)
1	2	I LOVE TO LOVE	Tina Charles (CBS)
2	3	LOVE REALLY HURTS WITHOUT YOU	Billy Ocean (GTO)
11	4	YOU SEE THE TROUBLE WITH ME	Barry White (20th Century)
7	5	I WANNA STAY WITH YOU	Gallagher & Lyle (A&M)
3	6	CONVOY	C W McCall (MGM)
5	7	PEOPLE LIKE YOU, PEOPLE LIKE ME	Glitter Band (Bell)
12	8	YOU DON'T HAVE TO SAY YOU LOVE ME	Guys & Dolls (Magnet)
14	9	FALLING APART AT THE SEAMS	Marmalade (Target)
21	10	YESTERDAY	Beatles (Apple)
6	11	DECEMBER '63 (OH WHAT A NIGHT)	Four Seasons (Warner Bros)
-	12	MUSIC	John Miles (Decca)
10	13	(DO THE) SPANISH HUSTLE	Fatback Band (Polydor)
18	14	CONCRETE AND CLAY	Randy Edelman (20th Century)
-	15	I'M MANDY FLY ME	10 c.c. (Mercury)
9	16	IT SHOULD HAVE BEEN ME	Yvonne Fair (Tamla Motown)
15	17	FUNKY WEEKEND	Stylistics (Avco)
-	18	HELLO HAPPINESS	Drifters (Bell)
13	19	RODRIGO'S GUITAR CONCERTO DE ARANJUEZ	Manuel & the Music Of The Mountains (EMI)
-	20	PINBALL WIZARD	Elton John (DJM)
8	21	RAIN	Status Quo (Vertigo)
29	22	HEY MR MUSIC MAN	Peters & Lee (Philips)
16	23	MISS YOU NIGHTS	Cliff Richard (EMI)
24	24	TAKE IT TO THE LIMIT	Eagles (Asylum)
23	25	WAKE UP EVERYBODY	Harold Melvin & the Blue Notes (Philadelpia)
19	26	SQUEEZE BOX	Who (Polydor)
20	27	I LOVE MUSIC	O'Jays (Philadelphia Int.)
-	28	JUNGLE ROCK	Hank Mizell (Charly)
27	29	SHIPS IN THE NIGHT	Be-Bop Deluxe (Harvest)
-	30	DON'T STOP IT NOW	Hot Chocolate (RAK)

3 April 1976

LW	TW	Title	Artist
1	1	SAVE YOUR KISSES FOR ME	Brotherhood Of Man (Pye)
4	2	YOU SEE THE TROUBLE WITH ME	Barry White (20th Century)
3	3	LOVE REALLY HURTS WITHOUT YOU	Billy Ocean (GTO)
12	4	MUSIC	John Miles (Decca)
10	5	YESTERDAY	Beatles (Apple)
2	6	I LOVE TO LOVE	Tina Charles (CBS)
5	7	I WANNA STAY WITH YOU	Gallagher & Lyle (A&M)
8	8	PEOPLE LIKE YOU, PEOPLE LIKE ME	Glitter Band (Bell)
9	9	FALLING APART AT THE SEAMS	Marmalade (Target)
8	10	YOU DON'T HAVE TO SAY YOU LOVE ME	Guys & Dolls (Magnet)
24	11	TAKE IT TO THE LIMIT	Eagles (Asylum)
14	12	CONCRETE AND CLAY	Randy Edelman (20th Century)
15	13	I'M MANDY FLY ME	10 c.c. (Mercury)
20	14	PINBALL WIZARD	Elton John (DJM)
6	15	CONVOY	C W McCall (MGM)
18	16	HELLO HAPPINESS	Drifters (Bell)
-	17	GIRLS GIRLS GIRLS	Sailor (Epic)
28	18	JUNGLE ROCK	Hank Mizell (Charly)
30	19	DON'T STOP IT NOW	Hot Chocolate (RAK)
-	20	CITY LIGHTS	David Essex (CBS)
11	21	DECEMBER '63	Four Seasons (Warner Bros)
23	22	MISS YOU NIGHTS	Cliff Richard (EMI)
-	23	FERNANDO	Abba (Epic)
13	24	(DO THE) SPANISH HUSTLE	Fatback Band (Polydor)
29	25	SHIPS IN THE NIGHT	Be-Bop Deluxe (Harvest)
22	26	HEY MR MUSIC MAN	Peters & Lee (Philips)
-	27	PAPERBACK WRITER	Beatles (Apple)
-	28	LET'S DO THE LATIN HUSTLE	M & O Band (Creole)
-	29	SPANISH WINE	Chris White (Charisma)
-	30	DO YOU KNOW WHERE YOU'RE GOING TO	Diana Ross (Tamla Motown)

10 April 1976

LW	TW	Title	Artist
1	1	SAVE YOUR KISSES FOR ME	Brotherhood Of Man (Pye)
4	2	MUSIC	John Miles (Decca)
2	3	YOU SEE THE TROUBLE WITH ME	Barry White (20th Century)
14	4	PINBALL WIZARD	Elton John (DJM)
23	5	FERNANDO	Abba (Epic)
3	6	LOVE REALLY HURTS WITHOUT YOU	Billy Ocean (GTO)
5	7	YESTERDAY	Beatles (Apple)
13	8	I'M MANDY FLY ME	10 c.c. (Mercury)
7	9	I WANNA STAY WITH YOU	Gallagher & Lyle (A&M)
9	10	FALLING APART AT THE SEAMS	Marmalade (Target)
17	11	GIRLS GIRLS GIRLS	Sailor (Epic)
6	12	I LOVE TO LOVE	Tina Charles (CBS)
18	13	JUNGLE ROCK	Hank Mizell (Charly)
8	14	PEOPLE LIKE YOU, PEOPLE LIKE ME	Glitter Band (Bell)
30	15	DO YOU KNOW WHERE YOU'RE GOING TO	Diana Ross (Tamla Motown)
-	16	HEY JUDE	Beatles (Apple)
16	17	HELLO HAPPINESS	Drifters (Bell)
11	18	TAKE IT TO THE LIMIT	Eagles (Asylum)
12	19	CONCRETE AND CLAY	Randy Edelman (20th Century)
19	20	DON'T STOP IT NOW	Hot Chocolate (RAK)
10	21	YOU DON'T HAVE TO SAY YOU LOVE ME	Guys & Dolls (Magnet)
26	22	HEY MR MUSIC MAN	Peters & Lee (Philips)
27	23	PAPERBACK WRITER	Beatles (Apple)
-	24	DISCO CONNECTION	Isaac Hayes Movement (ABC)
25	25	THERE'S A KIND OF HUSH (ALL OVER THE WORLD)	Carpenters (A&M)
-	26	LOVE ME LIKE I LOVE YOU	Bay City Rollers (Bell)
15	27	CONVOY	C W McCall (MGM)
-	28	MOVIN'	Brass Construction (United Artists)
-	29	GET UP AND BOOGIE	Silver Convention (Magnet)
20	30	CITY LIGHTS	David Essex (CBS)

17 April 1976

LW	TW	Title	Artist
1	1	SAVE YOUR KISSES FOR ME	Brotherhood Of Man (Pye)
5	2	FERNANDO	Abba (Epic)
2	3	MUSIC	John Miles (Decca)
3	4	YOU SEE THE TROUBLE WITH ME	Barry White (20th Century)
13	5	JUNGLE ROCK	Hank Mizell (Charly)
8	6	I'M MANDY FLY ME	10 c.c. (Mercury)
4	7	PINBALL WIZARD	Elton John (DJM)
11	8	GIRLS GIRLS GIRLS	Sailor (Epic)
15	9	DO YOU KNOW WHERE YOU'RE GOING TO	Diana Ross (Tamla Motown)
7	10	YESTERDAY	Beatles (Apple)
6	11	LOVE REALLY HURTS WITHOUT YOU	Billy Ocean (GTO)
26	12	LOVE ME LIKE I LOVE YOU	Bay City Rollers (Bell)
16	13	HEY JUDE	Beatles (Apple)
10	14	FALLING APART AT THE SEAMS	Marmalade (Target)
17	15	HELLO HAPPINESS	Drifters (Bell)
20	16	DON'T STOP IT NOW	Hot Chocolate (RAK)
24	17	DISCO CONNECTION	Isaac Hayes Movement (ABC)
23	18	PAPERBACK WRITER	Beatles (Apple)
9	19	I WANNA STAY WITH YOU	Gallagher & Lyle (A&M)
29	20	GET UP AND BOOGIE	Silver Convention (Magnet)
14	21	PEOPLE LIKE YOU, PEOPLE LIKE ME	Glitter Band (Bell)
25	22	THERE'S A KIND OF HUSH (ALL OVER THE WORLD)	Carpenters (A&M)
28	23	MOVIN'	Brass Construction (United Artists)
18	24	TAKE IT TO THE LIMIT	Eagles (Asylum)
19	25	CONCRETE AND CLAY	Randy Edelman (20th Century)
-	26	S-S-S-SINGLE BED	Fox (GTO)
-	27	ALL BY MYSELF	Eric Carmen (Arista)
-	28	HONKY TONK TRAIN BLUES	Keith Emerson (Manticore)
12	29	I LOVE TO LOVE	Tina Charles (CBS)
-	30	GET BACK	Beatles (Apple)

Britain actually won the 1976 Eurovision Song Contest, thanks to the all-age appeal (it was about a small child, and thus guaranteed to charm the over-50s) of *Save Your Kisses For Me*. Brotherhood Of Man, who sang the song at Eurovision and sold 1,001,400 copies of it during a five-week Number One run, had completely changed in personnel since the group which had charted with *United We Stand* in 1970, but was still drawn from the ranks of the UK's session singing elite.

24 April 1976

last week	this week	entry
1	1	SAVE YOUR KISSES FOR ME — Brotherhood Of Man (Pye)
2	2	FERNANDO — Abba (Epic)
5	3	JUNGLE ROCK — Hank Mizell (Charly)
3	4	MUSIC — John Miles (Decca)
9	5	DO YOU KNOW WHERE YOU'RE GOING TO — Diana Ross (Tamla Motown)
4	6	YOU SEE THE TROUBLE WITH ME — Barry White (20th Century)
6	7	I'M MANDY FLY ME — 10 c.c. (Mercury)
8	8	GIRLS GIRLS GIRLS — Sailor (Epic)
12	9	LOVE ME LIKE I LOVE YOU — Bay City Rollers (Bell)
26	10	S-S-S-SINGLE BED — Fox (GTO)
7	11	PINBALL WIZARD — Elton John (DJM)
17	12	DISCO CONNECTION — Isaac Hayes Movement (ABC)
13	13	HEY JUDE — Beatles (Apple)
20	14	GET UP AND BOOGIE — Silver Convention (Magnet)
10	15	YESTERDAY — Beatles (Apple)
16	16	DON'T STOP IT NOW — Hot Chocolate (RAK)
23	17	MOVIN' — Brass Construction (United Artists)
-	18	LIFE IS TOO SHORT GIRL — Sheer Elegance (Pye)
15	19	HELLO HAPPINESS — Drifters (Bell)
14	20	FALLING APART AT THE SEAMS — Marmalade (Target)
19	21	I WANNA STAY WITH YOU — Gallagher & Lyle (A&M)
28	22	HONKY TONK TRAIN BLUES — Keith Emerson (Manticore)
11	23	LOVE REALLY HURTS WITHOUT YOU — Billy Ocean (GTO)
27	24	ALL BY MYSELF — Eric Carmen (Arista)
-	25	FALLEN ANGEL — Frankie Valli (Private Stock)
22	26	THERE'S A KIND OF HUSH (ALL OVER THE WORLD) — Carpenters (A&M)
30	27	GET BACK — Beatles (Apple)
-	28	ARMS OF MARY — Sutherland Brothers & Quiver (CBS)
-	29	BABY I'M YOURS — Linda Lewis (Arista)
25	30	CONCRETE AND CLAY — Randy Edelman (20th Century)

1 May 1976

last week	this week	entry
2	1	FERNANDO — Abba (Epic)
1	2	SAVE YOUR KISSES FOR ME — Brotherhood Of Man (Pye)
3	3	JUNGLE ROCK — Hank Mizell (Charly)
5	4	DO YOU KNOW WHERE YOU'RE GOING TO — Diana Ross (Tamla Motown)
10	5	S-S-S-SINGLE BED — Fox (GTO)
4	6	MUSIC — John Miles (Decca)
8	7	GIRLS GIRLS GIRLS — Sailor (Epic)
9	8	LOVE ME LIKE I LOVE YOU — Bay City Rollers (Bell)
7	9	I'M MANDY FLY ME — 10 c.c. (Mercury)
14	10	GET UP AND BOOGIE — Silver Convention (Magnet)
12	11	DISCO CONNECTION — Isaac Hayes Movement (ABC)
6	12	YOU SEE THE TROUBLE WITH ME — Barry White (20th Century)
18	13	LIFE IS TOO SHORT GIRL — Sheer Elegance (Pye)
-	14	SILVER STAR — Four Seasons (Warner Bros)
13	15	HEY JUDE — Beatles (Apple)
-	16	CONVOY GB — Laurie Lingo & the Dipsticks (State)
16	17	DON'T STOP IT NOW — Hot Chocolate (RAK)
25	18	FALLEN ANGEL — Frankie Valli (Private Stock)
24	19	ALL BY MYSELF — Eric Carmen (Arista)
11	20	PINBALL WIZARD — Elton John (DJM)
22	21	HONKY TONK TRAIN BLUES — Keith Emerson (Manticore)
-	22	CAN'T HELP FALLING IN LOVE — Stylistics (Avco)
19	23	HELLO HAPPINESS — Drifters (Bell)
-	24	LET YOUR LOVE FLOW — Bellamy Brothers (Warner Bros)
17	25	MOVIN' — Brass Construction (United Artists)
-	26	YOU SEXY SUGAR PLUM — Rodger Collins (Fantasy)
28	27	ARMS OF MARY — Sutherland Brothers & Quiver (CBS)
-	28	LOVE HANGOVER — Diana Ross (Tamla Motown)
29	29	BABY I'M YOURS — Linda Lewis (Arista)
-	30	MORE MORE MORE — Andrea True Connection (Buddah)

8 May 1976

last week	this week	entry
1	1	FERNANDO — Abba (Epic)
2	2	SAVE YOUR KISSES FOR ME — Brotherhood Of Man (Pye)
3	3	JUNGLE ROCK — Hank Mizell (Charly)
5	4	S-S-S-SINGLE BED — Fox (GTO)
10	5	GET UP AND BOOGIE — Silver Convention (Magnet)
14	6	SILVER STAR — Four Seasons (Warner Bros)
8	7	LOVE ME LIKE I LOVE YOU — Bay City Rollers (Bell)
11	8	DISCO CONNECTION — Isaac Hayes Movement (ABC)
19	9	ALL BY MYSELF — Eric Carmen (Arista)
16	10	CONVOY GB — Laurie Lingo & the Dipsticks (State)
7	11	GIRLS GIRLS GIRLS — Sailor (Epic)
4	12	DO YOU KNOW WHERE YOU'RE GOING TO — Diana Ross (Tamla Motown)
13	13	LIFE IS TOO SHORT GIRL — Sheer Elegance (Pye)
30	14	MORE MORE MORE — Andrea True Connection (Buddah)
22	15	CAN'T HELP FALLING IN LOVE — Stylistics (Avco)
27	16	ARMS OF MARY — Sutherland Brothers & Quiver (CBS)
9	17	I'M MANDY FLY ME — 10 c.c. (Mercury)
28	18	LOVE HANGOVER — Diana Ross (Tamla Motown)
18	19	FALLEN ANGEL — Frankie Valli (Private Stock)
-	20	FOOL TO CRY — Rolling Stones (Rolling Stones)
-	21	I'LL GO WHERE YOUR MUSIC TAKES ME — Jimmy James & the Vagabonds (Pye)
6	22	MUSIC — John Miles (Decca)
-	23	REGGAE LIKE IT USED TO BE — Paul Nicholas (RSO)
-	24	YOU'RE THE REASON WHY — Rubettes (State)
-	25	MOVIESTAR — Harpo (DJM)
24	26	LET YOUR LOVE FLOW — Bellamy Brothers (Warner Bros)
-	27	DEVIL WOMAN — Cliff Richard (EMI)
17	28	DON'T STOP IT NOW — Hot Chocolate (RAK)
-	29	I'M YOUR PUPPET — James & Bobby Purify (Mercury)
-	30	DISCO LADY — Johnny Taylor (CBS)

15 May 1976

last week	this week	entry
1	1	FERNANDO — Abba (Epic)
4	2	S-S-S-SINGLE BED — Fox (GTO)
2	3	SAVE YOUR KISSES FOR ME — Brotherhood Of Man (Pye)
6	4	SILVER STAR — Four Seasons (Warner Bros)
3	5	JUNGLE ROCK — Hank Mizell (Charly)
5	6	GET UP AND BOOGIE — Silver Convention (Magnet)
10	7	CONVOY GB — Laurie Lingo & the Dipsticks (State)
15	8	CAN'T HELP FALLING IN LOVE — Stylistics (Avco)
20	9	FOOL TO CRY — Rolling Stones (Rolling Stones)
13	10	LIFE IS TOO SHORT GIRL — Sheer Elegance (Pye)
9	11	ALL BY MYSELF — Eric Carmen (Arista)
16	12	ARMS OF MARY — Sutherland Brothers & Quiver (CBS)
19	13	FALLEN ANGEL — Frankie Valli (Private Stock)
12	14	DO YOU KNOW WHERE YOU'RE GOING TO — Diana Ross (Tamla Motown)
26	15	LET YOUR LOVE FLOW — Bellamy Brothers (Warner Bros)
18	16	LOVE HANGOVER — Diana Ross (Tamla Motown)
-	17	NO CHARGE — J J Barrie (Power Exchange)
8	18	DISCO CONNECTION — Isaac Hayes Movement (ABC)
14	19	MORE MORE MORE — Andrea True Connection (Buddah)
29	20	I'M YOUR PUPPET — James & Bobby Purify (Mercury)
21	21	MY RESISTANCE IS LOW — Robin Sarstedt (Decca)
25	22	MOVIESTAR — Harpo (DJM)
27	23	DEVIL WOMAN — Cliff Richard (EMI)
22	24	MUSIC — John Miles (Decca)
30	25	DISCO LADY — Johnny Taylor (CBS)
11	26	GIRLS GIRLS GIRLS — Sailor (Epic)
17	27	I'M MANDY FLY ME — 10 c.c. (Mercury)
23	28	REGGAE LIKE IT USED TO BE — Paul Nicholas (RSO)
7	29	LOVE ME LIKE I LOVE YOU — Bay City Rollers (Bell)
-	30	SHAKE IT DOWN — Mud (Private Stock)

The Stylistics became the third act in 15 years to put *Can't Help Falling In Love* into the Top 10 - their recording of the song (originally penned for Elvis' *Blue Hawaii* movie) may have had something to do with the fact that its writers, Hugo Peretti, Luigi Creatore and George David Weiss, were now the Stylistics' producers! Hank Mizell's *Jungle Rock* was a chance rediscovery of an obscure mid-1950s rockabilly track, and its UK and European success brought Mizell out of retirement to record again.

May – June 1976

22 May 1976

last week	this week	entry
1	1	FERNANDO Abba (Epic)
3	2	SAVE YOUR KISSES FOR ME Brotherhood Of Man (Pye)
2	3	S-S-S-SINGLE BED Fox (GTO)
5	4	JUNGLE ROCK Hank Mizell (Charly)
9	5	FOOL TO CRY Rolling Stones (Rolling Stones)
12	6	ARMS OF MARY Sutherland Brothers & Quiver (CBS)
17	7	NO CHARGE J J Barrie (Power Exchange)
6	8	GET UP AND BOOGIE Silver Convention (Magnet)
19	9	MORE MORE MORE Andrea True Connection (Buddah)
8	10	CAN'T HELP FALLING IN LOVE Stylistics (Avco)
21	11	MY RESISTANCE IS LOW Robin Sarstedt (Decca)
4	12	SILVER STAR Four Seasons (Warner Bros)
15	13	LET YOUR LOVE FLOW Bellamy Brothers (Warner Bros)
16	14	LOVE SONGS Diana Ross (Tamla Motown)
-	15	SILLY LOVE SONGS Wings (Parlophone)
13	16	FALLEN ANGEL Frankie Valli (Private Stock)
20	17	I'M YOUR PUPPET James & Bobby Purify (Mercury)
23	18	DEVIL WOMAN Cliff Richard (EMI)
10	19	LIFE IS TOO SHORT GIRL Sheer Elegance (Pye)
7	20	CONVOY GB Laurie Lingo & the Dipsticks (State)
28	21	REGGAE LIKE IT USED TO BE Paul Nicholas (RSO)
-	22	COMBINE HARVESTER (BRAND NEW KEY) Wurzels (EMI)
30	23	SHAKE IT DOWN Mud (Private Stock)
11	24	ALL BY MYSELF Eric Carmen (Arista)
-	25	I'LL GO WHERE YOUR MUSIC TAKES ME Jimmy James & the Vagabonds (Pye)
18	26	DISCO CONNECTION Isaac Hayes Movement (ABC)
-	27	REQUIEM Slik (Bell)
-	28	MIDNIGHT TRAIN TO GEORGIA Gladys Knight & the Pips (Buddah)
-	29	LOVE ME LIKE A LOVER Tina Charles (CBS)
14	30	DO YOU KNOW WHERE YOU'RE GOING TO Diana Ross (Tamla Motown)

29 May 1976

last week	this week	entry
1	1	FERNANDO Abba (Epic)
7	2	NO CHARGE J J Barrie (Power Exchange)
11	3	MY RESISTANCE IS LOW Robin Sarstedt (Decca)
5	4	FOOL TO CRY Rolling Stones (Rolling Stones)
12	5	SILVER STAR Four Seasons (Warner Bros)
22	6	COMBINE HARVESTER (BRAND NEW KEY) Wurzels (EMI)
6	7	ARMS OF MARY Sutherland Brothers & Quiver (CBS)
15	8	SILLY LOVE SONGS Wings (Parlophone)
10	9	CAN'T HELP FALLING IN LOVE Stylistics (Avco)
9	10	MORE MORE MORE Andrea True Connection (Buddah)
18	11	DEVIL WOMAN Cliff Richard (EMI)
2	12	SAVE YOUR KISSES FOR ME Brotherhood Of Man (Pye)
4	13	JUNGLE ROCK Hank Mizell (Charly)
13	14	LET YOUR LOVE FLOW Bellamy Brothers (Warner Bros)
14	15	LOVE HANGOVER Diana Ross (Tamla Motown)
3	16	S-S-S-SINGLE BED Fox (GTO)
23	17	SHAKE IT DOWN Mud (Private Stock)
-	18	THIS IS IT Melba Moore (Buddah)
-	19	SHOW ME THE WAY Peter Frampton (A&M)
8	20	GET UP AND BOOGIE Silver Convention (Magnet)
17	21	I'M YOUR PUPPET James & Bobby Purify (Mercury)
28	22	MIDNIGHT TRAIN TO GEORGIA Gladys Knight & the Pips (Buddah)
-	23	TVC 15 David Bowie (RCA)
-	24	HEART ON MY SLEEVE Gallagher & Lyle (A&M)
20	25	CONVOY GB Laurie Lingo & the Dipsticks (State)
-	26	JOLENE Dolly Parton (RCA)
16	27	FALLEN ANGEL Frankie Valli (Private Stock)
-	28	LET'S MAKE A BABY Billy Paul (Philadelphia)
19	29	LIFE IS TOO SHORT GIRL Sheer Elegance (Pye)
-	30	SOUL CITY WALK Archie Bell & the Drells (Philadelphia)

5 June 1976

last week	this week	entry
1	1	FERNANDO Abba (Epic)
6	2	COMBINE HARVESTER (BRAND NEW KEY) Wurzels (EMI)
3	3	MY RESISTANCE IS LOW Robin Sarstedt (Decca)
2	4	NO CHARGE J J Barrie (Power Exchange)
8	5	SILLY LOVE SONGS Wings (Parlophone)
4	6	FOOL TO CRY Rolling Stones (Rolling Stones)
11	7	DEVIL WOMAN Cliff Richard (EMI)
14	8	LET YOUR LOVE FLOW Bellamy Brothers (Warner Bros)
7	9	ARMS OF MARY Sutherland Brothers & Quiver (CBS)
10	10	MORE MORE MORE Andrea True Connection (Buddah)
15	11	LOVE HANGOVER Diana Ross (Tamla Motown)
19	12	SHOW ME THE WAY Peter Frampton (A&M)
22	13	MIDNIGHT TRAIN TO GEORGIA Gladys Knight & the Pips (Buddah)
24	14	HEART ON MY SLEEVE Gallagher & Lyle (A&M)
21	15	I'M YOUR PUPPET James & Bobby Purify (Mercury)
5	16	SILVER STAR Four Seasons (Warner Bros)
17	17	SHAKE IT DOWN Mud (Private Stock)
9	18	CAN'T HELP FALLING IN LOVE Stylistics (Avco)
18	19	THIS IS IT Melba Moore (Buddah)
13	20	JUNGLE ROCK Hank Mizell (Charly)
26	21	JOLENE Dolly Parton (RCA)
12	22	SAVE YOUR KISSES FOR ME Brotherhood Of Man (Pye)
16	23	S-S-S-SINGLE BED Fox (GTO)
23	24	TVC 15 David Bowie (RCA)
-	25	REGGAE LIKE IT USED TO BE Paul Nicholas (RSO)
-	26	REQUIEM Slik (Bell)
30	27	SOUL CITY WALK Archie Bell & the Drells (Philadelphia)
28	28	LET'S MAKE A BABY Billy Paul (Philadelphia)
-	29	YOU TO ME ARE EVERYTHING The Real Thing (Pye Int)
-	30	I'LL GO WHERE YOUR MUSIC TAKES ME Jimmy James & the Vagabonds (Pye)

12 June 1976

last week	this week	entry
4	1	NO CHARGE J J Barrie (Power Exchange)
5	2	SILLY LOVE SONGS Wings (Parlophone)
3	3	MY RESISTANCE IS LOW Robin Sarstedt (Decca)
1	4	FERNANDO Abba (Epic)
2	5	COMBINE HARVESTER (BRAND NEW KEY) Wurzels (EMI)
8	6	LET YOUR LOVE FLOW Bellamy Brothers (Warner Bros)
29	7	YOU TO ME ARE EVERYTHING The Real Thing (Pye Int)
6	8	FOOL TO CRY Rolling Stones (Rolling Stones)
12	9	SHOW ME THE WAY Peter Frampton (A&M)
7	10	DEVIL WOMAN Cliff Richard (EMI)
11	11	LOVE HANGOVER Diana Ross (Tamla Motown)
14	12	HEART ON MY SLEEVE Gallagher & Lyle (A&M)
21	13	JOLENE Dolly Parton (RCA)
13	14	MIDNIGHT TRAIN TO GEORGIA Gladys Knight & the Pips (Buddah)
9	15	ARMS OF MARY Sutherland Brothers & Quiver (CBS)
-	16	TONIGHT'S THE NIGHT Rod Stewart (Riva)
17	17	SHAKE IT DOWN Mud (Private Stock)
-	18	YOU JUST MIGHT SEE ME CRY Our Kid (Polydor)
10	19	MORE MORE MORE Andrea True Connection (Buddah)
15	20	I'M YOUR PUPPET James & Bobby Purify (Mercury)
27	21	SOUL CITY WALK Archie Bell & the Drells (Philadelphia)
28	22	LET'S MAKE A BABY Billy Paul (Philadelphia)
-	23	YOU'RE MY EVERYTHING Lee Garrett (Chrysalis)
-	24	YOUNG HEARTS RUN FREE Candi Staton (Warner Bros)
19	25	THIS IS IT Melba Moore (Buddah)
-	26	THE FLASHER Mistura with Lloyd Michels (Route)
-	27	THE BOYS ARE BACK IN TOWN Thin Lizzy (Vertigo)
18	28	CAN'T HELP FALLING IN LOVE Stylistics (Avco)
-	29	THE CONTINENTAL Maureen McGovern (20th Century)
25	30	REGGAE LIKE IT USED TO BE Paul Nicholas (RSO)

Robin Sarstedt (actual name Clive) became the third brother in his family to, over a 15-year period (Eden Kane topped the chart in 1961, and Peter Sarstedt in 1968), have a Top Three hit. He was the first of them to do so with a revived oldie, the standard *My Resistance Is Low*. The Wurzels' *Combine Harvester* added Somerset yokel lyrics to Melanie's *Brand New Key*, while *Devil Woman*, the second hit single from Cliff Richard's *I'm Nearly Famous* album, was also his first-ever US million-seller.

19 June 1976

last	this		
2	1	SILLY LOVE SONGS	Wings (Parlophone)
5	2	COMBINE HARVESTER (BRAND NEW KEY)	Wurzels (EMI)
7	3	YOU TO ME ARE EVERYTHING	The Real Thing (Pye Int)
16	4	TONIGHT'S THE NIGHT	Rod Stewart (Riva)
13	5	JOLENE	Dolly Parton (RCA)
4	6	FERNANDO	Abba (Epic)
6	7	LET YOUR LOVE FLOW	Bellamy Brothers (Warner Bros)
1	8	NO CHARGE	J J Barrie (Power Exchange)
3	9	MY RESISTANCE IS LOW	Robin Sarstedt (Decca)
25	10	THIS IS IT	Melba Moore (Buddah)
18	11	YOU JUST MIGHT SEE ME CRY	Our Kid (Polydor)
8	12	FOOL TO CRY	Rolling Stones (Rolling Stones)
12	13	HEART ON MY SLEEVE	Gallagher & Lyle (A&M)
-	14	LET'S STICK TOGETHER	Bryan Ferry (Island)
14	15	MIDNIGHT TRAIN TO GEORGIA	Gladys Knight & the Pips (Buddah)
10	16	DEVIL WOMAN	Cliff Richard (EMI)
9	17	SHOW ME THE WAY	Peter Frampton (A&M)
21	18	SOUL CITY WALK	Archie Bell & the Drells (Philadelphia)
15	19	ARMS OF MARY	Sutherland Brothers & Quiver (CBS)
27	20	THE BOYS ARE BACK IN TOWN	Thin Lizzy (Vertigo)
24	21	YOUNG HEARTS RUN FREE	Candi Staton (Warner Bros)
23	22	YOU'RE MY EVERYTHING	Lee Garrett (Chrysalis)
11	23	LOVE HANGOVER	Diana Ross (Tamla Motown)
29	24	THE CONTINENTAL	Maureen McGovern (20th Century)
20	25	I'M YOUR PUPPET	James & Bobby Purify (Mercury)
17	26	SHAKE IT DOWN	Mud (Private Stock)
-	27	THE WANDERER	Dion (Philips)
-	28	LEADER OF THE PACK	Shangri-Las (Charly/Cooltempo)
19	29	MORE MORE MORE	Andrea True Connection (Buddah)
-	30	DANCE THE BODY MUSIC	Osibisa (Bronze)

26 June 1976

last	this		
3	1	YOU TO ME ARE EVERYTHING	The Real Thing (Pye Int)
11	2	YOU JUST MIGHT SEE ME CRY	Our Kid (Polydor)
1	3	SILLY LOVE SONGS	Wings (Parlophone)
2	4	COMBINE HARVESTER (BRAND NEW KEY)	Wurzels (EMI)
4	5	TONIGHT'S THE NIGHT	Rod Stewart (Riva)
13	6	HEART ON MY SLEEVE	Gallagher & Lyle (A&M)
5	7	JOLENE	Dolly Parton (RCA)
14	8	LET'S STICK TOGETHER	Bryan Ferry (Island)
20	9	THE BOYS ARE BACK IN TOWN	Thin Lizzy (Vertigo)
21	10	YOUNG HEARTS RUN FREE	Candi Staton (Warner Bros)
17	11	SHOW ME THE WAY	Peter Frampton (A&M)
8	12	NO CHARGE	J J Barrie (Power Exchange)
10	13	THIS IS IT	Melba Moore (Buddah)
-	14	LET YOUR LOVE FLOW	Bellamy Brothers (Warner Bros)
29	15	LEADER OF THE PACK	Shangri-Las (Charly/Cooltempo)
26	16	SHAKE IT DOWN	Mud (Private Stock)
9	17	MY RESISTANCE IS LOW	Robin Sarstedt (Decca)
12	18	FOOL TO CRY	Rolling Stones (Rolling Stones)
16	19	DEVIL WOMAN	Cliff Richard (EMI)
27	20	THE WANDERER	Dion (Philips)
24	21	THE CONTINENTAL	Maureen McGovern (20th Century)
22	22	YOU'RE MY EVERYTHING	Lee Garrett (Chrysalis)
15	23	MIDNIGHT TRAIN TO GEORGIA	Gladys Knight & the Pips (Buddah)
18	24	SOUL CITY WALK	Archie Bell & the Drells (Philadelphia)
6	25	FERNANDO	Abba (Epic)
-	26	(WHAT A) WONDERFUL WORLD	Johnny Nash (Epic)
-	27	I LOVE TO BOOGIE	T. Rex (EMI)
-	28	KISS AND SAY GOODBYE	Manhattans (CBS)
-	29	MY SWEET ROSALIE	Brotherhood Of Man (Pye)
30	30	DANCE THE BODY MUSIC	Osibisa (Bronze)

3 July 1976

last	this		
1	1	YOU TO ME ARE EVERYTHING	The Real Thing (Pye Int)
10	2	YOUNG HEARTS RUN FREE	Candi Staton (Warner Bros)
2	3	YOU JUST MIGHT SEE ME CRY	Our Kid (Polydor)
8	4	LET'S STICK TOGETHER	Bryan Ferry (Island)
5	5	TONIGHT'S THE NIGHT	Rod Stewart (Riva)
3	6	SILLY LOVE SONGS	Wings (Parlophone)
9	7	THE BOYS ARE BACK IN TOWN	Thin Lizzy (Vertigo)
15	8	LEADER OF THE PACK	Shangri-Las (Charly/Cooltempo)
4	9	COMBINE HARVESTER (BRAND NEW KEY)	Wurzels (EMI)
7	10	JOLENE	Dolly Parton (RCA)
28	11	KISS AND SAY GOODBYE	Manhattans (CBS)
6	12	HEART ON MY SLEEVE	Gallagher & Lyle (A&M)
-	13	THE ROUSSOS PHENOMENON (EP)	Demis Roussos (Philips)
22	14	YOU'RE MY EVERYTHING	Lee Garrett (Chrysalis)
11	15	SHOW ME THE WAY	Peter Frampton (A&M)
20	16	THE WANDERER	Dion (Philips)
27	17	I LOVE TO BOOGIE	T. Rex (EMI)
-	18	THE BOSTON TEA PARTY	Sensational Alex Harvey Band (Mountain)
-	19	A LITTLE BIT MORE	Dr Hook (Capitol)
24	20	SOUL CITY WALK	Archie Bell & the Drells (Philadelphia)
26	21	(WHAT A) WONDERFUL WORLD	Johnny Nash (Epic)
21	22	THE CONTINENTAL	Maureen McGovern (20th Century)
13	23	THIS IS IT	Melba Moore (Buddah)
-	24	MISTY BLUE	Dorothy Moore (Contempo)
14	25	LET YOUR LOVE FLOW	Bellamy Brothers (Warner Bros)
-	26	YOU ARE MY LOVE	Liverpool Express (Warner Bros)
12	27	NO CHARGE	J J Barrie (Power Exchange)
-	28	MAN TO MAN	Hot Chocolate (RAK)
18	29	FOOL TO CRY	Rolling Stones (Rolling Stones)
30	30	YOU'RE MY BEST FRIEND	Queen (EMI)

10 July 1976

last	this		
2	1	YOUNG HEARTS RUN FREE	Candi Staton (Warner Bros)
1	2	YOU TO ME ARE EVERYTHING	The Real Thing (Pye Int)
4	3	LET'S STICK TOGETHER	Bryan Ferry (Island)
3	4	YOU JUST MIGHT SEE ME CRY	Our Kid (Polydor)
5	5	TONIGHT'S THE NIGHT	Rod Stewart (Riva)
13	6	THE ROUSSOS PHENOMENON (EP)	Demis Roussos (Philips)
19	7	A LITTLE BIT MORE	Dr Hook (Capitol)
7	8	THE BOYS ARE BACK IN TOWN	Thin Lizzy (Vertigo)
11	9	KISS AND SAY GOODBYE	Manhattans (CBS)
8	10	LEADER OF THE PACK	Shangri-Las (Charly/Cooltempo)
30	11	YOU'RE MY BEST FRIEND	Queen (EMI)
12	12	HEART ON MY SLEEVE	Gallagher & Lyle (A&M)
24	13	MISTY BLUE	Dorothy Moore (Contempo)
6	14	SILLY LOVE SONGS	Wings (Parlophone)
17	15	I LOVE TO BOOGIE	T. Rex (EMI)
-	16	DON'T GO BREAKING MY HEART	Elton John & Kiki Dee (Rocket)
-	17	IT ONLY TAKES A MINUTE	100 Ton & A Feather (UK)
22	18	THE CONTINENTAL	Maureen McGovern (20th Century)
21	19	(WHAT A) WONDERFUL WORLD	Johnny Nash (Epic)
18	20	THE BOSTON TEA PARTY	Sensational Alex Harvey Band (Mountain)
26	21	YOU ARE MY LOVE	Liverpool Express (Warner Bros)
9	22	COMBINE HARVESTER (BRAND NEW KEY)	Wurzels (EMI)
28	23	MAN TO MAN	Hot Chocolate (RAK)
14	24	YOU'RE MY EVERYTHING	Lee Garrett (Chrysalis)
-	25	I RECALL A GYPSY WOMAN	Don Williams (ABC)
15	26	SHOW ME THE WAY	Peter Frampton (A&M)
-	27	ME AND BABY BROTHER	War (Island)
10	28	JOLENE	Dolly Parton (RCA)
-	29	GOOD VIBRATIONS	Beach Boys (Capitol)
-	30	ONE PIECE AT A TIME	Johnny Cash & the Tennessee Three (CBS)

The selling point of Demis Roussos' *Roussos Phenomenon* EP, even though it never gained an individual chart credit, was the song *Forever And Ever*, which had been released earlier as a single to absolutely no reaction. This became the first-ever bona-fide four-track EP (as opposed to a 3-track maxi-single, like *In The Summertime*) to top the NME singles chart since its inception. Meanwhile, there was a sudden inrush of reissued former hits to the chart, by Dion, the Beach Boys and the Shangri-Las.

July – August 1976

last week	this	17 July 1976
6	1	THE ROUSSOS PHENOMENON (EP) Demis Roussos (Philips)
7	2	A LITTLE BIT MORE Dr Hook (Capitol)
1	3	YOUNG HEARTS RUN FREE Candi Staton (Warner Bros)
16	4	DON'T GO BREAKING MY HEART Elton John & Kiki Dee (Rocket)
2	5	YOU TO ME ARE EVERYTHING The Real Thing (Pye Int)
9	6	KISS AND SAY GOODBYE Manhattans (CBS)
3	7	LET'S STICK TOGETHER Bryan Ferry (Island)
13	8	MISTY BLUE Dorothy Moore (Contempo)
5	9	TONIGHT'S THE NIGHT Rod Stewart (Riva)
4	10	YOU JUST MIGHT SEE ME CRY Our Kid (Polydor)
11	11	YOU'RE MY BEST FRIEND Queen (EMI)
10	12	LEADER OF THE PACK Shangri-Las (Charly)
17	13	IT ONLY TAKES A MINUTE 100 Ton & A Feather (UK)
20	14	THE BOSTON TEA PARTY Sensational Alex Harvey Band (Mountain)
23	15	MAN TO MAN Hot Chocolate (RAK)
14	16	SILLY LOVE SONGS Wings (Parlophone)
8	17	THE BOYS ARE BACK IN TOWN Thin Lizzy (Vertigo)
21	18	YOU ARE MY LOVE Liverpool Express (Warner Bros)
15	19	I LOVE TO BOOGIE T. Rex (EMI)
29	20	GOOD VIBRATIONS Beach Boys (Capitol)
25	21	I RECALL A GYPSY WOMAN Don Williams (ABC)
12	22	HEART ON MY SLEEVE Gallagher & Lyle (A&M)
-	23	HEAVEN MUST BE MISSING AN ANGEL Tavares (Capitol)
-	24	BACK IN THE U.S.S.R. Beatles (Parlophone)
-	25	HARVEST FOR THE WORLD Isley Brothers (Epic)
28	26	JOLENE Dolly Parton (RCA)
-	27	WHO'D SHE COO Ohio Players (Mercury)
-	28	JEANS ON David Dundas (AIR)
-	29	ROCK AND ROLL MUSIC Beach Boys (Reprise)
19	30	(WHAT A) WONDERFUL WORLD Johnny Nash (Epic)

		24 July 1976
4	1	DON'T GO BREAKING MY HEART Elton John & Kiki Dee (Rocket)
1	2	THE ROUSSOS PHENOMENON (EP) Demis Roussos (Philips)
2	3	A LITTLE BIT MORE Dr Hook (Capitol)
6	4	KISS AND SAY GOODBYE Manhattans (CBS)
3	5	YOUNG HEARTS RUN FREE Candi Staton (Warner Bros)
8	6	MISTY BLUE Dorothy Moore (Contempo)
11	7	YOU'RE MY BEST FRIEND Queen (EMI)
7	8	LET'S STICK TOGETHER Bryan Ferry (Island)
5	9	YOU TO ME ARE EVERYTHING The Real Thing (Pye Int)
13	10	IT ONLY TAKES A MINUTE 100 Ton & A Feather (UK)
18	11	YOU ARE MY LOVE Liverpool Express (Warner Bros)
15	12	MAN TO MAN Hot Chocolate (RAK)
12	13	LEADER OF THE PACK Shangri-Las (Charly)
23	14	HEAVEN MUST BE MISSING AN ANGEL Tavares (Capitol)
19	15	I LOVE TO BOOGIE T. Rex (EMI)
9	16	TONIGHT'S THE NIGHT Rod Stewart (Riva)
10	17	YOU JUST MIGHT SEE ME CRY Our Kid (Polydor)
21	18	I RECALL A GYPSY WOMAN Don Williams (ABC)
17	19	THE BOYS ARE BACK IN TOWN Thin Lizzy (Vertigo)
14	20	THE BOSTON TEA PARTY Sensational Alex Harvey Band (Mountain)
-	21	LOVE ON DELIVERY Billy Ocean (GTO)
25	22	HARVEST FOR THE WORLD Isley Brothers (Epic)
-	23	MYSTERY SONG Status Quo (Vertigo)
-	24	NOW IS THE TIME Jimmy James & the Vagabonds (Pye)
30	25	(WHAT A) WONDERFUL WORLD Johnny Nash (Epic)
-	26	ME AND BABY BROTHER War (Island)
27	27	NO CHANCE Billy Connolly (Polydor)
24	28	BACK IN THE U.S.S.R. Beatles (Parlophone)
20	29	GOOD VIBRATIONS Beach Boys (Capitol)
28	30	JEANS ON David Dundas (AIR)

		31 July 1976
1	1	DON'T GO BREAKING MY HEART Elton John & Kiki Dee (Rocket)
3	2	A LITTLE BIT MORE Dr Hook (Capitol)
2	3	THE ROUSSOS PHENOMENON (EP) Demis Roussos (Philips)
6	4	MISTY BLUE Dorothy Moore (Contempo)
4	5	KISS AND SAY GOODBYE Manhattans (CBS)
14	6	HEAVEN MUST BE MISSING AN ANGEL Tavares (Capitol)
5	7	YOUNG HEARTS RUN FREE Candi Staton (Warner Bros)
10	8	IT ONLY TAKES A MINUTE 100 Ton & A Feather (UK)
7	9	YOU'RE MY BEST FRIEND Queen (EMI)
11	10	YOU ARE MY LOVE Liverpool Express (Warner Bros)
30	11	JEANS ON David Dundas (AIR)
24	12	NOW IS THE TIME Jimmy James & the Vagabonds (Pye)
29	13	GOOD VIBRATIONS Beach Boys (Capitol)
12	14	MAN TO MAN Hot Chocolate (RAK)
20	15	THE BOSTON TEA PARTY Sensational Alex Harvey Band (Mountain)
22	16	HARVEST FOR THE WORLD Isley Brothers (Epic)
8	17	LET'S STICK TOGETHER Bryan Ferry (Island)
28	18	BACK IN THE U.S.S.R. Beatles (Parlophone)
9	19	YOU TO ME ARE EVERYTHING The Real Thing (Pye Int)
21	20	LOVE ON DELIVERY Billy Ocean (GTO)
23	21	MYSTERY SONG Status Quo (Vertigo)
13	22	LEADER OF THE PACK Shangri-Las (Charly)
17	23	YOU JUST MIGHT SEE ME CRY Our Kid (Polydor)
-	24	DOCTOR KISS-KISS 5000 Volts (Philips)
27	25	NO CHANCE Billy Connolly (Polydor)
16	26	TONIGHT'S THE NIGHT Rod Stewart (Riva)
26	27	ME AND BABY BROTHER War (Island)
18	28	I RECALL A GYPSY WOMAN Don Williams (ABC)
-	29	A FIFTH OF BEETHOVEN Walter Murphy (Private Stock)
15	30	I LOVE TO BOOGIE T. Rex (EMI)

		7 August 1976
1	1	DON'T GO BREAKING MY HEART Elton John & Kiki Dee (Rocket)
2	2	A LITTLE BIT MORE Dr Hook (Capitol)
6	3	HEAVEN MUST BE MISSING AN ANGEL Tavares (Capitol)
3	4	THE ROUSSOS PHENOMENON (EP) Demis Roussos (Philips)
5	5	KISS AND SAY GOODBYE Manhattans (CBS)
11	6	JEANS ON David Dundas (AIR)
4	7	MISTY BLUE Dorothy Moore (Contempo)
7	8	YOUNG HEARTS RUN FREE Candi Staton (Warner Bros)
12	9	NOW IS THE TIME Jimmy James & the Vagabonds (Pye)
16	10	HARVEST FOR THE WORLD Isley Brothers (Epic)
8	11	IT ONLY TAKES A MINUTE 100 Ton & A Feather (UK)
9	12	YOU'RE MY BEST FRIEND Queen (EMI)
21	13	MYSTERY SONG Status Quo (Vertigo)
24	14	DOCTOR KISS-KISS 5000 Volts (Philips)
10	15	YOU ARE MY LOVE Liverpool Express (Warner Bros)
-	16	IN ZAIRE Johnny Wakelin (Pye)
28	17	I RECALL A GYPSY WOMAN Don Williams (ABC)
14	18	MAN TO MAN Hot Chocolate (RAK)
-	19	YOU SHOULD BE DANCING Bee Gees (RSO)
17	20	LET'S STICK TOGETHER Bryan Ferry (Island)
25	21	NO CHANCE Billy Connolly (Polydor)
20	22	LOVE ON DELIVERY Billy Ocean (GTO)
15	23	THE BOSTON TEA PARTY Sensational Alex Harvey Band (Mountain)
-	24	SHAKE YOUR BOOTY K C & The Sunshine Band (Jayboy)
19	25	YOU TO ME ARE EVERYTHING The Real Thing (Pye Int)
18	26	BACK IN THE U.S.S.R. Beatles (Parlophone)
-	27	HERE COMES THE SUN Steve Harley & Cockney Rebel (EMI)
13	28	GOOD VIBRATIONS Beach Boys (Capitol)
-	29	YOU'LL NEVER FIND ANOTHER LOVE LIKE MINE Lou Rawls (Philadelphia)
-	30	LET 'EM IN Wings (Parlophone)

Though Elton John had had Number One hits in the US by 1976, he had never achieved one in the UK. *Don't Go Breaking My Heart* both relieved and exacerbated this state of affairs: it certainly topped the chart, for over a month, but was a duet between Elton and Kiki Dee, and therefore only a shared Number One. He might have been quite despondent to know that it would take him exactly fourteen more years, and numerous attempts, to finally achieve a solo UK chart topper with *Sacrifice*.

14 August 1976

last week	this week	Title / Artist
1	1	DON'T GO BREAKING MY HEART — Elton John & Kiki Dee (Rocket)
6	2	JEANS ON — David Dundas (AIR)
2	3	A LITTLE BIT MORE — Dr Hook (Capitol)
7	4	MISTY BLUE — Dorothy Moore (Contempo)
16	5	IN ZAIRE — Johnny Wakelin (Pye)
3	6	HEAVEN MUST BE MISSING AN ANGEL — Tavares (Capitol)
9	7	NOW IS THE TIME — Jimmy James & the Vagabonds (Pye)
4	8	THE ROUSSOS PHENOMENON (EP) — Demis Roussos (Philips)
14	9	DOCTOR KISS-KISS — 5000 Volts (Philips)
10	10	HARVEST FOR THE WORLD — Isley Brothers (Epic)
5	11	KISS AND SAY GOODBYE — Manhattans (CBS)
30	12	LET 'EM IN — Wings (Parlophone)
13	13	MYSTERY SONG — Status Quo (Vertigo)
8	14	YOUNG HEARTS RUN FREE — Candi Staton (Warner Bros)
19	15	YOU SHOULD BE DANCING — Bee Gees (RSO)
27	16	HERE COMES THE SUN — Steve Harley & Cockney Rebel (EMI)
24	17	SHAKE YOUR BOOTY — KC & The Sunshine Band (Jayboy)
-	18	WHAT I'VE GOT IN MIND — Billie Joe Spears (United Artists)
-	19	EXTENDED PLAY (EP) — Bryan Ferry (Island)
15	20	YOU ARE MY LOVE — Liverpool Express (Warner Bros)
12	21	YOU'RE MY BEST FRIEND — Queen (EMI)
22	22	LOVE ON DELIVERY — Billy Ocean (GTO)
20	23	LET'S STICK TOGETHER — Bryan Ferry (Island)
11	24	IT ONLY TAKES A MINUTE — 100 Ton & A Feather (UK)
29	25	YOU'LL NEVER FIND ANOTHER LOVE LIKE MINE — Lou Rawls (Philadelphia)
-	26	YOU DON'T HAVE TO GO — Chi-Lites (Brunswick)
23	27	THE BOSTON TEA PARTY — Sensational Alex Harvey Band (Mountain)
14	28	MAN TO MAN — Hot Chocolate (RAK)
-	29	16 BARS — Stylistics (H&L)
17	30	I RECALL A GYPSY WOMAN — Don Williams (ABC)

21 August 1976

last week	this week	Title / Artist
1	1	DON'T GO BREAKING MY HEART — Elton John & Kiki Dee (Rocket)
3	2	A LITTLE BIT MORE — Dr Hook (Capitol)
2	3	JEANS ON — David Dundas (AIR)
5	4	IN ZAIRE — Johnny Wakelin (Pye)
7	5	NOW IS THE TIME — Jimmy James & the Vagabonds (Pye)
6	6	HEAVEN MUST BE MISSING AN ANGEL — Tavares (Capitol)
12	7	LET 'EM IN — Wings (Parlophone)
15	8	YOU SHOULD BE DANCING — Bee Gees (RSO)
9	9	DOCTOR KISS-KISS — 5000 Volts (Philips)
19	10	EXTENDED PLAY (EP) — Bryan Ferry (Island)
13	11	MYSTERY SONG — Status Quo (Vertigo)
4	12	MISTY BLUE — Dorothy Moore (Contempo)
16	13	HERE COMES THE SUN — Steve Harley & Cockney Rebel (EMI)
26	14	YOU DON'T HAVE TO GO — Chi-Lites (Brunswick)
8	15	THE ROUSSOS PHENOMENON (EP) — Demis Roussos (Philips)
25	16	YOU'LL NEVER FIND ANOTHER LOVE LIKE MINE — Lou Rawls (Philadelphia)
10	17	HARVEST FOR THE WORLD — Isley Brothers (Epic)
18	18	WHAT I'VE GOT IN MIND — Billie Joe Spears (United Artists)
29	19	16 BARS — Stylistics (H&L)
11	20	KISS AND SAY GOODBYE — Manhattans (CBS)
-	21	MORNING GLORY — James & Bobby Purify (Mercury)
22	22	LOVE ON DELIVERY — Billy Ocean (GTO)
17	23	SHAKE YOUR BOOTY — KC & The Sunshine Band (Jayboy)
-	24	AFTERNOON DELIGHT — Starland Vocal Band (RCA)
14	25	YOUNG HEARTS RUN FREE — Candi Staton (Warner Bros)
-	26	JAILBREAK — Thin Lizzy (Vertigo)
-	27	DANCING QUEEN — Abba (Epic)
-	28	NICE AND SLOW — Jesse Green (EMI)
-	29	THE KILLING OF GEORGIE — Rod Stewart (Riva)
30	30	HERE I GO AGAIN — Twiggy (Mercury)

28 August 1976

last week	this week	Title / Artist
1	1	DON'T GO BREAKING MY HEART — Elton John & Kiki Dee (Rocket)
4	2	IN ZAIRE — Johnny Wakelin (Pye)
7	3	LET 'EM IN — Wings (Parlophone)
2	4	A LITTLE BIT MORE — Dr. Hook (Capitol)
3	5	JEANS ON — David Dundas (AIR)
8	6	YOU SHOULD BE DANCING — Bee Gees (RSO)
5	7	NOW IS THE TIME — Jimmy James & the Vagabonds (Pye)
18	8	WHAT I'VE GOT IN MIND — Billie Jo Spears (United Artists)
9	9	DOCTOR KISS-KISS — 5000 Volts (Philips)
13	10	HERE COMES THE SUN — Steve Harley & Cockney Rebel (EMI)
6	11	HEAVEN MUST BE MISSING AN ANGEL — Tavares (Capitol)
27	12	DANCING QUEEN — Abba (Epic)
10	13	EXTENDED PLAY (EP) — Bryan Ferry (Island)
29	14	THE KILLING OF GEORGIE — Rod Stewart (Riva)
14	15	YOU DON'T HAVE TO GO — Chi-Lites (Brunswick)
11	16	MYSTERY SONG — Status Quo (Vertigo)
16	17	YOU'LL NEVER FIND ANOTHER LOVE LIKE MINE — Lou Rawls (Philadelphia)
19	18	16 BARS — Stylistics (H&L)
12	19	MISTY BLUE — Dorothy Moore (Contempo)
28	20	NICE AND SLOW — Jesse Green (EMI)
-	21	BABY, WE BETTER TRY AND GET IT TOGETHER — Barry White (20th Century)
17	22	HARVEST FOR THE WORLD — Isley Brothers (Epic)
15	23	THE ROUSSOS PHENOMENON (EP) — Demis Roussos (Philips)
24	24	AFTERNOON DELIGHT — Starland Vocal Band (RCA)
25	25	(LIGHT OF EXPERIENCE) DOINA DE JALE — Gheorghe Zamfir (Epic)
21	26	MORNING GLORY — James & Bobby Purify (Mercury)
-	27	I CAN'T ASK FOR ANYTHING MORE THAN YOU BABE — Cliff Richard (EMI)
30	28	HERE I GO AGAIN — Twiggy (Mercury)
22	29	LOVE ON DELIVERY — Billy Ocean (GTO)
-	30	ARIA — Mr Acker Bilk (Pye)

4 September 1976

last week	this week	Title / Artist
1	1	DON'T GO BREAKING MY HEART — Elton John & Kiki Dee (Rocket)
3	2	LET 'EM IN — Wings (Parlophone)
2	3	IN ZAIRE — Johnny Wakelin (Pye)
5	4	JEANS ON — David Dundas (AIR)
6	5	YOU SHOULD BE DANCING — Bee Gees (RSO)
4	6	A LITTLE BIT MORE — Dr. Hook (Capitol)
12	7	DANCING QUEEN — Abba (Epic)
9	8	DOCTOR KISS-KISS — 5000 Volts (Philips)
15	9	YOU DON'T HAVE TO GO — Chi-Lites (Brunswick)
18	10	16 BARS — Stylistics (H&L)
17	11	YOU'LL NEVER FIND ANOTHER LOVE LIKE MINE — Lou Rawls (Philadelphia)
13	12	EXTENDED PLAY (EP) — Bryan Ferry (Island)
11	13	HEAVEN MUST BE MISSING AN ANGEL — Tavares (Capitol)
14	14	THE KILLING OF GEORGIE — Rod Stewart (Riva)
8	15	WHAT I'VE GOT IN MIND — Billie Jo Spears (United Artists)
7	16	NOW IS THE TIME — Jimmy James & The Vagabonds (Pye)
10	17	HERE COMES THE SUN — Steve Harley & Cockney Rebel (EMI)
25	18	(LIGHT OF EXPERIENCE) DOINA DE JALE — Gheorghe Zamfir (Epic)
21	19	BABY, WE BETTER TRY AND GET IT TOGETHER — Barry White (20th Century)
-	20	BLINDED BY THE LIGHT — Manfred Mann's Earthband (Bronze)
20	21	NICE AND SLOW — Jesse Green (EMI)
28	22	HERE I GO AGAIN — Twiggy (Mercury)
16	23	MYSTERY SONG — Status Quo (Vertigo)
24	24	AFTERNOON DELIGHT — Starland Vocal Band (RCA)
26	25	MORNING GLORY — James & Bobby Purify (Mercury)
30	26	ARIA — Mr Acker Bilk (Sonet)
-	27	MISSISSIPPI — Pussycat (Sonet)
19	28	MISTY BLUE — Dorothy Moore (Contempo)
-	29	LOVING ON THE LOSING SIDE — Tommy Hunt (Spark)
23	30	THE ROUSSOS PHENOMENON (EP) — Demis Roussos (Philips)

The NME missed a couple of issues in August and September 1976, and the appropriate charts were not published at that time. Fortunately charts were compiled and kept in the NME archive, to be unearthed a week before this book went to press.

Unusual hits included a revival of a Country Joe & the Fish song by former model Twiggy, and the appearance of Romanian pipes player Georghe Zamfir with the theme of the religious TV programme *Light Of Experience*.

September – October 1976

Abba's *Dancing Queen,* the group's biggest-selling single, held Rod Stewart from the chart top with *The Killing Of Georgie,* but Rod sudenly found himself with two simultaneous Top 10 hits, as *Sailing,* his Number One single of the previous year was suddenly in huge demand again following its adoption as the theme to the TV documentary series about HMS Ark Royal, *Sailor.* Meanwhile, Manfred Mann's Earthband were the first to have a major hit with a Bruce Springsteen song, *Blinded By The Light.*

October 1976

last week	this	9 October 1976
1	1	DANCING QUEEN Abba (Epic)
2	2	MISSISSIPPI Pussycat (Sonet)
4	3	CAN'T GET BY WITHOUT YOU Real Thing (Pye)
12	4	DISCO DUCK Rick Dees & His Cast Of Idiots (RSO)
10	5	SAILING Rod Stewart (Warner Bros)
6	6	DANCE LITTLE LADY DANCE Tina Charles (CBS)
13	7	GIRL OF MY BEST FRIEND Elvis Presley (RCA)
5	8	I ONLY WANT TO BE WITH YOU Bay City Rollers (Bell)
3	9	I AM A CIDER DRINKER Wurzels (EMI)
9	10	ARIA Mr Acker Bilk (Pye)
20	11	HOWZAT Sherbet (Epic)
7	12	BLINDED BY THE LIGHT Manfed Mann's Earthband (Bronze)
11	13	LOVING AND FREE/AMOUREUSE Kiki Dee (Rocket)
15	14	BEST DISCO IN TOWN Ritchie Family (Polydor)
8	15	THE KILLING OF GEORGIE Rod Stewart (Riva)
14	16	(LIGHT OF EXPERIENCE) DOINA DE JALE Gheorghe Zamfir (Epic)
-	17	WHEN FOREVER HAS GONE Demis Roussos (Philips)
-	18	HURT Manhattans (CBS)
26	19	I'LL MEET YOU AT MIDNIGHT Smokie (RAK)
-	20	NICE AND SLOW Jesse Green (EMI)
17	21	16 BARS Stylistics (H&L)
23	22	GET UP OFFA THAT THING James Brown (Polydor)
24	23	I WANT MORE Can (Virgin)
21	24	HERE I GO AGAIN Twiggy (Mercury)
-	25	DISCO MUSIC (I LIKE IT) J A L N Band (Magnet)
18	26	LET 'EM IN Wings (Parlophone)
-	27	LOVING ON THE LOSING SIDE Tommy Hunt (Spark)
-	28	TEARS OF A CLOWN Smokey Robinson & the Miracles (Tamla Motown)
22	29	BABY WE BETTER TRY AND GET IT TOGETHER Barry White (20th Century)
27	30	UPTOWN, UPTEMPO WOMAN Randy Edelman (20th Century)

last week	this	16 October 1976
2	1	MISSISSIPPI Pussycat (Sonet)
1	2	DANCING QUEEN Abba (Epic)
5	3	SAILING Rod Stewart (Warner Bros)
4	4	DISCO DUCK Rick Dees & His Cast Of Idiots (RSO)
11	5	HOWZAT Sherbet (Epic)
3	6	CAN'T GET BY WITHOUT YOU Real Thing (Pye)
7	7	GIRL OF MY BEST FRIEND Elvis Presley (RCA)
6	8	DANCE LITTLE LADY DANCE Tina Charles (CBS)
18	9	HURT Manhattans (CBS)
8	10	I ONLY WANT TO BE WITH YOU Bay City Rollers (Bell)
19	11	I'LL MEET YOU AT MIDNIGHT Smokie (RAK)
17	12	WHEN FOREVER HAS GONE Demis Roussos (Philips)
14	13	BEST DISCO IN TOWN Ritchie Family (Polydor)
10	14	ARIA Acker Bilk (Pye)
13	15	LOVING AND FREE/AMOUREUSE Kiki Dee (Rocket)
9	16	I AM A CIDER DRINKER Wurzels (EMI)
12	17	BLINDED BY THE LIGHT Manfed Mann's Earthband (Bronze)
-	18	IF YOU LEAVE ME NOW Chicago (CBS)
-	19	DON'T TAKE AWAY THE MUSIC Tavares (Capitol)
-	20	THE SUMMER OF MY LIFE Simon May (Pye)
-	21	THE RUBBER BAND MAN Detroit Spinners (Atlantic)
22	22	PLAY THAT FUNKY MUSIC Wild Cherry (Epic)
-	23	I'D REALLY LOVE TO SEE YOU TONIGHT England Dan & John Ford Coley (Atlantic)
-	24	DANCING WITH THE CAPTAIN Paul Nicholas (RSO)
23	25	I WANT MORE Can (Virgin)
30	26	UPTOWN, UPTEMPO WOMAN Randy Edelman (20th Century)
22	27	GET UP OFFA THAT THING James Brown (Polydor)
25	28	DISCO MUSIC (I LIKE IT) J A L N Band (Magnet)
24	29	HERE I GO AGAIN Twiggy (Mercury)
16	30	(LIGHT OF EXPERIENCE) DOINA DE JALE Gheorghe Zamfir (Epic)

last week	this	23 October 1976
1	1	MISSISSIPPI Pussycat (Sonet)
5	2	HOWZAT Sherbet (Epic)
3	3	SAILING Rod Stewart (Warner Bros)
2	4	DANCING QUEEN Abba (Epic)
12	5	WHEN FOREVER HAS GONE Demis Roussos (Philips)
9	6	HURT Manhattans (CBS)
20	7	THE SUMMER OF MY LIFE Simon May (Pye)
18	8	IF YOU LEAVE ME NOW Chicago (CBS)
4	9	DISCO DUCK Rick Dees & His Cast Of Idiots (RSO)
8	10	DANCE LITTLE LADY DANCE Tina Charles (CBS)
6	11	CAN'T GET BY WITHOUT YOU Real Thing (Pye)
13	12	BEST DISCO IN TOWN Ritchie Family (Polydor)
19	13	DON'T TAKE AWAY THE MUSIC Tavares (Capitol)
7	14	GIRL OF MY BEST FRIEND Elvis Presley (RCA)
24	15	DANCING WITH THE CAPTAIN Paul Nicholas (RSO)
22	16	PLAY THAT FUNKY MUSIC Wild Cherry (Epic)
11	17	I'LL MEET YOU AT MIDNIGHT Smokie (RAK)
10	18	I ONLY WANT TO BE WITH YOU Bay City Rollers (Bell)
15	19	LOVING AND FREE/AMOUREUSE Kiki Dee (Rocket)
14	20	ARIA Acker Bilk (Pye)
-	21	LOVE AND AFFECTION Joan Armatrading (A& M)
17	22	BLINDED BY THE LIGHT Manfed Mann's Earthband (Bronze)
-	23	COULDN'T GET IT RIGHT Climax Blues Band (BTM)
16	24	I AM A CIDER DRINKER Wurzels (EMI)
28	25	THE RUBBER BAND MAN Detroit Spinners (Atlantic)
28	26	DISCO MUSIC (I LIKE IT) J A L N Band (Magnet)
27	27	QUEEN OF MY SOUL Average White Band (Atlantic)
28	28	JAWS Lalo Schifrin (CTI)
-	29	COMING HOME David Essex (CBS)
23	30	I'D REALLY LOVE TO SEE YOU TONIGHT England Dan & John Ford Coley (Atlantic)

last week	this	30 October 1976
1	1	MISSISSIPPI Pussycat (Sonet)
8	2	IF YOU LEAVE ME NOW Chicago (CBS)
5	3	WHEN FOREVER HAS GONE Demis Roussos (Philips)
6	4	HURT Manhattans (CBS)
7	5	THE SUMMER OF MY LIFE Simon May (Pye)
2	6	HOWZAT Sherbet (Epic)
13	7	DON'T TAKE AWAY THE MUSIC Tavares (Capitol)
3	8	SAILING Rod Stewart (Warner Bros)
4	9	DANCING QUEEN Abba (Epic)
15	10	DANCING WITH THE CAPTAIN Paul Nicholas (RSO)
17	11	I'LL MEET YOU AT MIDNIGHT Smokie (RAK)
14	12	GIRL OF MY BEST FRIEND Elvis Presley (RCA)
9	13	DISCO DUCK Rick Dees & His Cast Of Idiots (RSO)
16	14	PLAY THAT FUNKY MUSIC Wild Cherry (Epic)
23	15	COULDN'T GET IT RIGHT Climax Blues Band (BTM)
25	16	THE RUBBER BAND MAN Detroit Spinners (Atlantic)
11	17	CAN'T GET BY WITHOUT YOU Real Thing (Pye)
21	18	LOVE AND AFFECTION Joan Armatrading (A& M)
12	19	BEST DISCO IN TOWN Ritchie Family (Polydor)
28	20	JAWS Lalo Schifrin (CTI)
27	21	QUEEN OF MY SOUL Average White Band (Atlantic)
10	22	DANCE LITTLE LADY DANCE Tina Charles (CBS)
19	23	LOVING AND FREE/AMOUREUSE Kiki Dee (Rocket)
30	24	I'D REALLY LOVE TO SEE YOU TONIGHT England Dan & John Ford Coley (Atlantic)
29	25	COMING HOME David Essex (CBS)
18	26	I ONLY WANT TO BE WITH YOU Bay City Rollers (Bell)
-	27	BEAUTIFUL NOISE Neil Diamond (CBS)
-	28	WITHOUT YOU Nilsson (RCA)
24	29	I AM A CIDER DRINKER Wurzels (EMI)
-	30	SHE'S GONE Daryl Hall & John Oates (Atlantic)

Sweden's Abba were deposed from Number One by another mixed-sex group from Continental Europe, Holland's Pussycat. More by coincidence than anything else, the chart suddenly took on a very cosmopolitan look: the Top 10 of October 23 had six different nationalities in it, with Britishers, Americans, a Greek (Demis Roussos) and some Australians (Sherbet) joining the two abovementioned acts. The Wurzels' hit was based on the Jonathan King/George Baker hit *Una Paloma Blanca*.

November 1976

6 November 1976

last week	this	title
2	1	IF YOU LEAVE ME NOW Chicago (CBS)
1	2	MISSISSIPPI Pussycat (Sonet)
3	3	WHEN FOREVER HAS GONE Demis Roussos (Philips)
4	4	HURT Manhattans (CBS)
6	5	HOWZAT Sherbet (Epic)
5	6	THE SUMMER OF MY LIFE Simon May (Pye)
7	7	DON'T TAKE AWAY THE MUSIC Tavares (Capitol)
10	8	DANCING WITH THE CAPTAIN Paul Nicholas (RSO)
14	9	PLAY THAT FUNKY MUSIC Wild Cherry (Epic)
8	10	SAILING Rod Stewart (Warner Bros)
11	11	I'LL MEET YOU AT MIDNIGHT Smokie (RAK)
15	12	COULDN'T GET IT RIGHT Climax Blues Band (BTM)
9	13	DANCING QUEEN Abba (Epic)
18	14	LOVE AND AFFECTION Joan Armatrading (A&M)
12	15	GIRL OF MY BEST FRIEND Elvis Presley (RCA)
20	16	JAWS Lalo Schifrin (CTI)
-	17	YOU MAKE ME FEEL LIKE DANCING Leo Sayer (Chrysalis)
16	18	THE RUBBER BAND MAN Detroit Spinners (Atlantic)
-	19	IF NOT YOU Dr Hook (Capitol)
27	20	BEAUTIFUL NOISE Neil Diamond (CBS)
25	21	COMING HOME David Essex (CBS)
-	22	SUBSTITUTE Who (Polydor)
28	23	WITHOUT YOU Nilsson (RCA)
13	24	DISCO DUCK Rick Dees & His Cast Of Idiots (RSO)
19	25	BEST DISCO IN TOWN Ritchie Family (Polydor)
21	26	QUEEN OF MY SOUL Average White Band (Atlantic)
-	27	LOST IN FRANCE Bonnie Tyler (RCA)
17	28	CAN'T GET BY WITHOUT YOU Real Thing (Pye)
22	29	DANCE LITTLE LADY DANCE Tina Charles (CBS)
-	30	YOU'RE MY BEST FRIEND Don Williams (ABC)

13 November 1976

last week	this	title
1	1	IF YOU LEAVE ME NOW Chicago (CBS)
2	2	MISSISSIPPI Pussycat (Sonet)
4	3	HURT Manhattans (CBS)
4	4	WHEN FOREVER HAS GONE Demis Roussos (Philips)
12	5	COULDN'T GET IT RIGHT Climax Blues Band (BTM)
17	6	YOU MAKE ME FEEL LIKE DANCING Leo Sayer (Chrysalis)
9	7	PLAY THAT FUNKY MUSIC Wild Cherry (Epic)
7	8	DON'T TAKE AWAY THE MUSIC Tavares (Capitol)
5	9	HOWZAT Sherbet (Epic)
22	10	SUBSTITUTE Who (Polydor)
19	11	IF NOT YOU Dr Hook (Capitol)
6	12	THE SUMMER OF MY LIFE Simon May (Pye)
8	13	DANCING WITH THE CAPTAIN Paul Nicholas (RSO)
10	14	SAILING Rod Stewart (Warner Bros)
-	15	UNDER THE MOON OF LOVE Showaddywaddy (Bell)
14	16	LOVE AND AFFECTION Joan Armatrading (A&M)
16	17	JAWS Lalo Schifrin (CTI)
27	18	LOST IN FRANCE Bonnie Tyler (RCA)
-	19	ROCK 'N' ME Steve Miller Band (Mercury)
11	20	I'LL MEET YOU AT MIDNIGHT Smokie (RAK)
13	21	DANCING QUEEN Abba (Epic)
18	22	THE RUBBER BAND MAN Detroit Spinners (Atlantic)
-	23	LOWDOWN Boz Scaggs (CBS)
-	24	LOVE ME Yvonne Elliman (RSO)
20	25	BEAUTIFUL NOISE Neil Diamond (CBS)
23	26	WITHOUT YOU Nilsson (RCA)
15	27	GIRL OF MY BEST FRIEND Elvis Presley (RCA)
-	28	SPINNING ROCK BOOGIE Hank C Burnette (Sonet)
21	29	COMING HOME David Essex (CBS)
26	30	QUEEN OF MY SOUL Average White Band (Atlantic)

20 November 1976

last week	this	title
1	1	IF YOU LEAVE ME NOW Chicago (CBS)
6	2	YOU MAKE ME FEEL LIKE DANCING Leo Sayer (Chrysalis)
2	3	MISSISSIPPI Pussycat (Sonet)
8	4	DON'T TAKE AWAY THE MUSIC Tavares (Capitol)
7	5	PLAY THAT FUNKY MUSIC Wild Cherry (Epic)
15	6	UNDER THE MOON OF LOVE Showaddywaddy (Bell)
3	7	HURT Manhattans (CBS)
11	8	IF NOT YOU Dr Hook (Capitol)
4	9	WHEN FOREVER HAS GONE Demis Roussos (Philips)
16	10	LOVE AND AFFECTION Joan Armatrading (A&M)
5	11	COULDN'T GET IT RIGHT Climax Blues Band (BTM)
25	12	BEAUTIFUL NOISE Neil Diamond (CBS)
18	13	LOST IN FRANCE Bonnie Tyler (RCA)
10	14	SUBSTITUTE Who (Polydor)
19	15	ROCK 'N' ME Steve Miller Band (Mercury)
9	16	HOWZAT Sherbet (Epic)
12	17	THE SUMMER OF MY LIFE Simon May (Pye)
17	18	JAWS Lalo Schifrin (CTI)
13	19	DANCING WITH THE CAPTAIN Paul Nicholas (RSO)
24	20	LOVE ME Yvonne Elliman (RSO)
-	21	DON'T MAKE ME WAIT TOO LONG Barry White (20th Century)
14	22	SAILING Rod Stewart (Warner Bros)
28	23	SPINNING ROCK BOOGIE Hank C Burnette (Sonet)
-	24	LIVIN' THING Electric Light Orchestra (Jet)
23	25	LOWDOWN Boz Scaggs (CBS)
20	26	I'LL MEET YOU AT MIDNIGHT Smokie (RAK)
-	27	SORRY SEEMS TO BE THE HARDEST WORD Elton John (Rocket)
22	28	THE RUBBER BAND MAN Detroit Spinners (Atlantic)
-	29	STOP ME (IF YOU'VE HEARD IT ALL BEFORE) Billy Ocean (GTO)
-	30	TEENAGE DEPRESSION Eddie & the Hot Rods (Island)

27 November 1976

last week	this	title
1	1	IF YOU LEAVE ME NOW Chicago (CBS)
6	2	UNDER THE MOON OF LOVE Showaddywaddy (Bell)
2	3	YOU MAKE ME FEEL LIKE DANCING Leo Sayer (Chrysalis)
8	4	IF NOT YOU Dr Hook (Capitol)
13	5	LOST IN FRANCE Bonnie Tyler (RCA)
3	6	MISSISSIPPI Pussycat (Sonet)
14	7	SUBSTITUTE Who (Polydor)
7	8	HURT Manhattans (CBS)
24	9	LIVIN' THING Electric Light Orchestra (Jet)
5	10	PLAY THAT FUNKY MUSIC Wild Cherry (Epic)
4	11	DON'T TAKE AWAY THE MUSIC Tavares (Capitol)
10	12	LOVE AND AFFECTION Joan Armatrading (A&M)
11	13	COULDN'T GET IT RIGHT Climax Blues Band (BTM)
20	14	LOVE ME Yvonne Elliman (RSO)
-	15	MONEY MONEY MONEY Abba (Epic)
15	16	ROCK 'N' ME Steve Miller Band (Mercury)
12	17	BEAUTIFUL NOISE Neil Diamond (CBS)
27	18	SORRY SEEMS TO BE THE HARDEST WORD Elton John (Rocket)
9	19	WHEN FOREVER HAS GONE Demis Roussos (Philips)
-	20	SOMEBODY TO LOVE Queen (EMI)
21	21	GET BACK Rod Stewart (Riva)
21	22	DON'T MAKE ME WAIT TOO LONG Barry White (20th Century)
23	23	SPINNING ROCK BOOGIE Hank C Burnette (Sonet)
-	24	FAIRY TALE Dana (GTO)
-	25	WHEN A CHILD IS BORN Johnny Mathis (CBS)
26	26	JAWS Lalo Schifrin (CTI)
29	27	STOP ME (IF YOU'VE HEARD IT ALL BEFORE) Billy Ocean (GTO)
-	28	HOT VALVES (EP) Be-Bop Deluxe (Harvest)
30	29	TEENAGE DEPRESSION Eddie & The Hot Rods (Island)
-	30	LITTLE DOES SHE KNOW Kursaal Flyers (CBS)

Most of Chicago's string of US hits through the early 1970s had meant very little in the UK just as many later to come would bypass domestic taste; *If You Leave Me Now,* demonstrating the band's developing AOR ballad style rather than their earlier brass'n'guitars pyrotechnics, was a major exception, topping the chart for a month. The Who's reissue of *Substitute* was the first Top 20 hit on a commercially-released UK 12-inch single, while Bonnie Tyler and Steve Miller both made their British chart debuts.

December 1976

4 December 1976

last week	this	
2	1	UNDER THE MOON OF LOVE — Showaddywaddy (Bell)
1	2	IF YOU LEAVE ME NOW — Chicago (CBS)
20	3	SOMEBODY TO LOVE — Queen (EMI)
3	4	YOU MAKE ME FEEL LIKE DANCING — Leo Sayer (Chrysalis)
15	5	MONEY MONEY MONEY — Abba (Epic)
14	6	LOVE ME — Yvonne Elliman (RSO)
9	7	LIVIN' THING — Electric Light Orchestra (Jet)
4	8	IF NOT YOU — Dr Hook (Capitol)
5	9	LOST IN FRANCE — Bonnie Tyler (RCA)
16	10	ROCK 'N' ME — Steve Miller Band (Mercury)
21	11	GET BACK — Rod Stewart (Riva)
10	12	PLAY THAT FUNKY MUSIC — Wild Cherry (Epic)
18	13	SORRY SEEMS TO BE THE HARDEST WORD — Elton John (Rocket)
6	14	MISSISSIPPI — Pussycat (Sonet)
25	15	WHEN A CHILD IS BORN — Johnny Mathis (CBS)
-	16	SO SAD THE SONG — Gladys Knight & the Pips (Buddah)
11	17	DON'T TAKE AWAY THE MUSIC — Tavares (Capitol)
-	18	LEAN ON ME — Mud (Private Stock)
30	19	LITTLE DOES SHE KNOW — Kursaal Flyers (CBS)
7	20	SUBSTITUTE — Who (Polydor)
17	21	BEAUTIFUL NOISE — Neil Diamond (CBS)
27	22	STOP ME (IF YOU'VE HEARD IT ALL BEFORE) — Billy Ocean (GTO)
13	23	COULDN'T GET IT RIGHT — Climax Blues Band (BTM)
12	24	LOVE AND AFFECTION — Joan Armatrading (A& M)
24	25	FAIRY TALE — Dana (GTO)
-	26	PORTSMOUTH — Mike Oldfield (Virgin)
23	27	SPINNING ROCK BOOGIE — Hank C Burnette (Sonet)
8	28	HURT — Manhattans (CBS)
-	29	YOU'LL NEVER GET TO HEAVEN (EP) — Stylistics (H&L)
22	30	DON'T MAKE ME WAIT TOO LONG — Barry White (20th Century)

11 December 1976

last	this	
1	1	UNDER THE MOON OF LOVE — Showaddywaddy (Bell)
3	2	SOMEBODY TO LOVE — Queen (EMI)
7	3	LIVIN' THING — Electric Light Orchestra (Jet)
6	4	LOVE ME — Yvonne Elliman (RSO)
5	5	MONEY MONEY MONEY — Abba (Epic)
2	6	IF YOU LEAVE ME NOW — Chicago (CBS)
15	7	WHEN A CHILD IS BORN — Johnny Mathis (CBS)
4	8	YOU MAKE ME FEEL LIKE DANCING — Leo Sayer (Chrysalis)
18	9	LEAN ON ME — Mud (Private Stock)
11	10	GET BACK — Rod Stewart (Riva)
9	11	LOST IN FRANCE — Bonnie Tyler (RCA)
8	12	IF NOT YOU — Dr Hook (Capitol)
13	13	SORRY SEEMS TO BE THE HARDEST WORD — Elton John (Rocket)
26	14	PORTSMOUTH — Mike Oldfield (Virgin)
19	15	LITTLE DOES SHE KNOW — Kursaal Flyers (CBS)
10	16	ROCK 'N' ME — Steve Miller Band (Mercury)
-	17	LIVING NEXT DOOR TO ALICE — Smokie (RAK)
14	18	MISSISSIPPI — Pussycat (Sonet)
25	19	FAIRY TALE — Dana (GTO)
21	20	BEAUTIFUL NOISE — Neil Diamond (CBS)
-	21	DOCTOR LOVE — Tina Charles (CBS)
23	22	COULDN'T GET IT RIGHT — Climax Blues Band (BTM)
20	23	SUBSTITUTE — The Who (Polydor)
30	24	DON'T MAKE ME WAIT TOO LONG — Barry White (20th Century)
-	25	BIONIC SANTA — Chris Hill (Philips)
-	26	GRANDMA'S PARTY (EP) — Paul Nicholas (RSO)
29	27	YOU'LL NEVER GET TO HEAVEN (EP) — Stylistics (H&L)
27	28	SPINNING ROCK BOOGIE — Hank C Burnette (Sonet)
-	29	HEY MR DREAM MAKER — Cliff Richard (EMI)
-	30	HANG ON SLOOPY — Sandpipers (Satril)

18 December 1976

last	this	
1	1	UNDER THE MOON OF LOVE — Showaddywaddy (Bell)
5	2	MONEY MONEY MONEY — Abba (Epic)
7	3	WHEN A CHILD IS BORN — Johnny Mathis (CBS)
2	4	SOMEBODY TO LOVE — Queen (EMI)
3	5	LIVIN' THING — Electric Light Orchestra (Jet)
4	6	LOVE ME — Yvonne Elliman (RSO)
6	7	IF YOU LEAVE ME NOW — Chicago (CBS)
14	8	PORTSMOUTH — Mike Oldfield (Virgin)
-	9	STOP ME (IF YOU'VE HEARD IT ALL BEFORE) — Billy Ocean (GTO)
9	10	LEAN ON ME — Mud (Private Stock)
17	11	LIVING NEXT DOOR TO ALICE — Smokie (RAK)
10	12	GET BACK — Rod Stewart (Riva)
8	13	YOU MAKE ME FEEL LIKE DANCING — Leo Sayer (Chrysalis)
13	14	SORRY SEEMS TO BE THE HARDEST WORD — Elton John (Rocket)
15	15	LITTLE DOES SHE KNOW — Kursaal Flyers (CBS)
11	16	LOST IN FRANCE — Bonnie Tyler (RCA)
21	17	DOCTOR LOVE — Tina Charles (CBS)
12	18	IF NOT YOU — Dr Hook (Capitol)
19	19	FAIRY TALE — Dana (GTO)
-	20	WILD SIDE OF LIFE — Status Quo (Vertigo)
26	21	GRANDMA'S PARTY (EP) — Paul Nicholas RSO
25	22	BIONIC SANTA — Chris Hill (Philips)
-	23	THINGS WE DO FOR LOVE — 10cc (Mercury)
16	24	ROCK 'N' ME — Steve Miller Band (Mercury)
27	25	YOU'LL NEVER GET TO HEAVEN (EP) — Stylistics (H&L)
18	26	MISSISSIPPI — Pussycat (Sonet)
24	27	DON'T MAKE ME WAIT TOO LONG — Barry White (20th Century)
-	28	HAITIAN DIVORCE — Steely Dan (ABC)
29	29	HEY MR DREAM MAKER — Cliff Richard (EMI)
23	30	SUBSTITUTE — The Who (Polydor)

25 December 1976

last	this	
3	1	WHEN A CHILD IS BORN — Johnny Mathis (CBS)
1	2	UNDER THE MOON OF LOVE — Showaddywaddy (Bell)
4	3	SOMEBODY TO LOVE — Queen (EMI)
2	4	MONEY MONEY MONEY — Abba (Epic)
5	5	LIVIN' THING — Electric Light Orchestra (Jet)
8	6	PORTSMOUTH — Mike Oldfield (Virgin)
22	7	BIONIC SANTA — Chris Hill (Philips)
6	8	LOVE ME — Yvonne Elliman (RSO)
11	9	LIVING NEXT DOOR TO ALICE — Smokie (RAK)
10	10	LEAN ON ME — Mud (Private Stock)
17	11	DOCTOR LOVE — Tina Charles (CBS)
7	12	IF YOU LEAVE ME NOW — Chicago (CBS)
-	13	DON'T GIVE UP ON US — David Soul (Private Stock)
20	14	WILD SIDE OF LIFE — Status Quo (Vertigo)
21	15	GRANDMA'S PARTY (EP) — Paul Nicholas RSO
-	16	I WISH — Stevie Wonder (Motown)
23	17	THINGS WE DO FOR LOVE — 10cc (Mercury)
12	18	GET BACK — Rod Stewart (Riva)
15	19	LITTLE DOES SHE KNOW — Kursaal Flyers (CBS)
8	20	STOP ME (IF YOU'VE HEARD IT ALL BEFORE) — Billy Ocean (GTO)
13	21	YOU MAKE ME FEEL LIKE DANCING — Leo Sayer (Chrysalis)
28	22	HAITIAN DIVORCE — Steely Dan (ABC)
-	23	DON'T CRY FOR ME ARGENTINA — Julie Covington (MCA)
16	24	LOST IN FRANCE — Bonnie Tyler (RCA)
19	25	FAIRY TALE — Dana (GTO)
14	26	SORRY SEEMS TO BE THE HARDEST WORD — Elton John (Rocket)
-	27	ANARCHY IN THE UK — Sex Pistols (EMI)
-	28	SIDE SHOW — Barry Biggs (Dynamic)
-	29	RING OUT SOLSTICE BELLS — Jethro Tull (Chrysalis)
26	30	MISSISSIPPI — Pussycat (Sonet)

Showaddywaddy's *Under The Moon Of Love*, which sold 953,000 copies, was a revival of a 1961 Curtis Lee single which had sold modestly. Song revivals were almost the theme of the month, as Rod Stewart covered *Get Back*, the Sandpipers revived *Hang On Sloopy*, and the Stylistics rediscovered Bacharach & David's *You'll Never Get To Heaven*. The Sex Pistols' *Anarchy In The UK* was withdrawn by EMI (which cancelled the band's contract) almost as soon as it had made its Christmas week chart showing.

309

Punk

Social revolution, a
fashion gimmick, a
return to music basics or
just some anarchy in the
UK? The Sex Pistols'
career was carefully
nurtured in its early
stages for maximum
shock value. But there
was a lot else going on
besides- and a ready
audience for the music.
Punk rock was a
reaction to what went
before. As pop was either
vapid chart singles or
'dinosaurs' from the
sixties playing to
stadium-sized audiences,
punk took music back to
the clubs. A uniquely
British phenomenon,
punk gradually became
New Wave, taking
America by storm. As
often seems to happen a
flowering of talent
followed as people
realised that pop music
could once again be
dynamic, vibrant,
exciting and dangerous.
Not since audiences
ripped up the seats at
'The Blackboard Jungle'
or Jagger sang 'Let's
Spend The Night
Together' on TV had pop
been like this.

Top: the Sex Pistols'
Johnny Rotten; top left
Dave Vanian of the
Damned; centre The
Clash; left Siouxsie
Sioux

January 1977

last week	this week	8 January 1977
1	1	WHEN A CHILD IS BORN — Johnny Mathis (CBS)
2	2	UNDER THE MOON OF LOVE — Showaddywaddy (Bell)
4	3	MONEY MONEY MONEY — Abba (Epic)
13	4	DON'T GIVE UP ON US — David Soul (Private Stock)
6	5	PORTSMOUTH — Mike Oldfield (Virgin)
11	6	DOCTOR LOVE — Tina Charles (CBS)
9	7	LIVING NEXT DOOR TO ALICE — Smokie (Rak)
15	8	GRANDMA'S PARTY — Paul Nicholas RSO
3	9	SOMEBODY TO LOVE — Queen (EMI)
5	10	LIVIN' THING — Electric Light Orchestra (Jet)
17	11	THINGS WE DO FOR LOVE — 10 c.c. (Mercury)
14	12	WILD SIDE OF LIFE — Status Quo (Vertigo)
8	13	LOVE ME — Yvonne Ellman (RSO)
10	14	LEAN ON ME — Mud (Private Stock)
16	15	I WISH — Stevie Wonder (Motown)
25	16	FAIRY TALE — Dana (GTO)
7	17	BIONIC SANTA — Chris Hill (Philips)
23	18	DON'T CRY FOR ME ARGENTINA — Julie Covington (MCA)
22	19	HAITIAN DIVORCE — Steely Dan (ABC)
-	20	SIDE SHOW — Barry Biggs (Dynamic)
-	21	CAR WASH — Rose Royce (MCA)
-	22	HERE'S TO LOVE — John Christie (EMI)
19	23	LITTLE DOES SHE KNOW — Kursaal Flyers (CBS)
18	24	GET BACK — Rod Stewart (Riva)
20	25	STOP ME (IF YOU'VE HEARD IT ALL BEFORE) — Billy Ocean (GTO)
26	26	SORRY SEEMS TO BE THE HARDEST WORD — Elton John (Rocket)
-	27	YOU'RE MORE THAN A NUMBER IN MY LITTLE RED BOOK — Drifters (Arista)
-	28	DADDY COOL — Boney M (Atlantic)
29	29	RING OUT SOLSTICE BELLS (EP) — Jethro Tull (Chrysalis)
12	30	IF YOU LEAVE ME NOW — Chicago (CBS)

last week	this week	15 January 1977
4	1	DON'T GIVE UP ON US — David Soul (Private Stock)
2	2	UNDER THE MOON OF LOVE — Showaddywaddy (Bell)
3	3	MONEY MONEY MONEY — Abba (Epic)
1	4	WHEN A CHILD IS BORN — Johnny Mathis (CBS)
15	5	I WISH — Stevie Wonder (Motown)
5	6	PORTSMOUTH — Mike Oldfield (Virgin)
6	7	DOCTOR LOVE — Tina Charles (CBS)
18	8	DON'T CRY FOR ME ARGENTINA — Julie Covington (MCA)
7	9	LIVING NEXT DOOR TO ALICE — Smokie (Rak)
11	10	THINGS WE DO FOR LOVE — 10 c.c. (Mercury)
8	11	GRANDMA'S PARTY — Paul Nicholas RSO
10	12	LIVIN' THING — Electric Light Orchestra (Jet)
12	13	WILD SIDE OF LIFE — Status Quo (Vertigo)
9	14	SOMEBODY TO LOVE — Queen (EMI)
20	15	SIDE SHOW — Barry Biggs (Dynamic)
13	16	LOVE ME — Yvonne Ellman (RSO)
21	17	CAR WASH — Rose Royce (MCA)
23	18	LITTLE DOES SHE KNOW — Kursaal Flyers (CBS)
28	19	DADDY COOL — Boney M (Atlantic)
19	20	HAITIAN DIVORCE — Steely Dan (ABC)
27	21	YOU'RE MORE THAN A NUMBER IN MY LITTLE RED BOOK — Drifters (Arista)
22	22	HERE'S TO LOVE — John Christie (EMI)
16	23	FAIRY TALE — Dana (GTO)
30	24	IF YOU LEAVE ME NOW — Chicago (CBS)
25	25	STOP ME (IF YOU'VE HEARD IT ALL BEFORE) — Billy Ocean (GTO)
14	26	LEAN ON ME — Mud (Private Stock)
-	27	WINTER MELODY — Donna Summer (GTO)
-	28	FLIP — Jesse Green (EMI)
17	29	BIONIC SANTA — Chris Hill (Philips)
-	30	ISN'T SHE LOVELY — David Parton (Pye)

last week	this week	22 January 1977
1	1	DON'T GIVE UP ON US — David Soul (Private Stock)
8	2	DON'T CRY FOR ME ARGENTINA — Julie Covington (MCA)
15	3	SIDE SHOW — Barry Biggs (Dynamic)
5	4	I WISH — Stevie Wonder (Motown)
17	5	CAR WASH — Rose Royce (MCA)
3	6	MONEY MONEY MONEY — Abba (Epic)
10	7	THINGS WE DO FOR LOVE — 10 c.c. (Mercury)
13	8	WILD SIDE OF LIFE — Status Quo (Vertigo)
2	9	UNDER THE MOON OF LOVE — Showaddywaddy (Bell)
4	10	WHEN A CHILD IS BORN — Johnny Mathis (CBS)
19	11	DADDY COOL — Boney M (Atlantic)
7	12	DOCTOR LOVE — Tina Charles (CBS)
21	13	YOU'RE MORE THAN A NUMBER IN MY LITTLE RED BOOK — Drifters (Arista)
30	14	ISN'T SHE LOVELY — David Parton (Pye)
9	15	LIVING NEXT DOOR TO ALICE — Smokie (Rak)
11	16	GRANDMA'S PARTY — Paul Nicholas RSO
6	17	PORTSMOUTH — Mike Oldfield (Virgin)
-	18	SUSPICION — Elvis Presley (RCA)
-	19	NEW KID IN TOWN — Eagles (Asylum)
-	20	LOST WITHOUT YOUR LOVE — Bread (Elektra)
14	21	SOMEBODY TO LOVE — Queen (EMI)
-	22	DON'T BELIEVE A WORD — Thin Lizzy (Vertigo)
-	23	SMILE — Pussycat (Sonet)
20	24	HAITIAN DIVORCE — Steely Dan (ABC)
-	25	EVERY MAN MUST HAVE A DREAM — Liverpool Express (Warner Bros)
12	26	LIVIN' THING — Electric Light Orchestra (Jet)
18	27	LITTLE DOES SHE KNOW — Kursaal Flyers (CBS)
23	28	FAIRY TALE — Dana (GTO)
-	29	KEEP IT COMIN' LOVE — K C & the Sunshine Band (Jayboy)
28	30	FLIP — Jesse Green (EMI)

last week	this week	29 January 1977
2	1	DON'T CRY FOR ME ARGENTINA — Julie Covington (MCA)
1	2	DON'T GIVE UP ON US — David Soul (Private Stock)
3	3	SIDE SHOW — Barry Biggs (Dynamic)
13	4	YOU'RE MORE THAN A NUMBER IN MY LITTLE RED BOOK — Drifters (Arista)
4	5	I WISH — Stevie Wonder (Motown)
14	6	ISN'T SHE LOVELY — David Parton (Pye)
7	7	THINGS WE DO FOR LOVE — 10 c.c. (Mercury)
8	8	WILD SIDE OF LIFE — Status Quo (Vertigo)
11	9	DADDY COOL — Boney M (Atlantic)
5	10	CAR WASH — Rose Royce (MCA)
12	11	DOCTOR LOVE — Tina Charles (CBS)
22	12	DON'T BELIEVE A WORD — Thin Lizzy (Vertigo)
6	13	MONEY MONEY MONEY — Abba (Epic)
15	14	LIVING NEXT DOOR TO ALICE — Smokie (Rak)
18	15	SUSPICION — Elvis Presley (RCA)
19	16	NEW KID IN TOWN — Eagles (Asylum)
17	17	PORTSMOUTH — Mike Oldfield (Virgin)
9	18	UNDER THE MOON OF LOVE — Showaddywaddy (Bell)
24	19	HAITIAN DIVORCE — Steely Dan (ABC)
-	20	DON'T LEAVE ME THIS WAY — Harold Melvin & the Blue Notes (CBS)
-	21	WHEN I NEED YOU — Leo Sayer (Chrysalis)
16	22	GRANDMA'S PARTY — Paul Nicholas RSO
23	23	SMILE — Pussycat (Sonet)
25	24	EVERY MAN MUST HAVE A DREAM — Liverpool Express (Warner Bros)
28	25	FAIRY TALE — Dana (GTO)
20	26	LOST WITHOUT YOUR LOVE — Bread (Elektra)
-	27	IT TAKES ALL NIGHT LONG — Gary Glitter (Arista)
10	28	WHEN A CHILD IS BORN — Johnny Mathis (CBS)
30	29	FLIP — Jesse Green (EMI)
-	30	SING ME — Brothers (Bus Stop)

David Soul had his hit TV role as Ken Hutchinson in the police series *Starsky And Hutch* as a major promotional asset when he made his first single. He proved to be an above-average vocalist with an ear for a commercial song anyway, and would have an impressive string of hits. None was bigger than *Don't Give Up On Us* though: it sold over a million in the UK alone. David Parton had the opportunistic UK cover version of Stevie Wonder's LP track *Isn't She Lovely*.

311

February 1977

5 February 1977

last week	this week	
2	1	DON'T GIVE UP ON US — David Soul (Private Stock)
1	2	DON'T CRY FOR ME ARGENTINA — Julie Covington (MCA)
3	3	SIDE SHOW — Barry Biggs (Dynamic)
6	4	ISN'T SHE LOVELY — David Parton (Pye)
21	5	WHEN I NEED YOU — Leo Sayer (Chrysalis)
5	6	I WISH — Stevie Wonder (Motown)
9	7	DADDY COOL — Boney M (Atlantic)
4	8	YOU'RE MORE THAN A NUMBER IN MY LITTLE RED BOOK — Drifters (Arista)
10	9	CAR WASH — Rose Royce (MCA)
8	10	WILD SIDE OF LIFE — Status Quo (Vertigo)
15	11	SUSPICION — Elvis Presley (RCA)
7	12	THINGS WE DO FOR LOVE — 10 c.c. (Mercury)
12	13	DON'T BELIEVE A WORD — Thin Lizzy (Vertigo)
14	14	LIVING NEXT DOOR TO ALICE — Smokie (Rak)
20	15	DON'T LEAVE ME THIS WAY — Harold Melvin & the Blue Notes (CBS)
-	16	JACK IN THE BOX — Moments (All Platinum)
16	17	NEW KID IN TOWN — Eagles (Asylum)
11	18	DOCTOR LOVE — Tina Charles (CBS)
24	19	EVERY MAN MUST HAVE A DREAM — Liverpool Express (Warner Bros)
-	20	WHAT CAN I SAY — Boz Scaggs (CBS)
13	21	MONEY MONEY MONEY — Abba (Epic)
30	22	SING ME — Brothers (Bus Stop)
-	23	MORE THAN A FEELING — Boston (EMI)
-	24	BOOGIE NIGHTS — Heatwave (GTO)
23	25	SMILE — Pussycat (Sonet)
29	26	FLIP — Jesse Green (EMI)
26	27	LOST WITHOUT YOUR LOVE — Bread (Elektra)
-	28	DON'T LEAVE ME THIS WAY — Thelma Houston (Motown)
-	29	WAKE UP SUSAN — Detroit Spinners (Atlantic)
18	30	UNDER THE MOON OF LOVE — Showaddywaddy (Bell)

12 February 1977

last week	this week	
2	1	DON'T CRY FOR ME ARGENTINA — Julie Covington (MCA)
1	2	DON'T GIVE UP ON US — David Soul (Private Stock)
5	3	WHEN I NEED YOU — Leo Sayer (Chrysalis)
3	4	SIDE SHOW — Barry Biggs (Dynamic)
7	5	DADDY COOL — Boney M (Atlantic)
4	6	ISN'T SHE LOVELY — David Parton (Pye)
11	7	SUSPICION — Elvis Presley (RCA)
8	8	YOU'RE MORE THAN A NUMBER IN MY LITTLE RED BOOK — Drifters (Arista)
15	9	DON'T LEAVE ME THIS WAY — Harold Melvin & the Blue Notes (CBS)
9	10	CAR WASH — Rose Royce (MCA)
16	11	JACK IN THE BOX — Moments (All Platinum)
13	12	DON'T BELIEVE A WORD — Thin Lizzy (Vertigo)
6	13	I WISH — Stevie Wonder (Motown)
24	14	BOOGIE NIGHTS — Heatwave (GTO)
10	15	WILD SIDE OF LIFE — Status Quo (Vertigo)
12	16	THINGS WE DO FOR LOVE — 10 c.c. (Mercury)
22	17	SING ME — Brothers (Bus Stop)
17	18	NEW KID IN TOWN — Eagles (Asylum)
-	19	IT TAKES ALL NIGHT LONG — Gary Glitter (Arista)
28	20	DON'T LEAVE ME THIS WAY — Thelma Houston (Motown)
20	21	WHAT CAN I SAY — Boz Scaggs (CBS)
-	22	CHANSON D' AMOUR — Manhattan Transfer (Atlantic)
-	23	MIGHTY POWER OF LOVE — Tavares (Capitol)
18	24	DOCTOR LOVE — Tina Charles (CBS)
-	25	EVERYBODY'S TALKIN' BOUT LOVE — Silver Convention (Magnet)
23	26	MORE THAN A FEELING — Boston (EMI)
-	27	YEAR OF THE CAT — Al Stewart (RCA)
29	28	WAKE UP SUSAN — Detroit Spinners (Atlantic)
19	29	EVERY MAN MUST HAVE A DREAM — Liverpool Express (Warner Bros)
-	30	HA CHA CHA — Brass Construction (United Artists)

19 February 1977

last week	this week	
1	1	DON'T CRY FOR ME ARGENTINA — Julie Covington (MCA)
3	2	WHEN I NEED YOU — Leo Sayer (Chrysalis)
2	3	DON'T GIVE UP ON US — David Soul (Private Stock)
9	4	DON'T LEAVE ME THIS WAY — Harold Melvin & the Blue Notes (CBS)
4	5	SIDE SHOW — Barry Biggs (Dynamic)
5	6	DADDY COOL — Boney M (Atlantic)
6	7	ISN'T SHE LOVELY — David Parton (Pye)
11	8	JACK IN THE BOX — Moments (All Platinum)
14	9	BOOGIE NIGHTS — Heatwave (GTO)
22	10	CHANSON D' AMOUR — Manhattan Transfer (Atlantic)
10	11	CAR WASH — Rose Royce (MCA)
7	12	SUSPICION — Elvis Presley (RCA)
17	13	SING ME — Brothers (Bus Stop)
15	14	WILD SIDE OF LIFE — Status Quo (Vertigo)
8	15	YOU'RE MORE THAN A NUMBER IN MY LITTLE RED BOOK — Drifters (Arista)
-	16	THIS IS TOMORROW — Bryan Ferry (Polydor)
-	17	ROMEO — Mr Big (EMI)
20	18	DON'T LEAVE ME THIS WAY — Thelma Houston (Motown)
12	19	DON'T BELIEVE A WORD — Thin Lizzy (Vertigo)
13	20	I WISH — Stevie Wonder (Motown)
18	21	NEW KID IN TOWN — Eagles (Asylum)
26	22	MORE THAN A FEELING — Boston (EMI)
-	23	THEY SHOOT HORSES DON'T THEY — Racing Cars (Chrysalis)
24	24	EVERY MAN MUST HAVE A DREAM — Liverpool Express (Warner Bros)
21	25	WHAT CAN I SAY — Boz Scaggs (CBS)
19	26	IT TAKES ALL NIGHT LONG — Gary Glitter (Arista)
16	27	THINGS WE DO FOR LOVE — 10 c.c. (Mercury)
-	28	I WANNA GO BACK — New Seekers (CBS)
-	29	SOUND AND VISION — David Bowie (RCA)
27	30	YEAR OF THE CAT — Al Stewart (RCA)

26 February 1977

last week	this week	
2	1	WHEN I NEED YOU — Leo Sayer (Chrysalis)
3	2	DON'T GIVE UP ON US — David Soul (Private Stock)
1	3	DON'T CRY FOR ME ARGENTINA — Julie Covington (MCA)
9	4	BOOGIE NIGHTS — Heatwave (GTO)
10	5	CHANSON D' AMOUR — Manhattan Transfer (Atlantic)
4	6	DON'T LEAVE ME THIS WAY — Harold Melvin & the Blue Notes (CBS)
8	7	JACK IN THE BOX — Moments (All Platinum)
5	8	SIDE SHOW — Barry Biggs (Dynamic)
17	9	ROMEO — Mr Big (EMI)
13	10	SING ME — Brothers (Bus Stop)
6	11	DADDY COOL — Boney M (Atlantic)
7	12	ISN'T SHE LOVELY — David Parton (Pye)
16	13	THIS IS TOMORROW — Bryan Ferry (Polydor)
18	14	DON'T LEAVE ME THIS WAY — Thelma Houston (Motown)
12	15	SUSPICION — Elvis Presley (RCA)
23	16	THEY SHOOT HORSES DON'T THEY — Racing Cars (Chrysalis)
11	17	CAR WASH — Rose Royce (MCA)
-	18	TORN BETWEEN TWO LOVERS — Mary MacGregor (Ariola)
25	19	WHAT CAN I SAY — Boz Scaggs (CBS)
-	20	BABY I KNOW — Rubettes (State)
15	21	YOU'RE MORE THAN A NUMBER IN MY LITTLE RED BOOK — Drifters (Arista)
-	22	SATURDAY NITE — Earth Wind & Fire (CBS)
19	23	DON'T BELIEVE A WORD — Thin Lizzy (Vertigo)
29	24	SOUND AND VISION — David Bowie (RCA)
22	25	MORE THAN A FEELING — Boston (EMI)
-	26	ROCKARIA — Electric Light Orchestra (Jet)
-	27	YOU'LL NEVER KNOW WHAT YOU'RE MISSING — Real Thing (Pye)
-	28	MIGHTY POWER OF LOVE — Tavares (Capitol)
-	29	GO YOUR OWN WAY — Fleetwood Mac (Warner Bros)
21	30	NEW KID IN TOWN — Eagles (Asylum)

Julie Covington's hit was the public's first taste of Tim Rice and Andrew Lloyd-Webber's *Evita* – it came froom the album version with assorted guest singers, which preceded the stage show. It also became the biggest selling single yet in Britain by a solo female singer. Barry Biggs' *Side Show* was a reggae adaptation of a US million-seller by soul group Blue Magic. Elvis's *Suspicion* was a 1962 album track, and Harold Melvin's top tenner was also a re-issue – Thelma Houston's cover was new.

last week	this week	5 March 1977
1	1	WHEN I NEED YOU — Leo Sayer (Chrysalis)
4	2	BOOGIE NIGHTS — Heatwave (GTO)
5	3	CHANSON D' AMOUR — Manhattan Transfer (Atlantic)
3	4	DON'T CRY FOR ME ARGENTINA — Julie Covington (MCA)
9	5	ROMEO — Mr Big (EMI)
7	6	JACK IN THE BOX — Moments (All Platinum)
2	7	DON'T GIVE UP ON US — David Soul (Private Stock)
6	8	DON'T LEAVE ME THIS WAY — Harold Melvin & the Blue Notes (CBS)
13	9	THIS IS TOMORROW — Bryan Ferry (Polydor)
18	10	TORN BETWEEN TWO LOVERS — Mary MacGregor (Ariola)
10	11	SING ME — Brothers (Bus Stop)
24	12	SOUND AND VISION — David Bowie (RCA)
16	13	THEY SHOOT HORSES DON'T THEY — Racing Cars (Chrysalis)
19	14	WHAT CAN I SAY — Boz Scaggs (CBS)
8	15	SIDE SHOW — Barry Biggs (Dynamic)
14	16	DON'T LEAVE ME THIS WAY — Thelma Houston (Motown)
20	17	BABY I KNOW — Rubettes (State)
11	18	DADDY COOL — Boney M (Atlantic)
22	19	SATURDAY NITE — Earth Wind & Fire (CBS)
26	20	ROCKARIA — Electric Light Orchestra (Jet)
-	21	KNOWING ME KNOWING YOU — Abba (Epic)
25	22	MORE THAN A FEELING — Boston (EMI)
17	23	CAR WASH — Rose Royce (MCA)
28	24	MIGHTY POWER OF LOVE — Tavares (Capitol)
29	25	GO YOUR OWN WAY — Fleetwood Mac (Warner Bros)
-	26	DARLIN' DARLIN' BABY — O'Jays (Philadelphia)
-	27	MAYBE I'M AMAZED — Wings (Parlophone)
12	28	ISN'T SHE LOVELY — David Parton (Pye)
27	29	YOU'LL NEVER KNOW WHAT YOU'RE MISSING — Real Thing (Pye)
15	30	SUSPICION — Elvis Presley (RCA)

last week	this week	12 March 1977
3	1	CHANSON D' AMOUR — Manhattan Transfer (Atlantic)
1	2	WHEN I NEED YOU — Leo Sayer (Chrysalis)
2	3	BOOGIE NIGHTS — Heatwave (GTO)
5	4	ROMEO — Mr Big (EMI)
10	5	TORN BETWEEN TWO LOVERS — Mary MacGregor (Ariola)
12	6	SOUND AND VISION — David Bowie (RCA)
4	7	DON'T CRY FOR ME ARGENTINA — Julie Covington (MCA)
21	8	KNOWING ME KNOWING YOU — Abba (Epic)
8	9	DON'T LEAVE ME THIS WAY — Harold Melvin & the Blue Notes (CBS)
11	10	SING ME — Brothers (Bus Stop)
14	11	WHAT CAN I SAY — Boz Scaggs (CBS)
9	12	THIS IS TOMORROW — Bryan Ferry (Polydor)
7	13	DON'T GIVE UP ON US — David Soul (Private Stock)
6	14	JACK IN THE BOX — Moments (All Platinum)
13	15	THEY SHOOT HORSES DON'T THEY — Racing Cars (Chrysalis)
20	16	ROCKARIA — Electric Light Orchestra (Jet)
16	17	DON'T LEAVE ME THIS WAY — Thelma Houston (Motown)
-	18	WHEN — Showaddywaddy (Arista)
17	19	BABY I KNOW — Rubettes (State)
19	20	SATURDAY NITE — Earth Wind & Fire (CBS)
-	21	MOODY BLUE — Elvis Presley (RCA)
-	22	ANOTHER SUITCASE IN ANOTHER HALL — Barbara Dickson (MCA)
-	23	MY KINDA LIFE — Cliff Richard (EMI)
-	24	TEAR ME APART — Suzi Quatro (Rak)
15	25	SIDE SHOW — Barry Biggs (Dynamic)
-	26	CRAZY WATER — Elton John (Rocket)
27	27	MAYBE I'M AMAZED — Wings (Parlophone)
-	28	IN THE MOOD — Ray Stevens (Warner Bros)
-	29	I'M QUALIFIED TO SATISFY — Barry White (20th Century)
29	30	YOU'LL NEVER KNOW WHAT YOU'RE MISSING — Real Thing (Pye)

last week	this week	19 March 1977
1	1	CHANSON D' AMOUR — Manhattan Transfer (Atlantic)
3	2	BOOGIE NIGHTS — Heatwave (GTO)
8	3	KNOWING ME KNOWING YOU — Abba (Epic)
5	4	TORN BETWEEN TWO LOVERS — Mary MacGregor (Ariola)
2	5	WHEN I NEED YOU — Leo Sayer (Chrysalis)
6	6	SOUND AND VISION — David Bowie (RCA)
4	7	ROMEO — Mr Big (EMI)
18	8	WHEN — Showaddywaddy (Arista)
12	9	THIS IS TOMORROW — Bryan Ferry (Polydor)
19	10	BABY I KNOW — Rubettes (State)
16	11	ROCKARIA — Electric Light Orchestra (Jet)
21	12	MOODY BLUE — Elvis Presley (RCA)
11	13	WHAT CAN I SAY — Boz Scaggs (CBS)
9	14	DON'T LEAVE ME THIS WAY — Harold Melvin & the Blue Notes (CBS)
7	15	DON'T CRY FOR ME ARGENTINA — Julie Covington (MCA)
22	16	ANOTHER SUITCASE IN ANOTHER HALL — Barbara Dickson (MCA)
10	17	SING ME — Brothers (Bus Stop)
17	18	DON'T LEAVE ME THIS WAY — Thelma Houston (Motown)
13	19	DON'T GIVE UP ON US — David Soul (Private Stock)
20	20	SATURDAY NITE — Earth Wind & Fire (CBS)
30	21	YOU'LL NEVER KNOW WHAT YOU'RE MISSING — Real Thing (Pye)
28	22	IN THE MOOD — Ray Stevens (Warner Bros)
26	23	CRAZY WATER — Elton John (Rocket)
14	24	JACK IN THE BOX — Moments (All Platinum)
23	25	MY KINDA LIFE — Cliff Richard (EMI)
-	26	OH BOY (THE SHAPE I'M IN) — Brotherhood of Man (Pye)
15	27	THEY SHOOT HORSES DON'T THEY — Racing Cars (Chrysalis)
-	28	SUNNY — Boney M (Atlantic)
-	29	LOVE HIT ME — Maxine Nightingale (United Artists)
-	30	LAY BACK IN THE ARMS OF SOMEONE — Smokie (Rak)

last week	this week	26 March 1977
3	1	KNOWING ME KNOWING YOU — Abba (Epic)
1	2	CHANSON D' AMOUR — Manhattan Transfer (Atlantic)
8	3	WHEN — Showaddywaddy (Arista)
6	4	SOUND AND VISION — David Bowie (RCA)
12	5	MOODY BLUE — Elvis Presley (RCA)
2	6	BOOGIE NIGHTS — Heatwave (GTO)
4	7	TORN BETWEEN TWO LOVERS — Mary MacGregor (Ariola)
-	8	GOING IN WITH MY EYES OPEN — David Soul (Private Stock)
11	9	ROCKARIA — Electric Light Orchestra (Jet)
7	10	ROMEO — Mr Big (EMI)
25	11	MY KINDA LIFE — Cliff Richard (EMI)
28	12	SUNNY — Boney M (Atlantic)
-	13	I DON'T WANT TO PUT A HOLD ON YOU — Berni Flint (EMI)
10	14	BABY I KNOW — Rubettes (State)
29	15	LOVE HIT ME — Maxine Nightingale (United Artists)
9	16	THIS IS TOMORROW — Bryan Ferry (Polydor)
13	17	WHAT CAN I SAY — Boz Scaggs (CBS)
26	18	OH BOY (THE SHAPE I'M IN) — Brotherhood of Man (Pye)
-	19	RED LIGHT SPELLS DANGER — Billy Ocean (GTO)
20	20	SATURDAY NITE — Earth Wind & Fire (CBS)
18	21	DON'T LEAVE ME THIS WAY — Thelma Houston (Motown)
-	22	LOVE IN C MINOR — Cerrone (Atlantic)
17	23	SING ME — Brothers (Bus Stop)
30	24	LAY BACK IN THE ARMS OF SOMEONE — Smokie (Rak)
-	25	TIE YOUR MOTHER DOWN — Queen (EMI)
23	26	CRAZY WATER — Elton John (Rocket)
-	27	YOU DON'T HAVE TO BE A STAR — Marilyn McCoo /Billy Davis Jr (ABC)
19	28	DON'T GIVE UP ON US — David Soul (Private Stock)
-	29	HOLD BACK THE NIGHT — Graham Parker & the Rumour (Vertigo)
-	30	MORE THAN A LOVER — Bonnie Tyler (RCA)

An American group singing in French were succeeded atop the British chart by a Swedish group singing in English. Showaddywaddy revived the Kalin Twins' 1958 chart-topper *When*, and Boney M covered Bobby Hebb's *Sunny* from 1966, while Ray Stevens' version of the standard *In The Mood* was eccentric even by his standards. Barbara Dickson's *Another Suitcase In Another Hall* was the second extract from Evita. Chart newcomer Berni Flint was a winner from TV's *New Faces* talent show.

April 1977

2 April 1977

LW	TW	Title
1	1	KNOWING ME KNOWING YOU — Abba (Epic)
8	2	GOING IN WITH MY EYES OPEN — David Soul (Private Stock)
2	3	CHANSON D' AMOUR — Manhattan Transfer (Atlantic)
3	4	WHEN — Showaddywaddy (Arista)
4	5	SOUND AND VISION — David Bowie (RCA)
13	6	I DON'T WANT TO PUT A HOLD ON YOU — Bernie Flint (EMI)
7	7	TORN BETWEEN TWO LOVERS — Mary MacGregor (Ariola)
5	8	MOODY BLUE — Elvis Presley (RCA)
12	9	SUNNY — Boney M (Atlantic)
18	10	OH BOY (THE SHAPE I'M IN) — Brotherhood of Man (Pye)
6	11	BOOGIE NIGHTS — Heatwave (GTO)
19	12	RED LIGHT SPELLS DANGER — Billy Ocean (GTO)
9	13	ROCKARIA — Electric Light Orchestra (Jet)
27	14	YOU DON'T HAVE TO BE A STAR — Marilyn McCoo/ Billy Davis Jr (ABC)
15	15	LOVE HIT ME — Maxine Nightingale (United Artists)
24	16	LAY BACK IN THE ARMS OF SOMEONE — Smokie (Rak)
29	17	HOLD BACK THE NIGHT — Graham Parker & the Rumour (Vertigo)
10	18	ROMEO — Mr Big (EMI)
14	19	BABY I KNOW — Rubettes (State)
-	20	WHEN I NEED YOU — Leo Sayer (Chrysalis)
-	21	YOU'LL NEVER KNOW WHAT YOU'RE MISSING — Real Thing (Pye)
11	22	MY KINDA LIFE — Cliff Richard (EMI)
-	23	GIMME SOME — Brendon (Magnet)
-	24	TOGETHER — O C Smith (Caribou)
-	25	ANOTHER SUITCASE IN ANOTHER HALL — Barbara Dickson (MCA)
-	26	HAVE I THE RIGHT — Dead End Kids (CBS)
30	27	MORE THAN A LOVER — Bonnie Tyler (RCA)
-	28	RIO — Michael Nesmith (Island)
20	29	SATURDAY NITE — Earth Wind & Fire (CBS)
26	30	CRAZY WATER — Elton John (Rocket)

9 April 1977

LW	TW	Title
1	1	KNOWING ME KNOWING YOU — Abba (Epic)
2	2	GOING IN WITH MY EYES OPEN — David Soul (Private Stock)
3	3	CHANSON D' AMOUR — Manhattan Transfer (Atlantic)
6	4	I DON'T WANT TO PUT A HOLD ON YOU — Bernie Flint (EMI)
4	5	WHEN — Showaddywaddy (Arista)
8	6	MOODY BLUE — Elvis Presley (RCA)
9	7	SUNNY — Boney M (Atlantic)
5	8	SOUND AND VISION — David Bowie (RCA)
10	9	OH BOY (THE SHAPE I'M IN) — Brotherhood of Man (Pye)
12	10	RED LIGHT SPELLS DANGER — Billy Ocean (GTO)
7	11	TORN BETWEEN TWO LOVERS — Mary MacGregor (Ariola)
16	12	LAY BACK IN THE ARMS OF SOMEONE — Smokie (Rak)
14	13	YOU DON'T HAVE TO BE A STAR — Marilyn McCoo/ Billy Davis Jr (ABC)
15	14	LOVE HIT ME — Maxine Nightingale (United Artists)
11	15	BOOGIE NIGHTS — Heatwave (GTO)
22	16	MY KINDA LIFE — Cliff Richard (EMI)
-	17	FREE — Deniece Williams (CBS)
-	18	I WANNA GET NEXT TO YOU — Rose Royce (MCA)
-	19	ROCK BOTTOM — Lynsey de Paul/Mike Moran (Polydor)
13	20	ROCKARIA — Electric Light Orchestra (Jet)
24	21	TOGETHER — O C Smith (Caribou)
17	22	HOLD BACK THE NIGHT — Graham Parker & the Rumour (Vertigo)
18	23	ROMEO — Mr Big (EMI)
23	24	GIMME SOME — Brendon (Magnet)
28	25	RIO — Michael Nesmith (Island)
27	26	MORE THAN A LOVER — Bonnie Tyler (RCA)
-	27	SOUTHERN NIGHTS — Glen Campbell (Capitol)
-	28	HOW MUCH LOVE — Leo Sayer (Chrysalis)
-	29	WHITE RIOT — The Clash (CBS)
-	30	PEARL'S A SINGER — Elkie Brooks (A&M)

16 April 1977

LW	TW	Title
1	1	KNOWING ME KNOWING YOU — Abba (Epic)
2	2	GOING IN WITH MY EYES OPEN — David Soul (Private Stock)
5	3	WHEN — Showaddywaddy (Arista)
10	4	RED LIGHT SPELLS DANGER — Billy Ocean (GTO)
8	5	SOUND AND VISION — David Bowie (RCA)
4	6	I DON'T WANT TO PUT A HOLD ON YOU — Bernie Flint (EMI)
17	7	FREE — Deniece Williams (CBS)
13	8	YOU DON'T HAVE TO BE A STAR — Marilyn McCoo/ Billy Davis Jr (ABC)
7	9	SUNNY — Boney M (Atlantic)
3	10	CHANSON D' AMOUR — Manhattan Transfer (Atlantic)
9	11	OH BOY (THE SHAPE I'M IN) — Brotherhood of Man (Pye)
12	12	LAY BACK IN THE ARMS OF SOMEONE — Smokie (Rak)
6	13	MOODY BLUE — Elvis Presley (RCA)
30	14	PEARL'S A SINGER — Elkie Brooks (A&M)
14	15	LOVE HIT ME — Maxine Nightingale (United Artists)
-	16	LONELY BOY — Andrew Gold (Asylum)
-	17	SIR DUKE — Stevie Wonder (Motown)
21	18	TOGETHER — O C Smith (Caribou)
-	19	WHODUNIT — Tavares (Capitol)
-	20	HAVE I THE RIGHT — Dead End Kids (BDS)
19	21	ROCK BOTTOM — Lynsey de Paul/Mike Moran (Polydor)
24	22	GIMME SOME — Brendon (Magnet)
16	23	MY KINDA LIFE — Cliff Richard (EMI)
18	24	I WANNA GET NEXT TO YOU — Rose Royce (MCA)
28	25	HOW MUCH LOVE — Leo Sayer (Chrysalis)
-	26	SOLSBURY HILL — Peter Gabriel (Charisma)
11	27	TORN BETWEEN TWO LOVERS — Mary MacGregor (Ariola)
27	28	SOUTHERN NIGHTS — Glen Campbell (Capitol)
-	29	THE SHUFFLE — Van McCoy (H&L)
-	30	LOVE THEME FROM A STAR IS BORN (EVERGREEN) — Barbra Streisand (CBS)

23 April 1977

LW	TW	Title
1	1	KNOWING ME KNOWING YOU — Abba (Epic)
2	2	GOING IN WITH MY EYES OPEN — David Soul (Private Stock)
9	3	SUNNY — Boney M (Atlantic)
3	4	WHEN — Showaddywaddy (Arista)
4	5	RED LIGHT SPELLS DANGER — Billy Ocean (GTO)
17	6	SIR DUKE — Stevie Wonder (Motown)
7	7	FREE — Deniece Williams (CBS)
6	8	I DON'T WANT TO PUT A HOLD ON YOU — Bernie Flint (EMI)
8	9	YOU DON'T HAVE TO BE A STAR — Marilyn McCoo/ Billy Davis Jr (ABC)
11	10	OH BOY (THE SHAPE I'M IN) — Brotherhood of Man (Pye)
25	11	HOW MUCH LOVE — Leo Sayer (Chrysalis)
12	12	LAY BACK IN THE ARMS OF SOMEONE — Smokie (Rak)
13	13	MOODY BLUE — Elvis Presley (RCA)
14	14	PEARL'S A SINGER — Elkie Brooks (A&M)
16	15	LONELY BOY — Andrew Gold (Asylum)
19	16	WHODUNIT — Tavares (Capitol)
5	17	SOUND AND VISION — David Bowie (RCA)
26	18	SOLSBURY HILL — Peter Gabriel (Charisma)
24	19	I WANNA GET NEXT TO YOU — Rose Royce (MCA)
10	20	CHANSON D' AMOUR — Manhattan Transfer (Atlantic)
20	21	HAVE I THE RIGHT — Dead End Kids (CBS)
22	22	GIMME SOME — Brendon (Magnet)
15	23	LOVE HIT ME — Maxine Nightingale (United Artists)
-	24	HOTEL CALIFORNIA — Eagles (Asylum)
29	25	THE SHUFFLE — Van McCoy (H&L)
-	26	MARQUEE MOON — Television (Elektra)
-	27	SMOKE ON THE WATER — Deep Purple (Purple)
27	28	TORN BETWEEN TWO LOVERS — Mary MacGregor (Ariola)
30	29	LOVE THEME FROM A STAR IS BORN (EVERGREEN) — Barbra Streisand (CBS)
18	30	TOGETHER — O C Smith (Caribou)

After winning the previous year's competition, Britain's 1977 stab at the Eurovision Song Contest was Lynsey De Paul & Mike Moran's duet *Rock Bottom*, which proved only moderately successful both at Eurovision and in the chart. Despite public clamour Stevie Wonder refused to allow his original version of *Isn't She Lovely* to be lifted from the *Songs In The Key Of Life* album, and its first single was *Sir Duke*, a jazz-flavoured tribute to Duke Ellington, which made Number Two here and One in the US.

30 April 1977

last week	this week	
1	1	KNOWING ME KNOWING YOU Abba (Epic)
7	2	FREE Deniece Williams (CBS)
5	3	RED LIGHT SPELLS DANGER Billy Ocean (GTO)
21	4	HAVE I THE RIGHT Dead End Kids (CBS)
8	5	I DON'T WANT TO PUT A HOLD ON YOU Berni Flint (EMI)
6	6	SIR DUKE Stevie Wonder (Motown)
14	7	PEARL'S A SINGER Elkie Brooks (A&M)
4	8	WHEN Showaddywaddy (Arista)
2	9	GOING IN WITH MY EYES OPEN David Soul (Private Stock)
16	10	WHODUNIT Tavares (Capitol)
11	11	HOW MUCH LOVE Leo Sayer (Chrysalis)
3	12	SUNNY Boney M (Atlantic)
9	13	YOU DON'T HAVE TO BE A STAR Marilyn McCoo/ Billy Davis Jr (ABC)
15	14	LONELY BOY Andrew Gold (Asylum)
10	15	OH BOY (THE SHAPE I'M IN) Brotherhood of Man (Pye)
-	16	AIN'T GONNA BUMP NO MORE Joe Tex (Epic)
12	17	LAY BACK IN THE ARMS OF SOMEONE Smokie (Rak)
18	18	SOLSBURY HILL Peter Gabriel (Charisma)
24	19	HOTEL CALIFORNIA Eagles (Asylum)
-	20	I DON'T WANT TO TALK ABOUT IT/THE FIRST CUT IS THE DEEPEST Rod Stewart (Riva)
25	21	THE SHUFFLE Van McCoy (H&L)
17	22	SOUND AND VISION David Bowie (RCA)
22	23	GIMME SOME Brendon (Magnet)
30	24	TOGETHER O C Smith (Caribou)
29	25	LOVE THEME FROM A STAR IS BORN (EVERGREEN) Barbra Streisand (CBS)
27	26	SMOKE ON THE WATER Deep Purple (Purple)
-	27	ANOTHER FUNNY HONEYMOON David Dundas (Air)
-	28	GOOD MORNING JUDGE 10 c.c. (Philips)
-	29	SOUTHERN NIGHTS Glen Campbell (Capitol)
-	30	ROCK BOTTOM Lynsey De Paul & Mike Moran (Polydor)

7 May 1977

2	1	FREE Deniece Williams (CBS)
6	2	SIR DUKE Stevie Wonder (Motown)
1	3	KNOWING ME KNOWING YOU Abba (Epic)
4	4	HAVE I THE RIGHT Dead End Kids (CBS)
3	5	RED LIGHT SPELLS DANGER Billy Ocean (GTO)
20	6	I DON'T WANT TO TALK ABOUT IT/THE FIRST CUT IS THE DEEPEST Rod Stewart (Riva)
7	7	PEARL'S A SINGER Elkie Brooks (A&M)
10	8	WHODUNIT Tavares (Capitol)
19	9	HOTEL CALIFORNIA Eagles (Asylum)
16	10	AIN'T GONNA BUMP NO MORE Joe Tex (Epic)
-	11	I WANNA GET NEXT TO YOU Rose Royce (MCA)
21	12	THE SHUFFLE Van McCoy (H&L)
18	13	SOLSBURY HILL Peter Gabriel (Charisma)
13	14	YOU DON'T HAVE TO BE A STAR Marilyn McCoo/ Billy Davis Jr (ABC)
25	15	LOVE THEME FROM A STAR IS BORN (EVERGREEN) Barbra Streisand (CBS)
5	16	I DON'T WANT TO PUT A HOLD ON YOU Berni Flint (EMI)
14	17	LONELY BOY Andrew Gold (Asylum)
12	18	SUNNY Boney M (Atlantic)
28	19	GOOD MORNING JUDGE 10 c.c. (Philips)
26	20	SMOKE ON THE WATER Deep Purple (Purple)
9	21	GOING IN WITH MY EYES OPEN David Soul (Private Stock)
15	22	OH BOY (THE SHAPE I'M IN) Brotherhood of Man (Pye)
11	23	HOW MUCH LOVE Leo Sayer (Chrysalis)
-	24	LUCILLE Kenny Rogers (United Artists)
-	25	GONNA CAPTURE YOUR HEART Blue (Rocket)
17	26	LAY BACK IN THE ARMS OF SOMEONE Smokie (Rak)
8	27	WHEN Showaddywaddy (Arista)
-	28	MAH NA MAH NA Piero Umiliani (EMI Int)
-	29	LET 'EM IN Billy Paul (Philadelphia)
-	30	DON'T STOP Fleetwood Mac (Warner Bros)

14 May 1977

1	1	FREE Deniece Williams (CBS)
6	2	I DON'T WANT TO TALK ABOUT IT/THE FIRST CUT IS THE DEEPEST Rod Stewart (Riva)
2	3	SIR DUKE Stevie Wonder (Motown)
8	4	WHODUNIT Tavares (Capitol)
10	5	AIN'T GONNA BUMP NO MORE Joe Tex (Epic)
12	6	THE SHUFFLE Van McCoy (H&L)
15	7	LOVE THEME FROM A STAR IS BORN (EVERGREEN) Barbra Streisand (CBS)
9	8	HOTEL CALIFORNIA Eagles (Asylum)
5	9	RED LIGHT SPELLS DANGER Billy Ocean (GTO)
23	10	HOW MUCH LOVE Leo Sayer (Chrysalis)
4	11	HAVE I THE RIGHT Dead End Kids (CBS)
19	12	GOOD MORNING JUDGE 10 c.c. (Philips)
24	13	LUCILLE Kenny Rogers (United Artists)
28	14	MAH NA MAH NA Piero Umiliani (EMI Int)
17	15	LONELY BOY Andrew Gold (Asylum)
7	16	PEARL'S A SINGER Elkie Brooks (A&M)
-	17	GOT TO GIVE IT UP Marvin Gaye (Motown)
3	18	KNOWING ME KNOWING YOU Abba (Epic)
20	19	SMOKE ON THE WATER Deep Purple (Purple)
13	20	SOLSBURY HILL Peter Gabriel (Charisma)
16	21	I DON'T WANT TO PUT A HOLD ON YOU Berni Flint (EMI)
29	22	LET 'EM IN Billy Paul (Philadelphia)
-	23	TOO HOT TO HANDLE/SLIP YOUR DISC TO THIS Heatwave (GTO)
-	24	WHERE IS THE LOVE Delegation (State)
-	25	COULD IT BE I'M FALLING IN LOVE Detroit Spinners (Atlantic)
-	26	IT'S A GAME Bay City Rollers (Arista)
14	27	YOU DON'T HAVE TO BE A STAR Marilyn McCoo/ Billy Davis Jr (ABC)
30	28	DON'T STOP Fleetwood Mac (Warner Bros)
11	29	I WANNA GET NEXT TO YOU Rose Royce (MCA)
-	30	NAUGHTY NAUGHTY NAUGHTY Joy Sarney (Alaska)

21 May 1977

1	1	FREE Deniece Williams (CBS)
2	2	I DON'T WANT TO TALK ABOUT IT/THE FIRST CUT IS THE DEEPEST Rod Stewart (Riva)
5	3	AIN'T GONNA BUMP NO MORE Joe Tex (Epic)
6	4	THE SHUFFLE Van McCoy (H&L)
12	5	GOOD MORNING JUDGE 10 c.c. (Philips)
8	6	HOTEL CALIFORNIA Eagles (Asylum)
7	7	LOVE THEME FROM A STAR IS BORN (EVERGREEN) Barbra Streisand (CBS)
3	8	SIR DUKE Stevie Wonder (Motown)
14	9	MAH NA MAH NA Piero Umiliani (EMI Int)
13	10	LUCILLE Kenny Rogers (United Artists)
4	11	WHODUNIT Tavares (Capitol)
17	12	GOT TO GIVE IT UP Marvin Gaye (Motown)
20	13	SOLSBURY HILL Peter Gabriel (Charisma)
16	14	PEARL'S A SINGER Elkie Brooks (A&M)
26	15	IT'S A GAME Bay City Rollers (Arista)
11	16	HAVE I THE RIGHT Dead End Kids (CBS)
23	17	TOO HOT TO HANDLE/SLIP YOUR DISC TO THIS Heatwave (GTO)
22	18	LET 'EM IN Billy Paul (Philadelphia)
15	19	LONELY BOY Andrew Gold (Asylum)
18	20	KNOWING ME KNOWING YOU Abba (Epic)
-	21	LIDO SHUFFLE Boz Scaggs (CBS)
29	22	I WANNA GET NEXT TO YOU Rose Royce (MCA)
19	23	SMOKE ON THE WATER Deep Purple (Purple)
24	24	WHERE IS THE LOVE Delegation (State)
28	25	DON'T STOP Fleetwood Mac (Warner Bros)
9	26	RED LIGHT SPELLS DANGER Billy Ocean (GTO)
-	27	TOKYO JOE Bryan Ferry (Polydor)
-	28	GONNA CAPTURE YOUR HEART Blue (Rocket)
-	29	UPTOWN FESTIVAL Shalamar (RCA)
10	30	HOW MUCH LOVE Leo Sayer (Chrysalis)

One of the oddest hit records ever, Piero Umiliani's *Mah Na Mah Na*, a wordless vocal over an insidiously catchy rhythm track, was first issued on record in the early seventies when it was used on the soundtrack of a film titled *Sweden, Heaven And Hell*. The 1977 re-issue came about after it was revived in television's *The Muppet Show* as the regular backing music to a dance scene; interest from this exposure was the major factor in making the single a Top 10 hit.

May – June 1977

28 May 1977

last week	this week	title
2	1	I DON'T WANT TO TALK ABOUT IT/THE FIRST CUT IS THE DEEPEST Rod Stewart (Riva)
3	2	AIN'T GONNA BUMP NO MORE Joe Tex (Epic)
4	3	THE SHUFFLE Van McCoy (H&L)
7	4	LOVE THEME FROM A STAR IS BORN (EVERGREEN) Barbra Streisand (CBS)
10	5	LUCILLE Kenny Rogers (United Artists)
12	6	GOT TO GIVE IT UP Marvin Gaye (Motown)
5	7	GOOD MORNING JUDGE 10 c.c. (Philips)
1	8	FREE Deniece Williams (CBS)
9	9	MAH NA MAH NA Piero Umiliani (EMI Int)
6	10	HOTEL CALIFORNIA Eagles (Asylum)
21	11	LIDO SHUFFLE Boz Scaggs (CBS)
8	12	SIR DUKE Stevie Wonder (Motown)
11	13	WHODUNIT Tavares (Capitol)
17	14	TOO HOT TO HANDLE/SLIP YOUR DISC TO THIS Heatwave (GTO)
-	15	DISCO INFERNO Trammps (Atlantic)
13	16	SOLSBURY HILL Peter Gabriel (Charisma)
27	17	TOKYO JOE Bryan Ferry (Polydor)
-	18	O.K. Rock Follies (Polydor)
15	19	IT'S A GAME Bay City Rollers (Arista)
28	20	GONNA CAPTURE YOUR HEART Blue (Rocket)
24	21	WHERE IS THE LOVE Delegation (State)
-	22	HELLO STRANGER Yvonne Elliman (RSO)
-	23	TELEPHONE LINE Electric Light Orchestra (Jet)
-	24	PEACHES/GO BUDDY GO Stranglers (United Artists)
-	25	SHEENA IS A PUNK ROCKER Ramones (Sire)
30	26	HOW MUCH LOVE Leo Sayer (Chrysalis)
19	27	LONELY BOY Andrew Gold (Asylum)
16	28	HAVE I THE RIGHT Dead End Kids (CBS)
-	29	FEEL LIKE CALLING HOME Mr Big (EMI)
14	30	PEARL'S A SINGER Elkie Brooks (A&M)

4 June 1977

last week	this week	title
1	1	I DON'T WANT TO TALK ABOUT IT/THE FIRST CUT IS THE DEEPEST Rod Stewart (Riva)
2	2	AIN'T GONNA BUMP NO MORE Joe Tex (Epic)
5	3	LUCILLE Kenny Rogers (United Artists)
4	4	LOVE THEME FROM A STAR IS BORN (EVERGREEN) Barbra Streisand (CBS)
3	5	THE SHUFFLE Van McCoy (H&L)
6	6	GOT TO GIVE IT UP Marvin Gaye (Motown)
18	7	O.K. Rock Follies (Polydor)
7	8	GOOD MORNING JUDGE 10 c.c. (Philips)
-	9	HALFWAY DOWN THE STAIRS Muppets (Pye)
9	10	MAH NA MAH NA Piero Umiliani (EMI Int)
10	11	HOTEL CALIFORNIA Eagles (Asylum)
17	12	TOKYO JOE Bryan Ferry (Polydor)
-	13	WE CAN DO IT Liverpool Football Team (State)
8	14	FREE Deniece Williams (CBS)
11	15	LIDO SHUFFLE Boz Scaggs (CBS)
15	16	DISCO INFERNO Trammps (Atlantic)
23	17	TELEPHONE LINE Electric Light Orchestra (Jet)
12	18	SIR DUKE Stevie Wonder (Motown)
-	19	YOU'RE MOVING OUT TODAY Carole Bayer Sager (Elektra)
-	20	BABY DON'T CHANGE YOUR MIND Gladys Knight & the Pips (Buddah)
25	21	SHEENA IS A PUNK ROCKER Ramones (Sire)
20	22	GONNA CAPTURE YOUR HEART Blue (Rocket)
14	23	TOO HOT TO HANDLE/SLIP YOUR DISC TO THIS Heatwave (GTO)
19	24	IT'S A GAME Bay City Rollers (Arista)
13	25	WHODUNIT Tavares (Capitol)
24	26	PEACHES/GO BUDDY GO Stranglers (United Artists)
-	27	GOD SAVE THE QUEEN Sex Pistols (Virgin)
-	28	SPOT THE PIGEON (EP) Genesis (Charisma)
-	29	UPTOWN FESTIVAL Shalamar (RCA)
-	30	CALENDAR SONG Trinidad Oil Company (Harvest)

11 June 1977

last week	this week	title
1	1	I DON'T WANT TO TALK ABOUT IT/THE FIRST CUT IS THE DEEPEST Rod Stewart (Riva)
3	2	LUCILLE Kenny Rogers (United Artists)
4	3	LOVE THEME FROM A STAR IS BORN (EVERGREEN) Barbra Streisand (CBS)
2	4	AIN'T GONNA BUMP NO MORE Joe Tex (Epic)
9	5	HALFWAY DOWN THE STAIRS Muppets (Pye)
27	6	GOD SAVE THE QUEEN Sex Pistols (Virgin)
5	7	THE SHUFFLE Van McCoy (H&L)
8	8	GOOD MORNING JUDGE 10 c.c. (Philips)
19	9	YOU'RE MOVING OUT TODAY Carole Bayer Sager (Elektra)
6	10	GOT TO GIVE IT UP Marvin Gaye (Motown)
17	11	TELEPHONE LINE Electric Light Orchestra (Jet)
7	12	O.K. Rock Follies (Polydor)
-	13	SHOW YOU THE WAY TO GO Jacksons (Epic)
15	14	LIDO SHUFFLE Boz Scaggs (CBS)
28	15	SPOT THE PIGEON (EP) Genesis (Charisma)
20	16	BABY DON'T CHANGE YOUR MIND Gladys Knight & the Pips (Buddah)
23	17	TOO HOT TO HANDLE/SLIP YOUR DISC TO THIS Heatwave (GTO)
26	18	PEACHES/GO BUDDY GO Stranglers (United Artists)
10	19	MAH NA MAH NA Piero Umiliani (EMI Int)
-	20	GOOD OLD FASHIONED LOVERBOY Queen (EMI)
13	21	WE CAN DO IT Liverpool Football Team (State)
11	22	HOTEL CALIFORNIA Eagles (Asylum)
-	23	NATURE BOY George Benson (Warner Bros)
-	24	FANFARE FOR THE COMMON MAN Emerson Lake & Palmer (Atlantic)
-	25	BE GOOD TO YOURSELF Frankie Miller (Chrysalis)
16	26	DISCO INFERNO Trammps (Atlantic)
21	27	SHEENA IS A PUNK ROCKER Ramones (Sire)
12	28	TOKYO JOE Bryan Ferry (Polydor)
-	29	YOU'RE GONNA GET NEXT TO ME Bo Kirkland & Ruth Davies (EMI Int)
-	30	DON'T LET GO Manhattan Transfer (Atlantic)

18 June 1977

last week	this week	title
6	1	GOD SAVE THE QUEEN Sex Pistols (Virgin)
13	2	SHOW YOU THE WAY TO GO Jacksons (Epic)
1	3	I DON'T WANT TO TALK ABOUT IT/THE FIRST CUT IS THE DEEPEST Rod Stewart (Riva)
2	4	LUCILLE Kenny Rogers (United Artists)
9	5	YOU'RE MOVING OUT TODAY Carole Bayer Sager (Elektra)
3	6	LOVE THEME FROM A STAR IS BORN (EVERGREEN) Barbra Streisand (CBS)
11	7	TELEPHONE LINE Electric Light Orchestra (Jet)
5	8	HALFWAY DOWN THE STAIRS Muppets (Pye)
4	9	AIN'T GONNA BUMP NO MORE Joe Tex (Epic)
24	10	FANFARE FOR THE COMMON MAN Emerson Lake & Palmer (Atlantic)
7	11	THE SHUFFLE Van McCoy (H&L)
8	12	GOOD MORNING JUDGE 10 c.c. (Philips)
14	13	LIDO SHUFFLE Boz Scaggs (CBS)
12	14	O.K. Rock Follies (Polydor)
18	15	PEACHES/GO BUDDY GO Stranglers (United Artists)
16	16	BABY DON'T CHANGE YOUR MIND Gladys Knight & the Pips (Buddah)
10	17	GOT TO GIVE IT UP Marvin Gaye (Motown)
28	18	TOKYO JOE Bryan Ferry (Polydor)
29	19	YOU'RE GONNA GET NEXT TO ME Bo Kirkland & Ruth Davies (EMI Int)
-	20	SAM Olivia Newton-John (EMI)
-	21	OH LORI Alessi (A&M)
15	22	SPOT THE PIGEON (EP) Genesis (Charisma)
26	23	DISCO INFERNO Trammps (Atlantic)
25	24	BE GOOD TO YOURSELF Frankie Miller (Chrysalis)
20	25	GOOD OLD FASHIONED LOVERBOY Queen (EMI)
-	26	GONNA CAPTURE YOUR HEART Blue (Rocket)
-	27	JOIN THE PARTY Honky (Creole)
17	28	TOO HOT TO HANDLE/SLIP YOUR DISC TO THIS Heatwave (GTO)
-	29	SO YOU WIN AGAIN Hot Chocolate (Rak)
23	30	NATURE BOY George Benson (Warner Bros)

Barbara Streisand's self-penned *Love Theme* from the remake of *A Star Is Born*, in which she co-starred with Kris Kristofferson, was her first ever UK Top Five entry, while Kenny Rogers' *Lucille* was his first success here after two hits with the First Edition seven years previously. The Sex Pistols' *God Save The Queen*, released non-coincidentally at the height of the Silver Jubilee celebrations, not only got a universal airplay ban, but was not stocked by major retailers like W. H. Smith – but still made the top.

last week	this week	25 June 1977		2 July 1977		9 July 1977		16 July 1977

25 June 1977

last week	this week	title
2	1	SHOW YOU THE WAY TO GO Jacksons (Epic)
4	2	LUCILLE Kenny Rogers (United Artists)
1	3	GOD SAVE THE QUEEN Sex Pistols (Virgin)
5	4	YOU'RE MOVING OUT TODAY Carole Bayer Sager (Elektra)
3	5	I DON'T WANT TO TALK ABOUT IT/THE FIRST CUT IS THE DEEPEST Rod Stewart (Riva)
7	6	TELEPHONE LINE Electric Light Orchestra (Jet)
6	7	LOVE THEME FROM A STAR IS BORN (EVERGREEN) Barbra Streisand (CBS)
8	8	HALFWAY DOWN THE STAIRS Muppets (Pye)
29	9	SO YOU WIN AGAIN Hot Chocolate (Rak)
10	10	FANFARE FOR THE COMMON MAN Emerson Lake & Palmer (Atlantic)
15	11	PEACHES/GO BUDDY GO Stranglers (United Artists)
11	12	THE SHUFFLE Van McCoy (H&L)
9	13	AIN'T GONNA BUMP NO MORE Joe Tex (Epic)
16	14	BABY DON'T CHANGE YOUR MIND Gladys Knight & the Pips (Buddah)
20	15	SAM Olivia Newton-John (EMI)
13	16	LIDO SHUFFLE Boz Scaggs (CBS)
17	17	GOT TO GIVE IT UP Marvin Gaye (Motown)
12	18	GOOD MORNING JUDGE 10 c.c. (Philips)
22	19	SPOT THE PIGEON (EP) Genesis (Charisma)
21	20	OH LORI Alessi (A&M)
25	21	GOOD OLD FASHIONED LOVERBOY Queen (EMI)
19	22	YOU'RE GONNA GET NEXT TO ME Bo Kirkland & Ruth Davies (EMI Int)
28	23	TOO HOT TO HANDLE/SLIP YOUR DISC TO THIS Heatwave (GTO)
-	24	DO WHAT YOU WANNA DO T Connection (TK)
27	25	JOIN THE PARTY Honky (Creole)
14	26	O.K. Rock Follies (Polydor)
-	27	ANYTHING BUT ROCK 'N' ROLL Tom Petty & the Heartbreakers (Island)
30	28	NATURE BOY George Benson (Warner Bros)
-	29	SLOW DOWN John Miles (Decca)
-	30	BITE YOUR LIP/CHICAGO Elton John/Kiki Dee (Rocket)

2 July 1977

this week	last week	title
1	1	SHOW YOU THE WAY TO GO Jacksons (Epic)
10	2	FANFARE FOR THE COMMON MAN Emerson Lake & Palmer (Atlantic)
9	3	SO YOU WIN AGAIN Hot Chocolate (Rak)
2	4	LUCILLE Kenny Rogers (United Artists)
3	5	GOD SAVE THE QUEEN Sex Pistols (Virgin)
4	6	YOU'RE MOVING OUT TODAY Carole Bayer Sager (Elektra)
7	7	LOVE THEME FROM A STAR IS BORN (EVERGREEN) Barbra Streisand (CBS)
11	8	PEACHES/GO BUDDY GO Stranglers (United Artists)
14	9	BABY DON'T CHANGE YOUR MIND Gladys Knight & the Pips (Buddah)
15	10	SAM Olivia Newton-John (EMI)
6	11	TELEPHONE LINE Electric Light Orchestra (Jet)
22	12	YOU'RE GONNA GET NEXT TO ME Bo Kirkland & Ruth Davies (EMI Int)
5	13	I DON'T WANT TO TALK ABOUT IT/THE FIRST CUT IS THE DEEPEST Rod Stewart (Riva)
-	14	MA BAKER Boney M (Atlantic)
24	15	DO WHAT YOU WANNA DO T Connection (TK)
20	16	OH LORI Alessi (A&M)
8	17	HALFWAY DOWN THE STAIRS Muppets (Pye)
27	18	ANYTHING BUT ROCK 'N' ROLL Tom Petty & the Heartbreakers (Island)
-	19	EXODUS Bob Marley & the Wailers (Island)
28	20	NATURE BOY George Benson (Warner Bros)
17	21	GOT TO GIVE IT UP Marvin Gaye (Motown)
30	22	BITE YOUR LIP/CHICAGO Elton John/Kiki Dee (Rocket)
16	23	LIDO SHUFFLE Boz Scaggs (CBS)
-	24	I JUST WANNA BE YOUR EVERYTHING Andy Gibb (Polydor)
13	25	AIN'T GONNA BUMP NO MORE Joe Tex (Epic)
-	26	FEEL THE NEED Detroit Emeralds (Atlantic)
19	27	SPOT THE PIGEON (EP) Genesis (Charisma)
-	28	COME WITH ME Jesse Green (EMI)
-	29	WE'RE ALL ALONE Rita Coolidge (A&M)
23	30	TOO HOT TO HANDLE/SLIP YOUR DISC TO THIS Heatwave (GTO)

9 July 1977

this week	last week	title
3	1	SO YOU WIN AGAIN Hot Chocolate (Rak)
2	2	FANFARE FOR THE COMMON MAN Emerson Lake & Palmer (Atlantic)
1	3	SHOW YOU THE WAY TO GO Jacksons (Epic)
9	4	BABY DON'T CHANGE YOUR MIND Gladys Knight & the Pips (Buddah)
14	5	MA BAKER Boney M (Atlantic)
10	6	SAM Olivia Newton-John (EMI)
8	7	PEACHES/GO BUDDY GO Stranglers (United Artists)
6	8	YOU'RE MOVING OUT TODAY Carole Bayer Sager (Elektra)
7	9	LOVE THEME FROM A STAR IS BORN (EVERGREEN) Barbra Streisand (CBS)
4	10	LUCILLE Kenny Rogers (United Artists)
11	11	TELEPHONE LINE Electric Light Orchestra (Jet)
5	12	GOD SAVE THE QUEEN Sex Pistols (Virgin)
12	13	YOU'RE GONNA GET NEXT TO ME Bo Kirkland & Ruth Davies (EMI Int)
15	14	DO WHAT YOU WANNA DO T Connection (TK)
16	15	OH LORI Alessi (A&M)
-	16	SLOW DOWN John Miles (Decca)
19	17	EXODUS Bob Marley & the Wailers (Island)
17	18	HALFWAY DOWN THE STAIRS Muppets (Pye)
-	19	GOOD OLD FASHIONED LOVERBOY Queen (EMI)
-	20	PRETTY VACANT Sex Pistols (Virgin)
26	21	FEEL THE NEED Detroit Emeralds (Atlantic)
23	22	LIDO SHUFFLE Boz Scaggs (CBS)
18	23	ANYTHING BUT ROCK 'N' ROLL Tom Petty & the Heartbreakers (Island)
13	24	I DON'T WANT TO TALK ABOUT IT/THE FIRST CUT IS THE DEEPEST Rod Stewart (Riva)
-	25	EASY Commodores (Motown)
28	26	COME WITH ME Jesse Green (EMI)
29	27	WE'RE ALL ALONE Rita Coolidge (A&M)
-	28	CENTRE CITY Fat Larry Band (Atlantic)
-	29	I KNEW THE BRIDE Dave Edmunds (Swan Song)
24	30	I JUST WANNA BE YOUR EVERYTHING Andy Gibb (Polydor)

16 July 1977

this week	last week	title
5	1	MA BAKER Boney M (Atlantic)
1	2	SO YOU WIN AGAIN Hot Chocolate (Rak)
2	3	FANFARE FOR THE COMMON MAN Emerson Lake & Palmer (Atlantic)
-	4	I FEEL LOVE Donna Summer (GTO)
3	5	SHOW YOU THE WAY TO GO Jacksons (Epic)
4	6	BABY DON'T CHANGE YOUR MIND Gladys Knight & the Pips (Buddah)
7	7	PEACHES/GO BUDDY GO Stranglers (United Artists)
20	8	PRETTY VACANT Sex Pistols (Virgin)
9	9	LOVE THEME FROM A STAR IS BORN (EVERGREEN) Barbra Streisand (CBS)
14	10	DO WHAT YOU WANNA DO T Connection (TK)
-	11	ANGELO Brotherhood Of Man (Pye)
16	12	SLOW DOWN John Miles (Decca)
13	13	YOU'RE GONNA GET NEXT TO ME Bo Kirkland & Ruth Davies (EMI Int)
15	14	OH LORI Alessi (A&M)
6	15	SAM Olivia Newton-John (EMI)
25	16	EASY Commodores (Motown)
10	17	LUCILLE Kenny Rogers (United Artists)
17	18	EXODUS Bob Marley & the Wailers (Island)
11	19	TELEPHONE LINE Electric Light Orchestra (Jet)
12	20	GOD SAVE THE QUEEN Sex Pistols (Virgin)
21	21	FEEL THE NEED Detroit Emeralds (Atlantic)
8	22	YOU'RE MOVING OUT TODAY Carole Bayer Sager (Elektra)
-	23	ONE STEP AWAY Tavares (Capitol)
27	24	WE'RE ALL ALONE Rita Coolidge (A&M)
-	25	THE CRUNCH Rah Band (Good Earth)
-	26	STRAWBERRY LETTER 23 Brothers Johnson (A&M)
-	27	I CAN PROVE IT Tony Etoria (GTO)
30	28	I JUST WANNA BE YOUR EVERYTHING Andy Gibb (Polydor)
-	29	ROAD RUNNER Jonathan Richman & the Modern Lovers (Beserkley)
29	30	I KNEW THE BRIDE Dave Edmunds (Swan Song)

ELP's *Fanfare For The Common Man* was a fast-paced keyboard-led workout on Aaron Copeland's familiar classical piece, continuing a tradition Keith Emerson had established in the sixties with the Nice's interpretations of Sibelius' *Karelia Suite* and Bernstein's *America*. It was ELP's only hit single but Emerson and Greg Lake had already scored solo. The Jacksons (they dropped the '5' from their name when they departed Motown and left Jermaine there) had their first UK Number One since their debut.

July – August 1977

23 July 1977

last week	this week	
4	1	I FEEL LOVE — Donna Summer (GTO)
1	2	MA BAKER — Boney M (Atlantic)
3	3	FANFARE FOR THE COMMON MAN — Emerson Lake & Palmer (Atlantic)
2	4	SO YOU WIN AGAIN — Hot Chocolate (Rak)
8	5	PRETTY VACANT — Sex Pistols (Virgin)
6	6	BABY DON'T CHANGE YOUR MIND — Gladys Knight & the Pips (Buddah)
11	7	ANGELO — Brotherhood Of Man (Pye)
14	8	OH LORI — Alessi (A&M)
15	9	SAM — Olivia Newton-John (EMI)
5	10	SHOW YOU THE WAY TO GO — Jacksons (Epic)
7	11	PEACHES — Stranglers (United Artists)
21	12	FEEL THE NEED — Detroit Emeralds (Atlantic)
12	13	SLOW DOWN — John Miles (Decca)
16	14	EASY — Commodores (Motown)
10	15	DO WHAT YOU WANNA DO — T Connection (TK)
9	16	LOVE THEME FROM A STAR IS BORN (EVERGREEN) — Barbra Streisand (CBS)
24	17	WE'RE ALL ALONE — Rita Coolidge (A&M)
13	18	YOU'RE GONNA GET NEXT TO ME — Bo Kirkland & Ruth Davies (EMI Int)
18	19	EXODUS — Bob Marley & the Wailers (Island)
-	20	DREAMS — Fleetwood Mac (Warner Bros)
29	21	ROAD RUNNER — Jonathan Richman & the Modern Lovers (Beserkley)
-	22	ROCKY MOUNTAIN WAY — Joe Walsh (ABC)
22	23	YOU'RE MOVING OUT TODAY — Carole Bayer Sager (Elektra)
30	24	I KNEW THE BRIDE — Dave Edmunds (Swan Song)
25	25	THE CRUNCH — Rah Band (Good Earth)
-	26	GOOD OLD FASHIONED LOVERBOY — Queen (EMI)
-	27	GIVE A LITTLE BIT — Supertramp (A&M)
-	28	IT'S YOUR LIFE — Smokie (Rak)
28	29	I JUST WANNA BE YOUR EVERYTHING — Andy Gibb (Polydor)
23	30	ONE STEP AWAY — Tavares (Capitol)

30 July 1977

last week	this week	
1	1	I FEEL LOVE — Donna Summer (GTO)
2	2	MA BAKER — Boney M (Atlantic)
4	3	SO YOU WIN AGAIN — Hot Chocolate (Rak)
3	4	FANFARE FOR THE COMMON MAN — Emerson Lake & Palmer (Atlantic)
7	5	ANGELO — Brotherhood Of Man (Pye)
5	6	PRETTY VACANT — Sex Pistols (Virgin)
8	7	OH LORI — Alessi (A&M)
6	8	BABY DON'T CHANGE YOUR MIND — Gladys Knight & the Pips (Buddah)
13	9	SLOW DOWN — John Miles (Decca)
11	10	PEACHES — Stranglers (United Artists)
9	11	SAM — Olivia Newton-John (EMI)
17	12	WE'RE ALL ALONE — Rita Coolidge (A&M)
21	13	ROAD RUNNER — Jonathan Richman & the Modern Lovers (Beserkley)
28	14	IT'S YOUR LIFE — Smokie (Rak)
20	15	DREAMS — Fleetwood Mac (Warner Bros)
15	16	DO WHAT YOU WANNA DO — T Connection (TK)
25	17	THE CRUNCH — Rah Band (Good Earth)
16	18	LOVE THEME FROM A STAR IS BORN (EVERGREEN) — Barbra Streisand (CBS)
-	19	YOU GOT WHAT IT TAKES — Showaddywaddy (Arista)
-	20	ALL AROUND THE WORLD — The Jam (Polydor)
14	21	EASY — Commodores (Motown)
12	22	FEEL THE NEED — Detroit Emeralds (Atlantic)
-	23	FLOAT ON — Floaters (ABC)
-	23	GOD SAVE THE QUEEN — Sex Pistols (Virgin)
10	25	SHOW YOU THE WAY TO GO — Jacksons (Epic)
30	26	ONE STEP AWAY — Tavares (Capitol)
-	27	THREE RING CIRCUS — Barry Biggs (Dynamic)
19	28	EXODUS — Bob Marley & the Wailers (Island)
22	29	ROCKY MOUNTAIN WAY — Joe Walsh (ABC)
-	30	A LITTLE BOOGIE WOOGIE IN THE BACK OF MY MIND — Gary Glitter (Arista)

6 August 1977

last week	this week	
1	1	I FEEL LOVE — Donna Summer (GTO)
2	2	MA BAKER — Boney M (Atlantic)
5	3	ANGELO — Brotherhood Of Man (Pye)
4	4	FANFARE FOR THE COMMON MAN — Emerson Lake & Palmer (Atlantic)
6	5	PRETTY VACANT — Sex Pistols (Virgin)
12	6	WE'RE ALL ALONE — Rita Coolidge (A&M)
3	7	SO YOU WIN AGAIN — Hot Chocolate (Rak)
19	8	YOU GOT WHAT IT TAKES — Showaddywaddy (Arista)
7	9	OH LORI — Alessi (A&M)
8	10	BABY DON'T CHANGE YOUR MIND — Gladys Knight & the Pips (Buddah)
23	11	FLOAT ON — Floaters (ABC)
21	12	EASY — Commodores (Motown)
14	13	IT'S YOUR LIFE — Smokie (Rak)
9	14	SLOW DOWN — John Miles (Decca)
17	15	THE CRUNCH — Rah Band (Good Earth)
28	16	EXODUS — Bob Marley & the Wailers (Island)
-	17	SOMETHING BETTER CHANGE — Stranglers (United Artists)
22	18	FEEL THE NEED — Detroit Emeralds (Atlantic)
-	19	NIGHTS ON BROADWAY — Candi Staton (Warner Bros)
-	20	THAT'S WHAT FRIENDS ARE FOR — Deniece Williams (CBS)
13	21	ROAD RUNNER — Jonathan Richman & the Modern Lovers (Beserkley)
11	22	SAM — Olivia Newton-John (EMI)
20	23	ALL AROUND THE WORLD — The Jam (Polydor)
-	24	PROVE IT — Television (Elektra)
25	25	ONE STEP AWAY — Tavares (Capitol)
-	26	I KNEW THE BRIDE — Dave Edmunds (Swan Song)
27	27	THREE RING CIRCUS — Barry Biggs (Dynamic)
15	28	DREAMS — Fleetwood Mac (Warner Bros)
-	29	DANCIN' EASY — Danny Williams (Ensign)
30	30	A LITTLE BOOGIE WOOGIE IN THE BACK OF MY MIND — Gary Glitter (Arista)

13 August 1977

last week	this week	
1	1	I FEEL LOVE — Donna Summer (GTO)
3	2	ANGELO — Brotherhood Of Man (Pye)
2	3	MA BAKER — Boney M (Atlantic)
8	4	YOU GOT WHAT IT TAKES — Showaddywaddy (Arista)
17	5	SOMETHING BETTER CHANGE — Stranglers (United Artists)
6	6	WE'RE ALL ALONE — Rita Coolidge (A&M)
11	7	FLOAT ON — Floaters (ABC)
13	8	IT'S YOUR LIFE — Smokie (Rak)
15	9	THE CRUNCH — Rah Band (Good Earth)
7	10	SO YOU WIN AGAIN — Hot Chocolate (Rak)
4	11	FANFARE FOR THE COMMON MAN — Emerson Lake & Palmer (Atlantic)
12	12	EASY — Commodores (Motown)
9	13	OH LORI — Alessi (A&M)
5	14	PRETTY VACANT — Sex Pistols (Virgin)
23	15	ALL AROUND THE WORLD — The Jam (Polydor)
21	16	ROAD RUNNER — Jonathan Richman & the Modern Lovers (Beserkley)
20	17	THAT'S WHAT FRIENDS ARE FOR — Deniece Williams (CBS)
-	18	NOBODY DOES IT BETTER — Carly Simon (Elektra)
24	19	PROVE IT — Television (Elektra)
14	20	SLOW DOWN — John Miles (Decca)
19	21	NIGHTS ON BROADWAY — Candi Staton (Warner Bros)
27	22	THREE RING CIRCUS — Barry Biggs (Dynamic)
16	23	EXODUS — Bob Marley & the Wailers (Island)
-	24	SWALLOW MY PRIDE — Ramones (Sire)
-	25	SPANISH STROLL — Mink De Ville (Capitol)
29	26	DANCIN' EASY — Danny Williams (Ensign)
-	27	IF I HAVE TO GO AWAY — Jigsaw (Splash)
26	28	I KNEW THE BRIDE — Dave Edmunds (Swan Song)
18	29	FEEL THE NEED — Detroit Emeralds (Atlantic)
-	30	TULANE — Steve Gibbons Band (Polydor)

Euro-disco reigned supreme as Donna Summers' *I Feel Love*, with its juddering electronic backing by Giorgio Moroder, was an almost instant chart-topper, with Boney M's *Ma Baker* (also Moroder-produced) close behind. The Sex Pistols' *Pretty Vacant* was slightly less successful than *God Save The Queen*, possibly because of being less controversial, but it was just safe enough to allow the group some media exposure – including an appearance on *Top Of The Pops*, which passed without incident.

August – September 1977

20 August 1977

last week	this week	Title / Artist (Label)
1	1	I FEEL LOVE — Donna Summer (GTO)
2	2	ANGELO — Brotherhood Of Man (Pye)
7	3	FLOAT ON — Floaters (ABC)
4	4	YOU GOT WHAT IT TAKES — Showaddywaddy (Arista)
9	5	THE CRUNCH — Rah Band (Good Earth)
3	6	MA BAKER — Boney M (Atlantic)
5	7	SOMETHING BETTER CHANGE — Stranglers (United Artists)
18	8	NOBODY DOES IT BETTER — Carly Simon (Elekra)
16	9	ROAD RUNNER — Jonathan Richman & the Modern Lovers (Beserkley)
6	10	WE'RE ALL ALONE — Rita Coolidge (A&M)
12	11	EASY — Commodores (Motown)
8	12	IT'S YOUR LIFE — Smokie (Rak)
21	13	NIGHTS ON BROADWAY — Candi Staton (Warner Bros)
17	14	THAT'S WHAT FRIENDS ARE FOR — Deniece Williams (CBS)
15	15	PRETTY VACANT — Sex Pistols (Virgin)
-	16	DANCIN' IN THE MOONLIGHT — Thin Lizzy (Vertigo)
11	17	FANFARE FOR THE COMMON MAN — Emerson Lake & Palmer (Atlantic)
10	18	SO YOU WIN AGAIN — Hot Chocolate (Rak)
-	19	DO ANYTHING YOU WANNA DO — Rods (Island)
13	20	OH LORI — Alessi (A&M)
-	21	AMERICAN GIRL — Tom Petty and the Heartbreakers (Island)
-	22	LET'S CLEAN UP THE GHETTO — Philadelphia Int. All Stars (Philadelphia)
15	23	ALL AROUND THE WORLD — The Jam (Polydor)
-	24	MAGIC FLY — Space (Pye)
25	25	SPANISH STROLL — Mink De Ville (Capitol)
24	26	SWALLOW MY PRIDE — Ramones (Sire)
23	27	EXODUS — Bob Marley & the Wailers (Island)
-	28	DREAMER — Jacksons (Epic)
20	29	SLOW DOWN — John Miles (Decca)
19	30	PROVE IT — Television (Elektra)

27 August 1977

last week	this week	Title / Artist (Label)
2	1	ANGELO — Brotherhood Of Man (Pye)
3	2	FLOAT ON — Floaters (ABC)
4	3	YOU GOT WHAT IT TAKES — Showaddywaddy (Arista)
5	4	THE CRUNCH — Rah Band (Good Earth)
1	5	I FEEL LOVE — Donna Summer (GTO)
8	6	NOBODY DOES IT BETTER — Carly Simon (Elekra)
10	7	WE'RE ALL ALONE — Rita Coolidge (A&M)
7	8	SOMETHING BETTER CHANGE — Stranglers (United Artists)
14	9	THAT'S WHAT FRIENDS ARE FOR — Deniece Williams (CBS)
6	10	MA BAKER — Boney M (Atlantic)
-	11	WAY DOWN — Elvis Presley (RCA)
9	12	ROAD RUNNER — Jonathan Richman & the Modern Lovers (Beserkley)
13	13	NIGHTS ON BROADWAY — Candi Staton (Warner Bros)
23	14	ALL AROUND THE WORLD — The Jam (Polydor)
12	15	IT'S YOUR LIFE — Smokie (Rak)
11	16	EASY — Commodores (Motown)
24	17	MAGIC FLY — Space (Pye)
16	18	DANCIN' IN THE MOONLIGHT — Thin Lizzy (Vertigo)
25	19	SPANISH STROLL — Mink De Ville (Capitol)
-	20	TULANE — Steve Gibbons Band (Polydor)
15	21	PRETTY VACANT — Sex Pistols (Virgin)
20,	22	OH LORI — Alessi (A&M)
19	23	DO ANYTHING YOU WANNA DO — Rods (Island)
18	24	SO YOU WIN AGAIN — Hot Chocolate (Rak)
-	25	DEEP DOWN INSIDE — Donna Summer (GTO)
-	26	MOODY BLUE — Elvis Presley (RCA)
-	27	I CAN'T GET YOU OUTTA MY MIND — Yvonne Elliman (RSO)
-	28	DREAMS — Fleetwood Mac (Warner Bros)
21	29	AMERICAN GIRL — Tom Petty & the Heartbreakers (Island)
27	30	EXODUS — Bob Marley & the Wailers (Island)

3 September 1977

last week	this week	Title / Artist (Label)
11	1	WAY DOWN — Elvis Presley (RCA)
2	2	FLOAT ON — Floaters (ABC)
6	3	NOBODY DOES IT BETTER — Carly Simon (Elekra)
1	4	ANGELO — Brotherhood Of Man (Pye)
17	5	MAGIC FLY — Space (Pye)
-	6	OXYGENE — Jean Michel Jarre (Polydor)
9	7	THAT'S WHAT FRIENDS ARE FOR — Deniece Williams (CBS)
13	8	NIGHTS ON BROADWAY — Candi Staton (Warner Bros)
4	9	THE CRUNCH — Rah Band (Good Earth)
25	10	DEEP DOWN INSIDE — Donna Summer (GTO)
7	11	WE'RE ALL ALONE — Rita Coolidge (A&M)
20	12	TULANE — Steve Gibbons Band (Polydor)
3	13	YOU GOT WHAT IT TAKES — Showaddywaddy (Arista)
-	14	SILVER LADY — David Soul (Private Stock)
5	15	I FEEL LOVE — Donna Summer (GTO)
23	16	DO ANYTHING YOU WANNA DO — Rods (Island)
-	17	TELEPHONE MAN — Meri Wilson (Pye)
-	18	GARY GILMORE'S EYES — Adverts (Anchor)
18	19	DANCIN' IN THE MOONLIGHT — Thin Lizzy (Vertigo)
8	20	SOMETHING BETTER CHANGE — Stranglers (United Artists)
10	21	MA BAKER — Boney M (Atlantic)
19	22	SPANISH STROLL — Mink De Ville (Capitol)
-	23	SUNSHINE AFTER THE RAIN — Elkie Brooks (A&M)
12	24	ROAD RUNNER — Jonathan Richman & the Modern Lovers (Beserkley)
-	25	LOOKING AFTER NUMBER ONE — Boomtown Rats (Ensign)
14	26	ALL AROUND THE WORLD — The Jam (Polydor)
27	27	I CAN'T GET YOU OUTTA MY MIND — Yvonne Elliman (RSO)
-	28	JAILHOUSE ROCK — Elvis Presley (RCA)
26	29	MOODY BLUE — Elvis Presley (RCA)
28	30	DREAMS — Fleetwood Mac (Warner Bros)

10 September 1977

last week	this week	Title / Artist (Label)
5	1	MAGIC FLY — Space (Pye)
1	2	WAY DOWN — Elvis Presley (RCA)
2	3	FLOAT ON — Floaters (ABC)
6	4	OXYGENE — Jean Michel Jarre (Polydor)
9	5	DEEP DOWN INSIDE — Donna Summer (GTO)
8	6	NIGHTS ON BROADWAY — Candi Staton (Warner Bros)
13	7	YOU GOT WHAT IT TAKES — Showaddywaddy (Arista)
14	8	SILVER LADY — David Soul (Private Stock)
3	9	NOBODY DOES IT BETTER — Carly Simon (Elekra)
17	10	TELEPHONE MAN — Meri Wilson (Pye)
4	11	ANGELO — Brotherhood Of Man (Pye)
7	12	THAT'S WHAT FRIENDS ARE FOR — Deniece Williams (CBS)
12	13	TULANE — Steve Gibbons Band (Polydor)
9	14	THE CRUNCH — Rah Band (Good Earth)
22	15	SPANISH STROLL — Mink De Ville (Capitol)
25	16	LOOKING AFTER NUMBER ONE — Boomtown Rats (Ensign)
18	17	GARY GILMORE'S EYES — Adverts (Anchor)
19	18	DANCIN' IN THE MOONLIGHT — Thin Lizzy (Vertigo)
28	19	JAILHOUSE ROCK — Elvis Presley (RCA)
-	20	ALL SHOOK UP — Elvis Presley (RCA)
-	21	THINK I'M GONNA FALL IN LOVE WITH YOU — Dooleys (GTO)
23	22	SUNSHINE AFTER THE RAIN — Elkie Brooks (A&M)
-	23	IT'S NOW OR NEVER — Elvis Presley (RCA)
16	24	DO ANYTHING YOU WANNA DO — Rods (Island)
20	25	SOMETHING BETTER CHANGE — Stranglers (United Artists)
-	26	RETURN TO SENDER — Elvis Presley (RCA)
11	27	WE'RE ALL ALONE — Rita Coolidge (A&M)
15	28	I FEEL LOVE — Donna Summer (GTO)
-	29	CRYING IN THE CHAPEL — Elvis Presley (RCA)
26	30	ALL AROUND THE WORLD — The Jam (Polydor)

When Elvis Presley suddenly died in mid-August the immediate reaction, apart from the unprecedented amount of worldwide media coverage the death generated, was that sales of his records went through the roof. All over the world RCA's stocks, back catalogue and all, were wiped out and the company's pressing plants simply could not cope with the demand. *Way Down* crashed its way to Number One and the biggest of his old singles began to reappear in the Top 30 – six in all on September 10.

September – October 1977

last / this week

17 September 1977

last	this		
1	1	MAGIC FLY	Space (Pye)
4	2	OXYGENE	Jean Michel Jarre (Polydor)
2	3	WAY DOWN	Elvis Presley (RCA)
5	4	DEEP DOWN INSIDE	Donna Summer (GTO)
8	5	SILVER LADY	David Soul (Private Stock)
10	6	TELEPHONE MAN	Meri Wilson (Pye)
3	7	FLOAT ON	Floaters (ABC)
6	8	NIGHTS ON BROADWAY	Candi Staton (Warner Bros)
24	9	DO ANYTHING YOU WANNA DO	Rods (Island)
9	10	NOBODY DOES IT BETTER	Carly Simon (Elektra)
12	11	THAT'S WHAT FRIENDS ARE FOR	Deniece Wiliams (CBS)
-	12	BEST OF MY LOVE	Emotions (CBS)
18	13	DANCIN' IN THE MOONLIGHT	Thin Lizzy (Vertigo)
16	14	LOOKING AFTER NUMBER ONE	Boomtown Rats (Ensign)
13	15	TULANE	Steve Gibbons Band (Polydor)
17	16	GARY GILMORE'S EYES	Adverts (Anchor)
15	17	SPANISH STROLL	Mink De Ville (Capitol)
-	18	BLACK BETTY	Ram Jam (Epic)
22	19	SUNSHINE AFTER THE RAIN	Elkie Brooks (A&M)
11	20	ANGELO	Brotherhood Of Man (Pye)
-	21	ANOTHER STAR	Stevie Wonder (Motown)
-	22	DREAMER	Jacksons (Epic)
-	23	I CAN'T GET YOU OUTTA MY MIND	Yvonne Elliman (RSO)
7	24	YOU GOT WHAT IT TAKES	Showaddywaddy (Arista)
-	25	WAITING IN VAIN	Bob Marley & The Wailers (Island)
14	26	THE CRUNCH	Rah Band (Good Earth)
-	27	BLACK IS BLACK	La Belle Epoque (Harvest)
21	28	THINK I'M GONNA FALL IN LOVE WITH YOU	Dooleys (GTO)
-	29	THUNDER IN MY HEART	Leo Sayer (Chrysalis)
-	30	FROM NEW YORK TO L.A.	Patsy Gallant (EMI)

24 September 1977

last	this		
1	1	MAGIC FLY	Space (Pye)
3	2	WAY DOWN	Elvis Presley (RCA)
5	3	SILVER LADY	David Soul (Private Stock)
2	4	OXYGENE	Jean Michel Jarre (Polydor)
4	5	DEEP DOWN INSIDE	Donna Summer (GTO)
6	6	TELEPHONE MAN	Meri Wilson (Pye)
12	7	BEST OF MY LOVE	Emotions (CBS)
8	8	NIGHTS ON BROADWAY	Candi Staton (Warner Bros)
10	9	NOBODY DOES IT BETTER	Carly Simon (Elektra)
14	10	LOOKING AFTER NUMBER ONE	Boomtown Rats (Ensign)
19	11	SUNSHINE AFTER THE RAIN	Elkie Brooks (A&M)
30	12	FROM NEW YORK TO L.A.	Patsy Gallant (EMI)
15	13	TULANE	Steve Gibbons Band (Polydor)
23	14	I CAN'T GET YOU OUTTA MY MIND	Yvonne Elliman (RSO)
11	15	THAT'S WHAT FRIENDS ARE FOR	Deniece Wiliams (CBS)
7	16	FLOAT ON	Floaters (ABC)
9	17	DO ANYTHING YOU WANNA DO	Rods (Island)
29	18	THUNDER IN MY HEART	Leo Sayer (Chrysalis)
27	19	BLACK IS BLACK	La Belle Epoque (Harvest)
18	20	BLACK BETTY	Ram Jam (Epic)
13	21	DANCIN' IN THE MOONLIGHT	Thin Lizzy (Vertigo)
28	22	THINK I'M GONNA FALL IN LOVE WITH YOU	Dooleys (GTO)
16	23	GARY GILMORE'S EYES	Adverts (Anchor)
-	24	WONDEROUS STORIES	Yes (Atlantic)
26	25	THE CRUNCH	Rah Band (Good Earth)
21	26	ANOTHER STAR	Stevie Wonder (Motown)
25	27	WAITING IN VAIN	Bob Marley & The Wailers (Island)
-	28	I REMEMBER ELVIS PRESLEY	Danny Mirror (Stone)
22	29	DREAMER	Jacksons (Epic)
17	30	SPANISH STROLL	Mink De Ville (Capitol)

1 October 1977

last	this		
2	1	WAY DOWN	Elvis Presley (RCA)
3	2	SILVER LADY	David Soul (Private Stock)
1	3	MAGIC FLY	Space (Pye)
6	4	TELEPHONE MAN	Meri Wilson (Pye)
19	5	BLACK IS BLACK	La Belle Epoque (Harvest)
4	6	OXYGENE	Jean Michel Jarre (Polydor)
7	7	BEST OF MY LOVE	Emotions (CBS)
5	8	DEEP DOWN INSIDE	Donna Summer (GTO)
12	9	FROM NEW YORK TO L.A.	Patsy Gallant (EMI)
10	10	LOOKING AFTER NUMBER ONE	Boomtown Rats (Ensign)
9	11	NOBODY DOES IT BETTER	Carly Simon (Elektra)
24	12	WONDEROUS STORIES	Yes (Atlantic)
17	13	DO ANYTHING YOU WANNA DO	Rods (Island)
28	14	I REMEMBER ELVIS PRESLEY	Danny Mirror (Stone)
11	15	SUNSHINE AFTER THE RAIN	Elkie Brooks (A&M)
-	16	I REMEMBER YESTERDAY	Donna Summer (GTO)
23	17	GARY GILMORE'S EYES	Adverts (Anchor)
14	18	I CAN'T GET YOU OUTTA MY MIND	Yvonne Elliman (RSO)
-	19	NO MORE HEROES	Stranglers (United Artists)
15	20	THAT'S WHAT FRIENDS ARE FOR	Deniece Williams (CBS)
20	21	BLACK BETTY	Ram Jam (Epic)
27	22	WAITING IN VAIN	Bob Marley & The Wailers (Island)
8	23	NIGHTS ON BROADWAY	Candi Staton (Warner Bros)
21	24	DANCIN' IN THE MOONLIGHT	Thin Lizzy (Vertigo)
-	25	YES SIR I CAN BOOGIE	Baccara (RCA)
-	26	FROM HERE TO ETERNITY	Giorgio (Oasis)
-	27	SHE'S A WINDUP	Dr Feelgood (United Artists)
18	28	THUNDER IN MY HEART	Leo Sayer (Chrysalis)
-	29	DO YOUR DANCE	Rose Royce (Warner Bros)
16	30	FLOAT ON	Floaters (ABC)

8 October 1977

last	this		
1	1	WAY DOWN	Elvis Presley (RCA)
2	2	SILVER LADY	David Soul (Private Stock)
3	3	MAGIC FLY	Space (Pye)
5	4	BLACK IS BLACK	La Belle Epoque (Harvest)
4	5	TELEPHONE MAN	Meri Wilson (Pye)
7	6	BEST OF MY LOVE	Emotions (CBS)
6	7	OXYGENE	Jean Michel Jarre (Polydor)
14	8	I REMEMBER ELVIS PRESLEY	Danny Mirror (Stone)
8	9	DEEP DOWN INSIDE	Donna Summer (GTO)
9	10	FROM NEW YORK TO L.A.	Patsy Gallant (EMI)
19	11	NO MORE HEROES	Stranglers (United Artists)
15	12	SUNSHINE AFTER THE RAIN	Elkie Brooks (A&M)
15	13	I REMEMBER YESTERDAY	Donna Summer (GTO)
21	14	BLACK BETTY	Ram Jam (Epic)
10	15	LOOKING AFTER NUMBER ONE	Boomtown Rats (Ensign)
12	16	WONDEROUS STORIES	Yes (Atlantic)
11	17	NOBODY DOES IT BETTER	Carly Simon (Elektra)
25	18	YES SIR I CAN BOOGIE	Baccara (RCA)
18	19	I CAN'T GET YOU OUTTA MY MIND	Yvonne Elliman (RSO)
26	20	FROM HERE TO ETERNITY	Giorgio (Oasis)
-	21	STAR WARS THEME/CANTINA BAND	Meco (RCA)
-	22	THINK I'M GONNA FALL IN LOVE WITH YOU	Dooleys (GTO)
28	23	THUNDER IN MY HEART	Leo Sayer (Chrysalis)
29	24	DO YOUR DANCE	Rose Royce (Warner Bros)
-	25	GREATEST LOVE OF ALL	George Benson (Arista)
-	26	COMPLETE CONTROL	Clash (CBS)
-	27	COOL OUT TONIGHT	David Essex (CBS)
13	28	DO ANYTHING YOU WANNA DO	Rods (Island)
22	29	WAITING IN VAIN	Bob Marley & The Wailers (Island)
27	30	SHE'S A WINDUP	Dr Feelgood (United Artists)

September opened with the unprecedented spectacle of two electronic keyboard instrumentals from the Continent at One and Two on the chart, until Elvis's posthumous smash reasserted itself. The inevitable Presley tribute hit came from the unexpected source of a Dutch DJ, who became a moderately passable Elvis soundalike on *I Remember...* Curiously the Sonet label, which issued the single, seemed cagey about its involvement and the Stone label (an obvious anagram of Sonet) was created especially for it.

October – November 1977

15 October 1977

last week	this week		
2	1	SILVER LADY	David Soul (Private Stock)
4	2	BLACK IS BLACK	La Belle Epoque (Harvest)
8	3	I REMEMBER ELVIS PRESLEY	Danny Mirror (Stone)
1	4	WAY DOWN	Elvis Presley (RCA)
18	5	YES SIR I CAN BOOGIE	Baccara (RCA)
11	6	NO MORE HEROES	Stranglers (United Artists)
6	7	BEST OF MY LOVE	Emotions (CBS)
16	8	WONDEROUS STORIES	Yes (Atlantic)
3	9	MAGIC FLY	Space (Pye)
10	10	FROM NEW YORK TO L.A.	Patsy Gallant (EMI)
21	11	STAR WARS THEME/CANTINA BAND	Meco (RCA)
13	12	I REMEMBER YESTERDAY	Donna Summer (GTO)
20	13	FROM HERE TO ETERNITY	Giorgio (Oasis)
-	14	ROCKIN' ALL OVER THE WORLD	Status Quo (Vertigo)
14	15	BLACK BETTY	Ram Jam (Epic)
12	16	SUNSHINE AFTER THE RAIN	Elkie Brooks (A&M)
5	17	TELEPHONE MAN	Meri Wilson (Pye)
7	18	OXYGENE	Jean Michel Jarre (Polydor)
26	19	COMPLETE CONTROL	Clash (CBS)
23	20	THUNDER IN MY HEART	Leo Sayer (Chrysalis)
9	21	DEEP DOWN INSIDE	Donna Summer (GTO)
15	22	LOOKING AFTER NUMBER ONE	Boomtown Rats (Ensign)
-	23	YOU'RE IN MY HEART	Rod Stewart (Riva)
-	24	CALLING OCCUPANTS OF INTERPLANETARY CRAFT	Carpenters (A&M)
-	25	HEROES	David Bowie (RCA)
17	26	NOBODY DOES IT BETTER	Carly Simon (Elekra)
-	27	PROBLEM CHILD	Damned (Stiff)
27	28	COOL OUT TONIGHT	David Essex (CBS)
25	29	GREATEST LOVE OF ALL	George Benson (Arista)
-	30	HAPPY DAYS	Pratt & McLain (Reprise)

22 October 1977

last week	this week		
5	1	YES SIR I CAN BOOGIE	Baccara (RCA)
2	2	BLACK IS BLACK	La Belle Epoque (Harvest)
1	3	SILVER LADY	David Soul (Private Stock)
23	4	YOU'RE IN MY HEART	Rod Stewart (Riva)
3	5	I REMEMBER ELVIS PRESLEY	Danny Mirror (Stone)
11	6	STAR WARS THEME/CANTINA BAND	Meco (RCA)
6	7	NO MORE HEROES	Stranglers (United Artists)
7	8	BEST OF MY LOVE	Emotions (CBS)
15	9	BLACK BETTY	Ram Jam (Epic)
14	10	ROCKIN' ALL OVER THE WORLD	Status Quo (Vertigo)
10	11	FROM NEW YORK TO L.A.	Patsy Gallant (EMI)
4	12	WAY DOWN	Elvis Presley (RCA)
25	13	HEROES	David Bowie (RCA)
8	14	WONDEROUS STORIES	Yes (Atlantic)
12	15	I REMEMBER YESTERDAY	Donna Summer (GTO)
13	16	FROM HERE TO ETERNITY	Giorgio (Oasis)
24	17	CALLING OCCUPANTS OF INTERPLANETARY CRAFT	Carpenters (A&M)
-	18	NAME OF THE GAME	Abba (CBS)
-	19	LOVE HURTS	Nazareth (Mountain)
16	20	TELEPHONE MAN	Meri Wilson (Pye)
9	21	MAGIC FLY	Space (Pye)
20	22	THUNDER IN MY HEART	Leo Sayer (Chrysalis)
19	23	COMPLETE CONTROL	Clash (CBS)
-	24	HOLIDAYS IN THE SUN	Sex Pistols (Virgin)
29	25	GREATEST LOVE OF ALL	George Benson (Arista)
21	26	DEEP DOWN INSIDE	Donna Summer (GTO)
-	27	ANGEL OF THE MORNING/ANYWAY YOU WANT ME	Mary Mason (Epic)
-	28	2-4-6-8 MOTORWAY	Tom Robinson Band (EMI)
-	29	NEEDLES AND PINS	Smokie (Rak)
16	30	SUNSHINE AFTER THE RAIN	Elkie Brooks (A&M)

29 October 1977

last week	this week		
4	1	YOU'RE IN MY HEART	Rod Stewart (Riva)
1	2	YES SIR I CAN BOOGIE	Baccara (RCA)
2	3	BLACK IS BLACK	La Belle Epoque (Harvest)
3	4	SILVER LADY	David Soul (Private Stock)
18	5	NAME OF THE GAME	Abba (CBS)
24	6	HOLIDAYS IN THE SUN	Sex Pistols (Virgin)
10	7	ROCKIN' ALL OVER THE WORLD	Status Quo (Vertigo)
6	8	STAR WARS THEME/CANTINA BAND	Meco (RCA)
7	9	NO MORE HEROES	Stranglers (United Artists)
9	10	BLACK BETTY	Ram Jam (Epic)
5	11	I REMEMBER ELVIS PRESLEY	Danny Mirror (Stone)
8	12	BEST OF MY LOVE	Emotions (CBS)
17	13	CALLING OCCUPANTS OF INTERPLANETARY CRAFT	Carpenters (A&M)
-	14	VIRGINIA PLAIN	Roxy Music (Polydor)
-	15	WE ARE THE CHAMPIONS	Queen (EMI)
16	16	FROM HERE TO ETERNITY	Giorgio (Oasis)
29	17	NEEDLES AND PINS	Smokie (Rak)
12	18	WAY DOWN	Elvis Presley (RCA)
28	19	2-4-6-8 MOTORWAY	Tom Robinson Band (EMI)
11	20	FROM NEW YORK TO L.A.	Patsy Gallant (EMI)
14	21	WONDEROUS STORIES	Yes (Atlantic)
19	22	LOVE HURTS	Nazareth (Mountain)
15	23	I REMEMBER YESTERDAY	Donna Summer (GTO)
13	24	HEROES	David Bowie (RCA)
-	25	NEW LIVE & RARE (EP)	Deep Purple (Purple)
-	26	I BELIEVE YOU	Dorothy Moore (Epic)
25	27	GREATEST LOVE OF ALL	George Benson (Arista)
27	28	ANGEL OF THE MORNING/ANYWAY YOU WANT ME	Mary Mason (Epic)
22	29	THUNDER IN MY HEART	Leo Sayer (Chrysalis)
-	30	WATER MARGIN	Pete Mac Junior/Godiego (BBC)

5 November 1977

last week	this week		
2	1	YES SIR I CAN BOOGIE	Baccara (RCA)
1	2	YOU'RE IN MY HEART	Rod Stewart (Riva)
5	3	NAME OF THE GAME	Abba (CBS)
3	4	BLACK IS BLACK	La Belle Epoque (Harvest)
7	5	ROCKIN' ALL OVER THE WORLD	Status Quo (Vertigo)
6	6	HOLIDAYS IN THE SUN	Sex Pistols (Virgin)
15	7	WE ARE THE CHAMPIONS	Queen (EMI)
19	8	2-4-6-8 MOTORWAY	Tom Robinson Band (EMI)
10	9	BLACK BETTY	Ram Jam (Epic)
4	10	SILVER LADY	David Soul (Private Stock)
8	11	STAR WARS THEME/CANTINA BAND	Meco (RCA)
13	12	CALLING OCCUPANTS OF INTERPLANETARY CRAFT	Carpenters (A&M)
14	13	VIRGINIA PLAIN	Roxy Music (Polydor)
17	14	NEEDLES AND PINS	Smokie (Rak)
9	15	NO MORE HEROES	Stranglers (United Artists)
22	16	LOVE HURTS	Nazareth (Mountain)
11	17	I REMEMBER ELVIS PRESLEY	Danny Mirror (Stone)
-	18	SHE'S NOT THERE	Santana (CBS)
12	19	BEST OF MY LOVE	Emotions (CBS)
-	20	TURN TO STONE	Electric Light Orchestra (Jet)
-	21	HOW DEEP IS YOUR LOVE	Bee Gees (RSO)
26	22	I BELIEVE YOU	Dorothy Moore (Epic)
-	23	LIVE IN TROUBLE	Barron Knights (Epic)
24	24	HEROES	David Bowie (RCA)
-	25	MODERN WORLD	Jam (Polydor)
16	26	FROM HERE TO ETERNITY	Giorgio (Oasis)
28	27	ANGEL OF THE MORNING/ANYWAY YOU WANT ME	Mary Mason (Epic)
-	28	EGYPTIAN REGGAE	Jonathan Richman (Beserkley)
21	29	WONDEROUS STORIES	Yes (Atlantic)
30	30	WATER MARGIN	Pete Mac Junior/Godiego (BBC)

La Belle Epoque's *Black Is Black* was the French female trio's interpretation of the 1965 hit by Spanish group Los Bravos. Curiously it was overtaken to the top by not only more Euro-disco ladies, but Spanish ones – the duo Baccara. The Damned made a brief chart debut with *Problem Child,* one of their handful of early singles for Stiff, and the Tom Robinson Band were notable New Wave newcomers. Pratt & McClain's *Happy Days* was the theme of the TV series starring Henry Winkler as The Fonz.

November 1977

12 November 1977

last week / this week

3	1	NAME OF THE GAME — Abba (CBS)
2	2	YOU'RE IN MY HEART — Rod Stewart (Riva)
1	3	YES SIR I CAN BOOGIE — Baccara (RCA)
5	4	ROCKIN' ALL OVER THE WORLD — Status Quo (Vertigo)
7	5	WE ARE THE CHAMPIONS — Queen (EMI)
8	5	2-4-6-8 MOTORWAY — Tom Robinson Band (EMI)
4	7	BLACK IS BLACK — La Belle Epoque (Harvest)
12	8	CALLING OCCUPANTS OF INTERPLANETARY CRAFT — Carpenters (A&M)
6	9	HOLIDAYS IN THE SUN — Sex Pistols (Virgin)
14	10	NEEDLES AND PINS — Smokie (Rak)
9	11	BLACK BETTY — Ram Jam (Epic)
10	12	SILVER LADY — David Soul (Private Stock)
13	12	VIRGINIA PLAIN — Roxy Music (Polydor)
21	14	HOW DEEP IS YOUR LOVE — Bee Gees (RSO)
23	15	LIVE IN TROUBLE — Barron Knights (Epic)
-	16	DANCIN' PARTY — Showaddywaddy (Arista)
11	17	STAR WARS THEME/CANTINA BAND — Meco (RCA)
20	18	TURN TO STONE — Electric Light Orchestra (Jet)
22	19	I BELIEVE YOU — Dorothy Moore (Epic)
18	20	SHE'S NOT THERE — Santana (CBS)
15	21	NO MORE HEROES — Stranglers (United Artists)
-	22	WATCHIN' THE DETECTIVES — Elvis Costello (Stiff)
28	23	EGYPTIAN REGGAE — Jonathan Richman (Beserkley)
25	24	MODERN WORLD — Jam (Polydor)
26	25	FROM HERE TO ETERNITY — Giorgio (Oasis)
-	26	BELFAST — Boney M (Atlantic/Hansa)
16	27	LOVE HURTS — Nazareth (Mountain)
-	28	GOIN' PLACES — Jacksons (Epic)
-	29	I WILL — Ruby Winters (Creole)
29	30	WONDEROUS STORIES — Yes (Atlantic)

19 November 1977

1	1	NAME OF THE GAME — Abba (CBS)
2	2	YOU'RE IN MY HEART — Rod Stewart (Riva)
4	3	ROCKIN' ALL OVER THE WORLD — Status Quo (Vertigo)
5	4	2-4-6-8 MOTORWAY — Tom Robinson Band (EMI)
5	5	WE ARE THE CHAMPIONS — Queen (EMI)
3	6	YES SIR I CAN BOOGIE — Baccara (RCA)
14	7	HOW DEEP IS YOUR LOVE — Bee Gees (RSO)
16	8	DANCIN' PARTY — Showaddywaddy (Arista)
10	9	NEEDLES AND PINS — Smokie (Rak)
8	10	CALLING OCCUPANTS OF INTERPLANETARY CRAFT — Carpenters (A&M)
7	11	BLACK IS BLACK — La Belle Epoque (Harvest)
15	12	LIVE IN TROUBLE — Barron Knights (Epic)
12	13	VIRGINIA PLAIN — Roxy Music (Polydor)
-	14	DADDY COOL/THE GIRL CAN'T HELP IT — Darts (Magnet)
11	15	BLACK BETTY — Ram Jam (Epic)
23	16	EGYPTIAN REGGAE — Jonathan Richman (Beserkley)
9	17	HOLIDAYS IN THE SUN — Sex Pistols (Virgin)
26	18	BELFAST — Boney M (Atlantic/Hansa)
20	19	SHE'S NOT THERE — Santana (CBS)
29	20	I WILL — Ruby Winters (Creole)
18	21	TURN TO STONE — Electric Light Orchestra (Jet)
-	22	DON'T IT MAKE MY BROWN EYES BLUE — Crystal Gayle (United Artists)
21	23	NO MORE HEROES — Stranglers (United Artists)
22	23	WATCHIN' THE DETECTIVES — Elvis Costello (Stiff)
28	25	GOIN' PLACES — Jacksons (Epic)
12	26	SILVER LADY — David Soul (Private Stock)
-	27	CAPTAIN KREMMEN — Kenny Everett/Mike Vickers (DJM)
-	28	THE FLORAL DANCE — Brighouse & Rastrick Band (Transatlantic))
-	29	DON'T LET ME BE MISUNDERSTOOD — Santa Esmeralda (Philips)
27	30	LOVE HURTS — Nazareth (Mountain)

26 November 1977

3	1	ROCKIN' ALL OVER THE WORLD — Status Quo (Vertigo)
1	2	NAME OF THE GAME — Abba (CBS)
5	3	WE ARE THE CHAMPIONS — Queen (EMI)
4	4	2-4-6-8 MOTORWAY — Tom Robinson Band (EMI)
2	5	YOU'RE IN MY HEART — Rod Stewart (Riva)
8	6	DANCIN' PARTY — Showaddywaddy (Arista)
7	7	HOW DEEP IS YOUR LOVE — Bee Gees (RSO)
6	8	YES SIR I CAN BOOGIE — Baccara (RCA)
12	9	LIVE IN TROUBLE — Barron Knights (Epic)
14	10	DADDY COOL/THE GIRL CAN'T HELP IT — Darts (Magnet)
-	11	MULL OF KINTYRE — Wings (Parlophone)
19	12	SHE'S NOT THERE — Santana (CBS)
9	13	NEEDLES AND PINS — Smokie (Rak)
10	14	CALLING OCCUPANTS OF INTERPLANETARY CRAFT — Carpenters (A&M)
16	15	EGYPTIAN REGGAE — Jonathan Richman (Beserkley)
20	16	I WILL — Ruby Winters (Creole)
28	17	THE FLORAL DANCE — Brighouse & Rastrick Brass Band (Transatlantic))
13	18	VIRGINIA PLAIN — Roxy Music (Polydor)
23	19	WATCHIN' THE DETECTIVES — Elvis Costello (Stiff)
17	20	HOLIDAYS IN THE SUN — Sex Pistols (Virgin)
30	21	LOVE HURTS — Nazareth (Mountain)
-	22	MARY OF THE FOURTH FORM — Boomtown Rats (Ensign)
18	23	BELFAST — Boney M (Atlantic/Hansa)
21	24	TURN TO STONE — Electric Light Orchestra (Jet)
-	25	YOU'RE FABULOUS BABE — Kenny Williams (Decca)
11	26	BLACK IS BLACK — La Belle Epoque (Harvest)
-	27	WHITE PUNKS ON DOPE — Tubes (A&M)
-	28	I BELIEVE YOU — Dorothy Moore (Epic)
22	29	DON'T IT MAKE MY BROWN EYES BLUE — Crystal Gayle (United Artists)
-	30	MODERN WORLD — Jam (Polydor)

3 December 1977

11	1	MULL OF KINTYRE — Wings (Parlophone)
3	2	WE ARE THE CHAMPIONS — Queen (EMI)
7	3	HOW DEEP IS YOUR LOVE — Bee Gees (RSO)
2	4	NAME OF THE GAME — Abba (CBS)
1	5	ROCKIN' ALL OVER THE WORLD — Status Quo (Vertigo)
10	6	DADDY COOL/THE GIRL CAN'T HELP IT — Darts (Magnet)
17	7	THE FLORAL DANCE — Brighouse & Rastrick Brass Band (Transatlantic))
6	8	DANCIN' PARTY — Showaddywaddy (Arista)
12	9	SHE'S NOT THERE — Santana (CBS)
9	10	LIVE IN TROUBLE — Barron Knights (Epic)
15	11	EGYPTIAN REGGAE — Jonathan Richman (Beserkley)
16	12	I WILL — Ruby Winters (Creole)
14	13	2-4-6-8 MOTORWAY — Tom Robinson Band (EMI)
5	14	YOU'RE IN MY HEART — Rod Stewart (Riva)
23	15	BELFAST — Boney M (Atlantic/Hansa)
22	16	MARY OF THE FOURTH FORM — Boomtown Rats (Ensign)
8	17	YES SIR I CAN BOOGIE — Baccara (RCA)
19	18	WATCHIN' THE DETECTIVES — Elvis Costello (Stiff)
24	19	TURN TO STONE — Electric Light Orchestra (Jet)
-	19	PUT YOUR LOVE IN ME — Hot Chocolate (Rak)
27	21	WHITE PUNKS ON DOPE — Tubes (A&M)
13	22	NEEDLES AND PINS — Smokie (Rak)
29	23	DON'T IT MAKE MY BROWN EYES BLUE — Crystal Gayle (United Artists)
14	24	CALLING OCCUPANTS OF INTERPLANETARY CRAFT — Carpenters (A&M)
-	25	LOVE OF MY LIFE — Dooleys (GTO)
-	26	GETTIN' READY FOR LOVE — Diana Ross (Motown)
-	27	WONDEROUS STORIES — Yes (Atlantic)
-	28	REALLY FREE — John Otway & Wild Willy Barrett (Polydor)
-	29	DANCE, DANCE, DANCE — Chic (Atlantic)
-	30	CAPTAIN KREMMEN — Kenny Everett/Mike Vickers (DJM)

Status Quo's *Rockin' All Over The World*, although it became one of the songs most closely associated with the band, was actually a cover of a US solo hit single by John Fogerty, former leader of Creedence Clearwater Revival. Chart newcomers Darts were a British vocal group with a tight mastery of the 1950s US black doo-wop vocal group tradition. Their debut hit was a medley of the original B-side of *Silhouettes* by the Rays from 1957, and Little Richard's better known hit from the same year.

10 December 1977

last week	this week		
1	1	MULL OF KINTYRE	Wings (Parlophone)
3	2	HOW DEEP IS YOUR LOVE	Bee Gees (RSO)
7	3	THE FLORAL DANCE	Brighouse & Rastrick Brass Band (Transatlantic))
12	4	I WILL	Ruby Winters (Creole)
2	5	WE ARE THE CHAMPIONS	Queen (EMI)
5	6	ROCKIN' ALL OVER THE WORLD	Status Quo (Vertigo)
11	7	EGYPTIAN REGGAE	Jonathan Richman (Beserkley)
6	8	DADDY COOL/THE GIRL CAN'T HELP IT	Darts (Magnet)
8	9	DANCIN' PARTY	Showaddywaddy (Arista)
18	10	WATCHIN' THE DETECTIVES	Elvis Costello (Stiff)
4	11	NAME OF THE GAME	Abba (CBS)
19	11	PUT YOUR LOVE IN ME	Hot Chocolate (Rak)
9	13	SHE'S NOT THERE	Santana (CBS)
10	14	LIVE IN TROUBLE	Barron Knights (Epic)
16	15	MARY OF THE FOURTH FORM	Boomtown Rats (Ensign)
-	16	IT'S A HEARTACHE	Bonnie Tyler (RCA)
25	17	LOVE OF MY LIFE	Dooleys (GTO)
-	17	LOVE'S UNKIND	Donna Summer (GTO)
29	19	DANCE, DANCE, DANCE	Chic (Atlantic)
23	20	DON'T IT MAKE MY BROWN EYES BLUE	Crystal Gayle (United Artists)
13	21	2-4-6-8 MOTORWAY	Tom Robinson Band (EMI)
27	22	WONDEROUS STORIES	Yes (Atlantic)
21	23	WHITE PUNKS ON DOPE	Tubes (A&M)
17	24	YES SIR I CAN BOOGIE	Baccara (RCA)
15	25	BELFAST	Boney M (Atlantic/Hansa)
14	26	YOU'RE IN MY HEART	Rod Stewart (Riva)
-	27	ONLY WOMEN BLEED	Julie Covington (Virgin)
-	28	L. A. RUN	Carvells (Creole)
22	29	NEEDLES AND PINS	Smokie (Rak)
19	30	TURN TO STONE	Electric Light Orchestra (Jet)

17 December 1977

1	1	MULL OF KINTYRE	Wings (Parlophone)
2	2	HOW DEEP IS YOUR LOVE	Bee Gees (RSO)
3	3	THE FLORAL DANCE	Brighouse & Rastrick Brass Band (Transatlantic))
7	4	EGYPTIAN REGGAE	Jonathan Richman (Beserkley)
4	5	I WILL	Ruby Winters (Creole)
9	6	DANCIN' PARTY	Showaddywaddy (Arista)
11	7	PUT YOUR LOVE IN ME	Hot Chocolate (Rak)
6	8	ROCKIN' ALL OVER THE WORLD	Status Quo (Vertigo)
8	9	DADDY COOL/THE GIRL CAN'T HELP IT	Darts (Magnet)
17	10	LOVE'S UNKIND	Donna Summer (GTO)
25	11	BELFAST	Boney M (Atlantic/Hansa)
-	12	WHITE CHRISTMAS	Bing Crosby (MCA)
16	13	IT'S A HEARTACHE	Bonnie Tyler (RCA)
15	14	MARY OF THE FOURTH FORM	Boomtown Rats (Ensign)
-	15	MY WAY	Elvis Presley (RCA)
19	16	DANCE, DANCE, DANCE	Chic (Atlantic)
20	17	DON'T IT MAKE MY BROWN EYES BLUE	Crystal Gayle (United Artists)
17	18	LOVE OF MY LIFE	Dooleys (GTO)
5	19	WE ARE THE CHAMPIONS	Queen (EMI)
10	20	WATCHIN' THE DETECTIVES	Elvis Costello (Stiff)
13	21	SHE'S NOT THERE	Santana (CBS)
-	22	I LOVE YOU	Donna Summer (Casablanca)
-	23	JAMMING/PUNKY REGGAE PARTY	Bob Marley & the Wailers (Island)
14	24	LIVE IN TROUBLE	Barron Knights (Epic)
11	25	NAME OF THE GAME	Abba (CBS)
27	26	ONLY WOMEN BLEED	Julie Covington (Virgin)
23	27	WHITE PUNKS ON DOPE	Tubes (A&M)
-	28	AS TIME GOES BY	Dooley Wilson (United Artists)
21	29	2-4-6-8 MOTORWAY	Tom Robinson Band (EMI)
30	30	TURN TO STONE	Electric Light Orchestra (Jet)

24 December 1977

1	1	MULL OF KINTYRE	Wings (Parlophone)
3	2	THE FLORAL DANCE	Brighouse & Rastrick Brass Band (Transatlantic))
2	3	HOW DEEP IS YOUR LOVE	Bee Gees (RSO)
5	4	I WILL	Ruby Winters (Creole)
4	5	EGYPTIAN REGGAE	Jonathan Richman (Beserkley)
9	6	DADDY COOL/THE GIRL CAN'T HELP IT	Darts (Magnet)
12	7	WHITE CHRISTMAS	Bing Crosby (MCA)
10	8	LOVE'S UNKIND	Donna Summer (GTO)
13	9	IT'S A HEARTACHE	Bonnie Tyler (RCA)
6	10	DANCIN' PARTY	Showaddywaddy (Arista)
18	11	LOVE OF MY LIFE	Dooleys (GTO)
11	12	BELFAST	Boney M (Atlantic/Hansa)
8	13	ROCKIN' ALL OVER THE WORLD	Status Quo (Vertigo)
20	14	WATCHIN' THE DETECTIVES	Elvis Costello (Stiff)
7	15	PUT YOUR LOVE IN ME	Hot Chocolate (Rak)
26	16	ONLY WOMEN BLEED	Julie Covington (Virgin)
17	17	DON'T IT MAKE MY BROWN EYES BLUE	Crystal Gayle (United Artists)
14	18	MARY OF THE FOURTH FORM	Boomtown Rats (Ensign)
15	19	MY WAY	Elvis Presley (RCA)
28	20	AS TIME GOES BY	Dooley Wilson (United Artists)
-	21	LET'S HAVE A QUIET NIGHT IN	David Soul (Private Stock)
16	22	DANCE, DANCE, DANCE	Chic (Atlantic)
19	23	WE ARE THE CHAMPIONS	Queen (EMI)
23	24	JAMMING/PUNKY REGGAE PARTY	Bob Marley & the Wailers (Island)
22	25	I LOVE YOU	Donna Summer (Casablanca)
-	26	LITTLE GIRL	Banned (Harvest)
-	27	WHO PAYS THE FERRYMAN	Yannis Markopoulos (BBC)
-	28	REALLY FREE	John Otway & Wild Willy Barrett (Polydor)
24	29	LIVE IN TROUBLE	Barron Knights (Epic)
-	30	GETTIN' READY FOR LOVE	Diana Ross (Motown)

Wings' *Mull Of Kintyre* did not have absolutely universal appeal – in America it was deemed a no-hjoper and relegated to the B-side of *Girls School*, which was the B-side here. However the bagpipe-accompanied hymn-like tribute to the corner of Scotland where the McCartneys had a farm home, sold on the sentimental UK Christams market in quantities unknown at EMI since the heydays of the Beatles. Even before Christmas the single had soared past a million sales and demand kept on growing.

January 1978

7 January 1978

Last	This	Title	Artist (Label)
1	1	MULL OF KINTYRE	Wings (Parlophone)
2	2	THE FLORAL DANCE	Brighouse & Rastrick Brass Band (Transatlantic)
3	3	HOW DEEP IS YOUR LOVE	Bee Gees (RSO)
9	4	IT'S A HEARTACHE	Bonnie Tyler (RCA)
7	5	WHITE CHRISTMAS	Bing Crosby (MCA)
4	6	I WILL	Ruby Winters (Creole)
8	6	LOVE'S UNKIND	Donna Summer (GTO)
5	8	EGYPTIAN REGGAE	Jonathan Richman (Beserkley)
6	9	DADDY COOL/THE GIRL CAN'T HELP IT	Darts (Magnet)
17	10	DON'T IT MAKE MY BROWN EYES BLUE	Crystal Gayle (United Artists)
10	11	DANCIN' PARTY	Showaddywaddy (Arista)
22	12	DANCE, DANCE, DANCE	Chic (Atlantic)
13	13	MY WAY	Elvis Presley (RCA)
20	14	AS TIME GOES BY	Dooley Wilson (United Artists)
15	15	PUT YOUR LOVE IN ME	Hot Chocolate (RAK)
21	16	LET'S HAVE A QUIET NIGHT IN	David Soul (Private Stock)
12	17	BELFAST	Boney M (Atlantic/Hansa)
13	18	ROCKIN' ALL OVER THE WORLD	Status Quo (Vertigo)
27	19	WHO PAYS THE FERRYMAN	Yannis Markopoulos (BBC)
28	20	REALLY FREE	John Otway & Wild Willy Barrett (Polydor)
18	20	MARY OF THE FOURTH FORM	Boomtown Rats (Ensign)
13	22	WATCHING THE DETECTIVES	Elvis Costello (Stiff)
16	23	ONLY WOMEN BLEED	Julie Covington (Virgin)
-	24	UP TOWN TOP RANKING	Althia & Donna (Lightning)
11	25	LOVE OF MY LIFE	Dooleys (GTO)
24	26	JAMMING/PUNKY REGGAE PARTY	Bob Marley & the Wailers (Island)
23	27	WE ARE THE CHAMPIONS	Queen (EMI)
25	28	I LOVE YOU	Donna Summer (Casablanca)
26	29	LITTLE GIRL	Banned (Harvest)
29	30	LIVE IN TROUBLE	Barron Knights (Epic)

14 January 1978

Last	This	Title	Artist (Label)
1	1	MULL OF KINTYRE	Wings (Parlophone)
6	2	LOVE'S UNKIND	Donna Summer (GTO)
2	3	THE FLORAL DANCE	Brighouse & Rastrick Brass Band (Transatlantic)
3	4	HOW DEEP IS YOUR LOVE	Bee Gees (RSO)
4	5	IT'S A HEARTACHE	Bonnie Tyler (RCA)
16	6	LET'S HAVE A QUIET NIGHT IN	David Soul (Private Stock)
10	7	DON'T IT MAKE MY BROWN EYES BLUE	Crystal Gayle (United Artists)
24	8	UP TOWN TOP RANKING	Althia & Donna (Lightning)
6	9	I WILL	Ruby Winters (Creole)
12	10	DANCE, DANCE, DANCE	Chic (Atlantic)
17	11	BELFAST	Boney M (Atlantic/Hansa)
19	12	WHO PAYS THE FERRYMAN	Yannis Markopoulos (BBC)
13	13	MY WAY	Elvis Presley (RCA)
23	14	ONLY WOMEN BLEED	Julie Covington (Virgin)
26	15	JAMMING/PUNKY REGGAE PARTY	Bob Marley & the Wailers (Island)
-	16	NATIVE NEW YORKER	Odyssey (RCA)
25	17	LOVE OF MY LIFE	Dooleys (GTO)
9	18	DADDY COOL/THE GIRL CAN'T HELP IT	Darts (Magnet)
8	19	EGYPTIAN REGGAE	Jonathan Richman (Beserkley)
-	20	RUN BACK	Carl Douglas (Pye)
11	21	DANCIN' PARTY	Showaddywaddy (Arista)
15	22	PUT YOUR LOVE IN ME	Hot Chocolate (RAK)
20	23	MARY OF THE FOURTH FORM	Boomtown Rats (Ensign)
27	24	WE ARE THE CHAMPIONS	Queen (EMI)
18	25	ROCKIN' ALL OVER THE WORLD	Status Quo (Vertigo)
22	26	WATCHING THE DETECTIVES	Elvis Costello (Stiff)
28	27	I LOVE YOU	Donna Summer (Casablanca)
-	28	THE FLORAL DANCE	Terry Wogan (Phonogram)
29	29	LITTLE GIRL	The Banned (Harvest)
14	30	AS TIME GOES BY	Dooley Wilson (United Artists)

21 January 1978

Last	This	Title	Artist (Label)
1	1	MULL OF KINTYRE	Wings (Parlophone)
2	2	LOVE'S UNKIND	Donna Summer (GTO)
5	3	IT'S A HEARTACHE	Bonnie Tyler (RCA)
8	4	UP TOWN TOP RANKING	Althia & Donna (Lightning)
7	5	DON'T IT MAKE MY BROWN EYES BLUE	Crystal Gayle (United Artists)
10	6	DANCE, DANCE, DANCE	Chic (Atlantic)
3	7	THE FLORAL DANCE	Brighouse & Rastrick Brass Band (Transatlantic)
6	8	LET'S HAVE A QUIET NIGHT IN	David Soul (Private Stock)
16	9	NATIVE NEW YORKER	Odyssey (RCA)
4	10	HOW DEEP IS YOUR LOVE	Bee Gees (RSO)
15	11	JAMMING/PUNKY REGGAE PARTY	Bob Marley & the Wailers (Island)
14	12	ONLY WOMEN BLEED	Julie Covington (Virgin)
27	13	I LOVE YOU	Donna Summer (Casablanca)
9	14	I WILL	Ruby Winters (Creole)
-	15	ON FIRE	T-Connection (TK)
-	16	LOVELY DAY	Bill Withers (CBS)
12	17	WHO PAYS THE FERRYMAN	Yannis Markopoulos (BBC)
-	18	GALAXY	War (MCA)
19	19	DADDY COOL/THE GIRL CAN'T HELP IT	Darts (Magnet)
30	20	AS TIME GOES BY	Dooley Wilson (United Artists)
21	21	MY WAY	Elvis Presley (RCA)
20	22	RUN BACK	Carl Douglas (Pye)
-	23	THE GROOVE LINE	Heatwave (GTO)
-	24	COCOMOTION	El Coco (Pye)
-	25	WHO'S GONNA LOVE ME	Imperials (Power Exchange)
-	26	REALLY FREE	John Otway & Wild Willy Barrett (Polydor)
-	27	IF I HAD WORDS	Scott Fitzgerald & Yvonne Keely (Pepper)
-	28	FIGARO	Brotherhood Of Man (Pye)
-	29	SORRY, I'M A LADY	Baccara (RCA)
11	30	BELFAST	Boney M (Atlantic/Hansa)

28 January 1978

Last	This	Title	Artist (Label)
1	1	MULL OF KINTYRE	Wings (Parlophone)
4	2	UP TOWN TOP RANKING	Althia & Donna (Lightning)
9	3	NATIVE NEW YORKER	Odyssey (RCA)
2	4	LOVE'S UNKIND	Donna Summer (GTO)
5	5	IT'S A HEARTACHE	Bonnie Tyler (RCA)
5	6	DON'T IT MAKE MY BROWN EYES BLUE	Crystal Gayle (United Artists)
28	7	FIGARO	Brotherhood Of Man (Pye)
11	8	JAMMING/PUNKY REGGAE PARTY	Bob Marley & the Wailers (Island)
16	9	LOVELY DAY	Bill Withers (CBS)
8	10	LET'S HAVE A QUIET NIGHT IN	David Soul (Private Stock)
6	11	DANCE, DANCE, DANCE	Chic (Atlantic)
7	12	THE FLORAL DANCE	Brighouse & Rastrick Brass Band (Transatlantic)
12	13	ONLY WOMEN BLEED	Julie Covington (Virgin)
10	14	HOW DEEP IS YOUR LOVE	Bee Gees (RSO)
27	15	IF I HAD WORDS	Scott Fitzgerald & Yvonne Keely (Pepper)
23	16	THE GROOVE LINE	Heatwave (GTO)
18	17	GALAXY	War (MCA)
14	18	I WILL	Ruby Winters (Creole)
19	19	DADDY COOL/THE GIRL CAN'T HELP IT	Darts (Magnet)
15	20	ON FIRE	T-Connection (TK)
17	21	WHO PAYS THE FERRYMAN	Yannis Markopoulos (BBC)
13	22	I LOVE YOU	Donna Summer (Casablanca)
25	23	WHO'S GONNA LOVE ME	Imperials (Power Exchange)
-	24	JAM, JAM, JAM	People's Choice (Philadelphia Int.)
29	25	SORRY, I'M A LADY	Baccara (RCA)
-	26	MORNING OF OUR LIVES	Jonathan Richman & the Modern Lovers (Beserkley)
21	27	MY WAY	Elvis Presley (RCA)
22	28	RUN BACK	Carl Douglas (Pye)
-	29	MR BLUE SKY	Electric Light Orchestra (Jet)
-	30	BEAUTY AND THE BEAST	David Bowie (RCA)

By the end of its nine-week spell at Number One, *Mull Of Kintyre* had reached two million sales, and thus wrested away the title of Britain's all-time best-selling single which the Beatles' *She Loves You* had held since 1963. Donna Summer continued to find success on two different labels: her older GTO single *Love's Unkind* offered the closest challenge to Wings for two weeks. *The Floral Dance*, meanwhile, was joined briefly in the Top 30 by a 'vocal' rendition by Radio 2 DJ Terry Wogan.

February 1978

4 February 1978

last week	this week		
2	1	UP TOWN TOP RANKING	Althia & Donna (Lightning)
1	2	MULL OF KINTYRE	Wings (Parlophone)
9	3	LOVELY DAY	Bill Withers (CBS)
3	4	NATIVE NEW YORKER	Odyssey (RCA)
7	5	FIGARO	Brotherhood Of Man (Pye)
15	6	IF I HAD WORDS	Scott Fitzgerald & Yvonne Keely (Pepper)
4	7	LOVE'S UNKIND	Donna Summer (GTO)
5	8	IT'S A HEARTACHE	Bonnie Tyler (RCA)
8	8	JAMMING/PUNKY REGGAE PARTY	Bob Marley & the Wailers (Island)
17	10	GALAXY	War (MCA)
16	11	THE GROOVE LINE	Heatwave (GTO)
11	12	DANCE, DANCE, DANCE	Chic (Atlantic)
6	13	DON'T IT MAKE MY BROWN EYES BLUE	Crystal Gayle (United Artists)
25	14	SORRY, I'M A LADY	Baccara (RCA)
20	15	ON FIRE	T-Connection (TK)
-	16	TAKE A CHANCE ON ME	Abba (Epic)
29	17	MR BLUE SKY	Electric Light Orchestra (Jet)
-	18	RICH KIDS	Rich Kids (EMI)
13	19	ONLY WOMEN BLEED	Julie Covington (Virgin)
-	20	HOT LEGS/I WAS ONLY JOKING	Rod Stewart (Riva)
10	21	LET'S HAVE A QUIET NIGHT IN	David Soul (Private Stock)
-	22	COME BACK MY LOVE	Darts (Magnet)
14	23	HOW DEEP IS YOUR LOVE	Bee Gees (RSO)
-	24	WISHING ON A STAR	Rose Royce (Whitfield)
30	25	BEAUTY AND THE BEAST	David Bowie (RCA)
-	26	THEME FROM WHICH WAY IS UP	Stargard (MCA)
26	27	MORNING OF OUR LIVES	Jonathan Richman & the Modern Lovers (Beserkley)
12	28	THE FLORAL DANCE	Brighouse & Rastrick Brass Band (Transatlantic)
23	29	WHO'S GONNA LOVE ME	Imperials (Power Exchange)
-	30	LOVE IS LIKE OXYGEN	Sweet (Polydor)

11 February 1978

1	1	UP TOWN TOP RANKING	Althia & Donna (Lightning)
6	2	IF I HAD WORDS	Scott Fitzgerald & Yvonne Keely (Pepper)
5	3	FIGARO	Brotherhood Of Man (Pye)
16	4	TAKE A CHANCE ON ME	Abba (Epic)
4	5	NATIVE NEW YORKER	Odyssey (RCA)
2	6	MULL OF KINTYRE	Wings (Parlophone)
3	7	LOVELY DAY	Bill Withers (CBS)
17	8	MR BLUE SKY	Electric Light Orchestra (Jet)
20	9	HOT LEGS/I WAS ONLY JOKING	Rod Stewart (Riva)
11	10	THE GROOVE LINE	Heatwave (GTO)
14	11	SORRY, I'M A LADY	Baccara (RCA)
8	12	JAMMING/PUNKY REGGAE PARTY	Bob Marley & the Wailers (Island)
22	13	COME BACK MY LOVE	Darts (Magnet)
7	14	LOVE'S UNKIND	Donna Summer (GTO)
10	15	GALAXY	War (MCA)
30	16	LOVE IS LIKE OXYGEN	Sweet (Polydor)
8	17	IT'S A HEARTACHE	Bonnie Tyler (RCA)
-	18	5 MINUTES	Stranglers (United Artists)
18	19	RICH KIDS	Rich Kids (EMI)
12	20	DANCE, DANCE, DANCE	Chic (Atlantic)
-	21	STAYIN' ALIVE	Bee Gees (RSO)
29	22	WHO'S GONNA LOVE ME	Imperials (Power Exchange)
26	23	THEME FROM WHICH WAY IS UP	Stargard (MCA)
24	24	WISHING ON A STAR	Rose Royce (Warner Bros)
-	25	JUST ONE MORE NIGHT	Yellow Dog (Virgin)
-	26	EMOTION	Samantha Sang (Private Stock)
-	27	NO TIME TO BE 21	Adverts (Bright)
-	28	SHOT BY BOTH SIDES	Magazine (Virgin)
27	29	MORNING OF OUR LIVES	Jonathan Richman & the Modern Lovers (Beserkley)
-	30	FOR A FEW DOLLARS MORE	Smokie (RAK)

18 February 1978

4	1	TAKE A CHANCE ON ME	Abba (Epic)
3	2	FIGARO	Brotherhood Of Man (Pye)
2	3	IF I HAD WORDS	Scott Fitzgerald & Yvonne Keely (Pepper)
1	4	UP TOWN TOP RANKING	Althia & Donna (Lightning)
24	5	WISHING ON A STAR	Rose Royce (Warner Bros)
13	6	COME BACK MY LOVE	Darts (Magnet)
7	7	LOVELY DAY	Bill Withers (CBS)
8	8	MR BLUE SKY	Electric Light Orchestra (Jet)
11	9	SORRY, I'M A LADY	Baccara (RCA)
5	10	NATIVE NEW YORKER	Odyssey (RCA)
6	11	MULL OF KINTYRE	Wings (Parlophone)
9	12	HOT LEGS/I WAS ONLY JOKING	Rod Stewart (Riva)
16	13	LOVE IS LIKE OXYGEN	Sweet (Polydor)
25	14	JUST ONE MORE NIGHT	Yellow Dog (Virgin)
10	15	THE GROOVE LINE	Heatwave (GTO)
18	16	5 MINUTES	Stranglers (United Artists)
12	17	JAMMING/PUNKY REGGAE PARTY	Bob Marley & the Wailers (Island)
-	18	DRUMMER MAN	Tonight (TDS)
15	19	GALAXY	War (MCA)
-	20	WUTHERING HEIGHTS	Kate Bush (EMI)
14	21	LOVE'S UNKIND	Donna Summer (GTO)
-	22	FANTASY	Earth, Wind & Fire (CBS)
-	23	JUST THE WAY YOU ARE	Billy Joel (CBS)
21	24	STAYIN' ALIVE	Bee Gees (RSO)
26	25	EMOTION	Samantha Sang (Private Stock)
-	26	CLOSER TO THE HEART	Rush (Mercury Rush)
28	27	SHOT BY BOTH SIDES	Magazine (Virgin)
-	28	WHAT DO I GET	Buzzcocks (United Artists)
-	29	HEARTSONG	Gordon Giltrap (Electric)
-	30	ALL RIGHT NOW (EP)	Free (Island)

25 February 1978

1	1	TAKE A CHANCE ON ME	Abba (Epic)
6	2	COME BACK MY LOVE	Darts (Magnet)
5	3	WISHING ON A STAR	Rose Royce (Warner Bros)
2	4	FIGARO	Brotherhood Of Man (Pye)
3	5	IF I HAD WORDS	Scott Fitzgerald & Yvonne Keely (Pepper)
8	6	MR BLUE SKY	Electric Light Orchestra (Jet)
12	7	HOT LEGS/I WAS ONLY JOKING	Rod Stewart (Riva)
13	8	LOVE IS LIKE OXYGEN	Sweet (Polydor)
14	9	JUST ONE MORE NIGHT	Yellow Dog (Virgin)
24	10	STAYIN' ALIVE	Bee Gees (RSO)
9	11	SORRY, I'M A LADY	Baccara (RCA)
20	12	WUTHERING HEIGHTS	Kate Bush (EMI)
4	13	UP TOWN TOP RANKING	Althia & Donna (Lightning)
7	14	LOVELY DAY	Bill Withers (CBS)
18	15	DRUMMER MAN	Tonight (TDS)
25	16	EMOTION	Samantha Sang (Private Stock)
30	17	ALL RIGHT NOW (EP)	Free (Island)
10	18	NATIVE NEW YORKER	Odyssey (RCA)
16	18	5 MINUTES	Stranglers (United Artists)
11	20	MULL OF KINTYRE	Wings (Parlophone)
-	21	FOR A FEW DOLLARS MORE	Smokie (RAK)
-	22	I CAN'T STAND THE RAIN	Eruption (Atlantic)
15	23	THE GROOVE LINE	Heatwave (GTO)
-	24	THEME FROM WHICH WAY IS UP	Stargard (MCA)
-	25	RISING FREE (EP)	Tom Robinson Band (EMI)
23	26	JUST THE WAY YOU ARE	Billy Joel (CBS)
-	27	BAKER STREET	Gerry Rafferty (United Artists)
22	28	FANTASY	Earth, Wind & Fire (CBS)
-	29	WALK IN LOVE	Manhattan Transfer (Atlantic)
-	30	IS THIS LOVE	Bob Marley & the Wailers (Island)

Althia & Donna, to whom the honour finally fell of dethroning Wings' *Mull Of Kintyre* from Number One, were two Jamaican teenagers, both of whom helped write this rare reggae Number One (including the dialect lyrics). Against the odds for Continental acts, Baccara also made the Top Ten with the follow-up to their recent chart-topper, while Darts outsold their initial hit with *Come Back My Love,* a revival of an obscure 1955 single by US doo-wop group the Wrens.

March 1978

4 March 1978

last week	this week	
1	1	TAKE A CHANCE ON ME — Abba (Epic)
3	2	WISHING ON A STAR — Rose Royce (Warner Bros)
2	3	COME BACK MY LOVE — Darts (Magnet)
12	4	WUTHERING HEIGHTS — Kate Bush (EMI)
6	5	MR BLUE SKY — Electric Light Orchestra (Jet)
10	6	STAYIN' ALIVE — Bee Gees (RSO)
9	7	JUST ONE MORE NIGHT — Yellow Dog (Virgin)
4	8	FIGARO — Brotherhood Of Man (Pye)
7	9	HOT LEGS/I WAS ONLY JOKING — Rod Stewart (Riva)
17	10	ALL RIGHT NOW (EP) — Free (Island)
8	11	LOVE IS LIKE OXYGEN — Sweet (Polydor)
18	12	5 MINUTES — Stranglers (United Artists)
27	13	BAKER STREET — Gerry Rafferty (United Artists)
5	14	IF I HAD WORDS — Scott Fitzgerald & Yvonne Keely (Pepper)
30	15	IS THIS LOVE — Bob Marley & The Wailers (Island)
11	16	SORRY, I'M A LADY — Baccara (RCA)
16	17	EMOTION — Samantha Sang (Private Stock)
-	18	DENIS — Blondie (Chrysalis)
25	19	RISING FREE (EP) — Tom Robinson Band (EMI)
28	20	FANTASY — Earth, Wind & Fire (CBS)
15	21	DRUMMER MAN — Tonight (TDS)
14	22	LOVELY DAY — Bill Withers (CBS)
22	23	I CAN'T STAND THE RAIN — Eruption (Atlantic)
26	24	JUST THE WAY YOU ARE — Billy Joel (CBS)
21	25	FOR A FEW DOLLARS MORE — Smokie (RAK)
18	26	NATIVE NEW YORKER — Odyssey (RCA)
-	27	CLASH CITY ROCKERS — Clash (CBS)
-	28	RUMOUR HAS IT — Donna Summer (Casablanca)
24	29	THEME FROM WHICH WAY IS UP — Stargard (MCA)
-	30	SPREAD YOUR WINGS — Queen (EMI)

11 March 1978

last week	this week	
4	1	WUTHERING HEIGHTS — Kate Bush (EMI)
2	2	WISHING ON A STAR — Rose Royce (Warner Bros)
1	3	TAKE A CHANCE ON ME — Abba (Epic)
17	4	DENIS — Blondie (Chrysalis)
6	5	STAYIN' ALIVE — Bee Gees (RSO)
3	6	COME BACK MY LOVE — Darts (Magnet)
5	7	MR BLUE SKY — Electric Light Orchestra (Jet)
10	8	ALL RIGHT NOW (EP) — Free (Island)
7	9	JUST ONE MORE NIGHT — Yellow Dog (Virgin)
13	10	BAKER STREET — Gerry Rafferty (United Artists)
15	11	IS THIS LOVE — Bob Marley & the Wailers (Island)
23	12	I CAN'T STAND THE RAIN — Eruption (Atlantic)
11	13	LOVE IS LIKE OXYGEN — Sweet (Polydor)
17	14	EMOTION — Samantha Sang (Private Stock)
8	15	FIGARO — Brotherhood Of Man (Pye)
20	16	FANTASY — Earth, Wind & Fire (CBS)
19	17	RISING FREE (EP) — Tom Robinson Band (EMI)
9	18	HOT LEGS/I WAS ONLY JOKING — Rod Stewart (Riva)
14	19	IF I HAD WORDS — Scott Fitzgerald & Yvonne Keely (Pepper)
27	20	CLASH CITY ROCKERS — Clash (CBS)
12	20	5 MINUTES — Stranglers (United Artists)
24	22	JUST THE WAY YOU ARE — Billy Joel (CBS)
-	23	LILAC WINE — Elkie Brooks (A&M)
28	24	RUMOUR HAS IT — Donna Summer (Casablanca)
-	25	EVERY ONE'S A WINNER — Hot Chocolate (RAK)
-	26	WORDS — Rita Coolidge (A&M)
-	27	BIG BLOW — Manu Dibango (Decca)
-	28	WHENEVER YOU WANT MY LOVE — Real Thing (Pye)
21	29	DRUMMER MAN — Tonight (TDS)
-	30	WALK IN LOVE — Manhattan Transfer (Atlantic)

18 March 1978

last week	this week	
1	1	WUTHERING HEIGHTS — Kate Bush (EMI)
4	2	DENIS — Blondie (Chrysalis)
6	3	COME BACK MY LOVE — Darts (Magnet)
10	4	BAKER STREET — Gerry Rafferty (United Artists)
3	5	TAKE A CHANCE ON ME — Abba (Epic)
2	6	WISHING ON A STAR — Rose Royce (Warner Bros)
5	7	STAYIN' ALIVE — Bee Gees (RSO)
12	8	I CAN'T STAND THE RAIN — Eruption (Atlantic)
11	9	IS THIS LOVE — Bob Marley & The Wailers (Island)
7	10	MR BLUE SKY — Electric Light Orchestra (Jet)
8	11	ALL RIGHT NOW (EP) — Free (Island)
9	12	JUST ONE MORE NIGHT — Yellow Dog (Virgin)
14	13	EMOTION — Samantha Sang (Private Stock)
16	14	FANTASY — Earth, Wind & Fire (CBS)
-	15	MATCHSTALK MEN AND MATCHSTALK CATS AND DOGS — Brian & Michael (Pye)
-	16	I LOVE THE SOUND OF BREAKING GLASS — Nick Lowe (Radar)
23	17	LILAC WINE — Elkie Brooks (A&M)
25	18	EVERY ONE'S A WINNER — Hot Chocolate (RAK)
-	19	(I DON'T WANT TO GO TO) CHELSEA — Elvis Costello (Radar)
-	20	FOLLOW YOU, FOLLOW ME — Genesis (Charisma)
15	21	FIGARO — Brotherhood Of Man (Pye)
-	22	ALLY'S TARTAN ARMY — Andy Cameron (Klub)
24	23	RUMOUR HAS IT — Donna Summer (Casablanca)
-	24	NEWS OF THE WORLD — Jam (Polydor)
17	25	RISING FREE (EP) — Tom Robinson Band (EMI)
20	26	5 MINUTES — Stranglers (United Artists)
27	27	WE'VE GOT THE WHOLE WORLD — Nottm Forest & Paper Lace (Warner Bros)
28	28	WHENEVER YOU WANT MY LOVE — Real Thing (Pye)
30	29	WALK IN LOVE — Manhattan Transfer (Atlantic)
-	30	RHIANNON — Fleetwood Mac (Reprise)

25 March 1978

last week	this week	
1	1	WUTHERING HEIGHTS — Kate Bush (EMI)
2	2	DENIS — Blondie (Chrysalis)
4	3	BAKER STREET — Gerry Rafferty (United Artists)
8	4	I CAN'T STAND THE RAIN — Eruption (Atlantic)
3	5	COME BACK MY LOVE — Darts (Magnet)
6	6	WISHING ON A STAR — Rose Royce (Warner Bros)
9	7	IS THIS LOVE — Bob Marley & the Wailers (Island)
5	8	TAKE A CHANCE ON ME — Abba (Epic)
15	9	MATCHSTALK MEN AND MATCHSTALK CATS AND DOGS — Brian & Michael (Pye)
10	10	MR BLUE SKY — Electric Light Orchestra (Jet)
7	11	STAYIN' ALIVE — Bee Gees (RSO)
13	12	EMOTION — Samantha Sang (Private Stock)
16	13	I LOVE THE SOUND OF BREAKING GLASS — Nick Lowe (Radar)
18	14	EVERY ONE'S A WINNER — Hot Chocolate (RAK)
14	15	FANTASY — Earth, Wind & Fire (CBS)
17	16	LILAC WINE — Elkie Brooks (A&M)
22	17	ALLY'S TARTAN ARMY — Andy Cameron (Klub)
-	18	IF YOU CAN'T GIVE ME LOVE — Suzi Quatro (RAK)
23	19	RUMOUR HAS IT — Donna Summer (Casablanca)
11	20	ALL RIGHT NOW (EP) — Free (Island)
19	20	(I DON'T WANT TO GO TO) CHELSEA — Elvis Costello (Radar)
29	22	WALK IN LOVE — Manhattan Transfer (Atlantic)
12	23	JUST ONE MORE NIGHT — Yellow Dog (Virgin)
24	24	NEWS OF THE WORLD — Jam (Polydor)
27	25	WE'VE GOT THE WHOLE WORLD — Nottm Forest & Paper Lace (Warner Bros)
20	26	FOLLOW YOU, FOLLOW ME — Genesis (Charisma)
-	27	WHAT'S YOUR NAME, WHAT'S YOUR NUMBER — Andrea True Connection (Buddah)
-	28	SINGIN' IN THE RAIN — Sheila B Devotion (Carrere)
-	29	I WONDER WHY — Showaddywaddy (Arista)
-	30	JUST THE WAY YOU ARE — Billy Joel (CBS)

Sweet's ultra-slick top tenner, far removed from their early glam bubblegum, was the group's first chart entry for over two years. Free's *All Right Now* made the Top 20 for the third occasion in eight years, this time as lead track on the first of a new Island series of classic hits EPs. Tom Robinson's *Rising Free* EP sold largely on the strength of its controversial anthem *Glad To Be Gay*, while Blondie's chart debut revived fellow New Yorkers Randy & the Rainbows' 1963 hit Denise.

April 1978

1 April 1978

last	this	
2	1	DENIS — Blondie (Chrysalis)
3	2	BAKER STREET — Gerry Rafferty (United Artists)
1	3	WUTHERING HEIGHTS — Kate Bush (EMI)
9	4	MATCHSTALK MEN AND MATCHSTALK CATS AND DOGS — Brian & Michael (Pye)
4	5	I CAN'T STAND THE RAIN — Eruption (Atlantic)
6	6	WISHING ON A STAR — Rose Royce (Warner Bros)
13	7	I LOVE THE SOUND OF BREAKING GLASS — Nick Lowe (Radar)
5	8	COME BACK MY LOVE — Darts (Magnet)
8	9	TAKE A CHANCE ON ME — Abba (Epic)
14	10	EVERY ONE'S A WINNER — Hot Chocolate (RAK)
12	11	EMOTION — Samantha Sang (Private Stock)
18	11	IF YOU CAN'T GIVE ME LOVE — Suzi Quatro (RAK)
11	13	STAYIN' ALIVE — Bee Gees (RSO)
7	14	IS THIS LOVE — Bob Marley & the Wailers (Island)
26	15	FOLLOW YOU, FOLLOW ME — Genesis (Charisma)
-	16	WHENEVER YOU WANT MY LOVE — Real Thing (Pye)
16	17	LILAC WINE — Elkie Brooks (A&M)
20	18	(I DON'T WANT TO GO TO) CHELSEA — Elvis Costello (Radar)
15	19	FANTASY — Earth, Wind & Fire (CBS)
19	20	RUMOUR HAS IT — Donna Summer (Casablanca)
29	21	I WONDER WHY — Showaddywaddy (Arista)
10	22	MR BLUE SKY — Electric Light Orchestra (Jet)
22	23	WALK IN LOVE — Manhattan Transfer (Atlantic)
-	24	NEVER LET HER SLIP AWAY — Andrew Gold (Asylum)
17	25	ALLY'S TARTAN ARMY — Andy Cameron (Klub)
-	26	TOO MUCH TOO LITTLE TOO LATE — Johnny Mathis & Deniece Williams (CBS)
-	27	THE GHOST OF LOVE — Tavares (Capitol)
-	28	SOMETIMES WHEN WE TOUCH — Dan Hill (20th Century)
-	29	I'LL GO WHERE YOUR MUSIC TAKES ME — Tina Charles (CBS)
28	30	SINGIN' IN THE RAIN — Sheila B Devotion (EMI)

8 April 1978

last	this	
1	1	DENIS — Blondie (Chrysalis)
2	2	BAKER STREET — Gerry Rafferty (United Artists)
3	3	WUTHERING HEIGHTS — Kate Bush (EMI)
11	4	IF YOU CAN'T GIVE ME LOVE — Suzi Quatro (RAK)
4	5	MATCHSTALK MEN AND MATCHSTALK CATS AND DOGS — Brian & Michael (Pye)
21	6	I WONDER WHY — Showaddywaddy (Arista)
5	7	I CAN'T STAND THE RAIN — Eruption (Atlantic)
7	8	I LOVE THE SOUND OF BREAKING GLASS — Nick Lowe (Radar)
24	9	NEVER LET HER SLIP AWAY — Andrew Gold (Asylum)
14	10	IS THIS LOVE — Bob Marley & the Wailers (Island)
25	11	ALLY'S TARTAN ARMY — Andy Cameron (Klub)
15	12	FOLLOW YOU, FOLLOW ME — Genesis (Charisma)
10	13	EVERY ONE'S A WINNER — Hot Chocolate (RAK)
8	14	(I DON'T WANT TO GO TO) CHELSEA — Elvis Costello (Radar)
13	15	STAYIN' ALIVE — Bee Gees (RSO)
11	16	EMOTION — Samantha Sang (Private Stock)
-	17	WITH A LITTLE LUCK — Wings (Parlophone)
8	18	COME BACK MY LOVE — Darts (Magnet)
23	19	WALK IN LOVE — Manhattan Transfer (Atlantic)
19	20	FANTASY — Earth, Wind & Fire (CBS)
6	21	WISHING ON A STAR — Rose Royce (Warner Bros)
26	22	TOO MUCH TOO LITTLE TOO LATE — Johnny Mathis & Deniece Williams (CBS)
28	23	SOMETIMES WHEN WE TOUCH — Dan Hill (20th Century)
-	24	EVERYBODY DANCE — Chic (Atlantic)
-	25	MORE LIKE THE MOVIES — Dr Hook (Capitol)
9	26	TAKE A CHANCE ON ME — Abba (Epic)
30	27	SINGIN' IN THE RAIN — Sheila B Devotion (EMI)
22	28	MR BLUE SKY — Electric Light Orchestra (Jet)
16	29	WHENEVER YOU WANT MY LOVE — Real Thing (Pye)
17	30	LILAC WINE — Elkie Brooks (A&M)

15 April 1978

last	this	
6	1	I WONDER WHY — Showaddywaddy (Arista)
4	2	IF YOU CAN'T GIVE ME LOVE — Suzi Quatro (RAK)
1	3	DENIS — Blondie (Chrysalis)
5	4	MATCHSTALK MEN AND MATCHSTALK CATS AND DOGS — Brian & Michael (Pye)
2	5	BAKER STREET — Gerry Rafferty (United Artists)
12	6	FOLLOW YOU, FOLLOW ME — Genesis (Charisma)
9	7	NEVER LET HER SLIP AWAY — Andrew Gold (Asylum)
17	7	WITH A LITTLE LUCK — Wings (Parlophone)
22	9	TOO MUCH TOO LITTLE TOO LATE — Johnny Mathis & Deniece Williams (CBS)
3	10	WUTHERING HEIGHTS — Kate Bush (EMI)
19	11	WALK IN LOVE — Manhattan Transfer (Atlantic)
-	12	NIGHT FEVER — Bee Gees (RSO)
7	13	I CAN'T STAND THE RAIN — Eruption (Atlantic)
8	14	I LOVE THE SOUND OF BREAKING GLASS — Nick Lowe (Radar)
10	15	IS THIS LOVE — Bob Marley & the Wailers (Island)
13	16	EVERY ONE'S A WINNER — Hot Chocolate (RAK)
25	17	MORE LIKE THE MOVIES — Dr Hook (Capitol)
11	18	ALLY'S TARTAN ARMY — Andy Cameron (Klub)
23	19	SOMETIMES WHEN WE TOUCH — Dan Hill (20th Century)
27	20	SINGIN' IN THE RAIN — Sheila B Devotion (EMI)
24	21	EVERYBODY DANCE — Chic (Atlantic)
15	22	STAYIN' ALIVE — Bee Gees (RSO)
14	23	(I DON'T WANT TO GO TO) CHELSEA — Elvis Costello (Radar)
16	24	EMOTION — Samantha Sang (Private Stock)
-	25	SHE'S SO MODERN — Boomtown Rats (Ensign)
18	26	COME BACK MY LOVE — Darts (Magnet)
-	27	HEY SENORITA — War (MCA)
-	28	IT TAKES TWO TO TANGO — Richard Myhill (Mercury)
-	29	I LOVE MUSIC — O' Jays (Philadelphia)
20	30	FANTASY — Earth, Wind & Fire (CBS)

22 April 1978

last	this	
12	1	NIGHT FEVER — Bee Gees (RSO)
1	2	I WONDER WHY — Showaddywaddy (Arista)
7	3	NEVER LET HER SLIP AWAY — Andrew Gold (Asylum)
4	4	MATCHSTALK MEN AND MATCHSTALK CATS AND DOGS — Brian & Michael (Pye)
2	5	IF YOU CAN'T GIVE ME LOVE — Suzi Quatro (RAK)
5	6	BAKER STREET — Gerry Rafferty (United Artists)
7	7	WITH A LITTLE LUCK — Wings (Parlophone)
6	8	FOLLOW YOU, FOLLOW ME — Genesis (Charisma)
9	9	TOO MUCH TOO LITTLE TOO LATE — Johnny Mathis & Deniece Williams (CBS)
3	10	DENIS — Blondie (Chrysalis)
11	11	WALK IN LOVE — Manhattan Transfer (Atlantic)
19	12	SOMETIMES WHEN WE TOUCH — Dan Hill (20th Century)
10	13	WUTHERING HEIGHTS — Kate Bush (EMI)
17	14	MORE LIKE THE MOVIES — Dr Hook (Capitol)
21	15	EVERYBODY DANCE — Chic (Atlantic)
25	15	SHE'S SO MODERN — Boomtown Rats (Ensign)
14	17	I LOVE THE SOUND OF BREAKING GLASS — Nick Lowe (Radar)
20	18	SINGIN' IN THE RAIN — Sheila B Devotion (EMI)
23	19	(I DON'T WANT TO GO TO) CHELSEA — Elvis Costello (Radar)
-	20	LET'S ALL CHANT — Michael Zager Band (Private Stock)
13	21	I CAN'T STAND THE RAIN — Eruption (Atlantic)
16	22	EVERY ONE'S A WINNER — Hot Chocolate (RAK)
-	23	EGO — Elton John (Rocket)
27	24	HEY SENORITA — War (MCA)
28	25	IT TAKES TWO TO TANGO — Richard Myhill (Mercury)
22	26	STAYIN' ALIVE — Bee Gees (RSO)
15	27	IS THIS LOVE — Bob Marley & the Wailers (Island)
-	28	TAKE ME I'M YOURS — Squeeze (A&M)
-	29	LONG LIVE ROCK'N'ROLL — Rainbow (Polydor)
-	30	AUTOMATIC LOVER — Dee D Jackson (Mercury)

The Radar label, formed by a splinter group of the former Stiff hierarchy, got off to a cracking start as both of its first single releases, by Nick Lowe and Elvis Costello, cracked the Top 20 almost simultaneously. Brian & Michael's oddly-titled hit was a hymn to the solid Northern England values of painter L.S. Lowry (whose works were, indeed, populated by matchstick figures). Ally's Tartan Army, from further north still, was the Scotland football team's fans' anthem.

April – May 1978

last week / this week

29 April 1978

last week	this week	entry
1	1	NIGHT FEVER — Bee Gees (RSO)
9	2	TOO MUCH TOO LITTLE TOO LATE — Johnny Mathis & Deniece Williams (CBS)
5	3	IF YOU CAN'T GIVE ME LOVE — Suzi Quatro (RAK)
4	4	MATCHSTALK MEN AND MATCHSTALK CATS AND DOGS — Brian & Michael (Pye)
2	5	I WONDER WHY — Showaddywaddy (Arista)
3	6	NEVER LET HER SLIP AWAY — Andrew Gold (Asylum)
7	7	WITH A LITTLE LUCK — Wings (Parlophone)
8	8	FOLLOW YOU, FOLLOW ME — Genesis (Charisma)
18	9	SINGIN' IN THE RAIN — Sheila B Devotion (EMI)
6	10	BAKER STREET — Gerry Rafferty (United Artists)
15	11	SHE'S SO MODERN — Boomtown Rats (Ensign)
30	12	AUTOMATIC LOVER — Dee D Jackson (Mercury)
14	13	MORE LIKE THE MOVIES — Dr Hook (Capitol)
15	14	EVERYBODY DANCE — Chic (Atlantic)
20	15	LET'S ALL CHANT — Michael Zager Band (Private Stock)
11	16	WALK IN LOVE — Manhattan Transfer (Atlantic)
10	17	DENIS — Blondie (Chrysalis)
12	18	SOMETIMES WHEN WE TOUCH — Dan Hill (20th Century)
25	19	IT TAKES TWO TO TANGO — Richard Myhill (Mercury)
-	20	RIVERS OF BABYLON — Boney M (Atlantic)
28	21	TAKE ME I'M YOURS — Squeeze (A&M)
21	22	I CAN'T STAND THE RAIN — Eruption (Atlantic)
-	23	(I CAN'T GET NO) SATISFACTION — Devo (Stiff)
-	24	THE BEAT GOES ON AND ON — Ripple (Salsoul)
-	25	BAD OLD DAYS — CoCo (Ariola Hansa)
-	26	BACK IN LOVE AGAIN — Donna Summer (GTO)
22	27	EVERY ONE'S A WINNER — Hot Chocolate (RAK)
13	28	WUTHERING HEIGHTS — Kate Bush (EMI)
23	29	EGO — Elton John (Rocket)
26	30	STAYIN' ALIVE — Bee Gees (RSO)

6 May 1978

last week	this week	entry
1	1	NIGHT FEVER — Bee Gees (RSO)
6	2	NEVER LET HER SLIP AWAY — Andrew Gold (Asylum)
2	3	TOO MUCH TOO LITTLE TOO LATE — Johnny Mathis & Deniece Williams (CBS)
3	4	IF YOU CAN'T GIVE ME LOVE — Suzi Quatro (RAK)
12	5	AUTOMATIC LOVER — Dee D Jackson (Mercury)
4	6	MATCHSTALK MEN AND MATCHSTALK CATS AND DOGS — Brian & Michael (Pye)
8	7	FOLLOW YOU, FOLLOW ME — Genesis (Charisma)
5	8	I WONDER WHY — Showaddywaddy (Arista)
20	9	RIVERS OF BABYLON — Boney M (Atlantic)
9	10	SINGIN' IN THE RAIN — Sheila B Devotion (EMI)
15	11	LET'S ALL CHANT — Michael Zager Band (Private Stock)
7	12	WITH A LITTLE LUCK — Wings (Parlophone)
14	13	EVERYBODY DANCE — Chic (Atlantic)
11	14	SHE'S SO MODERN — Boomtown Rats (Ensign)
13	15	MORE LIKE THE MOVIES — Dr Hook (Capitol)
25	16	BAD OLD DAYS — CoCo (Ariola Hansa)
21	17	TAKE ME I'M YOURS — Squeeze (A&M)
18	18	SOMETIMES WHEN WE TOUCH — Dan Hill (20th Century)
-	19	THE DAY THE WORLD TURNED DAYGLO — X Ray Spex (EMI Int)
10	20	BAKER STREET — Gerry Rafferty (United Artists)
-	21	BECAUSE THE NIGHT — Patti Smith (Arista)
19	22	IT TAKES TWO TO TANGO — Richard Myhill (Mercury)
23	23	JACK AND JILL — Raydio (Arista)
23	24	(I CAN'T GET NO) SATISFACTION — Devo (Stiff)
16	25	WALK IN LOVE — Manhattan Transfer (Atlantic)
-	26	WHAT A WASTE — Ian Dury (Stiff)
27	27	DO IT DO IT AGAIN — Rafaella Carra (Epic)
17	28	DENIS — Blondie (Chrysalis)
-	29	HEY LORD DON'T ASK ME QUESTIONS — Graham Parker & The Rumour (Vertigo)
-	30	DANCE A LITTLE BIT CLOSER — Charo & the Salsoul Orchestra (Salsoul)

13 May 1978

last week	this week	entry
1	1	NIGHT FEVER — Bee Gees (RSO)
9	2	RIVERS OF BABYLON — Boney M (Atlantic)
3	3	TOO MUCH TOO LITTLE TOO LATE — Johnny Mathis & Deniece Williams (CBS)
2	4	NEVER LET HER SLIP AWAY — Andrew Gold (Asylum)
5	5	AUTOMATIC LOVER — Dee D Jackson (Mercury)
11	6	LET'S ALL CHANT — Michael Zager Band (Private Stock)
23	7	JACK AND JILL — Raydio (Arista)
21	8	BECAUSE THE NIGHT — Patti Smith (Arista)
8	9	I WONDER WHY — Showaddywaddy (Arista)
4	10	IF YOU CAN'T GIVE ME LOVE — Suzi Quatro (RAK)
13	11	EVERYBODY DANCE — Chic (Atlantic)
6	12	MATCHSTALK MEN AND MATCHSTALK CATS AND DOGS — Brian & Michael (Pye)
10	13	SINGIN' IN THE RAIN — Sheila B Devotion (EMI)
-	14	(I'M ALWAYS TOUCHED BY YOUR) PRESENCE DEAR — Blondie (Chrysalis)
7	15	FOLLOW YOU, FOLLOW ME — Genesis (Charisma)
14	16	SHE'S SO MODERN — Boomtown Rats (Ensign)
16	17	BAD OLD DAYS — CoCo (Ariola Hansa)
12	18	WITH A LITTLE LUCK — Wings (Parlophone)
17	19	TAKE ME I'M YOURS — Squeeze (A&M)
-	20	THE BOY FROM NEW YORK CITY — Darts (Magnet)
-	21	NICE 'N' SLEAZY — Stranglers (United Artists)
-	22	MORE THAN A WOMAN — Tavares (Capitol)
19	23	THE DAY THE WORLD TURNED DAYGLO — X Ray Spex (EMI Int)
-	24	LOVE IS IN THE AIR — John Paul Young (Ariola)
-	25	IF I CAN'T HAVE YOU — Yvonne Elliman (RSO)
27	26	DO IT DO IT AGAIN — Rafaella Carra (Epic)
-	27	HI TENSION — Hi Tension (Island)
15	28	MORE LIKE THE MOVIES — Dr Hook (Capitol)
26	29	WHAT A WASTE — Ian Dury (Stiff)
24	30	(I CAN'T GET NO) SATISFACTION — Devo (Stiff)

20 May 1978

last week	this week	entry
2	1	RIVERS OF BABYLON — Boney M (Atlantic)
1	2	NIGHT FEVER — Bee Gees (RSO)
8	3	BECAUSE THE NIGHT — Patti Smith (Arista)
3	4	TOO MUCH TOO LITTLE TOO LATE — Johnny Mathis & Deniece Williams (CBS)
5	5	AUTOMATIC LOVER — Dee D Jackson (Mercury)
4	6	NEVER LET HER SLIP AWAY — Andrew Gold (Asylum)
20	7	THE BOY FROM NEW YORK CITY — Darts (Magnet)
14	8	(I'M ALWAYS TOUCHED BY YOUR) PRESENCE DEAR — Blondie (Chrysalis)
6	9	LET'S ALL CHANT — Michael Zager Band (Private Stock)
25	10	IF I CAN'T HAVE YOU — Yvonne Elliman (RSO)
7	11	JACK AND JILL — Raydio (Arista)
16	12	SHE'S SO MODERN — Boomtown Rats (Ensign)
11	13	EVERYBODY DANCE — Chic (Atlantic)
24	14	LOVE IS IN THE AIR — John Paul Young (Ariola)
23	15	THE DAY THE WORLD TURNED DAYGLO — X Ray Spex (EMI Int)
22	16	MORE THAN A WOMAN — Tavares (Capitol)
27	17	HI TENSION — Hi Tension (Island)
26	18	DO IT DO IT AGAIN — Rafaella Carra (Epic)
21	19	NICE 'N' SLEAZY — Stranglers (United Artists)
10	20	IF YOU CAN'T GIVE ME LOVE — Suzi Quatro (RAK)
29	21	WHAT A WASTE — Ian Dury (Stiff)
12	22	MATCHSTALK MEN AND MATCHSTALK CATS AND DOGS — Brian & Michael (Pye)
19	23	TAKE ME I'M YOURS — Squeeze (A&M)
-	24	UP AGAINST THE WALL — Tom Robinson Band (EMI)
17	25	BAD OLD DAYS — CoCo (Ariola Hansa)
-	26	A-BA-NI-BI — Izhar Cohen & The Alphabeta (Polydor)
13	27	SINGIN' IN THE RAIN — Sheila B Devotion (EMI)
-	28	ANGELS WITH DIRTY FACES — Sham 69 (Polydor)
18	29	WITH A LITTLE LUCK — Wings (Parlophone)
-	30	CA PLANE POUR MOI — Plastic Bertrand (Sire)

Neither the Bee Gees' *How Deep Is Your Love* nor *Stayin' Alive* had quite equalled their US success (where both reached Number One) for the Bee Gees, but *Night Fever,* the third of the *Saturday Night Fever* movie triumvirate, redressed the balance by becoming the Gibb brothers' biggest UK seller. *What A Waste* finally put Ian Dury in the chart after two earlier critically-rated singles, while Richard Myhill's *It Takes Two To Tango* was one of the year's sillier marketing gimmicks: a square-shaped record.

27 May 1978

last week	this week	
1	1	RIVERS OF BABYLON Boney M (Atlantic)
2	2	NIGHT FEVER Bee Gees (RSO)
7	3	THE BOY FROM NEW YORK CITY Darts (Magnet)
3	4	BECAUSE THE NIGHT Patti Smith (Arista)
10	5	IF I CAN'T HAVE YOU Yvonne Elliman (RSO)
14	6	LOVE IS IN THE AIR John Paul Young (Ariola)
4	7	TOO MUCH TOO LITTLE TOO LATE Johnny Mathis & Deniece Williams (CBS)
16	8	MORE THAN A WOMAN Tavares (Capitol)
5	9	AUTOMATIC LOVER Dee D Jackson (Mercury)
6	10	NEVER LET HER SLIP AWAY Andrew Gold (Asylum)
21	11	WHAT A WASTE Ian Dury (Stiff)
11	12	JACK AND JILL Raydio (Arista)
17	13	HI TENSION Hi Tension (Island)
-	14	IT MAKES YOU FEEL LIKE DANCIN' Rose Royce (Warner Bros)
18	15	DO IT DO IT AGAIN Rafaella Carra (Epic)
9	16	LET'S ALL CHANT Michael Zager Band (Private Stock)
19	17	NICE 'N' SLEAZY Stranglers (United Artists)
30	18	CA PLANE POUR MOI Plastic Bertrand (Sire)
8	19	(I'M ALWAYS TOUCHED BY YOUR) PRESENCE DEAR Blondie (Chrysalis)
-	20	COME TO ME Ruby Winters (Creole)
12	21	SHE'S SO MODERN Boomtown Rats (Ensign)
26	22	A-BA-NI-BI Izhar Cohen & TheAlphabeta (Polydor)
15	23	THE DAY THE WORLD TURNED DAYGLO X Ray Spex (EMI Int)
-	24	ON A LITTLE STREET IN SINGAPORE Manhattan Transfer (Atlantic)
-	25	YOU'RE THE ONE THAT I WANT John Travolta/ Olivia Newton-John (RSO)
13	26	EVERYBODY DANCE Chic (Atlantic)
-	27	OH CAROL Smokie (RAK)
28	28	ANGELS WITH DIRTY FACES Sham 69 (Polydor)
-	29	SHAME Evelyn 'Champagne' King (RCA)
20	30	IF YOU CAN'T GIVE ME LOVE Suzi Quatro (RAK)

3 June 1978

1	1	RIVERS OF BABYLON Boney M (Atlantic)
3	2	THE BOY FROM NEW YORK CITY Darts (Magnet)
2	3	NIGHT FEVER Bee Gees (RSO)
4	4	BECAUSE THE NIGHT Patti Smith (Arista)
5	5	IF I CAN'T HAVE YOU Yvonne Elliman (RSO)
11	6	WHAT A WASTE Ian Dury (Stiff)
19	7	(I'M ALWAYS TOUCHED BY YOUR) PRESENCE DEAR Blondie (Chrysalis)
6	8	LOVE IS IN THE AIR John Paul Young (Ariola)
8	9	MORE THAN A WOMAN Tavares (Capitol)
18	10	CA PLANE POUR MOI Plastic Bertrand (Sire)
17	11	NICE 'N' SLEAZY Stranglers (United Artists)
15	12	DO IT DO IT AGAIN Rafaella Carra (Epic)
25	13	YOU'RE THE ONE THAT I WANT John Travolta/ Olivia Newton-John (RSO)
13	14	HI TENSION Hi Tension (Island)
20	15	COME TO ME Ruby Winters (Creole)
12	16	JACK AND JILL Raydio (Arista)
28	17	ANGELS WITH DIRTY FACES Sham 69 (Polydor)
10	18	NEVER LET HER SLIP AWAY Andrew Gold (Asylum)
-	19	DAVY'S ON THE ROAD AGAIN Manfred Mann's Earth Band (Bronze)
7	20	TOO MUCH TOO LITTLE TOO LATE Johnny Mathis & Deniece Williams (CBS)
21	21	SHE'S SO MODERN Boomtown Rats (Ensign)
14	22	IT MAKES YOU FEEL LIKE DANCIN' Rose Royce (Warner Bros)
27	23	OH CAROL Smokie (RAK)
9	24	AUTOMATIC LOVER Dee D Jackson (Mercury)
23	25	THE DAY THE WORLD TURNED DAYGLO X Ray Spex (EMI Int)
-	26	ROSALIE Thin Lizzy (Vertigo)
-	27	(DON'T FEAR) THE REAPER Blue Oyster Cult (CBS)
-	28	UP AGAINST THE WALL Tom Robinson Band (EMI)
29	29	OLE OLA Rod Stewart (Riva)
-	30	ANNIE'S SONG James Galway (RCA)

10 June 1978

1	1	RIVERS OF BABYLON Boney M (Atlantic)
13	2	YOU'RE THE ONE THAT I WANT John Travolta/ Olivia Newton-John (RSO)
2	3	THE BOY FROM NEW YORK CITY Darts (Magnet)
3	4	NIGHT FEVER Bee Gees (RSO)
5	5	IF I CAN'T HAVE YOU Yvonne Elliman (RSO)
6	6	WHAT A WASTE Ian Dury (Stiff)
10	7	CA PLANE POUR MOI Plastic Bertrand (Sire)
8	8	LOVE IS IN THE AIR John Paul Young (Ariola)
23	9	OH CAROL Smokie (RAK)
4	10	BECAUSE THE NIGHT Patti Smith (Arista)
29	11	OLE OLA Rod Stewart (Riva)
19	12	DAVY'S ON THE ROAD AGAIN Manfred Mann's Earth Band (Bronze)
9	13	MORE THAN A WOMAN Tavares (Capitol)
7	14	(I'M ALWAYS TOUCHED BY YOUR) PRESENCE DEAR Blondie (Chrysalis)
15	15	COME TO ME Ruby Winters (Creole)
14	16	HI TENSION Hi Tension (Island)
-	17	MISS YOU Rolling Stones (EMI)
30	18	ANNIE'S SONG James Galway (RCA)
17	19	ANGELS WITH DIRTY FACES Sham 69 (Polydor)
-	20	PUMP IT UP Elvis Costello (Radar)
-	21	NEVER SAY DIE Black Sabbath (Vertigo)
12	22	DO IT DO IT AGAIN Rafaella Carra (Epic)
27	23	(DON'T FEAR) THE REAPER Blue Oyster Cult (CBS)
11	24	NICE 'N' SLEAZY Stranglers (United Artists)
-	25	A-BA-NI-BI Izhar Cohen & The Alphabeta (Polydor)
-	26	MAKING UP AGAIN Goldie (Bronze)
26	27	ROSALIE Thin Lizzy (Vertigo)
16	28	JACK AND JILL Raydio (Arista)
-	29	AIN'T GOT A CLUE Lurkers (Beggars Banquet)
-	30	ON A LITTLE STREET IN SINGAPORE Manhattan Transfer (Atlantic)

17 June 1978

1	1	YOU'RE THE ONE THAT I WANT John Travolta/ Olivia Newton-John (RSO)
1	2	RIVERS OF BABYLON Boney M (Atlantic)
3	3	THE BOY FROM NEW YORK CITY Darts (Magnet)
18	4	ANNIE'S SONG James Galway (RCA)
11	5	OLE OLA Rod Stewart (Riva)
13	6	MORE THAN A WOMAN Tavares (Capitol)
5	7	IF I CAN'T HAVE YOU Yvonne Elliman (RSO)
12	8	DAVY'S ON THE ROAD AGAIN Manfred Mann's Earth Band (Bronze)
4	9	NIGHT FEVER Bee Gees (RSO)
17	10	MISS YOU Rolling Stones (EMI)
7	11	CA PLANE POUR MOI Plastic Bertrand (Sire)
8	12	LOVE IS IN THE AIR John Paul Young (Ariola)
9	13	OH CAROL Smokie (RAK)
16	14	HI TENSION Hi Tension (Island)
6	15	WHAT A WASTE Ian Dury (Stiff)
10	16	BECAUSE THE NIGHT Patti Smith (Arista)
26	17	MAKING UP AGAIN Goldie (Bronze)
-	18	IT SURE BRINGS OUT THE LOVE IN YOUR EYES David Soul (Private Stock)
-	19	AIRPORT Motors (Virgin)
27	20	ROSALIE Thin Lizzy (Vertigo)
-	21	MIND BLOWING DECISIONS Heatwave (GTO)
-	22	THE SMURF SONG Father Abraham (Decca)
-	23	DANCING IN THE CITY Marshall Hain (Harvest)
21	24	NEVER SAY DIE Black Sabbath (Vertigo)
19	25	ANGELS WITH DIRTY FACES Sham 69 (Polydor)
15	26	COME TO ME Ruby Winters (Creole)
22	27	DO IT DO IT AGAIN Rafaella Carra (Epic)
-	28	MAN WITH THE CHILD IN HIS EYES Kate Bush (EMI)
-	29	BEAUTIFUL LOVER Brotherhood of Man (Pye)
-	30	WILD WEST HERO Electric Light Orchestra (Jet)

Boney M's *Rivers Of Babylon,* a cover of a fairly obscure reggae release by the Melodians, was not only the biggest hit in the group's lengthy chart run, but also one of the UK's all-time top sellers. Following a second run of success by its B-side later in the year, the single sold only a few thousand short of two million, making it second only to *Mull Of Kintyre* in total UK sales. Darts' second Number Two, meanwhile, revived another US oldie, by the Ad Libs from1965.

June – July 1978

24 June 1978

last	this		
1	1	YOU'RE THE ONE THAT I WANT	John Travolta/ Olivia Newton-John (RSO)
10	2	MISS YOU	Rolling Stones (EMI)
2	3	RIVERS OF BABYLON	Boney M (Atlantic)
4	4	ANNIE'S SONG	James Galway (RCA)
13	5	OH CAROL	Smokie (RAK)
8	6	DAVY'S ON THE ROAD AGAIN	Manfred Mann's Earth Band (Bronze)
22	7	THE SMURF SONG	Father Abraham (Decca)
11	8	CA PLANE POUR MOI	Plastic Bertrand (Sire)
3	9	THE BOY FROM NEW YORK CITY	Darts (Magnet)
19	10	AIRPORT	Motors (Virgin)
23	11	DANCING IN THE CITY	Marshall Hain (Harvest)
7	12	IF I CAN'T HAVE YOU	Yvonne Elliman (RSO)
17	13	MAKING UP AGAIN	Goldie (Bronze)
28	14	MAN WITH THE CHILD IN HIS EYES	Kate Bush (EMI)
21	15	MIND BLOWING DECISIONS	Heatwave (GTO)
9	16	NIGHT FEVER	Bee Gees (RSO)
15	17	WHAT A WASTE	Ian Dury (Stiff)
-	18	LIKE CLOCKWORK	Boomtown Rats (Ensign)
12	19	LOVE IS IN THE AIR	John Paul Young (Ariola)
14	20	HI TENSION	Hi Tension (Island)
5	21	OLE OLA	Rod Stewart (Riva)
18	22	IT SURE BRINGS OUT THE LOVE IN YOUR EYES	David Soul (Private Stock)
-	23	(DON'T FEAR) THE REAPER	Blue Oyster Cult (CBS)
29	24	BEAUTIFUL LOVER	Brotherhood of Man (Pye)
24	25	NEVER SAY DIE	Black Sabbath (Vertigo)
-	26	SATISFY MY SOUL	Bob Marley & the Wailers (Island)
-	27	USED TA BE MY GIRL	O'Jays (Warner Bros)
26	28	COME TO ME	Ruby Winters (Creole)
6	29	MORE THAN A WOMAN	Tavares (Capitol)
25	30	ANGELS WITH DIRTY FACES	Sham 69 (Polydor)

1 July 1978

1	1	YOU'RE THE ONE THAT I WANT	John Travolta/ Olivia Newton-John (RSO)
7	2	THE SMURF SONG	Father Abraham (Decca)
2	3	MISS YOU	Rolling Stones (EMI)
10	4	AIRPORT	Motors (Virgin)
4	5	ANNIE'S SONG	James Galway (RCA)
6	6	DAVY'S ON THE ROAD AGAIN	Manfred Mann's Earth Band (Bronze)
13	7	MAKING UP AGAIN	Goldie (Bronze)
3	8	RIVERS OF BABYLON	Boney M (Atlantic)
14	9	MAN WITH THE CHILD IN HIS EYES	Kate Bush (EMI)
11	10	DANCING IN THE CITY	Marshall Hain (Harvest)
8	11	CA PLANE POUR MOI	Plastic Bertrand (Sire)
18	12	LIKE CLOCKWORK	Boomtown Rats (Ensign)
5	13	OH CAROL	Smokie (RAK)
15	14	MIND BLOWING DECISIONS	Heatwave (GTO)
27	15	USED TA BE MY GIRL	O'Jays (Warner Bros)
9	16	THE BOY FROM NEW YORK CITY	Darts (Magnet)
24	17	BEAUTIFUL LOVER	Brotherhood of Man (Pye)
12	18	IF I CAN'T HAVE YOU	Yvonne Elliman (RSO)
-	19	ARGENTINE MELODY	San Jose (MCA)
19	20	LOVE IS IN THE AIR	John Paul Young (Ariola)
21	21	BOOGIE OOGIE OOGIE	A Taste Of Honey (Capitol)
23	22	(DON'T FEAR) THE REAPER	Blue Oyster Cult (CBS)
25	23	NEVER SAY DIE	Black Sabbath (Vertigo)
-	24	SUBSTITUTE	Clout (Carrere)
22	25	IT SURE BRINGS OUT THE LOVE IN YOUR EYES	David Soul (Private Stock)
-	26	ROSALIE	Thin Lizzy (Vertigo)
-	27	FROM EAST TO WEST	Voyage (GTO/Hansa)
16	28	NIGHT FEVER	Bee Gees (RSO)
-	29	A LITTLE BIT OF SOAP	Showaddywaddy (Arista)
-	30	FLYING HIGH	Commodores (Motown)

8 July 1978

1	1	YOU'RE THE ONE THAT I WANT	John Travolta/ Olivia Newton-John (RSO)
2	2	THE SMURF SONG	Father Abraham (Decca)
3	3	MISS YOU	Rolling Stones (EMI)
4	4	AIRPORT	Motors (Virgin)
9	5	MAN WITH THE CHILD IN HIS EYES	Kate Bush (EMI)
5	6	ANNIE'S SONG	James Galway (RCA)
12	7	LIKE CLOCKWORK	Boomtown Rats (Ensign)
10	8	DANCING IN THE CITY	Marshall Hain (Harvest)
7	9	MAKING UP AGAIN	Goldie (Bronze)
14	10	MIND BLOWING DECISIONS	Heatwave (GTO)
8	11	RIVERS OF BABYLON	Boney M (Atlantic)
6	12	DAVY'S ON THE ROAD AGAIN	Manfred Mann's Earth Band (Bronze)
29	13	A LITTLE BIT OF SOAP	Showaddywaddy (Arista)
15	14	USED TA BE MY GIRL	O'Jays (Warner Bros)
19	15	ARGENTINE MELODY	San Jose (MCA)
21	16	BOOGIE OOGIE OOGIE	A Taste Of Honey (Capitol)
13	17	OH CAROL	Smokie (RAK)
22	18	(DON'T FEAR) THE REAPER	Blue Oyster Cult (CBS)
17	19	BEAUTIFUL LOVER	Brotherhood of Man (Pye)
-	20	(WHITE MAN) IN HAMMERSMITH PALAIS	Clash (CBS)
27	21	FROM EAST TO WEST	Voyage (GTO/Hansa)
11	22	CA PLANE POUR MOI	Plastic Bertrand (Sire)
24	23	SUBSTITUTE	Clout (Carrere)
28	24	NIGHT FEVER	Bee Gees (RSO)
26	25	ROSALIE	Thin Lizzy (Vertigo)
-	26	RUN FOR HOME	Lindisfarne (Mercury)
-	27	COME ON DANCE DANCE	Saturday Night Band (CBS)
-	28	THE BIGGEST BLOW: NO ONE IS INNOCENT	Sex Pistols (Virgin)
-	29	ROCK AND ROLL DAMNATION	AC/DC (Atlantic)
-	30	WILD WEST HERO	Electric Light Orchestra (Jet)

15 July 1978

1	1	YOU'RE THE ONE THAT I WANT	John Travolta/ Olivia Newton-John (RSO)
2	2	THE SMURF SONG	Father Abraham (Decca)
4	3	AIRPORT	Motors (Virgin)
8	4	DANCING IN THE CITY	Marshall Hain (Harvest)
5	5	MAN WITH THE CHILD IN HIS EYES	Kate Bush (EMI)
7	6	LIKE CLOCKWORK	Boomtown Rats (Ensign)
13	7	A LITTLE BIT OF SOAP	Showaddywaddy (Arista)
3	8	MISS YOU	Rolling Stones (EMI)
6	9	ANNIE'S SONG	James Galway (RCA)
28	10	BIGGEST BLOW	Sex Pistols (Virgin)
16	11	BOOGIE OOGIE OOGIE	A Taste Of Honey (Capitol)
23	12	SUBSTITUTE	Clout (Carrere)
14	13	USED TA BE MY GIRL	O'Jays (Warner Bros)
10	14	MIND BLOWING DECISIONS	Heatwave (GTO)
9	15	MAKING UP AGAIN	Goldie (Bronze)
15	16	ARGENTINE MELODY	San Jose (MCA)
30	17	WILD WEST HERO	Electric Light Orchestra (Jet)
18	18	(DON'T FEAR) THE REAPER	Blue Oyster Cult (CBS)
27	19	COME ON DANCE DANCE	Saturday Night Band (CBS)
21	20	FROM EAST TO WEST	Voyage (GTO/Hansa)
11	21	RIVERS OF BABYLON	Boney M (Atlantic)
-	22	MANY TOO MANY	Genesis (Charisma)
12	23	DAVY'S ON THE ROAD AGAIN	Manfred Mann's Earth Band (Bronze)
26	24	RUN FOR HOME	Lindisfarne (Mercury)
20	25	(WHITE MAN) IN HAMMERSMITH PALAIS	Clash (CBS)
17	26	OH CAROL	Smokie (RAK)
-	27	SHAME	Evelyn 'Champagne' King (RCA)
-	28	CARRY ON WAYWARD SON	Kansas (Kirschner)
-	29	FOREVER AUTUMN	Justin Hayward (CBS)
-	30	STAY	Jackson Browne (Asylum)

You're The One That I Want was not an original song from the stage production of *Grease*, but was written for the film version by Australian former Shadows member John Farrar, who also produced the recording. The single continued the very high sales shown by 1978's biggest hits – as well as spending 10 weeks at Number One, equal to the second-longest run on record (David Whitfield's *Cara Mia*), it amassed total sales of over 1,850,000 and became the UK's all-time number three best-seller.

July – August 1978

22 July 1978

last	this	title / artist (label)
1	1	YOU'RE THE ONE THAT I WANT John Travolta/ Olivia Newton-John (RSO)
2	2	THE SMURF SONG Father Abraham (Decca)
4	3	DANCING IN THE CITY Marshall Hain (Harvest)
10	4	THE BIGGEST BLOW Sex Pistols (Virgin)
6	5	LIKE CLOCKWORK Boomtown Rats (Ensign)
3	6	AIRPORT Motors (Virgin)
5	7	MAN WITH THE CHILD IN HIS EYES Kate Bush (EMI)
11	8	BOOGIE OOGIE OOGIE A Taste Of Honey (Capitol)
7	9	A LITTLE BIT OF SOAP Showaddywaddy (Arista)
12	10	SUBSTITUTE Clout (Carrere)
17	11	WILD WEST HERO Electric Light Orchestra (Jet)
24	12	RUN FOR HOME Lindisfarne (Mercury)
9	13	ANNIE'S SONG James Galway (RCA)
8	14	MISS YOU Rolling Stones (EMI)
13	15	USED TA BE MY GIRL O'Jays (Warner Bros)
14	16	MIND BLOWING DECISIONS Heatwave (GTO)
20	17	FROM EAST TO WEST Voyage (GTO/Hansa)
-	18	5-7-0-5 City Boy (Vertigo)
18	19	(DON'T FEAR) THE REAPER Blue Oyster Cult (CBS)
29	20	FOREVER AUTUMN Justin Hayward (CBS)
19	21	COME ON DANCE DANCE Saturday Night Band (CBS)
-	22	LOVE YOU MORE Buzzcocks (United Artists)
-	23	SATISFY MY SOUL Bob Marley & the Wailers (Island)
-	24	PRODIGAL SON Steel Pulse (Island)
25	25	(WHITE MAN) IN HAMMERSMITH PALAIS Clash (CBS)
30	26	STAY Jackson Browne (Asylum)
-	27	LIFE'S BEEN GOOD Joe Walsh (Asylum)
21	28	RIVERS OF BABYLON Boney M (Atlantic)
22	29	MANY TOO MANY Genesis (Charisma)
-	30	HOW CAN THIS BE LOVE Andrew Gold (Asylum)

29 July 1978

last	this	title / artist (label)
1	1	YOU'RE THE ONE THAT I WANT John Travolta/ Olivia Newton-John (RSO)
10	2	SUBSTITUTE Clout (Carrere)
3	3	DANCING IN THE CITY Marshall Hain (Harvest)
2	4	THE SMURF SONG Father Abraham (Decca)
8	5	BOOGIE OOGIE OOGIE A Taste Of Honey (Capitol)
5	6	LIKE CLOCKWORK Boomtown Rats (Ensign)
11	7	WILD WEST HERO Electric Light Orchestra (Jet)
9	8	A LITTLE BIT OF SOAP Showaddywaddy (Arista)
4	8	THE BIGGEST BLOW Sex Pistols (Virgin)
6	10	AIRPORT Motors (Virgin)
7	11	MAN WITH THE CHILD IN HIS EYES Kate Bush (EMI)
15	12	USED TA BE MY GIRL O'Jays (Warner Bros)
18	13	5-7-0-5 City Boy (Vertigo)
21	14	COME ON DANCE DANCE Saturday Night Band (CBS)
20	15	FOREVER AUTUMN Justin Hayward (CBS)
12	16	RUN FOR HOME Lindisfarne (Mercury)
27	17	LIFE'S BEEN GOOD Joe Walsh (Asylum)
13	18	ANNIE'S SONG James Galway (RCA)
28	19	RIVERS OF BABYLON Boney M (Atlantic)
16	20	MIND BLOWING DECISIONS Heatwave (GTO)
17	21	FROM EAST TO WEST Voyage (GTO/Hansa)
14	22	MISS YOU Rolling Stones (EMI)
26	23	STAY Jackson Browne (Asylum)
19	24	(DON'T FEAR) THE REAPER Blue Oyster Cult (CBS)
22	25	LOVE YOU MORE Buzzcocks (United Artists)
-	26	IS THIS A LOVE THING Raydio (Arista)
-	27	NORTHERN LIGHTS Renaissance (Warner Bros)
24	28	PRODIGAL SON Steel Pulse (Island)
-	29	IDENTITY X Ray Spex (EMI Int)
23	30	SATISFY MY SOUL Bob Marley & the Wailers (Island)

5 August 1978

last	this	title / artist (label)
1	1	YOU'RE THE ONE THAT I WANT John Travolta/ Olivia Newton-John (RSO)
2	2	SUBSTITUTE Clout (Carrere)
5	3	BOOGIE OOGIE OOGIE A Taste Of Honey (Capitol)
3	4	DANCING IN THE CITY Marshall Hain (Harvest)
6	5	LIKE CLOCKWORK Boomtown Rats (Ensign)
4	6	THE SMURF SONG Father Abraham (Decca)
7	7	WILD WEST HERO Electric Light Orchestra (Jet)
21	8	FROM EAST TO WEST Voyage (GTO/Hansa)
16	9	RUN FOR HOME Lindisfarne (Mercury)
23	10	STAY Jackson Browne (Asylum)
8	11	A LITTLE BIT OF SOAP Showaddywaddy (Arista)
15	12	FOREVER AUTUMN Justin Hayward (CBS)
9	13	THE BIGGEST BLOW Sex Pistols (Virgin)
12	14	USED TA BE MY GIRL O'Jays (Warner Bros)
13	15	5-7-0-5 City Boy (Vertigo)
10	16	AIRPORT Motors (Virgin)
-	17	IF THE KIDS ARE UNITED Sham 69 (Polydor)
17	18	LIFE'S BEEN GOOD Joe Walsh (Asylum)
-	19	HOW CAN THIS BE LOVE Andrew Gold (Asylum)
-	20	BABY STOP CRYING Bob Dylan (CBS)
19	21	RIVERS OF BABYLON Boney M (Atlantic)
14	22	COME ON DANCE DANCE Saturday Night Band (CBS)
-	23	THREE TIMES A LADY Commodores (Motown)
27	24	NORTHERN LIGHTS Renaissance (Warner Bros)
11	25	MAN WITH THE CHILD IN HIS EYES Kate Bush (EMI)
29	26	IDENTITY X Ray Spex (EMI Int)
-	27	COME BACK AND FINISH WHAT YOU STARTED Gladys Knight & the Pips (Buddah)
-	28	STUFF LIKE THAT Quincy Jones (A&M)
26	29	IS THIS A LOVE THING Raydio (Arista)
-	30	SUPER NATURE Cerrone (Atlantic)

12 August 1978

last	this	title / artist (label)
1	1	YOU'RE THE ONE THAT I WANT John Travolta/ Olivia Newton-John (RSO)
2	2	SUBSTITUTE Clout (Carrere)
3	3	BOOGIE OOGIE OOGIE A Taste Of Honey (Capitol)
12	4	FOREVER AUTUMN Justin Hayward (CBS)
17	5	IF THE KIDS ARE UNITED Sham 69 (Polydor)
23	5	THREE TIMES A LADY Commodores (Motown)
21	7	BROWN GIRL IN THE RING/RIVERS OF BABYLON Boney M (Atlantic/Hansa)
4	8	DANCING IN THE CITY Marshall Hain (Harvest)
6	9	THE SMURF SONG Father Abraham (Decca)
10	10	5-7-0-5 City Boy (Vertigo)
18	11	LIFE'S BEEN GOOD Joe Walsh (Asylum)
7	12	WILD WEST HERO Electric Light Orchestra (Jet)
20	13	BABY STOP CRYING Bob Dylan (CBS)
10	14	STAY Jackson Browne (Asylum)
27	15	COME BACK AND FINISH WHAT YOU STARTED Gladys Knight & the Pips (Buddah)
11	16	A LITTLE BIT OF SOAP Showaddywaddy (Arista)
5	17	LIKE CLOCKWORK Boomtown Rats (Ensign)
30	18	SUPER NATURE Cerrone (Atlantic)
24	19	NORTHERN LIGHTS Renaissance (Warner Bros)
9	20	RUN FOR HOME Lindisfarne (Mercury)
26	21	IDENTITY X Ray Spex (EMI Int)
8	22	FROM EAST TO WEST Voyage (GTO/Hansa)
-	23	IT'S RAINING Darts (Magnet)
14	24	USED TA BE MY GIRL O'Jays (Warner Bros)
-	25	WHO ARE YOU Who (Polydor)
-	26	IT'S ONLY MAKE BELIEVE Child (Ariola Hansa)
-	27	JILTED JOHN Jilted John (EMI Int)
-	28	I DON'T NEED TO TELL HER Lurkers (Beggars Banquet)
13	29	THE BIGGEST BLOW Sex Pistols (Virgin)
-	30	HOT SHOT Karen Young (Atlantic)

Clout's *Substitute* was not a revival of the Who's 1965 hit, although it was a cover version – of a mid-1970s recording by the Righteous Brothers. The group were an all-girl aggregation from South Africa. The Sex Pistols' single was their first release without the departed Johnny Rotten (though did feature train robber Ronnie Biggs). Justin Hayward's *Forever Autumn* was extracted from Jeff Wayne's musical adaptation of H.G. Wells' *The War Of The Worlds*, one of the year's biggest-selling albums.

August – September 1978

By mid-summer, discos across the country were turning over Boney M's *Rivers Of Babylon* and playing the nursery rhyme-like but extremely danceable B-side *Brown Girl In The Ring*. Promotional efforts (and airplay) on the record were promptly switched to this, and the single reversed its slow slide from the top to leap back into the Top 3. It's entirely probable that some purchasers of *Rivers* who had never flipped it, bought the record a second time, assuming *Brown Girl* to be the follow-up.

16 September 1978

last week	this week	entry
1	1	THREE TIMES A LADY — Commodores (Motown)
4	2	BROWN GIRL IN THE RING/RIVERS OF BABYLON — Boney M (Atlantic/Hansa)
2	3	DREADLOCK HOLIDAY — 10 c.c. (Mercury)
5	4	OH WHAT A CIRCUS — David Essex (Mercury)
6	5	JILTED JOHN — Jilted John (EMI Int)
3	6	IT'S RAINING — Darts (Magnet)
9	7	BRITISH HUSTLE — Hi Tension (Island)
12	8	HONG KONG GARDEN — Siouxsie & the Banshees (Polydor)
8	9	SUPER NATURE — Cerrone (Atlantic)
10	10	PICTURE THIS — Blondie (Chrysalis)
16	11	AN EVERLASTING LOVE — Andy Gibb (RSO)
7	12	YOU'RE THE ONE THAT I WANT — John Travolta/Olivia Newton-John (RSO)
16	13	KISS YOU ALL OVER — Exile (RAK)
24	14	FORGET ABOUT YOU — Motors (Virgin)
28	15	AGAIN AND AGAIN — Status Quo (Vertigo)
13	16	TOP OF THE POPS — Rezillos (Sire)
29	17	GREASE — Frankie Valli (RSO)
14	18	IT'S ONLY MAKE BELIEVE — Child (Ariola Hansa)
11	19	FOREVER AUTUMN — Justin Hayward (CBS)
15	20	BABY STOP CRYING — Bob Dylan (CBS)
23	21	I THOUGHT IT WAS YOU — Herbie Hancock (CBS)
21	22	GALAXY OF LOVE — Crown Heights Affair (Philips)
30	23	(YOU MAKE ME FEEL) MIGHTY REAL — Sylvester (Fantasy)
–	24	SUMMER NIGHT CITY — Abba (Epic)
26	25	DAVID WATTS — Jam (Polydor)
–	26	A ROSE HAS TO DIE — Dooleys (GTO)
18	27	WHO ARE YOU — Who (Polydor)
–	28	YOU'RE THE ONE THAT I WANT — Hylda Baker & Arthur Mullard (Pye)
–	29	WHAT YOU WAITING FOR — Stargard (MCA)
19	30	BOOGIE OOGIE OOGIE — A Taste Of Honey (Capitol)

23 September 1978

last week	this week	entry
3	1	DREADLOCK HOLIDAY — 10 c.c. (Mercury)
2	2	BROWN GIRL IN THE RING/RIVERS OF BABYLON — Boney M (Atlantic/Hansa)
1	3	THREE TIMES A LADY — Commodores (Motown)
13	4	KISS YOU ALL OVER — Exile (RAK)
5	5	JILTED JOHN — Jilted John (EMI Int)
4	6	OH WHAT A CIRCUS — David Essex (Mercury)
6	7	IT'S RAINING — Darts (Magnet)
8	8	HONG KONG GARDEN — Siouxsie & the Banshees (Polydor)
15	9	AGAIN AND AGAIN — Status Quo (Vertigo)
7	10	BRITISH HUSTLE — Hi Tension (Island)
–	11	LOVE DON'T LIVE HERE ANYMORE — Rose Royce (Whitfield)
10	12	PICTURE THIS — Blondie (Chrysalis)
–	13	SUMMER NIGHTS — John Travolta & Olivia Newton-John (RSO)
17	14	GREASE — Frankie Valli (RSO)
9	15	SUPER NATURE — Cerrone (Atlantic)
24	16	SUMMER NIGHT CITY — Abba (Epic)
11	17	AN EVERLASTING LOVE — Andy Gibb (RSO)
14	18	FORGET ABOUT YOU — Motors (Virgin)
21	19	I THOUGHT IT WAS YOU — Herbie Hancock (CBS)
12	20	YOU'RE THE ONE THAT I WANT — John Travolta/Olivia Newton-John (RSO)
23	21	(YOU MAKE ME FEEL) MIGHTY REAL — Sylvester (Fantasy)
22	22	GALAXY OF LOVE — Crown Heights Affair (Philips)
16	23	TOP OF THE POPS — Rezillos (Sire)
–	24	THE WINKER'S SONG (MISPRINT) — Ivor Biggun (Beggars Banquet)
–	25	NOW THAT WE FOUND LOVE — Third World (Island)
26	26	A ROSE HAS TO DIE — Dooleys (GTO)
18	27	IT'S ONLY MAKE BELIEVE — Child (Ariola Hansa)
–	28	LUCKY STARS — Dean Friedman (Lifesong)
28	29	YOU'RE THE ONE THAT I WANT — Hylda Baker & Arthur Mullard (Pye)
–	30	TALKING IN YOUR SLEEP — Crystal Gayle (United Artists)

30 September 1978

last week	this week	entry
1	1	DREADLOCK HOLIDAY — 10 c.c. (Mercury)
13	2	SUMMER NIGHTS — John Travolta & Olivia Newton-John (RSO)
3	3	THREE TIMES A LADY — Commodores (Motown)
14	4	GREASE — Frankie Valli (RSO)
4	5	KISS YOU ALL OVER — Exile (RAK)
6	6	OH WHAT A CIRCUS — David Essex (Mercury)
5	7	JILTED JOHN — Jilted John (EMI Int)
16	8	SUMMER NIGHT CITY — Abba (Epic)
11	9	LOVE DON'T LIVE HERE ANYMORE — Rose Royce (Whitfield)
12	10	PICTURE THIS — Blondie (Chrysalis)
10	11	BRITISH HUSTLE — Hi Tension (Island)
28	12	LUCKY STARS — Dean Friedman (Lifesong)
21	13	(YOU MAKE ME FEEL) MIGHTY REAL — Sylvester (Fantasy)
8	14	HONG KONG GARDEN — Siouxsie & the Banshees (Polydor)
2	15	BROWN GIRL IN THE RING/RIVERS OF BABYLON — Boney M (Atlantic/Hansa)
25	16	NOW THAT WE FOUND LOVE — Third World (Island)
9	17	AGAIN AND AGAIN — Status Quo (Vertigo)
7	18	IT'S RAINING — Darts (Magnet)
–	19	I CAN'T STOP LOVIN' YOU — Leo Sayer (Chrysalis)
18	20	FORGET ABOUT YOU — Motors (Virgin)
–	21	RASPUTIN — Boney M (Atlantic/Hansa)
17	22	AN EVERLASTING LOVE — Andy Gibb (RSO)
–	23	EVER FALLEN IN LOVE (WITH SOMEONE YOU SHOULDN'T'VE) — Buzzcocks (United Artists)
24	24	THE WINKER'S SONG (MISPRINT) — Ivor Biggun (Beggars Banquet)
–	25	BLAME IT ON THE BOOGIE — Jacksons (Epic)
26	26	A ROSE HAS TO DIE — Dooleys (GTO)
18	27	I THOUGHT IT WAS YOU — Herbie Hancock (CBS)
30	28	TALKING IN YOUR SLEEP — Crystal Gayle (United Artists)
20	29	YOU'RE THE ONE THAT I WANT — John Travolta/Olivia Newton-John (RSO)
23	30	TOP OF THE POPS — Rezillos (Sire)

7 October 1978

last week	this week	entry
2	1	SUMMER NIGHTS — John Travolta & Olivia Newton-John (RSO)
9	2	LOVE DON'T LIVE HERE ANYMORE — Rose Royce (Whitfield)
4	3	GREASE — Frankie Valli (RSO)
1	4	DREADLOCK HOLIDAY — 10 c.c. (Mercury)
19	5	I CAN'T STOP LOVIN' YOU — Leo Sayer (Chrysalis)
5	6	KISS YOU ALL OVER — Exile (RAK)
3	7	THREE TIMES A LADY — Commodores (Motown)
6	8	OH WHAT A CIRCUS — David Essex (Mercury)
12	9	LUCKY STARS — Dean Friedman (Lifesong)
7	10	JILTED JOHN — Jilted John (EMI Int)
8	11	SUMMER NIGHT CITY — Abba (Epic)
21	12	RASPUTIN — Boney M (Atlantic/Hansa)
13	13	(YOU MAKE ME FEEL) MIGHTY REAL — Sylvester (Fantasy)
10	14	PICTURE THIS — Blondie (Chrysalis)
4	15	HONG KONG GARDEN — Siouxsie & the Banshees (Polydor)
26	16	A ROSE HAS TO DIE — Dooleys (GTO)
16	17	NOW THAT WE FOUND LOVE — Third World (Island)
25	18	BLAME IT ON THE BOOGIE — Jacksons (Epic)
17	19	AGAIN AND AGAIN — Status Quo (Vertigo)
23	20	EVER FALLEN IN LOVE (WITH SOMEONE YOU SHOULDN'T'VE) — Buzzcocks (United Artists)
24	21	THE WINKER'S SONG (MISPRINT) — Ivor Biggun (Beggars Banquet)
28	22	TALKING IN YOUR SLEEP — Crystal Gayle (United Artists)
15	23	BROWN GIRL IN THE RING/RIVERS OF BABYLON — Boney M (Atlantic/Hansa)
11	24	BRITISH HUSTLE — Hi Tension (Island)
–	25	SANDY — John Travolta (RSO)
–	26	BAMA BOOGIE WOOGIE — Cleveland Eaton (Gull)
–	27	L A CONNECTION — Rainbow (Polydor)
–	28	DOWN AT THE DOCTOR'S — Dr Feelgood (United Artists)
–	29	DIPPETY DAY — Father Abraham & the Smurfs (Decca)
22	30	EVERLASTING LOVE — Andy Gibb (RSO)

The Commodores' *Three Times A Lady* was Motown's first UK chart-topper since Diana Ross' *I'm Still Waiting* in 1971, and became the label's biggest British seller to date. *Jilted John* was a novelty punk offering created by the alter-ego of actor Graham Fellows (later to be see in *Coronation Street*), while more comedy raised its head as Hylda Baker and Arthur Mullard spoofed John and Olivia, and Ivor Biggun was guaranteed a BBC ban for his hands-on effort on *The Winker's Song (Misprint)*.

333

14 October 1978

last week	this week	title / artist
1	1	SUMMER NIGHTS — John Travolta & Olivia Newton-John (RSO)
2	2	LOVE DON'T LIVE HERE ANYMORE — Rose Royce (Whitfield)
9	3	LUCKY STARS — Dean Friedman (Lifesong)
3	4	GREASE — Frankie Valli (RSO)
11	5	RASPUTIN — Boney M (Atlantic/Hansa)
5	6	I CAN'T STOP LOVIN' YOU — Leo Sayer (Chrysalis)
4	7	DREADLOCK HOLIDAY — 10 c.c. (Mercury)
-	8	SWEET TALKIN' WOMAN — Electric Light Orchestra (Jet)
13	9	(YOU MAKE ME FEEL) MIGHTY REAL — Sylvester (Fantasy)
10	10	SUMMER NIGHT CITY — Abba (Epic)
22	11	TALKING IN YOUR SLEEP — Crystal Gayle (United Artists)
6	12	KISS YOU ALL OVER — Exile (RAK)
17	13	NOW THAT WE FOUND LOVE — Third World (Island)
14	14	PICTURE THIS — Blondie (Chrysalis)
25	15	SANDY — John Travolta (RSO)
10	16	JILTED JOHN — Jilted John (EMI Int)
7	17	THREE TIMES A LADY — Commodores (Motown)
8	18	OH WHAT A CIRCUS — David Essex (Mercury)
21	19	THE WINKER'S SONG (MISPRINT) — Ivor Biggun (Beggars Banquet)
18	20	BLAME IT ON THE BOOGIE — Jacksons (Epic)
16	21	A ROSE HAS TO DIE — Dooleys (GTO)
-	22	RESPECTABLE — Rolling Stones (EMI)
20	23	EVER FALLEN IN LOVE (WITH SOMEONE YOU SHOULDN'T'VE) — Buzzcocks (United Artists)
-	24	MEXICAN GIRL — Smokie (RAK)
19	25	AGAIN AND AGAIN — Status Quo (Vertigo)
-	26	BLAME IT ON THE BOOGIE — Mick Jackson (Atlantic)
15	27	HONG KONG GARDEN — Siouxsie & the Banshees (Polydor)
28	28	DOWN AT THE DOCTOR'S — Dr Feelgood (United Artists)
27	29	L A CONNECTION — Rainbow (Polydor)
-	30	NEW LIVE AND RARE 2 (EP) — Deep Purple (Purple)

21 October 1978

last week	this week	title / artist
1	1	SUMMER NIGHTS — John Travolta & Olivia Newton-John (RSO)
2	2	LOVE DON'T LIVE HERE ANYMORE — Rose Royce (Whitfield)
3	3	LUCKY STARS — Dean Friedman (Lifesong)
5	4	RASPUTIN — Boney M (Atlantic/Hansa)
15	5	SANDY — John Travolta (RSO)
8	6	SWEET TALKIN' WOMAN — Electric Light Orchestra (Jet)
6	7	I CAN'T STOP LOVIN' YOU — Leo Sayer (Chrysalis)
4	8	GREASE — Frankie Valli (RSO)
13	9	NOW THAT WE FOUND LOVE — Third World (Island)
9	10	(YOU MAKE ME FEEL) MIGHTY REAL — Sylvester (Fantasy)
11	11	TALKING IN YOUR SLEEP — Crystal Gayle (United Artists)
-	12	RAT TRAP — Boomtown Rats (Ensign)
20	13	BLAME IT ON THE BOOGIE — Jacksons (Epic)
-	14	DARLIN' — Frankie Miller (Chrysalis)
-	15	MACARTHUR PARK — Donna Summer (Casablanca)
24	16	MEXICAN GIRL — Smokie (RAK)
21	17	A ROSE HAS TO DIE — Dooleys (GTO)
23	18	EVER FALLEN IN LOVE (WITH SOMEONE YOU SHOULDN'T'VE) — Buzzcocks (United Artists)
7	19	DREADLOCK HOLIDAY — 10 c.c. (Mercury)
-	20	HURRY UP HARRY — Sham 69 (Polydor)
12	21	KISS YOU ALL OVER — Exile (RAK)
10	22	SUMMER NIGHT CITY — Abba (Epic)
19	23	THE WINKER'S SONG (MISPRINT) — Ivor Biggun (Beggars Banquet)
-	24	GIVIN' UP GIVIN' IN — Three Degrees (Ariola)
14	25	PICTURE THIS — Blondie (Chrysalis)
-	26	DOWN IN THE TUBE STATION AT MIDNIGHT — Jam (Polydor)
22	27	RESPECTABLE — Rolling Stones (EMI)
28	28	BRANDY — O'Jays (Philadelphia)
-	29	GET IT WHILE YOU CAN — Olympic Runners (Polydor)
16	30	JILTED JOHN — Jilted John (EMI Int)

28 October 1978

last week	this week	title / artist
1	1	SUMMER NIGHTS — John Travolta & Olivia Newton-John (RSO)
4	2	RASPUTIN — Boney M (Atlantic/Hansa)
3	3	LUCKY STARS — Dean Friedman (Lifesong)
5	4	SANDY — John Travolta (RSO)
15	5	MACARTHUR PARK — Donna Summer (Casablanca)
2	6	LOVE DON'T LIVE HERE ANYMORE — Rose Royce (Whitfield)
12	7	RAT TRAP — Boomtown Rats (Ensign)
7	8	I CAN'T STOP LOVIN' YOU — Leo Sayer (Chrysalis)
6	9	SWEET TALKIN' WOMAN — Electric Light Orchestra (Jet)
20	10	HURRY UP HARRY — Sham 69 (Polydor)
8	11	GREASE — Frankie Valli (RSO)
13	12	BLAME IT ON THE BOOGIE — Jacksons (Epic)
9	13	NOW THAT WE FOUND LOVE — Third World (Island)
11	14	TALKING IN YOUR SLEEP — Crystal Gayle (United Artists)
10	15	(YOU MAKE ME FEEL) MIGHTY REAL — Sylvester (Fantasy)
18	16	EVER FALLEN IN LOVE (WITH SOMEONE YOU SHOULDNT'VE) — Buzzcocks (United Artists)
-	17	PUBLIC IMAGE — Public Image Ltd (Virgin)
26	18	DOWN IN THE TUBE STATION AT MIDNIGHT — Jam (Polydor)
14	19	DARLIN' — Frankie Miller (Chrysalis)
-	20	BLAME IT ON THE BOOGIE — Mick Jackson (Atlantic)
16	21	MEXICAN GIRL — Smokie (RAK)
-	22	ONE FOR YOU ONE FOR ME — Jonathan King (GTO)
-	23	INSTANT REPLAY — Dan Hartman (Blue Sky)
24	24	GIVIN' UP GIVIN' IN — Three Degrees (Ariola)
-	25	GET ON UP GET ON DOWN — Roy Ayers (Polydor)
-	26	DIPPETY DAY — Father Abraham & the Smurfs (Decca)
28	27	BRANDY — O'Jays (Philadelphia)
17	28	A ROSE HAS TO DIE — Dooleys (GTO)
29	29	GET IT WHILE YOU CAN — Olympic Runners (Polydor)
-	30	GOT TO GET YOU INTO MY LIFE — Earth Wind & Fire (CBS)

4 November 1978

last week	this week	title / artist
1	1	SUMMER NIGHTS — John Travota & Olivia Newton-John (RSO)
2	2	RASPUTIN — Boney M (Atlantic/Hansa)
5	3	MACARTHUR PARK — Donna Summer (Casablanca)
7	4	RAT TRAP — Boomtown Rats (Ensign)
4	5	SANDY — John Travolta (RSO)
3	6	LUCKY STARS — Dean Friedman (Lifesong)
17	7	PUBLIC IMAGE — Public Image Ltd (Virgin)
9	8	SWEET TALKIN' WOMAN — Electric Light Orchestra (Jet)
12	9	BLAME IT ON THE BOOGIE — Jacksons (Epic)
19	10	DARLIN' — Frankie Miller (Chrysalis)
8	11	I CAN'T STOP LOVIN' YOU — Leo Sayer (Chrysalis)
6	12	LOVE DON'T LIVE HERE ANYMORE — Rose Royce (Whitfield)
15	13	HAVE YOU EVER FALLEN IN LOVE — Buzzcocks (United Artists)
10	14	HURRY UP HARRY — Sham 69 (Polydor)
13	15	NOW THAT WE FOUND LOVE — Third World (Island)
14	16	TALKING IN YOUR SLEEP — Crystal Gayle (United Artists)
-	17	BICYCLE RACE/FAT BOTTOMED GIRLS — Queen (EMI)
18	18	DOWN IN THE TUBE STATION AT MIDNIGHT — Jam (Polydor)
24	19	GIVIN' UP GIVIN' IN — Three Degrees (Ariola)
23	20	INSTANT REPLAY — Dan Hartman (Blue Sky)
27	21	BRANDY — O'Jays (Philadelphia)
-	22	HOPELESSLY DEVOTED TO YOU — Olivia Newton-John (RSO)
21	23	MEXICAN GIRL — Smokie (RAK)
-	24	PART TIME LOVE — Elton John (Rocket)
20	25	BLAME IT ON THE BOOGIE — Mick Jackson (Atlantic)
29	26	GET IT WHILE YOU CAN — Olympic Runners (Polydor)
26	27	DIPPETY DAY — Father Abraham (Decca)
-	28	SILVER MACHINE — Hawkwind (United Artists)
11	29	GREASE — Frankie Valli (RSO)
-	30	RADIO RADIO — Elvis Costello (Radar)

The second Travolta/Newton-John duet from *Grease*, this time one of the original production songs *Summer Nights*, almost matched the enormous achievement of their first, with UK sales exceeding 1,500,000. Not since the Beatles had an act topped the UK chart with successive million sellers. *Grease* holds the record for spinning off more major hit singles than any other film, and they were now charting in force, as Frankie Valli's title song and John Travolta's solo *Sandy* both made the Top Five.

November – December 1978

11 November 1978

Last	This	Title	Artist (Label)
1	1	SUMMER NIGHTS	John Travolta & Olivia Newton-John (RSO)
4	2	RAT TRAP	Boomtown Rats (Ensign)
5	3	SANDY	John Travolta (RSO)
3	4	MACARTHUR PARK	Donna Summer (Casablanca)
10	5	DARLIN'	Frankie Miller (Chrysalis)
9	6	BLAME IT ON THE BOOGIE	Jacksons (Epic)
7	7	PUBLIC IMAGE	Public Image Ltd (Virgin)
22	8	HOPELESSLY DEVOTED TO YOU	Olivia Newton-John (RSO)
2	9	RASPUTIN	Boney M (Atlantic/Hansa)
20	10	INSTANT REPLAY	Dan Hartman (Blue Sky)
14	11	HURRY UP HARRY	Sham 69 (Polydor)
8	12	SWEET TALKIN' WOMAN	Electric Light Orchestra (Jet)
19	13	GIVIN' UP GIVIN' IN	Three Degrees (Ariola)
6	14	LUCKY STARS	Dean Friedman (Lifesong)
-	15	PRETTY LITTLE ANGEL EYES	Showaddywaddy (Arista)
17	16	BICYCLE RACE/FAT BOTTOMED GIRLS	Queen (EMI)
13	17	EVER FALLEN IN LOVE (WITH SOMEONE YOU SHOULDN'T'VE)	Buzzcocks (United Artists)
18	18	DOWN IN THE TUBE STATION AT MIDNIGHT	Jam (Polydor)
27	19	DIPPETY DAY	Father Abraham (Decca)
30	20	RADIO RADIO	Elvis Costello (Radar)
-	21	I LOVE AMERICA	Patrick Juvet (Casablanca)
-	22	ALWAYS AND FOREVER/MIND BLOWING DECISIONS	Heatwave (GTO)
11	23	I CAN'T STOP LOVIN' YOU	Leo Sayer (Chrysalis)
-	24	TOAST	Street Band (Logo)
16	25	TALKING IN YOUR SLEEP	Crystal Gayle (United Artists)
-	26	EAST RIVER	Brecker Brothers (Arista)
-	27	TEENAGE KICKS	Undertones (Sire)
28	28	SILVER MACHINE	Hawkwind (United Artists)
15	29	NOW THAT WE FOUND LOVE	Third World (Island)
21	30	BRANDY	O'Jays (Philadelphia)

18 November 1978

Last	This	Title	Artist (Label)
2	1	RAT TRAP	Boomtown Rats (Ensign)
8	2	HOPELESSLY DEVOTED TO YOU	Olivia Newton-John (RSO)
1	3	SUMMER NIGHTS	John Travolta & Olivia Newton-John (RSO)
4	4	MACARTHUR PARK	Donna Summer (Casablanca)
5	5	DARLIN'	Frankie Miller (Chrysalis)
3	6	SANDY	John Travolta (RSO)
7	7	MY BEST FRIEND'S GIRL	Cars (Elektra)
15	8	PRETTY LITTLE ANGEL EYES	Showaddywaddy (Arista)
10	9	INSTANT REPLAY	Dan Hartman (Blue Sky)
-	10	HANGING ON THE TELEPHONE	Blondie (Chrysalis)
13	11	GIVIN' UP GIVIN' IN	Three Degrees (Ariola)
6	12	BLAME IT ON THE BOOGIE	Jacksons (Epic)
9	13	RASPUTIN	Boney M (Atlantic/Hansa)
16	14	BICYCLE RACE/FAT BOTTOMED GIRLS	Queen (EMI)
7	15	PUBLIC IMAGE	Public Image Ltd (Virgin)
12	16	SWEET TALKIN' WOMAN	Electric Light Orchestra (Jet)
21	17	I LOVE AMERICA	Patrick Juvet (Casablanca)
14	18	LUCKY STARS	Dean Friedman (Lifesong)
24	19	TOAST	Street Band (Logo)
22	20	ALWAYS AND FOREVER/MIND BLOWING DECISIONS	Heatwave (GTO)
-	21	PART TIME LOVE	Elton John (Rocket)
11	22	HURRY UP HARRY	Sham 69 (Polydor)
18	23	DOWN IN THE TUBE STATION AT MIDNIGHT	Jam (Polydor)
-	24	GERM FREE ADOLESCENCE	X Ray Spex (EMI Int)
19	25	DIPPETY DAY	Father Abraham (Decca)
-	26	DON'T LET IT FADE AWAY	Darts (Magnet)
-	27	DA YA THINK I'M SEXY	Rod Stewart (Riva)
-	28	GIVING IT BACK	Phil Hurtt (Fantasy)
30	29	BRANDY	O'Jays (Philadelphia)
20	30	RADIO RADIO	Elvis Costello (Radar)

25 November 1978

Last	This	Title	Artist (Label)
1	1	RAT TRAP	Boomtown Rats (Ensign)
2	2	HOPELESSLY DEVOTED TO YOU	Olivia Newton-John (RSO)
9	3	INSTANT REPLAY	Dan Hartman (Blue Sky)
27	4	DA YA THINK I'M SEXY	Rod Stewart (Riva)
7	5	MY BEST FRIEND'S GIRL	Cars (Elektra)
8	6	PRETTY LITTLE ANGEL EYES	Showaddywaddy (Arista)
5	7	DARLIN'	Frankie Miller (Chrysalis)
6	8	SANDY	John Travolta (RSO)
3	9	SUMMER NIGHTS	John Travolta & Olivia Newton-John (RSO)
10	10	HANGING ON THE TELEPHONE	Blondie (Chrysalis)
4	11	MACARTHUR PARK	Donna Summer (Casablanca)
14	12	BICYCLE RACE/FAT BOTTOMED GIRLS	Queen (EMI)
17	13	I LOVE AMERICA	Patrick Juvet (Casablanca)
20	14	ALWAYS AND FOREVER/MIND BLOWING DECISIONS	Heatwave (GTO)
11	15	GIVIN' UP GIVIN' IN	Three Degrees (Ariola)
12	16	BLAME IT ON THE BOOGIE	Jacksons (Epic)
-	17	LE FREAK	Chic (Atlantic)
26	18	DON'T LET IT FADE AWAY	Darts (Magnet)
13	19	RASPUTIN	Boney M (Atlantic/Hansa)
19	20	TOAST	Street Band (Logo)
-	21	I LOST MY HEART TO A STARSHIP TROOPER	Sarah Brightman & Hot Gossip (Ariola Hansa)
-	22	DON'T CRY OUT LOUD	Elkie Brooks (A&M)
21	23	PART TIME LOVE	Elton John (Rocket)
-	24	IT SEEMS TO HANG ON	Ashford & Simpson (Warner Bros)
25	25	IN THE BUSH	Musique (CBS)
25	26	DIPPETY DAY	Father Abraham (Decca)
-	27	DANCE (DISCO HEAT)	Sylvester (Fantasy)
24	28	GERM FREE ADOLESCENCE	X Ray Spex (EMI Int)
15	29	PUBLIC IMAGE	Public Image Ltd (Virgin)
-	30	LYDIA	Dean Friedman (Lifesong)

2 December 1978

Last	This	Title	Artist (Label)
1	1	RAT TRAP	Boomtown Rats (Ensign)
4	2	DA YA THINK I'M SEXY	Rod Stewart (Riva)
2	3	HOPELESSLY DEVOTED TO YOU	Olivia Newton-John (RSO)
7	4	DARLIN'	Frankie Miller (Chrysalis)
6	5	PRETTY LITTLE ANGEL EYES	Showaddywaddy (Arista)
5	6	MY BEST FRIEND'S GIRL	Cars (Elektra)
3	7	INSTANT REPLAY	Dan Hartman (Blue Sky)
10	8	HANGING ON THE TELEPHONE	Blondie (Chrysalis)
-	9	TOO MUCH HEAVEN	Bee Gees (RSO)
13	10	I LOVE AMERICA	Patrick Juvet (Casablanca)
14	11	ALWAYS AND FOREVER/MIND BLOWING DECISIONS	Heatwave (GTO)
17	12	LE FREAK	Chic (Atlantic)
12	13	BICYCLE RACE/FAT BOTTOMED GIRLS	Queen (EMI)
23	14	PART TIME LOVE	Elton John (Rocket)
-	15	MARY'S BOY CHILD/OH MY LORD	Boney M (Atlantic/Hansa)
-	16	Y. M. C. A.	Village People (Mercury)
9	17	SUMMER NIGHTS	John Travolta & Olivia Newton-John (RSO)
-	18	GREASED LIGHTNING	John Travolta (Midsong)
25	19	IN THE BUSH	Musique (CBS)
8	20	SANDY	John Travolta (RSO)
21	21	I LOST MY HEART TO A STARSHIP TROOPER	Sarah Brightman & Hot Gossip (Ariola Hansa)
27	22	DANCE (DISCO HEAT)	Sylvester (Fantasy)
28	23	GERM FREE ADOLESCENCE	X Ray Spex (EMI Int)
20	24	TOAST	Street Band (Logo)
15	25	BLAME IT ON THE BOOGIE	Jacksons (Epic)
-	26	SHOOTING STAR	Dollar (EMI)
-	27	PROMISES	Buzzcocks (United Artists)
30	28	LYDIA	Dean Friedman (Lifesong)
-	29	LAY YOUR LOVE ON ME	Racay (RAK)
-	30	RAINING IN MY HEART	Leo Sayer (Chrysalis)

The last of the *Grease* hits moved into contention, as Olivia's solo on *Hopelessly Devoted To You* peaked at two behind the Boomtown Rats' first chart-topper, and John Travolta's *Greased Lightning* made the Top 20. Showaddywaddy revived *Pretty Little Angel Eyes*, the other 1961 US hit by Curtis Lee (whose *Under The Moon Of Love* had already given them a Number One), also taking this into the Top Five. The Cars' *My Best Friend's Girl* was the first major hit marketed as a picture disc.

December 1978

	9 December 1978		16 December 1978		23 December 1978
2	1 DA YA THINK I'M SEXY Rod Stewart (Riva)	2	1 MARY'S BOY CHILD/OH MY LORD Boney M (Atlantic/Hansa)	1	1 MARY'S BOY CHILD/OH MY LORD Boney M (Atlantic/Hansa)
15	2 MARY'S BOY CHILD/OH MY LORD Boney M (Atlantic/Hansa)	1	2 DA YA THINK I'M SEXY Rod Stewart (Riva)	5	2 Y. M. C. A. Village People (Mercury)
1	3 RAT TRAP Boomtown Rats (Ensign)	5	3 A TASTE OF AGGRO Barron Knights (Epic)	3	3 A TASTE OF AGGRO Barron Knights (Epic)
8	4 HANGING ON THE TELEPHONE Blondie (Chrysalis)	8	4 TOO MUCH HEAVEN Bee Gees (RSO)	4	4 TOO MUCH HEAVEN Bee Gees (RSO)
-	5 A TASTE OF AGGRO Barron Knights (Epic)	13	5 Y. M. C. A. Village People (Mercury)	2	5 DA YA THINK I'M SEXY Rod Stewart (Riva)
3	6 HOPELESSLY DEVOTED TO YOU Olivia Newton-John (RSO)	7	6 I LOST MY HEART TO A STARSHIP TROOPER Sarah Brightman & Hot Gossip (Ariola Hansa)	14	6 YOU DON'T BRING ME FLOWERS Barbra Streisand & Neil Diamond (CBS)
21	7 I LOST MY HEART TO A STARSHIP TROOPER Sarah Brightman & Hot Gossip (Ariola Hansa)	12	7 ALWAYS AND FOREVER/MIND BLOWING DECISIONS Heatwave (GTO)	6	7 I LOST MY HEART TO A STARSHIP TROOPER Sarah Brightman & Hot Gossip (Ariola Hansa)
9	8 TOO MUCH HEAVEN Bee Gees (RSO)	10	8 LE FREAK Chic (Atlantic)	8	8 LE FREAK Chic (Atlantic)
5	9 PRETTY LITTLE ANGEL EYES Showaddywaddy (Arista)	3	9 RAT TRAP Boomtown Rats (Ensign)	11	9 LAY YOUR LOVE ON ME Racey (RAK)
12	10 LE FREAK Chic (Atlantic)	26	10 IN THE BUSH Musique (CBS)	17	10 SONG FOR GUY Elton John (Rocket)
7	11 INSTANT REPLAY Dan Hartman (Blue Sky)	-	11 LAY YOUR LOVE ON ME Racey (RAK)	7	11 ALWAYS AND FOREVER/MIND BLOWING DECISIONS Heatwave (GTO)
11	12 ALWAYS AND FOREVER/MIND BLOWING DECISIONS Heatwave (GTO)	4	12 HANGING ON THE TELEPHONE Blondie (Chrysalis)	16	12 GREASED LIGHTNING John Travolta (Midsong)
16	13 Y. M. C. A. Village People (Mercury)	18	13 DON'T CRY OUT LOUD Elkie Brooks (A&M)	13	13 DON'T CRY OUT LOUD Elkie Brooks (A&M)
6	14 MY BEST FRIEND'S GIRL Cars (Elektra)	23	14 YOU DON'T BRING ME FLOWERS Barbra Streisand & Neil Diamond (CBS)	12	14 HANGING ON THE TELEPHONE Blondie (Chrysalis)
4	15 DARLIN' Frankie Miller (Chrysalis)	14	15 MY BEST FRIEND'S GIRL Cars (Elektra)	-	15 SHOOTING STAR Dollar (Carrere/EMI)
18	16 GREASED LIGHTNING John Travolta (Midsong)	16	16 GREASED LIGHTNING John Travolta (Midsong)	29	16 I'LL PUT YOU TOGETHER AGAIN Hot Chocolate (RAK)
-	17 TOMMY GUN Clash (CBS)	28	17 SONG FOR GUY Elton John (Rocket)	-	17 SEPTEMBER Earth Wind & Fire (CBS)
-	18 DON'T CRY OUT LOUD Elkie Brooks (A&M)	17	18 TOMMY GUN Clash (CBS)	21	18 PRETTY LITTLE ANGEL EYES Showaddywaddy (Arista)
13	19 BICYCLE RACE/FAT BOTTOMED GIRLS Queen (EMI)	25	19 DON'T LET IT FADE AWAY Darts (Magnet)	9	19 RAT TRAP Boomtown Rats (Ensign)
10	20 I LOVE AMERICA Patrick Juvet (Casablanca)	15	20 DARLIN' Frankie Miller (Chrysalis)	25	20 HIT ME WITH YOUR RHYTHM STICK Ian Dury & the Blockheads (Stiff)
14	21 PART TIME LOVE Elton John (Rocket)	-	21 RAINING IN MY HEART Leo Sayer (Chrysalis)	30	21 DR WHO Mankind (Pinnacle)
26	22 SHOOTING STAR Dollar (EMI)	9	22 PRETTY LITTLE ANGEL EYES Showaddywaddy (Arista)	18	22 TOMMY GUN Clash (CBS)
-	23 YOU DON'T BRING ME FLOWERS Barbra Streisand & Neil Diamond (CBS)	19	23 BICYCLE RACE/FAT BOTTOMED GIRLS Queen (EMI)	-	23 PLEASE COME HOME FOR CHRISTMAS Eagles (Asylum)
-	24 I'M EVERY WOMAN Chaka Khan (Warner Bros)	6	24 HOPELESSLY DEVOTED TO YOU Olivia Newton-John (RSO)	10	24 IN THE BUSH Musique (CBS)
-	25 DON'T LET IT FADE AWAY Darts (Magnet)	-	25 HIT ME WITH YOUR RHYTHM STICK Ian Dury & The Blockheads(Stiff)	19	25 DON'T LET IT FADE AWAY Darts (Magnet)
19	26 IN THE BUSH Musique (CBS)	24	26 I'M EVERY WOMAN Chaka Khan (Warner Bros)	-	26 A LITTLE MORE LOVE Olivia Newton-John (EMI)
23	27 GERM FREE ADOLESCENCE X Ray Spex (EMI Int)	21	27 PART TIME LOVE Elton John (Rocket)	26	27 I'M EVERY WOMAN Chaka Khan (Warner Bros)
-	28 SONG FOR GUY Elton John (Rocket)	11	28 INSTANT REPLAY Dan Hartman (Blue Sky)	27	28 PART TIME LOVE Elton John (Rocket)
-	29 I'LL PUT YOU TOGETHER AGAIN Hot Chocolate (RAK)	29	29 I'LL PUT YOU TOGETHER AGAIN Hot Chocolate (RAK)	20	29 DARLIN' Frankie Miller (Chrysalis)
-	30 DR WHO Mankind (Pinnacle)	30	30 DR WHO Mankind (Pinnacle)	-	30 MY LIFE Billy Joel (CBS)

Boney M's *Mary's Boy Child* marked the first time a Christmas song had reached Number One in different versions on two different occasions. The group's version (a medley with producer Frank Farian's *Oh My Lord,* which guaranteed him a slice of the royalties) came 21 years after Harry Belafonte's million-seller, and actually outsold the original, moving nearly 1,800,000 copies by the New Year. It was thus the fifth UK seven-figure seller in a 12-month period, giving 1978 a record very hard to beat.

Disco Fever

Top: Earth, Wind & Fire; right: Barry White; bottom right:Tavares; below: Donna Summer

The impact of the film 'Saturday Night Fever' and its accompanying soundtrack took most people by surprise. But disco had been a growing cult in clubs in America and Britain for a number of years. Dance clubs played obscure hardcore soul tracks to packed audiences of all night dancers. Rare and treasured cuts changed hands for large sums. Eventually the music, greatly watered down, crossed over into mainstream pop and John Travolta became the model for a new generation of disco-dancers. The Bee Gees wrote the music for the film and performed most of the songs. They'd been out of the limelight, but now became the hottest property in music and suddenly everyone was dancing again! Euro-disco hit the spot, principally through the influence of Giorgio Moroder who produced Donna Summers' early records among others.

January 1979

last this
week

6 January 1979

last	this	
2	1	Y. M. C. A. — Village People (Mercury)
1	2	MARY'S BOY CHILD — Boney M (Atlantic Hansa)
3	3	A TASTE OF AGGRO — Baron Knights (Epic)
6	4	YOU DON'T BRING ME FLOWERS — Barbra Streisand & Neil Diamond (CBS)
9	5	LAY YOUR LOVE ON ME — Racey (RAK)
10	6	SONG FOR GUY — Elton John (Rocket)
4	7	TOO MUCH HEAVEN — Bee Gees (RSO)
20	8	HIT ME WITH YOUR RHYTHM STICK — Ian Dury & The Blockheads (Stiff)
8	9	LE FREAK — Chic (Atlantic)
7	10	I LOST MY HEART TO A STARSHIP TROOPER — Sarah Brightman & Hot Gossip (Ariola Hansa)
5	11	DO YA THINK I'M SEXY — Rod Stewart (Riva)
12	12	GREASED LIGHTNING — John Travolta (Midsong)
27	13	I'M EVERY WOMAN — Chaka Khan (Warner Bros)
16	14	I'LL PUT YOU TOGETHER AGAIN — Hot Chocolate (RAK)
15	15	SHOOTING STAR — Dollar (Carrere/EMI)
22	16	TOMMY GUN — Clash (CBS)
24	17	IN THE BUSH — Musique (CBS)
17	18	SEPTEMBER — Earth Wind & Fire (CBS)
13	19	DON'T CRY OUT LOUD — Elkie Brooks (A&M)
21	20	DR WHO — Mankind (Pinnacle)
11	21	ALWAYS AND FOREVER/MIND BLOWING DECISIONS — Heatwave (GTO)
-	22	RAINING IN MY HEART — Leo Sayer (Chrysalis)
26	23	A LITTLE MORE LOVE — Olivia Newton-John (EMI)
25	24	DON'T LET IT FADE AWAY — Darts (Magnet)
14	25	HANGING ON THE TELEPHONE — Blondie (Chrysalis)
30	26	MY LIFE — Billy Joel (CBS)
-	27	ONE NATION UNDER A GROOVE — Funkadelic (Warner Bros)
23	28	PLEASE COME HOME FOR CHRISTMAS — Eagles (Asylum)
-	29	MIRRORS — Sally Oldfield (Bronze)
-	30	HELLO THIS IS JOANIE (THE TELEPHONE ANSWERING MACHINE SONG) — Paul Evans (Spring)

13 January 1979

last	this	
1	1	Y. M. C. A. — Village People (Mercury)
6	2	SONG FOR GUY — Elton John (Rocket)
5	3	LAY YOUR LOVE ON ME — Racey (RAK)
8	4	HIT ME WITH YOUR RHYTHM STICK — Ian Dury & The Blockheads (Stiff)
2	5	MARY'S BOY CHILD — Boney M (Atlantic Hansa)
9	6	LE FREAK — Chic (Atlantic)
3	7	A TASTE OF AGGRO — Baron Knights (Epic)
4	8	YOU DON'T BRING ME FLOWERS — Barbra Streisand & Neil Diamond (CBS)
7	9	TOO MUCH HEAVEN — Bee Gees (RSO)
10	10	I LOST MY HEART TO A STARSHIP TROOPER — Sarah Brightman & Hot Gossip (Ariola Hansa)
18	11	SEPTEMBER — Earth Wind & Fire (CBS)
15	12	SHOOTING STAR — Dollar (Carrere/EMI)
14	13	I'LL PUT YOU TOGETHER AGAIN — Hot Chocolate (RAK)
23	14	A LITTLE MORE LOVE — Olivia Newton-John (EMI)
11	15	DO YA THINK I'M SEXY — Rod Stewart (Riva)
13	16	I'M EVERY WOMAN — Chaka Khan (Warner Bros)
12	17	GREASED LIGHTNING — John Travolta (Midsong)
30	18	HELLO THIS IS JOANIE (THE TELEPHONE ANSWERING MACHINE SONG) — Paul Evans (Spring)
16	19	TOMMY GUN — Clash (CBS)
21	20	ALWAYS AND FOREVER/MIND BLOWING DECISIONS — Heatwave (GTO)
-	21	JUST THE WAY YOU ARE — Barry White (20th Century)
-	22	YOU NEEDED ME — Anne Murray (Capitol)
25	23	HANGING ON THE TELEPHONE — Blondie (Chrysalis)
17	24	IN THE BUSH — Musique (CBS)
20	25	DR WHO — Mankind (Pinnacle)
26	26	MY LIFE — Billy Joel (CBS)
-	27	PROMISES — Buzzcocks (United Artists)
22	28	RAINING IN MY HEART — Leo Sayer (Chrysalis)
29	29	MIRRORS — Sally Oldfield (Bronze)
19	30	DON'T CRY OUT LOUD — Elkie Brooks (A&M)

20 January 1979

last	this	
1	1	Y. M. C. A. — Village People (Mercury)
4	2	HIT ME WITH YOUR RHYTHM STICK — Ian Dury & The Blockheads (Stiff)
3	3	LAY YOUR LOVE ON ME — Racey (RAK)
2	4	SONG FOR GUY — Elton John (Rocket)
6	5	LE FREAK — Chic (Atlantic)
11	6	SEPTEMBER — Earth Wind & Fire (CBS)
18	7	HELLO THIS IS JOANIE (THE TELEPHONE ANSWERING MACHINE SONG) — Paul Evans (Spring)
14	8	A LITTLE MORE LOVE — Olivia Newton-John (EMI)
8	9	YOU DON'T BRING ME FLOWERS — Barbra Streisand & Neil Diamond (CBS)
9	10	TOO MUCH HEAVEN — Bee Gees (RSO)
16	11	I'M EVERY WOMAN — Chaka Khan (Warner Bros)
-	12	ONE NATION UNDER A GROOVE — Funkadelic (Warner Bros)
5	13	MARY'S BOY CHILD — Boney M (Atlantic Hansa)
21	14	JUST THE WAY YOU ARE — Barry White (20th Century)
10	15	I LOST MY HEART TO A STARSHIP TROOPER — Sarah Brightman & Hot Gossip (Ariola Hansa)
13	16	I'LL PUT YOU TOGETHER AGAIN — Hot Chocolate (RAK)
7	17	A TASTE OF AGGRO — Baron Knights (Epic)
-	18	CAR 67 — Driver 67 (Logo)
-	19	RAMA LAMA DING DONG — Rocky Sharpe & the Replays (Chiswick)
25	20	DR WHO — Mankind (Pinnacle)
26	21	MY LIFE — Billy Joel (CBS)
-	22	TAKE THAT TO THE BANK — Shalamar (RCA)
23	23	MIRRORS — Sally Oldfield (Bronze)
24	24	IN THE BUSH — Musique (CBS)
-	25	COOL MEDITATION — Third World (Island)
22	26	YOU NEEDED ME — Anne Murray (Capitol)
15	27	DO YA THINK I'M SEXY — Rod Stewart (Riva)
20	28	ALWAYS AND FOREVER/MIND BLOWING DECISIONS — Heatwave (GTO)
-	29	THIS IS IT — Dan Hartman (Blue Sky)
-	30	EVERY NIGHT — Phoebe Snow (CBS)

27 January 1979

last	this	
2	1	HIT ME WITH YOUR RHYTHM STICK — Ian Dury & The Blockheads (Stiff)
1	2	Y. M. C. A. — Village People (Mercury)
6	3	SEPTEMBER — Earth Wind & Fire (CBS)
8	4	A LITTLE MORE LOVE — Olivia Newton-John (EMI)
7	5	HELLO THIS IS JOANIE (THE TELEPHONE ANSWERING MACHINE SONG) — Paul Evans (Spring)
3	6	LAY YOUR LOVE ON ME — Racey (RAK)
5	7	LE FREAK — Chic (Atlantic)
18	8	CAR 67 — Driver 67 (Logo)
12	9	ONE NATION UNDER A GROOVE — Funkadelic (Warner Bros)
4	10	SONG FOR GUY — Elton John (Rocket)
-	11	WOMAN IN LOVE — Three Degrees (Ariola)
14	12	JUST THE WAY YOU ARE — Barry White (20th Century)
11	13	I'M EVERY WOMAN — Chaka Khan (Warner Bros)
23	14	MIRRORS — Sally Oldfield (Bronze)
19	15	RAMA LAMA DING DONG — Rocky Sharpe & the Replays (Chiswick)
16	16	I'LL PUT YOU TOGETHER AGAIN — Hot Chocolate (RAK)
10	17	TOO MUCH HEAVEN — Bee Gees (RSO)
21	18	MY LIFE — Billy Joel (CBS)
-	19	DON'T CRY FOR ME ARGENTINA — Shadows (EMI)
29	20	THIS IS IT — Dan Hartman (Blue Sky)
9	21	YOU DON'T BRING ME FLOWERS — Barbra Streisand & Neil Diamond (CBS)
22	22	TAKE THAT TO THE BANK — Shalamar (RCA)
26	23	YOU NEEDED ME — Anne Murray (Capitol)
25	24	COOL MEDITATION — Third World (Island)
-	25	HEART OF GLASS — Blondie (Chrysalis)
30	26	EVERY NIGHT — Phoebe Snow (CBS)
-	27	GOT MY MIND MADE UP — Instant Funk (Salsoul)
20	28	DR WHO — Mankind (Pinnacle)
15	29	I LOST MY HEART TO A STARSHIP TROOPER — Sarah Brightman & Hot Gossip (Ariola Hansa)
17	30	A TASTE OF AGGRO — Baron Knights (Epic)

1978's high singles sales, boosted by the disco music boom as well as the the commercial flowering of the punk-injected New Wave of rock, carried over into 1979. The Village People's disco smash *Y.M.C.A.*, with its gay overtones, was yet another million-plus UK seller. Elton John's *Song For Guy* was, almost uniquely for him, largely a piano solo: the poignant melody was written by Elton in tribute to an employee of his Rocket record label, who had been tragically killed in an accident.

last week	this	3 February 1979
1	1	HIT ME WITH YOUR RHYTHM STICK Ian Dury & the Blockheads (Stiff)
2	2	Y. M. C. A. Village People (Mercury)
25	3	HEART OF GLASS Blondie (Chrysalis)
3	4	SEPTEMBER Earth Wind & Fire (CBS)
11	5	WOMAN IN LOVE Three Degrees (Ariola)
4	6	A LITTLE MORE LOVE Olivia Newton-John (EMI)
19	7	DON'T CRY FOR ME ARGENTINA Shadows (EMI)
5	8	HELLO THIS IS JOANIE (THE TELEPHONE ANSWERING MACHINE SONG) Paul Evans (Spring)
8	9	CAR 67 Driver 67 (Logo)
7	10	LE FREAK Chic (Atlantic)
6	11	LAY YOUR LOVE ON ME Racey (RAK)
12	12	JUST THE WAY YOU ARE Barry White (20th Century)
18	13	MY LIFE Billy Joel (CBS)
15	14	RAMA LAMA DING DONG Rocky Sharpe & the Replays (Chiswick)
9	15	ONE NATION UNDER A GROOVE Funkadelic (Warner Bros)
23	16	YOU NEEDED ME Anne Murray (Capitol)
13	17	I'M EVERY WOMAN Chaka Khan (Warner Bros)
20	17	THIS IS IT Dan Hartman (Blue Sky)
22	19	TAKE THAT TO THE BANK Shalamar (RCA)
10	20	SONG FOR GUY Elton John (Rocket)
16	21	I'LL PUT YOU TOGETHER AGAIN Hot Chocolate (RAK)
14	22	MIRRORS Sally Oldfield (Bronze)
-	23	MILK AND ALCOHOL Dr Feelgood (United Artists)
17	24	TOO MUCH HEAVEN Bee Gees (RSO)
-	25	COULD IT BE MAGIC Barry Manilow (Arista)
24	26	COOL MEDITATION Third World (Island)
-	27	I WAS MADE FOR DANCIN' Leif Garrett (Atlantic)
-	28	KING ROCKER Generation X (Chrysalis)
-	29	WE'VE GOT TONIGHT Bob Seger (Capitol)
-	30	SIR DANCEALOT Olympic Runners (Polydor)

		10 February 1979
3	1	HEART OF GLASS Blondie (Chrysalis)
1	2	HIT ME WITH YOUR RHYTHM STICK Ian Dury & The Blockheads (Stiff)
5	3	WOMAN IN LOVE Three Degrees (Ariola)
-	4	CHIQUITITA Abba (Epic)
2	5	Y. M. C. A. Village People (Mercury)
4	6	SEPTEMBER Earth Wind & Fire (CBS)
9	7	CAR 67 Driver 67 (Logo)
6	8	A LITTLE MORE LOVE Olivia Newton-John (EMI)
7	8	DON'T CRY FOR ME ARGENTINA Shadows (EMI)
13	10	MY LIFE Billy Joel (CBS)
8	11	HELLO THIS IS JOANIE (THE TELEPHONE ANSWERING MACHINE SONG) Paul Evans (Spring)
23	12	MILK AND ALCOHOL Dr Feelgood (United Artists)
12	13	JUST THE WAY YOU ARE Barry White (20th Century)
26	14	COOL MEDITATION Third World (Island)
10	15	LE FREAK Chic (Atlantic)
-	16	CONTACT Edwin Starr (20th Century)
27	17	I WAS MADE FOR DANCIN' Leif Garrett (Atlantic)
11	18	LAY YOUR LOVE ON ME Racey (RAK)
22	19	MIRRORS Sally Oldfield (Bronze)
16	20	YOU NEEDED ME Anne Murray (Capitol)
-	21	I WILL SURVIVE Gloria Gaynor (Polydor)
28	22	KING ROCKER Generation X (Chrysalis)
19	23	TAKE THAT TO THE BANK Shalamar (RCA)
17	24	THIS IS IT Dan Hartman (Blue Sky)
-	25	GOT MY MIND MADE UP Instant Funk (Salsoul)
-	26	GET DOWN Gene Chandler (20th Century)
-	27	AIN'T LOVE A BITCH Rod Stewart (Riva)
-	28	SHAKE YOUR GROOVE THING Peaches & Herb (Polydor)
29	29	WE'VE GOT TONIGHT Bob Seger (Capitol)
30	30	SIR DANCEALOT Olympic Runners (Polydor)

		17 February 1979
4	1	CHIQUITITA Abba (Epic)
1	2	HEART OF GLASS Blondie (Chrysalis)
3	3	WOMAN IN LOVE Three Degrees (Ariola)
8	4	DON'T CRY FOR ME ARGENTINA Shadows (EMI)
2	5	HIT ME WITH YOUR RHYTHM STICK Ian Dury & The Blockheads (Stiff)
17	6	I WAS MADE FOR DANCIN' Leif Garrett (Atlantic)
16	7	CONTACT Edwin Starr (20th Century)
7	8	CAR 67 Driver 67 (Logo)
12	9	MILK AND ALCOHOL Dr Feelgood (United Artists)
10	10	MY LIFE Billy Joel (CBS)
22	11	KING ROCKER Generation X (Chrysalis)
6	12	SEPTEMBER Earth Wind & Fire (CBS)
5	13	Y. M. C. A. Village People (Mercury)
8	14	A LITTLE MORE LOVE Olivia Newton-John (EMI)
13	15	JUST THE WAY YOU ARE Barry White (20th Century)
-	16	TAKE ON THE WORLD Judas Priest (CBS)
-	17	SOUND OF THE SUBURBS Members (Virgin)
26	18	GET DOWN Gene Chandler (20th Century)
24	19	THIS IS IT Dan Hartman (Blue Sky)
11	20	HELLO THIS IS JOANIE (THE TELEPHONE ANSWERING MACHINE SONG) Paul Evans (Spring)
27	21	AIN'T LOVE A BITCH Rod Stewart (Riva)
14	22	COOL MEDITATION Third World (Island)
-	23	YOU BET YOUR LOVE Herbie Hancock (CBS)
-	24	OLIVER'S ARMY Elvis Costello (Radar)
23	25	TAKE THAT TO THE BANK Shalamar (RCA)
-	26	BAT OUT OF HELL Meat Loaf (Epic)
19	27	MIRRORS Sally Oldfield (Bronze)
21	28	I WILL SURVIVE Gloria Gaynor (Polydor)
15	29	LE FREAK Chic (Atlantic)
-	30	COULD IT BE MAGIC Barry Manilow (Arista)

		24 February 1979
2	1	HEART OF GLASS Blondie (Chrysalis)
1	2	CHIQUITITA Abba (Epic)
-	3	TRAGEDY Bee Gees (RSO)
7	4	CONTACT Edwin Starr (20th Century)
3	5	WOMAN IN LOVE Three Degrees (Ariola)
6	6	I WAS MADE FOR DANCIN' Leif Garrett (Atlantic)
4	7	DON'T CRY FOR ME ARGENTINA Shadows (EMI)
24	8	OLIVER'S ARMY Elvis Costello (Radar)
9	9	MILK AND ALCOHOL Dr Feelgood (United Artists)
11	10	KING ROCKER Generation X (Chrysalis)
5	11	HIT ME WITH YOUR RHYTHM STICK Ian Dury & the Blockheads (Stiff)
10	12	MY LIFE Billy Joel (CBS)
28	13	I WILL SURVIVE Gloria Gaynor (Polydor)
21	14	AIN'T LOVE A BITCH Rod Stewart (Riva)
16	15	TAKE ON THE WORLD Judas Priest (CBS)
18	16	GET DOWN Gene Chandler (20th Century)
17	17	SOUND OF THE SUBURBS Members (Virgin)
8	18	CAR 67 Driver 67 (Logo)
15	19	JUST THE WAY YOU ARE Barry White (20th Century)
-	20	GET IT Darts (Magnet)
12	21	SEPTEMBER Earth Wind & Fire (CBS)
13	22	Y. M. C. A. Village People (Mercury)
22	23	COOL MEDITATION Third World (Island)
14	24	A LITTLE MORE LOVE Olivia Newton-John (EMI)
-	25	DON'T STOP ME NOW Queen (EMI)
-	26	YOU NEEDED ME Anne Murray (Capitol)
-	27	SHAKE YOUR GROOVE THING Peaches & Herb (Polydor)
-	28	WHAT A FOOL BELIEVES Doobie Brothers (Warner Bros)
-	29	HOLD THE LINE Toto (CBS)
23	30	YOU BET YOUR LOVE Herbie Hancock (CBS)

Ian Dury gave Stiff Records its first Number One and biggest seller to date. The label announced in typically maverick fashion that the single would be deleted as soon as the one millionth copy was pressed: it didn't happen, because Dury's sales peaked a little above 900,000 – unlike those of Blondie's *Heart Of Glass,* which was yet another release to reach seven figures in the UK alone. Abba's *Chiquitita* was dedicated to UNICEF, which received all the royalties.

March 1979

3 March 1979

last week	this week		
1	1	HEART OF GLASS	Blondie (Chrysalis)
3	2	TRAGEDY	Bee Gees (RSO)
2	3	CHIQUITITA	Abba (Epic)
8	4	OLIVER'S ARMY	Elvis Costello (Radar)
13	5	I WILL SURVIVE	Gloria Gaynor (Polydor)
5	6	WOMAN IN LOVE	Three Degrees (Ariola)
6	7	I WAS MADE FOR DANCIN'	Leif Garrett (Atlantic)
4	8	CONTACT	Edwin Starr (20th Century)
16	9	GET DOWN	Gene Chandler (20th Century)
14	10	AIN'T LOVE A BITCH	Rod Stewart (Riva)
-	11	CAN YOU FEEL THE FORCE	Real Thing (Pye)
7	12	DON'T CRY FOR ME ARGENTINA	Shadows (EMI)
9	13	MILK AND ALCOHOL	Dr Feelgood (United Artists)
-	14	LUCKY NUMBER	Lene Lovich (Stiff)
17	15	SOUND OF THE SUBURBS	Members (Virgin)
15	16	TAKE ON THE WORLD	Judas Priest (CBS)
10	17	KING ROCKER	Generation X (Chrysalis)
-	18	INTO THE VALLEY	Skids (Virgin)
20	19	GET IT	Darts (Magnet)
27	20	SHAKE YOUR GROOVE THING	Peaches & Herb (Polydor)
-	21	BAT OUT OF HELL	Meat Loaf (Epic)
-	22	HEAVEN KNOWS	Donna Summer (Casablanca)
30	23	YOU BET YOUR LOVE	Herbie Hancock (CBS)
-	24	I WANT YOUR LOVE	Chic (Atlantic)
23	25	COOL MEDITATION	Third World (Island)
-	26	KEEP ON DANCIN'	Gary's Gang (CBS)
11	27	HIT ME WITH YOUR RHYTHM STICK	Ian Dury & The Blockheads (Stiff)
12	28	MY LIFE	Billy Joel (CBS)
-	29	STOP YOUR SOBBING	Pretenders (Real)
-	30	WEEKEND	Mick Jackson (Atlantic)

10 March 1979

2	1	TRAGEDY	Bee Gees (RSO)
1	2	HEART OF GLASS	Blondie (Chrysalis)
4	3	OLIVER'S ARMY	Elvis Costello (Radar)
5	4	I WILL SURVIVE	Gloria Gaynor (Polydor)
14	5	LUCKY NUMBER	Lene Lovich (Stiff)
8	6	CONTACT	Edwin Starr (20th Century)
3	7	CHIQUITITA	Abba (Epic)
19	8	GET IT	Darts (Magnet)
11	9	CAN YOU FEEL THE FORCE	Real Thing (Pye)
6	10	WOMAN IN LOVE	Three Degrees (Ariola)
9	11	GET DOWN	Gene Chandler (20th Century)
7	12	I WAS MADE FOR DANCIN'	Leif Garrett (Atlantic)
15	13	SOUND OF THE SUBURBS	Members (Virgin)
-	14	SOMETHING ELSE	Sex Pistols (Virgin)
10	15	AIN'T LOVE A BITCH	Rod Stewart (Riva)
24	16	I WANT YOUR LOVE	Chic (Atlantic)
18	17	INTO THE VALLEY	Skids (Virgin)
21	18	BAT OUT OF HELL	Meat Loaf (Epic)
26	19	KEEP ON DANCIN'	Gary's Gang (CBS)
-	20	PAINTER MAN	Boney M (Atlantic/Hansa)
-	21	HOLD THE LINE	Toto (CBS)
-	22	MONEY IN MY POCKET	Dennis Brown (Atlantic)
16	23	TAKE ON THE WORLD	Judas Priest (CBS)
13	24	MILK AND ALCOHOL	Dr Feelgood (United Artists)
-	25	JUST WHAT I NEEDED	Cars (Elektra)
-	26	DON'T STOP ME NOW	Queen (EMI)
-	27	WHAT A FOOL BELIEVES	Doobie Brothers (Warner Bros)
17	28	KING ROCKER	Generation X (Chrysalis)
22	29	HEAVEN KNOWS	Donna Summer (Casablanca)
-	30	ENGLISH CIVIL WAR	Clash (CBS)

17 March 1979

3	1	OLIVER'S ARMY	Elvis Costello (Radar)
1	2	TRAGEDY	Bee Gees (RSO)
4	3	I WILL SURVIVE	Gloria Gaynor (Polydor)
5	4	LUCKY NUMBER	Lene Lovich (Stiff)
9	5	CAN YOU FEEL THE FORCE	Real Thing (Pye)
14	6	SOMETHING ELSE	Sex Pistols (Virgin)
20	7	PAINTER MAN	Boney M (Atlantic/Hansa)
2	8	HEART OF GLASS	Blondie (Chrysalis)
16	9	I WANT YOUR LOVE	Chic (Atlantic)
19	10	KEEP ON DANCIN'	Gary's Gang (CBS)
6	11	CONTACT	Edwin Starr (20th Century)
11	12	GET DOWN	Gene Chandler (20th Century)
17	13	INTO THE VALLEY	Skids (Virgin)
8	14	GET IT	Darts (Magnet)
7	15	CHIQUITITA	Abba (Epic)
22	16	MONEY IN MY POCKET	Dennis Brown (Atlantic)
-	17	WAITING FOR AN ALIBI	Thin Lizzy (Vertigo)
26	18	DON'T STOP ME NOW	Queen (EMI)
-	19	YOU BET YOUR LOVE	Herbie Hancock (CBS)
13	20	SOUND OF THE SUBURBS	Members (Virgin)
-	21	CLOG DANCE	Violinski (Jet)
30	22	ENGLISH CIVIL WAR	Clash (CBS)
12	23	I WAS MADE FOR DANCIN'	Leif Garrett (Atlantic)
10	24	WOMAN IN LOVE	Three Degrees (Ariola)
-	25	FOREVER IN BLUE JEANS	Neil Diamond (CBS)
-	26	HONEY I'M LOST	Dooleys (GTO)
15	27	AIN'T LOVE A BITCH	Rod Stewart (Riva)
21	28	HOLD THE LINE	Toto (CBS)
-	29	TURN THE MUSIC UP	Players Association (Vanguard)
-	30	SULTANS OF SWING	Dire Straits (Vertigo)

24 March 1979

3	1	I WILL SURVIVE	Gloria Gaynor (Polydor)
1	2	OLIVER'S ARMY	Elvis Costello (Radar)
2	3	TRAGEDY	Bee Gees (RSO)
4	4	LUCKY NUMBER	Lene Lovich (Stiff)
5	5	CAN YOU FEEL THE FORCE	Real Thing (Pye)
9	6	I WANT YOUR LOVE	Chic (Atlantic)
6	7	SOMETHING ELSE	Sex Pistols (Virgin)
10	8	KEEP ON DANCIN'	Gary's Gang (CBS)
11	9	CONTACT	Edwin Starr (20th Century)
6	10	PAINTER MAN	Boney M (Atlantic/Hansa)
17	11	WAITING FOR AN ALIBI	Thin Lizzy (Vertigo)
28	12	HOLD THE LINE	Toto (CBS)
13	13	INTO THE VALLEY	Skids (Virgin)
-	14	IN THE NAVY	Village People (Mercury)
8	15	HEART OF GLASS	Blondie (Chrysalis)
12	16	GET DOWN	Gene Chandler (20th Century)
16	17	MONEY IN MY POCKET	Dennis Brown (Atlantic)
-	18	STRANGE TOWN	Jam (Polydor)
30	19	SULTANS OF SWING	Dire Straits (Vertigo)
29	20	TURN THE MUSIC UP	Players Association (Vanguard)
19	21	YOU BET YOUR LOVE	Herbie Hancock (CBS)
25	22	FOREVER IN BLUE JEANS	Neil Diamond (CBS)
14	23	GET IT	Darts (Magnet)
-	24	JUST WHAT I NEEDED	Cars (Elektra)
15	25	CHIQUITITA	Abba (Epic)
21	26	CLOG DANCE	Violinski (Jet)
18	27	DON'T STOP ME NOW	Queen (EMI)
20	28	SOUND OF THE SUBURBS	Members (Virgin)
-	29	EVERYBODY'S HAPPY NOWADAYS	Buzzcocks (United Artists)
-	30	DISCO NIGHTS (ROCK FREAK)	G.Q. (Arista)

Disco was bringing several veteran soul stars renewed success: both Edwin Starr and Gene Chandler returned with Top 10 hits, while former smooth UK soulsters the Real Thing also adapted with success to the rhythm of the day on *Can You Feel The Force*.

The Sex Pistols went back to Eddie Cochran in search of a cover, and Boney M had an unlikely revival of the Creation's mid-60s psychedelic workout *Painter Man*. Dire Straits made their debut with the several-month-old single *Sultans Of Swing*.

March – April 1979

31 March 1979

last week	this week	title	artist (label)
1	1	I WILL SURVIVE	Gloria Gaynor (Polydor)
4	2	LUCKY NUMBER	Lene Lovich (Stiff)
2	3	OLIVER'S ARMY	Elvis Costello (Radar)
6	4	I WANT YOUR LOVE	Chic (Atlantic)
5	5	CAN YOU FEEL THE FORCE	Real Thing (Pye)
7	6	SOMETHING ELSE	Sex Pistols (Virgin)
11	7	WAITING FOR AN ALIBI	Thin Lizzy (Vertigo)
14	8	IN THE NAVY	Village People (Mercury)
8	9	KEEP ON DANCIN'	Gary's Gang (CBS)
3	10	TRAGEDY	Bee Gees (RSO)
27	11	DON'T STOP ME NOW	Queen (EMI)
17	12	MONEY IN MY POCKET	Dennis Brown (Atlantic)
13	13	INTO THE VALLEY	Skids (Virgin)
19	14	SULTANS OF SWING	Dire Straits (Vertigo)
12	15	HOLD THE LINE	Toto (CBS)
26	16	CLOG DANCE	Violinski (Jet)
18	17	STRANGE TOWN	Jam (Polydor)
20	18	TURN THE MUSIC UP	Players Association (Vanguard)
16	19	GET DOWN	Gene Chandler (20th Century)
10	20	PAINTER MAN	Boney M (Atlantic/Hansa)
-	21	BRIGHT EYES	Art Garfunkel (CBS)
21	22	YOU BET YOUR LOVE	Herbie Hancock (CBS)
-	23	COOL FOR CATS	Squeeze (A&M)
-	24	WOW	Kate Bush (EMI)
9	25	CONTACT	Edwin Starr (20th Century)
24	26	JUST WHAT I NEEDED	Cars (Elektra)
22	27	FOREVER IN BLUE JEANS	Neil Diamond (CBS)
15	28	HEART OF GLASS	Blondie (Chrysalis)
-	29	FIRE	Pointer Sisters (Planet)
-	30	ENGLISH CIVIL WAR	Clash (CBS)

7 April 1979

last week	this week	title	artist (label)
8	1	IN THE NAVY	Village People (Mercury)
1	2	I WILL SURVIVE	Gloria Gaynor (Polydor)
4	3	I WANT YOUR LOVE	Chic (Atlantic)
6	4	SOMETHING ELSE	Sex Pistols (Virgin)
3	5	OLIVER'S ARMY	Elvis Costello (Radar)
5	6	CAN YOU FEEL THE FORCE	Real Thing (Pye)
2	7	LUCKY NUMBER	Lene Lovich (Stiff)
18	8	TURN THE MUSIC UP	Players Association (Vanguard)
14	9	SULTANS OF SWING	Dire Straits (Vertigo)
23	10	COOL FOR CATS	Squeeze (A&M)
11	11	DON'T STOP ME NOW	Queen (EMI)
21	12	BRIGHT EYES	Art Garfunkel (CBS)
9	13	KEEP ON DANCIN'	Gary's Gang (CBS)
7	14	WAITING FOR AN ALIBI	Thin Lizzy (Vertigo)
12	15	MONEY IN MY POCKET	Dennis Brown (Atlantic)
10	16	TRAGEDY	Bee Gees (RSO)
16	17	CLOG DANCE	Violinski (Jet)
24	18	WOW	Kate Bush (EMI)
27	19	FOREVER IN BLUE JEANS	Neil Diamond (CBS)
-	20	HE'S THE GREATEST DANCER	Sister Sledge (Atlantic)
-	21	THE RUNNER	Three Degrees (Ariola)
15	22	HOLD THE LINE	Toto (CBS)
17	23	STRANGE TOWN	Jam (Polydor)
26	24	JUST WHAT I NEEDED	Cars (Elektra)
20	25	PAINTER MAN	Boney M (Atlantic/Hansa)
13	26	INTO THE VALLEY	Skids (Virgin)
-	27	QUESTIONS AND ANSWERS	Sham 69 (Polydor)
-	28	SHAKE YOUR BODY	Jacksons (Epic)
29	29	SOME GIRLS	Racey (RAK)
-	30	THE STAIRCASE (MYSTERY)	Siouxsie & the Banshees (Polydor)

14 April 1979

last week	this week	title	artist (label)
12	1	BRIGHT EYES	Art Garfunkel (CBS)
2	2	I WILL SURVIVE	Gloria Gaynor (Polydor)
1	3	IN THE NAVY	Village People (Mercury)
10	4	COOL FOR CATS	Squeeze (A&M)
3	5	I WANT YOUR LOVE	Chic (Atlantic)
29	6	SOME GIRLS	Racey (RAK)
9	7	SULTANS OF SWING	Dire Straits (Vertigo)
20	8	HE'S THE GREATEST DANCER	Sister Sledge (Atlantic)
4	9	SOMETHING ELSE	Sex Pistols (Virgin)
-	10	SILLY THING/WHO KILLED BAMBI	Sex Pistols (Virgin)
7	11	LUCKY NUMBER	Lene Lovich (Stiff)
8	12	TURN THE MUSIC UP	Players Association (Vanguard)
6	13	CAN YOU FEEL THE FORCE	Real Thing (Pye)
28	14	SHAKE YOUR BODY	Jacksons (Epic)
5	15	OLIVER'S ARMY	Elvis Costello (Radar)
21	16	THE RUNNER	Three Degrees (Ariola)
-	17	I DON'T WANNA LOSE YOU	Kandidate (RAK)
15	18	MONEY IN MY POCKET	Dennis Brown (Atlantic)
23	19	STRANGE TOWN	Jam (Polydor)
13	20	KEEP ON DANCIN'	Gary's Gang (CBS)
30	21	THE STAIRCASE (MYSTERY)	Siouxsie & the Banshees (Polydor)
18	22	WOW	Kate Bush (EMI)
11	23	DON'T STOP ME NOW	Queen (EMI)
-	24	GOODNIGHT TONIGHT	Wings (Parlophone)
19	25	FOREVER IN BLUE JEANS	Neil Diamond (CBS)
14	26	WAITING FOR AN ALIBI	Thin Lizzy (Vertigo)
-	27	LET'S FLY AWAY	Voyage (GTO/Hansa)
-	28	FIRE	Pointer Sisters (Planet)
-	29	THE LOGICAL SONG	Supertramp (A&M)
22	30	HOLD THE LINE	Toto (CBS)

21 April 1979

last week	this week	title	artist (label)
1	1	BRIGHT EYES	Art Garfunkel (CBS)
4	2	COOL FOR CATS	Squeeze (A&M)
6	3	SOME GIRLS	Racey (RAK)
8	4	HE'S THE GREATEST DANCER	Sister Sledge (Atlantic)
10	5	SILLY THING/WHO KILLED BAMBI	Sex Pistols (Virgin)
2	6	I WILL SURVIVE	Gloria Gaynor (Polydor)
14	7	SHAKE YOUR GROOVE THING	Peaches & Herb (Polydor)
16	8	THE RUNNER	Three Degrees (Ariola)
3	9	IN THE NAVY	Village People (Mercury)
7	10	SULTANS OF SWING	Dire Straits (Vertigo)
5	11	I WANT YOUR LOVE	Chic (Atlantic)
9	12	SOMETHING ELSE	Sex Pistols (Virgin)
19	13	STRANGE TOWN	Jam (Polydor)
22	14	WOW	Kate Bush (EMI)
17	15	I DON'T WANNA LOSE YOU	Kandidate (RAK)
29	16	THE LOGICAL SONG	Supertramp (A&M)
-	17	QUESTIONS AND ANSWERS	Sham 69 (Polydor)
24	18	GOODNIGHT TONIGHT	Wings (Parlophone)
12	19	TURN THE MUSIC UP	Players Association (Vanguard)
23	20	DON'T STOP ME NOW	Queen (EMI)
-	21	POP MUZIK	M (MCA)
11	22	LUCKY NUMBER	Lene Lovich (Stiff)
-	23	REMEMBER THEN	Showaddywaddy (Arista)
-	24	VALLEY OF THE DOLLS	Generation X (Chrysalis)
15	25	OLIVER'S ARMY	Elvis Costello (Radar)
-	26	HALLELUJAH	Milk & Honey (Polydor)
-	27	LOVE YOU INSIDE OUT	Bee Gees (RSO)
25	28	FOREVER IN BLUE JEANS	Neil Diamond (CBS)
-	29	JUST WHAT I NEEDED	Cars (Elektra)
26	30	WAITING FOR AN ALIBI	Thin Lizzy (Vertigo)

Art Garfunkel's *Bright Eyes*, the haunting Mike Batt-composed theme song from the animated film *Watership Down*, suddenly accelerated to the top after a few weeks of slighter sales outside the Top 30. By half-way through the year it had sold over a million, completing a lengthy purple patch of seven-figure achievements which had begun with *Mull Of Kintyre* at the end of 1977. Strangely, Garfunkel's single was not a hit at all in the US, where he was generally a much more consistent chartmaker.

April – May 1979

last week	this week	28 April 1979		this	5 May 1979		this	12 May 1979		this	19 May 1979
1	1	BRIGHT EYES — Art Garfunkel (CBS)	1	1	BRIGHT EYES — Art Garfunkel (CBS)	1	1	BRIGHT EYES — Art Garfunkel (CBS)	2	1	POP MUZIK — M (MCA)
3	2	SOME GIRLS — Racey (RAK)	2	2	SOME GIRLS — Racey (RAK)	3	2	POP MUZIK — M (MCA)	1	2	BRIGHT EYES — Art Garfunkel (CBS)
2	3	COOL FOR CATS — Squeeze (A&M)	9	3	POP MUZIK — M (MCA)	9	3	HOORAY HOORAY IT'S A HOLI HOLIDAY — Boney M (Atlantic/Hansa)	3	3	HOORAY HOORAY IT'S A HOLI HOLIDAY — Boney M (Atlantic/Hansa)
26	4	HALLELUJAH — Milk & Honey (Polydor)	3	4	COOL FOR CATS — Squeeze (A&M)	2	4	SOME GIRLS — Racey (RAK)	14	4	DOES YOUR MOTHER KNOW — Abba (Epic)
7	5	SHAKE YOUR BODY — Jacksons (Epic)	5	5	SHAKE YOUR BODY — Jacksons (Epic)	13	5	KNOCK ON WOOD — Amii Stewart (Atlantic/Hansa)	13	5	REUNITED — Peaches & Herb (Polydor)
15	6	I DON'T WANNA LOSE YOU — Kandidate (RAK)	18	6	THE LOGICAL SONG — Supertramp (A&M)	8	6	GOODNIGHT TONIGHT — Wings (Parlophone)	5	6	KNOCK ON WOOD — Amii Stewart (Atlantic/Hansa)
5	7	SILLY THING/WHO KILLED BAMBI — Sex Pistols (Virgin)	4	7	HALLELUJAH — Milk & Honey (Polydor)	5	7	SHAKE YOUR BODY — Jacksons (Epic)	4	7	SOME GIRLS — Racey (RAK)
4	8	HE'S THE GREATEST DANCER — Sister Sledge (Atlantic)	12	8	GOODNIGHT TONIGHT — Wings (Parlophone)	6	8	THE LOGICAL SONG — Supertramp (A&M)	11	8	ONE WAY TICKET — Eruption (Atlantic)
21	9	POP MUZIK — M (MCA)	-	9	HOORAY HOORAY IT'S A HOLI HOLIDAY — Boney M (Atlantic/Hansa)	15	9	LOVE YOU INSIDE OUT — Bee Gees (RSO)	6	9	GOODNIGHT TONIGHT — Wings (Parlophone)
8	10	THE RUNNER — Three Degrees (Ariola)	10	10	THE RUNNER — Three Degrees (Ariola)	4	10	COOL FOR CATS — Squeeze (A&M)	18	10	BANANA SPLITS — Dickies (A&M)
9	11	IN THE NAVY — Village People (Mercury)	8	11	HE'S THE GREATEST DANCER — Sister Sledge (Atlantic)	23	11	ONE WAY TICKET — Eruption (Atlantic)	8	11	THE LOGICAL SONG — Supertramp (A&M)
18	12	GOODNIGHT TONIGHT — Wings (Parlophone)	6	12	I DON'T WANNA LOSE YOU — Kandidate (RAK)	7	12	HALLELUJAH — Milk & Honey (Polydor)	7	12	SHAKE YOUR BODY — Jacksons (Epic)
6	13	I WILL SURVIVE — Gloria Gaynor (Polydor)	17	13	KNOCK ON WOOD — Amii Stewart (Atlantic/Hansa)	16	13	REUNITED — Peaches & Herb (Polydor)	19	13	ROXANNE — Police (A&M)
14	14	WOW — Kate Bush (EMI)	7	14	SILLY THING/WHO KILLED BAMBI — Sex Pistols (Virgin)	-	14	DOES YOUR MOTHER KNOW — Abba (Epic)	23	14	BOYS KEEP SWINGIN' — David Bowie (RCA)
28	15	FOREVER IN BLUE JEANS — Neil Diamond (CBS)	21	15	LOVE YOU INSIDE OUT — Bee Gees (RSO)	12	15	I DON'T WANNA LOSE YOU — Kandidate (RAK)	9	15	LOVE YOU INSIDE OUT — Bee Gees (RSO)
10	16	SULTANS OF SWING — Dire Straits (Vertigo)	-	16	REUNITED — Peaches & Herb (Polydor)	10	16	THE RUNNER — Three Degrees (Ariola)	15	16	I DON'T WANNA LOSE YOU — Kandidate (RAK)
-	17	KNOCK ON WOOD — Amii Stewart (Atlantic/Hansa)	14	17	WOW — Kate Bush (EMI)	19	17	HAVEN'T STOPPED DANCIN' YET — Gonzalez (Sidewalk)	-	17	DANCE AWAY — Roxy Music (Polydor)
16	18	THE LOGICAL SONG — Supertramp (A&M)	16	18	SULTANS OF SWING — Dire Straits (Vertigo)	22	18	BANANA SPLITS — Dickies (A&M)	12	18	HALLELUJAH — Milk & Honey (Polydor)
23	19	REMEMBER THEN — Showaddywaddy (Arista)	22	19	HAVEN'T STOPPED DANCIN' YET — Gonzalez (Sidewalk)	24	19	ROXANNE — Police (A&M)	20	19	PARISIENNE WALKWAYS — Gary Moore (MCA)
11	20	I WANT YOUR LOVE — Chic (Atlantic)	15	20	FOREVER IN BLUE JEANS — Neil Diamond (CBS)	27	20	PARISIENNE WALKWAYS — Gary Moore (MCA)	27	20	GUILTY — Mike Oldfield (Virgin)
27	21	LOVE YOU INSIDE OUT — Bee Gees (RSO)	19	21	REMEMBER THEN — Showaddywaddy (Arista)	14	21	SILLY THING/WHO KILLED BAMBI — Sex Pistols (Virgin)	17	21	HAVEN'T STOPPED DANCIN' YET — Gonzalez (Sidewalk)
-	22	HAVEN'T STOPPED DANCIN' YET — Gonzalez (Sidewalk)	-	22	BANANA SPLITS — Dickies (A&M)	11	22	HE'S THE GREATEST DANCER — Sister Sledge (Atlantic)	25	22	JIMMY JIMMY — Undertones (Sire)
12	23	SOMETHING ELSE — Sex Pistols (Virgin)	28	23	ONE WAY TICKET — Eruption (Atlantic)	-	23	BOYS KEEP SWINGIN' — David Bowie (RCA)	10	23	COOL FOR CATS — Squeeze (A&M)
17	24	QUESTIONS AND ANSWERS — Sham 69 (Polydor)	24	24	ROXANNE — Police (A&M)	17	24	WOW — Kate Bush (EMI)	-	24	BOOGIE WONDERLAND — Earth, Wind & Fire with the Emotions (CBS)
-	25	OFFSHORE BANKING BUSINESS — Members (Virgin)	26	25	STRANGE TOWN — Jam (Polydor)	-	25	JIMMY JIMMY — Undertones (Sire)	28	25	LOVE BALLAD — George Benson (Warner Bros)
13	26	STRANGE TOWN — Jam (Polydor)	-	26	ONLY YOU — Child (Ariola/Hansa)	20	26	FOREVER IN BLUE JEANS — Neil Diamond (CBS)	-	26	LOVE SONG — The Damned (Chiswick)
-	27	MONEY IN MY POCKET — Dennis Brown (Atlantic)	-	27	PARISIENNE WALKWAYS — Gary Moore (MCA)	-	27	GUILTY — Mike Oldfield (Virgin)	29	27	NICE LEGS SHAME ABOUT HER FACE — Monks (Carrere)
-	28	ONE WAY TICKET — Eruption (Atlantic)	24	28	QUESTIONS AND ANSWERS — Sham 69 (Polydor)	-	28	LOVE BALLAD — George Benson (Warner Bros)	26	28	FOREVER IN BLUE JEANS — Neil Diamond (CBS)
19	29	TURN THE MUSIC UP — Players Association (Vanguard)	11	29	IN THE NAVY — Village People (Mercury)	-	29	NICE LEGS SHAME ABOUT HER FACE — Monks (Carrere)	24	29	WOW — Kate Bush (EMI)
-	30	HERE COMES THE NIGHT — Beach Boys (Caribou)	13	30	I WILL SURVIVE — Gloria Gaynor (Polydor)	-	30	THEME FROM THE DEER HUNTER (CAVATINA) — Shadows (EMI)	-	30	BRIDGE OVER TROUBLED WATER — Linda Clifford (RSO)

Milk And Honey's *Hallelujah* was the Israeli winner of the 1979 Eurovision song contest– the British entry, *Mary Ann* by Black Lace (which came an ignominious 12th, the lowest UK placing to date), had failed to chart. M, the most succinct chart name of all time, was actually vocalist Robin Scott; his chart-topper *Pop Musik* would eventually return to the Top 10 just over 10 years later, in a remixed version. More revived oldies included Amii Stewart's discofied *Knock On Wood* and Child's *Only You*.

May – June 1979

26 May 1979

last week	this week		
2	1	BRIGHT EYES	Art Garfunkel (CBS)
1	2	POP MUZIK	M (MCA)
5	3	REUNITED	Peaches & Herb (Polydor)
17	4	DANCE AWAY	Roxy Music (Polydor)
3	5	HOORAY HOORAY IT'S A HOLI HOLIDAY	Boney M (Atlantic/Hansa)
4	6	DOES YOUR MOTHER KNOW	Abba (Epic)
6	7	KNOCK ON WOOD	Amii Stewart (Atlantic/Hansa)
-	8	SUNDAY GIRL	Blondie (Chrysalis)
8	9	ONE WAY TICKET	Eruption (Atlantic)
19	10	PARISIENNE WALKWAYS	Gary Moore (MCA)
13	11	ROXANNE	Police (A&M)
11	12	THE LOGICAL SONG	Supertramp (A&M)
10	13	BANANA SPLITS	Dickies (A&M)
24	14	BOOGIE WONDERLAND	Earth, Wind & Fire with the Emotions(CBS)
14	15	BOYS KEEP SWINGIN'	David Bowie (RCA)
22	16	JIMMY JIMMY	Undertones (Sire)
9	17	GOODNIGHT TONIGHT	Wings (Parlophone)
-	18	I FOUGHT THE LAW	Clash (CBS)
-	19	THEME FROM THE DEER HUNTER (CAVATINA)	Shadows (EMI)
-	20	HOT STUFF	Donna Summer (Casablanca)
7	21	SOME GIRLS	Racey (RAK)
-	22	SHINE A LITTLE LOVE	Electric Light Orchestra (Jet)
15	23	LOVE YOU INSIDE OUT	Bee Gees (RSO)
27	24	NICE LEGS SHAME ABOUT HER FACE	Monks (Carrere)
-	25	AIN'T NO STOPPIN' US NOW	McFadden & Whitehead (Philadelphia)
12	26	SHAKE YOUR BODY	Jacksons (Epic)
21	27	HAVEN'T STOPPED DANCIN' YET	Gonzalez (Sidewalk)
16	28	I DON'T WANNA LOSE YOU	Kandidate (RAK)
-	29	THE NUMBER ONE SONG IN HEAVEN	Sparks (Virgin)
26	30	LOVE SONG	The Damned (Chiswick)

2 June 1979

8	1	SUNDAY GIRL	Blondie (Chrysalis)
4	2	DANCE AWAY	Roxy Music (Polydor)
3	3	REUNITED	Peaches & Herb (Polydor)
2	4	POP MUZIK	M (MCA)
14	5	BOOGIE WONDERLAND	Earth, Wind & Fire with the Emotions (CBS)
6	6	DOES YOUR MOTHER KNOW	Abba (Epic)
1	7	BRIGHT EYES	Art Garfunkel (CBS)
10	8	PARISIENNE WALKWAYS	Gary Moore (MCA)
15	9	BOYS KEEP SWINGIN'	David Bowie (RCA)
22	10	SHINE A LITTLE LOVE	Electric Light Orchestra (Jet)
11	11	ROXANNE	Police (A&M)
7	12	KNOCK ON WOOD	Amii Stewart (Atlantic/Hansa)
5	13	HOORAY HOORAY IT'S A HOLI HOLIDAY	Boney M (Atlantic/Hansa)
19	14	THEME FROM THE DEER HUNTER (CAVATINA)	Shadows (EMI)
9	15	ONE WAY TICKET	Eruption (Atlantic)
25	16	AIN'T NO STOPPIN' US NOW	McFadden & Whitehead (Philadelphia)
18	17	I FOUGHT THE LAW	Clash (CBS)
20	18	HOT STUFF	Donna Summer (Casablanca)
16	19	JIMMY JIMMY	Undertones (Sire)
29	20	THE NUMBER ONE SONG IN HEAVEN	Sparks (Virgin)
-	21	RING MY BELL	Anita Ward (TK)
24	22	NICE LEGS SHAME ABOUT HER FACE	Monks (Carrere)
-	23	MASQUERADE	Skids (Virgin)
13	24	BANANA SPLITS	Dickies (A&M)
-	25	BRIDGE OVER TROUBLED WATER	Linda Clifford (RSO)
26	26	GERTCHA	Chas & Dave (EMI)
27	27	H.A.P.P.Y. RADIO	Edwin Starr (RCA)
12	28	THE LOGICAL SONG	Supertramp (A&M)
-	29	ARE FRIENDS ELECTRIC	Tubeway Army (Beggars Banquet)
30	30	LOVE SONG	The Damned (Chiswick)

9 June 1979

2	1	DANCE AWAY	Roxy Music (Polydor)
1	2	SUNDAY GIRL	Blondie (Chrysalis)
3	3	REUNITED	Peaches & Herb (Polydor)
5	4	BOOGIE WONDERLAND	Earth, Wind & Fire with the Emotions (CBS)
4	5	POP MUZIK	M (MCA)
14	6	THEME FROM THE DEER HUNTER (CAVATINA)	Shadows (EMI)
21	7	RING MY BELL	Anita Ward (TK)
9	8	BOYS KEEP SWINGIN'	David Bowie (RCA)
7	9	BRIGHT EYES	Art Garfunkel (CBS)
6	10	DOES YOUR MOTHER KNOW	Abba (Epic)
16	11	AIN'T NO STOPPIN' US NOW	McFadden & Whitehead (Philadelphia)
10	12	SHINE A LITTLE LOVE	Electric Light Orchestra (Jet)
8	13	PARISIENNE WALKWAYS	Gary Moore (MCA)
17	14	HOT STUFF	Donna Summer (Casablanca)
15	15	ONE WAY TICKET	Eruption (Atlantic)
11	16	ROXANNE	Police (A&M)
20	17	THE NUMBER ONE SONG IN HEAVEN	Sparks (Virgin)
27	18	H.A.P.P.Y. RADIO	Edwin Starr (RCA)
23	19	MASQUERADE	Skids (Virgin)
29	20	ARE FRIENDS ELECTRIC	Tubeway Army (Beggars Banquet)
26	21	GERTCHA	Chas & Dave (EMI)
17	22	I FOUGHT THE LAW	Clash (CBS)
-	23	WE ARE FAMILY	Sister Sledge (Atlantic)
12	24	KNOCK ON WOOD	Amii Stewart (Atlantic/Hansa)
19	25	JIMMY JIMMY	Undertones (Sire)
13	26	HOORAY HOORAY IT'S A HOLI HOLIDAY	Boney M (Atlantic/Hansa)
-	27	I WANT YOU TO WANT ME	Cheap Trick (Epic)
-	28	THE LONE RANGER	Quantum Jump (Electric)
29	29	WHO WERE YOU WITH IN THE MOONLIGHT	Dollar (Carrere)
24	30	BANANA SPLITS	Dickies (A&M)

16 June 1979

7	1	RING MY BELL	Anita Ward (TK)
2	2	SUNDAY GIRL	Blondie (Chrysalis)
1	3	DANCE AWAY	Roxy Music (Polydor)
4	4	BOOGIE WONDERLAND	Earth, Wind & Fire with the Emotions (CBS)
6	5	THEME FROM THE DEER HUNTER (CAVATINA)	Shadows (EMI)
12	6	SHINE A LITTLE LOVE	Electric Light Orchestra (Jet)
3	7	REUNITED	Peaches & Herb (Polydor)
11	8	AIN'T NO STOPPIN' US NOW	McFadden & Whitehead (Philadelphia)
9	9	BOYS KEEP SWINGIN'	David Bowie (RCA)
5	10	POP MUZIK	M (MCA)
20	11	ARE FRIENDS ELECTRIC	Tubeway Army (Beggars Banquet)
23	12	WE ARE FAMILY	Sister Sledge (Atlantic)
14	13	HOT STUFF	Donna Summer (Casablanca)
-	14	UP THE JUNCTION	Squeeze (A&M)
18	15	H.A.P.P.Y. RADIO	Edwin Starr (RCA)
13	16	PARISIENNE WALKWAYS	Gary Moore (MCA)
10	17	DOES YOUR MOTHER KNOW	Abba (Epic)
19	18	MASQUERADE	Skids (Virgin)
9	19	BRIGHT EYES	Art Garfunkel (CBS)
17	20	THE NUMBER ONE SONG IN HEAVEN	Sparks (Virgin)
15	21	ONE WAY TICKET	Eruption (Atlantic)
16	22	ROXANNE	Police (A&M)
29	23	WHO WERE YOU WITH IN THE MOONLIGHT	Dollar (Carrere)
28	24	THE LONE RANGER	Quantum Jump (Electric)
-	25	NIGHT OWL	Gerry Rafferty (United Artists)
26	26	GERTCHA	Chas & Dave (EMI)
22	27	I FOUGHT THE LAW	Clash (CBS)
25	28	JIMMY JIMMY	Undertones (Sire)
-	29	CAVATINA	John Williams (Cube)
27	30	I WANT YOU TO WANT ME	Cheap Trick (Epic)

After a long inactive period during which its members (notably Bryan Ferry) had pursued solo recording careers, Roxy Music returned in no uncertain fashion with the chart-topping *Dance Away*. The Shadows cemented their recent chart comeback with a second Top 10 hit in *Theme From The Deer Hunter* – actually Stanley Myers' composition *Cavatina* – under which title John Williams' version joined the Shads in the chart. The Clash's *I Fought The Law* was originally recorded by the Crickets in 1959.

June – July 1979

23 June 1979

last	this	
1	1	RING MY BELL — Anita Ward (TK)
3	2	DANCE AWAY — Roxy Music (Polydor)
4	3	BOOGIE WONDERLAND — Earth, Wind & Fire with the Emotions (CBS)
2	4	SUNDAY GIRL — Blondie (Chrysalis)
11	5	ARE FRIENDS ELECTRIC — Tubeway Army (Beggars Banquet)
8	6	AIN'T NO STOPPIN' US NOW — McFadden & Whitehead (Philadelphia)
6	7	SHINE A LITTLE LOVE — Electric Light Orchestra (Jet)
12	8	WE ARE FAMILY — Sister Sledge (Atlantic)
5	9	THEME FROM THE DEER HUNTER (CAVATINA) — Shadows (EMI)
14	10	UP THE JUNCTION — Squeeze (A&M)
15	11	H.A.P.P.Y. RADIO — Edwin Starr (RCA)
24	12	THE LONE RANGER — Quantum Jump (Electric)
18	13	MASQUERADE — Skids (Virgin)
23	14	WHO WERE YOU WITH IN THE MOONLIGHT — Dollar (Carrere)
13	15	HOT STUFF — Donna Summer (Casablanca)
7	16	REUNITED — Peaches & Herb (Polydor)
9	17	BOYS KEEP SWINGIN' — David Bowie (RCA)
25	18	NIGHT OWL — Gerry Rafferty (United Artists)
26	19	GERTCHA — Chas & Dave (EMI)
-	20	LIVING ON THE FRONT LINE — Eddy Grant (Ice/Ensign)
20	21	THE NUMBER ONE SONG IN HEAVEN — Sparks (Virgin)
-	22	GO WEST — Village People (Mercury)
-	23	SAY WHEN — Lene Lovich (Stiff)
19	24	BRIGHT EYES — Art Garfunkel (CBS)
-	25	LIGHT MY FIRE/137 DISCO HEAVEN — Amii Stewart (Atlantic/Hansa)
-	26	SPACE BASS — Slick (Fantasy)
16	27	PARISIENNE WALKWAYS — Gary Moore (MCA)
29	28	CAVATINA — John Williams (Cube)
10	29	POP MUZIK — M (MCA)
27	30	I FOUGHT THE LAW — Clash (CBS)

30 June 1979

last	this	
1	1	RING MY BELL — Anita Ward (TK)
5	2	ARE FRIENDS ELECTRIC — Tubeway Army (Beggars Banquet)
10	3	UP THE JUNCTION — Squeeze (A&M)
3	4	BOOGIE WONDERLAND — Earth, Wind & Fire with the Emtions (CBS)
4	5	SUNDAY GIRL — Blondie (Chrysalis)
2	6	DANCE AWAY — Roxy Music (Polydor)
12	7	THE LONE RANGER — Quantum Jump (Electric)
6	8	AIN'T NO STOPPIN' US NOW — McFadden & Whitehead (Philadelphia)
18	9	NIGHT OWL — Gerry Rafferty (United Artists)
9	10	THEME FROM THE DEER HUNTER (CAVATINA) — Shadows (EMI)
11	11	H.A.P.P.Y. RADIO — Edwin Starr (RCA)
7	12	SHINE A LITTLE LOVE — Electric Light Orchestra (Jet)
8	13	WE ARE FAMILY — Sister Sledge (Atlantic)
20	14	LIVING ON THE FRONT LINE — Eddy Grant (Ice/Ensign)
28	15	CAVATINA — John Williams (Cube)
13	16	MASQUERADE — Skids (Virgin)
25	17	LIGHT MY FIRE/137 DISCO HEAVEN — Amii Stewart (Atlantic/Hansa)
22	18	GO WEST — Village People (Mercury)
14	19	WHO WERE YOU WITH IN THE MOONLIGHT — Dollar (Carrere)
19	20	GERTCHA — Chas & Dave (EMI)
15	21	HOT STUFF — Donna Summer (Casablanca)
-	22	LADY LYNDA — Beach Boys (Caribou)
-	23	SILLY GAMES — Janet Kay (Scope)
23	24	SAY WHEN — Lene Lovich (Stiff)
-	25	BABYLON BURNING — Ruts (Virgin)
26	26	SPACE BASS — Slick (Fantasy)
-	27	OLD SIAM SIR — Wings (Parlophone)
-	28	CHUCK E'S IN LOVE — Rickie Lee Jones (Warner Bros)
21	29	THE NUMBER ONE SONG IN HEAVEN — Sparks (Virgin)
16	30	REUNITED — Peaches & Herb (Polydor)

7 July 1979

last	this	
2	1	ARE FRIENDS ELECTRIC — Tubeway Army (Beggars Banquet)
3	2	UP THE JUNCTION — Squeeze (A&M)
1	3	RING MY BELL — Anita Ward (TK)
4	4	BOOGIE WONDERLAND — Earth, Wind & Fire with the Emotions (CBS)
7	5	THE LONE RANGER — Quantum Jump (Electric)
9	6	NIGHT OWL — Gerry Rafferty (United Artists)
15	7	CAVATINA — John Williams (Cube)
14	8	LIVING ON THE FRONT LINE — Eddy Grant (Ice/Ensign)
13	9	WE ARE FAMILY — Sister Sledge (Atlantic)
6	10	DANCE AWAY — Roxy Music (Polydor)
8	11	AIN'T NO STOPPIN' US NOW — McFadden & Whitehead (Philadelphia)
10	12	THEME FROM THE DEER HUNTER (CAVATINA) — Shadows (EMI)
11	13	H.A.P.P.Y. RADIO — Edwin Starr (RCA)
5	14	SUNDAY GIRL — Blondie (Chrysalis)
17	15	LIGHT MY FIRE/137 DISCO HEAVEN — Amii Stewart (Atlantic/Hansa)
19	16	WHO WERE YOU WITH IN THE MOONLIGHT — Dollar (Carrere)
-	17	C'MON EVERYBODY — Sex Pistols (Virgin)
25	18	BABYLON BURNING — Ruts (Virgin)
23	19	SILLY GAMES — Janet Kay (Scope)
18	20	GO WEST — Village People (Mercury)
12	21	SHINE A LITTLE LOVE — Electric Light Orchestra (Jet)
22	22	LADY LYNDA — Beach Boys (Caribou)
16	23	MASQUERADE — Skids (Virgin)
20	24	GERTCHA — Chas & Dave (EMI)
24	25	SAY WHEN — Lene Lovich (Stiff)
26	26	SPACE BASS — Slick (Fantasy)
-	27	MAYBE — Thom Pace (RSO)
-	28	DO ANYTHING YOU WANT TO DO — Thin Lizzy (Vertigo)
27	29	OLD SIAM SIR — Wings (Parlophone)
-	30	MY SHARONA — Knack (Capitol)

14 July 1979

last	this	
1	1	ARE FRIENDS ELECTRIC — Tubeway Army (Beggars Banquet)
2	2	UP THE JUNCTION — Squeeze (A&M)
19	3	SILLY GAMES — Janet Kay (Scope)
15	4	LIGHT MY FIRE/137 DISCO HEAVEN — Amii Stewart (Atlantic/Hansa)
6	5	NIGHT OWL — Gerry Rafferty (United Artists)
3	6	RING MY BELL — Anita Ward (TK)
17	7	C'MON EVERYBODY — Sex Pistols (Virgin)
8	8	LIVING ON THE FRONT LINE — Eddy Grant (Ice/Ensign)
5	9	THE LONE RANGER — Quantum Jump (Electric)
10	10	GOOD TIMES — Chic (Atlantic)
4	11	BOOGIE WONDERLAND — Earth, Wind & Fire with the Emotions (CBS)
27	12	MAYBE — Thom Pace (RSO)
16	13	WHO WERE YOU WITH IN THE MOONLIGHT — Dollar (Carrere)
10	14	DANCE AWAY — Roxy Music (Polydor)
18	15	BABYLON BURNING — Ruts (Virgin)
7	16	CAVATINA — John Williams (Cube)
-	17	GIRLS TALK — Dave Edmunds (Swan Song)
9	18	WE ARE FAMILY — Sister Sledge (Atlantic)
26	19	SPACE BASS — Slick (Fantasy)
30	20	MY SHARONA — Knack (Capitol)
20	21	GO WEST — Village People (Mercury)
22	22	LADY LYNDA — Beach Boys (Caribou)
28	23	DO ANYTHING YOU WANT TO DO — Thin Lizzy (Vertigo)
-	24	BAD GIRLS — Donna Summer (Casablanca)
-	25	DEATH DISCO — Public Image Ltd (Virgin)
14	26	SUNDAY GIRL — Blondie (Chrysalis)
11	27	AIN'T NO STOPPIN' US NOW — McFadden & Whitehead (Philadelphia)
12	28	THEME FROM THE DEER HUNTER (CAVATINA) — Shadows (EMI)
-	29	BREAKFAST IN AMERICA — Supertramp (A&M)
-	30	BORN TO BE ALIVE — Patrick Hernandez (Gem/Aquarius)

Anita Ward's *Ring My Bell* was a huge seller in disco-orientated record shops as an import for weeks before its UK release saw it to Number One, as was McFadden & Whitehead's top tenner *Ain't No Stoppin' Us Now* (now further immortalised by building society ads!) Squeeze scored their second Number Two hit in a row with *Up The Junction*, the Sex Pistols revived another Eddie Cochran oldie, and the chart-topping Tubeway Army was actually the soon-to-be-credited-personally Gary Numan.

21 July 1979

last week	this week		
3	1	SILLY GAMES	Janet Kay (Scope)
1	2	ARE FRIENDS ELECTRIC	Tubeway Army (Beggars Banquet)
7	3	C'MON EVERYBODY	Sex Pistols (Virgin)
4	4	LIGHT MY FIRE/137 DISCO HEAVEN	Amii Stewart (Atlantic/Hansa)
10	5	GOOD TIMES	Chic (Atlantic)
22	6	LADY LYNDA	Beach Boys (Caribou)
8	7	LIVING ON THE FRONT LINE	Eddy Grant (Ice/Ensign)
5	8	NIGHT OWL	Gerry Rafferty (United Artists)
15	9	BABYLON BURNING	Ruts (Virgin)
2	10	UP THE JUNCTION	Squeeze (A&M)
17	11	GIRLS TALK	Dave Edmunds (Swan Song)
-	12	WANTED	Dooleys (GTO)
9	13	THE LONE RANGER	Quantum Jump (Electric)
12	14	MAYBE	Thom Pace (RSO)
20	15	MY SHARONA	Knack (Capitol)
19	16	SPACE BASS	Slick (Fantasy)
21	17	GO WEST	Village People (Mercury)
6	18	RING MY BELL	Anita Ward (TK)
24	19	BAD GIRLS	Donna Summer (Casablanca)
29	20	BREAKFAST IN AMERICA	Supertramp (A&M)
23	21	DO ANYTHING YOU WANT TO DO	Thin Lizzy (Vertigo)
-	22	CHUCK E'S IN LOVE	Rickie Lee Jones (Warner Bros)
16	23	CAVATINA	John Williams (Cube)
-	24	CAN'T STAND LOSING YOU	Police (A&M)
25	25	DEATH DISCO	Public Image Ltd (Virgin)
-	26	IF I HAD YOU	Korgis (Rialto)
30	27	BORN TO BE ALIVE	Patrick Hernandez (Gem/Aquarius)
-	28	H.A.P.P.Y. RADIO	Edwin Starr (RCA)
-	29	I'M A SUCKER FOR YOUR LOVE	Teena Marie (Motown)
-	30	ANGEL EYES/VOULEZ VOUS	Abba (Epic)

28 July 1979

last week	this week		
2	1	ARE FRIENDS ELECTRIC	Tubeway Army (Beggars Banquet)
1	2	SILLY GAMES	Janet Kay (Scope)
11	3	GIRLS TALK	Dave Edmunds (Swan Song)
3	4	C'MON EVERYBODY	Sex Pistols (Virgin)
5	5	GOOD TIMES	Chic (Atlantic)
6	6	LADY LYNDA	Beach Boys (Caribou)
-	7	I DON'T LIKE MONDAYS	Boomtown Rats (Ensign)
20	8	BREAKFAST IN AMERICA	Supertramp (A&M)
12	9	WANTED	Dooleys (GTO)
8	10	NIGHT OWL	Gerry Rafferty (United Artists)
4	11	LIGHT MY FIRE/137 DISCO HEAVEN	Amii Stewart (Atlantic/Hansa)
27	12	BORN TO BE ALIVE	Patrick Hernandez (Gem/Aquarius)
10	13	UP THE JUNCTION	Squeeze (A&M)
24	14	CAN'T STAND LOSING YOU	Police (A&M)
9	15	BABYLON BURNING	Ruts (Virgin)
19	16	BAD GIRLS	Donna Summer (Casablanca)
15	17	MY SHARONA	Knack (Capitol)
14	18	MAYBE	Thom Pace (RSO)
21	19	DO ANYTHING YOU WANT TO DO	Thin Lizzy (Vertigo)
7	20	LIVING ON THE FRONT LINE	Eddy Grant (Ice/Ensign)
30	21	ANGEL EYES/VOULEZ VOUS	Abba (Epic)
16	22	SPACE BASS	Slick (Fantasy)
-	23	WE DON'T TALK ANYMORE	Cliff Richard (EMI)
26	24	IF I HAD YOU	Korgis (Rialto)
25	25	DEATH DISCO	Public Image Ltd (Virgin)
22	26	CHUCK E'S IN LOVE	Rickie Lee Jones (Warner Bros)
-	27	D.J.	David Bowie (RCA)
17	28	GO WEST	Village People (Mercury)
-	29	KID	Pretenders (Real)
-	30	DUKE OF EARL	Darts (Magnet)

4 August 1979

last week	this week		
7	1	I DON'T LIKE MONDAYS	Boomtown Rats (Ensign)
3	2	GIRLS TALK	Dave Edmunds (Swan Song)
2	3	SILLY GAMES	Janet Kay (Scope)
1	4	ARE FRIENDS ELECTRIC	Tubeway Army (Beggars Banquet)
5	5	GOOD TIMES	Chic (Atlantic)
9	6	WANTED	Dooleys (GTO)
17	7	MY SHARONA	Knack (Capitol)
8	8	BREAKFAST IN AMERICA	Supertramp (A&M)
21	9	ANGEL EYES/VOULEZ VOUS	Abba (Epic)
14	10	CAN'T STAND LOSING YOU	Police (A&M)
12	11	BORN TO BE ALIVE	Patrick Hernandez (Gem/Aquarius)
6	12	LADY LYNDA	Beach Boys (Caribou)
4	13	C'MON EVERYBODY	Sex Pistols (Virgin)
16	14	BAD GIRLS	Donna Summer (Casablanca)
23	15	WE DON'T TALK ANYMORE	Cliff Richard (EMI)
-	16	BEAT THE CLOCK	Sparks (Virgin)
24	17	IF I HAD YOU	Korgis (Rialto)
-	18	AFTER THE LOVE HAS GONE	Earth Wind & Fire (CBS)
26	19	CHUCK E'S IN LOVE	Rickie Lee Jones (Warner Bros)
11	20	LIGHT MY FIRE/137 DISCO HEAVEN	Amii Stewart (Atlantic/Hansa)
-	21	THE DIARY OF HORACE WIMP	Electric Light Orchestra (Jet)
18	22	MAYBE	Thom Pace (RSO)
-	23	MORNING DANCE	Spyro Gyra (Infinity)
-	24	STAY WITH ME TILL DAWN	Judy Tzuke (Rocket)
-	25	BOOGIE DOWN	Real Thing (Pye)
15	26	BABYLON BURNING	Ruts (Virgin)
30	27	DUKE OF EARL	Darts (Magnet)
10	28	NIGHT OWL	Gerry Rafferty (United Artists)
-	29	LADY WRITER	Dire Straits (Vertigo)
-	30	HERE COMES THE SUMMER	Undertones (Sire)

11 August 1979

last week	this week		
1	1	I DON'T LIKE MONDAYS	Boomtown Rats (Ensign)
10	2	CAN'T STAND LOSING YOU	Police (A&M)
2	3	GIRLS TALK	Dave Edmunds (Swan Song)
6	4	WANTED	Dooleys (GTO)
9	5	ANGEL EYES/VOULEZ VOUS	Abba (Epic)
16	6	BEAT THE CLOCK	Sparks (Virgin)
15	7	WE DON'T TALK ANYMORE	Cliff Richard (EMI)
7	8	MY SHARONA	Knack (Capitol)
4	9	ARE FRIENDS ELECTRIC	Tubeway Army (Beggars Banquet)
3	10	SILLY GAMES	Janet Kay (Scope)
17	11	IF I HAD YOU	Korgis (Rialto)
11	12	BORN TO BE ALIVE	Patrick Hernandez (Gem/Aquarius)
8	13	BREAKFAST IN AMERICA	Supertramp (A&M)
21	14	THE DIARY OF HORACE WIMP	Electric Light Orchestra (Jet)
18	15	AFTER THE LOVE HAS GONE	Earth Wind & Fire (CBS)
5	16	GOOD TIMES	Chic (Atlantic)
-	17	HERSHAM BOYS	Sham 69 (Polydor)
27	18	DUKE OF EARL	Darts (Magnet)
23	19	MORNING DANCE	Spyro Gyra (Infinity)
14	20	BAD GIRLS	Donna Summer (Casablanca)
-	21	REASONS TO BE CHEERFUL (PT.3)	Ian Dury & The Blockheads (Stiff)
19	22	CHUCK E'S IN LOVE	Rickie Lee Jones (Warner Bros)
24	23	STAY WITH ME TILL DAWN	Judy Tzuke (Rocket)
-	24	SWEET LITTLE ROCK 'N' ROLLER	Showaddywaddy (Arista)
-	25	YOU NEVER KNOW WHAT YOU'VE GOT	Me & You (Laser)
13	26	C'MON EVERYBODY	Sex Pistols (Virgin)
20	27	LIGHT MY FIRE/137 DISCO HEAVEN	Amii Stewart (Atlantic/Hansa)
-	28	JUST WHEN I NEEDED YOU MOST	Randy Vanwarmer (Island)
12	29	LADY LYNDA	Beach Boys (Caribou)
-	30	THE BOSS	Diana Ross (Motown)

Dave Edmunds had his biggest hit since *I Hear You Knocking* with *Girls Talk*, but couldn't get to Number One ahead of the Boomtown Rats' *I Don't Like Mondays*, a song inspired by a California teenager who had gone on a motiveless shooting spree and used the title phrase as her reason. Meanwhile, the Police built upon the success of *Roxanne* to score their first Top Five hit with *Can't Stand Losing You,* which had originally been released the previous year to considerably less reaction.

August – September 1979

More than 11 years after *Congratulations,* Cliff Richard finally got another Number One hit with *We Don't Talk Anymore,* a record produced by Bruce Welch of the Shadows. It became, internationally, Cliff biggest-selling single of all time, reaching the US Top 10 and those of a host of other countries. Ian Dury adopted a funky dance idiom for *Reasons To Be Cheerful (Pt.3),* while Roxy Music's *Dance Away* was also solidly in a dance groove - and was not the same song as Abba's *Angel Eyes.*

18 August 1979

last week	this week	title / artist
1	1	I DON'T LIKE MONDAYS — Boomtown Rats (Ensign)
7	2	WE DON'T TALK ANYMORE — Cliff Richard (EMI)
21	3	REASONS TO BE CHEERFUL (PT.3) — Ian Dury & the Blockheads (Stiff)
2	4	CAN'T STAND LOSING YOU — Police (A&M)
13	5	THE DIARY OF HORACE WIMP — Electric Light Orchestra (Jet)
5	6	ANGEL EYES/VOULEZ VOUS — Abba (Epic)
17	7	HERSHAM BOYS — Sham 69 (Polydor)
15	8	AFTER THE LOVE HAS GONE — Earth Wind & Fire (CBS)
4	9	WANTED — Dooleys (GTO)
6	10	BEAT THE CLOCK — Sparks (Virgin)
18	11	DUKE OF EARL — Darts (Magnet)
19	12	MORNING DANCE — Spyro Gyra (Infinity)
23	13	STAY WITH ME TILL DAWN — Judy Tzuke (Rocket)
3	14	GIRLS TALK — Dave Edmunds (Swan Song)
-	15	GANGSTERS — Special AKA (2 Tone)
16	16	GOOD TIMES — Chic (Atlantic)
-	17	OOH WHAT A LIFE — Gibson Brothers (Island)
-	18	BANG BANG — B A Robertson (Asylum)
8	19	MY SHARONA — Knack (Capitol)
12	20	BORN TO BE ALIVE — Patrick Hernandez (Gem/Aquarius)
-	21	ANGEL EYES — Roxy Music (Polydor)
11	22	IF I HAD YOU — Korgis (Rialto)
13	23	BREAKFAST IN AMERICA — Supertramp (A&M)
-	24	GOTTA GO HOME — Boney M (Atlantic/Hansa)
-	25	IS SHE REALLY GOING OUT WITH HIM — Joe Jackson (A&M)
28	26	JUST WHEN I NEEDED YOU MOST — Randy Vanwarmer (Island)
-	27	GIRLS GIRLS GIRLS — Kandidate (RAK)
20	28	BAD GIRLS — Donna Summer (Casablanca)
-	29	TEENAGE WARNING — Angelic Upstarts (Warner Bros)
-	30	SWEET LITTLE ROCK 'N' ROLLER — Showaddywaddy (Arista)

25 August 1979

last week	this week	title / artist
1	1	I DON'T LIKE MONDAYS — Boomtown Rats (Ensign)
2	2	WE DON'T TALK ANYMORE — Cliff Richard (EMI)
3	3	REASONS TO BE CHEERFUL (PT.3) — Ian Dury & the Blockheads (Stiff)
8	4	AFTER THE LOVE HAS GONE — Earth Wind & Fire (CBS)
7	5	HERSHAM BOYS — Sham 69 (Polydor)
11	6	DUKE OF EARL — Darts (Magnet)
18	7	BANG BANG — B A Robertson (Asylum)
15	8	GANGSTERS — Special AKA (2 Tone)
21	9	ANGEL EYES — Roxy Music (Polydor)
6	10	ANGEL EYES/VOULEZ VOUS — Abba (Epic)
5	11	THE DIARY OF HORACE WIMP — Electric Light Orchestra (Jet)
9	12	WANTED — Dooleys (GTO)
13	13	STAY WITH ME TILL DAWN — Judy Tzuke (Rocket)
4	14	CAN'T STAND LOSING YOU — Police (A&M)
17	15	OOH WHAT A LIFE — Gibson Brothers (Island)
12	16	MORNING DANCE — Spyro Gyra (Infinity)
30	17	SWEET LITTLE ROCK 'N' ROLLER — Showaddywaddy (Arista)
10	18	BEAT THE CLOCK — Sparks (Virgin)
25	19	IS SHE REALLY GOING OUT WITH HIM — Joe Jackson (A&M)
24	20	GOTTA GO HOME — Boney M (Atlantic/Hansa)
14	21	GIRLS TALK — Dave Edmunds (Swan Song)
20	22	BORN TO BE ALIVE — Patrick Hernandez (Gem/Aquarius)
-	23	STREET LIFE — Crusaders (MCA)
-	24	MONEY — Flying Lizards (Virgin)
26	25	JUST WHEN I NEEDED YOU MOST — Randy Vanwarmer (Island)
-	26	DUCHESS — Stranglers (United Artists)
-	27	LOST IN MUSIC — Sister Sledge (Atlantic)
29	28	TEENAGE WARNING — Angelic Upstarts (Warner Bros)
22	29	IF I HAD YOU — Korgis (Rialto)
27	30	GIRLS GIRLS GIRLS — Kandidate (RAK)

1 September 1979

last week	this week	title / artist
2	1	WE DON'T TALK ANYMORE — Cliff Richard (EMI)
1	2	I DON'T LIKE MONDAYS — Boomtown Rats (Ensign)
3	3	REASONS TO BE CHEERFUL (PT.3) — Ian Dury & the Blockheads (Stiff)
7	4	BANG BANG — B A Robertson (Asylum)
4	5	AFTER THE LOVE HAS GONE — Earth Wind & Fire (CBS)
6	6	DUKE OF EARL — Darts (Magnet)
9	7	ANGEL EYES — Roxy Music (Polydor)
8	8	GANGSTERS — Special AKA (2 Tone)
15	9	OOH WHAT A LIFE — Gibson Brothers (Island)
18	10	IS SHE REALLY GOING OUT WITH HIM — Joe Jackson (A&M)
11	11	THE DIARY OF HORACE WIMP — Electric Light Orchestra (Jet)
5	12	HERSHAM BOYS — Sham 69 (Polydor)
24	13	MONEY — Flying Lizards (Virgin)
17	14	SWEET LITTLE ROCK 'N' ROLLER — Showaddywaddy (Arista)
23	15	STREET LIFE — Crusaders (MCA)
-	16	WHEN YOU'RE YOUNG — Jam (Polydor)
16	17	MORNING DANCE — Spyro Gyra (Infinity)
-	18	GONE GONE GONE — Johnny Mathis (CBS)
10	19	ANGEL EYES/VOULEZ VOUS — Abba (Epic)
13	20	STAY WITH ME TILL DAWN — Judy Tzuke (Rocket)
20	21	GOTTA GO HOME — Boney K. (Atlantic/Hansa)
26	22	DUCHESS — Stranglers (United Artists)
18	23	BEAT THE CLOCK — Sparks (Virgin)
27	24	LOST IN MUSIC — Sister Sledge (Atlantic)
-	25	STRUT YOUR FUNKY STUFF — Frantique (Philadelphia)
12	26	WANTED — Dooleys (GTO)
25	27	JUST WHEN I NEEDED YOU MOST — Randy Vanwarmer (Island)
-	28	REGGAE FOR IT NOW — Bill Lovelady (Charisma)
14	29	CAN'T STAND LOSING YOU — Police (A&M)
-	30	IF I SAID YOU HAD A BEAUTIFUL BODY, WOULD YOU HOLD IT AGAINST ME... — Bellamy Brothers (Warner Bros)

8 September 1979

last week	this week	title / artist
1	1	WE DON'T TALK ANYMORE — Cliff Richard (EMI)
4	2	BANG BANG — B A Robertson (Asylum)
2	3	I DON'T LIKE MONDAYS — Boomtown Rats (Ensign)
7	4	ANGEL EYES — Roxy Music (Polydor)
5	5	AFTER THE LOVE HAS GONE — Earth Wind & Fire (CBS)
13	6	MONEY — Flying Lizards (Virgin)
8	7	GANGSTERS — Special AKA (2 Tone)
9	8	OOH WHAT A LIFE — Gibson Brothers (Island)
6	9	DUKE OF EARL — Darts (Magnet)
27	10	JUST WHEN I NEEDED YOU MOST — Randy Vanwarmer (Island)
3	11	REASONS TO BE CHEERFUL (PT.3) — Ian Dury & the Blockheads (Stiff)
15	12	STREET LIFE — Crusaders (MCA)
10	13	IS SHE REALLY GOING OUT WITH HIM — Joe Jackson (A&M)
-	14	CARS — Gary Numan (Beggars Banquet)
21	15	GOTTA GO HOME — Boney M (Atlantic/Hansa)
24	16	LOST IN MUSIC — Sister Sledge (Atlantic)
16	17	WHEN YOU'RE YOUNG — Jam (Polydor)
30	18	IF I SAID YOU HAD A BEAUTIFUL BODY, WOULD YOU HOLD IT AGAINST ME...
28	19	REGGAE FOR IT NOW — Bill Lovelady (Charisma)
12	20	HERSHAM BOYS — Sham 69 (Polydor)
19	21	ANGEL EYES/VOULEZ VOUS — Abba (Epic)
22	22	DUCHESS — Stranglers (United Artists)
17	23	MORNING DANCE — Spyro Gyra (Infinity)
18	24	GONE GONE GONE — Johnny Mathis (CBS)
-	25	DON'T BRING ME DOWN — Electric Light Orchestra (Jet)
25	26	STRUT YOUR FUNKY STUFF — Frantique (Philadelphia)
-	27	LOVE'S GOTTA HOLD ON ME — Dollar (Carrere)
11	28	THE DIARY OF HORACE WIMP — Electric Light Orchestra (Jet)
20	29	STAY WITH ME TILL DAWN — Judy Tzuke (Rocket)
14	30	SWEET LITTLE ROCK 'N' ROLLER — Showaddywaddy (Arista)

September – October 1979

15 September 1979

last week	this week	Title	Artist
1	1	WE DON'T TALK ANYMORE	Cliff Richard (EMI)
14	2	CARS	Gary Numan (Beggars Banquet)
2	3	BANG BANG	B A Robertson (Asylum)
6	4	MONEY Flying Lizards (Virgin)	
12	5	STREET LIFE	Crusaders (MCA)
4	6	ANGEL EYES	Roxy Music (Polydor)
10	7	JUST WHEN I NEEDED YOU MOST	Randy Vanwarmer (Island)
7	8	GANGSTERS	Special AKA (2 Tone)
25	9	DON'T BRING ME DOWN	Electric Light Orchestra (Jet)
18	10	IF I SAID YOU HAD A BEAUTIFUL BODY, WOULD YOU HOLD IT AGAINST ME...	Bellamy Brothers (Warner Bros)
15	11	GOTTA GO HOME	Boney M (Atlantic/Hansa)
27	12	LOVE'S GOTTA HOLD ON ME	Dollar (Carrere)
22	13	DUCHESS	Stranglers (United Artists)
24	14	GONE GONE GONE	Johnny Mathis (CBS)
8	15	OOH WHAT A LIFE	Gibson Brothers (Island)
3	16	I DON'T LIKE MONDAYS	Boomtown Rats (Ensign)
5	17	AFTER THE LOVE HAS GONE	Earth Wind & Fire (CBS)
26	18	STRUT YOUR FUNKY STUFF	Frantique (Philadelphia)
16	19	LOST IN MUSIC	Sister Sledge (Atlantic)
17	20	WHEN YOU'RE YOUNG	Jam (Polydor)
13	21	IS SHE REALLY GOING OUT WITH HIM	Joe Jackson (A&M)
19	22	REGGAE FOR IT NOW	Bill Lovelady (Charisma)
-	23	SAIL ON	Commodores (Motown)
-	24	CRUEL TO BE KIND	Nick Lowe (Radar)
9	25	DUKE OF EARL	Darts (Magnet)
23	26	MORNING DANCE	Spyro Gyra (Infinity)
-	27	TIME FOR ACTION	Secret Affair (I Spy)
-	28	LOOKIN' FOR LOVE TONIGHT	Fat Larry's Band (Fantasy)
11	29	REASONS TO BE CHEERFUL (PT.3)	Ian Dury & the Blockheads (Stiff)
-	30	BOY OH BOY	Racey (RAK)

22 September 1979

last week	this week	Title	Artist
2	1	CARS	Gary Numan (Beggars Banquet)
1	2	WE DON'T TALK ANYMORE	Cliff Richard (EMI)
9	3	DON'T BRING ME DOWN	Electric Light Orchestra (Jet)
5	4	STREET LIFE	Crusaders (MCA)
10	5	IF I SAID YOU HAD A BEAUTIFUL BODY, WOULD YOU HOLD IT AGAINST ME...	Bellamy Brothers (Warner Bros)
3	6	BANG BANG	B A Robertson (Asylum)
12	7	LOVE'S GOTTA HOLD ON ME	Dollar (Carrere)
6	8	ANGEL EYES	Roxy Music (Polydor)
7	9	JUST WHEN I NEEDED YOU MOST	Randy Vanwarmer (Island)
4	10	MONEY Flying Lizards (Virgin)	
11	11	GOTTA GO HOME	Boney M (Atlantic/Hansa)
22	12	REGGAE FOR IT NOW	Bill Lovelady (Charisma)
18	13	STRUT YOUR FUNKY STUFF	Frantique (Philadelphia)
8	14	GANGSTERS	Special AKA (2 Tone)
19	15	LOST IN MUSIC	Sister Sledge (Atlantic)
13	16	DUCHESS	Stranglers (United Artists)
23	17	SAIL ON	Commodores (Motown)
24	18	CRUEL TO BE KIND	Nick Lowe (Radar)
14	19	GONE GONE GONE	Johnny Mathis (CBS)
15	20	OOH WHAT A LIFE	Gibson Brothers (Island)
-	21	KATE BUSH ON STAGE (EP)	Kate Bush (EMI)
-	22	THE PRINCE	Madness (2 Tone)
27	23	TIME FOR ACTION	Secret Affair (I Spy)
-	24	MESSAGE IN A BOTTLE	Police (A&M)
30	25	BOY OH BOY	Racey (RAK)
-	26	SINCE YOU'VE BEEN GONE	Rainbow (Polydor)
-	27	TOMORROW'S GIRLS	UK Subs (Gem)
-	28	DON'T STOP TILL YOU GET ENOUGH	Michael Jackson (Epic)
17	29	AFTER THE LOVE HAS GONE	Earth Wind & Fire (CBS)
-	30	SLAP AND TICKLE	Squeeze (A&M)

29 September 1979

last week	this week	Title	Artist
1	1	CARS	Gary Numan (Beggars Banquet)
5	2	IF I SAID YOU HAD A BEAUTIFUL BODY, WOULD YOU HOLD IT AGAINST ME...	Bellamy Brothers (Warner Bros)
2	3	WE DON'T TALK ANYMORE	Cliff Richard (EMI)
24	4	MESSAGE IN A BOTTLE	Police (A&M)
7	5	LOVE'S GOTTA HOLD ON ME	Dollar (Carrere)
4	6	STREET LIFE	Crusaders (MCA)
3	7	DON'T BRING ME DOWN	Electric Light Orchestra (Jet)
17	8	SAIL ON	Commodores (Motown)
13	9	STRUT YOUR FUNKY STUFF	Frantique (Philadelphia)
12	10	REGGAE FOR IT NOW	Bill Lovelady (Charisma)
6	11	BANG BANG	B A Robertson (Asylum)
9	12	JUST WHEN I NEEDED YOU MOST	Randy Vanwarmer (Island)
19	13	GONE GONE GONE	Johnny Mathis (CBS)
18	14	CRUEL TO BE KIND	Nick Lowe (Radar)
23	15	TIME FOR ACTION	Secret Affair (I Spy)
11	16	GOTTA GO HOME	Boney M (Atlantic/Hansa)
22	17	THE PRINCE	Madness (2 Tone)
8	18	ANGEL EYES	Roxy Music (Polydor)
14	19	GANGSTERS	Special AKA (2 Tone)
-	20	DREAMING	Blondie (Crysalis)
15	21	LOST IN MUSIC	Sister Sledge (Atlantic)
-	22	WHATEVER YOU WANT	Status Quo (Vertigo)
30	23	SLAP AND TICKLE	Squeeze (A&M)
28	24	MONEY Flying Lizards (Virgin)	
26	25	DON'T STOP TILL YOU GET ENOUGH	Michael Jackson (Epic)
26	26	SINCE YOU'VE BEEN GONE	Rainbow (Polydor)
21	27	KATE BUSH ON STAGE (EP)	Kate Bush (EMI)
25	28	BOY OH BOY	Racey (RAK)
-	29	YOU CAN DO IT	Al Hudson (MCA)
20	30	OOH WHAT A LIFE	Gibson Brothers (Island)

6 October 1979

last week	this week	Title	Artist
4	1	MESSAGE IN A BOTTLE	Police (A&M)
2	2	IF I SAID YOU HAD A BEAUTIFUL BODY, WOULD YOU HOLD IT AGAINST ME...	Bellamy Brothers (Warner Bros)
1	3	CARS	Gary Numan (Beggars Banquet)
20	4	DREAMING Blondie (Crysalis)	
8	5	SAIL ON	Commodores (Motown)
5	6	LOVE'S GOTTA HOLD ON ME	Dollar (Carrere)
9	7	STRUT YOUR FUNKY STUFF	Frantique (Philadelphia)
22	8	WHATEVER YOU WANT	Status Quo (Vertigo)
6	9	STREET LIFE Crusaders (MCA)	
3	10	WE DON'T TALK ANYMORE	Cliff Richard (EMI)
14	11	CRUEL TO BE KIND	Nick Lowe (Radar)
26	12	SINCE YOU'VE BEEN GONE	Rainbow (Polydor)
7	13	DON'T BRING ME DOWN	Electric Light Orchestra (Jet)
25	14	DON'T STOP TILL YOU GET ENOUGH	Michael Jackson (Epic)
15	15	TIME FOR ACTION	Secret Affair (I Spy)
27	16	KATE BUSH ON STAGE (EP)	Kate Bush (EMI)
-	17	VIDEO KILLED THE RADIO STAR	Buggles (Island)
17	18	THE PRINCE	Madness (2 Tone)
29	19	YOU CAN DO IT	Al Hudson (MCA)
10	20	REGGAE FOR IT NOW	Bill Lovelady (Charisma)
-	21	QUEEN OF HEARTS	Dave Edmunds Swan Song)
23	22	SLAP AND TICKLE	Squeeze (A&M)
12	23	JUST WHEN I NEEDED YOU MOST	Randy Vanwarmer (Island)
-	24	EVERY DAY HURTS	Sad Cafe (RCA)
11	25	BANG BANG	B A Robertson (Asylum)
-	26	BACK OF MY HAND	Jags (Island)
13	27	GONE GONE GONE	Johnny Mathis (CBS)
16	28	GOTTA GO HOME	Boney M (Atlantic/Hansa)
18	29	ANGEL EYES	Roxy Music (Polydor)
-	30	THE DEVIL WENT DOWN TO GEORGIA	Charlie Daniels Band (Epic)

Gary Numan dropped his previous nom-du-disque on his second chart-topper *Cars,* and was to record under his own name from now on, though he would not have any further Number One hits. The Bellamy brothers made a very commercial and successful song out of an outrageous pun, while the Flying Lizards' tongues were even further in cheek turning an old Motown/Beatles favourite into a percussive showcase for the most deadpan female vocal (narrated in bored Sloane tones) yet committed to vinyl.

October – November 1979

13 October 1979

last week	this week	
1	1	MESSAGE IN A BOTTLE — Police (A&M)
4	2	DREAMING Blondie (Crysalis)
14	3	DON'T STOP TILL YOU GET ENOUGH — Michael Jackson (Epic)
17	4	VIDEO KILLED THE RADIO STAR — Buggles (Island)
16	5	KATE BUSH ON STAGE (EP) — Kate Bush (EMI)
8	6	WHATEVER YOU WANT — Status Quo (Vertigo)
3	7	CARS — Gary Numan (Beggars Banquet)
2	8	IF I SAID YOU HAD A BEAUTIFUL BODY, WOULD YOU HOLD IT AGAINST ME... — Bellamy Brothers (Warner Bros)
12	9	SINCE YOU'VE BEEN GONE — Rainbow (Polydor)
5	10	SAIL ON — Commodores (Motown)
6	11	LOVE'S GOTTA HOLD ON ME — Dollar (Carrere)
11	12	CRUEL TO BE KIND — Nick Lowe (Radar)
21	13	QUEEN OF HEARTS — Dave Edmunds Swan Song)
7	14	STRUT YOUR FUNKY STUFF — Frantique (Philadelphia)
18	15	THE PRINCE Madness (2 Tone)
19	16	YOU CAN DO IT — Al Hudson (MCA)
15	17	TIME FOR ACTION — Secret Affair (I Spy)
24	18	EVERY DAY HURTS — Sad Cafe (RCA)
-	19	CHOSEN FEW Dooleys (GTO)
13	20	DON'T BRING ME DOWN — Electric Light Orchestra (Jet)
-	21	ONE DAY AT A TIME — Lena Martell (Pye)
-	22	OK FRED — Erroll Dunkley (Scope)
26	23	BACK OF MY HAND — Jags (Island)
10	24	WE DON'T TALK ANYMORE — Cliff Richard (EMI)
20	25	REGGAE FOR IT NOW — Bill Lovelady (Charisma)
30	26	THE DEVIL WENT DOWN TO GEORGIA — Charlie Daniels Band (Epic)
22	27	SLAP AND TICKLE — Squeeze (A&M)
9	28	STREET LIFE — Crusaders (MCA)
-	29	GONNA GET ALONG WITHOUT YOU NOW — Viola Wills (Ariola/Hansa)
-	30	CHARADE — Skids (Virgin)

20 October 1979

4	1	VIDEO KILLED THE RADIO STAR — Buggles (Island)
1	2	MESSAGE IN A BOTTLE — Police (A&M)
3	3	DON'T STOP TILL YOU GET ENOUGH — Michael Jackson (Epic)
6	4	WHATEVER YOU WANT — Status Quo (Vertigo)
21	5	ONE DAY AT A TIME — Lena Martell (Pye)
2	6	DREAMING Blondie (Crysalis)
18	7	EVERY DAY HURTS — Sad Cafe (RCA)
9	8	SINCE YOU'VE BEEN GONE — Rainbow (Polydor)
5	9	KATE BUSH ON STAGE (EP) — Kate Bush (EMI)
8	10	IF I SAID YOU HAD A BEAUTIFUL BODY, WOULD YOU HOLD IT AGAINST ME... — Bellamy Brothers (Warner Bros)
13	11	QUEEN OF HEARTS — Dave Edmunds Swan Song
19	12	CHOSEN FEW Dooleys (GTO)
16	13	YOU CAN DO IT — Al Hudson (MCA)
7	14	CARS — Gary Numan (Beggars Banquet)
-	15	WHEN YOU'RE IN LOVE WITH A BEAUTIFUL WOMAN — Dr Hook (Capitol)
11	16	LOVE'S GOTTA HOLD ON ME — Dollar (Carrere)
22	17	OK FRED — Erroll Dunkley (Scope)
-	18	TUSK — Fleetwood Mac (Warner Bros)
10	19	SAIL ON — Commodores (Motown)
-	20	GREAT ROCK 'N' ROLL SWINDLE — Sex Pistols (Virgin)
17	21	TIME FOR ACTION — Secret Affair (I Spy)
26	22	THE DEVIL WENT DOWN TO GEORGIA — Charlie Daniels Band (Epic)
12	23	CRUEL TO BE KIND — Nick Lowe (Radar)
23	24	BACK OF MY HAND — Jags (Island)
15	25	THE PRINCE Madness (2 Tone)
-	26	STAR — Earth Wind & Fire (CBS)
14	27	STRUT YOUR FUNKY STUFF — Frantique (Philadelphia)
-	28	MY FORBIDDEN LOVER — Chic (Atlantic)
28	29	STREET LIFE — Crusaders (MCA)
-	30	LUTON AIRPORT — Cats UK (WEA)

27 October 1979

1	1	VIDEO KILLED THE RADIO STAR — Buggles (Island)
3	2	DON'T STOP TILL YOU GET ENOUGH — Michael Jackson (Epic)
2	3	MESSAGE IN A BOTTLE — Police (A&M)
5	4	ONE DAY AT A TIME — Lena Martell (Pye)
7	5	EVERY DAY HURTS — Sad Cafe (RCA)
15	6	WHEN YOU'RE IN LOVE WITH A BEAUTIFUL WOMAN — Dr Hook (Capitol)
6	7	DREAMING Blondie (Crysalis)
12	8	CHOSEN FEW Dooleys (GTO)
4	9	WHATEVER YOU WANT — Status Quo (Vertigo)
11	10	QUEEN OF HEARTS — Dave Edmunds Swan Song)
8	11	SINCE YOU'VE BEEN GONE — Rainbow (Polydor)
17	12	OK FRED — Erroll Dunkley (Scope)
18	13	TUSK — Fleetwood Mac (Warner Bros)
28	14	MY FORBIDDEN LOVER — Chic (Atlantic)
-	15	GIMME GIMME GIMME (A MAN AFTER MIDNIGHT) — Abba (Epic)
26	16	STAR Earth Wind & Fire (CBS)
22	17	THE DEVIL WENT DOWN TO GEORGIA — Charlie Daniels Band (Epic)
13	18	YOU CAN DO IT — Al Hudson (MCA)
9	19	KATE BUSH ON STAGE (EP) — Kate Bush (EMI)
-	20	GONNA GET ALONG WITHOUT YOU NOW — Viola Wills (Ariola/Hansa)
-	21	CRAZY LITTLE THING CALLED LOVE — Queen (EMI)
20	22	GREAT ROCK 'N' ROLL SWINDLE — Sex Pistols (Virgin)
-	23	SHE'S IN LOVE WITH YOU — Suzi Quatro (RAK)
-	24	MAKING PLANS FOR NIGEL — XTC (Virgin)
-	25	LET ME KNOW (I HAVE A RIGHT) — Gloria Gaynor (Polydor)
24	26	BACK OF MY HAND — Jags (Island)
30	27	LUTON AIRPORT — Cats UK (WEA)
-	28	SPIRIT BODY & SOUL — Nolan Sisters (Epic)
-	29	RISE — Herb Alpert (A&M)
14	30	CARS — Gary Numan (Beggars Banquet)

3 November 1979

4	1	ONE DAY AT A TIME — Lena Martell (Pye)
6	2	WHEN YOU'RE IN LOVE WITH A BEAUTIFUL WOMAN — Dr Hook (Capitol)
5	3	EVERY DAY HURTS — Sad Cafe (RCA)
1	4	VIDEO KILLED THE RADIO STAR — Buggles (Island)
2	5	DON'T STOP TILL YOU GET ENOUGH — Michael Jackson (Epic)
15	6	GIMME GIMME GIMME (A MAN AFTER MIDNIGHT) — Abba (Epic)
13	7	TUSK — Fleetwood Mac (Warner Bros)
8	8	CHOSEN FEW Dooleys (GTO)
12	9	OK FRED — Erroll Dunkley (Scope)
3	10	MESSAGE IN A BOTTLE — Police (A&M)
20	11	GONNA GET ALONG WITHOUT YOU NOW — Viola Wills (Ariola/Hansa)
14	12	MY FORBIDDEN LOVER — Chic (Atlantic)
24	13	MAKING PLANS FOR NIGEL — XTC (Virgin)
11	14	SINCE YOU'VE BEEN GONE — Rainbow (Polydor)
21	15	CRAZY LITTLE THING CALLED LOVE — Queen (EMI)
17	16	THE DEVIL WENT DOWN TO GEORGIA — Charlie Daniels Band (Epic)
7	17	DREAMING Blondie (Crysalis)
23	18	SHE'S IN LOVE WITH YOU — Suzi Quatro (RAK)
9	19	WHATEVER YOU WANT — Status Quo (Vertigo)
-	20	ON MY RADIO — Selecter (2 Tone)
-	21	MESSAGE TO YOU RUDY — Specials (2 Tone)
27	22	LUTON AIRPORT — Cats UK (WEA)
18	23	YOU CAN DO IT — Al Hudson (MCA)
10	24	QUEEN OF HEARTS — Dave Edmunds Swan Song)
-	25	THE SPARROW — Ramblers (Decca)
29	26	RISE — Herb Alpert (A&M)
16	27	STAR Earth Wind & Fire (CBS)
-	28	LADIES NIGHT — Kool & the Gang (Mercury)
26	29	BACK OF MY HAND — Jags (Island)
22	30	GREAT ROCK 'N' ROLL SWINDLE — Sex Pistols (Virgin)

The first EP to make the Top 10 for some time was Kate Bush's live souvenir of her one-and-only UK concert tour. Buggles, who scored a surprise Number One with the gimmicky *Video Killed The Radio Star*, consisted of Trevor Horn and Geoff Downes, both of whom would later join Yes, while Horn would also become one of the most successful record producers of the 1980s. MOR vocalist Lena Martell had an even more surprising chart-topper with Kris Kristofferson's *One Day At A Time*.

November – December 1979

last week	this week	10 November 1979
2	1	WHEN YOU'RE IN LOVE WITH A BEAUTIFUL WOMAN — Dr Hook (Capitol)
1	2	ONE DAY AT A TIME — Lena Martell (Pye)
6	3	GIMME GIMME GIMME (A MAN AFTER MIDNIGHT) — Abba (Epic)
3	4	EVERY DAY HURTS — Sad Cafe (RCA)
7	5	TUSK — Fleetwood Mac (Warner Bros)
5	6	DON'T STOP TILL YOU GET ENOUGH — Michael Jackson (Epic)
4	7	VIDEO KILLED THE RADIO STAR — Buggles (Island)
15	8	CRAZY LITTLE THING CALLED LOVE — Queen (EMI)
8	9	CHOSEN FEW — Dooleys (GTO)
20	10	ON MY RADIO — Selecter (2 Tone)
12	11	MY FORBIDDEN LOVER — Chic (Atlantic)
11	12	GONNA GET ALONG WITHOUT YOU NOW — Viola Wills (Ariola/Hansa)
26	13	STAR — Earth Wind & Fire (CBS)
18	14	SHE'S IN LOVE WITH YOU — Suzi Quatro (RAK)
21	15	MESSAGE TO YOU RUDY — Specials (2 Tone)
16	16	THE DEVIL WENT DOWN TO GEORGIA — Charlie Daniels Band (Epic)
-	17	STILL — Commodores (Motown)
9	18	OK FRED — Erroll Dunkley (Scope)
-	19	ETON RIFLES — Jam (Polydor)
28	20	LADIES NIGHT — Kool & the Gang (Mercury)
13	21	MAKING PLANS FOR NIGEL — XTC (Virgin)
26	22	RISE — Herb Alpert (A&M)
10	23	MESSAGE IN A BOTTLE — Police (A&M)
19	24	WHATEVER YOU WANT — Status Quo (Vertigo)
22	25	LUTON AIRPORT — Cats UK (WEA)
17	26	DREAMING — Blondie (Chrysalis)
24	27	QUEEN OF HEARTS — Dave Edmunds Swan Song
25	28	THE SPARROW — Ramblers (Decca)
14	29	SINCE YOU'VE BEEN GONE — Rainbow (Polydor)
-	30	I DON'T WANT TO BE A FREAK — Dynasty (Solar)

last week	this week	17 November 1979
1	1	WHEN YOU'RE IN LOVE WITH A BEAUTIFUL WOMAN — Dr Hook (Capitol)
3	2	GIMME GIMME GIMME (A MAN AFTER MIDNIGHT) — Abba (Epic)
2	3	ONE DAY AT A TIME — Lena Martell (Pye)
17	4	STILL — Commodores (Motown)
8	5	CRAZY LITTLE THING CALLED LOVE — Queen (EMI)
4	6	EVERY DAY HURTS — Sad Cafe (RCA)
5	7	TUSK — Fleetwood Mac (Warner Bros)
19	8	ETON RIFLES — Jam (Polydor)
10	9	ON MY RADIO — Selecter (2 Tone)
14	10	SHE'S IN LOVE WITH YOU — Suzi Quatro (RAK)
12	11	GONNA GET ALONG WITHOUT YOU NOW — Viola Wills (Ariola/Hansa)
28	12	THE SPARROW — Ramblers (Decca)
15	13	MESSAGE TO YOU RUDY — Specials (2 Tone)
20	14	LADIES NIGHT — Kool & the Gang (Mercury)
22	15	RISE — Herb Alpert (A&M)
-	16	NO MORE TEARS (ENOUGH IS ENOUGH) — Donna Summer/Barbra Streisand (Casablanca/CBS)
-	17	KNOCKED IT OFF — B A Robertson (Asylum)
18	18	OK FRED — Erroll Dunkley (Scope)
6	19	DON'T STOP TILL YOU GET ENOUGH — Michael Jackson (Epic)
21	20	MAKING PLANS FOR NIGEL — XTC (Virgin)
7	21	VIDEO KILLED THE RADIO STAR — Buggles (Island)
11	22	MY FORBIDDEN LOVER — Chic (Atlantic)
9	23	CHOSEN FEW — Dooleys (GTO)
30	24	I DON'T WANT TO BE A FREAK — Dynasty (Solar)
13	25	STAR — Earth Wind & Fire (CBS)
25	26	LUTON AIRPORT — Cats UK (WEA)
-	27	IT'S A DISCO NIGHT — Isley Brothers (Epic)
-	28	ONE STEP BEYOND — Madness (Stiff)
-	29	HE WAS BEAUTIFUL — Iris Williams (Columbia)
-	30	BIRD SONG — Lene Lovich (Stiff)

last week	this week	24 November 1979
1	1	WHEN YOU'RE IN LOVE WITH A BEAUTIFUL WOMAN — Dr Hook (Capitol)
8	2	ETON RIFLES — Jam (Polydor)
3	3	STILL — Commodores (Motown)
5	4	CRAZY LITTLE THING CALLED LOVE — Queen (EMI)
3	5	ONE DAY AT A TIME — Lena Martell (Pye)
9	6	ON MY RADIO — Selecter (2 Tone)
13	7	MESSAGE TO YOU RUDY — Specials (2 Tone)
2	8	GIMME GIMME GIMME (A MAN AFTER MIDNIGHT) — Abba (Epic)
16	9	NO MORE TEARS (ENOUGH IS ENOUGH) — Donna Summer/Barbra Streisand (Casablanca/CBS)
14	10	LADIES NIGHT — Kool & the Gang (Mercury)
6	11	EVERY DAY HURTS — Sad Cafe (RCA)
7	12	TUSK — Fleetwood Mac (Warner Bros)
17	13	KNOCKED IT OFF — B A Robertson (Asylum)
10	14	SHE'S IN LOVE WITH YOU — Suzi Quatro (RAK)
28	15	ONE STEP BEYOND — Madness (Stiff)
15	16	RISE — Herb Alpert (A&M)
27	17	IT'S A DISCO NIGHT — Isley Brothers (Epic)
11	18	GONNA GET ALONG WITHOUT YOU NOW — Viola Wills (Ariola/Hansa)
29	19	HE WAS BEAUTIFUL — Iris Williams (Columbia)
24	20	I DON'T WANNA BE A FREAK — Dynasty (Solar)
12	21	THE SPARROW — Ramblers (Decca)
-	22	QUE SERA MI VIDA — Gibson Brothers (Island)
-	23	SARAH — Thin Lizzy (Vertigo)
-	24	CONFUSION — Electric Light Orchestra (Jet)
-	25	MONKEY CHOPS — Dan I (Island)
-	26	DIAMOND SMILES — Boomtown Rats (Ensign)
-	27	ROCKABILLY REBEL — Matchbox (Magnet)
24	28	STAR — Earth Wind & Fire (CBS)
-	29	FALL OUT — Police (Illegal)
-	30	LET YOUR HEART DANCE — Secret Affair (I Spy)

last week	this week	1 December 1979
1	1	WHEN YOU'RE IN LOVE WITH A BEAUTIFUL WOMAN — Dr Hook (Capitol)
9	2	NO MORE TEARS (ENOUGH IS ENOUGH) — Donna Summer (Casablanca/CBS)
2	3	ETON RIFLES — Jam (Polydor)
4	4	STILL — Commodores (Motown)
5	5	CRAZY LITTLE THING CALLED LOVE — Queen (EMI)
10	6	LADIES NIGHT — Kool & the Gang (Mercury)
13	7	KNOCKED IT OFF — B A Robertson (Asylum)
-	8	COMPLEX — Gary Numan (Beggars Banquet)
15	9	ONE STEP BEYOND — Madness (Stiff)
5	10	ONE DAY AT A TIME — Lena Martell (Pye)
24	11	CONFUSION — Electric Light Orchestra (Jet)
16	12	RISE — Herb Alpert (A&M)
21	13	THE SPARROW — Ramblers (Decca)
8	14	GIMME GIMME GIMME (A MAN AFTER MIDNIGHT) — Abba (Epic)
22	15	QUE SERA MI VIDA — Gibson Brothers (Island)
17	16	IT'S A DISCO NIGHT — Isley Brothers (Epic)
7	17	MESSAGE TO YOU RUDY — Specials (2 Tone)
26	18	DIAMOND SMILES — Boomtown Rats (Ensign)
-	19	UNION CITY BLUE — Blondie (Chrysalis)
14	20	SHE'S IN LOVE WITH YOU — Suzi Quatro (RAK)
27	21	ROCKABILLY REBEL — Matchbox (Magnet)
-	22	OFF THE WALL — Michael Jackson (Epic)
-	23	WALKING ON THE MOON — Police (A&M)
20	24	I DON'T WANT TO BE A FREAK — Dynasty (Solar)
-	25	MONKEY CHOP — Dan-I (Island)
29	26	FALL OUT — Police (Illegal)
-	27	WORKING FOR THE YANKEE DOLLAR — Skids (Virgin)
-	28	IS IT LOVE YOU'RE AFTER — Rose Royce (Whitfield)
-	29	MELLOW MELLOW RIGHT ON — Lowrell (AVI)
-	30	I ONLY WANT TO BE WITH YOU — Tourists (Logo)

More than seven years after their debut with *Sylvia's Mother*, Dr Hook had their all-time UK best-seller with *When You're In Love With A Beautiful Woman*. This managed to hold from Number One the Jam's first top tenner *The Eton Rifles*, a savage Paul Weller swipe at the militaristic aspects of some public schools. Donna Summer and Barbra Streisand made an unexpected, successful one-off team, while Queen were barely recognisable in their echoey mid-50s rockabilly style on *Crazy Little Thing Called Love*.

December 1979

		8 December 1979			15 December 1979			22 December 1979
23	1	WALKING ON THE MOON Police (A&M)	11	1	ANOTHER BRICK IN THE WALL, PART II Pink Floyd (Harvest)	1	1	ANOTHER BRICK IN THE WALL, PART II Pink Floyd (Harvest)
2	2	NO MORE TEARS (ENOUGH IS ENOUGH) Donna Summer /Barbra Streisand (Casablanca/CBS)	1	2	WALKING ON THE MOON Police (A&M)	6	2	RAPPER'S DELIGHT Sugar Hill Gang (Sugar Hill)
1	3	WHEN YOU'RE IN LOVE WITH A BEAUTIFUL WOMAN Dr Hook (Capitol)	9	3	QUE SERA MI VIDA Gibson Brothers (Island)	4	3	I ONLY WANT TO BE WITH YOU Tourists (Logo)
11	4	CONFUSION Electric Light Orchestra (Jet)	9	4	I ONLY WANT TO BE WITH YOU Tourists (Logo)	2	4	WALKING ON THE MOON Police (A&M)
8	5	COMPLEX Gary Numan (Beggars Banquet)	2	5	NO MORE TEARS (ENOUGH IS ENOUGH) Donna Summer/ Barbra Streisand (Casablanca/CBS)	15	5	OFF THE WALL Michael Jackson (Epic)
5	6	CRAZY LITTLE THING CALLED LOVE Queen (EMI)	15	6	RAPPERS DELIGHT Sugar Hill Gang (Sugar Hill)	5	6	NO MORE TEARS (ENOUGH IS ENOUGH) Donna Summer/Barbra Streisand (Casablanca/CBS)
4	7	STILL Commodores (Motown)	3	7	WHEN YOU'RE IN LOVE WITH A BEAUTIFUL WOMAN Dr Hook (Capitol)	23	7	HAVE A DREAM Abba (Epic)
9	8	ONE STEP BEYOND Madness (Stiff)	4	8	CONFUSION Electric Light Orchestra (Jet)	20	8	DAY TRIP TO BANGOR Fiddlers Dram (Dingles)
15	9	QUE SERA MI VIDA Gibson Brothers (Island)	29	9	NIGHTS IN WHITE SATIN Moody Blues (Deram)	3	9	QUE SERA MI VIDA Gibson Brothers (Island)
3	10	ETON RIFLES Jam (Polydor)	5	10	COMPLEX Gary Numan (Beggars Banquet)	19	10	MY SIMPLE HEART Three Degrees (Ariola)
-	11	ANOTHER BRICK IN THE WALL, PART II Pink Floyd (Harvest)	17	11	UNION CITY BLUE Blondie (Chrysalis)	13	11	ONE STEP BEYOND Madness (Stiff)
6	12	LADIES NIGHT Kool & the Gang (Mercury)	6	12	CRAZY LITTLE THING CALLED LOVE Queen (EMI)	9	12	NIGHTS IN WHITE SATIN Moody Blues (Deram)
16	13	IT'S A DISCO NIGHT Isley Brothers (Epic)	8	13	ONE STEP BEYOND Madness (Stiff)	11	13	UNION CITY BLUE Blondie (Chrysalis)
18	14	DIAMOND SMILES Boomtown Rats (Ensign)	7	14	STILL Commodores (Motown)	8	14	CONFUSION Electric Light Orchestra (Jet)
-	15	RAPPERS DELIGHT Sugar Hill Gang (Sugar Hill)	16	15	OFF THE WALL Michael Jackson (Epic)	7	15	WHEN YOU'RE IN LOVE WITH A BEAUTIFUL WOMAN Dr Hook (Capitol)
22	16	OFF THE WALL Michael Jackson (Epic)	13	16	IT'S A DISCO NIGHT Isley Brothers (Epic)	-	16	JOHN I'M ONLY DANCIN' (AGAIN) David Bowie (RCA)
19	17	UNION CITY BLUE Blondie (Chrysalis)	10	17	ETON RIFLES Jam (Polydor)	27	17	LIVING ON AN ISLAND Status Quo (Vertigo)
17	18	KNOCKED IT OFF B A Robertson (Asylum)	14	18	DIAMOND SMILES Boomtown Rats (Ensign)	24	18	WONDERFUL CHRISTMAS TIME Paul McCartney (Parlophone)
30	19	I ONLY WANT TO BE WITH YOU Tourists (Logo)	27	19	MY SIMPLE HEART Three Degrees (Ariola)	12	19	CRAZY LITTLE THING CALLED LOVE Queen (EMI)
21	20	ROCKABILLY REBEL Matchbox (Magnet)	-	20	DAY TRIP TO BANGOR Fiddlers Dram (Dingles)	22	20	ROCKABILLY REBEL Matchbox (Magnet)
14	21	GIMME GIMME GIMME (A MAN AFTER MIDNIGHT) Abba (Epic)	12	21	LADIES NIGHT Kool & the Gang (Mercury)	30	21	IS IT LOVE YOU'RE AFTER Rose Royce (Whitfield)
13	22	THE SPARROW Ramblers (Decca)	20	22	ROCKABILLY REBEL Matchbox (Magnet)	18	22	DIAMOND SMILES Boomtown Rats (Ensign)
12	23	RISE Herb Alpert (A&M)	-	23	HAVE A DREAM Abba (Epic)	10	23	COMPLEX Gary Numan (Beggars Banquet)
28	24	IS IT LOVE YOU'RE AFTER Rose Royce (Whitfield)	-	24	WONDERFUL CHRISTMAS TIME Paul McCartney (Parlophone)	14	24	STILL Commodores (Motown)
25	25	MONKEY CHOP Dan I (Island)	22	25	THE SPARROW Ramblers (Decca)	-	25	TEARS OF A CLOWN Beat (2 Tone)
10	26	ONE DAY AT A TIME Lena Martell (Pye)	-	26	SARAH Thin Lizzy (Vertigo)	29	26	MY FEET KEEP DANCING Chic (Atlantic)
-	27	MY SIMPLE HEART Three Degrees (Ariola)	-	27	LIVING ON AN ISLAND Status Quo (Vertigo)	16	27	IT'S A DISCO NIGHT Isley Brothers (Epic)
-	28	DON'T BRING HARRY Stranglers (United Artists)	-	28	IT'S MY HOUSE Diana Ross (Motown)	-	28	LONDON CALLING Clash (CBS)
-	29	NIGHTS IN WHITE SATIN Moody Blues (Deram)	-	29	MY FEET KEEP DANCING Chic (Atlantic)	-	29	BLUE PETER Mike Oldfield (Virgin)
17	30	MESSAGE TO YOU RUDY Specials (2 Tone)	24	30	IS IT LOVE YOU'RE AFTER Rose Royce (Whitfield)	-	30	CHRISTMAS RAPPIN' Kurtis Blow (Mercury)

Pink Floyd's *Another Brick In The Wall*, a two-sided extract from their huge-selling double LP *The Wall,* was their first single since December 1968, when they had renounced the format in favour of an album-only approach. The track featured backup vocals by a children's choir from an Islington secondary school, whose only payment initially was a free copy of the album apiece! The Tourists, debuting with a revival of Dusty Springfield's first hit, included Annie Lennox and Dave Stewart, later the Eurythmics.

January – February 1980

After peaking at Number 29 with both their first hits the previous year, the Pretenders hit the big-time with their self-penned chart-topper *Brass In Pocket*, while Madness also hit Number One with their third release, *My Girl*. Billy Preston and Syreeta (Stevie Wonder's former wife) had had one Top 20 hit apiece (not including Preston's credit on the Beatles' *Get Back*) before teaming up on *With You I'm Born Again*, but this duetted ballad hit was by far the biggest either had in the UK.

351

February – March 1980

The Specials live EP, highlighted by the track *Too Much, Too Young*, which got extensive airplay (the other items were early 1970s reggae hit covers like *The Liquidator* and *Long Shot Kick De Bucket*), became the second EP to top the UK singles chart, following Demis Roussos in 1976. Booker T & the MGs' 1962 US hit *Green Onions* made the UK chart now because, as a '60s mod anthem, it featured on the soundtrack of the film *Quadrophenia*, based on the Who's 1973 concept album.

March 1980

8 March 1980

last week	this week		
1	1	ATOMIC	Blondie (Chrysalis)
9	2	I CAN'T STAND UP FOR FALLING DOWN	Elvis Costello (F.Beat)
3	3	CARRIE	Cliff Richard (EMI)
8	4	TAKE THAT LOOK OFF YOUR FACE	Marti Webb (Polydor)
2	5	COWARD OF THE COUNTY	Kenny Rogers (United Artists)
14	6	TOGETHER WE ARE BEAUTIFUL	Fern Kinney (WEA)
5	7	AND THE BEAT GOES ON	Whispers (Solar)
6	8	ROCK WITH YOU	Michael Jackson (Epic)
13	9	RIDERS IN THE SKY	Shadows (EMI)
12	10	SO GOOD TO BE BACK HOME AGAIN	Tourists (Logo)
18	11	GAMES WITHOUT FRONTIERS	Peter Gabriel (Charisma)
20	12	SO LONELY	Police (A&M)
24	13	HANDS OFF ... SHE'S MINE	Beat (Go Feet)
7	14	CAPTAIN BEAKY	Keith Michell (Polydor)
10	15	BABY I LOVE YOU	Ramones (Sire)
15	16	THE PLASTIC AGE	Buggles (Island)
-	17	ALABAMA SONG/SPACE ODDITY	David Bowie (RCA)
4	18	THE SPECIAL A.K.A. LIVE! (EP)	Specials (2 Tone)
-	19	ALL NIGHT LONG	Rainbow (Polydor)
27	20	STOMP	Brothers Johnson (A&M)
17	21	I'M IN THE MOOD FOR DANCING	Nolans (Epic)
-	22	TURNING JAPANESE	Vapors (United Artists)
30	23	CUBA/BETTER DO IT SALSA	Gibson Brothers (Island)
11	24	SOMEONE'S LOOKING AT YOU	Boomtown Rats (Ensign)
-	25	TONIGHT I'M ALRIGHT	Narada Michael Walden (Atlantic)
25	26	DO THAT TO ME ONE MORE TIME	Captain & Tennille (Casablanca)
16	27	I HEAR YOU NOW	Jon & Vangelis (Polydor)
-	28	JANE	Jefferson Starship (Grunt)
-	29	RUNNING FREE	Iron Maiden (EMI)
28	30	HOLDIN' ON	Tony Rallo & the Midnight Band (Calibre)

15 March 1980

last week	this week		
1	1	ATOMIC	Blondie (Chrysalis)
6	2	TOGETHER WE ARE BEAUTIFUL	Fern Kinney (WEA)
4	3	TAKE THAT LOOK OFF YOUR FACE	Marti Webb (Polydor)
11	4	GAMES WITHOUT FRONTIERS	Peter Gabriel (Charisma)
2	5	I CAN'T STAND UP FOR FALLING DOWN	Elvis Costello (F.Beat)
12	6	SO LONELY	Police (A&M)
3	7	CARRIE	Cliff Richard (EMI)
7	8	AND THE BEAT GOES ON	Whispers (Solar)
19	9	ALL NIGHT LONG	Rainbow (Polydor)
13	10	HANDS OFF ... SHE'S MINE	Beat (Go Feet)
5	11	COWARD OF THE COUNTY	Kenny Rogers (United Artists)
22	12	TURNING JAPANESE	Vapors (United Artists)
-	13	AT THE EDGE	Stiff Little Fingers (Chrysalis)
8	14	ROCK WITH YOU	Michael Jackson (Epic)
9	15	RIDERS IN THE SKY	Shadows (EMI)
-	16	DANCE YOURSELF DIZZY	Liquid Gold (Polo)
23	17	CUBA/BETTER DO IT SALSA	Gibson Brothers (Island)
10	18	SO GOOD TO BE BACK HOME AGAIN	Tourists (Logo)
26	19	DO THAT TO ME ONE MORE TIME	Captain & Tennille (Casablanca)
14	20	CAPTAIN BEAKY	Keith Michell (Polydor)
15	21	BABY I LOVE YOU	Ramones (Sire)
-	22	WORKING MY WAY BACK TO YOU	Detroit Spinners (Atlantic)
20	23	STOMP	Brothers Johnson (A&M)
16	24	THE PLASTIC AGE	Buggles (Island)
17	25	ALABAMA SONG/SPACE ODDITY	David Bowie (RCA)
25	26	TONIGHT I'M ALRIGHT	Narada Michael Walden (Atlantic)
-	27	HOT DOG	Shakin' Stevens (Epic)
-	28	SINGING THE BLUES	Dave Edmunds (Swan Song)
-	29	ECHO BEACH	Martha & the Muffins (Dindisc)
-	30	WARHEAD	U.K. Subs (Gem)

22 March 1980

last week	this week		
2	1	TOGETHER WE ARE BEAUTIFUL	Fern Kinney (WEA)
1	2	ATOMIC	Blondie (Chrysalis)
4	3	GAMES WITHOUT FRONTIERS	Peter Gabriel (Charisma)
3	4	TAKE THAT LOOK OFF YOUR FACE	Marti Webb (Polydor)
19	5	DO THAT TO ME ONE MORE TIME	Captain & Tennille (Casablanca)
6	6	SO LONELY	Police (A&M)
12	7	TURNING JAPANESE	Vapors (United Artists)
10	8	HANDS OFF ... SHE'S MINE	Beat (Go Feet)
9	9	ALL NIGHT LONG	Rainbow (Polydor)
16	10	DANCE YOURSELF DIZZY	Liquid Gold (Polo)
17	11	CUBA/BETTER DO IT SALSA	Gibson Brothers (Island)
8	12	AND THE BEAT GOES ON	Whispers (Solar)
23	13	STOMP	Brothers Johnson (A&M)
22	14	WORKING MY WAY BACK TO YOU	Detroit Spinners (Atlantic)
29	15	ECHO BEACH	Martha & the Muffins (Dindisc)
7	16	CARRIE	Cliff Richard (EMI)
-	17	GOING UNDERGROUND	Jam (Polydor)
5	18	I CAN'T STAND UP FOR FALLING DOWN	Elvis Costello (F.Beat)
14	19	ROCK WITH YOU	Michael Jackson (Epic)
-	20	THE SPIRIT OF RADIO	Rush (Mercury)
-	21	HOLDIN' ON	Tony Rallo & the Midnight Band (Calibre)
-	22	POISON IVY	Lambrettas (Rocket)
-	23	ANOTHER NAIL IN MY HEART	Squeeze (A&M)
11	24	COWARD OF THE COUNTY	Kenny Rogers (United Artists)
18	25	SO GOOD TO BE BACK HOME AGAIN	Tourists (Logo)
26	26	TONIGHT I'M ALRIGHT	Narada Michael Walden (Atlantic)
-	27	DON'T PUSH IT, DON'T FORCE IT	Leon Haywood (20th Century)
-	28	TURN IT ON AGAIN	Genesis (Charisma)
15	29	RIDERS IN THE SKY	Shadows (EMI)
-	30	HELLO I AM YOUR HEART	Bette Bright (Korova)

29 March 1980

last week	this week		
17	1	GOING UNDERGOUND	Jam (Polydor)
1	2	TOGETHER WE ARE BEAUTIFUL	Fern Kinney (WEA)
10	3	DANCE YOURSELF DIZZY	Liquid Gold (Polo)
4	4	TAKE THAT LOOK OFF YOUR FACE	Marti Webb (Polydor)
7	5	TURNING JAPANESE	Vapors (United Artists)
13	6	WORKING MY WAY BACK TO YOU	Detroit Spinners (Atlantic)
3	7	GAMES WITHOUT FRONTIERS	Peter Gabriel (Charisma)
13	8	STOMP	Brothers Johnson (A&M)
2	9	ATOMIC	Blondie (Chrysalis)
5	10	DO THAT TO ME ONE MORE TIME	Captain & Tennille (Casablanca)
15	11	ECHO BEACH	Martha & the Muffins (Dindisc)
11	12	CUBA/BETTER DO IT SALSA	Gibson Brothers (Island)
8	13	HANDS OFF ... SHE'S MINE	Beat (Go Feet)
6	14	SO LONELY	Police (A&M)
28	15	TURN IT ON AGAIN	Genesis (Charisma)
20	16	THE SPIRIT OF RADIO	Rush (Mercury)
9	17	ALL NIGHT LONG	Rainbow (Polydor)
-	18	HAPPY HOUSE	Siouxsie & the Banshees (Polydor)
-	19	JANUARY FEBRUARY	Barbara Dickson (Epic)
27	20	DON'T PUSH IT, DON'T FORCE IT	Leon Haywood (20th Century)
22	21	POISON IVY	Lambrettas (Rocket)
12	22	AND THE BEAT GOES ON	Whispers (Solar)
-	23	AT THE EDGE	Stiff Little Fingers (Chrysalis)
23	24	ANOTHER NAIL IN MY HEART	Squeeze (A&M)
26	25	TONIGHT I'M ALRIGHT	Narada Michael (Atlantic)
-	26	LOVE PATROL	Dooleys (GTO)
-	27	HOT DOG	Shakin' Stevens (Epic)
-	28	LET'S DO ROCK STEADY	Bodysnatchers (2 Tone)
18	29	I CAN'T STAND UP FOR FALLING DOWN	Elvis Costello (F.Beat)
21	30	HOLDIN' ON	Tony Rallo & the Midnight Band (Calibre)

Elvis Costello achieved his second-highest chart placing (*Oliver's Army* had made No.1 a year earlier) not with another of his own songs, but with a cover of a comparatively obscure Sam & Dave song from the 1960s. The revitalised Shadows also had their third top tenner in a row with a cover – the original intrumental hit version of *Riders In The Sky* by the Ramrods had been a hit early in 1961, contemporary with the Shads' *FBI*. The Lambrettas' *Poison Ivy* was also, obviously, a revival.

April 1980

last week	this week	5 April 1980
1	1	GOING UNDERGROUND Jam (Polydor)
2	2	TOGETHER WE ARE BEAUTIFUL Fern Kinney (WEA)
3	3	DANCE YOURSELF DIZZY Liquid Gold (Polo)
5	4	TURNING JAPANESE Vapors (United Artists)
6	5	WORKING MY WAY BACK TO YOU Detroit Spinners (Atlantic)
11	6	ECHO BEACH Martha & the Muffins (Dindisc)
10	7	DO THAT TO ME ONE MORE TIME Captain & Tennille (Casablanca)
4	8	TAKE THAT LOOK OFF YOUR FACE Marti Webb (Polydor)
8	9	STOMP Brothers Johnson (A&M)
21	10	POISON IVY Lambrettas (Rocket)
17	11	ALL NIGHT LONG Rainbow (Polydor)
24	12	ANOTHER NAIL IN MY HEART Squeeze (A&M)
-	13	KING/FOOD FOR THOUGHT UB40 (Graduate)
7	14	GAMES WITHOUT FRONTIERS Peter Gabriel (Charisma)
19	15	JANUARY FEBRUARY Barbara Dickson (Epic)
12	16	CUBA/BETTER DO IT SALSA Gibson Brothers (Island)
15	17	TURN IT ON AGAIN Genesis (Charisma)
16	18	THE SPIRIT OF RADIO Rush (Mercury)
13	19	HANDS OFF ... SHE'S MINE Beat (Go Feet)
18	20	HAPPY HOUSE Siouxsie & the Banshees (Polydor)
20	21	DON'T PUSH IT, DON'T FORCE IT Leon Haywood (20th Century)
-	22	LIVING AFTER MIDNIGHT Judas Priest (CBS)
14	23	SO LONELY Police (A&M)
-	24	NO-ONE DRIVING John Foxx (Virgin)
9	25	ATOMIC Blondie (Chrysalis)
-	26	KOOL IN THE KAFTAN B.A. Robertson (Asylum)
28	27	LET'S DO ROCK STEADY Bodysnatchers (2 Tone)
-	28	HIM Rupert Holmes (MCA)
-	29	SEXY EYES Dr. Hook (Capitol)
-	30	MY WORLD Secret Affair (I-SPy)

last week	this week	12 April 1980
3	1	DANCE YOURSELF DIZZY Liquid Gold (Polo)
1	2	GOING UNDERGOUND Jam (Polydor)
5	3	WORKING MY WAY BACK TO YOU Detroit Spinners (Atlantic)
4	4	TURNING JAPANESE Vapors (United Artists)
13	5	KING/FOOD FOR THOUGHT UB40 (Graduate)
29	6	SEXY EYES Dr. Hook (Capitol)
2	7	TOGETHER WE ARE BEAUTIFUL Fern Kinney (WEA)
10	8	POISON IVY Lambrettas (Rocket)
9	9	STOMP Brothers Johnson (A&M)
-	10	WORK REST AND PLAY (EP) Madness (Stiff)
17	11	TURN IT ON AGAIN Genesis (Charisma)
6	12	ECHO BEACH Martha & the Muffins (Dindisc)
15	13	JANUARY FEBRUARY Barbara Dickson (Epic)
-	14	TALK OF THE TOWN Pretenders (Real)
7	15	DO THAT TO ME ONE MORE TIME Captain & Tennille (Casablanca)
21	16	DON'T PUSH IT, DON'T FORCE IT Leon Haywood (20th Century)
22	17	LIVING AFTER MIDNIGHT Judas Priest (CBS)
11	18	ALL NIGHT LONG Rainbow (Polydor)
8	19	TAKE THAT LOOK OFF YOUR FACE Marti Webb (Polydor)
20	20	HAPPY HOUSE Siouxsie & the Banshees (Polydor)
30	21	MY WORLD Secret Affair (I-SPy)
28	22	HIM Rupert Holmes (MCA)
12	23	ANOTHER NAIL IN MY HEART Squeeze (A&M)
14	24	GAMES WITHOUT FRONTIERS Peter Gabriel (Charisma)
-	25	CALL ME Blondie (Chrysalis)
24	26	NO-ONE DRIVING John Foxx (Virgin)
26	27	KOOL IN THE KAFTAN B.A. Robertson (Asylum)
27	28	LET'S DO ROCK STEADY Bodysnatchers (2 Tone)
18	29	THE SPIRIT OF RADIO Rush (Mercury)
-	30	SILVER DREAM MACHINE (PART 1) David Essex (Mercury)

last week	this week	19 April 1980
1	1	DANCE YOURSELF DIZZY Liquid Gold (Polo)
6	2	SEXY EYES Dr. Hook (Capitol)
3	3	WORKING MY WAY BACK TO YOU Detroit Spinners (Atlantic)
5	4	KING/FOOD FOR THOUGHT UB40 (Graduate)
10	5	WORK REST AND PLAY (EP) Madness (Stiff)
2	6	GOING UNDERGOUND Jam (Polydor)
14	7	TALK OF THE TOWN Pretenders (Real)
25	8	CALL ME Blondie (Chrysalis)
13	9	JANUARY FEBRUARY Barbara Dickson (Epic)
8	10	POISON IVY Lambrettas (Rocket)
9	11	STOMP Brothers Johnson (A&M)
11	12	TURN IT ON AGAIN Genesis (Charisma)
30	13	SILVER DREAM MACHINE (PART 1) David Essex (Mercury)
4	14	TURNING JAPANESE Vapors (United Artists)
20	15	HAPPY HOUSE Siouxsie & the Banshees (Polydor)
17	16	LIVING AFTER MIDNIGHT Judas Priest (CBS)
16	17	DON'T PUSH IT, DON'T FORCE IT Leon Haywood (20th Century)
21	18	MY WORLD Secret Affair (I-SPy)
12	19	ECHO BEACH Martha & the Muffins (Dindisc)
28	20	LET'S DO ROCK STEADY Bodysnatchers (2 Tone)
7	21	TOGETHER WE ARE BEAUTIFUL Fern Kinney (WEA)
-	22	MY OH MY Sad Cafe (RCA)
27	23	KOOL IN THE KAFTAN B.A. Robertson (Asylum)
-	24	MISSING WORDS Selecter (2 Tone)
22	25	HIM Rupert Holmes (MCA)
-	26	CHECK OUT THE GROOVE Bobby Thurston (Epic)
-	27	GENO Dexy's Midnight Runners (Late Night Feelings)
-	28	CLEAN CLEAN Buggles (Island)
-	29	SO GOOD SO RIGHT/IN THE THICK OF IT Brenda Russell (A&M)
18	30	ALL NIGHT LONG Rainbow (Polydor)

last week	this week	26 April 1980
8	1	CALL ME Blondie (Chrysalis)
4	2	KING/FOOD FOR THOUGHT UB40 (Graduate)
3	3	WORKING MY WAY BACK TO YOU Detroit Spinners (Atlantic)
2	4	SEXY EYES Dr. Hook (Capitol)
13	5	SILVER DREAM MACHINE (PART 1) David Essex (Mercury)
1	6	DANCE YOURSELF DIZZY Liquid Gold (Polo)
7	7	TALK OF THE TOWN Pretenders (Real)
6	8	GOING UNDERGOUND Jam (Polydor)
5	9	WORK REST AND PLAY (EP) Madness (Stiff)
27	10	GENO Dexy's Midnight Runners (Late Night Feelings)
9	11	JANUARY FEBRUARY Barbara Dickson (Epic)
10	12	POISON IVY Lambrettas (Rocket)
-	13	TOCCATA Sky (Ariola)
17	14	DON'T PUSH IT, DON'T FORCE IT Leon Haywood (20th Century)
12	15	TURN IT ON AGAIN Genesis (Charisma)
23	16	KOOL IN THE KAFTAN B.A. Robertson (Asylum)
11	17	STOMP Brothers Johnson (A&M)
26	18	CHECK OUT THE GROOVE Bobby Thurston (Epic)
14	19	TURNING JAPANESE Vapors (United Artists)
16	20	LIVING AFTER MIDNIGHT Judas Priest (CBS)
-	21	MY PERFECT COUSIN Undertones (Sire)
22	22	MY OH MY Sad Cafe (RCA)
-	23	THE GROOVE Rodney Franklin (CBS)
-	24	DON'T MAKE WAVES Nolans (Epic)
24	25	MISSING WORDS Selecter (2 Tone)
-	26	COMING UP Paul McCartney (Parlophone)
-	27	HI FIDELITY Elvis Costello (F.Beat)
20	28	LET'S DO ROCK STEADY Bodysnatchers (2 Tone)
29	29	SO GOOD SO RIGHT/IN THE THICK OF IT Brenda Russell (A&M)
-	30	WHEELS OF STEEL Saxon (Carrere)

After three years of chart entries, the Jam finally made No.1 with *Going Underground*. Madness emulated the Specials' recent EP success with *Work, Rest And Play* (the plug track was *Night Boat To Cairo*), while Blondie teamed with disco producer Giorgio Moroder for *Call Me*, from the film *American Gigolo*. David Essex' hit was also a film theme, from *Silver Dream Racer*, in which Essex himslf starred. Major chart debutantes were UB40 with double A-side *King/Food For Thought*.

3 April 1980

last week	this week	Title	Artist (Label)
1	1	CALL ME	Blondie (Chrysalis)
10	2	GENO	Dexy's Midnight Runners (Late Night Feelings)
2	3	KING/FOOD FOR THOUGHT	UB40 (Graduate)
26	4	COMING UP	Paul McCartney (Parlophone)
4	5	SEXY EYES	Dr. Hook (Capitol)
13	6	TOCCATA	Sky (Ariola)
5	7	SILVER DREAM MACHINE (PART 1)	David Essex (Mercury)
3	8	WORKING MY WAY BACK TO YOU	Detroit Spinners (Atlantic)
7	9	TALK OF THE TOWN	Pretenders (Real)
14	10	DON'T PUSH IT, DON'T FORCE IT	Leon Haywood (20th Century)
9	11	WORK REST AND PLAY (EP)	Madness (Stiff)
23	12	THE GROOVE	Rodney Franklin (CBS)
18	13	CHECK OUT THE GROOVE	Bobby Thurston (Epic)
11	14	JANUARY FEBRUARY	Barbara Dickson (Epic)
6	15	DANCE YOURSELF DIZZY	Liquid Gold (Polo)
16	16	KOOL IN THE KAFTAN	B.A. Robertson (Asylum)
24	17	DON'T MAKE WAVES	Nolans (Epic)
22	18	MY OH MY	Sad Cafe (RCA)
21	19	MY PERFECT COUSIN	Undertones (Sire)
-	20	STARING AT THE RUDE BOYS	Ruts (Virgin)
27	21	HI FIDELITY	Elvis Costello (F.Beat)
25	22	MISSING WORDS	Selecter (2 Tone)
-	23	I SHOULDA LOVED YA	Narada Walden (Atlantic)
15	24	TURN IT ON AGAIN	Genesis (Charisma)
-	25	BREATHING	Kate Bush (EMI)
12	26	POISON IVY	Lambrettas (Rocket)
-	27	IN THE CITY	Jam (Polydor)
17	28	STOMP	Brothers Johnson (A&M)
20	29	LIVING AFTER MIDNIGHT	Judas Priest (CBS)
30	30	WHEELS OF STEEL	Saxon (Carrere)

10 May 1980

last week	this week	Title	Artist (Label)
2	1	GENO	Dexy's Midnight Runners (Late Night Feelings)
4	2	COMING UP	Paul McCartney (Parlophone)
6	3	TOCCATA	Sky (Ariola)
7	4	SILVER DREAM MACHINE (PART 1)	David Essex (Mercury)
1	5	CALL ME	Blondie (Chrysalis)
13	6	CHECK OUT THE GROOVE	Bobby Thurston (Epic)
-	7	WHAT'S ANOTHER YEAR	Johnny Logan (Epic)
3	8	KING/FOOD FOR THOUGHT	UB40 (Graduate)
5	9	SEXY EYES	Dr. Hook (Capitol)
12	10	THE GROOVE	Rodney Franklin (CBS)
19	11	MY PERFECT COUSIN	Undertones (Sire)
10	12	DON'T PUSH IT, DON'T FORCE IT	Leon Haywood (20th Century)
8	13	WORKING MY WAY BACK TO YOU	Detroit Spinners (Atlantic)
23	14	I SHOULDA LOVED YA	Narada Walden (Atlantic)
-	15	NO DOUBT ABOUT IT	Hot Chocolate (RAK)
9	16	TALK OF THE TOWN	Pretenders (Real)
25	17	BREATHING	Kate Bush (EMI)
-	18	THE GOLDEN YEARS (EP)	Motorhead (Bronze)
30	19	WHEELS OF STEEL	Saxon (Carrere)
18	20	MY OH MY	Sad Cafe (RCA)
11	21	WORK REST AND PLAY (EP)	Madness (Stiff)
17	22	DON'T MAKE WAVES	Nolans (Epic)
-	23	NE-NE NA-NA NA-NA NU-NU	Bad Manners (Magnet)
24	24	HOLD ON TO MY LOVE	Jimmy Ruffin (RSO)
-	25	THIS WORLD OF WATER	New Musik (GTO)
-	26	SHE'S OUT OF MY LIFE	Michael Jackson (Epic)
-	27	DOWN IN THE TUBE STATION AT MIDNIGHT	Jam (Polydor)
-	28	FOOL FOR YOUR LOVING	Whitesnake (United Artists)
26	29	POISON IVY	Lambrettas (Rocket)
-	30	LET'S GO ROUND AGAIN PT 1	Average White Band (RCA)

17 May 1980

last week	this week	Title	Artist (Label)
7	1	WHAT'S ANOTHER YEAR	Johnny Logan (Epic)
1	2	GENO	Dexy's Midnight Runners (Late Night Feelings)
2	3	COMING UP	Paul McCartney (Parlophone)
3	4	TOCCATA	Sky (Ariola)
4	5	SILVER DREAM MACHINE (PART 1)	David Essex (Mercury)
5	6	CALL ME	Blondie (Chrysalis)
10	7	THE GROOVE	Rodney Franklin (CBS)
24	8	HOLD ON TO MY LOVE	Jimmy Ruffin (RSO)
15	9	NO DOUBT ABOUT IT	Hot Chocolate (RAK)
18	10	THE GOLDEN YEARS (EP)	Motorhead (Bronze)
14	11	I SHOULDA LOVED YA	Narada Walden (Atlantic)
6	12	CHECK OUT THE GROOVE	Bobby Thurston (Epic)
11	13	MY PERFECT COUSIN	Undertones (Sire)
26	14	SHE'S OUT OF MY LIFE	Michael Jackson (Epic)
-	15	MIRROR IN THE BATHROOM	Beat (Go Feet)
22	16	DON'T MAKE WAVES	Nolans (Epic)
8	17	KING/FOOD FOR THOUGHT	UB40 (Graduate)
17	18	BREATHING	Kate Bush (EMI)
-	19	JUST CAN'T GIVE YOU UP	Mystic Merlin (Capitol)
30	20	LET'S GO ROUND AGAIN PT 1	Average White Band (RCA)
-	21	THEME FROM M*A*S*H (SUICIDE IS PAINLESS)	MASH (CBS)
-	22	YOU GAVE ME LOVE	Crown Heights Affair (De-Lite)
28	23	FOOL FOR YOUR LOVE	Whitesnake (United Artists)
12	24	DON'T PUSH IT, DON'T FORCE IT	Leon Haywood (20th Century)
9	25	SEXY EYES	Dr. Hook (Capitol)
13	26	WORKING MY WAY BACK TO YOU	Detroit Spinners (Atlantic)
-	27	POLICE AND THIEVES	Junior Murvin (Island)
19	28	WHEELS OF STEEL	Saxon (Carrere)
25	29	THIS WORLD OF WATER	New Musik (GTO)
-	30	STARING AT THE RUDE BOYS	Ruts (Virgin)

24 May 1980

last week	this week	Title	Artist (Label)
1	1	WHAT'S ANOTHER YEAR	Johnny Logan (Epic)
9	2	NO DOUBT ABOUT IT	Hot Chocolate (RAK)
14	3	SHE'S OUT OF MY LIFE	Michael Jackson (Epic)
2	4	GENO	Dexy's Midnight Runners (Late Night Feelings)
15	5	MIRROR IN THE BATHROOM	Beat (Go Feet)
8	6	HOLD ON TO MY LOVE	Jimmy Ruffin (RSO)
3	7	COMING UP	Paul McCartney (Parlophone)
11	8	I SHOULDA LOVED YA	Narada Walden (Atlantic)
-	9	OVER YOU	Roxy Music (Polydor)
16	10	DON'T MAKE WAVES	Nolans (Epic)
5	11	SILVER DREAM MACHINE (PART 1)	David Essex (Mercury)
21	12	THEME FROM M*A*S*H (SUICIDE IS PAINLESS)	MASH (CBS)
7	13	THE GROOVE	Rodney Franklin (CBS)
20	14	LET'S GO ROUND AGAIN PT 1	Average White Band (RCA)
4	15	TOCCATA	Sky (Ariola)
19	16	JUST CAN'T GIVE YOU UP	Mystic Merlin (Capitol)
18	17	BREATHING	Kate Bush (EMI)
10	18	THE GOLDEN YEARS (EP)	Motorhead (Bronze)
13	19	MY PERFECT COUSIN	Undertones (Sire)
-	20	YOU'LL ALWAYS FIND ME IN THE KITCHEN AT PARTIES	Jona Lewie (Stiff)
6	21	CALL ME	Blondie (Chrysalis)
12	22	CHECK OUT THE GROOVE	Bobby Thurston (Epic)
-	23	BACK TOGETHER AGAIN	Roberta Flack & Donny Hathaway (Atlantic)
22	24	YOU GAVE ME LOVE	Crown Heights Affair (De-Lite)
-	25	TEENAGE	UK Subs (Gem)
-	26	LET'S GET SERIOUS	Jermaine Jackson (Motown)
29	27	THIS WORLD OF WATER	New Musik (GTO)
23	28	FOOL FOR YOUR LOVING	Whitesnake (United Artists)
-	29	CRYING	Don McLean (EMI)
30	30	STARING AT THE RUDE BOYS	Ruts (Virgin)

British soul band Dexy's Midnight Runners, led by vocalist Kevin Rowland, made an impressive Number One debut with their tribute to Geno Washington, an American who had been probably the most popular performer on the UK dancehall circuit of the mid-60s.

Johnny Logan's chart-topping *What's Another Year* was the second Irish winner of the Eurovision song contest (Dana's *All Kinds Of Everything* had been the first, exactly 10 years previously); the third-placed British entry by Prima Donna failed to chart.

May – June 1980

last this week

31 May 1980

2 1 NO DOUBT ABOUT IT / Hot Chocolate (RAK)
1 2 WHAT'S ANOTHER YEAR / Johnny Logan (Epic)
3 3 SHE'S OUT OF MY LIFE / Michael Jackson (Epic)
5 4 MIRROR IN THE BATHROOM / Beat (Go Feet)
12 5 THEME FROM M*A*S*H (SUICIDE IS PAINLESS) / MASH (CBS)
9 6 OVER YOU / Roxy Music (Polydor)
- 7 WE ARE GLASS / Gary Numan (Beggars Banquet)
6 8 HOLD ON TO MY LOVE / Jimmy Ruffin (RSO)
4 9 GENO / Dexy's Midnight Runners (Late Night Feelings)
- 10 RAT RACE/RUDE BOYS OUTA JAIL / Specials (2 Tone)
28 11 FOOL FOR YOUR LOVING / Whitesnake (United Artists)
24 12 YOU GAVE ME LOVE / Crown Heights Affair (De-Lite)
7 13 COMING UP / Paul McCartney (Parlophone)
10 14 DON'T MAKE WAVES / Nolans (Epic)
14 15 LET'S GO ROUND AGAIN PT 1 / Average White Band (RCA)
29 16 CRYING / Don McLean (EMI)
26 17 LET'S GET SERIOUS / Jermaine Jackson (Motown)
8 18 I SHOULDA LOVED YA / Narada Walden (Atlantic)
23 19 BACK TOGETHER AGAIN / Roberta Flack & Donny Hathaway (Atlantic)
20 20 YOU'LL ALWAYS FIND ME IN THE KITCHEN AT PARTIES / Jona Lewie (Stiff)
- 21 FUNKYTOWN / Lipps Inc. (Casablanca)
- 22 I'M ALIVE / Electric Light Orchestra (Jet)
17 23 BREATHING / Kate Bush (EMI)
16 24 JUST CAN'T GIVE YOU UP / Mystic Merlin (Capitol)
13 25 THE GROOVE / Rodney Franklin (CBS)
11 26 SILVER DREAM MACHINE (PART 1) / David Essex (Mercury)
- 27 D-A-A-ANCE / Lambrettas (Rocket)
- 28 POLICE AND THIEVES / Junior Murvin (Island)
25 29 TEENAGE / UK Subs (Gem)
- 30 MIDIGHT DYNAMOS / Matchbox (Magnet)

7 June 1980

5 1 THEME FROM M*A*S*H (SUICIDE IS PAINLESS) / MASH (CBS)
1 2 NO DOUBT ABOUT IT / Hot Chocolate (RAK)
7 3 WE ARE GLASS / Gary Numan (Beggars Banquet)
3 4 SHE'S OUT OF MY LIFE / Michael Jackson (Epic)
6 5 OVER YOU / Roxy Music (Polydor)
4 6 MIRROR IN THE BATHROOM / Beat (Go Feet)
10 7 RAT RACE/RUDE BOYS OUTA JAIL / Specials (2 Tone)
2 8 WHAT'S ANOTHER YEAR / Johnny Logan (Epic)
21 9 FUNKYTOWN / Lipps Inc. (Casablanca)
16 10 CRYING / Don McLean (EMI)
8 11 HOLD ON TO MY LOVE / Jimmy Ruffin (RSO)
27 12 D-A-A-ANCE / Lambrettas (Rocket)
17 13 LET'S GET SERIOUS / Jermaine Jackson (Motown)
9 14 GENO / Dexy's Midnight Runners (Late Night Feelings)
19 15 BACK TOGETHER AGAIN / Roberta Flack & Donny Hathaway (Atlantic)
15 16 LET'S GO ROUND AGAIN PT 1 / Average White Band (RCA)
20 17 YOU'LL ALWAYS FIND ME IN THE KITCHEN AT PARTIES / Jona Lewie (Stiff)
12 18 YOU GAVE ME LOVE / Crown Heights Affair (De-Lite)
30 19 MIDIGHT DYNAMOS / Matchbox (Magnet)
22 20 I'M ALIVE / Electric Light Orchestra (Jet)
14 21 DON'T MAKE WAVES / Nolans (Epic)
11 22 FOOL FOR YOUR LOVING / Whitesnake (United Artists)
- 23 BEHIND THE GROOVE / Teena Marie (Motown)
- 24 EVERYBODY'S GOT TO LEARN SOME TIME / Korgis (Rialto)
25 25 NO SELF CONTROL / Peter Gabriel (Charisma)
24 26 JUST CAN'T GIVE YOU UP / Mystic Merlin (Capitol)
- 27 CHINATOWN / Thin Lizzy (Vertigo)
- 28 TWILGHT ZONE - TWIGHLIGHT TONE / Manhattan Transfer (Atlantic)
- 29 SUBSTITUTE / Liquid Gold (Polo)
28 30 POLICE AND THIEVES / Junior Murvin (Island)

14 June 1980

1 1 THEME FROM M*A*S*H (SUICIDE IS PAINLESS) / MASH (CBS)
9 2 FUNKYTOWN / Lipps Inc. (Casablanca)
2 3 NO DOUBT ABOUT IT / Hot Chocolate (RAK)
10 4 CRYING / Don McLean (EMI)
5 5 OVER YOU / Roxy Music (Polydor)
6 6 RAT RACE/RUDE BOYS OUTA JAIL / Specials (2 Tone)
15 7 BACK TOGETHER AGAIN / Roberta Flack & Donny Hathaway (Atlantic)
13 8 LET'S GET SERIOUS / Jermaine Jackson (Motown)
3 9 WE ARE GLASS / Gary Numan (Beggars Banquet)
18 10 YOU GAVE ME LOVE / Crown Heights Affair (De-Lite)
6 11 MIRROR IN THE BATHROOM / Beat (Go Feet)
16 12 LET'S GO ROUND AGAIN PT 1 / Average White Band (RCA)
8 13 WHAT'S ANOTHER YEAR / Johnny Logan (Epic)
12 14 D-A-A-ANCE / Lambrettas (Rocket)
- 15 BREAKING THE LAW / Judas Priest (CBS)
4 16 SHE'S OUT OF MY LIFE / Michael Jackson (Epic)
11 17 HOLD ON TO MY LOVE / Jimmy Ruffin (RSO)
20 18 I'M ALIVE / Electric Light Orchestra (Jet)
23 19 BEHIND THE GROOVE / Teena Marie (Motown)
19 20 MIDIGHT DYNAMOS / Matchbox (Magnet)
26 21 JUST CAN'T GIVE YOU UP / Mystic Merlin (Capitol)
17 22 YOU'LL ALWAYS FIND ME IN THE KITCHEN AT PARTIES / Jona Lewie (Stiff)
- 23 THE SCRATCH / Surface Noise (WEA)
14 24 GENO / Dexy's Midnight Runners (Late Night Feelings)
27 25 CHINATOWN / Thin Lizzy (Vertigo)
24 26 EVERYBODY'S GOT TO LEARN SOME TIME / Korgis (Rialto)
30 27 POLICE AND THIEVES / Junior Murvin (Island)
29 28 SUBSTITUTE / Liquid Gold (Polo)
- 29 CHRISTINE / Siouxsie & the Banshees (Polydor)
22 30 FOOL FOR YOUR LOVING / Whitesnake (United Artists)

21 June 1980

2 1 FUNKYTOWN / Lipps Inc. (Casablanca)
4 2 CRYING / Don McLean (EMI)
1 3 THEME FROM M*A*S*H (SUICIDE IS PAINLESS) / MASH (CBS)
5 4 OVER YOU / Roxy Music (Polydor)
7 5 BACK TOGETHER AGAIN / Roberta Flack & Donny Hathaway (Atlantic)
3 6 NO DOUBT ABOUT IT / Hot Chocolate (RAK)
6 7 RAT RACE/RUDE BOYS OUTA JAIL / Specials (2 Tone)
8 8 LET'S GET SERIOUS / Jermaine Jackson (Motown)
10 9 YOU GAVE ME LOVE / Crown Heights Affair (De-Lite)
9 10 WE ARE GLASS / Gary Numan (Beggars Banquet)
19 11 BEHIND THE GROOVE / Teena Marie (Motown)
14 12 D-A-A-ANCE / Lambrettas (Rocket)
20 13 MIDIGHT DYNAMOS / Matchbox (Magnet)
26 14 EVERYBODY'S GOT TO LEARN SOME TIME / Korgis (Rialto)
16 15 SHE'S OUT OF MY LIFE / Michael Jackson (Epic)
- 16 MESSAGES / Orchestral Manoeuvres In The Dark (Dindisc)
12 17 LET'S GO ROUND AGAIN PT 1 / Average White Band (RCA)
22 18 YOU'LL ALWAYS FIND ME IN THE KITCHEN AT PARTIES / Jona Lewie (Stiff)
18 19 I'M ALIVE / Electric Light Orchestra (Jet)
15 20 BREAKING THE LAW / Judas Priest (CBS)
- 21 SIX PACK / Police (A&M)
- 22 (IF LOVING YOU IS WRONG) I DON'T WANT TO BE RIGHT / Rod Stewart (Riva)
11 23 MIRROR IN THE BATHROOM / Beat (Go Feet)
29 24 CHRISTINE / Siouxsie & the Banshees (Polydor)
- 25 PLAY THE GAME / Queen (EMI)
- 26 JUMP TO THE BEAT / Stacy Lattisaw (Atlantic/Cotillion)
23 27 THE SCRATCH / Surface Noise (WEA)
- 28 LITTLE JEANNIE / Elton John (Rocket)
28 29 SUBSTITUTE / Liquid Gold (Polo)
24 30 GENO / Dexy's Midnight Runners (Late Night Feelings)

The *Theme From M*A*S*H* had originally been released by CBS as a single in 1970, when the original movie was on the circuit, and long before the advent of the hit TV series (which also made use of a non-vocal version of the tune). At that time, it had hardly sold at all, which made the reissue's Number One success a decade later a major surprise – a combination of public awareness, remorseless plugging, lucky hunch and spot-on promotion all coming together positively when least expected.

June – July 1980

last week	this week	28 June 1980
2	1	CRYING Don McLean (EMI)
1	2	FUNKYTOWN Lipps Inc. (Casablanca)
5	3	BACK TOGETHER AGAIN Roberta Flack & Donny Hathaway (Atlantic)
3	4	THEME FROM M*A*S*H (SUICIDE IS PAINLESS) MASH (CBS)
14	5	EVERYBODY'S GOT TO LEARN SOME TIME Korgis (Rialto)
10	6	BEHIND THE GROOVE Teena Marie (Motown)
4	7	OVER YOU Roxy Music (Polydor)
8	8	LET'S GET SERIOUS Jermaine Jackson (Motown)
9	9	YOU GAVE ME LOVE Crown Heights Affair (De-Lite)
6	10	NO DOUBT ABOUT IT Hot Chocolate (RAK)
29	11	SUBSTITUTE Liquid Gold (Polo)
25	12	PLAY THE GAME Queen (EMI)
20	13	BREAKING THE LAW Judas Priest (CBS)
16	14	MESSAGES Orchestral Manoeuvres In The Dark (Dindisc)
7	15	RAT RACE/RUDE BOYS OUTA JAIL Specials (2 Tone)
12	16	D-A-A-ANCE Lambrettas (Rocket)
13	17	MIDIGHT DYNAMOS Matchbox (Magnet)
21	18	SIX PACK Police (A&M)
-	19	SIMON TEMPLAR/TWO PINTS OF LAGER AND A PACKET OF CRISPS PLEASE Splodgenessabounds (Deram)
-	19	MY WAY OF THINKING/I THINK IT'S GOING TO RAIN UB40 (Graduate)
27	21	THE SCRATCH Surface Noise (WEA)
10	22	WE ARE GLASS Gary Numan (Beggars Banquet)
19	23	I'M ALIVE Electric Light Orchestra (Jet)
22	24	(IF LOVING YOU IS WRONG) I DON'T WANT TO BE RIGHT Rod Stewart (Riva)
26	25	JUMP TO THE BEAT Stacy Lattisaw (Atlantic/Cotillion)
18	26	YOU'LL ALWAYS FIND ME IN THE KITCHEN AT PARTIES Jona Lewie (Stiff)
-	27	(I'M NOT YOUR) STEPPING STONE Sex Pistols (Virgin)
-	28	KING'S CALL Phil Lynott (Vertigo)
-	29	COULD YOU BE LOVED Bob Marley & the Wailers (Island)
-	30	POLICE AND THIEVES Junior Murvin (Island)

last week	this week	5 July 1980
1	1	CRYING Don McLean (EMI)
2	2	FUNKYTOWN Lipps Inc. (Casablanca)
3	3	BACK TOGETHER AGAIN Roberta Flack & Donny Hathaway (Atlantic)
5	4	EVERYBODY'S GOT TO LEARN SOME TIME Korgis (Rialto)
19	5	SIMON TEMPLAR/TWO PINTS OF LAGER AND A PACKET OF CRISPS PLEASE Splodgenessabounds (Deram)
25	6	JUMP TO THE BEAT Stacy Lattisaw (Atlantic/Cotillion)
6	7	BEHIND THE GROOVE Teena Marie (Motown)
-	8	XANADU Olivia Newton-John & Electric Light Orchestra (Jet)
-	9	WATERFALLS Paul McCartney (Parlophone)
4	10	THEME FROM M*A*S*H (SUICIDE IS PAINLESS) MASH (CBS)
11	11	SUBSTITUTE Liquid Gold (Polo)
8	12	LET'S GET SERIOUS Jermaine Jackson (Motown)
12	13	PLAY THE GAME Queen (EMI)
9	14	YOU GAVE ME LOVE Crown Heights Affair (De-Lite)
19	15	MY WAY OF THINKING/I THINK IT'S GOING TO RAIN UB40 (Graduate)
29	16	COULD YOU BE LOVED Bob Marley & the Wailers (Island)
15	17	RAT RACE/RUDE BOYS OUTA JAIL Specials (2 Tone)
-	18	USE IT UP AND WEAR IT OUT Odyssey (RCA)
14	19	MESSAGES Orchestral Manoeuvres In The Dark (Dindisc)
7	20	OVER YOU Roxy Music (Polydor)
21	21	THE SCRATCH Surface Noise (WEA)
-	22	COMPUTER GAME (THEME FROM THE INVADERS) Yellow Magic Orchestra (A&M)
10	23	NO DOUBT ABOUT IT Hot Chocolate (RAK)
-	24	BIG TEASER/RAINBOW THEME Saxon (Carrere)
-	25	TO BE OR NOT TO BE B.A. Robertson (Asylum)
-	26	CHRISTINE Siouxsie & the Banshees (Polydor)
27	27	(I'M NOT YOUR) STEPPING STONE Sex Pistols (Virgin)
13	29	BREAKING THE LAW Judas Priest (CBS)
-	30	WHOLE LOTTA ROSIE AC/DC (Atlantic)

last week	this week	12 July 1980
8	1	XANADU Olivia Newton-John & Electric Light Orchestra (Jet)
6	2	JUMP TO THE BEAT Stacy Lattisaw (Atlantic/Cotillion)
1	3	CRYING Don McLean (EMI)
2	4	FUNKYTOWN Lipps Inc. (Casablanca)
4	5	EVERYBODY'S GOT TO LEARN SOME TIME Korgis (Rialto)
18	6	USE IT UP AND WEAR IT OUT Odyssey (RCA)
3	7	BACK TOGETHER AGAIN Roberta Flack & Donny Hathaway (Atlantic)
15	8	MY WAY OF THINKING/I THINK IT'S GOING TO RAIN UB40 (Graduate)
9	9	WATERFALLS Paul McCartney (Parlophone)
5	10	SIMON TEMPLAR/TWO PINTS OF LAGER AND A PACKET OF CRISPS PLEASE Splodgenessabounds (Deram)
7	11	BEHIND THE GROOVE Teena Marie (Motown)
25	12	TO BE OR NOT TO BE B.A. Robertson (Asylum)
28	13	CUPID - I'VE LOVED YOU FOR LONG TIME (MEDLEY) Detroit Spinners (Atlantic)
16	14	COULD YOU BE LOVED Bob Marley & the Wailers (Island)
13	15	PLAY THE GAME Queen (EMI)
11	16	SUBSTITUTE Liquid Gold (Polo)
-	17	LOVE WILL TEAR US APART Joy Division (Factory)
10	18	THEME FROM M*A*S*H (SUICIDE IS PAINLESS) MASH (CBS)
22	19	COMPUTER GAME (THEME FROM THE INVADERS) Yellow Magic Orchestra (A&M)
-	20	MIDIGHT DYNAMOS Matchbox (Magnet)
24	21	BIG TEASER/RAINBOW THEME Saxon (Carrere)
12	22	LET'S GET SERIOUS Jermaine Jackson (Motown)
-	23	EMOTIONAL RESCUE Rolling Stones (Rolling Stones)
-	24	(IF LOVING YOU IS WRONG) I DON'T WANT TO BE RIGHT Rod Stewart (Riva)
19	25	MESSAGES Orchestral Manoeuvres In The Dark (Dindisc)
-	26	DOES SHE HAVE A FRIEND Gene Chandler (20th Century)
27	27	A LOVER'S HOLIDAY/GLOW OF LOVE Change (WEA)
-	28	CHINATOWN Thin Lizzy (Vertigo)
29	29	BABOOSHKA Kate Bush (EMI)
-	30	MORE THAN I CAN SAY Leo Sayer (Chrysalis)

last week	this week	19 July 1980
1	1	XANADU Olivia Newton-John & Electric Light Orchestra (Jet)
6	2	USE IT UP AND WEAR IT OUT Odyssey (RCA)
13	3	CUPID - I'VE LOVED YOU FOR LONG TIME (MEDLEY) Detroit Spinners (Atlantic)
2	4	JUMP TO THE BEAT Stacy Lattisaw (Atlantic/Cotillion)
14	5	COULD YOU BE LOVED Bob Marley & the Wailers (Island)
3	6	CRYING Don McLean (EMI)
9	7	WATERFALLS Paul McCartney (Parlophone)
8	8	MY WAY OF THINKING/I THINK IT'S GOING TO RAIN UB40 (Graduate)
4	9	FUNKYTOWN Lipps Inc. (Casablanca)
29	10	BABOOSHKA Kate Bush (EMI)
5	11	EVERYBODY'S GOT TO LEARN SOME TIME Korgis (Rialto)
23	12	EMOTIONAL RESCUE Rolling Stones (Rolling Stones)
30	13	MORE THAN I CAN SAY Leo Sayer (Chrysalis)
12	14	TO BE OR NOT TO BE B.A. Robertson (Asylum)
17	15	LOVE WILL TEAR US APART Joy Division (Factory)
10	16	SIMON TEMPLAR/TWO PINTS OF LAGER AND A PACKET OF CRISPS PLEASE Splodgenessabounds (Deram)
21	17	BIG TEASER/RAINBOW THEME Saxon (Carrere)
7	18	BACK TOGETHER AGAIN Roberta Flack & Donny Hathaway (Atlantic)
19	19	COMPUTER GAME (THEME FROM THE INVADERS) Yellow Magic Orchestra (A&M)
15	20	PLAY THE GAME Queen (EMI)
11	21	BEHIND THE GROOVE Teena Marie (Motown)
27	22	A LOVER'S HOLIDAY/GLOW OF LOVE Change (WEA)
-	23	ME MYSELF I Joan Armatrading (A&M)
-	24	LET'S HANG ON Darts (Magnet)
26	25	DOES SHE HAVE A FRIEND Gene Chandler (20th Century)
-	26	THERE THERE MY DEAR Dexy's Midnight Runners (Late Night Feelings)
16	27	SUBSTITUTE Liquid Gold (Polo)
-	28	LIP UP FATTY Bad Manners (Magnet)
-	29	WEDNESDAY WEEK Undertones (Sire)
24	30	(IF LOVING YOU IS WRONG) I DON'T WANT TO BE RIGHT Rod Stewart (Riva)

Don McLean's revival of Roy Orbison's *Crying*, recorded in 1978 for his album *Chain Lightning*, was one of his own favourite performances, though was only belatedly released as a single after selling well in Europe following a sensationally-received TV performance – and only issued in McLean's native USA after its UK No.1 success. Meanwhile, covers of other oldies were also scoring, as the Detroit Spinners (*Cupid*), Leo Sayer (*More Than I Can Say*) and Darts (*Let's Hang On*) all took the revival route to success.

July – August 1980

last this week

26 July 1980

LW	TW	Title
1	1	XANADU — Olivia Newton-John & Electric Light Orchestra (Jet)
2	2	USE IT UP AND WEAR IT OUT — Odyssey (RCA)
5	3	COULD YOU BE LOVED — Bob Marley & the Wailers (Island)
4	4	JUMP TO THE BEAT — Stacy Lattisaw (Atlantic/Cotillion)
10	5	BABOOSHKA — Kate Bush (EMI)
3	6	CUPID - I'VE LOVED YOU FOR LONG TIME (MEDLEY) — Detroit Spinners (Atlantic)
13	7	MORE THAN I CAN SAY — Leo Sayer (Chrysalis)
8	8	MY WAY OF THINKING/I THINK IT'S GOING TO RAIN — UB40 (Graduate)
7	9	WATERFALLS — Paul McCartney (Parlophone)
12	10	EMOTIONAL RESCUE — Rolling Stones (Rolling Stones)
6	11	CRYING — Don McLean (EMI)
15	12	LOVE WILL TEAR US APART — Joy Division (Factory)
-	13	UPSIDE DOWN — Diana Ross (Motown)
26	14	THERE THERE MY DEAR — Dexy's Midnight Runners (Late Night Feelings)
9	15	FUNKYTOWN — Lipps Inc. (Casablanca)
14	16	TO BE OR NOT TO BE — B.A. Robertson (Asylum)
24	17	LET'S HANG ON — Darts (Magnet)
22	18	A LOVER'S HOLIDAY/GLOW OF LOVE — Change (WEA)
17	19	BIG TEASER/RAINBOW THEME — Saxon (Carrere)
20	20	PLAY THE GAME — Queen (EMI)
19	21	COMPUTER GAME (THEME FROM THE INVADERS) — Yellow Magic Orchestra (A&M)
25	22	DOES SHE HAVE A FRIEND — Gene Chandler (20th Century)
-	23	MY GIRL — Whispers (Solar)
-	24	NEON KNIGHTS — Black Sabbath (Vertigo)
-	25	MARIANA — Gibson Brothers (Island)
23	26	ME MYSELF I — Joan Armatrading (A&M)
16	27	SIMON TEMPLAR/TWO PINTS OF LAGER AND A PACKET OF CRISPS PLEASE — Splodgenessabounds (Deram)
-	28	OOPS UPSIDE YOUR HEAD — Gap Band (Mercury)
-	29	9 TO 5 — Sheena Easton (EMI)
-	30	BRAZILIAN LOVE AFFAIR — George Duke (Epic)

2 August 1980

LW	TW	Title
2	1	USE IT UP AND WEAR IT OUT — Odyssey (RCA)
7	2	MORE THAN I CAN SAY — Leo Sayer (Chrysalis)
1	3	XANADU — Olivia Newton-John & Electric Light Orchestra (Jet)
13	4	UPSIDE DOWN — Diana Ross (Motown)
5	5	BABOOSHKA — Kate Bush (EMI)
3	6	COULD YOU BE LOVED — Bob Marley & the Wailers (Island)
4	7	JUMP TO THE BEAT — Stacy Lattisaw (Atlantic/Cotillion)
10	8	EMOTIONAL RESCUE — Rolling Stones (Rolling Stones)
6	9	CUPID - I'VE LOVED YOU FOR LONG TIME (MEDLEY) — Detroit Spinners (Atlantic)
14	10	THERE THERE MY DEAR — Dexy's Midnight Runners (Late Night Feelings)
17	11	LET'S HANG ON — Darts (Magnet)
12	12	LOVE WILL TEAR US APART — Joy Division (Factory)
8	13	MY WAY OF THINKING/I THINK IT'S GOING TO RAIN — UB40 (Graduate)
18	14	A LOVER'S HOLIDAY/GLOW OF LOVE — Change (WEA)
25	15	MARIANA — Gibson Brothers (Island)
-	16	ARE YOU GETTING ENOUGH OF WHAT MAKES YOU HAPPY — Hot Chocolate (RAK)
-	17	FUNKIN' FOR JAMAICA — Tom Browne (Arista)
-	18	LIP UP FATTY — Bad Manners (Magnet)
21	19	COMPUTER GAME (THEME FROM THE INVADERS) — Yellow Magic Orchestra (A&M)
29	20	9 TO 5 — Sheena Easton (EMI)
-	21	GIVE ME THE NIGHT — George Benson (Warner Bros)
9	22	WATERFALLS — Paul McCartney (Parlophone)
-	23	BURNIN' HOT — Jermaine Jackson (Motown)
28	24	OOPS UPSIDE YOUR HEAD — Gap Band (Mercury)
30	25	BRAZILIAN LOVE AFFAIR — George Duke (Epic)
23	26	MY GIRL — Whispers (Solar)
-	27	SHINING STAR — Manhattans (CBS)
-	28	WEDNESDAY WEEK — Undertones (Sire)
20	29	PLAY THE GAME — Queen (EMI)
26	30	ME MYSELF I — Joan Armatrading (A&M)

9 August 1980

LW	TW	Title
4	1	UPSIDE DOWN — Diana Ross (Motown)
1	2	USE IT UP AND WEAR IT OUT — Odyssey (RCA)
2	3	MORE THAN I CAN SAY — Leo Sayer (Chrysalis)
6	4	COULD YOU BE LOVED — Bob Marley & the Wailers (Island)
-	5	THE WINNER TAKES IT ALL — Abba (Epic)
5	6	BABOOSHKA — Kate Bush (EMI)
3	7	XANADU — Olivia Newton-John & Electric Light Orchestra (Jet)
10	8	THERE THERE MY DEAR — Dexy's Midnight Runners (Late Night Feelings)
9	9	CUPID - I'VE LOVED YOU FOR LONG TIME (MEDLEY) — Detroit Spinners (Atlantic)
20	10	9 TO 5 — Sheena Easton (EMI)
24	11	OOPS UPSIDE YOUR HEAD — Gap Band (Mercury)
7	12	JUMP TO THE BEAT — Stacy Lattisaw (Atlantic/Cotillion)
21	13	GIVE ME THE NIGHT — George Benson (Warner Bros)
18	14	LIP UP FATTY — Bad Manners (Magnet)
11	15	LET'S HANG ON — Darts (Magnet)
28	16	WEDNESDAY WEEK — Undertones (Sire)
17	17	FUNKIN' FOR JAMAICA — Tom Browne (Arista)
8	18	EMOTIONAL RESCUE — Rolling Stones (Rolling Stones)
14	19	A LOVER'S HOLIDAY/GLOW OF LOVE — Change (WEA)
13	20	MY WAY OF THINKING/I THINK IT'S GOING TO RAIN — UB40 (Graduate)
23	21	BURNIN' HOT — Jermaine Jackson (Motown)
-	22	OH YEAH (ON THE RADIO) — Roxy Music (Polydor)
15	23	MARIANA — Gibson Brothers (Island)
-	24	DOES SHE HAVE A FRIEND — Gene Chandler (20th Century)
-	25	PRIVATE LIFE — Grace Jones (Island)
16	26	ARE YOU GETTING ENOUGH OF WHAT MAKES YOU HAPPY — Hot Chocolate (RAK)
27	27	SHINING STAR — Manhattans (CBS)
19	28	COMPUTER GAME (THEME FROM THE INVADERS) — Yellow Magic Orchestra (A&M)
12	29	LOVE WILL TEAR US APART — Joy Division (Factory)
-	30	GIRLFRIEND — Michael Jackson (Epic)

16 August 1980

LW	TW	Title
5	1	THE WINNER TAKES IT ALL — Abba (Epic)
1	2	UPSIDE DOWN — Diana Ross (Motown)
9	3	9 TO 5 — Sheena Easton (EMI)
2	4	USE IT UP AND WEAR IT OUT — Odyssey (RCA)
11	5	OOPS UPSIDE YOUR HEAD — Gap Band (Mercury)
3	6	MORE THAN I CAN SAY — Leo Sayer (Chrysalis)
13	7	GIVE ME THE NIGHT — George Benson (Warner Bros)
6	8	BABOOSHKA — Kate Bush (EMI)
22	9	OH YEAH (ON THE RADIO) — Roxy Music (Polydor)
4	10	COULD YOU BE LOVED — Bob Marley & the Wailers (Island)
17	11	FUNKIN' FOR JAMAICA — Tom Browne (Arista)
23	12	MARIANA — Gibson Brothers (Island)
8	13	THERE THERE MY DEAR — Dexy's Midnight Runners (Late Night Feelings)
7	14	XANADU — Olivia Newton-John & Electric Light Orchestra (Jet)
14	15	LIP UP FATTY — Bad Manners (Magnet)
25	16	PRIVATE LIFE — Grace Jones (Island)
26	17	ARE YOU GETTING ENOUGH OF WHAT MAKES YOU HAPPY — Hot Chocolate (RAK)
-	18	TOM HARK — Piranhas (Sire)
-	19	ASHES TO ASHES — David Bowie (RCA)
16	20	WEDNESDAY WEEK — Undertones (Sire)
21	21	BURNIN' HOT — Jermaine Jackson (Motown)
-	22	ALL OVER THE WORLD — Electric Light Orchestra (Jet)
-	23	BANKROBBER — Clash (CBS)
12	24	JUMP TO THE BEAT — Stacy Lattisaw (Atlantic/Cotillion)
29	25	LOVE WILL TEAR US APART — Joy Division (Factory)
18	26	EMOTIONAL RESCUE — Rolling Stones (Rolling Stones)
-	27	LONELY DESIRE — Teena Marie (Motown)
-	28	SLEEPWALK — Ultravox (Chrysalis)
20	29	MY WAY OF THINKING/I THINK IT'S GOING TO RAIN — UB40 (Graduate)
-	30	BACKSTROKIN' — Fatback (Spring)

Odyssey's chart-topping *Use It Up And Wear It Out* was a huge dancefloor and radio success in the UK without achieving anything at all in the group's native US. Oddly, the same fate befell Paul McCartney's *Waterfalls,* a UK Top 10 hit – in America, it could only bubble under the Top 100, despite its predecessor *Coming Up* having reached Number One there. Meanwhile, Sheena Easton, aspiring pop singer subject of Esther Rantzen's Big Time TV show, hit that big time for real with *9 To 5*.

23 August 1980

last week	this week		
1	1	THE WINNER TAKES IT ALL	Abba (Epic)
2	2	UPSIDE DOWN	Diana Ross (Motown)
3	3	9 TO 5	Sheena Easton (EMI)
19	4	ASHES TO ASHES	David Bowie (RCA)
9	5	OH YEAH (ON THE RADIO)	Roxy Music (Polydor)
5	6	OOPS UPSIDE YOUR HEAD	Gap Band (Mercury)
7	7	GIVE ME THE NIGHT	George Benson (Warner Bros)
11	8	FUNKIN' FOR JAMAICA	Tom Browne (Arista)
18	9	TOM HARK	Piranhas (Sire)
6	10	MORE THAN I CAN SAY	Leo Sayer (Chrysalis)
12	11	MARIANA	Gibson Brothers (Island)
4	12	USE IT UP AND WEAR IT OUT	Odyssey (RCA)
-	13	FEELS LIKE I'M IN LOVE	Kelly Marie (Calibre)
22	14	ALL OVER THE WORLD	Electric Light Orchestra (Jet)
17	15	ARE YOU GETTING ENOUGH OF WHAT MAKES YOU HAPPY	Hot Chocolate (RAK)
15	16	LIP UP FATTY	Bad Manners (Magnet)
8	17	BABOOSHKA	Kate Bush (EMI)
-	18	THE SUNSHINE OF YOUR SMILE	Mike Berry (Polydor)
10	19	COULD YOU BE LOVED	Bob Marley & the Wailers (Island)
16	20	PRIVATE LIFE	Grace Jones (Island)
-	21	CAN'T STOP THE MUSIC	Village People (Mercury)
28	22	SLEEPWALK	Ultravox (Chrysalis)
-	23	DREAMIN'	Cliff Richard (EMI)
-	24	IT'S STILL ROCK AND ROLL TO ME	Billy Joel (CBS)
23	25	BANKROBBER	Clash (CBS)
-	26	MODERN GIRL	Sheena Easton (EMI)
-	27	CIRCUS GAMES	Skids (Virgin)
-	28	A LOVER'S HOLIDAY/GLOW OF LOVE	Change (WEA)
14	29	XANADU	Olivia Newton-John & Electric Light Orchestra (Jet)
-	30	PARANOID	Black Sabbath (Vertigo)

30 August 1980

4	1	ASHES TO ASHES	David Bowie (RCA)
-	2	START	Jam (Polydor)
1	3	THE WINNER TAKES IT ALL	Abba (Epic)
3	4	9 TO 5	Sheena Easton (EMI)
9	5	TOM HARK	Piranhas (Sire)
2	6	UPSIDE DOWN	Diana Ross (Motown)
6	7	OOPS UPSIDE YOUR HEAD	Gap Band (Mercury)
13	8	FEELS LIKE I'M IN LOVE	Kelly Marie (Calibre)
5	9	OH YEAH (ON THE RADIO)	Roxy Music (Polydor)
18	10	THE SUNSHINE OF YOUR SMILE	Mike Berry (Polydor)
7	11	GIVE ME THE NIGHT	George Benson (Warner Bros)
14	12	ALL OVER THE WORLD	Electric Light Orchestra (Jet)
8	13	FUNKIN' FOR JAMAICA	Tom Browne (Arista)
23	14	DREAMIN'	Cliff Richard (EMI)
11	15	MARIANA	Gibson Brothers (Island)
20	16	PRIVATE LIFE	Grace Jones (Island)
10	17	MORE THAN I CAN SAY	Leo Sayer (Chrysalis)
26	18	MODERN GIRL	Sheena Easton (EMI)
21	19	CAN'T STOP THE MUSIC	Village People (Mercury)
16	20	LIP UP FATTY	Bad Manners (Magnet)
-	21	BIKO	Peter Gabriel (Charisma)
25	22	BANKROBBER	Clash (CBS)
-	23	YOU GOTTA BE A HUSTLER IF YOU WANNA GET ON	Sue Wilkinson (Cheapskate)
-	24	I DIE: YOU DIE	Gary Numan (Beggars Banquet)
-	25	BEST FRIEND/STAND DOWN MARGARET	Beat (Go Feet)
-	26	THERE THERE MY DEAR	Dexy's Midnight Runners (Late Night Feelings)
-	27	MARIE MARIE	Shakin' Stevens (Epic)
-	28	A WALK IN THE PARK	Nick Straker Band (CBS)
-	29	EIGHTH DAY	Hazel O'Connor (A&M)
24	30	IT'S STILL ROCK AND ROLL TO ME	Billy Joel (CBS)

6 September 1980

1	1	ASHES TO ASHES	David Bowie (RCA)
2	2	START	Jam (Polydor)
4	3	9 TO 5	Sheena Easton (EMI)
8	4	FEELS LIKE I'M IN LOVE	Kelly Marie (Calibre)
24	5	I DIE: YOU DIE	Gary Numan (Beggars Banquet)
5	6	TOM HARK	Piranhas (Sire)
10	7	THE SUNSHINE OF YOUR SMILE	Mike Berry (Polydor)
6	8	UPSIDE DOWN	Diana Ross (Motown)
7	9	OOPS UPSIDE YOUR HEAD	Gap Band (Mercury)
3	10	THE WINNER TAKES IT ALL	Abba (Epic)
29	11	EIGHTH DAY	Hazel O'Connor (A&M)
14	12	DREAMIN'	Cliff Richard (EMI)
11	13	GIVE ME THE NIGHT	George Benson (Warner Bros)
18	14	MODERN GIRL	Sheena Easton (EMI)
22	15	BANKROBBER	Clash (CBS)
19	16	CAN'T STOP THE MUSIC	Village People (Mercury)
9	17	OH YEAH (ON THE RADIO)	Roxy Music (Polydor)
12	18	ALL OVER THE WORLD	Electric Light Orchestra (Jet)
30	19	IT'S STILL ROCK AND ROLL TO ME	Billy Joel (CBS)
13	20	FUNKIN' FOR JAMAICA	Tom Browne (Arista)
25	21	BEST FRIEND/STAND DOWN MARGARET	Beat (Go Feet)
-	22	I WANT TO BE STRAIGHT	Ian Dury & the Blockheads (Stiff)
20	23	LIP UP FATTY	Bad Manners (Magnet)
27	24	MARIE MARIE	Shakin' Stevens (Epic)
-	25	IT'S ONLY LOVE/BEYOND THE REEF	Elvis Presley (RCA)
-	26	I OWE YOU ONE	Shalamar (Solar)
-	27	MAGIC	Olivia Newton-John (Jet)
17	28	MORE THAN I CAN SAY	Leo Sayer (Chrysalis)
-	29	PARANOID	Black Sabbath (Vertigo)
23	30	YOU GOTTA BE A HUSTLER IF YOU WANNA GET ON	Sue Wilkinson (Cheapskate)

13 September 1980

2	1	START	Jam (Polydor)
1	2	ASHES TO ASHES	David Bowie (RCA)
4	3	FEELS LIKE I'M IN LOVE	Kelly Marie (Calibre)
11	4	EIGHTH DAY	Hazel O'Connor (A&M)
3	5	9 TO 5	Sheena Easton (EMI)
5	6	I DIE: YOU DIE	Gary Numan (Beggars Banquet)
7	7	THE SUNSHINE OF YOUR SMILE	Mike Berry (Polydor)
6	8	TOM HARK	Piranhas (Sire)
12	9	DREAMIN'	Cliff Richard (EMI)
14	10	MODERN GIRL	Sheena Easton (EMI)
16	11	CAN'T STOP THE MUSIC	Village People (Mercury)
15	12	BANKROBBER	Clash (CBS)
10	13	THE WINNER TAKES IT ALL	Abba (Epic)
-	14	ONE DAY I'LL FLY AWAY	Randy Crawford (Warner Bros)
25	15	IT'S ONLY LOVE/BEYOND THE REEF	Elvis Presley (RCA)
19	16	IT'S STILL ROCK AND ROLL TO ME	Billy Joel (CBS)
13	17	GIVE ME THE NIGHT	George Benson (Warner Bros)
22	18	I WANT TO BE STRAIGHT	Ian Dury & the Blockheads (Stiff)
9	19	OOPS UPSIDE YOUR HEAD	Gap Band (Mercury)
24	20	MARIE MARIE	Shakin' Stevens (Epic)
8	21	UPSIDE DOWN	Diana Ross (Motown)
18	22	ALL OVER THE WORLD	Electric Light Orchestra (Jet)
29	23	PARANOID	Black Sabbath (Vertigo)
-	24	A WALK IN THE PARK	Nick Straker Band (CBS)
26	25	I OWE YOU ONE	Shalamar (Solar)
21	26	BEST FRIEND/STAND DOWN MARGARET	Beat (Go Feet)
17	27	OH YEAH (ON THE RADIO)	Roxy Music (Polydor)
-	28	SEARCHING	Change (WEA)
-	29	UNITED	Judas Priest (CBS)
30	30	YOU GOTTA BE A HUSTLER IF YOU WANNA GET ON	Sue Wilkinson (Cheapskate)

David Bowie's *Ashes To Ashes*, which continued – albeit obliquely – his Major Tom saga from *Space Oddity*, gave him his first chart-topper since the latter title's 1975 reissue. An unlikely return to the Top 30 came from Mike Berry, who had last charted in 1963; his ballad *The Sunshine Of Your Smile* was produced by one-time member of his Outlaws backing group Chas Hodges, now half of Chas & Dave. Berry was more normally found acting in 1980, moving from TV's *Worzel Gummidge* to *Are You Being Served?*

September – October 1980

last week	this week	20 September 1980
14	1	ONE DAY I'LL FLY AWAY — Randy Crawford (Warner Bros)
3	2	FEELS LIKE I'M IN LOVE — Kelly Marie (Calibre)
1	3	START — Jam (Polydor)
2	4	ASHES TO ASHES — David Bowie (RCA)
15	5	IT'S ONLY LOVE/BEYOND THE REEF — Elvis Presley (RCA)
4	6	EIGHTH DAY — Hazel O'Connor (A&M)
5	7	9 TO 5 — Sheena Easton (EMI)
9	8	DREAMIN' — Cliff Richard (EMI)
7	9	THE SUNSHINE OF YOUR SMILE — Mike Berry (Polydor)
12	10	BANKROBBER — Clash (CBS)
6	11	I DIE: YOU DIE — Gary Numan (Beggars Banquet)
10	12	MODERN GIRL — Sheena Easton (EMI)
-	13	MASTERBLASTER (JAMMIN') — Stevie Wonder (Motown)
7	14	TOM HARK — Piranhas (Sire)
-	15	ANOTHER ONE BITES THE DUST — Queen (EMI)
16	16	IT'S STILL ROCK AND ROLL TO ME — Billy Joel (CBS)
11	17	CAN'T STOP THE MUSIC — Village People (Mercury)
18	18	I WANT TO BE STRAIGHT — Ian Dury & the Blockheads (Stiff)
23	19	PARANOID — Black Sabbath (Vertigo)
25	20	I OWE YOU ONE — Shalamar (Solar)
13	21	THE WINNER TAKES IT ALL — Abba (Epic)
-	22	BIG TIME — Rick James (Motown)
-	23	BAGGY TROUSERS — Madness (Stiff)
-	24	DON'T MAKE ME WAIT TOO LONG — Roberta Flack (Atlantic)
19	25	OOPS UPSIDE YOUR HEAD — Gap Band (Mercury)
20	26	MARIE MARIE — Shakin' Stevens (Epic)
24	27	A WALK IN THE PARK — Nick Straker Band (CBS)
28	28	SEARCHING — Change (WEA)
-	29	I GOT YOU — Split Enz (A&M)
21	30	UPSIDE DOWN — Diana Ross (Motown)

last	this	27 September 1980
1	1	ONE DAY I'LL FLY AWAY — Randy Crawford (Warner Bros)
13	2	MASTERBLASTER (JAMMIN') — Stevie Wonder (Motown)
5	3	IT'S ONLY LOVE/BEYOND THE REEF — Elvis Presley (RCA)
2	4	FEELS LIKE I'M IN LOVE — Kelly Marie (Calibre)
12	5	MODERN GIRL — Sheena Easton (EMI)
15	6	ANOTHER ONE BITES THE DUST — Queen (EMI)
6	7	EIGHTH DAY — Hazel O'Connor (A&M)
4	8	ASHES TO ASHES — David Bowie (RCA)
3	9	START — Jam (Polydor)
8	10	DREAMIN' — Cliff Richard (EMI)
23	11	BAGGY TROUSERS — Madness (Stiff)
9	12	THE SUNSHINE OF YOUR SMILE — Mike Berry (Polydor)
7	13	9 TO 5 — Sheena Easton (EMI)
19	14	PARANOID — Black Sabbath (Vertigo)
17	15	CAN'T STOP THE MUSIC — Village People (Mercury)
-	16	DON'T STAND SO CLOSE TO ME — Police (A&M)
16	17	IT'S STILL ROCK AND ROLL TO ME — Billy Joel (CBS)
-	18	MY OLD PIANO — Diana Ross (Motown)
-	19	D.I.S.C.O. — Ottawan (Carrere)
10	20	BANKROBBER — Clash (CBS)
11	21	I DIE: YOU DIE — Gary Numan (Beggars Banquet)
14	22	TOM HARK — Piranhas (Sire)
29	23	I GOT YOU — Split Enz (A&M)
22	24	BIG TIME — Rick James (Motown)
-	25	BEST FRIEND/STAND DOWN MARGARET — Beat (Go Feet)
18	26	I WANT TO BE STRAIGHT — Ian Dury & the Blockheads (Stiff)
20	27	I OWE YOU ONE — Shalamar (Solar)
26	28	MARIE MARIE — Shakin' Stevens (Epic)
28	29	SEARCHING — Change (WEA)
-	30	GENERALS & MAJORS/DON'T LOSE YOUR TEMPER — XTC (Virgin)

last	this	4 October 1980
16	1	DON'T STAND SO CLOSE TO ME — Police (A&M)
2	2	MASTERBLASTER (JAMMIN') — Stevie Wonder (Motown)
1	3	ONE DAY I'LL FLY AWAY — Randy Crawford (Warner Bros)
11	4	BAGGY TROUSERS — Madness (Stiff)
18	5	MY OLD PIANO — Diana Ross (Motown)
4	6	FEELS LIKE I'M IN LOVE — Kelly Marie (Calibre)
6	7	ANOTHER ONE BITES THE DUST — Queen (EMI)
19	8	D.I.S.C.O. — Ottawan (Carrere)
3	9	IT'S ONLY LOVE/BEYOND THE REEF — Elvis Presley (RCA)
5	10	MODERN GIRL — Sheena Easton (EMI)
10	11	DREAMIN' — Cliff Richard (EMI)
7	12	EIGHTH DAY — Hazel O'Connor (A&M)
9	13	START — Jam (Polydor)
17	14	IT'S STILL ROCK AND ROLL TO ME — Billy Joel (CBS)
-	15	THREE LITTLE BIRDS — Bob Marley & the Wailers (Island)
27	16	I OWE YOU ONE — Shalamar (Solar)
-	17	AMIGO — Black Slate (Ensign)
29	18	SEARCHING — Change (WEA)
12	19	THE SUNSHINE OF YOUR SMILE — Mike Berry (Polydor)
-	20	STEREOTYPE/INTERNATIONAL JET SET — Specials (2 Tone)
8	21	ASHES TO ASHES — David Bowie (RCA)
14	22	PARANOID — Black Sabbath (Vertigo)
13	23	9 TO 5 — Sheena Easton (EMI)
23	24	I GOT YOU — Split Enz (A&M)
-	25	KILLER ON THE LOOSE — Thin Lizzy (Vertigo)
-	26	THE WANDERER — Donna Summer (Warner Bros./Geffen)
-	27	IF YOU'RE LOOKIN' FOR A WAY OUT — Odyssey (RCA)
-	28	YOU'RE LYING — Linx (Chrysalis)
-	29	WHAT'S IN A KISS — Gilbert O'Sullivan (CBS)
-	30	LOVE X LOVE — George Benson (Warner Bros)

last	this	11 October 1980
1	1	DON'T STAND SO CLOSE TO ME — Police (A&M)
2	2	MASTERBLASTER (JAMMIN') — Stevie Wonder (Motown)
8	3	D.I.S.C.O. — Ottawan (Carrere)
5	4	MY OLD PIANO — Diana Ross (Motown)
4	5	BAGGY TROUSERS — Madness (Stiff)
3	6	ONE DAY I'LL FLY AWAY — Randy Crawford (Warner Bros)
17	7	AMIGO — Black Slate (Ensign)
7	8	ANOTHER ONE BITES THE DUST — Queen (EMI)
18	9	SEARCHING — Change (WEA)
-	10	CASANOVA — Coffee (De-Lite)
15	11	THREE LITTLE BIRDS — Bob Marley & the Wailers (Island)
16	12	I OWE YOU ONE — Shalamar (Solar)
28	13	YOU'RE LYING — Linx (Chrysalis)
25	14	KILLER ON THE LOOSE — Thin Lizzy (Vertigo)
9	15	IT'S ONLY LOVE/BEYOND THE REEF — Elvis Presley (RCA)
24	16	I GOT YOU — Split Enz (A&M)
6	17	FEELS LIKE I'M IN LOVE — Kelly Marie (Calibre)
30	18	LOVE X LOVE — George Benson (Warner Bros)
-	19	TROUBLE — Gillan (Virgin)
27	20	IF YOU'RE LOOKIN' FOR A WAY OUT — Odyssey (RCA)
-	21	ALL OUT OF LOVE — Air Supply (Arista)
20	22	STEREOTYPE/INTERNATIONAL JET SET — Specials (2 Tone)
14	23	IT'S STILL ROCK AND ROLL TO ME — Billy Joel (CBS)
-	24	WHEN YOU ASK ABOUT LOVE — Matchbox (Magnet)
-	25	WOMAN IN LOVE — Barbra Streisand (CBS)
12	26	EIGHTH DAY — Hazel O'Connor (A&M)
-	27	ET LES OISEAUX CHATAIENT (AND THE BIRDS WERE SINGING) — Sweet People (Polydor)
11	28	DREAMIN' — Cliff Richard (EMI)
-	29	PARTY LIGHTS — Gap Band (Mercury)
-	30	GOTTA PULL MYSELF TOGETHER — Nolans (Epic)

Elvis Presley had his biggest posthumous hit since *Way Down* with the double-sider *It's Only Love/Beyond The Reef*. Curiously, *It's Only Love* had originally been such a poor seller when issued as a single in the US in 1971, that it had been thought not worthy of UK release at that time! Sheena Easton, meanwhile, joined the tiny elite of female artists to enjoy two simultaneous Top 10 hits, when her reactivated first single *Modern Girl* joined *9 To 5* in the winner's circle.

October – November 1980

last week	this week	18 October 1980
1	1	DON'T STAND SO CLOSE TO ME Police (A&M)
5	2	BAGGY TROUSERS Madness (Stiff)
3	3	D.I.S.C.O. Ottawan (Carrere)
2	4	MASTERBLASTER (JAMMIN') Stevie Wonder (Motown)
4	5	MY OLD PIANO Diana Ross (Motown)
20	6	IF YOU'RE LOOKIN' FOR A WAY OUT Odyssey (RCA)
7	7	AMIGO Black Slate (Ensign)
27	8	ET LES OISEAUX CHATAIENT (AND THE BIRDS WERE SINGING) Sweet People (Polydor)
24	9	WHEN YOU ASK ABOUT LOVE Matchbox (Magnet)
14	10	KILLER ON THE LOOSE Thin Lizzy (Vertigo)
19	11	TROUBLE Gillan (Virgin)
25	12	WOMAN IN LOVE Barbra Streisand (CBS)
6	13	ONE DAY I'LL FLY AWAY Randy Crawford (Warner Bros)
22	14	STEREOTYPE/INTERNATIONAL JET SET Specials (2 Tone)
-	15	WHAT YOU'RE PROPOSING Status Quo (Vertigo)
9	16	SEARCHING Change (WEA)
11	17	THREE LITTLE BIRDS Bob Marley & the Wailers (Island)
10	18	CASANOVA Coffee (De-Lite)
16	19	I GOT YOU Split Enz (A&M)
17	20	FEELS LIKE I'M IN LOVE Kelly Marie (Calibre)
21	21	LOVE X LOVE George Benson (Warner Bros)
8	22	ANOTHER ONE BITES THE DUST Queen (EMI)
-	23	ENOLA GAY Orchestral Manoeuvres In The Dark (Dindisc)
-	24	ARMY DREAMERS Kate Bush (EMI)
29	25	PARTY LIGHTS Gap Band (Mercury)
13	26	YOU'RE LYING Linx (Chrysalis)
-	27	SHE'S SO COLD Rolling Stones (Rolling Stones)
30	28	GOTTA PULL MYSELF TOGETHER Nolans (Epic)
15	29	IT'S ONLY LOVE/BEYOND THE REEF Elvis Presley (RCA)
12	30	I OWE YOU ONE Shalamar (Solar)

last week	this week	25 October 1980
1	1	DON'T STAND SO CLOSE TO ME Police (A&M)
2	2	D.I.S.C.O. Ottawan (Carrere)
8	3	ET LES OISEAUX CHATAIENT (AND THE BIRDS WERE SINGING) Sweet People (Polydor)
12	4	WOMAN IN LOVE Barbra Streisand (CBS)
2	5	BAGGY TROUSERS Madness (Stiff)
15	6	WHAT YOU'RE PROPOSING Status Quo (Vertigo)
4	7	MASTERBLASTER (JAMMIN') Stevie Wonder (Motown)
6	8	IF YOU'RE LOOKIN' FOR A WAY OUT Odyssey (RCA)
9	9	WHEN YOU ASK ABOUT LOVE Matchbox (Magnet)
7	10	AMIGO Black Slate (Ensign)
18	11	CASANOVA Coffee (De-Lite)
5	12	MY OLD PIANO Diana Ross (Motown)
28	13	GOTTA PULL MYSELF TOGETHER Nolans (Epic)
26	14	YOU'RE LYING Linx (Chrysalis)
10	15	KILLER ON THE LOOSE Thin Lizzy (Vertigo)
21	16	LOVE X LOVE George Benson (Warner Bros)
23	17	ENOLA GAY Orchestral Manoeuvres In The Dark (Dindisc)
-	18	ALL OUT OF LOVE Air Supply (Arista)
16	19	SEARCHING Change (WEA)
24	20	ARMY DREAMERS Kate Bush (EMI)
17	21	THREE LITTLE BIRDS Bob Marley & the Wailers (Island)
-	22	WHAT'S IN A KISS Gilbert O'Sullivan (CBS)
14	23	STEREOTYPE/INTERNATIONAL JET SET Specials (2 Tone)
-	24	LET ME TALK Earth Wind & Fire (CBS)
25	25	SPECIAL BREW Bad Manners (Magnet)
11	26	TROUBLE Gillan (Virgin)
25	27	PARTY LIGHTS Gap Band (Mercury)
13	28	ONE DAY I'LL FLY AWAY Randy Crawford (Warner Bros)
-	29	LOVELY ONE Jacksons (Epic)
-	30	I NEED YOUR LOVIN' Teena Marie (Motown)

last week	this week	1 November 1980
4	1	WOMAN IN LOVE Barbra Streisand (CBS)
6	2	WHAT YOU'RE PROPOSING Status Quo (Vertigo)
2	3	D.I.S.C.O. Ottawan (Carrere)
9	4	WHEN YOU ASK ABOUT LOVE Matchbox (Magnet)
5	5	BAGGY TROUSERS Madness (Stiff)
1	6	DON'T STAND SO CLOSE TO ME Police (A&M)
16	7	LOVE X LOVE George Benson (Warner Bros)
8	8	IF YOU'RE LOOKIN' FOR A WAY OUT Odyssey (RCA)
3	9	ET LES OISEAUX CHATAIENT (AND THE BIRDS WERE SINGING) Sweet People (Polydor)
25	10	SPECIAL BREW Bad Manners (Magnet)
17	10	ENOLA GAY Orchestral Manoeuvres In The Dark (Dindisc)
13	12	GOTTA PULL MYSELF TOGETHER Nolans (Epic)
11	13	CASANOVA Coffee (De-Lite)
-	14	DOG EAT DOG Adam & the Ants (CBS)
12	15	MY OLD PIANO Diana Ross (Motown)
18	16	ALL OUT OF LOVE Air Supply (Arista)
20	17	ARMY DREAMERS Kate Bush (EMI)
24	18	LET ME TALK Earth Wind & Fire (CBS)
-	19	ONE MAN WOMAN Sheena Easton (EMI)
7	20	MASTERBLASTER (JAMMIN') Stevie Wonder (Motown)
-	21	LONDON TOWN Light Of The World (Ensign)
21	22	THREE LITTLE BIRDS Bob Marley & the Wailers (Island)
29	23	LOVELY ONE Jacksons (Epic)
-	24	TOWERS OF LONDON XTC (Virgin)
-	25	SUDDENLY Olivia Newton-John & Cliff Richard (Jet)
-	26	NEVER KNEW LOVE LIKE THIS BEFORE Stephanie Mills (20th Century)
14	27	YOU'RE LYING Linx (Chrysalis)
22	28	WHAT'S IN A KISS Gilbert O'Sullivan (CBS)
30	29	I NEED YOUR LOVIN' Teena Marie (Motown)
-	30	WHY DO LOVERS BREAK EACH OTHERS HEARTS Showaddywaddy (Arista)

last week	this week	8 November 1980
1	1	WOMAN IN LOVE Barbra Streisand (CBS)
2	2	WHAT YOU'RE PROPOSING Status Quo (Vertigo)
4	3	WHEN YOU ASK ABOUT LOVE Matchbox (Magnet)
10	4	ENOLA GAY Orchestral Manoeuvres In The Dark (Dindisc)
10	5	SPECIAL BREW Bad Manners (Magnet)
3	6	D.I.S.C.O. Ottawan (Carrere)
14	7	DOG EAT DOG Adam & the Ants (CBS)
5	8	BAGGY TROUSERS Madness (Stiff)
-	9	FASHION David Bowie (RCA)
8	10	IF YOU'RE LOOKIN' FOR A WAY OUT Odyssey (RCA)
16	11	ALL OUT OF LOVE Air Supply (Arista)
12	12	GOTTA PULL MYSELF TOGETHER Nolans (Epic)
7	13	LOVE X LOVE George Benson (Warner Bros)
19	14	ONE MAN WOMAN Sheena Easton (EMI)
6	15	DON'T STAND SO CLOSE TO ME Police (A&M)
17	16	ARMY DREAMERS Kate Bush (EMI)
25	17	SUDDENLY Olivia Newton-John & Cliff Richard (Jet)
13	18	CASANOVA Coffee (De-Lite)
28	19	WHAT'S IN A KISS Gilbert O'Sullivan (CBS)
-	20	LOVING JUST FOR FUN Kelly Marie (Calibre)
9	21	ET LES OISEAUX CHATAIENT (AND THE BIRDS WERE SINGING) Sweet People (Polydor)
-	22	THE EARTH DIES SCREAMING /DREAM A LIE UB40 (Graduate)
23	23	LOVELY ONE Jacksons (Epic)
27	24	YOU'RE LYING Linx (Chrysalis)
30	25	WHY DO LOVERS BREAK EACH OTHERS HEARTS Showaddywaddy (Arista)
-	26	FALCON RAH Band (DJM)
-	27	THE TIDE IS HIGH Blondie (Chrysalis)
26	28	NEVER KNEW LOVE LIKE THIS BEFORE Stephanie Mills (20th Century)
18	29	LET ME TALK Earth Wind & Fire (CBS)
-	30	CELEBRATION Kool & the Gang (De-Lite)

The Police had their biggest seller yet with *Don't Stand So Close To Me*, a song with a heavyweight lyric concerning a teacher compromised by feelings for a pupil. In outrageous contrast, Ottowan's *D.I.S.C.O.* was the most mindless expression of Euro-bopping dancefloor hedonism yet to enrage the music press. Barbra Streisand's chart-topping *Woman In Love*, was not the former Frankie Laine Number One, but was a song taken from her album *Guilty*, a project written and co-produced by the Bee Gees.

November – December 1980

15 November 1980

Last	This	Title	Artist (Label)
1	1	WOMAN IN LOVE	Barbra Streisand (CBS)
27	2	THE TIDE IS HIGH	Blondie (Chrysalis)
5	3	SPECIAL BREW	Bad Manners (Magnet)
7	4	DOG EAT DOG	Adam & the Ants (CBS)
2	5	WHAT YOU'RE PROPOSING	Status Quo (Vertigo)
9	6	FASHION	David Bowie (RCA)
3	7	WHEN YOU ASK ABOUT LOVE	Matchbox (Magnet)
4	8	ENOLA GAY	Orchestral Manoeuvres In The Dark (Dindisc)
17	9	SUDDENLY	Olivia Newton-John & Cliff Richard (Jet)
10	10	IF YOU'RE LOOKIN' FOR A WAY OUT	Odyssey (RCA)
14	11	ONE MAN WOMAN	Sheena Easton (EMI)
28	12	NEVER KNEW LOVE LIKE THIS BEFORE	Stephanie Mills (20th Century)
-	13	(JUST LIKE) STARTING OVER	John Lennon (Geffen)
-	14	I COULD BE SO GOOD FOR YOU	Dennis Waterman (EMI)
11	15	ALL OUT OF LOVE	Air Supply (Arista)
-	16	THE SAME OLD SCENE	Roxy Music (Polydor)
-	17	PASSION	Rod Stewart (Riva)
6	18	D.I.S.C.O.	Ottawan (Carrere)
-	19	ACE OF SPADES	Motorhead (Bronze)
22	20	THE EARTH DIES SCREAMING /DREAM A LIE	UB40 (Graduate)
12	21	GOTTA PULL MYSELF TOGETHER	Nolans (Epic)
8	22	BAGGY TROUSERS	Madness (Stiff)
23	23	LOVELY ONE	Jacksons (Epic)
15	24	DON'T STAND SO CLOSE TO ME	Police (A&M)
20	25	LOVING JUST FOR FUN	Kelly Marie (Calibre)
16	26	ARMY DREAMERS	Kate Bush (EMI)
13	27	LOVE X LOVE	George Benson (Warner Bros)
30	28	CELEBRATION	Kool & the Gang (De-Lite)
-	29	SUPER TROUPER	Abba (Epic)
-	30	MILES AWAY	John Foxx (Virgin)

22 November 1980

Last	This	Title	Artist (Label)
2	1	THE TIDE IS HIGH	Blondie (Chrysalis)
14	2	I COULD BE SO GOOD FOR YOU	Dennis Waterman (EMI)
1	3	WOMAN IN LOVE	Barbra Streisand (CBS)
3	4	SPECIAL BREW	Bad Manners (Magnet)
29	5	SUPER TROUPER	Abba (Epic)
6	6	FASHION	David Bowie (RCA)
4	7	DOG EAT DOG	Adam & the Ants (CBS)
12	8	NEVER KNEW LOVE LIKE THIS BEFORE	Stephanie Mills (20th Century)
16	9	THE SAME OLD SCENE	Roxy Music (Polydor)
5	10	WHAT YOU'RE PROPOSING	Status Quo (Vertigo)
8	11	ENOLA GAY	Orchestral Manoeuvres In The Dark (Dindisc)
20	12	THE EARTH DIES SCREAMING /DREAM A LIE	UB40 (Graduate)
28	13	CELEBRATION	Kool & the Gang (De-Lite)
10	14	IF YOU'RE LOOKIN' FOR A WAY OUT	Odyssey (RCA)
13	15	(JUST LIKE) STARTING OVER	John Lennon (Geffen)
19	16	ACE OF SPADES	Motorhead (Bronze)
7	17	WHEN YOU ASK ABOUT LOVE	Matchbox (Magnet)
-	18	I'M COMING OUT	Diana Ross (Motown)
17	19	PASSION	Rod Stewart (Riva)
-	20	I LIKE (WHAT YOU'RE DOING TO ME)	Young & Company (Excalibur)
-	21	FEELS LIKE THE RIGHT TIME	Shakatak (Polydor)
11	22	ONE MAN WOMAN	Sheena Easton (EMI)
-	23	TO CUT A LONG STORY SHORT	Spandau Ballet (Reformation)
9	24	SUDDENLY	Olivia Newton-John & Cliff Richard (Jet)
15	25	ALL OUT OF LOVE	Air Supply (Arista)
21	26	GOTTA PULL MYSELF TOGETHER	Nolans (Epic)
-	27	BOURGIE BOURGIE	Gladys Knight & the Pips (CBS)
-	28	DO YOU FEEL MY LOVE?	Eddy Grant (Ensign)
-	29	LADY	Kenny Rogers (United Artists)
18	30	D.I.S.C.O.	Ottawan (Carrere)

29 November 1980

Last	This	Title	Artist (Label)
1	1	THE TIDE IS HIGH	Blondie (Chrysalis)
5	2	SUPER TROUPER	Abba (Epic)
8	3	NEVER KNEW LOVE LIKE THIS BEFORE	Stephanie Mills (20th Century)
2	4	I COULD BE SO GOOD FOR YOU	Dennis Waterman (EMI)
6	5	FASHION	David Bowie (RCA)
3	6	WOMAN IN LOVE	Barbra Streisand (CBS)
13	7	CELEBRATION	Kool & the Gang (De-Lite)
4	8	SPECIAL BREW	Bad Manners (Magnet)
7	9	DOG EAT DOG	Adam & the Ants (CBS)
15	10	(JUST LIKE) STARTING OVER	John Lennon (Geffen)
-	11	BANANA REPUBLIC	Boomtown Rats (Ensign)
11	12	ENOLA GAY	Orchestral Manoeuvres In Th Dark (Dindisc)
-	13	EMBARRASSMENT	Madness (Stiff)
18	14	I'M COMING OUT	Diana Ross (Motown)
23	15	TO CUT A LONG STORY SHORT	Spandau Ballet (Reformation)
9	16	THE SAME OLD SCENE	Roxy Music (Polydor)
10	17	WHAT YOU'RE PROPOSING	Status Quo (Vertigo)
16	18	ACE OF SPADES	Motorhead (Bronze)
19	19	PASSION	Rod Stewart (Riva)
12	20	THE EARTH DIES SCREAMING/ DREAM A LIE	UB40 (Graduate)
20	21	I LIKE (WHAT YOU'RE DOING TO ME)	Young & Company (Excalibur)
28	22	DO YOU FEEL MY LOVE?	Eddy Grant (Ensign)
29	23	LADY	Kenny Rogers (United Artists)
24	24	SUDDENLY	Olivia Newton-John & Cliff Richard (Jet)
17	25	WHEN YOU ASK ABOUT LOVE	Matchbox (Magnet)
-	26	DON'T WALK AWAY	Electric Light Orchestra (Jet)
14	27	IF YOU'RE LOOKIN' FOR A WAY OUT	Odyssey (RCA)
-	28	HUNGRY HEART	Bruce Springsteen (CBS)
-	29	FALCON	RAH Band (DJM)
25	30	ALL OUT OF LOVE	Air Supply (Arista)

6 December 1980

Last	This	Title	Artist (Label)
2	1	SUPER TROUPER	Abba (Epic)
1	2	THE TIDE IS HIGH	Blondie (Chrysalis)
4	3	I COULD BE SO GOOD FOR YOU	Dennis Waterman (EMI)
11	4	BANANA REPUBLIC	Boomtown Rats (Ensign)
7	5	CELEBRATION	Kool & the Gang (De-Lite)
3	6	NEVER KNEW LOVE LIKE THIS BEFORE	Stephanie Mills (20th Century)
5	7	FASHION	David Bowie (RCA)
15	8	TO CUT A LONG STORY SHORT	Spandau Ballet (Reformation)
13	9	EMBARRASSMENT	Madness (Stiff)
6	10	WOMAN IN LOVE	Barbra Streisand (CBS)
9	11	(JUST LIKE) STARTING OVER	John Lennon (Geffen)
22	12	DO YOU FEEL MY LOVE?	Eddy Grant (Ensign)
19	13	PASSION	Rod Stewart (Riva)
23	14	LADY	Kenny Rogers (United Artists)
14	15	I'M COMING OUT	Diana Ross (Motown)
20	16	THE EARTH DIES SCREAMING /DREAM A LIE	UB40 (Graduate)
21	17	I LIKE (WHAT YOU'RE DOING TO ME)	Young & Company (Excalibur)
26	18	DON'T WALK AWAY	Electric Light Orchestra (Jet)
16	19	THE SAME OLD SCENE	Roxy Music (Polydor)
8	20	SPECIAL BREW	Bad Manners (Magnet)
12	21	ENOLA GAY	Orchestral Manoeuvres In The Dark (Dindisc)
9	22	DOG EAT DOG	Adam & the Ants (CBS)
-	23	LOVE ON THE ROCKS	Neil Diamond (Capitol)
-	24	RABBIT	Chas & Dave (Rockney)
-	25	ROCK 'N' ROLL AIN'T NO NOISE POLLUTION	AC/DC (Atlantic)
-	26	LONELY TOGETHER	Barry Manilow (Arista)
25	27	WHEN YOU ASK ABOUT LOVE	Matchbox (Magnet)
27	28	IF YOU'RE LOOKIN' FOR A WAY OUT	Odyssey (RCA)
-	29	BLUE MOON	Showaddywaddy (Arista)
-	30	RUNAWAY BOYS	Stray Cats (Arista)

While Blondie and Abba, not for the first time, collided at the chart-top, actor Dennis Waterman very nearly also had a Number One hit with *I Could Be So Good For You*, the song written by himself and Gerard Kenny as the theme to the hugely successful TV series *Minder*, in which Waterman starred with George Cole. Spandau Ballet, the trendiest new group among stylish name-droppers, debuted with *To Cut A Long Story Short*, as did Bruce Springsteen with *Hungry Heart*.

last week	this week	13 December 1980
1	1	SUPER TROUPER Abba (Epic)
4	2	BANANA REPUBLIC Boomtown Rats (Ensign)
9	3	EMBARRASSMENT Madness (Stiff)
2	4	THE TIDE IS HIGH Blondie (Chrysalis)
3	5	I COULD BE SO GOOD FOR YOU Dennis Waterman (EMI)
-	6	STOP THE CAVALRY Jona Lewie (Stiff)
8	7	TO CUT A LONG STORY SHORT Spandau Ballet (Reformation)
12	8	DO YOU FEEL MY LOVE? Eddy Grant (Ensign)
5	9	CELEBRATION Kool & the Gang (De-Lite)
11	10	(JUST LIKE) STARTING OVER John Lennon (Geffen)
16	11	THE EARTH DIES SCREAMING /DREAM A LIE UB40 (Graduate)
-	12	THERE'S NO ONE QUITE LIKE GRANDMA St. Winifred's School Choir (MFP)
6	13	NEVER KNEW LOVE LIKE THIS BEFORE Stephanie Mills (20th Century)
15	14	I'M COMING OUT Diana Ross (Motown)
14	15	LADY Kenny Rogers (United Artists)
30	16	RUNAWAY BOYS Stray Cats (Arista)
-	17	LIES/DON'T DRIVE MY CAR Status Quo (Vertigo)
-	18	FLASH Queen (EMI)
25	19	ROCK 'N' ROLL AIN'T NO NOISE POLLUTION AC/DC (Atlantic)
-	20	DE DO DO DO, DE DA DA DA Police (A&M)
7	21	FASHION David Bowie (RCA)
10	22	WOMAN IN LOVE Barbra Streisand (CBS)
18	23	DON'T WALK AWAY Electric Light Orchestra (Jet)
-	24	ACE OF SPADES Motorhead (Bronze)
-	25	THE CALL UP Clash (CBS)
17	26	I LIKE (WHAT YOU'RE GIVING ME) Young & Company (Excalibur)
22	27	DOG EAT DOG Adam & the Ants (CBS)
23	28	LOVE ON THE ROCKS Neil Diamond (Capitol)
24	29	RABBIT Chas & Dave (Rockney)
-	30	DIE YOUNG Black Sabbath (Vertigo)

		20 December 1980
6	1	STOP THE CAVALRY Jona Lewie (Stiff)
1	2	SUPER TROUPER Abba (Epic)
12	3	THERE'S NO ONE QUITE LIKE GRANDMA St. Winifred's School Choir (MFP)
10	4	(JUST LIKE) STARTING OVER John Lennon (Geffen)
3	5	EMBARRASSMENT Madness (Stiff)
20	6	DE DO DO DO, DE DA DA DA Police (A&M)
16	7	RUNAWAY BOYS Stray Cats (Arista)
2	8	BANANA REPUBLIC Boomtown Rats (Ensign)
7	9	TO CUT A LONG STORY SHORT Spandau Ballet (Reformation)
8	10	DO YOU FEEL MY LOVE? Eddy Grant (Ensign)
15	11	LADY Kenny Rogers (United Artists)
4	12	THE TIDE IS HIGH Blondie (Chrysalis)
17	13	LIES/DON'T DRIVE MY CAR Status Quo (Vertigo)
18	14	FLASH Queen (EMI)
-	15	ANTMUSIC Adam & the Ants (CBS)
9	16	CELEBRATION Kool & the Gang (De-Lite)
28	17	LOVE ON THE ROCKS Neil Diamond (Capitol)
5	18	I COULD BE SO GOOD FOR YOU Dennis Waterman (EMI)
29	19	RABBIT Chas & Dave (Rockney)
19	20	ROCK 'N' ROLL AIN'T NO NOISE POLLUTION AC/DC (Atlantic)
-	21	LONELY TOGETHER Barry Manilow (Arista)
13	22	NEVER KNEW LOVE LIKE THIS BEFORE Stephanie Mills (20th Century)
14	23	I'M COMING OUT Diana Ross (Motown)
23	24	DON'T WALK AWAY Electric Light Orchestra (Jet)
-	25	DECEMBER WILL BE MAGIC AGAIN Kate Bush (EMI)
-	26	TOO NICE TO TALK TO Beat (Go Feet)
11	27	THE EARTH DIES SCREAMING/DREAM A LIE UB40 (Graduate)
21	28	FASHION David Bowie (RCA)
-	29	HEARTBREAK HOTEL Jacksons (Epic)
-	30	MY GIRL Rod Stewart (Riva)

Charting in 1980 and 81 – Generation X

Jona Lewie's *Stop The Cavalry*, a song with just a fleeting reference to Christmas in its lyric, nonetheless seemed to catch the Yuletide mood, and went to Number One. Early Christmas spirit, however, was shattered by the murder of John Lennon on December 8; the immediate chart result was to reverse the decline of his *(Just Like) Starting Over*, which headed for the top. Meanwhile, the big silent majority hit was the St Winifred's school choir song, which filled many a granny's Christmas stocking.

January 1981

John Lennon dominated the first weeks of 1981. EMI reported orders of 300,000 for his 1975 hit single *Imagine* in the wake of his death, and only a week after the current *(Just Like) Starting Over* had moved to the top of the chart, *Imagine* vaulted over it to take four weeks at Number One, with *Happy Xmas (War Is Over)* in hot pursuit, reaching the Top Three. Meanwhile, Queen made the Top 10 with their theme song from the film *Flash Gordon*, for which they wrote the soundtrack.

January – February 1981

31 January 1981

last week	this week		
1	1	IMAGINE	John Lennon (Apple)
2	2	ANTMUSIC	Adam & the Ants (CBS)
-	3	WOMAN	John Lennon (Geffen)
12	4	IN THE AIR TONIGHT	Phil Collins (Virgin)
13	5	YOUNG PARISIANS	Adam & the Ants (Decca)
3	6	DO NOTHING/MAGGIE'S FARM	Specials (2 Tone)
7	7	I AM THE BEAT	Look (MCA)
-	8	RAPTURE	Blondie (Chrysalis)
4	9	TOO NICE TO TALK TO	Beat (Go Feet)
14	10	DON'T STOP THE MUSIC	Yarbrough & Peoples (Mercury)
6	11	FLASH	Queen (EMI)
5	12	I AIN'T GONNA STAND FOR IT	Stevie Wonder (Motown)
-	13	VIENNA	Ultravox (Chrysalis)
17	14	RUNAROUND SUE	Racey (RAK)
18	15	SCARY MONSTERS (AND SUPER CREEPS)	David Bowie (RCA)
8	16	HAPPY XMAS (WAR IS OVER)	John & Yoko/Plastic Ono Band (Apple)
27	17	FADE TO GREY	Visage (Polydor)
20	18	IT'S MY TURN	Diana Ross (Motown)
21	19	OVER THE RAINBOW/YOU BELONG TO ME	Matchbox (Magnet)
15	20	LIES/DON'T DRIVE MY CAR	Status Quo (Vertigo)
9	21	RABBIT	Chas & Dave (Rockney)
-	22	A LITTLE IN LOVE	Cliff Richard (EMI)
25	23	GANGSTERS OF THE GROOVE	Heatwave (GTO)
-	24	ROMEO AND JULIET	Dire Straits (Vertigo)
-	25	THE RETURN OF THE LAS PALMAS 7	Madness (Stiff)
-	26	HITSVILLE UK	Clash (CBS)
11	27	WHO'S GONNA ROCK YOU	Nolans (Epic)
28	28	LORRAINE	Bad Manners (Magnet)
16	29	STOP THE CAVALRY	Jona Lewie (Stiff)
-	30	TWILIGHT CAFE	Susan Fassbender (CBS)

7 February 1981

last week	this week		
4	1	IN THE AIR TONIGHT	Phil Collins (Virgin)
3	2	WOMAN	John Lennon (Geffen)
1	3	IMAGINE	John Lennon (Apple)
8	4	RAPTURE	Blondie (Chrysalis)
13	5	VIENNA	Ultravox (Chrysalis)
10	6	DON'T STOP THE MUSIC	Yarbrough & Peoples (Mercury)
2	7	ANTMUSIC	Adam & the Ants (CBS)
17	8	FADE TO GREY	Visage (Polydor)
7	9	I AM THE BEAT	Look (MCA)
5	10	YOUNG PARISIANS	Adam & the Ants (Decca)
12	11	I AIN'T GONNA STAND FOR IT	Stevie Wonder (Motown)
22	12	A LITTLE IN LOVE	Cliff Richard (EMI)
24	13	ROMEO AND JULIET	Dire Straits (Vertigo)
25	14	THE RETURN OF THE LAS PALMAS 7	Madness (Stiff)
23	15	GANGSTERS OF THE GROOVE	Heatwave (GTO)
-	16	THE FREEZE	Spandau Ballet (Reformation)
-	17	I SURRENDER	Rainbow (Polydor)
14	18	RUNAROUND SUE	Racey (RAK)
6	19	DO NOTHING/MAGGIE'S FARM	Specials (2 Tone)
9	20	TOO NICE TO TALK TO	Beat (Go Feet)
30	21	TWILIGHT CAFE	Susan Fassbender (CBS)
18	22	IT'S MY TURN	Diana Ross (Motown)
-	23	BURN RUBBER ON ME (WHY YOU WANNA HURT ME)	Gap Band (Mercury)
15	24	SCARY MONSTERS (AND SUPER CREEPS)	David Bowie (RCA)
-	25	LORRAINE	Bad Manners (Magnet)
11	26	FLASH	Queen (EMI)
-	27	THE ELEPHANT'S GRAVEYARD (GUILTY)	Boomtown Rats (Ensign)
-	28	JUST WHEN I NEEDED YOU MOST	Barbara Jones (Sonet)
-	29	SGT. ROCK (IS GOING TO HELP ME)	XTC (Virgin)
26	30	HITSVILLE UK	Clash (CBS)

14 February 1981

last week	this week		
1	1	IN THE AIR TONIGHT	Phil Collins (Virgin)
2	2	WOMAN	John Lennon (Geffen)
5	3	VIENNA	Ultravox (Chrysalis)
4	4	RAPTURE	Blondie (Chrysalis)
6	5	DON'T STOP THE MUSIC	Yarbrough & Peoples (Mercury)
3	6	IMAGINE	John Lennon (Apple)
8	7	FADE TO GREY	Visage (Polydor)
-	8	OLDEST SWINGER IN TOWN	Fred Wedlock (Rocket)
13	9	ROMEO AND JULIET	Dire Straits (Vertigo)
10	10	YOUNG PARISIANS	Adam & the Ants (Decca)
14	11	THE RETURN OF THE LAS PALMAS 7	Madness (Stiff)
16	12	THE FREEZE	Spandau Ballet (Reformation)
7	13	ANTMUSIC	Adam & the Ants (CBS)
17	14	I SURRENDER	Rainbow (Polydor)
9	15	I AM THE BEAT	Look (MCA)
-	16	SHADDAP YOU FACE	Joe Dolce Music Theatre (Epic)
12	17	A LITTLE IN LOVE	Cliff Richard (EMI)
21	18	TWILIGHT CAFE	Susan Fassbender (CBS)
23	19	BURN RUBBER ON ME (WHY YOU WANNA HURT ME)	Gap Band (Mercury)
20	20	ROCK THIS TOWN	Stray Cats (Arista)
22	21	IT'S MY TURN	Diana Ross (Motown)
27	22	THE ELEPHANT'S GRAVEYARD (GUILTY)	Boomtown Rats (Ensign)
15	23	GANGSTERS OF THE GROOVE	Heatwave (GTO)
29	24	SGT. ROCK (IS GOING TO HELP ME)	XTC (Virgin)
11	25	I AIN'T GONNA STAND FOR IT	Stevie Wonder (Motown)
-	26	THAT'S ENTERTAINMENT	Jam (Metronome)
28	27	JUST WHEN I NEEDED YOU MOST	Barbara Jones (Sonet)
-	28	I'M IN LOVE WITH A GERMAN FILM STAR	Passions (Polydor)
-	29	SOUTHERN FREEEZ	Freeez (Beggars Banquet)
26	30	FLASH	Queen (EMI)

21 February 1981

last week	this week		
3	1	VIENNA	Ultravox (Chrysalis)
2	2	WOMAN	John Lennon (Geffen)
16	3	SHADDAP YOU FACE	Joe Dolce Music Theatre (Epic)
1	4	IN THE AIR TONIGHT	Phil Collins (Virgin)
8	5	OLDEST SWINGER IN TOWN	Fred Wedlock (Rocket)
14	6	I SURRENDER	Rainbow (Polydor)
4	7	RAPTURE	Blondie (Chrysalis)
6	8	IMAGINE	John Lennon (Apple)
10	9	THE RETURN OF THE LAS PALMAS 7	Madness (Stiff)
9	10	ROMEO AND JULIET	Dire Straits (Vertigo)
20	11	ROCK THIS TOWN	Stray Cats (Arista)
13	12	ANTMUSIC	Adam & the Ants (CBS)
5	13	DON'T STOP THE MUSIC	Yarbrough & Peoples (Mercury)
7	14	FADE TO GREY	Visage (Polydor)
-	15	WE'LL BRING THE HOUSE DOWN	Slade (Cheapskate)
-	16	MESSAGE OF LOVE	Pretenders (Real)
10	17	YOUNG PARISIANS	Adam & the Ants (Decca)
24	18	SGT. ROCK (IS GOING TO HELP ME)	XTC (Virgin)
28	19	I'M IN LOVE WITH A GERMAN FILM STAR	Passions (Polydor)
12	20	THE FREEZE	Spandau Ballet (Reformation)
17	21	A LITTLE IN LOVE	Cliff Richard (EMI)
15	22	I AM THE BEAT	Look (MCA)
19	23	BURN RUBBER ON ME (WHY YOU WANNA HURT ME)	Gap Band (Mercury)
29	24	SOUTHERN FREEEZ	Freeez (Beggars Banquet)
26	25	THAT'S ENTERTAINMENT	Jam (Metronome)
27	26	JUST WHEN I NEEDED YOU MOST	Barbara Jones (Sonet)
-	27	THE BED'S TOO BIG WITHOUT YOU	Sheila Hylton (Island)
25	28	I AIN'T GONNA STAND FOR IT	Stevie Wonder (Motown)
-	29	ONCE IN A LIFETIME	Talking Heads (Sire)
23	30	GANGSTERS OF THE GROOVE	Heatwave (GTO)

In the wake of two chart toppers, Lennon's posthumously-released *Woman*, the second single from his last album *Double Fantasy,* despite a breakneck debut at Number Three, was not quite able to capture the top slot either from *In The Air Tonight,* Phil Collins' first solo hit outside Genesis, or from Ultravox's first major success (*Sleepwalk* had peaked at only 28 the previous August), *Vienna*. The latter hit was the first dramatic indication of the input of new writer/singer Midge Ure into Ultravox.

February – March 1981

28 February 1981

last week	this week	Title
3	1	SHADDAP YOU FACE — Joe Dolce Music Theatre (Epic)
1	2	VIENNA — Ultravox (Chrysalis)
6	3	I SURRENDER — Rainbow (Polydor)
2	4	WOMAN — John Lennon (Geffen)
5	5	OLDEST SWINGER IN TOWN — Fred Wedlock (Rocket)
4	6	IN THE AIR TONIGHT — Phil Collins (Virgin)
16	7	MESSAGE OF LOVE — Pretenders (Real)
9	8	THE RETURN OF THE LAS PALMAS 7 — Madness (Stiff)
11	9	ROCK THIS TOWN — Stray Cats (Arista)
10	10	ROMEO AND JULIET — Dire Straits (Vertigo)
-	11	ST. VALENTINE'S DAY MASSACRE (EP) — Motorhead/Girlschool (Bronze)
14	12	FADE TO GREY — Visage (Polydor)
15	13	WE'LL BRING THE HOUSE DOWN — Slade (Cheapskate)
-	14	JEALOUS GUY — Roxy Music (EG)
-	15	(DO) THE HUCKLEBUCK — Coast To Coast (Polydor)
24	16	SOUTHERN FREEEZ — Freeez (Beggars Banquet)
18	17	SGT. ROCK (IS GOING TO HELP ME) — XTC (Virgin)
12	18	ANTMUSIC — Adam & the Ants (CBS)
21	19	A LITTLE IN LOVE — Cliff Richard (EMI)
7	20	RAPTURE — Blondie (Chrysalis)
-	21	KING OF THE WILD FRONTIER — Adam & the Ants (CBS)
-	22	FOUR FROM TOYAH (EP) — Toyah (Safari)
25	23	THAT'S ENTERTAINMENT — Jam (Metronome)
19	24	I'M IN LOVE WITH A GERMAN FILM STAR — Passions (Polydor)
8	25	IMAGINE — John Lennon (Apple)
-	26	(SOMEBODY) HELP ME OUT — Beggar & Co. (Ensign)
20	27	THE FREEZE — Spandau Ballet (Reformation)
28	28	ONCE IN A LIFETIME — Talking Heads (Sire)
17	29	YOUNG PARISIANS — Adam & the Ants (Decca)
30	30	GANGSTERS OF THE GROOVE — Heatwave (GTO)

7 March 1981

last week	this week	Title
1	1	SHADDAP YOU FACE — Joe Dolce Music Theatre (Epic)
2	2	VIENNA — Ultravox (Chrysalis)
3	3	I SURRENDER — Rainbow (Polydor)
14	4	JEALOUS GUY — Roxy Music (EG)
11	5	ST. VALENTINE'S DAY MASSACRE (EP) — Motorhead/Girlschool (Bronze)
16	6	SOUTHERN FREEEZ — Freeez (Beggars Banquet)
4	7	WOMAN — John Lennon (Geffen)
8	8	THE RETURN OF THE LAS PALMAS 7 — Madness (Stiff)
15	9	(DO) THE HUCKLEBUCK — Coast To Coast (Polydor)
9	10	ROCK THIS TOWN — Stray Cats (Arista)
5	11	OLDEST SWINGER IN TOWN — Fred Wedlock (Rocket)
-	12	SOMETHING 'BOUT YOU BABY I LIKE — Status Quo (Vertigo)
21	13	KING OF THE WILD FRONTIER — Adam & the Ants (CBS)
13	14	WE'LL BRING THE HOUSE DOWN — Slade (Cheapskate)
7	15	MESSAGE OF LOVE — Pretenders (Real)
6	16	IN THE AIR TONIGHT — Phil Collins (Virgin)
12	17	FADE TO GREY — Visage (Polydor)
10	18	ROMEO AND JULIET — Dire Straits (Vertigo)
26	19	(SOMEBODY) HELP ME OUT — Beggar & Co. (Ensign)
28	20	ONCE IN A LIFETIME — Talking Heads (Sire)
23	21	THAT'S ENTERTAINMENT — Jam (Metronome)
17	22	SGT. ROCK (IS GOING TO HELP ME) — XTC (Virgin)
22	23	FOUR FROM TOYAH (EP) — Toyah (Safari)
24	24	I'M IN LOVE WITH A GERMAN FILM STAR — Passions (Polydor)
-	25	REWARD — Teardrop Explodes (Vertigo)
19	26	A LITTLE IN LOVE — Cliff Richard (EMI)
-	27	STAR — Kiki Dee (Ariola)
18	28	ANTMUSIC — Adam & the Ants (CBS)
-	29	HOT LOVE — Kelly Marie (Calibre)
25	30	IMAGINE — John Lennon (Apple)

14 March 1981

last week	this week	Title
4	1	JEALOUS GUY — Roxy Music (EG)
2	2	VIENNA — Ultravox (Chrysalis)
1	3	SHADDAP YOU FACE — Joe Dolce Music Theatre (Epic)
13	4	KING OF THE WILD FRONTIER — Adam & the Ants (CBS)
9	5	(DO) THE HUCKLEBUCK — Coast To Coast (Polydor)
6	6	SOUTHERN FREEEZ — Freeez (Beggars Banquet)
12	7	SOMETHING 'BOUT YOU BABY I LIKE — Status Quo (Vertigo)
5	8	ST. VALENTINE'S DAY MASSACRE (EP) — Motorhead/Girlschool (Bronze)
3	9	I SURRENDER — Rainbow (Polydor)
20	10	ONCE IN A LIFETIME — Talking Heads (Sire)
-	10	KIDS IN AMERICA — Kim Wilde (RAK)
19	12	(SOMEBODY) HELP ME OUT — Beggar & Co. (Ensign)
8	13	THE RETURN OF THE LAS PALMAS 7 — Madness (Stiff)
23	14	FOUR FROM TOYAH (EP) — Toyah (Safari)
27	15	STAR — Kiki Dee (Ariola)
25	16	REWARD — Teardrop Explodes (Vertigo)
10	17	ROCK THIS TOWN — Stray Cats (Arista)
7	18	WOMAN — John Lennon (Geffen)
-	19	YOU BETTER YOU BET — Who (Polydor)
11	20	OLDEST SWINGER IN TOWN — Fred Wedlock (Rocket)
21	21	THAT'S ENTERTAINMENT — Jam (Metronome)
22	22	I MISSED AGAIN — Phil Collins (Virgin)
-	23	JONES VS. JONES/SUMMER MADNESS — Kool & the Gang (De-Lite)
29	24	HOT LOVE — Kelly Marie (Calibre)
-	25	THIS OLE HOUSE — Shakin' Stevens (Epic)
14	26	WE'LL BRING THE HOUSE DOWN — Slade (Cheapskate)
-	27	LATELY — Stevie Wonder (Motown)
17	28	FADE TO GREY — Visage (Polydor)
-	29	CEREMONY — New Order (Factory)
15	30	MESSAGE OF LOVE — Pretenders (Real)

21 March 1981

last week	this week	Title
1	1	JEALOUS GUY — Roxy Music (EG)
4	2	KING OF THE WILD FRONTIER — Adam & the Ants (CBS)
10	3	KIDS IN AMERICA — Kim Wilde (RAK)
25	4	THIS OLE HOUSE — Shakin' Stevens (Epic)
5	5	(DO) THE HUCKLEBUCK — Coast To Coast (Polydor)
2	6	VIENNA — Ultravox (Chrysalis)
16	7	REWARD — Teardrop Explodes (Vertigo)
14	8	FOUR FROM TOYAH (EP) — Toyah (Safari)
7	9	SOMETHING 'BOUT YOU BABY I LIKE — Status Quo (Vertigo)
6	10	SOUTHERN FREEEZ — Freeez (Beggars Banquet)
3	11	SHADDAP YOU FACE — Joe Dolce Music Theatre (Epic)
10	12	ONCE IN A LIFETIME — Talking Heads (Sire)
8	13	ST. VALENTINE'S DAY MASSACRE (EP) — Motorhead/Girlschool (Bronze)
19	14	YOU BETTER YOU BET — Who (Polydor)
15	15	STAR — Kiki Dee (Ariola)
22	16	I MISSED AGAIN — Phil Collins (Virgin)
12	17	(SOMEBODY) HELP ME OUT — Beggar & Co. (Ensign)
23	18	JONES VS. JONES/SUMMER MADNESS — Kool & the Gang (De-Lite)
-	19	MIND OF A TOY — Visage (Polydor)
29	20	CEREMONY — New Order (Factory)
27	21	LATELY — Stevie Wonder (Motown)
-	22	NAGASAKI NIGHTMARE — Crass (Crass)
24	23	HOT LOVE — Kelly Marie (Calibre)
17	24	ROCK THIS TOWN — Stray Cats (Arista)
-	25	PLANET EARTH — Duran Duran (EMI)
9	26	I SURRENDER — Rainbow (Polydor)
-	27	TWILIGHT ZONE/WRATH CHILD — Iron Maiden (EMI)
-	28	IT'S A LOVE THING — Whispers (Solar)
29	29	CAN YOU HANDLE IT — Sharon Redd (Epic)
-	30	NEW ORLEANS — Gillan (Virgin)

Comedy lyrics sudenly hit double paydirt, as Joe Dolce's Australian/Italian romp dethroned *Vienna* at Number One, while folky Fred Wedlock's wry comments on the disguising of old age ("when it takes you all night to do what you used to do all night") simultaneously made the Top Five. Even Madness' latest, *The Return Of The Las Palmas 7*, was basically a joke instrumental. On a more serious note, Roxy Music's cover of John Lennon's *Jealous Guy* was conceived as a sincere Lennon tribute.

28 March 1981

last week	this week	Title	Artist (Label)
4	1	THIS OLE HOUSE	Shakin' Stevens (Epic)
1	2	JEALOUS GUY	Roxy Music (EG)
3	3	KIDS IN AMERICA	Kim Wilde (RAK)
8	4	FOUR FROM TOYAH (EP)	Toyah (Safari)
7	5	REWARD	Teardrop Explodes (Vertigo)
2	6	KING OF THE WILD FRONTIER	Adam & the Ants (CBS)
5	7	(DO) THE HUCKLEBUCK	Coast To Coast (Polydor)
14	8	YOU BETTER YOU BET	Who (Polydor)
6	9	VIENNA	Ultravox (Chrysalis)
15	10	STAR	Kiki Dee (Ariola)
16	11	I MISSED AGAIN	Phil Collins (Virgin)
21	12	LATELY	Stevie Wonder (Motown)
9	13	SOMETHING 'BOUT YOU BABY I LIKE	Status Quo (Vertigo)
10	14	SOUTHERN FREEEZ	Freeez (Beggars Banquet)
18	15	JONES VS. JONES/SUMMER MADNESS	Kool & the Gang (De-Lite)
11	16	SHADDAP YOU FACE	Joe Dolce Music Theatre (Epic)
19	17	MIND OF A TOY	Visage (Polydor)
25	18	PLANET EARTH	Duran Duran (EMI)
12	19	ONCE IN A LIFETIME	Talking Heads (Sire)
-	20	EINSTEIN A GO-GO	Landscape (RCA)
20	21	CEREMONY	New Order (Factory)
-	22	INTUITION	Linx (Chrysalis)
-	23	D-DAYS	Hazel O'Connor (Albion)
28	24	IT'S A LOVE THING	Whispers (Solar)
22	25	NAGASAKI NIGHTMARE	Crass (Crass)
-	26	(WE DON'T NEED THIS) FASCIST GROOVE THANG	Heaven 17 (Virgin)
13	27	ST. VALENTINE'S DAY MASSACRE (EP)	Motorhead/Girlschool (Bronze)
17	28	(SOMEBODY) HELP ME OUT	Beggar & Co. (Ensign)
26	29	I SURRENDER	Rainbow (Polydor)
-	30	WHAT BECOMES OF THE BROKEN HEARTED?	Dave Stewart with Colin Blunstone (Stiff)

4 April 1981

		Title	Artist (Label)
1	1	THIS OLE HOUSE	Shakin' Stevens (Epic)
4	2	FOUR FROM TOYAH (EP)	Toyah (Safari)
3	3	KIDS IN AMERICA	Kim Wilde (RAK)
12	4	LATELY	Stevie Wonder (Motown)
2	5	JEALOUS GUY	Roxy Music (EG)
6	6	KING OF THE WILD FRONTIER	Adam & the Ants (CBS)
-	7	THE SHEFFIELD GRINDER /CAPSTICK COMES HOME	Tony Capstick & the Carlton Main /Frickley Colliery Band (Dingles)
8	8	YOU BETTER YOU BET	Who (Polydor)
20	9	EINSTEIN A GO-GO	Landscape (RCA)
7	10	(DO) THE HUCKLEBUCK	Coast To Coast (Polydor)
5	11	REWARD	Teardrop Explodes (Vertigo)
18	12	PLANET EARTH	Duran Duran (EMI)
22	13	INTUITION	Linx (Chrysalis)
17	14	MIND OF A TOY	Visage (Polydor)
-	15	MAKING YOUR MIND UP	Bucks Fizz (RCA)
24	16	IT'S A LOVE THING	Whispers (Solar)
30	17	WHAT BECOMES OF THE BROKEN HEARTED?	Dave Stewart with Colin Blunstone (Stiff)
-	18	SLOW MOTION	Ultravox (Island)
11	19	I MISSED AGAIN	Phil Collins (Virgin)
23	20	D-DAYS	Hazel O'Connor (Albion)
10	21	STAR	Kiki Dee (Ariola)
15	22	JONES VS. JONES/SUMMER MADNESS	Kool & the Gang (De-Lite)
-	23	GOOD THING GOING	Sugar Minott (RCA)
-	24	I SAW HER STANDING THERE	Elton John Band featuring John Lennon and the Muscle Shoals Horns (DJM)
-	25	JUST FADE AWAY	Stiff Little Fingers (Chrysalis)
-	26	POOR OLD SOLE	Orange Juice (Polydor)
21	27	CEREMONY	New Order (Factory)
-	28	FLOWERS OF ROMANCE	Public Image Ltd. (Virgin)
-	29	UP THE HILL BACKWARDS	David Bowie (RCA)
9	30	VIENNA	Ultravox (Chrysalis)

11 April 1981

		Title	Artist (Label)
1	1	THIS OLE HOUSE	Shakin' Stevens (Epic)
4	2	LATELY	Stevie Wonder (Motown)
3	3	KIDS IN AMERICA	Kim Wilde (RAK)
7	4	THE SHEFFIELD GRINDER /CAPSTICK COMES HOME	Tony Capstick & the Carlton Main /Frickley Colliery Band (Dingles)
15	5	MAKING YOUR MIND UP	Bucks Fizz (RCA)
9	6	EINSTEIN A GO-GO	Landscape (RCA)
2	7	FOUR FROM TOYAH (EP)	Toyah (Safari)
13	8	INTUITION	Linx (Chrysalis)
20	9	D-DAYS	Hazel O'Connor (Albion)
16	10	IT'S A LOVE THING	Whispers (Solar)
5	11	JEALOUS GUY	Roxy Music (EG)
17	12	WHAT BECOMES OF THE BROKEN HEARTED?	Dave Stewart with Colin Blunstone (Stiff)
8	13	YOU BETTER YOU BET	Who (Polydor)
14	14	MIND OF A TOY	Visage (Polydor)
10	15	(DO) THE HUCKLEBUCK	Coast To Coast (Polydor)
11	16	REWARD	Teardrop Explodes (Vertigo)
-	17	NIGHT GAMES	Graham Bonnet (Vertigo)
-	18	ATTENTION TO ME	Nolans (Epic)
6	19	KING OF THE WILD FRONTIER	Adam & the Ants (CBS)
12	20	PLANET EARTH	Duran Duran (EMI)
-	21	MUSCLEBOUND/GLOW	Spandau Ballet (Reformation)
-	22	JUST A FEELING	Bad Manners (Magnet)
-	23	NEW ORLEANS	Gillan (Virgin)
28	24	FLOWERS OF ROMANCE	Public Image Ltd. (Virgin)
29	25	UP THE HILL BACKWARDS	David Bowie (RCA)
-	26	CAN YOU FEEL IT	Jacksons (Epic)
-	27	PRIMARY	Cure (Fiction)
21	28	STAR	Kiki Dee (Ariola)
23	29	GOOD THING GOING	Sugar Minott (RCA)
18	30	SLOW MOTION	Ultravox (Island)

18 April 1981

		Title	Artist (Label)
5	1	MAKING YOUR MIND UP	Bucks Fizz (RCA)
1	2	THIS OLE HOUSE	Shakin' Stevens (Epic)
2	3	LATELY	Stevie Wonder (Motown)
6	4	EINSTEIN A GO-GO	Landscape (RCA)
8	5	INTUITION	Linx (Chrysalis)
3	6	KIDS IN AMERICA	Kim Wilde (RAK)
10	7	IT'S A LOVE THING	Whispers (Solar)
-	8	CHI MAI (THEME FROM THE LIFE AND TIMES OF LLOYD GEORGE)	Ennio Morricone (BBC)
26	9	CAN YOU FEEL IT	Jacksons (Epic)
17	10	NIGHT GAMES	Graham Bonnet (Vertigo)
29	11	GOOD THING GOING	Sugar Minott (RCA)
12	12	WHAT BECOMES OF THE BROKEN HEARTED?	Dave Stewart with Colin Blunstone (Stiff)
7	13	FOUR FROM TOYAH (EP)	Toyah (Safari)
9	14	D-DAYS	Hazel O'Connor (Albion)
18	15	ATTENTION TO ME	Nolans (Epic)
4	16	THE SHEFFIELD GRINDER/CAPSTICK COMES HOME	Tony Capstick & the Carlton Main /Frickley Colliery Band (Dingles)
24	17	FLOWERS OF ROMANCE	Public Image Ltd. (Virgin)
21	18	MUSCLEBOUND/GLOW	Spandau Ballet (Reformation)
22	19	JUST A FEELING	Bad Manners (Magnet)
-	20	AND THE BANDS PLAYED ON	Saxon (Carrere)
20	21	PLANET EARTH	Duran Duran (EMI)
14	22	MIND OF A TOY	Visage (Polydor)
15	23	(DO) THE HUCKLEBUCK	Coast To Coast (Polydor)
-	24	DON'T BREAK MY HEART AGAIN	Whitesnake (Liberty)
-	25	CROCODILES	Echo & the Bunnymen (Korova)
23	26	NEW ORLEANS	Gillan (Virgin)
-	27	WATCHING THE WHEELS	John Lennon (Geffen)
13	28	YOU BETTER YOU BET	Who (Polydor)
-	29	(WE DON'T NEED THIS) FASCIST GROOVE THANG	Heaven 17 (Virgin)
-	30	BERMUDA TRIANGLE	Barry Manilow (Arista)

Rock'n'roll revivalist Shakin' Stevens had been recording for over a decade, but had found his biggest success to date in the West End production *Elvis*, when he hit – along with new producer Stuart Colman – on just the right combination of sound and material to inaugurate one of the 1980s' most consistent hit runs. 1980's *Hot Dog* (Number 27) and *Marie, Marie* (Number 20) had almost broken him big, but the clever update of Rosemary Clooney's oldie *This Ole House* was the track that really launched Shaky.

April – May 1981

25 April 1981

last	this		
1	1	MAKING YOUR MIND UP	Bucks Fizz (RCA)
8	2	CHI MAI (THEME FROM THE LIFE AND TIMES OF LLOYD GEORGE)	Ennio Morricone (BBC)
3	3	LATELY Stevie Wonder (Motown)	Graham Bonnet (Vertigo)
10	4	NIGHT GAMES	Graham Bonnet (Vertigo)
11	5	GOOD THING GOING	Sugar Minott (RCA)
2	6	THIS OLE HOUSE	Shakin' Stevens (Epic)
4	7	EINSTEIN A GO-GO	Landscape (RCA)
5	8	INTUITION	Linx (Chrysalis)
9	9	CAN YOU FEEL IT	Jacksons (Epic)
7	10	IT'S A LOVE THING	Whispers (Solar)
18	11	MUSCLEBOUND/GLOW	Spandau Ballet (Reformation)
17	12	FLOWERS OF ROMANCE	Public Image Ltd. (Virgin)
19	13	JUST A FEELING	Bad Manners (Magnet)
14	14	D-DAYS	Hazel O'Connor (Albion)
15	15	ATTENTION TO ME	Nolans (Epic)
6	16	KIDS IN AMERICA	Kim Wilde (RAK)
12	17	WHAT BECOMES OF THE BROKEN HEARTED?	Dave Stewart with Colin Blunstone (Stiff)
20	18	AND THE BANDS PLAYED ON	Saxon (Carrere)
30	19	BERMUDA TRIANGLE	Barry Manilow (Arista)
26	20	NEW ORLEANS	Gillan (Virgin)
25	21	CROCODILES	Echo & the Bunnymen (Korova)
24	22	DON'T BREAK MY HEART AGAIN	Whitesnake (Liberty)
-	23	ONLY CRYING	Keith Marshall (Arrival)
13	24	FOUR FROM TOYAH (EP)	Toyah (Safari)
-	25	HIT AND RUN	Girlschool (Bronze)
-	26	DROWNING/ALL OUT FOR YOU	Beat (Go Feet)
16	27	THE SHEFFIELD GRINDER/CAPSTICK COMES HOME	Tony Capstick & the Carlton Main /Frickley Colliery Band (Dingles)
-	28	PRIMARY	Cure (Fiction)
-	29	THE MAGNIFICENT SEVEN	Clash (CBS)
22	30	MIND OF A TOY	Visage (Polydor)

2 May 1981

last	this		
2	1	CHI MAI (THEME FROM THE LIFE AND TIMES OF LLOYD GEORGE)	Ennio Morricone (BBC)
1	2	MAKING YOUR MIND UP	Bucks Fizz (RCA)
5	3	GOOD THING GOING	Sugar Minott (RCA)
9	4	CAN YOU FEEL IT	Jacksons (Epic)
6	5	THIS OLE HOUSE	Shakin' Stevens (Epic)
3	6	LATELY	Stevie Wonder (Motown)
-	7	GREY DAY	Madness (Stiff)
4	8	NIGHT GAMES	Graham Bonnet (Vertigo)
7	9	EINSTEIN A GO-GO	Landscape (RCA)
15	10	ATTENTION TO ME	Nolans (Epic)
11	11	MUSCLEBOUND/GLOW	Spandau Ballet (Reformation)
13	12	JUST A FEELING	Bad Manners (Magnet)
10	13	IT'S A LOVE THING	Whispers (Solar)
18	14	AND THE BANDS PLAYED ON	Saxon (Carrere)
-	15	STARS ON 45	Starsound (CBS)
8	16	INTUITION	Linx (Chrysalis)
22	17	DON'T BREAK MY HEART AGAIN	Whitesnake (Liberty)
21	18	CROCODILES	Echo & the Bunnymen (Korova)
12	19	FLOWERS OF ROMANCE	Public Image Ltd. (Virgin)
-	20	CAN'T GET ENOUGH OF YOU	Eddy Grant (Ensign)
20	21	NEW ORLEANS	Gillan (Virgin)
26	22	DROWNING/ALL OUT TO GET YOU	Beat (Go Feet)
19	23	BERMUDA TRIANGLE	Barry Manilow (Arista)
28	24	PRIMARY	Cure (Fiction)
-	25	KEEP ON RUNNIN' (TILL YOU BURN)	UK Subs (Gem)
23	26	ONLY CRYING	Keith Marshall (Arrival)
17	27	WHAT BECOMES OF THE ` BROKEN HEARTED?	Dave Stewart with Colin Blunstone (Stiff)
-	28	AI NO CORRIDA	Quincy Jones (A&M)
-	29	DOGS OF WAR	Exploited (Secret)
-	30	CANDY SKIN	Fire Engines

9 May 1981

last	this		
15	1	STARS ON 45	Starsound (CBS)
1	2	CHI MAI (THEME FROM THE LIFE AND TIMES OF LLOYD GEORGE)	Ennio Morricone (BBC)
2	3	MAKING YOUR MIND UP	Bucks Fizz (RCA)
7	4	GREY DAY	Madness (Stiff)
3	5	GOOD THING GOING	Sugar Minott (RCA)
4	6	CAN YOU FEEL IT	Jacksons (Epic)
10	7	ATTENTION TO ME	Nolans (Epic)
-	8	STAND AND DELIVER	Adam & the Ants (CBS)
11	9	MUSCLEBOUND/GLOW	Spandau Ballet (Reformation)
6	10	LATELY	Stevie Wonder (Motown)
-	11	YOU DRIVE ME CRAZY	Shakin' Stevens (Epic)
9	12	EINSTEIN A GO-GO	Landscape (RCA)
26	13	ONLY CRYING	Keith Marshall (Arrival)
8	14	NIGHT GAMES	Graham Bonnet (Vertigo)
20	15	CAN'T GET ENOUGH OF YOU	Eddy Grant (Ensign)
13	16	IT'S A LOVE THING	Whispers (Solar)
22	17	DROWNING/ALL OUT TO GET YOU	Beat (Go Feet)
21	18	NEW ORLEANS	Gillan (Virgin)
5	19	THIS OLE HOUSE	Shakin' Stevens (Epic)
23	20	BERMUDA TRIANGLE	Barry Manilow (Arista)
12	21	JUST A FEELING	Bad Manners (Magnet)
-	22	STRAY CAT STRUT	Stray Cats (Arista)
18	23	CROCODILES	Echo & the Bunnymen (Korova)
19	24	FLOWERS OF ROMANCE	Public Image Ltd. (Virgin)
14	25	AND THE BANDS PLAYED ON	Saxon (Carrere)
28	26	AI NO CORRIDA	Quincy Jones (A&M)
-	27	KEEP ON LOVING YOU	REO Speedwagon (Epic)
-	28	IS VIC THERE?	Department S (Demon)
-	29	HIT AND RUN	Girlschool (Bronze)
-	30	SWORDS OF A THOUSAND MEN	Tenpole Tudor (Stiff)

16 May 1981

last	this		
8	1	STAND AND DELIVER	Adam & the Ants (CBS)
1	2	STARS ON 45	Starsound (CBS)
2	3	CHI MAI (THEME FROM THE LIFE AND TIMES OF LLOYD GEORGE)	Ennio Morricone (BBC)
11	4	YOU DRIVE ME CRAZY	Shakin' Stevens (Epic)
4	5	GREY DAY	Madness (Stiff)
3	6	MAKING YOUR MIND UP	Bucks Fizz (RCA)
5	7	GOOD THING GOING	Sugar Minott (RCA)
6	8	CAN YOU FEEL IT	Jacksons (Epic)
9	9	MUSCLEBOUND/GLOW	Spandau Ballet (Reformation)
7	10	ATTENTION TO ME	Nolans (Epic)
30	11	SWORDS OF A THOUSAND MEN	Tenpole Tudor (Stiff)
13	12	ONLY CRYING	Keith Marshall (Arrival)
15	13	CAN'T GET ENOUGH OF YOU	Eddy Grant (Ensign)
14	14	NIGHT GAMES	Graham Bonnet (Vertigo)
20	15	BERMUDA TRIANGLE	Barry Manilow (Arista)
22	16	STRAY CAT STRUT	Stray Cats (Arista)
-	17	CHEQUERED LOVE	Kim Wilde (RAK)
-	18	DON'T BREAK MY HEART AGAIN	Whitesnake (Liberty)
26	19	AI NO CORRIDA	Quincy Jones (A&M)
-	20	TREASON (IT'S JUST A STORY)	Teardrop Explodes (Mercury)
27	21	KEEP ON LOVING YOU	REO Speedwagon (Epic)
19	22	THIS OLE HOUSE	Shakin' Stevens (Epic)
-	23	WHEN HE SHINES	Sheena Easton (EMI)
-	24	THE SOUND OF THE CROWD	Human League (Virgin)
-	25	THE ART OF PARTIES	Japan (Virgin)
16	26	IT'S A LOVE THING	Whispers (Solar)
28	27	IS VIC THERE?	Department S (Demon)
-	28	OSSIE'S DREAM (SPURS ARE ON THEIR WAY TO WEMBLEY)	Tottenham Hotspur F.A. Cup Final Squad 1981 (Rockney)
-	29	KILLERS LIVE (EP)	Thin Lizzy (Vertigo)
-	30	BETTE DAVIS EYES	Kim Carnes (EMI America)

Britain won the Eurovision Song contest for the first time since 1976, via a mixed-sex group of session singers named, for the occasion, Buck Fizz. (One of the girls, Cheryl Baker, had also been in a previous Euro-hopeful outfit, Co-Co, in 1978). The winning song, *Making Your Mind Up*, hit Number One, and the quartet stayed together to have a very consistent run of successes through most of the '80s. Other key chart debutantes were Holland's Starsound, whose *Stars On 45* soundalike medley started a whole fad.

last week	this week	23 May 1981			

23 May 1981

last	this	Title / Artist (Label)
1	1	STAND AND DELIVER — Adam & the Ants (CBS)
4	2	YOU DRIVE ME CRAZY — Shakin' Stevens (Epic)
17	3	CHEQUERED LOVE — Kim Wilde (RAK)
2	4	STARS ON 45 Starsound (CBS)
5	5	GREY DAY Madness (Stiff)
11	6	SWORDS OF A THOUSAND MEN — Tenpole Tudor (Stiff)
28	7	OSSIE'S DREAM (SPURS ARE ON THEIR WAY TO WEMBLEY) — Tottenham Hotspur F.A. Cup Final Squad 1981 (Rockney)
21	8	KEEP ON LOVING YOU — REO Speedwagon (Epic)
16	9	STRAY CAT STRUT — Stray Cats (Arista)
3	10	CHI MAI (THEME FROM THE LIFE AND TIMES OF LLOYD GEORGE) — Ennio Morricone (BBC)
19	11	AI NO CORRIDA — Quincy Jones (A&M)
30	12	BETTE DAVIS EYES — Kim Carnes (EMI America)
-	13	I WANT TO BE FREE — Toyah (Safari)
6	14	MAKING YOUR MIND UP — Bucks Fizz (RCA)
8	15	CAN YOU FEEL IT — Jacksons (Epic)
-	16	IT'S GOING TO HAPPEN! — Undertones (Ardeck)
20	17	TREASON (IT'S JUST A STORY) — Teardrop Explodes (Mercury)
10	18	ATTENTION TO ME — Nolans (Epic)
12	19	ONLY CRYING — Keith Marshall (Arrival)
27	20	IS VIC THERE? — Department S (Demon)
9	21	MUSCLEBOUND/GLOW — Spandau Ballet (Reformation)
24	22	THE SOUND OF THE CROWD — Human League (Virgin)
23	23	WHEN HE SHINES — Sheena Easton (EMI)
-	24	DROWNING/ALL OUT TO GET YOU — Beat (Go Feet)
15	25	BERMUDA TRIANGLE — Barry Manilow (Arista)
-	26	ABOUT THE WEATHER — Magazine (Virgin)
13	27	CAN'T GET ENOUGH OF YOU — Eddy Grant (Ensign)
-	28	BEING WITH YOU — Smokey Robinson (Motown)
-	29	THEME FROM CHARIOTS OF FIRE — Vangelis (Polydor)
29	30	KILLERS LIVE (EP) — Thin Lizzy (Vertigo)

30 May 1981

last	this	Title / Artist (Label)
1	1	STAND AND DELIVER — Adam & the Ants (CBS)
3	2	CHEQUERED LOVE — Kim Wilde (RAK)
2	3	YOU DRIVE ME CRAZY — Shakin' Stevens (Epic)
4	4	STARS ON 45 Starsound (CBS)
6	5	SWORDS OF A THOUSAND MEN — Tenpole Tudor (Stiff)
7	6	OSSIE'S DREAM (SPURS ARE ON THEIR WAY TO WEMBLEY) — Tottenham Hotspur F.A. Cup Final Squad 1981 (Rockney)
12	7	BETTE DAVIS EYES — Kim Carnes (EMI America)
13	8	I WANT TO BE FREE — Toyah (Safari)
8	9	KEEP ON LOVING YOU — REO Speedwagon (Epic)
9	10	STRAY CAT STRUT — Stray Cats (Arista)
23	11	WHEN HE SHINES — Sheena Easton (EMI)
-	12	DON'T SLOW DOWN/DON'T LET IT PASS YOU BY — UB40 (DEP International)
5	13	GREY DAY Madness (Stiff)
16	14	IT'S GOING TO HAPPEN! — Undertones (Ardeck)
10	15	CHI MAI (THEME FROM THE LIFE AND TIMES OF LLOYD GEORGE) — Ennio Morricone (BBC)
22	16	THE SOUND OF THE CROWD — Human League (Virgin)
28	17	BEING WITH YOU — Smokey Robinson (Motown)
17	18	TREASON (IT'S JUST A STORY) — Teardrop Explodes (Mercury)
-	19	HOW 'BOUT US — Champaign (CBS)
20	20	AIN'T NO STOPPING - DISCO MIX '81 — Enigma (Creole)
30	21	KILLERS LIVE (EP) — Thin Lizzy (Vertigo)
11	22	AI NO CORRIDA — Quincy Jones (A&M)
-	23	THE ART OF PARTIES — Japan (Virgin)
24	24	DROWNING/ALL OUT TO GET YOU — Beat (Go Feet)
29	25	THEME FROM CHARIOTS OF FIRE — Vangelis (Polydor)
-	26	ALL THOSE YEARS GO — George Harrison (Dark Horse)
26	27	ABOUT THE WEATHER — Magazine (Virgin)
-	28	ROCKABILLY GUY — Polecats (Mercury)
18	29	ATTENTION TO ME — Nolans (Epic)
-	30	CARELESS MEMORIES — Duran Duran (EMI)

6 June 1981

last	this	Title / Artist (Label)
1	1	STAND AND DELIVER — Adam & the Ants (CBS)
3	2	YOU DRIVE ME CRAZY — Shakin' Stevens (Epic)
4	3	STARS ON 45 Starsound (CBS)
2	4	CHEQUERED LOVE — Kim Wilde (RAK)
17	5	BEING WITH YOU — Smokey Robinson (Motown)
8	6	I WANT TO BE FREE — Toyah (Safari)
5	7	SWORDS OF A THOUSAND MEN — Tenpole Tudor (Stiff)
7	8	BETTE DAVIS EYES — Kim Carnes (EMI America)
26	9	ALL THOSE YEARS GO — George Harrison (Dark Horse)
9	10	KEEP ON LOVING YOU — REO Speedwagon (Epic)
16	11	THE SOUND OF THE CROWD — Human League (Virgin)
12	12	DON'T SLOW DOWN/DON'T LET IT PASS YOU BY — UB40 (DEP International)
19	13	HOW 'BOUT US — Champaign (CBS)
6	14	OSSIE'S DREAM (SPURS ARE ON THEIR WAY TO WEMBLEY) — Tottenham Hotspur F.A. Cup Final Squad 1981 (Rockney)
-	15	TOO DRUNK TO FUCK — Dead Kennedys (Cherry Red)
-	16	WILL YOU — Hazel O'Connor (A&M)
14	17	IT'S GOING TO HAPPEN! — Undertones (Ardeck)
18	18	TREASON (IT'S JUST A STORY) — Teardrop Explodes (Mercury)
10	19	STRAY CAT STRUT — Stray Cats (Arista)
-	20	FUNERAL PYRE — Jam (Polydor)
20	21	AIN'T NO STOPPING - DISCO MIX '81 — Enigma (Creole)
25	22	THEME FROM CHARIOTS OF FIRE — Vangelis (Polydor)
-	23	ONE DAY IN YOUR LIFE — Michael Jackson (Motown)
13	24	GREY DAY Madness (Stiff)
-	25	FOLLOW THE LEADERS — Killing Joke (Malicious Damage)
-	26	MORE THAN IN LOVE — Kate Robbins (RCA)
-	27	SPELLBOUND — Siouxsie & the Banshees (Polydor)
11	28	WHEN HE SHINES — Sheena Easton (EMI)
-	29	GOING BACK TO MY ROOTS — Odyssey (RCA)
-	30	PAPA'S GOT A BRAND NEW PIGBAG — Pigbag (Y)

13 June 1981

last	this	Title / Artist (Label)
5	1	BEING WITH YOU — Smokey Robinson (Motown)
1	2	STAND AND DELIVER — Adam & the Ants (CBS)
20	3	FUNERAL PYRE — Jam (Polydor)
2	4	YOU DRIVE ME CRAZY — Shakin' Stevens (Epic)
13	5	HOW 'BOUT US — Champaign (CBS)
6	6	I WANT TO BE FREE — Toyah (Safari)
16	7	WILL YOU — Hazel O'Connor (A&M)
23	8	ONE DAY IN YOUR LIFE — Michael Jackson (Motown)
26	9	MORE THAN IN LOVE — Kate Robbins (RCA)
3	10	STARS ON 45 Starsound (CBS)
7	11	SWORDS OF A THOUSAND MEN — Tenpole Tudor (Stiff)
22	12	THEME FROM CHARIOTS OF FIRE — Vangelis (Polydor)
4	13	CHEQUERED LOVE — Kim Wilde (RAK)
9	14	ALL THOSE YEARS GO — George Harrison (Dark Horse)
29	15	GOING BACK TO MY ROOTS — Odyssey (RCA)
12	16	DON'T SLOW DOWN/DON'T LET IT PASS YOU BY — UB40 (DEP International)
15	17	TOO DRUNK TO FUCK — Dead Kennedys (Cherry Red)
8	18	BETTE DAVIS EYES — Kim Carnes (EMI America)
21	19	AIN'T NO STOPPING - DISCO MIX — Enigma (Creole)
11	20	THE SOUND OF THE CROWD — Human League (Virgin)
10	21	KEEP ON LOVING YOU — REO Speedwagon (Epic)
-	22	ALL STOOD STILL — Ultravox (Chrysalis)
27	23	SPELLBOUND — Siouxsie & the Banshees (Polydor)
30	24	PAPA'S GOT A BRAND NEW PIGBAG — Pigbag (Y)
25	25	FOLLOW THE LEADERS — Killing Joke (Malicious Damage)
-	26	IF LEAVING ME IS EASY — Phil Collins (Virgin)
17	27	IT'S GOING TO HAPPEN! — Undertones (Ardeck)
-	28	THROW AWAY THE KEY — Linx (Chrysalis)
-	29	WOULD I LIE TO YOU — Whitesnake (Liberty)
-	30	ROCKABILLY GUY — Polecats (Mercury)

After two Number Twos with *Antmusic* and *Kings Of The Wild Frontier*, Adam & the Ants topped the chart convincingly with *Stand And Deliver*; for the next few months, Adam would be the top teen star in the country. Meanwhile, Spurs went to the 1981 Cup Final to the accompaniment of their own Top 10 single, George Harrison's song paid his own tribute to John Lennon, and the Dead Kennedys hit the Top 20 with a single of which hardly anyone would print the title, let alone give airplay to.

June – July 1981

20 June 1981	27 June 1981	4 July 1981	11 July 1981

20 June 1981 (last week / this week)

1 1 BEING WITH YOU
   Smokey Robinson (Motown)
9 2 MORE THAN IN LOVE
   Kate Robbins (RCA)
3 3 FUNERAL PYRE
   Jam (Polydor)
8 4 ONE DAY IN YOUR LIFE
   Michael Jackson (Motown)
15 5 GOING BACK TO MY ROOTS
   Odyssey (RCA)
7 6 WILL YOU
   Hazel O'Connor (A&M)
5 7 HOW 'BOUT US
   Champaign (CBS)
2 8 STAND AND DELIVER
   Adam & the Ants (CBS)
4 9 YOU DRIVE ME CRAZY
   Shakin' Stevens (Epic)
12 10 THEME FROM CHARIOTS OF
   FIRE Vangelis (Polydor)
22 11 ALL STOOD STILL
   Ultravox (Chrysalis)
16 12 DON'T SLOW DOWN/DON'T LET
   IT PASS YOU BY
   UB40 (DEP International)
19 13 AIN'T NO STOPPING - DISCO MIX
   '81 Enigma (Creole)
23 14 SPELLBOUND
   Siouxsie & the Banshees
   (Polydor)
14 15 ALL THOSE YEARS GO
   George Harrison (Dark Horse)
10 15 STARS ON 45
   Starsound (CBS)
- 17 TEDDY BEAR
   Red Sovine (Starday)
17 18 TOO DRUNK TO FUCK
   Dead Kennedys (Cherry Red)
18 19 BETTE DAVIS EYES
   Kim Carnes (EMI America)
25 20 FOLLOW THE LEADERS
   Killing Joke (Malicious Damage)
13 20 CHEQUERED LOVE
   Kim Wilde (RAK)
- 22 NEW LIFE
   Depeche Mode (Mute)
- 23 PIECE OF THE ACTION
   Bucks Fizz (RCA)
11 24 SWORDS OF A THOUSAND MEN
   Tenpole Tudor (Stiff)
26 25 IF LEAVING ME IS EASY
   Phil Collins (Virgin)
20 26 THE SOUND OF THE CROWD
   Human League (Virgin)
- 27 MEMORY
   Elaine Paige (Polydor)
28 28 THROW AWAY THE KEY
   Linx (Chrysalis)
- 29 TAKE IT TO THE TOP (CLIMBING)
   Kool & the Gang (De-Lite)
- 30 YOUTH OF NATION OF FIRE
   Bill Nelson (Mercury)

27 June 1981

4 1 ONE DAY IN YOUR LIFE
   Michael Jackson (Motown)
1 2 BEING WITH YOU
   Smokey Robinson (Motown)
2 3 MORE THAN IN LOVE
   Kate Robbins (RCA)
11 4 ALL STOOD STILL
   Ultravox (Chrysalis)
17 5 TEDDY BEAR
   Red Sovine (Starday)
5 6 GOING BACK TO MY ROOTS
   Odyssey (RCA)
7 7 HOW 'BOUT US
   Champaign (CBS)
6 8 WILL YOU
   Hazel O'Connor (A&M)
- 9 GHOST TOWN
   Specials (2 Tone)
- 10 I WANT TO BE FREE
   Toyah (Safari)
3 11 FUNERAL PYRE
   Jam (Polydor)
27 12 MEMORY
   Elaine Paige (Polydor)
8 13 STAND AND DELIVER
   Adam & the Ants (CBS)
23 14 PIECE OF THE ACTION
   Bucks Fizz (RCA)
10 15 THEME FROM CHARIOTS OF
   FIRE Vangelis (Polydor)
14 16 SPELLBOUND
   Siouxsie & the Banshees
   (Polydor)
25 17 IF LEAVING ME IS EASY
   Phil Collins (Virgin)
- 18 BODY TALK Imagination (R&B)
12 19 DON'T SLOW DOWN/DON'T LET
   IT PASS YOU BY
   UB40 (DEP International)
- 20 NO LAUGHING IN HEAVEN
   Gillan (Virgin)
18 21 TOO DRUNK TO FUCK
   Dead Kennedys (Cherry Red)
9 22 YOU DRIVE ME CRAZY
   Shakin' Stevens (Epic)
- 23 DANCING ON THE FLOOR
   (HOOKED ON LOVE)
   Third World (CBS)
28 24 THROW AWAY THE KEY
   Linx (Chrysalis)
23 25 SWORDS OF A THOUSAND MEN
   Tenpole Tudor (Stiff)
29 26 TAKE IT TO THE TOP (CLIMBING)
   Kool & the Gang (De-Lite)
- 27 THE RIVER
   Bruce Springsteen (CBS)
- 28 DOORS OF YOUR HEART
   Beat (Go Feet)
13 29 AIN'T NO STOPPING - DISCO MIX
   '81 Enigma (Creole)
- 30 NO WOMAN NO CRY
   Bob Marley & the Wailers (Island)

4 July 1981

1 1 ONE DAY IN YOUR LIFE
   Michael Jackson (Motown)
9 2 GHOST TOWN
   Specials (2 Tone)
2 3 BEING WITH YOU
   Smokey Robinson (Motown)
6 4 GOING BACK TO MY ROOTS
   Odyssey (RCA)
5 5 TEDDY BEAR
   Red Sovine (Starday)
18 6 BODY TALK Imagination (R&B)
- 7 CAN CAN
   Bad Manners (Magnet)
4 8 ALL STOOD STILL
   Ultravox (Chrysalis)
3 9 MORE THAN IN LOVE
   Kate Robbins (RCA)
12 10 MEMORY
   Elaine Paige (Polydor)
7 11 HOW 'BOUT US
   Champaign (CBS)
14 12 PIECE OF THE ACTION
   Bucks Fizz (RCA)
8 13 WILL YOU
   Hazel O'Connor (A&M)
24 14 THROW AWAY THE KEY
   Linx (Chrysalis)
30 15 NO WOMAN NO CRY
   Bob Marley & the Wailers (Island)
- 16 RAZZAMATAZZ
   Quincy Jones (A&M)
26 17 TAKE IT TO THE TOP (CLIMBING)
   Kool & the Gang (De-Lite)
17 18 IF LEAVING ME IS EASY
   Phil Collins (Virgin)
- 19 WIKKA WRAP
   Evasions (Groove)
- 20 WORDY RAPPINGHOOD
   Tom Tom Club (Island)
13 21 STAND AND DELIVER
   Adam & the Ants (CBS)
23 22 DANCING ON THE FLOOR
   (HOOKED ON LOVE)
   Third World (CBS)
10 23 I WANT TO BE FREE
   Toyah (Safari)
21 24 TOO DRUNK TO FUCK
   Dead Kennedys (Cherry Red)
28 25 DOORS OF YOUR HEART
   Beat (Go Feet)
- 26 PRETTY IN PINK
   Psychedelic Furs (CBS)
15 27 THEME FROM CHARIOTS OF
   FIRE Vangelis (Polydor)
16 28 SPELLBOUND
   Siouxsie & the Banshees
   (Polydor)
19 29 DON'T SLOW DOWN/DON'T LET
   IT PASS YOU BY
   UB40 (DEP International)
- 30 CAN'T HAPPEN HERE
   Rainbow (Polydor)

11 July 1981

1 1 ONE DAY IN YOUR LIFE
   Michael Jackson (Motown)
2 2 GHOST TOWN
   Specials (2 Tone)
7 3 CAN CAN
   Bad Manners (Magnet)
4 4 GOING BACK TO MY ROOTS
   Odyssey (RCA)
6 5 BODY TALK Imagination (R&B)
10 6 MEMORY
   Elaine Paige (Polydor)
15 7 NO WOMAN NO CRY
   Bob Marley & the Wailers (Island)
3 8 BEING WITH YOU
   Smokey Robinson (Motown)
- 9 STARS ON 45, VOLUME 2
   Starsound (CBS)
16 10 RAZZAMATAZZ
   Quincy Jones (A&M)
5 11 TEDDY BEAR
   Red Sovine (Starday)
9 12 MORE THAN IN LOVE
   Kate Robbins (RCA)
8 13 ALL STOOD STILL
   Ultravox (Chrysalis)
11 14 HOW 'BOUT US
   Champaign (CBS)
20 15 WORDY RAPPINGHOOD
   Tom Tom Club (Island)
19 16 WIKKA WRAP
   Evasions (Groove)
- 17 YOU MIGHT NEED SOMEBODY
   Randy Crawford (Warner Bros)
12 18 PIECE OF THE ACTION
   Bucks Fizz (RCA)
- 19 THERE'S A GUY WORKS DOWN
   THE CHIP SHOP SWEARS HE'S
   ELVIS
   Kirsty MacColl (Polydor)
14 20 THROW AWAY THE KEY
   Linx (Chrysalis)
17 21 TAKE IT TO THE TOP (CLIMBING)
   Kool & the Gang (De-Lite)
22 22 DANCING ON THE FLOOR
   (HOOKED ON LOVE)
   Third World (CBS)
- 23 NEW LIFE
   Depeche Mode (Mute)
- 24 FOR YOUR EYES ONLY
   Sheena Easton (EMI)
- 25 BEACH BOY GOLD
   Gidea Park (Stone)
25 26 DOORS OF YOUR HEART
   Beat (Go Feet)
18 27 IF LEAVING ME IS EASY
   Phil Collins (Virgin)
- 28 THE PASSIONS OF LOVERS
   Bauhaus (Beggars Banquet)
- 29 THE RIVER
   Bruce Springsteen (CBS)
30 30 CAN'T HAPPEN HERE
   Rainbow (Polydor)

For the first time in many years, Motown dominated the top of the chart, as Smokey Robinson yielded to a Michael Jackson song which had actually been around, unpromoted, for years. Kate Robbins, a cousin of Paul McCartney (and in later years one of the key voices behind *Spitting Image*), also challenged hard for the top with a song introduced while she was taking the role of a fictional pop singer in the TV soap *Crossroads*. Meanwhile, Elaine Paige introduced Lloyd-Webber's *Cats* with *Memory*.

18 July 1981

last week	this week	Title / Artist (Label)
2	1	GHOST TOWN — Specials (2 Tone)
3	2	CAN CAN — Bad Manners (Magnet)
1	3	ONE DAY IN YOUR LIFE — Michael Jackson (Motown)
9	4	STARS ON 45, VOLUME 2 — Starsound (CBS)
5	5	BODY TALK — Imagination (R&B)
15	6	WORDY RAPPINGHOOD — Tom Tom Club (Island)
-	7	MOTORHEAD LIVE — Motorhead (Bronze)
4	8	GOING BACK TO MY ROOTS — Odyssey (RCA)
7	9	NO WOMAN NO CRY — Bob Marley & the Wailers (Island)
6	10	MEMORY — Elaine Paige (Polydor)
10	11	RAZZAMATAZZ — Quincy Jones (A&M)
22	12	DANCING ON THE FLOOR (HOOKED ON LOVE) — Third World (CBS)
8	13	BEING WITH YOU — Smokey Robinson (Motown)
17	14	YOU MIGHT NEED SOMEBODY — Randy Crawford (Warner Bros)
-	15	SAT IN YOUR LAP — Kate Bush (EMI)
19	16	THERE'S A GUY WORKS DOWN THE CHIP SHOP SWEARS HE'S ELVIS — Kirsty MacColl (Polydor)
23	17	NEW LIFE — Depeche Mode (Mute)
30	18	CAN'T HAPPEN HERE — Rainbow (Polydor)
-	19	VISAGE — Visage (Polydor)
18	20	PIECE OF THE ACTION — Bucks Fizz (RCA)
20	21	THROW AWAY THE KEY — Linx (Chrysalis)
12	22	MORE THAN IN LOVE — Kate Robbins (RCA)
14	23	HOW 'BOUT US — Champaign (CBS)
13	24	ALL STOOD STILL — Ultravox (Chrysalis)
24	25	FOR YOUR EYES ONLY — Sheena Easton (EMI)
11	26	TEDDY BEAR — Red Sovine (Starday)
21	27	TAKE IT TO THE TOP (CLIMBING) — Kool & the Gang (De-Lite)
16	28	WIKKA WRAP — Evasions (Groove)
29	29	BEACH BOY GOLD — Gidea Park (Stone)
-	30	ME NO POP I — Kid Creole & the Coconuts presents Coati Mundi (Ze)

25 July 1981

last week	this week	Title / Artist (Label)
1	1	GHOST TOWN — Specials (2 Tone)
4	2	STARS ON 45, VOLUME 2 — Starsound (CBS)
2	3	CAN CAN — Bad Manners (Magnet)
5	4	BODY TALK — Imagination (R&B)
3	5	ONE DAY IN YOUR LIFE — Michael Jackson (Motown)
6	6	WORDY RAPPINGHOOD — Tom Tom Club (Island)
9	7	NO WOMAN NO CRY — Bob Marley & the Wailers (Island)
12	8	DANCING ON THE FLOOR (HOOKED ON LOVE) — Third World (CBS)
7	9	MOTORHEAD LIVE — Motorhead (Bronze)
-	10	LAY ALL YOUR LOVE ON ME — Abba (Epic)
15	11	SAT IN YOUR LAP — Kate Bush (EMI)
14	12	YOU MIGHT NEED SOMEBODY — Randy Crawford (Warner Bros)
-	13	CHANT NO.1 (I DON'T NEED THIS PRESSURE ON) — Spandau Ballet (Reformation)
8	14	GOING BACK TO MY ROOTS — Odyssey (RCA)
10	15	MEMORY — Elaine Paige (Polydor)
11	16	RAZZAMATAZZ — Quincy Jones (A&M)
16	17	THERE'S A GUY WORKS DOWN THE CHIP SHOP SWEARS HE'S ELVIS — Kirsty MacColl (Polydor)
19	18	VISAGE — Visage (Polydor)
25	19	FOR YOUR EYES ONLY — Sheena Easton (EMI)
17	20	NEW LIFE — Depeche Mode (Mute)
-	21	NEVER SURRENDER — Saxon (Carrere)
-	22	WALK RIGHT NOW — Jacksons (Epic)
-	23	HAPPY BIRTHDAY — Stevie Wonder (Motown)
-	24	SHOW ME — Dexy's Midnight Runners (Mercury)
18	25	CAN'T HAPPEN HERE — Rainbow (Polydor)
26	26	I'M IN LOVE — Evelyn King (RCA)
20	27	PIECE OF THE ACTION — Bucks Fizz (RCA)
-	28	A PROMISE — Echo & the Bunnymen (Korova)
28	29	WIKKA WRAP — Evasions (Groove)
13	30	BEING WITH YOU — Smokey Robinson (Motown)

1 August 1981

last week	this week	Title / Artist (Label)
13	1	CHANT NO.1 (I DON'T NEED THIS PRESSURE ON) — Spandau Ballet (Reformation)
1	2	GHOST TOWN — Specials (2 Tone)
23	3	HAPPY BIRTHDAY — Stevie Wonder (Motown)
2	4	STARS ON 45, VOLUME 2 — Starsound (CBS)
10	5	LAY ALL YOUR LOVE ON ME — Abba (Epic)
3	6	CAN CAN — Bad Manners (Magnet)
4	7	BODY TALK — Imagination (R&B)
8	8	DANCING ON THE FLOOR (HOOKED ON LOVE) — Third World (CBS)
11	9	SAT IN YOUR LAP — Kate Bush (EMI)
-	10	GREEN DOOR — Shakin' Stevens (Epic)
-	11	HOOKED ON CLASSICS — Royal Philharmonic Orchestra arranged and conducted by Louis Clark (RCA)
9	12	MOTORHEAD LIVE — Motorhead (Bronze)
6	13	WORDY RAPPINGHOOD — Tom Tom Club (Island)
7	14	NO WOMAN NO CRY — Bob Marley & the Wailers (Island)
19	15	FOR YOUR EYES ONLY — Sheena Easton (EMI)
20	16	NEW LIFE — Depeche Mode (Mute)
5	17	ONE DAY IN YOUR LIFE — Michael Jackson (Motown)
21	18	NEVER SURRENDER — Saxon (Carrere)
22	19	WALK RIGHT NOW — Jacksons (Epic)
-	20	GIRLS ON FILM — Duran Duran (EMI)
24	21	SHOW ME — Dexy's Midnight R (Mercury)
18	22	VISAGE — Visage (Polydor)
12	23	YOU MIGHT NEED SOMEBODY — Randy Crawford (Warner Bros)
15	24	MEMORY — Elaine Paige (Polydor)
-	25	CARIBBEAN DISCO SHOW — Lobo (Polydor)
26	26	I'M IN LOVE — Evelyn King (RCA)
14	27	GOING BACK TO MY ROOTS — Odyssey (RCA)
28	28	A PROMISE — Echo & the Bunnymen (Korova)
16	29	RAZZAMATAZZ — Quincy Jones (A&M)
-	30	TEMPTED — Squeeze (A&M)

8 August 1981

last week	this week	Title / Artist (Label)
10	1	GREEN DOOR — Shakin' Stevens (Epic)
1	2	CHANT NO.1 (I DON'T NEED THIS PRESSURE ON) — Spandau Ballet (Reformation)
11	3	HOOKED ON CLASSICS — Royal Philharmonic Orchestra arranged and conducted by Louis Clark (RCA)
2	4	GHOST TOWN — Specials (2 Tone)
3	5	HAPPY BIRTHDAY — Stevie Wonder (Motown)
4	6	STARS ON 45, VOLUME 2 — Starsound (CBS)
5	7	LAY ALL YOUR LOVE ON ME — Abba (Epic)
15	8	FOR YOUR EYES ONLY — Sheena Easton (EMI)
16	9	NEW LIFE — Depeche Mode (Mute)
6	10	CAN CAN — Bad Manners (Magnet)
-	11	BACK TO THE SIXTIES — Tight Fit (Jive)
8	12	DANCING ON THE FLOOR (HOOKED ON LOVE) — Third World (CBS)
19	13	WALK RIGHT NOW — Jacksons (Epic)
7	14	BODY TALK — Imagination (R&B)
20	15	GIRLS ON FILM — Duran Duran (EMI)
-	16	BEACH BOY GOLD — Gidea Park (Stone)
-	17	WATER ON GLASS/BOYS — Kim Wilde (RAK)
22	18	VISAGE — Visage (Polydor)
14	19	NO WOMAN NO CRY — Bob Marley & the Wailers (Island)
9	20	SAT IN YOUR LAP — Kate Bush (EMI)
12	21	MOTORHEAD LIVE — Motorhead (Bronze)
21	22	SHOW ME — Dexy's Midnight Runners (Mercury)
23	23	YOU MIGHT NEED SOMEBODY — Randy Crawford (Warner Bros)
-	24	ARABIAN NIGHTS — Siouxsie & the Banshees (Polydor)
25	25	CARIBBEAN DISCO SHOW — Lobo (Polydor)
13	26	WORDY RAPPINGHOOD — Tom Tom Club (Island)
-	27	TAKE IT ON THE RUN — REO Spe..wagon (Epic)
-	28	MOTORHEAD — Hawkwind (Bronze)
-	29	JULIE OCEAN — Undertones (Ardeck)
-	30	HOLD ON TIGHT — Electric Light Orchestra (Jet)

Stevie Wonder's *Happy Birthday* was a song to the late Martin Luther King, and part of Wonder's widely publicised efforts to have King's birthday recognised as a national holiday in the US – a goal he eventually attained. Abba's *Lay All Your Love On Me*, a dancefloor-orientated track, was unique among their releases in being only available in a extended version on a 12-inch single, with no standard 7-inch equivalent pressed. Meanwhile, the medley fad sparked by Stars On 45 was now in full flow.

August – September 1981

15 August 1981

last	this	title / artist
5	1	HAPPY BIRTHDAY — Stevie Wonder (Motown)
1	2	GREEN DOOR — Shakin' Stevens (Epic)
3	3	HOOKED ON CLASSICS — Royal Philharmonic Orchestra arranged and conducted by Louis Clark (RCA)
2	4	CHANT NO.1 (I DON'T NEED THIS PRESSURE ON) — Spandau Ballet (Reformation)
11	5	BACK TO THE SIXTIES — Tight Fit (Jive)
13	6	WALK RIGHT NOW — Jacksons (Epic)
4	7	GHOST TOWN — Specials (2 Tone)
15	8	GIRLS ON FILM — Duran Duran (EMI)
17	9	WATER ON GLASS/BOYS — Kim Wilde (RAK)
8	10	FOR YOUR EYES ONLY — Sheena Easton (EMI)
10	11	CAN CAN — Bad Manners (Magnet)
30	12	HOLD ON TIGHT — Electric Light Orchestra (Jet)
9	13	NEW LIFE — Depeche Mode (Mute)
16	14	BEACH BOY GOLD — Gidea Park (Stone)
22	15	SHOW ME — Dexy's Midnight Runners (Mercury)
6	16	STARS ON 45, VOLUME 2 — Starsound (CBS)
7	17	LAY ALL YOUR LOVE ON ME — Abba (Epic)
-	18	(SI, SI) JE SUIS UN ROCK STAR — Bill Wyman (A&M)
12	19	DANCING ON THE FLOOR (HOOKED ON LOVE) — Third World (CBS)
14	20	BODY TALK — Imagination (R&B)
-	21	LOVE ACTION (I BELIEVE IN LOVE) — Human League (Virgin)
25	22	CARIBBEAN DISCO SHOW — Lobo (Polydor)
20	23	SAT IN YOUR LAP — Kate Bush (EMI)
-	24	JAPANESE BOY — Aneka (Hansa)
-	25	BACKFIRED — Debbie Harry (Chrysalis)
-	26	ONE IN TEN — UB40 (DEP International)
18	27	VISAGE — Visage (Polydor)
-	28	FIRE — U2 (Island)
-	29	STARTRAX CLUB DISCO — Startrax (Picksy)
-	30	WE'RE ALMOST THERE — Michael Jackson (Motown)

22 August 1981

last	this	title / artist
2	1	GREEN DOOR — Shakin' Stevens (Epic)
3	2	HOOKED ON CLASSICS — Royal Philharmonic Orchestra arranged and conducted by Louis Clark (RCA)
1	3	HAPPY BIRTHDAY — Stevie Wonder (Motown)
21	4	LOVE ACTION (I BELIEVE IN LOVE) — Human League (Virgin)
8	5	GIRLS ON FILM — Duran Duran (EMI)
12	6	HOLD ON TIGHT — Electric Light Orchestra (Jet)
5	7	BACK TO THE SIXTIES — Tight Fit (Jive)
4	8	CHANT NO.1 (I DON'T NEED THIS PRESSURE ON) — Spandau Ballet (Reformation)
22	9	CARIBBEAN DISCO SHOW — Lobo (Polydor)
24	10	JAPANESE BOY — Aneka (Hansa)
9	11	WATER ON GLASS/BOYS — Kim Wilde (RAK)
14	12	BEACH BOY GOLD — Gidea Park (Stone)
6	13	WALK RIGHT NOW — Jacksons (Epic)
-	14	WUNDERBAR — Tenpole Tudor (Stiff)
10	15	FOR YOUR EYES ONLY — Sheena Easton (EMI)
26	16	ONE IN TEN — UB40 (DEP International)
-	17	TAINTED LOVE — Soft Cell (Some Bizzare)
7	18	GHOST TOWN — Specials (2 Tone)
18	19	(SI, SI) JE SUIS UN ROCK STAR — Bill Wyman (A&M)
13	20	NEW LIFE — Depeche Mode (Mute)
17	21	LAY ALL YOUR LOVE ON ME — Abba (Epic)
28	22	FIRE — U2 (Island)
25	23	BACKFIRED — Debbie Harry (Chrysalis)
15	24	SHOW ME — Dexy's Midnight Runners (Mercury)
16	25	STARS ON 45, VOLUME 2 — Starsound (CBS)
19	26	DANCING ON THE FLOOR (HOOKED ON LOVE) — Third World (CBS)
-	27	LOVE SONG — Simple Minds (Virgin)
29	28	STARTRAX CLUB DISCO — Startrax (Picksy)
-	29	STOP DRAGGIN' MY HEART AROUND — Stevie Nicks with Tom Petty & the Heartbreakers (WEA)
-	30	I LOVE MUSIC — Enigma (Creole)

29 August 1981

last	this	title / artist
1	1	GREEN DOOR — Shakin' Stevens (Epic)
4	2	LOVE ACTION (I BELIEVE IN LOVE) — Human League (Virgin)
10	3	JAPANESE BOY — Aneka (Hansa)
2	4	HOOKED ON CLASSICS — Royal Philharmonic Orchestra arranged and conducted by Louis Clark (RCA)
5	5	GIRLS ON FILM — Duran Duran (EMI)
6	6	HOLD ON TIGHT — Electric Light Orchestra (Jet)
17	7	TAINTED LOVE — Soft Cell (Some Bizzare)
9	8	CARIBBEAN DISCO SHOW — Lobo (Polydor)
11	9	WATER ON GLASS/BOYS — Kim Wilde (RAK)
3	10	HAPPY BIRTHDAY — Stevie Wonder (Motown)
19	11	(SI, SI) JE SUIS UN ROCK STAR — Bill Wyman (A&M)
7	12	BACK TO THE SIXTIES — Tight Fit (Jive)
-	13	ABACAB — Genesis (Charisma)
16	14	ONE IN TEN — UB40 (DEP International)
12	15	BEACH BOY GOLD — Gidea Park (Stone)
14	16	WUNDERBAR — Tenpole Tudor (Stiff)
8	17	CHANT NO.1 (I DON'T NEED THIS PRESSURE ON) — Spandau Ballet (Reformation)
-	18	CHEMISTRY — Nolans (Epic)
-	19	TAKE IT ON THE RUN — REO Speedwagon (Epic)
22	20	FIRE — U2 (Island)
-	21	THE THIN WALL — Ultravox (Chrysalis)
28	22	STARTRAX CLUB DISCO — Startrax (Picksy)
15	23	FOR YOUR EYES ONLY — Sheena Easton (EMI)
13	24	WALK RIGHT NOW — Jacksons (Epic)
30	25	I LOVE MUSIC — Enigma (Creole)
20	26	NEW LIFE — Depeche Mode (Mute)
27	27	RAINY NIGHT IN GEORGIA — Randy Crawford (Warner Bros)
-	28	WIRED FOR SOUND — Cliff Richard (EMI)
-	29	ARABIAN NIGHTS — Siouxsie & the Banshees (Polydor)
-	30	START ME UP — Rolling Stones (Rolling Stones)

5 September 1981

last	this	title / artist
3	1	JAPANESE BOY — Aneka (Hansa)
7	2	TAINTED LOVE — Soft Cell (Some Bizzare)
6	3	HOLD ON TIGHT — Electric Light Orchestra (Jet)
-	4	SHE'S GOT CLAWS — Gary Numan (Beggars Banquet)
13	5	ABACAB — Genesis (Charisma)
2	6	LOVE ACTION (I BELIEVE IN LOVE) — Human League (Virgin)
8	7	CARIBBEAN DISCO SHOW — Lobo (Polydor)
14	8	ONE IN TEN — UB40 (DEP International)
4	9	HOOKED ON CLASSICS — Royal Philharmonic Orchestra arranged and conducted by Louis Clark (RCA)
1	10	GREEN DOOR — Shakin' Stevens (Epic)
5	11	GIRLS ON FILM — Duran Duran (EMI)
12	12	BACK TO THE SIXTIES — Tight Fit (Jive)
28	13	WIRED FOR SOUND — Cliff Richard (EMI)
21	14	THE THIN WALL — Ultravox (Chrysalis)
30	15	START ME UP — Rolling Stones (Rolling Stones)
16	16	WUNDERBAR — Tenpole Tudor (Stiff)
27	17	RAINY NIGHT IN GEORGIA — Randy Crawford (Warner Bros)
10	18	HAPPY BIRTHDAY — Stevie Wonder (Motown)
22	19	STARTRAX CLUB DISCO — Startrax (Picksy)
11	20	(SI, SI) JE SUIS UN ROCK STAR — Bill Wyman (A&M)
-	21	SOUVENIR — Orchestral Manoeuvres In The Dark (Dindisc)
25	22	I LOVE MUSIC — Enigma (Creole)
9	23	WATER ON GLASS/BOYS — Kim Wilde (RAK)
15	24	BEACH BOY GOLD — Gidea Park (Stone)
18	25	CHEMISTRY — Nolans (Epic)
20	26	FIRE — U2 (Island)
-	27	PASSIONATE FRIEND — Teardrop Explodes (Zoo)
-	28	HANDS UP (GIVE ME YOUR HEART) — Ottawan (Carrere)
19	29	TAKE IT ON THE RUN — REO Speedwagon (Epic)
-	30	EVERYBODY SALSA — Modern Romance (WEA)

Amid the medleys with a dance beat (*Hooked On Classics, Beach Boy Gold, Caribbean Disco Show, Back To The Sixties, Startrax Club Disco*, etc.), Bill Wyman scored a solo hit outside the Stones, and Debbie Harry did likewise without Blondie, Aneka (Scottish singer Mary Sandeman) made the top with her debut, the shameless oriental pastiche *Japanese Boy*, and the Human League reached the Top 10 for the first time with *Love Action*. Meanwhile, UB40's 'one in ten' were Britain's unemployed.

12 September 1981

last	this		
2	1	TAINTED LOVE	Soft Cell (Some Bizzare)
6	2	LOVE ACTION (I BELIEVE IN LOVE)	Human League (Virgin)
3	3	HOLD ON TIGHT	Electric Light Orchestra (Jet)
1	4	JAPANESE BOY	Aneka (Hansa)
4	5	SHE'S GOT CLAWS	Gary Numan (Beggars Banquet)
13	6	WIRED FOR SOUND	Cliff Richard (EMI)
5	7	ABACAB	Genesis (Charisma)
15	8	START ME UP	Rolling Stones (Rolling Stones)
8	9	ONE IN TEN	UB40 (DEP International)
14	10	THE THIN WALL	Ultravox (Chrysalis)
9	11	HOOKED ON CLASSICS	Royal Philharmonic Orchestra arranged and conducted by Louis Clark (RCA)
7	12	CARIBBEAN DISCO SHOW	Lobo (Polydor)
30	13	EVERYBODY SALSA	Modern Romance (WEA)
11	14	GIRLS ON FILM	Duran Duran (EMI)
25	15	CHEMISTRY	Nolans (Epic)
-	16	PRINCE CHARMING	Adam & the Ants (CBS)
10	17	GREEN DOOR	Shakin' Stevens (Epic)
21	18	SOUVENIR	Orchestral Manoeuvres In The Dark (Dindisc)
17	19	RAINY NIGHT IN GEORGIA	Randy Crawford (Warner Bros)
28	20	HANDS UP (GIVE ME YOUR HEART)	Ottawan (Carrere)
16	21	WUNDERBAR	Tenpole Tudor (Stiff)
-	22	PRETEND	Alvin Stardust (Stiff)
-	23	YOU'LL NEVER KNOW	Hi-Gloss (Epic)
20	24	(SI, SI) JE SUIS UN ROCK STAR	Bill Wyman (A&M)
12	25	BACK TO THE SIXTIES	Tight Fit (Jive)
18	26	HAPPY BIRTHDAY	Stevie Wonder (Motown)
-	27	SLOW HAND	Pointer Sisters (Planet)
26	28	FIRE	U2 (Island)
27	29	PASSIONATE FRIEND	Teardrop Explodes (Zoo)
23	30	WATER ON GLASS/BOYS	Kim Wilde (RAK)

19 September 1981

last	this		
16	1	PRINCE CHARMING	Adam & the Ants (CBS)
1	2	TAINTED LOVE	Soft Cell (Some Bizzare)
6	3	WIRED FOR SOUND	Cliff Richard (EMI)
8	4	START ME UP	Rolling Stones (Rolling Stones)
4	5	JAPANESE BOY	Aneka (Hansa)
18	6	SOUVENIR	Orchestral Manoeuvres In The Dark (Dindisc)
3	7	HOLD ON TIGHT	Electric Light Orchestra (Jet)
20	8	HANDS UP (GIVE ME YOUR HEART)	Ottawan (Carrere)
2	9	LOVE ACTION (I BELIEVE IN LOVE)	Human League (Virgin)
8	10	ONE IN TEN	UB40 (DEP International)
13	11	EVERYBODY SALSA	Modern Romance (WEA)
27	12	SLOW HAND	Pointer Sisters (Planet)
5	13	SHE'S GOT CLAWS	Gary Numan (Beggars Banquet)
19	14	RAINY NIGHT IN GEORGIA	Randy Crawford (Warner Bros)
7	15	ABACAB	Genesis (Charisma)
10	16	THE THIN WALL	Ultravox (Chrysalis)
23	17	YOU'LL NEVER KNOW	Hi-Gloss (Epic)
-	18	THE BIRDIE SONG	Tweets (PRT)
-	19	IN AND OUT OF LOVE	Imagination (R&B)
-	20	ENDLESS LOVE	Diana Ross & Lionel Richie (Motown)
22	21	PRETEND	Alvin Stardust (Stiff)
-	22	SO THIS IS ROMANCE	Linx (Chrysalis)
11	23	HOOKED ON CLASSICS	Royal Philharmonic Orchestra arranged and conducted by Louis Clark (RCA)
-	24	ONE OF THOSE NIGHTS	Bucks Fizz (RCA)
-	25	HAND HELD IN BLACK AND WHITE	Dollar (WEA)
29	26	PASSIONATE FRIEND	Teardrop Explodes (Zoo)
-	27	AS THE TIME GOES BY	Funkapolitan (London)
14	28	GIRLS ON FILM	Duran Duran (EMI)
17	29	GREEN DOOR	Shakin' Stevens (Epic)
15	30	CHEMISTRY	Nolans (Epic)

26 September 1981

last	this		
1	1	PRINCE CHARMING	Adam & the Ants (CBS)
2	2	TAINTED LOVE	Soft Cell (Some Bizzare)
6	3	SOUVENIR	Orchestral Manoeuvres In The Dark (Dindisc)
8	4	HANDS UP (GIVE ME YOUR HEART)	Ottawan (Carrere)
3	5	WIRED FOR SOUND	Cliff Richard (EMI)
21	6	PRETEND	Alvin Stardust (Stiff)
20	7	ENDLESS LOVE	Diana Ross & Lionel Richie (Motown)
5	8	JAPANESE BOY	Aneka (Hansa)
12	9	SLOW HAND	Pointer Sisters (Planet)
7	10	HOLD ON TIGHT	Electric Light Orchestra (Jet)
22	11	SO THIS IS ROMANCE	Linx (Chrysalis)
4	12	START ME UP	Rolling Stones (Rolling Stones)
18	13	THE BIRDIE SONG	Tweets (PRT)
17	14	YOU'LL NEVER KNOW	Hi-Gloss (Epic)
9	15	LOVE ACTION (I BELIEVE IN LOVE)	Human League (Virgin)
16	16	IN AND OUT OF LOVE	Imagination (R&B)
15	17	ABACAB	Genesis (Charisma)
16	18	THE THIN WALL	Ultravox (Chrysalis)
10	19	ONE IN TEN	UB40 (DEP International)
11	20	EVERYBODY SALSA	Modern Romance (WEA)
-	21	INVISIBLE SUN	Police (A&M)
13	22	SHE'S GOT CLAWS	Gary Numan (Beggars Banquet)
24	23	ONE OF THOSE NIGHTS	Bucks Fizz (RCA)
-	24	STARS ON 45, VOLUME 3	Starsound (CBS)
-	25	UNDER YOUR THUMB	Godley & Creme (Polydor)
14	26	RAINY NIGHT IN GEORGIA	Randy Crawford (Warner Bros)
25	27	HAND HELD IN BLACK AND WHITE	Dollar (WEA)
-	28	JUST CAN'T GET ENOUGH	Depeche Mode (Mute)
-	29	HOLLIEDAZE (MEDLEY)	Hollies (EMI)
26	30	PASSIONATE FRIEND	Teardrop Explodes (Zoo)

3 October 1981

last	this		
1	1	PRINCE CHARMING	Adam & the Ants (CBS)
21	2	INVISIBLE SUN	Police (A&M)
2	3	TAINTED LOVE	Soft Cell (Some Bizzare)
4	4	HANDS UP (GIVE ME YOUR HEART)	Ottawan (Carrere)
7	5	ENDLESS LOVE	Diana Ross & Lionel Richie (Motown)
5	6	PRETEND	Alvin Stardust (Stiff)
13	7	THE BIRDIE SONG	Tweets (PRT)
3	8	SOUVENIR	Orchestral Manoeuvres In The Dark (Dindisc)
25	9	UNDER YOUR THUMB	Godley & Creme (Polydor)
-	10	SHUT UP	Madness (Stiff)
5	11	WIRED FOR SOUND	Cliff Richard (EMI)
9	12	SLOW HAND	Pointer Sisters (Planet)
14	13	YOU'LL NEVER KNOW	Hi-Gloss (Epic)
24	14	STARS ON 45, VOLUME 3	Starsound (CBS)
11	15	SO THIS IS ROMANCE	Linx (Chrysalis)
28	16	JUST CAN'T GET ENOUGH	Depeche Mode (Mute)
10	17	HOLD ON TIGHT	Electric Light Orchestra (Jet)
27	18	HAND HELD IN BLACK AND WHITE	Dollar (WEA)
16	19	IN AND OUT OF LOVE	Imagination (R&B)
8	20	JAPANESE BOY	Aneka (Hansa)
19	21	ONE IN TEN	UB40 (DEP International)
-	22	LET'S HANG ON	Barry Manilow (Arista)
15	23	LOVE ACTION (I BELIEVE IN LOVE)	Human League (Virgin)
12	24	START ME UP	Rolling Stones (Rolling Stones)
23	25	ONE OF THOSE NIGHTS	Bucks Fizz (RCA)
-	26	WALKING IN THE SUNSHINE	Bad Manners (Magnet)
29	27	HOLLIEDAZE (MEDLEY)	Hollies (EMI)
20	28	EVERYBODY SALSA	Modern Romance (WEA)
-	29	PLAY TO WIN	Heaven 17 (Virgin)
-	30	SEASONS OF GOLD	Gidea Park (Polo)

Soft Cell's *Tainted Love*, the duo's debut hit, became the year's biggest selling single, despite spending only a week at Number One. Such was the impact of this sharp cover version (of a 1960s song originally cut by Gloria Jones, the late Marc Bolan's girlfriend) in Britain's clubs and discos that the record just kept on selling even after it had left the chart – and did the same in America, where it still holds the all-time record of 43 consecutive weeks on the Billboard Top 100.

October – November 1981

10 October 1981

last week	this week		
1	1	PRINCE CHARMING	Adam & the Ants (CBS)
2	2	INVISIBLE SUN	Police (A&M)
10	3	SHUT UP	Madness (Stiff)
9	4	UNDER YOUR THUMB	Godley & Creme (Polydor)
6	5	PRETEND	Alvin Stardust (Stiff)
8	6	SOUVENIR	Orchestral Manoeuvres In The Dark (Dindisc)
4	7	HANDS UP (GIVE ME YOUR HEART)	Ottawan (Carrere)
3	8	TAINTED LOVE	Soft Cell (Some Bizzare)
5	9	ENDLESS LOVE	Diana Ross & Lionel Richie (Motown)
7	10	THE BIRDIE SONG	Tweets (PRT)
16	11	JUST CAN'T GET ENOUGH	Depeche Mode (Mute)
-	12	IT'S MY PARTY	Dave Stewart with Barbara Gaskin (Broken)
15	13	SO THIS IS ROMANCE	Linx (Chrysalis)
12	14	SLOW HAND	Pointer Sisters (Planet)
13	15	YOU'LL NEVER KNOW	Hi-Gloss (Epic)
-	16	THUNDER IN THE MOUNTAINS	Toyah (Safari)
19	17	IN AND OUT OF LOVE	Imagination (R&B)
26	18	WALKING IN THE SUNSHINE	Bad Manners (Magnet)
-	19	MAD EYED SCREAMER	Creatures (Polydor)
11	20	WIRED FOR SOUND	Cliff Richard (EMI)
-	21	PASSIONATE FRIEND	Teardrop Explodes (Zoo)
23	22	LOVE ACTION (I BELIEVE IN LOVE)	Human League (Virgin)
-	23	GOOD YEAR FOR THE ROSES	Elvis Costello & the Attractions (F.Beat)
-	24	PROCESSION/EVERYTHING'S GONE GREEN	New Order (Factory)
-	25	QUIET LIFE	Japan (Hansa)
22	26	LET'S HANG ON	Barry Manilow (Arista)
14	27	STARS ON 45, VOLUME 3	Starsound (CBS)
-	28	LOCK UP YOUR DAUGHTERS	Slade (RCA)
30	29	SEASONS OF GOLD	Gidea Park (Polo)
18	30	HAND HELD IN BLACK AND WHITE	Dollar (WEA)

17 October 1981

1	1	PRINCE CHARMING	Adam & the Ants (CBS)
2	2	INVISIBLE SUN	Police (A&M)
4	3	UNDER YOUR THUMB	Godley & Creme (Polydor)
3	4	SHUT UP	Madness (Stiff)
12	5	IT'S MY PARTY	Dave Stewart with Barbara Gaskin (Broken)
10	6	THE BIRDIE SONG	Tweets (PRT)
7	7	HANDS UP (GIVE ME YOUR HEART)	Ottawan (Carrere)
5	8	PRETEND	Alvin Stardust (Stiff)
16	9	THUNDER IN THE MOUNTAINS	Toyah (Safari)
6	10	SOUVENIR	Orchestral Manoeuvres In The Dark (Dindisc)
11	11	JUST CAN'T GET ENOUGH	Depeche Mode (Mute)
23	12	GOOD YEAR FOR THE ROSES	Elvis Costello & the Attractions (F.Beat)
18	13	WALKING IN THE SUNSHINE	Bad Manners (Magnet)
9	14	ENDLESS LOVE	Diana Ross & Lionel Richie (Motown)
8	15	TAINTED LOVE	Soft Cell (Some Bizzare)
25	16	QUIET LIFE	Japan (Hansa)
-	17	OPEN YOUR HEART	Human League (Virgin)
19	18	MAD EYED SCREAMER	Creatures (Polydor)
17	19	IN AND OUT OF LOVE	Imagination (R&B)
-	20	HAPPY BIRTHDAY	Altered Images (Epic)
14	21	SLOW HAND	Pointer Sisters (Planet)
-	22	IT'S RAINING	Shakin' Stevens (Epic)
13	23	SO THIS IS ROMANCE	Linx (Chrysalis)
22	24	LOVE ACTION (I BELIEVE IN LOVE)	Human League (Virgin)
15	25	YOU'LL NEVER KNOW	Hi-Gloss (Epic)
24	26	PROCESSION/EVERYTHING'S GONE GREEN	New Order (Factory)
-	27	O SUPERMAN	Laurie Anderson (Warner Bros)
-	28	GLORIA	U2 (Island)
26	29	LET'S HANG ON	Barry Manilow (Arista)
28	30	LOCK UP YOUR DAUGHTERS	Slade (RCA)

24 October 1981

5	1	IT'S MY PARTY	Dave Stewart with Barbara Gaskin (Broken)
6	2	THE BIRDIE SONG	Tweets (PRT)
3	3	UNDER YOUR THUMB	Godley & Creme (Polydor)
9	4	THUNDER IN THE MOUNTAINS	Toyah (Safari)
22	5	IT'S RAINING	Shakin' Stevens (Epic)
1	6	PRINCE CHARMING	Adam & the Ants (CBS)
17	7	OPEN YOUR HEART	Human League (Virgin)
27	8	O SUPERMAN	Laurie Anderson (Warner Bros)
11	9	JUST CAN'T GET ENOUGH	Depeche Mode (Mute)
20	10	HAPPY BIRTHDAY	Altered Images (Epic)
13	11	WALKING IN THE SUNSHINE	Bad Manners (Magnet)
12	12	GOOD YEAR FOR THE ROSES	Elvis Costello & the Attractions (F.Beat)
4	13	SHUT UP	Madness (Stiff)
2	14	INVISIBLE SUN	Police (A&M)
7	15	HANDS UP (GIVE ME YOUR HEART)	Ottawan (Carrere)
14	16	ENDLESS LOVE	Diana Ross & Lionel Richie (Motown)
29	17	LET'S HANG ON	Barry Manilow (Arista)
10	18	SOUVENIR	Orchestral Manoeuvres In The Dark (Dindisc)
16	19	QUIET LIFE	Japan (Hansa)
8	20	PRETEND	Alvin Stardust (Stiff)
-	21	HOLD ME	B.A. Robertson & Maggie Bell (Swan Song)
15	22	TAINTED LOVE	Soft Cell (Some Bizzare)
28	23	GLORIA	U2 (Island)
-	24	ABSOLUTE BEGINNERS	Jam (Polydor)
-	25	LABELLED WITH LOVE	Squeeze (A&M)
-	26	WHEN YOU WERE SWEET SIXTEEN	Fureys & Davey Arthur (Ritz)
-	27	DEAD CITIES	Exploited (Secret)
18	28	MAD EYED SCREAMER	Creatures (Polydor)
-	29	TONIGHT I'M YOURS (DON'T HURT ME)	Rod Stewart (Riva)
21	30	SLOW HAND	Pointer Sisters (Planet)

31 October 1981

1	1	IT'S MY PARTY	Dave Stewart with Barbara Gaskin (Broken)
10	2	HAPPY BIRTHDAY	Altered Images (Epic)
8	3	O SUPERMAN	Laurie Anderson (Warner Bros)
24	4	ABSOLUTE BEGINNERS	Jam (Polydor)
12	5	GOOD YEAR FOR THE ROSES	Elvis Costello & the Attractions (F.Beat)
4	6	THUNDER IN THE MOUNTAINS	Toyah (Safari)
7	7	OPEN YOUR HEART	Human League (Virgin)
2	8	THE BIRDIE SONG	Tweets (PRT)
3	9	UNDER YOUR THUMB	Godley & Creme (Polydor)
-	10	EVERY LITTLE THING SHE DOES IS MAGIC	Police (A&M)
5	11	IT'S RAINING	Shakin' Stevens (Epic)
25	12	LABELLED WITH LOVE	Squeeze (A&M)
11	13	WALKING IN THE SUNSHINE	Bad Manners (Magnet)
17	14	LET'S HANG ON	Barry Manilow (Arista)
21	15	HOLD ME	B.A. Robertson & Maggie Bell (Swan Song)
18	16	SOUVENIR	Orchestral Manoeuvres In The Dark (Dindisc)
9	17	JUST CAN'T GET ENOUGH	Depeche Mode (Mute)
15	18	HANDS UP (GIVE ME YOUR HEART)	Ottawan (Carrere)
13	19	SHUT UP	Madness (Stiff)
14	20	INVISIBLE SUN	Police (A&M)
-	21	WHEN SHE WAS MY GIRL	Four Tops (Casablanca)
6	22	PRINCE CHARMING	Adam & the Ants (CBS)
29	23	TONIGHT I'M YOURS (DON'T HURT ME)	Rod Stewart (Riva)
19	24	QUIET LIFE	Japan (Hansa)
26	25	WHEN YOU WERE SWEET SIXTEEN	Fureys & Davey Arthur (Ritz)
-	26	WHY DO FOOLS FALL IN LOVE	Diana Ross (Capitol)
-	27	LOVE ME TONIGHT	Trevor Walters (Magnet)
28	28	MAD EYED SCREAMER	Creatures (Polydor)
22	29	TAINTED LOVE	Soft Cell (Some Bizzare)
-	30	TWILIGHT	Electric Light Orchestra (Jet)

Adam & The Ants' five weeks at Number One with *Prince Charming* was the year's longest run at the top beating their own *Stand And Deliver* by a week. Ottowan's *Hands Up* was an even more banal vehicle for this group's instructions on how to dance like the Continentals do than had been their earlier *D.I.S.C.O.*, but it still flowered into comparative intellectuality alongside the Tweets' dafter-than-a-brush *Birdie Song*, which mobile discos would still be playing to excited uproar at children's parties 10 years later.

November 1981

last week	this week	**7 November 1981**
2	1	HAPPY BIRTHDAY — Altered Images (Epic)
1	2	IT'S MY PARTY — Dave Stewart with Barbara Gaskin (Broken)
4	3	ABSOLUTE BEGINNERS — Jam (Polydor)
10	4	EVERY LITTLE THING SHE DOES IS MAGIC — Police (A&M)
3	5	O SUPERMAN — Laurie Anderson (Warner Bros)
5	6	GOOD YEAR FOR THE ROSES — Elvis Costello & the Attractions (F.Beat)
6	7	THUNDER IN THE MOUNTAINS — Toyah (Safari)
8	8	THE BIRDIE SONG — Tweets (PRT)
21	9	WHEN SHE WAS MY GIRL — Four Tops (Casablanca)
12	10	LABELLED WITH LOVE — Squeeze (A&M)
14	11	LET'S HANG ON — Barry Manilow (Arista)
15	12	HOLD ME — B.A. Robertson & Maggie Bell (Swan Song)
7	13	OPEN YOUR HEART — Human League (Virgin)
11	14	IT'S RAINING — Shakin' Stevens (Epic)
23	15	TONIGHT I'M YOURS (DON'T HURT ME) — Rod Stewart (Riva)
-	16	JOAN OF ARC — Orchestral Manoeuvres In The Dark (Dindisc)
9	17	UNDER YOUR THUMB — Godley & Creme (Polydor)
25	18	WHEN YOU WERE SWEET SIXTEEN — Fureys & Davey Arthur (Ritz)
-	19	TOM SAWYER (LIVE) — Rush (Exit)
16	20	SOUVENIR — Orchestral Manoeuvres In The Dark (Dindisc)
-	21	PHYSICAL — Olivia Newton-John (EMI)
13	22	WALKING IN THE SUNSHINE — Bad Manners (Magnet)
19	23	SHUT UP — Madness (Stiff)
26	24	WHY DO FOOLS FALL IN LOVE — Diana Ross (Capitol)
20	25	INVISIBLE SUN — Police (A&M)
-	26	BEGIN THE BEGUINE (VOLVER A EMPEZAR) — Julio Iglesias (CBS)
18	27	HANDS UP (GIVE ME YOUR HEART) — Ottawan (Carrere)
22	28	PRINCE CHARMING — Adam & the Ants (CBS)
17	29	JUST CAN'T GET ENOUGH — Depeche Mode (Mute)
30	30	TWILIGHT — Electric Light Orchestra (Jet)

last	this	**14 November 1981**
4	1	EVERY LITTLE THING SHE DOES IS MAGIC — Police (A&M)
1	2	HAPPY BIRTHDAY — Altered Images (Epic)
9	3	WHEN SHE WAS MY GIRL — Four Tops (Casablanca)
2	4	IT'S MY PARTY — Dave Stewart with Barbara Gaskin (Broken)
10	5	LABELLED WITH LOVE — Squeeze (A&M)
6	6	GOOD YEAR FOR THE ROSES — Elvis Costello & the Attractions (F.Beat)
16	7	JOAN OF ARC — Orchestral Manoeuvres In The Dark (Dindisc)
15	8	TONIGHT I'M YOURS (DON'T HURT ME) — Rod Stewart (Riva)
12	9	HOLD ME — B.A. Robertson & Maggie Bell (Swan Song)
3	10	ABSOLUTE BEGINNERS — Jam (Polydor)
-	11	FAVOURITE SHIRTS (BOY MEETS GIRL) — Haircut 100 (Arista)
18	12	WHEN YOU WERE SWEET SIXTEEN — Fureys & Davey Arthur (Ritz)
21	13	PHYSICAL — Olivia Newton-John (EMI)
26	14	BEGIN THE BEGUINE (VOLVER A EMPEZAR) — Julio Iglesias (CBS)
13	15	OPEN YOUR HEART — Human League (Virgin)
11	16	LET'S HANG ON — Barry Manilow (Arista)
8	17	THE BIRDIE SONG — Tweets (PRT)
-	18	LET'S GROOVE — Earth Wind & Fire (CBS)
-	19	STEPPIN' OUT — Kool & the Gang (De-Lite)
14	20	IT'S RAINING — Shakin' Stevens (Epic)
-	21	LOVE ME TONIGHT — Trevor Walters (Magnet)
19	22	TOM SAWYER (LIVE) — Rush (Exit)
24	23	WHY DO FOOLS FALL IN LOVE — Diana Ross (Capitol)
30	24	TWILIGHT — Electric Light Orchestra (Jet)
22	25	WALKING IN THE SUNSHINE — Bad Manners (Magnet)
5	26	O SUPERMAN — Laurie Anderson (Warner Bros)
7	27	THUNDER IN THE MOUNTAINS — Toyah (Safari)
-	28	FLASHBACK — Imagination (R&B)
-	29	UNDER PRESSURE — Queen & David Bowie (EMI)
-	30	THE VOICE — Ultravox (Chrysalis)

last	this	**21 November 1981**
1	1	EVERY LITTLE THING SHE DOES IS MAGIC — Police (A&M)
3	2	WHEN SHE WAS MY GIRL — Four Tops (Casablanca)
7	3	JOAN OF ARC — Orchestral Manoeuvres In The Dark (Dindisc)
29	4	UNDER PRESSURE — Queen & David Bowie (EMI)
2	5	HAPPY BIRTHDAY — Altered Images (Epic)
14	6	BEGIN THE BEGUINE (VOLVER A EMPEZAR) — Julio Iglesias (CBS)
11	7	FAVOURITE SHIRTS (BOY MEETS GIRL) — Haircut 100 (Arista)
5	8	LABELLED WITH LOVE — Squeeze (A&M)
9	9	TONIGHT I'M YOURS (DON'T HURT ME) — Rod Stewart (Riva)
13	10	PHYSICAL — Olivia Newton-John (EMI)
4	11	IT'S MY PARTY — Dave Stewart with Barbara Gaskin (Broken)
6	12	GOOD YEAR FOR THE ROSES — Elvis Costello & the Attractions (F.Beat)
18	13	LET'S GROOVE — Earth Wind & Fire (CBS)
23	14	WHY DO FOOLS FALL IN LOVE — Diana Ross (Capitol)
12	15	WHEN YOU WERE SWEET SIXTEEN — Fureys & Davey Arthur (Ritz)
-	16	BEDSITTER — Soft Cell (Some Bizzare)
15	17	OPEN YOUR HEART — Human League (Virgin)
16	18	LET'S HANG ON — Barry Manilow (Arista)
9	19	HOLD ME — B.A. Robertson & Maggie Bell (Swan Song)
-	20	I GO TO SLEEP — Pretenders (Real)
17	21	THE BIRDIE SONG — Tweets (PRT)
20	22	IT'S RAINING — Shakin' Stevens (Epic)
30	23	THE VOICE — Ultravox (Chrysalis)
-	24	AY AY AY AY MOOSEY — Modern Romance (WEA)
19	25	STEPPIN' OUT — Kool & the Gang (De-Lite)
-	26	VISIONS OF CHINA — Japan (Virgin)
27	27	THUNDER IN THE MOUNTAINS — Toyah (Safari)
10	28	ABSOLUTE BEGINNERS — Jam (Polydor)
-	29	PAINT ME DOWN — Spandau Ballet (Chrysalis)
24	30	TWILIGHT — Electric Light Orchestra (Jet)

last	this	**28 November 1981**
4	1	UNDER PRESSURE — Queen & David Bowie (EMI)
6	2	BEGIN THE BEGUINE (VOLVER A EMPEZAR) — Julio Iglesias (CBS)
7	3	FAVOURITE SHIRTS (BOY MEETS GIRL) — Haircut 100 (Arista)
1	4	EVERY LITTLE THING SHE DOES IS MAGIC — Police (A&M)
3	5	JOAN OF ARC — Orchestral Manoeuvres In The Dark (Dindisc)
10	6	PHYSICAL — Olivia Newton-John (EMI)
9	7	TONIGHT I'M YOURS (DON'T HURT ME) — Rod Stewart (Riva)
13	8	LET'S GROOVE — Earth Wind & Fire (CBS)
2	9	WHEN SHE WAS MY GIRL — Four Tops (Casablanca)
20	10	I GO TO SLEEP — Pretenders (Real)
16	11	BEDSITTER — Soft Cell (Some Bizzare)
24	12	AY AY AY AY MOOSEY — Modern Romance (WEA)
8	13	LABELLED WITH LOVE — Squeeze (A&M)
14	14	WHY DO FOOLS FALL IN LOVE — Diana Ross (Capitol)
25	15	STEPPIN' OUT — Kool & the Gang (De-Lite)
5	16	HAPPY BIRTHDAY — Altered Images (Epic)
15	17	WHEN YOU WERE SWEET SIXTEEN — Fureys & Davey Arthur (Ritz)
-	18	DADDY'S HOME — Cliff Richard (EMI)
-	19	TEARS ARE NOT ENOUGH — ABC (Neutron)
12	20	GOOD YEAR FOR THE ROSES — Elvis Costello & the Attractions (F.Beat)
18	21	LET'S HANG ON — Barry Manilow (Arista)
11	22	IT'S MY PARTY — Dave Stewart with Barbara Gaskin (Broken)
-	23	THE LUNATICS (HAVE TAKEN OVER THE ASYLUM) — Fun Boy Three (Chrysalis)
-	24	CAMBODIA — Kim Wilde (RAK)
17	25	OPEN YOUR HEART — Human League (Virgin)
-	26	YES, TONIGHT JOSEPHINE — Jets (EMI)
22	27	IT'S RAINING — Shakin' Stevens (Epic)
22	28	THE VOICE — Ultravox (Chrysalis)
26	29	VISIONS OF CHINA — Japan (Virgin)
27	30	THUNDER IN THE MOUNTAINS — Toyah (Safari)

Altered Images' *Happy Birthday* chart-topper was a completely different song from Stevie Wonder's identical title of earlier in the year. This group's lead singer, diminutive Scottish lass Clare Grogan, had already found a bite of fame via a role in the film *Gregory's Girl*; when Altered Images hits went off the boil, she would turn to full-time acting. Latin idol Julio Iglesias finally found UK chart success with *Begin The Beguine;* but made no compromise to his usual style – it was sung almost entirely in Spanish!

December 1981

5 December 1981

Last	This	Title	Artist (Label)
1	1	UNDER PRESSURE	Queen & David Bowie (EMI)
2	2	BEGIN THE BEGUINE (VOLVER A EMPEZAR)	Julio Iglesias (CBS)
8	3	LET'S GROOVE	Earth Wind & Fire (CBS)
11	4	BEDSITTER	Soft Cell (Some Bizzare)
3	5	FAVOURITE SHIRTS (BOY MEETS GIRL)	Haircut 100 (Arista)
14	6	WHY DO FOOLS FALL IN LOVE	Diana Ross (Capitol)
10	7	I GO TO SLEEP	Pretenders (Real)
17	8	DADDY'S HOME	Cliff Richard (EMI)
6	9	PHYSICAL	Olivia Newton-John (EMI)
5	10	JOAN OF ARC	Orchestral Manoeuvres In The Dark (Dindisc)
15	11	STEPPIN' OUT	Kool & the Gang (De-Lite)
30	12	THUNDER IN THE MOUNTAINS	Toyah (Safari)
12	13	AY AY AY AY MOOSEY	Modern Romance (WEA)
28	14	THE VOICE	Ultravox (Chrysalis)
23	15	THE LUNATICS (HAVE TAKEN OVER THE ASYLUM)	Fun Boy Three (Chrysalis)
4	16	EVERY LITTLE THING SHE DOES IS MAGIC	Police (A&M)
7	17	TONIGHT I'M YOURS (DON'T HURT ME)	Rod Stewart (Riva)
19	18	TEARS ARE NOT ENOUGH	ABC (Neutron)
9	19	WHEN SHE WAS MY GIRL	Four Tops (Casablanca)
13	20	LABELLED WITH LOVE	Squeeze (A&M)
-	21	WEDDING BELLS	Godley & Creme (Polydor)
24	22	CAMBODIA	Kim Wilde (RAK)
-	23	LET'S ALL SING LIKE THE BIRDIES SING	Tweets (PRT)
-	24	FLASHBACK	Imagination (R&B)
16	25	HAPPY BIRTHDAY	Altered Images (Epic)
-	26	PAINT ME DOWN	Spandau Ballet (Chrysalis)
-	27	MY OWN WAY	Duran Duran (EMI)
26	28	YES, TONIGHT JOSEPHINE	Jets (EMI)
25	29	OPEN YOUR HEART	Human League (Virgin)
27	30	IT'S RAINING	Shakin' Stevens (Epic)

12 December 1981

Last	This	Title	Artist (Label)
2	1	BEGIN THE BEGUINE (VOLVER A EMPEZAR)	Julio Iglesias (CBS)
8	2	DADDY'S HOME	Cliff Richard (EMI)
1	3	UNDER PRESSURE	Queen & David Bowie (EMI)
6	4	WHY DO FOOLS FALL IN LOVE	Diana Ross (Capitol)
3	5	LET'S GROOVE	Earth Wind & Fire (CBS)
4	6	BEDSITTER	Soft Cell (Some Bizzare)
-	7	DON'T YOU WANT ME	Human League (Virgin)
7	8	I GO TO SLEEP	Pretenders (Real)
-	9	IT MUST BE LOVE	Madness (Stiff)
12	10	THUNDER IN THE MOUNTAINS	Toyah (Safari)
5	11	FAVOURITE SHIRTS (BOY MEETS GIRL)	Haircut 100 (Arista)
13	12	AY AY AY AY MOOSEY	Modern Romance (WEA)
22	13	CAMBODIA	Kim Wilde (RAK)
11	14	STEPPIN' OUT	Kool & the Gang (De-Lite)
9	15	PHYSICAL	Olivia Newton-John (EMI)
14	16	THE VOICE	Ultravox (Chrysalis)
21	17	WEDDING BELLS	Godley & Creme (Polydor)
10	18	JOAN OF ARC	Orchestral Manoeuvres In The Dark (Dindisc)
17	19	TONIGHT I'M YOURS (DON'T HURT ME)	Rod Stewart (Riva)
15	20	THE LUNATICS (HAVE TAKEN OVER THE ASYLUM)	Fun Boy Three (Chrysalis)
24	21	FLASHBACK	Imagination (R&B)
23	22	LET'S ALL SING LIKE THE BIRDIES SING	Tweets (PRT)
27	23	MY OWN WAY	Duran Duran (EMI)
18	24	TEARS ARE NOT ENOUGH	ABC (Neutron)
29	25	OPEN YOUR HEART	Human League (Virgin)
28	26	YES, TONIGHT JOSEPHINE	Jets (EMI)
-	27	WILD IS THE WIND	David Bowie (RCA)
-	28	LOVE NEEDS NO DISGUISE	Gary Numan & Dramatis (Beggars Banquet)
-	29	SPIRITS IN THE MATERIAL WORLD	Police (A&M)
-	30	ROCK 'N' ROLL	Status Quo (Vertigo)

19 December 1981

Last	This	Title	Artist (Label)
7	1	DON'T YOU WANT ME	Human League (Virgin)
2	2	DADDY'S HOME	Cliff Richard (EMI)
-	3	ANT RAP	Adam & the Ants (CBS)
-	4	ONE OF US	Abba (Epic)
1	5	BEGIN THE BEGUINE (VOLVER A EMPEZAR)	Julio Iglesias (CBS)
9	6	IT MUST BE LOVE	Madness (Stiff)
4	7	WHY DO FOOLS FALL IN LOVE	Diana Ross (Capitol)
5	8	LET'S GROOVE	Earth Wind & Fire (CBS)
3	9	UNDER PRESSURE	Queen & David Bowie (EMI)
17	10	WEDDING BELLS	Godley & Creme (Polydor)
6	11	BEDSITTER	Soft Cell (Some Bizzare)
29	12	SPIRITS IN THE MATERIAL WORLD	Police (A&M)
30	13	ROCK 'N' ROLL	Status Quo (Vertigo)
13	14	CAMBODIA	Kim Wilde (RAK)
8	15	I GO TO SLEEP	Pretenders (Real)
10	16	THUNDER IN THE MOUNTAINS	Toyah (Safari)
23	17	MY OWN WAY	Duran Duran (EMI)
21	18	FLASHBACK	Imagination (R&B)
-	19	THE LAND OF MAKE BELIEVE	Bucks Fizz (RCA)
27	20	WILD IS THE WIND	David Bowie (RCA)
12	21	AY AY AY AY MOOSEY	Modern Romance (WEA)
22	22	LET'S ALL SING LIKE THE BIRDIES SING	Tweets (PRT)
19	23	TONIGHT I'M YOURS (DON'T HURT ME)	Rod Stewart (Riva)
-	24	BUONA SERA	Bad Manners (Magnet)
-	25	I COULD BE HAPPY	Altered Images (Epic)
20	26	THE LUNATICS (HAVE TAKEN OVER THE ASYLUM)	Fun Boy Three (Chrysalis)
14	27	STEPPIN' OUT	Kool & the Gang (De-Lite)
15	28	PHYSICAL	Olivia Newton-John (EMI)
-	29	MIRROR MIRROR (MON AMOUR)	Dollar (WEA)
16	30	THE VOICE	Ultravox (Chrysalis)

Under Pressure was recorded during a chance studio encounter between Queen and David Bowie while the group were recording in Germany. In 1990, its distinctive bassline would be lifted wholesale by rapper Vanilla Ice for his *Ice Ice Baby*. Cliff Richard's revival of Shep & the Limelites' 1961 US doo-wop hit *Daddy's Home* fulfilled an ambition to cut a version of one of the singer's all-time favourite songs – though it was not done in a studio, but taped during a live concert performance for the BBC.

Top:Madness; left: the Specials; bottom right: the Jam

Elvis did it. The Stones did it. Now these guys did it: listening to black music and liking it. They grew up with the sounds of sixties soul and when reggae and ska were making their mark. The Specials were the hottest band on the Two-Tone label, which had an amazing run of success with its distinctive brand of heavily ska-based music. The Police started out playing their own style of reggae (an early album was titled Regatta De Blanc), as did UB40 and numerous other bands with black and white members. The Beat created a wonderfully dancey sound, and then there was the Jam. Led by Paul Weller they played punchy, hypnotic white soul and sold by the truckload.

January 1982

2 January 1982

4	1	ONE OF US	Abba (Epic)
1	2	DON'T YOU WANT ME	
			Human League (Virgin)
2	3	DADDY'S HOME	
			Cliff Richard (EMI)
3	4	ANT RAP	
			Adam & the Ants (CBS)
6	5	IT MUST BE LOVE	
			Madness (Stiff)
19	6	THE LAND OF MAKE BELIEVE	
			Bucks Fizz (RCA)
10	7	WEDDING BELLS	
			Godley & Creme (Polydor)
5	8	BEGIN THE BEGUINE (VOLVER A	
		EMPEZAR)	Julio Iglesias (CBS)
13	9	ROCK 'N' ROLL	
			Status Quo (Vertigo)
12	10	SPIRITS IN THE MATERIAL	
		WORLD	Police (A&M)
7	11	WHY DO FOOLS FALL IN LOVE	
			Diana Ross (Capitol)
8	12	LET'S GROOVE	
			Earth Wind & Fire (CBS)
11	13	BEDSITTER	
			Soft Cell (Some Bizzare)
29	14	MIRROR MIRROR (MON AMOUR)	
			Dollar (WEA)
17	15	MY OWN WAY	
			Duran Duran (EMI)
8	16	UNDER PRESSURE	
			Queen & David Bowie (EMI)
-	17	YOUNG TURKS	
			Rod Stewart (Riva)
-	18	I'LL FIND MY WAY HOME	
			Jon & Vangelis (Polydor)
18	19	FLASHBACK	
			Imagination (R&B)
23	20	TONIGHT I'M YOURS (DON'T	
		HURT ME)	Rod Stewart (Riva)
22	21	LET'S ALL SING LIKE THE	
		BIRDIES SING	Tweets (PRT)
26	22	THE LUNATICS (HAVE TAKEN	
		OVER THE ASYLUM)	
			Fun Boy Three (Chrysalis)
-	23	WAITING FOR A GIRL LIKE YOU	
			Foreigner (Atlantic)
14	24	CAMBODIA	
			Kim Wilde (RAK)
-	25	STARS OVER 45	
			Chas & Dave (Rockney)
21	26	AY AY AY AY MOOSEY	
			Modern Romance (WEA)
15	27	I GO TO SLEEP	
			Pretenders (Real)
-	28	HOKEY COKEY	
			Snowmen (Stiff)
25	29	I COULD BE HAPPY	
			Altered Images (Epic)
-	30	MERRY XMAS EVERYBODY	
			Slade (Polydor)

9 January 1982

2	1	DON'T YOU WANT ME	
			Human League (Virgin)
1	2	ONE OF US	Abba (Epic)
4	3	ANT RAP	
			Adam & the Ants (CBS)
5	4	IT MUST BE LOVE	
			Madness (Stiff)
6	5	THE LAND OF MAKE BELIEVE	
			Bucks Fizz (RCA)
3	6	DADDY'S HOME	
			Cliff Richard (EMI)
7	7	WEDDING BELLS	
			Godley & Creme (Polydor)
18	8	I'LL FIND MY WAY HOME	
			Jon & Vangelis (Polydor)
14	9	MIRROR MIRROR (MON AMOUR)	
			Dollar (WEA)
17	10	YOUNG TURKS	
			Rod Stewart (Riva)
9	11	ROCK 'N' ROLL	
			Status Quo (Vertigo)
10	12	SPIRITS IN THE MATERIAL	
		WORLD	Police (A&M)
15	13	MY OWN WAY	
			Duran Duran (EMI)
29	14	I COULD BE HAPPY	
			Altered Images (Epic)
28	15	HOKEY COKEY	
			Snowmen (Stiff)
23	16	WAITING FOR A GIRL LIKE YOU	
			Foreigner (Atlantic)
8	17	BEGIN THE BEGUINE (VOLVER A	
		EMPEZAR)	Julio Iglesias (CBS)
11	18	WHY DO FOOLS FALL IN LOVE	
			Diana Ross (Capitol)
13	19	BED SITTER	
			Soft Cell (Some Bizzare)
24	20	CAMBODIA	Kim Wilde (RAK)
-	21	GET DOWN ON IT	
			Kool & the Gang (De-Lite)
21	21	LET'S ALL SING LIKE THE	
		BIRDIES SING	
			Tweets (PRT)
25	23	STARS OVER 45	
			Chas & Dave (Rockney)
12	24	LET'S GROOVE	
			Earth Wind & Fire (CBS)
16	25	UNDER PRESSURE	
			Queen & David Bowie (EMI)
19	26	FLASHBACK	
			Imagination (R&B)
-	27	BRIDESHEAD REVISITED	
			Original Soundtrack (Chrysalis)
-	28	WILD AS THE WIND	
			David Bowie (RCA)
22	29	THE LUNATICS (HAVE TAKEN	
		OVER THE ASYLUM)	
			Fun Boy Three (Chrysalis)
30	30	MERRY XMAS EVERYBODY	
			Slade (Polydor)

16 January 1982

5	1	THE LAND OF MAKE BELIEVE	
			Bucks Fizz (RCA)
1	2	DON'T YOU WANT ME	
			Human League (Virgin)
21	3	GET DOWN ON IT	
			Kool & the Gang (De-Lite)
8	4	I'LL FIND MY WAY HOME	
			Jon & Vangelis (Polydor)
4	5	IT MUST BE LOVE	
			Madness (Stiff)
3	6	ANT RAP	
			Adam & the Ants (CBS)
6	7	DADDY'S HOME	
			Cliff Richard (EMI)
9	8	MIRROR MIRROR (MON AMOUR)	
			Dollar (WEA)
2	9	ONE OF US	Abba (Epic)
7	10	WEDDING BELLS	
			Godley & Creme (Polydor)
14	11	I COULD BE HAPPY	
			Altered Images (Epic)
16	12	WAITING FOR A GIRL LIKE YOU	
			Foreigner (Atlantic)
21	13	LET'S ALL SING LIKE THE	
		BIRDIES SING	Tweets (PRT)
-	14	THE MODEL/COMPUTER LOVE	
			Kraftwerk (EMI)
12	15	SPIRITS IN THE MATERIAL	
		WORLD	Police (A&M)
10	16	YOUNG TURKS	
			Rod Stewart (Riva)
11	17	ROCK 'N' ROLL	
			Status Quo (Vertigo)
-	18	YELLOW PEARL	
			Phil Lynott (Vertigo)
-	19	DEADRINGER	
			Meatloaf (Epic)
-	20	OH JULIE	
			Shakin' Stevens (Epic)
-	21	TENDERNESS	
			Diana Ross (Capitol)
13	22	MY OWN WAY	
			Duran Duran (EMI)
17	23	BEGIN THE BEGUINE	
			Julio Iglesias (CBS)
20	24	CAMBODIA	Kim Wilde (RAK)
19	25	BEDSITTER	
			Soft Cell (Some Bizzare)
15	26	HOKEY COKEY	
			Snowmen (Stiff)
23	27	STARS OVER 45	
			Chas & Dave (Rockney)
24	28	LET'S GROOVE	
			Earth Wind & Fire (CBS)
26	29	FLASHBACK	
			Imagination (R&B)
-	30	DON'T WALK AWAY	
			Four Tops (Casablanca)

23 January 1982

1	1	THE LAND OF MAKE BELIEVE	
			Bucks Fizz (RCA)
3	2	GET DOWN ON IT	
			Kool & the Gang (De-Lite)
8	3	MIRROR MIRROR (MON AMOUR)	
			Dollar (WEA)
2	4	DON'T YOU WANT ME	
			Human League (Virgin)
20	5	OH JULIE	
			Shakin' Stevens (Epic)
14	6	THE MODEL/COMPUTER LOVE	
			Kraftwerk (EMI)
9	7	ONE OF US	Abba (Epic)
-	8	BEING BOILED	
			Human League (EMI)
11	9	I COULD BE HAPPY	
			Altered Images (Epic)
4	10	I'LL FIND MY WAY HOME	
			Jon & Vangelis (Polydor)
5	11	IT MUST BE LOVE	
			Madness (Stiff)
12	12	WAITING FOR A GIRL LIKE YOU	
			Foreigner (Atlantic)
6	13	ANT RAP	
			Adam & the Ants (CBS)
-	14	GOLDEN BROWN	
			Stranglers (Liberty)
16	15	YOUNG TURKS	
			Rod Stewart (Riva)
7	16	DADDY'S HOME	
			Cliff Richard (EMI)
18	17	YELLOW PEARL	
			Phil Lynott (Vertigo)
30	18	DON'T WALK AWAY	
			Four Tops (Casablanca)
-	19	I WANNA BE A WINNER	
			Brown Sauce (BBC)
-	20	ARTHUR'S THEME (BEST THAT	
		YOU CAN DO)	
			Christopher Cross
			(Warner Brothers)
-	21	DROWNING IN BERLIN	
			Mobiles (Rialto)
19	22	DEADRINGER	Meatloaf (Epic)
17	23	ROCK 'N' ROLL	
			Status Quo (Vertigo)
-	24	I WANNA SPEND SOME TIME	
		WITH YOU	
			Alton Edwards (Streetwave)
13	25	LET'S ALL SING LIKE THE	
		BIRDIES SING	Tweets (PRT)
22	26	MY OWN WAY	
			Duran Duran (EMI)
25	27	BED SITTER	
			Soft Cell (Some Bizzare)
10	28	WEDDING BELLS	
			Godley & Creme (Polydor)
-	29	MAID OF ORLEANS	
			Orchestral Manoeuvres In The
			Dark (Dindisc)
-	30	LOVE PLUS ONE	
			Haircut 100 (Arista)

Human League's *Don't You Want Me*, a massive seller over Christmas, continued strongly into the New Year to eventually sell some 1.4 million copies, making it Virgin's biggest-ever single. Its success prompted EMI to reissue *Being Boiled*, the group's first-ever single, originally recorded for the independent Fast Products label in 1978, when the band's line-up was materially different. Vintage sound nothwithstanding, the reissue immediately made the Top 10 alongside *Don't You Want Me*.

January – February 1982

last week	this week	30 January 1982
6	1	THE MODEL/COMPUTER LOVE Kraftwerk (EMI)
1	2	THE LAND OF MAKE BELIEVE Bucks Fizz (RCA)
5	3	OH JULIE Shakin' Stevens (Epic)
8	4	BEING BOILED Human League (EMI)
2	5	GET DOWN ON IT Kool & the Gang (De-Lite)
14	6	GOLDEN BROWN Stranglers (Liberty)
10	7	I'LL FIND MY WAY HOME Jon & Vangelis (Polydor)
22	8	DEADRINGER Meatloaf (Epic)
4	9	DON'T YOU WANT ME Human League (Virgin)
21	10	DROWNING IN BERLIN Mobiles (Rialto)
12	11	WAITING FOR A GIRL LIKE YOU Foreigner (Atlantic)
3	12	MIRROR MIRROR (MON AMOUR) Dollar (WEA)
9	13	I COULD BE HAPPY Altered Images (Epic)
17	14	YELLOW PEARL Phil Lynott (Vertigo)
29	15	MAID OF ORLEANS Orchestral Manoeuvres In The Dark (Dindisc)
20	16	ARTHUR'S THEME (BEST THAT YOU CAN DO) Christopher Cross (Warner Brothers)
11	17	IT MUST BE LOVE Madness (Stiff)
24	18	I WANNA SPEND SOME TIME WITH YOU Alton Edwards (Streetwave)
18	19	DON'T WALK AWAY Four Tops (Casablanca)
-	20	EASIER SAID THAN DONE Shakatak (Polydor)
13	21	ANT RAP Adam & the Ants (CBS)
7	22	ONE OF US Abba (Epic)
28	23	WEDDING BELLS Godley & Creme (Polydor)
-	24	HERE IS THE NEWS Electric Light Orchestra (Jet)
19	25	I WANNA BE A WINNER Brown Sauce (BBC)
16	26	DADDY'S HOME Cliff Richard (EMI)
-	27	SENSES WORKING OVERTIME XTC (Virgin)
-	28	RESTLESS Gillan (Virgin)
-	29	EUROPEAN SON Japan (Hansa)
-	30	NEVER GIVE UP ON A GOOD THING George Benson (Warner Brothers)

		6 February 1982
1	1	THE MODEL/COMPUTER LOVE Kraftwerk (EMI)
3	2	OH JULIE Shakin' Stevens (Epic)
6	3	GOLDEN BROWN Stranglers (Liberty)
16	4	ARTHUR'S THEME (BEST THAT YOU CAN DO) Christopher Cross (Warner Brothers)
2	5	THE LAND OF MAKE BELIEVE Bucks Fizz (RCA)
5	6	GET DOWN ON IT Kool & the Gang (De-Lite)
4	7	BEING BOILED Human League (EMI)
8	8	DEADRINGER Meatloaf (Epic)
15	9	MAID OF ORLEANS Orchestral Manoeuvres In The Dark (Dindisc)
10	10	DROWNING IN BERLIN Mobiles (Rialto)
7	11	I'LL FIND MY WAY HOME Jon & Vangelis (Polydor)
12	12	MIRROR MIRROR (MON AMOUR) Dollar (WEA)
11	13	WAITING FOR A GIRL LIKE YOU Foreigner (Atlantic)
19	14	DON'T WALK AWAY Four Tops (Casablanca)
25	15	I WANNA BE A WINNER Brown Sauce (BBC)
-	16	LOVE PLUS ONE Haircut 100 (Arista)
18	17	I WANNA SPEND SOME TIME WITH YOU Alton Edwards (Streetwave)
9	18	DON'T YOU WANT ME Human League (Virgin)
20	19	EASIER SAID THAN DONE Shakatak (Polydor)
24	20	HERE IS THE NEWS Electric Light Orchestra (Jet)
13	21	I COULD BE HAPPY Altered Images (Epic)
30	22	NEVER GIVE UP ON A GOOD THING George Benson (Warner Brothers)
-	23	FOOL IF YOU THINK IT'S OVER Elkie Brooks (A&M)
22	24	ONE OF US Abba (Epic)
27	25	SENSES WORKING OVERTIME XTC (Virgin)
-	26	COMIN' IN AND OUT OF YOUR LIFE Barbra Streisand (CBS)
-	27	I CAN'T GO FOR THAT (NO CAN DO) Daryl Hall & John Oates (RCA)
14	28	YELLOW PEARL Phil Lynott (Vertigo)
-	29	TROUBLE Lindsey Buckingham (Mercury)
-	30	THEME FROM HILL STREET BLUES Mike Post & Larry Carlton (Elektra)

		13 February 1982
1	1	THE MODEL/COMPUTER LOVE Kraftwerk (EMI)
3	2	GOLDEN BROWN Stranglers (Liberty)
2	3	OH JULIE Shakin' Stevens (Epic)
9	4	MAID OF ORLEANS Orchestral Manoeuvres In The Dark (Dindisc)
4	5	ARTHUR'S THEME (BEST THAT YOU CAN DO) Christopher Cross (Warner Brothers)
8	6	DEADRINGER Meatloaf (Epic)
-	7	SAY HELLO WAVE GOODBYE Soft Cell (Some Bizzare)
-	8	A TOWN CALLED MALICE Jam (Polydor)
19	9	EASIER SAID THAN DONE Shakatak (Polydor)
10	10	DROWNING IN BERLIN Mobiles (Rialto)
6	11	GET DOWN ON IT Kool & the Gang (De-Lite)
7	12	BEING BOILED Human League (EMI)
5	13	THE LAND OF MAKE BELIEVE Bucks Fizz (RCA)
-	14	LET'S GET IT UP AC/DC (Atlantic)
25	15	SENSES WORKING OVERTIME XTC (Virgin)
13	16	WAITING FOR A GIRL LIKE YOU Foreigner (Atlantic)
11	17	I'LL FIND MY WAY HOME Jon & Vangelis (Polydor)
-	18	THE LION SLEEPS TONIGHT Tight Fit (Jive)
27	19	I CAN'T GO FOR THAT (NO CAN DO) Daryl Hall & John Oates (RCA)
16	20	LOVE PLUS ONE Haircut 100 (Arista)
22	21	NEVER GIVE UP ON A GOOD THING George Benson (Warner Brothers)
-	22	RESTLESS Gillan (Virgin)
12	23	MIRROR MIRROR Dollar (WEA)
-	24	THE BOILER Rhoda & the Special AKA (2 Tone)
18	25	DON'T YOU WANT ME Human League (Virgin)
21	26	I COULD BE HAPPY Altered Images (Epic)
15	27	I WANNA BE A WINNER Brown Sauce (BBC)
17	28	I WANNA SPEND SOME TIME WITH YOU Alton Edwards (Streetwave)
-	29	DO YOU BELIEVE IN THE WESTWORLD Theatre Of Hate (Burning Rome)
28	30	YELLOW PEARL Phil Lynott (Vertigo)

		20 February 1982
8	1	A TOWN CALLED MALICE Jam (Polydor)
2	2	GOLDEN BROWN Stranglers (Liberty)
1	3	THE MODEL/COMPUTER LOVE Kraftwerk (EMI)
4	4	MAID OF ORLEANS Orchestral Manoeuvres In The Dark (Dindisc)
18	5	THE LION SLEEPS TONIGHT Tight Fit (Jive)
20	6	LOVE PLUS ONE Haircut 100 (Arista)
5	7	ARTHUR'S THEME (BEST THAT YOU CAN DO) Christopher Cross (Warner Brothers)
3	8	OH JULIE Shakin' Stevens (Epic)
6	9	DEADRINGER Meatloaf (Epic)
15	10	SENSES WORKING OVERTIME XTC (Virgin)
19	11	I CAN'T GO FOR THAT (NO CAN DO) Daryl Hall & John Oates (RCA)
7	12	SAY HELLO WAVE GOODBYE Soft Cell (Some Bizzare)
-	13	CENTREFOLD J. Geils Band (EMI America)
10	14	DROWNING IN BERLIN Mobiles (Rialto)
9	15	EASIER SAID THAN DONE Shakatak (Polydor)
-	16	T'AIN'T WHAT YOU DO Fun Boy Three & Bananarama (Chrysalis)
13	17	THE LAND OF MAKE BELIEVE Bucks Fizz (RCA)
12	18	BEING BOILED Human League (EMI)
-	19	SEE YOU Depeche Mode (Mute)
21	20	NEVER GIVE UP ON A GOOD THING George Benson (Warner Brothers)
-	21	CARDIAC ARREST Madness (Stiff)
14	22	LET'S GET IT UP AC/DC (Atlantic)
16	23	WAITING FOR A GIRL LIKE YOU Foreigner (Atlantic)
11	24	GET DOWN ON IT Kool & the Gang (De-Lite)
-	25	POISON ARROW ABC (Neutron)
17	26	I'LL FIND MY WAY HOME Jon & Vangelis (Polydor)
-	27	TONIGHT I'M GONNA LOVE YOU ALL OVER Four Tops (Casablanca)
23	28	MIRROR MIRROR Dollar (WEA)
-	29	I WON'T CLOSE MY EYES UB40 (DEP International)
30	30	FOOL IF YOU THINK IT'S OVER Elkie Brooks (A&M)

Kraftwerk's *The Model* was a 1978 track whose popularity had grown steadily, mainly through club play, until reaction to its almost incidental inclusion on the B-side of *Computer Love* finally alerted EMI to the fact that the wrong side of the single was being promoted. The Jam's *A Town Called Malice* made their No.1 hat-trick, while *Golden Brown,* unusually based around a harpsichord riff, was the Stranglers' all-time biggest UK hit. OMD, meanwhile, followed *Joan Of Arc* thematically with *Maid Of Orleans.*

February – March 1982

27 February 1982

last week	this week	
1	1	A TOWN CALLED MALICE — Jam (Polydor)
5	2	THE LION SLEEPS TONIGHT — Tight Fit (Jive)
2	3	GOLDEN BROWN — Stranglers (Liberty)
12	4	SAY HELLO WAVE GOODBYE — Soft Cell (Some Bizzare)
4	5	MAID OF ORLEANS — Orchestral Manoeuvres In The Dark (Dindisc)
13	6	CENTREFOLD — J. Geils Band (EMI America)
6	7	LOVE PLUS ONE — Haircut 100 (Arista)
10	8	SENSES WORKING OVERTIME — XTC (Virgin)
7	9	ARTHUR'S THEME (BEST THAT YOU CAN DO) — Christopher Cross (Warner Brothers)
3	10	THE MODEL/COMPUTER LOVE — Kraftwerk (EMI)
11	11	I CAN'T GO FOR THAT (NO CAN DO) — Daryl Hall & John Oates (RCA)
8	12	OH JULIE — Shakin' Stevens (Epic)
9	13	DEADRINGER — Meatloaf (Epic)
21	14	CARDIAC ARREST — Madness (Stiff)
20	15	NEVER GIVE UP ON A GOOD THING — George Benson (Warner Brothers)
14	16	DROWNING IN BERLIN — Mobiles (Rialto)
-	17	MICKEY — Toni Basil (Radialchoice)
16	18	T'AIN'T WHAT YOU DO — Fun Boy Three & Bananarama (Chrysalis)
22	19	LET'S GET IT UP — AC/DC (Atlantic)
-	20	LANDSLIDE — Olivia Newton-John (EMI)
-	21	RUN TO THE HILLS — Iron Maiden (EMI)
30	22	FOOL IF YOU THINK IT'S OVER — Elkie Brooks (A&M)
-	23	HEAD OVER HEELS — Abba (Epic)
19	24	SEE YOU — Depeche Mode (Mute)
15	25	EASIER SAID THAN DONE — Shakatak (Polydor)
-	26	YOU'RE THE ONE FOR ME — D Train (Epic)
25	27	POISON ARROW — ABC (Neutron)
-	28	GO WILD IN THE COUNTRY — Bow Wow Wow (RCA)
23	29	WAITING FOR A GIRL LIKE YOU — Foreigner (Atlantic)
24	30	GET DOWN ON IT — Kool & the Gang (De-Lite)

6 March 1982

last week	this week	
1	1	A TOWN CALLED MALICE — Jam (Polydor)
2	2	THE LION SLEEPS TONIGHT — Tight Fit (Jive)
7	3	LOVE PLUS ONE — Haircut 100 (Arista)
6	4	CENTREFOLD — J. Geils Band (EMI America)
18	5	T'AIN'T WHAT YOU DO — Fun Boy Three & Bananarama (Chrysalis)
4	6	SAY HELLO WAVE GOODBYE — Soft Cell (Some Bizzare)
17	7	MICKEY — Toni Basil (Radialchoice)
24	8	SEE YOU — Depeche Mode (Mute)
3	9	GOLDEN BROWN — Stranglers (Liberty)
11	10	I CAN'T GO FOR THAT (NO CAN DO) — Daryl Hall & John Oates (RCA)
5	11	MAID OF ORLEANS — Orchestral Manoeuvres In The Dark (Dindisc)
-	12	DEUTSCHER GIRLS — Adam & the Ants (Ego)
22	13	FOOL IF YOU THINK IT'S OVER — Elkie Brooks (A&M)
-	14	STARS ON STEVIE — Starsound (CBS)
9	15	ARTHUR'S THEME (BEST THAT YOU CAN DO) — Christopher Cross (Warner Brothers)
14	16	CARDIAC ARREST — Madness (Stiff)
21	17	RUN TO THE HILLS — Iron Maiden (EMI)
-	18	CLASSIC — Adrian Gurvitz (RAK)
28	19	GO WILD IN THE COUNTRY — Bow Wow Wow (RCA)
15	20	NEVER GIVE UP ON A GOOD THING — George Benson (Warner Brothers)
8	21	SENSES WORKING OVERTIME — XTC (Virgin)
-	22	THEME FROM HILL STREET BLUES — Mike Post & Larry Carlton (Elektra)
-	23	SOME GUYS HAVE ALL THE LUCK — Robert Palmer (Island)
12	24	OH JULIE — Shakin' Stevens (Epic)
27	25	POISON ARROW — ABC (Neutron)
23	26	HEAD OVER HEELS — Abba (Epic)
-	27	SHOWROOM DUMMIES — Kraftwerk (EMI)
13	28	DEADRINGER — Meatloaf (Epic)
-	29	I WON'T CLOSE MY EYES — UB40 (DEP International)
25	30	EASIER SAID THAN DONE — Shakatak (Polydor)

13 March 1982

last week	this week	
2	1	THE LION SLEEPS TONIGHT — Tight Fit (Jive)
7	2	MICKEY — Toni Basil (Radialchoice)
3	3	LOVE PLUS ONE — Haircut 100 (Arista)
4	4	CENTREFOLD — J. Geils Band (EMI America)
5	5	T'AIN'T WHAT YOU DO — Fun Boy Three & Bananarama (Chrysalis)
1	6	A TOWN CALLED MALICE — Jam (Polydor)
8	7	SEE YOU — Depeche Mode (Mute)
12	8	DEUTSCHER GIRLS — Adam & the Ants (Ego)
6	9	SAY HELLO WAVE GOODBYE — Soft Cell (Some Bizzare)
16	10	CARDIAC ARREST — Madness (Stiff)
18	11	CLASSIC — Adrian Gurvitz (RAK)
17	12	RUN TO THE HILLS — Iron Maiden (EMI)
19	13	GO WILD IN THE COUNTRY — Bow Wow Wow (RCA)
25	14	POISON ARROW — ABC (Neutron)
10	15	I CAN'T GO FOR THAT (NO CAN DO) — Daryl Hall & John Oates (RCA)
14	16	STARS ON STEVIE — Starsound (CBS)
11	17	MAID OF ORLEANS — Orchestral Manoeuvres In The Dark (Dindisc)
9	18	GOLDEN BROWN — Stranglers (Liberty)
23	19	SOME GUYS HAVE ALL THE LUCK — Robert Palmer (Island)
-	20	SEVEN TEARS — Goombay Dance Band (Epic)
20	21	NEVER GIVE UP ON A GOOD THING — George Benson (Warner Brothers)
-	22	MUSIC FOR CHAMELEONS — Gary Numan (Beggars Banquet)
-	23	JUST AN ILLUSION — Imagination (R&B)
-	24	QUIEREME MUCHO (YOURS) — Julio Iglesias (CBS)
-	25	BAAL'S HYMN — David Bowie (RCA)
15	26	ARTHUR'S THEME (BEST THAT YOU CAN DO) — Christopher Cross (Warner Brothers)
-	27	LOVE MAKES THE WORLD GO ROUND — Jets (EMI)
21	28	SENSES WORKING OVERTIME — XTC (Virgin)
22	29	THEME FROM HILL STREET BLUES — Mike Post & Larry Carlton (Elektra)
26	30	HEAD OVER HEELS — Abba (Epic)

20 March 1982

last week	this week	
1	1	THE LION SLEEPS TONIGHT — Tight Fit (Jive)
2	2	MICKEY — Toni Basil (Radialchoice)
3	3	LOVE PLUS ONE — Haircut 100 (Arista)
5	4	T'AIN'T WHAT YOU DO — Fun Boy Three & Bananarama (Chrysalis)
20	5	SEVEN TEARS — Goombay Dance Band (Epic)
4	6	CENTREFOLD — J. Geils Band (EMI America)
7	7	SEE YOU — Depeche Mode (Mute)
13	8	GO WILD IN THE COUNTRY — Bow Wow Wow (RCA)
12	9	RUN TO THE HILLS — Iron Maiden (EMI)
14	10	POISON ARROW — ABC (Neutron)
11	11	CLASSIC — Adrian Gurvitz (RAK)
6	12	A TOWN CALLED MALICE — Jam (Polydor)
16	13	STARS ON STEVIE — Starsound (CBS)
23	14	JUST AN ILLUSION — Imagination (R&B)
8	15	DEUTSCHER GIRLS — Adam & the Ants (Ego)
24	16	QUIEREME MUCHO (YOURS) — Julio Iglesias (CBS)
10	17	CARDIAC ARREST — Madness (Stiff)
19	18	SOME GUYS HAVE ALL THE LUCK — Robert Palmer (Island)
17	19	MAID OF ORLEANS — Orchestral Manoeuvres In The Dark (Dindisc)
27	20	LOVE MAKES THE WORLD GO ROUND — Jets (EMI)
22	21	MUSIC FOR CHAMELEONS — Gary Numan (Beggars Banquet)
18	22	GOLDEN BROWN — Stranglers (Liberty)
9	23	SAY HELLO WAVE GOODBYE — Soft Cell (Some Bizzare)
-	24	PARTY FEARS TWO — Associates (Associates)
25	25	BAAL'S HYMN — David Bowie (RCA)
15	26	I CAN'T GO FOR THAT (NO CAN DO) — Daryl Hall & John Oates (RCA)
30	27	HEAD OVER HEELS — Abba (Epic)
-	28	DAMNED DON'T CRY — Visage (Polydor)
-	29	AIN'T NO PLEASING YOU — Chas & Dave (Rockney)
-	30	HAVE YOU EVER BEEN IN LOVE — Leo Sayer (Chrysalis)

Tight Fit, a studio trio who had already hit with one of 1981's many medley singles, *Back To The Sixties*, came fully into their own with a full revival of a '60s hit, the Tokens' *The Lion Sleeps Tonight* from 1962. It denied Number One to Toni Basil's *Mickey*, a commercial if totally daft song by one of the entertainment world's top dance choreographers. It did top the chart in Basil's native USA , no doubt aided by possibly the most exhausting dance video ever.

March – April 1982

27 March 1982

last week	this week	title / artist (label)
1	1	THE LION SLEEPS TONIGHT — Tight Fit (Jive)
5	2	SEVEN TEARS — Goombay Dance Band (Epic)
2	3	MICKEY — Toni Basil (Radialchoice)
3	4	LOVE PLUS ONE — Haircut 100 (Arista)
10	5	POISON ARROW — ABC (Neutron)
4	6	T'AIN'T WHAT YOU DO — Fun Boy Three & Bananarama (Chrysalis)
14	7	JUST AN ILLUSION — Imagination (R&B)
16	8	QUIEREME MUCHO (YOURS) — Julio Iglesias (CBS)
8	9	GO WILD IN THE COUNTRY — Bow Wow Wow (RCA)
-	10	LAYLA — Derek & the Dominoes (RSO)
11	11	CLASSIC — Adrian Gurvitz (RAK)
7	12	SEE YOU — Depeche Mode (Mute)
24	13	PARTY FEARS TWO — Associates (Associates)
28	14	DAMNED DON'T CRY — Visage (Polydor)
6	15	CENTREFOLD — J. Geils Band (EMI America)
9	16	RUN TO THE HILLS — Iron Maiden (EMI)
13	17	STARS ON STEVIE — Starsound (CBS)
12	18	A TOWN CALLED MALICE — Jam (Polydor)
18	19	SOME GUYS HAVE ALL THE LUCK — Robert Palmer (Island)
-	20	YOUR HONOUR — Pluto (KR)
29	21	AIN'T NO PLEASING YOU — Chas & Dave (Rockney)
21	22	MUSIC FOR CHAMELEONS — Gary Numan (Beggars Banquet)
17	23	CARDIAC ARREST — Madness (Stiff)
-	24	GHOSTS — Japan (Virgin)
27	25	HEAD OVER HEELS — Abba (Epic)
25	26	BAAL'S HYMN — David Bowie (RCA)
19	27	MAID OF ORLEANS — Orchestral Manoeuvres in The Dark (Dindisc)
-	28	ARE YOU LONESOME TONIGHT — Elvis Presley (RCA)
-	29	A BUNCH OF THYME — Foster & Allen (Ritz)
15	30	DEUTSCHER GIRLS — Adam & the Ants (Ego)

3 April 1982

last week	this week	title / artist (label)
2	1	SEVEN TEARS — Goombay Dance Band (Epic)
7	2	JUST AN ILLUSION — Imagination (R&B)
8	3	QUIEREME MUCHO (YOURS) — Julio Iglesias (CBS)
1	4	THE LION SLEEPS TONIGHT — Tight Fit (Jive)
5	5	POISON ARROW — ABC (Neutron)
10	6	LAYLA — Derek & the Dominoes (RSO)
3	7	MICKEY — Toni Basil (Radialchoice)
21	8	AIN'T NO PLEASING YOU — Chas & Dave (Rockney)
13	9	PARTY FEARS TWO — Associates (Associates)
11	10	CLASSIC — Adrian Gurvitz (RAK)
9	11	GO WILD IN THE COUNTRY — Bow Wow Wow (RCA)
24	12	GHOSTS — Japan (Virgin)
4	13	LOVE PLUS ONE — Haircut 100 (Arista)
-	14	HAVE YOU EVER BEEN IN LOVE — Leo Sayer (Chrysalis)
14	15	DAMNED DON'T CRY — Visage (Polydor)
-	16	MY CAMERA NEVER LIES — Bucks Fizz (RCA)
12	17	SEE YOU — Depeche Mode (Mute)
29	18	A BUNCH OF THYME — Foster & Allen (Ritz)
6	19	T'AIN'T WHAT YOU DO — Fun Boy Three & Bananarama (Chrysalis)
20	20	YOUR HONOUR — Pluto (KR)
-	21	GIVE ME BACK MY HEART — Dollar (WEA)
-	22	SEE THOSE EYES — Altered Images (Epic)
28	23	ARE YOU LONESOME TONIGHT — Elvis Presley (RCA)
16	24	RUN TO THE HILLS — Iron Maiden (EMI)
-	25	IS IT A DREAM — Classix Nouveaux (Liberty)
-	26	DON'T LOVE ME TOO HARD — Nolans (Epic)
-	27	EMPIRE SONG — Killing Joke (Malicious Damage)
15	28	CENTREFOLD — J. Geils Band (EMI America)
-	29	DEAR JOHN — Status Quo (Vertigo)
22	30	MUSIC FOR CHAMELEONS — Gary Numan (Beggars Banquet)

10 April 1982

last week	this week	title / artist (label)
1	1	SEVEN TEARS — Goombay Dance Band (Epic)
3	2	QUIEREME MUCHO (YOURS) — Julio Iglesias (CBS)
2	3	JUST AN ILLUSION — Imagination (R&B)
8	4	AIN'T NO PLEASING YOU — Chas & Dave (Rockney)
12	5	GHOSTS — Japan (Virgin)
5	6	POISON ARROW — ABC (Neutron)
16	7	MY CAMERA NEVER LIES — Bucks Fizz (RCA)
6	8	LAYLA — Derek & the Dominoes (RSO)
14	9	HAVE YOU EVER BEEN IN LOVE — Leo Sayer (Chrysalis)
-	10	MORE THAN THIS — Roxy Music (EG)
22	11	SEE THOSE EYES — Altered Images (Epic)
9	12	PARTY FEARS TWO — Associates (Associates)
10	13	CLASSIC — Adrian Gurvitz (RAK)
15	14	DAMNED DON'T CRY — Visage (Polydor)
4	15	THE LION SLEEPS TONIGHT — Tight Fit (Jive)
29	16	DEAR JOHN — Status Quo (Vertigo)
21	17	GIVE ME BACK MY HEART — Dollar (WEA)
25	18	IS IT A DREAM — Classix Nouveaux (Liberty)
26	19	DON'T LOVE ME TOO HARD — Nolans (Epic)
18	20	A BUNCH OF THYME — Foster & Allen (Ritz)
7	21	MICKEY — Toni Basil (Radialchoice)
20	22	YOUR HONOUR — Pluto (KR)
-	23	IRON FIST — Motorhead (Bronze)
13	24	LOVE PLUS ONE — Haircut 100 (Arista)
-	25	NIGHT BIRDS — Shakatak (Polydor)
-	26	STONE COLD — Rainbow (Polydor)
11	27	GO WILD IN THE COUNTRY — Bow Wow Wow (RCA)
-	28	MEMORY — Barbra Streisand (CBS)
-	29	STREETPLAYER-MECHANIK — Fashion (Arista)
-	30	PAPA'S GOT A BRAND NEW PIGBAG — Pigbag (Y)

17 April 1982

last week	this week	title / artist (label)
7	1	MY CAMERA NEVER LIES — Bucks Fizz (RCA)
4	2	AIN'T NO PLEASING YOU — Chas & Dave (Rockney)
1	3	SEVEN TEARS — Goombay Dance Band (Epic)
10	4	MORE THAN THIS — Roxy Music (EG)
5	5	GHOSTS — Japan (Virgin)
3	6	JUST AN ILLUSION — Imagination (R&B)
17	7	GIVE ME BACK MY HEART — Dollar (WEA)
9	8	HAVE YOU EVER BEEN IN LOVE — Leo Sayer (Chrysalis)
-	9	EBONY AND IVORY — Paul McCartney & Stevie Wonder (Parlophone)
16	10	DEAR JOHN — Status Quo (Vertigo)
8	11	LAYLA — Derek & the Dominoes (RSO)
25	12	NIGHT BIRDS — Shakatak (Polydor)
18	13	IS IT A DREAM — Classix Nouveaux (Liberty)
2	14	QUIEREME MUCHO (YOURS) — Julio Iglesias (CBS)
19	15	DON'T LOVE ME TOO HARD — Nolans (Epic)
11	16	SEE THOSE EYES — Altered Images (Epic)
-	17	FANTASTIC DAY — Haircut 100 (Arista)
14	18	DAMNED DON'T CRY — Visage (Polydor)
-	19	BLUE EYES — Elton John (Rocket)
-	20	HOUSE ON FIRE — Boomtown Rats (Mercury)
20	21	A BUNCH OF THYME — Foster & Allen (Ritz)
-	22	REALLY SAYING SOMETHING — Bananarama & the Fun Boy Three (Deram)
6	23	POISON ARROW — ABC (Neutron)
-	24	ONE STEP FURTHER — Bardo (Epic)
-	25	CAT PEOPLE (PUTTING OUT FIRE) — David Bowie (MCA)
-	26	THIS TIME (WE'LL GET IT RIGHT) — England World Cup (England)
30	27	PAPA'S GOT A BRAND NEW PIGBAG — Pigbag (Y)
12	28	PARTY FEARS TWO — Associates (Associates)
-	29	A CELEBRATION — U2 (Island)
23	30	IRON FIST — Motorhead (Bronze)

The Goombay Dance Band appeared to have inherited the mantle of Boney M on *Seven Tears*, which bore most of the hallmarks of the Frank Farian group's hits, including the ability to top the chart with apparent ease. Meanwhile, *Layla* was a Top 10 hit for the second time (10 years after the first), Bucks Fizz made it two Number One singles in succession, and Elvis' *Are You Lonesome Tonight* was a live version of his 1961 hit, during which he cracked up with laughter halfway though.

April – May 1982

24 April 1982

Last	This	Title / Artist
1	1	MY CAMERA NEVER LIES — Bucks Fizz (RCA)
9	2	EBONY AND IVORY — Paul McCartney & Stevie Wonder (Parlophone)
2	3	AIN'T NO PLEASING YOU — Chas & Dave (Rockney)
7	4	GIVE ME BACK MY HEART — Dollar (WEA)
3	5	SEVEN TEARS — Goombay Dance Band (Epic)
4	6	MORE THAN THIS — Roxy Music (EG)
5	7	GHOSTS — Japan (Virgin)
27	8	PAPA'S GOT A BRAND NEW PIGBAG — Pigbag (Y)
16	9	SEE THOSE EYES — Altered Images (Epic)
19	10	BLUE EYES — Elton John (Rocket)
17	11	FANTASTIC DAY — Haircut 100 (Arista)
6	12	JUST AN ILLUSION — Imagination (R&B)
10	13	DEAR JOHN — Status Quo (Vertigo)
24	14	ONE STEP FURTHER — Bardo (Epic)
12	15	NIGHT BIRDS — Shakatak (Polydor)
-	16	I CAN MAKE YOU FEEL GOOD — Shalamar (Solar)
15	17	DON'T LOVE ME TOO HARD — Nolans (Epic)
13	18	IS IT A DREAM — Classix Nouveaux (Liberty)
22	19	REALLY SAYING SOMETHING — Bananarama & the Fun Boy Three (Deram)
8	20	HAVE YOU EVER BEEN IN LOVE — Leo Sayer (Chrysalis)
26	21	THIS TIME (WE'LL GET IT RIGHT) — England World Cup Squad (England)
11	22	LAYLA — Derek & the Dominoes (RSO)
20	23	HOUSE ON FIRE — Boomtown Rats (Mercury)
-	24	EVER SO LONELY — Monsoon (Mobile Suit Corp)
21	25	A BUNCH OF THYME — Foster & Allen (Ritz)
18	26	DAMNED DON'T CRY — Visage (Polydor)
-	27	FREEZE-FRAME — J. Geils Band (EMI America)
14	28	QUIEREME MUCHO (YOURS) — Julio Iglesias (CBS)
25	29	CAT PEOPLE (PUTTING OUT FIRE) — David Bowie (MCA)
-	30	NOBODY — Toni Basil (Radialchoice)

1 May 1982

Last	This	Title / Artist
2	1	EBONY AND IVORY — Paul McCartney & Stevie Wonder (Parlophone)
1	2	MY CAMERA NEVER LIES — Bucks Fizz (RCA)
8	3	PAPA'S GOT A BRAND NEW PIGBAG — Pigbag (Y)
14	4	ONE STEP FURTHER — Bardo (Epic)
10	5	BLUE EYES — Elton John (Rocket)
3	6	AIN'T NO PLEASING YOU — Chas & Dave (Rockney)
4	7	GIVE ME BACK MY HEART — Dollar (WEA)
15	8	NIGHT BIRDS — Shakatak (Polydor)
21	9	THIS TIME (WE'LL GET IT RIGHT) — England World Cup Squad (England)
-	10	SHIRLEY — Shakin' Stevens (Epic)
6	11	MORE THAN THIS — Roxy Music (EG)
24	12	EVER SO LONELY — Monsoon (Mobile Suit Corp)
11	13	FANTASTIC DAY — Haircut 100 (Arista)
19	14	REALLY SAYING SOMETHING — Bananarama & the Fun Boy Three (Deram)
16	15	I CAN MAKE YOU FEEL GOOD — Shalamar (Solar)
13	16	DEAR JOHN — Status Quo (Vertigo)
7	17	GHOSTS — Japan (Virgin)
5	18	SEVEN TEARS — Goombay Dance Band (Epic)
-	19	VIEW FROM A BRIDGE — Kim Wilde (RAK)
12	20	JUST AN ILLUSION — Imagination (R&B)
-	21	I LOVE ROCK'N'ROLL — Joan Jett & the Blackhearts (Epic)
29	22	CAT PEOPLE (PUTTING OUT FIRE) — David Bowie (MCA)
-	23	PROMISED YOU A MIRACLE — Simple Minds (Virgin)
20	24	HAVE YOU EVER BEEN IN LOVE — Leo Sayer (Chrysalis)
17	25	DON'T LOVE ME TOO HARD — Nolans (Epic)
-	26	WE HAVE A DREAM — Scottish World Cup Squad (WEA)
-	27	I WON'T LET YOU DOWN — PhD (WEA)
-	28	BLACK COFFEE IN BED — Squeeze (A&M)
9	29	SEE THOSE EYES — Altered Images (Epic)
-	30	TOTTENHAM TOTTENHAM — Tottenham Hotspur F.A. Cup Squad (Rockney)

8 May 1982

Last	This	Title / Artist
1	1	EBONY AND IVORY — Paul McCartney & Stevie Wonder (Parlophone)
10	2	SHIRLEY — Shakin' Stevens (Epic)
4	3	ONE STEP FURTHER — Bardo (Epic)
3	4	PAPA'S GOT A BRAND NEW PIGBAG — Pigbag (Y)
9	5	THIS TIME (WE'LL GET IT RIGHT) — England World Cup Squad (England)
14	6	REALLY SAYING SOMETHING — Bananarama & the Fun Boy Three (Deram)
27	7	I WON'T LET YOU DOWN — PhD (WEA)
15	8	I CAN MAKE YOU FEEL GOOD — Shalamar (Solar)
13	9	FANTASTIC DAY — Haircut 100 (Arista)
7	10	GIVE ME BACK MY HEART — Dollar (WEA)
21	11	I LOVE ROCK'N'ROLL — Joan Jett & the Blackhearts (Epic)
5	12	BLUE EYES — Elton John (Rocket)
13	13	EVER SO LONELY — Monsoon (Mobile Suit Corp)
19	14	VIEW FROM A BRIDGE — Kim Wilde (RAK)
6	15	AIN'T NO PLEASING YOU — Chas & Dave (Rockney)
26	16	WE HAVE A DREAM — Scottish World Cup Squad (WEA)
2	17	MY CAMERA NEVER LIES — Bucks Fizz (RCA)
23	18	PROMISED YOU A MIRACLE — Simple Minds (Virgin)
-	19	GIRL CRAZY — Hot Chocolate (RAK)
11	20	MORE THAN THIS — Roxy Music (EG)
8	21	NIGHT BIRDS — Shakatak (Polydor)
-	22	BODY LANGUAGE — Queen (EMI)
-	23	SHOUT! SHOUT! — Rocky Sharpe & the Replays (Chiswick)
-	24	STAY — Barry Manilow (Arista)
-	25	KNOW YOUR RIGHTS — Clash (CBS)
-	26	INSTINCTION — Spandau Ballet (Chrysalis)
-	27	FANTASY ISLAND — Tight Fit (Jive)
-	28	A LITTLE PEACE — Nicole (CBS)
-	29	THE SONG THAT I SING — Stutz Bear Cats (Multi-Media Tapes)
-	30	GOT NO BRAINS — Bad Manners (Magnet)

15 May 1982

Last	This	Title / Artist
7	1	I WON'T LET YOU DOWN — PhD (WEA)
5	2	THIS TIME (WE'LL GET IT RIGHT) — England World Cup Squad (England)
1	3	EBONY AND IVORY — Paul McCartney & Stevie Wonder (Parlophone)
28	4	A LITTLE PEACE — Nicole (CBS)
11	5	I LOVE ROCK'N'ROLL — Joan Jett & the Blackhearts (Epic)
16	6	WE HAVE A DREAM — Scottish World Cup Squad (WEA)
6	7	REALLY SAYING SOMETHING — Bananarama & the Fun Boy Three (Deram)
4	8	PAPA'S GOT A BRAND NEW PIGBAG — Pigbag (Y)
-	9	ONLY YOU — Yazoo (Mute)
3	10	ONE STEP FURTHER — Bardo (Epic)
13	11	EVER SO LONELY — Monsoon (Mobile Suit Corp)
8	12	I CAN MAKE YOU FEEL GOOD — Shalamar (Solar)
9	13	FANTASTIC DAY — Haircut 100 (Arista)
14	14	VIEW FROM A BRIDGE — Kim Wilde (RAK)
19	15	GIRL CRAZY — Hot Chocolate (RAK)
23	16	SHOUT! SHOUT! — Rocky Sharpe & the Replays (Chiswick)
2	17	SHIRLEY — Shakin' Stevens (Epic)
26	18	INSTINCTION — Spandau Ballet (Chrysalis)
18	19	PROMISED YOU A MIRACLE — Simple Minds (Virgin)
-	20	FORGET ME NOT — Patrice Rushen (Elektra)
22	21	BODY LANGUAGE — Queen (EMI)
-	22	ISLAND OF LOST SOULS — Blondie (Chrysalis)
-	22	THE MEANING OF LOVE — Depeche Mode (Mute)
12	24	BLUE EYES — Elton John (Rocket)
24	25	STAY — Barry Manilow (Arista)
-	26	TOTTENHAM TOTTENHAM — Tottenham Hotspur F.A. Cup Squad (Rockney)
27	27	FANTASY ISLAND — Tight Fit (Jive)
21	28	NIGHT BIRDS — Shakatak (Polydor)
10	29	GIVE ME BACK MY HEART — Dollar (WEA)
20	30	MORE THAN THIS — Roxy Music (EG)

Shakin' Stevens' unbelievably brief chart run with *Shirley* (10-2-17-out!) seemed to suggest a record pulled off the market while in mid-flight. There is no evidence, though, that this was the case: more simply, it seems only hardcore Stevens fans bought this particular single, and since there were plenty of them, it shot high in the chart – but since they also tended to buy in the first week, the single then dropped catastrophically thereafter, through having exhausted all its support base. Or WAS it withdrawn....

22 May 1982

last week	this week	
4	1	A LITTLE PEACE Nicole (CBS)
5	2	I LOVE ROCK'N'ROLL Joan Jett & the Blackhearts (Epic)
1	3	I WON'T LET YOU DOWN PhD (WEA)
9	4	ONLY YOU Yazoo (Mute)
6	5	WE HAVE A DREAM Scottish World Cup Squad (WEA)
3	6	EBONY AND IVORY Paul McCartney & Stevie Wonder (Parlophone)
15	7	GIRL CRAZY Hot Chocolate (RAK)
7	8	REALLY SAYING SOMETHING Bananarama & the Fun Boy Three (Deram)
27	9	FANTASY ISLAND Tight Fit (Jive)
2	10	THIS TIME (WE'LL GET IT RIGHT) England World Cup Squad (England)
18	11	INSTINCTION Spandau Ballet (Chrysalis)
19	12	PROMISED YOU A MIRACLE Simple Minds (Virgin)
20	13	FORGET ME NOT Patrice Rushen (Elektra)
22	14	THE MEANING OF LOVE Depeche Mode (Mute)
-	15	MAMA USED TO SAY Junior (Mercury)
-	16	GOODY TWO SHOES Adam Ant (CBS)
-	17	THE LOOK OF LOVE ABC (Neutron)
26	18	TOTTENHAM TOTTENHAM Tottenham Hotspur F.A. Cup Squad (Rockney)
-	19	HOUSE OF FUN Madness (Stiff)
22	20	ISLAND OF LOST SOULS Blondie (Chrysalis)
13	21	FANTASTIC DAY Haircut 100 (Arista)
16	22	SHOUT! SHOUT! Rocky Sharpe & the Replays (Chiswick)
11	23	EVER SO LONELY Monsoon (Mobile Suit Corp)
8	24	PAPA'S GOT A BRAND NEW PIGBAG Pigbag (Y)
-	25	CLUB COUNTRY Associates (Associates)
12	26	I CAN MAKE YOU FEEL GOOD Shalamar (Solar)
-	27	HUNGRY LIKE THE WOLF Duran Duran (EMI)
-	28	THE TELEPHONE Fun Boy Three (Chrysalis)
-	29	SUSPICIOUS MINDS Candi Staton (Sugarhill)
-	30	THE NUMBER OF THE BEAST Iron Maiden (EMI)

29 May 1982

last week	this week	
16	1	GOODY TWO SHOES Adam Ant (CBS)
1	2	A LITTLE PEACE Nicole (CBS)
3	3	I WON'T LET YOU DOWN PhD (WEA)
4	4	ONLY YOU Yazoo (Mute)
19	5	HOUSE OF FUN Madness (Stiff)
2	6	I LOVE ROCK'N'ROLL Joan Jett & the Blackhearts (Epic)
9	7	FANTASY ISLAND Tight Fit (Jive)
17	8	THE LOOK OF LOVE ABC (Neutron)
7	9	GIRL CRAZY Hot Chocolate (RAK)
5	10	WE HAVE A DREAM Scottish World Cup Squad (WEA)
15	11	MAMA USED TO SAY Junior (Mercury)
13	12	FORGET ME NOT Patrice Rushen (Elektra)
6	13	EBONY AND IVORY Paul McCartney & Stevie Wonder (Parlophone)
27	14	HUNGRY LIKE THE WOLF Duran Duran (EMI)
20	15	ISLAND OF LOST SOULS Blondie (Chrysalis)
10	16	THIS TIME (WE'LL GET IT RIGHT) England World Cup Squad (England)
8	17	REALLY SAYING SOMETHING Bananarama & the Fun Boy Three (Deram)
14	18	THE MEANING OF LOVE Depeche Mode (Mute)
12	19	PROMISED YOU A MIRACLE Simple Minds (Virgin)
-	20	CANTONESE BOY Japan (Virgin)
11	21	INSTINCTION Spandau Ballet (Chrysalis)
18	22	TOTTENHAM TOTTENHAM Tottenham Hotspur F.A. Cup Squad (Rockney)
28	23	THE TELEPHONE Fun Boy Three (Chrysalis)
24	24	3 X 3 (EP) Genesis (Charisma)
25	25	CLUB COUNTRY Associates (Associates)
-	26	TEMPTATION New Order (Factory)
29	27	SUSPICIOUS MINDS Candi Staton (Sugarhill)
30	28	THE NUMBER OF THE BEAST Iron Maiden (EMI)
22	29	SHOUT! SHOUT! Rocky Sharpe & the Replays (Chiswick)
21	30	FANTASTIC DAY Haircut 100 (Arista)

5 June 1982

last week	this week	
5	1	HOUSE OF FUN Madness (Stiff)
1	2	GOODY TWO SHOES Adam Ant (CBS)
7	3	FANTASY ISLAND Tight Fit (Jive)
4	4	ONLY YOU Yazoo (Mute)
8	5	THE LOOK OF LOVE ABC (Neutron)
-	6	TORCH Soft Cell (Some Bizzare)
14	7	HUNGRY LIKE THE WOLF Duran Duran (EMI)
11	8	MAMA USED TO SAY Junior (Mercury)
2	9	A LITTLE PEACE Nicole (CBS)
12	10	FORGET ME NOT Patrice Rushen (Elektra)
3	11	I WON'T LET YOU DOWN PhD (WEA)
15	12	ISLAND OF LOST SOULS Blondie (Chrysalis)
9	13	GIRL CRAZY Hot Chocolate (RAK)
6	14	I LOVE ROCK'N'ROLL Joan Jett & the Blackhearts (Epic)
28	15	THE NUMBER OF THE BEAST Iron Maiden (EMI)
24	16	3 X 3 (EP) Genesis (Charisma)
17	17	THE MEANING OF LOVE Depeche Mode (Mute)
10	18	WE HAVE A DREAM Scottish World Cup Squad (WEA)
20	19	CANTONESE BOY Japan (Virgin)
-	20	THE BACK OF LOVE Echo & the Bunnymen (Korova)
-	21	FIREWORKS Siouxsie & the Banshees (Polydor)
25	22	CLUB COUNTRY Associates (Associates)
26	23	TEMPTATION New Order (Factory)
23	24	THE TELEPHONE Fun Boy Three (Chrysalis)
27	25	SUSPICIOUS MINDS Candi Staton (Sugarhill)
-	26	BRAVE NEW WORLD Toyah (Safari)
-	27	I'VE NEVER BEEN TO ME Charlene (Motown)
-	28	LOVE IS ALRIGHT UB40 (DEP International)
22	29	TOTTENHAM TOTTENHAM Tottenham Hotspur F.A. Cup Squad (Rockney)
21	30	INSTINCTION Spandau Ballet (Chrysalis)

12 June 1982

last week	this week	
1	1	HOUSE OF FUN Madness (Stiff)
2	2	GOODY TWO SHOES Adam Ant (CBS)
6	3	TORCH Soft Cell (Some Bizzare)
5	4	THE LOOK OF LOVE ABC (Neutron)
4	5	ONLY YOU Yazoo (Mute)
3	6	FANTASY ISLAND Tight Fit (Jive)
8	7	MAMA USED TO SAY Junior (Mercury)
7	8	HUNGRY LIKE THE WOLF Duran Duran (EMI)
27	9	I'VE NEVER BEEN TO ME Charlene (Motown)
22	10	CLUB COUNTRY Associates (Associates)
12	11	ISLAND OF LOST SOULS Blondie (Chrysalis)
11	12	I WON'T LET YOU DOWN PhD (WEA)
10	13	FORGET ME NOT Patrice Rushen (Elektra)
16	14	3 X 3 (EP) Genesis (Charisma)
9	15	A LITTLE PEACE Nicole (CBS)
13	16	GIRL CRAZY Hot Chocolate (RAK)
18	17	WE HAVE A DREAM Scottish World Cup Squad (WEA)
-	18	I'M A WONDERFUL THING (BABY) Kid Creole & the Coconuts (Ze)
14	19	I LOVE ROCK'N'ROLL Joan Jett & the Blackhearts (Epic)
21	20	FIREWORKS Siouxsie & the Banshees (Polydor)
24	21	THE TELEPHONE Fun Boy Three (Chrysalis)
15	22	THE NUMBER OF THE BEAST Iron Maiden (EMI)
20	23	THE BACK OF LOVE Echo & the Bunnymen (Korova)
-	24	WORK THAT BODY Diana Ross (Capitol)
-	25	DO I DO Stevie Wonder (Motown)
-	26	PINKY BLUE Altered Images (Epic)
17	27	THE MEANING OF LOVE Depeche Mode (Mute)
-	28	I WANT CANDY Bow Wow Wow (RCA)
-	29	THE BEATLES MOVIE MEDLEY Beatles (Parlophone)
26	30	BRAVE NEW WORLD Toyah (Safari)

Adam & The Ants broke up early in 1982, with Adam Ant himself continuing as a solo act; *Goody Two Shoes* was the singer's first post-group single, and had no trouble keeping up the hit momentum. The song it replaced at Number One was the English version of Germany's winner of the Eurovision Song Contest, sung by teenager Nicole. Meanwhile, newcomers Yazoo, featuring Alison Moyet and ex-Depeche Mode member Vince Clarke, just missed the Top Three with their debut single *Only You*.

June – July 1982

19 June 1982

last week	this week	Title	Artist (Label)
2	1	GOODY TWO SHOES	Adam Ant (CBS)
3	2	TORCH	Soft Cell (Some Bizzare)
1	3	HOUSE OF FUN	Madness (Stiff)
4	4	THE LOOK OF LOVE	ABC (Neutron)
8	5	HUNGRY LIKE THE WOLF	Duran Duran (EMI)
9	6	I'VE NEVER BEEN TO ME	Charlene (Motown)
6	7	FANTASY ISLAND	Tight Fit (Jive)
7	8	MAMA USED TO SAY	Junior (Mercury)
5	9	ONLY YOU	Yazoo (Mute)
14	10	3 X 3 (EP)	Genesis (Charisma)
28	11	I WANT CANDY	Bow Wow Wow (RCA)
18	12	I'M A WONDERFUL THING (BABY)	Kid Creole & the Coconuts (Ze)
11	13	ISLAND OF LOST SOULS	Blondie (Chrysalis)
21	14	THE TELEPHONE	Fun Boy Three (Chrysalis)
12	15	I WON'T LET YOU DOWN	PhD (WEA)
13	16	FORGET ME NOT	Patrice Rushen (Elektra)
10	17	CLUB COUNTRY	Associates (Associates)
24	18	WORK THAT BODY	Diana Ross (Capitol)
22	19	THE NUMBER OF THE BEAST	Iron Maiden (EMI)
20	20	FIREWORKS	Siouxsie & the Banshees (Polydor)
30	21	BRAVE NEW WORLD	Toyah (Safari)
-	22	TEMPTATION	New Order (Factory)
16	23	GIRL CRAZY	Hot Chocolate (RAK)
25	24	DO I DO	Stevie Wonder (Motown)
23	25	THE BACK OF LOVE	Echo & the Bunnymen (Korova)
-	26	GOING TO A GO GO	Rolling Stones (Rolling Stones)
15	27	A LITTLE PEACE	Nicole (CBS)
29	28	THE BEATLES MOVIE MEDLEY	Beatles (Parlophone)
-	29	IKO IKO	Belle Stars (Stiff)
-	30	SHE DON'T FOOL ME	Status Quo (Vertigo)

26 June 1982

last week	this week	Title	Artist (Label)
1	1	GOODY TWO SHOES	Adam Ant (CBS)
6	2	I'VE NEVER BEEN TO ME	Charlene (Motown)
2	3	TORCH	Soft Cell (Some Bizzare)
5	4	HUNGRY LIKE THE WOLF	Duran Duran (EMI)
4	5	THE LOOK OF LOVE	ABC (Neutron)
12	6	I'M A WONDERFUL THING (BABY)	Kid Creole & the Coconuts (Ze)
3	7	HOUSE OF FUN	Madness (Stiff)
18	8	WORK THAT BODY	Diana Ross (Capitol)
-	9	WE TAKE MYSTERY	Gary Numan (Beggars Banquet)
11	10	I WANT CANDY	Bow Wow Wow (RCA)
24	11	DO I DO	Stevie Wonder (Motown)
7	12	FANTASY ISLAND	Tight Fit (Jive)
-	13	INSIDE OUT	Odyssey (RCA)
-	14	NO REGRETS	Midge Ure (Chrysalis)
-	15	AVALON	Roxy Music (EG)
26	16	GOING TO A GO GO	Rolling Stones (Rolling Stones)
28	17	THE BEATLES MOVIE MEDLEY	Beatles (Parlophone)
10	18	3 X 3 (EP)	Genesis (Charisma)
8	19	MAMA USED TO SAY	Junior (Mercury)
-	20	FREE BIRD	Lynyrd Skynyrd (MCA)
21	21	BRAVE NEW WORLD	Toyah (Safari)
-	22	IKO IKO	Natasha (Towerbell)
9	23	ONLY YOU	Yazoo (Mute)
13	24	ISLAND OF LOST SOULS	Blondie (Chrysalis)
14	25	THE TELEPHONE	Fun Boy Three (Chrysalis)
-	26	ABRACADABRA	Steve Miller Band (Mercury)
-	27	LAS PALABRAS DE AMOUR	Queen (EMI)
25	28	THE BACK OF LOVE	Echo & the Bunnymen (Korova)
20	29	FIREWORKS	Siouxsie & the Banshees (Polydor)
-	30	YOU LITTLE FOOL	Elvis Costello (F.Beat)

3 July 1982

last week	this week	Title	Artist (Label)
2	1	I'VE NEVER BEEN TO ME	Charlene (Motown)
3	2	TORCH	Soft Cell (Some Bizzare)
1	3	GOODY TWO SHOES	Adam Ant (CBS)
13	4	INSIDE OUT	Odyssey (RCA)
6	5	I'M A WONDERFUL THING (BABY)	Kid Creole & the Coconuts (Ze)
10	6	I WANT CANDY	Bow Wow Wow (RCA)
8	7	WORK THAT BODY	Diana Ross (Capitol)
15	8	AVALON	Roxy Music (EG)
26	9	ABRACADABRA	Steve Miller Band (Mercury)
5	10	THE LOOK OF LOVE	ABC (Neutron)
11	11	DO I DO	Stevie Wonder (Motown)
17	12	THE BEATLES MOVIE MEDLEY	Beatles (Parlophone)
-	13	HAPPY TALK	Captain Sensible (A&M)
22	14	IKO IKO	Natasha (Towerbell)
4	15	HUNGRY LIKE THE WOLF	Duran Duran (EMI)
14	16	NO REGRETS	Midge Ure (Chrysalis)
27	17	LAS PALABRAS DE AMOUR	Queen (EMI)
-	18	A NIGHT TO REMEMBER	Shalamar (Solar)
9	19	WE TAKE MYSTERY	Gary Numan (Beggars Banquet)
7	20	HOUSE OF FUN	Madness (Stiff)
16	21	GOING TO A GO GO	Rolling Stones (Rolling Stones)
18	22	3 X 3 (EP)	Genesis (Charisma)
-	23	MUSIC AND LIGHT	Imagination (R&B)
19	24	MAMA USED TO SAY	Junior (Mercury)
-	25	HEART (STOP BEATING IN TIME)	Leo Sayer (Chrysalis)
-	26	JUST WHO IS THE 5 O'CLOCK HERO	Jam (Polydor)
-	27	NOW THOSE DAYS ARE GONE	Bucks Fizz (RCA)
28	28	THE BACK OF LOVE	Echo & the Bunnymen (Korova)
21	29	BRAVE NEW WORLD	Toyah (Safari)
-	30	MURPHY'S LAW	Cherie (Polydor)

10 July 1982

last week	this week	Title	Artist (Label)
13	1	HAPPY TALK	Captain Sensible (A&M)
4	2	INSIDE OUT	Odyssey (RCA)
9	3	ABRACADABRA	Steve Miller Band (Mercury)
23	4	MUSIC AND LIGHT	Imagination (R&B)
1	5	I'VE NEVER BEEN TO ME	Charlene (Motown)
5	6	I'M A WONDERFUL THING (BABY)	Kid Creole & the Coconuts (Ze)
26	7	JUST WHO IS THE 5 O'CLOCK HERO	Jam (Polydor)
7	8	WORK THAT BODY	Diana Ross (Capitol)
16	9	NO REGRETS	Midge Ure (Chrysalis)
12	10	THE BEATLES MOVIE MEDLEY	Beatles (Parlophone)
14	11	IKO IKO	Natasha (Towerbell)
2	12	TORCH	Soft Cell (Some Bizzare)
18	13	A NIGHT TO REMEMBER	Shalamar (Solar)
3	14	GOODY TWO SHOES	Adam Ant (CBS)
15	15	HUNGRY LIKE THE WOLF	Duran Duran (EMI)
8	16	AVALON	Roxy Music (EG)
27	17	NOW THOSE DAYS ARE GONE	Bucks Fizz (RCA)
30	18	MURPHY'S LAW	Cherie (Polydor)
-	19	FOR THOSE ABOUT TO ROCK	AC/DC (Atlantic)
6	20	I WANT CANDY	Bow Wow Wow (RCA)
10	21	THE LOOK OF LOVE	ABC (Neutron)
11	22	DO I DO	Stevie Wonder (Motown)
17	23	LAS PALABRAS DE AMOUR	Queen (EMI)
25	24	HEART (STOP BEATING IN TIME)	Leo Sayer (Chrysalis)
-	25	FAME	Irene Cara (RSO)
-	26	FREE BIRD	Lynyrd Skynyrd (MCA)
28	27	THE BACK OF LOVE	Echo & the Bunnymen (Korova)
-	28	SHY BOY	Bananarama (London)
19	29	WE TAKE MYSTERY	Gary Numan (Beggars Banquet)
-	30	VIDEOTHEQUE	Dollar (WEA)

With their second chart EP *3x3* (the first had been *Spot The Pigeon* in 1977), Genesis joined the select club of those who had put an EP into the Top 10. Its lead track, which got the airplay, was *Paperlate*. The Beatles returned to the chart, at least by proxy, with a medley of excerpts from several film songs, spliced together from the original recordings. They were joined by the Rolling Stones, who also looked backwards with a live cover of a 1960s Temptations hit.

last week	this week	17 July 1982		24 July 1982		31 July 1982		7 August 1982	
3	1	ABRACADABRA	Steve Miller Band (Mercury)	2	1 FAME — Irene Cara (RSO)		1	1 FAME — Irene Cara (RSO)	4	1 COME ON EILEEN — Dexy's Midnight Runners (Mercury)

17 July 1982

last week	this week	Title
3	1	ABRACADABRA — Steve Miller Band (Mercury)
25	2	FAME — Irene Cara (RSO)
2	3	INSIDE OUT — Odyssey (RCA)
1	4	HAPPY TALK — Captain Sensible (A&M)
4	5	MUSIC AND LIGHT — Imagination (R&B)
13	6	A NIGHT TO REMEMBER — Shalamar (Solar)
7	7	JUST WHO IS THE 5 O'CLOCK HERO — Jam (Polydor)
17	8	NOW THOSE DAYS ARE GONE — Bucks Fizz (RCA)
9	9	NO REGRETS — Midge Ure (Chrysalis)
5	10	I'VE NEVER BEEN TO ME — Charlene (Motown)
10	11	THE BEATLES MOVIE MEDLEY — Beatles (Parlophone)
11	12	IKO IKO — Natasha (Towerbell)
19	13	FOR THOSE ABOUT TO ROCK — AC/DC (Atlantic)
23	14	LAS PALABRAS DE AMOUR — Queen (EMI)
8	15	WORK THAT BODY — Diana Ross (Capitol)
18	16	MURPHY'S LAW — Cherie (Polydor)
28	17	SHY BOY — Bananarama (London)
-	18	IT STARTED WITH A KISS — Hot Chocolate (RAK)
16	19	AVALON — Roxy Music (EG)
6	20	I'M A WONDERFUL THING (BABY) — Kid Creole & the Coconuts (Ze)
-	21	DA DA DA — Trio (Mobile Suit Corporation)
26	22	FREE BIRD — Lynyrd Skynyrd (MCA)
15	23	HUNGRY LIKE THE WOLF — Duran Duran (EMI)
-	24	ME AND MY GIRL (NIGHT CLUBBING) — David Essex (Mercury)
24	25	HEART (STOP BEATING IN TIME) — Leo Sayer (Chrysalis)
-	26	TAKE IT AWAY — Paul McCartney (Parlophone)
-	27	NIGHT TRAIN — Visage (Polydor)
22	28	DO I DO — Stevie Wonder (Motown)
20	29	I WANT CANDY — Bow Wow Wow (RCA)
30	30	VIDEOTHEQUE — Dollar (WEA)

24 July 1982

last week	this week	Title
2	1	FAME — Irene Cara (RSO)
21	2	DA DA DA — Trio (Mobile Suit Corporation)
1	3	ABRACADABRA — Steve Miller Band (Mercury)
17	4	SHY BOY — Bananarama (London)
6	5	A NIGHT TO REMEMBER — Shalamar (Solar)
3	6	INSIDE OUT — Odyssey (RCA)
18	7	IT STARTED WITH A KISS — Hot Chocolate (RAK)
5	8	MUSIC AND LIGHT — Imagination (R&B)
4	9	HAPPY TALK — Captain Sensible (A&M)
8	10	NOW THOSE DAYS ARE GONE — Bucks Fizz (RCA)
12	11	IKO IKO — Natasha (Towerbell)
-	12	DON'T GO — Yazoo (Mute)
-	13	I SECOND THAT EMOTION — Japan (Hansa)
27	14	NIGHT TRAIN — Visage (Polydor)
16	15	MURPHY'S LAW — Cherie (Polydor)
9	16	NO REGRETS — Midge Ure (Chrysalis)
7	17	JUST WHO IS THE 5 O'CLOCK HERO — Jam (Polydor)
22	18	FREE BIRD — Lynyrd Skynyrd (MCA)
-	19	THE ONLY WAY OUT — Cliff Richard (EMI)
24	20	ME AND MY GIRL (NIGHT CLUBBING) — David Essex (Mercury)
13	21	FOR THOSE ABOUT TO ROCK — AC/DC (Atlantic)
14	22	LAS PALABRAS DE AMOUR — Queen (EMI)
-	23	DRIVING IN MY CAR — Madness (Stiff)
25	24	HEART (STOP BEATING IN TIME) — Leo Sayer (Chrysalis)
15	25	WORK THAT BODY — Diana Ross (Capitol)
11	26	THE BEATLES MOVIE MEDLEY — Beatles (Parlophone)
30	27	VIDEOTHEQUE — Dollar (WEA)
23	28	HUNGRY LIKE THE WOLF — Duran Duran (EMI)
-	29	COME ON EILEEN — Dexy's Midnight Runners (Mercury)
26	30	TAKE IT AWAY — Paul McCartney (Parlophone)

31 July 1982

last week	this week	Title
1	1	FAME — Irene Cara (RSO)
23	2	DRIVING IN MY CAR — Madness (Stiff)
2	3	DA DA DA — Trio (Mobile Suit Corporation)
29	4	COME ON EILEEN — Dexy's Midnight Runners (Mercury)
12	5	DON'T GO — Yazoo (Mute)
4	6	SHY BOY — Bananarama (London)
3	7	ABRACADABRA — Steve Miller Band (Mercury)
7	8	IT STARTED WITH A KISS — Hot Chocolate (RAK)
19	9	THE ONLY WAY OUT — Cliff Richard (EMI)
14	10	NIGHT TRAIN — Visage (Polydor)
5	11	A NIGHT TO REMEMBER — Shalamar (Solar)
13	12	I SECOND THAT EMOTION — Japan (Hansa)
6	13	INSIDE OUT — Odyssey (RCA)
20	14	ME AND MY GIRL (NIGHT CLUBBING) — David Essex (Mercury)
-	15	STOOL PIGEON — Kid Creole & the Coconuts (Ze)
10	16	NOW THOSE DAYS ARE GONE — Bucks Fizz (RCA)
8	17	MUSIC AND LIGHT — Imagination (R&B)
-	18	STRANGE LITTLE GIRL — Stranglers (Liberty)
15	19	MURPHY'S LAW — Cherie (Polydor)
11	20	IKO IKO — Natasha (Towerbell)
30	21	TAKE IT AWAY — Paul McCartney (Parlophone)
9	22	HAPPY TALK — Captain Sensible (A&M)
-	23	TOO LATE — Junior (Mercury)
27	24	VIDEOTHEQUE — Dollar (WEA)
16	25	NO REGRETS — Midge Ure (Chrysalis)
-	26	THE HANGING GARDEN — Cure (Fiction)
26	27	THE BEATLES MOVIE MEDLEY — Beatles (Parlophone)
-	28	MY GIRL LOLLIPOP — Bad Manners (Magnet)
-	29	WAR CHILD — Blondie (Chrysalis)
24	30	HEART (STOP BEATING IN TIME) — Leo Sayer (Chrysalis)

7 August 1982

last week	this week	Title
4	1	COME ON EILEEN — Dexy's Midnight Runners (Mercury)
1	2	FAME — Irene Cara (RSO)
2	3	DRIVING IN MY CAR — Madness (Stiff)
5	4	DON'T GO — Yazoo (Mute)
8	5	IT STARTED WITH A KISS — Hot Chocolate (RAK)
15	6	STOOL PIGEON — Kid Creole & the Coconuts (Ze)
6	7	SHY BOY — Bananarama (London)
3	8	DA DA DA — Trio (Mobile Suit Corporation)
7	9	ABRACADABRA — Steve Miller Band (Mercury)
12	10	I SECOND THAT EMOTION — Japan (Hansa)
9	11	THE ONLY WAY OUT — Cliff Richard (EMI)
10	12	NIGHT TRAIN — Visage (Polydor)
14	13	ME AND MY GIRL (NIGHT CLUBBING) — David Essex (Mercury)
18	14	STRANGE LITTLE GIRL — Stranglers (Liberty)
11	15	A NIGHT TO REMEMBER — Shalamar (Solar)
13	16	INSIDE OUT — Odyssey (RCA)
21	17	TAKE IT AWAY — Paul McCartney (Parlophone)
-	18	THE CLAPPING SONG — Belle Stars (Stiff)
24	19	VIDEOTHEQUE — Dollar (WEA)
28	20	MY GIRL LOLLIPOP — Bad Manners (Magnet)
-	21	ALWAYS ON MY MIND — Willie Nelson (CBS)
23	22	TOO LATE — Junior (Mercury)
-	23	SUMMERTIME — Fun Boy Three (Chrysalis)
16	24	NOW THOSE DAYS ARE GONE — Bucks Fizz (RCA)
-	25	CHALK DUST - THE UMPIRE STRIKES BACK — Brat (Hansa)
-	26	ARTHUR DALEY — Firm (Bark)
-	27	LOVE IS IN CONTROL — Donna Summer (Warner Brothers)
-	28	EYE OF THE TIGER — Survivor (Scotti Brothers)
-	29	LOVE MY WAY — Psychedelic Furs (CBS)
26	30	THE HANGING GARDEN — Cure (Fiction)

The theme from *Fame* had been a US hit two years earlier when the original film was in the cinemas. Its belated British success was spurred by the huge success in the UK of the spin-off *Fame* TV series. July 1982 was unique in chart history, in that for three weeks running, a record hit Number Two from a previous week's position outside the Top 20. Oddly, two of the three (*Fame,* going to Number One, was the exception), dropped back to Number Three the following week.

August – September 1982

	14 August 1982		21 August 1982		28 August 1982		4 September 1982
1	1 COME ON EILEEN — Dexy's Midnight Runners (Mercury)	1	1 COME ON EILEEN — Dexy's Midnight Runners (Mercury)	1	1 COME ON EILEEN — Dexy's Midnight Runners (Mercury)	2	1 EYE OF THE TIGER — Survivor (Scotti Brothers)
2	2 FAME — Irene Cara (RSO)	21	2 EYE OF THE TIGER — Survivor (Scotti Brothers)	2	2 EYE OF THE TIGER — Survivor (Scotti Brothers)	1	2 COME ON EILEEN — Dexy's Midnight Runners (Mercury)
5	3 IT STARTED WITH A KISS — Hot Chocolate (RAK)	5	3 DON'T GO — Yazoo (Mute)	13	3 CAN'T TAKE MY EYES OFF YOU — Boys Town (ERC)	5	3 WHAT — Soft Cell (Some Bizzare)
3	4 DRIVING IN MY CAR — Madness (Stiff)	2	4 FAME — Irene Cara (RSO)	4	4 FAME — Irene Cara (RSO)	3	4 CAN'T TAKE MY EYES OFF YOU — Boys Town (ERC)
4	5 DON'T GO — Yazoo (Mute)	3	5 IT STARTED WITH A KISS — Hot Chocolate (RAK)	-	5 WHAT — Soft Cell (Some Bizzare)	16	5 SAVE A PRAYER — Duran Duran (EMI)
6	6 STOOL PIGEON — Kid Creole & the Coconuts (Ze)	7	6 STRANGE LITTLE GIRL — Stranglers (Liberty)	5	6 IT STARTED WITH A KISS — Hot Chocolate (RAK)	17	6 HI FIDELITY — Kids From Fame (RCA)
14	7 STRANGE LITTLE GIRL — Stranglers (Liberty)	4	7 DRIVING IN MY CAR — Madness (Stiff)	26	7 I EAT CANNIBALS — Toto Coelo (Radialchoice)	7	7 I EAT CANNIBALS — Toto Coelo (Radialchoice)
7	8 SHY BOY — Bananarama (London)	6	8 STOOL PIGEON — Kid Creole & the Coconuts (Ze)	6	8 STRANGE LITTLE GIRL — Stranglers (Liberty)	21	8 NOBODY'S FOOL — Haircut 100 (Arista)
13	9 ME AND MY GIRL (NIGHT CLUBBING) — David Essex (Mercury)	13	9 MY GIRL LOLLIPOP — Bad Manners (Magnet)	3	9 DON'T GO — Yazoo (Mute)	4	9 FAME — Irene Cara (RSO)
11	10 THE ONLY WAY OUT — Cliff Richard (EMI)	16	10 THE CLAPPING SONG — Belle Stars (Stiff)	10	10 THE CLAPPING SONG — Belle Stars (Stiff)	6	10 IT STARTED WITH A KISS — Hot Chocolate (RAK)
10	11 I SECOND THAT EMOTION — Japan (Hansa)	15	11 ARTHUR DALEY — Firm (Bark)	7	11 DRIVING IN MY CAR — Madness (Stiff)	9	11 DON'T GO — Yazoo (Mute)
9	12 ABRACADABRA — Steve Miller Band (Mercury)	10	12 THE ONLY WAY OUT — Cliff Richard (EMI)	8	12 STOOL PIGEON — Kid Creole & the Coconuts (Ze)	19	12 JOHN WAYNE IS BIG LEGGY — Haysi Fantayzee (Regard)
20	13 MY GIRL LOLLIPOP — Bad Manners (Magnet)	-	13 CAN'T TAKE MY EYES OFF YOU — Boys Town (ERC)	9	13 MY GIRL LOLLIPOP — Bad Manners (Magnet)	-	13 WALKING ON SUNSHINE — Rockers Revenge (London)
8	14 DA DA DA — Trio (Mobile Suit Corporation)	17	14 TAKE IT AWAY — Paul McCartney (Parlophone)	29	14 HURRY HOME — Wavelength (Ariola)	18	14 BIG FUN — Kool & the Gang (De-Lite)
26	15 ARTHUR DALEY — Firm (Bark)	22	15 JOHN WAYNE IS BIG LEGGY — Haysi Fantayzee (Regard)	24	15 SUMMERTIME — Fun Boy Three (Chrysalis)	27	15 CHERRY PINK AND APPLE BLOSSOM WHITE — Modern Romance (WEA)
18	16 THE CLAPPING SONG — Belle Stars (Stiff)	18	16 LOVE IS IN CONTROL — Donna Summer (Warner Brothers)	-	16 SAVE A PRAYER — Duran Duran (EMI)	-	16 WHITE BOYS AND HEROES — Gary Numan (Beggars Banquet)
17	17 TAKE IT AWAY — Paul McCartney (Parlophone)	-	17 BIG FUN — Kool & the Gang (De-Lite)	21	17 HI FIDELITY — Kids From Fame (RCA)	8	17 STRANGE LITTLE GIRL — Stranglers (Liberty)
27	18 LOVE IS IN CONTROL — Donna Summer (Warner Brothers)	25	18 18 CARAT LOVE AFFAIR — Associates (Associates)	17	18 BIG FUN — Kool & the Gang (De-Lite)	13	18 MY GIRL LOLLIPOP — Bad Manners (Magnet)
19	19 VIDEOTHEQUE — Dollar (WEA)	14	19 DA DA DA — Trio (Mobile Suit Corporation)	15	19 JOHN WAYNE IS BIG LEGGY — Haysi Fantayzee (Regard)	-	19 UNDER THE BOARDWALK — Tom Tom Club (Island)
25	20 CHALK DUST - THE UMPIRE STRIKES BACK — Brat (Hansa)	8	20 SHY BOY — Bananarama (London)	11	20 ARTHUR DALEY — Firm (Bark)	-	20 THE MESSAGE — Grandmaster Flash (Sugarhill)
28	21 EYE OF THE TIGER — Survivor (Scotti Brothers)	24	21 HI FIDELITY — Kids From Fame (RCA)	-	21 NOBODY'S FOOL — Haircut 100 (Arista)	12	21 STOOL PIGEON — Kid Creole & the Coconuts (Ze)
-	22 JOHN WAYNE IS BIG LEGGY — Haysi Fantayzee (Regard)	20	22 CHALK DUST - THE UMPIRE STRIKES BACK — Brat (Hansa)	18	22 18 CARAT LOVE AFFAIR — Associates (Associates)	10	22 THE CLAPPING SONG — Belle Stars (Stiff)
15	23 A NIGHT TO REMEMBER — Shalamar (Solar)	11	23 I SECOND THAT EMOTION — Japan (Hansa)	16	23 LOVE IS IN CONTROL — Donna Summer (Warner Brothers)	-	23 GIVE ME YOUR HEART TONIGHT — Shakin' Stevens (Epic)
-	24 HI FIDELITY — Kids From Fame (RCA)	28	24 SUMMERTIME — Fun Boy Three (Chrysalis)	14	24 TAKE IT AWAY — Paul McCartney (Parlophone)	11	24 DRIVING IN MY CAR — Madness (Stiff)
-	25 18 CARAT LOVE AFFAIR — Associates (Associates)	-	25 BAMBOO HOUSES — Sylvian Sakamoto (Virgin)	20	25 SHY BOY — Bananarama (London)	26	25 SPREAD A LITTLE HAPPINESS — Sting (A&M)
22	26 TOO LATE — Junior (Mercury)	-	26 I EAT CANNIBALS — Toto Coelo (Radialchoice)	27	26 SPREAD A LITTLE HAPPINESS — Sting (A&M)	-	26 TODAY — Talk Talk (EMI)
12	27 NIGHT TRAIN — Visage (Polydor)	-	27 SPREAD A LITTLE HAPPINESS — Sting (A&M)	-	27 CHERRY PINK AND APPLE BLOSSOM WHITE — Modern Romance (WEA)	22	27 18 CARAT LOVE AFFAIR — Associates (Associates)
23	28 SUMMERTIME — Fun Boy Three (Chrysalis)	9	28 ME AND MY GIRL (NIGHT CLUBBING) — David Essex (Mercury)	12	28 THE ONLY WAY OUT — Cliff Richard (EMI)	14	28 HURRY HOME — Wavelength (Ariola)
-	29 DREAMING — Kate Bush (EMI)	-	29 HURRY HOME — Wavelength (Ariola)	23	29 I SECOND THAT EMOTION — Japan (Hansa)	15	29 SUMMERTIME — Fun Boy Three (Chrysalis)
-	30 WHEN THE TIGERS BROKE FREE — Pink Floyd (Harvest)	26	30 TOO LATE — Junior (Mercury)	-	30 BACKCHAT — Queen (EMI)	-	30 GLITTERING PRIZE — Simple Minds (Virgin)

Survivor's *Eye Of The Tiger* was the theme to the Sylvester Stallone film *Rocky 3*, the smash success of both record and movie being mutually beneficial. Several more revivals charted, with Fun Boy Three revamping Gershwin's *Summertime*, Bad Manners changing the sex of *My Girl (Boy) Lollipop*, Japan covering the Miracles' *I Second That Emotion*, the Boystown gang reviving Andy Williams' *Can't Take My Eyes Off You*, and oddest of all, Modern Romance resurrecting *Cherry Pink And Apple Blossom White*.

September – October 1982

11 September 1982

last week	this week		
1	1	EYE OF THE TIGER	Survivor (Scotti Brothers)
5	2	SAVE A PRAYER	Duran Duran (EMI)
2	3	COME ON EILEEN	Dexy's Midnight Runners (Mercury)
3	4	WHAT	Soft Cell (Some Bizzare)
6	5	HI FIDELITY	Kids From Fame (RCA)
4	6	CAN'T TAKE MY EYES OFF YOU	Boys Town (ERC)
13	7	WALKING ON SUNSHINE	Rockers Revenge (London)
7	8	I EAT CANNIBALS	Toto Coelo (Radialchoice)
23	9	GIVE ME YOUR HEART TONIGHT	Shakin' Stevens (Epic)
-	10	PRIVATE INVESTIGATIONS	Dire Straits (Vertigo)
8	11	NOBODY'S FOOL	Haircut 100 (Arista)
26	12	TODAY	Talk Talk (EMI)
9	13	FAME	Irene Cara (RSO)
20	14	THE MESSAGE	Grandmaster Flash (Sugarhill)
15	15	CHERRY PINK AND APPLE BLOSSOM WHITE	Modern Romance (WEA)
12	16	JOHN WAYNE IS BIG LEGGY	Haysi Fantayzee (Regard)
25	17	SPREAD A LITTLE HAPPINESS	Sting (A&M)
-	18	ALL OF MY HEART	ABC (Neutron)
14	19	BIG FUN	Kool & the Gang (De-Lite)
16	20	WHITE BOYS AND HEROES	Gary Numan (Beggars Banquet)
11	21	DON'T GO	Yazoo (Mute)
10	22	IT STARTED WITH A KISS	Hot Chocolate (RAK)
19	23	UNDER THE BOARDWALK	Tom Tom Club (Island)
28	24	HURRY HOME	Wavelength (Ariola)
22	25	THE CLAPPING SONG	Belle Stars (Stiff)
-	26	LEAVE IN SILENCE	Depeche Mode (Mute)
-	27	THERE IT IS	Shalamar (Solar)
-	28	SO HERE I AM	UB40 (DEP International)
18	29	MY GIRL LOLLIPOP	Bad Manners (Magnet)
-	30	SADDLE UP	David Christie (KR)

18 September 1982

last week	this week		
1	1	EYE OF THE TIGER	Survivor (Scotti Brothers)
10	2	PRIVATE INVESTIGATIONS	Dire Straits (Vertigo)
2	3	SAVE A PRAYER	Duran Duran (EMI)
7	4	WALKING ON SUNSHINE	Rockers Revenge (London)
3	5	COME ON EILEEN	Dexy's Midnight Runners (Mercury)
18	6	ALL OF MY HEART	ABC (Neutron)
9	7	GIVE ME YOUR HEART TONIGHT	Shakin' Stevens (Epic)
5	8	HI FIDELITY	Kids From Fame (RCA)
14	9	THE MESSAGE	Grandmaster Flash (Sugarhill)
4	10	WHAT	Soft Cell (Some Bizzare)
11	11	NOBODY'S FOOL	Haircut 100 (Arista)
8	12	I EAT CANNIBALS	Toto Coelo (Radialchoice)
27	13	THERE IT IS	Shalamar (Solar)
17	14	SPREAD A LITTLE HAPPINESS	Sting (A&M)
12	15	TODAY	Talk Talk (EMI)
6	16	CAN'T TAKE MY EYES OFF YOU	Boys Town (ERC)
30	17	SADDLE UP	David Christie (KR)
-	18	WHY	Carly Simon (WEA)
16	19	JOHN WAYNE IS BIG LEGGY	Haysi Fantayzee (Regard)
-	20	THE BITTEREST PILL	Jam (Polydor)
26	21	LEAVE IN SILENCE	Depeche Mode (Mute)
15	22	CHERRY PINK AND APPLE BLOSSOM WHITE	Modern Romance (WEA)
28	23	SO HERE I AM	UB40 (DEP International)
-	24	ZOOM	Fat Larry's Band (Virgin)
-	25	INVITATIONS	Shakatak (Polydor)
-	26	HALFWAY UP, HALFWAY DOWN	Dennis Brown (A&M)
13	27	FAME	Irene Cara (RSO)
23	28	UNDER THE BOARDWALK	Tom Tom Club (Island)
-	29	LOVE COME DOWN	Evelyn King (RCA)
-	30	WINDPOWER	Thomas Dolby (Venice In Peril)

25 September 1982

last week	this week		
2	1	PRIVATE INVESTIGATIONS	Dire Straits (Vertigo)
1	2	EYE OF THE TIGER	Survivor (Scotti Brothers)
3	3	SAVE A PRAYER	Duran Duran (EMI)
20	4	THE BITTEREST PILL	Jam (Polydor)
6	5	ALL OF MY HEART	ABC (Neutron)
4	6	WALKING ON SUNSHINE	Rockers Revenge (London)
9	7	THE MESSAGE	Grandmaster Flash (Sugarhill)
13	8	THERE IT IS	Shalamar (Solar)
-	9	FRIEND OR FOE	Adam Ant (CBS)
18	10	WHY	Carly Simon (WEA)
17	11	SADDLE UP	David Christie (KR)
8	12	HI FIDELITY	Kids From Fame (RCA)
5	13	COME ON EILEEN	Dexy's Midnight Runners (Mercury)
29	14	LOVE COME DOWN	Evelyn King (RCA)
15	15	TODAY	Talk Talk (EMI)
7	16	GIVE ME YOUR HEART TONIGHT	Shakin' Stevens (Epic)
25	17	INVITATIONS	Shakatak (Polydor)
24	18	ZOOM	Fat Larry's Band (Virgin)
-	19	AND I'M TELLING YOU I'M NOT GOING	Jennifer Holliday (Geffen)
12	20	I EAT CANNIBALS	Toto Coelo (Radialchoice)
10	21	WHAT	Soft Cell (Some Bizzare)
-	22	HARD TO SAY I'M SORRY	Chicago (Full Moon)
23	23	SO HERE I AM	UB40 (DEP International)
-	24	GLITTERING PRIZE	Simple Minds (Virgin)
16	25	CAN'T TAKE MY EYES OFF YOU	Boys Town (ERC)
14	26	SPREAD A LITTLE HAPPINESS	Sting (A&M)
-	27	GIVE ME SOME KINDA MUSIC	Dollar (WEA)
30	28	WINDPOWER	Thomas Dolby (Venice In Peril)
-	29	JUST WHAT I ALWAYS WANTED	Mari Wilson (Compact)
11	30	NOBODY'S FOOL	Haircut 100 (Arista)

2 October 1982

last week	this week		
4	1	THE BITTEREST PILL	Jam (Polydor)
1	2	PRIVATE INVESTIGATIONS	Dire Straits (Vertigo)
3	3	EYE OF THE TIGER	Survivor (Scotti Brothers)
6	4	WALKING ON SUNSHINE	Rockers Revenge (London)
5	5	ALL OF MY HEART	ABC (Neutron)
9	6	FRIEND OR FOE	Adam Ant (CBS)
11	7	SADDLE UP	David Christie (KR)
8	8	THERE IT IS	Shalamar (Solar)
18	9	ZOOM	Fat Larry's Band (Virgin)
3	10	SAVE A PRAYER	Duran Duran (EMI)
10	11	WHY	Carly Simon (WEA)
14	12	LOVE COME DOWN	Evelyn King (RCA)
7	13	THE MESSAGE	Grandmaster Flash (Sugarhill)
-	14	PASS THE DUTCHIE	Musical Youth (MCA)
16	15	GIVE ME YOUR HEART TONIGHT	Shakin' Stevens (Epic)
29	16	JUST WHAT I ALWAYS WANTED	Mari Wilson (Compact)
12	17	HI FIDELITY	Kids From Fame (RCA)
15	18	TODAY	Talk Talk (EMI)
24	19	GLITTERING PRIZE	Simple Minds (Virgin)
-	20	TAKE A CHANCE ON ME	Roxy Music (EG)
22	21	HARD TO SAY I'M SORRY	Chicago (Full Moon)
-	22	LEAVE IN SILENCE	Depeche Mode (Mute)
-	23	DO YOU REALLY WANT TO HURT ME	Culture Club (Virgin)
-	24	JACKIE WILSON SAYS (I'M IN HEAVEN WHEN YOU SMILE)	Dexy's Midnight Runners (Mercury)
13	25	COME ON EILEEN	Dexy's Midnight Runners (Mercury)
-	26	IN THE HEAT OF THE NIGHT	Imagination (R&B)
17	27	INVITATIONS	Shakatak (Polydor)
30	28	NOBODY'S FOOL	Haircut 100 (Arista)
25	29	CAN'T TAKE MY EYES OFF YOU	Boys Town (ERC)
20	30	I EAT CANNIBALS	Toto Coelo (Radialchoice)

Dire Straits' first chart-topping single *Private Investigations* was notable for its exceptional length, almost six minutes – a fact which did not seem to lose it any airplay. Grandmaster Flash's *The Message* was the first of the big rap hits which would characterise the later 1980s, and was itself highly influential, while Dexy's Midnight Runners' *Come On Eileen*, their first Number One since Geno, proved to be their biggest seller, and would pass the million sales mark in the UK before year's end.

October 1982

9 October 1982

last week	this week	title	artist
14	1	PASS THE DUTCHIE	Musical Youth (MCA)
9	2	ZOOM	Fat Larry's Band (Virgin)
1	3	THE BITTEREST PILL	Jam (Polydor)
12	4	LOVE COME DOWN	Evelyn King (RCA)
8	5	THERE IT IS	Shalamar (Solar)
11	6	WHY	Carly Simon (WEA)
21	7	HARD TO SAY I'M SORRY	Chicago (Full Moon)
23	8	DO YOU REALLY WANT TO HURT ME	Culture Club (Virgin)
6	9	FRIEND OR FOE	Adam Ant (CBS)
3	10	EYE OF THE TIGER	Survivor (Scotti Brothers)
4	11	WALKING ON SUNSHINE	Rockers Revenge (London)
16	12	JUST WHAT I ALWAYS WANTED	Mari Wilson (Compact)
2	13	PRIVATE INVESTIGATIONS	Dire Straits (Vertigo)
24	14	JACKIE WILSON SAYS (I'M IN HEAVEN WHEN YOU SMILE)	Dexy's Midnight Runners (Mercury)
5	15	ALL OF MY HEART	ABC (Neutron)
7	16	SADDLE UP	David Christie (KR)
19	17	GLITTERING PRIZE	Simple Minds (Virgin)
20	18	TAKE A CHANCE ON ME	Roxy Music (EG)
-	19	STARMAKER	Kids From Fame (RCA)
26	20	IN THE HEAT OF THE NIGHT	Imagination (R&B)
13	21	THE MESSAGE	Grandmaster Flash (Sugarhill)
-	22	REAP THE WILD WIND	Ultravox (Chrysalis)
-	23	THE HOUSE OF THE RISING SUN	Animals (RAK)
27	24	INVITATIONS	Shakatak (Polydor)
15	25	GIVE ME YOUR HEART TONIGHT	Shakin' Stevens (Epic)
22	26	LEAVE IN SILENCE	Depeche Mode (Mute)
-	27	CHANCES	Hot Chocolate (RAK)
-	28	DO YA WANNA FUNK	Sylvester (London)
10	29	SAVE A PRAYER	Duran Duran (EMI)
17	30	HI FIDELITY	Kids From Fame (RCA)

16 October 1982

last week	this week	title	artist
1	1	PASS THE DUTCHIE	Musical Youth (MCA)
8	2	DO YOU REALLY WANT TO HURT ME	Culture Club (Virgin)
2	3	ZOOM	Fat Larry's Band (Virgin)
4	4	LOVE COME DOWN	Evelyn King (RCA)
14	5	JACKIE WILSON SAYS (I'M IN HEAVEN WHEN YOU SMILE)	Dexy's Midnight Runners (Mercury)
7	6	HARD TO SAY I'M SORRY	Chicago (Full Moon)
19	7	STARMAKER	Kids From Fame (RCA)
12	8	JUST WHAT I ALWAYS WANTED	Mari Wilson (Compact)
5	9	THERE IT IS	Shalamar (Solar)
9	10	FRIEND OR FOE	Adam Ant (CBS)
3	11	THE BITTEREST PILL	Jam (Polydor)
17	12	GLITTERING PRIZE	Simple Minds (Virgin)
23	13	THE HOUSE OF THE RISING SUN	Animals (RAK)
22	14	REAP THE WILD WIND	Ultravox (Chrysalis)
6	15	WHY	Carly Simon (WEA)
10	16	EYE OF THE TIGER	Survivor (Scotti Brothers)
11	17	WALKING ON SUNSHINE	Rockers Revenge (London)
16	18	SADDLE UP	David Christie (KR)
20	19	IN THE HEAT OF THE NIGHT	Imagination (R&B)
18	20	TAKE A CHANCE ON ME	Roxy Music (EG)
15	21	ALL OF MY HEART	ABC (Neutron)
13	22	PRIVATE INVESTIGATIONS	Dire Straits (Vertigo)
-	23	BACK ON THE CHAIN GANG	Pretenders (Real)
-	24	SHOULD I STAY OR SHOULD I GO	Clash (CBS)
25	25	ZIGGY STARDUST	Bauhaus (Beggars Banquet)
-	26	LIFELINE	Spandau Ballet (Chrysalis)
-	27	ANNIE I'M NOT YOUR DADDY	Kid Creole & the Coconuts (Ze)
27	28	CHANCES	Hot Chocolate (RAK)
25	29	GIVE ME YOUR HEART TONIGHT	Shakin' Stevens (Epic)
-	30	AMOR	Julio Iglesias (CBS)

23 October 1982

last week	this week	title	artist
2	1	DO YOU REALLY WANT TO HURT ME	Culture Club (Virgin)
1	2	PASS THE DUTCHIE	Musical Youth (MCA)
7	3	STARMAKER	Kids From Fame (RCA)
3	4	ZOOM	Fat Larry's Band (Virgin)
-	5	LOVE ME DO	Beatles (Parlophone)
6	6	JACKIE WILSON SAYS (I'M IN HEAVEN WHEN YOU SMILE)	Dexy's Midnight Runners (Mercury)
4	7	LOVE COME DOWN	Evelyn King (RCA)
6	8	HARD TO SAY I'M SORRY	Chicago (Full Moon)
26	9	LIFELINE	Spandau Ballet (Chrysalis)
8	10	JUST WHAT I ALWAYS WANTED	Mari Wilson (Compact)
27	11	ANNIE I'M NOT YOUR DADDY	Kid Creole & the Coconuts (Ze)
14	12	REAP THE WILD WIND	Ultravox (Chrysalis)
15	13	WHY	Carly Simon (WEA)
13	14	THE HOUSE OF THE RISING SUN	Animals (RAK)
9	15	THERE IT IS	Shalamar (Solar)
25	16	ZIGGY STARDUST	Bauhaus (Beggars Banquet)
10	17	FRIEND OR FOE	Adam Ant (CBS)
-	18	I WANNA DO IT WITH YOU	Barry Manilow (Arista)
12	19	GLITTERING PRIZE	Simple Minds (Virgin)
-	20	I'LL BE SATISFIED	Shakin' Stevens (Epic)
11	21	THE BITTEREST PILL	Jam (Polydor)
23	22	BACK ON THE CHAIN GANG	Pretenders (Real)
17	23	WALKING ON SUNSHINE	Rockers Revenge (London)
24	24	SHOULD I STAY OR SHOULD I GO	Clash (CBS)
-	25	DANGER GAMES	Pinkees (Creole)
18	26	SADDLE UP	David Christie (KR)
16	27	EYE OF THE TIGER	Survivor (Scotti Brothers)
20	28	TAKE A CHANCE ON ME	Roxy Music (EG)
19	29	IN THE HEAT OF THE NIGHT	Imagination (R&B)
-	30	I DON'T WANNA DANCE	Eddy Grant (Ice)

30 October 1982

last week	this week	title	artist
1	1	DO YOU REALLY WANT TO HURT ME	Culture Club (Virgin)
3	2	STARMAKER	Kids From Fame (RCA)
5	3	LOVE ME DO	Beatles (Parlophone)
11	4	ANNIE I'M NOT YOUR DADDY	Kid Creole & the Coconuts (Ze)
4	5	ZOOM	Fat Larry's Band (Virgin)
2	6	PASS THE DUTCHIE	Musical Youth (MCA)
18	7	I WANNA DO IT WITH YOU	Barry Manilow (Arista)
9	8	LIFELINE	Spandau Ballet (Chrysalis)
8	9	HARD TO SAY I'M SORRY	Chicago (Full Moon)
14	10	THE HOUSE OF THE RISING SUN	Animals (RAK)
12	11	REAP THE WILD WIND	Ultravox (Chrysalis)
-	12	MAD WORLD	Tears For Fears (Mercury)
25	13	DANGER GAMES	Pinkees (Creole)
20	14	I'LL BE SATISFIED	Shakin' Stevens (Epic)
15	15	ZIGGY STARDUST	Bauhaus (Beggars Banquet)
6	16	JACKIE WILSON SAYS (I'M IN HEAVEN WHEN YOU SMILE)	Dexy's Midnight Runners (Mercury)
7	17	LOVE COME DOWN	Evelyn King (RCA)
30	18	I DON'T WANNA DANCE	Eddy Grant (Ice)
24	19	SHOULD I STAY OR SHOULD I GO	Clash (CBS)
10	20	JUST WHAT I ALWAYS WANTED	Mari Wilson (Compact)
29	21	IN THE HEAT OF THE NIGHT	Imagination (R&B)
17	22	FRIEND OR FOE	Adam Ant (CBS)
23	23	WALKING ON SUNSHINE	Rockers Revenge (London)
22	24	BACK ON THE CHAIN GANG	Pretenders (Real)
-	25	THE DAY BEFORE YOU CAME	Abba (Epic)
-	26	LOVE'S COMIN' AT YA	Melba Moore (EMI America)
-	27	NEVER GIVE YOU UP	Sharon Redd (Prelude)
13	28	WHY	Carly Simon (WEA)
-	29	ZAMBEZI	Piranhas (Dakota)
-	30	AMOR	Julio Iglesias (CBS)

Dexy's followed *Eileen* quickly with a spirited revival of Van Morrison's *Jackie Wilson Says (I'm In Heaven When You Smile)*, which brought about an hilarious situation on TV's *Top Of The Pops*, when either ill-informed researchers or mischief-minded studio wags were responsible for displaying a huge portrait of darts player JOCKY Wilson as the backdrop to Dexys' performance. Teenage group Musical Youth arrived from total obscurity at No.1, and Boy George & Culture Club also made their chart-topping debut.

November 1982

6 November 1982

last week	this week	
1	1	DO YOU REALLY WANT TO HURT ME — Culture Club (Virgin)
2	2	STARMAKER — Kids From Fame (RCA)
4	3	ANNIE I'M NOT YOUR DADDY — Kid Creole & the Coconuts (Ze)
12	4	MAD WORLD — Tears For Fears (Mercury)
18	5	I DON'T WANNA DANCE — Eddy Grant (Ice)
3	6	LOVE ME DO — Beatles (Parlophone)
8	7	LIFELINE — Spandau Ballet (Chrysalis)
7	8	I WANNA DO IT WITH YOU — Barry Manilow (Arista)
6	9	PASS THE DUTCHIE — Musical Youth (MCA)
-	10	OOH LA LA LA — Kool & the Gang (De-Lite)
5	11	ZOOM — Fat Larry's Band (Virgin)
14	12	I'LL BE SATISFIED — Shakin' Stevens (Epic)
9	13	HARD TO SAY I'M SORRY — Chicago (Full Moon)
15	14	ZIGGY STARDUST — Bauhaus (Beggars Banquet)
-	15	HEARTBREAKER — Dionne Warwick (Arista)
11	16	REAP THE WILD WIND — Ultravox (Chrysalis)
26	17	LOVE'S COMIN' AT YA — Melba Moore (EMI America)
29	18	ZAMBEZI — Piranhas (Dakota)
13	19	DANGER GAMES — Pinkees (Creole)
10	20	THE HOUSE OF THE RISING SUN — Animals (RAK)
-	21	CAROLINE — Status Quo (Vertigo)
16	22	JACKIE WILSON SAYS (I'M IN HEAVEN WHEN YOU SMILE) — Dexy's Midnight Runners (Mercury)
22	23	FRIEND OR FOE — Adam Ant (CBS)
27	24	NEVER GIVE YOU UP — Sharon Redd (Prelude)
17	25	LOVE COME DOWN — Evelyn King (RCA)
30	26	AMOR — Julio Iglesias (CBS)
21	27	IN THE HEAT OF THE NIGHT — Imagination (R&B)
24	28	BACK ON THE CHAIN GANG — Pretenders (Real)
-	29	ANNIE GET YOUR GUN — Squeeze (A&M)
-	30	OLD FLAMES — Foster & Allen (Ritz)

13 November 1982

last week	this week	
5	1	I DON'T WANNA DANCE — Eddy Grant (Ice)
15	2	HEARTBREAKER — Dionne Warwick (Arista)
4	3	MAD WORLD — Tears For Fears (Mercury)
1	4	DO YOU REALLY WANT TO HURT ME — Culture Club (Virgin)
3	5	ANNIE I'M NOT YOUR DADDY — Kid Creole & the Coconuts (Ze)
2	6	STARMAKER — Kids From Fame (RCA)
8	7	I WANNA DO IT WITH YOU — Barry Manilow (Arista)
10	8	OOH LA LA LA — Kool & the Gang (De-Lite)
12	9	I'LL BE SATISFIED — Shakin' Stevens (Epic)
-	10	(SEXUAL) HEALING — Marvin Gaye (CBS)
-	11	MANEATER — Daryl Hall & John Oates (RCA)
21	12	CAROLINE — Status Quo (Vertigo)
6	13	LOVE ME DO — Beatles (Parlophone)
7	14	LIFELINE — Spandau Ballet (Chrysalis)
-	15	THE GIRL IS MINE — Michael Jackson & Paul McCartney (Epic)
17	16	LOVE'S COMIN' AT YA — Melba Moore (EMI America)
18	17	ZAMBEZI — Piranhas (Dakota)
13	18	HARD TO SAY I'M SORRY — Chicago (Full Moon)
9	19	PASS THE DUTCHIE — Musical Youth (MCA)
28	20	BACK ON THE CHAIN GANG — Pretenders (Real)
24	21	NEVER GIVE YOU UP — Sharon Redd (Prelude)
11	22	ZOOM — Fat Larry's Band (Virgin)
-	23	MUSCLES — Diana Ross (Capitol)
-	24	THEME FROM HARRY'S GAME — Clannad (RCA)
16	25	REAP THE WILD WIND — Ultravox (Chrysalis)
-	26	STATE OF INDEPENDENCE — Donna Summer (Warner Brothers)
26	27	AMOR — Julio Iglesias (CBS)
-	28	LIVING ON THE CEILING — Blancmange (London)
-	29	JACK AND DIANE — John Cougar (Riva)
14	30	ZIGGY STARDUST — Bauhaus (Beggars Banquet)

20 November 1982

last week	this week	
1	1	I DON'T WANNA DANCE — Eddy Grant (Ice)
2	2	HEARTBREAKER — Dionne Warwick (Arista)
3	3	MAD WORLD — Tears For Fears (Mercury)
15	4	THE GIRL IS MINE — Michael Jackson & Paul McCartney (Epic)
10	5	(SEXUAL) HEALING — Marvin Gaye (CBS)
11	6	MANEATER — Daryl Hall & John Oates (RCA)
8	7	OOH LA LA LA — Kool & the Gang (De-Lite)
24	8	THEME FROM HARRY'S GAME — Clannad (RCA)
4	9	DO YOU REALLY WANT TO HURT ME — Culture Club (Virgin)
7	10	I WANNA DO IT WITH YOU — Barry Manilow (Arista)
17	11	ZAMBEZI — Piranhas (Dakota)
6	12	STARMAKER — Kids From Fame (RCA)
23	13	MUSCLES — Diana Ross (Capitol)
12	14	CAROLINE — Status Quo (Vertigo)
-	15	RIO — Duran Duran (EMI)
21	16	NEVER GIVE YOU UP — Sharon Redd (Prelude)
-	17	CRY BOY CRY — Blue Zoo (Magnet)
-	18	YOUNG GUNS (GO FOR IT) — Wham! (Innervision)
8	19	I'LL BE SATISFIED — Shakin' Stevens (Epic)
29	20	JACK AND DIANE — John Cougar (Riva)
28	21	LIVING ON THE CEILING — Blancmange (London)
16	22	LOVE'S COMIN' AT YA — Melba Moore (EMI America)
13	23	LOVE ME DO — Beatles (Parlophone)
26	24	STATE OF INDEPENDENCE — Donna Summer (Warner Brothers)
-	25	IT'S RAINING AGAIN — Supertramp (A&M)
5	26	ANNIE I'M NOT YOUR DADDY — Kid Creole & the Coconuts (Ze)
-	27	LOVE — John Lennon (Parlophone)
-	28	DO IT TO THE MUSIC — Raw Silk (KR)
-	29	MIRROR MAN — Human League (Virgin)
-	30	SAVE YOUR LOVE — Renee & Renato (Hollywood)

27 November 1982

last week	this week	
2	1	HEARTBREAKER — Dionne Warwick (Arista)
1	2	I DON'T WANNA DANCE — Eddy Grant (Ice)
29	3	MIRROR MAN — Human League (Virgin)
5	4	(SEXUAL) HEALING — Marvin Gaye (CBS)
8	5	THEME FROM HARRY'S GAME — Clannad (RCA)
3	6	MAD WORLD — Tears For Fears (Mercury)
4	7	THE GIRL IS MINE — Michael Jackson & Paul McCartney (Epic)
18	8	YOUNG GUNS (GO FOR IT) — Wham! (Innervision)
6	9	MANEATER — Daryl Hall & John Oates (RCA)
13	10	MUSCLES — Diana Ross (Capitol)
15	11	RIO — Duran Duran (EMI)
21	12	LIVING ON THE CEILING — Blancmange (London)
24	13	STATE OF INDEPENDENCE — Donna Summer (Warner Brothers)
9	14	DO YOU REALLY WANT TO HURT ME — Culture Club (Virgin)
7	15	OOH LA LA LA — Kool & the Gang (De-Lite)
28	16	DO IT TO THE MUSIC — Raw Silk (KR)
17	17	CRY BOY CRY — Blue Zoo (Magnet)
-	18	YOUTH OF TODAY — Musical Youth (MCA)
-	19	TRULY — Lionel Richie (Motown)
30	20	SAVE YOUR LOVE — Renee & Renato (Hollywood)
-	21	WISHING (IF I HAD A PHOTOGRAPH OF YOU) — Flock Of Seagulls (Jive)
11	22	ZAMBEZI — Piranhas (Dakota)
14	23	CAROLINE — Status Quo (Vertigo)
-	24	THE OTHER SIDE OF LOVE — Yazoo (Mute)
12	25	STARMAKER — Kids From Fame (RCA)
-	26	BEST YEARS OF OUR LIVES — Modern Romance (WEA)
26	27	ANNIE I'M NOT YOUR DADDY — Kid Creole & the Coconuts (Ze)
10	28	I WANNA DO IT WITH YOU — Barry Manilow (Arista)
-	29	BACK TO LOVE — Evelyn King (RCA)
20	30	JACK AND DIANE — John Cougar (Riva)

After an 18-month chart absence, Eddy Grant returned with his biggest success to date *I Don't Wanna Dance*. Replacing this with her first-ever UK No.1 was veteran chartmaker Dionne Warwick, whose *Heartbreaker* was written and produced by the Bee Gees in much the same way as Barbra Streisand's *Woman In Love* had been in 1980. The Gibb Brothers also sang prominent back-up vocals on the single. Clannad's debut, the haunting *Theme From Harry's Game*, was from a TV drama of that title.

December 1982

4 December 1982

last week	this week		
3	1	MIRROR MAN	Human League (Virgin)
2	2	I DON'T WANNA DANCE	Eddy Grant (Ice)
8	3	YOUNG GUNS (GO FOR IT)	Wham! (Innervision)
1	4	HEARTBREAKER	Dionne Warwick (Arista)
4	5	(SEXUAL) HEALING	Marvin Gaye (CBS)
20	6	SAVE YOUR LOVE	Renee & Renato (Hollywood)
12	7	LIVING ON THE CEILING	Blancmange (London)
6	8	MAD WORLD	Tears For Fears (Mercury)
11	9	RIO	Duran Duran (EMI)
21	10	WISHING (IF I HAD A PHOTOGRAPH OF YOU)	Flock Of Seagulls (Jive)
19	11	TRULY	Lionel Richie (Motown)
17	12	CRY BOY CRY	Blue Zoo (Magnet)
5	13	THEME FROM HARRY'S GAME	Clannad (RCA)
-	14	BEAT SURRENDER	Jam (Polydor)
18	15	YOUTH OF TODAY	Musical Youth (MCA)
9	16	MANEATER	Daryl Hall & John Oates (RCA)
24	17	THE OTHER SIDE OF LOVE	Yazoo (Mute)
7	18	THE GIRL IS MINE	Michael Jackson & Paul McCartney (Epic)
26	19	BEST YEARS OF OUR LIVES	Modern Romance (WEA)
-	20	OUR HOUSE	Madness (Stiff)
-	21	HYMN	Ultravox (Chrysalis)
13	22	STATE OF INDEPENDENCE	Donna Summer (Warner Brothers)
-	23	TIME (CLOCK OF THE HEART)	Culture Club (Virgin)
10	24	MUSCLES	Diana Ross (Capitol)
14	25	DO YOU REALLY WANT TO HURT ME	Culture Club (Virgin)
25	26	STARMAKER	Kids From Fame (RCA)
16	27	DO IT TO THE MUSIC	Raw Silk (KR)
-	28	WHERE THE HEART IS	Soft Cell (Some Bizzare)
-	29	TALK TALK	Talk Talk (EMI)
-	30	IT'S RAINING AGAIN	Supertramp (A&M)

11 December 1982

last week	this week		
14	1	BEAT SURRENDER	Jam (Polydor)
1	2	MIRROR MAN	Human League (Virgin)
3	3	YOUNG GUNS (GO FOR IT)	Wham! (Innervision)
6	4	SAVE YOUR LOVE	Renee & Renato (Hollywood)
11	5	TRULY	Lionel Richie (Motown)
23	6	TIME (CLOCK OF THE HEART)	Culture Club (Virgin)
7	7	LIVING ON THE CEILING	Blancmange (London)
9	8	RIO	Duran Duran (EMI)
2	9	I DON'T WANNA DANCE	Eddy Grant (Ice)
21	10	HYMN	Ultravox (Chrysalis)
10	11	WISHING (IF I HAD A PHOTOGRAPH OF YOU)	Flock Of Seagulls (Jive)
15	12	YOUTH OF TODAY	Musical Youth (MCA)
17	13	THE OTHER SIDE OF LOVE	Yazoo (Mute)
20	14	OUR HOUSE	Madness (Stiff)
4	15	HEARTBREAKER	Dionne Warwick (Arista)
19	16	BEST YEARS OF OUR LIVES	Modern Romance (WEA)
28	17	WHERE THE HEART IS	Soft Cell (Some Bizzare)
-	18	LET'S GET THIS STRAIGHT (FROM THE START)/OLD	Kevin Rowland & Dexy's Midnight Runners (Mercury)
5	19	(SEXUAL) HEALING	Marvin Gaye (CBS)
8	20	MAD WORLD	Tears For Fears (Mercury)
-	21	FRIENDS	Shalamar (Solar)
22	22	STATE OF INDEPENDENCE	Donna Summer (Warner Brothers)
12	23	CRY BOY CRY	Blue Zoo (Magnet)
-	24	I CONFESS	Beat (Go Feet)
13	25	THEME FROM HARRY'S GAME	Clannad (RCA)
-	26	YOU CAN'T HURRY LOVE	Phil Collins (Virgin)
-	27	BUFFALO GALS	Malcolm McLaren & the World's Famous Supreme Team (Charisma)
30	28	IT'S RAINING AGAIN	Supertramp (A&M)
29	29	TALK TALK	Talk Talk (EMI)
-	30	PEACE ON EARTH/LITTLE DRUMMER BOY	David Bowie & Bing Crosby (RCA)

18 December 1982

last week	this week		
1	1	BEAT SURRENDER	Jam (Polydor)
6	2	TIME (CLOCK OF THE HEART)	Culture Club (Virgin)
2	3	MIRROR MAN	Human League (Virgin)
4	4	SAVE YOUR LOVE	Renee & Renato (Hollywood)
5	5	TRULY	Lionel Richie (Motown)
14	6	OUR HOUSE	Madness (Stiff)
10	7	HYMN	Ultravox (Chrysalis)
3	8	YOUNG GUNS (GO FOR IT)	Wham! (Innervision)
8	9	RIO	Duran Duran (EMI)
18	10	LET'S GET THIS STRAIGHT (FROM THE START)/OLD	Kevin Rowland & Dexy's Midnight Runners (Mercury)
16	11	BEST YEARS OF OUR LIVES	Modern Romance (WEA)
7	12	LIVING ON THE CEILING	Blancmange (London)
30	13	PEACE ON EARTH/LITTLE DRUMMER BOY	David Bowie & Bing Crosby (RCA)
11	14	WISHING (IF I HAD A PHOTOGRAPH OF YOU)	Flock Of Seagulls (Jive)
17	15	WHERE THE HEART IS	Soft Cell (Some Bizzare)
13	16	THE OTHER SIDE OF LOVE	Yazoo (Mute)
21	17	FRIENDS	Shalamar (Solar)
9	18	I DON'T WANNA DANCE	Eddy Grant (Ice)
-	19	THE SHAKIN' STEVENS EP (EP)	Shakin' Stevens (Epic)
26	20	YOU CAN'T HURRY LOVE	Phil Collins (Virgin)
15	21	HEARTBREAKER	Dionne Warwick (Arista)
27	22	BUFFALO GALS	Malcolm McLaren & the World's Famous Supreme Team (Charisma)
-	23	UNDER ATTACK	Abba (Epic)
12	24	YOUTH OF TODAY	Musical Youth (MCA)
-	25	IF YOU CAN'T STAND THE HEAT	Bucks Fizz (RCA)
22	26	STATE OF INDEPENDENCE	Donna Summer (Warner Brothers)
20	27	MAD WORLD	Tears For Fears (Mercury)
19	28	(SEXUAL) HEALING	Marvin Gaye (CBS)
28	29	IT'S RAINING AGAIN	Supertramp (A&M)
-	30	MELT	Siouxsie & the Banshees (Polydor)

25 December 1982

last week	this week		
2	1	TIME (CLOCK OF THE HEART)	Culture Club (Virgin)
4	2	SAVE YOUR LOVE	Renee & Renato (Hollywood)
1	3	BEAT SURRENDER	Jam (Polydor)
19	4	THE SHAKIN' STEVENS EP (EP)	Shakin' Stevens (Epic)
6	5	OUR HOUSE	Madness (Stiff)
13	6	PEACE ON EARTH/LITTLE DRUMMER BOY	David Bowie & Bing Crosby (RCA)
11	7	BEST YEARS OF OUR LIVES	Modern Romance (WEA)
17	8	FRIENDS	Shalamar (Solar)
8	9	YOUNG GUNS (GO FOR IT)	Wham! (Innervision)
20	10	YOU CAN'T HURRY LOVE	Phil Collins (Virgin)
16	11	THE OTHER SIDE OF LOVE	Yazoo (Mute)
3	12	MIRROR MAN	Human League (Virgin)
22	13	BUFFALO GALS	Malcolm McLaren & the World's Famous Supreme Team (Charisma)
-	14	LITTLE TOWN	Cliff Richard (EMI)
7	15	HYMN	Ultravox (Chrysalis)
12	16	LIVING ON THE CEILING	Blancmange (London)
10	17	LET'S GET THIS STRAIGHT (FROM THE START)/OLD	Kevin Rowland & Dexy's Midnight Runners (Mercury)
9	18	RIO	Duran Duran (EMI)
-	19	A WINTER'S TALE	David Essex (Mercury)
21	20	HEARTBREAKER	Dionne Warwick (Arista)
26	21	STATE OF INDEPENDENCE	Donna Summer (Warner Brothers)
-	22	THEME FROM E.T. (THE EXTRA TERRESTRIAL)	John Williams (MCA)
25	23	IF YOU CAN'T STAND THE HEAT	Bucks Fizz (RCA)
23	24	UNDER ATTACK	Abba (Epic)
-	25	SINGALONGA-A-SANTA MEDLEY	Santa Claus & the Christmas Trees (Polydor)
-	26	HI DE HI, HI DE HO	Kool & the Gang (De-Lite)
-	27	ORVILLE'S SONG	Keith Harris & Orville (BBC)
29	28	IT'S RAINING AGAIN	Supertramp (A&M)
-	29	DEAR ADDY	Kid Creole & the Coconuts (Ze)

Beat Surrender's Number One success saw the Jam off in fine style – they were playing their final tour before splitting up, as the single was released. Newcomers Wham! made a strong impact with their dancefloor-orientated *Young Guns (Go For It)*, peaking at No.3. Also new, though destined for rather lesser things, were another duo, Rene & Renato, whose corny Neopolitan-style ballad *Save Your Love* was Christmas' silly season hit. Culture Club, meanwhile, snatched a second successive No. 1.

January 1983

last week	this	8 January 1983
2	1	SAVE YOUR LOVE Renee & Renato (Hollywood)
20	2	A WINTER'S TALE David Essex (Mercury)
4	3	THE SHAKIN' STEVENS EP (EP) Shakin' Stevens (Epic)
11	4	YOU CAN'T HURRY LOVE Phil Collins (Virgin)
1	5	TIME (CLOCK OF THE HEART) Culture Club (Virgin)
8	6	BEST YEARS OF OUR LIVES Modern Romance (WEA)
6	7	PEACE ON EARTH/LITTLE DRUMMER BOY David Bowie & Bing Crosby (RCA)
5	8	OUR HOUSE Madness (Stiff)
7	9	TRULY Lionel Richie (Motown)
18	10	LET'S GET THIS STRAIGHT (FROM THE START)/OLD Kevin Rowland & Dexy's Midnight Runners (Mercury)
3	11	BEAT SURRENDER Jam (Polydor)
-	12	ALL THE LOVE IN THE WORLD Dionne Warwick (Arista)
14	13	BUFFALO GALS Malcolm McLaren & the World's Famous Supreme Team(Charisma)
13	14	MIRROR MAN Human League (Virgin)
15	15	LITTLE TOWN Cliff Richard (EMI)
9	16	FRIENDS Shalamar (Solar)
28	17	ORVILLE'S SONG Keith Harris & Orville (BBC)
24	18	IF YOU CAN'T STAND THE HEAT Bucks Fizz (RCA)
16	19	HYMN Ultravox (Chrysalis)
10	20	YOUNG GUNS (GO FOR IT) Wham! (Innervision)
-	21	CACHARPAYA (ANDES PUMPSA DESI) Incantation (Beggars Banquet)
17	22	LIVING ON THE CEILING Blancmange (London)
23	23	THEME FROM E.T. (THE EXTRA TERRESTRIAL) John Williams (MCA)
22	24	STATE OF INDEPENDENCE Donna Summer (Warner Brothers)
25	25	UNDER ATTACK Abba (Epic)
30	26	DEAR ADDY Kid Creole & the Coconuts (Ze)
-	27	WISHING (IF I HAD A PHOTOGRAPH OF YOU) A Flock Of Seagulls (Jive)
-	28	HEARTACHE AVENUE Maisonettes (Ready Steady Go!)
19	29	RIO Duran Duran (EMI)
-	30	FAT MAN Southern Death Cult (Situation 2)

		15 January 1983
4	1	YOU CAN'T HURRY LOVE Phil Collins (Virgin)
2	2	A WINTER'S TALE David Essex (Mercury)
1	3	SAVE YOUR LOVE Renee & Renato (Hollywood)
6	4	BEST YEARS OF OUR LIVES Modern Romance (WEA)
12	5	ALL THE LOVE IN THE WORLD Dionne Warwick (Arista)
17	6	ORVILLE'S SONG Keith Harris & Orville (BBC)
8	7	OUR HOUSE Madness (Stiff)
5	8	TIME (CLOCK OF THE HEART) Culture Club (Virgin)
21	9	CACHARPAYA (ANDES PUMPSA DESI) Incantation (Beggars Banquet)
13	10	BUFFALO GALS Malcolm McLaren & the World's Famous Supreme Team (Charisma)
18	11	IF YOU CAN'T STAND THE HEAT Bucks Fizz (RCA)
19	12	HYMN Ultravox (Chrysalis)
3	13	THE SHAKIN' STEVENS EP (EP) Shakin' Stevens (Epic)
20	14	YOUNG GUNS (GO FOR IT) Wham! (Innervision)
23	15	THEME FROM E.T. (THE EXTRA TERRESTRIAL) John Williams (MCA)
16	16	FRIENDS Shalamar (Solar)
9	17	TRULY Lionel Richie (Motown)
-	18	EUROPEAN FEMALE Stranglers (Epic)
11	19	BEAT SURRENDER Jam (Polydor)
-	20	DOWN UNDER Men At Work (Epic)
10	21	LET'S GET THIS STRAIGHT (FROM THE START)/OLD Kevin Rowland & Dexy's Midnight Runners (Mercury)
-	22	STEPPIN' OUT Joe Jackson (A&M)
24	23	STATE OF INDEPENDENCE Donna Summer (Warner Brothers)
14	24	MIRROR MAN Human League (Virgin)
7	25	PEACE ON EARTH/LITTLE DRUMMER BOY David Bowie & Bing Crosby (RCA)
28	26	HEARTACHE AVENUE Maisonettes (Ready Steady Go!)
29	27	RIO Duran Duran (EMI)
25	28	UNDER ATTACK Abba (Epic)
22	29	LIVING ON THE CEILING Blancmange (London)
15	30	LITTLE TOWN Cliff Richard (EMI)

		22 January 1983
1	1	YOU CAN'T HURRY LOVE Phil Collins (Virgin)
6	2	ORVILLE'S SONG Keith Harris & Orville (BBC)
2	3	A WINTER'S TALE David Essex (Mercury)
-	4	THE STORY OF THE BLUES Wah! (Eternal)
20	5	DOWN UNDER Men At Work (Epic)
3	6	SAVE YOUR LOVE Renee & Renato (Hollywood)
10	7	BUFFALO GALS Malcolm McLaren & the World's Famous Supreme Team (Charisma)
4	8	BEST YEARS OF OUR LIVES Modern Romance (WEA)
11	9	IF YOU CAN'T STAND THE HEAT Bucks Fizz (RCA)
18	10	EUROPEAN FEMALE Stranglers (Epic)
9	11	CACHARPAYA (ANDES PUMPSA DESI) Incantation (Beggars Banquet)
26	12	HEARTACHE AVENUE Maisonettes (Ready Steady Go!)
8	13	TIME (CLOCK OF THE HEART) Culture Club (Virgin)
-	14	ELECTRIC AVENUE Eddy Grant (Ice)
12	15	HYMN Ultravox (Chrysalis)
22	16	STEPPIN' OUT Joe Jackson (A&M)
5	17	ALL THE LOVE IN THE WORLD Dionne Warwick (Arista)
28	18	OUR HOUSE Madness (Stiff)
15	19	THEME FROM E.T. (THE EXTRA TERRESTRIAL) John Williams (MCA)
14	20	YOUNG GUNS (GO FOR IT) Wham! (Innervision)
-	21	OH DIANE Fleetwood Mac (Warner Brothers)
27	22	RIO Duran Duran (EMI)
28	23	UNDER ATTACK Abba (Epic)
23	24	STATE OF INDEPENDENCE Donna Summer (Warner Brothers)
-	25	UP WHERE WE BELONG Joe Cocker & Jennifer Warnes (Island)
-	26	DEAR ADDY Kid Creole & the Coconuts (Ze)
-	27	MIND UP TONIGHT Melba Moore (Capitol)
-	28	GLORIA Laura Branigan (Atlantic)
21	29	LET'S GET THIS STRAIGHT (FROM THE START)/OLD Kevin Rowland & Dexy's Midnight Runners (Mercury)
16	30	FRIENDS Shalamar (Solar)

David Essex's *A Winter's Tale* was the third UK Top 10 hit to share its title with a Shakespeare Play – Adam Faith's *As You Like It* and Dire Straits' *Romeo And Juliet* had been the previous examples. The lead track on the *Shakin' Stevens EP* was a revival of Elvis Presley's *Blue Christmas*.

January – February 1983

29 January 1983

last	this	Title / Artist (Label)
5	1	DOWN UNDER — Men At Work (Epic)
1	2	YOU CAN'T HURRY LOVE — Phil Collins (Virgin)
14	3	ELECTRIC AVENUE — Eddy Grant (Ice)
16	4	STEPPIN' OUT — Joe Jackson (A&M)
10	5	EUROPEAN FEMALE — Stranglers (Epic)
12	6	HEARTACHE AVENUE — Maisonettes (Ready Steady Go!)
4	7	THE STORY OF THE BLUES — Wah! (Eternal)
2	8	ORVILLE'S SONG — Keith Harris & Orville (BBC)
3	9	A WINTER'S TALE — David Essex (Mercury)
11	10	CACHARPAYA (ANDES PUMPSA DESI) — Incantation (Beggars Banquet)
-	11	TWISTING BY THE POOL — Dire Straits (Vertigo)
-	12	NEW YEAR'S DAY — U2 (Island)
-	13	SIGN OF THE TIMES — Belle Stars (Stiff)
18	14	OUR HOUSE — Madness (Stiff)
28	15	GLORIA — Laura Branigan (Atlantic)
7	16	BUFFALO GALS — Malcolm McLaren & the World's Famous Supreme Team (Charisma)
20	17	YOUNG GUNS (GO FOR IT) — Wham! (Innervision)
17	18	ALL THE LOVE IN THE WORLD — Dionne Warwick (Arista)
21	19	OH DIANE — Fleetwood Mac (Warner Brothers)
9	20	IF YOU CAN'T STAND THE HEAT — Bucks Fizz (RCA)
8	21	BEST YEARS OF OUR LIVES — Modern Romance (WEA)
13	22	TIME (CLOCK OF THE HEART) — Culture Club (Virgin)
6	23	SAVE YOUR LOVE — Renee & Renato (Hollywood)
27	24	MIND UP TONIGHT — Melba Moore (Capitol)
-	25	HOLD ME TIGHTER IN THE RAIN — Billy Griffin (CBS)
-	26	TOO SHY — Kajagoogoo (EMI)
-	27	THE CUTTER — Echo & the Bunnymen (Korova)
15	28	HYMN — Ultravox (Chrysalis)
30	29	FRIENDS — Shalamar (Solar)
25	30	UP WHERE WE BELONG — Joe Cocker & Jennifer Warnes (Island)

5 February 1983

last	this	Title / Artist (Label)
1	1	DOWN UNDER — Men At Work (Epic)
3	2	ELECTRIC AVENUE — Eddy Grant (Ice)
13	3	SIGN OF THE TIMES — Belle Stars (Stiff)
4	4	STEPPIN' OUT — Joe Jackson (A&M)
2	5	YOU CAN'T HURRY LOVE — Phil Collins (Virgin)
6	6	HEARTACHE AVENUE — Maisonettes (Ready Steady Go!)
26	7	TOO SHY — Kajagoogoo (EMI)
15	8	GLORIA — Laura Branigan (Atlantic)
7	9	THE STORY OF THE BLUES — Wah! (Eternal)
11	10	TWISTING BY THE POOL — Dire Straits (Vertigo)
12	11	NEW YEAR'S DAY — U2 (Island)
27	12	THE CUTTER — Echo & the Bunnymen (Korova)
19	13	OH DIANE — Fleetwood Mac (Warner Brothers)
25	14	HOLD ME TIGHTER IN THE RAIN — Billy Griffin (CBS)
5	15	EUROPEAN FEMALE — Stranglers (Epic)
30	16	UP WHERE WE BELONG — Joe Cocker & Jennifer Warnes (Island)
8	17	ORVILLE'S SONG — Keith Harris & Orville (BBC)
17	18	YOUNG GUNS (GO FOR IT) — Wham! (Innervision)
10	19	CACHARPAYA (ANDES PUMPSA DESI) — Incantation (Beggars Banquet)
-	20	LAST NIGHT A D.J. SAVED MY LIFE — Indeep (Sound of New York)
24	21	MIND UP TONIGHT — Melba Moore (Capitol)
9	22	A WINTER'S TALE — David Essex (Mercury)
16	23	BUFFALO GALS — Malcolm McLaren & the World's Famous Supreme Team (Charisma)
18	24	ALL THE LOVE IN THE WORLD — Dionne Warwick (Arista)
-	25	IN THE NAME OF LOVE — Sharon Redd (Prelude)
-	26	THE CHINESE WAY — Level 42 (Polydor)
14	27	OUR HOUSE — Madness (Stiff)
-	28	NATURE BOY — Central Line (Mercury)
23	29	SAVE YOUR LOVE — Renee & Renato (Hollywood)
-	30	BILLIE JEAN — Michael Jackson (Epic)

12 February 1983

last	this	Title / Artist (Label)
1	1	DOWN UNDER — Men At Work (Epic)
3	2	SIGN OF THE TIMES — Belle Stars (Stiff)
7	3	TOO SHY — Kajagoogoo (EMI)
2	4	ELECTRIC AVENUE — Eddy Grant (Ice)
8	5	GLORIA — Laura Branigan (Atlantic)
16	6	UP WHERE WE BELONG — Joe Cocker & Jennifer Warnes (Island)
12	7	THE CUTTER — Echo & the Bunnymen (Korova)
5	8	YOU CAN'T HURRY LOVE — Phil Collins (Virgin)
11	9	NEW YEAR'S DAY — U2 (Island)
-	10	WHAM RAP! — Wham! (Innervision)
20	11	LAST NIGHT A D.J. SAVED MY LIFE — Indeep (Sound of New York)
4	12	STEPPIN' OUT — Joe Jackson (A&M)
10	13	TWISTING BY THE POOL — Dire Straits (Vertigo)
-	14	CHANGE — Tears For Fears (Mercury)
13	15	OH DIANE — Fleetwood Mac (Warner Brothers)
30	16	BILLIE JEAN — Michael Jackson (Epic)
9	17	THE STORY OF THE BLUES — Wah! (Eternal)
14	18	HOLD ME TIGHTER IN THE RAIN — Billy Griffin (CBS)
6	19	HEARTACHE AVENUE — Maisonettes (Ready Steady Go!)
-	20	CHRISTIAN — China Crisis (Virgin)
28	21	NATURE BOY — Central Line (Mercury)
-	22	GOING UNDERGROUND/THE DREAMS OF CHILDREN — Jam (Polydor)
26	23	THE CHINESE WAY — Level 42 (Polydor)
-	24	AFRICA — Toto (CBS)
19	25	CACHARPAYA (ANDES PUMPSA DESI) — Incantation (Beggars Banquet)
-	26	THE HARDER THEY COME — Rockers Revenge featuring Donnie Calvin (London)
21	27	MIND UP TONIGHT — Melba Moore (Capitol)
-	28	TUNNEL OF LOVE — Fun Boy Three (Chrysalis)
17	29	ORVILLE'S SONG — Keith Harris & Orville (BBC)
-	30	SHINY SHINY — Haysi Fantayzee (Regard)

19 February 1983

last	this	Title / Artist (Label)
3	1	TOO SHY — Kajagoogoo (EMI)
1	2	DOWN UNDER — Men At Work (Epic)
2	3	SIGN OF THE TIMES — Belle Stars (Stiff)
14	4	CHANGE — Tears For Fears (Mercury)
6	5	UP WHERE WE BELONG — Joe Cocker & Jennifer Warnes (Island)
10	6	WHAM RAP! — Wham! (Innervision)
4	7	ELECTRIC AVENUE — Eddy Grant (Ice)
15	8	OH DIANE — Fleetwood Mac (Warner Brothers)
5	9	GLORIA — Laura Branigan (Atlantic)
11	10	LAST NIGHT A D.J. SAVED MY LIFE — Indeep (Sound of New York)
16	11	BILLIE JEAN — Michael Jackson (Epic)
8	12	YOU CAN'T HURRY LOVE — Phil Collins (Virgin)
9	13	NEW YEAR'S DAY — U2 (Island)
13	14	TWISTING BY THE POOL — Dire Straits (Vertigo)
7	15	THE CUTTER — Echo & the Bunnymen (Korova)
24	16	AFRICA — Toto (CBS)
20	17	CHRISTIAN — China Crisis (Virgin)
21	18	NATURE BOY — Central Line (Mercury)
12	19	STEPPIN' OUT — Joe Jackson (A&M)
28	20	TUNNEL OF LOVE — Fun Boy Three (Chrysalis)
17	21	THE STORY OF THE BLUES — Wah! (Eternal)
23	22	THE CHINESE WAY — Level 42 (Polydor)
-	23	COLD SWEAT — Thin Lizzy (Vertigo)
-	24	GET THE BALANCE RIGHT — Depeche Mode (Mute)
-	25	LOVE ON YOUR SIDE — Thompson Twins (Arista)
-	26	COMMUNICATION — Spandau Ballet (Reformation)
30	27	SHINY SHINY — Haysi Fantayzee (Regard)
-	28	JAILHOUSE ROCK — Elvis Presley (RCA)
26	29	THE HARDER THEY COME — Rockers Revenge featuring Donnie Calvin (London)
25	30	CACHARPAYA (ANDES PUMPSA DESI) — Incantation (Beggars Banquet)

Dire Straits' *Twisting By The Pool* was not, unusually, extracted from one of the group's albums, but a new track in traditional rock'n'roll mode. *Down Under* hitmakers Men At Work, were, appropriately, an Australian group, who also had gigantic success in the US - there, this was their second Number One hit after *Who Can It Be Now*, which had sold only moderately here.

26 February 1983

last week	this week		
1	1	TOO SHY	Kajagoogoo (EMI)
3	2	SIGN OF THE TIMES	Belle Stars (Stiff)
16	3	AFRICA	Toto (CBS)
11	4	BILLIE JEAN	Michael Jackson (Epic)
4	5	CHANGE	Tears For Fears (Mercury)
2	6	DOWN UNDER	Men At Work (Epic)
5	7	UP WHERE WE BELONG	Joe Cocker & Jennifer Warnes (Island)
20	8	TUNNEL OF LOVE	Fun Boy Three (Chrysalis)
17	9	CHRISTIAN	China Crisis (Virgin)
-	10	TOMORROW'S (JUST ANOTHER DAY)/MADNESS (IS ALL IN THE MIND)	Madness (Stiff)
10	11	LAST NIGHT A D.J. SAVED MY LIFE	Indeep (Sound of New York)
8	12	OH DIANE	Fleetwood Mac (Warner Brothers)
25	13	LOVE ON YOUR SIDE	Thompson Twins (Arista)
9	14	GLORIA	Laura Branigan (Atlantic)
6	15	WHAM RAP!	Wham! (Innervision)
7	16	ELECTRIC AVENUE	Eddy Grant (Ice)
-	17	NEVER GONNA GIVE YOU UP	Musical Youth (MCA)
21	18	THE STORY OF THE BLUES	Wah! (Eternal)
27	19	SHINY SHINY	Haysi Fantayzee (Regard)
14	20	TWISTING BY THE POOL	Dire Straits (Vertigo)
13	21	NEW YEAR'S DAY	U2 (Island)
15	22	THE CUTTER	Echo & the Bunnymen (Korova)
-	23	SHE MEANS NOTHING TO ME	Phil Everly & Cliff Richard (Capitol)
23	24	COLD SWEAT	Thin Lizzy (Vertigo)
18	25	NATURE BOY	Central Line (Mercury)
12	26	YOU CAN'T HURRY LOVE	Phil Collins (Virgin)
-	27	WAVES	Blancmange (London)
28	28	GENETIC ENGINEERING	Orchestral Manoeuvres In The Dark (Virgin)
24	29	GET THE BALANCE RIGHT	Depeche Mode (Mute)
26	30	COMMUNICATION	Spandau Ballet (Reformation)

5 March 1983

last week	this week		
4	1	BILLIE JEAN	Michael Jackson (Epic)
1	2	TOO SHY	Kajagoogoo (EMI)
3	3	AFRICA	Toto (CBS)
5	4	CHANGE	Tears For Fears (Mercury)
10	5	TOMORROW'S (JUST ANOTHER DAY)/MADNESS (IS ALL IN THE MIND)	Madness (Stiff)
-	6	TOTAL ECLIPSE OF THE HEART	Bonnie Tyler (CBS)
17	7	NEVER GONNA GIVE YOU UP	Musical Youth (MCA)
8	8	TUNNEL OF LOVE	Fun Boy Three (Chrysalis)
13	9	LOVE ON YOUR SIDE	Thompson Twins (Arista)
2	10	SIGN OF THE TIMES	Belle Stars (Stiff)
7	11	UP WHERE WE BELONG	Joe Cocker & Jennifer Warnes (Island)
15	12	WHAM RAP!	Wham! (Innervision)
6	13	DOWN UNDER	Men At Work (Epic)
9	14	CHRISTIAN	China Crisis (Virgin)
-	15	BABY COME TO ME	Patti Austin & James Ingram (Qwest)
-	16	HEY LITTLE GIRL	Icehouse (Chrysalis)
19	17	SHINY SHINY	Haysi Fantayzee (Regard)
28	18	GENETIC ENGINEERING	Orchestral Manoeuvres In The Dark (Virgin)
-	19	SWEET DREAMS (ARE MADE OF THIS)	Eurythmics (RCA)
12	20	OH DIANE	Fleetwood Mac (Warner Brothers)
-	21	NA NA NA HEY HEY KISS HIM GOODBYE	Bananarama (London)
23	22	SHE MEANS NOTHING TO ME	Phil Everly & Cliff Richard (Capitol)
11	23	LAST NIGHT A D.J. SAVED MY LIFE	Indeep (Sound of New York)
-	24	ROCK THE BOAT	Forrest (CBS)
29	25	GET THE BALANCE RIGHT	Depeche Mode (Mute)
30	26	COMMUNICATION	Spandau Ballet (Reformation)
24	27	COLD SWEAT	Thin Lizzy (Vertigo)
-	28	MIDNIGHT SUMMER DREAM	Stranglers (Epic)
14	29	GLORIA	Laura Branigan (Atlantic)
16	30	ELECTRIC AVENUE	Eddy Grant (Ice)

12 March 1983

last week	this week		
1	1	BILLIE JEAN	Michael Jackson (Epic)
6	2	TOTAL ECLIPSE OF THE HEART	Bonnie Tyler (CBS)
19	3	SWEET DREAMS (ARE MADE OF THIS)	Eurythmics (RCA)
3	4	AFRICA	Toto (CBS)
5	5	TOMORROW'S (JUST ANOTHER DAY)/MADNESS (IS ALL IN THE MIND)	Madness (Stiff)
24	6	ROCK THE BOAT	Forrest (CBS)
7	7	NEVER GONNA GIVE YOU UP	Musical Youth (MCA)
9	8	LOVE ON YOUR SIDE	Thompson Twins (Arista)
2	9	TOO SHY	Kajagoogoo (EMI)
26	10	COMMUNICATION	Spandau Ballet (Reformation)
22	11	SHE MEANS NOTHING TO ME	Phil Everly & Cliff Richard (Capitol)
4	12	CHANGE	Tears For Fears (Mercury)
8	13	TUNNEL OF LOVE	Fun Boy Three (Chrysalis)
16	14	HEY LITTLE GIRL	Icehouse (Chrysalis)
15	15	BABY COME TO ME	Patti Austin & James Ingram (Qwest)
11	16	UP WHERE WE BELONG	Joe Cocker & Jennifer Warnes (Island)
21	17	NA NA NA HEY HEY KISS HIM GOODBYE	Bananarama (London)
25	18	GET THE BALANCE RIGHT	Depeche Mode (Mute)
-	19	WAVES	Blancmange (London)
18	20	GENETIC ENGINEERING	Orchestral Manoeuvres In The Dark (Virgin)
13	21	DOWN UNDER	Men At Work (Epic)
10	22	SIGN OF THE TIMES	Belle Stars (Stiff)
28	23	MIDNIGHT SUMMER DREAM	Stranglers (Epic)
-	24	NUMBERS/BARRIERS	Soft Cell (Some Bizzare)
17	25	SHINY SHINY	Haysi Fantayzee (Regard)
20	26	OH DIANE	Fleetwood Mac (Warner Brothers)
-	27	HIGH LIFE	Modern Romance (WEA)
12	28	WHAM RAP!	Wham! (Innervision)
14	29	CHRISTIAN	China Crisis (Virgin)
27	30	COLD SWEAT	Thin Lizzy (Vertigo)

19 March 1983

last week	this week		
2	1	TOTAL ECLIPSE OF THE HEART	Bonnie Tyler (CBS)
1	2	BILLIE JEAN	Michael Jackson (Epic)
3	3	SWEET DREAMS (ARE MADE OF THIS)	Eurythmics (RCA)
6	4	ROCK THE BOAT	Forrest (CBS)
17	5	NA NA HEY HEY KISS HIM GOODBYE	Bananarama (London)
4	6	AFRICA	Toto (CBS)
8	7	LOVE ON YOUR SIDE	Thompson Twins (Arista)
9	8	TOO SHY	Kajagoogoo (EMI)
5	9	TOMORROW'S (JUST ANOTHER DAY)/MADNESS (IS ALL IN THE MIND)	Madness (Stiff)
11	10	SHE MEANS NOTHING TO ME	Phil Everly & Cliff Richard (Capitol)
15	11	BABY COME TO ME	Patti Austin & James Ingram (Qwest)
10	12	COMMUNICATION	Spandau Ballet (Reformation)
13	13	TUNNEL OF LOVE	Fun Boy Three (Chrysalis)
20	14	GENETIC ENGINEERING	Orchestral Manoeuvres In The Dark (Virgin)
27	15	HIGH LIFE	Modern Romance (WEA)
7	16	NEVER GONNA GIVE YOU UP	Musical Youth (MCA)
12	17	CHANGE	Tears For Fears (Mercury)
-	18	SPEAK LIKE A CHILD	Style Council (Polydor)
14	19	HEY LITTLE GIRL	Icehouse (Chrysalis)
-	20	YOU CAN'T HIDE (YOUR LOVE FROM ME)	David Joseph (Island)
19	21	WAVES	Blancmange (London)
-	22	RIP IT UP	Orange Juice (Polydor)
18	23	GET THE BALANCE RIGHT	Depeche Mode (Mute)
16	24	UP WHERE WE BELONG	Joe Cocker & Jennifer Warnes (Island)
-	25	RUN FOR YOUR LIFE	Bucks Fizz (RCA)
24	26	NUMBERS/BARRIERS	Soft Cell (Some Bizzare)
-	27	DROP THE PILOT	Joan Armatrading (A&M)
-	28	WE'VE GOT TONIGHT	Kenny Rogers & Sheena Easton (Liberty)
-	29	SOWETO	Malcolm McLaren with the McLarenettes (Charisma)
-	30	ALL TOMORROW'S PARTIES	Japan (Hansa)

Th one-off teaming of Phil Everly and Cliff Richard produced, in *She Means Nothing To Me*, a Top 10 hit with almost the traditional Everly rock'n'roll sound. Its producer was Stuart Colman, the man behind most of Shakin' Stevens' hits to date. Bonnie Tyler's chart topper was from the pen of Jim Steinman, who had also been responsible for Meat Loaf's *Bat Out Of Hell*; this single had similar melodramatic hallmarks.

March – April 1983

26 March 1983

last	this		
1	1	TOTAL ECLIPSE OF THE HEART	Bonnie Tyler (CBS)
3	2	SWEET DREAMS (ARE MADE OF THIS)	Eurythmics (RCA)
4	3	ROCK THE BOAT	Forrest (CBS)
18	4	SPEAK LIKE A CHILD	Style Council (Polydor)
5	5	NA NA HEY HEY KISS HIM GOODBYE	Bananarama (London)
2	6	BILLIE JEAN	Michael Jackson (Epic)
15	7	HIGH LIFE	Modern Romance (WEA)
22	8	RIP IT UP	Orange Juice (Polydor)
10	9	SHE MEANS NOTHING TO ME	Phil Everly & Cliff Richard (Capitol)
6	10	AFRICA	Toto (CBS)
-	11	IS THERE SOMETHING I SHOULD KNOW?	Duran Duran (EMI)
7	12	LOVE ON YOUR SIDE	Thompson Twins (Arista)
11	13	BABY COME TO ME	Patti Austin & James Ingram (Qwest)
25	14	RUN FOR YOUR LIFE	Bucks Fizz (RCA)
9	15	TOMORROW'S (JUST ANOTHER DAY)/MADNESS (IS ALL IN THE MIND)	Madness (Stiff)
20	16	YOU CAN'T HIDE (YOUR LOVE FROM ME)	David Joseph (Island)
-	17	LET'S DANCE	David Bowie (EMI America)
-	18	VISIONS IN BLUE	Ultravox (Chrysalis)
21	19	WAVES	Blancmange (London)
12	20	COMMUNICATION	Spandau Ballet (Reformation)
16	21	NEVER GONNA GIVE YOU UP	Musical Youth (MCA)
-	22	JOY	Band A.K.A. (Epic)
13	23	TUNNEL OF LOVE	Fun Boy Three (Chrysalis)
-	24	BLUE MONDAY	New Order (Factory)
19	25	HEY LITTLE GIRL	Icehouse (Chrysalis)
27	26	DROP THE PILOT	Joan Armatrading (A&M)
8	27	TOO SHY	Kajagoogoo (EMI)
-	28	DON'T TALK TO ME ABOUT LOVE	Altered Images (Epic)
-	29	GARDEN PARTY	Mezzoforte (Steinar)
14	30	GENETIC ENGINEERING	Orchestral Manoeuvres In The Dark (Virgin)

2 April 1983

11	1	IS THERE SOMETHING I SHOULD KNOW? Duran Duran (EMI)
17	2	LET'S DANCE David Bowie (EMI America)
4	3	SPEAK LIKE A CHILD Style Council (Polydor)
1	4	TOTAL ECLIPSE OF THE HEART Bonnie Tyler (CBS)
2	5	SWEET DREAMS (ARE MADE OF THIS) Eurythmics (RCA)
28	6	DON'T TALK TO ME ABOUT LOVE Altered Images (Epic)
8	7	RIP IT UP Orange Juice (Polydor)
3	8	ROCK THE BOAT Forrest (CBS)
5	9	NA NA HEY HEY KISS HIM GOODBYE Bananarama (London)
6	10	BILLIE JEAN Michael Jackson (Epic)
26	11	DROP THE PILOT Joan Armatrading (A&M)
14	12	RUN FOR YOUR LIFE Bucks Fizz (RCA)
16	13	YOU CAN'T HIDE (YOUR LOVE FROM ME) David Joseph (Island)
18	14	VISIONS IN BLUE Ultravox (Chrysalis)
29	15	GARDEN PARTY Mezzoforte (Steinar)
7	16	HIGH LIFE Modern Romance (WEA)
24	17	BLUE MONDAY New Order (Factory)
-	18	BOXERBEAT Joboxers (RCA)
-	19	ORCHARD ROAD Leo Sayer (Chrysalis)
-	20	CRY ME A RIVER Mari Wilson (Compact)
-	21	WHISTLE DOWN THE WIND Nick Heyward (Arista)
-	22	FIELDS OF FIRE (400 MILES) Big Country (Mercury)
20	23	COMMUNICATION Spandau Ballet (Reformation)
12	24	LOVE ON YOUR SIDE Thompson Twins (Arista)
19	25	WAVES Blancmange (London)
9	26	SHE MEANS NOTHING TO ME Phil Everly & Cliff Richard (Capitol)
-	27	I AM ME (I'M ME) Twisted Sister (Atlantic)
-	28	THE HOUSE THAT JACK BUILT Tracie (Respond)
10	29	AFRICA Toto (CBS)
30	30	GENETIC ENGINEERING Orchestral Manoeuvres In The Dark (Virgin)

9 April 1983

1	1	IS THERE SOMETHING I SHOULD KNOW? Duran Duran (EMI)
2	2	LET'S DANCE David Bowie (EMI America)
6	3	DON'T TALK TO ME ABOUT LOVE Altered Images (Epic)
7	4	RIP IT UP Orange Juice (Polydor)
18	5	BOXERBEAT Joboxers (RCA)
3	5	SPEAK LIKE A CHILD Style Council (Polydor)
5	7	SWEET DREAMS (ARE MADE OF THIS) Eurythmics (RCA)
4	8	TOTAL ECLIPSE OF THE HEART Bonnie Tyler (CBS)
8	9	ROCK THE BOAT Forrest (CBS)
-	10	OOH TO BE AH Kajagoogoo (EMI)
19	11	ORCHARD ROAD Leo Sayer (Chrysalis)
9	12	NA NA HEY HEY KISS HIM GOODBYE Bananarama (London)
22	13	FIELDS OF FIRE (400 MILES) Big Country (Mercury)
10	14	BILLIE JEAN Michael Jackson (Epic)
21	15	WHISTLE DOWN THE WIND Nick Heyward (Arista)
11	16	DROP THE PILOT Joan Armatrading (A&M)
17	17	BLUE MONDAY New Order (Factory)
-	18	TWO HEARTS BEAT AS ONE U2 (Island)
13	19	YOU CAN'T HIDE (YOUR LOVE FROM ME) David Joseph (Island)
-	20	BREAKAWAY Tracey Ullman (Stiff)
12	21	RUN FOR YOUR LIFE Bucks Fizz (RCA)
14	22	VISIONS IN BLUE Ultravox (Chrysalis)
15	23	GARDEN PARTY Mezzoforte (Steinar)
-	24	SNOT RAP Kenny Everett (RCA)
-	25	THE CELTIC SOUL BROTHERS Kevin Rowland & Dexy's Midnight Runners (Mercury)
25	26	WAVES Blancmange (London)
16	28	HIGH LIFE Modern Romance (WEA)
27	29	I AM ME (I'M ME) Twisted Sister (Atlantic)
28	30	THE HOUSE THAT JACK BUILT Tracie (Respond)

16 April 1983

2	1	LET'S DANCE David Bowie (EMI America)
1	2	IS THERE SOMETHING I SHOULD KNOW? Duran Duran (EMI)
5	3	BOXERBEAT Joboxers (RCA)
-	4	CHURCH OF THE POISON MIND Culture Club (Virgin)
10	5	OOH TO BE AH Kajagoogoo (EMI)
20	6	BREAKAWAY Tracey Ullman (Stiff)
3	7	SPEAK LIKE A CHILD Style Council (Polydor)
17	8	BLUE MONDAY New Order (Factory)
7	9	SWEET DREAMS (ARE MADE OF THIS) Eurythmics (RCA)
24	10	SNOT RAP Kenny Everett (RCA)
13	11	FIELDS OF FIRE (400 MILES) Big Country (Mercury)
15	12	WHISTLE DOWN THE WIND Nick Heyward (Arista)
18	13	TWO HEARTS BEAT AS ONE U2 (Island)
3	14	DON'T TALK TO ME ABOUT LOVE Altered Images (Epic)
27	15	WORDS F.R. David (Carrere)
30	16	THE HOUSE THAT JACK BUILT Tracie (Respond)
14	17	BILLIE JEAN Michael Jackson (Epic)
8	18	TOTAL ECLIPSE OF THE HEART Bonnie Tyler (CBS)
4	19	RIP IT UP Orange Juice (Polydor)
25	20	THE CELTIC SOUL BROTHERS Kevin Rowland & Dexy's Midnight Runners (Mercury)
-	21	LOVE IS A STRANGER Eurythmics (RCA)
-	22	BEAT IT Michael Jackson (Epic)
-	23	JOHNNY B. GOODE Peter Tosh (EMI)
-	24	SHE'S IN PARTIES Bauhaus (Beggars Banquet)
29	25	I AM ME (I'M ME) Twisted Sister (Atlantic)
11	26	ORCHARD ROAD Leo Sayer (Chrysalis)
-	27	CRY ME A RIVER Mari Wilson (Compact)
16	28	DROP THE PILOT Joan Armatrading (A&M)
9	29	ROCK THE BOAT Forrest (CBS)
22	30	VISIONS IN BLUE Ultravox (Chrysalis)

Duran Duran finally scored a Number One with their seventh hit single, *Is There Something I Should Know,* while David Bowie's new deal with EMI and studio teaming with former Chic member Nile Rodgers gave him worldwide chart-topping success with both the single *Let's Dance* (not the old Chris Montez hit), and the parent album of the same title. Paul Weller (ex-Jam) debuted srongly with new band Style Council.

last week	this week	23 April 1983	
1	1	LET'S DANCE	David Bowie (EMI America)
4	2	CHURCH OF THE POISON MIND	Culture Club (Virgin)
22	3	BEAT IT	Michael Jackson (Epic)
15	4	WORDS	F.R. David (Carrere)
6	5	BREAKAWAY	Tracey Ullman (Stiff)
5	6	OOH TO BE AH	Kajagoogoo (EMI)
2	7	IS THERE SOMETHING I SHOULD KNOW?	Duran Duran (EMI)
8	8	BLUE MONDAY	New Order (Factory)
16	9	THE HOUSE THAT JACK BUILT	Tracie (Respond)
3	10	BOXERBEAT	Joboxers (RCA)
11	11	FIELDS OF FIRE (400 MILES)	Big Country (Mercury)
10	12	SNOT RAP	Kenny Everett (RCA)
21	13	LOVE IS A STRANGER	Eurythmics (RCA)
7	14	SPEAK LIKE A CHILD	Style Council (Polydor)
12	15	WHISTLE DOWN THE WIND	Nick Heyward (Arista)
-	16	TRUE	Spandau Ballet (Reformation)
-	17	WE ARE DETECTIVE	Thompson Twins (Arista)
-	18	TRUE LOVE WAYS	Cliff Richard & the London Philharmonic Orchestra (EMI)
-	19	TEMPTATION	Heaven 17 (Virgin)
25	20	I AM ME (I'M ME)	Twisted Sister (Atlantic)
-	21	(KEEP FEELING) FASCINATION	Human League (Virgin)
13	22	TWO HEARTS BEAT AS ONE	U2 (Island)
20	23	THE CELTIC SOUL BROTHERS	Kevin Rowland & Dexy's Midnight Runners (Mercury)
18	24	TOTAL ECLIPSE OF THE HEART	Bonnie Tyler (CBS)
24	25	SHE'S IN PARTIES	Bauhaus (Beggars Banquet)
-	26	YOUNG FREE AND SINGLE	Sunfire (Warner Brothers)
9	27	SWEET DREAMS (ARE MADE OF THIS)	Eurythmics (RCA)
17	28	BILLIE JEAN	Michael Jackson (Epic)
19	29	RIP IT UP	Orange Juice (Polydor)
14	30	DON'T TALK TO ME ABOUT LOVE	Altered Images (Epic)
-	31	LAST FILM	Kissing The Pink (Magnet)
-	32	TWIST (ROUND 'N' ROUND)	Chill Fac-torr (Philly World)
-	33	FLIGHT OF ICARUS	Iron Maiden (EMI)
-	34	OVERKILL	Men At Work (Epic)
-	35	CRY ME A RIVER	Julie London (Edsel)
-	36	SWEET MEMORY	Belle Stars (Stiff)
-	37	ROSANNA	Toto (CBS)
-	38	I'M NEVER GIVING UP	Sweet Dreams (Ariola)
23	39	JOHNNY B. GOODE	Peter Tosh (EMI)
-	40	CANDY GIRL	New Edition (London)
-	41	OUT OF SIGHT OUT OF MIND	Level 42 (Polydor)
-	42	DANCING TIGHT	Galaxy featuring Phil Fearon (Ensign)
26	43	ORCHARD ROAD	Leo Sayer (Chrysalis)
-	44	FROM ME TO YOU	Beatles (Parlophone)
-	45	MARKET SQUARE HEROES	Marillion (EMI)
-	46	TELEGRAPH	Orchestral Manoeuvres In The Dark (Virgin)
-	47	MINEFIELD	I-Level (Virgin)
-	48	YOU ARE IN MY SYSTEM	System (Polydor)
-	49	MUCK IT OUT!	Farmer's Boys (EMI)
-	50	MISS THE GIRL	Creatures (Wonderland)

	30 April 1983	
1	1 LET'S DANCE	David Bowie (EMI America)
2	2 CHURCH OF THE POISON MIND	Culture Club (Virgin)
3	3 BEAT IT	Michael Jackson (Epic)
4	4 WORDS	F.R. David (Carrere)
13	5 LOVE IS A STRANGER	Eurythmics (RCA)
16	6 TRUE	Spandau Ballet (Reformation)
21	7 (KEEP FEELING) FASCINATION	Human League (Virgin)
8	8 BLUE MONDAY	New Order (Factory)
9	9 THE HOUSE THAT JACK BUILT	Tracie (Respond)
5	10 BREAKAWAY	Tracey Ullman (Stiff)
17	11 WE ARE DETECTIVE	Thompson Twins (Arista)
18	12 TRUE LOVE WAYS	Cliff Richard & the London Philharmonic Orchestra (EMI)
10	13 BOXERBEAT	Joboxers (RCA)
6	14 OOH TO BE AH	Kajagoogoo (EMI)
33	15 FLIGHT OF ICARUS	Iron Maiden (EMI)
19	16 TEMPTATION	Heaven 17 (Virgin)
37	17 ROSANNA	Toto (CBS)
7	18 IS THERE SOMETHING I SHOULD KNOW?	Duran Duran (EMI)
25	19 SHE'S IN PARTIES	Bauhaus (Beggars Banquet)
26	20 YOUNG FREE AND SINGLE	Sunfire (Warner Brothers)
42	21 DANCING TIGHT	Galaxy featuring Phil Fearon (Ensign)
11	22 FIELDS OF FIRE (400 MILES)	Big Country (Mercury)
20	23 I AM ME (I'M ME)	Twisted Sister (Atlantic)
34	24 OVERKILL	Men At Work (Epic)
15	25 WHISTLE DOWN THE WIND	Nick Heyward (Arista)
50	26 MISS THE GIRL	Creatures (Wonderland)
12	27 SNOT RAP	Kenny Everett (RCA)
-	28 PRICE YOU PAY	Questions (Respond)
31	29 LAST FILM	Kissing The Pink (Magnet)
24	30 TOTAL ECLIPSE OF THE HEART	Bonnie Tyler (CBS)
27	31 SWEET DREAMS (ARE MADE OF THIS)	Eurythmics (RCA)
47	32 MINEFIELD	I-Level (Virgin)
32	33 TWIST (ROUND 'N' ROUND)	Chill Fac-torr (Philly World)
23	34 THE CELTIC SOUL BROTHERS	Kevin Rowland & Dexy's Midnight Runners (Mercury)
44	35 FROM ME TO YOU	Beatles (Parlophone)
-	36 FRIDAY NIGHT (LIVE VERSION)	Kids From Fame (RCA)
-	37 PALE SHELTER	Tears For Fears (Mercury)
29	38 RIP IT UP	Orange Juice (Polydor)
40	39 SPEAK LIKE A CHILD	Style Council (Polydor)
40	40 CANDY GIRL	New Edition (London)
36	41 SWEET MEMORY	Belle Stars (Stiff)
22	42 TWO HEARTS BEAT AS ONE	U2 (Island)
-	43 THE STAND	Alarm (IRS)
28	44 BILLIE JEAN	Michael Jackson (Epic)
-	45 OUR LIPS ARE SEALED	Fun Boy Three (Chrysalis)
38	46 I'M NEVER GIVING UP	Sweet Dreams (Ariola)
35	47 CRY ME A RIVER	Julie London (Edsel)
45	48 MARKET SQUARE HEROES	Marillion (EMI)
-	49 HEARTBREAKER	Musical Youth (MCA)
-	50 WAR PARTY	Eddy Grant (Ice)

	7 May 1983	
6	1 TRUE	Spandau Ballet (Reformation)
7	2 (KEEP FEELING) FASCINATION	Human League (Virgin)
4	3 WORDS	F.R. David (Carrere)
3	4 BEAT IT	Michael Jackson (Epic)
1	5 LET'S DANCE	David Bowie (EMI America)
2	6 CHURCH OF THE POISON MIND	Culture Club (Virgin)
16	7 TEMPTATION	Heaven 17 (Virgin)
11	8 WE ARE DETECTIVE	Thompson Twins (Arista)
5	9 LOVE IS A STRANGER	Eurythmics (RCA)
15	10 FLIGHT OF ICARUS	Iron Maiden (EMI)
12	11 TRUE LOVE WAYS	Cliff Richard & the Londo Philharmonic Orchestra (EMI)
8	12 BLUE MONDAY	New Order (Factory)
37	13 PALE SHELTER	Tears For Fears (Mercury)
17	14 ROSANNA	Toto (CBS)
21	15 DANCING TIGHT	Galaxy featuring Phil Fearon (Ensign)
10	16 BREAKAWAY	Tracey Ullman (Stiff)
45	17 OUR LIPS ARE SEALED	Fun Boy Three (Chrysalis)
18	18 I AM ME (I'M ME)	Twisted Sister (Atlantic)
24	19 OVERKILL	Men At Work (Epic)
20	20 YOUNG FREE AND SINGLE	Sunfire (Warner Brothers)
36	21 FRIDAY NIGHT (LIVE VERSION)	Kids From Fame (RCA)
26	22 MISS THE GIRL	Creatures (Wonderland)
9	23 THE HOUSE THAT JACK BUILT	Tracie (Respond)
29	24 LAST FILM	Kissing The Pink (Magnet)
19	25 SHE'S IN PARTIES	Bauhaus (Beggars Banquet)
46	26 I'M NEVER GIVING UP	Sweet Dreams (Ariola)
13	27 BOXERBEAT	Joboxers (RCA)
14	28 OOH TO BE AH	Kajagoogoo (EMI)
-	29 FUTURE GENERATION	B52's (Island)
-	30 CAN'T GET USED TO LOSING YOU	Beat (Go Feet)
33	31 TWIST (ROUND 'N' ROUND)	Chill Fac-torr (Philly World)
-	32 MUSIC (PART 1)	D Train (Prelude)
-	33 CREATURES OF THE NIGHT	Kiss (Casablanca)
-	34 BLIND VISION	Blancmange (London)
32	35 MINEFIELD	I-Level (Virgin)
18	36 IS THERE SOMETHING I SHOULD KNOW?	Duran Duran (EMI)
-	37 MUCK IT OUT!	Farmer's Boys (EMI)
35	38 FROM ME TO YOU	Beatles (Parlophone)
28	39 PRICE YOU PAY	Questions (Respond)
22	40 FIELDS OF FIRE (400 MILES)	Big Country (Mercury)
-	41 THUNDER AND LIGHTNING	Thin Lizzy (Vertigo)
-	42 FAMILY MAN	Daryl Hall & John Oates (RCA)
43	43 THE STAND	Alarm (IRS)
41	44 SWEET MEMORY	Belle Stars (Stiff)
31	45 SWEET DREAMS (ARE MADE OF THIS)	Eurythmics (RCA)
-	46 ZOMBIE CREEPING FLESH	Peter & the Test Tube Babies (Trapper)
50	47 WAR PARTY	Eddy Grant (Ice)
48	48 CANDY GIRL	New Edition (London)
34	49 THE CELTIC SOUL BROTHERS	Kevin Rowland & Dexy's Midnight Runners (Mercury)
-	50 I GUESS THAT'S WHY THEY CALL IT THE BLUES	Elton John (Rocket)

Only a few days after the 27th anniversary of it expanding from 20 to 30 positions, the NME singles chart was extended to a Top Fifty, in which form it has remained until the present day. The highest new entry in the first of the new charts was Spandau Ballet's *True,* which was to become the first of their two consecutive chart-toppers, and their all-time biggest selling single.

May 1983

14 May 1983

last week	this week	title	artist
1	1	TRUE	Spandau Ballet (Reformation)
2	2	(KEEP FEELING) FASCINATION	Human League (Virgin)
7	3	TEMPTATION	Heaven 17 (Virgin)
13	4	PALE SHELTER	Tears For Fears (Mercury)
3	5	WORDS	F.R. David (Carrere)
4	6	BEAT IT	Michael Jackson (Epic)
8	7	WE ARE DETECTIVE	Thompson Twins (Arista)
15	8	DANCING TIGHT	Galaxy featuring Phil Fearon (Ensign)
5	9	LET'S DANCE	David Bowie (EMI America)
12	10	BLUE MONDAY	New Order (Factory)
17	11	OUR LIPS ARE SEALED	Fun Boy Three (Chrysalis)
6	12	CHURCH OF THE POISON MIND	Culture Club (Virgin)
11	13	TRUE LOVE WAYS	Cliff Richard & the London Philharmonic Orchestra (EMI)
10	14	FLIGHT OF ICARUS	Iron Maiden (EMI)
9	15	LOVE IS A STRANGER	Eurythmics (RCA)
34	16	BLIND VISION	Blancmange (London)
21	17	FRIDAY NIGHT (LIVE VERSION)	Kids From Fame (RCA)
14	18	ROSANNA	Toto (CBS)
22	19	MISS THE GIRL	Creatures (Wonderland)
24	20	LAST FILM	Kissing The Pink (Magnet)
30	21	CAN'T GET USED TO LOSING YOU	Beat (Go Feet)
18	22	I AM ME (I'M ME)	Twisted Sister (Atlantic)
16	23	BREAKAWAY	Tracey Ullman (Stiff)
20	24	YOUNG FREE AND SINGLE	Sunfire (Warner Brothers)
19	25	OVERKILL	Men At Work (Epic)
-	26	SHIPBUILDING	Robert Wyatt (Rough Trade)
27	27	FUTURE GENERATION	B52's (Island)
33	28	CREATURES OF THE NIGHT	Kiss (Casablanca)
26	29	I'M NEVER GIVING UP	Sweet Dreams (Ariola)
-	30	NOT NOW JOHN	Pink Floyd (Harvest)
23	31	THE HOUSE THAT JACK BUILT	Tracie (Respond)
42	32	FAMILY MAN	Daryl Hall & John Oates (RCA)
-	33	BUFFALO SOLDIER	Bob Marley & the Wailers (Island/Tuff Gong)
48	34	CANDY GIRL	New Edition (London)
41	35	THUNDER AND LIGHTNING	Thin Lizzy (Vertigo)
32	36	MUSIC (PART 1)	D Train (Prelude)
-	37	STOP AND GO	David Grant (Chrysalis)
31	38	TWIST (ROUND 'N' ROUND)	Chill Fac-torr (Philly World)
44	39	SWEET MEMORY	Belle Stars (Stiff)
25	40	SHE'S IN PARTIES	Bauhaus (Beggars Banquet)
50	41	I GUESS THAT'S WHY THEY CALL IT THE BLUES	Elton John (Rocket)
-	42	COUNTDOWN	Rush (Mercury)
37	43	MUCK IT OUT!	Farmer's Boys (EMI)
35	44	MINEFIELD	I-Level (Virgin)
-	45	DON'T STOP THAT CRAZY RHYTHM	Modern Romance (WEA)
40	46	FIELDS OF FIRE (400 MILES)	Big Country (Mercury)
-	47	HEY!	Julio Iglesias (CBS)
28	48	OOH TO BE AH	Kajagoogoo (EMI)
46	49	ZOMBIE CREEPING FLESH	Peter & the Test Tube Babies (Trapper)
-	50	CATCH 23	GBH (Clay)

21 May 1983

last week	this week	title	artist
1	1	TRUE	Spandau Ballet (Reformation)
3	2	TEMPTATION	Heaven 17 (Virgin)
2	3	(KEEP FEELING) FASCINATION	Human League (Virgin)
8	4	DANCING TIGHT	Galaxy featuring Phil Fearon (Ensign)
11	5	OUR LIPS ARE SEALED	Fun Boy Three (Chrysalis)
34	6	CANDY GIRL	New Edition (London)
4	7	PALE SHELTER	Tears For Fears (Mercury)
21	8	CAN'T GET USED TO LOSING YOU	Beat (Go Feet)
5	9	WORDS	F.R. David (Carrere)
16	10	BLIND VISION	Blancmange (London)
7	11	WE ARE DETECTIVE	Thompson Twins (Arista)
10	12	BLUE MONDAY	New Order (Factory)
6	13	BEAT IT	Michael Jackson (Epic)
9	14	LET'S DANCE	David Bowie (EMI America)
20	15	LAST FILM	Kissing The Pink (Magnet)
-	16	BAD BOYS	Wham! (Innervision)
19	17	MISS THE GIRL	Creatures (Wonderland)
32	18	FAMILY MAN	Daryl Hall & John Oates (RCA)
13	19	TRUE LOVE WAYS	Cliff Richard & the London Philharmonic Orchestra (EMI)
33	20	BUFFALO SOLDIER	Bob Marley & the Wailers (Island/Tuff Gong)
25	21	OVERKILL	Men At Work (Epic)
17	22	FRIDAY NIGHT (LIVE VERSION)	Kids From Fame (RCA)
15	23	LOVE IS A STRANGER	Eurythmics (RCA)
12	24	CHURCH OF THE POISON MIND	Culture Club (Virgin)
26	25	SHIPBUILDING	Robert Wyatt (Rough Trade)
45	26	DON'T STOP THAT CRAZY RHYTHM	Modern Romance (WEA)
-	27	WHAT KINDA BOY YOU'RE LOOKIN' FOR (GIRL)	Hot Chocolate (RAK)
-	28	NOBODY'S DIARY	Yazoo (Mute)
30	29	NOT NOW JOHN	Pink Floyd (Harvest)
27	30	FUTURE GENERATION	B52's (Island)
36	31	MUSIC (PART 1)	D Train (Prelude)
50	32	CATCH 23	GBH (Clay)
14	33	FLIGHT OF ICARUS	Iron Maiden (EMI)
-	34	FEEL THE NEED IN ME	Forrest (CBS)
28	35	CREATURES OF THE NIGHT	Kiss (Casablanca)
42	36	COUNTDOWN	Rush (Mercury)
18	37	ROSANNA	Toto (CBS)
-	38	JUICY FRUIT	Mtume (Epic)
-	39	THAT'LL DO NICELY	Bad Manners (Magnet)
37	40	STOP AND GO	David Grant (Chrysalis)
-	41	IN THE BOTTLE	C.O.D. (Streetwave)
39	42	SWEET MEMORY	Belle Stars (Stiff)
43	43	MUCK IT OUT!	Farmer's Boys (EMI)
-	44	JUST GOT LUCKY	Joboxers (RCA)
23	45	BREAKAWAY	Tracey Ullman (Stiff)
35	46	THUNDER AND LIGHTNING	Thin Lizzy (Vertigo)
22	47	I AM ME (I'M ME)	Twisted Sister (Atlantic)
38	48	TWIST (ROUND 'N' ROUND)	Chill Fac-torr (Philly World)
31	49	THE HOUSE THAT JACK BUILT	Tracie (Respond)
24	50	YOUNG FREE AND SINGLE	Sunfire (Warner Brothers)

28 May 1983

last week	this week	title	artist
1	1	TRUE	Spandau Ballet (Reformation)
2	2	TEMPTATION	Heaven 17 (Virgin)
6	3	CANDY GIRL	New Edition (London)
8	4	CAN'T GET USED TO LOSING YOU	Beat (Go Feet)
4	5	DANCING TIGHT	Galaxy featuring Phil Fearon (Ensign)
5	6	OUR LIPS ARE SEALED	Fun Boy Three (Chrysalis)
3	7	(KEEP FEELING) FASCINATION	Human League (Virgin)
16	8	BAD BOYS	Wham! (Innervision)
10	9	BLIND VISION	Blancmange (London)
28	10	NOBODY'S DIARY	Yazoo (Mute)
20	11	BUFFALO SOLDIER	Bob Marley & the Wailers (Island/Tuff Gong)
7	12	PALE SHELTER	Tears For Fears (Mercury)
27	13	WHAT KINDA BOY YOU'RE LOOKIN' FOR (GIRL)	Hot Chocolate (RAK)
12	14	BLUE MONDAY	New Order (Factory)
-	15	EVERY BREATH YOU TAKE	Police (A&M)
18	16	FAMILY MAN	Daryl Hall & John Oates (RCA)
-	17	MONEY GO ROUND	Style Council (Polydor)
9	18	WORDS	F.R. David (Carrere)
11	19	WE ARE DETECTIVE	Thompson Twins (Arista)
25	20	SHIPBUILDING	Robert Wyatt (Rough Trade)
26	21	DON'T STOP THAT CRAZY RHYTHM	Modern Romance (WEA)
17	22	MISS THE GIRL	Creatures (Wonderland)
-	23	CANTON (LIVE)	Japan (Virgin)
15	24	LAST FILM	Kissing The Pink (Magnet)
44	25	JUST GOT LUCKY	Joboxers (RCA)
42	26	SWEET MEMORY	Belle Stars (Stiff)
13	27	BEAT IT	Michael Jackson (Epic)
21	28	Title	Artist Label
34	28	FEEL THE NEED IN ME	Forrest (CBS)
31	29	MUSIC (PART 1)	D Train (Prelude)
-	30	GLORY, GLORY, MAN UNITED	Manchester United Football Team (EMI)
14	31	LET'S DANCE	David Bowie (EMI America)
21	32	OVERKILL	Men At Work (Epic)
-	33	I GOT MINE	Motorhead (Bronze)
22	34	FRIDAY NIGHT (LIVE VERSION)	Kids From Fame (RCA)
40	35	STOP AND GO	David Grant (Chrysalis)
29	36	NOT NOW JOHN	Pink Floyd (Harvest)
33	37	FLIGHT OF ICARUS	Iron Maiden (EMI)
38	38	JUICY FRUIT	Mtume (Epic)
37	39	ROSANNA	Toto (CBS)
-	40	TRAGEDY AND MYSTERY	China Crisis (Virgin)
-	41	CANDY MAN	Mary Jane Girls (Motown)
30	42	FUTURE GENERATION	B52's (Island)
47	43	I AM ME (I'M ME)	Twisted Sister (Atlantic)
35	44	CREATURES OF THE NIGHT	Kiss (Casablanca)
23	45	LOVE IS A STRANGER	Eurythmics (RCA)
24	46	CHURCH OF THE POISON MIND	Culture Club (Virgin)
-	47	WAITING FOR A TRAIN	Flash & the Pan (Easybeat)
-	48	IN A BIG COUNTRY	Big Country (Mercury)
-	49	I GUESS THAT'S WHY THEY CALL IT THE BLUES	Elton John (Rocket)
-	50	MORNIN'	Al Jarreau (WEA)

New Order hit the top 10 for the first time with their 12-inch-only single *Blue Monday*. This would prove to be an almost perennial seller, re-charting on more than one occasion through the '80s, and eventually becomming the best-selling 12-inch of all time, with domestic sales nudging a million by 1990. Similarly-named New Edition, meanwhile, were a black teenage group with several future soul stars in their ranks.

4 June 1983

Last week	This week	Title	Artist
3	1	CANDY GIRL	New Edition (London)
15	2	EVERY BREATH YOU TAKE	Police (A&M)
8	3	BAD BOYS	Wham! (Innervision)
4	4	CAN'T GET USED TO LOSING YOU	Beat (Go Feet)
1	5	TRUE	Spandau Ballet (Reformation)
2	6	TEMPTATION	Heaven 17 (Virgin)
10	7	NOBODY'S DIARY	Yazoo (Mute)
17	8	MONEY GO ROUND	Style Council (Polydor)
11	9	BUFFALO SOLDIER	Bob Marley & the Wailers (Island/Tuff Gong)
13	10	WHAT KINDA BOY YOU'RE LOOKIN' FOR (GIRL)	Hot Chocolate (RAK)
5	11	DANCING TIGHT	Galaxy featuring Phil Fearon (Ensign)
25	12	JUST GOT LUCKY	Joboxers (RCA)
6	13	OUR LIPS ARE SEALED	Fun Boy Three (Chrysalis)
-	14	LOVE TOWN	Booker Newbury III (Polydor)
30	15	GLORY, GLORY, MAN UNITED	Manchester United Football Team (EMI)
9	16	BLIND VISION	Blancmange (London)
7	17	(KEEP FEELING) FASCINATION	Human League (Virgin)
48	18	IN A BIG COUNTRY	Big Country (Mercury)
20	19	SHIPBUILDING	Robert Wyatt (Rough Trade)
28	20	FEEL THE NEED IN ME	Forrest (CBS)
29	21	MUSIC (PART 1)	D Train (Prelude)
14	22	BLUE MONDAY	New Order (Factory)
12	23	PALE SHELTER	Tears For Fears (Mercury)
47	24	WAITING FOR A TRAIN	Flash & the Pan (Easybeat)
-	25	LADY LOVE ME (ONE MORE TIME)	George Benson (Warner Brothers)
-	26	BRING ME CLOSER	Altered Images (Epic)
18	27	WORDS	F.R. David (Carrere)
21	28	DON'T STOP THAT CRAZY RHYTHM	Modern Romance (WEA)
22	29	MISS THE GIRL	Creatures (Wonderland)
16	30	FAMILY MAN	Daryl Hall & John Oates (RCA)
35	31	STOP AND GO	David Grant (Chrysalis)
19	32	WE ARE DETECTIVE	Thompson Twins (Arista)
38	33	JUICY FRUIT	Mtume (Epic)
-	34	THE WHEEL	Spear of Destiny (Epic)
-	35	WE CAME TO DANCE	Ultravox (Chrysalis)
-	36	THE KIDS ARE BACK	Twisted Sister (Atlantic)
23	37	CANTON (LIVE)	Japan (Virgin)
-	38	BABY JANE	Rod Stewart (Warner Brothers)
-	39	CHINA GIRL	David Bowie (EMI America)
-	40	LET'S LIVE IT UP (NITE PEOPLE)	David Joseph (Island)
27	41	BEAT IT	Michael Jackson (Epic)
50	42	MORNIN'	Al Jarreau (WEA)
32	43	OVERKILL	Men At Work (Epic)
33	44	I GOT MINE	Motorhead (Bronze)
-	45	THE HEAT IS ON	Agnetha Faltskog (Epic)
-	46	LITTLE RED CORVETTE	Prince (Warner Brothers)
-	47	WALK OUT TO WINTER	Aztec Camera (Rough Trade)
-	48	FLESH OF MY FLESH	Orange Juice (Polydor)
-	49	COUNTDOWN	Rush (Mercury)
41	50	CANDY MAN	Mary Jane Girls (Motown)

11 June 1983

This week	Title	Artist
2 1	EVERY BREATH YOU TAKE	Police (A&M)
3 2	BAD BOYS	Wham! (Innervision)
7 3	NOBODY'S DIARY	Yazoo (Mute)
1 4	CANDY GIRL	New Edition (London)
12 5	JUST GOT LUCKY	Joboxers (RCA)
9 6	BUFFALO SOLDIER	Bob Marley & the Wailers (Island/Tuff Gong)
4 7	CAN'T GET USED TO LOSING YOU	Beat (Go Feet)
8 8	MONEY GO ROUND	Style Council (Polydor)
14 9	LOVE TOWN	Booker Newbury III (Polydor)
5 10	TRUE	Spandau Ballet (Reformation)
6 11	TEMPTATION	Heaven 17 (Virgin)
10 12	WHAT KINDA BOY YOU'RE LOOKIN' FOR (GIRL)	Hot Chocolate (RAK)
18 13	IN A BIG COUNTRY	Big Country (Mercury)
25 14	LADY LOVE ME (ONE MORE TIME)	George Benson (Warner Brothers)
13 15	OUR LIPS ARE SEALED	Fun Boy Three (Chrysalis)
39 16	CHINA GIRL	David Bowie (EMI America)
24 17	WAITING FOR A TRAIN	Flash & the Pan (Easybeat)
20 18	FEEL THE NEED IN ME	Forrest (CBS)
15 19	GLORY, GLORY, MAN UNITED	Manchester United Football Team (EMI)
- 20	FLASHDANCE ... WHAT A FEELING	Irene Cara (Casablanca)
11 21	DANCING TIGHT	Galaxy featuring Phil Fearon (Ensign)
35 22	WE CAME TO DANCE	Ultravox (Chrysalis)
- 23	PILLS AND SOAP	Imposter (Imp)
31 24	STOP AND GO	David Grant (Chrysalis)
38 25	BABY JANE	Rod Stewart (Warner Brothers)
26 26	BRING ME CLOSER	Altered Images (Epic)
- 27	I GUESS THAT'S WHY THEY CALL IT THE BLUES	Elton John (Rocket)
16 28	BLIND VISION	Blancmange (London)
19 29	SHIPBUILDING	Robert Wyatt (Rough Trade)
- 30	HANG ON NOW	Kajagoogoo (EMI)
22 31	BLUE MONDAY	New Order (Factory)
- 32	MOONLIGHT SHADOW	Mike Oldfield (Virgin)
23 33	PALE SHELTER	Tears For Fears (Mercury)
34 34	THE KIDS ARE BACK	Twisted Sister (Atlantic)
33 35	JUICY FRUIT	Mtume (Epic)
- 36	TAKE THAT SITUATION	Nick Heyward (Arista)
40 37	LET'S LIVE IT UP (NITE PEOPLE)	David Joseph (Island)
21 38	MUSIC (PART 1)	D Train (Prelude)
48 39	FLESH OF MY FLESH	Orange Juice (Polydor)
- 40	LOOKING AT MIDNIGHT	Imagination (R&B)
27 41	WORDS	F.R. David (Carrere)
- 42	SHEEPFARMING IN THE FALKLANDS	Crass (Crass)
34 43	THE WHEEL	Spear of Destiny (Epic)
17 44	(KEEP FEELING) FASCINATION	Human League (Virgin)
42 45	MORNIN'	Al Jarreau (WEA)
- 46	WANNA BE STARTIN' SOMETHIN'	Michael Jackson (Epic)
- 47	WALKIN' THE LINE	Brass Construction (Capitol)
28 48	DON'T STOP THAT CRAZY RHYTHM	Modern Romance (WEA)
30 49	FAMILY MAN	Daryl Hall & John Oates (RCA)
46 50	LITTLE RED CORVETTE	Prince (Warner Brothers)

18 June 1983

This week	Title	Artist
1 1	EVERY BREATH YOU TAKE	Police (A&M)
2 2	BAD BOYS	Wham! (Innervision)
16 3	CHINA GIRL	David Bowie (EMI America)
3 4	NOBODY'S DIARY	Yazoo (Mute)
6 5	BUFFALO SOLDIER	Bob Marley & the Wailers (Island/Tuff Gong)
20 6	FLASHDANCE ... WHAT A FEELING	Irene Cara (Casablanca)
9 7	LOVE TOWN	Booker Newbury III (Polydor)
5 8	JUST GOT LUCKY	Joboxers (RCA)
17 9	WAITING FOR A TRAIN	Flash & the Pan (Easybeat)
14 10	LADY LOVE ME (ONE MORE TIME)	George Benson (Warner Brothers)
23 11	PILLS AND SOAP	Imposter (Imp)
4 12	CANDY GIRL	New Edition (London)
27 13	I GUESS THAT'S WHY THEY CALL IT THE BLUES	Elton John (Rocket)
25 14	BABY JANE	Rod Stewart (Warner Brothers)
7 15	CAN'T GET USED TO LOSING YOU	Beat (Go Feet)
13 16	IN A BIG COUNTRY	Big Country (Mercury)
30 17	HANG ON NOW	Kajagoogoo (EMI)
8 18	MONEY GO ROUND	Style Council (Polydor)
22 19	WE CAME TO DANCE	Ultravox (Chrysalis)
46 20	WANNA BE STARTIN' SOMETHIN'	Michael Jackson (Epic)
11 21	TEMPTATION	Heaven 17 (Virgin)
32 22	MOONLIGHT SHADOW	Mike Oldfield (Virgin)
- 23	DEAD GIVEAWAY	Shalamar (Solar)
18 24	FEEL THE NEED IN ME	Forrest (CBS)
12 25	WHAT KINDA BOY YOU'RE LOOKIN' FOR (GIRL)	Hot Chocolate (RAK)
24 26	STOP AND GO	David Grant (Chrysalis)
21 27	DANCING TIGHT	Galaxy featuring Phil Fearon (Ensign)
- 28	DREAM TO SLEEP	H2O (RCA)
15 29	OUR LIPS ARE SEALED	Fun Boy Three (Chrysalis)
40 30	LOOKING AT MIDNIGHT	Imagination (R&B)
31 31	BLUE MONDAY	New Order (Factory)
- 32	DARK IS THE NIGHT	Shakatak (Polydor)
- 33	MARKET SQUARE HEROES	Marillion (EMI)
42 34	SHEEPFARMING IN THE FALKLANDS	Crass (Crass)
10 35	TRUE	Spandau Ballet (Reformation)
29 36	SHIPBUILDING	Robert Wyatt (Rough Trade)
19 37	GLORY, GLORY, MAN UNITED	Manchester United Football Team (EMI)
39 38	FLESH OF MY FLESH	Orange Juice (Polydor)
37 39	LET'S LIVE IT UP (NITE PEOPLE)	David Joseph (Island)
26 40	BRING ME CLOSER	Altered Images (Epic)
- 41	IT'S OVER	Funk Masters (Master Funk)
45 42	JUICY FRUIT	Mtume (Epic)
34 43	THE KIDS ARE BACK	Twisted Sister (Atlantic)
- 44	CONFUSION (HITS US EVERY TIME)	Truth (Formation)
45 45	MORNIN'	Al Jarreau (WEA)
- 46	WALK OUT TO WINTER	Aztec Camera (Rough Trade)
38 47	MUSIC (PART 1)	D Train (Prelude)
- 48	TRAGEDY AND MYSTERY	China Crisis (Virgin)
- 49	SURPRISE SURPRISE	Central Line (Mercury)
33 50	PALE SHELTER	Tears For Fears (Mercury)

Irene Cara reprised her exuberant *Fame* style for *Flashdance...What A Feeling*, which again was the theme for a film (*Flashdance*), but not, this time, one she starred in. Wham!, meanwhile, crept ever nearer the top as *Bad Boys* peaked at Two. George Michael was so embarrassed by the video to this single that he ensured its early disappearance and non-availability on the commercial video sales market.

June – July 1983

last week	this week	25 June 1983	
3	1	CHINA GIRL	David Bowie (EMI America)
1	2	EVERY BREATH YOU TAKE	Police (A&M)
6	3	FLASHDANCE ... WHAT A FEELING	Irene Cara (Casablanca)
14	4	BABY JANE	Rod Stewart (Warner Brothers)
2	5	BAD BOYS	Wham! (Innervision)
4	6	NOBODY'S DIARY	Yazoo (Mute)
13	7	I GUESS THAT'S WHY THEY CALL IT THE BLUES	Elton John (Rocket)
5	8	BUFFALO SOLDIER	Bob Marley & the Wailers (Island/Tuff Gong)
9	9	WAITING FOR A TRAIN	Flash & the Pan (Easybeat)
10	10	LADY LOVE ME (ONE MORE TIME)	George Benson (Warner Brothers)
20	11	WANNA BE STARTIN' SOMETHIN'	Michael Jackson (Epic)
12	12	PILLS AND SOAP	Imposter (Imp)
7	13	LOVE TOWN	Booker Newbury III (Polydor)
32	14	DARK IS THE NIGHT	Shakatak (Polydor)
23	15	DEAD GIVEAWAY	Shalamar (Solar)
28	16	DREAM TO SLEEP	H2O (RCA)
8	17	JUST GOT LUCKY	Joboxers (RCA)
17	18	HANG ON NOW	Kajagoogoo (EMI)
33	19	MARKET SQUARE HEROES	Marillion (EMI)
19	20	WE CAME TO DANCE	Ultravox (Chrysalis)
-	21	WHEN WE WERE YOUNG	Bucks Fizz (RCA)
22	22	MOONLIGHT SHADOW	Mike Oldfield (Virgin)
16	23	IN A BIG COUNTRY	Big Country (Mercury)
12	24	CANDY GIRL	New Edition (London)
30	25	LOOKING AT MIDNIGHT	Imagination (R&B)
44	26	CONFUSION (HITS US EVERY TIME)	Truth (Formation)
18	27	MONEY GO ROUND	Style Council (Polydor)
15	28	CAN'T GET USED TO LOSING YOU	Beat (Go Feet)
-	29	ROCK 'N' ROLL IS KING	Electric Light Orchestra (Jet)
-	30	LET'S ALL GO	Killing Joke (EG/Malicious Damage)
-	31	COME LIVE WITH ME	Heaven 17 (Virgin)
27	32	DANCING TIGHT	Galaxy featuring Phil Fearon (Ensign)
-	33	I WON'T HOLD YOU BACK	Toto (CBS)
42	34	JUICY FRUIT	Mtume (Epic)
-	35	THE HEAT IS ON	Agnetha Faltskog (Epic)
-	36	TAKE THAT SITUATION	Nick Heyward (Arista)
-	37	WHEREVER I LAY MY HAT (THAT'S MY HOME)	Paul Young (CBS)
40	38	BRING ME CLOSER	Altered Images (Epic)
39	39	LET'S LIVE IT UP (NITE PEOPLE)	David Joseph (Island)
26	40	STOP AND GO	David Grant (Chrysalis)
-	41	I.O.U.	Freeez (Beggars Banquet)
25	42	WHAT KINDA BOY YOU'RE LOOKIN' FOR (GIRL)	Hot Chocolate (RAK)
38	43	FLESH OF MY FLESH	Orange Juice (Polydor)
35	44	TRUE	Spandau Ballet (Reformation)
-	45	SHE WORKS HARD FOR THE MONEY	Donna Summer (Mercury)
31	46	BLUE MONDAY	New Order (Factory)
41	47	IT'S OVER	Funk Masters (Master Funk)
34	48	SHEEPFARMING IN THE FALKLANDS	Crass (Crass)
49	49	SURPRISE SURPRISE	Central Line (Mercury)
-	50	IT'S SO HIGH	Matt Fretton (Chrysalis)

last week	this week	2 July 1983	
2	1	EVERY BREATH YOU TAKE	Police (A&M)
4	2	BABY JANE	Rod Stewart (Warner Brothers)
1	3	CHINA GIRL	David Bowie (EMI America)
3	4	FLASHDANCE ... WHAT A FEELING	Irene Cara (Casablanca)
7	5	I GUESS THAT'S WHY THEY CALL IT THE BLUES	Elton John (Rocket)
9	6	WAITING FOR A TRAIN	Flash & the Pan (Easybeat)
11	7	WANNA BE STARTIN' SOMETHIN'	Michael Jackson (Epic)
5	8	BAD BOYS	Wham! (Innervision)
21	9	WHEN WE WERE YOUNG	Bucks Fizz (RCA)
15	10	DEAD GIVEAWAY	Shalamar (Solar)
6	11	NOBODY'S DIARY	Yazoo (Mute)
10	12	LADY LOVE ME (ONE MORE TIME)	George Benson (Warner Brothers)
41	13	I.O.U.	Freeez (Beggars Banquet)
14	14	DARK IS THE NIGHT	Shakatak (Polydor)
22	15	MOONLIGHT SHADOW	Mike Oldfield (Virgin)
-	16	WAR BABY	Tom Robinson (Panic)
19	17	MARKET SQUARE HEROES	Marillion (EMI)
16	18	DREAM TO SLEEP	H2O (RCA)
8	19	BUFFALO SOLDIER	Bob Marley & the Wailers (Island/Tuff Gong)
13	20	LOVE TOWN	Booker Newbury III (Polydor)
37	21	WHEREVER I LAY MY HAT (THAT'S MY HOME)	Paul Young (CBS)
31	22	COME LIVE WITH ME	Heaven 17 (Virgin)
26	23	CONFUSION (HITS US EVERY TIME)	Truth (Formation)
36	24	TAKE THAT SITUATION	Nick Heyward (Arista)
29	25	ROCK 'N' ROLL IS KING	Electric Light Orchestra (Jet)
12	26	PILLS AND SOAP	Imposter (Imp)
-	27	ALL NIGHT LONG	Mary Jane Girls (Gordy)
17	28	JUST GOT LUCKY	Joboxers (RCA)
20	29	WE CAME TO DANCE	Ultravox (Chrysalis)
47	30	IT'S OVER	Funk Masters (Master Funk)
45	31	SHE WORKS HARD FOR THE MONEY	Donna Summer (Mercury)
18	32	HANG ON NOW	Kajagoogoo (EMI)
25	33	LOOKING AT MIDNIGHT	Imagination (R&B)
23	34	IN A BIG COUNTRY	Big Country (Mercury)
30	35	LET'S ALL GO	Killing Joke (EG/Malicious Damage)
-	36	TEACHER	I-Level (Virgin)
35	37	THE HEAT IS ON	Agnetha Faltskog (Epic)
38	38	LET'S LIVE IT UP (NITE PEOPLE)	David Joseph (Island)
-	39	TRANSFER AFFECTION	A Flock Of Seagulls (Jive)
28	40	CAN'T GET USED TO LOSING YOU	Beat (Go Feet)
-	41	TANTALISE (WO WO EE YEH YEH)	Jimmy the Hoover (Innervision)
-	42	THE TROOPER	Iron Maiden (EMI)
-	43	HAVE YOU EVER SEEN THE RAIN?	Bonnie Tyler (CBS)
-	44	BRING IT ON ... BRING IT ON	James Brown (Sonet)
-	45	DON'T TRY TO STOP IT	Roman Holliday (Jive)
-	46	FORBIDDEN COLOURS	David Sylvian (Virgin)
-	47	BIRTHDAY	Icicle Works (Situation 2)
48	48	YOU CAN HAVE IT	Robert Palmer (Island)
-	49	SOME KIND OF FRIEND	Barry Manilow (Arista)
-	50	FEEL THE NEED IN ME	Forrest (CBS)

last week	this week	9 July 1983	
2	1	BABY JANE	Rod Stewart (Warner Brothers)
4	2	FLASHDANCE ... WHAT A FEELING	Irene Cara (Casablanca)
1	3	EVERY BREATH YOU TAKE	Police (A&M)
15	4	MOONLIGHT SHADOW	Mike Oldfield (Virgin)
5	5	I GUESS THAT'S WHY THEY CALL IT THE BLUES	Elton John (Rocket)
13	6	I.O.U.	Freeez (Beggars Banquet)
21	7	WHEREVER I LAY MY HAT (THAT'S MY HOME)	Paul Young (CBS)
3	8	CHINA GIRL	David Bowie (EMI America)
16	9	WAR BABY	Tom Robinson (Panic)
10	10	DEAD GIVEAWAY	Shalamar (Solar)
25	11	ROCK 'N' ROLL IS KING	Electric Light Orchestra (Jet)
22	12	COME LIVE WITH ME	Heaven 17 (Virgin)
8	13	BAD BOYS	Wham! (Innervision)
9	14	WHEN WE WERE YOUNG	Bucks Fizz (RCA)
6	15	WAITING FOR A TRAIN	Flash & the Pan (Easybeat)
7	16	WANNA BE STARTIN' SOMETHIN'	Michael Jackson (Epic)
24	17	TAKE THAT SITUATION	Nick Heyward (Arista)
46	18	FORBIDDEN COLOURS	David Sylvian (Virgin)
42	19	THE TROOPER	Iron Maiden (EMI)
30	20	IT'S OVER	Funk Masters (Master Funk)
12	21	LADY LOVE ME (ONE MORE TIME)	George Benson (Warner Brothers)
22	22	NOBODY'S DIARY	Yazoo (Mute)
27	23	ALL NIGHT LONG	Mary Jane Girls (Gordy)
18	24	DREAM TO SLEEP	H2O (RCA)
23	25	CONFUSION (HITS US EVERY TIME)	Truth (Formation)
-	26	DOUBLE DUTCH	Malcolm McLaren (Charisma)
14	27	DARK IS THE NIGHT	Shakatak (Polydor)
17	28	MARKET SQUARE HEROES	Marillion (EMI)
19	29	BUFFALO SOLDIER	Bob Marley & the Wailers (Island/Tuff Gong)
-	30	SHE WORKS HARD FOR THE MONEY	Donna Summer (Mercury)
45	31	DON'T TRY TO STOP IT	Roman Holliday (Jive)
39	32	TRANSFER AFFECTION	A Flock Of Seagulls (Jive)
41	33	TANTALISE (WO WO EE YEH YEH)	Jimmy the Hoover (Innervision)
26	34	PILLS AND SOAP	Imposter (Imp)
-	35	BLACK HEART	Marc & the Mambas (Some Bizzare)
-	36	GET DOWN SATURDAY NIGHT	Oliver Cheatham (MCA)
-	37	ACKEE 1-2-3	Beat (Go Feet)
35	38	LET'S ALL GO	Killing Joke (EG/Malicious Damage)
39	39	TELL ME WHY	Musical Youth (MCA)
-	40	THE WALK	Cure (Fiction)
42	41	JUICY FRUIT	Mtume (Epic)
-	42	LET'S LIVE FOR TODAY	Lords Of The New Church (I.R.S.)
43	43	YOU MAKE IT HEAVEN	Terry Wells (Philly World)
36	44	TEACHER	I-Level (Virgin)
33	45	LOOKING AT MIDNIGHT	Imagination (R&B)
-	46	EVERYDAY I WRITE THE BOOK	Elvis Costello & the Attractions (F.Beat)
-	47	WHO'S THAT GIRL?	Eurythmics (RCA)
44	48	BRING IT ON ... BRING IT ON	James Brown (Sonet)
20	49	LOVE TOWN	Booker Newbury III (Polydor)
-	50	NEW GRANGE	Clannad (RCA)

Rod Stewart's *Baby Jane* was his first UK number one since *Da Ya Think I'm Sexy?* in 1978. Oddly, it failed to make the Top 10 in the US, where most of his recent singles had fared better than in Britain. The Imposter, who made the Top 20 with *Pills And Soap*, was actually a masquerading Elvis Costello, while Agnetha Faltskog was one of the former Abba singers.

16 July 1983

last week	this week	Title	Artist
7	1	WHEREVER I LAY MY HAT (THAT'S MY HOME)	Paul Young (CBS)
1	2	BABY JANE	Rod Stewart (Warner Brothers)
4	3	MOONLIGHT SHADOW	Mike Oldfield (Virgin)
2	4	FLASHDANCE ... WHAT A FEELING	Irene Cara (Casablanca)
6	5	I.O.U.	Freeez (Beggars Banquet)
8	6	WAR BABY	Tom Robinson (Panic)
12	7	COME LIVE WITH ME	Heaven 17 (Virgin)
10	8	DEAD GIVEAWAY	Shalamar (Solar)
5	9	I GUESS THAT'S WHY THEY CALL IT THE BLUES	Elton John (Rocket)
19	10	THE TROOPER	Iron Maiden (EMI)
17	11	TAKE THAT SITUATION	Nick Heyward (Arista)
11	12	ROCK 'N' ROLL IS KING	Electric Light Orchestra (Jet)
3	13	EVERY BREATH YOU TAKE	Police (A&M)
20	14	IT'S OVER	Funk Masters (Master Funk)
26	15	DOUBLE DUTCH	Malcolm McLaren (Charisma)
16	16	FORBIDDEN COLOURS	David Sylvian (Virgin)
47	17	WHO'S THAT GIRL?	Eurythmics (RCA)
8	18	CHINA GIRL	David Bowie (EMI America)
40	19	THE WALK	Cure (Fiction)
3	20	ALL NIGHT LONG	Mary Jane Girls (Gordy)
14	21	WHEN WE WERE YOUNG	Bucks Fizz (RCA)
15	22	WAITING FOR A TRAIN	Flash & the Pan (Easybeat)
33	23	TANTALISE (WO WO EE YEH YEH)	Jimmy the Hoover (Innervision)
13	24	BAD BOYS	Wham! (Innervision)
46	25	EVERYDAY I WRITE THE BOOK	Elvis Costello & the Attractions (F.Beat)
25	26	CONFUSION (HITS US EVERY TIME)	Truth (Formation)
16	27	WANNA BE STARTIN' SOMETHIN'	Michael Jackson (Epic)
21	28	LADY LOVE ME (ONE MORE TIME)	George Benson (Warner Brothers)
-	29	CRUEL SUMMER	Bananarama (London)
-	30	NEVER STOP	Echo & the Bunnymen (Korova)
24	31	DREAM TO SLEEP	H2O (RCA)
32	32	NOBODY'S DIARY	Yazoo (Mute)
-	33	AFTER A FASHION	Midge Ure & Mick Karn (Musicfest)
-	34	RIGHT NOW	Creatures (Wonderland)
30	35	SHE WORKS HARD FOR THE MONEY	Donna Summer (Mercury)
39	36	TELL ME WHY	Musical Youth (MCA)
37	37	GET DOWN SATURDAY NIGHT	Oliver Cheatham (MCA)
31	38	DON'T TRY TO STOP IT	Roman Holliday (Jive)
-	39	THE FIRST PICTURE OF YOU	Lotus Eaters (Sylvan)
28	40	MARKET SQUARE HEROES	Marillion (EMI)
29	41	BUFFALO SOLDIER	Bob Marley & the Wailers (Island/Tuff Gong)
48	42	BRING IT ON ... BRING IT ON	James Brown (Sonet)
-	43	PIECES OF ICE	Diana Ross (Capitol)
44	44	MESSAGES FROM THE STARS	RAH Band (TMT)
-	45	BETWEEN THE SHEETS	Isley Brothers (Epic)
38	46	LET'S ALL GO	Killing Joke (EG/Malicious Damage)
37	47	ACKEE 1-2-3	Beat (Go Feet)
32	48	TRANSFER AFFECTION	A Flock Of Seagulls (Jive)
-	49	THE MAN WHOSE HEAD EXPANDED	Fall (Rough Trade)
-	50	IT'S A MISTAKE	Men At Work (Epic)

23 July 1983

last week	this week	Title	Artist
1	1	WHEREVER I LAY MY HAT (THAT'S MY HOME)	Paul Young (CBS)
5	2	I.O.U.	Freeez (Beggars Banquet)
2	3	BABY JANE	Rod Stewart (Warner Brothers)
3	4	MOONLIGHT SHADOW	Mike Oldfield (Virgin)
17	5	WHO'S THAT GIRL?	Eurythmics (RCA)
6	6	WAR BABY	Tom Robinson (Panic)
7	7	COME LIVE WITH ME	Heaven 17 (Virgin)
4	8	FLASHDANCE ... WHAT A FEELING	Irene Cara (Casablanca)
15	9	DOUBLE DUTCH	Malcolm McLaren (Charisma)
14	10	IT'S OVER	Funk Masters (Master Funk)
20	11	ALL NIGHT LONG	Mary Jane Girls (Gordy)
12	12	THE WALK	Cure (Fiction)
30	13	NEVER STOP	Echo & the Bunnymen (Korova)
12	14	ROCK 'N' ROLL IS KING	Electric Light Orchestra (Jet)
10	15	THE TROOPER	Iron Maiden (EMI)
16	16	FORBIDDEN COLOURS	David Sylvian (Virgin)
8	17	DEAD GIVEAWAY	Shalamar (Solar)
23	18	TANTALISE (WO WO EE YEH YEH)	Jimmy the Hoover (Innervision)
29	19	CRUEL SUMMER	Bananarama (London)
-	20	WRAPPED AROUND YOUR FINGER	Police (A&M)
11	21	TAKE THAT SITUATION	Nick Heyward (Arista)
9	22	I GUESS THAT'S WHY THEY CALL IT THE BLUES	Elton John (Rocket)
34	23	RIGHT NOW	Creatures (Wonderland)
24	24	EVERYDAY I WRITE THE BOOK	Elvis Costello & the Attractions (F.Beat)
38	25	DON'T TRY TO STOP IT	Roman Holliday (Jive)
33	26	AFTER A FASHION	Midge Ure & Mick Karn (Musicfest)
39	27	THE FIRST PICTURE OF YOU	Lotus Eaters (Sylvan)
24	28	BAD BOYS	Wham! (Innervision)
35	29	SHE WORKS HARD FOR THE MONEY	Donna Summer (Mercury)
22	30	WAITING FOR A TRAIN	Flash & the Pan (Easybeat)
-	31	THE CROWN	Gary Byrd & the G.B. Experience (Motown)
37	32	GET DOWN SATURDAY NIGHT	Oliver Cheatham (MCA)
-	33	FEEL LIKE MAKIN' LOVE	George Benson (Warner Brothers)
36	34	TELL ME WHY	Musical Youth (MCA)
-	35	GIVE IT SOME EMOTION	Tracie (Respond)
26	36	CONFUSION (HITS US EVERY TIME)	Truth (Formation)
-	37	GIVE IT UP	KC & the Sunshine Band (Epic)
-	38	DO IT AGAIN/BILLIE JEAN	Club House (Island)
44	39	MESSAGES FROM THE STARS	RAH Band (TMT)
-	40	IT'S LATE	Shakin' Stevens (Epic)
-	41	BIG LOG	Robert Plant (WEA)
-	42	BLUE MONDAY	New Order (Factory)
43	43	WATCHING	Thompson Twins (Arista)
-	44	YOU AIN'T REALLY DOWN	Status IV (TMT)
21	45	WHEN WE WERE YOUNG	Bucks Fizz (RCA)
-	46	IT'S A MISTAKE	Men At Work (Epic)
32	47	NOBODY'S DIARY	Yazoo (Mute)
-	48	NEVER GONNA LET YOU GO	Sergio Mendes featuring Joe Pizzulo & Leza Miller (A&M)
18	49	CHINA GIRL	David Bowie (EMI America)
-	50	EVERYTHING COUNTS	Depeche Mode (Mute)

30 July 1983

last week	this week	Title	Artist
1	1	WHEREVER I LAY MY HAT (THAT'S MY HOME)	Paul Young (CBS)
2	2	I.O.U.	Freeez (Beggars Banquet)
5	3	WHO'S THAT GIRL?	Eurythmics (RCA)
9	4	DOUBLE DUTCH	Malcolm McLaren (Charisma)
3	5	BABY JANE	Rod Stewart (Warner Brothers)
20	6	WRAPPED AROUND YOUR FINGER	Police (A&M)
7	7	COME LIVE WITH ME	Heaven 17 (Virgin)
4	8	MOONLIGHT SHADOW	Mike Oldfield (Virgin)
13	9	NEVER STOP	Echo & the Bunnymen (Korova)
8	10	FLASHDANCE ... WHAT A FEELING	Irene Cara (Casablanca)
6	11	WAR BABY	Tom Robinson (Panic)
19	12	CRUEL SUMMER	Bananarama (London)
31	13	THE CROWN	Gary Byrd & the G.B. Experience (Motown)
10	14	IT'S OVER	Funk Masters (Master Funk)
11	15	ALL NIGHT LONG	Mary Jane Girls (Gordy)
16	16	FORBIDDEN COLOURS	David Sylvian (Virgin)
38	17	DO IT AGAIN/BILLIE JEAN	Club House (Island)
12	18	THE WALK	Cure (Fiction)
18	19	TANTALISE (WO WO EE YEH YEH)	Jimmy the Hoover (Innervision)
23	20	RIGHT NOW	Creatures (Wonderland)
25	21	DON'T TRY TO STOP IT	Roman Holliday (Jive)
40	22	IT'S LATE	Shakin' Stevens (Epic)
28	23	BAD BOYS	Wham! (Innervision)
15	24	THE TROOPER	Iron Maiden (EMI)
27	25	THE FIRST PICTURE OF YOU	Lotus Eaters (Sylvan)
35	26	GIVE IT SOME EMOTION	Tracie (Respond)
14	27	ROCK 'N' ROLL IS KING	Electric Light Orchestra (Jet)
24	28	EVERYDAY I WRITE THE BOOK	Elvis Costello & the Attractions (F.Beat)
26	29	AFTER A FASHION	Midge Ure & Mick Karn (Musicfest)
22	30	I GUESS THAT'S WHY THEY CALL IT THE BLUES	Elton John (Rocket)
50	31	EVERYTHING COUNTS	Depeche Mode (Mute)
17	32	DEAD GIVEAWAY	Shalamar (Solar)
49	33	CHINA GIRL	David Bowie (EMI America)
37	34	GIVE IT UP	KC & the Sunshine Band (Epic)
33	35	FEEL LIKE MAKIN' LOVE	George Benson (Warner Brothers)
-	36	FREAK	Bruce Foxton (Arista)
29	37	SHE WORKS HARD FOR THE MONEY	Donna Summer (Mercury)
21	38	TAKE THAT SITUATION	Nick Heyward (Arista)
-	39	I'M STILL STANDING	Elton John (Rocket)
46	40	IT'S A MISTAKE	Men At Work (Epic)
45	41	WHEN WE WERE YOUNG	Bucks Fizz (RCA)
30	42	WAITING FOR A TRAIN	Flash & the Pan (Easybeat)
41	43	BIG LOG	Robert Plant (WEA)
42	44	BLUE MONDAY	New Order (Factory)
-	45	HAPPY	Michael Jackson (Motown)
36	46	CONFUSION (HITS US EVERY TIME)	Truth (Formation)
-	47	DEATH CULT (EP)	Death Cult (Situation 2)
-	48	LOVE TO STAY	Altered Images (Epic)
39	49	MESSAGES FROM THE STARS	RAH Band (TMT)
43	50	WATCHING	Thompson Twins (Arista)

Paul Young, former lead vocalist with the popular live soul band Q-Tips (and before that a member of Streetband, whose novelty *Toast* had charted in 1978), had waited some time for his solo success, but it finally arrived with the chart-topping *Wherever I Lay My Hat*. This was a cover of a Marvin Gaye number, originally found on the B-side of his hit *Too Busy Thinking About My Baby*.

August 1983

6 August 1983

last week	this week		
1	1	WHEREVER I LAY MY HAT (THAT'S MY HOME)	Paul Young (CBS)
3	2	WHO'S THAT GIRL?	Eurythmics (RCA)
2	3	I.O.U.	Freeez (Beggars Banquet)
13	4	THE CROWN	Gary Byrd and the G.B. Experience (Motown)
6	5	WRAPPED AROUND YOUR FINGER	Police (A&M)
4	6	DOUBLE DUTCH	Malcolm McLaren (Charisma)
7	7	COME LIVE WITH ME	Heaven 17 (Virgin)
17	8	DO IT AGAIN/BILLIE JEAN	Club House (Island)
12	9	CRUEL SUMMER	Bananarama (London)
22	10	IT'S LATE	Shakin' Stevens (Epic)
8	11	MOONLIGHT SHADOW	Mike Oldfield (Virgin)
21	12	DON'T TRY TO STOP IT	Roman Holliday (Jive)
34	13	GIVE IT UP	KC and the Sunshine Band (Epic)
5	14	BABY JANE	Rod Stewart (Warner Brothers)
18	15	THE WALK	Cure (Fiction)
36	16	FREAK	Bruce Foxton (Arista)
10	17	FLASHDANCE ... WHAT A FEELING	Irene Cara (Casablanca)
9	18	NEVER STOP	Echo and the Bunnymen (Korova)
-	19	CLUB TROPICANA	Wham! (Innervision)
14	20	IT'S OVER	Funk Masters (Master Funk)
31	21	EVERYTHING COUNTS	Depeche Mode (Mute)
25	22	THE FIRST PICTURE OF YOU	Lotus Eaters (Sylvan)
20	23	RIGHT NOW	Creatures (Wonderland)
16	24	FORBIDDEN COLOURS	David Sylvian (Virgin)
39	25	I'M STILL STANDING	Elton John (Rocket)
11	26	WAR BABY	Tom Robinson (Panic)
15	27	ALL NIGHT LONG	Mary Jane Girls (Gordy)
19	28	TANTALISE (WO WO EE YEH YEH)	Jimmy the Hoover (Innervision)
28	29	EVERYDAY I WRITE THE BOOK	Elvis Costello and the Attractions (F.Beat)
43	30	BIG LOG	Robert Plant (WEA)
-	31	ROCKIT	Herbie Hancock (CBS)
-	32	LOVE BLONDE	Kim Wilde (RAK)
27	33	ROCK 'N' ROLL IS KING	Electric Light Orchestra (Jet)
23	34	BAD BOYS	Wham! (Innervision)
35	35	FEEL LIKE MAKIN' LOVE	George Benson (Warner Brothers)
-	36	WAIT UNTIL TONIGHT	Galaxy featuring Phil Fearon (Ensign)
24	37	THE TROOPER	Iron Maiden (EMI)
-	38	FOR YOU	Farmers Boys (EMI)
-	39	THE SUN GOES DOWN (LIVING IT UP)	Level 42 (Polydor)
37	40	SHE WORKS HARD FOR THE MONEY	Donna Summer (Mercury)
50	41	WATCHING	Thompson Twins (Arista)
47	42	DEATH CULT (EP)	Death Cult (Situation 2)
-	43	HAVE YOU SEEN HER	Chi-Lites (SMP)
-	44	HIM	Sarah Brightman (Polydor)
-	45	GET IT RIGHT	Aretha Franklin (Arista)
-	46	SHINE	Motorhead (Bronze)
-	47	THE MAN WITH 4 WAY HIPS	Tom Tom Club (Island)
-	48	THE SUN GOES DOWN	Thin Lizzy (Vertigo)
-	49	CRAZY	Manhattans (CBS)
-	50	PUT OUR HEADS TOGETHER	O'Jays (Philadelphia International)

13 August 1983

1	1	WHEREVER I LAY MY HAT (THAT'S MY HOME)	Paul Young (CBS)
13	2	GIVE IT UP	KC and the Sunshine Band (Epic)
3	3	I.O.U.	Freeez (Beggars Banquet)
6	4	DOUBLE DUTCH	Malcolm McLaren (Charisma)
4	5	THE CROWN	Gary Byrd and the G.B. Experience (Motown)
2	6	WHO'S THAT GIRL?	Eurythmics (RCA)
19	7	CLUB TROPICANA	Wham! (Innervision)
5	8	WRAPPED AROUND YOUR FINGER	Police (A&M)
9	9	CRUEL SUMMER	Bananarama (London)
30	10	BIG LOG	Robert Plant (WEA)
8	11	DO IT AGAIN/BILLIE JEAN	Club House (Island)
21	12	EVERYTHING COUNTS	Depeche Mode (Mute)
10	13	IT'S LATE	Shakin' Stevens (Epic)
23	14	RIGHT NOW	Creatures (Wonderland)
25	15	I'M STILL STANDING	Elton John (Rocket)
7	16	COME LIVE WITH ME	Heaven 17 (Virgin)
31	17	ROCKIT	Herbie Hancock (CBS)
-	18	LONG HOT SUMMER	Style Council (Polydor)
11	19	MOONLIGHT SHADOW	Mike Oldfield (Virgin)
12	20	DON'T TRY TO STOP IT	Roman Holliday (Jive)
15	21	THE WALK	Cure (Fiction)
22	22	THE FIRST PICTURE OF YOU	Lotus Eaters (Sylvan)
16	23	FREAK	Bruce Foxton (Arista)
-	24	GOLD	Spandau Ballet (Reformation)
-	25	TOUR DE FRANCE	Kraftwerk (EMI)
17	26	FLASHDANCE ... WHAT A FEELING	Irene Cara (Casablanca)
18	27	NEVER STOP	Echo and the Bunnymen (Korova)
29	28	EVERYDAY I WRITE THE BOOK	Elvis Costello and the Attractions (F.Beat)
20	29	IT'S OVER	Funk Masters (Master Funk)
32	30	LOVE BLONDE	Kim Wilde (RAK)
34	31	BAD BOYS	Wham! (Innervision)
27	32	ALL NIGHT LONG	Mary Jane Girls (Gordy)
-	33	GIVE IT SOME EMOTION	Tracie (Respond)
-	34	COME DANCING	Kinks (Arista)
-	35	WALKING IN THE RAIN	Modern Romance (WEA)
14	36	BABY JANE	Rod Stewart (Warner Brothers)
-	37	BAD DAY	Carmel (London)
33	38	ROCK 'N' ROLL IS KING	Electric Light Orchestra (Jet)
48	39	THE SUN GOES DOWN	Thin Lizzy (Vertigo)
-	40	PARADISE	Stranglers (Epic)
26	41	WAR BABY	Tom Robinson (Panic)
41	42	WATCHING	Thompson Twins (Arista)
35	43	FEEL LIKE MAKIN' LOVE	George Benson (Warner Brothers)
-	44	NIGHTMARE	Saxon (Carrere)
24	45	FORBIDDEN COLOURS	David Sylvian (Virgin)
36	46	WAIT UNTIL TONIGHT	Galaxy featuring Phil Fearon (Ensign)
47	47	THE MAN WITH 4 WAY HIPS	Tom Tom Club (Island)
43	48	HAVE YOU SEEN HER	Chi-Lites (SMP)
-	49	PRIME TIME	Haircut One Hundred (Polydor)
-	50	NATIVE BOY	Animal Nightlife (Innervision)

20 August 1983

2	1	GIVE IT UP	KC and the Sunshine Band (Epic)
7	2	CLUB TROPICANA	Wham! (Innervision)
18	3	LONG HOT SUMMER	Style Council (Polydor)
5	4	THE CROWN	Gary Byrd and the G.B. Experience (Motown)
24	5	GOLD	Spandau Ballet (Reformation)
3	6	I.O.U.	Freeez (Beggars Banquet)
4	7	DOUBLE DUTCH	Malcolm McLaren (Charisma)
15	8	I'M STILL STANDING	Elton John (Rocket)
1	9	WHEREVER I LAY MY HAT (THAT'S MY HOME)	Paul Young (CBS)
10	10	BIG LOG	Robert Plant (WEA)
17	11	ROCKIT	Herbie Hancock (CBS)
12	12	EVERYTHING COUNTS	Depeche Mode (Mute)
6	13	WHO'S THAT GIRL?	Eurythmics (RCA)
14	14	RIGHT NOW	Creatures (Wonderland)
9	15	CRUEL SUMMER	Bananarama (London)
23	16	FREAK	Bruce Foxton (Arista)
22	17	THE FIRST PICTURE OF YOU	Lotus Eaters (Sylvan)
13	18	IT'S LATE	Shakin' Stevens (Epic)
30	19	LOVE BLONDE	Kim Wilde (RAK)
8	20	WRAPPED AROUND YOUR FINGER	Police (A&M)
19	21	MOONLIGHT SHADOW	Mike Oldfield (Virgin)
25	22	TOUR DE FRANCE	Kraftwerk (EMI)
11	23	DO IT AGAIN/BILLIE JEAN	Club House (Island)
16	24	COME LIVE WITH ME	Heaven 17 (Virgin)
-	25	GUILTY OF LOVE	Whitesnake (Liberty)
-	26	DISAPPEARING ACT	Shalamar (Solar)
46	27	WAIT UNTIL TONIGHT	Galaxy featuring Phil Fearon (Ensign)
21	28	THE WALK	Cure (Fiction)
27	29	NEVER STOP	Echo and the Bunnymen (Korova)
29	30	IT'S OVER	Funk Masters (Master Funk)
-	31	WATCHING YOU, WATCHING ME	David Grant (Chrysalis)
-	32	BALLERINA	Steve Harley (Stiletto)
-	33	BLUE MONDAY	New Order (Factory)
-	34	THE SUN GOES DOWN (LIVING IT UP)	Level 42 (Polydor)
37	35	BAD DAY	Carmel (London)
40	36	PARADISE	Stranglers (Epic)
33	37	GIVE IT SOME EMOTION	Tracie (Respond)
34	38	COME DANCING	Kinks (Arista)
26	39	FLASHDANCE ... WHAT A FEELING	Irene Cara (Casablanca)
-	40	MEAN STREAK	Y & T (A&M)
-	41	PUT OUR HEADS TOGETHER	O'Jays (Philadelphia International)
20	42	DON'T TRY TO STOP IT	Roman Holliday (Jive)
-	43	WINGS OF A DOVE	Madness (Stiff)
-	44	(SHE'S) SEXY AND 17	Stray Cats (Arista)
36	45	BABY JANE	Rod Stewart (Warner Brothers)
-	46	DON'T CRY	Asia (Geffen)
41	47	WAR BABY	Tom Robinson (Panic)
50	48	NATIVE BOY	Animal Nightlife (Innervision)
28	49	EVERYDAY I WRITE THE BOOK	Elvis Costello and the Attractions (F.Beat)
43	50	FEEL LIKE MAKIN' LOVE	George Benson (Warner Brothers)

Like just a couple of Top Ten hits before it, (Abba's *Lay All Your Love On Me* and New Order's *Blue Monday*) Gary Byrd's *The Crown* was available only in full-length form as a 12-inch single, while most of the sales of Freeez's *I.O.U.*, which was to be one of the biggest club and dancefloor successes of the year, were also on 12-inch vinyl, to dancers and mobile DJs.

August – September 1983

27 August 1983

last week	this week	title	artist (label)
5	1	GOLD	Spandau Ballet (Reformation)
1	2	GIVE IT UP	KC & the Sunshine Band (Epic)
3	3	LONG HOT SUMMER	Style Council (Polydor)
8	4	I'M STILL STANDING	Elton John (Rocket)
2	5	CLUB TROPICANA	Wham! (Innervision)
12	6	EVERYTHING COUNTS	Depeche Mode (Mute)
11	7	ROCKIT	Herbie Hancock (CBS)
43	8	WINGS OF A DOVE	Madness (Stiff)
10	9	BIG LOG	Robert Plant (WEA)
4	10	THE CROWN	Gary Byrd & the G.B. Experience (Motown)
7	11	DOUBLE DUTCH	Malcolm McLaren (Charisma)
14	12	RIGHT NOW	Creatures (Wonderland)
17	13	THE FIRST PICTURE OF YOU	Lotus Eaters (Sylvan)
9	14	WHEREVER I LAY MY HAT (THAT'S MY HOME)	Paul Young (CBS)
6	15	I.O.U.	Freeez (Beggars Banquet)
31	16	WATCHING YOU, WATCHING ME	David Grant (Chrysalis)
-	17	RED RED WINE	UB40 (DEP International)
38	18	COME DANCING	Kinks (Arista)
13	19	WHO'S THAT GIRL?	Eurythmics (RCA)
22	20	TOUR DE FRANCE	Kraftwerk (EMI)
27	21	WAIT UNTIL TONIGHT	Galaxy featuring Phil Fearon (Ensign)
19	22	LOVE BLONDE	Kim Wilde (RAK)
34	23	THE SUN GOES DOWN (LIVING IT UP)	Level 42 (Polydor)
35	24	BAD DAY	Carmel (London)
21	25	MOONLIGHT SHADOW	Mike Oldfield (Virgin)
-	26	LIKE AN ANIMAL	Glove (Wonderland)
15	27	CRUEL SUMMER	Bananarama (London)
37	28	GIVE IT SOME EMOTION	Tracie (Respond)
46	29	DON'T CRY	Asia (Geffen)
16	30	FREAK	Bruce Foxton (Arista)
28	31	THE WALK	Cure (Fiction)
33	32	BLUE MONDAY	New Order (Factory)
25	33	GUILTY OF LOVE	Whitesnake (Liberty)
26	34	DISAPPEARING ACT	Shalamar (Solar)
18	35	IT'S LATE	Shakin' Stevens (Epic)
-	36	WALKING IN THE RAIN	Modern Romance (WEA)
32	37	BALLERINA	Steve Harley (Stiletto)
49	38	EVERYDAY I WRITE THE BOOK	Elvis Costello & the Attractions (F.Beat)
-	39	POPCORN LOVE	New Edition (London)
-	40	WHAT AM I GONNA DO	Rod Stewart (Warner Brothers)
-	41	TONIGHT I CELEBRATE MY LOVE	Peabo Bryson & Roberta Flack (Capitol)
20	42	WRAPPED AROUND YOUR FINGER	Police (A&M)
24	43	COME LIVE WITH ME	Heaven 17 (Virgin)
-	44	STAY ON TOP	Uriah Heep (Bronze)
-	45	INDIAN SUMMER	Belle Stars (Stiff)
44	46	(SHE'S) SEXY AND 17	Stray Cats (Arista)
-	47	STREET OF DREAMS	Rainbow (Polydor)
-	48	JOHNNY FRIENDLY	Joboxers (RCA)
42	49	DON'T TRY TO STOP IT	Roman Holliday (Jive)
48	50	NATIVE BOY	Animal Nightlife (Innervision)

3 September 1983

last week	this week	title	artist (label)
1	1	GOLD	Spandau Ballet (Reformation)
3	2	LONG HOT SUMMER	Style Council (Polydor)
8	3	WINGS OF A DOVE	Madness (Stiff)
2	4	GIVE IT UP	KC & the Sunshine Band (Epic)
4	5	I'M STILL STANDING	Elton John (Rocket)
5	6	CLUB TROPICANA	Wham! (Innervision)
17	7	RED RED WINE	UB40 (DEP International)
7	8	ROCKIT	Herbie Hancock (CBS)
6	9	EVERYTHING COUNTS	Depeche Mode (Mute)
16	10	WATCHING YOU, WATCHING ME	David Grant (Chrysalis)
18	11	COME DANCING	Kinks (Arista)
23	12	THE SUN GOES DOWN (LIVING IT UP)	Level 42 (Polydor)
36	13	WALKING IN THE RAIN	Modern Romance (WEA)
40	14	WHAT AM I GONNA DO	Rod Stewart (Warner Brothers)
9	15	BIG LOG	Robert Plant (WEA)
11	16	DOUBLE DUTCH	Malcolm McLaren (Charisma)
10	17	THE CROWN	Gary Byrd & the G.B. Experience (Motown)
13	18	THE FIRST PICTURE OF YOU	Lotus Eaters (Sylvan)
15	19	I.O.U.	Freeez (Beggars Banquet)
20	20	TOUR DE FRANCE	Kraftwerk (EMI)
24	21	BAD DAY	Carmel (London)
21	22	WAIT UNTIL TONIGHT	Galaxy featuring Phil Fearon (Ensign)
22	23	LOVE BLONDE	Kim Wilde (RAK)
12	24	RIGHT NOW	Creatures (Wonderland)
14	25	WHEREVER I LAY MY HAT (THAT'S MY HOME)	Paul Young (CBS)
-	26	CONFUSION	New Order (Factory)
-	27	WAKE UP	Danse Society (Society)
-	28	A STEP IN THE RIGHT DIRECTION	Truth (Formation)
28	29	GIVE IT SOME EMOTION	Tracie (Respond)
34	30	DISAPPEARING ACT	Shalamar (Solar)
26	31	LIKE AN ANIMAL	Glove (Wonderland)
-	32	MAMA	Genesis (Virgin/Charisma)
41	33	WHO'S THAT GIRL?	Eurythmics (RCA)
-	34	TONIGHT I CELEBRATE MY LOVE	Peabo Bryson & Roberta Flack (Capitol)
47	35	STREET OF DREAMS	Rainbow (Polydor)
33	36	GUILTY OF LOVE	Whitesnake (Liberty)
-	37	TO A NATION OF ANIMAL LOVERS	Conflict (Crass)
27	38	CRUEL SUMMER	Bananarama (London)
25	39	MOONLIGHT SHADOW	Mike Oldfield (Virgin)
-	40	WARRIORS	Gary Numan (Beggars Banquet)
-	41	ROCK OF AGES	Def Leppard (Vertigo)
-	42	CHANCE	Big Country (Mercury)
-	43	IS IT LOVE	Gang of Four (EMI)
-	44	TREES AND FLOWERS	Strawberry Switchblade (92 Happy Customers)
45	45	LEAN ON ME!	Redskins (CNT)
32	46	BLUE MONDAY	New Order (Factory)
-	47	GIMME ALL YOUR LOVIN'	ZZ Top (Warner Brothers)
-	48	BLUE WORLD	Moody Blues (Threshold)
-	49	WILL YOU STAY TONIGHT	Comsat Angels (Jive)
31	50	THE WALK	Cure (Fiction)

10 September 1983

last week	this week	title	artist (label)
7	1	RED RED WINE	UB40 (DEP International)
3	2	WINGS OF A DOVE	Madness (Stiff)
1	3	GOLD	Spandau Ballet (Reformation)
4	4	GIVE IT UP	KC & the Sunshine Band (Epic)
14	5	WHAT AM I GONNA DO	Rod Stewart (Warner Brothers)
5	6	I'M STILL STANDING	Elton John (Rocket)
2	7	LONG HOT SUMMER	Style Council (Polydor)
26	8	CONFUSION	New Order (Factory)
12	9	THE SUN GOES DOWN (LIVING IT UP)	Level 42 (Polydor)
6	10	CLUB TROPICANA	Wham! (Innervision)
13	11	WALKING IN THE RAIN	Modern Romance (WEA)
21	12	BAD DAY	Carmel (London)
32	13	MAMA	Genesis (Virgin/Charisma)
34	14	TONIGHT I CELEBRATE MY LOVE	Peabo Bryson & Roberta Flack (Capitol)
10	15	WATCHING YOU, WATCHING ME	David Grant (Chrysalis)
42	16	CHANCE	Big Country (Mercury)
11	17	COME DANCING	Kinks (Arista)
9	18	EVERYTHING COUNTS	Depeche Mode (Mute)
8	19	ROCKIT	Herbie Hancock (CBS)
40	20	WARRIORS	Gary Numan (Beggars Banquet)
30	21	DISAPPEARING ACT	Shalamar (Solar)
-	22	NEVER SAY DIE (GIVE A LITTLE BIT MORE)	Cliff Richard (EMI)
15	23	BIG LOG	Robert Plant (WEA)
-	24	CRUSHED BY THE WHEELS OF INDUSTRY	Heaven 17 (Virgin)
28	25	A STEP IN THE RIGHT DIRECTION	Truth (Formation)
16	26	DOUBLE DUTCH	Malcolm McLaren (Charisma)
17	27	THE CROWN	Gary Byrd & the G.B. Experience (Motown)
20	28	TOUR DE FRANCE	Kraftwerk (EMI)
-	29	OL' RAG BLUES	Status Quo (Vertigo)
-	30	DOLCE VITA	Ryan Paris (Carrere)
27	31	WAKE UP	Danse Society (Society)
18	32	THE FIRST PICTURE OF YOU	Lotus Eaters (Sylvan)
24	33	RIGHT NOW	Creatures (Wonderland)
-	34	(SHE'S) SEXY AND 17	Stray Cats (Arista)
-	35	SECRET MESSAGES	Electric Light Orchestra (Jet)
41	36	ROCK OF AGES	Def Leppard (Vertigo)
19	37	I.O.U.	Freeez (Beggars Banquet)
-	38	SHE LOVES YOU	Beatles (Parlophone)
23	39	LOVE BLONDE	Kim Wilde (RAK)
-	40	DON'T CRY	Asia (Geffen)
-	41	HALF THE DAY'S GONE AND WE HAVEN'T EARNED A PENNY	Kenny Lynch (Satril)
-	42	RIDERS ON THE STORM	Annabel Lamb (A&M)
46	43	BLUE MONDAY	New Order (Factory)
31	44	LIKE AN ANIMAL	Glove (Wonderland)
-	45	RACIST FRIEND	Special AKA (2 Tone)
-	46	ONE MIND TWO HEARTS	Paradise (Priority)
47	47	GIMME ALL YOUR LOVIN'	ZZ Top (Warner Brothers)
36	48	GUILTY OF LOVE	Whitesnake (Liberty)
22	49	WAIT UNTIL TONIGHT	Galaxy featuring Phil Fearon (Ensign)
-	50	THERE'S SOMETHING WRONG IN PARADISE	Kid Creole & the Coconuts (Island)

The chart-topping *Red Red Wine*, although adapted by UB40 from the 1969 reggae styling by Tony Tribe, was actually a Neil Diamond song, and a track from his second album in 1968. Former Led Zeppelin vocalist Robert Plant, meanwhile, had a Top 10 hit (something Zeppelin always distained) with the oddly-titled *Big Log*, and the Kinks finally made the chart once again after an 11 year absence.

September – October 1983

17 September 1983

last week	this week	entry
1	1	RED RED WINE UB40 (DEP International)
13	2	MAMA Genesis (Virgin/Charisma)
2	3	WINGS OF A DOVE Madness (Stiff)
5	4	WHAT AM I GONNA DO Rod Stewart (Warner Brothers)
14	5	TONIGHT I CELEBRATE MY LOVE Peabo Bryson & Roberta Flack (Capitol)
8	6	CONFUSION New Order (Factory)
3	7	GOLD Spandau Ballet (Reformation)
9	8	THE SUN GOES DOWN (LIVING IT UP) Level 42 (Polydor)
4	9	GIVE IT UP KC & the Sunshine Band (Epic)
20	10	WARRIORS Gary Numan (Beggars Banquet)
11	11	WALKING IN THE RAIN Modern Romance (WEA)
6	12	I'M STILL STANDING Elton John (Rocket)
16	13	CHANCE Big Country (Mercury)
30	14	DOLCE VITA Ryan Paris (Carrere)
-	15	COME BACK AND STAY Paul Young (CBS)
12	16	BAD DAY Carmel (London)
7	17	LONG HOT SUMMER Style Council (Polydor)
29	18	OL' RAG BLUES Status Quo (Vertigo)
24	19	CRUSHED BY THE WHEELS OF INDUSTRY Heaven 17 (Virgin)
-	20	KARMA CHAMELEON Culture Club (Virgin)
10	21	CLUB TROPICANA Wham! (Innervision)
17	22	COME DANCING Kinks (Arista)
19	23	ROCKIT Herbie Hancock (CBS)
22	24	NEVER SAY DIE (GIVE A LITTLE BIT MORE) Cliff Richard (EMI)
15	25	WATCHING YOU, WATCHING ME David Grant (Chrysalis)
21	26	DISAPPEARING ACT Shalamar (Solar)
-	27	GO DEH YAKA (GO TO THE TOP) Monyaka (Polydor)
31	28	WAKE UP Danse Society (Society)
28	29	TOUR DE FRANCE Kraftwerk (EMI)
18	30	EVERYTHING COUNTS Depeche Mode (Mute)
43	31	BLUE MONDAY New Order (Factory)
-	32	BODY WORK Hot Streak (Polydor)
25	33	A STEP IN THE RIGHT DIRECTION Truth (Formation)
34	34	(SHE'S) SEXY AND 17 Stray Cats (Arista)
46	35	ONE MIND TWO HEARTS Paradise (Priority)
42	36	RIDERS ON THE STORM Annabel Lamb (A&M)
-	37	JOHNNY FRIENDLY Joboxers (RCA)
-	38	WHAT I WANT Dead Or Alive (Epic)
-	39	YOU'RE LOOKIN' HOT TONIGHT Barry Manilow (Arista)
-	40	IT'S RAINING MEN Weather Girls (CBS)
50	41	THERE'S SOMETHING WRONG IN PARADISE Kid Creole & the Coconuts (Island)
23	42	BIG LOG Robert Plant (WEA)
-	43	YOUR DRESS John Foxx (Virgin)
-	44	SUPERMAN (GIOCA JOUER) Black Lace (Flair)
-	45	DR. HECKYLL AND MR. JIVE Men At Work (Epic)
-	46	MIDNIGHT AT THE LOST AND FOUND Meat Loaf (Epic)
-	47	JUST BE GOOD TO ME S.O.S. Band (Tabu)
-	48	TAHITI (FROM "MUTINY ON THE BOUNTY") David Essex (Mercury)
-	49	JUST IN TIME Raw Silk (West End)
-	50	THE SHADOW OF YOUR SMILE D Train (Epic)

24 September 1983

last week	this week	entry
1	1	RED RED WINE UB40 (DEP International)
2	2	MAMA Genesis (Virgin/Charisma)
20	3	KARMA CHAMELEON Culture Club (Virgin)
5	4	TONIGHT I CELEBRATE MY LOVE Peabo Bryson & Roberta Flack (Capitol)
15	5	COME BACK AND STAY Paul Young (CBS)
14	6	DOLCE VITA Ryan Paris (Carrere)
4	7	WHAT AM I GONNA DO Rod Stewart (Warner Brothers)
18	8	OL' RAG BLUES Status Quo (Vertigo)
3	9	WINGS OF A DOVE Madness (Stiff)
19	10	CRUSHED BY THE WHEELS OF INDUSTRY Heaven 17 (Virgin)
11	11	WALKING IN THE RAIN Modern Romance (WEA)
8	12	THE SUN GOES DOWN (LIVING IT UP) Level 42 (Polydor)
13	13	CHANCE Big Country (Mercury)
6	14	CONFUSION New Order (Factory)
24	15	NEVER SAY DIE (GIVE A LITTLE BIT MORE) Cliff Richard (EMI)
-	16	MODERN LOVE David Bowie (EMI America)
12	17	I'M STILL STANDING Elton John (Rocket)
-	18	BIG APPLE Kajagoogoo (EMI)
10	19	WARRIORS Gary Numan (Beggars Banquet)
27	20	GO DEH YAKA (GO TO THE TOP) Monyaka (Polydor)
17	21	LONG HOT SUMMER Style Council (Polydor)
-	22	THIS IS NOT A LOVE SONG Public Image Ltd. (Virgin)
9	23	GIVE IT UP KC & the Sunshine Band (Epic)
7	24	GOLD Spandau Ballet (Reformation)
16	25	BAD DAY Carmel (London)
26	26	WATCHING YOU, WATCHING ME David Grant (Chrysalis)
36	27	RIDERS ON THE STORM Annabel Lamb (A&M)
31	28	BLUE MONDAY New Order (Factory)
21	29	CLUB TROPICANA Wham! (Innervision)
37	30	JOHNNY FRIENDLY Joboxers (RCA)
23	31	ROCKIT Herbie Hancock (CBS)
26	32	DISAPPEARING ACT Shalamar (Solar)
48	33	TAHITI (FROM "MUTINY ON THE BOUNTY") David Essex (Mercury)
32	34	BODY WORK Hot Streak (Polydor)
22	35	COME DANCING Kinks (Arista)
30	36	EVERYTHING COUNTS Depeche Mode (Mute)
34	37	(SHE'S) SEXY AND 17 Stray Cats (Arista)
33	38	A STEP IN THE RIGHT DIRECTION Truth (Formation)
46	39	MIDNIGHT AT THE LOST AND FOUND Meat Loaf (Epic)
-	40	SOUL INSIDE Soft Cell (Some Bizzare)
-	41	WHAT I GOT IS WHAT YOU NEED Unique (Prelude)
41	42	THERE'S SOMETHING WRONG IN PARADISE Kid Creole & the Coconuts (Island)
45	43	DR. HECKYLL AND MR. JIVE Men At Work (Epic)
44	44	SUPERMAN (GIOCA JOUER) Black Lace (Flair)
-	45	REBEL RUN Toyah (Safari)
49	46	JUST IN TIME Raw Silk (West End)
-	47	THE SAFETY DANCE Men Without Hats (Statik)
-	48	TEARS ON THE TELEPHONE Hot Chocolate (RAK)
35	49	ONE MIND TWO HEARTS Paradise (Priority)
-	50	NEW SONG Howard Jones (WEA)

1 October 1983

last week	this week	entry
3	1	KARMA CHAMELEON Culture Club (Virgin)
1	2	RED RED WINE UB40 (DEP International)
5	3	COME BACK AND STAY Paul Young (CBS)
4	4	TONIGHT I CELEBRATE MY LOVE Peabo Bryson & Roberta Flack (Capitol)
2	5	MAMA Genesis (Virgin/Charisma)
16	6	MODERN LOVE David Bowie (EMI America)
6	7	DOLCE VITA Ryan Paris (Carrere)
11	8	WALKING IN THE RAIN Modern Romance (WEA)
8	9	OL' RAG BLUES Status Quo (Vertigo)
13	10	CHANCE Big Country (Mercury)
18	11	BIG APPLE Kajagoogoo (EMI)
28	12	BLUE MONDAY New Order (Factory)
40	13	SOUL INSIDE Soft Cell (Some Bizzare)
20	14	GO DEH YAKA (GO TO THE TOP) Monyaka (Polydor)
7	15	WHAT AM I GONNA DO Rod Stewart (Warner Brothers)
15	16	NEVER SAY DIE (GIVE A LITTLE BIT MORE) Cliff Richard (EMI)
10	17	CRUSHED BY THE WHEELS OF INDUSTRY Heaven 17 (Virgin)
45	18	REBEL RUN Toyah (Safari)
22	19	THIS IS NOT A LOVE SONG Public Image Ltd. (Virgin)
33	20	TAHITI (FROM "MUTINY ON THE BOUNTY") David Essex (Mercury)
9	21	WINGS OF A DOVE Madness (Stiff)
14	22	CONFUSION New Order (Factory)
-	23	DEAR PRUDENCE Siouxsie & the Banshees (Wonderland)
12	24	THE SUN GOES DOWN (LIVING IT UP) Level 42 (Polydor)
34	25	BODY WORK Hot Streak (Polydor)
-	26	68 GUNS Alarm (IRS)
-	27	(YOU SAID) YOU'D GIMME SOME MORE KC & the Sunshine Band (Epic)
41	28	WHAT I GOT IS WHAT YOU NEED Unique (Prelude)
-	29	BLUE HAT FOR A BLUE DAY Nick Heyward (Arista)
-	30	THEY DON'T KNOW Tracey Ullman (Stiff)
24	31	GOLD Spandau Ballet (Reformation)
17	32	I'M STILL STANDING Elton John (Rocket)
44	33	SUPERMAN (GIOCA JOUER) Black Lace (Flair)
-	34	JAM ON REVENGE (THE WIKKI WIKKI SONG) Newcleus (Beckett)
35	35	COME DANCING Kinks (Arista)
27	36	RIDERS ON THE STORM Annabel Lamb (A&M)
-	37	SUPERSTAR Lydia Murdock (Korova)
42	38	THERE'S SOMETHING WRONG IN PARADISE Kid Creole & the Coconuts (Island)
43	39	DR. HECKYLL AND MR. JIVE Men At Work (Epic)
29	40	CLUB TROPICANA Wham! (Innervision)
19	41	WARRIORS Gary Numan (Beggars Banquet)
21	42	LONG HOT SUMMER Style Council (Polydor)
48	43	TEARS ON THE TELEPHONE Hot Chocolate (RAK)
47	44	THE SAFETY DANCE Men Without Hats (Statik)
38	45	A STEP IN THE RIGHT DIRECTION Truth (Formation)
32	46	DISAPPEARING ACT Shalamar (Solar)
39	47	MIDNIGHT AT THE LOST AND FOUND Meat Loaf (Epic)
-	48	UNCONDITIONAL LOVE Donna Summer (Mercury)
-	49	SOMEONE BELONGING TO SOMEONE Bee Gees (RSO)
-	50	BOOGIE DOWN Al Jarreau (WEA)

Genesis' *Mama* was the fourth song of that title to make the Top 20 since the chart began, and the highest-placed yet, peaking at Number Two. It was, however, a new song, different from any of its predecessors (by David Whitfield, Connie Francis and Dave Berry). Ryan Paris' top-tenner *Dolce Vita* originated - appropriately considering the artist's surname - from France, though it was sung in English.

last week	this week	8 October 1983	
1	1	KARMA CHAMELEON	Culture Club (Virgin)
6	2	MODERN LOVE	David Bowie (EMI America)
3	3	COME BACK AND STAY	Paul Young (CBS)
2	4	RED RED WINE	UB40 (DEP International)
4	5	MAMA	Genesis (Virgin/Charisma)
4	6	TONIGHT I CELEBRATE MY LOVE	
			Peabo Bryson & Roberta Flack (Capitol)
12	7	BLUE MONDAY	New Order (Factory)
11	8	BIG APPLE	Kajagoogoo (EMI)
10	9	CHANCE	Big Country (Mercury)
23	10	DEAR PRUDENCE	
			Siouxsie & the Banshees (Wonderland)
19	11	THIS IS NOT A LOVE SONG	
			Public Image Ltd. (Virgin)
7	12	DOLCE VITA	Ryan Paris (Carrere)
13	13	SOUL INSIDE	Soft Cell (Some Bizzare)
9	14	OL' RAG BLUES	Status Quo (Vertigo)
26	15	68 GUNS	Alarm (IRS)
20	16	TAHITI (FROM "MUTINY ON THE BOUNTY")	
			David Essex (Mercury)
14	17	GO DEH YAKA (GO TO THE TOP)	
			Monyaka (Polydor)
8	18	WALKING IN THE RAIN	Modern Romance (WEA)
25	19	BODY WORK	Hot Streak (Polydor)
18	20	REBEL RUN	Toyah (Safari)
-	21	NEW SONG	Howard Jones (WEA)
33	22	SUPERMAN (GIOCA JOUER)	Black Lace (Flair)
-	23	LOVE IN ITSELF.2	Depeche Mode (Mute)
17	24	CRUSHED BY THE WHEELS OF INDUSTRY	
			Heaven 17 (Virgin)
28	25	WHAT I GOT IS WHAT YOU NEED	Unique (Prelude)
30	26	THEY DON'T KNOW	Tracey Ullman (Stiff)
-	27	POP GOES MY LOVE	Freeez (Beggars Banquet)
29	28	BLUE HAT FOR A BLUE DAY	Nick Heyward (Arista)
16	29	NEVER SAY DIE (GIVE A LITTLE BIT MORE)	
			Cliff Richard (EMI)
22	30	CONFUSION	New Order (Factory)
15	31	WHAT AM I GONNA DO	
			Rod Stewart (Warner Brothers)
24	32	THE SUN GOES DOWN (LIVING IT UP)	
			Level 42 (Polydor)
-	33	IN YOUR EYES	George Benson (Warner Brothers)
-	34	(HEY YOU) THE ROCKSTEADY CREW	
			Rocksteady Crew (Charisma/Virgin)
-	35	KISSING WITH CONFIDENCE	
			Will Powers (Island)
-	36	ALL NIGHT LONG (ALL NIGHT)	
			Lionel Richie (Motown)
21	37	WINGS OF A DOVE	Madness (Stiff)
-	38	SONG TO THE SIREN	This Mortal Coil (4AD)
27	39	(YOU SAID) YOU'D GIMME SOME MORE	
			KC & the Sunshine Band (Epic)
37	40	SUPERSTAR	Lydia Murdock (Korova)
39	41	DR. HECKYLL AND MR. JIVE	Men At Work (Epic)
31	42	GOLD	Spandau Ballet (Reformation)
32	43	I'M STILL STANDING	Elton John (Rocket)
47	44	MIDNIGHT AT THE LOST AND FOUND	
			Meat Loaf (Epic)
-	45	YOU DON'T NEED SOMEONE NEW	
			Lotus Eaters (Sylvian)
-	46	KICKER CONSPIRACY	Fall (Rough Trade)
-	47	SHINE	Play Dead (Situation 2)
42	48	LONG HOT SUMMER	Style Council (Polydor)
35	49	COME DANCING	Kinks (Arista)
36	50	RIDERS ON THE STORM	Annabel Lamb (A&M)

		15 October 1983	
1	1	KARMA CHAMELEON	Culture Club (Virgin)
10	2	DEAR PRUDENCE	
			Siouxsie & the Banshees (Wonderland)
2	3	MODERN LOVE	David Bowie (EMI America)
11	4	THIS IS NOT A LOVE SONG	
			Public Image Ltd. (Virgin)
5	5	BLUE MONDAY	New Order (Factory)
4	6	RED RED WINE	UB40 (DEP International)
26	7	THEY DON'T KNOW	Tracey Ullman (Stiff)
16	8	TAHITI (FROM "MUTINY ON THE BOUNTY")	
			David Essex (Mercury)
3	9	COME BACK AND STAY	Paul Young (CBS)
6	10	TONIGHT I CELEBRATE MY LOVE	
			Peabo Bryson & Roberta Flack (Capitol)
21	11	NEW SONG	Howard Jones (WEA)
15	12	68 GUNS	Alarm (IRS)
5	13	MAMA	Genesis (Virgin/Charisma)
22	14	SUPERMAN (GIOCA JOUER)	Black Lace (Flair)
33	15	IN YOUR EYES	George Benson (Warner Brothers)
9	16	CHANCE	Big Country (Mercury)
8	17	BIG APPLE	Kajagoogoo (EMI)
23	18	LOVE IN ITSELF.2	Depeche Mode (Mute)
17	19	GO DEH YAKA (GO TO THE TOP)	
			Monyaka (Polydor)
12	20	DOLCE VITA	Ryan Paris (Carrere)
28	21	BLUE HAT FOR A BLUE DAY	Nick Heyward (Arista)
14	22	OL' RAG BLUES	Status Quo (Vertigo)
19	23	BODY WORK	Hot Streak (Polydor)
34	24	(HEY YOU) THE ROCKSTEADY CREW	
			Rocksteady Crew (Charisma/Virgin)
13	25	SOUL INSIDE	Soft Cell (Some Bizzare)
36	26	ALL NIGHT LONG (ALL NIGHT)	
			Lionel Richie (Motown)
25	27	WHAT I GOT IS WHAT YOU NEED	Unique (Prelude)
18	28	WALKING IN THE RAIN	Modern Romance (WEA)
-	29	LOVE WILL FIND A WAY	
			David Grant (Chrysalis)
27	30	POP GOES MY LOVE	Freeez (Beggars Banquet)
24	31	CRUSHED BY THE WHEELS OF INDUSTRY	
			Heaven 17 (Virgin)
44	32	MIDNIGHT AT THE LOST AND FOUND	
			Meat Loaf (Epic)
33	33	SAY SAY SAY	Paul McCartney
			& Michael Jackson (Parlophone)
35	34	KISSING WITH CONFIDENCE	Will Powers (Island)
-	35	AUTODRIVE	Herbie Hancock (CBS)
46	36	KICKER CONSPIRACY	Fall (Rough Trade)
-	37	THE SAFETY DANCE	Men Without Hats (Statik)
20	38	REBEL RUN	Toyah (Safari)
-	39	JINX	Peter & the Test Tube Babies (Trapper)
29	40	NEVER SAY DIE (GIVE A LITTLE BIT MORE)	
			Cliff Richard (EMI)
-	41	TEMPLE OF LOVE	
			Sisters of Mercy (Merciful Release)
-	42	TEDDY BEAR	Booker Newbury III (Polydor)
43	43	YOU REALLY GOT ME	Kinks (PRT)
-	44	ZULU BEAT	King Kurt (Thin Sliced)
43	45	I'M STILL STANDING	Elton John (Rocket)
31	46	WHAT AM I GONNA DO	
			Rod Stewart (Warner Brothers)
32	47	THE SUN GOES DOWN (LIVING IT UP)	
			Level 42 (Polydor)
-	48	ME OR YOU (EP)	Killing Joke (Polydor)
40	49	SUPERSTAR	Lydia Murdock (Korova)
-	50	TEARS ON THE TELEPHONE	
			Hot Chocolate (RAK)

		22 October 1983	
1	1	KARMA CHAMELEON	Culture Club (Virgin)
7	2	THEY DON'T KNOW	Tracey Ullman (Stiff)
2	3	DEAR PRUDENCE	
			Siouxsie & the Banshees (Wonderland)
11	4	NEW SONG	Howard Jones (WEA)
5	5	BLUE MONDAY	New Order (Factory)
3	6	MODERN LOVE	David Bowie (EMI America)
15	7	IN YOUR EYES	George Benson (Warner Brothers)
4	8	THIS IS NOT A LOVE SONG	
			Public Image Ltd. (Virgin)
24	9	(HEY YOU) THE ROCKSTEADY CREW	
			Rocksteady Crew (Charisma/Virgin)
14	10	SUPERMAN (GIOCA JOUER)	Black Lace (Flair)
26	11	ALL NIGHT LONG (ALL NIGHT)	
			Lionel Richie (Motown)
8	12	TAHITI (FROM "MUTINY ON THE BOUNTY")	
			David Essex (Mercury)
33	13	SAY SAY SAY	Paul McCartney
			& Michael Jackson (Parlophone)
13	14	MAMA	Genesis (Virgin/Charisma)
12	15	68 GUNS	Alarm (IRS)
6	16	RED RED WINE	UB40 (DEP International)
21	17	BLUE HAT FOR A BLUE DAY	Nick Heyward (Arista)
-	18	PLEASE DON'T MAKE ME CRY	
			UB40 (DEP International)
9	19	COME BACK AND STAY	Paul Young (CBS)
32	20	MIDNIGHT AT THE LOST AND FOUND	
			Meat Loaf (Epic)
37	21	THE SAFETY DANCE	Men Without Hats (Statik)
10	22	TONIGHT I CELEBRATE MY LOVE	
			Peabo Bryson & Roberta Flack (Capitol)
-	23	KISS THE BRIDE	Elton John (Rocket)
18	24	LOVE IN ITSELF.2	Depeche Mode (Mute)
29	25	LOVE WILL FIND A WAY	David Grant (Chrysalis)
49	26	SUPERSTAR	Lydia Murdock (Korova)
30	27	POP GOES MY LOVE	Freeez (Beggars Banquet)
34	28	KISSING WITH CONFIDENCE	
			Will Powers (Island)
-	29	OVER AND OVER	Shalamar (Solar)
35	30	AUTODRIVE	Herbie Hancock (CBS)
17	31	BIG APPLE	Kajagoogoo (EMI)
20	32	DOLCE VITA	Ryan Paris (Carrere)
33	33	DESTINATION ZULU LAND	King Kurt (Stiff)
16	34	CHANCE	Big Country (Mercury)
48	35	ME OR YOU (EP)	Killing Joke (Polydor)
41	36	TEMPLE OF LOVE	
			Sisters of Mercy (Merciful Release)
19	37	GO DEH YAKA (GO TO THE TOP)	
			Monyaka (Polydor)
-	38	UPTOWN GIRL	Billy Joel (CBS)
44	39	ZULU BEAT	King Kurt (Thin Sliced)
-	40	SONG TO THE SIREN	This Mortal Coil (4AD)
-	41	DANCE WITH ME	
			Lords Of The New Church (I.R.S.)
42	42	TEDDY BEAR	Booker Newbury III (Polydor)
-	43	UNCONDITIONAL LOVE	Donna Summer (Mercury)
-	44	LONDON TOWN	Bucks Fizz (RCA)
-	45	LOVE REACTION	
			Divine (Design Communications)
-	46	I WANT YOU (ALL TONIGHT)	
			Curtis Hairston (RCA)
47	47	LOVE ON A FARMBOY'S WAGES	XTC (Virgin)
45	48	I'M STILL STANDING	Elton John (Rocket)
22	49	OL' RAG BLUES	Status Quo (Vertigo)
-	50	WORKING WITH FIRE AND STEEL	
			China Crisis (Virgin)

Culture Club's *Karma Chameleon* was 1983's biggest-selling single, and also the group's top seller by far – in fact, its 1,400,000 sales made it the seventh biggest-selling hit of the 1980s. Siouxsie & The Banshees chased it closely for a week with their version of Lennon & McCartney's *Dear Prudence*, originally from the 1968 *White Album*, and one of the least-covered of all the Beatles' songs.

403

October – November 1983

Union Of The Snake utilised one of the first of Duran Duran's celebrated mega-budget fantasy videos, though this did not succeed in pushing it higher than Number Three. Beating it to the top was Billy Joel's affectionate pastiche of Frankie Valli & the Four Seasons, taken from his highly successful album *An Innocent Man*, which contained several such tributes to Joel's own roots and influences.

November – December 1983

19 November 1983

last week	this week	Title	Artist (Label)
1	1	UPTOWN GIRL	Billy Joel (CBS)
2	2	ALL NIGHT LONG (ALL NIGHT)	Lionel Richie (Motown)
14	3	SAY SAY SAY	Paul McCartney & Michael Jackson (Parlophone)
6	4	PUSS 'N BOOTS	Adam Ant (CBS)
13	5	CRY JUST A LITTLE BIT	Shakin' Stevens (Epic)
11	6	THE SUN AND THE RAIN	Madness (Stiff)
9	7	THE LOVE CATS	Cure (Fiction)
5	8	THE SAFETY DANCE	Men Without Hats (Statik)
3	9	UNION OF THE SNAKE	Duran Duran (EMI)
23	10	UNDERCOVER OF THE NIGHT	Rolling Stones (Rolling Stones)
4	11	KARMA CHAMELEON	Culture Club (Virgin)
15	12	THAT WAS THEN BUT THIS IS NOW	ABC (Neutron)
16	13	A MESS OF BLUES	Status Quo (Vertigo)
10	14	PLEASE DON'T MAKE ME CRY	UB40 (DEP International)
18	15	SYNCHRONICITY II	Police (A&M)
45	16	NEVER NEVER	Assembly (Mute)
30	17	UNCONDITIONAL LOVE	Donna Summer (Mercury)
7	18	THEY DON'T KNOW	Tracey Ullman (Stiff)
28	19	LOVE WILL TEAR US APART	Joy Division (Factory)
37	20	ONLY FOR LOVE	Limahl (EMI)
8	21	(HEY YOU) THE ROCKSTEADY CREW	Rocksteady Crew (Charisma/Virgin)
24	22	RIGHT BY YOUR SIDE	Eurythmics (RCA)
12	23	NEW SONG	Howard Jones (WEA)
44	24	OWNER OF A LONELY HEART	Yes (Atco)
36	25	CALLING YOUR NAME	Marilyn (Mercury)
-	26	A SOLID BOND IN YOUR HEART	Style Council (Polydor)
38	27	THIS CHARMING MAN	Smiths (Rough Trade)
19	28	BLUE MONDAY	New Order (Factory)
43	29	OBLIVIOUS	Aztec Camera (Rough Trade)
46	30	007	Musical Youth (MCA)
22	31	IN YOUR EYES	George Benson (Warner Brothers)
27	32	HEAVEN IS WAITING	Danse Society (Society)
-	33	LISTEN TO THE RADIO: ATMOSPHERICS	Tom Robinson & Crew (Panic)
39	34	LICK IT UP	Kiss (Vertigo)
21	35	KISSING WITH CONFIDENCE	Will Powers (Island)
17	36	KISS THE BRIDE	Elton John (Rocket)
-	37	LOVE OF THE COMMON PEOPLE	Paul Young (CBS)
40	38	STARFLEET	Brian May (EMI)
33	39	RED RED WINE	UB40 (DEP International)
-	40	SONG TO THE SIREN	This Mortal Coil (4AD)
31	41	THE SINGLES 1981-83	Bauhaus (Beggars Banquet)
26	42	SUPERSTAR	Lydia Murdock (Korova)
-	43	THAT'S ALL	Genesis (Charisma/Virgin)
35	44	THIS IS NOT A LOVE SONG	Public Image Ltd. (Virgin)
41	45	GUNS FOR HIRE	AC/DC (Atlantic)
-	46	THANK YOU FOR THE MUSIC	Abba (CBS)
-	47	ALL MY LIFE	Major Harris (London)
-	48	THRILLER	Michael Jackson (Epic)
-	49	TILL I CAN'T TAKE LOVE NO MORE	Eddy Grant (Ice)
-	50	SAY IT ISN'T SO	Daryl Hall & John Oates (RCA)

26 November 1983

last week	this week	Title	Artist (Label)
1	1	UPTOWN GIRL	Billy Joel (CBS)
3	2	SAY SAY SAY	Paul McCartney & Michael Jackson (Parlophone)
5	3	CRY JUST A LITTLE BIT	Shakin' Stevens (Epic)
2	4	ALL NIGHT LONG (ALL NIGHT)	Lionel Richie (Motown)
6	5	THE SUN AND THE RAIN	Madness (Stiff)
16	6	NEVER NEVER	Assembly (Mute)
26	7	A SOLID BOND IN YOUR HEART	Style Council (Polydor)
7	8	THE LOVE CATS	Cure (Fiction)
4	9	PUSS 'N BOOTS	Adam Ant (CBS)
10	10	UNDERCOVER OF THE NIGHT	Rolling Stones (Rolling Stones)
37	11	LOVE OF THE COMMON PEOPLE	Paul Young (CBS)
8	12	THE SAFETY DANCE	Men Without Hats (Statik)
11	13	KARMA CHAMELEON	Culture Club (Virgin)
48	14	THRILLER	Michael Jackson (Epic)
17	15	UNCONDITIONAL LOVE	Donna Summer (Mercury)
19	16	LOVE WILL TEAR US APART	Joy Division (Factory)
25	17	CALLING YOUR NAME	Marilyn (Mercury)
20	18	ONLY FOR LOVE	Limahl (EMI)
18	19	UNION OF THE SNAKE	Duran Duran (EMI)
13	20	A MESS OF BLUES	Status Quo (Vertigo)
12	21	THAT WAS THEN BUT THIS IS NOW	ABC (Neutron)
29	22	OBLIVIOUS	Aztec Camera (Rough Trade)
-	23	HOLD ME NOW	Thompson Twins (Arista)
22	24	RIGHT BY YOUR SIDE	Eurythmics (RCA)
14	25	PLEASE DON'T MAKE ME CRY	UB40 (DEP International)
-	26	LET'S STAY TOGETHER	Tina Turner (Capitol)
27	27	THIS CHARMING MAN	Smiths (Rough Trade)
43	28	THAT'S ALL	Genesis (Charisma/Virgin)
-	29	WATERFRONT	Simple Minds (Virgin)
15	30	SYNCHRONICITY II	Police (A&M)
21	31	(HEY YOU) THE ROCKSTEADY CREW	Rocksteady Crew (Charisma/Virgin)
24	32	OWNER OF A LONELY HEART	Yes (Atco)
-	33	LISTEN TO THE MUSIC PLAY	Shannon (Club)
-	34	BARK AT THE MOON	Ozzy Osbourne (Epic)
28	35	BLUE MONDAY	New Order (Factory)
18	36	THEY DON'T KNOW	Tracey Ullman (Stiff)
-	37	WHAT IS LOVE?	Howard Jones (WEA)
32	38	HEAVEN IS WAITING	Danse Society (Society)
-	39	DRESSING UP	Street Angels (Street Beat)
46	40	THANK YOU FOR THE MUSIC	Abba (CBS)
-	41	WHITE LINES (DON'T DO IT)	Grandmaster Flash (Sugarhill)
-	42	HAPPINESS IS JUST AROUND THE BEND	Cuba Gooding (Streetwise)
30	43	007	Musical Youth (MCA)
-	44	ISLANDS IN THE STREAM	Kenny Rogers & Dolly Parton (RCA)
31	45	IN YOUR EYES	George Benson (Warner Brothers)
-	46	FLAMING SWORD	Care (Arista)
33	47	LISTEN TO THE RADIO : ATMOSPHERICS	Tom Robinson & Crew (Panic)
36	48	KISS THE BRIDE	Elton John (Rocket)
-	49	REILLY	Olympic Orchestra (Red Bus)
-	50	MY OH MY	Slade (RCA)

3 December 1983

last week	this week	Title	Artist (Label)
6	1	NEVER NEVER	Assembly (Mute)
1	2	UPTOWN GIRL	Billy Joel (CBS)
2	3	SAY SAY SAY	Paul McCartney & Michael Jackson (Parlophone)
3	4	CRY JUST A LITTLE BIT	Shakin' Stevens (Epic)
11	5	LOVE OF THE COMMON PEOPLE	Paul Young (CBS)
14	6	THRILLER	Michael Jackson (Epic)
7	7	THE LOVE CATS	Cure (Fiction)
8	8	A SOLID BOND IN YOUR HEART	Style Council (Polydor)
17	9	CALLING YOUR NAME	Marilyn (Mercury)
5	10	THE SUN AND THE RAIN	Madness (Stiff)
26	11	LET'S STAY TOGETHER	Tina Turner (Capitol)
4	12	ALL NIGHT LONG (ALL NIGHT)	Lionel Richie (Motown)
23	13	HOLD ME NOW	Thompson Twins (Arista)
24	14	RIGHT BY YOUR SIDE	Eurythmics (RCA)
29	15	WATERFRONT	Simple Minds (Virgin)
22	16	OBLIVIOUS	Aztec Camera (Rough Trade)
9	17	PUSS 'N BOOTS	Adam Ant (CBS)
10	18	UNDERCOVER OF THE NIGHT	Rolling Stones (Rolling Stones)
27	19	THIS CHARMING MAN	Smiths (Rough Trade)
16	20	LOVE WILL TEAR US APART	Joy Division (Factory)
-	21	ONLY YOU	Flying Pickets (10)
-	22	THAT'S LOVE THAT IT IS	Blancmange (London)
34	23	BARK AT THE MOON	Ozzy Osbourne (Epic)
-	24	RUNNING WITH THE NIGHT	Lionel Richie (Motown)
25	25	THAT'S ALL	Genesis (Charisma/Virgin)
12	26	THE SAFETY DANCE	Men Without Hats (Statik)
-	27	PLEASE DON'T FALL IN LOVE	Cliff Richard (EMI)
32	28	OWNER OF A LONELY HEART	Yes (Atco)
20	29	A MESS OF BLUES	Status Quo (Vertigo)
13	30	KARMA CHAMELEON	Culture Club (Virgin)
18	31	ONLY FOR LOVE	Limahl (EMI)
37	32	WHAT IS LOVE?	Howard Jones (WEA)
-	33	2000 MILES	Pretenders (Real)
50	34	MY OH MY	Slade (RCA)
-	35	SHARP DRESSED MAN	ZZ Top (Warner Brothers)
-	36	I'M OUT OF YOUR LIFE	Arnie's Love (Streetwave)
15	37	UNCONDITIONAL LOVE	Donna Summer (Mercury)
21	38	THAT WAS THEN BUT THIS IS NOW	ABC (Neutron)
19	39	UNION OF THE SNAKE	Duran Duran (EMI)
31	40	(HEY YOU) THE ROCKSTEADY CREW	Rocksteady Crew (Charisma/Virgin)
47	41	LISTEN TO THE RADIO : ATMOSPHERICS	Tom Robinson & Crew (Panic)
-	42	SUNBURST AND SNOWBLIND	Cocteau Twins (4AD)
-	43	RELAX	Frankie Goes To Hollywood (ZTT)
25	44	PLEASE DON'T MAKE ME CRY	UB40 (DEP International)
33	45	LET THE MUSIC PLAY	Shannon (Club)
35	46	BLUE MONDAY	New Order (Factory)
49	47	REILLY	Olympic Orchestra (Red Bus)
44	48	ISLANDS IN THE STREAM	Kenny Rogers & Dolly Parton (RCA)
-	49	READY STEADY WHO (EP)	Who (Reaction)
-	50	MOVE OVER DARLING	Tracey Ullman (Stiff)

Paul McCartney's duet with Michael Jackson on *Say Say Say* was the second of their collaboartions, following the previous year's Top 5 hit *The Girl Is Mine*. Presumably as a condition of the reciprocal agreement, the earlier single had been on Jackson's label, Epic, and billed him first. *Say Say Say* reversed the billing, and appeared on McCartney's label, Parlophone – as had his duet with Stevie Wonder.

December 1983

10 December 1983

last	this	Title	Artist (Label)
5	1	LOVE OF THE COMMON PEOPLE	Paul Young (CBS)
21	2	ONLY YOU	Flying Pickets (10)
9	3	CALLING YOUR NAME	Marilyn (Mercury)
11	4	LET'S STAY TOGETHER	Tina Turner (Capitol)
2	5	UPTOWN GIRL	Billy Joel (CBS)
13	6	HOLD ME NOW	Thompson Twins (Arista)
1	7	NEVER NEVER	Assembly (Mute)
3	8	SAY SAY SAY	Paul McCartney & Michael Jackson (Parlophone)
15	9	WATERFRONT	Simple Minds (Virgin)
34	10	MY OH MY	Slade (RCA)
14	11	RIGHT BY YOUR SIDE	Eurythmics (RCA)
6	12	THRILLER	Michael Jackson (Epic)
4	13	CRY JUST A LITTLE BIT	Shakin' Stevens (Epic)
50	14	MOVE OVER DARLING	Tracey Ullman (Stiff)
8	15	A SOLID BOND IN YOUR HEART	Style Council (Polydor)
16	16	OBLIVIOUS	Aztec Camera (Rough Trade)
27	17	PLEASE DON'T FALL IN LOVE	Cliff Richard (EMI)
7	18	THE LOVE CATS	Cure (Fiction)
19	19	THIS CHARMING MAN	Smiths (Rough Trade)
-	20	CLUB FANTASTIC MEGAMIX	Wham! (Innervision)
23	21	BARK AT THE MOON	Ozzy Osbourne (Epic)
-	22	TELL HER ABOUT IT	Billy Joel (CBS)
-	23	VICTIMS	Culture Club (Virgin)
24	24	RUNNING WITH THE NIGHT	Lionel Richie (Motown)
48	25	ISLANDS IN THE STREAM	Kenny Rogers & Dolly Parton (RCA)
18	26	UNDERCOVER OF THE NIGHT	Rolling Stones (Rolling Stones)
25	27	THAT'S ALL	Genesis (Charisma/Virgin)
10	28	THE SUN AND THE RAIN	Madness (Stiff)
32	29	WHAT IS LOVE?	Howard Jones (WEA)
28	30	OWNER OF A LONELY HEART	Yes (Atco)
42	31	SUNBURST AND SNOWBLIND	Cocteau Twins (4AD)
-	32	METAL HEALTH	Quiet Riot (Epic)
12	33	ALL NIGHT LONG (ALL NIGHT)	Lionel Richie (Motown)
20	34	LOVE WILL TEAR US APART	Joy Division (Factory)
17	35	PUSS 'N BOOTS	Adam Ant (CBS)
22	36	THAT'S LOVE THAT IT IS	Blancmange (London)
-	37	THE WAY YOU ARE	Tears For Fears (Mercury)
-	38	RAT RAPPING	Roland Rat Superstar (Rodent)
-	39	MUTINY 1983	Birthday Party (Mute)
-	40	WHERE IS MY MAN	Eartha Kitt (Record Shack)
30	41	KARMA CHAMELEON	Culture Club (Virgin)
26	42	THE SAFETY DANCE	Men Without Hats (Statik)
33	43	2000 MILES	Pretenders (Real)
-	44	ROCK THE MIDNIGHT	David Grant (Chrysalis)
-	45	MY MELANCHOLY BABY	Chas & Dave (Rockney)
-	46	THANK YOU FOR THE MUSIC	Abba (CBS)
35	47	SHARP DRESSED MAN	ZZ Top (Warner Brothers)
-	48	THE VOW	Toyah (Safari)
-	49	MARGUERITA TIME	Status Quo (Vertigo)
-	50	ON A SUNDAY	Nick Heyward (Arista)

17 December 1983

last	this	Title	Artist (Label)
2	1	ONLY YOU	Flying Pickets (10)
1	2	LOVE OF THE COMMON PEOPLE	Paul Young (CBS)
10	3	MY OH MY	Slade (RCA)
6	4	HOLD ME NOW	Thompson Twins (Arista)
4	5	LET'S STAY TOGETHER	Tina Turner (Capitol)
14	6	MOVE OVER DARLING	Tracey Ullman (Stiff)
23	7	VICTIMS	Culture Club (Virgin)
5	8	UPTOWN GIRL	Billy Joel (CBS)
3	9	CALLING YOUR NAME	Marilyn (Mercury)
17	10	PLEASE DON'T FALL IN LOVE	Cliff Richard (EMI)
12	11	THRILLER	Michael Jackson (Epic)
7	12	NEVER NEVER	Assembly (Mute)
9	13	WATERFRONT	Simple Minds (Virgin)
11	14	RIGHT BY YOUR SIDE	Eurythmics (RCA)
22	15	TELL HER ABOUT IT	Billy Joel (CBS)
25	16	ISLANDS IN THE STREAM	Kenny Rogers & Dolly Parton (RCA)
20	17	CLUB FANTASTIC MEGAMIX	Wham! (Innervision)
8	18	SAY SAY SAY	Paul McCartney & Michael Jackson (Parlophone)
13	19	CRY JUST A LITTLE BIT	Shakin' Stevens (Epic)
16	20	OBLIVIOUS	Aztec Camera (Rough Trade)
21	21	BARK AT THE MOON	Ozzy Osbourne (Epic)
27	22	THAT'S ALL	Genesis (Charisma/Virgin)
19	23	THIS CHARMING MAN	Smiths (Rough Trade)
29	24	WHAT IS LOVE?	Howard Jones (WEA)
49	25	MARGUERITA TIME	Status Quo (Vertigo)
15	26	A SOLID BOND IN YOUR HEART	Style Council (Polydor)
24	27	RUNNING WITH THE NIGHT	Lionel Richie (Motown)
-	28	MANY RIVERS TO CROSS	UB40 (DEP International)
-	29	READ 'EM AND WEEP	Barry Manilow (Arista)
43	30	2000 MILES	Pretenders (Real)
38	31	RAT RAPPING	Roland Rat Superstar (Rodent)
18	32	THE LOVE CATS	Cure (Fiction)
37	33	THE WAY YOU ARE	Tears For Fears (Mercury)
-	34	PIPES OF PEACE	Paul McCartney (Parlophone)
31	35	SUNBURST AND SNOWBLIND	Cocteau Twins (4AD)
36	36	THAT'S LOVE THAT IT IS	Blancmange (London)
41	37	KARMA CHAMELEON	Culture Club (Virgin)
-	38	COLD AS CHRISTMAS	Elton John (Rocket)
32	39	METAL HEALTH	Quiet Riot (Epic)
40	40	WHERE IS MY MAN	Eartha Kitt (Record Shack)
30	41	OWNER OF A LONELY HEART	Yes (Atco)
28	42	THE SUN AND THE RAIN	Madness (Stiff)
39	43	MUTINY 1983	Birthday Party (Mute)
45	44	MY MELANCHOLY BABY	Chas & Dave (Rockney)
26	45	UNDERCOVER OF THE NIGHT	Rolling Stones (Rolling Stones)
-	46	I'M OUT OF YOUR LIFE	Arnie's Love (Streetwave)
47	47	MERRY XMAS EVERYBODY	Slade (Polydor)
-	48	I CAN HELP	Elvis Presley (RCA)
-	49	SINGALONG-A-SANTA AGAIN	Santa Claus & the Christmas Trees (Polydor)
-	50	SWEET SURRENDER	Rod Stewart (Warner Brothers)

24 December 1983

last	this	Title	Artist (Label)
1	1	ONLY YOU	Flying Pickets (10)
7	2	VICTIMS	Culture Club (Virgin)
3	3	MY OH MY	Slade (RCA)
2	4	LOVE OF THE COMMON PEOPLE	Paul Young (CBS)
4	5	HOLD ME NOW	Thompson Twins (Arista)
5	6	LET'S STAY TOGETHER	Tina Turner (Capitol)
10	7	PLEASE DON'T FALL IN LOVE	Cliff Richard (EMI)
15	8	TELL HER ABOUT IT	Billy Joel (CBS)
6	9	MOVE OVER DARLING	Tracey Ullman (Stiff)
16	10	ISLANDS IN THE STREAM	Kenny Rogers & Dolly Parton (RCA)
24	11	WHAT IS LOVE?	Howard Jones (WEA)
11	12	THRILLER	Michael Jackson (Epic)
8	13	UPTOWN GIRL	Billy Joel (CBS)
29	14	READ 'EM AND WEEP	Barry Manilow (Arista)
17	15	CLUB FANTASTIC MEGAMIX	Wham! (Innervision)
25	16	MARGUERITA TIME	Status Quo (Vertigo)
9	17	CALLING YOUR NAME	Marilyn (Mercury)
22	18	THAT'S ALL	Genesis (Charisma/Virgin)
13	19	WATERFRONT	Simple Minds (Virgin)
30	20	2000 MILES	Pretenders (Real)
28	21	MANY RIVERS TO CROSS	UB40 (DEP International)
14	22	RIGHT BY YOUR SIDE	Eurythmics (RCA)
19	23	CRY JUST A LITTLE BIT	Shakin' Stevens (Epic)
12	24	NEVER NEVER	Assembly (Mute)
47	25	MERRY XMAS EVERYBODY	Slade (Polydor)
34	26	PIPES OF PEACE	Paul McCartney (Parlophone)
18	27	SAY SAY SAY	Paul McCartney & Michael Jackson (Parlophone)
20	28	OBLIVIOUS	Aztec Camera (Rough Trade)
23	29	THIS CHARMING MAN	Smiths (Rough Trade)
-	30	STRAIGHT AHEAD	Kool & the Gang (De-Lite)
31	31	RAT RAPPING	Roland Rat Superstar (Rodent)
21	32	BARK AT THE MOON	Ozzy Osbourne (Epic)
27	33	RUNNING WITH THE NIGHT	Lionel Richie (Motown)
38	34	COLD AS CHRISTMAS	Elton John (Rocket)
50	35	SWEET SURRENDER	Rod Stewart (Warner Brothers)
33	36	THE WAY YOU ARE	Tears For Fears (Mercury)
40	37	WHERE IS MY MAN	Eartha Kitt (Record Shack)
-	38	CHRISTMAS SPECTRE	Jingle Belles (Passion)
35	39	SUNBURST AND SNOWBLIND	Cocteau Twins (4AD)
-	40	WHAT ARE WE GONNA GET 'ER INDOORS	Dennis Waterman & George Cole (EMI)
36	41	THAT'S LOVE THAT IT IS	Blancmange (London)
49	42	SINGALONG-A-SANTA AGAIN	Santa Claus & the Christmas Trees (Polydor)
43	43	MUTINY 1983	Birthday Party (Mute)
-	44	THERE AIN'T NO SANITY CLAUSE	Damned (Big Bear)
32	45	THE LOVE CATS	Cure (Fiction)
37	46	KARMA CHAMELEON	Culture Club (Virgin)
45	47	UNDERCOVER OF THE NIGHT	Rolling Stones (Rolling Stones)
-	48	PRIDE OF SILENCE	Discharge (Clay)
48	49	I CAN HELP	Elvis Presley (RCA)
-	50	TIME	Frida/B.A. Robertson (Epic)

The Flying Pickets' *Only You* was an acapella (no intrumental accompaniment) rendition of Yazoo's first hit, an early revival of a song which had only been in the chart itself 18 months earlier. Wham!, meanwhile, deeply in dispute with their label Innervision, were incensed by the appearance of the *Club Fantastic Megamix*, which was merely stitched-together portions from their earlier singles.

Techno-Pop

Musicians had been dabbling with synthesisers and electronic instruments for years, sometimes – as with Norman Greenbaum's 'Spirit In The Sky' – with great results. But Gary Numan really ushered in the age of Techno-Pop with 'Are Friends Electric', which went to Number One in 1979. Along came some people who really knew how to create great pop records using electronic wizardry. This was music for the electronic age – and classic pop.

Clockwise from top left: Gary Numan; Marc Almond, originally half of Soft Cell; the public face of Kraftwerk; Eurythmics

January 1984

7 January 1984

last	this	title	artist
1	1	ONLY YOU	Flying Pickets (10)
3	2	MY OH MY	Slade (RCA)
2	3	VICTIMS	Culture Club (Virgin)
10	4	ISLANDS IN THE STREAM	Kenny Rogers & Dolly Parton (RCA)
8	5	TELL HER ABOUT IT	Billy Joel (CBS)
16	6	MARGUERITA TIME	Status Quo (Vertigo)
4	7	LOVE OF THE COMMON PEOPLE	Paul Young (CBS)
5	8	HOLD ME NOW	Thompson Twins (Arista)
6	9	LET'S STAY TOGETHER	Tina Turner (Capitol)
20	10	2000 MILES	Pretenders (Real)
11	11	WHAT IS LOVE?	Howard Jones (WEA)
9	12	MOVE OVER DARLING	Tracey Ullman (Stiff)
12	13	THRILLER	Michael Jackson (Epic)
7	14	PLEASE DON'T FALL IN LOVE	Cliff Richard (EMI)
26	15	PIPES OF PEACE	Paul McCartney (Parlophone)
14	16	READ 'EM AND WEEP	Barry Manilow (Arista)
25	17	MERRY XMAS EVERYBODY	Slade (Polydor)
21	18	MANY RIVERS TO CROSS	UB40 (DEP International)
18	19	THAT'S ALL	Genesis (Charisma/Virgin)
-	20	CHRISTMAS COUNTDOWN	Frank Kelly (Ritz)
30	21	STRAIGHT AHEAD	Kool & the Gang (De-Lite)
19	22	WATERFRONT	Simple Minds (Virgin)
15	23	CLUB FANTASTIC MEGAMIX	Wham! (Innervision)
31	24	RAT RAPPING	Roland Rat Superstar (Rodent)
40	25	WHAT ARE WE GONNA DO WITH 'ER INDOORS	Dennis Waterman & George Cole (EMI)
13	26	UPTOWN GIRL	Billy Joel (CBS)
17	27	CALLING YOUR NAME	Marilyn (Mercury)
34	28	COLD AS CHRISTMAS	Elton John (Rocket)
-	29	COME TO NEVER	Keith Harris & Orville (BBC)
29	30	THIS CHARMING MAN	Smiths (Rough Trade)
-	31	RELAX	Frankie Goes To Hollywood (ZTT)
37	32	WHERE IS MY MAN	Eartha Kitt (Record Shack)
46	33	KARMA CHAMELEON	Culture Club (Virgin)
38	34	CHRISTMAS SPECTRE	Jingle Belles (Passion)
27	35	SAY SAY SAY	Paul McCartney & Michael Jackson (Parlophone)
35	36	SWEET SURRENDER	Rod Stewart (Warner Bros)
24	37	NEVER NEVER	Assembly (Mute)
36	38	THE WAY YOU ARE	Tears For Fears (Mercury)
33	39	RUNNING WITH THE NIGHT	Lionel Richie (Motown)
32	40	BARK AT THE MOON	Ozzy Osbourne (Epic)
43	41	MUTINY 1983	Birthday Party (Mute)
48	42	PRIDE OF SILENCE	Discharge (Clay)
39	43	SUNBURST AND SNOWBLIND	Cocteau Twins (4AD)
23	44	CRY JUST A LITTLE BIT	Shakin' Stevens (Epic)
22	45	RIGHT BY YOUR SIDE	Eurythmics (RCA)
42	46	SINGALONG-A-SANTA AGAIN	Santa Claus & the Christmas Trees (Polydor)
50	47	TIME	Frida & B.A. Robertson (Epic)
49	48	I CAN HELP	Elvis Presley (RCA)
-	49	I BELIEVE IN FATHER CHRISTMAS	Greg Lake (Manticore)
-	50	BIRD OF PARADISE	Snowy White (Towerbell)

14 January 1984

last	this	title	artist
1	1	ONLY YOU	Flying Pickets (10)
7	2	LOVE OF THE COMMON PEOPLE	Paul Young (CBS)
3	3	VICTIMS	Culture Club (Virgin)
5	4	TELL HER ABOUT IT	Billy Joel (CBS)
2	5	MY OH MY	Slade (RCA)
15	6	PIPES OF PEACE	Paul McCartney (Parlophone)
6	7	MARGUERITA TIME	Status Quo (Vertigo)
11	8	WHAT IS LOVE?	Howard Jones (WEA)
9	9	HOLD ME NOW	Thompson Twins (Arista)
13	10	THRILLER	Michael Jackson (Epic)
4	11	ISLANDS IN THE STREAM	Kenny Rogers & Dolly Parton (RCA)
9	12	LET'S STAY TOGETHER	Tina Turner (Capitol)
10	13	2000 MILES	Pretenders (Real)
18	14	MANY RIVERS TO CROSS	UB40 (DEP International)
21	15	STRAIGHT AHEAD	Kool & the Gang (De-Lite)
14	16	PLEASE DON'T FALL IN LOVE	Cliff Richard (EMI)
12	17	MOVE OVER DARLING	Tracey Ullman (Stiff)
50	18	BIRD OF PARADISE	Snowy White (Towerbell)
26	19	UPTOWN GIRL	Billy Joel (CBS)
20	20	CHRISTMAS COUNTDOWN	Frank Kelly (Ritz)
24	21	RAT RAPPING	Roland Rat Superstar (Rodent)
31	22	RELAX	Frankie Goes To Hollywood (ZTT)
39	23	RUNNING WITH THE NIGHT	Lionel Richie (Motown)
19	24	THAT'S ALL	Genesis (Charisma/Virgin)
25	25	WHAT ARE WE GONNA DO WITH 'ER INDOORS	Dennis Waterman & George Cole (EMI)
17	26	MERRY XMAS EVERYBODY	Slade (Polydor)
-	27	A ROCKIN' GOOD WAY	Shaky & Bonnie (Epic)
36	28	SWEET SURRENDER	Rod Stewart (Warner Bros)
29	29	THE WAY YOU ARE	Tears For Fears (Mercury)
23	30	CLUB FANTASTIC MEGAMIX	Wham! (Innervision)
48	31	I CAN HELP	Elvis Presley (RCA)
35	32	SAY SAY SAY	Paul McCartney & Michael Jackson (Parlophone)
33	33	KARMA CHAMELEON	Culture Club (Virgin)
22	34	WATERFRONT	Simple Minds (Virgin)
-	35	THAT'S LIVING ALRIGHT (FROM "AUF WIEDERSEHEN PET")	Joe Fagin (Towerbell)
-	36	DUCK FOR THE OYSTER	Malcolm McLaren (Charisma)
27	37	CALLING YOUR NAME	Marilyn (Mercury)
28	38	COLD AS CHRISTMAS	Elton John (Rocket)
16	39	READ 'EM AND WEEP	Barry Manilow (Arista)
-	40	KING OF PAIN	Police (A&M)
44	41	CRY JUST A LITTLE BIT	Shakin' Stevens (Epic)
30	42	THIS CHARMING MAN	Smiths (Rough Trade)
32	43	WHERE IS MY MAN	Eartha Kitt (Record Shack)
40	44	BARK AT THE MOON	Ozzy Osbourne (Epic)
43	45	SUNBURST AND SNOWBLIND	Cocteau Twins (4AD)
47	46	TIME	Frida & B.A. Robertson (Epic)
-	47	WHITE LINES (DON'T DON'T DO IT)	Grandmaster & Melle Mel (Sugarhill)
45	48	RIGHT BY YOUR SIDE	Eurythmics (RCA)
-	49	I AM WHAT I AM	Gloria Gaynor (Chrysalis)
-	50	BLUE MONDAY	New Order (Factory)

21 January 1984

last	this	title	artist
6	1	PIPES OF PEACE	Paul McCartney (Parlophone)
8	2	WHAT IS LOVE?	Howard Jones (WEA)
22	3	RELAX	Frankie Goes To Hollywood (ZTT)
4	4	TELL HER ABOUT IT	Billy Joel (CBS)
7	4	MARGUERITA TIME	Status Quo (Vertigo)
2	6	LOVE OF THE COMMON PEOPLE	Paul Young (CBS)
27	7	A ROCKIN' GOOD WAY	Shaky & Bonnie (Epic)
3	8	VICTIMS	Culture Club (Virgin)
10	9	THRILLER	Michael Jackson (Epic)
18	10	BIRD OF PARADISE	Snowy White (Towerbell)
1	11	ONLY YOU	Flying Pickets (10)
11	12	ISLANDS IN THE STREAM	Kenny Rogers & Dolly Parton (RCA)
9	13	HOLD ME NOW	Thompson Twins (Arista)
15	14	STRAIGHT AHEAD	Kool & the Gang (De-Lite)
35	15	THAT'S LIVING ALRIGHT (FROM "AUF WIEDERSEHEN PET")	Joe Fagin (Towerbell)
5	16	MY OH MY	Slade (RCA)
40	17	KING OF PAIN	Police (A&M)
12	18	LET'S STAY TOGETHER	Tina Turner (Capitol)
-	19	WISHFUL THNIKING	China Crisis (Virgin)
-	20	LOVE IS A WONDERFUL COLOUR	Icicle Works (Beggars Banquet)
21	21	RAT RAPPING	Roland Rat Superstar (Rodent)
-	22	WONDERLAND	Big Country (Mercury)
23	23	RUNNING WITH THE NIGHT	Lionel Richie (Motown)
-	24	GIVE ME MORE TIME	Whitesnake (Liberty)
-	25	NOBODY TOLD ME	John Lennon (Ono Music/Polydor)
49	26	I AM WHAT I AM	Gloria Gaynor (Chrysalis)
28	27	SWEET SURRENDER	Rod Stewart (Warner Bros)
14	28	MANY RIVERS TO CROSS	UB40 (DEP International)
-	29	GIRLS JUST WANT TO HAVE FUN	Cyndi Lauper (Portrait)
-	30	WHERE WERE YOU HIDING WHEN THE STORM BROKE	Alarm (IRS)
19	31	UPTOWN GIRL	Billy Joel (CBS)
42	32	THIS CHARMING MAN	Smiths (Rough Trade)
17	33	MOVE OVER DARLING	Tracey Ullman (Stiff)
-	34	THE SOUND OF MUSIC	Dayton (Capitol)
50	35	BLUE MONDAY	New Order (Factory)
13	36	2000 MILES	Pretenders (Real)
45	37	SUNBURST AND SNOWBLIND	Cocteau Twins (4AD)
43	38	WHERE IS MY MAN	Eartha Kitt (Record Shack)
47	39	WHITE LINES (DON'T DON'T DO IT)	Grandmaster & Melle Mel (Sugarhill)
34	40	WATERFRONT	Simple Minds (Virgin)
29	41	THE WAY YOU ARE	Tears For Fears (Mercury)
-	42	ANOTHER MAN	Barbara Mason (Streetwave)
-	43	A NIGHT IN NEW YORK	Elbow Bones & the Racketeers (EMI America)
30	44	CLUB FANTASTIC MEGAMIX	Wham! (Innervision)
-	45	RAZOR'S EDGE	Meat Loaf (Epic)
-	46	HOLIDAY	Madonna (Sire)
-	47	HUMAN TOUCH	Rick Springfield (RCA)
24	48	THAT'S ALL	Genesis (Charisma/Virgin)
25	49	WHAT ARE WE GONNA DO WITH 'ER INDOORS	Dennis Waterman & George Cole (EMI)
16	50	PLEASE DON'T FALL IN LOVE	Cliff Richard (EMI)

Paul McCartney's *Pipes Of Peace*, promoted by a video which linked the song's sentiments to the famous trenches Christmas truce of World War 1, was his first solo Number One since *Another Day* in 1971 and marked the beginning of one of his strongest sales years since the Beatles break-up. The rapping Roland Rat Superstar was the unlikely glove puppet saviour of TV-AM, now seeking new fields to conquer.

January – February 1984

28 January 1984

last week	this week	Title	Artist
3	1	RELAX	Frankie Goes To Hollywood (ZTT)
1	2	PIPES OF PEACE	Paul McCartney (Parlophone)
10	3	BIRD OF PARADISE	Snowy White (Towerbell)
2	4	WHAT IS LOVE?	Howard Jones (WEA)
15	5	THAT'S LIVING ALRIGHT (FROM "AUF WIEDERSEHEN PET")	Joe Fagin (Towerbell)
25	6	NOBODY TOLD ME	John Lennon (Ono Music/Polydor)
7	7	A ROCKIN' GOOD WAY	Shaky & Bonnie (Epic)
22	8	WONDERLAND	Big Country (Mercury)
23	9	RUNNING WITH THE NIGHT	Lionel Richie (Motown)
20	10	LOVE IS A WONDERFUL COLOUR	Icicle Works (Beggars Banquet)
4	11	MARGUERITA TIME	Status Quo (Vertigo)
-	12	HERE COMES THE RAIN AGAIN	Eurythmics (RCA)
5	13	TELL HER ABOUT IT	Billy Joel (CBS)
19	14	WISHFUL THNIKING	China Crisis (Virgin)
17	15	KING OF PAIN	Police (A&M)
13	16	HOLD ME NOW	Thompson Twins (Arista)
6	17	LOVE OF THE COMMON PEOPLE	Paul Young (CBS)
12	18	ISLANDS IN THE STREAM	Kenny Rogers & Dolly Parton (RCA)
26	19	I AM WHAT I AM	Gloria Gaynor (Chrysalis)
29	20	GIRLS JUST WANT TO HAVE FUN	Cyndi Lauper (Portrait)
14	21	STRAIGHT AHEAD	Kool & the Gang (De-Lite)
9	22	THRILLER	Michael Jackson (Epic)
-	23	THE KILLING MOON	Echo & the Bunnymen (Korova)
8	24	VICTIMS	Culture Club (Virgin)
40	25	WATERFRONT	Simple Minds (Virgin)
-	26	BREAK MY STRIDE	Matthew Wilder (Epic)
30	27	WHERE WERE YOU HIDING WHEN THE STORM BROKE	Alarm (IRS)
-	28	(FEELS LIKE) HEAVEN	Fiction Factory (CBS)
-	29	WHAT DIFFERENCE DOES IT MAKE?	Smiths (Rough Trade)
38	30	WHERE IS MY MAN	Eartha Kitt (Record Shack)
11	31	ONLY YOU	Flying Pickets (10)
-	32	THE COLOUR FIELD	Colour Field (Chrysalis)
18	33	LET'S STAY TOGETHER	Tina Turner (Capitol)
-	34	PRISONER OF LOVE	Spear Of Destiny (CBS)
43	35	A NIGHT IN NEW YORK	Elbow Bones & the Racketeers (EMI America)
27	36	SWEET SURRENDER	Rod Stewart (Warner Bros)
16	37	MY OH MY	Slade (RCA)
-	38	HYPERACTIVE!	Thomas Dolby (Parlophone Odeon)
24	39	GIVE ME MORE TIME	Whitesnake (Liberty)
46	40	HOLIDAY	Madonna (Sire)
21	41	RAT RAPPING	Roland Rat Superstar (Rodent)
-	42	S.O.S.	ABC (Neutron)
42	43	ANOTHER MAN	Barbara Mason (Streetwave)
-	44	LIONS IN MY OWN GARDEN	Prefab Sprout (Kitchenware)
-	45	SIXTEEN	Musical Youth (MCA)
-	46	LOVE IS A BATTLEFIELD	Pat Benatar (Chrysalis)
37	47	SUNBURST AND SNOWBLIND	Cocteau Twins (4AD)
-	48	STOP LOOK AND LISTEN	Donna Summer (Mercury)
39	49	WHITE LINES (DON'T DON'T DO IT)	Grandmaster & Melle Mel (Sugarhill)
-	50	THIS MUST BE THE PLACE	Talking Heads (EMI)

4 February 1984

last week	this week	Title	Artist
1	1	RELAX	Frankie Goes To Hollywood (ZTT)
6	2	NOBODY TOLD ME	John Lennon (Ono Music/Polydor)
5	3	THAT'S LIVING ALRIGHT (FROM "AUF WIEDERSEHEN PET")	Joe Fagin (Towerbell)
2	4	PIPES OF PEACE	Paul McCartney (Parlophone)
8	5	WONDERLAND	Big Country (Mercury)
20	6	GIRLS JUST WANT TO HAVE FUN	Cyndi Lauper (Portrait)
4	7	WHAT IS LOVE?	Howard Jones (WEA)
23	8	THE KILLING MOON	Echo & the Bunnymen (Korova)
3	9	BIRD OF PARADISE	Snowy White (Towerbell)
7	10	A ROCKIN' GOOD WAY	Shaky & Bonnie (Epic)
14	11	WISHFUL THNIKING	China Crisis (Virgin)
26	12	BREAK MY STRIDE	Matthew Wilder (Epic)
12	13	HERE COMES THE RAIN AGAIN	Eurythmics (RCA)
-	14	SPEED YOUR LOVE TO ME	Simple Minds (Virgin)
19	15	I AM WHAT I AM	Gloria Gaynor (Chrysalis)
28	16	(FEELS LIKE) HEAVEN	Fiction Factory (CBS)
29	17	WHAT DIFFERENCE DOES IT MAKE?	Smiths (Rough Trade)
27	18	WHERE WERE YOU HIDING WHEN THE STORM BROKE	Alarm (IRS)
-	19	RADIO GA GA	Queen (EMI)
10	20	LOVE IS A WONDERFUL COLOUR	Icicle Works (Beggars Banquet)
9	21	RUNNING WITH THE NIGHT	Lionel Richie (Motown)
15	22	KING OF PAIN	Police (A&M)
40	23	HOLIDAY	Madonna (Sire)
11	24	MARGUERITA TIME	Status Quo (Vertigo)
13	25	TELL HER ABOUT IT	Billy Joel (CBS)
-	26	DON'T SING	Prefab Sprout (Kitchenware)
-	27	NEW MOON ON MONDAY	Duran Duran (EMI)
34	28	PRISONER OF LOVE	Spear Of Destiny (CBS)
-	29	SPICE OF LIFE	Manhattan Transfer (Atlantic)
16	30	HOLD ME NOW	Thompson Twins (Arista)
-	31	HUMAN TOUCH	Rick Springfield (RCA)
-	32	THE POLITICS OF DANCING	Re-Flex (EMI)
32	33	THE COLOUR FIELD	Colour Field (Chrysalis)
-	34	LET THE MUSIC PLAY	Shannon (Club)
21	35	STRAIGHT AHEAD	Kool & the Gang (De-Lite)
38	36	HYPERACTIVE!	Thomas Dolby (Parlophone Odeon)
-	37	WOULDN'T IT BE GOOD	Nik Kershaw (MCA)
18	38	ISLANDS IN THE STREAM	Kenny Rogers & Dolly Parton (RCA)
-	39	SONG TO THE SIREN	This Mortal Coil (4AD)
42	40	S.O.S.	ABC (Neutron)
30	41	WHERE IS MY MAN	Eartha Kitt (Record Shack)
-	42	SHARE THE NIGHT	World Premiere (Epic)
35	43	A NIGHT IN NEW YORK	Elbow Bones & the Racketeers (EMI America)
43	44	ANOTHER MAN	Barbara Mason (Streetwave)
33	45	LET'S STAY TOGETHER	Tina Turner (Capitol)
39	46	GIVE ME MORE TIME	Whitesnake (Liberty)
47	47	SUNBURST AND SNOWBLIND	Cocteau Twins (4AD)
46	48	LOVE IS A BATTLEFIELD	Pat Benatar (Chrysalis)
50	49	THIS MUST BE THE PLACE	Talking Heads (EMI)
-	50	NAUGHTY MIRANDA	Indians In Moscow (Kennick)

11 February 1984

last week	this week	Title	Artist
1	1	RELAX	Frankie Goes To Hollywood (ZTT)
6	2	GIRLS JUST WANT TO HAVE FUN	Cyndi Lauper (Portrait)
19	3	RADIO GA GA	Queen (EMI)
12	4	BREAK MY STRIDE	Matthew Wilder (Epic)
16	5	(FEELS LIKE) HEAVEN	Fiction Factory (CBS)
8	6	THE KILLING MOON	Echo & the Bunnymen (Korova)
3	7	THAT'S LIVING ALRIGHT (FROM "AUF WIEDERSEHEN PET")	Joe Fagin (Towerbell)
27	8	NEW MOON ON MONDAY	Duran Duran (EMI)
13	9	HERE COMES THE RAIN AGAIN	Eurythmics (RCA)
-	10	DOCTOR! DOCTOR!	Thompson Twins (Arista)
23	11	HOLIDAY	Madonna (Sire)
5	12	WONDERLAND	Big Country (Mercury)
4	13	PIPES OF PEACE	Paul McCartney (Parlophone)
17	14	WHAT DIFFERENCE DOES IT MAKE?	Smiths (Rough Trade)
2	15	NOBODY TOLD ME	John Lennon (Ono Music/Polydor)
11	16	WISHFUL THNIKING	China Crisis (Virgin)
14	17	SPEED YOUR LOVE TO ME	Simple Minds (Virgin)
9	18	BIRD OF PARADISE	Snowy White (Towerbell)
15	19	I AM WHAT I AM	Gloria Gaynor (Chrysalis)
29	20	SPICE OF LIFE	Manhattan Transfer (Atlantic)
18	21	WHERE WERE YOU HIDING WHEN THE STORM BROKE	Alarm (IRS)
7	22	WHAT IS LOVE?	Howard Jones (WEA)
10	23	A ROCKIN' GOOD WAY	Shaky & Bonnie (Epic)
34	24	LET THE MUSIC PLAY	Shannon (Club)
36	25	HYPERACTIVE!	Thomas Dolby (Parlophone Odeon)
-	26	SOUL TRAIN	Swansway (Exit)
-	27	LOVE THEME FROM "THE THORN BIRDS"	Juan Martin (WEA)
31	28	HUMAN TOUCH	Rick Springfield (RCA)
-	29	PUNCH AND JUDY	Marillion (EMI)
44	30	ANOTHER MAN	Barbara Mason (Streetwave)
37	31	WOULDN'T IT BE GOOD	Nik Kershaw (MCA)
-	32	SIXTEEN	Musical Youth (MCA)
-	33	ONE SMALL DAY	Ultravox (Chrysalis)
-	34	MICHAEL CAINE	Madness (Stiff)
22	35	KING OF PAIN	Police (A&M)
-	36	STREET DANCE	Break Machine (Record Shack)
-	37	JUMP	Van Halen (Warner Bros)
-	38	ILLEGAL ALIEN	Genesis (Charisma/Virgin)
20	39	LOVE IS A WONDERFUL COLOUR	Icicle Works (Beggars Banquet)
42	40	SHARE THE NIGHT	World Premiere (Epic)
-	41	SHE WAS HOT	Rolling Stones (Rolling Stones)
21	42	RUNNING WITH THE NIGHT	Lionel Richie (Motown)
43	43	A NIGHT IN NEW YORK	Elbow Bones & the Racketeers (EMI America)
-	44	SOMEBODY'S WATCHING ME	Rockwell (Motown)
-	45	RUN RUNAWAY	Slade (RCA)
28	46	PRISONER OF LOVE	Spear Of Destiny (CBS)
39	47	SONG TO THE SIREN	This Mortal Coil (4AD)
-	48	99 RED BALLOONS	Nena (Epic)
-	49	AL-NAAYFISH (THE SOUL)	Hashim (Streetwave)
-	50	I GAVE YOU MY HEART (DIDN'T I)	Hot Chocolate (RAK)

Frankie Goes To Hollywood's *Relax* was the year's second-biggest-selling single, and undoubtedly its most controversial, its apparently sexually deviant lyric leading to a BBC ban after DJ Mike Read complained on air about what he was listening to. It was also an outstandingly strong dance track, and this fact, combined with natural curiosity over the ban, drew record buyers by the hundred thousand.

February – March 1984

Two ostensibly similar dance-orientated female singers, both chart newcomers from the US, found themselves together in the Top 10. But while Cyndi Lauper (who started the stronger with *Girls Just Want To Have Fun*) would prove an inconsistent hitmaker, Madonna's *Holiday* was her first comparatively modest step to becoming the most successful chart act of the decade on both sides of the Atlantic.

10 March 1984

last week	this week		
1	1	99 RED BALLOONS	Nena (Epic)
8	2	JOANNA	Kool & the Gang (De-Lite)
2	3	RELAX	Frankie Goes To Hollywood (ZTT)
7	4	WOULDN'T IT BE GOOD	Nik Kershaw (MCA)
6	5	SOMEBODY'S WATCHING ME	Rockwell (Motown)
3	6	DOCTOR! DOCTOR!	Thompson Twins (Arista)
11	7	AN INNOCENT MAN	Billy Joel (CBS)
5	8	RADIO GA GA	Queen (EMI)
16	9	STREET DANCE	Break Machine (Record Shack)
20	10	RUN RUNAWAY	Slade (RCA)
4	11	MY EVER CHANGING MOODS	Style Cou (Polydor)
13	12	HIDE AND SEEK	Howard Jones (WEA)
21	13	JUMP	Van Halen (Warner Bros)
10	14	BREAK MY STRIDE	Matthew Wilder (Epic)
18	15	GET OUT OF YOUR LAZY BED	Matt Bianco (WEA)
9	16	MICHAEL CAINE	Madness (Stiff)
14	17	LET THE MUSIC PLAY	Shannon (Club)
27	18	I GAVE YOU MY HEART (DIDN'T I)	Hot Chocolate (RAK)
36	19	MORE MORE MORE	Carmel (London)
12	20	GIRLS JUST WANT TO HAVE FUN	Cyndi Lauper (Portrait)
19	21	DOWN IN THE SUBWAY	Soft Cell (Some Bizzare)
15	22	HOLIDAY	Madonna (Sire)
17	23	WHAT DIFFERENCE DOES IT MAKE?	Smiths (Rough Trade)
30	24	YOUR LOVE IS KING	Sade (Epic)
-	25	BREAKIN' DOWN (SUGAR SAMBA)	Julia & Company (London)
29	26	ULLO JOHN! GOTTA NEW MOTOR!	Alexei Sayle (Island)
44	27	THE POLITICS OF DANCING	Re-Flex (EMI)
-	28	THE MUSIC OF TORVILL AND DEAN (EP)	Richard Hartley & the Michael Reed Orchestra (Safari)
-	29	WOOD BEEZ (PRAY LIKE ARETHA FRANKLIN)	Scritti Politti (Virgin)
43	30	THIS CHARMING MAN	Smiths (Rough Trade)
-	31	MY GUY	Tracey Ullman (Stiff)
28	32	DANCE HALL DAYS	Wang Chung (Geffen)
22	33	SOUL TRAIN	Swansway (Exit)
23	34	MAIN THEME FROM "THE THORN BIRDS"	Henry Mancini & His Orchestra (Warner Bros)
-	35	CHASING FOR THE BREEZE	Aswad (Island)
-	36	IT'S RAINING MEN	Weather Girls (CBS)
35	37	HELP	Tina Turner (Capitol)
32	38	NEW MOON ON MONDAY	Duran Duran (EMI)
33	39	SPICE OF LIFE	Manhattan Transfer (Atlantic)
-	40	YOU'RE ALREADY DEAD	Crass (Crass)
24	41	HYPERACTIVE!	Thomas Dolby (Parlophone Odeon)
-	42	TO BE OR NOT TO BE (THE HITLER RAP)	Mel Brooks (Island)
25	43	ONE SMALL DAY	Ultravox (Chrysalis)
37	44	SONG TO THE SIREN	This Mortal Coil (4AD)
50	45	YAH MO B THERE	James Ingram & Michael McDonald (Qwest)
26	46	THAT'S LIVING ALRIGHT (FROM "AUF WIEDERSEHEN PET")	Joe Fagin (Towerbell)
-	47	WALKING IN MY SLEEP	Roger Daltrey (WEA)
-	48	FRAGGLE ROCK THEME	Fraggles (RCA)
40	49	THE KILLING MOON	Echo & the Bunnymen (Korova)
-	50	CRY AND BE FREE	Marilyn (Mercury)

17 March 1984

1	1	99 RED BALLOONS	Nena (Epic)
2	2	JOANNA	Kool & the Gang (De-Lite)
9	3	STREET DANCE	Break Machine (Record Shack)
4	4	WOULDN'T IT BE GOOD	Nik Kershaw (MCA)
13	5	JUMP	Van Halen (Warner Bros)
5	6	SOMEBODY'S WATCHING ME	Rockwell (Motown)
3	7	RELAX	Frankie Goes To Hollywood (ZTT)
8	8	RUN RUNAWAY	Slade (RCA)
7	9	AN INNOCENT MAN	Billy Joel (CBS)
6	10	DOCTOR! DOCTOR!	Thompson Twins (Arista)
12	11	HIDE AND SEEK	Howard Jones (WEA)
15	12	GET OUT OF YOUR LAZY BED	Matt Bianco (WEA)
28	13	THE MUSIC OF TORVILL AND DEAN (EP)	Richard Hartley & the Michael Reed Orchestra (Safari)
18	14	I GAVE YOU MY HEART (DIDN'T I)	Hot Chocolate (RAK)
25	15	BREAKIN' DOWN (SUGAR SAMBA)	Julia & Company (London)
17	16	LET THE MUSIC PLAY	Shannon (Club)
-	17	HELLO	Lionel Richie (Motown)
26	18	ULLO JOHN! GOTTA NEW MOTOR!	Alexei Sayle (Island)
-	19	WHAT DO I DO?	Phil Fearon & Galaxy (Ensign)
11	20	MY EVER CHANGING MOODS	Style Council (Polydor)
8	21	RADIO GA GA	Queen (EMI)
24	22	YOUR LOVE IS KING	Sade (Epic)
19	23	MORE MORE MORE	Carmel (London)
36	24	IT'S RAINING MEN	Weather Girls (CBS)
21	25	DOWN IN THE SUBWAY	Soft Cell (Some Bizzare)
16	26	MICHAEL CAINE	Madness (Stiff)
-	27	RENEGADES OF FUNK	Afrika Bambaataa & Soulsonic Force (Tommy Boy)
29	28	WOOD BEEZ (PRAY LIKE ARETHA FRANKLIN)	Scritti Politti (Virgin)
31	29	MY GUY	Tracey Ullman (Stiff)
14	30	BREAK MY STRIDE	Matthew Wilder (Epic)
23	31	WHAT DIFFERENCE DOES IT MAKE?	Smiths (Rough Trade)
30	32	THIS CHARMING MAN	Smiths (Rough Trade)
27	33	THE POLITICS OF DANCING	Re-Flex (EMI)
42	34	TO BE OR NOT TO BE (THE HITLER RAP)	Mel Brooks (Island)
20	35	GIRLS JUST WANT TO HAVE FUN	Cyndi Lauper (Portrait)
-	36	NIGHT OF THE HAWKS	Hawkwind (Flicknife)
35	37	CHASING FOR THE BREEZE	Aswad (Island)
-	38	ROBERT DE NIRO'S WAITING	Bananarama (London)
37	39	HELP	Tina Turner (Capitol)
22	40	HOLIDAY	Madonna (Sire)
-	41	TUESDAY SUNSHINE	Questions (Respond)
-	42	BREAKING POINT	Bourgie Bourgie (MCA)
33	43	SOUL TRAIN	Swansway (Exit)
32	44	DANCE HALL DAYS	Wang Chung (Geffen)
-	45	BORROWED TIME	John Lennon (Polydor)
34	46	MAIN THEME FROM "THE THORN BIRDS"	Henry Mancini & His Orchestra (Warner Bros)
-	47	HANNA HANNA	China Crisis (Virgin)
48	48	FRAGGLE ROCK THEME	Fraggles (RCA)
50	49	CRY AND BE FREE	Marilyn (Mercury)
-	50	CHERRY OH BABY	UB40 (DEP International)

24 March 1984

1	1	99 RED BALLOONS	Nena (Epic)
17	2	HELLO	Lionel Richie (Motown)
2	3	JOANNA	Kool & the Gang (De-Lite)
3	4	STREET DANCE	Break Machine (Record Shack)
5	5	JUMP	Van Halen (Warner Bros)
4	6	WOULDN'T IT BE GOOD	Nik Kershaw (MCA)
24	7	IT'S RAINING MEN	Weather Girls (CBS)
19	8	WHAT DO I DO?	Phil Fearon & Galaxy (Ensign)
6	9	SOMEBODY'S WATCHING ME	Rockwell (Motown)
9	10	AN INNOCENT MAN	Billy Joel (CBS)
7	11	RELAX	Frankie Goes To Hollywood (ZTT)
15	12	BREAKIN' DOWN (SUGAR SAMBA)	Julia & Company (London)
22	13	YOUR LOVE IS KING	Sade (Epic)
13	14	THE MUSIC OF TORVILL AND DEAN (EP)	Richard Hartley & the Michael Reed Orchestra (Safari)
11	15	HIDE AND SEEK	Howard Jones (WEA)
34	16	TO BE OR NOT TO BE (THE HITLER RAP)	Mel Brooks (Island)
8	17	RUN RUNAWAY	Slade (RCA)
18	18	ULLO JOHN! GOTTA NEW MOTOR!	Alexei Sayle (Island)
27	19	RENEGADES OF FUNK	Afrika Bambaataa & Soulsonic Force (Tommy Boy)
14	20	I GAVE YOU MY HEART (DIDN'T I)	Hot Chocolate (RAK)
50	21	CHERRY OH BABY	UB40 (DEP International)
-	22	IT'S A MIRACLE	Culture Club (Virgin)
38	23	ROBERT DE NIRO'S WAITING	Bananarama (London)
28	24	WOOD BEEZ (PRAY LIKE ARETHA FRANKLIN)	Scritti Politti (Virgin)
29	25	MY GUY	Tracey Ullman (Stiff)
10	26	DOCTOR! DOCTOR!	Thompson Twins (Arista)
-	27	UP ON THE CATWALK	Simple Minds (Virgin)
44	28	DANCE HALL DAYS	Wang Chung (Geffen)
12	29	GET OUT OF YOUR LAZY BED	Matt Bianco (WEA)
45	30	BORROWED TIME	John Lennon (Polydor)
-	31	A LOVE WORTH WAITING FOR	Shakin' Stevens (Epic)
-	32	WHITE LINES (DON'T DON'T DO IT)	Grandmaster & Melle Mel (Sugarhill)
16	33	LET THE MUSIC PLAY	Shannon (Club)
30	34	BREAK MY STRIDE	Matthew Wilder (Epic)
-	35	DR. MABUSE	Propaganda (ZTT)
20	36	MY EVER CHANGING MOODS	Style Council (Polydor)
-	37	BIRD'S FLY	Icicle Works (Beggars Banquet)
-	38	LUCKY STAR	Madonna (Sire)
-	39	NELSON MANDELA	Special AKA (2 Tone)
-	40	2000 LIGHT YEARS AWAY FROM HOME	Danse Society (Society)
-	41	OUT COME THE FREAKS	Was (Not Was) (Ze/Geffen)
39	42	HELP	Tina Turner (Capitol)
21	43	RADIO GA GA	Queen (EMI)
-	44	PEOPLE ARE PEOPLE	Depeche Mode (Mute)
45	45	SONG TO THE SIREN	This Mortal Coil (4AD)
23	46	MORE MORE MORE	Carmel (London)
-	47	THAT'S THE WAY (I LIKE IT)	Dead Or Alive (Epic)
-	48	SWIMMING HORSES	Siouxsie & the Banshees (Wonderland)
-	49	THE GREATNESS AND PERFECTION OF LOVE	Julian Cope (Mercury)
33	50	THE POLITICS OF DANCING	Re-Flex (EMI)

99 Red Balloons by West Berlin-based Nena (the name of both the group and its female lead singer) was originally a German hit titled *99 Luftballons*, and it charted in the US in its German-language version. The UK hit, however, was an English translation. Singer/songwriter Nick Kershaw, meanwhile, had his first major success with *Wouldn't It Be Good,* which reached Number Four.

March – April 1984

31 March 1984

last week	this week	title	artist
2	1	HELLO	Lionel Richie (Motown)
7	2	IT'S RAINING MEN	Weather Girls (CBS)
4	3	STREET DANCE	Break Machine (Record Shack)
13	4	YOUR LOVE IS KING	Sade (Epic)
1	5	99 RED BALLOONS	Nena (Epic)
3	6	JOANNA	Kool & the Gang (De-Lite)
8	7	WHAT DO I DO?	Phil Fearon & Galaxy (Ensign)
22	8	IT'S A MIRACLE	Culture Club (Virgin)
23	9	ROBERT DE NIRO'S WAITING	Bananarama (London)
5	10	JUMP	Van Halen (Warner Bros)
6	11	WOULDN'T IT BE GOOD	Nik Kershaw (MCA)
16	12	TO BE OR NOT TO BE (THE HITLER RAP)	Mel Brooks (Island)
10	13	AN INNOCENT MAN	Billy Joel (CBS)
31	14	A LOVE WORTH WAITING FOR	Shakin' Stevens (Epic)
18	15	ULLO JOHN! GOTTA NEW MOTOR!	Alexei Sayle (Island)
48	16	SWIMMING HORSES	Siouxsie & the Banshees (Wonderland)
27	17	UP ON THE CATWALK	Simple Minds (Virgin)
44	18	PEOPLE ARE PEOPLE	Depeche Mode (Mute)
12	19	BREAKIN' DOWN (SUGAR SAMBA)	Julia & Company (London)
15	20	HIDE AND SEEK	Howard Jones (WEA)
21	21	CHERRY OH BABY	UB40 (DEP International)
14	22	THE MUSIC OF TORVILL AND DEAN (EP)	Richard Hartley & the Michael Reed Orchestra (Safari)
9	23	SOMEBODY'S WATCHING ME	Rockwell (Motown)
-	24	YOU TAKE ME UP	Thompson Twins (Arista)
11	25	RELAX	Frankie Goes To Hollywood (ZTT)
28	26	DANCE HALL DAYS	Wang Chung (Geffen)
24	27	WOOD BEEZ (PRAY LIKE ARETHA FRANKLIN)	Scritti Politti (Virgin)
39	28	NELSON MANDELA	Special AKA (2 Tone)
-	29	THE LION'S MOUTH	Kajagoogoo (EMI)
38	30	LUCKY STAR	Madonna (Sire)
47	31	THAT'S THE WAY (I LIKE IT)	Dead Or Alive (Epic)
17	32	RUN RUNAWAY	Slade (RCA)
25	33	MY GUY	Tracey Ullman (Stiff)
20	34	I GAVE YOU MY HEART (DIDN'T I)	Hot Chocolate (RAK)
30	35	BORROWED TIME	John Lennon (Polydor)
-	36	TV DINNERS	ZZ Top (Warner Bros)
35	37	DR. MABUSE	Propaganda (ZTT)
-	38	P.Y.T. (PRETTY YOUNG THING)	Michael Jackson (Epic)
42	39	HELP	Tina Turner (Capitol)
36	40	MY EVER CHANGING MOODS	Style Council (Polydor)
-	41	JESSIE'S GIRL	Rick Springfield (RCA)
-	42	TAXI	J. Blackfoot (Allegiance)
19	43	RENEGADES OF FUNK	Afrika Bambaataa & Soulsonic Force (Tommy Boy)
37	44	BIRD'S FLY	Icicle Works (Beggars Banquet)
46	45	MORE MORE MORE	Carmel (London)
29	46	GET OUT OF YOUR LAZY BED	Matt Bianco (WEA)
40	47	2000 LIGHT YEARS AWAY FROM HOME	Danse Society (Society)
-	48	DOWN IN THE SUBWAY	Soft Cell (Some Bizzare)
-	49	DON'T LOOK ANY FURTHER	Dennis Edwards featuring Siedah Garrett (Gordy)
-	50	DANCING IN THE SHEETS	Shalamar (CBS)

7 April 1984

this week	title	artist
1	HELLO	Lionel Richie (Motown)
2	IT'S RAINING MEN	Weather Girls (CBS)
3	IT'S A MIRACLE	Culture Club (Virgin)
4	ROBERT DE NIRO'S WAITING	Bananarama (London)
5	YOUR LOVE IS KING	Sade (Epic)
6	WHAT DO I DO?	Phil Fearon & Galaxy (Ensign)
7	A LOVE WORTH WAITING FOR	Shakin' Stevens (Epic)
8	PEOPLE ARE PEOPLE	Depeche Mode (Mute)
9	YOU TAKE ME UP	Thompson Twins (Arista)
10	STREET DANCE	Break Machine (Record Shack)
11	P.Y.T. (PRETTY YOUNG THING)	Michael Jackson (Epic)
12	JOANNA	Kool & the Gang (De-Lite)
13	CHERRY OH BABY	UB40 (DEP International)
14	99 RED BALLOONS	Nena (Epic)
15	NELSON MANDELA	Special AKA (2 Tone)
16	SWIMMING HORSES	Siouxsie & the Banshees (Wonderland)
17	THE MUSIC OF TORVILL AND DEAN (EP)	Richard Hartley & the Michael Reed Orchestra (Safari)
18	WOULDN'T IT BE GOOD	Nik Kershaw (MCA)
19	JUMP	Van Halen (Warner Bros)
20	AN INNOCENT MAN	Billy Joel (CBS)
21	TO BE OR NOT TO BE (THE HITLER RAP)	Mel Brooks (Island)
22	AIN'T NOBODY	Rufus & Chaka Khan (Warner Bros)
23	UP ON THE CATWALK	Simple Minds (Virgin)
24	DANCE HALL DAYS	Wang Chung (Geffen)
25	RELAX	Frankie Goes To Hollywood (ZTT)
26	LUCKY STAR	Madonna (Sire)
27	ULLO JOHN! GOTTA NEW MOTOR!	Alexei Sayle (Island)
28	WOOD BEEZ (PRAY LIKE ARETHA FRANKLIN)	Scritti Politti (Virgin)
29	HEAVEN	Psychedelic Furs (CBS)
30	GLAD IT'S ALL OVER/DAMNED ON 45	Captain Sensible (A&M)
31	HIDE AND SEEK	Howard Jones (WEA)
32	BREAKIN' DOWN (SUGAR SAMBA)	Julia & Company (London)
33	SOMEBODY'S WATCHING ME	Rockwell (Motown)
34	TV DINNERS	ZZ Top (Warner Bros)
35	BORROWED TIME	John Lennon (Polydor)
36	THE LION'S MOUTH	Kajagoogoo (EMI)
37	DR. MABUSE	Propaganda (ZTT)
38	SHE'S STRANGE	Cameo (Club)
39	DON'T LOOK ANY FURTHER	Dennis Edwards featuring Siedah Garrett (Gordy)
40	NO SELL OUT	Malcolm X (Tommy Boy)
41	THAT'S THE WAY (I LIKE IT)	Dead Or Alive (Epic)
42	BABY YOU'RE DYNAMITE	Cliff Richard (EMI)
43	TAXI	J. Blackfoot (Allegiance)
44	AGAINST ALL ODDS (TAKE A LOOK AT ME NOW)	Phil Collins (Virgin)
45	MY GUY	Tracey Ullman (Stiff)
46	DANCING IN THE SHEETS	Shalamar (CBS)
47	JESSIE'S GIRL	Rick Springfield (RCA)
48	EIGHTIES	Killing Joke (EG)
49	YOU'RE THE ONE FOR ME	Paul Hardcastle (Total Control)
50	THE DECEIVER	Alarm (IRS)

14 April 1984

this week	title	artist
1	HELLO	Lionel Richie (Motown)
2	YOU TAKE ME UP	Thompson Twins (Arista)
3	A LOVE WORTH WAITING FOR	Shakin' Stevens (Epic)
4	PEOPLE ARE PEOPLE	Depeche Mode (Mute)
5	ROBERT DE NIRO'S WAITING	Bananarama (London)
6	IT'S RAINING MEN	Weather Girls (CBS)
7	IT'S A MIRACLE	Culture Club (Virgin)
8	P.Y.T. (PRETTY YOUNG THING)	Michael Jackson (Epic)
9	NELSON MANDELA	Special AKA (2 Tone)
10	WHAT DO I DO?	Phil Fearon & Galaxy (Ensign)
11	YOUR LOVE IS KING	Sade (Epic)
12	GLAD IT'S ALL OVER/DAMNED ON 45	Captain Sensible (A&M)
13	CHERRY OH BABY	UB40 (DEP International)
14	AGAINST ALL ODDS (TAKE A LOOK AT ME NOW)	Phil Collins (Virgin)
15	AIN'T NOBODY	Rufus & Chaka Khan (Warner Bros)
16	LUCKY STAR	Madonna (Sire)
17	THE CATERPILLAR	Cure (Fiction)
18	WOOD BEEZ (PRAY LIKE ARETHA FRANKLIN)	Scritti Politti (Virgin)
19	THE MUSIC OF TORVILL AND DEAN (EP)	Richard Hartley & the Michael Reed Orchestra (Safari)
20	STREET DANCE	Break Machine (Record Shack)
21	HEAVEN	Psychedelic Furs (CBS)
22	UP ON THE CATWALK	Simple Minds (Virgin)
23	THAT'S THE WAY (I LIKE IT)	Dead Or Alive (Epic)
24	JOANNA	Kool & the Gang (De-Lite)
25	99 RED BALLOONS	Nena (Epic)
26	EIGHTIES	Killing Joke (EG)
27	JUMP	Van Halen (Warner Bros)
28	AN INNOCENT MAN	Billy Joel (CBS)
29	RELAX	Frankie Goes To Hollywood (ZTT)
30	BABY YOU'RE DYNAMITE	Cliff Richard (EMI)
31	LOCOMOTION	Orchestral Manoeuvres In The Dark (Virgin)
32	DON'T LOOK ANY FURTHER	Dennis Edwards featuring Siedah Garrett (Gordy)
33	DANCE HALL DAYS	Wang Chung (Geffen)
34	GIVE ME TONIGHT	Shannon (Club)
35	WOULDN'T IT BE GOOD	Nik Kershaw (MCA)
36	TO BE OR NOT TO BE (THE HITLER RAP)	Mel Brooks (Island)
37	TV DINNERS	ZZ Top (Warner Bros)
38	LIBERATOR	Spear Of Destiny (Epic)
39	SOMEDAY	Gap Band (Total Experience)
40	NO SELL OUT	Malcolm X (Tommy Boy)
41	SWIMMING HORSES	Siouxsie & the Banshees (Wonderland)
42	YOU'RE THE ONE FOR ME	Paul Hardcastle (Total Control)
43	SHE'S STRANGE	Cameo (Club)
44	BREAKIN' DOWN (SUGAR SAMBA)	Julia & Company (London)
45	I WANT TO BREAK FREE	Queen (EMI)
46	TO ALL THE GIRLS I'VE LOVED BEFORE	Julio Iglesias & Willie Nelson (CBS)
47	DANCING IN THE SHEETS	Shalamar (CBS)
48	DR. MABUSE	Propaganda (ZTT)
49	THE DECEIVER	Alarm (IRS)
50	BORROWED TIME	John Lennon (Polydor)

Lionel Richie's *Hello* was his biggest UK seller, and at this point, also Motown's biggest-selling single, overtaking the Commodores' *Three Times A Lady*, which Richie had also written and sung lead vocal on!

Unusually, two comedy records were in the Top 20, as movie star and director Mel Brooks rapped *To Be Or Not To Be*, and Alexei Sayle from The Young Ones politely enquired *Ullo John! Gotta New Motor?*

last week	this week	21 April 1984	
1	1	HELLO	Lionel Richie (Motown)
2	2	YOU TAKE ME UP	Thompson Twins (Arista)
4	3	PEOPLE ARE PEOPLE	Depeche Mode (Mute)
3	4	A LOVE WORTH WAITING FOR	Shakin' Stevens (Epic)
12	5	GLAD IT'S ALL OVER/DAMNED ON 45	Captain Sensible (A&M)
14	6	AGAINST ALL ODDS (TAKE A LOOK AT ME NOW)	Phil Collins (Virgin)
9	7	NELSON MANDELA	Special AKA (2 Tone)
5	8	ROBERT DE NIRO'S WAITING	Bananarama (London)
15	9	AIN'T NOBODY	Rufus & Chaka Khan (Warner Bros)
7	10	IT'S A MIRACLE	Culture Club (Virgin)
6	11	IT'S RAINING MEN	Weather Girls (CBS)
45	12	I WANT TO BREAK FREE	Queen (EMI)
18	13	WOOD BEEZ (PRAY LIKE ARETHA FRANKLIN)	Scritti Politti (Virgin)
8	14	P.Y.T. (PRETTY YOUNG THING)	Michael Jackson (Epic)
16	15	LUCKY STAR	Madonna (Sire)
17	16	THE CATERPILLAR	Cure (Fiction)
10	17	WHAT DO I DO?	Phil Fearon & Galaxy (Ensign)
11	18	YOUR LOVE IS KING	Sade (Epic)
13	19	CHERRY OH BABY	UB40 (DEP International)
31	20	LOCOMOTION	Orchestral Manoeuvres In The Dark (Virgin)
21	21	HEAVEN	Psychedelic Furs (CBS)
39	22	SOMEDAY	Gap Band (Total Experience)
-	23	JUST BE GOOD TO ME	S.O.S. Band (Tabu)
24	24	THAT'S THE WAY (I LIKE IT)	Dead Or Alive (Epic)
40	25	NO SELL OUT	Malcolm X (Tommy Boy)
38	26	LIBERATOR	Spear Of Destiny (Epic)
-	27	(WHEN YOU SAY YOU LOVE SOMEBODY) IN THE HEART	Kool & the Gang (De-Lite)
29	28	RELAX	Frankie Goes To Hollywood (ZTT)
34	29	GIVE ME TONIGHT	Shannon (Club)
26	30	EIGHTIES	Killing Joke (EG)
-	31	DON'T TELL ME	Blancmange (London)
20	32	STREET DANCE	Break Machine (Record Shack)
-	33	SILVER	Echo & the Bunnymen (Korova)
-	34	HAND IN GLOVE	Sandie Shaw (Rough Trade)
48	35	DR. MABUSE	Propaganda (ZTT)
-	36	AUTOMATIC	Pointer Sisters (Planet)
41	37	SWIMMING HORSES	Siouxsie & the Banshees (Wonderland)
30	38	BABY YOU'RE DYNAMITE	Cliff Richard (EMI)
29	39	DANCING GIRLS	Nik Kershaw (MCA)
-	40	WHEN YOU'RE YOUNG AND IN LOVE	Flying Pickets (10)
19	41	THE MUSIC OF TORVILL AND DEAN (EP)	Richard Hartley & the Michael Reed Orchestra (Safari)
42	42	YOU'RE THE ONE FOR ME	Paul Hardcastle (Total Control)
28	43	AN INNOCENT MAN	Billy Joel (CBS)
32	44	DON'T LOOK ANY FURTHER	Dennis Edwards featuring Siedah Garrett (Gordy)
49	45	THE DECEIVER	Alarm (IRS)
22	46	UP ON THE CATWALK	Simple Minds (Virgin)
-	47	BEAT BOX	Art Of Noise (ZTT)
43	48	SHE'S STRANGE	Cameo (Club)
46	49	TO ALL THE GIRLS I'VE LOVED BEFORE	Julio Iglesias & Willie Nelson (CBS)
44	50	BREAKIN' DOWN (SUGAR SAMBA)	Julia & Company (London)

last week	this week	28 April 1984	
1	1	HELLO	Lionel Richie (Motown)
6	2	AGAINST ALL ODDS (TAKE A LOOK AT ME NOW)	Phil Collins (Virgin)
2	3	YOU TAKE ME UP	Thompson Twins (Arista)
12	4	I WANT TO BREAK FREE	Queen (EMI)
9	5	AIN'T NOBODY	Rufus & Chaka Khan (Warner Bros)
5	6	GLAD IT'S ALL OVER/DAMNED ON 45	Captain Sensible (A&M)
4	7	A LOVE WORTH WAITING FOR	Shakin' Stevens (Epic)
3	8	PEOPLE ARE PEOPLE	Depeche Mode (Mute)
7	9	NELSON MANDELA	Special AKA (2 Tone)
13	10	WOOD BEEZ (PRAY LIKE ARETHA FRANKLIN)	Scritti Politti (Virgin)
27	11	(WHEN YOU SAY YOU LOVE SOMEBODY) IN THE HEART	Kool & the Gang (De-Lite)
16	12	THE CATERPILLAR	Cure (Fiction)
23	13	JUST BE GOOD TO ME	S.O.S. Band (Tabu)
20	14	LOCOMOTION	Orchestral Manoeuvres In The Dark (Virgin)
31	15	DON'T TELL ME	Blancmange (London)
22	16	SOMEDAY	Gap Band (Total Experience)
33	17	SILVER	Echo & the Bunnymen (Korova)
24	18	THAT'S THE WAY (I LIKE IT)	Dead Or Alive (Epic)
34	19	HAND IN GLOVE	Sandie Shaw (Rough Trade)
8	20	ROBERT DE NIRO'S WAITING	Bananarama (London)
10	21	IT'S A MIRACLE	Culture Club (Virgin)
-	22	THIEVES LIKE US	New Order (Factory)
-	23	THE REFLEX	Duran Duran (EMI)
14	24	P.Y.T. (PRETTY YOUNG THING)	Michael Jackson (Epic)
39	25	DANCING GIRLS	Nik Kershaw (MCA)
11	26	IT'S RAINING MEN	Weather Girls (CBS)
35	27	DR. MABUSE	Propaganda (ZTT)
-	28	ONE LOVE/PEOPLE GET READY	Bob Marley & the Wailers (Island)
29	29	GIVE ME TONIGHT	Shannon (Club)
15	30	LUCKY STAR	Madonna (Sire)
-	31	PEARLY DEWDROPS DROPS	Cocteau Twins (4AD)
40	32	WHEN YOU'RE YOUNG AND IN LOVE	Flying Pickets (10)
-	33	SOMEBODY ELSE'S GUY	Jocelyn Brown (Fourth & Broadway)
17	34	WHAT DO I DO?	Phil Fearon & Galaxy (Ensign)
35	35	YOUR LOVE IS KING	Sade (Epic)
36	36	AUTOMATIC	Pointer Sisters (Planet)
19	37	CHERRY OH BABY	UB40 (DEP International)
-	38	I'M FALLING	Bluebells (London)
-	39	SEARCHIN'	Hazell Dean (Proto)
44	40	DON'T LOOK ANY FURTHER	Dennis Edwards featuring Siedah Garrett (Gordy)
42	41	YOU'RE THE ONE FOR ME	Paul Hardcastle (Total Control)
25	42	NO SELL OUT	Malcolm X (Tommy Boy)
-	43	HI, HOW YA DOIN'?	Kenny G (Arista)
48	44	SHE'S STRANGE	Cameo (Club)
-	45	YOU DON'T LOVE ME	Marilyn (Mercury)
21	46	HEAVEN	Psychedelic Furs (CBS)
49	48	TO ALL THE GIRLS I'VE LOVED BEFORE	Julio Iglesias & Willie Nelson (CBS)
-	49	JESSE	Grandmaster & Melle Mel (Sugarhill)
-	50	EAT IT	Weird Al Yankovic (Scotti Brothers/Epic)

last week	this week	5 May 1984	
2	1	AGAINST ALL ODDS (TAKE A LOOK AT ME NOW)	Phil Collins (Virgin)
4	2	I WANT TO BREAK FREE	Queen (EMI)
1	3	HELLO	Lionel Richie (Motown)
23	4	THE REFLEX	Duran Duran (EMI)
3	5	YOU TAKE ME UP	Thompson Twins (Arista)
11	6	(WHEN YOU SAY YOU LOVE SOMEBODY) IN THE HEART	Kool & the Gang (De-Lite)
14	7	LOCOMOTION	Orchestral Manoeuvres In The Dark (Virgin)
6	8	GLAD IT'S ALL OVER/DAMNED ON 45	Captain Sensible (A&M)
32	9	WHEN YOU'RE YOUNG AND IN LOVE	Flying Pickets (10)
15	10	DON'T TELL ME	Blancmange (London)
7	11	A LOVE WORTH WAITING FOR	Shakin' Stevens (Epic)
22	12	THIEVES LIKE US	New Order (Factory)
5	13	AIN'T NOBODY	Rufus & Chaka Khan (Warner Bros)
38	14	I'M FALLING	Bluebells (London)
13	15	JUST BE GOOD TO ME	S.O.S. Band (Tabu)
8	16	PEOPLE ARE PEOPLE	Depeche Mode (Mute)
36	17	AUTOMATIC	Pointer Sisters (Planet)
10	18	WOOD BEEZ (PRAY LIKE ARETHA FRANKLIN)	Scritti Politti (Virgin)
9	19	NELSON MANDELA	Special AKA (2 Tone)
28	20	ONE LOVE/PEOPLE GET READY	Bob Marley & the Wailers (Island)
31	21	PEARLY DEWDROPS DROPS	Cocteau Twins (4AD)
25	22	DANCING GIRLS	Nik Kershaw (MCA)
33	23	SOMEBODY ELSE'S GUY	Jocelyn Brown (Fourth & Broadway)
12	24	THE CATERPILLAR	Cure (Fiction)
17	25	SILVER	Echo & the Bunnymen (Korova)
19	26	HAND IN GLOVE	Sandie Shaw (Rough Trade)
-	27	THE LEBANON	Human League (Virgin)
16	28	SOMEDAY	Gap Band (Total Experience)
24	29	P.Y.T. (PRETTY YOUNG THING)	Michael Jackson (Epic)
-	30	THE LONGEST TIME	Billy Joel (CBS)
-	31	PEACE IN OUR TIME	Imposter (Imposter)
39	32	SEARCHIN'	Hazell Dean (Proto)
18	33	THAT'S THE WAY (I LIKE IT)	Dead Or Alive (Epic)
-	34	LOVE WARS	Womack & Womack (Elektra)
48	35	TO ALL THE GIRLS I'VE LOVED BEFORE	Julio Iglesias & Willie Nelson (CBS)
-	36	LOVE GAMES	Belle & the Devotions (CBS)
-	37	STANDING IN THE SHADOW	Whitesnake (Liberty)
-	38	GOOD TECHNOLOGY	Red Guitars (Self Drive)
29	39	GIVE ME TONIGHT	Shannon (Club)
26	40	IT'S RAINING MEN	Weather Girls (CBS)
20	41	ROBERT DE NIRO'S WAITING	Bananarama (London)
30	42	LUCKY STAR	Madonna (Sire)
41	43	YOU'RE THE ONE FOR ME	Paul Hardcastle (Total Control)
43	44	HI, HOW YA DOIN'?	Kenny G (Arista)
45	45	FOOTLOOSE	Kenny Loggins (CBS)
45	46	YOU DON'T LOVE ME	Marilyn (Mercury)
49	47	JESSE	Grandmaster & Melle Mel (Sugarhill)
-	48	SONS AND DAUGHTERS THEME	Kerri & Mick (A1)
35	49	YOUR LOVE IS KING	Sade (Epic)
44	50	SHE'S STRANGE	Cameo (Club)

Phil Collins' chart-topper was the theme song to the film *Against All Odds*, though Collins merely sang over the soundtrack, and was not seen on screen. Madonna made the Top 20 with her second hit *Lucky Star*, while *P.Y.T. (Pretty Young Thing)*, the sixth UK single to be extracted from Michael Jackson's *Thriller* album, was, not surprisingly, the poorest seller of the six – though it did still reach the Top 10.

May 1984

12 May 1984

last	this	Title	Artist (Label)
4	1	THE REFLEX	Duran Duran (EMI)
1	2	AGAINST ALL ODDS (TAKE A LOOK AT ME NOW)	Phil Collins (Virgin)
2	3	I WANT TO BREAK FREE	Queen (EMI)
17	4	AUTOMATIC	Pointer Sisters (Planet)
3	5	HELLO	Lionel Richie (Motown)
7	6	LOCOMOTION	Orchestral Manoeuvres In The Dark (Virgin)
20	7	ONE LOVE/PEOPLE GET READY	Bob Marley & the Wailers (Island)
9	8	WHEN YOU'RE YOUNG AND IN LOVE	Flying Pickets (10)
10	9	DON'T TELL ME	Blancmange (London)
27	10	THE LEBANON	Human League (Virgin)
12	11	THIEVES LIKE US	New Order (Factory)
14	12	I'M FALLING	Bluebells (London)
5	13	YOU TAKE ME UP	Thompson Twins (Arista)
13	14	AIN'T NOBODY	Rufus & Chaka Khan (Warner Bros)
22	15	DANCING GIRLS	Nik Kershaw (MCA)
6	16	(WHEN YOU SAY YOU LOVE SOMEBODY) IN THE HEART	Kool & the Gang (De-Lite)
21	17	PEARLY DEWDROPS DROPS	Cocteau Twins (4AD)
16	18	LOVE GAMES	Belle & the Devotions (CBS)
15	19	JUST BE GOOD TO ME	S.O.S. Band (Tabu)
26	20	HAND IN GLOVE	Sandie Shaw (Rough Trade)
8	21	GLAD IT'S ALL OVER/DAMNED ON 45	Captain Sensible (A&M)
45	22	FOOTLOOSE	Kenny Loggins (CBS)
23	23	SOMEBODY ELSE'S GUY	Jocelyn Brown (Fourth & Broadway)
35	24	TO ALL THE GIRLS I'VE LOVED BEFORE	Julio Iglesias & Willie Nelson (CBS)
18	25	WOOD BEEZ (PRAY LIKE ARETHA FRANKLIN)	Scritti Politti (Virgin)
11	26	A LOVE WORTH WAITING FOR	Shakin' Stevens (Epic)
30	27	THE LONGEST TIME	Billy Joel (CBS)
25	28	SILVER	Echo & the Bunnymen (Korova)
24	29	THE CATERPILLAR	Cure (Fiction)
-	30	LET'S HEAR IT FOR THE BOY	Deniece Williams (CBS)
16	31	PEOPLE ARE PEOPLE	Depeche Mode (Mute)
19	32	NELSON MANDELA	Special AKA (2 Tone)
38	33	GOOD TECHNOLOGY	Red Guitars (Self Drive)
-	34	STAY WITH ME TONIGHT	Jeffrey Osborne (A&M)
-	35	ASSASSING	Marillion (EMI)
32	36	SEARCHIN'	Hazell Dean (Proto)
31	37	PEACE IN OUR TIME	Imposter (Imposter)
-	38	I'LL BE AROUND	Terri Wells (Phillyworld)
-	39	RELAX	Frankie Goes To Hollywood (ZTT)
47	40	JESSE	Grandmaster & Melle Mel (Sugarhill)
28	41	SOMEDAY	Gap Band (Total Experience)
33	42	THAT'S THE WAY (I LIKE IT)	Dead Or Alive (Epic)
34	43	LOVE WARS	Womack & Womack (Elektra)
-	44	I FEEL LIKE BUDDY HOLLY	Alvin Stardust (Chrysalis)
-	45	EACH AND EVERY ONE	Everything But The Girl (blanco y negro)
44	46	HI, HOW YA DOIN'?	Kenny G (Arista)
-	47	HIGH ENERGY	Evelyn Thomas (Record Shack)
41	48	ROBERT DE NIRO'S WAITING	Bananarama (London)
29	49	P.Y.T. (PRETTY YOUNG THING)	Michael Jackson (Epic)
-	50	DECEIVING GIRL	Dennis Brown (Yucca Ur)

19 May 1984

last	this	Title	Artist (Label)
1	1	THE REFLEX	Duran Duran (EMI)
2	2	AGAINST ALL ODDS (TAKE A LOOK AT ME NOW)	Phil Collins (Virgin)
4	3	AUTOMATIC	Pointer Sisters (Planet)
3	4	I WANT TO BREAK FREE	Queen (EMI)
5	5	LOCOMOTION	Orchestral Manoeuvres In The Dark (Virgin)
7	6	ONE LOVE/PEOPLE GET READY	Bob Marley & the Wailers (Island)
22	7	FOOTLOOSE	Kenny Loggins (CBS)
10	8	THE LEBANON	Human League (Virgin)
8	9	WHEN YOU'RE YOUNG AND IN LOVE	Flying Pickets (10)
9	10	DON'T TELL ME	Blancmange (London)
30	11	LET'S HEAR IT FOR THE BOY	Deniece Williams (CBS)
18	12	LOVE GAMES	Belle & the Devotions (CBS)
23	13	SOMEBODY ELSE'S GUY	Jocelyn Brown (Fourth & Broadway)
5	14	HELLO	Lionel Richie (Motown)
12	15	I'M FALLING	Bluebells (London)
15	16	DANCING GIRLS	Nik Kershaw (MCA)
35	17	ASSASSING	Marillion (EMI)
24	18	TO ALL THE GIRLS I'VE LOVED BEFORE	Julio Iglesias & Willie Nelson (CBS)
11	19	THIEVES LIKE US	New Order (Factory)
16	20	(WHEN YOU SAY YOU LOVE SOMEBODY) IN THE HEART	Kool & the Gang (De-Lite)
17	21	PEARLY DEWDROPS DROPS	Cocteau Twins (4AD)
38	22	I'LL BE AROUND	Terri Wells (Phillyworld)
34	23	STAY WITH ME TONIGHT	Jeffrey Osborne (A&M)
-	24	GOING DOWN TOWN TONIGHT	Status Quo (Vertigo)
14	25	AIN'T NOBODY	Rufus & Chaka Khan (Warner Bros)
27	26	THE LONGEST TIME	Billy Joel (CBS)
45	27	EACH AND EVERY ONE	Everything But The Girl (blanco y negro)
43	28	LOVE WARS	Womack & Womack (Elektra)
19	29	JUST BE GOOD TO ME	S.O.S. Band (Tabu)
-	30	BREAK DANCE PARTY	Break Machine (Record Shack)
13	31	YOU TAKE ME UP	Thompson Twins (Arista)
20	32	HAND IN GLOVE	Sandie Shaw (Rough Trade)
25	33	WOOD BEEZ (PRAY LIKE ARETHA FRANKLIN)	Scritti Politti (Virgin)
-	34	BAD LIFE	Public Image Ltd. (Virgin)
-	35	DANCING WITH TEARS IN MY EYES	Ultravox (Chrysalis)
39	36	RELAX	Frankie Goes To Hollywood (ZTT)
36	37	SEARCHIN'	Hazell Dean (Proto)
32	38	NELSON MANDELA	Special AKA (2 Tone)
-	39	ROBIN (THE HOODED MAN)	Clannad (RCA)
37	40	PEACE IN OUR TIME	Imposter (Imposter)
40	41	JESSE	Grandmaster & Melle Mel (Sugarhill)
42	42	SILVER	Echo & the Bunnymen (Korova)
44	43	I FEEL LIKE BUDDY HOLLY	Alvin Stardust (Chrysalis)
21	44	GLAD IT'S ALL OVER/DAMNED ON 45	Captain Sensible (A&M)
29	45	THE CATERPILLAR	Cure (Fiction)
-	46	LOVE LIES LOST	Helen Terry (London)
-	47	DON'T GIVE ME UP	Harold Melvin & the Blue Notes (London)
-	48	DON'T WASTE YOUR TIME	Yarbrough & Peoples (Total Experience)
-	49	PANAMA	Van Halen (Warner Bros)
-	50	SPIRIT WALKER	Cult (Situation Z)

26 May 1984

last	this	Title	Artist (Label)
3	1	AUTOMATIC	Pointer Sisters (Planet)
1	2	THE REFLEX	Duran Duran (EMI)
2	3	AGAINST ALL ODDS (TAKE A LOOK AT ME NOW)	Phil Collins (Virgin)
6	4	ONE LOVE/PEOPLE GET READY	Bob Marley & the Wailers (Island)
7	5	FOOTLOOSE	Kenny Loggins (CBS)
11	6	LET'S HEAR IT FOR THE BOY	Deniece Williams (CBS)
4	7	I WANT TO BREAK FREE	Queen (EMI)
5	8	LOCOMOTION	Orchestral Manoeuvres In The Dark (Virgin)
13	9	SOMEBODY ELSE'S GUY	Jocelyn Brown (Fourth & Broadway)
8	10	THE LEBANON	Human League (Virgin)
10	11	DON'T TELL ME	Blancmange (London)
30	12	BREAK DANCE PARTY	Break Machine (Record Shack)
22	13	I'LL BE AROUND	Terri Wells (Phillyworld)
12	14	LOVE GAMES	Belle & the Devotions (CBS)
28	15	LOVE WARS	Womack & Womack (Elektra)
23	16	STAY WITH ME TONIGHT	Jeffrey Osborne (A&M)
-	17	WAKE ME UP BEFORE YOU GO GO	Wham! (Epic)
35	18	DANCING WITH TEARS IN MY EYES	Ultravox (Chrysalis)
24	19	GOING DOWN TOWN TONIGHT	Status Quo (Vertigo)
17	20	ASSASSING	Marillion (EMI)
16	21	DANCING GIRLS	Nik Kershaw (MCA)
-	22	GROOVIN' (YOU'RE THE BEST/BIG BOSS GROOVE)	Style Council (Polydor)
14	23	HELLO	Lionel Richie (Motown)
37	24	SEARCHIN'	Hazell Dean (Proto)
29	25	JUST BE GOOD TO ME	S.O.S. Band (Tabu)
27	26	EACH AND EVERY ONE	Everything But The Girl (blanco y negro)
9	27	WHEN YOU'RE YOUNG AND IN LOVE	Flying Pickets (10)
25	28	AIN'T NOBODY	Rufus & Chaka Khan (Warner Bros)
18	29	TO ALL THE GIRLS I'VE LOVED BEFORE	Julio Iglesias & Willie Nelson (CBS)
21	30	PEARLY DEWDROPS DROPS	Cocteau Twins (4AD)
-	31	DANCING IN THE DARK	Bruce Springsteen (CBS)
19	32	THIEVES LIKE US	New Order (Factory)
36	33	RELAX	Frankie Goes To Hollywood (ZTT)
43	34	I FEEL LIKE BUDDY HOLLY	Alvin Stardust (Chrysalis)
34	35	BAD LIFE	Public Image Ltd. (Virgin)
15	36	I'M FALLING	Bluebells (London)
-	37	MURDER	New Order (Factory/Benelux)
26	38	THE LONGEST TIME	Billy Joel (CBS)
50	39	SPIRIT WALKER	Cult (Situation Z)
-	40	PEARL IN THE SHELL	Howard Jones (WEA)
20	41	(WHEN YOU SAY YOU LOVE SOMEBODY) IN THE HEART	Kool & the Gang (De-Lite)
-	42	SMALL TOWN CREED	Kane Gang (Kitchenware)
46	43	LOVE LIES LOST	Helen Terry (London)
41	44	JESSE	Grandmaster & Melle Mel (Sugarhill)
-	45	ROUGH JUSTICE	Bananarama (London)
-	46	EMERGENCY (DIAL 999)	Loose Ends (Virgn)
-	47	SWEETEST SWEETEST	Jermaine Jackson (Arista)
31	48	YOU TAKE ME UP	Thompson Twins (Arista)
-	49	WHAT PRESENCE?	Orange Juice (Polydor)
49	50	PANAMA	Van Halen (Warner Bros)

Bob Marley achieved a Top Five hit three years after his death with the double A-side *One Love/People Get Ready*. The single was taken from the commemorative Marley compilation album *Legend*, which was simultaneously topping the UK album chart. Meanwhile, the unlikely vocal combination of Latin balladeer Julio Iglesias and country star Willie Nelson proved to be commercially effective.

2 June 1984

last week	this week	Title	Artist (Label)
1	1	AUTOMATIC	Pointer Sisters (Planet)
6	2	LET'S HEAR IT FOR THE BOY	Deniece Williams (CBS)
17	3	WAKE ME UP BEFORE YOU GO GO	Wham! (Epic)
2	4	THE REFLEX	Duran Duran (EMI)
22	5	GROOVIN' (YOU'RE THE BEST/BIG BOSS GROOVE)	Style Council (Polydor)
4	6	ONE LOVE/PEOPLE GET READY	Bob Marley & the Wailers (Island)
5	7	FOOTLOOSE	Kenny Loggins (CBS)
18	8	DANCING WITH TEARS IN MY EYES	Ultravox (Chrysalis)
12	9	BREAK DANCE PARTY	Break Machine (Record Shack)
3	10	AGAINST ALL ODDS (TAKE A LOOK AT ME NOW)	Phil Collins (Virgin)
7	11	I WANT TO BREAK FREE	Queen (EMI)
24	12	SEARCHIN'	Hazell Dean (Proto)
15	13	LOVE WARS	Womack & Womack (Elektra)
34	14	I FEEL LIKE BUDDY HOLLY	Alvin Stardust (Chrysalis)
8	15	LOCOMOTION	Orchestral Manoeuvres In The Dark (Virgin)
40	16	PEARL IN THE SHELL	Howard Jones (WEA)
19	17	GOING DOWN TOWN TONIGHT	Status Quo (Vertigo)
31	18	DANCING IN THE DARK	Bruce Springsteen (CBS)
9	19	SOMEBODY ELSE'S GUY	Jocelyn Brown (Fourth & Broadway)
16	20	STAY WITH ME TONIGHT	Jeffrey Osborne (A&M)
26	21	EACH AND EVERY ONE	Everything But The Girl (blanco y negro)
33	22	RELAX	Frankie Goes To Hollywood (ZTT)
13	23	I'LL BE AROUND	Terri Wells (Phillyworld)
10	24	THE LEBANON	Human League (Virgin)
11	25	DON'T TELL ME	Blancmange (London)
27	26	WHEN YOU'RE YOUNG AND IN LOVE	Flying Pickets (10)
-	27	HIGH ENERGY	Evelyn Thomas (Record Shack)
-	28	HEAVEN KNOWS (I'M MISERABLE NOW)	Smiths (Rough Trade)
-	29	RED GUITAR	David Sylvian (Virgin)
37	30	MURDER	New Order (Factory/Benelux)
-	31	WHEN AM I GOING TO MAKE A LIVING	Sade (Epic)
-	32	INFATUATION	Rod Stewart (Warner Bros)
29	33	TO ALL THE GIRLS I'VE LOVED BEFORE	Julio Iglesias & Willie Nelson (CBS)
-	35	THINKING OF YOU	Sister Sledge (Cotillion/Atlantic)
-	36	SO TIRED	Ozzy Osbourne (Epic)
21	37	DANCING GIRLS	Nik Kershaw (MCA)
14	38	LOVE GAMES	Belle & the Devotions (CBS)
42	39	SMALL TOWN CREED	Kane Gang (Kitchenware)
39	40	SPIRIT WALKER	Cult (Situation Z)
-	41	DAZZLE	Siouxsie & the Banshees (Wonderland)
-	42	SAD SONGS (SAY SO MUCH)	Elton John (Rocket)
30	43	PEARLY DEWDROPS	Cocteau Twins (4AD)
44	44	EMERGENCY (DIAL 999)	Loose Ends (Virgn)
49	45	WHAT PRESENCE?	Orange Juice (Polydor)
45	46	ROUGH JUSTICE	Bananarama (London)
-	47	THE BODY ELECTRIC	Rush (Vertigo)
-	48	PERFECT SKIN	Lloyd Cole & the Commotions (Polydor)
43	49	LOVE LIES LOST	Helen Terry (Virgin)
-	50	WALK THROUGH THE FIRE	Peter Gabriel (Virgin)

9 June 1984

last week	this week	Title	Artist (Label)
3	1	WAKE ME UP BEFORE YOU GO GO	Wham! (Epic)
5	2	GROOVIN' (YOU'RE THE BEST/BIG BOSS GROOVE)	Style Council (Polydor)
2	3	LET'S HEAR IT FOR THE BOY	Deniece Williams (CBS)
8	4	DANCING WITH TEARS IN MY EYES	Ultravox (Chrysalis)
1	5	AUTOMATIC	Pointer Sisters (Planet)
4	6	THE REFLEX	Duran Duran (EMI)
12	7	SEARCHIN'	Hazell Dean (Proto)
14	8	I FEEL LIKE BUDDY HOLLY	Alvin Stardust (Chrysalis)
27	9	HIGH ENERGY	Evelyn Thomas (Record Shack)
28	10	HEAVEN KNOWS (I'M MISERABLE NOW)	Smiths (Rough Trade)
10	11	AGAINST ALL ODDS (TAKE A LOOK AT ME NOW)	Phil Collins (Virgin)
16	12	PEARL IN THE SHELL	Howard Jones (WEA)
6	13	ONE LOVE/PEOPLE GET READY	Bob Marley & the Wailers (Island)
29	14	RED GUITAR	David Sylvian (Virgin)
11	15	I WANT TO BREAK FREE	Queen (EMI)
9	16	BREAK DANCE PARTY	Break Machine (Record Shack)
36	17	SO TIRED	Ozzy Osbourne (Epic)
22	18	RELAX	Frankie Goes To Hollywood (ZTT)
13	19	LOVE WARS	Womack & Womack (Elektra)
7	20	FOOTLOOSE	Kenny Loggins (CBS)
-	21	SMALLTOWN BOY	Bronski Beat (Forbidden Fruit)
41	22	DAZZLE	Siouxsie & the Banshees (Wonderland)
-	23	ONE BETTER DAY	Madness (Stiff)
42	24	SAD SONGS (SAY SO MUCH)	Elton John (Rocket)
35	25	THINKING OF YOU	Sister Sledge (Cotillion/Atlantic)
18	26	DANCING IN THE DARK	Bruce Springsteen (CBS)
17	27	GOING DOWN TOWN TONIGHT	Status Quo (Vertigo)
-	28	ONLY WHEN YOU LEAVE	Spandau Ballet (Reformation)
21	29	EACH AND EVERY ONE	Everything But The Girl (blanco y negro)
19	30	SOMEBODY ELSE'S GUY	Jocelyn Brown (Fourth & Broadway)
-	31	ANIMAL (FUCK LIKE A BEAST)	W.A.S.P. (Music For Nations)
15	32	LOCOMOTION	Orchestral Manoeuvres In The Dark (Virgin)
23	33	I'LL BE AROUND	Terri Wells (Phillyworld)
30	34	MURDER	New Order (Factory/Benelux)
49	35	LOVE LIES LOST	Helen Terry (Virgin)
46	36	ROUGH JUSTICE	Bananarama (London)
20	37	STAY WITH ME TONIGHT	Jeffrey Osborne (A&M)
-	38	FAREWELL MY SUMMER LOVE	Michael Jackson (Motown)
-	39	WE'RE NOT GONNA TAKE IT	Twisted Sister (Atlantic)
40	40	SPIRIT WALKER	Cult (Situation Z)
-	41	THE BOY WHO CAME BACK	Marc Almond (Some Bizzarre)
-	42	SUSANNA	Art Company (Epic)
31	43	WHEN AM I GOING TO MAKE A LIVING	Sade (Epic)
32	44	INFATUATION	Rod Stewart (Warner Bros)
25	45	DON'T TELL ME	Blancmange (London)
50	46	WALK THROUGH THE FIRE	Peter Gabriel (Virgin)
47	47	THE BODY ELECTRIC	Rush (Vertigo)
48	48	PERFECT SKIN	Lloyd Cole & the Commotions (Polydor)
24	49	THE LEBANON	Human League (Virgin)
26	50	WHEN YOU'RE YOUNG AND IN LOVE	Flying Pickets (10)

16 June 1984

last week	this week	Title	Artist (Label)
1	1	WAKE ME UP BEFORE YOU GO GO	Wham! (Epic)
-	2	TWO TRIBES	Frankie Goes To Hollywood (ZTT)
28	3	ONLY WHEN YOU LEAVE	Spandau Ballet (Reformation)
21	4	SMALLTOWN BOY	Bronski Beat (Forbidden Fruit)
3	5	LET'S HEAR IT FOR THE BOY	Deniece Williams (CBS)
10	6	HEAVEN KNOWS (I'M MISERABLE NOW)	Smiths (Rough Trade)
12	7	PEARL IN THE SHELL	Howard Jones (WEA)
4	8	DANCING WITH TEARS IN MY EYES	Ultravox (Chrysalis)
9	9	HIGH ENERGY	Evelyn Thomas (Record Shack)
7	10	SEARCHIN'	Hazell Dean (Proto)
2	11	GROOVIN' (YOU'RE THE BEST/BIG BOSS GROOVE)	Style Council (Polydor)
24	12	SAD SONGS (SAY SO MUCH)	Elton John (Rocket)
6	13	THE REFLEX	Duran Duran (EMI)
14	14	RED GUITAR	David Sylvian (Virgin)
8	15	I FEEL LIKE BUDDY HOLLY	Alvin Stardust (Chrysalis)
25	16	THINKING OF YOU	Sister Sledge (Cotillion/Atlantic)
23	17	ONE BETTER DAY	Madness (Stiff)
17	18	SO TIRED	Ozzy Osbourne (Epic)
5	19	AUTOMATIC	Pointer Sisters (Planet)
18	20	RELAX	Frankie Goes To Hollywood (ZTT)
-	21	ABSOLUTE	Scritti Politti (Virgin)
38	22	FAREWELL MY SUMMER LOVE	Michael Jackson (Motown)
15	23	I WANT TO BREAK FREE	Queen (EMI)
42	24	SUSANNA	Art Company (Epic)
44	25	INFATUATION	Rod Stewart (Warner Bros)
-	26	CHANGE OF HEART	Change (WEA)
26	27	DANCING IN THE DARK	Bruce Springsteen (CBS)
-	28	THANKS FOR THE NIGHT	Damned (Damned)
-	29	LOVE ALL DAY	Nick Heyward (Arista)
22	30	DAZZLE	Siouxsie & the Banshees (Wonderland)
11	31	AGAINST ALL ODDS (TAKE A LOOK AT ME NOW)	Phil Collins (Virgin)
43	32	WHEN AM I GOING TO MAKE A LIVING	Sade (Epic)
16	33	BREAK DANCE PARTY	Break Machine (Record Shack)
27	34	GOING DOWN TOWN TONIGHT	Status Quo (Vertigo)
13	35	ONE LOVE/PEOPLE GET READY	Bob Marley & the Wailers (Island)
19	36	LOVE WARS	Womack & Womack (Elektra)
20	37	FOOTLOOSE	Kenny Loggins (CBS)
-	38	I WON'T LET THE SUN GO DOWN ON ME	Nik Kershaw (MCA)
31	39	ANIMAL (FUCK LIKE A BEAST)	W.A.S.P. (Music For Nations)
36	40	ROUGH JUSTICE	Bananarama (London)
37	41	STAY WITH ME TONIGHT	Jeffrey Osborne (A&M)
46	42	WALK THROUGH THE FIRE	Peter Gabriel (Virgin)
-	43	VENCEREMOS - WE WILL WIN	Working Week (Virgin)
-	44	THIN LINE BETWEEN LOVE AND HATE	Pretenders (Real)
48	45	PERFECT SKIN	Lloyd Cole & the Commotions (Polydor)
33	46	I'LL BE AROUND	Terri Wells (Phillyworld)
34	47	MURDER	New Order (Factory/Benelux)
30	48	SOMEBODY ELSE'S GUY	Jocelyn Brown (Fourth & Broadway)
-	49	FEELS SO REAL (WON'T LET GO)	Patrice Rushen (Elektra)
-	50	EUROPEAN QUEEN	Billy Ocean (Jive)

After an enforced absence from recording while contractual matters were resolved and a new deal with Epic was finalised, Wham! returned with the Number One hit they had always been promising. *Wake Me Up Before You Go Go* was stylistically a tribute to the great Motown pop-dance tracks with which George Michael had grown up, and it captured that classic Detroit groove and ambience exactly.

June – July 1984

23 June 1984

last	this		
2	1	TWO TRIBES Frankie Goes To Hollywood (ZTT)	
4	2	SMALLTOWN BOY Bronski Beat (Forbidden Fruit)	
1	3	WAKE ME UP BEFORE YOU GO GO Wham! (Epic)	
3	4	ONLY WHEN YOU LEAVE Spandau Ballet (Reformation)	
9	5	HIGH ENERGY Evelyn Thomas (Record Shack)	
12	6	SAD SONGS (SAY SO MUCH) Elton John (Rocket)	
7	7	PEARL IN THE SHELL Howard Jones (WEA)	
8	8	DANCING WITH TEARS IN MY EYES Ultravox (Chrysalis)	
20	9	RELAX Frankie Goes To Hollywood (ZTT)	
6	10	HEAVEN KNOWS (I'M MISERABLE NOW) Smiths (Rough Trade)	
16	11	THINKING OF YOU Sister Sledge (Cotillion/Atlantic)	
5	12	LET'S HEAR IT FOR THE BOY Deniece Williams (CBS)	
22	13	FAREWELL MY SUMMER LOVE Michael Jackson (Motown)	
10	14	SEARCHIN' Hazell Dean (Proto)	
38	15	I WON'T LET THE SUN GO DOWN ON ME Nik Kershaw (MCA)	
11	16	GROOVIN' (YOU'RE THE BEST/BIG BOSS GROOVE) Style Council (Polydor)	
15	17	I FEEL LIKE BUDDY HOLLY Alvin Stardust (Chrysalis)	
17	18	ONE BETTER DAY Madness (Stiff)	
24	19	SUSANNA Art Company (Epic)	
26	20	CHANGE OF HEART Change (WEA)	
21	21	ABSOLUTE Scritti Politti (Virgin)	
18	22	SO TIRED Ozzy Osbourne (Epic)	
13	23	THE REFLEX Duran Duran (EMI)	
19	24	AUTOMATIC Pointer Sisters (Planet)	
-	25	BODY AND SOUL/TRAIN Sisters Of Mercy (Merciful Release)	
-	26	I WANNA BE LOVED Elvis Costello (F Beat)	
25	27	INFATUATION Rod Stewart (Warner Bros)	
-	28	TALKING LOUD AND CLEAR Orchestral Manoeuvres In The Dark (Virgin)	
-	29	WAITING IN VAIN Bob Marley & the Wailers (Island)	
14	30	RED GUITAR David Sylvian (Virgin)	
-	31	WHAT I WANT Dead Or Alive (Epic)	
28	32	THANKS FOR THE NIGHT Damned (Damned)	
-	33	DOIN' IT IN A HAUNTED HOUSE Yvonne Gage (Epic)	
40	34	ROUGH JUSTICE Bananarama (London)	
23	35	I WANT TO BREAK FREE Queen (EMI)	
32	36	WHEN AM I GOING TO MAKE A LIVING Sade (Epic)	
-	37	TONIGHT IS WHAT IT MEANS TO BE YOUNG Jim Steinman (MCA)	
-	38	THOSE FIRST IMPRESSIONS Associates (WEA)	
-	39	DANCE ME UP Gary Glitter (Arista)	
-	40	I WANNA MAKE YOU FEEL GOOD System (Polydor)	
36	41	LOVE WARS Womack & Womack (Elektra)	
45	42	PERFECT SKIN Lloyd Cole & the Commotions (Polydor)	
31	43	AGAINST ALL ODDS (TAKE A LOOK AT ME NOW) Phil Collins (Virgin)	
27	44	DANCING IN THE DARK Bruce Springsteen (CBS)	
-	45	WHITE LINES (DON'T DON'T DO IT) Grandmaster & Melle Mel (Sugarhill)	
29	46	LOVE ALL DAY Nick Heyward (Arista)	
50	47	EUROPEAN QUEEN Billy Ocean (Jive)	
-	48	TIME AFTER TIME Cyndi Lauper (Portrait)	
30	49	DAZZLE Siouxsie & the Banshees (Wonderland)	
49	50	FEELS SO REAL (WON'T LET GO) Patrice Rushen (Elektra)	

30 June 1984

last	this		
1	1	TWO TRIBES Frankie Goes To Hollywood (ZTT)	
2	2	SMALLTOWN BOY Bronski Beat (Forbidden Fruit)	
15	3	I WON'T LET THE SUN GO DOWN ON ME Nik Kershaw (MCA)	
9	4	RELAX Frankie Goes To Hollywood (ZTT)	
3	5	WAKE ME UP BEFORE YOU GO GO Wham! (Epic)	
6	6	SAD SONGS (SAY SO MUCH) Elton John (Rocket)	
13	7	FAREWELL MY SUMMER LOVE Michael Jackson (Motown)	
4	8	ONLY WHEN YOU LEAVE Spandau Ballet (Reformation)	
19	9	SUSANNA Art Company (Epic)	
11	10	THINKING OF YOU Sister Sledge (Cotillion/Atlantic)	
5	11	HIGH ENERGY Evelyn Thomas (Record Shack)	
-	12	JUMP (FOR MY LOVE) Pointer Sisters (Planet)	
20	13	CHANGE OF HEART Change (WEA)	
7	14	PEARL IN THE SHELL Howard Jones (WEA)	
21	15	ABSOLUTE Scritti Politti (Virgin)	
10	16	HEAVEN KNOWS (I'M MISERABLE NOW) Smiths (Rough Trade)	
45	17	WHITE LINES (DON'T DON'T DO IT) Grandmaster & Melle Mel (Sugarhill)	
28	18	TALKING LOUD AND CLEAR Orchestral Manoeuvres In The Dark (Virgin)	
-	19	BREAKIN' ... THERE'S NO STOPPING US Ollie & Jerry (Polydor)	
22	20	SO TIRED Ozzy Osbourne (Epic)	
8	21	DANCING WITH TEARS IN MY EYES Ultravox (Chrysalis)	
26	22	I WANNA BE LOVED Elvis Costello (F Beat)	
23	23	STUCK ON YOU Lionel Richie (Motown)	
14	24	SEARCHIN' Hazell Dean (Proto)	
16	25	GROOVIN' (YOU'RE THE BEST/BIG BOSS GROOVE) Style Council (Polydor)	
-	26	LOVE RESURRECTION Alison Moyet (CBS)	
17	27	I FEEL LIKE BUDDY HOLLY Alvin Stardust (Chrysalis)	
27	28	INFATUATION Rod Stewart (Warner Bros)	
42	29	PERFECT SKIN Lloyd Cole & the Commotions (Polydor)	
48	30	TIME AFTER TIME Cyndi Lauper (Portrait)	
29	31	WAITING IN VAIN Bob Marley & the Wailers (Island)	
12	32	LET'S HEAR IT FOR THE BOY Deniece Williams (CBS)	
33	33	DOIN' IT IN A HAUNTED HOUSE Yvonne Gage (Epic)	
-	34	LEAVE A TENDER MOMENT ALONE Billy Joel (CBS)	
-	35	COME BACK Mighty Wah! (Beggars Banquet)	
18	36	ONE BETTER DAY Madness (Stiff)	
-	37	LIFE ON YOUR OWN Human League (Virgin)	
38	38	THOSE FIRST IMPRESSIONS Associates (WEA)	
40	39	DANCE ME UP Gary Glitter (Arista)	
46	40	LOVE ALL DAY Nick Heyward (Arista)	
-	41	ON THE WINGS OF LOVE Jeffrey Osborne (A&M)	
34	42	ROUGH JUSTICE Bananarama (London)	
44	43	DANCING IN THE DARK Bruce Springsteen (CBS)	
25	44	BODY AND SOUL Sisters Of Mercy (Merciful Release)	
30	45	RED GUITAR David Sylvian (Virgin)	
-	46	I FOUND LOVIN' Fatback Band (Master Mix)	
-	47	OH BROTHER Fall (Beggars Banquet)	
-	48	YOUNG AT HEART Bluebells (London)	
23	49	THE REFLEX Duran Duran (EMI)	
24	50	AUTOMATIC Pointer Sisters (Planet)	

7 July 1984

last	this		
1	1	TWO TRIBES Frankie Goes To Hollywood (ZTT)	
4	2	RELAX Frankie Goes To Hollywood (ZTT)	
12	3	JUMP (FOR MY LOVE) Pointer Sisters (Planet)	
3	4	I WON'T LET THE SUN GO DOWN ON ME Nik Kershaw (MCA)	
2	5	SMALLTOWN BOY Bronski Beat (Forbidden Fruit)	
30	6	TIME AFTER TIME Cyndi Lauper (Portrait)	
19	7	BREAKIN' ... THERE'S NO STOPPING US Ollie & Jerry (Polydor)	
7	8	FAREWELL MY SUMMER LOVE Michael Jackson (Motown)	
5	9	WAKE ME UP BEFORE YOU GO GO Wham! (Epic)	
17	10	WHITE LINES (DON'T DON'T DO IT) Grandmaster & Melle Mel (Sugarhill)	
6	11	SAD SONGS (SAY SO MUCH) Elton John (Rocket)	
10	12	THINKING OF YOU Sister Sledge (Cotillion/Atlantic)	
18	13	TALKING LOUD AND CLEAR Orchestral Manoeuvres In The Dark (Virgin)	
13	14	CHANGE OF HEART Change (WEA)	
9	15	SUSANNA Art Company (Epic)	
23	16	STUCK ON YOU Lionel Richie (Motown)	
22	17	I WANNA BE LOVED Elvis Costello (F Beat)	
15	18	ABSOLUTE Scritti Politti (Virgin)	
37	19	LIFE ON YOUR OWN Human League (Virgin)	
11	20	HIGH ENERGY Evelyn Thomas (Record Shack)	
38	21	DANCE ME UP Gary Glitter (Arista)	
8	22	ONLY WHEN YOU LEAVE Spandau Ballet (Reformation)	
26	23	LOVE RESURRECTION Alison Moyet (CBS)	
16	24	HEAVEN KNOWS (I'M MISERABLE NOW) Smiths (Rough Trade)	
29	25	PERFECT SKIN Lloyd Cole & the Commotions (Polydor)	
34	26	LEAVE A TENDER MOMENT ALONE Billy Joel (CBS)	
-	27	WHEN DOVES CRY Prince & The Revolution (Warner Bros)	
14	28	PEARL IN THE SHELL Howard Jones (WEA)	
24	29	SEARCHIN' Hazell Dean (Proto)	
48	30	YOUNG AT HEART Bluebells (London)	
21	31	DANCING WITH TEARS IN MY EYES Ultravox (Chrysalis)	
-	32	IN THE GHETTO Nick Cave (Mute)	
41	33	ON THE WINGS OF LOVE Jeffrey Osborne (A&M)	
34	34	COME BACK Mighty Wah! (Beggars Banquet)	
20	35	SO TIRED Ozzy Osbourne (Epic)	
33	36	DOIN' IT IN A HAUNTED HOUSE Yvonne Gage (Epic)	
39	37	THOSE FIRST IMPRESSIONS Associates (WEA)	
28	38	INFATUATION Rod Stewart (Warner Bros)	
31	39	WAITING IN VAIN Bob Marley & the Wailers (Island)	
-	40	WHEN YOUR 'EX' WANTS YOU BACK Surface (Salsoul)	
46	41	I FOUND LOVIN' Fatback Band (Master Mix)	
32	42	LET'S HEAR IT FOR THE BOY Deniece Williams (CBS)	
-	43	TO FRANCE Mike Oldfield (Virgin)	
-	44	UP AROUND THE BEND Hanoi Rocks (CBS)	
-	45	SWEET SOMEBODY Shannon (Club)	
-	46	AGADOO Black Lace (Flair)	
-	47	SISTER OF MERCY Thompson Twins (Arista)	
-	48	WHAT'S LOVE GOT TO DO WITH IT Tina Turner (Capitol)	
36	49	ONE BETTER DAY Madness (Stiff)	
-	50	DON'T LET NOBODY HOLD YOU DOWN L.J. Reynolds (Club)	

As *Two Tribes* gave Frankie Goes To Hollywood an instant second Number One, with its eight-week residency at the top being the longest since John Travolta and Olivia Newton-John's marathon in 1978, something akin to Frankie-mania broke out, and sales of *Relax,* which had surreptitiously re-entered the lower part of the chart, took off again, to send it back up to Number Two, behind *Two Tribes.*

14 July 1984

last week	this week	Title / Artist (Label)
1	1	TWO TRIBES Frankie Goes To Hollywood (ZTT)
2	2	RELAX Frankie Goes To Hollywood (ZTT)
6	3	TIME AFTER TIME Cyndi Lauper (Portrait)
4	4	I WON'T LET THE SUN GO DOWN ON ME Nik Kershaw (MCA)
7	5	BREAKIN' ... THERE'S NO STOPPING US Ollie & Jerry (Polydor)
3	6	JUMP (FOR MY LOVE) Pointer Sisters (Planet)
5	7	SMALLTOWN BOY Bronski Beat (Forbidden Fruit)
10	8	WHITE LINES (DON'T DON'T DO IT) Grandmaster & Melle Mel (Sugarhill)
8	9	FAREWELL MY SUMMER LOVE Michael Jackson (Motown)
16	10	STUCK ON YOU Lionel Richie (Motown)
13	11	TALKING LOUD AND CLEAR Orchestral Manoeuvres In The Dark (Virgin)
27	12	WHEN DOVES CRY Prince & The Revolution (Warner Bros)
23	13	LOVE RESURRECTION Alison Moyet (CBS)
48	14	WHAT'S LOVE GOT TO DO WITH IT Tina Turner (Capitol)
12	15	THINKING OF YOU Sister Sledge (Cotillion/Atlantic)
19	16	LIFE ON YOUR OWN Human League (Virgin)
30	17	YOUNG AT HEART Bluebells (London)
47	18	SISTER OF MERCY Thompson Twins (Arista)
9	19	WAKE ME UP BEFORE YOU GO GO Wham! (Epic)
-	20	HOLE IN MY SHOE Neil (WEA)
14	21	CHANGE OF HEART Change (WEA)
18	22	ABSOLUTE Scritti Politti (Virgin)
21	23	DANCE ME UP Gary Glitter (Arista)
-	24	STATE OF SHOCK Jacksons (Epic)
11	25	SAD SONGS (SAY SO MUCH) Elton John (Rocket)
-	26	LAMENT Ultravox (Chrysalis)
25	27	PERFECT SKIN Lloyd Cole & the Commotions (Polydor)
15	28	SUSANNA Art Company (Epic)
45	29	SWEET SOMEBODY Shannon (Club)
-	30	I LOVE MEN Eartha Kitt (Record Shack)
26	31	LEAVE A TENDER MOMENT ALONE Billy Joel (CBS)
-	32	SEVEN SEAS Echo & the Bunnymen (Korova)
20	33	HIGH ENERGY Evelyn Thomas (Record Shack)
-	34	PARTYLINE Brass Construction (Capitol)
-	35	CLOSEST THING TO HEAVEN Kane Gang (Kitchenware)
41	36	I FOUND LOVIN' Fatback Band (Master Mix)
44	37	UP AROUND THE BEND Hanoi Rocks (CBS)
34	38	COME BACK Mighty Wah! (Beggars Banquet)
33	39	ON THE WINGS OF LOVE Jeffrey Osborne (A&M)
39	40	WAITING IN VAIN Bob Marley & the Wailers (Island)
32	41	IN THE GHETTO Nick Cave (Mute)
17	42	I WANNA BE LOVED Elvis Costello (F Beat)
22	43	ONLY WHEN YOU LEAVE Spandau Ballet (Reformation)
40	44	WHEN YOUR 'EX' WANTS YOU BACK Surface (Salsoul)
-	45	BEAT STREET BREAKDOWN Grandmaster Flash (Atlantic)
-	46	EYES WITHOUT A FACE Billy Idol (Chrysalis)
-	47	JAMMIN' IN AMERICA Gap Band (Total Experience)
50	48	DON'T LET NOBODY HOLD YOU DOWN L.J. Reynolds (Club)
-	49	DOWN ON THE STREET Shakatak (Polydor)
46	50	AGADOO Black Lace (Flair)

21 July 1984

this week	Title / Artist (Label)
1	TWO TRIBES Frankie Goes To Hollywood (ZTT)
2	HOLE IN MY SHOE Neil (WEA)
3	RELAX Frankie Goes To Hollywood (ZTT)
4	TIME AFTER TIME Cyndi Lauper (Portrait)
5	WHEN DOVES CRY Prince & The Revolution (Warner Bros)
6	I WON'T LET THE SUN GO DOWN ON ME Nik Kershaw (MCA)
7	WHITE LINES (DON'T DON'T DO IT) Grandmaster & Melle Mel (Sugarhill)
8	WHAT'S LOVE GOT TO DO WITH IT Tina Turner (Capitol)
9	BREAKIN' ... THERE'S NO STOPPING US Ollie & Jerry (Polydor)
10	LOVE RESURRECTION Alison Moyet (CBS)
12	JUMP (FOR MY LOVE) Pointer Sisters (Planet)
13	YOUNG AT HEART Bluebells (London)
14	STATE OF SHOCK Jacksons (Epic)
15	SEVEN SEAS Echo & the Bunnymen (Korova)
16	SMALLTOWN BOY Bronski Beat (Forbidden Fruit)
17	STUCK ON YOU Lionel Richie (Motown)
18	TALKING LOUD AND CLEAR Orchestral Manoeuvres In The Dark (Virgin)
19	LAMENT Ultravox (Chrysalis)
20	FAREWELL MY SUMMER LOVE Michael Jackson (Motown)
21	YOU THINK YOU'RE A MAN Divine (Proto)
22	THINKING OF YOU Sister Sledge (Cotillion/Atlantic)
23	CLOSEST THING TO HEAVEN Kane Gang (Kitchenware)
24	EVERYBODY'S LAUGHING Phil Fearon & Galaxy (Ensign)
25	DOWN ON THE STREET Shakatak (Polydor)
26	BEAT STREET BREAKDOWN Grandmaster Flash (Atlantic)
27	LIFE ON YOUR OWN Human League (Virgin)
28	WAKE ME UP BEFORE YOU GO GO Wham! (Epic)
29	ABSOLUTE Scritti Politti (Virgin)
30	BREAK DANCE PARTY Break Machine (Record Shack)
31	COME BACK Mighty Wah! (Beggars Banquet)
32	I FOUND LOVIN' Fatback Band (Master Mix)
33	CHANGE OF HEART Change (WEA)
34	DANCE ME UP Gary Glitter (Arista)
35	SWEET SOMEBODY Shannon (Club)
36	SAD SONGS (SAY SO MUCH) Elton John (Rocket)
37	LEAVE A TENDER MOMENT ALONE Billy Joel (CBS)
38	AGADOO Black Lace (Flair)
39	ON THE WINGS OF LOVE Jeffrey Osborne (A&M)
40	I WANNA BE LOVED Elvis Costello (F Beat)
41	PERFECT SKIN Lloyd Cole & the Commotions (Polydor)
42	SUSANNA Art Company (Epic)
43	IN THE GHETTO Nick Cave (Mute)
44	TOSSING AND TURNING Windjammer (MCA)
45	JUST FOR OLD TIME'S SAKE Foster & Allen (Ritz)
46	ALL OF YOU Julio Iglesias & Diana Ross (CBS)
47	HOT HOT HOT Arrow (Chrysalis)
48	WAITING IN VAIN Bob Marley & the Wailers (Island)
49	HIGH ENERGY Evelyn Thomas (Record Shack)
50	I LOVE MEN Eartha Kitt (Record Shack)

28 July 1984

this week	Title / Artist (Label)
1	TWO TRIBES Frankie Goes To Hollywood (ZTT)
2	HOLE IN MY SHOE Neil (WEA)
3	WHEN DOVES CRY Prince & The Revolution (Warner Brothers)
4	RELAX Frankie Goes To Hollywood (ZTT)
5	WHAT'S LOVE GOT TO DO WITH IT Tina Turner (Capitol)
6	TIME AFTER TIME Cyndi Lauper (Portrait)
7	WHITE LINES (DON'T DON'T DO IT) Grandmaster & Melle Mel (Sugarhill)
8	I WON'T LET THE SUN GO DOWN ON ME Nik Kershaw (MCA)
9	LOVE RESURRECTION Alison Moyet (CBS)
10	YOUNG AT HEART Bluebells (London)
11	SEVEN SEAS Echo & the Bunnymen (Korova)
12	SISTER OF MERCY Thompson Twins (Arista)
13	YOU THINK YOU'RE A MAN Divine (Proto)
14	EVERYBODY'S LAUGHING Phil Fearon & Galaxy (Ensign)
15	STATE OF SHOCK Jacksons (Epic)
16	JUMP (FOR MY LOVE) Pointer Sisters (Planet)
17	DOWN ON THE STREET Shakatak (Polydor)
18	SMALLTOWN BOY Bronski Beat (Forbidden Fruit)
19	TALKING LOUD AND CLEAR Orchestral Manoeuvres In The Dark (Virgin)
20	CLOSEST THING TO HEAVEN Kane Gang (Kitchenware)
21	STUCK ON YOU Lionel Richie (Motown)
22	FAREWELL MY SUMMER LOVE Michael Jackson (Motown)
23	SWEET SOMEBODY Shannon (Club)
24	IT'S A HARD LIFE Queen (EMI)
25	COME BACK Mighty Wah! (Beggars Banquet)
26	THE DAY BEFORE YOU CAME Blancmange (London)
27	THINKING OF YOU Sister Sledge (Cotillion/Atlantic)
28	LAMENT Ultravox (Chrysalis)
29	WAKE ME UP BEFORE YOU GO GO Wham! (Epic)
30	BREAKIN' ... THERE'S NO STOPPING US Ollie & Jerry (Polydor)
31	MINE Everything But The Girl (blanco y negro)
32	EYES WITHOUT A FACE Billy Idol (Chrysalis)
33	TOSSING AND TURNING Windjammer (MCA)
34	BEAT STREET BREAKDOWN Grandmaster Flash (Atlantic)
35	CHANGE OF HEART Change (WEA)
36	LOVE SONGS ARE BACK AGAIN Band Of Gold (RCA)
37	ABSOLUTE Scritti Politti (Virgin)
38	A HARD DAY'S NIGHT Beatles (Parlophone)
39	TAKE Colour Field (Chrysalis)
40	A NEW DAY Killing Joke (EG)
41	SAD SONGS (SAY SO MUCH) Elton John (Rocket)
42	SELF CONTROL Laura Branigan (Atlantic)
43	LIFE ON YOUR OWN Human League (Virgin)
44	JUST FOR OLD TIME'S SAKE Foster & Allen (Ritz)
45	SUMMER GROOVE Tony Jackson (Cedar)
46	BREAK DANCE PARTY Break Machine (Record Shack)
47	ON THE WINGS OF LOVE Jeffrey Osborne (A&M)
48	IN THE GHETTO Nick Cave (Mute)
49	I'M STEPPING OUT John Lennon (Polydor)
50	MY MALE CURIOSITY Kid Creole & the Coconuts (Virgin)

Nobody but the Beatles (and, posthumously, John Lennon in January 1981) had ever held Numbers One and Two on the singles chart simultaneously before Frankie Goes To Hollywood. Their label, ZTT, craftily kept the pot boiling by issuing limited editions of new and varied mixes of both songs every couple of weeks, which addicted fans bought and re-bought, sending both singles over the million.

August 1984

4 August 1984

LW	TW	Title / Artist (Label)
1	1	TWO TRIBES Frankie Goes To Hollywood (ZTT)
2	2	HOLE IN MY SHOE Neil (WEA)
5	3	WHAT'S LOVE GOT TO DO WITH IT Tina Turner (Capitol)
3	4	WHEN DOVES CRY Prince & The Revolution (Warner Bros)
4	5	RELAX Frankie Goes To Hollywood (ZTT)
6	6	TIME AFTER TIME Cyndi Lauper (Portrait)
10	7	YOUNG AT HEART Bluebells (London)
9	8	LOVE RESURRECTION Alison Moyet (CBS)
7	9	WHITE LINES (DON'T DON'T DO IT) Grandmaster & Melle Mel (Sugarhill)
14	10	EVERYBODY'S LAUGHING Phil Fearon & Galaxy (Ensign)
13	11	YOU THINK YOU'RE A MAN Divine (Proto)
11	12	SEVEN SEAS Echo & the Bunnymen (Korova)
20	13	CLOSEST THING TO HEAVEN Kane Gang (Kitchenware)
17	14	DOWN ON THE STREET Shakatak (Polydor)
24	15	IT'S A HARD LIFE Queen (EMI)
8	16	I WON'T LET THE SUN GO DOWN ON ME Nik Kershaw (MCA)
12	17	SISTER OF MERCY Thompson Twins (Arista)
16	18	JUMP (FOR MY LOVE) Pointer Sisters (Planet)
32	19	EYES WITHOUT A FACE Billy Idol (Chrysalis)
25	20	COME BACK Mighty Wah! (Beggars Banquet)
30	21	BREAKIN' ... THERE'S NO STOPPING US Ollie & Jerry (Polydor)
15	22	STATE OF SHOCK Jacksons (Epic)
26	23	THE DAY BEFORE YOU CAME Blancmange (London)
19	24	TALKING LOUD AND CLEAR Orchestral Manoeuvres In The Dark (Virgin)
23	25	SWEET SOMEBODY Shannon (Club)
-	26	WHATEVER I DO (WHEREVER I GO) Hazell Dean (Proto)
33	27	TOSSING AND TURNING Windjammer (MCA)
28	28	SOME GUYS HAVE ALL THE LUCK Rod Stewart (Warner Bros)
-	29	AGADOO Black Lace (Flair)
21	30	STUCK ON YOU Lionel Richie (Motown)
38	31	A HARD DAY'S NIGHT Beatles (Parlophone)
-	32	SUNGLASSES Tracey Ullman (Stiff)
47	33	ON THE WINGS OF LOVE Jeffrey Osborne (A&M)
36	34	LOVE SONGS ARE BACK AGAIN Band Of Gold (RCA)
-	35	CARELESS WHISPER George Michael (Epic)
40	36	A NEW DAY Killing Joke (EG)
-	37	BROWN SUGAR Rolling Stones (Rolling Stones)
39	38	TAKE Colour Field (Chrysalis)
18	39	SMALLTOWN BOY Bronski Beat (Forbidden Fruit)
28	40	LAMENT Ultravox (Chrysalis)
22	41	FAREWELL MY SUMMER LOVE Michael Jackson (Motown)
42	42	SELF CONTROL Laura Branigan (Atlantic)
-	43	GUILTY Paul Hardcastle (Total Control)
34	44	BEAT STREET BREAKDOWN Grandmaster Flash (Atlantic)
29	45	WAKE ME UP BEFORE YOU GO GO Wham! (Epic)
27	46	THINKING OF YOU Sister Sledge (Cotillion/Atlantic)
41	47	SAD SONGS (SAY SO MUCH) Elton John (Rocket)
43	48	LIFE ON YOUR OWN Human League (Virgin)
-	49	AIN'T NO SUNSHINE Sivuca (London)
-	50	THERE ARE MORE SNAKES THAN LADDERS Captain Sensible (A&M)

11 August 1984

LW	TW	Title / Artist (Label)
1	1	TWO TRIBES Frankie Goes To Hollywood (ZTT)
4	2	WHEN DOVES CRY Prince & The Revolution (Warner Bros)
3	3	WHAT'S LOVE GOT TO DO WITH IT Tina Turner (Capitol)
5	4	RELAX Frankie Goes To Hollywood (ZTT)
2	5	HOLE IN MY SHOE Neil (WEA)
15	6	IT'S A HARD LIFE Queen (EMI)
9	7	WHITE LINES (DON'T DON'T DO IT) Grandmaster & Melle Mel (Sugarhill)
35	8	CARELESS WHISPER George Michael (Epic)
10	9	EVERYBODY'S LAUGHING Phil Fearon & Galaxy (Ensign)
14	10	DOWN ON THE STREET Shakatak (Polydor)
13	11	CLOSEST THING TO HEAVEN Kane Gang (Kitchenware)
26	12	WHATEVER I DO (WHEREVER I GO) Hazell Dean (Proto)
7	13	YOUNG AT HEART Bluebells (London)
11	14	YOU THINK YOU'RE A MAN Divine (Proto)
6	15	TIME AFTER TIME Cyndi Lauper (Portrait)
19	16	EYES WITHOUT A FACE Billy Idol (Chrysalis)
8	17	LOVE RESURRECTION Alison Moyet (CBS)
27	18	TOSSING AND TURNING Windjammer (MCA)
33	19	ON THE WINGS OF LOVE Jeffrey Osborne (A&M)
16	20	I WON'T LET THE SUN GO DOWN ON ME Nik Kershaw (MCA)
29	21	AGADOO Black Lace (Flair)
42	22	SELF CONTROL Laura Branigan (Atlantic)
23	23	THE DAY BEFORE YOU CAME Blancmange (London)
12	24	SEVEN SEAS Echo & the Bunnymen (Korova)
20	25	COME BACK Mighty Wah! (Beggars Banquet)
18	26	JUMP (FOR MY LOVE) Pointer Sisters (Planet)
17	27	SISTER OF MERCY Thompson Twins (Arista)
-	28	NERVOUS SHAKEDOWN AC/DC (Atlantic)
21	29	BREAKIN' ... THERE'S NO STOPPING US Ollie & Jerry (Polydor)
30	30	SOME GUYS HAVE ALL THE LUCK Rod Stewart (Warner Bros)
31	31	JUST THE WAY YOU LIKE IT S.O.S. Band (Tabu)
32	32	SUNGLASSES Tracey Ullman (Stiff)
-	33	THE FRIENDS AGAIN EP (EP) Friends Again (Mercury)
-	34	STUCK ON YOU Trevor Walters (Sanity)
-	35	BANANA BANANA King Kurt (Stiff)
-	36	PALE BLUE EYES Paul Quinn & Edwyn Collins (Swamplands)
37	37	99 1/2 Carol Lynn Townes (Polydor)
25	38	SWEET SOMEBODY Shannon (Club)
22	39	STATE OF SHOCK Jacksons (Epic)
-	40	JUST FOR OLD TIME'S SAKE Foster & Allen (Ritz)
-	41	IN THE COUNTRY Farmer's Boys (EMI)
-	42	CHOOSE ME (RESCUE ME) Loose Ends (Virgin)
-	43	THE MORE YOU LIVE THE MORE YOU LOVE A Flock Of Seagulls (Jive)
30	44	STUCK ON YOU Lionel Richie (Motown)
-	45	TODAY'S YOUR LUCKY DAY Harold Melvin and the Blue Notes (London)
43	46	GUILTY Paul Hardcastle (Total Control)
-	47	HARDROCK Herbie Hancock (CBS)
45	48	WAKE ME UP BEFORE YOU GO GO Wham! (Epic)
47	49	SAD SONGS (SAY SO MUCH) Elton John (Rocket)
50	50	THERE ARE MORE SNAKES THAN LADDERS Captain Sensible (A&M)

18 August 1984

LW	TW	Title / Artist (Label)
8	1	CARELESS WHISPER George Michael (Epic)
1	2	TWO TRIBES Frankie Goes To Hollywood (ZTT)
3	3	WHAT'S LOVE GOT TO DO WITH IT Tina Turner (Capitol)
21	4	AGADOO Black Lace (Flair)
2	5	WHEN DOVES CRY Prince & The Revolution (Warner Bros)
12	6	WHATEVER I DO (WHEREVER I GO) Hazell Dean (Proto)
6	7	IT'S A HARD LIFE Queen (EMI)
4	8	RELAX Frankie Goes To Hollywood (ZTT)
5	9	HOLE IN MY SHOE Neil (WEA)
11	10	CLOSEST THING TO HEAVEN Kane Gang (Kitchenware)
22	11	SELF CONTROL Laura Branigan (Atlantic)
7	12	WHITE LINES (DON'T DON'T DO IT) Grandmaster & Melle Mel (Sugarhill)
19	13	ON THE WINGS OF LOVE Jeffrey Osborne (A&M)
9	14	EVERYBODY'S LAUGHING Phil Fearon & Galaxy (Ensign)
10	15	DOWN ON THE STREET Shakatak (Polydor)
-	16	LIKE TO GET TO KNOW YOU WELL Howard Jones (WEA)
15	17	TIME AFTER TIME Cyndi Lauper (Portrait)
13	18	YOUNG AT HEART Bluebells (London)
14	19	YOU THINK YOU'RE A MAN Divine (Proto)
18	20	TOSSING AND TURNING Windjammer (MCA)
34	21	STUCK ON YOU Trevor Walters (Sanity)
16	22	EYES WITHOUT A FACE Billy Idol (Chrysalis)
30	23	SOME GUYS HAVE ALL THE LUCK Rod Stewart (Warner Bros)
17	24	LOVE RESURRECTION Alison Moyet (CBS)
28	25	NERVOUS SHAKEDOWN AC/DC (Atlantic)
-	26	TWO MINUTES TO MIDNIGHT Iron Maiden (EMI)
-	27	WE ROCK Dio (Vertigo)
23	28	THE DAY BEFORE YOU CAME Blancmange (London)
26	29	JUMP (FOR MY LOVE) Pointer Sisters (Planet)
32	30	SUNGLASSES Tracey Ullman (Stiff)
-	31	DR. BEAT Miami Sound Machine (Epic)
-	32	PASSENGERS Elton John (Rocket)
-	33	EMPTY ROOMS Gary Moore (10)
24	34	SEVEN SEAS Echo & the Bunnymen (Korova)
36	35	PALE BLUE EYES Paul Quinn & Edwyn Collins (Swamplands)
-	36	GIRL YOU'RE SO TOGETHER Michael Jackson (Motown)
37	37	ARE YOU READY Break Machine (Record Shack)
35	38	BANANA BANANA King Kurt (Stiff)
20	39	I WON'T LET THE SUN GO DOWN ON ME Nik Kershaw (MCA)
25	40	COME BACK Mighty Wah! (Beggars Banquet)
31	41	JUST THE WAY YOU LIKE IT S.O.S. Band (Tabu)
-	42	I NEED YOU Pointer Sisters (Planet)
-	43	I'LL WAIT Van Halen (Warner Bros)
27	44	SISTER OF MERCY Thompson Twins (Arista)
-	45	LOVE SONGS ARE BACK AGAIN Band Of Gold (RCA)
44	46	STUCK ON YOU Lionel Richie (Motown)
37	47	99 1/2 Carol Lynn Townes (Polydor)
-	48	BLACK STATIONS/WHITE STATIONS M&M (RCA)
-	49	YOU ARE MY MELODY Change (WEA)
45	50	TODAY'S YOUR LUCKY DAY Harold Melvin & the Blue Notes (London)

The *Young Ones* TV character neil (small 'n' to show his insignificance) was the hapless hippy of the quartet, so the notion of his alter-ego, actor Nigel Planer, reviving a suitably flowering hippy oldie and recording it in the neil persona, was an appropriate one. The song chosen was Traffic's 1967 Number Two hit *Hole In My Shoe,* and neil effortlessly equalled the chart achievement of the original.

25 August 1984

last week	this week		
1	1	CARELESS WHISPER	George Michael (Epic)
4	2	AGADOO	Black Lace (Flair)
2	3	TWO TRIBES	Frankie Goes To Hollywood (ZTT)
11	4	SELF CONTROL	Laura Branigan (Atlantic)
6	5	WHATEVER I DO (WHEREVER I GO)	
			Hazell Dean (Proto)
3	6	WHAT'S LOVE GOT TO DO WITH IT	
			Tina Turner (Capitol)
16	7	LIKE TO GET TO KNOW YOU WELL	
			Howard Jones (WEA)
5	8	WHEN DOVES CRY	
			Prince & The Revolution (Warner Bros)
13	9	ON THE WINGS OF LOVE	Jeffrey Osborne (A&M)
21	10	STUCK ON YOU	Trevor Walters (Sanity)
8	11	RELAX	Frankie Goes To Hollywood (ZTT)
12	12	WHITE LINES (DON'T DON'T DO IT)	
			Grandmaster & Melle Mel (Sugarhill)
7	13	IT'S A HARD LIFE	Queen (EMI)
10	14	CLOSEST THING TO HEAVEN	
			Kane Gang (Kitchenware)
20	15	TOSSING AND TURNING	Windjammer (MCA)
30	16	SUNGLASSES	Tracey Ullman (Stiff)
-	17	I JUST CALLED TO SAY I LOVE YOU	
			Stevie Wonder (Motown)
14	18	EVERYBODY'S LAUGHING	
			Phil Fearon & Galaxy (Ensign)
26	19	TWO MINUTES TO MIDNIGHT	Iron Maiden (EMI)
23	20	SOME GUYS HAVE ALL THE LUCK	
			Rod Stewart (Warner Bros)
9	21	HOLE IN MY SHOE	Neil (WEA)
-	22	THE INK IN THE WELL	David Sylvian (Virgin)
31	23	DR. BEAT	Miami Sound Machine (Epic)
15	24	DOWN ON THE STREET	Shakatak (Polydor)
19	25	YOU THINK YOU'RE A MAN	Divine (Proto)
32	26	PASSENGERS	Elton John (Rocket)
18	27	YOUNG AT HEART	Bluebells (London)
22	28	EYES WITHOUT A FACE	Billy Idol (Chrysalis)
42	29	I NEED YOU	Pointer Sisters (Planet)
45	30	LOVE SONGS ARE BACK AGAIN	Band Of Gold (RCA)
-	31	MOTHER'S TALK	Tears For Fears (Mercury)
25	32	NERVOUS SHAKEDOWN	AC/DC (Atlantic)
17	33	TIME AFTER TIME	Cyndi Lauper (Portrait)
41	34	JUST THE WAY YOU LIKE IT S.O.S. Band (Tabu)	
-	35	CASTLES IN SPAIN Armoury Show (Parlophone)	
28	36	THE DAY BEFORE YOU CAME Blancmange (London)	
-	37	I'LL FLY FOR YOU	Spandau Ballet (Reformation)
24	38	LOVE RESURRECTION	Alison Moyet (CBS)
48	39	BLACK STATIONS/WHITE STATIONS	M&M (RCA)
-	40	THE MORE YOU LIVE THE MORE YOU LOVE	
			A Flock Of Seagulls (Jive)
-	41	THE ONLY FLAME IN TOWN Elvis Costello (F.Beat)	
27	42	WE ROCK	Dio (Vertigo)
39	43	I WON'T LET THE SUN GO DOWN ON ME	
			Nik Kershaw (MCA)
29	44	JUMP (FOR MY LOVE)	Pointer Sisters (Planet)
33	45	EMPTY ROOMS	Gary Moore (10)
38	46	BANANA BANANA	King Kurt (Stiff)
37	47	ARE YOU READY	Break Machine (Record Shack)
36	48	GIRL YOU'RE SO TOGETHER	
			Michael Jackson (Motown)
-	49	YOU'RE NEVER TOO YOUNG	
			Cool Notes (Abstract Dance)
-	50	STATE OF INDEPENDENCE	
			Jon & Vangelis (Polydor)

1 September 1984

1	1	CARELESS WHISPER	George Michael (Epic)
17	2	I JUST CALLED TO SAY I LOVE YOU	
			Stevie Wonder (Motown)
2	3	AGADOO	Black Lace (Flair)
7	4	LIKE TO GET TO KNOW YOU WELL	
			Howard Jones (WEA)
4	5	SELF CONTROL	Laura Branigan (Atlantic)
3	6	TWO TRIBES	Frankie Goes To Hollywood (ZTT)
10	7	STUCK ON YOU	Trevor Walters (Sanity)
5	8	WHATEVER I DO (WHEREVER I GO)	
			Hazell Dean (Proto)
6	9	WHAT'S LOVE GOT TO DO WITH IT	
			Tina Turner (Capitol)
19	10	TWO MINUTES TO MIDNIGHT	Iron Maiden (EMI)
26	11	PASSENGERS	Elton John (Rocket)
23	12	DR. BEAT	Miami Sound Machine (Epic)
8	13	WHEN DOVES CRY	
			Prince & The Revolution (Warner Bros)
12	14	WHITE LINES (DON'T DON'T DO IT)	
			Grandmaster & Melle Mel (Sugarhill)
9	15	ON THE WINGS OF LOVE	Jeffrey Osborne (A&M)
11	16	RELAX	Frankie Goes To Hollywood (ZTT)
37	17	I'LL FLY FOR YOU	Spandau Ballet (Reformation)
13	18	IT'S A HARD LIFE	Queen (EMI)
16	19	SUNGLASSES	Tracey Ullman (Stiff)
20	20	SOME GUYS HAVE ALL THE LUCK	
			Rod Stewart (Warner Bros)
29	21	I NEED YOU	Pointer Sisters (Planet)
31	22	MOTHER'S TALK	Tears For Fears (Mercury)
14	23	CLOSEST THING TO HEAVEN	
			Kane Gang (Kitchenware)
-	24	WILLIAM, IT WAS REALLY NOTHING	
			Smiths (Rough Trade)
15	25	TOSSING AND TURNING	Windjammer (MCA)
21	26	HOLE IN MY SHOE	Neil (WEA)
18	27	EVERYBODY'S LAUGHING	
			Phil Fearon & Galaxy (Ensign)
24	28	DOWN ON THE STREET	Shakatak (Polydor)
-	29	GHOSTBUSTERS	Ray Parker Jr. (Arista)
32	30	NERVOUS SHAKEDOWN	AC/DC (Atlantic)
40	31	THE MORE YOU LIVE THE MORE YOU LOVE	
			A Flock Of Seagulls (Jive)
-	32	TOUR DE FRANCE	Kraftwerk (EMI)
45	33	EMPTY ROOMS	Gary Moore (10)
35	34	CASTLES IN SPAIN Armoury Show (Parlophone)	
49	35	YOU'RE NEVER TOO YOUNG	
			Cool Notes (Abstract Dance)
25	36	YOU THINK YOU'RE A MAN	Divine (Proto)
22	37	THE INK IN THE WELL	David Sylvian (Virgin)
41	38	THE ONLY FLAME IN TOWN	
			Elvis Costello (F.Beat)
-	39	MASTER AND SERVANT	Depeche Mode (Mute)
30	40	LOVE SONGS ARE BACK AGAIN	
			Band Of Gold (RCA)
27	41	YOUNG AT HEART	Bluebells (London)
-	42	MAGIC TOUCH	Rose Royce (Streetwave)
-	43	WAITING FOR THE LOVEBOAT	Associates (WEA)
34	44	JUST THE WAY IT S.O.S. Band (Tabu)	
-	45	SHE BOP	Cyndi Lauper (Portrait)
46	46	BIG IN JAPAN	Alphaville (WEA International)
-	47	LADY SHINE	Horn Section (Fourth & Broadway)
28	48	EYES WITHOUT A FACE	Billy Idol (Chrysalis)
42	49	WE ROCK	Dio (Vertigo)
-	50	MR. SOLITAIRE	Animal Nightlife (Island)

8 September 1984

2	1	I JUST CALLED TO SAY I LOVE YOU	
			Stevie Wonder (Motown)
1	2	CARELESS WHISPER	George Michael (Epic)
4	3	LIKE TO GET TO KNOW YOU WELL	
			Howard Jones (WEA)
3	4	AGADOO	Black Lace (Flair)
5	5	SELF CONTROL	Laura Branigan (Atlantic)
11	6	PASSENGERS	Elton John (Rocket)
12	7	DR. BEAT	Miami Sound Machine (Epic)
7	8	STUCK ON YOU	Trevor Walters (Sanity)
17	9	I'LL FLY FOR YOU	Spandau Ballet (Reformation)
6	10	TWO TRIBES	Frankie Goes To Hollywood (ZTT)
8	11	WHATEVER I DO (WHEREVER I GO)	
			Hazell Dean (Proto)
9	12	WHAT'S LOVE GOT TO DO WITH IT	
			Tina Turner (Capitol)
10	13	TWO MINUTES TO MIDNIGHT	Iron Maiden (EMI)
29	14	GHOSTBUSTERS	Ray Parker Jr. (Arista)
24	15	WILLIAM, IT WAS REALLY NOTHING	
			Smiths (Rough Trade)
14	16	WHITE LINES (DON'T DON'T DO IT)	
			Grandmaster & Melle Mel (Sugarhill)
-	17	MADAM BUTTERFLY (UN BEL DI VEDREMO)	
			Malcolm McLaren (Charisma)
20	18	SOME GUYS HAVE ALL THE LUCK	
			Rod Stewart (Warner Bros)
22	19	MOTHER'S TALK	Tears For Fears (Mercury)
39	20	MASTER AND SERVANT	Depeche Mode (Mute)
15	21	ON THE WINGS OF LOVE	Jeffrey Osborne (A&M)
46	22	BIG IN JAPAN	Alphaville (WEA International)
19	23	SUNGLASSES	Tracey Ullman (Stiff)
16	24	RELAX	Frankie Goes To Hollywood (ZTT)
13	25	WHEN DOVES CRY	
			Prince & The Revolution (Warner Bros)
-	26	SUNSET NOW	Heaven 17 (Virgin)
-	27	HOT WATER	Level 42 (Polydor)
18	28	IT'S A HARD LIFE	Queen (EMI)
32	29	TOUR DE FRANCE	Kraftwerk (EMI)
21	30	I NEED YOU	Pointer Sisters (Planet)
-	31	ARE YOU READY	Break Machine (Record Shack)
-	32	CATH	Bluebells (London)
40	33	LOVE SONGS ARE BACK AGAIN Band Of Gold (RCA)	
-	34	KILLED BY DEATH	Motorhead (Bronze)
27	35	EVERYBODY'S LAUGHING	
			Phil Fearon & Galaxy (Ensign)
42	36	MAGIC TOUCH	Rose Royce (Streetwave)
31	37	THE MORE YOU LIVE THE MORE YOU LOVE	
			A Flock Of Seagulls (Jive)
38	38	ALL I NEED IS EVERYTHING Aztec Camera (WEA)	
-	39	FOREST FIRE	
			Lloyd Cole & the Commotions (Polydor)
44	40	JUST THE WAY YOU LIKE IT S.O.S. Band (Tabu)	
28	41	DOWN ON THE STREET	Shakatak (Polydor)
25	42	TOSSING AND TURNING	Windjammer (MCA)
-	43	TALKING IN YOUR SLEEP	Bucks Fizz (RCA)
33	44	EMPTY ROOMS	Gary Moore (10)
34	45	CASTLES IN SPAIN Armoury Show (Parlophone)	
23	46	CLOSEST THING TO HEAVEN	
			Kane Gang (Kitchenware)
35	47	YOU'RE NEVER TOO YOUNG	
			Cool Notes (Abstract Dance)
47	48	LADY SHINE	Horn Section (Fourth & Broadway)
-	49	WHAT I LIKE MOST ABOUT YOU IS YOUR	
		GIRLFRIEND	Special AKA (2 Tone)
45	50	SHE BOP	Cyndi Lauper (Portrait)

Record sales in 1984, at least among the really big hits, were at the highest level of the decade. George Michael's *Careless Whisper* (not credited to Wham! to distiguish this ballad from Wham!'s uptempo repertoire) replaced the million-selling *Two Tribes* at Number One, and promply sold over a million itself, as did Stevie Wonder's single which, in turn, replaced it - a unique sequence in chart history.

September 1984

15 September 1984

last week	this week	entry
1	1	I JUST CALLED TO SAY I LOVE YOU — Stevie Wonder (Motown)
2	2	CARELESS WHISPER — George Michael (Epic)
14	3	GHOSTBUSTERS — Ray Parker Jr. (Arista)
3	4	LIKE TO GET TO KNOW YOU WELL — Howard Jones (WEA)
6	5	PASSENGERS — Elton John (Rocket)
7	6	DR. BEAT — Miami Sound Machine (Epic)
4	7	AGADOO — Black Lace (Flair)
5	8	SELF CONTROL — Laura Branigan (Atlantic)
22	9	BIG IN JAPAN — Alphaville (WEA International)
9	10	I'LL FLY FOR YOU — Spandau Ballet (Reformation)
17	11	MADAM BUTTERFLY (UN BEL DI VEDREMO) — Malcolm McLaren (Charisma)
20	12	MASTER AND SERVANT — Depeche Mode (Mute)
15	13	WILLIAM, IT WAS REALLY NOTHING — Smiths (Rough Trade)
-	14	PRIDE (IN THE NAME OF LOVE) — U2 (Island)
10	15	TWO TRIBES — Frankie Goes To Hollywood (ZTT)
11	16	WHATEVER I DO (WHEREVER I GO) — Hazell Dean (Proto)
17	17	MOTHER'S TALK — Tears For Fears (Mercury)
8	18	STUCK ON YOU — Trevor Walters (Sanity)
27	19	HOT WATER — Level 42 (Polydor)
12	20	WHAT'S LOVE GOT TO DO WITH IT — Tina Turner (Capitol)
18	21	SOME GUYS HAVE ALL THE LUCK — Rod Stewart (Warner Bros)
-	22	LOST IN MUSIC — Sister Sledge (Atlantic/Cotillion)
26	23	SUNSET NOW — Heaven 17 (Virgin)
13	24	TWO MINUTES TO MIDNIGHT — Iron Maiden (EMI)
43	25	TALKING IN YOUR SLEEP — Bucks Fizz (RCA)
16	26	WHITE LINES (DON'T DON'T DO IT) — Grandmaster & Melle Mel (Sugarhill)
-	27	HEAVEN'S ON FIRE — Kiss (Vertigo)
24	28	RELAX — Frankie Goes To Hollywood (ZTT)
30	29	I NEED YOU — Pointer Sisters (Planet)
-	30	TESLA GIRLS — Orchestral Manoeuvres In The Dark (Virgin)
36	31	MAGIC TOUCH — Rose Royce (Streetwave)
25	32	WHEN DOVES CRY — Prince & The Revolution (Warner Bros)
29	33	TOUR DE FRANCE — Kraftwerk (EMI)
34	34	KILLED BY DEATH — Motorhead (Bronze)
-	35	TORTURE — Jacksons (Epic)
-	36	GIRL YOU'RE SO TOGETHER — Michael Jackson (Motown)
37	37	ARE YOU READY — Break Machine (Record Shack)
-	38	ENCORE — Cheryl Lynn (Streetwave)
-	39	LAP OF LUXURY — Jethro Tull (Chrysalis)
38	40	ALL I NEED IS EVERYTHING — Aztec Camera (WEA)
21	41	ON THE WINGS OF LOVE — Jeffrey Osborne (A&M)
-	42	UNITY PART 1 — James Brown & Afrika Bambaataa (Tommy Boy)
37	43	THE MORE YOU LIVE THE MORE YOU LOVE — A Flock Of Seagulls (Jive)
23	44	SUNGLASSES — Tracey Ullman (Stiff)
47	45	YOU'RE NEVER TOO YOUNG — Cool Notes (Abstract Dance)
50	46	SHE BOP — Cyndi Lauper (Portrait)
39	47	FOREST FIRE — Lloyd Cole & the Commotions (Polydor)
-	48	ANOTHER SILENT DAY — Adventures (Chrysalis)
-	49	YOU GET THE BEST FROM ME — Alicia Myers (MCA)
49	50	WHAT I LIKE MOST ABOUT YOU IS YOUR GIRLFRIEND — Special AKA (2 Tone)

22 September 1984

last week	this week	entry
1	1	I JUST CALLED TO SAY I LOVE YOU — Stevie Wonder (Motown)
3	2	GHOSTBUSTERS — Ray Parker Jr. (Arista)
2	3	CARELESS WHISPER — George Michael (Epic)
9	4	BIG IN JAPAN — Alphaville (WEA International)
14	5	PRIDE (IN THE NAME OF LOVE) — U2 (Island)
6	6	DR. BEAT — Miami Sound Machine (Epic)
5	7	PASSENGERS — Elton John (Rocket)
4	8	LIKE TO GET TO KNOW YOU WELL — Howard Jones (WEA)
11	9	MADAM BUTTERFLY (UN BEL DI VEDREMO) — Malcolm McLaren (Charisma)
7	10	AGADOO — Black Lace (Flair)
12	11	MASTER AND SERVANT — Depeche Mode (Mute)
22	12	LOST IN MUSIC — Sister Sledge (Atlantic/Cotillion)
8	13	SELF CONTROL — Laura Branigan (Atlantic)
13	14	WILLIAM, IT WAS REALLY NOTHING — Smiths (Rough Trade)
25	15	TALKING IN YOUR SLEEP — Bucks Fizz (RCA)
10	16	I'LL FLY FOR YOU — Spandau Ballet (Reformation)
19	17	HOT WATER — Level 42 (Polydor)
-	18	A LETTER TO YOU — Shakin' Stevens (Epic)
-	19	BLUE JEAN — David Bowie (EMI America)
35	20	TORTURE — Jacksons (Epic)
17	21	MOTHER'S TALK — Tears For Fears (Mercury)
23	22	SUNSET NOW — Heaven 17 (Virgin)
15	23	TWO TRIBES — Frankie Goes To Hollywood (ZTT)
-	24	HAMMER TO FALL — Queen (EMI)
18	25	STUCK ON YOU — Trevor Walters (Sanity)
-	26	HUMAN RACING — Nik Kershaw (MCA)
16	27	WHATEVER I DO (WHEREVER I GO) — Hazell Dean (Proto)
33	28	TOUR DE FRANCE — Kraftwerk (EMI)
31	29	MAGIC TOUCH — Rose Royce (Streetwave)
-	30	BETTER BE GOOD TO ME — Tina Turner (Capitol)
30	31	TESLA GIRLS — Orchestral Manoeuvres In The Dark (Virgin)
-	32	SMOOTH OPERATOR — Sade (Epic)
26	33	WHITE LINES (DON'T DON'T DO IT) — Grandmaster & Melle Mel (Sugarhill)
40	34	ALL I NEED IS EVERYTHING — Aztec Camera (WEA)
20	35	WHAT'S LOVE GOT TO DO WITH IT — Tina Turner (Capitol)
-	36	WHY — Bronski Beat (Forbidden Fruit)
28	37	RELAX — Frankie Goes To Hollywood (ZTT)
42	38	UNITY PART 1 — James Brown & Afrika Bambaataa (Tommy Boy)
-	39	IF IT HAPPENS AGAIN — UB40 (DEP International)
21	40	SOME GUYS HAVE ALL THE LUCK — Rod Stewart (Warner Bros)
49	41	YOU GET THE BEST FROM ME — Alicia Myers (MCA)
-	42	LOVE KILLS — Freddie Mercury (CBS)
-	43	ACCELERATION — Bill Nelson (Cocteau)
39	44	LAP OF LUXURY — Jethro Tull (Chrysalis)
24	45	TWO MINUTES TO MIDNIGHT — Iron Maiden (EMI)
-	46	THE MEDICINE SONG — Stephanie Mills (Club)
27	47	HEAVEN'S ON FIRE — Kiss (Vertigo)
32	48	WHEN DOVES CRY — Prince & The Revolution (Warner Bros)
-	49	THE GIRL FROM IPANEMA — Astrud Gilberto (Verve)
50	50	WHAT I LIKE MOST ABOUT YOU IS YOUR GIRLFRIEND — Special AKA (2 Tone)

29 September 1984

last week	this week	entry
1	1	I JUST CALLED TO SAY I LOVE YOU — Stevie Wonder (Motown)
2	2	GHOSTBUSTERS — Ray Parker Jr. (Arista)
5	3	PRIDE (IN THE NAME OF LOVE) — U2 (Island)
12	4	LOST IN MUSIC — Sister Sledge (Atlantic/Cotillion)
3	5	CARELESS WHISPER — George Michael (Epic)
4	6	BIG IN JAPAN — Alphaville (WEA International)
19	7	BLUE JEAN — David Bowie (EMI America)
6	8	DR. BEAT — Miami Sound Machine (Epic)
18	9	A LETTER TO YOU — Shakin' Stevens (Epic)
11	10	MASTER AND SERVANT — Depeche Mode (Mute)
9	11	MADAM BUTTERFLY (UN BEL DI VEDREMO) — Malcolm McLaren (Charisma)
36	12	WHY — Bronski Beat (Forbidden Fruit)
10	13	AGADOO — Black Lace (Flair)
24	14	HAMMER TO FALL — Queen (EMI)
31	15	TESLA GIRLS — Orchestral Manoeuvres In The Dark (Virgin)
7	16	PASSENGERS — Elton John (Rocket)
42	17	LOVE KILLS — Freddie Mercury (CBS)
8	18	LIKE TO GET TO KNOW YOU WELL — Howard Jones (WEA)
-	19	PURPLE RAIN — Prince & The Revolution (Warner Bros)
17	20	HOT WATER — Level 42 (Polydor)
16	21	I'LL FLY FOR YOU — Spandau Ballet (Reformation)
13	22	SELF CONTROL — Laura Branigan (Atlantic)
26	23	HUMAN RACING — Nik Kershaw (MCA)
-	24	APOLLO 9 — Adam Ant (CBS)
39	25	IF IT HAPPENS AGAIN — UB40 (DEP International)
15	26	TALKING IN YOUR SLEEP — Bucks Fizz (RCA)
32	27	SMOOTH OPERATOR — Sade (Epic)
28	28	TOUR DE FRANCE — Kraftwerk (EMI)
14	29	WILLIAM, IT WAS REALLY NOTHING — Smiths (Rough Trade)
34	30	ALL I NEED IS EVERYTHING — Aztec Camera (WEA)
30	31	BETTER BE GOOD TO ME — Tina Turner (Capitol)
-	32	EAST OF EDEN — Big Country (Mercury)
-	33	I WISH YOU WOULD — Jocelyn Brown (Fourth & Broadway)
46	34	THE MEDICINE SONG — Stephanie Mills (Club)
29	35	MAGIC TOUCH — Rose Royce (Streetwave)
-	36	WE DON'T WORK FOR FREE — Grandmaster & Melle Mel (Sugarhill)
-	37	FOREST FIRE — Lloyd Cole & the Commotions (Polydor)
20	38	TORTURE — Jacksons (Epic)
22	39	SUNSET NOW — Heaven 17 (Virgin)
-	40	TOGETHER IN ELECTRIC DREAMS — Giorgio Moroder & Philip Oakey (Virgin)
23	41	TWO TRIBES — Frankie Goes To Hollywood (ZTT)
-	42	MR. SOLITAIRE — Animal Nightlife (Island)
43	43	RAIN FOREST — Paul Hardcastle (Bluebird)
-	44	LET HER FEEL IT — Simplicious (Fourth & Broadway)
-	45	WHAT IS LIFE — Black Uhuru (Island)
27	46	WHATEVER I DO (WHEREVER I GO) — Hazell Dean (Proto)
50	47	WHAT I LIKE MOST ABOUT YOU IS YOUR GIRLFRIEND — Special AKA (2 Tone)
-	48	DRIVE — Cars (Elektra)
49	49	THE GIRL FROM IPANEMA — Astrud Gilberto (Verve)
43	50	ACCELERATION — Bill Nelson (Cocteau)

I Just Called To Say I Love You was part of Stevie Wonder's soundtrack music for the Gene Wilder film *The Woman in Red*, but proved to be as strong a song as any Stevie had ever produced specifically for his own recording purposes. It easily broke Motown's UK sales record only recently established by Lionel Richie's *Hello,* selling a total of 1,775,000 copies before the end of the year.

6 October 1984

last week	this week	Title	Artist (Label)
1	1	I JUST CALLED TO SAY I LOVE YOU	Stevie Wonder (Motown)
3	2	PRIDE (IN THE NAME OF LOVE)	U2 (Island)
2	3	GHOSTBUSTERS	Ray Parker Jr. (Arista)
4	4	LOST IN MUSIC	Sister Sledge (Atlantic/Cotillion)
7	5	BLUE JEAN	David Bowie (EMI America)
12	6	WHY	Bronski Beat (Forbidden Fruit)
5	7	CARELESS WHISPER	George Michael (Epic)
17	8	LOVE KILLS	Freddie Mercury (CBS)
14	9	HAMMER TO FALL	Queen (EMI)
6	10	BIG IN JAPAN	Alphaville (WEA International)
9	11	A LETTER TO YOU	Shakin' Stevens (Epic)
19	12	PURPLE RAIN	Prince & The Revolution (Warner Bros)
8	13	DR. BEAT	Miami Sound Machine (Epic)
25	14	IF IT HAPPENS AGAIN	UB40 (DEP International)
24	15	APOLLO 9	Adam Ant (CBS)
13	16	AGADOO	Black Lace (Flair)
10	17	MASTER AND SERVANT	Depeche Mode (Mute)
11	18	MADAM BUTTERFLY (UN BEL DI VEDREMO)	Malcolm McLaren (Charisma)
32	19	EAST OF EDEN	Big Country (Mercury)
-	20	THE WAR SONG	Culture Club (Virgin)
23	21	HUMAN RACING	Nik Kershaw (MCA)
20	22	HOT WATER	Level 42 (Polydor)
48	23	DRIVE	Cars (Elektra)
15	24	TESLA GIRLS	Orchestral Manoeuvres In The Dark (Virgin)
16	25	PASSENGERS	Elton John (Rocket)
27	26	SMOOTH OPERATOR	Sade (Epic)
-	27	NO MORE LONELY NIGHTS	Paul McCartney (Parlophone)
-	28	MYSTERY	Dio (Vertigo)
28	29	TOUR DE FRANCE	Kraftwerk (EMI)
43	30	RAIN FOREST	Paul Hardcastle (Bluebird)
26	31	TALKING IN YOUR SLEEP	Bucks Fizz (RCA)
42	32	MR. SOLITAIRE	Animal Nightlife (Island)
45	33	WHAT IS LIFE	Black Uhuru (Island)
47	34	WHAT I LIKE MOST ABOUT YOU IS YOUR GIRLFRIEND	Special AKA (2 Tone)
21	35	I'LL FLY FOR YOU	Spandau Ballet (Reformation)
33	36	I WISH YOU WOULD	Jocelyn Brown (Fourth & Broadway)
34	37	THE MEDICINE SONG	Stephanie Mills (Club)
18	38	LIKE TO GET TO KNOW YOU WELL	Howard Jones (WEA)
35	39	MAGIC TOUCH	Rose Royce (Streetwave)
31	40	BETTER BE GOOD TO ME	Tina Turner (Capitol)
-	41	COVER ME	Bruce Springsteen (CBS)
-	42	FLESH FOR FANTASY	Billy Idol (Chrysalis)
-	43	I CAN'T LET YOU GO	Haywoode (CBS)
22	44	SELF CONTROL	Laura Branigan (Atlantic)
29	45	WILLIAM, IT WAS REALLY NOTHING	Smiths (Rough Trade)
37	46	FOREST FIRE	Lloyd Cole & the Commotions (Polydor)
41	47	TWO TRIBES	Frankie Goes To Hollywood (ZTT)
38	48	TORTURE	Jacksons (Epic)
-	49	SKIN DEEP	Stranglers (Epic)
40	50	TOGETHER IN ELECTRIC DREAMS	Giorgio Moroder & Philip Oakey (Virgin)

13 October 1984

last week	this week	Title	Artist (Label)
1	1	I JUST CALLED TO SAY I LOVE YOU	Stevie Wonder (Motown)
20	2	THE WAR SONG	Culture Club (Virgin)
3	3	GHOSTBUSTERS	Ray Parker Jr. (Arista)
2	4	PRIDE (IN THE NAME OF LOVE)	U2 (Island)
4	5	LOST IN MUSIC	Sister Sledge (Atlantic/Cotillion)
6	6	WHY	Bronski Beat (Forbidden Fruit)
5	7	BLUE JEAN	David Bowie (EMI America)
12	8	PURPLE RAIN	Prince & The Revolution (Warner Bros)
14	9	IF IT HAPPENS AGAIN	UB40 (DEP International)
23	10	DRIVE	Cars (Elektra)
8	11	LOVE KILLS	Freddie Mercury (CBS)
-	12	FREEDOM	Wham! (Epic)
19	13	EAST OF EDEN	Big Country (Mercury)
15	14	APOLLO 9	Adam Ant (CBS)
11	15	A LETTER TO YOU	Shakin' Stevens (Epic)
9	16	HAMMER TO FALL	Queen (EMI)
7	17	CARELESS WHISPER	George Michael (Epic)
26	18	SMOOTH OPERATOR	Sade (Epic)
10	19	BIG IN JAPAN	Alphaville (WEA International)
27	20	NO MORE LONELY NIGHTS	Paul McCartney (Parlophone)
13	21	DR. BEAT	Miami Sound Machine (Epic)
49	22	SKIN DEEP	Stranglers (Epic)
50	23	TOGETHER IN ELECTRIC DREAMS	Giorgio Moroder & Philip Oakey (Virgin)
32	24	MR. SOLITAIRE	Animal Nightlife (Island)
21	25	HUMAN RACING	Nik Kershaw (MCA)
17	26	MASTER AND SERVANT	Depeche Mode (Mute)
-	27	SHOUT IT TO THE TOP	Style Council (Polydor)
16	28	AGADOO	Black Lace (Flair)
37	29	THE MEDICINE SONG	Stephanie Mills (Club)
41	30	COVER ME	Bruce Springsteen (CBS)
18	31	MADAM BUTTERFLY (UN BEL DI VEDREMO)	Malcolm McLaren (Charisma)
-	32	MISSING YOU	John Waite (EMI America)
24	33	TESLA GIRLS	Orchestral Manoeuvres In The Dark (Virgin)
28	34	MYSTERY	Dio (Vertigo)
-	35	TUCH ME	Fonda Rae (Streetwave)
-	36	THE LUCKY ONE	Laura Branigan (Atlantic)
22	37	HOT WATER	Level 42 (Polydor)
-	38	I'M GONNA TEAR YOUR PLAYHOUSE DOWN	Paul Young (CBS)
29	39	TOUR DE FRANCE	Kraftwerk (EMI)
-	40	MODERN GIRL	Meat Loaf (Arista)
39	41	MAGIC TOUCH	Rose Royce (Streetwave)
38	42	LIKE TO GET TO KNOW YOU WELL	Howard Jones (WEA)
-	43	TOUCH BY TOUCH	Diana Ross (Capitol)
36	44	I WISH YOU WOULD	Jocelyn Brown (Fourth & Broadway)
33	45	WHAT IS LIFE	Black Uhuru (Island)
40	46	BETTER BE GOOD TO ME	Tina Turner (Capitol)
-	47	THE A TEAM	Mike Post (RCA)
-	48	LEAN PERIOD	Orange Juice (Polydor)
-	49	SONSORIA	Some Bizzare (Virgin)
42	50	FLESH FOR FANTASY	Billy Idol (Chrysalis)

20 October 1984

last week	this week	Title	Artist (Label)
2	1	THE WAR SONG	Culture Club (Virgin)
12	2	FREEDOM	Wham! (Epic)
1	3	I JUST CALLED TO SAY I LOVE YOU	Stevie Wonder (Motown)
10	4	DRIVE	Cars (Elektra)
20	5	NO MORE LONELY NIGHTS	Paul McCartney (Parlophone)
23	6	TOGETHER IN ELECTRIC DREAMS	Giorgio Moroder & Philip Oakey (Virgin)
3	7	GHOSTBUSTERS	Ray Parker Jr. (Arista)
6	8	WHY	Bronski Beat (Forbidden Fruit)
27	9	SHOUT IT TO THE TOP	Style Council (Polydor)
5	10	LOST IN MUSIC	Sister Sledge (Atlantic/Cotillion)
4	11	PRIDE (IN THE NAME OF LOVE)	U2 (Island)
8	12	PURPLE RAIN	Prince & The Revolution (Warner Bros)
9	13	IF IT HAPPENS AGAIN	UB40 (DEP International)
32	14	MISSING YOU	John Waite (EMI America)
11	15	LOVE KILLS	Freddie Mercury (CBS)
38	16	I'M GONNA TEAR YOUR PLAYHOUSE DOWN	Paul Young (CBS)
22	17	SKIN DEEP	Stranglers (Epic)
7	18	BLUE JEAN	David Bowie (EMI America)
18	19	SMOOTH OPERATOR	Sade (Epic)
-	20	ALL CRIED OUT	Alison Moyet (CBS)
14	21	APOLLO 9	Adam Ant (CBS)
13	22	EAST OF EDEN	Big Country (Mercury)
15	23	A LETTER TO YOU	Shakin' Stevens (Epic)
30	24	COVER ME	Bruce Springsteen (CBS)
16	25	HAMMER TO FALL	Queen (EMI)
-	26	TOO LATE FOR GOODBYES	Julian Lennon (Charisma)
17	27	CARELESS WHISPER	George Michael (Epic)
24	28	MR. SOLITAIRE	Animal Nightlife (Island)
21	29	DR. BEAT	Miami Sound Machine (Epic)
-	30	I FEEL FOR YOU	Chaka Khan (Warner Bros)
19	31	BIG IN JAPAN	Alphaville (WEA International)
-	32	GOTTA GET YOU HOME TONIGHT	Eugene Wilde (Fourth & Broadway)
36	33	THE LUCKY ONE	Laura Branigan (Atlantic)
29	34	THE MEDICINE SONG	Stephanie Mills (Club)
35	35	TUCH ME	Fonda Rae (Streetwave)
40	36	MODERN GIRL	Meat Loaf (Arista)
-	37	LISTEN TO YOUR FATHER	Feargal Sharkey (Zarjazz)
31	38	MADAM BUTTERFLY (UN BEL DI VEDREMO)	Malcolm McLaren (Charisma)
-	39	WEEKEND GIRL	S.O.S. Band (Tabu)
25	40	HUMAN RACING	Nik Kershaw (MCA)
-	41	GIMME ALL YOUR LOVIN'	ZZ Top (Warner Bros)
47	42	THE A TEAM	Mike Post (RCA)
33	43	TESLA GIRLS	Orchestral Manoeuvres In The Dark (Virgin)
28	44	AGADOO	Black Lace (Flair)
34	45	MYSTERY	Dio (Vertigo)
-	46	HIGHLY STRUNG	Spandau Ballet (Reformation)
47	47	THE SECOND TIME	Kim Wilde (MCA)
-	48	ON THE WINGS OF A NIGHTINGALE	Everly Brothers (Mercury)
26	49	MASTER AND SERVANT	Depeche Mode (Mute)
-	50	YOUR TOUCH	Bonnie Pointer (Epic)

Ray Parker Jr's *Ghostbusters* theme had its initial big-selling period in the Autumn of 1984 before the film itself was released in the UK, but it would also make a comeback and have a second Top 10 run in January the following year, boosted by the movie's nationwide box office success. Prince, meanwhile, scored his second Top 10 hit from his own first movie *Purple Rain*, this time with the title song.

October – November 1984

27 October 1984

last	this	title	artist
2	1	FREEDOM	Wham! (Epic)
1	2	THE WAR SONG	Culture Club (Virgin)
3	3	I JUST CALLED TO SAY I LOVE YOU	Stevie Wonder (Motown)
5	4	NO MORE LONELY NIGHTS	Paul McCartney (Parlophone)
6	5	TOGETHER IN ELECTRIC DREAMS	Giorgio Moroder & Philip Oakey (Virgin)
4	6	DRIVE	Cars (Elektra)
9	7	SHOUT IT TO THE TOP	Style Council (Polydor)
14	8	MISSING YOU	John Waite (EMI America)
16	9	I'M GONNA TEAR YOUR PLAYHOUSE DOWN	Paul Young (CBS)
17	10	SKIN DEEP	Stranglers (Epic)
20	11	ALL CRIED OUT	Alison Moyet (CBS)
7	12	GHOSTBUSTERS	Ray Parker Jr. (Arista)
8	13	WHY	Bronski Beat (Forbidden Fruit)
30	14	I FEEL FOR YOU	Chaka Khan (Warner Bros)
-	15	LOVE'S GREAT ADVENTURE	Ultravox (Chrysalis)
13	16	IF IT HAPPENS AGAIN	UB40 (DEP International)
11	17	PRIDE (IN THE NAME OF LOVE)	U2 (Island)
18	18	SMOOTH OPERATOR	Sade (Epic)
12	19	PURPLE RAIN	Prince & The Revolution (Warner Bros)
10	20	LOST IN MUSIC	Sister Sledge (Atlantic/Cotillion)
46	21	HIGHLY STRUNG	Spandau Ballet (Reformation)
26	22	TOO LATE FOR GOODBYES	Julian Lennon (Charisma)
-	23	PENNY LOVER	Lionel Richie (Motown)
36	24	MODERN GIRL	Meat Loaf (Arista)
15	25	LOVE KILLS	Freddie Mercury (CBS)
32	26	GOTTA GET YOU HOME TONIGHT	Eugene Wilde (Fourth & Broadway)
21	27	APOLLO 9	Adam Ant (CBS)
37	28	LISTEN TO YOUR FATHER	Feargal Sharkey (Zarjazz)
24	29	COVER ME	Bruce Springsteen (CBS)
34	30	THE MEDICINE SONG	Stephanie Mills (Club)
-	31	WALK AWAY	Sisters Of Mercy (Merciful Release)
41	32	GIMME ALL YOUR LOVIN'	ZZ Top (Warner Bros)
28	33	MR. SOLITAIRE	Animal Nightlife (Island)
27	34	CARELESS WHISPER	George Michael (Epic)
18	35	BLUE JEAN	David Bowie (EMI America)
-	36	WHO WEARS THESE SHOES	Elton John (Rocket)
47	37	THE SECOND TIME	Kim Wilde (MCA)
39	38	WEEKEND GIRL	S.O.S. Band (Tabu)
23	39	A LETTER TO YOU	Shakin' Stevens (Epic)
-	40	CARIBBEAN QUEEN (NO MORE LOVE ON THE RUN)	Billy Ocean (Jive)
43	41	TESLA GIRLS	Orchestral Manoeuvres In The Dark (Virgin)
44	42	AGADOO	Black Lace (Flair)
22	43	EAST OF EDEN	Big Country (Mercury)
35	44	TUCH ME	Fonda Rae (Streetwave)
-	45	THE WANDERER	Status Quo (Vertigo)
49	46	MASTER AND SERVANT	Depeche Mode (Mute)
48	47	ON THE WINGS OF A NIGHTINGALE	Everly Brothers (Mercury)
33	48	THE LUCKY ONE	Laura Branigan (Atlantic)
-	49	SLIPPERY PEOPLE	Staple Singers (Epic)
-	50	I'M SO BEAUTIFUL	Divine (Proto)

3 November 1984

last	this	title	artist
1	1	FREEDOM	Wham! (Epic)
4	2	NO MORE LONELY NIGHTS	Paul McCartney (Parlophone)
14	3	I FEEL FOR YOU	Chaka Khan (Warner Bros)
5	4	TOGETHER IN ELECTRIC DREAMS	Giorgio Moroder & Philip Oakey (Virgin)
11	5	ALL CRIED OUT	Alison Moyet (CBS)
3	6	I JUST CALLED TO SAY I LOVE YOU	Stevie Wonder (Motown)
22	7	TOO LATE FOR GOODBYES	Julian Lennon (Charisma)
8	8	MISSING YOU	John Waite (EMI America)
2	9	THE WAR SONG	Culture Club (Virgin)
6	10	DRIVE	Cars (Elektra)
9	11	I'M GONNA TEAR YOUR PLAYHOUSE DOWN	Paul Young (CBS)
15	12	LOVE'S GREAT ADVENTURE	Ultravox (Chrysalis)
7	13	SHOUT IT TO THE TOP	Style Council (Polydor)
45	14	THE WANDERER	Status Quo (Vertigo)
21	15	HIGHLY STRUNG	Spandau Ballet (Reformation)
10	16	SKIN DEEP	Stranglers (Epic)
40	17	CARIBBEAN QUEEN (NO MORE LOVE ON THE RUN)	Billy Ocean (Jive)
23	18	PENNY LOVER	Lionel Richie (Motown)
28	19	LISTEN TO YOUR FATHER	Feargal Sharkey (Zarjazz)
24	20	MODERN GIRL	Meat Loaf (Arista)
12	21	GHOSTBUSTERS	Ray Parker Jr. (Arista)
-	22	THE WILD BOYS	Duran Duran (EMI)
13	23	WHY	Bronski Beat (Forbidden Fruit)
18	24	SMOOTH OPERATOR	Sade (Epic)
19	25	PURPLE RAIN	Prince & The Revolution (Warner Bros)
26	26	GOTTA GET YOU HOME TONIGHT	Eugene Wilde (Fourth & Broadway)
32	27	GIMME ALL YOUR LOVIN'	ZZ Top (Warner Bros)
16	28	IF IT HAPPENS AGAIN	UB40 (DEP International)
37	29	THE SECOND TIME	Kim Wilde (MCA)
-	30	I'M SO EXCITED	Pointer Sisters (Planet)
44	31	TUCH ME	Fonda Rae (Streetwave)
17	32	PRIDE (IN THE NAME OF LOVE)	U2 (Island)
-	33	THE THORN (EP)	Siouxsie & the Banshees (Wonderland)
-	34	ACES HIGH	Iron Maiden (EMI)
20	35	LOST IN MUSIC	Sister Sledge (Atlantic/Cotillion)
31	36	WALK AWAY	Sisters Of Mercy (Merciful Release)
30	37	THE MEDICINE SONG	Stephanie Mills (Club)
-	38	THIS IS MINE	Heaven 17 (Virgin)
-	39	OUT OF TOUCH	Daryl Hall & John Oates (RCA)
47	40	ON THE WINGS OF A NIGHTINGALE	Everly Brothers (Mercury)
25	41	LOVE KILLS	Freddie Mercury (CBS)
38	42	WEEKEND GIRL	S.O.S. Band (Tabu)
35	43	BLUE JEAN	David Bowie (EMI America)
29	44	COVER ME	Bruce Springsteen (CBS)
36	45	WHO WEARS THESE SHOES	Elton John (Rocket)
34	46	CARELESS WHISPER	George Michael (Epic)
49	47	SLIPPERY PEOPLE	Staple Singers (Epic)
42	48	AGADOO	Black Lace (Flair)
27	49	APOLLO 9	Adam Ant (CBS)
50	50	I'M SO BEAUTIFUL	Divine (Proto)

10 November 1984

last	this	title	artist
3	1	I FEEL FOR YOU	Chaka Khan (Warner Bros)
1	2	FREEDOM	Wham! (Epic)
2	3	NO MORE LONELY NIGHTS	Paul McCartney (Parlophone)
22	4	THE WILD BOYS	Duran Duran (EMI)
7	5	TOO LATE FOR GOODBYES	Julian Lennon (Charisma)
14	6	THE WANDERER	Status Quo (Vertigo)
4	7	TOGETHER IN ELECTRIC DREAMS	Giorgio Moroder & Philip Oakey (Virgin)
17	8	CARIBBEAN QUEEN (NO MORE LOVE ON THE RUN)	Billy Ocean (Jive)
5	9	ALL CRIED OUT	Alison Moyet (CBS)
27	10	GIMME ALL YOUR LOVIN'	ZZ Top (Warner Bros)
8	11	MISSING YOU	John Waite (EMI America)
6	12	I JUST CALLED TO SAY I LOVE YOU	Stevie Wonder (Motown)
12	13	LOVE'S GREAT ADVENTURE	Ultravox (Chrysalis)
10	14	DRIVE	Cars (Elektra)
18	15	PENNY LOVER	Lionel Richie (Motown)
34	16	ACES HIGH	Iron Maiden (EMI)
19	17	LISTEN TO YOUR FATHER	Feargal Sharkey (Zarjazz)
9	18	THE WAR SONG	Culture Club (Virgin)
26	19	GOTTA GET YOU HOME TONIGHT	Eugene Wilde (Fourth & Broadway)
15	20	HIGHLY STRUNG	Spandau Ballet (Reformation)
-	21	THE NEVER ENDING STORY	Limahl (EMI)
30	22	I'M SO EXCITED	Pointer Sisters (Planet)
20	23	MODERN GIRL	Meat Loaf (Arista)
13	24	SHOUT IT TO THE TOP	Style Council (Polydor)
-	25	I SHOULD HAVE KNOWN BETTER	Jim Diamond (A&M)
-	26	BERSERKER	Gary Numan (Numa)
21	27	GHOSTBUSTERS	Ray Parker Jr. (Arista)
-	28	SEXCRIME (NINETEEN EIGHTY-FOUR)	Eurythmics (RCA)
11	29	I'M GONNA TEAR YOUR PLAYHOUSE DOWN	Paul Young (CBS)
-	30	BLASPHEMOUS RUMOURS (EP)	Depeche Mode (Mute)
-	31	LET IT ALL BLOW	Dazz Band (Motown)
-	32	WHEN LOVE BREAKS DOWN	Prefab Sprout (Kitchenware)
16	33	SKIN DEEP	Stranglers (Epic)
-	34	THE JUDGEMENT IS THE MIRROR	Dali's Car (Paradox)
-	35	PULLING PUNCHES	David Sylvian (Virgin)
-	36	HARD HABIT TO BREAK	Chicago (Full Moon)
28	37	IF IT HAPPENS AGAIN	UB40 (DEP International)
38	38	THIS IS MINE	Heaven 17 (Virgin)
23	39	WHY	Bronski Beat (Forbidden Fruit)
32	40	PRIDE (IN THE NAME OF LOVE)	U2 (Island)
-	41	THE CHANT HAS JUST BEGUN	Alarm (IRS)
-	42	SHOOTING FROM THE HEART	Cliff Richard (EMI)
-	43	PHEW WOW	Farmer's Boys (EMI)
40	44	ON THE WINGS OF A NIGHTINGALE	Everly Brothers (Mercury)
33	45	THE THORN (EP)	Siouxsie & the Banshees (Wonderland)
24	46	SMOOTH OPERATOR	Sade (Epic)
47	47	SLIPPERY PEOPLE	Staple Singers (Epic)
-	48	BACK IN MY ARMS (ONCE AGAIN)	Hazell Dean (Proto)
49	49	SLIPPERY PEOPLE	Talking Heads (EMI)
-	50	RATTLESNAKES	Lloyd Cole & the Commotions (Polydor)

In a chart heavy with film songs, more were making their mark, notably the one-off tie-up between Giorgio Moroder and Human League's vocalist Philip Oakey on *Together In Electric Dreams* (from *Electric Dreams*), and Paul McCartney's Number Two hit *No More Lonely Nights*, a song generally agreed to be the best thing about McCartney's ill-received feature, *Give My Regards To Broad Street*.

November 1984

17 November 1984

last week	this week	Title	Artist (Label)
1	1	I FEEL FOR YOU	Chaka Khan (Warner Bros)
2	2	FREEDOM	Wham! (Epic)
4	3	THE WILD BOYS	Duran Duran (EMI)
5	4	TOO LATE FOR GOODBYES	Julian Lennon (Charisma)
8	5	CARIBBEAN QUEEN (NO MORE LOVE ON THE RUN)	Billy Ocean (Jive)
10	6	GIMME ALL YOUR LOVIN'	ZZ Top (Warner Bros)
6	7	THE WANDERER	Status Quo (Vertigo)
3	8	NO MORE LONELY NIGHTS	Paul McCartney (Parlophone)
7	9	TOGETHER IN ELECTRIC DREAMS	Giorgio Moroder & Philip Oakey (Virgin)
9	10	ALL CRIED OUT	Alison Moyet (CBS)
21	11	THE NEVER ENDING STORY	Limahl (EMI)
25	12	I SHOULD HAVE KNOWN BETTER	Jim Diamond (A&M)
22	13	I'M SO EXCITED	Pointer Sisters (Planet)
13	14	LOVE'S GREAT ADVENTURE	Ultravox (Chrysalis)
11	15	MISSING YOU	John Waite (EMI America)
30	16	BLASPHEMOUS RUMOURS (EP)	Depeche Mode (Mute)
12	17	I JUST CALLED TO SAY I LOVE YOU	Stevie Wonder (Motown)
16	18	ACES HIGH	Iron Maiden (EMI)
15	19	PENNY LOVER	Lionel Richie (Motown)
19	20	GOTTA GET YOU HOME TONIGHT	Eugene Wilde (Fourth & Broadway)
36	21	HARD HABIT TO BREAK	Chicago (Full Moon)
14	22	DRIVE	Cars (Elektra)
17	23	LISTEN TO YOUR FATHER	Feargal Sharkey (Zarjazz)
23	24	MODERN GIRL	Meat Loaf (Arista)
27	25	GHOSTBUSTERS	Ray Parker Jr. (Arista)
26	26	BERSERKER	Gary Numan (Numa)
-	27	RESPECT YOURSELF	Kane Gang (Kitchenware)
28	28	SEXCRIME (NINETEEN EIGHTY-FOUR)	Eurythmics (RCA)
38	29	THIS IS MINE	Heaven 17 (Virgin)
24	30	SHOUT IT TO THE TOP	Style Council (Polydor)
31	31	LET IT ALL BLOW	Dazz Band (Motown)
-	32	KEEP ON KEEPIN' ON	Redskins (Decca)
-	33	THE PRICE	New Model Army (Abstract)
18	34	THE WAR SONG	Culture Club (Virgin)
-	35	HYPNOTIZE	Scritti Politti (Virgin)
-	36	THE RIDDLE	Nik Kershaw (MCA)
34	37	THE JUDGEMENT IS THE MIRROR	Dali's Car (Paradox)
33	38	SKIN DEEP	Stranglers (Epic)
20	39	HIGHLY STRUNG	Spandau Ballet (Reformation)
-	40	OFF AND ON LOVE	Champaign (CBS)
45	41	THE THORN (EP)	Siouxsie & the Banshees (Wonderland)
48	42	BACK IN MY ARMS (ONCE AGAIN)	Hazell Dean (Proto)
-	43	EST (TRIP TO THE MOON)	Alien Sex Fiend (Anagram)
-	44	LOUISE	Human League (Virgin)
32	45	WHEN LOVE BREAKS DOWN	Prefab Sprout (Kitchenware)
50	46	RATTLESNAKES	Lloyd Cole & the Commotions (Polydor)
47	47	SLIPPERY PEOPLE	Staple Singers (Epic)
39	48	WHY	Bronski Beat (Forbidden Fruit)
-	49	THE CHANT HAS BEGUN	Level 42 (Polydor)
-	50	HALF A MINUTE	Matt Bianco (WEA)

24 November 1984

last week	this week	Title	Artist (Label)
1	1	I FEEL FOR YOU	Chaka Khan (Warner Bros)
3	2	THE WILD BOYS	Duran Duran (EMI)
12	3	I SHOULD HAVE KNOWN BETTER	Jim Diamond (A&M)
2	4	FREEDOM	Wham! (Epic)
5	5	CARIBBEAN QUEEN (NO MORE LOVE ON THE RUN)	Billy Ocean (Jive)
11	6	THE NEVER ENDING STORY	Limahl (EMI)
6	7	GIMME ALL YOUR LOVIN'	ZZ Top (Warner Bros)
10	8	ALL CRIED OUT	Alison Moyet (CBS)
7	9	THE WANDERER	Status Quo (Vertigo)
21	10	HARD HABIT TO BREAK	Chicago (Full Moon)
4	11	TOO LATE FOR GOODBYES	Julian Lennon (Charisma)
36	12	THE RIDDLE	Nik Kershaw (MCA)
13	13	I'M SO EXCITED	Pointer Sisters (Planet)
16	14	BLASPHEMOUS RUMOURS (EP)	Depeche Mode (Mute)
14	15	LOVE'S GREAT ADVENTURE	Ultravox (Chrysalis)
8	16	NO MORE LONELY NIGHTS	Paul McCartney (Parlophone)
20	17	GOTTA GET YOU HOME TONIGHT	Eugene Wilde (Fourth & Broadway)
-	18	TREAT HER LIKE A LADY	Temptations (Motown)
28	19	SEXCRIME (NINETEEN EIGHTY-FOUR)	Eurythmics (RCA)
9	20	TOGETHER IN ELECTRIC DREAMS	Giorgio Moroder & Philip Oakey (Virgin)
31	21	LET IT ALL BLOW	Dazz Band (Motown)
18	22	ACES HIGH	Iron Maiden (EMI)
44	23	LOUISE	Human League (Virgin)
-	24	ALL JOIN HANDS	Slade (RCA)
25	25	WE ARE FAMILY	Sister Sledge (Cotillion/Atlantic)
15	26	MISSING YOU	John Waite (EMI America)
19	27	PENNY LOVER	Lionel Richie (Motown)
17	28	I JUST CALLED TO SAY I LOVE YOU	Stevie Wonder (Motown)
50	29	HALF A MINUTE	Matt Bianco (WEA)
29	30	THIS IS MINE	Heaven 17 (Virgin)
24	31	MODERN GIRL	Meat Loaf (Arista)
22	32	DRIVE	Cars (Elektra)
32	33	KEEP ON KEEPIN' ON	Redskins (Decca)
-	34	I WON'T RUN AWAY	Alvin Stardust (Chrysalis)
35	35	LIKE A VIRGIN	Madonna (Sire)
-	36	HYPNOTIZE	Scritti Politti (Virgin)
-	37	TEARDROPS	Shakin' Stevens (Epic)
-	38	PRIVATE DANCER	Tina Turner (Capitol)
47	39	SLIPPERY PEOPLE	Staple Singers (Epic)
33	40	THE PRICE	New Model Army (Abstract)
41	41	THE THORN (EP)	Siouxsie & the Banshees (Wonderland)
26	42	BERSERKER	Gary Numan (Numa)
-	43	IF THIS IS IT	Huey Lewis & the News (Chrysalis)
-	44	WARNING SIGN	Nick Heyward (Arista)
-	45	HOW TO BE A MILLIONAIRE	ABC (Neutron)
48	46	WHY	Bronski Beat (Forbidden Fruit)
-	47	ONE NIGHT IN BANGKOK	Murray Head (RCA)
-	48	I FORGOT	Cool Notes (Abstract Dance)
-	49	NEVER TURN AWAY	Orchestral Manoeuvres In The Dark (Virgin)
-	50	DO THE CONGA	Black Lace (Flair)

1 December 1984

last week	this week	Title	Artist (Label)
1	1	I FEEL FOR YOU	Chaka Khan (Warner Bros)
3	2	I SHOULD HAVE KNOWN BETTER	Jim Diamond (A&M)
12	3	THE RIDDLE	Nik Kershaw (MCA)
6	4	THE NEVER ENDING STORY	Limahl (EMI)
19	5	SEXCRIME (NINETEEN EIGHTY-FOUR)	Eurythmics (RCA)
2	6	THE WILD BOYS	Duran Duran (EMI)
5	7	CARIBBEAN QUEEN (NO MORE LOVE ON THE RUN)	Billy Ocean (Jive)
10	8	HARD HABIT TO BREAK	Chicago (Full Moon)
18	9	TREAT HER LIKE A LADY	Temptations (Motown)
9	10	THE WANDERER	Status Quo (Vertigo)
21	11	LET IT ALL BLOW	Dazz Band (Motown)
13	12	I'M SO EXCITED	Pointer Sisters (Planet)
4	13	FREEDOM	Wham! (Epic)
7	14	GIMME ALL YOUR LOVIN'	ZZ Top (Warner Bros)
34	15	I WON'T RUN AWAY	Alvin Stardust (Chrysalis)
24	16	ALL JOIN HANDS	Slade (RCA)
-	17	THE POWER OF LOVE	Frankie Goes To Hollywood (ZTT)
37	18	TEARDROPS	Shakin' Stevens (Epic)
15	19	LOVE'S GREAT ADVENTURE	Ultravox (Chrysalis)
23	20	LOUISE	Human League (Virgin)
29	21	HALF A MINUTE	Matt Bianco (WEA)
8	22	ALL CRIED OUT	Alison Moyet (CBS)
11	23	TOO LATE FOR GOODBYES	Julian Lennon (Charisma)
47	24	ONE NIGHT IN BANGKOK	Murray Head (RCA)
14	25	BLASPHEMOUS RUMOURS (EP)	Depeche Mode (Mute)
17	26	GOTTA GET YOU HOME TONIGHT	Eugene Wilde (Fourth & Broadway)
-	27	INVISIBLE	Alison Moyet (CBS)
38	28	PRIVATE DANCER	Tina Turner (Capitol)
-	29	FRESH	Kool & the Gang (De-Lite)
-	30	THE MEDAL SONG	Culture Club (Virgin)
25	31	WE ARE FAMILY	Sister Sledge (Cotillion/Atlantic)
35	32	LIKE A VIRGIN	Madonna (Sire)
50	33	DO THE CONGA	Black Lace (Flair)
-	34	RESPECT YOURSELF	Kane Gang (Kitchenware)
-	35	WE ALL STAND TOGETHER	Paul McCartney & the Frog Chorus (Parlophone)
20	36	TOGETHER IN ELECTRIC DREAMS	Giorgio Moroder & Philip Oakey (Virgin)
-	37	IT AIN'T NECESSARILY SO	Bronski Beat (Forbidden Fruit)
-	38	WHERE THE ROSE IS SOWN	Big Country (Mercury)
33	39	KEEP ON KEEPIN' ON	Redskins (Decca)
26	40	MISSING YOU	John Waite (EMI America)
43	41	IF THIS IS IT	Huey Lewis & the News (Chrysalis)
31	42	MODERN GIRL	Meat Loaf (Arista)
-	43	CLOSE (TO THE EDIT)	Art Of Noise (ZTT)
30	44	THIS IS MINE	Heaven 17 (Virgin)
16	45	NO MORE LONELY NIGHTS	Paul McCartney (Parlophone)
27	46	PENNY LOVER	Lionel Richie (Motown)
-	47	HOTLINE TO HEAVEN	Bananarama (London)
-	48	LOVELIGHT IN FLIGHT	Stevie Wonder (Motown)
28	49	I JUST CALLED TO SAY I LOVE YOU	Stevie Wonder (Motown)
-	50	MATT'S MOOD	Breakout Krew (London)

Chaka Khan's chart-topping *I Feel For You* featured guest appearances from Stevie Wonder (on harmonica) and rapper Grandmaster Melle Mel, who had himself been in the Top 10 earlier in the year with *White Lines (Don't Don't Do It)*. Billy Ocean's *Caribbean Queen* had previously been released as *European Queen*, sounding identical apart from the all-important place of origin.

December 1984

8 December 1984

2	1	I SHOULD HAVE KNOWN BETTER	Jim Diamond (A&M)
17	2	THE POWER OF LOVE	Frankie Goes To Hollywood (ZTT)
3	3	THE RIDDLE	Nik Kershaw (MCA)
1	4	I FEEL FOR YOU	Chaka Khan (Warner Bros)
5	5	SEXCRIME (NINETEEN EIGHTY-FOUR)	Eurythmics (RCA)
18	6	TEARDROPS	Shakin' Stevens (Epic)
4	7	THE NEVER ENDING STORY	Limahl (EMI)
8	8	HARD HABIT TO BREAK	Chicago (Full Moon)
15	9	I WON'T RUN AWAY	Alvin Stardust (Chrysalis)
20	10	LOUISE	Human League (Virgin)
16	11	ALL JOIN HANDS	Slade (RCA)
7	12	CARIBBEAN QUEEN (NO MORE LOVE ON THE RUN)	Billy Ocean (Jive)
6	13	THE WILD BOYS	Duran Duran (EMI)
9	14	TREAT HER LIKE A LADY	Temptations (Motown)
29	15	FRESH	Kool & the Gang (De-Lite)
24	16	ONE NIGHT IN BANGKOK	Murray Head (RCA)
27	17	INVISIBLE	Alison Moyet (CBS)
38	18	WHERE THE ROSE IS SOWN	Big Country (Mercury)
33	19	DO THE CONGA	Black Lace (Flair)
34	20	RESPECT YOURSELF	Kane Gang (Kitchenware)
35	21	WE ALL STAND TOGETHER	Paul McCartney & the Frog Chorus (Parlophone)
21	22	HALF A MINUTE	Matt Bianco (WEA)
10	23	THE WANDERER	Status Quo (Vertigo)
12	24	I'M SO EXCITED	Pointer Sisters (Planet)
48	25	LOVELIGHT IN FLIGHT	Stevie Wonder (Motown)
11	26	LET IT ALL BLOW	Dazz Band (Motown)
13	27	FREEDOM	Wham! (Epic)
30	28	THE MEDAL SONG	Culture Club (Virgin)
-	29	NO MERCY	Stranglers (Epic)
28	30	PRIVATE DANCER	Tina Turner (Capitol)
32	31	LIKE A VIRGIN	Madonna (Sire)
14	32	GIMME ALL YOUR LOVIN'	ZZ Top (Warner Bros)
-	33	WARNING SIGN	Nick Heyward (Arista)
-	34	NELLIE THE ELEPHANT	Toy Dolls (Volume)
-	35	THANK GOD IT'S CHRISTMAS	Queen (EMI)
-	36	SHOUT	Tears For Fears (Mercury)
-	37	LAY YOUR HANDS ON ME	Thompson Twins (Arista)
25	38	BLASPHEMOUS RUMOURS (EP)	Depeche Mode (Mute)
-	39	POLICE OFFICER	Smiley Culture (Fashion)
31	40	WE ARE FAMILY	Sister Sledge (Cotillion/Atlantic)
-	41	YOU SPIN ME ROUND (LIKE A RECORD)	Dead Or Alive (Epic)
-	42	THANK YOU MY LOVE	Imagination (R&B)
19	43	LOVE'S GREAT ADVENTURE	Ultravox (Chrysalis)
45	44	NO MORE LONELY NIGHTS	Paul McCartney (Parlophone)
43	45	CLOSE (TO THE EDIT)	Art Of Noise (ZTT)
39	46	KEEP ON KEEPIN' ON	Redskins (Decca)
41	47	IF THIS IS IT	Huey Lewis & the News (Chrysalis)
-	48	YOU USED TO HOLD ME SO TIGHT	Thelma Houston (MCA)
-	49	EVERY MAN HAS A WOMAN	John Lennon (Polydor)
37	50	IT AIN'T NECESSARILY SO	Bronski Beat (Forbidden Fruit)

15 December 1984

-	1	DO THEY KNOW IT'S CHRISTMAS?	Band Aid (Mercury)
2	2	THE POWER OF LOVE	Frankie Goes To Hollywood (ZTT)
1	3	I SHOULD HAVE KNOWN BETTER	Jim Diamond (A&M)
4	4	SEXCRIME (NINETEEN EIGHTY-FOUR)	Eurythmics (RCA)
3	5	THE RIDDLE	Nik Kershaw (MCA)
31	6	LIKE A VIRGIN	Madonna (Sire)
6	7	TEARDROPS	Shakin' Stevens (Epic)
21	8	WE ALL STAND TOGETHER	Paul McCartney & the Frog Chorus (Parlophone)
-	9	LAST CHRISTMAS	Wham! (Epic)
15	10	FRESH	Kool & the Gang (De-Lite)
9	11	I WON'T RUN AWAY	Alvin Stardust (Chrysalis)
10	12	LOUISE	Human League (Virgin)
16	13	ONE NIGHT IN BANGKOK	Murray Head (RCA)
-	14	ROUND AND ROUND	Spandau Ballet (Reformation)
8	15	HARD HABIT TO BREAK	Chicago (Full Moon)
19	16	DO THE CONGA	Black Lace (Flair)
17	17	INVISIBLE	Alison Moyet (CBS)
4	18	I FEEL FOR YOU	Chaka Khan (Warner Bros)
26	19	LET IT ALL BLOW	Dazz Band (Motown)
37	20	LAY YOUR HANDS ON ME	Thompson Twins (Arista)
-	21	EVERYTHING MUST CHANGE	Paul Young (CBS)
35	22	THANK GOD IT'S CHRISTMAS	Queen (EMI)
11	23	ALL JOIN HANDS	Slade (RCA)
14	24	TREAT HER LIKE A LADY	Temptations (Motown)
20	25	RESPECT YOURSELF	Kane Gang (Kitchenware)
7	26	THE NEVER ENDING STORY	Limahl (EMI)
29	27	NO MERCY	Stranglers (Epic)
12	28	CARIBBEAN QUEEN (NO MORE LOVE ON THE RUN)	Billy Ocean (Jive)
30	29	PRIVATE DANCER	Tina Turner (Capitol)
34	30	NELLIE THE ELEPHANT	Toy Dolls (Volume)
22	31	HALF A MINUTE	Matt Bianco (WEA)
41	32	YOU SPIN ME ROUND (LIKE A RECORD)	Dead Or Alive (Epic)
33	33	WARNING SIGN	Nick Heyward (Arista)
-	34	TONIGHT	David Bowie (EMI America)
25	35	LOVELIGHT IN FLIGHT	Stevie Wonder (Motown)
13	36	THE WILD BOYS	Duran Duran (EMI)
-	37	SEPTEMBER SONG	Ian McCulloch (Korova)
18	38	WHERE THE ROSE IS SOWN	Big Country (Mercury)
-	39	I WANT TO KNOW WHAT LOVE IS	Foreigner (Atlantic)
45	40	CLOSE (TO THE EDIT)	Art Of Noise (ZTT)
-	41	RATS	Subhumans (Bluurg)
39	42	POLICE OFFICER	Smiley Culture (Fashion)
24	43	I'M SO EXCITED	Pointer Sisters (Planet)
-	44	I FEEL FINE	Beatles (Parlophone)
50	45	IT AIN'T NECESSARILY SO	Bronski Beat (Forbidden Fruit)
28	46	THE MEDAL SONG	Culture Club (Virgin)
42	47	THANK YOU MY LOVE	Imagination (R&B)
-	48	ANOTHER ROCK AND ROLL CHRISTMAS	Gary Glitter (Arista)
-	49	MATT'S MOOD	Breakout Krew (London)
-	50	I WOULD DIE 4 U	Prince & The Revolution (Warner Bros)

22 December 1984

1	1	DO THEY KNOW IT'S CHRISTMAS?	Band Aid (Mercury)
9	2	LAST CHRISTMAS	Wham! (Epic)
2	3	THE POWER OF LOVE	Frankie Goes To Hollywood (ZTT)
6	4	LIKE A VIRGIN	Madonna (Sire)
8	5	WE ALL STAND TOGETHER	Paul McCartney & the Frog Chorus (Parlophone)
4	6	SEXCRIME (NINETEEN EIGHTY-FOUR)	Eurythmics (RCA)
5	7	THE RIDDLE	Nik Kershaw (MCA)
3	8	I SHOULD HAVE KNOWN BETTER	Jim Diamond (A&M)
7	9	TEARDROPS	Shakin' Stevens (Epic)
10	10	FRESH	Kool & the Gang (De-Lite)
30	11	NELLIE THE ELEPHANT	Toy Dolls (Volume)
11	12	I WON'T RUN AWAY	Alvin Stardust (Chrysalis)
21	13	EVERYTHING MUST CHANGE	Paul Young (CBS)
16	14	DO THE CONGA	Black Lace (Flair)
13	15	ONE NIGHT IN BANGKOK	Murray Head (RCA)
14	16	ROUND AND ROUND	Spandau Ballet (Reformation)
18	17	I FEEL FOR YOU	Chaka Khan (Warner Bros)
20	18	LAY YOUR HANDS ON ME	Thompson Twins (Arista)
22	19	THANK GOD IT'S CHRISTMAS	Queen (EMI)
48	20	ANOTHER ROCK AND ROLL CHRISTMAS	Gary Glitter (Arista)
17	21	INVISIBLE	Alison Moyet (CBS)
12	22	LOUISE	Human League (Virgin)
27	23	NO MERCY	Stranglers (Epic)
25	24	RESPECT YOURSELF	Kane Gang (Kitchenware)
26	25	THE NEVER ENDING STORY	Limahl (EMI)
-	26	GHOSTBUSTERS	Ray Parker Jr. (Arista)
15	27	HARD HABIT TO BREAK	Chicago (Full Moon)
19	28	LET IT ALL BLOW	Dazz Band (Motown)
23	29	ALL JOIN HANDS	Slade (RCA)
39	30	I WANT TO KNOW WHAT LOVE IS	Foreigner (Atlantic)
31	31	SEPTEMBER SONG	Ian McCulloch (Korova)
32	32	YOU SPIN ME ROUND (LIKE A RECORD)	Dead Or Alive (Epic)
24	33	TREAT HER LIKE A LADY	Temptations (Motown)
38	34	WHERE THE ROSE IS SOWN	Big Country (Mercury)
34	35	TONIGHT	David Bowie (EMI America)
36	36	THE WILD BOYS	Duran Duran (EMI)
42	37	POLICE OFFICER	Smiley Culture (Fashion)
50	38	I WOULD DIE 4 U	Prince & The Revolution (Warner Bros)
-	39	SHOUT	Tears For Fears (Mercury)
35	40	LOVELIGHT IN FLIGHT	Stevie Wonder (Motown)
31	41	HALF A MINUTE	Matt Bianco (WEA)
41	42	RATS	Subhumans (Bluurg)
45	43	IT AIN'T NECESSARILY SO	Bronski Beat (Forbidden Fruit)
29	44	PRIVATE DANCER	Tina Turner (Capitol)
-	45	I WISH IT COULD BE CHRISTMAS EVERYDAY	Wizzard (Harvest)
-	46	SHARP DRESSED MAN	ZZ Top (Warner Bros)
-	47	WHO DO YOU LOVE	Intruders (Streetwave)
40	48	CLOSE (TO THE EDIT)	Art Of Noise (ZTT)
47	49	THANK YOU MY LOVE	Imagination (R&B)
33	50	WARNING SIGN	Nick Heyward (Arista)

Bob Geldof conceived of the Charity record *Do They Know It's Christmas?* while watching TV reports of widespread starvation in Ethiopia. The cream of Britain's rock elite gave their services to the recording for free, record shops donated their profit, and only the Government (via VAT) took anything away from the money-raising effort. Entering at Number One, the single sold a million in a week.

January 1985

5 January 1985

last week	this week	Title	Artist (Label)
1	1	DO THEY KNOW IT'S CHRISTMAS?	Band Aid (Mercury)
2	2	EVERYTHING SHE WANTS/LAST CHRISTMAS	Wham! (Epic)
5	3	WE ALL STAND TOGETHER	Paul McCartney & the Frog Chorus (Parlophone)
4	4	LIKE A VIRGIN	Madonna (Sire)
11	5	NELLIE THE ELEPHANT	Toy Dolls (Volume)
3	6	THE POWER OF LOVE	Frankie Goes To Hollywood (ZTT)
13	7	EVERYTHING MUST CHANGE	Paul Young (CBS)
20	8	ANOTHER ROCK AND ROLL CHRISTMAS	Gary Glitter (Arista)
14	9	DO THE CONGA	Black Lace (Flair)
10	10	FRESH	Kool & the Gang (De-Lite)
9	11	TEARDROPS	Shakin' Stevens (Epic)
7	12	THE RIDDLE	Nik Kershaw (MCA)
8	13	I SHOULD HAVE KNOWN BETTER	Jim Diamond (A&M)
6	14	SEXCRIME (NINETEEN EIGHTY-FOUR)	Eurythmics (Virgin)
15	15	ONE NIGHT IN BANGKOK	Murray Head (RCA)
39	16	SHOUT	Tears For Fears (Mercury)
12	17	I WON'T RUN AWAY	Alvin Stardust (Chrysalis)
26	18	GHOSTBUSTERS	Ray Parker Jr. (Arista)
16	19	ROUND AND ROUND	Spandau Ballet (Reformation)
18	20	LAY YOUR HANDS ON ME	Thompson Twins (Arista)
21	21	INVISIBLE	Alison Moyet (CBS)
17	22	I FEEL FOR YOU	Chaka Khan (Warner Bros)
30	23	I WANT TO KNOW WHAT LOVE IS	Foreigner (Atlantic)
19	24	THANK GOD IT'S CHRISTMAS	Queen (EMI)
29	25	ALL JOIN HANDS	Slade (RCA)
45	26	I WISH IT COULD BE CHRISTMAS EVERYDAY	Wizzard (Harvest)
22	27	LOUISE	Human League (Virgin)
25	28	NEVER ENDING STORY	Limahl (EMI)
27	29	SOUL DEEP	Council Collective (Polydor)
27	30	HARD HABIT TO BREAK	Chicago (Full Moon)
43	31	IT AIN'T NECESSARILY SO	Bronski Beat (Forbidden Fruit)
-	32	MERRY XMAS EVERYBODY	Slade (Polydor)
28	33	LET IT ALL BLOW	Dazz Band (Motown)
24	34	RESPECT YOURSELF	Kane Gang (Kitchenware)
31	35	SEPTEMBER SONG	Ian McCulloch (Korova)
44	36	PRIVATE DANCER	Tina Turner (Capitol)
-	37	VALOTTE	Julian Lennon (Charisma)
	38	ABIDE WITH ME	Inspirational Choir (Epic)
40	39	LOVELIGHT IN FLIGHT	Stevie Wonder (Motown)
23	40	NO MERCY	Stranglers (Epic)
37	41	POLICE OFFICER	Smiley Culture (Fashion)
34	42	WHERE THE ROSE IS SOWN	Big Country (Mercury)
33	43	TREAT HER LIKE A LADY	Temptations (Motown)
44	44	SHARP DRESSED MAN	ZZ Top (Warner Bros)
36	45	THE WILD BOYS	Duran Duran (Parlophone)
-	46	ANYTHING?	Direct Drive (Polydor)
-	47	HAPPY XMAS (WAR IS OVER)	John & Yoko/Plastic Ono Band (Apple)
-	48	I'LL DO THE TALKING	Cruella DeVille (CPL Priority)
-	49	YOU USED TO HOLD ME	Thelma Houston (MCA)
-	50	BIG DEAL	Bobby G (BBC)

12 January 1985

Title	Artist (Label)
1 1 DO THEY KNOW IT'S CHRISTMAS?	Band Aid (Mercury)
2 2 EVERYTHING SHE WANTS/LAST CHRISTMAS	Wham! (Epic)
5 3 NELLIE THE ELEPHANT	Toy Dolls (Volume)
4 4 LIKE A VIRGIN	Madonna (Sire)
3 5 WE ALL STAND TOGETHER	Paul McCartney & the Frog Chorus (Parlophone)
7 6 EVERYTHING MUST CHANGE	Paul Young (CBS)
6 7 THE POWER OF LOVE	Frankie Goes To Hollywood (ZTT)
16 8 SHOUT	Tears For Fears (Mercury)
18 9 GHOSTBUSTERS	Ray Parker Jr. (Arista)
23 10 I WANT TO KNOW WHAT LOVE IS	Foreigner (Atlantic)
12 11 THE RIDDLE	Nik Kershaw (MCA)
8 12 ANOTHER ROCK AND ROLL CHRISTMAS	Gary Glitter (Arista)
10 13 FRESH	Kool & the Gang (De-Lite)
9 14 DO THE CONGA	Black Lace (Flair)
20 15 LAY YOUR HANDS ON ME	Thompson Twins (Arista)
15 16 ONE NIGHT IN BANGKOK	Murray Head (RCA)
11 17 TEARDROPS	Shakin' Stevens (Epic)
19 18 ROUND AND ROUND	Spandau Ballet (Reformation)
14 19 SEXCRIME (NINETEEN EIGHTY-FOUR)	Eurythmics (Virgin)
29 20 SOUL DEEP	Council Collective (Polydor)
21 21 INVISIBLE	Alison Moyet (CBS)
13 22 I SHOULD HAVE KNOWN BETTER	Jim Diamond (A&M)
22 23 I FEEL FOR YOU	Chaka Khan (Warner Bros)
17 24 I WON'T RUN AWAY	Alvin Stardust (Chrysalis)
41 25 POLICE OFFICER	Smiley Culture (Fashion)
- 26 WHO DO YOU LOVE?	Intruders (Streetwave)
- 27 STEP OFF	Grandmaster Melle Mel (Sugarhill)
- 28 FRIENDS	Amii Stewart (RCA)
29 29 SHARP DRESSED MAN	ZZ Top (Warner Bros)
39 30 LOVELIGHT IN FLIGHT	Stevie Wonder (Motown)
- 31 YAH MO B THERE	James Ingram (Qwest)
- 32 I JUST CALLED TO SAY I LOVE YOU	Stevie Wonder (Motown)
30 33 HARD HABIT TO BREAK	Chicago (Full Moon)
34 34 RESPECT YOURSELF	Kane Gang (Kitchenware)
27 35 LOUISE	Human League (Virgin)
- 36 THANK YOU MY LOVE	Imagination (R&B)
37 37 ALL JOIN HANDS	Slade (RCA)
36 38 PRIVATE DANCER	Tina Turner (Capitol)
43 39 TREAT HER LIKE A LADY	Temptations (Motown)
- 40 SAY YEAH	Limit (Portrait)
42 41 SOLID	Ashford & Simpson (Capitol)
24 42 THANK GOD IT'S CHRISTMAS	Queen (EMI)
37 43 VALOTTE	Julian Lennon (Charisma)
45 44 THE WILD BOYS	Duran Duran (Parlophone)
42 45 WHERE THE ROSE IS SOWN	Big Country (Mercury)
46 46 ANYTHING?	Direct Drive (Polydor)
50 47 BIG DEAL	Bobby G (BBC)
40 48 NO MERCY	Stranglers (Epic)
26 49 I WISH IT COULD BE CHRISTMAS EVERYDAY	Wizzard (Harvest)
31 50 IT AIN'T NECESSARILY SO	Bronski Beat (Forbidden Fruit)

19 January 1985

Title	Artist (Label)
2 1 EVERYTHING SHE WANTS/LAST CHRISTMAS	Wham! (Epic)
4 2 LIKE A VIRGIN	Madonna (Sire)
1 3 DO THEY KNOW IT'S CHRISTMAS?	Band Aid (Mercury)
10 4 I WANT TO KNOW WHAT LOVE IS	Foreigner (Atlantic)
8 5 SHOUT	Tears For Fears (Mercury)
5 6 WE ALL STAND TOGETHER	Paul McCartney & the Frog Chorus (Parlophone)
3 7 NELLIE THE ELEPHANT	Toy Dolls (Volume)
9 8 GHOSTBUSTERS	Ray Parker Jr. (Arista)
27 9 STEP OFF	Grandmaster Melle Mel (Sugarhill)
6 10 EVERYTHING MUST CHANGE	Paul Young (CBS)
25 11 POLICE OFFICER	Smiley Culture (Fashion)
12 12 FRESH	Kool & the Gang (De-Lite)
15 13 LAY YOUR HANDS ON ME	Thompson Twins (Arista)
- 14 SAN DAMIANO (HEART AND SOUL)	Sal Solo (MCA)
7 15 THE POWER OF LOVE	Frankie Goes To Hollywood (ZTT)
21 16 INVISIBLE	Alison Moyet (CBS)
50 17 IT AIN'T NECESSARILY SO	Bronski Beat (Forbidden Fruit)
11 18 THE RIDDLE	Nik Kershaw (MCA)
40 19 SAY YEAH	Limit (Portrait)
14 20 DO THE CONGA	Black Lace (Flair)
16 21 ONE NIGHT IN BANGKOK	Murray Head (RCA)
20 22 SOUL DEEP	Council Collective (Polydor)
18 23 ROUND AND ROUND	Spandau Ballet (Reformation)
23 24 I FEEL FOR YOU	Chaka Khan (Warner Bros)
28 25 FRIENDS	Amii Stewart (RCA)
19 26 SEXCRIME (NINETEEN EIGHTY-FOUR)	Eurythmics (Virgin)
29 27 SHARP DRESSED MAN	ZZ Top (Warner Bros)
44 28 THE WILD BOYS	Duran Duran (Parlophone)
- 29 SINCE YESTERDAY	Strawberry Switchblade (Korova)
- 30 DANCING IN THE DARK	Bruce Springsteen (CBS)
- 31 LOVE AND PRIDE	King (CBS)
32 32 I JUST CALLED TO SAY I LOVE YOU	Stevie Wonder (Motown)
- 33 ATMOSPHERE	Russ Abbott (Spirit)
17 34 TEARDROPS	Shakin' Stevens (Epic)
- 35 WASH IT ALL OFF	You've Got Foetus On Your Breath (Self Immolation)
30 36 LOVELIGHT IN FLIGHT	Stevie Wonder (Motown)
- 37 1999/LITTLE RED CORVETTE	Prince (Warner Bros)
31 38 YAH MO B THERE	James Ingram (Qwest)
- 39 ABIDE WITH ME	Inspirational Choir (Epic)
- 40 SEXOMATIC	Bar-Kays (Club)
- 41 I HEAR TALK	Bucks Fizz (RCA)
36 42 THANK YOU MY LOVE	Imagination (R&B)
39 43 TREAT HER LIKE A LADY	Temptations (Motown)
- 44 YOU SPIN ME ROUND (LIKE A RECORD)	Dead Or Alive (Epic)
- 45 NEUTRON DANCE	Pointer Sisters (Planet)
41 46 SOLID	Ashford & Simpson (Capitol)
22 47 I SHOULD HAVE KNOWN BETTER	Jim Diamond (A&M)
34 48 RESPECT YOURSELF Kane Gang (Kitchenware)	
45 49 WHERE THE ROSE IS SOWN Big Country (Mercury)	
- 50 LOVERBOY	Billy Ocean (Jive)

The Band Aid single became Britain's biggest-ever seller by New Year, heading for the three million mark. It also appeared to give a general boost to record sales over the 1984/5 holiday period: Wham!'s *Last Christmas* also went well over a million, while Paul McCartney's *We All Stand Together* and Madonna's *Like A Virgin* both exceeded 700,000. In all, 1984 produced seven million-sellers.

January – February 1985

26 January 1985

last week	this week	Title	Artist (Label)
4	1	I WANT TO KNOW WHAT LOVE IS	Foreigner (Atlantic)
5	2	SHOUT	Tears For Fears (Mercury)
2	3	LIKE A VIRGIN	Madonna (Sire)
1	4	EVERYTHING SHE WANTS/LAST CHRISTMAS	Wham! (Epic)
3	5	DO THEY KNOW IT'S CHRISTMAS?	Band Aid (Mercury)
–	6	I KNOW HIM SO WELL	Elaine Paige & Barbara Dickson (RCA)
37	7	1999/LITTLE RED CORVETTE	Prince (Warner Bros)
9	8	STEP OFF	Grandmaster Melle Mel (Sugarhill)
11	9	POLICE OFFICER	Smiley Culture (Fashion)
8	10	GHOSTBUSTERS	Ray Parker Jr. (Arista)
10	11	EVERYTHING MUST CHANGE	Paul Young (CBS)
29	12	SINCE YESTERDAY	Strawberry Switchblade (Korova)
14	13	SAN DAMIANO (HEART AND SOUL)	Sal Solo (MCA)
25	14	FRIENDS	Amii Stewart (RCA)
19	15	SAY YEAH	Limit (Portrait)
31	16	LOVE AND PRIDE	King (CBS)
17	17	IT AIN'T NECESSARILY SO	Bronski Beat (Forbidden Fruit)
7	18	NELLIE THE ELEPHANT	Toy Dolls (Volume)
6	19	WE ALL STAND TOGETHER	Paul McCartney & the Frog Chorus (Parlophone)
33	20	ATMOSPHERE	Russ Abbott (Spirit)
27	21	SHARP DRESSED MAN	ZZ Top (Warner Bros)
46	22	SOLID	Ashford & Simpson (Capitol)
15	23	THE POWER OF LOVE	Frankie Goes To Hollywood (ZTT)
–	24	JUST A SHADOW	Big Country (Mercury)
13	25	LAY YOUR HANDS ON ME	Thompson Twins (Arista)
12	26	FRESH	Kool & the Gang (De-Lite)
–	27	RUN TO YOU	Bryan Adams (A&M)
50	28	LOVERBOY	Billy Ocean (Jive)
30	29	DANCING IN THE DARK	Bruce Springsteen (CBS)
22	30	SOUL DEEP	Council Collective (Polydor)
42	31	THIS IS MY NIGHT	Chaka Khan (Warner Bros)
–	32	THANK YOU MY LOVE	Imagination (R&B)
–	33	CAN I	Cashmere (Fourth & Broadway)
38	34	YAH MO B THERE	James Ingram (Qwest)
–	35	20/20	George Benson (Warner Bros)
–	36	WORLD DESTRUCTION	Time Zone (Virgin)
–	37	SUSSUDIO	Phil Collins (Virgin)
16	38	INVISIBLE	Alison Moyet (CBS)
–	39	A NEW ENGLAND	Kirsty MacColl (Stiff)
23	40	ROUND AND ROUND	Spandau Ballet (Reformation)
–	41	CLOSE (TO THE EDIT)	Art Of Noise (ZTT)
–	42	JULIA	Eurythmics (Virgin)
21	43	ONE NIGHT IN BANGKOK	Murray Head (RCA)
45	44	NEUTRON DANCE	Pointer Sisters (Planet)
44	45	YOU SPIN ME ROUND (LIKE A RECORD)	Dead Or Alive (Epic)
–	46	WE CAN BE BRAVE AGAIN	Armoury Show (Parlophone)
–	47	WE BELONG	Pat Benatar (Chrysalis)
–	48	ANYTHING?	Direct Drive (Polydor)
–	49	SEE THAT GLOW	This Island Earth (Magnet)
–	50	CONTAGIOUS	Whispers (MCA)

2 February 1985

last week	this week	Title	Artist (Label)
1	1	I WANT TO KNOW WHAT LOVE IS	Foreigner (Atlantic)
7	2	1999/LITTLE RED CORVETTE	Prince (Warner Bros)
6	3	I KNOW HIM SO WELL	Elaine Paige & Barbara Dickson (RCA)
2	4	SHOUT	Tears For Fears (Mercury)
16	5	LOVE AND PRIDE	King (CBS)
12	6	SINCE YESTERDAY	Strawberry Switchblade (Korova)
3	7	LIKE A VIRGIN	Madonna (Sire)
20	8	ATMOSPHERE	Russ Abbott (Spirit)
14	9	FRIENDS	Amii Stewart (RCA)
22	10	SOLID	Ashford & Simpson (Capitol)
4	11	EVERYTHING SHE WANTS/LAST CHRISTMAS	Wham! (Epic)
8	12	STEP OFF	Grandmaster Melle Mel (Sugarhill)
31	13	THIS IS MY NIGHT	Chaka Khan (Warner Bros)
15	14	SAY YEAH	Limit (Portrait)
5	15	DO THEY KNOW IT'S CHRISTMAS?	Band Aid (Mercury)
9	16	POLICE OFFICER	Smiley Culture (Fashion)
34	17	YAH MO B THERE	James Ingram (Qwest)
29	18	DANCING IN THE DARK	Bruce Springsteen (CBS)
11	19	EVERYTHING MUST CHANGE	Paul Young (CBS)
10	20	GHOSTBUSTERS	Ray Parker Jr. (Arista)
27	21	RUN TO YOU	Bryan Adams (A&M)
37	22	SUSSUDIO	Phil Collins (Virgin)
28	23	LOVERBOY	Billy Ocean (Jive)
32	24	THANK YOU MY LOVE	Imagination (R&B)
17	25	IT AIN'T NECESSARILY SO	Bronski Beat (Forbidden Fruit)
13	26	SAN DAMIANO (HEART AND SOUL)	Sal Solo (MCA)
24	27	JUST A SHADOW	Big Country (Mercury)
33	28	CAN I	Cashmere (Fourth & Broadway)
47	29	WE BELONG	Pat Benatar (Chrysalis)
39	30	A NEW ENGLAND	Kirsty MacColl (Stiff)
–	31	THINKING OF YOU	Colour Field (Chrysalis)
–	32	PERFECT STRANGERS	Deep Purple (Polydor)
41	33	CLOSE (TO THE EDIT)	Art Of Noise (ZTT)
35	34	20/20	George Benson (Warner Bros)
21	35	SHARP DRESSED MAN	ZZ Top (Warner Bros)
42	36	JULIA	Eurythmics (Virgin)
45	37	YOU SPIN ME ROUND (LIKE A RECORD)	Dead Or Alive (Epic)
19	38	WE ALL STAND TOGETHER	Paul McCartney & the Frog Chorus (Parlophone)
–	39	SEA OF LOVE	Honeydrippers (Es Paranza)
–	40	LOVERIDE	Nuance (Fourth & Broadway)
–	41	THIS HOUSE (IS WHERE YOUR LOVE STANDS)	Big Sound Authority (Source)
–	42	NIGHTSHIFT	Commodores (Motown)
44	43	NEUTRON DANCE	Pointer Sisters (Planet)
18	44	NELLIE THE ELEPHANT	Toy Dolls (Volume)
50	45	CONTAGIOUS	Whispers (MCA)
49	46	SEE THAT GLOW	This Island Earth (Magnet)
36	47	WORLD DESTRUCTION	Time Zone (Virgin)
23	48	THE POWER OF LOVE	Frankie Goes To Hollywood (ZTT)
46	49	WE CAN BE BRAVE AGAIN	Armoury Show (Parlophone)
–	50	LOVE LIKE BLOOD	Killing Joke (EG)

9 February 1985

last week	this week	Title	Artist (Label)
3	1	I KNOW HIM SO WELL	Elaine Paige & Barbara Dickson (RCA)
1	2	I WANT TO KNOW WHAT LOVE IS	Foreigner (Atlantic)
5	3	LOVE AND PRIDE	King (CBS)
2	4	1999/LITTLE RED CORVETTE	Prince (Warner Bros)
10	5	SOLID	Ashford & Simpson (Capitol)
4	6	SHOUT	Tears For Fears (Mercury)
18	7	DANCING IN THE DARK	Bruce Springsteen (CBS)
17	8	YAH MO B THERE	James Ingram (Qwest)
8	9	ATMOSPHERE	Russ Abbott (Spirit)
6	10	SINCE YESTERDAY	Strawberry Switchblade (Korova)
9	11	FRIENDS	Amii Stewart (RCA)
23	12	LOVERBOY	Billy Ocean (Jive)
7	13	LIKE A VIRGIN	Madonna (Sire)
13	14	THIS IS MY NIGHT	Chaka Khan (Warner Bros)
22	15	SUSSUDIO	Phil Collins (Virgin)
21	16	RUN TO YOU	Bryan Adams (A&M)
11	17	EVERYTHING SHE WANTS/LAST CHRISTMAS	Wham! (Epic)
12	18	STEP OFF	Grandmaster Melle Mel (Sugarhill)
33	19	CLOSE (TO THE EDIT)	Art Of Noise (ZTT)
30	20	A NEW ENGLAND	Kirsty MacColl (Stiff)
14	21	SAY YEAH	Limit (Portrait)
29	22	WE BELONG	Pat Benatar (Chrysalis)
42	23	NIGHTSHIFT	Commodores (Motown)
31	24	THINKING OF YOU	Colour Field (Chrysalis)
15	25	DO THEY KNOW IT'S CHRISTMAS?	Band Aid (Mercury)
24	26	THANK YOU MY LOVE	Imagination (R&B)
–	27	THIS IS NOT AMERICA	David Bowie & Pat Metheny (EMI America)
41	28	THIS HOUSE (IS WHERE YOUR LOVE STANDS)	Big Sound Authority (Source)
20	29	GHOSTBUSTERS	Ray Parker Jr. (Arista)
27	30	JUST A SHADOW	Big Country (Mercury)
16	31	POLICE OFFICER	Smiley Culture (Fashion)
28	32	CAN I	Cashmere (Fourth & Broadway)
–	33	HOW SOON IS NOW?	Smiths (Rough Trade)
–	34	WHO COMES TO BOOGIE	Little Benny & the Masters (Bluebird)
34	35	20/20	George Benson (Warner Bros)
35	36	SHARP DRESSED MAN	ZZ Top (Warner Bros)
32	37	PERFECT STRANGERS	Deep Purple (Polydor)
50	38	LOVE LIKE BLOOD	Killing Joke (EG)
–	39	LAND OF HOPE AND GLORY	Ex Pistols (Virginia)
–	40	THINGS CAN ONLY GET BETTER	Howard Jones (WEA)
–	41	IT'S IT'S THE SWEET MIX	Sweet (Anagram)
–	42	YOU'RE THE INSPIRATION	Chicago (Warner Bros)
39	43	SEA OF LOVE	Honeydrippers (Es Paranza)
45	44	CONTAGIOUS	Whispers (MCA)
26	45	SAN DAMIANO (HEART AND SOUL)	Sal Solo (MCA)
19	46	EVERYTHING MUST CHANGE	Paul Young (CBS)
40	47	LOVERIDE	Nuance (Fourth & Broadway)
–	48	I HEAR TALK	Bucks Fizz (RCA)
–	49	PERSONALITY/LET HER FEEL IT	Eugene Wilde (Fourth & Broadway)
–	50	I SLEEP ALONE AT NIGHT	Jim Diamond (A&M)

Elaine Paige and Barbara Dickson's duet was the highlight ballad from the musical *Chess*, written by Tim Rice with Born Ulvaeus and Benny Andersson of Abba. It proved to be a vastly bigger seller than either singer ever had individually. Prince's Number Two hit, also his biggest to date, was a reissued pairing of two former A-sides from 1983; *Little Red Corvette* had earlier charted at a mere number 46.

16 February 1985

last week	this week	Title	Artist (Label)
3	1	LOVE AND PRIDE	King (CBS)
1	2	I KNOW HIM SO WELL	Elaine Paige & Barbara Dickson (RCA)
5	3	SOLID	Ashford & Simpson (Capitol)
7	4	DANCING IN THE DARK	Bruce Springsteen (CBS)
2	5	I WANT TO KNOW WHAT LOVE IS	Foreigner (Atlantic)
4	6	1999/LITTLE RED CORVETTE	Prince (Warner Bros)
19	7	CLOSE (TO THE EDIT)	Art Of Noise (ZTT)
15	8	SUSSUDIO	Phil Collins (Virgin)
16	9	RUN TO YOU	Bryan Adams (A&M)
9	10	ATMOSPHERE	Russ Abbott (Spirit)
20	11	A NEW ENGLAND	Kirsty MacColl (Stiff)
6	12	SHOUT	Tears For Fears (Mercury)
27	13	THIS IS NOT AMERICA	David Bowie & Pat Metheny (EMI America)
24	14	THINKING OF YOU	Colour Field (Chrysalis)
40	15	THINGS CAN ONLY GET BETTER	Howard Jones (WEA)
16	16	SINCE YESTERDAY	Strawberry Switchblade (Korova)
23	17	NIGHTSHIFT	Commodores (Motown)
8	18	YAH MO B THERE	James Ingram (Qwest)
11	19	LOVERBOY	Billy Ocean (Jive)
33	20	HOW SOON IS NOW?	Smiths (Rough Trade)
28	21	THIS HOUSE (IS WHERE YOUR LOVE STANDS)	Big Sound Authority (Source)
22	22	WE BELONG	Pat Benatar (Chrysalis)
38	23	LOVE LIKE BLOOD	Killing Joke (EG)
12	24	LIKE A VIRGIN	Madonna (Sire)
14	25	THIS IS MY NIGHT	Chaka Khan (Warner Bros)
32	26	CAN I	Cashmere (Fourth & Broadway)
13	27	FRIENDS	Amii Stewart (RCA)
-	28	HERE I COME	Barrington Levy (London)
42	29	YOU'RE THE INSPIRATION	Chicago (Warner Bros)
-	30	LOVE AIN'T NO STRANGER	Whitesnake (Liberty)
35	31	20/20	George Benson (Warner Bros)
39	32	LAND OF HOPE AND GLORY	Ex Pistols (Virginia)
-	33	CHANGE YOUR MIND	Sharpe & Numan (Polydor)
-	34	THE BOYS OF SUMMER	Don Henley (Geffen)
41	35	IT'S IT'S THE SWEET MIX	Sweet (Anagram)
17	36	EVERYTHING SHE WANTS/LAST CHRISTMAS	Wham! (Epic)
-	37	JUST ANOTHER NIGHT	Mick Jagger (CBS)
43	38	SEA OF LOVE	Honeydrippers (Es Paranza)
31	39	POLICE OFFICER	Smiley Culture (Fashion)
-	40	HOWLING AT THE MOON	Ramones (Beggars Banquet)
49	41	PERSONALITY/LET HER FEEL IT	Eugene Wilde (Fourth & Broadway)
-	42	BREAKFAST	Associates (WEA)
21	43	SAY YEAH	Limit (Portrait)
-	44	METHOD OF MODERN LOVE	Daryl Hall & John Oates (RCA)
26	45	THANK YOU MY LOVE	Imagination (R&B)
-	46	MY GIRL LOVES ME	Shalamar (MCA)
-	47	WORLD DESTRUCTION	Time Zone (Virgin)
-	48	DO YOU REALLY (WANT MY LOVE)	Junior (London)
18	49	STEP OFF	Grandmaster Melle Mel (Sugarhill)
-	50	MISLED	Kool & the Gang (De-Lite)

23 February 1985

last week	this week	Title	Artist (Label)
2	1	I KNOW HIM SO WELL	Elaine Paige & Barbara Dickson (RCA)
1	2	LOVE AND PRIDE	King (CBS)
3	3	SOLID	Ashford & Simpson (Capitol)
4	4	DANCING IN THE DARK	Bruce Springsteen (CBS)
15	5	THINGS CAN ONLY GET BETTER	Howard Jones (WEA)
7	6	CLOSE (TO THE EDIT)	Art Of Noise (ZTT)
11	7	A NEW ENGLAND	Kirsty MacColl (Stiff)
8	8	SUSSUDIO	Phil Collins (Virgin)
5	9	I WANT TO KNOW WHAT LOVE IS	Foreigner (Atlantic)
9	10	RUN TO YOU	Bryan Adams (A&M)
6	11	1999/LITTLE RED CORVETTE	Prince (Warner Bros)
14	12	THINKING OF YOU	Colour Field (Chrysalis)
13	13	THIS IS NOT AMERICA	David Bowie & Pat Metheny (EMI America)
17	14	NIGHTSHIFT	Commodores (Motown)
-	15	YOU SPIN ME ROUND (LIKE A RECORD)	Dead Or Alive (Epic)
10	16	ATMOSPHERE	Russ Abbott (Spirit)
19	17	LOVERBOY	Billy Ocean (Jive)
20	18	HOW SOON IS NOW?	Smiths (Rough Trade)
29	19	YOU'RE THE INSPIRATION	Chicago (Warner Bros)
23	20	LOVE LIKE BLOOD	Killing Joke (EG)
12	21	SHOUT	Tears For Fears (Mercury)
21	22	THIS HOUSE (IS WHERE YOUR LOVE STANDS)	Big Sound Authority (Source)
-	23	LET'S GO CRAZY/TAKE ME WITH YOU	Prince & the Revolution (Warner Bros)
33	24	CHANGE YOUR MIND	Sharpe & Numan (Polydor)
22	25	WE BELONG	Pat Benatar (Chrysalis)
16	26	SINCE YESTERDAY	Strawberry Switchblade (Korova)
37	27	JUST ANOTHER NIGHT	Mick Jagger (CBS)
34	28	THE BOYS OF SUMMER	Don Henley (Geffen)
18	29	YAH MO B THERE	James Ingram (Qwest)
31	30	20/20	George Benson (Warner Bros)
-	31	LET ME DOWN EASY	Stranglers (Epic)
41	32	PERSONALITY/LET HER FEEL IT	Eugene Wilde (Fourth & Broadway)
-	33	WHO COMES TO BOOGIE	Little Benny & the Masters (Bluebird)
25	34	THIS IS MY NIGHT	Chaka Khan (Warner Bros)
50	35	MISLED	Kool & the Gang (De-Lite)
35	36	IT'S IT'S THE SWEET MIX	Sweet (Anagram)
28	37	HERE I COME	Barrington Levy (London)
26	38	CAN I	Cashmere (Fourth & Broadway)
-	39	LEGS	ZZ Top (Warner Bros)
24	40	LIKE A VIRGIN	Madonna (Sire)
-	41	CALIFORNIA GIRLS	David Lee Roth (Warner Bros)
-	42	TAINTED LOVE	Soft Cell (Some Bizzare)
27	43	FRIENDS	Amii Stewart (RCA)
30	44	LOVE AIN'T NO STRANGER	Whitesnake (Liberty)
49	45	STEP OFF	Grandmaster Melle Mel (Sugarhill)
48	46	DO YOU REALLY (WANT MY LOVE)	Junior (London)
-	47	BETWEEN THE WARS (EP)	Billy Bragg (Go! Discs)
-	48	I DIDN'T MEAN IT AT ALL	Sasss (10)
-	49	SHAFT	Van Twist (Polydor)
40	50	HOWLING AT THE MOON	Ramones (Beggars Banquet)

2 March 1985

last week	this week	Title	Artist (Label)
1	1	I KNOW HIM SO WELL	Elaine Paige & Barbara Dickson (RCA)
2	2	LOVE AND PRIDE	King (CBS)
15	3	YOU SPIN ME ROUND (LIKE A RECORD)	Dead Or Alive (Epic)
3	4	SOLID	Ashford & Simpson (Capitol)
4	5	DANCING IN THE DARK	Bruce Springsteen (CBS)
5	6	THINGS CAN ONLY GET BETTER	Howard Jones (WEA)
14	7	NIGHTSHIFT	Commodores (Motown)
6	8	CLOSE (TO THE EDIT)	Art Of Noise (ZTT)
7	9	A NEW ENGLAND	Kirsty MacColl (Stiff)
10	10	RUN TO YOU	Bryan Adams (A&M)
19	11	YOU'RE THE INSPIRATION	Chicago (Warner Bros)
12	12	THINKING OF YOU	Colour Field (Chrysalis)
20	13	LOVE LIKE BLOOD	Killing Joke (EG)
9	14	I WANT TO KNOW WHAT LOVE IS	Foreigner (Atlantic)
23	15	LET'S GO CRAZY/TAKE ME WITH YOU	Prince & the Revolution (Warner Bros)
13	16	THIS IS NOT AMERICA	David Bowie & Pat Metheny (EMI America)
8	17	SUSSUDIO	Phil Collins (Virgin)
11	18	1999/LITTLE RED CORVETTE	Prince (Warner Bros)
17	19	LOVERBOY	Billy Ocean (Jive)
24	20	CHANGE YOUR MIND	Sharpe & Numan (Polydor)
28	21	THE BOYS OF SUMMER	Don Henley (Geffen)
18	22	HOW SOON IS NOW?	Smiths (Rough Trade)
-	23	THEME FROM SHAFT	Eddy & the Soulband (Club)
16	24	ATMOSPHERE	Russ Abbott (Spirit)
39	25	LEGS	ZZ Top (Warner Bros)
27	26	JUST ANOTHER NIGHT	Mick Jagger (CBS)
35	27	MISLED	Kool & the Gang (De-Lite)
21	28	SHOUT	Tears For Fears (Mercury)
26	29	SINCE YESTERDAY	Strawberry Switchblade (Korova)
40	30	LIKE A VIRGIN	Madonna (Sire)
22	31	THIS HOUSE (IS WHERE YOUR LOVE STANDS)	Big Sound Authority (Source)
49	32	SHAFT	Van Twist (Polydor)
-	33	NEVER UNDERSTAND	Jesus & Mary Chain (blanco y negro)
34	34	I'M SO HAPPY	Julia & Co. (Next Plateau)
32	35	PERSONALITY/LET HER FEEL IT	Eugene Wilde (Fourth & Broadway)
31	36	LET ME DOWN EASY	Stranglers (Epic)
-	37	SUNSPOTS	Julian Cope (Mercury)
-	38	MOVE CLOSER	Phyllis Nelson (Carrere)
25	39	WE BELONG	Pat Benatar (Chrysalis)
-	40	ABSOLUTE REALITY	Alarm (IRS)
30	41	20/20	George Benson (Warner Bros)
-	42	BREAKING UP MY HEART	Shakin' Stevens (Epic)
-	43	HANGIN' ON A STRING (CONTEMPLATING)	Loose Ends (Virgin)
44	44	HERE I COME	Barrington Levy (London)
29	45	YAH MO B THERE	James Ingram (Qwest)
33	46	WHO COMES TO BOOGIE	Little Benny & the Masters (Bluebird)
-	47	RADIOACTIVE	Firm (Bark)
42	48	TAINTED LOVE	Soft Cell (Some Bizzare)
46	49	DO YOU REALLY (WANT MY LOVE)	Junior (London)
-	50	WORLD DESTRUCTION	Time Zone (Virgin)

King, whose *Love And Pride* was both their first and biggest hit, were led by vocalist Paul King, who since the group's demise has become a presenter (or 'VJ') for MTV. The Commodores' *Nightshift* was a tribute record, namechecking departed soul stars like Marvin Gaye and Jackie Wilson, while David Bowie collaborated with jazzman Pat Metheny for the soundtrack of the film *The Falcon & The Snowman*.

March 1985

9 March 1985

last	this	title	artist
3	1	YOU SPIN ME ROUND (LIKE A RECORD)	Dead Or Alive (Epic)
1	2	I KNOW HIM SO WELL	Elaine Paige & Barbara Dickson (RCA)
7	3	NIGHTSHIFT	Commodores (Motown)
2	4	LOVE AND PRIDE	King (CBS)
5	5	DANCING IN THE DARK	Bruce Springsteen (CBS)
4	6	SOLID	Ashford & Simpson (Capitol)
15	7	LET'S GO CRAZY/TAKE ME WITH YOU	Prince & the Revolution (Warner Bros)
6	8	THINGS CAN ONLY GET BETTER	Howard Jones (WEA)
21	9	THE BOYS OF SUMMER	Don Henley (Geffen)
10	10	RUN TO YOU	Bryan Adams (A&M)
9	11	A NEW ENGLAND	Kirsty MacColl (Stiff)
23	12	THEME FROM SHAFT	Eddy & the Soulband (Club)
13	13	LOVE LIKE BLOOD	Killing Joke (EG)
8	14	CLOSE (TO THE EDIT)	Art Of Noise (ZTT)
-	15	KISS ME	Stephen 'Tintin' Duffy (10)
12	16	THINKING OF YOU	Colour Field (Chrysalis)
11	17	YOU'RE THE INSPIRATION	Chicago (Warner Bros)
-	18	MATERIAL GIRL	Madonna (Sire)
20	19	CHANGE YOUR MIND	Sharpe & Numan (Polydor)
25	20	LEGS	ZZ Top (Warner Bros)
33	21	NEVER UNDERSTAND	Jesus & Mary Chain (blanco y negro)
18	22	1999/LITTLE RED CORVETTE	Prince (Warner Bros)
22	23	HOW SOON IS NOW?	Smiths (Rough Trade)
-	24	THE LAST KISS	David Cassidy (Arista)
40	25	ABSOLUTE REALITY	Alarm (IRS)
42	26	BREAKING UP MY HEART	Shakin' Stevens (Epic)
19	27	LOVERBOY	Billy Ocean (Jive)
43	28	HANGIN' ON A STRING (CONTEMPLATING)	Loose Ends (Virgin)
37	29	SUNSPOTS	Julian Cope (Mercury)
-	30	EVERY TIME YOU GO AWAY	Paul Young (CBS)
26	31	JUST ANOTHER NIGHT	Mick Jagger (CBS)
24	32	ATMOSPHERE	Russ Abbott (Spirit)
50	33	WORLD DESTRUCTION	Time Zone (Virgin)
14	34	I WANT TO KNOW WHAT LOVE IS	Foreigner (Atlantic)
-	35	EASY LOVER	Philip Bailey & Phil Collins (CBS)
17	36	SUSSUDIO	Phil Collins (Virgin)
-	37	METHOD OF MODERN LOVE	Daryl Hall & John Oates (RCA)
46	38	WHO COMES TO BOOGIE	Little Benny & the Masters (Bluebird)
27	39	MISLED	Kool & the Gang (De-Lite)
16	40	THIS IS NOT AMERICA	David Bowie & Pat Metheny (EMI America)
-	41	DO WHAT YOU DO	Jermaine Jackson (Arista)
36	42	LET ME DOWN EASY	Stranglers (Epic)
31	43	THIS HOUSE (IS WHERE YOUR LOVE STANDS)	Big Sound Authority (Source)
32	44	SHAFT	Van Twist (Polydor)
39	45	WE BELONG	Pat Benatar (Chrysalis)
30	46	LIKE A VIRGIN	Madonna (Sire)
-	47	THE HEAT IS ON	Glenn Frey (MCA)
-	48	WE CLOSE OUR EYES	Go West (Chrysalis)
-	49	MR. TELEPHONE MAN	New Edition (MCA)
-	50	THE BELLE OF ST. MARK	Sheila E (Warner Bros)

16 March 1985

last	this	title	artist
1	1	YOU SPIN ME ROUND (LIKE A RECORD)	Dead Or Alive (Epic)
3	2	NIGHTSHIFT	Commodores (Motown)
18	3	MATERIAL GIRL	Madonna (Sire)
15	4	KISS ME	Stephen 'Tintin' Duffy (10)
2	5	I KNOW HIM SO WELL	Elaine Paige & Barbara Dickson (RCA)
7	6	LET'S GO CRAZY/TAKE ME WITH YOU	Prince & the Revolution (Warner Bros)
4	7	LOVE AND PRIDE	King (CBS)
5	8	DANCING IN THE DARK	Bruce Springsteen (CBS)
35	9	EASY LOVER	Philip Bailey & Phil Collins (CBS)
6	10	SOLID	Ashford & Simpson (Capitol)
24	11	THE LAST KISS	David Cassidy (Arista)
9	12	THE BOYS OF SUMMER	Don Henley (Geffen)
12	13	THEME FROM SHAFT	Eddy & the Soulband (Club)
8	14	THINGS CAN ONLY GET BETTER	Howard Jones (WEA)
20	15	LEGS	ZZ Top (Warner Bros)
26	16	BREAKING UP MY HEART	Shakin' Stevens (Epic)
13	17	LOVE LIKE BLOOD	Killing Joke (EG)
30	18	EVERY TIME YOU GO AWAY	Paul Young (CBS)
41	19	DO WHAT YOU DO	Jermaine Jackson (Arista)
10	20	RUN TO YOU	Bryan Adams (A&M)
-	21	THAT OLE DEVIL CALLED LOVE	Alison Moyet (CBS)
11	22	A NEW ENGLAND	Kirsty MacColl (Stiff)
37	23	METHOD OF MODERN LOVE	Daryl Hall & John Oates (RCA)
16	24	THINKING OF YOU	Colour Field (Chrysalis)
31	25	JUST ANOTHER NIGHT	Mick Jagger (CBS)
28	26	HANGIN' ON A STRING (CONTEMPLATING)	Loose Ends (Virgin)
21	27	NEVER UNDERSTAND	Jesus & Mary Chain (blanco y negro)
48	28	WE CLOSE OUR EYES	Go West (Chrysalis)
-	29	NO TIME TO CRY	Sisters Of Mercy (Merciful Release)
-	30	STARVATION/TAM-TAM POUR L'ETHIOPIE	Starvation (Zarjazz)
31	31	CLOSE (TO THE EDIT)	Art Of Noise (ZTT)
17	32	YOU'RE THE INSPIRATION	Chicago (Warner Bros)
19	33	CHANGE YOUR MIND	Sharpe & Numan (Polydor)
50	34	THE BELLE OF ST. MARK	Sheila E (Warner Bros)
49	35	MR. TELEPHONE MAN	New Edition (MCA)
33	36	WORLD DESTRUCTION	Time Zone (Virgin)
22	37	1999/LITTLE RED CORVETTE	Prince (Warner Bros)
-	38	SOME LIKE IT HOT	Power Station (Parlophone)
-	39	MOVE CLOSER	Phyllis Nelson (Carrere)
-	40	BETWEEN THE WARS (EP)	Billy Bragg (Go! Discs)
40	41	THIS IS NOT AMERICA	David Bowie & Pat Metheny (EMI America)
-	42	WIDE BOY	Nik Kershaw (MCA)
27	43	LOVERBOY	Billy Ocean (Jive)
29	44	SUNSPOTS	Julian Cope (Mercury)
25	45	ABSOLUTE REALITY	Alarm (IRS)
-	46	FALLING ANGELS RIDING	David Essex (Mercury)
23	47	HOW SOON IS NOW?	Smiths (Rough Trade)
-	48	SUPER GRAN	Billy Connolly (Stiff)
38	49	WHO COMES TO BOOGIE	Little Benny & the Masters (Bluebird)
-	50	FOREVER MAN	Eric Clapton (Warner Bros)

23 March 1985

last	this	title	artist
9	1	EASY LOVER	Philip Bailey & Phil Collins (CBS)
1	2	YOU SPIN ME ROUND (LIKE A RECORD)	Dead Or Alive (Epic)
3	3	MATERIAL GIRL	Madonna (Sire)
21	4	THAT OLE DEVIL CALLED LOVE	Alison Moyet (CBS)
4	5	KISS ME	Stephen 'Tintin' Duffy (10)
11	6	THE LAST KISS	David Cassidy (Arista)
2	7	NIGHTSHIFT	Commodores (Motown)
18	8	EVERY TIME YOU GO AWAY	Paul Young (CBS)
19	9	DO WHAT YOU DO	Jermaine Jackson (Arista)
42	10	WIDE BOY	Nik Kershaw (MCA)
28	11	WE CLOSE OUR EYES	Go West (Chrysalis)
5	12	I KNOW HIM SO WELL	Elaine Paige & Barbara Dickson (RCA)
40	13	BETWEEN THE WARS (EP)	Billy Bragg (Go! Discs)
6	14	LET'S GO CRAZY/TAKE ME WITH YOU	Prince & the Revolution (Warner Bros)
16	15	BREAKING UP MY HEART	Shakin' Stevens (Epic)
10	16	SOLID	Ashford & Simpson (Capitol)
26	17	HANGIN' ON A STRING (CONTEMPLATING)	Loose Ends (Virgin)
23	18	METHOD OF MODERN LOVE	Daryl Hall & John Oates (RCA)
34	19	THE BELLE OF ST. MARK	Sheila E (Warner Bros)
15	20	LEGS	ZZ Top (Warner Bros)
8	21	DANCING IN THE DARK	Bruce Springsteen (CBS)
-	22	COVER ME	Bruce Springsteen (CBS)
12	23	THE BOYS OF SUMMER	Don Henley (Geffen)
38	24	SOME LIKE IT HOT	Power Station (Parlophone)
45	25	ABSOLUTE REALITY	Alarm (IRS)
27	26	NEVER UNDERSTAND	Jesus & Mary Chain (blanco y negro)
37	27	1999/LITTLE RED CORVETTE	Prince (Warner Bros)
35	28	MR. TELEPHONE MAN	New Edition (MCA)
-	29	WON'T YOU HOLD MY HAND NOW	King (CBS)
39	30	MOVE CLOSER	Phyllis Nelson (Carrere)
30	31	STARVATION/TAM-TAM POUR L'ETHIOPIE	Starvation (Zarjazz)
13	32	THEME FROM SHAFT	Eddy & the Soulband (Club)
14	33	THINGS CAN ONLY GET BETTER	Howard Jones (WEA)
25	34	JUST ANOTHER NIGHT	Mick Jagger (CBS)
29	35	NO TIME TO CRY	Sisters Of Mercy (Merciful Release)
17	36	LOVE LIKE BLOOD	Killing Joke (EG)
50	37	FOREVER MAN	Eric Clapton (Warner Bros)
-	38	DANCING IN THE DARK (EP)	Big Daddy (Making Waves)
20	39	RUN TO YOU	Bryan Adams (A&M)
46	40	FALLING ANGELS RIDING	David Essex (Mercury)
22	41	A NEW ENGLAND	Kirsty MacColl (Stiff)
36	42	WORLD DESTRUCTION	Time Zone (Virgin)
48	43	SUPER GRAN	Billy Connolly (Stiff)
-	44	THE HEAT IS ON	Glenn Frey (MCA)
-	45	HYMN FROM A VILLAGE	James (Fontana)
-	46	NO FOOL (FOR LOVE)	Hazell Dean (Proto)
-	47	GUN LAW	Kane Gang (Kitchenware)
-	48	BELFAST	Barnbrack (Homespun)
7	49	LOVE AND PRIDE	King (CBS)
-	50	SPEND THE NIGHT	Cool Notes (Abstract Dance)

David Cassidy made his first UK chart appearance for nearly ten years with *The Last Kiss*, while the *Theme From Shaft*, originally a top tenner for its composer Isaac Hayes in 1971, returned via two different dancefloor interpretations. The Power Station, charting with *Some Like It Hot*, were Robert Palmer, John and Andy Taylor from Duran Duran, and Bernard Edwards and Tony Thompson from Chic.

30 March 1985

last	this	
1	1	EASY LOVER Philip Bailey & Phil Collins (CBS)
4	2	THAT OLE DEVIL CALLED LOVE Alison Moyet (CBS)
8	3	EVERY TIME YOU GO AWAY Paul Young (CBS)
3	4	MATERIAL GIRL Madonna (Sire)
2	5	YOU SPIN ME ROUND (LIKE A RECORD) Dead Or Alive (Epic)
9	6	DO WHAT YOU DO Jermaine Jackson (Arista)
11	7	WE CLOSE OUR EYES Go West (Chrysalis)
19	8	THE BELLE OF ST. MARK Sheila E (Warner Bros)
5	9	KISS ME Stephen 'Tintin' Duffy (10)
6	10	THE LAST KISS David Cassidy (Arista)
-	11	PIE JESU Sarah Brightman & Paul Miles-Kingston (HMV)
10	12	WIDE BOY Nik Kershaw (MCA)
13	13	BETWEEN THE WARS (EP) Billy Bragg (Go! Discs)
22	14	COVER ME Bruce Springsteen (CBS)
7	15	NIGHTSHIFT Commodores (Motown)
24	16	SOME LIKE IT HOT Power Station (Parlophone)
17	17	HANGIN' ON A STRING (CONTEMPLATING) Loose Ends (Virgin)
12	18	I KNOW HIM SO WELL Elaine Paige & Barbara Dickson (RCA)
28	19	MR. TELEPHONE MAN New Edition (MCA)
29	20	WON'T YOU HOLD MY HAND NOW King (CBS)
-	21	WELCOME TO THE PLEASUREDOME Frankie Goes To Hollywood (ZTT)
38	22	DANCING IN THE DARK (EP) Big Daddy (Making Waves)
30	23	MOVE CLOSER Phyllis Nelson (Carrere)
14	24	LET'S GO CRAZY/TAKE ME WITH YOU Prince & the Revolution (Warner Bros)
21	25	DANCING IN THE DARK Bruce Springsteen (CBS)
-	26	AIKEA GUINEA Cocteau Twins (4AD)
50	27	SPEND THE NIGHT Cool Notes (Abstract Dance)
48	28	BELFAST Barnbrack (Homespun)
-	29	SHAKESPEARE'S SISTER Smiths (Rough Trade)
-	30	LET'S GO TOGETHER Change (Cooltempo)
23	31	THE BOYS OF SUMMER Don Henley (Geffen)
18	32	METHOD OF MODERN LOVE Daryl Hall & John Oates (RCA)
-	33	COULD IT BE I'M FALLING IN LOVE David Grant & Jaki Graham (Chrysalis)
44	34	THE HEAT IS ON Glenn Frey (MCA)
26	35	NEVER UNDERSTAND Jesus & Mary Chain (blanco y negro)
-	36	MYZSTERIOUS MIZSTER JONES Slade (RCA)
15	37	BREAKING UP MY HEART Shakin' Stevens (Epic)
39	38	RUN TO YOU Bryan Adams (A&M)
27	39	1999/LITTLE RED CORVETTE Prince (Warner Bros)
-	40	PUMP ME UP Grandmaster Melle Mel (Sugarhill)
16	41	SOLID Ashford & Simpson (Capitol)
-	42	GRIMLY FIENDISH Damned (MCA)
-	43	LOVE IS A BATTLEFIELD Pat Benatar (Chrysalis)
-	44	EVERYBODY WANTS TO RULE THE WORLD Tears For Fears (Mercury)
-	45	SHE GOES TO FINOS Toy Dolls (Volume)
32	46	THEME FROM SHAFT Eddy & the Soulband (Club)
25	47	ABSOLUTE REALITY Alarm (IRS)
-	48	CAN'T FIGHT THE FEELING REO Speedwagon (Epic)
31	49	STARVATION/TAM-TAM POUR L'ETHIOPIE Starvation (Zarjazz)
20	50	LEGS ZZ Top (Warner Bros)

6 April 1985

last	this	
1	1	EASY LOVER Philip Bailey & Phil Collins (CBS)
2	2	THAT OLE DEVIL CALLED LOVE Alison Moyet (CBS)
11	3	PIE JESU Sarah Brightman & Paul Miles-Kingston (HMV)
21	4	WELCOME TO THE PLEASUREDOME Frankie Goes To Hollywood (ZTT)
3	5	EVERY TIME YOU GO AWAY Paul Young (CBS)
7	6	WE CLOSE OUR EYES Go West (Chrysalis)
6	7	DO WHAT YOU DO Jermaine Jackson (Arista)
4	8	WIDE BOY Nik Kershaw (MCA)
9	9	MATERIAL GIRL Madonna (Sire)
14	10	COVER ME Bruce Springsteen (CBS)
44	11	EVERYBODY WANTS TO RULE THE WORLD Tears For Fears (Mercury)
16	12	SOME LIKE IT HOT Power Station (Parlophone)
17	13	HANGIN' ON A STRING (CONTEMPLATING) Loose Ends (Virgin)
13	14	BETWEEN THE WARS (EP) Billy Bragg (Go! Discs)
5	15	YOU SPIN ME ROUND (LIKE A RECORD) Dead Or Alive (Epic)
10	16	THE LAST KISS David Cassidy (Arista)
29	17	SHAKESPEARE'S SISTER Smiths (Rough Trade)
9	18	KISS ME Stephen 'Tintin' Duffy (10)
33	19	COULD IT BE I'M FALLING IN LOVE David Grant & Jaki Graham (Chrysalis)
23	20	MOVE CLOSER Phyllis Nelson (Carrere)
22	21	DANCING IN THE DARK (EP) Big Daddy (Making Waves)
20	22	WON'T YOU HOLD MY HAND NOW King (CBS)
34	23	THE HEAT IS ON Glenn Frey (MCA)
19	24	MR. TELEPHONE MAN New Edition (MCA)
8	25	THE BELLE OF ST. MARK Sheila E (Warner Bros)
42	26	GRIMLY FIENDISH Damned (MCA)
26	27	AIKEA GUINEA Cocteau Twins (4AD)
-	28	NOW THAT WE'VE FOUND LOVE Third World (Island)
15	29	NIGHTSHIFT Commodores (Motown)
-	30	CLOUDS ACROSS THE MOON RAH Band (RCA)
27	31	SPEND THE NIGHT Cool Notes (Abstract Dance)
43	32	LOVE IS A BATTLEFIELD Pat Benatar (Chrysalis)
18	33	I KNOW HIM SO WELL Elaine Paige & Barbara Dickson (RCA)
25	34	DANCING IN THE DARK Bruce Springsteen (CBS)
48	35	CAN'T FIGHT THE FEELING REO Speedwagon (Epic)
-	36	KINGS AND QUEENS Killing Joke (EG)
-	37	SOMEBODY Bryan Adams (A&M)
-	38	LIFE IN A NORTHERN TOWN Dream Academy (blanco y negro)
-	39	A PAIR OF BROWN EYES Pogues (Stiff)
31	40	THE BOYS OF SUMMER Don Henley (Geffen)
30	41	LET'S GO TOGETHER Change (Cooltempo)
45	42	SHE GOES TO FINOS Toy Dolls (Volume)
32	43	METHOD OF MODERN LOVE Daryl Hall & John Oates (RCA)
-	44	CRY Godley & Creme (Polydor)
36	45	MYZSTERIOUS MIZSTER JONES Slade (RCA)
-	46	BAD HABITS Jenny Burton (Atlantic)
47	47	BLACK MAN RAY China Crisis (Virgin)
-	48	GUN LAW Kane Gang (Kitchenware)
-	49	PIECE OF THE ACTION Meat Loaf (Arista)
28	50	BELFAST Barnbrack (Homespun)

13 April 1985

last	this	
4	1	WELCOME TO THE PLEASUREDOME Frankie Goes To Hollywood (ZTT)
1	2	EASY LOVER Philip Bailey & Phil Collins (CBS)
3	3	PIE JESU Sarah Brightman & Paul Miles-Kingston (HMV)
2	4	THAT OLE DEVIL CALLED LOVE Alison Moyet (CBS)
11	5	EVERYBODY WANTS TO RULE THE WORLD Tears For Fears (Mercury)
6	6	WE CLOSE OUR EYES Go West (Chrysalis)
5	7	EVERY TIME YOU GO AWAY Paul Young (CBS)
7	8	DO WHAT YOU DO Jermaine Jackson (Arista)
8	9	WIDE BOY Nik Kershaw (MCA)
19	10	COULD IT BE I'M FALLING IN LOVE David Grant & Jaki Graham (Chrysalis)
10	11	COVER ME Bruce Springsteen (CBS)
20	12	MOVE CLOSER Phyllis Nelson (Carrere)
13	13	HANGIN' ON A STRING (CONTEMPLATING) Loose Ends (Virgin)
18	14	KISS ME Stephen 'Tintin' Duffy (10)
14	15	BETWEEN THE WARS (EP) Billy Bragg (Go! Discs)
9	16	MATERIAL GIRL Madonna (Sire)
12	17	SOME LIKE IT HOT Power Station (Parlophone)
16	18	THE LAST KISS David Cassidy (Arista)
23	19	THE HEAT IS ON Glenn Frey (MCA)
31	20	SPEND THE NIGHT Cool Notes (Abstract Dance)
17	21	SHAKESPEARE'S SISTER Smiths (Rough Trade)
26	22	GRIMLY FIENDISH Damned (MCA)
28	23	NOW THAT WE'VE FOUND LOVE Third World (Island)
21	24	DANCING IN THE DARK (EP) Big Daddy (Making Waves)
30	25	CLOUDS ACROSS THE MOON RAH Band (RCA)
27	26	AIKEA GUINEA Cocteau Twins (4AD)
-	27	WE ARE THE WORLD USA For Africa (CBS)
32	28	LOVE IS A BATTLEFIELD Pat Benatar (Chrysalis)
-	29	ONE MORE NIGHT Phil Collins (Virgin)
22	30	WON'T YOU HOLD MY HAND NOW King (CBS)
-	31	BE NEAR ME ABC (Neutron)
35	32	CAN'T FIGHT THE FEELING REO Speedwagon (Epic)
15	33	YOU SPIN ME ROUND (LIKE A RECORD) Dead Or Alive (Epic)
41	34	LET'S GO TOGETHER Change (Cooltempo)
24	35	MR. TELEPHONE MAN New Edition (MCA)
50	36	BELFAST Barnbrack (Homespun)
25	37	THE BELLE OF ST. MARK Sheila E (Warner Bros)
29	38	NIGHTSHIFT Commodores (Motown)
-	39	THAT WAS YESTERDAY Foreigner (Atlantic)
-	40	FREE YOURSELF Untouchables (Stiff)
38	41	LIFE IN A NORTHERN TOWN Dream Academy (blanco y negro)
47	42	BLACK MAN RAY China Crisis (Virgin)
42	43	SHE GOES TO FINOS Toy Dolls (Volume)
37	44	SOMEBODY Bryan Adams (A&M)
34	45	DANCING IN THE DARK Bruce Springsteen (CBS)
44	46	CRY Godley & Creme (Polydor)
-	47	THE ABC OF KISSING R.J. Smith (Jive)
-	48	WE NEED LOVE Cashmere (Fourth & Broadway)
43	49	METHOD OF MODERN LOVE Daryl Hall & John Oates (RCA)
49	50	PIECE OF THE ACTION Meat Loaf (Arista)

Having stalled, comparatively, at Number Two with *The Power Of Love* after their first two chart-toppers, Frankie Goes To Hollywood made pole position again with *Welcome To The Pleasuredome,* which was also the title track of their debut album. Big Daddy's version of *Dancing In The Dark,* following hard on Springsteen's, rearranged the song in the mode of Pat Boone's hit *Moody River* from 1961!

April – May 1985

last week	this	20 April 1985		
5	1	EVERYBODY WANTS TO RULE THE WORLD		Tears For Fears (Mercury)
2	2	EASY LOVER	Philip Bailey & Phil Collins (CBS)	
1	3	WELCOME TO THE PLEASUREDOME		Frankie Goes To Hollywood (ZTT)
3	4	PIE JESU		Sarah Brightman & Paul Miles-Kingston (HMV)
6	5	WE CLOSE OUR EYES	Go West (Chrysalis)	
27	6	WE ARE THE WORLD	USA For Africa (CBS)	
12	7	MOVE CLOSER	Phyllis Nelson (Carrere)	
4	8	THAT OLE DEVIL CALLED LOVE	Alison Moyet (CBS)	
10	9	COULD IT BE I'M FALLING IN LOVE		David Grant & Jaki Graham (Chrysalis)
7	10	EVERY TIME YOU GO AWAY	Paul Young (CBS)	
19	11	THE HEAT IS ON	Glenn Frey (MCA)	
20	12	SPEND THE NIGHT	Cool Notes (Abstract Dance)	
9	13	WIDE BOY	Nik Kershaw (MCA)	
8	14	DO WHAT YOU DO	Jermaine Jackson (Arista)	
11	15	COVER ME	Bruce Springsteen (CBS)	
13	16	HANGIN' ON A STRING (CONTEMPLATING)		Loose Ends (Virgin)
29	17	ONE MORE NIGHT	Phil Collins (Virgin)	
32	18	CAN'T FIGHT THE FEELING		REO Speedwagon (Epic)
31	19	BE NEAR ME	ABC (Neutron)	
25	20	CLOUDS ACROSS THE MOON	RAH Band (RCA)	
16	21	MATERIAL GIRL	Madonna (Sire)	
41	22	LIFE IN A NORTHERN TOWN		Dream Academy (blanco y negro)
14	23	KISS ME	Stephen 'Tintin' Duffy (10)	
30	24	WON'T YOU HOLD MY HAND NOW	King (CBS)	
28	25	LOVE IS A BATTLEFIELD	Pat Benatar (Chrysalis)	
17	26	SOME LIKE IT HOT	Power Station (Parlophone)	
33	27	YOU SPIN ME ROUND (LIKE A RECORD)		Dead Or Alive (Epic)
22	28	GRIMLY FIENDISH	Damned (MCA)	
21	29	SHAKESPEARE'S SISTER	Smiths (Rough Trade)	
23	30	NOW THAT WE'VE FOUND LOVE		Third World (Island)
-	31	I FEEL LOVE (MEDLEY)		Bronski Beat (Forbidden Fruit)
26	32	AIKEA GUINEA	Cocteau Twins (4AD)	
15	33	BETWEEN THE WARS (EP)	Billy Bragg (Go! Discs)	
36	34	BELFAST	Barnbrack (Homespun)	
39	35	THAT WAS YESTERDAY	Foreigner (Atlantic)	
42	36	BLACK MAN RAY	China Crisis (Virgin)	
-	37	DON'T COME AROUND HERE NO MORE		Tom Petty & the Heartbreakers (MCA)
24	38	DANCING IN THE DARK (EP)		Big Daddy (Making Waves)
-	39	DON'T WORRY BABY	Los Lobos (London)	
34	40	LET'S GO TOGETHER	Change (Cooltempo)	
46	41	CRY	Godley & Creme (Polydor)	
-	42	GOING DOWN TO LIVERPOOL	Bangles (CBS)	
-	43	DON'T YOU (FORGET ABOUT ME)		Simple Minds (Virgin)
-	44	STAINSBY GIRLS	Chris Rea (Magnet)	
-	45	CASTLES IN THE AIR	Colour Field (Chrysalis)	
-	46	THE COUNTRY OF THE BLIND	Faith Brothers (Siren)	
-	47	SO FAR AWAY	Dire Straits (Vertigo)	
49	48	METHOD OF MODERN LOVE		Daryl Hall & John Oates (RCA)
44	49	SOMEBODY	Bryan Adams (A&M)	
40	50	FREE YOURSELF	Untouchables (Stiff)	

27 April 1985		
1	1	EVERYBODY WANTS TO RULE THE WORLD Tears For Fears (Mercury)
6	2	WE ARE THE WORLD USA For Africa (CBS)
7	3	MOVE CLOSER Phyllis Nelson (Carrere)
2	4	EASY LOVER Philip Bailey & Phil Collins (CBS)
3	5	WELCOME TO THE PLEASUREDOME Frankie Goes To Hollywood (ZTT)
5	6	WE CLOSE OUR EYES Go West (Chrysalis)
9	7	COULD IT BE I'M FALLING IN LOVE David Grant & Jaki Graham (Chrysalis)
17	8	ONE MORE NIGHT Phil Collins (Virgin)
20	9	CLOUDS ACROSS THE MOON RAH Band (RCA)
12	10	SPEND THE NIGHT Cool Notes (Abstract Dance)
11	11	THE HEAT IS ON Glenn Frey (MCA)
22	12	LIFE IN A NORTHERN TOWN Dream Academy (blanco y negro)
4	13	PIE JESU Sarah Brightman & Paul Miles-Kingston (HMV)
-	14	LOOK MAMA Howard Jones (WEA)
10	15	EVERY TIME YOU GO AWAY Paul Young (CBS)
18	16	CAN'T FIGHT THE FEELING REO Speedwagon (Epic)
31	17	I FEEL LOVE (MEDLEY) Bronski Beat (Forbidden Fruit)
25	18	LOVE IS A BATTLEFIELD Pat Benatar (Chrysalis)
43	19	DON'T YOU (FORGET ABOUT ME) Simple Minds (Virgin)
36	20	BLACK MAN RAY China Crisis (Virgin)
21	21	THAT OLE DEVIL CALLED LOVE Alison Moyet (CBS)
-	22	LOVER COME BACK TO ME Dead Or Alive (Epic)
47	23	SO FAR AWAY Dire Straits (Vertigo)
-	24	WOULD I LIE TO YOU? Eurythmics (Virgin)
-	25	I WAS BORN TO LOVE YOU Freddie Mercury (EMI)
14	26	DO WHAT YOU DO Jermaine Jackson (Arista)
-	27	SUPER GRAN Billy Connolly (Stiff)
13	28	WIDE BOY Nik Kershaw (MCA)
15	29	COVER ME Bruce Springsteen (CBS)
-	30	EYE TO EYE Chaka Khan (Warner Bros)
16	31	HANGIN' ON A STRING (CONTEMPLATING) Loose Ends (Virgin)
19	32	BE NEAR ME ABC (Neutron)
24	33	WON'T YOU HOLD MY HAND NOW King (CBS)
37	34	DON'T COME AROUND HERE NO MORE Tom Petty & the Heartbreakers (MCA)
26	35	SOME LIKE IT HOT Power Station (Parlophone)
-	36	GROOVIN' War (Bluebird)
28	37	GRIMLY FIENDISH Damned (MCA)
35	38	THAT WAS YESTERDAY Foreigner (Atlantic)
39	39	DON'T WORRY BABY Los Lobos (London)
42	40	GOING DOWN TO LIVERPOOL Bangles (CBS)
30	41	NOW THAT WE'VE FOUND LOVE Third World (Island)
-	42	TICKET TO RIDE Beatles (Parlophone)
-	43	THINKING ABOUT YOUR LOVE Skipworth & Turner (Fourth & Broadway)
-	44	RHYTHM OF THE NIGHT DeBarge (Gordy)
27	45	YOU SPIN ME ROUND (LIKE A RECORD) Dead Or Alive (Epic)
34	46	BELFAST Barnbrack (Homespun)
41	47	CRY Godley & Creme (Polydor)
45	48	CASTLES IN THE AIR Colour Field (Chrysalis)
-	49	MEGAREX T. Rex (Marc On Wax)
-	50	BABIES Ashford & Simpson (Capitol)

4 May 1985		
1	1	EVERYBODY WANTS TO RULE THE WORLD Tears For Fears (Mercury)
3	2	MOVE CLOSER Phyllis Nelson (Carrere)
2	3	WE ARE THE WORLD USA For Africa (CBS)
8	4	ONE MORE NIGHT Phil Collins (Virgin)
17	5	I FEEL LOVE (MEDLEY) Bronski Beat (Forbidden Fruit)
9	6	CLOUDS ACROSS THE MOON RAH Band (RCA)
7	7	COULD IT BE I'M FALLING IN LOVE David Grant & Jaki Graham (Chrysalis)
19	8	DON'T YOU (FORGET ABOUT ME) Simple Minds (Virgin)
6	9	WE CLOSE OUR EYES Go West (Chrysalis)
22	10	LOVER COME BACK TO ME Dead Or Alive (Epic)
14	11	LOOK MAMA Howard Jones (WEA)
20	12	BLACK MAN RAY China Crisis (Virgin)
-	13	FEEL SO REAL Steve Arrington (Atlantic)
12	14	LIFE IN A NORTHERN TOWN Dream Academy (blanco y negro)
-	15	THE UNFORGETTABLE FIRE U2 (Island)
25	16	I WAS BORN TO LOVE YOU Freddie Mercury (EMI)
18	17	LOVE IS A BATTLEFIELD Pat Benatar (Chrysalis)
5	18	WELCOME TO THE PLEASUREDOME Frankie Goes To Hollywood (ZTT)
11	19	THE HEAT IS ON Glenn Frey (MCA)
4	20	EASY LOVER Philip Bailey & Phil Collins (CBS)
10	21	SPEND THE NIGHT Cool Notes (Abstract Dance)
16	22	CAN'T FIGHT THE FEELING REO Speedwagon (Epic)
30	23	EYE TO EYE Chaka Khan (Warner Bros)
24	24	WOULD I LIE TO YOU? Eurythmics (Virgin)
23	25	SO FAR AWAY Dire Straits (Vertigo)
-	26	NO REST New Model Army (EMI)
-	27	19 Paul Hardcastle (Chrysalis)
-	28	STAINSBY GIRLS Chris Rea (Magnet)
21	29	THAT OLE DEVIL CALLED LOVE Alison Moyet (CBS)
-	30	WALKING ON THE CHINESE WALL Philip Bailey (CBS)
-	31	DON'T FALL IN LOVE (I SAID) Toyah (Portrait)
13	32	PIE JESU Sarah Brightman & Paul Miles-Kingston (HMV)
-	33	WALK LIKE A MAN Divine (Proto)
15	34	EVERY TIME YOU GO AWAY Paul Young (CBS)
-	35	I WANT YOUR LOVIN' (JUST A LITTLE BIT) Curtis Hairston (London)
31	36	HANGIN' ON A STRING (CONTEMPLATING) Loose Ends (Virgin)
29	37	COVER ME Bruce Springsteen (CBS)
46	38	BELFAST Barnbrack (Homespun)
39	39	DON'T WORRY BABY Los Lobos (London)
38	40	THAT WAS YESTERDAY Foreigner (Atlantic)
37	41	GRIMLY FIENDISH Damned (MCA)
26	42	DO WHAT YOU DO Jermaine Jackson (Arista)
44	43	RHYTHM OF THE NIGHT DeBarge (Gordy)
-	44	NIGHTSHIFT Winston Groovy (Jive)
34	45	DON'T COME AROUND HERE NO MORE Tom Petty & the Heartbreakers (MCA)
36	46	GROOVIN' War (Bluebird)
40	47	GOING DOWN TO LIVERPOOL Bangles (CBS)
-	48	IMAGINATION Belouis Some (Parlophone)
-	49	BEYOND THE SEA George Benson (Warner Bros)
48	50	CASTLES IN THE AIR Colour Field (Chrysalis)

USA For Africa's *We Are The World* was the American response to Band Aid, initiated by Harry Belafonte, and written by Michael Jackson and Lionel Richie, along with the varied but perfectly-integrated likes of Stevie Wonder, Ray Charles, Bob Dylan, Paul Simon, Diana Ross, Dionne Warwick, Bruce Springsteen, Kenny Rogers, Tina Turner and Willie Nelson. It too raised millions for famine relief.

11 May 1985

last week	this week		
2	1	MOVE CLOSER	Phyllis Nelson (Carrere)
27	2	19	Paul Hardcastle (Chrysalis)
1	3	EVERYBODY WANTS TO RULE THE WORLD	Tears For Fears (Mercury)
15	4	THE UNFORGETTABLE FIRE	U2 (Island)
5	5	I FEEL LOVE (MEDLEY)	Bronski Beat (Forbidden Fruit)
3	6	WE ARE THE WORLD	USA For Africa (CBS)
8	7	DON'T YOU (FORGET ABOUT ME)	Simple Minds (Virgin)
4	8	ONE MORE NIGHT	Phil Collins (Virgin)
13	9	FEEL SO REAL	Steve Arrington (Atlantic)
6	10	CLOUDS ACROSS THE MOON	RAH Band (RCA)
16	11	I WAS BORN TO LOVE YOU	Freddie Mercury (CBS)
7	12	COULD IT BE I'M FALLING IN LOVE	David Grant & Jaki Graham (Chrysalis)
43	13	RHYTHM OF THE NIGHT	DeBarge (Gordy)
10	14	LOVER COME BACK TO ME	Dead Or Alive (Epic)
11	15	LOOK MAMA	Howard Jones (WEA)
12	16	BLACK MAN RAY	China Crisis (Virgin)
23	17	EYE TO EYE	Chaka Khan (Warner Bros)
25	18	SO FAR AWAY	Dire Straits (Vertigo)
9	19	WE CLOSE OUR EYES	Go West (Chrysalis)
-	20	WALLS COME TUMBLING DOWN	Style Council (Polydor)
35	21	I WANT YOUR LOVIN' (JUST A LITTLE BIT)	Curtis Hairston (London)
-	22	SLAVE TO LOVE	Bryan Ferry (EG)
28	23	STAINSBY GIRLS	Chris Rea (Magnet)
26	24	NO REST	New Model Army (EMI)
24	25	WOULD I LIE TO YOU?	Eurythmics (Virgin)
18	26	WELCOME TO THE PLEASUREDOME	Frankie Goes To Hollywood (ZTT)
20	27	EASY LOVER	Philip Bailey & Phil Collins (CBS)
-	28	CRY	Godley & Creme (Polydor)
14	29	LIFE IN A NORTHERN TOWN	Dream Academy (blanco y negro)
-	30	DUEL	Propaganda (ZTT)
17	31	LOVE IS A BATTLEFIELD	Pat Benatar (Chrysalis)
33	32	WALK LIKE A MAN	Divine (Proto)
19	33	THE HEAT IS ON	Glenn Frey (MCA)
-	34	SHAKE THE DISEASE	Depeche Mode (Mute)
-	35	WALKING ON SUNSHINE	Katrina & the Waves (Capitol)
-	36	MODERN ROMANCE	Francis Rossi & Bernard Frost (Vertigo)
-	37	RAGE TO LOVE	Kim Wilde (MCA)
-	38	I WONDER IF I TAKE YOU HOME	Lisa Lisa & Cult Jam (CBS)
36	39	HANGIN' ON A STRING (CONTEMPLATING)	Loose Ends (Virgin)
39	40	DON'T WORRY BABY	Los Lobos (London)
-	41	GIRLS ON MY MIND	Fatback (Atlantic/Cotillion)
-	42	GREEN SHIRT	Elvis Costello (F.Beat)
-	43	FROGGY MIX	James Brown (Boiling Point)
-	44	LOVE DON'T LIVE HERE ANYMORE	Jimmy Nail (Atlantic Starr (A&M)
-	45	FREAK-A-RISTIC	Atlantic Starr (A&M)
-	46	DANGEROUS	Pennye Ford (Total Experience)
30	47	WALKING ON THE CHINESE WALL	Philip Bailey (CBS)
31	48	DON'T FALL IN LOVE (I SAID)	Toyah (Portrait)
21	49	SPEND THE NIGHT	Cool Notes (Abstract Dance)
45	50	DON'T COME AROUND HERE NO MORE	Tom Petty & the Heartbreakers (MCA)

18 May 1985

2	1	19	Paul Hardcastle (Chrysalis)
1	2	MOVE CLOSER	Phyllis Nelson (Carrere)
5	3	I FEEL LOVE (MEDLEY)	Bronski Beat (Forbidden Fruit)
4	4	THE UNFORGETTABLE FIRE	U2 (Island)
3	5	EVERYBODY WANTS TO RULE THE WORLD	Tears For Fears (Mercury)
9	6	FEEL SO REAL	Steve Arrington (Atlantic)
20	7	WALLS COME TUMBLING DOWN	Style Council (Polydor)
6	8	WE ARE THE WORLD	USA For Africa (CBS)
7	9	DON'T YOU (FORGET ABOUT ME)	Simple Minds (Virgin)
13	10	RHYTHM OF THE NIGHT	DeBarge (Gordy)
11	11	I WAS BORN TO LOVE YOU	Freddie Mercury (CBS)
8	12	ONE MORE NIGHT	Phil Collins (Virgin)
21	13	I WANT YOUR LOVIN' (JUST A LITTLE BIT)	Curtis Hairston (London)
10	14	CLOUDS ACROSS THE MOON	RAH Band (RCA)
25	15	WOULD I LIE TO YOU?	Eurythmics (Virgin)
28	16	CRY	Godley & Creme (Polydor)
22	17	SLAVE TO LOVE	Bryan Ferry (EG)
12	18	COULD IT BE I'M FALLING IN LOVE	David Grant & Jaki Graham (Chrysalis)
14	19	LOVER COME BACK TO ME	Dead Or Alive (Epic)
44	20	LOVE DON'T LIVE HERE ANYMORE	Jimmy Nail (Virgin)
32	21	WALK LIKE A MAN	Divine (Proto)
34	22	SHAKE THE DISEASE	Depeche Mode (Mute)
48	23	DON'T FALL IN LOVE (I SAID)	Toyah (Portrait)
18	24	SO FAR AWAY	Dire Straits (Vertigo)
-	25	KAYLEIGH	Marillion (EMI)
-	26	CALL ME	Go West (Virgin)
17	27	EYE TO EYE	Chaka Khan (Warner Bros)
36	28	MODERN ROMANCE	Francis Rossi & Bernard Frost (Vertigo)
-	29	A VIEW TO A KILL	Duran Duran (Parlophone)
15	30	LOOK MAMA	Howard Jones (WEA)
-	31	LIKE A VIRGIN	Lords Of The New Church (Illegal)
-	32	OUT IN THE FIELDS	Gary Moore & Phil Lynott (10)
23	33	STAINSBY GIRLS	Chris Rea (Magnet)
-	34	MAGIC TOUCH	Loose Ends (Virgin)
35	35	WALKING ON SUNSHINE	Katrina & the Waves (Capitol)
-	36	FREE YOURSELF	Untouchables (Stiff)
24	37	NO REST	New Model Army (EMI)
-	38	GET IT ON	Power Station (Parlophone)
-	39	ALL FALL DOWN	Five Star (Tent)
37	40	RAGE TO LOVE	Kim Wilde (MCA)
16	41	BLACK MAN RAY	China Crisis (Virgin)
49	42	SPEND THE NIGHT	Cool Notes (Abstract Dance)
-	43	HERE WE GO	Everton 1985 (Columbia)
27	44	EASY LOVER	Philip Bailey & Phil Collins (CBS)
46	45	DANGEROUS	Pennye Ford (Total Experience)
-	46	THE WORD GIRL	Scritti Politti (Virgin)
-	47	THINKING ABOUT YOUR LOVE	Skipworth & Turner (Fourth & Broadway)
-	48	IMAGINATION	Belouis Some (Parlophone)
-	49	DEEP	March Violets (Rebirth)
42	50	GREEN SHIRT	Elvis Costello (F.Beat)

25 May 1985

1	1	19	Paul Hardcastle (Chrysalis)
2	2	MOVE CLOSER	Phyllis Nelson (Carrere)
3	3	I FEEL LOVE (MEDLEY)	Bronski Beat (Forbidden Fruit)
10	4	RHYTHM OF THE NIGHT	DeBarge (Gordy)
7	5	WALLS COME TUMBLING DOWN	Style Council (Polydor)
6	6	FEEL SO REAL	Steve Arrington (Atlantic)
29	7	A VIEW TO A KILL	Duran Duran (Parlophone)
20	8	LOVE DON'T LIVE HERE ANYMORE	Jimmy Nail (Virgin)
25	9	KAYLEIGH	Marillion (EMI)
11	10	I WAS BORN TO LOVE YOU	Freddie Mercury (CBS)
17	11	SLAVE TO LOVE	Bryan Ferry (EG)
4	12	THE UNFORGETTABLE FIRE	U2 (Island)
5	13	EVERYBODY WANTS TO RULE THE WORLD	Tears For Fears (Mercury)
9	14	DON'T YOU (FORGET ABOUT ME)	Simple Minds (Virgin)
13	15	I WANT YOUR LOVIN' (JUST A LITTLE BIT)	Curtis Hairston (London)
15	16	WOULD I LIE TO YOU?	Eurythmics (Virgin)
16	17	CRY	Godley & Creme (Polydor)
12	18	ONE MORE NIGHT	Phil Collins (Virgin)
32	19	OUT IN THE FIELDS	Gary Moore & Phil Lynott (10)
34	20	MAGIC TOUCH	Loose Ends (Virgin)
8	21	WE ARE THE WORLD	USA For Africa (CBS)
22	22	SHAKE THE DISEASE	Depeche Mode (Mute)
26	23	CALL ME	Go West (Chrysalis)
21	24	WALK LIKE A MAN	Divine (Proto)
40	25	RAGE TO LOVE	Kim Wilde (MCA)
14	26	CLOUDS ACROSS THE MOON	RAH Band (RCA)
-	27	WE ALL FOLLOW MAN. UNITED	Manchester United Football Team (Columbia)
39	28	ALL FALL DOWN	Five Star (Tent)
36	29	FREE YOURSELF	Untouchables (Stiff)
35	30	WALKING ON SUNSHINE	Katrina & the Waves (Capitol)
43	31	HERE WE GO	Everton 1985 (Columbia)
-	32	SANCTIFIED LADY	Marvin Gaye (CBS)
38	33	GET IT ON	Power Station (Parlophone)
19	34	LOVER COME BACK TO ME	Dead Or Alive (Epic)
46	35	THE WORD GIRL	Scritti Politti (Virgin)
23	36	DON'T FALL IN LOVE (I SAID)	Toyah (Portrait)
45	37	DANGEROUS	Pennye Ford (Total Experience)
28	38	MODERN ROMANCE	Francis Rossi & Bernard Frost (Vertigo)
18	39	COULD IT BE I'M FALLING IN LOVE	David Grant & Jaki Graham (Chrysalis)
33	40	STAINSBY GIRLS	Chris Rea (Magnet)
30	41	DUEL	Propaganda (ZTT)
30	42	LOOK MAMA	Howard Jones (WEA)
37	43	NO REST	New Model Army (EMI)
-	44	REMEMBER I LOVE YOU	Jim Diamond (A&M)
-	45	OBSESSION	Animotion (Mercury)
-	46	ICING ON THE CAKE	Stephen 'Tintin' Duffy (10)
24	47	SO FAR AWAY	Dire Straits (Vertigo)
27	48	EYE TO EYE	Chaka Khan (Warner Bros)
-	49	LIKE I LIKE IT	Aurra (10)
-	50	PAISLEY PARK	Prince & the Revolution (WEA)

19 was the average age of American soldiers who served in the Vietnam war, and the futility of that involvement was the subject of Paul Hardcastle's chart-topper, blending documentary voices over the backdrop of Hardcastle's dance-solid keyboard backing tracks. Simple Minds' *Don't You (Forget About Me)* was written for the film *The Breakfast Club*, and gave the group a US Number One.

June 1985

A View To A Kill was performd by Duran Duran over the credits of the James Bond film of the same title: the group shared its writing credits with veteran Bond composer John Barry. TV actor Jimmy Nail, meanwhile, made his musical debut in impressive style, with a top three revival of Love Don't Live Here Anymore, a song which was originally a number two hit for Rose Royce in October 1978.

June – July 1985

last week	this week	22 June 1985	
4	1	YOU'LL NEVER WALK ALONE	Crowd (Spartan)
2	2	KAYLEIGH	Marillion (EMI)
9	3	SUDDENLY	Billy Ocean (Jive)
1	4	19	Paul Hardcastle (Chrysalis)
5	5	OBSESSION	Animotion (Mercury)
16	6	CRAZY FOR YOU	Madonna (Geffen)
8	7	THE WORD GIRL	Scritti Politti (Virgin)
3	8	A VIEW TO A KILL	Duran Duran (Parlophone)
6	9	OUT IN THE FIELDS	Gary Moore & Phil Lynott (10)
29	10	FRANKIE	Sister Sledge (Atlantic)
14	11	HISTORY	Mai Tai (Virgin)
7	12	WALKING ON SUNSHINE	Katrina & the Waves (Capitol)
20	13	JOHNNY COME HOME	Fine Young Cannibals (London)
27	14	CHERISH	Kool & the Gang (De-Lite)
24	15	I'M ON FIRE/BORN IN THE USA	Bruce Springsteen (CBS)
19	16	ALL FALL DOWN	Five Star (Tent)
13	17	LOVING THE ALIEN	David Bowie (EMI America)
11	18	ICING ON THE CAKE	Stephen 'Tintin' Duffy (10)
40	19	BEN	Marti Webb (Starblend)
12	20	CALL ME	Go West (Chrysalis)
17	21	DUEL	Propaganda (ZTT)
41	22	PAISLEY PARK	Prince & the Revolution (WEA)
10	23	LOVE DON'T LIVE HERE ANYMORE	Jimmy Nail (Virgin)
26	24	SHE SELLS SANCTUARY	Cult (Beggars Banquet)
15	25	RHYTHM OF THE NIGHT	DeBarge (Gordy)
36	26	AXEL F	Harold Faltermeyer (MCA)
38	27	YOU TRIP ME UP	Jesus & Mary Chain (blanco y negro)
25	28	IF YOU LOVE SOMEBODY SET THEM FREE	Sting (A&M)
18	29	SLAVE TO LOVE	Bryan Ferry (EG)
22	30	I FEEL LOVE (MEDLEY)	Bronski Beat (Forbidden Fruit)
39	31	KING IN A CATHOLIC STYLE (WAKE UP)	China Crisis (Virgin)
28	32	SO IN LOVE	Orchestral Manoeuvres In The Dark (Virgin)
34	33	THINKING ABOUT YOUR LOVE	Skipworth & Turner (Fourth & Broadway)
48	34	SECRETS IN THE STREET	Nils Lofgren (Towerbell)
-	35	YOU DON'T NEED A REASON	Phil Fearon & Galaxy (Ensign)
21	36	MOVE CLOSER	Phyllis Nelson (Carrere)
7	37	SHADOW OF THE NIGHT	Pat Benatar (Chrysalis)
-	38	BUTTERCUP	Carl Anderson (Streetwave)
-	39	TIGHT CONNECTION TO MY HEART	Bob Dylan (CBS)
-	40	ACT OF WAR	Elton John & Millie Jackson (Rocket)
32	41	THE PERFECT KISS	New Order (Factory)
42	42	THE LADY DON'T MIND	Talking Heads (EMI)
35	43	DON'T YOU (FORGET ABOUT ME)	Simple Minds (Virgin)
50	43	ALL MY LOVE	Spear Of Destiny (Epic)
46	44	GET UP I FEEL LIKE BEING A SEX MACHINE	James Brown (Boiling Point)
-	46	EL VINO COLLAPSO	Black Lace (Flair)
-	47	LAURA	Nick Heyward (Arista)
-	48	SAVE YOUR LOVE	Rene & Angela (Club)
-	49	LAST TIME FOREVER	Squeeze (A&M)
47	50	THE MORE THEY KNOCK	Gloria D. Brown (10)

		29 June 1985	
6	1	CRAZY FOR YOU	Madonna (Geffen)
1	2	YOU'LL NEVER WALK ALONE	Crowd (Spartan)
10	3	FRANKIE	Sister Sledge (Atlantic)
2	4	KAYLEIGH	Marillion (EMI)
3	5	SUDDENLY	Billy Ocean (Jive)
6	6	THE WORD GIRL	Scritti Politti (Virgin)
26	7	AXEL F	Harold Faltermeyer (MCA)
14	8	CHERISH	Kool & the Gang (De-Lite)
15	9	I'M ON FIRE/BORN IN THE USA	Bruce Springsteen (CBS)
11	10	HISTORY	Mai Tai (Virgin)
5	11	OBSESSION	Animotion (Mercury)
13	12	JOHNNY COME HOME	Fine Young Cannibals (London)
19	13	BEN	Marti Webb (Starblend)
8	14	A VIEW TO A KILL	Duran Duran (Parlophone)
4	15	19	Paul Hardcastle (Chrysalis)
-	16	HEAD OVER HEELS	Tears For Fears (Mercury)
9	17	OUT IN THE FIELDS	Gary Moore & Phil Lynott (10)
-	18	TOMB OF MEMORIES	Paul Young (CBS)
12	19	WALKING ON SUNSHINE	Katrina & the Waves (Capitol)
17	20	LOVING THE ALIEN	David Bowie (EMI America)
-	21	(BURN IT UP) BRING IT DOWN!	Redskins (Decca)
16	22	ALL FALL DOWN	Five Star (Tent)
21	23	DUEL	Propaganda (ZTT)
-	24	THE SHADOW OF LOVE	Damned (MCA)
22	25	PAISLEY PARK	Prince & the Revolution (WEA)
28	26	IF YOU LOVE SOMEBODY SET THEM FREE	Sting (A&M)
24	27	SHE SELLS SANCTUARY	Cult (Beggars Banquet)
31	28	KING IN A CATHOLIC STYLE (WAKE UP)	China Crisis (Virgin)
39	29	TIGHT CONNECTION TO MY HEART	Bob Dylan (CBS)
18	30	ICING ON THE CAKE	Stephen 'Tintin' Duffy (10)
20	31	CALL ME	Go West (Chrysalis)
2	32	SMUGGLER'S BLUES	Glenn Frey (BBC)
-	33	N-N-NINETEEN NOT OUT	Commentators (Oval)
42	34	THE LADY DON'T MIND	Talking Heads (EMI)
35	35	SALLY MacLENNANE	Pogues (Stiff)
27	36	YOU TRIP ME UP	Jesus & Mary Chain (blanco y negro)
30	37	I FEEL LOVE (MEDLEY)	Bronski Beat (Forbidden Fruit)
40	38	ACT OF WAR	Elton John & Millie Jackson (Rocket)
35	39	YOU DON'T NEED A REASON	Phil Fearon & Galaxy (Ensign)
44	40	GET UP I FEEL LIKE BEING A SEX MACHINE	James Brown (Boiling Point)
41	41	THE PERFECT KISS	New Order (Factory)
50	42	THE MORE THEY KNOCK	Gloria D. Brown (10)
49	43	LAST TIME FOREVER	Squeeze (A&M)
-	44	TURN IT UP	Conway Brothers (10)
-	45	OUT OF TOUCH	Daryl Hall & John Oates (RCA)
-	46	COLD AS ICE	Foreigner (Atlantic)
47	47	LAURA	Nick Heyward (Arista)
34	48	SECRETS IN THE STREET	Nils Lofgren (Towerbell)
-	49	MONEY'S TOO TIGHT (TO MENTION)	Simply Red (Elektra)
43	50	ALL MY LOVE	Spear Of Destiny (Epic)

		6 July 1985	
3	1	FRANKIE	Sister Sledge (Atlantic)
1	2	CRAZY FOR YOU	Madonna (Geffen)
7	3	AXEL F	Harold Faltermeyer (MCA)
8	4	CHERISH	Kool & the Gang (De-Lite)
2	5	YOU'LL NEVER WALK ALONE	Crowd (Spartan)
4	6	KAYLEIGH	Marillion (EMI)
9	7	I'M ON FIRE/BORN IN THE USA	Bruce Springsteen (CBS)
5	8	SUDDENLY	Billy Ocean (Jive)
10	9	HISTORY	Mai Tai (Virgin)
12	10	JOHNNY COME HOME	Fine Young Cannibals (London)
13	11	BEN	Marti Webb (Starblend)
16	12	HEAD OVER HEELS	Tears For Fears (Mercury)
6	13	THE WORD GIRL	Scritti Politti (Virgin)
-	14	LIFE IN ONE DAY	Howard Jones (WEA)
18	15	TOMB OF MEMORIES	Paul Young (CBS)
11	16	OBSESSION	Animotion (Mercury)
14	17	A VIEW TO A KILL	Duran Duran (Parlophone)
28	18	KING IN A CATHOLIC STYLE (WAKE UP)	China Crisis (Virgin)
25	19	PAISLEY PARK	Prince & the Revolution (WEA)
33	20	N-N-NINETEEN NOT OUT	Commentators (Oval)
21	21	(BURN IT UP) BRING IT DOWN!	Redskins (Decca)
24	22	THE SHADOW OF LOVE	Damned (MCA)
27	23	SHE SELLS SANCTUARY	Cult (Beggars Banquet)
-	24	IN TOO DEEP	Dead Or Alive (Epic)
17	25	OUT IN THE FIELDS	Gary Moore & Phil Lynott (10)
26	26	IF YOU LOVE SOMEBODY SET THEM FREE	Sting (A&M)
32	27	SMUGGLER'S BLUES	Glenn Frey (BBC)
15	28	19	Paul Hardcastle (Chrysalis)
23	29	DUEL	Propaganda (ZTT)
22	30	ALL FALL DOWN	Five Star (Tent)
-	31	GOODBYE BAD TIMES	Phil Oakey & Giorgio Moroder (Virgin)
35	32	SALLY MacLENNANE	Pogues (Stiff)
20	33	LOVING THE ALIEN	David Bowie (EMI America)
-	34	SILVER SHADOW	Atlantic Starr (A&M)
44	35	TURN IT UP	Conway Brothers (10)
-	36	MY TOOT TOOT	Denise LaSalle (Epic)
-	37	COME TO MILTON KEYNES	Style Council (Polydor)
-	38	LIVE IS LIFE	Opus (Polydor)
-	39	THE POWER OF LOVE	Jennifer Rush (CBS)
-	40	LOVING YOU	Feargal Sharkey (Virgin)
38	41	ACT OF WAR	Elton John & Millie Jackson (Rocket)
42	42	LAST TIME FOREVER	Squeeze (A&M)
45	43	OUT OF TOUCH	Daryl Hall & John Oates (RCA)
31	44	CALL ME	Go West (Chrysalis)
19	45	WALKING ON SUNSHINE	Katrina & the Waves (Capitol)
-	46	MOVIN'	400 Blows (Illuminated)
-	47	WHO'S HOLDING DONNA NOW	DeBarge (Gordy)
-	48	SOUL PASSING THROUGH SOUL	Toyah (Portrait)
-	49	DON'T BREAK MY HEART	Affair (10)
46	50	COLD AS ICE	Foreigner (Atlantic)

Gerry Marsden became the first artist to perform on two different number one versions of the same song when the Crowd's revival of *You'll Never Walk Alone*, previously a 1963 chart topper for Gerry & The Pacemakers, also made the top. The new recording was made as a benefit effort to aid the families of victims of Bradford Football Club's recent stand fire disaster.

July 1985

13 July 1985

last week	this week	title	artist (label)
1	1	FRANKIE	Sister Sledge (Atlantic)
3	2	AXEL F	Harold Faltermeyer (MCA)
2	3	CRAZY FOR YOU	Madonna (Geffen)
7	4	I'M ON FIRE/BORN IN THE USA	Bruce Springsteen (CBS)
4	5	CHERISH	Kool & the Gang (De-Lite)
11	6	BEN	Marti Webb (Starblend)
8	7	SUDDENLY	Billy Ocean (Jive)
10	8	JOHNNY COME HOME	Fine Young Cannibals (London)
12	9	HEAD OVER HEELS	Tears For Fears (Mercury)
5	10	YOU'LL NEVER WALK ALONE	Crowd (Spartan)
6	11	KAYLEIGH	Marillion (EMI)
9	12	HISTORY	Mai Tai (Virgin)
14	13	LIFE IN ONE DAY	Howard Jones (WEA)
36	14	MY TOOT TOOT	Denise LaSalle (Epic)
13	15	THE WORD GIRL	Scritti Politti (Virgin)
15	16	TOMB OF MEMORIES	Paul Young (CBS)
24	17	IN TOO DEEP	Dead Or Alive (Epic)
20	18	N-N-NINETEEN NOT OUT	Commentators (Oval)
35	19	TURN IT UP	Conway Brothers (10)
18	20	KING IN A CATHOLIC STYLE (WAKE UP)	China Crisis (Virgin)
37	21	COME TO MILTON KEYNES	Style Council (Polydor)
22	22	THE SHADOW OF LOVE	Damned (MCA)
23	23	SHE SELLS SANCTUARY	Cult (Beggars Banquet)
-	24	THERE MUST BE AN ANGEL (PLAYING WITH MY HEART)	Eurythmics (Virgin)
16	25	OBSESSION	Animotion (Mercury)
26	26	MONEY FOR NOTHING	Dire Straits (Vertigo)
27	27	SMUGGLER'S BLUES	Glenn Frey (BBC)
21	28	(BURN IT UP) BRING IT DOWN!	Redskins (Decca)
19	29	PAISLEY PARK	Prince & the Revolution (WEA)
38	30	LIVE IS LIFE	Opus (Polydor)
17	31	A VIEW TO A KILL	Duran Duran (Parlophone)
28	32	19	Paul Hardcastle (Chrysalis)
-	33	GENIE	Brooklyn Bronx & Queens (Cooltempo)
46	34	MOVIN'	400 Blows (Illuminated)
-	35	DANGER	AC/DC (Atlantic)
-	36	ROUND AND ROUND	Jaki Graham (EMI)
-	37	LOVE IS JUST THE GREAT PRETENDER '85	Animal Nightlife (Island)
-	38	MONEY'S TOO TIGHT (TO MENTION)	Simply Red (Elektra)
26	39	IF YOU LOVE SOMEBODY SET THEM FREE	Sting (A&M)
40	40	LOVING YOU	Feargal Sharkey (Virgin)
-	41	BONZO GOES TO BITBURG	Ramones (Beggars Banquet)
-	42	THAT JOKE ISN'T FUNNY ANYMORE	Smiths (Rough Trade)
-	43	EXCITABLE	Amazulu (Island)
25	44	OUT IN THE FIELDS	Gary Moore & Phil Lynott (10)
39	45	THE POWER OF LOVE	Jennifer Rush (CBS)
42	46	LAST TIME FOREVER	Squeeze (A&M)
-	47	BUTTERCUP	Carl Anderson (Streetwave)
-	48	STAR ON FIRE	John Foxx (Virgin)
-	49	ROLLIN' DANY	Fall (Beggars Banquet)
-	50	ALL OF ME FOR ALL OF YOU	9.9 (RCA)

20 July 1985

last week	this week	title	artist (label)
1	1	FRANKIE	Sister Sledge (Atlantic)
2	2	AXEL F	Harold Faltermeyer (MCA)
4	3	I'M ON FIRE/BORN IN THE USA	Bruce Springsteen (CBS)
5	4	CHERISH	Kool & the Gang (De-Lite)
3	5	CRAZY FOR YOU	Madonna (Geffen)
14	6	MY TOOT TOOT	Denise LaSalle (Epic)
24	7	THERE MUST BE AN ANGEL (PLAYING WITH MY HEART)	Eurythmics (Virgin)
8	8	JOHNNY COME HOME	Fine Young Cannibals (London)
6	9	BEN	Marti Webb (Starblend)
9	10	HEAD OVER HEELS	Tears For Fears (Mercury)
30	11	LIVE IS LIFE	Opus (Polydor)
12	12	HISTORY	Mai Tai (Virgin)
17	13	IN TOO DEEP	Dead Or Alive (Epic)
19	14	TURN IT UP	Conway Brothers (10)
7	15	SUDDENLY	Billy Ocean (Jive)
11	16	KAYLEIGH	Marillion (EMI)
13	17	LIFE IN ONE DAY	Howard Jones (WEA)
21	18	COME TO MILTON KEYNES	Style Council (Polydor)
27	19	SMUGGLER'S BLUES	Glenn Frey (BBC)
18	20	N-N-NINETEEN NOT OUT	Commentators (Oval)
23	21	SHE SELLS SANCTUARY	Cult (Beggars Banquet)
10	22	YOU'LL NEVER WALK ALONE	Crowd (Spartan)
22	23	THE SHADOW OF LOVE	Damned (MCA)
16	24	TOMB OF MEMORIES	Paul Young (CBS)
42	25	THAT JOKE ISN'T FUNNY ANYMORE	Smiths (Rough Trade)
15	26	THE WORD GIRL	Scritti Politti (Virgin)
-	27	IN YOUR CAR	Cool Notes (Abstract Dance)
36	28	ROUND AND ROUND	Jaki Graham (EMI)
-	29	WHITE WEDDING	Billy Idol (Chrysalis)
37	30	LOVE IS JUST THE GREAT PRETENDER '85	Animal Nightlife (Island)
-	31	THE ZZ TOP SUMMER HOLIDAY	ZZ Top (Warner Bros)
39	32	IF YOU LOVE SOMEBODY SET THEM FREE	Sting (A&M)
33	33	LIVING ON VIDEO	Trans-X (Boiling Point)
-	34	SILVER SHADOW	Atlantic Starr (A&M)
25	35	OBSESSION	Animotion (Mercury)
35	36	DANGER	AC/DC (Atlantic)
33	37	GENIE	Brooklyn Bronx & Queens (Cooltempo)
26	38	MONEY FOR NOTHING	Dire Straits (Vertigo)
-	39	ALL NIGHT HOLIDAY	Russ Abbott (Spirit)
29	40	PAISLEY PARK	Prince & the Revolution (WEA)
40	41	LOVING YOU	Feargal Sharkey (Virgin)
-	42	DANCIN' IN THE KEY OF LIFE	Steve Arrington (Atlantic)
-	43	SEEING THROUGH MY EYES	Broken Bones (Fall Out)
20	44	KING IN A CATHOLIC STYLE (WAKE UP)	China Crisis (Virgin)
28	45	(BURN IT UP) BRING IT DOWN!	Redskins (Decca)
31	46	A VIEW TO A KILL	Duran Duran (Parlophone)
32	47	19	Paul Hardcastle (Chrysalis)
-	48	CONGA	Miami Sound Machine (Epic)
43	49	EXCITABLE	Amazulu (Island)
48	50	STAR ON FIRE	John Foxx (Virgin)

27 July 1985

last week	this week	title	artist (label)
7	1	THERE MUST BE AN ANGEL (PLAYING WITH MY HEART)	Eurythmics (Virgin)
2	2	AXEL F	Harold Faltermeyer (MCA)
1	3	FRANKIE	Sister Sledge (Atlantic)
4	4	CHERISH	Kool & the Gang (De-Lite)
6	5	MY TOOT TOOT	Denise LaSalle (Epic)
11	6	LIVE IS LIFE	Opus (Polydor)
3	7	I'M ON FIRE/BORN IN THE USA	Bruce Springsteen (CBS)
-	8	INTO THE GROOVE	Madonna (Sire)
14	9	TURN IT UP	Conway Brothers (10)
27	10	IN YOUR CAR	Cool Notes (Abstract Dance)
8	11	JOHNNY COME HOME	Fine Young Cannibals (London)
-	12	MONEY'S TOO TIGHT (TO MENTION)	Simply Red (Elektra)
28	13	ROUND AND ROUND	Jaki Graham (EMI)
14	14	IN TOO DEEP	Dead Or Alive (Epic)
5	15	CRAZY FOR YOU	Madonna (Geffen)
21	16	SHE SELLS SANCTUARY	Cult (Beggars Banquet)
33	17	LIVING ON VIDEO	Trans-X (Boiling Point)
9	18	BEN	Marti Webb (Starblend)
10	19	HEAD OVER HEELS	Tears For Fears (Mercury)
42	20	DANCIN' IN THE KEY OF LIFE	Steve Arrington (Atlantic)
29	21	WHITE WEDDING	Billy Idol (Chrysalis)
12	22	HISTORY	Mai Tai (Virgin)
-	23	DARE ME	Pointer Sisters (RCA)
-	24	WE DON'T NEED ANOTHER HERO	Tina Turner (Capitol)
16	25	KAYLEIGH	Marillion (EMI)
15	26	SUDDENLY	Billy Ocean (Jive)
30	27	LOVE IS JUST THE GREAT PRETENDER '85	Animal Nightlife (Island)
39	28	ALL NIGHT HOLIDAY	Russ Abbott (Spirit)
-	29	LET ME BE THE ONE	Five Star (Tent)
38	30	MONEY FOR NOTHING	Dire Straits (Vertigo)
-	31	MEMORY	Aled Jones (BBC)
32	32	THE SHADOW OF LOVE	Damned (MCA)
25	33	THAT JOKE ISN'T FUNNY ANYMORE	Smiths (Rough Trade)
19	34	SMUGGLER'S BLUES	Glenn Frey (BBC)
-	35	LONG TIME	Arrow (London)
37	36	GENIE	Brooklyn Bronx & Queens (Cooltempo)
41	37	LOVING YOU	Feargal Sharkey (Virgin)
-	38	VIVE LE ROCK	Adam Ant (CBS)
-	39	TWISTN' THE NIGHT AWAY	Divine (Proto)
-	40	TAKE ME HOME	Phil Collins (Virgin)
-	41	CAN'T GET THERE FROM HERE	R.E.M. (IRS)
-	42	STRONGER TOGETHER	Shannon (Club)
36	43	DANGER	AC/DC (Atlantic)
34	44	SILVER SHADOW	Atlantic Starr (A&M)
17	45	LIFE IN ONE DAY	Howard Jones (WEA)
-	46	SECRET	Orchestral Manoeuvres In The Dark (Virgin)
-	47	ATTACK ME WITH YOUR LOVE	Cameo (Club)
24	48	TOMB OF MEMORIES	Paul Young (CBS)
31	49	THE ZZ TOP SUMMER HOLIDAY	ZZ Top (Warner Bros)
-	50	TOO MANY GAMES	Maze featuring Frankie Beverly (Capitol)

Frankie was written by Joy Denny as a personal tribute to Frank Sinatra, but Sister Sledge's chart-topping version, in an arrangement redolent of early 1960s girl groups, de-personalised the song to encompass any old Frankie. Poised below it, chartwise Harold Faltermeyer's instrumental *Axel F* was the theme to Eddie Murphy's film *Beverly Hills Cop*, in which Murphy played the cop Axel Foley.

3 August 1985

last week	this week		
1	1	THERE MUST BE AN ANGEL (PLAYING WITH MY HEART)	Eurythmics (Virgin)
8	2	INTO THE GROOVE	Madonna (Sire)
2	3	AXEL F	Harold Faltermeyer (MCA)
3	4	FRANKIE	Sister Sledge (Atlantic)
24	5	WE DON'T NEED ANOTHER HERO	Tina Turner (Capitol)
6	6	LIVE IS LIFE	Opus (Polydor)
13	7	ROUND AND ROUND	Jaki Graham (EMI)
17	8	LIVING ON VIDEO	Trans-X (Boiling Point)
4	9	CHERISH	Kool & the Gang (De-Lite)
5	10	MY TOOT TOOT	Denise LaSalle (Epic)
15	11	CRAZY FOR YOU	Madonna (Geffen)
21	12	WHITE WEDDING	Billy Idol (Chrysalis)
10	13	IN YOUR CAR	Cool Notes (Abstract Dance)
30	14	MONEY FOR NOTHING	Dire Straits (Vertigo)
12	15	MONEY'S TOO TIGHT (TO MENTION)	Simply Red (Elektra)
7	16	I'M ON FIRE/BORN IN THE USA	Bruce Springsteen (CBS)
16	17	SHE SELLS SANCTUARY	Cult (Beggars Banquet)
23	18	DARE ME	Pointer Sisters (RCA)
-	19	IN BETWEEN DAYS	Cure (Fiction)
-	20	GLORY DAYS	Bruce Springsteen (CBS)
11	21	JOHNNY COME HOME	Fine Young Cannibals (London)
29	22	LET ME BE THE ONE	Five Star (Tent)
9	23	TURN IT UP	Conway Brothers (10)
28	24	ALL NIGHT HOLIDAY	Russ Abbott (Spirit)
-	25	EMPTY ROOMS	Gary Moore (10)
20	26	DANCIN' IN THE KEY OF LIFE	Steve Arrington (Atlantic)
42	27	STRONGER TOGETHER	Shannon (Club)
50	28	TOO MANY GAMES	Maze featuring Frankie Beverly (Capitol)
-	29	RASPBERRY BERET	Prince & the Revolution (WEA)
37	30	LOVING YOU	Feargal Sharkey (Virgin)
-	31	I GOT YOU BABE	UB40 guest vocals by Chrissie Hynde (DEP International)
14	32	IN TOO DEEP	Dead Or Alive (Epic)
40	33	TAKE ME HOME	Phil Collins (Virgin)
46	34	SECRET	Orchestral Manoeuvres In The Dark (Virgin)
-	35	YOU'RE THE ONE FOR ME	D Train (Epic)
19	36	HEAD OVER HEELS	Tears For Fears (Mercury)
36	37	GENIE	Brooklyn Bronx & Queens (Cooltempo)
39	38	TWISTN' THE NIGHT AWAY	Divine (Proto)
44	39	SILVER SHADOW	Atlantic Starr (A&M)
-	40	ON A CROWDED STREET	Barbara Pennington (Record Shack)
-	41	DRIVE	Cars (Elektra)
-	42	MUTUAL ATTRACTION	Change (Cooltempo)
-	43	SEVEN HORSES	Icicle Works (Beggars Banquet)
-	44	I SPY FOR THE F.B.I.	Untouchables (Stiff)
25	45	KAYLEIGH	Marillion (EMI)
27	46	LOVE IS JUST THE GREAT PRETENDER '85	Animal Nightlife (Island)
49	47	THE ZZ TOP SUMMER HOLIDAY	ZZ Top (Warner Bros)
43	48	DANGER	AC/DC (Atlantic)
41	49	CAN'T GET THERE FROM HERE	R.E.M. (IRS)
35	50	LONG TIME	Arrow (London)

10 August 1985

2	1	INTO THE GROOVE	Madonna (Sire)
1	2	THERE MUST BE AN ANGEL (PLAYING WITH MY HEART)	Eurythmics (Virgin)
5	3	WE DON'T NEED ANOTHER HERO	Tina Turner (Capitol)
6	4	LIVE IS LIFE	Opus (Polydor)
14	5	MONEY FOR NOTHING	Dire Straits (Vertigo)
12	6	WHITE WEDDING	Billy Idol (Chrysalis)
8	7	LIVING ON VIDEO	Trans-X (Boiling Point)
3	8	AXEL F	Harold Faltermeyer (MCA)
4	9	FRANKIE	Sister Sledge (Atlantic)
7	10	ROUND AND ROUND	Jaki Graham (EMI)
9	11	CHERISH	Kool & the Gang (De-Lite)
20	12	GLORY DAYS	Bruce Springsteen (CBS)
10	13	MY TOOT TOOT	Denise LaSalle (Epic)
31	14	I GOT YOU BABE	UB40 guest vocals by Chrissie Hynde (DEP International)
11	15	CRAZY FOR YOU	Madonna (Geffen)
19	16	IN BETWEEN DAYS	Cure (Fiction)
-	17	DON QUIXOTE	Nik Kershaw (MCA)
17	18	SHE SELLS SANCTUARY	Cult (Beggars Banquet)
18	19	DARE ME	Pointer Sisters (RCA)
-	20	HOLIDAY	Madonna (Sire)
13	21	IN YOUR CAR	Cool Notes (Abstract Dance)
22	22	LET ME BE THE ONE	Five Star (Tent)
15	23	MONEY'S TOO TIGHT (TO MENTION)	Simply Red (Elektra)
29	24	RASPBERRY BERET	Prince & the Revolution (WEA)
16	25	I'M ON FIRE/BORN IN THE USA	Bruce Springsteen (CBS)
25	26	EMPTY ROOMS	Gary Moore (10)
-	27	EXCITABLE	Amazulu (Island)
21	28	JOHNNY COME HOME	Fine Young Cannibals (London)
-	29	I WONDER IF I TAKE YOU HOME	Lisa Lisa & Cult Jam (CBS)
26	30	DANCIN' IN THE KEY OF LIFE	Steve Arrington (Atlantic)
28	31	TOO MANY GAMES	Maze featuring Frankie Beverly (Capitol)
-	32	SAY I'M YOUR NUMBER ONE	Princess (Supreme)
30	33	LOVING YOU	Feargal Sharkey (Virgin)
50	34	LONG TIME	Arrow (London)
24	35	ALL NIGHT HOLIDAY	Russ Abbott (Spirit)
33	36	TAKE ME HOME	Phil Collins (Virgin)
-	37	BETTER THAN THEM/NO SENSE	New Model Army (EMI)
-	38	GOODBYE GIRL	Go West (Chrysalis)
41	39	DRIVE	Cars (Elektra)
27	40	STRONGER TOGETHER	Shannon (Club)
46	41	LOVE IS JUST THE GREAT PRETENDER '85	Animal Nightlife (Island)
34	42	SECRET	Orchestral Manoeuvres In The Dark (Virgin)
38	43	TWISTN' THE NIGHT AWAY	Divine (Proto)
35	44	YOU'RE THE ONE FOR ME	D Train (Epic)
-	45	BODY AND SOUL	Mai Tai (Virgin)
-	46	P MACHINERY	Propaganda (ZTT)
47	47	THE ZZ TOP SUMMER HOLIDAY	ZZ Top (Warner Bros)
-	48	TUPELO	Nick Cave & the Bad Seeds (Mute)
-	49	ROCK 'N' ROLL CHILDREN	Dio (Vertigo)
40	50	ON A CROWDED STREET	Barbara Pennington (Record Shack)

17 August 1985

1	1	INTO THE GROOVE	Madonna (Sire)
6	2	WHITE WEDDING	Billy Idol (Chrysalis)
3	3	WE DON'T NEED ANOTHER HERO	Tina Turner (Capitol)
2	4	THERE MUST BE AN ANGEL (PLAYING WITH MY HEART)	Eurythmics (Virgin)
5	5	MONEY FOR NOTHING	Dire Straits (Vertigo)
20	6	HOLIDAY	Madonna (Sire)
14	7	I GOT YOU BABE	UB40 guest vocals by Chrissie Hynde (DEP International)
17	8	DON QUIXOTE	Nik Kershaw (MCA)
12	9	GLORY DAYS	Bruce Springsteen (CBS)
16	10	IN BETWEEN DAYS	Cure (Fiction)
9	11	FRANKIE	Sister Sledge (Atlantic)
4	12	LIVE IS LIFE	Opus (Polydor)
7	13	LIVING ON VIDEO	Trans-X (Boiling Point)
11	14	CHERISH	Kool & the Gang (De-Lite)
10	15	ROUND AND ROUND	Jaki Graham (EMI)
26	16	EMPTY ROOMS	Gary Moore (10)
8	17	AXEL F	Harold Faltermeyer (MCA)
18	18	SHE SELLS SANCTUARY	Cult (Beggars Banquet)
15	19	CRAZY FOR YOU	Madonna (Geffen)
-	20	RUNNING UP THAT HILL	Kate Bush (EMI)
39	21	DRIVE	Cars (Elektra)
24	22	RASPBERRY BERET	Prince & the Revolution (WEA)
13	23	MY TOOT TOOT	Denise LaSalle (Epic)
19	24	DARE ME	Pointer Sisters (RCA)
27	25	EXCITABLE	Amazulu (Island)
22	26	LET ME BE THE ONE	Five Star (Tent)
36	27	TAKE ME HOME	Phil Collins (Virgin)
-	28	YOUR FASCINATION	Gary Numan (Numa)
38	29	GOODBYE GIRL	Go West (Chrysalis)
25	30	I'M ON FIRE/BORN IN THE USA	Bruce Springsteen (CBS)
49	31	ROCK 'N' ROLL CHILDREN	Dio (Vertigo)
32	32	SAY I'M YOUR NUMBER ONE	Princess (Supreme)
23	33	MONEY'S TOO TIGHT (TO MENTION)	Simply Red (Elektra)
46	34	P MACHINERY	Propaganda (ZTT)
21	35	IN YOUR CAR	Cool Notes (Abstract Dance)
33	36	LOVING YOU	Feargal Sharkey (Virgin)
31	37	TOO MANY GAMES	Maze featuring Frankie Beverly (Capitol)
-	38	ALONE WITHOUT YOU	King (CBS)
-	39	COME BACK	Spear Of Destiny (Epic)
44	40	YOU'RE THE ONE FOR ME	D Train (Epic)
34	41	LONG TIME	Arrow (London)
45	42	BODY AND SOUL	Mai Tai (Virgin)
42	43	SECRET	Orchestral Manoeuvres In The Dark (Virgin)
29	44	I WONDER IF I TAKE YOU HOME	Lisa Lisa & Cult Jam (CBS)
-	45	TAKES A LITTLE TIME	Total Contrast (London)
37	46	BETTER THAN THEM/NO SENSE	New Model Army (EMI)
50	47	ON A CROWDED STREET	Barbara Pennington (Record Shack)
-	48	FREEWAY OF LOVE	Aretha Franklin (Arista)
-	49	SUMMER OF '69	Bryan Adams (A&M)
-	50	TARZAN BOY	Baltimora (Columbia)

Madonna's *Into The Groove*, from her film *Desperately Seeking Susan*, hit the Top Ten just as her previous single *Crazy For You* (also featured in a film, *Vision Quest*) left it. In the US, *Into The Groove* was only released on the 12-inch B-side of *Angel*, but in the UK became her first Number One. Also from a film - her own *Mad Max: Beyond Thunderdome* - was Tina Turner's *We Don't Need Another Hero*.

August – September 1985

24 August 1985

last week	this week		
1	1	INTO THE GROOVE	Madonna (Sire)
6	2	HOLIDAY	Madonna (Sire)
7	3	I GOT YOU BABE	UB40 guest vocals by Chrissie Hynde (DEP International)
20	4	RUNNING UP THAT HILL	Kate Bush (EMI)
5	5	MONEY FOR NOTHING	Dire Straits (Vertigo)
3	6	WE DON'T NEED ANOTHER HERO	Tina Turner (Capitol)
21	7	DRIVE	Cars (Elektra)
2	8	WHITE WEDDING	Billy Idol (Chrysalis)
4	9	THERE MUST BE AN ANGEL (PLAYING WITH MY HEART)	Eurythmics (Virgin)
32	10	SAY I'M YOUR NUMBER ONE	Princess (Supreme)
8	11	DON QUIXOTE	Nik Kershaw (MCA)
10	12	IN BETWEEN DAYS	Cure (Fiction)
25	13	EXCITABLE	Amazulu (Island)
11	14	FRANKIE	Sister Sledge (Atlantic)
12	15	LIVE IS LIFE	Opus (Polydor)
9	16	CRAZY FOR YOU	Madonna (Geffen)
14	17	CHERISH	Kool & the Gang (De-Lite)
16	18	EMPTY ROOMS	Gary Moore (10)
9	19	GLORY DAYS	Bruce Springsteen (CBS)
22	20	RASPBERRY BERET	Prince & the Revolution (WEA)
44	21	I WONDER IF I TAKE YOU HOME	Lisa Lisa & Cult Jam (CBS)
17	22	AXEL F	Harold Faltermeyer (MCA)
15	23	ROUND AND ROUND	Jaki Graham (EMI)
40	24	YOU'RE THE ONE FOR ME	D Train (Epic)
13	25	LIVING ON VIDEO	Trans-X (Boiling Point)
18	26	SHE SELLS SANCTUARY	Cult (Beggars Banquet)
50	27	TARZAN BOY	Baltimora (Columbia)
29	28	GOODBYE GIRL	Go West (Chrysalis)
26	29	LET ME BE THE ONE	Five Star (Tent)
-	30	STORIES OF JOHNNY	Marc Almond (Some Bizzare)
27	31	TAKE ME HOME	Phil Collins (Virgin)
38	32	ALONE WITHOUT YOU	King (CBS)
28	33	YOUR FASCINATION	Gary Numan (Numa)
24	34	DARE ME	Pointer Sisters (RCA)
42	35	BODY AND SOUL	Mai Tai (Virgin)
-	36	BACK ON THE STREETS	Saxon (Parlophone)
-	37	THE POWER OF LOVE	Jennifer Rush (CBS)
36	38	LOVING YOU	Feargal Sharkey (Virgin)
34	39	P MACHINERY	Propaganda (ZTT)
-	40	KNOCK ON WOOD/LIGHT MY FIRE	Amii Stewart (Sedition)
31	41	ROCK 'N' ROLL CHILDREN	Dio (Vertigo)
45	42	TAKES A LITTLE TIME	Total Contrast (London)
23	43	MY TOOT TOOT	Denise LaSalle (Epic)
-	44	DON'T YOU (FORGET ABOUT ME)	Simple Minds (Virgin)
-	45	ALWAYS ON MY MIND	Elvis Presley (RCA)
49	46	SUMMER OF '69	Bryan Adams (A&M)
-	47	MYSTERY LADY	Billy Ocean (Jive)
-	48	TUPELO	Nick Cave & the Bad Seeds (Mute)
-	49	WILD COLONIAL BOY	Ruefrex (Kasper)
41	50	LONG TIME	Arrow (London)

31 August 1985

1	1	INTO THE GROOVE	Madonna (Sire)
3	2	I GOT YOU BABE	UB40 guest vocals by Chrissie Hynde (DEP International)
4	3	RUNNING UP THAT HILL	Kate Bush (EMI)
2	4	HOLIDAY	Madonna (Sire)
7	5	DRIVE	Cars (Elektra)
5	6	MONEY FOR NOTHING	Dire Straits (Vertigo)
10	7	SAY I'M YOUR NUMBER ONE	Princess (Supreme)
8	8	WHITE WEDDING	Billy Idol (Chrysalis)
27	9	TARZAN BOY	Baltimora (Columbia)
6	10	WE DON'T NEED ANOTHER HERO	Tina Turner (Capitol)
32	11	ALONE WITHOUT YOU	King (CBS)
13	12	EXCITABLE	Amazulu (Island)
9	13	THERE MUST BE AN ANGEL (PLAYING WITH MY HEART)	Eurythmics (Virgin)
24	14	YOU'RE THE ONE FOR ME	D Train (Epic)
21	15	I WONDER IF I TAKE YOU HOME	Lisa Lisa & Cult Jam (CBS)
11	16	DON QUIXOTE	Nik Kershaw (MCA)
31	17	TAKE ME HOME	Phil Collins (Virgin)
30	18	STORIES OF JOHNNY	Marc Almond (Some Bizzare)
12	19	IN BETWEEN DAYS	Cure (Fiction)
42	20	TAKES A LITTLE TIME	Total Contrast (London)
15	21	LIVE IS LIFE	Opus (Polydor)
28	22	GOODBYE GIRL	Go West (Chrysalis)
41	23	ROCK 'N' ROLL CHILDREN	Dio (Vertigo)
17	24	CHERISH	Kool & the Gang (De-Lite)
16	25	LOVE IS THE SEVENTH WAVE	Sting (A&M)
16	26	CRAZY FOR YOU	Madonna (Geffen)
-	27	DON'T MESS WITH DR. DREAM	Thompson Twins (Arista)
20	28	RASPBERRY BERET	Prince & the Revolution (WEA)
19	29	GLORY DAYS	Bruce Springsteen (CBS)
49	30	WILD COLONIAL BOY	Ruefrex (Kasper)
14	31	FRANKIE	Sister Sledge (Atlantic)
-	32	I CAN DREAM ABOUT YOU	Dan Hartman (MCA)
22	33	AXEL F	Harold Faltermeyer (MCA)
-	34	DIRTY OLD TOWN	Pogues (Stiff)
-	35	DO NOT DISTURB	Bananarama (London)
18	36	EMPTY ROOMS	Gary Moore (10)
35	37	BODY AND SOUL	Mai Tai (Virgin)
-	38	YESTERDAY'S MEN	Madness (Zarjazz)
46	39	SUMMER OF '69	Bryan Adams (A&M)
40	40	KNOCK ON WOOD/LIGHT MY FIRE	Amii Stewart (Sedition)
-	41	CLOSE TO PERFECTION	Miquel Brown (Record Shack)
-	42	POWER OF LOVE	Huey Lewis & the News (Chrysalis)
29	43	LET ME BE THE ONE	Five Star (Tent)
23	44	ROUND AND ROUND	Jaki Graham (EMI)
39	45	P MACHINERY	Propaganda (ZTT)
37	46	THE POWER OF LOVE	Jennifer Rush (CBS)
26	47	SHE SELLS SANCTUARY	Cult (Beggars Banquet)
-	48	TEQUILA	No Way Jose (Fourth & Broadway)
25	49	LIVING ON VIDEO	Trans-X (Boiling Point)
43	50	MY TOOT TOOT	Denise LaSalle (Epic)

7 September 1985

2	1	I GOT YOU BABE	UB40 guest vocals by Chrissie Hynde (DEP International)
3	2	RUNNING UP THAT HILL	Kate Bush (EMI)
1	3	INTO THE GROOVE	Madonna (Sire)
5	4	DRIVE	Cars (Elektra)
9	5	TARZAN BOY	Baltimora (Columbia)
-	6	DANCING IN THE STREET	David Bowie & Mick Jagger (EMI America)
7	7	SAY I'M YOUR NUMBER ONE	Princess (Supreme)
4	8	HOLIDAY	Madonna (Sire)
11	9	ALONE WITHOUT YOU	King (CBS)
6	10	MONEY FOR NOTHING	Dire Straits (Vertigo)
8	11	WHITE WEDDING	Billy Idol (Chrysalis)
15	12	I WONDER IF I TAKE YOU HOME	Lisa Lisa & Cult Jam (CBS)
10	13	WE DON'T NEED ANOTHER HERO	Tina Turner (Capitol)
32	14	I CAN DREAM ABOUT YOU	Dan Hartman (MCA)
12	15	EXCITABLE	Amazulu (Island)
14	16	YOU'RE THE ONE FOR ME	D Train (Epic)
13	17	THERE MUST BE AN ANGEL (PLAYING WITH MY HEART)	Eurythmics (Virgin)
20	18	TAKES A LITTLE TIME	Total Contrast (London)
27	19	DON'T MESS WITH DR. DREAM	Thompson Twins (Arista)
38	20	YESTERDAY'S MEN	Madness (Zarjazz)
18	21	STORIES OF JOHNNY	Marc Almond (Some Bizzare)
37	22	BODY AND SOUL	Mai Tai (Virgin)
17	23	TAKE ME HOME	Phil Collins (Virgin)
-	24	HOLDING OUT FOR A HERO	Bonnie Tyler (CBS)
-	25	LAVENDER	Marillion (EMI)
16	26	DON QUIXOTE	Nik Kershaw (MCA)
-	27	PART TIME LOVER	Stevie Wonder (Motown)
40	28	KNOCK ON WOOD/LIGHT MY FIRE	Amii Stewart (Sedition)
24	29	CHERISH	Kool & the Gang (De-Lite)
19	30	IN BETWEEN DAYS	Cure (Fiction)
-	31	DON'T STOP THE DANCE	Bryan Ferry (EG)
42	32	POWER OF LOVE	Huey Lewis & the News (Chrysalis)
23	33	ROCK 'N' ROLL CHILDREN	Dio (Vertigo)
21	34	LIVE IS LIFE	Opus (Polydor)
25	35	LOVE IS THE SEVENTH WAVE	Sting (A&M)
22	36	GOODBYE GIRL	Go West (Chrysalis)
-	37	BODY ROCK	Maria Vidal (EMI America)
35	38	DO NOT DISTURB	Bananarama (London)
43	39	LET ME BE THE ONE	Five Star (Tent)
31	40	FRANKIE	Sister Sledge (Atlantic)
26	41	CRAZY FOR YOU	Madonna (Geffen)
46	42	THE POWER OF LOVE	Jennifer Rush (CBS)
-	43	HEAVEN KNOWS	Jaki Graham (EMI)
28	44	RASPBERRY BERET	Prince & the Revolution (WEA)
-	45	YOU DID CUT ME	China Crisis (Virgin)
-	46	TRAPPED	Colonel Abrams (MCA)
-	47	DANCING ON THE JAGGED EDGE	Sister Sledge (Atlantic)
45	48	P MACHINERY	Propaganda (ZTT)
34	49	DIRTY OLD TOWN	Pogues (Stiff)
-	50	LITTLE BY LITTLE	Robert Plant (Es Peranza)

On August 24, Madonna became only the fourth act in chart history to occupy Numbers One and Two in the chart simultaneously, as the re-promoted *Holiday* from 1984 lined up behind *Into The Groove*. She also had *Crazy For You* still showing at Number 16 that week, which made her the first female artist since Ruby Murray in 1955 to have more than two singles in the Top 20 together.

September 1985

14 September 1985 | 21 September 1985 | 28 September 1985

lw	tw	14 September 1985			21 September 1985			28 September 1985
6	1	DANCING IN THE STREET — David Bowie & Mick Jagger (EMI America)	1	1	DANCING IN THE STREET — David Bowie & Mick Jagger (EMI America)	1	1	DANCING IN THE STREET — David Bowie & Mick Jagger (EMI America)
1	2	I GOT YOU BABE — UB40 guest vocals by Chrissie Hynde (DEP International)	5	2	HOLDING OUT FOR A HERO — Bonnie Tyler (CBS)	2	2	HOLDING OUT FOR A HERO — Bonnie Tyler (CBS)
5	3	TARZAN BOY — Baltimora (Columbia)	10	3	PART TIME LOVER — Stevie Wonder (Motown)	3	3	PART TIME LOVER — Stevie Wonder (Motown)
2	4	RUNNING UP THAT HILL — Kate Bush (EMI)	3	4	TARZAN BOY — Baltimora (Columbia)	6	4	LAVENDER — Marillion (EMI)
24	5	HOLDING OUT FOR A HERO — Bonnie Tyler (CBS)	2	5	I GOT YOU BABE — UB40 guest vocals by Chrissie Hynde (DEP International)	22	5	ANGEL — Madonna (Sire)
3	6	INTO THE GROOVE — Madonna (Sire)	16	6	LAVENDER — Marillion (EMI)	4	6	IF I WAS — Midge Ure (Chrysalis)
4	7	DRIVE — Cars (Elektra)	7	7	DRIVE — Cars (Elektra)	7	7	TARZAN BOY — Baltimora (Columbia)
7	8	SAY I'M YOUR NUMBER ONE — Princess (Supreme)	4	8	RUNNING UP THAT HILL — Kate Bush (EMI)	13	8	POWER OF LOVE — Huey Lewis & the News (Chrysalis)
9	9	ALONE WITHOUT YOU — King (CBS)	15	9	KNOCK ON WOOD/LIGHT MY FIRE — Amii Stewart (Sedition)	9	9	KNOCK ON WOOD/LIGHT MY FIRE — Amii Stewart (Sedition)
27	10	PART TIME LOVER — Stevie Wonder (Motown)	13	10	BODY AND SOUL — Mai Tai (Virgin)	5	10	I GOT YOU BABE — UB40 guest vocals by Chrissie Hynde (DEP International)
14	11	I CAN DREAM ABOUT YOU — Dan Hartman (MCA)	6	11	INTO THE GROOVE — Madonna (Sire)	10	11	BODY AND SOUL — Mai Tai (Virgin)
10	12	MONEY FOR NOTHING — Dire Straits (Vertigo)	8	12	SAY I'M YOUR NUMBER ONE — Princess (Supreme)	25	12	BODY ROCK — Maria Vidal (EMI America)
22	13	BODY AND SOUL — Mai Tai (Virgin)	24	13	POWER OF LOVE — Huey Lewis & the News (Chrysalis)	39	13	LEAN ON ME (AH-LI-AYO) — Red Box (Sire)
19	14	DON'T MESS WITH DR. DREAM — Thompson Twins (Arista)	9	14	ALONE WITHOUT YOU — King (CBS)	7	14	DRIVE — Cars (Elektra)
28	15	KNOCK ON WOOD/LIGHT MY FIRE — Amii Stewart (Sedition)	11	15	I CAN DREAM ABOUT YOU — Dan Hartman (MCA)	21	15	SHE'S SO BEAUTIFUL — Cliff Richard (EMI)
25	16	LAVENDER — Marillion (EMI)	19	16	YESTERDAY'S MEN — Madness (Zarjazz)	24	16	REBEL YELL — Billy Idol (Chrysalis)
12	17	I WONDER IF I TAKE YOU HOME — Lisa Lisa & Cult Jam (CBS)	14	17	DON'T MESS WITH DR. DREAM — Thompson Twins (Arista)	11	17	INTO THE GROOVE — Madonna (Sire)
8	18	HOLIDAY — Madonna (Sire)	21	18	DON'T STOP THE DANCE — Bryan Ferry (EG)	8	18	RUNNING UP THAT HILL — Kate Bush (EMI)
20	19	YESTERDAY'S MEN — Madness (Zarjazz)	12	19	MONEY FOR NOTHING — Dire Straits (Vertigo)	14	19	ALONE WITHOUT YOU — King (CBS)
11	20	WHITE WEDDING — Billy Idol (Chrysalis)	40	20	IF I WAS — Midge Ure (Chrysalis)	12	20	SAY I'M YOUR NUMBER ONE — Princess (Supreme)
31	21	DON'T STOP THE DANCE — Bryan Ferry (EG)	45	21	SHE'S SO BEAUTIFUL — Cliff Richard (EMI)	23	21	BRAND NEW FRIEND — Lloyd Cole & the Commotions (Polydor)
13	22	WE DON'T NEED ANOTHER HERO — Tina Turner (Capitol)	-	22	ANGEL — Madonna (Sire)	16	22	YESTERDAY'S MEN — Madness (Zarjazz)
16	23	YOU'RE THE ONE FOR ME — D Train (Epic)	38	23	BRAND NEW FRIEND — Lloyd Cole & the Commotions (Polydor)	18	23	DON'T STOP THE DANCE — Bryan Ferry (EG)
32	24	POWER OF LOVE — Huey Lewis & the News (Chrysalis)	-	24	REBEL YELL — Billy Idol (Chrysalis)	34	24	IS IT A DREAM? — Damned (MCA)
21	25	STORIES OF JOHNNY — Marc Almond (Some Bizzare)	30	25	BODY ROCK — Maria Vidal (EMI America)	31	25	THE POWER OF LOVE — Jennifer Rush (CBS)
15	26	EXCITABLE — Amazulu (Island)	28	26	I'LL BE GOOD — Rene & Angela (Club)	40	26	MY HEART GOES BANG — Dead Or Alive (Epic)
18	27	TAKES A LITTLE TIME — Total Contrast (London)	20	27	WHITE WEDDING — Billy Idol (Chrysalis)	47	27	CLOSE TO ME — Cure (Fiction)
-	28	I'LL BE GOOD — Rene & Angela (Club)	17	28	I WONDER IF I TAKE YOU HOME — Lisa Lisa & Cult Jam (CBS)	-	28	THE LODGERS — Style Council (Polydor)
38	29	DO NOT DISTURB — Bananarama (London)	32	29	THE SHOW (THEME FROM 'CONNIE') — Rebecca Storm (Towerbell)	26	29	I'LL BE GOOD — Rene & Angela (Club)
37	30	BODY ROCK — Maria Vidal (EMI America)	-	30	SINGLE LIFE — Cameo (Club)	15	30	I CAN DREAM ABOUT YOU — Dan Hartman (MCA)
42	31	THE POWER OF LOVE — Jennifer Rush (CBS)	31	31	THE POWER OF LOVE — Jennifer Rush (CBS)	30	31	SINGLE LIFE — Cameo (Club)
-	32	THE SHOW (THEME FROM 'CONNIE') — Rebecca Storm (Towerbell)	29	32	DO NOT DISTURB — Bananarama (London)	19	32	MONEY FOR NOTHING — Dire Straits (Vertigo)
23	33	TAKE ME HOME — Phil Collins (Virgin)	25	33	STORIES OF JOHNNY — Marc Almond (Some Bizzare)	45	33	TRAPPED — Colonel Abrams (MCA)
17	34	THERE MUST BE AN ANGEL (PLAYING WITH MY HEART) — Eurythmics (Virgin)	-	34	IS IT A DREAM? — Damned (MCA)	37	34	ST. ELMO'S FIRE (MAN IN MOTION) — John Parr (London)
-	35	WHAT'S YOUR PROBLEM — Blancmange (London)	35	35	WHAT'S YOUR PROBLEM — Blancmange (London)	28	35	I WONDER IF I TAKE YOU HOME — Lisa Lisa & Cult Jam (CBS)
34	36	LIVE IS LIFE — Opus (Polydor)	18	36	HOLIDAY — Madonna (Sire)	17	36	DON'T MESS WITH DR. DREAM — Thompson Twins (Arista)
-	37	LEAN ON ME (AH-LI-AYO) — Red Box (Sire)	-	37	ST. ELMO'S FIRE (MAN IN MOTION) — John Parr (London)	-	37	LOVE TAKE OVER — Five Star (Tent)
-	38	BRAND NEW FRIEND — Lloyd Cole & the Commotions (Polydor)	50	38	ONE LOVE — Atlantic Starr (A&M)	-	38	CALL OUT THE DOGS — Gary Numan (Numa)
39	39	SUMMER OF '69 — Bryan Adams (A&M)	37	39	LEAN ON ME (AH-LI-AYO) — Red Box (Sire)	41	39	I'LL BE A FREAK FOR YOU — Royal Delite (Streetwave)
-	40	IF I WAS — Midge Ure (Chrysalis)	-	40	MY HEART GOES BANG — Dead Or Alive (Epic)	-	40	IT'S CALLED A HEART — Depeche Mode (Mute)
43	41	HEAVEN KNOWS — Jaki Graham (EMI)	-	41	I'LL BE A FREAK FOR YOU — Royal Delite (Streetwave)	-	41	SOMETHING ABOUT YOU — Level 42 (Polydor)
33	42	ROCK 'N' ROLL CHILDREN — Dio (Vertigo)	-	42	MAKES NO SENSE AT ALL — Husker Du (SST)	42	42	WHITE WEDDING — Billy Idol (Chrysalis)
39	43	LET ME BE THE ONE — Five Star (Tent)	-	43	PERFECT WAY — Scritti Politti (Virgin)	-	43	A NIGHT AT THE APOLLO LIVE! — Daryl Hall & John Oates & Ruffin & Kendrick (RCA)
35	44	LOVE IS THE SEVENTH WAVE — Sting (A&M)	48	44	YOU DID CUT ME — China Crisis (Virgin)	42	44	MAKES NO SENSE AT ALL — Husker Du (SST)
-	45	SHE'S SO BEAUTIFUL — Cliff Richard (EMI)	49	45	TRAPPED — Colonel Abrams (MCA)	-	45	JOLENE — Strawberry Switchblade (Korova)
-	46	APPETITE — Prefab Sprout (Kitchenware)	23	46	YOU'RE THE ONE FOR ME — D Train (Epic)	-	46	DAY AND NIGHT — Balaam & the Angel (Virgin)
-	47	PALE SHELTER — Tears For Fears (Mercury)	-	47	CLOSE TO ME — Cure (Fiction)	29	47	THE SHOW (THEME FROM 'CONNIE') — Rebecca Storm (Towerbell)
45	48	YOU DID CUT ME — China Crisis (Virgin)	-	48	ROAD TO RACK AND RUIN — King Kurt (Stiff)	-	48	JAMES BOND LIVES DOWN OUR STREET — Toy Dolls (Volume)
46	49	TRAPPED — Colonel Abrams (MCA)	22	49	WE DON'T NEED ANOTHER HERO — Tina Turner (Capitol)	-	49	AFTER THE FIRE — Roger Daltrey (10)
-	50	ONE LOVE — Atlantic Starr (A&M)	-	50	COME TO MY AID — Simply Red (Elektra)	-	50	ROMEO WHERE'S JULIET? — Collage (MCA)

Following the return of the Cars' *Drive* to the Top 10 a year after its original flutter, after its high-profile use during the Live Aid broadcast in July, David Bowie & Mick Jagger's revival of *Dancing In The Street*, a number premiered on video at Live Aid, similarly benefited from its association with the year's major charity event, racing to Number One. All its royalties went to the Band Aid Trust.

October 1985

last week	this	5 October 1985
6	1	IF I WAS — Midge Ure (Chrysalis)
3	2	PART TIME LOVER — Stevie Wonder (Motown)
1	3	DANCING IN THE STREET — David Bowie & Mick Jagger (EMI America)
2	4	HOLDING OUT FOR A HERO — Bonnie Tyler (CBS)
5	5	ANGEL — Madonna (Sire)
13	6	LEAN ON ME (AH-LI-AYO) — Red Box (Sire)
4	7	LAVENDER — Marillion (EMI)
16	8	REBEL YELL — Billy Idol (Chrysalis)
28	9	THE LODGERS — Style Council (Polydor)
12	10	BODY ROCK — Maria Vidal (EMI America)
25	11	THE POWER OF LOVE — Jennifer Rush (CBS)
8	12	POWER OF LOVE — Huey Lewis & the News (Chrysalis)
9	13	KNOCK ON WOOD/LIGHT MY FIRE — Amii Stewart (Sedition)
33	14	TRAPPED — Colonel Abrams (MCA)
40	15	IT'S CALLED A HEART — Depeche Mode (Mute)
11	16	BODY AND SOUL — Mai Tai (Virgin)
7	17	TARZAN BOY — Baltimora (Columbia)
10	18	I GOT YOU BABE — UB40 guest vocals by Chrissie Hynde (DEP International)
21	19	BRAND NEW FRIEND — Lloyd Cole & the Commotions (Polydor)
15	20	SHE'S SO BEAUTIFUL — Cliff Richard (EMI)
31	21	SINGLE LIFE — Cameo (Club)
27	22	CLOSE TO ME — Cure (Fiction)
29	23	I'LL BE GOOD — Rene & Angela (Club)
-	24	RAIN — Cult (Beggars Banquet)
14	25	DRIVE — Cars (Elektra)
39	26	I'LL BE A FREAK FOR YOU — Royal Delite (Streetwave)
26	27	MY HEART GOES BANG — Dead Or Alive (Epic)
24	28	IS IT A DREAM? — Damned (MCA)
18	29	RUNNING UP THAT HILL — Kate Bush (EMI)
20	30	SAY I'M YOUR NUMBER ONE — Princess (Supreme)
-	31	STRENGTH — Alarm (IRS)
46	32	DAY AND NIGHT — Balaam & the Angel (Virgin)
37	33	LOVE TAKE OVER — Five Star (Tent)
-	34	RUNNING FREE — Iron Maiden (EMI)
35	35	I WONDER IF I TAKE YOU HOME — Lisa Lisa & Cult Jam (CBS)
-	36	LOOKING FOR LEWIS AND CLARK — Long Ryders (Island)
17	37	INTO THE GROOVE — Madonna (Sire)
34	38	ST. ELMO'S FIRE (MAN IN MOTION) — John Parr (London)
-	39	THE BOY WITH THE THORN IN HIS SIDE — Smiths (Rough Trade)
22	40	YESTERDAY'S MEN — Madness (Zarjazz)
32	41	MONEY FOR NOTHING — Dire Straits (Vertigo)
48	42	JAMES BOND LIVES DOWN OUR STREET — Toy Dolls (Volume)
43	43	A NIGHT AT THE APOLLO LIVE! — Daryl Hall & John Oates & Ruffin & Kendrick (RCA)
44	44	MAKES NO SENSE AT ALL — Husker Du (SST)
-	45	TAKE ON ME — A-ha (Warner Bros)
-	46	LIVING ON MY OWN — Freddie Mercury (CBS)
-	47	HARD TIME FOR LOVERS — Jennifer Holliday (Geffen)
50	48	ROMEO WHERE'S JULIET? — Collage (MCA)
23	49	DON'T STOP THE DANCE — Bryan Ferry (EG)
30	50	I CAN DREAM ABOUT YOU — Dan Hartman (MCA)

last week	this	12 October 1985
11	1	THE POWER OF LOVE — Jennifer Rush (CBS)
1	2	IF I WAS — Midge Ure (Chrysalis)
6	3	LEAN ON ME (AH-LI-AYO) — Red Box (Sire)
2	4	PART TIME LOVER — Stevie Wonder (Motown)
3	5	DANCING IN THE STREET — David Bowie & Mick Jagger (EMI America)
8	6	REBEL YELL — Billy Idol (Chrysalis)
4	7	HOLDING OUT FOR A HERO — Bonnie Tyler (CBS)
5	8	ANGEL — Madonna (Sire)
14	9	TRAPPED — Colonel Abrams (MCA)
7	10	LAVENDER — Marillion (EMI)
12	11	POWER OF LOVE — Huey Lewis & the News (Chrysalis)
9	12	THE LODGERS — Style Council (Polydor)
10	13	BODY ROCK — Maria Vidal (EMI America)
34	14	RUNNING FREE — Iron Maiden (EMI)
15	15	IT'S CALLED A HEART — Depeche Mode (Mute)
19	16	BRAND NEW FRIEND — Lloyd Cole & the Commotions (Polydor)
39	17	THE BOY WITH THE THORN IN HIS SIDE — Smiths (Rough Trade)
13	18	KNOCK ON WOOD/LIGHT MY FIRE — Amii Stewart (Sedition)
20	19	SHE'S SO BEAUTIFUL — Cliff Richard (EMI)
-	20	ALIVE AND KICKING — Simple Minds (Virgin)
23	21	I'LL BE GOOD — Rene & Angela (Club)
24	22	RAIN — Cult (Beggars Banquet)
16	23	BODY AND SOUL — Mai Tai (Virgin)
21	24	SINGLE LIFE — Cameo (Club)
27	25	MY HEART GOES BANG — Dead Or Alive (Epic)
38	26	ST. ELMO'S FIRE (MAN IN MOTION) — John Parr (London)
17	27	TARZAN BOY — Baltimora (Columbia)
22	28	CLOSE TO ME — Cure (Fiction)
-	29	THIS IS ENGLAND — Clash (CBS)
-	30	GAMBLER — Madonna (Geffen)
-	31	JUST LIKE HONEY — Jesus & Mary Chain (blanco y negro)
-	32	THE HEAVEN I NEED — Three Degrees (Supreme)
-	33	SWEETEST TABOO — Sade (Epic)
-	34	ONE OF THE LIVING — Tina Turner (Capitol)
-	35	YEH YEH — Matt Bianco (WEA)
36	36	LOOKING FOR LEWIS AND CLARK — Long Ryders (Island)
30	37	SAY I'M YOUR NUMBER ONE — Princess (Supreme)
-	38	I BELIEVE — Tears For Fears (Mercury)
33	39	ROMEO WHERE'S JULIET? — Collage (MCA)
48	40	LOVE TAKE OVER — Five Star (Tent)
26	41	DRIVE — Cars (Elektra)
42	42	I'LL BE A FREAK FOR YOU — Royal Delite (Streetwave)
45	43	TAKE ON ME — A-ha (Warner Bros)
49	44	DON'T STOP THE DANCE — Bryan Ferry (EG)
31	45	STRENGTH — Alarm (Geffen)
35	46	I WONDER IF I TAKE YOU HOME — Lisa Lisa & Cult Jam (CBS)
37	47	INTO THE GROOVE — Madonna (Sire)
-	48	PREACHER PREACHER — Animal Nightlife (Island)
29	49	RUNNING UP THAT HILL — Kate Bush (EMI)
18	50	I GOT YOU BABE — UB40 guest vocals by Chrissie Hynde (DEP International)

last week	this	19 October 1985
1	1	THE POWER OF LOVE — Jennifer Rush (CBS)
2	2	IF I WAS — Midge Ure (Chrysalis)
3	3	LEAN ON ME (AH-LI-AYO) — Red Box (Sire)
9	4	TRAPPED — Colonel Abrams (MCA)
6	5	REBEL YELL — Billy Idol (Chrysalis)
26	6	ST. ELMO'S FIRE (MAN IN MOTION) — John Parr (London)
20	7	ALIVE AND KICKING — Simple Minds (Virgin)
4	8	PART TIME LOVER — Stevie Wonder (Motown)
8	9	ANGEL — Madonna (Sire)
43	10	TAKE ON ME — A-ha (Warner Bros)
7	11	HOLDING OUT FOR A HERO — Bonnie Tyler (CBS)
13	12	BODY ROCK — Maria Vidal (EMI America)
5	13	DANCING IN THE STREET — David Bowie & Mick Jagger (EMI America)
30	14	GAMBLER — Madonna (Geffen)
14	15	RUNNING FREE — Iron Maiden (EMI)
17	16	THE BOY WITH THE THORN IN HIS SIDE — Smiths (Rough Trade)
24	17	SINGLE LIFE — Cameo (Club)
22	18	RAIN — Cult (Beggars Banquet)
-	19	MIAMI VICE THEME — Jan Hammer (MCA)
11	20	POWER OF LOVE — Huey Lewis & the News (Chrysalis)
-	21	SLAVE TO THE RHYTHM — Grace Jones (ZTT)
29	22	THIS IS ENGLAND — Clash (CBS)
10	23	LAVENDER — Marillion (EMI)
31	24	JUST LIKE HONEY — Jesus & Mary Chain (blanco y negro)
21	25	I'LL BE GOOD — Rene & Angela (Club)
12	26	THE LODGERS — Style Council (Polydor)
28	27	CLOSE TO ME — Cure (Fiction)
19	28	SHE'S SO BEAUTIFUL — Cliff Richard (EMI)
33	29	SWEETEST TABOO — Sade (Epic)
38	30	I BELIEVE — Tears For Fears (Mercury)
-	31	THE BIG MONEY — Rush (Vertigo)
-	32	NIKITA — Elton John (Rocket)
35	33	YEH YEH — Matt Bianco (WEA)
36	34	LOOKING FOR LEWIS AND CLARK — Long Ryders (Island)
23	35	BODY AND SOUL — Mai Tai (Virgin)
-	36	SOMETHING ABOUT YOU — Level 42 (Polydor)
18	37	KNOCK ON WOOD/LIGHT MY FIRE — Amii Stewart (Sedition)
-	38	BRING ON THE DANCING HORSES — Echo & the Bunnymen (Korova)
-	39	LIPSTICK, POWDER AND PAINT — Shakin' Stevens (Epic)
25	40	MY HEART GOES BANG — Dead Or Alive (Epic)
41	41	DRIVE — Cars (Elektra)
27	42	TARZAN BOY — Baltimora (Columbia)
40	43	LOVE TAKE OVER — Five Star (Tent)
-	44	WENDELL GEE — R.E.M. (IRS)
15	45	IT'S CALLED A HEART — Depeche Mode (Mute)
45	46	STRENGTH — Alarm (IRS)
42	47	I'LL BE A FREAK FOR YOU — Royal Delite (Streetwave)
-	48	ROAD TO NOWHERE — Talking Heads (EMI)
-	49	SLEEPING BAG — ZZ Top (Warner Bros)
16	50	BRAND NEW FRIEND — Lloyd Cole & the Commotions (Polydor)

Following an initially slow chart climb, Jennifer Rush's *The Power Of Love*, untroubled by the identically-titled (but different) Frankie Goes To Hollywood hit of the previous Christmas, or indeed by Huey Lewis & The News' also different song *Power Of Love* (from the film *Back To The Future*) in the current chart, zoomed to Number One. It would be the year's biggest-selling single.

October – November 1985

26 October 1985

last week	this week		
1	1	THE POWER OF LOVE	Jennifer Rush (CBS)
4	2	TRAPPED	Colonel Abrams (MCA)
10	3	TAKE ON ME	A-ha (Warner Bros)
2	4	IF I WAS	Midge Ure (Chrysalis)
3	5	LEAN ON ME (AH-LI-AYO)	Red Box (Sire)
7	6	ALIVE AND KICKING	Simple Minds (Virgin)
14	7	GAMBLER	Madonna (Geffen)
6	8	ST. ELMO'S FIRE (MAN IN MOTION)	John Parr (London)
19	9	MIAMI VICE THEME	Jan Hammer (MCA)
5	10	REBEL YELL	Billy Idol (Chrysalis)
18	11	RAIN	Cult (Beggars Banquet)
21	12	SLAVE TO THE RHYTHM	Grace Jones (ZTT)
39	13	LIPSTICK, POWDER AND PAINT	Shakin' Stevens (Epic)
32	14	NIKITA	Elton John (Rocket)
8	15	PART TIME LOVER	Stevie Wonder (Motown)
22	16	THIS IS ENGLAND	Clash (CBS)
11	17	HOLDING OUT FOR A HERO	Bonnie Tyler (CBS)
36	18	SOMETHING ABOUT YOU	Level 42 (Polydor)
9	19	ANGEL	Madonna (Sire)
17	20	SINGLE LIFE	Cameo (Club)
38	21	BRING ON THE DANCING HORSES	Echo & the Bunnymen (Korova)
13	22	DANCING IN THE STREET	David Bowie & Mick Jagger (EMI America)
49	23	SLEEPING BAG	ZZ Top (Warner Bros)
30	24	I BELIEVE	Tears For Fears (Mercury)
-	25	THE TASTE OF YOUR TEARS	King (CBS)
29	26	SWEETEST TABOO	Sade (Epic)
12	27	BODY ROCK	Maria Vidal (EMI America)
-	28	ELECTION DAY	Arcadia (Odeon)
43	29	LOVE TAKE OVER	Five Star (Tent)
33	30	YEH YEH	Matt Bianco (WEA)
34	31	LOOKING FOR LEWIS AND CLARK	Long Ryders (Island)
-	32	CLOUDBURSTING	Kate Bush (EMI)
-	33	CITIES IN DUST	Siouxsie & the Banshees (Wonderland)
25	34	SHE'S SO BEAUTIFUL	Cliff Richard (EMI)
16	35	THE BOY WITH THE THORN IN HIS SIDE	Smiths (Rough Trade)
20	36	POWER OF LOVE	Huey Lewis & the News (Chrysalis)
24	37	JUST LIKE HONEY	Jesus & Mary Chain (blanco y negro)
-	38	KING FOR A DAY	Thompson Twins (Arista)
44	39	WENDELL GEE	R.E.M. (IRS)
15	40	RUNNING FREE	Iron Maiden (EMI)
31	41	THE BIG MONEY	Rush (Vertigo)
26	42	THE LODGERS	Style Council (Polydor)
-	43	THE HEAVEN I NEED	Three Degrees (Supreme)
-	44	CHIEF INSPECTOR	Wally Badarou (Fourth & Broadway)
-	45	INVINCIBLE	Pat Benatar (Chrysalis)
23	46	LAVENDER	Marillion (EMI)
48	47	ROAD TO NOWHERE	Talking Heads (EMI)
-	48	HIT AND RUN	Total Contrast (London)
27	49	CLOSE TO ME	Cure (Fiction)
-	50	THEY SAY IT'S GONNA RAIN	Hazell Dean (Parlophone)

2 November 1985

3	1	TAKE ON ME	A-ha (Warner Bros)
1	2	THE POWER OF LOVE	Jennifer Rush (CBS)
2	3	TRAPPED	Colonel Abrams (MCA)
9	4	MIAMI VICE THEME	Jan Hammer (MCA)
7	5	GAMBLER	Madonna (Geffen)
6	6	ALIVE AND KICKING	Simple Minds (Virgin)
8	7	ST. ELMO'S FIRE (MAN IN MOTION)	John Parr (London)
14	8	NIKITA	Elton John (Rocket)
12	9	SLAVE TO THE RHYTHM	Grace Jones (ZTT)
5	10	LEAN ON ME (AH-LI-AYO)	Red Box (Sire)
4	11	IF I WAS	Midge Ure (Chrysalis)
28	12	ELECTION DAY	Arcadia (Odeon)
18	13	SOMETHING ABOUT YOU	Level 42 (Polydor)
13	14	LIPSTICK, POWDER AND PAINT	Shakin' Stevens (Epic)
10	15	REBEL YELL	Billy Idol (Chrysalis)
11	16	RAIN	Cult (Beggars Banquet)
32	17	CLOUDBURSTING	Kate Bush (EMI)
25	18	THE TASTE OF YOUR TEARS	King (CBS)
21	19	BRING ON THE DANCING HORSES	Echo & the Bunnymen (Korova)
23	20	SLEEPING BAG	ZZ Top (Warner Bros)
-	21	DON'T BREAK MY HEART	UB40 (DEP International)
15	22	PART TIME LOVER	Stevie Wonder (Motown)
33	23	CITIES IN DUST	Siouxsie & the Banshees (Wonderland)
17	24	HOLDING OUT FOR A HERO	Bonnie Tyler (CBS)
30	25	YEH YEH	Matt Bianco (WEA)
-	26	A GOOD HEART	Feargal Sharkey (Virgin)
16	27	THIS IS ENGLAND	Clash (CBS)
26	28	SWEETEST TABOO	Sade (Epic)
-	29	HOWARD'S WAY	Simon May Orchestra (BBC)
-	30	UNCLE SAM	Madness (Zarjazz)
-	31	SISTERS ARE DOIN' IT FOR THEMSELVES	Eurythmics & Aretha Franklin (RCA)
38	32	KING FOR A DAY	Thompson Twins (Arista)
20	33	SINGLE LIFE	Cameo (Club)
22	34	DANCING IN THE STREET	David Bowie & Mick Jagger (EMI America)
47	35	ROAD TO NOWHERE	Talking Heads (EMI)
27	36	BODY ROCK	Maria Vidal (EMI America)
48	37	HIT AND RUN	Total Contrast (London)
50	38	THEY SAY IT'S GONNA RAIN	Hazell Dean (Parlophone)
-	39	LE FEMME ACCIDENT	Orchestral Manoeuvres In The Dark (Virgin)
24	40	I BELIEVE	Tears For Fears (Mercury)
31	41	LOOKING FOR LEWIS AND CLARK	Long Ryders (Island)
34	42	SHE'S SO BEAUTIFUL	Cliff Richard (EMI)
19	43	ANGEL	Madonna (Sire)
44	44	CHIEF INSPECTOR	Wally Badarou (Fourth & Broadway)
-	45	FORTRESS AROUND YOUR HEART	Sting (A&M)
-	46	PROFOUNDLY IN LOVE WITH PANDORA	Ian Dury (EMI)
-	47	LOVE LETTER	Marc Almond (Some Bizzare)
-	48	I'VE GOT YOU UNDER MY SKIN	Julio Iglesias (CBS)
-	49	STAIRWAY TO HEAVEN	Far Corporation (Arista)
41	50	THE BIG MONEY	Rush (Vertigo)

9 November 1985

2	1	THE POWER OF LOVE	Jennifer Rush (CBS)
1	2	TAKE ON ME	A-ha (Warner Bros)
8	3	NIKITA	Elton John (Rocket)
3	4	TRAPPED	Colonel Abrams (MCA)
12	5	ELECTION DAY	Arcadia (Odeon)
4	6	MIAMI VICE THEME	Jan Hammer (MCA)
6	7	ALIVE AND KICKING	Simple Minds (Virgin)
13	8	SOMETHING ABOUT YOU	Level 42 (Polydor)
5	9	GAMBLER	Madonna (Geffen)
7	10	ST. ELMO'S FIRE (MAN IN MOTION)	John Parr (London)
26	11	A GOOD HEART	Feargal Sharkey (Virgin)
18	12	THE TASTE OF YOUR TEARS	King (CBS)
14	13	LIPSTICK, POWDER AND PAINT	Shakin' Stevens (Epic)
9	14	SLAVE TO THE RHYTHM	Grace Jones (ZTT)
17	15	CLOUDBURSTING	Kate Bush (EMI)
21	16	DON'T BREAK MY HEART	UB40 (DEP International)
25	17	YEH YEH	Matt Bianco (WEA)
10	18	LEAN ON ME (AH-LI-AYO)	Red Box (Sire)
23	19	CITIES IN DUST	Siouxsie & the Banshees (Wonderland)
19	20	BRING ON THE DANCING HORSES	Echo & the Bunnymen (Korova)
11	21	IF I WAS	Midge Ure (Chrysalis)
31	22	SISTERS ARE DOIN' IT FOR THEMSELVES	Eurythmics & Aretha Franklin (RCA)
15	23	REBEL YELL	Billy Idol (Chrysalis)
20	24	SLEEPING BAG	ZZ Top (Warner Bros)
49	25	STAIRWAY TO HEAVEN	Far Corporation (Arista)
35	26	ROAD TO NOWHERE	Talking Heads (EMI)
32	27	KING FOR A DAY	Thompson Twins (Arista)
30	28	UNCLE SAM	Madness (Zarjazz)
16	29	RAIN	Cult (Beggars Banquet)
-	30	CAN YOU PUSSY DO THE DOG	Cramps (Big Beat)
29	31	HOWARD'S WAY	Simon May Orchestra (BBC)
-	32	SECRET RENDEZVOUS	Rene & Angela (Club)
28	33	SWEETEST TABOO	Sade (Epic)
-	34	THE WHOLE OF THE MOON	Waterboys (Ensign)
-	35	SUB CULTURE	New Order (Factory)
46	36	PROFOUNDLY IN LOVE WITH PANDORA	Ian Dury (EMI)
37	37	BROTHERS IN ARMS	Dire Straits (Vertigo)
-	38	JUST FOR MONEY	Paul Hardcastle (Chrysalis)
39	39	TELL ME HOW IT FEELS	52nd Street (10)
22	40	PART TIME LOVER	Stevie Wonder (Motown)
45	41	FORTRESS AROUND YOUR HEART	Sting (A&M)
-	42	CHIEF INSPECTOR	Wally Badarou (Fourth & Broadway)
-	43	IT'S ONLY LOVE	Bryan Adams & Tina Turner (A&M)
-	44	WINDS OF CHANGE	Robert Wyatt (Rough Trade)
24	45	HOLDING OUT FOR A HERO	Bonnie Tyler (CBS)
39	46	LE FEMME ACCIDENT	Orchestral Manoeuvres In The Dark (Virgin)
-	47	EMERGENCY	Kool & the Gang (De-Lite)
-	48	CRUISER'S CREEK	Fall (Beggars Banquet)
-	49	OH SHEILA	Ready For The World (MCA)
-	50	BLUE	Fine Young Cannibals (London)

Madonna's *Gambler* was her second single to be lifted from the film *Vision Quest* - which was retitled *Crazy For You* (presumably to cash in on the Madonna connection) when it was released on video in the UK. John Parr's *St. Elmo's Fire* was also a theme song, from the Brat Pack movie of the same title, while Jan Hammer's instrumental *Miami Vice Theme* was from the TV cop series of the same title.

November 1985

last this
week   **16 November 1985**

3	1	NIKITA	Elton John (Rocket)
1	2	THE POWER OF LOVE	Jennifer Rush (CBS)
11	3	A GOOD HEART	Feargal Sharkey (Virgin)
2	4	TAKE ON ME	A-ha (Warner Bros)
8	5	SOMETHING ABOUT YOU	Level 42 (Polydor)
16	6	DON'T BREAK MY HEART	UB40 (DEP International)
4	7	TRAPPED	Colonel Abrams (MCA)
10	8	ST. ELMO'S FIRE (MAN IN MOTION)	John Parr (London)
25	9	STAIRWAY TO HEAVEN	Far Corporation (Arista)
5	10	ELECTION DAY	Arcadia (Odeon)
26	11	ROAD TO NOWHERE	Talking Heads (EMI)
22	12	SISTERS ARE DOIN' IT FOR THEMSELVES	Eurythmics & Aretha Franklin (RCA)
17	13	YEH YEH	Matt Bianco (WEA)
9	14	GAMBLER	Madonna (Geffen)
12	15	THE TASTE OF YOUR TEARS	King (CBS)
7	16	ALIVE AND KICKING	Simple Minds (Virgin)
13	17	LIPSTICK, POWDER AND PAINT	Shakin' Stevens (Epic)
6	18	MIAMI VICE THEME	Jan Hammer (MCA)
14	19	SLAVE TO THE RHYTHM	Grace Jones (ZTT)
15	20	CLOUDBURSTING	Kate Bush (EMI)
31	21	HOWARD'S WAY	Simon May Orchestra (BBC)
19	22	CITIES IN DUST	Siouxsie & the Banshees (Wonderland)
37	23	BROTHERS IN ARMS	Dire Straits (Vertigo)
-	24	LOST WEEKEND	Lloyd Cole & the Commotions (Polydor)
-	25	ONE VISION	Queen (EMI)
-	26	THE SHOW	Doug E. Fresh (Cooltempo)
20	27	BRING ON THE DANCING HORSES	Echo & the Bunnymen (Korova)
28	28	UNCLE SAM	Madness (Zarjazz)
38	29	JUST FOR MONEY	Paul Hardcastle (Chrysalis)
30	30	CAN YOU PUSSY DO THE DOG	Cramps (Big Beat)
24	31	SLEEPING BAG	ZZ Top (Warner Bros)
-	32	THAT CERTAIN SMILE	Midge Ure (Chrysalis)
33	33	THE WHOLE OF THE MOON	Waterboys (Ensign)
18	34	LEAN ON ME (AH-LI-AYO)	Red Box (Sire)
-	35	YOU ARE MY WORLD	Communards (London)
43	36	IT'S ONLY LOVE	Bryan Adams & Tina Turner (A&M)
50	37	BLUE	Fine Young Cannibals (London)
38	38	SEE THE DAY	Dee C. Lee (CBS)
44	39	WINDS OF CHANGE	Robert Wyatt (Rough Trade)
-	40	THIS IS ENGLAND	Clash (CBS)
-	41	THAT'S WHAT FRIENDS ARE FOR	Dionne Warwick (Arista)
-	42	YOU DON'T KNOW	Serious Intentions (Important)
32	43	SECRET RENDEZVOUS	Rene & Angela (Club)
27	44	KING FOR A DAY	Thompson Twins (Arista)
23	45	REBEL YELL	Billy Idol (Chrysalis)
35	46	SUB CULTURE	New Order (Factory)
42	47	CHIEF INSPECTOR	Wally Badarou (Fourth & Broadway)
46	48	LE FEMME ACCIDENT	Orchestral Manoeuvres In The Dark (Virgin)
-	49	YOUR PERSONAL TOUCH	Evelyn 'Champagne' King (RCA)
-	50	WHEN LOVE BREAKS DOWN	Prefab Sprout (Kitchenware)

23 November 1985

3	1	A GOOD HEART	Feargal Sharkey (Virgin)
6	2	DON'T BREAK MY HEART	UB40 (DEP International)
5	3	SOMETHING ABOUT YOU	Level 42 (Polydor)
2	4	THE POWER OF LOVE	Jennifer Rush (CBS)
1	5	NIKITA	Elton John (Rocket)
9	6	STAIRWAY TO HEAVEN	Far Corporation (Arista)
4	7	TAKE ON ME	A-ha (Warner Bros)
12	8	SISTERS ARE DOIN' IT FOR THEMSELVES	Eurythmics & Aretha Franklin (RCA)
25	9	ONE VISION	Queen (EMI)
11	10	ROAD TO NOWHERE	Talking Heads (EMI)
7	11	TRAPPED	Colonel Abrams (MCA)
26	12	THE SHOW	Doug E. Fresh (Cooltempo)
15	13	THE TASTE OF YOUR TEARS	King (CBS)
29	14	JUST FOR MONEY	Paul Hardcastle (Chrysalis)
24	15	LOST WEEKEND	Lloyd Cole & the Commotions (Polydor)
13	16	YEH YEH	Matt Bianco (WEA)
10	17	ELECTION DAY	Arcadia (Odeon)
-	18	I'M YOUR MAN	Wham! (Epic)
14	19	GAMBLER	Madonna (Geffen)
16	20	ALIVE AND KICKING	Simple Minds (Virgin)
8	21	ST. ELMO'S FIRE (MAN IN MOTION)	John Parr (London)
22	22	BROTHERS IN ARMS	Dire Straits (Vertigo)
21	23	HOWARD'S WAY	Simon May Orchestra (BBC)
28	24	UNCLE SAM	Madness (Zarjazz)
33	25	THE WHOLE OF THE MOON	Waterboys (Ensign)
-	26	SAY YOU SAY ME	Lionel Richie (Motown)
17	27	LIPSTICK, POWDER AND PAINT	Shakin' Stevens (Epic)
41	28	THAT'S WHAT FRIENDS ARE FOR	Dionne Warwick (Arista)
36	29	IT'S ONLY LOVE	Bryan Adams & Tina Turner (A&M)
32	30	THAT CERTAIN SMILE	Midge Ure (Chrysalis)
20	31	CLOUDBURSTING	Kate Bush (EMI)
19	32	SLAVE TO THE RHYTHM	Grace Jones (ZTT)
22	33	CITIES IN DUST	Siouxsie & the Banshees (Wonderland)
18	34	MIAMI VICE THEME	Jan Hammer (MCA)
27	35	BRING ON THE DANCING HORSES	Echo & the Bunnymen (Korova)
38	36	SEE THE DAY	Dee C. Lee (CBS)
47	37	CHIEF INSPECTOR	Wally Badarou (Fourth & Broadway)
37	38	BLUE	Fine Young Cannibals (London)
35	39	YOU ARE MY WORLD	Communards (London)
-	40	MATED	David Grant & Jaki Graham (EMI)
31	41	SLEEPING BAG	ZZ Top (Warner Bros)
43	42	SECRET RENDEZVOUS	Rene & Angela (Club)
-	43	SUN CITY	Artists United Against Apartheid (Manhattan)
50	44	WHEN LOVE BREAKS DOWN	Prefab Sprout (Kitchenware)
-	45	RSVP	Five Star (Tent)
49	46	YOUR PERSONAL TOUCH	Evelyn 'Champagne' King (RCA)
47	47	WE BUILT THIS CITY	Starship (RCA)
-	48	DAY BY DAY	Shakatak (Polydor)
39	49	WINDS OF CHANGE	Robert Wyatt (Rough Trade)
-	50	SAVING ALL MY LOVE FOR YOU	Whitney Houston (Arista)

30 November 1985

1	1	A GOOD HEART	Feargal Sharkey (Virgin)
18	2	I'M YOUR MAN	Wham! (Epic)
2	3	DON'T BREAK MY HEART	UB40 (DEP International)
9	4	ONE VISION	Queen (EMI)
4	5	THE POWER OF LOVE	Jennifer Rush (CBS)
8	6	SISTERS ARE DOIN' IT FOR THEMSELVES	Eurythmics & Aretha Franklin (RCA)
5	7	NIKITA	Elton John (Rocket)
3	8	SOMETHING ABOUT YOU	Level 42 (Polydor)
7	9	TAKE ON ME	A-ha (Warner Bros)
6	10	STAIRWAY TO HEAVEN	Far Corporation (Arista)
10	11	ROAD TO NOWHERE	Talking Heads (EMI)
26	12	SAY YOU SAY ME	Lionel Richie (Motown)
12	13	THE SHOW	Doug E. Fresh (Cooltempo)
28	14	THAT'S WHAT FRIENDS ARE FOR	Dionne Warwick (Arista)
15	15	SEE THE DAY	Dee C. Lee (CBS)
50	16	SAVING ALL MY LOVE FOR YOU	Whitney Houston (Arista)
15	17	LOST WEEKEND	Lloyd Cole & the Commotions (Polydor)
-	18	SEPARATE LIVES	Phil Collins & Marilyn Martin (Virgin)
22	19	BROTHERS IN ARMS	Dire Straits (Vertigo)
11	20	TRAPPED	Colonel Abrams (MCA)
13	21	THE TASTE OF YOUR TEARS	King (CBS)
14	22	JUST FOR MONEY	Paul Hardcastle (Chrysalis)
25	23	THE WHOLE OF THE MOON	Waterboys (Ensign)
30	24	THAT CERTAIN SMILE	Midge Ure (Chrysalis)
29	25	IT'S ONLY LOVE	Bryan Adams & Tina Turner (A&M)
43	26	SUN CITY	Artists United Against Apartheid (Manhattan)
44	27	WHEN LOVE BREAKS DOWN	Prefab Sprout (Kitchenware)
23	28	HOWARD'S WAY	Simon May Orchestra (BBC)
-	29	HEART OF LOTHIAN	Marillion (EMI)
24	30	UNCLE SAM	Madness (Zarjazz)
16	31	YEH YEH	Matt Bianco (WEA)
-	32	SPIES LIKE US	Paul McCartney (Parlophone)
19	33	GAMBLER	Madonna (Geffen)
47	34	WE BUILT THIS CITY	Starship (RCA)
-	35	REVOLUTION (EP)	Cult (Beggars Banquet)
21	36	ST. ELMO'S FIRE (MAN IN MOTION)	John Parr (London)
-	37	DON'T YOU JUST KNOW IT	Amazulu (Island)
-	38	AFTER THE LOVE HAS GONE	Princess (Supreme)
-	39	DON'T LOOK DOWN	Go West (Chrysalis)
-	40	CARAVAN OF LOVE	Isley Jasper Isley (Epic)
38	41	BLUE	Fine Young Cannibals (London)
46	42	YOUR PERSONAL TOUCH	Evelyn 'Champagne' King (RCA)
-	43	JEALOUS GUY	John Lennon (Parlophone)
-	44	TINY DYNAMINE	Cocteau Twins (4AD)
-	45	CAN YOU PUSSY DO THE DOG	Cramps (Big Beat)
-	46	TELL ME HOW IT FEELS	52nd Street (10)
39	47	YOU ARE MY WORLD	Communards (London)
33	48	CITIES IN DUST	Siouxsie & the Banshees (Wonderland)
40	49	MATED	David Grant & Jaki Graham (EMI)
-	50	GO HOME	Stevie Wonder (Motown)

The Far Corporation, a studio aggregation put together in Germany by former Boney M producer Frank Farian, capitalised upon the facts that Led Zeppelin had never released their best-loved track *Stairway To Heaven* as a single, and that the remaining members of Zeppelin had played it at Live Aid, by releasing a cover. Enough people thought this sounded as good as the original, to make it a hit.

last week	this week	7 December 1985	
2	1	I'M YOUR MAN	Wham! (Epic)
1	2	A GOOD HEART	Feargal Sharkey (Virgin)
15	3	SEE THE DAY	Dee C. Lee (CBS)
3	4	DON'T BREAK MY HEART	UB40 (DEP International)
16	5	SAVING ALL MY LOVE FOR YOU	Whitney Houston (Arista)
11	6	ROAD TO NOWHERE	Talking Heads (EMI)
12	7	SAY YOU SAY ME	Lionel Richie (Motown)
5	8	THE POWER OF LOVE	Jennifer Rush (CBS)
18	9	SEPARATE LIVES	Phil Collins & Marilyn Martin (Virgin)
13	10	THE SHOW	Doug E. Fresh (Cooltempo)
4	11	ONE VISION	Queen (EMI)
8	12	SOMETHING ABOUT YOU	Level 42 (Polydor)
6	13	SISTERS ARE DOIN' IT FOR THEMSELVES	Eurythmics & Aretha Franklin (RCA)
14	14	THAT'S WHAT FRIENDS ARE FOR	Dionne Warwick (Arista)
7	15	NIKITA	Elton John (Rocket)
9	16	TAKE ON ME	A-ha (Warner Bros)
29	17	HEART OF LOTHIAN	Marillion (EMI)
32	18	SPIES LIKE US	Paul McCartney (Parlophone)
17	19	LOST WEEKEND	Lloyd Cole & the Commotions (Polydor)
49	20	MATED	David Grant & Jaki Graham (EMI)
26	21	SUN CITY	Artists United Against Apartheid (Manhattan)
19	22	BROTHERS IN ARMS	Dire Straits (Vertigo)
10	23	STAIRWAY TO HEAVEN	Far Corporation (Arista)
27	24	WHEN LOVE BREAKS DOWN	Prefab Sprout (Kitchenware)
39	25	DON'T LOOK DOWN	Go West (Chrysalis)
35	26	REVOLUTION (EP)	Cult (Beggars Banquet)
23	27	THE WHOLE OF THE MOON	Waterboys (Ensign)
30	28	UNCLE SAM	Madness (Zarjazz)
-	29	WHEN A HEART BEATS	Nik Kershaw (MCA)
-	30	HIT THAT PERFECT BEAT	Bronski Beat (Forbidden Fruit)
-	31	MUSIC IS THE ANSWER	Colonel Abrams (MCA)
34	32	WE BUILT THIS CITY	Starship (RCA)
-	33	BRAVE NEW WORLD	New Model Army (EMI)
25	34	IT'S ONLY LOVE	Bryan Adams & Tina Turner (A&M)
21	35	THE TASTE OF YOUR TEARS	King (CBS)
43	36	JEALOUS GUY	John Lennon (Parlophone)
40	37	CARAVAN OF LOVE	Isley Jasper Isley (Epic)
24	38	THAT CERTAIN SMILE	Midge Ure (Chrysalis)
42	39	YOUR PERSONAL TOUCH	Evelyn 'Champagne' King (RCA)
50	40	GO HOME	Stevie Wonder (Motown)
38	41	AFTER THE LOVE HAS GONE	Princess (Supreme)
37	42	DON'T YOU JUST KNOW IT	Amazulu (Island)
-	43	WEST END GIRLS	Pet Shop Boys (Parlophone)
-	44	HEART AND SOUL (EP)	Huey Lewis & the News (Chrysalis)
45	45	DRESS YOU UP	Madonna (Sire)
-	46	EDIE	Adult Net (Beggars Banquet)
-	47	AGAIN	Jimmy Tarbuck (Safari)
20	48	TRAPPED	Colonel Abrams (MCA)
28	49	HOWARD'S WAY	Simon May Orchestra (BBC)
-	50	DO YOU BELIEVE IN MIRACLES	Slade (RCA)

last week	this week	14 December 1985	
1	1	I'M YOUR MAN	Wham! (Epic)
5	2	SAVING ALL MY LOVE FOR YOU	Whitney Houston (Arista)
3	3	SEE THE DAY	Dee C. Lee (CBS)
9	4	SEPARATE LIVES	Phil Collins & Marilyn Martin (Virgin)
2	5	A GOOD HEART	Feargal Sharkey (Virgin)
4	6	DON'T BREAK MY HEART	UB40 (DEP International)
45	7	DRESS YOU UP	Madonna (Sire)
7	8	SAY YOU SAY ME	Lionel Richie (Motown)
10	9	THE SHOW	Doug E. Fresh (Cooltempo)
6	10	ROAD TO NOWHERE	Talking Heads (EMI)
8	11	THE POWER OF LOVE	Jennifer Rush (CBS)
25	12	DON'T LOOK DOWN	Go West (Chrysalis)
18	13	SPIES LIKE US	Paul McCartney (Parlophone)
32	14	WE BUILT THIS CITY	Starship (RCA)
14	15	THAT'S WHAT FRIENDS ARE FOR	Dionne Warwick (Arista)
15	16	NIKITA	Elton John (Rocket)
21	17	SUN CITY	Artists United Against Apartheid (Manhattan)
-	18	WRAP HER UP	Elton John (Rocket)
-	19	DO THEY KNOW IT'S CHRISTMAS?	Band Aid (Mercury)
20	20	MATED	David Grant & Jaki Graham (EMI)
43	21	WEST END GIRLS	Pet Shop Boys (Parlophone)
11	22	ONE VISION	Queen (EMI)
13	23	SISTERS ARE DOIN' IT FOR THEMSELVES	Eurythmics & Aretha Franklin (RCA)
16	24	TAKE ON ME	A-ha (Warner Bros)
24	25	WHEN LOVE BREAKS DOWN	Prefab Sprout (Kitchenware)
-	26	SHE'S STRANGE	Cameo (Club)
-	27	MERRY CHRISTMAS EVERYONE	Shakin' Stevens (Epic)
-	28	LEAVING ME NOW (REMIX)	Level 42 (Polydor)
17	29	HEART OF LOTHIAN	Marillion (EMI)
12	30	SOMETHING ABOUT YOU	Level 42 (Polydor)
26	31	REVOLUTION (EP)	Cult (Beggars Banquet)
-	32	MY HOMETOWN	Bruce Springsteen (CBS)
-	33	LAST CHRISTMAS	Wham! (Epic)
23	34	STAIRWAY TO HEAVEN	Far Corporation (Arista)
-	35	ALL THE LOVE IN THE WORLD	Rose Marie (A.I.)
31	36	MUSIC IS THE ANSWER	Colonel Abrams (MCA)
42	37	DON'T YOU JUST KNOW IT	Amazulu (Island)
22	38	BROTHERS IN ARMS	Dire Straits (Vertigo)
-	39	RUN TO THE HILLS	Iron Maiden (EMI)
-	40	KICK OVER THE STATUES	Redskins (Abstract Dance)
28	41	UNCLE SAM	Madness (Zarjazz)
29	42	WHEN A HEART BEATS	Nik Kershaw (MCA)
41	43	AFTER THE LOVE HAS GONE	Princess (Supreme)
-	44	GIRLIE GIRLIE	Sophia George (Winner)
30	45	HIT THAT PERFECT BEAT	Bronski Beat (Forbidden Fruit)
46	46	RUSSIANS	Sting (A&M)
47	47	WINDSWEPT	Bryan Ferry (EG)
48	48	DO YOU BELIEVE IN MIRACLES	Slade (RCA)
19	49	LOST WEEKEND	Lloyd Cole & the Commotions (Polydor)
36	50	JEALOUS GUY	John Lennon (Parlophone)

last week	this week	21 December 1985	
2	1	SAVING ALL MY LOVE FOR YOU	Whitney Houston (Arista)
4	2	SEPARATE LIVES	Phil Collins & Marilyn Martin (Virgin)
3	3	SEE THE DAY	Dee C. Lee (CBS)
7	4	DRESS YOU UP	Madonna (Sire)
19	5	DO THEY KNOW IT'S CHRISTMAS?	Band Aid (Mercury)
8	6	SAY YOU SAY ME	Lionel Richie (Motown)
33	7	LAST CHRISTMAS	Wham! (Epic)
27	8	MERRY CHRISTMAS EVERYONE	Shakin' Stevens (Epic)
1	9	I'M YOUR MAN	Wham! (Epic)
21	10	WEST END GIRLS	Pet Shop Boys (Parlophone)
5	11	A GOOD HEART	Feargal Sharkey (Virgin)
32	12	MY HOMETOWN	Bruce Springsteen (CBS)
14	13	WE BUILT THIS CITY	Starship (RCA)
13	14	SPIES LIKE US	Paul McCartney (Parlophone)
6	15	DON'T BREAK MY HEART	UB40 (DEP International)
10	16	ROAD TO NOWHERE	Talking Heads (EMI)
12	17	DON'T LOOK DOWN	Go West (Chrysalis)
9	18	THE SHOW	Doug E. Fresh (Cooltempo)
26	19	SHE'S STRANGE	Cameo (Club)
18	20	WRAP HER UP	Elton John (Rocket)
17	21	SUN CITY	Artists United Against Apartheid (Manhattan)
37	22	DON'T YOU JUST KNOW IT	Amazulu (Island)
20	23	MATED	David Grant & Jaki Graham (EMI)
15	24	THAT'S WHAT FRIENDS ARE FOR	Dionne Warwick (Arista)
16	25	NIKITA	Elton John (Rocket)
11	26	THE POWER OF LOVE	Jennifer Rush (CBS)
45	27	HIT THAT PERFECT BEAT	Bronski Beat (Forbidden Fruit)
39	28	RUN TO THE HILLS	Iron Maiden (EMI)
-	29	RING OF ICE	Jennifer Rush (CBS)
-	30	WALKING IN THE AIR	Aled Jones (HMV)
28	31	LEAVING ME NOW (REMIX)	Level 42 (Polydor)
-	32	MR D.J.	Concept (Fourth & Broadway)
23	33	SISTERS ARE DOIN' IT FOR THEMSELVES	Eurythmics & Aretha Franklin (RCA)
22	34	ONE VISION	Queen (EMI)
25	35	WHEN LOVE BREAKS DOWN	Prefab Sprout (Kitchenware)
43	36	AFTER THE LOVE HAS GONE	Princess (Supreme)
44	37	GIRLIE GIRLIE	Sophia George (Winner)
40	38	KICK OVER THE STATUES	Redskins (Abstract Dance)
47	39	WINDSWEPT	Bryan Ferry (EG)
-	40	CHRISTMAS TIME	Bryan Adams (A&M)
-	41	ABIDE WITH ME	Inspirational Choir (Portrait)
-	42	HOKEY COKEY	Black Lace (Flair)
42	43	WHEN A HEART BEATS	Nik Kershaw (MCA)
-	44	BECAUSE	Julian Lennon (EMI)
49	45	LOST WEEKEND	Lloyd Cole & the Commotions (Polydor)
29	46	HEART OF LOTHIAN	Marillion (EMI)
46	47	RUSSIANS	Sting (A&M)
38	48	BROTHERS IN ARMS	Dire Straits (Vertigo)
31	49	REVOLUTION (EP)	Cult (Beggars Banquet)
36	50	MUSIC IS THE ANSWER	Colonel Abrams (MCA)

Whitney Houston, a younger cousin of Dionne Warwick, made her first real impact in the UK when *Saving All My Love For You* was lifted from her eponymous debut album to become the final chart-topper of 1985. *Separate Lives,* one place below it, was duetted by Phil Collins and Marilyn Martin on the soundtrack of the film *White Nights,* from which also came Lionel Richie's *Say You, Say Me.*

January 1986

The year opened with not only 1985's batch of Christmas and holiday discs (Shakin' Stevens, Aled Jones, Bryan Adams, Keith Harris, Black Lace) in the chart, but also 1984's second-time-around biggies.

last week	this week	4 January 1986	
1	1	SAVING ALL MY LOVE FOR YOU	Whitney Houston (Arista)
8	2	MERRY CHRISTMAS EVERYONE	Shakin' Stevens (Epic)
10	3	WEST END GIRLS	Pet Shop Boys (Parlophone)
5	4	DO THEY KNOW IT'S CHRISTMAS	Band Aid (Mercury)
12	5	MY HOMETOWN	Bruce Springsteen (CBS)
7	6	LAST CHRISTMAS	Wham! (Epic)
2	7	SEPARATE LIVES	Phil Collins & Marilyn Martin (Virgin)
3	8	SEE THE DAY	Dee C. Lee (CBS)
4	9	DRESS YOU UP	Madonna (Sire)
6	10	SAY YOU SAY ME	Lionel Richie (Motown)
30	11	WALKING IN THE AIR	Aled Jones (HMV)
9	12	I'M YOUR MAN	Wham! (Epic)
13	13	WE BUILT THIS CITY	Starship (RCA)
27	14	HIT THAT PERFECT BEAT	Bronski Beat (Forbidden Fruit)
22	15	DON'T YOU JUST KNOW IT	Amazulu (Island)
11	16	A GOOD HEART	Feargal Sharkey (Virgin)
14	17	SPIES LIKE US	Paul McCartney (Parlophone)
17	18	DON'T LOOK DOWN	Go West (Chrysalis)
37	19	GIRLIE GIRLIE	Sophie George (Winner)
20	20	SHE'S STRANGE	Cameo (Club)
32	21	MR. DJ	Concept (Fourth & Broadway)
47	22	RUSSIANS	Sting (A&M)
26	23	THE POWER OF LOVE	Jennifer Rush (CBS)
31	24	LEAVING ME NOW	Level 42 (Polydor)
18	25	THE SHOW	Doug E. Fresh (Cooltempo)
15	26	DON'T BREAK MY HEART	UB40 (DEP International)
29	27	RING OF ICE	Jennifer Rush (CBS)
20	28	WRAP HER UP	Elton John (Rocket)
25	29	NIKITA	Elton John (Rocket)
16	30	ROAD TO NOWHERE	Talking Heads (EMI)
-	31	SATURDAY LOVE	Cherelle & Alexander O'Neal (Tabu)
-	32	ALICE I WANT YOU JUST FOR ME!	Full Force (CBS)
28	33	RUN TO THE HILLS	Iron Maiden (EMI)
-	34	WE ALL STAND TOGETHER	Paul McCartney & the Frog Chorus (Parlophone)
23	35	MATED	David Grant & Jaki Graham (EMI)
42	36	HOKEY COKEY	Black Lace (Flair)
-	37	WHITE CHRISTMAS	Keith Harris & Orville (Columbia)
36	38	AFTER THE LOVE HAS GONE	Princess (Supreme)
-	39	DAYS LIKE THESE	Billy Bragg (Go! Discs)
-	40	WHO'S ZOOMIN' WHO?	Aretha Franklin (Arista)
-	41	THE SUN ALWAYS SHINES ON TV	A-ha (Warner Bros)
40	42	CHRISTMAS TIME	Bryan Adams (A&M)
38	43	KICK OVER THE STATUES	Redskins (Abstract Dance)
35	44	WHEN LOVE BREAKS DOWN	Prefab Sprout (Kitchenware)
44	45	BECAUSE	Julian Lennon (EMI)
-	46	TONIGHT SHE COMES	Cars (Elektra)
21	47	SUN CITY	Artists United Against Apartheid (Manhattan)
34	48	ONE VISION	Queen (EMI)
24	50	THAT'S WHAT FRIENDS ARE FOR	Dionne Warwick & Friends (Arista)

		11 January 1986	
3	1	WEST END GIRLS	Pet Shop Boys (Parlophone)
1	2	SAVING ALL MY LOVE FOR YOU	Whitney Houston (Arista)
2	3	MERRY CHRISTMAS EVERYONE	Shakin' Stevens (Epic)
4	4	DO THEY KNOW IT'S CHRISTMAS	Band Aid (Mercury)
12	5	I'M YOUR MAN	Wham! (Epic)
11	6	WALKING IN THE AIR	Aled Jones (HMV)
9	7	DRESS YOU UP	Madonna (Sire)
14	8	HIT THAT PERFECT BEAT	Bronski Beat (Forbidden Fruit)
7	9	SEPARATE LIVES	Phil Collins & Marilyn Martin (Virgin)
6	10	LAST CHRISTMAS	Wham! (Epic)
8	11	SEE THE DAY	Dee C. Lee (CBS)
19	12	GIRLIE GIRLIE	Sophie George (Winner)
5	13	MY HOMETOWN	Bruce Springsteen (CBS)
13	14	WE BUILT THIS CITY	Starship (RCA)
31	15	SATURDAY LOVE	Cherelle & Alexander O'Neal (Tabu)
15	16	DON'T YOU JUST KNOW IT	Amazulu (Island)
10	17	SAY YOU SAY ME	Lionel Richie (Motown)
28	18	WRAP HER UP	Elton John (Rocket)
16	19	A GOOD HEART	Feargal Sharkey (Virgin)
24	20	LEAVING ME NOW	Level 42 (Polydor)
21	21	MR. DJ	Concept (Fourth & Broadway)
17	22	SPIES LIKE US	Paul McCartney (Parlophone)
18	23	DON'T LOOK DOWN	Go West (Chrysalis)
22	24	RUSSIANS	Sting (A&M)
32	25	ALICE I WANT YOU JUST FOR ME!	Full Force (CBS)
41	26	THE SUN ALWAYS SHINES ON TV	A-ha (Warner Bros)
20	27	SHE'S STRANGE	Cameo (Club)
27	28	RING OF ICE	Jennifer Rush (CBS)
39	29	DAYS LIKE THESE	Billy Bragg (Go! Discs)
-	30	SUSPICIOUS MINDS	Fine Young Cannibals (London)
26	31	DON'T BREAK MY HEART	UB40 (DEP International)
-	32	THE HOUSE IS HAUNTED	Marc Almond (Some Bizzare)
38	33	AFTER THE LOVE HAS GONE	Princess (Supreme)
-	34	BROKEN WINGS	Mr. Mister (RCA)
-	35	YOU LITTLE THIEF	Feargal Sharkey (Virgin)
-	36	TORTURE	King (CBS)
29	37	NIKITA	Elton John (Rocket)
30	38	ROAD TO NOWHERE	Talking Heads (EMI)
25	39	THE SHOW	Doug E. Fresh (Cooltempo)
23	40	THE POWER OF LOVE	Jennifer Rush (CBS)
37	41	WHITE CHRISTMAS	Keith Harris & Orville (Columbia)
36	42	HOKEY COKEY	Black Lace (Flair)
-	43	IS IT A CRIME	Sade (Epic)
-	44	EDGE OF DARKNESS	Eric Clapton (BBC)
40	45	WHO'S ZOOMIN' WHO?	Aretha Franklin (Arista)
46	46	BECAUSE	Julian Lennon (EMI)
33	47	RUN TO THE HILLS	Iron Maiden (EMI)
34	48	WE ALL STAND TOGETHER	Paul McCartney & the Frog Chorus (Parlophone)
-	49	PICTURES IN THE DARK	Mike Oldfield (Virgin)
-	50	NEW YORK EYES	Nicole (Portrait)

The Band Aid single's eventual UK sale after repeated success was over 3.5 million, making it probably impossible for anything to ever outsell it, while Wham!'s *Last Christmas* sold over 1.4 million.

		18 January 1986	
1	1	WEST END GIRLS	Pet Shop Boys (Parlophone)
8	2	HIT THAT PERFECT BEAT	Bronski Beat (Forbidden Fruit)
26	3	THE SUN ALWAYS SHINES ON TV	A-ha (Warner Bros)
2	4	SAVING ALL MY LOVE FOR YOU	Whitney Houston (Arista)
12	5	GIRLIE GIRLIE	Sophie George (Winner)
15	6	SATURDAY LOVE	Cherelle & Alexander O'Neal (Tabu)
7	7	DRESS YOU UP	Madonna (Sire)
8	8	WALK OF LIFE	Dire Straits (Vertigo)
3	9	MERRY CHRISTMAS EVERYONE	Shakin' Stevens (Epic)
18	10	WRAP HER UP	Elton John (Rocket)
5	11	I'M YOUR MAN	Wham! (Epic)
24	12	RUSSIANS	Sting (A&M)
35	13	YOU LITTLE THIEF	Feargal Sharkey (Virgin)
9	14	SEPARATE LIVES	Phil Collins & Marilyn Martin (Virgin)
20	15	LEAVING ME NOW	Level 42 (Polydor)
14	16	WE BUILT THIS CITY	Starship (RCA)
28	17	RING OF ICE	Jennifer Rush (CBS)
25	18	ALICE I WANT YOU JUST FOR ME!	Full Force (CBS)
23	19	DON'T LOOK DOWN	Go West (Chrysalis)
45	20	WHO'S ZOOMIN' WHO?	Aretha Franklin (Arista)
30	21	SUSPICIOUS MINDS	Fine Young Cannibals (London)
16	22	DON'T YOU JUST KNOW IT	Amazulu (Island)
22	23	SPIES LIKE US	Paul McCartney (Parlophone)
6	24	WALKING IN THE AIR	Aled Jones (HMV)
11	25	SEE THE DAY	Dee C. Lee (CBS)
34	26	BROKEN WINGS	Mr. Mister (RCA)
-	27	IT'S ALRIGHT (BABY'S COMIN' BACK)	Eurythmics (RCA)
36	28	TORTURE	King (CBS)
19	29	A GOOD HEART	Feargal Sharkey (Virgin)
17	30	SAY YOU SAY ME	Lionel Richie (Motown)
4	31	DO THEY KNOW IT'S CHRISTMAS	Band Aid (Mercury)
10	32	LAST CHRISTMAS	Wham! (Epic)
-	33	SYSTEM ADDICT	Five Star (Tent)
38	34	ROAD TO NOWHERE	Talking Heads (EMI)
-	35	SPIRIT OF '76	Alarm (IRS)
33	36	AFTER THE LOVE HAS GONE	Princess (Supreme)
37	37	SHAKE YOUR FOUNDATIONS	AC/DC (Atlantic)
50	38	NEW YORK EYES	Nicole (Portrait)
9	39	PULL UP TO THE BUMPER	Grace Jones (Island)
-	40	TAKE ON ME	A-ha (Warner Bros)
-	41	RIPTIDE	Robert Palmer (Island)
27	42	SHE'S STRANGE	Cameo (Club)
39	43	THE SHOW	Doug E. Fresh (Cooltempo)
32	44	THE HOUSE IS HAUNTED	Marc Almond (Some Bizzare)
43	45	IS IT A CRIME	Sade (Epic)
13	46	MY HOMETOWN	Bruce Springsteen (CBS)
29	47	DAYS LIKE THESE	Billy Bragg (Go! Discs)
48	48	WE ALL STAND TOGETHER	Paul McCartney & the Frog Chorus (Parlophone)
-	49	ONE NATION	Masquerade (Streetwave)
-	50	ONLY LOVE	Nana Mouskouri (Philips)

January – February 1986

25 January 1986

last week	this week	title	artist (label)
3	1	THE SUN ALWAYS SHINES ON TV	A-ha (Warner Bros)
1	2	WEST END GIRLS	Pet Shop Boys (Parlophone)
8	3	WALK OF LIFE	Dire Straits (Vertigo)
6	4	SATURDAY LOVE	Cherelle & Alexander O'Neal (Tabu)
13	5	YOU LITTLE THIEF	Feargal Sharkey (Virgin)
2	6	HIT THAT PERFECT BEAT	Bronski Beat (Forbidden Fruit)
5	7	GIRLIE GIRLIE	Sophie George (Winner)
20	8	WHO'S ZOOMIN' WHO?	Aretha Franklin (Arista)
26	9	BROKEN WINGS	Mr. Mister (RCA)
18	10	ALICE I WANT YOU JUST FOR ME!	Full Force (CBS)
12	11	RUSSIANS	Sting (A&M)
27	12	IT'S ALRIGHT (BABY'S COMIN' BACK)	Eurythmics (RCA)
4	13	SAVING ALL MY LOVE FOR YOU	Whitney Houston (Arista)
21	14	SUSPICIOUS MINDS	Fine Young Cannibals (London)
17	15	RING OF ICE	Jennifer Rush (CBS)
15	16	LEAVING ME NOW	Level 42 (Polydor)
50	17	ONLY LOVE	Nana Mouskouri (Philips)
33	18	SYSTEM ADDICT	Five Star (Tent)
28	19	TORTURE	King (CBS)
35	20	SPIRIT OF '76	Alarm (IRS)
10	21	WRAP HER UP	Elton John (Rocket)
14	22	SEPARATE LIVES	Phil Collins & Marilyn Martin (Virgin)
-	23	PHANTOM OF THE OPERA	Sarah Brightman & Steve Harley (Polydor)
39	24	PULL UP TO THE BUMPER	Grace Jones (Island)
7	25	DRESS YOU UP	Madonna (Sire)
16	26	WE BUILT THIS CITY	Starship (RCA)
-	27	CUT ME DOWN	Lloyd Cole & the Commotions (Polydor)
37	28	SHAKE YOUR FOUNDATIONS	AC/DC (Atlantic)
-	29	LIFE'S WHAT YOU MAKE IT	Talk Talk (EMI)
22	30	DON'T YOU JUST KNOW IT	Amazulu (Island)
24	31	WALKING IN THE AIR	Aled Jones (HMV)
11	32	I'M YOUR MAN	Wham! (Epic)
23	33	SPIES LIKE US	Paul McCartney (Parlophone)
34	34	SAY YOU SAY ME	Lionel Richie (Motown)
-	35	IMAGINATION	Belouis Some (Parlophone)
-	36	IF I RULED THE WORLD	Kurtis Blow (Club)
-	37	LEADER OF THE PACK	Twisted Sister (Atlantic)
38	38	WHEN THE GOING GETS TOUGH, THE TOUGH GET GOING	Billy Ocean (Jive)
-	39	GUILTY	Yarbrough & Peoples (Total Experience)
49	40	ONE NATION	Masquerade (Streetwave)
38	41	NEW YORK EYES	Nicole (Portrait)
47	42	DAYS LIKE THESE	Billy Bragg (Go! Discs)
25	43	SEE THE DAY	Dee C. Lee (CBS)
45	44	IS IT A CRIME	Sade (Epic)
36	45	AFTER THE LOVE HAS GONE	Princess (Supreme)
19	46	DON'T LOOK DOWN	Go West (Chrysalis)
-	47	YOU'RE MY LAST CHANCE	52nd Street (10)
-	48	GLENN MILLER MEDLEY	John Anderson (Modern)
-	49	OCEAN BLUE	ABC (Neutron)
-	50	GIRLS ARE MORE FUN	Ray Parker Jr. (Arista)

1 February 1986

last week	this week	title	artist (label)
1	1	THE SUN ALWAYS SHINES ON TV	A-ha (Warner Bros)
3	2	WALK OF LIFE	Dire Straits (Vertigo)
9	3	BROKEN WINGS	Mr. Mister (RCA)
17	4	ONLY LOVE	Nana Mouskouri (Philips)
2	5	WEST END GIRLS	Pet Shop Boys (Parlophone)
4	6	SATURDAY LOVE	Cherelle & Alexander O'Neal (Tabu)
5	7	YOU LITTLE THIEF	Feargal Sharkey (Virgin)
10	8	ALICE I WANT YOU JUST FOR ME!	Full Force (CBS)
6	9	HIT THAT PERFECT BEAT	Bronski Beat (Forbidden Fruit)
18	10	SYSTEM ADDICT	Five Star (Tent)
12	11	IT'S ALRIGHT (BABY'S COMIN' BACK)	Eurythmics (RCA)
8	12	WHO'S ZOOMIN' WHO?	Aretha Franklin (Arista)
14	13	SUSPICIOUS MINDS	Fine Young Cannibals (London)
-	14	BORDERLINE	Madonna (Sire)
11	15	RUSSIANS	Sting (A&M)
24	16	PULL UP TO THE BUMPER	Grace Jones (Island)
38	17	WHEN THE GOING GETS TOUGH, THE TOUGH GET GOING	Billy Ocean (Jive)
-	18	IN A LIFETIME	Clannad & Bono (RCA)
20	19	SPIRIT OF '76	Alarm (IRS)
23	20	PHANTOM OF THE OPERA	Sarah Brightman & Steve Harley (Polydor)
7	21	GIRLIE GIRLIE	Sophie George (Winner)
29	22	LIFE'S WHAT YOU MAKE IT	Talk Talk (EMI)
-	23	SANCTIFY YOURSELF	Simple Minds (Virgin)
16	24	LEAVING ME NOW	Level 42 (Polydor)
-	25	LIVING IN AMERICA	James Brown (Scotti Brothers)
15	26	RING OF ICE	Jennifer Rush (CBS)
-	27	HOW WILL I KNOW	Whitney Houston (Arista)
27	28	CUT ME DOWN	Lloyd Cole & the Commotions (Polydor)
35	29	IMAGINATION	Belouis Some (Parlophone)
28	30	SHAKE YOUR FOUNDATIONS	AC/DC (Atlantic)
25	31	DRESS YOU UP	Madonna (Sire)
36	32	IF I RULED THE WORLD	Kurtis Blow (Club)
-	33	SHOT IN THE DARK	Ozzy Osbourne (Epic)
40	34	ONE NATION	Masquerade (Streetwave)
-	35	I CAN'T WAIT	Stevie Nicks (Parlophone)
-	36	DON'T LET ME BE MISUNDERSTOOD	Elvis Costello (F.Beat)
37	37	FUNKY SENSATION	Ladies Choice (Sure Delight)
37	38	LEADER OF THE PACK	Twisted Sister (Atlantic)
-	39	CHAIN REACTION	Diana Ross (Capitol)
21	40	WRAP HER UP	Elton John (Rocket)
19	41	TORTURE	King (CBS)
-	42	IF YOU'RE READY (COME GO WITH ME)	Ruby Turner (Jive)
50	43	GIRLS ARE MORE FUN	Ray Parker Jr. (Arista)
26	44	WE BUILT THIS CITY	Starship (RCA)
-	45	RISE	Public Image Ltd. (Virgin)
-	46	THE PROMISE	Arcadia (Odeon)
22	47	SEPARATE LIVES	Phil Collins & Marilyn Martin (Virgin)
48	48	GLENN MILLER MEDLEY	John Anderson (Modern)
13	49	SAVING ALL MY LOVE FOR YOU	Whitney Houston (Arista)
-	50	SMALL BLUE THING	Suzanne Vega (A&M)

8 February 1986

last week	this week	title	artist (label)
1	1	THE SUN ALWAYS SHINES ON TV	A-ha (Warner Bros)
4	2	ONLY LOVE	Nana Mouskouri (Philips)
14	3	BORDERLINE	Madonna (Sire)
17	4	WHEN THE GOING GETS TOUGH, THE TOUGH GET GOING	Billy Ocean (Jive)
2	5	WALK OF LIFE	Dire Straits (Vertigo)
3	6	BROKEN WINGS	Mr. Mister (RCA)
10	7	SYSTEM ADDICT	Five Star (Tent)
13	8	SUSPICIOUS MINDS	Fine Young Cannibals (London)
23	9	SANCTIFY YOURSELF	Simple Minds (Virgin)
6	10	SATURDAY LOVE	Cherelle & Alexander O'Neal (Tabu)
7	11	YOU LITTLE THIEF	Feargal Sharkey (Virgin)
20	12	PHANTOM OF THE OPERA	Sarah Brightman & Steve Harley (Polydor)
16	13	PULL UP TO THE BUMPER	Grace Jones (Island)
8	14	ALICE I WANT YOU JUST FOR ME!	Full Force (CBS)
18	15	IN A LIFETIME	Clannad & Bono (RCA)
25	16	LIVING IN AMERICA	James Brown (Scotti Brothers)
5	17	WEST END GIRLS	Pet Shop Boys (Parlophone)
11	18	IT'S ALRIGHT (BABY'S COMIN' BACK)	Eurythmics (RCA)
22	19	LIFE'S WHAT YOU MAKE IT	Talk Talk (EMI)
33	20	SHOT IN THE DARK	Ozzy Osbourne (Epic)
-	21	MY MAGIC MAN	Rochelle (Warner Bros)
12	22	WHO'S ZOOMIN' WHO?	Aretha Franklin (Arista)
9	23	HIT THAT PERFECT BEAT	Bronski Beat (Forbidden Fruit)
27	24	HOW WILL I KNOW	Whitney Houston (Arista)
45	25	RISE	Public Image Ltd. (Virgin)
19	26	SPIRIT OF '76	Alarm (IRS)
29	27	IMAGINATION	Belouis Some (Parlophone)
-	28	ONE DANCE WON'T DO	Audrey Hall (Germain)
36	29	DON'T LET ME BE MISUNDERSTOOD	Elvis Costello (F.Beat)
-	30	ELOISE	Damned (MCA)
32	31	IF I RULED THE WORLD	Kurtis Blow (Club)
-	32	THE CAPTAIN OF HER HEART	Double (Polydor)
24	33	LEAVING ME NOW	Level 42 (Polydor)
15	34	RUSSIANS	Sting (A&M)
21	35	GIRLIE GIRLIE	Sophie George (Winner)
37	36	FUNKY SENSATION	Ladies Choice (Sure Delight)
42	37	IF YOU'RE READY (COME GO WITH ME)	Ruby Turner (Jive)
-	38	GIVING GROUND	Sisterhood
-	39	BABY LOVE	Regina (Funkin' Marvellous)
-	40	TURNING AWAY	Shakin' Stevens (Epic)
39	41	CHAIN REACTION	Diana Ross (Capitol)
26	42	RING OF ICE	Jennifer Rush (CBS)
46	43	THE PROMISE	Arcadia (Odeon)
47	44	SEPARATE LIVES	Phil Collins & Marilyn Martin (Virgin)
-	45	AND SHE WAS	Talking Heads (EMI)
-	46	BURNING HEART	Survivor (Scotti Brothers)
-	47	SMALL TOWN	John Cougar Mellencamp (Riva)
-	48	THE SWEETEST GIRL	Madness (Zarjazz)
-	49	JOHNNY JOHNNY	Prefab Sprout (Kitchenware)
28	50	CUT ME DOWN	Lloyd Cole & the Commotions (Polydor)

Norwegian trio A-ha made it two Number Ones in a row, while Dire Straits had their biggest single from the huge-selling *Brothers In Arms* album with *Walk Of Life*, which peaked at Two. Nana Mouskouri's unexpected chart appearance was due to *Only Love* being the theme to the TV mini-series *Mistral*, while Madonna's *Borderline* was a reissue of a previously unsuccesful 1984 single.

443

February – March 1986

15 February 1986

		Title	Artist (label)
4	1	WHEN THE GOING GETS TOUGH, THE TOUGH GET GOING	Billy Ocean (Jive)
3	2	BORDERLINE	Madonna (Sire)
1	3	THE SUN ALWAYS SHINES ON TV	A-ha (Warner Bros)
2	4	ONLY LOVE	Nana Mouskouri (Philips)
16	5	LIVING IN AMERICA	James Brown (Scotti Brothers)
7	6	SYSTEM ADDICT	Five Star (Tent)
12	7	PHANTOM OF THE OPERA	Sarah Brightman & Steve Harley (Polydor)
9	8	SANCTIFY YOURSELF	Simple Minds (Virgin)
5	9	WALK OF LIFE	Dire Straits (Vertigo)
8	10	SUSPICIOUS MINDS	Fine Young Cannibals (London)
32	11	THE CAPTAIN OF HER HEART	Double (Polydor)
6	12	BROKEN WINGS	Mr. Mister (RCA)
13	13	PULL UP TO THE BUMPER	Grace Jones (Island)
30	14	ELOISE	Damned (MCA)
10	15	SATURDAY LOVE	Cherelle & Alexander O'Neal (Tabu)
19	16	LIFE'S WHAT YOU MAKE IT	Talk Talk (EMI)
17	17	HOW WILL I KNOW	Whitney Houston (Arista)
25	18	RISE	Public Image Ltd. (Virgin)
20	19	SHOT IN THE DARK	Ozzy Osbourne (Epic)
15	20	IN A LIFETIME	Clannad & Bono (RCA)
11	21	YOU LITTLE THIEF	Feargal Sharkey (Virgin)
18	22	IT'S ALRIGHT (BABY'S COMIN' BACK)	Eurythmics (RCA)
31	23	IF I RULED THE WORLD	Kurtis Blow (Club)
27	24	IMAGINATION	Belouis Some (Parlophone)
21	25	MY MAGIC MAN	Rochelle (Warner Bros)
29	26	DON'T LET ME BE MISUNDERSTOOD	Costello (F.Beat)
46	27	BURNING HEART	Survivor (Scotti Brothers)
45	28	AND SHE WAS	Talking Heads (EMI)
41	29	CHAIN REACTION	Diana Ross (Capitol)
37	30	IF YOU'RE READY (COME GO WITH ME)	Ruby Turner (Jive)
-	31	RADIO AFRICA	Latin Quarter (Rockin' Horse)
14	32	ALICE I WANT YOU JUST FOR ME!	Full Force (CBS)
22	33	WHO'S ZOOMIN' WHO?	Aretha Franklin (Arista)
17	34	WEST END GIRLS	Pet Shop Boys (Parlophone)
28	35	ONE DANCE WON'T DO	Audrey Hall (Germain)
43	36	THE PROMISE	Arcadia (Odeon)
-	37	STARTING TOGETHER	Su Pollard (Rainbow)
-	38	SMOKIN' IN THE BOYS ROOM	Motley Crue (Elektra)
40	39	MY MAGIC MAN	Shakin' Stevens (Epic)
-	40	SIDEWALK TALK	Jellybean (EMI America)
-	41	DON'T WASTE MY TIME	Paul Hardcastle (Chrysalis)
23	42	HIT THAT PERFECT BEAT	Bronski Beat (Forbidden Fruit)
38	43	GIVING GROUND	Sisterhood (Merciful Release)
-	44	PAIN	Betty Wright (Cooltempo)
-	45	SOUL KISS	Olivia Newton-John
-	46	YEARS LATER	Cactus World News (MCA)
39	47	BABY LOVE	Regina (Funkin' Marvellous)
35	48	GIRLIE GIRLIE	Sophie George (Winner)
-	49	WASTELANDS	Midge Ure (Chrysalis)
48	50	THE SWEETEST GIRL	Madness (Zarjazz)

22 February 1986

		Title	Artist (label)
1	1	WHEN THE GOING GETS TOUGH, THE TOUGH GET GOING	Billy Ocean (Jive)
14	2	ELOISE	Damned (MCA)
3	3	BORDERLINE	Madonna (Sire)
5	4	LIVING IN AMERICA	James Brown (Scotti Brothers)
6	5	SYSTEM ADDICT	Five Star (Tent)
37	6	STARTING TOGETHER	Su Pollard (Rainbow)
11	7	THE CAPTAIN OF HER HEART	Double (Polydor)
3	8	THE SUN ALWAYS SHINES ON TV	A-ha (Warner Bros)
17	9	HOW WILL I KNOW	Whitney Houston (Arista)
18	10	RISE	Public Image Ltd. (Virgin)
29	11	ONLY LOVE	Nana Mouskouri (Philips)
27	12	CHAIN REACTION	Diana Ross (Capitol)
27	13	BURNING HEART	Survivor (Scotti Brothers)
7	14	PHANTOM OF THE OPERA	Sarah Brightman & Steve Harley (Polydor)
9	15	WALK OF LIFE	Dire Straits (Vertigo)
8	16	SANCTIFY YOURSELF	Simple Minds (Virgin)
13	17	PULL UP TO THE BUMPER	Grace Jones (Island)
28	18	AND SHE WAS	Talking Heads (EMI)
24	19	IMAGINATION	Belouis Some (Parlophone)
31	20	RADIO AFRICA	Latin Quarter (Rockin' Horse)
19	21	SHOT IN THE DARK	Ozzy Osbourne (Epic)
41	22	DON'T WASTE MY TIME	Paul Hardcastle (Chrysalis)
10	23	SUSPICIOUS MINDS	Fine Young Cannibals (London)
16	24	LIFE'S WHAT YOU MAKE IT	Talk Talk (EMI)
39	25	TURNING AWAY	Shakin' Stevens (Epic)
12	26	BROKEN WINGS	Mr. Mister (RCA)
-	27	MANIC MONDAY	Bangles (CBS)
21	28	YOU LITTLE THIEF	Feargal Sharkey (Virgin)
23	29	IF I RULED THE WORLD	Kurtis Blow (Club)
26	30	DON'T LET ME BE MISUNDERSTOOD	Elvis Costello (F.Beat)
30	31	IF YOU'RE READY (COME GO WITH ME)	Ruby Turner (Jive)
-	32	MOON OVER BOURBON STREET	Sting (A&M)
15	33	SATURDAY LOVE	Cherelle & Alexander O'Neal (Tabu)
20	34	IN A LIFETIME	Clannad & Bono (RCA)
22	35	IT'S ALRIGHT (BABY'S COMIN' BACK)	Eurythmics (RCA)
-	36	STRIPPED	Depeche Mode (Mute)
-	37	STAGES	ZZ Top (Warner Bros)
44	38	PAIN	Betty Wright (Cooltempo)
25	39	MY MAGIC MAN	Rochelle (Warner Bros)
35	40	ONE DANCE WON'T DO	Audrey Hall (Germain)
50	41	THE SWEETEST GIRL	Madness (Zarjazz)
-	42	IF YOU WERE HERE TONIGHT	Alexander O'Neal (Tabu)
-	43	I'M NOT GONNA LET YOU	Colonel Abrams (MCA)
-	44	HOLD ME	Teddy Pendergrass & Whitney Houston (Asylum)
-	45	SILENT RUNNING	Mike & the Mechanics (WEA)
33	46	WHO'S ZOOMIN' WHO?	Aretha Franklin (Arista)
36	47	THE PROMISE	Arcadia (Odeon)
38	48	SMOKIN' IN THE BOYS ROOM	Motley Crue (Elektra)
46	49	YEARS LATER	Cactus World News (MCA)
49	50	WASTELANDS	Midge Ure (Chrysalis)

1 March 1986

		Title	Artist (label)
1	1	WHEN THE GOING GETS TOUGH, THE TOUGH GET GOING	Billy Ocean (Jive)
6	2	STARTING TOGETHER	Su Pollard (Rainbow)
12	3	CHAIN REACTION	Diana Ross (Capitol)
2	4	ELOISE	Damned (MCA)
9	5	HOW WILL I KNOW	Whitney Houston (Arista)
13	6	BURNING HEART	Survivor (Scotti Brothers)
3	7	BORDERLINE	Madonna (Sire)
5	8	SYSTEM ADDICT	Five Star (Tent)
10	9	RISE	Public Image Ltd. (Virgin)
7	10	THE CAPTAIN OF HER HEART	Double (Polydor)
4	11	LIVING IN AMERICA	James Brown (Scotti Brothers)
11	12	ONLY LOVE	Nana Mouskouri (Philips)
12	13	DON'T WASTE MY TIME	Paul Hardcastle (Chrysalis)
20	14	RADIO AFRICA	Latin Quarter (Rockin' Horse)
36	15	STRIPPED	Depeche Mode (Mute)
15	16	WALK OF LIFE	Dire Straits (Vertigo)
27	17	MANIC MONDAY	Bangles (CBS)
25	18	TURNING AWAY	Shakin' Stevens (Epic)
18	19	AND SHE WAS	Talking Heads (EMI)
24	20	LIFE'S WHAT YOU MAKE IT	Talk Talk (EMI)
16	21	SANCTIFY YOURSELF	Simple Minds (Virgin)
8	22	THE SUN ALWAYS SHINES ON TV	A-ha (Warner Bros)
19	23	IMAGINATION	Belouis Some (Parlophone)
23	24	SUSPICIOUS MINDS	Fine Young Cannibals (London)
-	25	LOVE MISSILE F1-11	Sigue Sigue Sputnik (Parlophone)
14	26	PHANTOM OF THE OPERA	Sarah Brightman & Steve Harley (Polydor)
40	27	ONE DANCE WON'T DO	Audrey Hall (Germain)
-	28	LOVE IS THE DRUG	Grace Jones (Island)
39	29	MY MAGIC MAN	Rochelle (Warner Bros)
-	30	HOUNDS OF LOVE	Kate Bush (EMI)
31	31	NEW YORK NEW YORK	Frank Sinatra (Reprise)
41	32	THE SWEETEST GIRL	Madness (Zarjazz)
21	33	SHOT IN THE DARK	Ozzy Osbourne (Epic)
33	34	SATURDAY LOVE	Cherelle & Alexander O'Neal (Tabu)
-	35	HEAVEN MUST BE MISSING AN ANGEL	Tavares (Capitol)
26	36	BROKEN WINGS	Mr. Mister (RCA)
43	37	I'M NOT GONNA LET YOU	Colonel Abrams (MCA)
28	38	YOU LITTLE THIEF	Feargal Sharkey (Virgin)
-	39	THE POWER IS YOURS	Redskins (Decca)
-	40	ANOTHER NIGHT	Aretha Franklin (Arista)
38	41	PAIN	Betty Wright (Cooltempo)
-	42	LADIES	Mantronix (10)
-	43	HI HO SILVER	Jim Diamond (A&M)
34	44	IN A LIFETIME	Clannad & Bono (RCA)
31	45	IF YOU'RE READY (COME GO WITH ME)	Ruby Turner (Jive)
17	46	PULL UP TO THE BUMPER	Grace Jones (Island)
30	47	DON'T LET ME BE MISUNDERSTOOD	Elvis Costello (F.Beat)
-	48	THIS TIME	Bryan Adams (A&M)
32	49	MOON OVER BOURBON STREET	Sting (A&M)
37	50	STAGES	ZZ Top (Warner Bros)

Movie tie-ins once again made their presence heavily felt in the chart: Billy Ocean's chart-topper was the theme from the Michael Douglas/Kathleen Turner blockbuster *The Jewel Of The Nile*, while James Brown's *Living In America* – his all-time biggest UK success – was the theme from Sylvester Stallone's *Rocky 4*. Extraordinarily, former punks the Damned revived Barry Ryan's 1968 Number One.

8 March 1986

last week	this week		
1	1	WHEN THE GOING GETS TOUGH, THE TOUGH GET GOING	Billy Ocean (Jive)
3	2	CHAIN REACTION	Diana Ross (Capitol)
2	3	STARTING TOGETHER	Su Pollard (Rainbow)
4	4	ELOISE	Damned (MCA)
25	5	LOVE MISSILE F1-11	Sigue Sigue Sputnik (Parlophone)
5	6	HOW WILL I KNOW	Whitney Houston (Arista)
6	7	BURNING HEART	Survivor (Scotti Brothers)
17	8	MANIC MONDAY	Bangles (CBS)
13	9	DON'T WASTE MY TIME	Paul Hardcastle (Chrysalis)
9	10	RISE	Public Image Ltd. (Virgin)
15	11	STRIPPED	Depeche Mode (Mute)
19	12	AND SHE WAS	Talking Heads (EMI)
8	13	SYSTEM ADDICT	Five Star (Tent)
-	14	THE POWER OF LOVE/DO YOU BELIEVE IN LOVE	Huey Lewis & the News (Chrysalis)
7	15	BORDERLINE	Madonna (Sire)
30	16	HOUNDS OF LOVE	Kate Bush (EMI)
-	17	IF YOU WERE HERE TONIGHT	Alexander O'Neal (Tabu)
35	18	HEAVEN MUST BE MISSING AN ANGEL	Tavares (Capitol)
11	19	LIVING IN AMERICA	James Brown (Scotti Brothers)
14	20	RADIO AFRICA	Latin Quarter (Rockin' Horse)
31	21	NEW YORK NEW YORK	Frank Sinatra (Reprise)
10	22	THE CAPTAIN OF HER HEART	Double (Polydor)
18	23	TURNING AWAY	Shakin' Stevens (Epic)
22	24	THE SUN ALWAYS SHINES ON TV	A-ha (Warner Bros)
12	25	ONLY LOVE	Nana Mouskouri (Philips)
23	26	IMAGINATION	Belouis Some (Parlophone)
28	27	LOVE IS THE DRUG	Grace Jones (Island)
16	28	WALK OF LIFE	Dire Straits (Vertigo)
-	29	SUGAR FREE	Juicy (Epic)
-	30	GET UP I FEEL LIKE BEING A SEX MACHINE	James Brown (Boiling Point)
-	31	(NOTHIN' SERIOUS) JUST BUGGIN'	Whistle (Champion)
27	32	ONE DANCE WON'T DO	Audrey Hall (Germain)
39	33	THE POWER IS YOURS	Redskins (Decca)
42	34	LADIES	Mantronix (10)
37	35	I'M NOT GONNA LET YOU	Colonel Abrams (MCA)
36	36	BROKEN WINGS	Mr. Mister (RCA)
43	37	HI HO SILVER	Jim Diamond (A&M)
-	38	THE RIVER	Total Contrast (London)
-	39	ROCK ME TONIGHT	Freddie Jackson (Capitol)
48	40	THIS TIME	Bryan Adams (A&M)
21	41	SANCTIFY YOURSELF	Simple Minds (Virgin)
-	42	CALLING AMERICA	Electric Light Orchestra (Epic)
-	43	DIGGING YOUR SCENE	Blow Monkeys (RCA)
44	44	IN A LIFETIME	Clannad & Bono (RCA)
26	45	PHANTOM OF THE OPERA	Sarah Brightman & Steve Harley (Polydor)
-	46	FACES OF FREEDOM	Test Dept. (Ministry Of Power!)
-	47	UNDER A RAGING MOON	Roger Daltrey (10)
-	48	KISS	Prince (Paisley Park)
49	49	MOON OVER BOURBON STREET	Sting (A&M)
40	50	ANOTHER NIGHT	Aretha Franklin (Arista)

15 March 1986

2	1	CHAIN REACTION	Diana Ross (Capitol)
5	2	LOVE MISSILE F1-11	Sigue Sigue Sputnik (Parlophone)
8	3	MANIC MONDAY	Bangles (CBS)
1	4	WHEN THE GOING GETS TOUGH, THE TOUGH GET GOING	Billy Ocean (Jive)
3	5	STARTING TOGETHER	Su Pollard (Rainbow)
21	6	NEW YORK NEW YORK	Frank Sinatra (Reprise)
7	7	BURNING HEART	Survivor (Scotti Brothers)
14	8	THE POWER OF LOVE/DO YOU BELIEVE IN LOVE	Huey Lewis & the News (Chrysalis)
4	9	ELOISE	Damned (MCA)
9	10	DON'T WASTE MY TIME	Paul Hardcastle (Chrysalis)
6	11	HOW WILL I KNOW	Whitney Houston (Arista)
18	12	HEAVEN MUST BE MISSING AN ANGEL	Tavares (Capitol)
17	13	IF YOU WERE HERE TONIGHT	Alexander O'Neal (Tabu)
37	14	HI HO SILVER	Jim Diamond (A&M)
31	15	(NOTHIN' SERIOUS) JUST BUGGIN'	Whistle (Champion)
16	16	HOUNDS OF LOVE	Kate Bush (EMI)
-	17	ABSOLUTE BEGINNERS	David Bowie (Virgin)
10	18	RISE	Public Image Ltd. (Virgin)
12	19	AND SHE WAS	Talking Heads (EMI)
48	20	KISS	Prince (Paisley Park)
32	21	ONE DANCE WON'T DO	Audrey Hall (Germain)
11	22	STRIPPED	Depeche Mode (Mute)
-	23	HARLEM SHUFFLE	Rolling Stones (Rolling Stones)
43	24	DIGGING YOUR SCENE	Blow Monkeys (RCA)
19	25	LIVING IN AMERICA	James Brown (Scotti Brothers)
-	26	SILENT RUNNING	Mike & the Mechanics (WEA)
13	27	SYSTEM ADDICT	Five Star (Tent)
-	28	POGUETRY IN MOTION (EP)	Pogues (Stiff)
35	29	I'M NOT GONNA LET YOU	Colonel Abrams (MCA)
15	30	BORDERLINE	Madonna (Sire)
38	31	THE RIVER	Total Contrast (London)
-	32	MOVE AWAY	Culture Club (Virgin)
25	33	ONLY LOVE	Nana Mouskouri (Philips)
29	34	SUGAR FREE	Juicy (Epic)
22	35	THE CAPTAIN OF HER HEART	Double (Polydor)
-	36	KYRIE	Mr. Mister (RCA)
30	37	GET UP I FEEL LIKE BEING A SEX MACHINE	James Brown (Boiling Point)
-	38	TRUMPTON RIOTS	Half Man Half Biscuit
26	39	IMAGINATION	Belouis Some (Parlophone)
23	40	TURNING AWAY	Shakin' Stevens (Epic)
33	41	THE POWER IS YOURS	Redskins (Decca)
-	42	LOVE COMES QUICKLY	Pet Shop Boys (Parlophone)
-	43	CANDYMAN	Siouxsie & the Banshees (Wonderland)
27	44	LOVE IS THE DRUG	Grace Jones (Island)
-	45	THE HONEYTHIEF	Hipsway (Mercury)
-	46	NO ONE IS TO BLAME	Howard Jones (WEA)
39	47	ROCK ME TONIGHT	Freddie Jackson (Capitol)
-	48	OVERJOYED	Stevie Wonder (Motown)
47	49	UNDER A RAGING MOON	Roger Daltrey (10)
49	50	MOON OVER BOURBON STREET	Sting (A&M)

22 March 1986

1	1	CHAIN REACTION	Diana Ross (Capitol)
3	2	MANIC MONDAY	Bangles (CBS)
6	3	NEW YORK NEW YORK	Frank Sinatra (Reprise)
17	4	ABSOLUTE BEGINNERS	David Bowie (Virgin)
14	5	HI HO SILVER	Jim Diamond (A&M)
8	6	THE POWER OF LOVE/DO YOU BELIEVE IN LOVE	Huey Lewis & the News (Chrysalis)
2	7	LOVE MISSILE F1-11	Sigue Sigue Sputnik (Parlophone)
15	8	(NOTHIN' SERIOUS) JUST BUGGIN'	Whistle (Champion)
4	9	WHEN THE GOING GETS TOUGH, THE TOUGH GET GOING	Billy Ocean (Jive)
32	10	MOVE AWAY	Culture Club (Virgin)
36	11	KYRIE	Mr. Mister (RCA)
20	12	KISS	Prince (Paisley Park)
23	13	HARLEM SHUFFLE	Rolling Stones (Rolling Stones)
7	14	BURNING HEART	Survivor (Scotti Brothers)
11	15	HOW WILL I KNOW	Whitney Houston (Arista)
12	16	HEAVEN MUST BE MISSING AN ANGEL	Tavares (Capitol)
13	17	IF YOU WERE HERE TONIGHT	Alexander O'Neal (Tabu)
5	18	STARTING TOGETHER	Su Pollard (Rainbow)
24	19	DIGGING YOUR SCENE	Blow Monkeys (RCA)
10	20	DON'T WASTE MY TIME	Paul Hardcastle (Chrysalis)
26	21	SILENT RUNNING	Mike & the Mechanics (WEA)
46	22	NO ONE IS TO BLAME	Howard Jones (WEA)
45	23	THE HONEYTHIEF	Hipsway (Mercury)
16	24	HOUNDS OF LOVE	Kate Bush (EMI)
9	25	ELOISE	Damned (MCA)
-	26	LIVING DOLL	Cliff Richard and the Young Ones (WEA)
43	27	CANDYMAN	Siouxsie & the Banshees (Wonderland)
28	28	SHEEP	Housemartins (Go! Discs)
-	29	TOUCH ME (I WANT YOUR BODY)	Samantha Fox (Jive)
38	30	TRUMPTON RIOTS	Half Man Half Biscuit (Probe Plus)
42	31	LOVE COMES QUICKLY	Pet Shop Boys (Parlophone)
49	32	UNDER A RAGING MOON	Roger Daltrey (10)
-	33	YOU TO ME ARE EVERYTHING	Real Thing (PRT)
28	34	POGUETRY IN MOTION (EP)	Pogues (Stiff)
-	35	CALLING AMERICA	Electric Light Orchestra (Epic)
21	36	ONE DANCE WON'T DO	Audrey Hall (Germain)
19	37	AND SHE WAS	Talking Heads (EMI)
47	38	ROCK ME TONIGHT	Freddie Jackson (Capitol)
-	39	DARE TO DREAM	Viola Wills (Streetwave)
-	40	I CAN'T LET YOU GO	52nd Street (10)
-	41	LIVING IN ANOTHER WORLD	Talk Talk (EMI)
-	42	DON'T WANT TO KNOW IF YOU ARE LONELY	Husker Du (Warner Bros)
-	43	LOVE'S GONNA GET YOU	Jocelyn Brown (Warner Bros)
48	44	OVERJOYED	Stevie Wonder (Motown)
18	45	RISE	Public Image Ltd. (Virgin)
25	46	LIVING IN AMERICA	James Brown (Scotti Brothers)
29	47	I'M NOT GONNA LET YOU	Colonel Abrams (MCA)
44	48	LOVE IS THE DRUG	Grace Jones (Island)
-	49	SO MACHO	Sinitta (Fanfare)
-	50	DO WHAT I DO	John Taylor (Parlophone)

Like *Ghostbusters* a year before, Huey Lewis & The News' *Power Of Love* leapt back into contention once the film featuring it – Michael J Fox's *Back To The Future* – had general release here. This time, the song was a double A-side with another former US Top 10 hit for Lewis, *Do You Believe In Love?* The Bangles' debut hit *Manic Monday* was written by Prince, under the oblique pseudonym of 'Christopher'.

March – April 1986

last this week

29 March 1986

last	this		
4	1	ABSOLUTE BEGINNERS	David Bowie (Virgin)
1	2	CHAIN REACTION	Diana Ross (Capitol)
26	3	LIVING DOLL	Cliff Richard & the Young Ones (WEA)
2	4	MANIC MONDAY	Bangles (CBS)
12	5	KISS	Prince (Paisley Park)
5	6	HI HO SILVER	Jim Diamond (A&M)
10	7	MOVE AWAY	Culture Club (Virgin)
19	8	DIGGING YOUR SCENE	Blow Monkeys (RCA)
13	9	HARLEM SHUFFLE	Rolling Stones (Rolling Stones)
3	10	NEW YORK NEW YORK	Frank Sinatra (Reprise)
8	11	(NOTHIN' SERIOUS) JUST BUGGIN'	Whistle (Champion)
6	12	THE POWER OF LOVE/DO YOU BELIEVE IN LOVE	Huey Lewis & the News (Chrysalis)
7	13	LOVE MISSILE F1-11	Sigue Sigue Sputnik (Parlophone)
33	14	YOU TO ME ARE EVERYTHING	Real Thing (PRT)
22	15	NO ONE IS TO BLAME	Howard Jones (WEA)
11	16	KYRIE	Mr. Mister (RCA)
-	17	WONDERFUL WORLD	Sam Cooke (RCA)
9	18	WHEN THE GOING GETS TOUGH, THE TOUGH GET GOING	Billy Ocean (Jive)
23	19	THE HONEYTHIEF	Hipsway (Mercury)
29	20	TOUCH ME (I WANT YOUR BODY)	Samantha Fox (Jive)
38	21	ROCK ME TONIGHT	Freddie Jackson (Capitol)
-	22	PETER GUNN	Art of Noise & Duane Eddy (China)
31	23	LOVE COMES QUICKLY	Pet Shop Boys (Parlophone)
17	24	IF YOU WERE HERE TONIGHT	Alexander O'Neal (Tabu)
-	25	SHELL SHOCK	New Order (Factory)
-	26	A KIND OF MAGIC	Queen (EMI)
21	27	SILENT RUNNING	Mike & the Mechanics (WEA)
27	28	CANDYMAN	Siouxsie & the Banshees (Wonderland)
15	29	HOW WILL I KNOW	Whitney Houston (Arista)
34	30	POGUETRY IN MOTION (EP)	Pogues (Stiff)
14	31	BURNING HEART	Survivor (Scotti Brothers)
16	32	HEAVEN MUST BE MISSING AN ANGEL	Tavares (Capitol)
30	33	TRUMPTON RIOTS	Half Man Half Biscuit (Probe Plus)
-	34	HELLO DARLING	Tippa Irie (Greensleeves/UK Bubblers)
-	35	E=MC2	Big Audio Dynamite (CBS)
18	36	STARTING TOGETHER	Su Pollard (Rainbow)
39	37	DARE TO DREAM	Viola Wills (Streetwave)
49	38	SO MACHO	Sinitta (Fanfare)
44	39	OVERJOYED	Stevie Wonder (Motown)
-	40	SECRET LOVERS	Atlantic Starr (A&M)
40	41	I CAN'T LET YOU GO	52nd Street (10)
32	42	UNDER A RAGING MOON	Roger Daltrey (10)
20	43	DON'T WASTE MY TIME	Paul Hardcastle (Chrysalis)
35	44	CALLING AMERICA	Electric Light Orchestra (Epic)
36	45	ONE DANCE WON'T DO	Audrey Hall (Germain)
24	46	HOUNDS OF LOVE	Kate Bush (EMI)
-	47	ROCK ME AMADEUS	Falco (A&M)
-	48	MARLENA ON THE WALL	Suzanne Vega (A&M)
-	49	GALVESTON BAY	Lonnie Hill (10)
-	50	C'MON C'MON	Bronski Beat (Forbidden Fruit)

5 April 1986

last	this		
3	1	LIVING DOLL	Cliff Richard & the Young Ones (WEA)
1	2	ABSOLUTE BEGINNERS	David Bowie (Virgin)
17	3	WONDERFUL WORLD	Sam Cooke (RCA)
20	4	TOUCH ME (I WANT YOUR BODY)	Samantha Fox (Jive)
2	5	CHAIN REACTION	Diana Ross (Capitol)
14	6	YOU TO ME ARE EVERYTHING	Real Thing (PRT)
22	7	PETER GUNN	Art of Noise & Duane Eddy (China)
6	8	HI HO SILVER	Jim Diamond (A&M)
4	9	MANIC MONDAY	Bangles (CBS)
5	10	KISS	Prince (Paisley Park)
16	11	KYRIE	Mr. Mister (RCA)
7	12	MOVE AWAY	Culture Club (Virgin)
8	13	DIGGING YOUR SCENE	Blow Monkeys (RCA)
26	14	A KIND OF MAGIC	Queen (EMI)
9	15	HARLEM SHUFFLE	Rolling Stones (Rolling Stones)
11	16	(NOTHIN' SERIOUS) JUST BUGGIN'	Whistle (Champion)
-	17	A DIFFERENT CORNER	George Michael (Epic)
23	18	LOVE COMES QUICKLY	Pet Shop Boys (Parlophone)
13	19	LOVE MISSILE F1-11	Sigue Sigue Sputnik (Parlophone)
12	20	THE POWER OF LOVE/DO YOU BELIEVE IN LOVE	Huey Lewis & the News (Chrysalis)
15	21	NO ONE IS TO BLAME	Howard Jones (WEA)
25	22	SHELL SHOCK	New Order (Factory)
19	23	THE HONEYTHIEF	Hipsway (Mercury)
21	24	ROCK ME TONIGHT	Freddie Jackson (Capitol)
10	25	NEW YORK NEW YORK	Frank Sinatra (Reprise)
35	26	E=MC2	Big Audio Dynamite (CBS)
40	27	SECRET LOVERS	Atlantic Starr (A&M)
34	28	HELLO DARLING	Tippa Irie (Greensleeves/UK Bubblers)
47	29	ROCK ME AMADEUS	Falco (A&M)
39	30	OVERJOYED	Stevie Wonder (Motown)
18	31	WHEN THE GOING GETS TOUGH, THE TOUGH GET GOING	Billy Ocean (Jive)
-	32	HAVE YOU EVER HAD IT BLUE	Style Council (Polydor)
37	33	DARE TO DREAM	Viola Wills (Streetwave)
49	34	GALVESTON BAY	Lonnie Hill (10)
24	35	IF YOU WERE HERE TONIGHT	Alexander O'Neal (Tabu)
38	36	SO MACHO	Sinitta (Fanfare)
-	37	TRAIN OF THOUGHT	A-ha (Warner Bros)
-	38	IS YOUR LOVE STRONG ENOUGH?	Bryan Ferry (EG)
32	39	HEAVEN MUST BE MISSING AN ANGEL	Tavares (Capitol)
50	40	C'MON C'MON	Bronski Beat (Forbidden Fruit)
30	41	POGUETRY IN MOTION (EP)	Pogues (Stiff)
-	42	SOMEONE TO SOMEBODY	Feargal Sharkey (Virgin)
-	43	DO WHAT I DO	John Taylor (Parlophone)
-	44	STROLLIN' ON	Maxi Priest (10)
-	45	HIGH HORSE	Evelyn 'Champagne' King (RCA)
33	46	TRUMPTON RIOTS	Half Man Half Biscuit (Probe Plus)
28	47	CANDYMAN	Siouxsie & the Banshees (Wonderland)
42	48	UNDER A RAGING MOON	Roger Daltrey (10)
-	49	GODSTAR	Psychic TV (Temple)
-	50	WHAT HAVE YOU DONE FOR ME LATELY	Janet Jackson (A&M)

12 April 1986

last	this		
1	1	LIVING DOLL	Cliff Richard & the Young Ones (WEA)
3	2	WONDERFUL WORLD	Sam Cooke (RCA)
4	3	TOUCH ME (I WANT YOUR BODY)	Samantha Fox (Jive)
17	4	A DIFFERENT CORNER	George Michael (Epic)
6	5	YOU TO ME ARE EVERYTHING	Real Thing (PRT)
14	6	A KIND OF MAGIC	Queen (EMI)
2	7	ABSOLUTE BEGINNERS	David Bowie (Virgin)
5	8	CHAIN REACTION	Diana Ross (Capitol)
7	9	PETER GUNN	Art of Noise & Duane Eddy (China)
29	10	ROCK ME AMADEUS	Falco (A&M)
11	11	KYRIE	Mr. Mister (RCA)
10	12	KISS	Prince (Paisley Park)
8	13	HI HO SILVER	Jim Diamond (A&M)
27	14	SECRET LOVERS	Atlantic Starr (A&M)
12	15	MOVE AWAY	Culture Club (Virgin)
26	16	E=MC2	Big Audio Dynamite (CBS)
13	17	DIGGING YOUR SCENE	Blow Monkeys (RCA)
9	18	MANIC MONDAY	Bangles (CBS)
22	19	SHELL SHOCK	New Order (Factory)
30	20	OVERJOYED	Stevie Wonder (Motown)
15	21	HARLEM SHUFFLE	Rolling Stones (Rolling Stones)
18	22	LOVE COMES QUICKLY	Pet Shop Boys (Parlophone)
37	23	TRAIN OF THOUGHT	A-ha (Warner Bros)
32	24	HAVE YOU EVER HAD IT BLUE	Style Council (Polydor)
20	25	THE POWER OF LOVE/DO YOU BELIEVE IN LOVE	Huey Lewis & the News (Chrysalis)
28	26	HELLO DARLING	Tippa Irie (Greensleeves/UK Bubblers)
16	27	(NOTHIN' SERIOUS) JUST BUGGIN'	Whistle (Champion)
-	28	LOOK AWAY	Big Country (Mercury)
-	29	ALL THE THINGS SHE SAID	Simple Minds (Virgin)
-	30	THERE'LL BE SAD SONGS	Billy Ocean (Jive)
38	31	IS YOUR LOVE STRONG ENOUGH?	Bryan Ferry (EG)
40	32	C'MON C'MON	Bronski Beat (Forbidden Fruit)
21	33	NO ONE IS TO BLAME	Howard Jones (WEA)
39	34	HEAVEN MUST BE MISSING AN ANGEL	Tavares (Capitol)
34	35	GALVESTON BAY	Lonnie Hill (10)
25	36	NEW YORK NEW YORK	Frank Sinatra (Reprise)
-	37	THE FINEST	S.O.S. Band (Tabu)
33	38	DARE TO DREAM	Viola Wills (Streetwave)
24	39	ROCK ME TONIGHT	Freddie Jackson (Capitol)
23	40	THE HONEYTHIEF	Hipsway (Mercury)
-	41	FUNNY HOW LOVE CAN BE	Fine Young Cannibals (London)
36	42	SO MACHO	Sinitta (Fanfare)
19	43	LOVE MISSILE F1-11	Sigue Sigue Sputnik (Parlophone)
-	44	A BROKEN HEART CAN MEND	Alexander O'Neal (Tabu)
50	45	WHAT HAVE YOU DONE FOR ME LATELY	Janet Jackson (A&M)
-	46	THE THINGS THE LONELY DO	Amazulu (Island)
-	47	COME ON NORTHERN IRELAND	Northern Ireland World Cup Squad (Haxx)
48	48	UNDER A RAGING MOON	Roger Daltrey (10)
45	49	HIGH HORSE	Evelyn 'Champagne' King (RCA)
42	50	SOMEONE TO SOMEBODY	Feargal Sharkey (Virgin)

With the Comic Relief charity version of *Living Doll*, Cliff Richard became the second person (after Gerry Marsden) to perform on two different Number One versions of the same song, and the first ever to receive top billing on both. Hank Marvin, who had played guitar on the 1959 hit, obliged with a guitar solo on the new version, while the Young Ones added typically manic touches to the record.

April – May 1986

last week	this week	19 April 1986
1	1	LIVING DOLL Cliff Richard & the Young Ones (WEA)
4	2	A DIFFERENT CORNER George Michael (Epic)
10	3	ROCK ME AMADEUS Falco (A&M)
2	4	WONDERFUL WORLD Sam Cooke (RCA)
6	5	A KIND OF MAGIC Queen (EMI)
3	6	TOUCH ME (I WANT YOUR BODY) Samantha Fox (Jive)
5	7	YOU TO ME ARE EVERYTHING Real Thing (PRT)
23	8	TRAIN OF THOUGHT A-ha (Warner Bros)
16	9	E=MC2 Big Audio Dynamite (CBS)
9	10	PETER GUNN Art of Noise & Duane Eddy (China)
14	11	SECRET LOVERS Atlantic Starr (A&M)
24	12	HAVE YOU EVER HAD IT BLUE Style Council (Polydor)
28	13	LOOK AWAY Big Country (Mercury)
29	14	ALL THE THINGS SHE SAID Simple Minds (Virgin)
8	15	CHAIN REACTION Diana Ross (Capitol)
7	16	ABSOLUTE BEGINNERS David Bowie (Virgin)
13	17	HI HO SILVER Jim Diamond (A&M)
11	18	KYRIE Mr. Mister (RCA)
37	19	THE FINEST S.O.S. Band (Tabu)
18	20	MANIC MONDAY Bangles (CBS)
20	21	OVERJOYED Stevie Wonder (Motown)
17	22	DIGGING YOUR SCENE Blow Monkeys (RCA)
15	23	MOVE AWAY Culture Club (Virgin)
19	24	SHELL SHOCK New Order (Factory)
22	25	LOVE COMES QUICKLY Pet Shop Boys (Parlophone)
12	26	KISS Prince (Paisley Park)
26	27	HELLO DARLING Tippa Irie (Greensleeves/UK Bubblers)
30	28	THERE'LL BE SAD SONGS Billy Ocean (Jive)
42	29	SO MACHO Sinitta (Fanfare)
32	30	C'MON C'MON Bronski Beat (Forbidden Fruit)
-	31	CAN'T WAIT ANOTHER MINUTE Five Star (Tent)
-	32	GREATEST LOVE OF ALL Whitney Houston (Arista)
31	33	IS YOUR LOVE STRONG ENOUGH? Bryan Ferry (EG)
-	34	MARLENA ON THE WALL Suzanne Vega (A&M)
25	35	THE POWER OF LOVE/DO YOU BELIEVE IN LOVE Huey Lewis & the News (Chrysalis)
-	36	TENDER LOVE Force MD's (Tommy Boy)
38	37	DARE TO DREAM Viola Wills (Streetwave)
45	38	WHAT HAVE YOU DONE FOR ME LATELY Janet Jackson (A&M)
-	39	JUST SAY NO Grange Hill (BBC)
-	40	SOME PEOPLE Belouis Some (Parlophone)
-	41	AFTER ALL THESE YEARS Foster & Allen (Ritz)
32	42	NO ONE IS TO BLAME Howard Jones (WEA)
-	43	ROUGH BOY ZZ Top (Warner Bros)
-	44	STROLLIN' ON Maxi Priest (10)
-	45	DRIVING AWAY FROM HOME It's Immaterial (Siren)
-	46	PRISONER OF LOVE Millie Scott (Fourth & Broadway)
21	47	HARLEM SHUFFLE Rolling Stones (Rolling Stones)
41	48	FUNNY HOW LOVE CAN BE Fine Young Cannibals (London)
39	49	ROCK ME TONIGHT Freddie Jackson (Capitol)
-	50	WHY CAN'T THIS BE LOVE Van Halen (Warner Bros)

last	this	26 April 1986
2	1	A DIFFERENT CORNER George Michael (Epic)
3	2	ROCK ME AMADEUS Falco (A&M)
1	3	LIVING DOLL Cliff Richard & the Young Ones (WEA)
5	4	A KIND OF MAGIC Queen (EMI)
6	5	TOUCH ME (I WANT YOUR BODY) Samantha Fox (Jive)
14	6	ALL THE THINGS SHE SAID Simple Minds (Virgin)
4	7	WONDERFUL WORLD Sam Cooke (RCA)
13	8	LOOK AWAY Big Country (Mercury)
8	9	TRAIN OF THOUGHT A-ha (Warner Bros)
7	10	YOU TO ME ARE EVERYTHING Real Thing (PRT)
11	11	SECRET LOVERS Atlantic Starr (A&M)
9	12	E=MC2 Big Audio Dynamite (CBS)
31	13	CAN'T WAIT ANOTHER MINUTE Five Star (Tent)
39	14	JUST SAY NO Grange Hill (BBC)
19	15	THE FINEST S.O.S. Band (Tabu)
12	16	HAVE YOU EVER HAD IT BLUE Style Council (Polydor)
38	17	WHAT HAVE YOU DONE FOR ME LATELY Janet Jackson (A&M)
10	18	PETER GUNN Art of Noise & Duane Eddy (China)
30	19	C'MON C'MON Bronski Beat (Forbidden Fruit)
-	20	STARS Hear 'N' Aid (Vertigo)
15	21	CHAIN REACTION Diana Ross (Capitol)
45	22	DRIVING AWAY FROM HOME It's Immaterial (Siren)
-	23	LIVE TO TELL Madonna (Sire)
17	24	HI HO SILVER Jim Diamond (A&M)
33	25	IS YOUR LOVE STRONG ENOUGH? Bryan Ferry (EG)
-	26	A QUESTION OF LUST Depeche Mode (Mute)
34	27	MARLENA ON THE WALL Suzanne Vega (A&M)
16	28	ABSOLUTE BEGINNERS David Bowie (Virgin)
-	29	THIS IS LOVE Gary Numan (Numa)
18	30	KYRIE Mr. Mister (RCA)
27	31	HELLO DARLING Tippa Irie (Greensleeves/UK Bubblers)
32	32	YOU AND ME TONIGHT Aurra (10)
-	33	ALL AND ALL Joyce Sims (London)
-	34	SLEDGEHAMMER Peter Gabriel (Virgin)
21	35	OVERJOYED Stevie Wonder (Motown)
43	36	ROUGH BOY ZZ Top (Warner Bros)
-	37	I'LL KEEP ON LOVING YOU Princess (Supreme)
26	38	KISS Prince (Paisley Park)
22	39	DIGGING YOUR SCENE Blow Monkeys (RCA)
46	40	PRISONER OF LOVE Millie Scott (Fourth & Broadway)
29	41	SO MACHO Sinitta (Fanfare)
25	42	LOVE COMES QUICKLY Pet Shop Boys (Parlophone)
-	43	WE'VE GOT THE WHOLE WORLD AT OUR FEET England World Cup Squad 1986 (Columbia)
32	44	GREATEST LOVE OF ALL Whitney Houston (Arista)
24	45	SHELL SHOCK New Order (Factory)
44	46	STROLLIN' ON Maxi Priest (10)
50	47	WHY CAN'T THIS BE LOVE Van Halen (Warner Bros)
48	48	FUNNY HOW LOVE CAN BE Fine Young Cannibals (London)
20	49	MANIC MONDAY Bangles (CBS)
28	50	THERE'LL BE SAD SONGS Billy Ocean (Jive)

last	this	3 May 1986
1	1	A DIFFERENT CORNER George Michael (Epic)
2	2	ROCK ME AMADEUS Falco (A&M)
17	3	WHAT HAVE YOU DONE FOR ME LATELY Janet Jackson (A&M)
4	4	A KIND OF MAGIC Queen (EMI)
14	5	JUST SAY NO Grange Hill (BBC)
8	6	LOOK AWAY Big Country (Mercury)
23	7	LIVE TO TELL Madonna (Sire)
6	8	ALL THE THINGS SHE SAID Simple Minds (Virgin)
13	9	CAN'T WAIT ANOTHER MINUTE Five Star (Tent)
3	10	LIVING DOLL Cliff Richard & the Young Ones (WEA)
44	11	GREATEST LOVE OF ALL Whitney Houston (Arista)
5	12	TOUCH ME (I WANT YOUR BODY) Samantha Fox (Jive)
22	13	DRIVING AWAY FROM HOME It's Immaterial (Siren)
7	14	WONDERFUL WORLD Sam Cooke (RCA)
9	15	TRAIN OF THOUGHT A-ha (Warner Bros)
11	16	SECRET LOVERS Atlantic Starr (A&M)
10	17	YOU TO ME ARE EVERYTHING Real Thing (PRT)
12	18	E=MC2 Big Audio Dynamite (CBS)
27	19	MARLENA ON THE WALL Suzanne Vega (A&M)
15	20	THE FINEST S.O.S. Band (Tabu)
-	21	LESSONS IN LOVE Level 42 (Polydor)
32	22	YOU AND ME TONIGHT Aurra (10)
26	23	A QUESTION OF LUST Depeche Mode (Mute)
-	24	I HEARD IT THROUGH THE GRAPEVINE Marvin Gaye (Tamla Motown)
20	25	STARS Hear 'N' Aid (Vertigo)
16	26	HAVE YOU EVER HAD IT BLUE Style Council (Polydor)
-	27	KNIFE EDGE Alarm (IRS)
18	28	PETER GUNN Art of Noise & Duane Eddy (China)
34	29	SLEDGEHAMMER Peter Gabriel (Virgin)
19	30	C'MON C'MON Bronski Beat (Forbidden Fruit)
37	31	I'LL KEEP ON LOVING YOU Princess (Supreme)
33	32	ALL AND ALL Joyce Sims (London)
46	33	STROLLIN' ON Maxi Priest (10)
29	34	THIS IS LOVE Gary Numan (Numa)
21	35	CHAIN REACTION Diana Ross (Capitol)
25	36	IS YOUR LOVE STRONG ENOUGH? Bryan Ferry (EG)
-	37	BOYS DON'T CRY Cure (Fiction)
-	38	WORLDS APART Cactus World News (MCA)
-	39	ON MY OWN Patti LaBelle & Michael McDonald (MCA)
-	40	HOME Public Image Ltd. (Virgin)
-	41	IF YOU LEAVE Orchestral Manoeuvres In The Dark (Virgin)
42	42	IF SHE KNEW WHAT SHE WANTS Bangles (CBS)
-	43	HEADLINE NEWS William Bell (Absolute)
47	44	WHY CAN'T THIS BE LOVE Van Halen (Warner Bros)
40	45	PRISONER OF LOVE Millie Scott (Fourth & Broadway)
24	46	HI HO SILVER Jim Diamond (A&M)
-	47	YOUR LATEST TRICK Dire Straits (Vertigo)
-	48	DO FRIES GO WITH THAT SHAKE George Clinton (Capitol)
5	49	TENDER LOVE Force MD's (Tommy Boy)
-	50	A NIGHT TO REMEMBER Shalamar (MCA)

George Michael's *A Different Corner,* though recorded while Wham! were still together (and included on the duo's final album), was a solo project in all respects - as well as writing and singing the song, Michael also played all the instruments himself and produced the session, and the resulting record was unusual in having no drums or percussion in the arrangement.

447

May 1986

10 May 1986

last week	this week	Title	Artist (Label)
1	1	A DIFFERENT CORNER	George Michael (Epic)
2	2	ROCK ME AMADEUS	Falco (A&M)
3	3	WHAT HAVE YOU DONE FOR ME LATELY	Janet Jackson (A&M)
5	4	JUST SAY NO	Grange Hill (BBC)
7	5	LIVE TO TELL	Madonna (Sire)
9	6	CAN'T WAIT ANOTHER MINUTE	Five Star (Tent)
21	7	LESSONS IN LOVE	Level 42 (Polydor)
4	8	A KIND OF MAGIC	Queen (EMI)
24	9	I HEARD IT THROUGH THE GRAPEVINE	Marvin Gaye (Tamla Motown)
6	10	LOOK AWAY	Big Country (Mercury)
39	11	ON MY OWN	Patti LaBelle & Michael McDonald (MCA)
11	12	GREATEST LOVE OF ALL	Whitney Houston (Arista)
10	13	LIVING DOLL	Cliff Richard & the Young Ones (WEA)
22	14	YOU AND ME TONIGHT	Aurra (10)
13	15	DRIVING AWAY FROM HOME	It's Immaterial (Siren)
20	16	THE FINEST	S.O.S. Band (Tabu)
29	17	SLEDGEHAMMER	Peter Gabriel (Virgin)
8	18	ALL THE THINGS SHE SAID	Simple Minds (Virgin)
19	19	MARLENA ON THE WALL	Suzanne Vega (A&M)
12	20	TOUCH ME (I WANT YOUR BODY)	Samantha Fox (Jive)
16	21	SECRET LOVERS	Atlantic Starr (A&M)
25	22	STARS	Hear 'N' Aid (Vertigo)
23	23	I'LL KEEP ON LOVING YOU	Princess (Supreme)
15	24	TRAIN OF THOUGHT	A-ha (Warner Bros)
14	25	WONDERFUL WORLD	Sam Cooke (RCA)
32	26	ALL AND ALL	Joyce Sims (London)
-	27	THERE'LL BE SAD SONGS	Billy Ocean (Jive)
47	28	YOUR LATEST TRICK	Dire Straits (Vertigo)
23	29	A QUESTION OF LUST	Depeche Mode (Mute)
44	30	WHY CAN'T THIS BE LOVE	Van Halen (Warner Bros)
37	31	BOYS DON'T CRY	Cure (Fiction)
17	32	YOU TO ME ARE EVERYTHING	Real Thing (PRT)
42	33	IF SHE KNEW WHAT SHE WANTS	Bangles (CBS)
-	34	THE BIG SKY	Kate Bush (EMI)
-	35	EXPERIENCE	Diana Ross (Capitol)
-	36	ROUGH BOY	ZZ Top (Warner Bros)
45	37	PRISONER OF LOVE	Millie Scott (Fourth & Broadway)
49	38	TENDER LOVE	Force MD's (Tommy Boy)
26	39	HAVE YOU EVER HAD IT BLUE	Style Council (Polydor)
18	40	E=MC2	Big Audio Dynamite (CBS)
30	41	C'MON C'MON	Bronski Beat (Forbidden Fruit)
-	42	SOMETHING TO BELIEVE IN	Ramones (Beggars Banquet)
28	43	PETER GUNN	Art of Noise & Duane Eddy (China)
-	44	ROCK LOBSTER	B52's (Island)
-	45	HALLEY'S COMET	Chas & Dave (Rockney)
34	46	THIS IS LOVE	Gary Numan (Numa)
27	47	KNIFE EDGE	Alarm (IRS)
33	48	STROLLIN' ON	Maxi Priest (10)
48	49	DO FRIES GO WITH THAT SHAKE	George Clinton (Capitol)
40	50	HOME	Public Image Ltd. (Virgin)

17 May 1986

last week	this week	Title	Artist (Label)
2	1	ROCK ME AMADEUS	Falco (A&M)
11	2	ON MY OWN	Patti LaBelle & Michael McDonald (MCA)
5	3	LIVE TO TELL	Madonna (Sire)
3	4	WHAT HAVE YOU DONE FOR ME LATELY	Janet Jackson (A&M)
7	5	LESSONS IN LOVE	Level 42 (Polydor)
9	6	I HEARD IT THROUGH THE GRAPEVINE	Marvin Gaye (Tamla Motown)
-	7	THE CHICKEN SONG	Spitting Image (Virgin)
1	8	A DIFFERENT CORNER	George Michael (Epic)
6	9	CAN'T WAIT ANOTHER MINUTE	Five Star (Tent)
12	10	GREATEST LOVE OF ALL	Whitney Houston (Arista)
17	11	SLEDGEHAMMER	Peter Gabriel (Virgin)
10	12	LOOK AWAY	Big Country (Mercury)
8	13	A KIND OF MAGIC	Queen (EMI)
14	14	YOU AND ME TONIGHT	Aurra (10)
4	15	JUST SAY NO	Grange Hill (BBC)
30	16	WHY CAN'T THIS BE LOVE	Van Halen (Warner Bros)
26	17	ALL AND ALL	Joyce Sims (London)
31	18	BOYS DON'T CRY	Cure (Fiction)
23	19	I'LL KEEP ON LOVING YOU	Princess (Supreme)
21	20	SECRET LOVERS	Atlantic Starr (A&M)
16	21	THE FINEST	S.O.S. Band (Tabu)
44	22	YOUR LATEST TRICK	Dire Straits (Vertigo)
-	23	ROCK LOBSTER	B52's (Island)
13	24	LIVING DOLL	Cliff Richard & the Young Ones (WEA)
27	25	THERE'LL BE SAD SONGS	Billy Ocean (Jive)
-	26	SPIRIT IN THE SKY	Dr. & the Medics (IRS)
-	27	FUZZBOX (EP)	We've Got A Fuzzbox And We're Gonna Use It (Vindaloo)
18	28	ALL THE THINGS SHE SAID	Simple Minds (Virgin)
20	29	TOUCH ME (I WANT YOUR BODY)	Samantha Fox (Jive)
15	30	DRIVING AWAY FROM HOME	It's Immaterial (Siren)
29	31	A QUESTION OF LUST	Depeche Mode (Mute)
34	32	THE BIG SKY	Kate Bush (EMI)
25	33	WONDERFUL WORLD	Sam Cooke (RCA)
22	34	STARS	Hear 'N' Aid (Vertigo)
-	35	SNOOKER LOOPY	Matchroom Mob with Chas & Dave (Rockney)
24	36	TRAIN OF THOUGHT	A-ha (Warner Bros)
-	37	SITTING ON TOP OF THE WORLD	Liverpool FC (Columbia)
48	38	STROLLIN' ON	Maxi Priest (10)
33	39	IF SHE KNEW WHAT SHE WANTS	Bangles (CBS)
35	40	EXPERIENCE	Diana Ross (Capitol)
36	41	ROUGH BOY	ZZ Top (Warner Bros)
38	42	TENDER LOVE	Force MD's (Tommy Boy)
50	43	HOME	Public Image Ltd. (Virgin)
-	44	THE HEART OF ROCK AND ROLL	Huey Lewis & the News (Chrysalis)
45	45	HALLEY'S COMET	Chas & Dave (Rockney)
-	46	ESP	Hazell Dean (EMI)
-	47	WHAT ARE YOU GONNA DO ABOUT IT	Total Contrast (London)
-	48	BIG TRIP TO MEXICO	Scottish World Cup Team (Columbia)
-	49	A NIGHT TO REMEMBER	Shalamar (MCA)
19	50	MARLENA ON THE WALL	Suzanne Vega (A&M)

24 May 1986

last week	this week	Title	Artist (Label)
7	1	THE CHICKEN SONG	Spitting Image (Virgin)
2	2	ON MY OWN	Patti LaBelle & Michael McDonald (MCA)
5	3	LESSONS IN LOVE	Level 42 (Polydor)
11	4	SLEDGEHAMMER	Peter Gabriel (Virgin)
1	5	ROCK ME AMADEUS	Falco (A&M)
3	6	LIVE TO TELL	Madonna (Sire)
4	7	WHAT HAVE YOU DONE FOR ME LATELY	Janet Jackson (A&M)
10	8	GREATEST LOVE OF ALL	Whitney Houston (Arista)
6	9	I HEARD IT THROUGH THE GRAPEVINE	Marvin Gaye (Tamla Motown)
26	10	SPIRIT IN THE SKY	Dr. & the Medics (IRS)
9	11	CAN'T WAIT ANOTHER MINUTE	Five Star (Tent)
16	12	WHY CAN'T THIS BE LOVE	Van Halen (Warner Bros)
23	13	ROCK LOBSTER	B52's (Island)
17	14	ALL AND ALL	Joyce Sims (London)
8	15	A DIFFERENT CORNER	George Michael (Epic)
-	16	ROLLIN' HOME	Status Quo (Vertigo)
35	17	SNOOKER LOOPY	Matchroom Mob with Chas & Dave (Rockney)
25	18	THERE'LL BE SAD SONGS	Billy Ocean (Jive)
13	19	A KIND OF MAGIC	Queen (EMI)
14	20	YOU AND ME TONIGHT	Aurra (10)
18	21	BOYS DON'T CRY	Cure (Fiction)
19	22	I'LL KEEP ON LOVING YOU	Princess (Supreme)
-	23	WHO MADE WHO	AC/DC (Atlantic)
12	24	LOOK AWAY	Big Country (Mercury)
22	25	YOUR LATEST TRICK	Dire Straits (Vertigo)
27	26	FUZZBOX (EP)	We've Got A Fuzzbox And We're Gonna Use It (Vindaloo)
20	27	SECRET LOVERS	Atlantic Starr (A&M)
15	28	JUST SAY NO	Grange Hill (BBC)
42	29	TENDER LOVE	Force MD's (Tommy Boy)
21	30	THE FINEST	S.O.S. Band (Tabu)
41	31	ROUGH BOY	ZZ Top (Warner Bros)
-	32	ADDICTED TO LOVE	Robert Palmer (Island)
-	33	SINFUL	Pete Wylie (Eternal)
-	34	HUNGRY FOR HEAVEN	Dio (Vertigo)
32	35	THE BIG SKY	Kate Bush (EMI)
-	36	YOU CAN'T BLAME LOVE	Thomas & Taylor (Cooltempo)
-	37	LOVE TOUCH	Rod Stewart (Warner Bros)
-	38	BASSLINE	Mantronix (10)
-	39	IT CAN BE DONE	Redskins (Decca)
39	40	IF SHE KNEW WHAT SHE WANTS	Bangles (CBS)
-	41	THERE AIN'T NO SANITY CLAUSE	Damned (Big Beat)
-	42	WHAT YOU NEED	INXS (Mercury)
-	43	PRIVATE LIFE	Grace Jones (Island)
-	44	I CAN'T WAIT	Nu Shooz (Atlantic)
-	45	MINE ALL MINE	Cashflow (Club)
45	46	HALLEY'S COMET	Chas & Dave (Rockney)
28	47	ALL THE THINGS SHE SAID	Simple Minds (Virgin)
24	48	LIVING DOLL	Cliff Richard & the Young Ones (WEA)
37	49	SITTING ON TOP OF THE WORLD	Liverpool FC (Columbia)
33	50	WONDERFUL WORLD	Sam Cooke (RCA)

Marvin Gaye's posthumous return to the Top 10 with his 1969 chart-topper *I Heard It Through The Grapevine* was due to the song's use in a Levi Jeans commercal on TV. Many other oldies would have similar usage and major chart success in the next few years. *The Chicken Song* was also heard first on TV, the record being a spin-off from the savage latex-likeness satirical comedy show *Spitting Image*.

31 May 1986

last week	this week		
1	1	THE CHICKEN SONG	Spitting Image (Virgin)
3	2	LESSONS IN LOVE	Level 42 (Polydor)
2	3	ON MY OWN	Patti LaBelle & Michael McDonald (MCA)
4	4	SLEDGEHAMMER	Peter Gabriel (Virgin)
10	5	SPIRIT IN THE SKY	Dr. & the Medics (IRS)
16	6	ROLLIN' HOME	Status Quo (Vertigo)
12	7	WHY CAN'T THIS BE LOVE	Van Halen (Warner Bros)
13	8	ROCK LOBSTER	B52's (Island)
32	9	ADDICTED TO LOVE	Robert Palmer (Island)
17	10	SNOOKER LOOPY	Matchroom Mob with Chas & Dave (Rockney)
5	11	ROCK ME AMADEUS	Falco (A&M)
18	12	THERE'LL BE SAD SONGS	Billy Ocean (Jive)
-	13	HOLDING BACK THE YEARS	Simply Red (WEA)
6	14	LIVE TO TELL	Madonna (Sire)
8	15	GREATEST LOVE OF ALL	Whitney Houston (Arista)
14	16	ALL AND ALL	Joyce Sims (London)
7	17	WHAT HAVE YOU DONE FOR ME LATELY	Janet Jackson (A&M)
11	18	CAN'T WAIT ANOTHER MINUTE	Five Star (Tent)
23	19	WHO MADE WHO	AC/DC (Atlantic)
-	20	SET ME FREE	Jaki Graham (EMI)
31	21	ROUGH BOY	ZZ Top (Warner Bros)
45	22	MINE ALL MINE	Cashflow (Club)
33	23	SINFUL	Pete Wylie (Eternal)
21	24	BOYS DON'T CRY	Cure (Fiction)
37	25	LOVE TOUCH	Rod Stewart (Warner Bros)
9	26	I HEARD IT THROUGH THE GRAPEVINE	Marvin Gaye (Tamla Motown)
38	27	BASSLINE	Mantronix (10)
-	28	INVISIBLE TOUCH	Genesis (Virgin)
44	29	I CAN'T WAIT	Nu Shooz (Atlantic)
20	30	YOU AND ME TONIGHT	Aurra (10)
-	31	BIG MOUTH STRIKES AGAIN	Smiths (Rough Trade)
22	32	I'LL KEEP ON LOVING YOU	Princess (Supreme)
26	33	FUZZBOX (EP)	We've Got A Fuzzbox And We're Gonna Use It (Vindaloo)
15	34	A DIFFERENT CORNER	George Michael (Epic)
29	35	TENDER LOVE	Force MD's (Tommy Boy)
35	36	THE BIG SKY	Kate Bush (EMI)
-	37	SERPENT'S KISS	Mission (Chapter 22)
41	38	THERE AIN'T NO SANITY CLAUSE	Damned (Big Beat)
-	39	BAD BOY	Miami Sound Machine (Epic)
40	40	IF SHE KNEW WHAT SHE WANTS	Bangles (CBS)
-	41	TIME	Freddie Mercury (EMI)
-	42	COMPUTER LOVE	Zapp Band (Warner Bros)
-	43	CAN'T GET BY WITHOUT YOU	Real Thing (PRT)
39	44	IT CAN BE DONE	Redskins (Decca)
24	45	LOOK AWAY	Big Country (Mercury)
19	46	A KIND OF MAGIC	Queen (EMI)
34	47	HUNGRY FOR HEAVEN	Dio (Vertigo)
36	48	YOU CAN'T BLAME LOVE	Thomas & Taylor (Cooltempo)
43	49	PRIVATE LIFE	Grace Jones (Island)
25	50	YOUR LATEST TRICK	Dire Straits (Vertigo)

7 June 1986

last week	this week		
5	1	SPIRIT IN THE SKY	Dr. & the Medics (IRS)
4	2	SLEDGEHAMMER	Peter Gabriel (Virgin)
1	3	THE CHICKEN SONG	Spitting Image (Virgin)
3	4	ON MY OWN	Patti LaBelle & Michael McDonald (MCA)
2	5	LESSONS IN LOVE	Level 42 (Polydor)
13	6	HOLDING BACK THE YEARS	Simply Red (WEA)
9	7	ADDICTED TO LOVE	Robert Palmer (Island)
7	8	WHY CAN'T THIS BE LOVE	Van Halen (Warner Bros)
-	9	EVERYBODY WANTS TO RUN THE WORLD	Tears For Fears (Mercury)
20	10	SET ME FREE	Jaki Graham (EMI)
6	11	ROLLIN' HOME	Status Quo (Vertigo)
19	12	WHO MADE WHO	AC/DC (Atlantic)
8	13	ROCK LOBSTER	B52's (Island)
23	14	SINFUL	Pete Wylie (Eternal)
10	15	SNOOKER LOOPY	Matchroom Mob with Chas & Dave (Rockney)
12	16	THERE'LL BE SAD SONGS	Billy Ocean (Jive)
28	17	INVISIBLE TOUCH	Genesis (Virgin)
31	18	BIG MOUTH STRIKES AGAIN	Smiths (Rough Trade)
22	19	MINE ALL MINE	Cashflow (Club)
29	20	I CAN'T WAIT	Nu Shooz (Atlantic)
43	21	CAN'T GET BY WITHOUT YOU	Real Thing (PRT)
25	22	LOVE TOUCH	Rod Stewart (Warner Bros)
39	23	BAD BOY	Miami Sound Machine (Epic)
15	24	GREATEST LOVE OF ALL	Whitney Houston (Arista)
41	25	TIME	Freddie Mercury (EMI)
-	26	OPPORTUNITIES	Pet Shop Boys (Parlophone)
14	27	LIVE TO TELL	Madonna (Sire)
16	28	ALL AND ALL	Joyce Sims (London)
11	29	ROCK ME AMADEUS	Falco (A&M)
-	30	VIENNA CALLING	Falco (A&M)
-	31	NASTY	Janet Jackson (A&M)
-	32	21ST CENTURY BOY	Sigue Sigue Sputnik (Parlophone)
-	33	DISENCHANTED	Communards (London)
37	34	SERPENT'S KISS	Mission (Chapter 22)
18	35	CAN'T WAIT ANOTHER MINUTE	Five Star (Tent)
24	36	BOYS DON'T CRY	Cure (Fiction)
26	37	I HEARD IT THROUGH THE GRAPEVINE	Marvin Gaye (Tamla Motown)
33	38	FUZZBOX (EP)	We've Got A Fuzzbox And We're Gonna Use It (Vindaloo)
-	39	ONE HIT TO THE BODY	Rolling Stones (Rolling Stones)
27	40	BASSLINE	Mantronix (10)
21	41	ROUGH BOY	ZZ Top (Warner Bros)
-	42	SWEET BIRD OF YOUTH	The The (Some Bizzare)
43	43	ON THE BEACH	Chris Rea (Magnet)
49	44	PRIVATE LIFE	Grace Jones (Island)
46	45	A KIND OF MAGIC	Queen (EMI)
42	46	COMPUTER LOVE	Zapp Band (Warner Bros)
32	47	I'LL KEEP ON LOVING YOU	Princess (Supreme)
-	48	GOD THANK YOU WOMAN	Culture Club (Virgin)
-	49	JUMP BACK	Dhar Braxton (Fourth & Broadway)
-	50	DANCING IN THE STREET	Matt Bianco (WEA)

14 June 1986

last week	this week		
1	1	SPIRIT IN THE SKY	Dr. & the Medics (IRS)
6	2	HOLDING BACK THE YEARS	Simply Red (WEA)
2	3	SLEDGEHAMMER	Peter Gabriel (Virgin)
9	4	EVERYBODY WANTS TO RUN THE WORLD	Tears For Fears (Mercury)
7	5	ADDICTED TO LOVE	Robert Palmer (Island)
3	6	THE CHICKEN SONG	Spitting Image (Virgin)
5	7	LESSONS IN LOVE	Level 42 (Polydor)
4	8	ON MY OWN	Patti LaBelle & Michael McDonald (MCA)
20	9	I CAN'T WAIT	Nu Shooz (Atlantic)
10	10	SET ME FREE	Jaki Graham (EMI)
14	11	SINFUL	Pete Wylie (Eternal)
21	12	CAN'T GET BY WITHOUT YOU	Real Thing (PRT)
17	13	INVISIBLE TOUCH	Genesis (Virgin)
30	14	VIENNA CALLING	Falco (A&M)
26	15	OPPORTUNITIES	Pet Shop Boys (Parlophone)
8	16	WHY CAN'T THIS BE LOVE	Van Halen (Warner Bros)
18	17	BIG MOUTH STRIKES AGAIN	Smiths (Rough Trade)
19	18	MINE ALL MINE	Cashflow (Club)
32	19	21ST CENTURY BOY	Sigue Sigue Sputnik (Parlophone)
16	20	THERE'LL BE SAD SONGS	Billy Ocean (Jive)
23	21	BAD BOY	Miami Sound Machine (Epic)
15	22	SNOOKER LOOPY	Matchroom Mob with Chas & Dave (Rockney)
-	23	MEDICINE SHOW	Big Audio Dynamite (CBS)
11	24	ROLLIN' HOME	Status Quo (Vertigo)
31	25	NASTY	Janet Jackson (A&M)
12	26	WHO MADE WHO	AC/DC (Atlantic)
-	27	TOO GOOD TO BE FORGOTTEN	Amazulu (Island)
13	28	ROCK LOBSTER	B52's (Island)
33	29	DISENCHANTED	Communards (London)
-	30	HUNTING HIGH AND LOW	A-ha (Warner Bros)
-	31	MY FAVOURITE WASTE OF TIME	Owen Paul (Epic)
34	32	SERPENT'S KISS	Mission (Chapter 22)
-	33	CALL OF THE WILD	Midge Ure (Chrysalis)
22	34	LOVE TOUCH	Rod Stewart (Warner Bros)
48	35	GOD THANK YOU WOMAN	Culture Club (Virgin)
-	36	HEARTACHE	Gene Loves Jezebel (Beggars Banquet)
-	37	VENUS	Bananarama (London)
-	38	LEFT OF CENTRE	Suzanne Vega (A&M)
-	39	JUNCTION SIGNAL	Blyth Power (All The Madmen)
-	40	MOUNTAINS	Prince (Paisley Park)
-	41	AMITYVILLE (THE HOUSE ON THE HILL)	Lovebug Starski (Epic)
28	42	ALL AND ALL	Joyce Sims (London)
49	43	JUMP BACK	Dhar Braxton (Fourth & Broadway)
35	44	CAN'T WAIT ANOTHER MINUTE	Five Star (Tent)
25	45	TIME	Freddie Mercury (EMI)
27	46	LIVE TO TELL	Madonna (Sire)
43	47	ON THE BEACH	Chris Rea (Magnet)
29	48	ROCK ME AMADEUS	Falco (A&M)
-	49	ALL I NEED IS A MIRACLE	Mike & the Mechanics (WEA)
-	50	NEW BEGINNING	Bucks Fizz (Polydor)

Spirit In The Sky became one of the still select number of songs to have two different Number One versions, with 16 years between Norman Greenbaum's original and the UK revival by Dr. & the Medics. *Everybody Wants To Run The World* by Tears For Fears was a rather different kind of revival – essentially their chart-topper of the previous year, with slightly amended lyrics for its charity cause.

June – July 1986

Wham!'s final Number One hit *The Edge Of Heaven* reached the chart top as the duo played a farewell concert to a packed Wembley Stadium, prior to going their separate ways. David Bowie's *Underground*, meanwhile, was a song from the fantasy film *Labyrinth*, in which he played the part of the Goblin King, while Falco became the first Austrian to have two successive UK Top 10 hits!

12 July 1986

last week	this week		
5	1	PAPA DON'T PREACH	Madonna (Sire)
2	2	HAPPY HOUR	Housemartins (Go! Discs)
1	3	THE EDGE OF HEAVEN	Wham! (Epic)
6	4	MY FAVOURITE WASTE OF TIME	Owen Paul (Epic)
4	5	TOO GOOD TO BE FORGOTTEN	Amazulu (Island)
3	6	I CAN'T WAIT	Nu Shooz (Atlantic)
12	7	VENUS	Bananarama (London)
9	8	NEW BEGINNING	Bucks Fizz (Polydor)
17	9	DO YA DO YA (WANNA PLEASE ME)	Samantha Fox (Jive)
8	10	HUNTING HIGH AND LOW	A-ha (Warner Bros)
14	11	FRIENDS WILL BE FRIENDS	Queen (EMI)
20	12	HEADLINES	Midnight Star (Solar)
16	13	CAN'T GET BY WITHOUT YOU	Real Thing (PRT)
24	14	BANG ZOOM LET'S GO-GO	Real Roxanne (Cooltempo)
13	15	AMITYVILLE (THE HOUSE ON THE HILL)	Lovebug Starski (Epic)
7	16	SPIRIT IN THE SKY	Dr. & the Medics (IRS)
10	17	HOLDING BACK THE YEARS	Simply Red (WEA)
31	18	LET'S GO ALL THE WAY	Sly Fox (Capitol)
15	19	UNDERGROUND	David Bowie (EMI America)
26	20	PARANOIMIA	Art of Noise & Max Headroom (China)
25	21	IT'S 'ORRIBLE BEING IN LOVE	Claire & Friends (BBC)
11	22	ADDICTED TO LOVE	Robert Palmer (Island)
19	23	BAD BOY	Miami Sound Machine (Epic)
36	24	BRILLIANT MIND	Furniture (Stiff)
30	25	I CAN'T STOP	Gary Numan (Numa)
38	26	NASTY	Janet Jackson (A&M)
27	27	LEVI STUBBS' TEARS	Billy Bragg (Go! Discs)
18	28	SLEDGEHAMMER	Peter Gabriel (Virgin)
-	29	HIGHER LOVE	Steve Winwood (Island)
21	30	VIENNA CALLING	Falco (A&M)
-	31	CAMOUFLAGE	Stan Ridgway (IRS)
22	32	THE TEACHER	Big Country (Mercury)
-	33	TELL ME TOMORROW	Princess (Supreme)
41	34	LEFT OF CENTRE	Suzanne Vega (A&M)
-	35	THE PROMISE YOU MADE	Cock Robin (CBS)
-	36	EVERY BEAT OF MY HEART	Rod Stewart (Warner Bros)
48	37	ON MY OWN	Patti LaBelle & Michael McDonald (MCA)
34	38	WHEN TOMORROW COMES	Eurythmics (RCA)
37	39	ROSES	Haywoode (CBS)
46	40	GOING DOWN TO LIVERPOOL	Bangles (CBS)
44	41	DON'T LET LOVE GET YOU DOWN	Archie Bell & the Drells (Portrait)
-	42	BORROWED LOVE	S.O.S. Band (Tabu)
35	43	SERPENT'S KISS	Mission (Chapter 22)
27	44	INVISIBLE TOUCH	Genesis (Virgin)
23	45	OPPORTUNITIES	Pet Shop Boys (Parlophone)
32	46	JUMP BACK	Dhar Braxton (Fourth & Broadway)
33	47	DEAF FOREVER	Motorhead (GWR)
-	48	SET FIRE TO ME	Willie Colon (A&M)
-	49	DREAMS	Van Halen (Warner Bros)
-	50	SING OUR OWN SONG	UB40 (DEP International)

19 July 1986

1	1	PAPA DON'T PREACH	Madonna (Sire)
3	2	THE EDGE OF HEAVEN	Wham! (Epic)
2	3	HAPPY HOUR	Housemartins (Go! Discs)
4	4	MY FAVOURITE WASTE OF TIME	Owen Paul (Epic)
18	5	LET'S GO ALL THE WAY	Sly Fox (Capitol)
5	6	TOO GOOD TO BE FORGOTTEN	Amazulu (Island)
9	7	DO YA DO YA (WANNA PLEASE ME)	Samantha Fox (Jive)
7	8	VENUS	Bananarama (London)
6	9	I CAN'T WAIT	Nu Shooz (Atlantic)
14	10	BANG ZOOM LET'S GO-GO	Real Roxanne (Cooltempo)
36	11	EVERY BEAT OF MY HEART	Rod Stewart (Warner Bros)
8	12	NEW BEGINNING	Bucks Fizz (Polydor)
10	13	HUNTING HIGH AND LOW	A-ha (Warner Bros)
50	14	SING OUR OWN SONG	UB40 (DEP International)
20	15	PARANOIMIA	Art of Noise & Max Headroom (China)
12	16	HEADLINES	Midnight Star (Solar)
21	17	IT'S 'ORRIBLE BEING IN LOVE	Claire & Friends (BBC)
29	18	HIGHER LOVE	Steve Winwood (Island)
13	19	CAN'T GET BY WITHOUT YOU	Real Thing (PRT)
11	20	FRIENDS WILL BE FRIENDS	Queen (EMI)
16	21	SPIRIT IN THE SKY	Dr. & the Medics (IRS)
39	22	ROSES	Haywoode (CBS)
-	23	THE LADY IN RED	Chris De Burgh (A&M)
22	24	ADDICTED TO LOVE	Robert Palmer (Island)
31	25	CAMOUFLAGE	Stan Ridgway (IRS)
27	26	LEVI STUBBS' TEARS	Billy Bragg (Go! Discs)
23	27	BAD BOY	Miami Sound Machine (Epic)
43	28	SERPENT'S KISS	Mission (Chapter 22)
17	29	HOLDING BACK THE YEARS	Simply Red (WEA)
15	30	AMITYVILLE (THE HOUSE ON THE HILL)	Lovebug Starski (Epic)
19	31	UNDERGROUND	David Bowie (EMI America)
24	32	BRILLIANT MIND	Furniture (Stiff)
48	33	SET FIRE TO ME	Willie Colon (A&M)
41	34	DON'T LET LOVE GET YOU DOWN	Archie Bell & the Drells (Portrait)
35	35	THE PROMISE YOU MADE	Cock Robin (CBS)
33	36	TELL ME TOMORROW	Princess (Supreme)
37	37	I CAN'T STOP	Gary Numan (Numa)
34	38	LEFT OF CENTRE	Suzanne Vega (A&M)
26	39	NASTY	Janet Jackson (A&M)
28	40	SLEDGEHAMMER	Peter Gabriel (Virgin)
-	41	SMILE	Audrey Hall (Germain)
-	42	LISTEN LIKE THIEVES	INXS (Mercury)
-	43	LOVE OF A LIFETIME	Chaka Khan (Warner Bros)
45	44	OPPORTUNITIES	Pet Shop Boys (Parlophone)
49	45	DREAMS	Van Halen (Warner Bros)
-	46	ROCKIN' WITH RITA	Vindaloo Summer Special (Vindaloo)
-	47	(SOLUTION) TO THE PROBLEM	Masquerade (Streetwave)
-	48	MY ADIDAS	Run DMC (London)
-	49	THE SINGER	Nick Cave (Mute)
-	50	IVORY TOWER	Van Morrison (Mercury)

26 July 1986

1	1	PAPA DON'T PREACH	Madonna (Sire)
11	2	EVERY BEAT OF MY HEART	Rod Stewart (Warner Bros)
5	3	LET'S GO ALL THE WAY	Sly Fox (Capitol)
14	4	SING OUR OWN SONG UB40	(DEP International)
23	5	THE LADY IN RED	Chris De Burgh (A&M)
4	6	MY FAVOURITE WASTE OF TIME	Owen Paul (Epic)
2	7	THE EDGE OF HEAVEN	Wham! (Epic)
8	8	VENUS	Bananarama (London)
3	9	HAPPY HOUR	Housemartins (Go! Discs)
18	10	HIGHER LOVE	Steve Winwood (Island)
6	11	TOO GOOD TO BE FORGOTTEN	Amazulu (Island)
10	12	BANG ZOOM LET'S GO-GO	Real Roxanne (Cooltempo)
15	13	PARANOIMIA	Art of Noise & Max Headroom (China)
25	14	CAMOUFLAGE	Stan Ridgway (IRS)
22	15	ROSES	Haywoode (CBS)
7	16	DO YA DO YA (WANNA PLEASE ME)	Samantha Fox (Jive)
9	17	I CAN'T WAIT	Nu Shooz (Atlantic)
-	18	I DIDN'T MEAN TO TURN YOU ON	Robert Palmer (Island)
12	19	NEW BEGINNING	Bucks Fizz (Polydor)
17	20	IT'S 'ORRIBLE BEING IN LOVE	Claire & Friends (BBC)
-	21	WHAT'S THE COLOUR OF MONEY?	Hollywood Beyond (WEA)
16	22	HEADLINES	Midnight Star (Solar)
41	23	SMILE	Audrey Hall (Germain)
32	24	BRILLIANT MIND	Furniture (Stiff)
20	25	FRIENDS WILL BE FRIENDS	Queen (EMI)
19	26	CAN'T GET BY WITHOUT YOU	Real Thing (PRT)
29	27	HOLDING BACK THE YEARS	Simply Red (WEA)
36	28	TELL ME TOMORROW	Princess (Supreme)
13	29	HUNTING HIGH AND LOW	A-ha (Warner Bros)
-	30	SO MACHO	Sinitta (Fanfare)
-	31	AIN'T NOTHIN' GOIN' ON BUT THE RENT	Gwen Guthrie (Boiling Point)
-	32	SOME CANDY TALKING	Jesus & Mary Chain (blanco y negro)
46	33	ROCKIN' WITH RITA	Vindaloo Summer Special (Vindaloo)
-	34	GARDEN OF DELIGHT/LIKE A HURRICANE	Mission (Chapter 22)
33	35	SET FIRE TO ME	Willie Colon (A&M)
26	36	LEVI STUBBS' TEARS	Billy Bragg (Go! Discs)
38	37	LEFT OF CENTRE	Suzanne Vega (A&M)
24	38	ADDICTED TO LOVE	Robert Palmer (Island)
42	39	LISTEN LIKE THIEVES	INXS (Mercury)
40	40	SLEDGEHAMMER	Peter Gabriel (Virgin)
34	41	DON'T LET LOVE GET YOU DOWN	Archie Bell & the Drells (Portrait)
45	42	DREAMS	Van Halen (Warner Bros)
-	43	PRESS	Paul McCartney (Parlophone)
-	44	THE FLAME	Arcadia (Odeon)
21	45	SPIRIT IN THE SKY	Dr. & the Medics (IRS)
35	46	THE PROMISE YOU MADE	Cock Robin (CBS)
47	47	MY ADIDAS	Run DMC (London)
48	48	SUN STREET	Katrina & the Waves (Capitol)
-	49	DANCING ON THE CEILING	Lionel Richie (Motown)
-	50	BORROWED LOVE	S.O.S. Band (Tabu)

Bananarama's *Venus* was a dance-beat revival of Shocking Blue's 1970 hit. Like the Dutch group's original version, it was a solid Top 10 hit in Britain, but went one better in the US by topping the chart and selling over a million. Billy Bragg's *Levi Stubbs' Tears* referred to the lead singer of the Four Tops, while Claire & Friends were a group of pre-teen kids who had found fame on BBC Saturday morning TV.

August 1986

2 August 1986

last week	this week	title	artist (label)
5	1	THE LADY IN RED	Chris De Burgh (A&M)
1	2	PAPA DON'T PREACH	Madonna (Sire)
2	3	EVERY BEAT OF MY HEART	Rod Stewart (Warner Bros)
3	4	LET'S GO ALL THE WAY	Sly Fox (Capitol)
4	5	SING OUR OWN SONG	UB40 (DEP International)
14	6	CAMOUFLAGE	Stan Ridgway (IRS)
21	7	WHAT'S THE COLOUR OF MONEY?	Hollywood Beyond (WEA)
18	8	I DIDN'T MEAN TO TURN YOU ON	Robert Palmer (Island)
32	9	SOME CANDY TALKING	Jesus & Mary Chain (blanco y negro)
10	10	HIGHER LOVE	Steve Winwood (Island)
30	11	SO MACHO	Sinitta (Fanfare)
6	12	MY FAVOURITE WASTE OF TIME	Owen Paul (Epic)
9	13	HAPPY HOUR	Housemartins (Go! Discs)
15	14	ROSES	Haywoode (CBS)
-	15	FIND THE TIME	Five Star (Tent)
8	16	VENUS	Bananarama (London)
23	17	SMILE	Audrey Hall (Germain)
12	18	BANG ZOOM LET'S GO-GO	Real Roxanne (Cooltempo)
7	19	THE EDGE OF HEAVEN	Wham! (Epic)
31	20	AIN'T NOTHIN' GOIN' ON BUT THE RENT	Gwen Guthrie (Boiling Point)
-	21	FIGHT FOR OURSELVES	Spandau Ballet (Reformation)
13	22	PARANOIMIA	Art of Noise & Max Headroom (China)
11	23	TOO GOOD TO BE FORGOTTEN	Amazulu (Island)
43	24	PRESS	Paul McCartney (Parlophone)
-	25	PANIC	Smiths (Rough Trade)
49	26	DANCING ON THE CEILING	Lionel Richie (Motown)
-	27	RED SKY	Status Quo (Vertigo)
34	28	GARDEN OF DELIGHT/LIKE A HURRICANE	Mission (Chapter 22)
-	29	UNDERSTANDING JANE	Icicle Works (Beggars Banquet)
-	30	POINT OF NO RETURN	Nu Shooz (Atlantic)
22	31	HEADLINES	Midnight Star (Solar)
16	32	DO YA DO YA (WANNA PLEASE ME)	Samantha Fox (Jive)
24	33	BRILLIANT MIND	Furniture (Stiff)
33	34	ROCKIN' WITH RITA	Vindaloo Summer Special (Vindaloo)
46	35	THE PROMISE YOU MADE	Cock Robin (CBS)
48	36	SUN STREET	Katrina & the Waves (Capitol)
-	37	I WANT TO WAKE UP WITH YOU	Boris Gardiner (Revue)
25	38	FRIENDS WILL BE FRIENDS	Queen (EMI)
-	39	SHOUT	Lulu & the Luvvers (Jive/Decca)
20	40	IT'S 'ORRIBLE BEING IN LOVE	Claire & Friends (BBC)
-	41	LOVE KILLS	Joe Strummer (CBS)
47	42	MY ADIDAS	Run DMC (London)
-	43	ED'S FUNKY DINER	It's Immaterial (Siren)
-	44	CALLING ALL THE HEROES	It Bites (Virgin)
40	45	SLEDGEHAMMER	Peter Gabriel (Virgin)
37	46	LEFT OF CENTRE	Suzanne Vega (A&M)
35	47	SET FIRE TO ME	Willie Colon (A&M)
41	48	DON'T LET LOVE GET YOU DOWN	Archie Bell & the Drells (Portrait)
42	49	DREAMS	Van Halen (Warner Bros)
44	50	THE FLAME	Arcadia (Odeon)

9 August 1986

last week	this week	title	artist (label)
1	1	THE LADY IN RED	Chris De Burgh (A&M)
2	2	PAPA DON'T PREACH	Madonna (Sire)
4	3	LET'S GO ALL THE WAY	Sly Fox (Capitol)
6	4	CAMOUFLAGE	Stan Ridgway (IRS)
11	5	SO MACHO	Sinitta (Fanfare)
3	6	EVERY BEAT OF MY HEART	Rod Stewart (Warner Bros)
8	7	I DIDN'T MEAN TO TURN YOU ON	Robert Palmer (Island)
7	8	WHAT'S THE COLOUR OF MONEY?	Hollywood Beyond (WEA)
5	9	SING OUR OWN SONG	UB40 (DEP International)
15	10	FIND THE TIME	Five Star (Tent)
14	11	ROSES	Haywoode (CBS)
9	12	SOME CANDY TALKING	Jesus & Mary Chain (blanco y negro)
25	13	PANIC	Smiths (Rough Trade)
21	14	FIGHT FOR OURSELVES	Spandau Ballet (Reformation)
17	15	SMILE	Audrey Hall (Germain)
27	16	RED SKY	Status Quo (Vertigo)
20	17	AIN'T NOTHIN' GOIN' ON BUT THE RENT	Gwen Guthrie (Boiling Point)
37	18	I WANT TO WAKE UP WITH YOU	Boris Gardiner (Revue)
12	19	MY FAVOURITE WASTE OF TIME	Owen Paul (Epic)
26	20	DANCING ON THE CEILING	Lionel Richie (Motown)
13	21	HAPPY HOUR	Housemartins (Go! Discs)
39	22	SHOUT	Lulu & the Luvvers (Jive/Decca)
10	23	HIGHER LOVE	Steve Winwood (Island)
16	24	VENUS	Bananarama (London)
18	25	BANG ZOOM LET'S GO-GO	Real Roxanne (Cooltempo)
36	26	SUN STREET	Katrina & the Waves (Capitol)
-	27	THE WAY IT IS	Bruce Hornsby & the Range (RCA)
28	28	GARDEN OF DELIGHT/LIKE A HURRICANE	Mission (Chapter 22)
24	29	PRESS	Paul McCartney (Parlophone)
-	30	PRETTY IN PINK	Psychedelic Furs (CBS)
19	31	THE EDGE OF HEAVEN	Wham! (Epic)
-	32	HEARTLAND	The The (Some Bizzare)
22	33	PARANOIMIA	Art of Noise & Max Headroom (China)
44	34	CALLING ALL THE HEROES	It Bites (Virgin)
-	35	OH PEOPLE	Patti LaBelle (MCA)
23	36	TOO GOOD TO BE FORGOTTEN	Amazulu (Island)
-	37	CAN YOU FEEL THE FORCE?	Real Thing (PRT)
34	38	ROCKIN' WITH RITA	Vindaloo Summer Special (Vindaloo)
-	39	DREAMTIME	Daryl Hall (RCA)
-	40	OPEN UP THE RED BOX	Simply Red (WEA)
-	41	BURN	Dr. & the Medics (IRS)
35	42	THE PROMISE YOU MADE	Cock Robin (CBS)
43	43	LOVE KILLS	Joe Strummer (CBS)
-	44	THE ULTIMATE SIN	Ozzy Osbourne (Epic)
29	45	UNDERSTANDING JANE	Icicle Works (Beggars Banquet)
-	46	GOLDRUSH	Yello (Mercury)
-	47	I CAN PROVE IT	Phil Fearon & Galaxy (Ensign)
-	48	CRUMMY STUFF	Ramones (Beggars Banquet)
33	49	BRILLIANT MIND	Furniture (Stiff)
31	50	HEADLINES	Midnight Star (Solar)

16 August 1986

last week	this week	title	artist (label)
1	1	THE LADY IN RED	Chris De Burgh (A&M)
5	2	SO MACHO	Sinitta (Fanfare)
18	3	I WANT TO WAKE UP WITH YOU	Boris Gardiner (Revue)
2	4	PAPA DON'T PREACH	Madonna (Sire)
4	5	CAMOUFLAGE	Stan Ridgway (IRS)
3	6	LET'S GO ALL THE WAY	Sly Fox (Capitol)
13	7	PANIC	Smiths (Rough Trade)
10	8	FIND THE TIME	Five Star (Tent)
8	9	WHAT'S THE COLOUR OF MONEY?	Hollywood Beyond (WEA)
17	10	AIN'T NOTHIN' GOIN' ON BUT THE RENT	Gwen Guthrie (Boiling Point)
6	11	EVERY BEAT OF MY HEART	Rod Stewart (Warner Bros)
22	12	SHOUT	Lulu & the Luvvers (Jive/Decca)
-	13	ANYONE CAN FALL IN LOVE	Anita Dobson (BBC)
14	14	FIGHT FOR OURSELVES	Spandau Ballet (Reformation)
9	15	SING OUR OWN SONG	UB40 (DEP International)
16	16	RED SKY	Status Quo (Vertigo)
7	17	I DIDN'T MEAN TO TURN YOU ON	Robert Palmer (Island)
34	18	CALLING ALL THE HEROES	It Bites (Virgin)
12	19	SOME CANDY TALKING	Jesus & Mary Chain (blanco y negro)
11	20	ROSES	Haywoode (CBS)
15	21	SMILE	Audrey Hall (Germain)
26	22	SUN STREET	Katrina & the Waves (Capitol)
20	23	DANCING ON THE CEILING	Lionel Richie (Motown)
29	24	PRESS	Paul McCartney (Parlophone)
28	25	GARDEN OF DELIGHT/LIKE A HURRICANE	Mission (Chapter 22)
27	26	THE WAY IT IS	Bruce Hornsby & the Range (RCA)
32	27	HEARTLAND	The The (Some Bizzare)
41	28	BURN	Dr. & the Medics (IRS)
30	29	PRETTY IN PINK	Psychedelic Furs (CBS)
19	30	MY FAVOURITE WASTE OF TIME	Owen Paul (Epic)
47	31	I CAN PROVE IT	Phil Fearon & Galaxy (Ensign)
21	32	HAPPY HOUR	Housemartins (Go! Discs)
-	33	TAKING THE VEIL	David Sylvian (Virgin)
-	34	GLORY OF LOVE	Peter Cetera (Full Moon)
31	35	THE EDGE OF HEAVEN	Wham! (Epic)
24	36	VENUS	Bananarama (London)
35	37	OH PEOPLE	Patti LaBelle (MCA)
44	38	THE ULTIMATE SIN	Ozzy Osbourne (Epic)
-	39	YOU GIVE LOVE A BAD NAME	Bon Jovi (Vertigo)
-	40	BREAKING AWAY	Jaki Graham (EMI)
39	41	DREAMTIME	Daryl Hall (RCA)
23	42	HIGHER LOVE	Steve Winwood (Island)
-	43	WHEN I THINK OF YOU	Janet Jackson (A&M)
43	44	LOVE KILLS	Joe Strummer (CBS)
-	45	FOOL'S PARADISE	Meli'sa Morgan (Capitol)
46	46	SOWETO	Jeffrey Osborne (A&M)
-	47	GOLDRUSH	Yello (Mercury)
40	48	OPEN UP THE RED BOX	Simply Red (WEA)
25	49	BANG ZOOM LET'S GO-GO	Real Roxanne (Cooltempo)
45	50	UNDERSTANDING JANE	Icicle Works (Beggars Banquet)

Lulu's first-ever hit *Shout*, from 1964 – always a perennial mobile disco favourite – became the latest oldie to gain re-admittance to the big time after she recorded a new, updated version for Jive Records. Decca promptly re-promoted the still-on-catalogue original, and both versions proceeded to sell equally well, sales on each being combined in chart calculations to send Lulu back into the Top 10.

August – September 1986

23 August 1986

last week	this week	Title	Artist (Label)
3	1	I WANT TO WAKE UP WITH YOU	Boris Gardiner (Revue)
1	2	THE LADY IN RED	Chris De Burgh (A&M)
2	3	SO MACHO	Sinitta (Fanfare)
13	4	ANYONE CAN FALL IN LOVE	Anita Dobson (BBC)
10	5	AIN'T NOTHIN' GOIN' ON BUT THE RENT	Gwen Guthrie (Boiling Point)
18	6	CALLING ALL THE HEROES	It Bites (Virgin)
12	7	SHOUT	Lulu & the Luvvers (Jive/Decca)
8	8	FIND THE TIME	Five Star (Tent)
4	9	PAPA DON'T PREACH	Madonna (Sire)
5	10	CAMOUFLAGE	Stan Ridgway (IRS)
7	11	PANIC	Smiths (Rough Trade)
-	12	GIRLS AND BOYS	Prince (Paisley Park)
31	13	I CAN PROVE IT	Phil Fearon & Galaxy (Ensign)
9	14	WHAT'S THE COLOUR OF MONEY?	Hollywood Beyond (WEA)
23	15	DANCING ON THE CEILING	Lionel Richie (Motown)
17	16	I DIDN'T MEAN TO TURN YOU ON	Robert Palmer (Island)
16	17	RED SKY	Status Quo (Vertigo)
11	18	EVERY BEAT OF MY HEART	Rod Stewart (Warner Bros)
6	19	LET'S GO ALL THE WAY	Sly Fox (Capitol)
-	20	BROTHER LOUIE	Modern Talking (RCA)
14	21	FIGHT FOR OURSELVES	Spandau Ballet (Reformation)
40	22	BREAKING AWAY	Jaki Graham (EMI)
-	23	HUMAN	Human League (Virgin)
43	24	WHEN I THINK OF YOU	Janet Jackson (A&M)
-	25	NICE IN NICE	Stranglers (Epic)
34	26	GLORY OF LOVE	Peter Cetera (Full Moon)
-	27	CAN YOU FEEL THE FORCE?	Real Thing (PRT)
-	28	ADORATIONS	Killing Joke (EG)
26	29	THE WAY IT IS	Bruce Hornsby & the Range (RCA)
37	30	OH PEOPLE	Patti LaBelle (MCA)
-	31	WE DON'T HAVE TO	Jermaine Stewart (10)
24	32	PRESS	Paul McCartney (Parlophone)
39	33	YOU GIVE LOVE A BAD NAME	Bon Jovi (Vertigo)
45	34	FOOL'S PARADISE	Meli'sa Morgan (Capitol)
27	35	HEARTLAND	The The (Some Bizzare)
20	36	ROSES	Haywoode (CBS)
41	37	DREAMTIME	Daryl Hall (RCA)
36	38	VENUS	Bananarama (London)
21	39	SMILE	Audrey Hall (Germain)
22	40	SUN STREET	Katrina & the Waves (Capitol)
15	41	SING OUR OWN SONG	UB40 (DEP International)
-	42	BAND OF THE HAND	Bob Dylan & the Heartbreakers (MCA)
33	43	TAKING THE VEIL	David Sylvian (Virgin)
28	44	BURN	Dr. & the Medics (IRS)
25	45	GARDEN OF DELIGHT/LIKE A HURRICANE	Mission (Chapter 22)
29	46	PRETTY IN PINK	Psychedelic Furs (CBS)
19	47	SOME CANDY TALKING	Jesus & Mary Chain (blanco y negro)
-	48	DON'T LEAVE ME THIS WAY	Communards (London)
-	49	TYPICAL MALE	Tina Turner (Capitol)
-	50	KISSES IN THE MOONLIGHT	George Benson (Warner Bros)

30 August 1986

last week	this week	Title	Artist (Label)
1	1	I WANT TO WAKE UP WITH YOU	Boris Gardiner (Revue)
2	2	THE LADY IN RED	Chris De Burgh (A&M)
3	3	SO MACHO	Sinitta (Fanfare)
5	4	AIN'T NOTHIN' GOIN' ON BUT THE RENT	Gwen Guthrie (Boiling Point)
4	5	ANYONE CAN FALL IN LOVE	Anita Dobson (BBC)
6	6	CALLING ALL THE HEROES	It Bites (Virgin)
13	7	I CAN PROVE IT	Phil Fearon & Galaxy (Ensign)
15	8	DANCING ON THE CEILING	Lionel Richie (Motown)
12	9	GIRLS AND BOYS	Prince (Paisley Park)
20	10	BROTHER LOUIE	Modern Talking (RCA)
23	11	HUMAN	Human League (Virgin)
10	12	CAMOUFLAGE	Stan Ridgway (IRS)
7	13	SHOUT	Lulu & the Luvvers (Jive/Decca)
26	14	GLORY OF LOVE	Peter Cetera (Full Moon)
22	15	BREAKING AWAY	Jaki Graham (EMI)
31	16	WE DON'T HAVE TO	Jermaine Stewart (10)
11	17	PANIC	Smiths (Rough Trade)
-	18	A QUESTION OF TIME	Depeche Mode (Mute)
48	19	DON'T LEAVE ME THIS WAY	Communards (London)
9	20	PAPA DON'T PREACH	Madonna (Sire)
8	21	FIND THE TIME	Five Star (Tent)
24	22	WHEN I THINK OF YOU	Janet Jackson (A&M)
29	23	THE WAY IT IS	Bruce Hornsby & the Range (RCA)
25	24	NICE IN NICE	Stranglers (Epic)
33	25	YOU GIVE LOVE A BAD NAME	Bon Jovi (Vertigo)
35	26	HEARTLAND	The The (Some Bizzare)
14	27	WHAT'S THE COLOUR OF MONEY?	Hollywood Beyond (WEA)
49	28	TYPICAL MALE	Tina Turner (Capitol)
37	29	DREAMTIME	Daryl Hall (RCA)
-	30	LOVE CAN'T TURN AROUND	Farley 'Jackmaster' Funk (D.J. International)
19	31	LET'S GO ALL THE WAY	Sly Fox (Capitol)
28	32	ADORATIONS	Killing Joke (EG)
34	33	FOOL'S PARADISE	Meli'sa Morgan (Capitol)
46	34	PRETTY IN PINK	Psychedelic Furs (CBS)
21	35	FIGHT FOR OURSELVES	Spandau Ballet (Reformation)
16	36	I DIDN'T MEAN TO TURN YOU ON	Robert Palmer (Island)
44	37	BURN	Dr. & the Medics (IRS)
27	38	CAN YOU FEEL THE FORCE?	Real Thing (PRT)
-	39	HAUNTED	Pogues (MCA)
-	40	TOKYO STORM WARNING	Elvis Costello (Imp)
32	41	PRESS	Paul McCartney (Parlophone)
-	42	YOU SHOOK ME ALL NIGHT LONG	AC/DC (Atlantic)
43	43	TAKING THE VEIL	David Sylvian (Virgin)
17	44	RED SKY	Status Quo (Vertigo)
18	45	EVERY BEAT OF MY HEART	Rod Stewart (Warner Bros)
-	46	AUTOMATIC	Millie Scott (Fourth & Broadway)
39	47	SMILE	Audrey Hall (Germain)
42	48	BAND OF THE HAND	Bob Dylan & the Heartbreakers (MCA)
-	49	DUOTONES	Kenny G (Arista)
-	50	COME ON HOME	Everything But The Girl (blanco y negro)

6 September 1986

last week	this week	Title	Artist (Label)
1	1	I WANT TO WAKE UP WITH YOU	Boris Gardiner (Revue)
10	2	BROTHER LOUIE	Modern Talking (RCA)
19	3	DON'T LEAVE ME THIS WAY	Communards (London)
2	4	THE LADY IN RED	Chris De Burgh (A&M)
3	5	SO MACHO	Sinitta (Fanfare)
11	6	HUMAN	Human League (Virgin)
14	7	GLORY OF LOVE	Peter Cetera (Full Moon)
16	8	WE DON'T HAVE TO	Jermaine Stewart (10)
6	9	CALLING ALL THE HEROES	It Bites (Virgin)
5	10	ANYONE CAN FALL IN LOVE	Anita Dobson (BBC)
4	11	AIN'T NOTHIN' GOIN' ON BUT THE RENT	Gwen Guthrie (Boiling Point)
9	12	GIRLS AND BOYS	Prince (Paisley Park)
8	13	DANCING ON THE CEILING	Lionel Richie (Motown)
22	14	WHEN I THINK OF YOU	Janet Jackson (A&M)
18	15	A QUESTION OF TIME	Depeche Mode (Mute)
7	16	I CAN PROVE IT	Phil Fearon & Galaxy (Ensign)
23	17	THE WAY IT IS	Bruce Hornsby & the Range (RCA)
25	18	YOU GIVE LOVE A BAD NAME	Bon Jovi (Vertigo)
30	19	LOVE CAN'T TURN AROUND	Farley 'Jackmaster' Funk (D.J. International)
24	20	NICE IN NICE	Stranglers (Epic)
-	21	RAGE HARD	Frankie Goes To Hollywood (ZTT)
15	22	BREAKING AWAY	Jaki Graham (EMI)
12	23	CAMOUFLAGE	Stan Ridgway (IRS)
13	24	PANIC	Smiths (Rough Trade)
25	25	SHOUT	Lulu & the Luvvers (Jive/Decca)
26	26	HEARTLAND	The The (Some Bizzare)
-	27	(I JUST) DIED IN YOUR ARMS	Cutting Crew (Siren)
20	28	PAPA DON'T PREACH	Madonna (Sire)
-	29	IN TOO DEEP	Genesis (Virgin)
29	30	DREAMTIME	Daryl Hall (RCA)
34	31	PRETTY IN PINK	Psychedelic Furs (CBS)
21	32	FIND THE TIME	Five Star (Tent)
-	33	OH PEOPLE	Patti LaBelle (MCA)
-	34	WASTED YEARS	Iron Maiden (EMI)
42	35	YOU SHOOK ME ALL NIGHT LONG	AC/DC (Atlantic)
-	36	STUCK WITH YOU	Huey Lewis & the News (Chrysalis)
-	37	HOLIDAY RAP	MC Miker 'G' & Deejay Sven (Debut)
28	38	TYPICAL MALE	Tina Turner (Capitol)
39	39	HAUNTED	Pogues (MCA)
32	40	ADORATIONS	Killing Joke (EG)
40	41	TOKYO STORM WARNING	Elvis Costello (Imp)
35	42	FIGHT FOR OURSELVES	Spandau Ballet (Reformation)
27	43	WHAT'S THE COLOUR OF MONEY?	Hollywood Beyond (WEA)
45	44	EVERY BEAT OF MY HEART	Rod Stewart (Warner Bros)
-	45	IF PUSH COMES TO A SHOVE	Sly Fox (Capitol)
-	46	DEAR BOOPSIE	Pam Hall (Bluemountain)
47	47	BURN	Dr. & the Medics (IRS)
36	48	I DIDN'T MEAN TO TURN YOU ON	Robert Palmer (Island)
-	49	ROCK'N'ROLL MERCENARIES	Meat Loaf & John Parr (Arista)
33	50	FOOL'S PARADISE	Meli'sa Morgan (Capitol)

Reggae hits had become rare and reggae Number Ones unknown by 1986, but Boris Gardiner's *I Want To Wake Up With You*, over 16 years after his original chart success with *Elizabethan Reggae*, was sufficiently a mainstream romantic song, and sufficiently commercial, to break the mould. Anita Dobson's hit, meanwhile, was a vocal version of the theme from TV's *East Enders*, in which she starred.

September 1986

13 September 1986

last	this	title	artist
3	1	DON'T LEAVE ME THIS WAY	Communards (London)
1	2	I WANT TO WAKE UP WITH YOU	Boris Gardiner (Revue)
8	3	WE DON'T HAVE TO	Jermaine Stewart (10)
2	4	BROTHER LOUIE	Modern Talking (RCA)
6	5	HUMAN	Human League (Virgin)
21	6	RAGE HARD Frankie Goes To Hollywood (ZTT)	
7	7	GLORY OF LOVE	Peter Cetera (Full Moon)
5	8	SO MACHO	Sinitta (Fanfare)
14	9	WHEN I THINK OF YOU	Janet Jackson (A&M)
27	10	(I JUST) DIED IN YOUR ARMS	Cutting Crew (Siren)
19	11	LOVE CAN'T TURN AROUND	Farley 'Jackmaster' Funk (D.J. International)
4	12	THE LADY IN RED	Chris De Burgh (A&M)
17	13	THE WAY IT IS	Bruce Hornsby & the Range (RCA)
12	14	GIRLS AND BOYS	Prince (Paisley Park)
11	15	AIN'T NOTHIN' GOIN' ON BUT THE RENT	Gwen Guthrie (Boiling Point)
34	16	WASTED YEARS	Iron Maiden (EMI)
37	17	HOLIDAY RAP	MC Miker 'G' & Deejay Sven (Debut)
18	18	YOU GIVE LOVE A BAD NAME	Bon Jovi (Vertigo)
13	19	DANCING ON THE CEILING	Lionel Richie (Motown)
-	20	THORN IN MY SIDE	Eurythmics (RCA)
21	21	WALK THIS WAY	Run DMC (London)
20	22	NICE IN NICE	Stranglers (Epic)
10	23	ANYONE CAN FALL IN LOVE	Anita Dobson (BBC)
26	24	HEARTLAND	The The (Some Bizzare)
15	25	A QUESTION OF TIME	Depeche Mode (Mute)
9	26	CALLING ALL THE HEROES	It Bites (Virgin)
-	27	WORD UP	Cameo (Club)
22	28	BREAKING AWAY	Jaki Graham (EMI)
29	29	IN TOO DEEP	Genesis (Virgin)
31	30	PRETTY IN PINK	Psychedelic Furs (CBS)
30	31	DREAMTIME	Daryl Hall (RCA)
39	32	HAUNTED	Pogues (MCA)
16	33	I CAN PROVE IT Phil Fearon & Galaxy (Ensign)	
36	34	STUCK WITH YOU	Huey Lewis & the News (Chrysalis)
40	35	ADORATIONS	Killing Joke (EG)
-	36	RAIN OR SHINE	Five Star (Tent)
-	37	SWEET FREEDOM	Michael McDonald (MCA)
-	38	WILD WILD LIFE	Talking Heads (EMI)
35	39	YOU SHOOK ME ALL NIGHT LONG	AC/DC (Atlantic)
-	40	WHAT DOES IT TAKE	Kenny G (Arista)
-	41	DIAMOND GIRL	Pete Wylie (Eternal)
-	42	HOLD ON TIGHT	Samantha Fox (Jive)
-	43	MR. PHARMACIST	Fall (Beggars Banquet)
49	44	ROCK'N'ROLL MERCENARIES	Meatloaf & John Parr (Arista)
-	45	(FOREVER) LIVE AND DIE	Orchestral Manoeuvres In The Dark (Virgin)
-	46	MORE THAN PHYSICAL	Bananarama (London)
23	47	CAMOUFLAGE	Stan Ridgway (IRS)
38	48	TYPICAL MALE	Tina Turner (Capitol)
45	49	IF PUSH COMES TO A SHOVE	Sly Fox (Capitol)
50	50	FOOL'S PARADISE	Meli'sa Morgan (Capitol)

20 September 1986

last	this	title	artist
1	1	DON'T LEAVE ME THIS WAY	Communards (London)
6	2	RAGE HARD Frankie Goes To Hollywood (ZTT)	
3	3	WE DON'T HAVE TO	Jermaine Stewart (10)
2	4	I WANT TO WAKE UP WITH YOU	Boris Gardiner (Revue)
10	5	(I JUST) DIED IN YOUR ARMS	Cutting Crew (Siren)
7	6	GLORY OF LOVE	Peter Cetera (Full Moon)
17	7	HOLIDAY RAP	MC Miker 'G' & Deejay Sven (Debut)
5	8	HUMAN	Human League (Virgin)
11	9	LOVE CAN'T TURN AROUND	Farley 'Jackmaster' Funk (D.J. International)
21	10	WALK THIS WAY	Run DMC (London)
18	11	YOU GIVE LOVE A BAD NAME	Bon Jovi (Vertigo)
4	12	BROTHER LOUIE	Modern Talking (RCA)
27	13	WORD UP	Cameo (Club)
20	14	THORN IN MY SIDE	Eurythmics (RCA)
9	15	WHEN I THINK OF YOU	Janet Jackson (A&M)
16	16	WASTED YEARS	Iron Maiden (EMI)
13	17	THE WAY IT IS	Bruce Hornsby & the Range (RCA)
8	18	SO MACHO	Sinitta (Fanfare)
12	19	THE LADY IN RED	Chris De Burgh (A&M)
37	20	SWEET FREEDOM	Michael McDonald (MCA)
34	21	STUCK WITH YOU	Huey Lewis & the News (Chrysalis)
32	22	PRETTY IN PINK	Psychedelic Furs (CBS)
36	23	RAIN OR SHINE	Five Star (Tent)
14	24	GIRLS AND BOYS	Prince (Paisley Park)
-	25	RUMOURS	Timex Social Club (Cooltempo)
29	26	IN TOO DEEP	Genesis (Virgin)
15	27	AIN'T NOTHIN' GOIN' ON BUT THE RENT	Gwen Guthrie (Boiling Point)
42	28	HOLD ON TIGHT	Samantha Fox (Jive)
45	29	(FOREVER) LIVE AND DIE	Orchestral Manoeuvres In The Dark (Virgin)
19	30	DANCING ON THE CEILING	Lionel Richie (Motown)
24	31	HEARTLAND	The The (Some Bizzare)
26	32	CALLING ALL THE HEROES	It Bites (Virgin)
22	33	NICE IN NICE	Stranglers (Epic)
-	34	YOU CAN CALL ME AL	Paul Simon (Warner Bros)
38	35	WILD WILD LIFE	Talking Heads (EMI)
48	36	TYPICAL MALE	Tina Turner (Capitol)
-	37	ROMAN P/GOOD VIBRATONS	Psychic TV (Temple)
-	38	THE OTHER SIDE OF YOU	Mighty Lemon Drops (Blue Guitar)
28	39	BREAKING AWAY	Jaki Graham (EMI)
44	40	ROCK'N'ROLL MERCENARIES	Meatloaf & John Parr (Arista)
-	41	(I'M A DREAMER)	BB&Q (Cooltempo)
32	42	HAUNTED	Pogues (MCA)
33	43	I CAN PROVE IT Phil Fearon & Galaxy (Ensign)	
25	44	A QUESTION OF TIME	Depeche Mode (Mute)
-	45	MONTEGO BAY	Amazulu (Island)
-	46	WALK LIKE AN EGYPTIAN	Bangles (CBS)
35	47	ADORATIONS	Killing Joke (EG)
43	48	MR. PHARMACIST	Fall (Beggars Banquet)
-	49	YIN AND YANG	Love & Rockets (Beggars Banquet)
-	50	SEVENTH HEAVEN	Gwen Guthrie (Fourth & Broadway)

27 September 1986

last	this	title	artist
1	1	DON'T LEAVE ME THIS WAY	Communards (London)
3	2	WE DON'T HAVE TO	Jermaine Stewart (10)
6	3	GLORY OF LOVE	Peter Cetera (Full Moon)
5	4	(I JUST) DIED IN YOUR ARMS	Cutting Crew (Siren)
13	5	WORD UP	Cameo (Club)
10	6	WALK THIS WAY	Run DMC (London)
4	7	I WANT TO WAKE UP WITH YOU	Boris Gardiner (Revue)
23	8	RAIN OR SHINE	Five Star (Tent)
7	9	HOLIDAY RAP	MC Miker 'G' & Deejay Sven (Debut)
14	10	THORN IN MY SIDE	Eurythmics (RCA)
2	11	RAGE HARD Frankie Goes To Hollywood (ZTT)	
11	12	YOU GIVE LOVE A BAD NAME	Bon Jovi (Vertigo)
9	13	LOVE CAN'T TURN AROUND	Farley 'Jackmaster' Funk (D.J. International)
20	14	SWEET FREEDOM	Michael McDonald (MCA)
25	15	RUMOURS	Timex Social Club (Cooltempo)
22	16	PRETTY IN PINK	Psychedelic Furs (CBS)
12	17	BROTHER LOUIE	Modern Talking (RCA)
8	18	HUMAN	Human League (Virgin)
-	19	ONE GREAT THING	Big Country (Mercury)
29	20	(FOREVER) LIVE AND DIE	Orchestral Manoeuvres In The Dark (Virgin)
18	21	SO MACHO	Sinitta (Fanfare)
21	22	STUCK WITH YOU	Huey Lewis & the News (Chrysalis)
-	23	STATE OF THE NATION	New Order (Factory)
16	24	WASTED YEARS	Iron Maiden (EMI)
25	25	BRAND NEW LOVER	Dead Or Alive (Epic)
31	26	HEARTLAND	The The (Some Bizzare)
15	27	WHEN I THINK OF YOU	Janet Jackson (A&M)
-	28	SLOW DOWN	Loose Ends (Virgin)
17	29	THE WAY IT IS	Bruce Hornsby & the Range (RCA)
40	30	ROCK'N'ROLL MERCENARIES	Meatloaf & John Parr (Arista)
41	31	(I'M A DREAMER)	BB&Q (Cooltempo)
28	32	HOLD ON TIGHT	Samantha Fox (Jive)
-	33	PEEL SESSION	New Order (Strange Fruit)
-	34	ALWAYS THERE	Marti Webb (BBC)
34	35	YOU CAN CALL ME AL	Paul Simon (Warner Bros)
45	36	MONTEGO BAY	Amazulu (Island)
-	37	WORLD SHUT YOUR MOUTH	Julian Cope (Island)
-	38	FATAL HESITATION	Chris De Burgh (A&M)
-	39	TRUE COLORS	Cyndi Lauper (Portrait)
50	40	SEVENTH HEAVEN	Gwen Guthrie (Fourth & Broadway)
32	41	CALLING ALL THE HEROES	It Bites (Virgin)
37	42	ROMAN P/GOOD VIBRATONS	Psychic TV (Temple)
30	43	DANCING ON THE CEILING	Lionel Richie (Motown)
24	44	GIRLS AND BOYS	Prince (Paisley Park)
-	45	ANOTHER HEARTACHE	Rod Stewart (Warner Bros)
-	46	WHO WANTS TO LIVE FOREVER	Queen (EMI)
46	47	WALK LIKE AN EGYPTIAN	Bangles (CBS)
26	48	IN TOO DEEP	Genesis (Virgin)
27	49	AIN'T NOTHIN' GOIN' ON BUT THE RENT	Gwen Guthrie (Boiling Point)
-	50	NO MORE TEARS	Hollywood Beyond (WEA)

Don't Leave Me This Way had originally been a simultaneous Top 20 hit for both Harold Melvin & the Blue Notes and Thelma Houston in 1977. The Communards' revival turned it into a Hi-NRG dance track, Jimi Somerville being joined on the vocals by guest Sarah Jane Morris. Its five-week Number One run was the year's longest, and it was also 1986's second-best-selling single.

4 October 1986

last week	this week	title	artist (label)
1	1	DON'T LEAVE ME THIS WAY	Communards (London)
8	2	RAIN OR SHINE	Five Star (Tent)
5	3	WORD UP	Cameo (Club)
2	4	WE DON'T HAVE TO	Jermaine Stewart (10)
10	5	THORN IN MY SIDE	Eurythmics (RCA)
4	6	(I JUST) DIED IN YOUR ARMS	Cutting Crew (Siren)
6	7	WALK THIS WAY	Run DMC (London)
3	8	GLORY OF LOVE	Peter Cetera (Full Moon)
20	9	(FOREVER) LIVE AND DIE	Orchestral Manoeuvres In The Dark (Virgin)
15	10	RUMOURS	Timex Social Club (Cooltempo)
14	11	SWEET FREEDOM	Michael McDonald (MCA)
19	12	TRUE BLUE	Madonna (Sire)
13	13	ONE GREAT THING	Big Country (Mercury)
35	14	YOU CAN CALL ME AL	Paul Simon (Warner Bros)
13	15	LOVE CAN'T TURN AROUND	Farley 'Jackmaster' Funk (D.J. International)
16	16	PRETTY IN PINK	Psychedelic Furs (CBS)
23	17	STATE OF THE NATION	New Order (Factory)
7	18	I WANT TO WAKE UP WITH YOU	Boris Gardiner (Revue)
22	19	STUCK WITH YOU	Huey Lewis & the News (Chrysalis)
9	20	HOLIDAY RAP	MC Miker 'G' & Deejay Sven (Debut)
-	21	I'VE BEEN LOSING YOU	A-ha (Warner Bros)
46	22	WHO WANTS TO LIVE FOREVER	Queen (EMI)
36	23	MONTEGO BAY	Amazulu (Island)
11	24	RAGE HARD	Frankie Goes To Hollywood (ZTT)
39	25	TRUE COLORS	Cyndi Lauper (Portrait)
34	26	ALWAYS THERE	Marti Webb (BBC)
-	27	SAME OLD STORY	Ultravox (Chrysalis)
28	28	SLOW DOWN	Loose Ends (Virgin)
25	29	BRAND NEW LOVER	Dead Or Alive (Epic)
12	30	YOU GIVE LOVE A BAD NAME	Bon Jovi (Vertigo)
17	31	BROTHER LOUIE	Modern Talking (RCA)
18	32	HUMAN	Human League (Virgin)
26	33	HEARTLAND	The The (Some Bizzare)
47	34	WALK LIKE AN EGYPTIAN	Bangles (CBS)
37	35	WORLD SHUT YOUR MOUTH	Julian Cope (Island)
-	36	SUBURBIA	Pet Shop Boys (Parlophone)
21	37	SO MACHO	Sinitta (Fanfare)
-	38	ALL I WANT TO DO	UB40 (DEP International)
-	39	WONDERLAND	Paul Young (CBS)
-	40	THINK FOR A MINUTE	Housemartins (Go! Discs)
-	41	ATLANTIS IS CALLING (SOS FOR LOVE)	Modern Talking (RCA)
31	42	(I'M A DREAMER)	BB&Q (Cooltempo)
-	43	ALL I WANT	Howard Jones (WEA)
27	44	WHEN I THINK OF YOU	Janet Jackson (A&M)
33	45	PEEL SESSION	New Order (Strange Fruit)
-	46	IN THE ARMY NOW	Status Quo (Vertigo)
42	47	ROMAN P/GOOD VIBRATONS	Psychic TV (Temple)
29	48	THE WAY IT IS	Bruce Hornsby & the Range (RCA)
48	49	IN TOO DEEP	Genesis (Virgin)
-	50	BE A LOVER	Billy Idol (Chrysalis)

11 October 1986

this week	title	artist (label)
1	DON'T LEAVE ME THIS WAY	Communards (London)
2	RAIN OR SHINE	Five Star (Tent)
3	TRUE BLUE	Madonna (Sire)
4	THORN IN MY SIDE	Eurythmics (RCA)
5	WORD UP	Cameo (Club)
6	YOU CAN CALL ME AL	Paul Simon (Warner Bros)
7	I'VE BEEN LOSING YOU	A-ha (Warner Bros)
8	WE DON'T HAVE TO	Jermaine Stewart (10)
9	WALK THIS WAY	Run DMC (London)
10	(FOREVER) LIVE AND DIE	Orchestral Manoeuvres In The Dark (Virgin)
11	(I JUST) DIED IN YOUR ARMS	Cutting Crew (Siren)
12	STUCK WITH YOU	Huey Lewis & the News (Chrysalis)
13	GLORY OF LOVE	Peter Cetera (Full Moon)
14	TRUE COLORS	Cyndi Lauper (Portrait)
15	ALWAYS THERE	Marti Webb (BBC)
16	SUBURBIA	Pet Shop Boys (Parlophone)
17	MONTEGO BAY	Amazulu (Island)
18	IN THE ARMY NOW	Status Quo (Vertigo)
19	WONDERLAND	Paul Young (CBS)
20	RUMOURS	Timex Social Club (Cooltempo)
21	LOVE CAN'T TURN AROUND	Farley 'Jackmaster' Funk (D.J. International)
22	WALK LIKE AN EGYPTIAN	Bangles (CBS)
23	SWEET FREEDOM	Michael McDonald (MCA)
24	ONE GREAT THING	Big Country (Mercury)
25	WORLD SHUT YOUR MOUTH	Julian Cope (Island)
26	EVERY LOSER WINS	Nick Berry (BBC)
27	ALL I WANT	Howard Jones (WEA)
28	STATE OF THE NATION	New Order (Factory)
29	MIDAS TOUCH	Midnight Star (Solar)
30	WHO WANTS TO LIVE FOREVER	Queen (EMI)
31	BE A LOVER	Billy Idol (Chrysalis)
32	PRETTY IN PINK	Psychedelic Furs (CBS)
33	SAME OLD STORY	Ultravox (Chrysalis)
34	IN TOO DEEP	Genesis (Virgin)
35	BRAND NEW LOVER	Dead Or Alive (Epic)
36	SLOW DOWN	Loose Ends (Virgin)
37	YOU MAKE ME FEEL BRAND NEW	Boris Gardiner (Trojan)
38	ATLANTIS IS CALLING (SOS FOR LOVE)	Modern Talking (RCA)
39	DON'T STAND SO CLOSE TO ME '86	Police (A&M)
40	RAGE HARD	Frankie Goes To Hollywood (ZTT)
41	THINK FOR A MINUTE	Housemartins (Go! Discs)
42	HEARTACHE ALL OVER THE WORLD	Elton John (Rocket)
43	YOU GIVE LOVE A BAD NAME	Bon Jovi (Vertigo)
44	(I'M A DREAMER)	BB&Q (Cooltempo)
45	BROTHER LOUIE	Modern Talking (RCA)
46	HOLIDAY RAP	MC Miker 'G' & Deejay Sven (Debut)
47	ALL I WANT TO DO	UB40 (DEP International)
48	ALL I ASK OF YOU	Cliff Richard & Sarah Brightman (Polydor)
49	NOBODY KNOWS	Nik Kershaw (MCA)
50	GIRLS AIN'T NOTHING BUT TROUBLE	DJ Jazzy Jeff & Fresh Prince (Champion)

18 October 1986

this week	title	artist (label)
1	TRUE BLUE	Madonna (Sire)
2	EVERY LOSER WINS	Nick Berry (BBC)
3	RAIN OR SHINE	Five Star (Tent)
4	YOU CAN CALL ME AL	Paul Simon (Warner Bros)
5	DON'T LEAVE ME THIS WAY	Communards (London)
6	I'VE BEEN LOSING YOU	A-ha (Warner Bros)
7	SUBURBIA	Pet Shop Boys (Parlophone)
8	IN THE ARMY NOW	Status Quo (Vertigo)
9	WORD UP	Cameo (Club)
10	THORN IN MY SIDE	Eurythmics (RCA)
11	(FOREVER) LIVE AND DIE	Orchestral Manoeuvres In The Dark (Virgin)
12	TRUE COLORS	Cyndi Lauper (Portrait)
13	ALL I ASK OF YOU	Cliff Richard & Sarah Brightman (Polydor)
14	WALK LIKE AN EGYPTIAN	Bangles (CBS)
15	WALK THIS WAY	Run DMC (London)
16	(I JUST) DIED IN YOUR ARMS	Cutting Crew (Siren)
17	STUCK WITH YOU	Huey Lewis & the News (Chrysalis)
18	WE DON'T HAVE TO	Jermaine Stewart (10)
19	MONTEGO BAY	Amazulu (Island)
20	WONDERLAND	Paul Young (CBS)
21	ALWAYS THERE	Marti Webb (BBC)
22	DON'T STAND SO CLOSE TO ME '86	Police (A&M)
23	RUMOURS	Timex Social Club (Cooltempo)
24	WORLD SHUT YOUR MOUTH	Julian Cope (Island)
25	MIDAS TOUCH	Midnight Star (Solar)
26	SLOW DOWN	Loose Ends (Virgin)
27	LOVE CAN'T TURN AROUND	Farley 'Jackmaster' Funk (D.J. International)
28	THE WIZARD	Paul Hardcastle (Chrysalis)
29	ALL I WANT	Howard Jones (WEA)
30	BE A LOVER	Billy Idol (Chrysalis)
31	WHO WANTS TO LIVE FOREVER	Queen (EMI)
32	C'MON EVERY BEATBOX	Big Audio Dynamite (CBS)
33	STATE OF THE NATION	New Order (Factory)
34	SAME OLD STORY	Ultravox (Chrysalis)
35	NOBODY KNOWS	Nik Kershaw (MCA)
36	DON'T GET ME WRONG	Pretenders (Real)
37	STAY WITH ME	Mission (Mercury)
38	GIRLS AIN'T NOTHING BUT TROUBLE	DJ Jazzy Jeff & Fresh Prince (Champion)
39	THINK FOR A MINUTE	Housemartins (Go! Discs)
40	SWEET FREEDOM	Michael McDonald (MCA)
41	FEELS LIKE THE FIRST TIME	Sinitta (Fanfare)
42	YOU MAKE ME FEEL BRAND NEW	Boris Gardiner (Trojan)
43	WHO DO YOU WANT FOR YOUR LOVE	Icicle Works (Beggars Banquet)
44	IN TOO DEEP	Genesis (Virgin)
45	ONE GREAT THING	Big Country (Mercury)
46	ALWAYS THE SUN	Stranglers (Epic)
47	GLORY OF LOVE	Peter Cetera (Full Moon)
48	PRETTY IN PINK	Psychedelic Furs (CBS)
49	WHOLE NEW WORLD	It Bites (Virgin)
50	ATLANTIS IS CALLING (SOS FOR LOVE)	Modern Talking (RCA)

Paul Simon's *You Can Call Me Al* was the first single from his critically-rated and huge-selling album *Graceland*. Curiously, though a Top Five hit here, the single was only a moderate seller in the US, despite an exceptional video in which Simon deliberately allowed himself to be upstaged by comedy actor Chevy Chase. Namesake Paul Hardcastle's *The Wizard* was the new theme for *Top Of The Pops*.

October – November 1986

25 October 1986

last week	this week		
2	1	EVERY LOSER WINS	Nick Berry (BBC)
1	2	TRUE BLUE	Madonna (Sire)
8	3	IN THE ARMY NOW	Status Quo (Vertigo)
4	4	YOU CAN CALL ME AL	Paul Simon (Warner Bros)
13	5	ALL IS ASK OF YOU	Cliff Richard & Sarah Brightman (Polydor)
3	6	RAIN OR SHINE	Five Star (Tent)
7	7	SUBURBIA	Pet Shop Boys (Parlophone)
14	8	WALK LIKE AN EGYPTIAN	Bangles (CBS)
5	9	DON'T LEAVE ME THIS WAY	Communards (London)
12	10	TRUE COLORS	Cyndi Lauper (Portrait)
6	11	I'VE BEEN LOSING YOU	A-ha (Warner Bros)
24	12	WORLD SHUT YOUR MOUTH	Julian Cope (Island)
10	13	THORN IN MY SIDE	Eurythmics (RCA)
21	14	ALWAYS THERE	Marti Webb (BBC)
11	15	(FOREVER) LIVE AND DIE	Orchestral Manoeuvres In The Dark (Virgin)
9	16	WORD UP	Cameo (Club)
19	17	MONTEGO BAY	Amazulu (Island)
28	18	THE WIZARD	Paul Hardcastle (Chrysalis)
36	19	DON'T GET ME WRONG	Pretenders (Real)
30	20	BE A LOVER	Billy Idol (Chrysalis)
22	21	DON'T STAND SO CLOSE TO ME '86	Police (A&M)
25	22	MIDAS TOUCH	Midnight Star (Solar)
17	23	STUCK WITH YOU	Huey Lewis & the News (Chrysalis)
39	24	THINK FOR A MINUTE	Housemartins (Go! Discs)
42	25	YOU MAKE ME FEEL BRAND NEW	Boris Gardiner (Trojan)
15	26	WALK THIS WAY	Run DMC (London)
37	27	STAY WITH ME	Mission (Mercury)
18	28	WE DON'T HAVE TO	Jermaine Stewart (10)
-	29	LOVE'S EASY TEARS	Cocteau Twins (4AD)
16	30	(I JUST) DIED IN YOUR ARMS	Cutting Crew (Siren)
38	31	GIRLS AIN'T NOTHING BUT TROUBLE	DJ Jazzy Jeff & Fresh Prince (Champion)
20	32	WONDERLAND	Paul Young (CBS)
46	33	ALWAYS THE SUN	Stranglers (Epic)
32	34	C'MON EVERY BEATBOX	Big Audio Dynamite (CBS)
29	35	ALL I WANT	Howard Jones (WEA)
26	36	SLOW DOWN	Loose Ends (Virgin)
-	37	HEARTACHE ALL OVER THE WORLD	Elton John (Rocket)
34	38	SAME OLD STORY	Ultravox (Chrysalis)
-	39	LIVING ON A PRAYER	Bon Jovi (Vertigo)
23	40	RUMOURS	Timex Social Club (Cooltempo)
-	41	(THEY LONG TO BE) CLOSE TO YOU	Gwen Guthrie (Boiling Point)
43	42	WHO DO YOU WANT FOR YOUR LOVE	Icicle Works (Beggars Banquet)
41	43	FEELS LIKE THE FIRST TIME	Sinitta (Fanfare)
33	44	STATE OF THE NATION	New Order (Factory)
-	45	TAKE MY BREATH AWAY	Berlin (CBS)
-	46	SHOWING OUT	Mel & Kim (Supreme)
49	47	WHOLE NEW WORLD	It Bites (Virgin)
35	48	NOBODY KNOWS	Nik Kershaw (MCA)
40	49	SWEET FREEDOM	Michael McDonald (MCA)
-	50	RUBY RED	Marc Almond (Some Bizzare)

1 November 1986

1	1	EVERY LOSER WINS	Nick Berry (BBC)
5	2	ALL IS ASK OF YOU	Cliff Richard & Sarah Brightman (Polydor)
2	3	TRUE BLUE	Madonna (Sire)
3	4	IN THE ARMY NOW	Status Quo (Vertigo)
8	5	WALK LIKE AN EGYPTIAN	Bangles (CBS)
4	6	YOU CAN CALL ME AL	Paul Simon (Warner Bros)
7	7	SUBURBIA	Pet Shop Boys (Parlophone)
6	8	RAIN OR SHINE	Five Star (Tent)
19	9	DON'T GET ME WRONG	Pretenders (Real)
-	10	YOU ARE EVERYTHING TO ME	Boris Gardiner (Revue)
22	11	MIDAS TOUCH	Midnight Star (Solar)
10	12	TRUE COLORS	Cyndi Lauper (Portrait)
12	13	WORLD SHUT YOUR MOUTH	Julian Cope (Island)
11	14	I'VE BEEN LOSING YOU	A-ha (Warner Bros)
18	15	THE WIZARD	Paul Hardcastle (Chrysalis)
14	16	ALWAYS THERE	Marti Webb (BBC)
27	17	STAY WITH ME	Mission (Mercury)
-	18	TO HAVE AND TO HOLD	Catherine Stock (Sierra)
45	19	TAKE MY BREATH AWAY	Berlin (CBS)
9	20	DON'T LEAVE ME THIS WAY	Communards (London)
21	21	BE A LOVER	Billy Idol (Chrysalis)
24	22	THINK FOR A MINUTE	Housemartins (Go! Discs)
31	23	GIRLS AIN'T NOTHING BUT TROUBLE	DJ Jazzy Jeff & Fresh Prince (Champion)
39	24	LIVING ON A PRAYER	Bon Jovi (Vertigo)
-	25	ASK	Smiths (Rough Trade)
13	26	THORN IN MY SIDE	Eurythmics (RCA)
-	27	NOTORIOUS	Duran Duran (EMI)
33	28	ALWAYS THE SUN	Stranglers (Epic)
15	29	(FOREVER) LIVE AND DIE	Orchestral Manoeuvres In The Dark (Virgin)
16	30	WORD UP	Cameo (Club)
41	31	(THEY LONG TO BE) CLOSE TO YOU	Gwen Guthrie (Boiling Point)
-	32	YOU KEEP ME HANGIN' ON	Kim Wilde (MCA)
29	33	LOVE'S EASY TEARS	Cocteau Twins (4AD)
-	34	DON'T GIVE UP	Peter Gabriel & Kate Bush (Virgin)
34	35	C'MON EVERY BEATBOX	Big Audio Dynamite (CBS)
28	36	WE DON'T HAVE TO	Jermaine Stewart (10)
23	37	STUCK WITH YOU	Huey Lewis & the News (Chrysalis)
21	38	DON'T STAND SO CLOSE TO ME '86	Police (A&M)
-	39	HEARTBEAT	Don Johnson (Epic)
26	40	WALK THIS WAY	Run DMC (London)
32	41	WONDERLAND	Paul Young (CBS)
-	42	ANOTHERLOVERHOLENYOHEAD	Prince (Paisley Park)
-	43	SOMETHING OUTA NOTHING	Banned (Harvest)
-	44	FOR AMERICA	Red Box (Sire)
30	45	(I JUST) DIED IN YOUR ARMS	Cutting Crew (Siren)
17	46	MONTEGO BAY	Amazulu (Island)
35	47	ALL I WANT	Howard Jones (WEA)
-	48	HE'S BACK (THE MAN BEHIND THE MASK)	Alice Cooper (MCA)
-	49	BREAKOUT	Swing Out Sister (Mercury)
46	50	SHOWING OUT	Mel & Kim (Supreme)

8 November 1986

1	1	EVERY LOSER WINS	Nick Berry (BBC)
4	2	IN THE ARMY NOW	Status Quo (Vertigo)
2	3	ALL IS ASK OF YOU	Cliff Richard & Sarah Brightman (Polydor)
19	4	TAKE MY BREATH AWAY	Berlin (CBS)
5	5	WALK LIKE AN EGYPTIAN	Bangles (CBS)
9	6	DON'T GET ME WRONG	Pretenders (Real)
3	7	TRUE BLUE	Madonna (Sire)
6	8	YOU CAN CALL ME AL	Paul Simon (Warner Bros)
11	9	MIDAS TOUCH	Midnight Star (Solar)
27	10	NOTORIOUS	Duran Duran (EMI)
32	11	YOU KEEP ME HANGIN' ON	Kim Wilde (MCA)
25	12	ASK	Smiths (Rough Trade)
7	13	SUBURBIA	Pet Shop Boys (Parlophone)
12	14	TRUE COLORS	Cyndi Lauper (Portrait)
10	15	YOU ARE EVERYTHING TO ME	Boris Gardiner (Revue)
18	16	TO HAVE AND TO HOLD	Catherine Stock (Sierra)
8	17	RAIN OR SHINE	Five Star (Tent)
24	18	LIVING ON A PRAYER	Bon Jovi (Vertigo)
34	19	DON'T GIVE UP	Peter Gabriel & Kate Bush (Virgin)
43	20	SOMETHING OUTA NOTHING	Banned (Harvest)
28	21	ALWAYS THE SUN	Stranglers (Epic)
-	22	BECAUSE I LOVE YOU	Shakin' Stevens (Epic)
-	23	THIS IS THE WORLD CALLING	Bob Geldof (Mercury)
50	24	SHOWING OUT	Mel & Kim (Supreme)
21	25	BE A LOVER	Billy Idol (Chrysalis)
44	26	FOR AMERICA	Red Box (Sire)
15	27	THE WIZARD	Paul Hardcastle (Chrysalis)
23	28	GIRLS AIN'T NOTHING BUT TROUBLE	DJ Jazzy Jeff & Fresh Prince (Champion)
14	29	I'VE BEEN LOSING YOU	A-ha (Warner Bros)
17	30	STAY WITH ME	Mission (Mercury)
20	31	DON'T LEAVE ME THIS WAY	Communards (London)
22	32	THINK FOR A MINUTE	Housemartins (Go! Discs)
16	33	ALWAYS THERE	Marti Webb (BBC)
31	34	(THEY LONG TO BE) CLOSE TO YOU	Gwen Guthrie (Boiling Point)
13	35	WORLD SHUT YOUR MOUTH	Julian Cope (Island)
42	36	ANOTHERLOVERHOLENYOHEAD	Prince (Paisley Park)
-	37	THROUGH THE BARRICADES	Spandau Ballet (Reformation)
49	38	BREAKOUT	Swing Out Sister (Mercury)
-	39	(WAITING FOR THE) GHOST TRAIN	Madness (Zarjazz)
-	40	DESIRE (COME ANDGET IT)	Gene Loves Jezebel (Beggars Banquet)
-	41	WHEN THE WIND BLOWS	David Bowie (Virgin)
-	42	THE FINAL COUNTDOWN	Europe (Epic)
-	43	SOMETIMES	Erasure (Mute)
-	44	I'VE BEEN IN LOVE BEFORE	Cutting Crew (Siren)
-	45	PRETTY LITTLE HEAD	Paul McCartney (Parlophone)
-	46	DON'T FORGET ME	Glass Tiger (Manhattan)
-	47	INFECTED	The The (Some Bizzare)
-	48	JACK THE GROOVE	Raze (Champion)
-	49	THE NIGHT	Communards
36	50	WE DON'T HAVE TO	Jermaine Stewart (10)

East Enders actor Nick Berry outdid the success of fellow cast member Anita Dobson's hit by a considerable margin, as his ballad *Every Loser Wins* topped the chart for three weeks and became the year's top-selling single, its sales only a fraction short of 800,000. Berry denied a Number One slot to the *Phantom Of The Opera* ballad *All I Ask Of You*, Cliff Richard's second major hit duet this year.

November 1986

15 November 1986

last week	this week	title	artist (label)
4	1	TAKE MY BREATH AWAY	Berlin (CBS)
5	2	WALK LIKE AN EGYPTIAN	Bangles (CBS)
1	3	EVERY LOSER WINS	Nick Berry (BBC)
2	4	IN THE ARMY NOW	Status Quo (Vertigo)
11	5	YOU KEEP ME HANGIN' ON	Kim Wilde (MCA)
24	6	SHOWING OUT	Mel & Kim (Supreme)
10	7	NOTORIOUS	Duran Duran (EMI)
3	8	ALL IS ASK OF YOU	Cliff Richard & Sarah Brightman (Polydor)
6	9	DON'T GET ME WRONG	Pretenders (Real)
9	10	MIDAS TOUCH	Midnight Star (Solar)
12	11	ASK	Smiths (Rough Trade)
19	12	DON'T GIVE UP	Peter Gabriel & Kate Bush (Virgin)
18	13	LIVING ON A PRAYER	Bon Jovi (Vertigo)
7	14	TRUE BLUE	Madonna (Sire)
20	15	SOMETHING OUTA NOTHING	Banned (Harvest)
8	16	YOU CAN CALL ME AL	Paul Simon (Warner Bros)
37	17	THROUGH THE BARRICADES	Spandau Ballet (Reformation)
38	18	BREAKOUT	Swing Out Sister (Mercury)
39	19	(WAITING FOR THE) GHOST TRAIN	Madness (Zarjazz)
14	20	TRUE COLORS	Cyndi Lauper (Portrait)
22	21	BECAUSE I LOVE YOU	Shakin' Stevens (Epic)
42	22	THE FINAL COUNTDOWN	Europe (Epic)
26	23	FOR AMERICA	Red Box (Sire)
23	24	THIS IS THE WORLD CALLING	Bob Geldof (Mercury)
13	25	SUBURBIA	Pet Shop Boys (Parlophone)
-	26	EXPERIMENT IV	Kate Bush (EMI)
34	27	(THEY LONG TO BE) CLOSE TO YOU	Gwen Guthrie (Boiling Point)
15	28	YOU ARE EVERYTHING TO ME	Boris Gardiner (Revue)
29	29	BE A LOVER	Billy Idol (Chrysalis)
36	30	ANOTHERLOVERHOLENYOHEAD	Prince (Paisley Park)
-	31	BIZARRE LOVE TRIANGLE	New Order (Factory)
21	32	ALWAYS THE SUN	Stranglers (Epic)
43	33	SOMETIMES	Erasure (Mute)
32	34	THINK FOR A MINUTE	Housemartins (Go! Discs)
17	35	RAIN OR SHINE	Five Star (Tent)
46	36	DON'T FORGET ME	Glass Tiger (Manhattan)
-	37	AMERICA	King Kurt (Polydor)
41	38	WHEN THE WIND BLOWS	David Bowie (Virgin)
16	39	TO HAVE AND TO HOLD	Catherine Stock (Sierra)
-	40	GHOSTDANCING	Simple Minds (Virgin)
40	41	DESIRE (COME AND GET IT)	Gene Loves Jezebel (Beggars Banquet)
28	42	GIRLS AIN'T NOTHING BUT TROUBLE	DJ Jazzy Jeff & Fresh Prince (Champion)
47	43	INFECTED	The The (Some Bizzare)
33	44	ALWAYS THERE	Marti Webb (BBC)
-	45	GOIN' TO THE BANK	Commodores (Polydor)
46	46	I WANT YOU	Elvis Costello (Imp)
-	47	51ST STATE	New Model Army (EMI)
27	48	THE WIZARD	Paul Hardcastle (Chrysalis)
45	49	PRETTY LITTLE HEAD	Paul McCartney (Parlophone)
-	50	FALLING IN LOVE	Sybil (Champion)

22 November 1986

last week	this week	title	artist (label)
1	1	TAKE MY BREATH AWAY	Berlin (CBS)
5	2	YOU KEEP ME HANGIN' ON	Kim Wilde (MCA)
6	3	SHOWING OUT	Mel & Kim (Supreme)
18	4	BREAKOUT	Swing Out Sister (Mercury)
2	5	WALK LIKE AN EGYPTIAN	Bangles (CBS)
12	6	DON'T GIVE UP	Peter Gabriel & Kate Bush (Virgin)
17	7	THROUGH THE BARRICADES	*Spandau Ballet (Reformation)
13	8	LIVING ON A PRAYER	Bon Jovi (Vertigo)
22	9	THE FINAL COUNTDOWN	Europe (Epic)
3	10	EVERY LOSER WINS	Nick Berry (BBC)
4	11	IN THE ARMY NOW	Status Quo (Vertigo)
23	12	FOR AMERICA	Red Box (Sire)
7	13	NOTORIOUS	Duran Duran (EMI)
8	14	ALL IS ASK OF YOU	Cliff Richard & Sarah Brightman (Polydor)
40	15	GHOSTDANCING	Simple Minds (Virgin)
-	16	FRENCH KISSIN' IN THE USA	Debbie Harry (Chrysalis)
26	17	EXPERIMENT IV	Kate Bush (EMI)
9	18	DON'T GET ME WRONG	Pretenders (Real)
19	19	(WAITING FOR THE) GHOST TRAIN	Madness (Zarjazz)
21	20	BECAUSE I LOVE YOU	Shakin' Stevens (Epic)
33	21	SOMETIMES	Erasure (Mute)
10	22	MIDAS TOUCH	Midnight Star (Solar)
24	23	THIS IS THE WORLD CALLING	Bob Geldof (Mercury)
11	24	ASK	Smiths (Rough Trade)
-	25	EACH TIME YOU BREAK MY HEART	Nick Kamen (WEA)
31	26	BIZARRE LOVE TRIANGLE	New Order (Factory)
15	27	SOMETHING OUTA NOTHING	Banned (Harvest)
36	28	DON'T FORGET ME	Glass Tiger (Manhattan)
14	29	TRUE BLUE	Madonna (Sire)
-	30	ANYTHING	Damned (MCA)
-	31	SWEET LOVE	Anita Baker (Elektra)
-	32	LOVE IS THE SLUG	Fuzzbox (Vindaloo)
16	33	YOU CAN CALL ME AL	Paul Simon (Warner Bros)
43	34	INFECTED	The The (Some Bizzare)
20	35	TRUE COLORS	Cyndi Lauper (Portrait)
-	36	STRANGER IN A STRANGE LAND	Iron Maiden (EMI)
38	37	WHEN THE WIND BLOWS	David Bowie (Virgin)
-	38	IF I SAY YES	Five Star (Tent)
-	39	GREETINGS TO THE NEW BRUNETTE	Billy Bragg (Go! Discs)
-	40	CRAZY LOVE	Maxi Priest (10)
27	41	(THEY LONG TO BE) CLOSE TO YOU	Gwen Guthrie (Boiling Point)
37	42	AMERICA	King Kurt (Polydor)
-	43	WALKING IN THE AIR	Aled Jones (HMV)
-	44	THE SKYE BOAT SONG	Roger Whittaker & Des O'Connor (Tembo)
-	45	ALL FALL DOWN	Ultravox (Chrysalis)
-	46	AIN'T NOTHING BUT A HOUSEPARTY	Phil Fearon (Ensign)
47	47	JODY	Jermaine Stewart (10)
-	48	GYPSY	Suzanne Vega (A&M)
-	49	THE RAIN	Oran 'Juice' Jones (Def Jam)
-	50	I'M NOT PERFECT	Grace Jones (Manhattan)

29 November 1986

last week	this week	title	artist (label)
1	1	TAKE MY BREATH AWAY	Berlin (CBS)
2	2	YOU KEEP ME HANGIN' ON	Kim Wilde (MCA)
4	3	BREAKOUT	Swing Out Sister (Mercury)
3	4	SHOWING OUT	Mel & Kim (Supreme)
9	5	THE FINAL COUNTDOWN	Europe (Epic)
8	6	LIVING ON A PRAYER	Bon Jovi (Vertigo)
7	7	THROUGH THE BARRICADES	Spandau Ballet (Reformation)
6	8	DON'T GIVE UP	Peter Gabriel & Kate Bush (Virgin)
16	9	FRENCH KISSIN' IN THE USA	Debbie Harry (Chrysalis)
5	10	WALK LIKE AN EGYPTIAN	Bangles (CBS)
25	11	EACH TIME YOU BREAK MY HEART	Nick Kamen (WEA)
12	12	FOR AMERICA	Red Box (Sire)
15	13	GHOSTDANCING	Simple Minds (Virgin)
21	14	SOMETIMES	Erasure (Mute)
31	15	SWEET LOVE	Anita Baker (Elektra)
19	16	(WAITING FOR THE) GHOST TRAIN	Madness (Zarjazz)
20	17	BECAUSE I LOVE YOU	Shakin' Stevens (Epic)
38	18	IF I SAY YES	Five Star (Tent)
44	19	THE SKYE BOAT SONG	Roger Whittaker & Des O'Connor (Tembo)
36	20	STRANGER IN A STRANGE LAND	Iron Maiden (EMI)
14	21	ALL IS ASK OF YOU	Cliff Richard & Sarah Brightman (Polydor)
13	22	NOTORIOUS	Duran Duran (EMI)
-	23	WARRIORS OF THE WASTELAND	Frankie Goes To Hollywood (ZTT)
11	24	IN THE ARMY NOW	Status Quo (Vertigo)
30	25	ANYTHING	Damned (MCA)
10	26	EVERY LOSER WINS	Nick Berry (BBC)
-	27	LAND OF CONFUSION	Genesis (Virgin)
32	28	LOVE IS THE SLUG	Fuzzbox (Vindaloo)
28	29	DON'T FORGET ME	Glass Tiger (Manhattan)
17	30	EXPERIMENT IV	Kate Bush (EMI)
18	31	DON'T GET ME WRONG	Pretenders (Real)
-	32	WAR (WHAT IS IT GOOD FOR)	Bruce Springsteen (CBS)
49	33	THE RAIN	Oran 'Juice' Jones (Def Jam)
23	34	THIS IS THE WORLD CALLING	Bob Geldof (Mercury)
22	35	MIDAS TOUCH	Midnight Star (Solar)
-	36	IS THIS LOVE	Alison Moyet (CBS)
45	37	ALL FALL DOWN	Ultravox (Chrysalis)
-	38	HIP TO BE SQUARE	Huey Lewis & the News (Chrysalis)
39	39	GREETINGS TO THE NEW BRUNETTE	Billy Bragg (Go! Discs)
-	40	I'VE BEEN IN LOVE BEFORE	Cutting Crew (Siren)
-	41	JE T'AIME (ALLO ALLO)/RENE	DMC Rene & Yvette (Sedition)
-	42	BECAUSE OF YOU	Dexy's Midnight Runners (Mercury)
-	43	WATERLOO	Dr. & the Medics (IRS)
-	44	I NEED YOUR LOVING	Human League (Virgin)
-	45	HOLD THE HEART	Big Country (Mercury)
-	46	SOME PEOPLE	Paul Young (CBS)
-	47	HELLO FRIEND	Chris Rea (Magnet)
37	48	WHEN THE WIND BLOWS	David Bowie (Virgin)
50	49	I'M NOT PERFECT	Grace Jones (Manhattan)
24	50	ASK	Smiths (Rough Trade)

Berlin's *Take My Breath Away* was helped to the top by its high-profile inclusion in the hugely successful Tom Cruise film *Top Gun*. Kim Wilde's revival of the Supremes' *You Keep Me Hangin' On* was her highest-placed UK single, at Number Two, but fared even better in the US, where it topped the chart. Meanwhile, ex-Blondie singer Deborah Harry scored her first major hit since the group's demise.

December 1986

6 December 1986

last	this		
5	1	THE FINAL COUNTDOWN	Europe (Epic)
1	2	TAKE MY BREATH AWAY	Berlin (CBS)
2	3	YOU KEEP ME HANGIN' ON	Kim Wilde (MCA)
14	4	SOMETIMES	Erasure (Mute)
4	5	SHOWING OUT	Mel & Kim (Supreme)
6	6	LIVING ON A PRAYER	Bon Jovi (Vertigo)
3	7	BREAKOUT	Swing Out Sister (Mercury)
9	8	FRENCH KISSIN' IN THE USA	Debbie Harry (Chrysalis)
11	9	EACH TIME YOU BREAK MY HEART	Nick Kamen (WEA)
15	10	SWEET LOVE	Anita Baker (Elektra)
12	11	FOR AMERICA	Red Box (Sire)
7	12	THROUGH THE BARRICADES	Spandau Ballet (Reformation)
18	13	IF I SAY YES	Five Star (Tent)
8	14	DON'T GIVE UP	Peter Gabriel & Kate Bush (Virgin)
13	15	GHOSTDANCING	Simple Minds (Virgin)
19	16	THE SKYE BOAT SONG	Roger Whittaker & Des O'Connor (Tembo)
32	17	WAR (WHAT IS IT GOOD FOR)	Bruce Springsteen (CBS)
-	18	SO COLD THE NIGHT	Communards (London)
10	19	WALK LIKE AN EGYPTIAN	Bangles (CBS)
23	20	WARRIORS OF THE WASTELAND	Frankie Goes To Hollywood (ZTT)
27	21	LAND OF CONFUSION	Genesis (Virgin)
20	22	STRANGER IN A STRANGE LAND	Iron Maiden (EMI)
33	23	THE RAIN	Oran 'Juice' Jones (Def Jam)
-	24	THE MIRACLE OF LOVE	Eurythmics (RCA)
16	25	(WAITING FOR THE) GHOST TRAIN	Madness (Zarjazz)
21	26	ALL IS ASK OF YOU	Cliff Richard & Sarah Brightman (Polydor)
-	27	SHAKE YOU DOWN	Gregory Abbott (CBS)
-	28	CANDY	Cameo (Club)
45	29	HOLD THE HEART	Big Country (Mercury)
-	30	SHIVER	George Benson (Warner Bros)
17	31	BECAUSE I LOVE YOU	Shakin' Stevens (Epic)
25	32	ANYTHING	Damned (MCA)
29	33	DON'T FORGET ME	Glass Tiger (Manhattan)
-	34	CARAVAN OF LOVE	Housemartins (Go! Discs)
-	35	NIGHTS OF PLEASURE	Loose Ends (Virgin)
40	36	I'VE BEEN IN LOVE BEFORE	Cutting Crew (Siren)
37	37	ALL FALL DOWN	Ultravox (Chrysalis)
36	38	IS THIS LOVE	Alison Moyet (CBS)
28	39	LOVE IS THE SLUG	Fuzzbox (Vindaloo)
42	40	BECAUSE OF YOU	Dexy's Midnight Runners (Mercury)
49	41	I'M NOT PERFECT	Grace Jones (Manhattan)
-	42	DREAMIN'	Status Quo (Vertigo)
24	43	IN THE ARMY NOW	Status Quo (Vertigo)
-	44	STEP RIGHT UP	Jaki Graham (EMI)
48	45	WHEN THE WIND BLOWS	David Bowie (Virgin)
-	46	CRY WOLF	A-ha (Warner Bros)
39	47	GREETINGS TO THE NEW BRUNETTE	Billy Bragg (Go! Discs)
30	48	EXPERIMENT IV	Kate Bush (EMI)
41	49	JE T'AIME (ALLO ALLO)/RENE DMC	Rene & Yvette (Sedition)
-	50	TRUE COLOURS	Go West (Chrysalis)

13 December 1986

last	this		
1	1	THE FINAL COUNTDOWN	Europe (Epic)
4	2	SOMETIMES	Erasure (Mute)
2	3	TAKE MY BREATH AWAY	Berlin (CBS)
9	4	EACH TIME YOU BREAK MY HEART	Nick Kamen (WEA)
6	5	LIVING ON A PRAYER	Bon Jovi (Vertigo)
8	6	FRENCH KISSIN' IN THE USA	Debbie Harry (Chrysalis)
7	7	BREAKOUT	Swing Out Sister (Mercury)
16	8	THE SKYE BOAT SONG	Roger Whittaker & Des O'Connor (Tembo)
23	9	THE RAIN	Oran 'Juice' Jones (Def Jam)
27	10	SHAKE YOU DOWN	Gregory Abbott (CBS)
3	11	YOU KEEP ME HANGIN' ON	Kim Wilde (MCA)
5	12	SHOWING OUT	Mel & Kim (Supreme)
18	13	SO COLD THE NIGHT	Communards (London)
10	14	SWEET LOVE	Anita Baker (Elektra)
11	15	FOR AMERICA	Red Box (Sire)
34	16	CARAVAN OF LOVE	Housemartins (Go! Discs)
17	17	WAR (WHAT IS IT GOOD FOR)	Bruce Springsteen (CBS)
13	18	IF I SAY YES	Five Star (Tent)
30	19	SHIVER	George Benson (Warner Bros)
20	20	WARRIORS OF THE WASTELAND	Frankie Goes To Hollywood (ZTT)
21	21	LAND OF CONFUSION	Genesis (Virgin)
12	22	THROUGH THE BARRICADES	Spandau Ballet (Reformation)
28	23	CANDY	Cameo (Club)
46	24	CRY WOLF	A-ha (Warner Bros)
24	25	THE MIRACLE OF LOVE	Eurythmics (RCA)
38	26	IS THIS LOVE	Alison Moyet (CBS)
-	27	OPEN YOUR HEART	Madonna (Sire)
32	28	ANYTHING	Damned (MCA)
15	29	GHOSTDANCING	Simple Minds (Virgin)
44	30	STEP RIGHT UP	Jaki Graham (EMI)
31	31	BECAUSE I LOVE YOU	Shakin' Stevens (Epic)
26	32	ALL IS ASK OF YOU	Cliff Richard & Sarah Brightman (Polydor)
14	33	DON'T GIVE UP	Peter Gabriel & Kate Bush (Virgin)
22	34	STRANGER IN A STRANGE LAND	Iron Maiden (EMI)
35	35	HOLD THE HEART	Big Country (Mercury)
42	36	DREAMIN'	Status Quo (Vertigo)
50	37	TRUE COLOURS	Go West (Chrysalis)
37	38	ALL FALL DOWN	Ultravox (Chrysalis)
25	39	(WAITING FOR THE) GHOST TRAIN	Madness (Zarjazz)
33	40	DON'T FORGET ME	Glass Tiger (Manhattan)
-	41	CHILLIN' OUT	Curtis Hairston (Atlantic)
-	42	REET PETITE	Jackie Wilson (SMP)
-	43	HYMN TO HER	Pretenders (Real)
-	44	ONLY LOVE REMAINS	Paul McCartney (Parlophone)
39	45	LOVE IS THE SLUG	Fuzzbox (Vindaloo)
40	46	BECAUSE OF YOU	Dexy's Midnight Runners (Mercury)
19	47	WALK LIKE AN EGYPTIAN	Bangles (CBS)
36	48	I'VE BEEN IN LOVE BEFORE	Cutting Crew (Siren)
-	49	SLOW RIVERS	Elton John & Cliff Richard (Rocket)
-	50	REAL WILD CHILD (WILD ONE)	Iggy Pop (A&M)

20 December 1986

last	this		
16	1	CARAVAN OF LOVE	Housemartins (Go! Discs)
1	2	THE FINAL COUNTDOWN	Europe (Epic)
2	3	SOMETIMES	Erasure (Mute)
27	4	OPEN YOUR HEART	Madonna (Sire)
9	5	THE RAIN	Oran 'Juice' Jones (Def Jam)
10	6	SHAKE YOU DOWN	Gregory Abbott (CBS)
13	7	SO COLD THE NIGHT	Communards (London)
42	8	REET PETITE	Jackie Wilson (SMP)
3	9	TAKE MY BREATH AWAY	Berlin (CBS)
5	10	LIVING ON A PRAYER	Bon Jovi (Vertigo)
4	11	EACH TIME YOU BREAK MY HEART	Nick Kamen (WEA)
6	12	FRENCH KISSIN' IN THE USA	Debbie Harry (Chrysalis)
24	13	CRY WOLF	A-ha (Warner Bros)
8	14	THE SKYE BOAT SONG	Roger Whittaker & Des O'Connor (Tembo)
7	15	BREAKOUT	Swing Out Sister (Mercury)
19	16	SHIVER	George Benson (Warner Bros)
11	17	YOU KEEP ME HANGIN' ON	Kim Wilde (MCA)
21	18	LAND OF CONFUSION	Genesis (Virgin)
-	19	BIG FUN	Gap Band (Total Experience)
12	20	SHOWING OUT	Mel & Kim (Supreme)
26	21	IS THIS LOVE	Alison Moyet (CBS)
17	22	WAR (WHAT IS IT GOOD FOR)	Bruce Springsteen (CBS)
30	23	STEP RIGHT UP	Jaki Graham (EMI)
46	24	BECAUSE OF YOU	Dexy's Midnight Runners (Mercury)
15	25	FOR AMERICA	Red Box (Sire)
14	26	SWEET LOVE	Anita Baker (Elektra)
23	27	CANDY	Cameo (Club)
25	28	THE MIRACLE OF LOVE	Eurythmics (RCA)
-	29	OH MY FATHER HAD A RABBIT	Ray Moore (Play)
18	30	IF I SAY YES	Five Star (Tent)
36	31	DREAMIN'	Status Quo (Vertigo)
44	32	ONLY LOVE REMAINS	Paul McCartney (Parlophone)
32	33	ALL IS ASK OF YOU	Cliff Richard & Sarah Brightman (Polydor)
28	34	ANYTHING	Damned (MCA)
22	35	THROUGH THE BARRICADES	Spandau Ballet (Reformation)
-	36	NIGHTS OF PLEASURE	Loose Ends (Virgin)
20	37	WARRIORS OF THE WASTELAND	Frankie Goes To Hollywood (ZTT)
43	38	HYMN TO HER	Pretenders (Real)
29	39	GHOSTDANCING	Simple Minds (Virgin)
31	40	BECAUSE I LOVE YOU	Shakin' Stevens (Epic)
41	41	BIG IN AMERICA	Stranglers (Epic)
-	42	THE BOY IN THE BUBBLE	Paul Simon (Warner Bros)
-	43	OVER THE HILLS AND FAR AWAY	Gary Moore (10)
-	44	I'M ALL YOU NEED	Samantha Fox (Jive)
-	45	A SPACEMAN CAME TRAVELLING	Chris De Burgh (A&M)
-	46	LAST CHRISTMAS	Wham! (Epic)
47	47	DON'T GIVE UP	Peter Gabriel & Kate Bush (Virgin)
35	48	HOLD THE HEART	Big Country (Mercury)
45	49	LOVE IS THE SLUG	Fuzzbox (Vindaloo)
47	50	WALK LIKE AN EGYPTIAN	Bangles (CBS)

The Final Countdown hitmakers Europe came from Sweden, and were only the second Swedish act to top the UK chart since Abba (fellow Scandinavians A-ha being Norwegian). Newcomer Nick Kamen was a former male model and star of Levi's TV ads, while the year-end silly season hit was from chart veterans Roger Whittaker and Des O'Connor, duetting on a remake of the traditional *Skye Boat Song*.

3 January 1987

last week	this week	title	artist
1	1	CARAVAN OF LOVE	Housemartins (Go! Discs)
8	2	REET PETITE	Jackie Wilson (SMP)
4	3	OPEN YOUR HEART	Madonna (Sire)
2	4	THE FINAL COUNTDOWN	Europe (Epic)
3	5	SOMETIMES	Erasure (Mute)
7	6	SO COLD THE NIGHT	Communards (London)
6	7	SHAKE YOU DOWN	Gregory Abbott (CBS)
5	8	THE RAIN	Oran 'Juice' Jones (Def Jam)
13	9	CRY WOLF	A-ha (Warner Bros)
10	10	LIVING ON A PRAYER	Bon Jovi (Vertigo)
21	11	IS THIS LOVE	Alison Moyet (CBS)
19	12	BIG FUN	Gap Band (Total Experience)
9	13	TAKE MY BREATH AWAY	Berlin (CBS)
24	14	BECAUSE OF YOU	Dexy's Midnight Runners (Mercury)
23	15	STEP RIGHT UP	Jaki Graham (EMI)
18	16	LAND OF CONFUSION	Genesis (Virgin)
31	17	DREAMIN'	Status Quo (Vertigo)
12	18	FRENCH KISSIN' IN THE USA	Debbie Harry (Chrysalis)
14	19	THE SKYE BOAT SONG	Roger Whittaker & Des O'Connor (Tembo)
11	20	EACH TIME YOU BREAK MY HEART	Nick Kamen (WEA)
16	21	SHIVER	George Benson (Warner Bros)
43	22	OVER THE HILLS AND FAR AWAY	Gary Moore (10)
28	23	THE MIRACLE OF LOVE	Eurythmics (RCA)
38	24	HYMN TO HER	Pretenders (Real)
15	25	BREAKOUT	Swing Out Sister (Mercury)
27	26	CANDY	Cameo (Club)
26	27	SWEET LOVE	Anita Baker (Elektra)
	28	SANTA CLAUS IS ON THE DOLE	Spitting Image (Virgin)
32	29	ONLY LOVE REMAINS	Paul McCartney (Parlophone)
42	30	THE BOY IN THE BUBBLE	Paul Simon (Warner Bros)
-	31	BALLERINA GIRL	Lionel Richie (Motown)
-	32	NO MORE THE FOOL	Elkie Brooks (Legend)
17	33	YOU KEEP ME HANGIN' ON	Kim Wilde (MCA)
34	34	IF I SAY YES	Five Star (Tent)
46	35	LAST CHRISTMAS	Wham! (Epic)
20	36	SHOWING OUT	Mel & Kim (Supreme)
29	37	OH MY FATHER HAD A RABBIT	Ray Moore (Play)
44	38	I'M ALL YOU NEED	Samantha Fox (Jive)
33	39	ALL I ASK OF YOU	Cliff Richard & Sarah Brightman (Polydor)
22	40	WAR (WHAT IS IT GOOD FOR)	Bruce Springsteen (CBS)
50	41	WALK LIKE AN EGYPTIAN	Bangles (CBS)
25	42	FOR AMERICA	Red Box (Sire)
35	43	THROUGH THE BARRICADES	Spandau Ballet (Reformation)
39	44	GHOSTDANCING	Simple Minds (Virgin)
48	45	HOLD THE HEART	Big Country (Mercury)
-	46	HEY! LUCIANI	Fall (Beggars Banquet)
47	47	REAL WILD CHILD	Iggy Pop (A&M)
36	48	NIGHTS OF PLEASURE	Loose Ends (Virgin)
41	49	BIG IN AMERICA	Stranglers (Epic)
45	50	A SPACEMAN CAME TRAVELLING	Chris De Burgh (A&M)

10 January 1987

last week	this week	title	artist
2	1	REET PETITE	Jackie Wilson (SMP)
1	2	CARAVAN OF LOVE	Housemartins (Go! Discs)
3	3	OPEN YOUR HEART	Madonna (Sire)
4	4	THE FINAL COUNTDOWN	Europe (Epic)
9	5	CRY WOLF	A-ha (Warner Bros)
11	6	IS THIS LOVE	Alison Moyet (CBS)
5	7	SOMETIMES	Erasure (Mute)
6	8	SO COLD THE NIGHT	Communards (London)
8	9	THE RAIN	Oran 'Juice' Jones (Def Jam)
7	10	SHAKE YOU DOWN	Gregory Abbott (CBS)
12	11	BIG FUN	Gap Band (Total Experience)
10	12	LIVING ON A PRAYER	Bon Jovi (Vertigo)
14	13	BECAUSE OF YOU	Dexy's Midnight Runners (Mercury)
13	14	TAKE MY BREATH AWAY	Berlin (CBS)
16	15	LAND OF CONFUSION	Genesis (Virgin)
32	16	NO MORE THE FOOL	Elkie Brooks (Legend)
15	17	STEP RIGHT UP	Jaki Graham (EMI)
23	18	THE MIRACLE OF LOVE	Eurythmics (RCA)
17	19	DREAMIN'	Status Quo (Vertigo)
24	20	HYMN TO HER	Pretenders (Real)
22	21	OVER THE HILLS AND FAR AWAY	Gary Moore (10)
18	22	FRENCH KISSIN' IN THE USA	Debbie Harry (Chrysalis)
21	23	SHIVER	George Benson (Warner Bros)
29	24	ONLY LOVE REMAINS	Paul McCartney (Parlophone)
20	25	EACH TIME YOU BREAK MY HEART	Nick Kamen (WEA)
19	26	THE SKYE BOAT SONG	Roger Whittaker & Des O'Connor (Tembo)
30	27	THE BOY IN THE BUBBLE	Paul Simon (Warner Bros)
41	28	WALK LIKE AN EGYPTIAN	Bangles (CBS)
26	29	CANDY	Cameo (Club)
39	30	ALL I ASK OF YOU	Cliff Richard & Sarah Brightman (Polydor)
25	31	BREAKOUT	Swing Out Sister (Mercury)
33	32	YOU KEEP ME HANGIN' ON	Kim Wilde (MCA)
31	33	BALLERINA GIRL	Lionel Richie (Motown)
-	34	YOU CAN DANCE	Go Go Lorenzo & the Davis Pinkney Project (Boiling Point)
42	35	FOR AMERICA	Red Box (Sire)
37	36	OH MY FATHER HAD A RABBIT	Ray Moore (Play)
36	37	SHOWING OUT	Mel & Kim (Supreme)
28	38	SANTA CLAUS IS ON THE DOLE	Spitting Image (Virgin)
27	39	SWEET LOVE	Anita Baker (Elektra)
34	40	IF I SAY YES	Five Star (Tent)
50	41	A SPACEMAN CAME TRAVELLING	Chris De Burgh (A&M)
40	42	WAR (WHAT IS IT GOOD FOR)	Bruce Springsteen (CBS)
-	43	HIP TO BE SQUARE	Huey Lewis & the News (Chrysalis)
47	44	REAL WILD CHILD	Iggy Pop (A&M)
-	45	C'EST LA VIE	Robbie Nevil (Manhattan)
-	46	ALMAZ	Randy Crawford (Warner Bros)
-	47	MUSIC OF THE NIGHT	Michael Crawford & Sarah Brightman (Polydor)
-	48	EVERY LOSER WINS	Nick Berry (BBC)
49	49	BIG IN AMERICA	Stranglers (Epic)
46	50	HEY! LUCIANI	Fall (Beggars Banquet)

17 January 1987

last week	this week	title	artist
1	1	REET PETITE	Jackie Wilson (SMP)
6	2	IS THIS LOVE	Alison Moyet (CBS)
2	3	CARAVAN OF LOVE	Housemartins (Go! Discs)
5	4	CRY WOLF	A-ha (Warner Bros)
11	5	BIG FUN	Gap Band (Total Experience)
3	6	OPEN YOUR HEART	Madonna (Sire)
7	7	SOMETIMES	Erasure (Mute)
16	8	NO MORE THE FOOL	Elkie Brooks (Legend)
4	9	THE FINAL COUNTDOWN	Europe (Epic)
-	10	JACK YOUR BODY	Steve 'Silk' Hurley (DJ International)
9	11	THE RAIN	Oran 'Juice' Jones (Def Jam)
12	12	LIVING ON A PRAYER	Bon Jovi (Vertigo)
10	13	SHAKE YOU DOWN	Gregory Abbott (CBS)
20	14	HYMN TO HER	Pretenders (Real)
8	15	SO COLD THE NIGHT	Communards (London)
17	16	STEP RIGHT UP	Jaki Graham (EMI)
21	17	OVER THE HILLS AND FAR AWAY	Gary Moore (10)
33	18	BALLERINA GIRL	Lionel Richie (Motown)
27	19	THE BOY IN THE BUBBLE	Paul Simon (Warner Bros)
18	20	THE MIRACLE OF LOVE	Eurythmics (RCA)
19	21	DREAMIN'	Status Quo (Vertigo)
45	22	C'EST LA VIE	Robbie Nevil (Manhattan)
44	23	REAL WILD CHILD	Iggy Pop (A&M)
15	24	LAND OF CONFUSION	Genesis (Virgin)
-	25	WALKING DOWN YOUR STREET	Bangles (CBS)
22	26	FRENCH KISSIN' IN THE USA	Debbie Harry (Chrysalis)
-	27	SOMETHING IN MY HOUSE	Dead Or Alive (Epic)
14	28	TAKE MY BREATH AWAY	Berlin (CBS)
13	29	BECAUSE OF YOU	Dexy's Midnight Runners (Mercury)
-	30	THIS WHEEL'S ON FIRE	Siouxsie & the Banshees (Wonderland)
-	31	WASTELAND	Mission (Mercury)
40	32	IF I SAY YES	Five Star (Tent)
23	33	SHIVER	George Benson (Warner Bros)
-	34	TRAMPOLENE	Julian Cope (Island)
-	35	SURRENDER	Swing Out Sister (Mercury)
-	36	ONCE BITTEN TWICE SHY	Vesta Williams (A&M)
32	37	YOU KEEP ME HANGIN' ON	Kim Wilde (MCA)
24	38	ONLY LOVE REMAINS	Paul McCartney (Parlophone)
-	39	IT DIDN'T MATTER	Style Council (Polydor)
-	40	KISS	Age of Chance (Fon)
25	41	EACH TIME YOU BREAK MY HEART	Nick Kamen (WEA)
37	42	SHOWING OUT	Mel & Kim (Supreme)
-	43	I LOVE MY RADIO	Taffy (Transglobal)
-	44	BEHIND THE MASK	Eric Clapton (Duck)
29	45	CANDY	Cameo (Club)
-	46	RAT IN MI KITCHEN	UB40 (DEP International)
31	47	BREAKOUT	Swing Out Sister (Mercury)
34	48	YOU CAN DANCE	Go Go Lorenzo & the Davis Pinkney Project (Boiling Point)
46	49	ALMAZ	Randy Crawford (Warner Bros)
47	50	MUSIC OF THE NIGHT	Michael Crawford & Sarah Brightman (Polydor)

The Housemartins' *Caravan Of Love* was a cover of a small US hit of a year earlier by Isley Jasper Isley, the breakaway younger three ex-members of the Isley Brothers. Jackie Wilson's *Reet Petite*, meanwhile, was a straight reissue of his first hit single from 1957, when it had peaked at Number Six. This time, Wilson had three posthumous weeks at the top of the chart and sales of over 750,000.

January – February 1987

24 January 1987

last week	this week		
1	1	REET PETITE	Jackie Wilson (SMP)
10	2	JACK YOUR BODY	Steve 'Silk' Hurley (DJ International)
2	3	IS THIS LOVE	Alison Moyet (CBS)
22	4	C'EST LA VIE	Robbie Nevil (Manhattan)
5	5	BIG FUN	Gap Band (Total Experience)
35	6	SURRENDER	Swing Out Sister (Mercury)
8	7	NO MORE THE FOOL	Elkie Brooks (Legend)
14	8	HYMN TO HER	Pretenders (Real)
39	9	IT DIDN'T MATTER	Style Council (Polydor)
7	10	SOMETIMES	Erasure (Mute)
23	11	REAL WILD CHILD	Iggy Pop (A&M)
3	12	CARAVAN OF LOVE	Housemartins (Go! Discs)
4	13	CRY WOLF	A-ha (Warner Bros)
17	14	OVER THE HILLS AND FAR AWAY	Gary Moore (10)
11	15	THE RAIN	Oran 'Juice' Jones (Def Jam)
31	16	WASTELAND	Mission (Mercury)
6	17	OPEN YOUR HEART	Madonna (Sire)
18	18	BALLERINA GIRL	Lionel Richie (Motown)
9	19	THE FINAL COUNTDOWN	Europe (Epic)
13	20	SHAKE YOU DOWN	Gregory Abbott (CBS)
12	21	LIVING ON A PRAYER	Bon Jovi (Vertigo)
34	22	TRAMPOLENE	Julian Cope (Island)
30	23	THIS WHEEL'S ON FIRE	Siouxsie & the Banshees (Wonderland)
27	24	SOMETHING IN MY HOUSE	Dead Or Alive (Epic)
19	25	THE BOY IN THE BUBBLE	Paul Simon (Warner Bros)
16	26	STEP RIGHT UP	Jaki Graham (EMI)
25	27	WALKING DOWN YOUR STREET	Bangles (CBS)
46	28	RAT IN MI KITCHEN	UB40 (DEP International)
15	29	SO COLD THE NIGHT	Communards (London)
43	30	I LOVE MY RADIO	Taffy (Transglobal)
24	31	LAND OF CONFUSION	Genesis (Virgin)
40	32	KISS	Age of Chance (Fon)
21	33	DREAMIN'	Status Quo (Vertigo)
36	34	ONCE BITTEN TWICE SHY	Vesta Williams (A&M)
-	35	YOU SEXY THING	Hot Chocolate (EMI)
-	36	VICTORY	Kool & the Gang (Club)
-	37	JACK THE GROOVE	Raze (Champion)
49	38	ALMAZ	Randy Crawford (Warner Bros)
-	39	YOU DON'T KNOW	Berlin (Mercury)
-	40	DOWN TO EARTH	Curiosity Killed The Cat (Mercury)
-	41	I.O.U.	Freeez (Citybeat)
20	42	THE MIRACLE OF LOVE	Eurythmics (RCA)
45	43	CANDY	Cameo (Club)
32	44	IF I SAY YES	Five Star (Tent)
-	45	HEARTACHE	Pepsi & Shirlie (Polydor)
-	46	MAGIC SMILE	Rosie Vela (A&M)
-	47	LOVE IS FOREVER	Billy Ocean (Jive)
-	48	SOUL MAN	Sam Moore & Lou Reed (A&M)
-	49	CHAMP	Mohawks (Pama)
47	50	BREAKOUT	Swing Out Sister (Mercury)

31 January 1987

last week	this week		
4	1	C'EST LA VIE	Robbie Nevil (Manhattan)
2	2	JACK YOUR BODY	Steve 'Silk' Hurley (DJ International)
1	3	REET PETITE	Jackie Wilson (SMP)
3	4	IS THIS LOVE	Alison Moyet (CBS)
6	5	SURRENDER	Swing Out Sister (Mercury)
7	6	NO MORE THE FOOL	Elkie Brooks (Legend)
5	7	BIG FUN	Gap Band (Total Experience)
8	8	HYMN TO HER	Pretenders (Real)
9	9	IT DIDN'T MATTER	Style Council (Polydor)
16	10	WASTELAND	Mission (Mercury)
11	11	REAL WILD CHILD	Iggy Pop (A&M)
24	12	SOMETHING IN MY HOUSE	Dead Or Alive (Epic)
23	13	THIS WHEEL'S ON FIRE	Siouxsie & the Banshees (Wonderland)
27	14	WALKING DOWN YOUR STREET	Bangles (CBS)
28	15	RAT IN MI KITCHEN	UB40 (DEP International)
40	16	DOWN TO EARTH	Curiosity Killed The Cat (Mercury)
45	17	HEARTACHE	Pepsi & Shirlie (Polydor)
22	18	TRAMPOLENE	Julian Cope (Island)
38	19	ALMAZ	Randy Crawford (Warner Bros)
-	20	I KNEW YOU WERE WAITING	Aretha Franklin & George Michael (Epic)
30	21	I LOVE MY RADIO	Taffy (Transglobal)
10	22	SOMETIMES	Erasure (Mute)
41	23	I.O.U.	Freeez (Citybeat)
14	24	OVER THE HILLS AND FAR AWAY	Gary Moore (10)
37	25	JACK THE GROOVE	Raze (Champion)
18	26	BALLERINA GIRL	Lionel Richie (Motown)
35	27	YOU SEXY THING	Hot Chocolate (EMI)
12	28	CARAVAN OF LOVE	Housemartins (Go! Discs)
32	29	KISS	Age of Chance (Fon)
31	30	LAND OF CONFUSION	Genesis (Virgin)
34	31	ONCE BITTEN TWICE SHY	Vesta Williams (A&M)
25	32	THE BOY IN THE BUBBLE	Paul Simon (Warner Bros)
13	33	CRY WOLF	A-ha (Warner Bros)
46	34	MAGIC SMILE	Rosie Vela (A&M)
48	35	SOUL MAN	Sam Moore & Lou Reed (A&M)
-	36	BEST KEPT SECRET	China Crisis (Virgin)
-	37	BEHIND THE MASK	Eric Clapton (Duck)
-	38	SLOW TRAIN TO DAWN	The The (Some Bizzare)
29	39	SO COLD THE NIGHT	Communards (London)
20	40	SHAKE YOU DOWN	Gregory Abbott (CBS)
15	41	THE RAIN	Oran 'Juice' Jones (Def Jam)
-	42	BACK IN THE HIGH LIFE	Steve Winwood (Island)
36	43	VICTORY	Kool & the Gang (Club)
19	44	THE FINAL COUNTDOWN	Europe (Epic)
42	45	THE MIRACLE OF LOVE	Eurythmics (RCA)
-	46	TROUBLE TOWN	Daintees (Kitchenware)
-	47	FACTS AND FIGURES	Hugh Cornwell (Virgin)
-	48	MUSIC OF THE NIGHT	Michael Crawford & Sarah Brightman (Polydor)
-	49	CROSS THAT BRIDGE	Ward Brothers (Siren)
17	50	OPEN YOUR HEART	Madonna (Sire)

7 February 1987

last week	this week		
20	1	I KNEW YOU WERE WAITING	Aretha Franklin & George Michael (Epic)
2	2	JACK YOUR BODY	Steve 'Silk' Hurley (DJ International)
1	3	C'EST LA VIE	Robbie Nevil (Manhattan)
17	4	HEARTACHE	Pepsi & Shirlie (Polydor)
16	5	DOWN TO EARTH	Curiosity Killed The Cat (Mercury)
19	6	ALMAZ	Randy Crawford (Warner Bros)
6	7	NO MORE THE FOOL	Elkie Brooks (Legend)
5	8	SURRENDER	Swing Out Sister (Mercury)
4	9	IS THIS LOVE	Alison Moyet (CBS)
15	10	RAT IN MI KITCHEN	UB40 (DEP International)
10	11	WASTELAND	Mission (Mercury)
3	12	REET PETITE	Jackie Wilson (SMP)
21	13	I LOVE MY RADIO	Taffy (Transglobal)
7	14	BIG FUN	Gap Band (Total Experience)
12	15	SOMETHING IN MY HOUSE	Dead Or Alive (Epic)
-	16	SHOPLIFTERS OF THE WORLD UNITE	Smiths (Rough Trade)
-	17	IT DOESN'T HAVE TO BE THAT WAY	Blow Monkeys (RCA)
27	18	YOU SEXY THING	Hot Chocolate (EMI)
11	19	REAL WILD CHILD	Iggy Pop (A&M)
25	20	JACK THE GROOVE	Raze (Champion)
13	21	THIS WHEEL'S ON FIRE	Siouxsie & the Banshees (Wonderland)
8	22	HYMN TO HER	Pretenders (Real)
14	23	WALKING DOWN YOUR STREET	Bangles (CBS)
9	24	IT DIDN'T MATTER	Style Council (Polydor)
34	25	MAGIC SMILE	Rosie Vela (A&M)
23	26	I.O.U.	Freeez (Citybeat)
48	27	MUSIC OF THE NIGHT	Michael Crawford & Sarah Brightman (Polydor)
18	28	TRAMPOLENE	Julian Cope (Island)
37	29	BEHIND THE MASK	Eric Clapton (Duck)
31	30	ONCE BITTEN TWICE SHY	Vesta Williams (A&M)
-	31	ROCK THE NIGHT	Europe (Epic)
-	32	STRANGERS IN OUR TOWN	Spear of Destiny (10)
22	33	SOMETIMES	Erasure (Mute)
43	34	VICTORY	Kool & the Gang (Club)
-	35	STAY OUT OF MY LIFE	Five Star (Tent)
-	36	THE FUTURE'S SO BRIGHT I GOTTA WEAR GLASSES	Timbuk 3 (IRS)
36	37	BEST KEPT SECRET	China Crisis (Virgin)
-	38	FROZEN HEART	FM (Portrait)
35	39	SOUL MAN	Sam Moore & Lou Reed (A&M)
24	40	OVER THE HILLS AND FAR AWAY	Gary Moore (10)
49	41	CROSS THAT BRIDGE	Ward Brothers (Siren)
-	42	ELDORADO	Drum Theatre (Epic)
-	43	GIGOLO	Damned (MCA)
-	44	FORGOTTEN TOWN	Christians (Island)
41	45	THE RAIN	Oran 'Juice' Jones (Def Jam)
28	46	CARAVAN OF LOVE	Housemartins (Go! Discs)
26	47	BALLERINA GIRL	Lionel Richie (Motown)
-	48	LOVE IS FOREVER	Billy Ocean (Jive)
47	49	FACTS AND FIGURES	Hugh Cornwell (Virgin)
40	50	SHAKE YOU DOWN	Gregory Abbott (CBS)

For once, duetting with Aretha Franklin on *I Knew You Were Waiting (For Me)*, George Michael topped the chart with a song he had not written – it was penned by Dennis Morgan and Simon Climie, the latter being half of the hit duo Climie Fisher. This was the first time Aretha had topped the chart in Britain, though she was no stranger to the US Number One slot – and hit it again with this song.

460

14 February 1987

last week	this week		
1	1	I KNEW YOU WERE WAITING	Aretha Franklin & George Michael (Epic)
4	2	HEARTACHE	Pepsi & Shirlie (Polydor)
6	3	ALMAZ	Randy Crawford (Warner Bros)
5	4	DOWN TO EARTH	Curiosity Killed The Cat (Mercury)
2	5	JACK YOUR BODY	Steve 'Silk' Hurley (DJ International)
17	6	IT DOESN'T HAVE TO BE THAT WAY	Blow Monkeys (RCA)
3	7	C'EST LA VIE	Robbie Nevil (Manhattan)
16	8	SHOPLIFTERS OF THE WORLD UNITE	Smiths (Rough Trade)
13	9	I LOVE MY RADIO	Taffy (Transglobal)
7	10	NO MORE THE FOOL	Elkie Brooks (Legend)
8	11	SURRENDER	Swing Out Sister (Mercury)
18	12	YOU SEXY THING	Hot Chocolate (EMI)
9	13	IS THIS LOVE	Alison Moyet (CBS)
10	14	RAT IN MI KITCHEN	UB40 (DEP International)
30	15	ONCE BITTEN TWICE SHY	Vesta Williams (A&M)
11	16	WASTELAND	Mission (Mercury)
-	17	MALE STRIPPER	Man 2 Man (Bolts)
35	18	STAY OUT OF MY LIFE	Five Star (Tent)
12	19	REET PETITE	Jackie Wilson (SMP)
27	20	MUSIC OF THE NIGHT	Michael Crawford & Sarah Brightman (Polydor)
43	21	GIGOLO	Damned (MCA)
14	22	BIG FUN	Gap Band (Total Experience)
25	23	MAGIC SMILE	Rosie Vela (A&M)
29	24	BEHIND THE MASK	Eric Clapton (Duck)
28	25	TRAMPOLENE	Julian Cope (Island)
36	26	THE FUTURE'S SO BRIGHT I GOTTA WEAR GLASSES	Timbuk 3 (IRS)
15	27	SOMETHING IN MY HOUSE	Dead Or Alive (Epic)
20	28	JACK THE GROOVE	Raze (Champion)
31	29	ROCK THE NIGHT	Europe (Epic)
22	30	HYMN TO HER	Pretenders (Real)
19	31	REAL WILD CHILD	Iggy Pop (A&M)
21	32	THIS WHEEL'S ON FIRE	Siouxsie & the Banshees (Wonderland)
41	33	CROSS THAT BRIDGE	Ward Brothers (Siren)
-	34	RUNNING IN THE FAMILY	Level 42 (Polydor)
-	35	STAND BY ME	Ben E. King (Atlantic)
37	36	BEST KEPT SECRET	China Crisis (Virgin)
-	37	I FOUND LOVE	Darlene Davis (Serious)
24	38	IT DIDN'T MATTER	Style Council (Polydor)
32	39	STRANGERS IN OUR TOWN	Spear of Destiny (10)
-	40	HEAD GOES ASTRAY	Soup Dragons (Raw)
-	41	CRUSH ON YOU	Jets (MCA)
-	42	COMING AROUND AGAIN	Carly Simon (Arista)
44	43	FORGOTTEN TOWN	Christians (Island)
-	44	YOU BE ILLIN'	Run DMC (Profile)
39	45	SOUL MAN	Sam Moore & Lou Reed (A&M)
23	46	WALKING DOWN YOUR STREET	Bangles (CBS)
38	47	FROZEN HEART	FM (Portrait)
26	48	I.O.U.	Freeez (Citybeat)
47	49	BALLERINA GIRL	Lionel Richie (Motown)
-	50	HOW MANY LIES?	Spandau Ballet (Reformation)

21 February 1987

1	1	I KNEW YOU WERE WAITING	Aretha Franklin & George Michael (Epic)
2	2	HEARTACHE	Pepsi & Shirlie (Polydor)
4	3	DOWN TO EARTH	Curiosity Killed The Cat (Mercury)
6	4	IT DOESN'T HAVE TO BE THAT WAY	Blow Monkeys (RCA)
3	5	ALMAZ	Randy Crawford (Warner Bros)
17	6	MALE STRIPPER	Man 2 Man (Bolts)
9	7	I LOVE MY RADIO	Taffy (Transglobal)
35	8	STAND BY ME	Ben E. King (Atlantic)
12	9	YOU SEXY THING	Hot Chocolate (EMI)
20	10	MUSIC OF THE NIGHT	Michael Crawford & Sarah Brightman (Polydor)
18	11	STAY OUT OF MY LIFE	Five Star (Tent)
8	12	SHOPLIFTERS OF THE WORLD UNITE	Smiths (Rough Trade)
34	13	RUNNING IN THE FAMILY	Level 42 (Polydor)
24	14	BEHIND THE MASK	Eric Clapton (Duck)
5	15	JACK YOUR BODY	Steve 'Silk' Hurley (DJ International)
-	16	WHEN A MAN LOVES A WOMAN	Percy Sledge (Atlantic)
15	17	ONCE BITTEN TWICE SHY	Vesta Williams (A&M)
10	18	NO MORE THE FOOL	Elkie Brooks (Legend)
26	19	THE FUTURE'S SO BRIGHT I GOTTA WEAR GLASSES	Timbuk 3 (IRS)
13	20	IS THIS LOVE	Alison Moyet (CBS)
29	21	ROCK THE NIGHT	Europe (Epic)
7	22	C'EST LA VIE	Robbie Nevil (Manhattan)
23	23	MAGIC SMILE	Rosie Vela (A&M)
42	24	THE RIGHT THING	Simply Red (WEA)
-	25	COMING AROUND AGAIN	Carly Simon (Arista)
21	26	GIGOLO	Damned (MCA)
43	27	FORGOTTEN TOWN	Christians (Island)
11	28	SURRENDER	Swing Out Sister (Mercury)
27	29	SOMETHING IN MY HOUSE	Dead Or Alive (Epic)
-	30	LIVE IT UP	Mental As Anything (Epic)
14	31	RAT IN MI KITCHEN	UB40 (DEP International)
32	32	THIS WHEEL'S ON FIRE	Siouxsie & the Banshees (Wonderland)
50	33	HOW MANY LIES?	Spandau Ballet (Reformation)
16	34	WASTELAND	Mission (Mercury)
37	35	I FOUND LOVE	Darlene Davis (Serious)
38	36	IT DIDN'T MATTER	Style Council (Polydor)
-	37	EVANGELINE	Icicle Works (Beggars Banquet)
-	38	SHIP OF FOOLS	World Party (Ensign)
44	39	YOU BE ILLIN'	Run DMC (Profile)
-	40	YOU ARE MY WORLD	Communards (London)
19	41	REET PETITE	Jackie Wilson (SMP)
22	42	BIG FUN	Gap Band (Total Experience)
40	43	HEAD GOES ASTRAY	Soup Dragons (Raw)
30	44	HYMN TO HER	Pretenders (Real)
31	45	REAL WILD CHILD	Iggy Pop (A&M)
45	46	SOUL MAN	Sam Moore & Lou Reed (A&M)
-	47	GOOD TO GO LOVER	Gwen Guthrie (Boiling Point)
48	48	WHO IS IT?	Mantronix (10)
-	49	SKIN TRADE	Duran Duran (EMI)
-	50	WHEN LOVE COMES CALLING	Paul Johnson (CBS)

28 February 1987

8	1	STAND BY ME	Ben E. King (Atlantic)
16	2	WHEN A MAN LOVES A WOMAN	Percy Sledge (Atlantic)
1	3	I KNEW YOU WERE WAITING	Aretha Franklin & George Michael (Epic)
3	4	DOWN TO EARTH	Curiosity Killed The Cat (Mercury)
6	5	MALE STRIPPER	Man 2 Man (Bolts)
2	6	HEARTACHE	Pepsi & Shirlie (Polydor)
13	7	RUNNING IN THE FAMILY	Level 42 (Polydor)
11	8	STAY OUT OF MY LIFE	Five Star (Tent)
4	9	IT DOESN'T HAVE TO BE THAT WAY	Blow Monkeys (RCA)
5	10	ALMAZ	Randy Crawford (Warner Bros)
-	11	SONIC BOOM BOY	Westworld (RCA)
9	12	YOU SEXY THING	Hot Chocolate (EMI)
14	13	BEHIND THE MASK	Eric Clapton (Duck)
30	14	LIVE IT UP	Mental As Anything (Epic)
10	15	MUSIC OF THE NIGHT	Michael Crawford & Sarah Brightman (Polydor)
7	16	I LOVE MY RADIO	Taffy (Transglobal)
25	17	COMING AROUND AGAIN	Carly Simon (Arista)
-	18	CRUSH ON YOU	Jets (MCA)
-	19	LOVE REMOVAL MACHINE	Cult (Beggars Banquet)
24	20	THE RIGHT THING	Simply Red (WEA)
49	21	SKIN TRADE	Duran Duran (EMI)
17	22	ONCE BITTEN TWICE SHY	Vesta Williams (A&M)
21	23	ROCK THE NIGHT	Europe (Epic)
12	24	SHOPLIFTERS OF THE WORLD UNITE	Smiths (Rough Trade)
40	25	YOU ARE MY WORLD	Communards (London)
19	26	THE FUTURE'S SO BRIGHT I GOTTA WEAR GLASSES	Timbuk 3 (IRS)
-	27	I GET THE SWEETEST FEELING	Jackie Wilson (SMP)
-	28	STRANGERS IN OUR TOWN	Spear of Destiny (10)
29	29	FORGOTTEN TOWN	Christians (Island)
-	30	MANHATTAN SKYLINE	A-ha (Warner Bros)
-	31	I AM THE LAW	Anthrax (Island)
15	32	JACK YOUR BODY	Steve 'Silk' Hurley (DJ International)
-	33	EV'RY LITTLE BIT	Millie Scott (Fourth & Broadway)
-	34	V THIRTEEN	Big Audio Dynamite (CBS)
-	35	IT DOESN'T HAVE TO BE	Erasure (Mute)
33	36	HOW MANY LIES?	Spandau Ballet (Reformation)
18	37	NO MORE THE FOOL	Elkie Brooks (Legend)
26	38	GIGOLO	Damned (MCA)
35	39	I FOUND LOVE	Darlene Davis (Serious)
-	40	MISSIONARY MAN	Eurythmics (RCA)
46	41	SOUL MAN	Sam Moore & Lou Reed (A&M)
39	42	YOU BE ILLIN'	Run DMC (Profile)
36	43	IT DIDN'T MATTER	Style Council (Polydor)
45	44	REAL WILD CHILD	Iggy Pop (A&M)
48	45	WHO IS IT?	Mantronix (10)
-	46	IT'S MY BEAT	Sweet Tee & Jazzy Joyce (Cooltempo)
47	47	(YOU'VE GOTTA) FIGHT FOR YOUR RIGHT	Beastie Boys (Def Jam)
29	48	SOMETHING IN MY HOUSE	Dead Or Alive (Epic)
34	49	WASTELAND	Mission (Mercury)
38	50	SHIP OF FOOLS	World Party (Ensign)

Early in 1987, Levi's launched two new TV ads, each using a soul hit of the 60s from the Atlantic stable as its soundtrack. Both records – Ben E King's 1961 hit *Stand By Me* (which had only reached Number 27 originally) and Percy Sledge's *When A Man Loves A Woman* (Top Five in 1966) – were reissued to benefit from the valuable promotion, and rapidly bounded to Numbers One and Two respectively.

March 1987

7 March 1987

last week	this week	title	artist (label)
1	1	STAND BY ME	Ben E. King (Atlantic)
2	2	WHEN A MAN LOVES A WOMAN	Percy Sledge (Atlantic)
5	3	MALE STRIPPER	Man 2 Man (Bolts)
7	4	RUNNING IN THE FAMILY	Level 42 (Polydor)
4	5	DOWN TO EARTH	Curiosity Killed The Cat (Mercury)
14	6	LIVE IT UP	Mental As Anything (Epic)
18	7	CRUSH ON YOU	Jets (MCA)
6	8	HEARTACHE	Pepsi & Shirlie (Polydor)
11	9	SONIC BOOM BOY	Westworld (RCA)
3	10	I KNEW YOU WERE WAITING	Aretha Franklin & George Michael (Epic)
19	11	LOVE REMOVAL MACHINE	Cult (Beggars Banquet)
30	12	MANHATTAN SKYLINE	A-ha (Warner Bros)
20	13	THE RIGHT THING	Simply Red (WEA)
17	14	COMING AROUND AGAIN	Carly Simon (Arista)
23	15	ROCK THE NIGHT	Europe (Epic)
27	16	I GET THE SWEETEST FEELING	Jackie Wilson (SMP)
-	17	THE GREAT PRETENDER	Freddie Mercury (Parlophone)
-	18	EVERYTHING I OWN	Boy George (Virgin)
13	19	BEHIND THE MASK	Eric Clapton (Duck)
8	20	STAY OUT OF MY LIFE	Five Star (Tent)
1	21	IT DOESN'T HAVE TO BE THAT WAY	Blow Monkeys (RCA)
25	22	YOU ARE MY WORLD	Communards (London)
47	23	(YOU'VE GOTTA) FIGHT FOR YOUR RIGHT	Beastie Boys (Def Jam)
35	24	IT DOESN'T HAVE TO BE	Erasure (Mute)
31	25	I AM THE LAW	Anthrax (Island)
21	26	SKIN TRADE	Duran Duran (EMI)
-	27	WILD FRONTIER	Gary Moore (10)
-	28	PENNY LANE/STRAWBERRY FIELDS FOREVER	Beatles (Parlophone)
-	29	WATCHING THE WILDLIFE	Frankie Goes To Hollywood (ZTT)
16	30	I LOVE MY RADIO	Taffy (Transglobal)
10	31	ALMAZ	Randy Crawford (Warner Bros)
12	32	YOU SEXY THING	Hot Chocolate (EMI)
26	33	THE FUTURE'S SO BRIGHT I GOTTA WEAR GLASSES	Timbuk 3 (IRS)
33	34	EV'RY LITTLE BIT	Millie Scott (Fourth & Broadway)
29	35	FORGOTTEN TOWN	Christians (Island)
41	36	SOUL MAN	Sam Moore & Lou Reed (A&M)
-	37	DON'T NEED A GUN	Billy Idol (Chrysalis)
15	38	MUSIC OF THE NIGHT	Michael Crawford & Sarah Brightman (Polydor)
-	39	SHADES	Iggy Pop (A&M)
-	40	WEAK IN THE PRESENCE OF BEAUTY	Alison Moyet (CBS)
22	41	ONCE BITTEN TWICE SHY	Vesta Williams (A&M)
36	42	HOW MANY LIES?	Spandau Ballet (Reformation)
-	43	TOWN TO TOWN	Microdisney (Virgin)
-	44	WHEN LOVE COMES CALLING	Paul Johnson (CBS)
24	45	SHOPLIFTERS OF THE WORLD UNITE	Smiths (Rough Trade)
39	46	I FOUND LOVE	Darlene Davis (Serious)
40	47	MISSIONARY MAN	Eurythmics (RCA)
-	48	POISON STREET	New Model Army (EMI)
-	49	TRICK OF THE NIGHT	Bananarama (London)
-	50	IF YOU LET ME STAY	Terence Trent D'Arby (CBS)

14 March 1987

last week	this week	title	artist (label)
1	1	STAND BY ME	Ben E. King (Atlantic)
2	2	WHEN A MAN LOVES A WOMAN	Percy Sledge (Atlantic)
6	3	LIVE IT UP	Mental As Anything (Epic)
17	4	THE GREAT PRETENDER	Freddie Mercury (Parlophone)
18	5	EVERYTHING I OWN	Boy George (Virgin)
16	6	I GET THE SWEETEST FEELING	Jackie Wilson (SMP)
7	7	CRUSH ON YOU	Jets (MCA)
3	8	MALE STRIPPER	Man 2 Man (Bolts)
4	9	RUNNING IN THE FAMILY	Level 42 (Polydor)
13	10	THE RIGHT THING	Simply Red (WEA)
11	11	LOVE REMOVAL MACHINE	Cult (Beggars Banquet)
12	12	MANHATTAN SKYLINE	A-ha (Warner Bros)
9	13	SONIC BOOM BOY	Westworld (RCA)
5	14	DOWN TO EARTH	Curiosity Killed The Cat (Mercury)
14	15	COMING AROUND AGAIN	Carly Simon (Arista)
-	16	MOONLIGHTING	Al Jarreau (WEA)
23	17	(YOU'VE GOTTA) FIGHT FOR YOUR RIGHT	Beastie Boys (Def Jam)
-	18	RESPECTABLE	Mel & Kim (Supreme)
25	19	I AM THE LAW	Anthrax (Island)
24	20	IT DOESN'T HAVE TO BE	Erasure (Mute)
15	21	ROCK THE NIGHT	Europe (Epic)
26	22	SKIN TRADE	Duran Duran (EMI)
8	23	HEARTACHE	Pepsi & Shirlie (Polydor)
27	24	WILD FRONTIER	Gary Moore (10)
29	25	WATCHING THE WILDLIFE	Frankie Goes To Hollywood (ZTT)
40	26	WEAK IN THE PRESENCE OF BEAUTY	Alison Moyet (CBS)
10	27	I KNEW YOU WERE WAITING	Aretha Franklin & George Michael (Epic)
-	28	RESPECT YOURSELF	Bruce Willis (Motown)
-	29	SEVERINE	Mission (Mercury)
22	30	YOU ARE MY WORLD	Communards (London)
20	31	STAY OUT OF MY LIFE	Five Star (Tent)
37	32	DON'T NEED A GUN	Billy Idol (Chrysalis)
21	33	IT DOESN'T HAVE TO BE THAT WAY	Blow Monkeys (RCA)
47	34	MISSIONARY MAN	Eurythmics (RCA)
19	35	BEHIND THE MASK	Eric Clapton (Duck)
35	36	FORGOTTEN TOWN	Christians (Island)
45	37	SHOPLIFTERS OF THE WORLD UNITE	Smiths (Rough Trade)
30	38	I LOVE MY RADIO	Taffy (Transglobal)
-	39	SIGN O' THE TIMES	Prince (Paisley Park)
36	40	SOUL MAN	Sam Moore & Lou Reed (A&M)
-	41	WAITING	Style Council (Polydor)
-	42	LOVING YOU IS SWEETER THAN EVER	Nick Kamen (WEA)
43	43	WORKING UP A SWEAT	Full Circle (EMI America)
-	44	LET THE MUSIC TAKE CONTROL	J.M. Silk (RCA)
-	45	TONIGHT TONIGHT TONIGHT	Genesis (Virgin)
31	46	ALMAZ	Randy Crawford (Warner Bros)
-	47	HAPPY	Surface (CBS)
38	48	MUSIC OF THE NIGHT	Michael Crawford & Sarah Brightman (Polydor)
-	49	LET THE MUSIC MOVE U	Raze (Champion)
-	50	JIMMY LEE	Aretha Franklin (Arista)

21 March 1987

last week	this week	title	artist (label)
5	1	EVERYTHING I OWN	Boy George (Virgin)
4	2	THE GREAT PRETENDER	Freddie Mercury (Parlophone)
3	3	STAND BY ME	Ben E. King (Atlantic)
6	4	I GET THE SWEETEST FEELING	Jackie Wilson (SMP)
2	5	WHEN A MAN LOVES A WOMAN	Percy Sledge (Atlantic)
18	6	RESPECTABLE	Mel & Kim (Supreme)
3	7	LIVE IT UP	Mental As Anything (Epic)
16	8	MOONLIGHTING	Al Jarreau (WEA)
7	9	CRUSH ON YOU	Jets (MCA)
39	10	SIGN O' THE TIMES	Prince (Paisley Park)
8	11	MALE STRIPPER	Man 2 Man (Bolts)
9	12	RUNNING IN THE FAMILY	Level 42 (Polydor)
26	13	WEAK IN THE PRESENCE OF BEAUTY	Alison Moyet (CBS)
20	14	IT DOESN'T HAVE TO BE	Erasure (Mute)
10	15	THE RIGHT THING	Simply Red (WEA)
11	16	LOVE REMOVAL MACHINE	Cult (Beggars Banquet)
45	17	TONIGHT TONIGHT TONIGHT	Genesis (Virgin)
15	18	COMING AROUND AGAIN	Carly Simon (Arista)
29	19	SEVERINE	Mission (Mercury)
12	20	MANHATTAN SKYLINE	A-ha (Warner Bros)
17	21	(YOU'VE GOTTA) FIGHT FOR YOUR RIGHT	Beastie Boys (Def Jam)
13	22	SONIC BOOM BOY	Westworld (RCA)
28	23	RESPECT YOURSELF	Bruce Willis (Motown)
14	24	DOWN TO EARTH	Curiosity Killed The Cat (Mercury)
25	25	WATCHING THE WILDLIFE	Frankie Goes To Hollywood (ZTT)
42	26	LOVING YOU IS SWEETER THAN EVER	Nick Kamen (WEA)
36	27	FORGOTTEN TOWN	Christians (Island)
24	28	WILD FRONTIER	Gary Moore (10)
22	29	SKIN TRADE	Duran Duran (EMI)
32	30	DON'T NEED A GUN	Billy Idol (Chrysalis)
43	31	WORKING UP A SWEAT	Full Circle (EMI America)
21	32	ROCK THE NIGHT	Europe (Epic)
34	33	MISSIONARY MAN	Eurythmics (RCA)
-	34	I FOUND LOVE	Lone Justice (Geffen)
40	35	SOUL MAN	Sam Moore & Lou Reed (A&M)
30	36	YOU ARE MY WORLD	Communards (London)
-	37	SHAKIN' LIKE A LEAF	Stranglers (Epic)
-	38	LIKE FLAMES	Berlin (Mercury)
-	39	LET MY PEOPLE GO-GO	Rainmakers (Mercury)
47	40	HAPPY	Surface (CBS)
-	41	GET THAT LOVE	Thompson Twins (Arista)
41	42	WAITING	Style Council (Polydor)
50	43	JIMMY LEE	Aretha Franklin (Arista)
-	44	THIS BRUTAL HOUSE	Nitro Deluxe (Cooltempo)
-	45	WHAT YOU GET IS WHAT YOU SEE	Tina Turner (Capitol)
-	46	STOP BAJON ... PRIMAVERA	Tullio De Piscopo (Greyhound)
-	47	IF YOU LET ME STAY	Terence Trent D'Arby (CBS)
-	48	I'D RATHER GO BLIND	Ruby Turner (Jive)
-	49	THERESE	Bodines (Creation)
44	50	LET THE MUSIC TAKE CONTROL	J.M. Silk (RCA)

Australian group Mental As Anything had their Top 10 hit boosted by its use in the smash hit film *Crocodile Dundee*, starring their fellow Aussie Paul Hogan. Both Queen's Freddie Mercury and former Culture Club lead singer hit with oldies, Mercury going back to the '50s with a Platters original, and George covering David Gates' *Everything I Own* – though his model was Ken Boothe's 1974 hit.

28 March 1987

last week	this week		
6	1	RESPECTABLE	Mel & Kim (Supreme)
1	2	EVERYTHING I OWN	Boy George (Virgin)
4	3	I GET THE SWEETEST FEELING	
			Jackie Wilson (SMP)
2	4	THE GREAT PRETENDER	
			Freddie Mercury (Parlophone)
8	5	MOONLIGHTING	Al Jarreau (WEA)
13	6	WEAK IN THE PRESENCE OF BEAUTY	
			Alison Moyet (CBS)
23	7	RESPECT YOURSELF	Bruce Willis (Motown)
3	8	STAND BY ME	Ben E. King (Atlantic)
7	9	LIVE IT UP	Mental As Anything (Epic)
21	10	(YOU'VE GOTTA) FIGHT FOR YOUR RIGHT	
			Beastie Boys (Def Jam)
10	11	SIGN O' THE TIMES	Prince (Paisley Park)
14	12	IT DOESN'T HAVE TO BE	Erasure (Mute)
12	13	RUNNING IN THE FAMILY	Level 42 (Polydor)
–	14	WITH OR WITHOUT YOU	U2 (Island)
5	15	WHEN A MAN LOVES A WOMAN	
			Percy Sledge (Atlantic)
19	16	SEVERINE	Mission (Mercury)
9	17	CRUSH ON YOU	Jets (MCA)
17	18	TONIGHT TONIGHT TONIGHT	Genesis (Virgin)
–	19	LET'S WAIT A WHILE	Janet Jackson (Breakout)
–	20	SEXY GIRL	Lillo Thomas (Capitol)
26	21	LOVING YOU IS SWEETER THAN EVER	
			Nick Kamen (WEA)
11	22	MALE STRIPPER	Man 2 Man (Bolts)
15	23	THE RIGHT THING	Simply Red (WEA)
47	24	IF YOU LET ME STAY	
			Terence Trent D'Arby (CBS)
16	25	LOVE REMOVAL MACHINE	
			Cult (Beggars Banquet)
–	26	BIG TIME	Peter Gabriel (Charisma)
–	27	EVER FALLEN IN LOVE	
			Fine Young Cannibals (London)
30	28	DON'T NEED A GUN	Billy Idol (Chrysalis)
43	29	JIMMY LEE	Aretha Franklin (Arista)
34	30	I FOUND LOVE	Lone Justice (Geffen)
31	31	WORKING UP A SWEAT	
			Full Circle (EMI America)
45	32	WHAT YOU GET IS WHAT YOU SEE	
			Tina Turner (Capitol)
20	33	MANHATTAN SKYLINE	A-ha (Warner Bros)
–	34	KEEP YOUR EYE ON ME	Herb Alpert (Breakout)
25	35	WATCHING THE WILDLIFE	
			Frankie Goes To Hollywood (ZTT)
–	36	STILL OF THE NIGHT	Whitesnake (EMI)
27	37	FORGOTTEN TOWN	Christians (Island)
39	38	LET MY PEOPLE GO-GO	Rainmakers (Mercury)
40	39	HAPPY	Surface (CBS)
18	40	COMING AROUND AGAIN	Carly Simon (Arista)
–	41	STONE LOVE	Kool & the Gang (Club)
22	42	SONIC BOOM BOY	Westworld (RCA)
49	43	THERESE	Bodines (Creation)
38	44	LIKE FLAMES	Berlin (Mercury)
48	45	I'D RATHER GO BLIND	Ruby Turner (Jive)
24	46	DOWN TO EARTH	
			Curiosity Killed The Cat (Mercury)
–	47	HOW MUSIC CAME ABOUT	
			Gap Band (Total Experience)
–	48	LEAN ON ME	Club Nouveau (King Jay)
50	49	LET THE MUSIC TAKE CONTROL	J.M. Silk (RCA)
33	50	MISSIONARY MAN	Eurythmics (RCA)

4 April 1987

last week	this week		
1	1	RESPECTABLE	Mel & Kim (Supreme)
14	2	WITH OR WITHOUT YOU	U2 (Island)
2	3	EVERYTHING I OWN	Boy George (Virgin)
19	4	LET'S WAIT A WHILE	Janet Jackson (Breakout)
7	5	RESPECT YOURSELF	Bruce Willis (Motown)
3	6	I GET THE SWEETEST FEELING	
			Jackie Wilson (SMP)
–	7	LET IT BE	Ferry Aid (The Sun)
6	8	WEAK IN THE PRESENCE OF BEAUTY	
			Alison Moyet (CBS)
11	9	SIGN O' THE TIMES	Prince (Paisley Park)
4	10	THE GREAT PRETENDER	
			Freddie Mercury (Parlophone)
26	11	BIG TIME	Peter Gabriel (Charisma)
10	12	(YOU'VE GOTTA) FIGHT FOR YOUR RIGHT	
			Beastie Boys (Def Jam)
5	13	MOONLIGHTING	Al Jarreau (WEA)
9	14	LIVE IT UP	Mental As Anything (Epic)
12	15	IT DOESN'T HAVE TO BE	Erasure (Mute)
24	16	IF YOU LET ME STAY	Terence Trent D'Arby (CBS)
48	17	LEAN ON ME	Club Nouveau (King Jay)
20	18	SEXY GIRL	Lillo Thomas (Capitol)
27	19	EVER FALLEN IN LOVE	
			Fine Young Cannibals (London)
21	20	LOVING YOU IS SWEETER THAN EVER	
			Nick Kamen (WEA)
8	21	STAND BY ME	Ben E. King (Atlantic)
–	22	LA ISLA BONITA	Madonna (Sire)
23	23	THE IRISH ROVER	Pogues & the Dubliners (Stiff)
15	24	WHEN A MAN LOVES A WOMAN	
			Percy Sledge (Atlantic)
18	25	TONIGHT TONIGHT TONIGHT	Genesis (Virgin)
34	26	KEEP YOUR EYE ON ME	Herb Alpert (Breakout)
36	27	STILL OF THE NIGHT	Whitesnake (EMI)
16	28	SEVERINE	Mission (Mercury)
13	29	RUNNING IN THE FAMILY	Level 42 (Polydor)
35	30	WATCHING THE WILDLIFE	
			Frankie Goes To Hollywood (ZTT)
32	31	WHAT YOU GET IS WHAT YOU SEE	
			Tina Turner (Capitol)
23	32	THE RIGHT THING	Simply Red (WEA)
25	33	LOVE REMOVAL MACHINE	Cult (Beggars Banquet)
43	34	THERESE	Bodines (Creation)
17	35	CRUSH ON YOU	Jets (MCA)
22	36	MALE STRIPPER	Man 2 Man (Bolts)
46	37	DOWN TO EARTH	
			Curiosity Killed The Cat (Mercury)
–	38	THE PASSENGER	
			Siouxsie & the Banshees (Wonderland)
39	39	HEAT OF THE NIGHT	Bryan Adams (A&M)
40	40	OUT WITH HER	Blow Monkeys (RCA)
–	41	SIMPLE AS THAT	
			Huey Lewis and the News (Chrysalis)
–	42	CAN'T BE WITH YOU TONIGHT	
			Judy Boucher (Orbitone)
–	43	DAY IN DAY OUT	David Bowie (EMI America)
28	44	DON'T NEED A GUN	Billy Idol (Chrysalis)
33	45	MANHATTAN SKYLINE	A-ha (Warner Bros)
45	46	I'D RATHER GO BLIND	Ruby Turner (Jive)
31	47	WORKING UP A SWEAT	Full Circle (EMI America)
40	48	COMING AROUND AGAIN	Carly Simon (Arista)
–	49	AND THE BEAT GOES ON	Whispers (Solar)
–	50	SHE COMES FROM THE RAIN	
			Weather Prophets (Elevation)

11 April 1987

last week	this week		
7	1	LET IT BE	Ferry Aid (The Sun)
1	2	RESPECTABLE	Mel & Kim (Supreme)
4	3	LET'S WAIT A WHILE	Janet Jackson (Breakout)
2	4	WITH OR WITHOUT YOU	U2 (Island)
22	5	LA ISLA BONITA	Madonna (Sire)
17	6	LEAN ON ME	Club Nouveau (King Jay)
11	7	BIG TIME	Peter Gabriel (Charisma)
3	8	EVERYTHING I OWN	Boy George (Virgin)
9	9	SIGN O' THE TIMES	Prince (Paisley Park)
16	10	IF YOU LET ME STAY	Terence Trent D'Arby (CBS)
8	11	WEAK IN THE PRESENCE OF BEAUTY	
			Alison Moyet (CBS)
23	12	THE IRISH ROVER	Pogues & the Dubliners (Stiff)
6	13	I GET THE SWEETEST FEELING	
			Jackie Wilson (SMP)
5	14	RESPECT YOURSELF	Bruce Willis (Motown)
–	15	ORDINARY DAY	
			Curiosity Killed The Cat (Mercury)
10	16	THE GREAT PRETENDER	
			Freddie Mercury (Parlophone)
19	17	EVER FALLEN IN LOVE	
			Fine Young Cannibals (London)
43	18	DAY IN DAY OUT	David Bowie (EMI America)
12	19	(YOU'VE GOTTA) FIGHT FOR YOUR RIGHT	
			Beastie Boys (Def Jam)
27	20	STILL OF THE NIGHT	Whitesnake (EMI)
14	21	LIVE IT UP	Mental As Anything (Epic)
–	22	WANTED DEAD OR ALIVE	Bon Jovi (Vertigo)
–	23	LIVING IN A BOX	Living In A Box (Chrysalis)
15	24	IT DOESN'T HAVE TO BE	Erasure (Mute)
20	25	LOVING YOU IS SWEETER THAN EVER	
			Nick Kamen (WEA)
13	26	MOONLIGHTING	Al Jarreau (WEA)
18	27	SEXY GIRL	Lillo Thomas (Capitol)
42	28	CAN'T BE WITH YOU TONIGHT	
			Judy Boucher (Orbitone)
46	29	I'D RATHER GO BLIND	Ruby Turner (Jive)
–	30	EVE'S VOLCANO	Julian Cope (Island)
40	31	OUT WITH HER	Blow Monkeys (RCA)
26	32	KEEP YOUR EYE ON ME	Herb Alpert (Breakout)
21	33	STAND BY ME	Ben E. King (Atlantic)
39	34	HEAT OF THE NIGHT	Bryan Adams (A&M)
31	35	WHAT YOU GET IS WHAT YOU SEE	
			Tina Turner (Capitol)
–	36	LET MY PEOPLE GO-GO	Rainmakers (Mercury)
25	37	TONIGHT TONIGHT TONIGHT	Genesis (Virgin)
–	38	ANOTHER STEP	Kim Wilde & Junior (MCA)
49	39	AND THE BEAT GOES ON	Whispers (Solar)
50	40	SHE COMES FROM THE RAIN	
			Weather Prophets (Elevation)
38	41	THE PASSENGER	
			Siouxsie & the Banshees (Wonderland)
24	42	WHEN A MAN LOVES A WOMAN	
			Percy Sledge (Atlantic)
47	43	WORKING UP A SWEAT	Full Circle (EMI America)
–	44	SAILING	Rod Stewart (Warner Bros)
–	45	SOMETHING INSIDE (SO STRONG)	
			Labi Siffre (China)
–	46	BOOPS (HERE TO GO)	
			Sly & Robbie (Fourth & Broadway)
–	47	NEVER TAKE ME ALIVE	Spear of Destiny (10)
–	48	REMEMBRANCE DAY	B-Movie (Deram)
28	49	SEVERINE	Mission (Mercury)
32	50	THE RIGHT THING	Simply Red (WEA)

Just under two years after the Crowd's *You'll Never Walk Alone*, another multi-artist revival of an old song in aid of a disaster fund topped the chart. Ferry Aid's *Let It Be* was instigated by *The Sun* newspaper, in the wake of the *Herald Of Free Enterprise* ferry disaster at Zeebrugge during March. Paul McCartney, who had sung lead on the Beatles' original, was one of the Ferry Aid performers.

April – May 1987

last week	this week	18 April 1987	
1	1	LET IT BE	Ferry Aid (The Sun)
5	2	LA ISLA BONITA	Madonna (Sire)
3	3	LET'S WAIT A WHILE	Janet Jackson (Breakout)
2	4	RESPECTABLE	Mel & Kim (Supreme)
4	5	WITH OR WITHOUT YOU	U2 (Island)
6	6	LEAN ON ME	Club Nouveau (King Jay)
10	7	IF YOU LET ME STAY	Terence Trent D'Arby (CBS)
8	8	THE IRISH ROVER	Pogues & the Dubliners (Stiff)
15	9	ORDINARY DAY	Curiosity Killed The Cat (Mercury)
17	10	EVER FALLEN IN LOVE	Fine Young Cannibals (London)
22	11	WANTED DEAD OR ALIVE	Bon Jovi (Vertigo)
28	12	CAN'T BE WITH YOU TONIGHT	Judy Boucher (Orbitone)
11	13	WEAK IN THE PRESENCE OF BEAUTY	Alison Moyet (CBS)
18	14	DAY IN DAY OUT	David Bowie (EMI America)
20	15	STILL OF THE NIGHT	Whitesnake (EMI)
7	16	BIG TIME	Peter Gabriel (Charisma)
23	17	LIVING IN A BOX	Living In A Box (Chrysalis)
9	18	SIGN O' THE TIMES	Prince (Paisley Park)
8	19	EVERYTHING I OWN	Boy George (Virgin)
13	20	I GET THE SWEETEST FEELING	Jackie Wilson (SMP)
19	21	(YOU'VE GOTTA) FIGHT FOR YOUR RIGHT	Beastie Boys (Def Jam)
14	22	RESPECT YOURSELF.	Bruce Willis (Motown)
32	23	KEEP YOUR EYE ON ME	Herb Alpert (Breakout)
16	24	THE GREAT PRETENDER	Freddie Mercury (Parlophone)
31	25	OUT WITH HER	Blow Monkeys (RCA)
36	26	LET MY PEOPLE GO-GO	Rainmakers (Mercury)
38	27	ANOTHER STEP	Kim Wilde & Junior (MCA)
-	28	WHY CAN'T I BE YOU	Cure (Fiction)
21	29	LIVE IT UP	Mental As Anything (Epic)
-	30	BIG DECISION	That Petrol Emotion (Polydor)
47	31	NEVER TAKE ME ALIVE	Spear of Destiny (10)
39	32	I'D RATHER GO BLIND	Ruby Turner (Jive)
30	33	EVE'S VOLCANO	Julian Cope (Island)
46	34	BOOPS (HERE TO GO)	Sly & Robbie (Fourth & Broadway)
-	35	RADIO HEART	Gary Numan & Radio Heart (GFM)
-	36	NOTHING'S GONNA STOP US NOW	Starship (Grunt)
25	37	LOVING YOU IS SWEETER THAN EVER	Nick Kamen (WEA)
-	38	BIG LOVE	Fleetwood Mac (Warner Bros)
-	39	FOLLOWING	Bangles (CBS)
40	40	SHE COMES FROM THE RAIN	Weather Prophets (Elevation)
-	41	THE SLIGHTEST TOUCH	Five Star (Tent)
45	42	SOMETHING INSIDE (SO STRONG)	Labi Siffre (China)
-	43	IT'S THE WAY YOU USE IT	Eric Clapton (Duck)
-	44	HOOKED ON LOVE	Dead Or Alive (Epic)
50	45	THE RIGHT THING	Simply Red (WEA)
34	46	HEAT OF THE NIGHT	Bryan Adams (A&M)
27	47	SEXY GIRL	Lillo Thomas (Capitol)
35	48	WHAT YOU GET IS WHAT YOU SEE	Tina Turner (Capitol)
-	49	TWILIGHT WORLD	Swing Out Sister (Mercury)
24	50	IT DOESN'T HAVE TO BE	Erasure (Mute)

		25 April 1987	
2	1	LA ISLA BONITA	Madonna (Sire)
6	2	LEAN ON ME	Club Nouveau (King Jay)
1	3	LET IT BE	Ferry Aid (The Sun)
12	4	CAN'T BE WITH YOU TONIGHT	Judy Boucher (Orbitone)
7	5	IF YOU LET ME STAY	Terence Trent D'Arby (CBS)
3	6	LET'S WAIT A WHILE	Janet Jackson (Breakout)
4	7	RESPECTABLE	Mel & Kim (Supreme)
17	8	LIVING IN A BOX	Living In A Box (Chrysalis)
5	9	WITH OR WITHOUT YOU	U2 (Island)
8	10	THE IRISH ROVER	Pogues & the Dubliners (Stiff)
10	11	EVER FALLEN IN LOVE	Fine Young Cannibals (London)
11	12	WANTED DEAD OR ALIVE	Bon Jovi (Vertigo)
41	13	THE SLIGHTEST TOUCH	Five Star (Tent)
9	14	ORDINARY DAY	Curiosity Killed The Cat (Mercury)
28	15	WHY CAN'T I BE YOU	Cure (Fiction)
15	16	STILL OF THE NIGHT	Whitesnake (EMI)
14	17	DAY IN DAY OUT	David Bowie (EMI America)
26	18	LET MY PEOPLE GO-GO	Rainmakers (Mercury)
-	19	A BOY FROM NOWHERE	Tom Jones (Epic)
27	20	ANOTHER STEP	Kim Wilde & Junior (MCA)
-	21	DIAMOND LIGHTS	Glenn & Chris (Record Shack)
-	22	SHEILA TAKE A BOW	Smiths (Rough Trade)
18	23	SIGN O' THE TIMES	Prince (Paisley Park)
23	24	KEEP YOUR EYE ON ME	Herb Alpert (Breakout)
42	25	SOMETHING INSIDE (SO STRONG)	Labi Siffre (China)
13	26	WEAK IN THE PRESENCE OF BEAUTY	Alison Moyet (CBS)
36	27	NOTHING'S GONNA STOP US NOW	Starship (Grunt)
-	28	CARRIE	Europe (Epic)
30	29	BIG DECISION	That Petrol Emotion (Polydor)
22	30	RESPECT YOURSELF	Bruce Willis (Motown)
16	31	BIG TIME	Peter Gabriel (Charisma)
34	32	BOOPS (HERE TO GO)	Sly & Robbie (Fourth & Broadway)
38	33	BIG LOVE	Fleetwood Mac (Warner Bros)
31	34	NEVER TAKE ME ALIVE	Spear of Destiny (10)
19	35	EVERYTHING I OWN	Boy George (Virgin)
32	36	I'D RATHER GO BLIND	Ruby Turner (Jive)
39	37	FOLLOWING	Bangles (CBS)
-	38	MEET EL PRESIDENTE	Duran Duran (EMI)
-	39	ALONE AGAIN OR	Damned (MCA)
49	40	TWILIGHT WORLD	Swing Out Sister (Mercury)
33	41	EVE'S VOLCANO	Julian Cope (Island)
29	42	LIVE IT UP	Mental As Anything (Epic)
-	43	TO BE WITH YOU AGAIN	Level 42 (Polydor)
-	44	WATCH OUT!	Patrice Rushen (Elektra)
-	45	I GET THE SWEETEST FEELING	Jackie Wilson (SMP)
47	46	SEXY GIRL	Lillo Thomas (Capitol)
24	47	THE GREAT PRETENDER	Freddie Mercury (Parlophone)
25	48	OUT WITH HER	Blow Monkeys (RCA)
-	49	WISHING I WAS LUCKY	Wet Wet Wet (Precious)
35	50	RADIO HEART	Gary Numan & Radio Heart (GFM)

		2 May 1987	
1	1	LA ISLA BONITA	Madonna (Sire)
4	2	CAN'T BE WITH YOU TONIGHT	Judy Boucher (Orbitone)
8	3	LIVING IN A BOX	Living In A Box (Chrysalis)
2	4	LEAN ON ME	Club Nouveau (King Jay)
3	5	LET IT BE	Ferry Aid (The Sun)
5	6	IF YOU LET ME STAY	Terence Trent D'Arby (CBS)
13	7	THE SLIGHTEST TOUCH	Five Star (Tent)
7	8	RESPECTABLE	Mel & Kim (Supreme)
22	9	SHEILA TAKE A BOW	Smiths (Rough Trade)
19	10	A BOY FROM NOWHERE	Tom Jones (Epic)
6	11	LET'S WAIT A WHILE	Janet Jackson (Breakout)
11	12	EVER FALLEN IN LOVE	Fine Young Cannibals (London)
27	13	NOTHING'S GONNA STOP US NOW	Starship (Grunt)
25	14	SOMETHING INSIDE (SO STRONG)	Labi Siffre (China)
15	15	WHY CAN'T I BE YOU	Cure (Fiction)
20	16	ANOTHER STEP	Kim Wilde & Junior (MCA)
9	17	WITH OR WITHOUT YOU	U2 (Island)
12	18	WANTED DEAD OR ALIVE	Bon Jovi (Vertigo)
43	19	TO BE WITH YOU AGAIN	Level 42 (Polydor)
21	20	DIAMOND LIGHTS	Glenn & Chris (Record Shack)
34	21	NEVER TAKE ME ALIVE	Spear of Destiny (10)
33	22	BIG LOVE	Fleetwood Mac (Warner Bros)
-	23	LIL' DEVIL	Cult (Beggars Banquet)
-	24	APRIL SKIES	Jesus & Mary Chain (blanco y negro)
18	25	LET MY PEOPLE GO-GO	Rainmakers (Mercury)
10	26	THE IRISH ROVER	Pogues & the Dubliners (Stiff)
16	27	STILL OF THE NIGHT	Whitesnake (EMI)
14	28	ORDINARY DAY	Curiosity Killed The Cat (Mercury)
-	29	BACK AND FORTH	Cameo (Club)
17	30	DAY IN DAY OUT	David Bowie (EMI America)
39	31	ALONE AGAIN OR	Damned (MCA)
24	32	KEEP YOUR EYE ON ME	Herb Alpert (Breakout)
32	33	BOOPS (HERE TO GO)	Sly & Robbie (Fourth & Broadway)
38	34	MEET EL PRESIDENTE	Duran Duran (EMI)
23	35	SIGN O' THE TIMES	Prince (Paisley Park)
-	36	LET YOURSELF GO	Sybil (Champion)
29	37	BIG DECISION	That Petrol Emotion (Polydor)
40	38	TWILIGHT WORLD	Swing Out Sister (Mercury)
41	39	EVE'S VOLCANO	Julian Cope (Island)
-	40	LET ME KNOW	Maxi Priest (10)
-	41	WET MY WHISTLE	Midnight Star (Solar)
26	42	WEAK IN THE PRESENCE OF BEAUTY	Alison Moyet (CBS)
28	43	CARRIE	Europe (Epic)
-	44	ECHO BEACH	Toyah (EG)
-	45	YOU'RE THE VOICE	John Farnham (Wheatley)
-	46	MOVE OVER DARLING	Doris Day (CBS)
-	47	BEN	Toni Warne (Mute)
-	48	SHAME	Orchestral Manoeuvres In The Dark (Virgin)
-	49	HELLO TO MY BABY	Ladysmith Black Mambazo (Warner Bros)
-	50	LOVE AND MONEY	Love & Money (Mercury)

Judy Boucher's lovers' rock (a smoochy reggae style) version of *Can't Be With You Tonight* was a surprise crossover hit, held from Number One only by the strength of Madonna's latin-ish *La Isla Bonita*.

Female performers had had a strong few weeks in the Top Three, with girl duo Mel & Kim reaching Number One before Ferry Aid, and Janet Jackson's *Let's Wait A While* hitting Number Three.

9 May 1987

last week	this week		
1	1	LA ISLA BONITA	Madonna (Sire)
13	2	NOTHING'S GONNA STOP US NOW	Starship (Grunt)
2	3	CAN'T BE WITH YOU TONIGHT	Judy Boucher (Orbitone)
7	4	THE SLIGHTEST TOUCH	Five Star (Tent)
3	5	LIVING IN A BOX	Living In A Box (Chrysalis)
10	6	A BOY FROM NOWHERE	Tom Jones (Epic)
4	7	LEAN ON ME	Club Nouveau (King Jay)
9	8	SHEILA TAKE A BOW	Smiths (Rough Trade)
6	9	IF YOU LET ME STAY	Terence Trent D'Arby (CBS)
16	10	ANOTHER STEP	Kim Wilde & Junior (MCA)
14	11	SOMETHING INSIDE (SO STRONG)	Labi Siffre (China)
20	12	DIAMOND LIGHTS	Glenn & Chris (Record Shack)
19	13	TO BE WITH YOU AGAIN	Level 42 (Polydor)
24	14	APRIL SKIES	Jesus & Mary Chain (blanco y negro)
8	15	RESPECTABLE	Mel & Kim (Supreme)
12	16	EVER FALLEN IN LOVE	Fine Young Cannibals (London)
11	17	LET'S WAIT A WHILE	Janet Jackson (Breakout)
23	18	LIL' DEVIL	Cult (Beggars Banquet)
5	19	LET IT BE	Ferry Aid (The Sun)
21	20	NEVER TAKE ME ALIVE	Spear of Destiny (10)
22	21	BIG LOVE	Fleetwood Mac (Warner Bros)
33	22	BOOPS (HERE TO GO)	Sly & Robbie (Fourth & Broadway)
15	23	WHY CAN'T I BE YOU	Cure (Fiction)
18	24	WANTED DEAD OR ALIVE	Bon Jovi (Vertigo)
17	25	WITH OR WITHOUT YOU	U2 (Island)
31	26	ALONE AGAIN OR	Damned (MCA)
34	27	MEET EL PRESIDENTE	Duran Duran (EMI)
28	28	ORDINARY DAY	Curiosity Killed The Cat (Mercury)
29	29	BACK AND FORTH	Cameo (Club)
37	30	BIG DECISION	That Petrol Emotion (Polydor)
25	31	LET MY PEOPLE GO-GO	Rainmakers (Mercury)
43	32	CARRIE	Europe (Epic)
32	33	KEEP YOUR EYE ON ME	Herb Alpert (Breakout)
-	34	THERE'S GHOST IN MY HOUSE	Fall (Beggars Banquet)
36	35	LET YOURSELF GO	Sybil (Champion)
26	36	THE IRISH ROVER	Pogues & the Dubliners (Stiff)
27	37	STILL OF THE NIGHT	Whitesnake (EMI)
-	38	REAL FASHION REGGAE STYLE	Carey Johnson (Oval)
-	39	SHATTERED DREAMS	Johnny Hates Jazz (Virgin)
-	40	WISHING I WAS LUCKY	Wet Wet Wet (Precious)
-	41	STRANGE LOVE	Depeche Mode (Mute)
-	42	THE LAND OF RING DANG DO	King Kurt (Polydor)
47	43	BEN	Toni Warne (Mute)
30	44	DAY IN DAY OUT	David Bowie (EMI America)
-	45	PRIME MOVER	Zodiac Mindwarp & the Love Reaction (Mercury)
-	46	FRIDAY ON MY MIND	Gary Moore (10)
47	47	I WANT TO HEAR IT FROM YOU	Go West (Chrysalis)
-	48	AIN'T THAT LOVIN' YOU BABY	Elvis Presley (RCA)
-	49	RADIO HEAD	Talking Heads (EMI)
35	50	SIGN O' THE TIMES	Prince (Paisley Park)

16 May 1987

2	1	NOTHING'S GONNA STOP US NOW	Starship (Grunt)
3	2	CAN'T BE WITH YOU TONIGHT	Judy Boucher (Orbitone)
1	3	LA ISLA BONITA	Madonna (Sire)
14	4	APRIL SKIES	Jesus & Mary Chain (blanco y negro)
6	5	A BOY FROM NOWHERE	Tom Jones (Epic)
5	6	LIVING IN A BOX	Living In A Box (Chrysalis)
4	7	THE SLIGHTEST TOUCH	Five Star (Tent)
11	8	SOMETHING INSIDE (SO STRONG)	Labi Siffre (China)
13	9	TO BE WITH YOU AGAIN	Level 42 (Polydor)
10	10	ANOTHER STEP	Kim Wilde & Junior (MCA)
21	11	BIG LOVE	Fleetwood Mac (Warner Bros)
18	12	LIL' DEVIL	Cult (Beggars Banquet)
20	13	NEVER TAKE ME ALIVE	Spear of Destiny (10)
7	14	LEAN ON ME	Club Nouveau (King Jay)
9	15	IF YOU LET ME STAY	Terence Trent D'Arby (CBS)
29	16	BACK AND FORTH	Cameo (Club)
8	17	SHEILA TAKE A BOW	Smiths (Rough Trade)
22	18	BOOPS (HERE TO GO)	Sly & Robbie (Fourth & Broadway)
12	19	DIAMOND LIGHTS	Glenn & Chris (Record Shack)
41	20	STRANGE LOVE	Depeche Mode (Mute)
34	21	THERE'S GHOST IN MY HOUSE	Fall (Beggars Banquet)
38	22	REAL FASHION REGGAE STYLE	Carey Johnson (Oval)
15	23	RESPECTABLE	Mel & Kim (Supreme)
45	24	PRIME MOVER	Zodiac Mindwarp & the Love Reaction (Mercury)
27	25	MEET EL PRESIDENTE	Duran Duran (EMI)
17	26	LET'S WAIT A WHILE	Janet Jackson (Breakout)
32	27	CARRIE	Europe (Epic)
40	28	WISHING I WAS LUCKY	Wet Wet Wet (Precious)
23	29	WHY CAN'T I BE YOU	Cure (Fiction)
24	30	WANTED DEAD OR ALIVE	Bon Jovi (Vertigo)
39	31	SHATTERED DREAMS	Johnny Hates Jazz (Virgin)
16	32	EVER FALLEN IN LOVE	Fine Young Cannibals (London)
30	33	BIG DECISION	That Petrol Emotion (Polydor)
-	34	BA-NA-NA-BAM-BOO	Westworld (RCA)
26	35	ALONE AGAIN OR	Damned (MCA)
19	36	LET IT BE	Ferry Aid (The Sun)
25	37	WITH OR WITHOUT YOU	U2 (Island)
49	38	RADIO HEAD	Talking Heads (EMI)
35	39	LET YOURSELF GO	Sybil (Champion)
37	40	STILL OF THE NIGHT	Whitesnake (EMI)
31	41	LET MY PEOPLE GO-GO	Rainmakers (Mercury)
28	42	ORDINARY DAY	Curiosity Killed The Cat (Mercury)
-	43	TWILIGHT WORLD	Swing Out Sister (Mercury)
36	44	THE IRISH ROVER	Pogues & the Dubliners (Stiff)
-	45	HOUSENATION	Housemaster Boyz (Magnetic Dance)
42	46	THE LAND OF RING DANG DO	King Kurt (Polydor)
44	47	DAY IN DAY OUT	David Bowie (EMI America)
-	48	LOOKING FOR A NEW LOVE	Jody Watley (MCA)
-	49	WET MY WHISTLE	Midnight Star (Solar)
-	50	IN LOVE WITH LOVE	Debbie Harry (Chrysalis)

23 May 1987

1	1	NOTHING'S GONNA STOP US NOW	Starship (Grunt)
5	2	A BOY FROM NOWHERE	Tom Jones (Epic)
8	3	SOMETHING INSIDE (SO STRONG)	Labi Siffre (China)
2	4	CAN'T BE WITH YOU TONIGHT	Judy Boucher (Orbitone)
6	5	LIVING IN A BOX	Living In A Box (Chrysalis)
18	6	BOOPS (HERE TO GO)	Sly & Robbie (Fourth & Broadway)
11	7	BIG LOVE	Fleetwood Mac (Warner Bros)
10	8	ANOTHER STEP	Kim Wilde & Junior (MCA)
12	9	LIL' DEVIL	Cult (Beggars Banquet)
4	10	APRIL SKIES	Jesus & Mary Chain (blanco y negro)
3	11	LA ISLA BONITA	Madonna (Sire)
16	12	BACK AND FORTH	Cameo (Club)
7	13	THE SLIGHTEST TOUCH	Five Star (Tent)
13	14	NEVER TAKE ME ALIVE	Spear of Destiny (10)
31	15	SHATTERED DREAMS	Johnny Hates Jazz (Virgin)
20	16	STRANGE LOVE	Depeche Mode (Mute)
22	17	REAL FASHION REGGAE STYLE	Carey Johnson (Oval)
21	18	THERE'S GHOST IN MY HOUSE	Fall (Beggars Banquet)
-	19	INCOMMUNICADO	Marillion (EMI)
9	20	TO BE WITH YOU AGAIN	Level 42 (Polydor)
24	21	PRIME MOVER	Zodiac Mindwarp & the Love Reaction (Mercury)
28	22	WISHING I WAS LUCKY	Wet Wet Wet (Precious)
-	23	DOMINOES	Robbie Nevil (Manhattan)
27	24	CARRIE	Europe (Epic)
15	25	IF YOU LET ME STAY	Terence Trent D'Arby (CBS)
-	26	I WANNA DANCE WITH SOMEBODY (WHO LOVES ME)	Whitney Houston (Arista)
-	27	SERIOUS	Donna Allen (Portrait)
14	28	LEAN ON ME	Club Nouveau (King Jay)
-	29	JACK MIX II	Mirage (Debut)
17	30	RESPECTABLE	Mel & Kim (Supreme)
-	31	SHEILA TAKE A BOW	Smiths (Rough Trade)
39	32	LET YOURSELF GO	Sybil (Champion)
-	33	BATTLESHIP CHAINS	Georgia Satellites (Elektra)
-	34	FIVE GET OVEREXCITED	Housemartins (Go! Discs)
-	35	GO FOR IT!	Coventry F.C. (Sky Blue)
-	36	INFIDELITY	Simply Red (Elektra)
-	37	CROSS THE TRACKS	Maceo & the Macs (Urban)
-	38	BORN TO RUN	Bruce Springsteen (CBS)
45	39	HOUSENATION	Housemaster Boyz (Magnetic Dance)
-	40	YOU'RE THE VOICE	John Farnham (Wheatley)
34	41	BA-NA-NA-BAM-BOO	Westworld (RCA)
35	42	ALONE AGAIN OR	Damned (MCA)
19	43	DIAMOND LIGHTS	Glenn & Chris (Record Shack)
33	44	BIG DECISION	That Petrol Emotion (Polydor)
37	45	WITH OR WITHOUT YOU	U2 (Island)
-	46	NOSEDIVE KARMA (EP)	Gaye Bykers On Acid (Purple Fluid)
-	47	ROCK STEADY	Whispers (Solar)
29	48	WHY CAN'T I BE YOU	Cure (Fiction)
-	49	TALK DIRTY TO ME	Poison (Music For Nations)
41	50	LET MY PEOPLE GO-GO	Rainmakers (Mercury)

Neither Starship nor their linear predecessors Jefferson Starship and Jefferson Airplane had ever had a UK Top 10 single before *Nothing's Gonna Stop Us Now*, despite several in the US since the mid-60s.

This song was from the hit film *Mannequin*, and was one of the year's biggest hits, selling 740,000. Tom Jones' first hit for 15 years was a song from the projected stage musical *Matador*, about El Cordobes.

May – June 1987

last this
week

30 May 1987

1	1	NOTHING'S GONNA STOP US NOW	Starship (Grunt)
2	2	A BOY FROM NOWHERE	Tom Jones (Epic)
15	3	SHATTERED DREAMS	Johnny Hates Jazz (Virgin)
3	4	SOMETHING INSIDE (SO STRONG)	Labi Siffre (China)
19	5	INCOMMUNICADO	Marillion (EMI)
26	6	I WANNA DANCE WITH SOMEBODY (WHO LOVES ME)	Whitney Houston (Arista)
4	7	CAN'T BE WITH YOU TONIGHT	Judy Boucher (Orbitone)
7	8	BIG LOVE	Fleetwood Mac (Warner Bros)
6	9	BOOPS (HERE TO GO)	Sly & Robbie (Fourth & Broadway)
5	10	LIVING IN A BOX	Living In A Box (Chrysalis)
-	11	HOLD ME NOW	Johnny Logan (Epic)
9	12	LIL' DEVIL	Cult (Beggars Banquet)
12	13	BACK AND FORTH	Cameo (Club)
22	14	WISHING I WAS LUCKY	Wet Wet Wet (Precious)
21	15	PRIME MOVER	Zodiac Mindwarp & the Love Reaction (Mercury)
8	16	ANOTHER STEP	Kim Wilde & Junior (MCA)
38	17	BORN TO RUN	Bruce Springsteen (CBS)
29	18	JACK MIX II	Mirage (Debut)
34	19	FIVE GET OVEREXCITED	Housemartins (Go! Discs)
10	20	APRIL SKIES	Jesus & Mary Chain (blanco y negro)
14	21	NEVER TAKE ME ALIVE	Spear of Destiny (10)
11	22	LA ISLA BONITA	Madonna (Sire)
13	23	THE SLIGHTEST TOUCH	Five Star (Tent)
16	24	STRANGE LOVE	Depeche Mode (Mute)
18	25	THERE'S GHOST IN MY HOUSE	Fall (Beggars Banquet)
27	26	SERIOUS	Donna Allen (Portrait)
40	27	YOU'RE THE VOICE	John Farnham (Wheatley)
17	28	REAL FASHION REGGAE STYLE	Carey Johnson (Oval)
23	29	DOMINOES	Robbie Nevil (Manhattan)
-	30	FRIDAY ON MY MIND	Gary Moore (10)
32	31	LET YOURSELF GO	Sybil (Champion)
36	32	INFIDELITY	Simply Red (Elektra)
-	33	WHO'S AFRAID OF THE BIG BAD NOISE	Age of Chance (Fon)
35	34	GO FOR IT!	Coventry F.C. (Sky Blue)
28	35	LEAN ON ME	Club Nouveau (King Jay)
-	36	WATCHDOGS	UB40 (DEP International)
33	37	BATTLESHIP CHAINS	Georgia Satellites (Elektra)
47	38	ROCK STEADY	Whispers (Solar)
-	39	VICTIM OF LOVE	Erasure (Mute)
-	40	STAR TREKKIN'	Firm (Bark)
-	41	NO SLEEP TILL BROOKLYN	Beastie Boys (Def Jam)
-	42	THE DAY AFTER YOU	Blow Monkeys (RCA)
-	43	HOT SHOT TOTTENHAM	Tottenham F.C. (Rainbow)
-	44	WET MY WHISTLE	Midnight Star (Solar)
43	45	DIAMOND LIGHTS	Glenn & Chris (Record Shack)
37	46	CROSS THE TRACKS	Maceo & the Macs (Urban)
20	47	TO BE WITH YOU AGAIN	Level 42 (Polydor)
24	48	CARRIE	Europe (Epic)
-	49	ORDINARY GIRL	Alison Moyet (CBS)
-	50	GOODBYE STRANGER	Pepsi & Shirlie (Polydor)

6 June 1987

6	1	I WANNA DANCE WITH SOMEBODY (WHO LOVES ME)	Whitney Houston (Arista)
1	2	NOTHING'S GONNA STOP US NOW	Starship (Grunt)
11	3	HOLD ME NOW	Johnny Logan (Epic)
5	4	INCOMMUNICADO	Marillion (EMI)
3	5	SHATTERED DREAMS	Johnny Hates Jazz (Virgin)
18	6	JACK MIX II	Mirage (Debut)
2	7	A BOY FROM NOWHERE	Tom Jones (Epic)
14	8	WISHING I WAS LUCKY	Wet Wet Wet (Precious)
4	9	SOMETHING INSIDE (SO STRONG)	Labi Siffre (China)
7	10	CAN'T BE WITH YOU TONIGHT	Judy Boucher (Orbitone)
19	11	FIVE GET OVEREXCITED	Housemartins (Go! Discs)
13	12	BACK AND FORTH	Cameo (Club)
15	13	PRIME MOVER	Zodiac Mindwarp & the Love Reaction (Mercury)
8	14	BIG LOVE	Fleetwood Mac (Warner Bros)
17	15	BORN TO RUN	Bruce Springsteen (CBS)
26	16	SERIOUS	Donna Allen (Portrait)
10	17	LIVING IN A BOX	Living In A Box (Chrysalis)
-	18	I STILL HAVEN'T FOUND WHAT I'M LOOKING FOR	U2 (Island)
50	19	GOODBYE STRANGER	Pepsi & Shirlie (Polydor)
9	20	BOOPS (HERE TO GO)	Sly & Robbie (Fourth & Broadway)
21	21	NEVER TAKE ME ALIVE	Spear of Destiny (10)
12	22	LIL' DEVIL	Cult (Beggars Banquet)
39	23	VICTIM OF LOVE	Erasure (Mute)
-	24	KEEP ME IN MIND	Boy George (Virgin)
24	25	STRANGE LOVE	Depeche Mode (Mute)
-	26	IS THIS LOVE	Whitesnake (EMI)
-	27	LUKA	Suzanne Vega (A&M)
41	28	NO SLEEP TILL BROOKLYN	Beastie Boys (Def Jam)
27	29	YOU'RE THE VOICE	John Farnham (Wheatley)
30	30	FRIDAY ON MY MIND	Gary Moore (10)
28	31	REAL FASHION REGGAE STYLE	Carey Johnson (Oval)
32	32	INFIDELITY	Simply Red (Elektra)
-	33	LOOKING FOR A NEW LOVE	Jody Watley (MCA)
-	34	IT'S NOT UNUSUAL	Tom Jones (Decca)
22	35	LA ISLA BONITA	Madonna (Sire)
-	36	UNDER THE BOARDWALK	Bruce Willis (Motown)
-	37	CRIMINALLY INSANE	Slayer (Def Jam)
16	38	ANOTHER STEP	Kim Wilde & Junior (MCA)
38	39	ROCK STEADY	Whispers (Solar)
49	40	ORDINARY GIRL	Alison Moyet (CBS)
33	41	WHO'S AFRAID OF THE BIG BAD NOISE	Age of Chance (Fon)
-	42	NOTHING'S GONNA STOP ME NOW	Samantha Fox (Jive)
42	43	THE DAY AFTER YOU	Blow Monkeys (RCA)
23	44	THE SLIGHTEST TOUCH	Five Star (Tent)
29	45	DOMINOES	Robbie Nevil (Manhattan)
48	46	CARRIE	Europe (Epic)
-	47	I'M IN LOVE	Lillo Thomas (Capitol)
-	48	BITTER SWEET	Little Steven (Manhattan)
-	49	LOVE MISSILE F1-11	Pop Will Eat Itself (Chapter 22)
-	50	ALONE	Heart (Capitol)

13 June 1987

1	1	I WANNA DANCE WITH SOMEBODY (WHO LOVES ME)	Whitney Houston (Arista)
2	2	NOTHING'S GONNA STOP US NOW	Starship (Grunt)
3	3	HOLD ME NOW	Johnny Logan (Epic)
6	4	JACK MIX II	Mirage (Debut)
5	5	SHATTERED DREAMS	Johnny Hates Jazz (Virgin)
8	6	WISHING I WAS LUCKY	Wet Wet Wet (Precious)
19	7	GOODBYE STRANGER	Pepsi & Shirlie (Polydor)
23	8	VICTIM OF LOVE	Erasure (Mute)
4	9	INCOMMUNICADO	Marillion (EMI)
18	10	I STILL HAVEN'T FOUND WHAT I'M LOOKING FOR	U2 (Island)
16	11	SERIOUS	Donna Allen (Portrait)
28	12	NO SLEEP TILL BROOKLYN	Beastie Boys (Def Jam)
11	13	FIVE GET OVEREXCITED	Housemartins (Go! Discs)
-	14	I WANT YOUR SEX	George Michael (Epic)
7	15	A BOY FROM NOWHERE	Tom Jones (Epic)
27	16	LUKA	Suzanne Vega (A&M)
42	17	NOTHING'S GONNA STOP ME NOW	Samantha Fox (Jive)
26	18	IS THIS LOVE	Whitesnake (EMI)
9	19	SOMETHING INSIDE (SO STRONG)	Labi Siffre (China)
29	20	YOU'RE THE VOICE	John Farnham (Wheatley)
-	21	WHEN SMOKEY SINGS	ABC (Neutron)
10	22	CAN'T BE WITH YOU TONIGHT	Judy Boucher (Orbitone)
32	23	INFIDELITY	Simply Red (Elektra)
-	24	LET'S DANCE	Chris Rea (Magnet)
14	25	BIG LOVE	Fleetwood Mac (Warner Bros)
12	26	BACK AND FORTH	Cameo (Club)
-	27	IT'S TRICKY	Run DMC (Profile)
33	28	LOOKING FOR A NEW LOVE	Jody Watley (MCA)
13	29	PRIME MOVER	Zodiac Mindwarp & the Love Reaction (Mercury)
-	30	THE GAME	Echo & the Bunnymen (WEA)
34	31	IT'S NOT UNUSUAL	Tom Jones (Decca)
20	32	BOOPS (HERE TO GO)	Sly & Robbie (Fourth & Broadway)
36	33	UNDER THE BOARDWALK	Bruce Willis (Motown)
17	34	LIVING IN A BOX	Living In A Box (Chrysalis)
24	35	KEEP ME IN MIND	Boy George (Virgin)
15	36	BORN TO RUN	Bruce Springsteen (CBS)
39	37	ROCK STEADY	Whispers (Solar)
-	38	CROSS THE TRACKS	Maceo & the Macs (Urban)
-	39	DIAMONDS	Herb Alpert (Breakout)
38	40	ANOTHER STEP	Kim Wilde & Junior (MCA)
25	41	STRANGE LOVE	Depeche Mode (Mute)
43	42	THE DAY AFTER YOU	Blow Monkeys (RCA)
-	43	FAKE	Alexander O'Neal (Tabu)
41	44	WHO'S AFRAID OF THE BIG BAD NOISE	Age of Chance (Fon)
44	45	THE SLIGHTEST TOUCH	Five Star (Tent)
31	46	REAL FASHION REGGAE STYLE	Carey Johnson (Oval)
40	47	ORDINARY GIRL	Alison Moyet (CBS)
-	48	PLEASURE PRINCIPLE	Janet Jackson (Breakout)
-	49	BATTLESHIP CHAINS	Georgia Satellites (Elektra)
35	50	LA ISLA BONITA	Madonna (Sire)

Johnny Logan, who had won the Eurovision song contest for Ireland in 1980, repeated the feat in 1987 with *Hold Me Now,* and once again had a major UK hit with it, reaching Number Three. Wet Wet Wet's debut single made the Top 10, as did that of Johnny Hates Jazz, while Whitney Houston scored a second chart-topper with the first single from her second album, *I Wanna Dance With Somebody.*

June – July 1987

20 June 1987

last	this	Title	Artist (Label)
1	1	I WANNA DANCE WITH SOMEBODY (WHO LOVES ME)	Whitney Houston (Arista)
14	2	I WANT YOUR SEX	George Michael (Epic)
3	3	HOLD ME NOW	Johnny Logan (Epic)
–	4	STAR TREKKIN'	Firm (Bark)
10	5	I STILL HAVEN'T FOUND WHAT I'M LOOKING FOR	U2 (Island)
4	6	JACK MIX II	Mirage (Debut)
7	7	GOODBYE STRANGER	Pepsi & Shirlie (Polydor)
2	8	NOTHING'S GONNA STOP US NOW	Starship (Grunt)
17	9	NOTHING'S GONNA STOP ME NOW	Samantha Fox (Jive)
8	10	VICTIM OF LOVE	Erasure (Mute)
6	11	WISHING I WAS LUCKY	Wet Wet Wet (Precious)
5	12	SHATTERED DREAMS	Johnny Hates Jazz (Virgin)
11	13	SERIOUS	Donna Allen (Portrait)
21	14	WHEN SMOKEY SINGS	ABC (Neutron)
33	15	UNDER THE BOARDWALK	Bruce Willis (Motown)
12	16	NO SLEEP TILL BROOKLYN	Beastie Boys (Def Jam)
27	17	IT'S TRICKY	Run DMC (Profile)
28	18	LOOKING FOR A NEW LOVE	Jody Watley (MCA)
20	19	YOU'RE THE VOICE	John Farnham (Wheatley)
30	20	THE GAME	Echo & the Bunnymen (WEA)
31	21	IT'S NOT UNUSUAL	Tom Jones (Decca)
16	22	LUKA	Suzanne Vega (A&M)
18	23	IS THIS LOVE	Whitesnake (EMI)
13	24	FIVE GET OVEREXCITED	Housemartins (Go! Discs)
–	25	PROMISED YOU A MIRACLE	Simple Minds (Virgin)
15	26	A BOY FROM NOWHERE	Tom Jones (Epic)
24	27	LET'S DANCE	Chris Rea (Magnet)
–	28	LIFETIME LOVE	Joyce Sims (London)
39	29	DIAMONDS	Herb Alpert (Breakout)
35	30	KEEP ME IN MIND	Boy George (Virgin)
9	31	INCOMMUNICADO	Marillion (EMI)
–	32	I BELIEVE IN MIRACLES	Jackson Sisters (Urban)
37	33	ROCK STEADY	Whispers (Solar)
43	34	FAKE	Alexander O'Neal (Tabu)
–	35	NO WAY BACK/DO IT PROPERLY	Adonis (London)
–	36	WISHING WELL	Terence Trent D'Arby (CBS)
–	37	IF I WAS YOUR GIRLFRIEND	Prince (Paisley Park)
–	38	THE JACK THAT HOUSE BUILT	Jack & Chill (Oval)
22	39	CAN'T BE WITH YOU TONIGHT	Judy Boucher (Orbitone)
–	40	CRIMINALLY INSANE	Slayer (Def Jam)
41	41	BREAK EVERY RULE	Tina Turner (Capitol)
–	42	GET READY	Carol Hitchcock (A&M)
–	43	NOSEDIVE KARMA (EP)	Gaye Bykers On Acid (Purple Fluid)
–	44	THROWING IT ALL AWAY	Genesis (Virgin)
44	45	WHO'S AFRAID OF THE BIG BAD NOISE	Age of Chance (Fon)
–	46	DON'T DREAM IT'S OVER	Crowded House (Capitol)
48	47	PLEASURE PRINCIPLE	Janet Jackson (Breakout)
42	48	THE DAY AFTER YOU	Blow Monkeys (RCA)
49	49	CAN'T TAKE IT NO MORE	Soup Dragons (Raw)
–	50	SCALES OF JUSTICE	Living In A Box (Chrysalis)

27 June 1987

last	this	Title	Artist (Label)
4	1	STAR TREKKIN'	Firm (Bark)
1	2	I WANNA DANCE WITH SOMEBODY (WHO LOVES ME)	Whitney Houston (Arista)
2	3	I WANT YOUR SEX	George Michael (Epic)
3	4	HOLD ME NOW	Johnny Logan (Epic)
15	5	UNDER THE BOARDWALK	Bruce Willis (Motown)
5	6	I STILL HAVEN'T FOUND WHAT I'M LOOKING FOR	U2 (Island)
9	7	NOTHING'S GONNA STOP ME NOW	Samantha Fox (Jive)
8	8	NOTHING'S GONNA STOP US NOW	Starship (Grunt)
19	9	YOU'RE THE VOICE	John Farnham (Wheatley)
14	10	WHEN SMOKEY SINGS	ABC (Neutron)
7	11	GOODBYE STRANGER	Pepsi & Shirlie (Polydor)
18	12	LOOKING FOR A NEW LOVE	Jody Watley (MCA)
10	13	VICTIM OF LOVE	Erasure (Mute)
–	14	MISFIT	Curiosity Killed The Cat (Mercury)
23	15	IS THIS LOVE	Whitesnake (EMI)
6	16	JACK MIX II	Mirage (Debut)
25	17	PROMISED YOU A MIRACLE	Simple Minds (Virgin)
–	18	IT'S A SIN	Pet Shop Boys (Parlophone)
36	19	WISHING WELL	Terence Trent D'Arby (CBS)
17	20	IT'S TRICKY	Run DMC (Profile)
11	21	WISHING I WAS LUCKY	Wet Wet Wet (Precious)
21	22	IT'S NOT UNUSUAL	Tom Jones (Decca)
37	23	IF I WAS YOUR GIRLFRIEND	Prince (Paisley Park)
–	24	TIME WILL CRAWL	David Bowie (EMI America)
26	25	A BOY FROM NOWHERE	Tom Jones (Epic)
20	26	THE GAME	Echo & the Bunnymen (WEA)
27	27	LET'S DANCE	Chris Rea (Magnet)
47	28	PLEASURE PRINCIPLE	Janet Jackson (Breakout)
16	29	NO SLEEP TILL BROOKLYN	Beastie Boys (Def Jam)
12	30	SHATTERED DREAMS	Johnny Hates Jazz (Virgin)
22	31	LUKA	Suzanne Vega (A&M)
34	32	FAKE	Alexander O'Neal (Tabu)
13	33	SERIOUS	Donna Allen (Portrait)
–	34	COMIN' ON STRONG	Broken English (EMI)
29	35	DIAMONDS	Herb Alpert (Breakout)
28	36	LIFETIME LOVE	Joyce Sims (London)
32	37	I BELIEVE IN MIRACLES	Jackson Sisters (Urban)
49	38	CAN'T TAKE IT NO MORE	Soup Dragons (Raw)
33	39	ROCK STEADY	Whispers (Solar)
35	40	NO WAY BACK/DO IT PROPERLY	Adonis (London)
–	41	FLAMES OF PARADISE	Elton John & Jennifer Rush (CBS)
45	42	WHO'S AFRAID OF THE BIG BAD NOISE	Age of Chance (Fon)
–	43	MY PRETTY ONE	Cliff Richard (EMI)
50	44	SCALES OF JUSTICE	Living In A Box (Chrysalis)
–	45	ALWAYS	Atlantic Starr (Warner Bros)
46	46	DON'T DREAM IT'S OVER	Crowded House (Capitol)
44	47	THROWING IT ALL AWAY	Genesis (Virgin)
–	48	RIGHT NEXT DOOR	Robert Cray Band (Mercury)
–	49	TEARING US APART	Eric Clapton & Tina Turner (Duck)
43	50	NOSEDIVE KARMA (EP)	Gaye Bykers On Acid (Purple Fluid)

4 July 1987

last	this	Title	Artist (Label)
1	1	STAR TREKKIN'	Firm (Bark)
18	2	IT'S A SIN	Pet Shop Boys (Parlophone)
5	3	UNDER THE BOARDWALK	Bruce Willis (Motown)
2	4	I WANNA DANCE WITH SOMEBODY (WHO LOVES ME)	Whitney Houston (Arista)
3	5	I WANT YOUR SEX	George Michael (Epic)
14	6	MISFIT	Curiosity Killed The Cat (Mercury)
10	7	WHEN SMOKEY SINGS	ABC (Neutron)
7	8	NOTHING'S GONNA STOP ME NOW	Samantha Fox (Jive)
9	9	YOU'RE THE VOICE	John Farnham (Wheatley)
15	10	IS THIS LOVE	Whitesnake (EMI)
19	11	WISHING WELL	Terence Trent D'Arby (CBS)
4	12	HOLD ME NOW	Johnny Logan (Epic)
12	13	LOOKING FOR A NEW LOVE	Jody Watley (MCA)
8	14	NOTHING'S GONNA STOP US NOW	Starship (Grunt)
23	15	IF I WAS YOUR GIRLFRIEND	Prince (Paisley Park)
6	16	I STILL HAVEN'T FOUND WHAT I'M LOOKING FOR	U2 (Island)
27	17	LET'S DANCE	Chris Rea (Magnet)
13	18	VICTIM OF LOVE	Erasure (Mute)
17	19	PROMISED YOU A MIRACLE	Simple Minds (Virgin)
34	20	COMIN' ON STRONG	Broken English (EMI)
43	21	MY PRETTY ONE	Cliff Richard (EMI)
22	22	IT'S NOT UNUSUAL	Tom Jones (Decca)
–	23	THE LIVING DAYLIGHTS	A-ha (Warner Bros)
36	24	LIFETIME LOVE	Joyce Sims (London)
44	25	SCALES OF JUSTICE	Living In A Box (Chrysalis)
–	26	SWEETEST SMILE	Black (A&M)
29	27	NO SLEEP TILL BROOKLYN	Beastie Boys (Def Jam)
46	28	DON'T DREAM IT'S OVER	Crowded House (Capitol)
45	29	ALWAYS	Atlantic Starr (Warner Bros)
20	30	IT'S TRICKY	Run DMC (Profile)
11	31	GOODBYE STRANGER	Pepsi & Shirlie (Polydor)
48	32	RIGHT NEXT DOOR	Robert Cray Band (Mercury)
–	33	INDIANS	Anthrax (Island)
25	34	A BOY FROM NOWHERE	Tom Jones (Epic)
31	35	LUKA	Suzanne Vega (A&M)
28	36	PLEASURE PRINCIPLE	Janet Jackson (Breakout)
–	37	SWEET SIXTEEN	Billy Idol (Chrysalis)
24	38	TIME WILL CRAWL	David Bowie (EMI America)
–	39	ALONE	Heart (Capitol)
16	40	JACK MIX II	Mirage (Debut)
37	41	I BELIEVE IN MIRACLES	Jackson Sisters (Urban)
–	42	I KNOW YOU GOT SOUL	Eric B. (Cooltempo)
–	43	A LITTLE BOOGIE WOOGIE	Shakin' Stevens (Epic)
32	44	FAKE	Alexander O'Neal (Tabu)
35	45	DIAMONDS	Herb Alpert (Breakout)
21	46	WISHING I WAS LUCKY	Wet Wet Wet (Precious)
47	47	THROWING IT ALL AWAY	Genesis (Virgin)
40	48	NO WAY BACK/DO IT PROPERLY	Adonis (London)
38	49	CAN'T TAKE IT NO MORE	Soup Dragons (Raw)
–	50	CATCH	Cure (Fiction)

The Firm, anonymous pranksters who previous hit had been *Arthur Daley ('E's Alright)*, spoofed the *Star Trek* TV series and movies in almost music-hall style on *Star Trekkin'* – it appealed hugely to children, and possibly many of the copies which saw it to Number One were bought by parents for their offspring. They certainly would not have given them George Michael's BBC-banned *I Want Your Sex*.

July 1987

last
week   this

11 July 1987

Last	This	Title	Artist (Label)
2	1	IT'S A SIN	Pet Shop Boys (Parlophone)
3	2	UNDER THE BOARDWALK	Bruce Willis (Motown)
11	3	WISHING WELL	Terence Trent D'Arby (CBS)
1	4	STAR TREKKIN'	Firm (Bark)
4	5	I WANNA DANCE WITH SOMEBODY (WHO LOVES ME)	Whitney Houston (Arista)
6	6	YOU'RE THE VOICE	John Farnham (Wheatley)
7	7	MISFIT	Curiosity Killed The Cat (Mercury)
8	8	WHEN SMOKEY SINGS	ABC (Neutron)
21	9	MY PRETTY ONE	Cliff Richard (EMI)
23	10	THE LIVING DAYLIGHTS	A-ha (Warner Bros)
17	11	LET'S DANCE	Chris Rea (Magnet)
10	12	IS THIS LOVE	Whitesnake (EMI)
5	13	I WANT YOUR SEX	George Michael (Epic)
29	14	ALWAYS	Atlantic Starr (Warner Bros)
26	15	SWEETEST SMILE	Black (A&M)
15	16	IF I WAS YOUR GIRLFRIEND	Prince (Paisley Park)
39	17	ALONE	Heart (Capitol)
9	18	NOTHING'S GONNA STOP ME NOW	Samantha Fox (Jive)
20	19	COMIN' ON STRONG	Broken English (EMI)
19	20	SWEET SIXTEEN	Billy Idol (Chrysalis)
12	21	HOLD ME NOW	Johnny Logan (Epic)
-	22	(YOUR LOVE KEEPS LIFTING ME) HIGHER AND HIGHER	Jackie Wilson (SMP)
16	23	I STILL HAVEN'T FOUND WHAT I'M LOOKING FOR	U2 (Island)
19	24	PROMISED YOU A MIRACLE	Simple Minds (Virgin)
50	25	CATCH	Cure (Fiction)
14	26	NOTHING'S GONNA STOP US NOW	Starship (Grunt)
24	27	LIFETIME LOVE	Joyce Sims (London)
-	28	F.L.M.	Mel & Kim (Supreme)
33	29	INDIANS	Anthrax (Island)
-	30	SONGBIRD	Kenny G (Arista)
38	31	TIME WILL CRAWL	David Bowie (EMI America)
47	32	THROWING IT ALL AWAY	Genesis (Virgin)
-	33	HOOVERVILLE	Christians (Island)
-	34	RED RAIN	Peter Gabriel (Charisma)
28	35	DON'T DREAM IT'S OVER	Crowded House (Capitol)
-	36	WOMAN OF PRINCIPLE	Trouble Funk (Fourth & Broadway)
18	37	VICTIM OF LOVE	Erasure (Mute)
13	38	LOOKING FOR A NEW LOVE	Jody Watley (MCA)
-	39	FOOLED BY A SMILE	Swing Out Sister (Mercury)
27	40	NO SLEEP TILL BROOKLYN	Beastie Boys (Def Jam)
25	41	SCALES OF JUSTICE	Living In A Box (Chrysalis)
-	42	JUST DON'T WANT TO BE LONELY	Freddie McGregor (Germain)
-	43	JIVE TALKIN	Boogie Box High (Hardback)
45	44	DIAMONDS	Herb Alpert (Breakout)
43	45	A LITTLE BOOGIE WOOGIE	Shakin' Stevens (Epic)
22	46	IT'S NOT UNUSUAL	Tom Jones (Decca)
-	47	SCREAM	Mantronix (10)
-	48	DON'T LOOK ANY FURTHER	Dennis Edwards (Gordy)
-	49	I NEED A MAN	Man To Man (Bolts)
-	50	SWAMP	That Petrol Emotion (Polydor)

18 July 1987

Last	This	Title	Artist (Label)
1	1	IT'S A SIN	Pet Shop Boys (Parlophone)
2	2	UNDER THE BOARDWALK	Bruce Willis (Motown)
3	3	WISHING WELL	Terence Trent D'Arby (CBS)
10	4	THE LIVING DAYLIGHTS	A-ha (Warner Bros)
14	5	ALWAYS	Atlantic Starr (Warner Bros)
9	6	MY PRETTY ONE	Cliff Richard (EMI)
4	7	STAR TREKKIN'	Firm (Bark)
15	8	SWEETEST SMILE	Black (A&M)
17	9	ALONE	Heart (Capitol)
5	10	I WANNA DANCE WITH SOMEBODY (WHO LOVES ME)	Whitney Houston (Arista)
6	11	YOU'RE THE VOICE	John Farnham (Wheatley)
-	12	WHO'S THAT GIRL	Madonna (Sire)
28	13	F.L.M.	Mel & Kim (Supreme)
11	14	LET'S DANCE	Chris Rea (Magnet)
20	15	SWEET SIXTEEN	Billy Idol (Chrysalis)
8	16	WHEN SMOKEY SINGS	ABC (Neutron)
7	17	MISFIT	Curiosity Killed The Cat (Mercury)
12	18	IS THIS LOVE	Whitesnake (EMI)
19	19	COMIN' ON STRONG	Broken English (EMI)
32	20	THROWING IT ALL AWAY	Genesis (Virgin)
30	21	SONGBIRD	Kenny G (Arista)
22	22	(YOUR LOVE KEEPS LIFTING ME) HIGHER AND HIGHER	Jackie Wilson (SMP)
43	23	JIVE TALKIN	Boogie Box High (Hardback)
16	24	IF I WAS YOUR GIRLFRIEND	Prince (Paisley Park)
25	25	CATCH	Cure (Fiction)
45	26	A LITTLE BOOGIE WOOGIE	Shakin' Stevens (Epic)
13	27	I WANT YOUR SEX	George Michael (Epic)
33	28	HOOVERVILLE	Christians (Island)
34	29	RED RAIN	Peter Gabriel (Charisma)
24	30	PROMISED YOU A MIRACLE	Simple Minds (Virgin)
27	31	LIFETIME LOVE	Joyce Sims (London)
23	32	I STILL HAVEN'T FOUND WHAT I'M LOOKING FOR	U2 (Island)
-	33	I HEARD A RUMOUR	Bananarama (London)
-	34	SOMEWHERE OUT THERE	Linda Ronstadt & James Ingram (MCA)
26	35	NOTHING'S GONNA STOP US NOW	Starship (Grunt)
21	36	HOLD ME NOW	Johnny Logan (Epic)
42	37	JUST DON'T WANT TO BE LONELY	Freddie McGregor (Germain)
29	38	INDIANS	Anthrax (Island)
18	39	NOTHING'S GONNA STOP ME NOW	Samantha Fox (Jive)
35	40	DON'T DREAM IT'S OVER	Crowded House (Capitol)
41	41	VICTIM OF LOVE	Erasure (Mute)
47	42	SCREAM	Mantronix (10)
-	43	OOPS UPSIDE YOUR HEAD	Gap Band (Total Experience)
-	44	DRAGNET	Art Of Noise (China)
38	45	LOOKING FOR A NEW LOVE	Jody Watley (MCA)
49	46	I NEED A MAN	Man To Man (Bolts)
48	47	DON'T LOOK ANY FURTHER	Dennis Edwards (Gordy)
50	48	SWAMP	That Petrol Emotion (Polydor)
36	49	WOMAN OF PRINCIPLE	Trouble Funk (Fourth & Broadway)
39	50	FOOLED BY A SMILE	Swing Out Sister (Mercury)

25 July 1987

Last	This	Title	Artist (Label)
1	1	IT'S A SIN	Pet Shop Boys (Parlophone)
3	2	WISHING WELL	Terence Trent D'Arby (CBS)
12	3	WHO'S THAT GIRL	Madonna (Sire)
2	4	UNDER THE BOARDWALK	Bruce Willis (Motown)
8	5	SWEETEST SMILE	Black (A&M)
13	6	F.L.M.	Mel & Kim (Supreme)
4	7	THE LIVING DAYLIGHTS	A-ha (Warner Bros)
5	8	ALWAYS	Atlantic Starr (Warner Bros)
23	9	JIVE TALKIN	Boogie Box High (Hardback)
26	10	A LITTLE BOOGIE WOOGIE	Shakin' Stevens (Epic)
6	11	MY PRETTY ONE	Cliff Richard (EMI)
-	12	LA BAMBA	Los Lobos (Slash)
22	13	(YOUR LOVE KEEPS LIFTING ME) HIGHER AND HIGHER	Jackie Wilson (SMP)
9	14	ALONE	Heart (Capitol)
15	15	SWEET SIXTEEN	Billy Idol (Chrysalis)
28	16	HOOVERVILLE	Christians (Island)
-	17	SHE'S ON IT	Beastie Boys (Def Jam)
17	18	MISFIT	Curiosity Killed The Cat (Mercury)
7	19	STAR TREKKIN'	Firm (Bark)
10	20	I WANNA DANCE WITH SOMEBODY (WHO LOVES ME)	Whitney Houston (Arista)
21	21	SONGBIRD	Kenny G (Arista)
25	22	CATCH	Cure (Fiction)
33	23	I HEARD A RUMOUR	Bananarama (London)
-	24	ALL YOU NEED IS LOVE	Beatles (Parlophone)
14	25	LET'S DANCE	Chris Rea (Magnet)
37	26	JUST DON'T WANT TO BE LONELY	Freddie McGregor (Germain)
11	27	YOU'RE THE VOICE	John Farnham (Wheatley)
18	28	IS THIS LOVE	Whitesnake (EMI)
-	29	SUGAR MICE	Marillion (EMI)
20	30	THROWING IT ALL AWAY	Genesis (Virgin)
-	31	LABOUR OF LOVE	Hue & Cry (Circa)
43	32	OOPS UPSIDE YOUR HEAD	Gap Band (Total Experience)
48	33	SWAMP	That Petrol Emotion (Polydor)
30	34	PROMISED YOU A MIRACLE	Simple Minds (Virgin)
27	35	I WANT YOUR SEX	George Michael (Epic)
41	36	VICTIM OF LOVE	Erasure (Mute)
-	37	SOLD	Boy George (Virgin)
42	38	SCREAM	Mantronix (10)
-	39	WAS THAT YOU?	Spear of Destiny (10)
50	40	FOOLED BY A SMILE	Swing Out Sister (Mercury)
-	41	I REALLY DIDN'T MEAN IT	Luther Vandross (Epic)
-	42	TOM'S DINER	Suzanne Vega (A&M)
32	43	I STILL HAVEN'T FOUND WHAT I'M LOOKING FOR	U2 (Island)
35	44	NOTHING'S GONNA STOP US NOW	Starship (Grunt)
29	45	RED RAIN	Peter Gabriel (Charisma)
19	46	COMIN' ON STRONG	Broken English (EMI)
24	47	IF I WAS YOUR GIRLFRIEND	Prince (Paisley Park)
36	48	HOLD ME NOW	Johnny Logan (Epic)
-	49	SEVEN WONDERS	Fleetwood Mac (Warner Bros)
-	50	SPY IN THE HOUSE OF LOVE	Was (Not Was) (Fontana)

Actor Bruce Willis, of the *Moonlighting* TV series, got support from the Temptations on his revival of the Drifters' 1964 song *Under The Boardwalk*, while ABC made the Top 10 at the same time with a song about another Motown luminary. Chris Rea became the third act (following Chris Montez and David Bowie) to have a major hit titled *Let's Dance* – all three songs were unconnected and unsimilar.

1 August 1987

last week	this week	title	artist
3	1	WHO'S THAT GIRL	Madonna (Sire)
12	2	LA BAMBA	Los Lobos (Slash)
1	3	IT'S A SIN	Pet Shop Boys (Parlophone)
8	4	ALWAYS	Atlantic Starr (Warner Bros)
14	5	ALONE	Heart (Capitol)
4	6	UNDER THE BOARDWALK	Bruce Willis (Motown)
9	7	JIVE TALKIN	Boogie Box High (Hardback)
6	8	F.L.M.	Mel & Kim (Supreme)
2	9	WISHING WELL	Terence Trent D'Arby (CBS)
5	10	SWEETEST SMILE	Black (A&M)
23	11	I HEARD A RUMOUR	Bananarama (London)
26	12	JUST DON'T WANT TO BE LONELY	Freddie McGregor (Germain)
7	13	THE LIVING DAYLIGHTS	A-ha (Warner Bros)
31	14	LABOUR OF LOVE	Hue & Cry (Circa)
17	15	SHE'S ON IT	Beastie Boys (Def Jam)
10	16	A LITTLE BOOGIE WOOGIE	Shakin' Stevens (Epic)
21	17	SONGBIRD	Kenny G (Arista)
29	18	SUGAR MICE	Marillion (EMI)
13	19	(YOUR LOVE KEEPS LIFTING ME) HIGHER AND HIGHER	Jackie Wilson (SMP)
32	20	OOPS UPSIDE YOUR HEAD	Gap Band (Total Experience)
20	21	I WANNA DANCE WITH SOMEBODY (WHO LOVES ME)	Whitney Houston (Arista)
16	22	HOOVERVILLE	Christians (Island)
-	23	ROADBLOCK	Stock Aitken & Waterman (Breakout)
41	24	I REALLY DIDN'T MEAN IT	Luther Vandross (Epic)
-	25	TRUE FAITH	New Order (Factory)
15	26	SWEET SIXTEEN	Billy Idol (Chrysalis)
-	27	TOY BOY	Sinitta (Fanfare)
-	28	YOU CAUGHT MY EYE	Judy Boucher (Orbitone)
-	29	I SURRENDER	Samantha Fox (Jive)
37	30	SOLD	Boy George (Virgin)
-	31	SONG FROM THE EDGE OF THE WORLD	Siouxsie & the Banshees (Wonderland)
19	32	STAR TREKKIN'	Firm (Bark)
25	33	LET'S DANCE	Chris Rea (Magnet)
22	34	CATCH	Cure (Fiction)
-	35	SERIOUS MIX	Mirage (Debut)
-	36	ANIMAL	Def Leppard (Bludgeon Riffola)
-	37	LAST NIGHT	Kid 'n' Play (Cooltempo)
39	38	WAS THAT YOU?	Spear of Destiny (10)
28	39	IS THIS LOVE	Whitesnake (EMI)
11	40	MY PRETTY ONE	Cliff Richard (EMI)
-	41	GIRLS GIRLS GIRLS	Motley Crue (Elektra)
-	42	STEP BY STEP	Taffy (Transglobal)
-	43	CALL ME	Spagna (CBS)
50	44	SPY IN THE HOUSE OF LOVE	Was (Not Was) (Fontana)
33	45	SWAMP	That Petrol Emotion (Polydor)
18	46	MISFIT	Curiosity Killed The Cat (Mercury)
-	47	PERSONAL TOUCH	Errol Brown (WEA)
-	48	LIPS LIKE SUGAR	Echo & the Bunnymen (WEA)
-	49	TALKING OF LOVE	Anita Dobson (Parlophone)
24	50	ALL YOU NEED IS LOVE	Beatles (Parlophone)

8 August 1987

last week	this week	title	artist
2	1	LA BAMBA	Los Lobos (Slash)
1	2	WHO'S THAT GIRL	Madonna (Sire)
4	3	ALWAYS	Atlantic Starr (Warner Bros)
5	4	ALONE	Heart (Capitol)
7	5	JIVE TALKIN	Boogie Box High (Hardback)
3	6	IT'S A SIN	Pet Shop Boys (Parlophone)
15	7	SHE'S ON IT	Beastie Boys (Def Jam)
12	8	JUST DON'T WANT TO BE LONELY	Freddie McGregor (Germain)
6	9	UNDER THE BOARDWALK	Bruce Willis (Motown)
8	10	F.L.M.	Mel & Kim (Supreme)
25	11	TRUE FAITH	New Order (Factory)
11	12	I HEARD A RUMOUR	Bananarama (London)
14	13	LABOUR OF LOVE	Hue & Cry (Circa)
9	14	WISHING WELL	Terence Trent D'Arby (CBS)
16	15	A LITTLE BOOGIE WOOGIE	Shakin' Stevens (Epic)
24	16	I REALLY DIDN'T MEAN IT	Luther Vandross (Epic)
43	17	CALL ME	Spagna (CBS)
-	18	I JUST CAN'T STOP LOVING YOU	Michael Jackson (Epic)
18	19	SUGAR MICE	Marillion (EMI)
36	20	ANIMAL	Def Leppard (Bludgeon Riffola)
28	21	YOU CAUGHT MY EYE	Judy Boucher (Orbitone)
10	22	SWEETEST SMILE	Black (A&M)
23	23	ROADBLOCK	Stock Aitken & Waterman (Breakout)
20	24	OOPS UPSIDE YOUR HEAD	Gap Band (Total Experience)
13	25	THE LIVING DAYLIGHTS	A-ha (Warner Bros)
27	26	TOY BOY	Sinitta (Fanfare)
47	27	PERSONAL TOUCH	Errol Brown (WEA)
30	28	SOLD	Boy George (Virgin)
41	29	GIRLS GIRLS GIRLS	Motley Crue (Elektra)
17	30	SONGBIRD	Kenny G (Arista)
29	31	I SURRENDER	Samantha Fox (Jive)
-	32	SOMEWHERE OUT THERE	Linda Ronstadt & James Ingram (MCA)
-	33	SWEET LTTLE MYSTERY	Wet Wet Wet (Precious)
-	34	I COULD HAVE BEEN A DREAMER	Dio (Vertigo)
22	35	HOOVERVILLE	Christians (Island)
21	36	I WANNA DANCE WITH SOMEBODY (WHO LOVES ME)	Whitney Houston (Arista)
-	37	FUNKY TOWN	Pseudo Echo (RCA)
48	38	LIPS LIKE SUGAR	Echo & the Bunnymen (WEA)
35	39	SERIOUS MIX	Mirage (Debut)
19	40	(YOUR LOVE KEEPS LIFTING ME) HIGHER AND HIGHER	Jackie Wilson (SMP)
-	41	HAVE A NICE DAY	Roxanne Shante (Breakout)
-	42	JUST CALL	Sherrick (Warner Bros)
38	43	WAS THAT YOU?	Spear of Destiny (10)
42	44	STEP BY STEP	Taffy (Transglobal)
31	45	SONG FROM THE EDGE OF THE WORLD	Siouxsie & the Banshees (Wonderland)
40	46	MY PRETTY ONE	Cliff Richard (EMI)
-	47	DON'T SHILLY-SHALLY	Edwyn Collins (WEA)
-	48	SAY YOU REALLY WANT ME	Kim Wilde (MCA)
-	49	SHATTERED GLASS	Laura Branigan (Atlantic)
49	50	TALKING OF LOVE	Anita Dobson (Parlophone)

15 August 1987

last week	this week	title	artist
1	1	LA BAMBA	Los Lobos (Slash)
4	2	ALONE	Heart (Capitol)
18	3	I JUST CAN'T STOP LOVING YOU	Michael Jackson (Epic)
2	4	WHO'S THAT GIRL	Madonna (Sire)
11	5	TRUE FAITH	New Order (Factory)
17	6	CALL ME	Spagna (CBS)
13	7	LABOUR OF LOVE	Hue & Cry (Circa)
3	8	ALWAYS	Atlantic Starr (Warner Bros)
20	9	ANIMAL	Def Leppard (Bludgeon Riffola)
23	10	ROADBLOCK	Stock Aitken & Waterman (Breakout)
5	11	JIVE TALKIN	Boogie Box High (Hardback)
7	12	SHE'S ON IT	Beastie Boys (Def Jam)
12	13	I HEARD A RUMOUR	Bananarama (London)
8	14	JUST DON'T WANT TO BE LONELY	Freddie McGregor (Germain)
6	15	IT'S A SIN	Pet Shop Boys (Parlophone)
26	16	TOY BOY	Sinitta (Fanfare)
32	17	SOMEWHERE OUT THERE	Linda Ronstadt & James Ingram (MCA)
19	18	SUGAR MICE	Marillion (EMI)
29	19	GIRLS GIRLS GIRLS	Motley Crue (Elektra)
16	20	I REALLY DIDN'T MEAN IT	Luther Vandross (Epic)
10	21	F.L.M.	Mel & Kim (Supreme)
9	22	UNDER THE BOARDWALK	Bruce Willis (Motown)
-	23	NEVER GONNA GIVE YOU UP	Rick Astley (RCA)
21	24	YOU CAUGHT MY EYE	Judy Boucher (Orbitone)
15	25	A LITTLE BOOGIE WOOGIE	Shakin' Stevens (Epic)
-	26	BRIDGE TO YOUR HEART	Wax (RCA)
42	27	JUST CALL	Sherrick (Warner Bros)
33	28	SWEET LTTLE MYSTERY	Wet Wet Wet (Precious)
37	29	FUNKY TOWN	Pseudo Echo (RCA)
24	30	OOPS UPSIDE YOUR HEAD	Gap Band (Total Experience)
14	31	WISHING WELL	Terence Trent D'Arby (CBS)
22	32	SWEETEST SMILE	Black (A&M)
27	33	PERSONAL TOUCH	Errol Brown (WEA)
-	34	MY BOY LOLLIPOP	Millie (Island)
44	35	STEP BY STEP	Taffy (Transglobal)
28	36	SOLD	Boy George (Virgin)
38	37	LIPS LIKE SUGAR	Echo & the Bunnymen (WEA)
31	38	I SURRENDER	Samantha Fox (Jive)
-	39	U GOT THE LOOK	Prince & Sheena Easton (Paisley Park)
-	40	THE MOTIVE	Then Jerico (London)
45	41	SONG FROM THE EDGE OF THE WORLD	Siouxsie & the Banshees (Wonderland)
39	42	SERIOUS MIX	Mirage (Debut)
-	43	JUST GIVE THE DJ A BREAK	Dynamix 11 (Cooltempo)
-	44	LA BAMBA	Ritchie Valens (RCA)
-	45	JUMP START	Natalie Cole (Manhattan)
34	46	I COULD HAVE BEEN A DREAMER	Dio (Vertigo)
41	47	HAVE A NICE DAY	Roxanne Shante (Breakout)
43	48	WAS THAT YOU?	Spear of Destiny (10)
48	49	SAY YOU REALLY WANT ME	Kim Wilde (MCA)
-	50	PAPA WAS A ROLLING STONE	Temptations (Motown)

When Madonna's *Who's That Girl*, Los Lobos' *La Bamba* and Michael Jackson's *I Just Can't Stop Loving You* were successively Number One during August, they made up a unique sequence, because with a three-week delay, those same three singles, in the same order, then topped the US chart – something which had never happened before. All three were US records, even though their UK success came earlier.

469

August – September 1987

22 August 1987

Last	This	Title	Artist (Label)
3	1	I JUST CAN'T STOP LOVING YOU	Michael Jackson (Epic)
6	2	CALL ME	Spagna (CBS)
1	3	LA BAMBA	Los Lobos (Slash)
5	4	TRUE FAITH	New Order (Factory)
9	5	ANIMAL	Def Leppard (Bludgeon Riffola)
7	6	LABOUR OF LOVE	Hue & Cry (Circa)
2	7	ALONE	Heart (Capitol)
23	8	NEVER GONNA GIVE YOU UP	Rick Astley (RCA)
8	9	ALWAYS	Atlantic Starr (Warner Bros)
17	10	SOMEWHERE OUT THERE	Linda Ronstadt & James Ingram (MCA)
10	11	ROADBLOCK	Stock Aitken & Waterman (Breakout)
28	12	SWEET LTTLE MYSTERY	Wet Wet Wet (Precious)
4	13	WHO'S THAT GIRL	Madonna (Sire)
–	14	GIRLFRIEND IN A COMA	Smiths (Rough Trade)
–	15	WHAT HAVE I DONE TO DESERVE THIS	Pet Shop Boys & Dusty Springfield (Parlophone)
11	16	JIVE TALKIN	Boogie Box High (Hardback)
13	17	I HEARD A RUMOUR	Bananarama (London)
–	18	NEVER SAY GOODBYE	Bon Jovi (Vertigo)
29	19	FUNKY TOWN	Pseudo Echo (RCA)
16	20	TOY BOY	Sinitta (Fanfare)
–	21	HAPPY WHEN IT RAINS	Jesus & Mary Chain (blanco y negro)
14	22	JUST DON'T WANT TO BE LONELY	Freddie McGregor (Germain)
12	23	SHE'S ON IT	Beastie Boys (Def Jam)
19	24	GIRLS GIRLS GIRLS	Motley Crue (Elektra)
–	25	GARAGE DAYS REVISITED (EP)	Metallica (Vertigo)
–	26	WHENEVER YOU'RE READY	Five Star (Tent)
–	27	DIDN'T WE ALMOST HAVE IT ALL	Whitney Houston (Arista)
21	28	F.L.M.	Mel & Kim (Supreme)
39	29	U GOT THE LOOK	Prince & Sheena Easton (Paisley Park)
22	30	UNDER THE BOARDWALK	Bruce Willis (Motown)
20	31	I REALLY DIDN'T MEAN IT	Luther Vandross (Epic)
15	32	IT'S A SIN	Pet Shop Boys (Parlophone)
24	33	YOU CAUGHT MY EYE	Judy Boucher (Orbitone)
37	34	LIPS LIKE SUGAR	Echo & the Bunnymen (WEA)
38	35	I SURRENDER	Samantha Fox (Jive)
27	36	JUST CALL	Sherrick (Warner Bros)
26	37	BRIDGE TO YOUR HEART	Wax (RCA)
32	38	SWEETEST SMILE	Black (A&M)
49	39	SAY YOU REALLY WANT ME	Kim Wilde (MCA)
–	40	WILD FLOWER	Cult (Beggars Banquet)
46	41	I COULD HAVE BEEN A DREAMER	Dio (Vertigo)
25	42	A LITTLE BOOGIE WOOGIE	Shakin' Stevens (Epic)
50	43	PAPA WAS A ROLLING STONE	Temptations (Motown)
40	44	THE MOTIVE	Then Jerico (London)
–	45	LOVE POWER	Dionne Warwick (Arista)
31	46	WISHING WELL	Terence Trent D'Arby (CBS)
–	47	IF THERE WAS A MAN	Pretenders (Real)
43	48	JUST GIVE THE DJ A BREAK	Dynamix 11 (Cooltempo)
45	49	JUMP START	Natalie Cole (Manhattan)
47	50	HAVE A NICE DAY	Roxanne Shante (Breakout)

29 August 1987

Last	This	Title	Artist (Label)
1	1	I JUST CAN'T STOP LOVING YOU	Michael Jackson (Epic)
8	2	NEVER GONNA GIVE YOU UP	Rick Astley (RCA)
2	3	CALL ME	Spagna (CBS)
5	4	ANIMAL	Def Leppard (Bludgeon Riffola)
15	5	WHAT HAVE I DONE TO DESERVE THIS	Pet Shop Boys & Dusty Springfield (Parlophone)
4	6	TRUE FAITH	New Order (Factory)
20	7	TOY BOY	Sinitta (Fanfare)
12	8	SWEET LTTLE MYSTERY	Wet Wet Wet (Precious)
3	9	LA BAMBA	Los Lobos (Slash)
14	10	GIRLFRIEND IN A COMA	Smiths (Rough Trade)
10	11	SOMEWHERE OUT THERE	Linda Ronstadt & James Ingram (MCA)
26	12	WHENEVER YOU'RE READY	Five Star (Tent)
19	13	FUNKY TOWN	Pseudo Echo (RCA)
6	14	LABOUR OF LOVE	Hue & Cry (Circa)
25	15	GARAGE DAYS REVISITED (EP)	Metallica (Vertigo)
29	16	U GOT THE LOOK	Prince & Sheena Easton (Paisley Park)
27	17	DIDN'T WE ALMOST HAVE IT ALL	Whitney Houston (Arista)
13	18	WHO'S THAT GIRL	Madonna (Sire)
40	19	WILD FLOWER	Cult (Beggars Banquet)
37	20	BRIDGE TO YOUR HEART	Wax (RCA)
36	21	JUST CALL	Sherrick (Warner Bros)
11	22	ROADBLOCK	Stock Aitken & Waterman (Breakout)
–	23	WIPE OUT	Fat Boys & the Beach Boys (Urban)
38	24	SWEETEST SMILE	Black (A&M)
18	25	NEVER SAY GOODBYE	Bon Jovi (Vertigo)
7	26	ALONE	Heart (Capitol)
–	27	SEATTLE	Public Image Ltd (Virgin)
9	28	ALWAYS	Atlantic Starr (Warner Bros)
21	29	HAPPY WHEN IT RAINS	Jesus & Mary Chain (blanco y negro)
44	30	THE MOTIVE	Then Jerico (London)
–	31	HEART AND SOUL	T'Pau (Siren)
24	32	GIRLS GIRLS GIRLS	Motley Crue (Elektra)
17	33	I HEARD A RUMOUR	Bananarama (London)
–	34	THRU THE FLOWERS	Primitives (Lazy)
–	35	HOUR GLASS	Squeeze (A&M)
39	36	SAY YOU REALLY WANT ME	Kim Wilde (MCA)
–	37	CASANOVA	Levert (Atlantic)
43	38	PAPA WAS A ROLLING STONE	Temptations (Motown)
–	39	SOME PEOPLE	Cliff Richard (EMI)
–	40	THE RHYTHM DIVINE	Yello & Shirley Bassey (Mercury)
49	41	JUMP START	Natalie Cole (Manhattan)
28	42	F.L.M.	Mel & Kim (Supreme)
35	43	I SURRENDER	Samantha Fox (Jive)
–	44	THE LONER	Gary Moore (10)
47	45	IF THERE WAS A MAN	Pretenders (Real)
22	46	JUST DON'T WANT TO BE LONELY	Freddie McGregor (Germain)
16	47	JIVE TALKIN	Boogie Box High (Hardback)
–	48	I'M NOT IN LOVE	Johnny Logan (Epic)
–	49	LOVE ME TENDER	Elvis Presley (RCA)
–	50	GIVE TO LIVE	Sammy Hagar (Geffen)

5 September 1987

Last	This	Title	Artist (Label)
2	1	NEVER GONNA GIVE YOU UP	Rick Astley (RCA)
5	2	WHAT HAVE I DONE TO DESERVE THIS	Pet Shop Boys & Dusty Springfield (Parlophone)
3	3	I JUST CAN'T STOP LOVING YOU	Michael Jackson (Epic)
7	4	TOY BOY	Sinitta (Fanfare)
8	5	SWEET LTTLE MYSTERY	Wet Wet Wet (Precious)
3	6	CALL ME	Spagna (CBS)
12	7	WHENEVER YOU'RE READY	Five Star (Tent)
13	8	FUNKY TOWN	Pseudo Echo (RCA)
6	9	TRUE FAITH	New Order (Factory)
4	10	ANIMAL	Def Leppard (Bludgeon Riffola)
11	11	SOMEWHERE OUT THERE	Linda Ronstadt & James Ingram (MCA)
16	12	U GOT THE LOOK	Prince & Sheena Easton (Paisley Park)
17	13	DIDN'T WE ALMOST HAVE IT ALL	Whitney Houston (Arista)
20	14	BRIDGE TO YOUR HEART	Wax (RCA)
23	15	WIPE OUT	Fat Boys & the Beach Boys (Urban)
–	16	WONDERFUL LIFE	Black (A&M)
9	17	LA BAMBA	Los Lobos (Slash)
19	18	WILD FLOWER	Cult (Beggars Banquet)
39	19	SOME PEOPLE	Cliff Richard (EMI)
15	20	GARAGE DAYS REVISITED (EP)	Metallica (Vertigo)
14	21	LABOUR OF LOVE	Hue & Cry (Circa)
10	22	GIRLFRIEND IN A COMA	Smiths (Rough Trade)
21	23	JUST CALL	Sherrick (Warner Bros)
22	24	ROADBLOCK	Stock Aitken & Waterman (Breakout)
30	25	THE MOTIVE	Then Jerico (London)
31	26	HEART AND SOUL	T'Pau (Siren)
25	27	NEVER SAY GOODBYE	Bon Jovi (Vertigo)
37	28	CASANOVA	Levert (Atlantic)
35	29	HOUR GLASS	Squeeze (A&M)
36	30	SAY YOU REALLY WANT ME	Kim Wilde (MCA)
18	31	WHO'S THAT GIRL	Madonna (Sire)
28	32	ALWAYS	Atlantic Starr (Warner Bros)
38	33	PAPA WAS A ROLLING STONE	Temptations (Motown)
26	34	ALONE	Heart (Capitol)
–	35	ME AND THE FARMER	Housemartins (Go! Discs)
48	36	I'M NOT IN LOVE	Johnny Logan (Epic)
–	37	IT'S THE END OF THE WORLD	R.E.M. (IRS)
27	38	SEATTLE	Public Image Ltd (Virgin)
29	39	HAPPY WHEN IT RAINS	Jesus & Mary Chain (blanco y negro)
–	40	MARY'S PRAYER	Danny Wilson (Virgin)
46	41	JUST DON'T WANT TO BE LONELY	Freddie McGregor (Germain)
–	42	NEVER LET ME DOWN	Depeche Mode (Mute)
–	43	THE NIGHT YOU MURDERED LOVE	ABC (Neutron)
44	44	JUMP START	Natalie Cole (Manhattan)
32	45	GIRLS GIRLS GIRLS	Motley Crue (Elektra)
24	46	SWEETEST SMILE	Black (A&M)
34	47	THRU THE FLOWERS	Primitives (Lazy)
44	48	THE LONER	Gary Moore (10)
49	49	LOVE ME TENDER	Elvis Presley (RCA)
50	50	GIVE TO LIVE	Sammy Hagar (Geffen)

Rick Astley's *Never Gonna Give You Up* was 1987's biggest-selling single in the UK, as well as being the biggest hit to date for the hot-streak writing and production team of Stock/Aitken/Waterman, and (jointly with T'Pau's later *China In Your Hand*) it also had the year's longest Number One run. Peter Waterman had talent-scouted Astley after spotting him singing in a club in his own Lancashire locality.

September 1987

12 September 1987

last week	this week	title	artist
1	1	NEVER GONNA GIVE YOU UP	Rick Astley (RCA)
2	2	WHAT HAVE I DONE TO DESERVE THIS	Pet Shop Boys & Dusty Springfield (Parlophone)
15	3	WIPE OUT	Fat Boys & the Beach Boys (Urban)
4	4	TOY BOY	Sinitta (Fanfare)
16	5	WONDERFUL LIFE	Black (A&M)
5	6	SWEET LTTLE MYSTERY	Wet Wet Wet (Precious)
26	7	HEART AND SOUL	T'Pau (Siren)
3	8	I JUST CAN'T STOP LOVING YOU	Michael Jackson (Epic)
14	9	BRIDGE TO YOUR HEART	Wax (RCA)
6	10	CALL ME	Spagna (CBS)
8	11	FUNKY TOWN	Pseudo Echo (RCA)
7	12	WHENEVER YOU'RE READY	Five Star (Tent)
12	13	U GOT THE LOOK	Prince & Sheena Easton (Paisley Park)
19	14	SOME PEOPLE	Cliff Richard (EMI)
13	15	DIDN'T WE ALMOST HAVE IT ALL	Whitney Houston (Arista)
9	16	TRUE FAITH	New Order (Factory)
10	17	ANIMAL	Def Leppard (Bludgeon Riffola)
25	18	THE MOTIVE	Then Jerico (London)
28	19	CASANOVA	Levert (Atlantic)
-	20	WHERE THE STREETS HAVE NO NAME	U2 (Island)
29	21	PUMP UP THE VOLUME	M/A/R/R/S (4AD)
22	22	HOUR GLASS	Squeeze (A&M)
42	23	NEVER LET ME DOWN	Depeche Mode (Mute)
18	24	WILD FLOWER	Cult (Beggars Banquet)
11	25	SOMEWHERE OUT THERE	Linda Ronstadt & James Ingram (MCA)
35	26	ME AND THE FARMER	Housemartins (Go! Discs)
27	27	GIRLFRIEND IN A COMA	Smiths (Rough Trade)
23	28	JUST CALL	Sherrick (Warner Bros)
17	29	LA BAMBA	Los Lobos (Slash)
33	30	PAPA WAS A ROLLING STONE	Temptations (Motown)
21	31	LABOUR OF LOVE	Hue & Cry (Circa)
27	32	NEVER SAY GOODBYE	Bon Jovi (Vertigo)
-	33	I DON'T WANT TO BE A HERO	Johnny Hates Jazz (Virgin)
-	34	LIES	Jonathan Butler (Jive)
-	35	HOUSENATION	Housemaster Boyz (Magnetic Dance)
-	36	THE MOTION OF LOVE	Gene Loves Jezebel (Beggars Banquet)
-	37	YOU'RE PUTTIN' A RUSH ON ME	Stephanie Mills (MCA)
24	38	ROADBLOCK	Stock Aitken & Waterman (Breakout)
43	39	THE NIGHT YOU MURDERED LOVE	ABC (Neutron)
31	40	WHO'S THAT GIRL	Madonna (Sire)
-	41	LOVING YOU AGAIN	Chris Rea (Magnet)
-	42	STOP TO LOVE	Luther Vandross (Epic)
-	43	I FOUND LOVING	Steve Walsh (A1)
-	44	MY LOVE IS GUARANTEED	Sybil (Champion)
-	45	TROUBLE	Trouble Funk (Fourth & Broadway)
20	46	GARAGE DAYS REVISITED (EP)	Metallica (Vertigo)
34	47	ALONE	Heart (Capitol)
40	48	MARY'S PRAYER	Danny Wilson (Virgin)
48	49	THE LONER	Gary Moore (10)
44	50	JUMP START	Natalie Cole (Manhattan)

19 September 1987

last week	this week	title	artist
1	1	NEVER GONNA GIVE YOU UP	Rick Astley (RCA)
3	2	WIPE OUT	Fat Boys & the Beach Boys (Urban)
20	3	WHERE THE STREETS HAVE NO NAME	U2 (Island)
2	4	WHAT HAVE I DONE TO DESERVE THIS	Pet Shop Boys & Dusty Springfield (Parlophone)
7	5	HEART AND SOUL	T'Pau (Siren)
21	6	PUMP UP THE VOLUME	M/A/R/R/S (4AD)
14	7	SOME PEOPLE	Cliff Richard (EMI)
4	8	TOY BOY	Sinitta (Fanfare)
19	9	CASANOVA	Levert (Atlantic)
5	10	WONDERFUL LIFE	Black (A&M)
6	11	SWEET LTTLE MYSTERY	Wet Wet Wet (Precious)
22	12	HOUR GLASS	Squeeze (A&M)
26	13	ME AND THE FARMER	Housemartins (Go! Discs)
9	14	BRIDGE TO YOUR HEART	Wax (RCA)
-	15	IT'S OVER	Level 42 (Polydor)
33	16	I DON'T WANT TO BE A HERO	Johnny Hates Jazz (Virgin)
18	17	THE MOTIVE	Then Jerico (London)
35	18	HOUSENATION	Housemaster Boyz (Magnetic Dance)
13	19	U GOT THE LOOK	Prince & Sheena Easton (Paisley Park)
8	20	I JUST CAN'T STOP LOVING YOU	Michael Jackson (Epic)
10	21	CALL ME	Spagna (CBS)
-	22	CAUSING A COMMOTION	Madonna (Sire)
16	23	TRUE FAITH	New Order (Factory)
-	24	POUR SOME SUGAR ON ME	Def Leppard (Bludgeon Riffola)
15	25	DIDN'T WE ALMOST HAVE IT ALL	Whitney Houston (Arista)
11	26	FUNKY TOWN	Pseudo Echo (RCA)
-	27	TOMORROW	Communards (London)
23	28	NEVER LET ME DOWN	Depeche Mode (Mute)
-	29	HEY MATTHEW	Karel Fialka (IRS)
27	30	GIRLFRIEND IN A COMA	Smiths (Rough Trade)
25	31	SOMEWHERE OUT THERE	Linda Ronstadt & James Ingram (MCA)
12	32	WHENEVER YOU'RE READY	Five Star (Tent)
34	33	LIES	Jonathan Butler (Jive)
-	34	SCREAM UNTIL YOU LIKE IT	W.A.S.P. (Capitol)
-	35	CARS	Gary Numan (Beggars Banquet)
36	36	THE MOTION OF LOVE	Gene Loves Jezebel (Beggars Banquet)
37	37	YOU'RE PUTTIN' A RUSH ON ME	Stephanie Mills (MCA)
39	38	THE NIGHT YOU MURDERED LOVE	ABC (Neutron)
42	39	STOP TO LOVE	Luther Vandross (Epic)
-	40	FREE	Curiosity Killed The Cat (Mercury)
29	41	LA BAMBA	Los Lobos (Slash)
-	42	BOHEMIAN RHAPSODY	Bad News (EMI)
-	43	SOFT AS YOUR FACE	Soup Dragons (Raw)
24	44	WILD FLOWER	Cult (Beggars Banquet)
17	45	ANIMAL	Def Leppard (Bludgeon Riffola)
-	46	I KNOW YOU GOT SOUL	Bobby Byrd (Urban)
-	47	WATERFALL	Wendy & Lisa (Virgin)
-	48	I NEED LOVE	LL Cool J (Def Jam)
31	49	LABOUR OF LOVE	Hue & Cry (Circa)
43	50	I FOUND LOVING	Steve Walsh (A1)

26 September 1987

last week	this week	title	artist
1	1	NEVER GONNA GIVE YOU UP	Rick Astley (RCA)
6	2	PUMP UP THE VOLUME	M/A/R/R/S (4AD)
5	3	HEART AND SOUL	T'Pau (Siren)
2	4	WIPE OUT	Fat Boys & the Beach Boys (Urban)
22	5	CAUSING A COMMOTION	Madonna (Sire)
3	6	WHERE THE STREETS HAVE NO NAME	U2 (Island)
7	7	SOME PEOPLE	Cliff Richard (EMI)
15	8	IT'S OVER	Level 42 (Polydor)
9	9	CASANOVA	Levert (Atlantic)
18	10	HOUSENATION	Housemaster Boyz (Magnetic Dance)
4	11	WHAT HAVE I DONE TO DESERVE THIS	Pet Shop Boys & Dusty Springfield (Parlophone)
10	12	WONDERFUL LIFE	Black (A&M)
16	13	I DON'T WANT TO BE A HERO	Johnny Hates Jazz (Virgin)
8	14	TOY BOY	Sinitta (Fanfare)
29	15	HEY MATTHEW	Karel Fialka (IRS)
-	16	BAD	Michael Jackson (Epic)
14	17	BRIDGE TO YOUR HEART	Wax (RCA)
11	18	SWEET LTTLE MYSTERY	Wet Wet Wet (Precious)
48	19	I NEED LOVE	LL Cool J (Def Jam)
33	20	LIES	Jonathan Butler (Jive)
12	21	HOUR GLASS	Squeeze (A&M)
24	22	POUR SOME SUGAR ON ME	Def Leppard (Bludgeon Riffola)
13	23	ME AND THE FARMER	Housemartins (Go! Discs)
27	24	TOMORROW	Communards (London)
39	25	STOP TO LOVE	Luther Vandross (Epic)
21	26	CALL ME	Spagna (CBS)
-	27	JACK LE FREAK	Chic (Atlantic)
19	28	U GOT THE LOOK	Prince & Sheena Easton (Paisley Park)
-	29	CROCKETT'S THEME	Jan Hammer (MCA)
35	30	CARS	Gary Numan (Beggars Banquet)
26	31	FUNKY TOWN	Pseudo Echo (RCA)
17	32	THE MOTIVE	Then Jerico (London)
38	33	THE NIGHT YOU MURDERED LOVE	ABC (Neutron)
23	34	TRUE FAITH	New Order (Factory)
50	35	I FOUND LOVING	Steve Walsh (A1)
-	36	MY LOVE IS GUARANTEED	Sybil (Champion)
30	37	GIRLFRIEND IN A COMA	Smiths (Rough Trade)
-	38	COME SEE ABOUT ME	Shakin' Stevens (Epic)
-	39	LET'S WORK	Mick Jagger (CBS)
28	40	NEVER LET ME DOWN	Depeche Mode (Mute)
37	41	YOU'RE PUTTIN' A RUSH ON ME	Stephanie Mills (MCA)
43	42	SOFT AS YOUR FACE	Soup Dragons (Raw)
25	43	DIDN'T WE ALMOST HAVE IT ALL	Whitney Houston (Arista)
20	44	I JUST CAN'T STOP LOVING YOU	Michael Jackson (Epic)
-	45	NEVER LET ME DOWN	David Bowie (EMI America)
46	46	I FOUND LOVIN'	Fatback Band (Master Mix)
-	47	SECRET AGENT MAN	Bruce Willis (Motown)
-	48	THE OPERA HOUSE	Jack Mokassa (Champion)
31	49	SOMEWHERE OUT THERE	Linda Ronstadt & James Ingram (MCA)
-	50	REAL COOL TIME	Ramones (Beggars Banquet)

Two acts who first charted in the 1960s, Dusty Springfield and the Beach Boys, both reappeared in the Top Three via singles made in collaboration with current artists. Dusty duetted with her fan Neil Tennant on the Pet Shop Boys' *What Have I Done To Deserve This*, while the Beach Boys provided the surf music accompaniment and vocal back-up to the Fat Boys' rap revival of the Surfaris' *Wipe Out*.

October 1987

3 October 1987

Last	This	Title	Artist (Label)
2	1	PUMP UP THE VOLUME	M/A/R/R/S (4AD)
1	2	NEVER GONNA GIVE YOU UP	Rick Astley (RCA)
16	3	BAD	Michael Jackson (Epic)
5	4	CAUSING A COMMOTION	Madonna (Sire)
7	5	SOME PEOPLE	Cliff Richard (EMI)
4	6	WIPE OUT	Fat Boys & the Beach Boys (Urban)
10	7	HOUSENATION	Housemaster Boyz (Magnetic Dance)
15	8	HEY MATTHEW	Karel Fialka (IRS)
19	9	I NEED LOVE	LL Cool J (Def Jam)
3	10	HEART AND SOUL	T'Pau (Siren)
29	11	CROCKETT'S THEME	Jan Hammer (MCA)
8	12	IT'S OVER	Level 42 (Polydor)
13	13	I DON'T WANT TO BE A HERO	Johnny Hates Jazz (Virgin)
9	14	CASANOVA	Levert (Atlantic)
6	15	WHERE THE STREETS HAVE NO NAME	U2 (Island)
-	16	THIS CORROSION	Sisters of Mercy (Merciful Release)
22	17	POUR SOME SUGAR ON ME	Def Leppard (Bludgeon Riffola)
14	18	TOY BOY	Sinitta (Fanfare)
20	19	LIES	Jonathan Butler (Jive)
27	20	JACK LE FREAK	Chic (Atlantic)
11	21	WHAT HAVE I DONE TO DESERVE THIS	Pet Shop Boys & Dusty Springfield (Parlophone)
-	22	FULL METAL JACKET	Abigail Mead & Nigel Goulding (Warner Bros)
12	23	WONDERFUL LIFE	Black (A&M)
24	24	TOMORROW	Communards (London)
-	25	BRILLIANT DISGUISE	Bruce Springsteen (CBS)
30	26	CARS	Gary Numan (Beggars Banquet)
25	27	STOP TO LOVE	Luther Vandross (Epic)
-	28	WHO WILL YOU RUN TO	Heart (Capitol)
-	29	WHITE COATS (EP)	New Model Army (EMI)
18	30	SWEET LTTLE MYSTERY	Wet Wet Wet (Precious)
23	31	ME AND THE FARMER	Housemartins (Go! Discs)
33	32	THE NIGHT YOU MURDERED LOVE	ABC (Neutron)
17	33	BRIDGE TO YOUR HEART	Wax (RCA)
-	34	CRAZY CRAZY NIGHT	Kiss (Vertigo)
38	35	COME SEE ABOUT ME	Shakin' Stevens (Epic)
46	36	I FOUND LOVIN'	Fatback Band (Master Mix)
-	37	VALERIE	Steve Winwood (Island)
28	38	U GOT THE LOOK	Prince & Sheena Easton (Paisley Park)
43	39	DIDN'T WE ALMOST HAVE IT ALL	Whitney Houston (Arista)
35	40	I FOUND LOVING	Steve Walsh (A1)
-	41	THE REAL THING	Jellybean (Chrysalis)
-	42	THE CIRCUS	Erasure (Mute)
-	43	COME ON LET'S GO	Los Lobos (Slash)
-	44	WHEN THE FINGERS POINT	Christians (Island)
21	45	HOUR GLASS	Squeeze (A&M)
26	46	CALL ME	Spagna (CBS)
39	47	LET'S WORK	Mick Jagger (CBS)
50	48	REAL COOL TIME	Ramones (Beggars Banquet)
-	49	YOU WIN AGAIN	Bee Gees (Warner Bros)
36	50	MY LOVE IS GUARANTEED	Sybil (Champion)

10 October 1987

Last	This	Title	Artist (Label)
1	1	PUMP UP THE VOLUME	M/A/R/R/S (4AD)
3	2	BAD	Michael Jackson (Epic)
2	3	NEVER GONNA GIVE YOU UP	Rick Astley (RCA)
11	4	CROCKETT'S THEME	Jan Hammer (MCA)
22	5	FULL METAL JACKET	Abigail Mead & Nigel Goulding (Warner Bros)
9	6	I NEED LOVE	LL Cool J (Def Jam)
5	7	SOME PEOPLE	Cliff Richard (EMI)
8	8	CAUSING A COMMOTION	Madonna (Sire)
16	9	THIS CORROSION	Sisters of Mercy (Merciful Release)
7	10	HOUSENATION	Housemaster Boyz (Magnetic Dance)
25	11	BRILLIANT DISGUISE	Bruce Springsteen (CBS)
8	12	HEY MATTHEW	Karel Fialka (IRS)
10	13	HEART AND SOUL	T'Pau (Siren)
26	14	CARS	Gary Numan (Beggars Banquet)
6	15	WIPE OUT	Fat Boys & the Beach Boys (Urban)
49	16	YOU WIN AGAIN	Bee Gees (Warner Bros)
13	17	I DON'T WANT TO BE A HERO	Johnny Hates Jazz (Virgin)
34	18	CRAZY CRAZY NIGHT	Kiss (Vertigo)
12	19	IT'S OVER	Level 42 (Polydor)
20	20	JACK LE FREAK	Chic (Atlantic)
14	21	CASANOVA	Levert (Atlantic)
24	22	TOMORROW	Communards (London)
17	23	POUR SOME SUGAR ON ME	Def Leppard (Bludgeon Riffola)
23	24	WONDERFUL LIFE	Black (A&M)
32	25	THE NIGHT YOU MURDERED LOVE	ABC (Neutron)
35	26	COME SEE ABOUT ME	Shakin' Stevens (Epic)
18	27	TOY BOY	Sinitta (Fanfare)
-	28	THE TRAVELLER	Spear of Destiny (10)
29	29	WHITE COATS (EP)	New Model Army (EMI)
37	30	VALERIE	Steve Winwood (Island)
28	31	WHO WILL YOU RUN TO	Heart (Capitol)
41	32	THE REAL THING	Jellybean (Chrysalis)
47	33	LET'S WORK	Mick Jagger (CBS)
-	34	SHE'S CRAZY	Beastie Boys (Def Jam)
-	36	MY BAG	Lloyd Cole & the Commotions (Polydor)
-	37	WELCOME TO THE JUNGLE	Guns 'N Roses (Geffen)
36	38	I FOUND LOVIN'	Fatback Band (Master Mix)
30	39	SWEET LTTLE MYSTERY	Wet Wet Wet (Precious)
27	40	STOP TO LOVE	Luther Vandross (Epic)
15	41	WHERE THE STREETS HAVE NO NAME	U2 (Island)
42	42	THE CIRCUS	Erasure (Mute)
-	43	MONY MONY	Billy Idol (Chrysalis)
21	44	WHAT HAVE I DONE TO DESERVE THIS	Pet Shop Boys & Dusty Springfield (Parlophone)
-	45	WALK THE DINOSAUR	Was (Not Was) (Fontana)
-	46	LOVE WILL FIND A WAY	Yes (Atco)
40	47	I FOUND LOVING	Steve Walsh (A1)
33	48	BRIDGE TO YOUR HEART	Wax (RCA)
43	49	COME ON LET'S GO	Los Lobos (Slash)
-	50	LITTLE LIES	Fleetwood Mac (Warner Bros)

17 October 1987

Last	This	Title	Artist (Label)
5	1	FULL METAL JACKET	Abigail Mead & Nigel Goulding (Warner Bros)
1	2	PUMP UP THE VOLUME	M/A/R/R/S (4AD)
2	3	BAD	Michael Jackson (Epic)
4	4	CROCKETT'S THEME	Jan Hammer (MCA)
16	5	YOU WIN AGAIN	Bee Gees (Warner Bros)
3	6	NEVER GONNA GIVE YOU UP	Rick Astley (RCA)
18	7	CRAZY CRAZY NIGHT	Kiss (Vertigo)
6	8	I NEED LOVE	LL Cool J (Def Jam)
7	9	SOME PEOPLE	Cliff Richard (EMI)
38	10	I FOUND LOVIN'	Fatback Band (Master Mix)
8	11	CAUSING A COMMOTION	Madonna (Sire)
9	12	THIS CORROSION	Sisters of Mercy (Merciful Release)
11	13	BRILLIANT DISGUISE	Bruce Springsteen (CBS)
10	14	HOUSENATION	Housemaster Boyz (Magnetic Dance)
12	15	HEY MATTHEW	Karel Fialka (IRS)
47	16	I FOUND LOVING	Steve Walsh (A1)
33	17	THE REAL THING	Jellybean (Chrysalis)
17	18	I DON'T WANT TO BE A HERO	Johnny Hates Jazz (Virgin)
19	19	IT'S OVER	Level 42 (Polydor)
14	20	CARS	Gary Numan (Beggars Banquet)
15	21	WIPE OUT	Fat Boys & the Beach Boys (Urban)
30	22	VALERIE	Steve Winwood (Island)
-	23	STRONG AS STEEL	Five Star (Tent)
26	24	COME SEE ABOUT ME	Shakin' Stevens (Epic)
43	25	MONY MONY	Billy Idol (Chrysalis)
20	26	JACK LE FREAK	Chic (Atlantic)
45	27	WALK THE DINOSAUR	Was (Not Was) (Fontana)
36	28	MY BAG	Lloyd Cole & the Commotions (Polydor)
34	29	LET'S WORK	Mick Jagger (CBS)
35	30	SHE'S CRAZY	Beastie Boys (Def Jam)
50	31	LITTLE LIES	Fleetwood Mac (Warner Bros)
37	32	WELCOME TO THE JUNGLE	Guns 'N Roses (Geffen)
32	33	WHO WILL YOU RUN TO	Heart (Capitol)
49	34	COME ON LET'S GO	Los Lobos (Slash)
23	35	POUR SOME SUGAR ON ME	Def Leppard (Bludgeon Riffola)
24	36	WONDERFUL LIFE	Black (A&M)
-	37	LOVE IN THE FIRST DEGREE	Bananarama (London)
-	38	THE RIGHT STUFF	Bryan Ferry (Virgin)
29	39	CASANOVA	Levert (Atlantic)
28	40	LIES	Jonathan Butler (Jive)
-	41	MONY MONY	Amazulu (EMI)
-	42	LET THE HAPPINESS IN	David Sylvian (Virgin)
-	43	I WANT TO BE YOUR PROPERTY	Blue Mercedes (MCA)
46	44	LOVE WILL FIND A WAY	Yes (Atco)
40	45	STOP TO LOVE	Luther Vandross (Epic)
-	46	DON'T GONNA (JAMMIN')	L.A. Mix (Breakout)
28	47	THE TRAVELLER	Spear of Destiny (10)
-	48	DANCE LITTLE SISTER	Terence Trent D'Arby (CBS)
48	49	BRIDGE TO YOUR HEART	Wax (RCA)
39	50	SWEET LTTLE MYSTERY	Wet Wet Wet (Precious)

Dance act M/A/R/R/S, wilful one-hit wonders who came together for just their No.1 *Pump Up The Volume* and then split, were actually an amalgam of talents, notably DJ/mixer C.J. Mackintosh, A.R. Kane, and Martin Young of Colourbox - the latter two acts being signed to the 4 AD label which released *Pump Up The Volume*. It sold more copies than anything else in 1987 on 12-inch.

24 October 1987

last week	this week	Title	Artist (Label)
5	1	YOU WIN AGAIN	Bee Gees (Warner Bros)
1	2	FULL METAL JACKET	Abigail Mead & Nigel Goulding (Warner Bros)
7	3	CRAZY CRAZY NIGHT	Kiss (Vertigo)
2	4	PUMP UP THE VOLUME	M/A/R/R/S (4AD)
4	5	CROCKETT'S THEME	Jan Hammer (MCA)
10	6	I FOUND LOVIN'	Fatback Band (Master Mix)
16	7	I FOUND LOVING	Steve Walsh (A1)
3	8	BAD	Michael Jackson (Epic)
17	9	THE REAL THING	Jellybean (Chrysalis)
-	10	CIRCUS (EP)	Erasure (Mute)
8	11	I NEED LOVE	LL Cool J (Def Jam)
27	12	WALK THE DINOSAUR	Was (Not Was) (Fontana)
-	13	RAIN IN THE SUMMERTIME	Alarm (IRS)
12	14	THIS CORROSION	Sisters of Mercy (Merciful Release)
6	15	NEVER GONNA GIVE YOU UP	Rick Astley (RCA)
25	16	MONY MONY	Billy Idol (Chrysalis)
22	17	VALERIE	Steve Winwood (Island)
23	18	STRONG AS STEEL	Five Star (Tent)
-	19	JUST LIKE HEAVEN	Cure (Fiction)
37	20	LOVE IN THE FIRST DEGREE	Bananarama (London)
31	21	LITTLE LIES	Fleetwood Mac (Warner Bros)
11	22	CAUSING A COMMOTION	Madonna (Sire)
9	23	SOME PEOPLE	Cliff Richard (EMI)
34	24	COME ON LET'S GO	Los Lobos (Slash)
-	25	MAYBE TOMORROW	UB40 (DEP International)
-	26	DUDE	Aerosmith (Geffen)
48	27	DANCE LITTLE SISTER	Terence Trent D'Arby (CBS)
13	28	BRILLIANT DISGUISE	Bruce Springsteen (CBS)
-	29	FAITH	George Michael (Epic)
28	30	MY BAG	Lloyd Cole & the Commotions (Polydor)
20	31	CARS	Gary Numan (Beggars Banquet)
18	32	I DON'T WANT TO BE A HERO	Johnny Hates Jazz (Virgin)
-	33	RENT	Pet Shop Boys (Parlophone)
19	34	IT'S OVER	Level 42 (Polydor)
33	35	WHO WILL YOU RUN TO	Heart (Capitol)
36	36	THE RIGHT STUFF	Bryan Ferry (Virgin)
-	37	SHE'S MINE	Cameo (Club)
24	38	COME SEE ABOUT ME	Shakin' Stevens (Epic)
-	39	I DON'T THINK	Ray Parker Jr. (Geffen)
30	40	SHE'S CRAZY	Beastie Boys (Def Jam)
-	41	BEAVER PATROL	Pop Will Eat Itself (Chapter 22)
14	42	HOUSENATION	Housemaster Boyz (Magnetic Dance)
29	43	LET'S WORK	Mick Jagger (CBS)
15	44	HEY MATTHEW	Karel Fialka (IRS)
32	45	WELCOME TO THE JUNGLE	Guns 'N Roses (Geffen)
-	46	BEETHOVEN	Eurythmics (RCA)
-	47	WHEN THE FINGERS POINT	Christians (Island)
26	48	JACK LE FREAK	Chic (Atlantic)
-	49	GENIUS MOVE	That Petrol Emotion (Polydor)
-	50	TOMORROW	Communards (London)

31 October 1987

last week	this week	Title	Artist (Label)
1	1	YOU WIN AGAIN	Bee Gees (Warner Bros)
20	2	LOVE IN THE FIRST DEGREE	Bananarama (London)
3	3	CRAZY CRAZY NIGHT	Kiss (Vertigo)
5	4	CROCKETT'S THEME	Jan Hammer (MCA)
10	5	CIRCUS (EP)	Erasure (Mute)
2	6	FULL METAL JACKET	Abigail Mead & Nigel Goulding (Warner Bros)
7	7	MONY MONY	Billy Idol (Chrysalis)
8	8	FAITH	George Michael (Epic)
12	9	WALK THE DINOSAUR	Was (Not Was) (Fontana)
4	10	PUMP UP THE VOLUME	M/A/R/R/S (4AD)
11	11	LITTLE LIES	Fleetwood Mac (Warner Bros)
6	12	I FOUND LOVIN'	Fatback Band (Master Mix)
33	13	RENT	Pet Shop Boys (Parlophone)
9	14	THE REAL THING	Jellybean (Chrysalis)
46	15	BEETHOVEN	Eurythmics (RCA)
7	16	I FOUND LOVING	Steve Walsh (A1)
13	17	RAIN IN THE SUMMERTIME	Alarm (IRS)
27	18	DANCE LITTLE SISTER	Terence Trent D'Arby (CBS)
25	19	MAYBE TOMORROW	UB40 (DEP International)
24	20	COME ON LET'S GO	Los Lobos (Slash)
18	21	STRONG AS STEEL	Five Star (Tent)
11	22	I NEED LOVE	LL Cool J (Def Jam)
19	23	JUST LIKE HEAVEN	Cure (Fiction)
8	24	BAD	Michael Jackson (Epic)
17	25	VALERIE	Steve Winwood (Island)
39	26	I DON'T THINK	Ray Parker Jr. (Geffen)
15	27	NEVER GONNA GIVE YOU UP	Rick Astley (RCA)
-	28	BLUE WATER	Fields of the Nephilim (Situation Two)
29	29	HERE I GO AGAIN	Whitesnake (EMI)
-	30	NO MEMORY	Scarlet Fantastic (Arista)
-	31	GOT MY MIND SET ON YOU	George Harrison (Dark Horse)
-	32	CHINA IN YOUR HAND	T'Pau (Siren)
-	33	MUSCLE DEEP	Then Jerico (London)
-	34	I'M NOT AFRAID	Black (A&M)
37	35	SHE'S MINE	Cameo (Club)
-	36	TIME STANDS STILL	Rush (Vertigo)
14	37	THIS CORROSION	Sisters of Mercy (Merciful Release)
-	38	I DON'T NEED NO DOCTOR	W.A.S.P. (Capitol)
-	39	GIT DOWN	Gaye Bykers On Acid (Purple Fluid)
-	40	BIRTHDAY	Sugarcubes (One Little Indian)
-	41	NEED YOU TONIGHT	INXS (Mercury)
47	42	WHEN THE FINGERS POINT	Christians (Island)
23	43	SOME PEOPLE	Cliff Richard (EMI)
36	44	THE RIGHT STUFF	Bryan Ferry (Virgin)
-	45	SO THE STORY GOES	Living In A Box (Chrysalis)
-	46	HIT THE NORTH	Fall (Beggars Banquet)
31	47	CARS	Gary Numan (Beggars Banquet)
-	48	WANTED	Style Council (Polydor)
-	49	I WANT TO BE YOUR PROPERTY	Blue Mercedes (MCA)
-	50	I WANT TO BE YOUR MAN	Roger (Reprise)

7 November 1987

last week	this week	Title	Artist (Label)
8	1	FAITH	George Michael (Epic)
1	2	YOU WIN AGAIN	Bee Gees (Warner Bros)
2	3	LOVE IN THE FIRST DEGREE	Bananarama (London)
11	4	LITTLE LIES	Fleetwood Mac (Warner Bros)
-	5	WHENEVER YOU NEED SOMEBODY	Rick Astley (RCA)
13	6	RENT	Pet Shop Boys (Parlophone)
4	7	CROCKETT'S THEME	Jan Hammer (MCA)
5	8	CIRCUS (EP)	Erasure (Mute)
9	9	WALK THE DINOSAUR	Was (Not Was) (Fontana)
3	10	CRAZY CRAZY NIGHT	Kiss (Vertigo)
32	11	CHINA IN YOUR HAND	T'Pau (Siren)
26	12	I DON'T THINK	Ray Parker Jr. (Geffen)
7	13	MONY MONY	Billy Idol (Chrysalis)
31	14	GOT MY MIND SET ON YOU	George Harrison (Dark Horse)
29	15	HERE I GO AGAIN	Whitesnake (EMI)
20	16	COME ON LET'S GO	Los Lobos (Slash)
19	17	MAYBE TOMORROW	UB40 (DEP International)
6	18	FULL METAL JACKET	Abigail Mead & Nigel Goulding (Warner Bros)
18	19	DANCE LITTLE SISTER	Terence Trent D'Arby (CBS)
14	20	THE REAL THING	Jellybean (Chrysalis)
-	21	BARCELONA	Freddie Mercury & Montserrat Caballe (Polydor)
36	22	TIME STANDS STILL	Rush (Vertigo)
15	23	BEETHOVEN	Eurythmics (RCA)
10	24	PUMP UP THE VOLUME	M/A/R/R/S (4AD)
48	25	WANTED	Style Council (Polydor)
-	26	NEVER CAN SAY GOODBYE	Communards (London)
38	27	I DON'T NEED NO DOCTOR	W.A.S.P. (Capitol)
12	28	I FOUND LOVIN'	Fatback Band (Master Mix)
46	29	HIT THE NORTH	Fall (Beggars Banquet)
30	30	MY BABY JUST CARES FOR ME	Nina Simone (Charly)
30	31	NO MEMORY	Scarlet Fantastic (Arista)
44	32	THE RIGHT STUFF	Bryan Ferry (Virgin)
22	33	I NEED LOVE	LL Cool J (Def Jam)
-	34	TEARS FROM HEAVEN	Heartbeat (Priority)
33	35	MUSCLE DEEP	Then Jerico (London)
-	36	WARM WET CIRCLES	Marillion (EMI)
-	37	REMEMBER ME	Cliff Richard (EMI)
-	38	MONY MONY	Amazulu (EMI)
17	39	RAIN IN THE SUMMERTIME	Alarm (IRS)
39	40	GIT DOWN	Gaye Bykers On Acid (Purple Fluid)
-	41	(I'VE HAD) THE TIME OF MY LIFE	Bill Medley & Jennifer Warnes (RCA)
-	42	DUDE	Aerosmith (Geffen)
16	43	I FOUND LOVING	Steve Walsh (A1)
25	44	VALERIE	Steve Winwood (Island)
-	45	SILVERMAC	Westworld (RCA)
28	46	BLUE WATER	Fields of the Nephilim (Situation Two)
27	47	NEVER GONNA GIVE YOU UP	Rick Astley (RCA)
50	48	I WANT TO BE YOUR MAN	Roger (Reprise)
23	49	JUST LIKE HEAVEN	Cure (Fiction)
40	50	BIRTHDAY	Sugarcubes (One Little Indian)

The Bee Gees' *You Win Again* was their first Number One since Tragedy in 1979, and their first hit of any kind since *Spirits (Having Flown)* in the same year; oddly, it was only a minor success in the US, where the trio's 1970s success had been far greater than in Britain. Jan Hammer's *Crockett's Theme* was his second instrumental hit from Miami Vice, and was later appropriated by NatWest Bank TV ads!

November 1987

14 November 1987

last week	this week	title	artist (label)
2	1	YOU WIN AGAIN	Bee Gees (Warner Bros)
5	2	WHENEVER YOU NEED SOMEBODY	Rick Astley (RCA)
1	3	FAITH	George Michael (Epic)
11	4	CHINA IN YOUR HAND	T'Pau (Siren)
14	5	GOT MY MIND SET ON YOU	George Harrison (Dark Horse)
3	6	LOVE IN THE FIRST DEGREE	Bananarama (London)
21	7	BARCELONA	Freddie Mercury & Montserrat Caballe (Polydor)
4	8	LITTLE LIES	Fleetwood Mac (Warner Bros)
26	9	NEVER CAN SAY GOODBYE	Communards (London)
13	10	MONY MONY	Billy Idol (Chrysalis)
15	11	HERE I GO AGAIN	Whitesnake (EMI)
12	12	I DON'T THINK	Ray Parker Jr. (Geffen)
9	13	WALK THE DINOSAUR	Was (Not Was) (Fontana)
41	14	(I'VE HAD) THE TIME OF MY LIFE	Bill Medley & Jennifer Warnes (RCA)
7	15	CROCKETT'S THEME	Jan Hammer (MCA)
30	16	MY BABY JUST CARES FOR ME	Nina Simone (Charly)
6	17	RENT	Pet Shop Boys (Parlophone)
25	18	WANTED	Style Council (Polydor)
–	19	JACK MIX IV	Mirage (Debut)
–	20	PAID IN FULL	Eric B. & Rakim (Fourth & Broadway)
10	21	CRAZY CRAZY NIGHT	Kiss (Vertigo)
–	22	DARKLANDS	Jesus & Mary Chain (blanco y negro)
8	23	CIRCUS (EP)	Erasure (Mute)
16	24	COME ON LET'S GO	Los Lobos (Slash)
20	25	THE REAL THING	Jellybean (Chrysalis)
36	26	WARM WET CIRCLES	Marillion (EMI)
18	27	FULL METAL JACKET	Abigail Mead & Nigel Goulding (Warner Bros)
–	28	DINNER WITH GERSHWIN	Donna Summer (Warner Bros)
17	29	MAYBE TOMORROW	UB40 (DEP International)
37	30	REMEMBER ME	Cliff Richard (EMI)
–	31	I STARTED SOMETHING I COULDN'T FINISH	Smiths (Rough Trade)
32	32	NO MEMORY	Scarlet Fantastic (Arista)
–	33	WE'LL BE TOGETHER	Sting (A&M)
23	34	BEETHOVEN	Eurythmics (RCA)
19	35	DANCE LITTLE SISTER	Terence Trent D'Arby (CBS)
26	36	CRITICIZE	Alexander O'Neal (Tabu)
27	37	I DON'T NEED NO DOCTOR	W.A.S.P. (Capitol)
28	38	I FOUND LOVIN'	Fatback Band (Master Mix)
34	39	TEARS FROM HEAVEN	Heartbeat (Priority)
48	40	I WANT TO BE YOUR MAN	Roger (Reprise)
–	41	BACKSEAT EDUCATION	Zodiac Mindwarp (Mercury)
–	42	SO EMOTIONAL	Whitney Houston (Arista)
–	43	SOME GUYS HAVE ALL THE LUCK	Maxi Priest (10)
42	44	DUDE	Aerosmith (Geffen)
32	45	THE RIGHT STUFF	Bryan Ferry (Virgin)
–	46	STRONG AS STEEL	Five Star (Tent)
29	47	HIT THE NORTH	Fall (Beggars Banquet)
38	48	MONY MONY	Amazulu (EMI)
46	49	BLUE WATER	Fields of the Nephilim (Situation Two)
22	50	TIME STANDS STILL	Rush (Vertigo)

21 November 1987

last week	this week	title	artist (label)
4	1	CHINA IN YOUR HAND	T'Pau (Siren)
5	2	GOT MY MIND SET ON YOU	George Harrison (Dark Horse)
9	3	NEVER CAN SAY GOODBYE	Communards (London)
2	4	WHENEVER YOU NEED SOMEBODY	Rick Astley (RCA)
1	5	YOU WIN AGAIN	Bee Gees (Warner Bros)
16	6	MY BABY JUST CARES FOR ME	Nina Simone (Charly)
7	7	BARCELONA	Freddie Mercury & Montserrat Caballe (Polydor)
14	8	(I'VE HAD) THE TIME OF MY LIFE	Bill Medley & Jennifer Warnes (RCA)
3	9	FAITH	George Michael (Epic)
8	10	LITTLE LIES	Fleetwood Mac (Warner Bros)
11	11	HERE I GO AGAIN	Whitesnake (EMI)
19	12	JACK MIX IV	Mirage (Debut)
6	13	LOVE IN THE FIRST DEGREE	Bananarama (London)
20	14	PAID IN FULL	Eric B. & Rakim (Fourth & Broadway)
42	15	SO EMOTIONAL	Whitney Houston (Arista)
28	16	DINNER WITH GERSHWIN	Donna Summer (Warner Bros)
31	17	I STARTED SOMETHING I COULDN'T FINISH	Smiths (Rough Trade)
26	18	WARM WET CIRCLES	Marillion (EMI)
–	19	SHO' YOU RIGHT	Barry White (Breakout)
22	20	DARKLANDS	Jesus & Mary Chain (blanco y negro)
–	21	BUILD	Housemartins (Go! Discs)
12	22	I DON'T THINK	Ray Parker Jr. (Geffen)
41	23	BACKSEAT EDUCATION	Zodiac Mindwarp (Mercury)
10	24	MONY MONY	Billy Idol (Chrysalis)
15	25	CROCKETT'S THEME	Jan Hammer (MCA)
13	26	WALK THE DINOSAUR	Was (Not Was) (Fontana)
43	27	SOME GUYS HAVE ALL THE LUCK	Maxi Priest (10)
–	28	IN THE CLOUDS	All About Eve (Mercury)
37	29	I DON'T NEED NO DOCTOR	W.A.S.P. (Capitol)
–	30	LETTER FROM AMERICA	Proclaimers (Chrysalis)
36	31	CRITICIZE	Alexander O'Neal (Tabu)
47	32	HIT THE NORTH	Fall (Beggars Banquet)
32	33	NO MEMORY	Scarlet Fantastic (Arista)
17	34	RENT	Pet Shop Boys (Parlophone)
21	35	CRAZY CRAZY NIGHT	Kiss (Vertigo)
23	36	CIRCUS (EP)	Erasure (Mute)
49	37	BLUE WATER	Fields of the Nephilim (Situation Two)
–	38	REBEL WITHOUT A PAUSE	Public Enemy (Def Jam)
–	39	TO BE REBORN	Boy George (Virgin)
18	40	WANTED	Style Council (Polydor)
–	41	FUNNY HOW TIME FLIES	Janet Jackson (Breakout)
24	42	COME ON LET'S GO	Los Lobos (Slash)
–	43	CAN U DANCE	Kenny 'Jammin' Jason & 'Fast' Eddie Smith (Champion)
25	44	THE REAL THING	Jellybean (Chrysalis)
–	45	GO CUT CREATOR	LL Cool J (Def Jam)
–	46	SOLITUDE STANDING	Suzanne Vega (A&M)
50	47	TIME STANDS STILL	Rush (Vertigo)
33	48	WE'LL BE TOGETHER	Sting (A&M)
27	49	FULL METAL JACKET	Abigail Mead & Nigel Goulding (Warner Bros)
–	50	BIRTHDAY	Sugarcubes (One Little Indian)

28 November 1987

last week	this week	title	artist (label)
1	1	CHINA IN YOUR HAND	T'Pau (Siren)
2	2	GOT MY MIND SET ON YOU	George Harrison (Dark Horse)
3	3	NEVER CAN SAY GOODBYE	Communards (London)
6	4	MY BABY JUST CARES FOR ME	Nina Simone (Charly)
4	5	WHENEVER YOU NEED SOMEBODY	Rick Astley (RCA)
15	6	SO EMOTIONAL	Whitney Houston (Arista)
8	7	(I'VE HAD) THE TIME OF MY LIFE	Bill Medley & Jennifer Warnes (RCA)
12	8	JACK MIX IV	Mirage (Debut)
5	9	YOU WIN AGAIN	Bee Gees (Warner Bros)
7	10	BARCELONA	Freddie Mercury & Montserrat Caballe (Polydor)
31	11	CRITICIZE	Alexander O'Neal (Tabu)
11	12	HERE I GO AGAIN	Whitesnake (EMI)
14	13	PAID IN FULL	Eric B. & Rakim (Fourth & Broadway)
27	14	SOME GUYS HAVE ALL THE LUCK	Maxi Priest (10)
30	15	LETTER FROM AMERICA	Proclaimers (Chrysalis)
10	16	LITTLE LIES	Fleetwood Mac (Warner Bros)
19	17	SHO' YOU RIGHT	Barry White (Breakout)
16	18	DINNER WITH GERSHWIN	Donna Summer (Warner Bros)
17	19	I STARTED SOMETHING I COULDN'T FINISH	Smiths (Rough Trade)
21	20	BUILD	Housemartins (Go! Discs)
39	21	TO BE REBORN	Boy George (Virgin)
9	22	FAITH	George Michael (Epic)
13	23	LOVE IN THE FIRST DEGREE	Bananarama (London)
32	24	HIT THE NORTH	Fall (Beggars Banquet)
–	25	SO AMAZING	Luther Vandross (Epic)
38	26	REBEL WITHOUT A PAUSE	Public Enemy (Def Jam)
24	27	MONY MONY	Billy Idol (Chrysalis)
29	28	I DON'T NEED NO DOCTOR	W.A.S.P. (Capitol)
45	29	GO CUT CREATOR	LL Cool J (Def Jam)
18	30	WARM WET CIRCLES	Marillion (EMI)
23	31	BACKSEAT EDUCATION	Zodiac Mindwarp (Mercury)
–	32	I WANT TO BE YOUR PROPERTY	Blue Mercedes (MCA)
–	33	I'VE BEEN IN LOVE BEFORE	Cutting Crew (Siren)
22	34	I DON'T THINK	Ray Parker Jr. (Geffen)
35	35	DARKLANDS	Jesus & Mary Chain (blanco y negro)
34	36	RENT	Pet Shop Boys (Parlophone)
–	37	BIKO	Peter Gabriel (Charisma)
–	38	ONCE UPON A LONG AGO	Paul McCartney (Parlophone)
–	39	THE ONE I LOVE	R.E.M. (IRS)
–	40	THERE AIN'T NOTHIN' LIKE SHAGGIN'	Tams (Virgin)
26	41	WALK THE DINOSAUR	Was (Not Was) (Fontana)
–	42	SATELLITE	Hooters (CBS)
43	43	THE REAL THING	Jellybean (Chrysalis)
35	44	CRAZY CRAZY NIGHT	Kiss (Vertigo)
33	45	NO MEMORY	Scarlet Fantastic (Arista)
–	46	I COULD NEVER TAKE THE PLACE OF YOUR MAN	Prince (Paisley Park)
48	47	WE'LL BE TOGETHER	Sting (A&M)
25	48	CROCKETT'S THEME	Jan Hammer (MCA)
41	49	FUNNY HOW TIME FLIES	Janet Jackson (Breakout)
37	50	BLUE WATER	Fields of the Nephilim (Situation Two)

After reaching Number Three in September with their chart debut *Heart And Soul*, T'Pau (named after a Vulcan elder in the *Star Trek* TV series) made the top with the follow-up *China In Your Hand*, which shared the year's longest Number One residency of four weeks. The single it held at Two was George Harrison's biggest hit since *My Sweet Lord*, a revival of an obscure early '60s number by James Ray.

last this week

5 December 1987

Last	This	Title	Artist
1	1	CHINA IN YOUR HAND	T'Pau (Siren)
5	2	WHENEVER YOU NEED SOMEBODY	Rick Astley (RCA)
2	3	GOT MY MIND SET ON YOU	George Harrison (Dark Horse)
15	4	LETTER FROM AMERICA	Proclaimers (Chrysalis)
4	5	MY BABY JUST CARES FOR ME	Nina Simone (Charly)
3	6	NEVER CAN SAY GOODBYE	Communards (London)
6	7	SO EMOTIONAL	Whitney Houston (Arista)
11	8	CRITICIZE	Alexander O'Neal (Tabu)
7	9	(I'VE HAD) THE TIME OF MY LIFE	Bill Medley & Jennifer Warnes (RCA)
12	10	HERE I GO AGAIN	Whitesnake (EMI)
14	11	SOME GUYS HAVE ALL THE LUCK	Maxi Priest (10)
17	12	SHO' YOU RIGHT	Barry White (Breakout)
18	13	DINNER WITH GERSHWIN	Donna Summer (Warner Bros)
38	14	ONCE UPON A LONG AGO	Paul McCartney (Parlophone)
8	15	JACK MIX IV	Mirage (Debut)
20	16	BUILD	Housemartins (Go! Discs)
-	17	WHAT DO YOU WANT TO	Shakin' Stevens (Epic)
21	18	TO BE REBORN	Boy George (Virgin)
13	19	PAID IN FULL	Eric B. & Rakim (Fourth & Broadway)
9	20	YOU WIN AGAIN	Bee Gees (Warner Bros)
-	21	WHO FOUND WHO	Jellybean & Elissa Fiorello (Chrysalis)
46	22	I COULD NEVER TAKE THE PLACE OF YOUR MAN	Prince (Paisley Park)
-	23	HYSTERIA	Def Leppard (Bludgeon Riffola)
23	24	LOVE IN THE FIRST DEGREE	Bananarama (London)
10	25	BARCELONA	Freddie Mercury & Montserrat Caballe (Polydor)
32	26	I WANT TO BE YOUR PROPERTY	Blue Mercedes (MCA)
40	27	THERE AIN'T NOTHIN' LIKE SHAGGIN'	Tams (Virgin)
-	28	I'M THE MAN	Anthrax (Island)
22	29	FAITH	George Michael (Epic)
42	30	SATELLITE	Hooters (CBS)
16	31	LITTLE LIES	Fleetwood Mac (Warner Bros)
-	32	KING WITHOUT A CROWN	ABC (Neutron)
37	33	BIKO	Peter Gabriel (Charisma)
-	34	FAIRYTALE OF NEW YORK	Pogues (Pogue Mahone)
-	35	I WON'T CRY	Glen Goldsmith (Reproduction)
-	36	THE WAY YOU MAKE ME FEEL	Michael Jackson (Epic)
-	37	EVERY TIME WE SAY GOODBYE	Simply Red (Elektra)
26	38	REBEL WITHOUT A PAUSE	Public Enemy (Def Jam)
33	39	I'VE BEEN IN LOVE BEFORE	Cutting Crew (Siren)
-	40	TURN BACK THE CLOCK	Johnny Hates Jazz (Virgin)
19	41	I STARTED SOMETHING I COULDN'T FINISH	Smiths (Rough Trade)
-	42	UNCHAIN MY HEART	Joe Cocker (Capitol)
-	43	I SAY NOTHING	Voice of the Beehive (London)
25	44	SO AMAZING	Luther Vandross (Epic)
31	45	BACKSEAT EDUCATION	Zodiac Mindwarp (Mercury)
47	46	WE'LL BE TOGETHER	Sting (A&M)
-	47	LOVE LETTERS	Alison Moyet (CBS)
-	48	GORGEOUS	Gene Loves Jezebel (Beggars Banquet)
-	49	BIRTHDAY	Sugarcubes (One Little Indian)
39	50	THE ONE I LOVE	R.E.M. (IRS)

12 December 1987

Last	This	Title	Artist
1	1	CHINA IN YOUR HAND	T'Pau (Siren)
4	2	LETTER FROM AMERICA	Proclaimers (Chrysalis)
3	3	GOT MY MIND SET ON YOU	George Harrison (Dark Horse)
8	4	CRITICIZE	Alexander O'Neal (Tabu)
17	5	WHAT DO YOU WANT TO	Shakin' Stevens (Epic)
6	6	NEVER CAN SAY GOODBYE	Communards (London)
14	7	ONCE UPON A LONG AGO	Paul McCartney (Parlophone)
36	8	THE WAY YOU MAKE ME FEEL	Michael Jackson (Epic)
7	9	SO EMOTIONAL	Whitney Houston (Arista)
21	10	WHO FOUND WHO	Jellybean & Elissa Fiorello (Chrysalis)
-	11	WHEN I FALL IN LOVE	Rick Astley (RCA)
30	12	SATELLITE	Hooters (CBS)
5	13	MY BABY JUST CARES FOR ME	Nina Simone (Charly)
9	14	(I'VE HAD) THE TIME OF MY LIFE	Bill Medley & Jennifer Warnes (RCA)
15	15	TO BE REBORN	Boy George (Virgin)
10	16	HERE I GO AGAIN	Whitesnake (EMI)
-	17	ALWAYS ON MY MIND	Pet Shop Boys (Parlophone)
11	18	SOME GUYS HAVE ALL THE LUCK	Maxi Priest (10)
12	19	SHO' YOU RIGHT	Barry White (Breakout)
16	20	BUILD	Housemartins (Go! Discs)
27	21	I'VE BEEN IN LOVE BEFORE	Cutting Crew (Siren)
39	22	THERE AIN'T NOTHIN' LIKE SHAGGIN'	Tams (Virgin)
23	23	I'M THE MAN	Anthrax (Island)
22	24	I COULD NEVER TAKE THE PLACE OF YOUR MAN	Prince (Paisley Park)
2	25	WHENEVER YOU NEED SOMEBODY	Rick Astley (RCA)
47	26	LOVE LETTERS	Alison Moyet (CBS)
40	27	TURN BACK THE CLOCK	Johnny Hates Jazz (Virgin)
-	28	SOMEWHERE SOMEBODY	Five Star (Tent)
-	29	LOOK OF LOVE	Madonna (Sire)
26	30	I WANT TO BE YOUR PROPERTY	Blue Mercedes (MCA)
13	31	DINNER WITH GERSHWIN	Donna Summer (Warner Bros)
34	32	FAIRYTALE OF NEW YORK	Pogues (Pogue Mahone)
32	33	KING WITHOUT A CROWN	ABC (Neutron)
19	34	PAID IN FULL	Eric B. & Rakim (Fourth & Broadway)
23	35	HYSTERIA	Def Leppard (Bludgeon Riffola)
-	36	REASON TO LIVE	Kiss (Vertigo)
31	37	I WON'T CRY	Glen Goldsmith (Reproduction)
31	38	LITTLE LIES	Fleetwood Mac (Warner Bros)
15	39	JACK MIX IV	Mirage (Debut)
-	40	VOYAGE VOYAGE	Desireless (CBS)
-	41	ROCKIN' AROUND THE CHRISTMAS TREE	Mel Smith & Kim Wilde (10)
24	42	LOVE IN THE FIRST DEGREE	Bananarama (London)
33	43	BIKO	Peter Gabriel (Charisma)
38	44	REBEL WITHOUT A PAUSE	Public Enemy (Def Jam)
45	45	IDEAL WORLD	Christians (Island)
48	46	GORGEOUS	Gene Loves Jezebel (Beggars Banquet)
37	47	EVERY TIME WE SAY GOODBYE	Simply Red (Elektra)
20	48	YOU WIN AGAIN	Bee Gees (Warner Bros)
-	49	HELLO GOODBYE	Beatles (Parlophone)
29	50	FAITH	George Michael (Epic)

19 December 1987

Last	This	Title	Artist
11	1	WHEN I FALL IN LOVE	Rick Astley (RCA)
8	2	THE WAY YOU MAKE ME FEEL	Michael Jackson (Epic)
17	3	ALWAYS ON MY MIND	Pet Shop Boys (Parlophone)
5	4	WHAT DO YOU WANT TO	Shakin' Stevens (Epic)
2	5	LETTER FROM AMERICA	Proclaimers (Chrysalis)
1	6	CHINA IN YOUR HAND	T'Pau (Siren)
26	7	LOVE LETTERS	Alison Moyet (CBS)
7	8	ONCE UPON A LONG AGO	Paul McCartney (Parlophone)
29	9	LOOK OF LOVE	Madonna (Sire)
32	10	FAIRYTALE OF NEW YORK	Pogues (Pogue Mahone)
4	11	CRITICIZE	Alexander O'Neal (Tabu)
10	12	WHO FOUND WHO	Jellybean & Elissa Fiorello (Chrysalis)
41	13	ROCKIN' AROUND THE CHRISTMAS TREE	Mel Smith & Kim Wilde (10)
3	14	GOT MY MIND SET ON YOU	George Harrison (Dark Horse)
28	15	SOMEWHERE SOMEBODY	Five Star (Tent)
12	16	SATELLITE	Hooters (CBS)
6	17	NEVER CAN SAY GOODBYE	Communards (London)
23	18	I'M THE MAN	Anthrax (Island)
9	19	SO EMOTIONAL	Whitney Houston (Arista)
18	20	SOME GUYS HAVE ALL THE LUCK	Maxi Priest (10)
20	21	BUILD	Housemartins (Go! Discs)
-	22	TURN BACK THE CLOCK	Johnny Hates Jazz (Virgin)
-	23	CHILDREN SAY	Level 42 (Polydor)
47	24	EVERY TIME WE SAY GOODBYE	Simply Red (Elektra)
22	25	THERE AIN'T NOTHIN' LIKE SHAGGIN'	Tams (Virgin)
-	26	TOUCHED BY THE HAND OF GOD	New Order (Factory)
15	27	TO BE REBORN	Boy George (Virgin)
16	28	HERE I GO AGAIN	Whitesnake (EMI)
14	29	(I'VE HAD) THE TIME OF MY LIFE	Bill Medley & Jennifer Warnes (RCA)
21	30	I'VE BEEN IN LOVE BEFORE	Cutting Crew (Siren)
-	31	LAST NIGHT I DREAMT THAT SOMEBODY LOVED ME	Smiths (Rough Trade)
24	32	I COULD NEVER TAKE THE PLACE OF YOUR MAN	Prince (Paisley Park)
-	33	WHEN I FALL IN LOVE	Nat King Cole (Capitol)
-	34	BOG EYED JOG	Ray Moore (Play)
44	35	REBEL WITHOUT A PAUSE	Public Enemy (Def Jam)
35	36	HYSTERIA	Def Leppard (Bludgeon Riffola)
19	37	SHO' YOU RIGHT	Barry White (Breakout)
-	38	ANGEL EYES	Wet Wet Wet (Precious)
25	39	WHENEVER YOU NEED SOMEBODY	Rick Astley (RCA)
-	40	HEAVEN IS A PLACE ON EARTH	Belinda Carlisle (Virgin)
37	41	I WON'T CRY	Glen Goldsmith (Reproduction)
-	42	RESCUE ME	Alarm (IRS)
13	43	MY BABY JUST CARES FOR ME	Nina Simone (Charly)
-	44	G.T.O.	Sinitta (Fanfare)
36	45	REASON TO LIVE	Kiss (Vertigo)
46	46	LOVE IN THE FIRST DEGREE	Bananarama (London)
46	47	GORGEOUS	Gene Loves Jezebel (Beggars Banquet)
30	48	I WANT TO BE YOUR PROPERTY	Blue Mercedes (MCA)
31	49	DINNER WITH GERSHWIN	Donna Summer (Warner Bros)
-	50	TIGHTEN UP	Wally Jump Jr. (Breakout)

Rick Astley's *Whenever You Need Somebody* and *When I Fall In Love* were released within six weeks of each other, the latter being necessarily rushed to catch the Christmas market: in contrast to Astley's first two uptempo hits, it was a virtual carbon copy of his mother's favourite ballad performance, by Nat King Cole. Only two weeks after *Whenever* fell from Number Two, *Fall* shot to the top slot.

Dance To It!

Another case of a musical cult gathering a following and exploding into mainstream pop. DJs and 'Sound Systems' had been using techniques like sampling and toasting in rap in clubs in Britain and America for some time. Add to this the growing popularity of house music in clubs, particularly in Chicago and New York, and something had to give. Rap and House became the biggest new style in the mid to late eighties, and is still racking up hits.

Top: De La Soul; left:the man behind Soul II Soul, Jazzie B; far left:D-Mob's Danny D

last week	this	9 January 1988	
3	1	ALWAYS ON MY MIND	Pet Shop Boys (Parlophone)
1	2	WHEN I FALL IN LOVE	Rick Astley (RCA)
7	3	LOVE LETTERS	Alison Moyet (CBS)
2	4	THE WAY YOU MAKE ME FEEL	Michael Jackson (Epic)
10	5	FAIRYTALE OF NEW YORK	Pogues (Pogue Mahone)
6	6	CHINA IN YOUR HAND	T'Pau (Siren)
13	7	ROCKIN' AROUND THE CHRISTMAS TREE	Mel Smith & Kim Wilde (10)
9	8	LOOK OF LOVE	Madonna (Sire)
4	9	WHAT DO YOU WANT TO MAKE THOSE EYES AT ME FOR	Shakin' Stevens (Epic)
12	10	WHO FOUND WHO	Jellybean/Elissa Fiorello (Chrysalis)
40	11	HEAVEN IS A PLACE ON EARTH	Belinda Carlisle (Virgin)
33	12	WHEN I FALL IN LOVE	Nat King Cole (Capitol)
24	13	EVERY TIME WE SAY GOODBYE	Simply Red (Elektra)
5	14	LETTER FROM AMERICA	Proclaimers (Chrysalis)
11	15	CRITICIZE	Alexander O'Neal (Tabu)
26	16	TOUCHED BY THE HAND OF GOD	New Order (Factory)
23	17	CHILDREN SAY	Level 42 (Polydor)
22	18	TURN BACK THE CLOCK	Johnny Hates Jazz (Virgin)
8	19	ONCE UPON A LONG AGO	Paul McCartney (Parlophone)
14	20	GOT MY MIND SET ON YOU	George Harrison (Dark Horse)
31	21	LAST NIGHT I DREAMT THAT SOMEBODY LOVED ME	Smiths (Rough Trade)
38	22	ANGEL EYES	Wet Wet Wet (Precious)
-	23	JINGO	Jellybean (Chrysalis)
17	24	NEVER CAN SAY GOODBYE	Communards (London)
18	25	I'M THE MAN	Anthrax (Island)
19	26	SO EMOTIONAL	Whitney Houston (Arista)
-	27	IDEAL WORLD	Christians (Island)
44	28	G.T.O.	Sinitta (Fanfare)
-	29	PACKJAMMED	Stock Aitken Waterman (Breakout)
30	30	I'VE BEEN IN LOVE BEFORE	Cutting Crew (Siren)
16	31	SATELLITE	Hooters (CBS)
-	32	TUNNEL OF LOVE	Bruce Springsteen (CBS)
-	33	THE ONE I LOVE	R.E.M. (IRS)
29	34	(I'VE HAD) THE TIME OF MY LIFE	Bill Medley & Jennifer Warnes (RCA)
-	35	HOUSE ARREST	Krush (Club)
45	36	REASON TO LIVE	Kiss (Vertigo)
21	37	BUILD	Housemartins (Go! Discs)
20	38	SOME GUYS HAVE ALL THE LUCK	Maxi Priest (10)
50	39	TIGHTEN UP	Wally Jump Jr. (Breakout)
15	40	SOMEWHERE SOMEBODY	Five Star (Tent)
27	41	TO BE REBORN	Boy George (Virgin)
-	42	TRUE DEVOTION	Samantha Fox (Jive)
-	43	I FOUND SOMEONE	Cher (Geffen)
-	44	CHRISTMAS IN HOLLIS	Run DMC (Profile)
-	45	ON THE TURNING AWAY	Pink Floyd (EMI)
43	46	MY BABY JUST CARES FOR ME	Nina Simone (Charly)
-	47	THERE'S THE GIRL	Heart (Capitol)
28	48	HERE I GO AGAIN	Whitesnake (EMI)
32	49	I COULD NEVER TAKE THE PLACE OF YOUR MAN	Prince (Paisley Park)
42	50	RESCUE ME	Alarm (IRS)

		16 January 1988	
1	1	ALWAYS ON MY MIND	Pet Shop Boys (Parlophone)
11	2	HEAVEN IS A PLACE ON EARTH	Belinda Carlisle (Virgin)
5	3	FAIRYTALE OF NEW YORK	Pogues (Pogue Mahone)
35	4	HOUSE ARREST	Krush (Club)
4	5	THE WAY YOU MAKE ME FEEL	Michael Jackson (Epic)
22	6	ANGEL EYES	Wet Wet Wet (Precious)
3	7	LOVE LETTERS	Alison Moyet (CBS)
43	8	I FOUND SOMEONE	Cher (Geffen)
-	9	STUTTER RAP	Morris Minor & the Majors (10)
-	10	ALL DAY AND ALL OF THE NIGHT	Stranglers (Epic)
2	11	COME INTO MY LIFE	Joyce Sims (London)
2	12	WHEN I FALL IN LOVE	Rick Astley (RCA)
-	13	SIGN YOUR NAME	Terence Trent D'Arby (CBS)
18	14	TURN BACK THE CLOCK	Johnny Hates Jazz (Virgin)
12	15	WHEN I FALL IN LOVE	Nat King Cole (Capitol)
6	16	CHINA IN YOUR HAND	T'Pau (Siren)
-	17	FATHER FIGURE	George Michael (Epic)
23	18	JINGO	Jellybean (Chrysalis)
7	19	ROCKIN' AROUND THE CHRISTMAS TREE	Mel Smith & Kim Wilde (10)
28	20	G.T.O.	Sinitta (Fanfare)
-	21	BEHIND THE WHEEL	Depeche Mode (Mute)
-	22	RISE TO THE OCCASION	Climie Fisher (EMI)
-	23	BRING THE NOISE	Public Enemy (Def Jam)
15	24	CRITICIZE	Alexander O'Neal (Tabu)
-	25	IN GOD'S COUNTRY	U2 (Island)
13	26	EVERY TIME WE SAY GOODBYE	Simply Red (Elektra)
16	27	TOUCHED BY THE HAND OF GOD	New Order (Factory)
26	28	SO EMOTIONAL	Whitney Houston (Arista)
8	29	LOOK OF LOVE	Madonna (Sire)
10	30	WHO FOUND WHO	Jellybean/Elissa Fiorello (Chrysalis)
20	31	GOT MY MIND SET ON YOU	George Harrison (Dark Horse)
27	32	IDEAL WORLD	Christians (Island)
33	33	JENNIFER SHE SAID	Lloyd Cole (Polydor)
-	34	ROK DA HOUSE	Cookie Crew/Beatmasters (Rhythm King)
-	35	I CAN'T HELP IT	Bananarama (London)
39	36	TIGHTEN UP	Wally Jump Jr. (Breakout)
-	37	NEW SENSATION	INXS (Mercury)
-	38	THE JACK THAT HOUSE BUILT	Jack & Chill (Oval)
9	39	WHAT DO YOU WANT TO MAKE THOSE EYES AT ME FOR	Shakin' Stevens (Epic)
14	40	LETTER FROM AMERICA	Proclaimers (Chrysalis)
-	41	I THINK WE'RE ALONE NOW	Tiffany (MCA)
21	42	LAST NIGHT I DREAMT THAT SOMEBODY LOVED ME	Smiths (Rough Trade)
4	43	MORE LOVE	Feargal Sharkey (Virgin)
17	44	CHILDREN SAY	Level 42 (Polydor)
31	45	SATELLITE	Hooters (CBS)
36	46	REASON TO LIVE	Kiss (Vertigo)
47	47	THERE'S THE GIRL	Heart (Capitol)
-	48	SIDE SHOW	Wendy & Lisa (Virgin)
-	49	THE TIME WARP II	Damien (Jive)
-	50	THE WISHING WELL	Gosh (MBS)

		23 January 1988	
2	1	HEAVEN IS A PLACE ON EARTH	Belinda Carlisle (Virgin)
4	2	HOUSE ARREST	Krush (Club)
8	3	I FOUND SOMEONE	Cher (Geffen)
10	4	ALL DAY AND ALL OF THE NIGHT	Stranglers (Epic)
9	5	STUTTER RAP	Morris Minor & the Majors (10)
13	6	SIGN YOUR NAME	Terence Trent D'Arby (CBS)
11	7	COME INTO MY LIFE	Joyce Sims (London)
41	8	I THINK WE'RE ALONE NOW	Tiffany (MCA)
1	9	ALWAYS ON MY MIND	Pet Shop Boys (Parlophone)
17	10	FATHER FIGURE	George Michael (Epic)
22	12	RISE TO THE OCCASION	Climie Fisher (EMI)
-	13	HEATSEEKER	AC/DC (Atlantic)
18	14	JINGO	Jellybean (Chrysalis)
35	15	I CAN'T HELP IT	Bananarama (London)
20	16	G.T.O.	Sinitta (Fanfare)
21	17	BEHIND THE WHEEL	Depeche Mode (Mute)
34	18	ROK DA HOUSE	Cookie Crew/Beatmasters (Rhythm King)
12	19	WHEN I FALL IN LOVE	Rick Astley (RCA)
32	20	IDEAL WORLD	Christians (Island)
3	21	FAIRYTALE OF NEW YORK	Pogues (Pogue Mahone)
23	22	BRING THE NOISE	Public Enemy (Def Jam)
5	23	THE WAY YOU MAKE ME FEEL	Michael Jackson (Epic)
-	24	YOU'RE ALL I NEED	Motley Crue (Elektra)
14	25	TURN BACK THE CLOCK	Johnny Hates Jazz (Virgin)
33	26	JENNIFER SHE SAID	Lloyd Cole (Polydor)
50	27	THE WISHING WELL	Gosh (MBS)
-	28	L'AMOUR	Dollar (London)
37	29	NEW SENSATION	INXS (Mercury)
7	30	LOVE LETTERS	Alison Moyet (CBS)
-	31	TIRED OF GETTING PUSHED AROUND	Two Men, A Drum Machine & A Trumpet (London)
-	32	WILD HEARTED WOMAN	All About Eve (Mercury)
-	33	MANDINKA	Sinead O'Connor (Ensign)
-	34	I GOT DA FEELIN'	Sweet Tee (Cooltempo)
27	35	TOUCHED BY THE HAND OF GOD	New Order (Factory)
30	36	WHO FOUND WHO	Jellybean/Elissa Fiorello (Chrysalis)
15	37	WHEN I FALL IN LOVE	Nat King Cole (Capitol)
-	38	PARADISE	Black (A&M)
16	39	CHINA IN YOUR HAND	T'Pau (Siren)
-	40	WHEN WILL I BE FAMOUS	Bros (CBS)
24	41	CRITICIZE	Alexander O'Neal (Tabu)
-	42	SAY IT AGAIN	Jermaine Stewart (10)
43	43	LOVE OVERBOARD	Gladys Knight (MCA)
36	44	TIGHTEN UP	Wally Jump Jr. (Breakout)
40	45	LETTER FROM AMERICA	Proclaimers (Chrysalis)
38	46	THE JACK THAT HOUSE BUILT	Jack & Chill (Oval)
-	47	I WANNA BE A FLINTSTONE	Screaming Blue Messiahs (WEA)
49	48	THE TIME WARP II	Damien (Jive)
29	49	LOOK OF LOVE	Madonna (Sire)
-	50	CANDLE IN THE WIND	Elton John (Rocket)

The Pet Shop Boys had first performed *Always On My Mind* the previous August during a TV celebration of Elvis Presley's music on the occasion of the 10th anniversary of his death. When eventually released on record, it proved more successful than Elvis' original version of the song, which had reached the Top10 in 1972 (though had been relegated to a B-side in the US).

January – February 1988

30 January 1988

last	this	title	artist (label)
1	1	HEAVEN IS A PLACE ON EARTH	Belinda Carlisle (Virgin)
8	2	I THINK WE'RE ALONE NOW	Tiffany (MCA)
6	3	SIGN YOUR NAME	Terence Trent D'Arby (CBS)
2	4	HOUSE ARREST	Krush (Club)
4	5	ALL DAY AND ALL OF THE NIGHT	Stranglers (Epic)
7	6	COME INTO MY LIFE	Joyce Sims (London)
3	7	I FOUND SOMEONE	Cher (Geffen)
5	8	STUTTER RAP	Morris Minor & the Majors (10)
13	9	HEATSEEKER	AC/DC (Atlantic)
12	10	RISE TO THE OCCASION	Climie Fisher (EMI)
18	11	ROK DA HOUSE	Cookie Crew/Beatmasters (Rhythm King)
10	12	FATHER FIGURE	George Michael (Epic)
40	13	WHEN WILL I BE FAMOUS	Bros (CBS)
28	14	L'AMOUR	Dollar (London)
11	15	ANGEL EYES	Wet Wet Wet (Precious)
20	16	IDEAL WORLD	Christians (Island)
15	17	I CAN'T HELP IT	Bananarama (London)
24	18	YOU'RE ALL I NEED	Motley Crue (Elektra)
9	19	HOT IN THE CITY	Billy Idol (Chrysalis)
9	20	ALWAYS ON MY MIND	Pet Shop Boys (Parlophone)
31	21	TIRED OF GETTING PUSHED AROUND	Two Men, A Drum Machine & A Trumpet (London)
29	22	NEW SENSATION	INXS (Mercury)
14	23	JINGO	Jellybean (Chrysalis)
50	24	CANDLE IN THE WIND	Elton John (Rocket)
42	25	SAY IT AGAIN	Jermaine Stewart (10)
26	26	JENNIFER SHE SAID	Lloyd Cole (Polydor)
22	27	BRING THE NOISE	Public Enemy (Def Jam)
33	28	MANDINKA	Sinead O'Connor (Ensign)
19	29	WHEN I FALL IN LOVE	Rick Astley (RCA)
17	30	BEHIND THE WHEEL	Depeche Mode (Mute)
27	31	THE WISHING WELL	Gosh (MBS)
-	32	SHAKE YOUR LOVE	Debbie Gibson (Atlantic)
46	33	THE JACK THAT HOUSE BUILT	Jack & Chill (Oval)
34	34	I GOT DA FEELIN'	Sweet Tee (Cooltempo)
-	35	THERE IS NO LOVE BETWEEN US	Pop Will Eat Itself (Chapter 22)
32	36	WILD HEARTED WOMAN	All About Eve (Mercury)
16	37	G.T.O.	Sinitta (Fanfare)
-	38	TELL IT TO MY HEART	Taylor Dayne (Arista)
38	39	PARADISE	Black (A&M)
-	40	I SHOULD BE SO LUCKY	Kylie Minogue (PWL)
47	41	I WANNA BE A FLINTSTONE	Screaming Blue Messiahs (WEA)
-	42	PROMISES	Basia (Epic)
-	43	GIVE ME THE REASON	Luther Vandross (Epic)
23	44	THE WAY YOU MAKE ME FEEL	Michael Jackson (Epic)
25	45	TURN BACK THE CLOCK	Johnny Hates Jazz (Virgin)
-	46	VICTORIA	Fall (Beggars Banquet)
-	47	VALENTINE	T'Pau (Siren)
30	48	LOVE LETTERS	Alison Moyet (CBS)
-	49	A TRICK OF THE LIGHT	Triffids (Island)
43	50	LOVE OVERBOARD	Gladys Knight (MCA)

6 February 1988

last	this	title	artist (label)
2	1	I THINK WE'RE ALONE NOW	Tiffany (MCA)
3	2	SIGN YOUR NAME	Terence Trent D'Arby (CBS)
1	3	HEAVEN IS A PLACE ON EARTH	Belinda Carlisle (Virgin)
4	4	HOUSE ARREST	Krush (Club)
13	5	WHEN WILL I BE FAMOUS	Bros (CBS)
6	6	COME INTO MY LIFE	Joyce Sims (London)
11	7	ROK DA HOUSE	Cookie Crew/Beatmasters (Rhythm King)
14	8	L'AMOUR	Dollar (London)
8	9	STUTTER RAP	Morris Minor & the Majors (10)
10	10	RISE TO THE OCCASION	Climie Fisher (EMI)
32	11	SHAKE YOUR LOVE	Debbie Gibson (Atlantic)
9	12	HEATSEEKER	AC/DC (Atlantic)
19	13	HOT IN THE CITY	Billy Idol (Chrysalis)
24	14	CANDLE IN THE WIND	Elton John (Rocket)
21	15	TIRED OF GETTING PUSHED AROUND	Two Men, A Drum Machine & A Trumpet (London)
7	16	I FOUND SOMEONE	Cher (Geffen)
5	17	ALL DAY AND ALL OF THE NIGHT	Stranglers (Epic)
16	18	IDEAL WORLD	Christians (Island)
33	19	THE JACK THAT HOUSE BUILT	Jack & Chill (Oval)
38	20	TELL IT TO MY HEART	Taylor Dayne (Arista)
47	21	VALENTINE	T'Pau (Siren)
25	22	SAY IT AGAIN	Jermaine Stewart (10)
15	23	ANGEL EYES	Wet Wet Wet (Precious)
22	24	NEW SENSATION	INXS (Mercury)
28	25	MANDINKA	Sinead O'Connor (Ensign)
18	26	YOU'RE ALL I NEED	Motley Crue (Elektra)
40	27	I SHOULD BE SO LUCKY	Kylie Minogue (PWL)
20	28	ALWAYS ON MY MIND	Pet Shop Boys (Parlophone)
46	29	VICTORIA	Fall (Beggars Banquet)
34	30	I GOT DA FEELIN'	Sweet Tee (Cooltempo)
36	31	WILD HEARTED WOMAN	All About Eve (Mercury)
17	32	I CAN'T HELP IT	Bananarama (London)
12	33	FATHER FIGURE	George Michael (Epic)
-	34	SHE'S THE ONE	James Brown (Urban)
-	35	NO MORE LIES	Sharpe & Numan (Polydor)
-	36	GIVE ME ALL YOUR LOVE	Whitesnake (EMI)
-	37	SING A SONG (BREAK IT DOWN)	Mantronix (10)
-	38	IF I GIVE MY HEART	John McLean
-	39	NEVER KNEW LOVE LIKE THIS	Alexander O'Neal & Cherelle (Tabu)
-	40	COLD SWEAT	Sugarcubes (One Little Indian)
-	41	I REFUSE	Hue & Cry (Circa)
43	42	GIVE ME THE REASON	Luther Vandross (Epic)
-	43	HEAVEN KNOWS	Robert Plant (Es Paranza)
37	44	G.T.O.	Sinitta (Fanfare)
35	45	THERE IS NO LOVE BETWEEN US	Pop Will Eat Itself (Chapter 22)
23	46	JINGO	Jellybean (Chrysalis)
-	47	GIMME HOPE JO'ANNA	Eddy Grant (Ice)
41	48	I WANNA BE A FLINTSTONE	Screaming Blue Messiahs (WEA)
26	49	JENNIFER SHE SAID	Lloyd Cole (Polydor)
27	50	BRING THE NOISE	Public Enemy (Def Jam)

13 February 1988

last	this	title	artist (label)
1	1	I THINK WE'RE ALONE NOW	Tiffany (MCA)
5	2	WHEN WILL I BE FAMOUS	Bros (CBS)
20	3	TELL IT TO MY HEART	Taylor Dayne (Arista)
7	4	ROK DA HOUSE	Cookie Crew/Beatmasters (Rhythm King)
2	5	SIGN YOUR NAME	Terence Trent D'Arby (CBS)
11	6	SHAKE YOUR LOVE	Debbie Gibson (Atlantic)
3	7	HEAVEN IS A PLACE ON EARTH	Belinda Carlisle (Virgin)
8	8	L'AMOUR	Dollar (London)
27	9	I SHOULD BE SO LUCKY	Kylie Minogue (PWL)
14	10	CANDLE IN THE WIND	Elton John (Rocket)
19	11	THE JACK THAT HOUSE BUILT	Jack & Chill (Oval)
6	12	COME INTO MY LIFE	Joyce Sims (London)
22	13	SAY IT AGAIN	Jermaine Stewart (10)
13	14	HOT IN THE CITY	Billy Idol (Chrysalis)
4	15	HOUSE ARREST	Krush (Club)
21	16	VALENTINE	T'Pau (Siren)
36	17	GIVE ME ALL YOUR LOVE	Whitesnake (EMI)
15	18	TIRED OF GETTING PUSHED AROUND	Two Men, A Drum Machine & A Trumpet (London)
10	19	RISE TO THE OCCASION	Climie Fisher (EMI)
18	20	IDEAL WORLD	Christians (Island)
16	21	I FOUND SOMEONE	Cher (Geffen)
-	22	GET OUTTA MY DREAMS AND INTO MY CAR	Billy Ocean (Jive)
12	23	HEATSEEKER	AC/DC (Atlantic)
30	24	I GOT DA FEELIN'	Sweet Tee (Cooltempo)
9	25	STUTTER RAP	Morris Minor & the Majors (10)
-	26	LET'S GET BRUTAL	Nitro Deluxe (Cooltempo)
29	27	VICTORIA	Fall (Beggars Banquet)
25	28	MANDINKA	Sinead O'Connor (Ensign)
42	29	GIVE ME THE REASON	Luther Vandross (Epic)
48	30	I WANNA BE A FLINTSTONE	Screaming Blue Messiahs (WEA)
39	31	NEVER KNEW LOVE LIKE THIS	Alexander O'Neal & Cherelle (Tabu)
17	32	ALL DAY AND ALL OF THE NIGHT	Stranglers (Epic)
31	33	WILD HEARTED WOMAN	All About Eve (Mercury)
34	34	SHE'S THE ONE	James Brown (Urban)
40	35	COLD SWEAT	Sugarcubes (One Little Indian)
47	36	GIMME HOPE JO'ANNA	Eddy Grant (Ice)
-	37	SPY IN THE HOUSE OF LOVE	Was (Not Was) (Fontana)
-	38	TOWER OF STRENGTH	Mission (Mercury)
-	39	WE CARE A LOT	Faith No More (Slash)
24	40	NEW SENSATION	INXS (Mercury)
35	41	NO MORE LIES	Sharpe & Numan (Polydor)
43	42	HEAVEN KNOWS	Robert Plant (Es Paranza)
23	43	ANGEL EYES	Wet Wet Wet (Precious)
-	44	DREAMING	Orchestral Manoeuvres In The Dark (Virgin)
32	45	I CAN'T HELP IT	Bananarama (London)
-	46	A HAZY SHADE OF WINTER	Bangles (Def Jam)
-	47	WHEN WE WAS FAB	George Harrison (Dark Horse)
-	48	KISS AND TELL	Bryan Ferry (Virgin)
-	49	DIGNITY	Deacon Blue (CBS)
28	50	ALWAYS ON MY MIND	Pet Shop Boys (Parlophone)

In an unusually strong month for girl singers (which would be a hallmark of 1988), US vocalists Belinda Carlisle and Tiffany, both with their first hits, had successive weeks at Number One, while fellow American Taylor Dayne reached Number Three with her debut, Joyce Sims made Six, and female rappers the Cookie Crew got to Four with *Rok Da House*. Most significant debut, though, was Kylie Minogue.

February – March 1988

20 February 1988

last week	this week	title	artist
9	1	I SHOULD BE SO LUCKY	Kylie Minogue (PWL)
1	2	I THINK WE'RE ALONE NOW	Tiffany (MCA)
3	3	TELL IT TO MY HEART	Taylor Dayne (Arista)
2	4	WHEN WILL I BE FAMOUS	Bros (CBS)
22	5	GET OUTTA MY DREAMS AND INTO MY CAR	Billy Ocean (Jive)
10	6	CANDLE IN THE WIND	Elton John (Rocket)
6	7	SHAKE YOUR LOVE	Debbie Gibson (Atlantic)
11	8	THE JACK THAT HOUSE BUILT	Jack & Chill (Oval)
13	9	SAY IT AGAIN	Jermaine Stewart (10)
16	10	VALENTINE	T'Pau (Siren)
4	11	ROK DA HOUSE	Cookie Crew/Beatmasters (Rhythm King)
38	12	TOWER OF STRENGTH	Mission (Mercury)
17	13	GIVE ME ALL YOUR LOVE	Whitesnake (EMI)
8	14	L'AMOUR	Dollar (London)
5	15	SIGN YOUR NAME	Terence Trent D'Arby (CBS)
-	16	BEAT DIS	Bomb The Bass (Mister-ron)
14	17	HOT IN THE CITY	Billy Idol (Chrysalis)
37	18	SPY IN THE HOUSE OF LOVE	Was (Not Was) (Fontana)
28	19	MANDINKA	Sinead O'Connor (Ensign)
36	20	GIMME HOPE JO'ANNA	Eddy Grant (Ice)
18	21	TIRED OF GETTING PUSHED AROUND	Two Men, A Drum Machine & A Trumpet (London)
26	22	LET'S GET BRUTAL	Nitro Deluxe (Cooltempo)
15	23	HOUSE ARREST	Krush (Club)
7	24	HEAVEN IS A PLACE ON EARTH	Belinda Carlisle (Virgin)
12	25	COME INTO MY LIFE	Joyce Sims (London)
31	26	NEVER KNEW LOVE LIKE THIS	Alexander O'Neal & Cherelle (Tabu)
29	27	GIVE ME THE REASON	Luther Vandross (Epic)
-	28	GOING BACK TO CALI	LL Cool J (Def Jam)
42	29	HEAVEN KNOWS	Robert Plant (Es Paranza)
35	30	COLD SWEAT	Sugarcubes (One Little Indian)
20	31	IDEAL WORLD	Christians (Island)
27	32	VICTORIA	Fall (Beggars Banquet)
33	33	WILD HEARTED WOMAN	All About Eve (Mercury)
24	34	I GOT DA FEELIN'	Sweet Tee (Cooltempo)
-	35	CARS AND GIRLS	Prefab Sprout (Kitchenware)
34	36	SHE'S THE ONE	James Brown (Urban)
-	37	MAN IN THE MIRROR	Michael Jackson (Epic)
-	38	C'MON EVERYBODY	Eddie Cochran (Liberty)
49	39	DIGNITY	Deacon Blue (CBS)
23	40	HEATSEEKER	AC/DC (Atlantic)
-	41	FOR A FRIEND	Communards (London)
47	42	WHEN WE WAS FAB	George Harrison (Dark Horse)
-	43	THESE EARLY DAYS	Everything But The Girl (blanco y negro)
-	44	TAKE MY BREATH AWAY	Berlin (CBS)
46	45	A HAZY SHADE OF WINTER	Bangles (Def Jam)
39	46	WE CARE A LOT	Faith No More (Slash)
19	47	RISE TO THE OCCASION	Climie Fisher (EMI)
41	48	NO MORE LIES	Sharpe & Numan (Polydor)
30	49	I WANNA BE A FLINTSTONE	Screaming Blue Messiahs (WEA)
48	50	KISS AND TELL	Bryan Ferry (Virgin)

27 February 1988

last week	this week	title	artist
1	1	I SHOULD BE SO LUCKY	Kylie Minogue (PWL)
3	2	TELL IT TO MY HEART	Taylor Dayne (Arista)
16	3	BEAT DIS	Bomb The Bass (Mister-ron)
5	4	GET OUTTA MY DREAMS AND INTO MY CAR	Billy Ocean (Jive)
2	5	I THINK WE'RE ALONE NOW	Tiffany (MCA)
20	6	GIMME HOPE JO'ANNA	Eddy Grant (Ice)
10	7	VALENTINE	T'Pau (Siren)
9	8	SAY IT AGAIN	Jermaine Stewart (10)
4	9	WHEN WILL I BE FAMOUS	Bros (CBS)
12	10	TOWER OF STRENGTH	Mission (Mercury)
7	11	SHAKE YOUR LOVE	Debbie Gibson (Atlantic)
6	12	CANDLE IN THE WIND	Elton John (Rocket)
-	13	DOCTORIN' THE HOUSE	Coldcut (Ahead Of Our Time)
14	14	SUEDEHEAD	Morrissey (HMV)
8	15	THE JACK THAT HOUSE BUILT	Jack & Chill (Oval)
19	16	MANDINKA	Sinead O'Connor (Ensign)
37	17	MAN IN THE MIRROR	Michael Jackson (Epic)
-	18	DOMINION	Sisters Of Mercy (Merciful Release)
18	19	SPY IN THE HOUSE OF LOVE	Was (Not Was) (Fontana)
15	20	SIGN YOUR NAME	Terence Trent D'Arby (CBS)
-	21	JOE LE TAXI	Vanessa Paradis (FA Productions)
-	22	PEOPLE ARE STRANGE	Echo & the Bunnymen (WEA)
13	23	GIVE ME ALL YOUR LOVE	Whitesnake (EMI)
11	24	ROK DA HOUSE	Cookie Crew/Beatmasters (Rhythm King)
24	25	HEAVEN IS A PLACE ON EARTH	Belinda Carlisle (Virgin)
45	26	A HAZY SHADE OF WINTER	Bangles (Def Jam)
-	27	ANIMAL	W.A.S.P. (Music For Nations)
22	28	LET'S GET BRUTAL	Nitro Deluxe (Cooltempo)
-	29	HOT HOT HOT!!!	Cure (Fiction)
17	30	HOT IN THE CITY	Billy Idol (Chrysalis)
14	31	L'AMOUR	Dollar (London)
28	32	GOING BACK TO CALI	LL Cool J (Def Jam)
26	33	NEVER KNEW LOVE LIKE THIS	Alexander O'Neal & Cherelle (Tabu)
-	34	CRASH	Primitives (Lazy)
39	35	DIGNITY	Deacon Blue (CBS)
42	36	WHEN WE WAS FAB	George Harrison (Dark Horse)
29	37	HEAVEN KNOWS	Robert Plant (Es Paranza)
-	38	AN ENGLISHMAN IN NEW YORK	Sting (A&M)
-	39	WHEN I FALL IN LOVE	Rick Astley (RCA)
44	40	TAKE MY BREATH AWAY	Berlin (Club)
23	41	HOUSE ARREST	Krush (Club)
25	42	COME INTO MY LIFE	Joyce Sims (London)
30	43	COLD SWEAT	Sugarcubes (One Little Indian)
-	44	I WALK THE EARTH	Voice Of The Beehive (London)
41	45	FOR A FRIEND	Communards (London)
-	46	I DON'T MIND AT ALL	Bourgeois Tagg (Island)
38	47	C'MON EVERYBODY	Eddie Cochran (Liberty)
-	48	RECKLESS	Afrika Bambaataa (EMI)
-	49	THAT'S THE WAY IT IS	Mel & Kim (Supreme)
-	50	MOVE THE CROWD	Eric B. & Rakim (Fourth & Broadway)

5 March 1988

last week	this week	title	artist
3	1	BEAT DIS	Bomb The Bass (Mister-ron)
1	2	I SHOULD BE SO LUCKY	Kylie Minogue (PWL)
4	3	GET OUTTA MY DREAMS AND INTO MY CAR	Billy Ocean (Jive)
14	4	SUEDEHEAD	Morrissey (HMV)
2	5	TELL IT TO MY HEART	Taylor Dayne (Arista)
-	6	TOGETHER FOREVER	Rick Astley (RCA)
13	7	DOCTORIN' THE HOUSE	Coldcut (Ahead Of Our Time)
6	8	GIMME HOPE JO'ANNA	Eddy Grant (Ice)
5	9	I THINK WE'RE ALONE NOW	Tiffany (MCA)
21	10	JOE LE TAXI	Vanessa Paradis (FA Productions)
18	11	DOMINION	Sisters Of Mercy (Merciful Release)
10	12	TOWER OF STRENGTH	Mission (Mercury)
8	13	SAY IT AGAIN	Jermaine Stewart (10)
26	14	A HAZY SHADE OF WINTER	Bangles (Def Jam)
34	15	CRASH	Primitives (Lazy)
49	16	THAT'S THE WAY IT IS	Mel & Kim (Supreme)
17	17	MAN IN THE MIRROR	Michael Jackson (Epic)
9	18	WHEN WILL I BE FAMOUS	Bros (CBS)
-	19	GOOD GROOVE	Derek B (Music Of Life)
12	20	CANDLE IN THE WIND	Elton John (Rocket)
47	21	C'MON EVERYBODY	Eddie Cochran (Liberty)
11	22	SHAKE YOUR LOVE	Debbie Gibson (Atlantic)
7	23	VALENTINE	T'Pau (Siren)
35	24	DIGNITY	Deacon Blue (CBS)
19	25	SPY IN THE HOUSE OF LOVE	Was (Not Was) (Fontana)
36	26	WHEN WE WAS FAB	George Harrison (Dark Horse)
-	27	LOVE IS CONTAGIOUS	Taja Sevelle (Paisley Park)
-	28	HEART OF GOLD	Johnny Hates Jazz (Virgin)
-	29	ANARCHY IN THE UK	Megadeth (Capitol)
-	30	SHIP OF FOOLS	Erasure (Mute)
33	31	NEVER KNEW LOVE LIKE THIS	Alexander O'Neal & Cherelle (Tabu)
16	32	MANDINKA	Sinead O'Connor (Ensign)
-	33	NOBODY'S TWISTING YOUR ARM	Wedding Present (Reception)
15	34	THE JACK THAT HOUSE BUILT	Jack & Chill (Oval)
23	35	GIVE ME ALL YOUR LOVE	Whitesnake (EMI)
-	36	I GET WEAK	Belinda Carlisle (Virgin)
-	37	LOVEY DOVEY	Tony Terry (Epic)
-	38	I WANT HER	Keith Sweat (Vintertainment)
20	39	SIGN YOUR NAME	Terence Trent D'Arby (CBS)
30	40	HOT IN THE CITY	Billy Idol (Chrysalis)
22	41	PEOPLE ARE STRANGE	Echo & the Bunnymen (WEA)
32	42	GOING BACK TO CALI	LL Cool J (Def Jam)
27	43	ANIMAL	W.A.S.P. (Music For Nations)
24	44	ROK DA HOUSE	Cookie Crew/Beatmasters (Rhythm King)
25	45	HEAVEN IS A PLACE ON EARTH	Belinda Carlisle (Virgin)
31	46	L'AMOUR	Dollar (London)
41	47	HOUSE ARREST	Krush (Club)
-	48	DON'T TURN AROUND	Aswad (Mango)
-	49	JUST LIKE PARADISE	David Lee Roth (Warner Bros)
-	50	I'M NOT SCARED	Eighth Wonder (CBS)

Kylie Minogue was still acting (at least as far as British audiences were concerned) in the Aussie soap *Neighbours* when her Stock/Aitken/Waterman-written and produced *I Should Be So Lucky* topped the chart within a month of release, completing a trio of consecutive girl singer Number Ones. Kylie's chart career would be one of the most successful by any artist over the next four years.

479

March 1988

12 March 1988

last week	this week	title	artist
1	1	BEAT DIS	Bomb The Bass (Mister-ron)
2	2	I SHOULD BE SO LUCKY	Kylie Minogue (PWL)
10	3	JOE LE TAXI	Vanessa Paradis (FA Productions)
4	4	SUEDEHEAD	Morrissey (HMV)
6	5	TOGETHER FOREVER	Rick Astley (RCA)
3	6	GET OUTTA MY DREAMS AND INTO MY CAR	Billy Ocean (Jive)
7	7	DOCTORIN' THE HOUSE	Coldcut (Ahead Of Our Time)
14	8	A HAZY SHADE OF WINTER	Bangles (Def Jam)
8	9	GIMME HOPE JO'ANNA	Eddy Grant (Ice)
5	10	TELL IT TO MY HEART	Taylor Dayne (Arista)
15	11	CRASH	Primitives (Lazy)
9	12	GOOD GROOVE	Derek B (Music Of Life)
16	13	THAT'S THE WAY IT IS	Mel & Kim (Supreme)
11	14	DOMINION	Sisters Of Mercy (Merciful Release)
30	15	SHIP OF FOOLS	Erasure (Mute)
21	16	C'MON EVERYBODY	Eddie Cochran (Liberty)
36	17	I GET WEAK	Belinda Carlisle (Virgin)
9	18	I THINK WE'RE ALONE NOW	Tiffany (MCA)
27	19	LOVE IS CONTAGIOUS	Taja Sevelle (Paisley Park)
12	20	TOWER OF STRENGTH	Mission (Mercury)
13	21	SAY IT AGAIN	Jermaine Stewart (10)
-	22	NEVER/THESE DREAMS	Heart (Capitol)
25	23	SPY IN THE HOUSE OF LOVE	Was (Not Was) (Fontana)
28	24	HEART OF GOLD	Johnny Hates Jazz (Virgin)
33	25	NOBODY'S TWISTING YOUR	Wedding Present (Reception)
48	26	DON'T TURN AROUND	Aswad (Mango)
-	27	I KNOW YOU GOT SOUL	Eric B. & Rakim (Cooltempo)
23	28	VALENTINE	T'Pau (Siren)
20	29	CANDLE IN THE WIND	Elton John (Rocket)
-	30	FOR A FRIEND	Communards (London)
17	31	MAN IN THE MIRROR	Michael Jackson (Epic)
-	32	RECKLESS	Afrika Bambaataa (EMI)
-	33	DEVIL INSIDE	INXS (Mercury)
41	34	PEOPLE ARE STRANGE	Echo & the Bunnymen (WEA)
29	35	ANARCHY IN THE UK	Megadeth (Capitol)
22	36	SHAKE YOUR LOVE	Debbie Gibson (Atlantic)
18	37	WHEN WILL I BE FAMOUS	Bros (CBS)
50	38	I'M NOT SCARED	Eighth Wonder (CBS)
26	39	WHEN WE WAS FAB	George Harrison (Dark Horse)
34	40	THE JACK THAT HOUSE BUILT	Jack & Chill (Oval)
-	41	IF I SHOULD FALL FROM GRACE WITH GOD	Pogues (Pogue Mahone)
-	42	HOW MEN ARE	Aztec Camera (WEA)
-	43	CRAZY	Icehouse (Chrysalis)
31	44	NEVER KNEW LOVE LIKE THIS	Alexander O'Neal & Cherelle (Tabu)
37	45	LOVEY DOVEY	Tony Terry (Epic)
-	46	WHERE DO BROKEN HEARTS GO	Whitney Houston (Arista)
24	47	DIGNITY	Deacon Blue (CBS)
38	48	I WANT HER	Keith Sweat (Vintertainment)
49	49	JUST LIKE PARADISE	David Lee Roth (Warner Bros)
-	50	I FOUGHT THE LAW	Clash (CBS)

19 March 1988

last week	this week	title	artist
5	1	TOGETHER FOREVER	Rick Astley (RCA)
3	2	JOE LE TAXI	Vanessa Paradis (FA Productions)
1	3	BEAT DIS	Bomb The Bass (Mister-ron)
2	4	I SHOULD BE SO LUCKY	Kylie Minogue (PWL)
11	5	CRASH	Primitives (Lazy)
7	6	DOCTORIN' THE HOUSE	Coldcut (Ahead Of Our Time)
13	7	THAT'S THE WAY IT IS	Mel & Kim (Supreme)
9	8	GIMME HOPE JO'ANNA	Eddy Grant (Ice)
15	9	SHIP OF FOOLS	Erasure (Mute)
4	10	SUEDEHEAD	Morrissey (HMV)
19	11	LOVE IS CONTAGIOUS	Taja Sevelle (Paisley Park)
6	12	GET OUTTA MY DREAMS AND INTO MY CAR	Billy Ocean (Jive)
17	13	I GET WEAK	Belinda Carlisle (Virgin)
27	14	I KNOW YOU GOT SOUL	Eric B. & Rakim (Cooltempo)
22	15	NEVER/THESE DREAMS	Heart (Capitol)
8	16	A HAZY SHADE OF WINTER	Bangles (Def Jam)
26	17	DON'T TURN AROUND	Aswad (Mango)
12	18	GOOD GROOVE	Derek B (Music Of Life)
46	19	WHERE DO BROKEN HEARTS GO	Whitney Houston (Arista)
10	20	TELL IT TO MY HEART	Taylor Dayne (Arista)
14	21	DOMINION	Sisters Of Mercy (Merciful Release)
42	22	HOW MEN ARE	Aztec Camera (WEA)
16	23	C'MON EVERYBODY	Eddie Cochran (Liberty)
49	24	JUST LIKE PARADISE	David Lee Roth (Warner Bros)
24	25	HEART OF GOLD	Johnny Hates Jazz (Virgin)
32	26	RECKLESS	Afrika Bambaataa (EMI)
50	27	I FOUGHT THE LAW	Clash (CBS)
33	28	DEVIL INSIDE	INXS (Mercury)
-	29	I WALK THE EARTH	Voice Of The Beehive (London)
48	30	I WANT HER	Keith Sweat (Vintertainment)
45	31	LOVEY DOVEY	Tony Terry (Epic)
-	32	COULD'VE BEEN	Tiffany (MCA)
38	33	I'M NOT SCARED	Eighth Wonder (CBS)
-	34	DROP THE BOY	Bros (CBS)
-	35	DREAMING	Glen Goldsmith (Reproduction)
41	36	IF I SHOULD FALL FROM GRACE WITH GOD	Pogues (Pogue Mahone)
20	37	TOWER OF STRENGTH	Mission (Mercury)
21	38	SAY IT AGAIN	Jermaine Stewart (10)
43	39	CRAZY	Icehouse (Chrysalis)
-	40	LOVE CHANGES EVERYTHING	Climie Fisher (EMI)
-	41	FAITH	Wee Papa Girl Rappers (Jive)
34	42	PEOPLE ARE STRANGE	Echo & the Bunnymen (WEA)
-	43	MAJESTIC HEAD	Soup Dragons (Raw)
-	44	SIMPLE SIMON	Mantronix (10)
-	45	SHIMMER	Flatmates
-	46	JUST A MIRAGE	Jellybean (Chrysalis)
-	47	HOW CAN WE EASE THE PAIN	Maxi Priest (10)
25	48	NOBODY'S TWISTING YOUR ARM	Wedding Present (Reception)
35	49	ANARCHY IN THE UK	Megadeth (Capitol)
30	50	FOR A FRIEND	Communards (London)

26 March 1988

last week	this week	title	artist
17	1	DON'T TURN AROUND	Aswad (Mango)
5	2	CRASH	Primitives (Lazy)
1	3	TOGETHER FOREVER	Rick Astley (RCA)
2	4	JOE LE TAXI	Vanessa Paradis (FA Productions)
4	5	I SHOULD BE SO LUCKY	Kylie Minogue (PWL)
9	6	SHIP OF FOOLS	Erasure (Mute)
11	7	LOVE IS CONTAGIOUS	Taja Sevelle (Paisley Park)
15	8	NEVER/THESE DREAMS	Heart (Capitol)
3	9	BEAT DIS	Bomb The Bass (Mister-ron)
13	10	I GET WEAK	Belinda Carlisle (Virgin)
34	11	DROP THE BOY	Bros (CBS)
14	12	I KNOW YOU GOT SOUL	Eric B. & Rakim (Cooltempo)
6	13	DOCTORIN' THE HOUSE	Coldcut (Ahead Of Our Time)
-	14	CAN I PLAY WITH MADNESS	Iron Maiden (EMI)
19	15	WHERE DO BROKEN HEARTS GO	Whitney Houston (Arista)
12	16	GET OUTTA MY DREAMS AND INTO MY CAR	Billy Ocean (Jive)
-	17	DAYS OF NO TRUST	Magnum (Polydor)
32	18	COULD'VE BEEN	Tiffany (MCA)
33	19	I'M NOT SCARED	Eighth Wonder (CBS)
24	20	JUST LIKE PARADISE	David Lee Roth (Warner Bros)
7	21	THAT'S THE WAY IT IS	Mel & Kim (Supreme)
8	22	GIMME HOPE JO'ANNA	Eddy Grant (Ice)
25	23	HEART OF GOLD	Johnny Hates Jazz (Virgin)
-	24	BASS	Simon Harris (ffrr)
5	25	PROVE YOUR LOVE	Taylor Dayne (Arista)
18	26	GOOD GROOVE	Derek B (Music Of Life)
26	27	RECKLESS	Afrika Bambaataa (EMI)
10	28	SUEDEHEAD	Morrissey (HMV)
-	29	ON THESE ROADS	A-ha (Warner Bros)
27	30	I FOUGHT THE LAW	Clash (CBS)
-	31	CROSS MY BROKEN HEART	Sinitta (Fanfare)
21	32	DOMINION	Sisters Of Mercy (Merciful Release)
-	33	TEMPTATION	Wet Wet Wet (Precious)
22	34	HOW MEN ARE	Aztec Camera (WEA)
29	35	I WALK THE EARTH	Voice Of The Beehive (London)
28	36	DEVIL INSIDE	INXS (Mercury)
-	37	SHAKE	Gene & Jim (Rough Trade)
30	38	I WANT HER	Keith Sweat (Vintertainment)
-	39	GIRLFRIEND	Pebbles (MCA)
16	40	A HAZY SHADE OF WINTER	Bangles (Def Jam)
44	41	SIMPLE SIMON	Mantronix (10)
35	42	DREAMING	Glen Goldsmith (Reproduction)
36	43	IF I SHOULD FALL FROM GRACE WITH GOD	Pogues (Pogue Mahone)
23	44	C'MON EVERYBODY	Eddie Cochran (Liberty)
31	45	LOVEY DOVEY	Tony Terry (Epic)
-	46	ONLY IN MY DREAMS	Debbie Gibson (Atlantic)
40	47	LOVE CHANGES EVERYTHING	Climie Fisher (EMI)
43	48	MAJESTIC HEAD	Soup Dragons (Raw)
48	49	NOBODY'S TWISTING YOUR ARM	Wedding Present (Reception)
-	50	I PRONOUNCE YOU	Madness (Virgin)

Rick Astley scored his third Number One from four releases with *Together Forever*, while teenage French singer Vanessa Paradis (later to make her mark as a movie actress) made Number Two with her only UK hit *Joe Le Taxi*. Eddie Cochran's 1959 oldie *C'mon Everybody* found itself back in the Top 20 following its adoption as the latest Levi's TV ad soundtrack, and the Clash hit the Top 30 with a reissue.

April 1988

2 April 1988

last week	this week	title	artist (label)
1	1	DON'T TURN AROUND	Aswad (Mango)
11	2	DROP THE BOY	Bros (CBS)
14	3	CAN I PLAY WITH MADNESS	Iron Maiden (EMI)
18	4	COULD'VE BEEN	Tiffany (MCA)
5	5	I SHOULD BE SO LUCKY	Kylie Minogue (PWL)
8	6	NEVER/THESE DREAMS	Heart (Capitol)
2	7	CRASH	Primitives (Lazy)
10	8	I GET WEAK	Belinda Carlisle (Virgin)
31	9	CROSS MY BROKEN HEART	Sinitta (Fanfare)
4	10	JOE LE TAXI	Vanessa Paradis (FA Productions)
29	11	ON THESE ROADS	A-ha (Warner Bros)
7	12	LOVE IS CONTAGIOUS	Taja Sevelle (Paisley Park)
19	13	I'M NOT SCARED	Eighth Wonder (CBS)
6	14	SHIP OF FOOLS	Erasure (Mute)
24	15	BASS	Simon Harris (ffrr)
3	16	TOGETHER FOREVER	Rick Astley (RCA)
15	17	WHERE DO BROKEN HEARTS GO	Whitney Houston (Arista)
46	18	ONLY IN MY DREAMS	Debbie Gibson (Atlantic)
33	19	TEMPTATION	Wet Wet Wet (Precious)
27	20	RECKLESS	Afrika Bambaataa (EMI)
47	21	LOVE CHANGES EVERYTHING	Climie Fisher (EMI)
-	22	HEART	Pet Shop Boys (Parlophone)
23	23	HEART OF GOLD	Johnny Hates Jazz (Virgin)
38	24	I WANT HER	Keith Sweat (Vintertainment)
39	25	GIRLFRIEND	Pebbles (MCA)
-	26	AIN'T COMPLAINING	Status Quo (Vertigo)
12	27	I KNOW YOU GOT SOUL	Eric B. & Rakim (Cooltempo)
16	28	GET OUTTA MY DREAMS AND INTO MY CAR	Billy Ocean (Jive)
9	29	BEAT DIS	Bomb The Bass (Mister-ron)
17	30	DAYS OF NO TRUST	Magnum (Polydor)
30	31	I FOUGHT THE LAW	Clash (CBS)
13	32	DOCTORIN' THE HOUSE	Coldcut (Ahead Of Our Time)
42	33	DREAMING	Glen Goldsmith (Reproduction)
50	34	I PRONOUNCE YOU	Madness (Virgin)
25	35	PROVE YOUR LOVE	Taylor Dayne (Arista)
-	36	PINK CADILLAC	Natalie Cole (Manhattan)
20	37	JUST LIKE PARADISE	David Lee Roth (Warner Bros)
21	38	THAT'S THE WAY IT IS	Mel & Kim (Supreme)
49	39	NOBODY'S TWISTING YOUR ARM	Wedding Present (Reception)
-	40	JUST A MIRAGE	Jellybean (Chrysalis)
48	41	MAJESTIC HEAD	Soup Dragons (Raw)
22	42	GIMME HOPE JO'ANNA	Eddy Grant (Ice)
26	43	GOOD GROOVE	Derek B (Music Of Life)
-	44	LOVE IS STRONGER THAN PRIDE	Sade (Epic)
-	45	LADY MADONNA	Beatles (Parlophone)
-	46	SWEET LIES	Robert Palmer (Island)
-	47	SHE'S LIKE THE WIND	Patrick Swayze (RCA)
-	48	NOBODY CAN LOVE ME	Tongue In Cheek (Criminal)
36	49	DEVIL INSIDE	INXS (Mercury)
-	50	OOO LA LA LA	Teena Marie (Epic)

9 April 1988

last week	this week	title	artist (label)
1	1	DON'T TURN AROUND	Aswad (Mango)
3	2	CAN I PLAY WITH MADNESS	Iron Maiden (EMI)
2	3	DROP THE BOY	Bros (CBS)
4	4	COULD'VE BEEN	Tiffany (MCA)
22	5	HEART	Pet Shop Boys (Parlophone)
11	6	ON THESE ROADS	A-ha (Warner Bros)
9	7	CROSS MY BROKEN HEART	Sinitta (Fanfare)
13	8	I'M NOT SCARED	Eighth Wonder (CBS)
6	9	NEVER/THESE DREAMS	Heart (Capitol)
15	10	BASS	Simon Harris (ffrr)
5	11	I SHOULD BE SO LUCKY	Kylie Minogue (PWL)
21	12	LOVE CHANGES EVERYTHING	Climie Fisher (EMI)
18	13	ONLY IN MY DREAMS	Debbie Gibson (Atlantic)
17	14	WHERE DO BROKEN HEARTS GO	Whitney Houston (Arista)
19	15	TEMPTATION	Wet Wet Wet (Precious)
7	16	CRASH	Primitives (Lazy)
26	17	AIN'T COMPLAINING	Status Quo (Vertigo)
-	18	EVERYWHERE	Fleetwood Mac (Warner Bros)
33	19	DREAMING	Glen Goldsmith (Reproduction)
14	20	SHIP OF FOOLS	Erasure (Mute)
20	21	RECKLESS	Afrika Bambaataa (EMI)
35	22	PROVE YOUR LOVE	Taylor Dayne (Arista)
8	23	I GET WEAK	Belinda Carlisle (Virgin)
10	24	JOE LE TAXI	Vanessa Paradis (FA Productions)
-	25	THAT'S THE WAY I WANNA ROCK 'N' ROLL	AC/DC (Atlantic)
-	26	WHO'S LEAVING WHO	Hazell Dean (EMI)
36	27	PINK CADILLAC	Natalie Cole (Manhattan)
44	28	LOVE IS STRONGER THAN PRIDE	Sade (Epic)
-	29	A LOVE SUPREME	Will Downing (Fourth & Broadway)
-	30	SEX TALK	T'Pau (Siren)
24	31	I WANT HER	Keith Sweat (Vintertainment)
25	32	GIRLFRIEND	Pebbles (MCA)
16	33	TOGETHER FOREVER	Rick Astley (RCA)
-	34	I WANT YOU BACK	Bananarama (London)
37	35	JUST LIKE PARADISE	David Lee Roth (Warner Bros)
40	36	JUST A MIRAGE	Jellybean (Chrysalis)
31	37	I FOUGHT THE LAW	Clash (CBS)
12	38	LOVE IS CONTAGIOUS	Taja Sevelle (Paisley Park)
34	39	I PRONOUNCE YOU	Madness (Virgin)
-	40	PIANO IN THE DARK	Brenda Russell (Breakout)
41	41	I NEED A MAN	Eurythmics (RCA)
27	42	I KNOW YOU GOT SOUL	Eric B. & Rakim (Cooltempo)
47	43	SHE'S LIKE THE WIND	Patrick Swayze (RCA)
30	44	DAYS OF NO TRUST	Magnum (Polydor)
28	45	GET OUTTA MY DREAMS AND INTO MY CAR	Billy Ocean (Jive)
-	46	GET LUCKY	Jermaine Stewart (Siren)
-	47	WE ALL SLEEP ALONE	Cher (Geffen)
46	48	SWEET LIES	Robert Palmer (Island)
50	49	OOO LA LA LA	Teena Marie (Epic)
-	50	STORYBOOK LOVE	Mark Knopfler & Willy DeVille (Barry)

16 April 1988

last week	this week	title	artist (label)
5	1	HEART	Pet Shop Boys (Parlophone)
3	2	DROP THE BOY	Bros (CBS)
1	3	DON'T TURN AROUND	Aswad (Mango)
4	4	COULD'VE BEEN	Tiffany (MCA)
12	5	LOVE CHANGES EVERYTHING	Climie Fisher (EMI)
7	6	CROSS MY BROKEN HEART	Sinitta (Fanfare)
2	7	CAN I PLAY WITH MADNESS	Iron Maiden (EMI)
18	8	EVERYWHERE	Fleetwood Mac (Warner Bros)
6	9	ON THESE ROADS	A-ha (Warner Bros)
26	10	WHO'S LEAVING WHO	Hazell Dean (EMI)
-	11	ARMAGEDDON IT	Def Leppard (Bludgeon Riffola)
15	12	TEMPTATION	Wet Wet Wet (Precious)
8	13	I'M NOT SCARED	Eighth Wonder (CBS)
9	14	NEVER/THESE DREAMS	Heart (Capitol)
11	15	I SHOULD BE SO LUCKY	Kylie Minogue (PWL)
22	16	PROVE YOUR LOVE	Taylor Dayne (Arista)
13	17	ONLY IN MY DREAMS	Debbie Gibson (Atlantic)
-	18	SIDEWALKING	Jesus & Mary Chain (blanco y negro)
19	19	DREAMING	Glen Goldsmith (Reproduction)
25	20	THAT'S THE WAY I WANNA ROCK 'N' ROLL	AC/DC (Atlantic)
27	21	PINK CADILLAC	Natalie Cole (Manhattan)
32	22	GIRLFRIEND	Pebbles (MCA)
34	23	I WANT YOU BACK	Bananarama (London)
41	24	I NEED A MAN	Eurythmics (RCA)
14	25	WHERE DO BROKEN HEARTS GO	Whitney Houston (Arista)
17	26	AIN'T COMPLAINING	Status Quo (Vertigo)
36	27	JUST A MIRAGE	Jellybean (Chrysalis)
10	28	BASS	Simon Harris (ffrr)
-	29	EVERY ANGEL	All About Eve (Mercury)
24	30	CRASH	Primitives (Lazy)
-	31	DEUS	Sugarcubes (One Little Indian)
40	32	PIANO IN THE DARK	Brenda Russell (Breakout)
-	33	LET'S ALL CHANT	Pat & Mick (PWL)
30	34	SEX TALK	T'Pau (Siren)
-	35	THEME FROM S-EXPRESS	S-Express (Rhythm King)
-	36	PUSH IT/I AM DOWN	Salt 'N' Pepa (ffrr)
24	37	JOE LE TAXI	Vanessa Paradis (FA Productions)
20	38	SHIP OF FOOLS	Erasure (Mute)
33	39	TOGETHER FOREVER	Rick Astley (RCA)
31	40	I WANT HER	Keith Sweat (Vintertainment)
46	41	GET LUCKY	Jermaine Stewart (Siren)
-	42	FREEDOM	Alice Cooper (MCA)
-	43	BROKEN LAND	Adventures (Elektra)
44	44	LOVE IS STRONGER THAN PRIDE	Sade (Epic)
39	45	I PRONOUNCE YOU	Madness (Virgin)
38	46	LOVE IS CONTAGIOUS	Taja Sevelle (Paisley Park)
29	47	A LOVE SUPREME	Will Downing (Fourth & Broadway)
23	48	I GET WEAK	Belinda Carlisle (Virgin)
-	49	RECKLESS	Afrika Bambaataa (EMI)
37	50	I FOUGHT THE LAW	Clash (CBS)

UK reggae group Aswad had had just one chart hit before *Don't Turn Around* topped the chart – *Chasing For The Breeze,* which had stalled at Number 35 in 1984. The new success raised their subsequent profile tremendously – they even recorded (and appeared at Wembley) with Cliff Richard the following year. Bros, meanwhile, had their second Number Two in a row with with *Drop The Boy.*

April – May 1988

last week	this week	23 April 1988	
1	1	HEART	Pet Shop Boys (Parlophone)
5	2	LOVE CHANGES EVERYTHING	Climie Fisher (EMI)
8	3	EVERYWHERE	Fleetwood Mac (Warner Bros)
2	4	DROP THE BOY	Bros (CBS)
10	5	WHO'S LEAVING WHO	Hazell Dean (EMI)
21	6	PINK CADILLAC	Natalie Cole (Manhattan)
22	7	GIRLFRIEND	Pebbles (MCA)
4	8	COULD'VE BEEN	Tiffany (MCA)
16	9	PROVE YOUR LOVE	Taylor Dayne (Arista)
19	10	DREAMING	Glen Goldsmith (Reproduction)
13	11	I'M NOT SCARED	Eighth Wonder (CBS)
6	12	CROSS MY BROKEN HEART	Sinitta (Fanfare)
35	13	THEME FROM S-EXPRESS	S-Express (Rhythm King)
23	14	I WANT YOU BACK	Bananarama (London)
11	15	ARMAGEDDON IT	Def Leppard (Bludgeon Riffola)
3	16	DON'T TURN AROUND	Aswad (Mango)
27	17	JUST A MIRAGE	Jellybean (Chrysalis)
12	18	TEMPTATION	Wet Wet Wet (Precious)
-	19	I WANT YOU BACK '88	Michael Jackson/Jackson Five (Motown)
33	20	LET'S ALL CHANT	Pat & Mick (PWL)
47	21	A LOVE SUPREME	Will Downing (Fourth & Broadway)
18	22	SIDEWALKING	Jesus & Mary Chain (blanco y negro)
24	23	I NEED A MAN	Eurythmics (RCA)
41	24	GET LUCKY	Jermaine Stewart (Siren)
-	25	MARY'S PRAYER	Danny Wilson (Virgin)
32	26	PIANO IN THE DARK	Brenda Russell (Breakout)
9	27	ON THESE ROADS	A-ha (Warner Bros)
34	28	SEX TALK	T'Pau (Siren)
29	29	EVERY ANGEL	All About Eve (Mercury)
-	30	BEYOND THE PALE	Mission (Mercury)
17	31	ONLY IN MY DREAMS	Debbie Gibson (Atlantic)
7	32	CAN I PLAY WITH MADNESS	Iron Maiden (EMI)
20	33	THAT'S THE WAY I WANNA ROCK 'N' ROLL	AC/DC (Atlantic)
-	34	WHEN WILL YOU MAKE MY TELEPHONE RING	Deacon Blue (CBS)
14	35	NEVER/THESE DREAMS	Heart (Capitol)
-	36	ANGEL	Aerosmith (Geffen)
-	37	ONE MORE TRY	George Michael (Epic)
-	38	SHE'S LIKE THE WIND	Patrick Swayze (RCA)
-	39	ALWAYS SOMETHING THERE TO REMIND ME	Housemartins (Go! Discs)
-	40	NITE AND DAY	Al B. Sure! (Uptown)
15	41	I SHOULD BE SO LUCKY	Kylie Minogue (PWL)
-	42	I GAVE IT UP	Luther Vandross (Epic)
42	43	FREEDOM	Alice Cooper (MCA)
26	44	AIN'T COMPLAINING	Status Quo (Vertigo)
-	45	IT TAKES TWO	Rob Base & DJ E-Z Rock (Citybeat)
-	46	PLAY BACKMIX PART 1	James Brown (Urban)
-	47	PRIME MOVER	Rush (Vertigo)
-	48	PERFECT	Fairground Attraction (RCA)
-	49	DON'T LOOK ANY FURTHER	Kane Gang (Kitchenware)
31	50	DEUS	Sugarcubes (One Little Indian)

last week	this week	30 April 1988	
13	1	THEME FROM S-EXPRESS	S-Express (Rhythm King)
1	2	HEART	Pet Shop Boys (Parlophone)
2	3	LOVE CHANGES EVERYTHING	Climie Fisher (EMI)
6	4	PINK CADILLAC	Natalie Cole (Manhattan)
5	5	WHO'S LEAVING WHO	Hazell Dean (EMI)
19	6	I WANT YOU BACK '88	Michael Jackson/Jackson Five (Motown)
3	7	EVERYWHERE	Fleetwood Mac (Warner Bros)
7	8	GIRLFRIEND	Pebbles (MCA)
14	9	I WANT YOU BACK	Bananarama (London)
37	10	ONE MORE TRY	George Michael (Epic)
25	11	MARY'S PRAYER	Danny Wilson (Virgin)
4	12	DROP THE BOY	Bros (CBS)
20	13	LET'S ALL CHANT	Pat & Mick (PWL)
24	14	GET LUCKY	Jermaine Stewart (Siren)
17	15	JUST A MIRAGE	Jellybean (Chrysalis)
9	16	PROVE YOUR LOVE	Taylor Dayne (Arista)
46	17	PLAY IT BACK PART 1	James Brown (Urban)
10	18	DREAMING	Glen Goldsmith (Reproduction)
21	19	A LOVE SUPREME	Will Downing (Fourth & Broadway)
8	20	COULD'VE BEEN	Tiffany (MCA)
38	21	SHE'S LIKE THE WIND	Patrick Swayze (RCA)
48	22	PERFECT	Fairground Attraction (RCA)
30	23	BEYOND THE PALE	Mission (Mercury)
11	24	I'M NOT SCARED	Eighth Wonder (CBS)
12	25	CROSS MY BROKEN HEART	Sinitta (Fanfare)
16	26	DON'T TURN AROUND	Aswad (Mango)
26	27	PIANO IN THE DARK	Brenda Russell (Breakout)
28	28	SEX TALK	T'Pau (Siren)
45	29	IT TAKES TWO	Rob Base & DJ E-Z Rock (Citybeat)
-	30	DIVINE EMOTIONS	Narada (Reprise)
-	31	OUT OF REACH	Primitives (Lazy)
47	32	PRIME MOVER	Rush (Vertigo)
50	33	DEUS	Sugarcubes (One Little Indian)
34	34	WHEN WILL YOU MAKE MY TELEPHONE RING	Deacon Blue (CBS)
42	35	I GAVE IT UP	Luther Vandross (Epic)
29	36	EVERY ANGEL	All About Eve (Mercury)
-	37	BROKEN LAND	Adventures (Elektra)
40	38	NITE AND DAY	Al B. Sure! (Uptown)
-	39	WALK AWAY	Joyce Sims (London)
39	40	ALWAYS SOMETHING THERE TO REMIND ME	Housemartins (Go! Discs)
23	41	I NEED A MAN	Eurythmics (RCA)
15	42	ARMAGEDDON IT	Def Leppard (Bludgeon Riffola)
31	43	ONLY IN MY DREAMS	Debbie Gibson (Atlantic)
49	44	DON'T LOOK ANY FURTHER	Kane Gang (Kitchenware)
-	45	IM NIN' ALU	Ofra Haza (WEA)
22	46	SIDEWALKING	Jesus & Mary Chain (blanco y negro)
32	47	CAN I PLAY WITH MADNESS	Iron Maiden (EMI)
-	48	SOMETHIN' ELSE	Eddie Cochran (Liberty)
18	49	TEMPTATION	Wet Wet Wet (Precious)
-	50	AIRHEAD	Thomas Dolby (Manhattan)

last week	this week	7 May 1988	
1	1	THEME FROM S-EXPRESS	S-Express (Rhythm King)
11	2	MARY'S PRAYER	Danny Wilson (Virgin)
5	3	WHO'S LEAVING WHO	Hazell Dean (EMI)
9	4	I WANT YOU BACK	Bananarama (London)
10	5	ONE MORE TRY	George Michael (Epic)
22	6	PERFECT	Fairground Attraction (RCA)
2	7	HEART	Pet Shop Boys (Parlophone)
4	8	PINK CADILLAC	Natalie Cole (Manhattan)
3	9	LOVE CHANGES EVERYTHING	Climie Fisher (EMI)
6	10	I WANT YOU BACK '88	Michael Jackson/Jackson Five (Motown)
17	11	PLAY IT BACK PART 1	James Brown (Urban)
7	12	EVERYWHERE	Fleetwood Mac (Warner Bros)
19	13	A LOVE SUPREME	Will Downing (Fourth & Broadway)
13	14	LET'S ALL CHANT	Pat & Mick (PWL)
14	15	GET LUCKY	Jermaine Stewart (Siren)
8	16	GIRLFRIEND	Pebbles (MCA)
21	17	SHE'S LIKE THE WIND	Patrick Swayze (RCA)
31	18	OUT OF REACH	Primitives (Lazy)
16	19	PROVE YOUR LOVE	Taylor Dayne (Arista)
-	20	ALPHABET STREET	Prince (Paisley Park)
-	21	BLUE MONDAY (88 REMIX)	New Order (Factory)
15	22	JUST A MIRAGE	Jellybean (Chrysalis)
-	23	PUMP UP THE BITTER	Star Turn On 45 (Pacific)
29	24	IT TAKES TWO	Rob Base & DJ E-Z Rock (Citybeat)
27	25	PIANO IN THE DARK	Brenda Russell (Breakout)
37	26	BROKEN LAND	Adventures (Elektra)
23	27	BEYOND THE PALE	Mission (Mercury)
39	28	WALK AWAY	Joyce Sims (London)
40	29	ALWAYS SOMETHING THERE TO REMIND ME	Housemartins (Go! Discs)
30	30	DIVINE EMOTIONS	Narada (Reprise)
34	31	WHEN WILL YOU MAKE MY TELEPHONE RING	Deacon Blue (CBS)
24	32	I'M NOT SCARED	Eighth Wonder (CBS)
33	33	DEUS	Sugarcubes (One Little Indian)
-	34	BORN AGAIN	Christians (Island)
12	35	DROP THE BOY	Bros (CBS)
-	36	THE KING OF ROCK 'N' ROLL	Prefab Sprout (Kitchenware)
41	37	I NEED A MAN	Eurythmics (RCA)
18	38	DREAMING	Glen Goldsmith (Reproduction)
-	39	LITTLE GIRL LOST	Icicle Works (Beggars Banquet)
38	40	NITE AND DAY	Al B. Sure! (Uptown)
45	41	IM NIN' ALU	Ofra Haza (WEA)
-	42	FINEST WORKSONG	R.E.M. (IRS)
-	43	LOADSAMONEY (DOIN' UP THE HOUSE)	Harry Enfield (Mercury)
-	44	GIVE GIVE GIVE ME MORE MORE MORE	Wonder Stuff (Polydor)
35	45	I GAVE IT UP	Luther Vandross (Epic)
36	46	EVERY ANGEL	All About Eve (Mercury)
47	47	SIDEWALKING	Jesus & Mary Chain (blanco y negro)
25	48	CROSS MY BROKEN HEART	Sinitta (Fanfare)
-	49	START TALKING LOVE	Magnum (Polydor)
20	50	COULD'VE BEEN	Tiffany (MCA)

As Bananarama made the Top 10 with *I Want You Back*, in too came Michael Jackson & the Jackson 5 (as their Motown billing rewrote history to call them) with a remixed version of their very first hit, its title now amended to *I Want You Back '88*. Despite the apparent tight competition, these were completely different songs. Pat (Sharp) and Mick (Brown)'s *Let's All Chant* aided the Help A London Child appeal.

May 1988

14 May 1988

last	this	Title	Artist (Label)
6	1	PERFECT	Fairground Attraction (RCA)
1	2	THEME FROM S-EXPRESS	S-Express (Rhythm King)
2	3	MARY'S PRAYER	Danny Wilson (Virgin)
21	4	BLUE MONDAY (88 REMIX)	New Order (Factory)
8	5	PINK CADILLAC	Natalie Cole (Manhattan)
3	6	WHO'S LEAVING WHO	Hazell Dean (EMI)
4	7	I WANT YOU BACK	Bananarama (London)
7	8	HEART	Pet Shop Boys (Parlophone)
43	9	LOADSAMONEY (DOIN' UP THE HOUSE)	Harry Enfield (Mercury)
20	10	ALPHABET STREET	Prince (Paisley Park)
23	11	PUMP UP THE BITTER	Star Turn On 45 (Pacific)
5	12	ONE MORE TRY	George Michael (Epic)
10	13	I WANT YOU BACK '88	Michael Jackson/Jackson Five (Motown)
11	14	PLAY IT BACK PART 1	James Brown (Urban)
30	15	DIVINE EMOTIONS	Narada (Reprise)
14	16	LET'S ALL CHANT	Pat & Mick (PWL)
13	17	A LOVE SUPREME	Will Downing (Fourth & Broadway)
9	18	LOVE CHANGES EVERYTHING	Climie Fisher (EMI)
18	19	OUT OF REACH	Primitives (Lazy)
12	20	EVERYWHERE	Fleetwood Mac (Warner Bros)
16	21	GIRLFRIEND	Pebbles (MCA)
49	22	START TALKING LOVE	Magnum (Polydor)
-	23	NOTHIN' BUT A GOOD TIME	Poison (Capitol)
-	24	YOUNG BROTHER	Derek B (Tuff Audio)
17	25	SHE'S LIKE THE WIND	Patrick Swayze (RCA)
15	26	GET LUCKY	Jermaine Stewart (Siren)
28	27	WALK AWAY	Joyce Sims (London)
25	28	PIANO IN THE DARK	Brenda Russell (Breakout)
36	29	THE KING OF ROCK 'N' ROLL	Prefab Sprout (Kitchenware)
-	30	CIRCLE IN THE SAND	Belinda Carlisle (Virgin)
-	31	COLLISION	Loop
34	32	BORN AGAIN	Christians (Island)
26	33	BROKEN LAND	Adventures (Elektra)
-	34	ANFIELD RAP	Liverpool Football Club (Virgin)
-	35	GOT TO BE CERTAIN	Kylie Minogue (PWL)
-	36	I'LL SEE YOU ALONG THE WAY	Rick Clarke (WA)
-	37	WITH A LITTLE HELP FROM MY FRIENDS/SHE'S LEAVING HOME	Wet Wet Wet /Billy Bragg with Cara Tivey (Childline)
41	38	IM NIN' ALU	Ofra Haza (WEA)
42	39	FINEST WORKSONG	R.E.M. (IRS)
-	40	CALYPSO CRAZY	Billy Ocean (Jive)
22	41	JUST A MIRAGE	Jellybean (Chrysalis)
24	42	IT TAKES TWO	Rob Base & DJ E-Z Rock (Citybeat)
27	43	BEYOND THE PALE	Mission (Mercury)
-	44	ALL THIS LOVE THAT I'M GIVING	Gwen McCrae (Flame)
-	45	OUT COME THE FREAKS (AGAIN)	Was (Not Was) (Fontana)
38	46	DREAMING	Glen Goldsmith (Reproduction)
-	47	OH PATTI	Scritti Politti (Virgin)
40	48	NITE AND DAY	Al B. Sure! (Uptown)
29	49	ALWAYS SOMETHING THERE TO REMIND ME	Housemartins (Go! Discs)
19	50	PROVE YOUR LOVE	Taylor Dayne (Arista)

21 May 1988

last	this	Title	Artist (Label)
37	1	WITH A LITTLE HELP FROM MY FRIENDS/SHE'S LEAVING HOME	Wet Wet Wet /Billy Bragg with Cara Tivey (Childline)
1	2	PERFECT	Fairground Attraction (RCA)
4	3	BLUE MONDAY (88 REMIX)	New Order (Factory)
9	4	LOADSAMONEY (DOIN' UP THE HOUSE)	Harry Enfield (Mercury)
2	5	THEME FROM S-EXPRESS	S-Express (Rhythm King)
10	6	ALPHABET STREET	Prince (Paisley Park)
34	7	ANFIELD RAP	Liverpool Football Club (Virgin)
35	8	GOT TO BE CERTAIN	Kylie Minogue (PWL)
3	9	MARY'S PRAYER	Danny Wilson (Virgin)
7	10	I WANT YOU BACK	Bananarama (London)
11	11	PUMP UP THE BITTER	Star Turn On 45 (Pacific)
6	12	WHO'S LEAVING WHO	Hazell Dean (EMI)
5	13	PINK CADILLAC	Natalie Cole (Manhattan)
15	14	DIVINE EMOTIONS	Narada (Reprise)
33	15	BROKEN LAND	Adventures (Elektra)
29	16	THE KING OF ROCK 'N' ROLL	Prefab Sprout (Kitchenware)
17	17	A LOVE SUPREME	Will Downing (Fourth & Broadway)
16	18	LET'S ALL CHANT	Pat & Mick (PWL)
13	19	I WANT YOU BACK '88	Michael Jackson/Jackson Five (Motown)
24	20	YOUNG BROTHER	Derek B (Tuff Audio)
30	21	CIRCLE IN THE SAND	Belinda Carlisle (Virgin)
38	22	IM NIN' ALU	Ofra Haza (WEA)
14	23	PLAY IT BACK PART 1	James Brown (Urban)
22	24	START TALKING LOVE	Magnum (Polydor)
-	25	SOMEWHERE IN MY HEART	Aztec Camera (WEA)
8	26	HEART	Pet Shop Boys (Parlophone)
23	27	NOTHIN' BUT A GOOD TIME	Poison (Capitol)
-	28	DON'T GO	Hothouse Flowers (London)
12	29	ONE MORE TRY	George Michael (Epic)
47	30	OH PATTI	Scritti Politti (Virgin)
-	31	ENDLESS SUMMER NIGHTS	Richard Marx (Manhattan)
25	32	SHE'S LIKE THE WIND	Patrick Swayze (RCA)
18	33	LOVE CHANGES EVERYTHING	Climie Fisher (EMI)
20	34	EVERYWHERE	Fleetwood Mac (Warner Bros)
40	35	CALYPSO CRAZY	Billy Ocean (Jive)
-	36	OUT OF THE BLUE	Debbie Gibson (Atlantic)
27	37	WALK AWAY	Joyce Sims (London)
32	38	BORN AGAIN	Christians (Island)
39	39	MY ONE TEMPTATION	Mica Paris (Fourth & Broadway)
-	40	WHAT ABOUT LOVE	Heart (Capitol)
-	41	MARY JANE	Megadeth (Capitol)
45	42	OUT COME THE FREAKS (AGAIN)	Was (Not Was) (Fontana)
21	43	GIRLFRIEND	Pebbles (MCA)
48	44	NITE AND DAY	Al B. Sure! (Uptown)
-	45	HEY MR HEARTACHE	Kim Wilde (MCA)
-	46	LONDON CALLING	Clash (CBS)
19	47	OUT OF REACH	Primitives (Lazy)
-	48	VOYAGE VOYAGE	Desireless (CBS)
-	49	DON'T CALL ME BABY	Voice Of The Beehive (London)
-	50	SOMETHING JUST AIN'T RIGHT	Keith Sweat (Vintertainment)

28 May 1988

last	this	Title	Artist (Label)
1	1	WITH A LITTLE HELP FROM MY FRIENDS/SHE'S LEAVING HOME	Wet Wet Wet /Billy Bragg with Cara Tivey (Childline)
2	2	PERFECT	Fairground Attraction (RCA)
8	3	GOT TO BE CERTAIN	Kylie Minogue (PWL)
3	4	BLUE MONDAY (88 REMIX)	New Order (Factory)
7	5	ANFIELD RAP	Liverpool Football Club (Virgin)
6	6	DIVINE EMOTIONS	Narada (Reprise)
6	7	ALPHABET STREET	Prince (Paisley Park)
16	8	THE KING OF ROCK 'N' ROLL	Prefab Sprout (Kitchenware)
4	9	LOADSAMONEY (DOIN' UP THE HOUSE)	Harry Enfield (Mercury)
21	10	CIRCLE IN THE SAND	Belinda Carlisle (Virgin)
5	11	THEME FROM S-EXPRESS	S-Express (Rhythm King)
28	12	DON'T GO	Hothouse Flowers (London)
25	13	SOMEWHERE IN MY HEART	Aztec Camera (WEA)
10	14	I WANT YOU BACK	Bananarama (London)
20	15	YOUNG BROTHER	Derek B (Tuff Audio)
40	16	WHAT ABOUT LOVE	Heart (Capitol)
9	17	MARY'S PRAYER	Danny Wilson (Virgin)
22	18	IM NIN' ALU	Ofra Haza (WEA)
15	19	BROKEN LAND	Adventures (Elektra)
-	20	CHECK THIS OUT	L.A. Mix (Breakout)
13	21	PINK CADILLAC	Natalie Cole (Manhattan)
12	22	WHO'S LEAVING WHO	Hazell Dean (EMI)
-	23	THIS IS ME	Climie Fisher (EMI)
30	24	OH PATTI	Scritti Politti (Virgin)
11	25	PUMP UP THE BITTER	Star Turn On 45 (Pacific)
39	26	MY ONE TEMPTATION	Mica Paris (Fourth & Broadway)
41	27	MARY JANE	Megadeth (Capitol)
-	28	GIVE A LITTLE LOVE	Aswad (Mango)
36	29	OUT OF THE BLUE	Debbie Gibson (Atlantic)
19	30	I WANT YOU BACK '88	Michael Jackson/Jackson Five (Motown)
-	31	RUNS HOUSE	Run DMC (Profile)
32	32	A LOVE SUPREME	Will Downing (Fourth & Broadway)
18	33	LET'S ALL CHANT	Pat & Mick (PWL)
49	34	DON'T CALL ME BABY	Voice Of The Beehive (London)
-	35	WHO GET THE LOVE?	Status Quo (Vertigo)
29	36	ONE MORE TRY	George Michael (Epic)
-	37	FAIRPLAY	Soul II Soul (10)
38	38	BORN AGAIN	Christians (Island)
46	39	LONDON CALLING	Clash (CBS)
33	40	LOVE CHANGES EVERYTHING	Climie Fisher (EMI)
45	41	HEY MR HEARTACHE	Kim Wilde (MCA)
43	42	GIRLFRIEND	Pebbles (MCA)
-	43	LOVE WILL SAVE THE DAY	Whitney Houston (Arista)
-	44	LIFE AT A TOP PEOPLE'S HEALTH CLUB	Style Council (Polydor)
-	45	FOREVER AND EVER AMEN	Randy Travis (Warner Bros)
35	46	CALYPSO CRAZY	Billy Ocean (Jive)
32	47	SHE'S LIKE THE WIND	Patrick Swayze (RCA)
26	48	HEART	Pet Shop Boys (Parlophone)
48	49	VOYAGE VOYAGE	Desireless (CBS)
31	50	ENDLESS SUMMER NIGHTS	Richard Marx (Manhattan)

New Order's *Blue Monday*, a consistently good seller ever since its pair of 1983 Top 10 runs (when it peaked at Number Five). made a spectacular return to the upper table following a US remix supervised by Quincy Jones, attaining a new chart high of Number Three. Meanwhile, TV comedian found huge record success with his *Loadsamoney* alter ego, for whom the House idiom was a godsend!

June 1988

4 June 1988

last week	this week	Title	Artist
1	1	WITH A LITTLE HELP FROM MY FRIENDS/SHE'S LEAVING HOME	Wet Wet Wet /Billy Bragg with Cara Tivey (Childline)
3	2	GOT TO BE CERTAIN	Kylie Minogue (PWL)
2	3	PERFECT	Fairground Attraction (RCA)
10	4	CIRCLE IN THE SAND	Belinda Carlisle (Virgin)
5	5	THE KING OF ROCK 'N' ROLL	Prefab Sprout (Kitchenware)
12	6	DON'T GO	Hothouse Flowers (London)
13	7	SOMEWHERE IN MY HEART	Aztec Camera (WEA)
4	8	BLUE MONDAY (88 REMIX)	New Order (Factory)
20	9	CHECK THIS OUT	L.A. Mix (Breakout)
6	10	DIVINE EMOTIONS	Narada (Reprise)
5	11	ANFIELD RAP	Liverpool Football Club (Virgin)
24	12	OH PATTI	Scritti Politti (Virgin)
18	13	IM NIN' ALU	Ofra Haza (WEA)
16	14	WHAT ABOUT LOVE	Heart (Capitol)
23	15	THIS IS ME	Climie Fisher (EMI)
43	16	LOVE WILL SAVE THE DAY	Whitney Houston (Arista)
25	17	MY ONE TEMPTATION	Mica Paris (Fourth & Broadway)
11	18	THEME FROM S-EXPRESS	S-Express (Rhythm King)
28	19	GIVE A LITTLE LOVE	Aswad (Mango)
29	20	OUT OF THE BLUE	Debbie Gibson (Atlantic)
15	21	YOUNG BROTHER	Derek B (Tuff Audio)
49	22	VOYAGE VOYAGE	Desireless (CBS)
35	23	WHO GET THE LOVE?	Status Quo (Vertigo)
-	24	ANOTHER WEEKEND	Five Star (Tent)
-	25	LOST IN YOU	Rod Stewart (Warner Bros)
9	26	LOADSAMONEY (DOIN' UP THE HOUSE)	Harry Enfield (Mercury)
19	27	BROKEN LAND	Adventures (Elektra)
34	28	DON'T CALL ME BABY	Voice Of The Beehive (London)
44	29	LIFE AT A TOP PEOPLE'S HEALTH CLUB	Style Council (Polydor)
-	30	THE LOVERS	Alexander O'Neal (Tabu)
-	31	I SAW HIM STANDING THERE	Tiffany (MCA)
14	32	I WANT YOU BACK	Bananarama (London)
-	33	MOONCHILD (SECOND SEAL)	Fields Of The Nephilim (Situation Two)
-	34	PARADISE	Sade (Epic)
-	35	GET IT	Stevie Wonder & Michael Jackson (Motown)
17	36	MARY'S PRAYER	Danny Wilson (Virgin)
-	37	DOCTORIN' THE TARDIS	Timelords (KLF)
38	38	BORN AGAIN	Christians (Island)
-	39	JOY	Teddy Pendergrass (Elektra)
31	40	RUNS HOUSE	Run DMC (Profile)
7	41	ALPHABET STREET	Prince (Paisley Park)
-	42	MOVIN' 1988	Brass Construction (Syncopate)
41	43	HEY MR HEARTACHE	Kim Wilde (MCA)
-	44	LITTLE 15	Depeche Mode (Mute)
-	45	TELL ME	Nick Kamen (WEA)
27	46	MARY JANE	Megadeth (Capitol)
45	47	FOREVER AND EVER AMEN	Randy Travis (Warner Bros)
30	48	I WANT YOU BACK '88	Michael Jackson/Jackson Five (Motown)
-	49	MERCEDES BOY	Pebbles (MCA)
50	50	ENDLESS SUMMER NIGHTS	Richard Marx (Manhattan)

11 June 1988

last week	this week	Title	Artist
1	1	WITH A LITTLE HELP FROM MY FRIENDS/SHE'S LEAVING HOME	Wet Wet Wet /Billy Bragg with Cara Tivey (Childline)
2	2	GOT TO BE CERTAIN	Kylie Minogue (PWL)
7	3	SOMEWHERE IN MY HEART	Aztec Camera (WEA)
22	4	VOYAGE VOYAGE	Desireless (CBS)
9	5	CHECK THIS OUT	L.A. Mix (Breakout)
4	6	CIRCLE IN THE SAND	Belinda Carlisle (Virgin)
17	7	MY ONE TEMPTATION	Mica Paris (Fourth & Broadway)
16	8	LOVE WILL SAVE THE DAY	Whitney Houston (Arista)
6	9	DON'T GO	Hothouse Flowers (London)
3	10	PERFECT	Fairground Attraction (RCA)
5	11	THE KING OF ROCK 'N' ROLL	Prefab Sprout (Kitchenware)
37	12	DOCTORIN' THE TARDIS	Timelords (KLF)
8	13	BLUE MONDAY (88 REMIX)	New Order (Factory)
12	14	OH PATTI	Scritti Politti (Virgin)
-	15	EVERYDAY IS LIKE SUNDAY	Morrissey (HMV)
19	16	GIVE A LITTLE LOVE	Aswad (Mango)
-	17	CHAINS OF LOVE	Erasure (Mute)
13	18	IM NIN' ALU	Ofra Haza (WEA)
31	19	I SAW HIM STANDING THERE	Tiffany (MCA)
25	20	LOST IN YOU	Rod Stewart (Warner Bros)
10	21	DIVINE EMOTIONS	Narada (Reprise)
42	22	MOVIN' 1988	Brass Construction (Syncopate)
24	23	ANOTHER WEEKEND	Five Star (Tent)
18	24	THEME FROM S-EXPRESS	S-Express (Rhythm King)
25	25	WHAT ABOUT LOVE	Heart (Capitol)
-	26	WILD WORLD	Maxi Priest (10)
-	27	TRIBUTE (RIGHT ON)	Pasadenas (CBS)
-	28	BOYS (SUMMERTIME LOVE)	Sabrina (Ibiza)
20	29	OUT OF THE BLUE	Debbie Gibson (Atlantic)
15	30	THIS IS ME	Climie Fisher (EMI)
33	31	MOONCHILD (SECOND SEAL)	Fields Of The Nephilim (Situation Two)
11	32	ANFIELD RAP	Liverpool Football Club (Virgin)
28	33	DON'T CALL ME BABY	Voice Of The Beehive (London)
30	34	THE LOVERS	Alexander O'Neal (Tabu)
35	35	GET IT	Stevie Wonder & Michael Jackson (Motown)
-	36	I'M REAL	James Brown (Scotti Brothers)
34	37	PARADISE	Sade (Epic)
-	38	THERE'S MORE TO LOVE	Communards (London)
29	39	LIFE AT A TOP PEOPLE'S HEALTH CLUB	Style Council (Polydor)
-	40	NAUGHTY GIRLS	Samantha Fox (Jive)
21	41	YOUNG BROTHER	Derek B (Tuff Audio)
45	42	TELL ME	Nick Kamen (WEA)
-	43	YOU HAVE PLACED A CHILL IN MY HEART	Eurythmics (RCA)
23	44	WHO GET THE LOVE?	Status Quo (Vertigo)
26	45	LOADSAMONEY (DOIN' UP THE HOUSE)	Harry Enfield (Mercury)
41	46	ALPHABET STREET	Prince (Paisley Park)
-	47	WHAT YOU SEE IS WHAT YOU GOT	Glen Goldsmith (Reproduction)
-	48	JUST PLAY MUSIC	Big Audio Dynamite (CBS)
44	49	LITTLE 15	Depeche Mode (Mute)
-	50	MR. BACHELOR	Loose Ends (Virgin)

18 June 1988

last week	this week	Title	Artist
12	1	DOCTORIN' THE TARDIS	Timelords (KLF)
1	2	WITH A LITTLE HELP FROM MY FRIENDS/SHE'S LEAVING HOME	Wet Wet Wet /Billy Bragg with Cara Tivey (Childline)
4	3	VOYAGE VOYAGE	Desireless (CBS)
2	4	GOT TO BE CERTAIN	Kylie Minogue (PWL)
-	5	I OWE YOU NOTHING	Bros (CBS)
28	6	BOYS (SUMMERTIME LOVE)	Sabrina (Ibiza)
19	7	I SAW HIM STANDING THERE	Tiffany (MCA)
3	8	SOMEWHERE IN MY HEART	Aztec Camera (WEA)
15	9	EVERYDAY IS LIKE SUNDAY	Morrissey (HMV)
7	10	MY ONE TEMPTATION	Mica Paris (Fourth & Broadway)
26	11	WILD WORLD	Maxi Priest (10)
17	12	CHAINS OF LOVE	Erasure (Mute)
16	13	GIVE A LITTLE LOVE	Aswad (Mango)
23	14	ANOTHER WEEKEND	Five Star (Tent)
5	15	CHECK THIS OUT	L.A. Mix (Breakout)
6	16	CIRCLE IN THE SAND	Belinda Carlisle (Virgin)
8	17	LOVE WILL SAVE THE DAY	Whitney Houston (Arista)
10	18	PERFECT	Fairground Attraction (RCA)
11	19	THE KING OF ROCK 'N' ROLL	Prefab Sprout (Kitchenware)
43	20	YOU HAVE PLACED A CHILL IN MY HEART	Eurythmics (RCA)
14	21	OH PATTI	Scritti Politti (Virgin)
33	22	DON'T CALL ME BABY	Voice Of The Beehive (London)
27	23	TRIBUTE (RIGHT ON)	Pasadenas (CBS)
9	24	DON'T GO	Hothouse Flowers (London)
31	25	MOONCHILD (SECOND SEAL)	Fields Of The Nephilim (Situation Two)
-	26	WAP - BAM - BOOGIE/DON'T BLAME IT ON THAT GIRL	Matt Bianco (WEA)
-	27	LUCRETIA MY REFLECTION	Sisters Of Mercy (Merciful Release)
13	28	BLUE MONDAY (88 REMIX)	New Order (Factory)
37	29	PARADISE	Sade (Epic)
-	30	CAR WASH/IS IT LOVE YOU'RE AFTER	Rose Royce (MCA)
22	31	MOVIN' 1988	Brass Construction (Syncopate)
-	32	THE BLOOD THAT MOVES THE BODY	A-ha (Warner Bros)
36	33	I'M REAL	James Brown (Scotti Brothers)
20	34	LOST IN YOU	Rod Stewart (Warner Bros)
38	35	THERE'S MORE TO LOVE	Communards (London)
34	36	THE LOVERS	Alexander O'Neal (Tabu)
47	37	WHAT YOU SEE IS WHAT YOU GOT	Glen Goldsmith (Reproduction)
-	38	I DON'T WANNA GO ON WITH YOU LIKE THAT	Elton John (Rocket)
25	39	WHAT ABOUT LOVE	Heart (Capitol)
-	40	SIMPLY IRRESISTIBLE	Robert Palmer (EMI)
29	41	OUT OF THE BLUE	Debbie Gibson (Atlantic)
42	42	TELL ME	Nick Kamen (WEA)
24	43	THEME FROM S-EXPRESS	S-Express (Rhythm King)
30	44	THIS IS ME	Climie Fisher (EMI)
-	45	I'LL ALWAYS LOVE YOU	Taylor Dayne (Arista)
-	46	FOREVER AND EVER AMEN	Randy Travis (Warner Bros)
-	47	BREAKFAST IN BED	UB40 with Chrissie Hynde (DEP International)
-	48	STOP	Sam Brown (A&M)
-	49	FAST CAR	Tracy Chapman (Elektra)
-	50	NO CLAUSE 28	Boy George (Virgin)

The chart-topping double A-side of Beatles covers by Wet Wet Wet and Billy Bragg was taken from the NME-originated album *Sgt Pepper Knew My Father*, which consisted of the entire content of the Beatles' 1967 milestone re-interpreted by contemporary acts. All proceeds from the single were donated to the Childline charity for abused children founded by Esther Rantzen, hence the label.

25 June 1988

last week	this week	title	artist
5	1	I OWE YOU NOTHING	Bros (CBS)
1	2	DOCTORIN' THE TARDIS	Timelords (KLF)
6	3	BOYS (SUMMERTIME LOVE)	Sabrina (Ibiza)
3	4	VOYAGE VOYAGE	Desireless (CBS)
11	5	WILD WORLD	Maxi Priest (10)
2	6	WITH A LITTLE HELP FROM MY FRIENDS/SHE'S LEAVING HOME	Wet Wet Wet /Billy Bragg with Cara Tivey (Childline)
-	7	THE TWIST (YO TWIST)	Fat Boys & Chubby Checker (Urban)
12	8	CHAINS OF LOVE	Erasure (Mute)
23	9	TRIBUTE (RIGHT ON)	Pasadenas (CBS)
9	10	EVERYDAY IS LIKE SUNDAY	Morrissey (HMV)
4	11	GOT TO BE CERTAIN	Kylie Minogue (PWL)
8	12	SOMEWHERE IN MY HEART	Aztec Camera (WEA)
7	13	I SAW HIM STANDING THERE	Tiffany (MCA)
-	14	IN THE AIR TONIGHT '88	Phil Collins (Virgin)
26	15	WAP - BAM - BOOGIE/DON'T BLAME IT ON THAT GIRL	Matt Bianco (WEA)
30	16	CAR WASH/IS IT LOVE YOU'RE AFTER	Rose Royce (MCA)
20	17	YOU HAVE PLACED A CHILL IN MY HEART	Eurythmics (RCA)
27	18	LUCRETIA MY REFLECTION	Sisters Of Mercy (Merciful Release)
22	19	DON'T CALL ME BABY	Voice Of The Beehive (London)
32	20	THE BLOOD THAT MOVES THE BODY	A-ha (Warner Bros)
47	21	BREAKFAST IN BED	UB40 with Chrissie Hynde (DEP International)
10	22	MY ONE TEMPTATION	Mica Paris (Fourth & Broadway)
16	23	CIRCLE IN THE SAND	Belinda Carlisle (Virgin)
-	24	TOUGHER THAN THE REST	Bruce Springsteen (CBS)
13	25	GIVE A LITTLE LOVE	Aswad (Mango)
35	26	THERE'S MORE TO LOVE	Communards (London)
29	27	PARADISE	Sade (Epic)
15	28	CHECK THIS OUT	L.A. Mix (Breakout)
18	29	PERFECT	Fairground Attraction (RCA)
17	30	LOVE WILL SAVE THE DAY	Whitney Houston (Arista)
14	31	ANOTHER WEEKEND	Five Star (Tent)
37	32	WHAT YOU SEE IS WHAT YOU GOT	Glen Goldsmith (Reproduction)
49	33	FAST CAR	Tracy Chapman (Elektra)
-	34	ATMOSPHERE	Joy Division (Factory)
19	35	THE KING OF ROCK 'N' ROLL	Prefab Sprout (Kitchenware)
21	36	OH PATTI	Scritti Politti (Virgin)
38	37	I DON'T WANNA GO ON WITH YOU LIKE THAT	Elton John (Rocket)
40	38	SIMPLY IRRESISTIBLE	Robert Palmer (EMI)
24	39	DON'T GO	Hothouse Flowers (London)
-	40	PUSH IT/TRAMP	Salt 'N' Pepa (Champion/ffrr)
45	41	I'LL ALWAYS LOVE YOU	Taylor Dayne (Arista)
28	42	BLUE MONDAY (88 REMIX)	New Order (Factory)
-	43	MAYBE (WE SHOULD CALL IT A DAY)	Hazell Dean (EMI)
48	44	STOP	Sam Brown (A&M)
-	45	POP MUSIK	All Systems Go (Un1que)
42	46	TELL ME	Nick Kamen (WEA)
-	47	ISN'T IT MIDNIGHT	Fleetwood Mac (Warner Bros)
50	48	NO CLAUSE 28	Boy George (Virgin)
-	49	NOTHING'S GONNA CHANGE MY LOVE FOR YOU	Glenn Medeiros (London)
33	50	I'M REAL	James Brown (Scotti Brothers)

2 July 1988

last week	this week	title	artist
1	1	I OWE YOU NOTHING	Bros (CBS)
7	2	THE TWIST (YO TWIST)	Fat Boys & Chubby Checker (Urban)
3	3	BOYS (SUMMERTIME LOVE)	Sabrina (Ibiza)
9	4	TRIBUTE (RIGHT ON)	Pasadenas (CBS)
14	5	IN THE AIR TONIGHT '88	Phil Collins (Virgin)
2	6	DOCTORIN' THE TARDIS	Timelords (KLF)
21	7	BREAKFAST IN BED	UB40 with Chrissie Hynde (DEP International)
5	8	WILD WORLD	Maxi Priest (10)
4	9	VOYAGE VOYAGE	Desireless (CBS)
40	10	PUSH IT/TRAMP	Salt 'N' Pepa (Champion/ffrr)
24	11	TOUGHER THAN THE REST	Bruce Springsteen (CBS)
8	12	CHAINS OF LOVE	Erasure (Mute)
49	13	NOTHING'S GONNA CHANGE MY LOVE FOR YOU	Glenn Medeiros (London)
33	14	FAST CAR	Tracy Chapman (Elektra)
16	15	CAR WASH/IS IT LOVE YOU'RE AFTER	Rose Royce (MCA)
6	16	WITH A LITTLE HELP FROM MY FRIENDS/SHE'S LEAVING HOME	Wet Wet Wet /Billy Bragg with Cara Tivey (Childline)
17	17	YOU HAVE PLACED A CHILL IN MY HEART	Eurythmics (RCA)
15	18	WAP - BAM - BOOGIE/DON'T BLAME IT ON THAT GIRL	Matt Bianco (WEA)
10	19	EVERYDAY IS LIKE SUNDAY	Morrissey (HMV)
43	20	MAYBE (WE SHOULD CALL IT A DAY)	Hazell Dean (EMI)
11	21	GOT TO BE CERTAIN	Kylie Minogue (PWL)
26	22	THERE'S MORE TO LOVE	Communards (London)
-	23	I WILL BE WITH YOU	T'Pau (Siren)
12	24	SOMEWHERE IN MY HEART	Aztec Camera (WEA)
19	25	DON'T CALL ME BABY	Voice Of The Beehive (London)
-	26	NEVER TEAR US APART	INXS (Mercury)
20	27	THE BLOOD THAT MOVES THE BODY	A-ha (Warner Bros)
34	28	ATMOSPHERE	Joy Division (Factory)
-	29	DON'T BELIEVE THE HYPE	Public Enemy (Def Jam)
-	30	EVERLASTING	Natalie Cole (Manhattan)
13	31	I SAW HIM STANDING THERE	Tiffany (MCA)
32	32	WHAT YOU SEE IS WHAT YOU GOT	Glen Goldsmith (Reproduction)
27	33	PARADISE	Sade (Epic)
18	34	LUCRETIA MY REFLECTION	Sisters Of Mercy (Merciful Release)
-	35	ROSES ARE RED	Mac Band (MCA)
37	36	I DON'T WANNA GO ON WITH YOU LIKE THAT	Elton John (Rocket)
-	37	CROSS MY HEART	Eighth Wonder (CBS)
23	38	CIRCLE IN THE SAND	Belinda Carlisle (Virgin)
25	39	GIVE A LITTLE LOVE	Aswad (Mango)
22	40	MY ONE TEMPTATION	Mica Paris (Fourth & Broadway)
41	41	I'LL ALWAYS LOVE YOU	Taylor Dayne (Arista)
-	42	IN MY DREAMS	Will Downing (Fourth & Broadway)
-	43	HEAT IT UP	Wee Papa Girl Rappers (Jive)
29	44	FOLLOW THE LEADER	Eric B. & Rakim (MCA)
29	45	PERFECT	Fairground Attraction (RCA)
38	46	SIMPLY IRRESISTIBLE	Robert Palmer (EMI)
45	47	POP MUSIK	All Systems Go (Un1que)
28	48	CHECK THIS OUT	L.A. Mix (Breakout)
-	49	WE'VE GOT THE JUICE	Derek B (Tuff Audio)
-	50	THE BEST OF MY LOVE	Dee Lewis (Mercury)

9 July 1988

last week	this week	title	artist
2	1	THE TWIST (YO TWIST)	Fat Boys & Chubby Checker (Urban)
13	2	NOTHING'S GONNA CHANGE MY LOVE FOR YOU	Glenn Medeiros (London)
1	3	I OWE YOU NOTHING	Bros (CBS)
10	4	PUSH IT/TRAMP	Salt 'N' Pepa (Champion/ffrr)
4	5	TRIBUTE (RIGHT ON)	Pasadenas (CBS)
5	6	IN THE AIR TONIGHT '88	Phil Collins (Virgin)
3	7	BOYS (SUMMERTIME LOVE)	Sabrina (Ibiza)
7	8	FAST CAR	Tracy Chapman (Elektra)
-	9	BREAKFAST IN BED	UB40 with Chrissie Hynde (DEP International)
11	10	TOUGHER THAN THE REST	Bruce Springsteen (CBS)
29	11	DON'T BELIEVE THE HYPE	Public Enemy (Def Jam)
6	12	DOCTORIN' THE TARDIS	Timelords (KLF)
18	13	WAP - BAM - BOOGIE/DON'T BLAME IT ON THAT GIRL	Matt Bianco (WEA)
8	14	WILD WORLD	Maxi Priest (10)
20	15	MAYBE (WE SHOULD CALL IT A DAY)	Hazell Dean (EMI)
-	16	ROSES ARE RED	Mac Band (MCA)
23	17	I WILL BE WITH YOU	T'Pau (Siren)
12	18	CHAINS OF LOVE	Erasure (Mute)
17	19	YOU HAVE PLACED A CHILL IN MY HEART	Eurythmics (RCA)
26	20	NEVER TEAR US APART	INXS (Mercury)
22	21	THERE'S MORE TO LOVE	Communards (London)
44	22	FOLLOW THE LEADER	Eric B. & Rakim (MCA)
9	23	VOYAGE VOYAGE	Desireless (CBS)
37	24	CROSS MY HEART	Eighth Wonder (CBS)
15	25	CAR WASH/IS IT LOVE YOU'RE AFTER	Rose Royce (MCA)
30	26	EVERLASTING	Natalie Cole (Manhattan)
36	27	I DON'T WANNA GO ON WITH YOU LIKE THAT	Elton John (Rocket)
16	28	WITH A LITTLE HELP FROM MY FRIENDS/SHE'S LEAVING HOME	Wet Wet Wet /Billy Bragg with Cara Tivey (Childline)
21	29	GOT TO BE CERTAIN	Kylie Minogue (PWL)
28	30	ATMOSPHERE	Joy Division (Factory)
19	31	EVERYDAY IS LIKE SUNDAY	Morrissey (HMV)
24	32	SOMEWHERE IN MY HEART	Aztec Camera (WEA)
25	33	DON'T CALL ME BABY	Voice Of The Beehive (London)
-	34	ALL FIRED UP	Pat Benatar (Chrysalis)
42	35	IN MY DREAMS	Will Downing (Fourth & Broadway)
-	36	IT MUST HAVE BEEN LOVE	Magnum (Polydor)
43	37	HEAT IT UP	Wee Papa Girl Rappers (Jive)
33	38	PARADISE	Sade (Epic)
-	39	I DON'T WANT TO TALK ABOUT IT	Everything But The Girl (blanco y negro)
-	40	I WANT YOUR LOVE	Transvision Vamp (MCA)
41	41	I'LL ALWAYS LOVE YOU	Taylor Dayne (Arista)
32	42	WHAT YOU SEE IS WHAT YOU GOT	Glen Goldsmith (Reproduction)
49	43	WE'VE GOT THE JUICE	Derek B (Tuff Audio)
31	44	I SAW HIM STANDING THERE	Tiffany (MCA)
-	45	DROWNING IN A SEA OF LOVE	Adventures (Elektra)
-	46	TOMORROW PEOPLE	Ziggy Marley & the Makers (Virgin)
27	47	THE BLOOD THAT MOVES THE BODY	A-ha (Warner Bros)
-	48	I KNOW YOU'RE OUT THERE SOMEWHERE	Moody Blues (Polydor)
-	49	PAINTED MOON	Silencers (RCA)
-	50	BIG BUBBLES ON TROUBLES	Ellis Beggs & Howard (RCA)

Bros, rapidly emerging as the new teen sensation of the moment, made Number One with their third entry after scoring a pair of Number Two hits. *I Owe You Nothing* was actually a reissue of their previously unsuccessful single prior to *When Will I Be Famous*. The Timelords, whose gimmicky *Doctorin' The Tardis* Bros succeeded at the top, were those enigmatics also known as the JAMS and the KLF.

July 1988

16 July 1988

last	this		
2	1	NOTHING'S GONNA CHANGE MY LOVE FOR YOU	Glenn Medeiros (London)
4	2	PUSH IT/TRAMP	Salt 'N' Pepa (Champion/ffrr)
1	3	THE TWIST (YO TWIST)	Fat Boys & Chubby Checker (Urban)
8	4	FAST CAR	Tracy Chapman (Elektra)
16	5	ROSES ARE RED	Mac Band (MCA)
3	6	I OWE YOU NOTHING	Bros (CBS)
7	7	IN THE AIR TONIGHT '88	Phil Collins (Virgin)
39	8	I DON'T WANT TO TALK ABOUT IT	Everything But The Girl (blanco y negro)
7	9	BOYS (SUMMERTIME LOVE)	Sabrina (Ibiza)
13	10	WAP - BAM - BOOGIE/DON'T BLAME IT ON THAT GIRL	Matt Bianco (WEA)
5	11	TRIBUTE (RIGHT ON)	Pasadenas (CBS)
10	12	TOUGHER THAN THE REST	Bruce Springsteen (CBS)
9	13	BREAKFAST IN BED	UB40 with Chrissie Hynde (DEP International)
14	14	MAYBE (WE SHOULD CALL IT A DAY)	Hazell Dean (EMI)
24	15	CROSS MY HEART	Eighth Wonder (CBS)
22	16	FOLLOW THE LEADER	Eric B. & Rakim (MCA)
17	17	I WILL BE WITH YOU	T'Pau (Siren)
-	18	DIRTY DIANA	Michael Jackson (Epic)
11	19	DON'T BELIEVE THE HYPE	Public Enemy (Def Jam)
20	20	NEVER TEAR US APART	INXS (Mercury)
21	21	THERE'S MORE TO LOVE	Communards (London)
-	22	MONKEY	George Michael (Epic)
-	23	FOOLISH BEAT	Debbie Gibson (Atlantic)
14	24	WILD WORLD	Maxi Priest (10)
26	25	EVERLASTING	Natalie Cole (Manhattan)
12	26	DOCTORIN' THE TARDIS	Timelords (KLF)
34	27	ALL FIRED UP	Pat Benatar (Chrysalis)
19	28	YOU HAVE PLACED A CHILL IN MY HEART	Eurythmics (RCA)
27	29	I DON'T WANNA GO ON WITH YOU LIKE THAT	Elton John (Rocket)
40	30	I WANT YOUR LOVE	Transvision Vamp (MCA)
23	31	VOYAGE VOYAGE	Desireless (CBS)
46	32	TOMORROW PEOPLE	Ziggy Marley & the Makers (Virgin)
36	33	IT MUST HAVE BEEN LOVE	Magnum (Polydor)
-	34	LOVE BITES	Def Leppard (Bludgeon Riffola)
37	35	HEAT IT UP	Wee Papa Girl Rappers (Jive)
18	36	CHAINS OF LOVE	Erasure (Mute)
35	37	IN MY DREAMS	Will Downing (Fourth & Broadway)
45	38	DROWNING IN A SEA OF LOVE	Adventures (Elektra)
25	39	CAR WASH/IS IT LOVE YOU'RE AFTER	Rose Royce (MCA)
-	40	BEATIN' THE HEAT	Jack 'n' Chill (10)
41	41	I'LL ALWAYS LOVE YOU	Taylor Dayne (Arista)
-	42	FIESTA	Pogues (Pogue Mahone)
-	43	DON'T SAY IT'S LOVE	Johnny Hates Jazz (Virgin)
28	44	WITH A LITTLE HELP FROM MY FRIENDS/SHE'S LEAVING HOME	Wet Wet Wet /Billy Bragg with Cara Tivey (Childline)
-	45	HAPPY EVER AFTER	Julia Fordham (Circa)
48	46	I KNOW YOU'RE OUT THERE SOMEWHERE	Moody Blues (Polydor)
29	47	GOT TO BE CERTAIN	Kylie Minogue (PWL)
50	48	BIG BUBBLES ON TROUBLES	Ellis Beggs & Howard (RCA)
-	49	I'M TOO SCARED	Steven Dante (Cooltempo)
32	50	SOMEWHERE IN MY HEART	Aztec Camera (WEA)

23 July 1988

this		
1	NOTHING'S GONNA CHANGE MY LOVE FOR YOU	Glenn Medeiros (London)
18	2 DIRTY DIANA	Michael Jackson (Epic)
2	3 PUSH IT/TRAMP	Salt 'N' Pepa (Champion/ffrr)
8	4 I DON'T WANT TO TALK ABOUT IT	Everything But The Girl (blanco y negro)
5	5 ROSES ARE RED	Mac Band (MCA)
4	6 FAST CAR	Tracy Chapman (Elektra)
3	7 THE TWIST (YO TWIST)	Fat Boys & Chubby Checker (Urban)
6	8 I OWE YOU NOTHING	Bros (CBS)
22	9 MONKEY	George Michael (Epic)
30	10 I WANT YOUR LOVE	Transvision Vamp (MCA)
15	11 CROSS MY HEART	Eighth Wonder (CBS)
23	12 FOOLISH BEAT	Debbie Gibson (Atlantic)
9	13 BOYS (SUMMERTIME LOVE)	Sabrina (Ibiza)
34	14 LOVE BITES	Def Leppard (Bludgeon Riffola)
13	15 BREAKFAST IN BED	UB40 with Chrissie Hynde (DEP International)
7	16 IN THE AIR TONIGHT '88	Phil Collins (Virgin)
32	17 TOMORROW PEOPLE	Ziggy Marley & the Makers (Virgin)
10	18 WAP - BAM - BOOGIE/DON'T BLAME IT ON THAT GIRL	Matt Bianco (WEA)
11	19 TRIBUTE (RIGHT ON)	Pasadenas (CBS)
42	20 FIESTA	Pogues (Pogue Mahone)
12	21 TOUGHER THAN THE REST	Bruce Springsteen (CBS)
35	22 HEAT IT UP	Wee Papa Girl Rappers (Jive)
20	23 NEVER TEAR US APART	INXS (Mercury)
27	24 ALL FIRED UP	Pat Benatar (Chrysalis)
21	25 THERE'S MORE TO LOVE	Communards (London)
-	26 GLAM SLAM	Prince (Paisley Park)
14	27 MAYBE (WE SHOULD CALL IT A DAY)	Hazell Dean (EMI)
-	28 YOU CAME	Kim Wilde (MCA)
17	29 I WILL BE WITH YOU	T'Pau (Siren)
24	30 WILD WORLD	Maxi Priest (10)
16	31 FOLLOW THE LEADER	Eric B. & Rakim (MCA)
-	32 SUPERFLY GUY	S'Express (Rhythm King)
37	33 IN MY DREAMS	Will Downing (Fourth & Broadway)
19	34 DON'T BELIEVE THE HYPE	Public Enemy (Def Jam)
49	35 I'M TOO SCARED	Steven Dante (Cooltempo)
38	36 DROWNING IN A SEA OF LOVE	Adventures (Elektra)
26	37 DOCTORIN' THE TARDIS	Timelords (KLF)
40	38 BEATIN' THE HEAT	Jack 'n' Chill (10)
25	39 EVERLASTING	Natalie Cole (Manhattan)
43	40 DON'T SAY IT'S LOVE	Johnny Hates Jazz (Virgin)
-	41 A WISH AWAY	Wonder Stuff (Polydor)
28	42 YOU HAVE PLACED A CHILL IN MY HEART	Eurythmics (RCA)
31	43 VOYAGE VOYAGE	Desireless (CBS)
-	44 ANYTHING FOR YOU	Gloria Estefan & the Miami Sound Machine (Epic)
45	45 TURN IT UP	Richie Rich (Club)
-	46 I'M SORRY	Hothouse Flowers (London)
29	47 I DON'T WANNA GO ON WITH YOU LIKE THAT	Elton John (Rocket)
-	48 CHOCOLATE GIRL	Deacon Blue (CBS)
-	49 IT'S NATURE'S WAY	Dollar (London)
-	50 I NEED YOU	B.V.S.M.P. (Debut)

30 July 1988

this		
1	NOTHING'S GONNA CHANGE MY LOVE FOR YOU	Glenn Medeiros (London)
2	2 DIRTY DIANA	Michael Jackson (Epic)
4	3 I DON'T WANT TO TALK ABOUT IT	Everything But The Girl (blanco y negro)
10	4 I WANT YOUR LOVE	Transvision Vamp (MCA)
3	5 PUSH IT/TRAMP	Salt 'N' Pepa (Champion/ffrr)
12	6 FOOLISH BEAT	Debbie Gibson (Atlantic)
28	7 YOU CAME	Kim Wilde (MCA)
32	8 SUPERFLY GUY	S'Express (Rhythm King)
9	9 MONKEY	George Michael (Epic)
5	10 ROSES ARE RED	Mac Band (MCA)
14	11 LOVE BITES	Def Leppard (Bludgeon Riffola)
6	12 FAST CAR	Tracy Chapman (Elektra)
7	13 THE TWIST (YO TWIST)	Fat Boys & Chubby Checker (Urban)
-	14 THE ONLY WAY IS UP	Yazz & the Plastic Population (Big Life)
17	15 TOMORROW PEOPLE	Ziggy Marley & the Makers (Virgin)
8	16 I OWE YOU NOTHING	Bros (CBS)
20	17 FIESTA	Pogues (Pogue Mahone)
22	18 HEAT IT UP	Wee Papa Girl Rappers (Jive)
11	19 CROSS MY HEART	Eighth Wonder (CBS)
26	20 GLAM SLAM	Prince (Paisley Park)
-	21 REACH OUT I'LL BE THERE	Four Tops (Motown)
15	22 BREAKFAST IN BED	UB40 with Chrissie Hynde (DEP International)
24	23 ALL FIRED UP	Pat Benatar (Chrysalis)
13	24 BOYS (SUMMERTIME LOVE)	Sabrina (Ibiza)
-	25 FEEL THE NEED IN ME	Shakin' Stevens (Epic)
18	26 WAP - BAM - BOOGIE/DON'T BLAME IT ON THAT GIRL	Matt Bianco (WEA)
19	27 TRIBUTE (RIGHT ON)	Pasadenas (CBS)
16	28 IN THE AIR TONIGHT '88	Phil Collins (Virgin)
-	29 WHAT CAN I SAY TO MAKE YOU LOVE ME	Alexander O'Neal (Tabu)
21	30 TOUGHER THAN THE REST	Bruce Springsteen (CBS)
23	31 NEVER TEAR US APART	INXS (Mercury)
50	32 I NEED YOU	B.V.S.M.P. (Debut)
33	33 IN MY DREAMS	Will Downing (Fourth & Broadway)
35	34 I'M TOO SCARED	Steven Dante (Cooltempo)
-	35 HOW SHE THREW IT ALL AWAY	Style Council (Polydor)
-	36 PEEK A BOO	Siouxsie & the Banshees (Wonderland)
30	37 WILD WORLD	Maxi Priest (10)
46	38 I'M SORRY	Hothouse Flowers (London)
27	39 MAYBE (WE SHOULD CALL IT A DAY)	Hazell Dean (EMI)
-	40 YE KE KE KE	Mory Kante (London)
41	41 A WISH AWAY	Wonder Stuff (Polydor)
-	42 I SAY NOTHING	Voice Of The Beehive (London)
44	43 ANYTHING FOR YOU	Gloria Estefan & the Miami Sound Machine (Epic)
49	44 IT'S NATURE'S WAY	Dollar (London)
25	45 THERE'S MORE TO LOVE	Communards (London)
-	46 MARTHA'S HARBOUR	All About Eve (Mercury)
38	47 BEATIN' THE HEAT	Jack 'n' Chill (10)
-	48 HUSTLE TO THE MUSIC	Funky Worm (Fon)
-	49 LIKE DREAMERS DO	Mica Paris featuring Courtney Pine (Fourth & Broadway)
-	50 HOLD ON TO WHAT YOU'VE GOT	Evelyn 'Champagne' King (Manhattan)

Hawaii-born Glenn Medeiros' chart-topper had been a major seller in the US and all over Continental Europe many months before it finally caught on in the UK. Persistent airplay, particularly around the ILR network in Britain, for whom this single was a laid-back godsend, laid the groundwork for its eventual success here. Salt'n'Pepa's disc, as a result of confused licensing deals, was released on two labels.

6 August 1988

last week	this week	title	artist
1	1	NOTHING'S GONNA CHANGE MY LOVE FOR YOU	Glenn Medeiros (London)
8	2	SUPERFLY GUY	S'Express (Rhythm King)
-	3	THE LOCO-MOTION	Kylie Minogue (PWL)
14	4	THE ONLY WAY IS UP	Yazz & the Plastic Population (Big Life)
3	5	I DON'T WANT TO TALK ABOUT IT	Everything But The Girl (blanco y negro)
4	6	I WANT YOUR LOVE	Transvision Vamp (MCA)
7	7	YOU CAME	Kim Wilde (MCA)
5	8	PUSH IT/TRAMP	Salt 'N' Pepa (Champion/ffrr)
2	9	DIRTY DIANA	Michael Jackson (Epic)
21	10	REACH OUT I'LL BE THERE	Four Tops (Motown)
10	11	ROSES ARE RED	Mac Band (MCA)
32	12	I NEED YOU	B.V.S.M.P. (Debut)
6	13	FOOLISH BEAT	Debbie Gibson (Atlantic)
11	14	LOVE BITES	Def Leppard (Bludgeon Riffola)
9	15	MONKEY	George Michael (Epic)
-	16	FIND MY LOVE	Fairground Attraction (RCA)
25	17	FEEL THE NEED IN ME	Shakin' Stevens (Epic)
48	18	HUSTLE TO THE MUSIC	Funky Worm (Fon)
13	19	THE TWIST (YO TWIST)	Fat Boys & Chubby Checker (Urban)
20	20	GLAM SLAM	Prince (Paisley Park)
36	21	PEEK A BOO	Siouxsie & the Banshees (Wonderland)
12	22	FAST CAR	Tracy Chapman (Elektra)
23	23	ALL FIRED UP	Pat Benatar (Chrysalis)
18	24	HEAT IT UP	Wee Papa Girl Rappers (Jive)
29	25	WHAT CAN I SAY TO MAKE YOU LOVE ME	Alexander O'Neal (Tabu)
26	26	I OWE YOU NOTHING	Bros (CBS)
42	27	I SAY NOTHING	Voice Of The Beehive (London)
46	28	MARTHA'S HARBOUR	All About Eve (Mercury)
15	29	TOMORROW PEOPLE	Ziggy Marley & the Makers (Virgin)
34	30	I'M TOO SCARED	Steven Dante (Cooltempo)
26	31	WAP - BAM - BOOGIE/DON'T BLAME IT ON THAT GIRL	Matt Bianco (WEA)
22	32	BREAKFAST IN BED	UB40 with Chrissie Hynde (DEP International)
49	33	LIKE DREAMERS DO	Mica Paris featuring Courtney Pine (Fourth & Broadway)
17	34	FIESTA	Pogues (Pogue Mahone)
24	35	BOYS (SUMMERTIME LOVE)	Sabrina (Ibiza)
40	36	YE KE KE KE	Mory Kante (London)
-	37	THE HARDER I TRY	Brother Beyond (Parlophone)
-	38	SOMEWHERE DOWN THE CRAZY RIVER	Robbie Robertson (Geffen)
19	39	CROSS MY HEART	Eighth Wonder (CBS)
-	40	HAPPY EVER AFTER	Julia Fordham (Circa)
27	41	TRIBUTE (RIGHT ON)	Pasadenas (CBS)
-	42	ROCK MY WORLD	Five Star (Tent)
43	43	ANYTHING FOR YOU	Gloria Estefan & the Miami Sound Machine (Epic)
-	44	LOVE IS THE GUN	Blue Mercedes (MCA)
-	45	AIN'T NO STOPPIN' US NOW (PARTY FOR THE WORLD)	Steve Walsh (A1)
50	46	HOLD ON TO WHAT YOU'VE GOT	Evelyn 'Champagne' King (Manhattan)
-	47	MANNISH BOY	Muddy Waters (Epic)
-	48	FEELINGS OF FOREVER	Tiffany (MCA)
41	49	A WISH AWAY	Wonder Stuff (Polydor)
-	50	I GOT YOU (I FEEL GOOD)/NOWHERE TO RUN	James Brown/Martha & the Vandellas (A&M)

13 August 1988

last week	this week	title	artist
4	1	THE ONLY WAY IS UP	Yazz & the Plastic Population (Big Life)
3	2	THE LOCO-MOTION	Kylie Minogue (PWL)
12	3	I NEED YOU	B.V.S.M.P. (Debut)
2	4	SUPERFLY GUY	S'Express (Rhythm King)
1	5	NOTHING'S GONNA CHANGE MY LOVE FOR YOU	Glenn Medeiros (London)
6	6	THE EVIL THAT MEN DO	Iron Maiden (EMI)
7	7	YOU CAME	Kim Wilde (MCA)
16	8	FIND MY LOVE	Fairground Attraction (RCA)
10	9	REACH OUT I'LL BE THERE	Four Tops (Motown)
18	10	HUSTLE TO THE MUSIC	Funky Worm (Fon)
8	11	PUSH IT/TRAMP	Salt 'N' Pepa (Champion/ffrr)
5	12	I DON'T WANT TO TALK ABOUT IT	Everything But The Girl (blanco y negro)
6	13	I WANT YOUR LOVE	Transvision Vamp (MCA)
11	14	ROSES ARE RED	Mac Band (MCA)
21	15	PEEK A BOO	Siouxsie & the Banshees (Wonderland)
28	16	MARTHA'S HARBOUR	All About Eve (Mercury)
9	17	DIRTY DIANA	Michael Jackson (Epic)
27	18	I SAY NOTHING	Voice Of The Beehive (London)
13	19	FOOLISH BEAT	Debbie Gibson (Atlantic)
33	20	LIKE DREAMERS DO	Mica Paris featuring Courtney Pine (Fourth & Broadway)
23	21	ALL FIRED UP	Pat Benatar (Chrysalis)
-	22	HANDS TO HEAVEN	Breathe (Siren)
14	23	LOVE BITES	Def Leppard (Bludgeon Riffola)
-	24	GOOD TRADITION	Tanita Tikaram (WEA)
25	25	WHAT CAN I SAY TO MAKE YOU LOVE ME	Alexander O'Neal (Tabu)
40	26	HAPPY EVER AFTER	Julia Fordham (Circa)
19	27	THE TWIST (YO TWIST)	Fat Boys & Chubby Checker (Urban)
15	28	MONKEY	George Michael (Epic)
17	29	FEEL THE NEED IN ME	Shakin' Stevens (Epic)
22	30	FAST CAR	Tracy Chapman (Elektra)
37	31	THE HARDER I TRY	Brother Beyond (Parlophone)
30	32	I'M TOO SCARED	Steven Dante (Cooltempo)
26	33	I OWE YOU NOTHING	Bros (CBS)
42	34	ROCK MY WORLD	Five Star (Tent)
-	35	WORKING IN A GOLDMINE	Aztec Camera (WEA)
31	36	WAP - BAM - BOOGIE/DON'T BLAME IT ON THAT GIRL	Matt Bianco (WEA)
38	37	SOMEWHERE DOWN THE CRAZY RIVER	Robbie Robertson (Geffen)
-	38	JIBARO	Electra (ffrr)
35	39	BOYS (SUMMERTIME LOVE)	Sabrina (Ibiza)
-	40	CHOCOLATE GIRL	Deacon Blue (CBS)
-	41	MY LOVE	Julio Iglesias featuring Stevie Wonder (CBS)
24	42	HEAT IT UP	Wee Papa Girl Rappers (Jive)
-	43	GYPSY ROAD	Cinderella (Vertigo)
-	44	WHEN IT'S LOVE	Van Halen (Warner Bros)
-	45	CATCH MY FALL	Billy Idol (Chrysalis)
48	46	FEELINGS OF FOREVER	Tiffany (MCA)
36	47	YE KE KE KE	Mory Kante (London)
32	48	BREAKFAST IN BED	UB40 with Chrissie Hynde (DEP International)
45	49	AIN'T NO STOPPIN' US NOW (PARTY FOR THE WORLD)	Steve Walsh (A1)
49	50	A WISH AWAY	Wonder Stuff (Polydor)

20 August 1988

last week	this week	title	artist
1	1	THE ONLY WAY IS UP	Yazz & the Plastic Population (Big Life)
2	2	THE LOCO-MOTION	Kylie Minogue (PWL)
3	3	I NEED YOU	B.V.S.M.P. (Debut)
6	4	THE EVIL THAT MEN DO	Iron Maiden (EMI)
4	5	SUPERFLY GUY	S'Express (Rhythm King)
8	6	FIND MY LOVE	Fairground Attraction (RCA)
22	7	HANDS TO HEAVEN	Breathe (Siren)
7	8	YOU CAME	Kim Wilde (MCA)
9	9	REACH OUT I'LL BE THERE	Four Tops (Motown)
5	10	NOTHING'S GONNA CHANGE MY LOVE FOR YOU	Glenn Medeiros (London)
10	11	HUSTLE TO THE MUSIC	Funky Worm (Fon)
16	12	MARTHA'S HARBOUR	All About Eve (Mercury)
24	13	GOOD TRADITION	Tanita Tikaram (WEA)
41	14	MY LOVE	Julio Iglesias featuring Stevie Wonder (CBS)
11	15	PUSH IT/TRAMP	Salt 'N' Pepa (Champion/ffrr)
31	16	THE HARDER I TRY	Brother Beyond (Parlophone)
20	17	LIKE DREAMERS DO	Mica Paris featuring Courtney Pine (Fourth & Broadway)
18	18	I SAY NOTHING	Voice Of The Beehive (London)
13	19	I WANT YOUR LOVE	Transvision Vamp (MCA)
12	20	I DON'T WANT TO TALK ABOUT IT	Everything But The Girl (blanco y negro)
26	21	HAPPY EVER AFTER	Julia Fordham (Circa)
-	22	ON THE BEACH SUMMER '88	Chris Rea (WEA)
14	23	ROSES ARE RED	Mac Band (MCA)
21	24	ALL FIRED UP	Pat Benatar (Chrysalis)
15	25	PEEK A BOO	Siouxsie & the Banshees (Wonderland)
35	26	WORKING IN A GOLDMINE	Aztec Camera (WEA)
34	27	ROCK MY WORLD	Five Star (Tent)
17	28	DIRTY DIANA	Michael Jackson (Epic)
44	29	WHEN IT'S LOVE	Van Halen (Warner Bros)
-	30	RUSH HOUR	Jane Wiedlin (Manhattan)
-	31	SOMEWHERE DOWN THE CRAZY RIVER	Robbie Robertson (Geffen)
19	32	FOOLISH BEAT	Debbie Gibson (Atlantic)
-	33	KING OF EMOTION	Big Country (Mercury)
47	34	YE KE KE KE	Mory Kante (London)
-	35	SOLDIER OF LOVE	Donny Osmond (Virgin)
23	36	LOVE BITES	Def Leppard (Bludgeon Riffola)
-	37	SWEET CHILD OF MINE	Guns N' Roses (Geffen)
40	38	CHOCOLATE GIRL	Deacon Blue (CBS)
27	39	THE TWIST (YO TWIST)	Fat Boys & Chubby Checker (Urban)
45	40	CATCH MY FALL	Billy Idol (Chrysalis)
36	41	WAP - BAM - BOOGIE/DON'T BLAME IT ON THAT GIRL	Matt Bianco (WEA)
-	42	DON'T BE CRUEL	Bobby Brown (MCA)
38	43	JIBARO	Electra (ffrr)
-	44	I WON'T BLEED FOR YOU	Climie Fisher (EMI)
-	45	TEARDROPS	Womack & Womack (Fourth & Broadway)
25	46	WHAT CAN I SAY TO MAKE YOU LOVE ME	Alexander O'Neal (Tabu)
-	47	ANYTHING FOR YOU	Gloria Estefan & the Miami Sound Machine (Epic)
-	48	BLIND	Talking Heads (EMI)
30	49	FAST CAR	Tracy Chapman (Elektra)
-	50	LOVE IS THE GUN	Blue Mercedes (MCA)

Kylie Minogue's revival of Little Eva's 1962 smash *The Loco-Motion*, a revamped version of a single which Kylie had previously cut in Australia before her work with Stock/Aitken/Waterman in London, was one of the highest first-week entry, at Number Three, but nevertheless peaked at Two, just as the original had. It was Kylie's only Top 10 hit in America, where it also climbed to Number Two.

August – September 1988

27 August 1988

last	this	title	artist
1	1	THE ONLY WAY IS UP	Yazz & the Plastic Population (Big Life)
3	2	I NEED YOU	B.V.S.M.P. (Debut)
7	3	HANDS TO HEAVEN	Breathe (Siren)
2	4	THE LOCO-MOTION	Kylie Minogue (PWL)
16	5	THE HARDER I TRY	Brother Beyond (Parlophone)
6	6	FIND MY LOVE	Fairground Attraction (RCA)
14	7	MY LOVE	Julio Iglesias featuring Stevie Wonder (CBS)
4	8	THE EVIL THAT MEN DO	Iron Maiden (EMI)
8	9	YOU CAME	Kim Wilde (MCA)
13	10	GOOD TRADITION	Tanita Tikaram (WEA)
12	11	MARTHA'S HARBOUR	All About Eve (Mercury)
22	12	ON THE BEACH SUMMER '88	Chris Rea (WEA)
5	13	SUPERFLY GUY	S'Express (Rhythm King)
11	14	HUSTLE TO THE MUSIC	Funky Worm (Fon)
9	15	REACH OUT I'LL BE THERE	Four Tops (Motown)
33	16	KING OF EMOTION	Big Country (Mercury)
31	17	SOMEWHERE DOWN THE CRAZY RIVER	Robbie Robertson (Geffen)
10	18	NOTHING'S GONNA CHANGE MY LOVE FOR YOU	Glenn Medeiros (London)
-	19	RUNNING ALL OVER THE WORLD	Status Quo (Vertigo)
37	20	SWEET CHILD OF MINE	Guns N' Roses (Geffen)
47	21	ANYTHING FOR YOU	Gloria Estefan & the Miami Sound Machine (Epic)
29	22	WHEN IT'S LOVE	Van Halen (Warner Bros)
-	23	DON'T MAKE ME WAIT/MEGABLAST	Bomb The Bass (Mister-ron)
15	24	PUSH IT/TRAMP	Salt 'N' Pepa (Champion/ffrr)
25	25	YE KE KE KE	Mory Kante (London)
23	26	ROSES ARE RED	Mac Band (MCA)
45	27	TEARDROPS	Womack & Womack (Fourth & Broadway)
26	28	WORKING IN A GOLDMINE	Aztec Camera (WEA)
30	29	RUSH HOUR	Jane Wiedlin (Manhattan)
-	30	JUMP START	Natalie Cole (Manhattan)
19	31	I WANT YOUR LOVE	Transvision Vamp (MCA)
-	32	SUPERSTITIOUS	Europe (Epic)
17	33	LIKE DREAMERS DO	Mica Paris featuring Courtney Pine (Fourth & Broadway)
44	34	I WON'T BLEED FOR YOU	Climie Fisher (EMI)
18	35	I SAY NOTHING	Voice Of The Beehive (London)
42	36	DON'T BE CRUEL	Bobby Brown (MCA)
35	37	SOLDIER OF LOVE	Donny Osmond (Virgin)
20	38	I DON'T WANT TO TALK ABOUT IT	Everything But The Girl (blanco y negro)
-	39	EVERY GIRL AND BOY	Spagna (CBS)
-	40	EASY	Commodores (Motown)
-	41	WHERE DID I GO WRONG	UB40 (DEP International)
-	42	THE RACE	Yello (Mercury)
21	43	HAPPY EVER AFTER	Julia Fordham (Circa)
-	44	TOUCHY	A-ha (Warner Bros)
24	45	ALL FIRED UP	Pat Benatar (Chrysalis)
-	46	COMING BACK FOR MORE	Richard Darbyshire (Chrysalis)
32	47	FOOLISH BEAT	Debbie Gibson (Atlantic)
-	48	I HATE MYSELF FOR LOVING YOU	Joan Jett and the Blackhearts (London)
41	49	WAP - BAM - BOOGIE/DON'T BLAME IT ON THAT GIRL	Matt Bianco (WEA)
-	50	FOREVER YOUNG	Rod Stewart (Warner Bros)

3 September 1988

last	this	title	artist
1	1	THE ONLY WAY IS UP	Yazz & the Plastic Population (Big Life)
5	2	THE HARDER I TRY	Brother Beyond (Parlophone)
7	3	MY LOVE	Julio Iglesias featuring Stevie Wonder (CBS)
3	4	HANDS TO HEAVEN	Breathe (Siren)
4	5	THE LOCO-MOTION	Kylie Minogue (PWL)
6	6	FIND MY LOVE	Fairground Attraction (RCA)
2	7	I NEED YOU	B.V.S.M.P. (Debut)
23	8	DON'T MAKE ME WAIT/MEGABLAST	Bomb The Bass (Mister-ron)
10	9	GOOD TRADITION	Tanita Tikaram (WEA)
12	10	ON THE BEACH SUMMER '88	Chris Rea (WEA)
17	11	SOMEWHERE DOWN THE CRAZY RIVER	Robbie Robertson (Geffen)
27	12	TEARDROPS	Womack & Womack (Fourth & Broadway)
16	13	KING OF EMOTION	Big Country (Mercury)
42	14	THE RACE	Yello (Mercury)
44	15	TOUCHY	A-ha (Warner Bros)
20	16	SWEET CHILD OF MINE	Guns N' Roses (Geffen)
9	17	YOU CAME	Kim Wilde (MCA)
19	18	RUNNING ALL OVER THE WORLD	Status Quo (Vertigo)
-	19	A GROOVY KIND OF LOVE	Phil Collins (Virgin)
21	20	ANYTHING FOR YOU	Gloria Estefan & the Miami Sound Machine (Epic)
29	21	RUSH HOUR	Jane Wiedlin (Manhattan)
8	22	THE EVIL THAT MEN DO	Iron Maiden (EMI)
25	23	YE KE KE KE	Mory Kante (London)
13	24	SUPERFLY GUY	S'Express (Rhythm King)
11	25	MARTHA'S HARBOUR	All About Eve (Mercury)
39	26	EVERY GIRL AND BOY	Spagna (CBS)
-	27	HARVESTER OF SORROW	Metallica (Vertigo)
32	28	SUPERSTITIOUS	Europe (Epic)
14	29	HUSTLE TO THE MUSIC	Funky Worm (Fon)
37	30	SOLDIER OF LOVE	Donny Osmond (Virgin)
15	31	REACH OUT I'LL BE THERE	Four Tops (Motown)
22	32	WHEN IT'S LOVE	Van Halen (Warner Bros)
34	33	I WON'T BLEED FOR YOU	Climie Fisher (EMI)
41	34	WHERE DID I GO WRONG	UB40 (DEP International)
30	35	JUMP START	Natalie Cole (Manhattan)
-	36	I'M GONNA BE (500 MILES)	Proclaimers (Chrysalis)
-	37	HE AIN'T HEAVY HE'S MY BROTHER	Bill Medley (Scotti Brothers)
-	38	HEAVEN IN MY HANDS	Level 42 (Polydor)
40	39	EASY	Commodores (Motown)
-	40	WAY BEHIND	Primitives (Lazy)
36	41	DON'T BE CRUEL	Bobby Brown (MCA)
46	42	COMING BACK FOR MORE	Jellybean featuring Richard Darbyshire (Chrysalis)
-	43	SHAKE YOUR THANG	Salt 'N' Pepa (ffrr)
18	44	NOTHING'S GONNA CHANGE MY LOVE FOR YOU	Glenn Medeiros (London)
48	45	I HATE MYSELF FOR LOVING YOU	Joan Jett and the Blackhearts (London)
24	46	PUSH IT/TRAMP	Salt 'N' Pepa (Champion/ffrr)
-	47	HE AIN'T HEAVY HE'S MY BROTHER	Hollies (EMI)
26	48	ROSES ARE RED	Mac Band (MCA)
28	49	WORKING IN A GOLDMINE	Aztec Camera (WEA)
-	50	LET'S DO IT AGAIN	George Benson (Warner Bros)

10 September 1988

last	this	title	artist
1	1	THE ONLY WAY IS UP	Yazz & the Plastic Population (Big Life)
2	2	THE HARDER I TRY	Brother Beyond (Parlophone)
19	3	A GROOVY KIND OF LOVE	Phil Collins (Virgin)
12	4	TEARDROPS	Womack & Womack (Fourth & Broadway)
8	5	DON'T MAKE ME WAIT/MEGABLAST	Bomb The Bass (Mister-ron)
14	6	THE RACE	Yello (Mercury)
3	7	MY LOVE	Julio Iglesias featuring Stevie Wonder (CBS)
4	8	HANDS TO HEAVEN	Breathe (Siren)
47	9	HE AIN'T HEAVY HE'S MY BROTHER	Hollies (EMI)
38	10	HEAVEN IN MY HANDS	Level 42 (Polydor)
5	11	THE LOCO-MOTION	Kylie Minogue (PWL)
21	12	RUSH HOUR	Jane Wiedlin (Manhattan)
15	13	TOUCHY	A-ha (Warner Bros)
7	14	I NEED YOU	B.V.S.M.P. (Debut)
27	15	HARVESTER OF SORROW	Metallica (Vertigo)
20	16	ANYTHING FOR YOU	Gloria Estefan & the Miami Sound Machine (Epic)
9	17	GOOD TRADITION	Tanita Tikaram (WEA)
6	18	FIND MY LOVE	Fairground Attraction (RCA)
-	19	TEARS RUN RINGS	Marc Almond (Parlophone)
26	20	EVERY GIRL AND BOY	Spagna (CBS)
11	21	SOMEWHERE DOWN THE CRAZY RIVER	Robbie Robertson (Geffen)
18	22	RUNNING ALL OVER THE WORLD	Status Quo (Vertigo)
37	23	HE AIN'T HEAVY HE'S MY BROTHER	Bill Medley (Scotti Brothers)
13	24	KING OF EMOTION	Big Country (Mercury)
30	25	SOLDIER OF LOVE	Donny Osmond (Virgin)
10	26	ON THE BEACH SUMMER '88	Chris Rea (WEA)
-	27	ANOTHER PART OF ME	Michael Jackson (Epic)
36	28	I'M GONNA BE (500 MILES)	Proclaimers (Chrysalis)
29	29	WAY BEHIND	Primitives (Lazy)
16	30	SWEET CHILD OF MINE	Guns N' Roses (Geffen)
31	31	YOU CAME	Kim Wilde (MCA)
-	32	BIG FUN	Inner City featuring Kevin Saunderson (10)
34	33	WHERE DID I GO WRONG	UB40 (DEP International)
39	34	EASY	Commodores (Motown)
-	35	MAKE ME LAUGH	Anthrax (Island)
-	36	LOVELY DAY	Bill Withers (CBS)
35	37	JUMP START	Natalie Cole (Manhattan)
-	38	STOP THIS CRAZY THING	Junior Reid & the Coldcut Orchestra (Ahead Of Our Time)
43	39	SHAKE YOUR THANG	Salt 'N' Pepa (ffrr)
24	40	SUPERFLY GUY	S'Express (Rhythm King)
22	41	THE EVIL THAT MEN DO	Iron Maiden (EMI)
28	42	SUPERSTITIOUS	Europe (Epic)
-	43	RAW	Spandau Ballet (CBS)
23	44	YE KE KE KE	Mory Kante (London)
29	45	HUSTLE TO THE MUSIC	Funky Worm (Fon)
-	46	ANSWERS TO NOTHING	Midge Ure (Chrysalis)
-	47	LONG AND LASTING LOVE	Glenn Medeiros (London)
50	48	LET'S DO IT AGAIN	George Benson (Warner Bros)
-	49	TALKIN' 'BOUT A REVOLUTION	Tracy Chapman (Elektra)
25	50	MARTHA'S HARBOUR	All About Eve (Mercury)

In much the same way as Tears For Fears had previously revamped a hit into "running" mode for a charity single, so Status Quo returned to their 1977 hit and recut it as *Running All Over The World*. Although the new version had but a fraction of the chart success of its original, its earnings still made valuable contributions to the Band Aid coffers. Chris Rea, meanwhile, also recut his own *On The Beach*.

September – October 1988

17 September 1988

last week	this week	Title	Artist
9	1	HE AIN'T HEAVY HE'S MY BROTHER	Hollies (EMI)
3	2	A GROOVY KIND OF LOVE	Phil Collins (Virgin)
4	3	TEARDROPS	Womack & Womack (Fourth & Broadway)
6	4	THE RACE	Yello (Mercury)
1	5	THE ONLY WAY IS UP	Yazz & the Plastic Population (Big Life)
2	6	THE HARDER I TRY	Brother Beyond (Parlophone)
36	7	LOVELY DAY	Bill Withers (CBS)
-	8	I QUIT	Bros (CBS)
5	9	DON'T MAKE ME WAIT/MEGABLAST	Bomb The Bass (Mister-ron)
10	10	HEAVEN IN MY HANDS	Level 42 (Polydor)
27	11	ANOTHER PART OF ME	Michael Jackson (Epic)
12	12	RUSH HOUR	Jane Wiedlin (Manhattan)
7	13	MY LOVE	Julio Iglesias featuring Stevie Wonder (CBS)
13	14	TOUCHY	George Benson (Warner Bros)
34	15	EASY	Commodores (Motown)
8	16	HANDS TO HEAVEN	Breathe (Siren)
19	17	TEARS RUN RINGS	Marc Almond (Parlophone)
32	18	BIG FUN	Inner City featuring Kevin Saunderson (Epic)
16	19	ANYTHING FOR YOU	Gloria Estefan & the Miami Sound Machine (Epic)
-	20	NOTHING CAN DIVIDE US	Jason Donovan (PWL)
23	21	HE AIN'T HEAVY HE'S MY BROTHER	Bill Medley (Scotti Brothers)
38	22	STOP THIS CRAZY THING	Coldcut featuring Junior Reid & the Coldcut Orchestra (Ahead Of Our Time)
35	23	MAKE ME LAUGH	Anthrax (Island)
28	24	I'M GONNA BE (500 MILES)	Proclaimers (Chrysalis)
11	25	THE LOCO-MOTION	Kylie Minogue (PWL)
20	26	EVERY GIRL AND BOY	Spagna (CBS)
14	27	I NEED YOU	B.V.S.M.P. (Debut)
17	28	GOOD TRADITION	Tanita Tikaram (WEA)
39	29	SHAKE YOUR THANG	Salt 'N' Pepa (ffrr)
18	30	FIND MY LOVE	Fairground Attraction (RCA)
15	31	HARVEST OF SORROW	Metallica (Vertigo)
30	32	SWEET CHILD OF MINE	Guns N' Roses (Geffen)
33	33	WHERE DID I GO WRONG	UB40 (DEP International)
-	34	RIDING ON A TRAIN	Pasadenas (CBS)
22	35	RUNNING ALL OVER THE WORLD	Status Quo (Vertigo)
21	36	SOMEWHERE DOWN THE CRAZY RIVER	Robbie Robertson (Geffen)
31	37	YOU CAME	Kim Wilde (MCA)
-	38	HEY JUDE	Beatles (Apple)
37	39	JUMP START	Natalie Cole (Manhattan)
-	40	STALEMATE	Mac Band (MCA)
25	41	SOLDIER OF LOVE	Donny Osmond (Virgin)
-	42	I HATE MYSELF FOR LOVING YOU	Joan Jett & the Blackhearts (London)
29	43	WAY BEHIND	Primitives (Lazy)
-	44	WORLD WITHOUT YOU	Belinda Carlisle (Virgin)
43	45	RAW	Spandau Ballet (CBS)
24	46	KING OF EMOTION	Big Country (Mercury)
40	47	SUPERFLY GUY	S'Express (Rhythm King)
-	48	CAN YOU PARTY	Royal House (Champion)
-	49	TURN ON THE NIGHT	Kiss (Vertigo)
-	50	GITTIN' FUNKY	Kid 'n' Play (Cooltempo)

24 September 1988

last week	this week	Title	Artist
1	1	HE AIN'T HEAVY HE'S MY BROTHER	Hollies (EMI)
2	2	A GROOVY KIND OF LOVE	Phil Collins (Virgin)
8	3	I QUIT	Bros (CBS)
7	4	LOVELY DAY	Bill Withers (CBS)
3	5	TEARDROPS	Womack & Womack (Fourth & Broadway)
20	6	NOTHING CAN DIVIDE US	Jason Donovan (PWL)
-	7	DOMINO DANCING	Pet Shop Boys (Parlophone)
4	8	THE RACE	Yello (Mercury)
6	9	THE HARDER I TRY	Brother Beyond (Parlophone)
15	10	EASY	Commodores (Motown)
19	11	ANYTHING FOR YOU	Gloria Estefan & the Miami Sound Machine (Epic)
5	12	THE ONLY WAY IS UP	Yazz & the Plastic Population (Big Life)
18	13	BIG FUN	Inner City featuring Kevin Saunderson (10)
24	14	I'M GONNA BE (500 MILES)	Proclaimers (Chrysalis)
34	15	RIDING ON A TRAIN	Pasadenas (CBS)
9	16	DON'T MAKE ME WAIT	Bomb The Bass (Mister-ron)
11	17	ANOTHER PART OF ME	Michael Jackson (Epic)
22	18	STOP THIS CRAZY THING	Coldcut featuring Junior Reid & the Coldcut Orchestra (Ahead Of Our Time)
12	19	RUSH HOUR	Jane Wiedlin (Manhattan)
29	20	SHAKE YOUR THANG	Salt 'N' Pepa (ffrr)
21	21	SHE WANTS TO DANCE WITH ME	Rick Astley (RCA)
-	22	BAD MEDICINE	Bon Jovi (Vertigo)
13	23	MY LOVE	Julio Iglesias featuring Stevie Wonder (CBS)
16	24	HANDS TO HEAVEN	Breathe (Siren)
-	25	ONE MOMENT IN TIME	Whitney Houston (Arista)
10	26	HEAVEN IN MY HANDS	Level 42 (Polydor)
17	27	TEARS RUN RINGS	Marc Almond (Parlophone)
44	28	WORLD WITHOUT YOU	Belinda Carlisle (Virgin)
-	29	BURN IT UP	Beatmasters featuring P.P. Arnold (Rhythm King)
21	30	HE AIN'T HEAVY HE'S MY BROTHER	Bill Medley (Scotti Brothers)
14	31	TOUCHY	A-ha (Warner Bros)
-	32	REVOLUTION BABY	Transvision Vamp (MCA)
26	33	EVERY GIRL AND BOY	Spagna (CBS)
27	34	I NEED YOU	B.V.S.M.P. (Debut)
25	35	THE LOCO-MOTION	Kylie Minogue (PWL)
40	36	STALEMATE	Mac Band (MCA)
-	37	FAKE '88	Alexander O'Neal (Tabu)
28	38	GOOD TRADITION	Tanita Tikaram (WEA)
43	39	WAY BEHIND	Primitives (Lazy)
-	40	LOVE TRUTH AND HONESTY	Bananarama (London)
41	41	TURN ON THE NIGHT	Kiss (Vertigo)
42	42	I HATE MYSELF FOR LOVING YOU	Joan Jett & the Blackhearts (London)
48	43	CAN YOU PARTY	Royal House (Champion)
30	44	FIND MY LOVE	Fairground Attraction (RCA)
-	45	HEART OF GLASS	Associates (WEA)
35	46	RUNNING ALL OVER THE WORLD	Status Quo (Vertigo)
47	47	SPARE PARTS	Bruce Springsteen (CBS)
50	48	GITTIN' FUNKY	Kid 'n' Play (Cooltempo)
-	49	IN THE NAME OF LOVE	Swan Lake (Champion)
-	50	TURN IT INTO LOVE	Hazell Dean (EMI)

1 October 1988

last week	this week	Title	Artist
1	1	HE AIN'T HEAVY HE'S MY BROTHER	Hollies (EMI)
4	2	LOVELY DAY	Bill Withers (CBS)
2	3	A GROOVY KIND OF LOVE	Phil Collins (Virgin)
-	4	DESIRE	U2 (Island)
7	5	DOMINO DANCING	Pet Shop Boys (Parlophone)
6	6	NOTHING CAN DIVIDE US	Jason Donovan (PWL)
5	7	TEARDROPS	Womack & Womack (Fourth & Broadway)
13	8	BIG FUN	Inner City featuring Kevin Saunderson (10)
21	9	SHE WANTS TO DANCE WITH ME	Rick Astley (RCA)
8	10	THE RACE	Yello (Mercury)
3	11	I QUIT	Bros (CBS)
15	12	RIDING ON A TRAIN	Pasadenas (CBS)
25	13	ONE MOMENT IN TIME	Whitney Houston (Arista)
22	14	BAD MEDICINE	Bon Jovi (Vertigo)
11	15	ANYTHING FOR YOU	Gloria Estefan & the Miami Sound Machine (Epic)
12	16	THE ONLY WAY IS UP	Yazz & the Plastic Population (Big Life)
18	17	STOP THIS CRAZY THING	Coldcut featuring Junior Reid & the Coldcut Orchestra (Ahead Of Our Time)
14	18	I'M GONNA BE (500 MILES)	Proclaimers (Chrysalis)
10	19	EASY	Commodores (Motown)
20	20	SHAKE YOUR THANG	Salt 'N' Pepa (ffrr)
40	21	LOVE TRUTH AND HONESTY	Bananarama (London)
9	22	THE HARDER I TRY	Brother Beyond (Parlophone)
37	23	FAKE '88	Alexander O'Neal (Tabu)
16	24	DON'T MAKE ME WAIT/MEGABLAST	Bomb The Bass (Mister-ron)
28	25	WORLD WITHOUT YOU	Belinda Carlisle (Virgin)
50	26	TURN IT INTO LOVE	Hazell Dean (EMI)
29	27	BURN IT UP	Beatmasters featuring P.P. Arnold (Rhythm King)
32	28	REVOLUTION BABY	Transvision Vamp (MCA)
17	29	ANOTHER PART OF ME	Michael Jackson (Epic)
47	30	SPARE PARTS	Bruce Springsteen (CBS)
19	31	RUSH HOUR	Jane Wiedlin (Manhattan)
-	32	IT'S YER MONEY I'M AFTER BABY	Wonder Stuff (Polydor)
-	33	I DON'T BELIEVE IN MIRACLES	Sinitta (Fanfare)
-	34	A LITTLE RESPECT	Erasure (Mute)
23	35	MY LOVE	Julio Iglesias featuring Stevie Wonder (CBS)
-	36	SECRET GARDEN	T'Pau (Siren)
24	37	HANDS TO HEAVEN	Breathe (Siren)
33	38	EVERY GIRL AND BOY	Spagna (CBS)
-	39	I DON'T WANT YOUR LOVE	Duran Duran (EMI)
27	40	TEARS RUN RINGS	Marc Almond (Parlophone)
43	41	CAN YOU PARTY	Royal House (Champion)
34	42	I NEED YOU	B.V.S.M.P. (Debut)
-	43	SO IN LOVE WITH YOU	Spear Of Destiny (Virgin)
-	44	DON'T WORRY BE HAPPY	Bobby McFerrin (Manhattan)
35	45	THE LOCO-MOTION	Kylie Minogue (PWL)
-	46	WEE RULE	Wee Papa Girl Rappers (Jive)
36	47	STALEMATE	Mac Band (MCA)
-	48	INDESTRUCTIBLE	Four Tops featuring Smokey Robinson (Arista)
49	49	ALL OF ME	Sabrina (PWL)
30	50	HE AIN'T HEAVY HE'S MY BROTHER	Bill Medley (Scotti Brothers)

When the Hollies' 1969 hit *He Ain't Heavy He's My Brother* was reissued to compete with the new recording of the song by Bill Medley (cut for the film *Rambo III*), it could not have been expected to tear the chart apart. However, despite the strong competition from Medley, the group's original soared to Number One, holding down Phil Collins' revival of *A Groovy Kind Of Love* (from *Buster*) in doing so.

489

October 1988

8 October 1988

last week	this week	Title	Artist
4	1	DESIRE	U2 (Island)
1	2	HE AIN'T HEAVY HE'S MY BROTHER	Hollies (EMI)
13	3	ONE MOMENT IN TIME	Whitney Houston (Arista)
5	4	DOMINO DANCING	Pet Shop Boys (Parlophone)
3	5	A GROOVY KIND OF LOVE	Phil Collins (Virgin)
2	6	LOVELY DAY	Bill Withers (CBS)
44	7	DON'T WORRY BE HAPPY	Bobby McFerrin (Manhattan)
9	8	SHE WANTS TO DANCE WITH ME	Rick Astley (RCA)
8	9	BIG FUN	Inner City featuring Kevin Saunderson (10)
34	10	A LITTLE RESPECT	Erasure (Mute)
7	11	TEARDROPS	Womack & Womack (Fourth & Broadway)
12	12	RIDING ON A TRAIN	Pasadenas (CBS)
6	13	NOTHING CAN DIVIDE US	Jason Donovan (PWL)
39	14	I DON'T WANT YOUR LOVE	Duran Duran (EMI)
23	15	FAKE '88	Alexander O'Neal (Tabu)
10	16	THE RACE	Yello (Mercury)
21	17	LOVE TRUTH AND HONESTY	Bananarama (London)
14	18	BAD MEDICINE	Bon Jovi (Vertigo)
19	19	I'M GONNA BE (500 MILES)	Proclaimers (Chrysalis)
46	20	WEE RULE	Wee Papa Girl Rappers (Jive)
11	21	I QUIT	Bros (CBS)
16	22	THE ONLY WAY IS UP	Yazz & the Plastic Population (Big Life)
15	23	ANYTHING FOR YOU	Gloria Estefan & the Miami Sound Machine (Epic)
26	24	TURN IT INTO LOVE	Hazell Dean (EMI)
19	25	EASY	Commodores (Motown)
27	26	BURN IT UP	Beatmasters featuring P.P. Arnold (Rhythm King)
20	27	SHAKE YOUR THANG	Salt 'N' Pepa (ffrr)
36	28	SECRET GARDEN	T'Pau (Siren)
28	29	REVOLUTION BABY	Transvision Vamp (MCA)
33	30	I DON'T BELIEVE IN MIRACLES	Sinitta (Fanfare)
17	31	STOP THIS CRAZY THING	Coldcut featuring Junior Reid & the Coldcut Orchestra (Ahead Of Our Time)
22	32	THE HARDER I TRY	Brother Beyond (Parlophone)
30	33	SPARE PARTS	Bruce Springsteen (CBS)
24	34	DON'T MAKE ME WAIT/MEGABLAST	Bomb The Bass (Mister-ron)
49	35	ALL OF ME	Sabrina (PWL)
25	36	WORLD WITHOUT YOU	Belinda Carlisle (Virgin)
31	37	RUSH HOUR	Jane Wiedlin (Manhattan)
-	38	NEVER TRUST A STRANGER	Kim Wilde (MCA)
-	39	ANY LOVE	Luther Vandross (Epic)
-	40	NEW ANGER	Gary Numan (Illegal)
-	41	DON'T WALK AWAY	Pat Benatar (Chrysalis)
-	42	WHY ARE YOU BEING SO REASONABLE NOW	Wedding Present (Reception)
29	43	ANOTHER PART OF ME	Michael Jackson (Epic)
43	44	SO IN LOVE WITH YOU	Spear Of Destiny (Virgin)
35	45	MY LOVE	Julio Iglesias featuring Stevie Wonder (CBS)
-	46	CHARLOTTE ANNE	Julian Cope (Island)
-	47	KILLING JAR	Siouxsie & the Banshees (Wonderland)
32	48	IT'S YER MONEY I'M AFTER BABY	Wonder Stuff (Polydor)
-	49	FREE	Will Downing (Fourth & Broadway)
-	50	GIVING YOU THE BEST THAT I GOT	Anita Baker (Elektra)

15 October 1988

last week	this week	Title	Artist
1	1	DESIRE	U2 (Island)
3	2	ONE MOMENT IN TIME	Whitney Houston (Arista)
7	3	DON'T WORRY BE HAPPY	Bobby McFerrin (Manhattan)
2	4	HE AIN'T HEAVY HE'S MY BROTHER	Hollies (EMI)
8	5	SHE WANTS TO DANCE WITH ME	Rick Astley (RCA)
10	6	A LITTLE RESPECT	Erasure (Mute)
5	7	A GROOVY KIND OF LOVE	Phil Collins (Virgin)
4	8	DOMINO DANCING	Pet Shop Boys (Parlophone)
20	9	WEE RULE	Wee Papa Girl Rappers (Jive)
9	10	BIG FUN	Inner City featuring Kevin Saunderson (10)
14	11	I DON'T WANT YOUR LOVE	Duran Duran (EMI)
15	12	FAKE '88	Alexander O'Neal (Tabu)
11	13	TEARDROPS	Womack & Womack (Fourth & Broadway)
6	14	LOVELY DAY	Bill Withers (CBS)
12	15	RIDING ON A TRAIN	Pasadenas (CBS)
13	16	NOTHING CAN DIVIDE US	Jason Donovan (PWL)
17	17	LOVE TRUTH AND HONESTY	Bananarama (London)
28	18	SECRET GARDEN	T'Pau (Siren)
24	19	TURN IT INTO LOVE	Hazell Dean (EMI)
30	20	I DON'T BELIEVE IN MIRACLES	Sinitta (Fanfare)
18	21	BAD MEDICINE	Bon Jovi (Vertigo)
26	22	BURN IT UP	Beatmasters featuring P.P. Arnold (Rhythm King)
16	23	THE RACE	Yello (Mercury)
38	24	NEVER TRUST A STRANGER	Kim Wilde (MCA)
19	25	I'M GONNA BE (500 MILES)	Proclaimers (Chrysalis)
-	26	HARVEST FOR THE WORLD	Christians (Island)
22	27	THE ONLY WAY IS UP	Yazz & the Plastic Population (Big Life)
35	28	ALL OF ME	Sabrina (PWL)
23	29	ANYTHING FOR YOU	Gloria Estefan & the Miami Sound Machine (Epic)
44	30	SO IN LOVE WITH YOU	Spear Of Destiny (Virgin)
21	31	I QUIT	Bros (CBS)
46	32	CHARLOTTE ANNE	Julian Cope (Island)
39	33	ANY LOVE	Luther Vandross (Epic)
25	34	EASY	Commodores (Motown)
47	35	KILLING JAR	Siouxsie & the Banshees (Wonderland)
29	36	REVOLUTION BABY	Transvision Vamp (MCA)
27	37	SHAKE YOUR THANG	Salt 'N' Pepa (ffrr)
34	38	DON'T MAKE ME WAIT/MEGABLAST	Bomb The Bass (Mister-ron)
41	39	DON'T WALK AWAY	Pat Benatar (Chrysalis)
32	40	THE HARDER I TRY	Brother Beyond (Parlophone)
-	41	GET REAL	Paul Rutherford (Fourth & Broadway)
-	42	WE CALL IT ACIEED	D Mob (ffrr)
50	43	GIVING YOU THE BEST THAT I GOT	Anita Baker (Elektra)
37	44	RUSH HOUR	Jane Wiedlin (Manhattan)
-	45	O-O-O	Adrenalin (MCA)
31	46	STOP THIS CRAZY THING	Coldcut featuring Junior Reid & the Coldcut Orchestra (Ahead Of Our Time)
-	47	ACID MAN	Jolly Roger (10)
-	48	HOW MANY TEARS CAN I HIDE	Shakin' Stevens (Epic)
-	49	THE BIG ONE	Black (A&M)
-	50	BURST	Darling Buds (Epic)

22 October 1988

last week	this week	Title	Artist
2	1	ONE MOMENT IN TIME	Whitney Houston (Arista)
3	2	DON'T WORRY BE HAPPY	Bobby McFerrin (Manhattan)
9	3	WEE RULE	Wee Papa Girl Rappers (Jive)
6	4	A LITTLE RESPECT	Erasure (Mute)
1	5	DESIRE	U2 (Island)
42	6	WE CALL IT ACIEED	D Mob (ffrr)
5	7	SHE WANTS TO DANCE WITH ME	Rick Astley (RCA)
22	8	BURN IT UP	Beatmasters featuring P.P. Arnold (Rhythm King)
26	9	HARVEST FOR THE WORLD	Christians (Island)
-	10	ORINOCO FLOW (SAIL AWAY)	Enya (WEA)
4	11	HE AIN'T HEAVY HE'S MY BROTHER	Hollies (EMI)
24	12	NEVER TRUST A STRANGER	Kim Wilde (MCA)
7	13	A GROOVY KIND OF LOVE	Phil Collins (Virgin)
13	14	TEARDROPS	Womack & Womack (Fourth & Broadway)
10	15	BIG FUN	Inner City featuring Kevin Saunderson (10)
17	16	LOVE TRUTH AND HONESTY	Bananarama (London)
18	17	SECRET GARDEN	T'Pau (Siren)
8	18	DOMINO DANCING	Pet Shop Boys (Parlophone)
-	19	JE NE SAIS PAS POURQUOI	Kylie Minogue (PWL)
20	20	I DON'T BELIEVE IN MIRACLES	Sinitta (Fanfare)
15	21	RIDING ON A TRAIN	Pasadenas (CBS)
16	22	NOTHING CAN DIVIDE US	Jason Donovan (PWL)
23	23	LOVELY DAY	Bill Withers (CBS)
12	24	FAKE '88	Alexander O'Neal (Tabu)
-	25	REAL GONE KID	Deacon Blue (CBS)
11	26	I DON'T WANT YOUR LOVE	Duran Duran (EMI)
28	27	ALL OF ME	Sabrina (PWL)
-	28	GIRL YOU KNOW IT'S TRUE	Milli Vanilli (Cooltempo)
19	29	TURN IT INTO LOVE	Hazell Dean (EMI)
33	30	ANY LOVE	Luther Vandross (Epic)
32	31	CHARLOTTE ANNE	Julian Cope (Island)
25	32	I'M GONNA BE (500 MILES)	Proclaimers (Chrysalis)
23	33	THE RACE	Yello (Mercury)
30	34	SO IN LOVE WITH YOU	Spear Of Destiny (Virgin)
27	35	THE ONLY WAY IS UP	Yazz & the Plastic Population (Big Life)
47	36	ACID MAN	Jolly Roger (10)
29	37	ANYTHING FOR YOU	Gloria Estefan & the Miami Sound Machine (Epic)
21	38	BAD MEDICINE	Bon Jovi (Vertigo)
45	39	O-O-O	Adrenalin (MCA)
-	40	CAN YOU PARTY	Royal House (Champion)
37	41	SHAKE YOUR THANG	Salt 'N' Pepa (ffrr)
-	42	CRAZY (FOR ME)	Freddie Jackson (Capitol)
41	43	GET REAL	Paul Rutherford (Fourth & Broadway)
-	44	STAYING TOGETHER	Debbie Gibson (Atlantic)
-	45	IN THE NAME OF LOVE '88	Thompson Twins (Arista)
-	46	I'LL HOUSE YOU	Richie Rich Meets the Jungle Brothers (Gee Street)
48	47	HOW MANY TEARS CAN I HIDE	Shakin' Stevens (Epic)
35	48	KILLING JAR	Siouxsie & the Banshees (Wonderland)
39	49	DON'T WALK AWAY	Pat Benatar (Chrysalis)
-	50	BREATHE LIFE INTO ME	Mica Paris (Fourth & Broadway)

Like the Hollies single which it failed to dislodge from the top, Bill Withers' *Lovely Day* had been a Top 10 hit before, in 1978. Like the Hollies, Withers progressed significantly higher second time around, though *Lovely Day* had been given a dance remix (by Dutch DJ Ben Liebrand) to encourage this new round of sales. Alexander O'Neal's *Fake '88* was also a remixed reissue.

29 October 1988

last week	this week	Title — Artist (Label)
6	1	WE CALL IT ACIEED — D Mob (ffrr)
10	2	ORINOCO FLOW (SAIL AWAY) — Enya (WEA)
1	3	ONE MOMENT IN TIME — Whitney Houston (Arista)
9	4	HARVEST FOR THE WORLD — Christians (Island)
19	5	JE NE SAIS PAS POURQUOI — Kylie Minogue (PWL)
2	6	DON'T WORRY BE HAPPY — Bobby McFerrin (Manhattan)
4	7	A LITTLE RESPECT — Erasure (Mute)
12	8	NEVER TRUST A STRANGER — Kim Wilde (MCA)
3	9	WEE RULE — Wee Papa Girl Rappers (Jive)
28	10	GIRL YOU KNOW IT'S TRUE — Milli Vanilli (Cooltempo)
8	11	BURN IT UP — Beatmasters featuring P.P. Arnold (Rhythm King)
7	12	SHE WANTS TO DANCE WITH ME — Rick Astley (RCA)
40	13	CAN YOU PARTY — Royal House (Champion)
14	14	TEARDROPS — Womack & Womack (Fourth & Broadway)
25	15	REAL GONE KID — Deacon Blue (CBS)
11	16	HE AIN'T HEAVY HE'S MY BROTHER — Hollies (EMI)
-	17	STAND UP FOR YOUR LOVE RIGHTS — Yazz & the Plastic Population (Big Life)
5	18	DESIRE — U2 (Island)
46	19	I'LL HOUSE YOU — Richie Rich Meets the Jungle Brothers (Gee Street)
13	20	A GROOVY KIND OF LOVE — Phil Collins (Virgin)
21	21	SHE MAKES MY DAY — Robert Palmer (EMI)
-	22	TWIST IN MY SOBRIETY — Tanita Tikaram (WEA)
17	23	SECRET GARDEN — T'Pau (Siren)
15	24	BIG FUN — Inner City featuring Kevin Saunderson (10)
36	25	ACID MAN — Jolly Roger (10)
27	26	ALL OF ME — Sabrina (PWL)
-	27	THE PARTY — Kraze (MCA)
22	28	NOTHING CAN DIVIDE US — Jason Donovan (PWL)
30	29	ANY LOVE — Luther Vandross (Epic)
16	30	LOVE TRUTH AND HONESTY — Bananarama (London)
20	31	I DON'T BELIEVE IN MIRACLES — Sinitta (Fanfare)
18	32	DOMINO DANCING — Pet Shop Boys (Parlophone)
33	33	WELCOME TO THE JUNGLE/NIGHT TRAIN — Guns N' Roses (Geffen)
21	34	RIDING ON A TRAIN — Pasadenas (CBS)
23	35	LOVELY DAY — Bill Withers (CBS)
-	36	NOTHIN' AT ALL — Heart (Capitol)
-	37	FIRST TIME — Robin Beck (Mercury)
24	38	FAKE '88 — Alexander O'Neal (Tabu)
-	39	1-2-3 — Gloria Estefan & the Miami Sound Machine (Epic)
-	40	KISS — Art Of Noise featuring Tom Jones (China)
-	41	LOVE IS ALL THAT MATTERS — Human League (Virgin)
50	42	BREATHE LIFE INTO ME — Mica Paris (Fourth & Broadway)
29	43	TURN IT INTO LOVE — Hazell Dean (EMI)
-	44	TAKE A LOOK — Level 42 (Polydor)
35	45	THE ONLY WAY IS UP — Yazz & the Plastic Population (Big Life)
45	46	IN THE NAME OF LOVE '88 — Thompson Twins (Arista)
-	47	ORDINARY ANGEL — Hue & Cry (Circa)
37	48	ANYTHING FOR YOU — Gloria Estefan & the Miami Sound Machine (Epic)
32	49	I'M GONNA BE (500 MILES) — Proclaimers (Chrysalis)
-	50	DECEMBER '63 (OH WHAT A NIGHT) — Frankie Valli & the Four Seasons (BR)

5 November 1988

last week	this week	Title — Artist (Label)
2	1	ORINOCO FLOW (SAIL AWAY) — Enya (WEA)
5	2	JE NE SAIS PAS POURQUOI — Kylie Minogue (PWL)
17	3	STAND UP FOR YOUR LOVE RIGHTS — Yazz & the Plastic Population (Big Life)
4	4	WE CALL IT ACIEED — D Mob (ffrr)
40	5	KISS — Art Of Noise featuring Tom Jones (China)
10	6	GIRL YOU KNOW IT'S TRUE — Milli Vanilli (Cooltempo)
4	7	HARVEST FOR THE WORLD — Christians (Island)
21	8	SHE MAKES MY DAY — Robert Palmer (EMI)
7	9	A LITTLE RESPECT — Erasure (Mute)
3	10	ONE MOMENT IN TIME — Whitney Houston (Arista)
13	11	CAN YOU PARTY — Royal House (Champion)
6	12	DON'T WORRY BE HAPPY — Bobby McFerrin (Manhattan)
15	13	REAL GONE KID — Deacon Blue (CBS)
11	14	BURN IT UP — Beatmasters featuring P.P. Arnold (Rhythm King)
9	15	WEE RULE — Wee Papa Girl Rappers (Jive)
19	16	I'LL HOUSE YOU — Richie Rich Meets the Jungle Brothers (Gee Street)
14	17	TEARDROPS — Womack & Womack (Fourth & Broadway)
8	18	NEVER TRUST A STRANGER — Kim Wilde (MCA)
37	19	FIRST TIME — Robin Beck (Mercury)
22	20	TWIST IN MY SOBRIETY — Tanita Tikaram (WEA)
39	21	1-2-3 — Gloria Estefan & the Miami Sound Machine (Epic)
12	22	SHE WANTS TO DANCE WITH ME — Rick Astley (RCA)
25	23	ACID MAN — Jolly Roger (10)
27	24	THE PARTY — Kraze (MCA)
33	25	WELCOME TO THE JUNGLE/NIGHT TRAIN — Guns N' Roses (Geffen)
24	26	BIG FUN — Inner City featuring Kevin Saunderson (10)
44	27	TAKE A LOOK — Level 42 (Polydor)
20	28	A GROOVY KIND OF LOVE — Phil Collins (Virgin)
-	29	I WISH U HEAVEN — Prince (Paisley Park)
16	30	HE AIN'T HEAVY HE'S MY BROTHER — Hollies (EMI)
36	31	NOTHIN' AT ALL — Heart (Capitol)
-	32	LET'S STICK TOGETHER — Bryan Ferry (EG)
18	33	DESIRE — U2 (Island)
28	34	NOTHING CAN DIVIDE US — Jason Donovan (PWL)
35	35	HERE COMES THAT SOUND — Simon Harris (ffrr)
41	36	LOVE IS ALL THAT MATTERS — Human League (Virgin)
23	37	SECRET GARDEN — T'Pau (Siren)
38	38	SHARP AS A KNIFE — Brandon Cooke featuring Roxanne Shante (Club)
-	39	HE AIN'T NO COMPETITION — Brother Beyond (Parlophone)
42	40	BREATHE LIFE INTO ME — Mica Paris (Fourth & Broadway)
47	41	ORDINARY ANGEL — Hue & Cry (Circa)
-	42	I WALK THE EARTH — Voice Of The Beehive (London)
50	43	DECEMBER '63 (OH WHAT A NIGHT) — Frankie Valli & the Four Seasons (BR)
26	44	ALL OF ME — Sabrina (PWL)
30	45	LOVE TRUTH AND HONESTY — Bananarama (London)
34	46	RIDING ON A TRAIN — Pasadenas (CBS)
-	47	BROKEN HEART (THIRTEEN VALLEYS) — Big Country (Mercury)
31	48	I DON'T BELIEVE IN MIRACLES — Sinitta (Fanfare)
-	49	YOU MAKE ME WORK — Cameo (Club)
35	50	LOVELY DAY — Bill Withers (CBS)

12 November 1988

last week	this week	Title — Artist (Label)
1	1	ORINOCO FLOW (SAIL AWAY) — Enya (WEA)
2	2	JE NE SAIS PAS POURQUOI — Kylie Minogue (PWL)
3	3	STAND UP FOR YOUR LOVE RIGHTS — Yazz & the Plastic Population (Big Life)
6	4	GIRL YOU KNOW IT'S TRUE — Milli Vanilli (Cooltempo)
5	5	KISS — Art Of Noise featuring Tom Jones (China)
19	6	FIRST TIME — Robin Beck (Mercury)
8	7	SHE MAKES MY DAY — Robert Palmer (EMI)
4	8	WE CALL IT ACIEED — D Mob (ffrr)
13	9	REAL GONE KID — Deacon Blue (CBS)
11	10	CAN YOU PARTY — Royal House (Champion)
21	11	1-2-3 — & the Miami Sound Machine (Epic)
10	12	ONE MOMENT IN TIME — Whitney Houston (Arista)
9	13	A LITTLE RESPECT — Erasure (Mute)
7	14	HARVEST FOR THE WORLD — Christians (Island)
39	15	HE AIN'T NO COMPETITION — Brother Beyond (Parlophone)
12	16	DON'T WORRY BE HAPPY — Bobby McFerrin (Manhattan)
32	17	LET'S STICK TOGETHER — Bryan Ferry (EG)
-	18	MISSING YOU — Chris De Burgh (A&M)
15	19	WEE RULE — Wee Papa Girl Rappers (Jive)
20	20	TWIST IN MY SOBRIETY — Tanita Tikaram (WEA)
25	21	WELCOME TO THE JUNGLE/NIGHT TRAIN — Guns N' Roses (Geffen)
17	22	TEARDROPS — Womack & Womack (Fourth & Broadway)
14	23	BURN IT UP — Beatmasters featuring P.P. Arnold (Rhythm King)
29	24	I WISH U HEAVEN — Prince (Paisley Park)
-	25	NEED YOU TONIGHT — INXS (Mercury)
18	26	NEVER TRUST A STRANGER — Kim Wilde (MCA)
23	27	ACID MAN — Jolly Roger (10)
24	28	THE PARTY — Kraze (MCA)
16	29	I'LL HOUSE YOU — Richie Rich Meets the Jungle Brothers (Gee Street)
28	30	A GROOVY KIND OF LOVE — Phil Collins (Virgin)
31	31	BIG FUN — Inner City featuring Kevin Saunderson (10)
35	32	HERE COMES THAT SOUND — Simon Harris (ffrr)
27	33	TAKE A LOOK — Level 42 (Polydor)
22	34	SHE WANTS TO DANCE WITH ME — Rick Astley (RCA)
43	35	DECEMBER '63 (OH WHAT A NIGHT) — Frankie Valli & the Four Seasons (BR)
40	36	BREATHE LIFE INTO ME — Mica Paris (Fourth & Broadway)
-	37	BITTERSWEET — Marc Almond (Some Bizzare)
34	38	NOTHING CAN DIVIDE US — Jason Donovan (PWL)
-	39	TWIST AND SHOUT/GET UP EVERYBODY — Salt 'N' Pepa (ffrr)
30	40	HE AIN'T HEAVY HE'S MY BROTHER — Hollies (EMI)
41	41	WHAT KIND OF FOOL — All About Eve (Mercury)
38	42	SHARP AS A KNIFE — Brandon Cooke featuring Roxanne Shante (Club)
-	43	COPPERHEAD ROAD — Steve Earle (MCA)
-	44	REVOLUTIONS — Jean Michel Jarre (Polydor)
47	45	BROKEN HEART (THIRTEEN VALLEYS) — Big Country (Mercury)
-	46	THE WAY YOU LOVE ME — Karyn White (Warner Bros)
-	47	SUNSHINE ON LEITH — Proclaimers (Chrysalis)
-	48	HEART OF STONE — Bucks Fizz (RCA)
-	49	PUT A LITTLE LOVE IN YOUR HEART — Annie Lennox & Al Green (A&M)
-	50	WEEKEND — Todd Terry Project (Sleeping Bag)

Enya's *Orinoco Flow* was the first major hit single to emerge from what was all-encompassingly termed New Age music, most of which consisted of ambient instrumental pieces. The singer herself was related to members of the Irish group Clannad (also sometimes considered on the fringes of New Age, despite their commercial profile), and had sung back-up on some of their early material.

November – December 1988

last week	this week	19 November 1988	
6	1	FIRST TIME	Robin Beck (Mercury)
1	2	ORINOCO FLOW (SAIL AWAY)	Enya (WEA)
15	3	HE AIN'T NO COMPETITION	Brother Beyond (Parlophone)
3	4	STAND UP FOR YOUR LOVE RIGHTS	Yazz & the Plastic Population (Big Life)
11	5	1-2-3	Gloria Estefan & the Miami Sound Machine (Epic)
2	6	JE NE SAIS PAS POURQUOI	Kylie Minogue (PWL)
18	7	MISSING YOU	Chris De Burgh (A&M)
4	8	GIRL YOU KNOW IT'S TRUE	Milli Vanilli (Cooltempo)
7	9	SHE MAKES MY DAY	Robert Palmer (EMI)
17	10	LET'S STICK TOGETHER	Bryan Ferry (EG)
25	11	NEED YOU TONIGHT	INXS (Mercury)
9	12	REAL GONE KID	Deacon Blue (CBS)
5	13	KISS	Art Of Noise featuring Tom Jones (China)
39	14	TWIST AND SHOUT/GET UP EVERYBODY	Salt 'N' Pepa (ffrr)
-	15	THE CLAIRVOYANT	Iron Maiden (EMI)
8	16	WE CALL IT ACIEED	D Mob (ffrr)
-	17	TIL I LOVED YOU	Barbra Streisand & Don Johnson (CBS)
12	18	ONE MOMENT IN TIME	Whitney Houston (Arista)
20	19	TWIST IN MY SOBRIETY	Tanita Tikaram (WEA)
24	20	I WISH U HEAVEN	Prince (Paisley Park)
10	21	CAN YOU PARTY	Royal House (Champion)
13	22	A LITTLE RESPECT	Erasure (Mute)
21	23	WELCOME TO THE JUNGLE/NIGHT TRAIN	Guns N' Roses (Geffen)
-	24	HANDLE WITH CARE	Traveling Wilburys (Wilbury)
14	25	HARVEST FOR THE WORLD	Christians (Island)
41	26	WHAT KIND OF FOOL	All About Eve (Mercury)
19	27	WEE RULE	Wee Papa Girl Rappers (Jive)
-	28	LIFE'S JUST A BALLGAME	Womack & Womack (Fourth & Broadway)
16	29	DON'T WORRY BE HAPPY	Bobby McFerrin (Manhattan)
36	30	BREATHE LIFE INTO ME	Mica Paris (Fourth & Broadway)
27	31	ACID MAN	Jolly Roger (10)
26	32	NEVER TRUST A STRANGER	Kim Wilde (MCA)
37	33	BITTERSWEET	Marc Almond (Some Bizzare)
22	34	TEARDROPS	Womack & Womack (Fourth & Broadway)
35	35	DECEMBER '63 (OH WHAT A NIGHT)	Frankie Valli and the Four Seasons (BR)
-	36	RADIO ROMANCE	Tiffany (MCA)
47	37	SUNSHINE ON LEITH	Proclaimers (Chrysalis)
23	38	BURN IT UP	Beatmasters featuring P.P. Arnold (Rhythm King)
32	39	HERE COMES THAT SOUND	Simon Harris (ffrr)
-	40	NATHAN JONES	Bananarama (London)
-	41	LOUIE LOUIE	Fat Boys (Urban)
-	42	IN YOUR ROOM	Bangles (CBS)
30	43	A GROOVY KIND OF LOVE	Phil Collins (Virgin)
-	44	ORDINARY ANGEL	Hue & Cry (Circa)
-	45	JACK TO THE SOUND OF THE UNDERGROUND	Hithouse (Supreme)
-	46	USELESS (I DON'T NEED YOU NOW)	Kym Mazelle (Syncopate)
50	47	WEEKEND	Todd Terry Project (Sleeping Bag)
46	48	THE WAY YOU LOVE ME	Karyn White (Warner Bros)
45	49	BROKEN HEART	(THIRTEEN VALLEYS) Big Country (Mercury)
31	50	BIG FUN	Inner City featuring Kevin Saunderson (10)

last week	this week	26 November 1988	
1	1	FIRST TIME	Robin Beck (Mercury)
11	2	NEED YOU TONIGHT	INXS (Mercury)
3	3	HE AIN'T NO COMPETITION	Brother Beyond (Parlophone)
4	4	STAND UP FOR YOUR LOVE RIGHTS	Yazz & the Plastic Population (Big Life)
7	5	MISSING YOU	Chris De Burgh (A&M)
14	6	TWIST AND SHOUT/GET UP EVERYBODY	Salt 'N' Pepa (ffrr)
6	7	JE NE SAIS PAS POURQUOI	Kylie Minogue (PWL)
2	8	ORINOCO FLOW (SAIL AWAY)	Enya (WEA)
15	9	THE CLAIRVOYANT	Iron Maiden (EMI)
17	10	TIL I LOVED YOU	Barbra Streisand & Don Johnson (CBS)
8	11	GIRL YOU KNOW IT'S TRUE	Milli Vanilli (Cooltempo)
24	12	HANDLE WITH CARE	Traveling Wilburys (Wilbury)
-	13	LEFT TO MY OWN DEVICES	Pet Shop Boys (Parlophone)
12	14	REAL GONE KID	Deacon Blue (CBS)
5	15	1-2-3	Gloria Estefan & the Miami Sound Machine (Epic)
40	16	NATHAN JONES	Bananarama (London)
9	17	SHE MAKES MY DAY	Robert Palmer (EMI)
10	18	LET'S STICK TOGETHER	Bryan Ferry (EG)
-	19	SUCCESS	Sigue Sigue Sputnik (Parlophone)
-	20	TAKE ME TO YOUR HEART	Rick Astley (RCA)
30	21	BREATHE LIFE INTO ME	Mica Paris (Fourth & Broadway)
13	22	KISS	Art Of Noise featuring Tom Jones (China)
16	23	WE CALL IT ACIEED	D Mob (ffrr)
36	24	RADIO ROMANCE	Tiffany (MCA)
-	25	TWO HEARTS	Phil Collins (Virgin)
28	26	LIFE'S JUST A BALLGAME	Womack & Womack (Fourth & Broadway)
18	27	ONE MOMENT IN TIME	Whitney Houston (Arista)
-	28	SMOOTH CRIMINAL	Michael Jackson (Epic)
19	29	TWIST IN MY SOBRIETY	Tanita Tikaram (WEA)
-	30	SAY A LITTLE PRAYER	Bomb The Bass featuring Maureen (Rhythm King)
26	31	WHAT KIND OF FOOL	All About Eve (Mercury)
20	32	I WISH U HEAVEN	Prince (Paisley Park)
-	33	LOVE HOUSE	Samantha Fox (Jive)
-	34	FREAKS (LIVE)	Marillion (EMI)
42	35	IN YOUR ROOM	Bangles (CBS)
45	36	JACK TO THE SOUND OF THE UNDERGROUND	Hithouse (Supreme)
-	37	SUDDENLY (THE WEDDING THEME FROM NEIGHBOURS)	Angry Anderson (Food For Thought)
32	38	NEVER TRUST A STRANGER	Kim Wilde (MCA)
21	39	CAN YOU PARTY	Royal House (Champion)
37	40	SUNSHINE ON LEITH	Proclaimers (Chrysalis)
29	41	DON'T WORRY BE HAPPY	Bobby McFerrin (Manhattan)
22	42	A LITTLE RESPECT	Erasure (Mute)
48	43	THE WAY YOU LOVE ME	Karyn White (Warner Bros)
-	44	ENCHANTED LADY	Pasadenas (CBS)
46	45	USELESS (I DON'T NEED YOU NOW)	Kym Mazelle (Syncopate)
27	46	WEE RULE	Wee Papa Girl Rappers (Jive)
23	47	WELCOME TO THE JUNGLE/NIGHT TRAIN	Guns N' Roses (Geffen)
34	48	TEARDROPS	Womack & Womack (Fourth & Broadway)
41	49	LOUIE LOUIE	Fat Boys (Urban)
-	50	DOWNTOWN '88	Petula Clark (PRT)

last week	this week	3 December 1988	
1	1	FIRST TIME	Robin Beck (Mercury)
2	2	NEED YOU TONIGHT	INXS (Mercury)
13	3	LEFT TO MY OWN DEVICES	Pet Shop Boys (Parlophone)
5	4	MISSING YOU	Chris De Burgh (A&M)
25	5	TWO HEARTS	Phil Collins (Virgin)
6	6	TWIST AND SHOUT/GET UP EVERYBODY	Salt 'N' Pepa (ffrr)
28	7	SMOOTH CRIMINAL	Michael Jackson (Epic)
20	8	TAKE ME TO YOUR HEART	Rick Astley (RCA)
30	9	SAY A LITTLE PRAYER	Bomb The Bass featuring Maureen (Rhythm King)
4	10	STAND UP FOR YOUR LOVE RIGHTS	Yazz & the Plastic Population (Big Life)
9	11	THE CLAIRVOYANT	Iron Maiden (EMI)
3	12	HE AIN'T NO COMPETITION	Brother Beyond (Parlophone)
16	13	NATHAN JONES	Bananarama (London)
-	14	CAT AMONG THE PIGEONS/SILENT NIGHT	Bros (CBS)
14	15	REAL GONE KID	Deacon Blue (CBS)
24	16	RADIO ROMANCE	Tiffany (MCA)
7	17	JE NE SAIS PAS POURQUOI	Kylie Minogue (PWL)
-	18	STAKKER HUMANOID	Humanoid (Westside)
36	19	JACK TO THE SOUND OF THE UNDERGROUND	Hithouse (Supreme)
8	20	ORINOCO FLOW (SAIL AWAY)	Enya (WEA)
37	21	SUDDENLY (THE WEDDING THEME FROM NEIGHBOURS)	Angry Anderson (Food For Thought)
34	22	FREAKS (LIVE)	Marillion (EMI)
10	23	TIL I LOVED YOU	Barbra Streisand & Don Johnson (CBS)
11	24	GIRL YOU KNOW IT'S TRUE	Milli Vanilli (Cooltempo)
-	25	MISTLETOE AND WINE	Cliff Richard (EMI)
-	26	KOKOMO	Beach Boys (Elektra)
19	27	SUCCESS	Sigue Sigue Sputnik (Parlophone)
12	28	HANDLE WITH CARE	Traveling Wilburys (Wilbury)
-	29	KISSING A FOOL	George Michael (Epic)
17	30	SHE MAKES MY DAY	Robert Palmer (EMI)
15	31	1-2-3	Gloria Estefan & the Miami Sound Machine (Epic)
50	32	DOWNTOWN '88	Petula Clark (PRT)
35	33	IN YOUR ROOM	Bangles (CBS)
26	34	LIFE'S JUST A BALLGAME	Womack & Womack (Fourth & Broadway)
44	35	ENCHANTED LADY	Pasadenas (CBS)
23	36	WE CALL IT ACIEED	D Mob (ffrr)
33	37	LOVE HOUSE	Samantha Fox (Jive)
18	38	LET'S STICK TOGETHER	Bryan Ferry (EG)
21	39	BREATHE LIFE INTO ME	Mica Paris (Fourth & Broadway)
-	40	MINNIE THE MOOCHER	Reggae Philharmonic Orchestra (Mango)
41	41	YOU ARE THE ONE	A-ha (Warner Bros)
22	42	KISS	Art Of Noise featuring Tom Jones (China)
40	43	SUNSHINE ON LEITH	Proclaimers (Chrysalis)
-	44	IT'S A TRIP (TUNE IN TURN ON DROP OUT)	Children Of The Night (Jive)
-	45	9 A.M. (THE COMFORT ZONE)	London Beat (AnXious)
-	46	ROAD TO OUR DREAM	T'Pau (Siren)
29	47	TWIST IN MY SOBRIETY	Tanita Tikaram (WEA)
-	48	BURNING BRIDGES (ON AND OFF AND ON AGAIN)	Status Quo (Vertigo)
27	49	ONE MOMENT IN TIME	Whitney Houston (Arista)
39	50	CAN YOU PARTY	Royal House (Champion)

After several major hits emerging from Levi's Jeans TV ads, it was finally the turn of a rival product to produce a winner – though in the case of Robin Beck's *First Time*, the process was the reverse of that of Levi's use of existing songs. Like its ancestor *I'd Like To Teach The World To Sing*, it was initially written as a Coca-Cola jingle, and turned into a full-blooded song after audience reaction to the advert.

492

December 1988

last week	this week	10 December 1988	
25	1	MISTLETOE AND WINE	Cliff Richard (EMI)
14	2	CAT AMONG THE PIGEONS/SILENT NIGHT	
			Bros (CBS)
21	3	SUDDENLY (THE WEDDING THEME FROM	
		NEIGHBOURS) Angry Anderson (Food For Thought)	
1	4	FIRST TIME	Robin Beck (Mercury)
3	5	LEFT TO MY OWN DEVICES	
			Pet Shop Boys (Parlophone)
-	6	ESPECIALLY FOR YOU	
			Kylie Minogue & Jason Donovan (PWL)
5	7	TWO HEARTS	Phil Collins (Virgin)
9	8	SAY A LITTLE PRAYER	Bomb The Bass
			featuring Maureen (Rhythm King)
7	9	SMOOTH CRIMINAL	Michael Jackson (Epic)
8	10	TAKE ME TO YOUR HEART	Rick Astley (RCA)
4	11	MISSING YOU	Chris De Burgh (A&M)
18	12	STAKKER HUMANOID	Humanoid (Westside)
2	13	NEED YOU TONIGHT	INXS (Mercury)
19	14	JACK TO THE SOUND OF THE UNDERGROUND	
			Hithouse (Supreme)
16	15	RADIO ROMANCE	Tiffany (MCA)
-	16	CRACKERS INTERNATIONAL (EP)	Erasure (Mute)
29	17	KISSING A FOOL	George Michael (Epic)
6	18	TWIST AND SHOUT/GET UP EVERYBODY	
			Salt 'N' Pepa (ffrr)
13	19	NATHAN JONES	Bananarama (London)
26	20	KOKOMO	Beach Boys (Elektra)
48	21	BURNING BRIDGES (ON AND OFF AND ON	
		AGAIN)	Status Quo (Vertigo)
-	22	FINE TIME	New Order (Factory)
15	23	REAL GONE KID	Deacon Blue (CBS)
32	24	DOWNTOWN '88	Petula Clark (PRT)
12	25	HE AIN'T NO COMPETITION	
			Brother Beyond (Parlophone)
35	26	ENCHANTED LADY	Pasadenas (CBS)
10	27	STAND UP FOR YOUR LOVE RIGHTS	
			Yazz & the Plastic Population (Big Life)
17	28	JE NE SAIS PAS POURQUOI	Kylie Minogue (PWL)
41	29	YOU ARE THE ONE	A-ha (Warner Bros)
24	30	GIRL YOU KNOW IT'S TRUE	Milli Vanilli (Cooltempo)
37	31	LOVE HOUSE	Samantha Fox (Jive)
11	32	THE CLAIRVOYANT	Iron Maiden (EMI)
45	33	9 A.M. (THE COMFORT ZONE)	London Beat (AnXious)
-	34	BORN TO BE MY BABY	Bon Jovi (Vertigo)
-	35	LOCO IN ACAPULCO	Four Tops (Arista)
-	36	FOUR LETTER WORD	Kim Wilde (MCA)
20	37	ORINOCO FLOW (SAIL AWAY)	Enya (WEA)
31	38	1-2-3	Gloria Estefan
			& the Miami Sound Machine (Epic)
46	39	ROAD TO OUR DREAM	T'Pau (Siren)
23	40	GOOD LIFE	Inner City (10)
42	41	TIL I LOVED YOU	
			Barbra Streisand & Don Johnson (CBS)
-	42	THE LAST BEAT OF MY HEART	
			Siouxsie & the Banshees (Wonderland)
30	43	SHE MAKES MY DAY	Robert Palmer (EMI)
22	44	FREAKS (LIVE)	Marillion (EMI)
33	45	IN YOUR ROOM	Bangles (CBS)
-	46	DENIS '88/RAPTURE '88	Blondie (Chrysalis)
39	47	BREATHE LIFE INTO ME	
			Mica Paris (Fourth & Broadway)
28	48	HANDLE WITH CARE	Traveling Wilburys (Wilbury)
-	49	THE CHRISTMAS SONG (CHESTNUTS ROASTING	
		ON AN OPEN FIRE)	Alexander O'Neal (Tabu)
-	50	WAITING FOR A STAR TO FALL	Boy Meets Girl (RCA)

		17 December 1988	
1	1	MISTLETOE AND WINE	Cliff Richard (EMI)
6	2	ESPECIALLY FOR YOU	
			Kylie Minogue & Jason Donovan (PWL)
3	3	SUDDENLY (THE WEDDING THEME FROM	
		NEIGHBOURS) Angry Anderson (Food For Thought)	
16	4	CRACKERS INTERNATIONAL (EP)	Erasure (Mute)
2	5	CAT AMONG THE PIGEONS/SILENT NIGHT	
			Bros (CBS)
7	6	TWO HEARTS	Phil Collins (Virgin)
40	7	GOOD LIFE	Inner City (10)
-	8	ANGEL OF HARLEM	U2 (Island)
4	9	FIRST TIME	Robin Beck (Mercury)
10	10	TAKE ME TO YOUR HEART	Rick Astley (RCA)
9	11	SMOOTH CRIMINAL	Michael Jackson (Epic)
8	12	SAY A LITTLE PRAYER	Bomb The Bass
			featuring Maureen (Rhythm King)
21	13	BURNING BRIDGES (ON AND OFF AND ON	
		AGAIN)	Status Quo (Vertigo)
24	14	DOWNTOWN '88	Petula Clark (PRT)
17	15	KISSING A FOOL	George Michael (Epic)
5	16	LEFT TO MY OWN DEVICES	
			Pet Shop Boys (Parlophone)
22	17	FINE TIME	New Order (Factory)
19	18	NATHAN JONES	Bananarama (London)
15	19	RADIO ROMANCE	Tiffany (MCA)
20	20	KOKOMO	Beach Boys (Elektra)
11	21	MISSING YOU	Chris De Burgh (A&M)
12	22	STAKKER HUMANOID	Humanoid (Westside)
35	23	LOCO IN ACAPULCO	Four Tops (Arista)
14	24	JACK TO THE SOUND OF THE UNDERGROUND	
			Hithouse (Supreme)
-	25	BUFFALO STANCE	Neneh Cherry (Circa)
34	26	BORN TO BE MY BABY	Bon Jovi (Vertigo)
13	27	NEED YOU TONIGHT	INXS (Mercury)
36	28	FOUR LETTER WORD	Kim Wilde (MCA)
29	29	YOU ARE THE ONE	A-ha (Warner Bros)
-	30	PUT A LITTLE LOVE IN YOUR HEART	
			Annie Lennox & Al Green (A&M)
33	31	9 A.M. (THE COMFORT ZONE)	London Beat (AnXious)
26	32	ENCHANTED LADY	Pasadenas (CBS)
49	33	THE CHRISTMAS SONG (CHESTNUTS	
		ROASTING ON AN OPEN FIRE)	
			Alexander O'Neal (Tabu)
18	34	TWIST AND SHOUT/GET UP EVERYBODY	Salt 'N'
			Pepa (ffrr)
23	35	REAL GONE KID	Deacon Blue (CBS)
25	36	HE AIN'T NO COMPETITION	
			Brother Beyond (Parlophone)
28	37	JE NE SAIS PAS POURQUOI	Kylie Minogue (PWL)
-	38	MINNIE THE MOOCHER	
			Reggae Philharmonic Orchestra (Mango)
46	39	KEEPING THE DREAM ALIVE	Freiheit (CBS)
-	40	REQUIEM	London Boys (WEA)
27	41	STAND UP FOR YOUR LOVE RIGHTS	
			Yazz & the Plastic Population (Big Life)
48	42	HANDLE WITH CARE	Traveling Wilburys (Wilbury)
-	43	YEAH YEAH YEAH YEAH	
			Pogues (Pogue Mahone)
30	44	GIRL YOU KNOW IT'S TRUE	Milli Vanilli (Cooltempo)
-	45	DON'T BELIEVE THE HYPE	Mista E (Urban)
-	46	LOVE NEVER DIES	Belinda Carlisle (Virgin)
37	47	ORINOCO FLOW (SAIL AWAY)	Enya (WEA)
-	48	I LIVE FOR YOUR LOVE	Natalie Cole (Manhattan)
-	49	TRUE LOVE	Shakin' Stevens (Epic)
43	50	SHE MAKES MY DAY	Robert Palmer (EMI)

		24 December 1988	
1	1	MISTLETOE AND WINE	Cliff Richard (EMI)
2	2	ESPECIALLY FOR YOU	
			Kylie Minogue & Jason Donovan (PWL)
3	3	SUDDENLY (THE WEDDING THEME FROM	
		NEIGHBOURS) Angry Anderson (Food For Thought)	
7	4	GOOD LIFE	Inner City (10)
4	5	CRACKERS INTERNATIONAL (EP)	Erasure (Mute)
13	6	BURNING BRIDGES (ON AND OFF AND ON	
		AGAIN)	Status Quo (Vertigo)
14	7	DOWNTOWN '88	Petula Clark (PRT)
8	8	ANGEL OF HARLEM	U2 (Island)
5	9	CAT AMONG THE PIGEONS/SILENT NIGHT	
			Bros (CBS)
6	10	TWO HEARTS	Phil Collins (Virgin)
10	11	TAKE ME TO YOUR HEART	Rick Astley (RCA)
17	12	FINE TIME	New Order (Factory)
23	13	LOCO IN ACAPULCO	Four Tops (Arista)
9	14	FIRST TIME	Robin Beck (Mercury)
25	15	BUFFALO STANCE	Neneh Cherry (Circa)
26	16	BORN TO BE MY BABY	Bon Jovi (Vertigo)
11	17	SMOOTH CRIMINAL	Michael Jackson (Epic)
18	18	NATHAN JONES	Bananarama (London)
31	19		
12	20	SAY A LITTLE PRAYER	Bomb The Bass
			featuring Maureen (Rhythm King)
28	21	FOUR LETTER WORD	Kim Wilde (MCA)
33	22	THE CHRISTMAS SONG (CHESTNUTS	
		ROASTING ON AN OPEN FIRE)	
			Alexander O'Neal (Tabu)
42	23	HANDLE WITH CARE	Traveling Wilburys (Wilbury)
16	24	LEFT TO MY OWN DEVICES	
			Pet Shop Boys (Parlophone)
49	25	TRUE LOVE	Shakin' Stevens (Epic)
30	26	PUT A LITTLE LOVE IN YOUR HEART	
			Annie Lennox & Al Green (A&M)
19	27	RADIO ROMANCE	Tiffany (MCA)
39	28	KEEPING THE DREAM ALIVE	Freiheit (CBS)
29	29	YOU ARE THE ONE	A-ha (Warner Bros)
15	30	KISSING A FOOL	George Michael (Epic)
21	31	MISSING YOU	Chris De Burgh (A&M)
43	32	YEAH YEAH YEAH YEAH	
			Pogues (Pogue Mahone)
22	33	STAKKER HUMANOID	Humanoid (Westside)
24	34	JACK TO THE SOUND OF THE UNDERGROUND	
			Hithouse (Supreme)
-	35	IMAGINE	John Lennon (Parlophone)
20	36	KOKOMO	Beach Boys (Elektra)
45	37	DON'T BELIEVE THE HYPE	Mista E (Urban)
38	38	MINNIE THE MOOCHER	
			Reggae Philharmonic Orchestra (Mango)
-	39	RHYTHM IS GONNA GET YOU	Gloria Estefan
			& the Miami Sound Machine (Epic)
-	40	IT'S PARTY TIME AGAIN	
			George Van Dusen (Bri-Tone)
27	41	NEED YOU TONIGHT	INXS (Mercury)
35	42	REAL GONE KID	Deacon Blue (CBS)
40	43	REQUIEM	London Boys (WEA)
48	44	I LIVE FOR YOUR LOVE	Natalie Cole (Manhattan)
-	45	HOW CAN I FALL	Breathe (Siren)
37	46	JE NE SAIS PAS POURQUOI	Kylie Minogue (PWL)
47	47	WAITING FOR A STAR TO FALL	Boy Meets Girl (RCA)
-	48	EVERLASTING LOVE	Sandra (Siren)
-	49	THINKIN' ABOUT YOUR BODY	
			Bobby McFerrin (Manhattan)
-	50	LOVE LIKE A RIVER	Climie Fisher (EMI)

Cliff Richard's *Mistletoe And Wine*, defying the pundits who mostly predicted Bros or Kylie & Jason's duet for the Christmas Number One, was his fastest-selling single since *The Young Ones* in 1962.

His first Number One since *We Don't Talk Anymore* in 1979, it meant Cliff was the only act to have topped the UK chart in the 1950s, '60s, '70s and now the 1980s. It was also his second UK million-seller.

The Age Of The Megastar

As the eighties drew to a close a few giants bestrode the music scene. Playing only in outdoor stadia with capacities in tens of thousands, selling albums in millions, they seemed likely to go on forever. But we've been here before, and while some might decry the ephemeral nature of pop music, its capacity for change is its most engaging feature. You're only as big as your last hit, or as good as your last show, and if the music gets too grand or too pretentious it will get blown away by the next bunch who can play red-hot music in a sweaty night club.

Clockwise from top left: Madonna; Prince; Elton John; U2; Bruce Springsteen

last this week

14 January 1989

last	this	Title — Artist (label)
2	1	ESPECIALLY FOR YOU — Kylie Minogue & Jason Donovan (PWL)
4	2	GOOD LIFE — Inner City (10)
15	3	BUFFALO STANCE — Neneh Cherry (Circa)
5	4	CRACKERS INTERNATIONAL (EP) — Erasure (Mute)
13	5	LOCO IN ACAPULCO — Four Tops (Arista)
21	6	FOUR LETTER WORD — Kim Wilde (MCA)
3	7	SUDDENLY (THE WEDDING THEME FROM NEIGHBOURS) — Angry Anderson (Food For Thought)
1	8	MISTLETOE AND WINE — Cliff Richard (EMI)
6	9	BURNING BRIDGES (ON AND OFF AND ON AGAIN) — Status Quo (Vertigo)
-	10	ALL SHE WANTS IS — Duran Duran (EMI)
28	11	KEEPING THE DREAM ALIVE — Freiheit (CBS)
29	12	YOU ARE THE ONE — A-ha (Warner Bros)
9	13	CAT AMONG THE PIGEONS/SILENT NIGHT — Bros (CBS)
17	14	SMOOTH CRIMINAL — Michael Jackson (Epic)
-	15	BABY I LOVE YOUR WAY/FREEBIRD (MEDLEY) — Will To Power (Epic)
39	16	RHYTHM IS GONNA GET YOU — Gloria Estefan & Miami Sound Machine (Epic)
10	17	TWO HEARTS — Phil Collins (Virgin)
47	18	WAITING FOR A STAR TO FALL — Boy Meets Girls (RCA)
-	19	SHE DRIVES ME CRAZY — Fine Young Cannibals (London)
7	20	DOWNTOWN '88 — Petula Clark (PRT)
18	21	NATHAN JONES — Bananarama (London)
12	22	FINE TIME — New Order (Factory)
8	23	ANGEL OF HARLEM — U2 (Island)
19	24	9 A.M. (THE COMFORT ZONE) — London Beat (AnXious)
11	25	TAKE ME TO YOUR HEART — Rick Astley (RCA)
-	26	JOHN KETTLEY (IS A WEATHERMAN) — A Tribe Of Toffs (Completely Different)
-	27	BORN THIS WAY (LET'S DANCE) — Cookie Crew (ffrr)
-	28	HIT THE GROUND — Darling Buds (CBS)
14	29	FIRST TIME — Robin Beck (Mercury)
50	30	LOVE LIKE A RIVER — Climie Fisher (EMI)
-	31	EVENING FALLS — Enya (WEA)
41	32	NEED YOU TONIGHT — INXS (Mercury)
20	33	SAY A LITTLE PRAYER — Bomb The Bass featuring Maureen (Rhythm King)
27	34	RADIO ROMANCE — Tiffany (MCA)
26	35	PUT A LITTLE LOVE IN YOUR HEART — Annie Lennox & Al Green (A&M)
24	36	LEFT TO MY OWN DEVICES — Pet Shop Boys (Parlophone)
16	37	BORN TO BE MY BABY — Bon Jovi (Vertigo)
-	38	BABY DON'T FORGET MY NUMBER — Milli Vanilli (Cooltempo)
-	39	CELEBRATION — Kool & the Gang (Club)
-	40	THE LIVING YEARS — Mike & the Mechanics (WEA)
-	41	YEAH! BUDDY — Royal House (Champion)
33	42	STAKKER HUMANOID — Humanoid (Westside)
25	43	TRUE LOVE — Shakin' Stevens (Epic)
-	44	GET ON THE DANCE FLOOR — Rob Base & DJ E-Z Rock (Supreme)
-	45	SOULMATE — Wee Papa Girl Rappers (Jive)
-	46	LONDON KID — Jean Michael Jarre featuring Hank Marvin (Polydor)
-	47	YOU GOT IT — Roy Orbison (Virgin)
-	48	CHIKKI CHIKKI AHH AHH — Baby Ford (Rhythm King)
44	49	I LIVE FOR YOUR LOVE — Natalie Cole (Manhattan)
23	50	HANDLE WITH CARE — Traveling Wilburys (Wilbury)

21 January 1989

last	this	Title — Artist (label)
1	1	ESPECIALLY FOR YOU — Kylie Minogue & Jason Donovan (PWL)
3	2	BUFFALO STANCE — Neneh Cherry (Circa)
4	3	CRACKERS INTERNATIONAL (EP) — Erasure (Mute)
40	4	THE LIVING YEARS — Mike & the Mechanics (WEA)
19	5	SHE DRIVES ME CRAZY — Fine Young Cannibals (London)
15	6	BABY I LOVE YOUR WAY/FREEBIRD (MEDLEY) — Will To Power (Epic)
2	7	GOOD LIFE — Inner City (10)
18	8	WAITING FOR A STAR TO FALL — Boy Meets Girls (RCA)
47	9	YOU GOT IT — Roy Orbison (Virgin)
10	10	ALL SHE WANTS IS — Duran Duran (EMI)
5	11	LOCO IN ACAPULCO — Four Tops (Arista)
-	12	SOMETHING'S GOTTEN HOLD OF MY HEART — Marc Almond featuring Gene Pitney (Parlophone)
6	13	FOUR LETTER WORD — Kim Wilde (MCA)
16	14	RHYTHM IS GONNA GET YOU — Gloria Estefan & Miami Sound Machine (Epic)
7	15	SUDDENLY (THE WEDDING THEME FROM NEIGHBOURS) — Angry Anderson (Food For Thought)
-	16	WAIT — Robert Howard & Kym Mazelle (RCA)
12	17	YOU ARE THE ONE — A-ha (Warner Bros)
-	18	RESPECT — Adeva (Cooltempo)
44	19	GET ON THE DANCE FLOOR — Rob Base & DJ E-Z Rock (Supreme)
27	20	BORN THIS WAY (LET'S DANCE) — Cookie Crew (ffrr)
-	21	CUDDLY TOY — Roachford (CBS)
11	22	KEEPING THE DREAM ALIVE — Freiheit (CBS)
30	23	LOVE LIKE A RIVER — Climie Fisher (EMI)
28	24	HIT THE GROUND — Darling Buds (CBS)
-	25	LOVE TRAIN — Holly Johnson (MCA)
9	26	BURNING BRIDGES (ON AND OFF AND ON AGAIN) — Status Quo (Vertigo)
17	27	TWO HEARTS — Phil Collins (Virgin)
38	28	BABY DON'T FORGET MY NUMBER — Milli Vanilli (Cooltempo)
-	29	BE MY TWIN — Brother Beyond (Parlophone)
14	30	SMOOTH CRIMINAL — Michael Jackson (Epic)
25	31	TAKE ME TO YOUR HEART — Rick Astley (RCA)
-	32	TRACIE — Level 42 (Polydor)
49	33	I LIVE FOR YOUR LOVE — Natalie Cole (Manhattan)
13	34	CAT AMONG THE PIGEONS/SILENT NIGHT — Bros (CBS)
41	35	YEAH! BUDDY — Royal House (Champion)
20	36	DOWNTOWN '88 — Petula Clark (PRT)
-	37	WHERE IS THE LOVE — Mica Paris & Will Downing (Fourth & Broadway)
22	38	FINE TIME — New Order (Factory)
24	39	9 A.M. (THE COMFORT ZONE) — London Beat (AnXious)
-	40	BREAK 4 LOVE — Raze (Champion)
-	41	AFTER THE WAR — Gary Moore (Virgin)
34	42	RADIO ROMANCE — Tiffany (MCA)
-	43	FISHERMAN'S BLUES — Waterboys (Ensign)
-	44	TENDER HANDS — Chris De Burgh (A&M)
23	45	ANGEL OF HARLEM — U2 (Island)
-	46	STRANGE KIND OF LOVE — Love & Money (Fontana)
-	47	EVERLASTING LOVE — Sandra (Siren)
-	48	THAT'S THE WAY LOVE IS — Ten City (Atlantic)
21	50	NATHAN JONES — Bananarama (London)

28 January 1989

last	this	Title — Artist (label)
4	1	THE LIVING YEARS — Mike & the Mechanics (WEA)
9	2	YOU GOT IT — Roy Orbison (Virgin)
12	3	SOMETHING'S GOTTEN HOLD OF MY HEART — Marc Almond featuring Gene Pitney (Parlophone)
5	4	SHE DRIVES ME CRAZY — Fine Young Cannibals (London)
1	5	ESPECIALLY FOR YOU — Kylie Minogue & Jason Donovan (PWL)
6	6	BABY I LOVE YOUR WAY/FREEBIRD (MEDLEY) — Will To Power (Epic)
21	7	CUDDLY TOY — Roachford (CBS)
2	8	BUFFALO STANCE — Neneh Cherry (Circa)
3	9	CRACKERS INTERNATIONAL (EP) — Erasure (Mute)
8	10	WAITING FOR A STAR TO FALL — Boy Meets Girls (RCA)
7	11	GOOD LIFE — Inner City (10)
25	12	LOVE TRAIN — Holly Johnson (MCA)
16	13	WAIT — Robert Howard & Kym Mazelle (RCA)
19	14	GET ON THE DANCE FLOOR — Rob Base & DJ E-Z Rock (Supreme)
18	15	RESPECT — Adeva (Cooltempo)
28	16	BABY DON'T FORGET MY NUMBER — Milli Vanilli (Cooltempo)
10	17	ALL SHE WANTS IS — Duran Duran (EMI)
37	18	WHERE IS THE LOVE — Mica Paris & Will Downing (Fourth & Broadway)
29	19	BE MY TWIN — Brother Beyond (Parlophone)
20	20	BORN THIS WAY (LET'S DANCE) — Cookie Crew (ffrr)
13	21	FOUR LETTER WORD — Kim Wilde (MCA)
49	22	THAT'S THE WAY LOVE IS — Ten City (Atlantic)
11	23	LOCO IN ACAPULCO — Four Tops (Arista)
14	24	RHYTHM IS GONNA GET YOU — Gloria Estefan & Miami Sound Machine (Epic)
24	25	HIT THE GROUND — Darling Buds (CBS)
43	26	MY PREROGATIVE — Bobby Brown (MCA)
22	27	KEEPING THE DREAM ALIVE — Freiheit (CBS)
17	28	YOU ARE THE ONE — A-ha (Warner Bros)
-	29	BIG AREA — Then Jerico (London)
32	30	TRACIE — Level 42 (Polydor)
31	31	BREAK 4 LOVE — Raze (Champion)
-	32	STUPID QUESTION — New Model Army (EMI)
35	33	YEAH! BUDDY — Royal House (Champion)
-	34	FISHERMAN'S BLUES — Waterboys (Ensign)
23	35	LOVE LIKE A RIVER — Climie Fisher (EMI)
33	36	I LIVE FOR YOUR LOVE — Natalie Cole (Manhattan)
15	37	SUDDENLY (THE WEDDING THEME FROM NEIGHBOURS) — Angry Anderson (Food For Thought)
27	38	TWO HEARTS — Phil Collins (Virgin)
41	39	AFTER THE WAR — Gary Moore (Virgin)
-	40	THE LOVER IN ME — Sheena Easton (MCA)
-	41	YOU'RE GONNA MISS ME — Turntable Orchestra (Republic)
-	42	I ONLY WANNA BE WITH YOU — Samantha Fox (Jive)
47	43	STRANGE KIND OF LOVE — Love & Money (Fontana)
-	44	5 O'CLOCK WORLD — Julian Cope (Island)
26	45	BURNING BRIDGES (ON AND OFF AND ON AGAIN) — Status Quo (Vertigo)
-	46	HIP HOUSE/I CAN DANCE — DJ Fast Eddie (DJ International)
-	47	LOVE CHANGES EVERYTHING — Michael Ball (Really Useful)
-	48	CATHEDRAL SONG — Tanita Tikaram (WEA)
48	49	EVERLASTING LOVE — Sandra (Siren)
-	50	IT'S ONLY LOVE — Simply Red (Elektra)

It was quite an inspired idea of Stock/Aitken/Waterman's to team Kylie Minogue with *Neighbours* co-star Jason Donovan, particularly as it tied in with their characters' TV wedding (accompanied on screen by Angry Anderson's song – hence its success), and also because PWL planned to launch Jason as a soloist in his own right during the year. It was the label's biggest-selling single – over 950,000.

February 1989

4 February 1989

last week	this week	title / artist (label)
3	1	SOMETHING'S GOTTEN HOLD OF MY HEART — Marc Almond featuring Gene Pitney (Parlophone)
1	2	THE LIVING YEARS — Mike & the Mechanics (WEA)
2	3	YOU GOT IT — Roy Orbison (Virgin)
7	4	CUDDLY TOY — Roachford (CBS)
4	5	SHE DRIVES ME CRAZY — Fine Young Cannibals (London)
12	6	LOVE TRAIN — Holly Johnson (MCA)
13	7	WAIT — Robert Howard & Kym Mazelle (RCA)
5	8	ESPECIALLY FOR YOU — Kylie Minogue & Jason Donovan (PWL)
9	9	BE MY TWIN — Brother Beyond (Parlophone)
22	10	THAT'S THE WAY LOVE IS — Ten City (Atlantic)
8	11	BUFFALO STANCE — Neneh Cherry (Circa)
6	12	BABY I LOVE YOUR WAY/FREEBIRD (MEDLEY) — Will To Power (Epic)
9	13	CRACKERS INTERNATIONAL (EP) — Erasure (Mute)
10	14	WAITING FOR A STAR TO FALL — Boy Meets Girls (RCA)
16	15	BABY DON'T FORGET MY NUMBER — Milli Vanilli (Cooltempo)
18	16	WHERE IS THE LOVE — Mica Paris & Will Downing (Fourth & Broadway)
29	17	BIG AREA — Then Jerico (London)
15	18	RESPECT — Adeva (Cooltempo)
14	19	GET ON THE DANCE FLOOR — Rob Base & DJ E-Z Rock (Supreme)
26	20	MY PREROGATIVE — Bobby Brown (MCA)
11	21	GOOD LIFE — Inner City (10)
40	22	THE LOVER IN ME — Sheena Easton (MCA)
36	23	I LIVE FOR YOUR LOVE — Natalie Cole (Manhattan)
31	24	BREAK 4 LOVE — Raze (Champion)
21	25	FOUR LETTER WORD — Kim Wilde (MCA)
42	26	I ONLY WANNA BE WITH YOU — Samantha Fox (Jive)
50	27	IT'S ONLY LOVE — Simply Red (Elektra)
30	28	TRACIE — Level 42 (Polydor)
-	29	FINE TIME — Yazz (Big Lie)
-	30	LOOKING FOR LINDA — Hue & Cry (Circa)
23	31	LOCO IN ACAPULCO — Four Tops (Arista)
24	32	RHYTHM IS GONNA GET YOU — Gloria Estefan & Miami Sound Machine (Epic)
34	33	FISHERMAN'S BLUES — Waterboys (Ensign)
32	34	STUPID QUESTION — New Model Army (EMI)
47	35	LOVE CHANGES EVERYTHING — Michael Ball (Really Useful)
17	36	ALL SHE WANTS IS — Duran Duran (EMI)
-	37	GRIP '89 — Stranglers (EMI)
27	38	KEEPING THE DREAM ALIVE — Freiheit (CBS)
39	39	AFTER THE WAR — Gary Moore (Virgin)
20	40	BORN THIS WAY (LET'S DANCE) — Cookie Crew (ffrr)
43	41	STRANGE KIND OF LOVE — Love & Money (Fontana)
37	42	SUDDENLY (THE WEDDING THEME FROM NEIGHBOURS) — Angry Anderson (Food For Thought)
-	43	PEACE IN OUR TIME — Big Country (Mercury)
-	44	TENDER HANDS — Chris De Burgh (A&M)
-	45	CLARE — Fairground Attraction (RCA)
25	46	HIT THE GROUND — Darling Buds (CBS)
44	47	5 O'CLOCK WORLD — Julian Cope (Island)
-	48	LOST IN YOUR EYES — Debbie Gibson (Atlantic)
41	49	YOU'RE GONNA MISS ME — Turntable Orchestra (Republic)
-	50	AMERICAN DREAM — Crosby Stills Nash & Young (Atlantic)

11 February 1989

last week	this week	title / artist (label)
1	1	SOMETHING'S GOTTEN HOLD OF MY HEART — Marc Almond featuring Gene Pitney (Parlophone)
6	2	LOVE TRAIN — Holly Johnson (MCA)
4	3	CUDDLY TOY — Roachford (CBS)
2	4	THE LIVING YEARS — Mike & the Mechanics (WEA)
3	5	YOU GOT IT — Roy Orbison (Virgin)
10	6	THAT'S THE WAY LOVE IS — Ten City (Atlantic)
7	7	WAIT — Robert Howard & Kym Mazelle (RCA)
8	8	THE LAST OF THE FAMOUS INTERNATIONAL PLAYBOYS — Morrissey (HMV)
5	9	SHE DRIVES ME CRAZY — Fine Young Cannibals (London)
20	10	MY PREROGATIVE — Bobby Brown (MCA)
35	11	LOVE CHANGES EVERYTHING — Michael Ball (Really Useful)
22	12	THE LOVER IN ME — Sheena Easton (MCA)
29	13	FINE TIME — Yazz (Big Lie)
17	14	BIG AREA — Then Jerico (London)
8	15	ESPECIALLY FOR YOU — Kylie Minogue & Jason Donovan (PWL)
27	16	IT'S ONLY LOVE — Simply Red (Elektra)
13	17	CRACKERS INTERNATIONAL (EP) — Erasure (Mute)
9	18	BE MY TWIN — Brother Beyond (Parlophone)
11	19	BUFFALO STANCE — Neneh Cherry (Circa)
26	20	I ONLY WANNA BE WITH YOU — Samantha Fox (Jive)
15	21	BABY DON'T FORGET MY NUMBER — Milli Vanilli (Cooltempo)
30	22	LOOKING FOR LINDA — Hue & Cry (Circa)
12	23	BABY I LOVE YOUR WAY/FREEBIRD (MEDLEY) — Will To Power (Epic)
18	24	RESPECT — Adeva (Cooltempo)
14	25	WAITING FOR A STAR TO FALL — Boy Meets Girls (RCA)
-	26	SHE WON'T TALK TO ME — Luther Vandross (Epic)
24	27	BREAK 4 LOVE — Raze (Champion)
-	28	EVERY ROSE HAS ITS THORN — Poison (Capitol)
16	29	WHERE IS THE LOVE — Mica Paris & Will Downing (Fourth & Broadway)
33	30	FISHERMAN'S BLUES — Waterboys (Ensign)
23	31	I LIVE FOR YOUR LOVE — Natalie Cole (Manhattan)
-	32	ROCKET — Def Leppard (Bludgeon Riffola)
-	33	I DON'T WANT A LOVER — Texas (Mercury)
28	34	TRACIE — Level 42 (Polydor)
35	35	HOLD ME IN YOUR ARMS — Rick Astley (RCA)
-	36	I CAN DO THIS — Monie Love (Cooltempo)
43	37	PEACE IN OUR TIME — Big Country (Mercury)
48	38	LOST IN YOUR EYES — Debbie Gibson (Atlantic)
21	39	GOOD LIFE — Inner City (10)
37	40	GRIP '89 — Stranglers (EMI)
19	41	GET ON THE DANCE FLOOR — Rob Base & DJ E-Z Rock (Supreme)
45	42	CLARE — Fairground Attraction (RCA)
25	43	FOUR LETTER WORD — Kim Wilde (MCA)
-	44	MAYOR OF SIMPLETON — XTC (Virgin)
-	45	HOW COME IT NEVER RAINS — Dogs D'Amour (China)
31	46	LOCO IN ACAPULCO — Four Tops (Arista)
47	47	NERVOUS/WAP BAM BOOGIE — Matt Bianco (WEA)
42	48	SUDDENLY (THE WEDDING THEME FROM NEIGHBOURS) — Angry Anderson (Food For Thought)
-	49	WHAT I AM — Edie Brickell & New Bohemians (Geffen)
-	50	CAN'T STAY AWAY FROM YOU — Gloria Estefan & Miami Sound Machine (Epic)

18 February 1989

last week	this week	title / artist (label)
1	1	SOMETHING'S GOTTEN HOLD OF MY HEART — Marc Almond featuring Gene Pitney (Parlophone)
-	2	BALLAD OF THE STREETS (EP) — Simple Minds (Virgin)
2	3	LOVE TRAIN — Holly Johnson (MCA)
8	4	THE LAST OF THE FAMOUS INTERNATIONAL PLAYBOYS — Morrissey (HMV)
4	5	THE LIVING YEARS — Mike & the Mechanics (WEA)
10	6	MY PREROGATIVE — Bobby Brown (MCA)
13	7	FINE TIME — Yazz (Big Lie)
11	8	LOVE CHANGES EVERYTHING — Michael Ball (Really Useful)
3	9	CUDDLY TOY — Roachford (CBS)
5	10	YOU GOT IT — Roy Orbison (Virgin)
12	11	THE LOVER IN ME — Sheena Easton (MCA)
16	12	IT'S ONLY LOVE — Simply Red (Elektra)
15	13	LOOKING FOR LINDA — Hue & Cry (Circa)
6	14	THAT'S THE WAY LOVE IS — Ten City (Atlantic)
20	16	I ONLY WANNA BE WITH YOU — Samantha Fox (Jive)
28	17	EVERY ROSE HAS ITS THORN — Poison (Capitol)
9	18	SHE DRIVES ME CRAZY — Fine Young Cannibals (London)
35	19	HOLD ME IN YOUR ARMS — Rick Astley (RCA)
-	20	STOP! — Sam Brown (A&M)
33	21	I DON'T WANT A LOVER — Texas (Mercury)
14	22	BIG AREA — Then Jerico (London)
32	23	ROCKET — Def Leppard (Bludgeon Riffola)
17	24	CRACKERS INTERNATIONAL (EP) — Erasure (Mute)
24	25	RESPECT — Adeva (Cooltempo)
15	26	ESPECIALLY FOR YOU — Kylie Minogue & Jason Donovan (PWL)
27	27	BREAK 4 LOVE — Raze (Champion)
26	28	SHE WON'T TALK TO ME — Luther Vandross (Epic)
21	29	BABY DON'T FORGET MY NUMBER — Milli Vanilli (Cooltempo)
19	30	BUFFALO STANCE — Neneh Cherry (Circa)
23	31	BABY I LOVE YOUR WAY/FREEBIRD (MEDLEY) — Will To Power (Epic)
18	32	BE MY TWIN — Brother Beyond (Parlophone)
38	33	LOST IN YOUR EYES — Debbie Gibson (Atlantic)
49	34	WHAT I AM — Edie Brickell & New Bohemians (Geffen)
29	35	WHERE IS THE LOVE — Mica Paris & Will Downing (Fourth & Broadway)
25	36	WAITING FOR A STAR TO FALL — Boy Meets Girls (RCA)
-	37	CAN U DIG IT — Pop Will Eat Itself (RCA)
-	38	HEY MUSIC LOVER — S'Express (Rhythm King)
36	39	I CAN DO THIS — Monie Love (Cooltempo)
45	40	HOW COME IT NEVER RAINS — Dogs D'Amour (China)
50	41	CAN'T STAY AWAY FROM YOU — Gloria Estefan & Miami Sound Machine (Epic)
41	42	GET ON THE DANCE FLOOR — Rob Base & DJ E-Z Rock (Supreme)
30	43	FISHERMAN'S BLUES — Waterboys (Ensign)
44	44	ALL THIS TIME — Tiffany (MCA)
31	45	I LIVE FOR YOUR LOVE — Natalie Cole (Manhattan)
-	46	THE PRICE OF LOVE — Bryan Ferry (EG)
-	47	PROMISED LAND — Style Council (Polydor)
-	48	STAND — R.E.M. (Warner Bros)
39	49	GOOD LIFE — Inner City (10)
37	50	PEACE IN OUR TIME — Big Country (Mercury)

Another inspired duet was that of Marc Almond on *Something's Gotten Hold Of My Heart* with the song's original 1967 hitmaker Gene Pitney. Almond's album version was recorded solo, but in an exact recreation of the Pitney original, so once Gene had agreed to add his vocals, the blending of the two vocal parts was relatively straightforward. Ironically, this became Pitney's first Number One.

25 February 1989

LW	TW	Title	Artist (Label)
2	1	BALLAD OF THE STREETS (EP)	Simple Minds (Virgin)
8	2	LOVE CHANGES EVERYTHING	Michael Ball (Really Useful)
1	3	SOMETHING'S GOTTEN HOLD OF MY HEART	Marc Almond featuring Gene Pitney (Parlophone)
6	4	MY PREROGATIVE	Bobby Brown (MCA)
20	5	STOP!	Sam Brown (A&M)
7	6	FINE TIME	Yazz (Big Life)
19	7	HOLD ME IN YOUR ARMS	Rick Astley (RCA)
5	8	THE LIVING YEARS	Mike & the Mechanics (WEA)
-	9	LEAVE ME ALONE	Michael Jackson (Epic)
3	10	LOVE TRAIN	Holly Johnson (MCA)
21	11	I DON'T WANT A LOVER	Texas (Mercury)
15	12	LOOKING FOR LINDA	Hue & Cry (Circa)
23	13	ROCKET	Def Leppard (Bludgeon Riffola)
17	14	EVERY ROSE HAS ITS THORN	Poison (Capitol)
13	15	WAIT	Robert Howard & Kym Mazelle (RCA)
4	16	THE LAST OF THE FAMOUS INTERNATIONAL PLAYBOYS	Morrissey (HMV)
12	17	IT'S ONLY LOVE	Simply Red (Elektra)
10	18	YOU GOT IT	Roy Orbison (Virgin)
11	19	THE LOVER IN ME	Sheena Easton (MCA)
41	20	CAN'T STAY AWAY FROM YOU	Gloria Estefan & Miami Sound Machine (Epic)
9	21	CUDDLY TOY	Roachford (CBS)
-	22	HELP!	Bananarama Lananeeneenoonoo (London)
38	23	HEY MUSIC LOVER	S'Express (Rhythm King)
16	24	I ONLY WANNA BE WITH YOU	Samantha Fox (Jive)
14	25	THAT'S THE WAY LOVE IS	Ten City (Atlantic)
-	26	WILD THING/LOC'ED AFTER DARK	Tone Loc (Fourth & Broadway)
-	27	NOTHING HAS BEEN PROVED	Dusty Springfield (Parlophone)
18	28	SHE DRIVES ME CRAZY	Fine Young Cannibals (London)
47	29	PROMISED LAND	Style Council (Polydor)
34	30	WHAT I AM	Edie Brickell & New Bohemians (Geffen)
22	31	BIG AREA	Then Jerico (London)
37	32	CAN U DIG IT	Pop Will Eat Itself (RCA)
33	33	LOST IN YOUR EYES	Debbie Gibson (Atlantic)
-	34	BLOW THE HOUSE DOWN	Living In A Box (Chrysalis)
24	35	CRACKERS INTERNATIONAL (EP)	Erasure (Mute)
26	36	ESPECIALLY FOR YOU	Kylie Minogue & Jason Donovan (PWL)
-	37	CAN'T BE SURE	Sundays (Rough Trade)
25	38	RESPECT	Adeva (Cooltempo)
27	39	BREAK 4 LOVE	Raze (Champion)
-	40	I'M ON MY WAY	Proclaimers (Chrysalis)
29	41	BABY DON'T FORGET MY NUMBER	Milli Vanilli (Cooltempo)
46	42	THE PRICE OF LOVE	Bryan Ferry (EG)
-	43	EVERYTHING COUNTS	Depeche Mode (Mute)
-	44	SECRET RENDEZVOUS	Karyn White (Warner Bros)
44	45	ALL THIS TIME	Tiffany (MCA)
30	46	BUFFALO STANCE	Neneh Cherry (Circa)
-	47	TURN UP THE BASS	Tyree featuring Kool Rock Steady (ffrr)
32	48	BE MY TWIN	Brother Beyond (Parlophone)
36	49	WAITING FOR A STAR TO FALL	Boy Meets Girls (RCA)
-	50	JEZEBEL	Shakin' Stevens (Epic)

4 March 1989

LW	TW	Title	Artist (Label)
1	1	BALLAD OF THE STREETS (EP)	Simple Minds (Virgin)
9	2	LEAVE ME ALONE	Michael Jackson (Epic)
5	3	STOP!	Sam Brown (A&M)
2	4	LOVE CHANGES EVERYTHING	Michael Ball (Really Useful)
22	5	HELP!	Bananarama Lananeeneenoonoo (London)
4	6	MY PREROGATIVE	Bobby Brown (MCA)
23	7	HEY MUSIC LOVER	S'Express (Rhythm King)
11	8	I DON'T WANT A LOVER	Texas (Mercury)
3	9	SOMETHING'S GOTTEN HOLD OF MY HEART	Marc Almond featuring Gene Pitney (Parlophone)
27	10	NOTHING HAS BEEN PROVED	Dusty Springfield (Parlophone)
7	11	HOLD ME IN YOUR ARMS	Rick Astley (RCA)
13	12	ROCKET	Def Leppard (Bludgeon Riffola)
12	13	LOOKING FOR LINDA	Hue & Cry (Circa)
8	14	THE LIVING YEARS	Mike & the Mechanics (WEA)
6	15	FINE TIME	Yazz (Big Life)
10	16	LOVE TRAIN	Holly Johnson (MCA)
20	17	CAN'T STAY AWAY FROM YOU	Gloria Estefan & Miami Sound Machine (Epic)
26	18	WILD THING/LOC'ED AFTER DARK	Tone Loc (Fourth & Broadway)
14	19	EVERY ROSE HAS ITS THORN	Poison (Capitol)
34	20	BLOW THE HOUSE DOWN	Living In A Box (Chrysalis)
29	21	PROMISED LAND	Style Council (Polydor)
18	22	YOU GOT IT	Roy Orbison (Virgin)
15	23	WAIT	Robert Howard & Kym Mazelle (RCA)
30	24	WHAT I AM	Edie Brickell & New Bohemians (Geffen)
47	25	TURN UP THE BASS	Tyree featuring Kool Rock Steady (ffrr)
17	26	IT'S ONLY LOVE	Simply Red (Elektra)
-	27	I'D RATHER JACK	Reynolds Girls (PWL)
25	28	THAT'S THE WAY LOVE IS	Ten City (Atlantic)
-	29	WAGES DAY	Deacon Blue (CBS)
24	30	I ONLY WANNA BE WITH YOU	Samantha Fox (Jive)
43	31	EVERYTHING COUNTS	Depeche Mode (Mute)
19	32	THE LOVER IN ME	Sheena Easton (MCA)
28	33	SHE DRIVES ME CRAZY	Fine Young Cannibals (London)
-	34	THIS TIME I KNOW IT'S FOR REAL	Donna Summer (Warner Bros)
-	35	CELEBRATE THE WORLD	Womack & Womack (Fourth & Broadway)
36	36	TOO MANY BROKEN HEARTS	Jason Donovan (PWL)
33	37	LOST IN YOUR EYES	Debbie Gibson (Atlantic)
21	38	CUDDLY TOY	Roachford (CBS)
37	39	CAN'T BE SURE	Sundays (Rough Trade)
32	40	CAN U DIG IT	Pop Will Eat Itself (RCA)
16	41	THE LAST OF THE FAMOUS INTERNATIONAL PLAYBOYS	Morrissey (HMV)
36	42	ESPECIALLY FOR YOU	Kylie Minogue & Jason Donovan (PWL)
-	43	HEARSAY	Alexander O'Neal (Tabu)
31	44	BIG AREA	Then Jerico (London)
-	45	INDESTRUCTIBLE	Four Tops (Arista)
-	46	MEAN MAN	W.A.S.P. (Capitol)
-	47	INFRO-FREAKO	Jesus Jones (Food)
38	48	RESPECT	Adeva (Cooltempo)
35	49	CRACKERS INTERNATIONAL (EP)	Erasure (Mute)
-	50	LOVE IN THE NATURAL WAY	Kim Wilde (MCA)

11 March 1989

LW	TW	Title	Artist (Label)
2	1	LEAVE ME ALONE	Michael Jackson (Epic)
1	2	BALLAD OF THE STREETS (EP)	Simple Minds (Virgin)
3	3	STOP!	Sam Brown (A&M)
5	4	HELP!	Bananarama Lananeeneenoonoo (London)
36	5	TOO MANY BROKEN HEARTS	Jason Donovan (PWL)
7	6	HEY MUSIC LOVER	S'Express (Rhythm King)
4	7	LOVE CHANGES EVERYTHING	Michael Ball (Really Useful)
17	8	CAN'T STAY AWAY FROM YOU	Gloria Estefan & Miami Sound Machine (Epic)
10	9	NOTHING HAS BEEN PROVED	Dusty Springfield (Parlophone)
25	10	TURN UP THE BASS	Tyree featuring Kool Rock Steady (ffrr)
8	11	I DON'T WANT A LOVER	Texas (Mercury)
20	12	BLOW THE HOUSE DOWN	Living In A Box (Chrysalis)
6	13	MY PREROGATIVE	Bobby Brown (MCA)
-	14	STRAIGHT UP	Paula Abdul (Siren)
29	15	WAGES DAY	Deacon Blue (CBS)
18	16	WILD THING/LOC'ED AFTER DARK	Tone Loc (Fourth & Broadway)
19	17	EVERY ROSE HAS ITS THORN	Poison (Capitol)
13	18	LOOKING FOR LINDA	Hue & Cry (Circa)
34	19	THIS TIME I KNOW IT'S FOR REAL	Donna Summer (Warner Bros)
46	20	MEAN MAN	W.A.S.P. (Capitol)
27	21	I'D RATHER JACK	Reynolds Girls (PWL)
9	22	SOMETHING'S GOTTEN HOLD OF MY HEART	Marc Almond featuring Gene Pitney (Parlophone)
31	23	EVERYTHING COUNTS	Depeche Mode (Mute)
11	24	HOLD ME IN YOUR ARMS	Rick Astley (RCA)
35	25	CELEBRATE THE WORLD	Womack & Womack (Fourth & Broadway)
16	26	LOVE TRAIN	Holly Johnson (MCA)
-	27	ROUND AND ROUND	New Order (Factory)
15	28	FINE TIME	Yazz (Big Life)
-	29	SLEEPTALK	Alyson Williams (Def Jam)
12	30	ROCKET	Def Leppard (Bludgeon Riffola)
14	31	THE LIVING YEARS	Mike & the Mechanics (WEA)
-	32	WHO WANTS TO BE THE DISCO KING?	Wonder Stuff (Far Out)
24	33	WHAT I AM	Edie Brickell & New Bohemians (Geffen)
-	34	VERONICA	Elvis Costello (Warner Bros)
-	35	CRYIN'	Vixen (EMI Manhattan)
23	36	WAIT	Robert Howard & Kym Mazelle (RCA)
50	37	LOVE IN THE NATURAL WAY	Kim Wilde (MCA)
22	38	YOU GOT IT	Roy Orbison (Virgin)
-	39	DON'T KNOW WHAT YOU'VE GOT (TIL IT'S GONE)	Cinderella (Vertigo)
-	40	ONE MAN	Chanelle (Cooltempo)
47	41	INFRO-FREAKO	Jesus Jones (Food)
-	42	INTERNATIONAL RESCUE	Fuzzbox (WEA)
-	43	WHERE DOES THE TIME GO?	Julia Fordham (Circa)
45	44	PROMISED LAND	Style Council (Polydor)
45	45	INDESTRUCTIBLE	Four Tops (Arista)
44	46	HEARSAY	Alexander O'Neal (Tabu)
28	47	THAT'S THE WAY LOVE IS	Ten City (Atlantic)
-	48	I BEG YOUR PARDON	Kon Kan (Atlantic)
26	49	IT'S ONLY LOVE	Simply Red (Elektra)
-	50	ETERNAL FLAME	Bangles (CBS)

Simple Minds added their name to the ultra-select list of those with a Number One EP. The notable track on the record, and the one which received the lion's share of airplay, was the epic *Belfast Child*. Michael Ball's debut hit *Love Changes Everything*, meanwhile, was from Andrew Lloyd-Webber's new hit musical *Aspects Of Love,* in the opening West End season of which, Ball starred.

March 1989

18 March 1989

last week	this week	Title	Artist (Label)
5	1	TOO MANY BROKEN HEARTS	Jason Donovan (PWL)
4	2	HELP!	Bananarama Lananeeneenoonoo (London)
-	3	LIKE A PRAYER	Madonna (Sire)
19	4	THIS TIME I KNOW IT'S FOR REAL	Donna Summer (Warner Bros)
1	5	LEAVE ME ALONE	Michael Jackson (Epic)
7	6	LOVE CHANGES EVERYTHING	Michael Ball (Really Useful)
3	7	STOP!	Sam Brown (A&M)
14	8	STRAIGHT UP	Paula Abdul (Siren)
12	9	BLOW THE HOUSE DOWN	Living In A Box (Chrysalis)
2	10	BALLAD OF THE STREETS (EP)	Simple Minds (Virgin)
6	11	HEY MUSIC LOVER	S'Express (Rhythm King)
21	12	I'D RATHER JACK	Reynolds Girls (PWL)
8	13	CAN'T STAY AWAY FROM YOU	Gloria Estefan & Miami Sound Machine (Epic)
9	14	NOTHING HAS BEEN PROVED	Dusty Springfield (Parlophone)
15	15	WAGES DAY	Deacon Blue (CBS)
10	16	TURN UP THE BASS	Tyree featuring Kool Rock Steady (ffrr)
11	17	I DON'T WANT A LOVER	Texas (Mercury)
20	18	MEAN MAN	W.A.S.P. (Capitol)
17	19	EVERY ROSE HAS ITS THORN	Poison (Capitol)
25	20	CELEBRATE THE WORLD	Womack & Womack (Fourth & Broadway)
13	21	MY PREROGATIVE	Bobby Brown (MCA)
32	22	WHO WANTS TO BE THE DISCO KING?	Wonder Stuff (Far Out)
29	23	SLEEPTALK	Alyson Williams (Def Jam)
42	24	INTERNATIONAL RESCUE	Fuzzbox (WEA)
27	25	ROUND AND ROUND	New Order (Factory)
35	26	CRYIN'	Vixen (EMI Manhattan)
40	27	ONE MAN	Chanelle (Cooltempo)
28	28	EVERYTHING COUNTS	Depeche Mode (Mute)
16	29	WILD THING/LOC'ED AFTER DARK	Tone Loc (Fourth & Broadway)
34	30	VERONICA	Elvis Costello (Warner Bros)
24	31	HOLD ME IN YOUR ARMS	Rick Astley (RCA)
32	32	LOVE IN THE NATURAL WAY	Kim Wilde (MCA)
18	33	LOOKING FOR LINDA	Hue & Cry (Circa)
48	34	I BEG YOUR PARDON	Kon Kan (Atlantic)
22	35	SOMETHING'S GOTTEN HOLD OF MY HEART	Marc Almond featuring Gene Pitney (Parlophone)
-	36	PARADISE CITY	Guns N' Roses (Geffen)
45	37	INDESTRUCTIBLE	Four Tops (Arista)
26	38	LOVE TRAIN	Holly Johnson (MCA)
-	39	KEEP ON MOVIN'	Soul II Soul featuring Caron Wheeler (10)
43	40	WHERE DOES THE TIME GO?	Julia Fordham (Circa)
-	41	VAGABONDS	New Model Army (EMI)
-	42	IT TAKES TWO	Rob Base & DJ E-Z Rock (Citybeat)
-	43	FAMILY MAN	Roachford (CBS)
31	44	THE LIVING YEARS	Mike & the Mechanics (WEA)
-	45	A LA VIE, A L'AMOUR	Jakie Quartz (PWL)
28	46	FINE TIME	Yazz (Big Lie)
-	47	THE RATTLER	Goodbye Mr. MacKenzie (Capitol)
38	48	YOU GOT IT	Roy Orbison (Virgin)
-	49	ANTI-SOCIAL	Anthrax (Island)
-	50	YOYO GET FUNKY	DJ Fast Eddie (DJ International)

25 March 1989

last week	this week	Title	Artist (Label)
3	1	LIKE A PRAYER	Madonna (Sire)
1	2	TOO MANY BROKEN HEARTS	Jason Donovan (PWL)
4	3	THIS TIME I KNOW IT'S FOR REAL	Donna Summer (Warner Bros)
8	4	STRAIGHT UP	Paula Abdul (Siren)
2	5	HELP!	Bananarama Lananeeneenoonoo (London)
39	6	KEEP ON MOVIN'	Soul II Soul featuring Caron Wheeler (10)
7	7	STOP!	Sam Brown (A&M)
9	8	BLOW THE HOUSE DOWN	Living In A Box (Chrysalis)
6	9	LOVE CHANGES EVERYTHING	Michael Ball (Really Useful)
12	10	I'D RATHER JACK	Reynolds Girls (PWL)
13	11	CAN'T STAY AWAY FROM YOU	Gloria Estefan & Miami Sound Machine (Epic)
11	12	HEY MUSIC LOVER	S'Express (Rhythm King)
25	13	ROUND AND ROUND	New Order (Factory)
36	14	PARADISE CITY	Guns N' Roses (Geffen)
5	15	LEAVE ME ALONE	Michael Jackson (Epic)
27	16	ONE MAN	Chanelle (Cooltempo)
20	17	CELEBRATE THE WORLD	Womack & Womack (Fourth & Broadway)
23	18	SLEEPTALK	Alyson Williams (Def Jam)
34	19	I BEG YOUR PARDON	Kon Kan (Atlantic)
24	20	INTERNATIONAL RESCUE	Fuzzbox (WEA)
10	21	BALLAD OF THE STREETS (EP)	Simple Minds (Virgin)
15	22	WAGES DAY	Deacon Blue (CBS)
14	23	NOTHING HAS BEEN PROVED	Dusty Springfield (Parlophone)
19	24	EVERY ROSE HAS ITS THORN	Poison (Capitol)
17	25	I DON'T WANT A LOVER	Texas (Mercury)
26	26	PEOPLE HOLD ON	Coldcut featuring Lisa Stansfield (Ahead Of Our Time)
16	27	TURN UP THE BASS	Tyree featuring Kool Rock Steady (ffrr)
30	28	VERONICA	Elvis Costello (Warner Bros)
22	29	WHO WANTS TO BE THE DISCO KING?	Wonder Stuff (Far Out)
43	30	FAMILY MAN	Roachford (CBS)
32	31	LOVE IN THE NATURAL WAY	Kim Wilde (MCA)
18	32	MEAN MAN	W.A.S.P. (Capitol)
37	33	INDESTRUCTIBLE	Four Tops (Arista)
21	34	MY PREROGATIVE	Bobby Brown (MCA)
26	35	CRYIN'	Vixen (EMI Manhattan)
-	36	BIG BUBBLES, NO TROUBLES	Ellis, Beggs & Howard (RCA)
47	37	THE RATTLER	Goodbye Mr. MacKenzie (Capitol)
-	38	DON'T BE CRUEL	Bobby Brown (MCA)
28	39	EVERYTHING COUNTS	Depeche Mode (Mute)
49	40	ANTI-SOCIAL	Anthrax (Island)
41	41	VAGABONDS	New Model Army (EMI)
45	42	A LA VIE, A L'AMOUR	Jakie Quartz (PWL)
40	43	WHERE DOES THE TIME GO?	Julia Fordham (Circa)
44	44	DAYS LIKE THIS	Sheena Easton (MCA)
29	45	WILD THING/LOC'ED AFTER DARK	Tone Loc (Fourth & Broadway)
35	46	SOMETHING'S GOTTEN HOLD OF MY HEART	Marc Almond featuring Gene Pitney (Parlophone)
-	47	ETERNAL FLAME	Bangles (CBS)
31	48	HOLD ME IN YOUR ARMS	Rick Astley (RCA)
-	49	WORLD OUTSIDE YOUR WINDOW	Tanita Tikaram (WEA)
-	50	DON'T TELL ME LIES	Breathe (Siren)

1 April 1989

last week	this week	Title	Artist (Label)
1	1	LIKE A PRAYER	Madonna (Sire)
3	2	THIS TIME I KNOW IT'S FOR REAL	Donna Summer (Warner Bros)
2	3	TOO MANY BROKEN HEARTS	Jason Donovan (PWL)
4	4	STRAIGHT UP	Paula Abdul (Siren)
6	5	KEEP ON MOVIN'	Soul II Soul featuring Caron Wheeler (10)
14	6	PARADISE CITY	Guns N' Roses (Geffen)
19	7	I BEG YOUR PARDON	Kon Kan (Atlantic)
10	8	I'D RATHER JACK	Reynolds Girls (PWL)
5	9	HELP!	Bananarama Lananeeneenoonoo (London)
16	10	ONE MAN	Chanelle (Cooltempo)
18	11	SLEEPTALK	Alyson Williams (Def Jam)
11	12	CAN'T STAY AWAY FROM YOU	Gloria Estefan & Miami Sound Machine (Epic)
7	13	STOP!	Sam Brown (A&M)
26	14	PEOPLE HOLD ON	Coldcut featuring Lisa Stansfield (Ahead Of Our Time)
20	15	INTERNATIONAL RESCUE	Fuzzbox (WEA)
-	16	HAVEN'T STOPPED DANCING YET	Pat & Mick (PWL)
38	17	DON'T BE CRUEL	Bobby Brown (MCA)
12	18	HEY MUSIC LOVER	S'Express (Rhythm King)
8	19	BLOW THE HOUSE DOWN	Living In A Box (Chrysalis)
13	20	ROUND AND ROUND	New Order (Factory)
30	21	FAMILY MAN	Roachford (CBS)
9	22	LOVE CHANGES EVERYTHING	Michael Ball (Really Useful)
-	23	FIRE WOMAN	Cult (Beggars Banquet)
47	24	ETERNAL FLAME	Bangles (CBS)
-	25	GOT TO GET YOU BACK	Kym Mazelle (Syncopate)
17	26	CELEBRATE THE WORLD	Womack & Womack (Fourth & Broadway)
33	27	INDESTRUCTIBLE	Four Tops (Arista)
15	28	LEAVE ME ALONE	Michael Jackson (Epic)
29	29	LOVE IN THE NATURAL WAY	Kim Wilde (MCA)
-	30	OF COURSE I'M LYING	Yello (Mercury)
28	31	VERONICA	Elvis Costello (Warner Bros)
-	32	ONLY THE LONELY	T'Pau (Siren)
37	33	THE RATTLER	Goodbye Mr. MacKenzie (Capitol)
-	34	MUSICAL FREEDOM (MOVING ON UP)	Paul Simpson featuring Adeva (Cooltempo)
25	35	I DON'T WANT A LOVER	Texas (Mercury)
36	36	BIG BUBBLES, NO TROUBLES	Ellis, Beggs & Howard (RCA)
-	37	THE BEAT(EN) GENERATION	The The (Epic)
21	38	BALLAD OF THE STREETS (EP)	Simple Minds (Virgin)
22	39	WAGES DAY	Deacon Blue (CBS)
40	40	AMERICANOS	Holly Johnson (MCA)
24	41	EVERY ROSE HAS ITS THORN	Poison (Capitol)
50	42	DON'T TELL ME LIES	Breathe (Siren)
23	43	NOTHING HAS BEEN PROVED	Dusty Springfield (Parlophone)
44	44	DAYS LIKE THIS	Sheena Easton (MCA)
-	45	DON'T WALK AWAY	Toni Childs (A&M)
34	46	MY PREROGATIVE	Bobby Brown (MCA)
-	47	CAN YOU KEEP A SECRET?	Brother Beyond (Parlophone)
-	48	JOCELYN SQUARE	Love & Money (Fontana)
27	49	TURN UP THE BASS	Tyree featuring Kool Rock Steady (ffrr)
-	50	LET'S GO ROUND THERE	Darling Buds (Epic)

Jason Donovan's debut romped easily to Number One, but was immediately dethroned by Madonna's *Like A Prayer*, the title track from her eagerly-awaited new album. Despite (or even because of) a major PR kerfuffle over the aborted use of the new song as a Pepsi-Cola promo, because its video was felt to be too controversial by the sponsor, *Like A Prayer* was a Number One all around the world.

8 April 1989

last week	this week		
1	1	LIKE A PRAYER	Madonna (Sire)
2	2	THIS TIME I KNOW IT'S FOR REAL	Donna Summer (Warner Bros)
4	3	STRAIGHT UP	Paula Abdul (Siren)
3	4	TOO MANY BROKEN HEARTS	Jason Donovan (PWL)
24	5	ETERNAL FLAME	Bangles (CBS)
7	6	I BEG YOUR PARDON	Kon Kan (Atlantic)
5	7	KEEP ON MOVIN'	Soul II Soul featuring Caron Wheeler (10)
6	8	PARADISE CITY	Guns N' Roses (Geffen)
16	9	HAVEN'T STOPPED DANCING YET	Pat & Mick (PWL)
14	10	PEOPLE HOLD ON	Coldcut featuring Lisa Stansfield (Ahead Of Our Time)
17	11	DON'T BE CRUEL	Bobby Brown (MCA)
8	12	I'D RATHER JACK	Reynolds Girls (PWL)
15	13	INTERNATIONAL RESCUE	Fuzzbox (WEA)
12	14	CAN'T STAY AWAY FROM YOU	Gloria Estefan & Miami Sound Machine (Epic)
23	15	FIRE WOMAN	Cult (Beggars Banquet)
9	16	HELP!	Bananarama Lananeeneenoonoo (London)
40	17	AMERICANOS	Holly Johnson (MCA)
37	18	THE BEAT(EN) GENERATION	The The (Epic)
11	19	SLEEPTALK	Alyson Williams (Def Jam)
10	20	ONE MAN	Chanelle (Cooltempo)
21	21	FAMILY MAN	Roachford (CBS)
13	22	STOP!	Sam Brown (A&M)
25	23	GOT TO GET YOU BACK	Kym Mazelle (Syncopate)
-	24	SHE'S A MYSTERY TO ME	Roy Orbison (Virgin)
47	25	CAN YOU KEEP A SECRET?	Brother Beyond (Parlophone)
18	26	HEY MUSIC LOVER	S'Express (Rhythm King)
34	27	MUSICAL FREEDOM (MOVING ON UP)	Paul Simpson featuring Adeva (Cooltempo)
30	28	OF COURSE I'M LYING	Yello (Mercury)
-	29	BABY I DON'T CARE	Transvision Vamp (MCA)
19	30	BLOW THE HOUSE DOWN	Living In A Box (Chrysalis)
33	31	THE RATTLER	Goodbye Mr. MacKenzie (Capitol)
26	32	CELEBRATE THE WORLD	Womack & Womack (Fourth & Broadway)
22	33	LOVE CHANGES EVERYTHING	Michael Ball (Really Useful)
32	34	ONLY THE LONELY	T'Pau (Siren)
-	35	MYSTIFY	INXS (Mercury)
36	36	LEAVE ME ALONE	Michael Jackson (Epic)
20	37	ROUND AND ROUND	New Order (Factory)
-	38	BEDS ARE BURNING	Midnight Oil (Sprint)
-	39	WHAT DOES IT TAKE?	Then Jerico (London)
-	40	GOT TO KEEP ON	Cookie Crew (ffrr)
-	41	REQUIEM	London Boys (WEA)
-	42	DEVOTION	Ten City (Atlantic)
-	43	BEAUTY IS ONLY SKIN DEEP	Aswad (Mango)
35	44	I DON'T WANT A LOVER	Texas (Mercury)
-	45	THE MONKEES EP (EP)	Monkees (Arista)
27	46	INDESTRUCTIBLE	Four Tops (Arista)
48	47	JOCELYN SQUARE	Love & Money (Fontana)
-	48	DANCERAMA	Sigue Sigue Sputnik (Parlophone)
50	49	LET'S GO ROUND THERE	Darling Buds (CBS)
29	50	LOVE IN THE NATURAL WAY	Kim Wilde (MCA)

15 April 1989

1	1	LIKE A PRAYER	Madonna (Sire)
5	2	ETERNAL FLAME	Bangles (CBS)
3	3	STRAIGHT UP	Paula Abdul (Siren)
6	4	I BEG YOUR PARDON	Kon Kan (Atlantic)
2	5	THIS TIME I KNOW IT'S FOR REAL	Donna Summer (Warner Bros)
-	6	IF YOU DON'T KNOW ME BY NOW	Simply Red (Elektra)
4	7	TOO MANY BROKEN HEARTS	Jason Donovan (PWL)
17	8	AMERICANOS	Holly Johnson (MCA)
7	9	KEEP ON MOVIN'	Soul II Soul featuring Caron Wheeler (10)
29	10	BABY I DON'T CARE	Transvision Vamp (MCA)
35	11	MYSTIFY	INXS (Mercury)
9	12	HAVEN'T STOPPED DANCING YET	Pat & Mick (PWL)
8	13	PARADISE CITY	Guns N' Roses (Geffen)
-	14	WHEN LOVE COMES TO TOWN	U2 with B.B. King (Island)
11	15	DON'T BE CRUEL	Bobby Brown (MCA)
25	16	CAN YOU KEEP A SECRET?	Brother Beyond (Parlophone)
18	17	THE BEAT(EN) GENERATION	The The (Epic)
10	18	PEOPLE HOLD ON	Coldcut featuring Lisa Stansfield (Ahead Of Our Time)
15	19	FIRE WOMAN	Cult (Beggars Banquet)
24	20	SHE'S A MYSTERY TO ME	Roy Orbison (Virgin)
12	21	I'D RATHER JACK	Reynolds Girls (PWL)
-	22	GOOD THING	Fine Young Cannibals (London)
27	23	MUSICAL FREEDOM (MOVING ON UP)	Paul Simpson featuring Adeva (Cooltempo)
14	24	CAN'T STAY AWAY FROM YOU	Gloria Estefan & Miami Sound Machine (Epic)
13	25	INTERNATIONAL RESCUE	Fuzzbox (WEA)
19	26	SLEEPTALK	Alyson Williams (Def Jam)
28	27	OF COURSE I'M LYING	Yello (Mercury)
20	28	ONE MAN	Chanelle (Cooltempo)
39	29	WHAT DOES IT TAKE?	Then Jerico (London)
42	30	DEVOTION	Ten City (Atlantic)
31	31	GOT TO KEEP ON	Cookie Crew (ffrr)
16	32	HELP!	Bananarama Lananeeneenoonoo (London)
43	33	BEAUTY IS ONLY SKIN DEEP	Aswad (Mango)
34	34	ONLY THE LONELY	T'Pau (Siren)
38	35	BEDS ARE BURNING	Midnight Oil (Sprint)
22	36	STOP!	Sam Brown (A&M)
41	37	REQUIEM	London Boys (WEA)
-	38	ONLY THE MOMENT	Marc Almond (Parlophone)
21	39	FAMILY MAN	Roachford (CBS)
37	40	ROUND AND ROUND	New Order (Factory)
-	41	PLEASE DON'T BE SCARED	Barry Manilow (Arista)
-	42	PLANET E	KC Flight (RCA)
-	43	THIS IS YOUR LIFE	Blow Monkeys (RCA)
-	44	WITH EVERY HEARTBEAT	Free Star (Tent)
45	45	ME MYSELF I	De La Soul (Big Life)
26	46	HEY MUSIC LOVER	S'Express (Rhythm King)
-	47	REAL LOVE	Jody Watley (MCA)
36	48	LEAVE ME ALONE	Michael Jackson (Epic)
-	49	VOODOO RAY	A Guy Called Gerald (Rham!)
-	50	YOU ON MY MIND	Swing Out Sister (Fontana)

22 April 1989

6	1	IF YOU DON'T KNOW ME BY NOW	Simply Red (Elektra)
2	2	ETERNAL FLAME	Bangles (CBS)
10	3	BABY I DON'T CARE	Transvision Vamp (MCA)
4	4	I BEG YOUR PARDON	Kon Kan (Atlantic)
1	5	LIKE A PRAYER	Madonna (Sire)
8	6	AMERICANOS	Holly Johnson (MCA)
14	7	WHEN LOVE COMES TO TOWN	U2 with B.B. King (Island)
3	8	STRAIGHT UP	Paula Abdul (Siren)
22	9	GOOD THING	Fine Young Cannibals (London)
-	10	THIS IS YOUR LAND	Simple Minds (Virgin)
11	11	MYSTIFY	INXS (Mercury)
7	12	TOO MANY BROKEN HEARTS	Jason Donovan (PWL)
5	13	THIS TIME I KNOW IT'S FOR REAL	Donna Summer (Warner Bros)
9	14	KEEP ON MOVIN'	Soul II Soul featuring Caron Wheeler (10)
31	15	GOT TO KEEP ON	Cookie Crew (ffrr)
12	16	HAVEN'T STOPPED DANCING YET	Pat & Mick (PWL)
23	17	MUSICAL FREEDOM (MOVING ON UP)	Paul Simpson featuring Adeva (Cooltempo)
13	18	PARADISE CITY	Guns N' Roses (Geffen)
27	19	OF COURSE I'M LYING	Yello (Mercury)
18	20	PEOPLE HOLD ON	Coldcut featuring Lisa Stansfield (Ahead Of Our Time)
-	21	LULLABY	Cure (Fiction)
15	22	DON'T BE CRUEL	Bobby Brown (MCA)
-	23	ONE	Metallica (Vertigo)
30	24	DEVOTION	Ten City (Atlantic)
45	25	ME MYSELF I	De La Soul (Big Life)
35	26	BEDS ARE BURNING	Midnight Oil (Sprint)
16	27	CAN YOU KEEP A SECRET?	Brother Beyond (Parlophone)
28	28	REQUIEM	London Boys (WEA)
47	29	REAL LOVE	Jody Watley (MCA)
-	30	AIN'T NOBODY BETTER	Inner City (10)
33	31	BEAUTY IS ONLY SKIN DEEP	Aswad (Mango)
29	32	WHAT DOES IT TAKE?	Then Jerico (London)
33	33	ONLY THE LONELY	T'Pau (Siren)
21	34	I'D RATHER JACK	Reynolds Girls (PWL)
43	35	THIS IS YOUR LIFE	Blow Monkeys (RCA)
-	36	WHO'S IN THE HOUSE	Beatmasters with Merlin (Rhythm King)
20	37	SHE'S A MYSTERY TO ME	Roy Orbison (Virgin)
41	38	PLEASE DON'T BE SCARED	Barry Manilow (Arista)
17	39	THE BEAT(EN) GENERATION	The The (Epic)
50	40	YOU ON MY MIND	Swing Out Sister (Fontana)
24	41	CAN'T STAY AWAY FROM YOU	Gloria Estefan & Miami Sound Machine (Epic)
26	42	SLEEPTALK	Alyson Williams (Def Jam)
-	43	NEVER	House Of Love (Fontana)
44	44	INTERNATIONAL RESCUE	Fuzzbox (WEA)
49	45	VOODOO RAY	A Guy Called Gerald (Rham!)
19	46	FIRE WOMAN	Cult (Beggars Banquet)
-	47	ORDINARY LIVES	Bee Gees (Warner Bros)
-	48	THAT'S HOW I'M LIVING	Toni Scott (Champion)
-	49	TYPICAL!	Frazier Chorus (Virgin)
28	50	ONE MAN	Chanelle (Cooltempo)

After an absence of more than a year from the chart, Donna Summer returned almost to the very top, thanks to the apparently magic writing and production touch of Stock/Aitken/Waterman, with whom she cut *This Time I Know It's For Real*. This was another strong period for female acts, with Madonna, Summer, Paula Abdul and the Bangles occupying an all-female Top Three for two weeks running.

April – May 1989

last week / **this week**

29 April 1989

last	this	title	artist
2	1	ETERNAL FLAME	Bangles (CBS)
1	2	IF YOU DON'T KNOW ME BY NOW	Simply Red (Elektra)
3	3	BABY I DON'T CARE	Transvision Vamp (MCA)
6	4	AMERICANOS	Holly Johnson (MCA)
9	5	GOOD THING	Fine Young Cannibals (London)
7	6	WHEN LOVE COMES TO TOWN	U2 with B.B. King (Island)
10	7	THIS IS YOUR LAND	Simple Minds (Virgin)
21	8	LULLABY	Cure (Fiction)
4	9	I BEG YOUR PARDON	Kon Kan (Atlantic)
30	10	AIN'T NOBODY BETTER	Inner City (10)
11	11	MYSTIFY	INXS (Mercury)
8	12	STRAIGHT UP	Paula Abdul (Siren)
23	13	ONE	Metallica (Vertigo)
-	14	INTERESTING DRUG	Morrissey (HMV)
5	15	LIKE A PRAYER	Madonna (Sire)
36	16	WHO'S IN THE HOUSE	Beatmasters with Merlin (Rhythm King)
28	17	REQUIEM	London Boys (WEA)
26	18	BEDS ARE BURNING	Midnight Oil (Sprint)
15	19	GOT TO KEEP ON	Cookie Crew (ffrr)
25	20	ME MYSELF I	De La Soul (Big Lie)
13	21	THIS TIME I KNOW IT'S FOR REAL	Donna Summer (Warner Bros)
12	22	TOO MANY BROKEN HEARTS	Jason Donovan (PWL)
14	23	KEEP ON MOVIN'	Soul II Soul featuring Caron Wheeler (10)
20	24	PEOPLE HOLD ON	Coldcut featuring Lisa Stansfield (Ahead Of Our Time)
-	25	DO YOU BELIEVE IN SHAME	Duranduran (EMI)
29	26	REAL LOVE	Jody Watley (MCA)
35	27	THIS IS YOUR LIFE	Blow Monkeys (RCA)
40	28	YOU ON MY MIND	Swing Out Sister (Fontana)
29	29	MISS YOU LIKE CRAZY	Natalie Cole (Manhattan)
17	30	MUSICAL FREEDOM (MOVING ON UP)	Paul Simpson featuring Adeva (Cooltempo)
19	31	OF COURSE I'M LYING	Yello (Mercury)
18	32	PARADISE CITY	Guns N' Roses (Geffen)
43	33	NEVER	House Of Love (Fontana)
-	34	MAKE MY BODY ROCK (FEEL IT)	Jomanda (RCA)
-	35	I'LL BE THERE FOR YOU	Bon Jovi (Vertigo)
38	36	PLEASE DON'T BE SCARED	Barry Manilow (Arista)
-	37	YOUR MAMA DON'T DANCE	Poison (Capitol)
16	38	HAVEN'T STOPPED DANCING YET	Pat & Mick (PWL)
22	39	DON'T BE CRUEL	Bobby Brown (MCA)
-	40	WHERE HAS ALL THE LOVE GONE?	Yazz (Big Lie)
24	41	DEVOTION	Ten City (Atlantic)
31	42	BEAUTY IS ONLY SKIN DEEP	Aswad (Mango)
32	43	WHAT DOES IT TAKE?	Then Jerico (London)
47	44	ORDINARY LIVES	Bee Gees (Warner Bros)
33	45	ONLY THE LONELY	T'Pau (Siren)
48	46	THAT'S HOW I'M LIVING	Toni Scott (Champion)
-	47	WISE UP! SUCKER	Pop Will Eat Itself (RCA)
-	48	ELECTRIC YOUTH	Debbie Gibson (Atlantic)
-	49	JOY AND PAIN/CHECK THIS OUT	Rob Base & DJ E-Z Rock (Supreme)
-	50	COME BACK	Luther Vandross (Epic)

6 May 1989

last	this	title	artist
1	1	ETERNAL FLAME	Bangles (CBS)
-	2	HAND ON YOUR HEART	Kylie Minogue (PWL)
2	3	IF YOU DON'T KNOW ME BY NOW	Simply Red (Elektra)
3	4	BABY I DON'T CARE	Transvision Vamp (MCA)
16	5	WHO'S IN THE HOUSE	Beatmasters with Merlin (Rhythm King)
5	6	GOOD THING	Fine Young Cannibals (London)
17	7	REQUIEM	London Boys (WEA)
8	8	LULLABY	Cure (Fiction)
4	9	AMERICANOS	Holly Johnson (MCA)
18	10	BEDS ARE BURNING	Midnight Oil (Sprint)
10	11	AIN'T NOBODY BETTER	Inner City (10)
14	12	INTERESTING DRUG	Morrissey (HMV)
29	13	MISS YOU LIKE CRAZY	Natalie Cole (Manhattan)
9	14	I BEG YOUR PARDON	Kon Kan (Atlantic)
40	15	WHERE HAS ALL THE LOVE GONE?	Yazz (Big Lie)
-	16	BRING ME EDELWEISS	Edelweiss (WEA)
13	17	ONE	Metallica (Vertigo)
37	18	YOUR MAMA DON'T DANCE	Poison (Capitol)
7	19	THIS IS YOUR LAND	Simple Minds (Virgin)
20	20	ME MYSELF I	De La Soul (Big Lie)
6	21	WHEN LOVE COMES TO TOWN	U2 with B.B. King (Island)
35	22	I'LL BE THERE FOR YOU	Bon Jovi (Vertigo)
48	23	ELECTRIC YOUTH	Debbie Gibson (Atlantic)
12	24	STRAIGHT UP	Paula Abdul (Siren)
28	25	YOU ON MY MIND	Swing Out Sister (Fontana)
11	26	MYSTIFY	INXS (Mercury)
19	27	GOT TO KEEP ON	Cookie Crew (ffrr)
15	28	LIKE A PRAYER	Madonna (Sire)
25	29	DO YOU BELIEVE IN SHAME	Duranduran (EMI)
-	30	THE LOOK	Roxette (EMI)
22	31	TOO MANY BROKEN HEARTS	Jason Donovan (PWL)
26	32	REAL LOVE	Jody Watley (MCA)
21	33	THIS TIME I KNOW IT'S FOR REAL	Donna Summer (Warner Bros)
-	34	MOVE CLOSER	Tom Jones (Jive)
23	35	KEEP ON MOVIN'	Soul II Soul featuring Caron Wheeler (10)
-	36	I'M EVERY WOMAN	Chaka Khan (Warner Bros)
-	37	HEAVEN HELP ME	Deon Estus (Mika)
34	38	MAKE MY BODY ROCK (FEEL IT)	Jomanda (RCA)
27	39	THIS IS YOUR LIFE	Blow Monkeys (RCA)
24	40	PEOPLE HOLD ON	Coldcut featuring Lisa Stansfield (Ahead Of Our Time)
-	41	THRILL HAS GONE	Texas (Mercury)
47	42	WISE UP! SUCKER	Pop Will Eat Itself (RCA)
32	43	PARADISE CITY	Guns N' Roses (Geffen)
38	44	HAVEN'T STOPPED DANCING YET	Pat & Mick (PWL)
-	45	FREE WORLD	Kirsty MacColl (Virgin)
31	46	OF COURSE I'M LYING	Yello (Mercury)
-	47	THROUGH THE STORM	Aretha Franklin & Elton John (Arista)
48	48	I CAN SEE CLEARLY NOW	Johnny Nash (Epic)
-	49	ROOMS ON FIRE	Stevie Nicks (EMI)
-	50	ON THE INSIDE (THEME FROM PRISONER : CELL BLOCK H)	Lynne Hamilton (A1)

13 May 1989

last	this	title	artist
2	1	HAND ON YOUR HEART	Kylie Minogue (PWL)
13	2	MISS YOU LIKE CRAZY	Natalie Cole (Manhattan)
1	3	ETERNAL FLAME	Bangles (CBS)
7	4	REQUIEM	London Boys (WEA)
-	5	I WANT IT ALL	Queen (Parlophone)
4	6	BABY I DON'T CARE	Transvision Vamp (MCA)
5	7	WHO'S IN THE HOUSE	Beatmasters with Merlin (Rhythm King)
10	8	BEDS ARE BURNING	Midnight Oil (Sprint)
3	9	IF YOU DON'T KNOW ME BY NOW	Simply Red (Elektra)
16	10	BRING ME EDELWEISS	Edelweiss (WEA)
15	11	WHERE HAS ALL THE LOVE GONE?	Yazz (Big Lie)
36	12	I'M EVERY WOMAN	Chaka Khan (Warner Bros)
18	13	YOUR MAMA DON'T DANCE	Poison (Capitol)
9	14	AMERICANOS	Holly Johnson (MCA)
22	15	I'LL BE THERE FOR YOU	Bon Jovi (Vertigo)
23	16	ELECTRIC YOUTH	Debbie Gibson (Atlantic)
6	17	GOOD THING	Fine Young Cannibals (London)
30	18	THE LOOK	Roxette (EMI)
8	19	LULLABY	Cure (Fiction)
11	20	AIN'T NOBODY BETTER	Inner City (10)
17	21	ONE	Metallica (Vertigo)
14	22	I BEG YOUR PARDON	Kon Kan (Atlantic)
12	23	INTERESTING DRUG	Morrissey (HMV)
-	24	DON'T IT MAKE YOU FEEL GOOD	Stefan Dennis (Sublime)
25	25	ME MYSELF I	De La Soul (Big Lie)
49	26	ROOMS ON FIRE	Stevie Nicks (EMI)
25	27	YOU ON MY MIND	Swing Out Sister (Fontana)
47	28	THROUGH THE STORM	Aretha Franklin & Elton John (Arista)
24	29	STRAIGHT UP	Paula Abdul (Siren)
-	30	VIOLENTLY	Hue & Cry (Circa)
27	31	GOT TO KEEP ON	Cookie Crew (ffrr)
34	32	MOVE CLOSER	Tom Jones (Jive)
32	33	REAL LOVE	Jody Watley (MCA)
-	34	HELYOM HALIB	Capella (Music Man)
41	35	THRILL HAS GONE	Texas (Mercury)
37	36	HEAVEN HELP ME	Deon Estus (Mika)
-	37	DISAPPOINTED	Public Image Ltd (Virgin)
-	38	MY LOVE IS SO RAW	Alyson Williams featuring Nikki-D (Def Jam)
28	39	LIKE A PRAYER	Madonna (Sire)
31	40	TOO MANY BROKEN HEARTS	Jason Donovan (PWL)
19	41	THIS IS YOUR LAND	Simple Minds (Virgin)
-	42	WORKIN' OVERTIME	Diana Ross (EMI)
-	43	THAT'S WHEN I THINK OF YOU	1927 (WEA)
21	44	WHEN LOVE COMES TO TOWN	U2 with B.B. King (Island)
29	45	DO YOU BELIEVE IN SHAME	Duranduran (EMI)
-	46	MY HEART CAN'T TELL YOU NO	Rod Stewart (Warner Bros)
48	47	I CAN SEE CLEARLY NOW	Johnny Nash (Epic)
33	48	THIS TIME I KNOW IT'S FOR REAL	Donna Summer (Warner Bros)
26	49	MYSTIFY	INXS (Mercury)
-	50	CAN I GET A WITNESS?	Sam Brown (A&M)

After a single-week stab by Simply Red with their revival Of Harold Melvin's *If You Don't Know My By Now*, the Bangles and then Kylie Minogue continued the distaff domination of the Number One slot.

Oddest new chart entry came from Edelweiss, a group from some mentally unstable Alpine region, whose *Bring Me Edelweiss* was a surreal forced marriage of Abba's *S.O.S.* and a yodelling competition.

May – June 1989

20 May 1989

last week	this week	Title	Artist (Label)
1	1	HAND ON YOUR HEART	Kylie Minogue (PWL)
-	2	FERRY CROSS THE MERSEY	Christians, Holly Johnson, Paul McCartney, Gerry Marsden & Stock Aitken Waterman (PWL)
5	3	I WANT IT ALL	Queen (Parlophone)
2	4	MISS YOU LIKE CRAZY	Natalie Cole (Manhattan)
10	5	BRING ME EDELWEISS	Edelweiss (WEA)
4	6	REQUIEM	London Boys (WEA)
12	7	I'M EVERY WOMAN	Chaka Khan (Warner Bros)
8	8	BEDS ARE BURNING	Midnight Oil (Sprint)
18	9	THE LOOK	Roxette (EMI)
3	10	ETERNAL FLAME	Bangles (CBS)
11	11	WHERE HAS ALL THE LOVE GONE?	Yazz (Big Lie)
16	12	ELECTRIC YOUTH	Debbie Gibson (Atlantic)
26	13	ROOMS ON FIRE	Stevie Nicks (EMI)
13	14	YOUR MAMA DON'T DANCE	Poison (Capitol)
6	15	BABY I DON'T CARE	Transvision Vamp (MCA)
7	16	WHO'S IN THE HOUSE	Beatmasters with Merlin (Rhythm King)
24	17	DON'T IT MAKE YOU FEEL GOOD	Stefan Dennis (Sublime)
30	18	VIOLENTLY	Hue & Cry (Circa)
9	19	IF YOU DON'T KNOW ME BY NOW	Simply Red (Elektra)
14	20	AMERICANOS	Holly Johnson (MCA)
15	21	I'LL BE THERE FOR YOU	Bon Jovi (Vertigo)
17	22	GOOD THING	Fine Young Cannibals (London)
34	23	HELYOM HALIB	Capella (Music Man)
-	24	MY BRAVE FACE	Paul McCartney (Parlophone)
-	25	EVERY LITTLE STEP	Bobby Brown (MCA)
20	26	AIN'T NOBODY BETTER	Inner City (10)
27	27	YOU ON MY MIND	Swing Out Sister (Fontana)
28	28	THROUGH THE STORM	Aretha Franklin & Elton John (Arista)
42	29	WORKIN' OVERTIME	Diana Ross (EMI)
22	30	I BEG YOUR PARDON	Kon Kan (Atlantic)
19	31	LULLABY	Cure (Fiction)
38	32	MY LOVE IS SO RAW	Alyson Williams featuring Nikki-D (Def Jam)
-	33	LOVE ATTACK	Shakin' Stevens (Epic)
21	34	ONE	Metallica (Vertigo)
35	35	ME MYSELF I	De La Soul (Big Life)
29	36	STRAIGHT UP	Paula Abdul (Siren)
-	37	FERGUS SINGS THE BLUES	Deacon Blue (CBS)
50	38	CAN I GET A WITNESS?	Sam Brown (A&M)
-	39	NOTHIN' (THAT COMPARES 2 U)	Jacksons (Epic)
43	40	THAT'S WHEN I THINK OF YOU	1927 (WEA)
31	41	GOT TO KEEP ON	Cookie Crew (ffrr)
37	42	DISAPPOINTED	Public Image Ltd (Virgin)
46	43	MY HEART CAN'T TELL YOU NO	Rod Stewart (Warner Bros)
36	44	HEAVEN HELP ME	Deon Estus (Mika)
33	45	REAL LOVE	Jody Watley (MCA)
23	46	INTERESTING DRUG	Morrissey (HMV)
-	47	MANCHILD	Neneh Cherry (Circa)
39	48	LIKE A PRAYER	Madonna (Sire)
-	49	CHANGE HIS WAYS	Robert Palmer (EMI)
-	50	THE WRATH OF KANE	Big Daddy Kane (Cold Chillin')

27 May 1989

last week	this week	Title	Artist (Label)
2	1	FERRY CROSS THE MERSEY	Christians, Holly Johnson, Paul McCartney, Gerry Marsden & Stock Aitken Waterman (PWL)
1	2	HAND ON YOUR HEART	Kylie Minogue (PWL)
4	3	MISS YOU LIKE CRAZY	Natalie Cole (Manhattan)
5	4	BRING ME EDELWEISS	Edelweiss (WEA)
7	5	I'M EVERY WOMAN	Chaka Khan (Warner Bros)
6	6	REQUIEM	London Boys (WEA)
9	7	THE LOOK	Roxette (EMI)
3	8	I WANT IT ALL	Queen (Parlophone)
25	9	EVERY LITTLE STEP	Bobby Brown (MCA)
23	10	HELYOM HALIB	Capella (Music Man)
13	11	ROOMS ON FIRE	Stevie Nicks (EMI)
17	12	DON'T IT MAKE YOU FEEL GOOD	Stefan Dennis (Sublime)
10	13	ETERNAL FLAME	Bangles (CBS)
37	14	FERGUS SINGS THE BLUES	Deacon Blue (CBS)
47	15	MANCHILD	Neneh Cherry (Circa)
8	16	BEDS ARE BURNING	Midnight Oil (Sprint)
18	17	VIOLENTLY	Hue & Cry (Circa)
24	18	MY BRAVE FACE	Paul McCartney (Parlophone)
-	19	ON THE INSIDE (THEME FROM PRISONER: CELL BLOCK H)	Lynne Hamilton (A1)
12	20	ELECTRIC YOUTH	Debbie Gibson (Atlantic)
49	21	CHANGE HIS WAYS	Robert Palmer (EMI)
16	22	WHO'S IN THE HOUSE	Beatmasters with Merlin (Rhythm King)
11	23	WHERE HAS ALL THE LOVE GONE?	Yazz (Big Lie)
38	24	CAN I GET A WITNESS?	Sam Brown (A&M)
15	25	BABY I DON'T CARE	Transvision Vamp (MCA)
-	26	FUNKY COLD MEDINA/ON FIRE	Tone Loc (Fourth & Broadway)
33	27	LOVE ATTACK	Shakin' Stevens (Epic)
28	28	WORKIN' OVERTIME	Diana Ross (EMI)
14	29	YOUR MAMA DON'T DANCE	Poison (Capitol)
19	30	IF YOU DON'T KNOW ME BY NOW	Simply Red (Elektra)
32	31	MY LOVE IS SO RAW	Alyson Williams featuring Nikki-D (Def Jam)
-	32	PINK SUNSHINE	Fuzzbox (WEA)
20	33	AMERICANOS	Holly Johnson (MCA)
-	34	THE REAL ME	W.A.S.P. (Capitol)
27	35	YOU ON MY MIND	Swing Out Sister (Fontana)
42	36	DISAPPOINTED	Public Image Ltd (Virgin)
22	37	GOOD THING	Fine Young Cannibals (London)
39	38	NOTHIN' (THAT COMPARES 2 U)	Jacksons (Epic)
30	39	I BEG YOUR PARDON	Kon Kan (Atlantic)
21	40	I'LL BE THERE FOR YOU	Bon Jovi (Vertigo)
-	41	I DON'T WANNA GET HURT	Donna Summer (Warner Bros)
26	42	AIN'T NOBODY BETTER	Inner City (10)
-	43	U + ME = LOVE	Funky Worm (Fon)
-	44	CLOSE MY EYES FOREVER	Lita Ford with Ozzy Osbourne (Dreamland)
45	45	I WON'T BACK DOWN	Tom Petty (MCA)
-	46	PSYCHONAUT LIB III	Fields Of The Nephilim (Situation Two)
-	47	DON'T YOU WANT ME BABY	Mandy Smith (PW)
-	48	GRACELAND	Bible (Chrysalis)
28	49	THROUGH THE STORM	Aretha Franklin & Elton John (Arista)
43	50	MY HEART CAN'T TELL YOU NO	Rod Stewart (Warner Bros)

3 June 1989

last week	this week	Title	Artist (Label)
1	1	FERRY CROSS THE MERSEY	Christians, Holly Johnson, Paul McCartney, Gerry Marsden & Stock Aitken Waterman (PWL)
9	2	EVERY LITTLE STEP	Bobby Brown (MCA)
3	3	MISS YOU LIKE CRAZY	Natalie Cole (Manhattan)
10	4	HELYOM HALIB	Capella (Music Man)
15	5	MANCHILD	Neneh Cherry (Circa)
2	6	HAND ON YOUR HEART	Kylie Minogue (PWL)
19	7	ON THE INSIDE (THEME FROM PRISONER: CELL BLOCK H)	Lynne Hamilton (A1)
6	8	REQUIEM	London Boys (WEA)
41	9	I DON'T WANNA GET HURT	Donna Summer (Warner Bros)
4	10	BRING ME EDELWEISS	Edelweiss (WEA)
-	11	EXPRESS YOURSELF	Madonna (Sire)
14	12	FERGUS SINGS THE BLUES	Deacon Blue (CBS)
7	13	THE LOOK	Roxette (EMI)
12	14	DON'T IT MAKE YOU FEEL GOOD	Stefan Dennis (Sublime)
5	15	I'M EVERY WOMAN	Chaka Khan (Warner Bros)
26	16	FUNKY COLD MEDINA/ON FIRE	Tone Loc (Fourth & Broadway)
24	17	CAN I GET A WITNESS?	Sam Brown (A&M)
18	18	MY BRAVE FACE	Paul McCartney (Parlophone)
-	19	SWEET CHILD O' MINE	Guns N' Roses (Geffen)
21	20	CHANGE HIS WAYS	Robert Palmer (EMI)
8	21	I WANT IT ALL	Queen (Parlophone)
-	22	I DROVE ALL NIGHT	Cyndi Lauper (Epic)
-	23	JUST KEEP ROCKIN'	Double Trouble & the Rebel MC (Desire)
32	24	PINK SUNSHINE	Fuzzbox (WEA)
34	25	THE REAL ME	W.A.S.P. (Capitol)
13	26	ETERNAL FLAME	Bangles (CBS)
-	27	FOREVER YOUR GIRL	Paula Abdul (Siren)
17	28	VIOLENTLY	Hue & Cry (Circa)
-	29	IT IS TIME TO GET FUNKY	D Mob featuring LRS & DC Sarome (ffrr)
11	30	ROOMS ON FIRE	Stevie Nicks (EMI)
16	31	BEDS ARE BURNING	Midnight Oil (Sprint)
-	32	ONE BETTER WORLD	ABC (Neutron)
33	33	NOTHIN' (THAT COMPARES 2 U)	Jacksons (Epic)
20	34	ELECTRIC YOUTH	Debbie Gibson (Atlantic)
46	35	PSYCHONAUT LIB III	Fields Of The Nephilim (Situation Two)
25	36	BABY I DON'T CARE	Transvision Vamp (MCA)
27	37	LOVE ATTACK	Shakin' Stevens (Epic)
-	38	RIGHT BACK WHERE WE STARTED FROM	Sinitta (Fanfare)
36	39	DISAPPOINTED	Public Image Ltd (Virgin)
43	40	U + ME = LOVE	Funky Worm (Fon)
45	41	I WON'T BACK DOWN	Tom Petty (MCA)
30	42	IF YOU DON'T KNOW ME BY NOW	Simply Red (Elektra)
23	43	WHERE HAS ALL THE LOVE GONE?	Yazz (Big Lie)
-	44	JOY AND PAIN	Donna Alien (BCM)
33	45	AMERICANOS	Holly Johnson (MCA)
-	46	SONG FOR WHOEVER	Beautiful South (Go! Discs)
22	47	WHO'S IN THE HOUSE	Beatmasters with Merlin (Rhythm King)
-	48	MY TELEPHONE	Coldcut (Ahead Of Our Time)
29	49	YOUR MAMA DON'T DANCE	Poison (Capitol)
-	50	LONG HOT SUMMER '89	Style Council (Polydor)

The Hillsborough football ground disaster once again sparked a charity single to raise money for victims' families. Since most of the latter were from Liverpool, the project, put together by Stock/Aitken /Waterman, utilised wholly Liverpudlian talent to perform Gerry Marsden's former hit song *Ferry Cross The Mersey* – Paul McCartney, Holly Johnson, the Christians and Gerry himself.

June 1989

10 June 1989

last week	this week	
1	1	FERRY CROSS THE MERSEY — Christians, Holly Johnson, Paul McCartney, Gerry Marsden & Stock Aitken Waterman (PWL)
7	2	ON THE INSIDE (THEME FROM PRISONER : CELL BLOCK H) Lynne Hamilton (A1)
11	3	EXPRESS YOURSELF Madonna (Sire)
-	4	SEALED WITH A KISS Jason Donovan (PWL)
5	5	MANCHILD Neneh Cherry (Circa)
9	6	I DON'T WANNA GET HURT Donna Summer (Warner Bros)
3	7	MISS YOU LIKE CRAZY Natalie Cole (Manhattan)
2	8	EVERY LITTLE STEP Bobby Brown (MCA)
38	9	RIGHT BACK WHERE WE STARTED FROM Sinitta (Fanfare)
-	10	THE BEST OF ME Cliff Richard (EMI)
19	11	SWEET CHILD O' MINE Guns N' Roses (Geffen)
4	12	HELYOM HALIB Capella (Music Man)
16	13	FUNKY COLD MEDINA/ON FIRE Tone Loc (Fourth & Broadway)
6	14	HAND ON YOUR HEART Kylie Minogue (PWL)
17	15	CAN I GET A WITNESS? Sam Brown (A&M)
8	16	REQUIEM London Boys (WEA)
10	17	BRING ME EDELWEISS Edelweiss (WEA)
12	18	FERGUS SINGS THE BLUES Deacon Blue (CBS)
23	19	JUST KEEP ROCKIN' Double Trouble & the Rebel MC (Desire)
22	20	I DROVE ALL NIGHT Cyndi Lauper (Epic)
29	21	IT IS TIME TO GET FUNKY D Mob featuring LRS & DC Sarome (ffrr)
24	22	PINK SUNSHINE Fuzzbox (WEA)
25	23	THE REAL ME W.A.S.P. (Capitol)
27	24	FOREVER YOUR GIRL Paula Abdul (Siren)
46	25	SONG FOR WHOEVER Beautiful South (Go! Discs)
13	26	THE LOOK Roxette (EMI)
-	27	BACK TO LIFE Soul II Soul featuring Caron Wheeler (10)
15	28	I'M EVERY WOMAN Chaka Khan (Warner Bros)
41	29	I WON'T BACK DOWN Tom Petty (MCA)
32	30	ONE BETTER WORLD ABC (Neutron)
20	31	CHANGE HIS WAYS Robert Palmer (EMI)
44	32	JOY AND PAIN Donna Allen (BCM)
14	33	DON'T IT MAKE YOU FEEL GOOD Stefan Dennis (Sublime)
21	34	I WANT IT ALL Queen (Parlophone)
-	35	THE ONLY ONE Transvision Vamp (MCA)
33	36	NOTHIN' (THAT COMPARES 2 U) Jacksons (Epic)
-	37	LOVE MADE ME Vixen (EMI-USA)
48	38	MY TELEPHONE Coldcut (Ahead Of Our Time)
-	39	ORANGE CRUSH R.E.M. (Warner Bros)
18	40	MY BRAVE FACE Paul McCartney (Parlophone)
26	41	ETERNAL FLAME Bangles (CBS)
34	42	ELECTRIC YOUTH Debbie Gibson (Atlantic)
-	43	I'M ON AUTOMATIC Sharpe & Numan (Polydor)
30	44	ROOMS ON FIRE Stevie Nicks (EMI)
-	45	WALTZ DARLING Malcolm McLaren & the Bootzilla Orchestra (Epic)
-	46	CRUEL SUMMER (SWINGBEAT VERSION) Bananarama (London)
-	47	GREEN AND GREY New Model Army (EMI)
-	48	WORK IT TO THE BONE L.N.R. (Kool Kat)
-	49	GATECRASHING Living In A Box (Chrysalis)
-	50	TILL I LOVED YOU Placido Domingo & Jennifer Rush (CBS)

17 June 1989

4	1	SEALED WITH A KISS Jason Donovan (PWL)
10	2	THE BEST OF ME Cliff Richard (EMI)
3	3	EXPRESS YOURSELF Madonna (Sire)
27	4	BACK TO LIFE Soul II Soul featuring Caron Wheeler (10)
9	5	RIGHT BACK WHERE WE STARTED FROM Sinitta (Fanfare)
11	6	SWEET CHILD O' MINE Guns N' Roses (Geffen)
1	7	FERRY CROSS THE MERSEY — Christians, Holly Johnson, Paul McCartney, Gerry Marsden & Stock Aitken Waterman (PWL)
7	8	MISS YOU LIKE CRAZY Natalie Cole (Manhattan)
2	9	ON THE INSIDE (THEME FROM PRISONER : CELL BLOCK H) Lynne Hamilton (A1)
6	10	I DON'T WANNA GET HURT Donna Summer (Warner Bros)
5	11	MANCHILD Neneh Cherry (Circa)
21	12	IT IS TIME TO GET FUNKY D Mob featuring LRS & DC Sarome (ffrr)
20	13	I DROVE ALL NIGHT Cyndi Lauper (Epic)
19	14	JUST KEEP ROCKIN' Double Trouble & the Rebel MC (Desire)
13	15	FUNKY COLD MEDINA/ON FIRE Tone Loc (Fourth & Broadway)
25	16	SONG FOR WHOEVER Beautiful South (Go! Discs)
35	17	THE ONLY ONE Transvision Vamp (MCA)
12	18	PINK SUNSHINE Fuzzbox (WEA)
8	19	EVERY LITTLE STEP Bobby Brown (MCA)
24	20	FOREVER YOUR GIRL Paula Abdul (Siren)
32	21	JOY AND PAIN Donna Allen (BCM)
46	22	CRUEL SUMMER (SWINGBEAT VERSION) Bananarama (London)
14	23	HAND ON YOUR HEART Kylie Minogue (PWL)
16	24	REQUIEM London Boys (WEA)
17	25	BRING ME EDELWEISS Edelweiss (WEA)
39	26	ORANGE CRUSH R.E.M. (Warner Bros)
50	27	TILL I LOVED YOU Placido Domingo & Jennifer Rush (CBS)
15	28	CAN I GET A WITNESS? Sam Brown (A&M)
12	29	HELYOM HALIB Capella (Music Man)
47	30	GREEN AND GREY New Model Army (EMI)
29	31	I WON'T BACK DOWN Tom Petty (MCA)
28	32	I'M EVERY WOMAN Chaka Khan (Warner Bros)
-	33	BE WITH YOU Bangles (CBS)
-	34	POP MUZIK (THE 1989 REMIX) M (Freestyle)
23	35	THE REAL ME W.A.S.P. (Capitol)
37	36	LOVE MADE ME Vixen (EMI-USA)
18	37	FERGUS SINGS THE BLUES Deacon Blue (CBS)
-	38	LICENCE TO KILL Gladys Knight (MCA)
-	39	WHY Carly Simon (WEA)
-	40	IF I'M NOT YOUR LOVER Al B. Sure! featuring Slick Rick (Warner Bros)
-	41	IN A LIFETIME Clannad (RCA)
31	42	CHANGE HIS WAYS Robert Palmer (EMI)
-	43	SUPERWOMAN Karyn White (Warner Bros)
26	44	THE LOOK Roxette (EMI)
45	45	WALTZ DARLING Malcolm McLaren & the Bootzilla Orchestra (Epic)
49	46	GATECRASHING Living In A Box (Chrysalis)
47	47	STORMS IN AFRICA Enya (WEA)
33	48	DON'T IT MAKE YOU FEEL GOOD Stefan Dennis (Sublime)
34	49	I WANT IT ALL Queen (Parlophone)
41	50	ETERNAL FLAME Bangles (CBS)

24 June 1989

1	1	SEALED WITH A KISS Jason Donovan (PWL)
4	2	BACK TO LIFE Soul II Soul featuring Caron Wheeler (10)
2	3	THE BEST OF ME Cliff Richard (EMI)
5	4	RIGHT BACK WHERE WE STARTED FROM Sinitta (Fanfare)
13	5	I DROVE ALL NIGHT Cyndi Lauper (Epic)
16	6	SONG FOR WHOEVER Beautiful South (Go! Discs)
6	7	SWEET CHILD O' MINE Guns N' Roses (Geffen)
3	8	EXPRESS YOURSELF Madonna (Sire)
-	9	ALL I WANT IS YOU U2 (Island)
12	10	IT IS TIME TO GET FUNKY D Mob featuring LRS & DC Sarome (ffrr)
21	11	JOY AND PAIN Donna Allen (BCM)
-	12	BATDANCE Prince (Warner Bros)
17	13	THE ONLY ONE Transvision Vamp (MCA)
14	14	JUST KEEP ROCKIN' Double Trouble & the Rebel MC (Desire)
8	15	MISS YOU LIKE CRAZY Natalie Cole (Manhattan)
18	16	PINK SUNSHINE Fuzzbox (WEA)
11	17	MANCHILD Neneh Cherry (Circa)
20	18	FOREVER YOUR GIRL Paula Abdul (Siren)
22	19	CRUEL SUMMER (SWINGBEAT VERSION) Bananarama (London)
10	20	I DON'T WANNA GET HURT Donna Summer (Warner Bros)
-	21	IN A LIFETIME Clannad (RCA)
26	22	ORANGE CRUSH R.E.M. (Warner Bros)
27	23	TILL I LOVED YOU Placido Domingo & Jennifer Rush (CBS)
9	24	ON THE INSIDE (THEME FROM PRISONER : CELL BLOCK H) Lynne Hamilton (A1)
15	25	FUNKY COLD MEDINA/ON FIRE Tone Loc (Fourth & Broadway)
38	26	LICENCE TO KILL Gladys Knight (MCA)
43	27	SUPERWOMAN Karyn White (Warner Bros)
33	28	BE WITH YOU Bangles (CBS)
31	29	I WON'T BACK DOWN Tom Petty (MCA)
34	30	POP MUZIK (THE 1989 REMIX) M (Freestyle)
19	31	EVERY LITTLE STEP Bobby Brown (MCA)
45	32	WALTZ DARLING Malcolm McLaren & the Bootzilla Orchestra (Epic)
7	33	FERRY CROSS THE MERSEY — Christians, Holly Johnson, Paul McCartney, Gerry Marsden & Stock Aitken Waterman (PWL)
46	34	GATECRASHING Living In A Box (Chrysalis)
-	35	LOOKING FOR A LOVE Joyce Sims (ffrr)
39	36	WHY Carly Simon (WEA)
47	37	STORMS IN AFRICA Enya (WEA)
-	38	TEARS Frankie Knuckles presenting Satoshi Tomiie featuring Robert Owens (ffrr)
-	39	DOWNTOWN One 2 Many (A&M)
-	40	ATOMIC CITY Holly Johnson (MCA)
23	41	HAND ON YOUR HEART Kylie Minogue (PWL)
40	42	IF I'M NOT YOUR LOVER Al B. Sure! featuring Slick Rick (Warner Bros)
29	43	HELYOM HALIB Capella (Music Man)
30	44	GREEN AND GREY New Model Army (EMI)
24	45	REQUIEM London Boys (WEA)
28	46	CAN I GET A WITNESS? Sam Brown (A&M)
-	47	I'M NOT THAT KIND OF GUY LL Cool J (Def Jam)
-	48	CRY Waterfront (Polydor)
-	49	CHILDREN OF THE REVOLUTION Baby Ford (Rhythm King)
-	50	THE WIND BENEATH MY WINGS Bette Midler (Atlantic)

The Best Of Me was, by EMI's reckoning (though it got complicated with various duet releases and best-selling imports), Cliff Richard's 100th single, and a huge publicity campaign was launched to push this aspect. Though Cliff was held at Number Two by Jason Donovan (for whom Bryan Hyland's *Sealed With A Kiss* was a smart change of pace), even the TV news carried the "100th single" story.

July 1989

1 July 1989

last week	this week	
2	1	BACK TO LIFE — Soul II Soul featuring Caron Wheeler (10)
12	2	BATDANCE — Prince (Warner Bros)
9	3	ALL I WANT IS YOU — U2 (Island)
6	4	SONG FOR WHOEVER — Beautiful South (Go! Discs)
1	5	SEALED WITH A KISS — Jason Donovan (PWL)
4	6	RIGHT BACK WHERE WE STARTED FROM — Sinitta (Fanfare)
5	7	I DROVE ALL NIGHT — Cyndi Lauper (Epic)
26	8	LICENCE TO KILL — Gladys Knight (MCA)
3	9	THE BEST OF ME — Cliff Richard (EMI)
11	10	JOY AND PAIN — Donna Allen (BCM)
10	11	IT IS TIME TO GET FUNKY — D Mob featuring LRS & DC Sarome (ffrr)
7	12	SWEET CHILD O' MINE — Guns N' Roses (Geffen)
21	13	IN A LIFETIME — Clannad (RCA)
14	14	JUST KEEP ROCKIN' — Double Trouble & the Rebel MC (Desire)
8	15	EXPRESS YOURSELF — Madonna (Sire)
40	16	ATOMIC CITY — Holly Johnson (MCA)
23	17	TILL I LOVED YOU — Placido Domingo & Jennifer Rush (CBS)
-	18	PATIENCE — Guns N' Roses (Geffen)
16	19	PINK SUNSHINE — Fuzzbox (WEA)
-	20	BREAKTHRU — Queen (Parlophone)
27	21	SUPERWOMAN — Karyn White (Warner Bros)
19	22	CRUEL SUMMER (SWINGBEAT VERSION) — Bananarama (London)
28	23	BE WITH YOU — Bangles (CBS)
15	24	MISS YOU LIKE CRAZY — Natalie Cole (Manhattan)
13	25	THE ONLY ONE — Transvision Vamp (MCA)
30	26	POP MUZIK (THE 1989 REMIX) — M (Freestyle)
-	27	FIGHT THE POWER — Public Enemy (Motown)
17	28	MANCHILD — Neneh Cherry (Circa)
20	29	I DON'T WANNA GET HURT — Donna Summer (Warner Bros)
34	30	GATECRASHING — Living In A Box (Chrysalis)
18	31	FOREVER YOUR GIRL — Paula Abdul (Siren)
32	32	WALTZ DARLING — Malcolm McLaren & the Bootzilla Orchestra (Epic)
29	33	I WON'T BACK DOWN — Tom Petty (MCA)
25	34	FUNKY COLD MEDINA/ON FIRE — Tone Loc (Fourth & Broadway)
-	35	GRANDPA'S PARTY — Monie Love (Cooltempo)
-	36	YOU'LL NEVER STOP ME LOVING YOU — Sonia (Chrysalis)
50	37	THE WIND BENEATH MY WINGS — Bette Midler (Atlantic)
48	38	CRY — Waterfront (Polydor)
35	39	LOOKING FOR A LOVE — Joyce Sims (ffrr)
-	40	VOODOO RAY — A Guy Called Gerald (Rham!)
-	41	THE SECOND SUMMER OF LOVE — Danny Wilson (Virgin)
22	42	ORANGE CRUSH — R.E.M. (Warner Bros)
39	43	DOWNTOWN — One 2 Many (A&M)
24	44	ON THE INSIDE (THEME FROM PRISONER : CELL BLOCK H) — Lynne Hamilton (A1)
-	45	LONDON NIGHTS — London Boys (WEA)
31	46	EVERY LITTLE STEP — Bobby Brown (MCA)
38	47	TEARS — Frankie Knuckles presenting Satoshi Tomiie featuring Robert Owens (ffrr)
-	48	CHINA DOLL — Julian Cope (Island)
37	49	STORMS IN AFRICA — Enya (WEA)
-	50	UNDER THE GOD — Tin Machine (EMI-USA)

8 July 1989

last week	this week	
1	1	BACK TO LIFE — Soul II Soul featuring Caron Wheeler (10)
2	2	BATDANCE — Prince (Warner Bros)
4	3	SONG FOR WHOEVER — Beautiful South (Go! Discs)
8	4	LICENCE TO KILL — Gladys Knight (MCA)
45	5	LONDON NIGHTS — London Boys (WEA)
3	6	ALL I WANT IS YOU — U2 (Island)
10	7	JOY AND PAIN — Donna Allen (BCM)
26	8	POP MUZIK (THE 1989 REMIX) — M (Freestyle)
6	10	RIGHT BACK WHERE WE STARTED FROM — Sinitta (Fanfare)
11	11	IT IS TIME TO GET FUNKY — D Mob featuring LRS & DC Sarome (ffrr)
18	12	PATIENCE — Guns N' Roses (Geffen)
5	13	SEALED WITH A KISS — Jason Donovan (PWL)
16	14	ATOMIC CITY — Holly Johnson (MCA)
-	15	IT'S ALRIGHT — Pet Shop Boys (Parlophone)
7	16	I DROVE ALL NIGHT — Cyndi Lauper (Epic)
14	17	JUST KEEP ROCKIN' — Double Trouble & the Rebel MC (Desire)
13	18	IN A LIFETIME — Clannad (RCA)
36	19	YOU'LL NEVER STOP ME LOVING YOU — Sonia (Chrysalis)
12	20	SWEET CHILD O' MINE — Guns N' Roses (Geffen)
23	21	BE WITH YOU — Bangles (CBS)
9	22	THE BEST OF ME — Cliff Richard (EMI)
21	23	SUPERWOMAN — Karyn White (Warner Bros)
27	24	FIGHT THE POWER — Public Enemy (Motown)
15	25	EXPRESS YOURSELF — Madonna (Sire)
38	26	CRY — Waterfront (Polydor)
17	27	TILL I LOVED YOU — Placido Domingo & Jennifer Rush (CBS)
-	28	SAY NO GO — De La Soul (Big Life)
19	29	PINK SUNSHINE — Fuzzbox (WEA)
35	30	GRANDPA'S PARTY — Monie Love (Cooltempo)
24	31	MISS YOU LIKE CRAZY — Natalie Cole (Manhattan)
-	32	AIN'T NOBODY — Rufus & Chaka Khan (Warner Bros)
29	33	I DON'T WANNA GET HURT — Donna Summer (Warner Bros)
40	34	VOODOO RAY — A Guy Called Gerald (Rham!)
37	35	THE WIND BENEATH MY WINGS — Bette Midler (Atlantic)
30	36	GATECRASHING — Living In A Box (Chrysalis)
22	37	CRUEL SUMMER (SWINGBEAT VERSION) — Bananarama (London)
43	38	DOWNTOWN — One 2 Many (A&M)
32	39	WALTZ DARLING — Malcolm McLaren & the Bootzilla Orchestra (Epic)
-	40	HERE COMES YOUR MAN — Pixies (4AD)
41	41	THE SECOND SUMMER OF LOVE — Danny Wilson (Virgin)
25	42	THE ONLY ONE — Transvision Vamp (MCA)
-	43	AND A BANG ON THE EAR — Waterboys (Ensign)
50	44	UNDER THE GOD — Tin Machine (EMI-USA)
28	45	MANCHILD — Neneh Cherry (Circa)
-	46	MISTY MORNING, ALBERT BRIDGE — Pogues (Pogue Mahone)
39	47	LOOKING FOR A LOVE — Joyce Sims (ffrr)
33	48	I WON'T BACK DOWN — Tom Petty (MCA)
-	49	A BIT OF — Kiss AMC (Syncopate)
-	50	I'M A MAN/YEKE YEKE — Clubhouse (Music Man)

15 July 1989

last week	this week	
1	1	BACK TO LIFE — Soul II Soul featuring Caron Wheeler (10)
5	2	LONDON NIGHTS — London Boys (WEA)
15	3	IT'S ALRIGHT — Pet Shop Boys (Parlophone)
19	4	YOU'LL NEVER STOP ME LOVING YOU — Sonia (Chrysalis)
3	5	SONG FOR WHOEVER — Beautiful South (Go! Discs)
6	6	BREAKTHRU — Queen (Parlophone)
2	7	BATDANCE — Prince (Warner Bros)
4	8	LICENCE TO KILL — Gladys Knight (MCA)
9	9	POP MUZIK (THE 1989 REMIX) — M (Freestyle)
32	10	AIN'T NOBODY — Rufus & Chaka Khan (Warner Bros)
12	11	PATIENCE — Guns N' Roses (Geffen)
-	12	ON OUR OWN — Bobby Brown (MCA)
6	13	ALL I WANT IS YOU — U2 (Island)
30	14	GRANDPA'S PARTY — Monie Love (Cooltempo)
7	15	JOY AND PAIN — Donna Allen (BCM)
34	16	VOODOO RAY — A Guy Called Gerald (Rham!)
10	17	RIGHT BACK WHERE WE STARTED FROM — Sinitta (Fanfare)
16	18	I DROVE ALL NIGHT — Cyndi Lauper (Epic)
23	19	SUPERWOMAN — Karyn White (Warner Bros)
26	20	CRY — Waterfront (Polydor)
17	21	JUST KEEP ROCKIN' — Double Trouble & the Rebel MC (Desire)
28	22	SAY NO GO — De La Soul (Big Life)
-	23	BLAME IT ON THE BASSLINE — Norman Cook featuring Mc Wildski (Go Beat)
-	24	LIBERIAN GIRL — Michael Jackson (Epic)
11	25	IT IS TIME TO GET FUNKY — D Mob featuring LRS & DC Sarome (ffrr)
35	26	THE WIND BENEATH MY WINGS — Bette Midler (Atlantic)
13	27	SEALED WITH A KISS — Jason Donovan (PWL)
14	28	ATOMIC CITY — Holly Johnson (MCA)
-	29	DAYS — Kirsty MacColl (Virgin)
21	30	BE WITH YOU — Bangles (CBS)
41	31	THE SECOND SUMMER OF LOVE — Danny Wilson (Virgin)
-	32	EDIE (CIAO BABY) — Cult (Beggars Banquet)
18	33	IN A LIFETIME — Clannad (RCA)
-	34	GET LOOSE — LA Mix featuring Jazzi P (Breakout)
20	35	SWEET CHILD O' MINE — Guns N' Roses (Geffen)
46	36	MISTY MORNING, ALBERT BRIDGE — Pogues (Pogue Mahone)
-	37	I DON'T WANNA LOSE YOU — Gloria Estefan (Epic)
-	38	A NEW FLAME — Simply Red (WEA)
24	39	FIGHT THE POWER — Public Enemy (Motown)
29	40	PINK SUNSHINE — Fuzzbox (WEA)
33	41	I DON'T WANNA GET HURT — Donna Summer (Warner Bros)
50	42	I'M A MAN/YEKE YEKE — Clubhouse (Music Man)
43	43	AND A BANG ON THE EAR — Waterboys (Ensign)
22	44	THE BEST OF ME — Cliff Richard (EMI)
25	45	EXPRESS YOURSELF — Madonna (Sire)
31	46	MISS YOU LIKE CRAZY — Natalie Cole (Manhattan)
-	47	NEVER ENOUGH — Jesus Jones (Food)
-	48	CHA CHA HEELS — Eartha Kitt & Bronski Beat (Arista)
-	49	LET ME LOVE YOU FOR TONIGHT — Kariya (Sleeping Bag)
27	50	TILL I LOVED YOU — Placido Domingo & Jennifer Rush (CBS)

Soul II Soul's *Back To Life*, the heavy rhythmic structure of which became a feature of virtually every other UK dance record for a while, proved strong enough to outsell Prince's equally polyrhythmic *Batdance*, performed in the movie *Batman*, and thus being heard in virtually every cinema in the country. Gladys Knight's *Licence To Kill* was also a celluloid theme – from the new James Bond film.

July – August 1989

22 July 1989

last	this		
4	1	YOU'LL NEVER STOP ME LOVING YOU	Sonia (Chrysalis)
2	2	LONDON NIGHTS	London Boys (WEA)
26	3	THE WIND BENEATH MY WINGS	Bette Midler (Atlantic)
1	4	BACK TO LIFE	Soul II Soul featuring Caron Wheeler (10)
12	5	ON OUR OWN	Bobby Brown (MCA)
10	6	AIN'T NOBODY	Rufus & Chaka Khan (Warner Bros)
3	7	IT'S ALRIGHT	Pet Shop Boys (Parlophone)
16	8	VOODOO RAY	A Guy Called Gerald (Rham!)
5	9	SONG FOR WHOEVER	Beautiful South (Go! Discs)
19	10	SUPERWOMAN	Karyn White (Warner Bros)
24	11	LIBERIAN GIRL	Michael Jackson (Epic)
14	12	GRANDPA'S PARTY	Monie Love (Cooltempo)
8	13	LICENCE TO KILL	Gladys Knight (MCA)
22	14	SAY NO GO	De La Soul (Big Life)
6	15	BREAKTHRU	Queen (Parlophone)
7	16	BATDANCE	Prince (Warner Bros)
23	17	BLAME IT ON THE BASSLINE	Norman Cook featuring Mc Wildski (Go Beat)
9	18	POP MUZIK (THE 1989 REMIX)	M (Freestyle)
37	19	I DON'T WANNA LOSE YOU	Gloria Estefan (Epic)
20	20	CRY	Waterfront (Polydor)
29	21	DAYS	Kirsty MacColl (Virgin)
38	22	A NEW FLAME	Simply Red (WEA)
11	23	PATIENCE	Guns N' Roses (Geffen)
34	24	GET LOOSE LA Mix featuring Jazzi P (Breakout)	
31	25	THE SECOND SUMMER OF LOVE	Danny Wilson (Virgin)
18	26	I DROVE ALL NIGHT	Cyndi Lauper (Epic)
-	27	CHOICE?	Blow Monkeys featuring Sylvia Tella (RCA)
17	28	RIGHT BACK WHERE WE STARTED FROM	Sinitta (Fanfare)
21	29	JUST KEEP ROCKIN'	Double Trouble & the Rebel MC (Desire)
32	30	EDIE (CIAO BABY)	Cult (Beggars Banquet)
15	31	JOY AND PAIN	Donna Allen (BCM)
27	32	SEALED WITH A KISS	Jason Donovan (PWL)
13	33	ALL I WANT IS YOU	U2 (Island)
-	34	LET IT ROLL	Doug Lazy (Atlantic)
25	35	IT IS TIME TO GET FUNKY	D Mob featuring LRS & DC Sarome (ffrr)
-	36	WHERE IN THE WORLD	Swing Out Sister (Fontana)
30	37	BE WITH YOU	Bangles (CBS)
33	38	IN A LIFETIME	Clannad (RCA)
49	39	LET ME LOVE YOU FOR TONIGHT	Kariya (Sleeping Bag)
35	40	SWEET CHILD O' MINE	Guns N' Roses (Geffen)
-	41	BLAME IT ON THE RAIN	Milli Vanilli (Cooltempo)
-	42	KATHLEEN	Roachford (CBS)
43	43	SWING THE MOOD	Jive Bunny & the Mastermixers (Music Factory Dance)
47	44	NEVER ENOUGH	Jesus Jones (Food)
-	45	COME AND GET SOME	Cookie Crew (ffrr)
48	46	CHA CHA HEELS	Eartha Kitt & Bronski Beat (Arista)
-	47	101	Sheena Easton (MCA)
-	48	DRESSED FOR SUCCESS	Roxette (EMI)
-	49	BETTER DAYS	Gun (A&M)
-	50	GRAVITATE TO ME	The The (Epic)

29 July 1989

last	this		
1	1	YOU'LL NEVER STOP ME LOVING YOU	Sonia (Chrysalis)
5	2	ON OUR OWN	Bobby Brown (MCA)
2	3	LONDON NIGHTS	London Boys (WEA)
-	4	TOO MUCH	Bros (CBS)
3	5	THE WIND BENEATH MY WINGS	Bette Midler (Atlantic)
19	6	I DON'T WANNA LOSE YOU	Gloria Estefan (Epic)
6	7	AIN'T NOBODY	Rufus & Chaka Khan (Warner Bros)
4	8	BACK TO LIFE	Soul II Soul featuring Caron Wheeler (10)
11	9	LIBERIAN GIRL	Michael Jackson (Epic)
10	10	SUPERWOMAN	Karyn White (Warner Bros)
43	11	SWING THE MOOD	Jive Bunny & the Mastermixers (Music Factory Dance)
21	12	DAYS	Kirsty MacColl (Virgin)
7	13	IT'S ALRIGHT	Pet Shop Boys (Parlophone)
8	14	VOODOO RAY	A Guy Called Gerald (Rham!)
22	15	A NEW FLAME	Simply Red (WEA)
12	16	GRANDPA'S PARTY	Monie Love (Cooltempo)
14	17	SAY NO GO	De La Soul (Big Life)
9	18	SONG FOR WHOEVER	Beautiful South (Go! Discs)
20	19	CRY	Waterfront (Polydor)
-	20	FRENCH KISS	Lil Louis (ffrr)
13	21	LICENCE TO KILL	Gladys Knight (MCA)
24	22	GET LOOSE LA Mix featuring Jazzi P (Breakout)	
25	23	THE SECOND SUMMER OF LOVE	Danny Wilson (Virgin)
27	24	CHOICE?	Blow Monkeys featuring Sylvia Tella (RCA)
17	25	BLAME IT ON THE BASSLINE	Norman Cook featuring Mc Wildski (Go Beat)
34	26	LET IT ROLL	Doug Lazy (Atlantic)
16	27	BATDANCE	Prince (Warner Bros)
30	28	EDIE (CIAO BABY)	Cult (Beggars Banquet)
15	29	BREAKTHRU	Queen (Parlophone)
23	30	PATIENCE	Guns N' Roses (Geffen)
26	31	I DROVE ALL NIGHT	Cyndi Lauper (Epic)
18	32	POP MUZIK (THE 1989 REMIX)	M (Freestyle)
45	33	COME AND GET SOME	Cookie Crew (ffrr)
-	34	KICK IT IN	Simple Minds (Virgin)
46	35	CHA CHA HEELS	Eartha Kitt & Bronski Beat (Arista)
29	36	JUST KEEP ROCKIN'	Double Trouble & the Rebel MC (Desire)
41	37	BLAME IT ON THE RAIN	Milli Vanilli (Cooltempo)
-	38	YOU'VE GOT TO CHOOSE	Darling Buds (CBS)
49	39	BETTER DAYS	Gun (A&M)
-	40	PURE	Lightning Seeds (Ghetto)
-	41	BLAZING SADDLES	Yello (Mercury)
-	42	SHE BANGS THE DRUMS	Stone Roses (Silvertone)
-	43	DO THE RIGHT THING	Redhead Kingpin & the FBI (10)
28	44	RIGHT BACK WHERE WE STARTED FROM	Sinitta (Fanfare)
48	45	DRESSED FOR SUCCESS	Roxette (EMI)
-	46	SATISFACTION	Wendy & Lisa (Virgin)
47	47	ON AND ON	Aswad (Mango)
32	48	SEALED WITH A KISS	Jason Donovan (PWL)
-	49	REST OF THE NIGHT	Natalie Cole (Manhattan)
-	50	DON'T MAKE ME OVER	Sybil (Champion)

5 August 1989

last	this		
11	1	SWING THE MOOD	Jive Bunny & the Mastermixers (Music Factory Dance)
4	2	TOO MUCH	Bros (CBS)
20	3	FRENCH KISS	Lil Louis (ffrr)
-	4	WOULDN'T CHANGE A THING	Kylie Minogue (PWL)
1	5	YOU'LL NEVER STOP ME LOVING YOU	Sonia (Chrysalis)
6	6	I DON'T WANNA LOSE YOU	Gloria Estefan (Epic)
3	7	LONDON NIGHTS	London Boys (WEA)
2	8	ON OUR OWN	Bobby Brown (MCA)
5	9	THE WIND BENEATH MY WINGS	Bette Midler (Atlantic)
7	10	AIN'T NOBODY	Rufus & Chaka Khan (Warner Bros)
15	11	A NEW FLAME	Simply Red (WEA)
12	12	DAYS	Kirsty MacColl (Virgin)
8	13	BACK TO LIFE	Soul II Soul featuring Caron Wheeler (10)
10	14	SUPERWOMAN	Karyn White (Warner Bros)
34	15	KICK IT IN	Simple Minds (Virgin)
-	16	DO YOU LOVE WHAT YOU FEEL	Inner City (10)
13	17	IT'S ALRIGHT	Pet Shop Boys (Parlophone)
24	18	CHOICE?	Blow Monkeys featuring Sylvia Tella (RCA)
19	19	CRY	Waterfront (Polydor)
-	20	POISON	Alice Cooper (Epic)
9	21	LIBERIAN GIRL	Michael Jackson (Epic)
14	22	VOODOO RAY	A Guy Called Gerald (Rham!)
26	23	LET IT ROLL	Doug Lazy (Atlantic)
42	24	SHE BANGS THE DRUMS	Stone Roses (Silvertone)
16	25	GRANDPA'S PARTY	Monie Love (Cooltempo)
17	26	SAY NO GO	De La Soul (Big Life)
39	27	BETTER DAYS	Gun (A&M)
-	28	TOY SOLDIERS	Martika (CBS)
21	29	LICENCE TO KILL	Gladys Knight (MCA)
-	30	LANDSLIDE OF LOVE	Transvision Vamp (MCA)
22	31	GET LOOSE LA Mix featuring Jazzi P (Breakout)	
-	32	SICK OF IT	Primitives (Lazy)
35	33	CHA CHA HEELS	Eartha Kitt & Bronski Beat (Arista)
-	34	THIS ONE	Paul McCartney (Parlophone)
18	35	SONG FOR WHOEVER	Beautiful South (Go! Discs)
46	36	SATISFACTION	Wendy & Lisa (Virgin)
27	37	BATDANCE	Prince (Warner Bros)
40	38	PURE	Lightning Seeds (Ghetto)
37	39	BLAME IT ON THE RAIN	Milli Vanilli (Cooltempo)
47	40	ON AND ON	Aswad (Mango)
-	41	YOU'RE HISTORY	Shakespears Sister (ffrr)
23	42	THE SECOND SUMMER OF LOVE	Danny Wilson (Virgin)
25	43	BLAME IT ON THE BASSLINE	Norman Cook featuring Mc Wildski (Go Beat)
-	44	THE END OF THE INNOCENCE	Don Henley (Geffen)
30	45	PATIENCE	Guns N' Roses (Geffen)
38	46	YOU'VE GOT TO CHOOSE	Darling Buds (CBS)
-	47	GOODWILL CITY/I'M SICK OF YOU	Goodbye Mr. MacKenzie (Capitol)
28	48	EDIE (CIAO BABY)	Cult (Beggars Banquet)
36	49	JUST KEEP ROCKIN'	Double Trouble & the Rebel MC (Desire)
-	50	PARADISE	Diana Ross (EMI)

Another major film hit, Bette Midler's *The Wind Beneath My Wings* – her first UK chart entry after years of American hits – was from *Beaches*, in which she also starred. Meanwhile, now remixed, Rufus & Chaka Khan's *Ain't Nobody* enjoyed a second Top 10 run more than five years after its original appearance, while M's *Pop Muzik* (also newly remixed) was back in the Top 10 after 10 years.

12 August 1989

last week	this week	Title	Artist (Label)
1	1	SWING THE MOOD	Jive Bunny & the Mastermixers (Music Factory Dance)
4	2	WOULDN'T CHANGE A THING	Kylie Minogue (PWL)
3	3	FRENCH KISS	Lil Louis (ffrr)
6	4	I DON'T WANNA LOSE YOU	Gloria Estefan (Epic)
20	5	POISON	Alice Cooper (Epic)
5	6	YOU'LL NEVER STOP ME LOVING YOU	Sonia (Chrysalis)
2	7	TOO MUCH	Bros (CBS)
16	8	DO YOU LOVE WHAT YOU FEEL	Inner City (10)
8	9	ON OUR OWN	Bobby Brown (MCA)
41	10	YOU'RE HISTORY	Shakespears Sister (ffrr)
30	11	LANDSLIDE OF LOVE	Transvision Vamp (MCA)
28	12	TOY SOLDIERS	Martika (CBS)
7	13	LONDON NIGHTS	London Boys (WEA)
15	14	KICK IT IN	Simple Minds (Virgin)
10	15	AIN'T NOBODY	Rufus & Chaka Khan (Warner Bros)
12	16	DAYS	Kirsty MacColl (Virgin)
11	17	A NEW FLAME	Simply Red (WEA)
13	18	BACK TO LIFE	Soul II Soul featuring Caron Wheeler (10)
9	19	THE WIND BENEATH MY WINGS	Bette Midler (Atlantic)
38	20	PURE	Lightning Seeds (Ghetto)
14	21	SUPERWOMAN	Karyn White (Warner Bros)
34	22	THIS ONE	Paul McCartney (Parlophone)
18	23	CHOICE?	Blow Monkeys featuring Sylvia Tella (RCA)
32	24	SICK OF IT	Primitives (Lazy)
27	25	BETTER DAYS	Gun (A&M)
-	26	SATELLITE KID	Dogs D'Amour (China)
22	27	VOODOO RAY	A Guy Called Gerald (Rham!)
17	28	IT'S ALRIGHT	Pet Shop Boys (Parlophone)
36	29	SATISFACTION	Wendy & Lisa (Virgin)
19	30	CRY	Waterfront (Polydor)
40	31	ON AND ON	Aswad (Mango)
29	32	LICENCE TO KILL	Gladys Knight (MCA)
-	33	DO THE RIGHT THING	Redhead Kingpin & the FBI (10)
37	34	BATDANCE	Prince (Warner Bros)
-	35	FRIENDS	Jody Watley with Eric B. & Rakim (MCA)
-	36	SELF!	Fuzzbox (WEA)
-	37	MY FIRST NIGHT WITHOUT YOU	Cyndi Lauper (Epic)
21	38	LIBERIAN GIRL	Michael Jackson (Epic)
44	39	THE END OF THE INNOCENCE	Don Henley (Geffen)
-	40	CHAINS	River Detectives (WEA)
-	41	LOSING MY MIND	Liza Minnelli (Epic)
26	42	SAY NO GO	De La Soul (Big Life)
-	43	HEY DJ/I CAN'T DANCE TO THE MUSIC YOU'RE PLAYING	Beatmasters featuring Betty Boo (Rhythm King)
25	44	GRANDPA'S PARTY	Monie Love (Cooltempo)
35	45	SONG FOR WHOEVER	Beautiful South (Go! Discs)
-	46	THIS IS THE RIGHT TIME	Lisa Stansfield (Arista)
-	47	I GOT IT GOIN' NOW	Tone Loc (Fourth & Broadway)
-	48	BLAME IT ON THE BOOGIE	Big Fun (Jive)
23	49	LET IT ROLL	Doug Lazy (Atlantic)
-	50	EVERYDAY NOW	Texas (Mercury)

19 August 1989

last week	this week	Title	Artist (Label)
1	1	SWING THE MOOD	Jive Bunny & the Mastermixers (Music Factory Dance)
2	2	WOULDN'T CHANGE A THING	Kylie Minogue (PWL)
3	3	FRENCH KISS	Lil Louis (ffrr)
5	4	POISON	Alice Cooper (Epic)
12	5	TOY SOLDIERS	Martika (CBS)
10	6	YOU'RE HISTORY	Shakespears Sister (ffrr)
4	7	I DON'T WANNA LOSE YOU	Gloria Estefan (Epic)
20	8	PURE	Lightning Seeds (Ghetto)
6	9	YOU'LL NEVER STOP ME LOVING YOU	Sonia (Chrysalis)
-	10	RIDE ON TIME	Black Box (deConstruction)
48	11	BLAME IT ON THE BOOGIE	Big Fun (Jive)
11	12	LANDSLIDE OF LOVE	Transvision Vamp (MCA)
9	13	ON OUR OWN	Bobby Brown (MCA)
41	14	LOSING MY MIND	Liza Minnelli (Epic)
46	15	THIS IS THE RIGHT TIME	Lisa Stansfield (Arista)
22	16	THIS ONE	Paul McCartney (Parlophone)
33	17	DO THE RIGHT THING	Redhead Kingpin & the FBI (10)
7	18	TOO MUCH	Bros (CBS)
43	19	HEY DJ/I CAN'T DANCE TO THE MUSIC YOU'RE PLAYING	Beatmasters featuring Betty Boo (Rhythm King)
8	20	DO YOU LOVE WHAT YOU FEEL	Inner City (10)
13	21	LONDON NIGHTS	London Boys (WEA)
26	22	SATELLITE KID	Dogs D'Amour (China)
19	23	THE WIND BENEATH MY WINGS	Bette Midler (Atlantic)
15	24	AIN'T NOBODY	Rufus & Chaka Khan (Warner Bros)
29	25	SATISFACTION	Wendy & Lisa (Virgin)
-	26	KISSES ON THE WIND	Neneh Cherry (Circa)
18	27	BACK TO LIFE	Soul II Soul featuring Caron Wheeler (10)
-	28	THE INVISIBLE MAN	Queen (Parlophone)
16	29	DAYS	Kirsty MacColl (Virgin)
31	30	ON AND ON	Aswad (Mango)
35	31	FRIENDS	Jody Watley with Eric B. & Rakim (MCA)
17	32	A NEW FLAME	Simply Red (WEA)
-	33	MENTAL	Manic MC's featuring Sara Carlson (RCA)
21	34	SUPERWOMAN	Karyn White (Warner Bros)
-	35	WARNING!	Adeva (Cooltempo)
36	36	SELF!	Fuzzbox (WEA)
-	37	SUGAR BOX	Then Jerico (London)
-	38	DON'T LOOK BACK	Fine Young Cannibals (London)
14	39	KICK IT IN	Simple Minds (Virgin)
34	40	BATDANCE	Prince (Warner Bros)
-	41	STAND	R.E.M. (Warner Bros)
25	42	BETTER DAYS	Gun (A&M)
39	43	THE END OF THE INNOCENCE	Don Henley (Geffen)
30	44	CRY	Waterfront (Polydor)
23	45	CHOICE?	Blow Monkeys featuring Sylvia Tella (RCA)
27	46	VOODOO RAY	A Guy Called Gerald (Rham!)
50	47	EVERYDAY NOW	Texas (Mercury)
40	48	CHAINS	River Detectives (WEA)
37	49	MY FIRST NIGHT WITHOUT YOU	Cyndi Lauper (Epic)
32	50	LICENCE TO KILL	Gladys Knight (MCA)

26 August 1989

last week	this week	Title	Artist (Label)
1	1	SWING THE MOOD	Jive Bunny & the Mastermixers (Music Factory Dance)
14	2	LOSING MY MIND	Liza Minnelli (Epic)
3	3	FRENCH KISS	Lil Louis (ffrr)
10	4	RIDE ON TIME	Black Box (deConstruction)
11	5	BLAME IT ON THE BOOGIE	Big Fun (Jive)
5	6	TOY SOLDIERS	Martika (CBS)
-	7	I JUST DON'T HAVE THE HEART	Cliff Richard (EMI)
2	8	WOULDN'T CHANGE A THING	Kylie Minogue (PWL)
4	9	POISON	Alice Cooper (Epic)
6	10	YOU'RE HISTORY	Shakespears Sister (ffrr)
15	11	THIS IS THE RIGHT TIME	Lisa Stansfield (Arista)
19	12	HEY DJ/I CAN'T DANCE TO THE MUSIC YOU'RE PLAYING	Beatmasters featuring Betty Boo (Rhythm King)
17	13	DO THE RIGHT THING	Redhead Kingpin & the FBI (10)
7	14	I DON'T WANNA LOSE YOU	Gloria Estefan (Epic)
8	15	PURE	Lightning Seeds (Ghetto)
26	16	KISSES ON THE WIND	Neneh Cherry (Circa)
9	17	YOU'LL NEVER STOP ME LOVING YOU	Sonia (Chrysalis)
28	18	THE INVISIBLE MAN	Queen (Parlophone)
13	19	ON OUR OWN	Bobby Brown (MCA)
-	20	NUMERO UNO	Starlight (Citybeat)
36	21	SELF!	Fuzzbox (WEA)
33	22	MENTAL	Manic MC's featuring Sara Carlson (RCA)
20	23	ON AND ON	Aswad (Mango)
12	24	LANDSLIDE OF LOVE	Transvision Vamp (MCA)
31	25	FRIENDS	Jody Watley with Eric B. & Rakim (MCA)
35	26	WARNING!	Adeva (Cooltempo)
-	27	I NEED YOUR LOVIN'	Alyson Williams (Def Jam)
-	28	LAY YOUR HANDS ON ME	Bon Jovi (Vertigo)
38	29	DON'T LOOK BACK	Fine Young Cannibals (London)
37	30	SUGAR BOX	Then Jerico (London)
18	31	TOO MUCH	Bros (CBS)
23	32	THE WIND BENEATH MY WINGS	Bette Midler (Atlantic)
16	33	THIS ONE	Paul McCartney (Parlophone)
-	34	REVIVAL	Eurythmics (RCA)
-	35	THE TIME WARP	Damian (Jive)
40	36	BATDANCE	Prince (Warner Bros)
-	37	WE COULD BE TOGETHER	Debbie Gibson (Atlantic)
21	38	LONDON NIGHTS	London Boys (WEA)
-	39	SOMETHING'S JUMPIN' IN YOUR SHIRT	Lisa Marie with Malcolm McLaren & the Bootzilla Orchestra (Epic)
20	40	DO YOU LOVE WHAT YOU FEEL	Inner City (10)
25	41	SATISFACTION	Wendy & Lisa (Virgin)
27	42	BACK TO LIFE	Soul II Soul featuring Caron Wheeler (10)
-	43	KNOCKED OUT	Paula Abdul (Siren)
24	44	AIN'T NOBODY	Rufus & Chaka Khan (Warner Bros)
45	45	EVERYDAY NOW	Texas (Mercury)
29	46	DAYS	Kirsty MacColl (Virgin)
34	47	SUPERWOMAN	Karyn White (Warner Bros)
32	48	A NEW FLAME	Simply Red (WEA)
-	49	LOVE'S ABOUT TO CHANGE MY HEART	Donna Summer (Warner Bros)
-	50	THE RIGHT STUFF	Vanessa Williams (Wing)

Jive Bunny & the Mastermixers' *Swing The Mood* was hardly a new idea – spliced excerpts from rock'n'roll oldies over an underlying rhythm track – but it had been a long time since the *Stars On 45* era, and the track was highly effective on dancefloors, hence its huge popularity. It eventually sold over 750,000 copies during and following its five weeks at Number One.

September 1989

2 September 1989

last week	this week	Title	Artist (Label)
1	1	SWING THE MOOD	Jive Bunny & the Mastermixers (Music Factory Dance)
4	2	RIDE ON TIME	Black Box (deConstruction)
7	3	I JUST DON'T HAVE THE HEART	Cliff Richard (EMI)
3	4	FRENCH KISS	Lil Louis (ffrr)
5	5	BLAME IT ON THE BOOGIE	Big Fun (Jive)
6	6	TOY SOLDIERS	Martika (CBS)
2	7	LOSING MY MIND	Liza Minnelli (Epic)
20	8	NUMERO UNO	Starlight (Citybeat)
12	9	HEY DJ/I CAN'T DANCE TO THE MUSIC YOU'RE PLAYING	Beatmasters featuring Betty Boo (Rhythm King)
9	10	POISON	Alice Cooper (Epic)
11	11	THIS IS THE RIGHT TIME	Lisa Stansfield (Arista)
8	12	WOULDN'T CHANGE A THING	Kylie Minogue (PWL)
18	13	THE INVISIBLE MAN	Queen (Parlophone)
26	14	WARNING!	Adeva (Cooltempo)
27	15	I NEED YOUR LOVIN'	Alyson Williams (Def Jam)
-	16	SOWING THE SEEDS OF LOVE	Tears For Fears (Fontana)
28	17	LAY YOUR HANDS ON ME	Bon Jovi (Vertigo)
10	18	YOU'RE HISTORY	Shakespears Sister (ffrr)
13	19	DO THE RIGHT THING	Redhead Kingpin & the FBI (10)
49	20	LOVE'S ABOUT TO CHANGE MY HEART	Donna Summer (Warner Bros)
25	21	FRIENDS	Jody Watley with Eric B. & Rakim (MCA)
16	22	KISSES ON THE WIND	Neneh Cherry (Circa)
30	23	SUGAR BOX	Then Jerico (London)
34	24	REVIVAL	Eurythmics (RCA)
-	25	NIGHTRAIN	Guns N' Roses (Geffen)
14	26	I DON'T WANNA LOSE YOU	Gloria Estefan (Epic)
29	27	DON'T LOOK BACK	Fine Young Cannibals (London)
17	28	YOU'LL NEVER STOP ME LOVING YOU	Sonia (Chrysalis)
37	29	WE COULD BE TOGETHER	Debbie Gibson (Atlantic)
-	30	IF ONLY I COULD	Sydney Youngblood (Circa)
21	31	SELF!	Fuzzbox (WEA)
15	32	PURE	Lightning Seeds (Ghetto)
33	33	THE TIME WARP	Damian (Jive)
39	34	SOMETHING'S JUMPIN' IN YOUR SHIRT	Lisa Marie with Malcolm McLaren & the Bootzilla Orchestra (Epic)
-	35	LOVE SONG	Cure (Fiction)
-	36	LOVE PAINS	Hazell Dean (Lisson)
-	37	MISS YOU MUCH	Janet Jackson (Breakout)
43	38	KNOCKED OUT	Paula Abdul (Siren)
22	39	MENTAL	Manic MC's featuring Sara Car (RCA)
-	40	THE BEST	Tina Turner (Capitol)
-	41	I AM THE MUSIC MAN	Black Lace (Flair)
19	42	ON OUR OWN	Bobby Brown (MCA)
-	43	RIGHT HERE WAITING	Richard Marx (EMI-USA)
-	44	BE FREE WITH YOUR LOVE	Spandau Ballet (CBS)
23	45	ON AND ON	Aswad (Mango)
24	46	LANDSLIDE OF LOVE	Transvision Vamp (MCA)
-	47	1-2-3	Chimes (CBS)
-	48	HEALING HANDS	Elton John (Rocket)
-	49	MIXED EMOTIONS	Rolling Stones (Rolling Stones)
-	50	PROUD TO FALL	Ian McCulloch (WEA)

9 September 1989

		Title	Artist (Label)
2	1	RIDE ON TIME	Black Box (deConstruction)
1	2	SWING THE MOOD	Jive Bunny & the Mastermixers (Music Factory Dance)
3	3	I JUST DON'T HAVE THE HEART	Cliff Richard (EMI)
16	4	SOWING THE SEEDS OF LOVE	Tears For Fears (Fontana)
5	5	BLAME IT ON THE BOOGIE	Big Fun (Jive)
8	6	NUMERO UNO	Starlight (Citybeat)
9	7	HEY DJ/I CAN'T DANCE TO THE MUSIC YOU'RE PLAYING	Beatmasters featuring Betty Boo (Rhythm King)
6	8	TOY SOLDIERS	Martika (CBS)
15	9	I NEED YOUR LOVIN'	Alyson Williams (Def Jam)
-	10	EVERY DAY (I LOVE YOU MORE)	Jason Donovan (PWL)
33	11	THE TIME WARP	Damian (Jive)
10	12	POISON	Alice Cooper (Epic)
4	13	FRENCH KISS	Lil Louis (ffrr)
43	14	RIGHT HERE WAITING	Richard Marx (EMI-USA)
14	15	WARNING!	Adeva (Cooltempo)
20	16	LOVE'S ABOUT TO CHANGE MY HEART	Donna Summer (Warner Bros)
25	17	NIGHTRAIN	Guns N' Roses (Geffen)
11	18	THIS IS THE RIGHT TIME	Lisa Stansfield (Arista)
17	19	LAY YOUR HANDS ON ME	Bon Jovi (Vertigo)
7	20	LOSING MY MIND	Liza Minnelli (Epic)
40	21	THE BEST	Tina Turner (Capitol)
12	22	WOULDN'T CHANGE A THING	Kylie Minogue (PWL)
24	23	REVIVAL	Eurythmics (RCA)
18	24	YOU'RE HISTORY	Shakespears Sister (ffrr)
37	25	MISS YOU MUCH	Janet Jackson (Breakout)
29	26	WE COULD BE TOGETHER	Debbie Gibson (Atlantic)
30	27	IF ONLY I COULD	Sydney Youngblood (Circa)
13	28	THE INVISIBLE MAN	Queen (Parlophone)
-	29	PARTYMAN	Prince (Warner Bros)
23	30	SUGAR BOX	Then Jerico (London)
19	31	DO THE RIGHT THING	Redhead Kingpin & the FBI (10)
34	32	SOMETHING'S JUMPIN' IN YOUR SHIRT	Lisa Marie with Malcolm McLaren & the Bootzilla Orchestra (Epic)
35	33	LOVE SONG	Cure (Fiction)
-	34	PERSONAL JESUS	Depeche Mode (Mute)
26	35	I DON'T WANNA LOSE YOU	Gloria Estefan (Epic)
27	36	DON'T LOOK BACK	Fine Young Cannibals (London)
28	37	YOU'LL NEVER STOP ME LOVING YOU	Sonia (Chrysalis)
22	38	KISSES ON THE WIND	Neneh Cherry (Circa)
44	39	BE FREE WITH YOUR LOVE	Spandau Ballet (CBS)
21	40	FRIENDS	Jody Watley with Eric B. & Rakim (MCA)
49	41	MIXED EMOTIONS	Rolling Stones (Rolling Stones)
-	42	AFRO DIZZI ACT	Cry Sisco! (Escape)
50	43	PROUD TO FALL	Ian McCulloch (WEA)
-	44	SALSA HOUSE	Richie Rich (ffrr)
-	45	FOREVER FREE	W.A.S.P. (Capitol)
41	46	I AM THE MUSIC MAN	Black Lace (Flair)
-	47	HONEY BE GOOD	Bible (Ensign)
-	48	PUMP UP THE JAM	Technotronic with Felly (Swanyard)
-	49	LOVE IN AN ELEVATOR	Aerosmith (Geffen)
36	50	LOVE PAINS	Hazell Dean (Lisson)

16 September 1989

		Title	Artist (Label)
1	1	RIDE ON TIME	Black Box (deConstruction)
10	2	EVERY DAY (I LOVE YOU MORE)	Jason Donovan (PWL)
2	3	SWING THE MOOD	Jive Bunny & the Mastermixers (Music Factory Dance)
14	4	RIGHT HERE WAITING	Richard Marx (EMI-USA)
4	5	SOWING THE SEEDS OF LOVE	Tears For Fears (Fontana)
6	6	NUMERO UNO	Starlight (Citybeat)
5	7	BLAME IT ON THE BOOGIE	Big Fun (Jive)
21	8	THE BEST	Tina Turner (Capitol)
3	9	I JUST DON'T HAVE THE HEART	Cliff Richard (EMI)
11	10	THE TIME WARP	Damian (Jive)
7	11	HEY DJ/I CAN'T DANCE TO THE MUSIC YOU'RE PLAYING	Beatmasters featuring Betty Boo (Rhythm King)
9	12	I NEED YOUR LOVIN'	Alyson Williams (Def Jam)
29	13	PARTYMAN	Prince (Warner Bros)
12	14	POISON	Alice Cooper (Epic)
-	15	CHERISH	Madonna (Sire)
8	16	TOY SOLDIERS	Martika (CBS)
17	17	NIGHTRAIN	Guns N' Roses (Geffen)
34	18	PERSONAL JESUS	Depeche Mode (Mute)
13	19	FRENCH KISS	Lil Louis (ffrr)
15	20	WARNING!	Adeva (Cooltempo)
26	21	WE COULD BE TOGETHER	Debbie Gibson (Atlantic)
25	22	MISS YOU MUCH	Janet Jackson (Breakout)
23	23	REVIVAL	Eurythmics (RCA)
48	24	PUMP UP THE JAM	Technotronic with Felly (Swanyard)
27	25	IF ONLY I COULD	Sydney Youngblood (Circa)
16	26	LOVE'S ABOUT TO CHANGE MY HEART	Donna Summer (Warner Bros)
49	27	LOVE IN AN ELEVATOR	Aerosmith (Geffen)
19	28	LAY YOUR HANDS ON ME	Bon Jovi (Vertigo)
33	29	LOVE SONG	Cure (Fiction)
22	30	WOULDN'T CHANGE A THING	Kylie Minogue (PWL)
-	31	HOOKS IN YOU	Marillion (Capitol)
18	32	THIS IS THE RIGHT TIME	Lisa Stansfield (Arista)
41	33	MIXED EMOTIONS	Rolling Stones (Rolling Stones)
24	34	YOU'RE HISTORY	Shakespears Sister (ffrr)
20	35	LOSING MY MIND	Liza Minnelli (Epic)
32	36	SOMETHING'S JUMPIN' IN YOUR SHIRT	Lisa Marie with Malcolm McLaren & the Bootzilla Orchestra (Epic)
-	37	IT ISN'T, IT WASN'T, IT AIN'T NEVER GONNA BE	Aretha Franklin & Whitney Houston (Arista)
31	38	DO THE RIGHT THING	Redhead Kingpin & the FBI (10)
-	39	MANTRA FOR A STATE OF MIND	S'Express (Rhythm King)
39	40	BE FREE WITH YOUR LOVE	Spandau Ballet (CBS)
42	41	AFRO DIZZI ACT	Cry Sisco! (Escape)
28	42	THE INVISIBLE MAN	Queen (Parlophone)
-	43	OYE MI CANTO (HEAR MY VOICE)	Gloria Estefan (Epic)
45	44	FOREVER FREE	W.A.S.P. (Capitol)
-	45	HARLEM DESIRE	London Boys (WEA)
-	46	SECRET RENDEZVOUS	Karyn White (Warner Bros)
30	47	SUGAR BOX	Then Jerico (London)
-	48	LOVE AND REGRET	Deacon Blue (CBS)
35	49	I DON'T WANNA LOSE YOU	Gloria Estefan (Epic)
-	50	EXPRESS YOURSELF	NWA (Fourth & Broadway)

The single which dethroned Jive Bunny was also the one track which had a more widespead disco and dancefloor reach in 1989 than *Swing The Mood*. *Ride On Time*, an Italian production which combined an irresistible keyboard riff with sampled vocal lines from US singer Loleatta Holloway, rode Number One for six weeks – longer than any other single for five years – and was this year's top seller.

23 September 1989

last week	this week	Title	Artist
1	1	RIDE ON TIME	Black Box (deConstruction)
4	2	RIGHT HERE WAITING	Richard Marx (EMI-USA)
2	3	EVERY DAY (I LOVE YOU MORE)	Jason Donovan (PWL)
8	4	THE BEST	Tina Turner (Capitol)
10	5	THE TIME WARP	Damian (Jive)
15	6	CHERISH	Madonna (Sire)
25	7	IF ONLY I COULD	Sydney Youngblood (Circa)
5	8	SOWING THE SEEDS OF LOVE	Tears For Fears (Fontana)
24	9	PUMP UP THE JAM	Technotronic with Felly (Swanyard)
3	10	SWING THE MOOD	Jive Bunny & the Mastermixers (Music Factory Dance)
6	11	NUMERO UNO	Starlight (Citybeat)
13	12	PARTYMAN	Prince (Warner Bros)
7	13	BLAME IT ON THE BOOGIE	Big Fun (Jive)
12	14	I NEED YOUR LOVIN'	Alyson Williams (Def Jam)
18	15	PERSONAL JESUS	Depeche Mode (Mute)
29	16	LOVE SONG	Cure (Fiction)
11	17	HEY DJ/I CAN'T DANCE TO THE MUSIC YOU'RE PLAYING	Beatmasters featuring Betty Boo (Rhythm King)
27	18	LOVE IN AN ELEVATOR	Aerosmith (Geffen)
14	19	POISON	Alice Cooper (Epic)
9	20	I JUST DON'T HAVE THE HEART	Cliff Richard (EMI)
45	21	HARLEM DESIRE	London Boys (WEA)
22	22	MISS YOU MUCH	Janet Jackson (Breakout)
39	23	MANTRA FOR A STATE OF MIND	S'Express (Rhythm King)
48	24	LOVE AND REGRET	Deacon Blue (CBS)
16	25	TOY SOLDIERS	Martika (CBS)
43	26	OYE MI CANTO (HEAR MY VOICE)	Gloria Estefan (Epic)
17	27	NIGHTRAIN	Guns N' Roses (Geffen)
44	28	FOREVER FREE	W.A.S.P. (Capitol)
37	29	IT ISN'T, IT WASN'T, IT AIN'T NEVER GONNA BE	Aretha Franklin & Whitney Houston (Arista)
21	30	WE COULD BE TOGETHER	Debbie Gibson (Atlantic)
19	31	FRENCH KISS	Lil Louis (ffrr)
28	32	LAY YOUR HANDS ON ME	Bon Jovi (Vertigo)
33	33	MIXED EMOTIONS	Rolling Stones (Rolling Stones)
31	34	HOOKS IN YOU	Marillion (Capitol)
-	35	DON'T LET ME DOWN, GENTLY	Wonder Stuff (Polydor)
26	36	LOVE'S ABOUT TO CHANGE MY HEART	Donna Summer (Warner Bros)
-	37	SOLD ME DOWN THE RIVER	Alarm (IRS)
30	38	WOULDN'T CHANGE A THING	Kylie Minogue (PWL)
46	39	SECRET RENDEZVOUS	Karyn White (Warner Bros)
-	40	ROCK WITH 'CHA	Bobby Brown (MCA)
23	41	REVIVAL	Eurythmics (RCA)
32	42	THIS IS THE RIGHT TIME	Lisa Stansfield (Arista)
20	43	WARNING!	Adeva (Cooltempo)
-	44	BLUES FROM A GUN	Jesus & Mary Chain (blanco y negro)
-	45	YOU KEEP IT ALL IN	Beautiful South (Go! Discs)
34	46	YOU'RE HISTORY	Shakespears Sister (ffrr)
-	47	LOVE TOGETHER	LA Mix featuring Kevin Henry (Breakout)
36	48	SOMETHING'S JUMPIN' IN YOUR SHIRT	Lisa Marie with Malcolm McLaren & the Bootzilla Orchestra (Epic)
-	49	NAME AND NUMBER	Curiosity Killed The Cat (Mercury)
38	50	DO THE RIGHT THING	Redhead Kingpin & the FBI (10)

30 September 1989

last week	this week	Title	Artist
1	1	RIDE ON TIME	Black Box (deConstruction)
2	2	RIGHT HERE WAITING	Richard Marx (EMI-USA)
9	3	PUMP UP THE JAM	Technotronic with Felly (Swanyard)
6	4	CHERISH	Madonna (Sire)
7	5	IF ONLY I COULD	Sydney Youngblood (Circa)
4	6	THE BEST	Tina Turner (Capitol)
-	7	DRAMA!	Erasure (Mute)
5	8	THE TIME WARP	Damian (Jive)
21	9	HARLEM DESIRE	London Boys (WEA)
3	10	EVERY DAY (I LOVE YOU MORE)	Jason Donovan (PWL)
8	11	SOWING THE SEEDS OF LOVE	Tears For Fears (Fontana)
18	12	LOVE IN AN ELEVATOR	Aerosmith (Geffen)
35	13	DON'T LET ME DOWN, GENTLY	Wonder Stuff (Polydor)
45	14	YOU KEEP IT ALL IN	Beautiful South (Go! Discs)
10	15	SWING THE MOOD	Jive Bunny & the Mastermixers (Music Factory Dance)
-	16	THE SENSUAL WORLD	Kate Bush (EMI)
23	17	MANTRA FOR A STATE OF MIND	S'Express (Rhythm King)
11	18	NUMERO UNO	Starlight (Citybeat)
15	19	PERSONAL JESUS	Depeche Mode (Mute)
24	20	LOVE AND REGRET	Deacon Blue (CBS)
12	21	PARTYMAN	Prince (Warner Bros)
26	22	OYE MI CANTO (HEAR MY VOICE)	Gloria Estefan (Epic)
14	23	I NEED YOUR LOVIN'	Alyson Williams (Def Jam)
28	24	FOREVER FREE	W.A.S.P. (Capitol)
13	25	BLAME IT ON THE BOOGIE	Big Fun (Jive)
22	26	MISS YOU MUCH	Janet Jackson (Breakout)
29	27	IT ISN'T, IT WASN'T, IT AIN'T NEVER GONNA BE	Aretha Franklin & Whitney Houston (Arista)
-	28	SWEET SURRENDER	Wet Wet Wet (Precious)
16	29	LOVE SONG	Cure (Fiction)
40	30	ROCK WITH 'CHA	Bobby Brown (MCA)
17	31	HEY DJ/I CAN'T DANCE TO THE MUSIC YOU'RE PLAYING	Beatmasters featuring Betty Boo (Rhythm King)
44	32	BLUES FROM A GUN	Jesus & Mary Chain (blanco y negro)
20	33	I JUST DON'T HAVE THE HEART	Cliff Richard (EMI)
-	34	ROAD TO YOUR SOUL	All About Eve (Mercury)
19	35	POISON	Alice Cooper (Epic)
-	36	SUENO LATINO (THE LATIN DREAM)	Sueno Latino (BCM)
49	37	NAME AND NUMBER	Curiosity Killed The Cat (Mercury)
39	38	SECRET RENDEZVOUS	Karyn White (Warner Bros)
30	39	WE COULD BE TOGETHER	Debbie Gibson (Atlantic)
-	40	IF I COULD TURN BACK TIME	Cher (Geffen)
25	41	TOY SOLDIERS	Martika (CBS)
37	42	SOLD ME DOWN THE RIVER	Alarm (IRS)
31	43	NOTHIN' BUT A GOOD TIME	Poison (Capitol)
-	44	FRENCH KISS	Lil Louis (ffrr)
-	45	FACTS OF LOVE	Climie Fisher (EMI)
36	46	LOVE'S ABOUT TO CHANGE MY HEART	Donna Summer (Warner Bros)
-	47	HANGIN' TOUGH	New Kids On The Block (CBS)
27	48	NIGHTRAIN	Guns N' Roses (Geffen)
38	49	WOULDN'T CHANGE A THING	Kylie Minogue (PWL)
-	50	ROOM IN YOUR HEART	Living In A Box (Chrysalis)

7 October 1989

last week	this week	Title	Artist
1	1	RIDE ON TIME	Black Box (deConstruction)
3	2	PUMP UP THE JAM	Technotronic with (Swanyard)
5	3	IF ONLY I COULD	Sydney Youngblood (Circa)
7	4	DRAMA!	Erasure (Mute)
14	5	YOU KEEP IT ALL IN	Beautiful South (Go! Discs)
2	6	RIGHT HERE WAITING	Richard Marx (EMI-USA)
28	7	SWEET SURRENDER	Wet Wet Wet (Precious)
6	8	THE BEST	Tina Turner (Capitol)
4	9	CHERISH	Madonna (Sire)
16	10	THE SENSUAL WORLD	Kate Bush (EMI)
-	11	CHOCOLATE BOX	Bros (CBS)
-	12	WE DIDN'T START THE FIRE	Billy Joel (CBS)
8	13	THE TIME WARP	Damian (Jive)
9	14	HARLEM DESIRE	London Boys (WEA)
12	15	LOVE IN AN ELEVATOR	Aerosmith (Geffen)
11	16	SOWING THE SEEDS OF LOVE	Tears For Fears (Fontana)
22	17	OYE MI CANTO (HEAR MY VOICE)	Gloria Estefan (Epic)
17	18	MANTRA FOR A STATE OF MIND	S'Express (Rhythm King)
15	19	SWING THE MOOD	Jive Bunny & the Mastermixers (Music Factory Dance)
10	20	EVERY DAY (I LOVE YOU MORE)	Jason Donovan (PWL)
18	21	NUMERO UNO	Starlight (Citybeat)
40	22	IF I COULD TURN BACK TIME	Cher (Geffen)
13	23	DON'T LET ME DOWN, GENTLY	Wonder Stuff (Polydor)
37	24	NAME AND NUMBER	Curiosity Killed The Cat (Mercury)
23	25	I NEED YOUR LOVIN'	Alyson Williams (Def Jam)
38	26	SECRET RENDEZVOUS	Karyn White (Warner Bros)
20	27	LOVE AND REGRET	Deacon Blue (CBS)
19	28	PERSONAL JESUS	Depeche Mode (Mute)
-	29	STREET TUFF	Rebel MC & Double Trouble (Desire)
50	30	ROOM IN YOUR HEART	Living In A Box (Chrysalis)
25	31	BLAME IT ON THE BOOGIE	Big Fun (Jive)
34	32	ROAD TO YOUR SOUL	All About Eve (Mercury)
26	33	MISS YOU MUCH	Janet Jackson (Breakout)
30	34	ROCK WITH 'CHA	Bobby Brown (MCA)
35	35	LOVE ON A MOUNTAIN TOP	Sinitta (Fanfare)
21	36	PARTYMAN	Prince (Warner Bros)
27	37	IT ISN'T, IT WASN'T, IT AIN'T NEVER GONNA BE	Aretha Franklin & Whitney Houston (Arista)
-	38	GIRL I'M GONNA MISS YOU	Milli Vanilli (Cooltempo)
31	39	HEY DJ/I CAN'T DANCE TO THE MUSIC YOU'RE PLAYING	Beatmasters featuring Betty Boo (Rhythm King)
36	40	SUENO LATINO (THE LATIN DREAM)	Sueno Latino (BCM)
-	41	KENNEDY	Wedding Present (RCA)
29	42	LOVE SONG	Cure (Fiction)
33	43	CAN'T FORGET YOU	Sonia (Chrysalis)
-	44	THE REAL WILD HOUSE	Raul Orellana (RCA)
24	45	FOREVER FREE	W.A.S.P. (Capitol)
-	46	I FEEL FOR YOU	Chaka Khan (Warner Bros)
47	47	HANGIN' TOUGH	New Kids On The Block (CBS)
-	48	BED OF NAILS	Alice Cooper (Epic)
-	49	THE DOWNTOWN LIGHTS	Blue Nile (Linn)
-	50	LEAVE A LIGHT ON	Belinda Carlisle (Virgin)

The singles which queued unsuccessfully at Number Two behind Black Box were varied: Jason Donovan's uptempo *Every Day (I Love You More)*, US teen idol Richard Marx' ballad *Right Here Waiting*, and the hot club dancer *Pump Up The Jam*, by Belgian act Technotronic. Another dancefloor-driven top-tenner was Damian's *The Time Warp*, a revival of a song from the cult *Rocky Horror Picture Show* movie.

October 1989

14 October 1989

LW	TW	Title	Artist (Label)
1	1	RIDE ON TIME	Black Box (deConstruction)
2	2	PUMP UP THE JAM	Technotronic with Felly (Swanyard)
4	3	DRAMA!	Erasure (Mute)
3	4	IF ONLY I COULD	Sydney Youngblood (Circa)
29	5	STREET TUFF	Rebel MC & Double Trouble (Desire)
12	6	WE DIDN'T START THE FIRE	Billy Joel (CBS)
7	7	SWEET SURRENDER	Wet Wet Wet (Precious)
5	8	YOU KEEP IT ALL IN	Beautiful South (Go! Discs)
11	9	CHOCOLATE BOX	Bros (CBS)
38	10	GIRL I'M GONNA MISS YOU	Milli Vanilli (Cooltempo)
6	11	RIGHT HERE WAITING	Richard Marx (EMI-USA)
-	12	THAT'S WHAT I LIKE	Jive Bunny & the Mastermixers (Music Factory Dance)
24	13	NAME AND NUMBER	Curiosity Killed The Cat (Mercury)
22	14	IF I COULD TURN BACK TIME	Cher (Geffen)
8	15	THE BEST	Tina Turner (Capitol)
17	16	OYE MI CANTO (HEAR MY VOICE)	Gloria Estefan (Epic)
43	17	CAN'T FORGET YOU	Sonia (Chrysalis)
50	18	LEAVE A LIGHT ON	Belinda Carlisle (Virgin)
9	19	CHERISH	Madonna (Sire)
10	20	THE SENSUAL WORLD	Kate Bush (EMI)
35	21	LOVE ON A MOUNTAIN TOP	Sinitta (Fanfare)
26	22	SECRET RENDEZVOUS	Karyn White (Warner Bros)
13	23	THE TIME WARP	Damian (Jive)
15	24	LOVE IN AN ELEVATOR	Aerosmith (Geffen)
-	25	WISHING ON A STAR	Fresh 4 With Lizz (10)
18	26	MANTRA FOR A STATE OF MIND	S'Express (Rhythm King)
14	27	HARLEM DESIRE	London Boys (WEA)
41	28	KENNEDY	Wedding Present (RCA)
30	29	ROOM IN YOUR HEART	Living In A Box (Chrysalis)
16	30	SOWING THE SEEDS OF LOVE	Tears For Fears (Fontana)
25	31	I NEED YOUR LOVIN'	Alyson Williams (Def Jam)
34	32	ROCK WITH 'CHA	Bobby Brown (MCA)
46	33	I FEEL FOR YOU	Chaka Khan (Warner Bros)
21	34	NUMERO UNO	Starlight (Citybeat)
48	35	BED OF NAILS	Alice Cooper (Epic)
44	36	THE REAL WILD HOUSE	Raul Orellana (RCA)
19	37	SWING THE MOOD	Jive Bunny & the Mastermixers (Music Factory Dance)
-	38	DON'T DROP THE BOMBS	Liza Minnelli (Epic)
32	39	ROAD TO YOUR SOUL	All About Eve (Mercury)
-	40	LEAN ON YOU	Cliff Richard (EMI)
20	41	EVERY DAY (I LOVE YOU MORE)	Jason Donovan (PWL)
-	42	I WANT THAT MAN	Deborah Harry (Chrysalis)
27	43	LOVE AND REGRET	Deacon Blue (CBS)
-	44	LOVE STRAIN	Kym Mazelle (Syncopate)
33	45	MISS YOU MUCH	Janet Jackson (Breakout)
-	46	I FEEL THE EARTH MOVE	Martika (CBS)
28	47	PERSONAL JESUS	Depeche Mode (Mute)
31	48	BLAME IT ON THE BOOGIE	Big Fun (Jive)
-	49	TRAIL OF TEARS	Dogs D'Amour (China)
-	50	THE ROAD TO HELL (PARTS 1 AND 2)	Chris Rea (WEA)

21 October 1989

LW	TW	Title	Artist (Label)
12	1	THAT'S WHAT I LIKE	Jive Bunny & the Mastermixers (Music Factory Dance)
1	2	RIDE ON TIME	Black Box (deConstruction)
2	3	PUMP UP THE JAM	Technotronic with Felly (Swanyard)
5	4	STREET TUFF	Rebel MC & Double Trouble (Desire)
10	5	GIRL I'M GONNA MISS YOU	Milli Vanilli (Cooltempo)
6	6	WE DIDN'T START THE FIRE	Billy Joel (CBS)
4	7	IF ONLY I COULD	Sydney Youngblood (Circa)
18	8	LEAVE A LIGHT ON	Belinda Carlisle (Virgin)
3	9	DRAMA!	Erasure (Mute)
14	10	IF I COULD TURN BACK TIME	Cher (Geffen)
7	11	SWEET SURRENDER	Wet Wet Wet (Precious)
25	12	WISHING ON A STAR	Fresh 4 With Lizz (10)
17	13	CAN'T FORGET YOU	Sonia (Chrysalis)
50	14	THE ROAD TO HELL (PARTS 1 AND 2)	Chris Rea (WEA)
21	15	LOVE ON A MOUNTAIN TOP	Sinitta (Fanfare)
29	16	ROOM IN YOUR HEART	Living In A Box (Chrysalis)
8	17	YOU KEEP IT ALL IN	Beautiful South (Go! Discs)
11	18	RIGHT HERE WAITING	Richard Marx (EMI-USA)
13	19	NAME AND NUMBER	Curiosity Killed The Cat (Mercury)
40	20	LEAN ON YOU	Cliff Richard (EMI)
15	21	THE BEST	Tina Turner (Capitol)
9	22	CHOCOLATE BOX	Bros (CBS)
42	23	I WANT THAT MAN	Deborah Harry (Chrysalis)
22	24	SECRET RENDEZVOUS	Karyn White (Warner Bros)
-	25	OH WELL	Oh Well (Parlophone)
16	26	OYE MI CANTO (HEAR MY VOICE)	Gloria Estefan (Epic)
-	27	SCANDAL	Queen (Parlophone)
19	28	CHERISH	Madonna (Sire)
26	29	MANTRA FOR A STATE OF MIND	S'Express (Rhythm King)
36	30	THE REAL WILD HOUSE	Raul Orellana (RCA)
20	31	THE SENSUAL WORLD	Kate Bush (EMI)
-	32	DON'T MAKE ME OVER	Sybil (Champion)
46	33	I FEEL THE EARTH MOVE	Martika (CBS)
-	34	C'MON AND GET MY LOVE	D Mob introducing Cathy Dennis (ffrr)
35	35	BED OF NAILS	Alice Cooper (Epic)
-	36	I THANK YOU	Adeva (Cooltempo)
37	37	EYE KNOW	De La Soul (Big Life)
28	38	KENNEDY	Wedding Present (RCA)
23	39	THE TIME WARP	Damian (Jive)
-	40	RUN SILENT	Shakespears Sister (ffrr)
27	41	HARLEM DESIRE	London Boys (WEA)
-	42	LET THE DAY BEGIN	Call (MCA)
24	43	LOVE IN AN ELEVATOR	Aerosmith (Geffen)
44	44	LOVE STRAIN	Kym Mazelle (Syncopate)
49	45	TRAIL OF TEARS	Dogs D'Amour (China)
30	46	SOWING THE SEEDS OF LOVE	Tears For Fears (Fontana)
31	47	I NEED YOUR LOVIN'	Alyson Williams (Def Jam)
37	48	SWING THE MOOD	Jive Bunny & the Mastermixers (Music Factory Dance)
-	49	WANTED	Halo James (Epic)
38	50	DON'T DROP THE BOMBS	Liza Minnelli (Epic)

28 October 1989

LW	TW	Title	Artist (Label)
1	1	THAT'S WHAT I LIKE	Jive Bunny & the Mastermixers (Music Factory Dance)
5	2	GIRL I'M GONNA MISS YOU	Milli Vanilli (Cooltempo)
4	3	STREET TUFF	Rebel MC & Double Trouble (Desire)
2	4	RIDE ON TIME	Black Box (deConstruction)
12	5	WISHING ON A STAR	Fresh 4 With Lizz (10)
6	6	WE DIDN'T START THE FIRE	Billy Joel (CBS)
8	7	LEAVE A LIGHT ON	Belinda Carlisle (Virgin)
3	8	PUMP UP THE JAM	Technotronic with Felly (Swanyard)
14	9	THE ROAD TO HELL (PARTS 1 AND 2)	Chris Rea (WEA)
10	10	IF I COULD TURN BACK TIME	Cher (Geffen)
36	11	I THANK YOU	Adeva (Cooltempo)
7	12	IF ONLY I COULD	Sydney Youngblood (Circa)
16	13	ROOM IN YOUR HEART	Living In A Box (Chrysalis)
37	14	EYE KNOW	De La Soul (Big Life)
23	15	I WANT THAT MAN	Deborah Harry (Chrysalis)
20	16	LEAN ON YOU	Cliff Richard (EMI)
15	17	LOVE ON A MOUNTAIN TOP	Sinitta (Fanfare)
-	18	ALL AROUND THE WORLD	Lisa Stansfield (Arista)
11	19	SWEET SURRENDER	Wet Wet Wet (Precious)
27	20	SCANDAL	Queen (Parlophone)
32	21	DON'T MAKE ME OVER	Sybil (Champion)
25	22	OH WELL	Oh Well (Parlophone)
9	23	DRAMA!	Erasure (Mute)
34	24	C'MON AND GET MY LOVE	D Mob introducing Cathy Dennis (ffrr)
19	25	NAME AND NUMBER	Curiosity Killed The Cat (Mercury)
17	26	YOU KEEP IT ALL IN	Beautiful South (Go! Discs)
13	27	CAN'T FORGET YOU	Sonia (Chrysalis)
33	28	I FEEL THE EARTH MOVE	Martika (CBS)
30	29	THE REAL WILD HOUSE	Raul Orellana (RCA)
21	30	THE BEST	Tina Turner (Capitol)
18	31	RIGHT HERE WAITING	Richard Marx (EMI-USA)
26	32	OYE MI CANTO (HEAR MY VOICE)	Gloria Estefan (Epic)
35	33	BED OF NAILS	Alice Cooper (Epic)
22	34	CHOCOLATE BOX	Bros (CBS)
-	35	THE MESSAGE IS LOVE	Arthur Baker & the Backbeat Disciples with Al Green (Breakout)
29	36	MANTRA FOR A STATE OF MIND	S'Express (Rhythm King)
-	37	THE SUN RISING	Beloved (WEA)
24	38	SECRET RENDEZVOUS	Karyn White (Warner Bros)
42	39	LET THE DAY BEGIN	Call (MCA)
28	40	CHERISH	Madonna (Sire)
49	41	WANTED	Halo James (Epic)
-	42	FOR SPACIOUS LIES	Norman Cook featuring Lester (Go Beat)
-	43	STATE OF MIND	Fish (EMI)
48	44	SWING THE MOOD	Jive Bunny & the Mastermixers (Music Factory Dance)
-	45	RESTLESS DAYS	And Why Not? (Island)
-	46	DRIVE ON	Brother Beyond (Parlophone)
31	47	THE SENSUAL WORLD	Kate Bush (EMI)
-	48	LISTEN TO YOUR HEART	Roxette (EMI)
39	49	THE TIME WARP	Damian (Jive)
-	50	TAKE CARE OF YOURSELF	Level 42 (Polydor)

So lengthy was Black Box's Number One tenure that Jive Bunny, having been deposed by it, took over again with their follow-up single, which milked exactly the same ingredients as before, while widening the excerpts' musical range into the '60s. Another UK dance act, D Mob, first introduced female vocalist Cathy Dennis on *C'mon And Get My Love*, which made the Top 20.

November 1989

4 November 1989

last week	this week	title	artist
1	1	THAT'S WHAT I LIKE	Jive Bunny & the Mastermixers (Music Factory Dance)
2	2	GIRL I'M GONNA MISS YOU	Milli Vanilli (Cooltempo)
3	3	STREET TUFF	Rebel MC & Double Trouble (Desire)
18	4	ALL AROUND THE WORLD	Lisa Stansfield (Arista)
7	5	LEAVE A LIGHT ON	Belinda Carlisle (Virgin)
13	6	ROOM IN YOUR HEART	Living In A Box (Chrysalis)
14	7	EYE KNOW	De La Soul (Big Life)
4	8	RIDE ON TIME	Black Box (deConstruction)
11	9	I THANK YOU	Adeva (Cooltempo)
10	10	IF I COULD TURN BACK TIME	Cher (Geffen)
9	11	THE ROAD TO HELL (PARTS 1 AND 2)	Chris Rea (WEA)
5	12	WISHING ON A STAR	Fresh 4 With Lizz (10)
15	13	I WANT THAT MAN	Deborah Harry (Chrysalis)
21	14	DON'T MAKE ME OVER	Sybil (Champion)
-	15	NEVER TOO LATE	Kylie Minogue (PWL)
28	16	I FEEL THE EARTH MOVE	Martika (CBS)
6	17	WE DIDN'T START THE FIRE	Billy Joel (CBS)
24	18	C'MON AND GET MY LOVE	D Mob introducing Cathy Dennis (ffrr)
-	19	ANOTHER DAY IN PARADISE	Phil Collins (Virgin)
8	20	PUMP UP THE JAM	Technotronic with Felly (Swanyard)
-	21	NEVER TOO MUCH	Luther Vandross (Epic)
22	22	OH WELL	Oh Well (Parlophone)
12	23	IF ONLY I COULD	Sydney Youngblood (Circa)
16	24	LEAN ON YOU	Cliff Richard (EMI)
-	25	TELL ME WHEN THE FEVER ENDED	Electribe 101 (Mercury)
20	26	SCANDAL	Queen (Parlophone)
-	27	GRAND PIANO	Mixmaster (BC)
19	28	SWEET SURRENDER	Wet Wet Wet (Precious)
35	29	THE MESSAGE IS LOVE	Arthur Baker & the Backbeat Disciples with Al Green (Breakout)
37	30	THE SUN RISING	Beloved (WEA)
43	31	STATE OF MIND	Fish (EMI)
17	32	LOVE ON A MOUNTAIN TOP	Sinitta (Fanfare)
29	33	THE REAL WILD HOUSE	Raul Orellana (RCA)
-	34	BORN TO BE SOLD	Transvision Vamp (MCA)
50	35	TAKE CARE OF YOURSELF	Level 42 (Polydor)
26	36	YOU KEEP IT ALL IN	Beautiful South (Go! Discs)
30	37	THE BEST	Tina Turner (Capitol)
46	38	DRIVE ON	Brother Beyond (Parlophone)
-	39	YOU'VE GOT IT	Simply Red (Elektra)
-	40	RHYTHM NATION	Janet Jackson (Breakout)
25	41	NAME AND NUMBER	Curiosity Killed The Cat (Mercury)
-	42	LAMBADA	Kaoma (CBS)
45	43	RESTLESS DAYS	And Why Not? (Island)
23	44	DRAMA!	Erasure (Mute)
48	45	LISTEN TO YOUR NATION	Roxette (EMI)
-	46	IT'S ALL COMING BACK TO ME NOW	Pandora's Box (Virgin)
41	47	WANTED	Halo James (Epic)
31	48	RIGHT HERE WAITING	Richard Marx (EMI-USA)
39	49	LET THE DAY BEGIN	Call (MCA)
-	50	NOT AT ALL	Status Quo (Vertigo)

11 November 1989

last week	this week	title	artist
4	1	ALL AROUND THE WORLD	Lisa Stansfield (Arista)
1	2	THAT'S WHAT I LIKE	Jive Bunny & the Mastermixers (Music Factory Dance)
2	3	GIRL I'M GONNA MISS YOU	Milli Vanilli (Cooltempo)
6	4	ROOM IN YOUR HEART	Living In A Box (Chrysalis)
3	5	STREET TUFF	Rebel MC & Double Trouble (Desire)
15	6	NEVER TOO LATE	Kylie Minogue (PWL)
5	7	LEAVE A LIGHT ON	Belinda Carlisle (Virgin)
27	8	GRAND PIANO	Mixmaster (BC)
7	9	EYE KNOW	De La Soul (Big Life)
21	10	NEVER TOO MUCH	Luther Vandross (Epic)
16	11	I FEEL THE EARTH MOVE	Martika (CBS)
11	12	THE ROAD TO HELL (PARTS 1 AND 2)	Chris Rea (WEA)
19	13	ANOTHER DAY IN PARADISE	Phil Collins (Virgin)
8	14	RIDE ON TIME	Black Box (deConstruction)
13	15	I WANT THAT MAN	Deborah Harry (Chrysalis)
10	16	IF I COULD TURN BACK TIME	Cher (Geffen)
17	17	WE DIDN'T START THE FIRE	Billy Joel (CBS)
18	18	C'MON AND GET MY LOVE	D Mob introducing Cathy Dennis (ffrr)
30	19	THE SUN RISING	Beloved (WEA)
34	20	BORN TO BE SOLD	Transvision Vamp (MCA)
9	21	I THANK YOU	Adeva (Cooltempo)
25	22	TELL ME WHEN THE FEVER ENDED	Electribe 101 (Mercury)
14	23	DON'T MAKE ME OVER	Sybil (Champion)
12	24	WISHING ON A STAR	Fresh 4 With Lizz (10)
20	25	PUMP UP THE JAM	Technotronic with Felly (Swanyard)
23	26	IF ONLY I COULD	Sydney Youngblood (Circa)
29	27	THE MESSAGE IS LOVE	Arthur Baker & the Backbeat Disciples with Al Green (Breakout)
22	28	OH WELL	Oh Well (Parlophone)
26	29	SCANDAL	Queen (Parlophone)
-	30	DON'T ASK ME WHY	Eurythmics (RCA)
40	31	RHYTHM NATION	Janet Jackson (Breakout)
24	32	LEAN ON YOU	Cliff Richard (EMI)
38	33	DRIVE ON	Brother Beyond (Parlophone)
-	34	GOLDEN GREEN/GET TGETHER	Wonder Stuff (Polydor)
33	35	THE REAL WILD HOUSE	Raul Orellana (RCA)
36	36	YOU'VE GOT IT	Simply Red (Elektra)
35	37	TAKE CARE OF YOURSELF	Level 42 (Polydor)
28	38	SWEET SURRENDER	Wet Wet Wet (Precious)
31	39	STATE OF MIND	Fish (EMI)
-	40	SWING THE MOOD	Jive Bunny & the Mastermixers (Music Factory Dance)
-	41	A NEW SOUTH WALES	Alarm featuring the Morriston Orpheus Male Voice Choir (IRS)
37	42	THE BEST	Tina Turner (Capitol)
43	43	RESTLESS DAYS	And Why Not? (Island)
42	44	LAMBADA	Kaoma (CBS)
-	45	LET THE RHYTHM PUMP	Doug Lazy (Atlantic)
36	46	YOU KEEP IT ALL IN	Beautiful South (Go! Discs)
-	47	7 O'CLOCK	Quireboys (Parlophone)
-	48	STRINGS OF LIFE '89	Rhythim Is Rhythim (Kool Kat)
-	49	DR. FEELGOOD	Motley Crue (Elektra)
-	50	DON'T KNOW MUCH	Linda Ronstadt featuring Aaron Neville (Elektra)

18 November 1989

last week	this week	title	artist
1	1	ALL AROUND THE WORLD	Lisa Stansfield (Arista)
6	2	NEVER TOO LATE	Kylie Minogue (PWL)
13	3	ANOTHER DAY IN PARADISE	Phil Collins (Virgin)
3	4	GIRL I'M GONNA MISS YOU	Milli Vanilli (Cooltempo)
2	5	THAT'S WHAT I LIKE	Jive Bunny & the Mastermixers (Music Factory Dance)
8	6	GRAND PIANO	Mixmaster (BC)
11	7	I FEEL THE EARTH MOVE	Martika (CBS)
50	8	DON'T KNOW MUCH	Linda Ronstadt featuring Aaron Neville (Elektra)
10	9	NEVER TOO MUCH	Luther Vandross (Epic)
5	10	STREET TUFF	Rebel MC & Double Trouble (Desire)
-	11	YOU GOT IT (THE RIGHT STUFF)	New Kids On The Block (CBS)
4	12	ROOM IN YOUR HEART	Living In A Box (Chrysalis)
-	13	INFINITE DREAMS	Iron Maiden (EMI)
7	14	LEAVE A LIGHT ON	Belinda Carlisle (Virgin)
14	15	RIDE ON TIME	Black Box (deConstruction)
12	16	THE ROAD TO HELL (PARTS 1 AND 2)	Chris Rea (WEA)
20	17	BORN TO BE SOLD	Transvision Vamp (MCA)
18	18	C'MON AND GET MY LOVE	D Mob introducing Cathy Dennis (ffrr)
9	19	EYE KNOW	De La Soul (Big Life)
15	20	I WANT THAT MAN	Deborah Harry (Chrysalis)
-	21	PACIFIC 707	808 State (ZTT)
22	22	TELL ME WHEN THE FEVER ENDED	Electribe 101 (Mercury)
16	23	IF I COULD TURN BACK TIME	Cher (Geffen)
30	24	DON'T ASK ME WHY	Eurythmics (RCA)
31	25	RHYTHM NATION	Janet Jackson (Breakout)
19	26	THE SUN RISING	Beloved (WEA)
17	27	WE DIDN'T START THE FIRE	Billy Joel (CBS)
41	28	A NEW SOUTH WALES	Alarm featuring the Morriston Orpheus Male Voice Choir (IRS)
25	29	PUMP UP THE JAM	Technotronic with Felly (Swanyard)
-	30	COMMENT TE DIRE ADIEU	Jimmy Somerville featuring June Miles Kingston (London)
23	31	I THANK YOU	Adeva (Cooltempo)
26	32	IF ONLY I COULD	Sydney Youngblood (Circa)
44	33	LAMBADA	Kaoma (CBS)
47	34	7 O'CLOCK	Quireboys (Parlophone)
34	35	GOLDEN GREEN/GET TGETHER	Wonder Stuff (Polydor)
23	36	DON'T MAKE ME OVER	Sybil (Champion)
-	37	I'M NOT THE MAN I USED TO BE	Fine Young Cannibals (London)
43	38	RESTLESS DAYS	And Why Not? (Island)
-	39	ANGELIA	Richard Marx (EMI-USA)
-	40	WHATCHA GONNA DO WITH MY LOVIN'	Inner City (10)
24	41	WISHING ON A STAR	Fresh 4 With Lizz (10)
28	42	OH WELL	Oh Well (Parlophone)
-	43	THE ARMS OF ORION	Prince with Sheena Easton (Warner Bros)
40	44	SWING THE MOOD	Jive Bunny & the Mastermixers (Music Factory Dance)
27	45	THE MESSAGE IS LOVE	Arthur Baker & the Backbeat Disciples with Al Green (Breakout)
-	46	SACRIFICE	Elton John (Rocket)
-	47	SUN KING/EDIE (CIAO BABY)	Cult (Beggars Banquet)
-	48	THIS OLD HEART OF MINE	Rod Stewart with Ronald Isley (Warner Bros)
35	49	THE REAL WILD HOUSE	Raul Orellana (RCA)
-	50	WOMAN IN CHAINS	Tears For Fears (Fontana)

After first hitting the chart as featured vocalist on Coldcut's *People Hold On*, then hitting the Top 20 in her own right with *This Is The Right Time*, Lisa Stansfield made Number One with the soulful *All Around The World* – an appropriate title for a record which would bring her global chart success, including a Top Three hit in the US, and a Number One placing on America's R&B chart.

November – December 1989

25 November 1989

last	this		
1	1	ALL AROUND THE WORLD	Lisa Stansfield (Arista)
11	2	YOU GOT IT (THE RIGHT STUFF)	New Kids On The Block (CBS)
3	3	ANOTHER DAY IN PARADISE	Phil Collins (Virgin)
8	4	DON'T KNOW MUCH	Linda Ronstadt featuring Aaron Neville (Elektra)
2	5	NEVER TOO LATE	Kylie Minogue (PWL)
6	6	GRAND PIANO	Mixmaster (BC)
21	7	PACIFIC 707	808 State (ZTT)
13	8	INFINITE DREAMS	Iron Maiden (EMI)
4	9	GIRL I'M GONNA MISS YOU	Milli Vanilli (Cooltempo)
7	10	I FEEL THE EARTH MOVE	Martika (CBS)
–	11	HOMELY GIRL	UB40 (DEP International)
9	12	NEVER TOO MUCH	Luther Vandross (Epic)
5	13	THAT'S WHAT I LIKE	Jive Bunny & the Mastermixers (Music Factory Dance)
40	14	WHATCHA GONNA DO WITH MY LOVIN'	Inner City (10)
10	15	STREET TUFF	Rebel MC & Double Trouble (Desire)
37	16	I'M NOT THE MAN I USED TO BE	Fine Young Cannibals (London)
18	17	C'MON AND GET MY LOVE	D Mob introducing Cathy Dennis (ffrr)
33	18	LAMBADA	Kaoma (CBS)
12	19	ROOM IN YOUR HEART	Living In A Box (Chrysalis)
–	20	OUIJA BOARD, OUIJA BOARD	Morrissey (HMV)
25	21	RHYTHM NATION	Janet Jackson (Breakout)
30	22	COMMENT TE DIRE ADIEU	Jimmy Somerville featuring June Miles Kingston (London)
24	23	DON'T ASK ME WHY	Eurythmics (RCA)
15	24	RIDE ON TIME	Black Box (deConstruction)
22	25	TELL ME WHEN THE FEVER ENDED	Electribe 101 (Mercury)
14	26	LEAVE A LIGHT ON	Belinda Carlisle (Virgin)
–	27	FOOLS GOLD/WHAT THE WORLD IS WAITING FOR	Stone Roses (Silvertone)
20	28	I WANT THAT MAN	Deborah Harry (Chrysalis)
43	29	THE ARMS OF ORION	Prince with Sheena Easton (Warner Bros)
16	30	THE ROAD TO HELL (PARTS 1 AND 2)	Chris Rea (WEA)
23	31	IF I COULD TURN BACK TIME	Cher (Geffen)
26	32	A NEW SOUTH WALES	Alarm featurin Morrisson Orpheus Male Voice Choir (IRS)
19	33	EYE KNOW	De La Soul (Big Life)
50	34	WOMAN IN CHAINS	Tears For Fears (Fontana)
29	35	PUMP UP THE JAM	Technotronic with Felly (Swanyard)
–	36	THE EVE OF THE WAR	Ben Liebrand/Jeff Wayne (CBS)
–	37	I SECOND THAT EMOTION	Alyson Williams (Def Jam)
47	38	SUN KING/EDIE (CIAO BABY)	Cult (Beggars Banquet)
27	39	WE DIDN'T START THE FIRE	Billy Joel (CBS)
17	40	BORN TO BE SOLD	Transvision Vamp (MCA)
36	41	RESTLESS DAYS	And Why Not? (Island)
32	42	IF ONLY I COULD	Sydney Youngblood (Circa)
–	43	WITH EVERY BEAT OF MY HEART	Taylor Dayne (Arista)
–	44	I DON'T WANNA LOSE YOU	Tina Turner (Capitol)
39	45	ANGELIA	Richard Marx (EMI-USA)
26	46	THE SUN RISING	Beloved (WEA)
–	47	I DON'T KNOW WHY I LOVE YOU	House Of Love (Fontana)
–	48	YOUTH GONE WILD	Skid Row (Atlantic)
48	49	THIS OLD HEART OF MINE	Rod Stewart with Ronald Isley (Warner Bros)
–	50	CAN'T SHAKE THE FEELING	Big Fun (Jive)

2 December 1989

last	this		
2	1	YOU GOT IT (THE RIGHT STUFF)	New Kids On The Block (CBS)
4	2	DON'T KNOW MUCH	Linda Ronstadt featuring Aaron Neville (Elektra)
1	3	ALL AROUND THE WORLD	Lisa Stansfield (Arista)
11	4	HOMELY GIRL	UB40 (DEP International)
27	5	FOOLS GOLD/WHAT THE WORLD IS WAITING FOR	Stone Roses (Silvertone)
18	6	LAMBADA	Kaoma (CBS)
7	7	PACIFIC 707	808 State (ZTT)
36	8	THE EVE OF THE WAR	Ben Liebrand/Jeff Wayne (CBS)
3	9	ANOTHER DAY IN PARADISE	Phil Collins (Virgin)
5	10	NEVER TOO LATE	Kylie Minogue (PWL)
6	11	GRAND PIANO	Mixmaster (BC)
14	12	WHATCHA GONNA DO WITH MY LOVIN'	Inner City (10)
8	13	INFINITE DREAMS	Iron Maiden (EMI)
22	14	COMMENT TE DIRE ADIEU	Jimmy Somerville featuring June Miles Kingston (London)
16	15	I'M NOT THE MAN I USED TO BE	Fine Young Cannibals (London)
50	16	CAN'T SHAKE THE FEELING	Big Fun (Jive)
–	17	RONI	Bobby Brown (MCA)
9	18	GIRL I'M GONNA MISS YOU	Milli Vanilli (Cooltempo)
10	19	I FEEL THE EARTH MOVE	Martika (CBS)
20	20	OUIJA BOARD, OUIJA BOARD	Morrissey (HMV)
21	21	GET ON YOUR FEET	Gloria Estefan (Epic)
15	22	STREET TUFF	Rebel MC & Double Trouble (Desire)
–	23	MADCHESTER RAVE ON (EP)	Happy Mondays (Factory)
13	24	THAT'S WHAT I LIKE	Jive Bunny & the Mastermixers (Music Factory Dance)
34	25	WOMAN IN CHAINS	Tears For Fears (Fontana)
17	26	C'MON AND GET MY LOVE	D Mob introducing Cathy Dennis (ffrr)
12	27	NEVER TOO MUCH	Luther Vandross (Epic)
29	28	THE ARMS OF ORION	Prince with Sheena Easton (Warner Bros)
19	29	ROOM IN YOUR HEART	Living In A Box (Chrysalis)
23	30	DON'T ASK ME WHY	Eurythmics (RCA)
24	31	RIDE ON TIME	Black Box (deConstruction)
26	32	LEAVE A LIGHT ON	Belinda Carlisle (Virgin)
21	33	RHYTHM NATION	Janet Jackson (Breakout)
–	34	LATINO MIX	Latino Rave (Deep Heat)
28	35	I WANT THAT MAN	Deborah Harry (Chrysalis)
–	36	GOT TO GET	Rob 'N' Raz featuring Leila K (Arista)
37	37	I SECOND THAT EMOTION	Alyson Williams (Def Jam)
30	38	THE ROAD TO HELL (PARTS 1 AND 2)	Chris Rea (WEA)
–	39	I'LL SAIL THIS SHIP ALONE	Beautiful South (Go! Discs)
–	40	ENCORE	Tongue 'N' Cheek (Syncopate)
31	41	IF I COULD TURN BACK TIME	Cher (Geffen)
–	42	FIGURE OF EIGHT	Paul McCartney (Parlophone)
–	43	MY LOVE	London Boys (WEA)
47	44	I DON'T KNOW WHY I LOVE YOU	House Of Love (Fontana)
48	45	YOUTH GONE WILD	Skid Row (Atlantic)
–	46	FOOL FOR YOUR LOVIN'	Whitesnake (EMI)
44	47	I DON'T WANNA LOSE YOU	Tina Turner (Capitol)
–	48	WITH GOD ON OUR SIDE	Neville Brothers (A&M)
49	49	THIS WOMAN'S WORK	Kate Bush (EMI)
25	50	TELL ME WHEN THE FEVER ENDED	Electribe 101 (Mercury)

9 December 1989

last	this		
8	1	THE EVE OF THE WAR	Ben Liebrand/Jeff Wayne (CBS)
1	2	YOU GOT IT (THE RIGHT STUFF)	New Kids On The Block (CBS)
2	3	DON'T KNOW MUCH	Linda Ronstadt featuring Aaron Neville (Elektra)
6	4	LAMBADA	Kaoma (CBS)
16	5	CAN'T SHAKE THE FEELING	Big Fun (Jive)
4	6	HOMELY GIRL	UB40 (DEP International)
7	7	PACIFIC 707	808 State (ZTT)
–	8	WHEN YOU COME BACK TO ME	Jason Donovan (PWL)
3	9	ALL AROUND THE WORLD	Lisa Stansfield (Arista)
–	10	GET A LIFE/JAZZIE'S GROOVE	Soul II Soul (10)
5	11	FOOLS GOLD/WHAT THE WORLD IS WAITING FOR	Stone Roses (Silvertone)
12	12	WHATCHA GONNA DO WITH MY LOVIN'	Inner City (10)
14	13	COMMENT TE DIRE ADIEU	Jimmy Somerville featuring June Miles Kingston (London)
9	14	ANOTHER DAY IN PARADISE	Phil Collins (Virgin)
21	15	GET ON YOUR FEET	Gloria Estefan (Epic)
17	16	RONI	Bobby Brown (MCA)
–	17	YOU SURROUND ME	Erasure (Mute)
23	18	MADCHESTER RAVE ON (EP)	Happy Mondays (Factory)
15	19	I'M NOT THE MAN I USED TO BE	Fine Young Cannibals (London)
–	20	IN PRIVATE	Dusty Springfield (Parlophone)
34	21	LATINO MIX	Latino Rave (Deep Heat)
36	22	GOT TO GET	Rob 'N' Raz featuring Leila K (Arista)
10	23	NEVER TOO LATE	Kylie Minogue (PWL)
49	24	THIS WOMAN'S WORK	Kate Bush (EMI)
25	25	WOMAN IN CHAINS	Tears For Fears (Fontana)
11	26	GRAND PIANO	Mixmaster (BC)
47	27	I DON'T WANNA LOSE YOU	Tina Turner (Capitol)
–	28	THE AMSTERDAM (EP)	Simple Minds (Virgin)
19	29	I FEEL THE EARTH MOVE	Martika (CBS)
18	30	GIRL I'M GONNA MISS YOU	Milli Vanilli (Cooltempo)
26	31	C'MON AND GET MY LOVE	D Mob introducing Cathy Dennis (ffrr)
24	32	THAT'S WHAT I LIKE	Jive Bunny & the Mastermixers (Music Factory Dance)
31	33	RIDE ON TIME	Black Box (deConstruction)
39	34	I'LL SAIL THIS SHIP ALONE	Beautiful South (Go! Discs)
43	35	MY LOVE	London Boys (WEA)
22	36	STREET TUFF	Rebel MC & Double Trouble (Desire)
13	37	INFINITE DREAMS	Iron Maiden (EMI)
–	38	LIVING IN SIN	Bon Jovi (Vertigo)
–	39	STORIES	Izit (ffrr)
48	40	WITH GOD ON OUR SIDE	Neville Brothers (A&M)
–	41	WARM LOVE	Beatmasters featuring Claudia Fontaine (Rhythm King)
–	42	THE MIRACLE	Queen (Parlophone)
28	43	THE ARMS OF ORION	Prince with Sheena Easton (Warner Bros)
46	44	FOOL FOR YOUR LOVIN'	Whitesnake (EMI)
–	45	BLAME IT ON THE RAIN	Milli Vanilli (Cooltempo)
40	46	ENCORE	Tongue 'N' Cheek (Syncopate)
–	47	WHENEVER GOD SHINES HIS LIGHT	Van Morrison with Cliff Richard (Polydor)
48	48	SIT AND WAIT	Sydney Youngblood (Circa)
–	49	HIT MIX (THE OFFICIAL BOOTLEG MEGAMIX)	Alexander O'Neal (Tabu)
–	50	BROKE AWAY	Wet Wet Wet (Precious)

The void awaiting a new teen sensation was suddenly filled at the end of 1989 by New Kids On The Block, a youthful, good-looking quintet from Boston, USA, who were able to close-harmonise, rap, and synchronise their dance movements equally well. The UK ignored their US hits at first, until a repromotion of *You Got It (The Right Stuff)* kick-started their career here from Number One.

16 December 1989

last week	this week	title	artist (label)
10	1	GET A LIFE/JAZZIE'S GROOVE	Soul II Soul (10)
1	2	THE EVE OF THE WAR	Ben Liebrand/Jeff Wayne (CBS)
2	3	YOU GOT IT (THE RIGHT STUFF)	New Kids On The Block (CBS)
8	4	WHEN YOU COME BACK TO ME	Jason Donovan (PWL)
4	5	LAMBADA	Kaoma (CBS)
3	6	DON'T KNOW MUCH	Linda Ronstadt featuring Aaron Neville (Elektra)
-	7	DONALD WHERE'S YOUR TROOSERS?	Andy Stewart (Stone)
-	8	LET'S PARTY	Jive Bunny & the Mastermixers (Music Factory Dance)
5	9	CAN'T SHAKE THE FEELING	Big Fun (Jive)
17	10	YOU SURROUND ME	Erasure (Mute)
27	11	I DON'T WANNA LOSE YOU	Tina Turner (Capitol)
22	12	GOT TO GET	Rob 'N' Raz featuring Leila K (Arista)
6	13	HOMELY GIRL	UB40 (DEP International)
-	14	DEAR JESSIE	Madonna (Sire)
28	15	THE AMSTERDAM (EP)	Simple Minds (Virgin)
20	16	IN PRIVATE	Dusty Springfield (Parlophone)
48	17	SIT AND WAIT	Sydney Youngblood (Circa)
9	18	ALL AROUND THE WORLD	Lisa Stansfield (Arista)
7	19	PACIFIC 707	808 State (ZTT)
47	20	WHENEVER GOD SHINES HIS LIGHT	Van Morrison with Cliff Richard (Polydor)
21	21	LATINO MIX	Latino Rave (Deep Heat)
11	22	FOOLS GOLD/WHAT THE WORLD IS WAITING FOR	Stone Roses (Silvertone)
49	23	HIT MIX (THE OFFICIAL BOOTLEG MEGAMIX)	Alexander O'Neal (Tabu)
42	24	THE MIRACLE	Queen (Parlophone)
24	25	THIS WOMAN'S WORK	Kate Bush (EMI)
12	26	WHATCHA GONNA DO WITH MY LOVIN'	Inner City (10)
14	27	ANOTHER DAY IN PARADISE	Phil Collins (Virgin)
-	28	GETTING AWAY WITH IT	Electronic (Factory)
13	29	COMMENT TE DIRE ADIEU	Jimmy Somerville featuring June Miles Kingston (London)
19	30	I'M NOT THE MAN I USED TO BE	Fine Young Cannibals (London)
15	31	GET ON YOUR FEET	Gloria Estefan (Epic)
50	32	BROKE AWAY	Wet Wet Wet (Precious)
25	33	WOMAN IN CHAINS	Tears For Fears (Fontana)
-	34	GOING BACK TO MY ROOTS	FPI Project present Rich In Paradise featuring Paolo Dini (Rumour)
-	35	LISTEN TO YOUR HEART	Sonia (Chrysalis)
16	36	RONI	Bobby Brown (MCA)
38	37	LIVING IN SIN	Bon Jovi (Vertigo)
-	38	SISTER	Bros (CBS)
18	39	MADCHESTER RAVE ON (EP)	Happy Mondays (Factory)
-	40	20 SECONDS TO COMPLY	Silver Bullet (Tam Tam)
23	41	NEVER TOO LATE	Kylie Minogue (PWL)
34	42	I'LL SAIL THIS SHIP ALONE	Beautiful South (Go! Discs)
-	43	LA LUNA	Belinda Carlisle (Virgin)
29	44	I FEEL THE EARTH MOVE	Martika (CBS)
32	45	THAT'S WHAT I LIKE	Jive Bunny & the Mastermixers (Music Factory Dance)
40	46	WITH GOD ON OUR SIDE	Neville Brothers (A&M)
30	47	GIRL I'M GONNA MISS YOU	Milli Vanilli (Cooltempo)
-	48	COLDCUT'S CHRISTMAS BREAK	Coldcut (Ahead Of Our Time)
33	49	RIDE ON TIME	Black Box (deConstruction)
45	50	BLAME IT ON THE RAIN	Milli Vanilli (Cooltempo)

23 December 1989

last week	this week	title	artist (label)
-	1	DO THEY KNOW IT'S CHRISTMAS?	Band Aid (PWL)
8	2	LET'S PARTY	Jive Bunny & the Mastermixers (Music Factory Dance)
4	3	WHEN YOU COME BACK TO ME	Jason Donovan (PWL)
1	4	GET A LIFE/JAZZIE'S GROOVE	Soul II Soul (10)
14	5	DEAR JESSIE	Madonna (Sire)
7	6	DONALD WHERE'S YOUR TROOSERS?	Andy Stewart (Stone)
11	7	I DON'T WANNA LOSE YOU	Tina Turner (Capitol)
5	8	LAMBADA	Kaoma (CBS)
2	9	THE EVE OF THE WAR	Ben Liebrand/Jeff Wayne (CBS)
17	10	SIT AND WAIT	Sydney Youngblood (Circa)
3	11	YOU GOT IT (THE RIGHT STUFF)	New Kids On The Block (CBS)
12	12	GOT TO GET	Rob 'N' Raz featuring Leila K (Arista)
6	13	DON'T KNOW MUCH	Linda Ronstadt featuring Aaron Neville (Elektra)
28	14	GETTING AWAY WITH IT	Electronic (Factory)
16	15	IN PRIVATE	Dusty Springfield (Parlophone)
23	16	HIT MIX (THE OFFICIAL BOOTLEG MEGAMIX)	Alexander O'Neal (Tabu)
10	17	YOU SURROUND ME	Erasure (Mute)
20	18	WHENEVER GOD SHINES HIS LIGHT	Van Morrison with Cliff Richard (Polydor)
21	19	LATINO MIX	Latino Rave (Deep Heat)
32	20	BROKE AWAY	Wet Wet Wet (Precious)
9	21	CAN'T SHAKE THE FEELING	Big Fun (Jive)
13	22	HOMELY GIRL	UB40 (DEP International)
15	23	THE AMSTERDAM (EP)	Simple Minds (Virgin)
38	24	SISTER	Bros (CBS)
18	25	ALL AROUND THE WORLD	Lisa Stansfield (Arista)
22	26	FOOLS GOLD/WHAT THE WORLD IS WAITING FOR	Stone Roses (Silvertone)
-	27	TOUCH ME	49ers (Fourth & Broadway)
-	28	BURNING THE GROUND	Duranduran (EMI)
24	29	THE MIRACLE	Queen (Parlophone)
27	30	ANOTHER DAY IN PARADISE	Phil Collins (Virgin)
19	31	PACIFIC 707	808 State (ZTT)
34	32	GOING BACK TO MY ROOTS	FPI Project present Rich In Paradise featuring Paolo Dini (Rumour)
35	33	LISTEN TO YOUR HEART	Sonia (Chrysalis)
40	34	20 SECONDS TO COMPLY	Silver Bullet (Tam Tam)
26	35	WHATCHA GONNA DO WITH MY LOVIN'	Inner City (10)
-	36	BUDDY/THE MAGIC NUMBER	De La Soul (Big Life)
29	37	COMMENT TE DIRE ADIEU	Jimmy Somerville featuring June Miles Kingston (London)
25	38	THIS WOMAN'S WORK	Kate Bush (EMI)
-	39	WORDS	Christians (Island)
-	40	WIG WAM BAM	Damian (Jive)
43	41	LA LUNA	Belinda Carlisle (Virgin)
30	42	I'M NOT THE MAN I USED TO BE	Fine Young Cannibals (London)
46	43	WITH GOD ON OUR SIDE	Neville Brothers (A&M)
-	44	INNA CITY MAMMA	Neneh Cherry (Circa)
-	45	DECEMBER	All About Eve (Mercury)
42	46	I'LL SAIL THIS SHIP ALONE	Beautiful South (Go! Discs)
31	47	GET ON YOUR FEET	Gloria Estefan (Epic)
45	48	THAT'S WHAT I LIKE	Jive Bunny & the Mastermixers (Music Factory Dance)
-	49	ITALO HOUSE	Rococco (Mercury)
-	50	WHEN WILL I SEE YOU AGAIN	Brother Beyond (Parlophone)

Jive Bunny introduced festive elements into the medley formula for *Let's Party*, but were beaten to the Christmas Number One slot by a new charity version of *Do They Know It's Christmas?*, this time produced by Stock/Aitken/Waterman, and including contributions from Cliff Richard, Kylie Minogue, Jason Donovan, Lisa Stansfield, Chris Rea and several others, as Band Aid II.

January 1990

13 January 1990

last week	this week		
1	1	DO THEY KNOW IT'S CHRISTMAS?	Band Aid II (PWL)
3	2	WHEN YOU COME BACK TO ME	Jason Donovan (PWL)
-	3	HANGIN' TOUGH New Kids On The Block (CBS)	
4	4	GET A LIFE/JAZZIE'S GROOVE	Soul II Soul (10)
5	5	DEAR JESSIE	Madonna (Sire)
36	6	BUDDY/THE MAGIC NUMBER	De La Soul (Big Life)
8	7	LAMBADA	Kaoma (CBS)
2	8	LET'S PARTY	Jive Bunny & the Mastermixers (Music Factory Dance)
24	9	SISTER	Bros (CBS)
12	10	GOT TO GET Rob 'N' Raz featuring Leila K (Arista)	
14	11	GETTING AWAY WITH IT	Electronic (Factory)
34	12	20 SECONDS TO COMPLY	Silver Bullet (Tam Tam)
6	13	DONALD WHERE'S YOUR TROOSERS?	Andy Stewart (Stone)
32	14	GOING BACK TO MY ROOTS FPI Project present Rich in Paradise featuring Paolo Dini (Rumour)	
11	15	YOU GOT IT (THE RIGHT STUFF)	New Kids On The Block (CBS)
33	16	LISTEN TO YOUR HEART	Sonia (Chrysalis)
10	17	SIT AND WAIT	Sydney Youngblood (Circa)
19	18	LATINO MIX	Latino Rave (Deep Heat)
27	19	TOUCH ME	49ers (Fourth & Broadway)
-	20	GOT TO HAVE YOUR LOVE	Mantronix featuring Wondress (Capitol)
7	21	DON'T WANNA LOSE YOU	Tina Turner (Capitol)
-	22	HEY YOU	Quireboys (Parlophone)
13	23	DON'T KNOW MUCH	Linda Ronstadt featuring Aaron Neville (Elektra)
-	24	BIG WEDGE	Fish (EMI)
-	25	QUEEN OF THE NEW YEAR	Deacon Blue (CBS)
9	26	THE EVE OF THE WAR	Ben Liebrand/Jeff Wayne (CBS)
39	27	WORDS	Christians (Island)
-	28	BUTTERFLY ON A WHEEL	Mission (Mercury)
21	29	CAN'T SHAKE THE FEELING	Big Fun (Jive)
-	30	PUT YOUR HANDS TOGETHER	D Mob featuring Nuff Juice (London)
17	31	YOU SURROUND ME	Erasure (Mute)
16	32	HIT MIX (THE OFFICIAL BOOTLEG MEGAMIX)	Alexander O'Neal (Tabu)
20	33	BROKE AWAY	Wet Wet Wet (Precious)
15	34	IN PRIVATE	Dusty Springfield (Parlophone)
-	35	MADCHESTER RAVE ON (EP)	Happy Mondays (Factory)
-	36	COULD HAVE TOLD HER SO	Halo James (Epic)
26	37	FOOL'S GOLD/WHAT THE WORLD IS WAITING FOR	Stone Roses (Silvertone)
-	38	YOU MAKE ME FEEL (MIGHTY REAL)	Jimmy Somerville (London)
-	39	HERE AND NOW	Luther Vandross (Epic)
25	40	ALL AROUND THE WORLD	Lisa Stansfield (Arista)
44	41	INNA CITY MAMMA	Neneh Cherry (Circa)
18	42	WHENEVER GOD SHINES HIS LIGHT	Van Morrison with Cliff Richard (Polydor)
46	43	I'LL SAIL THIS SHIP ALONE	Beautiful South (Go! Discs)
-	44	LIVING IN SIN	Bon Jovi (Vertigo)
-	45	I'LL BE GOOD TO YOU	Quincy Jones featuring Ray Charles & Chaka Khan (Qwest)
28	46	BURNING THE GROUND	Duran Duran (Parlophone)
-	47	I CALLED U	Lil Louis & the World (ffrr)
41	48	LA LUNA	Belinda Carlisle (Virgin)
22	49	HOMELY GIRL	UB40 (DEP International)
-	50	DESTINY/AUTUMN LOVE	Electra (London)

20 January 1990

last week	this week		
3	1	HANGIN' TOUGH New Kids On The Block (CBS)	
19	2	TOUCH ME	49ers (Fourth & Broadway)
20	3	GOT TO HAVE YOUR LOVE	Mantronix featuring Wondress (Capitol)
4	4	GET A LIFE/JAZZIE'S GROOVE	Soul II Soul (10)
14	5	GOING BACK TO MY ROOTS FPI Project present Rich in Paradise featuring Paolo Dini (Rumour)	
2	6	WHEN YOU COME BACK TO ME	Jason Donovan (PWL)
6	7	BUDDY/THE MAGIC NUMBER De La Soul (Big Life)	
16	8	LISTEN TO YOUR HEART	Sonia (Chrysalis)
-	9	TEARS ON MY PILLOW	Kylie Minogue (PWL)
10	10	GOT TO GET	Rob 'N' Raz featuring Leila K (Arista)
28	11	BUTTERFLY ON A WHEEL	Electronic (Factory)
12	12	20 SECONDS TO COMPLY	Silver Bullet (Tam Tam)
30	13	PUT YOUR HANDS TOGETHER	D Mob featuring Nuff Juice (London)
5	14	DEAR JESSIE	Madonna (Sire)
7	15	LAMBADA	Kaoma (CBS)
38	16	YOU MAKE ME FEEL (MIGHTY REAL)	Jimmy Somerville (London)
11	17	GETTING AWAY WITH IT	Electronic (Factory)
25	18	QUEEN OF THE NEW YEAR	Deacon Blue (CBS)
18	19	LATINO MIX	Latino Rave (Deep Heat)
1	20	DO THEY KNOW IT'S CHRISTMAS?	Band Aid II (PWL)
36	21	COULD HAVE TOLD HER SO	Halo James (Epic)
22	22	HEY YOU	Quireboys (Parlophone)
24	23	BIG WEDGE	Fish (EMI)
47	24	I CALLED U	Lil Louis & the World (ffrr)
17	25	SIT AND WAIT	Sydney Youngblood (Circa)
-	26	MORE THAN YOU KNOW	Martika (CBS)
15	27	YOU GOT IT (THE RIGHT STUFF)	New Kids On The Block (CBS)
35	28	MADCHESTER RAVE ON (EP)	Happy Mondays (Factory)
9	29	SISTER	Bros (CBS)
45	30	I'LL BE GOOD TO YOU	Quincy Jones featuring Ray Charles & Chaka Khan (Qwest)
-	31	NO MORE MR. NICE GUY	Megadeth (SBK)
-	32	N-R-G	Adamski (MCA)
-	33	AIN'T NO STOPPIN' US NOW	Big Daddy Kane (Cold Chillin')
-	34	WELCOME TO THE TERRORDOME	Public Enemy (Def Jam)
-	35	NOTHING COMPARES 2 U	Sinead O'Connor (Ensign)
21	36	I DON'T WANNA LOSE YOU	Tina Turner (Capitol)
-	37	JUICY	Wrecks 'N' Effect (Motown)
-	38	WELCOME	Gino Latino (ffrr)
31	39	YOU SURROUND ME	Erasure (Mute)
37	40	FOOL'S GOLD/WHAT THE WORLD IS WAITING FOR	Stone Roses (Silvertone)
-	41	JUST LIKE JESSE JAMES	Cher (Geffen)
42	42	THE FACE	And Why Not? (Island)
39	43	HERE AND NOW	Luther Vandross (Epic)
23	44	DON'T KNOW MUCH	Linda Ronstadt featuring Aaron Neville (Elektra)
27	45	WORDS	Christians (Island)
-	46	NOTHING EVER HAPPENS	Del Amitri (A&M)
-	47	WE ALMOST GOT IT TOGETHER Tanita Tikaram (WEA)	
13	48	DONALD WHERE'S YOUR TROOSERS?	Andy Stewart (Stone)
26	49	THE EVE OF THE WAR	Ben Liebrand/Jeff Wayne (CBS)
-	50	JAM IT JAM	She Rockers (Jive)

27 January 1990

last week	this week		
9	1	TEARS ON MY PILLOW	Kylie Minogue (PWL)
2	2	TOUCH ME	49ers (Fourth & Broadway)
1	3	HANGIN' TOUGH New Kids On The Block (CBS)	
3	4	GOT TO HAVE YOUR LOVE	Mantronix featuring Wondress (Capitol)
16	5	YOU MAKE ME FEEL (MIGHTY REAL)	Jimmy Somerville (London)
13	6	PUT YOUR HANDS TOGETHER D Mob featuring Nuff Juice (London)	
5	7	GOING BACK TO MY ROOTS FPI Project present Rich in Paradise featuring Paolo Dini (Rumour)	
21	8	COULD HAVE TOLD HER SO	Halo James (Epic)
4	9	GET A LIFE/JAZZIE'S GROOVE	Soul II Soul (10)
11	10	BUTTERFLY ON A WHEEL	Mission (Mercury)
32	11	N-R-G	Adamski (MCA)
24	12	I CALLED U	Lil Louis & the World (ffrr)
10	13	GOT TO GET	Rob 'N' Raz featuring Leila K (Arista)
35	14	NOTHING COMPARES 2 U	Sinead O'Connor (Ensign)
26	15	MORE THAN YOU KNOW	Martika (CBS)
31	16	NO MORE MR. NICE GUY	Megadeth (SBK)
6	17	WHEN YOU COME BACK TO ME	Jason Donovan (PWL)
8	18	LISTEN TO YOUR HEART	Sonia (Chrysalis)
38	19	WELCOME	Gino Latino (ffrr)
7	20	BUDDY/THE MAGIC NUMBER	De La Soul (Big Life)
30	21	I'LL BE GOOD TO YOU Quincy Jones featuring Ray Charles & Chaka Khan (Qwest)	
12	22	20 SECONDS TO COMPLY	Silver Bullet (Tam Tam)
22	23	HEY YOU	Quireboys (Parlophone)
15	24	LAMBADA	Kaoma (CBS)
14	25	DEAR JESSIE	Madonna (Sire)
37	26	JUICY	Wrecks 'N' Effect (Motown)
-	27	I WISH IT WOULD RAIN DOWN	Phil Collins (Virgin)
34	28	WELCOME TO THE TERRORDOME	Public Enemy (Def Jam)
-	29	WAS THAT ALL IT WAS? Kym Mazelle (Syncopate)	
-	30	INSTANT REPLAY	Yell! (Fanfare)
41	31	JUST LIKE JESSE JAMES	Cher (Geffen)
17	32	GETTING AWAY WITH IT	Electronic (Factory)
28	33	MADCHESTER RAVE ON (EP)	Happy Mondays (Factory)
46	34	NOTHING EVER HAPPENS	Del Amitri (A&M)
18	35	QUEEN OF THE NEW YEAR	Deacon Blue (CBS)
-	36	HAPPENIN' ALL OVER AGAIN	Lonnie Gordon (Supreme)
19	37	LATINO MIX	Latino Rave (Deep Heat)
38	38	DOWNTOWN TRAIN	Rod Stewart (Warner Bros)
33	39	AIN'T NO STOPPIN' US NOW	Big Daddy Kane (Cold Chillin')
42	40	THE FACE	And Why Not? (Island)
27	41	YOU GOT IT (THE RIGHT STUFF)	New Kids On The Block (CBS)
25	42	SIT AND WAIT	Sydney Youngblood (Circa)
-	43	WALK ON BY	Sybil (PWL)
44	44	INNA CITY MAMMA	Neneh Cherry (Circa)
23	45	BIG WEDGE	Fish (EMI)
-	46	HELLO	Beloved (WEA)
39	47	YOU SURROUND ME	Erasure (Mute)
-	48	IN PRIVATE	Dusty Springfield (Parlophone)
-	49	COME BACK TO ME	Janet Jackson (Breakout)
40	50	FOOL'S GOLD/WHAT THE WORLD IS WAITING FOR	Stone Roses (Silvertone)

Total sales of the Band Aid II single were 594,000, no way comparable to those of the original record, but a worthy contribution nonetheless to the Band Aid charity's funds. Cliff Richard's performance on the song also meant that he had been on two consecutive Christmas chart-toppers, each with a Christmas theme – a unique achievement which he would extend at the end of 1990.

3 February 1990

last week	this week	Title / Artist (Label)
14	1	NOTHING COMPARES 2 U — Sinead O'Connor (Ensign)
1	2	TEARS ON MY PILLOW — Kylie Minogue (PWL)
2	3	TOUCH ME — 49ers (Fourth & Broadway)
8	4	COULD HAVE TOLD HER SO — Halo James (Epic)
4	5	GOT TO HAVE YOUR LOVE — Mantronix featuring Wondress (Capitol)
11	6	N-R-G — Adamski (MCA)
3	7	HANGIN' TOUGH — New Kids On The Block (CBS)
36	8	HAPPENIN' ALL OVER AGAIN — Lonnie Gordon (Supreme)
5	9	YOU MAKE ME FEEL (MIGHTY REAL) — Jimmy Somerville (London)
7	10	GOING BACK TO MY ROOTS — FPI Project featuring Rich in Paradise featuring Paolo Dini (Rumour)
6	11	PUT YOUR HANDS TOGETHER — D Mob featuring Nuff Juice (London)
30	12	INSTANT REPLAY — Yell! (Fanfare)
34	13	NOTHING EVER HAPPENS — Del Amitri (A&M)
-	14	GET UP (BEFORE THE NIGHT IS OVER) — Technotronic featuring Ya Kid K (Swanyard)
15	15	MORE THAN YOU KNOW — Martika (CBS)
27	16	I WISH IT WOULD RAIN DOWN — Phil Collins (Virgin)
19	17	WELCOME — Gino Latino (ffrr)
18	18	NO MORE MR. NICE GUY — Megadeth (SBK)
21	19	I'LL BE GOOD TO YOU — Quincy Jones featuring Ray Charles & Chaka Khan (Qwest)
12	20	I CALLED U — Lil Louis & the World (ffrr)
9	21	GET A LIFE/JAZZIE'S GROOVE — Soul II Soul (10)
13	22	GOT TO GET — Rob 'N' Raz featuring Leila K (Arista)
28	23	WELCOME TO THE TERRORDOME — Public Enemy (Def Jam)
26	24	JUICY — Wrecks 'N' Effect (Motown)
29	25	WAS THAT ALL IT WAS? — Kym Mazelle (Syncopate)
23	26	HEY YOU — Quireboys (Parlophone)
43	27	WALK ON BY — Sybil (PWL)
17	28	WHEN YOU COME BACK TO ME — Jason Donovan (PWL)
-	29	ALL 4 LOVE (BREAK 4 LOVE '90) — Raze featuring Lady J & the Secretary of Ent (Champion)
31	30	JUST LIKE JESSE JAMES — Cher (Geffen)
10	31	BUTTERFLY ON A WHEEL — Mission (Mercury)
-	32	SHINE ON — House of Love (Fontana)
22	33	20 SECONDS TO COMPLY — Silver Bullet (Tam Tam)
46	34	HELLO — Beloved (WEA)
24	35	LAMBADA — Kaoma (CBS)
49	36	COME BACK TO ME — Janet Jackson (Breakout)
40	37	THE FACE — And Why Not? (Island)
18	38	LISTEN TO YOUR HEART — Sonia (Chrysalis)
3	39	SLEEP WITH ME (EP) — Birdland (Lazy)
-	40	HERE I AM (COME AND TAKE ME) — UB40 (DEP International)
38	41	DOWNTOWN TRAIN — Rod Stewart (Warner Bros)
-	42	THE KING AND QUEEN OF AMERICA — Eurythmics (RCA)
20	43	BUDDY/THE MAGIC NUMBER — De La Soul (Big Life)
32	44	GETTING AWAY WITH IT — Electronic (Factory)
-	45	18 AND LIFE — Skid Row (Atlantic)
25	46	DEAR JESSIE — Madonna (Sire)
-	47	BAD LOVE — Eric Clapton (Duck)
-	48	SALLY CINNAMON — Stone Roses (Silvertone)
-	49	BELFAST — Energy Orchard (MCA)
-	50	DANCANDO LAMBADA — Kaoma (CBS)

10 February 1990

last week	this week	Title / Artist (Label)
1	1	NOTHING COMPARES 2 U — Sinead O'Connor (Ensign)
14	2	GET UP (BEFORE THE NIGHT IS OVER) — Technotronic featuring Ya Kid K (Swanyard)
8	3	HAPPENIN' ALL OVER AGAIN — Lonnie Gordon (Supreme)
2	4	TEARS ON MY PILLOW — Kylie Minogue (PWL)
5	5	GOT TO HAVE YOUR LOVE — Mantronix featuring Wondress (Capitol)
16	6	I WISH IT WOULD RAIN DOWN — Phil Collins (Virgin)
3	7	TOUCH ME — 49ers (Fourth & Broadway)
4	8	COULD HAVE TOLD HER SO — Halo James (Epic)
27	9	WALK ON BY — Sybil (PWL)
12	10	INSTANT REPLAY — Yell! (Fanfare)
13	11	NOTHING EVER HAPPENS — Del Amitri (A&M)
7	12	HANGIN' TOUGH — New Kids On The Block (CBS)
9	13	YOU MAKE ME FEEL (MIGHTY REAL) — Jimmy Somerville (London)
-	14	LIVE TOGETHER — Lisa Stansfield (Arista)
6	15	N-R-G — Adamski (MCA)
32	16	SHINE ON — House of Love (Fontana)
10	17	GOING BACK TO MY ROOTS — FPI Project present Rich in Paradise featuring Paolo Dini (Rumour)
45	18	18 AND LIFE — Skid Row (Atlantic)
37	19	THE FACE — And Why Not? (Island)
19	20	I'LL BE GOOD TO YOU — Quincy Jones featuring Ray Charles & Chaka Khan (Qwest)
30	21	JUST LIKE JESSE JAMES — Cher (Geffen)
11	22	PUT YOUR HANDS TOGETHER — D Mob featuring Nuff Juice (London)
23	23	WELCOME — Gino Latino (ffrr)
24	24	JUICY — Wrecks 'N' Effect (Motown)
15	25	MORE THAN YOU KNOW — Martika (CBS)
29	26	ALL 4 LOVE (BREAK 4 LOVE '90) — Raze featuring Lady J & the Secretary of Ent (Champion)
42	27	THE KING AND QUEEN OF AMERICA — Eurythmics (RCA)
25	28	WAS THAT ALL IT WAS? — Kym Mazelle (Syncopate)
-	29	DUB BE GOOD TO ME — Beats International featuring Lindy Layton (Go Beat)
34	30	HELLO — Beloved (WEA)
22	31	GOT TO GET — Rob 'N' Raz featuring Leila K (Arista)
21	32	GET A LIFE/JAZZIE'S GROOVE — Soul II Soul (10)
39	33	SLEEP WITH ME (EP) — Birdland (Lazy)
36	34	COME BACK TO ME — Janet Jackson (Breakout)
-	35	PROBABLY A ROBBERY — Renegade Soundwave (Mute)
18	36	NO MORE MR. NICE GUY — Megadeth (SBK)
20	37	I CALLED U — Lil Louis & the World (ffrr)
28	38	WHEN YOU COME BACK TO ME — Jason Donovan (PWL)
41	39	DOWNTOWN TRAIN — Rod Stewart (Warner Bros)
47	40	BAD LOVE — Eric Clapton (Duck)
23	41	WELCOME TO THE TERRORDOME — Public Enemy (Def Jam)
40	42	HERE I AM (COME AND TAKE ME) — UB40 (DEP International)
26	43	HEY YOU — Quireboys (Parlophone)
48	44	SALLY CINNAMON — Stone Roses (Silvertone)
-	45	LOVE DON'T COME EASY — Alarm (IRS)
35	46	LAMBADA — Kaoma (CBS)
49	47	BELFAST — Energy Orchard (MCA)
-	48	LET THERE BE HOUSE — Deskee (Big One)
33	49	20 SECONDS TO COMPLY — Silver Bullet (Tam Tam)
31	50	BUTTERFLY ON A WHEEL — Mission (Mercury)

17 February 1990

last week	this week	Title / Artist (Label)
1	1	NOTHING COMPARES 2 U — Sinead O'Connor (Ensign)
2	2	GET UP (BEFORE THE NIGHT IS OVER) — Technotronic featuring Ya Kid K (Swanyard)
3	3	HAPPENIN' ALL OVER AGAIN — Lonnie Gordon (Supreme)
29	4	DUB BE GOOD TO ME — Beats International featuring Lindy Layton (Go Beat)
9	5	WALK ON BY — Sybil (PWL)
6	6	I WISH IT WOULD RAIN DOWN — Phil Collins (Virgin)
5	7	GOT TO HAVE YOUR LOVE — Mantronix featuring Wondress (Capitol)
14	8	LIVE TOGETHER — Lisa Stansfield (Arista)
-	9	I DON'T KNOW ANYBODY ELSE — Black Box (deConstruction)
4	10	TEARS ON MY PILLOW — Kylie Minogue (PWL)
11	11	NOTHING EVER HAPPENS — Del Amitri (A&M)
7	12	TOUCH ME — 49ers (Fourth & Broadway)
10	13	INSTANT REPLAY — Yell! (Fanfare)
18	14	18 AND LIFE — Skid Row (Atlantic)
19	15	THE FACE — And Why Not? (Island)
8	16	COULD HAVE TOLD HER SO — Halo James (Epic)
17	17	JUST LIKE JESSE JAMES — Cher (Geffen)
16	18	SHINE ON — House of Love (Fontana)
30	19	HELLO — Beloved (WEA)
34	20	COME BACK TO ME — Janet Jackson (Breakout)
12	21	HANGIN' TOUGH — New Kids On The Block (CBS)
20	22	I'LL BE GOOD TO YOU — Quincy Jones featuring Ray Charles & Chaka Khan (Qwest)
27	23	THE KING AND QUEEN OF AMERICA — Eurythmics (RCA)
23	24	WELCOME — Gino Latino (ffrr)
-	25	ENJOY THE SILENCE — Depeche Mode (Mute)
13	26	YOU MAKE ME FEEL (MIGHTY REAL) — Jimmy Somerville (London)
40	27	BAD LOVE — Eric Clapton (Duck)
15	28	N-R-G — Adamski (MCA)
39	29	DOWNTOWN TRAIN — Rod Stewart (Warner Bros)
17	30	GOING BACK TO MY ROOTS — FPI Project present Rich in Paradise featuring Paolo Dini (Rumour)
24	31	JUICY — Wrecks 'N' Effect (Motown)
-	32	BRASSNECK — Wedding Present (RCA)
22	33	PUT YOUR HANDS TOGETHER — D Mob featuring Nuff Juice (London)
35	34	PROBABLY A ROBBERY — Renegade Soundwave (Mute)
-	35	TELL ME THERE'S A HEAVEN — Chris Rea (East West)
-	36	BIKINI GIRLS WITH MACHINE GUNS — Cramps (Enigma)
26	37	ALL 4 LOVE (BREAK 4 LOVE '90) — Raze featuring Lady J & the Secretary of Ent (Champion)
-	38	EPIC — Faith No More (Slash)
25	39	MORE THAN YOU KNOW — Martika (CBS)
-	40	STEAMY WINDOWS — Tina Turner (Capitol)
31	41	GOT TO GET — Rob 'N' Raz featuring Leila K (Arista)
-	42	(CHERRY LIPS) DER ERDBEERMUND — Culture Beat (Epic)
28	43	WAS THAT ALL IT WAS? — Kym Mazelle (Syncopate)
-	44	NO BLUE SKIES — Lloyd Cole (Polydor)
32	45	GET A LIFE/JAZZIE'S GROOVE — Soul II Soul (10)
47	46	BELFAST — Energy Orchard (MCA)
-	47	WALK ON THE WILD SIDE — Jamie J. Morgan (Tabu)
33	48	SLEEP WITH ME (EP) — Birdland (Lazy)
45	49	LOVE DON'T COME EASY — Alarm (IRS)
-	50	PUT IT THERE — Paul McCartney (Parlophone)

Nothing Compares 2 U, a Prince song of some obscurity before Sinead O'Connor happened upon it, gave the Irish songstress the best-selling single of the first half of 1990, with an exceptional five-week run at the top. In the Wake of Kylie Minogue's revival of Little Anthony & the Imperials' *Tears On My Pillow*, new covers of the old hits *Instant Replay, Walk On By* and *Mighty Real* all made the Top 10.

February – March 1990

last week	this week	24 February 1990	
1	1	NOTHING COMPARES 2 U	Sinead O'Connor (Ensign)
4	2	DUB BE GOOD TO ME	Beats International featuring Lindy Layton (Go Beat)
9	3	I DON'T KNOW ANYBODY ELSE	Black Box (deConstruction)
2	4	GET UP (BEFORE THE NIGHT IS OVER)	Technotronic featuring Ya Kid K (Swanyard)
3	5	HAPPENIN' ALL OVER AGAIN	Lonnie Gordon (Supreme)
8	6	LIVE TOGETHER	Lisa Stansfield (Arista)
-	7	HOW AM I SUPPOSED TO LIVE WITHOUT YOU	Michael Bolton (CBS)
5	8	WALK ON BY	Sybil (PWL)
25	9	ENJOY THE SILENCE	Depeche Mode (Mute)
6	10	I WISH IT WOULD RAIN DOWN	Phil Collins (Virgin)
7	11	I GOT TO HAVE YOUR LOVE	Mantronix featuring Wondress (Capitol)
17	12	JUST LIKE JESSE JAMES	Cher (Geffen)
19	13	HELLO	Beloved (WEA)
29	14	DOWNTOWN TRAIN	Rod Stewart (Warner Bros)
13	15	INSTANT REPLAY	Yell! (Fanfare)
20	16	COME BACK TO ME	Janet Jackson (Breakout)
11	17	NOTHING EVER HAPPENS	Del Amitri (A&M)
40	18	STEAMY WINDOWS	Tina Turner (Capitol)
27	19	BAD LOVE	Eric Clapton (Duck)
14	20	18 AND LIFE	Skid Row (Atlantic)
-	21	96 TEARS	Stranglers (Epic)
12	22	TOUCH ME	49ers (Fourth & Broadway)
10	23	TEARS ON MY PILLOW	Kylie Minogue (PWL)
32	24	BRASSNECK	Wedding Present (RCA)
-	25	ROOM AT THE TOP	Adam Ant (MCA)
15	26	THE FACE	And Why Not? (Island)
35	27	TELL ME THERE'S A HEAVEN	Chris Rea (East West)
-	28	INFINITY	Guru Josh (deConstruction)
50	29	PUT IT THERE	Paul McCartney (Parlophone)
-	30	BLACK BETTY	Ram Jam (Epic)
16	31	COULD HAVE TOLD HER SO	Halo James (Epic)
24	32	WELCOME	Gino Latino (ffrr)
34	33	PROBABLY A ROBBERY	Renegade Soundwave (Mute)
21	34	HANGIN' TOUGH	New Kids On The Block (CBS)
18	35	SHINE ON	House of Love (Fontana)
38	36	EPIC	Faith No More (Slash)
47	37	WALK ON THE WILD SIDE	Jamie J. Morgan (Tabu)
-	38	STRONGER THAN THAT	Cliff Richard (EMI)
-	39	DIRTY LOVE	Thunder (EMI)
-	40	I'M NOT SATISFIED	Fine Young Cannibals (London)
22	41	I'LL BE GOOD TO YOU	Quincy Jones featuring Ray Charles & Chaka Khan (Qwest)
23	42	TALKING WITH MYSELF	Electribe 101 (Mercury)
23	43	THE KING AND QUEEN OF AMERICA	Eurythmics (RCA)
30	44	GOING BACK TO MY ROOTS	FPI Project present Rich in Paradise featuring Paolo Dini (Rumour)
-	45	GET BUSY	Mr. Lee (Jive)
42	46	(CHERRY LIPS) DER ERDBEERMUND	Culture Beat (Epic)
-	47	PRINCIPAL'S OFFICE	Young MC (Delicious Vinyl)
44	48	NO BLUE SKIES	Lloyd Cole (Polydor)
-	49	TAKING ON THE WORLD	Gun (A&M)
-	50	LILY WAS HERE	David A. Stewart featuring Candy Dulfer (RCA)

		3 March 1990	
1	1	NOTHING COMPARES 2 U	Sinead O'Connor (Ensign)
2	2	DUB BE GOOD TO ME	Beats International featuring Lindy Layton (Go Beat)
7	3	HOW AM I SUPPOSED TO LIVE WITHOUT YOU	Michael Bolton (CBS)
9	4	ENJOY THE SILENCE	Depeche Mode (Mute)
3	5	I DON'T KNOW ANYBODY ELSE	Black Box (deConstruction)
6	6	LIVE TOGETHER	Lisa Stansfield (Arista)
4	7	GET UP (BEFORE THE NIGHT IS OVER)	Technotronic featuring Ya Kid K (Swanyard)
18	8	STEAMY WINDOWS	Tina Turner (Capitol)
14	9	DOWNTOWN TRAIN	Rod Stewart (Warner Bros)
5	10	HAPPENIN' ALL OVER AGAIN	Lonnie Gordon (Supreme)
8	11	WALK ON BY	Sybil (PWL)
38	12	STRONGER THAN THAT	Cliff Richard (EMI)
28	13	INFINITY	Guru Josh (deConstruction)
10	14	I WISH IT WOULD RAIN DOWN	Phil Collins (Virgin)
-	15	ELEPHANT STONE	Stone Roses (Silvertone)
21	16	96 TEARS	Stranglers (Epic)
25	17	ROOM AT THE TOP	Adam Ant (MCA)
12	18	JUST LIKE JESSE JAMES	Cher (Geffen)
27	19	TELL ME THERE'S A HEAVEN	Chris Rea (East West)
42	20	TALKING WITH MYSELF	Electribe 101 (Mercury)
11	21	I GOT TO HAVE YOUR LOVE	Mantronix featuring Wondress (Capitol)
-	22	DUDE (LOOKS LIKE A LADY)	Aerosmith (Geffen)
-	23	THE BRITS 1990 (DANCE MEDLEY)	Various Artists (RCA)
15	24	INSTANT REPLAY	Yell! (Fanfare)
30	25	BLACK BETTY	Ram Jam (Epic)
16	26	COME BACK TO ME	Janet Jackson (Breakout)
40	27	I'M NOT SATISFIED	Fine Young Cannibals (London)
13	28	HELLO	Beloved (WEA)
50	29	LILY WAS HERE	David A. Stewart featuring Candy Dulfer (RCA)
37	30	WALK ON THE WILD SIDE	Jamie J. Morgan (Tabu)
17	31	NOTHING EVER HAPPENS	Del Amitri (A&M)
19	32	BAD LOVE	Eric Clapton (Duck)
-	33	I MIGHT	Shakin' Stevens (Epic)
23	34	TEARS ON MY PILLOW	Kylie Minogue (PWL)
22	35	TOUCH ME	49ers (Fourth & Broadway)
45	36	GET BUSY	Mr. Lee (Jive)
39	37	DIRTY LOVE	Thunder (EMI)
-	38	RUNAWAY HORSES	Belinda Carlisle (Virgin)
-	39	A LOVER SPURNED	Marc Almond (Some Bizzare)
20	40	18 AND LIFE	Skid Row (Atlantic)
41	41	NATURAL THING	Innocence (Cooltempo)
-	42	MOMENTS IN SOUL	JT & the Big Family (Champion)
29	43	PUT IT THERE	Paul McCartney (Parlophone)
31	44	COULD HAVE TOLD HER SO	Halo James (Epic)
47	45	PRINCIPAL'S OFFICE	Young MC (Delicious Vinyl)
-	46	HOUSE OF BROKEN LOVE	Great White (Capitol)
26	47	THE FACE	And Why Not? (Island)
-	48	COME TOGETHER AS ONE	Will Downing (Fourth & Broadway)
33	49	PROBABLY A ROBBERY	Renegade Soundwave (Mute)
24	50	BRASSNECK	Wedding Present (RCA)

		10 March 1990	
2	1	DUB BE GOOD TO ME	Beats International featuring Lindy Layton (Go Beat)
3	2	HOW AM I SUPPOSED TO LIVE WITHOUT YOU	Michael Bolton (CBS)
1	3	NOTHING COMPARES 2 U	Sinead O'Connor (Ensign)
23	4	THE BRITS 1990 (DANCE MEDLEY)	Various Artists (RCA)
4	5	ENJOY THE SILENCE	Depeche Mode (Mute)
9	6	DOWNTOWN TRAIN	Rod Stewart (Warner Bros)
15	7	ELEPHANT STONE	Stone Roses (Silvertone)
7	8	GET UP (BEFORE THE NIGHT IS OVER)	Technotronic featuring Ya Kid K (Swanyard)
42	9	MOMENTS IN SOUL	JT & the Big Family (Champion)
13	10	INFINITY	Guru Josh (deConstruction)
5	11	I DON'T KNOW ANYBODY ELSE	Black Box (deConstruction)
25	12	BLACK BETTY	Ram Jam (Epic)
17	13	ROOM AT THE TOP	Adam Ant (MCA)
-	14	BLUE SAVANNAH	Erasure (Mute)
12	15	STRONGER THAN THAT	Cliff Richard (EMI)
20	16	TALKING WITH MYSELF	Electribe 101 (Mercury)
10	17	HAPPENIN' ALL OVER AGAIN	Lonnie Gordon (Supreme)
8	18	STEAMY WINDOWS	Tina Turner (Capitol)
22	19	DUDE (LOOKS LIKE A LADY)	Aerosmith (Geffen)
29	20	LILY WAS HERE	David A. Stewart featuring Candy Dulfer (RCA)
41	21	NATURAL THING	Innocence (Cooltempo)
-	22	LOVE SHACK	B52's (Reprise)
30	23	WALK ON THE WILD SIDE	Jamie J. Morgan (Tabu)
6	24	LIVE TOGETHER	Lisa Stansfield (Arista)
39	25	A LOVER SPURNED	Marc Almond (Some Bizzare)
-	26	HERE WE ARE/DON'T LET THE SUN GO DOWN ON ME	Gloria Estefan (Epic)
11	27	WALK ON BY	Sybil (PWL)
33	28	I MIGHT	Shakin' Stevens (Epic)
-	29	ADVICE FOR THE YOUNG AT HEART	Tears For Fears (Fontana)
16	30	96 TEARS	Stranglers (Epic)
18	31	JUST LIKE JESSE JAMES	Cher (Geffen)
14	32	I WISH IT WOULD RAIN DOWN	Phil Collins (Virgin)
19	33	TELL ME THERE'S A HEAVEN	Chris Rea (East West)
-	34	MADLY IN LOVE	Bros (CBS)
21	35	GOT TO HAVE YOUR LOVE	Mantronix featuring Wondress (Capitol)
-	36	DELIVERANCE	Mission (Mercury)
38	37	RUNAWAY HORSES	Belinda Carlisle (Virgin)
-	38	SWEET SOUL SISTER	Cult (Beggars Banquet)
24	39	INSTANT REPLAY	Yell! (Fanfare)
-	40	LOADED	Primal Scream (Creation)
-	41	LOVE AND ANGER	Kate Bush (EMI)
27	42	I'M NOT SATISFIED	Fine Young Cannibals (London)
35	43	TOUCH ME	49ers (Fourth & Broadway)
-	44	WARRIOR	MC Wildski (Arista)
28	45	HELLO	Beloved (WEA)
-	46	AFTER THE RAIN	Titiyo (Arista)
48	47	COME TOGETHER AS ONE	Will Downing (Fourth & Broadway)
26	48	COME BACK TO ME	Janet Jackson (Breakout)
-	49	WALK ON THE WILD SIDE	Beat System (Fourth & Broadway)
-	50	THE DEEPER THE LOVE	Whitesnake (EMI)

Dub Be Good To Me was a re-styling of the SOS Band's 1984 hit *Just Be Good To Me*, with a new rap section interpolated, by Beats International leader and former Housemartins vocalist Norman Cook. The featured female vocalist was Lindy Layton, an actress/singer familiar to some from TV's *Grange Hill*, who would find further chart success under her own name.

17 March 1990

last week	this week	Title	Artist
1	1	DUB BE GOOD TO ME	Beats International featuring Lindy Layton (Go Beat)
4	2	THE BRITS 1990 (DANCE MEDLEY)	Various Artists (RCA)
9	3	MOMENTS IN SOUL	JT & the Big Family (Champion)
10	4	INFINITY	Guru Josh (deConstruction)
2	5	HOW AM I SUPPOSED TO LIVE WITHOUT YOU	Michael Bolton (CBS)
14	6	BLUE SAVANNAH	Erasure (Mute)
22	7	LOVE SHACK	B52's (Reprise)
20	8	LILY WAS HERE	David A. Stewart featuring Candy Dulfer (RCA)
-	9	THAT SOUNDS GOOD TO ME	Jive Bunny & the Mastermixers (Music Factory Dance)
3	10	NOTHING COMPARES 2 U	Sinead O'Connor (Ensign)
21	11	NATURAL THING	Innocence (Cooltempo)
8	12	GET UP (BEFORE THE NIGHT IS OVER)	Technotronic featuring Ya Kid K (Swanyard)
5	13	ENJOY THE SILENCE	Depeche Mode (Mute)
34	14	MADLY IN LOVE	Bros (CBS)
11	15	I DON'T KNOW ANYBODY ELSE	Black Box (deConstruction)
12	16	BLACK BETTY	Ram Jam (Epic)
28	17	I MIGHT	Shakin' Stevens (Epic)
6	18	DOWNTOWN TRAIN	Rod Stewart (Warner Bros)
-	19	I'LL BE LOVING YOU FOREVER	New Kids On The Block (CBS)
-	20	MADE OF STONE	Stone Roses (Silvertone)
26	21	HERE WE ARE/DON'T LET THE SUN GO DOWN ON ME	Gloria Estefan (Epic)
7	22	ELEPHANT STONE	Stone Roses (Silvertone)
16	23	TALKING WITH MYSELF	Electribe 101 (Mercury)
40	24	LOADED	Primal Scream (Creation)
25	25	STRAWBERRY FIELDS FOREVER	Candy Flip (Debu)
13	26	ROOM AT THE TOP	Adam Ant (MCA)
25	27	A LOVER SPURNED	Marc Almond (Some Bizzare)
36	28	DELIVERANCE	Mission (Mercury)
-	29	THIS IS HOW IT FEELS	Inspiral Carpets (Cow)
17	30	HAPPENIN' ALL OVER AGAIN	Lonnie Gordon (Supreme)
23	31	WALK ON THE WILD SIDE	Jamie J. Morgan (Tabu)
50	32	THE DEEPER THE LOVE	Whitesnake (EMI)
19	33	DUDE (LOOKS LIKE A LADY)	Aerosmith (Geffen)
-	34	HOLD BACK THE RIVER	Wet Wet Wet (Precious)
15	35	STRONGER THAN THAT	Cliff Richard (EMI)
38	36	SWEET SOUL SISTER	Cult (Beggars Banquet)
29	37	ADVICE FOR THE YOUNG AT HEART	Tears For Fears (Fontana)
41	38	LOVE AND ANGER	Kate Bush (EMI)
-	39	HANDFUL OF PROMISES	Big Fun (Jive)
18	40	STEAMY WINDOWS	Tina Turner (Capitol)
-	41	BIRDHOUSE IN YOUR SOUL	They Might Be Giants (Elektra)
-	42	DON'T YOU LOVE ME	49ers (Fourth & Broadway)
-	43	A GENTLEMAN'S EXCUSE ME	Fish (EMI)
37	44	RUNAWAY HORSES	Belinda Carlisle (Virgin)
-	45	LOVE PAINS	Liza Minnelli (Epic)
31	46	JUST LIKE JESSE JAMES	Cher (Geffen)
27	47	WALK ON BY	Sybil (PWL)
-	48	WITH A LITTLE LOVE	Sam Brown (A&M)
-	49	BRING FORTH THE GUILLOTINE	Silver Bullet (Tam Tam)
44	50	WARRIOR	MC Wildski (Arista)

24 March 1990

last week	this week	Title	Artist
1	1	DUB BE GOOD TO ME	Beats International featuring Lindy Layton (Go Beat)
9	2	THAT SOUNDS GOOD TO ME	Jive Bunny & the Mastermixers (Music Factory Dance)
7	3	LOVE SHACK	B52's (Reprise)
25	4	STRAWBERRY FIELDS FOREVER	Candy Flip (Debu)
6	5	BLUE SAVANNAH	Erasure (Mute)
4	6	INFINITY	Guru Josh (deConstruction)
19	7	I'LL BE LOVING YOU FOREVER	New Kids On The Block (CBS)
8	8	LILY WAS HERE	David A. Stewart featuring Candy Dulfer (RCA)
2	9	THE BRITS 1990 (DANCE MEDLEY)	Various Artists (RCA)
3	10	MOMENTS IN SOUL	JT & the Big Family (Champion)
5	11	HOW AM I SUPPOSED TO LIVE WITHOUT YOU	Michael Bolton (CBS)
11	12	NATURAL THING	Innocence (Cooltempo)
-	13	POWER	Snap! (Arista)
10	14	NOTHING COMPARES 2 U	Sinead O'Connor (Ensign)
29	15	THIS IS HOW IT FEELS	Inspiral Carpets (Cow)
42	16	DON'T YOU LOVE ME	49ers (Fourth & Broadway)
39	17	HANDFUL OF PROMISES	Big Fun (Jive)
24	18	LOADED	Primal Scream (Creation)
12	19	GET UP (BEFORE THE NIGHT IS OVER)	Technotronic featuring Ya Kid K (Swanyard)
14	20	MADLY IN LOVE	Bros (CBS)
-	21	EVERYTHING BEGINS WITH AN 'E'	E-Zee Posse (More Protein)
13	22	ENJOY THE SILENCE	Depeche Mode (Mute)
21	23	HERE WE ARE/DON'T LET THE SUN GO DOWN ON ME	Gloria Estefan (Epic)
41	24	BIRDHOUSE IN YOUR SOUL	They Might Be Giants (Elektra)
15	25	I DON'T KNOW ANYBODY ELSE	Black Box (deConstruction)
43	26	A GENTLEMAN'S EXCUSE ME	Fish (EMI)
28	27	DELIVERANCE	Mission (Mercury)
16	28	BLACK BETTY	Ram Jam (Epic)
18	29	DOWNTOWN TRAIN	Rod Stewart (Warner Bros)
-	30	READ MY LIPS (ENOUGH IS ENOUGH)	Jimmy Somerville (London)
17	31	I MIGHT	Shakin' Stevens (Epic)
20	32	MADE OF STONE	Stone Roses (Silvertone)
34	33	HOLD BACK THE RIVER	Wet Wet Wet (Precious)
-	34	CHIME	Orbital (ffrr)
26	35	ROOM AT THE TOP	Adam Ant (MCA)
-	36	ROK THE NATION	Rob 'N' Raz with Leila K (Arista)
23	37	TALKING WITH MYSELF	Electribe 101 (Mercury)
22	38	ELEPHANT STONE	Stone Roses (Silvertone)
-	39	ANOTHER DAY IN PARADISE	Jam Tronik (Debut)
30	40	HAPPENIN' ALL OVER AGAIN	Lonnie Gordo (Supreme)
38	41	LOVE AND ANGER	Kate Bush (EMI)
-	42	ALL I WANNA DO IS MAKE LOVE TO YOU	Heart (Capitol)
37	43	ADVICE FOR THE YOUNG AT HEART	Tears For Fears (Fontana)
-	44	MAMA GAVE BIRTH 2 THE SOUL CHILDREN	Queen Latifah & De La Soul (Gee Street)
32	45	THE DEEPER THE LOVE	Whitesnake (EMI)
-	46	YOUR LOVE TAKES ME HIGHER	Beloved (East West)
-	47	DEVOTION	Kicking Back With Taxman (10)
27	48	A LOVER SPURNED	Marc Almond (Some Bizzare)
-	49	KISS THIS THING GOODBYE	Del Amitri (A&M)
33	50	DUDE (LOOKS LIKE A LADY)	Aerosmith (Geffen)

31 March 1990

last week	this week	Title	Artist
3	1	LOVE SHACK	B52's (Reprise)
13	2	POWER	Snap! (Arista)
4	3	STRAWBERRY FIELDS FOREVER	Candy Flip (Debu)
5	4	BLUE SAVANNAH	Erasure (Mute)
1	5	DUB BE GOOD TO ME	Beats International featuring Lindy Layton (Go Beat)
8	6	LILY WAS HERE	David A. Stewart featuring Candy Dulfer (RCA)
7	7	I'LL BE LOVING YOU FOREVER	New Kids On The Block (CBS)
2	8	THAT SOUNDS GOOD TO ME	Jive Bunny & the Mastermixers (Music Factory Dance)
16	9	DON'T YOU LOVE ME	49ers (Fourth & Broadway)
24	10	BIRDHOUSE IN YOUR SOUL	They Might Be Giants (Elektra)
21	11	EVERYTHING BEGINS WITH AN 'E'	E-Zee Posse (More Protein)
18	12	LOADED	Primal Scream (Creation)
15	13	THIS IS HOW IT FEELS	Inspiral Carpets (Cow)
11	14	HOW AM I SUPPOSED TO LIVE WITHOUT YOU	Michael Bolton (CBS)
6	15	INFINITY	Guru Josh (deConstruction)
17	16	HANDFUL OF PROMISES	Big Fun (Jive)
34	17	CHIME	Orbital (ffrr)
10	18	MOMENTS IN SOUL	JT & the Big Family (Champion)
39	19	ANOTHER DAY IN PARADISE	Jam Tronik (Debut)
14	20	NOTHING COMPARES 2 U	Sinead O'Connor (Ensign)
9	21	THE BRITS 1990 (DANCE MEDLEY)	Various Artists (RCA)
12	22	NATURAL THING	Innocence (Cooltempo)
44	23	MAMA GAVE BIRTH 2 THE SOUL CHILDREN	Queen Latifah & De La Soul (Gee Street)
42	24	ALL I WANNA DO IS MAKE LOVE TO YOU	Heart (Capitol)
30	25	READ MY LIPS (ENOUGH IS ENOUGH)	Jimmy Somerville (London)
-	26	WHAT U WAITIN' 4?	Jungle Brothers (Eternal)
22	27	ENJOY THE SILENCE	Depeche Mode (Mute)
-	28	DON'T MISS THE PARTYLINE	Bizz Nizz (Cooltempo)
-	29	TOO LATE TO SAY GOODBYE	Richard Marx (EMI-USA)
23	30	HERE WE ARE/DON'T LET THE SUN GO DOWN ON ME	Gloria Estefan (Epic)
46	31	YOUR LOVE TAKES ME HIGHER	Beloved (East West)
-	32	SHE BANGS THE DRUMS	Stone Roses (Silvertone)
-	33	BLACK VELVET	Alannah Myles (East West)
19	34	GET UP (BEFORE THE NIGHT IS OVER)	Technotronic featuring Ya Kid K (Swanyard)
-	35	PICTURES OF YOU	Cure (Fiction)
-	36	ESCAPADE	Janet Jackson (Breakout)
49	37	KISS THIS THING GOODBYE	Del Amitri (A&M)
27	38	DELIVERANCE	Mission (Mercury)
26	39	A GENTLEMAN'S EXCUSE ME	Fish (EMI)
-	40	BETTER WORLD	Rebel MC (Desire)
-	41	GHETTO HEAVEN	Family Stand (East West)
25	42	I DON'T KNOW ANYBODY ELSE	Black Box (deConstruction)
20	43	MADLY IN LOVE	Bros (CBS)
-	44	I REMEMBER YOU	Skid Row (Atlantic)
-	45	SATURDAY LOVE	Cherelle with Alexander O'Neal (Tabu)
-	46	RHYTHM OF LIFE	Oleta Adams (Fontana)
47	47	DEVOTION	Kicking Back With Taxman (10)
-	48	BABY	Halo James (Epic)
-	49	KINGSTON TOWN	UB40 (DEP International)
31	50	I MIGHT	Shakin' Stevens (Epic)

The dominance of dance music on the UK singles scene was recognised by the *Brits 1990* single, which rolled together excerpts from 1989 club and chart hits by D Mob, S-Express, the Cookie Crew, the Beatmasters and others. Otherwise, oldie revivals were still making much of the running, with Candy Flip's remoulding of the Beatles' *Strawberry Fields Forever* among the most striking.

April 1990

7 April 1990

last	this	Title	Artist (Label)
2	1	POWER	Snap! (Arista)
3	2	STRAWBERRY FIELDS FOREVER	Candy Flip (Debu)
1	3	LOVE SHACK	B52's (Reprise)
4	4	BLUE SAVANNAH	Erasure (Mute)
10	5	BIRDHOUSE IN YOUR SOUL	They Might Be Giants (Elektra)
6	6	LILY WAS HERE	David A. Stewart featuring Candy Dulfer (RCA)
5	7	DUB BE GOOD TO ME	Beats International
9	8	DON'T YOU LOVE ME	49ers (Fourth & Broadway)
19	9	ANOTHER DAY IN PARADISE	Jam Tronik (Debut)
28	10	DON'T MISS THE PARTYLINE	Bizz Nizz (Cooltempo)
41	11	GHETTO HEAVEN	Family Stand (East West)
-	12	VOGUE	Madonna (Sire)
23	13	MAMA GAVE BIRTH 2 THE SOUL CHILDREN	Queen Latifah & De La Soul (Gee Street)
7	14	I'LL BE LOVING YOU FOREVER	New Kids On The Block (CBS)
-	15	STEP ON	Happy Mondays (Factory)
13	16	THIS IS HOW IT FEELS	Inspiral Carpets (Cow)
17	17	CHIME	Orbital (ffrr)
11	18	EVERYTHING BEGINS WITH AN 'E'	E-Zee Posse (More Protein)
-	19	HANG ON TO YOUR LOVE	Jason Donovan (PWL)
8	20	THAT SOUNDS GOOD TO ME	Jive Bunny & the Mastermixers (Music Factory Dance)
14	21	HOW AM I SUPPOSED TO LIVE WITHOUT YOU	Michael Bolton (CBS)
24	22	ALL I WANNA DO IS MAKE LOVE TO YOU	Heart (Capitol)
15	23	INFINITY	Guru Josh (deConstruction)
12	24	LOADED	Primal Scream (Creation)
26	25	WHAT U WAITIN' 4?	Jungle Brothers (Eternal)
40	26	BETTER WORLD	Rebel MC (Desire)
27	27	ESCAPADE	Janet Jackson (Breakout)
49	28	KINGSTON TOWN	UB40 (DEP International)
18	29	MOMENTS IN SOUL	JT & the Big Family (Champion)
33	30	BLACK VELVET	Alannah Myles (East West)
25	31	READ MY LIPS (ENOUGH IS ENOUGH)	Jimmy Somerville (London)
20	32	NOTHING COMPARES 2 U	Sinead O'Connor (Ensign)
33	33	PICTURES OF YOU	Cure (Fiction)
-	34	THIS BEAT IS TECHNOTRONIC	Technotronic featuring MC Eric (Swanyard)
21	35	THE BRITS 1990 (DANCE MEDLEY)	Various Artists (RCA)
44	36	I REMEMBER YOU	Skid Row (Atlantic)
-	37	FAME 90	David Bowie (EMI-USA)
16	38	HANDFUL OF PROMISES	Big Fun (Jive)
37	39	KISS THIS THING GOODBYE	Del Amitri (A&M)
-	40	THE BEATLES AND THE STONES	House of Love (Fontana)
-	41	911 IS A JOKE	Public Enemy (Def Jam)
-	42	I'D RATHER GO BLIND	Sydney Youngblood (Circa)
43	43	REAL REAL REAL	Jesus Jones (Food)
-	44	KILLER	Adamski (MCA)
25	45	TOO LATE TO SAY GOODBYE	Richard Marx (EMI-USA)
32	46	SHE BANGS THE DRUMS	Stone Roses (Silvertone)
-	47	I DON'T LOVE YOU ANYMORE	Quireboys (Parlophone)
22	48	NATURAL THING	Innocence (Cooltempo)
-	49	THAT'S THE WAY OF THE WORLD	D Mob featuring Cathy Dennis (ffrr)
27	50	ENJOY THE SILENCE	Depeche Mode (Mute)

14 April 1990

last	this	Title	Artist (Label)
1	1	POWER	Snap! (Arista)
12	2	VOGUE	Madonna (Sire)
2	3	STRAWBERRY FIELDS FOREVER	Candy Flip (Debu)
10	4	DON'T MISS THE PARTYLINE	Bizz Nizz (Cooltempo)
19	5	HANG ON TO YOUR LOVE	Jason Donovan (PWL)
15	6	STEP ON	Happy Mondays (Factory)
3	7	LOVE SHACK	B52's (Reprise)
11	8	GHETTO HEAVEN	Family Stand (East West)
28	9	KINGSTON TOWN	UB40 (DEP International)
30	10	BLACK VELVET	Alannah Myles (East West)
5	11	BIRDHOUSE IN YOUR SOUL	They Might Be Giants (Elektra)
4	12	BLUE SAVANNAH	Erasure (Mute)
22	13	ALL I WANNA DO IS MAKE LOVE TO YOU	Heart (Capitol)
6	14	LILY WAS HERE	David A. Stewart featuring Candy Dulfer (RCA)
13	15	MAMA GAVE BIRTH 2 THE SOUL CHILDREN	Queen Latifah & De La Soul (Gee Street)
34	16	THIS BEAT IS TECHNOTRONIC	Technotronic featuring MC Eric (Swanyard)
9	17	ANOTHER DAY IN PARADISE	Jam Tronik (Debut)
43	18	REAL REAL REAL	Jesus Jones (Food)
7	19	DUB BE GOOD TO ME	Beats International featuring Lindy Layton (Go Beat)
27	20	ESCAPADE	Janet Jackson (Breakout)
26	21	BETTER WORLD	Rebel MC (Desire)
-	22	OPPOSITES ATTRACT	Paula Abdul with the Wild Pair (Siren)
14	23	I'LL BE LOVING YOU FOREVER	New Kids On The Block (CBS)
37	24	FAME 90	David Bowie (EMI-USA)
8	25	DON'T YOU LOVE ME	49ers (Fourth & Broadway)
16	26	THIS IS HOW IT FEELS	Inspiral Carpets (Cow)
18	27	EVERYTHING BEGINS WITH AN 'E'	E-Zee Posse (More Protein)
25	28	WHAT U WAITIN' 4?	Jungle Brothers (Eternal)
33	29	PICTURES OF YOU	Cure (Fiction)
-	30	COUNTING EVERY MINUTE	Sonia (Chrysalis)
17	31	CHIME	Orbital (ffrr)
40	32	THE BEATLES AND THE STONES	House of Love (Fontana)
47	33	I DON'T LOVE YOU ANYMORE	Quireboys (Parlophone)
-	34	EVERYBODY NEEDS SOMEBODY TO LOVE	Blues Brothers (East West)
21	35	HOW AM I SUPPOSED TO LIVE WITHOUT YOU	Michael Bolton (CBS)
44	36	KILLER	Adamski (MCA)
49	37	THAT'S THE WAY OF THE WORLD	D Mob featuring Cathy Dennis (ffrr)
23	38	INFINITY	Guru Josh (deConstruction)
-	39	EASTER	Marillion (EMI)
29	40	MOMENTS IN SOUL	JT & the Big Family (Champion)
32	41	NOTHING COMPARES 2 U	Sinead O'Connor (Ensign)
-	42	RAG DOLL	Aerosmith (Geffen)
20	43	THAT SOUNDS GOOD TO ME	Jive Bunny & the Mastermixers (Music Factory Dance)
24	44	LOADED	Primal Scream (Creation)
31	45	READ MY LIPS (ENOUGH IS ENOUGH)	Jimmy Somerville (London)
42	46	I'D RATHER GO BLIND	Sydney Youngblood (Circa)
36	47	I REMEMBER YOU	Skid Row (Atlantic)
39	48	KISS THIS THING GOODBYE	Del Amitri (A&M)
-	49	HEART OF STONE	Cher (Geffen)
50	50	911 IS A JOKE	Public Enemy (Def Jam)

21 April 1990

last	this	Title	Artist (Label)
2	1	VOGUE	Madonna (Sire)
10	2	BLACK VELVET	Alannah Myles (East West)
9	3	KINGSTON TOWN	UB40 (DEP International)
1	4	POWER	Snap! (Arista)
6	5	STEP ON	Happy Mondays (Factory)
4	6	DON'T MISS THE PARTYLINE	Bizz Nizz (Cooltempo)
22	7	OPPOSITES ATTRACT	Paula Abdul with the Wild Pair (Siren)
8	8	GHETTO HEAVEN	Family Stand (East West)
7	9	LOVE SHACK	B52's (Reprise)
16	10	THIS BEAT IS TECHNOTRONIC	Technotronic featuring MC Eric (Swanyard)
13	11	ALL I WANNA DO IS MAKE LOVE TO YOU	Heart (Capitol)
5	12	HANG ON TO YOUR LOVE	Jason Donovan (PWL)
3	13	STRAWBERRY FIELDS FOREVER	Candy Flip (Debu)
11	14	BIRDHOUSE IN YOUR SOUL	They Might Be Giants (Elektra)
20	15	ESCAPADE	Janet Jackson (Breakout)
15	16	MAMA GAVE BIRTH 2 THE SOUL CHILDREN	Queen Latifah & De La Soul (Gee Street)
18	17	REAL REAL REAL	Jesus Jones (Food)
34	18	EVERYBODY NEEDS SOMEBODY TO LOVE	Blues Brothers (East West)
14	19	LILY WAS HERE	David A. Stewart featuring Candy Dulfer (RCA)
12	20	BLUE SAVANNAH	Erasure (Mute)
17	21	ANOTHER DAY IN PARADISE	Jam Tronik (Debut)
29	22	PICTURES OF YOU	Cure (Fiction)
33	23	I DON'T LOVE YOU ANYMORE	Quireboys (Parlophone)
24	24	FAME 90	David Bowie (EMI-USA)
21	25	BETTER WORLD	Rebel MC (Desire)
-	26	PLAY	Ride (Creation)
30	27	COUNTING EVERY MINUTE	Sonia (Chrysalis)
19	28	DUB BE GOOD TO ME	Beats International featuring Lindy Layton (Go Beat)
32	29	THE BEATLES AND THE STONES	House of Love (Fontana)
36	30	KILLER	Adamski (MCA)
23	31	I'LL BE LOVING YOU FOREVER	New Kids On The Block (CBS)
39	32	EASTER	Marillion (EMI)
-	33	TOMORROW	Tongue 'N' Cheek (Syncopate)
26	34	THIS IS HOW IT FEELS	Inspiral Carpets (Cow)
-	35	USE IT UP AND WEAR IT OUT	Pat & Mick (PWL)
-	36	FROM OUT OF NOWHERE	Faith No More (Slash)
27	37	EVERYTHING BEGINS WITH AN 'E'	E-Zee Posse (More Protein)
37	38	THAT'S THE WAY OF THE WORLD	D Mob featuring Cathy Dennis (ffrr)
42	39	RAG DOLL	Aerosmith (Geffen)
49	40	HEART OF STONE	Cher (Geffen)
-	41	MUSICAL MELODY/WEIGHT FOR THE BASS	Unique 3 (10)
25	42	DON'T YOU LOVE ME	49ers (Fourth & Broadway)
-	43	ELENI	Tol & Tol (Dover)
-	44	IT'S HERE	Kim Wilde (MCA)
28	45	WHAT U WAITIN' 4?	Jungle Brothers (Eternal)
-	46	SCARLET	All About Eve (Mercury)
38	47	INFINITY	Guru Josh (deConstruction)
-	48	DIRTY CASH	Adventures of Stevie V (Mercury)
-	49	NO ALIBIS	Eric Clapton (Duck)
31	50	CHIME	Orbital (ffrr)

David A Stewart (of the Eurythmics)'s *Lily Was Here* was the theme for a film which sank without trace by comparison with its arresting title tune, which – rarely these days for an instrumental – made the Top 10. Dutch female jazz saxophonist Candy Dulfer, who had previously played with Prince, was the featured soloist, along with Stewart's own guitar. Madonna was hitting the top regularly.

April – May 1990

28 April 1990

last week	this week	title / artist (label)
1	1	VOGUE — Madonna (Sire)
2	2	BLACK VELVET — Alannah Myles (East West)
7	3	OPPOSITES ATTRACT — Paula Abdul with the Wild Pair (Siren)
3	4	KINGSTON TOWN — UB40 (DEP International)
4	5	POWER — Snap! (Arista)
5	6	STEP ON — Happy Mondays (Factory)
11	7	ALL I WANNA DO IS MAKE LOVE TO YOU — Heart (Capitol)
6	8	DON'T MISS THE PARTYLINE — Bizz Nizz (Cooltempo)
18	9	EVERYBODY NEEDS SOMEBODY TO LOVE — Blues Brothers (East West)
8	10	GHETTO HEAVEN — Family Stand (East West)
30	11	KILLER — Adamski (MCA)
10	12	THIS BEAT IS TECHNOTRONIC — Technotronic featuring MC Eric (Swanyard)
15	13	ESCAPADE — Janet Jackson (Breakout)
12	14	HANG ON TO YOUR LOVE — Jason Donovan (PWL)
48	15	DIRTY CASH — Adventures of Stevie V (Mercury)
9	16	LOVE SHACK — B52's (Reprise)
27	17	COUNTING EVERY MINUTE — Sonia (Chrysalis)
14	18	BIRDHOUSE IN YOUR SOUL — They Might Be Giants (Elektra)
17	19	REAL REAL REAL — Jesus Jones (Food)
13	20	STRAWBERRY FIELDS FOREVER — Candy Flip (Debu)
16	21	MAMA GAVE BIRTH 2 THE SOUL CHILDREN — Queen Latifah & De La Soul (Gee Street)
19	22	LILY WAS HERE — David A. Stewart featuring Candy Dulfer (RCA)
35	23	USE IT UP AND WEAR IT OUT — Pat & Mick (PWL)
20	24	BLUE SAVANNAH — Erasure (Mute)
23	25	I DON'T LOVE YOU ANYMORE — Quireboys (Parlophone)
36	26	FROM OUT OF NOWHERE — Faith No More (Slash)
29	27	THE BEATLES AND THE STONES — House of Love (Fontana)
-	28	SOMETHING HAPPENED ON THE WAY TO HEAVEN — Phil Collins (Virgin)
22	29	PICTURES OF YOU — Cure (Fiction)
30	30	TOMORROW — Tongue 'N' Cheek (Syncopate)
28	31	DUB BE GOOD TO ME — Beats International featuring Lindy Layton (Go Beat)
21	32	ANOTHER DAY IN PARADISE — Jam Tronik (Debut)
41	33	MUSICAL MELODY/WEIGHT FOR THE BASS — Unique 3 (10)
25	34	BETTER WORLD — Rebel MC (Desire)
40	35	HEART OF STONE — Cher (Geffen)
-	36	HITCHIN' A RIDE — Sinitta (Fanfare)
37	37	I'LL BE LOVING YOU FOREVER — New Kids On The Block (CBS)
39	38	RAG DOLL — Aerosmith (Geffen)
26	39	PLAY — Ride (Creation)
24	40	FAME 90 — David Bowie (EMI-USA)
44	41	IT'S HERE — Kim Wilde (MCA)
-	42	EXPRESSION — Salt 'N' Pepa (London)
46	43	SCARLET — All About Eve (Mercury)
34	44	THIS IS HOW IT FEELS — Inspiral Carpets (Cow)
-	45	THE SEX OF IT — Kid Creole & the Coconuts (CBS)
37	46	EVERYTHING BEGINS WITH AN 'E' — E-Zee Posse (More Protein)
32	47	EASTER — Marillion (EMI)
-	48	TATTOOED MILLIONAIRE — Bruce Dickinson (EMI)
-	49	WILD WOMEN DO — Natalie Cole (EMI-USA)
-	50	LOVE CHILD — Goodbye Mr. MacKenzie (Parlophone)

5 May 1990

last week	this week	title / artist (label)
1	1	VOGUE — Madonna (Sire)
2	2	BLACK VELVET — Alannah Myles (East West)
3	3	OPPOSITES ATTRACT — Paula Abdul with the Wild Pair (Siren)
11	4	KILLER — Adamski (MCA)
-	5	A DREAM'S A DREAM — Soul II Soul (10)
15	6	DIRTY CASH — Adventures of Stevie V (Mercury)
7	7	STEP ON — Happy Mondays (Factory)
5	8	POWER — Snap! (Arista)
4	9	KINGSTON TOWN — UB40 (DEP International)
7	10	ALL I WANNA DO IS MAKE LOVE TO YOU — Heart (Capitol)
9	11	EVERYBODY NEEDS SOMEBODY TO LOVE — Blues Brothers (East West)
10	12	GHETTO HEAVEN — Family Stand (East West)
8	13	DON'T MISS THE PARTYLINE — Bizz Nizz (Cooltempo)
28	14	SOMETHING HAPPENED ON THE WAY TO HEAVEN — Phil Collins (Virgin)
-	15	NOVEMBER SPAWNED A MONSTER — Morrissey (HMV)
17	16	COUNTING EVERY MINUTE — Sonia (Chrysalis)
23	17	USE IT UP AND WEAR IT OUT — Pat & Mick (PWL)
12	18	THIS BEAT IS TECHNOTRONIC — Technotronic featuring MC Eric (Swanyard)
26	19	FROM OUT OF NOWHERE — Faith No More (Slash)
14	20	HANG ON TO YOUR LOVE — Jason Donovan (PWL)
49	21	WILD WOMEN DO — Natalie Cole (EMI-USA)
16	22	LOVE SHACK — B52's (Reprise)
13	23	ESCAPADE — Janet Jackson (Breakout)
33	24	MUSICAL MELODY/WEIGHT FOR THE BASS — Unique 3 (10)
19	25	REAL REAL REAL — Jesus Jones (Food)
-	26	SNAPPINESS — BBG featuring Dina Taylor (Urban)
30	27	TOMORROW — Tongue 'N' Cheek (Syncopate)
48	28	TATTOOED MILLIONAIRE — Bruce Dickinson (EMI)
18	29	BIRDHOUSE IN YOUR SOUL — They Might Be Giants (Elektra)
45	30	THE SEX OF IT — Kid Creole & the Coconuts (CBS)
20	31	STRAWBERRY FIELDS FOREVER — Candy Flip (Debu)
-	32	CRADLE OF LOVE — Billy Idol (Chrysalis)
36	33	HITCHIN' A RIDE — Sinitta (Fanfare)
43	34	SCARLET — All About Eve (Mercury)
-	35	THE SIXTH SENSE — Latino Rave (Deep Heat)
22	36	LILY WAS HERE — David A. Stewart featuring Candy Dulfer (RCA)
37	37	SOMETHING YOU GOT — And Why Not? (Island)
24	38	BLUE SAVANNAH — Erasure (Mute)
42	39	EXPRESSION — Salt 'N' Pepa (London)
21	40	MAMA GAVE BIRTH 2 THE SOUL CHILDREN — Queen Latifah & De La Soul (Gee Street)
25	41	I DON'T LOVE YOU ANYMORE — Quireboys (Parlophone)
-	42	I'LL BE YOUR SHELTER — Taylor Dayne (Arista)
31	43	DUB BE GOOD TO ME — Beats International featuring Lindy Layton (Go Beat)
41	44	IT'S HERE — Kim Wilde (MCA)
-	45	AFRIKA — History featuring Q Tee (SBK)
35	46	HEART OF STONE — Cher (Geffen)
37	47	I'LL BE LOVING YOU FOREVER — New Kids On The Block (CBS)
-	48	TRIPPIN' ON YOUR LOVE — A Way Of Life (Eternal)
-	49	CAN'T SET RULES ABOUT LOVE — Adam Ant (MCA)
-	50	HEAVEN GIVE ME WORDS — Propaganda (Virgin)

12 May 1990

last week	this week	title / artist (label)
1	1	VOGUE — Madonna (Sire)
3	2	OPPOSITES ATTRACT — Paula Abdul with the Wild Pair (Siren)
4	3	KILLER — Adamski (MCA)
5	4	A DREAM'S A DREAM — Soul II Soul (10)
6	5	DIRTY CASH — Adventures of Stevie V (Mercury)
2	6	BLACK VELVET — Alannah Myles (East West)
14	7	SOMETHING HAPPENED ON THE WAY TO HEAVEN — Phil Collins (Virgin)
-	8	BETTER THE DEVIL YOU KNOW — Kylie Minogue (PWL)
21	9	WILD WOMEN DO — Natalie Cole (EMI-USA)
15	10	NOVEMBER SPAWNED A MONSTER — Morrissey (HMV)
7	11	STEP ON — Happy Mondays (Factory)
12	12	GHETTO HEAVEN — Family Stand (East West)
-	13	HOLD ON — En Vogue (East West)
8	14	POWER — Snap! (Arista)
-	15	COVER GIRL — New Kids On The Block (CBS)
26	16	SNAPPINESS — BBG featuring Dina Taylor (Urban)
9	17	KINGSTON TOWN — UB40 (DEP International)
28	18	TATTOOED MILLIONAIRE — Bruce Dickinson (EMI)
11	19	EVERYBODY NEEDS SOMEBODY TO LOVE — Blues Brothers (East West)
10	20	ALL I WANNA DO IS MAKE LOVE TO YOU — Heart (Capitol)
33	21	HITCHIN' A RIDE — Sinitta (Fanfare)
27	22	TOMORROW — Tongue 'N' Cheek (Syncopate)
17	23	USE IT UP AND WEAR IT OUT — Pat & Mick (PWL)
13	24	DON'T MISS THE PARTYLINE — Bizz Nizz (Cooltempo)
30	25	THE SEX OF IT — Kid Creole & the Coconuts (CBS)
19	26	FROM OUT OF NOWHERE — Faith No More (Slash)
-	27	HEAVEN GIVE ME WORDS — Propaganda (Virgin)
25	28	REAL REAL REAL — Jesus Jones (Food)
16	29	COUNTING EVERY MINUTE — Sonia (Chrysalis)
-	30	WHAT DID I DO TO YOU? — Lisa Stansfield (Arista)
-	31	HOW CAN WE BE LOVERS — Michael Bolton (CBS)
32	32	CRADLE OF LOVE — Billy Idol (Chrysalis)
-	33	CIRCLESQUARE — Wonder Stuff (Polydor)
22	34	LOVE SHACK — B52's (Reprise)
18	35	THIS BEAT IS TECHNOTRONIC — Technotronic featuring MC Eric (Swanyard)
-	36	STEPPING STONE/FAMILY OF MAN — Farm (Produce)
37	37	WON'T TALK ABOUT IT — Beats International (Go Beat)
20	38	HANG ON TO YOUR LOVE — Jason Donovan (PWL)
45	39	AFRIKA — History featuring Q Tee (SBK)
-	40	BAKERMAN — Laid Back (Arista)
24	41	MUSICAL MELODY/WEIGHT FOR THE BASS — Unique 3 (10)
-	42	GLIDER (EP) — My Bloody Valentine (Creation)
-	43	KISSING GATE — Sam Brown (A&M)
23	44	ESCAPADE — Janet Jackson (Breakout)
35	45	THE SIXTH SENSE — Latino Rave (Deep Heat)
29	46	BIRDHOUSE IN YOUR SOUL — They Might Be Giants (Elektra)
-	47	TAKE YOUR TIME — Mantronix featuring Wondress (Capitol)
-	48	GIVE A LITTLE LOVE BACK TO THE WORLD — Emma (Big Wave)
39	49	EXPRESSION — Salt 'N' Pepa (London)
42	50	I'LL BE YOUR SHELTER — Taylor Dayne (Arista)

Once again, female singers dominated the top of the chart, as Madonna's *Vogue* (a commentary on a new hip dance/fashion trend, which was America's biggest-selling single this year), *Black Velvet* by Canadian hard-rocker Alannah Myles, and Paula Abdul's dance-and-rap duet *Opposites Attract*, hogged positions One to Three for the best part of a month.

19 May 1990

last	this	Title	Artist
3	1	KILLER	Adamski (MCA)
8	2	BETTER THE DEVIL YOU KNOW	Kylie Minogue (PWL)
5	3	DIRTY CASH	Adventures of Stevie V (Mercury)
15	4	COVER GIRL	New Kids On The Block (CBS)
1	5	VOGUE	Madonna (Sire)
2	6	OPPOSITES ATTRACT	Paula Abdul with the Wild Pair (Siren)
4	7	A DREAM'S A DREAM	Soul II Soul (10)
13	8	HOLD ON	En Vogue (East West)
6	9	BLACK VELVET	Alannah Myles (East West)
37	10	WON'T TALK ABOUT IT	Beats International (Go Beat)
9	11	WILD WOMEN DO	Natalie Cole (EMI-USA)
47	12	TAKE YOUR TIME	Mantronix featuring Wondress (Capitol)
7	13	SOMETHING HAPPENED ON THE WAY TO HEAVEN	Phil Collins (Virgin)
12	14	GHETTO HEAVEN	Family Stand (East West)
30	15	WHAT DID I DO TO YOU?	Lisa Stansfield (Arista)
11	16	STEP ON	Happy Mondays (Factory)
31	17	HOW CAN WE BE LOVERS	Michael Bolton (CBS)
14	18	POWER	Snap! (Arista)
33	19	CIRCLESQUARE	Wonder Stuff (Polydor)
17	20	KINGSTON TOWN	UB40 (DEP International)
21	21	HITCHIN' A RIDE	Sinitta (Fanfare)
-	22	LOVE THING	Pasadenas (CBS)
-	23	BACKSTREET SYMPHONY	Thunder (EMI)
20	24	ALL I WANNA DO IS MAKE LOVE TO YOU	Heart (Capitol)
16	25	SNAPPINESS	BBG featuring Dina Taylor (Urban)
-	26	SOFTLY WHISPERING I LOVE YOU	Paul Young (Epic)
27	27	HEAVEN GIVE ME WORDS	Propaganda (Virgin)
-	28	HOW WAS IT FOR YOU?	James (Fontana)
-	29	POLICY OF TRUTH	Depeche Mode (Mute)
19	30	EVERYBODY NEEDS SOMEBODY TO LOVE	Blues Brothers (East West)
24	31	DON'T MISS THE PARTYLINE	Bizz Nizz (Cooltempo)
10	32	NOVEMBER SPAWNED A MONSTER	Morrissey (HMV)
43	33	KISSING GATE	Sam Brown (A&M)
-	34	ANGEL	Eurythmics (RCA)
22	35	TOMORROW	Tongue 'N' Cheek (Syncopate)
18	36	TATTOOED MILLIONAIRE	Bruce Dickinson (EMI)
40	37	BAKERMAN	Laid Back (Arista)
-	38	I STILL HAVEN'T FOUND WHAT I'M LOOKING FOR	Chimes (CBS)
28	39	REAL REAL REAL	Jesus Jones (Food)
-	40	WITHOUT YOU	Motley Crue (Elektra)
-	41	DON'T WANNA FALL IN LOVE	Jane Child (Warner Bros)
25	42	THE SEX OF IT	Kid Creole & the Coconuts (CBS)
-	43	ROAM	B52's (Reprise)
-	44	SAVE ME	Big Country (Mercury)
48	45	GIVE A LITTLE LOVE BACK TO THE WORLD	Emma (Big Wave)
-	46	GIVE IT UP	Hothouse Flowers (London)
-	47	RADICAL YOUR LOVER (EP)	Little Angels (Polydor)
-	48	SAVE ME	Fleetwood Mac (Warner Bros)
23	49	USE IT UP AND WEAR IT OUT	Pat & Mick (PWL)
39	50	AFRIKA	History featuring Q Tee (SBK)

26 May 1990

last	this	Title	Artist
1	1	KILLER	Adamski (MCA)
2	2	BETTER THE DEVIL YOU KNOW	Kylie Minogue (PWL)
38	3	I STILL HAVEN'T FOUND WHAT I'M LOOKING FOR	Chimes (CBS)
3	4	DIRTY CASH	Adventures of Stevie V (Mercury)
4	5	COVER GIRL	New Kids On The Block (CBS)
8	6	HOLD ON	En Vogue (East West)
10	7	WON'T TALK ABOUT IT	Beats International (Go Beat)
6	8	OPPOSITES ATTRACT	Paula Abdul with the Wild Pair (Siren)
12	9	TAKE YOUR TIME	Mantronix featuring Wondress (Capitol)
5	10	VOGUE	Madonna (Sire)
17	11	HOW CAN WE BE LOVERS	Michael Bolton (CBS)
7	12	A DREAM'S A DREAM	Soul II Soul (10)
26	13	SOFTLY WHISPERING I LOVE YOU	Paul Young (Epic)
-	14	VENUS	Don Pablo's Animals (Rumour)
15	15	WHAT DID I DO TO YOU?	Lisa Stansfield (Arista)
9	16	BLACK VELVET	Alannah Myles (East West)
22	17	LOVE THING	Pasadenas (CBS)
34	18	ANGEL	Eurythmics (RCA)
29	19	POLICY OF TRUTH	Depeche Mode (Mute)
43	20	ROAM	B52's (Reprise)
18	21	POWER	Snap! (Arista)
16	22	STEP ON	Happy Mondays (Factory)
20	23	KINGSTON TOWN	UB40 (DEP International)
14	24	GHETTO HEAVEN	Family Stand (East West)
46	25	GIVE IT UP	Hothouse Flowers (London)
11	26	WILD WOMEN DO	Natalie Cole (EMI-USA)
19	27	CIRCLESQUARE	Wonder Stuff (Polydor)
33	28	KISSING GATE	Sam Brown (A&M)
24	29	ALL I WANNA DO IS MAKE LOVE TO YOU	Heart (Capitol)
13	30	SOMETHING HAPPENED ON THE WAY TO HEAVEN	Phil Collins (Virgin)
23	31	BACKSTREET SYMPHONY	Thunder (EMI)
28	32	HOW WAS IT FOR YOU?	James (Fontana)
31	33	DON'T MISS THE PARTYLINE	Bizz Nizz (Cooltempo)
47	34	RADICAL YOUR LOVER (EP)	Little Angels (Polydor)
25	35	SNAPPINESS	BBG featuring Dina Taylor (Urban)
-	36	JOY AND HEARTBREAK	Movement 98 (Circa)
21	37	HITCHIN' A RIDE	Sinitta (Fanfare)
-	38	IT'S MY LIFE	Talk Talk (Parlophone)
41	39	DON'T WANNA FALL IN LOVE	Jane Child (Warner Bros)
45	40	GIVE A LITTLE LOVE BACK TO THE WORLD	Emma (Big Wave)
-	41	IT'S HAPPENIN'	Plus One featuring Sirron (MCA)
-	42	DOIN' THE BOO	Betty Boo (Rhythm King)
27	43	HEAVEN GIVE ME WORDS	Propaganda (Virgin)
-	44	THE DESPERATE HOURS	Marc Almond (Some Bizzare)
30	45	EVERYBODY NEEDS SOMEBODY TO LOVE	Blues Brothers (East West)
-	46	PAPA WAS A ROLLING STONE	Was (Not Was) (Fontana)
-	47	GLAD ALL OVER	Crystal Palace F.C. Cup Squad featuring the Fab Four (Parkfield)
44	48	SAVE ME	Big Country (Mercury)
40	49	WITHOUT YOU	Motley Crue (Elektra)
-	50	JUST A FRIEND	Biz Markie (Cold Chillin')

2 June 1990

last	this	Title	Artist
1	1	KILLER	Adamski (MCA)
3	2	I STILL HAVEN'T FOUND WHAT I'M LOOKING FOR	Chimes (CBS)
6	3	HOLD ON	En Vogue (East West)
14	4	VENUS	Don Pablo's Animals (Rumour)
4	5	DIRTY CASH	Adventures of Stevie V (Mercury)
2	6	BETTER THE DEVIL YOU KNOW	Kylie Minogue (PWL)
-	7	WORLD IN MOTION	England/New Order (Factory)
7	8	WON'T TALK ABOUT IT	Beats International (Go Beat)
5	9	COVER GIRL	New Kids On The Block (CBS)
11	10	HOW CAN WE BE LOVERS	Michael Bolton (CBS)
46	11	PAPA WAS A ROLLING STONE	Was (Not Was) (Fontana)
20	12	ROAM	B52's (Reprise)
8	13	OPPOSITES ATTRACT	Paula Abdul with the Wild Pair (Siren)
19	14	POLICY OF TRUTH	Depeche Mode (Mute)
9	15	TAKE YOUR TIME	Mantronix featuring Wondress (Capitol)
10	16	VOGUE	Madonna (Sire)
-	17	STAR	Erasure (Mute)
18	18	ANGEL	Eurythmics (RCA)
13	19	SOFTLY WHISPERING I LOVE YOU	Paul Young (Epic)
16	20	BLACK VELVET	Alannah Myles (East West)
42	21	DOIN' THE BOO	Betty Boo (Rhythm King)
17	22	LOVE THING	Pasadenas (CBS)
39	23	DON'T WANNA FALL IN LOVE	Jane Child (Warner Bros)
28	24	KISSING GATE	Sam Brown (A&M)
25	25	GIVE IT UP	Hothouse Flowers (London)
36	26	JOY AND HEARTBREAK	Movement 98 (Circa)
21	27	POWER	Snap! (Arista)
12	28	A DREAM'S A DREAM	Soul II Soul (10)
15	29	WHAT DID I DO TO YOU?	Lisa Stansfield (Arista)
38	30	IT'S MY LIFE	Talk Talk (Parlophone)
23	31	KINGSTON TOWN	UB40 (DEP International)
-	32	EVERYBODY, EVERYBODY	Black Box (deConstruction)
-	33	STILL GOT THE BLUES (FOR YOU)	Gary Moore (Virgin)
34	34	RADICAL YOUR LOVER (EP)	Little Angels (Polydor)
29	35	ALL I WANNA DO IS MAKE LOVE TO YOU	Heart (Capitol)
-	36	REPUTATION	Dusty Springfield (Parlophone)
-	37	THE ONLY ONE I KNOW	Charlatans (Situation Two)
24	38	GHETTO HEAVEN	Family Stand (East West)
41	39	IT'S HAPPENIN'	Plus One featuring Sirron (MCA)
-	40	HEAR THE DRUMMER (GET WICKED)	Chad Jackson (Big Wave)
-	41	CUTS BOTH WAYS	Gloria Estefan (Epic)
22	42	STEP ON	Happy Mondays (Factory)
-	43	YAAAH	D-Shake (Cooltempo)
-	44	HOLD ON	Wilson Phillips (SBK)
50	45	JUST A FRIEND	Biz Markie (Cold Chillin')
-	46	USELESS (I DON'T NEED YOU NOW)	Kym Mazelle (Syncopate)
-	47	I'LL BE YOUR EVERYTHING	Tommy Page (Sire)
-	48	EXPRESS YOURSELF	NWA (Fourth & Broadway)
-	49	VISION OF YOU	Belinda Carlisle (Virgin)
-	50	FIND A WAY	Coldcut featuring Queen Latifah (Ahead Of Our Time)

Adamski, otherwise Adam Tinley, had once been part of a schoolboy duo named the Stupid Babies, but he put that well behind him by the chart-topping days of his soul/dance track *Killer*. Adamski was the instrumentalist on the single; the featured vocalist was London soul singer Seal, who would move on to chart success of his own – including an early solo revival of *Killer*.

9 June 1990 (last week / this week)

Last	This	Title	Artist (Label)
7	1	WORLD IN MOTION	England/New Order (Factory)
1	2	KILLER	Adamski (MCA)
40	3	HEAR THE DRUMMER (GET WICKED)	Chad Jackson (Big Wave)
4	4	VENUS	Don Pablo's Animals (Rumour)
2	5	I STILL HAVEN'T FOUND WHAT I'M LOOKING FOR	Chimes (CBS)
5	6	DIRTY CASH	Adventures of Stevie V (Mercury)
21	7	DOIN' THE BOO	Betty Boo (Rhythm King)
11	8	PAPA WAS A ROLLING STONE	Was (Not Was) (Fontana)
6	9	BETTER THE DEVIL YOU KNOW	Kylie Minogue (PWL)
3	10	HOLD ON	En Vogue (East West)
17	11	STAR	Erasure (Mute)
12	12	ROAM	B52's (Reprise)
10	13	HOW CAN WE BE LOVERS	Michael Bolton (CBS)
30	14	IT'S MY LIFE	Talk Talk (Parlophone)
37	15	THE ONLY ONE I KNOW	Charlatans (Situation Two)
32	16	EVERYBODY, EVERYBODY	Black Box (deConstruction)
9	17	COVER GIRL	New Kids On The Block (CBS)
23	18	DON'T WANNA FALL IN LOVE	Jane Child (Warner Bros)
16	19	VOGUE	Madonna (Sire)
8	20	WON'T TALK ABOUT IT	Beats International (Go Beat)
48	21	EXPRESS YOURSELF	NWA (Fourth & Broadway)
13	22	OPPOSITES ATTRACT	Paula Abdul with the Wild Pair (Siren)
26	23	JOY AND HEARTBREAK	Movement 98 (Circa)
-	24	IT MUST HAVE BEEN LOVE	Roxette (EMI)
14	25	POLICY OF TRUTH	Depeche Mode (Mute)
43	26	YAAAH	D-Shake (Cooltempo)
20	27	BLACK VELVET	Alannah Myles (East West)
44	28	HOLD ON	Wilson Phillips (SBK)
24	29	KISSING GATE	Sam Brown (A&M)
15	30	TAKE YOUR TIME	Mantronix featuring Wondress (Capitol)
27	31	POWER	Snap! (Arista)
-	32	INTO THE BLUE	Mission (Mercury)
33	33	STILL GOT THE BLUES (FOR YOU)	Gary Moore (Virgin)
-	34	THE ONLY RHYME THAT BITES	MC Tunes Vs. 808 State (ZTT)
-	35	THE MASTERPLAN	Diana Brown & Barrie K. Sharpe (ffrr)
18	36	ANGEL	Eurythmics (RCA)
36	37	REPUTATION	Dusty Springfield (Parlophone)
-	38	LAZYITIS - ONE ARMED BOXER/MAD CYRIL - HELLO GIRLS	Happy Mondays & Karl Denver (Factory)
-	39	NOTHING COMPARES 2 U	MXM (London)
-	40	TOUCHED BY THE HAND OF CICCIOLINA	Pop Will Eat Itself (RCA)
41	41	CUTS BOTH WAYS	Gloria Estefan (Epic)
-	42	SACRIFICE/HEALING HANDS	Elton John (Rocket)
25	43	GIVE IT UP	Hothouse Flowers (London)
28	44	A DREAM'S A DREAM	Soul II Soul (10)
49	45	VISION OF YOU	Belinda Carlisle (Virgin)
35	46	ALL I WANNA DO IS MAKE LOVE TO YOU	Heart (Capitol)
19	47	SOFTLY WHISPERING I LOVE YOU	Paul Young (Epic)
47	48	I'LL BE YOUR EVERYTHING	Tommy Page (Sire)
39	49	IT'S HAPPENIN'	Plus One featuring Sirron (MCA)
-	50	REBEL MUSIC	Rebel MC (Desire)

16 June 1990

This	Title	Artist (Label)
1	WORLD IN MOTION	England/New Order (Factory)
2	HEAR THE DRUMMER (GET WICKED)	Chad Jackson (Big Wave)
3	KILLER	Adamski (MCA)
4	VENUS	Don Pablo's Animals (Rumour)
5	THE ONLY ONE I KNOW	Charlatans (Situation Two)
6	DOIN' THE BOO	Betty Boo (Rhythm King)
7	DIRTY CASH	Adventures of Stevie V (Mercury)
8	SACRIFICE/HEALING HANDS	Elton John (Rocket)
9	STEP BY STEP	New Kids On The Block (CBS)
10	STAR	Erasure (Mute)
11	IT MUST HAVE BEEN LOVE	Roxette (EMI)
12	PAPA WAS A ROLLING STONE	Was (Not Was) (Fontana)
13	EVERYBODY, EVERYBODY	Black Box (deConstruction)
14	IT'S MY LIFE	Talk Talk (Parlophone)
15	I STILL HAVEN'T FOUND WHAT I'M LOOKING FOR	Chimes (CBS)
16	HOLD ON	Wilson Phillips (SBK)
17	BETTER THE DEVIL YOU KNOW	Kylie Minogue (PWL)
18	DON'T WANNA FALL IN LOVE	Jane Child (Warner Bros)
19	HOLD ON	En Vogue (East West)
20	YAAAH	D-Shake (Cooltempo)
21	THE ONLY RHYME THAT BITES	MC Tunes Vs. 808 State (ZTT)
22	ROAM	B52's (Reprise)
23	OOOPS UP	Snap! (Arista)
24	HOW CAN WE BE LOVERS	Michael Bolton (CBS)
25	TOUCHED BY THE HAND OF CICCIOLINA	Pop Will Eat Itself (RCA)
26	VOGUE	Madonna (Sire)
27	COVER GIRL	New Kids On The Block (CBS)
28	GIRL TO GIRL	49ers (Fourth & Broadway)
29	OPPOSITES ATTRACT	Paula Abdul with the Wild Pair (Siren)
30	THE FREE STYLE MEGAMIX	Bobby Brown (MCA)
31	KISSING GATE	Sam Brown (A&M)
32	WON'T TALK ABOUT IT	Beats International (Go Beat)
33	INTO THE BLUE	Mission (Mercury)
34	LAZYITIS - ONE ARMED BOXER/MAD CYRIL - HELLO GIRLS	Happy Mondays & Karl Denver (Factory)
35	THE MASTERPLAN	Diana Brown & Barrie K. Sharpe (ffrr)
36	EXPRESS YOURSELF	NWA (Fourth & Broadway)
37	POWER	Snap! (Arista)
38	REPUTATION	Dusty Springfield (Parlophone)
39	JOY AND HEARTBREAK	Movement 98 (Circa)
40	WHOSE LAW (IS IT ANYWAY?)	Guru Josh (deConstruction)
41	SHALL WE TAKE A TRIP	Northside (Factory)
42	STILL GOT THE BLUES (FOR YOU)	Gary Moore (Virgin)
43	BLACK VELVET	Alannah Myles (East West)
44	FEEL THE RHYTHM	Jazzi P (A&M)
45	POLICY OF TRUTH	Depeche Mode (Mute)
46	CLOSE TO YOU	Maxi Priest (10)
47	VISION OF YOU	Belinda Carlisle (Virgin)
48	ANGEL	Eurythmics (RCA)
49	DON'T TEST	Junior Tucker (10)
50	NOTHING COMPARES 2 U	MXM (London)

23 June 1990

This	Title	Artist (Label)
1	WORLD IN MOTION	England/New Order (Factory)
2	STEP BY STEP	New Kids On The Block (CBS)
3	SACRIFICE/HEALING HANDS	Elton John (Rocket)
4	NESSUN DORMA	Luciano Pavarotti (Decca)
5	IT MUST HAVE BEEN LOVE	Roxette (EMI)
6	OOOPS UP	Snap! (Arista)
7	HEAR THE DRUMMER (GET WICKED)	Chad Jackson (Big Wave)
8	HOLD ON	Wilson Phillips (SBK)
9	KILLER	Adamski (MCA)
10	THE ONLY ONE I KNOW	Charlatans (Situation Two)
11	DOIN' THE BOO	Betty Boo (Rhythm King)
12	THE ONLY RHYME THAT BITES	MC Tunes Vs. 808 State (ZTT)
13	VENUS	Don Pablo's Animals (Rumour)
14	DIRTY CASH	Adventures of Stevie V (Mercury)
15	STAR	Erasure (Mute)
16	THE FREE STYLE MEGAMIX	Bobby Brown (MCA)
17	YAAAH	D-Shake (Cooltempo)
18	IT'S MY LIFE	Talk Talk (Parlophone)
19	THINKING OF YOU	Maureen Walsh (Urban)
20	PAPA WAS A ROLLING STONE	Was (Not Was) (Fontana)
21	WHOSE LAW (IS IT ANYWAY?)	Guru Josh (deConstruction)
22	BETTER THE DEVIL YOU KNOW	Kylie Minogue (PWL)
23	HOLD ON	En Vogue (East West)
24	GIRL TO GIRL	49ers (Fourth & Broadway)
25	U CAN'T TOUCH THIS	MC Hammer (Capitol)
26	I STILL HAVEN'T FOUND WHAT I'M LOOKING FOR	Chimes (CBS)
27	DON'T WANNA FALL IN LOVE	Jane Child (Warner Bros)
28	YOU'VE GOT A FRIEND	Big Fun & Sonia featuring Gary Barnacle (Jive)
29	CLOSE TO YOU	Maxi Priest (10)
30	EVERYBODY, EVERYBODY	Black Box (deConstruction)
31	ROAM	B52's (Reprise)
32	TOUCHED BY THE HAND OF CICCIOLINA	Pop Will Eat Itself (RCA)
33	MONA	Craig McLachlan & Check 1-2 (Epic)
34	HOW CAN WE BE LOVERS	Michael Bolton (CBS)
35	VOGUE	Madonna (Sire)
36	TIME AFTER TIME	Beloved (East West)
37	VICTIMS OF SUCCESS	Dogs D'Amour (China)
38	THE MASTERPLAN	Diana Brown & Barrie K. Sharpe (ffrr)
39	ROCKIN' CHAIR	Magnum (Polydor)
40	MOVE AWAY JIMMY BLUE	Del Amitri (A&M)
41	TREAT ME GOOD	Yazz (Big Life)
42	OPPOSITES ATTRACT	Paula Abdul with the Wild Pair (Siren)
43	ALL THE YOUNG DUDES	Bruce Dickinson (EMI)
44	STILL GOT THE BLUES (FOR YOU)	Gary Moore (Virgin)
45	COVER GIRL	New Kids On The Block (CBS)
46	KISSING GATE	Sam Brown (A&M)
47	MESSAGE IN A BOX	World Party (Ensign)
48	THE GREAT SONG OF INDIFFERENCE	Bob Geldof (Mercury)
49	LOVING YOU	Massivo featuring Tracy (Debut)
50	REPUTATION	Dusty Springfield (Parlophone)

With the World Cup In Italy to be played in the summer of 1990, the release of a single by the England national team was almost a foregone conclusion. What was les expected, however, was that the project would be undertaken by hitmakers New Order, who produced what was probably the most credible football record of all time by combining their own talents with those of "the lads".

June – July 1990

last week / this week

30 June 1990

Last	This	Title	Artist (Label)
3	1	SACRIFICE/HEALING HANDS	Elton John (Rocket)
4	2	NESSUN DORMA	Luciano Pavarotti (Decca)
5	3	IT MUST HAVE BEEN LOVE	Roxette (EMI)
1	4	WORLD IN MOTION	England/New Order (Factory)
6	5	OOOPS UP	Snap! (Arista)
2	6	STEP BY STEP	New Kids On The Block (CBS)
12	7	THE ONLY RHYME THAT BITES	MC Tunes Vs. 808 State (ZTT)
8	8	HOLD ON	Wilson Phillips (SBK)
19	9	THINKING OF YOU	Maureen Walsh (Urban)
29	10	CLOSE TO YOU	Maxi Priest (10)
16	11	THE FREE STYLE MEGAMIX	Bobby Brown (MCA)
28	12	YOU'VE GOT A FRIEND	Big Fun & Sonia featuring Gary Barnacle (Jive)
7	13	HEAR THE DRUMMER (GET WICKED)	Chad Jackson (Big Wave)
33	14	MONA	Craig McLachlan & Check 1-2 (Epic)
25	15	U CAN'T TOUCH THIS	MC Hammer (Capitol)
10	16	THE ONLY ONE I KNOW	Charlatans (Situation Two)
9	17	KILLER	Adamski (MCA)
11	18	DOIN' THE BOO	Betty Boo (Rhythm King)
-	19	ANOTHER NIGHT	Jason Donovan (PWL)
41	20	TREAT ME GOOD	Yazz (Big Life)
21	21	WHOSE LAW (IS IT ANYWAY?)	Guru Josh (deConstruction)
13	22	VENUS	Don Pablo's Animals (Rumour)
43	23	ALL THE YOUNG DUDES	Bruce Dickinson (EMI)
14	24	DIRTY CASH	Adventures of Stevie V (Mercury)
18	25	IT'S MY LIFE	Talk Talk (Parlophone)
-	26	TASTE THE PAIN	Red Hot Chili Peppers (EMI-USA)
15	27	STAR	Erasure (Mute)
37	28	VICTIMS OF SUCCESS	Dogs D'Amour (China)
49	29	LOVING YOU	Massivo featuring Tracy (Debut)
20	30	PAPA WAS A ROLLING STONE	Was (Not Was) (Fontana)
17	31	YAAAH	D-Shake (Cooltempo)
39	32	ROCKIN' CHAIR	Magnum (Polydor)
-	33	SHE COMES IN THE FALL	Inspiral Carpets (Cow)
48	34	THE GREAT SONG OF INDIFFERENCE	Bob Geldof (Mercury)
22	35	BETTER THE DEVIL YOU KNOW	Kylie Minogue (PWL)
38	36	THE MASTERPLAN	Diana Brown & Barrie K. Sharpe (ffrr)
26	37	I STILL HAVEN'T FOUND WHAT I'M LOOKING FOR	Chimes (CBS)
40	38	MOVE AWAY JIMMY BLUE	Del Amitri (A&M)
23	39	HOLD ON	En Vogue (East West)
-	40	UNSKINNY BOP	Poison (Capitol)
47	41	MESSAGE IN A BOX	World Party (Ensign)
24	42	GIRL TO GIRL	49ers (Fourth & Broadway)
27	43	DON'T WANNA FALL IN LOVE	Jane Child (Warner Bros)
35	44	VOGUE	Madonna (Sire)
-	45	BROTHERS GONNA WORK IT OUT	Public Enemy (Def Jam)
-	46	LOVE DON'T LIVE HERE ANYMORE	Double Trouble (Desire)
31	47	ROAM	B52's (Reprise)
-	48	NOBODY'S CHILD	Traveling Wilburys (Wilbury)
36	49	TIME AFTER TIME	Beloved (East West)
-	50	SHE AIN'T WORTH IT	Glenn Medeiros featuring Bobby Brown (London)

7 July 1990

Last	This	Title	Artist (Label)
1	1	SACRIFICE/HEALING HANDS	Elton John (Rocket)
2	2	NESSUN DORMA	Luciano Pavarotti (Decca)
3	3	IT MUST HAVE BEEN LOVE	Roxette (EMI)
14	4	MONA	Craig McLachlan & Check 1-2 (Epic)
5	5	OOOPS UP	Snap! (Arista)
4	6	WORLD IN MOTION	England/New Order (Factory)
10	7	CLOSE TO YOU	Maxi Priest (10)
15	8	U CAN'T TOUCH THIS	MC Hammer (Capitol)
8	9	HOLD ON	Wilson Phillips (SBK)
7	10	THE ONLY RHYME THAT BITES	MC Tunes Vs. 808 State (ZTT)
9	11	THINKING OF YOU	Maureen Walsh (Urban)
12	12	YOU'VE GOT A FRIEND	Big Fun & Sonia featuring Gary Barnacle (Jive)
11	13	THE FREE STYLE MEGAMIX	Bobby Brown (MCA)
46	14	LOVE DON'T LIVE HERE ANYMORE	Double Trouble (Desire)
13	15	HEAR THE DRUMMER (GET WICKED)	Chad Jackson (Big Wave)
6	16	STEP BY STEP	New Kids On The Block (CBS)
20	17	TREAT ME GOOD	Yazz (Big Life)
19	18	ANOTHER NIGHT	Jason Donovan (PWL)
34	19	THE GREAT SONG OF INDIFFERENCE	Bob Geldof (Mercury)
18	20	DOIN' THE BOO	Betty Boo (Rhythm King)
29	21	LOVING YOU	Massivo featuring Tracy (Debut)
23	22	ALL THE YOUNG DUDES	Bruce Dickinson (EMI)
40	23	UNSKINNY BOP	Poison (Capitol)
17	24	KILLER	Adamski (MCA)
50	25	SHE AIN'T WORTH IT	Glenn Medeiros featuring Bobby Brown (London)
22	26	VENUS	Don Pablo's Animals (Rumour)
16	27	THE ONLY ONE I KNOW	Charlatans (Situation Two)
33	28	SHE COMES IN THE FALL	Inspiral Carpets (Cow)
-	29	THUNDERBIRDS ARE GO!	FAB featuring MC Parker (Brothers Organisation)
24	30	DIRTY CASH	Adventures of Stevie V (Mercury)
32	31	ROCKIN' CHAIR	Magnum (Polydor)
38	32	MOVE AWAY JIMMY BLUE	Del Amitri (A&M)
27	33	STAR	Erasure (Mute)
-	34	PSYKO FUNK	Boo Yaa Tribe (Fourth & Broadway)
28	35	VICTIMS OF SUCCESS	Dogs D'Amour (China)
-	36	COME HOME	James (Fontana)
25	37	IT'S MY LIFE	Talk Talk (Parlophone)
-	38	ALMOST HEAR YOU SIGH	Rolling Stones (Rolling Stones)
41	39	MESSAGE IN A BOX	World Party (Ensign)
-	40	I'M STILL WAITING	Diana Ross (Motown)
21	41	WHOSE LAW (IS IT ANYWAY?)	Guru Josh (deConstruction)
30	42	PAPA WAS A ROLLING STONE	Was (Not Was) (Fontana)
48	43	NOBODY'S CHILD	Traveling Wilburys (Wilbury)
-	44	DANGEROUS SEX	Tackhead (SBK)
-	45	CELEBRATE	An Emotional Fish (East West)
-	46	STRUNG OUT	Wendy & Lisa (Virgin)
36	47	THE MASTERPLAN	Diana Brown & Barrie K. Sharpe (ffrr)
-	48	CALIFORNIA DREAMIN'/CARRY THE BLAME	River City People (EMI)
-	49	BATTLE OF THE SEXES	Faith Hope & Charity (WEA)
26	50	TASTE THE PAIN	Red Hot Chili Peppers (EMI-USA)

14 July 1990

Last	This	Title	Artist (Label)
1	1	SACRIFICE/HEALING HANDS	Elton John (Rocket)
2	2	NESSUN DORMA	Luciano Pavarotti (Decca)
3	3	MONA	Craig McLachlan & Check 1-2 (Epic)
29	4	THUNDERBIRDS ARE GO!	FAB featuring MC Parker (Brothers Organisation)
-	5	ONE LOVE	Stone Roses (Silvertone)
8	6	U CAN'T TOUCH THIS	MC Hammer (Capitol)
3	7	IT MUST HAVE BEEN LOVE	Roxette (EMI)
7	8	CLOSE TO YOU	Maxi Priest (10)
6	9	WORLD IN MOTION	England/New Order (Factory)
5	10	OOOPS UP	Snap! (Arista)
11	11	THINKING OF YOU	Maureen Walsh (Urban)
14	12	LOVE DON'T LIVE HERE ANYMORE	Double Trouble (Desire)
10	13	THE ONLY RHYME THAT BITES	MC Tunes Vs. 808 State (ZTT)
19	14	THE GREAT SONG OF INDIFFERENCE	Bob Geldof (Mercury)
9	15	HOLD ON	Wilson Phillips (SBK)
25	16	SHE AIN'T WORTH IT	Glenn Medeiros featuring Bobby Brown (London)
23	17	UNSKINNY BOP	Poison (Capitol)
40	18	I'M STILL WAITING	Diana Ross (Motown)
-	19	ALRIGHT	Janet Jackson (A&M)
15	20	HEAR THE DRUMMER (GET WICKED)	Chad Jackson (Big Wave)
21	21	LOVING YOU	Massivo featuring Tracy (Debut)
18	22	ANOTHER NIGHT	Jason Donovan (PWL)
12	23	YOU'VE GOT A FRIEND	Big Fun & Sonia featuring Gary Barnacle (Jive)
20	24	DOIN' THE BOO	Betty Boo (Rhythm King)
28	25	SHE COMES IN THE FALL	Inspiral Carpets (Cow)
38	26	ALMOST HEAR YOU SIGH	Rolling Stones (Rolling Stones)
13	27	THE FREE STYLE MEGAMIX	Bobby Brown (MCA)
36	28	COME HOME	James (Fontana)
48	29	CALIFORNIA DREAMIN'/CARRY THE BLAME	River City People (EMI)
24	30	KILLER	Adamski (MCA)
17	31	TREAT ME GOOD	Yazz (Big Life)
32	32	MOVE AWAY JIMMY BLUE	Del Amitri (A&M)
22	33	ALL THE YOUNG DUDES	Bruce Dickinson (EMI)
39	34	MESSAGE IN A BOX	World Party (Ensign)
-	35	NAKED IN THE RAIN	Blue Pearl (Big Life)
16	36	STEP BY STEP	New Kids On The Block (CBS)
27	37	THE ONLY ONE I KNOW	Charlatans (Situation Two)
34	38	PSYKO FUNK	Boo Yaa Tribe (Fourth & Broadway)
26	39	VENUS	Don Pablo's Animals (Rumour)
-	40	FLOTATION	Grid (East West)
-	41	ROCKIN' OVER THE BEAT	Technotronic featuring Ya Kid K (Swanyard)
46	42	STRUNG OUT	Wendy & Lisa (Virgin)
45	43	CELEBRATE	An Emotional Fish (East West)
-	44	CHILDREN OF THE NIGHT	Richard Marx (EMI-USA)
30	45	DIRTY CASH	Adventures of Stevie V (Mercury)
-	46	FALLING TO PIECES	Faith No More (Slash)
-	47	OAKLAND STROKE	Tony! Toni! Tone! (Wing)
-	48	OH GIRL	Paul Young (CBS)
44	49	DANGEROUS SEX	Tackhead (SBK)
-	50	HEAVEN KNOWS	Cool Down Zone (10)

Pavarotti's rendition of *Nessun Dorma*, from Puccini's opera *Turandot*, was the inspired theme music choice for the BBC's World Cup coverage, and as a result the aria became the biggest-selling piece of unbowdlerised classical music ever in the UK. Pavarotti was only prevented from reaching Number One by Elton John's *Sacrifice*, his own all-time biggest UK seller.

July – August 1990

last week	this week	21 July 1990	
1	1	SACRIFICE/HEALING HANDS	Elton John (Rocket)
5	2	ONE LOVE	Stone Roses (Silvertone)
4	3	THUNDERBIRDS ARE GO!	FAB featuring MC Parker (Brothers Organisation)
2	4	NESSUN DORMA	Luciano Pavarotti (Decca)
3	5	MONA	Craig McLachlan & Check 1-2 (Epic)
6	6	U CAN'T TOUCH THIS	MC Hammer (Capitol)
16	7	SHE AIN'T WORTH IT	Glenn Medeiros featuring Bobby Brown (London)
7	8	IT MUST HAVE BEEN LOVE	Roxette (EMI)
8	9	CLOSE TO YOU	Maxi Priest (10)
19	10	ALRIGHT	Janet Jackson (A&M)
9	11	WORLD IN MOTION	England/New Order (Factory)
10	12	OOOPS UP	Snap! (Arista)
18	13	I'M STILL WAITING	Diana Ross (Motown)
12	14	LOVE DON'T LIVE HERE ANYMORE	Double Trouble (Desire)
17	15	UNSKINNY BOP	Poison (Capitol)
15	16	HOLD ON	Wilson Phillips (SBK)
41	17	ROCKIN' OVER THE BEAT	Technotronic featuring Ya Kid K (Swanyard)
13	18	THE ONLY RHYME THAT BITES	MC Tunes Vs. 808 State (ZTT)
–	19	I'M FREE	Soup Dragons (Raw TV)
–	20	HANKY PANKY	Madonna (Sire)
11	21	THINKING OF YOU	Maureen Walsh (Urban)
14	22	THE GREAT SONG OF INDIFFERENCE	Bob Geldof (Mercury)
35	23	NAKED IN THE RAIN	Blue Pearl (Big Life)
29	24	CALIFORNIA DREAMIN'/CARRY THE BLAME	River City People (EMI)
21	25	LOVING YOU	Massivo featuring Tracy (Debut)
26	26	ALMOST HEAR YOU SIGH	Rolling Stones (Rolling Stones)
24	27	DOIN' THE BOO	Betty Boo (Rhythm King)
20	28	SHAME ON YOU	Gun (A&M)
25	29	SHE COMES IN THE FALL	Inspiral Carpets (Cow)
30	30	KILLER	Adamski (MCA)
20	31	HEAR THE DRUMMER (GET WICKED)	Chad Jackson (Big Wave)
32	32	MOVE AWAY JIMMY BLUE	Del Amitri (A&M)
–	33	LFO	LFO (Warp)
22	34	ANOTHER NIGHT	Jason Donovan (PWL)
–	35	GIMME SOME LOVIN'	Thunder (EMI)
–	36	TURTLE POWER	Partners In Kryme (SBK)
48	37	OH GIRL	Paul Young (CBS)
42	38	STRUNG OUT	Wendy & Lisa (Virgin)
23	39	YOU'VE GOT A FRIEND	Big Fun & Sonia featuring Gary Barnacle (Jive)
46	40	FALLING TO PIECES	Faith No More (Slash)
–	41	POISON	Bell Biv Devoe (MCA)
–	42	WASH YOUR FACE IN MY SINK	Dream Warriors (Fourth & Broadway)
–	43	EMPEROR'S NEW CLOTHES	Sinead O'Connor (Ensign)
27	44	THE FREE STYLE MEGAMIX	Bobby Brown (MCA)
47	45	OAKLAND STROKE	Tony! Toni! Tone! (Wing)
36	46	STEP BY STEP	New Kids On The Block (CBS)
–	47	SILENT VOICE	Innocence (Cooltempo)
40	48	FLOTATION	Grid (East West)
–	49	MONIE IN THE MIDDLE	Monie Love (Cooltempo)
–	50	WHY CAN'T WE LIVE TOGETHER?	Timmy Thomas (TK)

		28 July 1990	
36	1	TURTLE POWER	Partners In Kryme (SBK)
1	2	SACRIFICE/HEALING HANDS	Elton John (Rocket)
5	3	MONA	Craig McLachlan & Check 1-2 (Epic)
3	4	THUNDERBIRDS ARE GO!	FAB featuring MC Parker (Brothers Organisation)
20	5	HANKY PANKY	Madonna (Sire)
6	6	U CAN'T TOUCH THIS	MC Hammer (Capitol)
4	7	NESSUN DORMA	Luciano Pavarotti (Decca)
7	8	SHE AIN'T WORTH IT	Glenn Medeiros featuring Bobby Brown (London)
23	9	NAKED IN THE RAIN	Blue Pearl (Big Life)
17	10	ROCKIN' OVER THE BEAT	Technotronic featuring Ya Kid K (Swanyard)
19	11	I'M FREE	Soup Dragons (Raw TV)
2	12	ONE LOVE	Stone Roses (Silvertone)
8	13	IT MUST HAVE BEEN LOVE	Roxette (EMI)
14	14	OOOPS UP	Snap! (Arista)
–	15	TOM'S DINER	DNA featuring Suzanne Vega (A&M)
24	16	CALIFORNIA DREAMIN'/CARRY THE BLAME	River City People (EMI)
9	17	CLOSE TO YOU	Maxi Priest (10)
11	18	WORLD IN MOTION	England/New Order (Factory)
16	19	HOLD ON	Wilson Phillips (SBK)
13	20	I'M STILL WAITING	Diana Ross (Motown)
–	21	KNOCKED OUT	Paula Abdul (Virgin America)
10	22	ALRIGHT	Janet Jackson (A&M)
42	23	WASH YOUR FACE IN MY SINK	Dream Warriors (Fourth & Broadway)
15	24	UNSKINNY BOP	Poison (Capitol)
21	25	THINKING OF YOU	Maureen Walsh (Urban)
41	26	POISON	Bell Biv Devoe (MCA)
18	27	THE ONLY RHYME THAT BITES	MC Tunes Vs. 808 State (ZTT)
14	28	LOVE DON'T LIVE HERE ANYMORE	Double Trouble (Desire)
29	29	SHE COMES IN THE FALL	Inspiral Carpets (Cow)
37	30	OH GIRL	Paul Young (CBS)
30	31	KILLER	Adamski (MCA)
27	32	DOIN' THE BOO	Betty Boo (Rhythm King)
33	33	LFO	LFO (Warp)
47	34	SILENT VOICE	Innocence (Cooltempo)
–	35	LIES	En Vogue (East West)
–	36	VELOURIA	Pixies (4AD)
28	37	SHAME ON YOU	Gun (A&M)
–	38	TRICKY DISCO	Tricky Disco (Warp)
43	39	EMPEROR'S NEW CLOTHES	Sinead O'Connor (Ensign)
26	40	ALMOST HEAR YOU SIGH	Rolling Stones (Rolling Stones)
–	41	DOUBLEBACK	ZZ Top (Warner Bros)
–	42	THAT'S JUST THE WAY IT IS	Phil Collins (Virgin)
25	43	LOVING YOU	Massivo featuring Tracy (Debut)
31	44	HEAR THE DRUMMER (GET WICKED)	Chad Jackson (Big Wave)
–	45	STARDATE 1990/RAINBOW CHILD	Dan Reed Network (Mercury)
–	46	DOIN' OUR OWN DANG	Jungle Brothers (Eternal)
35	47	GIMME SOME LOVIN'	Thunder (EMI)
48	48	I'M BACK ON MY FEET AGAIN	Michael Bolton (CBS)
49	49	MONIE IN THE MIDDLE	Monie Love (Cooltempo)
50	50	TRUE LOVE	Chimes (CBS)

		4 August 1990	
1	1	TURTLE POWER	Partners In Kryme (SBK)
5	2	HANKY PANKY	Madonna (Sire)
15	3	TOM'S DINER	DNA featuring Suzanne Vega (A&M)
2	4	SACRIFICE/HEALING HANDS	Elton John (Rocket)
9	5	NAKED IN THE RAIN	Blue Pearl (Big Life)
3	6	MONA	Craig McLachlan & Check 1-2 (Epic)
6	7	U CAN'T TOUCH THIS	MC Hammer (Capitol)
10	8	ROCKIN' OVER THE BEAT	Technotronic featuring Ya Kid K (Swanyard)
11	9	I'M FREE	Soup Dragons (Raw TV)
4	10	THUNDERBIRDS ARE GO!	FAB featuring MC Parker (Brothers Organisation)
23	11	WASH YOUR FACE IN MY SINK	Dream Warriors (Fourth & Broadway)
–	12	THIEVES IN THE TEMPLE	Prince (Paisley Park)
21	13	KNOCKED OUT	Paula Abdul (Virgin America)
13	14	IT MUST HAVE BEEN LOVE	Roxette (EMI)
33	15	LFO	LFO (Warp)
16	16	CALIFORNIA DREAMIN'/CARRY THE BLAME	River City People (EMI)
8	17	SHE AIN'T WORTH IT	Glenn Medeiros featuring Bobby Brown (London)
14	18	OOOPS UP	Snap! (Arista)
38	19	TRICKY DISCO	Tricky Disco (Warp)
7	20	NESSUN DORMA	Luciano Pavarotti (Decca)
39	21	EMPEROR'S NEW CLOTHES	Sinead O'Connor (Ensign)
–	22	ONLY YOUR LOVE	Bananarama (London)
17	23	CLOSE TO YOU	Maxi Priest (10)
26	24	POISON	Bell Biv Devoe (MCA)
36	25	VELOURIA	Pixies (4AD)
–	26	ITSY BITSY TEENY WEENY YELLOW POLKA DOT BIKINI	Bombalurina (Carpet)
18	27	WORLD IN MOTION	England/New Order (Factory)
42	28	THAT'S JUST THE WAY IT IS	Phil Collins (Virgin)
–	29	HARDCORE UPROAR	Together (ffrr)
41	30	DOUBLEBACK	ZZ Top (Warner Bros)
12	31	ONE LOVE	Stone Roses (Silvertone)
–	32	TONIGHT	New Kids On The Block (CBS)
45	33	STARDATE 1990/RAINBOW CHILD	Dan Reed Network (Mercury)
34	34	SILENT VOICE	Innocence (Cooltempo)
–	35	HOW MUCH LOVE	Vixen (EMI-USA)
50	36	TRUE LOVE	Chimes (CBS)
–	37	I CAN SEE CLEARLY NOW	Hothouse Flowers (London)
19	38	HOLD ON	Wilson Phillips (SBK)
30	39	OH GIRL	Paul Young (CBS)
–	40	KING OF WISHFUL THINKING	Go West (Chrysalis)
20	41	I'M STILL WAITING	Diana Ross (Motown)
–	42	I DIDN'T WANT TO NEED YOU	Heart (Capitol)
–	43	FOR HER LIGHT	Fields of the Nephilim (Beggars Banquet)
–	44	AMANDA	Craig McLachlan & Check 1-2 (Epic)
–	45	WEAR YOU TO THE BALL	UB40 (DEP International)
24	46	UNSKINNY BOP	Poison (Capitol)
–	47	LAMBORGHINI/CHANGE SOON COME	Shut Up And Dance (Shut Up And Dance)
31	48	KILLER	Adamski (MCA)
–	49	VIOLENCE OF SUMMER (LOVE'S TAKING OVER)	Duran Duran (Parlophone)
22	50	ALRIGHT	Janet Jackson (A&M)

Children's favourites found a hold on the mid-summer charts, as *Turtle Power* (from the kids' film *Teenage Mutant Ninja Turtles*) made an extraordinary leap to Number One, and FAB's *Thunderbirds Are Go!* (with Parker finding new fame as a rapper) also reached the Top 10. Rather more adult was Madonna's *Hanky Panky* (from the movie *Dick Tracy*), which had a mention or two of spanking!

521

August 1990

11 August 1990

last week	this week	Title	Artist
1	1	TURTLE POWER	Partners In Kryme (SBK)
3	2	TOM'S DINER	DNA featuring Suzanne Vega (A&M)
2	3	HANKY PANKY	Madonna (Sire)
5	4	NAKED IN THE RAIN	Blue Pearl (Big Life)
7	5	U CAN'T TOUCH THIS	MC Hammer (Capitol)
4	6	SACRIFICE/HEALING HANDS	Elton John (Rocket)
26	7	ITSY BITSY TEENY WEENY YELLOW POLKA DOT BIKINI	Bombalurina (Carpet)
12	8	THIEVES IN THE TEMPLE	Prince (Paisley Park)
9	9	I'M FREE	Soup Dragons (Raw TV)
10	10	LFO	LFO (Warp)
11	11	WASH YOUR FACE IN MY SINK	Dream Warriors (Fourth & Broadway)
6	12	MONA	Craig McLachlan & Check 1-2 (Epic)
8	13	ROCKIN' OVER THE BEAT	Technotronic featuring Ya Kid K (Swanyard)
19	14	TRICKY DISCO	Tricky Disco (Warp)
32	15	TONIGHT	New Kids On The Block (CBS)
16	16	CALIFORNIA DREAMIN'/CARRY THE BLAME	River City People (EMI)
24	17	POISON	Bell Biv Devoe (MCA)
29	18	HARDCORE UPROAR	Together (ffrr)
49	19	VIOLENCE OF SUMMER (LOVE'S TAKING OVER)	Duran Duran (Parlophone)
14	20	IT MUST HAVE BEEN LOVE	Roxette (EMI)
28	21	THAT'S JUST THE WAY IT IS	Phil Collins (Virgin)
22	22	ONLY YOUR LOVE	Bananarama (London)
44	23	AMANDA	Craig McLachlan & Check 1-2 (Epic)
-	24	BLAZE OF GLORY	Jon Bon Jovi (Vertigo)
-	25	SHE'S A LITTLE ANGEL	Little Angels (Polydor)
10	26	THUNDERBIRDS ARE GO!	FAB featuring MC Parker (Brothers Organisation)
30	27	DOUBLEBACK	ZZ Top (Warner Bros)
13	28	KNOCKED OUT	Paula Abdul (Virgin America)
37	29	I CAN SEE CLEARLY NOW	Hothouse Flowers (London)
18	30	OOOPS UP	Snap! (Arista)
21	31	EMPEROR'S NEW CLOTHES	Sinead O'Connor (Ensign)
17	32	SHE AIN'T WORTH IT	Glenn Medeiros featuring Bobby Brown (London)
31	33	ONE LOVE	Stone Roses (Silvertone)
34	34	SILENT VOICE	Innocence (Cooltempo)
-	35	NOBODY	Tongue 'N' Cheek (Syncopate)
20	36	NESSUN DORMA	Luciano Pavarotti (Decca)
-	37	WHAT TIME IS LOVE?	KLF featuring the Children of the Revolution (KLF Communications)
40	38	KING OF WISHFUL THINKING	Go West (Chrysalis)
-	39	DOIN' OUR OWN DANG	Jungle Brothers (Eternal)
27	40	WORLD IN MOTION	England/New Order (Factory)
23	41	CLOSE TO YOU	Maxi Priest (10)
-	42	LISTEN TO YOUR HEART/DANGEROUS	Roxette (EMI)
45	43	WEAR YOU TO THE BALL	UB40 (DEP International)
-	44	AN ENGLISHMAN IN NEW YORK	Sting (A&M)
33	45	STARDATE 1990/RAINBOW CHILD	Dan Reed Network (Mercury)
-	46	PURE	GTO (Cooltempo)
-	47	SILLY GAMES	Lindy Layton featuring Janet Kay (Arista)
42	48	I DIDN'T WANT TO NEED YOU	Heart (Capitol)
-	49	WHERE ARE YOU BABY?	Betty Boo (Rhythm King)
38	50	HOLD ON	Wilson Phillips (SBK)

18 August 1990

last week	this week	Title	Artist
2	1	TOM'S DINER	DNA featuring Suzanne Vega (A&M)
1	2	TURTLE POWER	Partners In Kryme (SBK)
4	3	NAKED IN THE RAIN	Blue Pearl (Big Life)
5	4	U CAN'T TOUCH THIS	MC Hammer (Capitol)
7	5	ITSY BITSY TEENY WEENY YELLOW POLKA DOT BIKINI	Bombalurina (Carpet)
15	6	TONIGHT	New Kids On The Block (CBS)
8	7	THIEVES IN THE TEMPLE	Prince (Paisley Park)
9	8	I'M FREE	Soup Dragons (Raw TV)
42	9	LISTEN TO YOUR HEART/DANGEROUS	Roxette (EMI)
10	10	LFO	LFO (Warp)
6	11	SACRIFICE/HEALING HANDS	Elton John (Rocket)
3	12	HANKY PANKY	Madonna (Sire)
13	13	ROCKIN' OVER THE BEAT	Technotronic featuring Ya Kid K (Swanyard)
44	14	AN ENGLISHMAN IN NEW YORK	Sting (A&M)
37	15	WHAT TIME IS LOVE?	KLF featuring the Children of the Revolution (KLF Communications)
14	16	TRICKY DISCO	Tricky Disco (Warp)
24	17	BLAZE OF GLORY	Jon Bon Jovi (Vertigo)
18	18	HARDCORE UPROAR	Together (ffrr)
11	19	WASH YOUR FACE IN MY SINK	Dream Warriors (Fourth & Broadway)
16	20	CALIFORNIA DREAMIN'/CARRY THE BLAME	River City People (EMI)
12	21	MONA	Craig McLachlan & Check 1-2 (Epic)
-	22	COME TOGETHER	Primal Scream (Creation)
23	23	AMANDA	Craig McLachlan & Check 1-2 (Epic)
49	24	WHERE ARE YOU BABY?	Betty Boo (Rhythm King)
29	25	I CAN SEE CLEARLY NOW	Hothouse Flowers (London)
17	26	POISON	Bell Biv Devoe (MCA)
19	27	VIOLENCE OF SUMMER (LOVE'S TAKING OVER)	Duran Duran (Parlophone)
-	28	STAY WITH ME HEARTACHE/I FEEL FINE	Wet Wet Wet (Precious)
20	29	IT MUST HAVE BEEN LOVE	Roxette (EMI)
-	30	LOOK ME IN THE HEART	Tina Turner (Capitol)
21	31	THAT'S JUST THE WAY IT IS	Phil Collins (Virgin)
38	32	KING OF WISHFUL THINKING	Go West (Chrysalis)
47	33	SILLY GAMES	Lindy Layton featuring Janet Kay (Arista)
35	34	NOBODY	Tongue 'N' Cheek (Syncopate)
27	35	DOUBLEBACK	ZZ Top (Warner Bros)
39	36	DOIN' OUR OWN DANG	Jungle Brothers (Eternal)
-	37	BEYOND YOUR WILDEST DREAMS	Lonnie Gordon (Supreme)
38	38	VISION OF LOVE	Mariah Carey (CBS)
-	39	LET LOVE RULE	Lenny Kravitz (Virgin America)
26	40	THUNDERBIRDS ARE GO!	FAB featuring MC Parker (Brothers Organisation)
-	41	I'M BACK ON MY FEET AGAIN	Michael Bolton (CBS)
43	42	WEAR YOU TO THE BALL	UB40 (DEP International)
-	43	BONITA APPLEBUM	A Tribe Called Quest (Jive)
30	44	OOOPS UP	Snap! (Arista)
25	45	SHE'S A LITTLE ANGEL	Little Angels (Polydor)
32	46	SHE AIN'T WORTH IT	Glenn Medeiros featuring Bobby Brown (London)
22	47	ONLY YOUR LOVE	Bananarama (London)
-	48	HOW THE HEART BEHAVES	Was (Not Was) (Fontana)
34	49	SILENT VOICE	Innocence (Cooltempo)
-	50	CLUB AT THE END OF THE STREET/WHISPERS	Elton John (Rocket)

25 August 1990

last week	this week	Title	Artist
1	1	TOM'S DINER	DNA featuring Suzanne Vega (A&M)
5	2	ITSY BITSY TEENY WEENY YELLOW POLKA DOT BIKINI	Bombalurina (Carpet)
2	3	TURTLE POWER	Partners In Kryme (SBK)
9	4	LISTEN TO YOUR HEART/DANGEROUS	Roxette (EMI)
3	5	NAKED IN THE RAIN	Blue Pearl (Big Life)
6	6	TONIGHT	New Kids On The Block (CBS)
4	7	U CAN'T TOUCH THIS	MC Hammer (Capitol)
8	8	I'M FREE	Soup Dragons (Raw TV)
24	9	WHERE ARE YOU BABY?	Betty Boo (Rhythm King)
14	10	AN ENGLISHMAN IN NEW YORK	Sting (A&M)
17	11	BLAZE OF GLORY	Jon Bon Jovi (Vertigo)
15	12	WHAT TIME IS LOVE?	KLF featuring the Children of the Revolution (KLF Communications)
-	13	PRAYING FOR TIME	George Michael (Epic)
7	14	THIEVES IN THE TEMPLE	Prince (Paisley Park)
18	15	HARDCORE UPROAR	Together (ffrr)
38	16	VISION OF LOVE	Mariah Carey (CBS)
16	17	TRICKY DISCO	Tricky Disco (Warp)
-	18	FOUR BACHARACH AND DAVID SONGS (EP)	Deacon Blue (CBS)
22	19	COME TOGETHER	Primal Scream (Creation)
10	20	LFO	LFO (Warp)
32	21	KING OF WISHFUL THINKING	Go West (Chrysalis)
12	22	HANKY PANKY	Madonna (Sire)
11	23	SACRIFICE/HEALING HANDS	Elton John (Rocket)
33	24	SILLY GAMES	Lindy Layton featuring Janet Kay (Arista)
25	25	I CAN SEE CLEARLY NOW	Hothouse Flowers (London)
23	26	AMANDA	Craig McLachlan & Check 1-2 (Epic)
-	27	HEART LIKE A WHEEL	Human League (Virgin)
26	28	POISON	Bell Biv Devoe (MCA)
13	29	ROCKIN' OVER THE BEAT	Technotronic featuring Ya Kid K (Swanyard)
30	30	LOOK ME IN THE HEART	Tina Turner (Capitol)
20	31	CALIFORNIA DREAMIN'/CARRY THE BLAME	River City People (EMI)
28	32	STAY WITH ME HEARTACHE/I FEEL FINE	Wet Wet Wet (Precious)
-	33	SILHOUETTES	Cliff Richard (EMI)
-	34	RELEASE ME	Wilson Phillips (SBK)
-	35	CAN YOU PARTY	Jive Bunny & the Mastermixers (Music Factory Dance)
-	36	THE JOKER	Steve Miller Band (Capitol)
-	37	LA SERENISSIMA	DNA (Raw Bass)
19	38	WASH YOUR FACE IN MY SINK	Dream Warriors (Fourth & Broadway)
39	39	NEXT TO YOU	Aswad featuring Long MC (Mango)
43	40	BONITA APPLEBUM	A Tribe Called Quest (Jive)
29	41	IT MUST HAVE BEEN LOVE	Roxette (EMI)
-	42	DIVE! DIVE! DIVE!	Bruce Dickinson (EMI)
36	43	DOIN' OUR OWN DANG	Jungle Brothers (Eternal)
-	44	LOOKING FOR ATLANTIS	Prefab Sprout (Kitchenware)
50	45	CLUB AT THE END OF THE STREET/WHISPERS	Elton John (Rocket)
34	46	NOBODY	Tongue 'N' Cheek (Syncopate)
21	47	MONA	Craig McLachlan & Check 1-2 (Epic)
41	48	I'M BACK ON MY FEET AGAIN	Michael Bolton (CBS)
48	49	HOW THE HEART BEHAVES	Was (Not Was) (Fontana)
-	50	GROOVE IS IN THE HEART/WHAT IS LOVE?	Deee-Lite (Elektra)

DNA's rhythm cut-up of Suzanne Vega's accoustic piece *Tom's Diner* was originally a bootleg, circulated to clubs and rave events where it created a sensation. When Vega got to hear the offending article via her record company, however, she approved of the project, and A&M took the recording over, restoring Vega's own name jointly to the record's credits, and hitting Number One.

1 September 1990

last week	this week	title / artist
2	1	ITSY BITSY TEENY WEENY YELLOW POLKA DOT BIKINI Bombalurina (Carpet)
1	2	TOM'S DINER DNA featuring Suzanne Vega (A&M)
13	3	PRAYING FOR TIME George Michael (Epic)
4	4	LISTEN TO YOUR HEART/DANGEROUS Roxette (EMI)
18	5	FOUR BACHARACH AND DAVID SONGS (EP) Deacon Blue (CBS)
9	6	WHERE ARE YOU BABY? Betty Boo (Rhythm King)
5	7	NAKED IN THE RAIN Blue Pearl (Big Life)
35	8	CAN CAN YOU PARTY Jive Bunny & the Mastermixers (Music Factory Dance)
3	9	TURTLE POWER Partners In Kryme (SBK)
6	10	TONIGHT New Kids On The Block (CBS)
12	11	WHAT TIME IS LOVE? KLF featuring the Children of the Revolution (KLF Communications)
7	12	U CAN'T TOUCH THIS MC Hammer (Capitol)
10	13	AN ENGLISHMAN IN NEW YORK Sting (A&M)
16	14	VISION OF LOVE Mariah Carey (CBS)
11	15	BLAZE OF GLORY Jon Bon Jovi (Vertigo)
33	16	SILHOUETTES Cliff Richard (EMI)
15	17	HARDCORE UPROAR Together (ffrr)
21	18	KING OF WISHFUL THINKING Go West (Chrysalis)
8	19	I'M FREE Soup Dragons (Raw TV)
27	20	HEART LIKE A WHEEL Human League (Virgin)
50	21	GROOVE IS IN THE HEART/WHAT IS LOVE? Deee-Lite (Elektra)
24	22	SILLY GAMES Lindy Layton featuring Janet Kay (Arista)
36	23	THE JOKER Steve Miller Band (Capitol)
17	24	TRICKY DISCO Tricky Disco (Warp)
30	25	LOOK ME IN THE HEART Tina Turner (Capitol)
26	26	AMANDA Craig McLachlan & Check 1-2 (Epic)
39	27	NEXT TO YOU Aswad featuring Long MC (Mango)
23	28	SACRIFICE/HEALING HANDS Elton John (Rocket)
-	29	NOW YOU'RE GONE Whitesnake (EMI)
34	30	RELEASE ME Wilson Phillips (SBK)
19	31	COME TOGETHER Primal Scream (Creation)
-	32	RHYTHM OF THE RAIN Jason Donovan (PWL)
-	33	END OF THE WORLD Sonia (Chrysalis/PWL)
14	34	THIEVES IN THE TEMPLE Prince (Paisley Park)
20	35	LFO LFO (Warp)
37	36	LA SERENISSIMA DNA (Raw Bass)
-	37	IN MY WORLD Anthrax (Island)
22	38	HANKY PANKY Madonna (Sire)
42	39	DIVE! DIVE! DIVE! Bruce Dickinson (EMI)
-	40	DON'T BE A FOOL Loose Ends (10)
45	41	CLUB AT THE END OF THE STREET/WHISPERS Elton John (Rocket)
25	42	I CAN SEE CLEARLY NOW Hothouse Flowers (London)
-	43	THE RIGHT COMBINATION Seiko & Donnie Wahlberg (Epic)
28	44	POISON Bell Biv Devoe (MCA)
-	45	GROOVY TRAIN Farm (Produce)
31	46	CALIFORNIA DREAMIN'/CARRY THE BLAME River City People (EMI)
29	47	ROCKIN' OVER THE BEAT Technotronic featuring Ya Kid K (Swanyard)
-	48	WALKING BY MYSELF Gary Moore (Virgin)
44	49	LOOKING FOR ATLANTIS Prefab Sprout (Kitchenware)
-	50	GANGSTA GANGSTA NWA (Fourth & Broadway)

8 September 1990

this week	title / artist
1	ITSY BITSY TEENY WEENY YELLOW POLKA DOT BIKINI Bombalurina (Carpet)
2	FOUR BACHARACH AND DAVID SONGS (EP) Deacon Blue (CBS)
3	GROOVE IS IN THE HEART/WHAT IS LOVE? Deee-Lite (Elektra)
4	PRAYING FOR TIME George Michael (Epic)
5	WHERE ARE YOU BABY? Betty Boo (Rhythm King)
6	THE JOKER Steve Miller Band (Capitol)
7	CAN CAN YOU PARTY Jive Bunny & the Mastermixers (Music Factory Dance)
8	SILHOUETTES Cliff Richard (EMI)
9	TOM'S DINER DNA featuring Suzanne Vega (A&M)
10	TONIGHT New Kids On The Block (CBS)
11	LISTEN TO YOUR HEART/DANGEROUS Roxette (EMI)
12	NAKED IN THE RAIN Blue Pearl (Big Life)
13	VISION OF LOVE Mariah Carey (CBS)
14	WHAT TIME IS LOVE? KLF featuring the Children of the Revolution (KLF Communications)
15	NEXT TO YOU Aswad featuring Long MC (Mango)
16	RHYTHM OF THE RAIN Jason Donovan (PWL)
17	TURTLE POWER Partners In Kryme (SBK)
18	KING OF WISHFUL THINKING Go West (Chrysalis)
19	SILLY GAMES Lindy Layton featuring Janet Kay (Arista)
20	END OF THE WORLD Sonia (Chrysalis/PWL)
21	IN MY WORLD Anthrax (Island)
22	U CAN'T TOUCH THIS MC Hammer (Capitol)
23	DON'T BE A FOOL Loose Ends (10)
24	AN ENGLISHMAN IN NEW YORK Sting (A&M)
25	BLAZE OF GLORY Jon Bon Jovi (Vertigo)
26	LIFE'S WHAT YOU MAKE IT Talk Talk (Parlophone)
27	I'M FREE Soup Dragons (Raw TV)
28	GROOVY TRAIN Farm (Produce)
29	THE SPACE JUNGLE Adamski (MCA)
30	HARDCORE UPROAR Together (ffrr)
31	NOW YOU'RE GONE Whitesnake (EMI)
32	COME TOGETHER Primal Scream (Creation)
33	HEART LIKE A WHEEL Human League (Virgin)
34	PEACE THROUGHOUT THE WORLD Maxi Priest featuring Jazzie B (10)
35	LOOK ME IN THE HEART Tina Turner (Capitol)
36	LA SERENISSIMA DNA (Raw Bass)
37	TRICKY DISCO Tricky Disco (Warp)
38	ICEBLINK LUCK Cocteau Twins (4AD)
39	RELEASE ME Wilson Phillips (SBK)
40	THE OTHER SIDE Aerosmith (Geffen)
41	I'VE BEEN THINKING ABOUT YOU Londonbeat (AnXious)
42	EPIC Faith No More (Slash)
43	THE RIGHT COMBINATION Seiko & Donnie Wahlberg (Epic)
44	SACRIFICE/HEALING HANDS Elton John (Rocket)
45	WALKING BY MYSELF Gary Moore (Virgin)
46	AMANDA Craig McLachlan & Check 1-2 (Epic)
47	ROLLERCOASTER (EP) Jesus & Mary Chain (blanco y negro)
48	HEY VENUS That Petrol Emotion (Virgin)
49	FASCINATING RHYTHM Bass-o-matic (Virgin)
50	THIEVES IN THE TEMPLE Prince (Paisley Park)

15 September 1990

last week	this week	title / artist
3	1	GROOVE IS IN THE HEART/WHAT IS LOVE? Deee-Lite (Elektra)
2	2	FOUR BACHARACH AND DAVID SONGS (EP) Deacon Blue (CBS)
1	3	ITSY BITSY TEENY WEENY YELLOW POLKA DOT BIKINI Bombalurina (Carpet)
6	4	THE JOKER Steve Miller Band (Capitol)
5	5	WHERE ARE YOU BABY? Betty Boo (Rhythm King)
14	6	WHAT TIME IS LOVE? KLF featuring the Children of the Revolution (KLF Communications)
16	7	RHYTHM OF THE RAIN Jason Donovan (PWL)
29	8	THE SPACE JUNGLE Adamski (MCA)
13	9	VISION OF LOVE Mariah Carey (CBS)
4	10	PRAYING FOR TIME George Michael (Epic)
23	11	DON'T BE A FOOL Loose Ends (10)
10	12	TONIGHT New Kids On The Block (CBS)
12	13	NAKED IN THE RAIN Blue Pearl (Big Life)
-	14	LIVIN' IN THE LIGHT Caron Wheeler (RCA)
15	15	NEXT TO YOU Aswad featuring Long MC (Mango)
7	16	CAN CAN YOU PARTY Jive Bunny & the Mastermixers (Music Factory Dance)
9	17	TOM'S DINER DNA featuring Suzanne Vega (A&M)
20	18	END OF THE WORLD Sonia (Chrysalis/PWL)
8	19	SILHOUETTES Cliff Richard (EMI)
-	20	SUICIDE BLONDE INXS (Mercury)
11	21	LISTEN TO YOUR HEART/DANGEROUS Roxette (EMI)
-	22	BLACK CAT Janet Jackson (A&M)
18	23	KING OF WISHFUL THINKING Go West (Chrysalis)
28	24	GROOVY TRAIN Farm (Produce)
26	25	LIFE'S WHAT YOU MAKE IT Talk Talk (Parlophone)
49	26	FASCINATING RHYTHM Bass-o-matic (Virgin)
38	27	ICEBLINK LUCK Cocteau Twins (4AD)
22	28	U CAN'T TOUCH THIS MC Hammer (Capitol)
42	29	EPIC Faith No More (Slash)
17	30	TURTLE POWER Partners In Kryme (SBK)
27	31	I'M FREE Soup Dragons (Raw TV)
36	32	LA SERENISSIMA DNA (Raw Bass)
19	33	SILLY GAMES Lindy Layton featuring Janet Kay (Arista)
34	34	PEACE THROUGHOUT THE WORLD Maxi Priest featuring Jazzie B (10)
25	35	BLAZE OF GLORY Jon Bon Jovi (Vertigo)
-	36	NOTHING TO LOSE S'Express (Rhythm King)
-	37	GET ME OUT New Model Army (EMI)
24	38	AN ENGLISHMAN IN NEW YORK Sting (A&M)
30	39	HARDCORE UPROAR Together (ffrr)
-	40	LOVER/MONEY Dan Reed Network (Mercury)
41	41	I'VE BEEN THINKING ABOUT YOU Londonbeat (AnXious)
47	42	ROLLERCOASTER (EP) Jesus & Mary Chain (blanco y negro)
32	43	COME TOGETHER Primal Scream (Creation)
-	44	BURUNDI BLUES Beats International featuring Janet Kay (Go Beat)
35	45	LOOK ME IN THE HEART Tina Turner (Capitol)
-	46	HARD TO HANDLE Black Crowes (Def American)
31	47	NOW YOU'RE GONE Whitesnake (EMI)
-	48	THERE SHE GOES AGAIN Quireboys (Parlophone)
33	49	HEART LIKE A WHEEL Human League (Virgin)
-	50	SHOW ME HEAVEN Maria McKee (Epic)

Bombalurina was a cover name for TV children's entertainer Timmy Mallet, whose lowest-common-denominator revival of Brian Hyland's 1960 debut hit turned enough heads during the summer holiday silly season to send it to Number One. Perched behind it, and the biggest-selling EP for a long time, was Deacon Blue's unexpected four-track set of covers of Bacharach/David '60s classics.

September – October 1990

22 September 1990

4	1	THE JOKER	Steve Miller Band (Capitol)
1	2	GROOVE IS IN THE HEART/WHAT IS LOVE?	Deee-Lite (Elektra)
8	3	THE SPACE JUNGLE	Adamski (MCA)
6	4	WHAT TIME IS LOVE?	KLF featuring the Children of the Revolution (KLF Communications)
2	5	FOUR BACHARACH AND DAVID SONGS (EP)	Deacon Blue (CBS)
24	6	GROOVY TRAIN	Farm (Produce)
-	7	HOLY SMOKE	Iron Maiden (EMI)
9	8	VISION OF LOVE	Mariah Carey (CBS)
14	9	LIVIN' IN THE LIGHT	Caron Wheeler (RCA)
20	10	SUICIDE BLONDE	INXS (Mercury)
11	11	DON'T BE A FOOL	Loose Ends (10)
3	12	ITSY BITSY TEENY WEENY YELLOW POLKA DOT BIKINI	Bombalurina (Carpet)
50	13	SHOW ME HEAVEN	Maria McKee (Epic)
22	14	BLACK CAT	Janet Jackson (A&M)
5	15	WHERE ARE YOU BABY?	Betty Boo (Rhythm King)
26	16	FASCINATING RHYTHM	Bass-o-matic (Virgin)
10	17	PRAYING FOR TIME	George Michael (Epic)
41	18	I'VE BEEN THINKING ABOUT YOU	Londonbeat (AnXious)
7	19	RHYTHM OF THE RAIN	Jason Donovan (PWL)
12	20	TONIGHT	New Kids On The Block (CBS)
25	21	LIFE'S WHAT YOU MAKE IT	Talk Talk (Parlophone)
13	22	NAKED IN THE RAIN	Blue Pearl (Big Life)
-	23	THEN	Charlatans (Situation Two)
18	24	END OF THE WORLD	Sonia (Chrysalis/PWL)
-	25	FOOL'S GOLD	Stone Roses (Silvertone)
29	26	EPIC	Faith No More (Slash)
-	27	THUNDERSTRUCK	AC/DC (Atco)
21	28	LISTEN TO YOUR HEART/DANGEROUS	Roxette (EMI)
36	29	NOTHING TO LOSE	S'Express (Rhythm King)
17	30	TOM'S DINER	DNA featuring Suzanne Vega (A&M)
32	31	LA SERENISSIMA	DNA (Raw Bass)
27	32	ICEBLINK LUCK	Cocteau Twins (4AD)
-	33	CULT OF SNAP	Snap! (Arista)
19	34	SILHOUETTES	Cliff Richard (EMI)
-	35	TUNES SPLIT THE ATOM	MC Tunes Vs. 808 State (ZTT)
16	36	CAN YOU PARTY	Jive Bunny & the Mastermixers (Music Factory Dance)
48	37	THERE SHE GOES AGAIN	Quireboys (Parlophone)
44	38	BURUNDI BLUES	Beats International featuring Janet Kay (Go Beat)
23	39	KING OF WISHFUL THINKING	Go West (Chrysalis)
31	40	I'M FREE	Soup Dragons (Raw TV)
15	41	NEXT TO YOU	Aswad featuring Long MC (Mango)
40	42	LOVER/MONEY	Dan Reed Network (Mercury)
28	43	U CAN'T TOUCH THIS	MC Hammer (Capitol)
-	44	I CAN'T STAND IT	24/7 featuring Captain Hollywood (BCM)
30	45	TURTLE POWER	Partners In Kryme (SBK)
46	46	HARD TO HANDLE	Black Crowes (Def American)
33	47	SILLY GAMES	Lindy Layton featuring Janet Kay (Arista)
-	48	WOW WOW - NA NA	Grand Plaz (Urban)
35	49	BLAZE OF GLORY	Jon Bon Jovi (Vertigo)
-	50	TIMELESS MELODY	La's (Go! Discs)

29 September 1990

1	1	THE JOKER	Steve Miller Band (Capitol)
13	2	SHOW ME HEAVEN	Maria McKee (Epic)
2	3	GROOVE IS IN THE HEART/WHAT IS LOVE?	Deee-Lite (Elektra)
7	4	HOLY SMOKE	Iron Maiden (EMI)
18	5	I'VE BEEN THINKING ABOUT YOU	Londonbeat (AnXious)
4	6	WHAT TIME IS LOVE?	KLF featuring the Children of the Revolution (KLF Communications)
16	7	FASCINATING RHYTHM	Bass-o-matic (Virgin)
10	8	SUICIDE BLONDE	INXS (Mercury)
6	9	GROOVY TRAIN	Farm (Produce)
3	10	THE SPACE JUNGLE	Adamski (MCA)
33	11	CULT OF SNAP	Snap! (Arista)
23	12	THEN	Charlatans (Situation Two)
5	13	FOUR BACHARACH AND DAVID SONGS (EP)	Deacon Blue (CBS)
14	14	BLACK CAT	Janet Jackson (A&M)
8	15	VISION OF LOVE	Mariah Carey (CBS)
44	16	I CAN'T STAND IT	24/7 featuring Captain Hollywood (BCM)
12	17	ITSY BITSY TEENY WEENY YELLOW POLKA DOT BIKINI	Bombalurina (Carpet)
27	18	THUNDERSTRUCK	AC/DC (Atco)
9	19	LIVIN' IN THE LIGHT	Caron Wheeler (RCA)
25	20	FOOL'S GOLD	Stone Roses (Silvertone)
11	21	DON'T BE A FOOL	Loose Ends (10)
15	22	WHERE ARE YOU BABY?	Betty Boo (Rhythm King)
35	23	TUNES SPLIT THE ATOM	MC Tunes Vs. 808 State (ZTT)
-	24	NEVER ENOUGH	Cure (Fiction)
26	25	EPIC	Faith No More (Slash)
-	26	IT'S A SHAME (MY SISTER)	Monie Love featuring True Image (Cooltempo)
29	27	NOTHING TO LOSE	S'Express (Rhythm King)
-	28	BLUE VELVET	Bobby Vinton (Epic)
-	29	(WHAT'S WRONG WITH) DREAMING	River City People (EMI)
-	30	WORLD IN MY EYES	Depeche Mode (Mute)
31	31	LA SERENISSIMA	DNA (Raw Bass)
20	32	TONIGHT	New Kids On The Block (CBS)
-	33	HOLY WARS ... THE PUNISHMENT DUE	Megadeth (Capitol)
22	34	NAKED IN THE RAIN	Blue Pearl (Big Life)
-	35	FALL (EP)	Ride (Creation)
48	36	WOW WOW - NA NA	Grand Plaz (Urban)
-	37	MAKE IT MINE	Shamen (One Little Indian)
17	38	PRAYING FOR TIME	George Michael (Epic)
-	39	3 SONGS	Wedding Present (RCA)
28	40	LISTEN TO YOUR HEART/DANGEROUS	Roxette (EMI)
-	41	I'VE GOT YOU UNDER MY SKIN	Neneh Cherry (Circa)
-	42	YOU'RE WALKING	Electribe 101 (Mercury)
19	43	RHYTHM OF THE RAIN	Jason Donovan (PWL)
24	44	END OF THE WORLD	Sonia (Chrysalis/PWL)
-	45	DO ME!	Bell Biv Devoe (MCA)
21	46	LIFE'S WHAT YOU MAKE IT	Talk Talk (Parlophone)
38	47	BURUNDI BLUES	Beats International featuring Janet Kay (Go Beat)
-	48	ROCK'N'ROLL NIGGER	Birdland (Lazy)
-	49	OMEN	Orbital (ffrr)
-	50	COMING BACK FOR MORE	LA Mix (A&M)

6 October 1990

2	1	SHOW ME HEAVEN	Maria McKee (Epic)
28	2	BLUE VELVET	Bobby Vinton (Epic)
5	3	I'VE BEEN THINKING ABOUT YOU	Londonbeat (AnXious)
1	4	THE JOKER	Steve Miller Band (Capitol)
16	5	I CAN'T STAND IT	24/7 featuring Captain Hollywood (BCM)
11	6	CULT OF SNAP	Snap! (Arista)
7	7	FASCINATING RHYTHM	Bass-o-matic (Virgin)
3	8	GROOVE IS IN THE HEART/WHAT IS LOVE?	Deee-Lite (Elektra)
9	9	GROOVY TRAIN	Farm (Produce)
-	10	SO HARD	Pet Shop Boys (Parlophone)
6	11	WHAT TIME IS LOVE?	KLF featuring the Children of the Revolution (KLF Communications)
12	12	THEN	Charlatans (Situation Two)
24	13	NEVER ENOUGH	Cure (Fiction)
4	14	HOLY SMOKE	Iron Maiden (EMI)
18	15	THUNDERSTRUCK	AC/DC (Atco)
23	16	TUNES SPLIT THE ATOM	MC Tunes Vs. 808 State (ZTT)
10	17	THE SPACE JUNGLE	Adamski (MCA)
8	18	SUICIDE BLONDE	INXS (Mercury)
26	19	IT'S A SHAME (MY SISTER)	Monie Love featuring True Image (Cooltempo)
30	20	WORLD IN MY EYES	Depeche Mode (Mute)
-	21	BODY LANGUAGE	Adventures of Stevie V (Mercury)
13	22	FOUR BACHARACH AND DAVID SONGS (EP)	Deacon Blue (CBS)
15	23	VISION OF LOVE	Mariah Carey (CBS)
-	24	THE ANNIVERSARY WALTZ	Status Quo (Vertigo)
20	25	FOOL'S GOLD	Stone Roses (Silvertone)
-	26	HEAVEN	Chimes (CBS)
33	27	HOLY WARS ... THE PUNISHMENT DUE	Megadeth (Capitol)
14	28	BLACK CAT	Janet Jackson (A&M)
35	29	FALL (EP)	Ride (Creation)
-	30	SPIN THAT WHEEL (TURTLES GET REAL)	Hi-Tek 3 featuring Ya Kid K (Brothers Organisation)
39	31	3 SONGS	Wedding Present (RCA)
-	32	MEGAMIX	Technotronic (Swanyard)
19	33	LIVIN' IN THE LIGHT	Caron Wheeler (RCA)
17	34	ITSY BITSY TEENY WEENY YELLOW POLKA DOT BIKINI	Bombalurina (Carpet)
41	35	I'VE GOT YOU UNDER MY SKIN	Neneh Cherry (Circa)
37	36	MAKE IT MINE	Shamen (One Little Indian)
21	37	DON'T BE A FOOL	Loose Ends (10)
-	38	SHE'S SO FINE	Thunder (EMI)
25	39	EPIC	Faith No More (Slash)
-	40	CAPTURE YOUR HEART (EP)	Runrig (Chrysalis)
-	41	HAVE YOU SEEN HER	MC Hammer (Capitol)
22	42	WHERE ARE YOU BABY?	Betty Boo (Rhythm King)
29	43	(WHAT'S WRONG WITH) DREAMING	River City People (EMI)
-	44	EVERYBODY (RAP)	Criminal Element Orchestra featuring Wendell Williams (deConstruction)
27	45	NOTHING TO LOSE	S'Express (Rhythm King)
-	46	FANTASY	Fantasy UFO (XL Recording)
32	47	LA SERENISSIMA	DNA (Raw Bass)
31	48	TONIGHT	New Kids On The Block (CBS)
-	49	HANG IN LONG ENOUGH	Phil Collins (Virgin)
-	50	COLD HEARTED	Paula Abdul (Virgin America)

Once again the power of the Levi's Jeans TV ad made a Number One record, as Steve Miller's 1973 US chart-topper *The Joker*, which had never been a UK hit before, romped to the top with ease. Maria McKee, who replaced it with *Show Me Heaven*, was former lead singer of the band Lone Justice, and also younger sister of Bryan McLean of legendary '60s band Love, writer of *Alone Again Or*.

October 1990

13 October 1990

last week	this week	Title	Artist
2	1	BLUE VELVET	Bobby Vinton (Epic)
1	2	SHOW ME HEAVEN	Maria McKee (Epic)
3	3	I'VE BEEN THINKING ABOUT YOU	Londonbeat (AnXious)
24	4	THE ANNIVERSARY WALTZ	Status Quo (Vertigo)
10	5	SO HARD	Pet Shop Boys (Parlophone)
5	6	I CAN'T STAND IT	24/7 featuring Captain Hollywood (BCM)
32	7	MEGAMIX	Technotronic (Swanyard)
7	8	FASCINATING RHYTHM	Bass-o-matic (Virgin)
41	9	HAVE YOU SEEN HER	MC Hammer (Capitol)
4	10	THE JOKER	Steve Miller Band (Capitol)
6	11	CULT OF SNAP	Snap! (Arista)
19	12	IT'S A SHAME (MY SISTER)	Monie Love featuring True Image (Cooltempo)
8	13	GROOVE IS IN THE HEART/WHAT IS LOVE?	Deee-Lite (Elektra)
13	14	NEVER ENOUGH	Cure (Fiction)
16	15	TUNES SPLIT THE ATOM	MC Tunes Vs. 808 State (ZTT)
9	16	GROOVY TRAIN	Farm (Produce)
30	17	SPIN THAT WHEEL (TURTLES GET REAL)	Hi-Tek 3 featuring Ya Kid K (Brothers Organisation)
20	18	WORLD IN MY EYES	Depeche Mode (Mute)
35	19	I'VE GOT YOU UNDER MY SKIN	Neneh Cherry (Circa)
26	20	HEAVEN	Chimes (CBS)
21	21	BODY LANGUAGE	Adventures of Stevie V (Mercury)
11	22	WHAT TIME IS LOVE?	KLF featuring the Children of the Revolution (KLF Communications)
-	23	A LITTLE TIME	Beautiful South (Go! Discs)
12	24	THEN	Charlatans (Situation Two)
44	25	EVERYBODY (RAP)	Criminal Element Orchestra featuring Wendell Williams (deConstruction)
17	26	THE SPACE JUNGLE	Adamski (MCA)
15	27	THUNDERSTRUCK	AC/DC (Atco)
-	28	MORE	Sisters of Mercy (Merciful Release)
-	29	CONTRIBUTION	Mica Paris featuring Rakim (Fourth & Broadway)
23	30	VISION OF LOVE	Mariah Carey (CBS)
31	31	3 SONGS	Wedding Present (RCA)
-	32	RIGHT HERE, RIGHT NOW	Jesus Jones (Food)
18	33	SUICIDE BLONDE	INXS (Mercury)
22	34	FOUR BACHARACH AND DAVID SONGS (EP)	Deacon Blue (CBS)
49	35	HANG IN LONG ENOUGH	Phil Collins (Virgin)
36	36	MAKE IT MINE	Shamen (One Little Indian)
14	37	HOLY SMOKE	Iron Maiden (EMI)
-	38	DIDN'T I (BLOW YOUR MIND)/LET'S TRY IT AGAIN	New Kids On The Block (CBS)
27	39	HOLY WARS ... THE PUNISHMENT DUE	Megadeth (Capitol)
-	40	GOOD MORNING BRITAIN	Aztec Camera & Mick Jones (WEA)
-	41	WORKING MAN	Rita MacNeil (Polydor)
-	42	ELEVATION	Xpansions (Optimism)
-	43	FROM A DISTANCE	Cliff Richard (EMI)
38	44	SHE'S SO FINE	Thunder (EMI)
50	45	COLD HEARTED	Paula Abdul (Virgin America)
29	46	FALL (EP)	Ride (Creation)
25	47	FOOL'S GOLD	Stone Roses (Silvertone)
-	48	SUPERFLY 1990	Curtis Mayfield & Ice T (Capitol)
28	49	BLACK CAT	Janet Jackson (A&M)
-	50	LET'S PUSH IT	Innocence (Cooltempo)

20 October 1990

last week	this week	Title	Artist
1	1	BLUE VELVET	Bobby Vinton (Epic)
2	2	SHOW ME HEAVEN	Maria McKee (Epic)
4	3	THE ANNIVERSARY WALTZ	Status Quo (Vertigo)
7	4	MEGAMIX	Technotronic (Swanyard)
9	5	HAVE YOU SEEN HER	MC Hammer (Capitol)
23	6	A LITTLE TIME	Beautiful South (Go! Discs)
3	7	I'VE BEEN THINKING ABOUT YOU	Londonbeat (AnXious)
6	8	I CAN'T STAND IT	24/7 featuring Captain Hollywood (BCM)
38	9	DIDN'T I (BLOW YOUR MIND)/LET'S TRY IT AGAIN	New Kids On The Block (CBS)
5	10	SO HARD	Pet Shop Boys (Parlophone)
43	11	FROM A DISTANCE	Cliff Richard (EMI)
17	12	SPIN THAT WHEEL (TURTLES GET REAL)	Hi-Tek 3 featuring Ya Kid K (Brothers Organisation)
8	13	FASCINATING RHYTHM	Bass-o-matic (Virgin)
18	14	WORLD IN MY EYES	Depeche Mode (Mute)
10	15	THE JOKER	Steve Miller Band (Capitol)
19	16	I'VE GOT YOU UNDER MY SKIN	Neneh Cherry (Circa)
-	17	KINKY AFRO	Happy Mondays (Factory)
12	18	IT'S A SHAME (MY SISTER)	Monie Love featuring True Image (Cooltempo)
11	19	CULT OF SNAP	Snap! (Arista)
40	20	GOOD MORNING BRITAIN	Aztec Camera & Mick Jones (WEA)
25	21	EVERYBODY (RAP)	Criminal Element Orchestra featuring Wendell Williams (deConstruction)
-	22	CRYING IN THE RAIN	A-ha (Warner Bros)
16	23	GROOVY TRAIN	Farm (Produce)
28	24	MORE	Sisters of Mercy (Merciful Release)
-	25	PICCADILLY PALARE	Morrissey (HMV)
41	26	WORKING MAN	Rita MacNeil (Polydor)
13	27	GROOVE IS IN THE HEART/WHAT IS LOVE?	Deee-Lite (Elektra)
-	28	I'M YOUR BABY TONIGHT	Whitney Houston (Arista)
20	29	HEAVEN	Chimes (CBS)
50	30	LET'S PUSH IT	Innocence (Cooltempo)
29	31	CONTRIBUTION	Mica Paris featuring Rakim (Fourth & Broadway)
35	32	HANG IN LONG ENOUGH	Phil Collins (Virgin)
32	33	RIGHT HERE, RIGHT NOW	Jesus Jones (Food)
-	34	BE TENDER WITH MY BABY	Tina Turner (Capitol)
21	35	BODY LANGUAGE	Adventures of Stevie V (Mercury)
36	36	DANCE OF THE MAD	Pop Will Eat Itself (RCA)
15	37	TUNES SPLIT THE ATOM	MC Tunes Vs. 808 State (ZTT)
-	38	(WE WANT) THE SAME THING	Belinda Carlisle (Virgin)
22	39	WHAT TIME IS LOVE?	KLF featuring the Children of the Revolution (KLF Communications)
14	40	NEVER ENOUGH	Cure (Fiction)
41	41	THAT MAN (HE'S ALL MINE)	Inner City (10)
24	42	THEN	Charlatans (Situation Two)
-	43	MOTHER UNIVERSE	Soup Dragons (Raw TV)
26	44	THE SPACE JUNGLE	Adamski (MCA)
-	45	FROM A DISTANCE	Bette Midler (Atlantic)
-	46	TAKE MY BREATH AWAY	Berlin (CBS)
30	47	VISION OF LOVE	Mariah Carey (CBS)
-	48	TOTAL CONFUSION	A Homeboy, A Hippie & A Funki Dredd (Tam Tam)
42	49	ELEVATION	Xpansions (Optimism)
-	50	BIRTHDAY	Paul McCartney (Parlophone)

27 October 1990

last week	this week	Title	Artist
3	1	THE ANNIVERSARY WALTZ	Status Quo (Vertigo)
6	2	A LITTLE TIME	Beautiful South (Go! Discs)
2	3	SHOW ME HEAVEN	Maria McKee (Epic)
1	4	BLUE VELVET	Bobby Vinton (Epic)
28	5	I'M YOUR BABY TONIGHT	Whitney Houston (Arista)
4	6	MEGAMIX	Technotronic (Swanyard)
9	7	DIDN'T I (BLOW YOUR MIND)/LET'S TRY IT AGAIN	New Kids On The Block (CBS)
11	8	FROM A DISTANCE	Cliff Richard (EMI)
7	9	I'VE BEEN THINKING ABOUT YOU	Londonbeat (AnXious)
-	10	UNCHAINED MELODY	Righteous Brothers (Verve/Polydor)
17	11	KINKY AFRO	Happy Mondays (Factory)
26	12	WORKING MAN	Rita MacNeil (Polydor)
8	13	I CAN'T STAND IT	24/7 featuring Captain Hollywood (BCM)
5	14	HAVE YOU SEEN HER	MC Hammer (Capitol)
22	15	CRYING IN THE RAIN	A-ha (Warner Bros)
10	16	SO HARD	Pet Shop Boys (Parlophone)
12	17	SPIN THAT WHEEL (TURTLES GET REAL)	Hi-Tek 3 featuring Ya Kid K (Brothers Organisation)
20	18	GOOD MORNING BRITAIN	Aztec Camera & Mick Jones (WEA)
24	19	MORE	Sisters of Mercy (Merciful Release)
38	20	(WE WANT) THE SAME THING	Belinda Carlisle (Virgin)
25	21	PICCADILLY PALARE	Morrissey (HMV)
46	22	TAKE MY BREATH AWAY	Berlin (CBS)
18	23	IT'S A SHAME (MY SISTER)	Monie Love featuring True Image (Cooltempo)
34	24	BE TENDER WITH MY BABY	Tina Turner (Capitol)
43	25	MOTHER UNIVERSE	Soup Dragons (Raw TV)
13	26	FASCINATING RHYTHM	Bass-o-matic (Virgin)
50	27	BIRTHDAY	Paul McCartney (Parlophone)
30	28	LET'S PUSH IT	Innocence (Cooltempo)
-	29	DON'T ASK ME	Public Image Ltd. (Virgin)
14	30	WORLD IN MY EYES	Depeche Mode (Mute)
29	31	HEAVEN	Chimes (CBS)
15	32	THE JOKER	Steve Miller Band (Capitol)
33	33	GROOVY TRAIN	Farm (Produce)
19	34	CULT OF SNAP	Snap! (Arista)
27	35	GROOVE IS IN THE HEART/WHAT IS LOVE?	Deee-Lite (Elektra)
-	36	THE OBVIOUS CHILD	Paul Simon (Warner Bros)
41	37	THAT MAN (HE'S ALL MINE)	Inner City (10)
16	38	I'VE GOT YOU UNDER MY SKIN	Neneh Cherry (Circa)
-	39	WAITING FOR THAT DAY	George Michael (Epic)
21	40	EVERYBODY (RAP)	Criminal Element Orchestra featuring Wendell Williams (deConstruction)
-	41	YOU GOTTA LOVE SOMEONE	Elton John (Rocket)
-	42	LOVE IS A KILLER	Vixen (EMI-USA)
31	43	CONTRIBUTION	Mica Paris featuring Rakim (Fourth & Broadway)
45	44	FROM A DISTANCE	Bette Midler (Atlantic)
-	45	ALL ALONG THE WATCHTOWER	Jimi Hendrix (Polydor)
-	46	AFTERMATH/I'M FOR REAL	Nightmares On Max (Warp)
48	47	TOTAL CONFUSION	A Homeboy, A Hippie & A Funki Dredd (Tam Tam)
-	48	THREE BABIES	Sinead O'Connor (Ensign)
-	49	THE PRISONER	FAB featuring MC Number 6 (Brothers Organisation)
32	50	HANG IN LONG ENOUGH	Phil Collins (Virgin)

Like *The Joker*, American balladeer Bobby Vinton's 1963 US chart-topper *Blue Velvet* had never been a British hit, and as with the Steve Miller single, it was its exposure on a TV advert (for skin cream) and the movie of the same title, which shot it to the top of the chart – Vinton's first success here, despite a long string of US chartmakers, since his *Roses Are Red* debut, 28 years earlier.

November 1990

3 November 1990

last	this		
10	1	UNCHAINED MELODY	Righteous Brothers (Verve/Polydor)
2	2	A LITTLE TIME	Beautiful South (Go! Discs)
11	3	KINKY AFRO	Happy Mondays (Factory)
5	4	I'M YOUR BABY TONIGHT	Whitney Houston (Arista)
22	5	TAKE MY BREATH AWAY	Berlin (CBS)
1	6	THE ANNIVERSARY WALTZ	Status Quo (Vertigo)
12	7	WORKING MAN	Rita MacNeil (Polydor)
3	8	SHOW ME HEAVEN	Maria McKee (Epic)
4	9	BLUE VELVET	Bobby Vinton (Epic)
20	10	(WE WANT) THE SAME THING	Belinda Carlisle (Virgin)
15	11	CRYING IN THE RAIN	A-ha (Warner Bros)
6	12	MEGAMIX	Technotronic (Swanyard)
9	13	I'VE BEEN THINKING ABOUT YOU	Londonbeat (AnXious)
18	14	GOOD MORNING BRITAIN	Aztec Camera & Mick Jones (WEA)
13	15	I CAN'T STAND IT	24/7 featuring Captain Hollywood (BCM)
16	16	THE OBVIOUS CHILD	Paul Simon (Warner Bros)
29	17	DON'T ASK ME	Public Image Ltd. (Virgin)
25	18	MOTHER UNIVERSE	Soup Dragons (Raw TV)
14	19	HAVE YOU SEEN HER	MC Hammer (Capitol)
7	20	DIDN'T I (BLOW YOUR MIND)/LET'S TRY IT AGAIN	New Kids On The Block (CBS)
28	21	LET'S PUSH IT	Innocence (Cooltempo)
39	22	WAITING FOR THAT DAY	George Michael (Epic)
8	23	FROM A DISTANCE	Cliff Richard (EMI)
-	24	FANTASY	Black Box (deConstruction)
-	25	DRESSED FOR SUCCESS	Roxette (EMI)
46	26	AFTERMATH/I'M FOR REAL	Nightmares On Max (Warp)
-	27	CLOSE TO ME	Cure (Fiction)
-	28	STEP BACK IN TIME	Kylie Minogue (PWL)
-	29	I'M DOING FINE	Jason Donovan (PWL)
41	30	YOU GOTTA LOVE SOMEONE	Elton John (Rocket)
-	31	LOVE WILL NEVER DO (WITHOUT YOU)	Janet Jackson (A&M)
23	32	IT'S A SHAME (MY SISTER)	Monie Love featuring True Image (Cooltempo)
27	33	BIRTHDAY	Paul McCartney (Parlophone)
16	34	SO HARD	Pet Shop Boys (Parlophone)
-	35	LITTLE BROTHER	Blue Pearl (Big Life)
-	36	SOMETHING TO BELIEVE IN	Poison (Enigma)
17	37	SPIN THAT WHEEL (TURTLES GET REAL)	Hi-Tek 3 featuring Ya kid K (Brothers Organisation)
26	38	FASCINATING RHYTHM	Bass-o-matic (Virgin)
24	39	BE TENDER WITH MY BABY	Tina Turner (Capitol)
-	40	ANTHEM	N-Joi (deConstruction)
19	41	MORE	Sisters of Mercy (Merciful Release)
44	42	FROM A DISTANCE	Bette Midler (Atlantic)
48	43	THREE BABIES	Sinead O'Connor (Ensign)
-	44	I'LL BE YOUR BABY TONIGHT	Robert Palmer & UB40 (EMI)
32	45	THE JOKER	Steve Miller Band (Capitol)
37	46	THAT MAN (HE'S ALL MINE)	Inner City (10)
21	47	PICCADILLY PALARE	Morrissey (HMV)
-	48	(CAN'T LIVE WITHOUT YOU) LOVE AND AFFECTION	Nelson (DGC)
-	49	WE LET THE STARS GO	Prefab Sprout (Kitchenware)
33	50	GROOVY TRAIN	Farm (Produce)

10 November 1990

last	this		
1	1	UNCHAINED MELODY	Righteous Brothers (Verve/Polydor)
2	2	A LITTLE TIME	Beautiful South (Go! Discs)
5	3	TAKE MY BREATH AWAY	Berlin (CBS)
10	4	(WE WANT) THE SAME THING	Belinda Carlisle (Virgin)
28	5	STEP BACK IN TIME	Kylie Minogue (PWL)
-	6	DON'T WORRY	Kim Appleby (Parlophone)
4	7	I'M YOUR BABY TONIGHT	Whitney Houston (Arista)
3	8	KINKY AFRO	Happy Mondays (Factory)
27	9	CLOSE TO ME	Cure (Fiction)
44	10	I'LL BE YOUR BABY TONIGHT	Robert Palmer & UB40 (EMI)
8	11	SHOW ME HEAVEN	Maria McKee (Epic)
7	12	WORKING MAN	Rita MacNeil (Polydor)
24	13	FANTASY	Black Box (deConstruction)
6	14	THE ANNIVERSARY WALTZ	Status Quo (Vertigo)
16	15	THE OBVIOUS CHILD	Paul Simon (Warner Bros)
11	16	CRYING IN THE RAIN	A-ha (Warner Bros)
9	17	BLUE VELVET	Bobby Vinton (Epic)
25	18	DRESSED FOR SUCCESS	Roxette (EMI)
29	19	I'M DOING FINE	Jason Donovan (PWL)
12	20	MEGAMIX	Technotronic (Swanyard)
14	21	GOOD MORNING BRITAIN	Aztec Camera & Mick Jones (WEA)
22	22	WAITING FOR THAT DAY	George Michael (Epic)
-	23	THERE SHE GOES	La's (Go! Discs)
35	24	LITTLE BROTHER	Blue Pearl (Big Life)
13	25	I'VE BEEN THINKING ABOUT YOU	Londonbeat (AnXious)
-	26	MY RISING STAR	Northside (Factory)
15	27	I CAN'T STAND IT	24/7 featuring Captain Hollywood (BCM)
-	28	TO LOVE SOMEBODY	Jimmy Somerville (London)
18	29	MOTHER UNIVERSE	Soup Dragons (Raw TV)
21	30	LET'S PUSH IT	Innocence (Cooltempo)
19	31	HAVE YOU SEEN HER	MC Hammer (Capitol)
31	32	LOVE WILL NEVER DO (WITHOUT YOU)	Janet Jackson (A&M)
17	33	DON'T ASK ME	Public Image Ltd. (Virgin)
-	34	SPIT IN THE RAIN	Del Amitri (A&M)
26	35	AFTERMATH/I'M FOR REAL	Nightmares On Max (Warp)
20	36	DIDN'T I (BLOW YOUR MIND)/LET'S TRY IT AGAIN	New Kids On The Block (CBS)
-	37	NEW POWER GENERATION	Prince (Paisley Park)
-	38	UNBELIEVABLE	EMF (Parlophone)
-	39	CUBIK/OLYMPIC	808 State (ZTT)
23	40	FROM A DISTANCE	Cliff Richard (EMI)
30	41	YOU GOTTA LOVE SOMEONE	Elton John (Rocket)
36	42	SOMETHING TO BELIEVE IN	Poison (Enigma)
-	43	FOG ON THE TYNE (REVISITED)	Gazza & Lindisfarne (Best)
42	44	FROM A DISTANCE	Bette Midler (Atlantic)
-	45	DIG FOR FIRE	Pixies (4AD)
40	46	ANTHEM	N-Joi (deConstruction)
48	47	(CAN'T LIVE WITHOUT YOU) LOVE AND AFFECTION	Nelson (DGC)
-	48	SHE'S SO HIGH	Blur (Food)
43	49	THREE BABIES	Sinead O'Connor (Ensign)
-	50	RHYTHM TAKES CONTROL	Unique 3 (10)

17 November 1990

last	this		
1	1	UNCHAINED MELODY	Righteous Brothers (Verve/Polydor)
6	2	DON'T WORRY	Kim Appleby (Parlophone)
2	3	A LITTLE TIME	Beautiful South (Go! Discs)
5	4	STEP BACK IN TIME	Kylie Minogue (PWL)
10	5	I'LL BE YOUR BABY TONIGHT	Robert Palmer & UB40 (EMI)
43	6	FOG ON THE TYNE (REVISITED)	Gazza & Lindisfarne (Best)
3	7	TAKE MY BREATH AWAY	Berlin (CBS)
13	8	FANTASY	Black Box (deConstruction)
4	9	(WE WANT) THE SAME THING	Belinda Carlisle (Virgin)
7	10	I'M YOUR BABY TONIGHT	Whitney Houston (Arista)
23	11	THERE SHE GOES	La's (Go! Discs)
9	12	CLOSE TO ME	Cure (Fiction)
38	13	UNBELIEVABLE	EMF (Parlophone)
18	14	DRESSED FOR SUCCESS	Roxette (EMI)
39	15	CUBIK/OLYMPIC	808 State (ZTT)
8	16	KINKY AFRO	Happy Mondays (Factory)
15	17	THE OBVIOUS CHILD	Paul Simon (Warner Bros)
11	18	SHOW ME HEAVEN	Maria McKee (Epic)
12	19	WORKING MAN	Rita MacNeil (Polydor)
28	20	TO LOVE SOMEBODY	Jimmy Somerville (London)
24	21	LITTLE BROTHER	Blue Pearl (Big Life)
34	22	SPIT IN THE RAIN	Del Amitri (A&M)
19	23	I'M DOING FINE	Jason Donovan (PWL)
22	24	WAITING FOR THAT DAY	George Michael (Epic)
-	25	TIME TO MAKE THE FLOOR BURN	Megabass (Megabass)
26	26	ISLAND HEAD (EP)	Inspiral Carpets (Cow)
17	27	BLUE VELVET	Bobby Vinton (Epic)
50	28	RHYTHM TAKES CONTROL	Unique 3 (10)
16	29	CRYING IN THE RAIN	A-ha (Warner Bros)
37	30	NEW POWER GENERATION	Prince (Paisley Park)
14	31	THE ANNIVERSARY WALTZ	Status Quo (Vertigo)
26	32	MY RISING STAR	Northside (Factory)
-	33	MIRACLE	Jon Bon Jovi (Vertigo)
-	34	UK BLAK	Caron Wheeler (RCA)
-	35	100 MILES AND RUNNIN'	NWA (Fourth & Broadway)
-	36	HANDS ACROSS THE OCEAN/AMELIA	Mission (Mercury)
20	37	MEGAMIX	Technotronic (Swanyard)
-	38	IMPULSIVE	Wilson Phillips (SBK)
21	39	GOOD MORNING BRITAIN	Aztec Camera & Mick Jones (WEA)
35	40	AFTERMATH/I'M FOR REAL	Nightmares On Max (Warp)
-	41	FALLING	Julee Cruise (Warner Bros)
27	42	I CAN'T STAND IT	24/7 featuring Captain Hollywood (BCM)
25	43	I'VE BEEN THINKING ABOUT YOU	Londonbeat (AnXious)
-	44	IT'S ALRIGHT NOW	Beloved (East West)
-	45	FLASHBACK JACK	Adamski (MCA)
46	46	RHYTHM OF LIFE	Oleta Adams (Fontana)
-	47	LET'S SWING AGAIN	Jive Bunny & the Mastermixers (Music Factory Dance)
46	48	ANTHEM	N-Joi (deConstruction)
30	49	LET'S PUSH IT	Innocence (Cooltempo)
-	50	ILLEGAL GUNSHOT/SPLIFFHEAD	Ragga Twins (Shut Up And Dance)

The major rival to TV advertising when it came to giving a hit record a special promotion boost, was its inclusion in a hit film. The Righteous Brothers' 1965 hit version of *Unchained Melody* was one of the musical highlights of the box-office winner *Ghost* – a key factor in the demand which shot it to four weeks at Number One, and made this 25-year-old recording 1990's biggest seller.

November – December 1990

24 November 1990

last	this	title	artist
1	1	UNCHAINED MELODY	Righteous Brothers (Verve/Polydor)
6	2	FOG ON THE TYNE (REVISITED)	Gazza & Lindisfarne (Best)
2	3	DON'T WORRY	Kim Appleby (Parlophone)
8	4	FANTASY	Black Box (deConstruction)
5	5	I'LL BE YOUR BABY TONIGHT	Robert Palmer & UB40 (EMI)
15	6	CUBIK/OLYMPIC	808 State (ZTT)
3	7	A LITTLE TIME	Beautiful South (Go! Discs)
13	8	UNBELIEVABLE	EMF (Parlophone)
11	9	THERE SHE GOES	La's (Go! Discs)
-	10	ICE ICE BABY	Vanilla Ice (SBK)
20	11	TO LOVE SOMEBODY	Jimmy Somerville (London)
4	12	STEP BACK IN TIME	Kylie Minogue (PWL)
7	13	TAKE MY BREATH AWAY	Berlin (CBS)
41	14	FALLING	Julee Cruise (Warner Bros)
10	15	I'M YOUR BABY TONIGHT	Whitney Houston (Arista)
9	16	(WE WANT) THE SAME THING	Belinda Carlisle (Virgin)
25	17	TIME TO MAKE THE FLOOR BURN	Megabass (Megabass)
22	18	SPIT IN THE RAIN	Del Amitri (A&M)
47	19	LET'S SWING AGAIN	Jive Bunny & the Mastermixers (Music Factory Dance)
14	20	DRESSED FOR SUCCESS	Roxette (EMI)
-	21	IT TAKES TWO	Rod Stewart & Tina Turner (Warner Bros)
26	22	ISLAND HEAD (EP)	Inspiral Carpets (Cow)
17	23	THE OBVIOUS CHILD	Paul Simon (Warner Bros)
12	24	CLOSE TO ME	Cure (Fiction)
-	25	MISSING YOU	Soul II Soul (10)
30	26	NEW POWER GENERATION	Prince (Paisley Park)
33	27	MIRACLE	Jon Bon Jovi (Vertigo)
-	28	KING OF THE ROAD (EP)	Proclaimers (Chrysalis)
-	29	SUCKER DJ	Dimples D (FBI)
-	30	BEING BORING	Pet Shop Boys (Parlophone)
36	31	HANDS ACROSS THE OCEAN/AMELIA	Mission (Mercury)
27	32	BLUE VELVET	Bobby Vinton (Epic)
16	33	KINKY AFRO	Happy Mondays (Factory)
19	34	WORKING MAN	Rita MacNeil (Polydor)
-	35	POWER OF LOVE/DEEE-LITE THEME	Deee-Lite (Elektra)
45	36	FLASHBACK JACK	Adamski (MCA)
18	37	SHOW ME HEAVEN	Maria McKee (Epic)
21	38	LITTLE BROTHER	Blue Pearl (Big Life)
34	39	UK BLAK	Caron Wheeler (RCA)
23	40	I'M DOING FINE	Jason Donovan (PWL)
28	41	RHYTHM TAKES CONTROL	Unique 3 (10)
-	42	STATE OF INDEPENDENCE	Donna Summer (Warner Bros)
24	43	WAITING FOR THAT DAY	George Michael (Epic)
-	44	I ALMOST FEEL LIKE CRYING	Craig McLachlan & Check 1-2 (Epic)
-	45	MY DEFINITION OF A BOOMBASTIC JAZZ STYLE	Dream Warriors (Fourth & Broadway)
38	46	IMPULSIVE	Wilson Phillips (SBK)
47	47	LOVE TAKES TIME	Mariah Carey (CBS)
-	48	SUMERLAND (EP)	Fields of the Nephilim (Beggars Banquet)
44	49	IT'S ALRIGHT NOW	Beloved (East West)
29	50	CRYING IN THE RAIN	A-ha (Warner Bros)

1 December 1990

last	this	title	artist
10	1	ICE ICE BABY	Vanilla Ice (SBK)
1	2	UNCHAINED MELODY	Righteous Brothers (Verve/Polydor)
3	3	DON'T WORRY	Kim Appleby (Parlophone)
8	4	UNBELIEVABLE	EMF (Parlophone)
14	5	FALLING	Julee Cruise (Warner Bros)
4	6	FANTASY	Black Box (deConstruction)
21	7	IT TAKES TWO	Rod Stewart & Tina Turner (Warner Bros)
28	8	KING OF THE ROAD (EP)	Proclaimers (Chrysalis)
5	9	I'LL BE YOUR BABY TONIGHT	Robert Palmer & UB40 (EMI)
6	10	CUBIK/OLYMPIC	808 State (ZTT)
2	11	FOG ON THE TYNE (REVISITED)	Gazza & Lindisfarne (Best)
11	12	TO LOVE SOMEBODY	Jimmy Somerville (London)
45	13	MY DEFINITION OF A BOOMBASTIC JAZZ STYLE	Dream Warriors (Fourth & Broadway)
7	14	A LITTLE TIME	Beautiful South (Go! Discs)
9	15	THERE SHE GOES	La's (Go! Discs)
25	16	MISSING YOU	Soul II Soul (10)
17	17	TIME TO MAKE THE FLOOR BURN	Megabass (Megabass)
19	18	LET'S SWING AGAIN	Jive Bunny & the Mastermixers (Music Factory Dance)
-	19	SEVEN LITTLE GIRLS SITTING IN THE BACK SEAT	Bombalurina featuring Timmy Mallett (Carpet)
22	20	ISLAND HEAD (EP)	Inspiral Carpets (Cow)
35	21	POWER OF LOVE/DEEE-LITE THEME	Deee-Lite (Elektra)
13	22	TAKE MY BREATH AWAY	Berlin (CBS)
29	23	SUCKER DJ	Dimples D (FBI)
-	24	ARE YOU DREAMING?	24/7 (BCM)
30	25	BEING BORING	Pet Shop Boys (Parlophone)
12	26	STEP BACK IN TIME	Kylie Minogue (PWL)
15	27	I'M YOUR BABY TONIGHT	Whitney Houston (Arista)
32	28	WICKED GAME	Chris Isaak (London)
18	29	SPIT IN THE RAIN	Del Amitri (A&M)
16	30	(WE WANT) THE SAME THING	Belinda Carlisle (Virgin)
27	31	MIRACLE	Jon Bon Jovi (Vertigo)
20	32	DRESSED FOR SUCCESS	Roxette (EMI)
-	33	MONEY TALKS	AC/DC (Atco)
23	34	THE OBVIOUS CHILD	Paul Simon (Warner Bros)
42	35	STATE OF INDEPENDENCE	Donna Summer (Warner Bros)
-	36	KINKY BOOTS	Patrick MacNee & Honor Blackman (Deram)
24	37	CLOSE TO ME	Cure (Fiction)
-	38	LOVE'S GOT ME	Loose Ends (10)
37	39	SHOW ME HEAVEN	Maria McKee (Epic)
32	40	BLUE VELVET	Bobby Vinton (Epic)
-	41	24 HOURS	Betty Boo (Rhythm King)
34	42	WORKING MAN	Rita MacNeil (Polydor)
26	43	NEW POWER GENERATION	Prince (Paisley Park)
48	44	SUMERLAND (EP)	Fields of the Nephilim (Beggars Banquet)
-	45	A BETTER LOVE	Londonbeat (AnXious)
33	46	KINKY AFRO	Happy Mondays (Factory)
-	47	CAREFUL	Horse (Capitol)
39	48	UK BLAK	Caron Wheeler (RCA)
-	49	DOWN TO EARTH	Monie Love (Cooltempo)
31	50	HANDS ACROSS THE OCEAN/AMELIA	Mission (Mercury)

8 December 1990

last	this	title	artist
1	1	ICE ICE BABY	Vanilla Ice (SBK)
2	2	UNCHAINED MELODY	Righteous Brothers (Verve/Polydor)
4	3	UNBELIEVABLE	EMF (Parlophone)
7	4	IT TAKES TWO	Rod Stewart & Tina Turner (Warner Bros)
3	5	DON'T WORRY	Kim Appleby (Parlophone)
36	6	KINKY BOOTS	Patrick MacNee & Honor Blackman (Deram)
8	7	KING OF THE ROAD (EP)	Proclaimers (Chrysalis)
5	8	FALLING	Julee Cruise (Warner Bros)
6	9	FANTASY	Black Box (deConstruction)
13	10	MY DEFINITION OF A BOOMBASTIC JAZZ STYLE	Dream Warriors (Fourth & Broadway)
28	11	WICKED GAME	Chris Isaak (London)
12	12	TO LOVE SOMEBODY	Jimmy Somerville (London)
19	13	SEVEN LITTLE GIRLS SITTING IN THE BACK SEAT	Bombalurina featuring Timmy Mallett (Carpet)
-	14	JUSTIFY MY LOVE	Madonna (Sire)
9	15	I'LL BE YOUR BABY TONIGHT	Robert Palmer & UB40 (EMI)
-	16	ALL TOGETHER NOW	Farm (Produce)
10	17	CUBIK/OLYMPIC	808 State (ZTT)
23	18	SUCKER DJ	Dimples D (FBI)
25	19	BEING BORING	Pet Shop Boys (Parlophone)
-	20	SAVIOUR'S DAY	Cliff Richard (EMI)
-	21	POWER OF LOVE/DEEE-LITE THEME	Deee-Lite (Elektra)
41	22	24 HOURS	Betty Boo (Rhythm King)
-	23	THIS ONE'S FOR THE CHILDREN	New Kids On The Block (CBS)
24	24	ARE YOU DREAMING?	24/7 (BCM)
16	25	MISSING YOU	Soul II Soul (10)
-	26	PRAY	MC Hammer (Capitol)
49	27	DOWN TO EARTH	Monie Love (Cooltempo)
17	28	TIME TO MAKE THE FLOOR BURN	Megabass (Megabass)
-	29	JUST THIS SIDE OF LOVE	Malandra Burrows (Yorkshire Television)
-	30	SITUATION	Yazoo (Mute)
14	31	A LITTLE TIME	Beautiful South (Go! Discs)
22	32	TAKE MY BREATH AWAY	Berlin (CBS)
15	33	THERE SHE GOES	La's (Go! Discs)
11	34	FOG ON THE TYNE (REVISITED)	Gazza & Lindisfarne (Best)
-	35	MARY HAD A LITTLE BOY	Snap! (Arista)
-	36	IMPOSSIBLE LOVE	UB40 (DEP International)
33	37	MONEY TALKS	AC/DC (Atco)
-	38	LOSE CONTROL	James (Fontana)
18	39	LET'S SWING AGAIN	Jive Bunny & the Mastermixers (Music Factory Dance)
-	40	I'M IN THE MOOD FOR LOVE	Lord Tanamo (Mooncrest)
38	41	LOVE'S GOT ME	Loose Ends (10)
-	42	LOVE TAKES TIME	Mariah Carey (CBS)
-	43	MY BOOK	Beautiful South (Go! Discs)
-	44	THE STORM	World of Twist (Circa)
27	45	I'M YOUR BABY TONIGHT	Whitney Houston (Arista)
-	46	DISAPPEAR	INXS (Mercury)
-	47	THE EXORCIST (THE REMIX)	Scientist (Kickin')
-	48	AROUND THE WAY GIRL/MAMA SAY KNOCK YOU OUT	LL Cool J (Def Jam)
26	49	STEP BACK IN TIME	Kylie Minogue (PWL)
20	50	ISLAND HEAD (EP)	Inspiral Carpets (Cow)

Ice Ice Baby was one of the biggest rap hits of all time, but much of its hook lay not in Vanilla Ice's vocal syncopations, but in the distinctive heavy bassline which the single lifted wholesale from Queen & David Bowie's 1981 chart-topper *Under Pressure*. More revived oldies crowding the Top 10 included *Fog On The Tyne*, *It Takes Two*, *King Of The Road* and *I'll Be Your Baby Tonight*.

December 1990

	15 December 1990			22 December 1990	
1	1	ICE ICE BABY Vanilla Ice (SBK)	1	1	ICE ICE BABY Vanilla Ice (SBK)
14	2	JUSTIFY MY LOVE Madonna (Sire)	2	2	JUSTIFY MY LOVE Madonna (Sire)
20	3	SAVIOUR'S DAY Cliff Richard (EMI)	3	3	SAVIOUR'S DAY Cliff Richard (EMI)
6	4	KINKY BOOTS Patrick MacNee & Honor Blackman (Deram)	6	4	ALL TOGETHER NOW Farm (Produce)
3	5	UNBELIEVABLE EMF (Parlophone)	24	5	YOU'VE LOST THAT LOVIN' FEELIN' Righteous Brothers (Verve/Polydor)
16	6	ALL TOGETHER NOW Farm (Produce)	10	6	PRAY MC Hammer (Capitol)
11	7	WICKED GAME Chris Isaak (London)	13	7	MARY HAD A LITTLE BOY Snap! (Arista)
2	8	UNCHAINED MELODY Righteous Brothers (Verve/Polydor)	9	8	THIS ONE'S FOR THE CHILDREN New Kids On The Block (CBS)
23	9	THIS ONE'S FOR THE CHILDREN New Kids On The Block (CBS)	12	9	SITUATION Yazoo (Mute)
26	10	PRAY MC Hammer (Capitol)	7	10	WICKED GAME Chris Isaak (London)
5	11	DON'T WORRY Kim Appleby (Parlophone)	47	11	SADNESS PART 1 Enigma (Virgin International)
30	12	SITUATION Yazoo (Mute)	29	12	THE TOTAL MIX Black Box (deConstruction)
35	13	MARY HAD A LITTLE BOY Snap! (Arista)	5	13	UNBELIEVABLE EMF (Parlophone)
4	14	IT TAKES TWO Rod Stewart & Tina Turner (Warner Bros)	11	14	DON'T WORRY Kim Appleby (Parlophone)
10	15	MY DEFINITION OF A BOOMBASTIC JAZZ STYLE Dream Warriors (Fourth & Broadway)	19	15	JUST THIS SIDE OF LOVE Malandra Burrows (Yorkshire Television)
7	16	KING OF THE ROAD (EP) Proclaimers (Chrysalis)	8	16	UNCHAINED MELODY Righteous Brothers (Verve/Polydor)
18	17	SUCKER DJ Dimples D (FBI)	4	17	KINKY BOOTS Patrick MacNee & Honor Blackman (Deram)
8	18	FALLING Julee Cruise (Warner Bros)	17	18	SUCKER DJ Dimples D (FBI)
29	19	JUST THIS SIDE OF LOVE Malandra Burrows (Yorkshire Television)	25	19	DISAPPEAR INXS (Mercury)
9	20	FANTASY Black Box (deConstruction)	50	20	THE ANNIVERSARY WALTZ Status Quo (Vertigo)
22	21	24 HOURS Betty Boo (Rhythm King)	-	21	THE GREASE MEGAMIX John Travolta & Olivia Newton-John (Polydor)
12	22	TO LOVE SOMEBODY Jimmy Somerville (London)	23	22	ARE YOU DREAMING? 24/7 (BCM)
24	23	ARE YOU DREAMING? 24/7 (BCM)	-	23	FREEDOM! George Michael (Epic)
-	24	YOU'VE LOST THAT LOVIN' FEELIN' Righteous Brothers (Verve/Polydor)	21	24	24 HOURS Betty Boo (Rhythm King)
46	25	DISAPPEAR INXS (Mercury)	39	25	CRAZY Seal (ZTT)
13	26	SEVEN LITTLE GIRLS SITTING IN THE BACK SEAT Bombalurina featuring Timmy Mallett (Carpet)	-	26	GONNA MAKE YOU SWEAT C&C Music Factory featuring Freedom Williams (CBS)
15	27	I'LL BE YOUR BABY TONIGHT Robert Palmer & UB40 (EMI)	18	27	FALLING Julee Cruise (Warner Bros)
-	28	ALL MY TRIALS Paul McCartney (Parlophone)	35	28	(THEY LONG TO BE) CLOSE TO YOU/MERRY CHRISTMAS DARLING Carpenters (A&M)
-	29	THE TOTAL MIX Black Box (deConstruction)	-	29	ALL THE MAN THAT I NEED Whitney Houston (Arista)
19	30	BEING BORING Pet Shop Boys (Parlophone)	41	30	CRAZY Patsy Cline (MCA)
21	31	POWER OF LOVE/DEEE-LITE THEME Deee-Lite (Elektra)	-	31	THE BEST CHRISTMAS OF THEM ALL Shakin' Stevens (Epic)
-	32	A MATTER OF FACT Innocence (Cooltempo)	15	32	MY DEFINITION OF A BOOMBASTIC JAZZ STYLE Dream Warriors (Fourth & Broadway)
27	33	DOWN TO EARTH Monie Love (Cooltempo)	37	33	MY BOOK Beautiful South (Go! Discs)
38	34	LOSE CONTROL James (Fontana)	-	34	TURN IT UP Technotronic (Swanyard)
-	35	(THEY LONG TO BE) CLOSE TO YOU/MERRY CHRISTMAS DARLING Carpenters (A&M)	32	35	A MATTER OF FACT Innocence (Cooltempo)
17	36	CUBIK/OLYMPIC 808 State (ZTT)	-	36	I CALL YOUR NAME A-ha (Warner Bros)
43	37	MY BOOK Beautiful South (Go! Discs)	14	37	IT TAKES TWO Rod Stewart & Tina Turner (Warner Bros)
28	38	TIME TO MAKE THE FLOOR BURN Megabass (Megabass)	-	38	TURTLE RHAPSODY Orchestra On The Half Shell (SBK)
-	39	CRAZY Seal (ZTT)	16	39	KING OF THE ROAD (EP) Proclaimers (Chrysalis)
25	40	MISSING YOU Soul II Soul (10)	-	40	(I'VE HAD) THE TIME OF MY LIFE Bill Medley & Jennifer Warnes (RCA)
-	41	CRAZY Patsy Cline (MCA)	-	41	THE CRAZY PARTY MIXES Jive Bunny & the Mastermixers (Music Factory Dance)
32	42	TAKE MY BREATH AWAY Berlin (CBS)	20	42	FANTASY Black Box (deConstruction)
-	43	MERRY XMAS EVERYBODY Metal Gurus (Mercury)	22	43	TO LOVE SOMEBODY Jimmy Somerville (London)
-	44	A BETTER LOVE Londonbeat (AnXious)	-	44	THE BEE Scientist (Kickin')
42	45	LOVE TAKES TIME Mariah Carey (CBS)	28	45	ALL MY TRIALS Paul McCartney (Parlophone)
31	46	A LITTLE TIME Beautiful South (Go! Discs)	-	46	DOCTOR JEEP Sisters of Mercy (Merciful Release)
-	47	SADNESS PART 1 Enigma (Virgin International)	27	47	I'LL BE YOUR BABY TONIGHT Robert Palmer & UB40 (EMI)
40	48	I'M IN THE MOOD FOR LOVE Lord Tanamo (Mooncrest)	26	48	SEVEN LITTLE GIRLS SITTING IN THE BACK SEAT Bombalurina featuring Timmy Mallett (Carpet)
33	49	THERE SHE GOES La's (Go! Discs)	38	49	TIME TO MAKE THE FLOOR BURN Megabass (Megabass)
-	50	THE ANNIVERSARY WALTZ Status Quo (Vertigo)	-	50	I CAN'T SAY GOODBYE Kim Wilde (MCA)

It was almost inevitable that the Righteous Brothers' *You've Lost That Lovin' Feelin'* would be reissued as the *Unchained Melody* follow-up. This made its third completely separate appearance in the UK Top 10 over a 25-year period, a record unequalled to date by any other single. Meanwhile, Cliff's *Saviour's Day* gave him his third (counting Band Aid II) Christmas Number One in a row.

January 1991

5 January 1991

Last	This	Title / Artist
3	1	SAVIOUR'S DAY — Cliff Richard (EMI)
5	2	YOU'VE LOST THAT LOVIN' FEELING/EBB TIDE — Righteous Brothers (Verve)
11	3	SADNESS PART 1 — Enigma (Virgin International)
1	4	ICE ICE BABY — Vanilla Ice (SBK)
21	5	THE GREASE MEGAMIX — John Travolta & Olivia Newton-John (Polydor)
2	6	JUSTIFY MY LOVE — Madonna (Sire)
4	7	ALL TOGETHER NOW — Farm (Produce)
7	8	MARY HAD A LITTE BOY — Snap (Arista)
6	9	PRAY — MC Hammer (Capitol)
12	10	THE TOTAL MIX — Black Box (deConstruction)
10	11	WICKED GAME — Chris Isaak (London)
15	12	JUST THIS SIDE OF LOVE — Malandra Burrows (YTV)
20	13	THE ANNIVERSARY WALTZ PART TWO — Status Quo (Vertigo)
-	14	ALL THE MAN THAT I NEED — Whitney Houston (Arista)
13	15	UNBELIEVABLE — EMF (Parlophone)
25	16	CRAZY — Seal (ZTT)
26	17	GONNA MAKE YOU SWEAT — C&C Music Factory featuring Freedom Williams (Columbia)
31	18	THE BEST CHRISTMAS OF THEM ALL — Shakin' Stevens (Epic)
16	19	UNCHAINED MELODY — Righteous Brothers (Verve)
41	20	THE CRAZY PARTY MIXES — Jive Bunny & the Mastermixers (Music Factory)
28	21	(THEY LONG TO BE) CLOSE TO YOU/MERRY CHRISTMAS DARLING — Carpenters (A&M)
9	22	SITUATION — Yazoo (Mute)
30	23	CRAZY — Patsy Cline (MCA)
8	24	THIS ONE'S FOR THE CHILDREN — New Kids On The Block (Columbia)
19	25	DISAPPEAR — INXS (Mercury)
14	26	DON'T WORRY — Kim Appleby (Parlophone)
22	27	ARE YOU DREAMING? — Twenty 4 Seven featuring Captain Hollywood (BCM)
23	28	FREEDOM! — George Michael (Epic)
18	29	SUCKER DJ — Dimples D (FBI)
24	30	24 HOURS — Betty Boo (Rhythm King)
17	31	KINKY BOOTS — Patrick MacNee & Honor Blackman (Deram)
27	32	FALLING — Julee Cruise (Warner Bros)
33	33	A MATTER OF FACT — Innocence (Cooltempo)
	34	DOCTOR JEEP — Sisters Of Mercy (Merciful Release)
40	35	(I'VE HAD) THE TIME OF MY LIFE — Bill Medley & Jennifer Warnes (RCA)
38	36	TURTLE RHAPSODY — Orchestra On The Half Shell (SBK)
	37	MY BOOK — Beautiful South (Go! Discs)
	38	I CAN'T TAKE THE POWER — Off-Shore (CBS)
36	39	I CALL YOUR NAME — A-ha (Warner Bros)
32	40	MY DEFINITION OF A BOOMBASTIC JAZZ STYLE — Dream Warriors (4th & Broadway)
	41	SUMMER RAIN — Belinda Carlisle (Virgin)
	42	FANTASY — Black Box (deConstruction)
	43	GEORDIE BOYS (GAZZA RAP) — Gazza (Best)
37	44	IT TAKES TWO — Rod Stewart & Tina Turner (Warner Bros)
34	46	TURN IT UP — Technotronic (Swanyard)
	47	ROCK THE BOAT — Delage (PWL)
	48	PRODIGAL BLUES — Billy Idol (Chrysalis)
39	49	KING OF THE ROAD (EP) — Proclaimers (Chrysalis)
	50	I'M NOT IN LOVE — Will To Power (Epic)
50	50	I CAN'T SAY GOOBYE — Kim Wilde (MCA)

12 January 1991

Last	This	Title / Artist
3	1	SADNESS PART 1 — Enigma (Virgin International)
-	2	BRING YOUR DAUGHTER ... TO THE SLAUGHTER — Iron Maiden (EMI)
4	3	ICE ICE BABY — Vanilla Ice (SBK)
5	4	THE GREASE MEGAMIX — John Travolta & Olivia Newton-John (Polydor)
2	5	YOU'VE LOST THAT LOVIN' FEELING/EBB TIDE — Righteous Brothers (Verve)
7	6	ALL TOGETHER NOW — Farm (Produce)
6	7	JUSTIFY MY LOVE — Madonna (Sire)
16	8	CRAZY — Seal (ZTT)
10	9	THE TOTAL MIX — Black Box (deConstruction)
1	10	SAVIOUR'S DAY — Cliff Richard (EMI)
8	11	MARY HAD A LITTE BOY — Snap (Arista)
14	12	ALL THE MAN THAT I NEED — Whitney Houston (Arista)
9	13	PRAY — MC Hammer (Capitol)
23	14	CRAZY — Patsy Cline (MCA)
17	15	GONNA MAKE YOU SWEAT — C&C Music Factory featuring Freedom Williams (Columbia)
15	16	UNBELIEVABLE — EMF (Parlophone)
13	17	THE ANNIVERSARY WALTZ PART TWO — Status Quo (Vertigo)
11	18	WICKED GAME — Chris Isaak (London)
19	19	UNCHAINED MELODY — Righteous Brothers (Verve)
35	20	(I'VE HAD) THE TIME OF MY LIFE — Bill Medley & Jennifer Warnes (RCA)
12	21	JUST THIS SIDE OF LOVE — Malandra Burrows (YTV)
27	22	ARE YOU DREAMING? — Twenty 4 Seven featuring Captain Hollywood (BCM)
25	23	DISAPPEAR — INXS (Mercury)
24	24	SITUATION — Yazoo (Mute)
30	25	24 HOURS — Betty Boo (Rhythm King)
26	26	FREEDOM! — George Michael (Epic)
	27	I CAN'T TAKE THE POWER — Off-Shore (CBS)
	28	GOT THE TIME — Anthrax (Island)
24	29	THIS ONE'S FOR THE CHILDREN — New Kids On The Block (Columbia)
	30	PREACHER MAN — Bananarama (London)
29	31	SUCKER DJ — Dimples D (FBI)
20	32	THE CRAZY PARTY MIXES — Jive Bunny & the Mastermixers (Music Factory)
	33	DON'T WORRY — Kim Appleby (Parlophone)
	34	I'M NOT IN LOVE — Will To Power (Epic)
	35	MERCY MERCY MERCY/I WANT YOU — Robert Palmer featuring Gilly G (EMI)
33	36	A MATTER OF FACT — Innocence (Cooltempo)
	37	SUMMER RAIN — Belinda Carlisle (Virgin)
	38	INTERNATIONAL BRIGHT YOUNG THING — Jesus Jones (Food)
21	39	(THEY LONG TO BE) CLOSE TO YOU/MERRY CHRISTMAS DARLING — Carpenters (A&M)
	40	GEORDIE BOYS (GAZZA RAP) — Gazza (Best)
31	41	KINKY BOOTS — Patrick MacNee & Honor Blackman (Deram)
36	42	TURTLE RHAPSODY — Orchestra On The Half Shell (SBK)
-	43	TELL ME WHERE YOU'RE GOING — Silje (EMI)
46	44	FANTASY — Black Box (deConstruction)
32	45	FALLING — Julee Cruise (Warner Bros)
40	46	MY DEFINITION OF A BOOMBASTIC JAZZ STYLE — Dream Warriors (4th & Broadway)
	47	ALWAYS THE SUN — Stranglers (Epic)
18	48	THE BEST CHRISTMAS OF THEM ALL — Shakin' Stevens (Epic)
39	49	I CALL YOUR NAME — A-ha (Warner Bros)
	50	ALL THIS TIME — Sting (A&M)

19 January 1991

Last	This	Title / Artist
1	1	SADNESS PART 1 — Enigma (Virgin International)
8	2	CRAZY — Seal (ZTT)
2	3	BRING YOUR DAUGHTER ... TO THE SLAUGHTER — Iron Maiden (EMI)
4	4	THE GREASE MEGAMIX — John Travolta & Olivia Newton-John (Polydor)
15	5	GONNA MAKE YOU SWEAT — C&C Music Factory featuring Freedom Williams (Columbia)
20	6	(I'VE HAD) THE TIME OF MY LIFE — Bill Medley & Jennifer Warnes (RCA)
3	7	ICE ICE BABY — Vanilla Ice (SBK)
38	8	INTERNATIONAL BRIGHT YOUNG THING — Jesus Jones (Food)
14	9	CRAZY — Patsy Cline (MCA)
6	10	ALL TOGETHER NOW — Farm (Produce)
11	11	PRAY — MC Hammer (Capitol)
27	12	I CAN'T TAKE THE POWER — Off-Shore (CBS)
12	13	ALL THE MAN THAT I NEED — Whitney Houston (Arista)
5	14	YOU'VE LOST THAT LOVIN' FEELING/EBB TIDE — Righteous Brothers (Verve)
-	15	3AM ETERNAL LIVE AT THE SSL — KLF featuring The Children Of The Revolution (KLF Communications)
16	16	X Y & ZEE — Pop Will Eat Itself (RCA)
7	17	JUSTIFY MY LOVE — Madonna (Sire)
11	18	MARY HAD A LITTE BOY — Snap (Arista)
	19	A LL TRUE MAN — Alexander O'Neal (Tabu)
50	20	ALL THIS TIME — Sting (A&M)
9	21	THE TOTAL MIX — Black Box (deConstruction)
30	22	PREACHER MAN — Bananarama (London)
35	23	MERCY MERCY MERCY/I WANT YOU — Robert Palmer featuring Gilly G (EMI)
16	24	UNBELIEVABLE — EMF (Parlophone)
	25	SENSITIVITY — Ralph Tresvant (MCA)
28	26	GOT THE TIME — Anthrax (Island)
	27	HIPPYCHICK — Soho (S&M)
	28	BOX SET GO — High (London)
	29	A LIL' AIN'T ENOUGH — David Lee Roth (Warner Bros)
22	30	ARE YOU DREAMING? — Twenty 4 Seven featuring Captain Hollywood (BCM)
18	31	WICKED GAME — Chris Isaak (London)
	32	CAN I KICK IT? — A Tribe Called Quest (Jive)
34	33	I'M NOT IN LOVE — Will To Power (Epic)
37	34	SUMMER RAIN — Belinda Carlisle (Virgin)
	35	JORDAN : THE EP (EP) — Prefab Sprout (Kitchenware)
24	36	SITUATION — Yazoo (Mute)
47	37	ALWAYS THE SUN — Stranglers (Epic)
23	38	DISAPPEAR — INXS (Mercury)
-	39	III — Orbital (FFRR)
19	40	UNCHAINED MELODY — Righteous Brothers (Verve)
	41	GET HERE — Oleta Adams (Fontana)
	42	MISS AMERICA — Big Dish (East West)
17	43	THE ANNIVERSARY WALTZ PART TWO — Status Quo (Vertigo)
	44	WELL, DID YOU EVAH! — Deborah Harry & Iggy Pop (Chrysalis)
25	45	24 HOURS — Betty Boo (Rhythm King)
43	46	TELL ME WHERE YOU'RE GOING — Silje (EMI)
47	47	FREEDOM! — George Michael (Epic)
31	48	SUCKER DJ — Dimples D (FBI)
	49	WHERE HAS ALL THE LOVE GONE — Maureen (Urban)
36	50	A MATTER OF FACT — Innocence (Cooltempo)

Bill Medley & Jennifer Warnes' duet on *(I've Had) The Time Of My Life,* from the film *Dirty Dancing,* had already reached Number Seven in the chart on its first release in 1987. Early 1991 saw it return with equal strength – in fact, peaking one place higher than originally. Patsy Cline's 30-year-old *Crazy* also making the Top 10 was a huge improvement on its 1961 showing, when it had missed the 30.

January – February 1991

last week / this week

26 January 1991

last	this		
1	1	SADNESS PART 1	Enigma (Virgin International)
15	2	3AM ETERNAL LIVE AT THE SSL	
		KLF featuring The Children Of The	
		Revolution (KLF Communications)	
2	3	CRAZY	Seal (ZTT)
5	4	GONNA MAKE YOU SWEAT	C&C Music Factory
		featuring Freedom Williams (Columbia)	
-	5	INNUENDO	Queen (Parlophone)
12	6	I CAN'T TAKE THE POWER	Off-Shore (CBS)
23	7	MERCY MERCY/I WANT YOU	
		Robert Palmer featuring Gilly G (EMI)	
8	8	INTERNATIONAL BRIGHT YOUNG THING	
		Jesus Jones (Food)	
25	9	SENSITIVITY	Ralph Tresvant (MCA)
6	10	(I'VE HAD) THE TIME OF MY LIFE	
		Bill Medley & Jennifer Warnes (RCA)	
4	11	THE GREASE MEGAMIX	John Travolta
		& Olivia Newton-John (Polydor)	
27	12	HIPPYCHICK	Soho (S&M)
19	13	ALL TRUE MAN	Alexander O'Neal (Tabu)
13	14	ALL THE MAN THAT I NEED	Whitney Houston (Arista)
9	15	CRAZY	Patsy Cline (MCA)
22	16	PREACHER MAN	Bananarama (London)
32	17	CAN I KICK IT?	A Tribe Called Quest (Jive)
7	18	ICE ICE BABY	Vanilla Ice (SBK)
10	19	ALL TOGETHER NOW	Farm (Produce)
3	20	BRING YOUR DAUGHTER ... TO THE	
		SLAUGHTER	Iron Maiden (EMI)
16	21	X Y & ZEE	Pop Will Eat Itself (RCA)
-	22	WIGGLE IT	2 In A Room (SBK)
20	23	ALL THIS TIME	Sting (A&M)
-	24	FORGET ME NOTS	Tongue 'N' Cheek (Syncopate)
41	25	GET HERE	Oleta Adams (Fontana)
11	26	PRAY	MC Hammer (Capitol)
34	27	SUMMER RAIN	Belinda Carlisle (Virgin)
-	28	CRY FOR HELP	Rick Astley (RCA)
18	29	MARY HAD A LITTE BOY	Snap (Arista)
33	30	I'M NOT IN LOVE	Will To Power (Epic)
17	31	JUSTIFY MY LOVE	Madonna (Sire)
39	32	Ill	Orbital (FFRR)
-	33	DO THE BARTMAN	Simpsons (Geffen)
24	34	A LIL' AIN'T ENOUGH	David Lee Roth (Warner Bros)
26	35	BOX SET GO	High (London)
42	36	MISS AMERICA	Big Dish (East West)
37	37	ALWAYS THE SUN	Stranglers (Epic)
21	38	THE TOTAL MIX	Black Box (deConstruction)
14	39	YOU'VE LOST THAT LOVIN' FEELING/EBB TIDE	
		Righteous Brothers (Verve)	
-	40	MYSTERIES OF LOVE	LA Mix (A&M)
-	41	COMING OUT OF THE DARK	
		Gloria Estefan (Epic)	
49	42	WHERE HAS ALL THE LOVE GONE	Maureen (Urban)
-	43	TWICE AS HARD	Black Crowes (Def American)
30	44	ARE YOU DREAMING?	Twenty 4 Seven
		featuring Captain Hollywood (BCM)	
35	45	JORDAN : THE EP (EP)Prefab Sprout (Kitchenware)	
44	46	WELL, DID YOU EVAH!	
		Deborah Harry & Iggy Pop (Chrysalis)	
-	47	THE GIRL I USED TO KNOW	
		Brother Beyond (Parlophone)	
-	48	OUTSTANDING	Kenny Thomas (Cooltempo)
31	49	WICKED GAME	Chris Isaak (London)
-	50	BREAKAWAY (REMIX)	
		Donna Summer (Warner Bros)	

2 February 1991

5	1	INNUENDO	Queen (Parlophone)
2	2	3AM ETERNAL LIVE AT THE SSL	
		KLF featuring The Children Of The	
		Revolution (KLF Communications)	
22	3	WIGGLE IT	2 In A Room (SBK)
1	4	SADNESS PART 1	Enigma (Virgin International)
4	5	GONNA MAKE YOU SWEAT	C&C Music Factory
		featuring Freedom Williams (Columbia)	
28	6	CRY FOR HELP	Rick Astley (RCA)
6	8	I CAN'T TAKE THE POWER	Off-Shore (CBS)
33	9	DO THE BARTMAN	Simpsons (Geffen)
12	10	HIPPYCHICK	Soho (S&M)
7	11	MERCY MERCY/I WANT YOU	
		Robert Palmer featuring Gilly G (EMI)	
9	12	SENSITIVITY	Ralph Tresvant (MCA)
10	13	(I'VE HAD) THE TIME OF MY LIFE	Bill Medley
		Jennifer Warnes (RCA)	
17	14	CAN I KICK IT?	A Tribe Called Quest (Jive)
25	15	GET HERE	Oleta Adams (Fontana)
-	16	I BELIEVE	EMF (Parlophone)
8	17	INTERNATIONAL BRIGHT YOUNG THING	
		Jesus Jones (Food)	
14	18	ALL THE MAN THAT I NEED	
		Whitney Houston (Arista)	
-	19	SUMMERS MAGIC	
		Mark Summers (4th & Broadway)	
41	20	COMING OUT OF THE DARK	
		Gloria Estefan (Epic)	
27	21	SUMMER RAIN	Belinda Carlisle (Virgin)
13	22	ALL TRUE MAN	Alexander O'Neal (Tabu)
24	23	FORGET ME NOTS	
		Tongue 'N' Cheek (Syncopate)	
-	24	WHAT DO I HAVE TO DO	Kylie Minogue (PWL)
11	25	THE GREASE MEGAMIX	John Travolta
		& Olivia Newton-John (Polydor)	
26	26	PLAY THAT FUNKY MUSIC	Vanilla Ice (SBK)
-	27	(I WANNA GIVE YOU) DEVOTION	Nomad
		featuring MC Mikee Freedom (Rumour)	
16	28	PREACHER MAN	Bananarama (London)
48	29	OUTSTANDING	Kenny Thomas (Cooltempo)
18	30	ICE ICE BABY	Vanilla Ice (SBK)
19	31	ALL TOGETHER NOW	Farm (Produce)
32	32	Ill	Orbital (FFRR)
15	33	CRAZY	Patsy Cline (MCA)
30	34	I'M NOT IN LOVE	Will To Power (Epic)
36	35	MISS AMERICA	Big Dish (East West)
21	36	X Y & ZEE	Pop Will Eat Itself (RCA)
37	37	DEDICATION	Thin Lizzy (Vertigo)
35	38	SOMEDAY	Mariah Carey (Columbia)
23	39	ALL THIS TIME	Sting (A&M)
-	40	MUST BEE THE MUSIC	
		King Bee featuring Michele (Columbia)	
26	41	PRAY	MC Hammer (Capitol)
-	42	ECHO MY HEART	Linda Layton (Arista)
39	43	YOU'VE LOST THAT LOVIN' FEELING/EBB TIDE	
		Righteous Brothers (Verve)	
-	44	COOL JERK	Go-Gos (I.R.S.)
40	45	MYSTERIES OF LOVE	LA Mix (A&M)
-	46	THE BEE (REMIX)	Scientist (Kickin')
29	47	GOOD TIMES	Jimmy Barnes & INXS (Atlantic)
29	48	MARY HAD A LITTE BOY	Snap (Arista)
35	49	BOX SET GO	High (London)
31	50	JUSTIFY MY LOVE	Madonna (Sire)

9 February 1991

2	1	3AM ETERNAL LIVE AT THE SSL	
		KLF featuring The Children Of The	
		Revolution (KLF Communications)	
9	2	DO THE BARTMAN	Simpsons (Geffen)
3	3	WIGGLE IT	2 In A Room (SBK)
1	4	INNUENDO	Queen (Parlophone)
6	5	CRY FOR HELP	Rick Astley (RCA)
27	6	(I WANNA GIVE YOU) DEVOTION	Nomad
		featuring MC Mikee Freedom (Rumour)	
16	7	I BELIEVE	EMF (Parlophone)
24	8	WHAT DO I HAVE TO DO	Kylie Minogue (PWL)
10	9	HIPPYCHICK	Soho (S&M)
-	10	ONLY YOU	Praise featuring Miriam Stockley (Epic)
5	11	GONNA MAKE YOU SWEAT	C&C Music Factory
		featuring Freedom Williams (Columbia)	
26	12	PLAY THAT FUNKY MUSIC	Vanilla Ice (SBK)
4	13	SADNESS PART 1	Enigma (Virgin International)
7	14	CRAZY	Seal (ZTT)
15	15	GET HERE	Oleta Adams (Fontana)
8	16	I CAN'T TAKE THE POWER	Off-Shore (CBS)
14	17	CAN I KICK IT?	A Tribe Called Quest (Jive)
11	18	MERCY MERCY/I WANT YOU	
		Robert Palmer featuring Gilly G (EMI)	
12	19	SENSITIVITY	Ralph Tresvant (MCA)
-	20	YOU GOT THE LOVE	
		Source featuring Candi Staton (Truelove)	
19	21	SUMMERS MAGIC	
		Mark Summers (4th & Broadway)	
29	22	OUTSTANDING	Kenny Thomas (Cooltempo)
20	23	COMING OUT OF THE DARK	Gloria Estefan (Epic)
-	24	GLAD	Kim Appleby (Parlophone)
13	25	(I'VE HAD) THE TIME OF MY LIFE	
		Bill Medley & Jennifer Warnes (RCA)	
-	26	GAMES	New Kids On The Block (Columbia)
-	27	THE NIGHT FEVER MEGAMIX	Mixmasters (I.Q.)
23	28	FORGET ME NOTS	Tongue 'N' Cheek (Syncopate)
-	29	BONEYARD	Little Angels (Polydor)
-	30	SMALLTOWN BOY	
		Jimmy Somerville with Bronski Beat (London)	
17	31	INTERNATIONAL BRIGHT YOUNG THING	
		Jesus Jones (Food)	
21	32	SUMMER RAIN	Belinda Carlisle (Virgin)
18	33	ALL THE MAN THAT I NEED	
		Whitney Houston (Arista)	
-	34	MY HEART, THE BEAT/DANCE THE NIGHT	
		AWAY	D Shake (Cooltempo)
38	35	SOMEDAY	Mariah Carey (Columbia)
31	36	ALL TOGETHER NOW	Farm (Produce)
28	37	PREACHER MAN	Bananarama (London)
-	38	BLUE HOTEL	Chris Isaak (Reprise)
33	39	CRAZY	Patsy Cline (MCA)
30	40	ICE ICE BABY	Vanilla Ice (SBK)
34	41	I'M NOT IN LOVE	Will To Power (Epic)
47	42	GOOD TIMES	Jimmy Barnes & INXS (Atlantic)
-	43	THE WAY YOU DO THE THINGS YOU DO	
		UB40 (DEP International)	
22	44	ALL TRUE MAN	Alexander O'Neal (Tabu)
25	45	THE GREASE MEGAMIX	John Travolta
		& Olivia Newton-John (Polydor)	
35	46	MISS AMERICA	Big Dish (East West)
-	47	EVERYBODY NEEDS SOMEBODY	Birdland (Lazy)
-	48	LOVE REARS ITS UGLY HEAD	Living Colour (Epic)
37	49	DEDICATION	Thin Lizzy (Vertigo)
-	50	ALL RIGHT NOW	Free (Island)

Seal's Number Two hit *Crazy* had no connection with Patsy Cline's vintage hit if the same title, even though both singles were in the top 10 together. *Innuendo* was the title track from Queen's similarly chart-topping album; these were the last Number One hits Freddie Mercury would have during his lifetime. Rick Astley also made the Top 10 again, after almost two years' absence.

February – March 1991

16 February 1991

		Title	Artist (Label)
1	1	3AM ETERNAL LIVE AT THE SSL	KLF featuring The Children Of The Revolution (KLF Communications)
2	2	DO THE BARTMAN	Simpsons (Geffen)
10	3	ONLY YOU	Praise featuring Miriam Stockley (Epic)
6	4	(I WANNA GIVE YOU) DEVOTION	featuring MC Mikee Freedom (Rumour)
3	5	WIGGLE IT	2 In A Room (SBK)
7	6	I BELIEVE	EMF (Parlophone)
8	7	WHAT DO I HAVE TO DO	Kylie Minogue (PWL)
9	8	HIPPYCHICK	Soho (S&M)
5	9	CRY FOR HELP	Rick Astley (RCA)
24	10	GLAD	Kim Appleby (Parlophone)
12	11	PLAY THAT FUNKY MUSIC	Vanilla Ice (SBK)
15	12	GET HERE	Oleta Adams (Fontana)
26	13	GAMES	New Kids On The Block (Columbia)
20	14	YOU GOT THE LOVE	Source featuring Candi Staton (Truelove)
22	15	OUTSTANDING	Kenny Thomas (Cooltempo)
11	16	GONNA MAKE YOU SWEAT	C&C Music Factory featuring Freedom Williams (Columbia)
27	17	THE NIGHT FEVER MEGAMIX	Mixmasters (I.Q.)
14	18	CRAZY	Seal (ZTT)
4	19	INNUENDO	Queen (Parlophone)
38	20	BLUE HOTEL	Chris Isaak (Reprise)
16	21	I CAN'T TAKE THE POWER	Off-Shore (CBS)
17	22	CAN I KICK IT?	A Tribe Called Quest (Jive)
13	23	SADNESS PART 1	Enigma (Virgin International)
21	24	SUMMERS MAGIC	Mark Summers (4th & Broadway)
18	25	MERCY MERCY MERCY/I WANT YOU	Robert Palmer featuring Gilly G (EMI)
23	26	COMING OUT OF THE DARK	Gloria Estefan (Epic)
19	27	SENSITIVITY	Ralph Tresvant (MCA)
50	28	ALL RIGHT NOW	Free (Island)
30	29	SMALLTOWN BOY	Jimmy Somerville with Bronski Beat (London)
-	30	EVERY BEAT OF MY HEART	Railway Children (Virgin)
42	31	GOOD TIMES	Jimmy Barnes & INXS (Atlantic)
-	32	THINKIN' ABOUT YOUR BODY	2 Mad (Big Life)
-	33	BEAUTIFUL LOVE	Julian Cope (Island)
-	34	IN YER FACE	808 State (ZTT)
-	35	AUBERGE	Chris Rea (East West)
32	36	SUMMER RAIN	Belinda Carlisle (Virgin)
-	37	THE KING IS HALF UNDRESSED	Jellyfish (Charisma)
-	38	HEAL THE PAIN	George Michael (Epic)
43	39	THE WAY YOU DO THE THINGS YOU DO	UB40 (DEP International)
35	40	SOMEDAY	Mariah Carey (Columbia)
33	41	ALL THE MAN THAT I NEED	Whitney Houston (Arista)
48	42	LOVE REARS ITS UGLY HEAD	Living Colour (Epic)
-	43	IT'S TOO LATE	Quartz introducing Dina Carroll (Mercury)
28	44	FORGET ME NOTS	Tongue 'N' Cheek (Syncopate)
25	45	(I'VE HAD) THE TIME OF MY LIFE	Bill Medley & Jennifer Warnes (RCA)
-	46	DON'T QUIT	Caron Wheeler (RCA)
29	47	BONEYARD	Little Angels (Polydor)
-	48	BABY DON'T CRY	Lalah Hathaway (Virgin America)
-	49	WHICH WAY SHOULD I JUMP?	Milltown Brothers (A&M)
36	50	ALL TOGETHER NOW	Farm (Produce)

23 February 1991

		Title	Artist (Label)
2	1	DO THE BARTMAN	Simpsons (Geffen)
1	2	3AM ETERNAL LIVE AT THE SSL	KLF featuring The Children Of The Revolution (KLF Communications)
3	3	ONLY YOU	Praise featuring Miriam Stockley (Epic)
4	4	(I WANNA GIVE YOU) DEVOTION	featuring MC Mikee Freedom (Rumour)
10	5	GLAD	Kim Appleby (Parlophone)
12	6	GET HERE	Oleta Adams (Fontana)
5	7	WIGGLE IT	2 In A Room (SBK)
14	8	YOU GOT THE LOVE	Source featuring Candi Staton (Truelove)
7	9	WHAT DO I HAVE TO DO	Kylie Minogue (PWL)
6	10	I BELIEVE	EMF (Parlophone)
34	11	IN YER FACE	808 State (ZTT)
28	12	ALL RIGHT NOW	Free (Island)
8	13	HIPPYCHICK	Soho (S&M)
9	14	CRY FOR HELP	Rick Astley (RCA)
15	15	OUTSTANDING	Kenny Thomas (Cooltempo)
20	16	BLUE HOTEL	Chris Isaak (Reprise)
11	17	PLAY THAT FUNKY MUSIC	Vanilla Ice (SBK)
13	18	GAMES	New Kids On The Block (Columbia)
31	19	GOOD TIMES	Jimmy Barnes & INXS (Atlantic)
-	20	THINK ABOUT	DJH featuring Stefy (RCA)
16	21	GONNA MAKE YOU SWEAT	C&C Music Factory featuring Freedom Williams (Columbia)
18	22	CRAZY	Seal (ZTT)
35	23	AUBERGE	Chris Rea (East West)
30	24	EVERY BEAT OF MY HEART	Railway Children (Virgin)
38	25	HEAL THE PAIN	George Michael (Epic)
33	26	BEAUTIFUL LOVE	Julian Cope (Island)
-	27	TREMELO (EP)	My Bloody Valentine (Creation)
24	28	SUMMERS MAGIC	Mark Summers (4th & Broadway)
-	29	OUR FRANK	Morrissey (HMV)
42	30	LOVE REARS ITS UGLY HEAD	Living Colour (Epic)
22	31	CAN I KICK IT?	A Tribe Called Quest (Jive)
23	32	SADNESS PART 1	Enigma (Virgin International)
17	33	THE NIGHT FEVER MEGAMIX	Mixmasters (I.Q.)
37	34	THE KING IS HALF UNDRESSED	Jellyfish (Charisma)
-	35	HERE COMES THE HAMMER	MC Hammer (Capitol)
27	36	SENSITIVITY	Ralph Tresvant (MCA)
25	37	MERCY MERCY MERCY/I WANT YOU	Robert Palmer featuring Gilly G (EMI)
-	38	FEELIN'	LAs (Go! Discs)
32	39	THINKIN' ABOUT YOUR BODY	2 Mad (Big Life)
49	40	WHICH WAY SHOULD I JUMP?	Milltown Brothers (A&M)
43	41	IT'S TOO LATE	Quartz introducing Dina Carroll (Mercury)
19	42	INNUENDO	Queen (Parlophone)
21	43	I CAN'T TAKE THE POWER	Off-Shore (CBS)
26	44	COMING OUT OF THE DARK	Gloria Estefan (Epic)
-	45	IF THIS IS LOVE	JJ (Columbia)
-	46	MOVE YOUR BODY (ELEVATION)	Xpansions (Arista)
29	47	SMALLTOWN BOY	Jimmy Somerville with Bronski Beat (London)
-	48	LOVE WALKED IN	Thunder (EMI)
41	49	ALL THE MAN THAT I NEED	Whitney Houston (Arista)
-	50	HOW DO YOU SAY ... LOVE/GROOVE IS IN THE HEART	Deee-Lite (Elektra)

2 March 1991

		Title	Artist (Label)
1	1	DO THE BARTMAN	Simpsons (Geffen)
4	2	(I WANNA GIVE YOU) DEVOTION	Nomad featuring MC Mikee Freedom (Rumour)
6	3	GET HERE	Oleta Adams (Fontana)
8	4	YOU GOT THE LOVE	Source featuring Candi Staton (Truelove)
2	5	3AM ETERNAL LIVE AT THE SSL	KLF featuring The Children Of The Revolution (KLF Communications)
5	6	GLAD	Kim Appleby (Parlophone)
12	7	ALL RIGHT NOW	Free (Island)
11	8	IN YER FACE	808 State (ZTT)
-	9	CRAZY FOR YOU	Madonna (Sire)
3	10	ONLY YOU	Praise featuring Miriam Stockley (Epic)
15	11	OUTSTANDING	Kenny Thomas (Cooltempo)
20	12	THINK ABOUT	DJH featuring Stefy (RCA)
7	13	WIGGLE IT	2 In A Room (SBK)
9	14	WHAT DO I HAVE TO DO	Kylie Minogue (PWL)
23	15	AUBERGE	Chris Rea (East West)
16	16	BLUE HOTEL	Chris Isaak (Reprise)
19	17	GOOD TIMES	Jimmy Barnes & INXS (Atlantic)
35	18	HERE COMES THE HAMMER	MC Hammer (Capitol)
46	19	MOVE YOUR BODY (ELEVATION)	Xpansions (Arista)
-	20	SHOULD I STAY OR SHOULD I GO/RUSH	Clash/BAD II (Columbia)
10	21	I BELIEVE	EMF (Parlophone)
48	22	LOVE WALKED IN	Thunder (EMI)
13	23	HIPPYCHICK	Soho (S&M)
24	24	EVERY BEAT OF MY HEART	Railway Children (Virgin)
25	25	HEAL THE PAIN	George Michael (Epic)
-	26	BECAUSE I LOVE YOU	Stevie B (Polydor)
29	27	OUR FRANK	Morrissey (HMV)
26	28	BEAUTIFUL LOVE	Julian Cope (Island)
22	29	CRAZY	Seal (ZTT)
14	30	CRY FOR HELP	Rick Astley (RCA)
31	31	LOVE REARS ITS UGLY HEAD	Living Colour (Epic)
17	32	PLAY THAT FUNKY MUSIC	Vanilla Ice (SBK)
-	33	UNFINISHED SYMPATHY	Massive (Wild Bunch)
18	34	GAMES	New Kids On The Block (Columbia)
41	35	IT'S TOO LATE	Quartz introducing Dina Carroll (Mercury)
40	36	WHICH WAY SHOULD I JUMP?	Milltown Brothers (A&M)
38	37	FEELIN'	LAs (Go! Discs)
-	38	APPARENTLY NOTHIN'	Young Disciples (Talkin' Loud)
21	39	GONNA MAKE YOU SWEAT	C&C Music Factory featuring Freedom Williams (Columbia)
-	40	GO FOR IT! (HEART AND FIRE)	Rocky V featuring Joey B. Ellis & Tynetta Hare (Capitol)
41	41	WHO? WHERE? WHY?	Jesus Jones (Food)
50	42	HOW DO YOU SAY ... LOVE/GROOVE IS IN THE HEART	Deee-Lite (Elektra)
-	43	TILL WE MEET AGAIN	Inner City (10)
32	44	SADNESS PART 1	Enigma (Virgin International)
-	45	THIS IS YOUR LIFE	Banderas (London)
-	46	THE ONE AND ONLY	Chesney Hawkes (Chrysalis)
28	47	SUMMERS MAGIC	Mark Summers (4th & Broadway)
39	48	THINKIN' ABOUT YOUR BODY	2 Mad (Big Life)
-	49	ADRENALIN (EP)	N-Joi (deConstruction)
36	50	SENSITIVITY	Ralph Tresvant (MCA)

The Number One novelty rap *Do The Bartman* was a spin-off from the hugely successful US animated comedy show *The Simpsons*, which chronicled the affairs of an eminently avoidable family, of whom son Bart was chief troublemaker. On Sky satellite TV in the UK, and therefore available only to a comparatively small audience, both show and characters still developed a cult following.

531

March 1991

The Clash, several years after disbanding, were the latest act to have a Number One courtesy of a Levi's commercial. *Should I Stay Or Should I Go*, originally released in 1982, had only managed to climb to Number 19 at that time. The B-side of the reissue featured not a Clash track, but *Rush*, a cut for ex-member Mick Jones' subsequent band BAD (Big Audio Dynamite) II.

30 March 1991

last week	this week	title
1	1	THE STONK/THE SMILE SONG Hale & Pace & the Stonkers/Victoria Wood (London)
8	2	RHYTHM OF MY HEART Rod Stewart (Warner Bros)
14	3	WHERE THE STREETS HAVE NO NAME/CAN'T TAKE MY EYES OFF YOU Pet Shop Boys (Parlophone)
3	4	JOYRIDE Roxette (EMI)
2	5	SHOULD I STAY OR SHOULD I GO/RUSH Clash/BAD II (Columbia)
15	6	THE ONE AND ONLY Chesney Hawkes (Chrysalis)
4	7	BECAUSE I LOVE YOU Stevie B (Polydor)
12	8	SECRET LOVE Bee Gees (Warner Bros)
5	9	IT'S TOO LATE Quartz introducing Dina Carroll (Mercury)
23	10	LET THERE BE LOVE Simple Minds (Virgin)
7	11	YOU GOT THE LOVE Source featuring Candi Staton (Truelove)
13	12	THIS IS YOUR LIFE Banderas (London)
10	13	UNFINISHED SYMPATHY Massive (Wild Bunch)
18	14	LOOSE FIT Happy Mondays (Factory)
17	15	LOSING MY RELIGION R.E.M. (Warner Bros)
12	16	LOVE REARS ITS UGLY HEAD Living Colour (Epic)
9	17	MOVE YOUR BODY (ELEVATION) Xpansions (Arista)
-	18	SIT DOWN James (Fontana)
27	19	I'VE GOT NEWS FOR YOU Feargal Sharkey (Virgin)
6	20	CRAZY FOR YOU Madonna (Sire)
24	21	I'M GOING SLIGHTLY MAD Queen (EMI)
29	22	SHE'S A WOMAN Scritti Politti/Shabba Ranks (Virgin)
-	23	OVER TO YOU JOHN (HERE WE GO AGAIN) Jive Bunny & the Mastermixers (Music Factory)
25	24	BOW DOWN MISTER Jesus Loves You (More Protein)
-	25	BEEN CAUGHT STEALING Jane's Addiction (Warner Bros)
16	26	DO THE BARTMAN Simpsons (Geffen)
-	27	SNAP MEGAMIX Snap (Arista)
38	28	WEAR YOUR LOVE LIKE HEAVEN Definition Of Sound (Circa)
45	29	CAN YOU DIG IT? Mock Turtles (Siren)
20	30	(I WANNA GIVE YOU) DEVOTION Nomad featuring MC Mikee Freedom (Rumour)
32	31	HANGAR 18 Megadeth (Capitol)
30	32	WHO? WHERE? WHY? Jesus Jones (Food)
-	33	SAY HELLO WAVE GOODBYE '91 Soft Cell/Marc Almond (Mercury)
19	34	OVER RISING (EP) Charlatans (Situation Two)
37	35	CHERRY PIE Warrant (Columbia)
21	36	ALL RIGHT NOW Free (Island)
-	37	HUMAN NATURE Gary Clail On-U Sound System (Perfecto)
-	38	PLAYING WITH KNIVES Bizarre Inc (Vinyl Solution)
-	39	CARAVAN Inspiral Carpets (Cow)
33	40	DON'T GO MESSIN' WITH MY HEART Mantronix (Capitol)
-	41	GREASE THE DREAM MIX Frankie Valli /John Travolta/Olivia Newton-John (PWL)
22	42	TODAY FOREVER (EP) Ride (Creation)
28	43	GET HERE Oleta Adams (Fontana)
39	44	AROUND THE WAY GIRL LL Cool J (Columbia)
-	45	WHAT IS THIS THING CALLED LOVE? Alexander O'Neal (Tabu)
-	46	WORD OF MOUTH Mike & the Mechanics (Virgin)
-	47	HERE WE GO C&C Music Factory (Columbia)
-	48	BY MY SIDE INXS (Mercury)
-	49	HIGHWIRE Rolling Stones (Columbia)
-	50	YESTERDAY TODAY Ocean Colour Scene (!Phfft)

6 April 1991

last week	this week	title
6	1	THE ONE AND ONLY Chesney Hawkes (Chrysalis)
3	2	WHERE THE STREETS HAVE NO NAME/CAN'T TAKE MY EYES OFF YOU Pet Shop Boys (Parlophone)
18	3	SIT DOWN James (Fontana)
2	4	RHYTHM OF MY HEART Rod Stewart (Warner Bros)
8	5	SECRET LOVE Bee Gees (Warner Bros)
10	6	LET THERE BE LOVE Simple Minds (Virgin)
4	7	JOYRIDE Roxette (EMI)
1	8	THE STONK/THE SMILE SONG Hale & Pace & the Stonkers/Victoria Wood (London)
9	9	IT'S TOO LATE Quartz introducing Dina Carroll (Mercury)
27	10	SNAP MEGAMIX Snap (Arista)
5	11	SHOULD I STAY OR SHOULD I GO/RUSH Clash/BAD II (Columbia)
12	12	THIS IS YOUR LIFE Banderas (London)
19	13	I'VE GOT NEWS FOR YOU Feargal Sharkey (Virgin)
37	14	HUMAN NATURE Gary Clail On-U Sound System (Perfecto)
15	15	LOSING MY RELIGION R.E.M. (Warner Bros)
11	16	YOU GOT THE LOVE Source featuring Candi Staton (Truelove)
22	17	SHE'S A WOMAN Scritti Politti/Shabba Ranks (Virgin)
14	18	LOOSE FIT Happy Mondays (Factory)
-	19	LOVE AND KISSES Dannii Minogue (MCA)
47	20	HERE WE GO C&C Music Factory (Columbia)
28	21	WEAR YOUR LOVE LIKE HEAVEN Definition Of Sound (Circa)
7	22	BECAUSE I LOVE YOU Stevie B (Polydor)
49	23	HIGHWIRE Rolling Stones (Columbia)
23	24	OVER TO YOU JOHN (HERE WE GO AGAIN) Jive Bunny & the Mastermixers (Music Factory)
13	25	UNFINISHED SYMPATHY Massive (Wild Bunch)
46	26	WORD OF MOUTH Mike & the Mechanics (Virgin)
17	27	MOVE YOUR BODY (ELEVATION) Xpansions (Arista)
16	28	LOVE REARS ITS UGLY HEAD Living Colour (Epic)
29	29	CAN YOU DIG IT? Mock Turtles (Siren)
48	30	BY MY SIDE INXS (Mercury)
-	31	MOVE RIGHT OUT Rick Astley (RCA)
24	32	BOW DOWN MISTER Jesus Loves You (More Protein)
25	33	BEEN CAUGHT STEALING Jane's Addiction (Warner Bros)
39	34	CARAVAN Inspiral Carpets (Cow)
21	35	I'M GOING SLIGHTLY MAD Queen (EMI)
-	36	THE WHOLE OF THE MOON Waterboys (Ensign)
33	37	SAY HELLO WAVE GOODBYE '91 Soft Cell/Marc Almond (Mercury)
-	38	WHERE LOVE LIVES (COME ON IN) Alison Limerick (Arista)
-	39	COWBOYS AND ANGELS George Michael (Epic)
20	40	CRAZY FOR YOU Madonna (Sire)
-	41	STRIKE IT UP Black Box (deConstruction)
32	42	WHO? WHERE? WHY? Jesus Jones (Food)
-	43	I LOVE YOU Vanilla Ice (SBK)
-	44	MEA CULPA PART II Enigma (Virgin International)
-	45	SENZA UNA DONNA (WITHOUT A WOMAN) Zucchero/Paul Young (London)
30	46	(I WANNA GIVE YOU) DEVOTION Nomad featuring MC Mikee Freedom (Rumour)
-	47	ANTHEM N-Joi (deConstruction)
-	48	TOO WICKED (EP) Aswad (Mango)
26	49	DO THE BARTMAN Simpsons (Geffen)
-	50	ALWAYS ON THE RUN Lenny Kravitz (Virgin America)

13 April 1991

last week	this week	title
3	1	SIT DOWN James (Fontana)
1	2	THE ONE AND ONLY Chesney Hawkes (Chrysalis)
36	3	THE WHOLE OF THE MOON Waterboys (Ensign)
4	4	RHYTHM OF MY HEART Rod Stewart (Warner Bros)
5	5	SECRET LOVE Bee Gees (Warner Bros)
19	6	LOVE AND KISSES Dannii Minogue (MCA)
14	7	HUMAN NATURE Gary Clail On-U Sound System (Perfecto)
10	8	SNAP MEGAMIX Snap (Arista)
7	9	JOYRIDE Roxette (EMI)
2	10	WHERE THE STREETS HAVE NO NAME/CAN'T TAKE MY EYES OFF YOU Pet Shop Boys (Parlophone)
41	11	STRIKE IT UP Black Box (deConstruction)
13	12	I'VE GOT NEWS FOR YOU Feargal Sharkey (Virgin)
6	13	LET THERE BE LOVE Simple Minds (Virgin)
-	14	RESCUE ME Madonna (Sire)
47	15	ANTHEM N-Joi (deConstruction)
20	16	HERE WE GO C&C Music Factory (Columbia)
12	17	THIS IS YOUR LIFE Banderas (London)
21	18	WEAR YOUR LOVE LIKE HEAVEN Definition Of Sound (Circa)
9	19	IT'S TOO LATE Quartz introducing Dina Carroll (Mercury)
-	20	DEEP, DEEP TROUBLE Simpsons featuring Bart & Homer (Geffen)
17	21	SHE'S A WOMAN Scritti Politti/Shabba Ranks (Virgin)
23	22	HIGHWIRE Rolling Stones (Columbia)
26	23	WORD OF MOUTH Mike & the Mechanics (Virgin)
-	24	THE SIZE OF A COW Wonder Stuff (Polydor)
15	25	LOSING MY RELIGION R.E.M. (Warner Bros)
29	26	CAN YOU DIG IT? Mock Turtles (Siren)
-	27	RING MY BELL Monie Love Vs. Adeva (Cooltempo)
34	28	CARAVAN Inspiral Carpets (Cow)
38	29	WHERE LOVE LIVES (COME ON IN) Alison Limerick (Arista)
11	30	SHOULD I STAY OR SHOULD I GO/RUSH Clash/BAD II (Columbia)
24	31	OVER TO YOU JOHN (HERE WE GO AGAIN) Jive Bunny & the Mastermixers (Music Factory)
39	32	COWBOYS AND ANGELS George Michael (Epic)
30	33	BY MY SIDE INXS (Mercury)
-	34	HYPERREAL Shamen (One Little Indian)
16	35	YOU GOT THE LOVE Source featuring Candi Staton (Truelove)
18	36	LOOSE FIT Happy Mondays (Factory)
45	37	SENZA UNA DONNA (WITHOUT A WOMAN) Zucchero/Paul Young (London)
-	38	HEAVEN Chris Rea (East West)
33	39	BEEN CAUGHT STEALING Jane's Addict (Warner Bros)
28	40	LOVE REARS ITS UGLY HEAD Living Colour (Epic)
-	41	SAILING ON THE SEVEN SEAS Orchestral Manoeuvres In The Dark (Virgin)
8	42	THE STONK/THE SMILE SONG Hale & Pace & the Stonkers/Victoria Wood (London)
22	43	BECAUSE I LOVE YOU Stevie B (Polydor)
25	44	UNFINISHED SYMPATHY Massive (Wild Bunch)
-	45	I'M ALRIGHT Katharine E (Dead Dead Good)
-	46	SEAL OUR FATE Gloria Estefan (Epic)
50	47	ALWAYS ON THE RUN Lenny Kravitz (Virg America)
-	48	(I JUST WANNA) B WITH U Transvision Vamp (MCA)
27	49	MOVE YOUR BODY (ELEVATION) Xpansions (Arista)
-	50	IT WON'T BE LONG Alison Moyet (Columbia)

Hale & Pace's *The Stonk*, a rock'n'roll mover in the classic style with lyrics about an absurdly silly dance was released - as had been Bananarama and French & Saunders' *Help!*, two years earlier - in aid of Comic Relief. Its chart ascendancy coincided with the charitable organisation's (literally) outrageously successful Red Nose Day – to the profits of which *The Stonk*'s waived royalties flowed.

April – May 1991

20 April 1991

last week	this	title	artist
3	1	THE WHOLE OF THE MOON	Waterboys (Ensign)
1	2	SIT DOWN	James (Fontana)
2	3	THE ONE AND ONLY	Chesney Hawkes (Chrysalis)
14	4	RESCUE ME	Madonna (Sire)
24	5	THE SIZE OF A COW	Wonder Stuff (Polydor)
6	6	LOVE AND KISSES	Dannii Minogue (MCA)
15	7	ANTHEM	N-Joi (deConstruction)
7	8	HUMAN NATURE	Gary Clail On-U Sound System (Perfecto)
4	9	RHYTHM OF MY HEART	Rod Stewart (Warner Bros)
20	10	DEEP, DEEP TROUBLE	Simpsons featuring Bart & Homer (Geffen)
11	11	STRIKE IT UP	Black Box (deConstruction)
9	12	JOYRIDE	Roxette (EMI)
5	13	SECRET LOVE	Bee Gees (Warner Bros)
27	14	RING MY BELL	Monie Love Vs. Adeva (Cooltempo)
29	15	WHERE LOVE LIES (COME ON IN)	Alison Limerick (Arista)
16	16	HERE WE GO	C&C Music Factory (Columbia)
12	17	I'VE GOT NEWS FOR YOU	Feargal Sharkey (Virgin)
8	18	SNAP MEGAMIX	Snap (Arista)
-	19	ROCK THE CASBAH	Clash (Columbia)
26	20	CAN YOU DIG IT?	Mock Turtles (Siren)
23	21	WORD OF MOUTH	Mike & the Mechanics (Virgin)
37	22	SENZA UNA DONNA (WITHOUT A WOMAN)	Zucchero/Paul Young (London)
48	23	(I JUST WANNA) B WITH U	Transvision Vamp (MCA)
10	24	WHERE THE STREETS HAVE NO NAME/CAN'T TAKE MY EYES OFF YOU	Pet Shop Boys (Parlophone)
13	25	LET THERE BE LOVE	Simple Minds (Virgin)
-	26	SINFUL!	Pete Wylie & the Farm (Siren)
18	27	WEAR YOUR LOVE LIKE HEAVEN	Definition Of Sound (Circa)
34	28	HYPERREAL	Shamen (One Little Indian)
41	29	SAILING ON THE SEVEN SEAS	Orchestral Manoeuvres In The Dark (Virgin)
-	30	THE SHOOP SHOOP SONG (IT'S IN HIS KISS)	Cher (Epic)
21	31	SHE'S A WOMAN	Scritti Politti/Shabba Ranks (Virgin)
19	32	IT'S TOO LATE	Quartz introducing Dina Carroll (Mercury)
17	33	THIS IS YOUR LIFE	Banderas (London)
-	34	QUADROPHONIA	Quadrophonia (Cow)
28	35	CARAVAN	Inspiral Carpets (Cow)
46	36	SEAL OUR FATE	Gloria Estefan (Epic)
-	37	FOOTSTEPS FOLLOWING ME	Frances Nero (Debut)
-	38	UNDERCOVER ANARCHIST	Silver Bullet (Parlophone)
-	39	HERE I STAND	Milltown Brothers (A&M)
50	40	IT WON'T BE LONG	Alison Moyet (Columbia)
25	41	LOSING MY RELIGION	R.E.M. (Warner Bros)
45	42	I'M ALRIGHT	Katharine E (Dead Dead Good)
-	43	SING YOUR LIFE	Morrissey (HMV)
-	44	YOU'VE GOT TO GIVE ME ROOM/RHYTHM OF LIFE	Oleta Adams (Fontana)
22	45	HIGHWIRE	Rolling Stones (Columbia)
-	46	LONG TRAIN RUNNING	Bananarama (London)
47	47	MY HEAD'S IN MISSISSIPPI	ZZ Top (Warner Bros)
-	48	GET READY!	Rochford (Columbia)
38	49	HEAVEN	Chris Rea (East West)
35	50	YOU GOT THE LOVE	Source featuring Candi Staton (Truelove)

27 April 1991

last week	this	title	artist
4	1	RESCUE ME	Madonna (Sire)
2	2	SIT DOWN	James (Fontana)
3	3	THE ONE AND ONLY	Chesney Hawkes (Chrysalis)
1	4	THE WHOLE OF THE MOON	Waterboys (Ensign)
5	5	THE SIZE OF A COW	Wonder Stuff (Polydor)
30	6	THE SHOOP SHOOP SONG (IT'S IN HIS KISS)	Cher (Epic)
6	7	LOVE AND KISSES	Dannii Minogue (MCA)
19	8	ROCK THE CASBAH	Clash (Columbia)
10	9	DEEP, DEEP TROUBLE	Simpsons featuring Bart & Homer (Geffen)
8	10	HUMAN NATURE	Gary Clail On-U Sound System (Perfecto)
21	11	WORD OF MOUTH	Mike & the Mechanics (Virgin)
7	12	ANTHEM	N-Joi (deConstruction)
9	13	RHYTHM OF MY HEART	Rod Stewart (Warner Bros)
11	14	STRIKE IT UP	Black Box (deConstruction)
22	15	SENZA UNA DONNA (WITHOUT A WOMAN)	Zucchero/Paul Young (London)
15	16	WHERE LOVE LIES (COME ON IN)	Alison Limerick (Arista)
12	17	JOYRIDE	Roxette (EMI)
14	18	RING MY BELL	Monie Love Vs. Adeva (Cooltempo)
20	19	CAN YOU DIG IT?	Mock Turtles (Siren)
29	20	SAILING ON THE SEVEN SEAS	Orchestral Manoeuvres In The Dark (Virgin)
34	21	QUADROPHONIA	Quadrophonia (ARS)
26	22	SINFUL!	Pete Wylie & the Farm (Siren)
46	23	LONG TRAIN RUNNING	Bananarama (London)
13	24	SECRET LOVE	Bee Gees (Warner Bros)
37	25	FOOTSTEPS FOLLOWING ME	Frances Nero (Debut)
-	26	GET THE MESSAGE	Electronic (Factory)
23	27	(I JUST WANNA) B WITH U	Transvision Vamp (MCA)
-	28	RING RING RING (HA HA HEY)	De La Soul (Big Life)
36	29	SEAL OUR FATE	Gloria Estefan (Epic)
-	30	CHILDREN	EMF (Parlophone)
47	31	MY HEAD'S IN MISSISSIPPI	ZZ Top (Warner Bros)
16	32	HERE WE GO	C&C Music Factory (Columbia)
28	33	HYPERREAL	Shamen (One Little Indian)
48	34	GET READY!	Rochford (Columbia)
17	35	I'VE GOT NEWS FOR YOU	Feargal Sharkey (Virgin)
-	36	ARE YOU READY	AC/DC (Atco)
18	37	SNAP MEGAMIX	Snap (Arista)
-	38	BORN FREE	Vic Reeves & the Roman Numerals (Sense)
32	39	IT'S TOO LATE	Quartz introducing Dina Carroll (Mercury)
25	40	LET THERE BE LOVE	Simple Minds (Virgin)
38	41	UNDERCOVER ANARCHIST	Silver Bullet (Parlophone)
-	42	OOOPS!	808 State featuring Bjork (ZTT)
44	43	YOU'VE GOT TO GIVE ME ROOM/RHYTHM OF LIFE	Oleta Adams (Fontana)
24	44	WHERE THE STREETS HAVE NO NAME/CAN'T TAKE MY EYES OFF YOU	Pet Shop Boys (Parlophone)
39	45	HERE I STAND	Milltown Brothers (A&M)
-	46	YOU'RE SO VAIN	Carly Simon (Elektra)
27	47	WEAR YOUR LOVE LIKE HEAVEN	Definition Of Sound (Circa)
-	48	LOVE IS A WONDERFUL THING	Michael Bolton (Columbia)
-	49	EAST EASY RIDER (EP)	Julian Cope (Island)
-	50	HOUSEFLY	Tricky Disco (Warp)

4 May 1991

last week	this	title	artist
6	1	THE SHOOP SHOOP SONG (IT'S IN HIS KISS)	Cher (Epic)
2	2	SIT DOWN	James (Fontana)
3	3	THE ONE AND ONLY	Chesney Hawkes (Chrysalis)
38	4	BORN FREE	Vic Reeves & the Roman Numerals (Sense)
1	5	RESCUE ME	Madonna (Sire)
28	6	RING RING RING (HA HA HEY)	De La Soul (Big Life)
26	7	GET THE MESSAGE	Electronic (Factory)
4	8	THE WHOLE OF THE MOON	Waterboys (Ensign)
-	9	LAST TRAIN TO TRANCENTRAL - LIVE FROM THE LOST CONTINENT/THE IRON HORSE	KLF (KLF Communications)
20	10	SAILING ON THE SEVEN SEAS	Orchestral Manoeuvres In The Dark (Virgin)
15	11	SENZA UNA DONNA (WITHOUT A WOMAN)	Zucchero/Paul Young (London)
5	12	THE SIZE OF A COW	Wonder Stuff (Polydor)
10	13	HUMAN NATURE	Gary Clail On-U Sound System (Perfecto)
25	14	FOOTSTEPS FOLLOWING ME	Frances Nero (Debut)
9	15	DEEP, DEEP TROUBLE	Simpsons featuring Bart & Homer (Geffen)
-	16	THERE'S NO OTHER WAY	Blur (Food)
8	17	ROCK THE CASBAH	Clash (Columbia)
21	18	QUADROPHONIA	Quadrophonia (ARS)
30	19	CHILDREN	EMF (Parlophone)
11	20	WORD OF MOUTH	Mike & the Mechanics (Virgin)
29	21	SEAL OUR FATE	Gloria Estefan (Epic)
7	22	LOVE AND KISSES	Dannii Minogue (MCA)
12	23	ANTHEM	N-Joi (deConstruction)
19	24	CAN YOU DIG IT?	Mock Turtles (Siren)
23	25	LONG TRAIN RUNNING	Bananarama (London)
48	26	LOVE IS A WONDERFUL THING	Michael Bolton (Columbia)
34	27	GET READY!	Rochford (Columbia)
13	28	RHYTHM OF MY HEART	Rod Stewart (Warner Bros)
-	29	DON'T LET ME DOWN	Farm (Produce)
-	30	FUTURE LOVE (EP)	Seal (ZTT)
22	31	SINFUL!	Pete Wylie & the Farm (Siren)
36	32	ARE YOU READY	AC/DC (Atco)
14	33	STRIKE IT UP	Black Box (deConstruction)
-	34	JUST A GROOVE	Nomad (Rumour)
16	35	WHERE LOVE LIES (COME ON IN)	Alison Limerick (Arista)
42	36	OOOPS!	808 State featuring Bjork (ZTT)
-	37	PROMISE ME	Beverley Craven (Epic)
-	38	TOUCH ME (ALL NIGHT LONG)	Cathy Dennis (Polydor)
31	39	MY HEAD'S IN MISSISSIPPI	ZZ Top (Warner Bros)
17	40	JOYRIDE	Roxette (EMI)
18	41	RING MY BELL	Monie Love Vs. Adeva (Cooltempo)
24	42	SECRET LOVE	Bee Gees (Warner Bros)
32	43	HERE WE GO	C&C Music Factory (Columbia)
-	44	POWER OF LOVE/LOVE POWER	Luther Vandross (Epic)
45	45	HERE I STAND	Milltown Brothers (A&M)
-	46	GOOD BEAT	Deee-Lite (Elektra)
33	47	HYPERREAL	Shamen (One Little Indian)
46	48	YOU'RE SO VAIN	Carly Simon (Elektra)
-	49	GONNA CATCH YOU	Lonnie Gordon (Supreme)
35	50	I'VE GOT NEWS FOR YOU	Feargal Sharkey (Virgin)

The Waterboys' chart-topping *The Whole Of The Moon* had originally been released late in 1985, when it had charted but peaked at a comparatively modest Number 23. Newcomer Chesney Hawkes' Number One song, meanwhile, came from the soundtrack of the film *Buddy's Song*, in which Chesney (son of the Tremeloes' Chip Hawkes) co-starred with Roger Daltrey.

May 1991

last this week

11 May 1991

last	this		
1	1	THE SHOOP SHOOP SONG (IT'S IN HIS KISS)	Cher (Epic)
9	2	LAST TRAIN TO TRANCENTRAL - LIVE FROM THE LOST CONTINENT/THE IRON HORSE	KLF (KLF Communications)
4	3	BORN FREE	Vic Reeves & the Roman Numerals (Sense)
3	4	THE ONE AND ONLY	Chesney Hawkes (Chrysalis)
6	5	RING RING RING (HA HA HEY)	De La Soul (Big Life)
7	6	GET THE MESSAGE	Electronic (Factory)
10	7	SAILING ON THE SEVEN SEAS	Orchestral Manoeuvres In The Dark (Virgin)
2	8	SIT DOWN	James (Fontana)
11	9	SENZA UNA DONNA (WITHOUT A WOMAN)	Zucchero/Paul Young (London)
38	10	TOUCH ME (ALL NIGHT LONG)	Cathy Dennis (Polydor)
16	11	THERE'S NO OTHER WAY	Blur (Food)
14	12	FOOTSTEPS FOLLOWING ME	Frances Nero (Debut)
30	13	FUTURE LOVE (EP)	Seal (ZTT)
8	14	THE WHOLE OF THE MOON	Waterboys (Ensign)
18	15	QUADROPHONIA	Quadrophonia (ARS)
34	16	JUST A GROOVE	Nomad (Rumour)
19	17	CHILDREN	EMF (Parlophone)
26	18	LOVE IS A WONDERFUL THING	Michael Bolton (Columbia)
13	19	HUMAN NATURE	Gary Clail On-U Sound System (Perfecto)
5	20	RESCUE ME	Madonna (Sire)
-	21	FADING LIKE A FLOWER (EVERY TIME YOU LEAVE)	Roxette (EMI)
29	22	DON'T LET ME DOWN	Farm (Produce)
49	23	GONNA CATCH YOU	Lonnie Gordon (Supreme)
37	24	PROMISE ME	Beverley Craven (Epic)
21	25	SEAL OUR FATE	Gloria Estefan (Epic)
27	26	GET READY!	Roachford (Columbia)
12	27	THE SIZE OF A COW	Wonder Stuff (Polydor)
15	28	DEEP, DEEP TROUBLE	Simpsons featuring Bart & Homer (Geffen)
23	29	ANTHEM	N-Joi (deConstruction)
25	30	LONG TRAIN RUNNING	Bananarama (London)
20	31	WORD OF MOUTH	Mike & the Mechanics (Virgin)
17	32	ROCK THE CASBAH	Clash (Columbia)
24	33	CAN YOU DIG IT?	Mock Turtles (Siren)
22	34	LOVE AND KISSES	Dannii Minogue (MCA)
-	35	ANASTHASIA	T99 (XL)
32	36	ARE YOU READY	AC/DC (Atco)
46	37	GOOD BEAT	Deee-Lite (Elektra)
-	38	THE OTHER SIDE OF SUMMER	Elvis Costello (Warner Bros)
-	39	I SAY YEAH	Secchi featuring Orlando Johnson (Epic)
28	40	RHYTHM OF MY HEART	Rod Stewart (Warner Bros)
36	41	OOOPS!	808 State featuring Bjork (ZTT)
-	42	DALLIANCE	Wedding Present (RCA)
33	43	STRIKE IT UP	Black Box (deConstruction)
-	44	DEVIL'S TOY	Almighty (Polydor)
-	45	ANOTHER SLEEPLESS NIGHT	Shawn Christopher (Arista)
-	46	FEEL LIKE CHANGE	Black (A&M)
-	47	HER	Guy (MCA)
-	48	YOU'RE IN LOVE	Wilson Phillips (SBK)
48	49	YOU'RE SO VAIN	Carly Simon (Elektra)
-	50	TAKE IT	Flowered Up (London)

18 May 1991

last	this		
1	1	THE SHOOP SHOOP SONG (IT'S IN HIS KISS)	Cher (Epic)
2	2	LAST TRAIN TO TRANCENTRAL - LIVE FROM THE LOST CONTINENT/THE IRON HORSE	KLF (KLF Communications)
10	3	TOUCH ME (ALL NIGHT LONG)	Cathy Dennis (Polydor)
7	4	SAILING ON THE SEVEN SEAS	Orchestral Manoeuvres In The Dark (Virgin)
9	5	SENZA UNA DONNA (WITHOUT A WOMAN)	Zucchero/Paul Young (London)
-	6	GYPSY WOMAN (LA DA DEE)	Crystal Waters (A&M)
6	7	GET THE MESSAGE	Electronic (Factory)
12	8	FOOTSTEPS FOLLOWING ME	Frances Nero (Debut)
24	9	PROMISE ME	Beverley Craven (Epic)
13	10	FUTURE LOVE (EP)	Seal (ZTT)
3	11	BORN FREE	Vic Reeves & the Roman Numerals (Sense)
5	12	RING RING RING (HA HA HEY)	De La Soul (Big Life)
16	13	JUST A GROOVE	Nomad (Rumour)
11	14	THERE'S NO OTHER WAY	Blur (Food)
21	15	FADING LIKE A FLOWER (EVERY TIME YOU LEAVE)	Roxette (EMI)
8	16	SIT DOWN	James (Fontana)
35	17	ANASTHASIA	T99 (XL)
18	18	LOVE IS A WONDERFUL THING	Michael Bolton (Columbia)
4	19	THE ONE AND ONLY	Chesney Hawkes (Chrysalis)
15	20	QUADROPHONIA	Quadrophonia (ARS)
-	21	BABY BABY	Amy Grant (A&M)
14	22	THE WHOLE OF THE MOON	Waterboys (Ensign)
23	23	GONNA CATCH YOU	Lonnie Gordon (Supreme)
26	24	GET READY!	Roachford (Columbia)
48	25	YOU'RE IN LOVE	Wilson Phillips (SBK)
17	26	CHILDREN	EMF (Parlophone)
19	27	HUMAN NATURE	Gary Clail On-U Sound System (Perfecto)
22	28	DON'T LET ME DOWN	Farm (Produce)
38	29	THE OTHER SIDE OF SUMMER	Elvis Costello (Warner Bros)
20	30	RESCUE ME	Madonna (Sire)
31	31	SUCCESS	Dannii Minogue (MCA)
42	32	DALLIANCE	Wedding Present (RCA)
25	33	SEAL OUR FATE	Gloria Estefan (Epic)
-	34	CALL IT WHAT YOU WANT	New Kids On The Block (Columbia)
-	35	TAINTED LOVE/WHERE DID OUR LOVE GO?	Soft Cell/Marc Almond (Mercury)
-	36	A MESSAGE TO YOUR HEART	Samantha Janus (Hollywood)
29	37	ANTHEM	N-Joi (deConstruction)
-	38	R.S.V.P.	Jason Donovan (PWL)
28	39	DEEP, DEEP TROUBLE	Simpsons featuring Bart & Homer (Geffen)
50	40	TAKE IT	Flowered Up (London)
30	41	LONG TRAIN RUNNING	Bananarama (London)
44	42	DEVIL'S TOY	Almighty (Polydor)
-	43	I DON'T KNOW IF I SHOULD CALL YOU BABY	Soul Family Sensation (One Little Indian)
-	44	SHINY HAPPY PEOPLE	R.E.M. (Warner Bros)
39	45	I SAY YEAH	Secchi featuring Orlando Johnson (Epic)
27	46	THE SIZE OF A COW	Wonder Stuff (Polydor)
47	47	HER	Guy (MCA)
-	48	POWER OF LOVE/LOVE POWER	Luther Vandross (Epic)
34	49	LOVE AND KISSES	Dannii Minogue (MCA)
-	50	WHENEVER YOU NEED ME	T'Pau (Siren)

25 May 1991

last	this		
6	1	GYPSY WOMAN (LA DA DEE)	Crystal Waters (A&M)
1	2	THE SHOOP SHOOP SONG (IT'S IN HIS KISS)	Cher (Epic)
2	3	LAST TRAIN TO TRANCENTRAL - LIVE FROM THE LOST CONTINENT/THE IRON HORSE	KLF (KLF Communications)
9	4	PROMISE ME	Beverley Craven (Epic)
3	5	TOUCH ME (ALL NIGHT LONG)	Cathy Dennis (Polydor)
35	6	TAINTED LOVE/WHERE DID OUR LOVE GO?	Soft Cell/Marc Almond (Mercury)
4	7	SAILING ON THE SEVEN SEAS	Orchestral Manoeuvres In The Dark (Virgin)
-	8	I WANNA SEX YOU UP	Color Me Badd (Giant)
15	9	FADING LIKE A FLOWER (EVERY TIME YOU LEAVE)	Roxette (EMI)
5	10	SENZA UNA DONNA (WITHOUT A WOMAN)	Zucchero/Paul Young (London)
44	11	SHINY HAPPY PEOPLE	R.E.M. (Warner Bros)
10	12	FUTURE LOVE (EP)	Seal (ZTT)
7	13	GET THE MESSAGE	Electronic (Factory)
17	14	ANASTHASIA	T99 (XL)
21	15	BABY BABY	Amy Grant (A&M)
14	16	THERE'S NO OTHER WAY	Blur (Food)
34	17	CALL IT WHAT YOU WANT	New Kids On The Block (Columbia)
8	18	FOOTSTEPS FOLLOWING ME	Frances Nero (Debut)
18	19	LOVE IS A WONDERFUL THING	Michael Bolton (Columbia)
20	20	CAUGHT IN MY SHADOW	Wonder Stuff (Polydor)
31	21	SUCCESS	Dannii Minogue (MCA)
12	22	RING RING RING (HA HA HEY)	De La Soul (Big Life)
-	23	YOUR SWAYING ARMS	Deacon Blue (Columbia)
38	24	R.S.V.P.	Jason Donovan (PWL)
13	25	JUST A GROOVE	Nomad (Rumour)
25	26	YOU'RE IN LOVE	Wilson Phillips (SBK)
50	27	WHENEVER YOU NEED ME	T'Pau (Siren)
16	28	SIT DOWN	James (Fontana)
19	29	THE ONE AND ONLY	Chesney Hawkes (Chrysalis)
-	30	HEADLONG	Queen (Parlophone)
-	31	THE SIMPLE TRUTH - CAMPAIGN FOR KURDISH REFUGEES	Chris De Burgh (A&M)
-	32	SEE THE LIGHTS	Simple Minds (Virgin)
-	33	INTO TOMORROW	Paul Weller Movement (Freedom High)
11	34	BORN FREE	Vic Reeves & the Roman Numerals (Sense)
-	35	FROZEN (EP)	Curve
40	36	TAKE IT	Flowered Up (London)
20	37	QUADROPHONIA	Quadrophonia (ARS)
22	38	THE WHOLE OF THE MOON	Waterboys (Ensign)
24	39	GET READY!	Roachford (Columbia)
-	40	KISS THEM FOR ME	Siouxsie & the Banshees (Wonderland)
-	41	HIGHWAY 5	Blessing (MCA)
-	42	I TOUCH MYSELF	Divinyls (Virgin America)
-	43	ONE LOVE - PEOPLE GET READY	Bob Marley & the Wailers (Tuff Gong)
23	44	GONNA CATCH YOU	Lonnie Gordon (Supreme)
30	45	RESCUE ME	Madonna (Sire)
29	46	THE OTHER SIDE OF SUMMER	Elvis Costello (Warner Bros)
-	47	NOTHING CAN STOP US	St Etienne (Heavenly)
43	48	I DON'T KNOW IF I SHOULD CALL YOU BABY	Soul Family Sensation (One Little Indian)
-	49	MOVE THAT BODY	Technotronic featuring Reggie (ARS)
26	50	CHILDREN	EMF (Parlophone)

Cher recorded *The Shoop Shoop Song*, originally a Top 10 hit in the US in 1964 for Betty Everett, and (as *It's In His Kiss*) a similar UK success for Linda Lewis in 1975, for her film *Mermaids*, which in turn provided a healthy promotional boost for the single. It proved to be her biggest-ever UK seller, and her first Number One in this country since her debut (with Sonny) hit *I Got You Babe*.

June 1991

1 June 1991

last	this	title	artist
1	1	GYPSY WOMAN (LA DA DEE)	Crystal Waters (A&M)
2	2	THE SHOOP SHOOP SONG (IT'S IN HIS KISS)	Cher (Epic)
4	3	PROMISE ME	Beverley Craven (Epic)
8	4	I WANNA SEX YOU UP	Color Me Badd (Giant)
6	5	TAINTED LOVE/WHERE DID OUR LOVE GO?	Soft Cell/Marc Almond (Mercury)
15	6	BABY BABY	Amy Grant (A&M)
5	7	TOUCH ME (ALL NIGHT LONG)	Cathy Dennis (Polydor)
11	8	SHINY HAPPY PEOPLE	R.E.M. (Warner Bros)
21	9	SUCCESS	Dannii Minogue (MCA)
3	10	LAST TRAIN TO TRANCENTRAL - LIVE FROM THE LOST CONTINENT/THE IRON HORSE	KLF (KLF Communications)
17	11	CALL IT WHAT YOU WANT	New Kids On The Block (Columbia)
24	12	R.S.V.P.	Jason Donovan (PWL)
-	13	SHOCKED	Kylie Minogue (PWL)
23	14	YOUR SWAYING ARMS	Deacon Blue (Columbia)
9	15	FADING LIKE A FLOWER (EVERY TIME YOU LEAVE)	Roxette (EMI)
7	16	SAILING ON THE SEVEN SEAS	Orchestral Manoeuvres In The Dark (Virgin)
32	17	SEE THE LIGHTS	Simple Minds (Virgin)
20	18	CAUGHT IN MY SHADOW	Wonder Stuff (Polydor)
14	19	ANASTHASIA	T99 (XL)
27	20	WHENEVER YOU NEED ME	T'Pau (Siren)
49	21	MOVE THAT BODY	Technotronic featuring Reggie (ARS)
30	22	HEADLONG	Queen (Parlophone)
19	23	LOVE IS A WONDERFUL THING	Michael Bolton (Columbia)
13	24	GET THE MESSAGE	Electronic (Factory)
10	25	SENZA UNA DONNA (WITHOUT A WOMAN)	Zucchero/Paul Young (London)
12	26	FUTURE LOVE (EP)	Seal (ZTT)
16	27	THERE'S NO OTHER WAY	Blur (Food)
26	28	YOU'RE IN LOVE	Wilson Phillips (SBK)
40	29	KISS THEM FOR ME	Siouxsie & the Banshees (Wonderland)
-	30	YO! SWEETNESS	MC Hammer (Capitol)
31	31	THE SIMPLE TRUTH - CAMPAIGN FOR KURDISH REFUGEES	Chris De Burgh (A&M)
-	32	92F BOILERHOUSE	Pop Will Eat Itself (RCA)
25	33	JUST A GROOVE	Nomad (Rumour)
-	34	MY SALT HEART	Hue & Cry (Circa)
-	35	WALKING DOWN MADISON	Kirsty MacColl (Virgin)
18	36	FOOTSTEPS FOLLOWING ME	Frances Nero (Debut)
-	37	ONLY FOOLS (NEVER FALL IN LOVE)	Sonia (IQ)
42	38	I TOUCH MYSELF	Divinyls (Virgin America)
22	39	RING RING RING (HA HA HEY)	De La Soul (Big Life)
-	40	YOUNG GODS	Little Angels (Polydor)
41	41	HIGHWAY 5	Blessing (MCA)
-	42	LOVESICK	Gang Starr (Cooltempo)
29	43	THE ONE AND ONLY	Chesney Hawkes (Chrysalis)
-	44	DO YOU WANT ME	Salt 'N' Pepa (ffrr)
35	45	FROZEN (EP)	Curve
36	46	TAKE IT	Flowered Up (London)
-	47	NOW IS TOMORROW	Definition Of Sound (Circa)
-	48	RECIPE FOR LOVE/IT HAD TO BE YOU	Harry Connick Jr. (Columbia)
28	49	SIT DOWN	James (Fontana)
-	50	WALKING IN MEMPHIS	Marc Cohn (Atlantic)

8 June 1991

last	this	title	artist
4	1	I WANNA SEX YOU UP	Color Me Badd (Giant)
2	2	THE SHOOP SHOOP SONG (IT'S IN HIS KISS)	Cher (Epic)
1	3	GYPSY WOMAN (LA DA DEE)	Crystal Waters (A&M)
6	4	BABY BABY	Amy Grant (A&M)
3	5	PROMISE ME	Beverley Craven (Epic)
13	6	SHOCKED	Kylie Minogue (PWL)
5	7	TAINTED LOVE/WHERE DID OUR LOVE GO?	Soft Cell/Marc Almond (Mercury)
8	8	SHINY HAPPY PEOPLE	R.E.M. (Warner Bros)
7	9	TOUCH ME (ALL NIGHT LONG)	Cathy Dennis (Polydor)
9	10	SUCCESS	Dannii Minogue (MCA)
-	11	HOLIDAY	Madonna (Sire)
21	12	MOVE THAT BODY	Technotronic featuring Reggie (ARS)
10	13	LAST TRAIN TO TRANCENTRAL - LIVE FROM THE LOST CONTINENT/THE IRON HORSE	KLF (KLF Communications)
22	14	HEADLONG	Queen (Parlophone)
30	15	YO! SWEETNESS	MC Hammer (Capitol)
37	16	ONLY FOOLS (NEVER FALL IN LOVE)	Sonia (IQ)
14	17	YOUR SWAYING ARMS	Deacon Blue (Columbia)
17	18	SEE THE LIGHTS	Simple Minds (Virgin)
-	19	JEALOUSY	Pet Shop Boys (Parlophone)
11	20	CALL IT WHAT YOU WANT	New Kids On The Block (Columbia)
20	21	WHENEVER YOU NEED ME	T'Pau (Siren)
-	22	THE ROBOTS	Kraftwerk (EMI)
-	23	LIGHT MY FIRE	Doors (Elektra)
18	24	CAUGHT IN MY SHADOW	Wonder Stuff (Polydor)
32	25	92F BOILERHOUSE	Pop Will Eat Itself (RCA)
12	26	R.S.V.P.	Jason Donovan (PWL)
35	27	WALKING DOWN MADISON	Kirsty MacColl (Virgin)
-	28	THINKING ABOUT YOUR LOVE	Kenny Thomas (Cooltempo)
15	29	FADING LIKE A FLOWER (EVERY TIME YOU LEAVE)	Roxette (EMI)
16	30	SAILING ON THE SEVEN SEAS	Orchestral Manoeuvres In The Dark (Virgin)
-	31	ESCAPE	Gary Clail On-U Sound System (Perfecto)
44	32	DO YOU WANT ME	Salt 'N' Pepa (ffrr)
29	33	KISS THEM FOR ME	Siouxsie & the Banshees (Wonderland)
48	34	RECIPE FOR LOVE/IT HAD TO BE YOU	Harry Connick Jr. (Columbia)
-	35	PLANET OF SOUND	Pixies (4AD)
-	36	ANASTHASIA	T99 (XL)
38	37	I TOUCH MYSELF	Divinyls (Virgin America)
24	38	GET THE MESSAGE	Electronic (Factory)
23	39	LOVE IS A WONDERFUL THING	Michael Bolton (Columbia)
-	40	SOLACE OF YOU	Living Colour (Epic)
-	41	SAFE FROM HARM	Massive Attack (Wild Bunch)
-	42	THERE'S GOT TO BE A WAY	Mariah Carey (Columbia)
27	43	THERE'S NO OTHER WAY	Blur (Food)
-	44	I LIKE THE WAY (THE KISSING GAME)	Hi-Five (Jive)
26	45	FUTURE LOVE (EP)	Seal (ZTT)
41	46	HIGHWAY 5	Blessing (MCA)
-	47	MY SPECIAL CHILD	Sinead O'Connor (Ensign)
40	48	YOUNG GODS	Little Angels (Polydor)
36	49	FOOTSTEPS FOLLOWING ME	Frances Nero (Debut)
-	50	RUBBERBANDMAN	Yello (Mercury)

15 June 1991

last	this	title	artist
1	1	I WANNA SEX YOU UP	Color Me Badd (Giant)
4	2	BABY BABY	Amy Grant (A&M)
2	3	THE SHOOP SHOOP SONG (IT'S IN HIS KISS)	Cher (Epic)
11	4	HOLIDAY	Madonna (Sire)
6	5	SHOCKED	Kylie Minogue (PWL)
23	6	LIGHT MY FIRE	Doors (Elektra)
3	7	GYPSY WOMAN (LA DA DEE)	Crystal Waters (A&M)
8	8	SHINY HAPPY PEOPLE	R.E.M. (Warner Bros)
19	9	JEALOUSY	Pet Shop Boys (Parlophone)
5	10	PROMISE ME	Beverley Craven (Epic)
16	11	ONLY FOOLS (NEVER FALL IN LOVE)	Sonia (IQ)
15	12	YO! SWEETNESS	MC Hammer (Capitol)
28	13	THINKING ABOUT YOUR LOVE	Kenny Thomas (Cooltempo)
10	14	SUCCESS	Dannii Minogue (MCA)
12	15	MOVE THAT BODY	Technotronic featuring Reggie (ARS)
22	16	THE ROBOTS	Kraftwerk (EMI)
9	17	TOUCH ME (ALL NIGHT LONG)	Cathy Dennis (Polydor)
13	18	LAST TRAIN TO TRANCENTRAL - LIVE FROM THE LOST CONTINENT/THE IRON HORSE	KLF (KLF Communications)
7	19	TAINTED LOVE/WHERE DID OUR LOVE GO?	Soft Cell/Marc Almond (Mercury)
32	20	DO YOU WANT ME	Salt 'N' Pepa (ffrr)
27	21	WALKING DOWN MADISON	Kirsty MacColl (Virgin)
37	22	I TOUCH MYSELF	Divinyls (Virgin America)
-	23	REMEMBER ME WITH LOVE	Gloria Estefan (Epic)
-	24	PEOPLE ARE STILL HAVING SEX	Latour (Polydor)
25	25	92F BOILERHOUSE	Pop Will Eat Itself (RCA)
31	26	ESCAPE	Gary Clail On-U Sound System (Perfecto)
41	27	SAFE FROM HARM	Massive Attack (Wild Bunch)
35	28	PLANET OF SOUND	Pixies (4AD)
40	29	SOLACE OF YOU	Living Colour (Epic)
14	30	HEADLONG	Queen (Parlophone)
-	31	COVER MY EYES (PAIN AND HEAVEN)	Marillion (EMI)
21	32	WHENEVER YOU NEED ME	T'Pau (Siren)
20	33	CALL IT WHAT YOU WANT	New Kids On The Block (Columbia)
34	34	RECIPE FOR LOVE/IT HAD TO BE YOU	Harry Connick Jr. (Columbia)
44	35	I LIKE THE WAY (THE KISSING GAME)	Hi-Five (Jive)
-	36	GET THE FUNK OUT	Extreme (A&M)
33	37	KISS THEM FOR ME	Siouxsie & the Banshees (Wonderland)
-	38	SPACE	New Model Army (EMI)
17	39	YOUR SWAYING ARMS	Deacon Blue (Columbia)
-	40	THE MOTOWN SONG	Rod Stewart (with the Temptations) (Warner Bros)
-	41	NOW IS TOMORROW	Definition Of Sound (Circa)
-	42	MONKEY BUSINESS	Skid Row (Atlantic)
-	43	TAKE 5	Northside (Factory)
-	44	IT AIN'T OVER 'TIL IT'S OVER	Lenny Kravitz (Virgin America)
-	45	GENERATIONS OF LOVE	Jesus Loves You More (More Protein)
47	46	MY SPECIAL CHILD	Sinead O'Connor (Ensign)
42	47	THERE'S GOT TO BE A WAY	Mariah Carey (Columbia)
50	48	RUBBERBANDMAN	Yello (Mercury)
-	49	FAREWELL MR. SORROW	All About Eve (Mercury)
46	50	HIGHWAY 5	Blessing (MCA)

Sisters Kylie and Dannii Minogue found themselves in the Top 10 simultaneously for the first time, while Soft Cell's 1981 million-seller *Tainted Love* returned to the charts in a remixed version, in association with a compilation album. Madonna's *Holiday* also revisited the top 10 - for the third separate time in eight years! The song was now almost a hardy summer perennial.

22 June 1991

last week	this week	Title	Artist (Label)
1	1	I WANNA SEX YOU UP	Color Me Badd (Giant)
2	2	BABY BABY	Amy Grant (A&M)
-	3	ANY DREAM WILL DO	Jason Donovan (Really Useful)
4	4	HOLIDAY	Madonna (Sire)
13	5	THINKING ABOUT YOUR LOVE	Kenny Thomas (Cooltempo)
3	6	THE SHOOP SHOOP SONG (IT'S IN HIS KISS)	Cher (Epic)
6	7	LIGHT MY FIRE	Doors (Elektra)
8	8	SHINY HAPPY PEOPLE	R.E.M. (Warner Bros)
11	9	ONLY FOOLS (NEVER FALL IN LOVE)	Sonia (IQ)
20	10	DO YOU WANT ME	Salt 'N' Pepa (ffrr)
9	11	JEALOUSY	Pet Shop Boys (Parlophone)
5	12	SHOCKED	Kylie Minogue (PWL)
-	13	FROM A DISTANCE	Bette Midler (Atlantic)
10	14	PROMISE ME	Beverley Craven (Epic)
15	15	PEOPLE ARE STILL HAVING SEX	Latour (Polydor)
40	16	THE MOTOWN SONG	Rod Stewart (with the Temptations) (Warner Bros)
7	17	GYPSY WOMAN (LA DA DEE)	Crystal Waters (A&M)
22	18	I TOUCH MYSELF	Divinyls (Virgin America)
44	19	IT AIN'T OVER 'TIL IT'S OVER	Lenny Kravitz (Virgin America)
23	20	REMEMBER ME WITH LOVE	Gloria Estefan (Epic)
21	21	WALKING DOWN MADISON	Kirsty MacColl (Virgin)
36	22	GET THE FUNK OUT	Extreme (A&M)
17	23	TOUCH ME (ALL NIGHT LONG)	Cathy Dennis (Polydor)
27	24	SAFE FROM HARM	Massive Attack (Wild Bunch)
42	25	MONKEY BUSINESS	Skid Row (Atlantic)
49	26	FAREWELL MR. SORROW	All About Eve (Mercury)
12	27	YO! SWEETNESS	MC Hammer (Capitol)
15	28	MOVE THAT BODY	Technotronic featuring Reggie (ARS)
29	29	SOLACE OF YOU	Living Colour (Epic)
-	30	NAKED LOVE (JUST SAY YOU WANT ME) PART 1	Quartz with Dina Carroll (Mercury)
-	31	TRIBAL BASE	Rebel MC featuring Tenor Fly & Barrington Levy (Desire)
34	32	RECIPE FOR LOVE/IT HAD TO BE YOU	Harry Connick Jr. (Columbia)
18	33	LAST TRAIN TO TRANCENTRAL - LIVE FROM THE LOST CONTINENT/THE IRON HORSE	KLF (KLF Communications)
19	34	TAINTED LOVE/WHERE DID OUR LOVE GO?	Soft Cell/Marc Almond (Mercury)
-	35	RUSH RUSH	Paula Abdul (Virgin America)
14	36	SUCCESS	Dannii Minogue (MCA)
-	37	WATCHER'S POINT OF VIEW	PM Dawn (Gee Street)
-	38	I'M A MAN NOT A BOY	Chesney Hawkes (Chrysalis)
46	39	MY SPECIAL CHILD	Sinead O'Connor (Ensign)
26	40	ESCAPE	Gary Clail On-U Sound System (Perfecto)
31	41	COVER MY EYES (PAIN AND HEAVEN)	Marillion (EMI)
16	42	THE ROBOTS	Kraftwerk (EMI)
45	43	GENERATIONS OF LOVE	Jesus Loves You More (More Protein)
-	44	CROCKETT'S THEME/CHANCER	Jan Hammer (MCA)
-	45	SHE SELLS	Banderas (London)
35	46	I LIKE THE WAY (THE KISSING GAME)	Hi-Five (Jive)
-	47	WHAT YOU WANT	Xpansions featuring Dale Joyner (Arista)
43	48	TAKE 5	Northside (Factory)
32	49	WHENEVER YOU NEED ME	T'Pau (Siren)
-	50	THERE'S NOTHING LIKE THIS	Omar (Talkin' Loud)

29 June 1991

last week	this week	Title	Artist (Label)
3	1	ANY DREAM WILL DO	Jason Donovan (Really Useful)
1	2	I WANNA SEX YOU UP	Color Me Badd (Giant)
5	3	THINKING ABOUT YOUR LOVE	Kenny Thomas (Cooltempo)
13	4	FROM A DISTANCE	Bette Midler (Atlantic)
10	5	DO YOU WANT ME	Salt 'N' Pepa (ffrr)
16	6	THE MOTOWN SONG	Rod Stewart (with the Temptations) (Warner Bros)
2	7	BABY BABY	Amy Grant (A&M)
19	8	IT AIN'T OVER 'TIL IT'S OVER	Lenny Kravitz (Virgin America)
15	9	PEOPLE ARE STILL HAVING SEX	Latour (Polydor)
-	10	CHORUS	Erasure (Mute)
9	11	ONLY FOOLS (NEVER FALL IN LOVE)	Sonia (IQ)
6	12	THE SHOOP SHOOP SONG (IT'S IN HIS KISS)	Cher (Epic)
18	13	I TOUCH MYSELF	Divinyls (Virgin America)
-	14	REAL LOVE	Driza Bone
8	15	SHINY HAPPY PEOPLE	R.E.M. (Warner Bros)
4	16	HOLIDAY	Madonna (Sire)
35	17	RUSH RUSH	Paula Abdul (Virgin America)
7	18	LIGHT MY FIRE	Doors (Elektra)
22	19	GET THE FUNK OUT	Extreme (A&M)
38	20	I'M A MAN NOT A BOY	Chesney Hawkes (Chrysalis)
31	21	TRIBAL BASE	Rebel MC featuring Tenor Fly & Barrington Levy (Desire)
14	22	PROMISE ME	Beverley Craven (Epic)
23	23	NIGHT IN MOTION	CUBIC 22 (XL)
50	24	THERE'S NOTHING LIKE THIS	Omar (Talkin' Loud)
24	25	SAFE FROM HARM	Massive Attack (Wild Bunch)
11	26	JEALOUSY	Pet Shop Boys (Parlophone)
27	27	HEY STOOPID	Alice Cooper (Epic)
12	28	SHOCKED	Kylie Minogue (PWL)
17	29	GYPSY WOMAN (LA DA DEE)	Crystal Waters (A&M)
-	30	EVERYTHING I DO (I DO IT FOR YOU)	Bryan Adams (A&M)
21	31	WALKING DOWN MADISON	Kirsty MacColl (Virgin)
37	32	WATCHER'S POINT OF VIEW	PM Dawn (Gee Street)
20	33	REMEMBER ME WITH LOVE	Gloria Estefan (Epic)
23	34	TOUCH ME (ALL NIGHT LONG)	Cathy Dennis (Polydor)
25	35	MONKEY BUSINESS	Skid Row (Atlantic)
30	36	NAKED LOVE (JUST SAY YOU WANT ME) PART 1	Quartz with Dina Carroll (Mercury)
43	37	GENERATIONS OF LOVE	Jesus Loves You More (More Protein)
28	38	MOVE THAT BODY	Technotronic featuring Reggie (ARS)
-	39	SHERIFF FATMAN	Carter USM (Big Cat)
-	40	SHE SELLS	Banderas (London)
41	41	COVER MY EYES (PAIN AND HEAVEN)	Marillion (EMI)
29	42	SOLACE OF YOU	Living Colour (Epic)
-	43	DEEP IN MY HEART/EVERYBODY REMIX	Clubhouse/Capella (ffrr)
34	44	TAINTED LOVE/WHERE DID OUR LOVE GO?	Soft Cell/Marc Almond (Mercury)
-	45	HIGHER THAN THE SUN	Primal Scream (Creation)
-	46	IF LOOKS COULD KILL	Transvision Vamp (MCA)
-	47	DEAD RINGER FOR LOVE	Meatloaf (Epic)
-	48	ALWAYS THERE	Incognito featuring Jocelyn Brown (Talkin' Loud)
49	49	MAMA	Kim Appleby (Parlophone)
-	50	UNFORGETTABLE	Natalie Cole with Nat King Cole (Elektra)

6 July 1991

last week	this week	Title	Artist (Label)
1	1	ANY DREAM WILL DO	Jason Donovan (Really Useful)
10	2	CHORUS	Erasure (Mute)
30	3	EVERYTHING I DO (I DO IT FOR YOU)	Bryan Adams (A&M)
3	4	THINKING ABOUT YOUR LOVE	Kenny Thomas (Cooltempo)
2	5	I WANNA SEX YOU UP	Color Me Badd (Giant)
4	6	FROM A DISTANCE	Bette Midler (Atlantic)
6	7	THE MOTOWN SONG	Rod Stewart (with the Temptations) (Warner Bros)
8	8	IT AIN'T OVER 'TIL IT'S OVER	Lenny Kravitz (Virgin America)
5	9	DO YOU WANT ME	Salt 'N' Pepa (ffrr)
14	10	REAL LOVE	Driza Bone
17	11	RUSH RUSH	Paula Abdul (Virgin America)
24	12	THERE'S NOTHING LIKE THIS	Omar (Talkin' Loud)
48	13	ALWAYS THERE	Incognito featuring Jocelyn Brown (Talkin' Loud)
9	14	PEOPLE ARE STILL HAVING SEX	Latour (Polydor)
13	15	I TOUCH MYSELF	Divinyls (Virgin America)
7	16	BABY BABY	Amy Grant (A&M)
27	17	HEY STOOPID	Alice Cooper (Epic)
23	18	NIGHT IN MOTION	CUBIC 22 (XL)
20	19	I'M A MAN NOT A BOY	Chesney Hawkes (Chrysalis)
11	20	ONLY FOOLS (NEVER FALL IN LOVE)	Sonia (IQ)
12	21	THE SHOOP SHOOP SONG (IT'S IN HIS KISS)	Cher (Epic)
19	22	GET THE FUNK OUT	Extreme (A&M)
15	23	SHINY HAPPY PEOPLE	R.E.M. (Warner Bros)
50	24	UNFORGETTABLE	Natalie Cole with Nat King Cole (Elektra)
-	25	7 WAYS TO LOVE	Cola Boy (Arista)
-	26	ROLLIN' IN MY 5.0	Vanilla Ice (SBK)
21	27	TRIBAL BASE	Rebel MC featuring Tenor Fly & Barrington Levy (Desire)
39	28	SHERIFF FATMAN	Carter USM (Big Cat)
37	29	GENERATIONS OF LOVE	Jesus Loves You More (More Protein)
49	30	MAMA	Kim Appleby (Parlophone)
-	31	GOT A LOVE FOR YOU	Jomanda (Giant)
-	32	BRING THE NOISE	Anthrax featuring Chuck D (Island)
18	33	LIGHT MY FIRE	Doors (Elektra)
25	34	SAFE FROM HARM	Massive Attack (Wild Bunch)
16	35	HOLIDAY	Madonna (Sire)
32	36	WATCHER'S POINT OF VIEW	PM Dawn (Gee Street)
-	37	GIRLS	Powercut featuring Nubian Prinz (Eternal)
40	38	SHE SELLS	Banderas (London)
-	39	THINGS THAT MAKE YOU GO HMMM...	C&C Music Factory (Columbia)
-	40	MY NAME IS NOT SUSAN	Whitney Houston (Arista)
-	41	KEEP WARM	Jinny (Virgin)
29	42	GYPSY WOMAN (LA DA DEE)	Crystal Waters (A&M)
-	43	LITTLE LOST SOMETIMES	Almighty (Polydor)
-	44	NOW THAT WE FOUND LOVE	Heavy D & the Boyz (MCA)
45	45	AND THEN SHE SMILES	Mock Turtles (Siren)
-	46	LOOKING FOR THE SUMMER	Chris Rea (East West)
-	47	LEARNING TO FLY	Tom Petty & the Heartbreakers (MCA)
22	48	PROMISE ME	Beverley Craven (Epic)
31	49	WALKING DOWN MADISON	Kirsty MacColl (Virgin)
-	50	DO IT AGAIN	Beach Boys (Capitol)

Jason Donovan's *Any Dream Will Do* came from his title role in the smash-hit stage revival of Andrew Lloyd-Webber and Tim Rice's first musical *Joseph And The Amazing Technicolor Dream Coat,* at the London Palladium. Meanwhile, the Doors' *Light My Fire,* never previously a UK hit, made the grade 24 years after first release with the help of Oliver Stone's *The Doors* movie.

July 1991

13 July 1991

last week	this week	Title	Artist (Label)
1	1	ANY DREAM WILL DO	Jason Donovan (Really Useful)
3	2	EVERYTHING I DO (I DO IT FOR YOU)	Bryan Adams (A&M)
2	3	CHORUS	Erasure (Mute)
25	4	7 WAYS TO LOVE	Cola Boy (Arista)
-	5	YOU COULD BE MINE	Guns N' Roses (Geffen)
13	6	ALWAYS THERE	Incognito featuring Jocelyn Brown (Talkin' Loud)
11	7	RUSH RUSH	Paula Abdul (Virgin America)
4	8	THINKING ABOUT YOUR LOVE	Kenny Thomas (Cooltempo)
10	9	REAL LOVE	Driza Bone
5	10	I WANNA SEX YOU UP	Color Me Badd (Giant)
44	11	NOW THAT WE FOUND LOVE	Heavy D & the Boyz (MCA)
8	12	IT AIN'T OVER 'TIL IT'S OVER	Lenny Kravitz (Virgin America)
6	13	FROM A DISTANCE	Bette Midler (Atlantic)
7	14	THE MOTOWN SONG	Rod Stewart (with the Temptations) (Warner Bros)
9	15	DO YOU WANT ME	Salt 'N' Pepa (ffrr)
12	16	THERE'S NOTHING LIKE THIS	Omar (Talkin' Loud)
17	17	NIGHT IN MOTION	CUBC 22 (XL)
15	18	I TOUCH MYSELF	Divinyls (Virgin America)
40	19	MY NAME IS NOT SUSAN	Whitney Houston (Arista)
32	20	BRING THE NOISE	Anthrax featuring Chuck D (Island)
17	21	HEY STOOPID	Alice Cooper (Epic)
24	22	UNFORGETTABLE	Natalie Cole with Nat King Cole (Elektra)
39	23	THINGS THAT MAKE YOU GO HMMM...	C&C Music Factory (Columbia)
30	24	MAMA	Kim Appleby (Parlophone)
16	25	BABY BABY	Amy Grant (A&M)
-	26	ARE YOU MINE?	Bros (Columbia)
27	27	LOVE AND UNDERSTANDING	Cher (Geffen)
28	28	SHERIFF FATMAN	Carter USM (Big Cat)
14	29	PEOPLE ARE STILL HAVING SEX	Latour (Polydor)
-	30	SEXUALITY	Billy Bragg (Go! Discs)
31	31	THE WAVE OF THE FUTURE	Quadrophonia (ARS)
26	32	ROLLIN' IN MY 5.0	Vanilla Ice (SBK)
-	33	PANDORA'S BOX	Orchestral Manoeuvres In The Dark (Virgin)
22	34	GET THE FUNK OUT	Extreme (A&M)
38	35	SHE SELLS	Banderas (London)
20	36	ONLY FOOLS (NEVER FALL IN LOVE)	Sonia (IQ)
-	37	BEST I CAN	Queensryche (EMI USA)
29	38	GENERATIONS OF LOVE	Jesus Loves You More (More Protein)
-	39	WE ARE BACK/NURTURE	LFO (Warp)
-	40	I LIKE IT	DJH featuring Stefy (RCA)
-	41	BITTER TEARS	INXS (Mercury)
23	42	SHINY HAPPY PEOPLE	R.E.M. (Warner Bros)
31	43	GOT A LOVE FOR YOU	Jomanda (Giant)
46	44	LOOKING FOR THE SUMMER	Chris Rea (East West)
47	45	LEARNING TO FLY	Tom Petty & the Heartbreakers (MCA)
45	46	AND THEN SHE SMILES	Mock Turtles (Siren)
21	47	THE SHOOP SHOOP SONG (IT'S IN HIS KISS)	Cher (Epic)
19	48	I'M A MAN NOT A BOY	Chesney Hawkes (Chrysalis)
33	49	LIGHT MY FIRE	Doors (Elektra)
27	50	TRIBAL BASE	Rebel MC featuring Tenor Fly & Barrington Levy (Desire)

20 July 1991

last week	this week	Title	Artist (Label)
2	1	EVERYTHING I DO (I DO IT FOR YOU)	Bryan Adams (A&M)
1	2	ANY DREAM WILL DO	Jason Donovan (Really Useful)
4	3	7 WAYS TO LOVE	Cola Boy (Arista)
5	4	YOU COULD BE MINE	Guns N' Roses (Geffen)
6	5	ALWAYS THERE	Incognito featuring Jocelyn Brown (Talkin' Loud)
11	6	NOW THAT WE FOUND LOVE	Heavy D & the Boyz (MCA)
7	7	RUSH RUSH	Paula Abdul (Virgin America)
3	8	CHORUS	Erasure (Mute)
26	9	ARE YOU MINE?	Bros (Columbia)
8	10	THINKING ABOUT YOUR LOVE	Kenny Thomas (Cooltempo)
23	11	THINGS THAT MAKE YOU GO HMMM...	C&C Music Factory (Columbia)
19	12	MY NAME IS NOT SUSAN	Whitney Houston (Arista)
40	13	I LIKE IT	DJH featuring Stefy (RCA)
27	14	LOVE AND UNDERSTANDING	Cher (Geffen)
33	15	PANDORA'S BOX	Orchestral Manoeuvres In The Dark (Virgin)
22	16	UNFORGETTABLE	Natalie Cole with Nat King Cole (Elektra)
20	17	BRING THE NOISE	Anthrax featuring Chuck D (Island)
12	18	IT AIN'T OVER 'TIL IT'S OVER	Lenny Kravitz (Virgin America)
15	19	DO YOU WANT ME	Salt 'N' Pepa (ffrr)
41	20	BITTER TEARS	INXS (Mercury)
24	21	MAMA	Kim Appleby (Parlophone)
16	22	THERE'S NOTHING LIKE THIS	Omar (Talkin' Loud)
-	23	LET THE BEAT HIT 'EM	Lisa Lisa & Cult Jam (Columbia)
9	24	REAL LOVE	Driza Bone
10	25	I WANNA SEX YOU UP	Color Me Badd (Giant)
30	26	SEXUALITY	Billy Bragg (Go! Discs)
27	27	I TOUCH MYSELF	Divinyls (Virgin America)
14	28	THE MOTOWN SONG	Rod Stewart (with the Temptations) (Warner Bros)
13	29	FROM A DISTANCE	Bette Midler (Atlantic)
-	30	THE BEGINNING	Seal (ZTT)
21	31	HEY STOOPID	Alice Cooper (Epic)
17	32	NIGHT IN MOTION	CUBC 22 (XL)
25	33	BABY BABY	Amy Grant (A&M)
-	34	JUST ANOTHER DREAM	Cathy Dennis (Polydor)
-	35	MONSTERS AND ANGELS	Voice Of The Beehive (London)
-	36	THE VERTIGO (EP)	Altern 8 (Network)
28	37	SHERIFF FATMAN	Carter USM (Big Cat)
-	38	APPLE GREEN	Milltown Brothers (A&M)
38	39	GENERATIONS OF LOVE	Jesus Loves You More (More Protein)
-	40	I AIN'T GONNA CRY	Little Angels (Polydor)
41	41	RIGHT HERE, RIGHT NOW	Jesus Jones (Food)
45	42	LEARNING TO FLY	Tom Petty & the Heartbreakers (MCA)
-	43	MIX IT UP	Dan Reed Network (Mercury)
-	44	(HAMMER HAMMER) THEY PUT ME IN THE DARK	Hammer (Capitol)
31	45	THE WAVE OF THE FUTURE	Quadrophonia (ARS)
29	46	PEOPLE ARE STILL HAVING SEX	Latour (Polydor)
46	47	AND THEN SHE SMILES	Mock Turtles (Siren)
34	48	GET THE FUNK OUT	Extreme (A&M)
-	49	THE SOUND OF EDEN (EVERY TIME I SEE HER)	Shades Of Rhythm (ZTT)
42	50	SHINY HAPPY PEOPLE	R.E.M. (Warner Bros)

27 July 1991

last week	this week	Title	Artist (Label)
1	1	EVERYTHING I DO (I DO IT FOR YOU)	Bryan Adams (A&M)
6	2	NOW THAT WE FOUND LOVE	Heavy D & the Boyz (MCA)
4	3	YOU COULD BE MINE	Guns N' Roses (Geffen)
2	4	ANY DREAM WILL DO	Jason Donovan (Really Useful)
11	5	THINGS THAT MAKE YOU GO HMMM...	C&C Music Factory (Columbia)
5	6	ALWAYS THERE	Incognito featuring Jocelyn Brown (Talkin' Loud)
7	7	RUSH RUSH	Paula Abdul (Virgin America)
3	8	7 WAYS TO LOVE	Cola Boy (Arista)
14	9	LOVE AND UNDERSTANDING	Cher (Geffen)
23	10	LET THE BEAT HIT 'EM	Lisa Lisa & Cult Jam (Columbia)
13	11	I LIKE IT	DJH featuring Stefy (RCA)
15	12	PANDORA'S BOX	Orchestral Manoeuvres In The Dark (Virgin)
9	13	ARE YOU MINE?	Bros (Columbia)
34	14	JUST ANOTHER DREAM	Cathy Dennis (Polydor)
-	15	MORE THAN WORDS	Extreme (A&M)
8	16	CHORUS	Erasure (Mute)
-	17	JUMP TO THE BEAT	Dannii Minogue (MCA)
10	18	THINKING ABOUT YOUR LOVE	Kenny Thomas (Cooltempo)
16	19	UNFORGETTABLE	Natalie Cole with Nat King Cole (Elektra)
44	20	(HAMMER HAMMER) THEY PUT ME IN THE DARK	Hammer (Capitol)
30	21	THE BEGINNING	Seal (ZTT)
21	22	MAMA	Kim Appleby (Parlophone)
19	23	DO YOU WANT ME	Salt 'N' Pepa (ffrr)
-	24	A BETTER LOVE	Londonbeat (AnXious)
40	25	I AIN'T GONNA CRY	Little Angels (Polydor)
49	26	THE SOUND OF EDEN (EVERY TIME I SEE HER)	Shades Of Rhythm (ZTT)
41	27	RIGHT HERE, RIGHT NOW	Jesus Jones (Food)
12	28	MY NAME IS NOT SUSAN	Whitney Houston (Arista)
-	29	MOVE ANY MOUNTAIN - PRO-GEN '91	Shamen (One Little Indian)
35	30	MONSTERS AND ANGELS	Voice Of The Beehive (London)
36	31	THE VERTIGO (EP)	Altern 8 (Network)
25	32	I WANNA SEX YOU UP	Color Me Badd (Giant)
20	33	BITTER TEARS	INXS (Mercury)
29	34	FROM A DISTANCE	Bette Midler (Atlantic)
18	35	IT AIN'T OVER 'TIL IT'S OVER	Lenny Kravitz (Virgin America)
-	36	THE WHISTLE SONG	Frankie Knuckles (Virgin America)
-	37	HOLDING ON	Beverley Craven (Epic)
-	38	WINTER IN JULY	Bomb The Bass (Rhythm King)
22	39	THERE'S NOTHING LIKE THIS	Omar (Talkin' Loud)
-	40	TAKE ME NOW	Tammy Payne (Talkin' Loud)
-	41	TWIST AND SHOUT	Deacon Blue (Columbia)
-	42	PREGNANT FOR THE LAST TIME	Morrissey (HMV)
-	43	HOT SUMMER SALSA	Jive Bunny & the Mastermixers (Music Factory)
44	44	LOVE CONQUERS ALL	ABC (Parlophone)
-	45	SHELTER ME	Circuit (Cooltempo)
24	46	REAL LOVE	Driza Bone
-	47	TIME, LOVE & TENDERNESS	Michael Bolton (Columbia)
26	48	SEXUALITY	Billy Bragg (Go! Discs)
17	49	BRING THE NOISE	Anthrax featuring Chuck D (Island)
28	50	THE MOTOWN SONG	Rod Stewart (with the Temptations) (Warner Bros)

When Bryan Adams' *Everything I Do (I Do It For You)*, the theme song from the Kevin Costner film *Robin Hood – Prince Of Thieves*, topped the UK chart on July 20, it took up the longest residency there in chart history, defeating the record of 11 consecutive weeks held for 36 years by Slim Whitman and *Rose Marie*. Adams would eventually step down on October 26, after 14 weeks.

3 August 1991

last	this	Title	Artist (Label)
1	1	EVERYTHING I DO (I DO IT FOR YOU)	Bryan Adams (A&M)
2	2	NOW THAT WE FOUND LOVE	Heavy D & the Boyz (MCA)
15	3	MORE THAN WORDS	Extreme (A&M)
5	4	THINGS THAT MAKE YOU GO HMMM...	C&C Music Factory (Columbia)
12	5	PANDORA'S BOX	Orchestral Manoeuvres In The Dark (Virgin)
17	6	JUMP TO THE BEAT	Dannii Minogue (MCA)
14	7	JUST ANOTHER DREAM	Cathy Dennis (Polydor)
29	8	MOVE ANY MOUNTAIN - PRO-GEN '91	Shamen (One Little Indian)
9	9	LOVE AND UNDERSTANDING	Cher (Geffen)
4	10	ANY DREAM WILL DO	Jason Donovan (Really Useful)
36	11	THE WHISTLE SONG	Frankie Knuckles (Virgin America)
10	12	LET THE BEAT HIT 'EM	Lisa Lisa & Cult Jam (Columbia)
7	13	RUSH RUSH	Paula Abdul (Virgin America)
24	14	A BETTER LOVE	Londonbeat (AnXious)
11	15	I LIKE IT	DJH featuring Stefy (RCA)
3	16	YOU COULD BE MINE	Guns N' Roses (Geffen)
6	17	ALWAYS THERE	Incognito featuring Jocelyn Brown (Talkin' Loud)
38	18	WINTER IN JULY	Bomb The Bass (Rhythm King)
21	19	THE BEGINNING	Seal (ZTT)
8	20	7 WAYS TO LOVE	Cola Boy (Arista)
16	21	CHORUS	Erasure (Mute)
22	22	MAMA	Kim Appleby (Parlophone)
-	23	I'M TOO SEXY	Right Said Fred (Tug)
31	24	THE VERTIGO (EP)	Altern 8 (Network)
30	25	MONSTERS AND ANGELS	Voice Of The Beehive (London)
26	26	THE SOUND OF EDEN (EVERY TIME I SEE HER)	Shades Of Rhythm (ZTT)
27	27	RIGHT HERE, RIGHT NOW	Jesus Jones (Food)
41	28	TWIST AND SHOUT	Deacon Blue (Columbia)
18	29	THINKING ABOUT YOUR LOVE	Kenny Thomas (Cooltempo)
37	30	HOLDING ON	Beverley Craven (Epic)
19	31	UNFORGETTABLE	Natalie Cole with Nat King Cole (Elektra)
20	32	(HAMMER HAMMER) THEY PUT ME IN THE DARK	Hammer (Capitol)
-	33	A ROLLER SKATING JAM NAMED "SATURDAYS"	De La Soul (Big Life)
13	34	ARE YOU MINE?	Bros (Columbia)
35	35	ALL 4 LOVE	Color Me Badd (Giant)
42	36	PREGNANT FOR THE LAST TIME	Morrissey (HMV)
44	37	LOVE CONQUERS ALL	ABC (Parlophone)
-	38	SUMMERTIME	DJ Jazzy Jeff & Fresh Prince (Jive)
-	39	FAMILY AFFAIR	BEF featuring Lalah Hathaway (10)
-	40	GO	Moby (Outer Rhythm)
-	41	LUCKY 7 MEGAMIX	UK Mixmasters (I.Q.)
-	42	APPARENTLY NOTHIN'	Young Disciples (Talkin' Loud)
-	43	SECRETS (OF SUCCESS)	Cookie Crew (ffrr)
23	44	DO YOU WANT ME	Salt 'N' Pepa (ffrr)
47	45	TIME, LOVE & TENDERNESS	Michael Bolton (Columbia)
-	46	REBEL WOMAN	DNA (DNA)
25	47	I AIN'T GONNA CRY	Little Angels (Polydor)
32	48	I WANNA SEX YOU UP	Color Me Badd (Giant)
34	49	FROM A DISTANCE	Bette Midler (Atlantic)
39	50	THERE'S NOTHING LIKE THIS	Omar (Talkin' Loud)

10 August 1991

last	this	Title	Artist (Label)
1	1	EVERYTHING I DO (I DO IT FOR YOU)	Bryan Adams (A&M)
3	2	MORE THAN WORDS	Extreme (A&M)
8	3	MOVE ANY MOUNTAIN - PRO-GEN '91	Shamen (One Little Indian)
2	4	NOW THAT WE FOUND LOVE	Heavy D & the Boyz (MCA)
4	5	THINGS THAT MAKE YOU GO HMMM...	C&C Music Factory (Columbia)
6	6	JUMP TO THE BEAT	Dannii Minogue (MCA)
23	7	I'M TOO SEXY	Right Said Fred (Tug)
-	8	ENTER SANDMAN	Metallica (Vertigo)
9	9	LOVE AND UNDERSTANDING	Cher (Geffen)
5	10	PANDORA'S BOX	Orchestral Manoeuvres In The Dark (Virgin)
18	11	WINTER IN JULY	Bomb The Bass (Rhythm King)
11	12	THE WHISTLE SONG	Frankie Knuckles (Virgin America)
7	13	JUST ANOTHER DREAM	Cathy Dennis (Polydor)
28	14	TWIST AND SHOUT	Deacon Blue (Columbia)
35	15	ALL 4 LOVE	Color Me Badd (Giant)
38	16	SUMMERTIME	DJ Jazzy Jeff & Fresh Prince (Jive)
10	17	ANY DREAM WILL DO	Jason Donovan (Really Useful)
19	18	THE BEGINNING	Seal (ZTT)
13	19	RUSH RUSH	Paula Abdul (Virgin America)
42	20	APPARENTLY NOTHIN'	Young Disciples (Talkin' Loud)
14	21	A BETTER LOVE	Londonbeat (AnXious)
33	22	A ROLLER SKATING JAM NAMED "SATURDAYS"	De La Soul (Big Life)
15	23	I LIKE IT	DJH featuring Stefy (RCA)
-	24	EVERY HEARTBEAT	Amy Grant (A&M)
12	25	LET THE BEAT HIT 'EM	Lisa Lisa & Cult Jam (Columbia)
30	26	HOLDING ON	Beverley Craven (Epic)
16	27	YOU COULD BE MINE	Guns N' Roses (Geffen)
25	28	MONSTERS AND ANGELS	Voice Of The Beehive (London)
17	29	ALWAYS THERE	Incognito featuring Jocelyn Brown (Talkin' Loud)
45	30	TIME, LOVE & TENDERNESS	Michael Bolton (Columbia)
46	31	REBEL WOMAN	DNA (DNA)
22	32	MAMA	Kim Appleby (Parlophone)
39	33	FAMILY AFFAIR	BEF featuring Lalah Hathaway (10)
34	34	NO ONE CAN	Marillion (EMI)
-	35	WORK	Technotronic featuring Reggie (ARS)
-	36	LOVE'S UNKIND	Sophie Lawrence (IQ)
21	37	CHORUS	Erasure (Mute)
-	38	BANG	Blur (Food)
24	39	THE VERTIGO (EP)	Altern 8 (Network)
36	40	PREGNANT FOR THE LAST TIME	Morrissey (HMV)
29	41	THINKING ABOUT YOUR LOVE	Kenny Thomas (Cooltempo)
20	42	7 WAYS TO LOVE	Cola Boy (Arista)
27	43	RIGHT HERE, RIGHT NOW	Jesus Jones (Food)
-	44	TAKE ME IN YOUR ARMS AND LOVE ME	Scritti Politti & Sweetie Irie (Virgin)
37	45	LOVE CONQUERS ALL	ABC (Parlophone)
26	46	THE SOUND OF EDEN (EVERY TIME I SEE HER)	Shades Of Rhythm (ZTT)
40	47	GO	Moby (Outer Rhythm)
-	48	THE SCARY-GO-ROUND	Jellyfish (Charisma)
-	49	SATISFACTION	Vanilla Ice (SBK)
31	50	UNFORGETTABLE	Natalie Cole with Nat King Cole (Elektra)

17 August 1991

last	this	Title	Artist (Label)
1	1	EVERYTHING I DO (I DO IT FOR YOU)	Bryan Adams (A&M)
2	2	MORE THAN WORDS	Extreme (A&M)
7	3	I'M TOO SEXY	Right Said Fred (Tug)
3	4	MOVE ANY MOUNTAIN - PRO-GEN '91	Shamen (One Little Indian)
11	5	WINTER IN JULY	Bomb The Bass (Rhythm King)
15	6	ALL 4 LOVE	Color Me Badd (Giant)
-	7	SET ADRIFT ON MEMORY BLISS	PM Dawn (Gee Street)
8	8	ENTER SANDMAN	Metallica (Vertigo)
4	9	NOW THAT WE FOUND LOVE	Heavy D & the Boyz (MCA)
16	10	SUMMERTIME	DJ Jazzy Jeff & Fresh Prince (Jive)
14	11	TWIST AND SHOUT	Deacon Blue (Columbia)
5	12	THINGS THAT MAKE YOU GO HMMM...	C&C Music Factory (Columbia)
6	13	JUMP TO THE BEAT	Dannii Minogue (MCA)
10	14	PANDORA'S BOX	Orchestral Manoeuvres In The Dark (Virgin)
20	15	APPARENTLY NOTHIN'	Young Disciples (Talkin' Loud)
22	16	A ROLLER SKATING JAM NAMED "SATURDAYS"	De La Soul (Big Life)
9	17	LOVE AND UNDERSTANDING	Cher (Geffen)
13	18	JUST ANOTHER DREAM	Cathy Dennis (Polydor)
24	19	EVERY HEARTBEAT	Amy Grant (A&M)
18	20	THE BEGINNING	Seal (ZTT)
12	21	THE WHISTLE SONG	Frankie Knuckles (Virgin America)
26	22	HOLDING ON	Beverley Craven (Epic)
28	23	MONSTERS AND ANGELS	Voice Of The Beehive (London)
38	24	BANG	Blur (Food)
30	25	TIME, LOVE & TENDERNESS	Michael Bolton (Columbia)
36	26	LOVE'S UNKIND	Sophie Lawrence (IQ)
49	27	SATISFACTION	Vanilla Ice (SBK)
17	28	ANY DREAM WILL DO	Jason Donovan (Really Useful)
19	29	RUSH RUSH	Paula Abdul (Virgin America)
-	30	NEAR WILD HEAVEN	R.E.M. (Warner Bros)
31	31	REBEL WOMAN	DNA (DNA)
35	32	WORK	Technotronic featuring Reggie (ARS)
-	33	GUARANTEED	Level 42 (RCA)
34	34	FAMILY AFFAIR	BEF featuring Lalah Hathaway (10)
21	35	A BETTER LOVE	Londonbeat (AnXious)
29	36	ALWAYS THERE	Incognito featuring Jocelyn Brown (Talkin' Loud)
27	37	YOU COULD BE MINE	Guns N' Roses (Geffen)
44	38	TAKE ME IN YOUR ARMS AND LOVE ME	Scritti Politti & Sweetie Irie (Virgin)
-	39	STAY BEAUTIFUL	Manic Street Preachers (Columbia)
23	40	I LIKE IT	DJH featuring Stefy (RCA)
25	41	LET THE BEAT HIT 'EM	Lisa Lisa & Cult Jam (Columbia)
34	42	NO ONE CAN	Marillion (EMI)
41	43	THINKING ABOUT YOUR LOVE	Kenny Thomas (Cooltempo)
-	44	LONG TERM LOVERS OF PAIN	Hue & Cry (Circa)
-	45	RUN FROM LOVE	Jimmy Somerville (London)
-	46	ROMANTIC	Karyn White (Warner Bros)
-	47	SILVER THUNDERBIRD	Marc Cohn (Atlantic)
-	48	COLD, COLD HEART	Midge Ure (Arista)
-	49	MIND, BODY, SOUL	Fantasy UFO featuring Jay Groove (Strictly Underground)
50	50	THE VERTIGO (EP)	Altern 8 (Network)

Extreme's first major hit single *More Than Words* belied their normal status as a heavy rock outfit in the Guns N' Roses mode, being an accoustically-backed vocal harmony piece redolent of the mid-period Beatles. This widening of the group's horizons took them to Number Two in the chart, heavily boosting sales of their far more histrionic album, from which the single was taken.

August – September 1991

24 August 1991

last	this	title / artist (label)
1	1	EVERYTHING I DO (I DO IT FOR YOU) Bryan Adams (A&M)
3	2	I'M TOO SEXY Right Said Fred (Tug)
7	3	SET ADRIFT ON MEMORY BLISS PM Dawn (Gee Street)
6	4	ALL 4 LOVE Color Me Badd (Giant)
2	5	MORE THAN WORDS Extreme (A&M)
4	6	MOVE ANY MOUNTAIN - PRO-GEN '91 Shamen (One Little Indian)
5	7	WINTER IN JULY Bomb The Bass (Rhythm King)
10	8	SUMMERTIME DJ Jazzy Jeff & Fresh Prince (Jive)
33	9	GUARANTEED Level 42 (RCA)
8	10	ENTER SANDMAN Metallica (Vertigo)
11	11	TWIST AND SHOUT Deacon Blue (Columbia)
15	12	APPARENTLY NOTHIN' Young Disciples (Talkin' Loud)
9	13	NOW THAT WE FOUND LOVE Heavy D & the Boyz (MCA)
-	14	CHARLY Prodigy (XL)
12	15	THINGS THAT MAKE YOU GO HMMM.. C&C Music Factory (Columbia)
46	16	ROMANTIC Karyn White (Warner Brothers)
30	17	NEAR WILD HEAVEN R.E.M. (Warner Brothers)
-	18	HAPPY TOGETHER Jason Donovan (PWL)
19	19	EVERY HEARTBEAT Amy Grant (A&M)
26	20	LOVE'S UNKIND Sophie Lawrence (IQ)
16	21	A ROLLER SKATING JAM NAMED "SATURDAYS" De La Soul (Big Life)
48	22	COLD, COLD HEART Midge Ure (Arista)
23	23	MONSTERS AND ANGELS Voice Of The Beehive (London)
25	24	TIME, LOVE & TENDERNESS Michael Bolton (Columbia)
24	25	BANG Blur (Food)
27	26	SATISFACTION Vanilla Ice (SBK)
-	27	LOVE ... THY WILL BE DONE Martika (Columbia)
14	28	PANDORA'S BOX Orchestral Manoeuvres In The Dark (Virgin)
22	29	HOLDING ON Beverley Craven (Epic)
-	30	SUNSHINE ON A RAINY DAY Zoe (M&G)
34	31	FAMILY AFFAIR BEF featuring Lalah Hathaway (10)
18	32	JUST ANOTHER DREAM Cathy Dennis (Polydor)
13	33	JUMP TO THE BEAT Dannii Minogue (MCA)
-	34	WHAT CAN YOU DO FOR ME Utah Saints (ffrr)
17	35	LOVE AND UNDERSTANDING Cher (Geffen)
37	36	YOU COULD BE MINE Guns N' Roses (Geffen)
-	37	IT'S ON/EGG RUSH Flowered Up (London)
41	38	LET THE BEAT HIT 'EM Lisa Lisa & Cult Jam (Columbia)
-	39	OPEN YOUR MIND 808 State (ZTT)
-	40	DON'T FIGHT IT FEEL IT Primal Scream featuring Denise Johnson (Creation)
28	41	ANY DREAM WILL DO Jason Donovan (Really Useful)
-	42	MIND Farm (Produce)
20	43	THE BEGINNING Seal (ZTT)
47	44	SILVER THUNDERBIRD Marc Cohn (Atlantic)
39	45	STAY BEAUTIFUL Manic Street Preachers (Columbia)
-	46	YOU BELONG IN ROCK 'N' ROLL Tin Machine (London)
42	47	NO ONE CAN Marillion (EMI)
21	48	THE WHISTLE SONG Frankie Knuckles (Virgin America)
-	49	20TH CENTURY BOY Marc Bolan & T. Rex (Marc On Wax)
49	50	MIND, BODY, SOUL Fantasy UFO featuring Jay Groove (Strictly Underground)

31 August 1991

	this	title / artist (label)
1	1	EVERYTHING I DO (I DO IT FOR YOU) Bryan Adams (A&M)
2	2	I'M TOO SEXY Right Said Fred (Tug)
3	3	SET ADRIFT ON MEMORY BLISS PM Dawn (Gee Street)
-	4	GETT OFF Prince & The New Power Generation (Paisley Park)
4	5	ALL 4 LOVE Color Me Badd (Giant)
5	6	MORE THAN WORDS Extreme (A&M)
30	7	SUNSHINE ON A RAINY DAY Zoe (M&G)
8	8	SUMMERTIME DJ Jazzy Jeff & Fresh Prince (Jive)
14	9	CHARLY Prodigy (XL)
18	10	HAPPY TOGETHER Jason Donovan (PWL)
-	11	STAND BY LOVE Simple Minds (Virgin)
7	12	WINTER IN JULY Bomb The Bass (Rhythm King)
27	13	LOVE ... THY WILL BE DONE Martika (Columbia)
-	14	I'LL BE BACK Arnee & the Terminators (Epic)
22	15	COLD, COLD HEART Midge Ure (Arista)
6	16	MOVE ANY MOUNTAIN - PRO-GEN '91 Shamen (One Little Indian)
-	17	CALLING ELVIS Dire Straits (Vertigo)
13	18	NOW THAT WE FOUND LOVE Heavy D & the Boyz (MCA)
34	19	WHAT CAN YOU DO FOR ME Utah Saints (ffrr)
9	20	GUARANTEED Level 42 (RCA)
20	21	LOVE'S UNKIND Sophie Lawrence (IQ)
-	22	INSANITY Oceanic (Dead Dead Good)
16	23	ROMANTIC Karyn White (Warner Bros)
12	24	TWIST AND SHOUT Deacon Blue (Columbia)
15	25	APPARENTLY NOTHIN' Young Disciples (Talkin' Loud)
-	26	THINGS THAT MAKE YOU GO HMMM... C&C Music Factory (Columbia)
49	27	20TH CENTURY BOY Marc Bolan & T. Rex (Marc On Wax)
23	28	MONSTERS AND ANGELS Voice Of The Beehive (London)
19	29	EVERY HEARTBEAT Amy Grant (A&M)
17	30	NEAR WILD HEAVEN R.E.M. (Warner Bros)
42	31	MIND Farm (Produce)
46	32	YOU BELONG IN ROCK 'N' ROLL Tin Machine (London)
-	33	SOMETIMES IT'S A BITCH Stevie Nicks (EMI)
-	34	REPUBLICAN PARTY PEOPLE Big Country (Vertigo)
-	35	CRUCIFIED Army Of Lovers (China)
-	36	LIES EMF (Parlophone)
40	37	DON'T FIGHT IT FEEL IT Primal Scream featuring Denise Johnson (Creation)
-	38	LET'S TALK ABOUT SEX Salt 'N' Pepa (ffrr)
36	39	YOU COULD BE MINE Guns N' Roses (Geffen)
-	40	HARD TO HANDLE Black Crowes (Def American)
-	41	GOOD VIBRATIONS Marky Mark & the Funky Bunch featuring Loleatta Holloway (Interscope)
-	42	BE YOUNG, BE FOOLISH, BE HAPPY Sonia (IQ)
39	43	OPEN YOUR MIND 808 State (ZTT)
10	44	ENTER SANDMAN Metallica (Vertigo)
41	45	ANY DREAM WILL DO Jason Donovan (Really Useful)
38	46	LET THE BEAT HIT 'EM Lisa Lisa & Cult Jam (Columbia)
-	47	HELLO MARY LOU (GOODBYE HEART) Ricky Nelson (Liberty)
24	48	TIME, LOVE & TENDERNESS Michael Bolton (Columbia)
-	49	THE PROMISE OF A NEW DAY Paula Abdul (Virgin America)
28	50	PANDORA'S BOX Orchestral Manoeuvres In The Dark (Virgin)

7 September 1991

	this	title / artist (label)
1	1	EVERYTHING I DO (I DO IT FOR YOU) Bryan Adams (A&M)
2	2	I'M TOO SEXY Right Said Fred (Tug)
9	3	CHARLY Prodigy (XL)
4	4	GETT OFF Prince & the New Power Generation (Paisley Park)
7	5	SUNSHINE ON A RAINY DAY Zoe (M&G)
3	6	SET ADRIFT ON MEMORY BLISS PM Dawn (Gee Street)
14	7	I'LL BE BACK Arnee & the Terminators (Epic)
13	8	LOVE ... THY WILL BE DONE Martika (Columbia)
22	9	INSANITY Oceanic (Dead Dead Good)
10	10	HAPPY TOGETHER Jason Donovan (PWL)
5	11	ALL 4 LOVE Color Me Badd (Giant)
6	12	MORE THAN WORDS Extreme (A&M)
11	13	STAND BY LOVE Simple Minds (Virgin)
19	14	WHAT CAN YOU DO FOR ME Utah Saints (ffrr)
15	15	COLD, COLD HEART Midge Ure (Arista)
17	16	CALLING ELVIS Dire Straits (Vertigo)
27	17	20TH CENTURY BOY Marc Bolan & T. Rex (Marc On Wax)
-	18	WORD IS OUT Kylie Minogue (PWL)
38	19	LET'S TALK ABOUT SEX Salt 'N' Pepa (ffrr)
41	20	GOOD VIBRATIONS Marky Mark & the Funky Bunch featuring Loleatta Holloway (Interscope)
8	21	SUMMERTIME DJ Jazzy Jeff & Fresh Prince (Jive)
12	22	WINTER IN JULY Bomb The Bass (Rhythm King)
42	23	BE YOUNG, BE FOOLISH, BE HAPPY Sonia (IQ)
16	24	MOVE ANY MOUNTAIN - PRO-GEN '91 Shamen (One Little Indian)
18	25	NOW THAT WE FOUND LOVE Heavy D & the Boyz (MCA)
36	26	LIES EMF (Parlophone)
40	27	HARD TO HANDLE Black Crowes (Def American)
31	28	MIND Farm (Produce)
24	29	TWIST AND SHOUT Deacon Blue (Columbia)
33	30	SOMETIMES IT'S A BITCH Stevie Nicks (EMI)
32	31	YOU BELONG IN ROCK 'N' ROLL Tin Machine (London)
21	32	LOVE'S UNKIND Sophie Lawrence (IQ)
-	33	PRIMAL SCREAM Motley Crue (Elektra)
-	34	HOUSECALL Shabba Ranks featuring Maxi Priest (Epic)
-	35	SLEEP ALONE Wonder Stuff (Polydor)
23	36	ROMANTIC Karyn White (Warner Bros)
47	37	HELLO MARY LOU (GOODBYE HEART) Ricky Nelson (Liberty)
49	38	THE PROMISE OF A NEW DAY Paula Abdul (Virgin America)
-	39	THE BIG L Roxette (EMI)
-	40	MAKIN' HAPPY Crystal Waters (A&M)
-	41	WHAT WOULD WE DO DSK (Boy's Own)
34	42	REPUBLICAN PARTY PEOPLE Big Country (Vertigo)
29	43	EVERY HEARTBEAT Amy Grant (A&M)
-	44	HEARTHAMMER Runrig (Chrysalis)
25	45	APPARENTLY NOTHIN' Young Disciples (Talkin' Loud)
-	46	SALTWATER Julian Lennon (Virgin)
39	47	YOU COULD BE MINE Guns N' Roses (Geffen)
-	48	JET CITY WOMAN Queensryche (EMI USA)
28	49	MONSTERS AND ANGELS Voice Of The Beehive (London)
43	50	OPEN YOUR MIND 808 State (ZTT)

Right Said Fred's debut *I'm Too Sexy* was widely reviewed as a novelty release, yet it began a string of hit singles which showed a group capable of a highly flexible approach. This apparently tongue-in-cheek song about a male model became 1991's second-biggest seller, beaten only by the ubiquitous Bryan Adams hit which kept it at Number Two for three straight weeks.

September 1991

14 September 1991

last	this		
1	1	EVERYTHING I DO (I DO IT FOR YOU)	Bryan Adams (A&M)
3	2	CHARLY	Prodigy (XL)
2	3	I'M TOO SEXY	Right Said Fred (Tug)
4	4	GETT OFF	Prince & the New Power Generation (Paisley Park)
5	5	SUNSHINE ON A RAINY DAY	Zoe (M&G)
7	6	I'LL BE BACK	Arnee & the Terminators (Epic)
9	7	INSANITY	Oceanic (Dead Dead Good)
19	8	LET'S TALK ABOUT SEX	Salt 'N' Pepa (ffrr)
8	9	LOVE ... THY WILL BE DONE	Martika (Columbia)
6	10	SET ADRIFT ON MEMORY BLISS	PM Dawn (Gee Street)
18	11	WORD IS OUT	Kylie Minogue (PWL)
20	12	GOOD VIBRATIONS	Marky Mark & the Funky Bunch featuring Loleatta Holloway (Interscope)
14	13	WHAT CAN YOU DO FOR ME	Utah Saints (ffrr)
17	14	20TH CENTURY BOY	Marc Bolan & T. Rex (Marc On Wax)
10	15	HAPPY TOGETHER	Jason Donovan (PWL)
11	16	ALL 4 LOVE	Color Me Badd (Giant)
39	17	THE BIG L	Roxette (EMI)
12	18	MORE THAN WORDS	Extreme (A&M)
-	19	PEACE	Sabrina Johnston (East West)
23	20	BE YOUNG, BE FOOLISH, BE HAPPY	Sonia (IQ)
40	21	MAKIN' HAPPY	Crystal Waters (A&M)
15	22	COLD, COLD HEART	Midge Ure (Arista)
13	23	STAND BY LOVE	Simple Minds (Virgin)
-	24	I WANNA BE ADORED	Stone Roses (Silvertone)
-	25	CAN'T STOP THIS THING WE STARTED	Bryan Adams (A&M)
21	26	SUMMERTIME	DJ Jazzy Jeff & Fresh Prince (Jive)
-	27	MORE TO LIFE	Cliff Richard (EMI)
16	28	CALLING ELVIS	Dire Straits (Vertigo)
44	29	HEARTHAMMER	Runrig (Chrysalis)
-	30	CAN'T GIVE YOU MORE	Status Quo (Vertigo)
-	31	EVERYBODY'S FREE (TO FEEL GOOD)	Rozalla (Pulse-8)
33	32	PRIMAL SCREAM	Motley Crue (Elektra)
34	33	HOUSECALL	Shabba Ranks featuring Maxi Priest (Epic)
-	34	WILD HEARTED SON	Cult (Beggars Banquet)
24	35	MOVE ANY MOUNTAIN - PRO-GEN '91	Shamen (One Little Indian)
26	36	LIES	EMF (Parlophone)
22	37	WINTER IN JULY	Bomb The Bass (Rhythm King)
46	38	SALTWATER	Julian Lennon (Virgin)
27	39	HARD TO HANDLE	Black Crowes (Def American)
35	40	SLEEP ALONE	Wonder Stuff (Polydor)
-	41	ONLY LOVE CAN BREAK YOUR HEART	St Etienne (Heavenly)
37	42	HELLO MARY LOU (GOODBYE HEART)	Ricky Nelson (Liberty)
-	43	BROKEN ARROW	Rod Stewart (Warner Bros)
48	44	JET CITY WOMAN	Queensryche (EMI USA)
-	45	SUCH A GOOD FEELING	Brothers In Rhythm (4th & Broadway)
25	46	NOW THAT WE FOUND LOVE	Heavy D & the Boyz (MCA)
-	47	THEN YOU TURN AWAY	Orchestral Manoeuvres In The Dark (Virgin)
29	48	TWIST AND SHOUT	Deacon Blue (Columbia)
-	49	SUCH A FEELING	Bizarre Inc (Vinyl Solution)
-	50	SLAVE TO THE GRIND	Skid Row (Atlantic)

21 September 1991

last	this		
1	1	EVERYTHING I DO (I DO IT FOR YOU)	Bryan Adams (A&M)
-	2	DON'T CRY	Guns N' Roses (Geffen)
3	3	I'M TOO SEXY	Right Said Fred (Tug)
5	4	SUNSHINE ON A RAINY DAY	Zoe (M&G)
7	5	INSANITY	Oceanic (Dead Dead Good)
8	6	LET'S TALK ABOUT SEX	Salt 'N' Pepa (ffrr)
2	7	CHARLY	Prodigy (XL)
19	8	PEACE	Sabrina Johnston (East West)
4	9	GETT OFF	Prince & the New Power Generation (Paisley Park)
-	10	LOVE TO HATE YOU	Erasure (Mute)
13	11	WHAT CAN YOU DO FOR ME	Utah Saints (ffrr)
25	12	CAN'T STOP THIS THING WE STARTED	Bryan Adams (A&M)
14	13	20TH CENTURY BOY	Marc Bolan & T. Rex (Marc On Wax)
11	14	WORD IS OUT	Kylie Minogue (PWL)
17	15	THE BIG L	Roxette (EMI)
-	16	CREAM	Prince & the New Power Generation (Paisley Park)
9	17	LOVE ... THY WILL BE DONE	Martika (Columbia)
31	18	EVERYBODY'S FREE (TO FEEL GOOD)	Rozalla (Pulse-8)
21	19	MAKIN' HAPPY	Crystal Waters (A&M)
27	20	MORE TO LIFE	Cliff Richard (EMI)
12	21	GOOD VIBRATIONS	Marky Mark & the Funky Bunch featuring Loleatta Holloway (Interscope)
-	22	SOMETHING GOT ME STARTED	Simply Red (East West)
10	23	SET ADRIFT ON MEMORY BLISS	PM Dawn (Gee Street)
24	24	I WANNA BE ADORED	Stone Roses (Silvertone)
-	25	TRUST	Ned's Atomic Dustbin (Columbia)
6	26	I'LL BE BACK	Arnee & the Terminators (Epic)
27	27	THE ONE I LOVE	R.E.M. (I.R.S.)
16	28	ALL 4 LOVE	Color Me Badd (Giant)
-	29	BRIDGE OVER TROUBLED WATER	PJB featuring Hannah & Her Sisters (Dance Pool)
20	30	BE YOUNG, BE FOOLISH, BE HAPPY	Sonia (IQ)
38	31	SALTWATER	Julian Lennon (Virgin)
15	32	HAPPY TOGETHER	Jason Donovan (PWL)
33	33	HOUSECALL	Shabba Ranks featuring Maxi Priest (Epic)
49	34	SUCH A FEELING	Bizarre Inc (Vinyl Solution)
45	35	SUCH A GOOD FEELING	Brothers In Rhythm (4th & Broadway)
47	36	THEN YOU TURN AWAY	Orchestral Manoeuvres In The Dark (Virgin)
-	37	NUTBUSH CITY LIMITS	Tina Turner (Capitol)
-	38	TRY	Bros (Columbia)
-	39	MAKE IT TONIGHT	Wet Wet Wet (Precious)
29	40	HEARTHAMMER	Runrig (Chrysalis)
41	41	ONLY LOVE CAN BREAK YOUR HEART	St Etienne (Heavenly)
-	42	FEEL EVERY BEAT	Electronic (Factory)
-	43	DOMINATOR	Human Resource (R&S)
18	44	MORE THAN WORDS	Extreme (A&M)
-	45	IVORY	Skin Up (Love)
-	46	HEAD LIKE A HOLE	Nine Inch Nails (TVT)
34	47	WILD HEARTED SON	Cult (Beggars Banquet)
-	48	CRAZY FOR YOU	Incognito featuring Chyna (Talkin' Loud)
-	49	STAND BY MY WOMAN	Lenny Kravitz (Virgin America)
43	50	BROKEN ARROW	Rod Stewart (Warner Bros)

28 September 1991

last	this		
1	1	EVERYTHING I DO (I DO IT FOR YOU)	Bryan Adams (A&M)
6	2	LET'S TALK ABOUT SEX	Salt 'N' Pepa (ffrr)
10	3	LOVE TO HATE YOU	Erasure (Mute)
3	4	I'M TOO SEXY	Right Said Fred (Tug)
5	5	INSANITY	Oceanic (Dead Dead Good)
8	6	PEACE	Sabrina Johnston (East West)
2	7	DON'T CRY	Guns N' Roses (Geffen)
4	8	SUNSHINE ON A RAINY DAY	Zoe (M&G)
18	9	EVERYBODY'S FREE (TO FEEL GOOD)	Rozalla (Pulse-8)
12	10	CAN'T STOP THIS THING WE STARTED	Bryan Adams (A&M)
11	11	WHAT CAN YOU DO FOR ME	Utah Saints (ffrr)
7	12	CHARLY	Prodigy (XL)
22	13	SOMETHING GOT ME STARTED	Simply Red (East West)
34	14	SUCH A FEELING	Bizarre Inc (Vinyl Solution)
16	15	CREAM	Prince & the New Power Generation (Paisley Park)
35	16	SUCH A GOOD FEELING	Brothers In Rhythm (4th & Broadway)
37	17	NUTBUSH CITY LIMITS	Tina Turner (Capitol)
27	18	THE ONE I LOVE	R.E.M. (I.R.S.)
13	19	20TH CENTURY BOY	Marc Bolan & T. Rex (Marc On Wax)
9	20	GETT OFF	Prince & the New Power Generation (Paisley Park)
17	21	LOVE ... THY WILL BE DONE	Martika (Columbia)
29	22	BRIDGE OVER TROUBLED WATER	PJB featuring Hannah & Her Sisters (Dance Pool)
19	23	MAKIN' HAPPY	Crystal Waters (A&M)
31	24	SALTWATER	Julian Lennon (Virgin)
15	25	THE BIG L	Roxette (EMI)
20	26	MORE TO LIFE	Cliff Richard (EMI)
21	27	WIND OF CHANGE	Scorpions (Vertigo)
28	28	GOOD VIBRATIONS	Marky Mark & the Funky Bunch featuring Loleatta Holloway (Interscope)
25	29	TRUST	Ned's Atomic Dustbin (Columbia)
42	30	FEEL EVERY BEAT	Electronic (Factory)
-	31	JACKY	Marc Almond (Some Bizzare)
38	32	TRY	Bros (Columbia)
-	33	DON'T LET THE SUN GO DOWN ON ME	Oleta Adams (Fontana)
23	34	SET ADRIFT ON MEMORY BLISS	PM Dawn (Gee Street)
36	35	THEN YOU TURN AWAY	Orchestral Manoeuvres In The Dark (Virgin)
-	36	LIVE YOUR LIFE BE FREE	Belinda Carlisle (Virgin)
14	37	WORD IS OUT	Kylie Minogue (PWL)
26	38	I'LL BE BACK	Arnee & the Terminators (Epic)
-	39	IS IT GOOD FOR YOU?	Heavy D & the Boyz (MCA)
-	40	LIVE FOR LOVING YOU	Gloria Estefan (Epic)
-	41	ALRIGHT	Urban Soul (Cooltempo)
-	42	INTERNAL EXILE	Fish (Polydor)
33	43	HOUSECALL	Shabba Ranks featuring Maxi Priest (Epic)
-	44	I BELONG TO YOU	Whitney Houston (Arista)
43	45	DOMINATOR	Human Resource (R&S)
41	46	ONLY LOVE CAN BREAK YOUR HEART	St Etienne (Heavenly)
24	47	I WANNA BE ADORED	Stone Roses (Silvertone)
49	48	STAND BY MY WOMAN	Lenny Kravitz (Virgin America)
-	49	GOT IT AT THE DELMAR	Senseless Things (Epic)
-	50	I THINK I LOVE YOU	Voice Of The Beehive (London)

Bryan Adams' follow-up single to his Number One smash reached Number 10, yet such was the longevity of *Everything I Do*, that *Can't Stop This Thing We Started* arrived, rose, peaked, fell and vanished from the chart while its predecessor was still at Nnumber One! Meanwhile, girl rappers Salt 'N' Pepa joined Right Said Fred in talking about sex in the chart's Top Five.

October 1991

5 October 1991

last	this	entry
1	1	EVERYTHING I DO (I DO IT FOR YOU) Bryan Adams (A&M)
3	2	LOVE TO HATE YOU Erasure (Mute)
2	3	LET'S TALK ABOUT SEX Salt 'N' Pepa (ffrr)
6	4	PEACE Sabrina Johnston (East West)
9	5	EVERYBODY'S FREE (TO FEEL GOOD) Rozalla (Pulse-8)
5	6	INSANITY Oceanic (Dead Dead Good)
27	7	WIND OF CHANGE Scorpions (Vertigo)
13	8	SOMETHING GOT ME STARTED Simply Red (East West)
14	9	SUCH A FEELING Bizarre Inc (Vinyl Solution)
10	10	CAN'T STOP THIS THING WE STARTED Bryan Adams (A&M)
24	11	SALTWATER Julian Lennon (Virgin)
16	12	SUCH A FEELING Brothers In Rhythm (4th & Broadway)
8	13	SUNSHINE ON A RAINY DAY Zoe (M&G)
17	14	NUTBUSH CITY LIMITS Tina Turner (Capitol)
31	15	JACKY Marc Almond (Some Bizzare)
18	16	THE ONE I LOVE R.E.M. (I.R.S.)
11	17	WHAT CAN YOU DO FOR ME Utah Saints (ffrr)
15	18	CREAM Prince & the New Power Generation (Paisley Park)
4	19	I'M TOO SEXY Right Said Fred (Tug)
-	20	BEST OF YOU Kenny Thomas (Cooltempo)
22	21	BRIDGE OVER TROUBLED WATER PJB featuring Hannah & Her Sisters (Dance Pool)
7	22	DON'T CRY Guns N' Roses (Geffen)
36	23	LIVE YOUR LIFE BE FREE Belinda Carlisle (Virgin)
12	24	CHARLY Prodigy (XL)
33	25	DON'T LET THE SUN GO DOWN ON ME Oleta Adams (Fontana)
50	26	I THINK I LOVE YOU Voice Of The Beehive (London)
32	27	TRY Bros (Columbia)
30	28	FEEL EVERY BEAT Electronic (Factory)
19	29	20TH CENTURY BOY Marc Bolan & T. Rex (Marc On Wax)
20	30	GETT OFF Prince & the New Power Generation (Paisley Park)
40	31	LIVE FOR LOVING YOU Gloria Estefan (Epic)
42	32	INTERNAL EXILE Fish (Polydor)
39	33	IS IT GOOD FOR YOU? Heavy D & the Boyz (MCA)
44	34	I BELONG TO YOU Whitney Houston (Arista)
21	35	LOVE ... THY WILL BE DONE Martika (Columbia)
-	36	TOO MANY WALLS Cathy Dennis (Polydor)
-	37	NO MORE TEARS Ozzy Osbourne (Epic)
-	38	LOVE'S A LOADED GUN Alice Cooper (Epic)
23	39	MAKIN' HAPPY Crystal Waters (A&M)
-	40	SPECIAL WAY River City People (EMI)
25	41	THE BIG L Roxette (EMI)
-	42	DRY LAND Marillion (EMI)
-	43	WORLD IN UNION Kiri Te Kanawa (Columbia)
-	44	EMOTIONS Mariah Carey (Columbia)
45	45	I WANT YOU (FOREVER) DJ Carl Cox (Perfecto)
41	46	ALRIGHT Urban Soul (Cooltempo)
26	47	MORE TO LIFE Cliff Richard (EMI)
29	48	TRUST Ned's Atomic Dustbin (Columbia)
-	49	COME INSIDE Thompson Twins (Warner Bros)
-	50	GET YOURSELF TOGETHER Young Disciples (Talkin' Loud)

12 October 1991

last	this	entry
1	1	EVERYTHING I DO (I DO IT FOR YOU) Bryan Adams (A&M)
7	2	WIND OF CHANGE Scorpions (Vertigo)
2	3	LOVE TO HATE YOU Erasure (Mute)
3	4	LET'S TALK ABOUT SEX Salt 'N' Pepa (ffrr)
5	5	EVERYBODY'S FREE (TO FEEL GOOD) Rozalla (Pulse-8)
6	6	INSANITY Oceanic (Dead Dead Good)
11	7	SALTWATER Julian Lennon (Virgin)
4	8	PEACE Sabrina Johnston (East West)
20	9	BEST OF YOU Kenny Thomas (Cooltempo)
8	10	SOMETHING GOT ME STARTED Simply Red (East West)
9	11	SUCH A FEELING Bizarre Inc (Vinyl Solution)
12	12	SUCH A GOOD FEELING Brothers In Rhythm (4th & Broadway)
15	13	JACKY Marc Almond (Some Bizzare)
23	14	LIVE YOUR LIFE BE FREE Belinda Carlisle (Virgin)
-	15	ALWAYS LOOK ON THE BRIGHT SIDE OF LIFE Monty Python (Virgin)
13	16	SUNSHINE ON A RAINY DAY Zoe (M&G)
10	17	CAN'T STOP THIS THING WE STARTED Bryan Adams (A&M)
18	18	THE ONE I LOVE R.E.M. (I.R.S.)
21	19	BRIDGE OVER TROUBLED WATER PJB featuring Hannah & Her Sisters (Dance Pool)
26	20	I THINK I LOVE YOU Voice Of The Beehive (London)
43	21	WORLD IN UNION Kiri Te Kanawa (Columbia)
14	22	NUTBUSH CITY LIMITS Tina Turner (Capitol)
25	23	DON'T LE' THE SUN GO DOWN ON ME Oleta Adams (Fontana)
19	24	I'M TOO SEXY Right Said Fred (Tug)
17	25	WHAT CAN YOU DO FOR ME Utah Saints (ffrr)
36	26	TOO MANY WALLS Cathy Dennis (Polydor)
18	27	CREAM Prince & the New Power Generation (Paisley Park)
27	28	TRY Bros (Columbia)
31	29	LIVE FOR LOVING YOU Gloria Estefan (Epic)
24	30	CHARLY Prodigy (XL)
45	31	I WANT YOU (FOREVER) DJ Carl Cox (Perfecto)
38	32	LOVE'S A LOADED GUN Alice Cooper (Epic)
44	33	EMOTIONS Mariah Carey (Columbia)
-	34	MY LOVE LIFE Morrissey (HMV)
30	35	GETT OFF Prince & the New Power Generation (Paisley Park)
22	36	DON'T CRY Guns N' Roses (Geffen)
37	37	NO MORE TEARS Ozzy Osbourne (Epic)
38	38	CAN'T TRUST IT Public Enemy (Def Jam)
29	39	20TH CENTURY BOY Marc Bolan & T. Rex (Marc On Wax)
-	40	DECADENCE DANCE Extreme (A&M)
-	41	GET READY FOR THIS 2 Unlimited (PWL Continental)
42	42	DRY LAND Marillion (EMI)
-	43	AMERICAN PIE Don McLean (Liberty)
34	44	I BELONG TO YOU Whitney Houston (Arista)
35	45	LOVE ... THY WILL BE DONE Martika (Columbia)
33	46	IS IT GOOD FOR YOU? Heavy D & the Boyz (MCA)
-	47	NEVER STOP Brand New Heavies featuring N'Dea Davenport (ffrr)
28	48	FEEL EVERY BEAT Electronic (Factory)
-	49	WOMAN TO WOMAN Beverley Craven (Epic)
-	50	I ADORE MI AMOR Color Me Badd (Giant)

19 October 1991

last	this	entry
1	1	EVERYTHING I DO (I DO IT FOR YOU) Bryan Adams (A&M)
2	2	WIND OF CHANGE Scorpions (Vertigo)
15	3	ALWAYS LOOK ON THE BRIGHT SIDE OF LIFE Monty Python (Virgin)
7	4	SALTWATER Julian Lennon (Virgin)
21	5	WORLD IN UNION Kiri Te Kanawa (Columbia)
9	6	BEST OF YOU Kenny Thomas (Cooltempo)
6	7	INSANITY Oceanic (Dead Dead Good)
4	8	LET'S TALK ABOUT SEX Salt 'N' Pepa (ffrr)
3	9	LOVE TO HATE YOU Erasure (Mute)
5	10	EVERYBODY'S FREE (TO FEEL GOOD) Rozalla (Pulse-8)
14	11	LIVE YOUR LIFE BE FREE Belinda Carlisle (Virgin)
41	12	GET READY FOR THIS 2 Unlimited (PWL Continental)
13	13	JACKY Marc Almond (Some Bizzare)
8	14	PEACE Sabrina Johnston (East West)
10	15	SOMETHING GOT ME STARTED Simply Red (East West)
-	16	WALKING IN MEMPHIS Marc Cohn (Atlantic)
11	17	SUCH A FEELING Bizarre Inc (Vinyl Solution)
16	18	SUNSHINE ON A RAINY DAY Zoe (M&G)
12	19	SUCH A GOOD FEELING Brothers in Rhythm (4th & Broadway)
26	20	TOO MANY WALLS Cathy Dennis (Polydor)
31	21	I WANT YOU (FOREVER) DJ Carl Cox (Perfecto)
23	22	DON'T LET THE SUN GO DOWN ON ME Oleta Adams (Fontana)
19	23	BRIDGE OVER TROUBLED WATER PJB featuring Hannah & Her Sisters (Dance Pool)
33	24	EMOTIONS Mariah Carey (Columbia)
34	25	MY LOVE LIFE Morrissey (HMV)
20	26	I THINK I LOVE YOU Voice Of The Beehive (London)
27	27	CHANGE Lisa Stansfield (Arista)
24	28	I'M TOO SEXY Right Said Fred (Tug)
18	29	THE ONE I LOVE R.E.M. (I.R.S.)
-	30	BABY LOVE Dannii Minogue (MCA)
17	31	CAN'T STOP THIS THING WE STARTED Bryan Adams (A&M)
38	32	CAN'T TRUSS IT Public Enemy (Def Jam)
-	33	FINALLY Ce Ce Peniston (A&M)
22	34	NUTBUSH CITY LIMITS Tina Turner (Capitol)
25	35	WHAT CAN YOU DO FOR ME Utah Saints (ffrr)
43	36	AMERICAN PIE Don McLean (Liberty)
47	37	NEVER STOP Brand New Heavies featuring N'Dea Davenport (ffrr)
27	38	CREAM Prince & the New Power Generation (Paisley Park)
-	39	I ADORE MI AMOR Color Me Badd (Giant)
40	40	DECADENCE DANCE Extreme (A&M)
-	41	OH NO WON'T DO Cud (A&M)
30	42	CHARLY Prodigy (XL)
-	43	CARIBBEAN BLUE Enya (Warner Bros)
-	44	THE DREAMER All About Eve (Mercury)
32	45	LOVE'S A LOADED GUN Alice Cooper (Epic)
49	46	WOMAN TO WOMAN Beverley Craven (Epic)
29	47	LIVE FOR LOVING YOU Gloria Estefan (Epic)
-	48	RADIO WALL OF SOUND Slade (Polydor)
-	49	CLOSING TIME Deacon Blue (Columbia)
-	50	COME BACK (FOR REAL LOVE) Alison Limerick (Arista)

Veteran German band the Scorpions, with their first UK top 30 entry, were the eighth act to almost, but not quite, topple Bryan Adams from number one. Their *Wind Of Change,* an optimistic anthem to post-communist international friendship, came late to British success, having already been a huge success across the Continent and in the US in the first half of the year.

October – November 1991

26 October 1991 (last week / this week)

last	this	title	artist (label)
5	1	WORLD IN UNION	Kiri Te Kanawa (Columbia)
3	2	ALWAYS LOOK ON THE BRIGHT SIDE OF LIFE	Monty Python (Virgin)
1	3	EVERYTHING I DO (I DO IT FOR YOU)	Bryan Adams (A&M)
2	4	WIND OF CHANGE	Scorpions (Vertigo)
12	5	GET READY FOR THIS	2 Unlimited (PWL Continental)
4	6	SALTWATER	Julian Lennon (Virgin)
7	7	INSANITY	Oceanic (Dead Dead Good)
27	8	CHANGE	Lisa Stansfield (Arista)
6	9	BEST OF YOU	Kenny Thomas (Cooltempo)
30	10	BABY LOVE	Dannii Minogue (MCA)
11	11	LIVE YOUR LIFE BE FREE	Belinda Carlisle (Virgin)
-	12	DIZZY	Vic Reeves & the Wonder Stuff (Sense)
16	13	WALKING IN MEMPHIS	Marc Cohn (Atlantic)
8	14	LET'S TALK ABOUT SEX	Salt 'N' Pepa (ffrr)
10	15	EVERYBODY'S FREE (TO FEEL GOOD)	Rozalla (Pulse-8)
20	16	TOO MANY WALLS	Cathy Dennis (Polydor)
24	17	EMOTIONS	Mariah Carey (Columbia)
-	18	DJ CULTURE	Pet Shop Boys (Parlophone)
43	19	CARIBBEAN BLUE	Enya (Warner Bros)
-	20	GO	Moby (Outer Rhythm)
9	21	LOVE TO HATE YOU	Erasure (Mute)
21	22	I WANT YOU (FOREVER)	DJ Carl Cox (Perfecto)
13	23	JACKY	Marc Almond (Some Bizzare)
33	24	FINALLY	Ce Ce Peniston (A&M)
17	25	SUCH A FEELING	Bizarre Inc (Vinyl Solution)
-	26	THE SHOW MUST GO ON	Queen (Parlophone)
36	27	AMERICAN PIE	Don McLean (Liberty)
48	28	RADIO WALL OF SOUND	Slade (Polydor)
-	29	AFTER THE WATERSHED (EARLY LEARNING THE HARD WAY)	Carter USM (Big Cat)
14	30	PEACE	Sabrina Johnston (East West)
19	31	SUCH A GOOD FEELING	Brothers In Rhythm (4th & Broadway)
22	32	DON'T LET THE SUN GO DOWN ON ME	Oleta Adams (Fontana)
15	33	SOMETHING GOT ME STARTED	Simply Red (East West)
-	34	SAVE UP ALL YOUR TEARS	Cher (Geffen)
46	35	WOMAN TO WOMAN	Beverley Craven (Epic)
-	36	IT SHOULD'VE BEEN ME	Adeva (Cooltempo)
37	37	IF YOU CARED	Kim Appleby (Parlophone)
18	38	SUNSHINE ON A RAINY DAY	Zoe (M&G)
-	39	NOCTURNE	T99 (Emphasis)
49	40	CLOSING TIME	Deacon Blue (Columbia)
-	41	REAL LIFE	Simple Minds (Virgin)
-	42	JUST GET UP AND DANCE	Afrika Bambaataa (EMI USA)
28	43	I'M TOO SEXY	Right Said Fred (Tug)
44	44	THE DREAMER	All About Eve (Mercury)
-	45	SWING LOW (RUN WITH THE BALL)	Union featuring England Rugby World Cup Squad (Columbia)
23	46	BRIDGE OVER TROUBLED WATER	PJB featuring Hannah & Her Sisters (Dance Pool)
32	47	CAN'T TRUSS IT	Public Enemy (Def Jam)
41	48	OH NO WON'T DO	Cud (A&M)
26	49	I THINK I LOVE YOU	Voice Of The Beehive (London)
40	50	DECADENCE DANCE	Extreme (A&M)

2 November 1991

last	this	title	artist (label)
-	1	THE FLY	U2 (Island)
12	2	DIZZY	Vic Reeves & the Wonder Stuff (Sense)
5	3	GET READY FOR THIS	2 Unlimited (PWL Continental)
1	4	WORLD IN UNION	Kiri Te Kanawa (Columbia)
2	5	ALWAYS LOOK ON THE BRIGHT SIDE OF LIFE	Monty Python (Virgin)
3	6	EVERYTHING I DO (I DO IT FOR YOU)	Bryan Adams (A&M)
4	7	WIND OF CHANGE	Scorpions (Vertigo)
8	8	CHANGE	Lisa Stansfield (Arista)
18	9	DJ CULTURE	Pet Shop Boys (Parlophone)
-	10	NO SON OF MINE	Genesis (Virgin)
11	11	CARIBBEAN BLUE	Enya (Warner Bros)
20	12	GO	Moby (Outer Rhythm)
10	13	BABY LOVE	Dannii Minogue (MCA)
28	14	RADIO WALL OF SOUND	Slade (Polydor)
6	15	SALTWATER	Julian Lennon (Virgin)
7	16	INSANITY	Oceanic (Dead Dead Good)
17	17	EMOTIONS	Mariah Carey (Columbia)
26	18	THE SHOW MUST GO ON	Queen (Parlophone)
-	19	DON'T DREAM IT'S OVER	Paul Young (Columbia)
29	20	AFTER THE WATERSHED (EARLY LEARNING THE HARD WAY)	Carter USM (Big Cat)
14	21	LET'S TALK ABOUT SEX	Salt 'N' Pepa (ffrr)
24	22	FINALLY	Ce Ce Peniston (A&M)
9	23	BEST OF YOU	Kenny Thomas (Cooltempo)
16	24	TOO MANY WALLS	Cathy Dennis (Polydor)
11	25	LIVE YOUR LIFE BE FREE	Belinda Carlisle (Virgin)
-	26	IF YOU WERE WITH ME NOW	Kylie Minogue & Keith Washington (PWL)
15	27	EVERYBODY'S FREE (TO FEEL GOOD)	Rozalla (Pulse-8)
13	28	WALKING IN MEMPHIS	Marc Cohn (Atlantic)
27	29	AMERICAN PIE	Don McLean (Liberty)
-	30	40 MILES	Congress (Inner Rhythm)
-	31	SHINING STAR	INXS (Mercury)
21	32	LOVE TO HATE YOU	Erasure (Mute)
-	33	DJS TAKE CONTROL	SL2 (XL)
41	34	REAL LIFE	Simple Minds (Virgin)
22	35	I WANT YOU (FOREVER)	DJ Carl Cox (Perfecto)
23	36	JACKY	Marc Almond (Some Bizzare)
-	37	NOCTURNE	T99 (Emphasis)
25	38	SUCH A FEELING	Bizarre Inc (Vinyl Solution)
39	39	LIGHTNING	Zoe (M&G)
-	40	THIS HOUSE	Alison Moyet (Columbia)
34	41	SAVE UP ALL YOUR TEARS	Cher (Geffen)
-	42	HEAVY FUEL	Dire Straits (Vertigo)
30	43	PEACE	Sabrina Johnston (East West)
37	44	IF YOU CARED	Kim Appleby (Parlophone)
36	45	IT SHOULD'VE BEEN ME	Adeva (Cooltempo)
-	46	PAPER DOLL	PM Dawn (Gee Street)
-	47	MOVE TO MEMPHIS	A-ha (Warner Bros)
-	48	HOW CAN I LIVE YOU MORE?	M-People (deConstruction)
33	49	SOMETHING GOT ME STARTED	Simply Red (East West)
-	50	CATCH THE FIRE	Driza Bone (Fourth & Broadway)

9 November 1991

last	this	title	artist (label)
2	1	DIZZY	Vic Reeves & the Wonder Stuff (Sense)
1	2	THE FLY	U2 (Island)
3	3	GET READY FOR THIS	2 Unlimited (PWL Continental)
4	4	WORLD IN UNION	Kiri Te Kanawa (Columbia)
10	5	NO SON OF MINE	Genesis (Virgin)
6	6	EVERYTHING I DO (I DO IT FOR YOU)	Bryan Adams (A&M)
5	7	ALWAYS LOOK ON THE BRIGHT SIDE OF LIFE	Monty Python (Virgin)
7	8	WIND OF CHANGE	Scorpions (Vertigo)
26	9	IF YOU WERE WITH ME NOW	Kylie Minogue & Keith Washington (PWL)
11	10	CARIBBEAN BLUE	Enya (Warner Bros)
12	11	GO	Moby (Outer Rhythm)
8	12	CHANGE	Lisa Stansfield (Arista)
20	13	AFTER THE WATERSHED (EARLY LEARNING THE HARD WAY)	Carter USM (Big Cat)
29	14	AMERICAN PIE	Don McLean (Liberty)
-	15	RHYTHM IS A MYSTERY	K-Klass (deConstruction)
19	16	DON'T DREAM IT'S OVER	Paul Young (Columbia)
17	17	EMOTIONS	Mariah Carey (Columbia)
18	18	THE SHOW MUST GO ON	Queen (Parlophone)
16	19	INSANITY	Oceanic (Dead Dead Good)
33	20	DJS TAKE CONTROL	SL2 (XL)
13	21	BABY LOVE	Dannii Minogue (MCA)
9	22	DJ CULTURE	Pet Shop Boys (Parlophone)
14	23	RADIO WALL OF SOUND	Slade (Polydor)
-	24	IT'S GRIM UP NORTH	Justified Ancients of Mu Mu (KLFCommunications)
21	25	LET'S TALK ABOUT SEX	Salt 'N' Pepa (ffrr)
15	26	SALTWATER	Julian Lennon (Virgin)
-	27	FALL AT YOUR FEET	Crowded House (Capitol)
-	28	THE UNFORGIVEN	Metallica (Vertigo)
39	29	LIGHTNING	Zoe (M&G)
30	30	40 MILES	Congress (Inner Rhythm)
31	31	SHINING STAR	INXS (Mercury)
24	32	TOO MANY WALLS	Cathy Dennis (Polydor)
22	33	FINALLY	Ce Ce Peniston (A&M)
-	34	ME IN TIME	Charlatans (Situation Two)
-	35	DANCE WITH ME (I'M YOUR ECSTASY)	Control (All Around The World)
27	36	EVERYBODY'S FREE (TO FEEL GOOD)	Rozalla (Pulse-8)
-	37	MY TOWN	Glass Tiger featuring Rod Stewart (EMI)
23	38	BEST OF YOU	Kenny Thomas (Cooltempo)
-	39	WILDSIDE	Marky Mark & the Funky Bunch (Interscope)
25	40	LIVE YOUR LIFE BE FREE	Belinda Carlisle (Virgin)
40	41	THIS HOUSE	Alison Moyet (Columbia)
-	42	CHERRY (EP)	Curve (Anxious)
32	43	LOVE TO HATE YOU	Erasure (Mute)
-	44	NOCTURNE	T99 (Emphasis)
42	45	HEAVY FUEL	Dire Straits (Vertigo)
38	46	SUCH A FEELING	Bizarre Inc (Vinyl Solution)
48	47	HOW CAN I LIVE YOU MORE?	M-People (deConstruction)
-	48	RADIOACTIVITY	Kraftwerk (EMI)
34	49	REAL LIFE	Simple Minds (Virgin)
-	50	BABY UNIVERSAL	Tin Machine (Victor)

The Rugby World Cup took place in Britain in 1991, and *World In Union*, an unusual crossover into the pop field for opera star Kiri Te Kanawa, was the theme of the TV coverage. The song actually had classical, if not operatic, roots, since its melody was taken from the *Jupiter* section of Holst's *Planets Suite* – a distinction it shared with Manfred Mann's Earthband's 1973 hit *Joybringer*.

November 1991

16 November 1991

last week	this week	
1	1	DIZZY Vic Reeves & the Wonder Stuff (Sense)
3	2	GET READY FOR THIS 2 Unlimited (PWL Continental)
15	3	RHYTHM IS A MYSTERY K-Klass (deConstruction)
2	4	THE FLY U2 (Island)
9	5	IF YOU WERE WITH ME NOW Kylie Minogue & Keith Washington (PWL)
5	6	NO SON OF MINE Genesis (Virgin)
4	7	WORLD IN UNION Kiri Te Kanawa (Columbia)
6	8	EVERYTHING I DO (I DO IT FOR YOU) Bryan Adams (A&M)
24	9	IT'S GRIM UP NORTH Justified Ancients Of Mu Mu (KLF Communications)
14	10	AMERICAN PIE Don McLean (Liberty)
11	11	GO Moby (Outer Rhythm)
-	12	IS THERE ANYBODY OUT THERE? Bassheads (deConstruction)
10	13	CARIBBEAN BLUE Enya (Warner Bros)
20	14	DJS TAKE CONTROL SL2 (XL)
28	15	THE UNFORGIVEN Metallica (Vertigo)
17	16	EMOTIONS Mariah Carey (Columbia)
7	17	ALWAYS LOOK ON THE BRIGHT SIDE OF LIFE Monty Python (Virgin)
27	18	FALL AT YOUR FEET Crowded House (Capitol)
8	19	WIND OF CHANGE Scorpions (Vertigo)
-	20	KILLER ... ON THE LOOSE Seal (ZTT)
35	21	DANCE WITH ME (I'M YOUR ECSTASY) Control (All Around The World)
-	22	SWING LOW (RUN WITH THE BALL) Union featuring England Rugby World Cup Squad (Columbia)
-	23	ACTIV 8 (COME WITH ME) Altern 8 (Network)
-	24	WINTER SONG Chris Rea (East West)
16	25	DON'T DREAM IT'S OVER Paul Young (Columbia)
29	26	LIGHTNING Zoe (M&G)
12	27	CHANGE Lisa Stansfield (Arista)
-	28	RADIO SONG R.E.M. (Warner Bros)
13	29	AFTER THE WATERSHED (EARLY LEARNING THE HARD WAY) Carter USM (Big Cat)
19	30	INSANITY Oceanic (Dead Dead Good)
18	31	THE SHOW MUST GO ON Queen (Parlophone)
32	32	MY TOWN Glass Tiger featuring Rod Stewart (EMI)
-	33	FAITH (IN THE POWER OF LOVE) Rozalla (Pulse-8)
21	34	BABY LOVE Dannii Minogue (MCA)
-	35	REPEAT/LOVE'S SWEET EXILE Manic Street Preachers (Columbia)
31	36	SHINING STAR INXS (Mercury)
47	37	HOW CAN I LIVE YOU MORE? M-People (deConstruction)
34	38	ME IN TIME Charlatans (Situation Two)
-	39	DO YOU FEEL LIKE I FEEL? Belinda Carlisle (Virgin)
-	40	WHEN A MAN LOVES A WOMAN Michael Bolton (Columbia)
30	41	40 MILES Congress (Inner Rhythm)
-	42	2 231 Anticapella (PWL Continental)
33	43	FINALLY Ce Ce Peniston (A&M)
-	44	YOU TO ME ARE EVERYTHING Sonia (IQ)
23	45	RADIO WALL OF SOUND Slade (Polydor)
26	46	SALTWATER Julian Lennon (Virgin)
47	47	SIN Nine Inch Nails (TVT)
42	48	CHERRY (EP) Curve
-	49	NEVER GOIN' DOWN! Adamski & Jimi Polo (MCA)
22	50	DJ CULTURE Pet Shop Boys (Parlophone)

23 November 1991

last week	this week	
1	1	BLACK OR WHITE Michael Jackson (Epic)
1	2	DIZZY Vic Reeves & the Wonder Stuff (Sense)
3	3	RHYTHM IS A MYSTERY K-Klass (deConstruction)
12	4	IS THERE ANYBODY OUT THERE? Bassheads (deConstruction)
5	5	IF YOU WERE WITH ME NOW Kylie Minogue & Keith Washington (PWL)
2	6	GET READY FOR THIS 2 Unlimited (PWL Continental)
20	7	KILLER ... ON THE LOOSE Seal (ZTT)
8	8	ACTIV 8 (COME WITH ME) Altern 8 (Network)
9	9	IT'S GRIM UP NORTH Justified Ancients Of Mu Mu (KLF Communications)
6	10	NO SON OF MINE Genesis (Virgin)
40	11	WHEN A MAN LOVES A WOMAN Michael Bolton (Columbia)
8	12	EVERYTHING I DO (I DO IT FOR YOU) Bryan Adams (A&M)
4	13	THE FLY U2 (Island)
18	14	FALL AT YOUR FEET Crowded House (Capitol)
10	15	AMERICAN PIE Don McLean (Liberty)
-	16	PLAYING WITH KNIVES Bizarre Inc (Vinyl Solution)
33	17	FAITH (IN THE POWER OF LOVE) Rozalla (Pulse-8)
15	18	THE UNFORGIVEN Metallica (Vertigo)
7	19	WORLD IN UNION Kiri Te Kanawa (Columbia)
14	20	DJS TAKE CONTROL SL2 (XL)
-	21	HOLE HEARTED Extreme (A&M)
11	22	GO Moby (Outer Rhythm)
21	23	DANCE WITH ME (I'M YOUR ECSTASY) Control (All Around The World)
32	24	MY TOWN Glass Tiger featuring Rod Stewart (EMI)
24	25	WINTER SONG Chris Rea (East West)
39	26	DO YOU FEEL LIKE I FEEL? Belinda Car (Virgin)
44	27	YOU TO ME ARE EVERYTHING Sonia (IQ)
16	28	EMOTIONS Mariah Carey (Columbia)
37	29	HOW CAN I LIVE YOU MORE? M-People (deConstruction)
-	30	SO REAL Love Decade (All Around The World)
13	31	CARIBBEAN BLUE Enya (Warner Bros)
26	32	LIGHTNING Zoe (M&G)
22	33	SWING LOW (RUN WITH THE BALL) Union featuring England Rugby World Cup Squad (Columbia)
28	34	RADIO SONG R.E.M. (Warner Bros)
-	35	WASTED TIME Skid Row (East West)
-	36	THERE WILL NEVER BE ANOTHER TONIGHT Bryan Adams (A&M)
42	37	2 231 Anticapella (PWL Continental)
35	38	REPEAT/LOVE'S SWEET EXILE Manic Street Preachers (Columbia)
-	39	SO TELL ME WHY Poison (Capitol)
40	40	WAY OF THE WORLD Tina Turner (Capitol)
47	41	SIN Nine Inch Nails (TVT)
-	42	JUST A TOUCH OF LOVE (EVERY DAY) C&C Music Factory (Columbia)
43	43	DO WHAT YOU FEEL Joey Negro (10)
30	44	INSANITY Oceanic (Dead Dead Good)
19	45	WIND OF CHANGE Scorpions (Vertigo)
17	46	ALWAYS LOOK ON THE BRIGHT SIDE OF LIFE Monty Python (Virgin)
27	47	CHANGE Lisa Stansfield (Arista)
-	48	THE AIR YOU BREATHE Bomb The Bass (Rhythm King)
-	49	WINTER Love & Money (Fontana)
25	50	DON'T DREAM IT'S OVER Paul Young (Columbia)

30 November 1991

last week	this week	
1	1	BLACK OR WHITE Michael Jackson (Epic)
2	2	DIZZY Vic Reeves & the Wonder Stuff (Sense)
8	3	ACTIV 8 (COME WITH ME) Altern 8 (Network)
4	4	IS THERE ANYBODY OUT THERE? Bassheads (deConstruction)
11	5	WHEN A MAN LOVES A WOMAN Michael Bolton (Columbia)
16	6	PLAYING WITH KNIVES Bizarre Inc (Vinyl Solution)
3	7	RHYTHM IS A MYSTERY K-Klass (deConstruction)
7	8	KILLER ... ON THE LOOSE Seal (ZTT)
6	9	GET READY FOR THIS 2 Unlimited (PWL Continental)
5	10	IF YOU WERE WITH ME NOW Kylie Minogue & Keith Washington (PWL)
40	11	WAY OF THE WORLD Tina Turner (Capitol)
-	12	RIDE LIKE THE WIND Eastside Beat (ffrr)
21	13	HOLE HEARTED Extreme (A&M)
27	14	YOU TO ME ARE EVERYTHING Sonia (IQ)
-	15	SMELLS LIKE TEEN SPIRIT Nirvana (DGC)
-	16	SOUND James (Fontana)
17	17	FAITH (IN THE POWER OF LOVE) Rozalla (Pulse-8)
30	18	SO REAL Love Decade (All Around The World)
14	19	FALL AT YOUR FEET Crowded House (Capitol)
-	20	SPENDING MY TIME Roxette (EMI)
36	21	THERE WILL NEVER BE ANOTHER TONIGHT Bryan Adams (A&M)
15	22	AMERICAN PIE Don McLean (Liberty)
42	23	JUST A TOUCH OF LOVE (EVERY DAY) C&C Music Factory (Columbia)
9	24	IT'S GRIM UP NORTH Justified Ancients Of Mu Mu (KLF Communications)
-	25	STARS Simply Red (East West)
26	26	DO YOU FEEL LIKE I FEEL? Belinda Carlisle (Vi:gin)
24	27	MY TOWN Glass Tiger featuring Rod Stewart (EMI)
29	28	HOW CAN I LIVE YOU MORE? M-People (deConstruction)
12	29	EVERYTHING I DO (I DO IT FOR YOU) Bryan Adams (A&M)
-	30	JUDGE FUDGE Happy Mondays (Factory)
13	31	THE FLY U2 (Island)
-	32	YOU SHOWED ME Salt 'N' Pepa (ffrr)
10	33	NO SON OF MINE Genesis (Virgin)
37	34	2 231 Anticapella (PWL Continental)
19	35	WORLD IN UNION Kiri Te Kanawa (Columbia)
-	36	WONDERFUL TONIGHT (LIVE) Eric Clapton (Reprise)
35	37	WASTED TIME Skid Row (East West)
38	38	WICKED LOVE Oceanic (Dead Dead Good)
-	39	EXTACY Shades Of Rhythm (ZTT)
-	40	WHEN YOU TELL ME THAT YOU LOVE ME Diana Ross (Capitol)
39	41	SO TELL ME WHY Poison (Capitol)
43	42	DO WHAT YOU FEEL Joey Negro (10)
23	43	DANCE WITH ME (I'M YOUR ECSTASY) Control (All Around The World)
-	44	PROMISES Take That (RCA)
-	45	ROCK 'N' ROLL DANCE PARTY Jive Bunny & the Mastermixers (Music Factory)
34	46	RADIO SONG R.E.M. (Warner Bros)
-	47	TENDER LOVE Kenny Thomas (Cooltempo)
18	48	THE UNFORGIVEN Metallica (Vertigo)
22	49	GO Moby (Outer Rhythm)
-	50	KEEP ON PUMPIN' IT Vision Masters & Tony King featuring Kylie Minogue (PWL)

Michael Jackson's 1991 album *Dangerous* proved not to have quite the same sales impact as its enormous predecessors, *Thriller* and *Bad*. However, this did not stop the first single to be taken from it – *Black Or White* – from leaping to Number One in its week of release, to dethrone comedian Vic Reeves' Wonder Stuff-backed revival of Tommy Roe's 1969 chart-topper *Dizzy*.

544

December 1991

last this week

7 December 1991

last	this		
1	1	BLACK OR WHITE	Michael Jackson (Epic)
-	2	DON'T LET THE SUN GO DOWN ON ME	George Michael/Elton John (Epic)
12	3	RIDE LIKE THE WIND	Eastside Beat (ffrr)
40	4	WHEN YOU TELL ME THAT YOU LOVE ME	Diana Ross (Capitol)
-	5	JUSTIFIED AND ANCIENT	KLF/Tammy Wynette (KLF Communications)
6	6	PLAYING WITH KNIVES	Bizarre Inc (Vinyl Solution)
15	7	SMELLS LIKE TEEN SPIRIT	Nirvana (DGC)
3	8	ACTIV 8 (COME WITH ME)	Altern 8 (Network)
2	9	DIZZY	Vic Reeves & the Wonder Stuff (Sense)
5	10	WHEN A MAN LOVES A WOMAN	Michael Bolton (Columbia)
-	11	ROCKET MAN (I THINK IT'S GONNA BE A LONG TIME)	Kate Bush (Mercury)
25	12	STARS	Simply Red (East West)
16	13	SOUND	James (Fontana)
11	14	WAY OF THE WORLD	Tina Turner (Capitol)
4	15	IS THERE ANYBODY OUT THERE?	Bassheads (deConstruction)
7	16	RHYTHM IS A MYSTERY	K-Klass (deConstruction)
-	17	AM I RIGHT?	Erasure (Mute)
32	18	YOU SHOWED ME	Salt 'N' Pepa (ffrr)
-	19	WE SHOULD BE TOGETHER	Cliff Richard (EMI)
13	20	HOLE HEARTED	Extreme (A&M)
9	21	GET READY FOR THIS	2 Unlimited (PWL Continental)
39	22	EXTACY	Shades Of Rhythm (ZTT)
-	23	DRIVEN BY YOU	Brian May (Parlophone)
38	24	WICKED LOVE	Oceanic (Dead Dead Good)
18	25	SO REAL	Love Decade (All Around The World)
-	26	DIAMONDS & PEARLS	Prince & the New Power Generation (Paisley Park)
36	27	WONDERFUL TONIGHT (LIVE)	Eric Clapton (Reprise)
-	28	SEND ME AN ANGEL	Scorpions (Vertigo)
14	29	YOU TO ME ARE EVERYTHING	Sonia (IQ)
8	30	KILLER ... ON THE LOOSE	Seal (ZTT)
20	31	SPENDING MY TIME	Roxette (EMI)
10	32	IF YOU WERE WITH ME NOW	Kylie Minogue & Keith Washington (PWL)
-	33	TOO BLIND TO SEE IT	Kym Sims (East West)
17	34	FAITH (IN THE POWER OF LOVE)	Rozalla (Pulse-8)
23	35	JUST A TOUCH OF LOVE (EVERY DAY)	C&C Music Factory (Columbia)
47	36	TENDER LOVE	Kenny Thomas (Cooltempo)
21	37	THERE WILL NEVER BE ANOTHER TONIGHT	Bryan Adams (A&M)
30	38	JUDGE FUDGE	Happy Mondays (Factory)
-	39	RUNNING OUT OF TIME	Digital Orgasm (Dead Dead Good)
28	40	HOW CAN I LIVE YOU MORE?	M-People (deConstruction)
-	41	EVERYBODY MOVE	Cathy Dennis (Polydor)
-	42	IN THE GHETTO	Beats International (Go. Beat)
-	43	MARTIKA'S KITCHEN	Martika (Columbia)
50	44	KEEP ON PUMPIN' IT	Vision Masters & Tony King featuring Kylie Minogue (PWL)
-	45	ME AND A GUN (EP)	Tori Amos (East West)
46	46	JOSEPH MEGA-REMIX	Jason Donovan (Really Useful)
34	47	2 231	Anticapella (PWL Continental)
-	48	DON'T TALK JUST KISS	Right Said Fred/Jocelyn Brown (Tug)
-	49	MAMA I'M COMING HOME	Ozzy Osbourne (Epic)
-	50	THE BARE NECESSITIES MEGAMIX	UK Mixmasters (Connect)

14 December 1991

2	1	DON'T LET THE SUN GO DOWN ON ME	George Michael/Elton John (Epic)
4	2	WHEN YOU TELL ME THAT YOU LOVE ME	Diana Ross (Capitol)
5	3	JUSTIFIED AND ANCIENT	KLF/Tammy Wynette (KLF Communications)
1	4	BLACK OR WHITE	Michael Jackson (Epic)
3	5	RIDE LIKE THE WIND	Eastside Beat (ffrr)
23	6	DRIVEN BY YOU	Brian May (Parlophone)
7	7	SMELLS LIKE TEEN SPIRIT	Nirvana (DGC)
11	8	ROCKET MAN (I THINK IT'S GONNA BE A LONG TIME)	Kate Bush (Mercury)
12	9	STARS	Simply Red (East West)
-	10	MYSTERIOUS WAYS	U2 (Island)
33	11	TOO BLIND TO SEE IT	Kym Sims (East West)
-	12	IF YOU GO AWAY	New Kids On The Block (Columbia)
13	13	SOUND	James (Fontana)
8	14	ACTIV 8 (COME WITH ME)	Altern 8 (Network)
18	15	YOU SHOWED ME	Salt 'N' Pepa (ffrr)
17	16	AM I RIGHT?	Erasure (Mute)
19	17	WE SHOULD BE TOGETHER	Cliff Richard (EMI)
6	18	PLAYING WITH KNIVES	Bizarre Inc (Vinyl Solution)
22	19	EXTACY	Shades Of Rhythm (ZTT)
9	20	DIZZY	Vic Reeves & the Wonder Stuff (Sense)
48	21	DON'T TALK JUST KISS	Right Said Fred/Jocelyn Brown (Tug)
22	22	TENDER LOVE	Kenny Thomas (Cooltempo)
14	23	WAY OF THE WORLD	Tina Turner (Capitol)
50	24	THE BARE NECESSITIES MEGAMIX	UK Mixmasters (Connect)
10	25	WHEN A MAN LOVES A WOMAN	Michael Bolton (Columbia)
46	26	JOSEPH MEGA-REMIX	Jason Donovan (Really Useful)
26	27	DIAMONDS & PEARLS	Prince & the New Power Generation (Paisley Park)
43	28	MARTIKA'S KITCHEN	Martika (Columbia)
24	29	WICKED LOVE	Oceanic (Dead Dead Good)
-	30	THE SHOW MUST GO ON	Queen (Parlophone)
21	31	GET READY FOR THIS	2 Unlimited (PWL Continental)
27	32	WONDERFUL TONIGHT (LIVE)	Eric Clapton (Reprise)
33	33	COVER FROM THE SKY	Deacon Blue (Columbia)
-	34	HOW CAN I KEEP FROM SINGING?	Enya (Warner Bros)
39	35	RUNNING OUT OF TIME	Digital Orgasm (Dead Dead Good)
41	36	EVERYBODY MOVE	Cathy Dennis (Polydor)
15	37	IS THERE ANYBODY OUT THERE?	Bassheads (deConstruction)
-	38	ABIDE WITH ME	Vic Reeves (Sense)
-	39	I DON'T WANNA TAKE THIS PAIN	Dannii Minogue (MCA)
20	40	HOLE HEARTED	Extreme (A&M)
-	41	IT'S THE END OF THE WORLD AS WE KNOW IT (AND I FEEL FINE)	R.E.M. (I.R.S.)
-	42	LOVE SEES NO COLOUR	Farm (Produce)
-	43	THE YODELING SONG (REMIX)	Frank Ifield featuring the Backroom Boys (EMI)
-	44	LOVE HURTS	Cher (Geffen)
-	45	SILENT NIGHT	Sinead O'Connor (Ensign)
16	46	RHYTHM IS A MYSTERY	K-Klass (deConstruction)
-	47	OPEN YOUR EYES	Black Box (deConstruction)
-	48	I'LL BE HOME FOR CHRISTMAS	Shakin' Stevens (Epic)
-	49	LET IT REIGN	Inner City (10)
-	50	FRIENDSHIP	Sabrina Johnston (East West)

21 December 1991

-	1	BOHEMIAN RHAPSODY/THESE ARE THE DAYS OF OUR LIVES	Queen (Parlophone)
1	2	DON'T LET THE SUN GO DOWN ON ME	George Michael/Elton John (Epic)
2	3	WHEN YOU TELL ME THAT YOU LOVE ME	Diana Ross (Capitol)
3	4	JUSTIFIED AND ANCIENT	KLF/Tammy Wynette (KLF Communications)
6	5	DRIVEN BY YOU	Brian May (Parlophone)
11	6	TOO BLIND TO SEE IT	Kym Sims (East West)
5	7	RIDE LIKE THE WIND	Eastside Beat (ffrr)
4	8	BLACK OR WHITE	Michael Jackson (Epic)
21	9	DON'T TALK JUST KISS	Right Said Fred/Jocelyn Brown (Tug)
-	10	LIVE AND LET DIE	Guns N' Roses (Geffen)
17	11	WE SHOULD BE TOGETHER	Cliff Richard (EMI)
9	12	STARS	Simply Red (East West)
12	13	IF YOU GO AWAY	New Kids On The Block (Columbia)
8	14	ROCKET MAN (I THINK IT'S GONNA BE A LONG TIME)	Kate Bush (Mercury)
10	15	MYSTERIOUS WAYS	U2 (Island)
24	16	THE BARE NECESSITIES MEGAMIX	UK Mixmasters (Connect)
15	17	YOU SHOWED ME	Salt 'N' Pepa (ffrr)
7	18	SMELLS LIKE TEEN SPIRIT	Nirvana (DGC)
-	19	ROOBARB & CUSTARD	Shaft (Ffrreedom)
16	20	AM I RIGHT?	Erasure (Mute)
28	21	MARTIKA'S KITCHEN	Martika (Columbia)
30	22	THE SHOW MUST GO ON	Queen (Parlophone)
-	23	WAS IT WORTH IT?	Pet Shop Boys (Parlophone)
33	24	COVER FROM THE SKY	Deacon Blue (Columbia)
35	25	RUNNING OUT OF TIME	Digital Orgasm (Dead Dead Good)
14	26	ACTIV 8 (COME WITH ME)	Altern 8 (Network)
-	27	SEVEN O'CLOCK SILENT NIGHT	Simon & Garfunkel (Columbia)
26	28	JOSEPH MEGA-REMIX	Jason Donovan (Really Useful)
36	29	EVERYBODY MOVE	Cathy Dennis (Polydor)
13	30	SOUND	James (Fontana)
34	31	HOW CAN I KEEP FROM SINGING?	Enya (Warner Bros)
38	32	ABIDE WITH ME	Vic Reeves (Sense)
-	33	THE COMPLETE DOMINATOR	Human Resource (R&S)
27	34	DIAMONDS & PEARLS	Prince & the New Power Generation (Paisley Park)
20	35	DIZZY	Vic Reeves & the Wonder Stuff (Sense)
19	36	EXTACY	Shades Of Rhythm (ZTT)
39	37	I DON'T WANNA TAKE THIS PAIN	Dannii Minogue (MCA)
-	38	ALL WOMAN	Lisa Stansfield (Arista)
41	39	IT'S THE END OF THE WORLD AS WE KNOW IT (AND I FEEL FINE)	R.E.M. (I.R.S.)
23	40	WAY OF THE WORLD	Tina Turner (Capitol)
47	41	OPEN YOUR EYES	Black Box (deConstruction)
43	42	THE YODELING SONG (REMIX)	Frank Ifield featuring the Backroom Boys (EMI)
48	43	I'LL BE HOME FOR CHRISTMAS	Shakin' Stevens (Epic)
-	44	ADDAMS GROOVE	Hammer (Capitol)
25	45	WHEN A MAN LOVES A WOMAN	Michael Bolton (Columbia)
42	46	LOVE SEES NO COLOUR	Farm (Produce)
44	47	LOVE HURTS	Cher (Geffen)
-	48	UHF	UHF (XL)
22	49	TENDER LOVE	Kenny Thomas (Cooltempo)
18	50	PLAYING WITH KNIVES	Bizarre Inc (Vinyl Solution)

George Michael and Elton John's live duet on Elton's 1974 hit *Don't Let The Sun Go Down On Me* was an effortless chart-topper, despite the fact that Oleta Adams had already been in the Top 30 with the song in October. The duo were soon eclipsed at the top, however, by Queen's 16-year-old classic *Bohemian Rhapsody*, reissued in the wake of the tragic death of Freddie Mercury.

January 1992

11 January 1992

last week	this week	Title	Artist (Label)
1	1	BOHEMIAN RHAPSODY/THESE ARE THE BEST DAYS OF OUR LIVES	Queen (Parlophone)
4	2	JUSTIFIED AND ANCIENT	KLF/Tammy Wynette (KLF Communications)
3	3	WHEN YOU TELL ME THAT YOU LOVE ME	Diana Ross (Capitol)
9	4	DON'T TALK JUST KISS	Right Said Fred featuring Jocelyn Brown (Tug)
44	5	ADDAMS GROOVE	Hammer (Capitol)
10	6	LIVE AND LET DIE	Guns N' Roses (Geffen)
2	7	DON'T LET THE SUN GO DOWN ON ME	George Michael/Elton John (Epic)
6	8	TOO BLIND TO SEE IT	Kym Sims (East West)
19	9	ROOBARB & CUSTARD	Shaft (Ffrreedom)
5	10	DRIVEN BY YOU	Brian May (Parlophone)
28	11	JOSEPH MEGA-MIX	Jason Donovan (Really Useful)
12	12	STARS	Simply Red (East West)
16	13	THE BARE NECESSITIES MEGAMIX	UK Mixmasters (Connect)
8	14	BLACK OR WHITE	Michael Jackson (Epic)
21	15	MARTIKA'S KITCHEN	Martika (Columbia)
38	16	ALL WOMAN	Lisa Stansfield (Arista)
7	17	RIDE LIKE THE WIND	East Side Beat (ffrr)
29	18	EVERYBODY MOVE	Cathy Dennis (Polydor)
33	19	THE COMPLETE DOMINATOR	Human Resource (R&S)
25	20	RUNNING OUT OF TIME	Digital Orgasm (Dead Dead Good)
14	21	ROCKET MAN (I THINK IT'S GONNA BE A LONG TIME)	Kate Bush (Mercury)
-	22	GOODNIGHT GIRL	Wet Wet Wet (Precious)
11	23	WE SHOULD BE TOGETHER	Cliff Richard (EMI)
17	24	YOU SHOWED ME	Salt 'N' Pepa (ffrr)
20	25	AM I RIGHT? (re-mix)	Erasure (Mute)
15	26	MYSTERIOUS WAYS	U2 (Island)
23	27	WAS IT WORTH IT?	Pet Shop Boys (Parlophone)
18	28	SMELLS LIKE TEEN SPIRIT	Nirvana (DGC)
27	29	SEVEN O'CLOCK SILENT NIGHT	Simon & Garfunkel (Columbia)
-	30	WE GOT A LOVE THING	Ce Ce Peniston (A&M)
26	31	ACTIV 8 (COME WITH ME)	Altern 8 (Network)
13	32	IF YOU GO AWAY	New Kids On The Block (Columbia)
-	33	THIS NEW YEAR	Cliff Richard (EMI)
-	34	FAIRYTALE OF NEW YORK	Pogues featuring Kirsty MacColl (PM)
-	35	I CAN'T DANCE	Genesis (Virgin)
35	36	DIZZY	Vic Reeves & the Wonder Stuff (Sense)
-	37	MAGIC'S BACK	Malcolm McLaren (RCA)
-	38	HOME SWEET HOME ('91 REMIX)	Motley Crue (Elektra)
-	39	EVERYBODY IN THE PLACE (EP)	Prodigy (XL)
-	40	OLD RED EYES IS BACK	Beautiful South (Go! Discs)
34	41	DIAMONDS & PEARLS	Prince & the New Power Generation (Paisley Park)
-	42	RUBBISH	Carter The Unstoppable Sex Machine (Big Cat)
37	43	I DON'T WANNA TAKE THIS PAIN	Dannii Minogue (MCA)
22	44	THE SHOW MUST GO ON	Queen (Parlophone)
-	45	COUNTING SHEEP	Airhead (Korova)
30	46	SOUND	James (Fontana)
-	47	MEGAMIX	Crystal Waters (A&M)
-	48	(CAN YOU) FEEL THE PASSION	Blue Pearl (Big Life)
43	49	I'LL BE HOME FOR CHRISTMAS	Shakin' Stevens (Epic)
40	50	WAY OF THE WORLD	Tina Turner (Capitol)

18 January 1992

last week	this week	Title	Artist (Label)
1	1	BOHEMIAN RHAPSODY/THESE ARE THE BEST DAYS OF OUR LIVES	Queen (Parlophone)
2	2	JUSTIFIED AND ANCIENT	KLF/Tammy Wynette (KLF Communications)
5	3	ADDAMS GROOVE	Hammer (Capitol)
39	4	EVERYBODY IN THE PLACE (EP)	Prodigy (XL)
4	5	DON'T TALK JUST KISS	Right Said Fred featuring Jocelyn Brown (Tug)
22	6	GOODNIGHT GIRL	Wet Wet Wet (Precious)
8	7	TOO BLIND TO SEE IT	Kym Sims (East West)
30	8	WE GOT A LOVE THING	Ce Ce Peniston (A&M)
3	9	WHEN YOU TELL ME THAT YOU LOVE ME	Diana Ross (Capitol)
9	10	ROOBARB & CUSTARD	Shaft (Ffrreedom)
14	11	BLACK OR WHITE	Michael Jackson (Epic)
-	12	GOD GAVE ROCK AND ROLL TO YOU II	Kiss (Interscope)
-	13	FEEL SO HIGH	Des'ree (Dusted Sound)
16	14	ALL WOMAN	Lisa Stansfield (Arista)
42	15	RUBBISH	Carter The Unstoppable Sex Machine (Big Cat)
48	16	(CAN YOU) FEEL THE PASSION	Blue Pearl (Big Life)
40	17	OLD RED EYES IS BACK	Beautiful South (Go! Discs)
-	18	DIFFERENT STROKES	Isotonik (Ffrreedom)
7	19	DON'T LET THE SUN GO DOWN ON ME	George Michael/Elton John (Epic)
35	20	I CAN'T DANCE	Genesis (Virgin)
-	21	EASY TO SMILE	Senseless Things (Epic)
6	22	LIVE AND LET DIE	Guns N' Roses (Geffen)
-	23	HIT	Sugarcubes (One Little Indian)
20	24	RUNNING OUT OF TIME	Digital Orgasm (Dead Dead Good)
-	25	BLUE EYES	Wedding Present (RCA)
10	26	DRIVEN BY YOU	Brian May (Parlophone)
15	27	MARTIKA'S KITCHEN	Martika (Columbia)
25	28	AM I RIGHT? (re-mix)	Erasure (Mute)
-	29	WATERFALL	Stone Roses (Silvertone)
-	30	PRIDE (IN THE NAME OF LOVE)	Clivilles & Cole (Columbia)
47	31	MEGAMIX	Crystal Waters (A&M)
19	32	THE COMPLETE DOMINATOR	Human Resource (R&S)
33	33	THIS NEW YEAR	Cliff Richard (EMI)
-	34	CAN'T LET GO	Mariah Carey (Columbia)
17	35	RIDE LIKE THE WIND	East Side Beat (ffrr)
12	36	STARS	Simply Red (East West)
-	37	CREDO	Fish (Polydor)
-	38	SAY IT	ABC (Parlophone)
-	39	THE TRUTH	Real People (Columbia)
-	40	ROCK 'TIL YOU DROP	Status Quo (Vertigo)
-	41	VIBEOLOGY	Paula Abdul (Virgin America)
-	42	PERFECT PLACE	Voice Of The Beehive (London)
-	43	FUNKIN' FOR JAMAICA	Tom Browne (Arista)
-	44	HALF THE WORLD	Belinda Carlisle (Virgin)
-	45	NIGHTBIRD	Convert (A&M)
11	46	JOSEPH MEGA-MIX	Jason Donovan (Really Useful)
-	47	TAKE ME AWAY	Capella featuring Loleatta Holloway (PWL Continental)
18	48	EVERYBODY MOVE	Cathy Dennis (Polydor)
38	49	HOME SWEET HOME ('91 REMIX)	Motley Crue (Elektra)
-	50	FOR LOVE	Lush (4AD)

25 January 1992

last week	this week	Title	Artist (Label)
1	1	BOHEMIAN RHAPSODY/THESE ARE THE BEST DAYS OF OUR LIVES	Queen (Parlophone)
6	2	GOODNIGHT GIRL	Wet Wet Wet (Precious)
4	3	EVERYBODY IN THE PLACE (EP)	Prodigy (XL)
8	4	WE GOT A LOVE THING	Ce Ce Peniston (A&M)
12	5	GOD GAVE ROCK AND ROLL TO YOU II	Kiss (Interscope)
-	6	WELCOME TO THE CHEAP SEATS - THE ORIGINAL SOUNDTRACK (EP)	Wonder Stuff (Polydor)
7	7	TOO BLIND TO SEE IT	Kym Sims (East West)
13	8	FEEL SO HIGH	Des'ree (Dusted Sound)
9	9	GIVE ME JUST A LITTLE MORE TIME	Kylie Minogue (PWL)
20	10	I CAN'T DANCE	Genesis (Virgin)
2	11	JUSTIFIED AND ANCIENT	KLF/Tammy Wynette (KLF Communications)
30	12	PRIDE (IN THE NAME OF LOVE)	Clivilles & Cole (Columbia)
17	13	OLD RED EYES IS BACK	Beautiful South (Go! Discs)
16	14	(CAN YOU) FEEL THE PASSION	Blue Pearl (Big Life)
5	15	DON'T TALK JUST KISS	Right Said Fred featuring Jocelyn Brown (Tug)
3	16	ADDAMS GROOVE	Hammer (Capitol)
11	17	BLACK OR WHITE	Michael Jackson (Epic)
-	18	TWILIGHT ZONE	2 Unlimited (PWL Continental)
9	19	WHEN YOU TELL ME THAT YOU LOVE ME	Diana Ross (Capitol)
23	20	HIT	Sugarcubes (One Little Indian)
18	21	DIFFERENT STROKES	Isotonik (Ffrreedom)
14	22	ALL WOMAN	Lisa Stansfield (Arista)
10	23	ROOBARB & CUSTARD	Shaft (Ffrreedom)
41	24	VIBEOLOGY	Paula Abdul (Virgin America)
21	25	EASY TO SMILE	Senseless Things (Epic)
47	26	TAKE ME AWAY	Capella featuring Loleatta Holloway (PWL Continental)
34	27	CAN'T LET GO	Mariah Carey (Columbia)
25	28	BLUE EYES	Wedding Present (RCA)
15	29	RUBBISH	Carter The Unstoppable Sex Machine (Big Cat)
44	30	HALF THE WORLD	Belinda Carlisle (Virgin)
42	31	PERFECT PLACE	Voice Of The Beehive (London)
40	32	ROCK 'TIL YOU DROP	Status Quo (Vertigo)
-	33	SHUT 'EM DOWN	Dream Frequency featuring Debbie Sharp (Citybeat)
-	34	I WONDER WHY	Curtis Stigers (Arista)
31	35	MEGAMIX	Crystal Waters (A&M)
-	36	FALL TO LOVE	Diesel Park West (Food)
-	37	IDIOTS AT THE WHEEL (EP)	Kingmaker (Chrysalis)
-	38	MY HAND OVER MY HEART	Marc Almond (Some Bizzare)
19	39	DON'T LET THE SUN GO DOWN ON ME	George Michael/Elton John (Epic)
-	40	HIGHWAY 5 '92	Blessing (A&M)
45	41	NIGHTBIRD	Convert (A&M)
-	42	SHUT 'EM DOWN	Public Enemy (Def Jam)
38	43	SAY IT	ABC (Parlophone)
29	44	WATERFALL	Stone Roses (Silvertone)
43	45	FUNKIN' FOR JAMAICA	Tom Browne (Arista)
24	46	RUNNING OUT OF TIME	Digital Orgasm (Dead Dead Good)
-	47	THEN I FEEL GOOD	Katherine E (PWL Continental)
-	48	I LIKE IT	Overweight Pooch featuring Ce Ce Peniston (A&M)
-	49	LOVE IS EVERYWHERE	Cicero (Spaghetti)
-	50	STAY	Shakespears Sister (London)

Eventual sales of the reissued *Bohemian Rhapsody* took it over the two million mark, making it only the third single in the UK ever to pass this target, after Band Aid's *Do They Know It's Christmas* and Wings' *Mull Of Kintyre*. Clivilles and Cole, the names behind the initials in C&C Music Factory, reasserted themselves with a radical reinterpretation of U2's former Top Three hit *Pride (In The Name Of Love)*.

1 February 1992

last week	this week	title / artist
2	1	GOODNIGHT GIRL Wet Wet Wet (Precious)
9	2	GIVE ME JUST A LITTLE MORE TIME Kylie Minogue (PWL)
18	3	TWILIGHT ZONE 2 Unlimited (PWL Continental)
1	4	BOHEMIAN RHAPSODY/THESE ARE THE BEST DAYS OF OUR LIVES Queen (Parlophone)
6	5	WELCOME TO THE CHEAP SEATS - THE ORIGINAL SOUNDTRACK (EP) Wonder Stuff (Polydor)
3	6	EVERYBODY IN THE PLACE (EP) Prodigy (XL)
10	7	I CAN'T DANCE Genesis (Virgin)
5	8	GOD GAVE ROCK AND ROLL TO YOU II Kiss (Interscope)
4	9	WE GOT A LOVE THING Ce Ce Peniston (A&M)
8	10	FEEL SO HIGH Des'ree (Dusted Sound)
34	11	I WONDER WHY Curtis Stigers (Arista)
50	12	STAY Shakespears Sister (London)
12	13	PRIDE (IN THE NAME OF LOVE) Clivilles & Cole (Columbia)
7	14	TOO BLIND TO SEE IT Kym Sims (East West)
14	15	(CAN YOU) FEEL THE PASSION Blue Pearl (Big Life)
24	16	VIBEOLOGY Paula Abdul (Virgin America)
11	17	JUSTIFIED AND ANCIENT KLF/Tammy Wynette (KLF Communications)
-	18	BORN OF FRUSTRATION James (Fontana)
-	19	I'M DOING FINE NOW Pasadenas (Columbia)
20	20	HIT Sugarcubes (One Little Indian)
26	21	TAKE ME AWAY Capella featuring Loleatta Holloway (PWL Continental)
13	22	OLD RED EYES IS BACK Beautiful South (Go! Discs)
-	23	THE BOUNCER Kicks Like A Mule (Tribal Bass)
16	24	ADDAMS GROOVE Hammer (Capitol)
40	25	HIGHWAY 5 '92 Blessing (MCA)
-	26	LOVESICK PLEASURE (EP) Daisy Chainsaw (Deva)
27	27	CAN'T LET GO Mariah Carey (Columbia)
38	28	MY HAND OVER MY HEART Marc Almond (Some Bizzare)
33	29	FEEL SO REAL Dream Frequency featuring Debbie Sharp (Citybeat)
19	30	WHEN YOU TELL ME THAT YOU LOVE ME Diana Ross (Capitol)
31	31	PERFECT PLACE Voice Of The Beehive (London)
-	32	YOU LOVE US Manic Street Preachers (Heavenly)
15	33	DON'T TALK JUST KISS Right Said Fred featuring Jocelyn Brown (Tug)
-	34	MOVIN' Marathon (10)
22	35	ALL WOMAN Lisa Stansfield (Arista)
42	36	SHUT 'EM DOWN Public Enemy (Def Jam)
49	37	LOVE IS EVERYWHERE Cicero (Spaghetti)
36	38	FALL TO LOVE Diesel Park West (Food)
-	39	CAN YOU HANDLE IT DNA featuring Sharon Redd (EMI)
21	40	DIFFERENT STROKES Isotonik (Ffrreedom)
17	41	BLACK OR WHITE Michael Jackson (Epic)
23	42	ROOBARB & CUSTARD Shaft (Ffrreedom)
30	43	HALF THE WORLD Belinda Carlisle (Virgin)
37	44	IDIOTS AT THE WHEEL (EP) Kingmaker (Chrysalis)
32	45	ROCK 'TIL YOU DROP Status Quo (Vertigo)
-	46	THE SAINT Thompson Twins (Warner Bros)
-	47	(LOVE MOVES IN) MYSTERIOUS WAYS Julia Fordham (Circa)
29	48	RUBBISH Carter The Unstoppable Sex Machine (Big Cat)
-	49	WHAT IS HOUSE (EP) LFO (Warp)
25	50	EASY TO SMILE Senseless Things (Epic)

8 February 1992

last week	this week	title / artist
1	1	GOODNIGHT GIRL Wet Wet Wet (Precious)
2	2	GIVE ME JUST A LITTLE MORE TIME Kylie Minogue (PWL)
3	3	TWILIGHT ZONE 2 Unlimited (PWL Continental)
19	4	I'M DOING FINE NOW Pasadenas (Columbia)
11	5	I WONDER WHY Curtis Stigers (Arista)
12	6	STAY Shakespears Sister (London)
5	7	WELCOME TO THE CHEAP SEATS - THE ORIGINAL SOUNDTRACK (EP) Wonder Stuff (Polydor)
23	8	THE BOUNCER Kicks Like A Mule (Tribal Bass)
6	9	EVERYBODY IN THE PLACE (EP) Prodigy (XL)
18	10	BORN OF FRUSTRATION James (Fontana)
-	11	DIXIE - NARCO (EP) Primal Scream (Creation)
4	12	BOHEMIAN RHAPSODY/THESE ARE THE BEST DAYS OF OUR LIVES Queen (Parlophone)
7	13	I CAN'T DANCE Genesis (Virgin)
8	14	GOD GAVE ROCK AND ROLL TO YOU II Kiss (Interscope)
9	15	WE GOT A LOVE THING Ce Ce Peniston (A&M)
-	16	FOR YOUR BABIES Simply Red (East West)
16	17	VIBEOLOGY Paula Abdul (Virgin America)
27	18	CAN'T LET GO Mariah Carey (Columbia)
10	19	FEEL SO HIGH Des'ree (Dusted Sound)
32	20	YOU LOVE US Manic Street Preachers (Heavenly)
39	21	CAN YOU HANDLE IT DNA featuring Sharon Redd (EMI)
26	22	LOVESICK PLEASURE (EP) Daisy Chainsaw (Deva)
15	23	(CAN YOU) FEEL THE PASSION Blue Pearl (Big Life)
47	24	(LOVE MOVES IN) MYSTERIOUS WAYS Julia Fordham (Circa)
29	25	FEEL SO REAL Dream Frequency featuring Debbie Sharp (Citybeat)
25	26	HIGHWAY 5 '92 Blessing (MCA)
-	27	STEEL BARS Michael Bolton (Columbia)
14	28	TOO BLIND TO SEE IT Kym Sims (East West)
17	29	JUSTIFIED AND ANCIENT KLF/Tammy Wynette (KLF Communications)
20	30	HIT Sugarcubes (One Little Indian)
37	31	LOVE IS EVERYWHERE Cicero (Spaghetti)
13	32	PRIDE (IN THE NAME OF LOVE) Clivilles & Cole (Columbia)
31	33	PERFECT PLACE Voice Of The Beehive (London)
-	34	SO WHAT! Ronny Jordan (Antilles)
-	35	WHAT YOU DO TO ME Teenage Fan Club (Creation)
-	36	DIAMANTE Zucchero featuring Randy Crawford (London)
-	37	WHEN YOU'RE IN LOVE WITH A BEAUTIFUL WOMAN Dr. Hook (Capitol)
21	38	TAKE ME AWAY Capella featuring Loleatta Holloway (PWL Continental)
-	39	ALONE WITH YOU Texas (Mercury)
-	40	CHINA Tori Amos (East West)
-	41	I'LL CRY FOR YOU Europe (Epic)
-	42	STOP Mega City Four (Big Life)
-	43	ANOTHER GIRL - ANOTHER PLANET/PRETTY IN PINK Only Ones/Psychedelic Furs (Columbia)
-	44	TEARS IN HEAVEN Eric Clapton (Reprise)
24	45	ADDAMS GROOVE Hammer (Capitol)
-	46	FREQUENCY Altern 8 (Network)
22	47	OLD RED EYES IS BACK Beautiful South (Go! Discs)
-	48	VISIONS OF YOU Jah Wobble's Invaders Of The Heart (Oval)
-	49	COMEUPPANCE (EP) Thousand Yard Stare (Stifled Aardvark)
34	50	MOVIN' Marathon (10)

15 February 1992

last week	this week	title / artist
4	1	I'M DOING FINE NOW Pasadenas (Columbia)
1	2	GOODNIGHT GIRL Wet Wet Wet (Precious)
6	3	STAY Shakespears Sister (London)
3	4	TWILIGHT ZONE 2 Unlimited (PWL Continental)
5	5	I WONDER WHY Curtis Stigers (Arista)
-	6	REMEMBER THE TIME Michael Jackson (Epic)
2	7	GIVE ME JUST A LITTLE MORE TIME Kylie Minogue (PWL)
8	8	THE BOUNCER Kicks Like A Mule (Tribal Bass)
16	9	FOR YOUR BABIES Simply Red (East West)
11	10	DIXIE - NARCO (EP) Primal Scream (Creation)
10	11	BORN OF FRUSTRATION James (Fontana)
27	12	STEEL BARS Michael Bolton (Columbia)
9	13	EVERYBODY IN THE PLACE (EP) Prodigy (XL)
13	14	I CAN'T DANCE Genesis (Virgin)
7	15	WELCOME TO THE CHEAP SEATS - THE ORIGINAL SOUNDTRACK (EP) Wonder Stuff (Polydor)
-	16	LEAVE THEM ALL BEHIND Ride (Creation)
21	17	CAN YOU HANDLE IT DNA featuring Sharon Redd (EMI)
24	18	(LOVE MOVES IN) MYSTERIOUS WAYS Julia Fordham (Circa)
31	19	LOVE IS EVERYWHERE Cicero (Spaghetti)
-	20	GO-GO DANCER Wedding Present (RCA)
14	21	GOD GAVE ROCK AND ROLL TO YOU II Kiss (Interscope)
22	22	YOU LOVE US Manic Street Preachers (Heavenly)
-	23	REVERENCE Jesus & Mary Chain (blanco y negro)
12	24	BOHEMIAN RHAPSODY/THESE ARE THE BEST DAYS OF OUR LIVES Queen (Parlophone)
15	25	WE GOT A LOVE THING Ce Ce Peniston (A&M)
41	26	I'LL CRY FOR YOU Europe (Epic)
25	27	FEEL SO REAL Dream Frequency featuring Debbie Sharp (Citybeat)
-	28	ALIVE Pearl Jam (Epic)
26	29	HIGHWAY 5 '92 Blessing (MCA)
18	30	CAN'T LET GO Mariah Carey (Columbia)
-	31	MY GIRL Temptations (Epic)
39	32	ALONE WITH YOU Texas (Mercury)
-	33	DREAM COME TRUE Brand New Heavies featuring N'Dea Davenport (ffrr)
36	34	DIAMANTE Zucchero featuring Randy Crawford (London)
34	35	SO WHAT! Ronny Jordan (Antilles)
-	36	THE FORCE BEHIND THE POWER Diana Ross (EMI)
-	37	LOVE THING Tina Turner (Capitol)
19	38	FEEL SO HIGH Des'ree (Dusted Sound)
-	39	MUTATIONS Orbital (ffrr)
-	40	MOIRA JANE'S CAFE Definition Of Sound (Circa)
48	41	VISIONS OF YOU Jah Wobble's Invaders Of The Heart (Oval)
-	42	THE BIG ONES GET AWAY Buffy Sainte-Marie (Ensign)
35	43	WHAT YOU DO TO ME Teenage Fan Club (Creation)
-	44	OPTIMISTIC Sounds Of Blackness (Perspective)
17	45	VIBEOLOGY Paula Abdul (Virgin America)
22	46	LOVESICK PLEASURE (EP) Daisy Chainsaw (Deva)
-	47	MONKEY BUSINESS Danger Danger (Epic)
-	48	CRUCIFIED Army Of Lovers (Ton Son Ton)
44	49	TEARS IN HEAVEN Eric Clapton (Reprise)
23	50	(CAN YOU) FEEL THE PASSION Blue Pearl (Big Life)

Kylie Minogue's Number Two success was a quite faithful revival of the Chairmen Of The Board's first hit from mid-1970 (when Kylie was two years old!), while the Pasadenas' *I'm Doing Fine Now* revived another soul group hit from a similar vintage: New York City's original version had charted in the summer of 1973. Meanwhile, three EPs in the Top 10 was almost reminiscent of the Beatles' 1963 heyday.

February – March 1992

22 February 1992

3	1	STAY Shakespears Sister (London)
1	2	I'M DOING FINE NOW Pasadenas (Columbia)
2	3	GOODNIGHT GIRL Wet Wet Wet (Precious)
6	4	REMEMBER THE TIME Michael Jackson (Epic)
5	5	I WONDER WHY Curtis Stigers (Arista)
31	6	MY GIRL Temptations (Epic)
9	7	FOR YOUR BABIES Simply Red (East West)
4	8	TWILIGHT ZONE 2 Unlimited (PWL Continental)
12	9	STEEL BARS Michael Bolton (Columbia)
-	10	I LOVE YOUR SMILE Shanice (Motown)
7	11	GIVE ME JUST A LITTLE MORE TIME Kylie Minogue (PWL)
23	12	REVERENCE Jesus & Mary Chain (blanco y negro)
8	13	THE BOUNCER Kicks Like A Mule (Tribal Bass)
10	14	DIXIE - NARCO (EP) Primal Scream (Creation)
-	15	IT'S A FINE DAY Opus III (PWL International)
16	16	LOVE IS EVERYWHERE Cicero (Spaghetti)
16	17	LEAVE THEM ALL BEHIND Ride (Creation)
14	18	I CAN'T DANCE Genesis (Virgin)
18	19	(LOVE MOVES IN) MYSTERIOUS WAYS Julia Fordham (Circa)
11	20	BORN OF FRUSTRATION James (Fontana)
-	21	I THOUGHT I'D DIED AND GONE TO HEAVEN Bryan Adams (A&M)
-	22	IT MUST BE LOVE Madness (Virgin)
28	23	ALIVE Pearl Jam (Epic)
37	24	LOVE THING Tina Turner (Capitol)
-	25	ARE YOU READY TO PLAY Rozalla (Pulse 8)
44	26	OPTIMISTIC Sounds Of Blackness (Perspective)
36	27	THE FORCE BEHIND THE POWER Diana Ross (EMI)
-	28	LAID SO LOW (TEARS ROLL DOWN) Tears For Fears (Fontana)
32	29	ALONE WITH YOU Texas (Mercury)
21	30	GOD GAVE ROCK AND ROLL TO YOU II Kiss (Interscope)
33	31	DREAM COME TRUE Brand New Heavies featuring N'Dea Davenport (ffrr)
26	32	I'LL CRY FOR YOU Europe (Epic)
-	33	LIVE IN MANCHESTER PARTS 1 + 2 N-Joi (deConstruction)
48	34	CRUCIFIED Army Of Lovers (Ton Son Ton)
17	35	CAN YOU HANDLE IT DNA featuring Sharon Redd (EMI)
-	36	MASSIVE ATTACK (EP) Massive Attack (Wild Bunch)
42	37	THE BIG ONES GET AWAY Buffy Sainte-Marie (Ensign)
-	38	CHIC MYSTIQUE Chic (Warner Bros)
-	39	HARDCORE HEAVEN/YOU AND ME DJ Seduction (Ffrreedom)
24	40	BOHEMIAN RHAPSODY/THESE ARE THE BEST DAYS OF OUR LIVES Queen (Parlophone)
40	41	MOIRA JANE'S CAFE Definition Of Sound (Circa)
-	42	FAR OUT Sonz Of A Loop De Loop Era (Suburban Base)
-	43	THE EP Zero B (Ffrreedom)
-	44	GOOD FOR ME Amy Grant (A&M)
-	45	COVERS (EP) Everything But The Girl (blanco y negro)
25	46	WE GOT A LOVE THING Ce Ce Peniston (A&M)
39	47	MUTATIONS Orbital (ffrr)
41	48	VISIONS OF YOU Jah Wobble's Invaders Of The Heart (Oval)
29	49	HIGHWAY 5 '92 Blessing (MCA)
20	50	GO-GO DANCER Wedding Present (RCA)

29 February 1992

1	1	STAY Shakespears Sister (London)
6	2	MY GIRL Temptations (Epic)
10	3	I LOVE YOUR SMILE Shanice (Motown)
4	4	REMEMBER THE TIME Michael Jackson (Epic)
15	5	IT'S A FINE DAY Opus III (PWL International)
2	6	I'M DOING FINE NOW Pasadenas (Columbia)
7	7	FOR YOUR BABIES Simply Red (East West)
3	8	GOODNIGHT GIRL Wet Wet Wet (Precious)
21	9	I THOUGHT I'D DIED AND GONE TO HEAVEN Bryan Adams (A&M)
5	10	I WONDER WHY Curtis Stigers (Arista)
25	11	ARE YOU READY TO FLY Rozalla (Pulse 8)
22	12	IT MUST BE LOVE Madness (Virgin)
9	13	STEEL BARS Michael Bolton (Columbia)
8	14	TWILIGHT ZONE 2 Unlimited (PWL Continental)
28	15	LAID SO LOW (TEARS ROLL DOWN) Tears For Fears (Fontana)
33	16	LIVE IN MANCHESTER PARTS 1 + 2 N-Joi (deConstruction)
-	17	DRAGGING ME DOWN Inspiral Carpets (Cow Dung)
34	18	CRUCIFIED Army Of Lovers (Ton Son Ton)
11	19	GIVE ME JUST A LITTLE MORE TIME Kylie Minogue (PWL)
-	20	I KNOW New Atlantic (3 Beat)
45	21	COVERS (EP) Everything But The Girl (blanco y negro)
19	22	(LOVE MOVES IN) MYSTERIOUS WAYS Julia Fordham (Circa)
23	23	ALIVE Pearl Jam (Epic)
26	24	OPTIMISTIC Sounds Of Blackness (Perspective)
-	25	VIOLET - ACOUSTIC (EP) Seal (ZTT)
31	26	DREAM COME TRUE Brand New Heavies featuring N'Dea Davenport (ffrr)
-	27	WEATHER WITH YOU Crowded House (Capitol)
13	28	THE BOUNCER Kicks Like A Mule (Tribal Bass)
36	29	MASSIVE ATTACK (EP) Massive Attack (Wild Bunch)
-	30	HEART OF SOUL Cult (Beggars Banquet)
12	31	REVERENCE Jesus & Mary Chain (blanco y negro)
-	32	MAKE IT ON MY OWN Alison Limerick (Arista)
16	33	LOVE IS EVERYWHERE Cicero (Spaghetti)
-	34	DON'T LET IT SHOW ON YOUR FACE Adeva (Cooltempo)
14	35	DIXIE - NARCO (EP) Primal Scream (Creation)
40	36	BOHEMIAN RHAPSODY/THESE ARE THE BEST DAYS OF OUR LIVES Queen (Parlophone)
39	37	HARDCORE HEAVEN/YOU AND ME DJ Seduction (Ffrreedom)
-	38	PURE PLEASURE Digital Excitation (R&S/Outer Rhythm)
-	39	COLOURED KISSES Martika (Columbia)
18	40	I CAN'T DANCE Genesis (Virgin)
-	41	REALITY USED TO BE A FRIEND OF MINE PM Dawn (Gee Street)
43	42	THE EP Zero B (Ffrreedom)
20	43	BORN OF FRUSTRATION James (Fontana)
27	44	THE FORCE BEHIND THE POWER Diana Ross (EMI)
38	45	CHIC MYSTIQUE Chic (Warner Bros)
24	46	LOVE THING Tina Turner (Capitol)
-	47	COLD DAY IN HELL Gary Moore (Virgin)
37	48	THE BIG ONES GET AWAY Buffy Sainte-Marie (Ensign)
-	49	SHADES OF PARANOIMIA Art Of Noise (China)
-	50	ON EVERY STREET Dire Straits (Vertigo)

7 March 1992

1	1	STAY Shakespears Sister (London)
2	2	MY GIRL Temptations (Epic)
3	3	I LOVE YOUR SMILE Shanice (Motown)
5	4	IT'S A FINE DAY Opus III (PWL International)
12	5	IT MUST BE LOVE Madness (Virgin)
-	6	NOVEMBER RAIN Guns N' Roses (Geffen)
9	7	I THOUGHT I'D DIED AND GONE TO HEAVEN Bryan Adams (A&M)
6	8	I'M DOING FINE NOW Pasadenas (Columbia)
4	9	REMEMBER THE TIME Michael Jackson (Epic)
-	10	AMERICA : WHAT TIME IS LOVE? KLF (KLF Communications)
7	11	FOR YOUR BABIES Simply Red (East West)
27	12	WEATHER WITH YOU Crowded House (Capitol)
20	13	I KNOW New Atlantic (3 Beat)
-	14	ONE U2 (Island)
15	15	DRAGGING ME DOWN Inspiral Carpets (Cow Dung)
11	16	ARE YOU READY TO FLY Rozalla (Pulse 8)
32	17	MAKE IT ON MY OWN Alison Limerick (Arista)
-	18	FAIT ACCOMPLI Curve (AnXious)
-	19	WEIRDO Charlatans (Situation Two)
21	20	COVERS (EP) Everything But The Girl (blanco y negro)
23	21	ALIVE Pearl Jam (Epic)
8	22	GOODNIGHT GIRL Wet Wet Wet (Precious)
10	23	I WONDER WHY Curtis Stigers (Arista)
15	24	LAID SO LOW (TEARS ROLL DOWN) Tears For Fears (Fontana)
47	25	COLD DAY IN HELL Gary Moore (Virgin)
16	26	LIVE IN MANCHESTER PARTS 1 + 2 N-Joi (deConstruction)
14	27	TWILIGHT ZONE 2 Unlimited (PWL Continental)
34	28	DON'T LET IT SHOW ON YOUR FACE Adeva (Cooltempo)
-	29	ACCIDENT WAITING TO HAPPEN Billy Bragg (Go! Discs)
41	30	REALITY USED TO BE A FRIEND OF MINE PM Dawn (Gee Street)
29	31	MASSIVE ATTACK (EP) Massive Attack (Wild Bunch)
-	32	STANDING IN THE NEED OF LOVE River City People (EMI)
18	33	CRUCIFIED Army Of Lovers (Ton Son Ton)
25	34	VIOLET - ACOUSTIC (EP) Seal (ZTT)
37	35	HARDCORE HEAVEN/YOU AND ME DJ Seduction (Ffrreedom)
13	36	STEEL BARS Michael Bolton (Columbia)
38	37	PURE PLEASURE Digital Excitation (R&S/Outer Rhythm)
39	38	COLOURED KISSES Martika (Columbia)
-	39	PLACES THAT BELONG TO YOU Barbra Streisand (Columbia)
-	40	LOVER, LOVER, LOVER Ian McCulloch (East West)
26	41	DREAM COME TRUE Brand New Heavies featuring N'Dea Davenport (ffrr)
22	42	(LOVE MOVES IN) MYSTERIOUS WAYS Julia Fordham (Circa)
36	43	BOHEMIAN RHAPSODY/THESE ARE THE BEST DAYS OF OUR LIVES Queen (Parlophone)
50	44	ON EVERY STREET Dire Straits (Vertigo)
19	45	GIVE ME JUST A LITTLE MORE TIME Kylie Minogue (PWL)
-	46	RAVE GENERATOR Toxic Two (PWL Continental)
30	47	HEART OF SOUL Cult (Beggars Banquet)
24	48	OPTIMISTIC Sounds Of Blackness (Perspective)
-	49	EVERY KINDA PEOPLE Robert Palmer (Island)
33	50	LOVE IS EVERYWHERE Cicero (Spaghetti)

Old titles: new songs – neither Shakespears Sister's *Stay* nor Curtis Stigers' *I Wonder Why* was the same song as the erstwhile Maurice Williams/Hollies/Jackson Browne hit or the former Showaddywaddy chart-topper respectively; both were brand-new numbers. The two-girl duo's hit certainly lived up to its title, however, staying in the Number One slot for longer than many singles were stopping in the chart.

14 March 1992

last week	this week	title	artist (label)
1	1	STAY	Shakespears Sister (London)
3	2	I LOVE YOUR SMILE	Shanice (Motown)
2	3	MY GIRL	Temptations (Epic)
6	4	NOVEMBER RAIN	Guns N' Roses (Geffen)
10	5	AMERICA : WHAT TIME IS LOVE?	KLF (KLF Communications)
4	6	IT'S A FINE DAY	Opus III (PWL International)
14	7	ONE	U2 (Island)
5	8	IT MUST BE LOVE	Madness (Virgin)
12	9	WEATHER WITH YOU	Crowded House (Capitol)
7	10	THOUGHT I'D DIED AND GONE TO HEAVEN	Bryan Adams (A&M)
8	11	I'M DOING FINE NOW	Pasadenas (Columbia)
-	12	COME AS YOU ARE	Nirvana (DGC)
13	13	I KNOW	New Atlantic (3 Beat)
15	14	DRAGGING ME DOWN	Inspiral Carpets (Cow Dung)
9	15	REMEMBER THE TIME	Michael Jackson (Epic)
11	16	FOR YOUR BABIES	Simply Red (East West)
20	17	COVERS (EP)	Everything But The Girl (blanco y negro)
-	18	THREE	Wedding Present (RCA)
17	19	MAKE IT ON MY OWN	Alison Limerick (Arista)
19	20	WEIRDO	Charlatans (Situation Two)
16	21	ARE YOU READY TO FLY	Rozalla (Pulse 8)
39	22	PLACES THAT BELONG TO YOU	Barbra Streisand (Columbia)
-	23	FEELS LIKE FOREVER	Joe Cocker (Capitol)
-	24	TEARS IN HEAVEN	Eric Clapton (Reprise)
25	25	COLD DAY IN HELL	Gary Moore (Virgin)
28	26	DON'T LET IT SHOW ON YOUR FACE	Adeva (Cooltempo)
24	27	LAID SO LOW (TEARS ROLL DOWN)	Tears For Fears (Fontana)
-	28	A DEEPER LOVE	Clivilles & Cole (Columbia)
18	29	FAIT ACCOMPLI	Curve (AnXious)
-	30	TIME TO MAKE YOU MINE	Lisa Stansfield (Arista)
-	31	TO BE WITH YOU	Mr. Big (Atlantic)
-	32	STEAL YOUR FIRE	Gun (A&M)
23	33	I WONDER WHY	Curtis Stigers (Arista)
-	34	WE ARE EACH OTHER	Beautiful South (Go! Discs)
46	35	RAVE GENERATOR	Toxic Two (PWL Continental)
-	36	COLOUR MY LIFE	M People (deConstruction)
29	37	ACCIDENT WAITING TO HAPPEN	Billy Bragg (Go! Discs)
27	38	TWILIGHT ZONE	2 Unlimited (PWL Continental)
-	39	LOST IN YOUR LOVE	Tony Hadley (EMI)
49	40	EVERY KINDA PEOPLE	Robert Palmer (Island)
-	41	WE'VE GOT TO LIVE TOGETHER/WE GONNA GET	RAF (PWL Continental)
21	42	ALIVE	Pearl Jam (Epic)
-	43	FREE RANGE	Fall (Fontana/Cog Sinister)
-	44	UNDER THE BRIDGE	Red Hot Chili Peppers (Warner Bros)
26	45	LIVE IN MANCHESTER PARTS 1 + 2	N-Joi (deConstruction)
-	46	FAR GONE AND OUT	Jesus & Mary Chain (blanco y negro)
30	47	REALITY USED TO BE A FRIEND OF MINE	PM Dawn (Gee Street)
22	48	GOODNIGHT GIRL	Wet Wet Wet (Precious)
-	49	LIFT EVERY VOICE (TAKE ME AWAY)	Mass Order (Columbia)
40	50	LOVER, LOVER, LOVER	Ian McCulloch (East West)

21 March 1992

last week	this week	title	artist (label)
1	1	STAY	Shakespears Sister (London)
2	2	I LOVE YOUR SMILE	Shanice (Motown)
5	3	AMERICA : WHAT TIME IS LOVE?	KLF (KLF Communications)
3	4	MY GIRL	Temptations (Epic)
-	5	HUMAN TOUCH	Bruce Springsteen (Columbia)
9	6	WEATHER WITH YOU	Crowded House (Capitol)
6	7	IT'S A FINE DAY	Opus III (PWL International)
7	8	ONE	U2 (Island)
4	9	NOVEMBER RAIN	Guns N' Roses (Geffen)
12	10	COME AS YOU ARE	Nirvana (DGC)
24	11	TEARS IN HEAVEN	Eric Clapton (Reprise)
31	12	TO BE WITH YOU	Mr. Big (Atlantic)
-	13	FINALLY	Ce Ce Peniston (A&M)
28	14	A DEEPER LOVE	Clivilles & Cole (Columbia)
13	15	I KNOW	New Atlantic (3 Beat)
8	16	IT MUST BE LOVE	Madness (Virgin)
34	17	WE ARE EACH OTHER	Beautiful South (Go! Discs)
30	18	TIME TO MAKE YOU MINE	Lisa Stansfield (Arista)
11	19	I'M DOING FINE NOW	Pasadenas (Columbia)
23	20	FEELS LIKE FOREVER	Joe Cocker (Capitol)
22	21	PLACES THAT BELONG TO YOU	Barbra Streisand (Columbia)
19	22	MAKE IT ON MY OWN	Alison Limerick (Arista)
10	23	THOUGHT I'D DIED AND GONE TO HEAVEN	Bryan Adams (A&M)
-	24	DEEPLY DIPPY	Right Said Fred (Tug)
-	25	MORE THAN LOVE	Wet Wet Wet (Precious)
32	26	STEAL YOUR FIRE	Gun (A&M)
35	27	RAVE GENERATOR	Toxic Two (PWL Continental)
16	28	FOR YOUR BABIES	Simply Red (East West)
41	29	WE'VE GOT TO LIVE TOGETHER/WE GONNA GET	RAF (PWL Continental)
-	30	DO NOT PASS ME BY	Hammer (Capitol)
49	31	LIFT EVERY VOICE (TAKE ME AWAY)	Mass Order (Columbia)
17	32	COVERS (EP)	Everything But The Girl (blanco y negro)
-	33	SWEET HARMONY	Liquid (XL)
14	34	DRAGGING ME DOWN	Inspiral Carpets (Cow Dung)
46	35	FAR GONE AND OUT	Jesus & Mary Chain (blanco y negro)
40	36	EVERY KINDA PEOPLE	Robert Palmer (Island)
44	37	UNDER THE BRIDGE	Red Hot Chili Peppers (Warner Bros)
39	38	LOST IN YOUR LOVE	Tony Hadley (EMI)
36	39	COLOUR MY LIFE	M People (deConstruction)
15	40	REMEMBER THE TIME	Michael Jackson (Epic)
-	41	DON'T LOSE THE MAGIC	Shawn Christopher (Arista)
-	42	A JUICY RED APPLE	Skin Up (Love)
18	43	THREE	Wedding Present (RCA)
21	44	ARE YOU READY TO FLY	Rozalla (Pulse 8)
-	45	PEOPLE GET READY	Jeff Beck & Rod Stewart (Epic)
-	46	MIND ADVENTURES	Des'ree (Dusted Sound)
20	47	WEIRDO	Charlatans (Situation Two)
-	48	NATURAL LIFE	Natural Life (Tribe)
26	49	DON'T LET IT SHOW ON YOUR FACE	Adeva (Cooltempo)
27	50	LAID SO LOW (TEARS ROLL DOWN)	Tears For Fears (Fontana)

28 March 1992

last week	this week	title	artist (label)
1	1	STAY	Shakespears Sister (London)
13	2	FINALLY	Ce Ce Peniston (A&M)
-	3	WHY	Annie Lennox (RCA)
-	4	LET'S GET ROCKED	Def Leppard (Bludgeon Riffola)
-	5	HIGH	Cure (Fiction)
12	6	TO BE WITH YOU	Mr. Big (Atlantic)
5	7	HUMAN TOUCH	Bruce Springsteen (Columbia)
6	8	WEATHER WITH YOU	Crowded House (Capitol)
11	9	TEARS IN HEAVEN	Eric Clapton (Reprise)
2	10	I LOVE YOUR SMILE	Shanice (Motown)
24	11	DEEPLY DIPPY	Right Said Fred (Tug)
3	12	AMERICA : WHAT TIME IS LOVE?	KLF (KLF Communications)
4	13	MY GIRL	Temptations (Epic)
14	14	A DEEPER LOVE	Clivilles & Cole (Columbia)
-	15	BREATH OF LIFE	Erasure (Mute)
30	16	DO NOT PASS ME BY	Hammer (Capitol)
18	17	TIME TO MAKE YOU MINE	Lisa Stansfield (Arista)
8	18	ONE	U2 (Island)
10	19	COME AS YOU ARE	Nirvana (DGC)
25	20	MORE THAN LOVE	Wet Wet Wet (Precious)
7	21	IT'S A FINE DAY	Opus III (PWL International)
9	22	NOVEMBER RAIN	Guns N' Roses (Geffen)
-	23	MONEY DON'T MATTER 2 NIGHT	Prince & the New Power Generation (Paisley Park)
41	24	DON'T LOSE THE MAGIC	Shawn Christopher (Arista)
20	25	FEELS LIKE FOREVER	Joe Cocker (Capitol)
33	26	SWEET HARMONY	Liquid (XL)
-	27	CHURCH OF YOUR HEART	Roxette (EMI)
27	28	RAVE GENERATOR	Toxic Two (PWL Continental)
17	29	WE ARE EACH OTHER	Beautiful South (Go! Discs)
15	30	I KNOW	New Atlantic (3 Beat)
26	31	STEAL YOUR FIRE	Gun (A&M)
-	32	SLASH 'N' BURN	Manic Street Preachers (Columbia)
16	33	IT MUST BE LOVE	Madness (Virgin)
-	34	THE LIFE OF RILEY	Lightning Seeds (Virgin)
-	35	SAVE THE BEST FOR LAST	Vanessa Williams (Polydor)
35	36	FAR GONE AND OUT	Jesus & Mary Chain (blanco y negro)
-	37	WINTER	Tori Amos (East West)
-	38	YOU	Ten Sharp (Columbia)
-	39	TAKE MY ADVICE	Kym Sims (Atco)
-	40	EXPRESSION	Salt 'N' Pepa (ffrr)
19	41	I'M DOING FINE NOW	Pasadenas (Columbia)
42	42	A JUICY RED APPLE	Skin Up (Love)
37	43	UNDER THE BRIDGE	Red Hot Chili Peppers (Warner Bros)
46	44	MIND ADVENTURES	Des'ree (Dusted Sound)
23	45	THOUGHT I'D DIED AND GONE TO HEAVEN	Bryan Adams (A&M)
-	46	YOU'RE ALL THAT MATTERS TO ME	Curtis Stigers (Arista)
47	47	MAKE IT ON MY OWN	Alison Limerick (Arista)
31	48	LIFT EVERY VOICE (TAKE ME AWAY)	Mass Order (Columbia)
29	49	WE'VE GOT TO LIVE TOGETHER/WE GONNA GET	RAF (PWL Continental)
50	50	HALFWAY TO HEAVEN	Europe (Epic)

Ironically for Motown, the Temptations' 27-year-old *My Girl* was finally a UK smash after being made the theme for the similarly-titled MacCauley Culkin movie, was issued as a single by Epic, which had the Movie's soundtrack rights. More than recompense, though, was the equally big success of *I Love Your Smile,* by one of Motown's more recent signings, Shanice.

April 1992

4 April 1992

last week	this week	title	artist
6	1	TO BE WITH YOU	Mr. Big (Atlantic)
4	2	LET'S GET ROCKED	Def Leppard (Bludgeon Riffola)
3	3	WHY	Annie Lennox (RCA)
11	4	DEEPLY DIPPY	Right Said Fred (Tug)
2	5	FINALLY	Ce Ce Peniston (A&M)
1	6	STAY	Shakespears Sister (London)
5	7	HIGH	Cure (Fiction)
15	8	BREATH OF LIFE	Erasure (Mute)
9	9	TEARS IN HEAVEN	Eric Clapton (Reprise)
8	10	WEATHER WITH YOU	Crowded House (Capitol)
23	11	MONEY DON'T MATTER 2 NIGHT	Prince & the New Power Generation (Paisley Park)
10	12	I LOVE YOUR SMILE	Shanice (Motown)
7	13	HUMAN TOUCH	Bruce Springsteen (Columbia)
27	14	CHURCH OF YOUR HEART	Roxette (EMI)
26	15	SWEET HARMONY	Liquid (XL)
17	16	TIME TO MAKE YOU MINE	Lisa Stansfield (Arista)
13	17	MY GIRL	Temptations (Epic)
-	18	CHAINSAW CHARLIE (MURDERS IN THE NEW MORGUE)	W.A.S.P. (Parlophone)
20	19	MORE THAN LOVE	Wet Wet Wet (Precious)
16	20	DO NOT PASS ME BY	Hammer (Capitol)
40	21	EXPRESSION	Salt 'N' Pepa (ffrr)
39	22	TAKE MY ADVICE	Kym Sims (Atco)
12	23	AMERICA : WHAT TIME IS LOVE?	KLF (KLF Communications)
37	24	WINTER	Tori Amos (East West)
32	25	SLASH 'N' BURN	Manic Street Preachers (Columbia)
24	26	DON'T LOSE THE MAGIC	Shawn Christopher (Arista)
34	27	THE LIFE OF RILEY	Lightning Seeds (Virgin)
-	28	JOY	Soul II Soul (10)
14	29	A DEEPER LOVE	Clivilles & Cole (Columbia)
-	30	(I WANT TO BE) ELECTED	Campaign featuring Bruce Dickinson (London)
35	31	SAVE THE BEST FOR LAST	Vanessa Williams (Polydor)
38	32	YOU	Ten Sharp (Columbia)
28	33	RAVE GENERATOR	Toxic Two (PWL Continental)
18	34	ONE	U2 (Island)
-	35	BITCH SCHOOL	Spinal Tap (MCA)
-	36	MAKE IT WITH YOU	Pasadenas (Columbia)
21	37	IT'S A FINE DAY	Opus III (PWL International)
46	38	YOU'RE ALL THAT MATTERS TO ME	Curtis Stigers (Arista)
-	39	ROCK ME STEADY	DJ Professor (PWL Continental)
50	40	HALFWAY TO HEAVEN	Europe (Epic)
25	41	FEELS LIKE FOREVER	Joe Cocker (Capitol)
19	42	COME AS YOU ARE	Nirvana (DGC)
22	43	NOVEMBER RAIN	Guns N' Roses (Geffen)
-	44	LOVE YOU ALL MY LIFETIME	Chaka Khan (Warner Bros)
30	45	I KNOW	New Atlantic (3 Beat)
-	46	ONE TRUE WOMAN	Yazz (Polydor)
-	47	RING THE BELLS	James (Fontana)
31	48	STEAL YOUR FIRE	Gun (A&M)
-	49	THROUGH THE ROOF	Cud (A&M)
-	50	HALLELUJAH '92	Inner City (Cow)

11 April 1992

last week	this week	title	artist
1	1	TO BE WITH YOU	Mr. Big (Atlantic)
4	2	DEEPLY DIPPY	Right Said Fred (Tug)
3	3	WHY	Annie Lennox (RCA)
2	4	LET'S GET ROCKED	Def Leppard (Bludgeon Riffola)
5	5	FINALLY	Ce Ce Peniston (A&M)
28	6	JOY	Soul II Soul (10)
7	7	STAY	Shakespears Sister (London)
8	8	BREATH OF LIFE	Erasure (Mute)
31	9	SAVE THE BEST FOR LAST	Vanessa Williams (Polydor)
30	10	(I WANT TO BE) ELECTED	Campaign featuring Bruce Dickinson (London)
9	11	TEARS IN HEAVEN	Eric Clapton (Reprise)
11	12	MONEY DON'T MATTER 2 NIGHT	Prince & the New Power Generation (Paisley Park)
14	13	CHURCH OF YOUR HEART	Roxette (EMI)
38	14	YOU'RE ALL THAT MATTERS TO ME	Curtis Stigers (Arista)
22	15	TAKE MY ADVICE	Kym Sims (Atco)
16	16	TIME TO MAKE YOU MINE	Lisa Stansfield (Arista)
36	17	MAKE IT WITH YOU	Pasadenas (Columbia)
21	18	EXPRESSION	Salt 'N' Pepa (ffrr)
10	19	WEATHER WITH YOU	Crowded House (Capitol)
18	20	CHAINSAW CHARLIE (MURDERS IN THE NEW MORGUE)	W.A.S.P. (Parlophone)
20	21	DO NOT PASS ME BY	Hammer (Capitol)
12	22	I LOVE YOUR SMILE	Shanice (Motown)
32	23	YOU	Ten Sharp (Columbia)
17	24	EVAPOR 8	Altern 8 (Network)
25	25	MY GIRL	Temptations (Epic)
7	26	HIGH	Cure (Fiction)
-	27	INJECTED WITH A POISON	Praga Khan featuring Jade 4 U (Profile)
15	28	SWEET HARMONY	Liquid (XL)
47	29	RING THE BELLS	James (Fontana)
13	30	HUMAN TOUCH	Bruce Springsteen (Columbia)
50	31	HALLELUJAH '92	Inner City (Cow)
-	32	HOLD IT DOWN	Senseless Things (Epic)
-	33	POPSCENE	Blur (Food)
-	34	TOO GOOD TO BE TRUE	Tom Petty & the Heartbreakers (MCA)
-	35	I AM THE RESURRECTION	Stone Roses (Silvertone)
26	36	DON'T LOSE THE MAGIC	Shawn Christopher (Arista)
25	37	SLASH 'N' BURN	Manic Street Preachers (Columbia)
38	38	VIVA LAS VEGAS	ZZ Top (Warner Bros)
19	39	MORE THAN LOVE	Wet Wet Wet (Precious)
27	40	THE LIFE OF RILEY	Lightning Seeds (Virgin)
40	41	HALFWAY TO HEAVEN	Europe (Epic)
44	42	LOVE YOU ALL MY LIFETIME	Chaka Khan (Warner Bros)
-	43	ALWAYS	Urban Soul (Cooltempo)
-	44	JESUS CHRIST POSE	Soundgarden (A&M)
-	45	THE DISAPPOINTED	XTC (Virgin)
24	46	WINTER	Tori Amos (East West)
-	47	WASTED IN AMERICA	Love/Hate (Columbia)
-	48	PRETEND WE'RE DEAD	L7 (Slash)
-	49	MAD ABOUT THE BOY	Dinah Washington (Mercury)
-	50	AM I THE SAME GIRL	Swing Out Sister (Fontana)

18 April 1992

last week	this week	title	artist
2	1	DEEPLY DIPPY	Right Said Fred (Tug)
1	2	TO BE WITH YOU	Mr. Big (Atlantic)
6	3	JOY	Soul II Soul (10)
3	4	WHY	Annie Lennox (RCA)
9	5	SAVE THE BEST FOR LAST	Vanessa Williams (Polydor)
5	6	FINALLY	Ce Ce Peniston (A&M)
4	7	LET'S GET ROCKED	Def Leppard (Bludgeon Riffola)
14	8	YOU'RE ALL THAT MATTERS TO ME	Curtis Stigers (Arista)
7	9	STAY	Shakespears Sister (London)
10	10	(I WANT TO BE) ELECTED	Mr. Bean & Smear Campaign featuring Bruce Dickinson (London)
24	11	EVAPOR 8	Altern 8 (Network)
23	12	YOU	Ten Sharp (Columbia)
8	13	BREATH OF LIFE	Erasure (Mute)
15	14	TAKE MY ADVICE	Kym Sims (Atco)
17	15	MAKE IT WITH YOU	Pasadenas (Columbia)
38	16	VIVA LAS VEGAS	ZZ Top (Warner Bros)
16	17	TIME TO MAKE YOU MINE	Lisa Stansfield (Arista)
11	18	TEARS IN HEAVEN	Eric Clapton (Reprise)
-	19	SILVER SHORTS/FALLING	Wedding Present (RCA)
27	20	INJECTED WITH A POISON	Praga Khan featuring Jade 4 U (Profile)
-	21	ON A RAGGA TIP	SL2 (XL)
31	22	HALLELUJAH '92	Inner City (Cow)
18	23	EXPRESSION	Salt 'N' Pepa (ffrr)
50	24	AM I THE SAME GIRL	Swing Out Sister (Fontana)
12	25	MONEY DON'T MATTER 2 NIGHT	Prince & the New Power Generation (Paisley Park)
-	26	SEPARATE TABLES	Chris De Burgh (A&M)
-	27	HOLD ON MY HEART	Genesis (Virgin)
13	28	CHURCH OF YOUR HEART	Roxette (EMI)
32	29	HOLD IT DOWN	Senseless Things (Epic)
48	30	PRETEND WE'RE DEAD	L7 (Slash)
-	31	MAKE IT HAPPEN	Mariah Carey (Columbia)
19	32	WEATHER WITH YOU	Crowded House (Capitol)
-	33	I FEEL YOU	Love Decade (All Around The World)
-	34	ULTIMATE TRUNK FUNK (EP)	Brand New Heavies (Acid Jazz/ffrr)
33	35	POPSCENE	Blur (Food)
-	36	EVEN FLOW	Pearl Jam (Epic)
-	37	COULD'VE BEEN YOU	Cher (Geffen)
-	38	YOUR SONG/BROKEN ARROW	Rod Stewart (Warner Bros)
21	39	DO NOT PASS ME BY	Hammer (Capitol)
-	40	CALEDONIA	Frankie Miller (MCS)
44	41	JESUS CHRIST POSE	Soundgarden (A&M)
22	42	I LOVE YOUR SMILE	Shanice (Motown)
-	43	STARTOUCHERS	Digital Orgasm (Dead Dead Good)
49	44	MAD ABOUT THE BOY	Dinah Washington (Mercury)
-	45	EVERYDAY	Anticapella (PWL)
47	46	WASTED IN AMERICA	Love/Hate (Columbia)
-	47	SOMEDAY	M People with Heather Small (deConstruction)
45	48	THE DISAPPOINTED	XTC (Virgin)
20	49	CHAINSAW CHARLIE (MURDERS IN THE NEW MORGUE)	W.A.S.P. (Parlophone)
-	50	THAT LOVING FEELING	Cicero (Spaghetti)

Def Leppard's Number Two placing for *Let's Get Rocked* (which contained the memorable tongue-in-cheek aside *"I suppose a little rock's out of the question?"*) was the highest-ever for a UK single by this Sheffield-based outfit. Meanwhile Mr Bean (Rowan Atkinson) and Iron Maiden singer Bruce Dickinson's revival of Alice Cooper's *Elected* reminded Britain it had to choose a new government.

25 April 1992

last week	this week	title	artist (label)
1	1	DEEPLY DIPPY	Right Said Fred (Tug)
-	2	BE QUICK OR BE DEAD	Iron Maiden (EMI)
5	3	SAVE THE BEST FOR LAST	Vanessa Williams (Polydor)
3	4	JOY	Soul II Soul (10)
8	5	YOU'RE ALL THAT MATTERS TO ME	Curtis Stigers (Arista)
16	6	VIVA LAS VEGAS	ZZ Top (Warner Bros)
12	7	YOU	Ten Sharp (Columbia)
4	8	WHY	Annie Lennox (RCA)
11	9	EVAPOR 8	Altern 8 (Network)
2	10	TO BE WITH YOU	Mr. Big (Atlantic)
21	11	ON A RAGGA TIP	SL2 (XL)
31	12	MAKE IT HAPPEN	Mariah Carey (Columbia)
9	13	STAY	Shakespears Sister (London)
27	14	HOLD ON MY HEART	Genesis (Virgin)
14	15	TAKE MY ADVICE	Kym Sims (Atco)
24	16	AM I THE SAME GIRL	Swing Out Sister (Fontana)
6	17	FINALLY	Ce Ce Peniston (A&M)
37	18	COULD'VE BEEN YOU	Cher (Geffen)
7	19	LET'S GET ROCKED	Def Leppard (Bludgeon Riffola)
-	20	FINER FEELINGS	Kylie Minogue (PWL International)
17	21	TIME TO MAKE YOU MINE	Lisa Stansfield (Arista)
10	22	(I WANT TO BE) ELECTED	Mr. Bean & Smear Campaign featuring Bruce Dickinson (London)
-	23	THE ONLY LIVING BOY IN NEW CROSS	Carter The Unstoppable Sex Machine (Chrysalis)
20	24	INJECTED WITH A POISON	Praga Khan featuring Jade 4 U (Profile)
13	25	BREATH OF LIFE	Erasure (Mute)
26	26	SEPARATE TABLES	Chris De Burgh (A&M)
34	27	ULTIMATE TRUNK FUNK (EP)	Brand New Heavies (Acid Jazz/ffrr)
43	28	STARTOUCHERS	Digital Orgasm (Dead Dead Good)
30	29	PRETEND WE'RE DEAD	L7 (Slash)
36	30	EVEN FLOW	Pearl Jam (Epic)
-	31	THE DAYS OF PEARLY SPENCER	Marc Almond (Some Bizzare)
15	32	MAKE IT WITH YOU	Pasadenas (Columbia)
18	33	TEARS IN HEAVEN	Eric Clapton (Reprise)
47	34	SOMEDAY	M People with Heather Small (deConstruction)
38	35	YOUR SONG/BROKEN ARROW	Rod Stewart (Warner Bros)
48	36	THE DISAPPOINTED	XTC (Virgin)
50	37	THAT LOVING FEELING	Cicero (Spaghetti)
-	38	NEVER AGAIN	Mission (Mercury)
-	39	TWISTERELLA	Ride (Creation)
-	40	LIFT ME UP	Howard Jones (East West)
45	41	EVERYDAY	Anticapella (PWL)
-	42	HOUSE OF FUN	Madness (Virgin)
-	43	SO RIGHT	K-Klass (deConstruction)
22	44	HALLELUJAH '92	Inner City (Cow)
29	45	I'M THE ONE YOU NEED	Jody Watley (MCA)
46	46	HOLD IT DOWN	Senseless Things (Epic)
-	47	TELL ME WHAT YOU WANT ME TO DO	Tevin Campbell (Qwest)
33	48	I FEEL YOU	Love Decade (All Around The World)
-	49	I WANT TO TOUCH YOU	Catherine Wheel (Fontana)
19	50	SILVER SHORTS/FALLING	Wedding Present (RCA)

2 May 1992

last week	this week	title	artist (label)
1	1	DEEPLY DIPPY	Right Said Fred (Tug)
11	2	ON A RAGGA TIP	SL2 (XL)
3	3	SAVE THE BEST FOR LAST	Vanessa Williams (Polydor)
5	4	YOU'RE ALL THAT MATTERS TO ME	Curtis Stigers (Arista)
31	5	THE DAYS OF PEARLY SPENCER	Marc Almond (Some Bizzare)
7	6	YOU	Ten Sharp (Columbia)
2	7	BE QUICK OR BE DEAD	Iron Maiden (EMI)
23	8	THE ONLY LIVING BOY IN NEW CROSS	Carter The Unstoppable Sex Machine (Chrysalis)
20	9	FINER FEELINGS	Kylie Minogue (PWL International)
6	10	VIVA LAS VEGAS	ZZ Top (Warner Bros)
-	11	IN THE CLOSET	Michael Jackson (Epic)
12	12	MAKE IT HAPPEN	Mariah Carey (Columbia)
10	13	TO BE WITH YOU	Mr. Big (Atlantic)
14	14	HOLD ON MY HEART	Genesis (Virgin)
-	15	HANG ON IN THERE BABY	Curiosity (RCA)
9	16	EVAPOR 8	Altern 8 (Network)
-	17	TEMPLE OF LOVE (1992)	Sisters Of Mercy (Merciful Release)
-	18	NOTHING ELSE MATTERS	Metallica (Vertigo)
13	19	STAY	Shakespears Sister (London)
8	20	WHY	Annie Lennox (RCA)
-	21	SONG FOR LOVE	Extreme (A&M)
4	22	JOY	Soul II Soul (10)
16	23	AM I THE SAME GIRL	Swing Out Sister (Fontana)
-	24	ONE STEP OUT OF TIME	Michael Ball (Polydor)
-	25	UNEXPLAINED (EP)	EMF (Parlophone)
18	26	COULD'VE BEEN YOU	Cher (Geffen)
29	27	PRETEND WE'RE DEAD	L7 (Slash)
27	28	ULTIMATE TRUNK FUNK (EP)	Brand New Heavies (Acid Jazz/ffrr)
-	29	PLEASE DON'T GO/GAME BOY	KWS (Network)
43	30	SO RIGHT	K-Klass (deConstruction)
19	31	LET'S GET ROCKED	Def Leppard (Bludgeon Riffola)
42	32	HOUSE OF FUN	Madness (Virgin)
33	33	YOUR SONG/BROKEN ARROW	Rod Stewart (Warner Bros)
-	34	DO YOU WANT IT RIGHT NOW	Degrees Of Motion featuring Biti (ffrr)
17	35	FINALLY	Ce Ce Peniston (A&M)
-	36	THRILL ME	Simply Red (East West)
15	37	TAKE MY ADVICE	Kym Sims (Atco)
34	38	SOMEDAY	M People with Heather Small (deConstruction)
-	39	REMEDY	Black Crowes (Def American)
21	40	TIME TO MAKE YOU MINE	Lisa Stansfield (Arista)
-	41	TAKE ME	Dream Frequency featuring Debbie Sharp (Citybeat)
38	42	NEVER AGAIN	Mission (Mercury)
28	43	STARTOUCHERS	Digital Orgasm (Dead Dead Good)
-	44	TIRED OF BEING ALONE	Texas (Mercury)
-	45	MAKE ME SMILE (COME UP AND SEE ME)	Steve Harley & Cockney Rebel (EMI)
30	46	EVEN FLOW	Pearl Jam (Epic)
39	47	TWISTERELLA	Ride (Creation)
24	48	WORKAHOLIC	2 Unlimited (PWL Continental)
24	49	INJECTED WITH A POISON	Praga Khan featuring Jade 4 U (Profile)
26	50	SEPARATE TABLES	Chris De Burgh (A&M)

9 May 1992

last week	this week	title	artist (label)
1	1	DEEPLY DIPPY	Right Said Fred (Tug)
2	2	ON A RAGGA TIP	SL2 (XL)
29	3	PLEASE DON'T GO/GAME BOY	KWS (Network)
5	4	THE DAYS OF PEARLY SPENCER	Marc Almond (Some Bizzare)
4	5	YOU'RE ALL THAT MATTERS TO ME	Curtis Stigers (Arista)
15	6	HANG ON IN THERE BABY	Curiosity (RCA)
17	7	TEMPLE OF LOVE (1992)	Sisters Of Mercy (Merciful Release)
11	8	IN THE CLOSET	Michael Jackson (Epic)
9	9	FINER FEELINGS	Kylie Minogue (PWL International)
21	10	SONG FOR LOVE	Extreme (A&M)
18	11	NOTHING ELSE MATTERS	Metallica (Vertigo)
6	12	YOU	Ten Sharp (Columbia)
3	13	SAVE THE BEST FOR LAST	Vanessa Williams (Polydor)
8	14	THE ONLY LIVING BOY IN NEW CROSS	Carter The Unstoppable Sex Machine (Chrysalis)
-	15	LOVE IS HOLY	Kim Wilde (MCA)
10	16	VIVA LAS VEGAS	ZZ Top (Warner Bros)
25	17	UNEXPLAINED (EP)	EMF (Parlophone)
13	18	TO BE WITH YOU	Mr. Big (Atlantic)
44	19	TIRED OF BEING ALONE	Texas (Mercury)
48	20	WORKAHOLIC	2 Unlimited (PWL Continental)
-	21	WE HATE IT WHEN OUR FRIENDS BECOME SUCCESSFUL	Morrissey (HMV)
24	22	ONE STEP OUT OF TIME	Michael Ball (Polydor)
39	23	REMEDY	Black Crowes (Def American)
14	24	HOLD ON MY HEART	Genesis (Virgin)
36	25	THRILL ME	Simply Red (East West)
-	26	WEEKENDER	Flowered Up (Heavenly)
-	27	UNHOLY	Kiss (Mercury)
16	28	EVAPOR 8	Altern 8 (Network)
-	29	ALWAYS THE LAST TO KNOW	Del Amitri (A&M)
12	30	MAKE IT HAPPEN	Mariah Carey (Columbia)
19	31	STAY	Shakespears Sister (London)
30	32	SO RIGHT	K-Klass (deConstruction)
28	33	ULTIMATE TRUNK FUNK (EP)	Brand New Heavies (Acid Jazz/ffrr)
-	34	MISSING YOU NOW	Michael Bolton (Columbia)
7	35	BE QUICK OR BE DEAD	Iron Maiden (EMI)
34	36	DO YOU WANT IT RIGHT NOW	Degrees Of Motion featuring Biti (ffrr)
-	37	DO IT TO ME	Lionel Richie (Motown)
22	38	JOY	Soul II Soul (10)
-	39	PLEASE DON'T GO	Double You (ZYX)
-	40	HAZARD	Richard Marx (Capitol)
-	41	THE ISOTONIK EP (EP)	Isotonik (Ffrreedom)
20	42	WHY	Annie Lennox (RCA)
-	43	GET A LIFE	Julian Lennon (Virgin)
-	44	NOW THAT THE MAGIC HAS GONE	Joe Cocker (Capitol)
42	45	NEVER AGAIN	Mission (Mercury)
-	46	HIGHER GROUND	Gun (A&M)
32	47	HOUSE OF FUN	Madness (Virgin)
-	48	CLOSE BUT NO CIGAR	Thomas Dolby (Virgin)
27	49	PRETEND WE'RE DEAD	L7 (Slash)
-	50	TALES FROM A DANCEOGRAPHIC OCEAN	Jam & Spoon (R&S/Outer Rhythm)

Having seen their debut hit hold at Two behind Bryan Adams despite it being 1991's second best-selling single, Right Said Fred proclaimed their staying power with a third single, *Deeply Dippy*, in a third different style, and this time took it right to the top for four weeks. Meanwhile, Z.Z. Top scored a top tenner with an Elvis cover which had stalled in the mid-teens when Presley himself released it in 1964.

May 1992

16 May 1992

last	this		
3	1	PLEASE DON'T GO/GAME BOY	KWS (Network)
2	2	ON A RAGGA TIP	SL2 (XL)
6	3	HANG ON IN THERE BABY	Curiosity (RCA)
4	4	THE DAYS OF PEARLY SPENCER	
			Marc Almond (Some Bizzare)
1	5	DEEPLY DIPPY	Right Said Fred (Tug)
5	6	YOU'RE ALL THAT MATTERS TO ME	
			Curtis Stigers (Arista)
8	7	IN THE CLOSET	Michael Jackson (Epic)
7	8	TEMPLE OF LOVE (1992)	
			Sisters Of Mercy (Merciful Release)
10	9	SONG FOR LOVE	Extreme (A&M)
29	10	ALWAYS THE LAST TO KNOW	
			Del Amitri (A&M)
20	11	WORKAHOLIC	2 Unlimited (PWL Continental)
11	12	NOTHING ELSE MATTERS	Metallica (Vertigo)
15	13	LOVE IS HOLY	Kim Wilde (MCA)
12	14	YOU	Ten Sharp (Columbia)
19	15	TIRED OF BEING ALONE	Texas (Mercury)
-	16	COME PLAY WITH ME	Wedding Present (RCA)
9	17	FINER FEELINGS	
			Kylie Minogue (PWL International)
-	18	I DON'T CARE	Shakespears Sister (London)
13	19	SAVE THE BEST FOR LAST	
			Vanessa Williams (Polydor)
-	20	MY LOVIN' (YOU'RE GONNA GET IT)	
			En Vogue (East West America)
-	21	THE BOY FROM NEW YORK CITY	
			Alison Jordan (Arista)
25	22	THRILL ME	Simply Red (East West)
34	23	MISSING YOU NOW	Michael Bolton (Columbia)
40	24	HAZARD	Richard Marx (Capitol)
26	25	WEEKENDER	Flowered Up (Heavenly)
-	26	LOVE MAKES THE WORLD GO ROUND	
			Don-E (Fourth & Broadway)
17	27	UNEXPLAINED (EP)	EMF (Parlophone)
37	28	DO IT TO ME	Lionel Richie (Motown)
-	29	JOIN OUR CLUB/PEOPLE GET REAL	
			St. Etienne (Heavenly)
14	30	THE ONLY LIVING BOY IN NEW CROSS	
			Carter The Unstoppable Sex Machine (Chrysalis)
21	31	WE HATE IT WHEN OUR FRIENDS BECOME	
			SUCCESSFUL	Morrissey (HMV)
-	32	EVERYTHING ABOUT YOU	
			Ugly Kid Joe (Mercury)
44	33	NOW THAT THE MAGIC HAS GONE	
			Joe Cocker (Capitol)
16	34	VIVA LAS VEGAS	ZZ Top (Warner Bros)
22	35	ONE STEP OUT OF TIME	Michael Ball (Polydor)
39	36	PLEASE DON'T GO	Double You (ZYX)
36	37	DO YOU WANT IT RIGHT NOW	
			Degrees Of Motion featuring Biti (ffrr)
48	38	CLOSE BUT NO CIGAR	Thomas Dolby (Virgin)
23	39	REMEDY	Black Crowes (Def American)
-	40	STAY WITH ME	John O'Kane (Circa)
27	41	UNHOLY	Kiss (Mercury)
-	42	SHIVERING SAND	Mega City Four (Big Life)
41	43	THE ISOTONIK EP (EP)	Isotonik (Ffrreedom)
-	44	LOVE BREAKDOWN	Rozalla (Pulse 8)
18	45	TO BE WITH YOU	Mr. Big (Atlantic)
24	46	HOLD ON MY HEART	Genesis (Virgin)
32	47	SO RIGHT	K-Klass (deConstruction)
-	48	SENTIMENTAL	Alexander O'Neal (Epic)
-	49	STORY OF THE BLUES	Gary Moore (Virgin)
33	50	ULTIMATE TRUNK FUNK (EP)	
			Brand New Heavies (Acid Jazz/ffrr)

23 May 1992

1	1	PLEASE DON'T GO/GAME BOY	KWS (Network)
3	2	HANG ON IN THERE BABY	Curiosity (RCA)
20	3	MY LOVIN' (YOU'RE GONNA GET IT)	
			En Vogue (East West America)
-	4	KNOCKIN' ON HEAVEN'S DOOR	
			Guns N' Roses (Geffen)
2	5	ON A RAGGA TIP	SL2 (XL)
-	6	BEAUTY AND THE BEAST	
			Celine Dion & Peabo Bryson (Epic)
18	7	I DON'T CARE	Shakespears Sister (London)
32	8	EVERYTHING ABOUT YOU	
			Ugly Kid Joe (Mercury)
10	9	ALWAYS THE LAST TO KNOW	Del Amitri (A&M)
11	10	WORKAHOLIC	2 Unlimited (PWL Continental)
4	11	THE DAYS OF PEARLY SPENCER	
			Marc Almond (Some Bizzare)
24	12	HAZARD	Richard Marx (Capitol)
5	13	DEEPLY DIPPY	Right Said Fred (Tug)
9	14	SONG FOR LOVE	Extreme (A&M)
-	15	KEEP ON WALKIN'	Ce Ce Peniston (A&M)
6	16	YOU'RE ALL THAT MATTERS TO ME	
			Curtis Stigers (Arista)
23	17	MISSING YOU NOW	Michael Bolton (Columbia)
33	18	NOW THAT THE MAGIC HAS GONE	
			Joe Cocker (Capitol)
13	19	LOVE IS HOLY	Kim Wilde (MCA)
38	20	CLOSE BUT NO CIGAR	Thomas Dolby (Virgin)
21	21	THE BOY FROM NEW YORK CITY	
			Alison Jordan (Arista)
26	22	LOVE MAKES THE WORLD GO ROUND	
			Don-E (Fourth & Broadway)
-	23	15 YEARS (EP)	Levellers (China)
29	24	JOIN OUR CLUB/PEOPLE GET REAL	
			St. Etienne (Heavenly)
14	25	YOU	Ten Sharp (Columbia)
35	26	ONE STEP OUT OF TIME	Michael Ball (Polydor)
12	27	NOTHING ELSE MATTERS	Metallica (Vertigo)
-	28	SYMPATHY	Marillion (EMI)
7	29	IN THE CLOSET	Michael Jackson (Epic)
-	30	YOU WON'T SEE ME CRY	Wilson Phillips (SBK)
28	31	DO IT TO ME	Lionel Richie (Motown)
15	32	TIRED OF BEING ALONE	Texas (Mercury)
-	33	KILLJOY WAS HERE (EP)	Kingmaker (Scorch)
40	34	STAY WITH ME	John O'Kane (Circa)
-	35	PAPUA NEW GUINEA	
			Future Sound Of London (Jumpin' & Pumpin')
19	36	SAVE THE BEST FOR LAST	
			Vanessa Williams (Polydor)
37	37	BETTER DAYS	Bruce Springsteen (Columbia)
17	38	FINER FEELINGS	
			Kylie Minogue (PWL International)
-	39	LISTEN LIKE THIEVES	Was (Not Was) (Fontana)
-	40	JUST TAKE MY HEART	Mr. Big (Atlantic)
22	41	THRILL ME	Simply Red (East West)
-	42	LET'S GET HAPPY	Mass Order (Columbia)
49	43	STORY OF THE BLUES	Gary Moore (Virgin)
8	44	TEMPLE OF LOVE (1992)	
			Sisters Of Mercy (Merciful Release)
37	45	DO YOU WANT IT RIGHT NOW	
			Degrees Of Motion featuring Biti (ffrr)
42	46	SHIVERING SAND	Mega City Four (Big Life)
36	47	PLEASE DON'T GO	Double You (ZYX)
-	48	TAKE ME BACK TO LOVE AGAIN	
			Kathy Sledge (Epic)
16	49	COME PLAY WITH ME	Wedding Present (RCA)
-	50	PASSION	Gat Decor (Effective)

30 May 1992

1	1	PLEASE DON'T GO/GAME BOY	KWS (Network)
-	2	RAVING I'M RAVING	Shut Up & Dance featuring
			Peter Bouncer (Shut Up And Dance)
4	3	KNOCKIN' ON HEAVEN'S DOOR	
			Guns N' Roses (Geffen)
8	4	EVERYTHING ABOUT YOU	
			Ugly Kid Joe (Mercury)
3	5	MY LOVIN' (YOU'RE GONNA GET IT)	
			En Vogue (East West America)
7	6	I DON'T CARE	Shakespears Sister (London)
12	7	HAZARD	Richard Marx (Capitol)
-	8	JUMP	Kris Kross (Columbia)
2	9	HANG ON IN THERE BABY	Curiosity (RCA)
-	10	FRIDAY, I'M IN LOVE	Cure (Fiction)
15	11	KEEP ON WALKIN'	Ce Ce Peniston (A&M)
6	12	BEAUTY AND THE BEAST	
			Celine Dion & Peabo Bryson (Epic)
9	13	ALWAYS THE LAST TO KNOW	Del Amitri (A&M)
5	14	ON A RAGGA TIP	SL2 (XL)
30	15	YOU WON'T SEE ME CRY	Wilson Phillips (SBK)
23	16	15 YEARS (EP)	Levellers (China)
28	17	SYMPATHY	Marillion (EMI)
10	18	WORKAHOLIC	2 Unlimited (PWL Continental)
20	19	CLOSE BUT NO CIGAR	Thomas Dolby (Virgin)
22	20	LOVE MAKES THE WORLD GO ROUND	
			Don-E (Fourth & Broadway)
11	21	THE DAYS OF PEARLY SPENCER	
			Marc Almond (Some Bizzare)
-	22	BACK TO THE OLD SCHOOL	
			Bassheads (deConstruction)
13	23	DEEPLY DIPPY	Right Said Fred (Tug)
16	24	YOU'RE ALL THAT MATTERS TO ME	
			Curtis Stigers (Arista)
18	25	NOW THAT THE MAGIC HAS GONE	
			Joe Cocker (Capitol)
40	26	JUST TAKE MY HEART	Mr. Big (Atlantic)
35	27	PAPUA NEW GUINEA	
			Future Sound Of London (Jumpin' & Pumpin')
24	28	JOIN OUR CLUB/PEOPLE GET REAL	
			St. Etienne (Heavenly)
33	29	KILLJOY WAS HERE (EP)	Kingmaker (Scorch)
14	30	SONG FOR LOVE	Extreme (A&M)
25	31	YOU	Ten Sharp (Columbia)
-	32	ONE REASON WHY	Craig McLachlan (Epic)
-	33	TWO WORLDS COLLIDE	Inspiral Carpets (Cow)
26	34	ONE STEP OUT OF TIME	Michael Ball (Polydor)
-	35	RICH AND STRANGE	Cud (A&M)
-	36	EVERGLADE	L7 (Slash)
34	37	STAY WITH ME	John O'Kane (Circa)
31	38	DO IT TO ME	Lionel Richie (Motown)
37	39	BETTER DAYS	Bruce Springsteen (Columbia)
-	40	CONSTANT CRAVING	kd lang (Sire)
-	41	A PRINCE AMONG ISLANDS (EP)	
			Capercaillie (Survival)
17	42	MISSING YOU NOW	Michael Bolton (Columbia)
19	43	LOVE IS HOLY	Kim Wilde (MCA)
50	44	PASSION	Gat Decor (Effective)
42	45	LET'S GET HAPPY	Mass Order (Columbia)
-	46	ERNIE (THE FASTEST MILKMAN IN THE WEST)	
			Benny Hill (EMI)
39	47	LISTEN LIKE THIEVES	Was (Not Was) (Fontana)
-	48	DUNNO WHAT IT IS (ABOUT YOU)	Beatmasters
			featuring Elaine Vassell (Rhythm King)
21	49	THE BOY FROM NEW YORK CITY	
			Alison Jordan (Arista)
-	50	BELIEVER	Real People (Columbia)

Newcomers KWS soared to the summit with a jittery dance reworking of the January 1980 hit by KC & the Sunshine Band, while more oldie revivals crowded behind it: *The Days Of Pearly Spencer* (originally by David McWilliams), *Hang On In There Baby* (a 1974 hit for Johnny Bristol), and *Knockin' On Heaven's Door* (Bob Dylan's 1974 song.) Past, present and future, the chart cycle goes around.

6 June 1992

last week	this week	title / artist
1	1	PLEASE DON'T GO/GAME BOY KWS (Network)
8	2	JUMP Kris Kross (Columbia)
3	3	KNOCKIN' ON HEAVEN'S DOOR Guns N' Roses (Geffen)
4	4	EVERYTHING ABOUT YOU Ugly Kid Joe (Mercury)
2	5	RAVING I'M RAVING Shut Up & Dance featuring Peter Bouncer (Shut Up And Dance)
7	6	HAZARD Richard Marx (Capitol)
5	7	MY LOVIN' (YOU'RE GONNA GET IT) En Vogue (East West America)
10	8	FRIDAY, I'M IN LOVE Cure (Fiction)
6	9	I DON'T CARE Shakespear's Sister (London)
11	10	KEEP ON WALKIN' Ce Ce Peniston (A&M)
22	11	BACK TO THE OLD SCHOOL Bassheads (deConstruction)
9	12	HANG ON IN THERE BABY Curiosity (RCA)
15	13	YOU WON'T SEE ME CRY Wilson Phillips (SBK)
20	14	LOVE MAKES THE WORLD GO ROUND Don-E (Fourth & Broadway)
12	15	BEAUTY AND THE BEAST Celine Dion & Peabo Bryson (Epic)
13	16	ALWAYS THE LAST TO KNOW Del Amitri (A&M)
-	17	THE ONE Elton John (Rocket)
14	18	ON A RAGGA TIP SL2 (XL)
16	19	15 YEARS (EP) Levellers (China)
-	20	MIDLIFE CRISIS Faith No More (Slash)
-	21	SOMETHING GOOD Utah Saints (ffrr)
26	22	JUST TAKE MY HEART Mr. Big (Atlantic)
27	23	PAPUA NEW GUINEA Future Sound Of London (Jumpin' & Pumpin')
46	24	ERNIE (THE FASTEST MILKMAN IN THE WEST) Benny Hill (EMI)
32	25	ONE REASON WHY Craig McLachlan (Epic)
-	26	SET YOUR LOVING FREE Lisa Stansfield (Arista)
18	27	WORKAHOLIC 2 Unlimited (PWL Continental)
17	28	SYMPATHY Marillion (EMI)
24	29	YOU'RE ALL THAT MATTERS TO ME Curtis Stigers (Arista)
-	30	KARMADROME Pop Will Eat Itself (RCA)
23	31	DEEPLY DIPPY Right Said Fred (Tug)
25	32	NOW THAT THE MAGIC HAS GONE Joe Cocker (Capitol)
-	33	PRECIOUS Annie Lennox (RCA)
-	34	I THOUGHT IT WAS YOU Julia Fordham (Circa)
-	35	FEED MY FRANKENSTEIN Alice Cooper (Epic)
36	36	EVERGLADE L7 (Slash)
39	37	BETTER DAYS Bruce Springsteen (Columbia)
-	38	IT ONLY TAKES A MINUTE Take That (RCA)
-	39	THE IDOL WASP (Parlophone)
31	40	YOU Ten Sharp (Columbia)
35	41	RICH AND STRANGE Cud (A&M)
-	42	SENSE Lightning Seeds (Virgin)
40	43	CONSTANT CRAVING kd lang (Sire)
33	44	TWO WORLDS COLLIDE Inspiral Carpets (Cow)
-	45	BALLROOM BLITZ Tia Carrere (Reprise)
-	46	I BELIEVE IN MIRACLES Pasadenas (Columbia)
38	47	DO IT TO ME Lionel Richie (Motown)
-	48	DON'T WORRY 'BOUT A THING Incognito (Talkin' Loud)
-	49	FIND 'EM, FOOL 'EM (EP) S'Express (Rhythm King)
-	50	SKUNK FUNK Galliano (Talkin' Loud)

13 June 1992

last week	this week	title / artist
-	1	ABBA-ESQUE Erasure (Mute)
2	2	JUMP Kris Kross (Columbia)
1	3	PLEASE DON'T GO/GAME BOY KWS (Network)
4	4	EVERYTHING ABOUT YOU Ugly Kid Joe (Mercury)
5	5	TOO FUNKY George Michael (Epic)
6	6	HAZARD Richard Marx (Capitol)
21	7	SOMETHING GOOD Utah Saints (ffrr)
17	8	THE ONE Elton John (Rocket)
3	9	KNOCKIN' ON HEAVEN'S DOOR Guns N' Roses (Geffen)
8	10	FRIDAY, I'M IN LOVE Cure (Fiction)
33	11	PRECIOUS Annie Lennox (RCA)
7	12	MY LOVIN' (YOU'RE GONNA GET IT) En Vogue (East West America)
-	13	CALIFORNIA Wedding Present (RCA)
38	14	IT ONLY TAKES A MINUTE Take That (RCA)
11	15	BACK TO THE OLD SCHOOL Bassheads (deConstruction)
9	16	I DON'T CARE Shakespear's Sister (London)
20	17	MIDLIFE CRISIS Faith No More (Slash)
26	18	SET YOUR LOVING FREE Lisa Stansfield (Arista)
-	19	I WANT YOU NEAR ME Tina Turner (Capitol)
-	20	THE WORLD IS STONE Cyndi Lauper (Epic)
-	21	HEARTBEAT Nick Berry (Columbia)
25	22	ONE REASON WHY Craig McLachlan (Epic)
10	23	KEEP ON WALKIN' Ce Ce Peniston (A&M)
13	24	YOU WON'T SEE ME CRY Wilson Phillips (SBK)
48	25	DON'T WORRY 'BOUT A THING Incognito (Talkin' Loud)
46	26	I BELIEVE IN MIRACLES Pasadenas (Columbia)
12	27	HANG ON IN THERE BABY Curiosity (RCA)
45	28	BALLROOM BLITZ Tia Carrere (Reprise)
-	29	MOTORCYCLE EMPTINESS Manic Street Preachers (Columbia)
16	30	ALWAYS THE LAST TO KNOW Del Amitri (A&M)
23	31	PAPUA NEW GUINEA Future Sound Of London (Jumpin' & Pumpin')
-	32	MOVE ME NO MOUNTAIN Soul II Soul (Ten)
18	33	ON A RAGGA TIP SL2 (XL)
30	34	KARMADROME Pop Will Eat Itself (RCA)
42	35	SENSE Lightning Seeds (Virgin)
35	37	FEED MY FRANKENSTEIN Alice Cooper (Epic)
-	38	TV CRIMES Black Sabbath (IRS)
24	39	ERNIE (THE FASTEST MILKMAN IN THE WEST) Benny Hill (EMI)
-	40	CONTROLLING ME Oceanic (Dead Dead Good)
-	41	GOT TO BE FREE 49ers (4th & Broadway)
14	42	LOVE MAKES THE WORLD GO ROUND Don-E (Fourth & Broadway)
-	43	BELL BOTTOMED TEAR Beautiful South (Go! Discs)
-	44	UNTIL YOU COME BACK TO ME Adeva (Cooltempo)
15	45	BEAUTY AND THE BEAST Celine Dion & Peabo Bryson (Epic)
22	46	JUST TAKE MY HEART Mr. Big (Atlantic)
-	47	RUNAWAY/RUBBER LOVE Deee-Lite (Elektra)
36	48	EVERGLADE L7 (Slash)
-	49	A LITTLE BIT MORE Dr Hook (Capitol)
-	50	THE SOUND OF CRYING Prefab Sprout (Kitchenware)

20 June 1992

last week	this week	title / artist
1	1	ABBA-ESQUE Erasure (Mute)
21	2	HEARTBEAT Nick Berry (Columbia)
5	3	TOO FUNKY George Michael (Epic)
3	4	PLEASE DON'T GO/GAME BOY KWS (Network)
6	5	HAZARD Richard Marx (Capitol)
7	6	SOMETHING GOOD Utah Saints (ffrr)
2	7	JUMP Kris Kross (Columbia)
8	8	THE ONE Elton John (Rocket)
14	9	IT ONLY TAKES A MINUTE Take That (RCA)
4	10	EVERYTHING ABOUT YOU Ugly Kid Joe (Mercury)
-	11	EVEN BETTER THAN THE REAL THING U2 (Island)
9	12	KNOCKIN' ON HEAVEN'S DOOR Guns N' Roses (Geffen)
20	13	THE WORLD IS STONE Cyndi Lauper (Epic)
11	14	PRECIOUS Annie Lennox (RCA)
10	15	FRIDAY, I'M IN LOVE Cure (Fiction)
19	16	I WANT YOU NEAR ME Tina Turner (Capitol)
43	17	BELL BOTTOMED TEAR Beautiful South (Go! Discs)
40	18	CONTROLLING ME Oceanic (Dead Dead Good)
29	19	MOTORCYCLE EMPTINESS Manic Street Preachers (Columbia)
-	20	BLUE ROOM Orb (WAU! Mr Moto)
25	21	DON'T WORRY 'BOUT A THING Incognito (Talkin' Loud)
12	22	MY LOVIN' (YOU'RE GONNA GET IT) En Vogue (East West America)
50	23	THE SOUND OF CRYING Prefab Sprout (Kitchenware)
18	24	SET YOUR LOVING FREE Lisa Stansfield (Arista)
34	25	PENNIES FROM HEAVEN Inner City (Ten)
-	26	ONE SHINING MOMENT Diana Ross (Capitol)
32	27	MOVE ME NO MOUNTAIN Soul II Soul (Ten)
28	28	BALLROOM BLITZ Tia Carrere (Reprise)
22	29	ONE REASON WHY Craig McLachlan (Epic)
-	30	LIKE A CHILD AGAIN Mission (Vertigo)
17	31	MIDLIFE CRISIS Faith No More (Slash)
16	32	I DON'T CARE Shakespear's Sister (London)
-	33	TEMPLE OF DREAMS Messiah (Kickin')
26	34	I BELIEVE IN MIRACLES Pasadenas (Columbia)
-	35	FOUR SEASONS IN ONE DAY Crowded House (Capitol)
36	36	SENSE Lightning Seeds (Virgin)
-	37	AIN'T 2 PROUD 2 BEG TLC (Arista)
-	38	RUSTY CAGE Soundgarden (A&M)
-	39	I'LL BE THERE Innocence (Cooltempo)
-	40	GOOD STUFF B-52s (Reprise)
15	41	BACK TO THE OLD SCHOOL Bassheads (deConstruction)
23	42	KEEP ON WALKIN' Ce Ce Peniston (A&M)
-	43	EXPRESS YOURSELF Family Foundation (380)
47	44	RUNAWAY/RUBBER LOVE Deee-Lite (Elektra)
33	45	ON A RAGGA TIP SL2 (XL)
-	46	HANGIN' ON A STRING Loose Ends (Ten)
37	47	TV CRIMES Black Sabbath (IRS)
24	48	YOU WON'T SEE ME CRY Wilson Phillips (SBK)
-	49	CRUCIFY Tori Amos (East West)
27	50	HANG ON IN THERE BABY Curiosity (RCA)

Rave I'm Raving was a new phenomenon. A classic rave tune put out in limited quantities by an independent label. It stayed in the chart for two weeks, then sold out. Copies were instant collectors' items changing hands for £50. Take That entered this month with their first Top Ten hit, while Erasure's camping up of Abba managed to keep Nick Berry from going all the way to the top with his TV theme.

June – July 1992

27 June 1992

Last	This	Title	Artist (Label)
1	1	ABBA-ESQUE	Erasure (Mute)
2	2	HEARTBEAT	Nick Berry (Columbia)
3	3	TOO FUNKY	George Michael (Epic)
5	4	HAZARD	Richard Marx (Capitol)
4	5	PLEASE DON'T GO/GAME BOY	KWS (Network)
6	6	SOMETHING GOOD	Utah Saints (ffrr)
9	7	IT ONLY TAKES A MINUTE	Take That (RCA)
11	8	EVEN BETTER THAN THE REAL THING	U2 (Island)
7	9	JUMP	Kris Kross (Columbia)
8	10	THE ONE	Elton John (Rocket)
26	11	ONE SHINING MOMENT	Diana Ross (Capitol)
13	12	THE WORLD IS STONE	Cyndi Lauper (Epic)
17	13	BELL BOTTOMED TEAR	Beautiful South (Go! Discs)
20	14	BLUE ROOM	Orb (WAU! Mr Moto)
-	15	I'LL BE THERE	Mariah Carey (Columbia)
23	16	THE SOUND OF CRYING	Prefab Sprout (Kitchenware)
18	17	CONTROLLING ME	Oceanic (Dead Dead Good)
37	18	AIN'T 2 PROUD 2 BEG	TLC (Arista)
35	19	FOUR SEASONS IN ONE DAY	Crowded House (Capitol)
-	20	MAKE LOVE LIKE A MAN	Def Leppard (Bludgeon Riffola)
12	21	KNOCKIN' ON HEAVEN'S DOOR	Guns N' Roses (Geffen)
19	22	MOTORCYCLE EMPTINESS	Manic Street Preachers (Columbia)
-	23	SYMPHONY OF DESTRUCTION	Megadeth (Capitol)
10	24	EVERYTHING ABOUT YOU	Ugly Kid Joe (Mercury)
49	25	CRUCIFY	Tori Amos (east east)
21	26	DON'T WORRY 'BOUT A THING	Incognito (Talkin' Loud)
40	27	GOOD STUFF	B-52s (Reprise)
15	28	FRIDAY, I'M IN LOVE	Cure (Fiction)
39	29	I'LL BE THERE	Innocence (Cooltempo)
-	30	THUNDER	Prince & the New Power Generation (Paisley Park)
27	31	MOVE ME NO MOUNTAIN	Soul II Soul (Ten)
25	32	PENNIES FROM HEAVEN	Inner City (Ten)
-	33	DOLPHINS MAKE ME CRY	Martin Joseph (Epic)
14	34	PRECIOUS	Annie Lennox (RCA)
46	35	HANGIN' ON A STRING	Loose Ends (Ten)
33	36	TEMPLE OF DREAMS	Messiah (Kickin')
30	37	LIKE A CHILD AGAIN	Mission (Vertigo)
28	38	BALLROOM BLITZ	Tia Carrere (Reprise)
22	39	MY LOVIN' (YOU'RE GONNA GET IT)	En Vogue (east west America)
-	40	A LITTLE BIT MORE	Kym Sims (Atco)
-	41	OPP	Naughty By Nature (Big Life)
-	42	YOU BRING ON THE SUN	Londonbeat (Anxious)
43	43	EXPRESS YOURSELF	Family Foundation (380)
29	44	ONE REASON WHY	Craig McLachlan (Epic)
36	45	SENSE	Lightning Seeds (Virgin)
16	46	I WANT YOU NEAR ME	Tina Turner (Capitol)
-	47	I TALK TO THE WIND	Opus III (PWL International)
31	48	MIDLIFE CRISIS	Faith No More (Slash)
-	49	WHY SHOULD I LOVE YOU	Des'Ree (Dusted Soul)
-	50	THE BUG	Dire Straits (Vertigo)

4 July 1992

Last	This	Title	Artist (Label)
1	1	ABBA-ESQUE	Erasure (Mute)
2	2	HEARTBEAT	Nick Berry (Columbia)
15	3	I'LL BE THERE	Mariah Carey (Columbia)
4	4	HAZARD	Richard Marx (Capitol)
6	5	SOMETHING GOOD	Utah Saints (ffrr)
3	6	TOO FUNKY	George Michael (Epic)
7	7	IT ONLY TAKES A MINUTE	Take That (RCA)
11	8	ONE SHINING MOMENT	Diana Ross (Capitol)
5	9	PLEASE DON'T GO/GAME BOY	KWS (Network)
8	10	EVEN BETTER THAN THE REAL THING	U2 (Island)
-	11	DISAPPOINTED	Electronic (Parlophone)
10	12	THE ONE	Elton John (Rocket)
25	13	CRUCIFY	Tori Amos (East West)
14	14	BLUE ROOM	Orb (WAU! Mr Moto)
18	15	AIN'T 2 PROUD 2 BEG	TLC (Arista)
20	16	MAKE LOVE LIKE A MAN	Def Leppard (Bludgeon Riffola)
19	17	FOUR SEASONS IN ONE DAY	Crowded House (Capitol)
27	18	GOOD STUFF	B-52s (Reprise)
9	19	JUMP	Kris Kross (Columbia)
-	20	RHYTHM IS A DANCER	Snap (Logic)
12	21	THE WORLD IS STONE	Cyndi Lauper (Epic)
17	22	CONTROLLING ME	Oceanic (Dead Dead Good)
23	23	SYMPHONY OF DESTRUCTION	Megadeth (Capitol)
35	24	HANGIN' ON A STRING	Loose Ends (Ten)
-	25	DO RE MI, SO FAR SO GOOD	Carter USM (Chrysalis)
26	26	HYPNOTIC ST-8	Altern 8 (Network)
40	27	A LITTLE BIT MORE	Kym Sims (Atco)
13	28	BELL BOTTOMED TEAR	Beautiful South (Go! Discs)
42	29	YOU BRING ON THE SUN	Londonbeat (Anxious)
36	30	TEMPLE OF DREAMS	Messiah (Kickin')
33	31	DOLPHINS MAKE ME CRY	Martin Joseph (Epic)
16	32	THE SOUND OF CRYING	Prefab Sprout (Kitchenware)
21	33	KNOCKIN' ON HEAVEN'S DOOR	Guns N' Roses (Geffen)
29	34	I'LL BE THERE	Innocence (Cooltempo)
22	35	MOTORCYCLE EMPTINESS	Manic Street Preachers (Columbia)
-	36	SOME JUSTICE	Urban Shakedown featuring Mickey Finn (Urban Shakedown)
24	37	EVERYTHING ABOUT YOU	Ugly Kid Joe (Mercury)
-	38	UNCHAIN MY HEART	Joe Cocker (Capitol)
-	39	ESCAPING	Asia Blue (Atomic)
-	40	DAMN I WISH I WAS YOUR LOVER	Sophie B Hawkins (Columbia)
-	41	RISING SUN	Farm (End Product)
26	42	DON'T WORRY 'BOUT A THING	Incognito (Talkin' Loud)
41	43	OPP	Naughty By Nature (Big Life)
47	44	I TALK TO THE WIND	Opus III (PWL International)
48	45	MIDLIFE CRISIS	Faith No More (Slash)
-	46	HEART OVER MIND	Kim Wilde (MCA)
-	47	ROUGH BOY	ZZ Top (Warner Bros.)
-	48	I DROVE ALL NIGHT	Roy Orbison (MCA)
28	49	FRIDAY, I'M IN LOVE	Cure (Fiction)
-	50	SHAME SHAME SHAME	Sinitta (Arista)

11 July 1992

Last	This	Title	Artist (Label)
3	1	I'LL BE THERE	Mariah Carey (Columbia)
1	2	ABBA-ESQUE	Erasure (Mute)
4	3	HAZARD	Richard Marx (Capitol)
11	4	DISAPPOINTED	Electronic (Parlophone)
2	5	HEARTBEAT	Nick Berry (Columbia)
20	6	RHYTHM IS A DANCER	Snap (Logic)
8	7	ONE SHINING MOMENT	Diana Ross (Capitol)
10	8	EVEN BETTER THAN THE REAL THING	U2 (Island)
5	9	SOMETHING GOOD	Utah Saints (ffrr)
6	10	TOO FUNKY	George Michael (Epic)
-	11	SESAME'S STREET	Smart Es (Suburban Base)
7	12	IT ONLY TAKES A MINUTE	Take That (RCA)
13	13	CRUCIFY	Tori Amos (East West)
16	14	MAKE LOVE LIKE A MAN	Def Leppard (Bludgeon Riffola)
12	15	THE ONE	Elton John (Rocket)
9	16	PLEASE DON'T GO/GAME BOY	KWS (Network)
26	17	HYPNOTIC ST-8	Altern 8 (Network)
18	18	GOOD STUFF	B-52s (Reprise)
-	19	A TRIP TO TRUMPTON	Urban Hype (Faze 2)
38	20	UNCHAIN MY HEART	Joe Cocker (Capitol)
40	21	DAMN I WISH I WAS YOUR LOVER	Sophie B Hawkins (Columbia)
48	22	I DROVE ALL NIGHT	Roy Orbison (MCA)
25	23	DO RE MI, SO FAR SO GOOD	Carter USM (Chrysalis)
14	24	BLUE ROOM	Orb (WAU! Mr Moto)
-	25	FROM HERE TO ETERNITY	Iron Maiden (EMI)
24	26	HANGIN' ON A STRING	Loose Ends (Ten)
-	27	SHAKE YOUR HEAD	Was (Not Was) (Fontana)
15	28	AIN'T 2 PROUD 2 BEG	TLC (Arista)
-	29	AIN'T NO DOUBT	Jimmy Nail (East West)
17	30	FOUR SEASONS IN ONE DAY	Crowded House (Capitol)
50	31	SHAME SHAME SHAME	Sinitta (Arista)
29	32	YOU BRING ON THE SUN	Londonbeat (Anxious)
-	33	LIP SERVICE	Wet Wet Wet (Precious Organisation)
27	34	A LITTLE BIT MORE	Kym Sims (Atco)
-	35	AIN'T NO MAN	Dina Carroll (A&M PM)
46	36	HEART OVER MIND	Kim Wilde (MCA)
36	37	SOME JUSTICE	Urban Shakedown featuring Mickey Finn (Urban Shakedown)
19	38	JUMP	Kris Kross (Columbia)
-	39	100%	Sonic Youth (DGC)
-	40	BE MY DOWNFALL	Del Amitri (A&M)
30	41	TEMPLE OF DREAMS	Messiah (Kickin')
41	42	RISING SUN	Farm (End Product)
45	43	MIDLIFE CRISIS	Faith No More (Slash)
-	44	RAVE ALERT!	Praga Khan (Profile)
23	45	SYMPHONY OF DESTRUCTION	Megadeth (Capitol)
-	46	COME ON	DJ Seduction (ffrreedom)
21	47	THE WORLD IS STONE	Cyndi Lauper (Epic)
28	48	BELL BOTTOMED TEAR	Beautiful South (Go! Discs)
39	49	ESCAPING	Asia Blue (Atomic)
22	50	CONTROLLING ME	Oceanic (Dead Dead Good)

Swingbeat arrived in the form of TLC – also first of a trend of girl groups with initial letter names. Dire Straits could only manage an entry at Number 50 – echoing disappointing album sales. Punk threatened to rear its ugly head again c/o the Manic Street Preachers. *Sesame's Street* was the first of many rave versions of kids' TV themes. Rave was splitting into 'pop' and 'underground' – a familiar story.

July – August 1992

18 July 1992

		Title	Artist (Label)
29	1	AIN'T NO DOUBT	Jimmy Nail (East West)
1	2	I'LL BE THERE	Mariah Carey (Columbia)
11	3	SESAME'S STREET	Smart Es (Suburban Base)
2	4	ABBA-ESQUE	Erasure (Mute)
6	5	RHYTHM IS A DANCER	Snap (Logic)
8	6	EVEN BETTER THAN THE REAL THING	U2 (Island)
3	7	HAZARD	Richard Marx (Capitol)
-	8	SEXY MF	Prince & the New Power Generation (Paisley Park)
4	9	DISAPPOINTED	Electronic (Parlophone)
22	10	I DROVE ALL NIGHT	Roy Orbison (MCA)
19	11	A TRIP TO TRUMPTON	Urban Hype (Faze 2)
27	12	SHAKE YOUR HEAD	Was (Not Was) (Fontana)
7	13	ONE SHINING MOMENT	Diana Ross (Capitol)
20	14	UNCHAIN MY HEART	Joe Cocker (Capitol)
-	15	LSI	Shamen (One Little Indian)
21	16	DAMN I WISH I WAS YOUR LOVER	Sophie B Hawkins (Columbia)
5	17	HEARTBEAT	Nick Berry (Columbia)
-	18	FLYING SAUCER	Wedding Present (RCA)
33	19	LIP SERVICE	Wet Wet Wet (Precious Organisation)
35	20	AIN'T NO MAN	Dina Carroll (A&M PM)
17	21	HYPNOTIC ST-8	Altern 8 (Network)
25	22	FROM HERE TO ETERNITY	Iron Maiden (EMI)
9	23	SOMETHING GOOD	Utah Saints (ffrr)
10	24	TOO FUNKY	George Michael (Epic)
40	25	BE MY DOWNFALL	Del Amitri (A&M)
12	26	IT ONLY TAKES A MINUTE	Take That (RCA)
-	27	AMIGOS PARA SIEMPRE (FRIENDS FOR LIFE)	Jose Carreras & Sarah Brightman (Really Useful)
16	28	PLEASE DON'T GO/GAME BOY	KWS (Network)
-	29	MISSION OF LOVE	Jason Donovan (Polydor)
-	30	HEAVEN SENT	INXS (Mercury)
14	31	MAKE LOVE LIKE A MAN	Def Leppard (Bludgeon Riffola)
13	32	CRUCIFY	Tori Amos (East West)
31	33	SHAME SHAME SHAME	Sinitta (Arista)
-	34	YOU'RE THE ONE FOR ME, FATTY	Morrissey (His Master's Voice)
-	35	HORROR HEAD	Curve (Anxious)
36	36	THE ONE	Elton John (Rocket)
18	37	GOOD STUFF	B-52s (Reprise)
-	38	SLEEPING WITH THE LIGHTS ON	Curtis Stigers (Arista)
-	39	SEVEN	James (Fontana)
-	40	GOODBYE CRUEL WORLD	Shakespears Sister (London)
44	41	RAVE ALERT!	Praga Khan (Profile)
-	42	LOVE U MORE	Sunscreem (Sony Soho Square)
46	43	COME ON	DJ Seduction (ffrreedom)
-	44	I WANNA SING	Sabrina Johnston (East West)
45	45	ALL IWANT IS YOU	Bryan Adams (A&M)
-	46	SHINE ON	Degrees Of Motion (Esquire)
-	47	TREMELO SONG	Charlatans (Situation Two)
39	48	100%	Sonic Youth (DGC)
-	49	LIVE AND LEARN	Joe Public (Columbia)
-	50	ENTER YOUR FANTASY	Joey Negro (Ten)

25 July 1992

		Title	Artist (Label)
1	1	AIN'T NO DOUBT	Jimmy Nail (East West)
3	2	SESAME'S STREET	Smart Es (Suburban Base)
5	3	RHYTHM IS A DANCER	Snap (Logic)
2	4	I'LL BE THERE	Mariah Carey (Columbia)
8	5	SEXY MF	Prince & the New Power Generation (Paisley Park)
-	6	THIS USED TO BE MY PLAYGROUND	Madonna (Sire)
6	7	EVEN BETTER THAN THE REAL THING	U2 (Island)
4	8	ABBA-ESQUE	Erasure (Mute)
10	9	I DROVE ALL NIGHT	Roy Orbison (MCA)
-	10	WHO IS IT?	Michael Jackson (Epic)
11	11	A TRIP TO TRUMPTON	Urban Hype (Faze 2)
12	12	SHAKE YOUR HEAD	Was (Not Was) (Fontana)
15	13	LSI	Shamen (One Little Indian)
7	14	HAZARD	Richard Marx (Capitol)
16	15	DAMN I WISH I WAS YOUR LOVER	Sophie B Hawkins (Columbia)
14	16	UNCHAIN MY HEART	Joe Cocker (Capitol)
19	17	LIP SERVICE	Wet Wet Wet (Precious Organisation)
20	18	AIN'T NO MAN	Dina Carroll (A&M PM)
13	19	ONE SHINING MOMENT	Diana Ross (Capitol)
29	20	MISSION OF LOVE	Jason Donovan (Polydor)
45	21	ALL IWANT IS YOU	Bryan Adams (A&M)
30	22	HEAVEN SENT	INXS (Mercury)
27	23	AMIGOS PARA SIEMPRE (FRIENDS FOR LIFE)	Jose Carreras & Sarah Brightman (Really Useful)
-	24	LITHIUM	Nirvana (DGC)
25	25	BE MY DOWNFALL	Del Amitri (A&M)
9	26	DISAPPOINTED	Electronic (Parlophone)
-	27	JESUS HE KNOWS ME	Genesis (Virgin)
34	28	YOU'RE THE ONE FOR ME, FATTY	Morrissey (His Master's Voice)
-	29	FACE TO FACE	Siouxsie & the Banshees (Polydor)
-	30	YOUR MIRROR	Simply Red (Electric)
40	31	GOODBYE CRUEL WORLD	Shakespears Sister (London)
38	32	SLEEPING WITH THE LIGHTS ON	Curtis Stigers (Arista)
42	33	LOVE U MORE	Sunscreem (Sony Soho Square)
-	34	I LOVE YOU GOODBYE	Thomas Dolby (Virgin)
33	35	SHAME SHAME SHAME	Sinitta (Arista)
-	36	57 CHANNELS (AND NOTHIN' ON)	Bruce Springsteen (Columbia)
22	37	FROM HERE TO ETERNITY	Iron Maiden (EMI)
23	38	SOMETHING GOOD	Utah Saints (ffrr)
28	39	PLEASE DON'T GO/GAME BOY	KWS (Network)
24	40	TOO FUNKY	George Michael (Epic)
17	41	HEARTBEAT	Nick Berry (Columbia)
50	42	ENTER YOUR FANTASY	Joey Negro (Ten)
46	43	SHINE ON	Degrees Of Motion (Esquire)
-	44	WARM IT UP	Kris Kross (Columbia)
45	45	MOTHER DAWN	Blue Pearl (Big Life)
43	46	COME ON	DJ Seduction (ffrreedom)
-	47	GETTING IT RIGHT	Alison Limerick (Arista)
39	48	SEVEN	James (Fontana)
48	49	100%	Sonis Youth (DGC)
-	50	FULLTERM LOVE	Monie Love (Cooltempo)

1 August 1992

		Title	Artist (Label)
1	1	AIN'T NO DOUBT	Jimmy Nail (East West)
3	2	RHYTHM IS A DANCER	Snap (Logic)
6	3	THIS USED TO BE MY PLAYGROUND	Madonna (Sire)
2	4	SESAME'S STREET	Smart Es (Suburban Base)
5	5	SEXY MF	Prince & the New Power Generation (Paisley Park)
13	6	LSI	Shamen (One Little Indian)
12	7	SHAKE YOUR HEAD	Was (Not Was) (Fontana)
9	8	I DROVE ALL NIGHT	Roy Orbison (MCA)
10	9	WHO IS IT?	Michael Jackson (Epic)
4	10	I'LL BE THERE	Mariah Carey (Columbia)
15	11	DAMN I WISH I WAS YOUR LOVER	Sophie B Hawkins (Columbia)
11	12	A TRIP TO TRUMPTON	Urban Hype (Faze 2)
7	13	EVEN BETTER THAN THE REAL THING	U2 (Island)
24	14	LITHIUM	Nirvana (DGC)
-	15	ACHY BREAKY HEART	Billy Ray Cyrus (Mercury)
30	16	YOUR MIRROR	Simply Red (Electric)
8	17	ABBA-ESQUE	Erasure (Mute)
18	18	AIN'T NO MAN	Dina Carroll (A&M PM)
21	19	ALL IWANT IS YOU	Bryan Adams (A&M)
33	20	LOVE U MORE	Sunscreem (Sony Soho Square)
36	21	57 CHANNELS AND NOTHIN' ON	Bruce Springsteen (Columbia)
27	22	JESUS HE KNOWS ME	Genesis (Virgin)
17	23	LIP SERVICE	Wet Wet Wet (Precious Organisation)
23	24	AMIGOS PARA SIEMPRE (FRIENDS FOR LIFE)	Jose Carreras & Sarah Brightman (Really Useful)
14	25	HAZARD	Richard Marx (Capitol)
29	26	FACE TO FACE	Siouxsie & the Banshees (Polydor)
44	27	WARM IT UP	Kris Kross (Columbia)
16	28	UNCHAIN MY HEART	Joe Cocker (Capitol)
-	29	THOSE SIMPLE THINGS/DAYDREAM	Right Said Fred (Tug)
20	30	MISSION OF LOVE	Jason Donovan (Polydor)
-	31	HOW DO YOU DO!	Roxette (EMI)
31	32	GOODBYE CRUEL WORLD	Shakespears Sister (London)
-	33	JUST ANOTHER DAY	Jon Secada (SBK)
-	34	NO ONE CAN	Marillion (EMI)
-	35	SHOW YOU THE WAY TO GO	Dannii Minogue (MCA)
22	36	HEAVEN SENT	INXS (Mercury)
50	37	FULLTERM LOVE	Monie Love (Cooltempo)
19	38	ONE SHINING MOMENT	Diana Ross (Capitol)
-	39	BOOK OF PAGES	Enya (WEA)
-	40	DON'T LET IT GO TO YOUR HEAD	Brand New Heavies featuring N'Dea Davenport (Acid Jazz)
34	41	I LOVE YOU GOODBYE	Thomas Dolby (Virgin)
-	42	PEACE IN THE WORLD	Don-E (4th & Broadway)
-	43	RUNAWAY TRAIN	Elton John & Eric Clapton (Rocket)
25	44	BE MY DOWNFALL	Del Amitri (A&M)
28	45	YOU'RE THE ONE FOR ME, FATTY	Morrissey (His Master's Voice)
45	46	MOTHER DAWN	Blue Pearl (Big Life)
-	47	WISHING ON A STAR	Cover Girls (Epic)
26	48	DISAPPOINTED	Electronic (Parlophone)
-	49	SPANISH HORSES	Aztec Camera (WEA)
32	50	SLEEPING WITH THE LIGHTS ON	Curtis Stigers (Arista)

Jimmy Nail's entry at 29 was a temporary blip on the way to the top. That soulful face, that soulful voice. Never fails. Further down, Roy Orbison, the man with *the* heartbreaking voice, was back in the charts with *I Drove All Night*, while Joe Cocker contributed a Ray Charles classic *Unchain My Heart*. Prince was back to form. *Sexy MF* was available in two mixes – one with the real words, 'Sexy motherfucker'.

August 1992

8 August 1992

last week	this week	Title	Artist (Label)
1	1	AIN'T NO DOUBT	Jimmy Nail (East West)
2	2	RHYTHM IS A DANCER	Snap (Logic)
3	3	THIS USED TO BE MY PLAYGROUND	Madonna (Sire)
9	4	WHO IS IT?	Michael Jackson (Epic)
-	5	BARCELONA	Freddie Mercury & Montserrat Caballe (Polydor)
7	6	SHAKE YOUR HEAD	Was (Not Was) (Fontana)
6	7	LSI	Shamen (One Little Indian)
15	8	ACHY BREAKY HEART	Billy Ray Cyrus (Mercury)
8	9	I DROVE ALL NIGHT	Roy Orbison (MCA)
39	10	BOOK OF PAGES	Enya (WEA)
4	11	SESAME'S STREET	Smart Es (Suburban Base)
5	12	SEXY MF	Prince & the New Power Generation (Paisley Park)
29	13	THOSE SIMPLE THINGS/DAYDREAM	Right Said Fred (Tug)
11	14	DAMN I WISH I WAS YOUR LOVER	Sophie B Hawkins (Columbia)
22	15	JESUS HE KNOWS ME	Genesis (Virgin)
31	16	HOW DO YOU DO!	Roxette (EMI)
33	17	JUST ANOTHER DAY	Jon Secada (SBK)
14	18	LITHIUM	Nirvana (DGC)
27	19	WARM IT UP	Kris Kross (Columbia)
24	20	AMIGOS PARA SIEMPRE (FRIENDS FOR LIFE)	Jose Carreras & Sarah Brightman (Really Useful)
20	21	LOVE U MORE	Sunscreem (Sony Soho Square)
18	22	AIN'T NO MAN	Dina Carroll (A&M PM)
10	23	I'LL BE THERE	Mariah Carey (Columbia)
16	24	YOUR MIRROR	Simply Red (Electric)
12	25	A TRIP TO TRUMPTON	Urban Hype (Faze 2)
17	26	ABBA-ESQUE	Erasure (Mute)
-	27	SILENT LUCIDITY	Queensryche (EMI USA)
13	28	EVEN BETTER THAN THE REAL THING	U2 (Island)
21	29	57 CHANNELS (AND NOTHIN' ON)	Bruce Springsteen (Columbia)
34	30	NO ONE CAN	Marillion (EMI)
43	31	RUNAWAY TRAIN	Elton John & Eric Clapton (Rocket)
25	32	HAZARD	Richard Marx (Capitol)
-	33	LET ME TAKE YOU THERE	Betty Boo (WEA)
-	34	DON'T YOU WANT ME	Felix (deConstruction)
40	35	DON'T LET IT GO TO YOUR HEAD	Brand New Heavies featuring N'Dea Davenport (Acid Jazz)
-	36	IF YOU DON'T LOVE ME	Prefab Sprout (Kitchenware)
35	37	SHOW YOU THE WAY TO GO	Dannii Minogue (MCA)
-	38	MY GIRL	Madness (Virgin)
-	39	SWEETEST CHILD	Maria McKee featuring Youth (Geffen)
19	40	ALL I WANT IS YOU	Bryan Adams (A&M)
-	41	MR LOVERMAN	Shabba Ranks (Epic)
47	42	WISHING ON A STAR	Cover Girls (Epic)
37	43	FULLTERM LOVE	Monie Love (Cooltempo)
-	44	ROFO'S THEME	Rofo (PWL Continental)
23	45	LIP SERVICE	Wet Wet Wet (Precious Organisation)
26	46	FACE TO FACE	Siouxsie & the Banshees (Polydor)
-	47	DOES IT FEEL GOOD TO YOU	DJ Carl Cox (Perfecto)
28	48	UNCHAIN MY HEART	Joe Cocker (Capitol)
38	49	ONE SHINING MOMENT	Diana Ross (Capitol)
30	50	MISSION OF LOVE	Jason Donovan (Polydor)

15 August 1992

this week	Title	Artist (Label)
2	1	RHYTHM IS A DANCER	Snap (Logic)
5	2	BARCELONA	Freddie Mercury & Montserrat Caballe (Polydor)
1	3	AIN'T NO DOUBT	Jimmy Nail (East West)
8	4	ACHY BREAKY HEART	Billy Ray Cyrus (Mercury)
3	5	THIS USED TO BE MY PLAYGROUND	Madonna (Sire)
6	6	SHAKE YOUR HEAD	Was (Not Was) (Fontana)
10	7	BOOK OF PAGES	Enya (WEA)
17	8	JUST ANOTHER DAY	Jon Secada (SBK)
7	9	LSI	Shamen (One Little Indian)
9	10	I DROVE ALL NIGHT	Roy Orbison (MCA)
4	11	WHO IS IT?	Michael Jackson (Epic)
-	12	I FOUND HEAVEN	Take That (RCA)
16	13	HOW DO YOU DO!	Roxette (EMI)
34	14	DON'T YOU WANT ME	Felix (deConstruction)
-	15	THIS CHARMING MAN	Smiths (WEA)
13	16	THOSE SIMPLE THINGS/DAYDREAM	Right Said Fred (Tug)
15	17	JESUS HE KNOWS ME	Genesis (Virgin)
-	18	THE BEST THINGS IN LIFE ARE FREE	Luther Vandross & Janet Jackson (Perspective)
27	19	SILENT LUCIDITY	Queensryche (EMI USA)
-	20	BOING!	Wedding Present (RCA)
11	21	SESAME'S STREET	Smart Es (Suburban Base)
36	22	IF YOU DON'T LOVE ME	Prefab Sprout (Kitchenware)
19	23	WARM IT UP	Kris Kross (Columbia)
14	24	DAMN I WISH I WAS YOUR LOVER	Sophie B Hawkins (Columbia)
31	25	RUNAWAY TRAIN	Elton John & Eric Clapton (Rocket)
33	26	LET ME TAKE YOU THERE	Betty Boo (WEA)
-	27	LOW LIFE IN HIGH PLACES	Thunder (EMI)
38	28	MY GIRL	Madness (Virgin)
-	29	BAKER STREET	Undercover (PWL International)
12	30	SEXY MF	Prince & the New Power Generation (Paisley Park)
20	31	AMIGOS PARA SIEMPRE (FRIENDS FOR LIFE)	Jose Carreras & Sarah Brightman (Really Useful)
35	32	DON'T LET IT GO TO YOUR HEAD	Brand New Heavies featuring N'Dea Davenport (Acid Jazz)
41	33	MR LOVERMAN	Shabba Ranks (Epic)
18	34	LITHIUM	Nirvana (DGC)
22	35	AIN'T NO MAN	Dina Carroll (A&M PM)
-	36	A SMALL VICTORY	Faith No More (Slash)
23	37	I'LL BE THERE	Mariah Carey (Columbia)
-	38	THE MAGIC FRIEND	2 Unlimited (PWL Continental)
21	39	LOVE U MORE	Sunscreem (Sony Soho Square)
-	40	UH HUH OH YEH	Paul Weller (Go! Discs)
25	41	A TRIP TO TRUMPTON	Urban Hype (Faze 2)
-	42	PURPLE LOVE BALLOON	Cud (A&M)
47	43	DOES IT FEEL GOOD TO YOU	DJ Carl Cox (Perfecto)
26	44	ABBA-ESQUE	Erasure (Mute)
30	45	NO ONE CAN	Marillion (EMI)
37	46	SHOW YOU THE WAY TO GO	Dannii Minogue (MCA)
-	47	BREAKING THE GIRL	Red Hot Chili Peppers (Warner Bros.)
24	48	YOUR MIRROR	Simply Red (Electric)
39	49	SWEETEST CHILD	Maria McKee featuring Youth (Geffen)
-	50	GIVE HIM SOMETHING HE CAN FEEL	En Vogue (East West)

22 August 1992

last	this	Title	Artist (Label)
1	1	RHYTHM IS A DANCER	Snap (Logic)
2	2	BARCELONA	Freddie Mercury & Montserrat Caballe (Polydor)
4	3	ACHY BREAKY HEART	Billy Ray Cyrus (Mercury)
18	4	THE BEST THINGS IN LIFE ARE FREE	Luther Vandross & Janet Jackson (Perspective)
8	5	JUST ANOTHER DAY	Jon Secada (SBK)
3	6	AIN'T NO DOUBT	Jimmy Nail (East West)
15	7	THIS CHARMING MAN	Smiths (WEA)
29	8	BAKER STREET	Undercover (PWL International)
14	9	DON'T YOU WANT ME	Felix (deConstruction)
12	10	I FOUND HEAVEN	Take That (RCA)
5	11	THIS USED TO BE MY PLAYGROUND	Madonna (Sire)
6	12	SHAKE YOUR HEAD	Was (Not Was) (Fontana)
7	13	BOOK OF PAGES	Enya (WEA)
10	14	I DROVE ALL NIGHT	Roy Orbison (MCA)
26	15	LET ME TAKE YOU THERE	Betty Boo (WEA)
27	16	LOW LIFE IN HIGH PLACES	Thunder (EMI)
-	17	ROCK YOUR BABY	KWS (Network)
9	18	LSI	Shamen (One Little Indian)
-	19	WHAT KIND OF FOOL	Kylie Minogue (PWL International)
38	20	THE MAGIC FRIEND	2 Unlimited (PWL Continental)
13	21	HOW DO YOU DO!	Roxette (EMI)
17	22	JESUS HE KNOWS ME	Genesis (Virgin)
40	23	UH HUH OH YEH	Paul Weller (Go! Discs)
19	24	SILENT LUCIDITY	Queensryche (EMI USA)
36	25	A SMALL VICTORY	Faith No More (Slash)
22	26	IF YOU DON'T LOVE ME	Prefab Sprout (Kitchenware)
-	27	CRYING	Roy Orbison & kd lang (Virgin America)
33	28	MR LOVERMAN	Shabba Ranks (Epic)
31	29	AMIGOS PARA SIEMPRE (FRIENDS FOR LIFE)	Jose Carreras & Sarah Brightman (Really Useful)
-	30	HUMPIN' AROUND	Bobby Brown (MCA)
11	31	WHO IS IT?	Michael Jackson (Epic)
16	32	THOSE SIMPLE THINGS/DAYDREAM	Right Said Fred (Tug)
-	33	WALKING ON BROKEN GLASS	Annie Lennox (RCA)
28	34	MY GIRL	Madness (Virgin)
-	35	MY DESTINY	Lionel Richie (Motown)
-	36	THEN CAME YOU	Junior (MCA)
-	37	NEIGHBOR	Ugly Kid Joe (MCA)
24	38	DAMN I WISH I WAS YOUR LOVER	Sophie B Hawkins (Columbia)
-	39	REAL COOL WORLD	David Bowie (Warner Bros.)
21	40	SESAME'S STREET	Smart Es (Suburban Base)
42	41	PURPLE LOVE BALLOON	Cud (A&M)
47	42	BREAKING THE GIRL	Red Hot Chili Peppers (Warner Bros.)
23	43	WARM IT UP	Kris Kross (Columbia)
43	44	DOES IT FEEL GOOD TO YOU	DJ Carl Cox (Perfecto)
32	45	DON'T LET IT GO TO YOUR HEAD	Brand New Heavies featuring N'Dea Davenport (Acid Jazz)
-	46	GIVE IT UP	Wilson Phillips (SBK)
-	47	IN 4 CHOONS LATER	Rozalla (Pulse 8)
34	48	LITHIUM	Nirvana (DGC)
50	49	GIVE HIM SOMETHING HE CAN FEEL	En Vogue (East West)
-	50	HEAVEN OR HELL	Stranglers (China)

Blimey these Olympic Games come round a bit quick. Let's wheel out another 'operatic' number. Over to Freddie and Montserrat. Snap continued to pump out the hits – now in danger of becoming the most successful dance group of the lot. Undercover's house version of *Baker Street* did nearly as well as Gerry Rafferty's original. Paul Weller's first solo single moved up and Take That got bigger all the time.

August – September 1992

29 August 1992

last	this		
1	1	RHYTHM IS A DANCER	Snap (Logic)
3	2	ACHY BREAKY HEART	
			Billy Ray Cyrus (Mercury)
4	3	THE BEST THINGS IN LIFE ARE FREE	Luther
			Vandross & Janet Jackson (Perspective)
2	4	BARCELONA	
			Freddie Mercury & Montserrat Caballe (Polydor)
5	5	JUST ANOTHER DAY	Jon Secada (SBK)
8	6	BAKER STREET	
			Undercover (PWL International)
17	7	ROCK YOUR BABY	KWS (Network)
9	8	DON'T YOU WANT ME	Felix (deConstruction)
20	9	THE MAGIC FRIEND	
			2 Unlimited (PWL Continental)
10	10	I FOUND HEAVEN	Take That (RCA)
33	11	WALKING ON BROKEN GLASS	
			Annie Lennox (RCA)
27	12	CRYING Roy Orbison & kd lang (Virgin America)	
15	13	LET ME TAKE YOU THERE	Betty Boo (WEA)
7	14	THIS CHARMING MAN	Smiths (WEA)
6	15	AIN'T NO DOUBT	Jimmy Nail (East West)
19	16	WHAT KIND OF FOOL	
			Kylie Minogue (PWL International)
30	17	HUMPIN' AROUND	Bobby Brown (MCA)
11	18	THIS USED TO BE MY PLAYGROUND	
			Madonna (Sire)
35	19	MY DESTINY	Lionel Richie (Motown)
12	20	SHAKE YOUR HEAD	Was (Not Was) (Fontana)
23	21	UH HUH OH YEH	Paul Weller (Go! Discs)
16	22	LOW LIFE IN HIGH PLACES	Thunder (EMI)
-	23	TAKE THIS HEART	Richard Marx (Capitol)
-	24	SILENT ALL THESE YEARS	
			Tori Amos (East West)
36	25	THEN CAME YOU	Junior (MCA)
29	26	AMIGOS PARA SIEMPRE (FRIENDS FOR LIFE)	
			Jose Carreras & Sarah Brightman (Really Useful)
14	27	I DROVE ALL NIGHT	Roy Orbison (MCA)
21	28	HOW DO YOU DO!	Roxette (EMI)
25	29	A SMALL VICTORY	Faith No More (Slash)
13	30	BOOK OF PAGES	Enya (WEA)
37	31	NEIGHBOR	Ugly Kid Joe (MCA)
-	32	MOVIN' ON	Bananarama (London)
-	33	YOU LIED TO ME	Cathy Dennis (Polydor)
18	34	LSI	Shamen (One Little Indian)
46	35	GIVE IT UP	Wilson Phillips (SBK)
-	36	IT'S PROBABLY ME	
			Sting & Eric Clapton (A&M)
-	37	YOUTH GONE WILD/DELIVERING THE GOODS	
			Skid Row (Atlantic)
28	38	MR LOVERMAN	Shabba Ranks (Epic)
-	39	BULLETPROOF!	Pop Will Eat Itself (RCA)
-	40	LITTLE BLACK BOOK Belinda Carlisle (Offside)	
-	41	I NEED YOUR LOVIN'	Curiosity (Arista)
22	42	JESUS HE KNOWS ME	Genesis (Virgin)
26	43	IF YOU DON'T LOVE ME	
			Prefab Sprout (Kitchenware)
50	44	HEAVEN OR HELL	Stranglers (China)
-	45	HIGH	Hyper Go Go (deConstruction)
31	46	WHO IS IT?	Michael Jackson (Epic)
24	47	SILENT LUCIDITY	Queensryche (EMI USA)
-	48	SUMMER BREEZE	Geoffrey Williams (EMI)
-	49	DON'T BE CRUEL	Elvis Presley (RCA)
39	50	REAL COOL WORLD	
			David Bowie (Warner Bros.)

5 September 1992

1	1	RHYTHM IS A DANCER	Snap (Logic)
2	2	ACHY BREAKY HEART	
			Billy Ray Cyrus (Mercury)
6	3	BAKER STREET	
			Undercover (PWL International)
3	4	THE BEST THINGS IN LIFE ARE FREE	Luther
			Vandross & Janet Jackson (Perspective)
5	5	JUST ANOTHER DAY	Jon Secada (SBK)
7	6	ROCK YOUR BABY	KWS (Network)
11	7	WALKING ON BROKEN GLASS	
			Annie Lennox (RCA)
23	8	TAKE THIS HEART	Richard Marx (Capitol)
-	9	EBENEEZER GOODE Shamen (One Little Indian)	
12	10	CRYING Roy Orbison & kd lang (Virgin America)	
-	11	TOO MUCH LOVE WILL KILL YOU	
			Brian May (Parlophone)
19	12	MY DESTINY	Lionel Richie (Motown)
10	13	I FOUND HEAVEN	Take That (RCA)
8	14	DON'T YOU WANT ME	Felix (deConstruction)
13	15	LET ME TAKE YOU THERE	Betty Boo (WEA)
9	16	THE MAGIC FRIEND	
			2 Unlimited (PWL Continental)
16	17	WHAT KIND OF FOOL	
			Kylie Minogue (PWL International)
17	18	HUMPIN' AROUND	Bobby Brown (MCA)
4	19	BARCELONA	
			Freddie Mercury & Montserrat Caballe (Polydor)
15	20	AIN'T NO DOUBT	Jimmy Nail (East West)
32	21	MOVIN' ON	Bananarama (London)
24	22	SILENT ALL THESE YEARS	
			Tori Amos (East West)
40	23	LITTLE BLACK BOOK Belinda Carlisle (Offside)	
-	24	DANCING QUEEN	Abba (Polydor)
33	25	YOU LIED TO ME	Cathy Dennis (Polydor)
25	26	THEN CAME YOU	Junior (MCA)
-	27	REST IN PEACE	Extreme (A&M)
18	28	THIS USED TO BE MY PLAYGROUND	
			Madonna (Sire)
-	29	ALL SHOOK UP	Billy Joel (Epic)
37	30	YOUTH GONE WILD/DELIVERING THE GOODS	
			Skid Row (Atlantic)
-	31	BABY DON'T CRY	INXS (Mercury)
36	32	IT'S PROBABLY ME Sting & Eric Clapton (A&M)	
-	33	IT'S MY LIFE	Dr Alban (Arista)
31	34	NEIGHBOR	Ugly Kid Joe (MCA)
39	35	BULLETPROOF!	Pop Will Eat Itself (RCA)
-	36	DAS BOOT	U96 (M&G)
20	37	SHAKE YOUR HEAD	Was (Not Was) (Fontana)
21	38	UH HUH OH YEH	Paul Weller (Go! Discs)
41	39	I NEED YOUR LOVIN'	Curiosity (Arista)
-	40	HOUSE OF LOVE	E17 (London)
14	41	THIS CHARMING MAN	Smiths (WEA)
-	42	MOVING IN THE RIGHT DIRECTION	
			Pasadenas (Columbia)
-	43	WHAT GOD WANTS, PART 1	
			Roger Waters (Columbia)
22	44	LOW LIFE IN HIGH PLACES	Thunder (EMI)
49	45	DON'T BE CRUEL	Elvis Presley (RCA)
26	46	AMIGOS PARA SIEMPRE (FRIENDS FOR LIFE)	
			Jose Carreras & Sarah Brightman (Really Useful)
27	47	I DROVE ALL NIGHT	Roy Orbison (MCA)
45	48	HIGH	Hyper Go Go (deConstruction)
28	49	HOW DO YOU DO!	Roxette (EMI)
35	50	GIVE IT UP	Wilson Phillips (SBK)

12 September 1992

1	1	RHYTHM IS A DANCER	Snap (Logic)
3	2	BAKER STREET	
			Undercover (PWL International)
9	3	EBENEEZER GOODE Shamen (One Little Indian)	
2	4	ACHY BREAKY HEART	
			Billy Ray Cyrus (Mercury)
4	5	THE BEST THINGS IN LIFE ARE FREE	Luther
			Vandross & Janet Jackson (Perspective)
7	6	WALKING ON BROKEN GLASS	
			Annie Lennox (RCA)
11	7	TOO MUCH LOVE WILL KILL YOU	
			Brian May (Parlophone)
5	8	JUST ANOTHER DAY	Jon Secada (SBK)
8	9	TAKE THIS HEART	Richard Marx (Capitol)
6	10	ROCK YOUR BABY	KWS (Network)
-	11	JAM	Michael Jackson (Epic)
33	12	IT'S MY LIFE	Dr Alban (Arista)
12	13	MY DESTINY	Lionel Richie (Motown)
24	14	DANCING QUEEN	Abba (Polydor)
27	15	REST IN PEACE	Extreme (A&M)
10	16	CRYING Roy Orbison & kd lang (Virgin America)	
31	17	BABY DON'T CRY	INXS (Mercury)
40	18	HOUSE OF LOVE	E17 (London)
15	19	LET ME TAKE YOU THERE	Betty Boo (WEA)
14	20	DON'T YOU WANT ME	Felix (deConstruction)
23	21	LITTLE BLACK BOOK Belinda Carlisle (Offside)	
13	22	I FOUND HEAVEN	Take That (RCA)
18	23	HUMPIN' AROUND	Bobby Brown (MCA)
16	24	THE MAGIC FRIEND	
			2 Unlimited (PWL Continental)
36	25	DAS BOOT	U96 (M&G)
-	26	HOW SOON IS NOW?	Smiths (WEA)
21	27	MOVIN' ON	Bananarama (London)
17	28	WHAT KIND OF FOOL	
			Kylie Minogue (PWL International)
20	29	AIN'T NO DOUBT	Jimmy Nail (East West)
-	30	WHAT'S IN A WORD	Christians (Island)
25	31	YOU LIED TO ME	Cathy Dennis (Polydor)
29	32	ALL SHOOK UP	Billy Joel (Epic)
32	33	IT'S PROBABLY ME Sting & Eric Clapton (A&M)	
19	34	BARCELONA	
			Freddie Mercury & Montserrat Caballe (Polydor)
30	35	YOUTH GONE WILD/DELIVERING THE GOODS	
			Skid Row (Atlantic)
-	36	END OF THE ROAD	Boyz II Men (Motown)
-	37	SUCCESS HAS MADE A FAILURE OF OUR	
			HOME	Sinead O'Connor (Ensign)
-	38	HAVE YOU EVER NEEDED SOMEONE SO BAD	
			Def Leppard (Bludgeon Riffola)
39	39	ME AND MRS JONES Freddie Jackson (Capitol)	
47	40	BOOGIE NIGHTS	Sonia (Arista)
-	41	CRAZY LOVE	Ce Ce Peniston (A&M PM)
26	42	THEN CAME YOU	Junior (MCA)
-	43	MONSTER	L7 (Slash)
28	44	THIS USED TO BE MY PLAYGROUND	
			Madonna (Sire)
-	45	JUST LIKE A MAN	Del Amitri ((A&M)
22	46	SILENT ALL THESE YEARS	
			Tori Amos (East West)
-	47	I JUST WANT TO DANCE Daniel O'Donnell (ritz)	
-	48	DANCING QUEEN	Abracadabra (PWL)
43	49	WHAT GOD WANTS, PART 1	
			Roger Waters (Columbia)
39	50	I NEED YOUR LOVIN'	Curiosity (Arista)

Snap managed to see off Michael Jackson, Madonna, and now Billy Ray Cyrus. With all these Abba imitators around, the real thing had to come back in. Their grooviest single made Top Ten all over again.

More 1970s covers by Freddie Jackson and Sonia. It was all rave tunes in the Top Three on 12 September. Lots of heavy metal further down the chart. And Sting copied Elton by teaming up with Eric.

557

September – October 1992

19 September 1992

last week	this week	Entry
3	1	EBENEEZER GOODE Shamen (One Little Indian)
1	2	RHYTHM IS A DANCER Snap (Logic)
2	3	BAKER STREET Undercover (PWL International)
7	4	TOO MUCH LOVE WILL KILL YOU Brian May (Parlophone)
12	5	IT'S MY LIFE Dr Alban (Arista)
4	6	ACHY BREAKY HEART Billy Ray Cyrus (Mercury)
5	7	THE BEST THINGS IN LIFE ARE FREE Luther Vandross & Janet Jackson (Perspective)
11	8	JAM Michael Jackson (Epic)
6	9	WALKING ON BROKEN GLASS Annie Lennox (RCA)
14	10	DANCING QUEEN Abba (Polydor)
26	11	HOW SOON IS NOW? Smiths (WEA)
37	12	SUCCESS HAS MADE A FAILURE OF OUR HOME Sinead O'Connor (Ensign)
13	13	MY DESTINY Lionel Richie (Motown)
18	14	HOUSE OF LOVE E17 (London)
15	15	REST IN PEACE Extreme (A&M)
8	16	JUST ANOTHER DAY Jon Secada (SBK)
-	17	THEME FROM MASH (SUICIDE IS PAINLESS)/EVERYTHING I DO (I DO FOR YOU) Manic Street Preachers/Fatima Mansions (Columbia)
10	18	ROCK YOUR BABY KWS (Network)
9	19	TAKE THIS HEART Richard Marx (Capitol)
17	20	BABY DON'T CRY INXS (Mercury)
-	21	LOVESLAVE Wedding Present (RCA)
25	22	DAS BOOT U96 (M&G)
30	23	WHAT'S IN A WORD Christians (Island)
45	24	JUST LIKE A MAN Del Amitri ((A&M)
-	25	IRON LION ZION Bob Marley (Tuff Gong)
20	26	DON'T YOU WANT ME Felix (deConstruction)
38	27	HAVE YOU EVER NEEDED SOMEONE SO BAD Def Leppard (Bludgeon Riffola)
-	28	DIGGING IN THE DIRT Peter Gabriel (Real World)
21	29	LITTLE BLACK BOOK Belinda Carlisle (Offside)
16	30	CRYING Roy Orbison & kd lang (Virgin America)
36	31	END OF THE ROAD Boyz II Men (Motown)
-	32	THE CRYING GAME Boy George (Spaghetti)
-	33	THEY'RE HERE EMF (Parlophone)
39	34	ME AND MRS JONES Freddie Jackson (Capitol)
-	35	GENERATIONS Inspiral Carpets (Mute)
40	36	BOOGIE NIGHTS Sonia (Arista)
19	37	LET ME TAKE YOU THERE Betty Boo (WEA)
-	38	SLEEPING SATELLITE Tasmin Archer (EMI)
-	39	STINKIN' THINKIN' Happy Mondays (Factory)
27	40	MOVIN' ON Bananarama (London)
43	41	MONSTER L7 (Slash)
47	42	I JUST WANT TO DANCE Daniel O'Donnell (ritz)
49	43	WHAT GOD WANTS, PART 1 Roger Waters (Columbia)
24	44	THE MAGIC FRIEND 2 Unlimited (PWL Continental)
29	45	AIN'T NO DOUBT Jimmy Nail (East West)
33	46	IT'S PROBABLY ME Sting & Eric Clapton (A&M)
22	47	I FOUND HEAVEN Take That (RCA)
48	48	ALL SHOOK UP Billy Joel (Epic)
23	49	HUMPIN' AROUND Bobby Brown (MCA)
-	50	TELL IT LIKE IT T-I-IS B-52s (Reprise)

26 September 1992

last week	this week	Entry
1	1	EBENEEZER GOODE Shamen (One Little Indian)
5	2	IT'S MY LIFE Dr Alban (Arista)
3	3	BAKER STREET Undercover (PWL International)
2	4	RHYTHM IS A DANCER Snap (Logic)
25	5	IRON LION ZION Bob Marley (Tuff Gong)
4	6	TOO MUCH LOVE WILL KILL YOU Brian May (Parlophone)
17	7	THEME FROM MASH (SUICIDE IS PAINLESS)/EVERYTHING I DO (I DO FOR YOU) Manic Street Preachers/Fatima Mansions (Columbia)
7	8	THE BEST THINGS IN LIFE ARE FREE Luther Vandross & Janet Jackson (Perspective)
13	9	MY DESTINY Lionel Richie (Motown)
27	10	HAVE YOU EVER NEEDED SOMEONE SO BAD Def Leppard (Bludgeon Riffola)
14	11	HOUSE OF LOVE E17 (London)
8	12	JAM Michael Jackson (Epic)
31	13	END OF THE ROAD Boyz II Men (Motown)
32	14	THE CRYING GAME Boy George (Spaghetti)
12	15	SUCCESS HAS MADE A FAILURE OF OUR HOME Sinead O'Connor (Ensign)
38	16	SLEEPING SATELLITE Tasmin Archer (EMI)
17	17	JUST ANOTHER DAY Jon Secada (SBK)
11	18	HOW SOON IS NOW? Smiths (WEA)
24	19	JUST LIKE A MAN Del Amitri ((A&M)
9	20	WALKING ON BROKEN GLASS Annie Lennox (RCA)
28	21	DIGGING IN THE DIRT Peter Gabriel (Real World)
10	22	DANCING QUEEN Abba (Polydor)
6	23	ACHY BREAKY HEART Billy Ray Cyrus (Mercury)
-	24	JEREMY Pearl Jam (Epic)
20	25	BABY DON'T CRY INXS (Mercury)
-	26	FIRE/JERICHO Prodigy (XL)
34	27	ME AND MRS JONES Freddie Jackson (Capitol)
33	28	THEY'RE HERE EMF (Parlophone)
42	29	I JUST WANT TO DANCE Daniel O'Donnell (ritz)
26	30	DON'T YOU WANT ME Felix (deConstruction)
-	31	METAL MICKEY Suede (Nude)
35	32	GENERATIONS Inspiral Carpets (Mute)
23	33	WHAT'S IN A WORD Christians (Island)
-	34	IT'S ONLY NATURAL Crowded House (Capitol)
15	35	REST IN PEACE Extreme (A&M)
39	36	STINKIN' THINKIN' Happy Mondays (Factory)
19	37	TAKE THIS HEART Richard Marx (Capitol)
-	38	DO I HAVE TO SAY THE WORDS? Bryan Adams (A&M)
39	39	POSSESSED Vegas (RCA)
18	40	ROCK YOUR BABY KWS (Network)
22	41	DAS BOOT U96 (M&G)
-	42	I FEEL LOVE Messiah (Kickin)
-	43	STING ME Black Crowes (Def American)
-	44	FOR ALL TIME Catherine Zeta Jones (Columbia)
-	45	36D Beautiful South (Go! Discs)
29	46	RADICCIO Orbital (Internal)
47	47	LITTLE BLACK BOOK Belinda Carlisle (Offside)
-	48	PRESSURE DROP Izzy Stradlin (Geffen)
-	49	JUST RIGHT Soul II Soul (Ten)
-	50	CALIFORNIA HERE I COME Sophie B Hawkins (Columbia)

3 October 1992

last week	this week	Entry
1	1	EBENEEZER GOODE Shamen (One Little Indian)
2	2	IT'S MY LIFE Dr Alban (Arista)
5	3	IRON LION ZION Bob Marley (Tuff Gong)
16	4	SLEEPING SATELLITE Tasmin Archer (EMI)
7	5	THEME FROM MASH (SUICIDE IS PAINLESS)/EVERYTHING I DO (I DO FOR YOU) Manic Street Preachers/Fatima Mansions (Columbia)
3	6	BAKER STREET Undercover (PWL International)
4	7	RHYTHM IS A DANCER Snap (Logic)
26	8	FIRE/JERICHO Prodigy (XL)
9	9	MY DESTINY Lionel Richie (Motown)
6	10	TOO MUCH LOVE WILL KILL YOU Brian May (Parlophone)
13	11	END OF THE ROAD Boyz II Men (Motown)
14	12	THE CRYING GAME Boy George (Spaghetti)
10	13	HAVE YOU EVER NEEDED SOMEONE SO BAD Def Leppard (Bludgeon Riffola)
8	14	THE BEST THINGS IN LIFE ARE FREE Luther Vandross & Janet Jackson (Perspective)
-	15	DRIVE REM (Warner Bros.)
11	16	HOUSE OF LOVE E17 (London)
21	17	DIGGING IN THE DIRT Peter Gabriel (Real World)
38	18	DO I HAVE TO SAY THE WORDS? Bryan Adams (A&M)
42	19	I FEEL LOVE Messiah (Kickin)
29	20	I JUST WANT TO DANCE Daniel O'Donnell (ritz)
17	21	JUST ANOTHER DAY Jon Secada (SBK)
24	22	JEREMY Pearl Jam (Epic)
-	23	CONNECTED Stereo MC's (Gee Street)
34	24	IT'S ONLY NATURAL Crowded House (Capitol)
31	25	METAL MICKEY Suede (Nude)
-	26	I'M GONNA GET YOU Bizarre Inc featuring Angie Brown (Vinyl Solution)
27	27	MONEY LOVE Neneh Cherry (Circa)
-	28	GOODBYE Sundays (Parlophone)
39	29	POSSESSED Vegas (RCA)
20	30	WALKING ON BROKEN GLASS Annie Lennox (RCA)
-	31	ABBA-ESQUE – THE REMIXES Erasure (Mute)
49	32	JUST RIGHT Soul II Soul (Ten)
19	33	JUST LIKE A MAN Del Amitri ((A&M)
-	34	KEEP IT COMIN' (DANCE TILL YOU CAN'T DANCE NO MORE!) C&C Music Factory featuring Q Unique & Deborah Cooper (Columbia)
25	35	BABY DON'T CRY INXS (Mercury)
-	36	ALL THE WORLD LOVES LOVERS Prefab Sprout (kitchenware)
12	37	JAM Michael Jackson (Epic)
-	38	SOMETIMES LOVE JUST AIN'T ENOUGH Patty Smyth with Don Henley (MCA)
-	39	SENTINEL (SINGLE RESTRUCTURE) Mike Oldfield (Virgin)
-	40	ANARCHY IN THE UK Sex Pistols (Virgin)
-	41	GROOVIN' IN THE MIDNIGHT Maxi Priest (Ten)
44	42	FOR ALL TIME Catherine Zeta Jones (Columbia)
-	43	START ME UP Salt 'N' Pepa (ffrr)
-	44	I'M ON MY WAY Betty Boo (WEA)
36	45	STINKIN' THINKIN' Happy Mondays (Factory)
28	46	THEY'RE HERE EMF (Parlophone)
15	47	SUCCESS HAS MADE A FAILURE OF OUR HOME Sinead O'Connor (Ensign)
-	48	TETRIS Doctor Spin (Carpet)
18	49	HOW SOON IS NOW? Smiths (WEA)
-	50	LAURA Jimmy Nail (East West)

A merry-go-round in the Top Three, which remained rave-based. Brian May paid tribute to Freddie Mercury with a rather clumsily-titled single. Queen had first entered the NME singles chart 18 years earlier with *The Seven Seas Of Rhye*. Bob Marley charted posthumously this month with *Iron Lion Zion* a recording which was thought to be lost. Cover of the MASH theme was a little tongue in cheek.

October 1992

10 October 1992

1	1	EBEENEZER GOODE Shamen (One Little Indian)
4	2	SLEEPING SATELLITE Tasmin Archer (EMI)
2	3	IT'S MY LIFE Dr Alban (Arista)
11	4	END OF THE ROAD Boyz II Men (Motown)
3	5	IRON LION ZION Bob Marley (Tuff Gong)
15	6	DRIVE REM (Warner Bros.)
-	7	MY NAME IS PRINCE Prince & the New Power Generation (Paisley Park)
6	8	BAKER STREET Undercover (PWL International)
9	9	MY DESTINY Lionel Richie (Motown)
5	10	THEME FROM MASH (SUICIDE IS PAINLESS)/EVERYTHING I DO (I DO FOR YOU) Manic Street Preachers/Fatima Mansions (Columbia)
39	11	SENTINEL (SINGLE RESTRUCTURE) Mike Oldfield (Virgin)
8	12	FIRE/JERICHO Prodigy (XL)
10	13	TOO MUCH LOVE WILL KILL YOU Brian May (Parlophone)
7	14	RHYTHM IS A DANCER Snap (Logic)
27	15	MONEY LOVE Neneh Cherry (Circa)
-	16	LOVE SONG/ALIVE AND KICKING Simple Minds (Virgin)
38	17	SOMETIMES LOVE JUST AIN'T ENOUGH Patty Smyth with Don Henley (MCA)
26	18	I'M GONNA GET YOU featuring Angie Brown (Vinyl Solution)
-	19	A MILLION LOVE SONGS Take That (RCA)
19	20	I FEEL LOVE Messiah (Kickin)
-	21	NO ORDINARY LOVE Sade (Epic)
22	22	CONNECTED Stereo MC's (Gee Street)
48	23	TETRIS Doctor Spin (Carpet)
-	24	COULD'VE BEEN Billy Ray Cyrus (Mercury)
-	25	NOT SLEEPING AROUND Ned's Atomic Dustbin (Sony Soho Square)
24	26	IT'S ONLY NATURAL Crowded House (Capitol)
14	27	THE BEST THINGS IN LIFE ARE FREE Luther Vandross & Janet Jackson (Perspective)
16	28	HOUSE OF LOVE E17 (London)
-	29	ROADHOUSE MELODY Status Quo (Polydor)
12	30	THE CRYING GAME Boy George (Spaghetti)
40	31	ANARCHY IN THE UK Sex Pistols (Virgin)
13	32	HAVE YOU EVER NEEDED SOMEONE SO BAD Def Leppard (Bludgeon Riffola)
43	33	START ME UP Salt 'N' Pepa (ffrr)
20	34	I JUST WANT TO DANCE Daniel O'Donnell (ritz)
21	35	JUST ANOTHER DAY Jon Secada (SBK)
-	36	EXCITED M People (deConstruction)
-	37	(TAKE A LITTLE) PIECE OF MY HEART Erma Franklin (Epic)
34	38	KEEP IT COMIN' (DANCE TILL YOU CAN'T DANCE NO MORE!) C&C Music Factory featuring Q Unique & Deborah Cooper (Columbia)
-	39	SPECIAL KIND OF LOVE Dina Carroll (A&M PM)
18	40	DO I HAVE TO SAY THE WORDS? Bryan Adams (A&M)
-	41	PHASED UP All About Eve (MCA)
22	42	JEREMY Pearl Jam (Epic)
28	43	GOODBYE Sundays (Parlophone)
42	44	FOR ALL TIME Catherine Zeta Jones (Columbia)
25	45	METAL MICKEY Suede (Nude)
-	46	GYPSY WOMAN/PEACE Crystal Waters/Sabrina Johnston (Epic)
-	47	RADIO Shaky (Epic)
44	48	I'M ON MY WAY Betty Boo (WEA)
29	49	POSSESSED Vegas (RCA)
-	50	EVERYBODY WANTS HER Thunder (EMI)

17 October 1992

2	1	SLEEPING SATELLITE Tasmin Archer (EMI)
1	2	EBEENEZER GOODE Shamen (One Little Indian)
4	3	END OF THE ROAD Boyz II Men (Motown)
3	4	IT'S MY LIFE Dr Alban (Arista)
7	5	MY NAME IS PRINCE Prince & the New Power Generation (Paisley Park)
16	6	LOVE SONG/ALIVE AND KICKING Simple Minds (Virgin)
18	7	I'M GONNA GET YOU featuring Angie Brown (Vinyl Solution)
5	8	IRON LION ZION Bob Marley (Tuff Gong)
-	9	EROTICA Madonna (Maverick)
8	10	BAKER STREET Undercover (PWL International)
-	11	STICKY Wedding Present (RCA)
11	12	SENTINEL (SINGLE RESTRUCTURE) Mike Oldfield (Virgin)
9	13	MY DESTINY Lionel Richie (Motown)
19	14	A MILLION LOVE SONGS Take That (RCA)
-	15	ASSASSIN Orb (Big Life)
6	16	DRIVE REM (Warner Bros.)
17	17	SOMETIMES LOVE JUST AIN'T ENOUGH Patty Smyth with Don Henley (MCA)
-	18	A LETTER TO ELISE Cure (Fiction)
23	19	TETRIS Doctor Spin (Carpet)
-	20	DON'T YOU WANT ME Farm (End Product)
-	21	PERFECT MOTION Sunscreem (Sony Soho Square)
37	22	(TAKE A LITTLE) PIECE OF MY HEART Erma Franklin (Epic)
29	23	ROADHOUSE MELODY Status Quo (Polydor)
24	24	COULD'VE BEEN Billy Ray Cyrus (Mercury)
21	25	NO ORDINARY LOVE Sade (Epic)
-	26	HIGHWAY TO HELL (LIVE) AC/DC (Atco)
10	27	THEME FROM MASH (SUICIDE IS PAINLESS)/EVERYTHING I DO (I DO FOR YOU) Manic Street Preachers/Fatima Mansions (Columbia)
14	28	RHYTHM IS A DANCER Snap (Logic)
13	29	TOO MUCH LOVE WILL KILL YOU Brian May (Parlophone)
15	30	MONEY LOVE Neneh Cherry (Circa)
39	31	SPECIAL KIND OF LOVE Dina Carroll (A&M PM)
22	32	CONNECTED Stereo MC's (Gee Street)
36	33	EXCITED M People (deConstruction)
12	34	FIRE/JERICHO Prodigy (XL)
-	35	JUMP AROUND House Of Pain (XL)
47	36	RADIO Shaky (Epic)
-	37	AVENUE Saint Etienne (Heavenly)
27	38	THE BEST THINGS IN LIFE ARE FREE Luther Vandross & Janet Jackson (Perspective)
-	39	SHADES OF GREEN Mission (Vertigo)
-	40	LOVE ME DO Beatles (Parlophone)
25	41	NOT SLEEPING AROUND Ned's Atomic Dustbin (Sony Soho Square)
50	42	EVERYBODY WANTS HER Thunder (EMI)
-	43	GOOD ENOUGH Bobby Brown (MCA)
31	44	ANARCHY IN THE UK Sex Pistols (Virgin)
-	45	FAITHFUL Go West (Chrysalis)
20	46	I FEEL LOVE Messiah (Kickin)
33	47	START ME UP Salt 'N' Pepa (ffrr)
-	48	TRAMPS AND THIEVES Quireboys (Parlophone)
41	49	PHASED UP All About Eve (MCA)
35	50	JUST ANOTHER DAY Jon Secada (SBK)

24 October 1992

1	1	SLEEPING SATELLITE Tasmin Archer (EMI)
3	2	END OF THE ROAD Boyz II Men (Motown)
9	3	EROTICA Madonna (Maverick)
7	4	I'M GONNA GET YOU featuring Angie Brown (Vinyl Solution)
2	5	EBEENEZER GOODE Shamen (One Little Indian)
6	6	LOVE SONG/ALIVE AND KICKING Simple Minds (Virgin)
4	7	IT'S MY LIFE Dr Alban (Arista)
-	8	KEEP THE FAITH Bon Jovi (Jambco)
14	9	A MILLION LOVE SONGS Take That (RCA)
5	10	MY NAME IS PRINCE Prince & the New Power Generation (Paisley Park)
15	11	ASSASSIN Orb (Big Life)
19	12	TETRIS Doctor Spin (Carpet)
-	13	SKIN O' MY TEETH Megadeth (Capitol)
8	14	IRON LION ZION Bob Marley (Tuff Gong)
-	15	NOTHING TO FEAR Chris Rea (East West)
-	16	PEOPLE EVERYDAY Arrested Development (Cooltempo)
31	17	SPECIAL KIND OF LOVE Dina Carroll (A&M PM)
21	18	PERFECT MOTION Sunscreem (Sony Soho Square)
26	19	HIGHWAY TO HELL (LIVE) AC/DC (Atco)
13	20	MY DESTINY Lionel Richie (Motown)
10	21	BAKER STREET Undercover (PWL International)
17	22	SOMETIMES LOVE JUST AIN'T ENOUGH Patty Smyth with Don Henley (MCA)
12	23	SENTINEL (SINGLE RESTRUCTURE) Mike Oldfield (Virgin)
45	24	FAITHFUL Go West (Chrysalis)
-	25	IT WILL MAKE ME CRAZY Felix (deConstruction)
-	26	ERASURE-ISH Bjorn Again (M&G)
20	27	DON'T YOU WANT ME Farm (End Product)
22	28	(TAKE A LITTLE) PIECE OF MY HEART Erma Franklin (Epic)
-	29	ALWAYS TOMORROW Gloria Estefan (Epic)
-	30	NEVER SAW A MIRACLE Curtis Stigers (Arista)
-	31	THERE IS A LIGHT THAT NEVER GOES OUT Smiths (WEA)
24	32	COULD'VE BEEN Billy Ray Cyrus (Mercury)
23	33	ROADHOUSE MELODY Status Quo (Polydor)
18	34	A LETTER TO ELISE Cure (Fiction)
-	35	BE MY BABY Vanessa Paradis (Remark)
-	36	FEAR LOVES THIS PLACE (EP) Julian Cope (Island)
16	37	DRIVE REM (Warner Bros.)
36	38	RADIO Shaky (Epic)
33	39	EXCITED M People (deConstruction)
28	40	RHYTHM IS A DANCER Snap (Logic)
29	41	TOO MUCH LOVE WILL KILL YOU Brian May (Parlophone)
43	42	GOOD ENOUGH Bobby Brown (MCA)
11	43	STICKY Wedding Present (RCA)
44	44	EVERYBODY WANTS HER Thunder (EMI)
25	45	NO ORDINARY LOVE Sade (Epic)
35	46	JUMP AROUND House Of Pain (XL)
32	47	CONNECTED Stereo MC's (Gee Street)
-	48	LEAP OF FAITH Bruce Springsteen (Columbia)
38	49	THE BEST THINGS IN LIFE ARE FREE Luther Vandross & Janet Jackson (Perspective)
-	50	SHE'S PLAYING HARD TO GET Hi-Five (Jive)

The success of the Manic Street Preachers and others brought on the re-release of *Anarchy In The UK*. Still sounds really nasty. *(Take A Little) Piece Of My Heart* was in the repertoire of female soul and blues singers since the 1960s. The version by Erma Franklin (Aretha's sister) was used on a jeans advert. This Abba business was out of control with Bjorn Again now doing Erasure covers. Enough. Enough.

October – November 1992

31 October 1992

Last	This	Title — Artist (Label)
1	1	SLEEPING SATELLITE Tasmin Archer (EMI)
3	2	EROTICA Madonna (Maverick)
2	3	END OF THE ROAD Boyz II Men (Motown)
8	4	KEEP THE FAITH Bon Jovi (Jambco)
4	5	I'M GONNA GET YOU Bizarre Inc featuring Angie Brown (Vinyl Solution)
16	6	PEOPLE EVERYDAY Arrested Development (Cooltempo)
12	7	TETRIS Doctor Spin (Carpet)
9	8	A MILLION LOVE SONGS Take That (RCA)
7	9	IT'S MY LIFE Dr Alban (Arista)
-	10	RUN TO YOU Rage (Pulse 8)
25	11	IT WILL MAKE ME CRAZY Felix (deConstruction)
-	12	COLD Annie Lennox (RCA)
24	13	FAITHFUL Go West (Chrysalis)
15	14	NOTHING TO FEAR Chris Rea (East West)
31	15	THERE IS A LIGHT THAT NEVER GOES OUT Smiths (WEA)
5	16	EBENEEZER GOODE Shamen (One Little Indian)
6	17	LOVE SONG/ALIVE AND KICKING Simple Minds (Virgin)
28	18	(TAKE A LITTLE) PIECE OF MY HEART Erma Franklin (Epic)
-	19	MISERERE Zucchero with Luciano Pavarotti (London)
-	20	WHEREVER I MAY ROAM Metallica (Vertigo)
26	21	ERASURE-ISH Bjorn Again (M&G)
18	22	PERFECT MOTION Sunscreem (Sony Soho Square)
35	23	BE MY BABY Vanessa Paradis (Remark)
-	24	TO LOVE SOMEBODY Michael Bolton (Columbia)
29	25	ALWAYS TOMORROW Gloria Estefan (Epic)
10	26	MY NAME IS PRINCE Prince & the New Power Generation (Paisley Park)
27	27	DON'T YOU WANT ME Farm (End Product)
-	28	BOOM BOOM John Lee Hooker (Virgin)
21	29	BAKER STREET Undercover (PWL International)
-	30	SUPERMARIOLAND Ambassadors Of Funk featuring MC Mario (Living Beat)
-	31	TEETHGRINDER Therapy? (A&M)
11	32	ASSASSIN Orb (Big Life)
20	33	MY DESTINY Lionel Richie (Motown)
30	34	NEVER SAW A MIRACLE Curtis Stigers (Arista)
14	35	IRON LION ZION Bob Marley (Tuff Gong)
22	36	SOMETIMES LOVE JUST AIN'T ENOUGH Patty Smyth with Don Henley (MCA)
13	37	SKIN O' MY TEETH Megadeth (Capitol)
48	38	LEAP OF FAITH Bruce Springsteen (Columbia)
-	39	GIVE ME YOUR BODY Chippendales (XS Rhythm)
17	40	SPECIAL KIND OF LOVE Dina Carroll (A&M PM)
19	41	HIGHWAY TO HELL (LIVE) AC/DC (Atco)
-	42	LIBERATION Liberation (ZYX)
-	43	DO YOU BELIEVE IN US? John Secada (SPK)
-	44	I AM ONE WASP (Parlophone)
-	45	WOULD I LIE TO YOU? Charles & Eddie (Capitol)
23	46	SENTINEL (SINGLE RESTRUCTURE) Mike Oldfield (Virgin)
-	47	SO DAMN COOL Ugly Kid Joe (Mercury)
-	48	ARMCHAIR ANARCHIST Kingmaker (Scorch)
42	49	GOOD ENOUGH Bobby Brown (MCA)
32	50	COULD'VE BEEN Billy Ray Cyrus (Mercury)

7 November 1992

Last	This	Title — Artist (Label)
3	1	END OF THE ROAD Boyz II Men (Motown)
1	2	SLEEPING SATELLITE Tasmin Archer (EMI)
6	3	PEOPLE EVERYDAY Arrested Development (Cooltempo)
2	4	EROTICA Madonna (Maverick)
-	5	BOSS DRUM Shamen (One Little Indian)
5	6	I'M GONNA GET YOU Bizarre Inc featuring Angie Brown (Vinyl Solution)
4	7	KEEP THE FAITH Bon Jovi (Jambco)
-	8	WHO NEEDS LOVE (LIKE THAT) Erasure (Mute)
10	9	RUN TO YOU Rage (Pulse 8)
8	10	A MILLION LOVE SONGS Take That (RCA)
18	11	(TAKE A LITTLE) PIECE OF MY HEART Erma Franklin (Epic)
13	12	FAITHFUL Go West (Chrysalis)
11	13	IT WILL MAKE ME CRAZY Felix (deConstruction)
7	14	TETRIS Doctor Spin (Carpet)
24	15	TO LOVE SOMEBODY Michael Bolton (Columbia)
45	16	WOULD I LIE TO YOU? Charles & Eddie (Capitol)
23	17	BE MY BABY Vanessa Paradis (Remark)
30	18	SUPERMARIOLAND Ambassadors Of Funk featuring MC Mario (Living Beat)
28	19	BOOM BOOM John Lee Hooker (Virgin)
9	20	IT'S MY LIFE Dr Alban (Arista)
19	21	MISERERE Zucchero with Luciano Pavarotti (London)
-	22	HELLO (TURN YOUR RADIO ON) Shakespears Sister (London)
23	23	COLD Annie Lennox (RCA)
14	24	NOTHING TO FEAR Chris Rea (East West)
-	25	FREE YOUR MIND/GIVE HIM SOMETHING HE CAN FEEL En Vogue (East West)
-	26	TOO MUCH TOO YOUNG Little Angels (Polydor)
27	27	ALWAYS TOMORROW Gloria Estefan (Epic)
39	28	GIVE ME YOUR BODY Chippendales (XS Rhythm)
43	29	DO YOU BELIEVE IN US? John Secada (SPK)
27	30	DON'T YOU WANT ME Farm (End Product)
20	31	WHEREVER I MAY ROAM Metallica (Vertigo)
-	32	THE LAST SONG Elton John (Rocket)
-	33	QUEEN OF RAIN Roxette (EMI)
21	34	ERASURE-ISH Bjorn Again (M&G)
-	35	THE FRED EP Flowered Up/St Etienne /Rockingbirds (Heavenly)
17	36	LOVE SONG/ALIVE AND KICKING Simple Minds (Virgin)
15	37	THERE IS A LIGHT THAT NEVER GOES OUT Smiths (WEA)
29	38	BAKER STREET Undercover (PWL International)
22	39	PERFECT MOTION Sunscreem (Sony Soho Square)
33	40	MY DESTINY Lionel Richie (Motown)
31	41	TEETHGRINDER Therapy? (A&M)
-	42	DON'T STOP K-Klass (deConstruction)
16	43	EBENEEZER GOODE Shamen (One Little Indian)
34	44	NEVER SAW A MIRACLE Curtis Stigers (Arista)
-	45	HEARTBREAK RADIO Roy Orbison (Virgin America)
-	46	I'D DIE WITHOUT YOU PM Dawn (Gee Street)
38	47	LEAP OF FAITH Bruce Springsteen (Columbia)
42	48	VOULEZ VOUS Abba (Polydor)
42	49	LIBERATION Liberation (ZYX)
-	50	SWEAT (A LA LA LA LA LONG) Inner Circle (WEA)

14 November 1992

Last	This	Title — Artist (Label)
1	1	END OF THE ROAD Boyz II Men (Motown)
3	2	PEOPLE EVERYDAY Arrested Development (Cooltempo)
9	3	RUN TO YOU Rage (Pulse 8)
16	4	WOULD I LIE TO YOU? Charles & Eddie (Capitol)
5	5	BOSS DRUM Shamen (One Little Indian)
2	6	SLEEPING SATELLITE Tasmin Archer (EMI)
8	7	WHO NEEDS LOVE (LIKE THAT) Erasure (Mute)
18	8	SUPERMARIOLAND Ambassadors Of Funk featuring MC Mario (Living Beat)
17	9	BE MY BABY Vanessa Paradis (Remark)
-	10	THE QUEEN OF OUTER SPACE Wedding Present (RCA)
6	11	I'M GONNA GET YOU Bizarre Inc featuring Angie Brown (Vinyl Solution)
4	12	EROTICA Madonna (Maverick)
-	13	NEVER LET HER SLIP AWAY Undercover (PWL)
15	14	TO LOVE SOMEBODY Michael Bolton (Columbia)
11	15	(TAKE A LITTLE) PIECE OF MY HEART Erma Franklin (Epic)
22	16	HELLO (TURN YOUR RADIO ON) Shakespears Sister (London)
7	17	KEEP THE FAITH Bon Jovi (Jambco)
13	18	IT WILL MAKE ME CRAZY Felix (deConstruction)
10	19	A MILLION LOVE SONGS Take That (RCA)
-	20	I WILL ALWAYS LOVE YOU Whitney Houston (Arista)
12	21	FAITHFUL Go West (Chrysalis)
14	22	TETRIS Doctor Spin (Carpet)
-	23	STOP THE WORLD Extreme (A&M)
25	24	FREE YOUR MIND/GIVE HIM SOMETHING HE CAN FEEL En Vogue (East West)
21	25	MISERERE Zucchero with Luciano Pavarotti (London)
26	26	TOO MUCH TOO YOUNG Little Angels (Polydor)
32	27	THE LAST SONG Elton John (Rocket)
-	28	TASTE IT INXS (Mercury)
33	29	QUEEN OF RAIN Roxette (EMI)
19	30	BOOM BOOM John Lee Hooker (Virgin)
42	31	DON'T STOP K-Klass (deConstruction)
-	32	POING Rotterdam Termination Source (SEP)
20	33	IT'S MY LIFE Dr Alban (Arista)
29	34	DO YOU BELIEVE IN US? John Secada (SPK)
35	35	THE FRED EP Flowered Up/St Etienne /Rockingbirds (Heavenly)
46	36	I'D DIE WITHOUT YOU PM Dawn (Gee Street)
-	37	WHO PAYS THE PIPER? Gary Clail/On-U Sound System (Perfecto)
45	38	HEARTBREAK RADIO Roy Orbison (Virgin America)
31	39	WHEREVER I MAY ROAM Metallica (Vertigo)
28	40	GIVE ME YOUR BODY Chippendales (XS Rhythm)
27	41	ALWAYS TOMORROW Gloria Estefan (Epic)
50	42	SWEAT (A LA LA LA LA LONG) Inner Circle (WEA)
-	43	GET ME Dinosaur Jr (Warner Bros.)
30	44	DON'T YOU WANT ME Farm (End Product)
-	45	OH NO NOT MY BABY Cher (Geffen)
-	46	LOVE CAN MOVE MOUNTAINS Celine Dion (Epic)
23	47	COLD Annie Lennox (RCA)
24	48	NOTHING TO FEAR Chris Rea (East West)
-	49	BITCHES BREW Inspiral Carpets (Mute)
38	50	BAKER STREET Undercover (PWL International)

Accompanied by an awful lot of hype Madonna gave us the book, *Sex*, the video and the music. All very rude. Someone uncharitably wrote that she had become so powerful that none of her underlings dared to point out to her that crawling around with a cucumber in your rectum made you seem a bit of a prat. Pavarotti mania continued, and *Supermarioland* followed *Tetris* as a computer-game-inspired hit.

November – December 1992

21 November 1992

last week	this week		
4	1	WOULD I LIE TO YOU?	Charles & Eddie (Capitol)
1	2	END OF THE ROAD	Boyz II Men (Motown)
2	3	PEOPLE EVERYDAY	Arrested Development (Cooltempo)
13	4	NEVER LET HER SLIP AWAY	Undercover (PWL)
20	5	I WILL ALWAYS LOVE YOU	Whitney Houston (Arista)
9	6	BE MY BABY	Vanessa Paradis (Remark)
5	7	BOSS DRUM	Shamen (One Little Indian)
-	8	INVISIBLE TOUCH (LIVE)	Genesis (Virgin)
3	9	RUN TO YOU	Rage (Pulse 8)
-	10	MONTREUX (EP)	Simply Red (East West)
8	11	SUPERMARIOLAND	Ambassadors Of Funk featuring MC Mario (Living Beat)
16	12	HELLO (TURN YOUR RADIO ON)	Shakespears Sister (London)
14	13	TO LOVE SOMEBODY	Michael Bolton (Columbia)
-	14	TEMPTATION (REMIX)	Heaven 17 (Virgin)
7	15	WHO NEEDS LOVE (LIKE THAT)	Erasure (Mute)
6	16	SLEEPING SATELLITE	Tasmin Archer (EMI)
-	17	YESTERDAYS/NOVEMBER RAIN	Guns N' Roses (Geffen)
15	18	(TAKE A LITTLE) PIECE OF MY HEART	Erma Franklin (Epic)
28	19	TASTE IT	INXS (Mercury)
23	20	STOP THE WORLD	Extreme (A&M)
24	21	FREE YOUR MIND/GIVE HIM SOMETHING HE CAN FEEL	En Vogue (East West)
11	22	I'M GONNA GET YOU	Bizarre Inc featuring Angie Brown (Vinyl Solution)
27	23	THE LAST SONG	Elton John (Rocket)
32	24	POING	Rotterdam Termination Source (SEP)
19	25	A MILLION LOVE SONGS	Take That (RCA)
45	26	OH NO NOT MY BABY	Cher (Geffen)
37	27	WHO PAYS THE PIPER?	Gary Clail/On-U Sound System (Perfecto)
-	28	OUT OF SPACE	Prodigy (XL)
36	29	I'D DIE WITHOUT YOU	PM Dawn (Gee Street)
-	30	LET'S STAY TOGETHER	Pasadenas (Columbia)
-	31	GOLD	East 17 (London)
-	32	BACK TO THE LIGHT	Brian May (Parlophone)
-	33	THE CELTS	Enya (WEA)
-	34	HOW DOES IT FEEL? (THEME FROM TECHNO BLUES)	Electroset (ffrr)
-	35	EVERYTHING'S RUINED	Faith No More (Slash)
29	36	QUEEN OF RAIN	Roxette (EMI)
12	37	EROTICA	Madonna (Maverick)
-	38	IRRESISTIBLE	Cathy Dennis (Polydor)
-	39	IT'S YOU	EMF (Parlophone)
-	40	LOVE IS IN THE AIR	John Paul Young (Columbia)
17	41	KEEP THE FAITH	Bon Jovi (Jambco)
18	42	IT WILL MAKE ME CRAZY	Felix (deConstruction)
21	43	FAITHFUL	Go West (Chrysalis)
-	44	LITTLE BABY NOTHING	Manic Street Preachers (Columbia)
-	45	FUNKY GUITAR	TC 1992 (Union City Recordings)
31	46	DON'T STOP	K-Klass (deConstruction)
22	47	TETRIS	Doctor Spin (Carpet)
-	48	OUTSHINED	Soundgarden (A&M)
25	49	MISERERE	Zucchero with Luciano Pavarotti (London)
46	50	LOVE CAN MOVE MOUNTAINS	Celine Dion (Epic)

28 November 1992

last	this		
1	1	WOULD I LIE TO YOU?	Charles & Eddie (Capitol)
5	2	I WILL ALWAYS LOVE YOU	Whitney Houston (Arista)
4	3	NEVER LET HER SLIP AWAY	Undercover (PWL)
2	4	END OF THE ROAD	Boyz II Men (Motown)
3	5	PEOPLE EVERYDAY	Arrested Development (Cooltempo)
14	6	TEMPTATION (REMIX)	Heaven 17 (Virgin)
8	7	INVISIBLE TOUCH (LIVE)	Genesis (Virgin)
10	8	MONTREUX (EP)	Simply Red (East West)
6	9	BE MY BABY	Vanessa Paradis (Remark)
17	10	YESTERDAYS/NOVEMBER RAIN	Guns N' Roses (Geffen)
7	11	BOSS DRUM	Shamen (One Little Indian)
-	12	YOUR TOWN	Deacon Blue (Columbia)
28	13	OUT OF SPACE	Prodigy (XL)
9	14	RUN TO YOU	Rage (Pulse 8)
12	15	HELLO (TURN YOUR RADIO ON)	Shakespears Sister (London)
21	16	FREE YOUR MIND/GIVE HIM SOMETHING HE CAN FEEL	En Vogue (East West)
30	17	LET'S STAY TOGETHER	Pasadenas (Columbia)
11	18	SUPERMARIOLAND	Ambassadors Of Funk featuring MC Mario (Living Beat)
-	19	CELEBRATION	Kylie Minogue (PWL International)
18	20	(TAKE A LITTLE) PIECE OF MY HEART	Erma Franklin (Epic)
13	21	TO LOVE SOMEBODY	Michael Bolton (Columbia)
-	22	AS TIME GOES BY	Jason Donovan (Polydor)
-	23	THE IMPOSSIBLE DREAM	Carter The Unstoppable Sex Machine (Chrysalis)
32	24	BACK TO THE LIGHT	Brian May (Parlophone)
-	25	IF WE HOLD ON TOGETHER	Diana Ross (EMI)
39	26	IT'S YOU	EMF (Parlophone)
29	27	I'D DIE WITHOUT YOU	PM Dawn (Gee Street)
38	28	IRRESISTIBLE	Cathy Dennis (Polydor)
44	29	LITTLE BABY NOTHING	Manic Street Preachers (Columbia)
15	30	WHO NEEDS LOVE (LIKE THAT)	Erasure (Mute)
34	31	HOW DOES IT FEEL? (THEME FROM TECHNO BLUES)	Electroset (ffrr)
33	32	THE CELTS	Enya (WEA)
19	33	TASTE IT	INXS (Mercury)
26	34	OH NO NOT MY BABY	Cher (Geffen)
-	35	MORNING HAS BROKEN	Neil Diamond (Columbia)
35	36	EVERYTHING'S RUINED	Faith No More (Slash)
-	37	MAN ON THE MOON	REM (Warner Bros.)
31	38	GOLD	East 17 (London)
-	39	SLOW AND SEXY	Shabba Ranks featuring Johnny Gill (Columbia)
-	40	THE HARDER THEY COME	Madness (Go! Discs)
-	41	JUST WANNA KNOW/FE REAL	Maxi Priest (Ten)
-	42	GOD'S GREAT BANANA SKIN	Chris Rea (East West)
16	43	SLEEPING SATELLITE	Tasmin Archer (EMI)
22	44	I'M GONNA GET YOU	Bizarre Inc featuring Angie Brown (Vinyl Solution)
23	45	THE LAST SONG	Elton John (Rocket)
24	46	POING	Rotterdam Termination Source (SEP)
45	47	FUNKY GUITAR	TC 1992 (Union City Recordings)
40	48	LOVE, OH LOVE	Lionel Richie (Motown)
-	49	WHO CAN MAKE ME FEEL GOOD?	Bassheads (deConstruction)
-	50	CHAINS AROUND MY HEART	Richard Marx (Capitol)

5 December 1992

last	this		
2	1	I WILL ALWAYS LOVE YOU	Whitney Houston (Arista)
1	2	WOULD I LIE TO YOU?	Charles & Eddie (Capitol)
6	3	TEMPTATION (REMIX)	Heaven 17 (Virgin)
-	4	HEAL THE WORLD	Michael Jackson (Epic)
3	5	NEVER LET HER SLIP AWAY	Undercover (PWL)
4	6	END OF THE ROAD	Boyz II Men (Motown)
-	7	I STILL BELIEVE IN YOU	Cliff Richard (EMI)
-	8	WHO'S GONNA RIDE YOUR WILD HORSES	U2 (Island)
13	9	OUT OF SPACE	Prodigy (XL)
5	10	PEOPLE EVERYDAY	Arrested Development (Cooltempo)
8	11	MONTREUX (EP)	Simply Red (East West)
12	12	YOUR TOWN	Deacon Blue (Columbia)
10	13	YESTERDAYS/NOVEMBER RAIN	Guns N' Roses (Geffen)
-	14	TOM TRAUBERT'S BLUES (WALTZING MATILDA)	Rod Stewart (Warner Bros.)
19	15	CELEBRATION	Kylie Minogue (PWL International)
7	16	INVISIBLE TOUCH (LIVE)	Genesis (Virgin)
11	17	BOSS DRUM	Shamen (One Little Indian)
25	18	IF WE HOLD ON TOGETHER	Diana Ross (EMI)
37	19	MAN ON THE MOON	REM (Warner Bros.)
39	20	SLOW AND SEXY	Shabba Ranks featuring Johnny Gill (Columbia)
22	21	AS TIME GOES BY	Jason Donovan (Polydor)
9	22	BE MY BABY	Vanessa Paradis (Remark)
-	23	7	Prince & the New Power Generation (Paisley Park)
-	24	STEP IT UP	Stereo MC's (4th & Broadway)
14	25	RUN TO YOU	Rage (Pulse 8)
20	26	(TAKE A LITTLE) PIECE OF MY HEART	Erma Franklin (Epic)
-	27	CLOSE EVERY DOOR	Phillip Schofield (R'lly Useful)
16	28	FREE YOUR MIND/GIVE HIM SOMETHING HE CAN FEEL	En Vogue (East West)
17	29	LET'S STAY TOGETHER	Pasadenas (Columbia)
-	30	SO CLOSE	Dina Carroll (A&M PM)
50	31	CHAINS AROUND MY HEART	Richard Marx (Capitol)
28	32	IRRESISTIBLE	Cathy Dennis (Polydor)
23	33	THE IMPOSSIBLE DREAM	Carter The Unstoppable Sex Machine (Chrysalis)
24	34	BACK TO THE LIGHT	Brian May (Parlophone)
41	35	JUST WANNA KNOW/FE REAL	Maxi Priest (Ten)
26	36	IT'S YOU	EMF (Parlophone)
18	37	SUPERMARIOLAND	Ambassadors Of Funk featuring MC Mario (Living Beat)
-	38	INTACT	Ned's Atomic Dustbin (Furtive)
42	39	GOD'S GREAT BANANA SKIN	Chris Rea (East West)
-	40	LET ME BE YOUR UNDERWEAR	Club 69 (ffrr)
15	41	HELLO (TURN YOUR RADIO ON)	Shakespears Sister (London)
27	42	I'D DIE WITHOUT YOU	PM Dawn (Gee Street)
49	43	WHO CAN MAKE ME FEEL GOOD?	Bassheads (deConstruction)
29	44	LITTLE BABY NOTHING	Manic Street Preachers (Columbia)
-	45	MRS ROBINSON/BEING AROUND	Lemonheads (Atlantic)
21	46	TO LOVE SOMEBODY	Michael Bolton (Columbia)
-	47	SHE	Vegas (RCA)
48	48	LOVE, OH LOVE	Lionel Richie (Motown)
-	49	HOTEL ILLNESS	Black Crowes (Def American)
-	50	HOMOPHOBIC ASSHOLE	Senseless Things (Epic)

Whitney Houston got to the top in four leaps with the song from her movie debut *Bodyguard*, made with Kev Kostner. The song was later the subject of a court case when a woman who played it incessantly and at large volume was imprisoned for noise nuisance. Should have seen a psychiatrist. Cliff Richard entered in the Top Ten, while *Mrs Robinson* and *As Time Goes By*, among others, were duly revived.

December 1992

<table>
<tr><th>last week</th><th>this</th><th colspan="2">12 December 1992</th></tr>
</table>

last	this	12 December 1992		19 December 1992

12 December 1992

last	this	title	artist
1	1	I WILL ALWAYS LOVE YOU	Whitney Houston (Arista)
2	2	WOULD I LIE TO YOU?	Charles & Eddie (Capitol)
4	3	HEAL THE WORLD	Michael Jackson (Epic)
-	4	SLAM JAM	WWF Superstars (Arista)
-	5	COULD IT BE MAGIC	Take That (RCA)
14	6	TOM TRAUBERT'S BLUES (WALTZING MATILDA)	Rod Stewart (Warner Bros.)
7	7	I STILL BELIEVE IN YOU	Cliff Richard (EMI)
3	8	TEMPTATION (REMIX)	Heaven 17 (Virgin)
9	9	OUT OF SPACE	Prodigy (XL)
8	10	WHO'S GONNA RIDE YOUR WILD HORSES	U2 (Island)
-	11	IN MY DEFENCE	Freddie Mercury (Parlophone)
-	12	DEEPER AND DEEPER	Madonna (Maverick)
5	13	NEVER LET HER SLIP AWAY	Undercover (PWL)
18	14	IF WE HOLD ON TOGETHER	Diana Ross (EMI)
6	15	END OF THE ROAD	Boyz II Men (Motown)
11	16	MONTREUX (EP)	Simply Red (East West)
-	17	MEGAMIX	Boney M (Arista)
24	18	STEP IT UP	Stereo MC's (4th & Broadway)
30	19	SO CLOSE	Dina Carroll (A&M PM)
12	20	YOUR TOWN	Deacon Blue (Columbia)
10	21	PEOPLE EVERYDAY	Arrested Development (Cooltempo)
13	22	YESTERDAYS/NOVEMBER RAIN	Guns N' Roses (Geffen)
23	23	7	Prince & the New Power Generation (Paisley Park)
45	24	MRS ROBINSON/BEING AROUND	Lemonheads (Atlantic)
-	25	MIAMI HIT MIX	Gloria Estefan (Epic)
19	26	MAN ON THE MOON	REM (Warner Bros.)
17	27	BOSS DRUM	Shamen (One Little Indian)
15	28	CELEBRATION	Kylie Minogue (PWL International)
31	29	CHAINS AROUND MY HEART	Richard Marx (Capitol)
-	30	ONE IN TEN	808 State & UB40 (ZTT)
22	31	BE MY BABY	Vanessa Paradis (Remark)
-	32	RUMP SHAKER	Wreckx-N-Effect (MCA)
20	33	SLOW AND SEXY	Shabba Ranks featuring Johnny Gill (Columbia)
48	34	LET ME BE YOUR UNDERWEAR	Club 69 (ffrr)
27	35	CLOSE EVERY DOOR	Phillip Schofield (Really Useful)
-	36	IN BLOOM	Nirvana (Geffen)
16	37	INVISIBLE TOUCH (LIVE)	Genesis (Virgin)
-	38	HOLD BACK THE NIGHT	KWS (features guest vocals from the Trammps) (Network)
21	39	AS TIME GOES BY	Jason Donovan (Polydor)
-	40	AS ALWAYS	Secret Life (Cowboy)
25	41	RUN TO YOU	Rage (Pulse 8)
-	42	BROKEN WINGS	Network (Chrysalis)
26	43	(TAKE A LITTLE) PIECE OF MY HEART	Erma Franklin (Epic)
-	44	SANTA CLAUS IS COMING TO TOWN/LITTLE DRUMMER BOY	Bjorn Again (M&G)
38	45	INTACT	Ned's Atomic Dustbin (Furtive)
39	46	GOD'S GREAT BANANA SKIN	Chris Rea (East West)
28	47	FREE YOUR MIND/GIVE HIM SOMETHING HE CAN FEEL	En Vogue (East West)
-	48	LOVE'S ON EVERY CORNER	Dannii Minogue (MCA)
32	49	IRRESISTIBLE	Cathy Dennis (Polydor)
-	50	SUPERSONIC	HWA featuring Sonic The Hedgehog (Internal Affairs)

19 December 1992

last	this	title	artist
1	1	I WILL ALWAYS LOVE YOU	Whitney Houston (Arista)
3	2	HEAL THE WORLD	Michael Jackson (Epic)
2	3	WOULD I LIE TO YOU?	Charles & Eddie (Capitol)
4	4	SLAM JAM	WWF Superstars (Arista)
5	5	COULD IT BE MAGIC	Take That (RCA)
12	6	DEEPER AND DEEPER	Madonna (Maverick)
6	7	TOM TRAUBERT'S BLUES (WALTZING MATILDA)	Rod Stewart (Warner Bros.)
11	8	IN MY DEFENCE	Freddie Mercury (Parlophone)
7	9	I STILL BELIEVE IN YOU	Cliff Richard (EMI)
17	10	MEGAMIX	Boney M (Arista)
-	11	PHOREVER PEOPLE	Shamen (One Little Indian)
8	12	TEMPTATION (REMIX)	Heaven 17 (Virgin)
9	13	OUT OF SPACE	Prodigy (XL)
14	14	IF WE HOLD ON TOGETHER	Diana Ross (EMI)
18	15	STEP IT UP	Stereo MC's (4th & Broadway)
25	16	MIAMI HIT MIX	Gloria Estefan (Epic)
-	17	SOMEDAY (I'M COMING BACK)	Lisa Stansfield (Arista)
30	18	ONE IN TEN	808 State & UB40 (ZTT)
16	19	MONTREUX (EP)	Simply Red (East West)
19	20	SO CLOSE	Dina Carroll (A&M PM)
10	21	WHO'S GONNA RIDE YOUR WILD HORSES	U2 (Island)
13	22	NEVER LET HER SLIP AWAY	Undercover (PWL)
-	23	NO CHRISTMAS/STEP INTO CHRISTMAS	Wedding Present (RCA)
15	24	END OF THE ROAD	Boyz II Men (Motown)
24	25	MRS ROBINSON/BEING AROUND	Lemonheads (Atlantic)
-	26	ALIVE AND KICKING	Eastside Beat (ffrr)
20	27	YOUR TOWN	Deacon Blue (Columbia)
21	28	PEOPLE EVERYDAY	Arrested Development (Cooltempo)
36	29	IN BLOOM	Nirvana (Geffen)
22	30	YESTERDAYS/NOVEMBER RAIN	Guns N' Roses (Geffen)
26	31	MAN ON THE MOON	REM (Warner Bros.)
23	32	7	Prince & the New Power Generation (Paisley Park)
-	33	CERTAIN PEOPLE I KNOW	Morrissey (His Master's Voice)
-	34	MOTOWNPHILLY	Boyz II Men (Motown)
32	35	RUMP SHAKER	Wreckx-N-Effect (MCA)
29	36	CHAINS AROUND MY HEART	Richard Marx (Capitol)
-	37	IT'S A SHAME	Kris Kross (Ruff House)
-	38	WAY IN MY BRAIN (REMIX)	SL2 (XL)
-	39	WE ARE RAVING – THE ANTHEM	Slipstream (Boogie Food)
28	40	CELEBRATION	Kylie Minogue (PWL International)
38	41	HOLD BACK THE NIGHT	KWS (features guest vocals from the Trammps) (Network)
31	42	BE MY BABY	Vanessa Paradis (Remark)
44	43	SANTA CLAUS IS COMING TO TOWN/LITTLE DRUMMER BOY	Bjorn Again (M&G)
34	44	LET ME BE YOUR UNDERWEAR	Club 69 (ffrr)
42	45	BROKEN WINGS	Network (Chrysalis)
40	46	AS ALWAYS	Secret Life (Cowboy)
33	47	SLOW AND SEXY	Shabba Ranks featuring Johnny Gill (Columbia)
48	48	LOVE'S ON EVERY CORNER	Dannii Minogue (MCA)
-	49	STAY THIS WAY	Brand New Heavies (featuring N'Dea Davenport) (Acid Jazz)
-	50	TATTOO	Mike Oldfield (WEA)

Michael Jackson came up with his very own charity record – he's planning to save the world on his own. Take That went straight into the Top Ten but were outdone in the affections of British youth by a bunch of wrestlers. Boney M continued the 70s revival, while a hedgehog pitched in for computer addicts.

9 January 1993

last week	this week		
1	1	I WILL ALWAYS LOVE YOU	Whitney Houston (Arista)
2	2	HEAL THE WORLD	Michael Jackson (Epic)
5	3	COULD IT BE MAGIC	Take That (RCA)
11	4	PHOREVER PEOPLE	Shamen (One Little Indian)
3	5	WOULD I LIE TO YOU?	Charles & Eddie (Capitol)
10	6	MEGAMIX	Boney M (Arista)
16	7	MIAMI HIT MIX	Gloria Estefan (Epic)
17	8	SOMEDAY (I'M COMING BACK)	Lisa Stansfield (Arista)
4	9	SLAM JAM	WWF Superstars (Arista)
-	10	DRIFT AWAY	Michael Bolton (Columbia)
7	11	TOM TRAUBERT'S BLUES (WALTZING MATILDA)	Rod Stewart (Warner Bros.)
14	12	IF WE HOLD ON TOGETHER	Diana Ross (EMI)
6	13	DEEPER AND DEEPER	Madonna (Maverick)
8	14	IN MY DEFENCE	Freddie Mercury (Parlophone)
34	15	MOTOWNPHILLY	Boyz II Men (Motown)
39	16	WE ARE RAVING – THE ANTHEM	Slipstream (Boogie Food)
9	17	I STILL BELIEVE IN YOU	Cliff Richard (EMI)
19	18	MONTREUX (EP)	Simply Red (East West)
-	19	ALL ALONE ON CHRISTMAS	Darlene Love (Arista)
15	20	STEP IT UP	Stereo MC's (4th & Broadway)
13	21	OUT OF SPACE	Prodigy (XL)
18	22	ONE IN TEN	808 State & UB40 (ZTT)
12	23	TEMPTATION (REMIX)	Heaven 17 (Virgin)
25	24	MRS ROBINSON/BEING AROUND	Lemonheads (Atlantic)
-	25	THE THOUGHT OF IT	Louie Louie (Hardback)
26	26	ALIVE AND KICKING	Eastside Beat (ffrr)
38	27	WAY IN MY BRAIN (REMIX)	SL2 (XL)
20	28	SO CLOSE	Dina Carroll (A&M PM)
50	29	TATTOO	Mike Oldfield (WEA)
24	30	END OF THE ROAD	Boyz II Men (Motown)
-	31	ARRANGED MARRIAGE	Apache Indian (Island)
37	32	IT'S A SHAME	Kris Kross (Ruff House)
29	33	IN BLOOM	Nirvana (Geffen)
-	34	IF I EVER FALL IN LOVE	Shai (MCA)
22	35	NEVER LET HER SLIP AWAY	Undercover (PWL)
-	36	I GOT MY EDUCATION	Uncanny Alliance (A&M PM)
28	37	PEOPLE EVERYDAY	Arrested Development (Cooltempo)
49	38	STAY THIS WAY	Brand New Heavies featuring N'Dea Davenport) (Acid Jazz)
21	39	WHO'S GONNA RIDE YOUR WILD HORSES	U2 (Island)
30	40	YESTERDAYS/NOVEMBER RAIN	Guns N' Roses (Geffen)
-	41	SHE'S GOT THAT VIBE	R Kelly & Public Announcement (Jive)
41	42	HOLD BACK THE NIGHT	KWS (features guest vocals from the Trampps) (Network)
-	43	TELEVISION, THE DRUG OF THE NATION	Disposable Heroes Of Hiphoprisy (4th & Broadway)
-	44	ACHY BREAKY HEART	Alvin & the Chipmunks (with Billy Ray Cyrus) (Chipmunk)
33	45	CERTAIN PEOPLE I KNOW	Morrissey (His Master's Voice)
43	46	SANTA CLAUS IS COMING TO TOWN/LITTLE DRUMMER BOY	Bjorn Again (M&G)
-	47	LOVE ME THE RIGHT WAY	Rapination featuring Kym Mazelle (Arista)
31	48	MAN ON THE MOON	REM (Warner Bros.)
-	49	IF YOU ASKED ME TO	Celine Dion (Epic)
27	50	YOUR TOWN	Deacon Blue (Columbia)

16 January 1993

1	1	I WILL ALWAYS LOVE YOU	Whitney Houston (Arista)
-	2	EXTERMINATE! Snap featuring Niki Harris (Arista)	
3	3	COULD IT BE MAGIC	Take That (RCA)
2	4	HEAL THE WORLD	Michael Jackson (Epic)
5	5	WOULD I LIE TO YOU?	Charles & Eddie (Capitol)
-	6	MR WENDAL/REVOLUTION	Arrested Development (Cooltempo)
-	7	I'M EASY/BE AGGRESSIVE (LIVE)	Faith No More (Slash)
4	8	PHOREVER PEOPLE	Shamen (One Little Indian)
-	9	THE DEVIL YOU KNOW	Jesus Jones (Food)
-	10	WOMANKIND	Little Angels (Polydor)
7	11	MIAMI HIT MIX	Gloria Estefan (Epic)
-	12	GET THE GIRL! KILL THE BADDIES!	Pop Will Eat Itself (RCA)
8	13	SOMEDAY (I'M COMING BACK)	Lisa Stansfield (Arista)
-	14	BROKEN ENGLISH	Sunscreem (Sony Soho Square)
15	15	STEAM	Peter Gabriel (Real World)
6	16	MEGAMIX	Boney M (Arista)
-	17	AFTER ALL	The Frank & Walters (Setanta)
20	18	STEP IT UP	Stereo MC's (4th & Broadway)
21	19	OUT OF SPACE	Prodigy (XL)
9	20	SLAM JAM	WWF Superstars (Arista)
-	21	DOGS OF LUST	The The (Epic)
13	22	DEEPER AND DEEPER	Madonna (Maverick)
-	23	HOPE OF DELIVERANCE	Paul McCartney (Parlophone)
12	24	IF WE HOLD ON TOGETHER	Diana Ross (EMI)
-	25	LIFE OF SURPRISES	Prefab Sprout (Columbia)
-	26	THE LOVE I LOST	West End ftring Sylvia (PWL Int)
-	27	YOU TALK TOO MUCH	Sultans of Ping FC (Rhythm King)
-	28	IT'S GONNA BE A LOVELY DAY Soul System introducing Michelle Visage (Arista)	
31	29	ARRANGED MARRIAGE	Apache Indian (Island)
-	30	GIVE IT UP, TURN IT LOOSE	En Vogue (East West America)
16	31	WE ARE RAVING – THE ANTHEM	Slipstream (Boogie Food)
15	32	MOTOWNPHILLY	Boyz II Men (Motown)
10	33	DRIFT AWAY	Michael Bolton (Columbia)
18	34	MONTREUX (EP)	Simply Red (East West)
22	35	ONE IN TEN	808 State & UB40 (ZTT)
-	36	MANY RIVERS TO CROSS – LIVE FROM THE MIRAGE	Cher (Geffen)
24	37	MRS ROBINSON/BEING AROUND	Lemonheads (Atlantic)
23	38	TEMPTATION (REMIX)	Heaven 17 (Virgin)
37	39	PEOPLE EVERYDAY	Arrested Development (Cooltempo)
-	40	WHAT YOU WON'T DO FOR LOVE	Go West (Chrysalis)
11	41	TOM TRAUBERT'S BLUES (WALTZING MATILDA)	Rod Stewart (Warner Bros.)
-	42	LOVE SEES NO COLOUR	Farm (End Product)
14	43	IN MY DEFENCE	Freddie Mercury (Parlophone)
-	44	TIME FREQUENCY (EP)	Time Frequency (Internal Affairs)
30	45	END OF THE ROAD	Boyz II Men (Motown)
26	46	ALIVE AND KICKING	Eastside Beat (ffrr)
28	47	SO CLOSE	Dina Carroll (A&M PM)
34	48	IF I EVER FALL IN LOVE	Shai (MCA)
25	49	THE THOUGHT OF IT	Louie Louie (Hardback)
47	50	LOVE ME THE RIGHT WAY	Rapination featuring Kym Mazelle (Arista)

23 January 1993

1	1	I WILL ALWAYS LOVE YOU	Whitney Houston (Arista)
2	2	EXTERMINATE! Snap featuring Niki Harris (Arista)	
7	3	I'M EASY/BE AGGRESSIVE (LIVE)	Faith No More (Slash)
6	4	MR WENDAL/REVOLUTION	Arrested Development (Cooltempo)
3	5	COULD IT BE MAGIC	Take That (RCA)
26	6	THE LOVE I LOST	West End featuring Sylvia (PWL International)
-	7	WE ARE FAMILY '93 REMIXES	Sister Sledge (Atlantic)
4	8	HEAL THE WORLD	Michael Jackson (Epic)
15	9	STEAM	Peter Gabriel (Real World)
17	10	AFTER ALL	The Frank & Walters (Setanta)
5	11	WOULD I LIE TO YOU?	Charles & Eddie (Capitol)
9	12	THE DEVIL YOU KNOW	Jesus Jones (Food)
21	13	DOGS OF LUST	The The (Epic)
8	14	PHOREVER PEOPLE	Shamen (One Little Indian)
-	15	WHEN YOU WERE YOUNG	Del Amitri (A&M)
40	16	WHAT YOU WON'T DO FOR LOVE	Go West (Chrysalis)
-	17	SWEET HARMONY	Beloved (East West)
-	18	BED OF ROSES	Bon Jovi (Jambco)
-	19	OPEN YOUR MIND	Ursura (deConstruction)
29	20	ARRANGED MARRIAGE	Apache Indian (Island)
10	21	WOMANKIND	Little Angels (Polydor)
-	22	WOULD?	Alice In Cahins (Columbia)
28	23	IT'S GONNA BE A LOVELY DAY Soul System introducing Michelle Visage (Arista)	
12	24	GET THE GIRL! KILL THE BADDIES!	Pop Will Eat Itself (RCA)
18	25	STEP IT UP	Stereo MC's (4th & Broadway)
23	26	HOPE OF DELIVERANCE	Paul McCartney (Parlophone)
14	27	BROKEN ENGLISH	Sunscreem (Sony Soho Sq)
30	28	GIVE IT UP, TURN IT LOOSE	En Vogue (East West America)
13	29	SOMEDAY (I'M COMING BACK)	Lisa Stansfield (Arista)
25	30	LIFE OF SURPRISES	Prefab Sprout (Columbia)
36	31	MANY RIVERS TO CROSS – LIVE FROM THE MIRAGE	Cher (Geffen)
11	32	MIAMI HIT MIX	Gloria Estefan (Epic)
19	33	OUT OF SPACE	Prodigy (XL)
24	34	IF WE HOLD ON TOGETHER	Diana Ross (EMI)
22	35	DEEPER AND DEEPER	Madonna (Maverick)
27	36	YOU TALK TOO MUCH	Sultans of Ping FC (Rhythm King)
31	37	WE ARE RAVING – THE ANTHEM	Slipstream (Boogie Food)
-	38	SAVING FOREVER FOR YOU	Shanice (Giant)
-	39	OPEN SESAME	Leila K (Polydor)
-	40	MUSIC	Fargetta & Anne-Marie Smith (Parlophone)
-	41	FEED THE TREE	Belly (4AD)
44	42	TIME FREQUENCY (EP)	Time Frequency (Internal Affairs)
50	43	LOVE ME THE RIGHT WAY	Rapination featuring Kym Mazelle (Arista)
-	44	SPIRITUAL HIGH	Moodswings (Arista)
45	45	ONE IN TEN	808 State & UB40 (ZTT)
37	46	MRS ROBINSON/BEING AROUND	Lemonheads (Atlantic)
42	47	LOVE SEES NO COLOUR	Farm (End Product)
16	48	MEGAMIX	Boney M (Arista)
-	49	PLEASE SIR	Martyn Joseph (Epic)
32	50	MOTOWNPHILLY	Boyz II Men (Motown)

Asian ragga arrived in the shape of Apache Indian, while Whitney Houston went on and on – preventing the consistently successful Snap from getting another Number One. The Chipmunks decided we hadn't had enough of *Achy Breaky Heart*. Darlene Love, of *White Christmas* fame, made it into the festive chart again.

January – February 1993

30 January 1993

Last	This	Title / Artist (Label)
1	1	I WILL ALWAYS LOVE YOU Whitney Houston (Arista)
2	2	EXTERMINATE! Snap featuring Niki Harris (Arista)
6	3	THE LOVE I LOST West End featuring Sylvia (PWL International)
3	4	I'M EASY/BE AGGRESSIVE (LIVE) Faith No More (Slash)
7	5	WE ARE FAMILY '93 REMIXES Sister Sledge (Atlantic)
-	6	ORDINARY WORLD Duran Duran (Parlophone)
-	7	NO LIMIT 2 Unlimited (PWL Continental)
17	8	SWEET HARMONY Beloved (East West)
4	9	MR WENDAL/REVOLUTION Arrested Development (Cooltempo)
5	10	COULD IT BE MAGIC Take That (RCA)
18	11	BED OF ROSES Bon Jovi (Jambco)
19	12	OPEN YOUR MIND Ursura (deConstruction)
9	13	STEAM Peter Gabriel (Real World)
-	14	INDEPENDENCE Lulu (Dome)
16	15	WHAT YOU WON'T DO FOR LOVE Go West (Chrysalis)
-	16	DEEP East 17 (London)
-	17	HEAVEN IS Def Leppard (Bludgeon Riffola)
-	18	SANCTUARY MCMXCIII Cult (Beggars Banquet)
8	19	HEAL THE WORLD Michael Jackson (Epic)
-	20	IF I CAN'T CHANGE YOUR MIND Sugar (Creation)
15	21	WHEN YOU WERE YOUNG Del Amitri (A&M)
20	22	ARRANGED MARRIAGE Apache Indian (Island)
14	23	PHOREVER PEOPLE Shamen (One Little Indian)
11	24	WOULD I LIE TO YOU? Charles & Eddie (Capitol)
-	25	START CHOPPIN' Dinosaur Jr (blanco y negro)
26	26	HOPE OF DELIVERANCE Paul McCartney (Parlophone)
10	27	AFTER ALL The Frank & Walters (Setanta)
23	28	IT'S GONNA BE A LOVELY DAY Soul System introducing Michelle Visage (Arista)
-	29	LOVE MAKES NO SENSE Alexander O'Neal (Tabu)
39	30	OPEN SESAME Leila K (Polydor)
13	31	DOGS OF LUST The The (Epic)
-	32	HIP HOP HOORAY Naughty By Nature (Big Life)
25	33	STEP IT UP Stereo MC's (4th & Broadway)
43	34	LOVE ME THE RIGHT WAY Rapination featuring Kym Mazelle (Arista)
-	35	SOFT TOP, HARD SHOULDER Chris Rea (East West)
-	36	REVIVAL Martine Girault (ffrr)
40	37	MUSIC Fargetta & Anne-Marie Smith (Parlophone)
12	38	THE DEVIL YOU KNOW Jesus Jones (Food)
-	39	THINGS CAN ONLY GET BETTER D-Ream (Magnet)
-	40	I WANNA BE IN LOVE AGAIN Beijing Spring (MCA)
29	41	SOMEDAY (I'M COMING BACK) Lisa Stansfield (Arista)
21	42	WOMANKIND Little Angels (Polydor)
22	43	WOULD? Alice In Cahins (Columbia)
28	44	GIVE IT UP, TURN IT LOOSE En Vogue (East West America)
24	45	GET THE GIRL! KILL THE BADDIES! Pop Will Eat Itself (RCA)
33	46	OUT OF SPACE Prodigy (XL)
47	47	PHOTOGRAPH OF MARY Trey Lopez (Epic)
41	48	FEED THE TREE Belly (4AD)
-	49	WE SAIL ON THE STORMY WATERS Gary Clark (Circa)
27	50	BROKEN ENGLISH Sunscreem (Sony Soho Square)

6 February 1993

Last	This	Title / Artist (Label)
1	1	I WILL ALWAYS LOVE YOU Whitney Houston (Arista)
3	2	THE LOVE I LOST West End featuring Sylvia (PWL International)
7	3	NO LIMIT 2 Unlimited (PWL Continental)
2	4	EXTERMINATE! Snap featuring Niki Harris (Arista)
6	5	ORDINARY WORLD Duran Duran (Parlophone)
-	6	HOW CAN I LOVE YOU MORE (REMIXES) M People (deConstruction)
8	7	SWEET HARMONY Beloved (East West)
5	8	WE ARE FAMILY '93 REMIXES Sister Sledge (Atlantic)
4	9	I'M EASY/BE AGGRESSIVE (LIVE) Faith No More (Slash)
14	10	INDEPENDENCE Lulu (Dome)
17	11	HEAVEN IS Def Leppard (Bludgeon Riffola)
12	12	OPEN YOUR MIND Ursura (deConstruction)
16	13	DEEP East 17 (London)
9	14	MR WENDAL/REVOLUTION Arrested Development (Cooltempo)
11	15	BED OF ROSES Bon Jovi (Jambco)
-	16	TRAGIC COMIC Extreme (A&M)
10	17	COULD IT BE MAGIC Take That (RCA)
18	18	SANCTUARY MCMXCIII Cult (Beggars Banquet)
-	19	ANGEL John Secada (SBK)
-	20	ALL YOU NEED IS LOVE Tom Jones (Childline)
13	21	STEAM Peter Gabriel (Real World)
-	22	VIENNA Ultravox (Chrysalis)
34	23	LOVE ME THE RIGHT WAY Rapination featuring Kym Mazelle (Arista)
-	24	THE GREAT PRETENDER Freddie Mercury (Parlophone)
15	25	WHAT YOU WON'T DO FOR LOVE Go West (Chrysalis)
-	26	I LIFT MY CUP Gloworm (Pulse 8)
-	27	FALLING Cathy Dennis (Polydor)
29	28	LOVE MAKES NO SENSE Alexander O'Neal (Tabu)
26	29	HOPE OF DELIVERANCE Paul McCartney (Parlophone)
-	30	SWEET THING Mick Jagger (Atlantic)
39	31	THINGS CAN ONLY GET BETTER D-Ream (Magnet)
24	32	WOULD I LIE TO YOU? Charles & Eddie (Capitol)
23	33	PHOREVER PEOPLE Shamen (One Little Indian)
-	34	I WANNA STAY WITH YOU Undercover (PWL International)
28	35	IT'S GONNA BE A LOVELY DAY Soul System introducing Michelle Visage (Arista)
49	36	WE SAIL ON THE STORMY WATERS Gary Clark (Circa)
25	37	START CHOPPIN' Dinosaur Jr (blanco y negro)
30	38	OPEN SESAME Leila K (Polydor)
35	39	SOFT TOP, HARD SHOULDER Chris Rea (East West)
21	40	WHEN YOU WERE YOUNG Del Amitri (A&M)
-	41	CONFETTI (REMIX)/ MY DRUG BUDDY Lemonheads (Atlantic)
19	42	HEAL THE WORLD Michael Jackson (Epic)
22	43	ARRANGED MARRIAGE Apache Indian (Island)
47	44	PHOTOGRAPH OF MARY Trey Lopez (Epic)
36	45	REVIVAL Martine Girault (ffrr)
32	46	HIP HOP HOORAY Naughty By Nature (Big Life)
40	47	I WANNA BE IN LOVE AGAIN Beijing Spring (MCA)
20	48	IF I CAN'T CHANGE YOUR MIND Sugar (Creation)
-	49	I WANT YOU Sophie B Hawkins (Columbia)
37	50	MUSIC Fargetta & Anne-Marie Smith (Parlophone)

13 February 1993

Last	This	Title / Artist (Label)
1	1	I WILL ALWAYS LOVE YOU Whitney Houston (Arista)
3	2	NO LIMIT 2 Unlimited (PWL Continental)
-	3	LITTLE BIRD/LOVE SONG FOR A VAMPIRE Annie Lennox (RCA)
2	4	THE LOVE I LOST West End featuring Sylvia (PWL International)
5	5	ORDINARY WORLD Duran Duran (Parlophone)
13	6	DEEP East 17 (London)
6	7	HOW CAN I LOVE YOU MORE (REMIXES) M People (deConstruction)
4	8	EXTERMINATE! Snap featuring Niki Harris (Arista)
7	9	SWEET HARMONY Beloved (East West)
-	10	STAIRWAY TO HEAVEN Rolf Harris (Vertigo)
10	11	INDEPENDENCE Lulu (Dome)
16	12	TRAGIC COMIC Extreme (A&M)
12	13	OPEN YOUR MIND Ursura (deConstruction)
22	14	VIENNA Ultravox (Chrysalis)
8	15	WE ARE FAMILY '93 REMIXES Sister Sledge (Atlantic)
-	16	YOU'RE IN A BAD WAY Saint Etienne (Heavenly)
-	17	A BETTER MAN Thunder (EMI)
-	18	IF I EVER LOSE MY FAITH IN YOU Sting (A&M)
9	19	I'M EASY/BE AGGRESSIVE (LIVE) Faith No More (Slash)
-	20	WILL WE BE LOVERS Deacon Blue (Columbia)
19	21	ANGEL John Secada (SBK)
11	22	HEAVEN IS Def Leppard (Bludgeon Riffola)
34	23	I WANNA STAY WITH YOU Undercover (PWL International)
30	24	SWEET THING Mick Jagger (Atlantic)
-	25	STAND Poison (Capitol)
15	26	BED OF ROSES Bon Jovi (Jambco)
14	27	MR WENDAL/REVOLUTION Arrested Development (Cooltempo)
20	28	ALL YOU NEED IS LOVE Tom Jones (Childline)
-	29	BEAUTIFUL GIRL INXS (Mercury)
26	30	I LIFT MY CUP Gloworm (Pulse 8)
31	31	THINGS CAN ONLY GET BETTER D-Ream (Magnet)
36	32	WE SAIL ON THE STORMY WATERS Gary Clark (Circa)
27	33	FALLING Cathy Dennis (Polydor)
17	34	COULD IT BE MAGIC Take That (RCA)
18	35	SANCTUARY MCMXCIII Cult (Beggars Banquet)
-	36	AN EMOTIONAL TIME Hothouse Flowers (London)
23	37	LOVE ME THE RIGHT WAY Rapination featuring Kym Mazelle (Arista)
24	38	THE GREAT PRETENDER Freddie Mercury (Parlophone)
-	39	7:7 EXPANSION System 7 (Big Life)
21	40	STEAM Peter Gabriel (Real World)
29	41	HOPE OF DELIVERANCE Paul McCartney (Parlophone)
-	42	HOW CAN YOU TELL ME IT'S OVER Lorraine Cato (Columbia)
28	43	LOVE MAKES NO SENSE Alexander O'Neal (Tabu)
25	44	WHAT YOU WON'T DO FOR LOVE Go West (Chrysalis)
-	45	I SEE YOUR SMILE Gloria Estefan (Epic)
33	46	PHOREVER PEOPLE Shamen (One Little Indian)
32	47	WOULD I LIE TO YOU? Charles & Eddie (Capitol)
-	48	PRESSURE Billy Ocean (Jive)
-	49	TAKE IT FROM ME Girlfriend (Arista)
41	50	CONFETTI (REMIX)/ MY DRUG BUDDY Lemonheads (Atlantic)

The last chart in January brought Duran Duran back into the Top Ten after a long lay off, together with 2 Unlimited – lyrics 'No No No No No Lyrics' (repeat).

Lulu went 'house' and made the chart thirty years on from *Shout*. She's managed to hit the Top Ten in each of the last 4 decades. What happened to the Luvvers?

20 February 1993

Last	This	Title / Artist (Label)
-	1	WHY CAN'T I WAKE UP WITH YOU? Take That (RCA)
2	2	NO LIMIT 2 Unlimited (PWL Continental)
3	3	LITTLE BIRD/LOVE SONG FOR A VAMPIRE Annie Lennox (RCA)
-	4	I'M EVERY WOMAN Whitney Houston (Arista)
1	5	I WILL ALWAYS LOVE YOU Whitney Houston (Arista)
4	6	THE LOVE I LOST West End featuring Sylvia (PWL International)
6	7	DEEP East 17 (London)
10	8	STAIRWAY TO HEAVEN Rolf Harris (Vertigo)
5	9	ORDINARY WORLD Duran Duran (Parlophone)
7	10	HOW CAN I LOVE YOU MORE (REMIXES) M People (deConstruction)
18	11	IF I EVER LOSE YOU FAITH IN YOU Sting (A&M)
9	12	SWEET HARMONY Beloved (East West)
-	13	ARE YOU GONNA GO MY WAY Lenny Kravitz (Virgin)
8	14	EXTERMINATE! Snap featuring Niki Harris (Arista)
17	15	A BETTER MAN Thunder (EMI)
13	16	OPEN YOUR MIND Ursura (deConstruction)
14	17	VIENNA Ultravox (Chrysalis)
16	18	YOU'RE IN A BAD WAY Saint Etienne (Heavenly)
29	19	BEAUTIFUL GIRL INXS (Mercury)
-	20	RUBY TUESDAY Rod Stewart (Warner Bros.)
11	21	INDEPENDENCE Lulu (Dome)
-	22	THE SIDEWINDER SLEEPS TONITE REM (Warner Bros.)
21	23	ANGEL John Secada (SBK)
-	24	OH CAROLINA Shaggy (Greensleeves)
12	25	TRAGIC COMIC Extreme (A&M)
-	26	GROUND LEVEL Stereo MC's (4th & Broadway)
-	27	SAD BUT TRUE Metallica (Virgin)
15	28	WE ARE FAMILY '93 REMIXES Sister Sledge (Atlantic)
-	29	HERE COMES THE WAR New Model Army (Epic)
20	30	WILL WE BE LOVERS Deacon Blue (Columbia)
-	31	LOVE HURTS Peter Polycarpou (EMI)
19	32	I'M EASY/BE AGGRESSIVE (LIVE) Faith No More (Slash)
25	33	STAND Poison (Capitol)
-	34	TELL ME WHY Genesis (Virgin)
-	35	THE NAMELESS ONE Wendy James (MCA)
-	36	LEAVE IT ALONE Living Colour (Epic)
30	37	I LIFT MY CUP Gloworm (Pulse 8)
27	38	MR WENDAL/REVOLUTION Arrested Development (Cooltempo)
-	39	IN YOUR CARE Tasmin Archer (EMI)
31	40	THINGS CAN ONLY GET BETTER D-Ream (Magnet)
36	41	AN EMOTIONAL TIME Hothouse Flowers (London)
23	42	I WANNA STAY WITH YOU Undercover (PWL International)
28	43	ALL YOU NEED IS LOVE Tom Jones (Childline)
24	44	SWEET THING Mick Jagger (Atlantic)
-	45	ALL THIS LOVE I'M GIVING Music & Mystery (KTDA)
37	46	LOVE ME THE RIGHT WAY Rapination featuring Kym Mazelle (Arista)
-	47	NYC (CAN YOU BELIEVE THIS CITY?) Charles & Eddie (Stateside)
-	48	FOR WHAT IT'S WORTH Oui 3 (MCA)
22	49	HEAVEN IS Def Leppard (Bludgeon Riffola)
26	50	BED OF ROSES Bon Jovi (Jambco)

27 February 1993

Last	This	Title / Artist (Label)
1	1	WHY CAN'T I WAKE UP WITH YOU? Take That (RCA)
2	2	NO LIMIT 2 Unlimited (PWL Continental)
3	3	LITTLE BIRD/LOVE SONG FOR A VAMPIRE Annie Lennox (RCA)
4	4	I'M EVERY WOMAN Whitney Houston (Arista)
-	5	I FEEL YOU Depeche Mode (Mute)
-	6	GIVE IN TO ME Michael Jackson (Epic)
7	7	DEEP East 17 (London)
5	8	I WILL ALWAYS LOVE YOU Whitney Houston (Arista)
13	9	ARE YOU GONNA GO MY WAY Lenny Kravitz (Virgin)
6	10	THE LOVE I LOST West End featuring Sylvia (PWL International)
8	11	STAIRWAY TO HEAVEN Rolf Harris (Vertigo)
9	12	ORDINARY WORLD Duran Duran (Parlophone)
24	13	OH CAROLINA Shaggy (Greensleeves)
20	14	RUBY TUESDAY Rod Stewart (Warner Bros.)
22	15	THE SIDEWINDER SLEEPS TONITE REM (Warner Bros.)
10	16	HOW CAN I LOVE YOU MORE (REMIXES) M People (deConstruction)
11	17	IF I EVER LOSE MY FAITH IN YOU Sting (A&M)
39	18	IN YOUR CARE Tasmin Archer (EMI)
-	19	STICK IT OUT Right Said Fred & Friends (Tug)
12	20	SWEET HARMONY Beloved (East West)
48	21	FOR WHAT IT'S WORTH Oui 3 (MCA)
18	22	YOU'RE IN A BAD WAY Saint Etienne (Heavenly)
19	23	BEAUTIFUL GIRL INXS (Mercury)
26	24	GROUND LEVEL Stereo MC's (4th & Broadway)
16	25	OPEN YOUR MIND Ursura (deConstruction)
-	26	THIS TIME Dina Carroll (A&M PM)
27	27	SAD BUT TRUE Metallica (Virgin)
-	28	TOOK MY LOVE Bizarre Inc featuring Angie Brown (Vinyl Solution)
31	29	LOVE HURTS Peter Polycarpou (EMI)
14	30	EXTERMINATE! Snap featuring Niki Harris (Arista)
-	31	TELL ME WHY Genesis (Virgin)
23	32	ANGEL John Secada (SBK)
-	33	IN THE STILL OF THE NITE (I'LL REMEMBER) Boyz II Men (Motown)
35	34	THE NAMELESS ONE Wendy James (MCA)
-	35	REMINISCE Mary J Blige (Motown)
36	36	KILLING IN THE NAME Rage Against The Machine (Epic)
17	37	VIENNA Ultravox (Chrysalis)
47	38	NYC (CAN YOU BELIEVE THIS CITY?) Charles & Eddie (Stateside)
15	39	A BETTER MAN Thunder (EMI)
30	40	WILL WE BE LOVERS Deacon Blue (Columbia)
-	41	BROTHER LOUIE Quireboys (Parlophone)
-	42	HARVEST MOON Neil Young (Reprise)
-	43	WALK Pantera (Atlantic)
29	44	HERE COMES THE WAR New Model Army (Epic)
36	45	LEAVE IT ALONE Living Colour (Epic)
-	46	NIGHT BOAT TO CAIRO Madness (Virgin)
21	47	INDEPENDENCE Lulu (Dome)
28	48	WE ARE FAMILY '93 REMIXES Sister Sledge (Atlantic)
41	49	AN EMOTIONAL TIME Hothouse Flowers (London)
-	50	MY 16TH APOLOGY Shakespears Sister (London)

6 March 1993

Last	This	Title / Artist (Label)
2	1	NO LIMIT 2 Unlimited (PWL Continental)
3	2	LITTLE BIRD/LOVE SONG FOR A VAMPIRE Annie Lennox (RCA)
9	3	ARE YOU GONNA GO MY WAY Lenny Kravitz (Virgin)
1	4	WHY CAN'T I WAKE UP WITH YOU? Take That (RCA)
-	5	ANIMAL NITRATE Suede (Nude)
6	6	GIVE IN TO ME Michael Jackson (Epic)
5	7	I FEEL YOU Depeche Mode (Mute)
4	8	I'M EVERY WOMAN Whitney Houston (Arista)
-	9	PUSS/OH, THE GUILT Jesus Lizard/Nirvana (Touch 'N' Go)
7	10	DEEP East 17 (London)
-	11	BAD GIRL Madonna (Maverick)
12	12	OH CAROLINA Shaggy (Greensleeves)
-	13	RE:EVOLUTION Shamen with Terence McKenna (One Little Indian)
19	14	STICK IT OUT Right Said Fred & Friends (Tug)
14	15	RUBY TUESDAY Rod Stewart (Warner Bros.)
10	16	THE LOVE I LOST West End featuring Sylvia (PWL International)
18	17	IN YOUR CARE Tasmin Archer (EMI)
8	18	I WILL ALWAYS LOVE YOU Whitney Houston (Arista)
12	19	ORDINARY WORLD Duran Duran (Parlophone)
20	20	CONSTANT CRAVING kd lang (Sire)
15	21	THE SIDEWINDER SLEEPS TONITE REM (Warner Bros.)
16	22	HOW CAN I LOVE YOU MORE (REMIXES) M People (deConstruction)
-	23	I PUT A SPELL ON YOU Bryan Ferry (Virgin)
-	24	WONDERFUL Runrig (Chrysalis)
11	25	STAIRWAY TO HEAVEN Rolf Harris (Vertigo)
26	26	THIS TIME Dina Carroll (A&M PM)
21	27	FOR WHAT IT'S WORTH Oui 3 (MCA)
-	28	C'MON PEOPLE Paul McCartney (Parlophone)
33	29	IN THE STILL OF THE NITE (I'LL REMEMBER) Boyz II Men (Motown)
28	30	TOOK MY LOVE Bizarre Inc featuring Angie Brown (Vinyl Solution)
36	31	KILLING IN THE NAME Rage Against The Machine (Epic)
20	32	SWEET HARMONY Beloved (East West)
24	33	GROUND LEVEL Stereo MC's (4th & Broadway)
17	34	IF I EVER LOSE MY FAITH IN YOU Sting (A&M)
42	35	HARVEST MOON Neil Young (Reprise)
27	36	SAD BUT TRUE Metallica (Virgin)
25	37	OPEN YOUR MIND Ursura (deConstruction)
30	38	EXTERMINATE! Snap featuring Niki Harris (Arista)
38	39	NYC (CAN YOU BELIEVE THIS CITY?) Charles & Eddie (Stateside)
22	40	YOU'RE IN A BAD WAY Saint Etienne (Heavenly)
23	41	BEAUTIFUL GIRL INXS (Mercury)
-	42	WHENEVER YOU'RE NEAR Cher (Geffen)
-	43	SHE HITS ME 4 Of Us (Columbia)
-	44	DIRTY DEEDS DONE CHEAP (LIVE) AC/DC (Atco)
-	45	THE BOTTLE Christians (Island)
-	46	ALL ABOUT EVE Marxman (Talkin' Loud)
-	47	NEARLY LOST YOU Screaming Trees (Epic)
-	48	CONQUISTADOR Espiritu (Heavenly)
-	49	(WE DON'T NEED THIS) FASCIST GROOVE THING Heaven 17 (Virgin)
-	50	WHY DON'T YOU Rage (Pulse 8)

Take That went straight in at Number One for the first time. But record of the month was undoubtedly Rolf Harris's *Stairway To Heaven*. Postmodern culturally iconoclastic bearded painterly Australian TV personality, lays bare the soul of 70s rock. How does it affect you fellas? Ooooooooooh, it makes us wonder.

March 1993

13 March 1993

last	this	Title	Artist (Label)
1	1	NO LIMIT	2 Unlimited (PWL Continental)
6	2	GIVE IN TO ME	Michael Jackson (Epic)
2	3	LITTLE BIRD/LOVE SONG FOR A VAMPIRE	Annie Lennox (RCA)
12	4	OH CAROLINA	Shaggy (Greensleeves)
3	5	ARE YOU GONNA GO MY WAY	Lenny Kravitz (Virgin)
-	6	FEAR OF THE DARK (LIVE)	Iron Maiden (Epic)
11	7	BAD GIRL	Madonna (Maverick)
8	8	I'M EVERY WOMAN	Whitney Houston (Arista)
5	9	ANIMAL NITRATE	Suede (Nude)
14	10	STICK IT OUT	Right Said Fred & Friends (Tug)
7	11	I FEEL YOU	Depeche Mode (Mute)
10	12	DEEP	East 17 (London)
4	13	WHY CAN'T I WAKE UP WITH YOU?	Take That (RCA)
23	14	I PUT A SPELL ON YOU	Bryan Ferry (Virgin)
-	15	TOO YOUNG TO DIE	Jamiroquai (Sony Soho Square)
-	16	MR LOVERMAN	Shabba Ranks (Epic)
17	17	IN YOUR CARE	Tasmin Archer (EMI)
-	18	LOST IN MUSIC (SURE IS PURE REMIXES)	Sister Sledge (Atlantic)
16	19	THE LOVE I LOST	West End featuring Sylvia (PWL International)
20	20	CONSTANT CRAVING	kd lang (Sire)
15	21	RUBY TUESDAY	Rod Stewart (Warner Bros.)
-	22	LOOKING THROUGH PATIENT EYES	PM Dawn (Gee Street)
9	23	PUSS/OH, THE GUILT	Jesus Lizard/Nirvana (Touch 'N' Go)
-	24	ALONE	Big Country (Compulsion)
18	25	I WILL ALWAYS LOVE YOU	Whitney Houston (Arista)
26	26	THIS TIME	Dina Carroll (A&M PM)
-	27	CAT'S IN THE CRADLE	Ugly Kid Joe (Mercury)
-	28	BORN 2 BREED	Monie Love (Cooltempo)
-	29	IT STARTED WITH A KISS	Hot Chocolate (EMI)
29	30	IN THE STILL OF THE NITE (I'LL REMEMBER)	Boyz II Men (Motown)
-	31	LABOUR OF LOVE (REMIXES)	Hue& Cry (Circa)
27	32	FOR WHAT IT'S WORTH	Qui 3 (MCA)
19	33	ORDINARY WORLD	Duran Duran (Parlophone)
43	34	SHE HITS ME	4 Of Us (Columbia)
-	35	CRYSTAL CLEAR	Grid (Virgin)
13	36	RE:EVOLUTION	Shamen with Terence McKenna (One Little Indian)
31	37	KILLING IN THE NAME	Rage Against The Machine (Epic)
30	38	TOOK MY LOVE	Bizarre Inc featuring Angie Brown (Vinyl Solution)
-	39	HEART (DON'T CHANGE MY MIND)	Diana Ross (EMI)
-	40	INFORMER	Snow (East West America)
28	41	C'MON PEOPLE	Paul McCartney (Parlophone)
46	42	ALL ABOUT EVE	Marxman (Talkin' Loud)
45	43	THE BOTTLE	Christians (Island)
21	44	THE SIDEWINDER SLEEPS TONITE	REM (Warner Bros.)
24	45	WONDERFUL	Runrig (Chrysalis)
35	46	HARVEST MOON	Neil Young (Reprise)
-	47	GIVE IT TO YOU	Martha Wash (RCA)
39	48	NYC (CAN YOU BELIEVE THIS CITY?)	Charles & Eddie (Stateside)
22	49	HOW CAN I LOVE YOU MORE (REMIXES)	M People (deConstruction)
34	50	IF I EVER LOSE MY FAITH IN YOU	Sting (A&M)

20 March 1993

last	this	Title	Artist (Label)
4	1	OH CAROLINA	Shaggy (Greensleeves)
1	2	NO LIMIT	2 Unlimited (PWL Continental)
2	3	GIVE IN TO ME	Michael Jackson (Epic)
3	4	LITTLE BIRD/LOVE SONG FOR A VAMPIRE	Annie Lennox (RCA)
5	5	ARE YOU GONNA GO MY WAY	Lenny Kravitz (Virgin)
16	6	MR LOVERMAN	Shabba Ranks (Epic)
10	7	STICK IT OUT	Right Said Fred & Friends (Tug)
8	8	I'M EVERY WOMAN	Whitney Houston (Arista)
6	9	FEAR OF THE DARK (LIVE)	Iron Maiden (Epic)
7	10	BAD GIRL	Madonna (Maverick)
9	11	ANIMAL NITRATE	Suede (Nude)
27	12	CAT'S IN THE CRADLE	Ugly Kid Joe (Mercury)
40	13	INFORMER	Snow (East West America)
22	14	LOOKING THROUGH PATIENT EYES	PM Dawn (Gee Street)
15	15	TOO YOUNG TO DIE	Jamiroquai (Sony Soho Square)
20	16	CONSTANT CRAVING	kd lang (Sire)
18	17	LOST IN MUSIC (SURE IS PURE REMIXES)	Sister Sledge (Atlantic)
12	18	DEEP	East 17 (London)
24	19	ALONE	Big Country (Compulsion)
-	20	SHORTSHARPSHOCK (EP)	Therapy? (A&M)
14	21	I PUT A SPELL ON YOU	Bryan Ferry (Virgin)
19	22	THE LOVE I LOST	West End featuring Sylvia (PWL International)
13	23	WHY CAN'T I WAKE UP WITH YOU?	Take That (RCA)
17	24	IN YOUR CARE	Tasmin Archer (EMI)
31	25	LABOUR OF LOVE (REMIXES)	Hue& Cry (Circa)
-	26	WHEN I'M GOOD AND READY	Sybil (PWL International)
28	27	BORN 2 BREED	Monie Love (Cooltempo)
39	28	HEART (DON'T CHANGE MY MIND)	Diana Ross (EMI)
29	29	IT STARTED WITH A KISS	Hot Chocolate (EMI)
26	30	THIS TIME	Dina Carroll (A&M PM)
35	31	CRYSTAL CLEAR	Grid (Virgin)
-	32	THEM BONES	Alice In Chains (Columbia)
21	33	RUBY TUESDAY	Rod Stewart (Warner Bros.)
25	34	I WILL ALWAYS LOVE YOU	Whitney Houston (Arista)
-	35	REACH OUT I'LL BE THERE	Michael Bolton (Columbia)
11	36	I FEEL YOU	Depeche Mode (Mute)
-	37	THE MORNING PAPERS	Prince & the New Power Generation (Paisley Park)
-	38	MORE, MORE, MORE	Bananarama (London)
32	39	FOR WHAT IT'S WORTH	Qui 3 (MCA)
34	40	SHE HITS ME	4 Of Us (Columbia)
30	41	IN THE STILL OF THE NITE (I'LL REMEMBER)	Boyz II Men (Motown)
-	42	TIME TO GET UP	Liquid (XL)
42	43	ALL ABOUT EVE	Marxman (Talkin' Loud)
33	44	ORDINARY WORLD	Duran Duran (Parlophone)
37	45	KILLING IN THE NAME	Rage Against The Machine (Epic)
-	46	THE WOMAN I LOVE	Hollies (EMI)
-	47	ONE MORE CHANCE	Maxi Priest (Ten)
38	48	TOOK MY LOVE	Bizarre Inc featuring Angie Brown (Vinyl Solution)
43	49	THE BOTTLE	Christians (Island)
47	50	GIVE IT TO YOU	Martha Wash (RCA)

27 March 1993

last	this	Title	Artist (Label)
1	1	OH CAROLINA	Shaggy (Greensleeves)
2	2	NO LIMIT	2 Unlimited (PWL Continental)
6	3	MR LOVERMAN	Shabba Ranks (Epic)
13	4	INFORMER	Snow (East West America)
-	5	JUMP THEY SAY	David Bowie (Arista)
3	6	GIVE IN TO ME	Michael Jackson (Epic)
-	7	PEACE IN OUR TIME	Cliff Richard (EMI)
4	8	LITTLE BIRD/LOVE SONG FOR A VAMPIRE	Annie Lennox (RCA)
5	9	ARE YOU GONNA GO MY WAY	Lenny Kravitz (Virgin)
15	10	TOO YOUNG TO DIE	Jamiroquai (Sony Soho Square)
14	11	LOOKING THROUGH PATIENT EYES	PM Dawn (Gee Street)
7	12	STICK IT OUT	Right Said Fred & Friends (Tug)
8	13	I'M EVERY WOMAN	Whitney Houston (Arista)
-	14	YOUNG AT HEART	Bluebells (London)
12	15	CAT'S IN THE CRADLE	Ugly Kid Joe (Mercury)
16	16	CONSTANT CRAVING	kd lang (Sire)
26	17	WHEN I'M GOOD AND READY	Sybil (PWL International)
10	18	BAD GIRL	Madonna (Maverick)
11	19	ANIMAL NITRATE	Suede (Nude)
17	20	LOST IN MUSIC (SURE IS PURE REMIXES)	Sister Sledge (Atlantic)
18	21	DEEP	East 17 (London)
20	22	SHORTSHARPSHOCK (EP)	Therapy? (A&M)
-	23	PRESSURE US	Sunscreem (Sony Soho Square)
38	24	MORE, MORE, MORE	Bananarama (London)
27	25	BORN 2 BREED	Monie Love (Cooltempo)
-	26	DON'T WALK AWAY	Jade (Giant)
9	27	FEAR OF THE DARK (LIVE)	Iron Maiden (Epic)
35	28	REACH OUT I'LL BE THERE	Michael Bolton (Columbia)
-	29	SHOW ME LOVE	Robin S (Champion)
22	30	THE LOVE I LOST	West End featuring Sylvia (PWL International)
-	31	HEAVEN MUST BE MISSING AN ANGEL	Worlds Apart (Arista)
21	32	I PUT A SPELL ON YOU	Bryan Ferry (Virgin)
25	33	LABOUR OF LOVE (REMIXES)	Hue& Cry (Circa)
32	34	THEM BONES	Alice In Chains (Columbia)
-	35	HERE WE GO AGAIN!	Portrait (Capitol)
-	36	JUMP (LIVE)	Van Halen (Warner Bros.)
47	37	ONE MORE CHANCE	Maxi Priest (Ten)
-	38	STILL IN LOVE	Go West (Chrysalis)
-	39	CHOK THERE	Apache Indian (Island)
23	40	WHY CAN'T I WAKE UP WITH YOU?	Take That (RCA)
19	41	ALONE	Big Country (Compulsion)
31	42	CRYSTAL CLEAR	Grid (Virgin)
-	43	I BELIEVE IN YOU	Our Tribe (ffrreedom)
-	44	IT WAS A GOOD DAY	Ice Cube (4th & Broadway)
-	45	LOVE THING	Evolution (deConstruction)
24	46	IN YOUR CARE	Tasmin Archer (EMI)
34	47	I WILL ALWAYS LOVE YOU	Whitney Houston (Arista)
28	48	HEART (DON'T CHANGE MY MIND)	Diana Ross (EMI)
29	49	IT STARTED WITH A KISS	Hot Chocolate (EMI)
30	50	THIS TIME	Dina Carroll (A&M PM)

Sister Sledge joined in the Boney M/Abba/Hot Chocolate 70s pop disco revival, but went down better in the clubs than their erstwhile rivals. Some controversy arose over the emergence of white ragga singers (e.g. Snow), while an old white singer, Bryan Ferry, took an even older blues song into the Top 20.

April 1993

3 April 1993

last week	this week	Title	Artist (Label)
1	1	OH CAROLINA	Shaggy (Greensleeves)
14	2	YOUNG AT HEART	Bluebells (London)
4	3	INFORMER	Snow (East West America)
3	4	MR LOVERMAN	Shabba Ranks (Epic)
5	5	JUMP THEY SAY	David Bowie (Arista)
7	6	PEACE IN OUR TIME	Cliff Richard (EMI)
2	7	NO LIMIT	2 Unlimited (PWL Continental)
17	8	WHEN I'M GOOD AND READY	Sybil (PWL International)
6	9	GIVE IN TO ME	Michael Jackson (Epic)
-	10	FEVER	Madonna (Maverick)
8	11	LITTLE BIRD/LOVE SONG FOR A VAMPIRE	Annie Lennox (RCA)
9	12	ARE YOU GONNA GO MY WAY	Lenny Kravitz (Virgin)
26	13	DON'T WALK AWAY	Jade (Giant)
10	14	TOO YOUNG TO DIE	Jamiroquai (Sony Soho Square)
15	15	CAT'S IN THE CRADLE	Ugly Kid Joe (Mercury)
29	16	SHOW ME LOVE	Robin S (Champion)
23	17	PRESSURE US	Sunscreem (Sony Soho Square)
-	18	GO AWAY	Gloria Estefan (Epic)
11	19	LOOKING THROUGH PATIENT EYES	PM Dawn (Gee Street)
13	20	I'M EVERY WOMAN	Whitney Houston (Arista)
-	21	WRESTLEMANIA	World Wrestling Federation Stars (Arista)
24	22	MORE, MORE, MORE	Bananarama (London)
-	23	TENNESSEE	Arrested Development (Cooltempo)
39	24	CHOK THERE	Apache Indian (Island)
22	25	SHORTSHARPSHOCK (EP)	Therapy? (A&M)
16	26	CONSTANT CRAVING	kd lang (Sire)
31	27	HEAVEN MUST BE MISSING AN ANGEL	Worlds Apart (Arista)
-	28	I NEVER FELT LIKE THIS BEFORE	Mica Paris (4th & Broadway)
25	29	BORN 2 BREED	Monie Love (Cooltempo)
44	30	IT WAS A GOOD DAY	Ice Cube (4th & Broadway)
-	31	U GOT 2 KNOW	Capella (Internal Dance)
-	32	ONE VOICE	Bill Tarney (Arista)
19	33	ANIMAL NITRATE	Suede (Nude)
-	34	ADDICTION	Almighty (Polydor)
38	35	STILL IN LOVE	Go West (Chrysalis)
-	36	SUGAR KANE	Sonic Youth (Geffen)
35	37	HERE WE GO AGAIN!	Portrait (Capitol)
12	38	STICK IT OUT	Right Said Fred & Friends (Tug)
-	39	CAN'T DO A THING (TO STOP ME)	Chris Isaak (Reprise)
-	40	HEARTATTACK & VINE	Screamin' Jay Hawkins (Columbia)
21	41	DEEP	East 17 (London)
-	42	BLOOD OF EDEN	Peter Gabriel (Virgin)
-	43	I'M BACK FOR MORE	Lulu & Bobby Womack (Dome)
28	44	REACH OUT I'LL BE THERE	Michael Bolton (Columbia)
-	45	LOVE THE LIFE	JTQ with Noel McKoy (Big Life)
30	46	THE LOVE I LOST	West End featuring Sylvia (PWL International)
33	47	LABOUR OF LOVE (REMIXES)	Hue& Cry (Circa)
34	48	THEM BONES	Alice in Chains (Columbia)
36	49	JUMP (LIVE)	Van Halen (Warner Bros.)
37	50	ONE MORE CHANCE	Maxi Priest (Ten)

10 April 1993

last week	this week	Title	Artist (Label)
2	1	YOUNG AT HEART	Bluebells (London)
1	2	OH CAROLINA	Shaggy (Greensleeves)
3	3	INFORMER	Snow (East West America)
4	4	MR LOVERMAN	Shabba Ranks (Epic)
10	5	FEVER	Madonna (Maverick)
8	6	WHEN I'M GOOD AND READY	Sybil (PWL International)
16	7	SHOW ME LOVE	Robin S (Champion)
7	8	NO LIMIT	2 Unlimited (PWL Continental)
13	9	DON'T WALK AWAY	Jade (Giant)
18	10	GO AWAY	Gloria Estefan (Epic)
5	11	JUMP THEY SAY	David Bowie (Arista)
-	12	AIN'T NO LOVE (AIN'T NO USE)	Sub Sub featuring Melanie Williams (Rob's)
9	13	GIVE IN TO ME	Michael Jackson (Epic)
-	14	COME UNDONE	Duran Duran (Parlophone)
32	15	ONE VOICE	Bill Tarney (Arista)
15	16	CAT'S IN THE CRADLE	Ugly Kid Joe (Mercury)
-	17	LIVIN' ON THE EDGE	Aerosmith (Geffen)
31	18	U GOT 2 KNOW	Capella (Internal Dance)
23	19	TENNESSEE	Arrested Development (Cooltempo)
6	20	PEACE IN OUR TIME	Cliff Richard (EMI)
-	21	IS IT LIKE TODAY?	World Party (Ensign)
28	22	I NEVER FELT LIKE THIS BEFORE	Mica Paris (4th & Broadway)
21	23	WRESTLEMANIA	World Wrestling Federation Stars (Arista)
11	24	LITTLE BIRD/LOVE SONG FOR A VAMPIRE	Annie Lennox (RCA)
12	25	ARE YOU GONNA GO MY WAY	Lenny Kravitz (Virgin)
17	26	PRESSURE US	Sunscreem (Sony Soho Square)
14	27	TOO YOUNG TO DIE	Jamiroquai (Sony Soho Square)
28	28	LOOKING THROUGH PATIENT EYES	PM Dawn (Gee Street)
-	29	SING HALLELUJAH	Dr Alban (Logic Light)
20	30	I'M EVERY WOMAN	Whitney Houston (Arista)
-	31	YOU'VE GOT ME THINKING	Beloved (East West)
43	32	I'M BACK FOR MORE	Lulu & Bobby Womack (Dome)
39	33	CAN'T DO A THING (TO STOP ME)	Chris Isaak (Reprise)
-	34	COPACABANA (AT THE COPA) – THE 1993 REMIX	Barry Manilow (Arista)
42	35	BLOOD OF EDEN	Peter Gabriel (Virgin)
36	36	SUGAR KANE	Sonic Youth (Geffen)
37	37	SLOW IT DOWN	East 17 (London)
-	38	IT'S A SHAME ABOUT RAY	Lemonheads (Atlantic)
24	39	CHOK THERE	Apache Indian (Island)
22	40	MORE, MORE, MORE	Bananarama (London)
-	41	HOW I'M COMIN'	LL Cool J (Def Jam)
-	42	A JAMAICAN IN NEW YORK	Shinehead (Elektra)
30	43	IT WAS A GOOD DAY	Ice Cube (4th & Broadway)
45	44	LOVE THE LIFE	JTQ with Noel McKoy (Big Life)
35	45	STILL IN LOVE	Go West (Chrysalis)
40	46	HEARTATTACK & VINE	Screamin' Jay Hawkins (Columbia)
-	47	THE RIGHT DECISION	Jesus Jones (Food)
-	48	LOVE DON'T LOVE YOU (REMIX)	En Vogue (East West America)
26	49	CONSTANT CRAVING	kd lang (Sire)
29	50	BORN 2 BREED	Monie Love (Cooltempo)

16 April 1993

last week	this week	Title	Artist (Label)
1	1	YOUNG AT HEART	Bluebells (London)
2	2	OH CAROLINA	Shaggy (Greensleeves)
12	3	AIN'T NO LOVE (AIN'T NO USE)	Sub Sub featuring Melanie Williams (Rob's)
3	4	INFORMER	Snow (East West America)
6	5	WHEN I'M GOOD AND READY	Sybil (PWL International)
5	6	FEVER	Madonna (Maverick)
7	7	SHOW ME LOVE	Robin S (Champion)
-	8	REGRET	New Order (London)
4	9	MR LOVERMAN	Shabba Ranks (Epic)
9	10	DON'T WALK AWAY	Jade (Giant)
10	11	GO AWAY	Gloria Estefan (Epic)
8	12	NO LIMIT	2 Unlimited (PWL Continental)
18	13	U GOT 2 KNOW	Capella (Internal Dance)
14	14	COME UNDONE	Duran Duran (Parlophone)
15	15	ONE VOICE	Bill Tarney (Arista)
22	16	I NEVER FELT LIKE THIS BEFORE	Mica Paris (4th & Broadway)
34	17	COPACABANA (AT THE COPA) – THE 1993 REMIX	Barry Manilow (Arista)
31	18	YOU'VE GOT ME THINKING	Beloved (East West)
16	19	CAT'S IN THE CRADLE	Ugly Kid Joe (Mercury)
29	20	SING HALLELUJAH	Dr Alban (Logic Light)
21	21	IS IT LIKE TODAY?	World Party (Ensign)
19	22	TENNESSEE	Arrested Development (Cooltempo)
17	23	LIVIN' ON THE EDGE	Aerosmith (Geffen)
37	24	SLOW IT DOWN	East 17 (London)
42	25	A JAMAICAN IN NEW YORK	Shinehead (Elektra)
23	26	WRESTLEMANIA	World Wrestling Federation Stars (Arista)
11	27	JUMP THEY SAY	David Bowie (Arista)
-	28	DO YOU LOVE ME LIKE YOU SAY?	Terence Trent D'Arby (Columbia)
-	29	WIND IT UP (REWOUND)	Prodigy (XL)
13	30	GIVE IN TO ME	Michael Jackson (Epic)
-	31	SHOTGUN WEDDING	Rod Stewart (Warner Bros.)
24	32	LITTLE BIRD/LOVE SONG FOR A VAMPIRE	Annie Lennox (RCA)
32	33	I'M BACK FOR MORE	Lulu & Bobby Womack (Dome)
-	34	SLOW EMOTION REPLAY	The The (Epic)
25	35	ARE YOU GONNA GO MY WAY	Lenny Kravitz (Virgin)
26	36	PRESSURE US	Sunscreem (Sony Soho Square)
-	37	EVERYBODY HURTS	REM (Warner Bros.)
33	38	CAN'T DO A THING (TO STOP ME)	Chris Isaak (Reprise)
35	39	BLOOD OF EDEN	Peter Gabriel (Virgin)
38	40	IT'S A SHAME ABOUT RAY	Lemonheads (Atlantic)
-	41	FASHION CRISIS HITS NEW YORK	Frank & Walters (Setanta)
-	42	LOOKS LIKE I'M IN LOVE AGAIN	Keywest featuring Erik (PWL Sanctuary)
47	43	THE RIGHT DECISION	Jesus Jones (Food)
41	44	HOW I'M COMIN'	LL Cool J (Def Jam)
-	45	SWEET FREEDOM	Positive Gang (PWL Continental)
-	46	AUSLANDER	Living Colour (Epic)
20	47	PEACE IN OUR TIME	Cliff Richard (EMI)
-	48	I'M A WONDERFUL THING, BABY (BROTHERS IN RHYTHM REMIXES)	Kid Creole & the Coconuts (Island)
-	49	BROWN GIRL IN THE RING REMIX '93	Boney M (Arista)
-	50	CANDY EVERYBODY WANTS	10,000 Maniacs (Elektra)

The Bluebells got a re-release and made it to the top on the strength of a TV tampon advert – made a change from jeans. Ragga was now everywhere.

Wrestlers came again with the interestingly-titled *Wrestlemania*. But entry of the month was the great Screamin' Jay Hawkins. Finally got there Jay YAAH!

April – May 1993

24 April 1993

last	this	Title	Artist (Label)
1	1	YOUNG AT HEART	Bluebells (London)
3	2	AIN'T NO LOVE (AIN'T NO USE)	Sub Sub featuring Melanie Williams (Rob's)
2	3	OH CAROLINA	Shaggy (Greensleeves)
4	4	INFORMER	Snow (East West America)
8	5	REGRET	New Order (London)
5	6	WHEN I'M GOOD AND READY	Sybil (PWL International)
7	7	SHOW ME LOVE	Robin S (Champion)
13	8	U GOT 2 KNOW	Capella (Internal Dance)
10	9	DON'T WALK AWAY	Jade (Giant)
-	10	I HAVE NOTHING	Whitney Houston (Arista)
24	11	SLOW IT DOWN	East 17 (London)
28	12	DO YOU LOVE ME LIKE YOU SAY?	Terence Trent D'Arby (Columbia)
9	13	MR LOVERMAN	Shabba Ranks (Epic)
14	14	COME UNDONE	Duran Duran (Parlophone)
37	15	EVERYBODY HURTS	REM (Warner Bros.)
11	16	GO AWAY	Gloria Estefan (Epic)
12	17	NO LIMIT	2 Unlimited (PWL Continental)
31	18	SHOTGUN WEDDING	Rod Stewart (Warner Bros.)
29	19	WIND IT UP (REWOUND)	Prodigy (XL)
6	20	FEVER	Madonna (Maverick)
19	21	CAT'S IN THE CRADLE	Ugly Kid Joe (Mercury)
22	22	SING HALLELUJAH	Dr Alban (Logic Light)
18	23	YOU'VE GOT ME THINKING	Beloved (East West)
-	24	GIMME SHELTER (EP)	Various Artists (Food)
21	25	IS IT LIKE TODAY?	World Party (Ensign)
22	26	TENNESSEE	Arrested Development (Cooltempo)
17	27	COPACABANA (AT THE COPA) – THE 1993 REMIX	Barry Manilow (Arista)
34	28	SLOW EMOTION REPLAY	The The (Epic)
-	29	ONLY TENDER LOVE	Deacon Blue (Columbia)
16	30	I NEVER FELT LIKE THIS BEFORE	Mica Paris (4th & Broadway)
-	31	TRUGANINI	Midnight Oil (Columbia)
-	32	SEVEN DAYS	Sting (A&M)
26	33	WRESTLEMANIA	World Wrestling Federation Stars (Arista)
23	34	LIVIN' ON THE EDGE	Aerosmith (Geffen)
25	35	A JAMAICAN IN NEW YORK	Shinehead (Elektra)
-	36	U R THE BEST THING	D:Ream (Magnet)
32	37	LITTLE BIRD/LOVE SONG FOR A VAMPIR	Annie Lennox (RCA)
-	38	UNTIL YOU SUFFER SOME (FIRE AND ICE)	Poison (Capitol)
-	39	P.OWER OF A.MERICAN N.ATIVES	Dance 2 Trance (Logic)
-	40	SOAPBOX	Little Angels (Polydor)
45	41	SWEET FREEDOM	Positive Gang (PWL Continental)
49	42	BROWN GIRL IN THE RING REMIX '93	Boney M (Arista)
35	43	ARE YOU GONNA GO MY WAY	Lenny Kravitz (Virgin)
33	44	I'M BACK FOR MORE	Lulu & Bobby Womack (Dome)
27	45	JUMP THEY SAY	David Bowie (Arista)
30	46	GIVE IN TO ME	Michael Jackson (Epic)
15	47	ONE VOICE	Bill Tarney (Arista)
40	48	IT'S A SHAME ABOUT RAY	Lemonheads (Atlantic)
-	49	WE GOT THE LOVE – THE '93 REMIXES	Lindy Layton (PWL International)
-	50	THE SUPREME (EP)	Sinitta (Arista)

1 May 1993

last	this	Title	Artist (Label)
-	1	FIVE LIVE (EP)	George Michael/Queen/Lisa Stansfield (Parlophone)
1	2	YOUNG AT HEART	Bluebells (London)
2	3	AIN'T NO LOVE (AIN'T NO USE)	Sub Sub featuring Melanie Williams (Rob's)
10	4	I HAVE NOTHING	Whitney Houston (Arista)
5	5	REGRET	New Order (London)
4	6	INFORMER	Snow (East West America)
6	7	WHEN I'M GOOD AND READY	Sybil (PWL International)
8	8	U GOT 2 KNOW	Capella (Internal Dance)
3	9	OH CAROLINA	Shaggy (Greensleeves)
15	10	EVERYBODY HURTS	REM (Warner Bros.)
9	11	DON'T WALK AWAY	Jade (Giant)
12	12	DO YOU LOVE ME LIKE YOU SAY?	Terence Trent D'Arby (Columbia)
7	13	SHOW ME LOVE	Robin S (Champion)
14	14	COME UNDONE	Duran Duran (Parlophone)
11	15	SLOW IT DOWN	East 17 (London)
29	16	ONLY TENDER LOVE	Deacon Blue (Columbia)
19	17	WIND IT UP (REWOUND)	Prodigy (XL)
13	18	MR LOVERMAN	Shabba Ranks (Epic)
32	19	SEVEN DAYS	Sting (A&M)
16	20	GO AWAY	Gloria Estefan (Epic)
17	21	NO LIMIT	2 Unlimited (PWL Continental)
18	22	SHOTGUN WEDDING	Rod Stewart (Warner Bros.)
-	23	I'M SO INTO YOU	SWV (RCA)
22	24	SING HALLELUJAH	Dr Alban (Logic Light)
-	25	50FT QUEENIE	P J Harvey (Island)
21	26	CAT'S IN THE CRADLE	Ugly Kid Joe (Mercury)
-	27	SHIPS (WHERE WERE YOU)	Big Country (Compulsion)
36	28	U R THE BEST THING	D:Ream (Magnet)
40	29	SOAPBOX	Little Angels (Polydor)
-	30	TONIGHT	Def Leppard (Bludgeon Riffola)
-	31	FOR TOMORROW	Blur (Food)
39	32	P.OWER OF A.MERICAN N.ATIVES	Dance 2 Trance (Logic)
38	33	UNTIL YOU SUFFER SOME (FIRE AND ICE)	Poison (Capitol)
-	34	SWEAT (A LA LA LA LONG)	Inner Circle (Magnet)
24	35	GIMME SHELTER (EP)	Various Artists (Food)
25	36	IS IT LIKE TODAY?	World Party (Ensign)
31	37	TRUGANINI	Midnight Oil (Columbia)
28	38	SLOW EMOTION REPLAY	The The (Epic)
-	39	BETTER THE DEVIL YOU KNOW	Sonia (Arista)
23	40	YOU'VE GOT ME THINKING	Beloved (East West)
41	41	SWEET FREEDOM	Positive Gang (PWL Continental)
49	42	WE GOT THE LOVE – THE '93 REMIXES	Lindy Layton (PWL International)
20	43	FEVER	Madonna (Maverick)
27	44	COPACABANA (AT THE COPA) – THE 1993 REMIX	Barry Manilow (Arista)
26	45	TENNESSEE	Arrested Development (Cooltempo)
-	46	THE GHOST AT NUMBER ONE	Jellyfish (Charisma)
-	47	GLAD ALL OVER	Dave Clark Five (EMI)
37	48	LITTLE BIRD/LOVE SONG FOR A VAMPIRE	Annie Lennox (RCA)
30	49	I NEVER FELT LIKE THIS BEFORE	Mica Paris (4th & Broadway)
33	50	WRESTLEMANIA	World Wrestling Federation Stars (Arista)

8 May 1993

last	this	Title	Artist (Label)
1	1	FIVE LIVE (EP)	George Michael/Queen/Lisa Stansfield (Parlophone)
4	2	I HAVE NOTHING	Whitney Houston (Arista)
-	3	THAT'S THE WAY LOVE GOES	Janet Jackson (Virgin)
2	4	YOUNG AT HEART	Bluebells (London)
3	5	AIN'T NO LOVE (AIN'T NO USE)	Sub Sub featuring Melanie Williams (Rob's)
-	6	TRIBAL DANCE	2 Unlimited (PWL International)
10	7	EVERYBODY HURTS	REM (Warner Bros.)
-	8	ALL THAT SHE WANTS	Ace Of Base (Metronome)
6	9	INFORMER	Snow (East West America)
34	10	SWEAT (A LA LA LA LONG)	Inner Circle (Magnet)
8	11	U GOT 2 KNOW	Capella (Internal Dance)
7	12	WHEN I'M GOOD AND READY	Sybil (PWL International)
-	13	BELIEVE IN ME	Utah Saints (ffrr)
5	14	REGRET	New Order (London)
14	15	COME UNDONE	Duran Duran (Parlophone)
13	16	SHOW ME LOVE	Robin S (Champion)
9	17	OH CAROLINA	Shaggy (Greensleeves)
17	18	WIND IT UP (REWOUND)	Prodigy (XL)
27	19	SHIPS (WHERE WERE YOU)	Big Country (Compulsion)
23	20	I'M SO INTO YOU	SWV (RCA)
11	21	DON'T WALK AWAY	Jade (Giant)
39	22	BETTER THE DEVIL YOU KNOW	Sonia (Arista)
-	23	BULLET IN THE HEAD	Rage Against The Machine (Epic)
18	24	MR LOVERMAN	Shabba Ranks (Epic)
28	25	U R THE BEST THING	D:Ream (Magnet)
24	26	SING HALLELUJAH	Dr Alban (Logic Light)
12	27	DO YOU LOVE ME LIKE YOU SAY?	Terence Trent D'Arby (Columbia)
30	28	TONIGHT	Def Leppard (Bludgeon Riffola)
32	29	P.OWER OF A.MERICAN N.ATIVES	Dance 2 Trance (Logic)
-	30	TEN YEARS ASLEEP (EP)	Kingmaker (Scorch)
16	31	ONLY TENDER LOVE	Deacon Blue (Columbia)
19	32	SEVEN DAYS	Sting (A&M)
15	33	SLOW IT DOWN	East 17 (London)
-	34	PACKET OF PEACE	Lionrock (deConstruction)
-	35	WALKING IN MY SHOES	Depeche Mode (Mute)
31	36	FOR TOMORROW	Blur (Food)
-	37	HOUSECALL	Shabba Ranks featuring Maxi Priest (Epic)
-	38	THE JUNGLE BOOK GROOVE	Various Artists (Hollywood)
-	39	I'M GOING ALL THE WAY	Sounds Of Blackness (A&M PM)
47	40	GLAD ALL OVER	Dave Clark Five (EMI)
21	41	NO LIMIT	2 Unlimited (PWL Continental)
-	42	29 PALMS	Robert Plant (Es Paranza)
22	43	SHOTGUN WEDDING	Rod Stewart (Warner Bros.)
-	44	ONLY	Anthrax (Elektra)
20	45	GO AWAY	Gloria Estefan (Epic)
-	46	THE LOVE IN YOUR EYES	Daniel O'Donnell (Ritz)
-	47	BLUE FOR YOU/THIS TIME (LIVE)	Wet Wet Wet (Precious Organisation)
-	48	PARISIENNE WALKWAYS '93	Gary Moore (Virgin)
-	49	FREAK ME	Silk (Keia)
26	50	CAT'S IN THE CRADLE	Ugly Kid Joe (Mercury)

Now Barry Manilow was getting the remix treatment – any connection with the show *Copacabana* (based on Baz's music) opening in London? Trance music arrived as a variation on house with Dance 2 Trance. The Swedish revival continued with Ace Of Base – but reggae in Sweden? Whatever next, Welsh rap?

15 May 1993

last week	this week		
1	1	FIVE LIVE (EP)	George Michael/Queen/Lisa Stansfield (Parlophone)
8	2	ALL THAT SHE WANTS	Ace Of Base (Metronome)
3	3	THAT'S THE WAY LOVE GOES	Janet Jackson (Virgin)
10	4	SWEAT (A LA LA LA LONG)	Inner Circle (Magnet)
6	5	TRIBAL DANCE	2 Unlimited (PWL International)
2	6	I HAVE NOTHING	Whitney Houston (Arista)
7	7	EVERYBODY HURTS	REM (Warner Bros.)
4	8	YOUNG AT HEART	Bluebells (London)
5	9	AIN'T NO LOVE (AIN'T NO USE)	Sub Sub featuring Melanie Williams (Rob's)
13	10	BELIEVE IN ME	Utah Saints (ffrr)
9	11	INFORMER	Snow (East West America)
35	12	WALKING IN MY SHOES	Depeche Mode (Mute)
11	13	U GOT 2 KNOW	Capella (Internal Dance)
37	14	HOUSECALL	Shabba Ranks featuring Maxi Priest (Epic)
12	15	WHEN I'M GOOD AND READY	Sybil (PWL International)
20	16	I'M SO INTO YOU	SWV (RCA)
42	17	29 PALMS	Robert Plant (Es Paranza)
16	18	SHOW ME LOVE	Robin S (Champion)
30	19	TEN YEARS ASLEEP (EP)	Kingmaker (Scorch)
17	20	OH CAROLINA	Shaggy (Greensleeves)
25	21	U R THE BEST THING	D:Ream (Magnet)
-	22	IN THESE ARMS	Bon Jovi (Jambco)
15	23	COME UNDONE	Duran Duran (Parlophone)
-	24	STAND ABOVE ME	Orchestral Manoeuvres In The Dark (Virgin)
22	25	BETTER THE DEVIL YOU KNOW	Sonia (Arista)
18	26	WIND IT UP (REWOUND)	Prodigy (XL)
23	27	BULLET IN THE HEAD	Rage Against The Machine (Epic)
-	28	THE RETURN OF PAN	Waterboys (Geffen)
38	29	THE JUNGLE BOOK GROOVE	Various Artists (Hollywood)
48	30	PARISIENNE WALKWAYS '93	Gary Moore (Virgin)
14	31	REGRET	New Order (London)
26	32	SING HALLELUJAH	Dr Alban (Logic Light)
19	33	SHIPS (WHERE WERE YOU)	Big Country (Compulsion)
34	34	PACKET OF PEACE	Lionrock (deConstruction)
-	35	EXPRESS	Dina Carroll (A&M PM)
39	36	I'M GOING ALL THE WAY	Sounds Of Blackness (A&M PM)
-	37	THE GREATEST FLAME	Runrig (Chrysalis)
-	38	GLORIA	Van Morrison & John Lee Hooker (Exile)
-	39	SHOUTING FOR THE GUNNERS	Arsenal FA Cup Final Squad '93 feturing Tippa Irie & Peter Hunnigate (London)
47	40	BLUE FOR YOU/THIS TIME (LIVE)	Wet Wet Wet (Precious Organisation)
44	41	ONLY	Anthrax (Elektra)
28	42	TONIGHT	Def Leppard (Bludgeon Riffola)
-	43	KISS OF LIFE	Sade (Epic)
-	44	THE ONLY LIVING BOY IN NEW YORK (EP)	Everything But The Girl (blanco y negro)
36	45	FOR TOMORROW	Blur (Food)
29	46	P.OWER OF A.MERICAN N.ATIVES	Dance 2 Trance (Logic)
24	47	MR LOVERMAN	Shabba Ranks (Epic)
27	48	DO YOU LOVE ME LIKE YOU SAY?	Terence Trent D'Arby (Columbia)
-	49	TWO PRINCES	Spin Doctors (Epic)
-	50	HERO	David Crosby featuring Phil Collins (Atlantic)

22 May 1993

last	this		
2	1	ALL THAT SHE WANTS	Ace Of Base (Metronome)
1	2	FIVE LIVE (EP)	George Michael/Queen/Lisa Stansfield (Parlophone)
-	3	(I CAN'T HELP) FALLING IN LOVE WITH YOU	UB40 (DEP International)
4	4	SWEAT (A LA LA LA LONG)	Inner Circle (Magnet)
3	5	THAT'S THE WAY LOVE GOES	Janet Jackson (Virgin)
5	6	TRIBAL DANCE	2 Unlimited (PWL International)
7	7	EVERYBODY HURTS	REM (Warner Bros.)
10	8	BELIEVE IN ME	Utah Saints (ffrr)
14	9	HOUSECALL	Shabba Ranks featuring Maxi Priest (Epic)
6	10	I HAVE NOTHING	Whitney Houston (Arista)
22	11	IN THESE ARMS	Bon Jovi (Jambco)
9	12	AIN'T NO LOVE (AIN'T NO USE)	Sub Sub featuring Melanie Williams (Rob's)
8	13	YOUNG AT HEART	Bluebells (London)
11	14	INFORMER	Snow (East West America)
35	15	EXPRESS	Dina Carroll (A&M PM)
13	16	U GOT 2 KNOW	Capella (Internal Dance)
17	17	29 PALMS	Robert Plant (Es Paranza)
24	18	STAND ABOVE ME	Orchestral Manoeuvres In The Dark (Virgin)
-	19	TOP O' THE MORNING TO YA (REMIX)/HOUSE OF PAIN	House Of Pain (XL)
-	20	I DON'T WANNA FIGHT	Tina Turner (Parlophone)
21	21	HOBART PAVING/WHO DO YOU THINK YOU ARE	Saint Etienne (Heavenly)
49	22	TWO PRINCES	Spin Doctors (Epic)
15	23	WHEN I'M GOOD AND READY	Sybil (PWL Int)
-	24	ENCORES	Dire Straits (Vertigo)
21	25	U R THE BEST THING	D:Ream (Magnet)
19	26	TEN YEARS ASLEEP (EP)	Kingmaker (Scorch)
12	27	WALKING IN MY SHOES	Depeche Mode (Mute)
29	28	THE JUNGLE BOOK GROOVE	Various Artists (Hollywood)
16	29	I'M SO INTO YOU	SWV (RCA)
-	30	STARS	Felix (deConstruction)
-	31	LITTLE MIRACLES (HAPPEN EVERY DAY)	Luther Vandross (Epic)
37	32	THE GREATEST FLAME	Runrig (Chrysalis)
18	33	SHOW ME LOVE	Robin S (Champion)
34	34	BETTER THE DEVIL YOU KNOW	Sonia (Arista)
38	35	GLORIA	Van Morrison & John Lee Hooker (Exile)
32	36	SING HALLELUJAH	Dr Alban (Logic Light)
20	37	OH CAROLINA	Shaggy (Greensleeves)
28	38	THE RETURN OF PAN	Waterboys (Geffen)
-	39	BELIEVE	Lenny Kravitz (Virgin America)
-	40	SIMPLY LIFE	Elton John (Rocket)
23	41	COME UNDONE	Duran Duran (Parlophone)
30	42	PARISIENNE WALKWAYS '93	Gary Moore (Virgin)
39	43	SHOUTING FOR THE GUNNERS	Arsenal FA Cup Final Squad '93 feturing Tippa Irie & Peter Hunnigate (London)
27	44	BULLET IN THE HEAD	Rage Against The Machine (Epic)
-	45	POP IS DEAD	Radiohead (Parlophone)
-	46	HOT HOT HOT	Pat & Mick (PWL International)
-	47	HOUSE IS NOT A HOME	Charles & Eddie (Stateside)
-	48	THESE ARE THE THINGS WORTH FIGHTING FOR	Gary Claill On-U Sound System (Perfecto)
50	49	HERO	David Crosby featuring Phil Collins (Atlantic)
36	50	I'M GOING ALL THE WAY	Sounds Of Blackness (A&M PM)

29 May 1993

last	this		
1	1	ALL THAT SHE WANTS	Ace Of Base (Metronome)
3	2	(I CAN'T HELP) FALLING IN LOVE WITH YOU	UB40 (DEP International)
4	3	SWEAT (A LA LA LA LONG)	Inner Circle (Magnet)
2	4	FIVE LIVE (EP)	George Michael/Queen/Lisa Stansfield (Parlophone)
-	5	THE CIVIL WAR (EP)	Guns N' Roses (Geffen)
5	6	THAT'S THE WAY LOVE GOES	Janet Jackson (Virgin)
20	7	I DON'T WANNA FIGHT	Tina Turner (Parlophone)
7	8	EVERYBODY HURTS	REM (Warner Bros.)
6	9	TRIBAL DANCE	2 Unlimited (PWL International)
9	10	HOUSECALL	Shabba Ranks featuring Maxi Priest (Epic)
11	11	IN THESE ARMS	Bon Jovi (Jambco)
22	12	TWO PRINCES	Spin Doctors (Epic)
19	13	TOP O' THE MORNING TO YA (REMIX)/HOUSE OF PAIN	House Of Pain (XL)
15	14	EXPRESS	Dina Carroll (A&M PM)
10	15	I HAVE NOTHING	Whitney Houston (Arista)
12	16	AIN'T NO LOVE (AIN'T NO USE)	Sub Sub featuring Melanie Williams (Rob's)
8	17	BELIEVE IN ME	Utah Saints (ffrr)
34	18	BETTER THE DEVIL YOU KNOW	Sonia (Arista)
-	19	SO YOUNG	Suede (Nude)
14	20	INFORMER	Snow (East West America)
28	21	THE JUNGLE BOOK GROOVE	Various Artists (Hollywood)
-	22	BREAK IT DOWN AGAIN	Tears For Fears (Mercury)
18	23	STAND ABOVE ME	Orchestral Manoeuvres In The Dark (Virgin)
31	24	LITTLE MIRACLES (HAPPEN EVERY DAY)	Luther Vandross (Epic)
-	25	SHOUT	Louchie Lou & Michie One (ffrr)
21	26	HOBART PAVING/WHO DO YOU THINK YOU ARE	Saint Etienne (Heavenly)
13	27	YOUNG AT HEART	Bluebells (London)
47	28	HOUSE IS NOT A HOME	Charles & Eddie (Stateside)
-	29	CREATION	Stereo MC's (4th & Broadway)
17	30	29 PALMS	Robert Plant (Es Paranza)
-	31	WILL YOU LOVE ME TOMORROW	Bryan Ferry (Virgin)
32	32	SWEATING BULLETS	Megadeth (Capitol)
16	33	U GOT 2 KNOW	Capella (Internal Dance)
-	34	LIVING IN THE PAST	Jethro Tull (Chrysalis)
30	35	STARS	Felix (deConstruction)
25	36	U R THE BEST THING	D:Ream (Magnet)
39	37	BELIEVE	Lenny Kravitz (Virgin America)
23	38	WHEN I'M GOOD AND READY	Sybil (PWL International)
-	39	LORDS OF THE NEW CHURCH	Tasmin Archer (EMI)
-	40	I'M GONNA SOOTHE YOU	Maria McKee (Geffen)
40	41	SIMPLY LIFE	Elton John (Rocket)
24	42	ENCORES	Dire Straits (Vertigo)
43	43	SHOUTING FOR THE GUNNERS	Arsenal FA Cup Final Squad '93 feturing Tippa Irie & Peter Hunnigate (London)
32	44	THE GREATEST FLAME	Runrig (Chrysalis)
26	45	TEN YEARS ASLEEP (EP)	Kingmaker (Scorch)
38	46	THE RETURN OF PAN	Waterboys (Geffen)
-	47	WALK THROUGH THE WORLD	Marc Cohn (Atlantic)
-	48	OUT OF SEASON	Almighty (Polydor)
29	49	I'M SO INTO YOU	SWV (RCA)
27	50	WALKING IN MY SHOES	Depeche Mode (Mute)

The Arsenal used a ragga lyric in an attempt to lose their 'boring Arsenal' tag. They beat Sheffield Wednesday in a replay, but remained dull. UB40 rode the new reggae wave back to the top, and *The Jungle Book Groove* cashed in on the release of the movie on video. Spin Doctors arrived – and weren't dull at all.

June 1993

5 June 1993

last week	this week	title / artist
1	1	ALL THAT SHE WANTS Ace Of Base (Metronome)
2	2	(I CAN'T HELP) FALLING IN LOVE WITH YOU UB40 (DEP International)
3	3	SWEAT (A LA LA LA LA LONG) Inner Circle (Magnet)
7	4	I DON'T WANNA FIGHT Tina Turner (Parlophone)
12	5	TWO PRINCES Spin Doctors (Epic)
4	6	FIVE LIVE (EP) George Michael/Queen/Lisa Stansfield (Parlophone)
6	7	THAT'S THE WAY LOVE GOES Janet Jackson (Virgin)
8	8	EVERYBODY HURTS REM (Warner Bros.)
13	9	TOP O' THE MORNING TO YA (REMIX)/HOUSE OF PAIN House Of Pain (XL)
-	10	THREE LITTLE PIGS Green Jelly (Zoo)
-	11	BLOW YOUR MIND Jamiroquai (Orenda)
9	12	TRIBAL DANCE 2 Unlimited (PWL International)
11	13	IN THESE ARMS Bon Jovi (Jambco)
-	14	IN ALL THE RIGHT PLACES Lisa Stansfield (MCA)
10	15	HOUSECALL Shabba Ranks featuring Maxi Priest (Epic)
25	16	SHOUT Louchie Lou & Michie One (ffrr)
22	17	BREAK IT DOWN AGAIN Tears For Fears (Mercury)
21	18	THE JUNGLE BOOK GROOVE Various Artists (Hollywood)
-	19	WHAT IS LOVE Haddaway (Logic)
15	20	I HAVE NOTHING Whitney Houston (Arista)
29	21	CREATION Stereo MC's (4th & Broadway)
5	22	THE CIVIL WAR (EP) Guns N' Roses (Geffen)
39	23	LORDS OF THE NEW CHURCH Tasmin Archer (EMI)
14	24	EXPRESS Dina Carroll (A&M PM)
31	25	WILL YOU LOVE ME TOMORROW Bryan Ferry (Virgin)
16	26	AIN'T NO LOVE (AIN'T NO USE) Sub Sub featuring Melanie Williams (Rob's)
-	27	NO ORDINARY LOVE Sade (Epic)
24	28	LITTLE MIRACLES (HAPPEN EVERY DAY) Luther Vandross (Epic)
17	29	BELIEVE IN ME Utah Saints (ffrr)
-	30	ANGRY CHAIR Alice In Chains (Columbia)
-	31	DARK IS THE NIGHT A-Ha (Warner Bros.)
47	32	WALK THROUGH THE WORLD Marc Cohn (Atlantic)
-	33	I WANNA HOLD ON TO YOU Mica Paris (4th & Broadway)
37	34	BELIEVE Lenny Kravitz (Virgin America)
18	35	BETTER THE DEVIL YOU KNOW Sonia (Arista)
19	36	SO YOUNG Suede (Nude)
20	37	INFORMER Snow (East West America)
-	38	WITH ONE LOOK Barbra Streisand (Columbia)
32	39	SWEATING BULLETS Megadeth (Capitol)
28	40	HOUSE IS NOT A HOME Charles & Eddie (Stateside)
23	41	STAND ABOVE ME Orchestral Manoeuvres In The Dark (Virgin)
26	42	HOBART PAVING/WHO DO YOU THINK YOU ARE Saint Etienne (Heavenly)
40	43	I'M GONNA SOOTHE YOU Maria McKee (Geffen)
34	44	LIVING IN THE PAST Jethro Tull (Chrysalis)
30	45	29 PALMS Robert Plant (De Paranza)
-	46	HIGHER AND HIGHER Unation (MCA)
33	47	U GOT 2 KNOW Capella (Internal Dance)
36	48	U R THE BEST THING D:Ream (Magnet)
41	49	SIMPLY LIFE Elton John (Rocket)
27	50	YOUNG AT HEART Bluebells (London)

12 June 1993

last week	this week	title / artist
1	1	ALL THAT SHE WANTS Ace Of Base (Metronome)
2	2	(I CAN'T HELP) FALLING IN LOVE WITH YOU UB40 (DEP International)
3	3	SWEAT (A LA LA LA LA LONG) Inner Circle (Magnet)
5	4	TWO PRINCES Spin Doctors (Epic)
10	5	THREE LITTLE PIGS Green Jelly (Zoo)
-	6	CAN YOU FORGIVE HER? Pet Shop Boys (Parlophone)
16	7	SHOUT Louchie Lou & Michie One (ffrr)
4	8	I DON'T WANNA FIGHT Tina Turner (Parlophone)
19	9	WHAT IS LOVE Haddaway (Logic)
14	10	IN ALL THE RIGHT PLACES Lisa Stansfield (MCA)
6	11	FIVE LIVE (EP) George Michael/Queen/Lisa Stansfield (Parlophone)
7	12	THAT'S THE WAY LOVE GOES Janet Jackson (Virgin)
9	13	TOP O' THE MORNING TO YA (REMIX)/HOUSE OF PAIN House Of Pain (XL)
12	14	TRIBAL DANCE 2 Unlimited (PWL International)
8	15	EVERYBODY HURTS REM (Warner Bros.)
11	16	BLOW YOUR MIND Jamiroquai (Orenda)
31	17	DARK IS THE NIGHT A-Ha (Warner Bros.)
-	18	DO YOU SEE THE LIGHT (LOOKING FOR) Snap (Logic)
13	19	FACE THE STRANGE (EP) Therapy? (A&M)
13	20	IN THESE ARMS Bon Jovi (Jambco)
21	21	TEASE ME Chaka Demus & Pliers (Mango)
17	22	BREAK IT DOWN AGAIN Tears For Fears (Mercury)
18	23	THE JUNGLE BOOK GROOVE Various Artists (Hollywood)
15	24	HOUSECALL Shabba Ranks featuring Maxi Priest (Epic)
27	25	NO ORDINARY LOVE Sade (Epic)
21	26	CREATION Stereo MC's (4th & Broadway)
25	27	WILL YOU LOVE ME TOMORROW Bryan Ferry (Virgin)
-	28	HUMAN WORK OF ART Cliff Richard (EMI)
23	29	LORDS OF THE NEW CHURCH Tasmin Archer (EMI)
33	30	I WANNA HOLD ON TO YOU Mica Paris (4th & Broadway)
-	31	FROM DESPAIR TO WHERE Manic Street Preachers (Columbia)
20	32	I HAVE NOTHING Whitney Houston (Arista)
34	33	BELIEVE Lenny Kravitz (Virgin America)
38	34	WITH ONE LOOK Barbra Streisand (Columbia)
-	35	BLACK TIE WHITE NOISE David Bowie featuring Al B Sure! (Savage)
-	36	THINKING OF YOU '93 REMIXES Sister Sledge (Atlantic)
24	37	EXPRESS Dina Carroll (A&M PM)
22	38	THE CIVIL WAR (EP) Guns N' Roses (Geffen)
32	39	WALK THROUGH THE WORLD Marc Cohn (Atlantic)
26	40	AIN'T NO LOVE (AIN'T NO USE) Sub Sub featuring Melanie Williams (Rob's)
-	41	GET HERE Q featuring Tracey Ackerman (Arista)
30	42	ANGRY CHAIR Alice In Chains (Columbia)
-	43	IN A WORD OR 2/THE POWER Monie Love (Cooltempo)
42	44	HOBART PAVING/WHO DO YOU THINK YOU ARE Saint Etienne (Heavenly)
-	45	RUSHING Loni Clark (A&M PM)
-	46	ALL FUNKED UP Mother (Bosting)
47	47	U GOT 2 KNOW Capella (Internal Dance)
28	48	LITTLE MIRACLES Luther Vandross (Epic)
39	49	SWEATING BULLETS Megadeth (Capitol)
29	50	BELIEVE IN ME Utah Saints (ffrr)

19 June 1993

last week	this week	title / artist
2	1	(I CAN'T HELP) FALLING IN LOVE WITH YOU UB40 (DEP International)
1	2	ALL THAT SHE WANTS Ace Of Base (Metronome)
9	3	WHAT IS LOVE Haddaway (Logic)
-	4	DREAMS Gabrielle (Go! Beat)
4	5	TWO PRINCES Spin Doctors (Epic)
6	6	CAN YOU FORGIVE HER? Pet Shop Boys (Parlophone)
3	7	SWEAT (A LA LA LA LA LONG) Inner Circle (Magnet)
21	8	TEASE ME Chaka Demus & Pliers (Mango)
18	9	DO YOU SEE THE LIGHT (LOOKING FOR) Snap (Logic)
10	10	IN ALL THE RIGHT PLACES Lisa Stansfield (MCA)
5	11	THREE LITTLE PIGS Green Jelly (Zoo)
7	12	SHOUT Louchie Lou & Michie One (ffrr)
8	13	I DON'T WANNA FIGHT Tina Turner (Parlophone)
-	14	FIELDS OF GOLD Sting (A&M)
25	15	NO ORDINARY LOVE Sade (Epic)
14	16	TRIBAL DANCE 2 Unlimited (PWL International)
16	17	BLOW YOUR MIND Jamiroquai (Orenda)
11	18	FIVE LIVE (EP) George Michael/Queen/Lisa Stansfield (Parlophone)
-	19	DELICATE Terence Trent D'Arby featuring Des'Ree (Columbia)
15	20	EVERYBODY HURTS REM (Warner Bros.)
13	21	TOP O' THE MORNING TO YA (REMIX)/HOUSE OF PAIN House Of Pain (XL)
28	22	HUMAN WORK OF ART Cliff Richard (EMI)
12	23	THAT'S THE WAY LOVE GOES Janet Jackson (Virgin)
-	24	LIKE A SATELLITE Thunder (EMI)
20	25	IN THESE ARMS Bon Jovi (Jambco)
19	26	FACE THE STRANGE (EP) Therapy? (A&M)
17	27	DARK IS THE NIGHT A-Ha (Warner Bros.)
36	28	THINKING OF YOU '93 REMIXES Sister Sledge (Atlantic)
-	29	RESURRECTION Brian May with Cozy Powell (Parlophone)
22	30	BREAK IT DOWN AGAIN Tears For Fears (Mercury)
31	31	FROM DESPAIR TO WHERE Manic Street Preachers (Columbia)
23	32	THE JUNGLE BOOK GROOVE Various (Hollywood)
24	33	HOUSECALL Shabba Ranks featuring Maxi Priest (Epic)
27	34	WILL YOU LOVE ME TOMORROW Bryan Ferry (Virgin)
-	35	QUEEN JANE Kingmaker (Scorch)
29	36	LORDS OF THE NEW CHURCH Tasmin Archer (EMI)
-	37	THE POWER ZONE (EP) Time Frequency (Internal Affairs)
38	38	IN YOUR EYES Niamh Kavanagh (Arista)
-	39	BUDDY X Neneh Cherry (Circa)
43	40	IN A WORD OR 2/THE POWER Monie Love (Cooltempo)
-	41	HUMAN BEHAVIOUR Bjork (One Little Indian)
-	42	MORE THAN LIKELY PM Dawn featuring Boy George (Gee Street)
35	43	BLACK TIE WHITE NOISE David Bowie featuring Al B Sure! (Savage)
44	44	ALL FUNKED UP Mother (Bosting)
26	45	CREATION Stereo MC's (4th & Broadway)
41	46	GET HERE Q featuring Tracey Ackerman (Arista)
30	47	I WANNA HOLD ON TO YOU Mica Paris (4th & Broadway)
32	48	I HAVE NOTHING Whitney Houston (Arista)
-	49	LOVE IS STRONGER THAN DEATH The The (Epic)
-	50	BUSY BEE Ugly Kid Joe (A&M)

Shout by Louchie Lou & Michie One was the first of a host of ragga versions (give it a reggae beat and insert some rap material in the middle) of 60s pop hits. Jamiroquai signed for a 6 album, zillion pound deal on the strength of one release, and hit with every single off the 1st album *Emergency On Planet Earth*.

26 June 1993

last week	this week	title	artist (label)
4	1	DREAMS	Gabrielle (Go! Beat)
1	2	(I CAN'T HELP) FALLING IN LOVE WITH YOU	UB40 (DEP International)
3	3	WHAT IS LOVE	Haddaway (Logic)
2	4	ALL THAT SHE WANTS	Ace Of Base (Metronome)
5	5	TWO PRINCES	Spin Doctors (Epic)
8	6	TEASE ME	Chaka Demus & Pliers (Mango)
10	7	IN ALL THE RIGHT PLACES	Lisa Stansfield (MCA)
6	8	CAN YOU FORGIVE HER?	Pet Shop Boys (Parlophone)
7	9	SWEAT (A LA LA LA LONG)	Inner Circle (Magnet)
-	10	HAVE I TOLD YOU LATELY (LIVE)	Rod Stewart (Warner Bros.)
9	11	DO YOU SEE THE LIGHT (LOOKING FOR)	Snap (Logic)
19	12	DELICATE	Terence Trent D'Arby featuring Des'Ree (Columbia)
14	13	FIELDS OF GOLD	Sting (A&M)
-	14	ONE NIGHT IN HEAVEN	M People (deConstruction)
-	15	WEST END GIRLS	East 17 (London)
16	16	NO ORDINARY LOVE	Sade (Epic)
-	17	I WILL SURVIVE (PHIL KELSEY REMIX)	Gloria Gaynor (Polydor Classics)
12	18	SHOUT	Louchie Lou & Michie One (ffrr)
13	19	I DON'T WANNA FIGHT	Tina Turner (Parlophone)
11	20	THREE LITTLE PIGS	Green Jelly (Zoo)
29	21	RESURRECTION	Brian May/Cozy Powell (Parl'ne)
28	22	THINKING OF YOU '93 REMIXES	Sister Sledge (Atlantic)
-	23	WHAT'CHA GONNA DO?	Shabba Ranks featuring Queen Latifah (Epic)
16	24	TRIBAL DANCE	2 Unlimited (PWL International)
25	25	IN YOUR EYES	Niamh Kavanagh (Arista)
17	26	BLOW YOUR MIND	Jamiroquai (Orenda)
18	27	FIVE LIVE (EP)	George Michael/Queen/Lisa Stansfield (Parlophone)
21	28	TOP O' THE MORNING TO YA (REMIX)/HOUSE OF PAIN	House Of Pain (XL)
-	29	WEAK	SWV (RCA)
37	30	THE POWER ZONE (EP)	Time Frequency (Internal Affairs)
20	31	EVERYBODY HURTS	REM (Warner Bros.)
23	32	THAT'S THE WAY LOVE GOES	Janet Jackson (Virgin)
25	33	IN THESE ARMS	Bon Jovi (Jambco)
31	34	FROM DESPAIR TO WHERE	Manic Street Preachers (Columbia)
35	35	QUEEN JANE	Kingmaker (Scorch)
22	36	HUMAN WORK OF ART	Cliff Richard (EMI)
27	37	DARK IS THE NIGHT	A-Ha (Warner Bros.)
26	38	FACE THE STRANGE (EP)	Therapy? (A&M)
39	39	BUDDY X	Neneh Cherry (Circa)
-	40	BEYOND YOUR WILDEST DREAMS	Sybil (PWL International)
49	41	LOVE IS STRONGER THAN DEATH	The The (Epic)
-	42	BABY BE MINE	Blackstreet f'trng Teddy Riley (MCA)
24	43	LIKE A SATELLITE	Thunder (EMI)
50	44	BUSY BEE	Ugly Kid Joe (A&M)
41	45	HUMAN BEHAVIOUR	Bjork (One Little Indian)
-	46	ISN'T IT AMAZING	Hothouse Flowers (London)
42	47	MORE THAN LIKELY	PM Dawn featuring Boy George (Gee Street)
-	48	UNITED WE LOVE YOU	Manchester United & the Champions (Living Beat)
-	49	SHOCK TO THE SYSTEM	Billy Idol (Chrysalis)
-	50	ALL OR NOTHING (EP)	Dogs D'Amour (China)

3 July 1993

this week	title	artist (label)
1	DREAMS	Gabrielle (Go! Beat)
2	WHAT IS LOVE	Haddaway (Logic)
3	(I CAN'T HELP) FALLING IN LOVE WITH YOU	UB40 (DEP International)
4	TEASE ME	Chaka Demus & Pliers (Mango)
5	HAVE I TOLD YOU LATELY (LIVE)	Rod Stewart (Warner Bros.)
6	ALL THAT SHE WANTS	Ace Of Base (Metronome)
7	I WILL SURVIVE (PHIL KELSEY REMIX)	Gloria Gaynor (Polydor Classics)
8	TWO PRINCES	Spin Doctors (Epic)
9	IN ALL THE RIGHT PLACES	Lisa Stansfield (MCA)
10	ONE NIGHT IN HEAVEN	M People (deConstruction)
11	WEST END GIRLS	East 17 (London)
12	DELICATE	Terence Trent D'Arby featuring Des'Ree (Columbia)
13	SWEAT (A LA LA LA LONG)	Inner Circle (Magnet)
14	FIELDS OF GOLD	Sting (A&M)
15	DO YOU SEE THE LIGHT (LOOKING FOR)	Snap (Logic)
16	CAN YOU FORGIVE HER?	Pet Shop Boys (Parlophone)
17	NO ORDINARY LOVE	Sade (Epic)
18	I WANNA LOVE YOU	Jade (Giant)
19	RUINED IN A DAY	New Order (London)
20	EVERYBODY DANCE	Evolution (deConstruction)
21	WHAT'CHA GONNA DO?	Shabba Ranks featuring Queen Latifah (Epic)
22	I CAN SEE CLEARLY	Deborah Harry (Chrysalis)
23	THE POWER ZONE (EP)	Time Frequency (Internal Affairs)
24	SHOUT	Louchie Lou & Michie One (ffrr)
25	I DON'T WANNA FIGHT	Tina Turner (Parlophone)
26	IN YOUR EYES	Niamh Kavanagh (Arista)
27	CAN'T GET ENOUGH OF YOUR LOVE	Taylor Dayne (Arista)
28	SHOCK TO THE SYSTEM	Billy Idol (Chrysalis)
29	THINKING OF YOU '93 REMIXES	Sister Sledge (Atlantic)
30	NOTHIN' MY LOVE CAN'T FIX	Joey Lawrence (EMI)
31	THREE LITTLE PIGS	Green Jelly (Zoo)
32	WEAK	SWV (RCA)
33	CHERUB ROCK	Smashing Pumpkins (Hut)
34	TAKE ME FOR A LITTLE WHILE	Coverdale Page (EMI)
35	WHAT'S UP	4 Non Blondes (Interscope)
36	RESURRECTION	Brian May with Cozy Powell (Parlophone)
37	EAT THE RICH	Aerosmith (Geffen)
38	BLOW YOUR MIND	Jamiroquai (Orenda)
39	BUDDY X	Neneh Cherry (Circa)
40	MI TIERRA	Gloria Estefan (Epic)
41	I FEEL IT/THOUSAND	Moby (Equator)
42	TRIBAL DANCE	2 Unlimited (PWL International)
43	FIVE LIVE (EP)	George Michael/Queen/Lisa Stansfield (Parlophone)
44	SUPERMODEL (YOU BETTER WORK)	RuPaul (Tommy Boy)
45	PERSUASION	Tim Finn (Capitol)
46	QUEEN JANE	Kingmaker (Scorch)
47	BABY BE MINE	Blackstreet featuring Teddy Riley (MCA)
48	MISS CATHERINE	kd lang (Sire)
49	RADIO	Teenage Fanclub (Creation)
50	TOP O' THE MORNING TO YA (REMIX)/HOUSE OF PAIN	House Of Pain (XL)

10 July 1993

this week	title	artist (label)
1	DREAMS	Gabrielle (Go! Beat)
2	WHAT IS LOVE	Haddaway (Logic)
3	TEASE ME	Chaka Demus & Pliers (Mango)
4	(I CAN'T HELP) FALLING IN LOVE WITH YOU	UB40 (DEP International)
5	I WILL SURVIVE (PHIL KELSEY REMIX)	Gloria Gaynor (Polydor Classics)
6	HAVE I TOLD YOU LATELY (LIVE)	Rod Stewart (Warner Bros.)
7	ONE NIGHT IN HEAVEN	M People (deConstruction)
8	ALL THAT SHE WANTS	Ace Of Base (Metronome)
9	TWO PRINCES	Spin Doctors (Epic)
10	IN ALL THE RIGHT PLACES	Lisa Stansfield (MCA)
11	WHAT'S UP	4 Non Blondes (Interscope)
12	WILL YOU BE THERE	Michael Jackson (Epic)
13	WEST END GIRLS	East 17 (London)
14	I WANNA LOVE YOU	Jade (Giant)
15	RUINED IN A DAY	New Order (London)
16	DELICATE	Terence Trent D'Arby featuring Des'Ree (Columbia)
17	NOTHIN' MY LOVE CAN'T FIX	Joey Lawrence (EMI)
18	BELARUSE	Levellers (China)
19	I CAN SEE CLEARLY	Deborah Harry (Chrysalis)
20	EVERYBODY DANCE	Evolution (deConstruction)
21	SWEAT (A LA LA LA LONG)	Inner Circle (Magnet)
22	DO YOU SEE THE LIGHT (LOOKING FOR)	Snap (Logic)
23	IF I CAN'T HAVE YOU	Kim Wilde (MCA)
24	CAN'T GET ENOUGH OF YOUR LOVE	Taylor Dayne (Arista)
25	THE POWER ZONE (EP)	Time Frequency (Internal Affairs)
26	FIELDS OF GOLD	Sting (A&M)
27	STAY	Kenny Thomas (Cooltempo)
28	BIG GUN	AC/DC (Atco)
29	NO ORDINARY LOVE	Sade (Epic)
30	SWEAT	Usura (deConstruction)
31	SOUND OF SPEED (EP)	Jesus and Mary Chain (blanco y negro)
32	CAN YOU FORGIVE HER?	Pet Shop Boys (Parlophone)
33	WHAT'CHA GONNA DO?	Shabba Ranks featuring Queen Latifah (Epic)
34	RIDDIM	Us3 featuring Tukka Yoot (Capitol)
35	ZEROES & ONES	Jesus Jones (Food)
36	SHOUT	Louchie Lou & Michie One (ffrr)
37	IN THE MIDDLE	Alexander O'Neal (Tabu)
38	THREE LITTLE PIGS	Green Jelly (Zoo)
39	MI TIERRA	Gloria Estefan (Epic)
40	GIVE ME LOVE (EENIE MEENIE MINY MO)	David Morales & the Bad Yard Club (Mercury)
41	SUPERMODEL (YOU BETTER WORK)	RuPaul (Tommy Boy)
42	CHEMICAL WORLD	Blur (Food)
43	I DON'T WANNA FIGHT	Tina Turner (Parlophone)
44	SHOCK TO THE SYSTEM	Billy Idol (Chrysalis)
45	EAT THE RICH	Aerosmith (Geffen)
46	IN YOUR EYES	Niamh Kavanagh (Arista)
47	I JUST HAD TO HEAR YOUR VOICE	Oleta Adams (Fontana)
48	I FEEL IT/THOUSAND	Moby (Equator)
49	CHERUB ROCK	Smashing Pumpkins (Hut)
50	PERSUASION	Tim Finn (Capitol)

Thousand by Moby made the Guiness Book Of Records as the fastest record of all time. It started at 1 beat per minute and ended up at 1,000. Rod Stewart just kept on charting, while RuPaul, the transvestite supermodel, entered lower down. Gloria Gaynor was back with the song that made Number One in 1979.

July 1993

17 July 1993

last week	this week	Title	Artist
-	1	PRAY	Take That (RCA)
1	2	DREAMS	Gabrielle (Go! Beat)
2	3	WHAT IS LOVE	Haddaway (Logic)
3	4	TEASE ME	Chaka Demus & Pliers (Mango)
5	5	I WILL SURVIVE (PHIL KELSEY REMIX)	Gloria Gaynor (Polydor Classics)
4	6	(I CAN'T HELP) FALLING IN LOVE WITH YOU	UB40 (DEP International)
11	7	WHAT'S UP	4 Non Blondes (Interscope)
7	8	ONE NIGHT IN HEAVEN	M People (deConstruction)
6	9	HAVE I TOLD YOU LATELY (LIVE)	Rod Stewart (Warner Bros.)
9	10	TWO PRINCES	Spin Doctors (Epic)
12	11	WILL YOU BE THERE	Michael Jackson (Epic)
8	12	ALL THAT SHE WANTS	Ace Of Base (Metronome)
10	13	IN ALL THE RIGHT PLACES	Lisa Stansfield (MCA)
23	14	IF I CAN'T HAVE YOU	Kim Wilde (MCA)
17	15	NOTHIN' MY LOVE CAN'T FIX	Joey Lawrence (EMI)
-	16	THIS IS IT	Dannii Minogue (MCA)
14	17	I WANNA LOVE YOU	Jade (Giant)
-	18	SUNFLOWER	Paul Weller (Go! Discs)
24	19	CAN'T GET ENOUGH OF YOUR LOVE	Taylor Dayne (Arista)
-	20	HANG YOUR HEAD	Deacon Blue (Columbia)
18	21	BELARUSE	Levellers (China)
13	22	WEST END GIRLS	East 17 (London)
27	23	STAY	Kenny Thomas (Cooltempo)
21	24	SWEAT (A LA LA LA LA LONG)	Inner Circle (Magnet)
20	25	EVERYBODY DANCE	Evolution (deConstruction)
35	26	ZEROES & ONES	Jesus Jones (Food)
25	27	THE POWER ZONE (EP)	Time Frequency (Internal Affairs)
16	28	DELICATE	Terence Trent D'Arby featuring Des'Ree (Columbia)
-	29	I WANT YOU	Utah Saints (ffrr)
42	30	CHEMICAL WORLD	Blur (Food)
-	31	BREAK FROM THE OLD ROUTINE	Oui 3 (MCA)
32	32	BIG GUN	AC/DC (Atco)
30	33	SWEAT	Usura (deConstruction)
-	34	THE KEY: THE SECRET	Urban Cookie Collective (Pulse 8)
22	35	DO YOU SEE THE LIGHT (LOOKING FOR)	Snap (Logic)
15	36	RUINED IN A DAY	New Order (London)
31	37	SOUND OF SPEED (EP)	Jesus And Mary Chain (blanco y negro)
-	38	DO YOU REALLY WANT ME	Jon Secada (SBK)
-	39	GIVE IT ALL AWAY	World Party (Ensign)
19	40	I CAN SEE CLEARLY	Deborah Harry (Chrysalis)
-	41	DREAM OF ME	Orchestral Manoeuvres In The Dark (Virgin)
34	42	RIDDIM	Us3 featuring Tukka Yoot (Capitol)
-	43	RUNAWAY TRAIN	Soul Asylum (Columbia)
40	44	GIVE ME LOVE (EENIE MEENIE MINY MO)	David Morales & the Bad Yard Club (Mercury)
38	45	THREE LITTLE PIGS	Green Jelly (Zoo)
37	46	IN THE MIDDLE	Alexander O'Neal (Tabu)
-	47	SOON BE DONE	Shaggy (Greensleeves)
-	48	SOMEWHERE	Efua (Virgin)
47	49	I JUST HAD TO HEAR YOUR VOICE	Oleta Adams (Fontana)
-	50	BUT I DO	Clarence 'Frogman' Henry (MCA)

24 July 1993

Title	Artist
1 1 PRAY	Take That (RCA)
2 2 DREAMS	Gabrielle (Go! Beat)
3 3 WHAT IS LOVE	Haddaway (Logic)
7 4 WHAT'S UP	4 Non Blondes (Interscope)
4 5 TEASE ME	Chaka Demus & Pliers (Mango)
5 6 I WILL SURVIVE (PHIL KELSEY REMIX)	Gloria Gaynor (Polydor Classics)
6 7 (I CAN'T HELP) FALLING IN LOVE WITH YOU	UB40 (DEP International)
8 8 ONE NIGHT IN HEAVEN	M People (deConstruction)
14 9 IF I CAN'T HAVE YOU	Kim Wilde (MCA)
11 10 WILL YOU BE THERE	Michael Jackson (Epic)
- 11 ALMOST UNREAL	Roxette (EMI)
19 12 CAN'T GET ENOUGH OF YOUR LOVE	Taylor Dayne (Arista)
16 13 THIS IS IT	Dannii Minogue (MCA)
9 14 HAVE I TOLD YOU LATELY (LIVE)	Rod Stewart (Warner Bros.)
10 15 TWO PRINCES	Spin Doctors (Epic)
12 16 ALL THAT SHE WANTS	Ace Of Base (Metronome)
13 17 IN ALL THE RIGHT PLACES	Lisa Stansfield (MCA)
34 18 THE KEY: THE SECRET	Urban Cookie Collective (Pulse 8)
15 19 NOTHIN' MY LOVE CAN'T FIX	Joey Lawrence (EMI)
- 20 YOU'RE THE ONE THAT I WANT	Craig McClachlan & Debbie Gibson (Epic)
20 21 HANG YOUR HEAD	Deacon Blue (Columbia)
17 22 I WANNA LOVE YOU	Jade (Giant)
18 23 SUNFLOWER	Paul Weller (Go! Discs)
- 24 NIGHTSWIMMING	REM (Warner Bros.)
23 25 STAY	Kenny Thomas (Cooltempo)
21 26 BELARUSE	Levellers (China)
- 27 DOWN THAT ROAD	Shara Nelson (Cooltempo)
31 28 BREAK FROM THE OLD ROUTINE	Oui 3 (MCA)
29 29 I WANT YOU	Utah Saints (ffrr)
- 30 GLASTONBURY SONG	Waterboys (Geffen)
22 31 WEST END GIRLS	East 17 (London)
38 32 DO YOU REALLY WANT ME	Jon Secada (SBK)
24 33 SWEAT (A LA LA LA LA LONG)	Inner Circle (Magnet)
30 34 CHEMICAL WORLD	Blur (Food)
- 35 LIVING IN THE ROSE – THE BALLADS (EP)	New Model Army (Epic)
41 36 DREAM OF ME	Orchestral Manoeuvres In The Dark (Virgin)
25 37 EVERYBODY DANCE	Evolution (deConstruction)
- 38 THE DRUMSTRUCK (EP)	N-Joi (deConstruction)
39 39 GIVE IT ALL AWAY	World Party (Ensign)
48 40 SOMEWHERE	Efua (Virgin)
- 41 THIRD RAIL	Squeeze (A&M)
26 42 ZEROES & ONES	Jesus Jones (Food)
33 43 SWEAT	Usura (deConstruction)
32 44 BIG GUN	AC/DC (Atco)
27 45 THE POWER ZONE (EP)	Time Frequency (Internal Affairs)
44 46 TAKE A FREE FALL	Dance To Trance (Logic)
- 47 GIVE ME LOVE (EENIE MEENIE MINY MO)	David Morales & the Bad Yard Club (Mercury)
43 48 RUNAWAY TRAIN	Soul Asylum (Columbia)
42 49 RIDDIM	Us3 featuring Tukka Yoot (Capitol)
45 50 THREE LITTLE PIGS	Green Jelly (Zoo)

31 July 1993

Title	Artist
1 1 PRAY	Take That (RCA)
4 2 WHAT'S UP	4 Non Blondes (Interscope)
2 3 DREAMS	Gabrielle (Go! Beat)
- 4 RAIN	Madonna (Maverick)
5 5 TEASE ME	Chaka Demus & Pliers (Mango)
3 6 WHAT IS LOVE	Haddaway (Logic)
11 7 ALMOST UNREAL	Roxette (EMI)
- 8 LIVING ON MY OWN	Freddie Mercury (Parlophone)
8 9 ONE NIGHT IN HEAVEN	M People (deConstruction)
13 10 THIS IS IT	Dannii Minogue (MCA)
7 11 (I CAN'T HELP) FALLING IN LOVE WITH YOU	UB40 (DEP International)
10 12 WILL YOU BE THERE	Michael Jackson (Epic)
6 13 I WILL SURVIVE (PHIL KELSEY REMIX)	Gloria Gaynor (Polydor Classics)
9 14 IF I CAN'T HAVE YOU	Kim Wilde (MCA)
20 15 YOU'RE THE ONE THAT I WANT	Craig McClachlan & Debbie Gibson (Epic)
- 16 LUV 4 LUV	Robin S (Champion)
12 17 CAN'T GET ENOUGH OF YOUR LOVE	Taylor Dayne (Arista)
- 18 RUN TO YOU	Whitney Houston (Arista)
14 19 HAVE I TOLD YOU LATELY (LIVE)	Rod Stewart (Warner Bros.)
18 20 THE KEY: THE SECRET	Urban Cookie Collective (Pulse 8)
28 21 BREAK FROM THE OLD ROUTINE	Oui 3 (MCA)
- 22 IF	Janet Jackson (Virgin)
24 23 NIGHTSWIMMING	REM (Warner Bros.)
27 24 DOWN THAT ROAD	Shara Nelson (Cooltempo)
- 25 LA TRISTESSE DURERA (SCREAM TO A SIGH)	Manic Street Preachers (Columbia)
16 26 ALL THAT SHE WANTS	Ace Of Base (Metronome)
15 27 TWO PRINCES	Spin Doctors (Epic)
36 28 DREAM OF ME	Orchestral Manoeuvres In The Dark (Virgin)
- 29 RIVER OF DREAMS	Billy Joel (Columbia)
17 30 IN ALL THE RIGHT PLACES	Lisa Stansfield (MCA)
25 31 STAY	Kenny Thomas (Cooltempo)
23 32 SUNFLOWER	Paul Weller (Go! Discs)
- 33 CAUGHT IN THE MIDDLE	Juliet Roberts (Cooltempo)
- 34 UNFORGIVEN	D:Ream (Magnet)
29 35 I WANT YOU	Utah Saints (ffrr)
30 36 GLASTONBURY SONG	Waterboys (Geffen)
22 37 I WANNA LOVE YOU	Jade (Giant)
- 38 INSANE IN THE BRAIN	Cypress Hill (Ruff House)
- 39 HOW LONG	Yazz & Aswad (Polydor)
41 40 THIRD RAIL	Squeeze (A&M)
32 41 DO YOU REALLY WANT ME	Jon Secada (SBK)
19 42 NOTHIN' MY LOVE CAN'T FIX	Joey Lawrence (EMI)
- 43 LIGHT OF THE WORLD	Kim Appleby (Parlophone)
21 44 HANG YOUR HEAD	Deacon Blue (Columbia)
40 45 SOMEWHERE	Efua (Virgin)
38 46 THE DRUMSTRUCK (EP)	N-Joi (deConstruction)
46 47 TAKE A FREE FALL	Dance To Trance (Logic)
- 48 CHERISH THE DAY	Sade (Epic)
- 49 IT KEEPS RAINING (TEARS FROM MY EYES)	Bitty McLean (Brilliant)
33 50 SWEAT (A LA LA LA LA LONG)	Inner Circle (Magnet)

Take That went straight in at Number One – again, while Craig McClachlan and Debbie Gibson revived one of the best selling singles of all time, as the musical *Grease* opened on the West End stage. Shara Nelson went solo from Massive Attack, and Paul Weller continued *his* solo success with *Sunflower*.

7 August 1993

last week	this week	Title	Artist (Label)
1	1	PRAY	Take That (RCA)
2	2	WHAT'S UP	4 Non Blondes (Interscope)
8	3	LIVING ON MY OWN	Freddie Mercury (Parlophone)
3	4	DREAMS	Gabrielle (Go! Beat)
5	5	TEASE ME	Chaka Demus & Pliers (Mango)
4	6	RAIN	Madonna (Maverick)
7	7	ALMOST UNREAL	Roxette (EMI)
6	8	WHAT IS LOVE	Haddaway (Logic)
16	9	LUV 4 LUV	Robin S (Champion)
9	10	ONE NIGHT IN HEAVEN	M People (deConstruction)
20	11	THE KEY: THE SECRET	Urban Cookie Collective (Pulse 8)
10	12	THIS IS IT	Dannii Minogue (MCA)
11	13	(I CAN'T HELP) FALLING IN LOVE WITH YOU	UB40 (DEP International)
18	14	RUN TO YOU	Whitney Houston (Arista)
15	15	YOU'RE THE THE ONE THAT I WANT	Craig McClachlan & Debbie Gibson (Epic)
29	16	RIVER OF DREAMS	Billy Joel (Columbia)
-	17	LOOKING UP	Michelle Gayle (1st Avenue)
-	18	I'LL SLEEP WHEN I'M DEAD	Bon Jovi (Jambco)
13	19	I WILL SURVIVE (PHIL KELSEY REMIX)	Gloria Gaynor (Polydor Classics)
24	20	DOWN THAT ROAD	Shara Nelson (Cooltempo)
34	21	UNFORGIVEN	D:Ream (Magnet)
14	22	IF I CAN'T HAVE YOU	Kim Wilde (MCA)
22	23	IF	Janet Jackson (Virgin)
21	24	BREAK FROM THE OLD ROUTINE	Oui 3 (MCA)
12	25	WILL YOU BE THERE	Michael Jackson (Epic)
49	26	IT KEEPS RAINING (TEARS FROM MY EYES)	Bitty McLean (Brilliant)
19	27	HAVE I TOLD YOU LATELY (LIVE)	Rod Stewart (Warner Bros.)
25	28	LA TRISTESSE DURERA (SCREAM TO A SIGH)	Manic Street Preachers (Columbia)
-	29	GIVE IT UP	Goodmen (ffrreedom)
-	30	WHATEVER HAPPENED TO OLD FASHIONED LOVE	Daniel O'Donnell (Ritz)
17	31	CAN'T GET ENOUGH OF YOUR LOVE	Taylor Dayne (Arista)
23	32	NIGHTSWIMMING	REM (Warner Bros.)
27	33	TWO PRINCES	Spin Doctors (Epic)
-	34	ALL AROUND THE WORLD	Jason Donovan (Polydor)
39	35	HOW LONG	Yazz & Aswad (Polydor)
28	36	DREAM OF ME	Orchestral Manoeuvres In The Dark (Virgin)
26	37	ALL THAT SHE WANTS	Ace Of Base (Metronome)
-	38	MR VAIN	Culture Beat (Epic)
38	39	INSANE IN THE BRAIN	Cypress Hill (Ruff House)
-	40	CHECK YO SELF	Ice Cube (4th & Broadway)
-	41	UPTOWN TOPRANKING	Ali & Frazier (Arista)
-	42	LOVE SO STRONG	Secret Life (Cowboy)
43	43	LIGHT OF THE WORLD	Kim Appleby (Parlophone)
-	44	SUNTAN	Stan (Hug)
32	45	SUNFLOWER	Paul Weller (Go! Discs)
33	46	CAUGHT IN THE MIDDLE	Juliet Roberts (Cooltempo)
-	47	WHITE LOVE	One Dove (Boy's Own)
48	48	CHERISH THE DAY	Sade (Epic)
-	49	BAD BOYS	Inner Circle (Magnet)
30	50	IN ALL THE RIGHT PLACES	Lisa Stansfield (MCA)

14 August 1993

last week	this week	Title	Artist (Label)
3	1	LIVING ON MY OWN	Freddie Mercury (Parlophone)
1	2	PRAY	Take That (RCA)
2	3	WHAT'S UP	4 Non Blondes (Interscope)
11	4	THE KEY: THE SECRET	Urban Cookie Collective (Pulse 8)
5	5	TEASE ME	Chaka Demus & Pliers (Mango)
4	6	DREAMS	Gabrielle (Go! Beat)
16	7	RIVER OF DREAMS	Billy Joel (Columbia)
7	8	ALMOST UNREAL	Roxette (EMI)
6	9	RAIN	Madonna (Maverick)
8	10	WHAT IS LOVE	Haddaway (Logic)
9	11	LUV 4 LUV	Robin S (Champion)
-	12	NUFF VIBES (EP)	Apache Indian (Island)
18	13	I'LL SLEEP WHEN I'M DEAD	Bon Jovi (Jambco)
17	14	LOOKING UP	Michelle Gayle (1st Avenue)
12	15	THIS IS IT	Dannii Minogue (MCA)
26	16	IT KEEPS RAINING (TEARS FROM MY EYES)	Bitty McLean (Brilliant)
14	17	RUN TO YOU	Whitney Houston (Arista)
38	18	MR VAIN	Culture Beat (Epic)
10	19	ONE NIGHT IN HEAVEN	M People (deConstruction)
15	20	YOU'RE THE THE ONE THAT I WANT	Craig McClachlan & Debbie Gibson (Epic)
13	21	(I CAN'T HELP) FALLING IN LOVE WITH YOU	UB40 (DEP International)
20	22	DOWN THAT ROAD	Shara Nelson (Cooltempo)
-	23	I WILL ALWAYS LOVE YOU	Sarah Washington (Almighty)
23	24	IF	Janet Jackson (Virgin)
30	25	WHATEVER HAPPENED TO OLD FASHIONED LOVE	Daniel O'Donnell (Ritz)
19	26	I WILL SURVIVE (PHIL KELSEY REMIX)	Gloria Gaynor (Polydor Classics)
27	27	GIVE IT UP	Goodmen (ffrreedom)
-	28	LITTLE MISS CAN'T BE WRONG	Spin Doctors (Epic)
-	29	DON'T TALK ABOUT LOVE	Bad Boys Inc (A&M)
25	30	WILL YOU BE THERE	Michael Jackson (Epic)
-	31	ANARCHY IN THE UK	Green Jelly (Zoo)
32	32	IF I CAN'T HAVE YOU	Kim Wilde (MCA)
24	33	BREAK FROM THE OLD ROUTINE	Oui 3 (MCA)
-	34	EMERGENCY ON PLANET EARTH	Jamiroquai (Orenda)
35	35	HOW LONG	Yazz & Aswad (Polydor)
28	36	LA TRISTESSE DURERA (SCREAM TO A SIGH)	Manic Street Preachers (Columbia)
34	37	ALL AROUND THE WORLD	Jason Donovan (Polydor)
27	38	HAVE I TOLD YOU LATELY (LIVE)	Rod Stewart (Warner Bros.)
40	39	CHECK YO SELF	Ice Cube (4th & Broadway)
21	40	UNFORGIVEN	D:Ream (Magnet)
41	41	UPTOWN TOPRANKING	Ali & Frazier (Arista)
37	42	ALL THAT SHE WANTS	Ace Of Base (Metronome)
42	43	LOVE SO STRONG	Secret Life (Cowboy)
-	44	IF WE WERE LOVERS/ CON LOS ANOS QUE ME QUEDAN	Gloria Estefan (Epic)
-	45	OUTER SPACE GIRL	Beloved (East West)
33	46	TWO PRINCES	Spin Doctors (Epic)
-	47	ROCKIN' TO THE MUSIC	Black Box (deConstruction)
39	48	INSANE IN THE BRAIN	Cypress Hill (Ruff House)
47	49	WHITE LOVE	One Dove (Boy's Own)
46	50	CAUGHT IN THE MIDDLE	Juliet Roberts (Cooltempo)

21 August 1993

last week	this week	Title	Artist (Label)
1	1	LIVING ON MY OWN	Freddie Mercury (Parlophone)
4	2	THE KEY: THE SECRET	Urban Cookie Collective (Pulse 8)
16	3	IT KEEPS RAINING (TEARS FROM MY EYES)	Bitty McLean (Brilliant)
7	4	RIVER OF DREAMS	Billy Joel (Columbia)
12	5	NUFF VIBES (EP)	Apache Indian (Island)
2	6	PRAY	Take That (RCA)
3	7	WHAT'S UP	4 Non Blondes (Interscope)
18	8	MR VAIN	Culture Beat (Epic)
5	9	TEASE ME	Chaka Demus & Pliers (Mango)
-	10	HIGHER GROUND	UB40 (DEP International)
6	11	DREAMS	Gabrielle (Go! Beat)
9	12	RAIN	Madonna (Maverick)
14	13	LOOKING UP	Michelle Gayle (1st Avenue)
23	14	I WILL ALWAYS LOVE YOU	Sarah Washington (Almighty)
-	15	DREAMLOVER	Mariah Carey (Columbia)
8	16	ALMOST UNREAL	Roxette (EMI)
11	17	LUV 4 LUV	Robin S (Champion)
10	18	WHAT IS LOVE	Haddaway (Logic)
15	19	THIS IS IT	Dannii Minogue (MCA)
-	20	SLAVE TO THE VIBE	Aftershock (Virgin)
13	21	I'LL SLEEP WHEN I'M DEAD	Bon Jovi (Jambco)
29	22	DON'T TALK ABOUT LOVE	Bad Boys Inc (A&M)
28	23	LITTLE MISS CAN'T BE WRONG	Spin Doctors (Epic)
25	24	WHATEVER HAPPENED TO OLD FASHIONED LOVE	Daniel O'Donnell (Ritz)
24	25	IF	Janet Jackson (Virgin)
27	26	GIVE IT UP	Goodmen (ffrreedom)
17	27	RUN TO YOU	Whitney Houston (Arista)
20	28	YOU'RE THE THE ONE THAT I WANT	Craig McClachlan & Debbie Gibson (Epic)
19	29	ONE NIGHT IN HEAVEN	M People (deConstruction)
-	30	TUESDAY MORNING	Pogues (Warner Bros.)
21	31	(I CAN'T HELP) FALLING IN LOVE WITH YOU	UB40 (DEP International)
31	32	ANARCHY IN THE UK	Green Jelly (Zoo)
34	33	EMERGENCY ON PLANET EARTH	Jamiroquai (Orenda)
-	34	PAYING THE PRICE OF LOVE	Bee Gees (Polydor)
35	35	HOW LONG	Yazz & Aswad (Polydor)
22	36	DOWN THAT ROAD	Shara Nelson (Cooltempo)
-	37	ARIENNE	Tasmin Archer (EMI)
-	38	TILTED	Sugar (Creation)
-	39	LUSH	Orbital (Internal)
41	40	UPTOWN TOPRANKING	Ali & Frazier (Arista)
44	41	IF WE WERE LOVERS/ CON LOS ANOS QUE ME QUEDAN	Gloria Estefan (Epic)
50	42	CAUGHT IN THE MIDDLE	Juliet Roberts (Cooltempo)
45	43	OUTER SPACE GIRL	Beloved (East West)
-	44	NEVER GIVE UP	Monie Love (Cooltempo)
26	45	I WILL SURVIVE (PHIL KELSEY REMIX)	Gloria Gaynor (Polydor Classics)
-	46	AIN'T NO CASANOVA	Sinclair (Dome)
47	47	ROCKIN' TO THE MUSIC	Black Box (deConstruction)
39	48	CHECK YO SELF	Ice Cube (4th & Broadway)
-	49	WILL YOU BE THERE	Michael Jackson (Epic)
-	50	U GOT 2 KNOW (REVISITED)	Capella (Internal)

Freddie Mercury had a posthumous Number One, while soap stars invaded the charts in increasing quantities. Michelle Gayle from Eastenders joined Dannii Minogue, Craig McClachlan and Jason Donovan. UB40 had two singles in the Top 30 and their studio engineer Bitty McClean was at No. 3.

August – September 1993

Paul Weller was enjoying his biggest solo hit so far, while Nirvana showed they were the biggest rock band of the time. Bad Boys Inc came on like a substitute Take That, without ever matching their popularity. And former teen idols Duran Duran were back – though only in the lower reaches of the chart.

18 September 1993

last week	this week	title	artist (label)
1	1	MR VAIN	Culture Beat (Epic)
-	2	GO WEST	Pet Shop Boys (Parlophone)
2	3	RIGHT HERE	SWV (RCA)
3	4	IT KEEPS RAINING (TEARS FROM MY EYES)	Bitty McLean (Brilliant)
5	5	RIVER OF DREAMS	Billy Joel (Columbia)
4	6	HEART-SHAPED BOX	Nirvana (Geffen)
-	7	RUBBERBAND GIRL	Kate Bush (EMI)
18	8	BOOM! SHAKE THE ROOM	Jazzy Jeff & Fresh Prince (Jive)
6	9	LIVING ON MY OWN	Freddie Mercury (Parlophone)
8	10	THE KEY: THE SECRET	Urban Cookie Collective (Pulse 8)
-	11	CREEP	Radiohead (Parlophone)
10	12	FACES	2 Unlimited (PWL Continental)
7	13	DREAMLOVER	Mariah Carey (Columbia)
14	14	WORLD (THE PRICE OF LOVE)	New Order (CentreDate)
9	15	NUFF VIBES (EP)	Apache Indian (Island)
11	16	HIGHER GROUND	UB40 (DEP International)
21	17	SHE KISSED ME	Terence Trent D'Arby (Columbia)
12	18	SLAVE TO THE VIBE	Aftershock (Virgin)
-	19	IT MUST HAVE BEEN LOVE	Roxette (EMI)
20	20	HEAVEN HELP	Lenny Kravitz (Virgin)
17	21	SOMETIMES	James (Fontana)
13	22	DISCO INFERNO	Tina Turner (Parlophone)
15	23	WHAT'S UP	4 Non Blondes (Interscope)
-	24	ONE WOMAN	Jade (Giant)
23	25	TRIPPIN' ON YOUR LOVE	Kenny Thomas (Cooltempo)
26	26	PLUSH	Stone temple Pilots (Atlantic)
35	27	ACE OF SPADES	Motorhead (WGAF)
32	28	SO CALLED FRIEND	Texas (Vertigo)
37	29	MOVE – THE EP	Moby (Mute)
-	30	ONE GOODBYE IN TEN	Shara Nelson (Cooltempo)
34	31	HEY MR DJ	Zhane (Epic)
-	32	TWO STEPS BEHIND	Def Leppard (Bludgeon Riffola)
33	33	VENUS AS A BOY	Bjork (One Little Indian)
16	34	WILD WOOD	Paul Weller (Go! Discs)
-	35	HEAVEN KNOWS	Luther Vandross (Epic)
-	36	SHE DON'T LET NOBODY	Chaka Demus & Pliers (Mango)
19	37	WHEEL OF FORTUNE	Ace Of Base (Metronome)
25	38	I WILL ALWAYS LOVE YOU	Sarah Washington (Almighty)
30	39	TOO MUCH INFORMATION	Duran Duran (Parlophone)
-	40	NEW BREAKADAWN	De La Soul (Big Life)
-	41	TOO MANY PEOPLE	Pauline Henry (Sony Soho Square)
-	42	STRONGER TOGETHER	Sybil (PWL International)
49	43	SOUND OF EDEN/SWEET SENSATION	Shades Of Rhythm (ZTT)
22	44	TEASE ME	Chaka Demus & Pliers (Mango)
-	45	TRUST ME	Guru featuring N'Dea Davenport (Cooltempo)
29	46	SOMEBODY TO SHOVE	Soul Asylum (Columbia)
28	47	PAYING THE PRICE OF LOVE	Bee Gees (Polydor)
26	48	PRAY	Take That (RCA)
-	49	STRIKE ME PINK	Deborah Harry (Chrysalis)
-	50	BACK TO MY ROOTS/HOUSE OF LOVE	RuPaul (Union)

25 September 1993

last week	this week	title	artist (label)
2	1	GO WEST	Pet Shop Boys (Parlophone)
1	2	MR VAIN	Culture Beat (Epic)
8	3	BOOM! SHAKE THE ROOM	Jazzy Jeff & Fresh Prince (Jive)
-	4	MOVING ON UP	M People (deConstruction)
3	5	RIGHT HERE	SWV (RCA)
4	6	IT KEEPS RAINING (TEARS FROM MY EYES)	Bitty McLean (Brilliant)
7	7	RUBBERBAND GIRL	Kate Bush (EMI)
5	8	RIVER OF DREAMS	Billy Joel (Columbia)
-	9	LIFE	Haddaway (Logic)
10	10	ON THE ROPES (EP)	Wonder Stuff (Polydor)
11	11	CREEP	Radiohead (Parlophone)
-	12	CONDEMNATION	Depeche Mode (Mute)
36	13	SHE DON'T LET NOBODY	Chaka Demus & Pliers (Mango)
9	14	LIVING ON MY OWN	Freddie Mercury (Parlophone)
19	15	IT MUST HAVE BEEN LOVE	Roxette (EMI)
13	16	DREAMLOVER	Mariah Carey (Columbia)
10	17	THE KEY: THE SECRET	Urban Cookie Collective (Pulse 8)
12	18	FACES	2 Unlimited (PWL Continental)
20	19	HEAVEN HELP	Lenny Kravitz (Virgin)
-	20	BIG SCARY ANIMAL	Belinda Carlisle (Offside)
15	21	NUFF VIBES (EP)	Apache Indian (Island)
17	22	SHE KISSED ME	Terence Trent D'Arby (Columbia)
24	23	ONE WOMAN	Jade (Giant)
27	24	ACE OF SPADES	Motorhead (WGAF)
32	25	TWO STEPS BEHIND	Def Leppard (Bludgeon Riffola)
-	26	HERE WE GO	Stakka Bo (Polydor)
18	27	SLAVE TO THE VIBE	Aftershock (Virgin)
30	28	ONE GOODBYE IN TEN	Shara Nelson (Cooltempo)
16	29	HIGHER GROUND	UB40 (DEP International)
-	30	WHEN YOU GONNA LEARN	Jamiroquai (Sony Soho Square)
-	31	EVERLASTING LOVE	Worlds Apart (Arista)
-	32	JEWEL	Cranes (Dedicated)
6	33	HEART-SHAPED BOX	Nirvana (Geffen)
14	34	WORLD (THE PRICE OF LOVE)	New Order (CentreDate)
29	35	MOVE – THE EP	Moby (Mute)
-	36	LOVE SCENES	Beverley Craven (Epic)
35	37	HEAVEN KNOWS	Luther Vandross (Epic)
-	38	(NOW I KNOW WHAT MADE) OTIS BLUE	Paul Young (Columbia)
31	39	HEY MR DJ	Zhane (Epic)
-	40	SAIL AWAY	Little Angels (Polydor)
21	41	SOMETIMES	James (Fontana)
25	42	TRIPPIN' ON YOUR LOVE	Kenny Thomas (Cooltempo)
26	43	PLUSH	Stone temple Pilots (Atlantic)
-	44	TODAY	Smashing Pumpkins (Hut)
45	45	DISCO INFERNO	Tina Turner (Parlophone)
33	46	VENUS AS A BOY	Bjork (One Little Indian)
50	47	BACK TO MY ROOTS/HOUSE OF LOVE	RuPaul (Union)
23	48	WHAT'S UP	4 Non Blondes (Interscope)
-	49	CANTALOOP	Us3 featuring Rahsaan (Capitol)
-	50	FASCINATED	Lisa B (ffrr)

2 October 1993

last week	this week	title	artist (label)
3	1	BOOM! SHAKE THE ROOM	Jazzy Jeff & Fresh Prince (Jive)
1	2	GO WEST	Pet Shop Boys (Parlophone)
4	3	MOVING ON UP	M People (deConstruction)
2	4	MR VAIN	Culture Beat (Epic)
13	5	SHE DON'T LET NOBODY	Chaka Demus & Pliers (Mango)
9	6	LIFE	Haddaway (Logic)
-	7	RELAX	Frankie Goes To Hollywood (ZTT)
5	8	RIGHT HERE	SWV (RCA)
6	9	IT KEEPS RAINING (TEARS FROM MY EYES)	Bitty McLean (Brilliant)
20	10	BIG SCARY ANIMAL	Belinda Carlisle (Offside)
-	11	GOING NOWHERE	Gabrielle (Go Beat)
-	12	ROSES IN THE HOSPITAL	Manic Street Preachers (Columbia)
11	13	CREEP	Radiohead (Parlophone)
15	14	IT MUST HAVE BEEN LOVE	Roxette (EMI)
8	15	RIVER OF DREAMS	Billy Joel (Columbia)
10	16	ON THE ROPES (EP)	Wonder Stuff (Polydor)
12	17	CONDEMNATION	Depeche Mode (Mute)
28	18	ONE GOODBYE IN TEN	Shara Nelson (Cooltempo)
26	19	HERE WE GO	Stakka Bo (Polydor)
-	20	WHEN THE SHIP GOES DOWN	Cypress Hill (Ruff House)
-	21	DISTANT SUN	Crowded House (Capitol)
16	22	DREAMLOVER	Mariah Carey (Columbia)
-	23	STAY	Eternal (1st Avenue)
49	24	CANTALOOP	Us3 featuring Rahsaan (Capitol)
7	25	RUBBERBAND GIRL	Kate Bush (EMI)
18	26	FACES	2 Unlimited (PWL Continental)
-	27	WHENEVER YOU NEED SOMEBODY	Bad Boys Inc (A&M)
38	28	(NOW I KNOW WHAT MADE) OTIS BLUE	Paul Young (Columbia)
-	29	NEVER LET GO	Cliff Richard (EMI)
14	30	LIVING ON MY OWN	Freddie Mercury (Parlophone)
-	31	THIS IS THE WAY	Dannii Minogue (MCA)
-	32	EVANGELINE	Cocteau Twins (Fontana)
31	33	EVERLASTING LOVE	Worlds Apart (Arista)
-	34	THE KEY: THE SECRET	Urban Cookie Collective (Pulse 8)
19	35	HEAVEN HELP	Lenny Kravitz (Virgin)
23	36	ONE WOMAN	Jade (Giant)
37	37	LOVE SCENES	Beverley Craven (Epic)
29	38	HIGHER GROUND	UB40 (DEP International)
21	39	NUFF VIBES (EP)	Apache Indian (Island)
30	40	WHEN YOU GONNA LEARN	Jamiroquai (Sony Soho Square)
-	41	TRACKS OF MY TEARS	Go West (Chrysalis)
-	42	I LIKE IT/STAR	D:Ream (FXU)
50	43	FASCINATED	Lisa B (ffrr)
25	44	TWO STEPS BEHIND	Def Leppard (Bludgeon Riffola)
-	45	JOY	Staxx (Champion)
-	46	NORMAN 3	Teenage Fanclub (Creation)
22	47	SHE KISSED ME	Terence Trent D'Arby (Columbia)
48	48	KISS THAT FROG	Peter Gabriel (Virgin)
24	49	ACE OF SPADES	Motorhead (WGAF)
27	50	SLAVE TO THE VIBE	Aftershock (Virgin)

Village People recorded *Go West* in 1979 as part of the Gay scene in America ('go west' to San Francisco). The Pet Shop Boys took it to Number One with an ironic cover version. M People had their biggest hit so far. Worlds Apart were another Take That-style boy group with a cover of an old classic.

October 1993

last week	this week	9 October 1993	
-	1	RELIGHT MY FIRE	Take That featuring Lulu (RCA)
1	2	BOOM! SHAKE THE ROOM	Jazzy Jeff & Fresh Prince (Jive)
3	3	MOVING ON UP	M People (deConstruction)
7	4	RELAX	Frankie Goes To Hollywood (ZTT)
5	5	SHE DON'T LET NOBODY	Chaka Demus & Pliers (Mango)
2	6	GO WEST	Pet Shop Boys (Parlophone)
6	7	LIFE	Haddaway (Logic)
4	8	MR VAIN	Culture Beat (Epic)
-	9	I'D DO ANYTHING FOR LOVE (BUT I WON'T DO THAT)	Meatloaf (Virgin)
11	10	GOING NOWHERE	Gabrielle (Go Beat)
8	11	RIGHT HERE	SWV (RCA)
19	12	HERE WE GO	Stakka Bo (Polydor)
23	13	STAY	Eternal (1st Avenue)
10	14	BIG SCARY ANIMAL	Belinda Carlisle (Offside)
14	15	IT MUST HAVE BEEN LOVE	Roxette (EMI)
28	16	(NOW I KNOW WHAT MADE) OTIS BLUE	Paul Young (Columbia)
21	17	DISTANT SUN	Crowded House (Capitol)
41	18	TRACKS OF MY TEARS	Go West (Chrysalis)
9	19	IT KEEPS RAINING (TEARS FROM MY EYES)	Bitty McLean (Brilliant)
12	20	ROSES IN THE HOSPITAL	Manic Street Preachers (Columbia)
-	21	CHAIN REACTION	Diana Ross (EMI)
15	22	RIVER OF DREAMS	Billy Joel (Columbia)
13	23	CREEP	Radiohead (Parlophone)
24	24	CANTALOOP	Us3 featuring Rahsaan (Capitol)
20	25	WHEN THE SHIP GOES DOWN	Cypress Hill (Ruff House)
-	26	RUNAWAY LOVE	En Vogue (East West America)
16	27	ON THE ROPES (EP)	Wonder Stuff (Polydor)
33	28	EVERLASTING LOVE	Worlds Apart (Arista)
27	29	WHENEVER YOU NEED SOMEBODY	Bad Boys Inc (A&M)
-	30	I BELIEVE	Bon Jovi (Jambco)
18	31	ONE GOODBYE IN TEN	Shara Nelson (Cooltempo)
22	32	DREAMLOVER	Mariah Carey (Columbia)
-	33	SHOOP	Salt 'N' Pepa (ffrr)
31	34	THIS IS THE WAY	Dannii Minogue (MCA)
29	35	NEVER LET GO	Cliff Richard (EMI)
-	36	JIMMY OLSON'S BLUES	Spin Doctors (Epic)
17	37	CONDEMNATION	Depeche Mode (Mute)
-	38	ALL I GAVE	World Party (Ensign)
42	39	I LIKE IT/STAR	D:Ream (FXU)
45	40	JOY	Staxx (Champion)
26	41	FACES	2 Unlimited (PWL Continental)
34	42	THE KEY: THE SECRET	Urban Cookie Collective (Pulse 8)
32	43	EVANGELINE	Cocteau Twins (Fontana)
30	44	LIVING ON MY OWN	Freddie Mercury (Parlophone)
37	45	LOVE SCENES	Beverley Craven (Epic)
48	46	KISS THAT FROG	Peter Gabriel (Virgin)
-	47	NEVER GONNA GIVE YOU UP	FKW (PWL International)
38	48	HIGHER GROUND	UB40 (DEP International)
-	49	2 TONE (EP)	Various Artists (2 Tone)
36	50	ONE WOMAN	Jade (Giant)

		16 October 1993	
1	1	RELIGHT MY FIRE	Take That featuring Lulu (RCA)
2	2	BOOM! SHAKE THE ROOM	Jazzy Jeff & Fresh Prince (Jive)
9	3	I'D DO ANYTHING FOR LOVE (BUT I WON'T DO THAT)	Meatloaf (Virgin)
3	4	MOVING ON UP	M People (deConstruction)
5	5	SHE DON'T LET NOBODY	Chaka Demus & Pliers (Mango)
4	6	RELAX	Frankie Goes To Hollywood (ZTT)
7	7	LIFE	Haddaway (Logic)
13	8	STAY	Eternal (1st Avenue)
6	9	GO WEST	Pet Shop Boys (Parlophone)
-	10	HALLOWED BE THY NAME (LIVE)	Iron Maiden (EMI)
8	11	MR VAIN	Culture Beat (Epic)
30	12	I BELIEVE	Bon Jovi (Jambco)
10	13	GOING NOWHERE	Gabrielle (Go Beat)
11	14	RIGHT HERE	SWV (RCA)
12	15	HERE WE GO	Stakka Bo (Polydor)
-	16	ONE LOVE	Prodigy (Boy's Own)
-	17	PEACH	Prince (Paisley Park)
16	18	(NOW I KNOW WHAT MADE) OTIS BLUE	Paul Young (Columbia)
-	19	INTO YOUR ARMS	Lemonheads (Atlantic)
-	20	DON'T BE A STRANGER	Dina Carroll (A&M PM)
21	21	CHAIN REACTION	Diana Ross (EMI)
18	22	TRACKS OF MY TEARS	Go West (Chrysalis)
17	23	DISTANT SUN	Crowded House (Capitol)
14	24	BIG SCARY ANIMAL	Belinda Carlisle (Offside)
15	25	IT MUST HAVE BEEN LOVE	Roxette (EMI)
-	26	SUNDAY SUNDAY	Blur (Food)
39	27	I LIKE IT/STAR	D:Ream (FXU)
22	28	RIVER OF DREAMS	Billy Joel (Columbia)
33	29	SHOOP	Salt 'N' Pepa (ffrr)
-	30	BREAKDOWN	One Dove (Boy's Own)
-	31	RSVP	Pop Will Eat Itself (Infectious)
24	32	CANTALOOP	Us3 featuring Rahsaan (Capitol)
40	33	JOY	Staxx (Champion)
19	34	IT KEEPS RAINING (TEARS FROM MY EYES)	Bitty McLean (Brilliant)
-	35	LENNY AND TERENCE	Carter USM (Chrysalis)
36	36	JIMMY OLSON'S BLUES	Spin Doctors (Epic)
49	37	2 TONE (EP)	Various Artists (2 Tone)
26	38	RUNAWAY LOVE	En Vogue (East West America)
25	39	WHEN THE SHIP GOES DOWN	Cypress Hill (Ruff House)
-	40	I'M FREE	Jon Secada (SBK)
-	41	FALLING	Alison Moyet (Columbia)
32	42	SPACEMAN	4 Non Blondes (Interscope)
31	43	ONE GOODBYE IN TEN	Shara Nelson (Cooltempo)
23	44	CREEP	Radiohead (Parlophone)
28	45	EVERLASTING LOVE	Worlds Apart (Arista)
29	46	WHENEVER YOU NEED SOMEBODY	Bad Boys Inc (A&M)
38	47	ALL I GAVE	World Party (Ensign)
-	48	BABY IT'S YOU	Silk (Keia)
-	49	DANCEHALL MOOD	Aswad (Bubblin')
-	50	SAY WHAT!	X-Press 2 (Junior Boy's Own)

		23 October 1993	
3	1	I'D DO ANYTHING FOR LOVE (BUT I WON'T DO THAT)	Meatloaf (Virgin)
1	2	RELIGHT MY FIRE	Take That featuring Lulu (RCA)
2	3	BOOM! SHAKE THE ROOM	Jazzy Jeff & Fresh Prince (Jive)
8	4	STAY	Eternal (1st Avenue)
4	5	MOVING ON UP	M People (deConstruction)
5	6	SHE DON'T LET NOBODY	Chaka Demus & Pliers (Mango)
-	7	THE GIFT	INXS (Mercury)
7	8	LIFE	Haddaway (Logic)
6	9	RELAX	Frankie Goes To Hollywood (ZTT)
20	10	DON'T BE A STRANGER	Dina Carroll (A&M PM)
17	11	PEACH	Prince (Paisley Park)
-	12	PLAY DEAD	Bjork with David Arnold (Island)
-	13	SO NATURAL	Lisa Stansfield (Arista)
16	14	ONE LOVE	Prodigy (Boy's Own)
9	15	GO WEST	Pet Shop Boys (Parlophone)
-	16	U GOT 2 LET THE MUSIC	Capella (Internal)
11	17	MR VAIN	Culture Beat (Epic)
10	18	HALLOWED BE THY NAME (LIVE)	Iron Maiden (EMI)
13	19	GOING NOWHERE	Gabrielle (Go Beat)
19	20	INTO YOUR ARMS	Lemonheads (Atlantic)
21	21	CHAIN REACTION	Diana Ross (EMI)
33	22	JOY	Staxx (Champion)
18	23	(NOW I KNOW WHAT MADE) OTIS BLUE	Paul Young (Columbia)
14	24	RIGHT HERE	SWV (RCA)
-	25	TONGUE TIED	Cat (EMI)
15	26	HERE WE GO	Stakka Bo (Polydor)
-	27	CARNIVAL	Lionrock (deConstruction)
12	28	I BELIEVE	Bon Jovi (Jambco)
-	29	JULIA	ChrisRea (East West)
22	30	TRACKS OF MY TEARS	Go West (Chrysalis)
-	31	GOTTA GET IT RIGHT	Lean Fiagbe (Mother)
30	32	BREAKDOWN	One Dove (Boy's Own)
-	33	MIRACLE GOODNIGHT	David Bowie (Arista)
-	34	BUMPED	Right Said Fred (Tug)
-	35	SUNSET AND BABYLON	WASP (Capitol)
26	36	SUNDAY SUNDAY	Blur (Food)
-	37	DOWN IN A HOLE	Alice In Chains (Columbia)
25	38	IT MUST HAVE BEEN LOVE	Roxette (EMI)
-	39	FOR WHAT IT'S WORTH	Oui 3 (MCA)
-	40	GIVE IT UP	Goodmen (Fresh Fruit)
37	41	2 TONE (EP)	Various Artists (2 Tone)
-	42	ALL ABOUT SOUL	Billy Joel (Columbia)
50	43	SAY WHAT!	X-Press 2 (Junior Boy's Own)
41	44	FALLING	Alison Moyet (Columbia)
-	45	TAKE A LOOK AT YOURSELF	Coverdale Page (EMI)
39	46	WHEN THE SHIP GOES DOWN	Cypress Hill (Ruff House)
-	47	MOVIN' ON	Apache Indian (Island)
24	48	BIG SCARY ANIMAL	Belinda Carlisle (Offside)
23	49	DISTANT SUN	Crowded House (Capitol)
27	50	I LIKE IT/STAR	D:Ream (FXU)

Take That came straight in at Number One again – showing a regularity that was previously exceeded only by the Beatles and Elvis Presley. They didn't have the staying power of their predecessors though – within six weeks they were out of the Top 50. Meatloaf *does* have staying power, as we will see.

October – November 1993

30 October 1993

last week	this week	title / artist
1	1	I'D DO ANYTHING FOR LOVE (BUT I WON'T DO THAT) Meatloaf (Virgin)
-	2	PLEASE FORGIVE ME Bryan Adams (A&M)
-	3	BOTH SIDES OF THE STORY Phil Collins (Virgin)
16	4	U GOT 2 LET THE MUSIC Capella (Internal)
4	5	STAY Eternal (1st Avenue)
10	6	DON'T BE A STRANGER Dina Carroll (A&M PM)
3	7	BOOM! SHAKE THE ROOM Jazzy Jeff & Fresh Prince (Jive)
2	8	RELIGHT MY FIRE Take That featuring Lulu (RCA)
14	9	ONE LOVE Prodigy (Boy's Own)
5	10	MOVING ON UP M People (deConstruction)
40	11	GIVE IT UP Goodmen (Fresh Fruit)
12	12	PLAY DEAD Bjork with David Arnold (Island)
13	13	SO NATURAL Lisa Stansfield (Arista)
6	14	SHE DON'T LET NOBODY Chaka Demus & Pliers (Mango)
8	15	LIFE Haddaway (Logic)
11	16	PEACH Prince (Paisley Park)
-	17	TEXAS COWBOYS Grid (deConstruction)
-	18	WHY MUST WE WAIT UNTIL TONIGHT? Tina Turner (Parlophone)
7	19	THE GIFT INXS (Mercury)
25	20	TONGUE TIED Cat (EMI)
17	21	MR VAIN Culture Beat (Epic)
-	22	THIS GARDEN Levellers (China)
29	23	JULIA ChrisRea (East West)
39	24	FOR WHAT IT'S WORTH Oui 3 (MCA)
9	25	RELAX Frankie Goes To Hollywood (ZTT)
15	26	GO WEST Pet Shop Boys (Parlophone)
-	27	SHAMROCKS AND SHENANIGANS House Of Pain (XL)
-	28	OVER THE EDGE Almighty (Polydor)
31	29	GOTTA GET IT RIGHT Lean Fiagbe (Mother)
-	30	FROM A TO H AND BACK AGAIN Sheep On Drugs (Island)
42	31	ALL ABOUT SOUL Billy Joel (Columbia)
21	32	CHAIN REACTION Diana Ross (EMI)
-	33	CRYIN' Aerosmith (Geffen)
34	34	BUMPED Right Said Fred (Tug)
19	35	GOING NOWHERE Gabrielle (Go Beat)
38	36	HALLOWED BE THY NAME (LIVE) Iron Maiden (EMI)
28	37	I BELIEVE Bon Jovi (Jambco)
26	38	HERE WE GO Stakka Bo (Polydor)
24	39	RIGHT HERE SWV (RCA)
27	40	CARNIVAL Lionrock (deConstruction)
20	41	INTO YOUR ARMS Lemonheads (Atlantic)
-	42	STAY FOREVER Joey Lawrence (EMI)
22	43	JOY Staxx (Champion)
23	44	(NOW I KNOW WHAT MADE) OTIS BLUE Paul Young (Columbia)
33	45	MIRACLE GOODNIGHT David Bowie (Arista)
-	46	YOU OWE IT ALL TO ME Texas (Vertigo)
-	47	NEW POLICY ONE Terrorvision (Total Vegas)
-	48	SOMEBODY'S BABY Pat Benatar (Chrysalis)
-	49	PASS IT ON Bitty McLean (Brilliant)
-	50	SATURDAY'S NOT WHAT IT USED TO BE Kingmaker (Scorch)

6 November 1993

last week	this week	title / artist
1	1	I'D DO ANYTHING FOR LOVE (BUT I WON'T DO THAT) Meatloaf (Virgin)
2	2	PLEASE FORGIVE ME Bryan Adams (A&M)
4	3	U GOT 2 LET THE MUSIC Capella (Internal)
6	4	DON'T BE A STRANGER Dina Carroll (A&M PM)
11	5	GIVE IT UP Goodmen (Fresh Fruit)
5	6	STAY Eternal (1st Avenue)
3	7	BOTH SIDES OF THE STORY Phil Collins (Virgin)
7	8	BOOM! SHAKE THE ROOM Jazzy Jeff & Fresh Prince (Jive)
-	9	GOT TO GET IT Culture Beat (Epic)
-	10	GO Pearl Jam (Epic)
8	11	RELIGHT MY FIRE Take That featuring Lulu (RCA)
-	12	HERO Mariah Carey (Columbia)
9	13	ONE LOVE Prodigy (Boy's Own)
10	14	MOVING ON UP M People (deConstruction)
22	15	THIS GARDEN Levellers (China)
12	16	PLAY DEAD Bjork with David Arnold (Island)
14	17	SHE DON'T LET NOBODY Chaka Demus & Pliers (Mango)
-	18	QUEEN OF THE NIGHT Whitney Houston (Arista)
-	19	SHED A TEAR Wet Wet Wet (Precious Organisation))
18	20	WHY MUST WE WAIT UNTIL TONIGHT? Tina Turner (Parlophone)
-	21	REAL LOVE '93 Time Frequency (Internal Affairs)
-	22	SHOW OF STRENGTH (EP) Shamen (One Little Indian)
13	23	SO NATURAL Lisa Stansfield (Arista)
15	24	LIFE Haddaway (Logic)
29	25	GOTTA GET IT RIGHT Lean Fiagbe (Mother)
23	26	JULIA ChrisRea (East West)
17	27	TEXAS COWBOYS Grid (deConstruction)
20	28	TONGUE TIED Cat (EMI)
-	29	FEEL LIKE MAKING LOVE Pauline Henry (Sony Soho Square)
-	30	FREE LOVE Juliet Roberts (Cooltempo)
33	31	CRYIN' Aerosmith (Geffen)
-	32	WISH Soul II Soul (Virgin)
-	33	ANOTHER BOY MURDERED Faith No More & Boo Yaa Tribe (Epic)
16	34	PEACH Prince (Paisley Park)
25	35	RELAX Frankie Goes To Hollywood (ZTT)
-	36	CASCADE Future Sound Of London (Virgin)
46	37	YOU OWE IT ALL TO ME Texas (Vertigo)
24	38	FOR WHAT IT'S WORTH Oui 3 (MCA)
-	39	MORE AND MORE Captain Hollywood Project (Pulse 8)
-	40	TURN ON, TUNE IN, COP OUT Freak Power (4th & Broadway)
49	41	PASS IT ON Bitty McLean (Brilliant)
42	42	STAY FOREVER Joey Lawrence (EMI)
21	43	MR VAIN Culture Beat (Epic)
31	44	ALL ABOUT SOUL Billy Joel (Columbia)
34	45	BUMPED Right Said Fred (Tug)
-	46	PIECE BY PIECE Kenny Thomas (Cooltempo)
-	47	SELFISH Other Two (CentreDate)
35	48	GOING NOWHERE Gabrielle (Go Beat)
19	49	THE GIFT INXS (Mercury)
27	50	SHAMROCKS AND SHENANIGANS House Of Pain (XL)

13 November 1993

last week	this week	title / artist
1	1	I'D DO ANYTHING FOR LOVE (BUT I WON'T DO THAT) Meatloaf (Virgin)
2	2	PLEASE FORGIVE ME Bryan Adams (A&M)
5	3	GIVE IT UP Goodmen (Fresh Fruit)
4	4	DON'T BE A STRANGER Dina Carroll (A&M PM)
3	5	U GOT 2 LET THE MUSIC Capella (Internal)
9	6	GOT TO GET IT Culture Beat (Epic)
12	7	HERO Mariah Carey (Columbia)
21	8	REAL LOVE '93 Time Frequency (Internal Affairs)
29	9	FEEL LIKE MAKING LOVE Pauline Henry (Sony Soho Square)
-	10	RUNAWAY TRAIN Soul Asylum (Columbia)
-	11	OPEN UP Lettfield/Lydon (Hard Hands)
-	12	SAID I LOVED YOU, BUT I LIED Michael Bolton (Columbia)
22	13	SHOW OF STRENGTH (EP) Shamen (One Little Indian)
-	14	FEELS LIKE HEAVEN Urban Cookie Collective (Pulse 8)
-	15	LITTLE FLUFFY CLOUDS Orb (Big Life)
-	16	THE WEAVER (EP) Paul Weller (Go! Discs)
18	17	QUEEN OF THE NIGHT Whitney Houston (Arista)
8	18	BOOM! SHAKE THE ROOM Jazzy Jeff & Fresh Prince (Jive)
6	19	STAY Eternal (1st Avenue)
16	20	PLAY DEAD Bjork with David Arnold (Island)
14	21	MOVING ON UP M People (deConstruction)
7	22	BOTH SIDES OF THE STORY Phil Collins (Virgin)
10	23	GO Pearl Jam (Epic)
11	24	RELIGHT MY FIRE Take That featuring Lulu (RCA)
31	25	CRYIN' Aerosmith (Geffen)
19	26	SHED A TEAR Wet Wet Wet (Precious Organisation))
-	27	SO IN LOVE (THE REAL DEAL) Judy Cheeks (Positiva)
33	28	ANOTHER BOY MURDERED Faith No More & Boo Yaa Tribe (Epic)
39	29	MORE AND MORE Captain Hollywood Project (Pulse 8)
32	30	WISH Soul II Soul (Virgin)
30	31	FREE LOVE Juliet Roberts (Cooltempo)
-	32	THAT'S WHAT I THINK Cyndi Lauper (Epic)
-	33	NO TIME TO PLAY Guru featuring D C Lee (Cooltempo)
20	34	WHY MUST WE WAIT UNTIL TONIGHT? Tina Turner (Parlophone)
-	35	HOPELESSLY Rick Astley (RCA)
15	36	THIS GARDEN Levellers (China)
13	37	ONE LOVE Prodigy (Boy's Own)
17	38	SHE DON'T LET NOBODY Chaka Demus & Pliers (Mango)
36	39	CASCADE Future Sound Of London (Virgin)
46	40	PIECE BY PIECE Kenny Thomas (Cooltempo)
24	41	LIFE Haddaway (Logic)
-	42	LAID James (Fontana)
-	43	IF I COULD ONLY SAY GOODBYE David Hasselhoff (Arista)
41	44	PASS IT ON Bitty McLean (Brilliant)
25	45	GOTTA GET IT RIGHT Lean Fiagbe (Mother)
23	46	SO NATURAL Lisa Stansfield (Arista)
27	47	TEXAS COWBOYS Grid (deConstruction)
26	48	JULIA ChrisRea (East West)
40	49	TURN ON, TUNE IN, COP OUT Freak Power (4th & Broadway)
-	50	HAPPY NATION Ace Of Base (Metronome)

I'd Do Anything For Love became the best-selling single of 1993, and stayed at the top of the NME chart for a total of seven weeks. Bryan Adams, a previous marathon chart-topper, mistimed his release this time around. Old hippies will remember Buffalo Springfield's original version of *For What It's Worth*.

November – December 1993

<table>
<tr><th colspan="2">last this
week</th><th>20 November 1993</th></tr>
</table>

20 November 1993

last	this	title	artist
1	1	I'D DO ANYTHING FOR LOVE (BUT I WON'T DO THAT)	Meatloaf (Virgin)
2	2	PLEASE FORGIVE ME	Bryan Adams (A&M)
4	3	DON'T BE A STRANGER	Dina Carroll (A&M PM)
6	4	GOT TO GET IT	Culture Beat (Epic)
5	5	U GOT 2 LET THE MUSIC	Capella (Internal)
3	6	GIVE IT UP	Goodmen (Fresh Fruit)
10	7	RUNAWAY TRAIN	Soul Asylum (Columbia)
7	8	HERO	Mariah Carey (Columbia)
14	9	FEELS LIKE HEAVEN	Urban Cookie Collective (Pulse 8)
9	10	FEEL LIKE MAKING LOVE	Pauline Henry (Sony Soho Square)
-	11	AIN'T IT FUN	Guns N' Roses (Geffen)
15	12	LITTLE FLUFFY CLOUDS	Orb (Big Life)
8	13	REAL LOVE '93	Time Frequency (Internal Affairs)
12	14	SAID I LOVED YOU, BUT I LIED	Michael Bolton (Columbia)
-	15	TRUE LOVE	Elton John & Kiki Dee (Rocket)
11	16	OPEN UP	Lettfield/Lydon (Hard Hands)
-	17	WELCOME TO THE PLEASUREDOME	Frankie Goes To Hollywood (ZTT)
-	18	AGAIN	Janet Jackson (Virgin)
-	19	MAXIMUM OVERDRIVE	2 Unlimited (PWL Continental)
25	20	CRYIN'	Aerosmith (Geffen)
-	21	DEMOLITION MAN	Sting (A&M)
-	22	LET HER DOWN EASY	Terence Trent D'Arby (Columbia)
18	23	BOOM! SHAKE THE ROOM	Jazzy Jeff & Fresh Prince (Jive)
-	24	WILL YOU BE THERE (IN THE MORNING)	Heart (Capitol)
13	25	SHOW OF STRENGTH (EP)	Shamen (One Little Indian)
17	26	QUEEN OF THE NIGHT	Whitney Houston (Arista)
-	27	I'M LOOKING FOR THE ONE(TO BE WITH ME)	Jazzy Jeff & Fresh Prince (Jive)
-	28	I'LL BE THERE FOR YOU	House Of Virginism (ffrr)
42	29	LAID	James (Fontana)
-	30	NAILS IN MY FEET	Crowded House (Capitol)
20	31	PLAY DEAD	Bjork with David Arnold (Island)
19	32	STAY	Eternal (1st Avenue)
21	33	MOVING ON UP	M People (deConstruction)
26	34	SHED A TEAR	Wet Wet Wet (Precious Organisation))
16	35	THE WEAVER (EP)	Paul Weller (Go! Discs)
32	36	THAT'S WHAT I THINK	Cyndi Lauper (Epic)
-	37	COULD IT BE MAGIC 1993	Barry Manilow (Arista)
29	38	MORE AND MORE	Captain Hollywood Project (Pulse 8)
30	39	WISH	Soul II Soul (Virgin)
43	40	IF I COULD ONLY SAY GOODBYE	David Hasselhoff (Arista)
-	41	DUSKY SAPPHO (EP)	Carleen Anderson (Circa)
33	42	NO TIME TO PLAY	Guru featuring D C Lee (Cooltempo)
27	43	SO IN LOVE (THE REAL DEAL)	Judy Cheeks (Positiva)
35	44	HOPELESSLY	Rick Astley (RCA)
-	45	GIVIN' IT UP	Incognito (Talkin' Loud)
-	46	STUPID THING	Aimee Mann (Imago)
22	47	BOTH SIDES OF THE STORY	Phil Collins (Virgin)
50	48	HAPPY NATION	Ace Of Base (Metronome)
-	49	NEVER	Jomanda (Big Beat)
23	50	GO	Pearl Jam (Epic)

27 November 1993

last	this	title	artist
1	1	I'D DO ANYTHING FOR LOVE (BUT I WON'T DO THAT)	Meatloaf (Virgin)
2	2	PLEASE FORGIVE ME	Bryan Adams (A&M)
15	3	TRUE LOVE	Elton John & Kiki Dee (Rocket)
3	4	DON'T BE A STRANGER	Dina Carroll (A&M PM)
18	5	AGAIN	Janet Jackson (Virgin)
7	6	RUNAWAY TRAIN	Soul Asylum (Columbia)
5	7	U GOT 2 LET THE MUSIC	Capella (Internal)
9	8	FEELS LIKE HEAVEN	Urban Cookie Collective (Pulse 8)
4	9	GOT TO GET IT	Culture Beat (Epic)
8	10	HERO	Mariah Carey (Columbia)
11	11	AIN'T IT FUN	Guns N' Roses (Geffen)
-	12	LONG TRAIN RUNNIN'	Doobie Brothers (Warner Bros.)
24	13	WILL YOU BE THERE (IN THE MORNING)	Heart (Capitol)
-	14	MOMENTS OF PLEASURE	Kate Bush (EMI)
6	15	GIVE IT UP	Goodmen (Fresh Fruit)
-	16	AVE MARIA	Lesley Garrett (Internal Affairs)
10	17	FEEL LIKE MAKING LOVE	Pauline Henry (Sony Soho Square)
18	18	LET ME SHOW YOU	K-Klass (deConstruction)
19	19	MAXIMUM OVERDIRVE	2 Unlimited (PWL Continental)
14	20	SAID I LOVED YOU, BUT I LIED	Michael Bolton (Columbia)
16	21	OPEN UP	Lettfield/Lydon (Hard Hands)
12	22	LITTLE FLUFFY CLOUDS	Orb (Big Life)
-	23	THE ESSENTIAL (EP)	Naughty By Nature (Big Life)
13	24	REAL LOVE '93	Time Frequency (Internal Affairs)
25	25	FULL OF LIFE	Wonder Stuff (Far Out)
26	26	ON	Aphex Twin (Warp)
17	27	WELCOME TO THE PLEASUREDOME	Frankie Goes To Hollywood (ZTT)
21	28	DEMOLITION MAN	Sting (A&M)
-	29	THROW YA GUNZ	Onyx (Columbia)
30	30	NAILS IN MY FEET	Crowded House (Capitol)
-	31	LENNY VALENTINO	Auteurs (Hut)
27	32	I'M LOOKING FOR THE ONE(TO BE WITH ME)	Jazzy Jeff & Fresh Prince (Jive)
22	33	LET HER DOWN EASY	Terence Trent D'Arby (Columbia)
-	34	LAY DOWN YOUR ARMS	Belinda Carlisle (Offside)
-	35	IT'S ABOUT TIME	Lemonheads (Atlantic)
29	36	LAID	James (Fontana)
-	37	FOR WHOM THE BELL TOLLS	Bee Gees (Polydor)
-	38	POWER	Nu Colours (Wild Card)
20	39	CRYIN'	Aerosmith (Geffen)
37	40	COULD IT BE MAGIC 1993	Barry Manilow (Arista)
28	41	I'LL BE THERE FOR YOU	House Of Virginism (ffrr)
38	42	MORE AND MORE	Captain Hollywood Project (Pulse 8)
23	43	BOOM! SHAKE THE ROOM	Jazzy Jeff & Fresh Prince (Jive)
-	44	LIP GLOSS	Pulp (Island)
-	45	HOPE IN A HOPELESS WORLD	Paul Young (Columbia)
26	46	QUEEN OF THE NIGHT	Whitney Houston (Arista)
25	47	SHOW OF STRENGTH (EP)	Shamen (One Little Indian)
-	48	A HARD DAY'S NIGHT	Peter Sellers (EMI)
31	49	PLAY DEAD	Bjork with David Arnold (Island)
-	50	THUNDERDOME	Messiah (WEA)

4 December 1993

last	this	title	artist
1	1	I'D DO ANYTHING FOR LOVE (BUT I WON'T DO THAT)	Meatloaf (Virgin)
3	2	TRUE LOVE	Elton John & Kiki Dee (Rocket)
2	3	PLEASE FORGIVE ME	Bryan Adams (A&M)
4	4	DON'T BE A STRANGER	Dina Carroll (A&M PM)
-	5	STAY/I'VE GOT YOU UNDER MY SKIM	U2/Bono/Frank Sinatra (Island)
5	6	AGAIN	Janet Jackson (Virgin)
-	7	DON'T LOOK ANY FURTHER	M People (deConstruction)
-	8	MR BLOBBY	Mr Blobby (Destiny)
16	9	AVE MARIA	Lesley Garrett (Internal Affairs)
12	10	LONG TRAIN RUNNIN'	Doobie Brothers (Warner Bros.)
6	11	RUNAWAY TRAIN	Soul Asylum (Columbia)
2	12	YMCA '93 REMIX	Village People (Arista)
13	13	BIG TIME SENSUALITY	Bjork (One Little Indian)
9	14	GOT TO GET IT	Culture Beat (Epic)
8	15	FEELS LIKE HEAVEN	Urban Cookie Collective (Pulse 8)
10	16	HERO	Mariah Carey (Columbia)
37	17	FOR WHOM THE BELL TOLLS	Bee Gees (Polydor)
18	18	LET ME SHOW YOU	K-Klass (deConstruction)
14	19	MOMENTS OF PLEASURE	Kate Bush (EMI0=)
7	20	U GOT 2 LET THE MUSIC	Capella (Internal)
15	21	GIVE IT UP	Goodmen (Fresh Fruit)
-	22	IT'S ALRIGHT	East 17 (London)
-	23	WHAT'S MY NAME?	Snoop Doggy Dogg (Death Row)
13	24	WILL YOU BE THERE (IN THE MORNING)	Heart (Capitol)
11	25	AIN'T IT FUN	Guns N' Roses (Geffen)
19	26	MAXIMUM OVERDIRVE	2 Unlimited (PWL Continental)
34	27	LAY DOWN YOUR ARMS	Belinda Carlisle (Offside)
20	28	SAID I LOVED YOU, BUT I LIED	Michael Bolton (Columbia)
17	29	FEEL LIKE MAKING LOVE	Pauline Henry (Sony Soho Square)
23	30	THE ESSENTIAL (EP)	Naughty By Nature (Big Life)
25	31	FULL OF LIFE	Wonder Stuff (Far Out)
30	32	NAILS IN MY FEET	Crowded House (Capitol)
50	33	THUNDERDOME	Messiah (WEA)
28	34	DEMOLITION MAN	Sting (A&M)
24	35	REAL LOVE '93	Time Frequency (Internal Affairs)
33	36	LET HER DOWN EASY	Terence Trent D'Arby (Columbia)
-	37	FUNK DAT	Sagat (ffrr)
-	38	LOVE IS ON THE WAY	Luther Vandross (Epic)
-	39	IS THERE ANY LOVE IN YOUR HEART	Lenny Kravitz (Virgin America)
21	40	OPEN UP	Lettfield/Lydon (Hard Hands)
-	41	HOW 'BOUT US	Lulu (Dome)
-	42	YOU DON'T HAVE TO WORRY	Mary J Blige (MCA)
22	43	LITTLE FLUFFY CLOUDS	Orb (Big Life)
-	44	THE BUDDHA OF SUBURBIA	David Bowie featuring Lenny Kravitz (Arista)
-	45	HEY MR DJ	Zhane (Flavor Unit)
-	46	CARELESS WHISPER	Sarah Washington (Almighty)
29	47	THROW YA GUNZ	Onyx (Columbia)
26	48	ON	Aphex Twin (Warp)
49	49	WE CLOSE OUR EYES '93	Go West (Chrysalis)
-	50	TIMEBOMB	Chumbawumba (One Little Indian)

Duet time with Elton and Kiki doing it again, and Sinatra teaming up with Bono (though the two of them never met). The Doobie Brothers had an unexpected bonus when a remix of *Long Train Runnin'* became a huge hit in dance clubs. *Funk Dat* was the clean version of the title of Sagat's single.

11 December 1993

last week	this week	title	artist (label)
8	1	MR BLOBBY	Mr Blobby (Destiny)
2	2	TRUE LOVE	Elton John & Kiki Dee (Rocket)
1	3	I'D DO ANYTHING FOR LOVE (BUT I WON'T DO THAT)	Meatloaf (Virgin)
3	4	PLEASE FORGIVE ME	Bryan Adams (A&M)
5	5	STAY/I'VE GOT YOU UNDER MY SKIN	U2/Bono/Frank Sinatra (Island)
4	6	DON'T BE A STRANGER	Dina Carroll (A&M PM)
17	7	FOR WHOM THE BELL TOLLS	Bee Gees (Polydor)
-	8	CONTROVERSY	Prince (Paisley Park)
6	9	AGAIN	Janet Jackson (Virgin)
7	10	DON'T LOOK ANY FURTHER	M People (deConstruction)
-	11	I WOULDN'T NORMALLY DO THIS KIND OF THING	Pet Shop Boys (Parlophone)
10	12	LONG TRAIN RUNNIN'	Doobie Brothers (Warner Bros.)
12	13	YMCA '93 REMIX	Village People (Arista)
-	14	THE PERFECT YEAR	Dina Carroll (A&M PM)
22	15	IT'S ALRIGHT	East 17 (London)
11	16	RUNAWAY TRAIN	Soul Asylum (Columbia)
9	17	AVE MARIA	Lesley Garrett (Internal Affairs)
13	18	BIG TIME SENSUALITY	Bjork (One Little Indian)
16	19	HERO	Mariah Carey (Columbia)
-	20	I AIN'T GOIN' OUT LIKE THAT	Cypress Hill (Ruff House)
-	21	NO RAIN	Blind Melon (Capitol)
18	22	LET ME SHOW YOU	K-Klass (deConstruction)
23	23	WHAT'S MY NAME?	Snoop Doggy Dogg (Death Row)
-	24	BRING ME YOUR CUP	UB40 (DEP International)
15	25	FEELS LIKE HEAVEN	Urban Cookie Collective (Pulse 8)
26	26	I WISH	Gabrielle (Go Beat)
14	27	GOT TO GET IT	Culture Beat (Epic)
37	28	FUNK DAT	Sagat (ffrr)
21	29	GIVE IT UP	Goodmen (Fresh Fruit)
-	30	WALKING ON AIR	Bad Boys Inc (A&M)
26	31	MAXIMUM OVERDIRVE	2 Unlimited (PWL Continental)
20	32	U GOT 2 LET THE MUSIC	Capella (Internal)
-	33	A WHOLE NEW WORLD (ALADDIN'S THEME)	Peabo Bryson & Regina Belle (Columbia)
28	34	SAID I LOVED YOU, BUT I LIED	Michael Bolton (Columbia)
44	35	THE BUDDHA OF SUBURBIA	David Bowie featuring Lenny Kravitz (Arista)
24	36	WILL YOU BE THERE (IN THE MORNING)	Heart (Capitol)
-	37	LITTLE BIT OF HEAVEN	Lisa Stansfield (Arista)
27	38	LAY DOWN YOUR ARMS	Belinda Carlisle (Offside)
36	39	LET HER DOWN EASY	Terence Trent D'Arby (Columbia)
-	40	WOPBABALUBOP	Funkdoobiest (Epic)
19	41	MOMENTS OF PLEASURE	Kate Bush (EMI0=)
29	42	FEEL LIKE MAKING LOVE	Pauline Henry (Sony Soho Square)
38	43	LOVE IS ON THE WAY	Luther Vandross (Epic)
49	44	WE CLOSE OUR EYES '93	Go West (Chrysalis)
33	45	THUNDERDOME	Messiah (WEA)
-	46	YOUR LOVE	Diana Ross (EMI)
47	47	RESPECT ('93)	Adeva (Network)
39	48	IS THERE ANY LOVE IN YOUR HEART	Lenny Kravitz (Virgin America)
-	49	CRY FOR YOU	Jodeci (MCA)
-	50	FIND THE RIVER	REM (Warner Bros.)

18 December 1993

last week	this week	title	artist (label)
-	1	BABE	Take That (RCA)
1	2	MR BLOBBY	Mr Blobby (Destiny)
2	3	TRUE LOVE	Elton John & Kiki Dee (Rocket)
3	4	I'D DO ANYTHING FOR LOVE (BUT I WON'T DO THAT)	Meatloaf (Virgin)
-	5	TWIST AND SHOUT	Chaka Demus & Pliers (Mango)
7	6	FOR WHOM THE BELL TOLLS	Bee Gees (Polydor)
15	7	IT'S ALRIGHT	East 17 (London)
4	8	PLEASE FORGIVE ME	Bryan Adams (A&M)
11	9	I WOULDN'T NORMALLY DO THIS KIND OF THING	Pet Shop Boys (Parlophone)
5	10	STAY/I'VE GOT YOU UNDER MY SKIN	U2/Bono/Frank Sinatra (Island)
6	11	DON'T BE A STRANGER	Dina Carroll (A&M PM)
10	12	DON'T LOOK ANY FURTHER	M People (deConstruction)
14	13	THE PERFECT YEAR	Dina Carroll (A&M PM)
8	14	CONTROVERSY	Prince (Paisley Park)
-	15	BAT OUT OF HELL	Meatloaf (Epic)
9	16	AGAIN	Janet Jackson (Virgin)
12	17	LONG TRAIN RUNNIN'	Doobie Brothers (Warner Bros.)
18	18	BIG TIME SENSUALITY	Bjork (One Little Indian)
19	19	HERO	Mariah Carey (Columbia)
13	20	YMCA '93 REMIX	Village People (Arista)
21	21	NO RAIN	Blind Melon (Capitol)
-	22	THE POWER OF LOVE	Frankie Goes To Hollywood (ZTT)
16	23	RUNAWAY TRAIN	Soul Asylum (Columbia)
20	24	I AIN'T GOIN' OUT LIKE THAT	Cypress Hill (Ruff House)
-	25	SPOOKY	New Order (CentreDate)
24	26	BRING ME YOUR CUP	UB40 (DEP International)
-	27	HEALING LOVE	Cliff Richard (EMI)
-	28	ALL APOLOGIES	Nirvana (Geffen)
22	29	LET ME SHOW YOU	K-Klass (deConstruction)
-	30	THAT'S HOW I'M LIVIN'	Ice-T (Rhythm Syndicate)
33	31	A WHOLE NEW WORLD (ALADDIN'S THEME)	Peabo Bryson & Regina Belle (Columbia)
26	32	I WISH	Gabrielle (Go Beat)
-	33	I MISS YOU	Haddaway (Logic)
-	34	GONE TOO SOON	Michael Jackson (Epic)
-	35	COME BABY COME	K7 (Big Life)
-	36	FEELIN' ALRIGHT	EYC (MCA)
30	37	WALKING ON AIR	Bad Boys Inc (A&M)
17	38	AVE MARIA	Lesley Garrett (Internal Affairs)
46	39	YOUR LOVE	Diana Ross (EMI)
23	40	WHAT'S MY NAME?	Snoop Doggy Dogg (Death Row)
37	41	LITTLE BIT OF HEAVEN	Lisa Stansfield (Arista)
-	42	LAST HORIZON	Brian May (Parlophone)
-	43	I WAS BORN ON CHRISTMAS DAY	Saint Etienne (Heavenly)
27	44	GOT TO GET IT	Culture Beat (Epic)
-	45	REALLY DOE	Ice Cube (4th & Broadway)
28	46	FUNK DAT	Sagat (ffrr)
25	47	FEELS LIKE HEAVEN	Urban Cookie Collective (Pulse 8)
-	48	I WILL ALWAYS LOVE YOU	Whitney Houston (Arista)
39	49	LET HER DOWN EASY	Terence Trent D'Arby (Columbia)
-	50	YOU'LL NEVER WALK ALONE	Cilla Black with Barry Manilow (Columbia)

25 December 1993

last week	this week	title	artist (label)
2	1	MR BLOBBY	Mr Blobby (Destiny)
1	2	BABE	Take That (RCA)
5	3	TWIST AND SHOUT	Chaka Demus & Pliers (Mango)
6	4	FOR WHOM THE BELL TOLLS	Bee Gees (Polydor)
4	5	I'D DO ANYTHING FOR LOVE (BUT I WON'T DO THAT)	Meatloaf (Virgin)
7	6	IT'S ALRIGHT	East 17 (London)
3	7	TRUE LOVE	Elton John & Kiki Dee (Rocket)
13	8	THE PERFECT YEAR	Dina Carroll (A&M PM)
22	9	THE POWER OF LOVE	Frankie Goes To Hollywood (ZTT)
8	10	PLEASE FORGIVE ME	Bryan Adams (A&M)
15	11	BAT OUT OF HELL	Meatloaf (Epic)
12	12	DON'T LOOK ANY FURTHER	M People (deConstruction)
31	13	A WHOLE NEW WORLD (ALADDIN'S THEME)	Peabo Bryson & Regina Belle (Columbia)
11	14	DON'T BE A STRANGER	Dina Carroll (A&M PM)
9	15	I WOULDN'T NORMALLY DO THIS KIND OF THING	Pet Shop Boys (Parlophone)
10	16	STAY/I'VE GOT YOU UNDER MY SKIN	U2/Bono/Frank Sinatra (Island)
16	17	AGAIN	Janet Jackson (Virgin)
27	18	HEALING LOVE	Cliff Richard (EMI)
19	19	HERO	Mariah Carey (Columbia)
14	20	CONTROVERSY	Prince (Paisley Park)
21	21	NO RAIN	Blind Melon (Capitol)
35	22	COME BABY COME	K7 (Big Life)
17	23	LONG TRAIN RUNNIN'	Doobie Brothers (Warner Bros.)
-	24	FAMILY AFFAIR	Shabba Ranks (Atlas)
18	25	BIG TIME SENSUALITY	Bjork (One Little Indian)
37	26	WALKING ON AIR	Bad Boys Inc (A&M)
30	27	THAT'S HOW I'M LIVIN'	Ice-T (Rhythm Syndicate)
39	28	YOUR LOVE	Diana Ross (EMI)
24	29	I AIN'T GOIN' OUT LIKE THAT	Cypress Hill (Ruff House)
23	30	RUNAWAY TRAIN	Soul Asylum (Columbia)
34	31	GONE TOO SOON	Michael Jackson (Epic)
20	32	YMCA '93 REMIX	Village People (Arista)
36	33	FEELIN' ALRIGHT	EYC (MCA)
28	34	ALL APOLOGIES	Nirvana (Geffen)
26	35	BRING ME YOUR CUP	UB40 (DEP International)
33	36	I MISS YOU	Haddaway (Logic)
25	37	SPOOKY	New Order (CentreDate)
32	38	I WISH	Gabrielle (Go Beat)
43	39	I WAS BORN ON CHRISTMAS DAY	Saint Etienne (Heavenly)
-	40	I'M THE LEADER OF THE GANG	Hulk Hogan with Green Jelly (Bell)
38	41	AVE MARIA	Lesley Garrett (Internal Affairs)
48	42	I WILL ALWAYS LOVE YOU	Whitney Houston (Arista)
42	43	LAST HORIZON	Brian May (Parlophone)
29	44	LET ME SHOW YOU	K-Klass (deConstruction)
-	45	GREASE	Craig McLachlan (Epic)
50	46	YOU'LL NEVER WALK ALONE	Cilla Black with Barry Manilow (Columbia)
45	47	REALLY DOE	Ice Cube (4th & Broadway)
40	48	WHAT'S MY NAME?	Snoop Doggy Dogg (Death Row)
41	49	LITTLE BIT OF HEAVEN	Lisa Stansfield (Arista)
-	50	READ MY LIPS	Alex Party (Cleveland City)

Teen idols fight it out with Mr Blobby for Christmas Number One spot. Right behind them the season of consuming brings out the big names. The original of *Bat Out Of Hell* cashed in on the Meatloaf revival while Chaka Demus & Pliers followed a well-worn path with a ragga version of 1960s classic pop song.

January 1994

15 January 1994

last	this		
3	1	TWIST AND SHOUT	
		Chaka Demus & Pliers (Mango)	
6	2	IT'S ALRIGHT	East 17 (London)
1	3	MR BLOBBY	Mr Blobby (Destiny)
2	4	BABE	Take That (RCA)
22	5	COME BABY COME	K7 (Big Life)
-	6	THINGS CAN ONLY GET BETTER	
		D:Ream (Magnet)	
8	7	THE PERFECT YEAR	Dina Carroll (A&M PM)
4	8	FOR WHOM THE BELL TOLLS	
		Bee Gees (Polydor)	
5	9	I'D DO ANYTHING FOR LOVE (BUT I WON'T DO THAT)	Meatloaf (Virgin)
36	10	I MISS YOU	Haddaway (Logic)
-	11	ANYTHING	Culture Beat (Epic)
11	12	BAT OUT OF HELL	Meatloaf (Epic)
-	13	ALL FOR LOVE	
		Bryan Adams, Rod Stewart, Sting (A&M)	
13	14	A WHOLE NEW WORLD (ALADDIN'S THEME)	
		Peabo Bryson & Regina Belle (Columbia)	
-	15	SAVE OUR LOVE	Eternal (EMI)
24	16	FAMILY AFFAIR	Shabba Ranks (Atlas)
-	17	COLD COLD HEART	Wet Wet Wet (Precious)
10	18	PLEASE FORGIVE ME	Bryan Adams (A&M)
19	19	BLOW YOUR WHISTLE	DJ Duke (ffrr)
12	20	DON'T LOOK ANY FURTHER	
		M People (deConstruction)	
19	21	HERO	Mariah Carey (Columbia)
4	22	I'M IN THE MOOD	Ce Ce Peniston (A&M)
-	23	DSINFECTED (EP)	The The (Epic)
7	24	TRUE LOVE	Elton John & Kiki Dee (Rocket)
17	25	AGAIN	Janet Jackson (Virgin)
-	26	ACTION	Def Leppard (Bludgeon Riffola)
33	27	FEELIN' ALRIGHT	EYC (MCA)
-	28	EVERYDAY	Phil Collins (Virgin)
28	29	YOUR LOVE	Diana Ross (EMI)
-	30	MY HOUSE	Terrorovision (Total Vegas)
-	31	DAUGHTER	Pearl Jam (Epic)
-	32	TOWER OF STRENGTH (REMIXES)	
		Mission (Vertigo)	
-	33	BREATHE AGAIN	Toni Braxton (Arista)
9	34	THE POWER OF LOVE	
		Frankie Goes To Hollywood (ZTT)	
-	35	SHIPBUILDING (EP)	Tasmin Archer (EMI)
-	36	WHOOMP! (THERE IT IS)	Tag Team (Club Tools)
-	37	HERE I STAND	Bitty McLean (Brilliant)
-	38	TIME OF OUR LIVES	Alison Limerick (Arista)
-	39	WHO LET IN THE RAIN	Cyndi Lauper (Epic)
-	40	STOP LOVING ME, STOP LOVING YOU	
		Daryl Hall (Epic)	
-	41	WHY DON'T YOU TAKE ME	
		One Dove (Boy's Own)	
-	42	I GOT YOU BABE	
		Cher with Beavis and Butt-head (Geffen)	
-	43	YOU AND ME	Lisa B (ffrr)
40	44	I'M THE LEADER OF THE GANG	
		Hulk Hogan with Green Jelly (Bell)	
27	45	THAT'S HOW I'M LIVIN'	Ice-T (Rhythm Syndicate)
15	46	I WOULDN'T NORMALLY DO THIS KIND OF THING	Pet Shop Boys (Parlophone)
-	47	THE MUSIC OF THE NIGHT	Barbra Streisand & Michael Crawford (Columbia)
-	48	ABANDON SHIP	Blaggers ITA (Parlophone)
30	49	RUNAWAY TRAIN	Soul Asylum (Columbia)
26	50	WALKING ON AIR	Bad Boys Inc (A&M)

22 January 1994

6	1	THINGS CAN ONLY GET BETTER	
		D:Ream (Magnet)	
1	2	TWIST AND SHOUT	
		Chaka Demus & Pliers (Mango)	
11	3	ANYTHING	Culture Beat (Epic)
2	4	IT'S ALRIGHT	East 17 (London)
5	5	COME BABY COME	K7 (Big Life)
		Bryan Adams, Rod Stewart, Sting (A&M)	
10	7	I MISS YOU	Haddaway (Logic)
7	8	THE PERFECT YEAR	Dina Carroll (A&M PM)
15	9	SAVE OUR LOVE	Eternal (EMI)
8	10	FOR WHOM THE BELL TOLLS	
		Bee Gees (Polydor)	
-	11	CORNFLAKE GIRL	Tori Amos (East West)
26	12	ACTION	
		Def Leppard (Bludgeon Riffola)	
13	13	IN YOUR ROOM	Depeche Mode (Mute)
28	14	EVERYDAY	Phil Collins (Virgin)
33	15	BREATHE AGAIN	Toni Braxton (Arista)
4	16	BABE	Take That (RCA)
3	17	MR BLOBBY	Mr Blobby (Destiny)
22	18	I'M IN THE MOOD	Ce Ce Peniston (A&M)
37	19	HERE I STAND	Bitty McLean (Brilliant)
-	20	SOMETHING IN COMMON	
		Bobby Brown with Whitney Houston (MCA)	
14	21	A WHOLE NEW WORLD (ALADDIN'S THEME)	
		Peabo Bryson & Regina Belle (Columbia)	
23	22	DSINFECTED (EP)	The The (Epic)
-	23	I'M IN LUV	Joe (Mercury)
-	24	SATURN 5	Inspiral Carpets (Mute)
19	25	BLOW YOUR WHISTLE	DJ Duke (ffrr)
16	26	FAMILY AFFAIR	Shabba Ranks (Atlas)
17	27	COLD COLD HEART	
		Wet Wet Wet (Precious)	
9	28	I'D DO ANYTHING FOR LOVE (BUT I WON'T DO THAT)	Meatloaf (Virgin)
-	29	NUTHIN' BUT A G THANG	
		Dr Dre (Death Row)	
-	30	U	Loni Clark (A&M)
12	31	BAT OUT OF HELL	Meatloaf (Epic)
-	32	THE RED STROKES	Garth Brooks (Capitol)
27	33	FEELIN' ALRIGHT	EYC (MCA)
40	34	STOP LOVING ME, STOP LOVING YOU	
		Daryl Hall (Epic)	
-	35	GETTO JAM	Domino (Columbia)
39	36	WHO LET IN THE RAIN	Cyndi Lauper (Epic)
43	37	YOU AND ME	Lisa B (ffrr)
41	38	WHY DON'T YOU TAKE ME	
		One Dove (Boy's Own)	
21	39	HERO	Mariah Carey (Columbia)
20	40	DON'T LOOK ANY FURTHER	
		M People (deConstruction)	
18	41	PLEASE FORGIVE ME	Bryan Adams (A&M)
30	42	MY HOUSE	Terrorovision (Total Vegas)
-	43	HYPERACTIVE!	Thomas Dolby (EMI)
-	44	ASTRAL AMERICA	Apollo 4 40 (Stealth)
-	45	AUTUMN LEAVES	Coldcut (Arista)
35	46	SHIPBUILDING (EP)	Tasmin Archer (EMI)
25	47	AGAIN	Janet Jackson (Virgin)
-	48	BLACK GOLD	Soul Asylum (Columbia)
36	49	WHOOMP! (THERE IT IS)	
		Tag Team (Club Tools)	
-	50	SUPERMODEL/LITTLE DRUMMER BOY	
		RuPaul (Union)	

29 January 1994

1	1	THINGS CAN ONLY GET BETTER	
		D:Ream (Magnet)	
6	2	ALL FOR LOVE	
		Bryan Adams, Rod Stewart, Sting (A&M)	
2	3	TWIST AND SHOUT	
		Chaka Demus & Pliers (Mango)	
5	4	COME BABY COME	K7 (Big Life)
3	5	ANYTHING	Culture Beat (Epic)
11	6	CORNFLAKE GIRL	Tori Amos (East West)
7	7	I MISS YOU	Haddaway (Logic)
15	8	BREATHE AGAIN	Toni Braxton (Arista)
13	9	IN YOUR ROOM	Depeche Mode (Mute)
4	10	IT'S ALRIGHT	East 17 (London)
-	11	RETURN TO INNOCENCE	
		Enigma (Virgin)	
9	12	SAVE OUR LOVE	Eternal (EMI)
19	13	HERE I STAND	Bitty McLean (Brilliant)
32	14	THE RED STROKES	
		Garth Brooks (Capitol)	
15	15	PINCUSHION	ZZ Top (RCA)
20	16	SOMETHING IN COMMON	
		Bobby Brown with Whitney Houston (MCA)	
14	17	EVERYDAY	Phil Collins (Virgin)
10	18	FOR WHOM THE BELL TOLLS	
		Bee Gees (Polydor)	
-	19	NOW AND FOREVER	Richard Marx (Capitol)
8	20	THE PERFECT YEAR	Dina Carroll (A&M PM)
-	21	NOWHERE	Therapy? (A&M)
24	22	SATURN 5	Inspiral Carpets (Mute)
12	23	ACTION	Def Leppard (Bludgeon Riffola)
-	24	THE POWER OF LOVE	
		Celine Dion (Epic)	
43	25	HYPERACTIVE!	Thomas Dolby (EMI)
48	26	BLACK GOLD	Soul Asylum (Columbia)
23	27	I'M IN LUV	Joe (Mercury)
18	28	I'M IN THE MOOD	Ce Ce Peniston (A&M)
22	29	DSINFECTED (EP)	The The (Epic)
30	30	U	Loni Clark (A&M)
21	31	A WHOLE NEW WORLD (ALADDIN'S THEME)	
		Peabo Bryson & Regina Belle (Columbia)	
16	32	BABE	Take That (RCA)
29	33	NUTHIN' BUT A G THANG	
		Dr Dre (Death Row)	
34	34	STOP LOVING ME, STOP LOVING YOU	
		Daryl Hall (Epic)	
35	35	GETTO JAM	Domino (Columbia)
17	36	MR BLOBBY	Mr Blobby (Destiny)
26	37	FAMILY AFFAIR	Shabba Ranks (Atlas)
-	38	CAN'T TAKE YOUR LOVE	
		Pauline Henry (Sony Soho Square)	
25	39	BLOW YOUR WHISTLE	DJ Duke (ffrr)
44	40	ASTRAL AMERICA	Apollo 4 40 (Stealth)
33	41	FEELIN' ALRIGHT	EYC (MCA)
-	42	A CUTE SWEET LOVE ADDICTION	
		Johnny Gill (Motown)	
-	43	FACT OF LIFE	Oui 3 (MCA)
36	44	WHO LET IN THE RAIN	Cyndi Lauper (Epic)
45	45	AUTUMN LEAVES	Coldcut (Arista)
27	46	COLD COLD HEART	
		Wet Wet Wet (Precious)	
37	47	YOU AND ME	Lisa B (ffrr)
39	48	HERO	Mariah Carey (Columbia)
-	49	GOT TO BE REAL	
		Erik (PWL International)	
-	50	YOUR GHOST	Kristin Hersh (4AD)

House music made it to the top again with D:Ream, staving off the challenge of Bryan Adams and friends on *All For Love*. Whitney Houston charted, this time with her husband Bobby Brown, while Garth Brooks kept the Country flag flying in the UK charts. The Bee Gees had evidently been reading John Donne.

February 1994

last week	this week	5 February 1994	
1	1	THINGS CAN ONLY GET BETTER	D:Ream (Magnet)
8	2	BREATHE AGAIN	Toni Braxton (Arista)
2	3	ALL FOR LOVE	Bryan Adams, Rod Stewart, Sting (A&M)
11	4	RETURN TO INNOCENCE	Enigma (Virgin)
4	5	COME BABY COME	K7 (Big Life)
6	6	CORNFLAKE GIRL	Tori Amos (East West)
7	7	I MISS YOU	Haddaway (Logic)
3	8	TWIST AND SHOUT	Chaka Demus & Pliers (Mango)
5	9	ANYTHING	Culture Beat (Epic)
19	10	NOW AND FOREVER	Richard Marx (Capitol)
24	11	THE POWER OF LOVE	Celine Dion (Epic)
-	12	GIVE IT AWAY	Red Hot Chilli Peppers (Warner Bros.)
-	13	PERPETUAL DAWN	Orb (Big Life)
10	14	IT'S ALRIGHT	East 17 (London)
14	15	THE RED STROKES	Garth Brooks (Capitol)
12	16	SAVE OUR LOVE	Eternal (EMI)
13	17	HERE I STAND	Bitty McLean (Brilliant)
-	18	I LOVE MUSIC	Rozalla (Epic)
-	19	SWEET LULLABY	Deep Forest (Columbia)
16	20	SOMETHING IN COMMON	Bobby Brown with Whitney Houston (MCA)
15	21	PINCUSHION	ZZ Top (RCA)
21	22	NOWHERE	Therapy? (A&M)
-	23	CAN'T GET OUT OF BED	Charlatans (Beggars Banquet)
9	24	IN YOUR ROOM	Depeche Mode (Mute)
17	25	EVERYDAY	Phil Collins (Virgin)
18	26	FOR WHOM THE BELL TOLLS	Bee Gees (Polydor)
-	27	LOVER	Joe Roberts (ffrr)
20	28	THE PERFECT YEAR	Dina Carroll (A&M PM)
-	29	COME IN OUT OF THE RAIN	Wendy Moten (EMI)
-	30	ALL THRU THE NIGHT	POV with Jade (Giant)
27	31	I'M IN LUV	Joe (Mercury)
22	32	SATURN 5	Inspiral Carpets (Mute)
23	33	ACTION	Def Leppard (Bludgeon Riffola)
38	34	CAN'T TAKE YOUR LOVE	Pauline Henry (Sony Soho Square)
31	35	A WHOLE NEW WORLD (ALADDIN'S THEME)	Peabo Bryson & Regina Belle (Columbia)
-	36	THE MUSIC'S GOT ME	Bass Bumpers (Vertigo)
25	37	HYPERACTIVE!	Thomas Dolby (EMI)
26	38	BLACK GOLD	Soul Asylum (Columbia)
-	39	BELLS OF NY	Slo Moshun (Six 6)
-	40	IMPOSSIBLE	Captain Hollywood (Pulse 8)
34	41	STOP LOVING ME, STOP LOVING YOU	Daryl Hall (Epic)
43	42	FACT OF LIFE	Oui 3 (MCA)
42	43	A CUTE SWEET LOVE ADDICTION	Johnny Gill (Motown)
28	44	I'M IN THE MOOD	Ce Ce Peniston (A&M)
35	45	GETTO JAM	Domino (Giant)
49	46	GOT TO BE REAL	Erik (PWL International)
-	47	HEY JEALOUSY	Gin Blossoms (Fontana)
-	48	STAY WITH ME BABY	Ruby Turner (M&G)
30	49	U	Loni Clark (A&M)
-	50	RAISE	Hyper Go Go (Posiiva)

12 February 1994	
- 1 THINGS CAN ONLY GET BETTER	D:Ream (Magnet)
2 2 BREATHE AGAIN	Toni Braxton (Arista)
4 3 RETURN TO INNOCENCE	Enigma (Virgin)
3 4 ALL FOR LOVE	Bryan Adams, Rod Stewart, Sting (A&M)
11 5 THE POWER OF LOVE	Celine Dion (Epic)
- 6 A DEEPER LOVE	Aretha Franklin (Arista)
7 7 I MISS YOU	Haddaway (Logic)
6 8 CORNFLAKE GIRL	Tori Amos (East West)
5 9 COME BABY COME	K7 (Big Life)
12 10 GIVE IT AWAY	Red Hot Chilli Peppers (Warner Bros.)
8 11 TWIST AND SHOUT	Chaka Demus & Pliers (Mango)
9 12 ANYTHING	Culture Beat (Epic)
10 13 NOW AND FOREVER	Richard Marx (Capitol)
13 14 PERPETUAL DAWN	Orb (Big Life)
29 15 COME IN OUT OF THE RAIN	Wendy Moten (EMI)
19 16 SWEET LULLABY	Deep Forest (Columbia)
- 17 I LIKE TO MOVE IT	Reel 2 Real featuring the Mad Stuntman (Positiva)
14 18 IT'S ALRIGHT	East 17 (London)
27 19 LOVER	Joe Roberts (ffrr)
- 20 LINGER	Cranberries (Island)
16 21 SAVE OUR LOVE	Eternal (EMI)
- 22 WHY?	D:Mob with Cathy Dennis (ffrr)
23 23 CAN'T GET OUT OF BED	Charlatans (Beggars Banquet)
- 24 NERVOUS BREAKDOWN	Carleen Anderson (Circa)
15 25 THE RED STROKES	Garth Brooks (Capitol)
26 26 SO IN LOVE WITH YOU	Texas (Vertigo)
36 27 THE MUSIC'S GOT ME	Bass Bumpers (Vertigo)
18 28 I LOVE MUSIC	Rozalla (Epic)
- 29 UPTIGHT	Shara Nelson (Cooltempo)
22 30 NOWHERE	Therapy? (A&M)
21 31 PINCUSHION	ZZ Top (RCA)
26 32 FOR WHOM THE BELL TOLLS	Bee Gees (Polydor)
17 33 HERE I STAND	Bitty McLean (Brilliant)
30 34 ALL THRU THE NIGHT	POV with Jade (Giant)
20 35 SOMETHING IN COMMON	Bobby Brown with Whitney Houston (MCA)
47 36 HEY JEALOUSY	Gin Blossoms (Fontana)
40 37 IMPOSSIBLE	Captain Hollywood (Pulse 8)
39 38 BELLS OF NY	Slo Moshun (Six 6)
- 39 NEUROTICA	Cud (A&M)
- 40 LIFE BECOMING A LANDSLIDE (EP)	Manic Street Preachers (Columbia)
- 41 SPIRITUAL LOVE	Urban Species (Talkin' Loud)
31 42 I'M IN LUV	Joe (Mercury)
28 43 THE PERFECT YEAR	Dina Carroll (A&M PM)
- 44 MUDDY WATERS BLUES	Paul Rodgers (Victory)
48 45 STAY WITH ME BABY	Ruby Turner (M&G)
25 46 EVERYDAY	Phil Collins (Virgin)
24 47 IN YOUR ROOM	Depeche Mode (Mute)
32 48 SATURN 5	Inspiral Carpets (Mute)
35 49 A WHOLE NEW WORLD (ALADDIN'S THEME)	Peabo Bryson & Regina Belle (Columbia)
50 50 RAISE	Hyper Go Go (Posiiva)

19 February 1994	
- 1 WITHOUT YOU	Mariah Carey (Columbia)
2 2 BREATHE AGAIN	Toni Braxton (Arista)
6 3 A DEEPER LOVE	Aretha Franklin (Arista)
1 4 THINGS CAN ONLY GET BETTER	D:Ream (Magnet)
3 5 RETURN TO INNOCENCE	Enigma (Virgin)
5 6 THE POWER OF LOVE	Celine Dion (Epic)
- 7 MOVE ON BABY	Cappella (Internal)
15 8 COME IN OUT OF THE RAIN	Wendy Moten (EMI)
4 9 ALL FOR LOVE	Bryan Adams, Rod Stewart, Sting (A&M)
17 10 I LIKE TO MOVE IT	Reel 2 Real featuring the Mad Stuntman (Positiva)
9 11 COME BABY COME	K7 (Big Life)
20 12 LINGER	Cranberries (Island)
- 13 ROCK AND ROLL DREAMS COME THROUGH	Meatloaf (Virgin)
7 14 I MISS YOU	Haddaway (Logic)
16 15 SWEET LULLABY	Deep Forest (Columbia)
- 16 LET THE BEAT CONTROL YOUR BODY	2 Unlimited (PWL Continental)
- 17 LOCKED OUT	Crowded House (Capitol)
- 18 HIGHER GROUND	Sasha (deConstruction)
29 19 UPTIGHT	Shara Nelson (Cooltempo)
12 20 ANYTHING	Culture Beat (Epic)
- 21 SAIL AWAY	Urban Cookie Collective (Pulse 8)
11 22 TWIST AND SHOUT	Chaka Demus & Pliers (Mango)
10 23 GIVE IT AWAY	Red Hot Chilli Peppers (Warner Bros.)
22 24 WHY?	D:Mob with Cathy Dennis (ffrr)
36 25 HEY JEALOUSY	Gin Blossoms (Fontana)
- 26 LET'S GET MARRIED	Proclaimers (Chrysalis)
24 27 NERVOUS BREAKDOWN	Carleen Anderson (Circa)
19 28 LOVER	Joe Roberts (ffrr)
14 29 PERPETUAL DAWN	Orb (Big Life)
- 30 DIRTY DAWG	NKOTB (Columbia)
13 31 NOW AND FOREVER	Richard Marx (Capitol)
- 32 PALE MOVIE	Saint Etienne (Heavenly)
8 33 CORNFLAKE GIRL	Tori Amos (East West)
- 34 LINE UP	Elastica (Deceptive)
- 35 WATERFALL	Atlantic Ocean (Eastern Bloc)
- 36 CAFFEINE BOMB	Wildhearts (Bronze)
26 37 SO IN LOVE WITH YOU	Texas (Vertigo)
28 38 I LOVE MUSIC	Rozalla (Epic)
18 39 IT'S ALRIGHT	East 17 (London)
41 40 SPIRITUAL LOVE	Urban Species (Talkin' Loud)
- 41 BEEN A LONG TIME	Fog (Columbia)
40 42 LIFE BECOMING A LANDSLIDE (EP)	Manic Street Preachers (Columbia)
- 43 CAN'T WAIT TO BE WITH YOU	Jazzy Jeff & the Fresh Prince (Jive)
37 44 IMPOSSIBLE	Captain Hollywood (Pulse 8)
39 45 NEUROTICA	Cud (A&M)
- 46 RESPECT	Sub Sub (Rob's)
- 47 YOU MADE ME THE THIEF OF YOUR HEART	Sinead O'Connor (Island)
- 48 THE WIND BENEATH MY WINGS	Bill Tarmey (EMI)
- 49 WAKE UP AND SCRATCH ME	Sultans Of Ping (Epic)
21 50 SAVE OUR LOVE	Eternal (EMI)

Aretha Franklin, whose original Atlantic recordings in the 1960s opened up a whole new kind of music, was back in the Top 3, with a cover of a C&C Music Factory song. Mariah Carey confirmed her status as the most popular female singer of the day. The Charlatans returned to 7 inch vinyl – limited edition.

581

February – March 1994

26 February 1994

last week	this week		
1	1	WITHOUT YOU	Mariah Carey (Columbia)
-	2	STAY TOGETHER	Suede (Nude)
7	3	MOVE ON BABY	Cappella (Internal)
4	4	THINGS CAN ONLY GET BETTER	D:Ream (Magnet)
2	5	BREATHE AGAIN	Toni Braxton (Arista)
5	6	RETURN TO INNOCENCE	Enigma (Virgin)
6	7	THE POWER OF LOVE	Celine Dion (Epic)
16	8	LET THE BEAT CONTROL YOUR BODY	2 Unlimited (PWL Continental)
9	9	ALL FOR LOVE	Bryan Adams, Rod Stewart, Sting (A&M)
13	10	ROCK AND ROLL DREAMS COME THROUGH	Meatloaf (Virgin)
-	11	THE SIGN	Ace Of Base (Metronome)
3	12	A DEEPER LOVE	Aretha Franklin (Arista)
-	13	DON'T GO BREAKING MY HEART	Elton John & RuPaul (Rocket)
10	14	I LIKE TO MOVE IT	Reel 2 Real featuring the Mad Stuntman (Positiva)
8	15	COME IN OUT OF THE RAIN	Wendy Moten (EMI)
17	16	LOCKED OUT	Crowded House (Capitol)
11	17	COME BABY COME	K7 (Big Life)
12	18	LINGER	Cranberries (Island)
26	19	LET'S GET MARRIED	Proclaimers (Chrysalis)
-	20	DOWNTOWN	SWV (RCA)
15	21	SWEET LULLABY	Deep Forest (Columbia)
-	22	SPOONMAN	Soundgarden (A&M)
-	23	FOREVER NOW	Level 42 (RCA)
-	24	TWO TRIBES	Frankie Goes To Hollywood (ZTT)
14	25	I MISS YOU	Haddaway (Logic)
-	26	BECAUSE OF YOU	Gabrielle (Go Beat)
35	27	WATERFALL	Atlantic Ocean (Eastern Bloc)
18	28	HIGHER GROUND	Sasha (deConstruction)
21	29	SAIL AWAY	Urban Cookie Collective (Pulse 8)
-	30	NOTHING 'BOUT ME	Sting (A&M)
-	31	INSANE IN THE BRAIN	Cypress Hill (Ruff House)
-	32	RIGHT IN THE NIGHT (FALL IN LOVE ...)	Jam & Spoon featuring Plavka (Epic)
19	33	UPTIGHT	Shara Nelson (Cooltempo)
30	34	DIRTY DAWG	NKOTB (Columbia)
20	35	ANYTHING	Culture Beat (Epic)
43	36	CAN'T WAIT TO BE WITH YOU	Jazzy Jeff & the Fresh Prince (Jive)
36	37	CAFFEINE BOMB	Wildhearts (Bronze)
-	38	BLUEBEARD	Cocteau Twins (Fontana)
-	39	OUT OF MY HEAD	Marradonna (PWL International)
32	40	PALE MOVIE	Saint Etienne (Heavenly)
47	41	YOU MADE ME THE THIEF OF YOUR HEART	Sinead O'Connor (Island)
22	42	TWIST AND SHOUT	Chaka Demus & Pliers (Mango)
28	43	LOVER	Joe Roberts (ffrr)
24	44	WHY?	D:Mob with Cathy Dennis (ffrr)
25	45	HEY JEALOUSY	Gin Blossoms (Fontana)
-	46	REFUSE/RESIST	Sepultura (Roadrunner)
-	47	SOUL OF MY SOUL	Michael Bolton (Columbia)
-	48	LOVE AND HAPPINESS	River Ocean featuring India (Cooltempo)
-	49	HEAR ME CALLING	2wo Third3 (Epic)
31	50	NOW AND FOREVER	Richard Marx (Capitol)

5 March 1994

last week	this week		
1	1	WITHOUT YOU	Mariah Carey (Columbia)
11	2	THE SIGN	Ace Of Base (Metronome)
4	3	THINGS CAN ONLY GET BETTER	D:Ream (Magnet)
3	4	MOVE ON BABY	Cappella (Internal)
5	5	BREATHE AGAIN	Toni Braxton (Arista)
6	6	RETURN TO INNOCENCE	Enigma (Virgin)
8	7	LET THE BEAT CONTROL YOUR BODY	2 Unlimited (PWL Continental)
2	8	STAY TOGETHER	Suede (Nude)
13	9	DON'T GO BREAKING MY HEART	Elton John & RuPaul (Rocket)
9	10	ALL FOR LOVE	Bryan Adams, Rod Stewart, Sting (A&M)
7	11	THE POWER OF LOVE	Celine Dion (Epic)
10	12	ROCK AND ROLL DREAMS COME THROUGH	Meatloaf (Virgin)
-	13	DISARM	Smashing Pumpkins (Hut)
-	14	I WANT YOU	Inspiral Carpets featuring Mark E Smith (Cow)
14	15	I LIKE TO MOVE IT	Reel 2 Real featuring the Mad Stuntman (Positiva)
23	16	FOREVER NOW	Level 42 (RCA)
15	17	COME IN OUT OF THE RAIN	Wendy Moten (EMI)
20	18	DOWNTOWN	SWV (RCA)
18	19	LINGER	Cranberries (Island)
24	20	TWO TRIBES	Frankie Goes To Hollywood (ZTT)
26	21	BECAUSE OF YOU	Gabrielle (Go Beat)
12	22	A DEEPER LOVE	Aretha Franklin (Arista)
17	23	COME BABY COME	K7 (Big Life)
31	24	INSANE IN THE BRAIN	Cypress Hill (Ruff House)
-	26	LOSER	Beck (Geffen)
-	27	SULKY GIRL	Elvis Costello (Warner Bros.)
16	28	LOCKED OUT	Crowded House (Capitol)
30	29	NOTHING 'BOUT ME	Sting (A&M)
27	30	WATERFALL	Atlantic Ocean (Eastern Bloc)
19	31	LET'S GET MARRIED	Proclaimers (Chrysalis)
32	32	RIGHT IN THE NIGHT (FALL IN LOVE ...)	Jam & Spoon featuring Plavka (Epic)
21	33	SWEET LULLABY	Deep Forest (Columbia)
22	34	SPOONMAN	Soundgarden (A&M)
-	35	BOW WOW WOW	Funkdoobiest (Epic)
-	36	JINGO	FKW (PWL International)
29	37	SAIL AWAY	Urban Cookie Collective (Pulse 8)
25	38	I MISS YOU	Haddaway (Logic)
47	39	SOUL OF MY SOUL	Michael Bolton (Columbia)
-	40	HOOLIGAN'S HOLIDAY	Motley Crue (Elektra)
38	41	BLUEBEARD	Cocteau Twins (Fontana)
39	42	OUT OF MY HEAD	Marradonna (PWL International)
-	43	THE WAY YOU WORK IT	EYC (MCA)
36	44	CAN'T WAIT TO BE WITH YOU	Jazzy Jeff & the Fresh Prince (Jive)
-	45	WITHOUT YOU	Nilsson (RCA)
-	46	IF I LOVE YA, THEN I NEED YA	Eartha Kitt (RAC)
28	47	HIGHER GROUND	Sasha (deConstruction)
-	48	SAXY LADY	Quivver (A&M)
-	49	WONDERFUL LIFE	Black (PolyGram TV)
41	50	YOU MADE ME THE THIEF OF YOUR HEART	Sinead O'Connor (Island)

12 March 1994

last week	this week		
1	1	WITHOUT YOU	Mariah Carey (Columbia)
2	2	THE SIGN	Ace Of Base (Metronome)
-	3	DOOP	Doop (Citybeat)
5	4	BREATHE AGAIN	Toni Braxton (Arista)
-	5	THE MORE YOU IGNORE ME, THE CLOSER I GET	Morrissey (Parlophone)
6	6	RETURN TO INNOCENCE	Enigma (Virgin)
7	7	ROCKS/FUNKY JAM	Primal Scream (Creation)
3	8	THINGS CAN ONLY GET BETTER	D:Ream (Magnet)
-	9	RENAISSANCE	M People (deConstruction)
9	10	DON'T GO BREAKING MY HEART	Elton John & RuPaul (Rocket)
4	11	MOVE ON BABY	Cappella (Internal)
7	12	LET THE BEAT CONTROL YOUR BODY	2 Unlimited (PWL Continental)
10	13	ALL FOR LOVE	Bryan Adams, Rod Stewart, Sting (A&M)
-	14	ICH BIEN EIN AUSLANDER	Pop Will Eat Itself (Infectious)
15	15	I LIKE TO MOVE IT	Reel 2 Real featuring the Mad Stuntman (Positiva)
-	16	TRIGGER INSIDE	Therapy? (A&M)
-	17	I BELIEVE	Marcella Detroit (London)
8	18	STAY TOGETHER	Suede (Nude)
26	19	LOSER	Beck (Geffen)
20	20	BECAUSE OF LOVE	Janet Jackson (Virgin)
11	21	THE POWER OF LOVE	Celine Dion (Epic)
13	22	DISARM	Smashing Pumpkins (Hut)
19	23	LINGER	Cranberries (Island)
-	24	GOOD AS GOLD	Beautiful South (Go! Discs)
12	25	ROCK AND ROLL DREAMS COME THROUGH	Meatloaf (Virgin)
-	26	GLAM ROCK COPS	Carter USM (Chrysalis)
17	27	COME IN OUT OF THE RAIN	Wendy Moten (EMI)
43	28	THE WAY YOU WORK IT	EYC (MCA)
-	29	MURDER SHE WROTE	Chaka Demus & Pliers (Mango)
-	30	TEENAGE SENSATION	Credit To The Nation (One Little Indian)
27	31	SULKY GIRL	Elvis Costello (Warner Bros.)
14	32	I WANT YOU	Inspiral Carpets featuring Mark E Smith (Cow)
-	33	PIECES OF A DREAM	Incognito (Talkin' Loud)
16	34	FOREVER NOW	Level 42 (RCA)
22	35	BEAUTIFUL PEOPLE	Barbara Tucker (Positiva)
21	36	BECAUSE OF YOU	Gabrielle (Go Beat)
18	37	DOWNTOWN	SWV (RCA)
-	38	THERE BUT FOR THE GRACE OF GOD GO I	Fire Island (Junior Boy's Own)
-	39	HOUSE OF LOVE	Skin (EMI)
-	40	WHISPERING YOUR NAME	Alison Moyet (Columbia)
25	41	INSANE IN THE BRAIN	Cypress Hill (Ruff House)
20	42	TWO TRIBES	Frankie Goes To Hollywood (ZTT)
49	43	WONDERFUL LIFE	Black (PolyGram TV)
24	44	COME BABY COME	K7 (Big Life)
32	45	RIGHT IN THE NIGHT (FALL IN LOVE ...)	Jam & Spoon featuring Plavka (Epic)
39	46	SOUL OF MY SOUL	Michael Bolton (Columbia)
23	47	A DEEPER LOVE	Aretha Franklin (Arista)
46	48	IF I LOVE YA, THEN I NEED YA	Eartha Kitt (RAC)
36	49	JINGO	FKW (PWL International)
33	50	SWEET LULLABY	Deep Forest (Columbia)

Suede were the great hope of indie pop. Big before they even got a record deal, they came in at Number Two, but then slid down the chart at an alarming rate.

Elton John remade his previous Number One with drag supermodel RuPaul, while M People charted with the theme to a different kind of soap.

19 March 1994

last week	this week	title	artist (label)
3	1	DOOP	Doop (Citybeat)
1	2	WITHOUT YOU	Mariah Carey (Columbia)
2	3	THE SIGN	Ace Of Base (Metronome)
-	4	STREETS OF PHILADELPHIA	Bruce Springsteen (Columbia)
4	5	BREATHE AGAIN	Toni Braxton (Arista)
9	6	RENAISSANCE	M People (deConstruction)
6	7	RETURN TO INNOCENCE	Enigma (Virgin)
-	8	PRETTY GOOD YEAR	Tori Amos (East West)
-	9	VIOLENTLY HAPPY	Bjork (One Little Indian)
-	10	GIRLS AND BOYS	Blur (Food)
7	11	I BELIEVE	Marcella Detroit (London)
15	12	I LIKE TO MOVE IT	Reel 2 Real featuring the Mad Stuntman (Positiva)
-	13	SHINE ON	Degrees Of Motion featuring Biti (ffrr)
7	14	ROCKS/FUNKY JAM	Primal Scream (Creation)
28	15	THE WAY YOU WORK IT	EYC (MCA)
-	16	WHATTA MAN	Salt 'N' Pepa with En Vogue (ffrr)
8	17	THINGS CAN ONLY GET BETTER	D:Ream (Magnet)
10	18	DON'T GO BREAKING MY HEART	Elton John & RuPaul (Rocket)
19	19	LOSER	Beck (Geffen)
20	20	BECAUSE OF LOVE	Janet Jackson (Virgin)
5	21	THE MORE YOU IGNORE ME, THE CLOSER I GET	Morrissey (Parlophone)
26	22	GLAM ROCK COPS	Carter USM (Chrysalis)
-	23	I'M BROKEN/SLAUGHTERED	Pantera (Atco)
12	24	LET THE BEAT CONTROL YOUR BODY	2 Unlimited (PWL Continental)
24	25	GOOD AS GOLD	Beautiful South (Go! Discs)
23	26	LINGER	Cranberries (Island)
11	27	MOVE ON BABY	Cappella (Internal)
-	28	I CAN SEE CLEARLY NOW	Jimmy Cliff (Columbia)
30	29	TEENAGE SENSATION	Credit To The Nation (One Little Indian)
13	30	ALL FOR LOVE	Bryan Adams, Rod Stewart, Sting (A&M)
40	31	WHISPERING YOUR NAME	Alison Moyet (Columbia)
18	32	STAY TOGETHER	Suede (Nude)
29	33	MURDER SHE WROTE	Chaka Demus & Pliers (Mango)
-	34	AGAIN/I WANT YOU	Juliet Roberts (Cooltempo)
27	35	COME IN OUT OF THE RAIN	Wendy Moten (EMI)
-	36	EASY LIFE	Charlatans (Beggars Banquet)
-	37	LOVE COME DOWN	Alison Limerick (Arista)
21	38	THE POWER OF LOVE	Celine Dion (Epic)
-	39	GROOVE THANG	Zhane (Motown)
-	40	LET'S FACE THE MUSIC AND DANCE	Nat 'King' Cole (EMI)
-	41	SWITCH	Senser (Ultimate)
16	42	TRIGGER INSIDE	Therapy? (A&M)
14	43	ICH BIEN EIN AUSLANDER	Pop Will Eat Itself (Infectious)
33	44	PIECES OF A DREAM	Incognito (Talkin' Loud)
38	45	THERE BUT FOR THE GRACE OF GOD GO I	Fire Island (Junior Boy's Own)
-	46	I WANT TO THANK YOU	Robin S (Champion)
22	47	DISARM	Smashing Pumpkins (Hut)
25	48	ROCK AND ROLL DREAMS COME THROUGH	Meatloaf (Virgin)
-	49	HOBO HUMPIN SLOBO BABE	Whale (East West)
-	50	ONLY TO BE WITH YOU	Roachford (Columbia)

26 March 1994

last week	this week	title	artist (label)
1	1	DOOP	Doop (Citybeat)
2	2	WITHOUT YOU	Mariah Carey (Columbia)
4	3	STREETS OF PHILADELPHIA	Bruce Springsteen (Columbia)
3	4	THE SIGN	Ace Of Base (Metronome)
10	5	GIRLS AND BOYS	Blur (Food)
16	6	WHATTA MAN	Salt 'N' Pepa with En Vogue (ffrr)
11	7	I BELIEVE	Marcella Detroit (London)
8	8	U R THE BEST THING	D:Ream (Magnet)
-	9	DRY COUNTY	Bon Jovi (Jambco)
13	10	SHINE ON	Degrees Of Motion featuring Biti (ffrr)
6	11	RENAISSANCE	M People (deConstruction)
8	12	PRETTY GOOD YEAR	Tori Amos (East West)
12	13	I LIKE TO MOVE IT	Reel 2 Real featuring the Mad Stuntman (Positiva)
7	14	RETURN TO INNOCENCE	Enigma (Virgin)
-	15	DREAM ON DREAMER	Brand New Heavies (ffrr)
-	16	SLEEPING IN MY CAR	Roxette (EMI)
9	17	VIOLENTLY HAPPY	Bjork (One Little Indian)
-	18	I BELIEVE	Sounds Of Blackness (A&M)
28	19	I CAN SEE CLEARLY NOW	Jimmy Cliff (Columbia)
5	20	BREATHE AGAIN	Toni Braxton (Arista)
31	21	WHISPERING YOUR NAME	Alison Moyet (Columbia)
-	22	HOT LOVE NOW (EP)	Wonder Stuff (Far Out)
-	23	COULD IT BE I'M FALLING IN LOVE	Worlds Apart (Arista)
15	24	THE WAY YOU WORK IT	EYC (MCA)
-	25	SHAPES THAT GO TOGETHER	A-Ha (Warner Bros.)
26	26	LINGER	Cranberries (Island)
25	27	GOOD AS GOLD	Beautiful South (Go! Discs)
-	28	THE HOLLOW MAN	Marillion (EMI)
-	29	LOOK WHO'S TALKING	Dr Alban (Logic)
14	30	ROCKS/FUNKY JAM	Primal Scream (Creation)
-	31	SOMEBODY TO SHOVE	Soul Asylum (Columbia)
24	32	LET THE BEAT CONTROL YOUR BODY	2 Unlimited (PWL Continental)
50	33	ONLY TO BE WITH YOU	Roachford (Columbia)
17	34	THINGS CAN ONLY GET BETTER	D:Ream (Magnet)
40	35	LET'S FACE THE MUSIC AND DANCE	Nat 'King' Cole (EMI)
23	36	I'M BROKEN/SLAUGHTERED	Pantera (Atco)
39	37	GROOVE THANG	Zhane (Motown)
34	38	AGAIN/I WANT YOU	Juliet Roberts (Cooltempo)
20	39	BECAUSE OF LOVE	Janet Jackson (Virgin)
22	40	GLAM ROCK COPS	Carter USM (Chrysalis)
18	41	DON'T GO BREAKING MY HEART	Elton John & RuPaul (Rocket)
19	42	LOSER	Beck (Geffen)
-	43	YOU KNOW HOW WE DO IT	Ice Cube (Priority)
37	44	LOVE COME DOWN	Alison Limerick (Arista)
-	45	SKIP TO MY LU	Lisa Lisa (Pendulum)
-	46	UNITY	Queen Latifah (Motown)
-	47	NEVER LET YOU GO	NKOTB (Columbia)
-	48	I'M IN A PHILLY MOOD	Daryl Hall (Epic)
33	49	MURDER SHE WROTE	Chaka Demus & Pliers (Mango)
30	50	ALL FOR LOVE	Bryan Adams, Rod Stewart, Sting (A&M)

2 April 1994

last week	this week	title	artist (label)
1	1	DOOP	Doop (Citybeat)
3	2	STREETS OF PHILADELPHIA	Bruce Springsteen (Columbia)
8	3	U R THE BEST THING	D:Ream (Magnet)
4	4	THE SIGN	Ace Of Base (Metronome)
2	5	WITHOUT YOU	Mariah Carey (Columbia)
6	6	WHATTA MAN	Salt 'N' Pepa with En Vogue (ffrr)
9	7	DRY COUNTY	Bon Jovi (Jambco)
5	8	GIRLS AND BOYS	Blur (Food)
13	9	I LIKE TO MOVE IT	Reel 2 Real featuring the Mad Stuntman (Positiva)
-	10	I'LL REMEMBER	Madonna (Maverick)
10	11	SHINE ON	Degrees Of Motion featuring Biti (ffrr)
7	12	I BELIEVE	Marcella Detroit (London)
-	13	SON OF A GUN	JX (Internal Dance)
16	14	SLEEPING IN MY CAR	Roxette (EMI)
-	15	ROCK MY HEART	Haddaway (Logic)
14	16	RETURN TO INNOCENCE	Enigma (Virgin)
22	17	HOT LOVE NOW (EP)	Wonder Stuff (Far Out)
21	18	WHISPERING YOUR NAME	Alison Moyet (Columbia)
11	19	RENAISSANCE	M People (deConstruction)
15	20	DREAM ON DREAMER	Brand New Heavies (ffrr)
18	21	I BELIEVE	Sounds Of Blackness (A&M)
33	22	ONLY TO BE WITH YOU	Roachford (Columbia)
23	23	COULD IT BE I'M FALLING IN LOVE	Worlds Apart (Arista)
19	24	I CAN SEE CLEARLY NOW	Jimmy Cliff (Columbia)
-	25	WORLD IN YOUR HANDS	Culture Beat (Epic)
-	26	JAM J/SAY SOMETHING	James (Fontana)
-	27	DO YOU REMEMBER THE FIRST TIME?	Pulp (Island)
29	28	LOOK WHO'S TALKING	Dr Alban (Logic)
26	29	LINGER	Cranberries (Island)
-	30	HI DE HO	K7 & the Swing Kids (Big Life)
-	31	I WAS RIGHT AND YOU WERE WRONG	Deacon Blue (Columbia)
31	32	SOMEBODY TO SHOVE	Soul Asylum (Columbia)
-	33	ANOTHER SAD LOVE SONG	Toni Braxton (LaFace)
17	34	VIOLENTLY HAPPY	Bjork (One Little Indian)
25	35	SHAPES THAT GO TOGETHER	A-Ha (Warner Bros.)
24	36	THE WAY YOU WORK IT	EYC (MCA)
32	37	LET THE BEAT CONTROL YOUR BODY	2 Unlimited (PWL Continental)
-	38	KEEP GIVIN' ME YOUR LOVE	Ce Ce Peniston (A&M)
-	39	THE BEST YEARS OF MY LIFE	Diana Ross (EMI)
45	40	SKIP TO MY LU	Lisa Lisa (Pendulum)
27	41	GOOD AS GOLD	Beautiful South (Go! Discs)
12	42	PRETTY GOOD YEAR	Tori Amos (East West)
28	43	THE HOLLOW MAN	Marillion (EMI)
35	44	LET'S FACE THE MUSIC AND DANCE	Nat 'King' Cole (EMI)
34	45	THINGS CAN ONLY GET BETTER	D:Ream (Magnet)
20	46	BREATHE AGAIN	Toni Braxton (Arista)
43	47	YOU KNOW HOW WE DO IT	Ice Cube (Priority)
47	48	NEVER LET YOU GO	NKOTB (Columbia)
-	49	MONEY	Backbeat Band (Virgin)
-	50	C'EST LA VIE	UB40 (DEP International)

Doop by Doop used a Charleston-based sample, and as a result started a new dance craze. Bruce Springsteen scored with a tie-in to the hit film *Philadelphia*. Jimmy Cliff, the greatest singer that reggae ever produced, was back with a cover of a Johnny Nash hit. Blur and Bjork were getting bigger.

April 1994

9 April 1994

last week	this week	Title	Artist (Label)
-	1	EVERYTHING CHANGES	Take That (RCA)
1	2	DOOP	Doop (Citybeat)
2	3	STREETS OF PHILADELPHIA	Bruce Springsteen (Columbia)
-	4	THE MOST BEAUTIFUL GIRL IN THE WORLD	Prince (NPG)
3	5	U R THE BEST THING	D:Ream (Magnet)
4	6	THE SIGN	Ace Of Base (Metronome)
10	7	I'LL REMEMBER	Madonna (Maverick)
15	8	ROCK MY HEART	Haddaway (Logic)
9	9	I LIKE TO MOVE IT	Reel 2 Real featuring the Mad Stuntman (Positiva)
5	10	WITHOUT YOU	Mariah Carey (Columbia)
6	11	WHATTA MAN	Salt 'N' Pepa with En Vogue (ffrr)
-	12	HUNG UP	Paul Weller (Go! Discs)
11	13	SHINE ON	Degrees Of Motion featuring Biti (ffrr)
13	14	SON OF A GUN	JX (Internal Dance)
8	15	GIRLS AND BOYS	Blur (Food)
-	16	THE REAL THING	Toni Di Bart (Cleveland City)
7	17	DRY COUNTY	Bon Jovi (Jambco)
16	18	RETURN TO INNOCENCE	Enigma (Virgin)
23	19	COULD IT BE I'M FALLING IN LOVE	Worlds Apart (Arista)
12	20	I BELIEVE	Marcella Detroit (London)
26	21	JAM J/SAY SOMETHING	James (Fontana)
39	22	THE BEST YEARS OF MY LIFE2	Diana Ross (EMI)
25	23	WORLD IN YOUR HANDS	Culture Beat (Epic)
30	24	HI DE HO	K7 & the Swing Kids (Big Life)
-	25	TEN MILES HIGH	Little Angels (Polydor)
22	26	ONLY TO BE WITH YOU	Roachford (Columbia)
14	27	SLEEPING IN MY CAR	Roxette (EMI)
-	28	YOU GOTTA BE	Des'ree (Sony Soho Square)
-	29	DEDICATED TO THE ONE I LOVE	Bitty McLean (Brilliant)
33	30	ANOTHER SAD LOVE SONG	Toni Braxton (LaFace)
31	31	I WAS RIGHT AND YOU WERE WRONG	Deacon Blue (Columbia)
18	32	WHISPERING YOUR NAME	Alison Moyet (Columbia)
17	33	HOT LOVE NOW (EP)	Wonder Stuff (Far Out)
-	34	HOW GEE	Black Machine (London)
29	35	LINGER	Cranberries (Island)
-	36	GOTTA LOTTA LOVE	Ice-T (Virgin)
19	37	RENAISSANCE	M People (deConstruction)
-	38	SEVENTEEN	Let Loose (Mercury)
24	39	I CAN SEE CLEARLY NOW	Jimmy Cliff (Columbia)
50	40	C'EST LA VIE	UB40 (DEP International)
20	41	DREAM ON DREAMER	Brand New Heavies (ffrr)
35	42	SHAPES THAT GO TOGETHER	A-Ha (Warner Bros.)
21	43	I BELIEVE	Sounds Of Blackness (A&M)
28	44	LOOK WHO'S TALKING	Dr Alban (Logic)
27	45	DO YOU REMEMBER THE FIRST TIME?	Pulp (Island)
-	46	PHILADELPHIA	Neil Young (Reprise)
-	47	IN THE NAME OF THE FATHER	Bono & Gavin Friday (Island)
-	48	TAP THE BOTTLE	Young Black Teenagers (MCA)
-	49	MARCH OF THE PIGS	Nine Inch Nails (Island)
36	50	THE WAY YOU WORK IT	EYC (MCA)

16 April 1994

last week	this week	Title	Artist (Label)
1	1	EVERYTHING CHANGES	Take That (RCA)
2	2	DOOP	Doop (Citybeat)
3	3	STREETS OF PHILADELPHIA	Bruce Springsteen (Columbia)
4	4	THE MOST BEAUTIFUL GIRL IN THE WORLD	Prince (NPG)
7	5	I'LL REMEMBER	Madonna (Maverick)
6	6	THE SIGN	Ace Of Base (Metronome)
5	7	U R THE BEST THING	D:Ream (Magnet)
9	8	I LIKE TO MOVE IT	Reel 2 Real featuring the Mad Stuntman (Positiva)
8	9	ROCK MY HEART	Haddaway (Logic)
16	10	THE REAL THING	Toni Di Bart (Cleveland City)
10	11	WITHOUT YOU	Mariah Carey (Columbia)
11	12	WHATTA MAN	Salt 'N' Pepa with En Vogue (ffrr)
13	13	SHINE ON	Degrees Of Motion featuring Biti (ffrr)
-	14	LIBERATION	Pet Shop Boys (Parlophone)
29	15	DEDICATED TO THE ONE I LOVE	Bitty McLean (Brilliant)
14	16	SON OF A GUN	JX (Internal Dance)
30	17	ANOTHER SAD LOVE SONG	Toni Braxton (LaFace)
-	18	LET THE MUSIC (LIFT YOU UP)	Loveland (Six6)
-	19	SINGING THE BLUES	Daniel O'Donnell (Ritz)
18	20	RETURN TO INNOCENCE	Enigma (Virgin)
15	21	GIRLS AND BOYS	Blur (Food)
12	22	HUNG UP	Paul Weller (Go! Discs)
34	23	HOW GEE	Black Machine (London)
19	24	COULD IT BE I'M FALLING IN LOVE	Worlds Apart (Arista)
36	25	GOTTA LOTTA LOVE	Ice-T (Virgin)
28	26	YOU GOTTA BE	Des'ree (Sony Soho Square)
-	27	LONELY SYMPHONY (WE WILL BE FREE)	Francis Ruffelle (Virgin)
26	28	ONLY TO BE WITH YOU	Roachford (Columbia)
17	29	DRY COUNTY	Bon Jovi (Jambco)
25	30	TEN MILES HIGH	Little Angels (Polydor)
31	31	OBLIVION	Terrorvision (Total Vegas)
-	32	THE RED SHOES	Kate Bush (EMI)
20	33	I BELIEVE	Marcella Detroit (London)
27	34	SLEEPING IN MY CAR	Roxette (EMI)
23	35	WORLD IN YOUR HANDS	Culture Beat (Epic)
24	36	HI DE HO	K7 & the Swing Kids (Big Life)
21	37	JAM J/SAY SOMETHING	James (Fontana)
22	38	THE BEST YEARS OF MY LIFE	Diana Ross (EMI)
35	39	LINGER	Cranberries (Island)
38	40	SEVENTEEN	Let Loose (Mercury)
-	41	I'LL WAIT	Taylor Dayne (Arista)
-	42	HOW TO FALL IN LOVE PART 1	Bee Gees (Polydor)
-	43	WHAT'S IT LIKE TO BE BEAUTIFUL	Lena Fiagbe (Mother)
48	44	TAP THE BOTTLE	Young Black Teenagers (MCA)
-	45	PULL UP TO THE BUMPER	AM City (Arista)
32	46	WHISPERING YOUR NAME	Alison Moyet (Columbia)
-	47	SORRY BUT I'M GONNA HAVE TO PASS	Coasters (Rhino)
-	48	FOUND OUT ABOUT YOU	Gin Blossoms (Fontana)
40	49	C'EST LA VIE	UB40 (DEP International)
47	50	IN THE NAME OF THE FATHER	Bono & Gavin Friday (Island)

23 April 1994

last week	this week	Title	Artist (Label)
-	1	ALWAYS	Erasure (Mute)
4	2	THE MOST BEAUTIFUL GIRL IN THE WORLD	Prince (NPG)
1	3	EVERYTHING CHANGES	Take That (RCA)
10	4	THE REAL THING	Toni Di Bart (Cleveland City)
-	5	MMM MMM MMM MMM	Crash Test Dummies (RCA)
3	6	STREETS OF PHILADELPHIA	Bruce Springsteen (Columbia)
15	7	DEDICATED TO THE ONE I LOVE	Bitty McLean (Brilliant)
8	8	I LIKE TO MOVE IT	Reel 2 Real featuring the Mad Stuntman (Positiva)
2	9	DOOP	Doop (Citybeat)
14	10	LIBERATION	Pet Shop Boys (Parlophone)
6	11	THE SIGN	Ace Of Base (Metronome)
5	12	I'LL REMEMBER	Madonna (Maverick)
9	13	ROCK MY HEART	Haddaway (Logic)
7	14	U R THE BEST THING	D:Ream (Magnet)
12	15	WHATTA MAN	Salt 'N' Pepa with En Vogue (ffrr)
11	16	WITHOUT YOU	Mariah Carey (Columbia)
17	17	ANOTHER SAD LOVE SONG	Toni Braxton (LaFace)
18	18	LET THE MUSIC (LIFT YOU UP)	Loveland (Six6)
26	19	YOU GOTTA BE	Des'ree (Sony Soho Square)
32	20	THE RED SHOES	Kate Bush (EMI)
16	21	SON OF A GUN	JX (Internal Dance)
-	22	100% PURE LOVE	Crystal Waters (A&M)
-	23	SWEETS FOR MY SWEET	C J Lewis (MCA)
31	24	OBLIVION	Terrorvision (Total Vegas)
23	25	HOW GEE	Black Machine (London)
19	26	SINGING THE BLUES	Daniel O'Donnell (Ritz)
27	27	LONELY SYMPHONY (WE WILL BE FREE)	Francis Ruffelle (Virgin)
-	28	STANDING OUTSIDE THE FIRE	Garth Brooks (Liberty)
13	29	SHINE ON	Degrees Of Motion featuring Biti (ffrr)
28	30	ONLY TO BE WITH YOU	Roachford (Columbia)
41	31	I'LL WAIT	Taylor Dayne (Arista)
-	32	WHY ME?	P J & Duncan (XSRhythm)
25	33	GOTTA LOTTA LOVE	Ice-T (Virgin)
-	34	SUPERSONIC	Oasis (Creation)
42	35	HOW TO FALL IN LOVE PART 1	Bee Gees (Polydor)
-	36	PRESSURE	Drizabone (4th & Broadway)
48	37	FOUND OUT ABOUT YOU	Gin Blossoms (Fontana)
-	38	BUBBLE	Fluke (Circa)
-	39	HIGH ON A HAPPY VIBE	Urban Cookie Collective (Pulse 8)
-	40	I'LL STAND BY YOU	Pretenders (WEA)
-	41	CHINESE BAKERY	Auteurs (Hut)
34	42	SLEEPING IN MY CAR	Roxette (EMI)
21	43	GIRLS AND BOYS	Blur (Food)
-	44	IT WILL BE YOU	Paul Young (Columbia)
-	45	WHAT MAKES YOU CRY	Proclaimers (Chrysalis)
24	46	COULD IT BE I'M FALLING IN LOVE	Worlds Apart (Arista)
20	47	RETURN TO INNOCENCE	Enigma (Virgin)
22	48	HUNG UP	Paul Weller (Go! Discs)
-	49	MISLED	Celine Dion (Epic)
-	50	EXPRESS	BT Express (PWL International)

Getting straight in at Number One was a habit for Take That, but they quickly got pushed out as Erasure repeated the trick. Some of this was to do with big advance promotion, meaning that everyone who wanted the record was waiting for it and bought it in the first week. After that it sinks slowly downwards.

30 April 1994

last week	this week	Title	Artist
2	1	THE MOST BEAUTIFUL GIRL IN THE WORLD	Prince (NPG)
1	2	ALWAYS	Erasure (Mute)
5	3	MMM MMM MMM MMM	Crash Test Dummies (RCA)
4	4	THE REAL THING	Toni Di Bart (Cleveland City)
23	5	SWEETS FOR MY SWEET	C J Lewis (MCA)
3	6	EVERYTHING CHANGES	Take That (RCA)
7	7	DEDICATED TO THE ONE I LOVE	Bitty McLean (Brilliant)
8	8	I LIKE TO MOVE IT	Reel 2 Real featuring the Mad Stuntman (Positiva)
6	9	STREETS OF PHILADELPHIA	Bruce Springsteen (Columbia)
-	10	JUST A STEP FROM HEAVEN	Eternal (EMI)
-	11	LIGHT MY FIRE (THE CAPPELLA REMIXES)	Club House featuring Carl (PWL International)
17	12	ANOTHER SAD LOVE SONG	Toni Braxton (LaFace)
40	13	I'LL STAND BY YOU	Pretenders (WEA)
13	14	ROCK MY HEART	Haddaway (Logic)
22	15	100% PURE LOVE	Crystal Waters (A&M)
11	16	THE SIGN	Ace Of Base (Metronome)
19	17	YOU GOTTA BE	Des'ree (Sony Soho Square)
-	18	UNDER THE BRIDGE	Red Hot Chili Peppers (Warner Bros.)
15	19	WHATTA MAN	Salt 'N' Pepa with En Vogue (ffrr)
9	20	DOOP	Doop (Citybeat)
-	21	ALL OVER YOU	Level 42 (RCA)
14	22	U R THE BEST THING	D:Ream (Magnet)
10	23	LIBERATION	Pet Shop Boys (Parlophone)
12	24	I'LL REMEMBER	Madonna (Maverick)
18	25	LET THE MUSIC (LIFT YOU UP)	Loveland (Six6)
-	26	AS IF WE NEVER SAID GOODBYE	Barbra Streisand (Columbia)
21	27	SON OF A GUN	JX (Internal Dance)
28	28	STANDING OUTSIDE THE FIRE	Garth Brooks (Liberty)
29	29	MR JONES	Counting Crows (Geffen)
20	30	THE RED SHOES	Kate Bush (EMI)
-	31	COME ON YOU REDS	Manchester United Football Squad (PolyGram TV)
-	32	THE MONEY (EP)	Skin (Parlophone)
39	33	HIGH ON A HAPPY VIBE	Urban Cookie Collective (Pulse 8)
24	34	OBLIVION	Terrorvision (Total Vegas)
-	35	HOLD THAT SUCKER DOWN	Q T Quartet (Cheeky)
32	36	WHY ME?	P J & Duncan (XSRhythm)
25	37	HOW GEE	Black Machine (London)
44	38	IT WILL BE YOU	Paul Young (Columbia)
16	39	WITHOUT YOU	Mariah Carey (Columbia)
-	40	BIRDMAN	Ride (Creation)
27	41	LONELY SYMPHONY (WE WILL BE FREE)	Francis Ruffelle (Virgin)
49	42	MISLED	Celine Dion (Epic)
-	43	THE DAY I TRIED TO LIVE	Soundgarden (A&M)
-	44	13 STEPS LEAD DOWN	Elvis Costello (Warner Bros.)
-	45	DIFFERENT TIME, DIFFERENT PLACE	Julia Fordham (Circa)
36	46	PRESSURE	Drizabone (4th & Broadway)
-	47	BECOMING MORE LIKE GOD	Jah Wobble's Invaders Of The Heart (Island)
-	48	SILENT SCREAM	Richard Marx (Capitol)
34	49	SUPERSONIC	Oasis (Creation)
-	50	15 WAYS	Fall (Permanent)

7 May 1994

last week	this week	Title	Artist
3	1	MMM MMM MMM MMM	Crash Test Dummies (RCA)
4	2	THE REAL THING	Toni Di Bart (Cleveland City)
1	3	THE MOST BEAUTIFUL GIRL IN THE WORLD	Prince (NPG)
5	4	SWEETS FOR MY SWEET	C J Lewis (MCA)
2	5	ALWAYS	Erasure (Mute)
11	6	LIGHT MY FIRE (THE CAPPELLA REMIXES)	Club House featuring Carl (PWL International)
-	7	INSIDE	Stiltskin (White Water)
7	8	DEDICATED TO THE ONE I LOVE	Bitty McLean (Brilliant)
13	9	I'LL STAND BY YOU	Pretenders (WEA)
10	10	JUST A STEP FROM HEAVEN	Eternal (EMI)
31	11	COME ON YOU REDS	Manchester United Football Squad (PolyGram TV)
8	12	I LIKE TO MOVE IT	Reel 2 Real featuring the Mad Stuntman (Positiva)
18	13	UNDER THE BRIDGE	Red Hot Chili Peppers (Warner Bros.)
26	14	AS IF WE NEVER SAID GOODBYE	Barbra Streisand (Columbia)
6	15	EVERYTHING CHANGES	Take That (RCA)
9	16	STREETS OF PHILADELPHIA	Bruce Springsteen (Columbia)
17	17	100% PURE LOVE	Crystal Waters (A&M)
-	18	SATURDAY NIGHT, SUNDAY MORNING	T-Empo (ffrr)
-	19	REACH	Judy Cheeks (Positiva)
14	20	ROCK MY HEART	Haddaway (Logic)
12	21	ANOTHER SAD LOVE SONG	Toni Braxton (LaFace)
17	22	YOU GOTTA BE	Des'ree (Sony Soho Square)
-	23	ROCKIN' FOR MYSELF	Motiv8 (WEA)
16	24	THE SIGN	Ace Of Base (Metronome)
-	25	LICK A SHOT	Cypress Hill (Ruff House)
32	26	THE MONEY (EP)	Skin (Parlophone)
21	27	ALL OVER YOU	Level 42 (RCA)
-	28	BULL IN THE HEATHER	Sonic Youth (Geffen)
48	29	SILENT SCREAM	Richard Marx (Capitol)
-	30	WRECKX SHOP	Wreckx 'N' Effect (MCA)
20	31	DOOP	Doop (Citybeat)
-	32	OBJECTS IN THE REAR VIEW MIRROR	Meatloaf (Virgin)
33	33	MILLENIUM	Killing Joke (Butterfly)
35	34	HOLD THAT SUCKER DOWN	Q T Quartet (Cheeky)
38	35	IT WILL BE YOU	Paul Young (Columbia)
-	36	SLAVE TO THE RHYTHM	Grace Jones (ZTT)
45	37	DIFFERENT TIME, DIFFERENT PLACE	Julia Fordham (Circa)
19	38	WHATTA MAN	Salt 'N' Pepa with En Vogue (ffrr)
29	39	MR JONES	Counting Crows (Geffen)
-	40	UNIFORM	Inspiral Carpets (Cow)
47	41	BECOMING MORE LIKE GOD	Jah Wobble's Invaders Of The Heart (Island)
-	42	MUST BE THE MUSIC	Hysterix (deConstruction)
-	43	DREAMS	Cranberries (Island)
22	44	U R THE BEST THING	D:Ream (Magnet)
24	45	I'LL REMEMBER	Madonna (Maverick)
33	46	HIGH ON A HAPPY VIBE	Urban Cookie Collective (Pulse 8)
41	47	LONELY SYMPHONY (WE WILL BE FREE)	Francis Ruffelle (Virgin)
-	48	WE WAIT AND WE WONDER	Phil Collins (Virgin)
23	49	LIBERATION	Pet Shop Boys (Parlophone)
36	50	WHY ME?	P J & Duncan (XSRhythm)

14 May 1994

last week	this week	Title	Artist
7	1	INSIDE	Stiltskin (White Water)
2	2	THE REAL THING	Toni Di Bart (Cleveland City)
4	3	SWEETS FOR MY SWEET	C J Lewis (MCA)
1	4	MMM MMM MMM MMM	Crash Test Dummies (RCA)
3	5	THE MOST BEAUTIFUL GIRL IN THE WORLD	Prince (NPG)
11	6	COME ON YOU REDS	Manchester United Football Squad (PolyGram TV)
6	7	LIGHT MY FIRE (THE CAPPELLA REMIXES)	Club House featuring Carl (PWL International)
-	8	AROUND THE WORLD	East 17 (London)
5	9	ALWAYS	Erasure (Mute)
10	10	JUST A STEP FROM HEAVEN	Eternal (EMI)
8	11	DEDICATED TO THE ONE I LOVE	Bitty McLean (Brilliant)
9	12	I'LL STAND BY YOU	Pretenders (WEA)
12	13	I LIKE TO MOVE IT	Reel 2 Real featuring the Mad Stuntman (Positiva)
13	14	UNDER THE BRIDGE	Red Hot Chili Peppers (Warner Bros.)
32	15	OBJECTS IN THE REAR VIEW MIRROR	Meatloaf (Virgin)
16	16	LEAN ON ME	Michael Bolton (Columbia)
23	17	ROCKIN' FOR MYSELF	Motiv6 (WEA)
15	18	EVERYTHING CHANGES	Take That (RCA)
16	19	STREETS OF PHILADELPHIA	Bruce Springsteen (Columbia)
18	20	SATURDAY NIGHT, SUNDAY MORNING	T-Empo (ffrr)
19	21	REACH	Judy Cheeks (Positiva)
17	22	100% PURE LOVE	Crystal Waters (A&M)
-	23	CARRY ME HOME	Gloworm (Go Beat)
-	24	NAZIS	Roger Taylor (Parlophone)
25	25	ROCK MY HEART	Haddaway (Logic)
-	26	JULIE (EP)	Levellers (China)
24	27	THE SIGN	Ace Of Base (Metronome)
47	28	LONELY SYMPHONY (WE WILL BE FREE)	Francis Ruffelle (Virgin)
25	29	LICK A SHOT	Cypress Hill (Ruff House)
14	30	AS IF WE NEVER SAID GOODBYE	Barbra Streisand (Columbia)
43	31	DREAMS	Cranberries (Island)
29	32	SILENT SCREAM	Richard Marx (Capitol)
21	33	ANOTHER SAD LOVE SONG	Toni Braxton (LaFace)
28	34	BULL IN THE HEATHER	Sonic Youth (Geffen)
30	35	WRECKX SHOP	Wreckx 'N' Effect (MCA)
-	36	BACK IN MY LIFE	Joe Roberts (ffrr)
-	37	THE EYES OF TRUTH	Enigma (Virgin)
22	38	YOU GOTTA BE	Des'ree (Sony Soho Square)
33	39	MILLENIUM	Killing Joke (Butterfly)
36	40	SLAVE TO THE RHYTHM	Grace Jones (ZTT)
31	41	DOOP	Doop (Citybeat)
-	42	AIN'T NOTHING LIKE THE REAL THING	Marcella Detroit & Elton John (London)
48	43	WE WAIT AND WE WONDER	Phil Collins (Virgin)
34	44	HOLD THAT SUCKER DOWN	Q T Quartet (Cheeky)
-	45	SWEET POTATO PIE	Domino (Outburst)
46	46	SO CLOSE TO LOVE	Wendy Moten (EMI)
38	47	WHATTA MAN	Salt 'N' Pepa with En Vogue (ffrr)
42	48	MUST BE THE MUSIC	Hysterix (deConstruction)
26	49	THE MONEY (EP)	Skin (Parlophone)
-	50	BIG GAY HEART	Lemonheads (Atalntic)

If it's May it must be the Cup Final. After a spate of reasonable soccer records, Man United returned to the traditional dire formaula – and went all the way to Number One. Chelsea, their opponents, entered the charts later and lost 4-1 on the day. Stiltskin took jeans adverts out of old soul and into new grunge.

May – June 1994

21 May 1994

last	this		
1	1	INSIDE	Stiltskin (White Water)
6	2	COME ON YOU REDS	Manchester United Football Squad (PolyGram TV)
8	3	AROUND THE WORLD	East 17 (London)
3	4	SWEETS FOR MY SWEET	C J Lewis (MCA)
2	5	THE REAL THING	Toni Di Bart (Cleveland City)
-	6	LOVE IS ALL AROUND	Wet Wet Wet (Precious)
4	7	MMM MMM MMM MMM	Crash Test Dummies (RCA)
5	8	THE MOST BEAUTIFUL GIRL IN THE WORLD	Prince (NPG)
7	9	LIGHT MY FIRE (THE CAPPELLA REMIXES)	Club House featuring Carl (PWL International)
10	10	JUST A STEP FROM HEAVEN	Eternal (EMI)
16	11	LEAN ON ME	Michael Bolton (Columbia)
-	12	MORE TO THE WORLD	Bad Boys Inc (A&M)
37	13	THE EYES OF TRUTH	Enigma (Virgin)
-	14	THE REAL THING 2 Unlimited (PWL Continental)
9	15	ALWAYS	Erasure (Mute)
23	16	CARRY ME HOME	Gloworm (Go Beat)
-	17	PRAYER FOR THE DYING	Seal (ZTT)
-	18	DEEP FOREST	Deep Forest (Columbia)
12	19	I'LL STAND BY YOU	Pretenders (WEA)
42	20	AIN'T NOTHING LIKE THE REAL THING	Marcella Detroit & Elton John (London)
26	21	JULIE (EP)	Levellers (China)
13	22	I LIKE TO MOVE IT	Reel 2 Real featuring the Mad Stuntman (Positiva)
-	23	YOUR BODY'S CALLIN'	R Kelly (Jive)
11	24	DEDICATED TO THE ONE I LOVE	Bitty McLean (Brilliant)
17	25	ROCKIN' FOR MYSELF	Motiv8 (WEA)
-	26	GET-A-WAY	Maxx (Pulse 8)
24	27	NAZIS	Roger Taylor (Parlophone)
-	28	NO ONE CAN STOP US NOW	Chelsea Football Club (RCA)
-	29	NUMBER 1	EYC (MCA)
20	30	SATURDAY NIGHT, SUNDAY MORNING	T-Empo (ffrr)
22	31	100% PURE LOVE	Crystal Waters (A&M)
-	32	THE RHYTHM/HOLDING ON	Clock (MCA)
15	33	OBJECTS IN THE REAR VIEW MIRROR	Meatloaf (Virgin)
31	34	DREAMS	Cranberries (Island)
-	35	IF YOU GO	Jon Secada (SBK)
36	36	BACK IN MY LIFE	Joe Roberts (ffrr)
-	37	WHEN A MAN LOVES A WOMAN	Jody Watley (MCA)
21	38	REACH	Judy Cheeks (Positiva)
14	39	UNDER THE BRIDGE	Red Hot Chili Peppers (Warner Bros.)
-	40	MY LOVE/REMINISCE (REMIXES)	Mary J Blige (MCA)
18	41	EVERYTHING CHANGES	Take That (RCA)
46	42	SO CLOSE TO LOVE	Wendy Moten (EMI)
19	43	STREETS OF PHILADELPHIA	Bruce Springsteen (Columbia)
27	44	THE SIGN	Ace Of Base (Metronome)
-	45	MOVE CLOSER	Phyllis Nelson (EMI)
25	46	ROCK MY HEART	Haddaway (Logic)
-	47	WONDERFUL EXCUSE	Family Cat (Dedicated)
-	48	IT'S A LOVING THING	CB Milton (Logic)
-	49	HEADACHE	Frank Black (4AD)
28	50	LONELY SYMPHONY (WE WILL BE FREE)	Francis Ruffelle (Virgin)

28 May 1994

2	1	COME ON YOU REDS	Manchester United Football Squad (PolyGram TV)
6	2	LOVE IS ALL AROUND	Wet Wet Wet (Precious)
3	3	AROUND THE WORLD	East 17 (London)
1	4	INSIDE	Stiltskin (White Water)
4	5	SWEETS FOR MY SWEET	C J Lewis (MCA)
26	6	GET-A-WAY	Maxx (Pulse 8)
14	7	THE REAL THING 2 Unlimited (PWL Continental)
17	8	PRAYER FOR THE DYING	Seal (ZTT)
7	9	MMM MMM MMM MMM	Crash Test Dummies (RCA)
-	10	DISSIDENT	Pearl Jam (Epic)
5	11	THE REAL THING	Toni Di Bart (Cleveland City)
12	12	MORE TO THE WORLD	Bad Boys Inc (A&M)
10	13	JUST A STEP FROM HEAVEN	Eternal (EMI)
16	14	CARRY ME HOME	Gloworm (Go Beat)
-	15	LONG TIME GONE	Galliano (Talkin Loud)
8	16	THE MOST BEAUTIFUL GIRL IN THE WORLD	Prince (NPG)
9	17	LIGHT MY FIRE (THE CAPPELLA REMIXES)	Club House featuring Carl (PWL International)
11	18	LEAN ON ME	Michael Bolton (Columbia)
18	19	DEEP FOREST	Deep Forest (Columbia)
-	20	NO GOOD (START THE DANCE)	Prodigy (XL)
-	21	DIGNITY	Deacon Blue (Columbia)
-	22	SHOOP	Salt 'N' Pepa (ffrr)
15	23	ALWAYS	Erasure (Mute)
-	24	WHAT YOU'RE MISSING	K-Klass (deConstruction)
-	25	TEARS OF THE DRAGON	Bruce Dickinson (EMI)
19	26	I'LL STAND BY YOU	Pretenders (WEA)
20	27	AIN'T NOTHING LIKE THE REAL THING	Marcella Detroit & Elton John (London)
-	28	MAMA SAID	Carleen Anderson (Circa)
13	29	THE EYES OF TRUTH	Enigma (Virgin)
-	30	LOST IN AMERICA	Alice Cooper (Epic)
-	31	HYMN	Moby (Mute)
22	32	I LIKE TO MOVE IT	Reel 2 Real featuring the Mad Stuntman (Positiva)
-	33	READ MY LIPS	Alice Party (Cleveland City)
28	34	NO ONE CAN STOP US NOW	Chelsea Football Club (RCA)
-	35	SUCH A PHANTASY (EP)	Time Frequency (Internal Affairs)
-	36	PAST THE MISSION	Tori Amos (East West)
45	37	MOVE CLOSER	Phyllis Nelson (EMI)
-	38	EASE MY MIND	Arrested Develpment (Cooltempo)
34	39	DREAMS	Cranberries (Island)
32	40	THE RHYTHM/HOLDING ON	Clock (MCA)
23	41	YOUR BODY'S CALLIN'	R Kelly (Jive)
42	42	SO CLOSE TO LOVE	Wendy Moten (EMI)
21	43	JULIE (EP)	Levellers (China)
29	44	NUMBER 1	EYC (MCA)
-	45	LIKE A MOTORWAY	Saint Etienne (Heavenly)
-	46	GETTING INTO SOMETHING	Alison Moyet (Columbia)
37	47	WHEN A MAN LOVES A WOMAN	Jody Watley (MCA)
-	48	IN THE NAVY – 1994 REMIXES	Village People (Arista)
48	49	IT'S A LOVING THING	CB Milton (Logic)
39	50	UNDER THE BRIDGE	Red Hot Chili Peppers (Warner Bros.)

4 June 1994

2	1	LOVE IS ALL AROUND	Wet Wet Wet (Precious)
1	2	COME ON YOU REDS	Manchester United Football Squad (PolyGram TV)
3	3	AROUND THE WORLD	East 17 (London)
6	4	GET-A-WAY	Maxx (Pulse 8)
4	5	INSIDE	Stiltskin (White Water)
-	6	BABY, I LOVE YOUR WAY	Big Mountain (RCA)
20	7	NO GOOD (START THE DANCE)	Prodigy (XL)
5	8	SWEETS FOR MY SWEET	C J Lewis (MCA)
7	9	THE REAL THING	2 Unlimited (PWL Continental)
10	10	DISSIDENT	Pearl Jam (Epic)
-	11	SWAMP THING	Grid (deConstruction)
12	12	MORE TO THE WORLD	Bad Boys Inc (A&M)
14	13	CARRY ME HOME	Gloworm (Go Beat)
8	14	PRAYER FOR THE DYING	Seal (ZTT)
22	15	SHOOP	Salt 'N' Pepa (ffrr)
13	16	JUST A STEP FROM HEAVEN	Eternal (EMI)
-	17	EVERYBODY'S TALKIN'	Beautiful South (Go! Discs)
11	18	THE REAL THING	Toni Di Bart (Cleveland City)
-	19	OMEN II	Magic Affair (EMI)
9	20	MMM MMM MMM MMM	Crash Test Dummies (RCA)
15	21	LONG TIME GONE	Galliano (Talkin Loud)
-	22	TAKE IT BACK	Pink Floyd (EMI)
17	23	LIGHT MY FIRE (THE CAPPELLA REMIXES)	Club House featuring Carl (PWL International)
24	24	WHAT YOU'RE MISSING	K-Klass (deConstruction)
28	25	MAMA SAID	Carleen Anderson (Circa)
36	26	PAST THE MISSION	Tori Amos (East West)
16	27	THE MOST BEAUTIFUL GIRL IN THE WORLD	Prince (NPG)
-	28	SINCE I DON'T HAVE YOU	Guns N' Roses (Geffen)
29	29	BEGGIN' TO BE WRITTEN	Worlds Apart (Arista)
-	30	THE SISTERS (EP)	Pulp (Island)
33	31	READ MY LIPS	Alice Party (Cleveland City)
35	32	SUCH A PHANTASY (EP)	Time Frequency (Internal Affairs)
21	33	DIGNITY	Deacon Blue (Columbia)
26	34	I'LL STAND BY YOU	Pretenders (WEA)
18	35	LEAN ON ME	Michael Bolton (Columbia)
25	36	TEARS OF THE DRAGON	Bruce Dickinson (EMI)
23	37	ALWAYS	Erasure (Mute)
30	38	LOST IN AMERICA	Alice Cooper (Epic)
38	39	EASE MY MIND	Arrested Develpment (Cooltempo)
19	40	DEEP FOREST	Deep Forest (Columbia)
31	41	HYMN	Moby (Mute)
32	42	I LIKE TO MOVE IT	Reel 2 Real featuring the Mad Stuntman (Positiva)
-	43	CRASH! BOOM! BANG!	Roxette (EMI)
37	44	MOVE CLOSER	Phyllis Nelson (EMI)
27	45	AIN'T NOTHING LIKE THE REAL THING	Marcella Detroit & Elton John (London)
-	46	SLAVE NEW WORLD	Sepultura (Roadrunner)
-	47	PATIENCE OF ANGELS	Eddi Reader (blanco y negro)
48	48	IN THE NAVY – 1994 REMIXES	Village People (Arista)
46	49	GETTING INTO SOMETHING	Alison Moyet (Columbia)
-	50	NOBODY	Shara Nelson (Cooltempo)

Love Is All Around entered at a respectable Six, went to Number One and stayed there until the band withdrew it – because they were fed up with hearing it. A 1967 hit for the Troggs (it got to Number Four), writer Reg Presley made a tidy sum out of the re-run, and was unhappy about the record being pulled.

June 1994

last week	this week	11 June 1994
1	1	LOVE IS ALL AROUND Wet Wet Wet (Precious)
2	2	COME ON YOU REDS Manchester United Football Squad (PolyGram TV)
3	3	AROUND THE WORLD East 17 (London)
4	4	GET-A-WAY Maxx (Pulse 8)
6	5	BABY, I LOVE YOUR WAY Big Mountain (RCA)
-	6	ABSOLUTELY FABULOUS Absolutely Fabulous (Spaghetti)
7	7	NO GOOD (START THE DANCE) Prodigy (XL)
5	8	INSIDE Stiltskin (White Water)
17	9	EVERYBODY'S TALKIN' Beautiful South (Go! Discs)
28	10	SINCE I DON'T HAVE YOU Guns N' Roses (Geffen)
-	11	YOU DON'T LOVE ME (NO, NO, NO) Dawn Penn (Atlantic)
8	12	SWEETS FOR MY SWEET C J Lewis (MCA)
11	13	SWAMP THING Grid (deConstruction)
13	14	CARRY ME HOME Gloworm (Go Beat)
15	15	SHOOP Salt 'N' Pepa (ffrr)
9	16	THE REAL THING 2 Unlimited (PWL Continental)
12	17	MORE TO THE WORLD Bad Boys Inc (A&M)
18	18	OMEN II Magic Affair (EMI)
-	19	NO MORE TEARS (ENOUGH IS ENOUGH) Kym Mazelle & Jocelyn Brown (Arista)
-	20	FASTER/PCP Manic Street Preachers (Epic)
-	21	DON'T TURN AROUND Ace Of Base (Metronome)
-	22	TO THE END Blur (Food)
16	23	JUST A STEP FROM HEAVEN Eternal (EMI)
10	24	DISSIDENT Pearl Jam (Epic)
43	25	CRASH! BOOM! BANG! Roxette (EMI)
22	26	TAKE IT BACK Pink Floyd (EMI)
30	27	THE SISTERS (EP) Pulp (Island)
14	28	PRAYER FOR THE DYING . Seal (ZTT)
-	29	FINGERS OF LOVE Crowded House (Capitol)
18	30	THE REAL THING Toni Di Bart (Cleveland City)
20	31	MMM MMM MMM MMM Crash Test Dummies (RCA)
32	32	SUCH A PHANTASY (EP) Time Frequency (Internal Affairs)
27	33	THE MOST BEAUTIFUL GIRL IN THE WORLD Prince (NPG)
24	34	WHAT YOU'RE MISSING K-Klass (deConstruction)
-	35	BACK TO LOVE Brand New Heavies (ffrr)
-	36	ANYTHING SWV (RCA)
-	37	DIE LAUGHING Therapy? (A&M)
47	38	PATIENCE OF ANGELS Eddie Reader (blanco y negro)
29	39	BEGGIN' TO BE WRITTEN Worlds Apart (Arista)
26	40	PAST THE MISSION Tori Amos (East West)
-	41	HOLD ON TO YOUR FRIENDS Morrissey (Parlophone)
34	42	I'LL STAND BY YOU Pretenders (WEA)
31	43	READ MY LIPS Alice Party (Cleveland City)
25	44	MAMA SAID Carleen Anderson (Circa)
21	45	LONG TIME GONE Galliano (Talkin Loud)
39	46	EASE MY MIND Arrested Develpment (Cooltempo)
23	47	LIGHT MY FIRE (THE CAPPELLA REMIXES) Club House featuring Carl (PWL International)
-	48	INSIDE YOUR DREAMS U96 (Logic)
36	49	TEARS OF THE DRAGON Bruce Dickinson (EMI)
50	50	NOBODY Shara Nelson (Cooltempo)

last	this	18 June 1994
1	1	LOVE IS ALL AROUND Wet Wet Wet (Precious)
5	2	BABY, I LOVE YOUR WAY Big Mountain (RCA)
11	3	YOU DON'T LOVE ME (NO, NO, NO) Dawn Penn (Atlantic)
4	4	GET-A-WAY Maxx (Pulse 8)
7	5	NO GOOD (START THE DANCE) Prodigy (XL)
6	6	ABSOLUTELY FABULOUS Absolutely Fabulous (Spaghetti)
-	7	ANYTIME YOU NEED A FRIEND Mariah Carey (Columbia)
3	8	AROUND THE WORLD East 17 (London)
2	9	COME ON YOU REDS Manchester United Football Squad (PolyGram TV)
21	10	DON'T TURN AROUND Ace Of Base (Metronome)
13	11	SWAMP THING Grid (deConstruction)
9	12	EVERYBODY'S TALKIN' Beautiful South (Go! Discs)
8	13	INSIDE Stiltskin (White Water)
19	14	NO MORE TEARS (ENOUGH IS ENOUGH) Kym Mazelle & Jocelyn Brown (Arista)
10	15	SINCE I DON'T HAVE YOU Guns N' Roses (Geffen)
22	16	TO THE END Blur (Food)
14	17	CARRY ME HOME Gloworm (Go Beat)
15	18	SHOOP Salt 'N' Pepa (ffrr)
29	19	FINGERS OF LOVE Crowded House (Capitol)
-	20	ANY TIME, ANY PLACE Janet Jackson (Virgin)
35	21	BACK TO LOVE Brand New Heavies (ffrr)
-	22	CLOSER TO GOD Nine Inch Nails (Island)
-	23	TAKE ME AWAY D:Ream (Magnet)
-	24	U & ME Cappella (Internal Dance)
-	25	CRAZY MAN Blast featuring VDC (MCA)
20	26	FASTER/PCP Manic Street Preachers (Epic)
16	27	THE REAL THING 2 Unlimited (PWL Continental)
28	28	ANYTHING SWV (RCA)
18	29	OMEN II Magic Affair (EMI)
-	30	I WANNA BE YOUR MAN Chaka Demus & Pliers (Mango)
12	31	SWEETS FOR MY SWEET C J Lewis (MCA)
-	32	I SWEAR All-4-One (Atlantic)
25	33	CRASH! BOOM! BANG! Roxette (EMI)
27	34	THE SISTERS (EP) Pulp (Island)
17	35	MORE TO THE WORLD Bad Boys Inc (A&M)
-	36	SHINE Aswad (Bubblin')
-	37	JAILBIRD Primal Scream (Creation)
38	38	PATIENCE OF ANGELS Eddi Reader (blanco y negro)
23	39	JUST A STEP FROM HEAVEN Eternal (EMI)
31	40	MMM MMM MMM MMM Crash Test Dummies (RCA)
37	41	DIE LAUGHING Therapy? (A&M)
26	42	TAKE IT BACK Pink Floyd (EMI)
-	43	HARMONICA MAN Bravado (Peach)
-	44	EASE THE PRESSURE 2wo Third3 (Epic)
30	45	THE REAL THING Toni Di Bart (Cleveland City)
33	46	THE MOST BEAUTIFUL GIRL IN THE WORLD Prince (NPG)
-	47	GET INTO YOU Dannii Minogue (Mushroom)
-	48	YOU Bonnie Rait (Capitol)
-	49	I AIN'T MOVIN' Des'ree (Dusted Sound)
-	50	ELEPHANT PAW (GET DOWN TO THE FUNK) Pan Position (Positiva)

last	this	25 June 1994
1	1	LOVE IS ALL AROUND Wet Wet Wet (Precious)
2	2	BABY, I LOVE YOUR WAY Big Mountain (RCA)
3	3	YOU DON'T LOVE ME (NO, NO, NO) Dawn Penn (Atlantic)
10	4	DON'T TURN AROUND Ace Of Base (Metronome)
5	5	NO GOOD (START THE DANCE) Prodigy (XL)
11	6	SWAMP THING Grid (deConstruction)
7	7	ANYTIME YOU NEED A FRIEND Mariah Carey (Columbia)
4	8	GET-A-WAY Maxx (Pulse 8)
6	9	ABSOLUTELY FABULOUS Absolutely Fabulous (Spaghetti)
32	10	I SWEAR All-4-One (Atlantic)
20	11	ANY TIME, ANY PLACE Janet Jackson (Virgin)
24	12	U & ME Cappella (Internal Dance)
14	13	NO MORE TEARS (ENOUGH IS ENOUGH) Kym Mazelle & Jocelyn Brown (Arista)
8	14	AROUND THE WORLD East 17 (London)
9	15	COME ON YOU REDS Manchester United Football Squad (PolyGram TV)
12	16	EVERYBODY'S TALKIN' Beautiful South (Go! Discs)
16	17	TO THE END Blur (Food)
13	18	INSIDE Stiltskin (White Water)
15	19	SINCE I DON'T HAVE YOU Guns N' Roses (Geffen)
23	20	TAKE ME AWAY D:Ream (Magnet)
-	21	CRAZY FOR YOU Let Loose (Mercury)
17	22	CARRY ME HOME Gloworm (Go Beat)
-	23	DO YOU WANT IT RIGHT NOW Degrees Of Motion (ffrr)
30	24	I WANNA BE YOUR MAN Chaka Demus & Pliers (Mango)
21	25	BACK TO LOVE Brand New Heavies (ffrr)
-	26	WILLING TO FORGIVE Aretha Franklin (Arista)
25	27	CRAZY MAN Blast featuring VDC (MCA)
-	28	DOLPHIN Shed Seven (Polydor)
-	29	CLEOPATRA'S CAT Spin Doctors (Epic)
36	30	SHINE Aswad (Bubblin')
-	31	MIDDLEMAN Terrorvision (Total Vegas)
18	32	SHOOP Salt 'N' Pepa (ffrr)
-	33	MOVE YOUR BODY Anticappella featuring MC Fixx It (MCA)
19	34	FINGERS OF LOVE Crowded House (Capitol)
-	35	I STILL THINK OF YOU Utah Saints (ffrr)
22	36	CLOSER TO GOD Nine Inch Nails (Island)
-	37	THE ONE FOR ME Joe (Mercury)
-	38	FEEL WHAT YOU WANT Kristine W (Champion)
28	39	ANYTHING SWV (RCA)
43	40	HARMONICA MAN Bravado (Peach)
27	41	THE REAL THING 2 Unlimited (PWL Continental)
-	42	LAY YOUR LOVE ON ME Roachford (Columbia)
49	43	I AIN'T MOVIN' Des'ree (Dusted Sound)
-	44	INCREDIBLE M-Beat featuring General Levy (Renk)
-	45	7 SECONDS Youssou N'Dour featuring Neneh Cherry (Columbia)
38	46	PATIENCE OF ANGELS Eddi Reader (blanco y negro)
37	47	JAILBIRD Primal Scream (Creation)
48	48	YOU Bonnie Rait (Capitol)
-	49	THE SUN DOES RISE (EP) Jah Wobble's Invaders Of The Heart (Island)
-	50	TWO CAN PLAY AT THAT GAME Bobby Brown (MCA)

The Number One single was given continuous exposure by being the title song of the hit film *Four Weddings And A Funeral*, while *Absolutely Fabulous* was an eponymous TV series based on a thin joke – the Pet Shop Boys contributed. Dawn Penn was an old ska singer back in the charts with an old ska song.

July 1994

	2 July 1994			9 July 1994			16 July 1994	
1	1	LOVE IS ALL AROUND Wet Wet Wet (Precious)	1	1	LOVE IS ALL AROUND Wet Wet Wet (Precious)	1	1	LOVE IS ALL AROUND Wet Wet Wet (Precious)
2	2	BABY, I LOVE YOUR WAY Big Mountain (RCA)	-	2	LOVE AIN'T HERE ANYMORE Take That (RCA)	2	2	LOVE AIN'T HERE ANYMORE Take That (RCA)
6	3	SWAMP THING Grid (deConstruction)	4	3	I SWEAR All-4- One (Atlantic)	3	3	I SWEAR All-4- One (Atlantic)
10	4	I SWEAR All-4- One (Atlantic)	3	4	SWAMP THING Grid (deConstruction)	7	4	(MEET) THE FLINTSTONES BC-52s (MCA)
3	5	YOU DON'T LOVE ME (NO, NO, NO) Dawn Penn (Atlantic)	2	5	BABY, I LOVE YOUR WAY Big Mountain (RCA)	4	5	SWAMP THING Grid (deConstruction)
4	6	DON'T TURN AROUND Ace Of Base (Metronome)	8	6	GO ON MOVE featuring the Mad Stuntman (Positiva) Reel 2 Real	10	6	SHINE Aswad (Bubblin')
7	7	ANYTIME YOU NEED A FRIEND Mariah Carey (Columbia)	-	7	(MEET) THE FLINTSTONES BC-52s (MCA)	11	7	WORD UP Gun (A&M)
-	8	GO ON MOVE featuring the Mad Stuntman (Positiva) Reel 2 Real	5	8	YOU DON'T LOVE ME (NO, NO, NO) Dawn Penn (Atlantic)	5	8	BABY, I LOVE YOUR WAY Big Mountain (RCA)
5	9	NO GOOD (START THE DANCE) Prodigy (XL)	6	9	DON'T TURN AROUND Ace Of Base (Metronome)	6	9	GO ON MOVE featuring the Mad Stuntman (Positiva) Reel 2 Real
8	10	GET-A-WAY Maxx (Pulse 8)	15	10	SHINE Aswad (Bubblin')	-	10	LOVE IS STRONG Rolling Stones (Virgin)
-	11	CAUGHT IN THE MIDDLE – THE '94 REMIXES Juliet Roberts (Cooltempo)	-	11	WORD UP Gun (A&M)	13	11	EVERYBODY GONFI GON 2 Cowboys (ffrreedom)
-	12	SHAKERMAKER Oasis (Creation)	9	12	NO GOOD (START THE DANCE) Prodigy (XL)	8	12	YOU DON'T LOVE ME (NO, NO, NO) Dawn Penn (Atlantic)
11	13	ANY TIME, ANY PLACE Janet Jackson (Virgin)	-	13	EVERYBODY GONFI GON 2 Cowboys (ffrreedom)	20	13	CAN YOU FEEL THE LOVE TONIGHT Elton John (Mercury)
26	14	WILLING TO FORGIVE Aretha Franklin (Arista)	11	14	CAUGHT IN THE MIDDLE – THE '94 REMIXES Juliet Roberts (Cooltempo)	19	14	CRAZY FOR YOU Let Loose (Mercury)
30	15	SHINE Aswad (Bubblin')	7	15	ANYTIME YOU NEED A FRIEND Mariah Carey (Columbia)	12	15	NO GOOD (START THE DANCE) Prodigy (XL)
12	16	U & ME Cappella (Internal Dance)	14	16	WILLING TO FORGIVE Aretha Franklin (Arista)	9	16	DON'T TURN AROUND Ace Of Base (Metronome)
14	17	AROUND THE WORLD East 17 (London)	16	17	U & ME Cappella (Internal Dance)	17	17	U & ME Cappella (Internal Dance)
-	18	BODY IN MOTION Atlantic Ocean (Eastern Bloc)	10	18	GET-A-WAY Maxx (Pulse 8)	16	18	WILLING TO FORGIVE Aretha Franklin (Arista)
21	19	CRAZY FOR YOU Let Loose (Mercury)	19	19	CRAZY FOR YOU Let Loose (Mercury)	14	19	CAUGHT IN THE MIDDLE – THE '94 REMIXES Juliet Roberts (Cooltempo)
24	20	I WANNA BE YOUR MAN Chaka Demus & Pliers (Mango)	-	20	CAN YOU FEEL THE LOVE TONIGHT Elton John (Mercury)	-	20	SEARCHING China Black (Wild Card)
13	21	NO MORE TEARS (ENOUGH IS ENOUGH) Kym Mazelle & Jocelyn Brown (Arista)	12	21	SHAKERMAKER Oasis (Creation)	29	21	YOU MEAN THE WORLD TO ME Toni Braxton (LaFace)
-	22	BACK AND FORTH Aaliyah (Jive)	18	22	BODY IN MOTION Atlantic Ocean (Eastern Bloc)	15	22	ANYTIME YOU NEED A FRIEND Mariah Carey (Columbia)
9	23	ABSOLUTELY FABULOUS Absolutely Fabulous (Spaghetti)	22	23	BACK AND FORTH Aaliyah (Jive)	23	23	GET IT TOGETHER Beastie Boys (Capitol)
15	24	COME ON YOU REDS Manchester United Football Squad (PolyGram TV)	27	24	SHUT UP AND DANCE Aerosmith (Geffen)	26	24	AIN'T NOBODY (LOVES ME BETTER) KWS & Gwen Dickey (X-Clusive)
16	25	EVERYBODY'S TALKIN' Beautiful South (Go! Discs)	-	25	GET IT TOGETHER Beastie Boys (Capitol)	18	25	GET-A-WAY Maxx (Pulse 8)
31	26	MIDDLEMAN Terrorvision (Total Vegas)	34	26	AIN'T NOBODY (LOVES ME BETTER) KWS & Gwen Dickey (X-Clusive)	-	26	ON POINT House Of Pain (Ruffness)
-	27	SHUT UP AND DANCE Aerosmith (Geffen)	-	27	NIGHT IN MY VEINS Pretenders (WEA)	-	27	FEENIN' Jodeci (MCA)
18	28	INSIDE Stiltskin (White Water)	20	28	I WANNA BE YOUR MAN Chaka Demus & Pliers (Mango)	28	28	NIGHT IN MY VEINS Pretenders (WEA)
33	29	MOVE YOUR BODY Anticappella featuring MC Fixx It (MCA)	-	29	YOU MEAN THE WORLD TO ME Toni Braxton (LaFace)	22	29	BODY IN MOTION Atlantic Ocean (Eastern Bloc)
19	30	SINCE I DON'T HAVE YOU Guns N' Roses (Geffen)	13	30	ANY TIME, ANY PLACE Janet Jackson (Virgin)	21	30	SHAKERMAKER Oasis (Creation)
20	31	TAKE ME AWAY D:ream (Magnet)	17	31	AROUND THE WORLD East 17 (London)	24	31	SHUT UP AND DANCE Aerosmith (Geffen)
23	32	DO YOU WANT IT RIGHT NOW Degrees Of Motion (ffrr)	24	32	COME ON YOU REDS Manchester United Football Squad (PolyGram TV)	-	32	AFTERNOONS AND COFFEESPOONS Crash Test Dummies (RCA)
28	33	DOLPHIN Shed Seven (Polydor)	26	33	MIDDLEMAN Terrorvision (Total Vegas)	28	33	I WANNA BE YOUR MAN Chaka Demus & Pliers (Mango)
-	34	AIN'T NOBODY (LOVES ME BETTER) KWS & Gwen Dickey (X-Clusive)	37	34	I DON'T LIKE MONDAYS Boomtown Rats (Vertigo)	-	34	'90s GIRL Blackgirl (RCA)
-	35	CAN'T IMAGINE THE WORLD WITHOUT ME Echobelly (Fauve)	-	35	GLORYLAND Daryl Hall & Sounds Of Blackness (Mercury)	-	35	I'M NO ANGEL Marcella Detroit (London)
22	36	CARRY ME HOME Gloworm (Go Beat)	-	36	HEY DJ Lighter Shade of Brown (Mercury)	36	36	HEY DJ Lighter Shade of Brown (Mercury)
-	37	I DON'T LIKE MONDAYS Boomtown Rats (Vertigo)	-	37	CHANGE Blind Melon (Capitol)	23	37	BACK AND FORTH Aaliyah (Jive)
49	38	THE SUN DOES RISE (EP) Jah Wobble's Invaders Of The Heart (Island)	-	38	ANDRES L7 (London)	35	38	GLORYLAND Daryl Hall & Sounds Of Blackness (Mercury)
45	39	7 SECONDS Youssou N'Dour featuring Neneh Cherry (Columbia)	46	39	MAYBE LOVE Stevie Nicks (EMI)	-	39	TURN IT UP DJ Duke (ffrr)
17	40	TO THE END Blur (Food)	21	40	NO MORE TEARS (ENOUGH IS ENOUGH) Kym Mazelle & Jocelyn Brown (Arista)	37	40	CHANGE Blind Melon (Capitol)
29	41	CLEOPATRA'S CAT Spin Doctors (Epic)	42	41	GHETTO DAY/WHAT I NEED Crystal Waters (A&M)	43	41	7 SECONDS Youssou N'Dour featuring Neneh Cherry (Columbia)
-	42	GHETTO DAY/WHAT I NEED Crystal Waters (A&M)	23	42	ABSOLUTELY FABULOUS Absolutely Fabulous (Spaghetti)	-	42	WHY DO FOOLS FALL IN LOVE Diana Ross (EMI)
37	43	THE ONE FOR ME Joe (Mercury)	39	43	7 SECONDS Youssou N'Dour featuring Neneh Cherry (Columbia)	31	43	AROUND THE WORLD East 17 (London)
38	44	FEEL WHAT YOU WANT Kristine W (Champion)	-	44	SUCKERPUNCH Wildhearts (Bronze)	38	44	ANDRES L7 (London)
27	45	CRAZY MAN Blast featuring VDC (MCA)	33	45	DOLPHIN Shed Seven (Polydor)	50	45	FEELING GOOD Nina Simone (Mercury)
-	46	MAYBE LOVE Stevie Nicks (EMI)	29	46	MOVE YOUR BODY Anticappella featuring MC Fixx It (MCA)	32	46	COME ON YOU REDS Manchester United Football Squad (PolyGram TV)
50	47	TWO CAN PLAY AT THAT GAME Bobby Brown (MCA)	32	47	DO YOU WANT IT RIGHT NOW Degrees Of Motion (ffrr)	44	47	SUCKERPUNCH Wildhearts (Bronze)
-	48	YOU MUST BE PREPARED TO DREAM Ian McNabb (This Way Up)	25	48	EVERYBODY'S TALKIN' Beautiful South (Go! Discs)	39	48	MAYBE LOVE Stevie Nicks (EMI)
-	49	JESUS HAIRDO Charlatans (Beggars Banquet)	38	49	THE SUN DOES RISE (EP) Jah Wobble's Invaders Of The Heart (Island)	41	49	GHETTO DAY/WHAT I NEED Crystal Waters (A&M)
-	50	LOVE TOWN Peter Gabriel (Epic)	-	50	FEELING GOOD Nina Simone (Mercury)	-	50	SOMEDAY Eddy (Positiva)

Wet Wet Wet managed the unprecedented feat of keeping Take That from going in at Number One. The B-52s changed their name to join in the fun on the film of the Flintstones, while the Rolling Stones were in the Top Ten again, thirty years after their debut. Their album *Voodoo Lounge* went in at Number One.

23 July 1994

last week	this week		
1	1	LOVE IS ALL AROUND	Wet Wet Wet (Precious)
3	2	I SWEAR	All-4-One (Atlantic)
4	3	(MEET) THE FLINTSTONES	BC-52s (MCA)
2	4	LOVE AIN'T HERE ANYMORE	Take That (RCA)
6	5	SHINE	Aswad (Bubblin')
11	6	EVERYBODY GONFI GON	2 Cowboys (ffrreedom)
5	7	SWAMP THING	Grid (deConstruction)
14	8	CRAZY FOR YOU	Let Loose (Mercury)
7	9	WORD UP	Gun (A&M)
8	10	BABY, I LOVE YOU WAY	Big Mountain (RCA)
9	11	GO ON MOVE	Reel 2 Real featuring the Mad Stuntman (Positiva)
12	12	LOVE IS STRONG	Rolling Stones (Virgin)
20	13	SEARCHING	China Black (Wild Card)
13	14	CAN YOU FEEL THE LOVE TONIGHT	Elton John (Mercury)
16	15	REGULATE	Warren G & Nate Dogg (Death Row)
12	16	YOU DON'T LOVE ME (NO, NO, NO)	Dawn Penn (Atlantic)
-	17	TAKE ME AWAY (I'LL FOLLOW YOU)	Bad Boys Inc (A&M)
16	18	DON'T TURN AROUND	Ace Of Base (Metronome)
-	19	LIVING IN SUNSHINE	Clubhouse (PWL Continental)
-	20	EVERYTHING'S ALRIGHT (UPTIGHT)	CJ Lewis (Black Market)
15	21	NO GOOD (START THE DANCE)	Prodigy (XL)
34	22	'90s GIRL	Blackgirl (RCA)
-	23	TOWER OF STRENGTH	Skin (Parlophone)
32	24	AFTERNOONS AND COFFEESPOONS	Crash Test Dummies (RCA)
-	25	SAVANNA DANCE	Deep Forest (Columbia)
26	26	WILLING TO FORGIVE	Aretha Franklin (Arista)
17	27	U & ME	Cappella (Internal Dance)
-	28	LET'S GET READY TO RHUMBLE	PJ & Duncan (Telstar)
26	29	ON POINT	House Of Pain (Ruffness)
-	30	MORE TO LOVE	Volcano (deConstruction)
41	31	7 SECONDS	Youssou N'Dour featuring Neneh Cherry (Columbia)
-	32	IT'S ME	Alice Cooper (Epic)
19	33	CAUGHT IN THE MIDDLE – THE '94 REMIXES	Juliet Roberts (Cooltempo)
-	34	AGE OF PANIC	Senser (Ultimate)
22	35	ANYTIME YOU NEED A FRIEND	Mariah Carey (Columbia)
-	36	SMELLS LIKE TEEN SPIRIT	Abigail (Klone)
27	37	FEENIN'	Jodeci (MCA)
35	38	I'M NO ANGEL	Marcella Detroit (London)
-	39	THE PANDEMONIUM SINGLE	Killing Joke (Butterfly)
21	40	YOU MEAN THE WORLD TO ME	Toni Braxton (LaFace)
42	41	WHY DO FOOLS FALL IN LOVE	Diana Ross (EMI)
25	42	GET-A-WAY	Maxx (Pulse 8)
-	43	GET OFF THIS	Cracker (Virgin)
-	44	OUTSIDE	Omar (RCA)
28	45	NIGHT IN MY VEINS	Pretenders (WEA)
-	46	WIPE OUT	Animal (BMG Kidz)
39	47	TURN IT UP	DJ Duke (ffrr)
-	48	I CAN'T HELP MYSELF	Julia Fordham (Circa)
-	49	NITE LIFE	Kim English (Hi-Life)
-	50	FANTASTIC VOYAGE	Coolio (Tommy Boy)

30 July 1994

1	1	LOVE IS ALL AROUND	Wet Wet Wet (Precious)
2	2	I SWEAR	All-4-One (Atlantic)
3	3	(MEET) THE FLINTSTONES	BC-52s (MCA)
8	4	CRAZY FOR YOU	Let Loose (Mercury)
5	5	SHINE	Aswad (Bubblin')
15	6	REGULATE	Warren G & Nate Dogg (Death Row)
13	7	SEARCHING	China Black (Wild Card)
20	8	EVERYTHING'S ALRIGHT (UPTIGHT)	CJ Lewis (Black Market)
7	9	SWAMP THING	Grid (deConstruction)
6	10	EVERYBODY GONFI GON	2 Cowboys (ffrreedom)
-	11	RUN TO THE SUN	Erasure (Mute)
4	12	LOVE AIN'T HERE ANYMORE	Take That (RCA)
10	13	BABY, I LOVE YOUR WAY	Big Mountain (RCA)
28	14	LET'S GET READY TO RHUMBLE	PJ & Duncan (Telstar)
14	15	CAN YOU FEEL THE LOVE TONIGHT	Elton John (Mercury)
9	16	WORD UP	Gun (A&M)
17	17	TAKE ME AWAY (I'LL FOLLOW YOU)	Bad Boys Inc (A&M)
-	18	BLACK BOOK	EYC (MCA)
11	19	GO ON MOVE	Reel 2 Real featuring the Mad Stuntman (Positiva)
-	20	COMPLIMENTS ON YOUR KISS	Red Dragon with Brian & Tony Gold (Mango)
18	21	DON'T TURN AROUND	Ace Of Base (Metronome)
19	22	LIVING IN SUNSHINE	Clubhouse (PWL Continental)
16	23	YOU DON'T LOVE ME (NO, NO, NO)	Dawn Penn (Atlantic)
24	24	AFTERNOONS AND COFFEESPOONS	Crash Test Dummies (RCA)
23	25	TOWER OF STRENGTH	Skin (Parlophone)
-	26	TROUBLE	Shampoo (Food)
-	27	SOMETIMES ALWAYS	Jesus & Mary Chain (blanco y negro)
-	28	LIBIAMO	Carreras, Domingo, Pavarotti, Mehta (Warner Classics)
31	29	7 SECONDS	Youssou N'Dour featuring Neneh Cherry (Columbia)
-	30	THE MAN I LOVE	Kate Bush & Larry Adler (Mercury)
-	31	KISS FROM A ROSE	Seal (ZTT)
30	32	MORE TO LOVE	Volcano (deConstruction)
25	33	SAVANNA DANCE	Deep Forest (Columbia)
22	34	'90s GIRL	Blackgirl (RCA)
12	35	LOVE IS STRONG	Rolling Stones (Virgin)
21	36	NO GOOD (START THE DANCE)	Prodigy (XL)
26	37	WILLING TO FORGIVE	Aretha Franklin (Arista)
-	38	FROM HERE TO ETERNITY	Michael Ball (Columbia)
36	39	SMELLS LIKE TEEN SPIRIT	Abigail (Klone)
46	40	WIPE OUT	Animal (BMG Kidz)
35	41	ANYTIME YOU NEED A FRIEND	Mariah Carey (Columbia)
-	42	TWYFORD DOWN	Galliano (Talkin' Loud)
43	43	GET OFF THIS	Cracker (Virgin)
29	44	ON POINT	House Of Pain (Ruffness)
38	45	I'M NO ANGEL	Marcella Detroit (London)
32	46	IT'S ME	Alice Cooper (Epic)
-	47	REACHIN'	House Of Virginism (ffrr)
-	48	PING PONG	Stereolab (Duophonic UHF)
49	49	NITE LIFE	Kim English (Hi-Life)
-	50	GOLDENBOOK	Family Cat (Dedicated)

6 August 1994

1	1	LOVE IS ALL AROUND	Wet Wet Wet (Precious)
2	2	I SWEAR	All-4-One (Atlantic)
3	3	(MEET) THE FLINTSTONES	BC-52s (MCA)
4	4	CRAZY FOR YOU	Let Loose (Mercury)
6	5	REGULATE	Warren G & Nate Dogg (Death Row)
7	6	SEARCHING	China Black (Wild Card)
5	7	SHINE	Aswad (Bubblin')
8	8	EVERYTHING'S ALRIGHT (UPTIGHT)	CJ Lewis (Black Market)
14	9	LET'S GET READY TO RHUMBLE	PJ & Duncan (Telstar)
9	10	SWAMP THING	Grid (deConstruction)
11	11	RUN TO THE SUN	Erasure (Mute)
18	12	BLACK BOOK	EYC (MCA)
-	13	NO MORE (I CAN'T STAND IT)	Maxx (Pulse 8)
10	14	EVERYBODY GONFI GON	2 Cowboys (ffrreedom)
13	15	BABY, I LOVE YOUR WAY	Big Mountain (RCA)
4	16	LOVE AIN'T HERE ANYMORE	Take That (RCA)
26	17	TROUBLE	Shampoo (Food)
20	18	COMPLIMENTS ON YOUR KISS	Red Dragon with Brian & Tony Gold (Mango)
17	19	TAKE ME AWAY (I'LL FOLLOW YOU)	Bad Boys Inc (A&M)
15	20	CAN YOU FEEL THE LOVE TONIGHT	Elton John (Mercury)
31	21	KISS FROM A ROSE	Seal (ZTT)
16	22	WORD UP	Gun (A&M)
19	23	GO ON MOVE	Reel 2 Real featuring the Mad Stuntman (Positiva)
21	24	DON'T TURN AROUND	Ace Of Base (Metronome)
-	25	I DIDN'T MEAN IT	Status Quo (Polydor)
-	26	GIRLS + BOYS	Hed Boys (deConstruction)
29	27	7 SECONDS	Youssou N'Dour featuring Neneh Cherry (Columbia)
28	28	LIBIAMO	Carreras, Domingo, Pavarotti, Mehta (Warner Classics)
27	29	SOMETIMES ALWAYS	Jesus & Mary Chain (blanco y negro)
23	30	YOU DON'T LOVE ME (NO, NO, NO)	Dawn Penn (Atlantic)
-	31	(I WANT TO) KILL SOMEBODY	S*M*A*S*H (Hi Rise)
22	32	LIVING IN SUNSHINE	Clubhouse (PWL Continental)
24	33	AFTERNOONS AND COFFEESPOONS	Crash Test Dummies (RCA)
30	34	THE MAN I LOVE	Kate Bush & Larry Adler (Mercury)
-	35	HIT BY LOVE	Ce Ce Peniston (A&M)
-	36	IS THIS LOVE	Whitesnake (EMI)
-	37	LOVE IN A PEACEFUL WORLD	Level 42 (RCA)
38	38	FROM HERE TO ETERNITY	Michael Ball (Columbia)
47	39	REACHIN'	House Of Virginism (ffrr)
-	40	I LIFT MY CUP	Gloworm (Pulse 8)
25	41	TOWER OF STRENGTH	Skin (Parlophone)
-	42	DUMMY CRUSHER	Kerbdog (Vertigo)
42	43	TWYFORD DOWN	Galliano (Talkin' Loud)
40	44	WIPE OUT	Animal (BMG Kidz)
-	45	THIS TIME I FOUND LOVE	Rozalla (Epic)
32	46	MORE TO LOVE	Volcano (deConstruction)
36	47	NO GOOD (START THE DANCE)	Prodigy (XL)
-	48	WHAT GOES AROUND	Bitty McLean (Brilliant)
-	49	GIVE ME LIFE	Mr V (Cheeky)
-	50	SUMMERTIME	DJ Jazzy Jeff & the Fresh Prince (Jive)

Smells Like Teen Spirit was a Nirvana song that was sampled by any number of House artists. Abigail came up with a complete cover version of the song instead. World Music charted in the form of Youssou N'Dour teamed up with Neneh Cherry. Diana Ross was a seeming ever-present in the charts.

589

August 1994

13 August 1994

last	this	title	artist (label)
1	1	LOVE IS ALL AROUND	Wet Wet Wet (Precious)
2	2	I SWEAR	All-4- One (Atlantic)
4	3	CRAZY FOR YOU	Let Loose (Mercury)
6	4	SEARCHING	China Black (Wild Card)
5	5	REGULATE	Warren G & Nate Dogg (Death Row)
3	6	(MEET) THE FLINTSTONES	BC-52s (MCA)
9	7	LET'S GET READY TO RUMBLE	PJ & Duncan (Telstar)
13	8	NO MORE (I CAN'T STAND IT)	Maxx (Pulse 8)
17	9	TROUBLE	Shampoo (Food)
18	10	COMPLIMENTS ON YOUR KISS	Red Dragon with Brian & Tony Gold (Mango)
7	11	SHINE	Aswad (Bubblin')
10	12	SWAMP THING	Grid (deConstruction)
8	13	EVERYTHING'S ALRIGHT (UPTIGHT)	CJ Lewis (Black Market)
12	14	BLACK BOOK	EYC (MCA)
-	15	WHAT'S UP	DJ Miko (Systematic)
25	16	I DIDN'T MEAN IT	Status Quo (Polydor)
-	17	MIDNIGHT AT THE OASIS	Brand New Heavies (ffrr)
-	18	LIFEFORMS	Future Sound Of London (Virgin)
27	19	7 SECONDS	Youssou N'Dour featuring Neneh Cherry (Columbia)
14	20	EVERYBODY GONFI GON	2 Cowboys (ffrreedom)
11	21	RUN TO THE SUN	Erasure (Mute)
21	22	KISS FROM A ROSE	Seal (ZTT)
-	23	REVOL	Manic Street Preachers (Epic)
15	24	BABY, I LOVE YOUR WAY	Big Mountain (RCA)
-	25	GIVE IT UP	Public Enemy (Def Jam)
26	26	GIRLS + BOYS	Hed Boys (deConstruction)
-	27	TRUE SPIRIT	Carleen Anderson (Circa)
36	28	IS THIS LOVE	Whitesnake (EMI)
20	29	CAN YOU FEEL THE LOVE TONIGHT	Elton John (Mercury)
-	30	THE SIMPLE THINGS	Joe Cocker (Capitol)
16	31	LOVE AIN'T HERE ANYMORE	Take That (RCA)
24	32	DON'T TURN AROUND	Ace Of Base (Metronome)
28	33	LIBIAMO	Carreras, Domingo, Pavarotti, Mehta (Warner Classics)
50	34	SUMMERTIME	DJ Jazzy Jeff & the Fresh Prince (Jive)
22	35	WORD UP	Gun (A&M)
19	36	TAKE ME AWAY (I'LL FOLLOW YOU)	Bad Boys Inc (A&M)
-	37	LUCAS WITH THE LID OFF	Lucas (WEA)
23	38	GO ON MOVE	Reel 2 Real featuring the Mad Stuntman (Positiva)
30	39	YOU DON'T LOVE ME (NO, NO, NO)	Dawn Penn (Atlantic)
37	40	LOVE IN A PEACEFUL WORLD	Level 42 (RCA)
45	41	THIS TIME I FOUND LOVE	Rozalla (Epic)
-	42	HIT BY LOVE	Ce Ce Peniston (A&M)
-	43	RIGHT BESIDE YOU	Sophie B Hawkins (Columbia)
-	44	RUMP SHAKER	Wreckx-N-Effect (MCA)
40	45	I LIFT MY CUP	Gloworm (Pulse 8)
-	46	I LIKE	Shanice (Motown)
-	47	WHAT GOES AROUND	Bitty McLean (Brilliant)
42	48	DUMMY CRUSHER	Kerbdog (Vertigo)
-	49	TWO FATT GUITARS (REVISITED)	Direkt (UFG)
-	50	THE WAY SHE LOVES ME	Richard Marx (Capitol)

20 August 1994

last	this	title	artist (label)
1	1	LOVE IS ALL AROUND	Wet Wet Wet (Precious)
2	2	I SWEAR	All-4- One (Atlantic)
3	3	CRAZY FOR YOU	Let Loose (Mercury)
4	4	SEARCHING	China Black (Wild Card)
5	5	REGULATE	Warren G & Nate Dogg (Death Row)
6	6	(MEET) THE FLINTSTONES	BC-52s (MCA)
15	7	WHAT'S UP	DJ Miko (Systematic)
10	8	COMPLIMENTS ON YOUR KISS	Red Dragon with Brian & Tony Gold (Mango)
19	9	7 SECONDS	featuring Neneh Cherry (Columbia)
8	10	NO MORE (I CAN'T STAND IT)	Maxx (Pulse 8)
-	11	EIGHTEEN STRINGS	Tinman ffrr)
-	12	LIVE FOREVER	Oasis (Creation)
7	13	LET'S GET READY TO RUMBLE	PJ & Duncan (Telstar)
17	14	MIDNIGHT AT THE OASIS	Brand New Heavies (ffrr)
9	15	TROUBLE	Shampoo (Food)
12	16	SWAMP THING	Grid (deConstruction)
11	17	SHINE	Aswad (Bubblin')
-	18	BLACK HOLE SUN	Soundgarden (A&M)
18	19	LIFEFORMS	Future Sound Of London (Virgin)
30	20	THE SIMPLE THINGS	Joe Cocker (Capitol)
21	21	BLACK BOOK	EYC (MCA)
25	22	GIVE IT UP	Public Enemy (Def Jam)
-	23	SO GOOD	Eternal (EMI)
23	24	REVOL	Manic Street Preachers (Epic)
-	25	SOMEONE TO LOVE	Sean Maguire (Parlophone)
13	26	EVERYTHING'S ALRIGHT (UPTIGHT)	CJ Lewis (Black Market)
16	27	I DIDN'T MEAN IT	Status Quo (Polydor)
-	28	DO IT	Tony Di Bart (Cleveland City Blues)
27	29	TRUE SPIRIT	Carleen Anderson (Circa)
-	30	INTERLUDE	Morrissey & Siouxsie (Parlophone)
43	31	RIGHT BESIDE YOU	Sophie B Hawkins (Columbia)
22	32	KISS FROM A ROSE	Seal (ZTT)
20	33	EVERYBODY GONFI GON	2 Cowboys (ffrreedom)
-	34	EVERYTHING IS GONNA BE ALRIGHT	Sounds Of Blackness (A&M)
29	35	CAN YOU FEEL THE LOVE TONIGHT	Elton John (Mercury)
21	36	RUN TO THE SUN	Erasure (Mute)
-	37	DOGGY DOGG WORLD	Snoop Doggy Dogg (Death Row)
34	38	SUMMERTIME	DJ Jazzy Jeff & the Fresh Prince (Jive)
50	39	THE WAY SHE LOVES ME	Richard Marx (Capitol)
28	40	IS THIS LOVE	Whitesnake (EMI)
26	41	GIRLS + BOYS	Hed Boys (deConstruction)
49	42	TWO FATT GUITARS (REVISITED)	Direckt (UFG)
24	43	BABY, I LOVE YOUR WAY	Big Mountain (RCA)
-	44	AGE OF LONELINESS	Enigma (Virgin)
-	45	AWAY FROM HOME	Dr Alban (Logic)
-	46	THE FEELING	Tin Tin Out featuring Sweet Tee (Deep Distraction)
46	47	I LIKE	Shanice (Motown)
-	48	WHO'S THE DARKMAN?	Darkman (Wild Card)
-	49	LUCKY YOU	Lightning Seeds (Epic)
-	50	VASOLINE	Stone Temple Pilots (Atlantic)

27 August 1994

last	this	title	artist (label)
1	1	LOVE IS ALL AROUND	Wet Wet Wet (Precious)
3	2	CRAZY FOR YOU	Let Loose (Mercury)
8	3	COMPLIMENTS ON YOUR KISS	Red Dragon with Brian & Tony Gold (Mango)
4	4	SEARCHING	China Black (Wild Card)
2	5	I SWEAR	All-4- One (Atlantic)
9	6	7 SECONDS	Youssou N'Dour featuring Neneh Cherry (Columbia)
7	7	WHAT'S UP	DJ Miko (Systematic)
5	8	REGULATE	Warren G & Nate Dogg (Death Row)
12	9	LIVE FOREVER	Oasis (Creation)
6	10	(MEET) THE FLINTSTONES	BC-52s (MCA)
11	11	EIGHTEEN STRINGS	Tinman ffrr)
18	12	BLACK HOLE SUN	Soundgarden (A&M)
23	13	SO GOOD	Eternal (EMI)
10	14	NO MORE (I CAN'T STAND IT)	Maxx (Pulse 8)
14	15	MIDNIGHT AT THE OASIS	Brand New Heavies (ffrr)
13	16	LET'S GET READY TO RUMBLE	PJ & Duncan (Telstar)
15	17	TROUBLE	Shampoo (Food)
25	18	SOMEONE TO LOVE	Sean Maguire (Parlophone)
16	19	SWAMP THING	Grid (deConstruction)
31	20	RIGHT BESIDE YOU	Sophie B Hawkins (Columbia)
17	21	SHINE	Aswad (Bubblin')
20	22	THE SIMPLE THINGS	Joe Cocker (Capitol)
44	23	AGE OF LONELINESS	Enigma (Virgin)
-	24	SPEAKEASY	Shed Seven (Polydor)
28	25	DO IT	Toni Di Bart (Cleveland City Blues)
-	26	BOP GUN (ONE NATION)	Ice Cube featuring George Clinton (Priority)
-	27	DO YOU WANT TO GET FUNKY	C&C Music Factory (Columbia)
-	28	FEEL THE PAIN	Dinosaur Jr (blanco y negro)
22	29	GIVE IT UP	Public Enemy (Def Jam)
-	30	GAL WINE	Chaka Demus & Pliers (Mango)
30	31	INTERLUDE	Morrissey & Siouxsie (Parlophone)
26	32	EVERYTHING'S ALRIGHT (UPTIGHT)	CJ Lewis (Black Market)
21	33	BLACK BOOK	EYC (MCA)
34	34	EVERYTHING IS GONNA BE ALRIGHT	Sounds Of Blackness (A&M)
19	35	LIFEFORMS	Future Sound Of London (Virgin)
-	36	MAGIC	Sasha (deConstruction)
-	37	REGGAE MUSIC	UB40 (DEP International)
37	38	DOGGY DOGG WORLD	Snoop Doggy Dogg (Death Row)
24	39	REVOL	Manic Street Preachers (Epic)
-	40	ON YA WAY	Helicopter (Helicopter)
49	41	LUCKY YOU	Lightning Seeds (Epic)
-	42	TRIPPIN' ON SUNSHINE	Pizzaman (Loaded)
-	43	EVERYBODY'S GOT SUMMER	Atlantic Starr (Arista)
-	44	LA LA (MEANS I LOVE YOU)	Swing Out Sister (Mercury)
-	45	GIVE ME ALL YOUR LOVE	Magic Affair (EMI)
39	46	THE WAY SHE LOVES ME	Richard Marx (Capitol)
27	47	I DIDN'T MEAN IT	Status Quo (Polydor)
33	48	EVERYBODY GONFI GON	2 Cowboys (ffrreedom)
-	49	TRIPWIRE	Lionrock (deConstruction)
29	50	TRUE SPIRIT	Carleen Anderson (Circa)

DJ Miko continued the crossover between house and grunge music, and in came the Brand New Heavies with a cover of Maria Muldaur's 1974 hit. *Lifeforms* by Future Sound Of London lasted comfortably over 20 minutes. Status Quo were still making hits dressed in denim, though they're older than your granny.

3 September 1994

last	this		
1	1	LOVE IS ALL AROUND	Wet Wet Wet (Precious)
6	2	7 SECONDS	Youssou N'Dour featuring Neneh Cherry (Columbia)
2	3	CRAZY FOR YOU	Let Loose (Mercury)
3	4	COMPLIMENTS ON YOUR KISS	Red Dragon with Brian & Tony Gold (Mango)
4	5	SEARCHING	China Black (Wild Card)
5	6	I SWEAR	All-4- One (Atlantic)
7	7	WHAT'S UP	DJ Miko (Systematic)
8	8	REGULATE	Warren G & Nate Dogg (Death Row)
11	9	EIGHTEEN STRINGS	Tinman ffrr
-	10	I'LL MAKE LOVE TO YOU	Boyz II Men (Motown)
-	11	PARKLIFE	Blur (Food)
9	12	LIVE FOREVER	Oasis (Creation)
18	13	SOMEONE TO LOVE	Sean Maguire (Parlophone)
13	14	SO GOOD	Eternal (EMI)
17	15	TROUBLE	Shampoo (Food)
12	16	BLACK HOLE SUN	Soundgarden (A&M)
20	17	RIGHT BESIDE YOU	Sophie B Hawkins (Columbia)
10	18	(MEET) THE FLINTSTONES	BC-52s (MCA)
16	19	LET'S GET READY TO RHUMBLE	PJ & Duncan (Telstar)
-	20	GAL WINE	Chaka Demus & Pliers (Mango)
15	21	MIDNIGHT AT THE OASIS	Brand New Heavies (ffrr)
14	22	NO MORE (I CAN'T STAND IT)	Maxx (Pulse 8)
-	23	DREAMER	Livin' Joy (MCA)
-	24	AGE OF LONELINESS	Enigma (Virgin)
-	25	SPEAKEASY	Shed Seven (Polydor)
19	26	SWAMP THING	Grid (deConstruction)
21	27	SHINE	Aswad (Bubblin')
26	28	BOP GUN (ONE NATION)	Ice Cube featuring George Clinton (Priority)
-	29	SUMMER BUNNIES	R Kelly (Jive)
-	30	PRETEND BEST FRIEND	Terrorvision (Total Vegas)
-	31	MAGIC	Sasha (deConstruction)
-	32	STAY (I MISSED YOU)	Lisa Loeb & Nine Stories (RCA)
28	33	FEEL THE PAIN	Dinosaur Jr (blanco y negro)
27	34	DO YOU WANT TO GET FUNKY	C&C Music Factory (Columbia)
-	35	SW LIVE (EP)	Peter Gabriel (Virgin)
22	36	THE SIMPLE THINGS	Joe Cocker (Capitol)
25	37	DO IT	Toni Di Bart (Cleveland City Blues)
-	38	PRETTIEST EYES	Beautiful South (Go! Discs)
-	39	SUGAR SUGAR	Duke Baysee (Arista)
44	40	LA LA (MEANS I LOVE YOU)	Swing Out Sister (Mercury)
-	41	WILD NIGHT	John Mellencamp & Me'shell Ndegeocello (Mercury)
45	42	GIVE ME ALL YOUR LOVE	Magic Affair (EMI)
-	43	KNOW BY NOW	Robert Palmer (EMI)
-	44	ONE DAY	D:Mob (ffrr)
37	45	REGGAE MUSIC	UB40 (DEP International)
-	46	ONE GIANT LOVE	Cud (A&M)
-	47	HOT HOT HOT	Arrow (The Hit Label)
-	48	SHINING ROAD	Cranes (Dedicated)
-	49	ONLY SAW TODAY/INSTANT KARMA	Amos (Positiva)
-	50	YOUR FAVOURITE THING	Sugar (Creation)

10 September 1994

last	this		
1	1	LOVE IS ALL AROUND	Wet Wet Wet (Precious)
-	2	CONFIDE IN ME	Kylie Minogue (deConstruction)
2	3	7 SECONDS	Youssou N'Dour featuring Neneh Cherry (Columbia)
10	4	I'LL MAKE LOVE TO YOU	Boyz II Men (Motown)
4	5	COMPLIMENTS ON YOUR KISS	Red Dragon with Brian & Tony Gold (Mango)
3	6	CRAZY FOR YOU	Let Loose (Mercury)
5	7	SEARCHING	China Black (Wild Card)
6	8	I SWEAR	All-4- One (Atlantic)
8	10	REGULATE	Warren G & Nate Dogg (Death Row)
11	11	PARKLIFE	Blur (Food)
-	12	YESTERDAY, WHEN I WAS MAD	Pet Shop Boys (Parlophone)
9	13	EIGHTEEN STRINGS	Tinman ffrr
13	14	SOMEONE TO LOVE	Sean Maguire (Parlophone)
15	15	TROUBLE	Shampoo (Food)
-	16	RHYTHM OF THE NIGHT	Corona (WEA)
17	17	RIGHT BESIDE YOU	Sophie B Hawkins (Columbia)
-	18	INCREDIBLE	M-Beat featuring General Levy (Rank)
14	19	SO GOOD	Eternal (EMI)
23	20	DREAMER	Livin' Joy (MCA)
21	21	UNBEARABLE	Wonder Stuff (Far Out)
-	22	ATOMIC (REMIXES)	Blondie (Chrysalis)
30	23	PRETEND BEST FRIEND	Terrorvision (Total Vegas)
16	24	BLACK HOLE SUN	Soundgarden (A&M)
32	25	STAY (I MISSED YOU)	Lisa Loeb & Nine Stories (RCA)
20	26	GAL WINE	Chaka Demus & Pliers (Mango)
19	27	LET'S GET READY TO RHUMBLE	PJ & Duncan (Telstar)
12	28	LIVE FOREVER	Oasis (Creation)
-	29	EVERYTHING'S COOL	Pop Will Eat Itself (Infectious)
-	30	LIAR/DISCONNECT	Rollins Band (Imago)
43	31	KNOW BY NOW	Robert Palmer (EMI)
-	32	LETITGO	Prince (Warner Bros.)
22	33	NO MORE (I CAN'T STAND IT)	Maxx (Pulse 8)
18	34	(MEET) THE FLINTSTONES	BC-52s (MCA)
39	35	SUGAR SUGAR	Duke Baysee (Arista)
38	36	PRETTIEST EYES	Beautiful South (Go! Discs)
29	37	SUMMER BUNNIES	R Kelly (Jive)
21	38	MIDNIGHT AT THE OASIS	Brand New Heavies (ffrr)
27	39	SHINE	Aswad (Bubblin')
47	40	HOT HOT HOT	Arrow (The Hit Label)
-	41	BLAME IT ON ME	D:Ream (Magnet)
41	42	WILD NIGHT	John Mellencamp & Me'shell Ndegeocello (Mercury)
25	43	SPEAKEASY	Shed Seven (Polydor)
-	44	HEART OF STONE	Dave Stewart (East West)
-	45	INSIDE OUT/DOWN THAT ROAD (REMIXES)	Shara Nelson (Cooltempo)
26	46	SWAMP THING	Grid (deConstruction)
-	47	YESTERDAY ONCE MORE/SUPERSTAR	Redd Kross/Sonic Youth (A&M)
49	48	ONLY SAW TODAY/INSTANT KARMA	Amos (Positiva)
24	49	AGE OF LONELINESS	Enigma (Virgin)
31	50	MAGIC	Sasha (deConstruction)

17 September 1994

last	this		
-	1	SATURDAY NIGHT	Whigfield (Systematic)
1	2	LOVE IS ALL AROUND	Wet Wet Wet (Precious)
2	3	CONFIDE IN ME	Kylie Minogue (deConstruction)
-	4	ENDLESS LOVE	Luther Vandross & Mariah Carey (Epic)
4	5	I'LL MAKE LOVE TO YOU	Boyz II Men (Motown)
16	6	RHYTHM OF THE NIGHT	Corona (WEA)
3	7	7 SECONDS	Youssou N'Dour featuring Neneh Cherry (Columbia)
5	8	COMPLIMENTS ON YOUR KISS	Red Dragon with Brian & Tony Gold (Mango)
-	9	WHAT'S THE FREQUENCY, KENNETH	REM (Warner Bros.)
18	10	INCREDIBLE	M-Beat featuring General Levy (Rank)
6	11	CRAZY FOR YOU	Let Loose (Mercury)
7	12	SEARCHING	China Black (Wild Card)
11	13	PARKLIFE	Blur (Food)
12	14	YESTERDAY, WHEN I WAS MAD	Pet Shop Boys (Parlophone)
10	15	REGULATE	Warren G & Nate Dogg (Death Row)
9	16	WHAT'S UP	DJ Miko (Systematic)
8	17	I SWEAR	All-4- One (Atlantic)
17	18	RIGHT BESIDE YOU	Sophie B Hawkins (Columbia)
25	19	STAY (I MISSED YOU)	Lisa Loeb & Nine Stories (RCA)
22	20	ATOMIC (REMIXES)	Blondie (Chrysalis)
-	21	ROLLERCOASTER	Grid (deConstruction)
15	22	TROUBLE	Shampoo (Food)
20	23	DREAMER	Livin' Joy (MCA)
14	24	SOMEONE TO LOVE	Sean Maguire (Parlophone)
-	25	HEY NOW (GIRLS JUST WANT TO HAVE...)	Cyndi Lauper (Epic)
26	26	LOVE HERE I COME	Bad Boys Inc (A&M)
13	27	EIGHTEEN STRINGS	Tinman ffrr
21	28	UNBEARABLE	Wonder Stuff (Far Out)
41	29	BLAME IT ON ME	D:Ream (Magnet)
31	30	KNOW BY NOW	Robert Palmer (EMI)
19	31	SO GOOD	Eternal (EMI)
-	32	FIREWORKS	Roxette (Warner Bros.)
32	33	LETITGO	Prince (Warner Bros.)
-	34	ELEGANTLY AMERICAN	M People (deConstruction)
30	35	LIAR/DISCONNECT	Rollins Band (Imago)
-	36	WELCOME TO TOMORROW	Snap featuring Summer (Arista)
23	37	PRETEND BEST FRIEND	Terrorvision (Total Vegas)
24	38	BLACK HOLE SUN	Soundgarden (A&M)
35	39	SUGAR SUGAR	Duke Baysee (Arista)
-	40	WARRIORS	Aswad (Bubblin')
45	41	INSIDE OUT/DOWN THAT ROAD (REMIXES)	Shara Nelson (Cooltempo)
29	42	EVERYTHING'S COOL	Pop Will Eat Itself (Infectious)
33	43	NO MORE (I CAN'T STAND IT)	Maxx (Pulse 8)
-	44	KEEP THE FIRES BURNING	Clock (Media)
-	45	WILMOT	Sabres of Paradise (Warp)
26	46	GAL WINE	Chaka Demus & Pliers (Mango)
-	47	GO INTO THE LIGHT	Ian McNabb (This Way Up)
27	48	LET'S GET READY TO RHUMBLE	PJ & Duncan (Telstar)
34	49	(MEET) THE FLINTSTONES	BC-52s (MCA)
40	50	HOT HOT HOT	Arrow (The Hit Label)

Kylie Minogue emerged from her previous guise as a novelty act/TV tie-in, to show she was a credible pop star. This involved numerous photo sessions in differing states of undress. We must also note the emergence of a new sound – *Incredible* by M-Beat was the first ever Jungle hit – you read it here first.

September – October 1994

24 September 1994

last	this	title	artist
1	1	SATURDAY NIGHT	Whigfield (Systematic)
2	2	LOVE IS ALL AROUND	Wet Wet Wet (Precious)
6	3	RHYTHM OF THE NIGHT	Corona (WEA)
4	4	ENDLESS LOVE	Luther Vandross & Mariah Carey (Epic)
3	5	CONFIDE IN ME	Kylie Minogue (deConstruction)
5	6	I'LL MAKE LOVE TO YOU	Boyz II Men (Motown)
10	7	INCREDIBLE	M-Beat featuring General Levy (Rank)
-	8	ALWAYS	Bon Jovi (Jambco)
9	9	WHAT'S THE FREQUENCY, KENNETH	REM (Warner Bros.)
7	10	7 SECONDS	Youssou N'Dour featuring Neneh Cherry (Columbia)
8	11	COMPLIMENTS ON YOUR KISS	Red Dragon with Brian & Tony Gold (Mango)
19	12	STAY (I MISSED YOU)	Lisa Loeb & Nine Stories (RCA)
25	13	HEY NOW (GIRLS JUST WANT TO HAVE...)	Cyndi Lauper (Epic)
-	14	WE ARE THE PIGS	Suede (Nude)
11	15	CRAZY FOR YOU	Let Loose (Mercury)
15	16	REGULATE	Warren G & Nate Dogg (Death Row)
18	17	RIGHT BESIDE YOU	Sophie B Hawkins (Columbia)
12	18	SEARCHING	China Black (Wild Card)
-	19	SWEETNESS	Michelle Gayle (RCA)
-	20	VOODOO PEOPLE	Prodigy (XL)
21	21	ROLLERCOASTER	Grid (deConstruction)
-	22	DON'T SAY IT'S OVER	Gun (A&M)
16	23	WHAT'S UP	DJ Miko (Systematic)
17	24	I SWEAR	All-4- One (Atlantic)
13	25	PARKLIFE	Blur (Food)
23	26	DREAMER	Livin' Joy (MCA)
32	27	FIREWORKS	Roxette (EMI)
26	28	LOVE HERE I COME	Bad Boys Inc (A&M)
20	29	ATOMIC (REMIXES)	Blondie (Chrysalis)
36	30	WELCOME TO TOMORROW	Snap featuring Summer (Arista)
-	31	PINEAPPLE HEAD	Crowded House (Capitol)
-	32	ARE WE HERE?	Orbital (Internal Dance)
29	33	BLAME IT ON ME	D:Ream (Magnet)
-	34	FIND ME	Jam & Spoon featuring Plavka (Epic)
-	35	WRENCH	Almighty (Chrysalis)
22	36	TROUBLE	Shampoo (Food)
-	37	FOOTSTEPS	Stiltskin (White Water)
34	38	ELEGANTLY AMERICAN	M People (deConstruction)
14	39	YESTERDAY, WHEN I WAS MAD	Pet Shop Boys (Parlophone)
30	40	KNOW BY NOW	Robert Palmer (EMI)
40	41	WARRIORS	Aswad (Bubblin')
45	42	WILMOT	Sabres of Paradise (Warp)
27	43	EIGHTEEN STRINGS	Tinman ffrr)
24	44	SOMEONE TO LOVE	Sean Maguire (Parlophone)
-	45	SWEET SENSUAL LOVE	Big Mountain (Giant)
41	46	INSIDE OUT/DOWN THAT ROAD (REMIXES)	Shara Nelson (Cooltempo)
-	47	LOVE AND TEARS	Naomi Campbell (Epic)
-	48	EVERYBODY	DJ Bobo (PWL Continental)
31	49	SO GOOD	Eternal (EMI)
28	50	UNBEARABLE	Wonder Stuff (Far Out)

1 October 1994

last	this	title	artist
1	1	SATURDAY NIGHT	Whigfield (Systematic)
2	2	RHYTHM OF THE NIGHT	Corona (WEA)
4	3	ENDLESS LOVE	Luther Vandross & Mariah Carey (Epic)
8	4	ALWAYS	Bon Jovi (Jambco)
5	5	LOVE IS ALL AROUND	Wet Wet Wet (Precious)
13	6	HEY NOW (GIRLS JUST WANT TO HAVE...)	Cyndi Lauper (Epic)
12	7	STAY (I MISSED YOU)	Lisa Loeb & Nine Stories (RCA)
6	8	I'LL MAKE LOVE TO YOU	Boyz II Men (Motown)
-	9	STEAM	East 17 (London)
10	10	CONFIDE IN ME	Kylie Minogue (deConstruction)
7	11	INCREDIBLE	M-Beat featuring General Levy (Rank)
9	12	WHAT'S THE FREQUENCY, KENNETH	
19	13	SWEETNESS	Michelle Gayle (RCA)
10	14	7 SECONDS	Youssou N'Dour featuring Neneh Cherry (Columbia)
20	15	VOODOO PEOPLE	Prodigy (XL)
16	16	CAN YOU FEEL IT?	Reel 2 Real featuring the Mad Stuntman (Positiva)
17	17	RIGHT BESIDE YOU	Sophie B Hawkins (Columbia)
11	18	COMPLIMENTS ON YOUR KISS	Red Dragon with Brian & Tony Gold (Mango)
14	19	WE ARE THE PIGS	Suede (Nude)
-	20	NO ONE	2 Unlimited (PWL Continental)
21	21	ROLLERCOASTER	Grid (deConstruction)
-	22	BABY COME BACK	Pato Banton (Virgin)
15	23	CRAZY FOR YOU	Let Loose (Mercury)
-	24	FOREIGN SAND	Roger Taylor & Yoshiki (Parlophone)
16	25	REGULATE	Warren G & Nate Dogg (Death Row)
22	26	DON'T SAY IT'S OVER	Gun (A&M)
-	27	ZOMBIE	Cranberries (Island)
30	28	WELCOME TO TOMORROW	Snap featuring Summer (Arista)
18	29	SEARCHING	China Black (Wild Card)
-	30	BUG POWDER DUST	Bomb The Bass featuring Justin Warfield (4th & Broadway)
24	31	I SWEAR	All-4- One (Atlantic)
23	32	WHAT'S UP	DJ Miko (Systematic)
31	33	FIND ME	Jam & Spoon featuring Plavka (Epic)
-	34	PINEAPPLE HEAD	Crowded House (Capitol)
-	35	HUG MY SOUL (EP)	Saint Etienne (Heavenly)
-	36	WHEN CAN I SEE YOU	Babyface (Epic)
35	37	WRENCH	Almighty (Chrysalis)
-	38	GROOVE OF LOVE	EVE (MCA)
47	39	LOVE AND TEARS	Naomi Campbell (Epic)
32	40	ARE WE HERE?	Orbital (Internal Dance)
48	41	EVERYBODY	DJ Bobo (PWL Continental)
42	42	FIREWORKS	Roxette (EMI)
33	43	BLAME IT ON ME	D:Ream (Magnet)
28	44	LOVE HERE I COME	Bad Boys Inc (A&M)
36	45	TROUBLE	Shampoo (Food)
-	46	STAYING OUT FOR THE SUMMER	Dodgy (A&M)
-	47	HERE COME THE GOOD TIMES	A House (Parlophone)
-	48	GOOD TIMES	Edie Brickell (Geffen)
-	49	ORIGINAL NUTTAH	UK Apachi with Shy FX (Sour)
37	50	FOOTSTEPS	Stiltskin (White Water)

8 October 1994

last	this	title	artist
1	1	SATURDAY NIGHT	Whigfield (Systematic)
2	2	RHYTHM OF THE NIGHT	Corona (WEA)
4	3	ALWAYS	Bon Jovi (Jambco)
6	4	HEY NOW (GIRLS JUST WANT TO HAVE...)	Cyndi Lauper (Epic)
9	5	STEAM	East 17 (London)
3	6	ENDLESS LOVE	Luther Vandross & Mariah Carey (Epic)
7	7	STAY (I MISSED YOU)	Lisa Loeb & Nine Stories (RCA)
-	8	SECRET	Madonna (Maverick)
13	9	SWEETNESS	Michelle Gayle (RCA)
22	10	BABY COME BACK	Pato Banton (Virgin)
5	11	LOVE IS ALL AROUND	Wet Wet Wet (Precious)
8	12	I'LL MAKE LOVE TO YOU	Boyz II Men (Motown)
27	13	ZOMBIE	Cranberries (Island)
11	14	INCREDIBLE	M-Beat featuring General Levy (Rank)
-	15	SPACE COWBOY	Jamiroquai (Sony Soho Square)
16	16	CAN YOU FEEL IT?	Reel 2 Real featuring the Mad Stuntman (Positiva)
20	17	NO ONE	2 Unlimited (PWL Continental)
14	18	7 SECONDS	Youssou N'Dour featuring Neneh Cherry (Columbia)
10	19	CONFIDE IN ME	Kylie Minogue (deConstruction)
12	20	WHAT'S THE FREQUENCY, KENNETH	REM (Warner Bros.)
-	21	BEST OF MY LOVE	CJ Lewis (MCA)
-	22	GIMME ALL YOUR LOVIN'	Jocelyn Brown & Kym Mazelle (Bell)
17	23	RIGHT BESIDE YOU	Sophie B Hawkins (Columbia)
-	24	IF I GIVE YOU MY NUMBER	PJ & Duncan (XSRhythm)
15	25	VOODOO PEOPLE	Prodigy (XL)
-	26	MY IRON LUNG (EP)	Radiohead (Parlophone)
-	27	CIRCLE OF LIFE	Elton John (Rocket)
-	28	YOU GOT ME ROCKING	Rolling Stones (Virgin)
28	29	WELCOME TO TOMORROW	Snap featuring Summer (Arista)
30	30	BUG POWDER DUST	Bomb The Bass featuring Justin Warfield (4th & Broadway)
23	31	CRAZY FOR YOU	Let Loose (Mercury)
-	32	DREAMSCAPE '94	Time Frequency (Internal Affairs)
-	33	BORN DEAD	Body Count (Rhyme Syndicate)
-	34	OOH AAH (G-SPOT)	Wayne Marshall (Soultown)
25	35	REGULATE	Warren G & Nate Dogg (Death Row)
18	36	COMPLIMENTS ON YOUR KISS	Red Dragon with Brian & Tony Gold (Mango)
-	37	I WANT THE WORLD	2wo Third3 (Epic)
26	38	DON'T SAY IT'S OVER	Gun (A&M)
31	39	I SWEAR	All-4- One (Atlantic)
-	40	THIS IS YOUR NIGHT	Heavy D & the Boyz (Uptown)
-	41	COMING DOWN	Cult (Beggars Banquet)
-	42	SHOOT ALL THE CLOWNS	Bruce Dickinson (EMI)
29	43	SEARCHING	China Black (Wild Card)
38	44	GROOVE OF LOVE	EVE (MCA)
45	45	WHEN CAN I SEE YOU	Babyface (Epic)
48	46	GOOD TIMES	Edie Brickell (Geffen)
24	47	FOREIGN SAND	Roger Taylor & Yoshiki (Parlophone)
35	48	HUG MY SOUL (EP)	Saint Etienne (Heavenly)
-	49	I DON'T KNOW WHERE IT COMES FROM	Ride (Creation)
47	50	HERE COME THE GOOD TIMES	A House (Parlophone)

So Wet Wet Wet voluntarily gave up the top spot after 15 weeks. Whigfield's *Saturday Night* was the archetypal Euro hit. Everyone heard it on their hols and bought it when they came back. REM were back with a new single and a follow up album to the hugeselling *Automatic For The People*.

October 1994

15 October 1994

last	this	Title	Artist (Label)
1	1	SATURDAY NIGHT	Whigfield (Systematic)
-	2	SURE	Take That (RCA)
3	3	ALWAYS	Bon Jovi (Jambco)
10	4	BABY COME BACK	Pato Banton (Virgin)
8	5	SECRET	Madonna (Maverick)
2	6	RHYTHM OF THE NIGHT	Corona (WEA)
4	7	HEY NOW (GIRLS JUST WANT TO HAVE...)	Cyndi Lauper (Epic)
5	8	STEAM	East 17 (London)
9	9	SWEETNESS	Michelle Gayle (RCA)
7	10	STAY (I MISSED YOU)	Lisa Loeb & Nine Stories (RCA)
6	11	ENDLESS LOVE	Luther Vandross & Mariah Carey (Epic)
27	12	CIRCLE OF LIFE	Elton John (Rocket)
21	13	BEST OF MY LOVE	CJ Lewis (MCA)
13	14	ZOMBIE	Cranberries (Island)
12	15	I'LL MAKE LOVE TO YOU	Boyz II Men (Motown)
15	16	SPACE COWBOY	Jamiroquai (Sony Soho Square)
24	17	IF I GIVE YOU MY NUMBER	PJ & Duncan (XSRhythm)
14	18	INCREDIBLE	M-Beat featuring General Levy (Rank)
11	19	LOVE IS ALL AROUND	Wet Wet Wet (Precious)
-	20	MOVE IT UP: BIG BEAT	Cappella (Internal Dance)
17	21	NO ONE	2 Unlimited (PWL Continental)
29	22	WELCOME TO TOMORROW	Snap featuring Summer (Arista)
16	23	CAN YOU FEEL IT?	Reel 2 Real featuring the Mad Stuntman (Positiva)
37	24	I WANT THE WORLD	2wo Third3 (Epic)
22	25	GIMME ALL YOUR LOVIN'	Jocelyn Brown & Kym Mazelle (Bell)
-	26	SHE IS SUFFERING	Manic Street Preachers (Epic)
18	27	7 SECONDS	Youssou N'Dour featuring Neneh Cherry (Columbia)
28	28	YOU GOT ME ROCKING	Rolling Stones (Virgin)
-	29	CAN'TGETAMAN, CAN'TGETAJOB (LIFE'S...)	Sister Bliss featuring Colette (Go Beat)
-	30	PUSH THE FEELING ON	Nightcrawlers (ffrr)
19	31	CONFIDE IN ME	Kylie Minogue (deConstruction)
-	32	THAT'S THE WAY YOU DO IT	Purple Kings (Positiva)
32	33	DREAMSCAPE '94	Time Frequency (Internal Affairs)
23	34	RIGHT BESIDE YOU	Sophie B Hawkins (Columbia)
26	35	MY IRON LUNG (EP)	Radiohead (Parlophone)
-	36	TURN THE BEAT AROUND	Gloria Estefan (Epic)
20	37	WHAT'S THE FREQUENCY, KENNETH	REM (Warner Bros.)
33	38	BORN DEAD	Body Count (Rhyme Syndicate)
40	39	THIS IS YOUR NIGHT	Heavy D & the Boyz (Uptown)
-	40	LOOK BUT DON'T TOUCH (EP)	Skin (Parlophone)
-	41	I WANT YOU	Juliet Roberts (Cooltempo)
-	42	VIVA LE MEGABABES	Shampoo (Food)
-	43	GOD	Tori Amos (East West)
-	44	THAT WOMAN'S GOT ME DRINKING	Shane MacGowan & the Popes (ZTT)
31	45	CRAZY FOR YOU	Let Loose (Mercury)
-	46	BRIGHTEST STAR	Driza Bone (4th & Broadway)
-	47	HAPPY NATION	Ace Of Base (Metronome)
-	48	AT YOUR BEST (YOU ARE LOVE)	Aaliyah (Jive)
-	49	YOUNG GIRL	Darren Day (Bell)
-	50	BRING IT ON HOME	Urban Cookie Collective (Pulse 8)

22 October 1994

last	this	Title	Artist (Label)
2	1	SURE	Take That (RCA)
4	2	BABY COME BACK	Pato Banton (Virgin)
1	3	SATURDAY NIGHT	Whigfield (Systematic)
3	4	ALWAYS	Bon Jovi (Jambco)
9	5	SWEETNESS	Michelle Gayle (RCA)
6	6	RHYTHM OF THE NIGHT	Corona (WEA)
7	7	HEY NOW (GIRLS JUST WANT TO HAVE...)	Cyndi Lauper (Epic)
-	8	CIGARETTES AND ALCOHOL	Oasis (Creation)
5	9	SECRET	Madonna (Maverick)
8	10	STEAM	East 17 (London)
10	11	STAY (I MISSED YOU)	Lisa Loeb & Nine Stories (RCA)
12	12	CIRCLE OF LIFE	Elton John (Rocket)
13	13	BEST OF MY LOVE	CJ Lewis (MCA)
22	14	WELCOME TO TOMORROW	Snap featuring Summer (Arista)
11	15	ENDLESS LOVE	Luther Vandross & Mariah Carey (Epic)
-	16	SEVENTEEN	Let Loose (Mercury)
-	17	SHE'S GOT THAT VIBE	R Kelly (Jive)
20	18	MOVE IT UP: BIG BEAT	Cappella (Internal Dance)
14	19	ZOMBIE	Cranberries (Island)
26	20	SHE IS SUFFERING	Manic Street Preachers (Epic)
-	21	THE STRANGEST PARTY	INXS (Mercury)
17	22	IF I GIVE YOU MY NUMBER	PJ & Duncan (XSRhythm)
15	23	I'LL MAKE LOVE TO YOU	Boyz II Men (Motown)
-	24	CONNECTION	Elastica (Deceptive)
30	25	PUSH THE FEELING ON	Nightcrawlers (ffrr)
16	26	SPACE COWBOY	Jamiroquai (Sony Soho Square)
24	27	I WANT THE WORLD	2wo Third3 (Epic)
-	28	PLANET CARAVAN	Pantera (Atlantic)
19	29	LOVE IS ALL AROUND	Wet Wet Wet (Precious)
18	30	INCREDIBLE	M-Beat featuring General Levy (Rank)
-	31	SOME GIRLS	Ultimate Kaos (Wild Card)
36	32	TURN THE BEAT AROUND	Gloria Estefan (Epic)
29	33	CAN'TGETAMAN, CAN'TGETAJOB (LIFE'S...)	Sister Bliss featuring Colette (Go Beat)
28	34	YOU GOT ME ROCKING	Rolling Stones (Virgin)
21	35	NO ONE	2 Unlimited (PWL Continental)
42	36	VIVA LE MEGABABES	Shampoo (Food)
41	37	I WANT YOU	Juliet Roberts (Cooltempo)
32	38	THAT'S THE WAY YOU DO IT	Purple Kings (Positiva)
-	39	SHERRI DON'T FAIL ME NOW	Status Quo (Polydor)
48	40	AT YOUR BEST (YOU ARE LOVE)	Aaliyah (Jive)
-	41	EL TRAGO (THE DRINK)	2 In A Room (Positiva)
23	42	CAN YOU FEEL IT?	Reel 2 Real featuring the Mad Stuntman (Positiva)
-	43	TURN UP THE POWER	N-Trance (All Around The World)
27	44	7 SECONDS	Youssou N'Dour featuring Neneh Cherry (Columbia)
40	45	LOOK BUT DON'T TOUCH (EP)	Skin (Parlophone)
47	46	HAPPY NATION	Ace Of Base (Metronome)
43	47	GOD	Tori Amos (East West)
-	48	SAY YOU'LL BE MINE	Amy Grant (A&M)
-	49	RAIN KING	Counting Crows (Geffen)
46	50	BRIGHTEST STAR	Driza Bone (4th & Broadway)

29 October 1994

last	this	Title	Artist (Label)
2	1	BABY COME BACK	Pato Banton (Virgin)
1	2	SURE	Take That (RCA)
3	3	SATURDAY NIGHT	Whigfield (Systematic)
5	4	SWEETNESS	Michelle Gayle (RCA)
4	5	ALWAYS	Bon Jovi (Jambco)
17	6	SHE'S GOT THAT VIBE	R Kelly (Jive)
7	7	HEY NOW (GIRLS JUST WANT TO HAVE...)	Cyndi Lauper (Epic)
8	8	CIGARETTES AND ALCOHOL	Oasis (Creation)
14	9	WELCOME TO TOMORROW	Snap featuring Summer (Arista)
-	10	WHEN WE DANCE	Sting (A&M)
11	11	STAY (I MISSED YOU)	Lisa Loeb & Nine Stories (RCA)
16	12	SEVENTEEN	Let Loose (Mercury)
6	13	RHYTHM OF THE NIGHT	Corona (WEA)
12	14	CIRCLE OF LIFE	Elton John (Rocket)
9	15	SECRET	Madonna (Maverick)
21	16	THE STRANGEST PARTY	INXS (Mercury)
10	17	STEAM	East 17 (London)
18	18	MOVE IT UP: BIG BEAT	Cappella (Internal Dance)
-	19	YOU NEVER LOVE THE SAME WAY TWICE	Rozalla (Epic)
-	20	HIGH HOPES/KEEP TALKING	Pink Floyd (EMI)
13	21	BEST OF MY LOVE	CJ Lewis (MCA)
31	22	SOME GIRLS	Ultimate Kaos (Wild Card)
-	23	SLY	Massive Attack (Circa)
24	24	CONNECTION	Elastica (Deceptive)
15	25	ENDLESS LOVE	Luther Vandross & Mariah Carey (Epic)
32	26	TURN THE BEAT AROUND	Gloria Estefan (Epic)
22	27	IF I GIVE YOU MY NUMBER	PJ & Duncan (XSRhythm)
-	28	WELCOME TO PARADISE	Green Day (Warner Bros.)
-	29	ALICE, WHAT'S THE MATTER	Terrorvision (Total Vegas)
27	30	I WANT THE WORLD	2wo Third3 (Epic)
-	31	STARS	China Black (Wild Card)
-	32	YOU CAN GET IT	Maxx (Pulse 8)
19	33	ZOMBIE	Cranberries (Island)
43	34	TURN UP THE POWER	N-Trance (All Around The World)
23	35	I'LL MAKE LOVE TO YOU	Boyz II Men (Motown)
25	36	PUSH THE FEELING ON	Nightcrawlers (ffrr)
-	37	TAKE ME HOME	Joe Cocker featuring Bekka Bramlett (Capitol)
38	38	FEELING SO REAL	Moby (Mute)
36	39	VIVA LE MEGABABES	Shampoo (Food)
28	40	PLANET CARAVAN	Pantera (Atlantic)
41	41	EL TRAGO (THE DRINK)	2 In A Room (Positiva)
26	42	SPACE COWBOY	Jamiroquai (Sony Soho Square)
20	43	SHE IS SUFFERING	Manic Street Preachers (Epic)
39	44	SHERRI DON'T FAIL ME NOW	Status Quo (Polydor)
-	45	WHEN DO I GET TO SING MY WAY	Sparks (Logic)
33	46	CAN'TGETAMAN, CAN'TGETAJOB (LIFE'S...)	Sister Bliss featuring Colette (Go Beat)
49	47	RAIN KING	Counting Crows (Geffen)
48	48	SAY YOU'LL BE MINE	Amy Grant (A&M)
29	49	LOVE IS ALL AROUND	Wet Wet Wet (Precious)
-	50	MARY JANE	Spin Doctors (Epic)

Take That again, though held up by Whigfield and to be overtaken by Pato Banton. *She's Got That Vibe* finally made it into the chart after being re-released constantly by R Kelly (one of the biggest record producers in the US) over the last three years. Madonna was in the Top Ten again but not at the top.

November 1994

5 November 1994

LW	TW	Title	Artist (Label)
1	1	BABY COME BACK	Pato Banton (Virgin)
3	2	SATURDAY NIGHT	Whigfield (Systematic)
4	3	SWEETNESS	Michelle Gayle (RCA)
5	4	ALWAYS	Bon Jovi (Jambco)
6	5	SHE'S GOT THAT VIBE	R Kelly (Jive)
2	6	SURE	Take That (RCA)
9	7	WELCOME TO TOMORROW	Snap featuring Summer (Arista)
7	8	HEY NOW (GIRLS JUST WANT TO HAVE...)	Cyndi Lauper (Epic)
-	9	OH BABY I...	Eternal (EMI)
10	10	WHEN WE DANCE	Sting (A&M)
22	11	SOME GIRLS	Ultimate Kaos (Wild Card)
11	12	STAY (I MISSED YOU)	Lisa Loeb & Nine Stories (RCA)
12	13	SEVENTEEN	Let Loose (Mercury)
14	14	OUT OF THE SINKING/SEXY SADIE	Paul Weller (Go! Discs)
-	15	ALL I WANNA DO	Sheryl Crow (A&M)
14	16	CIRCLE OF LIFE	Elton John (Rocket)
8	17	CIGARETTES AND ALCOHOL	Oasis (Creation)
13	18	RHYTHM OF THE NIGHT	Corona (WEA)
17	19	STEAM	East 17 (London)
-	20	CRAZY	Aerosmith (Geffen)
15	21	SECRET	Madonna (Maverick)
23	22	SLY	Massive Attack (Circa)
-	23	ANOTHER NIGHT	MC Sar & The Real McCoy (Logic)
16	24	THE STRANGEST PARTY	INXS (Mercury)
29	25	ALICE, WHAT'S THE MATTER	Terrorvision (Total Vegas)
-	26	IF ONLY I KNEW	Tom Jones (ZTT)
-	27	TAKE THIS TIME	Sean Maguire (Parlophone)
-	28	WHAT'S GOING ON	Music Relief '94 (Jive)
18	29	MOVE IT UP: BIG BEAT	Cappella (Internal Dance)
20	30	HIGH HOPES/KEEP TALKING	Pink Floyd (EMI)
28	31	WELCOME TO PARADISE	Green Day (Warner Bros.)
19	32	YOU NEVER LOVE THE SAME WAY TWICE	Rozalla (Epic)
33	33	STARS	China Black (Wild Card)
32	34	YOU CAN GET IT	Maxx (Pulse 8)
-	35	SPEND SOME TIME	Brand New Heavies (Acid Jazz)
26	36	TURN THE BEAT AROUND	Gloria Estefan (Epic)
-	37	LIQUID COOL	Apollo 440 (Epic)
25	38	ENDLESS LOVE	Luther Vandross & Mariah Carey (Epic)
21	39	BEST OF MY LOVE	CJ Lewis (MCA)
-	40	IN THE MIDDLE OF THE NIGHT	Magic Affair (EMI)
24	41	CONNECTION	Elastica (Deceptive)
27	42	IF I GIVE YOU MY NUMBER	PJ & Duncan (XSRhythm)
-	43	(KEEP ON) SHINING	Loveland (Eastern Bloc)
44	44	NEW BORN FRIEND	Seal (ZTT)
-	45	I BELIEVE IN THE WONDER	Jeanie Tracy (Pulse 8)
35	46	I'LL MAKE LOVE TO YOU	Boyz II Men (Motown)
-	47	DEAR JOHN	Eddie Reader (blanco y negro)
45	48	WHEN DO I GET TO SING MY WAY	Sparks (Logic)
-	49	CHRISTINE KEELER	Senseless Things (Epic)
-	50	BACK IT UP	Robin S (Champion)

12 November 1994

LW	TW	Title	Artist (Label)
1	1	BABY COME BACK	Pato Banton (Virgin)
5	2	SHE'S GOT THAT VIBE	R Kelly (Jive)
3	3	SWEETNESS	Michelle Gayle (RCA)
4	4	ALWAYS	Bon Jovi (Jambco)
2	5	SATURDAY NIGHT	Whigfield (Systematic)
9	6	OH BABY I...	Eternal (EMI)
7	7	WELCOME TO TOMORROW	Snap featuring Summer (Arista)
23	8	ANOTHER NIGHT	MC Sar & The Real McCoy (Logic)
15	9	ALL I WANNA DO	Sheryl Crow (A&M)
-	10	THIS DJ	Warren G (Island)
10	11	WHEN WE DANCE	Sting (A&M)
8	12	HEY NOW (GIRLS JUST WANT TO HAVE...)	Cyndi Lauper (Epic)
26	13	IF ONLY I KNEW	Tom Jones (ZTT)
11	14	SOME GIRLS	Ultimate Kaos (Wild Card)
-	15	BANG AND BLAME	REM (Warner Bros.)
12	16	STAY (I MISSED YOU)	Lisa Loeb & Nine Stories (RCA)
-	17	ONE LAST LOVE SONG	Beautiful South (Go! Discs)
16	18	CIRCLE OF LIFE	Elton John (Rocket)
-	19	MELODY OF LOVE (WANNA BE BELOVED)	Donna Summer (Mercury)
20	20	CRAZY	Aerosmith (Geffen)
35	21	SPEND SOME TIME	Brand New Heavies (Acid Jazz)
6	22	SURE	Take That (RCA)
13	23	SEVENTEEN	Let Loose (Mercury)
33	24	STARS	China Black (Wild Card)
14	25	OUT OF THE SINKING/SEXY SADIE	Paul Weller (Go! Discs)
18	26	RHYTHM OF THE NIGHT	Corona (WEA)
21	27	SECRET	Madonna (Maverick)
24	28	THE STRANGEST PARTY	INXS (Mercury)
27	29	TAKE THIS TIME	Sean Maguire (Parlophone)
-	30	NOE OF YOUR BUSINESS	Salt 'N' Pepa (ffrr)
-	31	SMALL BIT OF LOVE	Saw Doctors (Smalltown)
32	32	YOU NEVER LOVE THE SAME WAY TWICE	Rozalla (Epic)
25	33	ALICE, WHAT'S THE MATTER	Terrorvision (Total Vegas)
22	34	SLY	Massive Attack (Circa)
-	35	YOU CAN GO YOUR OWN WAY	Chris Rea (East West)
-	36	OCEAN PIE	Shed Seven (Polydor)
37	37	LIQUID COOL	Apollo 440 (Epic)
29	38	MOVE IT UP: BIG BEAT	Cappella (Internal Dance)
19	39	STEAM	East 17 (London)
40	40	IN THE MIDDLE OF THE NIGHT	Magic Affair (EMI)
36	41	TURN THE BEAT AROUND	Gloria Estefan (Epic)
-	42	THINK TWICE	Celine Dion (Epic)
17	43	CIGARETTES AND ALCOHOL	Oasis (Creation)
28	44	WHAT'S GOING ON	Music Relief '94 (Jive)
42	45	IF I GIVE YOU MY NUMBER	PJ & Duncan (XSRhythm)
43	46	(KEEP ON) SHINING	Loveland (Eastern Bloc)
47	47	IT AIN'T A CRIME	House Of Pain (XL)
-	48	PUSH	Moist (Chrysalis)
-	49	WOW AND FLUTTER	Stereolab (Duophonic UHF)
31	50	WELCOME TO PARADISE	Green Day (Warner Bros.)

19 November 1994

LW	TW	Title	Artist (Label)
1	1	BABY COME BACK	Pato Banton (Virgin)
8	2	ANOTHER NIGHT	MC Sar & The Real McCoy (Logic)
-	3	LET ME BE YOUR FANTASY	Baby D (Systematic)
-	4	TRUE FAITH '94	New Order (London)
2	5	SHE'S GOT THAT VIBE	R Kelly (Jive)
6	6	OH BABY I...	Eternal (EMI)
9	7	ALL I WANNA DO	Sheryl Crow (A&M)
4	8	ALWAYS	Bon Jovi (Jambco)
3	9	SWEETNESS	Michelle Gayle (RCA)
-	10	SIGHT FOR SORE EYES	M People (deConstruction)
13	11	IF ONLY I KNEW	Tom Jones (ZTT)
5	12	SATURDAY NIGHT	Whigfield (Systematic)
7	13	WELCOME TO TOMORROW	Snap featuring Summer (Arista)
10	14	THIS DJ	Warren G (Island)
14	15	SOME GIRLS	Ultimate Kaos (Wild Card)
-	16	END OF THE CENTURY	Blur (Food)
17	17	ONE LAST LOVE SONG	Beautiful South (Go! Discs)
15	18	BANG AND BLAME	REM (Warner Bros.)
30	19	NOE OF YOUR BUSINESS	Salt 'N' Pepa (ffrr)
18	20	CIRCLE OF LIFE	Elton John (Rocket)
-	21	THE WILD ONES	Suede (Nude)
11	22	WHEN WE DANCE	Sting (A&M)
16	23	STAY (I MISSED YOU)	Lisa Loeb & Nine Stories (RCA)
-	24	WE HAVE ALL THE TIME IN THE WORLD	Louis Armstrong (EMI)
-	25	AND SO IS LOVE	Kate Bush (EMI)
-	26	HALF THE MAN	Jamiroquai (Sony Soho Square)
24	27	STARS	China Black (Wild Card)
12	28	HEY NOW (GIRLS JUST WANT TO HAVE...)	Cyndi Lauper (Epic)
19	29	MELODY OF LOVE (WANNA BE BELOVED)	Donna Summer (Mercury)
42	30	THINK TWICE	Celine Dion (Epic)
35	31	YOU CAN GO YOUR OWN WAY	Chris Rea (East West)
20	32	CRAZY	Aerosmith (Geffen)
21	33	SPEND SOME TIME	Brand New Heavies (Acid Jazz)
31	34	SMALL BIT OF LOVE	Saw Doctors (Smalltown)
27	35	SECRET	Madonna (Maverick)
29	36	TAKE THIS TIME	Sean Maguire (Parlophone)
32	37	YOU NEVER LOVE THE SAME WAY TWICE	Rozalla (Epic)
22	38	SURE	Take That (RCA)
-	39	LET'S GET TATTOOS	Carter USM (Chrysalis)
-	40	DON'T BRING ME DOWN	Spirits (MCA)
48	41	PUSH	Moist (Chrysalis)
-	42	GIRL, YOU'LL BE A WOMAN SOON	Urge Overkill (MCA)
26	43	RHYTHM OF THE NIGHT	Corona (WEA)
36	44	OCEAN PIE	Shed Seven (Polydor)
23	45	SEVENTEEN	Let Loose (Mercury)
33	46	ALICE, WHAT'S THE MATTER	Terrorvision (Total Vegas)
-	47	THE MORE I GET, THE MORE I WANT	KWS & Teddy Prendergrass (X-Clusive)
-	48	SLEEP WELL TONIGHT	Gene (Costermonger)
47	49	IT AIN'T A CRIME	House Of Pain (XL)
-	50	YOUR LOVING ARMS	Billie Ray Martin (Magnet)

The Equals had taken *Baby Come Back* to Number One in 1968 – toppling the Rolling Stones in the process. Pato Banton had a little help from members of UB40. Other reminders of the sixties were Paul Weller's cover of *Sexy Sadie* (John Lennon's song about the Mahareshi) and the evergreen Tom Jones.

November – December 1994

26 November 1994

last	this	title	artist (label)
1	1	BABY COME BACK	Pato Banton (Virgin)
3	2	LET ME BE YOUR FANTASY	Baby D (Systematic)
2	3	ANOTHER NIGHT	MC Sar & The Real McCoy (Logic)
24	4	WE HAVE ALL THE TIME IN THE WORLD	Louis Armstrong (EMI)
7	5	ALL I WANNA DO	Sheryl Crow (A&M)
6	6	OH BABY I...	Eternal (EMI)
10	7	SIGHT FOR SORE EYES	M People (deConstruction)
5	8	SHE'S GOT THAT VIBE	R Kelly (Jive)
4	9	TRUE FAITH '94	New Order (London)
-	10	SPIN THE BLACK CIRCLE	Pearl Jam (Epic)
8	11	ALWAYS	Bon Jovi (Jambco)
-	12	PUT YOURSELF IN MY PLACE	Kylie Minogue (deConstruction)
9	13	SWEETNESS	Michelle Gayle (RCA)
12	14	SATURDAY NIGHT	Whigfield (Systematic)
-	15	YOU WANT THIS	Jant Jackson (Virgin)
11	16	IF ONLY I KNEW	Tom Jones (ZTT)
-	17	CROCODILE SHOES	Jimmy Nail (East West)
26	18	HALF THE MAN	Jamiroquai (Sony Soho Square)
30	19	THINK TWICE	Celine Dion (Epic)
13	20	WELCOME TO TOMORROW	Snap featuring Summer (Arista)
16	21	END OF THE CENTURY	Blur (Food)
14	22	THIS DJ	Warren G (Island)
-	23	THANK YOU FOR HEARING ME	Sinead O'Connor (Ensign)
17	24	ONE LAST LOVE SONG	Beautiful South (Go! Discs)
20	25	CIRCLE OF LIFE	Elton John (Rocket)
15	26	SOME GIRLS	Ultimate Kaos (Wild Card)
-	27	ON BENDED KNEE	Boyz II Men (Motown)
39	28	LET'S GET TATTOOS	Carter USM (Chrysalis)
-	29	HAPPINESS	Roger Taylor (Parlophone)
-	30	SHORT DICK MAN	20 Fingers featuring Gillette (Multiply)
-	31	SURE SHOT	Beastie Boys (Capitol)
27	32	STARS	China Black (Wild Card)
19	33	NOE OF YOUR BUSINESS	Salt 'N' Pepa (ffrr)
18	34	BANG AND BLAME	REM (Warner Bros.)
-	35	I GET LIFTED	Barbara Tucker (Positiva)
21	36	THE WILD ONES	Suede (Nude)
25	37	AND SO IS LOVE	Kate Bush (EMI)
23	38	STAY (I MISSED YOU)	Lisa Loeb & Nine Stories (RCA)
28	39	HEY NOW (GIRLS JUST WANT TO HAVE...)	Cyndi Lauper (Epic)
40	40	DON'T BRING ME DOWN	Spirits (MCA)
-	41	DON'T TELL ME NO	Sophie B Hawkins (Columbia)
-	42	LOVE THE ONE YOU'RE WITH	Luther Vandross (Epic)
-	43	THE SUNSHINE AFTER THE RAIN	New Atlantic/U4EA featuring Berri (ffrreedom)
42	44	GIRL, YOU'LL BE A WOMAN SOON	Urge Overkill (MCA)
50	45	YOUR LOVING ARMS	Billie Ray Martin (Magnet)
22	46	WHEN WE DANCE	Sting (A&M)
37	47	YOU NEVER LOVE THE SAME WAY TWICE	Rozalla (Epic)
31	48	YOU CAN GO YOUR OWN WAY	Chris Rea (East West)
-	49	EVERY WOMAN KNOWS	Lulu (Dome)
47	50	THE MORE I GET, THE MORE I LOVE	KWS & Teddy Prendergrass (X-Clusive)

3 December 1994

last	this	title	artist (label)
2	1	LET ME BE YOUR FANTASY	Baby D (Systematic)
-	2	LOVE SPREADS	Stone Roses (Geffen)
1	3	BABY COME BACK	Pato Banton (Virgin)
3	4	ANOTHER NIGHT	MC Sar & The Real McCoy (Logic)
4	5	WE HAVE ALL THE TIME IN THE WORLD	Louis Armstrong (EMI)
5	6	ALL I WANNA DO	Sheryl Crow (A&M)
17	7	CROCODILE SHOES	Jimmy Nail (East West)
7	8	SIGHT FOR SORE EYES	M People (deConstruction)
6	9	OH BABY I...	Eternal (EMI)
-	10	STAY ANOTHER DAY	East 17 (London)
-	11	PUT YOURSELF IN MY PLACE	Kylie Minogue (deConstruction)
9	12	TRUE FAITH '94	New Order (London)
10	13	SPIN THE BLACK CIRCLE	Pearl Jam (Epic)
11	14	ALWAYS	Bon Jovi (Jambco)
8	15	SHE'S GOT THAT VIBE	R Kelly (Jive)
15	16	YOU WANT THIS	Jant Jackson (Virgin)
23	17	THANK YOU FOR HEARING ME	Sinead O'Connor (Ensign)
18	18	HALF THE MAN	Jamiroquai (Sony Soho Square)
-	19	HOLD ME, THRILL ME, KISS ME	Gloria Estefan (Epic)
19	20	THINK TWICE	Celine Dion (Epic)
-	21	TEXAS COWBOYS	Grid (deConstruction)
14	22	SATURDAY NIGHT	Whigfield (Systematic)
-	23	I LOVE SATURDAY (EP)	Erasure (Mute)
30	24	SHORT DICK MAN	20 Fingers featuring Gillette (Multiply)
13	25	SWEETNESS	Michelle Gayle (RCA)
-	26	RAISE YOUR HANDS	Reel 2 Real featuring the mad Stuntman (Positiva)
27	27	ON BENDED KNEE	Boyz II Men (Motown)
22	28	THIS DJ	Warren G (Island)
43	29	THE SUNSHINE AFTER THE RAIN	New Atlantic/U4EA featuring Berri (ffrreedom)
31	30	ETERNAL LOVE	PJ & Duncan (XSRhythm)
31	31	SURE SHOT	Beastie Boys (Capitol)
-	32	LOVE SHOULDA BROUGHT YOU HOME	Toni Braxton (LaFace)
41	33	DON'T TELL ME NO	Sophie B Hawkins (Columbia)
42	34	LOVE THE ONE YOU'RE WITH	Luther Vandross (Epic)
-	35	RUN TO YOU	Roxette (EMI)
38	36	LET'S GET TATTOOS	Carter USM (Chrysalis)
16	37	IF ONLY I KNEW	Tom Jones (ZTT)
-	38	ODE TO MY FAMILY	Cranberries (Island)
-	39	RESTLESS	Status Quo (Polydor)
20	40	WELCOME TO TOMORROW	Snap featuring Summer (Arista)
-	41	ABC AND D	Blue Bamboo (Escapade)
-	42	INNER CITY LIFE	Goldie Presents Metalheads (ffrr)
21	43	END OF THE CENTURY	Blur (Food)
-	44	TRUE LOVE ALWAYS	David Essex with Catherine Zeta Jones (PolyGram TV)
39	45	HEY NOW (GIRLS JUST WANT TO HAVE...)	Cyndi Lauper (Epic)
29	46	HAPPINESS	Roger Taylor (Parlophone)
35	47	I GET LIFTED	Barbara Tucker (Positiva)
25	48	CIRCLE OF LIFE	Elton John (Rocket)
44	49	GIRL, YOU'LL BE A WOMAN SOON	Urge Overkill (MCA)
-	50	CRY FOR ME	Roachford (Columbia)

10 December 1994

last	this	title	artist (label)
10	1	STAY ANOTHER DAY	East 17 (London)
1	2	LET ME BE YOUR FANTASY	Baby D (Systematic)
2	3	LOVE SPREADS	Stone Roses (Geffen)
5	4	WE HAVE ALL THE TIME IN THE WORLD	Louis Armstrong (EMI)
7	5	CROCODILE SHOES	Jimmy Nail (East West)
4	6	ANOTHER NIGHT	MC Sar & the Real McCoy (Logic)
3	7	BABY COME BACK	Pato Banton (Virgin)
6	8	ALL I WANNA DO	Sheryl Crow (A&M)
19	9	HOLD ME, THRILL ME, KISS ME	Gloria Estefan (Epic)
-	10	ALL I WANT FOR CHRISTMAS IS YOU	Mariah Carey (Epic)
8	11	SIGHT FOR SORE EYES	M People (deConstruction)
11	12	PUT YOURSELF IN MY PLACE	Kylie Minogue (deConstruction)
-	13	LOVE ME FOR A REASON	Boyzone (Polydor)
-	14	ALL I HAVE TO DO IS DREAM/MISS YOU NIGHTS	Cliff Richard (featuring Phil Everly) (EMI)
-	15	ANOTHER DAY	Whigfield (Systematic)
20	16	THINK TWICE	Celine Dion (Epic)
9	17	OH BABY I...	Eternal (EMI)
17	18	THANK YOU FOR HEARING ME	Sinead O'Connor (Ensign)
30	19	ETERNAL LOVE	PJ & Duncan (XSRhythm)
14	20	ALWAYS	Bon Jovi (Jambco)
21	21	TEXAS COWBOYS	Grid (deConstruction)
26	22	RAISE YOUR HANDS	Reel 2 Real featuring the mad Stuntman (Positiva)
35	23	RUN TO YOU	Roxette (EMI)
23	24	I LOVE SATURDAY (EP)	Erasure (Mute)
15	25	SHE'S GOT THAT VIBE	R Kelly (Jive)
41	26	ABC AND D	Blue Bamboo (Escapade)
27	27	SATURDAY NIGHT	Whigfield (Systematic)
18	28	HALF THE MAN	Jamiroquai (Sony Soho Square)
12	29	TRUE FAITH '94	New Order (London)
38	30	ODE TO MY FAMILY	Cranberries (Island)
-	31	BE HAPPY	Mary J Blige (MCA)
32	32	LOVE SHOULDA BROUGHT YOU HOME	Toni Braxton (LaFace)
24	33	SHORT DICK MAN	20 Fingers/ Gillette (Multiply)
29	34	THE SUNSHINE AFTER THE RAIN	New Atlantic/U4EA featuring Berri (ffrreedom)
25	35	SWEETNESS	Michelle Gayle (RCA)
16	36	YOU WANT THIS	Jant Jackson (Virgin)
34	37	LOVE THE ONE YOU'RE WITH	Luther Vandross (Epic)
33	38	DON'T TELL ME NO	Sophie B Hawkins (Columbia)
13	39	SPIN THE BLACK CIRCLE	Pearl Jam (Epic)
-	40	ONE MORE CHANCE	EYC (MCA)
27	41	ON BENDED KNEE	Boyz II Men (Motown)
-	42	OUT OF TEARS	Rolling Stones (Virgin)
-	43	PASSING STRANGERS	Joe Longthorne & Liz Dawn (EMI)
-	44	YABBA DABBA DOO	Darkman (Wild Card)
-	45	GUAGLIONE	Perez Prado (RCA)
42	46	INNER CITY LIFE	Goldie Presents Metalheads (ffrr)
44	47	TRUE LOVE ALWAYS	David Essex with Catherine Zeta Jones (PolyGram TV)
-	48	(I'M GONNA) CRY MYSELF BLIND	Primal Scream (Creation)
-	49	BORN TO RAISE HELL	Motorhead with Ice-T & Whitfield Crane (Arista)
-	50	INTERSTATE LOVE SONG	Stone Temple Pilots (East West)

Love Spreads was the single off the Stone Roses very long-awaited second album *Second Coming* – coming five years after their first. Jimmy Nail charted with the title song of his TV series about a Geordie singer struggling to make it in the big bad music biz. Kylie Minogue's hit was a cover of an Isley Brothers song.

December 1994

last this
week

17 December 1994

1	1	STAY ANOTHER DAY	East 17 (London)
-	2	POWER RANGERS	
			Mighty Morph'n Power Rangers (RCA)
10	3	ALL I WANT FOR CHRISTMAS IS YOU	
			Mariah Carey (Epic)
13	4	LOVE ME FOR A REASON	Boyzone (Polydor)
5	5	CROCODILE SHOES	Jimmy Nail (East West)
4	6	WE HAVE ALL THE TIME IN THE WORLD	
			Louis Armstrong (EMI)
2	7	LET ME BE YOUR FANTASY	Baby D (Systematic)
16	8	THINK TWICE	Celine Dion (Epic)
14	9	ALL I HAVE TO DO IS DREAM/MISS YOU	
		NIGHTS	Cliff Richard (featuring Phil Everly) (EMI)
-	10	PLEASE COME HOME FOR CHRISTMAS	
			Bon Jovi (Jambco)
-	11	COTTON EYE JOE	Rednex (Internal Affairs)
15	12	ANOTHER DAY	Whigfield (Systematic)
6	13	ANOTHER NIGHT	
			MC Sar & The Real McCoy (Logic)
9	14	HOLD ME, THRILL ME, KISS ME	
			Gloria Estefan (Epic)
-	15	TAKE A BOW	Madonna (Maverick)
19	16	ETERNAL LOVE	PJ & Duncan (XSRhythm)
7	17	BABY COME BACK	Pato Banton (Virgin)
12	18	PUT YOURSELF IN MY PLACE	
			Kylie Minogue (deConstruction)
3	19	LOVE SPREADS	Stone Roses (Geffen)
8	20	ALL I WANNA DO	Sheryl Crow (A&M)
11	21	SIGHT FOR SORE EYES	
			M People (deConstruction)
18	22	THANK YOU FOR HEARING ME	
			Sinead O'Connor (Ensign)
17	23	OH BABY I...	Eternal (EMI)
20	24	ALWAYS	Bon Jovi (Jambco)
24	25	I LOVE SATURDAY (EP)	Erasure (Mute)
21	26	TEXAS COWBOYS	Grid (deConstruction)
27	27	SATURDAY NIGHT	Whigfield (Systematic)
40	28	ONE MORE CHANCE	EYC (MCA)
22	29	RAISE YOUR HANDS	Reel 2 Real
			featuring the mad Stuntman (Positiva)
23	30	RUN TO YOU	Roxette (EMI)
-	31	I'LL FIND YOU	Michelle Gale (RCA)
-	32	SWEET LOVE	M-Beat featuring Nazlyn (Renk)
-	33	I WANT TO BE ALONE	2wo Third3 (Epic)
42	34	OUT OF TEARS	Rolling Stones (Virgin)
30	35	ODE TO MY FAMILY	Cranberries (Island)
26	36	ABC AND D	Blue Bamboo (Escapade)
34	37	THE SUNSHINE AFTER THE RAIN	
			New Atlantic/U4EA featuring Berri (ffrreedom)
31	38	BE HAPPY	Mary J Blige (MCA)
35	39	SWEETNESS	Michelle Gayle (RCA)
43	40	PASSING STRANGERS	
			Joe Longthorne & Liz Dawn (EMI)
25	41	SHE'S GOT THAT VIBE	R Kelly (Jive)
45	42	GUAGLIONE	Perez Prado (RCA)
-	43	WHEN I'M CLEANING WINDOWS	
			2 In A Tent (Silly Money)
-	44	DARKHEART	Bomb The Bass (Stoned Heights)
-	45	GALLOWS POLE	
			Jimmy Page & RobertPlant (Fontana)
28	46	HALF THE MAN	Jamiroquai (Sony Soho Square)
48	47	(I'M GONNA) CRY MYSELF BLIND	
			Primal Scream (Creation)
29	48	TRUE FAITH '94	New Order (London)
-	49	NOTHING BUT LOVE	Optimystic (WEA)
-	50	LET THE HEALING BEGIN	Joe Cocker (Capitol)

24 December 1994

1	1	STAY ANOTHER DAY	East 17 (London)
3	2	ALL I WANT FOR CHRISTMAS IS YOU	
			Mariah Carey (Epic)
4	3	LOVE ME FOR A REASON	Boyzone (Polydor)
2	4	POWER RANGERS	
			Mighty Morph'n Power Rangers (RCA)
5	5	CROCODILE SHOES	Jimmy Nail (East West)
8	6	THINK TWICE	Celine Dion (Epic)
10	7	PLEASE COME HOME FOR CHRISTMAS	
			Bon Jovi (Jambco)
11	8	COTTON EYE JOE	Rednex (Internal Affairs)
6	9	WE HAVE ALL THE TIME IN THE WORLD	
			Louis Armstrong (EMI)
7	10	LET ME BE YOUR FANTASY	
			Baby D (Systematic)
-	11	THEM GIRLS, THEM GIRLS	Zig & Zag (RCA)
12	12	ANOTHER DAY	Whigfield (Systematic)
14	13	HOLD ME, THRILL ME, KISS ME	
			Gloria Estefan (Epic)
9	14	ALL I HAVE TO DO IS DREAM/MISS YOU	
		NIGHTS	Cliff Richard (featuring Phil Everly) (EMI)
15	15	TAKE A BOW	Madonna (Maverick)
-	16	CRAZY (EP)	Eternal (EMI)
16	17	ETERNAL LOVE	PJ & Duncan (XSRhythm)
17	18	BABY COME BACK	Pato Banton (Virgin)
13	19	ANOTHER NIGHT	
			MC Sar & The Real McCoy (Logic)
32	20	SWEET LOVE	M-Beat featuring Nazlyn (Renk)
18	21	PUT YOURSELF IN MY PLACE	
			Kylie Minogue (deConstruction)
31	22	I'LL FIND YOU	Michelle Gale (RCA)
23	23	OH BABY I...	Eternal (EMI)
20	24	ALL I WANNA DO	Sheryl Crow (A&M)
24	25	ALWAYS	Bon Jovi (Jambco)
27	26	SATURDAY NIGHT	Whigfield (Systematic)
33	27	IWANT TO BE ALONE	2wo Third3 (Epic)
21	28	SIGHT FOR SORE EYES	
			M People (deConstruction)
28	29	ONE MORE CHANCE	EYC (MCA)
19	30	LOVE SPREADS	Stone Roses (Geffen)
22	31	THANK YOU FOR HEARING ME	
			Sinead O'Connor (Ensign)
43	32	WHEN I'M CLEANING WINDOWS	
			2 In A Tent (Silly Money)
25	33	I LOVE SATURDAY (EP)	Erasure (Mute)
-	34	WHIGGLE IN LINE	Black Duck (Flying South)
45	35	GALLOWS POLE	
			Jimmy Page & RobertPlant (Fontana)
-	36	DOLLARS	CJ Lewis (MCA)
44	37	DARKHEART	Bomb The Bass (Stoned Heights)
34	38	OUT OF TEARS	Rolling Stones (Virgin)
50	39	LET THE HEALING BEGIN	Joe Cocker (Capitol)
39	40	SWEETNESS	Michelle Gayle (RCA)
-	41	U SURE DO	Strike (Fresh)
-	42	RIVERDANCE	Bill Whelan (Son)
29	43	RAISE YOUR HANDS	Reel 2 Real
			featuring the mad Stuntman (Positiva)
26	44	TEXAS COWBOYS	Grid (deConstruction)
42	45	GUAGLIONE	Perez Prado (RCA)
30	46	RUN TO YOU	Roxette (EMI)
37	47	THE SUNSHINE AFTER THE RAIN	
			New Atlantic/U4EA featuring Berri (ffrreedom)
-	48	HIBERNACULUM	Mike Oldfield (WEA)
36	49	ABC AND D	Blue Bamboo (Escapade)
-	50	TRYIN' TO GET THE FEELING	
		AGAIN	Carpenters (A&M)

East 17 stayed at Number One for Christmas and appeared on TV in
white parkas, round a white grand piano. Very touching. For the oldies
there was Louis Armstrong and for the kids, the awful Power Rangers.

Title Index

This index is intended as a guide to locating records in the charts in this book. It is not an exhaustive guide to record titles and artist names. Records are repeated only if they have are re-issued and have a chart-run significantly after their first issue. Titles that begin with numerals are placed at the end of the index.

Artist Index

The Artist Index is arranged in order of the first name of the group or artist, so for Elvis Presley, look under 'E'. *Group names that begin with numerals are placed at the end of the index.*

Artist index

Beatles PLEASE PLEASE ME 02/02/63
Beatles FROM ME TO YOU 20/04/63
Beatles TWIST AND SHOUT (EP) 20/07/63
Beatles SHE LOVES YOU 31/08/63
Beatles THE BEATLES' HITS (EP) 02/11/63
Beatles THE BEATLES NO. 1 (EP) 16/11/63
Beatles WITH THE BEATLES (LP) 30/11/63
Beatles I WANT TO HOLD YOUR HAND 07/12/63
Beatles ALL MY LOVING (EP) 08/02/64
Beatles CAN'T BUY ME LOVE 28/03/64
Beatles AIN'T SHE SWEET 06/06/64
Beatles LONG TALL SALLY (EP) 04/07/64
Beatles A HARD DAY'S NIGHT 18/07/64
Beatles A HARD DAY'S NIGHT (LP) 18/07/64
Beatles I FEEL FINE 05/12/64
Beatles BEATLES FOR SALE (LP) 12/12/64
Beatles TICKET TO RIDE 17/04/65
Beatles HELP! 31/07/65
Beatles HELP! (LP) 14/08/65
Beatles DAY TRIPPER/WE CAN WORK IT OUT 11/12/65
Beatles PAPERBACK WRITER 18/06/66
Beatles REVOLVER (LP) 13/08/66
Beatles YELLOW SUBMARINE/ELEANOR RIGBY 13/08/66
Beatles PENNY LANE/STRAWBERRY FIELDS FOREVER 25/02/67
Beatles SGT. PEPPER'S LONELY HEARTS CLUB BAND (LP) 03/06/67
Beatles ALL YOU NEED IS LOVE 15/07/67
Beatles HELLO GOODBYE 02/12/67
Beatles MAGICAL MYSTERY TOUR (EP) 16/12/67
Beatles LADY MADONNA 23/03/68
Beatles HEY JUDE 07/09/68
Beatles THE BEATLES (LP) 30/11/68
Beatles GET BACK 26/04/69
Beatles THE BALLAD OF JOHN AND YOKO 07/06/69
Beatles SOMETHING 08/11/69
Beatles LET IT BE 14/03/70
Beatles YESTERDAY 20/3/76
Beatles BACK IN THE U.S.S.R. 17/7/76
Beatles THE BEATLES MOVIE MEDLEY 12/06/82
Beatles LOVE ME DO 17/10/92
Beatmasters featuring Betty Boo HEY DJ/I CAN'T DANCE TO THE MUSIC YOU'RE PLAYING 12/08/89
Beatmasters featuring Claudia Fontaine WARM LOVE 09/12/89
Beatmasters featuring Elaine Vassell DUNNO WHAT IT IS (ABOUT YOU) 30/05/92
Beatmasters featuring P.P. Arnold BURN IT UP 24/09/88
Beatmasters with Merlin WHO'S IN THE HOUSE 22/04/89
Beats International WON'T TALK ABOUT IT 12/05/90
Beats International IN THE GHETTO 07/12/91
Beats International featuring Janet Kay BURUNDI BLUES 15/09/90
Beats International featuring Lindy Layton DUB BE GOOD TO ME 10/02/90
Beautiful South SONG FOR WHOEVER 03/06/89
Beautiful South YOU KEEP IT ALL IN 23/09/89
Beautiful South I'LL SAIL THIS SHIP ALONE 02/12/89
Beautiful South A LITTLE TIME 13/10/90
Beautiful South MY BOOK 08/12/90
Beautiful South LET LOVE SPEAK UP FOR ITSELF 23/03/91
Beautiful South OLD RED EYES IS BACK 11/01/92
Beautiful South WE ARE EACH OTHER 14/03/92
Beautiful South BELL BOTTOMED TEAR 13/06/92
Beautiful South 36D 26/09/92
Beautiful South GOOD AS GOLD 12/03/94
Beautiful South EVERYBODY'S TALKIN' 04/06/94
Beautiful South PRETTIEST EYES 03/09/94
Beautiful South ONE LAST LOVE SONG 12/11/94
Beck LOSER 05/03/94
Bedrocks OB-LA-DI, OB-LA-DA 21/12/68
Bee Gees NEW YORK MINING DISASTER 1941 06/05/67
Bee Gees MASSACHUSETTS 16/09/67
Bee Gees WORLD 25/11/67
Bee Gees WORDS 03/02/68
Bee Gees JUMBO 20/04/68
Bee Gees I'VE GOTTA MESSAGE TO YOU 10/08/68
Bee Gees FIRST OF MAY 01/03/69
Bee Gees TOMORROW TOMORROW 14/06/69
Bee Gees DON'T FORGET TO REMEMBER 23/08/69
Bee Gees LONELY DAYS 26/12/70
Bee Gees MY WORLD 5/2/72
Bee Gees RUN TO ME 12/8/72
Bee Gees JIVE TALKIN' 05/07/75
Bee Gees YOU SHOULD BE DANCING 7/8/76
Bee Gees HOW DEEP IS YOUR LOVE 5/11/77
Bee Gees STAYIN' ALIVE 11/2/78
Bee Gees NIGHT FEVER 15/4/78
Bee Gees TOO MUCH HEAVEN 2/12/78
Bee Gees TRAGEDY 24/2/79
Bee Gees LOVE YOU INSIDE OUT 21/4/79
Bee Gees SOMEONE BELONGING TO SOMEONE 01/10/83
Bee Gees YOU WIN AGAIN 03/10/87
Bee Gees ORDINARY LIVES 22/04/89
Bee Gees SECRET LOVE 09/03/91
Bee Gees PAYING THE PRICE OF LOVE 21/08/93
Bee Gees FOR WHOM THE BELL TOLLS 27/11/93
Bee Gees HOW TO FALL IN LOVE PART 1 16/04/94
BEF featuring Lalah Hathaway FAMILY AFFAIR 03/08/91
Beggar & Co. (SOMEBODY) HELP ME OUT 28/02/81
Beijing Spring I WANNA BE IN LOVE AGAIN 30/01/93
Belinda Carlisle HEAVEN IS A PLACE ON EARTH 19/12/87
Belinda Carlisle I GET WEAK 05/03/88
Belinda Carlisle CIRCLE IN THE SAND 14/05/88
Belinda Carlisle WORLD WITHOUT YOU 17/09/88
Belinda Carlisle LOVE NEVER DIES 17/12/88
Belinda Carlisle LEAVE A LIGHT ON 07/10/89
Belinda Carlisle LA LUNA 16/12/89
Belinda Carlisle RUNAWAY HORSES 03/03/90
Belinda Carlisle VISION OF YOU 02/06/90
Belinda Carlisle (WE WANT) THE SAME THING 20/10/90
Belinda Carlisle SUMMER RAIN 05/01/91
Belinda Carlisle LIVE YOUR LIFE BE FREE 28/09/91
Belinda Carlisle DO YOU FEEL LIKE I FEEL? 16/11/91
Belinda Carlisle HALF THE WORLD 18/01/92
Belinda Carlisle LITTLE BLACK BOOK 29/08/92
Belinda Carlisle BIG SCARY ANIMAL 25/09/93
Belinda Carlisle LAY DOWN YOUR ARMS 27/11/93
Bell Biv Devoe POISON 21/07/90
Bell Biv Devoe DO ME! 29/09/90
Bellamy Brothers LET YOUR LOVE FLOW 1/5/76
Bellamy Brothers IF I SAID YOU HAD A BEAUTIFUL BODY WOULD YOU HOLD IT AGAINST ME 1/9/79
Belle Stars IKO IKO 19/06/82
Belle Stars THE CLAPPING SONG 07/08/82
Belle Stars SIGN OF THE TIMES 29/01/83
Belle Stars SWEET MEMORY 23/04/83
Belle Stars INDIAN SUMMER 27/08/83
Belle & the Devotions LOVE GAMES 05/05/84
Belly FEED THE TREE 23/01/93
Belouis Some IMAGINATION 04/05/85
Belouis Some SOME PEOPLE 19/04/86
Beloved THE SUN RISING 28/10/89
Beloved HELLO 27/01/90
Beloved YOUR LOVE TAKES ME HIGHER 24/03/90
Beloved TIME AFTER TIME 23/06/90
Beloved IT'S ALRIGHT NOW 17/11/90
Beloved SWEET HARMONY 23/01/93
Beloved YOU'VE GOT ME THINKING 10/04/93
Beloved OUTER SPACE GIRL 14/08/93
Ben E. King FIRST TASTE OF LOVE 04/02/61
Ben E. King STAND BY ME 01/07/61
Ben E. King AMOR 30/09/61
Ben E. King STAND BY ME 14/02/87
Ben Liebrand/Jeff Wayne THE EVE OF THE WAR 25/11/89
Benny Hill GATHER IN THE MUSHROOMS 25/02/61
Benny Hill TRANSISTOR RADIO 10/06/61
Benny Hill HARVEST OF LOVE 25/05/63
Benny Hill ERNIE (THE FASTEST MILKMAN IN THE WEST) 13/11/71
Benny Hill ERNIE (THE FASTEST MILKMAN IN THE WEST) 30/05/92
Berlin TAKE MY BREATH AWAY 25/10/86
Berlin YOU DON'T KNOW 24/01/87
Berlin LIKE FLAMES 21/03/87
Bern Elliott & the Fenmen MONEY 23/11/63
Bernard Bresslaw MAD PASSIONATE LOVE 06/09/58
Bernard Cribbins A HOLE IN THE GROUND 24/02/62
Bernard Cribbins RIGHT SAID FRED 07/07/62
Bernard Cribbins GOSSIP CALYPSO 15/12/62
Berni Flint I DON'T WANT TO PUT A HOLD ON YOU 26/3/77
Bert Kaempfert BYE BYE BLUES 08/01/66
Bert Kaempfert BYE BYE BLUES 29/01/66
Bert Weedon GUITAR BOOGIE SHUFFLE 16/05/59
Bert Weedon NASHVILLE BOOGIE 21/11/59
Bert Weedon SORRY ROBBIE 05/11/60
Bert Weedon GINCHY 11/02/61
Beryl Marsden WHO YOU GONNA HURT 13/11/65
Bette Bright HELLO I AM YOUR HEART 22/03/80
Bette Midler THE WIND BENEATH MY WINGS 24/06/89
Bette Midler FROM A DISTANCE 20/10/90
Betty Boo DOIN' THE BOO 26/05/90
Betty Boo WHERE ARE YOU BABY? 11/08/90
Betty Boo 24 HOURS 01/12/90
Betty Boo LET ME TAKE YOU THERE 08/08/92
Betty Boo I'M ON MY WAY 03/10/92
Betty Everett GETTING MIGHTY CROWDED 16/01/65
Betty Everett IT'S IN HIS KISS 02/11/68
Betty Wright SHOORAH! SHOORAH! 1/2/75
Betty Wright WHERE IS THE LOVE 3/5/75
Betty Wright PAIN 15/02/86
Beverley Craven PROMISE ME 04/05/91
Beverley Craven HOLDING ON 27/07/91
Beverley Craven WOMAN TO WOMAN 12/10/91
Beverley Craven LOVE SCENES 25/09/93
Beverley Sisters I SAW MOMMY KISSING SANTA CLAUS 28/11/53
Beverley Sisters WILLIE CAN 14/04/56
Beverley Sisters I DREAMED 02/02/57
Beverley Sisters THE LITTLE DRUMMER BOY 14/02/59
Beverley Sisters LITTLE DONKEY 21/11/59
Beverley Sisters GREEN FIELDS 02/07/60
Bible GRACELAND 27/05/89
Bible HONEY BE GOOD 09/09/89
Biddu Orchestra SUMMER OF '42 16/8/75
Big Audio Dynamite E=MC2 29/03/86
Big Audio Dynamite MEDICINE SHOW 14/06/86
Big Audio Dynamite C'MON EVERY BEATBOX 18/10/86
Big Audio Dynamite V THIRTEEN 28/02/87
Big Audio Dynamite JUST PLAY MUSIC 11/06/88
Big Ben Banjo Band LET'S GET TOGETHER NO.1 11/12/54
Big Ben Banjo Band LET'S GET TOGETHER AGAIN 10/12/55
Big Bopper CHANTILLY LACE 27/12/58
Big Country FIELDS OF FIRE (400 MILES) 02/04/83
Big Country IN A BIG COUNTRY 28/05/83
Big Country CHANCE 03/09/83
Big Country WONDERLAND 21/01/84
Big Country EAST OF EDEN 29/09/84
Big Country WHERE THE ROSE IS SOWN 01/12/84
Big Country JUST A SHADOW 26/01/85
Big Country LOOK AWAY 12/04/86
Big Country THE TEACHER 21/06/86
Big Country ONE GREAT THING 27/09/86
Big Country HOLD THE HEART 29/11/86
Big Country KING OF EMOTION 20/08/88
Big Country BROKEN HEART (THIRTEEN VALLEYS) 05/11/88
Big Country PEACE IN OUR TIME 04/02/89
Big Country SAVE ME 19/05/90
Big Country REPUBLICAN PARTY PEOPLE 31/08/91
Big Country ALONE 13/03/93
Big Country SHIPS (WHERE WERE YOU) 01/05/93
Big Daddy DANCING IN THE DARK (EP) 23/03/85
Big Daddy Kane THE WRATH OF KANE 20/05/89
Big Daddy Kane AIN'T NO STOPPIN' US NOW 20/01/90
Big Dee Irwin SWINGING ON A STAR 14/12/63
Big Dish MISS AMERICA 19/01/91
Big Fun BLAME IT ON THE BOOGIE 12/08/89
Big Fun CAN'T SHAKE THE FEELING 25/11/89
Big Fun HANDFUL OF PROMISES 17/03/90
Big Fun & Sonia featuring Gary Barnacle YOU'VE GOT A FRIEND 23/06/90
Big Mountain BABY, I LOVE YOUR WAY 04/06/94
Big Mountain SWEET SENSUAL LOVE 24/09/94
Big Sound Authority THIS HOUSE (IS WHERE YOUR LOVE STANDS) 02/02/85
Big Three BY THE WAY 27/07/63
Bill Black's Combo DON'T BE CRUEL 19/11/60
Bill Forbes TOO YOUNG 16/01/60
Bill Haley & His Comets SHAKE RATTLE AND ROLL 18/12/54
Bill Haley & His Comets ROCK AROUND THE CLOCK 08/01/55
Bill Haley & His Comets MAMBO ROCK 16/04/55
Bill Haley & His Comets ROCK A BEATIN' BOOGIE 31/12/55
Bill Haley & His Comets SEE YOU LATER, ALLIGATOR 10/03/56
Bill Haley & His Comets THE SAINTS ROCK 'N' ROLL 26/05/56
Bill Haley & His Comets ROCKIN' THROUGH THE RYE 18/08/56
Bill Haley & His Comets RAZZLE DAZZLE 15/09/56
Bill Haley & His Comets RIP IT UP 10/11/56
Bill Haley & His Comets ROCK 'N' ROLL STAGE SHOW (LP) 10/11/56
Bill Haley & His Comets RUDY'S ROCK 24/11/56
Bill Haley & His Comets ROCK THE JOINT 02/02/57
Bill Haley & His Comets DON'T KNOCK THE ROCK 09/02/57
Bill Haley & His Comets ROCK AROUND THE CLOCK 13/04/68
Bill Haley & His Comets ROCK AROUND THE CLOCK 30/3/74
Bill Hayes BALLAD OF DAVY CROCKETT 07/01/56
Bill Howard KING OF THE COPS 27/12/75
Bill Justis RAUNCHY 11/01/58
Bill Justis RAUNCHY 01/02/58
Bill Lovelady REGGAE FOR IT NOW 1/9/79
Bill Medley HE AIN'T HEAVY HE'S MY BROTHER 03/09/88
Bill Medley & Jennifer Warnes (I'VE HAD THE) TIME OF MY LIFE 07/11/87
Bill Nelson YOUTH OF NATION OF FIRE 20/06/81
Bill Nelson ACCELERATION 22/09/84
Bill Parsons ALL-AMERICAN BOY 11/04/59
Bill Tarmey THE WIND BENEATH MY WINGS 19/02/94
Bill Tarney ONE VOICE 03/04/93
Bill Whelan RIVERDANCE 24/12/94
Bill Withers LEAN ON ME 19/8/72
Bill Withers LOVELY DAY 21/1/78
Bill Withers OH YEAH! 01/06/85
Bill Withers LOVELY DAY 10/09/88
Bill Wyman (SI, SI) JE SUIS UN ROCK STAR 15/08/81
Billie Anthony THIS OLE HOUSE 16/10/54
Billie Davis TELL HIM 09/02/63
Billie Jo Spears BLANKET ON THE GROUND 26/7/75
Billie Jo Spears WHAT I'VE GOT IN MIND 14/8/76
Billie Ray Martin YOUR LOVING ARMS 19/11/94
Billy Bland LET THE LITTLE GIRL DANCE 14/05/60
Billy Bragg BETWEEN THE WARS (EP) 23/02/85
Billy Bragg DAYS LIKE THESE 04/01/86
Billy Bragg LEVI STUBBS' TEARS 28/06/86
Billy Bragg GREETINGS TO THE NEW BRUNETTE 22/11/86
Billy Bragg SEXUALITY 13/07/91
Billy Bragg ACCIDENT WAITING TO HAPPEN 07/03/92
Billy Connolly D.I.V.O.R.C.E. 1/11/75
Billy Connolly NO CHANCE 24/7/76
Billy Connolly SUPER GRAN 16/03/85
Billy Cotton & His Band, vocals by Doreen Stephens IN A GOLDEN COACH 02/05/53
Billy Cotton & His Band, vocals by The Bandits FRIENDS AND NEIGHBOURS 01/05/54
Billy Cotton & His Band, vocals by the Mill Girls & the Bandits I SAW MOMMY KISSING SANTA CLAUS 19/12/53
Billy Eckstine NO ONE BUT YOU 13/11/54
Billy Eckstine GIGI 14/02/59
Billy Eckstine & Sarah Vaughan PASSING STRANGERS 28/09/57
Billy Fury MAYBE TOMORROW 28/02/59
Billy Fury MAYBE TOMORROW 28/03/59
Billy Fury MARGO, DON'T GO 27/06/59
Billy Fury COLETTE 12/03/60
Billy Fury THAT'S LOVE 28/05/60
Billy Fury WONDROUS PLACE 15/10/60
Billy Fury A THOUSAND STARS 21/01/61
Billy Fury HALFWAY TO PARADISE 20/05/61
Billy Fury JEALOUSY 07/09/61
Billy Fury I'D NEVER FIND ANOTHER YOU 16/12/61
Billy Fury LETTER FULL OF TEARS 10/03/62
Billy Fury LAST NIGHT WAS MADE FOR LOVE 12/05/62
Billy Fury ONCE UPON A DREAM 28/07/62
Billy Fury BECAUSE OF LOVE 27/10/62
Billy Fury LIKE I'VE NEVER BEEN GONE 16/02/63
Billy Fury WHEN WILL YOU SAY I LOVE YOU 18/05/63

Eddie Calvert MANDY 08/02/58
Eddie Calvert LITTLE SERENADE 21/06/58
Eddie Cochran SUMMERTIME BLUES 08/11/58
Eddie Cochran C'MON EVERYBODY 14/03/59
Eddie Cochran SOMETHIN' ELSE 11/10/59
Eddie Cochran HALLELUJAH, I LOVE HER SO 23/01/60
Eddie Cochran THREE STEPS TO HEAVEN 14/05/60
Eddie Cochran LONELY 22/10/60
Eddie Cochran WEEKEND 24/06/61
Eddie Cochran JEANNIE JEANNIE JEANNIE 02/12/61
Eddie Cochran MY WAY 04/05/63
Eddie Cochran C'MON EVERYBODY 20/02/88
Eddie Cochran SOMETHIN' ELSE 30/04/88
Eddie Drennon & B.B.S. Unlimited LET'S DO THE LATIN HUSTLE 13/03/76
Eddie Fisher OUTSIDE OF HEAVEN 03/01/53
Eddie Fisher DOWNHEARTED 02/05/53
Eddie Fisher I'M WALKING BEHIND YOU 23/05/53
Eddie Fisher WISH YOU WERE HERE 07/11/53
Eddie Fisher OH MEIN PAPA 23/01/54
Eddie Fisher I NEED YOU NOW 30/10/54
Eddie Fisher WEDDING BELLS 19/03/55
Eddie Fisher CINDY, OH CINDY 24/11/56
Eddie Floyd KNOCK ON WOOD 25/03/67
Eddie Hodges I'M GONNA KNOCK ON YOUR DOOR 23/09/61
Eddie Holman HEY THERE LONELY GIRL 26/10/74
Eddie Kendricks KEEP ON TRUCKIN' 10/11/73
Eddie Reader DEAR JOHN 05/11/94
Eddie & The Hot Rods TEENAGE DEPRESSION 20/11/76
Eddy SOMEDAY 16/07/94
Eddy Arnold MAKE THE WORLD GO AWAY 12/02/66
Eddy Grant LIVING ON THE FRONT LINE 23/6/79
Eddy Grant DO YOU FEEL MY LOVE? 22/11/80
Eddy Grant CAN'T GET ENOUGH OF YOU 02/05/81
Eddy Grant I DON'T WANNA DANCE 23/10/82
Eddy Grant ELECTRIC AVENUE 22/01/83
Eddy Grant WAR PARTY 30/04/83
Eddy Grant TILL I CAN'T TAKE LOVE NO MORE 19/11/83
Eddy Grant GIMME HOPE JO'ANNA 06/02/88
Eddy & the Soulband THEME FROM SHAFT 02/03/85
Edelweiss BRING ME EDELWEISS 06/05/89
Eden Kane WELL I ASK YOU 03/06/61
Eden Kane GET LOST 07/09/61
Eden Kane FORGET ME NOT 20/01/62
Eden Kane I DON'T KNOW WHY 19/05/62
Eden Kane BOYS CRY 15/02/64
Edgar Winter Group FRANKENSTEIN 2/6/73
Edie Brickell GOOD TIMES 01/10/94
Edie Brickell & New Bohemians WHAT I AM 11/02/89
Edison Lighthouse LOVE GROWS 24/01/70
Edison Lighthouse IT'S UP TO YOU PETULA 13/02/71
Edith Piaf MILORD 21/05/60
Edmund Hockridge YOUNG and FOOLISH 18/02/56
Edmund Hockridge NO OTHER LOVE 12/05/56
Edmund Hockridge BY THE FOUNTAINS OF ROME 01/09/56
Edna Savage ARRIVEDERCI DARLING 14/01/56
Edwin Hawkins Singers OH HAPPY DAY 31/05/69
Edwin Starr STOP HER ON SIGHT 04/06/66
Edwin Starr 25 MILES 20/09/69
Edwin Starr WAR 17/10/70
Edwin Starr CONTACT 10/2/79
Edwin Starr H.A.P.P.Y. RADIO 2/6/79
Edwyn Collins DON'T SHILLY-SHALLY 08/08/87
Efua SOMEWHERE 17/07/93
Eighth Wonder I'M NOT SCARED 05/03/88
Eighth Wonder CROSS MY HEART 02/07/88
El Coco COCOMOTION 21/1/78
Elaine Paige MEMORY 20/06/81
Elaine Paige & Barbara Dickson I KNOW HIM SO WELL 26/01/85
Elastica LINE UP 19/02/94
Elastica CONNECTION 22/10/94
Elbow Bones & the Racketeers A NIGHT IN NEW YORK 21/01/84
Electra JIBARO 13/08/88
Electra DESTINY/AUTUMN LOVE 13/01/90
Electribe 101 TELL ME WHEN THE FEVER ENDED 24/02/90
Electribe 101 TALKING WITH MYSELF 24/02/90
Electribe 101 YOU'RE WALKING 29/09/90
Electric Light Orchestra 10538 OVERTURE 5/8/72
Electric Light Orchestra ROLL OVER BEETHOVEN 27/1/73
Electric Light Orchestra SHOW DOWN 13/10/73
Electric Light Orchestra MA-MA-MA-BELLE 16/3/74
Electric Light Orchestra EVIL WOMAN 11/1/76
Electric Light Orchestra LIVIN' THING 20/11/76
Electric Light Orchestra ROCKARIA 26/2/77
Electric Light Orchestra TELEPHONE LINE 28/5/77
Electric Light Orchestra TURN TO STONE 5/11/77
Electric Light Orchestra MR BLUE SKY 28/1/78
Electric Light Orchestra WILD WEST HERO 17/6/78
Electric Light Orchestra SWEET TALKIN' WOMAN 14/10/78
Electric Light Orchestra SHINE A LITTLE LOVE 26/5/79
Electric Light Orchestra THE DIARY OF HORACE WIMP 4/8/79
Electric Light Orchestra DON'T BRING ME DOWN 8/9/79
Electric Light Orchestra CONFUSION 24/11/79
Electric Light Orchestra I'M ALIVE 31/05/80
Electric Light Orchestra ALL OVER THE WORLD 16/08/80
Electric Light Orchestra DON'T WALK AWAY 29/11/80
Electric Light Orchestra HOLD ON TIGHT 08/08/81
Electric Light Orchestra TWILIGHT 31/10/81
Electric Light Orchestra HERE IS THE NEWS 30/01/82
Electric Light Orchestra ROCK 'N' ROLL IS KING 25/06/83
Electric Light Orchestra SECRET MESSAGES 10/09/83

Electric Light Orchestra CALLING AMERICA 08/03/86
Electric Prunes GET ME TO THE WORLD ON TIME 06/05/67
Electronic GETTING AWAY WITH IT 16/12/89
Electronic GET THE MESSAGE 27/04/91
Electronic FEEL EVERY BEAT 21/09/91
Electronic DISAPPOINTED 04/07/92
Electroset HOW DOES IT FEEL? (THEME FROM TECHNO BLUES) 21/11/92
Elegants LITTLE STAR 27/09/58
Elgins HEAVEN MUST HAVE SENT YOU 08/05/71
Elgins PUT YOURSELF IN MY PLACE 13/11/71
Elias & His Zig Zag Jive Flutes TOM HARK 26/04/58
Elkie Brooks PEARL'S A SINGER 9/4/77
Elkie Brooks SUNSHINE AFTER THE RAIN 3/9/77
Elkie Brooks LILAC WINE 11/3/78
Elkie Brooks DON'T CRY OUT LOUD 25/11/78
Elkie Brooks FOOL IF YOU THINK IT'S OVER 06/02/82
Elkie Brooks NO MORE THE FOOL 24/05/58
Ella Fitzgerald SWINGIN' SHEPHERD BLUES 24/05/58
Ella Fitzgerald BUT NOT FOR ME 17/10/59
Ella Fitzgerald MACK THE KNIFE 23/04/60
Ella Fitzgerald CAN'T BUY ME LOVE 09/05/64
Elis Beggs & Howard BIG BUBBLES, NO TROUBLES 09/07/88
Elmer Bernstein STACCATO'S THEME 19/12/59
Elton John YOUR SONG 23/01/71
Elton John ROCKET MAN 22/4/72
Elton John HONKY CAT 09/09/72
Elton John CROCODILE ROCK 27/1/73
Elton John DANIEL 27/1/73
Elton John SATURDAY NIGHT'S ALRIGHT FOR FIGHTING 14/7/73
Elton John GOODBYE YELLOW BRICK ROAD 6/10/73
Elton John STEP INTO CHRISTMAS 15/12/73
Elton John CANDLE IN THE WIND 2/3/74
Elton John DON'T LET THE SUN GO DOWN ON ME 8/6/74
Elton John THE BITCH IS BACK 21/9/74
Elton John LUCY IN THE SKY WITH DIAMONDS 23/11/74
Elton John PHILADELPHIA FREEDOM 15/3/75
Elton John SOMEONE SAVED MY LIFE TONIGHT 05/07/75
Elton John ISLAND GIRL 11/10/75
Elton John PINBALL WIZARD 27/3/76
Elton John SORRY SEEMS TO BE THE HARDEST WORD 20/11/76
Elton John CRAZY WATER 12/3/77
Elton John EGO 22/4/78
Elton John PART TIME LOVE 4/11/78
Elton John SONG FOR GUY 9/12/78
Elton John LITTLE JEANNIE 21/06/80
Elton John BLUE EYES 17/04/82
Elton John I GUESS THAT'S WHY THEY CALL IT THE BLUES 07/05/83
Elton John I'M STILL STANDING 30/07/83
Elton John KISS THE BRIDE 22/10/83
Elton John COLD AS CHRISTMAS 17/12/83
Elton John SAD SONGS (SAY SO MUCH) 02/06/84
Elton John PASSENGERS 18/08/84
Elton John WHO WEARS THESE SHOES 27/10/84
Elton John NIKITA 19/10/85
Elton John WRAP HER UP 14/12/85
Elton John HEARTACHE ALL OVER THE WORLD 11/10/86
Elton John I DON'T WANNA GO ON WITH YOU LIKE THAT 18/06/88
Elton John HEALING HANDS 02/09/89
Elton John SACRIFICE 18/11/89
Elton John SACRIFICE/HEALING HANDS 09/06/90
Elton John CLUB AT THE END OF THE STREET/WHISPERS 18/08/90
Elton John YOU GOTTA LOVE SOMEONE 27/10/90
Elton John THE ONE 06/06/92
Elton John THE LAST SONG 07/11/92
Elton John SIMPLY LIFE 22/05/93
Elton John CAN YOU FEEL THE LOVE TONIGHT 09/07/94
Elton John CIRCLE OF LIFE 08/10/94
Elton John Band featuring John Lennon and the Muscle Shoals Horns I SAW HER STANDING THERE 04/04/81
Elton John & Cliff Richard SLOW RIVERS 27/12/86
Elton John & Eric Clapton RUNAWAY TRAIN 01/08/92
Elton John & Jennifer Rush FLAMES OF PARADISE 27/06/87
Elton John & Kiki Dee DON'T GO BREAKING MY HEART 10/7/76
Elton John & Kiki Dee TRUE LOVE 20/11/93
Elton John & Millie Jackson ACT OF WAR 22/06/85
Elton John & RuPaul DON'T GO BREAKING MY HEART 26/02/94
Elton John/Kiki Dee BITE YOUR LIP/CHICAGO 25/6/77
Elvis Costello WATCHIN' THE DETECTIVES 12/11/77
Elvis Costello (I DON'T WANT TO GO TO) CHELSEA 18/3/78
Elvis Costello PUMP IT UP 10/6/78
Elvis Costello RADIO RADIO 17/2/79
Elvis Costello OLIVER'S ARMY 17/2/79
Elvis Costello I CAN'T STAND UP FOR FALLING DOWN 23/02/80
Elvis Costello HI FIDELITY 26/04/80
Elvis Costello GOOD YEAR FOR THE ROSES 10/10/81
Elvis Costello YOU LITTLE FOOL 26/06/82
Elvis Costello EVERYDAY I WRITE THE BOOK 09/07/83
Elvis Costello I WANNA BE LOVED 23/06/84
Elvis Costello THE ONLY FLAME IN TOWN 25/08/84
Elvis Costello GREEN SHIRT 01/02/86
Elvis Costello DON'T LET ME BE MISUNDERSTOOD 01/02/86
Elvis Costello TOKYO STORM WARNING 30/08/86
Elvis Costello I WANT YOU 15/11/86

Elvis Costello VERONICA 11/03/89
Elvis Costello THE OTHER SIDE OF SUMMER 11/05/91
Elvis Costello SULKY GIRL 05/03/94
Elvis Costello 13 STEPS LEAD DOWN 30/04/94
Elvis Costello HEARTBREAK HOTEL 12/05/56
Elvis Presley BLUE SUEDE SHOES 26/05/56
Elvis Presley I WANT YOU, I NEED YOU, I LOVE YOU 21/07/56
Elvis Presley HOUND DOG 22/09/56
Elvis Presley BLUE MOON 17/11/56
Elvis Presley I DON'T CARE IF THE SUN DON'T SHINE 24/11/56
Elvis Presley LOVE ME TENDER 08/12/56
Elvis Presley MYSTERY TRAIN 16/02/57
Elvis Presley RIP IT UP 09/03/57
Elvis Presley TOO MUCH 11/05/57
Elvis Presley ALL SHOOK UP 15/06/57
Elvis Presley TEDDY BEAR 13/07/57
Elvis Presley PARALYSED 31/08/57
Elvis Presley PARTY 05/10/57
Elvis Presley GOT A LOT O' LIVIN' TO DO 19/10/57
Elvis Presley LOVING YOU 02/11/57
Elvis Presley TRYING TO GET TO YOU 02/11/57
Elvis Presley LAWDY MISS CLAWDY 09/11/57
Elvis Presley SANTA BRING MY BABY BACK TO ME 16/11/57
Elvis Presley I'M LEFT, YOU'RE RIGHT, SHE'S GONE 18/01/58
Elvis Presley JAILHOUSE ROCK 25/01/58
Elvis Presley DON'T 01/03/58
Elvis Presley WEAR MY RING AROUND YOUR NECK 03/05/58
Elvis Presley HARD HEADED WOMAN 26/07/58
Elvis Presley KING CREOLE 04/10/58
Elvis Presley I GOT STUNG/ONE NIGHT 24/01/59
Elvis Presley A FOOL SUCH AS I/I NEED YOUR LOVE TONIGHT 25/04/59
Elvis Presley A BIG HUNK O' LOVE 25/07/59
Elvis Presley STRICTLY ELVIS (EP) 13/02/60
Elvis Presley STUCK ON YOU 09/04/60
Elvis Presley ELVIS IS BACK (LP) 16/07/60
Elvis Presley A MESS OF BLUES 16/07/60
Elvis Presley THE GIRL OF MY BEST FRIEND 30/07/60
Elvis Presley IT'S NOW OR NEVER 05/11/60
Elvis Presley G.I. BLUES (LP) 10/12/60
Elvis Presley ARE YOU LONESOME TONIGHT 21/01/61
Elvis Presley WOODEN HEART 11/03/61
Elvis Presley SURRENDER 27/05/61
Elvis Presley WILD IN THE COUNTRY 07/09/61
Elvis Presley I FEEL SO BAD 16/09/61
Elvis Presley HIS LATEST FLAME 04/11/61
Elvis Presley LITTLE SISTER 04/11/61
Elvis Presley CAN'T HELP FALLING IN LOVE 03/02/62
Elvis Presley ROCK-A-HULA BABY 03/02/62
Elvis Presley GOOD LUCK CHARM 12/05/62
Elvis Presley FOLLOW THAT DREAM (EP) 16/06/62
Elvis Presley SHE'S NOT YOU 01/09/62
Elvis Presley KID GALAHAD (EP) 03/11/62
Elvis Presley RETURN TO SENDER 10/11/62
Elvis Presley ONE BROKEN HEART FOR SALE 02/03/63
Elvis Presley (YOU'RE THE) DEVIL IN DISGUISE 06/07/63
Elvis Presley BOSSA NOVA BABY 26/10/63
Elvis Presley KISS ME QUICK 21/12/63
Elvis Presley VIVA LAS VEGAS 21/03/64
Elvis Presley KISSIN' COUSINS 27/06/64
Elvis Presley SUCH A NIGHT 22/08/64
Elvis Presley AIN'T THAT LOVING YOU BABY 31/10/64
Elvis Presley BLUE CHRISTMAS 26/12/64
Elvis Presley DO THE CLAM 13/03/65
Elvis Presley CRYING IN THE CHAPEL 29/05/65
Elvis Presley TELL ME WHY 13/11/65
Elvis Presley BLUE RIVER 26/02/66
Elvis Presley FRANKIE AND JOHNNY 23/04/66
Elvis Presley LOVE LETTERS 09/07/66
Elvis Presley ALL THAT I AM 15/10/66
Elvis Presley IF EVERY DAY WAS LIKE CHRISTMAS 10/12/66
Elvis Presley INDESCRIBABLY BLUE 18/02/67
Elvis Presley GUITAR MAN 24/02/68
Elvis Presley U.S. MALE 18/05/68
Elvis Presley YOUR TIME HASN'T COME YET BABY 20/07/68
Elvis Presley IF I CAN DREAM 08/02/69
Elvis Presley IN THE GHETTO 21/06/69
Elvis Presley CLEAN UP YOUR OWN BACKYARD 06/09/69
Elvis Presley SUSPICIOUS MINDS 29/11/69
Elvis Presley DON'T CRY DADDY 28/02/70
Elvis Presley KENTUCKY RAIN 16/05/70
Elvis Presley THE WONDER OF YOU 11/07/70
Elvis Presley I'VE LOST YOU 21/11/70
Elvis Presley YOU DON'T HAVE TO SAY YOU LOVE ME 02/01/71
Elvis Presley THERE GOES MY EVERYTHING 20/03/71
Elvis Presley RAGS TO RICHES 22/05/71
Elvis Presley I JUST CAN'T HELP BELIEVING 18/12/71
Elvis Presley UNTIL IT'S TIME FOR YOU TO GO 1/4/72
Elvis Presley AN AMERICAN TRILOGY 24/6/72
Elvis Presley BURNING LOVE 30/9/72
Elvis Presley ALWAYS ON MY MIND 30/12/72
Elvis Presley POLK SALAD ANNIE 2/6/73
Elvis Presley FOOL 18/8/73
Elvis Presley MY BOY 23/11/74
Elvis Presley PROMISED LAND 18/1/75
Elvis Presley GREEN GREEN GRASS OF HOME 13/12/75
Elvis Presley SUSPICION 22/1/77

673

676